ArtScroll Mesorah Series®

מועדים
לשמחה
חגים
וזמנים
לששון

Rabbi Meir Zlotowitz / Rabbi Nosson Scherman

General Editors

מחזור
בית אהרן

מחזור
בית אהרן
לפסח

NUSACH ASHKENAZ — נוסח אשכנז

Published by

Mesorah Publications, ltd

The Complete ArtScroll machzor Pesach

A new translation and anthologized commentary

composed by

Rabbi Avie Gold

in collaboration with

Rabbi Meir Zlotowitz

and Rabbi Nosson Scherman

Designed by

Rabbi Sheah Brander

FIRST EDITION
First Impression . . . March, 1990

Published and Distributed by
MESORAH PUBLICATIONS, Ltd.
Brooklyn, New York 11223

Distributed in Israel by
MESORAH MAFITZIM / J. GROSSMAN
Rechov Harav Uziel 117
Jerusalem, Israel

Distributed in Europe by
J. LEHMANN HEBREW BOOKSELLERS
20 Cambridge Terrace
Gateshead, Tyne and Wear
England NE8 1RP

Distributed in Australia & New Zealand by
GOLD'S BOOK & GIFT CO.
36 William Street
Balaclava 3183, Vic., Australia

Distributed in South Africa by
KOLLEL BOOKSHOP
22 Muller Street
Yeoville 2198
South Africa

THE ARTSCROLL MESORAH SERIES®
"MACHZOR BAIS AHARON / THE COMPLETE ARTSCROLL MACHZOR"
Pesach — Nusach Ashkenaz

ISBN: 0-89906-696-8

Typography by CompuScribe at ArtScroll Studios, Ltd., Brooklyn, NY
Bound by **Sefercraft, Inc.**, Brooklyn, NY

In honor of

ARNOLD LEE

ר׳ אהרן בן ר׳ ישראל הלל הלוי שיחיה

in the year of his seventieth birthday

בית אהרן בטחו בה׳ עזרם ומגנם הוא

Wise in the teachings of halachah and law,
born into a hard-working and traditional Jewish family,
he reached the pinnacle of his chosen legal profession at a young age, before entering into the field of real estate.

He and his wife, HELEN
מרת קיילא בת ר׳ אברהם אבא שתחיה
have remained pious and observant Jews, wholeheartedly imbued with a love of Yiddishkeit and ארץ ישראל, and have become acknowledged leaders of the Anglo-Jewish community, particularly in the fields of communal welfare, Jewish education, and Israel.

We, their children and grandchildren, wish them many years of good health and happiness עד מאה ועשרים שנה ומעלה, and aspire to emulate the example of our parents in Torah and אהבת ישראל, as prescribed by the ancient prayer
וְתֵיהַב לִי בְּנִין דִּכְרִין דְּעָבְדִין רְעוּתָךְ
And give me sons who carry out Your will.
(Zohar, Vayakhel)

אלימלך ורחל בת ר׳ שלמה
Edward and Agnes Lee

אברהם ליב ומַשָה נוריה בת ר׳ אברהם
Alan and Marsha Lee
אילנה הללה יעטא, ישראל אריה,
גליה אראלה שרה
Ilana, Victor, and Julia

LONDON
Passover, 1990 / פסח תש״נ

TABLE OF CONTENTS

SABBATH OF CHOL HAMOED — שַׁבָּת חוֹל הַמּוֹעֵד

◆§ Publisher's Preface

Pesach is the "time of our freedom," the birthday of the Jewish nation. Like all festivals, Pesach is also a time when there are many relatively unfamiliar additions to the order of prayer. Based on the kind reception given the ArtScroll Siddur and the ArtScroll Machzorim for Rosh Hashanah, Yom Kippur and Succos, we are hopeful that this Pesach Machzor will help the public spend less time searching and seeking instructions for the services, and more time understanding them. Following is a brief description of the features of the Machzor:

◆§ **Contents** *The Machzor is as complete as possible. It includes translations and commentaries on all the prayers and Torah readings except for the piyutim that are omitted by virtually all congregations. Those have been included in the back of the Machzor for the convenience of the congregations that require them. In addition there are full services for the Sabbath and weekday Chol HaMoed. The services for each day are self-contained so that the reader will be spared the annoying chore of turning back and forth. The Overview provides a perspective on Pesach and the themes of exile and redemption.*

◆§ **Translation** *The translation seeks to balance the lofty beauty of the heavily nuanced text and a readily understood English rendering. Where a choice had to be made, we generally preferred fidelity to the text over inaccurate simplicity, but occasionally, we had to stray from the literal translation in order to capture the essence of a phrase in an accessible English idiom. Especially in the piyutim, we had to go beyond a strictly literal translation, and sometimes rely on the commentary to clarify the meaning of the text.*

◆§ **HASHEM's Name During Prayer** *We translate the Four-Letter Name of God as "HASHEM," the pronunciation traditionally used for the Name to avoid pronouncing it unnecessarily. However, if one prays using the English translation, he should say "God" or "Lord" or he should pronounce the Name in its proper Hebrew way "Adonoy," in accord with the ruling of most halachic authorities.*

◆§ **Commentary** *The commentary has two goals; to explain the difficult passages and to involve the reader in the emotional, spiritual, and inspirational experience of prayer. We have avoided purely technical or grammatical comments. Unattributed comments are sometimes the author's own, but usually distill the general trend of several authorities of the Scriptural or Talmudic sources on which a phrase is based.*

◆§ **Laws and Instructions** *Clear instructions are provided throughout. More complex or lengthy halachos are discussed in the 'Laws' section at the end of the Machzor, which the reader will find to be a very helpful guide. In addition to halachos that relate specifically to Pesach, the Laws section includes general halachos that are relevant to the regular prayer service. Throughout the Machzor, we refer to these laws by paragraph (§) number.*

◆§ **Layout and Typography** *While we have followed the pattern of the ArtScroll Siddur and Machzorim, which have been greatly praised for their* *ease of use and clarity of layout, this Machzor presents special challenges due to the fact that, many omit part or all of the special Pesach piyutim. Consequently, we have provided separate repetitions of the chazzan's Shemoneh Esrei, one with piyutim and one without. This Machzor, with its clear instructions, copious subtitles, and precise page headings, was designed to make the service easy for everyone to follow. In addition, it incorporates the following popular features of the Siddur: The first and last phrases of the translation on each page parallel the first and last phrases of the Hebrew text; paragraphs begin with bold-type words to facilitate finding the individual tefillos; each paragraph in the translation is introduced with the parallel Hebrew world to ease cross-checking; portions said aloud by the chazzan are indicated by either the symbol ⁘ or the word chazzan. An asterisk (*) after a word indicates that that word or phrase is treated in the commentary. Numbered footnotes give the Scriptural sources of countless verses that have been melded into the prayers. A footnote beginning 'Cf.' indicates that the Scriptural source is paraphrased.*

Hebrew Grammar *As a general rule in the Hebrew language, the accent is on the last syllable. Where the accent is on an earlier syllable, it is indicated with a messeg, a vertical line below the accented letter:* שִׁירוּ*. In the case of the Shema and the Song at the Sea, which are given with the cantillation [trop], the accent follows the trop. A* שְׁוָא נָע *[sh'va na] is indicated by a hyphen mark above the letter:* בָּרְכוּ*; except for a sh'va on the first letter of a word, which is always a sh'va na. In identifying a sh'va na, we have followed the rules of the Vilna Gaon and Rabbi Yaakov Emden.*

Acknowledgments

The ArtScroll Series has been privileged to benefit from the advice and support of the venerable Torah leaders of the previous and present generations. MARAN HAGAON HARAV MOSHE FEINSTEIN, MARAN HAGAON HARAV YAAKOV KAMINETZKY, MARAN HAGAON HARAV SHNEUR KOTLER זצ"ל. *Among today's gedolei Yisrael* להבחל"ח MARAN HAGAON HARAV MORDECHAI GIFTER שליט"א *has been a father and mentor from the start.*

The profound influence of MARAN HAGAON HARAV GEDALIA SCHORR זצ"ל *pervades the Overviews. Quietly and self-effacingly, he put a lasting stamp on two generations of American Torah life.*

We are deeply grateful to Maranan Hageonim HARAV DAVID FEINSTEIN, HARAV DAVID COHEN *and* HARAV HILLEL DAVID שליט"א *for their constant involvement and for placing their encyclopedic scholarship at our disposal whenever needed.*

It is a source of great pride that so outstanding a Torah scholar as HARAV HERSH GOLDWURM שליט"א *has been associated with the ArtScroll Series virtually since its inception. In this Machzor Rabbi Goldwurm has contributed the 'Laws,' reviewed most of the instructions, and been available for research and guidance.*

Among those whose guidance was invaluable are such leaders of organizational and rabbinic life as RABBI MOSHE SHERER, RABBI PINCHAS STOLPER,

RABBI BORUCH B. BORCHARDT, RABBI JOSHUA FISHMAN, RABBI FABIAN SCHONFELD, RABBI BENJAMIN WALFISH, RABBI YAAKOV MARCUS, MR. DAVID H. SCHWARTZ, RABBI SHLOMO LESIN, RABBI YISRAEL H. EIDELMAN, RABBI RAPHAEL BUTLER, RABBI BURTON JAFFA, RABBI MICHOEL LEVI, *and* MR. YAAKOV KORNREICH.

A huge investment of time and resources was required to make this Machzor a reality. Only through the generous support of many people was it possible not only to produce the work, but to keep it within reach of the average family and congregation. Among those to whom we are grateful are:

The sons of ARNOLD *and* HELEN LEE *who dedicated this Machzor* BAIS AHARON *in honor of his seventieth birthday. Mr. Lee is a respectable leader of British Jewry, a man who has earned the respect and affection of colleagues and the general public, both in his profession and in his public service. We are proud that this Machzor serves such a noble purpose for a very distinguished family;*

MR. *and* MRS. ELI STERN *and* MR. *and* MRS. JOSEPH STERN *who dedicated the Nusach Sefard Machzorim, for Rosh Hashanah,* ZICHRON MOSHE; *for Yom Kippur,* ZICHRON Z'EV; *and for Succos,* ZICHRON SHMUEL. *People of unassuming gentility and gracious generosity, they benefit a host of Torah causes with vigor, imagination, and unselfish dedication;*

MRS. EMMA GLICK *of Wilmington, Delaware and her sons* YITZCHOK (EDWARD) *and* NAFTALI (NORMAN), *who dedicated the Ashkenaz Rosh Hashanah Machzor* ZICHRON REUVEN *in memory of their late husband and father, Reb Reuven Glick* ז״ל;

MRS. LILLIE FEDER *and her children* NORMAN *and* MAUREEN *of Toronto, who dedicated the Ashkenaz Yom Kippur Machzor* ZICHRON YOSEF *in memory of their husband and father, Reb Yosef* ז״ל;

The KUSHNER *and* LAULICHT *families, who dedicated the Succos Ashkenaz Machzor* BAIS YOSEF, *in memory of their late husband and father Reb Yosef Kushner* ז״ל;

We are also grateful to the good and loyal friends who dedicated the various editions of the ArtScroll Siddur (in order of their publication): MR. *and* MRS. ZALMAN MARGULIES; MR. *and* MRS. JOSEPH BERLINER; MR. *and* MRS. AARON L. HEIMOWITZ; MRS. MALA WASSNER; MR. *and* MRS. HIRSH WOLF; *and* MR. *and* MRS. BEREL TENNENBAUM.

Many other people have provided the assistance needed to produce such Torah projects. In addition to those mentioned in previous editions of the Siddur and other ArtScroll works, we are grateful to MR. *and* MRS. LOUIS GLICK, *whose sponsorship of the ArtScroll Mishnah Series with the* YAD AVRAHAM *commentary (from which the commentary to Tractate Pesachim has been abridged for this Machzor) is a jewel in the crown of Torah dissemination;* MR. *and* MRS. DAN SUKENIK *and* MR. *and* MRS. MOSHE SUKENIK, *who are living legends — for what they do and for the way they do it. May their work for Torah be a z'chus for the* נשמות *of their parents* ר׳ שלמה זאב ב״ר יחיאל ע״ה והאשה רודא בת ר׳ דניאל ע״ה. JUDAH J. SEPTIMUS *and* NATHAN B. SILBERMAN *have always been friends, but in their efforts to make possible our relocation to new headquarters, they have given a new dimension to loyalty and selflessness.*

The following people have been particularly helpful in making possible the publication of this Machzor: MEL *and* NAOMI BRODY, לעילוי נשמות הרב דוד בונם ב״ר זאב ע״ה והאשה חוה בת הרב ישראל ע״ה; MR. *and* MRS. ABRAHAM FRUCHTHANDLER; MR. *and* MRS. HAROLD JACOBS, MR. *and* MRS. AVROHOM KLEIN; MR. *and* MRS. MORDECHAI KURANTZ; MR. *and* MRS. CHAIM LEIBEL; RABBI *and* MRS. YEHUDAH LEVI; MR. *and* MRS. MORDECAI LIPSCHITZ, לעילוי נשמות ר׳ גבריאל ב״ר ברוך ע״ה ור׳ רפאל יהודה אריה ב״ר מאיר ע״ה; RABBI MOSHE *and* RUTH MALINOWITZ; MR. *and* MRS. MOSES MARX; MR. *and* MRS. SHLOMO PERL; MR. *and* MRS. ALBERT REICHMANN; MR. *and* MRS. SHMUEL RIEDER; MR. *and* MRS. ABE SEPTIMUS; MR. *and* MRS. LAURENCE A. TISCH; MR. *and* MRS. JOSEPH WEINBERG; MR. *and* MRS. WILLY WIESNER; *and* MR. *and* MRS. HOWARD ZUCKERMAN.

RABBI AVIE GOLD, *Senior Editor, translated and commented on the piyutim and coordinated the editing and organization of the entire Machzor. His breadth and dedication are fixtures of the entire ArtScroll Series, and this Machzor is no exception. The balance of the Machzor was drawn from other works in the Series or was written by members of the ArtScroll staff especially for this work. With this Machzor, Reb Avie will earn the gratitude of the many thousands of people for whom the beauty of the Pesach tefillos is now revealed.*

Only a fellow craftsman can perceive the excruciating hours that REB SHEAH BRANDER *expended in designing the Machzor for the mispallel's maximum ease. In this project he has outdone even his own standard of excellence. Moreover, his learned and incisive comments improved every aspect of this work.*

RABBI AVROHOM YOSAIF ROSENBERG *reviewed the vowelization and accenting of the piyutim, and* RABBI YEHEZKEL DANZIGER *condensed the Mishnah commentary. We are grateful to them.*

MRS. MENUCHA SILVER, MRS. ZISSI LANDAU *and* BASSIE GOLDSTEIN *typed the manuscript diligently and conscientiously.* RABBI YOSEF GESSER *and* MRS. FAYGIE WEINBAUM *carefully proofread the entire work.*

All of ArtScroll's staff has a share in our service to the community, each in his or her area of responsibility: SHMUEL BLITZ, *director of ArtScroll Jerusalem;* SHIMON GOLDING, SHEILA TENNENBAUM, AVROHOM BIDERMAN, *of the sales staff;* YOSEF TIMINSKY, MICHAEL HOREN, MICHAEL ZIVITZ, SAID KOHAN FAID, YITZCHOK SAFTLAS, MRS. JUDI DICK, LEA FREIER, MRS. ESTHER FEIERSTEIN, MRS. ESTIE DICKER, FAIGIE ZLOTOWITZ *and* ESTIE KUSHNER. *We conclude with gratitude to Hashem Yisborach for His infinite blessings and for the opportunity to have been the quill that records His word. May He guide our work in the future for the benefit of His people.*

Adar 5750 — *Rabbis Meir Zlotowitz / Nosson Scherman*
Brooklyn, NY

Overviews

An Overview / Pesach — The Eternal Redemption

אָמַר ר׳ אֲבָהוּ, מִפְּנֵי מַה נֶּעֱנַשׁ אַבְרָהָם אָבִינוּ וְנִשְׁתַּעְבְּדוּ בָנָיו מָאתַיִם וְעֶשֶׂר שָׁנִים? מִפְּנֵי שֶׁעָשָׂה אַנְגַּרְיָא בְּתַלְמִידֵי חֲכָמִים . . . וּשְׁמוּאֵל אָמַר מִפְּנֵי שֶׁהִפְרִיז עַל מִדּוֹתָיו שֶׁל הקב״ה . . . וְר׳ יוֹחָנָן אָמַר שֶׁהִפְרִישׁ בְּנֵי אָדָם מִלְּהִכָּנֵס תַּחַת כַּנְפֵי הַשְּׁכִינָה . . .

R' Avuhu said: Why was Abraham punished so that his children were subjugated for two hundred ten years? Because he waged war using Torah scholars [as his soldiers, when he mobilized his students to save Lot (Genesis 14:14)]. . . Shmuel said: Because he tested the forbearance of the Holy One, Blessed is He [by asking how he could be assured that God would keep the promise to give the Land to his descendants (ibid. 15:8)] . . . R' Yochanan said: Because he prevented people from entering under the wings of the Divine Presence [when he acceded to the request of the king of Sodom to allow him to keep control over his subjects, instead of letting them become servants of Abraham, who would teach them the ways of God (ibid. 14:21)] (Nedarim 32a).

I. Abraham and Egypt*

The Sages wonder why the Jewish people were condemned to centuries of exile in Egypt, including slavery and persecution. In response, they give three reasons, all of which involve shortcomings of Abraham. Like the other sins of our greatest figures, they would hardly have been considered misdeeds if they had been committed by lesser human beings, but an Abraham is judged by higher standards. Nevertheless, we must investigate why these reasons are sufficient justification for the Egyptian exile. Were they such weighty sins as to justify such a severe, intense, and long-lasting punishment? Secondly, the Egyptian exile took place long after Abraham's death; it affected his descendants, not him. Why, therefore, should *they* have suffered?

* The first section of the Overview is based on *Gevuros Hashem* by *Maharal.*

NONE OF THE THREE SHORTCOMINGS the Sages ascribe to Abraham could be considered a major sin in and of itself, but each revealed a degree of insufficient faith in God. Since Torah study is the primary value and its students are the ultimate guarantors of God's benevolent providence, shouldn't Abraham have looked for other ways to do battle, instead of tearing his disciples away from their studies as a first recourse? Would a man of perfect faith have questioned God's absolute promise to give *Eretz Yisrael* to his offspring? How could a man of Abraham's greatness have permitted the people of Sodom to remain the subjects of a king whose city still remains the enduring symbol of cruelty and perversion, when the international law of the time gave Abraham the right to claim them as his own servants and thereby bring them under the wings of the *Shechinah?*

A Basic Flaw

The Jewish nation began with Abraham; he was the source. If there was a basic flaw in Abraham, then it would carry over to his descendants and affect them, as well. Because Jews are children of Abraham — and not, in the spiritual sense, of Adam or Noah — the character of Abraham, as of Isaac and Jacob, was part of Israel's moral genetic code. Just as the experiences of the three Patriarchs portended the history of their offspring — מַעֲשֵׂי אָבוֹת סִימָן לַבָּנִים, *the deeds of the Patriarchs are portents for the children* — so their spiritual and moral greatness became an eternal legacy. Conversely, if there was even a minor lapse, it would have to be remedied before it snowballed into a historic shortcoming of major proportions. True, Abraham's faith in God was monumental beyond our imagination and the lapses noted by the Sages are minor by our standards. Nevertheless, just as a child's imperfect posture will cause him great suffering as an adult unless it is corrected early, so too a small flaw in Abraham's faith had to be corrected while his nation was still in its infancy. When a root is diseased, its effects will show up in the branches; and Abraham was the root of the entire nation.

This principle would not apply to ordinary sins. A misdeed committed in a fit of passion or because of ignorance or misjudgment does not indicate a serious, underlying imperfection in the transgressor. But occasionally a sin is of such a nature that it is more meaningful, more indicative of internal rot than another deed — even of one that may be intrinsically more serious. Thus we find that the sin of robbery was the one that sealed the fate of Noah's generation. Not that stealing *per se* is worse than the equally prevalent sins of immorality and idolatry; it is not. But it reveals a perversion of character, a selfishness that shows its perpetrator to be callous to the suffering of others. Sabbath desecration is symbolic of a lack of belief that God created heaven and earth in six days and rested on the seventh, so the willful Sabbath desecrator who disregards the importance of the day and its holiness has the halachic status of one who does not believe in God.

The Imperative

IT IS TRUE THAT GOD DOES NOT PUNISH without a sin and, by and large, the punishment must fit the sin. If so, however, how can one justify the severe suffering imposed on millions of Jews in Egypt because of the relatively minor sin of their grandfather?

Theoretically, there should be no such thing as a 'trivial' sin. In absolutely logical terms, it could be argued that if someone abuses God's gift of life, it should be taken from him. Strict Justice would indeed dictate this, but God joined mercy to justice when He created the world. Otherwise man could not survive or even repent, because he could not undo what he had wrought. There are times, however, when God suspends His mercy. The Egyptian exile is an example of such an unusual phenomenon. God, in His wisdom, knew that the crucible of slavery and exile was a necessary precondition for the shaping of the nation of Israel. This was preordained. But since the Divine plan for the world does not allow a punishment without a sin, Israel could not be condemned to Egypt without a cause. The cause was Abraham's insufficient faith. In order to allow the exile to take place and perform its necessary function, God temporarily suspended His attribute of mercy, and allowed absolute, uncompromising justice to run its course. Even that was ultimately merciful, as we shall see below, but while it was happening, it undoubtedly seemed not only cruel but incomprehensible.

II. The Underlying Hand*

Two Ways

GOD'S GUIDANCE OF HISTORY as it moves toward His goal of Creation takes two primary forms: (1) מִדַּת מִשְׁפָּט, *The Attribute of Justice;* and (2) מִדַּת הַמֶּמְשָׁלָה הַיִּחוּדִית, *The Attribute of Domination of God's Oneness.* The first form is the logical one that we were raised with and is one of *Rambam's* Thirteen Principles of Faith. This is the rule of שָׂכָר וְעֹנֶשׁ, *Reward and Punishment*. We expect to see good rewarded and evil punished. When this happens, the righteous are exalted, for we see the efficacy of their behavior, and the wicked are downtrodden, for it is clear that their behavior is displeasing to God. Then, God's Name is sanctified, for we see His will upheld and reinforced in the functioning of His universe. Such Divine conduct in itself is a boon to humanity, because it controls evil and, if people are willing to learn from the obvious, it diminishes sinful behavior.

But if, instead of seeking to do good and learn the lessons of God's reward and punishment, people choose to gratify themselves against God's will, and they slip into the sloth of vegetating instead of striving for spiritual and moral advancement, then God withdraws, as it were, from close supervision of the world's affairs. If people are not deserving of God's intimate supervision of their

* This section of the Overview is based on *Da'as Tevunos* by *R' Moshe Chaim Luzzatto.*

deeds, He no longer rewards and punishes in an obvious way. When that happens, the world is clouded by הֶסְתֵּר פָּנִים, *Concealment of God's Countenance*. Those are the times when Jews wonder, 'Where is God?' and when there is fuel to feed the passions of those who blaspheme that there is no God ר״ל.

A classic time of such concealment was during the period of the Babylonian exile. It was the first time a Temple had been destroyed and the people driven on a stream of blood from their land into slavery and degradation. That was a new condition in Jewish history, and some of the nation's most distinguished young men came to the prophet Ezekiel to ask if they were still required to show allegiance to God. After all, they argued in all sincerity, had not God banished them from His Presence, like a husband who divorced his wife or a master who freed his slave? And if so, did this not mean that the covenant between God and Israel had been permanently severed and we were no longer His people? (*Sanhedrin* 105a).

Such is the pernicious effect of concealment of God's countenance, when He is too hidden to be perceived.

Wicked, dishonest people appear to be ascendant everywhere, degrading values that we hold dear and subjugating good and sincere people. Such times can drive good people to hopelessness and despair, can make them wonder whether there is any point in attempting to serve a seemingly uncaring God.

Unseen Presence

BUT, EVEN THEN, GOD DOES NOT CEASE to regulate the world and move it toward His ultimate goal. The Attribute of Judgment may not be visible, but beneath the surface, the Attribute of Domination of God's Oneness is always active.

The quintessential example of such an era in history is the first two thousand years of the world's existence. The Sages refer to it as שְׁנֵי אֲלָפִים תֹּהוּ, *two thousand years of desolation* (*Sanhedrin* 97a). The Torah had not yet been given, so the primary source of holiness was lacking in the world. In later times of spiritual degradation, Israel and its Torah were present to cast shafts of light here and there into the world, in times as dark as the Babylonian exile or the more recent traumatic terrors that have shattered Jewry, but not for those first two millennia. Abraham was born in the year 1948 from Creation, and at the end of the first two thousand, he began to usher in the next epoch, the two thousand years of Torah (ibid.). During those early years, the world lacked the merit that Torah study and *mitzvah* observance would give it in subsequent times, and humanity fell swiftly from its noble origins, as the early chapters of *Genesis* describe. Hardly was it a time of Divine inactivity, however. God was relatively invisible, but, as the Torah shows us, He was preparing the way for the emergence of Abraham and His Chosen People. Thus it always is when His countenance is hidden. Behind the scenes, God continues to provide sustenance to the world while He guides history toward His foreordained goal.

Chronologically, the Egyptian exile took place *after* the two thousand years of desolation — Jacob and his family descended to Egypt in 2238 — but those 210 years in Egypt were the most intense of all periods of Divine concealment and, therefore, of the Domination of God's Oneness. Even though God's Presence was so cloaked as to be invisible, He was covertly preparing the way for Israel's perfection, freedom, and the giving of the Torah. That is why the Sages place the period of Egyptian slavery into the two thousand years of Torah — because, amid the apparent absence of justice, God was paving the way for the emergence of His glory in the blinding brilliance of Mount Sinai.

Another period of such hiddenness, though less intense, was the period of the Babylonian exile, as noted above. Then, too, God was there, unnoticed, guiding events for the eventual downfall of Haman and the command to rebuild the Temple.

It is altogether common in the broad sweep of history that we do not understand the purpose of events until their entire sequence is complete and their interrelationship becomes known.

In the story of Pesach, for example, there is no doubt that Jews must have grieved that the infant boy of Amram and Yocheved, leaders of the people, should have been abandoned on the Sea of Reeds and then swallowed in Pharaoh's palace to be raised as an oppressor of his own people. Only eighty years later did it become known that God was using Pharaoh himself to raise Moses, the eventual redeemer of Israel. In the time of Purim, how revolted the Jewish people must have been that their sister Esther — righteous, chaste, virtuous Esther — should have been compelled to become the consort of Jew-hating Ahasuerus. Five years later she emerged as their savior, and years after that, her son Darius ordered the construction of the Second Temple — the same Temple whose construction Ahasuerus had once halted. Many other instances can be cited of how, during those two periods, events moved toward wholly unanticipated manifestations of God's providence. Those outcomes proved that God was actively involved at the very time that His presence was undetected.

God never disdains His handiwork. When it seems that He ignores His universe, He is actually creating new forms of good for the world, because everything He does is good and He constantly seeks to benefit His creatures. As the Sages said:

> וַיֹּאמֶר יִשְׂרָאֵל, לָמָּה הֲרֵעֹתֶם לִי. ר׳ לֵוִי בְּשֵׁם ר׳ חָמָא בַּר חֲנִינָא: מֵעוֹלָם לֹא אָמַר יַעֲקֹב אָבִינוּ דָּבָר שֶׁל בַּטָּלָה אֶלָּא כָאן. אָמַר הקב״ה: אֲנִי עוֹסֵק לְהַמְלִיךְ בְּנוֹ בְמִצְרַיִם וְהוּא אוֹמֵר לָמָּה הֲרֵעֹתֶם לִי?
>
> *Israel said [to his sons, when he learned that he was required to send Benjamin to Egypt] 'Why have you done evil to me?' (Genesis 43:6). Said R' Levi in the name of Chamah bar Chanina: Jacob never said anything in vain, except here. The Holy One Blessed Is He said: I am engaged in making his son the ruler of Egypt and he says, 'Why have you done evil to me?!'*
>
> *(Bereishis Rabbah 91:13)*

Clearly, the entire time that Jacob was suffering over his loss of Joseph, God was arranging the circumstances for Joseph to ease the way for his family when they went to their unavoidable exile in Egypt. His Presence was unseen, but He was working diligently behind the scenes, sowing the future with His mercy and forethought.

III. The Eternal Redemption*

Fruits of Suffering

THE SAGES TEACH THAT THREE PRECIOUS GIFTS come only through prior suffering: Torah, *Eretz Yisrael*, and the World to Come (*Berachos* 5a). The terrible suffering of the Egyptian exile should have brought all three of these gifts. Indeed, it nearly did. Shortly after emerging from Egypt, Israel received the Torah. At that time the way was clear for them to go to *Eretz Yisrael*, as the Torah states clearly. And if that had happened, the Temple would have been built and the world would have entered directly into the period of complete bliss foretold by the prophets. That would have been the World to Come, the world in its perfect state as it will exist after the coming of Messiah. But Israel in the Wilderness fell short of this level of greatness. Because of their sins, they had to wait forty years before they could enter *Eretz Yisrael*, and even then, they did not have a Temple for almost four centuries and were condemned to future exiles.

Nevertheless, as the *Zohar* teaches, all future *galus* experiences and redemptions are reflections of Egypt. It was there that Israel became purged of its national deficiencies so that it could be worthy of God's mantle. The word מִצְרַיִם, *Egypt*, alludes to every exile, for it carries the connotation of שֶׁמְּצִירִים אֶת יִשְׂרָאֵל, *they oppress Israel*, the underlying condition of all exiles. In microcosm, every Jewish exile was contained in the sojourn in Egypt, and every Jewish redemption was contained in the Exodus. We celebrate Pesach as the quintessential redemption because the seeds of all the others are contained in it, for if Israel had not sinned, Pesach would have been the final and all-inclusive redemption.

Why was the suffering in Egypt necessary and what did it accomplish? The Sages speak of suffering as 'cleansing' a person of his impurities and of improving him, just as salt — despite its bitterness — improves meat by removing its blood (see *Berachos* 5a). A person too accustomed to physical comfort and luxury becomes resistant to spiritual stimuli. Someone who learns to enjoy pleasure and satiety finds that there is an increasing conflict between his body and soul, and it is impossible to satisfy the desires of both. One who becomes addicted to pleasure and luxury — and it is very easy for this to happen to anyone — will battle against the higher calling that demands of him to recognize something higher than profit and pleasure, indulgence and license. Indeed, he will erect a fortress of rationalization to prove that his chosen course is just and proper, and even that it is the high road to the spirit.

* This section of the Overview is based on *Ohr Gedalyahu*, by *Rabbi Gedalyah Schorr*

Purpose of Exile

IN EGYPT, ISRAEL WAS STRIPPED of everything external to its essence. When the redemption came, it was clearly, indisputably the hand of God that plucked a hapless slave-nation from an abyss and planted it on a mountain of sanctity and intellect. If there had been an infinitesimal lack of faith on Abraham's part, the Egypt-experience removed it. A nation that had lost its independence and resources, that had sunk — in the expression of the Sages — to the forty-ninth level of impurity, could hardly fail to believe in the All-Powerful One Who had it raised to the sublime height of Sinai.

In the words of *R' Shimshon Rafael Hirsch*: The Deliverance of Israel from Egypt . . . stands . . . as an action brought into being, as it were by another Divine imperative: "Let there be," in the history of mankind. . . Do not deceive yourself that a new spirit invaded your fathers after a long slavery; that they arose of their own will and fought battles and, unaided, wrested freedom from their tyrants by their victory. . . It was God's word alone that burst open Israel's dungeon; and they that had been sunk in slavery, bereft of all power and personal freedom, went out free, borne aloft by God's word. And so, throughout the progress of time, they belong to God collectively as a nation. . .they had to prepare for their wanderings and await the call of Almighty God which would summon them to freedom. . . They had to earn their freedom by complete surrender to God. . . Indeed, their exodus was so little dependent on their own power and foresight that they neither could nor did prepare themselves with that most essential food, bread, for their awe-inspiring wanderings (*Horeb*).

If it is true that a lack of total faith precipitated the exile, with the purpose that Abraham's offspring would become imbued with a faith born of total dependence on God, then we can see the fulfillment of this goal at the climax of the Exodus: At the great miracle of the Splitting of the Sea, when Israel saw conclusively that Egypt's back had been broken and that God was supreme, the Torah declares וַיַּאֲמִינוּ בַּה׳ וּבְמשֶׁה עַבְדּוֹ, *and they had faith in HASHEM and in Moses His servant* (*Exodus* 14:31).

In the aftermath of the exile, a new kind of faith had been instilled in Jewish hearts: the faith that everything that had happened to them, even in the darkest times, was not haphazard. They saw in retrospect the providence that *Daas Tevunos* calls the Domination of God's Oneness, for it became clear to them that even in Egypt they had been the recipients of God's kindness. It was a kindness that they did not recognize as such until the bondage had been ended. When it was over, however, they realized the meaning of the Sages' term יִסּוּרִים שֶׁל אַהֲבָה. Although this is usually translated as *suffering of love*, i.e., suffering that God imposes out of love for the victim, *Maharal* translates differently. It refers to the sort of suffering that *leads* to love of God. For only after purging oneself of infatuation with oneself and one's personal desires, and after recognizing that he owes everything to God, can a person elevate himself to a love of Him.

Hope

R'TZADDOK HAKOHEN NOTES A DIFFICULTY in the assurance God gave Israel after the Splitting of the Sea: כָּל הַמַּחֲלָה אֲשֶׁר שַׂמְתִּי בְמִצְרַיִם לֹא אָשִׂים עָלֶיךָ כִּי אֲנִי ה׳ רֹפְאֶךָ, *the entire illness that I placed upon Egypt, I will not place upon you, for I am HASHEM, your Healer* (*Exodus* 15:26). *R' Tzaddok* wonders how God can be called a Healer for *not* imposing an illness;

someone who is not ill need not be healed. Rather, he explains, the Torah is not telling us that God will refrain from bringing the Ten Plagues upon us. The Torah is telling us something else entirely. It is *not* true that God never imposes suffering upon Israel; our history testifies all too eloquently to that. But the suffering that God brings upon Jews is of a different order than that which befell Egypt. The Egyptians were punished for their sins. God's purpose was not to refine or elevate them; it was simply to punish them for their outrages and thereby to sanctify the Name by showing the world that no one can sin with impunity.

Israel's pain is different. Surely God afflicts Israel, but only as a father afflicts a beloved child — to train him and make him better. God afflicts Israel not as a *Punisher*, but as a *Healer*, to purge them of impurities, so that they will become better, purer, holier, more worthy of their sacred calling.

People who have been forced to recognize the futility of striving for the comforts of This World are able to perceive the beautiful light of the spirit when God shines it upon them. God revealed Himself in Egypt, but the Egyptians never 'saw' him, because they were too sunk in what passed for culture in their perverted, immoral world view. Tragically, there were many Jews, as well, who did not really 'see' God because they succumbed to the life of Egypt, and they never lifted themselves out of Egyptian society.

Chiddushei HaRim comments that there were three kinds of Jews in Egypt. There were some who perceived God in everything; they were not in exile at all in the truest sense, because nothing impaired their awareness of God in all things. At the other extreme, there were other Jews who were equally not in exile, because they had so thoroughly assimilated into the beliefs of Egypt that they considered themselves to be Egyptians, albeit enslaved and persecuted. Their goal was not to leave Egypt, but to be accepted by their masters. For such people no redemption was possible, and they died during the plague of darkness. Finally, there was the mass of Jews in the middle. They *were* in exile because they were not part of Egypt nor did they wish to be. But they had sunk very low, almost as low as a Jew can sink without being utterly and irreparably lost. For them, the hidden hand of God was truly a healer.

In this there is a message for all Jews in whatever condition they may be, for all three categories of people are always present, and all three aspects may be in each of us to varying degrees. In some ways an individual may be unswervingly loyal to his roots, in others he may have become indistinguishable from his surroundings, and in yet others he may straddle the fence between conviction and doubt. If anything, however, the story of Pesach should encourage everyone to be confident that there is hardly a depth from which a Jew cannot escape.

S'fas Emes writes: '[Just as our ancestors did in Egypt] we should maintain hope in this bitter exile, not to become despondent when we see how downtrodden we are, inwardly and outwardly, not to feel that we can never approach even to a small degree the greatness of our forefathers, much less to become worthy of service in the Temple! . . . For when God will grant that we be redeemed, the inner goodness within us will be aroused to be transformed in an instant to the highest levels, as in ancient times — may God hasten our redemption.'

It happened in Egypt and it will happen again. There was once a lightning shaft of realization that every tribulation was for the good and that it was a veiled expression of God's mercy. That revelation brought every Jewish man and woman to the level of prophecy at the Sea and at Sinai. The first Pesach remains an eternal festival of redemption, an eternal harbinger of what every Jewish generation can anticipate, not a fleeting moment to be celebrated as a remembrance of times long gone and never to return. It remains the embodiment of all redemptions, and it bears within itself the seed of the one that we now await, may it come speedily in our time.

מחזור
בית אהרן

בדיקת חמץ

On the night of 14 Nissan, the night before the Pesach *Seder,* the search for *chametz* (leaven) is made. It should be done with a candle as soon as possible after nightfall. [When the first *Seder* is on Saturday night, the search is conducted on Thursday night (13 Nissan).]

Before the search is begun, the following blessing is recited. See *Laws* §1-3.

If several people assist in the search, only one recites the blessing for all.

בָּרוּךְ אַתָּה יהוה, אֱלֹהֵינוּ מֶלֶךְ הָעוֹלָם, אֲשֶׁר קִדְּשָׁנוּ בְּמִצְוֹתָיו, וְצִוָּנוּ עַל בִּעוּר חָמֵץ.*

After the search, the *chametz* is wrapped and put aside in a safe place to be burned in the morning. Then the following declaration is made:

כָּל חֲמִירָא* וַחֲמִיעָא דְּאִכָּא בִרְשׁוּתִי,* דְּלָא חֲמִתֵּהּ וּדְלָא בִעַרְתֵּהּ וּדְלָא יְדַעְנָא לֵהּ, לִבָּטֵל וְלֶהֱוֵי הֶפְקֵר כְּעַפְרָא דְאַרְעָא.

In the morning, after the *chametz* has been burned, the following declaration is made [see *Laws* §8-9].

כָּל חֲמִירָא וַחֲמִיעָא דְּאִכָּא בִרְשׁוּתִי,* דַּחֲזִתֵּהּ וּדְלָא חֲזִתֵּהּ, דַּחֲמִתֵּהּ וּדְלָא חֲמִתֵּהּ, דְּבִעַרְתֵּהּ וּדְלָא בִעַרְתֵּהּ,* לִבָּטֵל וְלֶהֱוֵי הֶפְקֵר כְּעַפְרָא דְאַרְעָא.

בְּדִיקַת חָמֵץ / THE SEARCH FOR CHAMETZ

בִּעוּר חָמֵץ — *The removal of chametz.* Aside from the commandment to eat matzah all of Pesach and the special observances of the *Seder* nights, the best-known feature of the festival is the requirement not to eat, or even to own, *chametz* all during the festival. For many Jews, one of the most vivid memories of their childhood is the seemingly endless cleaning and scrubbing of their homes during the weeks and days before Pesach.

Although no household can be thoroughly cleaned in only a short while, the Talmudic Sages ordained that a search for *chametz* be made in every home, office, business, and any other place where *chametz* may have been brought, on one night of the year.

The search begins upon nightfall of the fourteenth day of Nissan, the evening before Pesach. The purpose of the commandment is the removal of all *chametz,* and it requires a formal inspection of all areas where *chametz* may have been brought during the course of the year — despite the fact that a thorough cleaning was made before Pesach.

The Talmud derives from Scriptural implications that the search be made by candle light and therefore it is done at night when a candle's flame is noticeable (*Pesachim* 2a). Although the destruction of the *chametz* will take place on the next morning, the blessing is made now because the search is in preparation for, and part of the *mitzvah* of, the destruction.

A widespread custom calls for the distribution of ten pieces of *chametz* through the house before the search (by someone other than the person conducting the search). Of course, care should be taken that the pieces do not leave crumbs, thereby defeating the purpose of the search.

כָּל חֲמִירָא — *Any chametz.* It is essential that all *chametz* be declared ownerless so that one not be in possession of *chametz* without knowing it. The evening declaration carefully omits: (a) any *chametz* that one wishes to retain for that night's supper (which should not be eaten before the search) and the next day's breakfast; (b) the *chametz* that will be burned the next morning; and (c) the *chametz* that will be sold to a non-Jew in the morning. All such *chametz* must be set aside carefully. After eating, leftover *chametz* should be placed with whatever *chametz* may have been found in the evening. They will be burned the morning before Pesach (except when Pesach begins on Saturday night, in which case the *chametz* will be burned Friday morning).

The declaration nullifying one's ownership of the *chametz* has legal ramifications. Moreover, it must be understood by the person saying it. If one does not understand the Aramaic, he should recite it in a language he understands. It should be recited by all members of the family.

בִּרְשׁוּתִי — *In my possession.* An agent appointed to conduct the search or burn the *chametz* for another should say, '*... that is in so-and-so's possession ...*' Nevertheless, it is preferable that the owner of the *chametz* recite the declaration, at the proper time, wherever he may be.

דַּחֲמִתֵּהּ וּדְלָא חֲמִתֵּהּ דְּבִעַרְתֵּהּ וּדְלָא בִעַרְתֵּהּ — *Whether I have seen it or not, whether I have*

THE SEARCH FOR CHAMETZ/LEAVEN

On the night of 14 Nissan, the night before the Pesach *Seder,* the search for *chametz* (leaven) is made. It should be done with a candle as soon as possible after nightfall. [When the first *Seder* is on Saturday night, the search is conducted on Thursday night (13 Nissan).]

Before the search is begun, the following blessing is recited. See *Laws* §1-3.

If several people assist in the search, only one recites the blessing for all.

בָּרוּךְ *Blessed are You, HASHEM, our God, King of the universe, Who has sanctified us with His commandments and has commanded us concerning the removal of chametz.**

After the search, the *chametz* is wrapped and put aside in a safe place to be burned in the morning. Then the following declaration is made:

כָּל חֲמִירָא *Any chametz* or leaven that is in my possession* which I have not seen, have not removed and do not know about, should be annulled and become ownerless, like dust of the earth.*

In the morning, after the *chametz* has been burned, the following declaration is made [see *Laws* §8-9].

כָּל חֲמִירָא *Any chametz or leaven that is in my possession,* whether I have recognized it or not, whether I have seen it or not, whether I have removed it or not,* should be annulled and become ownerless, like dust of the earth.*

---

removed it or not. In the nighttime declaration, only unknown *chametz* is mentioned. This is done so that the nullification of ownership will not apply to the *chametz* held in reserve for consumption that night or the next morning.

The morning declaration, however, includes all *chametz* without exception. It should not be made until the leftover *chametz* has been burnt enough to be inedible. Like the nighttime declaration, that of the morning must be recited in a language which the person reciting it understands. When Pesach begins on Saturday night, this declaration is made on Sabbath morning. Any *chametz* remaining from the Sabbath morning meal should be flushed down the drain before the declaration is made.

Erev Pesach

☐ **Fast of the Firstborn.** *Erev Pesach* is a fast day for בְּכוֹרוֹת, *firstborn males.* It is, however, customary for them to participate in the meal served in celebration of a *mitzvah*, such as a *bris* (circumcision) or *siyum* (completion of the study of a tractate of the *Talmud*); after partaking of the food served in celebration of this event, they may eat during the rest of the day [see *Laws* §5].

If the day before Pesach is a Sabbath, the fast of the firstborn (or the celebration of the *siyum* in its place) is observed on the Thursday before Pesach [see *Laws* §142].

☐ **Matzah on Erev Pesach.** The eating of matzah is forbidden all day on *Erev Pesach.* Nevertheless, many customarily abstain from eating matzah as early as Purim or the beginning of Nissan [see *Laws* §7].

☐ **Eating in the Afternoon.** From the middle of the afternoon on, no meal may be eaten, so that the *Seder* meal can be eaten with a hearty appetite [see *Laws* §12].

☐ **Weekday Activities on Erev Pesach.** The afternoon before Pesach has a festive character, for it was the time when the *pesach* sacrifice was offered in the Temple. (Some Rabbinic authorities hold that the *Seder* matzos should preferably be baked on *Erev Pesach* afternoon — and many people therefore do so, in a spirit of rejoicing and while chanting chapters from *Hallel*.) In fact, the afternoon has the halachic status of *Chol HaMoed,* the Intermediate Days of Pesach, which are not full festival days with all the strictures of *Yom Tov,* but during which many everyday activities are forbidden, to preserve the festive spirit. For that reason, haircuts — for instance — should be taken before noon [see *Laws* §10-11].

☐ **Seder Preparations.** All that is needed for the Seder should be prepared in advance on *Erev* Pesach. If *Erev* Pesach is on the Sabbath, the necessary preparations should be made on Friday. Otherwise, the beginning of the *Seder* will be delayed and the children may fall asleep.

☐ **Erev Pesach that Falls on the Sabbath.** Many difficulties — both halachic and practical — arise when *Erev Pesach* falls on the Sabbath. It is therefore important that one study the pertinent laws and make all the appropriate preparations [see *Laws* §140-149.]

ערוב תבשילין

When Pesach falls on Thursday and Friday, an *eruv tavshilin* is made on Wednesday Erev Pesach [see commentary]. The *eruv*-foods are held while the following blessing and declaration are recited.

בָּרוּךְ אַתָּה יהוה אֱלֹהֵינוּ מֶלֶךְ הָעוֹלָם, אֲשֶׁר קִדְּשָׁנוּ בְּמִצְוֹתָיו, וְצִוָּנוּ עַל מִצְוַת עֵרוּב.

בַּהֲדֵין עֵרוּבָא יְהֵא שָׁרֵא לָנָא לַאֲפוּיֵי וּלְבַשּׁוּלֵי וּלְאַטְמוּנֵי וּלְאַדְלוּקֵי שְׁרָגָא וּלְתַקָּנָא וּלְמֶעְבַּד כָּל צָרְכָּנָא, מִיּוֹמָא טָבָא לְשַׁבְּתָא [לָנָא וּלְכָל יִשְׂרָאֵל* הַדָּרִים בָּעִיר הַזֹּאת].

ערובי תחומין

The *eruv*-food is put in a safe place [see commentary] and the following blessing and declaration are recited. The appropriate bracketed phrases should be added.

בָּרוּךְ אַתָּה יהוה אֱלֹהֵינוּ מֶלֶךְ הָעוֹלָם, אֲשֶׁר קִדְּשָׁנוּ בְּמִצְוֹתָיו, וְצִוָּנוּ עַל מִצְוַת עֵרוּב.

בְּזֶה הָעֵרוּב יְהֵא מֻתָּר [לִי/לָנוּ] לֵילֵךְ מִמָּקוֹם זֶה אַלְפַּיִם אַמָּה לְכָל רוּחַ בְּ[שַׁבָּת וּבְ]יוֹם טוֹב זֶה.

ערובי חצרות

This *eruv* is required for the Sabbath, but not for a weekday Festival [see commentary]. The *eruv*-foods are held while the following blessing and declaration are recited. [If the *eruv* is made for the entire year, the bracketed passage is added.]

בָּרוּךְ אַתָּה יהוה אֱלֹהֵינוּ מֶלֶךְ הָעוֹלָם, אֲשֶׁר קִדְּשָׁנוּ בְּמִצְוֹתָיו, וְצִוָּנוּ עַל מִצְוַת עֵרוּב.

בַּהֲדֵין עֵרוּבָא יְהֵא שָׁרֵא לָנָא לְאַפּוּקֵי וּלְעַיּוּלֵי מִן הַבָּתִּים לֶחָצֵר, וּמִן הֶחָצֵר לְבָתִּים, וּמִבַּיִת לְבַיִת, וּמֵחָצֵר לְחָצֵר, וּמִגַּג לְגַג, כָּל מַאי דִצְרִיךְ לָן, וּלְכָל יִשְׂרָאֵל הַדָּרִים בַּשְּׁכוּנָה זוּ [וּלְכָל מִי שֶׁיִּתּוֹסֵף בָּהּ, לְכָל שַׁבְּתוֹת הַשָּׁנָה, וּלְכָל יָמִים טוֹבִים].

עֵרוּב תַּבְשִׁילִין / ERUV TAVSHILIN

The Biblical prohibition against labor on the Festivals (*Exodus* 12:16) specifically excludes preparation of food. Still, it is forbidden to prepare food on a Festival for use on another day. When a Festival falls on Friday, however, it is permitted to prepare food needed for the Sabbath. But since this may lead people to think that they may even cook in preparation for a weekday, the Rabbis attached a condition to the preparation of Sabbath meals on a Festival — i.e., such preparations must be started before the Festival (*Pesachim* 46b). Thus, when Pesach falls on Thursday and Friday, preparations for the Sabbath meal must begin on Wednesday. This enactment is called *eruv tavshilin*, literally, *mingling of cooked foods*. It consists of a *matzah* along with any other cooked food (such as fish, meat or an egg), set aside on the day before the Festival to be eaten on the Sabbath. The *eruv*-foods are held in the hand (*Orach Chaim* 527:2) and a blessing is recited. Since the person setting the *eruv* must understand its purpose, the accompanying declaration [beginning בַּהֲדֵין, *'Through this ...'*] must be said in a language he understands.

וּלְכָל יִשְׂרָאֵל — *And for all Jews.* The bracketed phrase is recited only if the maker of the *eruv*

ERUV TAVSHILIN

When Pesach falls on Thursday and Friday, an *eruv tavshilin* is made on Wednesday Erev Pesach [see commentary]. The *eruv*-foods are held while the following blessing and declaration are recited.

בָּרוּךְ *Blessed are You, HASHEM, our God, King of the universe, Who has sanctified us with His commandments and has commanded us concerning the mitzvah of eruv.*

בַּהֲדֵין *Through this eruv may we be permitted to bake, cook, insulate, kindle flame, prepare, and do anything necessary on the Festival for the sake of the Sabbath [for ourselves and for all Jews* who live in this city].*

ERUVEI TECHUMIN

The *eruv*-food is put in a safe place [see commentary] and the following blessing and declaration are recited. The appropriate bracketed phrases should be added.

בָּרוּךְ *Blessed are You, HASHEM, our God, King of the universe, Who has sanctified us with His commandments and has commanded us concerning the mitzvah of eruv.*

בְּזֶה *Through this eruv may [I/we] be permitted to walk two thousand cubits in every direction from this place during this [Sabbath and] Festival.*

ERUVEI CHATZEIROS

This *eruv* is required for the Sabbath, but not for a weekday Festival [see commentary]. The *eruv*-foods are held while the following blessing and declaration are recited. [If the *eruv* is made for the entire year, the bracketed passage is added.]

בָּרוּךְ *Blessed are You, HASHEM, our God, King of the universe, Who has sanctified us with His commandments and has commanded us concerning the mitzvah of eruv.*

בַּהֲדֵין *Through this eruv may we be permitted to carry out or to carry in from the houses to the courtyard, and from the courtyard to the houses, from house to house, from courtyard to courtyard, and from roof to roof, all that we require, for ourselves and for all Jews who live in this area [and to all who will move into this area, for all the Sabbaths and Festivals of the year].*

---

wishes to include those who may not have made an *eruv* for themselves. If so, a second person (not the minor child of the maker) must act as agent for the townspeople and take possession of the *eruv*-foods on their behalf.

עֵרוּבֵי תְּחוּמִין /MERGING OF BOUNDARIES

On the Sabbath and Festivals, one is forbidden to go more than 2,000 cubits from his halachically defined dwelling. This limit is called his תְּחוּם, *boundary*. Ordinarily, this 'dwelling' is the town in which one resides, but one has the option of establishing his dwelling elsewhere. By placing a sufficient amount of food for two Sabbath meals in a place as much as 2,000 cubits from his 'dwelling,' one establishes *that* place as his 'dwelling,' and his 2,000-cubit radius is reckoned from there. [For a full discussion of *eruvei chatzeiros* and *techumin*, see the Introduction to the ArtScroll Mishnah *Eruvin*.]

עֵרוּבֵי חֲצֵרוֹת / MERGING OF COURTYARDS

The Sages forbade carrying from the private domain of one person to that of another on the Sabbath. Similarly a courtyard, hall, or staircase shared by the residents of houses or apartments is regarded as a separate domain, and it is forbidden to carry from the private dwellings into the shared area. The Sages also provided a procedure to remove this prohibition against carrying. Known as *eruvei chatzeiros*, or the 'merging of courtyards,' this procedure considers all houses opening into the shared area as

❧ הדלקת הנרות ❧

On the first two nights of Pesach two blessings are recited. When Pesach coincides with the Sabbath, light the candles, then cover the eyes and recite the blessings. Uncover the eyes and gaze briefly at the candles. When Pesach falls on a weekday, some follow the above procedure, while others recite the blessings before lighting the candles. When Pesach coincides with the Sabbath, the words in brackets are added.

[It is forbidden to create a new flame — for example, by striking a match — on *Yom Tov*. Therefore, on the second night (and on the first night when Erev Pesach falls on the Sabbath) the candles must be lit from a flame that has been burning from before *Yom Tov* (or the Sabbath).]

בָּרוּךְ אַתָּה יהוה אֱלֹהֵינוּ מֶלֶךְ הָעוֹלָם, אֲשֶׁר קִדְּשָׁנוּ בְּמִצְוֹתָיו, וְצִוָּנוּ לְהַדְלִיק נֵר* שֶׁל [שַׁבָּת וְשֶׁל] יוֹם טוֹב.*

בָּרוּךְ אַתָּה יהוה אֱלֹהֵינוּ מֶלֶךְ הָעוֹלָם, שֶׁהֶחֱיָנוּ* וְקִיְּמָנוּ וְהִגִּיעָנוּ לַזְּמַן הַזֶּה.

It is customary to recite the following prayer after the kindling. The words in brackets are included as they apply.

יְהִי רָצוֹן* לְפָנֶיךָ, יהוה אֱלֹהַי וֵאלֹהֵי אֲבוֹתַי, שֶׁתְּחוֹנֵן אוֹתִי [וְאֶת אִישִׁי, וְאֶת בָּנַי, וְאֶת בְּנוֹתַי, וְאֶת אָבִי, וְאֶת אִמִּי] וְאֶת כָּל קְרוֹבַי; וְתִתֶּן לָנוּ וּלְכָל יִשְׂרָאֵל חַיִּים טוֹבִים וַאֲרוּכִים; וְתִזְכְּרֵנוּ בְּזִכְרוֹן טוֹבָה וּבְרָכָה; וְתִפְקְדֵנוּ בִּפְקֻדַּת יְשׁוּעָה וְרַחֲמִים; וּתְבָרְכֵנוּ בְּרָכוֹת גְּדוֹלוֹת; וְתַשְׁלִים בָּתֵּינוּ; וְתַשְׁכֵּן שְׁכִינָתְךָ בֵּינֵינוּ. וְזַכֵּנִי לְגַדֵּל בָּנִים וּבְנֵי בָנִים חֲכָמִים וּנְבוֹנִים, אוֹהֲבֵי יהוה, יִרְאֵי אֱלֹהִים, אַנְשֵׁי אֱמֶת, זֶרַע קֹדֶשׁ, בַּיהוה דְּבֵקִים, וּמְאִירִים אֶת הָעוֹלָם בַּתּוֹרָה וּבְמַעֲשִׂים טוֹבִים, וּבְכָל מְלֶאכֶת עֲבוֹדַת הַבּוֹרֵא. אָנָּא שְׁמַע אֶת תְּחִנָּתִי בָּעֵת הַזֹּאת, בִּזְכוּת שָׂרָה וְרִבְקָה וְרָחֵל וְלֵאָה אִמּוֹתֵינוּ, וְהָאֵר נֵרֵנוּ שֶׁלֹּא יִכְבֶּה לְעוֹלָם וָעֶד, וְהָאֵר פָּנֶיךָ וְנִוָּשֵׁעָה. אָמֵן.

---

owned by a single consortium. This is done by collecting *matzah* from each of the families and placing all the *matzah* in one of the dwelling units. [Even if only one person supplies the *matzah*, it is still possible to make an *eruv*. In this case, a second person (not the minor child of the donor) must act as agent for all those involved and take possession of the *matzah* on their behalf.] This symbolizes that all the contributors are legal residents of the unit where they have deposited their *matzah* and the entire area is regarded as a single dwelling. All the residents may carry in all its parts on the Sabbath, as long as the *matzos* were available and edible at the onset of the Sabbath. [The declaration as given here may not be used if the *eruv* area includes a public thoroughfare. Such an area requires complex additional procedures which should not be undertaken by a layman.]

The restrictions on carrying apply only to the Sabbath and not to the Festivals. Thus, *eruvei chatzeiros* is only necessary for *Yom Tov* that falls on the Sabbath but not for the other days of the Festival.

❧ הַדְלָקַת הַנֵּרוֹת / KINDLING LIGHTS ❧

Since women generally look after household matters, the *mitzvah* of kindling the lights has devolved upon the mistress of the house (*Rambam*). Nevertheless, a man living alone is required to kindle the lights and recite the proper blessing. Similarly, if a woman is too ill to light, her husband should light the candles and recite the blessing (*Magen Avraham*).

There should be some light in every room where it will be needed—and indeed this is a

KINDLING LIGHTS

On the first two nights of Pesach two blessings are recited. When Pesach coincides with the Sabbath, light the candles, then cover the eyes and recite the blessings. Uncover the eyes and gaze briefly at the candles. When Pesach falls on a weekday, some follow the above procedure, while others recite the blessings before lighting the candles. When Pesach coincides with the Sabbath, the words in brackets are added.

[It is forbidden to create a new flame — for example, by striking a match — on *Yom Tov*. Therefore, on the second night (and on the first night when Erev Pesach falls on the Sabbath) the candles must be lit from a flame that has been burning from before *Yom Tov* (or the Sabbath).]

בָּרוּךְ *Blessed are You, HASHEM, our God, King of the universe, Who has sanctified us with His commandments, and has commanded us to kindle the light* of [the Sabbath and of] the Festival.**

בָּרוּךְ *Blessed are You, HASHEM, our God, King of the universe, Who has kept us alive,* sustained us, and brought us to this season.*

It is customary to recite the following prayer after the kindling. The words in brackets are included as they apply.

יְהִי רָצוֹן *May it be Your will,* HASHEM, my God and God of my forefathers, that You show favor to me [my husband, my sons, my daughters, my father, my mother] and all my relatives; and that You grant us and all Israel a good and long life; that You remember us with a beneficent memory and blessing; that You consider us with a consideration of salvation and compassion; that You bless us with great blessings; that You make our households complete; that You cause Your Presence to dwell among us. Privilege me to raise children and grandchildren who are wise and understanding, who love HASHEM and fear God, people of truth, holy offspring, attached to HASHEM, who illuminate the world with Torah and good deeds and with every labor in the service of the Creator. Please, hear my supplication at this time, in the merit of Sarah, Rebecca, Rachel, and Leah, our mothers, and cause our light to illuminate that it be not extinguished forever, and let Your countenance shine so that we are saved. Amen.*

---

halachic requirement—nevertheless, the blessing is recited upon the flames that are kindled in the dining room *(Mishnah Berurah)*. The lights honor the Sabbath and Festival by brightening and dignifying the festive meal *(Rashi)*.

נֵר — *The light.* Prevalent custom calls for at least two candles. According to *Eliyah Rabbah,* they symbolize man and wife. Nevertheless, since one can fulfill the *mitzvah* with a single candle [indeed, *Mishnah Berurah* advises one with extremely limited means to purchase one good candle rather than two inferior ones], the blessing is couched in the singular form, נֵר, *light*, and not נֵרוֹת, *lights*.

שֶׁל [שַׁבָּת וְשֶׁל] יוֹם טוֹב — *Of [the Sabbath and of] the Festival.* The Sabbath is mentioned first, following the Talmudic rule that a more frequently performed *mitzvah* takes precedence over a less frequent one.

שֶׁהֶחֱיָנוּ — *Who has kept us alive.* Some authorities rule that women should not recite the שֶׁהֶחֱיָנוּ blessing at this point, but instead should listen to the blessing during *Kiddush*, as does the rest of the family. However, it is a virtually universal custom that women do recite the blessing when kindling the lights.

יְהִי רָצוֹן — *May it be Your will.* It is customary to recite this prayer after the kindling. Because of the Talmudic declaration, 'One who is scrupulous in the kindling of lights will be blessed with children who are Torah scholars' *(Shabbos* 23b), the prayer stresses the supplication that the children of the home grow up learned and righteous.

מנחה לערב פסח

WHEN EREV PESACH FALLS ON THE SABBATH THE REGULAR MINCHAH FOR THE SABBATH IS RECITED

אַשְׁרֵי יוֹשְׁבֵי בֵיתֶךָ, עוֹד יְהַלְלוּךָ סֶּלָה.[1] אַשְׁרֵי הָעָם שֶׁכָּכָה לּוֹ, אַשְׁרֵי הָעָם שֶׁיהוה אֱלֹהָיו.[2]

תהלים קמה

תְּהִלָּה לְדָוִד,

אֲרוֹמִמְךָ* אֱלוֹהַי הַמֶּלֶךְ, וַאֲבָרְכָה שִׁמְךָ לְעוֹלָם וָעֶד.
בְּכָל יוֹם אֲבָרְכֶךָּ,* וַאֲהַלְלָה שִׁמְךָ לְעוֹלָם וָעֶד.
גָּדוֹל יהוה וּמְהֻלָּל מְאֹד, וְלִגְדֻלָּתוֹ אֵין חֵקֶר.*
דּוֹר לְדוֹר יְשַׁבַּח מַעֲשֶׂיךָ, וּגְבוּרֹתֶיךָ יַגִּידוּ.
הֲדַר כְּבוֹד הוֹדֶךָ, וְדִבְרֵי נִפְלְאֹתֶיךָ אָשִׂיחָה.
וֶעֱזוּז נוֹרְאוֹתֶיךָ יֹאמֵרוּ, וּגְדוּלָּתְךָ אֲסַפְּרֶנָּה.
זֵכֶר רַב טוּבְךָ יַבִּיעוּ, וְצִדְקָתְךָ יְרַנֵּנוּ.
חַנּוּן וְרַחוּם* יהוה, אֶרֶךְ אַפַּיִם וּגְדָל חָסֶד.
טוֹב יהוה לַכֹּל, וְרַחֲמָיו עַל כָּל מַעֲשָׂיו.
יוֹדוּךָ יהוה כָּל מַעֲשֶׂיךָ, וַחֲסִידֶיךָ יְבָרְכוּכָה.
כְּבוֹד מַלְכוּתְךָ יֹאמֵרוּ, וּגְבוּרָתְךָ יְדַבֵּרוּ.
לְהוֹדִיעַ לִבְנֵי הָאָדָם גְּבוּרֹתָיו, וּכְבוֹד הֲדַר מַלְכוּתוֹ.

מִנְחָה לְעֶרֶב פֶּסַח / MINCHAH FOR EREV PESACH

The Talmud tells us that *Minchah* corresponds to — and substitutes for — the *[tamid]* daily afternoon offering of the Temple service, and that this prayer was first introduced by the Patriarch Isaac (*Berachos* 26b). These two factors explain both the time and the mood of this prayer.

The daily afternoon *tamid* could be brought no earlier that half an hour after midday; consequently *Minchah* may be recited only from that time onward. It is preferable, however, not to begin *Minchah* earlier than three and a half hours after midday, because the *tamid* was customarily delayed until then (*Orach Chaim* 233:1). Another reason that *Minchah* is left for late afternoon is because that part of the day is a time of Divine mercy. It was then that God answered Elijah's prayer for vindication (*I Kings* 18:36) and that Isaac went out to the field to pray (*Genesis* 24:63).

Since Isaac originated the *Minchah* prayer, it is logical that we find in his life a clue to the prayer's significance. Unlike his father Abraham whose life was a story of uninterrupted success, ascension, and the gaining of universal respect, Isaac was envied and persecuted by the reigning kings and dominant peoples of Canaan, and ended his life in blindness, saddened by the conflicts that put an end to the domestic tranquility of his family. Thus, whereas Abraham's life is like the expectancy of a new day, Isaac's story is symbolized by the sun descending from its noontime zenith to the gloom and fear of night.

Abraham inaugurated the morning prayer, which is brightened by psalms of praise, the proclamation of God's Oneness and the blessings of the *Shema,* which acknowledge God as the Creator of light, wisdom, and salvation. In stark contrast, Isaac's *Minchah* prayer consists almost exclusively of the *Shemoneh Esrei* with its acknowledgment of our total dependence on God for all our personal and national needs.

אַשְׁרֵי / Ashrei

The Sages teach that one should pray in a state of joyous dedication to God's will. To accomplish this, they inserted *Ashrei* prior to *Shemoneh Esrei,* because *Ashrei* concludes with verses that express confidence in God's goodness and concern for His servants.

Psalm 145 begins with the verse תְּהִלָּה לְדָוִד;

MINCHAH FOR EREV PESACH

WHEN EREV PESACH FALLS ON THE SABBATH THE REGULAR MINCHAH FOR THE SABBATH IS RECITED

אַשְׁרֵי *Praiseworthy are those who dwell in Your house; may they always praise You, Selah!*[1] *Praiseworthy is the people for whom this is so, praiseworthy is the people whose God is* HASHEM.[2]

Psalm 145 *A psalm of praise by David:*

א *I will exalt You,* my God the King,*
and I will bless Your Name forever and ever.

ב *Every day I will bless You,**
and I will laud Your Name forever and ever.

ג HASHEM *is great and exceedingly lauded,*
*and His greatness is beyond investigation.**

ד *Each generation will praise Your deeds to the next*
and of Your mighty deeds they will tell;

ה *The splendrous glory of Your power*
and Your wondrous deeds I shall discuss.

ו *And of Your awesome power they will speak,*
and Your greatness I shall relate.

ז *A recollection of Your abundant goodness they will utter*
and of Your righteousness they will sing exultantly.

ח *Gracious and merciful* is* HASHEM,
slow to anger, and great in [bestowing] kindness.

ט HASHEM *is good to all; His mercies are on all His works.*

י *All Your works shall thank You,* HASHEM,
and Your devout ones will bless You.

כ *Of the glory of Your kingdom they will speak,*
and of Your power they will tell;

ל *To inform human beings of His mighty deeds,*
and the glorious splendor of His kingdom.

(1) *Psalms* 84:5. (2) 144:15.

---

the two preliminary verses, each beginning with the word אַשְׁרֵי, are affixed to תְּהִלָּה לְדָוִד for two reasons: (a) By expressing the idea that those who can dwell in God's house of prayer and service are praiseworthy, these verses set the stage for the succeeding psalm of praise, for we, the praiseworthy ones, are about to laud the God in Whose house we dwell; and (b) the word אַשְׁרֵי is found three times in these verses. This alludes to the Talmudic dictum that one who recites psalm 145 three times a day is assured of a share in the World to Come (*Berachos* 4b); thus, those who do so are indeed אַשְׁרֵי, *praiseworthy.*

תְּהִלָּה . . . אֲרוֹמִמְךָ — *A psalm . . . I will exalt You.* Beginning with the word אֲרוֹמִמְךָ, the initials of the respective verses follow the order of the *Aleph-Beis.* According to *Abudraham* the *Aleph-Beis* structure symbolizes that we praise God with every sound available to the organs of speech. *Midrash Tadshei* records that the Psalmists and Sages used the *Aleph-Beis* formula in chapters that they wanted people to follow more easily or memorize.

בְּכָל יוֹם אֲבָרְכֶךָּ — *Every day I will bless You.* True, no mortal can pretend to know God's essence, but each of us *is* equipped to appreciate life, health, sustenance, sunshine, rainfall, and so on. For them and their daily renewal, we give daily blessings *(Siach Yitzchak).*

וְלִגְדֻלָּתוֹ אֵין חֵקֶר — *And His greatness is beyond investigation.* Much though we may try, we can understand neither God's essence nor His ways through human analysis, for He is infinite. We *must* rely on the traditions that have come to us from earlier generations, as the next verse suggests *(Rama).*

חַנּוּן וְרַחוּם — *Gracious and merciful.* Because God is *merciful,* He is אֶרֶךְ אַפַּיִם, *slow to anger,* so that punishment, although deserved, is delayed

מַלְכוּתְךָ מַלְכוּת כָּל עֹלָמִים, וּמֶמְשַׁלְתְּךָ בְּכָל דּוֹר וָדֹר.
סוֹמֵךְ יהוה* לְכָל הַנֹּפְלִים, וְזוֹקֵף לְכָל הַכְּפוּפִים.
עֵינֵי כֹל אֵלֶיךָ יְשַׂבֵּרוּ,* וְאַתָּה נוֹתֵן לָהֶם אֶת אָכְלָם בְּעִתּוֹ.
פּוֹתֵחַ* אֶת יָדֶךָ, וּמַשְׂבִּיעַ לְכָל חַי רָצוֹן.

Concentrate intently while reciting the verse, פּוֹתֵחַ.

צַדִּיק יהוה בְּכָל דְּרָכָיו, וְחָסִיד* בְּכָל מַעֲשָׂיו.
קָרוֹב יהוה לְכָל קֹרְאָיו, לְכֹל אֲשֶׁר יִקְרָאֻהוּ בֶאֱמֶת.
רְצוֹן יְרֵאָיו יַעֲשֶׂה, וְאֶת שַׁוְעָתָם יִשְׁמַע וְיוֹשִׁיעֵם.
שׁוֹמֵר יהוה אֶת כָּל אֹהֲבָיו, וְאֵת כָּל הָרְשָׁעִים יַשְׁמִיד.
❖ תְּהִלַּת יהוה יְדַבֶּר פִּי, וִיבָרֵךְ כָּל בָּשָׂר שֵׁם קָדְשׁוֹ לְעוֹלָם
וָעֶד. וַאֲנַחְנוּ נְבָרֵךְ* יָהּ, מֵעַתָּה וְעַד עוֹלָם, הַלְלוּיָהּ.*[1]

Chazzan recites חֲצִי קַדִּישׁ.

יִתְגַּדַּל וְיִתְקַדַּשׁ שְׁמֵהּ רַבָּא. (Cong.– אָמֵן.) בְּעָלְמָא דִּי בְרָא כִרְעוּתֵהּ. וְיַמְלִיךְ מַלְכוּתֵהּ, בְּחַיֵּיכוֹן וּבְיוֹמֵיכוֹן וּבְחַיֵּי דְכָל בֵּית יִשְׂרָאֵל, בַּעֲגָלָא וּבִזְמַן קָרִיב. וְאִמְרוּ: אָמֵן.

(Cong.– אָמֵן. יְהֵא שְׁמֵהּ רַבָּא מְבָרַךְ לְעָלַם וּלְעָלְמֵי עָלְמַיָּא.)

יְהֵא שְׁמֵהּ רַבָּא מְבָרַךְ לְעָלַם וּלְעָלְמֵי עָלְמַיָּא.

יִתְבָּרַךְ וְיִשְׁתַּבַּח וְיִתְפָּאַר וְיִתְרוֹמַם וְיִתְנַשֵּׂא וְיִתְהַדָּר וְיִתְעַלֶּה וְיִתְהַלָּל שְׁמֵהּ דְּקֻדְשָׁא בְּרִיךְ הוּא (Cong.– בְּרִיךְ הוּא) — לְעֵלָּא מִן כָּל בִּרְכָתָא וְשִׁירָתָא תֻּשְׁבְּחָתָא וְנֶחֱמָתָא, דַּאֲמִירָן בְּעָלְמָא. וְאִמְרוּ: אָמֵן. (Cong.– אָמֵן.)

---

as long as possible to allow time for repentance. And because He is *gracious* He is גְּדָל חָסֶד, *great in bestowing kindness* (*Siach Yitzchak*).

סוֹמֵךְ ה׳ — *HASHEM supports.* No verse in *Ashrei* begins with a נ, because in the context of this verse that speaks of God supporting the fallen, the letter נ can be taken as an allusion to נְפִילָה, Israel's future *downfall*, ח״ו, and the Psalmist refused to use a letter that could suggest such tragedy. Nevertheless, knowing that downfalls would take place, the Psalmist comforted Israel by saying *God supports all the fallen ones.* This is an implied guarantee that even when a dreaded downfall happens, the people can look forward to His support (*Berachos* 4b). *Maharsha* comments that by omitting a direct mention of downfall, the Psalmist implies that even when Israel *does* suffer reverses, those reverses will never be complete. Rather, as the next verse declares, God will support the fallen.

עֵינֵי כֹל אֵלֶיךָ יְשַׂבֵּרוּ — *The eyes of all look to You with hope.* Even animals instinctively rely upon God for their sustenance [how much more so should man recognize the beneficence of his Maker!] (*Radak*).

פּוֹתֵחַ — *[You] open.* When reciting this verse, one must have in mind the translation of the words because this declaration of God's universal goodness is one of the two reasons the Sages required the thrice-daily recitation of this psalm. One who forgot to concentrate on the translation must recite the verse again (*Tur* and *Shulchan Aruch* 51:7). This verse should be recited with great joy at the knowledge that God cares for every creature (*Yesod V'Shoresh HaAvodah*).

צַדִּיק . . . וְחָסִיד — *Righteous . . . and magnanimous.* That God's ways are just and righteous means that He judges people only according to their deeds. Nevertheless, even when justice calls for grievous punishment He is *magnanimous* in softening the blow, for He is merciful (*Vilna Gaon*).

וַאֲנַחְנוּ נְבָרֵךְ — *We will bless.* After completing psalm 145 which holds an assurance of the World to Come, we append this verse in which we express the hope that we will bless God *forever* — that is, in both worlds (*Levush*).

הַלְלוּיָהּ — *Halleluyah.* This familiar word is a contraction of two words: הַלְלוּ יָהּ, *praise God.* The term הַלְלוּ denotes crying out in happy

מ *Your kingdom is a kingdom spanning all eternities,*
and Your dominion is throughout every generation.
ס *HASHEM supports* all the fallen ones and straightens all the bent.*
ע *The eyes of all look to You with hope**
and You give them their food in its proper time;
פ *You open* Your hand,* Concentrate intently while reciting the verse, *'You open...'*
and satisfy the desire of every living thing.
צ *Righteous is HASHEM in all His ways*
and magnanimous in all His deeds.*
ק *HASHEM is close to all who call upon Him —*
to all who call upon Him sincerely.
ר *The will of those who fear Him He will do;*
and their cry He will hear, and save them.
ש *HASHEM protects all who love Him;*
but all the wicked He will destroy.
ת Chazzan– *May my mouth declare the praise of HASHEM*
and may all flesh bless His Holy Name forever and ever.
We will bless God from this time and forever, Halleluyah!**[1]

Chazzan recites Half-*Kaddish:*

יִתְגַּדַּל *May His great Name grow exalted and sanctified* (Cong.– *Amen.*) *in the world that He created as He willed. May He give reign to His kingship in your lifetimes and in your days, and in the lifetimes of the entire Family of Israel, swiftly and soon. Now respond: Amen.*

(Cong.– *Amen. May His great Name be blessed forever and ever.*)
May His great Name be blessed forever and ever.

Blessed, praised, glorified, exalted, extolled, mighty, upraised, and lauded be the Name of the Holy One, Blessed is He (Cong.– *Blessed is He*) — *beyond any blessing and song, praise and consolation that are uttered in the world. Now respond: Amen.* (Cong.– *Amen.*)

(1) *Psalms* 115:18.

excitement, while the unique meaning implied by the Name יָהּ means 'the One Who is forever.' The Psalmist addresses everyone, saying: Use your energy to be *excited* over God and nothing else *(R' Avigdor Miller).*

❧ שְׁמוֹנֶה עֶשְׂרֵה / SHEMONEH ESREI ☙

The Talmud refers to *Shemoneh Esrei* simply as תְּפִלָּה, *The Prayer,* for it is only in *Shemoneh Esrei* that we formulate our needs and ask God to fulfill them. The three *Shemoneh Esrei* prayers of the day were instituted by the Patriarchs and they are in place of the daily Temple offerings *(Berachos* 26b).

The term *Shemoneh Esrei* means eighteen, and, indeed, the original *Shemoneh Esrei* consisted of eighteen blessings. The requirement that there be precisely eighteen is based on various Scriptural supports (*Megillah* 17b). The text of the individual blessings was composed by the Men of the Great Assembly at the beginning of the Second Temple period, and it was put into its final form under Rabban Gamliel II after the Destruction, over four centuries later (ibid.). A nineteenth blessing was added later (see commentary to וְלַמַּלְשִׁינִים, p. 18), but the name *Shemoneh Esrei* was left unchanged. The *Zohar* refers to the *Shemoneh Esrei* as the *Amidah* ['standing prayer'], and the two names are used interchangeably.

Shemoneh Esrei has three sections: (a) In the first three blessings, the supplicant pays homage to God, like a slave praising his master before he dares make a request; (b) the middle section of thirteen (originally, twelve) blessings contains the supplicant's requests; (c) in the last three blessings, he takes leave, expressing gratitude and confidence in his Master's graciousness *(Berachos* 34a).

Even the middle section is not merely a catalogue of selfish requests. In each blessing, we first acknowledge God's mastery, and only then make the request. Thus, each blessing is an affirmation of God's power *(Vilna Gaon).*

שמונה עשרה – עמידה

Take three steps backward, then three steps forward. Remain standing with feet together while reciting *Shemoneh Esrei*. Recite it with quiet devotion and without interruption, verbal or otherwise. Although it should not be audible to others, one must pray loudly enough to hear himself.

כִּי שֵׁם יהוה אֶקְרָא,* הָבוּ גֹדֶל לֵאלֹהֵינוּ.[1]
אֲדֹנָי שְׂפָתַי תִּפְתָּח,* וּפִי יַגִּיד תְּהִלָּתֶךָ.[2]

אבות

Bend the knees at בָּרוּךְ; bow at אַתָּה; straighten up at ה׳.

בָּרוּךְ אַתָּה* יהוה אֱלֹהֵינוּ וֵאלֹהֵי אֲבוֹתֵינוּ,* אֱלֹהֵי אַבְרָהָם, אֱלֹהֵי יִצְחָק, וֵאלֹהֵי יַעֲקֹב, הָאֵל הַגָּדוֹל הַגִּבּוֹר וְהַנּוֹרָא, אֵל עֶלְיוֹן,* גּוֹמֵל חֲסָדִים טוֹבִים וְקוֹנֵה הַכֹּל,* וְזוֹכֵר חַסְדֵי אָבוֹת, וּמֵבִיא גוֹאֵל* לִבְנֵי בְנֵיהֶם, לְמַעַן שְׁמוֹ בְּאַהֲבָה.

Bend the knees at בָּרוּךְ; bow at אַתָּה; straighten up at ה׳.

מֶלֶךְ עוֹזֵר וּמוֹשִׁיעַ וּמָגֵן.* בָּרוּךְ אַתָּה יהוה, מָגֵן אַבְרָהָם.*

גבורות

אַתָּה גִּבּוֹר לְעוֹלָם אֲדֹנָי, מְחַיֵּה מֵתִים* אַתָּה, רַב לְהוֹשִׁיעַ. מַשִּׁיב הָרוּחַ וּמוֹרִיד הַגֶּשֶׁם, מְכַלְכֵּל חַיִּים בְּחֶסֶד, מְחַיֵּה מֵתִים בְּרַחֲמִים רַבִּים, סוֹמֵךְ נוֹפְלִים, וְרוֹפֵא חוֹלִים, וּמַתִּיר אֲסוּרִים, וּמְקַיֵּם אֱמוּנָתוֹ לִישֵׁנֵי עָפָר. מִי כָמוֹךָ בַּעַל גְּבוּרוֹת, וּמִי דּוֹמֶה לָּךְ, מֶלֶךְ מֵמִית וּמְחַיֶּה וּמַצְמִיחַ יְשׁוּעָה.* וְנֶאֱמָן אַתָּה לְהַחֲיוֹת מֵתִים. בָּרוּךְ אַתָּה יהוה, מְחַיֵּה הַמֵּתִים.

◆§ Introductory Phrases

כִּי שֵׁם ה׳ אֶקְרָא — *When I call out the Name of* HASHEM. Moses introduced his final prophecies and prayers for Israel's redemption with this verse *[Deuteronomy* 32:3]. In effect he said to Israel, 'When I call out God's Name in prayer, do not respond that He has forsaken us. God will keep His promises despite your shortcomings' *(Sforno).*

אֲדֹנָי שְׂפָתַי תִּפְתָּח — *My Lord, open my lips . . . Ramban* notes that שְׂפָתַי, *my lips,* can also mean *my boundaries.* Thus we ask God to free us from our limitations so that we can praise Him properly.

◆§ אָבוֹת / Patriarchs

The first blessing of *Shemoneh Esrei* is known as אָבוֹת, *Patriarchs,* because it recalls the greatness of our forefathers in whose merit God pledged to help Israel throughout history, even if we are unworthy.

בָּרוּךְ אַתָּה — *Blessed are You.* [Since God is perfect by definition, what benefit can man's blessing confer upon Him?]

— This is a declaration of fact: God *is* blessed in the sense that He is perfect and complete *(Sefer HaChinuch* 430).

— God is the *Source* of inexhaustible blessing, and He has created the world in order to do good to His creatures. Since this is His will, we pray for the Redemption, when man will be worthy of His utmost blessing *(Rashba; R' Bachya).*

אֱלֹהֵינוּ וֵאלֹהֵי אֲבוֹתֵינוּ — *Our God and the God of our forefathers.* First we call Him *our God* because we are obligated to serve Him and know Him to the limit of *our* capacity. But there is much about His ways that we cannot understand. In response to such doubts we proclaim that He is *the God of our forefathers,* and we have faith in the tradition they transmitted *(Dover Shalom).*

אֵל עֶלְיוֹן — *The supreme God.* The word עֶלְיוֹן, *supreme,* means that God is so exalted that He is far beyond the comprehension of even the holiest angels. We can understand Him only superficially, by studying His deeds, i.e., that He *bestows beneficial kindnesses (Siach Yitzchak).*

SHEMONEH ESREI – AMIDAH

Take three steps backward, then three steps forward. Remain standing with feet together while reciting *Shemoneh Esrei*. Recite it with quiet devotion and without interruption, verbal or otherwise. Although it should not be audible to others, one must pray loudly enough to hear himself.

When I call out the Name of HASHEM, ascribe greatness to our God.*[1] *My Lord, open my lips,* that my mouth may declare Your praise.*[2]

PATRIARCHS

Bend the knees at *'Blessed'*; bow at *'You'*; straighten up at *'HASHEM.'*

בָּרוּךְ *Blessed are You,* HASHEM, our God and the God of our forefathers,* God of Abraham, God of Isaac, and God of Jacob; the great, mighty, and awesome God, the supreme God,* Who bestows beneficial kindnesses and creates everything,* Who recalls the kindnesses of the Patriarchs and brings a Redeemer* to their children's children, for His Name's sake, with love.*

Bend the knees at *'Blessed'*; bow at *'You'*; straighten up at *'HASHEM.'*

O King, Helper, Savior, and Shield. Blessed are You, HASHEM, Shield of Abraham.**

GOD'S MIGHT

אַתָּה *You are eternally mighty, my Lord, the Resuscitator of the dead* are You; abundantly able to save. He makes the wind blow and He makes the dew descend, He sustains the living with kindness, resuscitates the dead with abundant mercy, supports the fallen, heals the sick, releases the confined, and maintains His faith to those asleep in the dust. Who is like You, O Master of mighty deeds, and who is comparable to You, O King Who causes death and restores life and makes salvation sprout!* And You are faithful to resuscitate the dead. Blessed are You, HASHEM, Who resuscitates the dead.*

(1) *Deuteronomy* 32:3. (2) *Psalms* 51:17.

וְקוֹנֵה הַכֹּל — *And creates everything.* The translation is based on the consensus of commentators, both here and to *Genesis* 14:19. Some translate *the Owner of everything.* Either way, the sense of the phrase is that God is Master of all creation.

וּמֵבִיא גוֹאֵל — *And brings a Redeemer.* The phrase is in the present tense. Every event, no matter how terrible it may seem, is a step toward the ultimate redemption by the Messiah (*Siach Yitzchak*).

עוֹזֵר וּמוֹשִׁיעַ וּמָגֵן — *Helper, Savior, and Shield.* God 'helps' [עוֹזֵר] those who try to help themselves; He 'saves' [מוֹשִׁיעַ] even without the victim's participation; and 'shields' [מָגֵן] to prevent danger from approaching (*Iyun Tefillah*). In a different interpretation, *B'nai Yisas'char* comments that עוֹזֵר refers to the help that God gives without any prayer on the part of the victim, while מוֹשִׁיעַ refers to God's response to a prayer.

מָגֵן אַבְרָהָם — *Shield of Abraham.* God preserves the spark of Abraham within every Jew, no matter how far he may have strayed (*Chidushei HaRim*).

גְּבוּרוֹת / God's Might

מְחַיֵּה מֵתִים — *The Resuscitator of the dead.* The concept that God restores life is found three times in this section, alluding to the three kinds of resuscitation: man's awakening every morning after deathlike slumber; the rain that has the life-sustaining quality of making vegetation grow; and the literal resuscitation of the dead, that will take place in the Messianic age (*Abudraham*).

וּמַצְמִיחַ יְשׁוּעָה — *And makes salvation sprout.* Good deeds are like seeds that are planted and produce crops. People can earn resuscitation because of the good their children do or because of beneficial results of undertakings they initiated in their lifetimes (*Siach Yitzchak*).

During the *chazzan's* repetition, *Kedushah* (below) is recited at this point.

קדושת השם

אַתָּה קָדוֹשׁ וְשִׁמְךָ קָדוֹשׁ,* וּקְדוֹשִׁים* בְּכָל יוֹם יְהַלְּלוּךָ סֶּלָה. בָּרוּךְ אַתָּה יהוה, הָאֵל הַקָּדוֹשׁ.

בינה

אַתָּה חוֹנֵן לְאָדָם דַּעַת,* וּמְלַמֵּד לֶאֱנוֹשׁ בִּינָה. חָנֵּנוּ מֵאִתְּךָ דֵּעָה בִּינָה וְהַשְׂכֵּל. בָּרוּךְ אַתָּה יהוה, חוֹנֵן הַדָּעַת.

קדושה

When reciting *Kedushah,* one must stand with his feet together and avoid any interruptions. One should rise on his toes when saying the words קָדוֹשׁ, קָדוֹשׁ, קָדוֹשׁ; בָּרוּךְ (of בָּרוּךְ כְּבוֹד); and יִמְלֹךְ.

Cong. then *Chazzan* – **נְקַדֵּשׁ** אֶת שִׁמְךָ בָּעוֹלָם, כְּשֵׁם שֶׁמַּקְדִּישִׁים אוֹתוֹ בִּשְׁמֵי מָרוֹם, כַּכָּתוּב עַל יַד נְבִיאֶךָ, וְקָרָא זֶה אֶל זֶה וְאָמַר:

All – קָדוֹשׁ קָדוֹשׁ קָדוֹשׁ* יהוה צְבָאוֹת, מְלֹא כָל הָאָרֶץ כְּבוֹדוֹ.*[1]

Chazzan – לְעֻמָּתָם בָּרוּךְ יֹאמֵרוּ:*

All – בָּרוּךְ כְּבוֹד יהוה, מִמְּקוֹמוֹ.[2]

Chazzan – וּבְדִבְרֵי קָדְשְׁךָ כָּתוּב לֵאמֹר:

All – יִמְלֹךְ יהוה* לְעוֹלָם, אֱלֹהַיִךְ צִיּוֹן לְדֹר וָדֹר, הַלְלוּיָהּ.[3]

Chazzan only concludes – לְדוֹר וָדוֹר נַגִּיד גָּדְלֶךָ וּלְנֵצַח נְצָחִים קְדֻשָּׁתְךָ נַקְדִּישׁ, וְשִׁבְחֲךָ אֱלֹהֵינוּ מִפִּינוּ לֹא יָמוּשׁ לְעוֹלָם וָעֶד, כִּי אֵל מֶלֶךְ גָּדוֹל וְקָדוֹשׁ אָתָּה. בָּרוּךְ אַתָּה יהוה, הָאֵל הַקָּדוֹשׁ.

Chazzan continues . . . אַתָּה חוֹנֵן (above).

קְדוּשָּׁה / Kedushah

Kedushah, Sanctification, expresses the concept that God is exalted above and separated from the limitations of material existence. When a *minyan* (quorum of ten) is present, it becomes the representative of the nation and echoes the angels who sing God's praise by proclaiming His holiness and glory. We do this by reciting *Kedushah,* a prayer based on that of the angels themselves, and with feet together, in the manner of the angels (*Ezekiel* 1:7). When reciting the words קָדוֹשׁ, קָדוֹשׁ, קָדוֹשׁ; בָּרוּךְ (of בָּרוּךְ כְּבוֹד); and יִמְלֹךְ, we rise up on our toes to symbolize that we seek to break loose from the bonds of earth and unite our service with that of the angels.

Based on the teachings of *Arizal,* everyone recites the entire *Kedushah* (from נְקַדֵּשׁ until הַלְלוּיָהּ), even the parts labeled *'Chazzan.'* Many congregations, however, follow the custom recorded in *Shulchan Aruch* (ch. 125) that only the verses labeled 'Cong.' or 'All' are recited by everyone. Each congregation, of course, should maintain its own custom.

קָדוֹשׁ קָדוֹשׁ קָדוֹשׁ — *Holy, holy, holy.* God is *holy* with relation to the physical world, *holy* with relation to the spiritual world and *holy* with relation to the World to Come (*Targum Yonasan*).

מְלֹא כָל הָאָרֶץ כְּבוֹדוֹ — *The whole world is filled with His glory.* Man can bring God's holiness — awesome though it is — to earth, by fulfilling the Torah's commandments (*Zohar*).

לְעֻמָּתָם בָּרוּךְ יֹאמֵרוּ — *Those facing them say 'Blessed.'* They respond to קָדוֹשׁ, *Holy . . .,* with the verse . . . בָּרוּךְ כְּבוֹד, *Blessed is the glory,* which the congregation will now recite in full.

יִמְלֹךְ ה׳ — HASHEM *shall reign.* The Sages inserted this verse into *Kedushah* because they wanted all prayers to include an implied or

During the *chazzan's* repetition, *Kedushah* (below) is recited at this point.

HOLINESS OF GOD'S NAME

אַתָּה *You are holy and Your Name is holy,* and holy ones* praise You every day, forever. Blessed are You, HASHEM, the holy God.*

INSIGHT

אַתָּה *You graciously endow man with wisdom* and teach insight to a frail mortal. Endow us graciously from Yourself with wisdom, insight, and discernment. Blessed are You, HASHEM, gracious Giver of wisdom.*

KEDUSHAH

When reciting *Kedushah*, one must stand with his feet together and avoid any interruptions. One should rise on his toes when saying *Holy, holy, holy; Blessed is;* and *HASHEM shall reign.*

Cong. then Chazzan – **נְקַדֵּשׁ** *We shall sanctify Your Name in this world, just as they sanctify it in heaven above, as it is written by Your prophet, "And one [angel] will call another and say:*

All – *'Holy, holy, holy* is HASHEM, Master of Legions, the whole world is filled with His glory.' "*[1]*

Chazzan – *Those facing them say 'Blessed':**

All – *'Blessed is the glory of HASHEM from His place.'[2]*

Chazzan – *And in Your holy Writings the following is written:*

All – *'HASHEM shall reign* forever — your God, O Zion — from generation to generation, Halleluyah!'[3]*

Chazzan only concludes – *From generation to generation we shall relate Your greatness and for infinite eternities we shall proclaim Your holiness. Your praise, our God, shall not leave our mouth forever and ever, for You, O God, are a great and holy King. Blessed are You, HASHEM, the holy God.*

Chazzan continues אַתָּה חוֹנֵן, *You graciously endow* . . . (above).

(1) *Isaiah* 6:3. (2) *Ezekiel* 3:12. (3) *Psalms* 146:10.

---

direct plea for the rebuilding of Jerusalem [Zion] (*Abudraham*).

קְדוּשַּׁת הַשֵּׁם / Holiness of God's Name

See prefatory comment to *Kedushah*.

אַתָּה קָדוֹשׁ וְשִׁמְךָ קָדוֹשׁ — *You are holy and Your Name is holy.* The 'Name' of God refers to the manner in which we perceive His actions. The person who enjoys good health and prosperity perceives God as the 'Merciful One,' whereas the person who suffers pain and poverty sees Him as the God of Judgment.

וּקְדוֹשִׁים — *And holy ones.* The term may refer to the angels (*Iyun Tefillah*) or, as most commentators agree, to Israel (*Abudraham*). As *Ramban* (*Leviticus* 18:2) defines it, human holiness is measured by how well a person controls his permissible desires. Someone who seeks ways to indulge his lusts and passions without directly violating the law is described as a נָבָל בִּרְשׁוּת הַתּוֹרָה, *degenerate with the Torah's permission.*

בִּינָה / Insight

אַתָּה חוֹנֵן לְאָדָם דַּעַת — *You graciously endow man with wisdom.* [This blessing begins the middle section of the *Shemoneh Esrei,* in which man makes his requests of God. The first plea is for wisdom and understanding — because man's intelligence is his primary characteristic, the one that sets him apart from animals.] We ask for *wisdom* and for *insight,* so that we can draw proper conclusions and achieve intellectual *discernment* (*Vilna Gaon*).

Only wisdom that is in accord with God's will is our assurance that we will indeed act wisely (*Mei Marom*).

תשובה

הֲשִׁיבֵנוּ אָבִינוּ* לְתוֹרָתֶךָ, וְקָרְבֵנוּ מַלְכֵּנוּ לַעֲבוֹדָתֶךָ, וְהַחֲזִירֵנוּ* בִּתְשׁוּבָה שְׁלֵמָה לְפָנֶיךָ. בָּרוּךְ אַתָּה יהוה, הָרוֹצֶה בִּתְשׁוּבָה.

סליחה

Strike the left side of the chest with the right fist while reciting the words חָטָאנוּ and פָּשָׁעְנוּ.

סְלַח לָנוּ אָבִינוּ כִּי חָטָאנוּ, מְחַל לָנוּ מַלְכֵּנוּ* כִּי פָשָׁעְנוּ, כִּי מוֹחֵל וְסוֹלֵחַ אָתָּה. בָּרוּךְ אַתָּה יהוה, חַנּוּן הַמַּרְבֶּה לִסְלוֹחַ.

גאולה

רְאֵה בְעָנְיֵנוּ,* וְרִיבָה רִיבֵנוּ, וּגְאָלֵנוּ[1] מְהֵרָה לְמַעַן שְׁמֶךָ,* כִּי גוֹאֵל חָזָק אָתָּה. בָּרוּךְ אַתָּה יהוה, גּוֹאֵל יִשְׂרָאֵל.

רפואה

רְפָאֵנוּ יהוה וְנֵרָפֵא,* הוֹשִׁיעֵנוּ וְנִוָּשֵׁעָה, כִּי תְהִלָּתֵנוּ אָתָּה,[2] וְהַעֲלֵה רְפוּאָה שְׁלֵמָה לְכָל מַכּוֹתֵינוּ, °°כִּי אֵל מֶלֶךְ רוֹפֵא נֶאֱמָן וְרַחֲמָן אָתָּה. בָּרוּךְ אַתָּה יהוה, רוֹפֵא חוֹלֵי עַמּוֹ יִשְׂרָאֵל.

ברכת השנים

בָּרֵךְ עָלֵינוּ* יהוה אֱלֹהֵינוּ אֶת הַשָּׁנָה הַזֹּאת וְאֶת כָּל מִינֵי תְבוּאָתָהּ לְטוֹבָה, וְתֵן טַל וּמָטָר לִבְרָכָה עַל פְּנֵי הָאֲדָמָה, וְשַׂבְּעֵנוּ מִטּוּבֶךָ, וּבָרֵךְ שְׁנָתֵנוּ כַּשָּׁנִים הַטּוֹבוֹת. בָּרוּךְ אַתָּה יהוה, מְבָרֵךְ הַשָּׁנִים.

°°At this point one may interject a prayer for one who is ill:

יְהִי רָצוֹן מִלְּפָנֶיךָ יהוה אֱלֹהַי וֵאלֹהֵי אֲבוֹתַי, שֶׁתִּשְׁלַח מְהֵרָה רְפוּאָה שְׁלֵמָה מִן הַשָּׁמַיִם, רְפוּאַת הַנֶּפֶשׁ וּרְפוּאַת הַגּוּף

for a male—לַחוֹלֶה (patient's name) בֶּן (mother's name) בְּתוֹךְ שְׁאָר חוֹלֵי יִשְׂרָאֵל.

for a female—לַחוֹלָה (patient's name) בַּת (mother's name) בְּתוֹךְ שְׁאָר חוֹלֵי יִשְׂרָאֵל.

Continue—כִּי אֵל . . .

תְּשׁוּבָה / Repentance

הֲשִׁיבֵנוּ אָבִינוּ — *Bring us back, our Father.* Only in this prayer for repentance, and in the next one, for forgiveness, do we refer to God as *our Father.* A father has the responsibility to teach his son the proper way to live — but even if a son has rebelled and become estranged, the father's compassion will assert itself if his son repents (*Etz Yosef*).

וְהַחֲזִירֵנוּ — *And influence us to return.* God never *compels* anyone to repent, but if a person makes a sincere beginning, God makes his way easier.

סְלִיחָה / Forgiveness

סְלַח לָנוּ אָבִינוּ . . . מְחַל לָנוּ מַלְכֵּנוּ — *Forgive us, our Father . . . pardon us, our King.* סְלִיחָה, *forgiveness,* means giving up the right to punish for a wrong, but מְחִילָה, *pardon,* means not even harboring resentment or ill will (*Abudraham*).

גְּאוּלָה / Redemption

רְאֵה בְעָנְיֵנוּ — *Behold our affliction.* Though Israel suffers because of its own sins, our enemies have no right to claim that they are merely doing God's work, because they cause Israel to suffer

REPENTANCE

הֲשִׁיבֵנוּ *Bring us back, our Father,* to Your Torah, and bring us near, our King, to Your service, and influence us to return* in perfect repentance before You. Blessed are You,* HASHEM, *Who desires repentance.*

FORGIVENESS

Strike the left side of the chest with the right fist while reciting the words *'erred'* and *'sinned.'*

סְלַח *Forgive us, our Father, for we have erred; pardon us, our King,* for we have willfully sinned; for You pardon and forgive. Blessed are You,* HASHEM, *the gracious One Who pardons abundantly.*

REDEMPTION

רְאֵה *Behold our affliction,* take up our grievance, and redeem us*[1] *speedily for Your Name's sake,* for You are a powerful Redeemer. Blessed are You,* HASHEM, *Redeemer of Israel.*

HEALTH AND HEALING

רְפָאֵנוּ *Heal us,* HASHEM *— then we will be healed;* save us — then we will be saved, for You are our praise.*[2] *Bring complete recovery for all our ailments, °°for You are God, King, the faithful and compassionate Healer. Blessed are You,* HASHEM, *Who heals the sick of His people Israel.*

YEAR OF PROSPERITY

בָּרֵךְ *Bless on our behalf* — O* HASHEM, *our God — this year and all its kinds of crops for the best, and give dew and rain for a blessing on the face of the earth, and satisfy us from Your bounty, and bless our year like the best years. Blessed are You,* HASHEM, *Who blesses the years.*

°°At this point one may interject a prayer for one who is ill:

May it be Your will, HASHEM, *my God, and the God of my forefathers, that You quickly send a complete recovery from heaven, spiritual healing and physical healing to the patient* (name) *son/daughter of* (mother's name) *among the other patients of Israel.* Continue: *For You are God ...*

(1) Cf. *Psalms* 119:153-154. (2) Cf. *Jeremiah* 17:14.

much more than necessary. Similarly, many commentators explain that the Egyptians were punished for oppressing and enslaving the Jews, even though God had decreed slavery and suffering, because the Egyptians, in their wickedness, went far beyond God's decree (*Etz Yosef*).

לְמַעַן שְׁמֶךָ — *For Your Name's sake.* Israel's suffering is a reflection on our God, and, therefore, a desecration of His Name.

⊲§ רְפוּאָה / Health and Healing

רְפָאֵנוּ ה' וְנֵרָפֵא — *Heal us,* HASHEM *— then we will be healed.* Sometimes human beings or angels are God's agents to heal illness, but in that case, the cure may be only partial or temporary. [Or the pain or other symptoms may be relieved, while the illness itself remains uncured (*Siach Yitzchak*).] But if God *Himself* undertakes to cure the patient, we are confident that it will not be a temporary nor a partial measure: *then we will be healed* (*Etz Yosef* from *Zohar*).

⊲§ בִּרְכַּת הַשָּׁנִים / Year of Prosperity

בָּרֵךְ עָלֵינוּ — *Bless on our behalf.* We request a blessing on our general business activities and then go on to ask for abundant crops. Even in bad times some people prosper, and even in good times some farms and businesses fail. We ask not only for general prosperity, but that we be enabled to share in it (*R' S. R. Hirsch*).

קיבוץ גליות

תְּקַע בְּשׁוֹפָר גָּדוֹל* לְחֵרוּתֵנוּ, וְשָׂא נֵס לְקַבֵּץ גָּלֻיּוֹתֵינוּ, וְקַבְּצֵנוּ יַחַד מֵאַרְבַּע כַּנְפוֹת הָאָרֶץ.[1] בָּרוּךְ אַתָּה יהוה, מְקַבֵּץ נִדְחֵי עַמּוֹ יִשְׂרָאֵל.

דין

הָשִׁיבָה שׁוֹפְטֵינוּ כְּבָרִאשׁוֹנָה,* וְיוֹעֲצֵינוּ* כְּבַתְּחִלָּה,[2] וְהָסֵר מִמֶּנּוּ יָגוֹן וַאֲנָחָה,* וּמְלוֹךְ עָלֵינוּ אַתָּה יהוה לְבַדְּךָ בְּחֶסֶד וּבְרַחֲמִים, וְצַדְּקֵנוּ בַּמִּשְׁפָּט. בָּרוּךְ אַתָּה יהוה, מֶלֶךְ אוֹהֵב צְדָקָה וּמִשְׁפָּט.

ברכת המינים

וְלַמַּלְשִׁינִים* אַל תְּהִי תִקְוָה, וְכָל הָרִשְׁעָה כְּרֶגַע תֹּאבֵד, וְכָל אֹיְבֶיךָ* מְהֵרָה יִכָּרֵתוּ, וְהַזֵּדִים מְהֵרָה תְעַקֵּר וּתְשַׁבֵּר וּתְמַגֵּר וְתַכְנִיעַ בִּמְהֵרָה בְיָמֵינוּ. בָּרוּךְ אַתָּה יהוה, שׁוֹבֵר אֹיְבִים וּמַכְנִיעַ זֵדִים.

צדיקים

עַל הַצַּדִּיקִים וְעַל הַחֲסִידִים, וְעַל זִקְנֵי עַמְּךָ בֵּית יִשְׂרָאֵל, וְעַל פְּלֵיטַת סוֹפְרֵיהֶם,* וְעַל גֵּרֵי הַצֶּדֶק וְעָלֵינוּ, יֶהֱמוּ רַחֲמֶיךָ יהוה אֱלֹהֵינוּ, וְתֵן שָׂכָר טוֹב לְכָל הַבּוֹטְחִים בְּשִׁמְךָ בֶּאֱמֶת, וְשִׂים חֶלְקֵנוּ עִמָּהֶם לְעוֹלָם, וְלֹא נֵבוֹשׁ* כִּי בְךָ בָּטָחְנוּ. בָּרוּךְ אַתָּה יהוה, מִשְׁעָן וּמִבְטָח לַצַּדִּיקִים.

בנין ירושלים

וְלִירוּשָׁלַיִם* עִירְךָ בְּרַחֲמִים תָּשׁוּב, וְתִשְׁכּוֹן בְּתוֹכָהּ כַּאֲשֶׁר דִּבַּרְתָּ, וּבְנֵה אוֹתָהּ בְּקָרוֹב בְּיָמֵינוּ בִּנְיַן עוֹלָם,

---

קִיבּוּץ גָּלֻיּוֹת / Ingathering of Exiles

תְּקַע בְּשׁוֹפָר גָּדוֹל — *Sound the great shofar.* There are three differences between this prayer for redemption and the earlier one of גְּאוּלָה, *Redemption:* (a) The earlier blessing refers to God's *daily* help in all sorts of crises and suffering, while this one refers to the *future* Redemption from exile; (b) the earlier blessing refers only to *physical* salvation, while this one is a plea for *spiritual* deliverance; (c) this one specifies not only freedom from oppression, but the ingathering of all exiles to *Eretz Yisrael.*

דִּין / Restoration of Justice

הָשִׁיבָה שׁוֹפְטֵינוּ כְּבָרִאשׁוֹנָה — *Restore our judges as in earliest times.* When Elijah heralds Messiah's coming, he will first re-establish the Sanhedrin. A secondary theme of this prayer is the wish that God help all Jewish judges rule wisely and justly *(Yaaros D'vash).*

וְיוֹעֲצֵינוּ — *And our counselors,* i.e., the prophets who gave wise advice in both spiritual and temporal affairs *(Olas Tamid).*

יָגוֹן וַאֲנָחָה — *Sorrow and groan.* יָגוֹן, *sorrow,* results from actual want or pain, such as hunger or destruction. אֲנָחָה, *groan,* refers to inner turmoil, such as worry or fear *(Vilna Gaon).*

בִּרְכַּת הַמִּינִים / Against Heretics

וְלַמַּלְשִׁינִים — *And for slanderers.* Chronologically, this is the *nineteenth* blessing of *Shemoneh Esrei;* it was instituted in Yavneh, some time after the destruction of the Second Temple. The blessing was composed in response to the threats of such heretical Jewish sects as

INGATHERING OF EXILES

תְּקַע *Sound the great shofar* for our freedom, raise the banner to gather our exiles and gather us together from the four corners of the earth.*[1] *Blessed are You,* HASHEM, *Who gathers in the dispersed of His people Israel.*

RESTORATION OF JUSTICE

הָשִׁיבָה *Restore our judges as in earliest times* and our counselors* as at first;*[2] *remove from us sorrow and groan;* and reign over us — You,* HASHEM, *alone — with kindness and compassion, and justify us through judgment. Blessed are You,* HASHEM, *the King Who loves righteousness and judgment.*

AGAINST HERETICS

וְלַמַּלְשִׁינִים *And for slanderers* let there be no hope; and may all wickedness perish in an instant; and may all Your enemies* be cut down speedily. May You speedily uproot, smash, cast down, and humble the wanton sinners — speedily in our days. Blessed are You,* HASHEM, *Who breaks enemies and humbles wanton sinners.*

THE RIGHTEOUS

עַל הַצַּדִּיקִים *On the righteous, on the devout, on the elders of Your people the Family of Israel, on the remnant of their scholars,* on the righteous converts and on ourselves — may Your compassion be aroused,* HASHEM, *our God, and give goodly reward to all who sincerely believe in Your Name. Put our lot with them forever, and we will not feel ashamed,* for we trust in You. Blessed are You,* HASHEM, *Mainstay and Assurance of the righteous.*

REBUILDING JERUSALEM

וְלִירוּשָׁלַיִם *And to Jerusalem,* Your city, may You return in compassion, and may You rest within it, as You have spoken. May You rebuild it soon in our days as an eternal structure,*

(1) Cf. *Isaiah* 11:12. (2) Cf. 1:26.

the Sadducees, Boethusians, Essenes, and the early Christians. They tried to lead Jews astray through example and persuasion, and they used their political power to oppress observant Jews and to slander them to the anti-Semitic Roman government.

In this atmosphere, Rabban Gamliel felt the need for a prayer against the heretics and slanderers, and to incorporate it in the *Shemoneh Esrei* to make the populace aware of the danger.

Despite the disappearance from within Israel of the sects against whom it was directed, it is always relevant, because there are still non-believers and heretics who endanger the spiritual continuity of Israel (*Yaaros D'vash*).

אֹיְבֶיךָ — *Your enemies.* Any enemy of Israel is an enemy of God (*Tikun Tefillah*).

צַדִּיקִים / The Righteous

פְּלֵיטַת סוֹפְרֵיהֶם — *The remnant of their scholars.* The term סוֹפְרִים, *scholars,* refers to those who transmit the Oral Torah from generation to generation (*Avodas Yisrael*). These four categories of people — righteous, devout, elders, scholars — are the leaders of the nation. Because the nation needs them, the Sages instituted a special prayer for their welfare (*R' Yehudah ben Yakar*).

וְלֹא נֵבוֹשׁ — *And we will not feel ashamed.* One who puts his faith in people feels shamed — because he has been shown to be helpless on his own. But he is not ashamed to have trusted in God, because no one can succeed without His help (*Dover Shalom*).

בִּנְיַן יְרוּשָׁלַיִם / Rebuilding Jerusalem

וְלִירוּשָׁלַיִם — *And to Jerusalem.* After having sought God's blessing on Israel's leaders and righteous people, we seek His blessing for the Holy City. No blessing is complete until the seat

וְכִסֵּא דָוִד* מְהֵרָה לְתוֹכָהּ תָּכִין. בָּרוּךְ אַתָּה יהוה, בּוֹנֵה יְרוּשָׁלָיִם.

מלכות בית דוד

אֶת צֶמַח דָּוִד* עַבְדְּךָ מְהֵרָה תַצְמִיחַ, וְקַרְנוֹ תָּרוּם בִּישׁוּעָתֶךָ, כִּי לִישׁוּעָתְךָ קִוִּינוּ כָּל הַיּוֹם. בָּרוּךְ אַתָּה יהוה, מַצְמִיחַ קֶרֶן יְשׁוּעָה.

קבלת תפלה

שְׁמַע קוֹלֵנוּ יהוה אֱלֹהֵינוּ, חוּס וְרַחֵם* עָלֵינוּ, וְקַבֵּל בְּרַחֲמִים וּבְרָצוֹן אֶת תְּפִלָּתֵנוּ, כִּי אֵל שׁוֹמֵעַ תְּפִלּוֹת וְתַחֲנוּנִים* אָתָּה. וּמִלְּפָנֶיךָ מַלְכֵּנוּ רֵיקָם אַל תְּשִׁיבֵנוּ,°° כִּי אַתָּה שׁוֹמֵעַ תְּפִלַּת עַמְּךָ יִשְׂרָאֵל בְּרַחֲמִים. בָּרוּךְ אַתָּה יהוה, שׁוֹמֵעַ תְּפִלָּה.

עבודה

רְצֵה* יהוה אֱלֹהֵינוּ בְּעַמְּךָ יִשְׂרָאֵל וּבִתְפִלָּתָם, וְהָשֵׁב אֶת הָעֲבוֹדָה לִדְבִיר בֵּיתֶךָ. וְאִשֵּׁי יִשְׂרָאֵל* וּתְפִלָּתָם בְּאַהֲבָה

°°During the silent *Shemoneh Esrei* one may insert either or both of these personal prayers.

For forgiveness:

אָנָּא יהוה, חָטָאתִי עָוִיתִי וּפָשַׁעְתִּי לְפָנֶיךָ, מִיּוֹם הֱיוֹתִי עַל הָאֲדָמָה עַד הַיּוֹם הַזֶּה (וּבִפְרַט בַּחֵטְא ....). אָנָּא יהוה, עֲשֵׂה לְמַעַן שִׁמְךָ הַגָּדוֹל, וּתְכַפֶּר לִי עַל עֲוֹנַי וַחֲטָאַי וּפְשָׁעַי שֶׁחָטָאתִי וְשֶׁעָוִיתִי וְשֶׁפָּשַׁעְתִּי לְפָנֶיךָ, מִנְּעוּרַי עַד הַיּוֹם הַזֶּה. וּתְמַלֵּא כָּל הַשֵּׁמוֹת שֶׁפָּגַמְתִּי בְּשִׁמְךָ הַגָּדוֹל.

For livelihood:

אַתָּה הוּא יהוה הָאֱלֹהִים, הַזָּן וּמְפַרְנֵס וּמְכַלְכֵּל מִקַּרְנֵי רְאֵמִים עַד בֵּיצֵי כִנִּים. הַטְרִיפֵנִי לֶחֶם חֻקִּי, וְהַמְצֵא לִי וּלְכָל בְּנֵי בֵיתִי מְזוֹנוֹתַי קוֹדֶם שֶׁאֶצְטָרֵךְ לָהֶם, בְּנַחַת וְלֹא בְצַעַר, בְּהֶתֵּר וְלֹא בְאִסּוּר, בְּכָבוֹד וְלֹא בְבִזָּיוֹן, לְחַיִּים וּלְשָׁלוֹם, מִשֶּׁפַע בְּרָכָה וְהַצְלָחָה, וּמִשֶּׁפַע בְּרֵכָה עֶלְיוֹנָה, כְּדֵי שֶׁאוּכַל לַעֲשׂוֹת רְצוֹנֶךָ וְלַעֲסוֹק בְּתוֹרָתֶךָ וּלְקַיֵּם מִצְוֹתֶיךָ. וְאַל תַּצְרִיכֵנִי לִידֵי מַתְּנַת בָּשָׂר וָדָם. וִיקֻיַּם בִּי מִקְרָא שֶׁכָּתוּב: פּוֹתֵחַ אֶת יָדֶךָ, וּמַשְׂבִּיעַ לְכָל חַי רָצוֹן.[1] וְכָתוּב: הַשְׁלֵךְ עַל יהוה יְהָבְךָ וְהוּא יְכַלְכְּלֶךָ.[2]

Continue— כִּי אַתָּה . . .

of holiness, Jerusalem, is rebuilt in all its grandeur (*Iyun Tefillah*).

וְכִסֵּא דָוִד — *The throne of David.* Jerusalem cannot be considered rebuilt unless an heir of David sits on the throne (*R' Yitzchak Zev Soloveitchik*).

מַלְכוּת בֵּית דָּוִד / Davidic Reign

אֶת צֶמַח דָּוִד — *The offspring of ... David.* Messiah's name will be צֶמַח, *Tzemach,* literally, the *sprouting* or *flourishing* of a plant (*Zechariah* 6:12). Thus, the normal process of redemption is like a plant's barely noticeable daily growth (*Iyun Tefillah*). David has been mentioned in the previous blessing as well. There, Jerusalem's rebirth depends on the Davidic heir. Here we learn that Israel's ultimate salvation is possible only through the Davidic Messiah.

קַבָּלַת תְּפִלָּה / Acceptance of Prayer

[In the middle section of *Shemoneh Esrei* we

and may You speedily establish the throne of David within it. Blessed are You,* HASHEM, *the Builder of Jerusalem.*

DAVIDIC REIGN

אֶת צֶמַח *The offspring of Your servant David* may You speedily cause to flourish, and enhance his pride through Your salvation, for we hope for Your salvation all day long. Blessed are You,* HASHEM, *Who causes the pride of salvation to flourish.*

ACCEPTANCE OF PRAYER

שְׁמַע קוֹלֵנוּ *Hear our voice,* HASHEM *our God, pity and be compassionate* to us, and accept — with compassion and favor — our prayer, for God Who hears prayers and supplications* are You. From before Yourself, our King, turn us not away empty-handed,°° for You hear the prayer of Your people Israel with compassion. Blessed are You,* HASHEM, *Who hears prayer.*

TEMPLE SERVICE

רְצֵה *Be favorable,** HASHEM, *our God, toward Your people Israel and their prayer and restore the service to the Holy of Holies of Your Temple. The fire-offerings of Israel* and their prayer*

°°During the silent *Shemoneh Esrei* one may insert either or both of these personal prayers.

For forgiveness:

אָנָּא *Please, O* HASHEM, *I have erred, been iniquitous, and willfully sinned before You, from the day I have existed on earth until this very day (and especially with the sin of ...). Please,* HASHEM, *act for the sake of Your Great Name and grant me atonement for my iniquities, my errors, and my willful sins through which I have erred, been iniquitous, and willfully sinned before You, from my youth until this day. And make whole all the Names that I have blemished in Your Great Name.*

For livelihood:

אַתָּה *It is You,* HASHEM *the God, Who nourishes, sustains, and supports, from the horns of re'eimim to the eggs of lice. Provide me with my allotment of bread; and bring forth for me and all members of my household, my food, before I have need for it; in contentment but not in pain, in a permissible but not a forbidden manner, in honor but not in disgrace, for life and for peace; from the flow of blessing and success and from the flow of the Heavenly spring, so that I be enabled to do Your will and engage in Your Torah and fulfill Your commandments. Make me not needful of people's largesse; and may there be fulfilled in me the verse that states, 'You open Your hand and satisfy the desire of every living thing'[1] and that states, 'Cast Your burden upon* HASHEM *and He will support you.'[2]*

Continue: *For You hear the prayer ...*

(1) *Psalms* 145:16. (2) 55:23.

have asked God to grant our specific needs. We now close the section with a general plea that He take note of our call and grant our requests.]

חוּס וְרַחֵם — *Pity and be compassionate.* The term חוּס, *pity,* refers to an artisan's special regard for the product of his hands; while רַחֲמִים, *compassion,* describes the emotion aroused upon seeing someone who is pathetically helpless. O God — *pity* us because we are Your handiwork, and *be compassionate* because we are nothing without You! *(Vilna Gaon).*

תְּפִלּוֹת וְתַחֲנוּנִים — *Prayers and supplications.* תַּחֲנוּן is a request for מַתְּנַת חִנָּם, *an unearned gift (Rashi, Deut.* 3:23). The most righteous people use this expression because they are aware that no man can claim that God 'owes' him something. *Gur Aryeh* explains that the righteous use the term תַּחֲנוּן only when praying for themselves, but when praying for the community they use תְּפִלָּה, because Israel as a *community* deserves God's help.

עֲבוֹדָה / Temple Service

רְצֵה — *Be favorable.* This begins the final section of *Shemoneh Esrei.* Like a servant who is grateful for having had the opportunity to express himself before his master, we thank God

תְקַבֵּל בְּרָצוֹן, וּתְהִי לְרָצוֹן תָּמִיד עֲבוֹדַת יִשְׂרָאֵל עַמֶּךָ.

וְתֶחֱזֶינָה עֵינֵינוּ* בְּשׁוּבְךָ לְצִיּוֹן בְּרַחֲמִים. בָּרוּךְ אַתָּה יהוה, הַמַּחֲזִיר שְׁכִינָתוֹ לְצִיּוֹן.

הודאה

Bow at מוֹדִים; straighten up at 'ה. In his repetition the *chazzan* should recite the entire מוֹדִים aloud, while the congregation recites מוֹדִים דְּרַבָּנָן softly.

מוֹדִים אֲנַחְנוּ לָךְ, שָׁאַתָּה הוּא יהוה אֱלֹהֵינוּ וֵאלֹהֵי אֲבוֹתֵינוּ לְעוֹלָם וָעֶד. צוּר חַיֵּינוּ,* מָגֵן יִשְׁעֵנוּ אַתָּה הוּא לְדוֹר וָדוֹר. נוֹדֶה לְּךָ* וּנְסַפֵּר תְּהִלָּתֶךָ[1] עַל חַיֵּינוּ* הַמְּסוּרִים בְּיָדֶךָ, וְעַל נִשְׁמוֹתֵינוּ הַפְּקוּדוֹת לָךְ,* וְעַל נִסֶּיךָ שֶׁבְּכָל יוֹם עִמָּנוּ, וְעַל נִפְלְאוֹתֶיךָ* וְטוֹבוֹתֶיךָ שֶׁבְּכָל עֵת, עֶרֶב וָבֹקֶר וְצָהֳרָיִם. הַטּוֹב כִּי לֹא כָלוּ רַחֲמֶיךָ, וְהַמְּרַחֵם כִּי לֹא תַמּוּ חֲסָדֶיךָ,[2]* מֵעוֹלָם קִוִּינוּ לָךְ.

מודים דרבנן

מוֹדִים אֲנַחְנוּ לָךְ, שָׁאַתָּה הוּא יהוה אֱלֹהֵינוּ וֵאלֹהֵי אֲבוֹתֵינוּ, אֱלֹהֵי כָל בָּשָׂר, יוֹצְרֵנוּ, יוֹצֵר בְּרֵאשִׁית. בְּרָכוֹת וְהוֹדָאוֹת לְשִׁמְךָ הַגָּדוֹל וְהַקָּדוֹשׁ, עַל שֶׁהֶחֱיִיתָנוּ וְקִיַּמְתָּנוּ. כֵּן תְּחַיֵּנוּ וּתְקַיְּמֵנוּ, וְתֶאֱסוֹף גָּלֻיּוֹתֵינוּ לְחַצְרוֹת קָדְשֶׁךָ, לִשְׁמוֹר חֻקֶּיךָ וְלַעֲשׂוֹת רְצוֹנֶךָ, וּלְעָבְדְּךָ בְּלֵבָב שָׁלֵם, עַל שֶׁאֲנַחְנוּ מוֹדִים לָךְ. בָּרוּךְ אֵל הַהוֹדָאוֹת.

---

for hearing us out. As we conclude *Shemoneh Esrei,* which is our substitute for the Temple's sacrificial service, we ask that the *true* service be restored to the Temple *(Etz Yosef).*

וְאִשֵּׁי יִשְׂרָאֵל — *The fire-offerings of Israel.* Since the Temple is not standing this phrase is taken in an allegorical sense. It refers to: the souls and the deeds of the righteous, which are as pleasing as sacrifices; Jewish prayers that are like offerings; or the altar fires and sacrifices of Messianic times. Some repunctuate the blessing to read: . . . *and restore the service . . . and the fire-offerings of Israel. Their prayer accept with love . . .*

⁂ וְתֶחֱזֶינָה עֵינֵינוּ — *May our eyes behold.* There is a principle that a person may not witness the downfall of his enemies unless he is personally worthy. As we find in the case of Lot's wife *(Genesis* 19:26), although God sent an angel to save her from the destruction of Sodom, she did not deserve to see the destruction of her neighbors. Similarly, one does not see the splendor of the miracles bringing about his salvation unless he is personally worthy. Therefore we pray that *we* may be worthy to witness the return to Zion with our own eyes *(Yaaros D'vash).*

⁂ **הוֹדָאָה / Thanksgiving [Modim]**

צוּר חַיֵּינוּ — *Rock of our lives.* Our parents are the 'rocks' from whom our bodies are hewn, but from You we receive life itself *(Etz Yosef).*

נוֹדֶה לְּךָ — *We shall thank You.* Having described God's greatness and our relationship, we now specify what we thank Him for.

עַל חַיֵּינוּ — *For our lives.* Lest anyone think that he is master over his own life, we acknowledge that every breath and heartbeat is a direct result of God's mercy *(Olas Tamid).*

נִשְׁמוֹתֵינוּ הַפְּקוּדוֹת לָךְ — *Our souls that are entrusted to You.* The word נְשָׁמָה, *neshamah,* refers to the higher soul that gives man his holiness, as opposed to the lower soul that merely keeps him alive. During sleep, the animal soul remains in man; he remains alive and his body continues to function. But the *neshamah* leaves the body and ascends to higher spiritual *accept with love and favor, and may the service of Your people Israel always be favorable to You.*

וְתֶחֱזֶינָה *May our eyes behold* Your return to Zion in compassion. Blessed are You, HASHEM, Who restores His Presence unto Zion.*

THANKSGIVING [MODIM]

Bow at *'We gratefully thank You'*; straighten up at *'HASHEM.'* In his repetition the *chazzan* should recite the entire *Modim* aloud, while the congregation recites *Modim of the Rabbis* softly.

מוֹדִים *We gratefully thank You, for it is You Who are HASHEM, our God and the God of our forefathers for all eternity; Rock of our lives,* Shield of our salvation are You from generation to generation. We shall thank You* and relate Your praise[1] — for our lives,* which are committed to Your power and for our souls that are entrusted to You;* for Your miracles that are with us every day; and for Your wonders* and favors in every season — evening, morning, and afternoon. The Beneficent One, for Your compassions were never exhausted, and the Compassionate One, for Your kindnesses* never ended[2] — always have we put our hope in You.*

MODIM OF THE RABBIS

מוֹדִים *We gratefully thank You, for it is You Who are HASHEM, our God and the God of our forefathers, the God of all flesh, our Molder, the Molder of the universe. Blessings and thanks are due Your great and holy Name for You have given us life and sustained us. So may You continue to give us life and sustain us and gather our exiles to the Courtyards of Your Sanctuary, to observe Your decrees, to do Your will and to serve You wholeheartedly. [We thank You] for inspiring us to thank You. Blessed is the God of thanksgivings.*

(1) Cf. *Psalms* 79:13. (2) Cf. *Lamentations* 3:22.

realms where it can conceivably receive Divine communications. Occasionally such messages become known to a person through dreams that may seem to be intuitive, but may be messages from on high, such as the prophetic dreams found in Scripture. During slumber, the *neshamah* leaves the body and is, so to speak, entrusted to God's safekeeping, to be returned to man in the morning *(Derech Hashem)*.

נִסֶּיךָ . . . נִפְלְאוֹתֶיךָ — *Your miracles . . . Your wonders. Miracles* are the extraordinary events that everyone recognizes as the results of God's intervention. *Wonders* are the familiar things that we do not regard as miracles because we have grown accustomed to them, such as breathing, raining, and growing. We thank God for both *miracles* and *wonders,* because we know that He is their Creator *(Etz Yosef)*.

הַטּוֹב . . . רַחֲמֶיךָ . . . חֲסָדֶיךָ — *The Beneficent One . . . Your compassions . . . Your kindnesses.* The three Hebrew terms טוֹב, רַחֲמִים and חֶסֶד all refer to God's attribute of Mercy. Specifically: טוֹב, *goodness* or *beneficence,* is the kind deed that was actually done; רַחֲמִים is the *compassion* with which God softens the decision called for by strict Justice. Thus, compassion will cause an offender to receive less than his deserved punishment; but he may well be punished to some degree; חֶסֶד is God's infinite store of *kindness*. It can either overcome completely the dictates of Justice, or it can provide the רַחֲמִים that mitigates Justice *(R' Munk)*.

מוֹדִים דְּרַבָּנָן / Modim of the Rabbis

When the *chazzan* bows and recites *Modim* in the manner of a slave accepting the total authority of his master, the congregation must join him in accepting God's sovereignty. Therefore each member of the congregation must make his own declaration of submission

וְעַל כֻּלָּם יִתְבָּרַךְ וְיִתְרוֹמַם שִׁמְךָ מַלְכֵּנוּ תָּמִיד לְעוֹלָם וָעֶד.

Bend the knees at בָּרוּךְ; bow at אַתָּה; straighten up at ה׳.

וְכֹל הַחַיִּים* יוֹדְוּךָ סֶּלָה, וִיהַלְלוּ אֶת שִׁמְךָ בֶּאֱמֶת, הָאֵל יְשׁוּעָתֵנוּ וְעֶזְרָתֵנוּ סֶלָה. בָּרוּךְ אַתָּה יהוה, הַטּוֹב שִׁמְךָ וּלְךָ נָאֶה לְהוֹדוֹת.

שלום

שָׁלוֹם רָב עַל יִשְׂרָאֵל עַמְּךָ תָּשִׂים לְעוֹלָם, כִּי אַתָּה הוּא מֶלֶךְ אָדוֹן לְכָל הַשָּׁלוֹם. וְטוֹב בְּעֵינֶיךָ* לְבָרֵךְ אֶת עַמְּךָ יִשְׂרָאֵל בְּכָל עֵת וּבְכָל שָׁעָה בִּשְׁלוֹמֶךָ. בָּרוּךְ אַתָּה יהוה, הַמְּבָרֵךְ אֶת עַמּוֹ יִשְׂרָאֵל בַּשָּׁלוֹם.

יִהְיוּ לְרָצוֹן* אִמְרֵי פִי וְהֶגְיוֹן לִבִּי לְפָנֶיךָ, יהוה צוּרִי וְגֹאֲלִי.[1]

The *chazzan's* repetition of *Shemoneh Esrei* ends here. Individuals continue below.
See commentary for permissible responses while reciting this final paragraph of *Shemoneh Esrei*.

אֱלֹהַי, נְצוֹר לְשׁוֹנִי מֵרָע,* וּשְׂפָתַי מִדַּבֵּר מִרְמָה,[2] וְלִמְקַלְלַי נַפְשִׁי תִדּוֹם, וְנַפְשִׁי כֶּעָפָר* לַכֹּל תִּהְיֶה. פְּתַח לִבִּי בְּתוֹרָתֶךָ,* וּבְמִצְוֹתֶיךָ תִּרְדּוֹף נַפְשִׁי. וְכֹל הַחוֹשְׁבִים עָלַי רָעָה, מְהֵרָה הָפֵר עֲצָתָם וְקַלְקֵל מַחֲשַׁבְתָּם. עֲשֵׂה לְמַעַן שְׁמֶךָ, עֲשֵׂה לְמַעַן יְמִינֶךָ, עֲשֵׂה לְמַעַן קְדֻשָּׁתֶךָ, עֲשֵׂה לְמַעַן תּוֹרָתֶךָ. לְמַעַן יֵחָלְצוּן יְדִידֶיךָ, הוֹשִׁיעָה יְמִינְךָ וַעֲנֵנִי.[3]

Some recite verses pertaining to their names at this point. See page 1143.

(Abudraham). The Talmud *(Sotah* 40a and *Yerushalmi* 1:8) cites the personal declarations used by a number of rabbis, and concludes that the proper custom is to recite them all. This collection of prayers was thus given the name *Modim of the Rabbis.*

וְכֹל הַחַיִּים — *Everything alive.* As long as there is life, people can express their thanks to God. This prayer refers specifically to the universal praise that will come with the restoration of the Divine service in the rebuilt Temple.

שָׁלוֹם / Peace

אָדוֹן לְכָל הַשָּׁלוֹם וְטוֹב בְּעֵינֶיךָ — *Master of all peace. May it be good in Your eyes.* For a blessing to come true, there must be two conditions: (a) the one from whom the blessing is sought must have the power to confer it, and (b) he must be willing to do so. Therefore, we declare that God is *Master of all peace* and we pray that *it be good in [His] eyes* to bestow it upon us *(Acharis Shalom).*

יִהְיוּ לְרָצוֹן — *May . . . find favor.* We conclude *Shemoneh Esrei* with this brief prayer that our prayers find favor before God. Kabbalistic literature attaches great sanctity to this verse and stresses that it be recited slowly and fervently.

Some authorities maintain that since יִהְיוּ לְרָצוֹן closes the *Shemoneh Esrei* prayer, it should be recited before אֱלֹהַי נְצוֹר, which is not an integral part of *Shemoneh Esrei* (see below). Others hold that since the Sages have appended אֱלֹהַי נְצוֹר, *Shemoneh Esrei* is not over until the end of אֱלֹהַי נְצוֹר, at which point יִהְיוּ לְרָצוֹן should be said. To accommodate both views, some authorities hold that יִהְיוּ לְרָצוֹן should be said both before and after אֱלֹהַי נְצוֹר.

אֱלֹהַי נְצוֹר / Concluding Prayers

Many of the Talmudic Sages composed individual supplications that they would recite at the conclusion of the prayer. Some of these supplications are cited in *Berachos* 16b-17a. The prayer now in universal use is based on that of Mar, son of Rabina (ibid. 18a).

While one is reciting אֱלֹהַי נְצוֹר, he may not respond to blessings and the like except for the exceptions given below. In the case of those exceptions, it is preferable to recite יִהְיוּ לְרָצוֹן

For all these, may Your Name be blessed and exalted, our King, continually forever and ever.

Bend the knees at *'Blessed'*; bow at *'You'*; straighten up at *'HASHEM.'*

Everything alive will gratefully acknowledge You, Selah! and praise Your Name sincerely, O God of our salvation and help, Selah! Blessed are You, HASHEM, Your Name is 'The Beneficent One' and to You it is fitting to give thanks.*

PEACE

שָׁלוֹם רָב *Establish abundant peace upon Your people Israel forever, for You are King, Master of all peace. May it be good in Your eyes* to bless Your people Israel at every time and every hour with Your peace. Blessed are You, HASHEM, Who blesses His people Israel with peace.*

May the expressions of my mouth and the thoughts of my heart find favor before You, HASHEM, my Rock and my Redeemer.*[1]

The *chazzan's* repetition of *Shemoneh Esrei* ends here. Individuals continue below. See commentary for permissible responses while reciting this final paragraph of *Shemoneh Esrei*.

אֱלֹהַי *My God, guard my tongue from evil* and my lips from speaking deceitfully.*[2] *To those who curse me, let my soul be silent; and let my soul be like dust* to everyone. Open my heart to Your Torah,* then my soul will pursue Your commandments. As for all those who design evil against me, speedily nullify their counsel and disrupt their design. Act for Your Name's sake; act for Your right hand's sake; act for Your sanctity's sake; act for Your Torah's sake. That Your beloved ones may be given rest; let Your right hand save, and respond to me.*[3]

Some recite verses pertaining to their names at this point. See page 1143.

(1) *Psalms* 19:15. (2) Cf. *Psalms* 34:14. (3) 60:7; 108:7.

before responding, but if there is not enough time to do so, the responses should be said anyway. The responses are: *Borchu;* the *amens* after הָאֵל הַקָּדוֹשׁ and שׁוֹמֵעַ תְּפִלָּה; אָמֵן יְהֵא שְׁמֵהּ רַבָּא and the *amen* after דַּאֲמִירָן בְּעָלְמָא; in *Kedushah,* the two verses קָדוֹשׁ and בָּרוּךְ כְּבוֹד; and the three words מוֹדִים אֲנַחְנוּ לָךְ. [See *Orach Chaim* ch. 122.]

אֱלֹהַי נְצוֹר לְשׁוֹנִי מֵרָע — *My God, guard my tongue from evil.* We pray that God protect us from situations that would tempt us to speak ill of others *(Abudraham).*

The Midrash [*Vayikra Rabbah* 33:1] relates that Rabban Shimon ben Gamliel once sent his servant, Tavi, to buy 'good food.' Tavi, who was famous for his wisdom, brought back a tongue. Thereupon Rabban Shimon sent him to buy some 'bad food.' Again, he returned with a tongue. Rabban Shimon asked him to explain how the same food could be both good and bad. Tavi said, 'From a tongue can come good or bad. When a tongue speaks *good,* there is nothing better, but when a tongue speaks *ill,* there is nothing worse' *(Vayikra Rabbah* 33:1).

נַפְשִׁי תִדּוֹם . . . כֶּעָפָר — *Let my soul be silent . . . like dust.* We should ignore barbs and insults, because the less a person cares about his prestige, the less he will let selfishness interfere with his service of God and his efforts at self-improvement *(Ruach Chaim).*

פְּתַח לִבִּי בְּתוֹרָתֶךָ — *Open my heart to Your Torah.* Our goal is to serve God in a positive manner by studying Torah and fulfilling its commandments *(Abudraham).*

☙ Verses for People's Names

Kitzur Sh'lah teaches that it is a source of merit for people that before יִהְיוּ לְרָצוֹן they recite a Scriptural verse symbolizing their name. The verse should either contain the person's name or else begin and end with the first and last letters of his name. A list of such verses may be found on p. 1143.

יִהְיוּ לְרָצוֹן אִמְרֵי פִי וְהֶגְיוֹן לִבִּי לְפָנֶיךָ, יהוה צוּרִי וְגֹאֲלִי.[1]

Bow and take three steps back. Bow left and say ... עֹשֶׂה; bow right and say ... הוּא יַעֲשֶׂה; bow forward and say וְעַל כָּל ... אָמֵן.

עֹשֶׂה שָׁלוֹם בִּמְרוֹמָיו, הוּא יַעֲשֶׂה שָׁלוֹם עָלֵינוּ, וְעַל כָּל יִשְׂרָאֵל. וְאִמְרוּ: אָמֵן.

יְהִי רָצוֹן מִלְּפָנֶיךָ* יהוה אֱלֹהֵינוּ וֵאלֹהֵי אֲבוֹתֵינוּ, שֶׁיִּבָּנֶה בֵּית הַמִּקְדָּשׁ בִּמְהֵרָה בְיָמֵינוּ, וְתֵן חֶלְקֵנוּ בְּתוֹרָתֶךָ. וְשָׁם נַעֲבָדְךָ בְּיִרְאָה, כִּימֵי עוֹלָם וּכְשָׁנִים קַדְמוֹנִיּוֹת. וְעָרְבָה לַיהוה מִנְחַת יְהוּדָה וִירוּשָׁלָיִם, כִּימֵי עוֹלָם וּכְשָׁנִים קַדְמוֹנִיּוֹת.[2]

THE INDIVIDUAL'S RECITATION OF שְׁמוֹנֶה עֶשְׂרֵה ENDS HERE.

The individual remains standing in place until the *chazzan* reaches *Kedushah* — or at least until the *chazzan* begins his repetition — then he takes three steps forward. The *chazzan* himself, or one praying alone, should remain in place for a few moments before taking three steps forward.

קדיש שלם

The *chazzan* recites קַדִּישׁ שָׁלֵם.

יִתְגַּדַּל וְיִתְקַדַּשׁ שְׁמֵהּ רַבָּא. (Cong. – אָמֵן.) בְּעָלְמָא דִּי בְרָא כִרְעוּתֵהּ. וְיַמְלִיךְ מַלְכוּתֵהּ, בְּחַיֵּיכוֹן וּבְיוֹמֵיכוֹן וּבְחַיֵּי דְכָל בֵּית יִשְׂרָאֵל, בַּעֲגָלָא וּבִזְמַן קָרִיב. וְאִמְרוּ: אָמֵן.

(Cong. – אָמֵן. יְהֵא שְׁמֵהּ רַבָּא מְבָרַךְ לְעָלַם וּלְעָלְמֵי עָלְמַיָּא.)

יְהֵא שְׁמֵהּ רַבָּא מְבָרַךְ לְעָלַם וּלְעָלְמֵי עָלְמַיָּא.

יִתְבָּרַךְ וְיִשְׁתַּבַּח וְיִתְפָּאַר וְיִתְרוֹמַם וְיִתְנַשֵּׂא וְיִתְהַדָּר וְיִתְעַלֶּה וְיִתְהַלָּל שְׁמֵהּ דְּקֻדְשָׁא בְּרִיךְ הוּא (Cong. – בְּרִיךְ הוּא) — לְעֵלָּא מִן כָּל בִּרְכָתָא וְשִׁירָתָא תֻּשְׁבְּחָתָא וְנֶחֱמָתָא, דַּאֲמִירָן בְּעָלְמָא. וְאִמְרוּ: אָמֵן. (Cong. – אָמֵן.)

(Cong. – קַבֵּל בְּרַחֲמִים וּבְרָצוֹן אֶת תְּפִלָּתֵנוּ.)

תִּתְקַבַּל צְלוֹתְהוֹן וּבָעוּתְהוֹן דְּכָל בֵּית יִשְׂרָאֵל קֳדָם אֲבוּהוֹן דִּי בִשְׁמַיָּא. וְאִמְרוּ: אָמֵן. (Cong. – אָמֵן.)

(Cong. – יְהִי שֵׁם יהוה מְבֹרָךְ, מֵעַתָּה וְעַד עוֹלָם.[3])

יְהֵא שְׁלָמָא רַבָּא מִן שְׁמַיָּא, וְחַיִּים עָלֵינוּ וְעַל כָּל יִשְׂרָאֵל. וְאִמְרוּ: אָמֵן. (Cong. – אָמֵן.)

(Cong. – עֶזְרִי מֵעִם יהוה, עֹשֵׂה שָׁמַיִם וָאָרֶץ.[4])

Take three steps back. Bow left and say ... עֹשֶׂה; bow right and say ... הוּא; bow forward and say וְעַל כָּל ... אָמֵן. Remain standing in place for a few moments, then take three steps forward.

עֹשֶׂה שָׁלוֹם בִּמְרוֹמָיו, הוּא יַעֲשֶׂה שָׁלוֹם עָלֵינוּ, וְעַל כָּל יִשְׂרָאֵל. וְאִמְרוּ: אָמֵן. (Cong. – אָמֵן.)

May the expressions of my mouth and the thoughts of my heart find favor before You, HASHEM, *my Rock and my Redeemer.*[1]

Bow and take three steps back. Bow left and say, *'He Who makes peace . . .'*; bow right and say, *'may He make peace . . .'*; bow forward and say, *'and upon all Israel . . . Amen.'*

He Who makes peace in His heights, may He make peace upon us, and upon all Israel. Now respond: Amen.

יְהִי רָצוֹן *May it be Your will,** HASHEM, *our God and the God of our forefathers, that the Holy Temple be rebuilt, speedily in our days. Grant us our share in Your Torah, and may we serve You there with reverence, as in days of old and in former years. Then the offering of Judah and Jerusalem will be pleasing to* HASHEM, *as in days of old and in former years.*[2]

THE INDIVIDUAL'S RECITATION OF *SHEMONEH ESREI* ENDS HERE.

The individual remains standing in place until the *chazzan* reaches *Kedushah* — or at least until the *chazzan* begins his repetition — then he takes three steps forward. The *chazzan* himself, or one praying alone, should remain in place for a few moments before taking three steps forward.

FULL KADDISH

The *chazzan* recites the Full *Kaddish*.

יִתְגַּדַּל *May His great Name grow exalted and sanctified* (Cong.— *Amen.*) *in the world that He created as He willed. May He give reign to His kingship in your lifetimes and in your days, and in the lifetimes of the entire Family of Israel, swiftly and soon. Now respond: Amen.*

(Cong.— *Amen. May His great Name be blessed forever and ever.*)

May His great Name be blessed forever and ever.

Blessed, praised, glorified, exalted, extolled, mighty, upraised, and lauded be the Name of the Holy One, Blessed is He (Cong.— *Blessed is He*) — *beyond any blessing and song, praise and consolation that are uttered in the world. Now respond: Amen.* (Cong.— *Amen.*)

(Cong.— *Accept our prayers with mercy and favor.*)

May the prayers and supplications of the entire Family of Israel be accepted before their Father Who is in Heaven. Now respond: Amen. (Cong.— *Amen.*)

(Cong.— *Blessed be the Name of* HASHEM, *from this time and forever.*[3])

May there be abundant peace from Heaven, and life, upon us and upon all Israel. Now respond: Amen. (Cong.— *Amen.*)

(Cong.— *My help is from* HASHEM, *Maker of heaven and earth.*[4])

Take three steps back. Bow left and say, *'He Who makes peace . . .'*; bow right and say, *'may He . . .'*; bow forward and say, *'and upon all Israel . . .'* Remain standing in place for a few moments, then take three steps forward.

He Who makes peace in His heights, may He make peace upon us, and upon all Israel. Now respond: Amen. (Cong.— *Amen.*)

(1) *Psalms* 19:15. (2) *Malachi* 3:4. (3) *Psalms* 113:2. (4) 121:2.

יְהִי רָצוֹן מִלְּפָנֶיךָ — *May it be Your will.* As noted above, the *Shemoneh Esrei*, as the primary prayer, takes the place of the Temple Service. Thus it is appropriate to conclude with this plea (from *Avos* 5:23) that God permit the rebuilding of the *Beis HaMikdash* so that we can perform the Temple Service in actuality. We ask further that God give us our share in the Torah, both because of the extreme importance of Torah study and because the study of the laws of the offerings takes the place of the offerings themselves.

Stand while reciting עָלֵינוּ.

עָלֵינוּ לְשַׁבֵּחַ לַאֲדוֹן הַכֹּל, לָתֵת גְּדֻלָּה לְיוֹצֵר בְּרֵאשִׁית, שֶׁלֹּא עָשָׂנוּ כְּגוֹיֵי הָאֲרָצוֹת, וְלֹא שָׂמָנוּ כְּמִשְׁפְּחוֹת הָאֲדָמָה. שֶׁלֹּא שָׂם חֶלְקֵנוּ כָּהֶם, וְגוֹרָלֵנוּ* כְּכָל הֲמוֹנָם. (שֶׁהֵם מִשְׁתַּחֲוִים* לְהֶבֶל וָרִיק, וּמִתְפַּלְּלִים אֶל אֵל לֹא יוֹשִׁיעַ.[1])

Bow while reciting וַאֲנַחְנוּ כּוֹרְעִים וּמִשְׁתַּחֲוִים.

וַאֲנַחְנוּ כּוֹרְעִים וּמִשְׁתַּחֲוִים וּמוֹדִים, לִפְנֵי מֶלֶךְ מַלְכֵי הַמְּלָכִים הַקָּדוֹשׁ בָּרוּךְ הוּא. שֶׁהוּא נוֹטֶה שָׁמַיִם וְיֹסֵד אָרֶץ,[2] וּמוֹשַׁב יְקָרוֹ בַּשָּׁמַיִם מִמַּעַל, וּשְׁכִינַת עֻזּוֹ בְּגָבְהֵי מְרוֹמִים. הוּא אֱלֹהֵינוּ, אֵין עוֹד. אֱמֶת מַלְכֵּנוּ, אֶפֶס זוּלָתוֹ, כַּכָּתוּב בְּתוֹרָתוֹ: וְיָדַעְתָּ הַיּוֹם וַהֲשֵׁבֹתָ אֶל לְבָבֶךָ,* כִּי יהוה הוּא הָאֱלֹהִים בַּשָּׁמַיִם מִמַּעַל וְעַל הָאָרֶץ מִתָּחַת, אֵין עוֹד.[3]

עַל כֵּן נְקַוֶּה לְּךָ* יהוה אֱלֹהֵינוּ לִרְאוֹת מְהֵרָה בְּתִפְאֶרֶת עֻזֶּךָ, לְהַעֲבִיר גִּלּוּלִים מִן הָאָרֶץ, וְהָאֱלִילִים כָּרוֹת יִכָּרֵתוּן, לְתַקֵּן עוֹלָם בְּמַלְכוּת שַׁדַּי. וְכָל בְּנֵי בָשָׂר יִקְרְאוּ בִשְׁמֶךָ, לְהַפְנוֹת אֵלֶיךָ כָּל רִשְׁעֵי אָרֶץ. יַכִּירוּ וְיֵדְעוּ כָּל יוֹשְׁבֵי תֵבֵל, כִּי לְךָ תִּכְרַע כָּל בֶּרֶךְ, תִּשָּׁבַע כָּל לָשׁוֹן.[4] לְפָנֶיךָ יהוה אֱלֹהֵינוּ יִכְרְעוּ וְיִפֹּלוּ, וְלִכְבוֹד שִׁמְךָ יְקָר יִתֵּנוּ. וִיקַבְּלוּ כֻלָּם אֶת עוֹל מַלְכוּתֶךָ, וְתִמְלֹךְ עֲלֵיהֶם מְהֵרָה לְעוֹלָם וָעֶד. כִּי הַמַּלְכוּת שֶׁלְּךָ הִיא וּלְעוֹלְמֵי עַד תִּמְלוֹךְ בְּכָבוֹד, כַּכָּתוּב בְּתוֹרָתֶךָ: יהוה יִמְלֹךְ

עָלֵינוּ / Aleinu

According to many early sources, among them *Rokeach, Kol Bo,* and a Gaonic responsum attributed to *Rabbi Hai Gaon,* this declaration of faith and dedication was composed by Joshua after he led Israel across the Jordan. During the Talmudic era it was part of the Rosh Hashanah *Mussaf* service. At some point during medieval times it began to find its way into the daily service.

Bach (Orach Chaim 133) explains that *Aleinu* was added to the daily prayers to implant faith in the Oneness of God's kingship, and the conviction that He will one day *remove detestable idolatry from the earth ...,* thus preventing Jews from being tempted to follow the beliefs and lifestyles of the nations among whom they dwell (see *Iyun Tefillah* and *Emek Brachah).*

As we can surmise from its authorship and its placement at the conclusion of every service, its significance is profound. Its first paragraph [עָלֵינוּ] proclaims the difference between Israel's concept of God and that of the other nations. The second paragraph [עַל כֵּן] expresses our confidence that all humanity will eventually recognize His sovereignty and declare its obedience to His commandments. It should be clear, however, that this does not imply a belief or even a hope that they will convert to Judaism. Rather, they will accept Him as *the only God* and obey the universal Noachide laws that are incumbent upon all nations *(R' Hirsch).*

חֶלְקֵנוּ ... וְגוֹרָלֵנוּ — *Our portion ... our lot.* God does not punish gentile nations until they have reached the full quota of sin, beyond which He no longer extends mercy. Then He brings retribution upon them, often wiping them out. Such powerful ancient empires as Egypt, Persia, Greece, Rome, and Carthage have disappeared or become inconsequential. God does not act this

Stand while reciting עָלֵינוּ, *'It is our duty . . .'*

עָלֵינוּ *It is our duty to praise the Master of all, to ascribe greatness to the Molder of primeval creation, for He has not made us like the nations of the lands and has not emplaced us like the families of the earth; for He has not assigned our portion like theirs nor our lot* like all their multitudes. (For they bow* to vanity and emptiness and pray to a god which helps not.*[1]*) But we bend our knees, bow, and acknowledge our thanks before the King Who reigns over kings, the Holy One, Blessed is He. He stretches out heaven and establishes earth's foundation,*[2] *the seat of His homage is in the heavens above and His powerful Presence is in the loftiest heights. He is our God and there is none other. True is our King, there is nothing beside Him, as it is written in His Torah: 'You are to know this day and take to your heart* that* HASHEM *is the only God — in heaven above and on the earth below — there is none other.'*[3]

Bow while reciting *'But we bend our knees.'*

עַל כֵּן *Therefore we put our hope in You,** HASHEM, *our God, that we may soon see Your mighty splendor, to remove detestable idolatry from the earth, and false gods will be utterly cut off, to perfect the universe through the Almighty's sovereignty. Then all humanity will call upon Your Name, to turn all the earth's wicked toward You. All the world's inhabitants will recognize and know that to You every knee should bend, every tongue should swear.*[4] *Before You,* HASHEM, *our God, they will bend every knee and cast themselves down and to the glory of Your Name they will render homage, and they will all accept upon themselves the yoke of Your kingship that You may reign over them soon and eternally. For the kingdom is Yours and You will reign*

(1) *Isaiah* 45:20. (2) 51:13. (3) *Deuteronomy* 4:39. (4) Cf. *Isaiah* 45:23.

way with regard to Israel, however. The world survives whether or not there is a Roman Empire, but the world could not survive without Israel. Therefore, God punishes Israel piecemeal, so that it may never be destroyed *(Siach Yitzchak).*

שֶׁהֵם מִשְׁתַּחֲוִים ... — *For they bow* ... The inclusion of this verse follows the original version of *Aleinu.* In the year 1400, a baptized Jew, no doubt seeking to prove his loyalty to the Church, spread the slander that this passage was meant to slur Christianity. He 'proved' his contention by the coincidence that the numerical value of וָרִיק, *emptiness,* is 316, the same as יֵשׁוּ, the Hebrew name of their messiah. The charge was refuted time and again, particularly by Manasseh ben Israel, the seventeenth-century scholar, but repeated persecutions and Church insistence, backed by governmental enforcement, caused the line to be dropped from most Ashkenazic *siddurim.* While most congregations have not returned it to the *Aleinu* prayer, some prominent authorities, among them Rabbi Yehoshua Leib Diskin, insist that *Aleinu* be recited in its original form *(World of Prayer; Siach Yitzchak).*

וְיָדַעְתָּ הַיּוֹם וַהֲשֵׁבֹתָ אֶל לְבָבֶךָ — *You are to know this day and take to your heart.* The masters of *Mussar* explain that an abstract belief in God is not sufficient to make people observe the *mitzvos* as they should. After obtaining knowledge we must take it to heart; that is, develop an emotional commitment to act upon the knowledge.

☙ עַל כֵּן נְקַוֶּה לְךָ — *Therefore we put our hope in You.* Having stated that God chose us from among all the nations to serve Him, we are entitled to hope that He will speedily reveal His greatness and rid the earth of spiritual abomination *(Abudraham).*

לְעֹלָם וָעֶד.[1] ❖ וְנֶאֱמַר: וְהָיָה יהוה לְמֶלֶךְ עַל כָּל הָאָרֶץ, בַּיּוֹם הַהוּא יִהְיֶה יהוה אֶחָד וּשְׁמוֹ אֶחָד.[2]

Some congregations recite the following after עָלֵינוּ:

אַל תִּירָא* מִפַּחַד פִּתְאֹם, וּמִשֹּׁאַת רְשָׁעִים כִּי תָבֹא.[3] עֻצוּ עֵצָה וְתֻפָר, דַּבְּרוּ דָבָר וְלֹא יָקוּם, כִּי עִמָּנוּ אֵל.[4] וְעַד זִקְנָה אֲנִי הוּא, וְעַד שֵׂיבָה אֲנִי אֶסְבֹּל, אֲנִי עָשִׂיתִי וַאֲנִי אֶשָּׂא, וַאֲנִי אֶסְבֹּל וַאֲמַלֵּט.[5]

קדיש יתום

Mourners recite קַדִּישׁ יָתוֹם, the Mourner's *Kaddish* (see *Laws* §81-83).

יִתְגַּדַּל וְיִתְקַדַּשׁ שְׁמֵהּ רַבָּא.* (Cong. – אָמֵן.*) בְּעָלְמָא דִּי בְרָא כִרְעוּתֵהּ.* וְיַמְלִיךְ מַלְכוּתֵהּ, בְּחַיֵּיכוֹן* וּבְיוֹמֵיכוֹן וּבְחַיֵּי דְכָל בֵּית יִשְׂרָאֵל, בַּעֲגָלָא וּבִזְמַן קָרִיב.* וְאִמְרוּ: אָמֵן.

(Cong. – אָמֵן. יְהֵא שְׁמֵהּ רַבָּא* מְבָרַךְ לְעָלַם וּלְעָלְמֵי עָלְמַיָּא.)

יְהֵא שְׁמֵהּ רַבָּא מְבָרַךְ לְעָלַם וּלְעָלְמֵי עָלְמַיָּא.

יִתְבָּרַךְ* וְיִשְׁתַּבַּח וְיִתְפָּאַר וְיִתְרוֹמַם וְיִתְנַשֵּׂא וְיִתְהַדָּר וְיִתְעַלֶּה וְיִתְהַלָּל שְׁמֵהּ דְּקֻדְשָׁא בְּרִיךְ הוּא (Cong. – בְּרִיךְ הוּא) — לְעֵלָּא מִן כָּל בִּרְכָתָא* וְשִׁירָתָא תֻּשְׁבְּחָתָא וְנֶחֱמָתָא, דַּאֲמִירָן בְּעָלְמָא. וְאִמְרוּ: אָמֵן. (Cong. – אָמֵן.)

יְהֵא שְׁלָמָא רַבָּא מִן שְׁמַיָּא, וְחַיִּים עָלֵינוּ וְעַל כָּל יִשְׂרָאֵל. וְאִמְרוּ: אָמֵן. (Cong. – אָמֵן.)

Take three steps back. Bow left and say . . . עֹשֶׂה; bow right and say . . . הוּא; bow forward and say וְעַל כָּל . . . אָמֵן. Remain standing in place for a few moments, then take three steps forward.

עֹשֶׂה שָׁלוֹם בִּמְרוֹמָיו, הוּא יַעֲשֶׂה שָׁלוֹם עָלֵינוּ, וְעַל כָּל יִשְׂרָאֵל. וְאִמְרוּ: אָמֵן. (Cong. – אָמֵן.)

אַל תִּירָא — *Do not fear. Zichron Zion* cites the custom of reciting these three verses after *Aleinu.* They express confidence in God's protection and are regarded as auguries of deliverance: (a) Do not fear an evildoer's intention, no matter how dangerous it seems; (b) let the enemies of Israel conspire and plan — they will fail; (c) God remains the eternal protector of Israel, even though it has sinned.

קַדִּישׁ יָתוֹם / The Mourner's Kaddish

For the eleven months following the death of a parent and on the *yahrzeit,* or anniversary of the death, a son is obligated to recite *Kaddish* as a source of merit for the soul of the departed. A discussion of the concept and basis underlying the recitation of the Mourner's *Kaddish* appears in the ArtScroll *Kaddish.*

יִתְגַּדַּל וְיִתְקַדַּשׁ שְׁמֵהּ רַבָּא — *May His great Name grow exalted and sanctified.* The ultimate sanctification of God's Name will come when Israel is redeemed; in this sense *Kaddish* is a plea for the final Redemption. It is also an expression of Israel's mission to bring recognition of His sovereignty to all people on earth. This mission is incumbent primarily upon the community as a whole, and *Kaddish* is therefore recited only in the presence of a *minyan* [a quorum of ten males over *bar mitzvah*] *(R' Munk).*

אָמֵן — *Amen.* The word אָמֵן, *Amen,* is the listener's acknowledgment that he believes in what the reader has just said. It is derived from the same root as אֱמוּנָה, *faithfulness (Tur, Orach Chaim* 124). Additionally, it stands for אֵל מֶלֶךְ נֶאֱמָן, *God, the trustworthy King (Shabbos* 119b).

בְּעָלְמָא דִּי בְרָא כִרְעוּתֵהּ — *In the world that He created as He willed.* God had His concept of a perfect world before He began creation. Then He began to create in accordance with His prior will *(Ran).* Or it refers to the *future.* Only then *for all eternity in glory as it is written in Your Torah: HASHEM shall reign for all eternity.*[1] Chazzan– *And it is said: HASHEM will be King over all the world — on that day HASHEM will be One and His Name will be One.*[2]

Some congregations recite the following after *Aleinu:*

אַל תִּירָא *Do not fear* sudden terror, or the holocaust of the wicked when it comes.*[3] *Plan a conspiracy and it will be annulled; speak your piece and it shall not stand, for God is with us.*[4] *Even till your seniority, I remain unchanged; and even till your ripe old age, I shall endure. I created you and I shall bear you; I shall endure and rescue.*[5]

MOURNER'S KADDISH

Mourners recite the Mourner's *Kaddish* (see *Laws* §81-83).
[A transliteration of this *Kaddish* appears on page 1147.]

יִתְגַּדַּל *May His great Name grow exalted and sanctified** (Cong.– *Amen.**) *in the world that He created as He willed.* May He give reign to His kingship in your lifetimes* and in your days, and in the lifetimes of the entire Family of Israel, swiftly and soon.* Now respond: Amen.*

(Cong.– *Amen. May His great Name* be blessed forever and ever.*)
May His great Name be blessed forever and ever.

Blessed, praised, glorified, exalted, extolled, mighty, upraised, and lauded be the Name of the Holy One, Blessed is He* (Cong.– *Blessed is He*) *— beyond any blessing* and song, praise and consolation that are uttered in the world. Now respond: Amen.* (Cong.– *Amen*.)

May there be abundant peace from Heaven, and life, upon us and upon all Israel. Now respond: Amen. (Cong.– *Amen.*)

Take three steps back. Bow left and say, *'He Who makes peace . . .'*; bow right and say, *'may He . . .'*; bow forward and say, *'and upon all Israel . . .'* Remain standing in place for a few moments, then take three steps forward.

He Who makes peace in His heights, may He make peace upon us, and upon all Israel. Now respond: Amen. (Cong.– *Amen.*)

(1) *Exodus* 15:18. (2) *Zechariah* 14:9. (3) *Proverbs* 3:25. (4) *Isaiah* 8:10. (5) 46:4.

---

will mankind function in accordance with God's original intention *(R' Yehudah ben Yakar).*

בְּחַיֵּיכוֹן — *In your lifetimes.* The one reciting the *Kaddish* expresses the hope that his fellow congregants may all live to witness the Redemption of Israel and the sanctification of God's Name *(Abudraham).*

בַּעֲגָלָא וּבִזְמַן קָרִיב — *Swiftly and soon.* May the travail preceding the Messianic epoch be over swiftly and not be drawn out; and may it begin very soon *(Aruch HaShulchan).*

יְהֵא שְׁמֵהּ רַבָּא — *May His great Name . . .* The Talmud stresses in several places that the response, יְהֵא שְׁמֵהּ רַבָּא, *May His great Name. . .*, has an enormous cosmic effect. Indeed, the *halachah* states that an opportunity to respond to *Kaddish* takes precedence over an opportunity to respond to any other prayer, even *Kedushah* and *Borchu.* Consequently, if *Kaddish* is about to be recited in one room and *Kedushah* in another, one should go to hear *Kaddish (Mishnah Berurah* 56:6).

The Talmud *(Shabbos* 19b) teaches that one must respond יְהֵא שְׁמֵהּ רַבָּא 'with all his power,' meaning his total concentration *(Rashi, Tosafos).* Though it is preferable to raise one's voice when saying it, one should not say it so loudly that he will invite ridicule *(R' Yonah).* And it must be enunciated clearly *(Maharal).*

יִתְבָּרַךְ — *Blessed.* This begins a series of praises that continue the central theme of *Kaddish:* namely that in time to come God's greatness will be acknowledged by all of mankind *(Emek Berachah).*

לְעֵלָּא מִן כָּל בִּרְכָתָא — *Beyond any blessing.* No words or ideas can praise God adequately.

סֵדֶר אֲמִירַת קָרְבַּן פֶּסַח

After *Minchah,* many customarily recite the following passages that describe the קָרְבַּן פֶּסַח, *pesach* offering:

רִבּוֹן הָעוֹלָמִים, אַתָּה צִוִּיתָנוּ לְהַקְרִיב קָרְבַּן הַפֶּסַח בְּמוֹעֲדוֹ בְּאַרְבָּעָה עָשָׂר יוֹם לַחֹדֶשׁ הָרִאשׁוֹן, וְלִהְיוֹת כֹּהֲנִים בַּעֲבוֹדָתָם וּלְוִיִּם בְּדוּכָנָם וְיִשְׂרָאֵל בְּמַעֲמָדָם קוֹרְאִים אֶת הַהַלֵּל. וְעַתָּה בַּעֲוֹנוֹתֵינוּ חָרַב בֵּית הַמִּקְדָּשׁ וּבָטֵל קָרְבַּן הַפֶּסַח, וְאֵין לָנוּ לֹא כֹהֵן בַּעֲבוֹדָתוֹ וְלֹא לֵוִי בְדוּכָנוֹ וְלֹא יִשְׂרָאֵל בְּמַעֲמָדוֹ, וְלֹא נוּכַל לְהַקְרִיב הַיּוֹם קָרְבַּן פֶּסַח. אֲבָל אַתָּה אָמַרְתָּ וּנְשַׁלְּמָה פָרִים שְׂפָתֵינוּ.[1] לָכֵן יְהִי רָצוֹן מִלְּפָנֶיךָ יהוה אֱלֹהֵינוּ וֵאלֹהֵי אֲבוֹתֵינוּ שֶׁיִּהְיֶה שִׂיחַ שִׂפְתוֹתֵינוּ חָשׁוּב לְפָנֶיךָ כְּאִלּוּ הִקְרַבְנוּ אֶת הַפֶּסַח בְּמוֹעֲדוֹ וְעָמַדְנוּ עַל מַעֲמָדוֹ, וְדִבְּרוּ הַלְוִיִּם בְּשִׁיר וְהַלֵּל לְהוֹדוֹת לַיהוה. וְאַתָּה תְּכוֹנֵן מִקְדָּשְׁךָ עַל מְכוֹנוֹ, וְנַעֲשֶׂה וְנַקְרִיב לְפָנֶיךָ אֶת הַפֶּסַח בְּמוֹעֲדוֹ, כְּמוֹ שֶׁכָּתַבְתָּ עָלֵינוּ בְּתוֹרָתֶךָ עַל יְדֵי מֹשֶׁה עַבְדֶּךָ כָּאָמוּר:

שמות יב:א-יא

וַיֹּאמֶר יהוה אֶל מֹשֶׁה וְאֶל אַהֲרֹן בְּאֶרֶץ מִצְרַיִם לֵאמֹר. הַחֹדֶשׁ הַזֶּה לָכֶם רֹאשׁ חֳדָשִׁים רִאשׁוֹן הוּא לָכֶם לְחָדְשֵׁי הַשָּׁנָה. דַּבְּרוּ אֶל כָּל עֲדַת יִשְׂרָאֵל לֵאמֹר בֶּעָשֹׂר לַחֹדֶשׁ הַזֶּה וְיִקְחוּ לָהֶם אִישׁ שֶׂה לְבֵית אָבֹת שֶׂה לַבָּיִת. וְאִם יִמְעַט הַבַּיִת מִהְיוֹת מִשֶּׂה וְלָקַח הוּא וּשְׁכֵנוֹ הַקָּרֹב אֶל בֵּיתוֹ בְּמִכְסַת נְפָשֹׁת אִישׁ לְפִי אָכְלוֹ תָּכֹסּוּ עַל הַשֶּׂה. שֶׂה תָמִים זָכָר בֶּן שָׁנָה יִהְיֶה לָכֶם מִן הַכְּבָשִׂים וּמִן הָעִזִּים תִּקָּחוּ. וְהָיָה לָכֶם לְמִשְׁמֶרֶת עַד אַרְבָּעָה עָשָׂר יוֹם לַחֹדֶשׁ הַזֶּה וְשָׁחֲטוּ אֹתוֹ כֹּל קְהַל עֲדַת יִשְׂרָאֵל בֵּין הָעַרְבָּיִם. וְלָקְחוּ מִן הַדָּם וְנָתְנוּ עַל שְׁתֵּי הַמְּזוּזֹת וְעַל הַמַּשְׁקוֹף עַל הַבָּתִּים אֲשֶׁר יֹאכְלוּ אֹתוֹ בָּהֶם. וְאָכְלוּ אֶת הַבָּשָׂר בַּלַּיְלָה הַזֶּה צְלִי אֵשׁ וּמַצּוֹת עַל מְרֹרִים יֹאכְלֻהוּ. אַל תֹּאכְלוּ מִמֶּנּוּ נָא וּבָשֵׁל מְבֻשָּׁל בַּמָּיִם כִּי אִם צְלִי אֵשׁ רֹאשׁוֹ עַל כְּרָעָיו וְעַל קִרְבּוֹ. וְלֹא תוֹתִירוּ מִמֶּנּוּ עַד בֹּקֶר וְהַנֹּתָר מִמֶּנּוּ עַד בֹּקֶר בָּאֵשׁ תִּשְׂרֹפוּ. וְכָכָה תֹּאכְלוּ אֹתוֹ מָתְנֵיכֶם חֲגֻרִים נַעֲלֵיכֶם בְּרַגְלֵיכֶם וּמַקֶּלְכֶם בְּיֶדְכֶם וַאֲכַלְתֶּם אֹתוֹ בְּחִפָּזוֹן פֶּסַח הוּא לַיהוה.

(Some recite additional Scriptural passages that mention the *pesach* offering. The passages appear on page 1108).

סֵדֶר אֲמִירַת קָרְבַּן פֶּסַח / Recital of the Pesach Offering

Rambam, in his introductory notes to *Hilchos Korban Pesach*, lists sixteen *mitzvos*, four positive and twelve negative, associated with the *pesach* offering. We may omit the four of the sixteen that have to do with the *pesach sheni*, the 'second *pesach'* offered by those who could not — because of either *tumah* or their distance from the *Beis Hamikdash* — offer the *pesach* at its proper time. We may likewise discount one of these *mitzvos* which has to do with the *chagigah* offering, an offering brought in conjunction with the *pesach*, but distinct from it. Thus we have eleven *mitzvos* associated with the *pesach*.

These eleven are: (1) to slaughter the *pesach* offering at the proper time, during the afternoon of the fourteenth of Nissan; (2) not

RECITAL OF THE PESACH OFFERING

After *Minchah,* many customarily recite the following passages that describe the קָרְבַּן פֶּסַח, *pesach* offering:

רִבּוֹן הָעוֹלָמִים *Master of the universe, You commanded us to bring the pesach offering at its set time, on the fourteenth day of the first month; and that the Kohanim be at their assigned service, the Levites on their platform, and the Israelites at their station reciting the Hallel. But now, through our sins, the Holy Temple is destroyed, the pesach offering is discontinued, and we have neither Kohen at his service, nor Levite on his platform, nor Israelite at his station. So we are unable to bring the pesach offering today. But You said: 'Let our lips compensate for the bulls'*[1] *— therefore, may it be Your will,* HASHEM, *our God and the God of our forefathers, that the prayer of our lips be considered by You as if we had brought the pesach offering at its set time, had stood at its station, and the Levites had uttered song and Hallel, to thank* HASHEM. *And may You establish Your sanctuary on its prepared site, that we may ascend and bring the pesach offering before You at its set time — as You have prescribed for us in Your Torah, through Moses, Your servant, as it is said:*

Exodus 12:1-11

וַיֹּאמֶר *And* HASHEM *said to Moses and Aaron in the land of Egypt saying: This month is for you the beginning of the months, it is for you the first of the months of the year. Speak to the entire congregation of Israel saying: On the tenth of this month, they shall take unto themselves, each man, a lamb/kid to his fathers' household, a lamb/kid to a household. But if the household is too small for a lamb/kid, then he shall take with his neighbor who is close to his house, according to the number of souls; each man according to how much he can eat, shall you count upon a lamb/kid. An unblemished male lamb/kid in its first year shall it be to you; you may take it from the sheep or from the goats. It shall be for you as a safekeeping until the fourteenth day of this month; and you — the entire assembly of the congregation of Israel — shall slaughter it in the afternoon. And they shall take some of the blood and place it on the two doorposts and on the lintel, upon the houses in which they shall eat it. And they shall eat the meat on that night, roasted with fire, and matzah, with bitter herbs shall they eat it. You shall not eat it rare or cooked in water, but only roasted with fire, its head with its legs and with its innards. You shall not leave over from it until morning; and anything left of it until morning, you shall burn in the fire. Thus shall you eat it: your loins girded, your shoes on your feet, and your staves in your hands; you shall eat it in haste, it is a pesach offering to* HASHEM.

(Some recite additional Scriptural passages that mention the *pesach* offering. The passages appear on page 1108.)

(1) *Hoshea* 14:3.

to slaughter it while any *chametz* may be found in one's possession; (3) not to allow the night to pass without placing on the Altar those parts ordained by Scripture to be consumed by the Altar fire; (4) to eat the meat of the *pesach* with *matzah* and bitter herbs on the night of the fifteenth of Nissan; (5) not to eat the *pesach* when it is only partially roasted, or if it has been cooked in liquid; (6) not to remove the meat of the sacrifice from the group of people who have registered to eat that particular animal; (7) not to allow a Jewish idolater to eat the *pesach*; (8) not to allow a non-Jew to eat the *pesach*; (9) not to allow an uncircumcised male to eat the *pesach*; (10) not to break the bones of the *pesach*; and (11) not to leave the meat of the

כָּךְ הָיְתָה עֲבוֹדַת קָרְבַּן הַפֶּסַח בְּבֵית אֱלֹהֵינוּ בְּיוֹם אַרְבָּעָה עָשָׂר בְּנִיסָן:

אֵין שׁוֹחֲטִין אוֹתוֹ אֶלָּא אַחַר תָּמִיד שֶׁל בֵּין הָעַרְבָּיִם. עֶרֶב פֶּסַח, בֵּין בְּחֹל בֵּין בְּשַׁבָּת, הָיָה הַתָּמִיד נִשְׁחָט בְּשֶׁבַע וּמֶחֱצָה וְקָרֵב בִּשְׁמוֹנֶה וּמֶחֱצָה. וְאִם חָל עֶרֶב פֶּסַח לִהְיוֹת עֶרֶב שַׁבָּת הָיוּ שׁוֹחֲטִין אוֹתוֹ בְּשֵׁשׁ וּמֶחֱצָה וְקָרֵב בְּשֶׁבַע וּמֶחֱצָה. וְהַפֶּסַח אַחֲרָיו.

כָּל אָדָם מִיִּשְׂרָאֵל, אֶחָד הָאִישׁ וְאֶחָד הָאִשָּׁה, כָּל שֶׁיָּכוֹל לְהַגִּיעַ לִירוּשָׁלַיִם בִּשְׁעַת שְׁחִיטַת הַפֶּסַח חַיָּב בְּקָרְבַּן פֶּסַח.

מְבִיאוֹ מִן הַכְּבָשִׂים אוֹ מִן הָעִזִּים, זָכָר תָּמִים בֶּן שָׁנָה, וְשׁוֹחֲטוֹ בְּכָל מָקוֹם בָּעֲזָרָה, אַחַר גְּמַר עֲבוֹדַת תְּמִיד הָעֶרֶב וְאַחַר הֲטָבַת הַנֵּרוֹת.

וְאֵין שׁוֹחֲטִין הַפֶּסַח, וְלֹא זוֹרְקִין הַדָּם, וְלֹא מַקְטִירִין הַחֵלֶב, עַל הֶחָמֵץ.

שָׁחַט הַשּׁוֹחֵט, וְקִבֵּל דָּמוֹ הַכֹּהֵן שֶׁבְּרֹאשׁ הַשּׁוּרָה בִּכְלִי שָׁרֵת, וְנוֹתֵן לַחֲבֵרוֹ, וַחֲבֵרוֹ לַחֲבֵרוֹ. כֹּהֵן הַקָּרוֹב אֵצֶל הַמִּזְבֵּחַ זוֹרְקוֹ זְרִיקָה אַחַת כְּנֶגֶד הַיְסוֹד, וְחוֹזֵר הַכְּלִי רֵיקָן לַחֲבֵרוֹ, וַחֲבֵרוֹ לַחֲבֵרוֹ. מְקַבֵּל אֶת הַמָּלֵא וּמַחֲזִיר אֶת הָרֵיקָן. וְהָיוּ הַכֹּהֲנִים עוֹמְדִים שׁוּרוֹת וּבִידֵיהֶם בָּזִיכִין שֶׁכֻּלָּן כֶּסֶף אוֹ כֻּלָּן זָהָב. וְלֹא הָיוּ מְעֹרָבִים. וְלֹא הָיוּ לַבָּזִיכִין שׁוּלַיִם, שֶׁלֹּא יַנִּיחוּם וְיִקָּרֵשׁ הַדָּם.

אַחַר כָּךְ תּוֹלִין אֶת הַפֶּסַח בְּאֻנְקְלָיוֹת, וּמַפְשִׁיט אוֹתוֹ כֻּלּוֹ, וְקוֹרְעִין בִּטְנוֹ וּמוֹצִיאִין אֵמוּרָיו – הַחֵלֶב שֶׁעַל הַקֶּרֶב, וְיוֹתֶרֶת הַכָּבֵד, וּשְׁתֵּי הַכְּלָיוֹת, וְהַחֵלֶב שֶׁעֲלֵיהֶן, וְהָאַלְיָה לְעֻמַּת הֶעָצֶה. נוֹתְנָן בִּכְלִי שָׁרֵת וּמוֹלְחָן וּמַקְטִירָן הַכֹּהֵן עַל הַמַּעֲרָכָה, חֶלְבֵי כָל זֶבַח וָזֶבַח לְבַדּוֹ. בְּחֹל, בַּיּוֹם וְלֹא בַלַּיְלָה שֶׁהוּא יוֹם טוֹב. אֲבָל אִם חָל עֶרֶב פֶּסַח בְּשַׁבָּת, מַקְטִירִין וְהוֹלְכִין כָּל הַלַּיְלָה. וּמוֹצִיא קְרָבָיו וּמְמַחֶה אוֹתָן עַד שֶׁמֵּסִיר מֵהֶן הַפֶּרֶשׁ.

שְׁחִיטָתוֹ וּזְרִיקַת דָּמוֹ וּמִחוּי קְרָבָיו וְהֶקְטֵר חֲלָבָיו דּוֹחִין אֶת הַשַּׁבָּת, וּשְׁאָר עִנְיָנָיו אֵין דּוֹחִין.

בְּשָׁלֹשׁ כִּתּוֹת הַפֶּסַח נִשְׁחָט. וְאֵין כַּת פְּחוּתָה מִשְּׁלֹשִׁים אֲנָשִׁים. נִכְנְסָה כַּת אַחַת, נִתְמַלְּאָה הָעֲזָרָה, נוֹעֲלִין אוֹתָהּ. וּבְעוֹד שֶׁהֵם שׁוֹחֲטִין וּמַקְרִיבִין, הַכֹּהֲנִים תּוֹקְעִין, הֶחָלִיל מַכֶּה לִפְנֵי הַמִּזְבֵּחַ, וְהַלְוִיִּים קוֹרְאִין אֶת הַהַלֵּל. אִם גָּמְרוּ קֹדֶם שֶׁיַּקְרִיבוּ כֻּלָּם, שָׁנוּ; אִם שָׁנוּ, שִׁלֵּשׁוּ. עַל כָּל קְרִיאָה תָּקְעוּ הֵרִיעוּ וְתָקְעוּ. גָּמְרָה כַּת אַחַת לְהַקְרִיב, פּוֹתְחִין הָעֲזָרָה, יָצְאָה כַּת רִאשׁוֹנָה, נִכְנְסָה כַּת שְׁנִיָּה, נָעֲלוּ דַּלְתוֹת הָעֲזָרָה. גָּמְרָה, יָצְאָה שְׁנִיָּה וְנִכְנְסָה שְׁלִישִׁית. כְּמַעֲשֵׂה הָרִאשׁוֹנָה כָּךְ מַעֲשֵׂה הַשְּׁנִיָּה וְהַשְּׁלִישִׁית.

---

pesach uneaten until the morning.

After *Minchah* on *Erev Pesach,* many customarily recite the Biblical verses (*Exodus* 12:1-12) that discuss the *pesach* offering, along

כָּךְ *This was the service of the pesach offering on the fourteenth of Nissan:*

We may not slaughter it until after the afternoon tamid offering. On the eve of Pesach, whether on a weekday or on the Sabbath, the tamid offering would be slaughtered at seven and a half hours [after daybreak], and offered at eight and a half hours. But when the eve of Pesach fell on Friday, they would slaughter it at six and a half hours, and offer it at seven and a half. [In either case] the pesach offering [was slaughtered] after it.

Every Jew, male or female, whoever is able to reach Jerusalem in time to slaughter the pesach, is obligated to bring the pesach offering.

It may be brought from sheep or from goats, an unblemished male in its first year. It may be slaughtered anywhere in the Temple Courtyard, after the completion of the afternoon tamid offering, and after the kindling of the Menorah's lamps.

We may not slaughter the pesach, nor throw its blood [onto the Altar], nor burn its fats [on the Altar], if chametz is in our possession.

Someone [even a non-Kohen] would slaughter [the animal]. The Kohen at the head of the line [closest to the animal] would receive its blood in a sanctified vessel and pass it to his colleague, and he to his colleague. The Kohen closest to the Altar would throw it, with one throwing, at the base [of the Altar], then return the vessel to his colleague, and he to his colleague. He would first accept the full one, then return the empty one. The Kohanim would stand in lines, [all the Kohanim of each line] holding either silver or golden vessels. But they would not mix [two types of vessels in one line]. The vessels did not have flat bottoms, lest one would put down a vessel [and forget it], thus causing the blood to congeal.

Following this, they would suspend the pesach from hooks. They would skin it completely, tear open its stomach and remove the organs ordained for the Altar — the suet covering the stomach, the diaphragm with the liver, the two kidneys and the suet upon them, and [in the case of a lamb] the tail opposite the kidneys. They would place [these organs] in a sanctified vessel and salt them, then a Kohen would burn them on the Altar fire. The portions of each offering [would be placed on the fire] separately. On a weekday, [this would be done] by day and not at night when the festival had already begun. But when the eve of Pesach fell on the Sabbath, they would burn [the organs] during the entire night. They would remove the innards and squeeze them until all their wastes were removed.

Slaughtering it, throwing its blood, squeezing out its innards, and burning its fats [on the Altar] supersede the Sabbath; but its other requirements do not supersede [the Sabbath].

The pesach is slaughtered in three groups, no group comprising less than thirty men. The first entered, filling the Courtyard; then they closed the gates. For as long as they slaughtered and offered [the pesach], the Kohanim would blow the shofar, the flute would play before the Altar, and the Levites would recite Hallel. If they completed [Hallel] before all had brought their offerings, they repeated it. If they completed [Hallel] a second time, they would recite it a third time. For each recitation, they blew tekiah, teruah, tekiah. When the first group was done offering, they opened the Courtyard [gates]. The first group left, the second group entered, and the Courtyard gates were closed. When they were done, the second group left and the third group entered. Like the procedure of the first, so was the procedure of the second and third.

אַחַר שֶׁיָּצְאוּ כֻּלָּן רוֹחֲצִין הָעֲזָרָה מִלִּכְלוּכֵי הַדָּם, וַאֲפִלּוּ בְּשַׁבָּת. אַמַּת הַמַּיִם הָיְתָה עוֹבֶרֶת בָּעֲזָרָה, שֶׁכְּשֶׁרוֹצִין לְהָדִיחַ הָרִצְפָּה סוֹתְמִין מְקוֹם יְצִיאַת הַמַּיִם וְהִיא מִתְמַלֵּאת עַל כָּל גְּדוֹתֶיהָ, עַד שֶׁהַמַּיִם עוֹלִין וְצָפִין וּמְקַבְּצִין אֲלֵיהֶם כָּל דָּם וְלִכְלוּךְ שֶׁבָּעֲזָרָה. אַחַר כָּךְ פּוֹתְחִין הַסְּתִימָה וְיוֹצְאִין הַמַּיִם עִם הַלִּכְלוּךְ, נִמְצֵאת הָרִצְפָּה מְנֻקָּה, זֶהוּ כִּבּוּד הַבַּיִת.

יָצְאוּ כָּל אֶחָד עִם פִּסְחוֹ וְצָלוּ אוֹתָם. כֵּיצַד צוֹלִין אוֹתוֹ? מְבִיאִין שַׁפּוּד שֶׁל רִמּוֹן, תּוֹחֲבוֹ מִתּוֹךְ פִּיו עַד בֵּית נְקוּבָתוֹ, וְתוֹלֵהוּ לְתוֹךְ הַתַּנּוּר וְהָאֵשׁ לְמַטָּה, וְתוֹלֶה כְּרָעָיו וּבְנֵי מֵעָיו חוּצָה לוֹ, וְאֵין מְנַקְּרִין אֶת הַפֶּסַח כִּשְׁאָר בָּשָׂר.

בְּשַׁבָּת אֵינָן מוֹלִיכִין אֶת הַפֶּסַח לְבֵיתָם, אֶלָּא כַּת הָרִאשׁוֹנָה יוֹצְאִין בְּפִסְחֵיהֶן וְיוֹשְׁבִין בְּהַר הַבַּיִת, הַשְּׁנִיָּה יוֹצְאִין עִם פִּסְחֵיהֶן וְיוֹשְׁבִין בַּחֵיל, וְהַשְּׁלִישִׁית בִּמְקוֹמָהּ עוֹמֶדֶת. חָשֵׁכָה, יָצְאוּ וְצָלוּ אֶת פִּסְחֵיהֶן.

כְּשֶׁמַּקְרִיבִין אֶת הַפֶּסַח בָּרִאשׁוֹן מַקְרִיבִין עִמּוֹ בְּיוֹם אַרְבָּעָה עָשָׂר זֶבַח שְׁלָמִים, מִן הַבָּקָר אוֹ מִן הַצֹּאן, גְּדוֹלִים אוֹ קְטַנִּים, זְכָרִים אוֹ נְקֵבוֹת, וְהִיא נִקְרֵאת חֲגִיגַת אַרְבָּעָה עָשָׂר, עַל זֶה נֶאֱמַר בַּתּוֹרָה, וְזָבַחְתָּ פֶּסַח לַיהוה אֱלֹהֶיךָ צֹאן וּבָקָר.[1] וְלֹא קְבָעָהּ הַכָּתוּב חוֹבָה אֶלָּא רְשׁוּת בִּלְבָד, מִכָּל מָקוֹם הִיא כְחוֹבָה מִדִּבְרֵי סוֹפְרִים, כְּדֵי שֶׁיְּהֵא הַפֶּסַח נֶאֱכָל עַל הַשֹּׂבַע. אֵימָתַי מְבִיאִין עִמּוֹ חֲגִיגָה? בִּזְמַן שֶׁהוּא בָא בְחֹל, בְּטָהֳרָה וּבְמוּעָט. וְנֶאֱכֶלֶת לִשְׁנֵי יָמִים וְלַיְלָה אֶחָד, וְדִינָהּ כְּכָל תּוֹרַת זִבְחֵי שְׁלָמִים, טְעוּנָה סְמִיכָה וּנְסָכִים וּמַתַּן דָּמִים שְׁתַּיִם שֶׁהֵן אַרְבַּע וּשְׁפִיכַת שִׁירַיִם לַיְסוֹד.

זֶהוּ סֵדֶר עֲבוֹדַת קָרְבַּן פֶּסַח וַחֲגִיגָה שֶׁעִמּוֹ בְּבֵית אֱלֹהֵינוּ שֶׁיִּבָּנֶה בִּמְהֵרָה בְיָמֵינוּ, אָמֵן. אַשְׁרֵי הָעָם שֶׁכָּכָה לּוֹ, אַשְׁרֵי הָעָם שֶׁיהוה אֱלֹהָיו.[2]

אֱלֹהֵינוּ וֵאלֹהֵי אֲבוֹתֵינוּ, מֶלֶךְ רַחֲמָן רַחֵם עָלֵינוּ, טוֹב וּמֵטִיב הִדָּרֶשׁ לָנוּ. שׁוּבָה אֵלֵינוּ בַּהֲמוֹן רַחֲמֶיךָ בִּגְלַל אָבוֹת שֶׁעָשׂוּ רְצוֹנֶךָ. בְּנֵה בֵיתְךָ כְּבַתְּחִלָּה וְכוֹנֵן מִקְדָּשְׁךָ עַל מְכוֹנוֹ. וְהַרְאֵנוּ בְּבִנְיָנוֹ וְשַׂמְּחֵנוּ בְּתִקּוּנוֹ. וְהָשֵׁב שְׁכִינָתְךָ לְתוֹכוֹ, וְהָשֵׁב כֹּהֲנִים לַעֲבוֹדָתָם וּלְוִיִּם לְשִׁירָם וּלְזִמְרָם, וְהָשֵׁב יִשְׂרָאֵל לִנְוֵיהֶם. וְשָׁם נַעֲלֶה וְנֵרָאֶה וְנִשְׁתַּחֲוֶה לְפָנֶיךָ. וְנֹאכַל שָׁם מִן הַזְּבָחִים וּמִן הַפְּסָחִים אֲשֶׁר יַגִּיעַ דָּמָם עַל קִיר מִזְבַּחֲךָ לְרָצוֹן. יִהְיוּ לְרָצוֹן אִמְרֵי פִי וְהֶגְיוֹן לִבִּי לְפָנֶיךָ, יהוה צוּרִי וְגֹאֲלִי.[3]

---

with the detailed listing of the procedure through which it was brought. The passage presented here beginning כָּךְ הָיְתָה, *This was,* appears in some *machzorim* and *siddurim* with minor variations. We have followed the text given in the *siddur* of *R' Yaakov Emden.*

After all [three groups] had left, they [the Kohanim] would wash the [stone] Courtyard [floor] of the blood, even on the Sabbath. A channel of water passed through the Courtyard. When they wished to wash the floor, they would block the outlet, causing the water to overflow and gather all the bloods and other waste matter in the Courtyard. Then they would remove the blockage and the water with the waste would run out. Thus, the floor would be clean. And this is the manner of cleansing the Temple.

They left, each with his pesach, and roasted them. In what manner was it roasted? They would bring a pomegranate wood spit, thrust it through its mouth to its anus and suspend it inside the oven with the fire below it. Its legs and innards were suspended outside [its body cavity]. They would not purge the pesach in the same manner as other meat.

On the Sabbath they would not carry the pesach [meat] to their homes. Rather, the first group would go out [of the Courtyard] with their pesach offerings and remain on the Temple Mount. The second group would go out and remain within the Cheil [a ten-cubit wide area, just outside the Courtyard walls]. The third group would remain where they were. When it became dark, they would leave [for their homes] and roast their pesach offerings.

When they would bring the pesach offering, they would bring with it — on the fourteenth of Nissan — a peace-offering, either from the cattle herd or from the flock, old or young, male or female. This is called 'the festive offering of the fourteenth.' Regarding this the Torah states: And you shall slaughter the pesach offering to HASHEM, your God, flock and cattle.[1] Yet the Torah did not establish this as an obligation, but only as a voluntary offering. Nevertheless, it was made obligatory by the Rabbis, in order that the pesach offering be eaten in satiety. When may the festive-offering be brought with it [the pesach]? When it [the pesach] is brought on a weekday, in purity and there are few. It may be eaten for two days and the included night, its laws being the same as the laws of other peace-offerings. It requires semichah, libations, two [Altar] applications of blood that are equivalent to four, and pouring the remainder [of the blood] at the [Altar's] base.

This is the order of the pesach offering and the festive-offering brought with it in the Temple of our God — may it be rebuilt speedily, in our days — Amen. Praiseworthy is the people for whom this is so; praiseworthy is the people whose God is HASHEM.[2]

אֱלֹהֵינוּ *Our God and the God of our forefathers, O merciful King, have mercy on us; O good and beneficent One, let Yourself be sought out by us; return to us in Your yearning mercy for the sake of the forefathers who did Your will. Rebuild You House as it was at first, and establish Your Sanctuary on its prepared site; show us its rebuilding and gladden us in its perfection. Return Your Shechinah to it; restore the Kohanim to their service, the Levites to their song and music; and restore Israel to their dwellings. And there may we ascend and appear and prostrate ourselves before You. There we shall eat of the peace offerings and pesach offerings whose blood will gain the sides of Your Altar for favorable acceptance. May the expressions of my mouth and the thoughts of my heart find favor before You, HASHEM, my Rock and my Redeemer.[3]*

---

(1) *Deuteronomy* 16:2 (2) *Psalms* 144:15. (3) 19:15.

WHEN PESACH FALLS ON A WEEKDAY, TURN TO *MAARIV*, PAGE 42.

❦ קבלת שבת ❦

When the first day of Pesach coincides with the Sabbath, *Kabbalas Shabbos* [our acceptance upon ourselves of the holiness of the Sabbath] consists of Psalms 92 and 93.

תהלים צב

מִזְמוֹר שִׁיר לְיוֹם הַשַּׁבָּת.* טוֹב לְהֹדוֹת לַיהוה, וּלְזַמֵּר לְשִׁמְךָ עֶלְיוֹן. לְהַגִּיד בַּבֹּקֶר חַסְדֶּךָ, וֶאֱמוּנָתְךָ בַּלֵּילוֹת.* עֲלֵי עָשׂוֹר* וַעֲלֵי נָבֶל, עֲלֵי הִגָּיוֹן בְּכִנּוֹר. כִּי שִׂמַּחְתַּנִי יהוה בְּפָעֳלֶךָ, בְּמַעֲשֵׂי יָדֶיךָ אֲרַנֵּן. מַה גָּדְלוּ מַעֲשֶׂיךָ יהוה, מְאֹד עָמְקוּ מַחְשְׁבֹתֶיךָ.* אִישׁ בַּעַר לֹא יֵדָע, וּכְסִיל לֹא יָבִין אֶת זֹאת. בִּפְרֹחַ רְשָׁעִים* כְּמוֹ עֵשֶׂב, וַיָּצִיצוּ כָּל פֹּעֲלֵי אָוֶן, לְהִשָּׁמְדָם עֲדֵי עַד.* וְאַתָּה מָרוֹם לְעֹלָם יהוה. כִּי הִנֵּה אֹיְבֶיךָ יהוה, כִּי הִנֵּה אֹיְבֶיךָ יֹאבֵדוּ, יִתְפָּרְדוּ כָּל פֹּעֲלֵי אָוֶן. וַתָּרֶם כִּרְאֵים קַרְנִי,* בַּלֹּתִי בְּשֶׁמֶן רַעֲנָן.* וַתַּבֵּט עֵינִי בְּשׁוּרָי, בַּקָּמִים עָלַי מְרֵעִים, תִּשְׁמַעְנָה אָזְנָי. ❖ צַדִּיק כַּתָּמָר יִפְרָח, כְּאֶרֶז* בַּלְּבָנוֹן יִשְׂגֶּה. שְׁתוּלִים בְּבֵית יהוה,* בְּחַצְרוֹת אֱלֹהֵינוּ יַפְרִיחוּ. עוֹד יְנוּבוּן בְּשֵׂיבָה, דְּשֵׁנִים וְרַעֲנַנִּים יִהְיוּ. לְהַגִּיד כִּי יָשָׁר יהוה, צוּרִי וְלֹא עַוְלָתָה בּוֹ.

❦ קַבָּלַת שַׁבָּת / KABBALAS SHABBOS ❦

⊰ מִזְמוֹר שִׁיר לְיוֹם הַשַּׁבָּת / Psalm 92 ⊱

The custom of reciting psalms ninety-two and ninety-three at the arrival of the Sabbath is ancient. In a responsa, *Rambam* (*Pe'er HaDor* 116) implies clearly that it predated him by many generations. With our recitation of this song of praise to the Sabbath, we accept its holiness upon ourselves together with all its positive and negative *mitzvos*.

מִזְמוֹר שִׁיר לְיוֹם הַשַּׁבָּת — *A psalm, a song for the Sabbath day.* Although this psalm is identified as belonging particularly to the theme of the Sabbath — indeed, it was the Levites' song for the Sabbath Temple service (*Rashi*) — the text contains not a single direct reference to the Sabbath. What is the connection? Many explanations are given. Among them are:

— The psalm refers not to the weekly Sabbath, but to the World to Come, when man will achieve the spiritual perfection we only glimpse during the Sabbath. The psalm is thus well suited to the Sabbath which is a semblance of that future spiritual perfection (*Rashi*).

— Praise of God is necessary, but difficult in the weekdays when people must struggle for a livelihood. On the Sabbath when Jews are free from the strictures of the week, they can turn their minds and hearts to the perception of God's ways and His praise — which are the topics of this psalm (*Radak*).

בַּבֹּקֶר ... בַּלֵּילוֹת — *In the dawn ... in the nights.* Dawn is an allusion to redemption, while night symbolizes exile. We express our faith that even when God made us suffer, that too was kindness, because He did it for our ultimate benefit. Thus we *relate* His *kindness*, whether it was as clear and pleasant as the bright *dawn* or whether it was as hard to accept as the dark *night*. During the harsh night of exile, we call it אֱמוּנָתְךָ, *Your faith*, because we have faith that God is good, even if we do not understand some of the things He does.

עֲלֵי עָשׂוֹר — *Upon ten-stringed instrument.* The Sages teach that the lyre of Messianic times will be ten-stringed, representing a beautiful enhancement of music, which is now limited to the octave of eight notes. Every period in life calls for its own unique expression of praise, just as each day has its own song of praise and each part of creation serves God in its own way. The

WHEN PESACH FALLS ON A WEEKDAY, TURN TO *MAARIV,* PAGE 42.

KABBALAS SHABBOS

When the first day of Pesach coincides with the Sabbath, *Kabbalas Shabbos* [our acceptance upon ourselves of the holiness of the Sabbath] consists of Psalms 92 and 93.

Psalm 92

מִזְמוֹר שִׁיר *A psalm, a song for the Sabbath day.* It is good to thank* H*ASHEM and to sing praise to Your Name, O Exalted One; to relate Your kindness in the dawn and Your faith in the nights.* Upon ten-stringed instrument* and lyre, with singing accompanied by a harp. For You have gladdened me,* H*ASHEM, with Your deeds; at the works of Your Hands I sing glad song. How great are Your deeds,* H*ASHEM; exceedingly profound are Your thoughts.* A boor cannot know, nor can a fool understand this: when the wicked bloom* like grass and all the doers of iniquity blossom — it is to destroy them till eternity.* But You remain exalted forever,* H*ASHEM. For behold! — Your enemies,* H*ASHEM, for behold! — Your enemies shall perish, dispersed shall be all doers of iniquity. As exalted as a re'eim's shall be my pride,* I will be saturated with ever-fresh oil.* My eyes have seen my vigilant foes; when those who would harm me rise up against me, my ears have heard their doom.* Chazzan– *A righteous man will flourish like a date palm, like a cedar* in the Lebanon he will grow tall. Planted in the house of* H*ASHEM,* in the courtyards of our God they will flourish. They will still be fruitful in old age, vigorous and fresh they will be — to declare that* H*ASHEM is just, my Rock in Whom there is no wrong.*

---

enhanced spirituality of Messianic times will demand a heightened form of song (*Sfas Emes;* see *Overview,* ArtScroll *Tehillim*).

מַעֲשֶׂיךָ ... מַחְשְׁבֹתֶיךָ — *Your deeds ... Your thoughts.* God's *deeds* are the tangible parts of Creation and the events we perceive with our senses. His *thoughts* are His purposes and goals; they are profound beyond human comprehension (*Sfas Emes*).

בִּפְרֹחַ רְשָׁעִים — *When the wicked bloom.* Most people can find no answer to the eternal human dilemma: Why do the wicked prosper? If only these inquisitors could look beyond what their senses tell them, they would realize that ...

לְהִשָּׁמְדָם עֲדֵי עַד — *To destroy them till eternity.* God gives temporal success and happiness to the wicked as reward for whatever good deeds they may have done. Having been recompensed, they will sink to destruction, while the righteous gain eternal reward (*Rashi*).

וַתָּרֶם כִּרְאֵים קַרְנִי — *As exalted as a re'eim's shall be my pride* [lit. *my horn*]. The once-downtrodden pride of the righteous will rise and be as exalted as the upraised horns of the haughty *re'eim* [a beast of uncertain identity, variously translated as unicorn, rhinoceros, buffalo, antelope, and others]. In any case, its use in Scripture indicates that it has a long and powerful horn.

בְּשֶׁמֶן רַעֲנָן — *With ever-fresh oil.* Oil is a common Scriptural simile for blessing, prosperity, and supremacy (*Rashi*).

כַּתָּמָר ... כְּאֶרֶז — *Like a date palm, like a cedar.* The *tzaddik* will be as fruitful as a date palm, and as sturdy in health as a cedar (*Rashi*).

שְׁתוּלִים בְּבֵית ה׳ — *Planted in the house of* H*ASHEM.* The quality of a tree — described in the previous verse — is only half the formula for success; for maximum benefit it must be planted in luxuriant soil. The righteous will be firmly rooted in the spiritual riches of God's House. There they will blossom without limit (*Radak*).

תהלים צג

יהוה מָלָךְ גֵּאוּת לָבֵשׁ,* לָבֵשׁ יהוה עֹז הִתְאַזָּר, אַף תִּכּוֹן תֵּבֵל בַּל תִּמּוֹט. נָכוֹן כִּסְאֲךָ מֵאָז, מֵעוֹלָם אָתָּה. נָשְׂאוּ נְהָרוֹת, יהוה, נָשְׂאוּ נְהָרוֹת קוֹלָם,* יִשְׂאוּ נְהָרוֹת דָּכְיָם. ❖ מִקֹּלוֹת מַיִם רַבִּים* אַדִּירִים מִשְׁבְּרֵי יָם, אַדִּיר בַּמָּרוֹם יהוה. עֵדֹתֶיךָ* נֶאֶמְנוּ מְאֹד לְבֵיתְךָ נַאֲוָה קֹדֶשׁ, יהוה, לְאֹרֶךְ יָמִים.*

קדיש יתום

Mourners recite קַדִּישׁ יָתוֹם, the Mourner's *Kaddish* (see *Laws* §81-83).

יִתְגַּדַּל וְיִתְקַדַּשׁ שְׁמֵהּ רַבָּא. (Cong. – אָמֵן.) בְּעָלְמָא דִּי בְרָא כִרְעוּתֵהּ. וְיַמְלִיךְ מַלְכוּתֵהּ, בְּחַיֵּיכוֹן וּבְיוֹמֵיכוֹן וּבְחַיֵּי דְכָל בֵּית יִשְׂרָאֵל, בַּעֲגָלָא וּבִזְמַן קָרִיב. וְאִמְרוּ: אָמֵן.

(Cong. – אָמֵן. יְהֵא שְׁמֵהּ רַבָּא מְבָרַךְ לְעָלַם וּלְעָלְמֵי עָלְמַיָּא.)

יְהֵא שְׁמֵהּ רַבָּא מְבָרַךְ לְעָלַם וּלְעָלְמֵי עָלְמַיָּא.

יִתְבָּרַךְ וְיִשְׁתַּבַּח וְיִתְפָּאַר וְיִתְרוֹמַם וְיִתְנַשֵּׂא וְיִתְהַדָּר וְיִתְעַלֶּה וְיִתְהַלָּל שְׁמֵהּ דְּקֻדְשָׁא בְּרִיךְ הוּא (Cong. – בְּרִיךְ הוּא) — לְעֵלָּא מִן כָּל בִּרְכָתָא וְשִׁירָתָא תֻּשְׁבְּחָתָא וְנֶחֱמָתָא, דַּאֲמִירָן בְּעָלְמָא. וְאִמְרוּ: אָמֵן. (Cong. – אָמֵן.)

יְהֵא שְׁלָמָא רַבָּא מִן שְׁמַיָּא, וְחַיִּים עָלֵינוּ וְעַל כָּל יִשְׂרָאֵל. וְאִמְרוּ: אָמֵן. (Cong. – אָמֵן.)

Take three steps back. Bow left and say . . . עֹשֶׂה; bow right and say . . . הוּא; bow forward and say וְעַל כָּל . . . אָמֵן. Remain standing in place for a few moments, then take three steps forward.

עֹשֶׂה שָׁלוֹם בִּמְרוֹמָיו, הוּא יַעֲשֶׂה שָׁלוֹם עָלֵינוּ, וְעַל כָּל יִשְׂרָאֵל. וְאִמְרוּ: אָמֵן. (Cong. – אָמֵן.)

ה׳ מָלָךְ / Psalm 93

This psalm is a direct continuation of the previous theme that God's greatness will be recognized by all in the Messianic era. Accordingly, the past-tense syntax of the psalm should be understood as uttered in retrospect. Because it describes God in His full grandeur and power as He was when He completed the six days of Creation, and because it describes Him as 'donning' grandeur and 'girding' Himself like one dressing in Sabbath finery, the psalm was designated as the Levite's 'Song of the Day' for Friday, when the footsteps of the Sabbath begin to be heard *(R' Yaakov Emden).*

An alternative interpretation of this psalm ascribes it to the beginning of Creation:

On the sixth day Adam was created. God blew a breath of life into his nostrils and invested him with a Divine soul. When Adam stood and scrutinized God's amazing creation, he realized how awesome and wonderful it was. As he sang God's praises, Adam truly looked Divine, because he was a reflection of God's image. The creatures of the earth were filled with awe, for they imagined that Adam was their creator. When they gathered to bow to him in submission, however, Adam was incredulous. 'Why do you bow to me?' he asked. 'Let us go together to pay homage to God, Who truly reigns. Let us robe the Creator in majesty.' Then Adam led all the creatures in this song, *HASHEM . . . reigned, He . . . donned grandeur (Pirkei deR' Eliezer* 11).

גֵּאוּת לָבֵשׁ — *He will have donned grandeur.* The concept of *grandeur* represents God's revelation as the dominant force before Whom yield the mightiest natural forces. In man, grandeur — or arrogance — is a contemptible trait, because man's power is limited at best. But to God, *grandeur* is becoming because all forces owe their existence to Him while He is dependent on nothing *(Midrash Shocher Tov).*

Iggeres HaRamban explains that the arrogant man is a rebel who defies the sovereignty of God. Such a person steals the royal vestments which belong to God alone, for, as our verse states, *HASHEM . . . reigned, He . . . donned grandeur.*

God 'dons' grandeur — it is similar to a person donning a garment; our comprehension of him is guided by the contours and quality of the garment, but the garment is hardly his essence.

Psalm 93

יהוה מָלָךְ *HASHEM will have reigned, He will have donned grandeur;* He will have donned might and girded Himself; even firmed the world that it should not falter. Your throne was established from of old; eternal are You. Like rivers they raised, O HASHEM, like rivers they raised their voice;* like rivers they shall raise their destructiveness.* Chazzan– *More than the roars of many waters,* mightier than the waves of the sea — You are mighty on high, HASHEM. Your testimonies* are exceedingly trustworthy about Your House, the Sacred Dwelling — O HASHEM, may it be for long days.**

MOURNER'S KADDISH

Mourners recite the Mourner's *Kaddish* (see *Laws* §81-83).

[A transliteration of this *Kaddish* appears on page 1147.]

יִתְגַּדַּל *May His great Name grow exalted and sanctified* (Cong.– *Amen.*) *in the world that He created as He willed. May He give reign to His kingship in your lifetimes and in your days, and in the lifetimes of the entire Family of Israel, swiftly and soon. Now respond: Amen.*

(Cong.– *Amen. May His great Name be blessed forever and ever.*)

May His great Name be blessed forever and ever.

Blessed, praised, glorified, exalted, extolled, mighty, upraised, and lauded be the Name of the Holy One, Blessed is He (Cong.– *Blessed is He*) *— beyond any blessing and song, praise and consolation that are uttered in the world. Now respond: Amen.* (Cong. – *Amen.*)

May there be abundant peace from Heaven, and life, upon us and upon all Israel. Now respond: Amen. (Cong.– *Amen.*)

Take three steps back. Bow left and say, *'He Who makes peace . . .';* bow right and say, *'may He . . .';* bow forward and say, *'and upon all Israel . . .'* Remain standing in place for a few moments, then take three steps forward.

He Who makes peace in His heights, may He make peace upon us, and upon all Israel. Now respond: Amen. (Cong.– *Amen.*)

No matter how much of God's greatness we think we understand, our puny intellect grasps but the minutest fraction of His infinite greatness. He does us the favor of allowing mankind this degree of perception so that we can aspire to the privilege of praising Him.

נָשְׂאוּ נְהָרוֹת קוֹלָם — *Like rivers they raised their voice.* The enemies of Israel will roar against Israel like raging rivers at flood stage *(Radak).*

The repetition of the phrase represents the destruction of the two Temples *(Etz Yosef).*

מִקֹּלוֹת מַיִם רַבִּים . . . — *More than the roars of many waters . . .* You, O God, are beyond the threatening roars of the hostile nations who wish to drown us. You are mightier than the powerful waves of the sea, i.e., the mighty forces of evil among those who wish to crush us.

עֵדֹתֶיךָ — *Your testimonies.* The assurances of Your prophets regarding the eventual rebuilding of the Temple *(Rashi).*

ה׳ לְאֹרֶךְ יָמִים — *O HASHEM, may it be for long days.* The psalm closes with a plea that when the *trustworthy* prophecies of the Third Temple are finally fulfilled, may it stand for *long days,* a Scriptural idiom meaning forever *(Radak).*

מַעֲרִיב / THE EVENING SERVICE

Like *Shacharis* and *Minchah* (see page 8), *Maariv* has its basis in the Temple service. In the Temple, no sacrifices were offered in the evening, but any sacrificial parts that had not been burned on the Altar during the day could be burned at night. Thus, although no sacrificial service was *required* during the night, the Altar was usually in use. This explains why *Maariv* began as a voluntary service; unlike *Shacharis* and *Minchah* that took the place of required offerings, *Maariv* corresponds to a service optional in the sense that it was unnecessary if all parts were burned during the day. During Talmudic times, Jewry universally adopted *Maariv* as an obligatory service, so it now has the status of *Shacharis* and *Minchah.* (It should be noted that the original optional status of *Maariv* applied only to *Shemoneh Esrei;* the *Shema* reading is Scripturally required.)

מעריב לפסח

In some congregations the *chazzan* chants a melody during his recitation of בָּרְכוּ so that the congregation can then recite יִתְבָּרַךְ.

Chazzan bows at בָּרְכוּ and straightens up at ה׳.

בָּרְכוּ אֶת יהוה* הַמְּבֹרָךְ.

Congregation, followed by *chazzan*, responds, bowing at בָּרוּךְ and straightening up at ה׳.

בָּרוּךְ יהוה הַמְּבֹרָךְ* לְעוֹלָם וָעֶד.

יִתְבָּרַךְ[1] וְיִשְׁתַּבַּח וְיִתְפָּאַר וְיִתְרוֹמַם וְיִתְנַשֵּׂא שְׁמוֹ שֶׁל מֶלֶךְ מַלְכֵי הַמְּלָכִים, הַקָּדוֹשׁ בָּרוּךְ הוּא. שֶׁהוּא רִאשׁוֹן וְהוּא אַחֲרוֹן, וּמִבַּלְעָדָיו אֵין אֱלֹהִים.[2] סֹלּוּ, לָרֹכֵב בָּעֲרָבוֹת, בְּיָהּ שְׁמוֹ, וְעִלְזוּ לְפָנָיו.[3] וּשְׁמוֹ מְרוֹמָם עַל כָּל בְּרָכָה וּתְהִלָּה.[4] בָּרוּךְ שֵׁם כְּבוֹד מַלְכוּתוֹ לְעוֹלָם וָעֶד. יְהִי שֵׁם יהוה מְבֹרָךְ, מֵעַתָּה וְעַד עוֹלָם.[5]

ברכות קריאת שמע

בָּרוּךְ אַתָּה יהוה אֱלֹהֵינוּ מֶלֶךְ הָעוֹלָם, אֲשֶׁר בִּדְבָרוֹ* מַעֲרִיב עֲרָבִים, בְּחָכְמָה פּוֹתֵחַ שְׁעָרִים, וּבִתְבוּנָה מְשַׁנֶּה עִתִּים, וּמַחֲלִיף אֶת הַזְּמַנִּים, וּמְסַדֵּר אֶת הַכּוֹכָבִים בְּמִשְׁמְרוֹתֵיהֶם בָּרָקִיעַ כִּרְצוֹנוֹ. בּוֹרֵא יוֹם וָלָיְלָה, גּוֹלֵל אוֹר מִפְּנֵי חֹשֶׁךְ וְחֹשֶׁךְ מִפְּנֵי אוֹר. וּמַעֲבִיר יוֹם וּמֵבִיא לָיְלָה, וּמַבְדִּיל בֵּין יוֹם וּבֵין לָיְלָה, יהוה צְבָאוֹת* שְׁמוֹ. ❖ אֵל חַי וְקַיָּם, תָּמִיד יִמְלוֹךְ עָלֵינוּ, לְעוֹלָם וָעֶד.

> Many congregations recite *piyutim* (liturgical poems) that are inserted at various points in the synagogue service, often in the middle of a paragraph. Those who do not recite *piyutim* should not assume their appearance to indicate a stop, but should continue until the next new paragraph as indicated by bold type for the first word. This *Machzor* includes those *piyutim* that are commonly recited. A few *piyutim* that are omitted by a vast majority of congregations have been included in an appendix beginning on page 1108. The text will indicate where they may be recited.

בָּרְכוּ / Borchu

בָּרְכוּ אֶת ה׳ — *Bless HASHEM.* בָּרְכוּ is recited only in the presence of a *minyan*, a quorum of ten adult males. The *chazzan* summons them to join in the forthcoming prayers known as בִּרְכוֹת קְרִיאַת שְׁמַע, *Blessings of the Shema.* As Zohar states: All sacred acts require summoning.

With relation to God, the term *bless* cannot mean adding to His powers. Rather it is our declaration that He is the *source* of all blessing *(Kad HaKemach).* It represents our dedication to fulfill His will by our obedience to His commandments. Thus, in a sense we *do* confer something upon Him, for it is in our power to accomplish His goals for man *(R' Hirsch).*

בָּרוּךְ ה׳ הַמְּבֹרָךְ — *Blessed is HASHEM, the blessed One.* With or without our acknowledgment, God is constantly 'blessed' by all aspects of Creation — from the celestial beings to the humblest pebble — for they function in accordance with His will *(Kad HaKemach).*

Having called upon the congregation to bless God, the *chazzan* must not let it appear as though he excludes himself from the obligation. Therefore, when the congregation has concluded its response, he repeats it *(Tur).*

בִּרְכוֹת קְרִיאַת שְׁמַע / Blessings of the Shema

The four nighttime Blessings of the *Shema* are similar in theme to the morning three. The total of seven is based on the verse *(Psalms 119:164): Seven times a day I praise You (Berachos 11a, Rashi).* Of the evening blessings, the first describes God's control over nature, seasons, and the cycles of light. The second speaks of God's gift of the Torah, the very essence of Israel's survival. The third refers to the Exodus, but with emphasis on the future redemption. The fourth, described by the Talmud as an extension of the theme of redemption, stresses God's protection of His people from the terrors and dangers of night.

בָּרוּךְ אַתָּה . . . אֲשֶׁר בִּדְבָרוֹ — *Blessed are You . . . Who by His word.* The command of God created day just as it created night, for every moment has a purpose in God's plan. This recognition of God's everpresent will is especially important at night, which represents the period of fear, failure, and exile *(R' Hirsch).*

ה׳ צְבָאוֹת — *HASHEM, Master of Legions.* He takes

MAARIV FOR PESACH

In some congregations the *chazzan* chants a melody during his recitation of *Borchu* so that the congregation can then recite *'Blessed, praised . . .'*

Chazzan bows at *'Bless'* and straightens up at *'HASHEM.'*

Bless HASHEM,* the blessed One.

Congregation, followed by *chazzan,* responds, bowing at *'Blessed'* and straightening up at *'HASHEM.'*

Blessed is HASHEM, the blessed One,* for all eternity.

Blessed,[1] praised, glorified, exalted and upraised is the Name of the King Who rules over kings — the Holy One, Blessed is He. For He is the First and He is the Last and aside from Him there is no god.[2] Extol Him — Who rides the highest heavens — with His Name, YAH, and exult before Him.[3] His Name is exalted beyond every blessing and praise.[4] Blessed is the Name of His glorious kingdom for all eternity. Blessed be the Name of HASHEM from this time and forever.[5]

BLESSINGS OF THE SHEMA

בָּרוּךְ *Blessed are You, HASHEM, our God, King of the universe, Who by His word* brings on evenings, with wisdom opens gates, with understanding alters periods, changes the seasons, and orders the stars in their heavenly constellations as He wills. He creates day and night, removing light before darkness and darkness before light. He causes day to pass and brings night, and separates between day and night — HASHEM, Master of Legions,* is His Name.* Chazzan– *May the living and enduring God continuously reign over us, for all eternity.*

(1) See *Orach Chaim* 57:1 (2) Cf. *Isaiah* 44:6. (3) *Psalms* 68:5. (4) Cf. *Nehemiah* 9:5. (5) *Psalms* 113:2.

the infinite number of forces and conditions that form the universe and harmonizes them to perform His will *(R' Hirsch).*

פיוטים / Piyutim

Piyutim (liturgical poems) are inserted at various points in the synagogue service on the Festivals and on certain Sabbaths during the year. These *piyutim* express the mood and theme of the day, and many of them have become highlights of the day's service.

The composers of these *piyutim* include some of the outstanding figures of ancient times. The first and greatest was R' Elazar HaKalir who, according to tradition, lived in the time of the Mishnah. [According to *Tosafos* (*Chagigah* 13a) and *Rosh* (*Berachos* 5:21), he is the second-century Tanna R' Elazar son of R' Shimon bar Yochai.] The other *paytanim* (composers of *piyutim*) were among the *Geonim* (7th-10th-century Torah authorities) and *Rishonim* (11th-15th-century authorities). Consequently, it should be clear that their compositions are not merely inspired poetry.

The *piyutim* for the first two nights of Pesach are ascribed to *R' Meir ben Yitzchak Shliach Tzibbur* of eleventh-century Germany. A contemporary of *Rashi*, R' Meir is cited extensively by *Rashi* and his disciples. He composed forty-nine *piyutim* (forty in Hebrew, nine in Aramaic) of which about fifteen are extant. The most celebrated of these is *Akdamus* — an awesome exultation of God, the Torah, and Israel — recited on Shavuos.

Although the *paytanim* often signed their names to their compositions, usually in an acrostic, no such signature is evident in the *piyutim* for the first night. However, the name מֵאִיר does appear as an acrostic in the second night's *piyutim*.

Laws of Maariv (see also *Laws* §33-55 for the laws of *Shema*)

The ideal time for *Maariv* is after dark. However, one may recite *Maariv* earlier in which case he must repeat the three chapters of *Shema* after dark.

As a general rule, no אָמֵן, *Amen,* or other prayer response may be recited between *Borchu* and *Shemoneh Esrei,* but there are exceptions. The main exception is 'between chapters' [בֵּין הַפְּרָקִים] of the *Shema Blessings* — i.e., after each of the blessings, and between the three chapters of *Shema*. At those points, אָמֵן (but not בָּרוּךְ הוּא וּבָרוּךְ שְׁמוֹ) may be said in response to any blessing. Some responses, however, are so important that they are permitted at any point in the *Shema* blessings. They are: (a) In *Kaddish,* אָמֵן יְהֵא שְׁמֵהּ רַבָּא . . . עָלְמַיָּא and the אָמֵן after דַּאֲמִירָן בְּעָלְמָא; and (b) the response to בָּרְכוּ.

No interruptions whatever are permitted during the two verses of שְׁמַע and בָּרוּךְ שֵׁם.

ON THE SABBATH, NO PIYUTIM ARE RECITED AT MAARIV.

FIRST NIGHT

לֵיל שִׁמֻּרִים, אוֹתוֹ אֵל חָצָה,*
בַּחֲצוֹת לַיְלָה
בְּתוֹךְ מִצְרַיִם כְּיָצָא,
גִּבּוֹר עַל קָמָיו[1] יַחֲצֵנוּ כְּחָצָה,
דּוֹד מַעֲרִיב עֶרֶב*
וּנְזַמְּרֶנּוּ בְּנֶפֶשׁ חֲפֵצָה.

SECOND NIGHT

לֵיל שִׁמֻּרִים,
אוֹר יִשְׂרָאֵל* קָדוֹשׁ אֲיֻמָּה כַּנִּדְגָּלוֹת*.
בְּצִעַן[2] עֲצַת מַלְאָכָיו הִשְׁלִים[3]* בְּהִגָּלוֹת.
גְּדֻלָּתוֹ מֵאָז. יְרַנְּנוּ בְּמַקְהֵלוֹת הַלֵּילוֹת.
לְהַגִּיד בַּבֹּקֶר חַסְדֶּךָ.
וֶאֱמוּנָתְךָ בַּלֵּילוֹת[4].

בָּרוּךְ אַתָּה יהוה, הַמַּעֲרִיב עֲרָבִים. (Cong. — אָמֵן.)

אַהֲבַת עוֹלָם* בֵּית יִשְׂרָאֵל עַמְּךָ אָהָבְתָּ. תּוֹרָה וּמִצְוֹת, חֻקִּים וּמִשְׁפָּטִים, אוֹתָנוּ לִמַּדְתָּ. עַל כֵּן יהוה אֱלֹהֵינוּ, בְּשָׁכְבֵנוּ וּבְקוּמֵנוּ נָשִׂיחַ בְּחֻקֶּיךָ, וְנִשְׂמַח בְּדִבְרֵי תוֹרָתֶךָ, וּבְמִצְוֹתֶיךָ לְעוֹלָם וָעֶד. ❖ כִּי הֵם חַיֵּינוּ, וְאֹרֶךְ יָמֵינוּ, וּבָהֶם נֶהְגֶּה יוֹמָם וָלָיְלָה. וְאַהֲבָתְךָ, אַל תָּסִיר מִמֶּנּוּ לְעוֹלָמִים.

FIRST NIGHT

לֵיל שִׁמֻּרִים, הוּא זֶה הַלַּיְלָה,
וְעִתְּדוֹ אֵל בְּאֹמֶר בַּחֲצוֹת הַלַּיְלָה,
זֶה אֲשֶׁר הוּא לוֹ יוֹם וְלוֹ לַיְלָה,*
חֹק אַהֲבָתוֹ יִזְכֹּר לְנִינַי
חָלַק לוֹ לַיְלָה.*

SECOND NIGHT

לֵיל שִׁמֻּרִים. הִפְלִיא עֵצוֹת מֵרָחוֹק*
עָמוֹק וְנֶעְלָם.[5]
וּבוֹ כְּאָמֵן* נִינָיו מִשִּׁעְבּוּד הֶעֱלָם.
זַקַּת חֲטִיבָה אַחַת עֲשָׂאָם לְעַלָּם.
בְּאַהֲבַת יהוה אֶת יִשְׂרָאֵל לְעוֹלָם.[6]

⊱ **לֵיל שִׁמֻּרִים אוֹתוֹ אֵל חָצָה** — *A guarded night — our God split in half.* This *piyut* is divided into five sections, each recited during a different part of the *Maariv* service. The initial letters of the verses form an acrostic of the *aleph-beis*, but with the letters ט through נ omitted.

The *piyut* is based on the verse: לֵיל שִׁמֻּרִים הוּא לַה׳, לְהוֹצִיאָם מֵאֶרֶץ מִצְרָיִם, הוּא הַלַּיְלָה הַזֶּה לַה׳, שִׁמֻּרִים לְכָל בְּנֵי יִשְׂרָאֵל לְדֹרֹתָם, *It is a guarded night unto HASHEM, to bring them forth from the land of Egypt; this night it is unto HASHEM, a guarded night to all the Children of Israel, for their generations* (*Exodus* 12:42), which refers to both past and future. That is, it is a night that God guarded from the time He foretold Abraham about the Egyptian slavery (see *Genesis* 15:13), until the night of the Exodus. [According to one view, when God created the world, He set this night aside as a time of redemption. Thus, it is guarded since the six days of Creation (*Rosh Hashanah* 12b).] But more, it is watched with anticipation for the future redemption from our present exile. Thus the *piyut* juxtaposes what happened during the Exodus with what we pray will happen in our times.

מַעֲרִיב עֶרֶב — *Who brings on evening.* The final stich of each section returns the *piyut* to the theme of the blessing into which it is inserted.

⊱ **לֵיל שִׁמֻּרִים אוֹר יִשְׂרָאֵל** — *A guarded night — the Light of Israel.* The second night's *piyut* follows an alphabetical sequence (although not always obvious) and is divided into five sections. The final stich of each stanza is a Scriptural verse.

אֲיֻמָּה כַּנִּדְגָּלוֹת — *As awesome as the angels.* This phrase is taken from *Song of Songs* (6:4) and refers to Israel. Thus the verse speaks of Hashem as 'the Light of Israel, a nation whose holiness is as awesome as the holiness of the angels.'

An alternative reading has: קָדוֹשׁ אֲיֻמָּה נִדְגָּלוֹת, *Holy One, awesome to the angelic hosts.* This then refers to God, Who is Holy and of Whom even the angels are in awe (*R' Wolf Heidenheim*).

עֲצַת מַלְאָכָיו הִשְׁלִים — *He carried out the plan of His messengers.* God sent Moses and Aaron to forewarn Pharaoh of the dire consequences that would befall the Egyptian firstborn. Moses threatened that God would slay the firstborn at midnight (*Exodus* 11:4-5). God agreed and precisely at midnight He descended to Egypt (*ibid.* 12:29) where He carried out Moses and Aaron's plan.

⊱ **אַהֲבַת עוֹלָם** — [*With*] *an eternal love.* This blessing is an ecstatic expression of gratitude to God for the gift of Torah. Only after acknowledging our dependence on, and love for, the Torah, can we go on to express our undivided

ON THE SABBATH, NO PIYUTIM ARE RECITED AT MAARIV.

FIRST NIGHT	SECOND NIGHT
א *A guarded night — our God split it in half,** ב *When He went forth midnight throughout Egypt.* ג *He Who prevails over His opponents,*[1] *may He divide it now as He did then.* ד *Beloved One, who brings on evening,** *let us all sing to Him with willing heart.*	א *A guarded night — the Light of Israel,** *whose holiness is as awesome as the angelic hosts,** ב *When [Israel was] exiled in Zoan.*[2] *He carried out the plan of His messengers*[3]* גד *They sang of His greatness in nighttime assemblies — to relate Your kindness in the morning, and Your faith in the night.*[4]

Blessed are You, HASHEM, Who brings on evenings. (Cong.– *Amen.*)

אַהֲבַת *With an eternal love* have You loved the House of Israel, Your nation. Torah and commandments, decrees and ordinances have You taught us. Therefore HASHEM, our God, upon our retiring and arising, we will discuss Your decrees and we will rejoice with the words of Your Torah and with Your commandments for all eternity.* Chazzan– *For they are our life and the length of our days and about them we will meditate day and night. May You not remove Your love from us forever.*

FIRST NIGHT	SECOND NIGHT
ה *A guarded night — this night is [for Israel],* ו *Ordained by God when He said, "At midnight."* ז *The One to Whom both day and night belong,** ח *May He recall the measure of His love, for the offspring of 'for whom He split the night.'**	ה *A guarded night—wondrously He carried out ancient plans,** *deep and inscrutable.*[5] ו *On this night He lifted his [Abraham's] offspring from slavery as a suckling's father.** זח *He bound them as a unique object in order to elevate them, With HASHEM's eternal love for Israel.*[6]

(1) Early *machzorim* read עַל אֱדוֹם, *over Edom.* (2) See *Numbers* 13:22 and *Isaiah* 30:4. (3) Cf. *Isaiah* 44:26. (4) *Psalms* 92:3. (5) Cf. *Isaiah* 25:1; 28:29. (6) *I Kings* 10:9.

loyalty and dedication to the One and Only God, Who gave us this most precious gift.

אֲשֶׁר הוּא לוֹ יוֹם וְלוֹ לַיְלָה — *To Whom both day and night belong* [lit., *that the day is His, and the night is His*]. Although this stich is a paraphrase of the verse: לְךָ יוֹם אַף לְךָ לָיְלָה, *the day is Yours, even the night is Yours* (*Psalms* 74:16), the *paytan* possibly intended it as a play on the verse: וְהָיָה יוֹם אֶחָד ... לֹא יוֹם וְלֹא לָיְלָה, *And there will be one day .... [which will be] neither day nor night* (Zechariah 14:7), substituting the word לוֹ, *his*, for לֹא, *not*. Interestingly, R' Yosef Tuv Elem [of Limoges and Anjou, France], a contemporary of R' Meir Shliach Tzibbur, used the homophonous stich אֲשֶׁר הוּא לֹא יוֹם וְלֹא לַיְלָה, *which is neither day nor night,* in his *piyut* for the Sabbath before Pesach which has also been incorporated into the Ashkenazic version of the *Haggadah* (p. 122).

חָלַק לוֹ לַיְלָה — *'For whom He split the night.'* This is an allusion to Abraham. During his battle with the four kings, we are told וַיֵּחָלֵק עֲלֵיהֶם לַיְלָה, literally, *and was divided upon them night* (*Genesis* 14:15). According to the midrashic interpretation cited by *Rashi* there, the night was divided for Abraham. During the first half, he miraculously defeated the alliance of the four kings. The second half then was reserved for the miracle that would occur at midnight on behalf of his offspring in Egypt.

עֵצוֹת מֵרָחוֹק — *Ancient plans.* Four hundred years earlier, God had told Abraham that his offspring would be slaves in a foreign land, but He also promised that *at the end they would leave with great wealth* (*Genesis* 15:13-14).

כְּאֹמֵן — *As a suckling's father* [lit., *a male nurse*]. That is, God gently and protectively lifted the Jews out of Egypt as a father carrying his infant to safety (cf. *Numbers* 11:12; *Aruga HaBosem*). Alternatively: the word כְּאֹמֵן is cognate with אָמֵן, *verily*, i.e., when He verified His promise to Abraham.

בָּרוּךְ אַתָּה יהוה, אוֹהֵב עַמּוֹ יִשְׂרָאֵל. (—Cong. אָמֵן.)

שמע

Immediately before its recitation concentrate on fulfilling the positive commandment of reciting the *Shema* twice daily. It is important to enunciate each word clearly and not to run words together. For this reason, vertical lines have been placed between two words that are prone to be slurred into one and are not separated by a comma or a hyphen. See *Laws* §40-52.

When praying without a *minyan,* begin with the following three-word formula:

אֵל מֶלֶךְ נֶאֱמָן.*

Recite the first verse aloud, with the right hand covering the eyes, and concentrate intently upon accepting God's absolute sovereignty.

שְׁמַע | יִשְׂרָאֵל,* יהוה | אֱלֹהֵינוּ, יהוה | אֶחָד:*[1]

In an undertone — בָּרוּךְ שֵׁם* כְּבוֹד מַלְכוּתוֹ לְעוֹלָם וָעֶד.

While reciting the first paragraph (דברים ו:ה-ט), concentrate on accepting the commandment to love God.

וְאָהַבְתָּ* אֵת | יהוה | אֱלֹהֶיךָ, בְּכָל־לְבָבְךָ, וּבְכָל־נַפְשְׁךָ, וּבְכָל־מְאֹדֶךָ: וְהָיוּ הַדְּבָרִים הָאֵלֶּה, אֲשֶׁר | אָנֹכִי מְצַוְּךָ הַיּוֹם,* עַל־לְבָבֶךָ:* וְשִׁנַּנְתָּם לְבָנֶיךָ, וְדִבַּרְתָּ בָּם, בְּשִׁבְתְּךָ בְּבֵיתֶךָ, וּבְלֶכְתְּךָ בַדֶּרֶךְ, וּבְשָׁכְבְּךָ וּבְקוּמֶךָ: וּקְשַׁרְתָּם* לְאוֹת | עַל־יָדֶךָ, וְהָיוּ לְטֹטָפֹת בֵּין | עֵינֶיךָ: וּכְתַבְתָּם | עַל־מְזֻזוֹת בֵּיתֶךָ, וּבִשְׁעָרֶיךָ:

⁂ שְׁמַע / The Shema

The recitation of the three paragraphs of *Shema* is required by the Torah, and one must have in mind that he is about to fulfill this commandment. Although one should try to concentrate on the meaning of all three paragraphs, he must concentrate at least on the first (שְׁמַע, *Hear* ...) and the second verses (בָּרוּךְ שֵׁם, *Blessed* ...) because the recitation of *Shema* represents fulfillment of the paramount commandment of acceptance of God's absolute sovereignty [קַבָּלַת עוֹל מַלְכוּת שָׁמַיִם]. By declaring that God is One, Unique, and Indivisible, we subordinate every facet of our personalities, possessions — our very lives — to His will.

We have included the cantillation symbols *(trop)* for the convenience of those who recite שְׁמַע in the manner it is read from the Torah. Nevertheless, to enable those unfamiliar with this notation to group the words properly, commas have been inserted.

⁂ אֵל מֶלֶךְ נֶאֱמָן — *God, trustworthy King.* The Sages teach that there are both 248 organs in the human body and 248 positive commandments. This parallel number symbolizes that the purpose of physical existence is to obey the precepts of the Torah. The total number of words in the three paragraphs of *Shema* is 245. The Sages wished to convey the above symbolism in the recitation of the *Shema,* so they added three words to it. If a *minyan* is present, the congregation listens to the *chazzan's* repetition aloud of the three words ה׳ אֱלֹהֵיכֶם אֱמֶת. If there is no *minyan,* the three words אֵל מֶלֶךְ נֶאֱמָן are recited before *Shema* is begun. The initials of these words spell אָמֵן [literally, *it is true*], thus testifying to our faith in the truths we are about to recite.

The three words of the verse mean: He is אֵל, *God,* the All-Powerful Source of all mercy; He is the מֶלֶךְ, *King,* Who rules, leads, and exercises supervision over all; and He is נֶאֱמָן, *trustworthy,* i.e., fair, apportioning no more suffering nor less good than one deserves *(Anaf Yosef).*

⁂ שְׁמַע יִשְׂרָאֵל — *Hear, O Israel.* Although the commentators find many layers of profound meaning in this seminal verse, there is a consensus among the halachic authorities that *Rashi's* explanation is the minimum that one should have in mind. It is the basis of our translation: At this point in history, HASHEM is only *our* God, for He is not acknowledged universally, but ultimately all will recognize Him as the *One and Only* God.

אֶחָד — *The One and Only.* The word אֶחָד has two connotations: (a) There is no God other than HASHEM *(Rashbam);* and, (b) though we perceive God in many roles — kind, angry, merciful, wise, judging, and so on — these different attitudes are not contradictory, even though human intelligence does not comprehend their harmony. *Harav Gedaliah Schorr* likened this concept to a ray of light seen through a prism. Though it is seen as a myriad of different colors, it is a single ray of light. So, too, God's many manifestations

Blessed are You, HASHEM, *Who loves His nation Israel.* (Cong. – *Amen.*)

THE SHEMA

Immediately before its recitation concentrate on fulfilling the positive commandment of reciting the *Shema* twice daily. It is important to enunciate each word clearly and not to run words together. See *Laws* §40-52.

When praying without a *minyan,* begin with the following three-word formula:

*God, trustworthy King.**

Recite the first verse aloud, with the right hand covering the eyes, and concentrate intently upon accepting God's absolute sovereignty.

Hear, O Israel:* HASHEM is our God, HASHEM, the One and Only.*[1]

In an undertone— *Blessed is the Name* of His glorious kingdom for all eternity.*

While reciting the first paragraph (*Deuteronomy* 6:5-9), concentrate on accepting the commandment to love God.

וְאָהַבְתָּ *You shall love** HASHEM, *your God, with all your heart, with all your soul and with all your resources. Let these matters that I command you today* be upon your heart.* Teach them thoroughly to your children and speak of them while you sit in your home, while you walk on the way, when you retire and when you arise. Bind them* as a sign upon your arm and let them be tefillin between your eyes. And write them on the doorposts of your house and upon your gates.*

(1) *Deuteronomy* 6:4.

are truly one.

In saying the word אֶחָד, *the One and Only,* draw out the second syllable (חָ) a bit and emphasize the final consonant (ד). While drawing out the ח — a letter with the numerical value of eight — bear in mind that God is Master of the earth and the seven heavens. While clearly enunciating the final ד — which has the numerical value of four — bear in mind that God is Master in all four directions, meaning everywhere.

The enlarged ע and ד

In Torah scrolls, the letters ע of שְׁמַע and ד of אֶחָד are written large. Together they form the word עֵד, *witness.* The enlarged letters allude to the thought that every Jew, by pronouncing the *Shema,* bears witness to HASHEM's unity and declares it to all the world (*Rokeach; Kol Bo; Abudraham*).

בָּרוּךְ שֵׁם — *Blessed is the Name.* Having proclaimed God as our King, we are grateful for the privilege of serving the One Whose kingdom is eternal and unbounded (*Etz Yosef*).

The Sages give two reasons for saying this verse silently:

(a) At Jacob's deathbed his children affirmed their loyalty to God by proclaiming the verse *Shema* [the word 'Israel' in that context refers to Jacob]. Jacob responded with the words '*Blessed is the Name . . .*' The Sages taught: Should we say these words in our prayers because Jacob said them? Yes. But, on the other hand, Moses did not transmit them to us, for they are not found in the Torah. Therefore, let us say them silently (*Pesachim* 56a).

(b) Moses heard this beautiful prayer from the angels, and taught it to Israel. We dare not say it aloud, because we are sinful and therefore unworthy of using an angelic formula. On Yom Kippur, however, when Israel elevates itself to the sin-free level of angels, we may proclaim it loudly (*Devarim Rabbah* 2:36).

וְאָהַבְתָּ — *You shall love.* One should learn to fulfill the commandments out of love, rather than fear — and certainly not out of habit. The Mishnah (*Berachos* 9:5) explains that one should serve God with all his emotions and desires (*with all your heart*), even to the point of giving up his life for God (*with all your soul*), and even at the cost of his wealth (*with all your resources*).

אֲשֶׁר אָנֹכִי מְצַוְּךָ הַיּוֹם — *That I command you today.* But have they all been commanded today? — This teaches that although the Torah was given thousands of years ago, we are not to regard the *mitzvos* as ancient rites followed out of loyalty and habit. Rather, we are to regard them with as much freshness and enthusiasm as if God had given them today.

עַל לְבָבֶךָ — *Upon your heart.* Always be conscious of the demands of God and His Torah. Then, you will convey them to your children and *speak of them,* i.e., study, concentrate, and review them wherever you are.

וּקְשַׁרְתָּם — *Bind them. Tefillin* on the arm, next to the heart, and on the head consecrate one's physical, emotional, and intellectual capacities to

While reciting the second paragraph (דברים יא:יג-כא), concentrate on accepting all the commandments and the concept of reward and punishment.

וְהָיָה,* אִם־שָׁמֹעַ תִּשְׁמְעוּ אֶל־מִצְוֺתַי, אֲשֶׁר | אָנֹכִי מְצַוֶּה |
אֶתְכֶם הַיּוֹם, לְאַהֲבָה אֶת־יהוה | אֱלֹהֵיכֶם וּלְעָבְדוֹ,
בְּכָל־לְבַבְכֶם, וּבְכָל־נַפְשְׁכֶם: וְנָתַתִּי מְטַר־אַרְצְכֶם בְּעִתּוֹ, יוֹרֶה
וּמַלְקוֹשׁ, וְאָסַפְתָּ דְגָנֶךָ וְתִירשְׁךָ וְיִצְהָרֶךָ: וְנָתַתִּי | עֵשֶׂב | בְּשָׂדְךָ
לִבְהֶמְתֶּךָ, וְאָכַלְתָּ וְשָׂבָעְתָּ: הִשָּׁמְרוּ* לָכֶם, פֶּן־יִפְתֶּה לְבַבְכֶם,
וְסַרְתֶּם וַעֲבַדְתֶּם | אֱלֹהִים | אֲחֵרִים, וְהִשְׁתַּחֲוִיתֶם לָהֶם:* וְחָרָה |
אַף־יהוה בָּכֶם, וְעָצַר | אֶת־הַשָּׁמַיִם, וְלֹא־יִהְיֶה מָטָר, וְהָאֲדָמָה לֹא
תִתֵּן אֶת־יְבוּלָהּ, וַאֲבַדְתֶּם* | מְהֵרָה מֵעַל הָאָרֶץ הַטֹּבָה | אֲשֶׁר |
יהוה נֹתֵן לָכֶם: וְשַׂמְתֶּם | אֶת־דְּבָרַי | אֵלֶּה, עַל־לְבַבְכֶם וְעַל־
נַפְשְׁכֶם, וּקְשַׁרְתֶּם | אֹתָם לְאוֹת | עַל־יֶדְכֶם, וְהָיוּ לְטוֹטָפֹת בֵּין |
עֵינֵיכֶם: וְלִמַּדְתֶּם | אֹתָם | אֶת־בְּנֵיכֶם, לְדַבֵּר בָּם, בְּשִׁבְתְּךָ* בְּבֵיתֶךָ,
וּבְלֶכְתְּךָ בַדֶּרֶךְ, וּבְשָׁכְבְּךָ וּבְקוּמֶךָ: וּכְתַבְתָּם | עַל־מְזוּזוֹת בֵּיתֶךָ,
וּבִשְׁעָרֶיךָ: לְמַעַן | יִרְבּוּ | יְמֵיכֶם* וִימֵי בְנֵיכֶם, עַל הָאֲדָמָה | אֲשֶׁר
נִשְׁבַּע | יהוה לַאֲבֹתֵיכֶם לָתֵת לָהֶם, כִּימֵי הַשָּׁמַיִם | עַל־הָאָרֶץ:*

במדבר טו:לז-מא

וַיֹּאמֶר | יהוה* | אֶל־מֹשֶׁה לֵּאמֹר: דַּבֵּר | אֶל־בְּנֵי | יִשְׂרָאֵל,
וְאָמַרְתָּ אֲלֵהֶם, וְעָשׂוּ לָהֶם צִיצִת, עַל־כַּנְפֵי בִגְדֵיהֶם
לְדֹרֹתָם, וְנָתְנוּ | עַל־צִיצִת הַכָּנָף, פְּתִיל תְּכֵלֶת:* וְהָיָה לָכֶם לְצִיצִת,
וּרְאִיתֶם | אֹתוֹ, וּזְכַרְתֶּם | אֶת־כָּל־מִצְוֺת | יהוה, וַעֲשִׂיתֶם | אֹתָם,
וְלֹא תָתוּרוּ* | אַחֲרֵי לְבַבְכֶם וְאַחֲרֵי | עֵינֵיכֶם, אֲשֶׁר־אַתֶּם זֹנִים |
אַחֲרֵיהֶם: לְמַעַן תִּזְכְּרוּ, וַעֲשִׂיתֶם | אֶת־כָּל־מִצְוֺתָי, וִהְיִיתֶם קְדֹשִׁים
לֵאלֹהֵיכֶם: אֲנִי יהוה | אֱלֹהֵיכֶם, אֲשֶׁר
הוֹצֵאתִי | אֶתְכֶם | מֵאֶרֶץ מִצְרַיִם, לִהְיוֹת
לָכֶם לֵאלֹהִים, אֲנִי | יהוה | אֱלֹהֵיכֶם: אֱמֶת —

Concentrate on fulfilling the commandment of remembering the Exodus from Egypt.

God's service *(Ramban)*. The *mezuzah* on the doorpost consecrates one's home to Him.

☙ וְהָיָה — *And it will come to pass.* Unlike the first paragraph of *Shema,* this one specifies the duty to perform מִצְוֺתַי, *My commandments,* and teaches that when the nation is righteous, it will be rewarded with success and prosperity. When it sins, it must expect poverty and exile.

וְאָכַלְתָּ וְשָׂבָעְתָּ הִשָּׁמְרוּ — *And you will eat and be satisfied. Beware ...* Prosperity is often the greatest challenge to religious devotion. People who are rich in wealth but poor in sophistication often succumb to temptation *(Rashi).*

יִפְתֶּה . . . וְהִשְׁתַּחֲוִיתֶם לָהֶם — *Be seduced . . . and bow to them,* i.e., to strange gods. An imperceptible, seemingly innocent surrender to temptation can be the beginning of a course that will end in idolatry *(Rashi).*

וְלֹא יִהְיֶה מָטָר . . . וַאֲבַדְתֶּם — *So there will be no rain . . . and you will . . . be banished.* First will come famine. If that does not bring repentance, exile will follow *(Vilna Gaon).*

וְלִמַּדְתֶּם . . . בְּשִׁבְתְּךָ — *Teach them . . . while you sit.* In giving the command to educate children in the Torah, the verse speaks in the plural (וְלִמַּדְתֶּם), while the other words in the verse (בְּשִׁבְתְּךָ and so

While reciting the second paragraph (*Deuteronomy* 11:13-21), concentrate on accepting all the commandments and the concept of reward and punishment.

וְהָיָה *And it will come to pass* that if you continually hearken to My commandments that I command you today, to love* HASHEM, *your God, and to serve Him, with all your heart and with all your soul — then I will provide rain for your land in its proper time, the early and late rains, that you may gather in your grain, your wine, and your oil. I will provide grass in your field for your cattle and you will eat and be satisfied. Beware* lest your heart be seduced and you turn astray and serve gods of others and bow to them.* Then the wrath of* HASHEM *will blaze against you. He will restrain the heaven so there will be no rain and the ground will not yield its produce. And you will swiftly be banished* from the goodly land which* HASHEM *gives you. Place these words of Mine upon your heart and upon your soul; bind them for a sign upon your arm and let them be tefillin between your eyes. Teach them to your children, to discuss them, while you sit* in your home, while you walk on the way, when you retire and when you arise. And write them on the doorposts of your house and upon your gates. In order to prolong your days* and the days of your children upon the ground that* HASHEM *has sworn to your ancestors to give them, like the days of the heaven on the earth.**

Numbers 15:37-41

וַיֹּאמֶר *And* HASHEM *said* to Moses saying: Speak to the Children of Israel and say to them that they are to make themselves tzitzis on the corners of their garments, throughout their generations. And they are to place upon the tzitzis of each corner a thread of techeiles.* And it shall constitute tzitzis for you, that you may see it and remember all the commandments of* HASHEM *and perform them; and not explore* after your heart and after your eyes after which you stray. So that you may remember and perform all My commandments; and be holy to your God. I am* HASHEM, *your God, Who has removed you from the land of Egypt to be a God to you; I am* HASHEM *your God — it is true —*

Concentrate on fulfilling the commandment of remembering the Exodus from Egypt.

---

on) are in the singular. This alludes to a communal responsibility to arrange for the Torah education of children (*Iyun Tefillah*).

לְמַעַן יִרְבּוּ יְמֵיכֶם — *In order to prolong your days.* [Although many *siddurim* set this verse as a new paragraph, leading some to believe that there are *four* paragraphs in the *Shema,* the verse is part of the paragraph which begins וְהָיָה.]

כִּימֵי הַשָּׁמַיִם עַל הָאָרֶץ — *Like the days of the heaven on the earth. Eretz Yisrael* is the eternal heritage of the Jewish people, just as heaven will always remain above the earth. Alternatively, just as heaven always showers blessings upon the earth in the form of life-giving rain, so too Israel will be blessed in the land God has sworn to it.

ויאמר ה׳ — *And* HASHEM *said.* The third paragraph of *Shema* is recited to fulfill the commandment to recall the Exodus every day. By freeing Israel from Egypt, God laid claim to the nation's eternal allegiance. No Jew is free to absolve himself of that obligation (*Rashi*).

פְּתִיל תְּכֵלֶת — *A thread of techeiles. Techeiles* is sky-blue wool dyed with the secretion of an amphibian called *chilazon.* For many centuries the identity of the animal has been unknown. Even in the absence of the *techeiles* thread, however, the commandment of *tzitzis* remains binding (*Menachos* 38a).

וְלֹא תָתוּרוּ — *And not explore.* First the eye sees, then the heart covets, then the body sins (*Rashi*).

Although the word אֱמֶת belongs to the next paragraph, it is appended to the conclusion of the previous one, as explained in the commentary.

יהוה אֱלֹהֵיכֶם אֱמֶת.* —*Chazzan* repeats

וֶאֱמוּנָה* כָּל זֹאת, וְקַיָּם עָלֵינוּ, כִּי הוּא יהוה אֱלֹהֵינוּ וְאֵין זוּלָתוֹ, וַאֲנַחְנוּ יִשְׂרָאֵל עַמּוֹ. הַפּוֹדֵנוּ מִיַּד מְלָכִים, מַלְכֵּנוּ הַגּוֹאֲלֵנוּ מִכַּף כָּל הֶעָרִיצִים. הָאֵל הַנִּפְרָע לָנוּ מִצָּרֵינוּ, וְהַמְשַׁלֵּם גְּמוּל לְכָל אֹיְבֵי נַפְשֵׁנוּ. הָעֹשֶׂה גְדֹלוֹת עַד אֵין חֵקֶר,* וְנִפְלָאוֹת עַד אֵין מִסְפָּר.[1] הַשָּׂם נַפְשֵׁנוּ בַּחַיִּים,* וְלֹא נָתַן לַמּוֹט רַגְלֵנוּ.[2] הַמַּדְרִיכֵנוּ עַל בָּמוֹת אוֹיְבֵינוּ, וַיָּרֶם קַרְנֵנוּ עַל כָּל שֹׂנְאֵינוּ. הָעֹשֶׂה לָּנוּ נִסִּים וּנְקָמָה בְּפַרְעֹה, אוֹתוֹת וּמוֹפְתִים בְּאַדְמַת בְּנֵי חָם.* הַמַּכֶּה בְעֶבְרָתוֹ כָּל בְּכוֹרֵי מִצְרָיִם, וַיּוֹצֵא אֶת עַמּוֹ יִשְׂרָאֵל מִתּוֹכָם לְחֵרוּת עוֹלָם. הַמַּעֲבִיר בָּנָיו בֵּין גִּזְרֵי יַם סוּף, אֶת רוֹדְפֵיהֶם וְאֶת שׂוֹנְאֵיהֶם בִּתְהוֹמוֹת טִבַּע. וְרָאוּ בָנָיו גְּבוּרָתוֹ, שִׁבְּחוּ וְהוֹדוּ לִשְׁמוֹ. ❖ וּמַלְכוּתוֹ בְּרָצוֹן קִבְּלוּ עֲלֵיהֶם. מֹשֶׁה וּבְנֵי יִשְׂרָאֵל לְךָ עָנוּ שִׁירָה,

SECOND NIGHT	FIRST NIGHT
לֵיל שִׁמֻּרִים אַדִּיר* וְנָאֶה לִתְהִלּוֹתָיו.	פֶּסַח* אָכְלוּ פְחוּזִים,*
זֵכֶר עָשָׂה לְנִפְלְאוֹתָיו.[3] בְּלֵילֵי חַג פֶּסַח.	וְנִפְלָאוֹת חוֹזִים,
לֵיל שִׁמֻּרִים אַנְוֶה גּוֹמֵל חֲסָדִים.	בִּימֵי חַג פֶּסַח.
תְּהִלָּתוֹ בִּקְהַל חֲסִידִים.[4] בְּלֵילֵי חַג פֶּסַח.	פֶּסַח בָּנוּ לִשְׁמֹר לְדוֹרוֹת,
לֵיל שִׁמֻּרִים בָּא מִבְּרֵאשִׁית לְהִתְאַמָּר,	פְּנֵה לָנוּ לְהוֹרוֹת,
לָנוּ הַלַּיְלָה מִשְׁמָר,[5] בְּלֵילֵי חַג פֶּסַח.	כִּימֵי חַג פֶּסַח.

אֱמֶת ◆ — *True.* The law that one may not interrupt between the last words of the *Shema* and אֱמֶת is of ancient origin. The reason for it is so that we may declare, as did the prophet [*Jeremiah* 10:10]: וַה׳ אֱלֹהִים אֱמֶת, *HASHEM, God, is true* (*Berachos* 14a).

אֱמֶת וֶאֱמוּנָה ◆ — *True and faithful.* This paragraph continues our fulfillment of the obligation to recall the Exodus in the evening. The morning blessing of אֱמֶת וְיַצִּיב, *True and certain* (p. 308), concentrates on God's kindness in having redeemed us from Egypt, while אֱמֶת וֶאֱמוּנָה, *True and faithful,* recited at night, symbolizes exile and stresses our faith that God will redeem us from this exile just as He did at the time of the Exodus (*Berachos* 12a; *Rashi* and *Tosafos*).

Alternatively, the faithfulness of the nights refers to man's confidence that God will return his soul in the morning refreshed and rested after a night of sleep (*Talmidei R' Yonah; Tos., Berachos* 12a; *Rashi* in *Pardes*).

Chiddushei HaRim explains that אֱמֶת, *truth,* refers to something that we know to be true, either because our senses tell us so or because we have conclusive evidence. אֱמוּנָה, *faith,* refers to something that we *believe,* even though we have seen neither it nor proof that it happened. We know the Exodus to be *true,* because it was witnessed by millions of people, but the future redemption is not yet an accomplished fact. Nevertheless we have a perfect *faith* that God will bring it about, as He promised through the prophets. This is just as real for us as our *faith* in another phenomenon that has not yet taken place — that we will wake up from our sleep tomorrow morning.

גְּדֹלוֹת עַד אֵין חֵקֶר — *Great deeds that are beyond comprehension.* If our entire solar system were to disappear, the loss would not even be noticed in the vastness of space (*Malbim, Job* 9:10).

הַשָּׂם נַפְשֵׁנוּ בַּחַיִּים — *Who set our soul in life.* A reference to the night in Egypt when all

Although the word אֱמֶת, *'true,'* belongs to the next paragraph, it is appended to the conclusion of the previous one, as explained in the commentary.

Chazzan repeats: **HASHEM, your God, is true.***

וֶאֱמוּנָה *And faithful* is all this, and it is firmly established for us that He is HASHEM our God, and there is none but Him, and we are Israel, His nation. He redeems us from the power of kings, our King Who delivers us from the hand of all the cruel tyrants. He is the God Who exacts vengeance for us from our foes and Who brings just retribution upon all enemies of our soul; Who performs great deeds that are beyond comprehension,* and wonders beyond number.[1] Who set our soul in life* and did not allow our foot to falter.[2] Who led us upon the heights of our enemies and raised our pride above all who hate us; Who wrought for us miracles and vengeance upon Pharaoh; signs and wonders on the land of the offspring of Ham;* Who struck with His anger all the firstborn of Egypt and removed His nation Israel from their midst to eternal freedom; Who brought His children through the split parts of the Sea of Reeds while those who pursued them and hated them He caused to sink into the depths. When His children perceived His power, they lauded and gave grateful praise to His Name.* Chazzan— *And His Kingship they accepted upon themselves willingly. Moses and the Children of Israel raised their voices to You in song,*

FIRST NIGHT	SECOND NIGHT
א *Pesach:* the hasty ones* ate [the Pesach offering] and beheld wonders, in the days of the Pesach festival.*	א *A guarded night: the Mighty One,* fitting are His praises, He has made a memorial for His wonders,[3] on the nights of the Pesach festival.*
ב *Pesach: it is for us to guard for the generation; O turn to teach us [its laws], as in the days of the Pesach festival.*	א *A guarded night: I shall praise the Bestower of kindness, His praise in the congregation of the devout,[4] on the nights of the Pesach festival.*
	ב *A guarded night: from the beginning [of Creation] for exaltedness, has this night been a watch for us,[5] on the nights of the Pesach festival.*

(1) *Job* 9:10. (2) *Psalms* 66:9. (3) 111:4. (4) 149:1. (5) *Nehemiah* 4:16.

non-Jewish firstborn died, but Jewish souls were preserved (*Abudraham*). This also implies God's protection from the murderous designs of our enemies in all generations (*Siach Yitzchak*).

בְּנֵי חָם — *The offspring of Ham.* Mitzrayim, forerunner of the Egyptian nation, was a son of Ham [*Genesis* 10:6].

☙ פֶּסַח — *Pesach.* Descriptions of the redemption from Egypt alternate with prayers for the Final Redemption in this alphabetically arranged *piyut.* Each verse begins with the word *Pesach* [referring to the offering or to the festival], and ends with either בִּימֵי חַג פֶּסַח, in *the days of the Pesach festival* (or *offering*), a reference to the Exodus, or כִּימֵי חַג פֶּסַח, as in *the days ...*, alluding to our desire to witness the miracles promised by the prophet: כִּימֵי צֵאתְךָ מֵאֶרֶץ מִצְרָיִם אַרְאֶנּוּ נִפְלָאוֹת, *As in the days when you departed from the land of Egypt, I shall show them [Israel] wonders* (*Micah* 7:15).

פְּחוּזִים — *Hasty ones* ... an allusion to the Israelites who were commanded to eat the Pesach offering בְּחִפָּזוֹן, *in haste* (*Exodus* 12:11). The roots פחז and חפז both mean *hurry* or *haste.* Although not very common, there are other Hebrew roots in which two of the letters may be interchanged, e.g., כֶּבֶשׂ and כֶּשֶׂב both mean *sheep.*

☙ לֵיל שִׁמֻּרִים אַדִּיר — *A guarded night: the Mighty One.* The verses of this *piyut* form a double alphabetical acrostic followed by the author's name מֵאִיר, *Meir.* The *piyut* describes many events that occurred on Pesach through the generations. The second stich of each verse is from a Scriptural passage.

FIRST NIGHT

פֶּסַח גָּזַר עִנּוּי אֱמוּנִים,*
אַרְבַּע מֵאוֹת נִמְנִים,
בִּימֵי חַג פֶּסַח.
פֶּסַח דַּת שָׁבֻעִים*
יְמַלֵּא,
וְיוֹם נָקָם יְגַלֶּה,
כִּימֵי חַג פֶּסַח.
פֶּסַח הָרַג בְּכוֹרֵי חָם,
וּבֶן בְּכוֹרוֹ רִחַם,
בִּימֵי חַג פֶּסַח.
פֶּסַח וָעַד לִשְׁפֹּט
מַרְשִׁיעִים,
וּלְהַעֲלוֹת לְצִיּוֹן
מוֹשִׁיעִים,[1]
כִּימֵי חַג פֶּסַח.
פֶּסַח זֶמֶר* בְּנוֹף נִתַּן,
לִגְאוֹל בְּנֵי אֵיתָן,
בִּימֵי חַג פֶּסַח.
פֶּסַח חֶרֶב עַל רִשְׁעֵי
הֲדֹם,*[2]
בְּיַד צַח וְאָדֹם,[3]
כִּימֵי חַג פֶּסַח.

SECOND NIGHT

לֵיל שִׁמֻּרִים בְּגִין קָרְבַּן פִּסְחִי,
יֶעֱרַב עָלָיו שִׂיחִי,[4] בְּלֵילֵי חַג פֶּסַח.
לֵיל שִׁמֻּרִים גִּיהַּ עוֹלָם הִתְאִיר,*
פֶּתַח דְּבָרֶיךָ יָאִיר,[5] בְּלֵילֵי חַג פֶּסַח.
לֵיל שִׁמֻּרִים גָּשׁ רָצוּי לְכַהֵן,
מִבְּכוֹרוֹת צֹאנוֹ וּמֵחֶלְבֵיהֶן,[6]* בְּלֵילֵי חַג פֶּסַח.
לֵיל שִׁמֻּרִים דָּרַךְ כּוֹכָב מִזְרָחִי,
מַשְׂכִּיל לְאֵיתָן הָאֶזְרָחִי,[7] בְּלֵילֵי חַג פֶּסַח.
לֵיל שִׁמֻּרִים דָּלַק מְלָכִים וְלִבָּם,
חַרְבָּם תָּבוֹא בְלִבָּם,[8] בְּלֵילֵי חַג פֶּסַח.
לֵיל שִׁמֻּרִים הַלַּיְלָה יִסְכָּה בַּפֶּלֶךְ,
לְרִקְמוֹת תּוּבַל לַמֶּלֶךְ,[9] בְּלֵילֵי חַג פֶּסַח.
לֵיל שִׁמֻּרִים הֶדְחַף וְנִסְחַף אֲחוֹרָיִם,
מוֹפֵת עַל מִצְרָיִם,[10] בְּלֵילֵי חַג פֶּסַח.
לֵיל שִׁמֻּרִים וָעַד לִבְרֹא עֲלֵנוּ,
נִפְלְאֹתֶיךָ וּמַחְשְׁבוֹתֶיךָ אֵלֵינוּ,[11]*
בְּלֵילֵי חַג פֶּסַח.
לֵיל שִׁמֻּרִים וְכַח חֲשָׂאי בְּחִילָה,
אֲבִימֶלֶךְ בַּחֲלוֹם הַלָּיְלָה,[12]* בְּלֵילֵי חַג פֶּסַח.
לֵיל שִׁמֻּרִים זֵדִים רְדוּי שָׁפַךְ,
שָׁלַח יָדוֹ הָפַךְ,[13] בְּלֵילֵי חַג פֶּסַח.
לֵיל שִׁמֻּרִים זְרִיזָה בְּרָכוֹת כֻּוְּנָה,
אֶל יַעֲקֹב בְּנָהּ,[14] בְּלֵילֵי חַג פֶּסַח.

עִנּוּי אֱמוּנִים — *Affliction for the faithful.* At the בְּרִית בֵּין הַבְּתָרִים, *Covenant Between the Parts* (*Genesis* 15:7-21), God foretold Abraham that he would have offspring, and that his offspring would suffer four hundred years of servitude and oppression in a foreign land. According to the Midrash, this covenant took place on the night of Pesach (*Pirkei D'Rabbi Eliezer* 28).

דַּת שָׁבֻעִים — *The law of the weeks. Daniel* (9:24) describes a seventy-week exile period decreed upon Israel to expiate the sins committed during the First Temple era. Virtually all the commentators explain the seventy weeks as 'seventy weeks of years,' that is, 490 years (70×7).

This period was to begin with the destruction of the First Temple and span the seventy years until the Second Temple was built plus the first 420 years of the Second Temple. [During the Second Temple era, the Land was under foreign control almost continuously. Thus, the period could be reckoned as a time exile.]

Had the Jews not sinned during these 490 years, the Final Redemption would have come. The Land would have been rid of foreign domination and the Messianic era would have been ushered in. Instead, the nation's iniquities brought about the destruction of the Temple and the onset of the present exile.

We now pray that this centuries-long *galus* be deemed sufficient atonement and that we be worthy of the Final Redemption.

זֶמֶר — *A song*. The translation follows *Arugas HaBosem. R' Wolf Heidenheim* renders: *A pruning was instituted in Nof, to redeem the children of Eisan.*

הֲדֹם — *Footstool* ... i.e., the earth: *Thus said* HASHEM, *'The heavens are My throne, and the earth is My footstool'* (*Isaiah* 66:1).

גִּיהַּ עוֹלָם הִתְאִיר — *The light of the world* [*Adam*] *was kindled.* The *paytan* follows the view of R' Yehoshua (*Rosh Hashanah* 11a) that the world was created, and thus Adam's light was kindled, in Nissan. The Midrash (*Vayikra Rabbah* 20:2) states that the glow of Adam's countenance outshone the glare of the sun.

פֶּתַח דְּבָרֶיךָ יָאִיר — *The opening of Your words illuminates.* 'Your words' implies a direct quote.

FIRST NIGHT

ג *Pesach: He decreed affliction for the faithful;* four hundred years were counted,*
in the days of the Pesach festival.

ד *Pesach: may He fulfill the law of the weeks,* and reveal the day of vengeance,*
as in the days of the Pesach festival.

ה *Pesach: He killed the firstborn of Ham['s son Mitzrayim], but pitied His own firstborn son [Israel],*
in the days of the Pesach festival.

ו *Pesach: it is designated [as the time] to judge the evil-doers, and to cause [Israel's] saviors to ascend Mount Zion,*[1]
as in the days of the Pesach festival.

ז *Pesach: a song* was instituted in Nof [Egypt], to [accompany] the redemption of the children of Eisan [Abraham],*
in the days of the Pesach festival.

ח *Pesach: a sword upon the wicked of the footstool,**[2] *in the hand of Him Who is pure and ruddy,*[3]
as in the days of the Pesach festival.

SECOND NIGHT

ב *A guarded night: for the sake of my Pesach offering, may my words be sweet to Him*[4]
on the nights of the Pesach festival.

ג *A guarded night: the light of the world [Adam] was kindled,* the opening of Your words illuminates,*[5]
on the nights of the Pesach festival.

ג *A guarded night: he [Abel] approached, and was accepted as a Kohen, [when he offered] of the firstborn of his flock and of their choicest,*[6]*
on the nights of the Pesach festival.

ד *A guarded night: the star of the East [Abraham] set forth, [he is called] the wise one, the strong one of the East,*[7]
on the nights of the Pesach festival.

ד *A guarded night: he chased kings and disheartened them, their sword pierced their own heart,*[8]
on the nights of the Pesach festival.

ה *A guarded night: Iscah [Sarah] was praised in the king's palace, in embroidered dress she was brought to the king,*[9]
on the nights of the Pesach festival.

ה *A guarded night: He [Pharaoh] was pushed away from her and was plagued with tzaraas, a miracle wrought upon Egypt,*[10]
on the nights of the Pesach festival.

ו *A guarded night: it is appointed for the breaking of our yoke, Your wonders and Your thoughts are for us,*[11]*
on the nights of the Pesach festival.

ו *A guarded night: He admonished silently, but in tremble, Abimelech in a dream of the night,*[12]*
on the nights of the Pesach festival.

ז *A guarded night: He suppressed the wanton [Sodomites] when He poured out [his wrath], He sent forth His hand and overturned,*[13]
on the nights of the Pesach festival.

ז *A guarded night: the alacritous one [Rebecca] redirected the blessings to her son Jacob,*[14]
on the nights of the Pesach festival.

(1) See *Obadiah* 1:21. (2) *Arugas HaBosem* reads חֶרֶב חַדָּה עַל אֱדוֹם, *a sharp sword upon Edom.* (3) *Song of Songs* 5:10. (4) *Psalms* 104:34. (5) 119:130. (6) *Genesis* 4:4. (7) *Psalms* 89:1. (8) 37:15. (9) 45:15. (10) Cf. *Isaiah* 20:3. (11) *Psalms* 40:6. (12) *Genesis* 20:3. (13) *Job* 28:9. (14) *Genesis* 27:6.

The first quote of God's words that appears in the Torah is, *'Let there be light'* (*Genesis* 1:3).

גָּשׁ . . . וּמֵחֶלְבֵיהֶן — *He [Abel] approached . . . and of their choicest.* According to *Pirkei D'Rabbi Eliezer* (21), the incident related in *Genesis* (ch. 4) regarding the offerings of Cain and Abel — which led to Cain killing Abel — took place on the eve of Pesach.

נִפְלְאוֹתֶיךָ וּמַחְשְׁבוֹתֶיךָ אֵלֵינוּ — *Your wonders and Your thoughts are for us.* For 2448 years from Creation until the Exodus, God Himself made all the necessary calculations for setting the beginning of each month, and for intercalating leap years. After the Exodus, this task was assigned to Israel (see *Exodus* 12:1-2). Thus, *Your wonders* alludes to the marvelous workings of the heavenly bodies; and *Your thoughts* refers to the calculations (*Arugas HaBosem*, based on *Pesikta D' Rav Kahana* 15).

אֲבִימֶלֶךְ בַּחֲלוֹם הַלַּיְלָה — *Abimelech in a dream of the night.* Twice during Abraham's sojourn in foreign lands, his wife Sarah was taken to the royal palace as the king's prospective bride. The first time, in Egypt, this was done publicly

FIRST NIGHT

פֶּסַח טְבִיחַת נִינֵי כוּשׁ,*
לְהוֹצִיא עַמּוֹ
בִּרְכוּשׁ,
בִּימֵי חַג פֶּסַח.

פֶּסַח יְדִידוּת קַן שְׁדוּדָה,
כַּנֵּס אוֹם נְדוּדָה,
כִּימֵי חַג פֶּסַח.

פֶּסַח כָּרַת לְשָׂמוֹ מִסִּים,[1]
וְהוֹצִיא עַמּוֹ בְּנִסִּים,
בִּימֵי חַג פֶּסַח.

פֶּסַח לוֹחֲצֵינוּ יִלְחַץ,
וְיִרְפָּאֵנוּ מִמַּחַץ,
כִּימֵי חַג פֶּסַח.

פֶּסַח מִלֵּא הֲמוֹן הָרֵקָה,
וְהִסִּיעַ גֶּפֶן שׂוֹרֵקָה,[2]
בִּימֵי חַג פֶּסַח.

פֶּסַח נְגִינוֹת צַר יַשְׁפִּיל,
וְגִיל עַמּוֹ יַכְפִּיל,
כִּימֵי חַג פֶּסַח.

פֶּסַח סִגֵּר זֵדִים לַדֶּבֶר,
וְרִפֵּא עַמּוֹ מִשֶּׁבֶר,
בִּימֵי חַג פֶּסַח.

SECOND NIGHT

לֵיל שִׁמֻּרִים חָסַם בְּטוֹב לְאֵלוֹם,
לָבָן הָאֲרַמִּי בַּחֲלוֹם,[3] בְּלֵילֵי חַג פֶּסַח.
לֵיל שִׁמֻּרִים חָקוּק בְּהוֹד כִּסְאָךְ,*
וַיָּשַׂר אֶל מַלְאָךְ,[4] בְּלֵילֵי חַג פֶּסַח.
לֵיל שִׁמֻּרִים טוֹב הִסְכִּים עַל יָדוֹ,
מֵקִים דְּבַר עַבְדּוֹ,[5]* בְּלֵילֵי חַג פֶּסַח.
לֵיל שִׁמֻּרִים טָעֲמָה כִּי טוֹב סַחְרָהּ,
לֹא יִכְבֶּה בַּלַּיְלָה נֵרָהּ,[6]* בְּלֵילֵי חַג פֶּסַח.
לֵיל שִׁמֻּרִים יְלָלָה בְּנֹף* נָפְלָה,
וַתָּקָם בְּעוֹד לַיְלָה,[7] בְּלֵילֵי חַג פֶּסַח.
לֵיל שִׁמֻּרִים יוֹצְרוֹ חֲלָקוֹ בְּחָכְמָה,
יוֹדֵעַ עַד מָה,[8] בְּלֵילֵי חַג פֶּסַח.
לֵיל שִׁמֻּרִים כְּדָן וְשָׁבוּי* לְקָה,
שָׂמֵחַ לְאֵיד לֹא יִנָּקֶה,[9] בְּלֵילֵי חַג פֶּסַח.
לֵיל שִׁמֻּרִים כּוּכָם* נֶחֱטַט וְנִכְּאוּ,
הָפַךְ לַיְלָה וְיִדַּכָּאוּ,[10] בְּלֵילֵי חַג פֶּסַח.
לֵיל שִׁמֻּרִים לְהָדֵק נִשְׁחָק אִקּוּנָם,
רֵאשִׁית לְכָל אוֹנָם,[11] בְּלֵילֵי חַג פֶּסַח.
לֵיל שִׁמֻּרִים לְבַטָּה יִרְאָתָם וְלָקָה,
בּוּקָה וּמְבוּקָה וּמְבֻלָּקָה,[12] בְּלֵילֵי חַג פֶּסַח.
לֵיל שִׁמֻּרִים מְאוֹדֵי הוֹדָאוֹת לְאַדֶּרְךָ,
עַל מִשְׁפְּטֵי צִדְקֶךָ,[13] בְּלֵילֵי חַג פֶּסַח.
לֵיל שִׁמֻּרִים מְאוֹרֵי יֶשַׁע לְהַזְמִינִי,
אֲחַזְתָּ בְּיַד יְמִינִי[14] בְּלֵילֵי חַג פֶּסַח.

and with much fanfare. Therefore, God punished Pharaoh and his subjects openly with *tzaraas* (*Genesis* 12:15-17). The second time, in Gerar, she was taken quietly to Abimelech. Thus God admonished him in a dream (ibid. 20:1-8).

נִינֵי כוּשׁ — *Cush's [brother's] offspring. Arugas HaBosem* renders כוּשׁ as a proper noun. However, the allusion to Egypt as Cush's offspring is puzzling, for Cush was not a forebear of Mitzrayim (progenitor of Egypt), but his brother.

Perhaps כּוּשׁ is an adjective. Since the land of Cush is populated by members of the black race, כּוּשִׁי has come to mean *dark-skinned*. Thus, our verse describes Egypt as *the offspring of the dark-skinned one*, i.e., Mitzrayim brother of Cush. Interestingly, *Rashi* (*Gen.* 12:11) describes Egyptians as 'black men, brothers of the Cushites.'

חָקוּק בְּהוֹד כִּסְאָךְ — *[Jacob] engraved on Your glorious throne*. The Midrash teaches that the likeness of Jacob is engraved on the Divine Throne (*Bereishis Rabbah* 68:12).

מֵקִים דְּבַר עַבְדּוֹ — *He established His servant's word*. When Jacob prevailed over Esau's heavenly guardian, Jacob exacted a confession that Isaac's blessings were rightfully bestowed upon him, and that Esau no longer had any claim to them. At this time, God also acknowledged that the blessings were Jacob's (*Rashi* to *Genesis* 32:29 and *Hosea* 12:5).

טָעֲמָה . . . בַּלַּיְלָה נֵרָהּ — *She understood . . . her lamp . . . that night*. According to *Pesikta Rabbasi* this verse refers to Bisyah, daughter of Pharaoh. Her 'enterprise' refers to Moses — who was called טוֹב, *good* (see *Exodus* 2:2) — for when she found him, she saved his life and raised him as her own son. In the merit of this act, when the Egyptian firstborn were slain at midnight, and even the firstborn daughters died, Bisyah's lamp [i.e., her soul] was not extinguished.

בְּנֹף — *In Nof* [*Egypt*]. Nof was one of the major cities of Egypt (see e.g., *Isaiah* 19:13). It is also called מֹף, *Mof* (*Hosea* 9:6), and is identified as Memphis (see *Targum* and *Radak*).

FIRST NIGHT	SECOND NIGHT
ט *Pesach: a slaughter of Cush's [brother's] offspring,* to bring forth His people with wealth, in the days of the Pesach festival.*	ח *A guarded night: He sealed to remain silent even from speaking favorably, [the mouth of] Laban the Aramean in a dream,*[3] *on the nights of the Pesach festival.*
י *Pesach: [to] the beloved vanquished nest [Jerusalem], gather the wandering nation, as in the days of the Pesach festival.*	ח *A guarded night: [Jacob] engraved on Your glorious throne,* prevailed over an angel,*[4] *on the nights of the Pesach festival.*
כ *Pesach: He destroyed those who demanded tribute*[1] *[Egypt], and brought his people out with miracles, in the days of the Pesach festival.*	ט *A guarded night: the Good One agreed with him [Jacob], He established His servant's word,*[5]* *on the nights of the Pesach festival.*
ל *Pesach: may He oppress our oppressors, and heal us from crushing blows, as in the days of the Pesach festival.*	ט *A guarded night: she understood that her enterprise is good, so her lamp was not extinguished that night,*[6]* *on the nights of the Pesach festival.*
מ *Pesach: He filled [the coffers of] the impoverished multitudes, and caused the red-grape vine*[2] *[Israel] to journey, in the days of the Pesach festival.*	י *A guarded night: a wailing in Nof [Egypt],* and she arose while it was yet night,*[7] *on the nights of the Pesach festival.*
נ *Pesach: [may we sing] songs for He will have suppressed the oppressors, and He will have doubled His people's joy, as in the days of the Pesach festival.*	י *A guarded night: its Creator divided it with wisdom, He Who knows how long,*[8] *on the nights of the Pesach festival.*
ס *Pesach: He subjected the wanton ones to the plague, and healed His people from [their injury], in the days of the Pesach festival.*	כ *A guarded night: the enslaved and the captive* were smitten, for their joy in [Israel's] downfall will not be wiped clean,*[9] *on the nights of the Pesach festival.*
	כ *A guarded night: their tombs* were riddled and broken, He overturned night upon them and they were crushed,*[10] *on the nights of the Pesach festival.*
	ל *A guarded night: to grind their icons finely, the first of all their strength,*[11] *on the nights of the Pesach festival.*
	ל *A guarded night: their idols were humbled and beaten, emptied, looted and breached,*[12] *on the nights of the Pesach festival.*
	מ *A guarded night: to bind many thanksgivings to You, for Your righteous judgments,*[13] *on the nights of the Pesach festival.*
	מ *A guarded night: to prepare for me beacons of salvation, You have taken hold of my right hand,*[14] *on the nights of the Pesach festival.*

(1) See *Exodus* 1:11. (2) Cf. *Psalms* 80:9. (3) *Genesis* 31:24 (4) *Hosea* 12:5. (5) *Isaiah* 44:26. (6) *Proverbs* 31:18. (7) 31:15. (8) *Psalms* 74:9. (9) *Proverbs* 17:5. (10) *Job* 34:25. (11) *Psalms* 105:36. (12) *Nahum* 2:11. (13) *Psalms* 119:62,164. (14) 73:23.

כַּדָּן וְשָׁבוּי — *The enslaved and the captive*. Even the firstborn of the non-Jewish slaves and other foreign captives in Egypt were slain during the plague of the firstborn (*Exodus* 11:5; 12:25). *Rashi* explains that they were punished for the joy with which they greeted each new decree against the Jewish slaves.

כּוּכִם — *Their tombs*. The Midrash tells of the ancient Egyptian customs of burying their dead within their homes and of engraving the images of their dead firstborns on the beams of their houses. When God slew their firstborn, even those firstborn who had predeceased the plague suffered, for the beams with their images were turned to sawdust and dogs pulled them from their graves into the houses. This served as a double punishment for the Egyptians. Not only did the oldest living child in each family die, but the family was also reminded in vivid fashion of their previous losses (*Yalkut Shimoni* I:186; *Teshuvos Rashbatz* II:246).

FIRST NIGHT

פֶּסַח עֲבוּר כָּל צוֹרֵר
שָׁמוּר,
וְנָקַם עִמּוֹ כְּאָמוּר,
כִּימֵי חַג פֶּסַח.

פֶּסַח פִּחֵד בָּתֵּי
מִצְרַיִם,
וּבָן בְּעָנוּי
נוֹצָרִים,
בִּימֵי חַג פֶּסַח.

פֶּסַח צְפִירַת צַר
לַעֲלוּקָה,
כְּנֵס אוּם חֲקוּקָה,*
כִּימֵי חַג פֶּסַח.

פֶּסַח קָשַׁר לְצַר אָבְדָה,
וְגָאַל יְדִידִים
מַעֲבוּדָה,
בִּימֵי חַג פֶּסַח.

פֶּסַח רָמִים זֵדִים
תְּהָרֵס,
וְרַעְיָתְךָ תְּאָרֵשׂ,
כִּימֵי חַג פֶּסַח.

פֶּסַח שָׁת בְּכָל בֵּית יְלֵל,
בְּצֵאתוֹ בַּחֲצוֹת לֵיל,
בִּימֵי חַג פֶּסַח.

SECOND NIGHT

לֵיל שִׁמֻּרִים נוֹרָאוֹת בַּעֲשׂוֹתְךָ נִקְוֶה,
וְלַיְלָה לַלַּיְלָה יְחַוֶּה,[1] בְּלֵילֵי חַג פֶּסַח.
לֵיל שִׁמֻּרִים נִלְחֲמוּ כּוֹכְבֵי אוֹרִים,
לְעֶזְרַת יהוה בַּגִּבּוֹרִים,[2] בְּלֵילֵי חַג פֶּסַח.
לֵיל שִׁמֻּרִים סִיַּע צֶדֶק נְעוּרִים,
צְלִיל לֶחֶם שְׂעֹרִים,[3]* בְּלֵילֵי חַג פֶּסַח.
לֵיל שִׁמֻּרִים שֻׂגַּב בְּמִבְטָח וּמָעוֹז,
גֶּבֶר חָכָם* בָּעוֹז,[4] בְּלֵילֵי חַג פֶּסַח.
לֵיל שִׁמֻּרִים עָרִיצֵי פּוּל שָׁקַד,
וְתַחַת כְּבוֹדוֹ יֵקַד,[5] בְּלֵילֵי חַג פֶּסַח.
לֵיל שִׁמֻּרִים עֹמֶר חֶרְמֵשׁוֹ פִּלְּחָם,
וּבְמִלְחֲמוֹת תְּנוּפָה נִלְחָם,[6] בְּלֵילֵי חַג פֶּסַח.
לֵיל שִׁמֻּרִים פְּאַר עֶלְיוֹן בַּאֲמִירוֹת,
מִכְּנַף הָאָרֶץ זְמִירוֹת,[7]* בְּלֵילֵי חַג פֶּסַח.
לֵיל שִׁמֻּרִים פַּעְנֵחַ צָפְנַת מַעְבָּדָיו,
סוֹדוֹ אֶל עֲבָדָיו,[8] בְּלֵילֵי חַג פֶּסַח.
לֵיל שִׁמֻּרִים צָפִית סְדוּרָה וַאֲרוּחָה,
וְהִנֵּה יָד שְׁלוּחָה,[9] בְּלֵילֵי חַג פֶּסַח.
לֵיל שִׁמֻּרִים צָמַת בּוֹ בְּלִיל,
קֹדֶשׁ יהוה חִלֵּל,[10] בְּלֵילֵי חַג פֶּסַח.
לֵיל שִׁמֻּרִים קוֹמַת תָּמָר הַצָּלָה,
הַהֲדַסִּים אֲשֶׁר בַּמְּצֻלָה,[11]* בְּלֵילֵי חַג פֶּסַח.
לֵיל שִׁמֻּרִים קֹמֶץ* הִשְׂבִּיעַ לְשַׁנְּנָה,
יִתֵּן לִידִידוֹ שֵׁנָא,[12] בְּלֵילֵי חַג פֶּסַח.
לֵיל שִׁמֻּרִים רוּחִי יְחַפֵּשׂ לִמְלָלָה,
אֶזְכְּרָה נְגִינָתִי בַּלָּיְלָה,[13] בְּלֵילֵי חַג פֶּסַח.

אוּם חֲקוּקָה — *The engraved nation.* The translation follows *Arugas HaBosem* and alludes to God's declaration: *I shall not forget you; I have engraved you upon My palms* (*Isaiah* 49:15-16).

A different interpretation derives חֲקוּקָה from חֹק, *law* or *decree*, and describes Israel as crowned with laws and *mitzvos* (*R' Wolf Heidenheim*).

Or the phrase may refer to circumcision, with which the nation is 'engraved.'

צְלִיל לֶחֶם שְׂעֹרִים — *A loaf of barley bread.* The Midrash derives from this expression (*Judges* 7:13) that in the days of Gideon, the nation was devoid of great, righteous leaders. The masoretic text spells the word for loaf צְלוּל, but reads it צְלִיל. There is a difference between the two. צְלִיל means *loaf;* צְלוּל means *clarified, filtered,* and alludes to a generation whose righteous leaders have been removed as if with a filter. לֶחֶם שְׂעֹרִים, *barley bread,* signifies the *Omer*-offering, brought on the second day of Pesach, having been cut the previous night. Thus, in the merit of the *Omer*-offering, Gideon's army defeated Midian (see *Rashi* to *Judges* 7:13).

גֶּבֶר חָכָם — *The wise man.* When Ruth approached Boaz at his threshery in the middle of the night with a proposal of levirate marriage, Boaz resolved not to do so until he had determined that no closer relative of Machlon would perform the rite. Boaz then strengthened his resolve with a solemn oath, invoked by the formula, חַי ה׳, *as Hashem lives* (see *Ruth* 3:8-13). The Midrash finds an allusion to this act in the verse, גֶּבֶר חָכָם בָּעוֹז, *a wise man [restrains himself] with [the] strength [of an oath], and a man of knowledge grows increasingly strong* (*Proverbs* 24:5 as interpreted by *Yalkut Shimoni*).

[The *Yalkut* seemingly plays on the name בֹּעַז, *Boaz,* and the word בָּעוֹז, *with strength.* But

FIRST NIGHT

ע *Pesach: [may He bring forth] the anger awaiting all oppressors, and exact vengeance for His people, as it is said,*
as in the days of the Pesach festival.

פ *Pesach: He hurled fear on the Egyptian homes, and contemplated the observant ones' afflictions,*
in the days of the Pesach festival.

צ *Pesach: [may He toss] the oppressing masses into Gehinnom; and gather the engraved nation,**
as in the days of the Pesach festival.

ק *Pesach: He bound destruction to the oppressors, and redeemed His beloved ones from servitude,*
in the days of the Pesach festival.

ר *Pesach: May You uproot the haughty wanton ones; and may You betroth Your companion [Israel],*
as in the days of the Pesach festival.

ש *Pesach: He emplaced moaning in every [Egyptian] home, when He went forth at midnight,*
in the days of the Pesach festival.

SECOND NIGHT

נ *A guarded night: we hope for the awesome deeds that You will perform, night after night to declare,*[1]
on the nights of the Pesach festival.

נ *A guarded night: the brightly shining stars did battle, to help [the nation of] Hashem as with warriors,*[2] *on the nights of the Pesach festival.*

ס *A guarded night: assistance for those emptied of righteousness, [from] a loaf of barley bread,*[3]*
on the nights of the Pesach festival.

ס *A guarded night: exalted with fortification and strength, the wise man* [restrained himself] with strength,*[4] *on the nights of the Pesach festival.*

ע *A guarded night: [retribution] hastened against the Assyrian king Pul's warriors, in lieu of his glory, a burning,*[5]
on the nights of the Pesach festival.

ע *A guarded night: [the merit of] the scythe of the Omer cut them down, and their heave-offering fought their battles,*[6]
on the nights of the Pesach festival.

פ *A guarded night: the Exalted One's glory is in its recountings, from the end of the earth, songs,*[7]*
on the nights of the Pesach festival.

פ *A guarded night: He uncovered the mysteries of His acts, revealing His secrets to His servants,*[8]
on the nights of the Pesach festival.

צ *A guarded night: the candelabrum was prepared and there was dinner, then behold, a hand came forth,*[9] *on the nights of the Pesach festival.*

צ *A guarded night: he [Balshezzar] was destroyed on that night, for he desecrated Hashem's sanctified vessels,*[10] *on the nights of the Pesach festival.*

ק *A guarded night: the towering date palm [Israel] was saved, the myrtles by the deep waters,*[11]*
on the nights of the Pesach festival.

ק *A guarded night: teaching about the fistful* brought satisfaction, as he [Mordechai] relinquished sleep to his Beloved,*[12]
on the nights of the Pesach festival.

ר *A guarded night: my spirit seeks to speak [God's praises], as I recall my songs [of the Temple] at night,*[13] *on the nights of the Pesach festival.*

(1) *Psalms* 19:3. (2) Cf. *Judges* 5:20,23. (3) 7:13. (4) *Proverbs* 24:5. (5) *Isaiah* 10:16. (6) 30:32, see *Rashi* there. (7) 24:16. (8) *Amos* 3:7. (9) *Ezekiel* 2:9; see *Daniel* 5:5. (10) *Leviticus* 19:8. (11) *Zechariah* 1:8. (12) *Psalms* 127:2. (13) 77:7.

further consideration may show that the name Boaz is derived from the word בְּעוֹז. For the Talmud (*Bava Basra* 91a) identifies Ivtzan of Bethlehem (*Judges* 12:8-10) as Boaz. Now, we often find that when a Scriptural personality has two names, the Midrash considers one as his given name and the other as an allusion to his character or an event of his life. Thus, we propose that Ivtzan was dubbed Boaz as a result of his strengthened resolve, and that is the name by which he is called in the *Book of Ruth* which records that event. In the *Book of Judges*, however, he is called by his given name Ivtzan (cf. *Maharal* to *Bava Basra* 91a and ArtScroll edition of *Divrei HaYamim I*, p. 386).]

מִכְּנַף הָאָרֶץ זְמִירוֹת — *From the end of the earth, songs*. The Talmud relates that when the forces of Assyria were destroyed, the earth itself began to sing songs of praise (*Bava Basra* 94a).

הַהֲדַסִּים אֲשֶׁר בַּמְּצֻלָה — *The myrtles by the deep waters*. The Talmud explains that *myrtles*

FIRST NIGHT

פֶּֽסַח תְּכַּן וְהוּחַק לְאוֹת,
לְהַרְאֵֽנוּ בּוֹ נִפְלָאוֹת,
כִּימֵי חַג פֶּֽסַח.
פֶּֽסַח תְּהִלָּה לְשֵׁם
שׁוֹכֵן שְׁחָקִים,
תָּקְפּוֹ יַבִּֽיעוּ
קְרוֹבִים וּרְחוֹקִים,
תֹּֽקֶף כְּבוֹדוֹ
בַּיָּם מְחוּקָּקִים,
שִׁיר וְתִשְׁבָּחוֹת
מְשׁוֹרְרִים
וּמְשַׂחֲקִים,
בְּגִילָה בְּרִנָּה,

SECOND NIGHT

לֵיל שִׁמֻּרִים רֶֽוַח וְהַצָּלָה עָמְדָה,
בַּלַּֽיְלָה הַהוּא נָדְדָה,[1] בְּלֵילֵי חַג פֶּֽסַח.
לֵיל שִׁמֻּרִים שֵֽׁמַע מִצְרַֽיִם לִנְצֹר,
יָחִילוּ כְּשֵֽׁמַע צוֹר,[2] בְּלֵילֵי חַג פֶּֽסַח.
לֵיל שִׁמֻּרִים שָׁמוּר לִנְקָמָה נְטוּרָה,
עַל צוֹר הַמְּעֻטִּירָה,[3] בְּלֵילֵי חַג פֶּֽסַח.
לֵיל שִׁמֻּרִים תָּבוֹעַ מִסֵּֽפֶר הַתּוֹרָה,
אַחַת מֵהֵֽנָּה לֹא נֶעְדָּֽרָה,[4] בְּלֵילֵי חַג פֶּֽסַח.
לֵיל שִׁמֻּרִים תִּכְּֽנוּ לְיֶֽשַׁע וָנֵס,
נִדְחֵי יִשְׂרָאֵל יְכַנֵּס,[5] בְּלֵילֵי חַג פֶּֽסַח.
לֵיל שִׁמֻּרִים מַאֲמָרֵי יִרְצֶה לִשְׁעוֹת,
מִקֶּֽדֶם פּוֹעֵל יְשׁוּעוֹת,[6] בְּלֵילֵי חַג פֶּֽסַח.
לֵיל שִׁמֻּרִים אָז בַּהֲנִיחֲךָ שְׁלוּהִים,
הוֹדִֽינוּ לְךָ אֱלֹהִים,[7] בְּלֵילֵי חַג פֶּֽסַח.
לֵיל שִׁמֻּרִים יֶֽשַׁע לָֽנוּ תְּחַדֶּה,
וְשִׁמְךָ לְעוֹלָם נוֹדֶה,[8] בְּלֵילֵי חַג פֶּֽסַח.
לֵיל שִׁמֻּרִים רֶֽנֶן הַשִּׁיר בְּחַדְּשֶֽׁךָ,
לְהוֹדוֹת לְשֵׁם קָדְשֶֽׁךָ,[9] בְּלֵילֵי חַג פֶּֽסַח.

לֵיל שִׁמֻּרִים טֶֽכֶס פְּלָאֶֽיךָ
מִשִּׁירֵי הוֹדָאוֹת נִתְיַחַדְתָּ,
יוֹמָם לְחֶֽסֶד וְלַֽיְלָה לְשִׁיר[10]* נִתְוַעַדְתָּ,
כְּלוּלֶֽיךָ אָז בֶּאֱמוּנָה רוּחֲךָ הִסַּדְתָּ,
מִפִּי עוֹלְלִים וְיוֹנְקִים עֹז יִסַּדְתָּ.[11]
בְּגִילָה בְּרִנָּה,

בְּשִׂמְחָה רַבָּה וְאָמְרוּ כֻלָּם:

מִי כָמֹֽכָה בָּאֵלִם יהוה, מִי כָּמֹֽכָה נֶאְדָּר בַּקֹּֽדֶשׁ, נוֹרָא תְהִלֹּת,* עֹֽשֵׂה פֶֽלֶא.[12] ❖ מַלְכוּתְךָ רָאוּ בָנֶֽיךָ* בּוֹקֵֽעַ יָם לִפְנֵי מֹשֶׁה,

---

alludes to the righteous *tzaddikim* — specifically, Chananiah, Mishael and Azariah — while *deep waters* refers to Babylon (*Sanhedrin* 93a).

קֹֽמֶץ — *Fistful*. According to the Midrash, Mordechai remained awake the entire night teaching the laws regarding the fistful of the meal-offering on the Altar (*Pirkei D'Rabbi Eliezer* 50). Thus, he relinquished his sleep for the sake of God's Torah.

יוֹמָם לְחֶֽסֶד וְלַֽיְלָה לְשִׁיר — *The day for lovingkindness and the night for song*. According to the Talmud, God spends His days judging and feeding the world with kindness. At night, He sits and listens to the songs of the celestial beings (*Avodah Zarah* 3b).

נוֹרָא תְהִלֹּת — *Too awesome for praise*. We are too terrified to attempt a complete assessment of His greatness, because whatever we say is insufficient (*Rashi*). Alternatively, it is impossible for one to praise God adequately; the only way to laud Him is to recount His awe-inspiring deeds. Thus this phrase means: [God's] *awesomeness constitutes His praises* (*Ramban*).

FIRST NIGHT

ת *Pesach: may You prepare and decree a sign, to show us wonders on it, as in the days of the Pesach festival. Pesach: praise to the Name of Him Who dwells in heaven; may the near and far ones speak about His might; the power of His glory was established at the sea, Song and praise they sing and play, with mirth, with glad song,*

SECOND NIGHT

ר *A guarded night: relief and salvation stood by [the Jews], on this night [King Ahasuerus' sleep] was disturbed,*[1]
on the nights of the Pesach festival.

ש *A guarded night: the reports of Egypt['s destruction] to observe, they shall tremble at the reports from Tyre,*[2]
on the nights of the Pesach festival.

ש *A guarded night: guarded, watched, for vengeance, upon the becrowned Tyre,*[3]
on the nights of the Pesach festival.

ת *A guarded night: derived from the Books of Scripture, not one of these [events] is missing,*[4]
on the nights of the Pesach festival.

ת *A guarded night: prepared for salvation and miracle, to gather in the outcast of Israel,*[5]
on the nights of the Pesach festival.

מ *A guarded night: may He turn favorably to my words, He Who is the Worker of wonders from days of old,*[6]
on the nights of the Pesach festival.

א *A guarded night: thence, when You gave rest to the weary, we have thanked You, O God;*[7]
on the nights of the Pesach festival.

י *A guarded night: renew salvation for us, and Your Name we'll thank forever,*[8]
on the nights of the Pesach festival.

ר *A guarded night: joyous singing when You renew song, to give thanks to Your Holy Name,*[9]
on the nights of the Pesach festival.

ט *A guarded night: for the order of Your wonders, Your Oneness was declared through songs of praise,*

י *You appointed the day for lovingkindness and the night for song.*[10]*

כל *Then, thanks to their faithfulness, You established Your [Holy] Spirit in Your betrothed [Israel]. Out of the mouths of babes and sucklings You have established strength,*[11] *with mirth, with glad song,*

with abundant gladness — and said unanimously:

מִי כָמֹכָה *Who is like You among the heavenly powers,* HASHEM! *Who is like You, mighty in holiness, too awesome for praise,* doing wonders!*[12] Chazzan– *Your children beheld Your majesty,* as You split the sea before Moses,*

(1) *Esther* 6:1. (2) *Isaiah* 23:5, see *Rashi* there. (3) 23:8. (4) 34:16 (5) *Psalms* 147:2. (6) 74:12. (7) 75:2. (8) 44:9. (9) 106:47. (10) Cf. 42:9. (11) Cf. 8:3. (12) *Exodus* 15:11.

מַלְכוּתְךָ רָאוּ בָנֶיךָ — *Your children beheld Your majesty.* The Sages taught: A maidservant saw more [of God's majesty] at the Sea than did even Ezekiel in his prophecies!.

FIRST NIGHT	SECOND NIGHT
לֵיל שִׁמֻּרִים,	לֵיל שִׁמֻּרִים,
סִמָּן הוּא לֶעָתִיד לָבֹא,	מַלְכוּתְךָ רָאוּ בָנֶיךָ חַי וְקַיָּם,
עֶלְיוֹן כִּי בֹא יָבֹא,[1]	נִפְתַּח שִׁבְחֲךָ בִּלְשׁוֹן עָתִיד* וְנִסְתַּיָּם,
פָּקֹד יִפְקֹד* עַם קְרוֹבוֹ,	סָכוּ לִימִין מֹשֶׁה*[3] בּוֹקֵעַ יָם,
צוּרֵנוּ הוּא נָגִילָה וְנִשְׂמְחָה בוֹ.[2]	וְהֵנִיף יָדוֹ עַל הַנָּהָר בַּעְיָם.[4]*

זֶה צוּר יִשְׁעֵנוּ, פָּצוּ פֶה וְאָמְרוּ: Continue: ... ה׳ יִמְלֹךְ

זֶה אֵלִי[5] עָנוּ וְאָמְרוּ:

יהוה יִמְלֹךְ לְעֹלָם וָעֶד.[6] ❖ וְנֶאֱמַר: כִּי פָדָה יהוה אֶת יַעֲקֹב,* וּגְאָלוֹ מִיַּד חָזָק מִמֶּנּוּ.[7]

FIRST NIGHT	SECOND NIGHT
לֵיל שִׁמֻּרִים,	לֵיל שִׁמֻּרִים,
קָרְאוּ נוֹרָא עֲלִילָה,	עָטוּר פְּלָאֵי צִדְקָךְ בִּצְבָא וְאוֹת,*
כִּי בוֹ שָׁבַר מוֹטוֹת עֶגְלָה,*	קִרְבָתְךָ לִי טוֹב יְשׁוּעוֹת הַבָּאוֹת,
רָעוֹץ יִרְעַץ אוּם מְדַקָּה וְאָכְלָה,*	שַׁתִּי בְךָ מַחְסִי בְּמַלְאֲכוֹת[8] הַנְּבָאוֹת,[9]
יוֹסִיף שֵׁנִית בּוֹ לְהִגָּאֵלָה.	מֶלֶךְ יִשְׂרָאֵל וְגֹאֲלוֹ יהוה צְבָאוֹת.[10]

[Some conclude the blessing as follows; others conclude with בָּרוּךְ . . . גָּאַל יִשְׂרָאֵל.]

בָּרוּךְ אַתָּה יהוה, מֶלֶךְ צוּר יִשְׂרָאֵל וְגוֹאֲלוֹ. (.Cong. – אָמֵן)

בָּרוּךְ אַתָּה יהוה, גָּאַל יִשְׂרָאֵל.* (.Cong. – אָמֵן)

פָּקֹד יִפְקֹד — *Recall, may He recall.* This phrase appears three times in relation to the Exodus. Twice (*Genesis* 50:24-25) when Joseph encouraged his brothers before his death by assuring them that God will not forsake them (the phrase can also mean *He shall certainly recall*). And again (*Exodus* 13:19), when the Torah repeats Joseph's words during the Exodus.

According to *Rashi* (*Exodus* 3:18), the doubling of the root פקד was a code by which the nation would recognize the true savior. Thus when Moshe returned to Egypt, God told him to tell the nation that Hashem said, פָּקֹד פָּקַדְתִּי, *I have certainly recalled you and all that Egypt has done to you...and they will heed your voice* (*Exodus* 3:16,18). That is, when they hear the words פָּקֹד פָּקַדְתִּי, they will believe that you are truly God's messenger.

בִּלְשׁוֹן עָתִיד — *In the future tense.* The 'Song at the Sea,' a narrative of praise describing the Israelites' crossing of the sea and the Egyptians' drowning in it, is written in the past tense, as would be expected. However, the opening phrase, אָז יָשִׁיר מֹשֶׁה, literally, *then Moses shall sing*, and the closing verse, ה׳ יִמְלֹךְ לְעֹלָם וָעֶד, *Hashem shall reign for all eternity* (*Exodus* 15:1,18), are in the future tense. [The *paytan* agrees with *Ramban*, who does not consider the verse, כִּי בָא סוּס פַּרְעֹה, *when Pharaoh's cavalry came* ... (ibid. v. 19) as part of the Song. According to *Ibn Ezra*, however, that verse is the last verse of the Song.]

לִימִין מֹשֶׁה — *At Moses' right hand*, as the prophet states: *He brought His majestic arm to Moses' right; He split the Sea before them* (*Isaiah* 63:12).

וְהֵנִיף יָדוֹ עַל הַנָּהָר בַּעְיָם — *May He raise His hand powerfully over the river.* When God gathers the Jews from their present dispersion through the Diaspora, *He shall dry up the Egyptian Sea*, to enable the Jews there to return to the Holy Land, and *He shall raise His hand over the* [*Euphrates*] *River with His powerful wind*, to allow those exiled in that part of the world to return (*Isaiah* 11:15).

כִּי פָדָה ה׳ אֶת יַעֲקֹב — *For* HASHEM *has redeemed Jacob.* Jacob faced more dangerous situations than either Abraham or Isaac (*Acharis Shalom*).

One should recite this blessing with intense joy, confident that God is our past and future Redeemer (*Yesod V'Shoresh HaAvodah*).

מוֹטוֹת עֶגְלָה — *The yoke placed by the calf.* Although the literal meaning is *the calf's yoke*, it does not refer to the yoke worn by a calf. Rather, 'the calf' is an allusion to Egypt, which

FIRST NIGHT	SECOND NIGHT
ס *A guarded night: a sign for the future,*	מ *A guarded night: Your children behold Your majesty, O Living, Enduring One.*
ע *That the Exalted One shall surely come.*[1]	נ *They opened and closed Your praise in the future tense.**
פ *Recall, may He recall,* His people dear,*	ס *They observed the Splitter of the Sea at Moses' right hand.*[3]*
צ *Our Rock, let us rejoice and be glad with Him.*[2]	*May He raise His hand powerfully over the river.*[4]*

'He is the Rock of our salvation!' they opened their mouths and said:

Continue: *'HASHEM shall reign . . .'*

'This is my God!'[5] *they exclaimed, then they said:*

יהוה *'HASHEM shall reign for all eternity!'*[6] Chazzan– *And it is further said: 'For HASHEM has redeemed Jacob* and delivered him from a power mightier than he.'*[7]

FIRST NIGHT	SECOND NIGHT
ק *A guarded night: He awesome in deed named it, For them He broke the yoke placed by the calf.**	עפצ *A guarded night: crowned with the wonders of Your righteousness, in Israel as a sign.**
ר *Destroy, may He destroy, the [fourth] nation, that crushed, devoured* [His own nation Israel].*	קר *Your nearness to me is good, [an omen of] the coming salvations.*
	שת *I have placed my trust in You, in Your works*[8] *recounted by the prophets.*[9] *O King of Israel and its Redeemer, HASHEM, Master of Legions.*[10]

[Some conclude the blessing as follows; others conclude with *'Blessed . . . Who redeemed Israel'.*]

Blessed are You, HASHEM, King, Rock of Israel and its Redeemer.

*Blessed are You, HASHEM, Who redeemed Israel.** (Cong.– *Amen.*)

(1) *Habakkuk* 2:3. (2) *Psalms* 118:24. (3) Cf. *Isaiah* 63:12. (4) 11:15. (5) *Exodus* 15:2. (6) 15:18. (7) *Jeremiah* 31:10. (8) Cf. *Psalms* 73:28. (9) Cf. *Haggai* 1:13 (10) *Isaiah* 44:6.

the prophet calls, עֶגְלָה יְפֵה פִיָּה, *a very beautiful calf* (*Jeremiah* 46:20). Thus the phrase refers to the yoke placed upon Israel by the Egyptian calf (*Arugas HaBosem; R' Wolf Heidenheim*), and is based on the verse, בְּשִׁבְרִי שָׁם מֹטוֹת מִצְרַיִם, *when I break the Egyptian yoke* (*Ezekiel* 30:18).

Alternatively: the עֶגְלָה refers to the Covenant Between the Parts in which Abraham was told to take עֶגְלָה מְשֻׁלֶּשֶׁת, *three calves, three goats* . . . and cut them in half (hence the term Between the Parts). It was at this time that God told Abraham, *'Know with certainty that your offspring will be strangers in a land not their own, they will enslave them and they will oppress them for four hundred years'* (*Genesis* 15:9,13). But, the total period of their sojourn in Egypt was only two hundred and ten years! Thus the phrase שָׁבַר מוטות עֶגְלָה means: God broke the four-hundred-year yoke — decreed when Abraham was told to take three calves — and decreased its length by almost half.

אוֹם מְדַקָּה וְאָכְלָה — *The [fourth] nation, that crushed, devoured.* In his visions, Daniel (ch. 7) saw four beasts, each of which represented one of the exiles to which Israel had been or would be subjected to. The first, a lion, alluded to Babylon; the second, a bear, symbolized Persia; and the third, a leopard, represented Greece. The fourth beast is not identified by species, but was *excessively terrifying, awesome and strong; with iron teeth,* אָכְלָה וּמַדְּקָה, *it was eating and crushing* . . . (ibid. 7:7). This last beast refers to the fourth *galus*, that of the Roman Empire (in all its metamorphoses) from which we still seek redemption.

בְּצָבָא נָאוֹת — *In Israel* [lit., *In a host*] *as a sign.* Israel leaving Egypt is called צִבְאוֹת ה׳, *the hosts of Hashem* (*Exodus* 12:41).

The sign referred to here is the *omen of the coming salvations* of the next verse (*R' Wolf Heidenheim*).

Alternatively: God displayed His wonders בְּצָבָא, *with a host* of angels, נָאוֹת, and *with miraculous sign*.

In either case, the expression בְּצָבָא נָאוֹת seems to be a play on the word צְבָאוֹת which means *legions* or *hosts*, and which is also a Divine Name that describes God as the *Master of Legions.*

גָּאַל יִשְׂרָאֵל – *Who redeemed Israel.* Some *machzorim* follow the custom to substitute the

הַשְׁכִּיבֵנוּ* יהוה אֱלֹהֵינוּ לְשָׁלוֹם,* וְהַעֲמִידֵנוּ מַלְכֵּנוּ לְחַיִּים, וּפְרוֹשׂ עָלֵינוּ סֻכַּת שְׁלוֹמֶךָ, וְתַקְּנֵנוּ בְּעֵצָה טוֹבָה מִלְּפָנֶיךָ, וְהוֹשִׁיעֵנוּ לְמַעַן שְׁמֶךָ. וְהָגֵן בַּעֲדֵנוּ, וְהָסֵר מֵעָלֵינוּ אוֹיֵב, דֶּבֶר, וְחֶרֶב, וְרָעָב, וְיָגוֹן, וְהָסֵר שָׂטָן מִלְּפָנֵינוּ וּמֵאַחֲרֵינוּ,* וּבְצֵל כְּנָפֶיךָ* תַּסְתִּירֵנוּ,[1] כִּי אֵל שׁוֹמְרֵנוּ וּמַצִּילֵנוּ אָתָּה, כִּי אֵל מֶלֶךְ חַנּוּן וְרַחוּם אָתָּה.[2] ❖ וּשְׁמוֹר צֵאתֵנוּ וּבוֹאֵנוּ, לְחַיִּים וּלְשָׁלוֹם מֵעַתָּה וְעַד עוֹלָם.[3] וּפְרוֹשׂ עָלֵינוּ* סֻכַּת שְׁלוֹמֶךָ.

FIRST NIGHT

לֵיל שִׁמֻּרִים, שִׁמְעוּ לְעַם אֲהָבִים, אֲשֶׁר הִצִּיל מִיַּד לְהָבִים,*
תְּשׁוּעָה הִיא לְבַת רַבִּים,* בְּנַחַת וְשָׁלוֹם בְּלִי פַּחַד שׁוֹכְבִים.

Some congregations recite the prayer אֶזְכְּרָה שְׁנוֹת עוֹלָמִים (p. 1111) at this point.

SECOND NIGHT

אוֹר יוֹם* הֶנֶף סְפִירָה הַכְּשֵׁרָה בְּנוֹגְהִים,
לְצִיּוֹן נִדָּחָה קְרָא דְּרוּשָׁה עֲלוֹת גֵּהִים,[4]
בִּנְיַן מְפֹאָר כְּרַךְ מַחְמַד לֵב וְגֵהִים,
מִשְׁכְּנֵי עֶלְיוֹן בְּעֶשֶׂר מַעֲלוֹת* קֹדֶשׁ גְּבֹהִים,
גִּיל לְבָבוֹת לְבָנוֹן* הַמְלַבֵּן נְצוֹחִים שְׁלוּהִים,
נִכְבָּדוֹת מְדֻבָּר בָּךְ עִיר הָאֱלֹהִים.[5]
דְּרִישׁוּת לִדְרֹשׁ בְּשִׁכְנָךְ מְקוֹם כִּפּוּר שָׁלֵם,
סְלוּלֵי צִיּוֹן מְבַקְשִׁים תַּפְקִידָם הָרֵם מִכְשׁוֹלִים,[6]
הָמוֹן חוֹגֵג עֲלוֹת יֵרָאֶה הַתֵּר שַׁלְשְׁלִים,
עֵת כִּי בָא לְחֶנְנָהּ[7] בְּלִי רִשׁוּלִים,
וּמֵהַקָּרוֹב לָהּ בִּכּוּרֵי נְדָבָה לְהַקְרִיב בְּטֹהַר שׁוֹלִים,
פִּצְחוּ רַנְּנוּ יַחְדָּו חָרְבוֹת יְרוּשָׁלָיִם.[8]

phrase מֶלֶךְ צוּר יִשְׂרָאֵל וְגוֹאֲלוֹ, *King, Rock of Israel and its Redeemer*, whenever *piyutim* are recited. However, the halachic authorities disagree regarding the propriety of this change. *Mishnah Berurah* (66:33; 236:3) states that it is preferable that the conclusion not be altered.

☙ הַשְׁכִּיבֵנוּ — *Lay us down.* This blessing is an extension of the theme of redemption. Whereas the earlier blessing spoke of Israel's redemption from Egypt [and alluded to the future redemption], this one describes God as our Savior from the dangers and afflictions associated with the terrors of the night, literally and figuratively.

הַשְׁכִּיבֵנוּ . . . לְשָׁלוֹם — *Lay us down to sleep . . . in peace.* The purpose of sleep is to allow the body to rejuvenate itself, the better to serve God the next day *(R' Hirsch).*

מִלְּפָנֵינוּ וּמֵאַחֲרֵינוּ — *From before us and behind us.* Protect us from spiritual harm in the future *[before us]* and from the consequences of what has already occurred *[behind us] (R' Hirsch).*

וּבְצֵל כְּנָפֶיךָ — *And in the shadow of Your wings. Psalms* 91:4 likens God's protection to the wings of a mother bird sheltering her young.

וּפְרוֹשׂ עָלֵינוּ — *And spread over us.* This phrase was recited earlier in the paragraph, but it is repeated now because of its similarity to the closing of the blessing. There is a general rule that the conclusion of a blessing should be related to the content. Unlike the weekday הַשְׁכִּיבֵנוּ, which concludes with a request for Divine protection, the concluding blessing on the Sabbath and Festivals reflects the peace that comes with the holiness of the day *(Anaf Yosef).*

לְהָבִים — *Lehavim.* One of the eight families among the descendants of *Mitzrayim*, progen-

הַשְׁכִּיבֵנוּ *Lay us down* to sleep,* HASHEM, *our God, in peace,* raise us erect, our King, to life; and spread over us the shelter of Your peace. Set us aright with good counsel from before Your Presence, and save us for Your Name's sake. Shield us, remove from us foe, plague, sword, famine, and woe; and remove spiritual impediment from before us and behind us,* and in the shadow of Your wings* shelter us[1] — for God Who protects and rescues us are You; for God, the Gracious and Compassionate King, are You.[2]*
Chazzan— *Safeguard our going and coming, for life and for peace from now to eternity.[3] And spread over us* the shelter of Your peace.*

FIRST NIGHT

ש *A guarded night: may He gather the people beloved,*
*Whom He saved from the hand of Lehavim.**
ת *Salvation for [the city] Bas-Rabbim,**
In comfort and peace without fear may they sleep.
(A guarded night for the Guardian of Israel.)

Some congregations recite the prayer אַזְכָּרָה שְׁנוֹת עוֹלָמִים (p. 1111) at this point.

SECOND NIGHT

א *The evening before the day* of the omer waving is prepared for counting at dusk*
ל *So that Zion which has been called 'Outcast' be recalled and healing sought for her.[4]*
ב *Splendorous edifice, city of heart's and eyes' delight,*
מ *Dwelling of the Exalted One, superior in ten degrees* of holiness.*
ג *Joy of hearts, Lebanon,* cleanser of sins premeditated and inadvertent,*
נ *The most glorious things are spoken of you, O city of God.[5]*
ד *With all forms of searching, we seek out Your residence where sins are forgiven.*
ס *They strive to clear the cluttered roads to Zion, their goal, to remove the snares.[6]*
ה *From the multitudes of celebrants that wish to ascend, to appear — remove the chains,*
ע *The time to favor her has already come,[7] may there be no delay.*
ו *And from her neighboring towns may the first-fruit offering be brought — in cleansed garments,*
פ *Open wide and sing glad song together, O ruins of Jerusalem.[8]*

(1) Cf. *Psalms* 17:8. (2) Cf. *Nehemiah* 9:31. (3) Cf. *Psalms* 121:8. (4) Cf. *Jeremiah* 30:17. (5) *Psalms* 87:3. (6) Cf. *Isaiah* 57:14. (7) Cf. *Psalms* 102:14. (8) *Isaiah* 52:9.

itor of Egypt (see *Genesis* 10:13-14).

בַּת רַבִּים — *[The city] Bas-Rabbim.* This phrase (borrowed from *Song of Songs* 7:5) refers to Jerusalem. Literally the term means *daughter of multitudes,* idiomatically, *many-peopled.* A similar phrase to describe the Holy City, רַבָּתִי עָם, *great with people,* appears in the first verse of *Lamentations.*

אור יום — *The evening before the day.* Written especially for the eve of the *omer*-offering, this *piyut* prays for the rebuilding of Jerusalem and the *Beis HaMikdash,* describes the reaping and the Temple service of the *omer*-offering, and sings the praises of the rebuilt Holy City. Each of the nine six-line stanzas ends with a Scriptural verse. The verses of the first half of the *piyut* contain an alphabetical acrostic that follows the א״ל ב״ם arrangement of the *aleph-beis.* In this arrangement the eleven letters from א through כ are paired with the eleven letters ל through ת, respectively. Thus, the first verse begins with א and the second with ל; the third begins with ב and the fourth with מ.

The *paytan's* signature מֵאִיר חָזָק, *Meir, may he be strong,* appears in the third, fourth and fifth verses of the sixth stanza as indicated there by the bold type.

בְּעֶשֶׂר מַעֲלוֹת — *In ten degrees.* The Mishnah (*Keilim* 1:6-9) enumerates ten levels of holiness, beginning with the general holiness of *Eretz Yisrael* and culminating with the rarefied sanctity of the Holy of Holies in the *Beis HaMikdash.*

לְבָנוֹן — *Lebanon.* The *Beis HaMikdash* is called *Lebanon* (literally, whitener) because it whitens [the soil of] Israel's iniquities (*Yoma* 39b).

SECOND NIGHT

זָרְזוּ לְהַקְדִּים שְׁלוּחִים* דַּיָּנֵי גֵיא נְבוּאוֹת,*
צֵאת מִבָּעֶרֶב עֲשׂוֹת כְּרִיכוֹת מֵאֲבִיבֵי תְבוּאוֹת,
חוֹל וְשַׁבָּת כְּרַבִּים מְלַאכוֹתָיו בְּשָׁלוֹשׁ בָּאוֹת,
קִבְּצוּ עֲיָרוֹת הַסְּמוּכוֹת עֵסֶק גָּדוֹל לְנָאוֹת,
חֲשֵׁכָה קְצָרוּהוּ וּנְתָנוּהוּ בְּקֻפָּה וְלַעֲזָרָה מוּבָאוֹת,
מַה יְּדִידוֹת מִשְׁכְּנוֹתֶיךָ יהוה צְבָאוֹת,[1]
טוֹבָה כְּפוּלָה וּמְכֻפֶּלֶת לַמָּקוֹם עָלֵינוּ לֵאמֹר,
רִבָּה עֳמָרִים בַּמִּדְבָּר כְּנֶגְדָּם אֶחָד לִתְמֹר,*
יַחְבֵּט וְנִתַּן לְאַבּוּב הָאוּר בְּכֻלּוֹ לִגְמֹר,
שְׁטָחוּהוּ בָעֲזָרָה עֲמָלוֹ לְרוּחַ חַיִּים לִכְמֹר,
כַּמָּה כִּכְּרֵי מֹר לְסַנְטָר הַלָּז לִזְמֹר,
שְׁבֻעוֹת חֻקּוֹת קָצִיר לָנוּ יִשְׁמֹר.[2]
תֻּכַּן בְּלֶתֶת וְצִבּוּר וְנִגְרַס בְּלִי חִסָּרוֹן,
בִּשְׁלֹשׁ עֶשְׂרֵה נָפָה יוֹצִיאוּ מִמֶּנּוּ עִשָּׂרוֹן,
נָתַן שַׁמְנוֹ וּלְבוֹנָתוֹ, יָצַק וּבָלַל בְּהִדָּרוֹן,
הֵנִיף וְהִגִּישׁ קָמַץ וּמָלַח וְהִקְטִיר הַזִּכָּרוֹן,
מִזֵּר שֻׁלְחָן גָּבֹהַּ זָכוּ בִּשְׁיָרֵי הַדּוֹרוֹן,
כָּל זָכָר בִּבְנֵי אַהֲרֹן.[3]
קָרֵב הָעֹמֶר שׁוֹקֵי יְרוּשָׁלַיִם בַּפֵּרוֹת מְעֻטָּרִים,
בִּזְרִיזוּת בֵּית דִּין מֵחֲצוֹת רְחוֹקִים מֻתָּרִים,
מֵרָחוֹק אֶת יהוה מְעֻזְּכֶם[4] זִכְרוּ מַזְכִּירִים וְנוֹהֲרִים,
יְרוּשָׁלַיִם הַבְּנוּיָה תַּעֲלֶה עַל לְבַבְכֶם נִמְהָרִים,
חִזְקוּ וְתִזְכּוּ לִשְׁמֹעַ שִׁיר יְשׁוֹרֵר לְהָרִים,
הַר בֵּית יהוה בְּרֹאשׁ הֶהָרִים.[5]
לְבֵיתְךָ נַאֲוָה קֹּדֶשׁ[6] נְוֵה תְהִלָּה חוֹמֵל,
בֵּית יַעַר הַלְּבָנוֹן[7] מְלַבְלֵב מְגָדִים וְגוֹמֵל,
זְהַב פַּרְוַיִם פֵּרוֹת פִּרְחָיו* עוֹד מֵהָאָמֵל,
לְזַרְעוֹ שֶׁל יִצְחָק[8] חֶסֶד בְּיוֹם הִגָּמֵל,
אֲרוֹמִמְךָ בְּעִטּוּר בִּכּוּרֵי בְּקַלָּתוֹת מְזֻהָבוֹת וְלֹא בְּתוֹרְמֶל,
כְּבוֹד הַלְּבָנוֹן נִתַּן לָהּ הֲדַר הַכַּרְמֶל.[9]
יֵרָאֶה כִּפַּת הַמּוֹקֵד תַּשְׁלוּם שָׁלֵם סְבִיבֶיךָ,
שִׁמְךָ כְּשֵׁם מַלְכֵּךְ[10] שְׁעָרֶיךָ בְּשִׁבְטֶיךָ בַּהֲסִבֶּיךָ,[11]

זָרְזוּ לְהַקְדִּים שְׁלוּחִים — *They would hasten to send agents.* Here, the *paytan* begins his description of the omer-offering service. These rites are the subject matter of Mishnah *Menachos* (ch. 10; see page 182).

גֵּיא נְבוּאוֹת — *Valley of Prophecies.* Jerusalem is called גֵּיא חִזָּיוֹן, *Valley of Visions* (*Isaiah* 22:1), because the majority of Scriptural prophecies speak of Jerusalem (*Rashi*). Although situated on a mountain, Jerusalem is called a valley, because of its humbled status (*Radak*).

כְּנֶגְדָּם אֶחָד לִתְמֹר — *One omer in their stead.* The Midrash (*Yalkut Shimoni*) teaches the relationship between the manna and the *omer*-offering. When God commanded the *mitzvah* of the *omer*-offering, He said, 'My children,

SECOND NIGHT

ז *They would hasten to send agents* [to reap the omer-barley],*
*the judges of the "Valley of Prophecies,"**
צ *To go forth in the evening to bundle the ripened grain.*
ח *Weekday or Sabbath, its harvest was of three se'ah, as the majority ruled.*
ק *From the nearby cities they gathered to enhance [the mitzvah]*
with elaborate involvement.
חק *At nightfall they would reap it and placed it in baskets —*
to the Courtyard was it brought,
How beloved are Your dwelling places, O HASHEM, Master of Legions.[1]
ט *Of the Omnipresent's doubled and redoubled goodness we are beholden to relate,*
ר *In the Wilderness [He supplied] myriad omer-measures,*
*but required only one omer in their stead.**
י *The barley corns were threshed and placed in a perforated pipe*
for the fire to toast them well.
ש *They would spread it in the Courtyard for the lively wind would dry it out.*
כ *Oh! How many talents of myrrh are we indebted to this Guardian, to praise Him!*
During the weeks of the harvest decrees, may He protect us.[2]
ת *They would be prepared — washed, gathered, placed in a grist-mill —*
with thirteen sieves they would extract from it a tenth-ephah.
He would place its oil and its frankincense — pouring and mixing appropriately,
he would wave it and bring it near [to the Altar], separate a fistful,
salt it and burn it as a remembrance.
From the encrowned Divine Table they [the Kohanim] merited
the offering's remainder, every male of the descendants of Aaron.[3]
Once the omer-offering was brought, the streets of Jerusalem were full,
crowned with the new crop.
Trusting the Sanhedrin's alacrity, the distant towns were permitted
[to use the new crop] from noontime on.
מא *From the distance shall you remember HASHEM, your Strength,*[4]
O you who are drawn to Him.
יר *Raise [hope] in your hearts for the rebuilt Jerusalem, speedily.*
חזק *May you be encouraged and may you merit to hear the song*
to be sung on the mountaintops,
When HASHEM's Temple mount will be the chief of the mountains.[5]
May Your Temple, the sacred Dwelling[6] *become a house of prayer,*
O Compassionate One,
The 'Temple of Lebanon's Forest'[7] *where sweet fruit blossomed and ripened.*
The fruits of Parvah's gold and its blossoms will never again be bereaved,*
from the day that kindness will be restored upon Isaac's seed.[8]
I shall exalt You, with my crowned first-fruits, in baskets woven of gold, not sackcloth,
may Lebanon's honor and Carmel's beauty be given to you.[9]
May there be seen anew the domed fire chamber,
all of your surroundings rebuilt to completeness, O [Jeru]salem.
Your [new] name shall be like the Name of your King,[10]
your gates with [the names of] your tribes will surround you.[11]

(1) *Psalms* 84:2. (2) Cf. *Jeremiah* 5:24. (3) *Leviticus* 6:11. (4) Cf. *Nehemiah* 8:10.
(5) *Isaiah* 2:2. (6) *Psalms* 93:5. (7) *I Kings* 7:2; 10:21. (8) Cf. *Genesis* 21:8.
(9) Cf. *Isaiah* 35:2. (10) Cf. *Ezekiel* 48:35. (11) Cf. 48:31-34.

when you were in the Wilderness I gave each of you an *omer* of manna [per day]. Now all I require in return is that all of you together bring one *omer* [per year].'

בֵּית יַעַר הַלְּבָנוֹן ... וְזְהַב פַּרְוַיִם פֵּרוֹת פִּרְחָיו — *'The Temple of Lebanon's Forest' ... The fruit of Parvah's gold and its blossoms.* The Talmud explains why the *Beis HaMikdash* — Lebanon (see above) — is also called יַעַר, *a forest.* When King Solomon built the Temple, he planted in it many varieties of sweet fruit trees made of gold. Each produced its fruit at the appropriate

SECOND NIGHT

הָעֵת כַּעֲדִי תִלְבְּשִׁי הֲדַר סָבִיךְ בְּמִסְבָּבִיךְ,
שֵׁרוּת כֹּהֲנַיִךְ בַּאֲבִיבַיִךְ, נְעִימוֹת לְוִיַּיִךְ בְּאַבּוּבַיִךְ,
עוֹד תַּעְדִּי תֻפַּיִךְ,[1] טִלּוּל רוֹבַיִךְ בִּרְחוֹבַיִךְ,[2]
שַׁאֲלוּ שְׁלוֹם יְרוּשָׁלָיִם יִשְׁלָיוּ אֹהֲבָיִךְ.[3]
יְתֵרָה חִבָּתֵךְ יְרוּשָׁלַיִם כִּנּוּי שִׁבְעִים שְׁמוֹתַיִךְ,[4]
כְּעִיר שֶׁחֻבְּרָה לָהּ[5] הָפְקְדוּ שׁוֹמְרֵי חוֹמוֹתַיִךְ,[6]
מַזְכִּירִים לְרַחֲמֵךְ וּלְשׁוּמֵךְ תְּהִלָּה בָּאָרֶץ לְיַשֵּׁב שׁוֹמְמוֹתַיִךְ,
בְּאַחֲוָה וּבְרֵעוּת וּמִקְדַּשׁ אֵל בְּרָמָה נְוִיוֹתַיִךְ,
אֲדַבְּרָה וַאֲבַקְשָׁה טוֹב לָךְ וְשָׁלוֹם[7] בָּאֵר מְנוֹתַיִךְ,
יְהִי שָׁלוֹם בְּחֵילֵךְ שַׁלְוָה בְּאַרְמְנוֹתָיִךְ.[8]

בָּרוּךְ אַתָּה יהוה, הַפּוֹרֵשׂ סֻכַּת שָׁלוֹם עָלֵינוּ וְעַל כָּל עַמּוֹ יִשְׂרָאֵל וְעַל יְרוּשָׁלָיִם. (Cong. – אָמֵן.)

Congregation rises and remains standing until after *Shemoneh Esrei.*

On the Sabbath, the congregation, followed by the *chazzan,* recites:

וְשָׁמְרוּ* בְנֵי יִשְׂרָאֵל אֶת הַשַּׁבָּת, לַעֲשׂוֹת אֶת הַשַּׁבָּת* לְדֹרֹתָם בְּרִית עוֹלָם. בֵּינִי וּבֵין בְּנֵי יִשְׂרָאֵל* אוֹת הִיא לְעֹלָם, כִּי שֵׁשֶׁת יָמִים עָשָׂה יהוה אֶת הַשָּׁמַיִם וְאֶת הָאָרֶץ, וּבַיּוֹם הַשְּׁבִיעִי שָׁבַת וַיִּנָּפַשׁ.*[9]

Congregation, then *chazzan:*

וַיְדַבֵּר מֹשֶׁה* אֶת מֹעֲדֵי יהוה, אֶל בְּנֵי יִשְׂרָאֵל.[10]

The *chazzan* recites חֲצִי קַדִּישׁ.

יִתְגַּדַּל וְיִתְקַדַּשׁ שְׁמֵהּ רַבָּא. (Cong. – אָמֵן.) בְּעָלְמָא דִּי בְרָא כִרְעוּתֵהּ, וְיַמְלִיךְ מַלְכוּתֵהּ, בְּחַיֵּיכוֹן וּבְיוֹמֵיכוֹן וּבְחַיֵּי דְכָל בֵּית יִשְׂרָאֵל, בַּעֲגָלָא וּבִזְמַן קָרִיב. וְאִמְרוּ: אָמֵן.

(Cong. – אָמֵן. יְהֵא שְׁמֵהּ רַבָּא מְבָרַךְ לְעָלַם וּלְעָלְמֵי עָלְמַיָּא.)

יְהֵא שְׁמֵהּ רַבָּא מְבָרַךְ לְעָלַם וּלְעָלְמֵי עָלְמַיָּא.

---

time. When the wind would blow through these trees, their golden fruits would fall. From the proceeds of these fruits, the *Kohanim* would receive their livelihood. But when the idolaters captured and entered the Temple, these trees withered. Yet God will restore them for us in the future (*Yoma* 39b).

According to the Talmud (*Yoma* 45a), Parvayim gold was a blood-red color. The name פַּרְוַיִם derives from דַּם פָּרִים, oxen blood.

☙ וְשָׁמְרוּ — *And . . . shall keep.* As noted above, there should be no interruption between the theme of redemption and *Shemoneh Esrei.* However, this Scriptural statement of Israel's Sabbath observance is related to the theme of redemption, because Israel will be redeemed from exile in the merit of Sabbath observance (*Abudraham*).

This chapter of Sabbath observance appears in the Torah immediately after the commandment to commence the construction of the Tabernacle. This teaches that even for the sake of building the Temple, one may not desecrate the Sabbath (*Rashi* to *Exodus* 31:13). [By logical extension, this concept refutes those who may tend to relax the observance of the Sabbath or other *mitzvos* for the sake of what they consider to be noble spiritual causes.]

SECOND NIGHT

Then, you shall be adorned and clad with the beauty of your elders in your circle,
the service of your Kohanim offering your fruits,
the sweet songs of your Levites playing on your pipes.
You shall once again be adorned with your drums.[1]
Your youth shall stroll in your streets.[2]
Pray for the peace of Jerusalem, those who love you shall be serene.[3]
Your love is great, O Jerusalem, with your seventy beautiful names.[4]
As [in] a city [with its citizens] united together,[5]
the guardians of your walls have been appointed.[6]
We remember you to draw compassion upon you,
to make you praiseworthy in the world, to resettle your ruins, with brotherhood,
with friendship, and with God's Sanctuary rebuilt in your exalted beauty.
I shall speak and I shall request goodness for you,
and that pure peace[7] *shall be your portion.*
May there be peace within your wall, serenity within your palaces.[8]

Blessed are You, HASHEM, Who spreads the shelter of peace upon us, upon all of His people Israel and upon Jerusalem. (Cong.– *Amen.)*

Congregation rises and remains standing until after *Shemoneh Esrei.*

On the Sabbath, the congregation, followed by the *chazzan,* recites:

וְשָׁמְרוּ *And the Children of Israel shall keep* the Sabbath, to make the Sabbath* an eternal covenant for their generations. Between Me and the Children of Israel* it is a sign forever that in six days HASHEM made heaven and earth, and on the seventh day He rested and was refreshed.**[9]

Congregation, then *chazzan:*

And Moses declared* HASHEM's appointed festivals to the Children of Israel.[10]

The *chazzan* recites Half-*Kaddish.*

יִתְגַּדַּל *May His great Name grow exalted and sanctified* (Cong.– *Amen.) in the world that He created as He willed. May He give reign to His kingship in your lifetimes and in your days, and in the lifetimes of the entire Family of Israel, swiftly and soon. Now respond: Amen.*

(Cong.– *Amen. May His great Name be blessed forever and ever.)*
May His great Name be blessed forever and ever.

(1) *Jeremiah* 31:3. (2) Cf. *Zechariah* 8:5. (3) *Psalms* 122:6. (4) See Midrash *Bamidbar Rabbah* 14:12 and *Baal HaTurim* (ed. Reinitz) to *Bamidbar* 11:16. (5) *Psalms* 122:3. (6) Cf. *Isaiah* 62:6. (7) Cf. *Psalms* 122:8-9. (8) 122:7. (9) *Exodus* 31:16-17. (10) *Leviticus* 23:44.

לַעֲשׂוֹת אֶת הַשַּׁבָּת — *To make the Sabbath.* Each generation must *'make' the Sabbath,* by teaching its importance and holiness to those who are lax in sanctifying it because they fail to appreciate its importance (*Maor VaShemesh*).

בֵּינִי וּבֵין בְּנֵי יִשְׂרָאֵל — *Between Me and the Children of Israel.* Only Israel is commanded to observe the Sabbath, thereby bearing witness to God's creation of heaven and earth in six days. Consequently, the Sabbath is a *sign* of God's special relationship with Israel.

וַיִּנָּפַשׁ — *And was refreshed.* The translation follows *Rashi* who comments that this is an example of how God is described in human terms: God, of course, cannot become tired or refreshed, but a man would need a day of rest to refresh himself after six days of labor.

Other commentators, *Ramban* and *R' Yehudah HaChassid* among them, derive this word from נֶפֶשׁ, *soul.* They render וַיִּנָּפַשׁ, *and He gave them a soul,* i.e., the heaven and earth just mentioned *were given a soul,* as if to say that the creation of the Sabbath gave a new spiritual dimension to the universe.

וַיְדַבֵּר מֹשֶׁה — *And Moses declared.* This verse concludes a chapter that discusses the festivals. Thus, the verse alludes to all the specific laws and teachings of each of the festivals.

יִתְבָּרַךְ וְיִשְׁתַּבַּח וְיִתְפָּאַר וְיִתְרוֹמַם וְיִתְנַשֵּׂא וְיִתְהַדָּר וְיִתְעַלֶּה וְיִתְהַלָּל שְׁמֵהּ דְּקֻדְשָׁא בְּרִיךְ הוּא (.Cong – בְּרִיךְ הוּא) – לְעֵלָּא מִן כָּל בִּרְכָתָא וְשִׁירָתָא תֻּשְׁבְּחָתָא וְנֶחֱמָתָא, דַּאֲמִירָן בְּעָלְמָא. וְאִמְרוּ: אָמֵן. (.Cong – אָמֵן.)

שמונה עשרה – עמידה

Take three steps backward, then three steps forward. Remain standing with the feet together while reciting *Shemoneh Esrei*. Recite it with quiet devotion and without interruption, verbal or otherwise. Although its recitation should not be audible to others, one must pray loudly enough to hear himself.

אֲדֹנָי שְׂפָתַי תִּפְתָּח, וּפִי יַגִּיד תְּהִלָּתֶךָ.[1]

אבות

Bend the knees at בָּרוּךְ; bow at אַתָּה; straighten up at ה׳.

בָּרוּךְ אַתָּה יהוה אֱלֹהֵינוּ וֵאלֹהֵי אֲבוֹתֵינוּ, אֱלֹהֵי אַבְרָהָם, אֱלֹהֵי יִצְחָק, וֵאלֹהֵי יַעֲקֹב, הָאֵל הַגָּדוֹל הַגִּבּוֹר וְהַנּוֹרָא, אֵל עֶלְיוֹן, גּוֹמֵל חֲסָדִים טוֹבִים וְקוֹנֵה הַכֹּל, וְזוֹכֵר חַסְדֵי אָבוֹת, וּמֵבִיא גוֹאֵל לִבְנֵי בְנֵיהֶם, לְמַעַן שְׁמוֹ בְּאַהֲבָה.

Bend the knees at בָּרוּךְ; bow at אַתָּה; straighten up at ה׳.

מֶלֶךְ עוֹזֵר וּמוֹשִׁיעַ וּמָגֵן. בָּרוּךְ אַתָּה יהוה, מָגֵן אַבְרָהָם.

גבורות

אַתָּה גִּבּוֹר לְעוֹלָם אֲדֹנָי, מְחַיֵּה מֵתִים אַתָּה, רַב לְהוֹשִׁיעַ.

[On the first night – מַשִּׁיב הָרוּחַ וּמוֹרִיד הַגָּשֶׁם.]

מְכַלְכֵּל חַיִּים בְּחֶסֶד, מְחַיֵּה מֵתִים בְּרַחֲמִים רַבִּים, סוֹמֵךְ נוֹפְלִים, וְרוֹפֵא חוֹלִים, וּמַתִּיר אֲסוּרִים, וּמְקַיֵּם אֱמוּנָתוֹ לִישֵׁנֵי עָפָר. מִי כָמוֹךָ בַּעַל גְּבוּרוֹת, וּמִי דּוֹמֶה לָּךְ, מֶלֶךְ מֵמִית וּמְחַיֶּה וּמַצְמִיחַ יְשׁוּעָה. וְנֶאֱמָן אַתָּה לְהַחֲיוֹת מֵתִים. בָּרוּךְ אַתָּה יהוה, מְחַיֵּה הַמֵּתִים.

קדושת השם

אַתָּה קָדוֹשׁ וְשִׁמְךָ קָדוֹשׁ, וּקְדוֹשִׁים בְּכָל יוֹם יְהַלְלוּךָ סֶּלָה. בָּרוּךְ אַתָּה יהוה, הָאֵל הַקָּדוֹשׁ.

The Festival Shemoneh Esrei

The basic structure of the Festival *Shemoneh Esrei* is similar to that of the Sabbath in that it consists of seven blessings: the same three-blessing introduction and conclusion as those of every other *Shemoneh Esrei* all year round, and a single-blessing mid-section that contains the prayers of the day.

However, there are differences between the *Shemoneh Esrei* of the Sabbath and that of the Festivals. Unlike the *Shemoneh Esrei* prayers of the Sabbath that concentrate primarily on the sanctity of the day, the Festival prayers stress Israel's status as God's Chosen People. The Sabbath derives its holiness from God Who rested on the seventh day of creation; its holiness predated Israel and is in no way dependent on the Jewish people. The Festivals, on the other hand, commemorate the history of Israel. Although the Sabbath, as the testimony to God

Blessed, praised, glorified, exalted, extolled, mighty, upraised, and lauded be the Name of the Holy One, Blessed is He (Cong.– *Blessed is He*) — *beyond any blessing and song, praise and consolation that are uttered in the world. Now respond: Amen.* (Cong.– *Amen.*)

SHEMONEH ESREI — AMIDAH

Take three steps backward, then three steps forward. Remain standing with the feet together while reciting *Shemoneh Esrei.* Recite it with quiet devotion and without interruption, verbal or otherwise. Although its recitation should not be audible to others, one must pray loudly enough to hear himself.

My Lord, open my lips, that my mouth may declare Your praise.[1]

PATRIARCHS

Bend the knees at *'Blessed'*; bow at *'You'*; straighten up at *'HASHEM.'*

בָּרוּךְ *Blessed are You, HASHEM, our God and the God of our forefathers, God of Abraham, God of Isaac, and God of Jacob; the great, mighty, and awesome God, the supreme God, Who bestows beneficial kindnesses and creates everything, Who recalls the kindnesses of the Patriarchs and brings a Redeemer to their children's children, for His Name's sake, with love.*

Bend the knees at *'Blessed'*; bow at *'You'*; straighten up at *'HASHEM.'*

O King, Helper, Savior, and Shield. Blessed are You, HASHEM, Shield of Abraham.

GOD'S MIGHT

אַתָּה *You are eternally mighty, my Lord, the Resuscitator of the dead are You; abundantly able to save.*

[On the first night – *He makes the wind blow and He makes the rain descend.*]

He sustains the living with kindness, resuscitates the dead with abundant mercy, supports the fallen, heals the sick, releases the confined, and maintains His faith to those asleep in the dust. Who is like You, O Master of mighty deeds, and who is comparable to You, O King Who causes death and restores life and makes salvation sprout! And You are faithful to resuscitate the dead. Blessed are You, HASHEM, Who resuscitates the dead.

HOLINESS OF GOD'S NAME

אַתָּה *You are holy and Your Name is holy, and holy ones praise You every day, forever. Blessed are You, HASHEM, the holy God.*

(1) *Psalms* 51:17.

the Creator, could exist without the Jewish people, there could be no Festivals unless there had been a nation that was freed from Egypt, given the Torah and sheltered in the Wilderness. This emphasis is apparent from the very start of the middle section of the Festival *Shemoneh Esrei,* which declares that God has chosen Israel from among the nations, a concept that is absent from the Sabbath *Shemoneh Esrei.*

Furthermore, since the Festivals are dependent on the calendar and the sanctification of the months — which the Torah assigns to the Jewish people through their courts — the Festivals are creatures of the Jewish people, as it were.

Another feature unique to the Festivals is that joy is an integral part of their observance. Both of these features are reflected in the Festival *Shemoneh Esrei.*

There is yet another difference between the Festival and the Sabbath prayers. Each *Shemoneh Esrei* of the Sabbath refers to a different aspect of the day, and is therefore unique. These differences do not apply on Festivals with the result that all the *Shemoneh Esrei* services (with the exception of *Mussaf,* of course) are identical.

☙ The commentary for the first section of *Shemoneh Esrei* may be found on page 12.

קדושת היום

אַתָּה בְחַרְתָּנוּ* מִכָּל הָעַמִּים, אָהַבְתָּ אוֹתָנוּ, וְרָצִיתָ בָּנוּ, וְרוֹמַמְתָּנוּ מִכָּל הַלְּשׁוֹנוֹת,* וְקִדַּשְׁתָּנוּ בְּמִצְוֹתֶיךָ, וְקֵרַבְתָּנוּ מַלְכֵּנוּ לַעֲבוֹדָתֶךָ, וְשִׁמְךָ הַגָּדוֹל וְהַקָּדוֹשׁ עָלֵינוּ קָרָאתָ.*

On Saturday night add. [If forgotten, do not repeat *Shemoneh Esrei*. See *Laws* §91.]

וַתּוֹדִיעֵנוּ* יהוה אֱלֹהֵינוּ אֶת מִשְׁפְּטֵי צִדְקֶךָ, וַתְּלַמְּדֵנוּ לַעֲשׂוֹת חֻקֵּי רְצוֹנֶךָ. וַתִּתֶּן לָנוּ יהוה אֱלֹהֵינוּ מִשְׁפָּטִים יְשָׁרִים* וְתוֹרוֹת אֱמֶת חֻקִּים וּמִצְוֹת טוֹבִים. וַתַּנְחִילֵנוּ זְמַנֵּי שָׂשׂוֹן וּמוֹעֲדֵי קֹדֶשׁ וְחַגֵּי נְדָבָה.* וַתּוֹרִישֵׁנוּ קְדֻשַּׁת שַׁבָּת וּכְבוֹד מוֹעֵד וַחֲגִיגַת הָרֶגֶל. וַתַּבְדֵּל* יהוה אֱלֹהֵינוּ בֵּין קֹדֶשׁ לְחוֹל, בֵּין אוֹר לְחֹשֶׁךְ, בֵּין יִשְׂרָאֵל לָעַמִּים, בֵּין יוֹם הַשְּׁבִיעִי לְשֵׁשֶׁת יְמֵי הַמַּעֲשֶׂה. בֵּין קְדֻשַּׁת שַׁבָּת לִקְדֻשַּׁת יוֹם טוֹב הִבְדַּלְתָּ, וְאֶת יוֹם הַשְּׁבִיעִי מִשֵּׁשֶׁת יְמֵי הַמַּעֲשֶׂה קִדַּשְׁתָּ, הִבְדַּלְתָּ וְקִדַּשְׁתָּ אֶת עַמְּךָ יִשְׂרָאֵל בִּקְדֻשָּׁתֶךָ.

On the Sabbath add the words in brackets. [If forgotten, see *Laws* §86-90.]

וַתִּתֶּן לָנוּ יהוה אֱלֹהֵינוּ בְּאַהֲבָה* [שַׁבָּתוֹת לִמְנוּחָה וּ]מוֹעֲדִים* לְשִׂמְחָה* חַגִּים* וּזְמַנִּים לְשָׂשׂוֹן,

---

אַתָּה בְחַרְתָּנוּ ... – *You have chosen us. Anaf Yosef* gives this passage a different interpretation for each of the festivals. Regarding Pesach the passage means:

You have chosen us from all peoples at the time of the dispersion after the Tower of Babel (see *Genesis* 11:1-9);

You loved us and found favor in us at the time of the Patriarchs — as it is written, *I have loved you, says* HASHEM, *and if you ask, 'How have You loved us?'* [I shall answer,] *'Is Esau not Jacob's brother ... yet I have loved Jacob'* (*Malachi* 1:3);

You exalted us above all the tongues by performing miracles for our benefit in Egypt;

You sanctified us with Your commandments of the *pesach* offering and circumcision;

You drew us close, our King, to Your service — as it is written, *When You bring the nation forth from Egypt, you shall serve Me on this mountain* (*Exodus* 3:12).

מִכָּל הַלְּשׁוֹנוֹת – *Above all the tongues.* Human language can capture sublime thoughts and complex ideas, but Israel was granted the language of the Torah, which encompasses God's own wisdom and which is uniquely suited to expressing concepts of holiness.

וְשִׁמְךָ ... עָלֵינוּ קָרָאתָ – *And proclaimed Your ... Name upon us.* We are proud and grateful that God wished to be known as God of Israel.

The three expressions at the beginning of this paragraph — *chosen, loved,* and *found favor* — allude to the respective historical characteristics of the three pilgrimage Festivals, which will be named in וַתִּתֶּן לָנוּ, *And You gave us.* On Pesach, God chose us from among the Egyptians; on Shavuos, He showed His love for us by giving us His Torah; and on Succos, He showed us favor by forgiving the sin of the Golden Calf and bringing us under the Divine shelter which is symbolized by the *succah* (*Siach Yitzchak*).

These three terms are suited to their respective Festivals. The term "choose" implies that one selects one thing over others — not that it is perfect, but because it is the best of the lot, or because of its potential. Thus, Pesach marks the choice of an imperfect Israel that had enormous potential for good. One loves another because he is compatible emotionally or in deed. God showed His love on Shavuos by giving us the Torah. Favor is the highest of all levels, because it transcends logic. Even after Israel sinned with the Golden Calf, Israel found favor in God's eyes to such a degree that He forgave the sin on Yom Kippur and ushered in Succos, the most joyous of the Festivals (*Poras Yosef*).

☙ וַתּוֹדִיעֵנוּ – *You made known to us.* This paragraph, which was composed by the Talmudic sages, Rav and Shmuel (*Berachos* 33b), takes the place of אַתָּה חוֹנַנְתָּנוּ, *You have graced us,* the insertion at the conclusion of the regular

SANCTIFICATION OF THE DAY

אַתָּה בְחַרְתָּנוּ *You have chosen us* from all the peoples; You loved us and found favor in us; You exalted us above all the tongues* and You sanctified us with Your commandments. You drew us close, our King, to Your service and proclaimed Your great and Holy Name upon us.**

On Saturday night add. [If forgotten, do not repeat *Shemoneh Esrei.* See *Laws* §91.]

וַתּוֹדִיעֵנוּ *You made known to us,* HASHEM, our God, Your righteous ordinances, and You taught us to do the decrees of Your will. You gave us, HASHEM, our God, fair laws* and true teachings, good decrees and commandments. As a heritage You gave us seasons of joy, appointed festivals of holiness, and free-willed festive offerings.* You made us heir to the Sabbath holiness, the appointed festival glory, and festive offering of the pilgrimage. You distinguished,* O HASHEM, our God, between the sacred and secular, between light and darkness, between Israel and the peoples, between the seventh day and the six days of labor. Between the sanctity of the Sabbath and the sanctity of the holiday You have distinguished, and the seventh day, from among the six days of labor You have sanctified. You have distinguished and You have sanctified Your people Israel with Your holiness.*

On the Sabbath add the words in brackets. [If forgotten, see *Laws* §86-90.]

וַתִּתֶּן *And You gave us, HASHEM, our God, with love* [Sabbaths for rest], appointed festivals* for gladness,* Festivals* and times for joy,*

Sabbath that draws the distinction between the holy and the secular (see p. 666). Despite the great sanctity of the Festivals, they are less holy than the Sabbath; hence the requirement that *Havdalah* be recited here in *Shemoneh Esrei* and as part of the *Kiddush.*

נַתִּתֶּן לָנוּ ... מִשְׁפָּטִים יְשָׁרִים — *You gave us ... fair laws.* God gave us many commandments of various kinds — some that are comprehensible to the human mind, some that teach us to perceive our proper role in creation, some decrees that are above our comprehension, and commandments to regulate all facets of our behavior in a manner that will bring us closer to His service. The Sabbaths and Festivals are uniquely suited to inspire us with renewed sanctity to strive toward the fulfillment of the tasks God has set for us *(R' Hirsch).*

זְמַנֵּי שָׂשׂוֹן וּמוֹעֲדֵי קֹדֶשׁ וְחַגֵּי נְדָבָה — *Seasons of joy, appointed festivals of holiness, and free-willed festive offerings.* These three terms refer to three aspects of the Festivals. Firstly, they are seasons of joy as regards the agricultural cycle: Pesach comes in springtime; Shavuos ushers in the time of the first fruits; and Succos is the festive season of harvest. Secondly, they are appointed as Festivals because of their historical significance: Pesach commemorates the Exodus; Shavuos recalls the Revelation at Sinai; and Succos reminds us that God sheltered us in the Wilderness. Finally, these three terms recall the three kinds of offerings, expressing both devotion and joy, that were offered by the multitudes of Jews who came to Jerusalem for each of the three annual pilgrimage Festivals *(R' Hirsch).*

וַתַּבְדֵּל — *You distinguished.* The following list parallels the one found in the weekday *Shemoneh Esrei* recited at the conclusion of the Sabbath, except, of course, that this one includes the distinction betwen the Sabbath and Festival holiness.

⁂ וַתִּתֶּן לָנוּ ... בְּאַהֲבָה — *And You gave us ... with love.* Having chosen us, God gave us this special day. If the Festival falls on a Sabbath, that day, too, is mentioned here specifically. The difference in description between the Sabbath and the Festivals expresses a major difference between them. Although there is rest on the Festivals and gladness on the Sabbath, their primary features are, as we say here, Sabbath for *rest* and Festivals for *gladness.*

מוֹעֲדִים — *Appointed festivals.* This term for the Festivals has the connotation of meeting, i.e., God has designated times when Israel can greet His Presence.

מוֹעֲדִים לְשִׂמְחָה — *Appointed festivals for gladness.* The expression used here is *appointed festivals* **for** *gladness,* rather than **of** *gladness.* This tells us that *Yom Tov* is not only a day of rejoicing but a source from which to draw joy and inspiration for the rest of the year. In the same way, שַׁבָּתוֹת לִמְנוּחָה, *Sabbaths for rest,* teaches that the Sabbath furnishes us with the blessing of restfulness for the entire week *(Sfas Emes).*

חַגִּים — *Festivals.* The word חַג is sometimes used for the Festival day and sometimes to refer to

אֶת יוֹם [הַשַּׁבָּת הַזֶּה וְאֶת יוֹם] חַג הַמַּצּוֹת הַזֶּה, זְמַן חֵרוּתֵנוּ [בְּאַהֲבָה*], מִקְרָא קֹדֶשׁ,* זֵכֶר לִיצִיאַת מִצְרָיִם.*

אֱלֹהֵינוּ וֵאלֹהֵי אֲבוֹתֵינוּ, יַעֲלֶה, וְיָבֹא,* וְיַגִּיעַ, וְיֵרָאֶה, וְיֵרָצֶה, וְיִשָּׁמַע, וְיִפָּקֵד, וְיִזָּכֵר זִכְרוֹנֵנוּ וּפִקְדוֹנֵנוּ, וְזִכְרוֹן אֲבוֹתֵינוּ, וְזִכְרוֹן מָשִׁיחַ בֶּן דָּוִד עַבְדֶּךָ, וְזִכְרוֹן יְרוּשָׁלַיִם עִיר קָדְשֶׁךָ, וְזִכְרוֹן כָּל עַמְּךָ בֵּית יִשְׂרָאֵל לְפָנֶיךָ, לִפְלֵיטָה לְטוֹבָה לְחֵן וּלְחֶסֶד וּלְרַחֲמִים, לְחַיִּים וּלְשָׁלוֹם בְּיוֹם חַג הַמַּצּוֹת הַזֶּה. זָכְרֵנוּ יהוה אֱלֹהֵינוּ בּוֹ לְטוֹבָה, וּפָקְדֵנוּ בוֹ לִבְרָכָה, וְהוֹשִׁיעֵנוּ בוֹ לְחַיִּים. וּבִדְבַר יְשׁוּעָה וְרַחֲמִים, חוּס וְחָנֵּנוּ וְרַחֵם עָלֵינוּ וְהוֹשִׁיעֵנוּ, כִּי אֵלֶיךָ עֵינֵינוּ, כִּי אֵל מֶלֶךְ חַנּוּן וְרַחוּם אָתָּה.[1]

On the Sabbath add the words in brackets. [If forgotten, see *Laws* §86-90.]

וְהַשִּׂיאֵנוּ* יהוה אֱלֹהֵינוּ אֶת בִּרְכַּת מוֹעֲדֶיךָ לְחַיִּים וּלְשָׁלוֹם, לְשִׂמְחָה וּלְשָׂשׂוֹן, כַּאֲשֶׁר רָצִיתָ* וְאָמַרְתָּ לְבָרְכֵנוּ. [אֱלֹהֵינוּ וֵאלֹהֵי אֲבוֹתֵינוּ רְצֵה בִמְנוּחָתֵנוּ] קַדְּשֵׁנוּ בְּמִצְוֹתֶיךָ וְתֵן חֶלְקֵנוּ בְּתוֹרָתֶךָ, שַׂבְּעֵנוּ מִטּוּבֶךָ וְשַׂמְּחֵנוּ בִּישׁוּעָתֶךָ, וְטַהֵר לִבֵּנוּ לְעָבְדְּךָ בֶּאֱמֶת,* וְהַנְחִילֵנוּ יהוה אֱלֹהֵינוּ [בְּאַהֲבָה וּבְרָצוֹן*] בְּשִׂמְחָה וּבְשָׂשׂוֹן [שַׁבַּת וּ]מוֹעֲדֵי קָדְשֶׁךָ, וְיִשְׂמְחוּ בְךָ יִשְׂרָאֵל מְקַדְּשֵׁי שְׁמֶךָ. בָּרוּךְ אַתָּה יהוה, מְקַדֵּשׁ [הַשַּׁבָּת וְ]יִשְׂרָאֵל וְהַזְּמַנִּים.*

---

the קָרְבַּן חֲגִיגָה, *festive offering,* that pilgrims brought in celebration of the day.

בְּאַהֲבָה — *With love.* This extra expression of love, referring only to the Sabbath, denotes the particular affection with which Israel accepted the commandments of the Sabbath. Whereas the Festival observance represents our acknowledgment of God's kindness to our ancestors, the Sabbath shows our desire to honor Him as the Creator.

מִקְרָא קֹדֶשׁ — *A holy convocation.* On these days, the nation is gathered to pursue holiness, and to sanctify the Festival through prayer and praise to God *(Ramban; Sforno).*

זֵכֶר לִיצִיאַת מִצְרָיִם — *A memorial of the Exodus from Egypt.* There is a deep connection between all the Festivals and the Exodus. We are called upon constantly to renew our service of God. The key to doing so is our awareness that God revealed Himself at the Exodus, demonstrated His mastery over the universe, and made us His people. Our daily prayers stress our liberation from Egypt, and on Pesach we re-experience the initial self-revelation of God, and the creation of the Jewish people as a free nation. The freedom gained in Egypt is further unfolded on Shavuos, when we receive the Torah. It finds its final expression on Succos when we leave the temporal world, to take refuge in the *succah,* which symbolizes the sheltering wings of the *Shechinah,* the Divine Presence *(Maharal).*

⚘ אֱלֹהֵינוּ . . . יַעֲלֶה וְיָבֹא — *Our God . . . may there rise, come.* Our recollection of Israel's closeness to God brings home the poignant reality that we still lack the Temple. Therefore, we pray that He bring an end to the exile and reunite Israel, Jerusalem, and the Temple.

This prayer contains eight words [יַעֲלֶה . . . וְיִזָּכֵר] expressing the same general idea. *Rabbi S.R. Hirsch* interprets them: May our personal behavior and fortune *rise* [יַעֲלֶה] above ordinary human existence; and *come* [וְיָבֹא] before God to merit His interest; may nothing prevent them from *reaching* [וְיַגִּיעַ] God and gaining His acceptance; may they be *noted* [וְיֵרָאֶה] in the best possible light; may they be worthy of God's *favor* [וְיֵרָצֶה]; may God *hear* [וְיִשָּׁמַע] the impact these remembrances have on our lives; may God *consider* [וְיִפָּקֵד] our needs; and may He *remem-*

[this day of Sabbath and] this day of the Festival of Matzos the time of our freedom [with love], a holy convocation,* a memorial of the Exodus from Egypt.**

אֱלֹהֵינוּ *Our God and God of our forefathers, may there rise, come,* reach, be noted, be favored, be heard, be considered, and be remembered — the remembrance and consideration of ourselves; the remembrance of our forefathers; the remembrance of Messiah, son of David, Your servant; the remembrance of Jerusalem, the City of Your Holiness; the remembrance of Your entire people the Family of Israel — before You for deliverance, for goodness, for grace, for kindness, and for compassion, for life, and for peace on this day of the Festival of Matzos. Remember us on it,* Hashem*, our God, for goodness, consider us on it for blessing, and help us on it for life. In the matter of salvation and compassion, pity, be gracious and compassionate with us and help us, for our eyes are turned to You, because You are God, the gracious and compassionate King.*[1]

On the Sabbath add the words in brackets. [If forgotten, see *Laws* §86-90.]

וְהַשִּׂיאֵנוּ *Bestow upon us,* O HASHEM, our God, the blessing of Your appointed festivals for life and for peace, for gladness and for joy, as You desired* and promised to bless us. [Our God and the God of our forefathers, may You be pleased with our rest.] Sanctify us with Your commandments and grant us our share in Your Torah; satisfy us from Your goodness and gladden us with Your salvation, and purify our heart to serve You sincerely.* And grant us a heritage, O HASHEM, our God — [with love and with favor*] with gladness and with joy — [the Sabbath and] the appointed festivals of Your holiness, and may Israel, the sanctifiers of Your Name, rejoice in You. Blessed are You, HASHEM, Who sanctifies [the Sabbath,] Israel and the festive seasons.**

(1) Cf. *Nehemiah* 9:31.

---

ber [וְיִזָּכֵר] us and our relationship to Him.

וְהַשִּׂיאֵנוּ — *Bestow upon us.* In concluding the central portion of the *Shemoneh Esrei,* we ask God to give all the joyous blessings of the day and season.

כַּאֲשֶׁר רָצִיתָ — *As You desired.* God wishes to bless and help His people; it remains for us to be worthy of His blessings.

בֶּאֱמֶת — *Sincerely.* Human beings are all too prone to self-deception. Someone may *think* he is sincere in his service of God, while he is really acting out of habit or to impress others. 'God — purify us to serve You in *true* sincerity!' *(Yesod V'Shoresh HaAvodah).*

בְּאַהֲבָה וּבְרָצוֹן — *With love and with favor.* This term is uniquely associated with the Sabbath; it is not even recited on Festivals unless they fall on the Sabbath. As the eternal reminder that God is the Creator, the *mitzvah* of the Sabbath shows us that God wants us to remember Him and praise Him. Accordingly, the Sabbath expresses His love for us and ours for Him, because on it we become more conscious that He desires our homage *(R' Hirsch);* and He finds special *favor* in our Temple offerings *(Abudraham).*

מְקַדֵּשׁ יִשְׂרָאֵל וְהַזְּמַנִּים — *Who sanctifies Israel and the festive seasons.* The use of the word זְמַנִּים, *festive seasons,* rather than the Scriptural term מוֹעֲדִים, *appointed Festivals,* alludes to a special feature of the Jewish calendar. The Torah ordains that Pesach must fall in the springtime, thus the court must take the זְמַנִּים, *seasons,* into account in formulating the calendar *(R' Bachya).*

מְקַדֵּשׁ [הַשַּׁבָּת וְ]יִשְׂרָאֵל וְהַזְּמַנִּים — *Who sanctifies [the Sabbath,] Israel and the seasons.* The *Kiddush* recited on *Yom Tov* closes by blessing God Who *sanctifies the people of Israel and the*

עבודה

רְצֵה יהוה אֱלֹהֵינוּ בְּעַמְּךָ יִשְׂרָאֵל וּבִתְפִלָּתָם, וְהָשֵׁב אֶת הָעֲבוֹדָה לִדְבִיר בֵּיתֶךָ. וְאִשֵּׁי יִשְׂרָאֵל וּתְפִלָּתָם בְּאַהֲבָה תְקַבֵּל בְּרָצוֹן, וּתְהִי לְרָצוֹן תָּמִיד עֲבוֹדַת יִשְׂרָאֵל עַמֶּךָ.

וְתֶחֱזֶינָה עֵינֵינוּ בְּשׁוּבְךָ לְצִיּוֹן בְּרַחֲמִים. בָּרוּךְ אַתָּה יהוה, הַמַּחֲזִיר שְׁכִינָתוֹ לְצִיּוֹן.

הודאה

Bow at מוֹדִים; straighten up at 'ה.

מוֹדִים אֲנַחְנוּ לָךְ, שָׁאַתָּה הוּא יהוה אֱלֹהֵינוּ וֵאלֹהֵי אֲבוֹתֵינוּ לְעוֹלָם וָעֶד. צוּר חַיֵּינוּ, מָגֵן יִשְׁעֵנוּ אַתָּה הוּא לְדוֹר וָדוֹר. נוֹדֶה לְּךָ וּנְסַפֵּר תְּהִלָּתֶךָ[1] עַל חַיֵּינוּ הַמְּסוּרִים בְּיָדֶךָ, וְעַל נִשְׁמוֹתֵינוּ הַפְּקוּדוֹת לָךְ, וְעַל נִסֶּיךָ שֶׁבְּכָל יוֹם עִמָּנוּ, וְעַל נִפְלְאוֹתֶיךָ וְטוֹבוֹתֶיךָ שֶׁבְּכָל עֵת, עֶרֶב וָבֹקֶר וְצָהֳרָיִם. הַטּוֹב כִּי לֹא כָלוּ רַחֲמֶיךָ, וְהַמְּרַחֵם כִּי לֹא תַמּוּ חֲסָדֶיךָ,[2] מֵעוֹלָם קִוִּינוּ לָךְ.

וְעַל כֻּלָּם יִתְבָּרַךְ וְיִתְרוֹמַם שִׁמְךָ מַלְכֵּנוּ תָּמִיד לְעוֹלָם וָעֶד.

Bend the knees at בָּרוּךְ; bow at אַתָּה; straighten up at 'ה.

וְכֹל הַחַיִּים יוֹדְוּךָ סֶּלָה, וִיהַלְלוּ אֶת שִׁמְךָ בֶּאֱמֶת, הָאֵל יְשׁוּעָתֵנוּ וְעֶזְרָתֵנוּ סֶלָה. בָּרוּךְ אַתָּה יהוה, הַטּוֹב שִׁמְךָ וּלְךָ נָאֶה לְהוֹדוֹת.

שלום

שָׁלוֹם רָב* עַל יִשְׂרָאֵל עַמְּךָ תָּשִׂים לְעוֹלָם, כִּי אַתָּה הוּא מֶלֶךְ אָדוֹן לְכָל הַשָּׁלוֹם. וְטוֹב בְּעֵינֶיךָ לְבָרֵךְ אֶת עַמְּךָ יִשְׂרָאֵל, בְּכָל עֵת וּבְכָל שָׁעָה בִּשְׁלוֹמֶךָ. בָּרוּךְ אַתָּה יהוה, הַמְּבָרֵךְ אֶת עַמּוֹ יִשְׂרָאֵל בַּשָּׁלוֹם.

יִהְיוּ לְרָצוֹן אִמְרֵי פִי וְהֶגְיוֹן לִבִּי לְפָנֶיךָ, יהוה צוּרִי וְגֹאֲלִי.[3]

---

seasons — Israel is mentioned before the seasons. But if the *Yom Tov* coincides with a Sabbath, we mention the Sabbath before Israel: *God Who sanctifies the Sabbath and Israel and the seasons.* The seventh day of the week was sanctified at Creation, long before the Jewish nation was created. In the case of the Festivals, however, although the Torah ordains the date on which they are to be celebrated, this date actually depends on the Jewish people — represented by *Beis Din*, the Rabbinic Court — which the Torah assigns to regulate and fix the calendar. We can

TEMPLE SERVICE

רְצֵה *Be favorable, HASHEM, our God, toward Your people Israel and their prayer and restore the service to the Holy of Holies of Your Temple. The fire-offerings of Israel and their prayer accept with love and favor, and may the service of Your people Israel always be favorable to You.*

וְתֶחֱזֶינָה *May our eyes behold Your return to Zion in compassion. Blessed are You, HASHEM, Who restores His Presence to Zion.*

THANKSGIVING [MODIM]

Bow at *'We gratefully thank You'*; straighten up at *'HASHEM.'*

מוֹדִים *We gratefully thank You, for it is You Who are HASHEM, our God and the God of our forefathers for all eternity; Rock of our lives, Shield of our salvation are You from generation to generation. We shall thank You and relate Your praise*[1] *— for our lives, which are committed to Your power and for our souls that are entrusted to You; for Your miracles that are with us every day; and for Your wonders and favors in every season — evening, morning, and afternoon. The Beneficent One, for Your compassions were never exhausted, and the Compassionate One, for Your kindnesses never ended*[2] *— always have we put our hope in You.*

For all these, may Your Name be blessed and exalted, our King, continually forever and ever.

Bend the knees at *'Blessed'*; bow at *'You'*; straighten up at *'HASHEM.'*

Everything alive will gratefully acknowledge You, Selah! and praise Your Name sincerely, O God of our salvation and help, Selah! Blessed are You, HASHEM, Your Name is 'The Beneficent One' and to You it is fitting to give thanks.

PEACE

שָׁלוֹם *Establish abundant peace* upon Your people Israel forever, for You are King, Master of all peace. May it be good in Your eyes to bless Your people Israel at every time and every hour with Your peace. Blessed are You, HASHEM, Who blesses His people Israel with peace.*

May the expressions of my mouth and the thoughts of my heart find favor before You, HASHEM, my Rock and my Redeemer.[3]

(1) Cf. *Psalms* 79:13. (2) Cf. *Lamentations* 3:22. (3) *Psalms* 19:15.

therefore make mention ofthe festive seasons only *after* first proclaiming the sanctity of the Jewish people itself (*Beitzah* 17a).

שָׁלוֹם רָב — *Abundant peace.* The last blessing of *Shemoneh Esrei* is a prayer for peace, because R' Shimon ben Chalafta said:

אֱלֹהַי, נְצוֹר לְשׁוֹנִי מֵרָע, וּשְׂפָתַי מִדַּבֵּר מִרְמָה,[1] וְלִמְקַלְלַי נַפְשִׁי תִדּוֹם, וְנַפְשִׁי כֶּעָפָר לַכֹּל תִּהְיֶה. פְּתַח לִבִּי בְּתוֹרָתֶךָ, וּבְמִצְוֹתֶיךָ תִּרְדּוֹף נַפְשִׁי. וְכֹל הַחוֹשְׁבִים עָלַי רָעָה, מְהֵרָה הָפֵר עֲצָתָם וְקַלְקֵל מַחֲשַׁבְתָּם. עֲשֵׂה לְמַעַן שְׁמֶךָ, עֲשֵׂה לְמַעַן יְמִינֶךָ, עֲשֵׂה לְמַעַן קְדֻשָּׁתֶךָ, עֲשֵׂה לְמַעַן תּוֹרָתֶךָ. לְמַעַן יֵחָלְצוּן יְדִידֶיךָ, הוֹשִׁיעָה יְמִינְךָ וַעֲנֵנִי.[2]

Some recite verses pertaining to their names here. See p. 1143.

יִהְיוּ לְרָצוֹן אִמְרֵי פִי וְהֶגְיוֹן לִבִּי לְפָנֶיךָ, יהוה צוּרִי וְגֹאֲלִי.[3]

Bow and take three steps back. Bow left and say ... עֹשֶׂה; bow right and say ... הוּא יַעֲשֶׂה; bow forward and say וְעַל כָּל ... אָמֵן.

עֹשֶׂה שָׁלוֹם בִּמְרוֹמָיו, הוּא יַעֲשֶׂה שָׁלוֹם עָלֵינוּ, וְעַל כָּל יִשְׂרָאֵל. וְאִמְרוּ: אָמֵן.

יְהִי רָצוֹן מִלְּפָנֶיךָ יהוה אֱלֹהֵינוּ וֵאלֹהֵי אֲבוֹתֵינוּ, שֶׁיִּבָּנֶה בֵּית הַמִּקְדָּשׁ בִּמְהֵרָה בְיָמֵינוּ, וְתֵן חֶלְקֵנוּ בְּתוֹרָתֶךָ. וְשָׁם נַעֲבָדְךָ בְּיִרְאָה, כִּימֵי עוֹלָם וּכְשָׁנִים קַדְמוֹנִיּוֹת. וְעָרְבָה לַיהוה מִנְחַת יְהוּדָה וִירוּשָׁלָיִם, כִּימֵי עוֹלָם וּכְשָׁנִים קַדְמוֹנִיּוֹת.[4]

SHEMONEH ESREI ENDS HERE.

Remain standing in place for at least a few moments before taking three steps forward.

On Friday night, all present stand and recite וַיְכֻלּוּ aloud in unison.

וַיְכֻלּוּ* הַשָּׁמַיִם וְהָאָרֶץ וְכָל צְבָאָם. וַיְכַל אֱלֹהִים בַּיּוֹם הַשְּׁבִיעִי מְלַאכְתּוֹ אֲשֶׁר עָשָׂה, וַיִּשְׁבֹּת בַּיּוֹם הַשְּׁבִיעִי מִכָּל מְלַאכְתּוֹ אֲשֶׁר עָשָׂה. וַיְבָרֶךְ אֱלֹהִים אֶת יוֹם הַשְּׁבִיעִי, וַיְקַדֵּשׁ אֹתוֹ, כִּי בוֹ שָׁבַת מִכָּל מְלַאכְתּוֹ, אֲשֶׁר בָּרָא אֱלֹהִים לַעֲשׂוֹת.[5]

SOME CONGREGATIONS RECITE HALLEL (PAGE 348) AT THIS POINT.

The Holy One, Blessed is He, could find no container that holds Israel's blessings as well as peace (*Uktzin* 3:12). Peace is the cement that holds the nation together. When reciting this prayer, one should have in mind the plea that all Jews feel affection for one another. Likewise he should pray that he be freed from the curse of anger, because there can be no peace where there is anger (*Yaaros D'vash*). Furthermore, after the Morning and Afternoon Temple services, the *Kohanim* would bless the people with *Bircas Kohanim*, which concludes with a blessing for peace. This blessing in *Shemoneh Esrei* contains the word peace four times, alluding to a prayer for each of the Four Exiles (*Etz Yosef*).

וַיְכֻלּוּ — ... *were finished.* We stand and recite this paragraph aloud because it is a form of testimony that God created heaven and earth

אֱלֹהַי *My God, guard my tongue from evil and my lips from speaking deceitfully.*[1] *To those who curse me, let my soul be silent; and let my soul be like dust to everyone. Open my heart to Your Torah, then my soul will pursue Your commandments. As for all those who design evil against me, speedily nullify their counsel and disrupt their design. Act for Your Name's sake; act for Your right hand's sake; act for Your sanctity's sake; act for Your Torah's sake. That Your beloved ones may be given rest; let Your right hand save, and respond to me.*[2]

Some recite verses pertaining to their names at this point. See page 1143.

May the expressions of my mouth and the thoughts of my heart find favor before You, HASHEM, my Rock and my Redeemer.[3] *He Who makes peace in His heights, may He make peace upon us, and upon all Israel. Now respond: Amen.*

Bow and take three steps back. Bow left and say, *'He Who makes peace . . .'*; bow right and say, *'may He make peace . . .'*; bow forward and say, *'and upon . . . Amen.'*

יְהִי רָצוֹן *May it be Your will, HASHEM, our God and the God of our forefathers, that the Holy Temple be rebuilt, speedily in our days. Grant us our share in Your Torah, and may we serve You there with reverence, as in days of old and in former years. Then the offering of Judah and Jerusalem will be pleasing to HASHEM, as in days of old and in former years.*[4]

SHEMONEH ESREI ENDS HERE.

Remain standing in place for at least a few moments before taking three steps forward.

On Friday night, all present stand and recite וַיְכֻלּוּ, *'Thus the heavens . . .,'* aloud in unison.

וַיְכֻלּוּ *Thus the heavens and the earth were finished,* and all their legion. On the seventh day God completed His work which He had done, and He abstained on the seventh day from all His work which He had done. God blessed the seventh day and sanctified it, because on it He had abstained from all His work which God created to make.*[5]

SOME CONGREGATIONS RECITE HALLEL (PAGE 348) AT THIS POINT.

(1) Cf. 34:14. (2) 60:7; 108:7. (3) *Psalms* 19:15. (4) *Malachi* 3:4. (5) *Genesis* 2:1-3.

— and witnesses must give their testimony while standing and in a loud, clear voice (*Ibn Yarchi*).

Because of this paragraph's status as a testimony, it should preferably be said with the congregation, or at least in the company of one other person. However, it may be recited by an individual as well (*Orach Chaim* 268).

Tur (ibid.) notes that it is especially important not to speak during וַיְכֻלּוּ or during the recitation of the seven-faceted blessing.

The *chazzan* recites קדיש שלם.

יִתְגַּדַּל וְיִתְקַדַּשׁ שְׁמֵהּ רַבָּא. (.Cong. – אָמֵן.) בְּעָלְמָא דִּי בְרָא כִרְעוּתֵהּ. וְיַמְלִיךְ מַלְכוּתֵהּ, בְּחַיֵּיכוֹן וּבְיוֹמֵיכוֹן וּבְחַיֵּי דְכָל בֵּית יִשְׂרָאֵל, בַּעֲגָלָא וּבִזְמַן קָרִיב. וְאִמְרוּ: אָמֵן.

(.Cong. – אָמֵן. יְהֵא שְׁמֵהּ רַבָּא מְבָרַךְ לְעָלַם וּלְעָלְמֵי עָלְמַיָּא.)

יְהֵא שְׁמֵהּ רַבָּא מְבָרַךְ לְעָלַם וּלְעָלְמֵי עָלְמַיָּא.

יִתְבָּרַךְ וְיִשְׁתַּבַּח וְיִתְפָּאַר וְיִתְרוֹמַם וְיִתְנַשֵּׂא וְיִתְהַדָּר וְיִתְעַלֶּה וְיִתְהַלָּל שְׁמֵהּ דְּקֻדְשָׁא בְּרִיךְ הוּא (.Cong. – בְּרִיךְ הוּא) – לְעֵלָּא מִן כָּל בִּרְכָתָא וְשִׁירָתָא תֻּשְׁבְּחָתָא וְנֶחֱמָתָא, דַּאֲמִירָן בְּעָלְמָא. וְאִמְרוּ: אָמֵן. (.Cong. – אָמֵן.)

(.Cong. – קַבֵּל בְּרַחֲמִים וּבְרָצוֹן אֶת תְּפִלָּתֵנוּ.)

תִּתְקַבֵּל צְלוֹתְהוֹן וּבָעוּתְהוֹן דְּכָל בֵּית יִשְׂרָאֵל קֳדָם אֲבוּהוֹן דִּי בִשְׁמַיָּא. וְאִמְרוּ: אָמֵן. (.Cong. – אָמֵן.)

(.Cong. – יְהִי שֵׁם יהוה מְבֹרָךְ, מֵעַתָּה וְעַד עוֹלָם.[1])

יְהֵא שְׁלָמָא רַבָּא מִן שְׁמַיָּא, וְחַיִּים עָלֵינוּ וְעַל כָּל יִשְׂרָאֵל. וְאִמְרוּ: אָמֵן. (.Cong. – אָמֵן.)

(.Cong. – עֶזְרִי מֵעִם יהוה, עֹשֵׂה שָׁמַיִם וָאָרֶץ.[2])

Take three steps back. Bow left and say . . . עֹשֶׂה; bow right and say . . . הוּא; bow forward and say וְעַל כָּל . . . אָמֵן. Remain standing in place for a few moments, then take three steps forward.

עֹשֶׂה שָׁלוֹם בִּמְרוֹמָיו, הוּא יַעֲשֶׂה שָׁלוֹם עָלֵינוּ, וְעַל כָּל יִשְׂרָאֵל. וְאִמְרוּ: אָמֵן. (.Cong. – אָמֵן.)

ספירת העומר

The *Omer* is counted from the second night of Pesach until the night before Shavuos. Most congregations count the *Omer* at this point; some count after *Aleinu* (p. 84). See commentary for pertinent laws.

In some congregations the following Kabbalistic prayer precedes the counting of the *Omer*.

לְשֵׁם יִחוּד קוּדְשָׁא בְּרִיךְ הוּא וּשְׁכִינְתֵּיהּ, בִּדְחִילוּ וּרְחִימוּ לְיַחֵד שֵׁם יו״ד הֵ״א בְּוָא״ו הֵ״א בְּיִחוּדָא שְׁלִים, בְּשֵׁם כָּל יִשְׂרָאֵל. הִנְנִי מוּכָן וּמְזוּמָן לְקַיֵּם מִצְוַת עֲשֵׂה שֶׁל סְפִירַת הָעוֹמֶר, כְּמוֹ שֶׁכָּתוּב בַּתּוֹרָה: וּסְפַרְתֶּם לָכֶם מִמָּחֳרַת הַשַּׁבָּת, מִיּוֹם הֲבִיאֲכֶם אֶת עֹמֶר הַתְּנוּפָה, שֶׁבַע שַׁבָּתוֹת תְּמִימֹת תִּהְיֶינָה. עַד מִמָּחֳרַת הַשַּׁבָּת הַשְּׁבִיעִת תִּסְפְּרוּ חֲמִשִּׁים יוֹם, וְהִקְרַבְתֶּם מִנְחָה חֲדָשָׁה לַיהוה.[3] וִיהִי נֹעַם אֲדֹנָי אֱלֹהֵינוּ עָלֵינוּ, וּמַעֲשֵׂה יָדֵינוּ כּוֹנְנָה עָלֵינוּ, וּמַעֲשֵׂה יָדֵינוּ כּוֹנְנֵהוּ.[4]

ספירת העומר / Counting the Omer

The Torah commands that from the second day of Pesach — the day the *Omer* offering of new barley is brought in the Temple — forty-nine days are to be counted; and the festival of Shavuos celebrated on the fiftieth day. This period is called *Sefiras HaOmer,* the counting of the Omer. The *Sefirah* count also recalls an earlier event. During the seven weeks following the Exodus, our ancestors prepared themselves for receiving the Torah at Mount Sinai. This responsibility to prepare oneself to receive the Torah is present every year, as we relive the Exodus from bondage and materialism, and strive to be worthy of the gift of Torah. In ancient times, the *Sefirah* period was a time of rejoicing, but it is now observed as a time of semi-mourning because of several reasons: the

The *chazzan* recites the Full *Kaddish*.

יִתְגַּדַּל *May His great Name grow exalted and sanctified* (Cong.— *Amen.*) *in the world that He created as He willed. May He give reign to His kingship in your lifetimes and in your days, and in the lifetimes of the entire Family of Israel, swiftly and soon. Now respond: Amen.*

(Cong.— *Amen. May His great Name be blessed forever and ever.*)

May His great Name be blessed forever and ever.

Blessed, praised, glorified, exalted, extolled, mighty, upraised, and lauded be the Name of the Holy One, Blessed is He (Cong.— *Blessed is He*) — *beyond any blessing and song, praise and consolation that are uttered in the world. Now respond: Amen.* (Cong.— *Amen.*)

(Cong.— *Accept our prayers with mercy and favor.*)

May the prayers and supplications of the entire Family of Israel be accepted before their Father Who is in Heaven. Now respond: Amen. (Cong.— *Amen.*)

(Cong.— *Blessed be the Name of* HASHEM, *from this time and forever.*[1])

May there be abundant peace from Heaven, and life, upon us and upon all Israel. Now respond: Amen. (Cong.— *Amen.*)

(Cong.— *My help is from* HASHEM, *Maker of heaven and earth.*[2])

Take three steps back. Bow left and say, *'He Who makes peace . . .'*; bow right and say, *'may He . . .'*; bow forward and say, *'and upon all Israel . . .'* Remain standing in place for a few moments, then take three steps forward.

He Who makes peace in His heights, may He make peace upon us, and upon all Israel. Now respond: Amen. (Cong.— *Amen.*)

COUNTING THE OMER

The *Omer* is counted from the second night of Pesach until the night before Shavuos. Most congregations count the *Omer* at this point; some count after *Aleinu* (p. 84). See commentary for pertinent laws.

In some congregations the following Kabbalistic prayer precedes the counting of the *Omer*.

לְשֵׁם *For the sake of the unification of the Holy One, Blessed is He, and His Presence, in fear and love to unify the Name Yud-Kei with Vav-Kei in perfect unity, in the name of all Israel. Behold I am prepared and ready to perform the commandment of counting the Omer, as it is written in the Torah: 'You are to count from the morrow of the rest day, from the day you brought the Omer-offering that is waved — they are to be seven complete weeks — until the morrow of the seventh week you are to count fifty days, and then offer a new meal-offering to* HASHEM.'[3] *May the pleasantness of my Lord, our God, be upon us — may He establish our handiwork for us; our handiwork, may He establish.*[4]

(1) *Psalms* 113:2. (2) 121:2. (3) *Leviticus* 23:15-16. (4) *Psalms* 90:17.

☙ A Summary of Laws of Sefirah

The *Omer* is counted, standing, after nightfall. Before reciting the blessing, one should be careful *not* to say 'Today is the ————th day.' If he did so, for example, in response to someone who asked which day it is, he may not recite the blessing, since he has already counted that day. Where there are days and weeks, this does not apply unless he also mentioned the week. In both cases, he may recite the blessing on succeeding nights.

If one forgets to count at night, he counts during the next day *without* a blessing, but may recite the blessing on succeeding nights. But if one forgot to count all day, he counts without a blessing on succeeding nights.

Chazzan, followed by congregation, recites the blessing and counts.
One praying without a *minyan* should, nevertheless, recite the entire *Omer* service.

בָּרוּךְ אַתָּה יהוה אֱלֹהֵינוּ מֶלֶךְ הָעוֹלָם, אֲשֶׁר קִדְּשָׁנוּ בְּמִצְוֹתָיו וְצִוָּנוּ עַל סְפִירַת הָעוֹמֶר.

הַיּוֹם יוֹם אֶחָד לָעוֹמֶר.

הָרַחֲמָן הוּא יַחֲזִיר לָנוּ עֲבוֹדַת בֵּית הַמִּקְדָּשׁ לִמְקוֹמָהּ, בִּמְהֵרָה בְיָמֵינוּ. אָמֵן סֶלָה.

תהלים סז

לַמְנַצֵּחַ בִּנְגִינֹת מִזְמוֹר שִׁיר. אֱלֹהִים יְחָנֵּנוּ וִיבָרְכֵנוּ, יָאֵר פָּנָיו אִתָּנוּ סֶלָה. לָדַעַת בָּאָרֶץ דַּרְכֶּךָ, בְּכָל גּוֹיִם יְשׁוּעָתֶךָ. יוֹדוּךָ עַמִּים אֱלֹהִים, יוֹדוּךָ עַמִּים כֻּלָּם. יִשְׂמְחוּ וִירַנְּנוּ לְאֻמִּים, כִּי תִשְׁפֹּט עַמִּים מִישֹׁר, וּלְאֻמִּים בָּאָרֶץ תַּנְחֵם סֶלָה. יוֹדוּךָ עַמִּים, אֱלֹהִים, יוֹדוּךָ עַמִּים כֻּלָּם. אֶרֶץ נָתְנָה יְבוּלָהּ, יְבָרְכֵנוּ אֱלֹהִים אֱלֹהֵינוּ. יְבָרְכֵנוּ אֱלֹהִים, וְיִירְאוּ אוֹתוֹ כָּל אַפְסֵי אָרֶץ.

אָנָּא בְּכֹחַ גְּדֻלַּת יְמִינְךָ תַּתִּיר צְרוּרָה. אב״ג ית״ץ
קַבֵּל רִנַּת עַמְּךָ שַׂגְּבֵנוּ טַהֲרֵנוּ נוֹרָא. קר״ע שט״ן
נָא גִבּוֹר דּוֹרְשֵׁי יִחוּדְךָ כְּבָבַת שָׁמְרֵם. נג״ד יכ״ש
בָּרְכֵם טַהֲרֵם רַחֲמֵם צִדְקָתְךָ תָּמִיד גָּמְלֵם. בט״ר צת״ג
חֲסִין קָדוֹשׁ בְּרוֹב טוּבְךָ נַהֵל עֲדָתֶךָ. חק״ב טנ״ע
יָחִיד גֵּאֶה לְעַמְּךָ פְּנֵה זוֹכְרֵי קְדֻשָּׁתֶךָ. יג״ל פז״ק
שַׁוְעָתֵנוּ קַבֵּל וּשְׁמַע צַעֲקָתֵנוּ יוֹדֵעַ תַּעֲלֻמוֹת. שק״ו צי״ת
בָּרוּךְ שֵׁם כְּבוֹד מַלְכוּתוֹ לְעוֹלָם וָעֶד.

רִבּוֹנוֹ שֶׁל עוֹלָם, אַתָּה צִוִּיתָנוּ עַל יְדֵי מֹשֶׁה עַבְדֶּךָ לִסְפּוֹר סְפִירַת הָעוֹמֶר, כְּדֵי לְטַהֲרֵנוּ מִקְּלִפּוֹתֵינוּ וּמִטֻּמְאוֹתֵינוּ, כְּמוֹ שֶׁכָּתַבְתָּ בְּתוֹרָתֶךָ: וּסְפַרְתֶּם לָכֶם מִמָּחֳרַת הַשַּׁבָּת מִיּוֹם הֲבִיאֲכֶם אֶת עֹמֶר הַתְּנוּפָה, שֶׁבַע שַׁבָּתוֹת תְּמִימֹת תִּהְיֶינָה. עַד מִמָּחֳרַת הַשַּׁבָּת הַשְּׁבִיעִת תִּסְפְּרוּ חֲמִשִּׁים יוֹם.[1] כְּדֵי שֶׁיִּטָּהֲרוּ נַפְשׁוֹת עַמְּךָ יִשְׂרָאֵל מִזֻּהֲמָתָם. וּבְכֵן יְהִי רָצוֹן מִלְּפָנֶיךָ יהוה אֱלֹהֵינוּ וֵאלֹהֵי אֲבוֹתֵינוּ, שֶׁבִּזְכוּת סְפִירַת הָעוֹמֶר שֶׁסָּפַרְתִּי הַיּוֹם, יְתֻקַּן מַה שֶּׁפָּגַמְתִּי בִּסְפִירָה חֶסֶד שֶׁבְּחֶסֶד. וְאֶטָּהֵר וְאֶתְקַדֵּשׁ בִּקְדֻשָּׁה שֶׁל מַעְלָה, וְעַל יְדֵי זֶה יֻשְׁפַּע שֶׁפַע רַב בְּכָל הָעוֹלָמוֹת. וּלְתַקֵּן אֶת נַפְשׁוֹתֵינוּ, וְרוּחוֹתֵינוּ, וְנִשְׁמוֹתֵינוּ, מִכָּל סִיג וּפְגַם, וּלְטַהֲרֵנוּ וּלְקַדְּשֵׁנוּ בִּקְדֻשָּׁתְךָ הָעֶלְיוֹנָה. אָמֵן סֶלָה.

In some congregations, if a mourner is present, the Mourner's *Kaddish* (p. 82) is recited, followed by *Aleinu*. In others, *Aleinu* is recited immediately.

Chazzan, followed by congregation, recites the blessing and counts.
One praying without a *minyan* should, nevertheless, recite the entire *Omer* service.

בָּרוּךְ *Blessed are You, HASHEM, our God, King of the universe, Who has sanctified us with His commandments and has commanded us regarding the counting of the Omer.*

Today is one day of the Omer.

הָרַחֲמָן *The Compassionate One! May He return for us the service of the Temple to its place, speedily in our days. Amen, selah!*

Psalm 67

לַמְנַצֵּחַ *For the Conductor, upon Neginos, a psalm, a song. May God favor us and bless us, may He illuminate His countenance with us, Selah. To make known Your way on earth, among all the nations Your salvation. The peoples will acknowledge You, O God, the peoples will acknowledge You, all of them. Nations will be glad and sing for joy, because You will judge the people fairly and guide the nations on earth, Selah. The peoples will acknowledge You, O God, the peoples will acknowledge You, all of them. The earth has yielded its produce, may God, our own God, bless us. May God bless us and may all the ends of the earth fear him.*

אָנָּא *We beg You! With the strength of Your right hand's greatness, untie the bundled sins. Accept the prayer of Your nation; strengthen us, purify us, O Awesome One. Please, O Strong One — those who foster Your Oneness, guard them like the apple of an eye. Bless them, purify them, show them pity, may Your righteousness always recompense them. Powerful Holy One, with Your abundant goodness guide Your congregation. One and only Exalted One, turn to Your nation, which proclaims Your holiness. Accept our entreaty and hear our cry, O Knower of mysteries. Blessed is the Name of His glorious Kingdom for all eternity.*

רִבּוֹנוֹ שֶׁל עוֹלָם *Master of the universe, You commanded us through Moses, Your servant, to count the Omer Count in order to cleanse us from our encrustations of evil and from our contaminations, as You have written in Your Torah: You are to count from the morrow of the rest day, from the day you brought the Omer-offering that is waved — they are to be seven complete weeks. Until the morrow of the seventh week you are to count fifty days,[1] so that the souls of Your people Israel be cleansed from their contamination. Therefore, may it be Your will, HASHEM, our God and the God of our forefathers, that in the merit of the Omer Count that I have counted today, may there be corrected whatever blemish I have caused in the sefirah chesed shebechesed. May I be cleansed and sanctified with the holiness of Above, and through this may abundant bounty flow in all the worlds. And may it correct our lives, spirits, and souls from all sediment and blemish; may it cleanse us and sanctify us with Your exalted holiness. Amen, Selah!*

In some congregations, if a mourner is present, the Mourner's *Kaddish* (p. 82) is recited, followed by *Aleinu*. In others, *Aleinu* is recited immediately.

(1) *Leviticus* 23:15-16.

absence of the Temple; the death of R' Akiva's 24,000 students during thirty-three days of the *Sefirah*; and a string of bloody massacres of Jewish communities during the Crusades.

The congregation stands while reciting עָלֵינוּ.

עָלֵינוּ לְשַׁבֵּחַ לַאֲדוֹן הַכֹּל, לָתֵת גְּדֻלָּה לְיוֹצֵר בְּרֵאשִׁית, שֶׁלֹּא עָשָׂנוּ כְּגוֹיֵי הָאֲרָצוֹת, וְלֹא שָׂמָנוּ כְּמִשְׁפְּחוֹת הָאֲדָמָה. שֶׁלֹּא שָׂם חֶלְקֵנוּ כָּהֶם, וְגוֹרָלֵנוּ כְּכָל הֲמוֹנָם. (שֶׁהֵם מִשְׁתַּחֲוִים לְהֶבֶל וָרִיק, וּמִתְפַּלְּלִים אֶל אֵל לֹא יוֹשִׁיעַ.[1]) וַאֲנַחְנוּ כּוֹרְעִים וּמִשְׁתַּחֲוִים וּמוֹדִים, לִפְנֵי מֶלֶךְ מַלְכֵי הַמְּלָכִים הַקָּדוֹשׁ בָּרוּךְ הוּא. שֶׁהוּא נוֹטֶה שָׁמַיִם וְיֹסֵד אָרֶץ,[2] וּמוֹשַׁב יְקָרוֹ בַּשָּׁמַיִם מִמַּעַל, וּשְׁכִינַת עֻזּוֹ בְּגָבְהֵי מְרוֹמִים. הוּא אֱלֹהֵינוּ, אֵין עוֹד. אֱמֶת מַלְכֵּנוּ, אֶפֶס זוּלָתוֹ, כַּכָּתוּב בְּתוֹרָתוֹ: וְיָדַעְתָּ הַיּוֹם וַהֲשֵׁבֹתָ אֶל לְבָבֶךָ, כִּי יהוה הוּא הָאֱלֹהִים בַּשָּׁמַיִם מִמַּעַל וְעַל הָאָרֶץ מִתָּחַת, אֵין עוֹד.[3]

Bow while reciting וַאֲנַחְנוּ כּוֹרְעִים וּמִשְׁתַּחֲוִים.

עַל כֵּן נְקַוֶּה לְּךָ יהוה אֱלֹהֵינוּ לִרְאוֹת מְהֵרָה בְּתִפְאֶרֶת עֻזֶּךָ, לְהַעֲבִיר גִּלּוּלִים מִן הָאָרֶץ, וְהָאֱלִילִים כָּרוֹת יִכָּרֵתוּן, לְתַקֵּן עוֹלָם בְּמַלְכוּת שַׁדַּי. וְכָל בְּנֵי בָשָׂר יִקְרְאוּ בִשְׁמֶךָ, לְהַפְנוֹת אֵלֶיךָ כָּל רִשְׁעֵי אָרֶץ. יַכִּירוּ וְיֵדְעוּ כָּל יוֹשְׁבֵי תֵבֵל, כִּי לְךָ תִּכְרַע כָּל בֶּרֶךְ, תִּשָּׁבַע כָּל לָשׁוֹן.[4] לְפָנֶיךָ יהוה אֱלֹהֵינוּ יִכְרְעוּ וְיִפֹּלוּ, וְלִכְבוֹד שִׁמְךָ יְקָר יִתֵּנוּ. וִיקַבְּלוּ כֻלָּם אֶת עוֹל מַלְכוּתֶךָ, וְתִמְלֹךְ עֲלֵיהֶם מְהֵרָה לְעוֹלָם וָעֶד. כִּי הַמַּלְכוּת שֶׁלְּךָ הִיא וּלְעוֹלְמֵי עַד תִּמְלוֹךְ בְּכָבוֹד, כַּכָּתוּב בְּתוֹרָתֶךָ: יהוה יִמְלֹךְ לְעֹלָם וָעֶד.[5] ❖ וְנֶאֱמַר: וְהָיָה יהוה לְמֶלֶךְ עַל כָּל הָאָרֶץ, בַּיּוֹם הַהוּא יִהְיֶה יהוה אֶחָד וּשְׁמוֹ אֶחָד.[6]

Some recite the following after עָלֵינוּ:

אַל תִּירָא מִפַּחַד פִּתְאֹם, וּמִשֹּׁאַת רְשָׁעִים כִּי תָבֹא.[7] עֻצוּ עֵצָה וְתֻפָר, דַּבְּרוּ דָבָר וְלֹא יָקוּם, כִּי עִמָּנוּ אֵל.[8] וְעַד זִקְנָה אֲנִי הוּא, וְעַד שֵׂיבָה אֲנִי אֶסְבֹּל, אֲנִי עָשִׂיתִי וַאֲנִי אֶשָּׂא, וַאֲנִי אֶסְבֹּל וַאֲמַלֵּט.[9]

קדיש יתום

Mourners recite קַדִּישׁ יָתוֹם (see *Laws* §81-83).

יִתְגַּדַּל וְיִתְקַדַּשׁ שְׁמֵהּ רַבָּא. (Cong. – אָמֵן.) בְּעָלְמָא דִּי בְרָא כִרְעוּתֵהּ. וְיַמְלִיךְ מַלְכוּתֵהּ, בְּחַיֵּיכוֹן וּבְיוֹמֵיכוֹן וּבְחַיֵּי דְכָל בֵּית יִשְׂרָאֵל, בַּעֲגָלָא וּבִזְמַן קָרִיב. וְאִמְרוּ: אָמֵן.

(Cong. – אָמֵן. יְהֵא שְׁמֵהּ רַבָּא מְבָרַךְ לְעָלַם וּלְעָלְמֵי עָלְמַיָּא.)

יְהֵא שְׁמֵהּ רַבָּא מְבָרַךְ לְעָלַם וּלְעָלְמֵי עָלְמַיָּא.

יִתְבָּרַךְ וְיִשְׁתַּבַּח וְיִתְפָּאַר וְיִתְרוֹמַם וְיִתְנַשֵּׂא וְיִתְהַדָּר וְיִתְעַלֶּה וְיִתְהַלָּל שְׁמֵהּ דְּקֻדְשָׁא בְּרִיךְ הוּא (Cong. – בְּרִיךְ הוּא) — לְעֵלָּא מִן כָּל

The congregation stands while reciting עָלֵינוּ, *'It is our duty ...'*

עָלֵינוּ *It is our duty to praise the Master of all, to ascribe greatness to the Molder of primeval creation, for He has not made us like the nations of the lands, and has not emplaced us like the families of the earth; for He has not assigned our portion like theirs nor our lot like all their multitudes. (For they bow to vanity and emptiness and pray to a god which helps not.[1]) But we bend our knees, bow, and acknowledge our thanks before the King Who reigns over kings, the Holy One, Blessed is He. He stretches out heaven and establishes earth's foundation,[2] the seat of His homage is in the heavens above and His powerful Presence is in the loftiest heights. He is our God and there is none other. True is our King, there is nothing beside Him, as it is written in His Torah: 'You are to know this day and take to your heart that* HASHEM *is the only God — in heaven above and on the earth below — there is none other.'[3]*

Bow while reciting 'But we bend our knees.'

עַל כֵּן *Therefore we put our hope in You,* HASHEM *our God, that we may soon see Your mighty splendor, to remove detestable idolatry from the earth, and false gods will be utterly cut off, to perfect the universe through the Almighty's sovereignty. Then all humanity will call upon Your Name, to turn all the earth's wicked toward You. All the world's inhabitants will recognize and know that to You every knee should bend, every tongue should swear.[4] Before You,* HASHEM, *our God, they will bend every knee and cast themselves down and to the glory of Your Name they will render homage, and they will all accept upon themselves the yoke of Your kingship that You may reign over them soon and eternally. For the kingdom is Yours and You will reign for all eternity in glory as it is written in Your Torah:* HASHEM *shall reign for all eternity.[5] And it is said:* HASHEM *will be King over all the world — on that day* HASHEM *will be One and His Name will be One.[6]*

Some recite the following after *Aleinu:*

אַל תִּירָא *Do not fear sudden terror, or the holocaust of the wicked when it comes.[7] Plan a conspiracy and it will be annulled; speak your piece and it shall not stand, for God is with us.[8] Even till your seniority, I remain unchanged; and even till your ripe old age, I shall endure. I created you and I shall bear you; I shall endure and rescue.[9]*

MOURNER'S KADDISH

Mourners recite the Mourner's *Kaddish* (see *Laws* §81-83).

[A transliteration of this *Kaddish* appears on page 1147.]

יִתְגַּדַּל *May His great Name grow exalted and sanctified* (Cong.– *Amen.*) *in the world that He created as He willed. May He give reign to His kingship in your lifetimes and in your days, and in the lifetimes of the entire Family of Israel, swiftly and soon. Now respond: Amen.*

(Cong.– *Amen. May His great Name be blessed forever and ever.*)

May His great Name be blessed forever and ever.

Blessed, praised, glorified, exalted, extolled, mighty, upraised, and lauded be the Name of the Holy One, Blessed is He (Cong.– *Blessed is He*) *— beyond any*

(1) *Isaiah* 45:20. (2) 51:13. (3) *Deuteronomy* 4:39. (4) Cf. *Isaiah* 45:23.
(5) *Exodus* 15:18. (6) *Zechariah* 14:9. (7) *Proverbs* 3:25. (8) *Isaiah* 8:10. (9) 46:4.

בִּרְכָתָא וְשִׁירָתָא תֻּשְׁבְּחָתָא וְנֶחֱמָתָא, דַּאֲמִירָן בְּעָלְמָא. וְאִמְרוּ: אָמֵן. (.Cong— אָמֵן.)

יְהֵא שְׁלָמָא רַבָּא מִן שְׁמַיָּא, וְחַיִּים עָלֵינוּ וְעַל כָּל יִשְׂרָאֵל. וְאִמְרוּ: אָמֵן. (.Cong— אָמֵן.)

Take three steps back. Bow left and say . . . עֹשֶׂה; bow right and say . . . הוּא; bow forward and say וְעַל כָּל . . . אָמֵן. Remain standing in place for a few moments, then take three steps forward.

עֹשֶׂה שָׁלוֹם בִּמְרוֹמָיו, הוּא יַעֲשֶׂה שָׁלוֹם עָלֵינוּ, וְעַל כָּל יִשְׂרָאֵל. וְאִמְרוּ: אָמֵן. (.Cong— אָמֵן.)

SOME CONGREGATIONS COUNT THE *OMER* (PAGE 78) AT THIS POINT.

Many congregations recite either אֲדוֹן עוֹלָם or יִגְדַּל, or both, at this point.

אֲדוֹן עוֹלָם* אֲשֶׁר מָלַךְ, בְּטֶרֶם כָּל יְצִיר נִבְרָא.
לְעֵת נַעֲשָׂה בְחֶפְצוֹ כֹּל, אֲזַי מֶלֶךְ שְׁמוֹ נִקְרָא.
וְאַחֲרֵי כִּכְלוֹת הַכֹּל, לְבַדּוֹ יִמְלוֹךְ נוֹרָא.
וְהוּא הָיָה וְהוּא הֹוֶה, וְהוּא יִהְיֶה בְּתִפְאָרָה.
וְהוּא אֶחָד וְאֵין שֵׁנִי, לְהַמְשִׁיל לוֹ לְהַחְבִּירָה.
בְּלִי רֵאשִׁית בְּלִי תַכְלִית, וְלוֹ הָעֹז וְהַמִּשְׂרָה.
וְהוּא אֵלִי וְחַי גֹּאֲלִי, וְצוּר חֶבְלִי בְּעֵת צָרָה.
וְהוּא נִסִּי וּמָנוֹס לִי, מְנָת כּוֹסִי בְּיוֹם אֶקְרָא.
בְּיָדוֹ אַפְקִיד רוּחִי, בְּעֵת אִישַׁן וְאָעִירָה.
וְעִם רוּחִי גְּוִיָּתִי, יהוה לִי וְלֹא אִירָא.

יִגְדַּל אֱלֹהִים חַי* וְיִשְׁתַּבַּח, נִמְצָא וְאֵין עֵת אֶל מְצִיאוּתוֹ.
אֶחָד וְאֵין יָחִיד כְּיִחוּדוֹ, נֶעְלָם וְגַם אֵין סוֹף לְאַחְדוּתוֹ.
אֵין לוֹ דְמוּת הַגּוּף וְאֵינוֹ גוּף, לֹא נַעֲרוֹךְ אֵלָיו קְדֻשָּׁתוֹ.
קַדְמוֹן לְכָל דָּבָר אֲשֶׁר נִבְרָא, רִאשׁוֹן וְאֵין רֵאשִׁית לְרֵאשִׁיתוֹ.
הִנּוֹ אֲדוֹן עוֹלָם לְכָל נוֹצָר, יוֹרֶה גְדֻלָּתוֹ וּמַלְכוּתוֹ.
שֶׁפַע נְבוּאָתוֹ נְתָנוֹ, אֶל אַנְשֵׁי סְגֻלָּתוֹ וְתִפְאַרְתּוֹ.
לֹא קָם בְּיִשְׂרָאֵל כְּמֹשֶׁה עוֹד, נָבִיא וּמַבִּיט אֶת תְּמוּנָתוֹ.
תּוֹרַת אֱמֶת נָתַן לְעַמּוֹ אֵל, עַל יַד נְבִיאוֹ נֶאֱמַן בֵּיתוֹ.
לֹא יַחֲלִיף הָאֵל וְלֹא יָמִיר דָּתוֹ, לְעוֹלָמִים לְזוּלָתוֹ.
צוֹפֶה וְיוֹדֵעַ סְתָרֵינוּ, מַבִּיט לְסוֹף דָּבָר בְּקַדְמָתוֹ.
גּוֹמֵל לְאִישׁ חֶסֶד כְּמִפְעָלוֹ, נוֹתֵן לְרָשָׁע רָע כְּרִשְׁעָתוֹ.
יִשְׁלַח לְקֵץ הַיָּמִין מְשִׁיחֵנוּ, לִפְדּוֹת מְחַכֵּי קֵץ יְשׁוּעָתוֹ.
מֵתִים יְחַיֶּה אֵל בְּרֹב חַסְדּוֹ, בָּרוּךְ עֲדֵי עַד שֵׁם תְּהִלָּתוֹ.

⸎ אֲדוֹן עוֹלָם — *Master of the universe.* This inspiring song of praise is attributed to R' Shlomo ibn Gabirol, one of the greatest early *paytanim* [liturgical poets], who flourished in the eleventh century. See commentary on page 192.

⸎ יִגְדַּל אֱלֹהִים חַי — *Exalted be the Living God.* This song of uncertain authorship summarizes *blessing and song, praise and consolation that are uttered in the world. Now respond: Amen.* (Cong.– *Amen.*)

May there be abundant peace from Heaven, and life, upon us and upon all Israel. Now respond: Amen. (Cong.– *Amen.*)

Take three steps back. Bow left and say, *'He Who makes peace . . .'*; bow right and say, *'may He . . .'*; bow forward and say, *'and upon all Israel . . .'* Remain standing in place for a few moments, then take three steps forward.

He Who makes peace in His heights, may He make peace upon us, and upon all Israel. Now respond: Amen. (Cong.– *Amen.*)

SOME CONGREGATIONS COUNT THE *OMER* (PAGE 78) AT THIS POINT.

Many congregations recite either אֲדוֹן עוֹלָם, *Master of the universe,* or יִגְדַּל, *Exalted be,* or both.

אֲדוֹן עוֹלָם *Master of the universe,* Who reigned before any form was created,*
At the time when His will brought all into being —
then as 'King' was His Name proclaimed.
After all has ceased to be, He, the Awesome One, will reign alone.
It is He Who was, He Who is, and He Who shall remain, in splendor.
He is One — there is no second to compare to Him, to declare as His equal.
Without beginning, without conclusion — His is the power and dominion.
He is my God, my living Redeemer, Rock of my pain in time of distress.
He is my banner, a refuge for me, the portion in my cup on the day I call.
Into His hand I shall entrust my spirit when I go to sleep — and I shall awaken!
With my spirit shall my body remain. HASHEM is with me, I shall not fear.

יִגְדַּל *Exalted be the Living God* and praised,*
He exists — unbounded by time is His existence.
He is One — and there is no unity like His Oneness.
Inscrutable and infinite is His Oneness.
He has no semblance of a body nor is He corporeal;
nor has His holiness any comparison.
He preceded every being that was created —
the First, and nothing precedes His precedence.
Behold! He is Master of the universe to every creature,
He demonstrates His greatness and His sovereignty.
He granted His flow of prophecy
to His treasured splendrous people.
In Israel none like Moses arose again —
a prophet who perceived His vision clearly.
God gave His people a Torah of truth,
by means of His prophet, the most trusted of His household.
God will never amend nor exchange His law
for any other one, for all eternity.
He scrutinizes and knows our hiddenmost secrets;
He perceives a matter's outcome at its inception.
He recompenses man with kindness according to his deed;
He places evil on the wicked according to his wickedness.
By the End of Days He will send our Messiah,
to redeem those longing for His final salvation.
God will revive the dead in His abundant kindness —
Blessed forever is His praised Name.

---

the 'Thirteen Principles of Faith' expounded by *Rambam* and stated succinctly in the famous *Ani Maamin* prayer. See commentary on page 192.

❧ הגדה של פסח ☙

קדש. ורחץ. כרפס. יחץ. מגיד. רחצה. מוציא. מצה. מרור. כורך. שלחן עורך. צפון. ברך. הלל. נרצה.

קדש

Kiddush should be recited and the *Seder* begun as soon after synagogue services as possible — however, not before nightfall. Each participant's cup should be poured by someone else to symbolize the majesty of the evening, as though each participant had a servant.

On Friday night begin here:

(וַיְהִי עֶרֶב וַיְהִי בֹקֶר)

יוֹם הַשִּׁשִּׁי: וַיְכֻלּוּ הַשָּׁמַיִם וְהָאָרֶץ וְכָל צְבָאָם. וַיְכַל אֱלֹהִים בַּיּוֹם הַשְּׁבִיעִי מְלַאכְתּוֹ אֲשֶׁר עָשָׂה, וַיִּשְׁבֹּת בַּיּוֹם הַשְּׁבִיעִי מִכָּל מְלַאכְתּוֹ אֲשֶׁר עָשָׂה. וַיְבָרֶךְ אֱלֹהִים אֶת יוֹם הַשְּׁבִיעִי וַיְקַדֵּשׁ אֹתוֹ, כִּי בוֹ שָׁבַת מִכָּל מְלַאכְתּוֹ אֲשֶׁר בָּרָא אֱלֹהִים לַעֲשׂוֹת.[1]

On all nights other than Friday, begin here;
on Friday night include all passages in parentheses.

סַבְרִי מָרָנָן וְרַבָּנָן וְרַבּוֹתַי:

בָּרוּךְ אַתָּה יהוה אֱלֹהֵינוּ מֶלֶךְ הָעוֹלָם, בּוֹרֵא פְּרִי הַגָּפֶן:

בָּרוּךְ אַתָּה יהוה אֱלֹהֵינוּ מֶלֶךְ הָעוֹלָם, אֲשֶׁר בָּחַר בָּנוּ מִכָּל עָם, וְרוֹמְמָנוּ מִכָּל לָשׁוֹן, וְקִדְּשָׁנוּ בְּמִצְוֹתָיו. וַתִּתֶּן לָנוּ יהוה אֱלֹהֵינוּ בְּאַהֲבָה [שַׁבָּתוֹת לִמְנוּחָה וּ]מוֹעֲדִים לְשִׂמְחָה, חַגִּים וּזְמַנִּים לְשָׂשׂוֹן, אֶת יוֹם [הַשַּׁבָּת הַזֶּה וְאֶת יוֹם] חַג הַמַּצּוֹת הַזֶּה, זְמַן חֵרוּתֵנוּ [בְּאַהֲבָה] מִקְרָא קֹדֶשׁ, זֵכֶר לִיצִיאַת מִצְרָיִם, כִּי בָנוּ בָחַרְתָּ וְאוֹתָנוּ קִדַּשְׁתָּ מִכָּל הָעַמִּים, [וְשַׁבָּת] וּמוֹעֲדֵי קָדְשֶׁךָ [בְּאַהֲבָה וּבְרָצוֹן] בְּשִׂמְחָה וּבְשָׂשׂוֹן הִנְחַלְתָּנוּ. בָּרוּךְ אַתָּה יהוה, מְקַדֵּשׁ [הַשַּׁבָּת וְ]יִשְׂרָאֵל וְהַזְּמַנִּים.

On Saturday night, add the following two paragraphs:

בָּרוּךְ אַתָּה יהוה אֱלֹהֵינוּ מֶלֶךְ הָעוֹלָם, בּוֹרֵא מְאוֹרֵי הָאֵשׁ.

בָּרוּךְ אַתָּה יהוה אֱלֹהֵינוּ מֶלֶךְ הָעוֹלָם, הַמַּבְדִּיל בֵּין קֹדֶשׁ לְחוֹל, בֵּין אוֹר לְחֹשֶׁךְ, בֵּין יִשְׂרָאֵל לָעַמִּים, בֵּין יוֹם הַשְּׁבִיעִי לְשֵׁשֶׁת יְמֵי הַמַּעֲשֶׂה. בֵּין קְדֻשַּׁת שַׁבָּת לִקְדֻשַּׁת יוֹם טוֹב הִבְדַּלְתָּ, וְאֶת יוֹם הַשְּׁבִיעִי מִשֵּׁשֶׁת יְמֵי הַמַּעֲשֶׂה קִדַּשְׁתָּ, הִבְדַּלְתָּ וְקִדַּשְׁתָּ אֶת עַמְּךָ יִשְׂרָאֵל בִּקְדֻשָּׁתֶךָ. בָּרוּךְ אַתָּה יהוה, הַמַּבְדִּיל בֵּין קֹדֶשׁ לְקֹדֶשׁ.

On all nights conclude here:

בָּרוּךְ אַתָּה יהוה אֱלֹהֵינוּ מֶלֶךְ הָעוֹלָם, שֶׁהֶחֱיָנוּ וְקִיְּמָנוּ וְהִגִּיעָנוּ לַזְּמַן הַזֶּה.

The wine should be drunk without delay while reclining on the left side.
It is preferable to drink the entire cup, but at the very least, most of the cup should be drained.

THE HAGGADAH

KADDESH. URECHATZ. KARPAS. YACHATZ. MAGGID. RACHTZAH. MOTZI. MATZAH. MAROR. KORECH. SHULCHAN ORECH. TZAFUN. BARECH. HALLEL. NIRTZAH.

KADDESH

Kiddush should be recited and the *Seder* begun as soon after synagogue services as possible – however, not before nightfall. Each participant's cup should be poured by someone else to symbolize the majesty of the evening, as though each participant had a servant.

On Friday night begin here:

(And there was evening and there was morning)

יוֹם הַשִּׁשִּׁי: *The sixth day. Thus the heaven and the earth were finished, and all their array. On the seventh day God completed His work which He had done, and He abstained on the seventh day from all His work which He had done. God blessed the seventh day and hallowed it, because on it He abstained from all His work which God created to make.*[1]

On all nights other than Friday, begin here;
on Friday night include all passages in parentheses.

By your leave, my masters and teachers:

בָּרוּךְ *Blessed are You, HASHEM, our God, King of the universe, Who creates the fruit of the vine.*

בָּרוּךְ *Blessed are You, HASHEM, our God, King of the universe, Who has chosen us from all nations, exalted us above all tongues, and sanctified us with His commandments. And You, HASHEM, our God, have lovingly given us (Sabbaths for rest), appointed times for gladness, feasts and seasons for joy, (this Sabbath and) this Feast of Matzos, the season of our freedom (in love,) a holy convocation in memoriam of the Exodus from Egypt. For You have chosen and sanctified us above all peoples, (and the Sabbath) and Your holy festivals (in love and favor), in gladness and joy have You granted us as a heritage. Blessed are You, HASHEM, Who sanctifies (the Sabbath,) Israel, and the festive seasons.*

On Saturday night, add the following two paragraphs:

בָּרוּךְ *Blessed are You, HASHEM, our God, King of the universe, Who creates the illumination of the fire.*

בָּרוּךְ *Blessed are You, HASHEM, our God, King of the universe, Who distinguishes between sacred and secular, between light and darkness, between Israel and the nations, between the seventh day and the six days of activity. You have distinguished between the holiness of the Sabbath and the holiness of a Festival, and have sanctified the seventh day above the six days of activity. You distinguished and sanctified Your nation, Israel, with Your holiness. Blessed are You, HASHEM, who distinguishes between holiness and holiness.*

On all nights conclude here:

בָּרוּךְ *Blessed are You, HASHEM, our God, King of the universe, Who has kept us alive, sustained us, and brought us to this season.*

The wine should be drunk without delay while reclining on the left side.
It is preferable to drink the entire cup, but at the very least, most of the cup should be drained.

1. *Bereishis* 1:31-2:3.

ורחץ

The head of the household — according to many opinions, all participants in the *Seder* — washes his hands as if to eat bread, [pouring water from a cup, twice on the right hand and twice on the left] but without reciting a blessing.

כרפס

All participants take a vegetable other than *maror* and dip it into salt-water. A piece smaller in volume than half an egg should be used. The following blessing is recited [with the intention that it also applies to the *maror* which will be eaten during the meal] before the vegetable is eaten.

בָּרוּךְ אַתָּה יהוה אֱלֹהֵינוּ מֶלֶךְ הָעוֹלָם, בּוֹרֵא פְּרִי הָאֲדָמָה.

יחץ

The head of the household breaks the middle matzah in two. He puts the smaller part back between the two whole matzos, and wraps up the larger part for later use as the Afikoman. Some briefly place the *Afikoman* portion on their shoulders, in accordance with the Biblical verse recounting that Israel left Egypt carrying their matzos on their shoulders, and say בִּבְהִלוּ יָצָאנוּ מִמִּצְרָיִם, *'In haste we went out of Egypt.'*

מגיד

The broken matzah is lifted for all to see as the head of the household begins with the following brief explanation of the proceedings.

הָא לַחְמָא עַנְיָא דִי אֲכָלוּ אַבְהָתָנָא בְּאַרְעָא דְמִצְרָיִם. כָּל דִּכְפִין יֵיתֵי וְיֵכוֹל, כָּל דִּצְרִיךְ יֵיתֵי וְיִפְסַח. הָשַׁתָּא הָכָא, לְשָׁנָה הַבָּאָה בְּאַרְעָא דְיִשְׂרָאֵל. הָשַׁתָּא עַבְדֵי, לְשָׁנָה הַבָּאָה בְּנֵי חוֹרִין.

The *Seder* plate is removed and the second of the four cups of wine is poured. The youngest present asks the reasons for the unusual proceedings of the evening.

מַה נִּשְׁתַּנָּה הַלַּיְלָה הַזֶּה מִכָּל הַלֵּילוֹת?

שֶׁבְּכָל הַלֵּילוֹת אָנוּ אוֹכְלִין חָמֵץ וּמַצָּה, הַלַּיְלָה הַזֶּה — כֻּלּוֹ מַצָּה.

שֶׁבְּכָל הַלֵּילוֹת אָנוּ אוֹכְלִין שְׁאָר יְרָקוֹת, הַלַּיְלָה הַזֶּה — מָרוֹר.

שֶׁבְּכָל הַלֵּילוֹת אֵין אָנוּ מַטְבִּילִין אֲפִילוּ פַּעַם אֶחָת, הַלַּיְלָה הַזֶּה — שְׁתֵּי פְעָמִים.

שֶׁבְּכָל הַלֵּילוֹת אָנוּ אוֹכְלִין בֵּין יוֹשְׁבִין וּבֵין מְסֻבִּין, הַלַּיְלָה הַזֶּה — כֻּלָּנוּ מְסֻבִּין.

The *Seder* plate is returned. The matzos are kept uncovered as the *Haggadah* is recited in unison. The *Haggadah* should be translated if necessary, and the story of the Exodus should be amplified upon.

עֲבָדִים הָיִינוּ לְפַרְעֹה בְּמִצְרָיִם, וַיּוֹצִיאֵנוּ יהוה אֱלֹהֵינוּ מִשָּׁם בְּיָד חֲזָקָה וּבִזְרוֹעַ נְטוּיָה. וְאִלּוּ לֹא הוֹצִיא הַקָּדוֹשׁ בָּרוּךְ הוּא אֶת אֲבוֹתֵינוּ מִמִּצְרָיִם, הֲרֵי אָנוּ וּבָנֵינוּ וּבְנֵי בָנֵינוּ מְשֻׁעְבָּדִים הָיִינוּ לְפַרְעֹה בְּמִצְרָיִם. וַאֲפִילוּ כֻּלָּנוּ חֲכָמִים, כֻּלָּנוּ נְבוֹנִים, כֻּלָּנוּ זְקֵנִים, כֻּלָּנוּ יוֹדְעִים אֶת הַתּוֹרָה, מִצְוָה עָלֵינוּ לְסַפֵּר בִּיצִיאַת מִצְרָיִם. וְכָל הַמַּרְבֶּה לְסַפֵּר בִּיצִיאַת מִצְרַיִם, הֲרֵי זֶה מְשֻׁבָּח.

URECHATZ

The head of the household — according to many opinions, all participants in the *Seder* — washes his hands as if to eat bread, [pouring water from a cup, twice on the right hand and twice on the left] but without reciting a blessing.

KARPAS

All participants take a vegetable other than *maror* and dip it into salt-water. A piece smaller in volume than half an egg should be used. The following blessing is recited [with the intention that it also applies to the *maror* which will be eaten during the meal] before the vegetable is eaten.

בָּרוּךְ *Blessed are You, HASHEM, our God, King of the universe, Who creates the fruits of the earth.*

YACHATZ

The head of the household breaks the middle matzah in two. He puts the smaller part back between the two whole matzos, and wraps up the larger part for later use as the Afikoman. Some briefly place the *Afikoman* portion on their shoulders, in accordance with the Biblical verse recounting that Israel left Egypt carrying their matzos on their shoulders, and say בְּבְהִלוּ יָצָאנוּ מִמִּצְרָיִם, *'In haste we went out of Egypt.'*

MAGGID

The broken matzah is lifted for all to see as the head of the household begins with the following brief explanation of the proceedings.

הָא *This is the bread of affliction that our fathers ate in the land of Egypt. Whoever is hungry — let him come and eat! Whoever is needy — let him come and celebrate Pesach! Now, we are here; next year may we be in the Land of Israel! Now, we are slaves; next year may we be free men!*

The *Seder* plate is removed and the second of the four cups of wine is poured. The youngest present asks the reasons for the unusual proceedings of the evening.

מַה נִּשְׁתַּנָּה *Why is this night different from all other nights?*

1. *On all other nights we may eat chametz and matzah, but on this night only matzah.*
2. *On all other nights we eat many vegetables, but on this night — we eat maror.*
3. *On all other nights we do not dip even once, but on this night — twice.*
4. *On all other nights we eat either sitting or reclining, but on this night — we all recline.*

The *Seder* plate is returned. The matzos are kept uncovered as the *Haggadah* is recited in unison. The *Haggadah* should be translated if necessary, and the story of the Exodus should be amplified upon.

עֲבָדִים *We were slaves to Pharaoh in Egypt, but HASHEM our God took us out from there with a mighty hand and an outstretched arm. Had not the Holy One, Blessed is He, taken our fathers out from Egypt, then we, our children, and our children's children would have remained enslaved to Pharaoh in Egypt. Even if we were all men of wisdom, understanding, experience, and knowledge of the Torah, it would still be an obligation upon us to tell about the Exodus from Egypt. The more one tells about the Exodus, the more he is praiseworthy.*

מַעֲשֶׂה בְּרַבִּי אֱלִיעֶזֶר וְרַבִּי יְהוֹשֻׁעַ וְרַבִּי אֶלְעָזָר בֶּן עֲזַרְיָה וְרַבִּי עֲקִיבָא וְרַבִּי טַרְפוֹן שֶׁהָיוּ מְסֻבִּין בִּבְנֵי בְרַק, וְהָיוּ מְסַפְּרִים בִּיצִיאַת מִצְרַיִם כָּל אוֹתוֹ הַלַּיְלָה. עַד שֶׁבָּאוּ תַלְמִידֵיהֶם וְאָמְרוּ לָהֶם, רַבּוֹתֵינוּ הִגִּיעַ זְמַן קְרִיאַת שְׁמַע שֶׁל שַׁחֲרִית.

אָמַר רַבִּי אֶלְעָזָר בֶּן עֲזַרְיָה, הֲרֵי אֲנִי כְּבֶן שִׁבְעִים שָׁנָה, וְלֹא זָכִיתִי שֶׁתֵּאָמֵר יְצִיאַת מִצְרַיִם בַּלֵּילוֹת, עַד שֶׁדְּרָשָׁהּ בֶּן זוֹמָא, שֶׁנֶּאֱמַר, לְמַעַן תִּזְכֹּר אֶת יוֹם צֵאתְךָ מֵאֶרֶץ מִצְרַיִם כֹּל יְמֵי חַיֶּיךָ.[1] יְמֵי חַיֶּיךָ הַיָּמִים, כֹּל יְמֵי חַיֶּיךָ הַלֵּילוֹת. וַחֲכָמִים אוֹמְרִים, יְמֵי חַיֶּיךָ הָעוֹלָם הַזֶּה, כֹּל יְמֵי חַיֶּיךָ לְהָבִיא לִימוֹת הַמָּשִׁיחַ.

בָּרוּךְ הַמָּקוֹם, בָּרוּךְ הוּא. בָּרוּךְ שֶׁנָּתַן תּוֹרָה לְעַמּוֹ יִשְׂרָאֵל, בָּרוּךְ הוּא. כְּנֶגֶד אַרְבָּעָה בָנִים דִּבְּרָה תוֹרָה: אֶחָד חָכָם, וְאֶחָד רָשָׁע, וְאֶחָד תָּם, וְאֶחָד שֶׁאֵינוֹ יוֹדֵעַ לִשְׁאוֹל.

חָכָם מָה הוּא אוֹמֵר? מָה הָעֵדֹת וְהַחֻקִּים וְהַמִּשְׁפָּטִים אֲשֶׁר צִוָּה יהוה אֱלֹהֵינוּ אֶתְכֶם?[2] וְאַף אַתָּה אֱמָר לוֹ כְּהִלְכוֹת הַפֶּסַח, אֵין מַפְטִירִין אַחַר הַפֶּסַח אֲפִיקוֹמָן.

רָשָׁע מָה הוּא אוֹמֵר? מָה הָעֲבֹדָה הַזֹּאת לָכֶם?[3] לָכֶם וְלֹא לוֹ, וּלְפִי שֶׁהוֹצִיא אֶת עַצְמוֹ מִן הַכְּלָל, כָּפַר בְּעִקָּר – וְאַף אַתָּה הַקְהֵה אֶת שִׁנָּיו וֶאֱמָר לוֹ, בַּעֲבוּר זֶה עָשָׂה יהוה לִי בְּצֵאתִי מִמִּצְרָיִם.[4] לִי וְלֹא לוֹ, אִלּוּ הָיָה שָׁם לֹא הָיָה נִגְאָל.

תָּם מָה הוּא אוֹמֵר? מַה זֹּאת? וְאָמַרְתָּ אֵלָיו, בְּחֹזֶק יָד הוֹצִיאָנוּ יהוה מִמִּצְרַיִם מִבֵּית עֲבָדִים.[5]

וְשֶׁאֵינוֹ יוֹדֵעַ לִשְׁאוֹל, אַתְּ פְּתַח לוֹ. שֶׁנֶּאֱמַר, וְהִגַּדְתָּ לְבִנְךָ בַּיּוֹם הַהוּא לֵאמֹר, בַּעֲבוּר זֶה עָשָׂה יהוה לִי בְּצֵאתִי מִמִּצְרָיִם.[6]

יָכוֹל מֵרֹאשׁ חֹדֶשׁ, תַּלְמוּד לוֹמַר בַּיּוֹם הַהוּא. אִי בַּיּוֹם הַהוּא, יָכוֹל מִבְּעוֹד יוֹם, תַּלְמוּד לוֹמַר בַּעֲבוּר זֶה. בַּעֲבוּר זֶה לֹא אָמַרְתִּי אֶלָּא בְּשָׁעָה שֶׁיֵּשׁ מַצָּה וּמָרוֹר מֻנָּחִים לְפָנֶיךָ.

מִתְּחִלָּה, עוֹבְדֵי עֲבוֹדָה זָרָה הָיוּ אֲבוֹתֵינוּ, וְעַכְשָׁו קֵרְבָנוּ הַמָּקוֹם לַעֲבֹדָתוֹ. שֶׁנֶּאֱמַר, וַיֹּאמֶר יְהוֹשֻׁעַ אֶל כָּל הָעָם, כֹּה אָמַר יהוה אֱלֹהֵי יִשְׂרָאֵל, בְּעֵבֶר הַנָּהָר יָשְׁבוּ אֲבוֹתֵיכֶם מֵעוֹלָם, תֶּרַח אֲבִי אַבְרָהָם וַאֲבִי נָחוֹר, וַיַּעַבְדוּ אֱלֹהִים אֲחֵרִים. וָאֶקַּח אֶת אֲבִיכֶם אֶת

(1) *Deuteronomy* 16:3. (2) 6:20. (3) *Exodus* 12:26. (4) 13:8. (5) 13:14. (6) 13:8.

מַעֲשֶׂה *It happened that Rabbi Eliezer, Rabbi Yehoshua, Rabbi Elazar ben Azaryah, Rabbi Akiva, and Rabbi Tarfon were reclining (at the Seder) in Bnei Brak. They discussed the Exodus all that night until their students came and said to them: 'Our teachers, it is [daybreak] time for the reading of the morning Shema.'*

אָמַר *Rabbi Elazar ben Azaryah said: I am like a seventy-year-old man, but I could not succeed in having the Exodus from Egypt mentioned every night, until Ben Zoma expounded it: 'In order that you may remember the day you left Egypt all the days of your life.'[1] The phrase 'the days of your life' would have indicated only the days; the addition of the word 'all' includes the nights as well. But the Sages declare that 'the days of your life' would mean only the present world; the addition of 'all' includes the era of the Messiah.*

בָּרוּךְ *Blessed is the Omnipresent; Blessed is He. Blessed is the One Who has given the Torah to His people Israel; Blessed is He. Concerning four sons does the Torah speak: a wise one, a wicked one, a simple one, and one who is unable to ask.*

חָכָם *The wise son — what does he say? 'What are the testimonies, decrees, and ordinances which* HASHEM, *our God, has commanded you?'[2] Therefore explain to him the laws of the Pesach offering: that one may not eat dessert after the final taste of the Pesach offering.*

רָשָׁע *The wicked son — what does he say? 'Of what purpose is this work to you?'[3] He says, 'To you,' thereby excluding himself. By excluding himself from the community of believers, he denies the basic principle of Judaism. Therefore, blunt his teeth and tell him: 'It is because of this that* HASHEM *did so for me when I went out of Egypt.'[4] 'For me,' but not for him — had he been there, he would not have been redeemed.*

תָּם *The simple son — what does he say? 'What is this?' Tell him: 'With a strong hand did* HASHEM *take us out of Egypt, from the house of bondage.'[5]*

וְשֶׁאֵינוֹ יוֹדֵעַ לִשְׁאוֹל *As for the son who is unable to ask, you must initiate the subject for him, as it is stated: You shall tell your son on that day: 'It is because of this that* HASHEM *did so for me when I went out of Egypt.'[6]*

יָכוֹל *One might think that the obligation to discuss the Exodus commences with the first day of the month of Nissan, but the Torah says: 'You shall tell your son on that day.' But the expression 'on that day' could be understood to mean only during the daytime; therefore the Torah adds: 'It is because of this that* HASHEM *did so for me when I went out of Egypt.' The pronoun 'this' implies something tangible, thus, 'You shall tell your son' applies only when matzah and maror lie before you — at the Seder.*

מִתְּחִלָּה *Originally our ancestors were idol worshipers, but now the Omnipresent has brought us near to His service, as it is written: Joshua said to all the people, 'So says* HASHEM, *God of Israel: Your fathers always lived beyond the Euphrates River, Terach the father of Abraham and Nachor, and they served other gods. Then I took your father Abraham*

אַבְרָהָם מֵעֵבֶר הַנָּהָר, וָאוֹלֵךְ אוֹתוֹ בְּכָל אֶרֶץ כְּנָעַן, וָאַרְבֶּה אֶת זַרְעוֹ, וָאֶתֶּן לוֹ אֶת יִצְחָק. וָאֶתֵּן לְיִצְחָק אֶת יַעֲקֹב וְאֶת עֵשָׂו, וָאֶתֵּן לְעֵשָׂו אֶת הַר שֵׂעִיר לָרֶשֶׁת אוֹתוֹ, וְיַעֲקֹב וּבָנָיו יָרְדוּ מִצְרָיִם.[1]

בָּרוּךְ שׁוֹמֵר הַבְטָחָתוֹ לְיִשְׂרָאֵל, בָּרוּךְ הוּא. שֶׁהַקָּדוֹשׁ בָּרוּךְ הוּא חִשַּׁב אֶת הַקֵּץ, לַעֲשׂוֹת כְּמָה שֶׁאָמַר לְאַבְרָהָם אָבִינוּ בִּבְרִית בֵּין הַבְּתָרִים, שֶׁנֶּאֱמַר, וַיֹּאמֶר לְאַבְרָם, יָדֹעַ תֵּדַע כִּי גֵר יִהְיֶה זַרְעֲךָ בְּאֶרֶץ לֹא לָהֶם, וַעֲבָדוּם וְעִנּוּ אֹתָם, אַרְבַּע מֵאוֹת שָׁנָה. וְגַם אֶת הַגּוֹי אֲשֶׁר יַעֲבֹדוּ דָּן אָנֹכִי, וְאַחֲרֵי כֵן יֵצְאוּ בִּרְכֻשׁ גָּדוֹל.[2]

The matzos are covered and the cups lifted as the following paragraph is proclaimed joyously. Upon its conclusion, the cups are put down and the matzos are uncovered.

וְהִיא שֶׁעָמְדָה לַאֲבוֹתֵינוּ וְלָנוּ, שֶׁלֹּא אֶחָד בִּלְבָד עָמַד עָלֵינוּ לְכַלּוֹתֵנוּ. אֶלָּא שֶׁבְּכָל דּוֹר וָדוֹר עוֹמְדִים עָלֵינוּ לְכַלּוֹתֵנוּ, וְהַקָּדוֹשׁ בָּרוּךְ הוּא מַצִּילֵנוּ מִיָּדָם.

צֵא וּלְמַד מַה בִּקֵּשׁ לָבָן הָאֲרַמִּי לַעֲשׂוֹת לְיַעֲקֹב אָבִינוּ, שֶׁפַּרְעֹה לֹא גָזַר אֶלָּא עַל הַזְּכָרִים, וְלָבָן בִּקֵּשׁ לַעֲקוֹר אֶת הַכֹּל. שֶׁנֶּאֱמַר:

אֲרַמִּי אֹבֵד אָבִי, וַיֵּרֶד מִצְרַיְמָה וַיָּגָר שָׁם בִּמְתֵי מְעָט, וַיְהִי שָׁם לְגוֹי, גָּדוֹל עָצוּם וָרָב.[3]

וַיֵּרֶד מִצְרַיְמָה — אָנוּס עַל פִּי הַדִּבּוּר.

וַיָּגָר שָׁם — מְלַמֵּד שֶׁלֹּא יָרַד יַעֲקֹב אָבִינוּ לְהִשְׁתַּקֵּעַ בְּמִצְרַיִם, אֶלָּא לָגוּר שָׁם. שֶׁנֶּאֱמַר, וַיֹּאמְרוּ אֶל פַּרְעֹה, לָגוּר בָּאָרֶץ בָּאנוּ, כִּי אֵין מִרְעֶה לַצֹּאן אֲשֶׁר לַעֲבָדֶיךָ, כִּי כָבֵד הָרָעָב בְּאֶרֶץ כְּנָעַן, וְעַתָּה יֵשְׁבוּ נָא עֲבָדֶיךָ בְּאֶרֶץ גֹּשֶׁן.[4]

בִּמְתֵי מְעָט — כְּמָה שֶׁנֶּאֱמַר, בְּשִׁבְעִים נֶפֶשׁ יָרְדוּ אֲבֹתֶיךָ מִצְרָיְמָה, וְעַתָּה שָׂמְךָ יהוה אֱלֹהֶיךָ כְּכוֹכְבֵי הַשָּׁמַיִם לָרֹב.[5]

וַיְהִי שָׁם לְגוֹי — מְלַמֵּד שֶׁהָיוּ יִשְׂרָאֵל מְצֻיָּנִים שָׁם.

גָּדוֹל עָצוּם — כְּמָה שֶׁנֶּאֱמַר, וּבְנֵי יִשְׂרָאֵל פָּרוּ וַיִּשְׁרְצוּ וַיִּרְבּוּ וַיַּעַצְמוּ בִּמְאֹד מְאֹד, וַתִּמָּלֵא הָאָרֶץ אֹתָם.[6]

וָרָב — כְּמָה שֶׁנֶּאֱמַר, רְבָבָה כְּצֶמַח הַשָּׂדֶה נְתַתִּיךְ, וַתִּרְבִּי וַתִּגְדְּלִי וַתָּבֹאִי בַּעֲדִי עֲדָיִים, שָׁדַיִם נָכֹנוּ וּשְׂעָרֵךְ צִמֵּחַ, וְאַתְּ עֵרֹם וְעֶרְיָה; וָאֶעֱבֹר עָלַיִךְ וָאֶרְאֵךְ מִתְבּוֹסֶסֶת בְּדָמָיִךְ, וָאֹמַר לָךְ, בְּדָמַיִךְ חֲיִי, וָאֹמַר לָךְ, בְּדָמַיִךְ חֲיִי.[7]

וַיָּרֵעוּ אֹתָנוּ הַמִּצְרִים, וַיְעַנּוּנוּ, וַיִּתְּנוּ עָלֵינוּ עֲבֹדָה קָשָׁה.[8]

from beyond the river and led him through all the land of Canaan. I multiplied his offspring and gave him Isaac. To Isaac I gave Jacob and Esau; to Esau I gave Mount Seir to inherit, but Jacob and his children went down to Egypt.'[1]

בָּרוּךְ *Blessed is He Who keeps His pledge to Israel; Blessed is He! For the Holy One, Blessed is He, calculated the end of bondage in order to do as He said to our father Abraham at the Covenant between the Parts, as it is stated: He said to Abram, 'Know with certainty that your offspring will be aliens in a land not their own, they will serve them and they will oppress them four hundred years; but also upon the nation which they shall serve will I execute judgment, and afterwards they shall leave with great possessions.'*[2]

The matzos are covered and the cups lifted as the following paragraph is proclaimed joyously. Upon its conclusion, the cups are put down and the matzos are uncovered.

וְהִיא *It is this that has stood by our fathers and us. For not only one has risen against us to annihilate us, but in every generation they rise against us to annihilate us. But the Holy One, Blessed is He, rescues us from their hand.*

צֵא *Go and learn what Laban the Aramean attempted to do to our father Jacob! For Pharaoh decreed only against the males, Laban attempted to uproot everything, as it is said:*

An Aramean attempted to destroy my father. Then he descended to Egypt and sojourned there, with few people; and there he became a nation — great, mighty and numerous.[3]

Then he descended to Egypt — compelled by Divine decree.

He sojourned there — this teaches that our father Jacob did not descend to Egypt to settle, but only to sojourn temporarily, as it says: They (the sons of Jacob) said to Pharaoh: 'We have come to sojourn in this land because there is no pasture for the flocks of your servants, because the famine is severe in the land of Canaan. And now, please let your servants dwell in the land of Goshen.'[4]

With few people — as it is written: With seventy persons, your forefathers descended to Egypt, and now HASHEM, *your God, has made you as numerous as the stars of heaven.*[5]

There he became a nation — this teaches that the Israelites were distinctive there.

Great, mighty — as it says: And the Children of Israel were fruitful, increased greatly, multiplied, and became very, very mighty; and the land was filled with them.[6]

Numerous — as it says: I made you as numerous as the plants of the field; you grew and developed, and became charming, beautiful of figure; and your hair grown long; but you were naked and bare. And I passed over you and saw you downtrodden in your blood and I said to you: 'Through your blood shall you live!' And I said to you: 'Through your blood shall you live!'.[7]

וַיָּרֵעוּ *The Egyptians did evil to us and afflicted us; and imposed hard labor upon us.*[8]

---

(1) *Joshua* 24:2-4. (2) *Genesis* 15:13-14. (3) *Deuteronomy* 26:5. (4) *Genesis* 47:4.
(5) *Deuteronomy* 10:22. (6) *Exodus* 1:7. (7) *Ezekiel* 16:7,6. (8) *Deuteronomy* 26:6.

וַיָּרֵעוּ אֹתָנוּ הַמִּצְרִים — כְּמָה שֶׁנֶּאֱמַר, הָבָה נִתְחַכְּמָה לוֹ, פֶּן יִרְבֶּה, וְהָיָה כִּי תִקְרֶאנָה מִלְחָמָה, וְנוֹסַף גַּם הוּא עַל שֹׂנְאֵינוּ, וְנִלְחַם בָּנוּ, וְעָלָה מִן הָאָרֶץ.[1]

וַיְעַנּוּנוּ — כְּמָה שֶׁנֶּאֱמַר, וַיָּשִׂימוּ עָלָיו שָׂרֵי מִסִּים, לְמַעַן עַנֹּתוֹ בְּסִבְלֹתָם, וַיִּבֶן עָרֵי מִסְכְּנוֹת לְפַרְעֹה, אֶת פִּתֹם וְאֶת רַעַמְסֵס.[2]

וַיִּתְּנוּ עָלֵינוּ עֲבֹדָה קָשָׁה — כְּמָה שֶׁנֶּאֱמַר, וַיַּעֲבִדוּ מִצְרַיִם אֶת בְּנֵי יִשְׂרָאֵל בְּפָרֶךְ.[3]

וַנִּצְעַק אֶל יהוה אֱלֹהֵי אֲבֹתֵינוּ, וַיִּשְׁמַע יהוה אֶת קֹלֵנוּ, וַיַּרְא אֶת עָנְיֵנוּ, וְאֶת עֲמָלֵנוּ, וְאֶת לַחֲצֵנוּ.[4]

וַנִּצְעַק אֶל יהוה אֱלֹהֵי אֲבֹתֵינוּ — כְּמָה שֶׁנֶּאֱמַר, וַיְהִי בַיָּמִים הָרַבִּים הָהֵם, וַיָּמָת מֶלֶךְ מִצְרַיִם, וַיֵּאָנְחוּ בְנֵי יִשְׂרָאֵל מִן הָעֲבֹדָה, וַיִּזְעָקוּ, וַתַּעַל שַׁוְעָתָם אֶל הָאֱלֹהִים מִן הָעֲבֹדָה.[5]

וַיִּשְׁמַע יהוה אֶת קֹלֵנוּ — כְּמָה שֶׁנֶּאֱמַר, וַיִּשְׁמַע אֱלֹהִים אֶת נַאֲקָתָם, וַיִּזְכֹּר אֱלֹהִים אֶת בְּרִיתוֹ אֶת אַבְרָהָם, אֶת יִצְחָק, וְאֶת יַעֲקֹב.[6]

וַיַּרְא אֶת עָנְיֵנוּ — זוֹ פְּרִישׁוּת דֶּרֶךְ אֶרֶץ, כְּמָה שֶׁנֶּאֱמַר, וַיַּרְא אֱלֹהִים אֶת בְּנֵי יִשְׂרָאֵל, וַיֵּדַע אֱלֹהִים.[7]

וְאֶת עֲמָלֵנוּ — אֵלּוּ הַבָּנִים, כְּמָה שֶׁנֶּאֱמַר, כָּל הַבֵּן הַיִּלּוֹד הַיְאֹרָה תַּשְׁלִיכֻהוּ, וְכָל הַבַּת תְּחַיּוּן.[8]

וְאֶת לַחֲצֵנוּ — זוֹ הַדְּחַק, כְּמָה שֶׁנֶּאֱמַר, וְגַם רָאִיתִי אֶת הַלַּחַץ אֲשֶׁר מִצְרַיִם לֹחֲצִים אֹתָם.[9]

וַיּוֹצִאֵנוּ יהוה מִמִּצְרַיִם בְּיָד חֲזָקָה, וּבִזְרֹעַ נְטוּיָה, וּבְמֹרָא גָּדֹל, וּבְאֹתוֹת וּבְמֹפְתִים.[10]

וַיּוֹצִאֵנוּ יהוה מִמִּצְרַיִם — לֹא עַל יְדֵי מַלְאָךְ, וְלֹא עַל יְדֵי שָׂרָף, וְלֹא עַל יְדֵי שָׁלִיחַ, אֶלָּא הַקָּדוֹשׁ בָּרוּךְ הוּא בִּכְבוֹדוֹ וּבְעַצְמוֹ. שֶׁנֶּאֱמַר, וְעָבַרְתִּי בְאֶרֶץ מִצְרַיִם בַּלַּיְלָה הַזֶּה, וְהִכֵּיתִי כָל בְּכוֹר בְּאֶרֶץ מִצְרַיִם מֵאָדָם וְעַד בְּהֵמָה, וּבְכָל אֱלֹהֵי מִצְרַיִם אֶעֱשֶׂה שְׁפָטִים, אֲנִי יהוה.[11]

וְעָבַרְתִּי בְאֶרֶץ מִצְרַיִם בַּלַּיְלָה הַזֶּה — אֲנִי וְלֹא מַלְאָךְ. וְהִכֵּיתִי כָל בְּכוֹר בְּאֶרֶץ מִצְרַיִם — אֲנִי וְלֹא שָׂרָף. וּבְכָל אֱלֹהֵי מִצְרַיִם אֶעֱשֶׂה שְׁפָטִים — אֲנִי וְלֹא הַשָּׁלִיחַ. אֲנִי יהוה — אֲנִי הוּא, וְלֹא אַחֵר.

בְּיָד חֲזָקָה — זוֹ הַדֶּבֶר, כְּמָה שֶׁנֶּאֱמַר, הִנֵּה יַד יהוה הוֹיָה בְּמִקְנְךָ אֲשֶׁר בַּשָּׂדֶה, בַּסּוּסִים בַּחֲמֹרִים בַּגְּמַלִּים בַּבָּקָר וּבַצֹּאן, דֶּבֶר כָּבֵד מְאֹד.[12]

וּבִזְרֹעַ נְטוּיָה — זוֹ הַחֶרֶב, כְּמָה שֶׁנֶּאֱמַר, וְחַרְבּוֹ שְׁלוּפָה בְּיָדוֹ, נְטוּיָה עַל יְרוּשָׁלָיִם.[13]

וּבְמֹרָא גָּדֹל — זוֹ גִּלּוּי שְׁכִינָה, כְּמָה שֶׁנֶּאֱמַר, אוֹ הֲנִסָּה אֱלֹהִים לָבוֹא לָקַחַת לוֹ גוֹי מִקֶּרֶב גּוֹי, בְּמַסֹּת, בְּאֹתֹת, וּבְמוֹפְתִים, וּבְמִלְחָמָה,

The Egyptians did evil to us — as it says: Let us deal with them wisely lest they multiply and, if we happen to be at war, they may join our enemies and fight against us and then leave the country.[1]

And afflicted us — as it says: They set taskmasters over them in order to oppress them with their burdens; and they built Pisom and Raamses as treasure cities for Pharaoh.[2]

They imposed hard labor upon us — as it says: The Egyptians subjugated the Children of Israel with hard labor.[3]

וַנִּצְעַק *We cried out to* HASHEM, *the God of our fathers; and* HASHEM *heard our cry and saw our affliction, our burden and our oppression.*[4]

We cried out to HASHEM, *the God of our fathers — as it says: It happened in the course of those many days that the king of Egypt died; and the children of Israel groaned because of the servitude and cried; their cry because of the servitude rose up to God.*[5]

HASHEM *heard our cry — as it says: God heard their groaning, and God recalled His covenant with Abraham, with Isaac, and with Jacob.*[6]

And saw our affliction — that is the disruption of family life, as it says: God saw the Children of Israel and God took note.[7]

Our burden — refers to the children, as it says: Every son that is born you shall cast into the river, but every daughter you shall let live.[8]

Our oppression — refers to the pressure expressed in the words: I have also seen how the Egyptians are oppressing them.[9]

וַיּוֹצִאֵנוּ HASHEM *brought us out of Egypt with a mighty hand and with an outstretched arm, with great awe, with signs and wonders.*[10]

HASHEM *brought us out of Egypt — not through an angel, not through a seraph, not through a messenger, but the Holy One, Blessed is He, in His glory, Himself, as it says: I will pass through the land of Egypt on that night; I will slay all the firstborn in the land of Egypt from man to beast; and upon all the gods of Egypt will I execute judgments; I,* HASHEM.[11]

'I will pass through the land of Egypt on that night' — I and no angel; 'I will slay all the firstborn in the land of Egypt' — I and no seraph; 'And upon all the gods of Egypt will I execute judgments' — I and no messenger; 'I, HASHEM*' — it is I and no other.*

With a mighty hand — refers to the pestilence, as it is stated: Behold, the hand of HASHEM *shall strike your cattle which are in the field, the horses, the donkeys, the camels, the herds, and the flocks — a very severe pestilence.*[12]

With an outstretched arm — refers to the sword, as it says: His drawn sword in His hand, outstretched over Jerusalem.[13]

With great awe — alludes to the revelation of the Shechinah, as it says: Has God ever attempted to take unto Himself a nation from the midst of another nation by trials, miraculous signs, and wonders, by war and

---

(1) *Exodus* 1:10. (2) 1:11. (3) 1:13. (4) *Deuteronomy* 26:7. (5) *Exodus* 2:23.
(6) 2:24. (7) 2:25. (8) *Exodus* 1:22. (9) 3:9. (10) *Deuteronomy* 26:8.
(11) *Exodus* 12:12. (12) 9:3. (13) *I Chronicles* 21:16.

וּבְיָד חֲזָקָה, וּבִזְרֹעַ נְטוּיָה, וּבְמוֹרָאִים גְּדֹלִים, כְּכֹל אֲשֶׁר עָשָׂה לָכֶם יהוה אֱלֹהֵיכֶם בְּמִצְרַיִם לְעֵינֶיךָ.[1]

וּבְאֹתוֹת — זֶה הַמַּטֶּה, כְּמָה שֶׁנֶּאֱמַר, וְאֶת הַמַּטֶּה הַזֶּה תִּקַּח בְּיָדֶךָ, אֲשֶׁר תַּעֲשֶׂה בּוֹ אֶת הָאֹתֹת.[2]

וּבְמֹפְתִים — זֶה הַדָּם, כְּמָה שֶׁנֶּאֱמַר, וְנָתַתִּי מוֹפְתִים בַּשָּׁמַיִם וּבָאָרֶץ

As each of the words דָּם, אֵשׁ, and עָשָׁן, is said, a bit of wine is removed from the cup, with the finger or by pouring.

דָּם וָאֵשׁ וְתִמְרוֹת עָשָׁן.[3]

דָּבָר אַחֵר — בְּיָד חֲזָקָה, שְׁתַּיִם. וּבִזְרֹעַ נְטוּיָה, שְׁתַּיִם. וּבְמֹרָא גָּדֹל, שְׁתַּיִם. וּבְאֹתוֹת, שְׁתַּיִם. וּבְמֹפְתִים, שְׁתַּיִם. אֵלּוּ עֶשֶׂר מַכּוֹת שֶׁהֵבִיא הַקָּדוֹשׁ בָּרוּךְ הוּא עַל הַמִּצְרִים בְּמִצְרַיִם, וְאֵלּוּ הֵן:

As each of the plagues is mentioned, a bit of wine is removed from the cup. The same is done by each word of Rabbi Yehudah's mnemonic.

דָּם. צְפַרְדֵּעַ. כִּנִּים. עָרוֹב. דֶּבֶר. שְׁחִין. בָּרָד.
אַרְבֶּה. חֹשֶׁךְ. מַכַּת בְּכוֹרוֹת.

רַבִּי יְהוּדָה הָיָה נוֹתֵן בָּהֶם סִמָּנִים:

דְּצַ״ךְ • עַדַ״שׁ • בְּאַחַ״ב.

The cups are refilled. The wine that was removed is not used.

רַבִּי יוֹסֵי הַגְּלִילִי אוֹמֵר: מִנַּיִן אַתָּה אוֹמֵר שֶׁלָּקוּ הַמִּצְרִים בְּמִצְרַיִם עֶשֶׂר מַכּוֹת וְעַל הַיָּם לָקוּ חֲמִשִּׁים מַכּוֹת? בְּמִצְרַיִם מָה הוּא אוֹמֵר, וַיֹּאמְרוּ הַחַרְטֻמִּם אֶל פַּרְעֹה, אֶצְבַּע אֱלֹהִים הִוא.[4] וְעַל הַיָּם מָה הוּא אוֹמֵר, וַיַּרְא יִשְׂרָאֵל אֶת הַיָּד הַגְּדֹלָה אֲשֶׁר עָשָׂה יהוה בְּמִצְרַיִם, וַיִּירְאוּ הָעָם אֶת יהוה, וַיַּאֲמִינוּ בַּיהוה וּבְמֹשֶׁה עַבְדּוֹ.[5] כַּמָּה לָקוּ בְּאֶצְבַּע? עֶשֶׂר מַכּוֹת. אֱמוֹר מֵעַתָּה, בְּמִצְרַיִם לָקוּ עֶשֶׂר מַכּוֹת, וְעַל הַיָּם לָקוּ חֲמִשִּׁים מַכּוֹת.

רַבִּי אֱלִיעֶזֶר אוֹמֵר. מִנַּיִן שֶׁכָּל מַכָּה וּמַכָּה שֶׁהֵבִיא הַקָּדוֹשׁ בָּרוּךְ הוּא עַל הַמִּצְרִים בְּמִצְרַיִם הָיְתָה שֶׁל אַרְבַּע מַכּוֹת? שֶׁנֶּאֱמַר, יְשַׁלַּח בָּם חֲרוֹן אַפּוֹ — עֶבְרָה, וָזַעַם, וְצָרָה, מִשְׁלַחַת מַלְאֲכֵי רָעִים.[6] עֶבְרָה, אַחַת. וָזַעַם, שְׁתַּיִם. וְצָרָה, שָׁלֹשׁ. מִשְׁלַחַת מַלְאֲכֵי רָעִים, אַרְבַּע. אֱמוֹר מֵעַתָּה, בְּמִצְרַיִם לָקוּ אַרְבָּעִים מַכּוֹת, וְעַל הַיָּם לָקוּ מָאתַיִם מַכּוֹת.

רַבִּי עֲקִיבָא אוֹמֵר. מִנַּיִן שֶׁכָּל מַכָּה וּמַכָּה שֶׁהֵבִיא הַקָּדוֹשׁ בָּרוּךְ הוּא עַל הַמִּצְרִים בְּמִצְרַיִם הָיְתָה שֶׁל חָמֵשׁ מַכּוֹת? שֶׁנֶּאֱמַר, יְשַׁלַּח בָּם חֲרוֹן אַפּוֹ, עֶבְרָה, וָזַעַם, וְצָרָה, מִשְׁלַחַת מַלְאֲכֵי רָעִים.[6] חֲרוֹן אַפּוֹ, אַחַת. עֶבְרָה, שְׁתַּיִם. וָזַעַם, שָׁלֹשׁ. וְצָרָה, אַרְבַּע. מִשְׁלַחַת מַלְאֲכֵי רָעִים, חָמֵשׁ. אֱמוֹר מֵעַתָּה, בְּמִצְרַיִם לָקוּ חֲמִשִּׁים מַכּוֹת, וְעַל הַיָּם לָקוּ חֲמִשִּׁים וּמָאתַיִם מַכּוֹת.

with a mighty hand and outstretched arm and by awesome revelations, as all that H*ASHEM your God did for you in Egypt, before your eyes?*[1]

With signs — refers to the miracles performed with the staff as it says: Take this staff in your hand, that you may perform the miraculous signs with it.[2]

With wonders — alludes to the blood, as it says: I will show wonders in the heavens and on the earth

As each of the words 'blood,' 'fire,' and 'smoke,' is said,
a bit of wine is removed from the cup, with the finger or by pouring.

Blood, fire, and columns of smoke.[3]

Another explanation of the preceding verse: [Each phrase represents two plagues,] hence: mighty hand — two; outstretched arm — two; great awe — two; signs — two; wonders — two. These are the ten plagues which the Holy One, Blessed is He, brought upon the Egyptians in Egypt, namely:

As each of the plagues is mentioned, a bit of wine is removed from the cup.
The same is done by each word of Rabbi Yehudah's mnemonic.

1. Blood 2. Frogs 3. Vermin 4. Wild Beasts
5. Pestilence 6. Boils 7. Hail 8. Locusts 9. Darkness
10. Plague of the Firstborn.

Rabbi Yehudah abbreviated them by their Hebrew initials:

D'TZACH, ADASH, B'ACHAB

The cups are refilled. The wine that was removed is not used.

רַבִּי יוֹסֵי *Rabbi Yose the Galilean said: How does one derive that the Egyptians were struck with ten plagues in Egypt, but with fifty plagues at the Sea? — Concerning the plagues in Egypt the Torah states: The magicians said to Pharaoh, 'It is the finger of God.'*[4] *However, of those at the Sea, the Torah relates: Israel saw the great 'hand' which* H*ASHEM laid upon the Egyptians, the people feared* H*ASHEM and they believed in* H*ASHEM and in His servant Moshe.*[5] *How many plagues did they receive with the finger? Ten! Then conclude that if they suffered ten plagues in Egypt [where they were struck with a finger], they must have been made to suffer fifty plagues at the sea [where they were struck with a whole hand].*

רַבִּי אֱלִיעֶזֶר *Rabbi Eliezer said: How does one derive that every plague that the Holy One, Blessed is He, inflicted upon the Egyptians in Egypt was equal to four plagues? — for it is written: He sent upon them his fierce anger: wrath, fury, and trouble, a band of emissaries of evil.*[6] *[Since each plague in Egypt consisted of] (a) wrath, (b) fury, (c) trouble and (d) a band of emissaries of evil, therefore conclude that in Egypt they were struck by forty plagues and by the sea two hundred!*

רַבִּי עֲקִיבָא *Rabbi Akiva said: How does one derive that each plague that the Holy One, Blessed is He, inflicted upon the Egyptians in Egypt was equal to five plagues? — For it is written: He sent upon them His fierce anger, wrath, fury, trouble, and a band of emissaries of evil.*[6] *[Since each plague in Egypt consisted of] (a) fierce anger, (b) wrath, (c) fury, (d) trouble and (e) a band of emissaries of evil, therefore conclude that in Egypt they were struck by fifty plagues and by the sea two hundred and fifty!*

---

(1) *Deuteronomy* 4:34. (2) *Exodus* 4:17. (3) *Joel* 3:3. (4) *Exodus* 8:15. (5) 14:31. (6) *Psalms* 78:49.

כַּמָּה מַעֲלוֹת טוֹבוֹת לַמָּקוֹם עָלֵינוּ.

אִלּוּ הוֹצִיאָנוּ מִמִּצְרַיִם, וְלֹא עָשָׂה בָהֶם שְׁפָטִים, **דַּיֵּנוּ.**
אִלּוּ עָשָׂה בָהֶם שְׁפָטִים, וְלֹא עָשָׂה בֵאלֹהֵיהֶם, **דַּיֵּנוּ.**
אִלּוּ עָשָׂה בֵאלֹהֵיהֶם, וְלֹא הָרַג אֶת בְּכוֹרֵיהֶם, **דַּיֵּנוּ.**
אִלּוּ הָרַג אֶת בְּכוֹרֵיהֶם, וְלֹא נָתַן לָנוּ אֶת מָמוֹנָם, **דַּיֵּנוּ.**
אִלּוּ נָתַן לָנוּ אֶת מָמוֹנָם, וְלֹא קָרַע לָנוּ אֶת הַיָּם, **דַּיֵּנוּ.**
אִלּוּ קָרַע לָנוּ אֶת הַיָּם, וְלֹא הֶעֱבִירָנוּ בְתוֹכוֹ בֶּחָרָבָה, **דַּיֵּנוּ.**
אִלּוּ הֶעֱבִירָנוּ בְתוֹכוֹ בֶּחָרָבָה, וְלֹא שִׁקַּע צָרֵינוּ בְּתוֹכוֹ, **דַּיֵּנוּ.**
אִלּוּ שִׁקַּע צָרֵינוּ בְּתוֹכוֹ,
וְלֹא סִפֵּק צָרְכֵּנוּ בַּמִּדְבָּר אַרְבָּעִים שָׁנָה, **דַּיֵּנוּ.**
אִלּוּ סִפֵּק צָרְכֵּנוּ בַּמִּדְבָּר אַרְבָּעִים שָׁנָה,
וְלֹא הֶאֱכִילָנוּ אֶת הַמָּן, **דַּיֵּנוּ.**
אִלּוּ הֶאֱכִילָנוּ אֶת הַמָּן, וְלֹא נָתַן לָנוּ אֶת הַשַּׁבָּת, **דַּיֵּנוּ.**
אִלּוּ נָתַן לָנוּ אֶת הַשַּׁבָּת, וְלֹא קֵרְבָנוּ לִפְנֵי הַר סִינַי, **דַּיֵּנוּ.**
אִלּוּ קֵרְבָנוּ לִפְנֵי הַר סִינַי, וְלֹא נָתַן לָנוּ אֶת הַתּוֹרָה, **דַּיֵּנוּ.**
אִלּוּ נָתַן לָנוּ אֶת הַתּוֹרָה, וְלֹא הִכְנִיסָנוּ לְאֶרֶץ יִשְׂרָאֵל, **דַּיֵּנוּ.**
אִלּוּ הִכְנִיסָנוּ לְאֶרֶץ יִשְׂרָאֵל,
וְלֹא בָנָה לָנוּ אֶת בֵּית הַבְּחִירָה, **דַּיֵּנוּ.**

עַל אַחַת כַּמָּה, וְכַמָּה טוֹבָה כְפוּלָה וּמְכֻפֶּלֶת לַמָּקוֹם עָלֵינוּ. שֶׁהוֹצִיאָנוּ מִמִּצְרַיִם, וְעָשָׂה בָהֶם שְׁפָטִים, וְעָשָׂה בֵאלֹהֵיהֶם, וְהָרַג אֶת בְּכוֹרֵיהֶם, וְנָתַן לָנוּ אֶת מָמוֹנָם, וְקָרַע לָנוּ אֶת הַיָּם, וְהֶעֱבִירָנוּ בְתוֹכוֹ בֶּחָרָבָה, וְשִׁקַּע צָרֵינוּ בְּתוֹכוֹ, וְסִפֵּק צָרְכֵּנוּ בַּמִּדְבָּר אַרְבָּעִים שָׁנָה, וְהֶאֱכִילָנוּ אֶת הַמָּן, וְנָתַן לָנוּ אֶת הַשַּׁבָּת, וְקֵרְבָנוּ לִפְנֵי הַר סִינַי, וְנָתַן לָנוּ אֶת הַתּוֹרָה, וְהִכְנִיסָנוּ לְאֶרֶץ יִשְׂרָאֵל, וּבָנָה לָנוּ אֶת בֵּית הַבְּחִירָה, לְכַפֵּר עַל כָּל עֲוֹנוֹתֵינוּ.

רַבָּן גַּמְלִיאֵל הָיָה אוֹמֵר. כָּל שֶׁלֹּא אָמַר שְׁלֹשָׁה דְּבָרִים אֵלּוּ בַּפֶּסַח, לֹא יָצָא יְדֵי חוֹבָתוֹ, וְאֵלּוּ הֵן,

פֶּסַח. מַצָּה. וּמָרוֹר.

פֶּסַח שֶׁהָיוּ אֲבוֹתֵינוּ אוֹכְלִים בִּזְמַן שֶׁבֵּית הַמִּקְדָּשׁ הָיָה קַיָּם, עַל שׁוּם מָה? עַל שׁוּם שֶׁפָּסַח הַקָּדוֹשׁ בָּרוּךְ הוּא עַל בָּתֵּי אֲבוֹתֵינוּ בְּמִצְרַיִם. שֶׁנֶּאֱמַר, וַאֲמַרְתֶּם, זֶבַח פֶּסַח הוּא לַיהוה, אֲשֶׁר פָּסַח עַל בָּתֵּי בְנֵי יִשְׂרָאֵל בְּמִצְרַיִם בְּנָגְפּוֹ אֶת מִצְרַיִם, וְאֶת בָּתֵּינוּ הִצִּיל, וַיִּקֹּד הָעָם וַיִּשְׁתַּחֲווּ.[1]

The Omnipresent has bestowed so many favors upon us!

Had He brought us out of Egypt, but not executed judgments against the Egyptians, it would have sufficed us.
Had He executed judgments against them, but not upon their gods, it would have sufficed us.
Had He executed judgments against their gods, but not slain their firstborn, it would have sufficed us.
Had He slain their firstborn, but not given us their wealth, it would have sufficed us.
Had He given us their wealth, but not split the Sea for us, it would have sufficed us.
Had He split the Sea for us, but not led us through it on dry land, it would have sufficed us.
Had He led us through on dry land, but not drowned our oppressors in it, it would have sufficed us.
Had He drowned our oppressors in it, but not provided for our needs in the desert for forty years, it would have sufficed us.
Had He provided for our needs in the desert for forty years, but not fed us the Manna, it would have sufficed us.
Had He fed us the Manna, but not given us the Shabbos, it would have sufficed us.
Had He given us the Shabbos, but not brought us before Mount Sinai, it would have sufficed us.
Had He brought us before Mount Sinai, but not given us the Torah, it would have sufficed us.
Had He given us the Torah, but not brought us into the Land of Israel, it would have sufficed us.
Had He brought us into the Land of Israel, but not built the Temple for us, it would have sufficed us.

עַל *Thus, how much more so, should we be grateful to the Omnipresent for all the numerous favors He showered upon us: He brought us out of Egypt; executed judgments against the Egyptians; and against their gods; slew their firstborn; gave us their wealth; split the Sea for us; led us through it on dry land; drowned our oppressors in it; provided for our needs in the desert for forty years; fed us the Manna; gave us the Shabbos; brought us before Mount Sinai; gave us the Torah; brought us to the Land of Israel; and built us the Temple, to atone for our sins.*

רַבָּן גַּמְלִיאֵל *Rabban Gamliel used to say: Whoever has not explained the following three things on Passover has not fulfilled his duty, namely;* **PESACH** *— the Pesach offering;* **MATZAH** *— the unleavened bread;* **MAROR** *— the bitter herbs.*

פֶּסַח *Pesach — Why did our fathers eat a Pesach offering during the period when the Temple stood? — Because the Holy One, Blessed is He, passed over the houses of our fathers in Egypt, as it is written: You shall say: 'It is a Pesach offering for* HASHEM, *Who passed over the houses of the Children of Israel in Egypt when He struck the Egyptians and spared our houses; and the people bowed down and prostrated themselves.'*[1]

(1) *Exodus* 12:27.

The middle matzah is lifted and displayed while the following paragraph is recited.

מַצָּה זוּ שֶׁאָנוּ אוֹכְלִים, עַל שׁוּם מָה? עַל שׁוּם שֶׁלֹּא הִסְפִּיק בְּצֵקָם שֶׁל אֲבוֹתֵינוּ לְהַחֲמִיץ, עַד שֶׁנִּגְלָה עֲלֵיהֶם מֶלֶךְ מַלְכֵי הַמְּלָכִים הַקָּדוֹשׁ בָּרוּךְ הוּא וּגְאָלָם. שֶׁנֶּאֱמַר, וַיֹּאפוּ אֶת הַבָּצֵק אֲשֶׁר הוֹצִיאוּ מִמִּצְרַיִם עֻגֹת מַצּוֹת כִּי לֹא חָמֵץ, כִּי גֹרְשׁוּ מִמִּצְרַיִם, וְלֹא יָכְלוּ לְהִתְמַהְמֵהַּ, וְגַם צֵדָה לֹא עָשׂוּ לָהֶם.[1]

The maror is lifted and displayed while the following paragraph is recited.

מָרוֹר זֶה שֶׁאָנוּ אוֹכְלִים, עַל שׁוּם מָה? עַל שׁוּם שֶׁמֵּרְרוּ הַמִּצְרִים אֶת חַיֵּי אֲבוֹתֵינוּ בְּמִצְרַיִם. שֶׁנֶּאֱמַר, וַיְמָרְרוּ אֶת חַיֵּיהֶם, בַּעֲבֹדָה קָשָׁה, בְּחֹמֶר וּבִלְבֵנִים, וּבְכָל עֲבֹדָה בַּשָּׂדֶה, אֵת כָּל עֲבֹדָתָם אֲשֶׁר עָבְדוּ בָהֶם בְּפָרֶךְ.[2]

בְּכָל דּוֹר וָדוֹר חַיָּב אָדָם לִרְאוֹת אֶת עַצְמוֹ כְּאִלּוּ הוּא יָצָא מִמִּצְרָיִם. שֶׁנֶּאֱמַר, וְהִגַּדְתָּ לְבִנְךָ בַּיּוֹם הַהוּא לֵאמֹר, בַּעֲבוּר זֶה עָשָׂה יהוה לִי, בְּצֵאתִי מִמִּצְרָיִם.[3] לֹא אֶת אֲבוֹתֵינוּ בִּלְבָד גָּאַל הַקָּדוֹשׁ בָּרוּךְ הוּא, אֶלָּא אַף אֹתָנוּ גָּאַל עִמָּהֶם. שֶׁנֶּאֱמַר, וְאוֹתָנוּ הוֹצִיא מִשָּׁם, לְמַעַן הָבִיא אֹתָנוּ לָתֶת לָנוּ אֶת הָאָרֶץ אֲשֶׁר נִשְׁבַּע לַאֲבוֹתֵינוּ.[4]

The matzos are covered and the cup is lifted and held until it is to be drunk. According to some customs, however, the cup is put down after the following paragraph, in which case the matzos should once more be uncovered.

לְפִיכָךְ אֲנַחְנוּ חַיָּבִים לְהוֹדוֹת, לְהַלֵּל, לְשַׁבֵּחַ, לְפָאֵר, לְרוֹמֵם, לְהַדֵּר, לְבָרֵךְ, לְעַלֵּה, וּלְקַלֵּס, לְמִי שֶׁעָשָׂה לַאֲבוֹתֵינוּ וְלָנוּ אֶת כָּל הַנִּסִּים הָאֵלּוּ, הוֹצִיאָנוּ מֵעַבְדוּת לְחֵרוּת, מִיָּגוֹן לְשִׂמְחָה, וּמֵאֵבֶל לְיוֹם טוֹב, וּמֵאֲפֵלָה לְאוֹר גָּדוֹל, וּמִשִּׁעְבּוּד לִגְאֻלָּה, וְנֹאמַר לְפָנָיו שִׁירָה חֲדָשָׁה, הַלְלוּיָהּ.

הַלְלוּיָהּ הַלְלוּ עַבְדֵי יהוה, הַלְלוּ אֶת שֵׁם יהוה. יְהִי שֵׁם יהוה מְבֹרָךְ, מֵעַתָּה וְעַד עוֹלָם. מִמִּזְרַח שֶׁמֶשׁ עַד מְבוֹאוֹ, מְהֻלָּל שֵׁם יהוה. רָם עַל כָּל גּוֹיִם יהוה, עַל הַשָּׁמַיִם כְּבוֹדוֹ. מִי כַּיהוה אֱלֹהֵינוּ, הַמַּגְבִּיהִי לָשָׁבֶת. הַמַּשְׁפִּילִי לִרְאוֹת, בַּשָּׁמַיִם וּבָאָרֶץ. מְקִימִי מֵעָפָר דָּל, מֵאַשְׁפֹּת יָרִים אֶבְיוֹן. לְהוֹשִׁיבִי עִם נְדִיבִים, עִם נְדִיבֵי עַמּוֹ. מוֹשִׁיבִי עֲקֶרֶת הַבַּיִת, אֵם הַבָּנִים שְׂמֵחָה, הַלְלוּיָהּ.[5]

בְּצֵאת יִשְׂרָאֵל מִמִּצְרָיִם, בֵּית יַעֲקֹב מֵעַם לֹעֵז. הָיְתָה יְהוּדָה לְקָדְשׁוֹ, יִשְׂרָאֵל מַמְשְׁלוֹתָיו. הַיָּם רָאָה וַיָּנֹס, הַיַּרְדֵּן יִסֹּב לְאָחוֹר. הֶהָרִים רָקְדוּ כְאֵילִים, גְּבָעוֹת כִּבְנֵי צֹאן. מַה לְּךָ הַיָּם כִּי תָנוּס, הַיַּרְדֵּן תִּסֹּב לְאָחוֹר. הֶהָרִים תִּרְקְדוּ כְאֵילִים, גְּבָעוֹת כִּבְנֵי צֹאן. מִלִּפְנֵי אָדוֹן חוּלִי אָרֶץ, מִלִּפְנֵי אֱלוֹהַּ יַעֲקֹב. הַהֹפְכִי הַצּוּר אֲגַם מָיִם, חַלָּמִישׁ לְמַעְיְנוֹ מָיִם.[6]

The middle matzah is lifted and displayed while the following paragraph is recited.

מַצָּה *Matzah — Why do we eat this unleavened bread? — Because the dough of our fathers did not have time to become leavened before the King of Kings, the Holy One, Blessed is He, revealed Himself to them and redeemed them, as it is written: They baked the dough which they had brought out of Egypt into unleavened bread, for it had not fermented, because they were driven out of Egypt and could not delay, nor had they prepared any provisions for the way.*[1]

The maror is lifted and displayed while the following paragraph is recited.

מָרוֹר *Maror — Why do we eat this bitter herb? — Because the Egyptians embittered the lives of our fathers in Egypt, as it says: They embittered their lives with hard labor, with mortar and bricks, and with all manner of labor in the field: whatever service they made them perform was with hard labor.*[2]

בְּכָל דּוֹר *In every generation it is one's duty to regard himself as though he personally had gone out of Egypt, as it is written: You shall tell your son on that day: 'It was because of this that* HASHEM *did for "me" when I went out of Egypt.'*[3] *It was not only our fathers whom the Holy One redeemed from slavery; we, too, were redeemed with them, as it is written: He brought "us" out from there so that He might take us to the land which He had promised to our fathers.*[4]

The matzos are covered and the cup is lifted and held until it is to be drunk. According to some customs, however, the cup is put down after the following paragraph, in which case the matzos should once more be uncovered.

לְפִיכָךְ *Therefore it is our duty to thank, praise, pay tribute, glorify, exalt, honor, bless, extol, and acclaim Him Who performed all these miracles for our fathers and for us. He brought us forth from slavery to freedom, from grief to joy, from mourning to festivity, from darkness to great light, and from servitude to redemption. Let us, therefore, recite a new song before Him! Halleluyah!*

הַלְלוּיָהּ *Halleluyah! Praise, you servants of* HASHEM, *praise the Name of* HASHEM. *Blessed be the Name of* HASHEM *from now and forever. From the rising of the sun to its setting,* HASHEM'*s Name is praised. High above all nations is* HASHEM, *above the heavens is His glory. Who is like* HASHEM, *our God, Who is enthroned on high, yet deigns to look, upon the heaven and earth? He raises the destitute from the dust, from the trash heaps He lifts the needy — to seat them with nobles, with nobles of His people. He transforms the barren wife into a glad mother of children. Halleluyah!*[5]

בְּצֵאת *When Israel went forth from Egypt, Yaakov's household from a people of alien tongue, Yehudah became His sanctuary, Israel His dominion. The Sea saw and fled; the Jordan turned backward. The mountains skipped like rams, and the hills like young lambs. What ails you, O Sea, that you flee? O Jordan, that you turn backward? O mountains, that you skip like rams? O hills, like young lambs? Before* HASHEM'*s presence — tremble, O earth, before the presence of the God of Yaakov, Who turns the rock into a pond of water, the flint into a flowing fountain.*[6]

---

(1) *Exodus* 12:39. (2) 1:14. (3) 13:8. (4) *Deuteronomy* 6:23. (5) *Psalms* 113. (6) 114.

According to all customs the cup is lifted and the matzos covered during the recitation of this blessing.
(On *Motzaei Shabbos* the phrase in parentheses substitutes for the preceding phrase.)

בָּרוּךְ אַתָּה יהוה אֱלֹהֵינוּ מֶלֶךְ הָעוֹלָם, אֲשֶׁר גְּאָלָנוּ וְגָאַל אֶת אֲבוֹתֵינוּ מִמִּצְרַיִם, וְהִגִּיעָנוּ הַלַּיְלָה הַזֶּה לֶאֱכָל בּוֹ מַצָּה וּמָרוֹר. כֵּן יהוה אֱלֹהֵינוּ וֵאלֹהֵי אֲבוֹתֵינוּ, יַגִּיעֵנוּ לְמוֹעֲדִים וְלִרְגָלִים אֲחֵרִים הַבָּאִים לִקְרָאתֵנוּ לְשָׁלוֹם, שְׂמֵחִים בְּבִנְיַן עִירֶךָ וְשָׂשִׂים בַּעֲבוֹדָתֶךָ, וְנֹאכַל שָׁם מִן הַזְּבָחִים וּמִן הַפְּסָחִים [מִן הַפְּסָחִים וּמִן הַזְּבָחִים] אֲשֶׁר יַגִּיעַ דָּמָם עַל קִיר מִזְבַּחֲךָ לְרָצוֹן. וְנוֹדֶה לְךָ שִׁיר חָדָשׁ עַל גְּאֻלָּתֵנוּ וְעַל פְּדוּת נַפְשֵׁנוּ. בָּרוּךְ אַתָּה יהוה, גָּאַל יִשְׂרָאֵל.

בָּרוּךְ אַתָּה יהוה אֱלֹהֵינוּ מֶלֶךְ הָעוֹלָם, בּוֹרֵא פְּרִי הַגָּפֶן.

The second cup is drunk while leaning on the left side — preferably the entire cup, but at least most of it.

רחצה

The hands are washed for matzah and the following blessing is recited.
It is preferable to bring water and a basin to the head of the household at the *Seder* table.

בָּרוּךְ אַתָּה יהוה אֱלֹהֵינוּ מֶלֶךְ הָעוֹלָם, אֲשֶׁר קִדְּשָׁנוּ בְּמִצְוֹתָיו, וְצִוָּנוּ עַל נְטִילַת יָדָיִם.

מוציא

The following two blessings are recited over matzah; the first is recited over matzah as food, and the second for the special *mitzvah* of eating matzah on the night of Pesach. [The latter blessing is to be made with the intention that it also apply to the 'sandwich' and the *afikoman*.]
The head of the household raises all the matzos on the *Seder* plate and recites the following blessing:

בָּרוּךְ אַתָּה יהוה אֱלֹהֵינוּ מֶלֶךְ הָעוֹלָם, הַמּוֹצִיא לֶחֶם מִן הָאָרֶץ.

The bottom matzah is put down and the following blessing is recited while the top (whole) matzah and the middle (broken) piece are still raised.

מצה

בָּרוּךְ אַתָּה יהוה אֱלֹהֵינוּ מֶלֶךְ הָעוֹלָם, אֲשֶׁר קִדְּשָׁנוּ בְּמִצְוֹתָיו, וְצִוָּנוּ עַל אֲכִילַת מַצָּה.

Each participant is required to eat an amount of matzah equal in volume to an egg. Since it is usually impossible to provide a sufficient amount of matzah from the two matzos for all members of the household, the other matzos should be available at the head of the table from which to complete the required amounts. However, each participant should receive a piece from each of the top two matzos. The matzos are to be eaten while reclining on the left side and without delay; they need not be dipped in salt.

מרור

The head of the household takes a half-egg volume of *maror,* dips it into *charoses,* and gives each participant a like amount. The following blessing is recited with the intention that it also apply to the *maror* of the 'sandwich'. The *maror* is eaten without reclining, and without delay.

According to all customs the cup is lifted and the matzos covered during the recitation of this blessing.
(On *Motzaei Shabbos* the phrase in parentheses substitutes for the preceding phrase.)

בָּרוּךְ *Blessed are You, HASHEM, our God, King of the universe, Who redeemed our ancestors from Egypt and enabled us to reach this night that we may eat matzah and maror. So, HASHEM, our God and God of our fathers, bring us also to future Festivals and holidays in peace, gladdened in the rebuilding of Your city, and joyful at Your service. There we shall eat of the offerings and Pesach sacrifices* (of the Pesach sacrifices and offerings) *whose blood will gain the sides of Your altar for gracious acceptance. We shall then sing a new song of praise to You for our redemption and for the liberation of our souls. Blessed are You, HASHEM, Who has redeemed Israel.*

בָּרוּךְ *Bessed are You, HASHEM, our God, King of the universe, Who creates the fruit of vine.*

The second cup is drunk while leaning on the left side — preferably the entire cup, but at least most of it.

RACHTZAH

The hands are washed for matzah and the following blessing is recited.
It is preferable to bring water and a basin to the head of the household at the *Seder* table.

בָּרוּךְ *Blessed are You, HASHEM, our God, King of the universe, Who has sanctified us with His commandments, and has commanded us concerning the washing of the hands.*

MOTZI

The following two blessings are recited over matzah; the first is recited over matzah as food, and the second for the special *mitzvah* of eating matzah on the night of Pesach. [The latter blessing is to be made with the intention that it also apply to the 'sandwich' and the *afikoman.]*

The head of the household raises all the matzos on the *Seder* plate and recites the following blessing:

בָּרוּךְ *Blessed are You, HASHEM, our God, King of the universe, Who brings forth bread from the earth.*

The bottom matzah is put down and the following blessing is recited while the top (whole) matzah and the middle (broken) piece are still raised.

MATZAH

בָּרוּךְ *Blessed are You, HASHEM, our God, King of the universe, Who has sanctified us with His commandments, and has commanded us concerning the eating of the matzah.*

Each participant is required to eat an amount of matzah equal in volume to an egg. Since it is usually impossible to provide a sufficient amount of matzah from the two matzos for all members of the household, the other matzos should be available at the head of the table from which to complete the required amounts. However, each participant should receive a piece from each of the top two matzos. The matzos are to be eaten while reclining on the left side and without delay; they need not be dipped in salt.

MAROR

The head of the household takes a half-egg volume of *maror,* dips it into *charoses,* and gives each participant a like amount. The following blessing is recited with the intention that it also apply to the *maror* of the 'sandwich'. The *maror* is eaten without reclining, and without delay.

בָּרוּךְ אַתָּה יהוה אֱלֹהֵינוּ מֶלֶךְ הָעוֹלָם, אֲשֶׁר קִדְּשָׁנוּ בְּמִצְוֹתָיו, וְצִוָּנוּ עַל אֲכִילַת מָרוֹר.

כורך

The bottom (thus far unbroken) matzah is now taken. From it, with the addition of other matzos, each participant receives a half-egg volume of matzah with an equal volume portion of *maror* (dipped into *charoses* which is shaken off). The following paragraph is recited and the 'sandwich' is eaten while reclining.

זֵכֶר לְמִקְדָּשׁ כְּהִלֵּל. כֵּן עָשָׂה הִלֵּל בִּזְמַן שֶׁבֵּית הַמִּקְדָּשׁ הָיָה קַיָּם. הָיָה כּוֹרֵךְ (פֶּסַח) מַצָּה וּמָרוֹר וְאוֹכֵל בְּיַחַד. לְקַיֵּם מַה שֶּׁנֶּאֱמַר, עַל מַצּוֹת וּמְרֹרִים יֹאכְלֻהוּ.[1]

שלחן עורך

The meal should be eaten in a combination of joy and solemnity, for the meal, too, is a part of the *Seder* service. While it is desirable that *zemiros* and discussion of the laws and events of Pesach be part of the meal, extraneous conversation should be avoided. It should be remembered that the *afikoman* must be eaten while there is still some appetite for it. In fact, if one is so sated that he must literally force himself to eat it, he is not credited with the performance of the *mitzvah* of *afikoman*. Therefore, it is unwise to eat more than a moderate amount during the meal.

צפון

From the *afikoman* matzah (and from additional matzos to make up the required amount) a half-egg volume portion — according to some, a full egg's volume portion — is given to each participant. It should be eaten before midnight, while reclining, without delay, and uninterruptedly. Nothing may be eaten or drunk after the *afikoman* (with the exception of water and the like) except for the last two *Seder* cups of wine.

ברך

The third cup is poured and *Bircas HaMazon* (Grace After Meals) is recited. According to some customs, the Cup of Eliahu is poured at this point.

תהלים קכו

שִׁיר הַמַּעֲלוֹת, בְּשׁוּב יהוה אֶת שִׁיבַת צִיּוֹן, הָיִינוּ כְּחֹלְמִים. אָז יִמָּלֵא שְׂחוֹק פִּינוּ וּלְשׁוֹנֵנוּ רִנָּה, אָז יֹאמְרוּ בַגּוֹיִם, הִגְדִּיל יהוה לַעֲשׂוֹת עִם אֵלֶּה. הִגְדִּיל יהוה לַעֲשׂוֹת עִמָּנוּ, הָיִינוּ שְׂמֵחִים. שׁוּבָה יהוה אֶת שְׁבִיתֵנוּ, כַּאֲפִיקִים בַּנֶּגֶב. הַזֹּרְעִים בְּדִמְעָה בְּרִנָּה יִקְצֹרוּ. הָלוֹךְ יֵלֵךְ וּבָכֹה נֹשֵׂא מֶשֶׁךְ הַזָּרַע, בֹּא יָבֹא בְרִנָּה, נֹשֵׂא אֲלֻמֹּתָיו.

תְּהִלַּת יהוה יְדַבֶּר פִּי, וִיבָרֵךְ כָּל בָּשָׂר שֵׁם קָדְשׁוֹ לְעוֹלָם וָעֶד.[2] וַאֲנַחְנוּ נְבָרֵךְ יָהּ, מֵעַתָּה וְעַד עוֹלָם, הַלְלוּיָהּ.[3] הוֹדוּ לַיהוה כִּי טוֹב, כִּי לְעוֹלָם חַסְדּוֹ.[4] מִי יְמַלֵּל גְּבוּרוֹת יהוה, יַשְׁמִיעַ כָּל תְּהִלָּתוֹ.[5]

בָּרוּךְ *Blessed are You, HASHEM, our God, King of the universe, Who has sanctified us with His commandments, and has commanded us concerning the eating of maror.*

KORECH

The bottom (thus far unbroken) matzah is now taken. From it, with the addition of other matzos, each participant receives a half-egg volume of matzah with an equal volume portion of *maror* (dipped into *charoses* which is shaken off). The following paragraph is recited and the 'sandwich' is eaten while reclining.

זֵכֶר *In remembrance of the Temple we do as Hillel did in Temple times: he would combine (the Pesach offering,) matzah and maror in a sandwich and eat them together, to fulfill what is written in the Torah: They shall eat it with matzos and bitter herbs.*[1]

SHULCHAN ORECH

The meal should be eaten in a combination of joy and solemnity, for the meal, too, is a part of the *Seder* service. While it is desirable that *zemiros* and discussion of the laws and events of Pesach be part of the meal, extraneous conversation should be avoided. It should be remembered that the *afikoman* must be eaten while there is still some appetite for it. In fact, if one is so sated that he must literally force himself to eat it, he is not credited with the performance of the *mitzvah* of *afikoman*. Therefore, it is unwise to eat more than a moderate amount during the meal.

TZAFUN

From the *afikoman* matzah (and from additional matzos to make up the required amount) a half-egg volume portion — according to some, a full egg's volume portion — is given to each participant. It should be eaten before midnight, while reclining, without delay, and uninterruptedly. Nothing may be eaten or drunk after the *afikoman* (with the exception of water and the like) except for the last two *Seder* cups of wine.

BARECH

The third cup is poured and *Bircas HaMazon* (Grace After Meals) is recited.
According to some customs, the Cup of Eliahu is poured at this point.

Psalm 126

שִׁיר הַמַּעֲלוֹת *A song of ascents. When HASHEM will return the captivity of Zion, we will be like dreamers. Then our mouth will be filled with laughter and our tongue with glad song. Then they will declare among the nations, 'HASHEM has done greatly with these.' HASHEM has done greatly with us, we were gladdened. O HASHEM — return our captivity like springs in the desert. Those who tearfully sow will reap in glad song. He who bears the measure of seeds walks along weeping, but will return in exultation, a bearer of his sheaves.*

תְּהִלַּת *May my mouth declare the praise of HASHEM and may all flesh bless His Holy Name forever.*[2] *We will bless HASHEM from this time and forever, Halleluyah!*[3] *Give thanks to God for He is good, His kindness endures forever.*[4] *Who can express the mighty acts of HASHEM? Who can declare all His praise?*[5]

---

(1) *Numbers* 9:11. (2) *Psalms* 145:21. (3) 115:18. (4) 118:1. (5) 106:2.

זימון

If three or more males, aged thirteen or older, participate in a meal, a leader is appointed to formally invite the others to join him in the recitation of *Bircas HaMazon*. This invitation is called *zimun*.

Leader – רַבּוֹתַי נְבָרֵךְ.

Others – יְהִי שֵׁם יהוה מְבֹרָךְ מֵעַתָּה וְעַד עוֹלָם.[1]

If ten men join in the *zimun*, the words in parentheses are added.

Leader – יְהִי שֵׁם יהוה מְבֹרָךְ מֵעַתָּה וְעַד עוֹלָם.[1]

בִּרְשׁוּת מָרָנָן וְרַבָּנָן וְרַבּוֹתַי, נְבָרֵךְ (אֱלֹהֵינוּ) שֶׁאָכַלְנוּ מִשֶּׁלּוֹ.

Others° – בָּרוּךְ (אֱלֹהֵינוּ) שֶׁאָכַלְנוּ מִשֶּׁלּוֹ וּבְטוּבוֹ חָיִינוּ.

°Those who have not eaten respond:
בָּרוּךְ (אֱלֹהֵינוּ) וּמְבֹרָךְ שְׁמוֹ תָּמִיד לְעוֹלָם וָעֶד.

Leader – בָּרוּךְ (אֱלֹהֵינוּ) שֶׁאָכַלְנוּ מִשֶּׁלּוֹ וּבְטוּבוֹ חָיִינוּ.

בָּרוּךְ הוּא וּבָרוּךְ שְׁמוֹ.

The *zimun* leader should recite *Bircas HaMazon* (or, at least, the first blessing) aloud. Other than to respond *Amen* at the conclusion of each blessing, it is forbidden to interrupt *Bircas HaMazon* for any response other than those permitted during the *Shema*.

ברכת הזן

בָּרוּךְ אַתָּה יהוה אֱלֹהֵינוּ מֶלֶךְ הָעוֹלָם, הַזָּן אֶת הָעוֹלָם כֻּלּוֹ, בְּטוּבוֹ, בְּחֵן בְּחֶסֶד וּבְרַחֲמִים, הוּא נֹתֵן לֶחֶם לְכָל בָּשָׂר, כִּי לְעוֹלָם חַסְדּוֹ.[2] וּבְטוּבוֹ הַגָּדוֹל, תָּמִיד לֹא חָסַר לָנוּ, וְאַל יֶחְסַר לָנוּ מָזוֹן לְעוֹלָם וָעֶד. בַּעֲבוּר שְׁמוֹ הַגָּדוֹל, כִּי הוּא אֵל זָן וּמְפַרְנֵס לַכֹּל, וּמֵטִיב לַכֹּל, וּמֵכִין מָזוֹן לְכָל בְּרִיּוֹתָיו אֲשֶׁר בָּרָא. ❖ בָּרוּךְ אַתָּה יהוה, הַזָּן אֶת הַכֹּל.

(Others – אָמֵן.)

ברכת הארץ

נוֹדֶה לְּךָ יהוה אֱלֹהֵינוּ, עַל שֶׁהִנְחַלְתָּ לַאֲבוֹתֵינוּ אֶרֶץ חֶמְדָּה טוֹבָה וּרְחָבָה. וְעַל שֶׁהוֹצֵאתָנוּ יהוה אֱלֹהֵינוּ מֵאֶרֶץ מִצְרַיִם, וּפְדִיתָנוּ מִבֵּית עֲבָדִים, וְעַל בְּרִיתְךָ שֶׁחָתַמְתָּ בִּבְשָׂרֵנוּ, וְעַל תּוֹרָתְךָ שֶׁלִּמַּדְתָּנוּ, וְעַל חֻקֶּיךָ שֶׁהוֹדַעְתָּנוּ, וְעַל חַיִּים חֵן וָחֶסֶד שֶׁחוֹנַנְתָּנוּ, וְעַל אֲכִילַת מָזוֹן שָׁאַתָּה זָן וּמְפַרְנֵס אוֹתָנוּ תָּמִיד, בְּכָל יוֹם וּבְכָל עֵת וּבְכָל שָׁעָה.

וְעַל הַכֹּל יהוה אֱלֹהֵינוּ אֲנַחְנוּ מוֹדִים לָךְ, וּמְבָרְכִים אוֹתָךְ, יִתְבָּרַךְ שִׁמְךָ בְּפִי כָּל חַי תָּמִיד לְעוֹלָם וָעֶד. כַּכָּתוּב, וְאָכַלְתָּ וְשָׂבָעְתָּ, וּבֵרַכְתָּ אֶת יהוה אֱלֹהֶיךָ, עַל הָאָרֶץ הַטֹּבָה אֲשֶׁר נָתַן לָךְ.[3] ❖ בָּרוּךְ אַתָּה יהוה, עַל הָאָרֶץ וְעַל הַמָּזוֹן.

(Others – אָמֵן.)

בנין ירושלים

רַחֵם יהוה אֱלֹהֵינוּ עַל יִשְׂרָאֵל עַמֶּךָ, וְעַל יְרוּשָׁלַיִם עִירֶךָ, וְעַל צִיּוֹן מִשְׁכַּן כְּבוֹדֶךָ, וְעַל מַלְכוּת בֵּית דָּוִד מְשִׁיחֶךָ, וְעַל הַבַּיִת הַגָּדוֹל וְהַקָּדוֹשׁ שֶׁנִּקְרָא שִׁמְךָ עָלָיו. אֱלֹהֵינוּ אָבִינוּ רְעֵנוּ זוּנֵנוּ פַּרְנְסֵנוּ

ZIMUN/INVITATION

If three or more males, aged thirteen or older, participate in a meal, a leader is appointed to formally invite the others to join him in the recitation of Grace after Meals. This invitation is called *zimun.*

Leader – *Gentlemen, let us bless.*

Others – *Blessed be the Name of* HASHEM *from this time and forever!*[1]

If ten men join in the *zimun,* the words in brackets are added.

Leader– *Blessed be the Name of* HASHEM *from this time and forever!*[1]
With the permission of the distinguished people present,
let us bless [our God,] He of Whose we have eaten.

Others° – *Blessed is [our God,] He of Whose we have eaten and through Whose goodness we live.*

°Those who have not eaten respond: *Blessed is He [our God] and blessed is His Name continuously forever.*

Leader– *Blessed is [our God,] He of Whose we have eaten and through Whose goodness we live.*
Blessed is He and Blessed is His Name.

The *zimun* leader should recite Grace after Meals (or, at least, the first blessing) aloud. Other than to respond *Amen* at the conclusion of each blessing, it is forbidden to interrupt Grace after Meals for any response other than those permitted during the *Shema.*

FIRST BLESSING: FOR THE NOURISHMENT

בָּרוּךְ *Blessed are You,* HASHEM, *our God, King of the universe, Who nourishes the entire world, in His goodness — with grace, with kindness, and with mercy. He gives nourishment to all flesh, for His kindness is eternal.*[2] *And through His great goodness, we have never lacked, and may we never lack, nourishment, for all eternity. For the sake of His great Name, because He is God Who nourishes and sustains all, and benefits all, and He prepares food for all of His creatures which He has created.* Leader– *Blessed are You,* HASHEM, *Who nourishes all.* (Others– *Amen.*)

SECOND BLESSING: FOR THE LAND

נוֹדֶה *We thank You,* HASHEM, *our God, because You have given to our forefathers as a heritage a desirable, good and spacious land; because You removed us,* HASHEM, *our God, from the land of Egypt and You redeemed us from the house of bondage; for Your covenant which You sealed in our flesh; for Your Torah which You taught us and for Your statutes which You made known to us; for life, grace, and lovingkindness which You granted us; and for the provision of food with which You nourish and sustain us constantly, in every day, in every season, and in every hour.*

וְעַל הַכֹּל *For all,* HASHEM, *our God, we thank You and bless You. May Your Name be blessed by the mouth of all the living, continuously for all eternity. As it is written: 'And you shall eat and you shall be satisfied and you shall bless* HASHEM, *your God, for the good land which He gave you.'*[3] Leader– *Blessed are You,* HASHEM, *for the land and for the nourishment.* (Others– *Amen.*)

THIRD BLESSING: FOR JERUSALEM

רַחֵם *Have mercy,* HASHEM, *our God, on Israel Your people; on Jerusalem, Your city; on Zion, the resting place of Your Glory; on the monarchy of the house of David, Your anointed; and on the great and holy House upon which Your Name is called. Our God, our Father — tend us, nourish us, sustain us,*

(1) *Psalms* 113:2. (2) 136:25. (3) *Deuteronomy* 8:10.

וְכַלְכְּלֵנוּ וְהַרְוִיחֵנוּ, וְהַרְוַח לָנוּ יהוה אֱלֹהֵינוּ מְהֵרָה מִכָּל צָרוֹתֵינוּ. וְנָא אַל תַּצְרִיכֵנוּ יהוה אֱלֹהֵינוּ, לֹא לִידֵי מַתְּנַת בָּשָׂר וָדָם, וְלֹא לִידֵי הַלְוָאָתָם, כִּי אִם לְיָדְךָ הַמְּלֵאָה הַפְּתוּחָה הַקְּדוֹשָׁה וְהָרְחָבָה, שֶׁלֹּא נֵבוֹשׁ וְלֹא נִכָּלֵם לְעוֹלָם וָעֶד.

On the Sabbath add the following. [If forgotten, see box below.]

רְצֵה וְהַחֲלִיצֵנוּ יהוה אֱלֹהֵינוּ בְּמִצְוֹתֶיךָ, וּבְמִצְוַת יוֹם הַשְּׁבִיעִי הַשַּׁבָּת הַגָּדוֹל וְהַקָּדוֹשׁ הַזֶּה, כִּי יוֹם זֶה גָּדוֹל וְקָדוֹשׁ הוּא לְפָנֶיךָ, לִשְׁבָּת בּוֹ וְלָנוּחַ בּוֹ בְּאַהֲבָה כְּמִצְוַת רְצוֹנֶךָ, וּבִרְצוֹנְךָ הָנִיחַ לָנוּ יהוה אֱלֹהֵינוּ, שֶׁלֹּא תְהֵא צָרָה וְיָגוֹן וַאֲנָחָה בְּיוֹם מְנוּחָתֵנוּ, וְהַרְאֵנוּ יהוה אֱלֹהֵינוּ בְּנֶחָמַת צִיּוֹן עִירֶךָ, וּבְבִנְיַן יְרוּשָׁלַיִם עִיר קָדְשֶׁךָ, כִּי אַתָּה הוּא בַּעַל הַיְשׁוּעוֹת וּבַעַל הַנֶּחָמוֹת.

אֱלֹהֵינוּ וֵאלֹהֵי אֲבוֹתֵינוּ, יַעֲלֶה, וְיָבֹא, וְיַגִּיעַ, וְיֵרָאֶה, וְיֵרָצֶה, וְיִשָּׁמַע, וְיִפָּקֵד, וְיִזָּכֵר זִכְרוֹנֵנוּ וּפִקְדוֹנֵנוּ, וְזִכְרוֹן אֲבוֹתֵינוּ, וְזִכְרוֹן מָשִׁיחַ בֶּן דָּוִד עַבְדֶּךָ, וְזִכְרוֹן יְרוּשָׁלַיִם עִיר קָדְשֶׁךָ, וְזִכְרוֹן כָּל עַמְּךָ בֵּית יִשְׂרָאֵל לְפָנֶיךָ, לִפְלֵיטָה לְטוֹבָה לְחֵן וּלְחֶסֶד וּלְרַחֲמִים, לְחַיִּים וּלְשָׁלוֹם בְּיוֹם חַג הַמַּצּוֹת הַזֶּה. זָכְרֵנוּ יהוה אֱלֹהֵינוּ בּוֹ לְטוֹבָה, וּפָקְדֵנוּ בוֹ לִבְרָכָה, וְהוֹשִׁיעֵנוּ בוֹ לְחַיִּים. וּבִדְבַר יְשׁוּעָה וְרַחֲמִים, חוּס וְחָנֵּנוּ וְרַחֵם עָלֵינוּ וְהוֹשִׁיעֵנוּ, כִּי אֵלֶיךָ עֵינֵינוּ, כִּי אֵל חַנּוּן וְרַחוּם אָתָּה.[1]

❖ **וּבְנֵה** יְרוּשָׁלַיִם עִיר הַקֹּדֶשׁ בִּמְהֵרָה בְיָמֵינוּ. בָּרוּךְ אַתָּה יהוה, בּוֹנֵה (בְּרַחֲמָיו) יְרוּשָׁלָיִם. אָמֵן. (Others – אָמֵן.)

[When required, the compensatory blessing is recited here.]

⊸§ If One Omitted יַעֲלֶה וְיָבֹא or רְצֵה

If one omitted יַעֲלֶה וְיָבֹא on Pesach (and/or רְצֵה on Pesach that falls on the Sabbath):

(a) If he realizes his omission after having recited the word בּוֹנֵה, *Who rebuilds,* of the next paragraph, but has not yet begun the following blessing, he completes the blessing until אָמֵן, and then makes up for the omission by reciting the appropriate Compensatory Blessing (facing page).

(b) If he realizes his omission after reciting the words בָּרוּךְ אַתָּה ה׳, *Blessed are You, HASHEM,* but had not yet said the word בּוֹנֵה, *Who rebuilds,* he concludes with the phrase, לַמְּדֵנִי חֻקֶּיךָ, *teach me Your statutes;* then recites the omitted paragraph and continues from there. [This ruling is based on the fact that בָּרוּךְ אַתָּה ה׳ לַמְּדֵנִי חֻקֶּיךָ, *Blessed are You, HASHEM; teach me Your statutes,* is a verse in *Psalms* (119:12) and not a blessing. Only if one has recited the next blessing of *Bircas HaMazon* is it forbidden to go back to a previous blessing, but if one has merely inserted a verse from *Psalms,* he is still in the middle of the prayer and may go back to correct an omission.]

(c) If he realizes his omission after having recited the first six words of the fourth blessing, he may still switch immediately into the compensatory blessing since the words בָּרוּךְ אַתָּה . . . הָעוֹלָם are identical in both blessings.

(d) If he realizes his omission after having recited the word הָאֵל, *the Almighty,* of the fourth blessing, it is too late for the compensatory blessing to be recited. In that case, at the first two meals of *Shabbos* and *Yom Tov* (but not *Chol HaMoed*), *Bircas HaMazon* must be repeated in its entirety; at the third meal, nothing need be done.

support us, relieve us; HASHEM, our God, grant us speedy relief from all our troubles. Please, make us not needful — HASHEM, our God — of the gifts of human hands nor of their loans, but only of Your Hand that is full, open, holy, and generous, that we not feel inner shame nor be humiliated for ever and ever.

On the Sabbath add the following. [If forgotten, see box below.]

רְצֵה *May it please You, HASHEM, our God — give us rest through Your commandments and through the commandment of the seventh day, this great and holy Sabbath. For this day is great and holy before You to rest on it and be content on it in love, as ordained by Your will. May it be Your will, HASHEM, our God, that there be no distress, grief, or lament on this day of our contentment. And show us, HASHEM, our God, the consolation of Zion, Your city, and the rebuilding of Jerusalem, City of Your holiness, for You are the Master of salvations and Master of consolations.*

אֱלֹהֵינוּ *Our God and God of our forefathers, may there rise, come, reach, be noted, be favored, be heard, be considered, and be remembered — the remembrance and consideration of ourselves; the remembrance of our forefathers; the remembrance of Messiah, son of David, Your servant; the remembrance of Jerusalem, the City of Your Holiness; the remembrance of Your entire people the Family of Israel — before You for deliverance, for goodness, for grace, for kindness, and for compassion, for life, and for peace on this Day of the Festival of Matzos. Remember us on it, HASHEM, our God, for goodness; consider us on it for blessing; and help us on it for life. In the matter of salvation and compassion, pity, be gracious and compassionate with us and help us, for our eyes are turned to You, because You are God, gracious and compassionate.*[1]

✣ **וּבְנֵה** *Rebuild Jerusalem, the Holy City, soon in our days. Blessed are You, HASHEM, Who rebuilds Jerusalem (in His mercy). Amen.*

(Others— *Amen.*)

[When required, the compensatory blessing is recited here.]

(1) Cf. *Nehemiah* 9:31.

Compensatory Blessings (see facing page)

If יַעֲלֶה וְיָבֹא was omitted on any day other than the Sabbath:

בָּרוּךְ אַתָּה יהוה אֱלֹהֵינוּ מֶלֶךְ הָעוֹלָם, אֲשֶׁר נָתַן יָמִים טוֹבִים לְעַמּוֹ יִשְׂרָאֵל לְשָׂשׂוֹן וּלְשִׂמְחָה, אֶת יוֹם חַג הַמַּצּוֹת הַזֶּה. בָּרוּךְ אַתָּה יהוה, מְקַדֵּשׁ יִשְׂרָאֵל וְהַזְּמַנִּים.

Blessed are You, HASHEM, our God, King of the universe, Who gave festivals to His people Israel for happiness and gladness, this day of the Festival of Matzos. Blessed are You, HASHEM, Who sanctifies Israel and the seasons.

If both רְצֵה and יַעֲלֶה וְיָבֹא were omitted on Pesach that falls on the Sabbath:

בָּרוּךְ אַתָּה יהוה אֱלֹהֵינוּ מֶלֶךְ הָעוֹלָם, אֲשֶׁר נָתַן שַׁבָּתוֹת לִמְנוּחָה לְעַמּוֹ יִשְׂרָאֵל בְּאַהֲבָה, לְאוֹת וְלִבְרִית, וְיָמִים טוֹבִים לְשָׂשׂוֹן וּלְשִׂמְחָה, אֶת יוֹם חַג הַמַּצּוֹת הַזֶּה. בָּרוּךְ אַתָּה יהוה, מְקַדֵּשׁ הַשַּׁבָּת וְיִשְׂרָאֵל וְהַזְּמַנִּים.

Blessed are You, HASHEM, our God, King of the universe, Who gave Sabbaths for contentment to His people Israel with love as a sign and as a covenant, and festivals for happiness and gladness, this day of the Festival of Matzos. Blessed are You, HASHEM, Who sanctifies the Sabbath, Israel, and the seasons.

If יַעֲלֶה וְיָבֹא was recited, but רְצֵה was omitted on the Sabbath:

בָּרוּךְ אַתָּה יהוה אֱלֹהֵינוּ מֶלֶךְ הָעוֹלָם, אֲשֶׁר נָתַן שַׁבָּתוֹת לִמְנוּחָה לְעַמּוֹ יִשְׂרָאֵל בְּאַהֲבָה, לְאוֹת וְלִבְרִית. בָּרוּךְ אַתָּה יהוה, מְקַדֵּשׁ הַשַּׁבָּת.

Blessed are You, HASHEM, our God, King of the universe, Who gave Sabbaths for contentment to His people Israel with love, as a sign and as a covenant. Blessed are You, HASHEM, Who sanctifies the Sabbath.

הטוב והמטיב

בָּרוּךְ אַתָּה יהוה אֱלֹהֵינוּ מֶלֶךְ הָעוֹלָם, הָאֵל אָבִינוּ מַלְכֵּנוּ אַדִּירֵנוּ בּוֹרְאֵנוּ גּוֹאֲלֵנוּ יוֹצְרֵנוּ קְדוֹשֵׁנוּ קְדוֹשׁ יַעֲקֹב, רוֹעֵנוּ רוֹעֵה יִשְׂרָאֵל, הַמֶּלֶךְ הַטּוֹב וְהַמֵּטִיב לַכֹּל, שֶׁבְּכָל יוֹם וָיוֹם הוּא הֵטִיב, הוּא מֵטִיב, הוּא יֵיטִיב לָנוּ. הוּא גְמָלָנוּ הוּא גוֹמְלֵנוּ הוּא יִגְמְלֵנוּ לָעַד, לְחֵן וּלְחֶסֶד וּלְרַחֲמִים וּלְרֶוַח הַצָּלָה וְהַצְלָחָה, בְּרָכָה וִישׁוּעָה נֶחָמָה פַּרְנָסָה וְכַלְכָּלָה ❖ וְרַחֲמִים וְחַיִּים וְשָׁלוֹם וְכָל טוֹב, וּמִכָּל טוּב לְעוֹלָם אַל יְחַסְּרֵנוּ. (Others — אָמֵן.)

הָרַחֲמָן הוּא יִמְלוֹךְ עָלֵינוּ לְעוֹלָם וָעֶד. הָרַחֲמָן הוּא יִתְבָּרַךְ בַּשָּׁמַיִם וּבָאָרֶץ. הָרַחֲמָן הוּא יִשְׁתַּבַּח לְדוֹר דּוֹרִים, וְיִתְפָּאַר בָּנוּ לָעַד וּלְנֵצַח נְצָחִים, וְיִתְהַדַּר בָּנוּ לָעַד וּלְעוֹלְמֵי עוֹלָמִים. הָרַחֲמָן הוּא יְפַרְנְסֵנוּ בְּכָבוֹד. הָרַחֲמָן הוּא יִשְׁבּוֹר עֻלֵּנוּ מֵעַל צַוָּארֵנוּ, וְהוּא יוֹלִיכֵנוּ קוֹמְמִיּוּת לְאַרְצֵנוּ. הָרַחֲמָן הוּא יִשְׁלַח לָנוּ בְּרָכָה מְרֻבָּה בַּבַּיִת הַזֶּה, וְעַל שֻׁלְחָן זֶה שֶׁאָכַלְנוּ עָלָיו. הָרַחֲמָן הוּא יִשְׁלַח לָנוּ אֶת אֵלִיָּהוּ הַנָּבִיא זָכוּר לַטּוֹב, וִיבַשֶּׂר לָנוּ בְּשׂוֹרוֹת טוֹבוֹת יְשׁוּעוֹת וְנֶחָמוֹת.

The Talmud (*Berachos* 46a) gives a rather lengthy text of the blessing that a guest inserts here for the host. It is quoted with minor variations in *Shulchan Aruch* (*Orach Chaim* 201) and many authorities are at a loss to explain why the prescribed text has fallen into disuse in favor of the briefer version commonly used. The text found in *Shulchan Aruch* is:

יְהִי רָצוֹן שֶׁלֹּא יֵבוֹשׁ וְלֹא יִכָּלֵם בַּעַל הַבַּיִת הַזֶּה, לֹא בָעוֹלָם הַזֶּה וְלֹא בָעוֹלָם הַבָּא, וְיַצְלִיחַ בְּכָל נְכָסָיו, וְיִהְיוּ נְכָסָיו מוּצְלָחִים וּקְרוֹבִים לָעִיר, וְאַל יִשְׁלוֹט שָׂטָן בְּמַעֲשֵׂה יָדָיו, וְאַל יִזְדַּקֵּק לְפָנָיו שׁוּם דְּבַר חֵטְא וְהִרְהוּר עָוֹן, מֵעַתָּה וְעַד עוֹלָם.

Those eating at their own table recite (including the words in parentheses that apply):

הָרַחֲמָן הוּא יְבָרֵךְ אוֹתִי (וְאֶת אִשְׁתִּי / בַּעְלִי וְאֶת זַרְעִי) וְאֶת כָּל אֲשֶׁר לִי.

Guests recite the following (children at their parents' table include the words in parentheses):

הָרַחֲמָן הוּא יְבָרֵךְ אֶת (אָבִי מוֹרִי) בַּעַל הַבַּיִת הַזֶּה, וְאֶת (אִמִּי מוֹרָתִי) בַּעֲלַת הַבַּיִת הַזֶּה, אוֹתָם וְאֶת בֵּיתָם וְאֶת זַרְעָם וְאֶת כָּל אֲשֶׁר לָהֶם.

אוֹתָנוּ וְאֶת כָּל אֲשֶׁר לָנוּ, כְּמוֹ שֶׁנִּתְבָּרְכוּ אֲבוֹתֵינוּ אַבְרָהָם יִצְחָק וְיַעֲקֹב בַּכֹּל מִכֹּל כֹּל,[1] כֵּן יְבָרֵךְ אוֹתָנוּ כֻּלָּנוּ יַחַד בִּבְרָכָה שְׁלֵמָה, וְנֹאמַר, אָמֵן.

בַּמָּרוֹם יְלַמְּדוּ עֲלֵיהֶם וְעָלֵינוּ זְכוּת, שֶׁתְּהֵא לְמִשְׁמֶרֶת שָׁלוֹם. וְנִשָּׂא בְרָכָה מֵאֵת יהוה, וּצְדָקָה מֵאֱלֹהֵי יִשְׁעֵנוּ, וְנִמְצָא חֵן וְשֵׂכֶל טוֹב בְּעֵינֵי אֱלֹהִים וְאָדָם.[2]

On the Sabbath add:

הָרַחֲמָן הוּא יַנְחִילֵנוּ יוֹם שֶׁכֻּלּוֹ שַׁבָּת וּמְנוּחָה לְחַיֵּי הָעוֹלָמִים.

FOURTH BLESSING: GOD'S GOODNESS

בָּרוּךְ *Blessed are You, HASHEM, our God, King of the universe, the Almighty, our Father, our King, our Sovereign, our Creator, our Redeemer, our Maker, our Holy One, Holy One of Jacob, our Shepherd, the Shepherd of Israel, the King Who is good and Who does good for all. For every single day He did good, He does good, and He will do good to us. He was bountiful with us, He is bountiful with us, and He will forever be bountiful with us — with grace and with kindness and with mercy, with relief, salvation, success, blessing, help, consolation, sustenance, support,* Leader— *mercy, life, peace, and all good; and of all good things may He never deprive us.* (Others— *Amen.*)

הָרַחֲמָן *The compassionate One! May He reign over us forever. The compassionate One! May He be blessed in heaven and on earth. The compassionate One! May He be praised throughout all generations, may He be glorified through us forever to the ultimate ends, and be honored through us forever and for all eternity. The compassionate One! May He sustain us in honor. The compassionate One! May He break the yoke of oppression from our necks and guide us erect to our Land. The compassionate One! May He send us abundant blessing to this house and upon this table at which we have eaten. The compassionate One! May He send us Elijah, the Prophet — he is remembered for good — to proclaim to us good tidings, salvations, and consolations.*

The Talmud (*Berachos* 46a) gives a rather lengthy text of the blessing that a guest inserts here for the host. It is quoted with minor variations in *Shulchan Aruch* (*Orach Chaim* 201) and many authorities are at a loss to explain why the prescribed text has fallen into disuse in favor of the briefer version commonly used. The text found in *Shulchan Aruch* is:

יְהִי רָצוֹן *May it be God's will that this host not be shamed nor humiliated in This World or in the World to Come. May he be successful in all his dealings. May his dealings be successful and conveniently close at hand. May no evil impediment reign over his handiwork, and may no semblance of sin or iniquitous thought attach itself to him from this time and forever.*

Those eating at their own table recite (including the words in parentheses that apply):

The compassionate One! May He bless me (my wife/husband and my children) and all that is mine.

Guests recite the following (children at their parents' table include the words in parentheses):

The compassionate One! May He bless (my father, my teacher) the master of this house, and (my mother, my teacher) lady of this house, them, their house, their family, and all that is theirs.

Ours and all that is ours — just as our forefathers Abraham, Isaac, and Jacob were blessed in everything, from everything, with everything.[1] *So may He bless us all together with a perfect blessing. And let us say: Amen!*

בַּמָּרוֹם *On high, may merit be pleaded upon them and upon us, for a safeguard of peace. May we receive a blessing from HASHEM and just kindness from the God of our salvation, and find favor and good understanding in the eyes of God and man.*[2]

On the Sabbath add:

The compassionate One! May He cause us to inherit the day which will be completely a Sabbath and rest day for eternal life.

(1) Cf. *Genesis* 24:1; 27:33; 33:11. (2) Cf. *Proverbs* 3:4.

Some add the words in parentheses on the two *Seder* nights.

הָרַחֲמָן הוּא יַנְחִילֵנוּ יוֹם שֶׁכֻּלּוֹ טוֹב (יוֹם שֶׁכֻּלּוֹ אָרוּךְ, יוֹם שֶׁצַּדִּיקִים יוֹשְׁבִים וְעַטְרוֹתֵיהֶם בְּרָאשֵׁיהֶם וְנֶהֱנִים מִזִּיו הַשְּׁכִינָה, וִיהִי חֶלְקֵנוּ עִמָּהֶם).

הָרַחֲמָן הוּא יְזַכֵּנוּ לִימוֹת הַמָּשִׁיחַ וּלְחַיֵּי הָעוֹלָם הַבָּא. מִגְדּוֹל יְשׁוּעוֹת מַלְכּוֹ וְעֹשֶׂה חֶסֶד לִמְשִׁיחוֹ לְדָוִד וּלְזַרְעוֹ עַד עוֹלָם.[1] עֹשֶׂה שָׁלוֹם בִּמְרוֹמָיו, הוּא יַעֲשֶׂה שָׁלוֹם עָלֵינוּ וְעַל כָּל יִשְׂרָאֵל. וְאִמְרוּ, אָמֵן.

יְראוּ אֶת יהוה קְדֹשָׁיו, כִּי אֵין מַחְסוֹר לִירֵאָיו. כְּפִירִים רָשׁוּ וְרָעֵבוּ, וְדֹרְשֵׁי יהוה לֹא יַחְסְרוּ כָל טוֹב.[2] הוֹדוּ לַיהוה כִּי טוֹב, כִּי לְעוֹלָם חַסְדּוֹ.[3] פּוֹתֵחַ אֶת יָדֶךָ, וּמַשְׂבִּיעַ לְכָל חַי רָצוֹן.[4] בָּרוּךְ הַגֶּבֶר אֲשֶׁר יִבְטַח בַּיהוה, וְהָיָה יהוה מִבְטַחוֹ.[5] נַעַר הָיִיתִי גַּם זָקַנְתִּי, וְלֹא רָאִיתִי צַדִּיק נֶעֱזָב, וְזַרְעוֹ מְבַקֶּשׁ לָחֶם.[6] יהוה עֹז לְעַמּוֹ יִתֵּן, יהוה יְבָרֵךְ אֶת עַמּוֹ בַשָּׁלוֹם.[7]

Upon completion of *Bircas* HaMazon the blessing over wine is recited and the third cup is drunk while reclining on the left side. It is preferable to drink the entire cup, but at the very least, most of the cup should be drained.

בָּרוּךְ אַתָּה יהוה אֱלֹהֵינוּ מֶלֶךְ הָעוֹלָם, בּוֹרֵא פְּרִי הַגָּפֶן.

The fourth cup is poured. According to most customs, the cup of Eliahu is poured at this point, after which the door is opened in accordance with the verse, 'It is a guarded night.' Then the following paragraph is recited.

שְׁפֹךְ חֲמָתְךָ אֶל הַגּוֹיִם אֲשֶׁר לֹא יְדָעוּךָ וְעַל מַמְלָכוֹת אֲשֶׁר בְּשִׁמְךָ לֹא קָרָאוּ. כִּי אָכַל אֶת יַעֲקֹב וְאֶת נָוֵהוּ הֵשַׁמּוּ.[8] שְׁפָךְ עֲלֵיהֶם זַעְמֶךָ וַחֲרוֹן אַפְּךָ יַשִּׂיגֵם.[9] תִּרְדֹּף בְּאַף וְתַשְׁמִידֵם מִתַּחַת שְׁמֵי יהוה.[10]

הלל

The door is closed and the recitation of the *Haggadah* is continued.

לֹא לָנוּ יהוה לֹא לָנוּ, כִּי לְשִׁמְךָ תֵּן כָּבוֹד, עַל חַסְדְּךָ עַל אֲמִתֶּךָ. לָמָּה יֹאמְרוּ הַגּוֹיִם, אַיֵּה נָא אֱלֹהֵיהֶם. וֵאלֹהֵינוּ בַשָּׁמָיִם, כֹּל אֲשֶׁר חָפֵץ עָשָׂה. עֲצַבֵּיהֶם כֶּסֶף וְזָהָב, מַעֲשֵׂה יְדֵי אָדָם. פֶּה לָהֶם וְלֹא יְדַבֵּרוּ, עֵינַיִם לָהֶם וְלֹא יִרְאוּ. אָזְנַיִם לָהֶם וְלֹא יִשְׁמָעוּ, אַף לָהֶם וְלֹא יְרִיחוּן. יְדֵיהֶם וְלֹא יְמִישׁוּן, רַגְלֵיהֶם וְלֹא יְהַלֵּכוּ, לֹא יֶהְגּוּ בִּגְרוֹנָם. כְּמוֹהֶם יִהְיוּ עֹשֵׂיהֶם, כֹּל אֲשֶׁר בֹּטֵחַ בָּהֶם. יִשְׂרָאֵל בְּטַח בַּיהוה, עֶזְרָם וּמָגִנָּם הוּא. בֵּית אַהֲרֹן בִּטְחוּ בַיהוה, עֶזְרָם וּמָגִנָּם הוּא. יִרְאֵי יהוה בִּטְחוּ בַיהוה, עֶזְרָם וּמָגִנָּם הוּא.

Some add the words in parentheses on the two *Seder* nights.

הָרַחֲמָן *The compassionate One! May He cause us to inherit the day which is completely good, (that everlasting day, the day when the just will sit with crowns on their heads, enjoying the reflection of God's majesty — and may our portion be with them!).*

הָרַחֲמָן *The compassionate One! May He make us worthy of the days of Messiah and the life of the World to Come. He Who is a tower of salvations to His king and does kindness for His anointed, to David and to his descendants forever.[1] He Who makes peace in His heights, may He make peace upon us and upon all Israel. Now respond: Amen!*

יְראוּ *Fear* HASHEM, *you — His holy ones — for there is no deprivation for His reverent ones. Young lions may want and hunger, but those who seek* HASHEM *will not lack any good.[2] Give thanks to God for He is good; His kindness endures forever.[3] You open Your hand and satisfy the desire of every living thing.[4] Blessed is the man who trusts in* HASHEM, *then* HASHEM *will be his security.[5] I was a youth and also have aged, and I have not seen a righteous man forsaken, with his children begging for bread.[6]* HASHEM *will give might to His people;* HASHEM *will bless His people with peace.[7]*

Upon completion of *Bircas HaMazon* the blessing over wine is recited and the third cup is drunk while reclining on the left side. It is preferable to drink the entire cup, but at the very least, most of the cup should be drained.

בָּרוּךְ *Blessed are You,* HASHEM, *our God, King of the universe, Who creates the fruit of the vine.*

The fourth cup is poured. According to most customs, the cup of Eliahu is poured at this point, after which the door is opened in accordance with the verse, 'It is a guarded night.' Then the following paragraph is recited.

שְׁפֹךְ *Pour Your wrath upon the nations that do not recognize You and upon the kingdoms that do not invoke Your Name. For they have devoured Yaakov and destroyed His habitation.[8] Pour Your anger upon them and let Your fiery wrath overtake them.[9] Pursue them with wrath and annihilate them from beneath the heavens of* HASHEM.[10]

HALLEL

The door is closed and the recitation of the *Haggadah* is continued.

לֹא לָנוּ *Not for our sake,* HASHEM, *not for our sake, but for Your Name's sake give glory, for Your kindness and for Your truth! Why should the nations say, 'Where is their God now?' Our God is in the heavens; whatever He pleases, He does! Their idols are silver and gold, the handiwork of man. They have a mouth, but cannot speak; they have eyes, but cannot see. They have ears, but cannot hear; they have a nose, but cannot smell. Their hands — they cannot feel; their feet — they cannot walk; they cannot utter a sound from their throat. Those who make them should become like them, whoever trusts in them! O Israel, trust in* HASHEM; *— their help and their shield is He! House of Aaron, trust in* HASHEM; *their help and their shield is He! You who fear* HASHEM, *trust in* HASHEM; *their help and their shield is He!*

---

(1) *Psalms* 18:51. (2) 34:10-11. (3) 136:1 et al. (4) 145:16. (5) *Jeremiah* 17:7. (6) *Psalms* 37:25. (7) 29:11. (8) 79:6-7. (9) 69:25. (10) *Lamentations* 3:66.

יְהוָה זְכָרָנוּ יְבָרֵךְ, יְבָרֵךְ אֶת בֵּית יִשְׂרָאֵל, יְבָרֵךְ אֶת בֵּית אַהֲרֹן. יְבָרֵךְ יִרְאֵי יְהוָה, הַקְּטַנִּים עִם הַגְּדֹלִים. יֹסֵף יְהוָה עֲלֵיכֶם, עֲלֵיכֶם וְעַל בְּנֵיכֶם. בְּרוּכִים אַתֶּם לַיהוָה, עֹשֵׂה שָׁמַיִם וָאָרֶץ. הַשָּׁמַיִם שָׁמַיִם לַיהוָה, וְהָאָרֶץ נָתַן לִבְנֵי אָדָם. לֹא הַמֵּתִים יְהַלְלוּ יָהּ, וְלֹא כָּל יֹרְדֵי דוּמָה. וַאֲנַחְנוּ נְבָרֵךְ יָהּ, מֵעַתָּה וְעַד עוֹלָם, הַלְלוּיָהּ.

אָהַבְתִּי כִּי יִשְׁמַע יְהוָה, אֶת קוֹלִי תַּחֲנוּנָי. כִּי הִטָּה אָזְנוֹ לִי, וּבְיָמַי אֶקְרָא. אֲפָפוּנִי חֶבְלֵי מָוֶת, וּמְצָרֵי שְׁאוֹל מְצָאוּנִי, צָרָה וְיָגוֹן אֶמְצָא. וּבְשֵׁם יְהוָה אֶקְרָא, אָנָּה יְהוָה מַלְּטָה נַפְשִׁי. חַנּוּן יְהוָה וְצַדִּיק, וֵאלֹהֵינוּ מְרַחֵם. שֹׁמֵר פְּתָאיִם יְהוָה, דַּלּוֹתִי וְלִי יְהוֹשִׁיעַ. שׁוּבִי נַפְשִׁי לִמְנוּחָיְכִי, כִּי יְהוָה גָּמַל עָלָיְכִי. כִּי חִלַּצְתָּ נַפְשִׁי מִמָּוֶת, אֶת עֵינִי מִן דִּמְעָה, אֶת רַגְלִי מִדֶּחִי. אֶתְהַלֵּךְ לִפְנֵי יְהוָה, בְּאַרְצוֹת הַחַיִּים. הֶאֱמַנְתִּי כִּי אֲדַבֵּר, אֲנִי עָנִיתִי מְאֹד. אֲנִי אָמַרְתִּי בְחָפְזִי, כָּל הָאָדָם כֹּזֵב.

מָה אָשִׁיב לַיהוָה, כָּל תַּגְמוּלוֹהִי עָלָי. כּוֹס יְשׁוּעוֹת אֶשָּׂא, וּבְשֵׁם יְהוָה אֶקְרָא. נְדָרַי לַיהוָה אֲשַׁלֵּם, נֶגְדָה נָּא לְכָל עַמּוֹ. יָקָר בְּעֵינֵי יְהוָה, הַמָּוְתָה לַחֲסִידָיו. אָנָּה יְהוָה כִּי אֲנִי עַבְדֶּךָ, אֲנִי עַבְדְּךָ, בֶּן אֲמָתֶךָ, פִּתַּחְתָּ לְמוֹסֵרָי. לְךָ אֶזְבַּח זֶבַח תּוֹדָה, וּבְשֵׁם יְהוָה אֶקְרָא. נְדָרַי לַיהוָה אֲשַׁלֵּם, נֶגְדָה נָּא לְכָל עַמּוֹ. בְּחַצְרוֹת בֵּית יְהוָה, בְּתוֹכֵכִי יְרוּשָׁלָיִם הַלְלוּיָהּ.

הַלְלוּ אֶת יְהוָה, כָּל גּוֹיִם, שַׁבְּחוּהוּ כָּל הָאֻמִּים. כִּי גָבַר עָלֵינוּ חַסְדּוֹ, וֶאֱמֶת יְהוָה לְעוֹלָם, הַלְלוּיָהּ.

הוֹדוּ לַיהוָה כִּי טוֹב,   כִּי לְעוֹלָם חַסְדּוֹ.
יֹאמַר נָא יִשְׂרָאֵל,   כִּי לְעוֹלָם חַסְדּוֹ.
יֹאמְרוּ נָא בֵית אַהֲרֹן,   כִּי לְעוֹלָם חַסְדּוֹ.
יֹאמְרוּ נָא יִרְאֵי יְהוָה,   כִּי לְעוֹלָם חַסְדּוֹ.

מִן הַמֵּצַר קָרָאתִי יָּהּ, עָנָנִי בַמֶּרְחָב יָהּ. יְהוָה לִי לֹא אִירָא, מַה יַּעֲשֶׂה לִי אָדָם. יְהוָה לִי בְּעֹזְרָי, וַאֲנִי אֶרְאֶה בְשֹׂנְאָי. טוֹב לַחֲסוֹת בַּיהוָה, מִבְּטֹחַ בָּאָדָם. טוֹב לַחֲסוֹת בַּיהוָה, מִבְּטֹחַ בִּנְדִיבִים. כָּל גּוֹיִם סְבָבוּנִי, בְּשֵׁם יְהוָה כִּי אֲמִילַם. סַבּוּנִי גַם סְבָבוּנִי, בְּשֵׁם יְהוָה כִּי אֲמִילַם. סַבּוּנִי כִדְבֹרִים דֹּעֲכוּ כְּאֵשׁ קוֹצִים, בְּשֵׁם יְהוָה כִּי אֲמִילַם. דָּחֹה דְחִיתַנִי לִנְפֹּל, וַיהוָה עֲזָרָנִי. עָזִּי וְזִמְרָת יָהּ, וַיְהִי לִי לִישׁוּעָה. קוֹל רִנָּה וִישׁוּעָה, בְּאָהֳלֵי צַדִּיקִים, יְמִין יְהוָה עֹשָׂה חָיִל. יְמִין יְהוָה רוֹמֵמָה, יְמִין יְהוָה עֹשָׂה חָיִל. לֹא אָמוּת כִּי אֶחְיֶה, וַאֲסַפֵּר מַעֲשֵׂי יָהּ. יַסֹּר יִסְּרַנִּי יָּהּ, וְלַמָּוֶת לֹא נְתָנָנִי. פִּתְחוּ לִי שַׁעֲרֵי צֶדֶק, אָבֹא בָם אוֹדֶה יָהּ. זֶה הַשַּׁעַר לַיהוָה, צַדִּיקִים יָבֹאוּ בוֹ. אוֹדְךָ כִּי עֲנִיתָנִי, וַתְּהִי לִי לִישׁוּעָה. אוֹדְךָ כִּי עֲנִיתָנִי, וַתְּהִי לִי לִישׁוּעָה. אֶבֶן מָאֲסוּ הַבּוֹנִים,

יהוה *HASHEM Who has remembered us will bless — He will bless the House of Israel; He will bless the House of Aharon; He will bless those who fear HASHEM, the small as well as the great. May HASHEM increase upon you, upon you and upon your children! You are blessed of HASHEM, maker of heaven and earth. As for the heavens — the heavens are HASHEM's, but the earth He has given to mankind. Neither the dead can praise God, nor any who descend into silence; but we will bless God from this time and forever. Halleluyah!*

אָהַבְתִּי *I love Him, for HASHEM hears my voice, my supplications. As He has inclined His ear to me, so in my days shall I call. The pains of death encircled me; the confines of the grave have found me; trouble and sorrow I would find. Then I would invoke the Name of HASHEM: 'Please HASHEM, save my soul.' Gracious is HASHEM and righteous, our God is merciful. HASHEM protects the simple; I was brought low, but He saved me. Return, my soul, to your rest; for HASHEM has been kind to you. For You have delivered my soul from death, my eyes from tears, my feet from stumbling. I shall walk before HASHEM in the lands of the living. I have kept faith although I say: 'I suffer exceedingly.' I said in my haste: 'All mankind is deceitful.'*

מָה אָשִׁיב *How can I repay HASHEM for all His kindness to me? I will raise the cup of salvations and the Name of HASHEM I will invoke. My vows to HASHEM I will pay, in the presence, now, of His entire people. Difficult in the eyes of HASHEM is the death of His devout ones. Please, HASHEM — for I am Your servant, I am Your servant, son of Your handmaid — You have released my bonds. To You I will sacrifice thanksgiving offerings, and the name of HASHEM I will invoke. My vows to HASHEM I will pay, in the presence, now, of His entire people. In the courtyards of the House of HASHEM, in your midst, O Jerusalem, Halleluyah!*

הַלְלוּ *Praise HASHEM, all nations; praise Him, all the states! For His kindness has overwhelmed us, and the truth of HASHEM is eternal, Halleluyah!*

הודו *Give thanks to HASHEM for He is good;*	*His kindness endures forever!*
Let Israel say:	*His kindness endures forever!*
Let the House of Aharon say:	*His kindness endures forever!*
Let those who fear HASHEM say:	*His kindness endures forever!*

מִן הַמֵּצַר *From the straits did I call upon God; God answered me with expansiveness. HASHEM is with me, I have no fear; how can man affect me? HASHEM is with me through my helpers; therefore I can face my foes. It is better to take refuge in HASHEM than to rely on man. It is better to take refuge in HASHEM than to rely on nobles. All the nations surround me; in the Name of HASHEM I cut them down! They encircle me, they also surround me; in the Name of HASHEM I cut them down! They encircle me like bees, but they are extinguished as a fire does thorns; in the Name of HASHEM I cut them down! You pushed me hard that I might fall, but HASHEM assisted me. God is my might and my praise, and He was a salvation for me. The sound of rejoicing and salvation is in the tents of the righteous: 'HASHEM's right hand does valiantly. HASHEM's right hand is raised triumphantly; HASHEM's right hand does valiantly!' I shall not die! But I shall live and relate the deeds of God. God has chastened me exceedingly, but He did not let me die. Open for me the gates of righteousness, I will enter them and thank God. This is the gate of HASHEM; the righteous shall enter through it. I thank You for You have answered me and become my salvation. I thank You for You have answered me and become my salvation. The stone the builders despised has*

הָיְתָה לְרֹאשׁ פִּנָּה. אֶבֶן מָאֲסוּ הַבּוֹנִים, הָיְתָה לְרֹאשׁ פִּנָּה. מֵאֵת יהוה הָיְתָה זֹּאת, הִיא נִפְלָאת בְּעֵינֵינוּ. מֵאֵת יהוה הָיְתָה זֹּאת, הִיא נִפְלָאת בְּעֵינֵינוּ. זֶה הַיּוֹם עָשָׂה יהוה, נָגִילָה וְנִשְׂמְחָה בוֹ. זֶה הַיּוֹם עָשָׂה יהוה, נָגִילָה וְנִשְׂמְחָה בוֹ.

אָנָּא יהוה הוֹשִׁיעָה נָּא. אָנָּא יהוה הוֹשִׁיעָה נָּא.
אָנָּא יהוה הַצְלִיחָה נָא. אָנָּא יהוה הַצְלִיחָה נָא.

בָּרוּךְ הַבָּא בְּשֵׁם יהוה, בֵּרַכְנוּכֶם מִבֵּית יהוה. בָּרוּךְ הַבָּא בְּשֵׁם יהוה, בֵּרַכְנוּכֶם מִבֵּית יהוה. אֵל יהוה וַיָּאֶר לָנוּ, אִסְרוּ חַג בַּעֲבֹתִים, עַד קַרְנוֹת הַמִּזְבֵּחַ. אֵל יהוה וַיָּאֶר לָנוּ, אִסְרוּ חַג בַּעֲבֹתִים, עַד קַרְנוֹת הַמִּזְבֵּחַ. אֵלִי אַתָּה וְאוֹדֶךָּ, אֱלֹהַי אֲרוֹמְמֶךָּ. אֵלִי אַתָּה וְאוֹדֶךָּ, אֱלֹהַי אֲרוֹמְמֶךָּ. הוֹדוּ לַיהוה כִּי טוֹב, כִּי לְעוֹלָם חַסְדּוֹ. הוֹדוּ לַיהוה כִּי טוֹב, כִּי לְעוֹלָם חַסְדּוֹ.

יְהַלְלוּךָ יהוה אֱלֹהֵינוּ כָּל מַעֲשֶׂיךָ, וַחֲסִידֶיךָ צַדִּיקִים עוֹשֵׂי רְצוֹנֶךָ, וְכָל עַמְּךָ בֵּית יִשְׂרָאֵל בְּרִנָּה יוֹדוּ וִיבָרְכוּ וִישַׁבְּחוּ וִיפָאֲרוּ וִירוֹמְמוּ וְיַעֲרִיצוּ וְיַקְדִּישׁוּ וְיַמְלִיכוּ אֶת שִׁמְךָ מַלְכֵּנוּ, כִּי לְךָ טוֹב לְהוֹדוֹת וּלְשִׁמְךָ נָאֶה לְזַמֵּר, כִּי מֵעוֹלָם וְעַד עוֹלָם אַתָּה אֵל.

הוֹדוּ לַיהוה כִּי טוֹב — כִּי לְעוֹלָם חַסְדּוֹ.
הוֹדוּ לֵאלֹהֵי הָאֱלֹהִים — כִּי לְעוֹלָם חַסְדּוֹ.
הוֹדוּ לַאֲדֹנֵי הָאֲדֹנִים — כִּי לְעוֹלָם חַסְדּוֹ.
לְעֹשֵׂה נִפְלָאוֹת גְּדֹלוֹת לְבַדּוֹ — כִּי לְעוֹלָם חַסְדּוֹ.
לְעֹשֵׂה הַשָּׁמַיִם בִּתְבוּנָה — כִּי לְעוֹלָם חַסְדּוֹ.
לְרֹקַע הָאָרֶץ עַל הַמָּיִם — כִּי לְעוֹלָם חַסְדּוֹ.
לְעֹשֵׂה אוֹרִים גְּדֹלִים — כִּי לְעוֹלָם חַסְדּוֹ.
אֶת הַשֶּׁמֶשׁ לְמֶמְשֶׁלֶת בַּיּוֹם — כִּי לְעוֹלָם חַסְדּוֹ.
אֶת הַיָּרֵחַ וְכוֹכָבִים לְמֶמְשְׁלוֹת בַּלָּיְלָה — כִּי לְעוֹלָם חַסְדּוֹ.
לְמַכֵּה מִצְרַיִם בִּבְכוֹרֵיהֶם — כִּי לְעוֹלָם חַסְדּוֹ.
וַיּוֹצֵא יִשְׂרָאֵל מִתּוֹכָם — כִּי לְעוֹלָם חַסְדּוֹ.
בְּיָד חֲזָקָה וּבִזְרוֹעַ נְטוּיָה — כִּי לְעוֹלָם חַסְדּוֹ.
לְגֹזֵר יַם סוּף לִגְזָרִים — כִּי לְעוֹלָם חַסְדּוֹ.
וְהֶעֱבִיר יִשְׂרָאֵל בְּתוֹכוֹ — כִּי לְעוֹלָם חַסְדּוֹ.
וְנִעֵר פַּרְעֹה וְחֵילוֹ בְיַם סוּף — כִּי לְעוֹלָם חַסְדּוֹ.
לְמוֹלִיךְ עַמּוֹ בַּמִּדְבָּר — כִּי לְעוֹלָם חַסְדּוֹ.
לְמַכֵּה מְלָכִים גְּדֹלִים — כִּי לְעוֹלָם חַסְדּוֹ.
וַיַּהֲרֹג מְלָכִים אַדִּירִים — כִּי לְעוֹלָם חַסְדּוֹ.

become the cornerstone. The stone the builders despised has become the cornerstone. This emanated from HASHEM; it is wondrous in our eyes. This emanated from HASHEM; it is wondrous in our eyes. This is the day HASHEM has made; let us rejoice and be glad on it. This is the day HASHEM has made; let us rejoice and be glad on it.

אָנָּא *Please, HASHEM, save now! Please, HASHEM, save now!*
Please, HASHEM, bring success now! Please, HASHEM, bring success now!

בָּרוּךְ *Blessed is he who comes in the Name of HASHEM; we bless you from the House of HASHEM. Blessed is he who comes in the Name of HASHEM; we bless you from the House of HASHEM. HASHEM is God, He illuminated for us; bind the festival offering with cords until the corners of the Altar. HASHEM is God, He illuminated for us; bind the festival offering with cords until the corners of the Altar. You are my God, and I will thank You; my God, I will exalt You. You are my God, and I will thank You; my God, I will exalt You. Give thanks to HASHEM, for He is good; His kindness endures forever. Give thanks to HASHEM, for He is good; His kindness endures forever.*

יְהַלְלוּךָ *All Your works shall praise You, HASHEM our God. And Your devout ones, the righteous, who do Your will, and Your entire people, the House of Israel, with glad song will thank, bless, praise, glorify, exalt, extol, sanctify, and proclaim the sovereignty of Your Name, our King. For to You it is fitting to give thanks, and unto Your Name it is proper to sing praises, for from This World to the World to Come You are God.*

הוֹדוּ *Give thanks to HASHEM for He is good,*
for His kindness endures forever.
Give thanks to the God of the heavenly powers,
for His kindness endures forever.
Give thanks to the Lord of the lords, for His kindness endures forever.
To Him Who alone performs great wonders, for His kindness endures forever.
To Him Who made the heavens with understanding,
for His kindness endures forever.
To Him Who spread out the earth upon the waters,
for His kindness endures forever.
To Him Who made great lights, for His kindness endures forever.
The sun for the reign of the day, for His kindness endures forever.
The moon and the stars for the reign of the night,
for His kindness endures forever.
To Him Who smote Egypt through their firstborn,
for His kindness endures forever.
And brought Israel forth from their midst, for His kindness endures forever.
With strong hand and outstretched arm, for His kindness endures forever.
To Him Who divided the Sea of Reeds into parts,
for His kindness endures forever.
And caused Israel to pass through it, for His kindness endures forever.
And threw Pharaoh and his army into the Sea of Reeds,
for His kindness endures forever.
To Him Who led His people through the wilderness,
for His kindness endures forever.
To Him Who smote great kings, for His kindness endures forever.
And slew mighty kings, for His kindness endures forever.

לְסִיחוֹן מֶלֶךְ הָאֱמֹרִי כִּי לְעוֹלָם חַסְדּוֹ.
וּלְעוֹג מֶלֶךְ הַבָּשָׁן כִּי לְעוֹלָם חַסְדּוֹ.
וְנָתַן אַרְצָם לְנַחֲלָה כִּי לְעוֹלָם חַסְדּוֹ.
נַחֲלָה לְיִשְׂרָאֵל עַבְדּוֹ כִּי לְעוֹלָם חַסְדּוֹ.
שֶׁבְּשִׁפְלֵנוּ זָכַר לָנוּ כִּי לְעוֹלָם חַסְדּוֹ.
וַיִּפְרְקֵנוּ מִצָּרֵינוּ כִּי לְעוֹלָם חַסְדּוֹ.
נֹתֵן לֶחֶם לְכָל בָּשָׂר כִּי לְעוֹלָם חַסְדּוֹ.
הוֹדוּ לְאֵל הַשָּׁמָיִם כִּי לְעוֹלָם חַסְדּוֹ.

נִשְׁמַת כָּל חַי תְּבָרֵךְ אֶת שִׁמְךָ יהוה אֱלֹהֵינוּ וְרוּחַ כָּל בָּשָׂר תְּפָאֵר וּתְרוֹמֵם זִכְרְךָ מַלְכֵּנוּ תָּמִיד. מִן הָעוֹלָם וְעַד הָעוֹלָם אַתָּה אֵל וּמִבַּלְעָדֶיךָ אֵין לָנוּ מֶלֶךְ גּוֹאֵל וּמוֹשִׁיעַ פּוֹדֶה וּמַצִּיל וּמְפַרְנֵס וּמְרַחֵם בְּכָל עֵת צָרָה וְצוּקָה. אֵין לָנוּ מֶלֶךְ אֶלָּא אָתָּה. אֱלֹהֵי הָרִאשׁוֹנִים וְהָאַחֲרוֹנִים אֱלוֹהַּ כָּל בְּרִיּוֹת אֲדוֹן כָּל תּוֹלָדוֹת הַמְּהֻלָּל בְּרֹב הַתִּשְׁבָּחוֹת הַמְנַהֵג עוֹלָמוֹ בְּחֶסֶד וּבְרִיּוֹתָיו בְּרַחֲמִים וַיהוה לֹא יָנוּם וְלֹא יִישָׁן הַמְּעוֹרֵר יְשֵׁנִים וְהַמֵּקִיץ נִרְדָּמִים וְהַמֵּשִׂיחַ אִלְּמִים וְהַמַּתִּיר אֲסוּרִים וְהַסּוֹמֵךְ נוֹפְלִים וְהַזּוֹקֵף כְּפוּפִים לְךָ לְבַדְּךָ אֲנַחְנוּ מוֹדִים. אִלּוּ פִינוּ מָלֵא שִׁירָה כַּיָּם, וּלְשׁוֹנֵנוּ רִנָּה כַּהֲמוֹן גַּלָּיו, וְשִׂפְתוֹתֵינוּ שֶׁבַח כְּמֶרְחֲבֵי רָקִיעַ, וְעֵינֵינוּ מְאִירוֹת כַּשֶּׁמֶשׁ וְכַיָּרֵחַ, וְיָדֵינוּ פְרוּשׂוֹת כְּנִשְׁרֵי שָׁמָיִם, וְרַגְלֵינוּ קַלּוֹת כָּאַיָּלוֹת, אֵין אֲנַחְנוּ מַסְפִּיקִים לְהוֹדוֹת לְךָ יהוה אֱלֹהֵינוּ וֵאלֹהֵי אֲבוֹתֵינוּ, וּלְבָרֵךְ אֶת שְׁמֶךָ עַל אַחַת מֵאָלֶף אֶלֶף אַלְפֵי אֲלָפִים וְרִבֵּי רְבָבוֹת פְּעָמִים הַטּוֹבוֹת שֶׁעָשִׂיתָ עִם אֲבוֹתֵינוּ וְעִמָּנוּ. מִמִּצְרַיִם גְּאַלְתָּנוּ יהוה אֱלֹהֵינוּ, וּמִבֵּית עֲבָדִים פְּדִיתָנוּ, בְּרָעָב זַנְתָּנוּ, וּבְשָׂבָע כִּלְכַּלְתָּנוּ, מֵחֶרֶב הִצַּלְתָּנוּ, וּמִדֶּבֶר מִלַּטְתָּנוּ, וּמֵחֳלָיִם רָעִים וְנֶאֱמָנִים דִּלִּיתָנוּ. עַד הֵנָּה עֲזָרוּנוּ רַחֲמֶיךָ, וְלֹא עֲזָבוּנוּ חֲסָדֶיךָ, וְאַל תִּטְּשֵׁנוּ יהוה אֱלֹהֵינוּ לָנֶצַח. עַל כֵּן אֵבָרִים שֶׁפִּלַּגְתָּ בָּנוּ, וְרוּחַ וּנְשָׁמָה שֶׁנָּפַחְתָּ בְּאַפֵּינוּ, וְלָשׁוֹן אֲשֶׁר שַׂמְתָּ בְּפִינוּ, הֵן הֵם יוֹדוּ וִיבָרְכוּ וִישַׁבְּחוּ וִיפָאֲרוּ וִירוֹמְמוּ וְיַעֲרִיצוּ וְיַקְדִּישׁוּ וְיַמְלִיכוּ אֶת שִׁמְךָ מַלְכֵּנוּ. כִּי כָל פֶּה לְךָ יוֹדֶה, וְכָל לָשׁוֹן לְךָ תִשָּׁבַע, וְכָל בֶּרֶךְ לְךָ תִכְרַע, וְכָל קוֹמָה לְפָנֶיךָ תִשְׁתַּחֲוֶה, וְכָל לְבָבוֹת יִירָאוּךָ, וְכָל קֶרֶב וּכְלָיוֹת יְזַמְּרוּ לִשְׁמֶךָ. כַּדָּבָר שֶׁכָּתוּב, כָּל עַצְמֹתַי תֹּאמַרְנָה, יהוה מִי כָמוֹךָ. מַצִּיל עָנִי מֵחָזָק מִמֶּנּוּ, וְעָנִי וְאֶבְיוֹן מִגֹּזְלוֹ. מִי יִדְמֶה לָּךְ, וּמִי יִשְׁוֶה לָּךְ, וּמִי יַעֲרָךְ לָךְ, הָאֵל הַגָּדוֹל הַגִּבּוֹר וְהַנּוֹרָא אֵל עֶלְיוֹן קֹנֵה שָׁמַיִם וָאָרֶץ. נְהַלֶּלְךָ וּנְשַׁבֵּחֲךָ וּנְפָאֶרְךָ וּנְבָרֵךְ אֶת שֵׁם קָדְשֶׁךָ, כָּאָמוּר, לְדָוִד בָּרְכִי נַפְשִׁי אֶת יהוה, וְכָל קְרָבַי אֶת שֵׁם קָדְשׁוֹ.

הָאֵל בְּתַעֲצֻמוֹת עֻזֶּךָ, הַגָּדוֹל בִּכְבוֹד שְׁמֶךָ, הַגִּבּוֹר לָנֶצַח וְהַנּוֹרָא בְּנוֹרְאוֹתֶיךָ, הַמֶּלֶךְ הַיּוֹשֵׁב עַל כִּסֵּא רָם וְנִשָּׂא.

שׁוֹכֵן עַד מָרוֹם וְקָדוֹשׁ שְׁמוֹ. וְכָתוּב רַנְּנוּ צַדִּיקִים בַּיהוה לַיְשָׁרִים נָאוָה תְהִלָּה. בְּפִי יְשָׁרִים תִּתְהַלָּל, וּבְדִבְרֵי צַדִּיקִים תִּתְבָּרַךְ,

Sichon, king of the Emorites, — for His kindness endures forever.
And Og, king of Bashan, — for His kindness endures forever.
And presented their land as a heritage, — for His kindness endures forever.
A heritage for Israel, His servant, — for His kindness endures forever.
In our lowliness He remembered us, — for His kindness endures forever.
And released us from our tormentors, — for His kindness endures forever.
He gives nourishment to all flesh, — for His kindness endures forever.
Give thanks to God of the heavens, — for His kindness endures forever.

נִשְׁמַת *The soul of every living being shall bless Your Name, HASHEM our God; the spirit of all flesh shall always glorify and exalt Your remembrance, our King. From This World to the World to Come, You are God, and other than You we have no king, redeemer or savior. Liberator, Rescuer, Sustainer and Merciful One in every time of distress and anguish, we have no king but You! — God of the first and of the last, God of all creatures, Master of all generations, Who is extolled through a multitude of praises, Who guides His world with kindness and His creatures with mercy. HASHEM neither slumbers nor sleeps. He Who rouses the sleepers and awakens the slumberers, Who makes the mute speak and releases the bound; Who supports the fallen and straightens the bent. To You alone we give thanks. Were our mouth as full of song as the sea, and our tongue as full of joyous song as its multitude of waves, and our lips as full of praise as the breadth of the heavens, and our eyes as brilliant as the sun and the moon, and our hands as outspread as eagles of the sky and our feet as swift as hinds — we still could not thank You sufficiently, HASHEM our God and God of our forefathers, and to bless Your Name for even one of the thousand thousand, thousands of thousands and myriad myriads of favors that You performed for our ancestors and for us. You redeemed us from Egypt, HASHEM our God, and liberated us from the house of bondage. In famine You nourished us and in plenty You sustained us. From sword You saved us; from plague You let us escape; and from severe and enduring diseases You spared us. Until now Your mercy has helped us, and Your kindness has not forsaken us. Do not abandon us, HASHEM our God, forever. Therefore, the organs that You set within us, and the spirit and soul that You breathed into our nostrils, and the tongue that You placed in our mouth — all of them shall thank and bless, praise and glorify, exalt and revere, sanctify and declare the sovereignty of Your Name, our King. For every mouth shall offer thanks to You; every tongue shall vow allegiance to You; every knee shall bend to You; every erect spine shall prostrate itself before You; all hearts shall fear You, and all innermost feelings and thoughts shall sing praises to Your name, as it is written: "All my bones shall say: 'HASHEM, who is like You?' You save the poor man from one stronger than he, the poor and destitute from one who would rob him." Who is like unto You? Who is equal to You? Who can be compared to You? O great, mighty, and awesome God, the supreme God, Creator of heaven and earth. We shall laud, praise, and glorify You and bless Your holy Name, as it is said: 'Of David: Bless HASHEM, O my soul, and let all my innermost being bless His holy Name!'*

הָאֵל *O God, in the omnipotence of Your strength, great in the glory of Your Name, mighty forever and awesome through Your awesome deeds, O King enthroned upon a high and lofty throne!*

שׁוֹכֵן עַד *He Who abides forever, exalted and holy is His Name. And it is written: 'Sing joyfully, O righteous, before HASHEM; for the upright, praise is fitting.' By the mouth of the upright shall You be lauded; by the words of*

וּבִלְשׁוֹן חֲסִידִים תִּתְרוֹמָם, וּבְקֶרֶב קְדוֹשִׁים תִּתְקַדָּשׁ.

וּבְמַקְהֲלוֹת רִבְבוֹת עַמְּךָ בֵּית יִשְׂרָאֵל, בְּרִנָּה יִתְפָּאַר שִׁמְךָ מַלְכֵּנוּ בְּכָל דּוֹר וָדוֹר, שֶׁכֵּן חוֹבַת כָּל הַיְּצוּרִים לְפָנֶיךָ יהוה אֱלֹהֵינוּ וֵאלֹהֵי אֲבוֹתֵינוּ, לְהוֹדוֹת לְהַלֵּל לְשַׁבֵּחַ לְפָאֵר לְרוֹמֵם לְהַדֵּר לְבָרֵךְ לְעַלֵּה וּלְקַלֵּס, עַל כָּל דִּבְרֵי שִׁירוֹת וְתִשְׁבְּחוֹת דָּוִד בֶּן יִשַׁי עַבְדְּךָ מְשִׁיחֶךָ.

יִשְׁתַּבַּח שִׁמְךָ לָעַד מַלְכֵּנוּ, הָאֵל הַמֶּלֶךְ הַגָּדוֹל וְהַקָּדוֹשׁ בַּשָּׁמַיִם וּבָאָרֶץ, כִּי לְךָ נָאֶה, יהוה אֱלֹהֵינוּ וֵאלֹהֵי אֲבוֹתֵינוּ, שִׁיר וּשְׁבָחָה הַלֵּל וְזִמְרָה עֹז וּמֶמְשָׁלָה נֶצַח גְּדֻלָּה וּגְבוּרָה תְּהִלָּה וְתִפְאֶרֶת קְדֻשָּׁה וּמַלְכוּת, בְּרָכוֹת וְהוֹדָאוֹת מֵעַתָּה וְעַד עוֹלָם. בָּרוּךְ אַתָּה יהוה, אֵל מֶלֶךְ גָּדוֹל בַּתִּשְׁבָּחוֹת, אֵל הַהוֹדָאוֹת, אֲדוֹן הַנִּפְלָאוֹת, הַבּוֹחֵר בְּשִׁירֵי זִמְרָה, מֶלֶךְ אֵל חֵי הָעוֹלָמִים.

The blessing over wine is recited and the fourth cup is drunk while reclining to the left side. It is preferable that the entire cup be drunk.

בָּרוּךְ אַתָּה יהוה אֱלֹהֵינוּ מֶלֶךְ הָעוֹלָם, בּוֹרֵא פְּרִי הַגָּפֶן.

After drinking the fourth cup, the concluding blessing is recited. On Shabbos include the passage in parentheses.

בָּרוּךְ אַתָּה יהוה אֱלֹהֵינוּ מֶלֶךְ הָעוֹלָם, עַל הַגֶּפֶן וְעַל פְּרִי הַגֶּפֶן, וְעַל תְּנוּבַת הַשָּׂדֶה, וְעַל אֶרֶץ חֶמְדָּה טוֹבָה וּרְחָבָה שֶׁרָצִיתָ וְהִנְחַלְתָּ לַאֲבוֹתֵינוּ לֶאֱכוֹל מִפִּרְיָהּ וְלִשְׂבּוֹעַ מִטּוּבָהּ. רַחֶם נָא יהוה אֱלֹהֵינוּ עַל יִשְׂרָאֵל עַמֶּךָ, וְעַל יְרוּשָׁלַיִם עִירֶךָ, וְעַל צִיּוֹן מִשְׁכַּן כְּבוֹדֶךָ, וְעַל מִזְבְּחֶךָ וְעַל הֵיכָלֶךָ. וּבְנֵה יְרוּשָׁלַיִם עִיר הַקֹּדֶשׁ בִּמְהֵרָה בְיָמֵינוּ, וְהַעֲלֵנוּ לְתוֹכָהּ, וְשַׂמְּחֵנוּ בְּבִנְיָנָהּ, וְנֹאכַל מִפִּרְיָהּ, וְנִשְׂבַּע מִטּוּבָהּ, וּנְבָרֶכְךָ עָלֶיהָ בִּקְדֻשָּׁה וּבְטָהֳרָה. [וּרְצֵה וְהַחֲלִיצֵנוּ בְּיוֹם הַשַּׁבָּת הַזֶּה] וְשַׂמְּחֵנוּ בְּיוֹם חַג הַמַּצּוֹת הַזֶּה. כִּי אַתָּה יהוה טוֹב וּמֵטִיב לַכֹּל, וְנוֹדֶה לְּךָ עַל הָאָרֶץ וְעַל פְּרִי הַגָּפֶן. בָּרוּךְ אַתָּה יהוה, עַל הָאָרֶץ וְעַל פְּרִי הַגָּפֶן.

נרצה

חֲסַל סִדּוּר פֶּסַח כְּהִלְכָתוֹ, כְּכָל מִשְׁפָּטוֹ וְחֻקָּתוֹ, כַּאֲשֶׁר זָכִינוּ לְסַדֵּר אוֹתוֹ, כֵּן נִזְכֶּה לַעֲשׂוֹתוֹ. זָךְ שׁוֹכֵן מְעוֹנָה, קוֹמֵם קְהַל עֲדַת מִי מָנָה, בְּקָרוֹב נַהֵל נִטְעֵי כַנָּה, פְּדוּיִם לְצִיּוֹן בְּרִנָּה.

לְשָׁנָה הַבָּאָה בִּירוּשָׁלָיִם.

On the first night recite the following. On the second night continue on page 122.

וּבְכֵן וַיְהִי בַּחֲצִי הַלַּיְלָה:

אָז רוֹב נִסִּים הִפְלֵאתָ בַּלַּיְלָה.
בְּרֹאשׁ אַשְׁמוֹרֶת זֶה הַלַּיְלָה.
גֵּר צֶדֶק נִצַּחְתּוֹ כְּנֶחֱלַק לוֹ לַיְלָה.
וַיְהִי בַּחֲצִי הַלַּיְלָה.

the righteous shall You be blessed; by the tongue of the devout shall You be exalted; and amid the holy shall You be sanctified.

וּבְמַקְהֲלוֹת *And in the assemblies of the myriads of Your people, the House of Israel, with joyous song shall Your Name be glorified, our King, throughout every generation. For such is the duty of all creatures — before You, HASHEM, our God, God of our forefathers, to thank, laud, praise, glorify, exalt, adore, bless, raise high, and sing praises — even beyond all expressions of the songs and praises of David the son of Yishai, Your servant, Your anointed.*

יִשְׁתַּבַּח *May Your Name be praised forever — our King, the God, the great and holy King — in heaven and on earth. Because for You is fitting — O HASHEM, our God, and the God of our forefathers — song and praise, lauding and hymns, power and dominion, triumph, greatness and strength, praise and splendor, holiness and sovereignty, blessings and thanksgivings from this time and forever. Blessed are You, HASHEM, God, King exalted through praises, God of thanksgivings, Master of wonders, Who chooses musical songs of praise — King, God, Life-giver of the world.*

The blessing over wine is recited and the fourth cup is drunk while reclining to the left side. It is preferable that the entire cup be drunk.

בָּרוּךְ *Blessed are You, HASHEM, our God, King of the universe, Who creates the fruit of the vine.*

After drinking the fourth cup, the concluding blessing is recited. On Shabbos include the passage in parentheses.

בָּרוּךְ *Blessed are You, HASHEM, our God, King of the universe, for the vine and the fruit of the vine, and for the produce of the field. For the desirable, good, and spacious land that You were pleased to give our forefathers as a heritage, to eat of its fruit and to be satisfied with its goodness. Have mercy, we beg You, HASHEM, our God, on Israel Your people; on Jerusalem, Your city; on Zion, resting place of Your glory; Your Altar, and Your Temple. Rebuild Jerusalem the city of holiness, speedily in our days. Bring us up into it and gladden us in its rebuilding and let us eat from its fruit and be satisfied with its goodness and bless You upon it in holiness and purity. (Favor us and strengthen us on this Shabbos day) and grant us happiness on this Festival of Matzos; for You, HASHEM, are good and do good to all, and we thank You for the land and for the fruit of the vine. Blessed are You, HASHEM, for the land and for the fruit of the vine.*

NIRTZAH

חֲסַל *The Seder is now concluded in accordance with its laws, with all its ordinances and statutes. Just as we were privileged to arrange it, so may we merit to perform it. O Pure One, Who dwells on high, raise up the countless congregation, soon — guide the offshoots of Your plants, redeemed, to Zion with glad song.*

NEXT YEAR IN JERUSALEM

On the first night recite the following. On the second night continue on page 122.

It came to pass at midnight.

You have, of old, performed many wonders — *by night.*
At the head of the watches of — *this night.*
To the righteous convert (Avraham),
You gave triumph by dividing for him — *the night.*
It came to pass at midnight.

דַּנְתָּ מֶלֶךְ גְּרָר בַּחֲלוֹם הַלַּיְלָה.
הִפְחַדְתָּ אֲרַמִּי בְּאֶמֶשׁ לַיְלָה.
וַיָּשַׂר יִשְׂרָאֵל לְמַלְאָךְ וַיּוּכַל לוֹ לַיְלָה.
וַיְהִי בַּחֲצִי הַלַּיְלָה.

זֶרַע בְּכוֹרֵי פַתְרוֹס מָחַצְתָּ בַּחֲצִי הַלַּיְלָה.
חֵילָם לֹא מָצְאוּ בְּקוּמָם בַּלַּיְלָה.
טִיסַת נְגִיד חֲרוֹשֶׁת סִלִּיתָ בְּכוֹכְבֵי לַיְלָה.
וַיְהִי בַּחֲצִי הַלַּיְלָה.

יָעַץ מְחָרֵף לְנוֹפֵף אִוּוּי הוֹבַשְׁתָּ פְגָרָיו בַּלַּיְלָה.
כָּרַע בֵּל וּמַצָּבוֹ בְּאִישׁוֹן לַיְלָה.
לְאִישׁ חֲמוּדוֹת נִגְלָה רָז חֲזוֹת לַיְלָה.
וַיְהִי בַּחֲצִי הַלַּיְלָה.

מִשְׁתַּכֵּר בִּכְלֵי קֹדֶשׁ נֶהֱרַג בּוֹ בַּלַּיְלָה.
נוֹשַׁע מִבּוֹר אֲרָיוֹת פּוֹתֵר בִּעֲתוּתֵי לַיְלָה.
שִׂנְאָה נָטַר אֲגָגִי וְכָתַב סְפָרִים בַּלַּיְלָה.
וַיְהִי בַּחֲצִי הַלַּיְלָה.

עוֹרַרְתָּ נִצְחֲךָ עָלָיו בְּנֶדֶד שְׁנַת לַיְלָה.
פּוּרָה תִדְרוֹךְ לְשֹׁמֵר מַה מִּלַּיְלָה.
צָרַח כַּשּׁוֹמֵר וְשָׂח אָתָא בֹקֶר וְגַם לַיְלָה.
וַיְהִי בַּחֲצִי הַלַּיְלָה.

קָרֵב יוֹם אֲשֶׁר הוּא לֹא יוֹם וְלֹא לַיְלָה.
רָם הוֹדַע כִּי לְךָ הַיּוֹם אַף לְךָ הַלַּיְלָה.
שׁוֹמְרִים הַפְקֵד לְעִירְךָ כָּל הַיּוֹם וְכָל הַלַּיְלָה.
תָּאִיר כְּאוֹר יוֹם חֶשְׁכַּת לַיְלָה.
וַיְהִי בַּחֲצִי הַלַּיְלָה.

On the second night recite the following. On the first night continue on page 124.

וּבְכֵן וַאֲמַרְתֶּם זֶבַח פֶּסַח:

אֹמֶץ גְּבוּרוֹתֶיךָ הִפְלֵאתָ בַּפֶּסַח.
בְּרֹאשׁ כָּל מוֹעֲדוֹת נִשֵּׂאתָ פֶּסַח.
גִּלִּיתָ לְאֶזְרָחִי חֲצוֹת לֵיל פֶּסַח.
וַאֲמַרְתֶּם זֶבַח פֶּסַח.

דְּלָתָיו דָּפַקְתָּ כְּחֹם הַיּוֹם בַּפֶּסַח.
הִסְעִיד נוֹצְצִים עֻגוֹת מַצּוֹת בַּפֶּסַח.
וְאֶל הַבָּקָר רָץ זֵכֶר לְשׁוֹר עֵרֶךְ פֶּסַח.
וַאֲמַרְתֶּם זֶבַח פֶּסַח.

זוֹעֲמוּ סְדוֹמִים וְלוֹהֲטוּ בָּאֵשׁ בַּפֶּסַח.
חֻלַּץ לוֹט מֵהֶם וּמַצּוֹת אָפָה בְּקֵץ פֶּסַח.

You judged the king of Gerar (Avimelech), in a dream — *by night.*
You frightened the Aramean (Lavan), in the dark — *of night.*
Israel (Yaakov) fought with an angel and overcame him — *by night.*
It came to pass at midnight.

Egypt's first-born You crushed — *at midnight.*
Their host they found not upon arising — *at night.*
The army of the prince of Charoshes (Sisera)
You swept away with stars of — *the night.*
It came to pass at midnight.

The blasphemer (Sennacherib) planned to raise his hand
against Jerusalem — but You withered his corpses — *by night.*
Bel was overturned with its pedestal, in the darkness — *of night.*
To the man of Your delights (Daniel),
was revealed the mystery of the visions — *of night.*
It came to pass at midnight.

He (Belshazzar) who caroused from the holy vessels was killed that very — *night.*
From the lion's den was rescued he (Daniel)
who interpreted the 'terrors' of — *the night.*
The Agagite (Haman) nursed hatred and wrote decrees — *at night.*
It came to pass at midnight.

You began Your triumph over him when You disturbed
(Ahaseurus') sleep — *at night.*
Trample the wine-press to help those who ask the
watchman, 'What of the long — *night?'*
He will shout, like a watchman, and say: 'Morning shall come — *after night.'*
It came to pass at midnight.

Hasten the day (of Messiah), that is neither day nor — *night.*
Most High — make known that Yours are day and — *night.*
Appoint guards for Your city, all the day and all the — *night.*
Brighten like the light of day the darkness of — *night.*
It came to pass at midnight.

On the second night recite the following. On the first night continue on page 124.

And you shall say: This is the feast of Passover.

You displayed wondrously Your mighty powers — *on Passover.*
Above all festivals You elevated — *Passover.*
To the Oriental (Avraham) You revealed the future midnight — *of Passover.*
And you shall say: This is the feast of Passover.

At his door You knocked in the heat of the day — *on Passover;*
He satiated the angels with matzah-cakes — *on Passover.*
And he ran to the herd — symbolic of the sacrificial beast — *of Passover.*
And you shall say: This is the feast of Passover.

The Sodomites provoked (God) and were devoured by fire — *on Passover;*
Lot was withdrawn from them — he had baked
matzos at the time — *of Passover.*

טִאטֵאתָ אַדְמַת מוֹף וְנוֹף בְּעָבְרְךָ בַּפֶּסַח.
וַאֲמַרְתֶּם זֶבַח פֶּסַח.
יָהּ רֹאשׁ כָּל אוֹן מָחַצְתָּ בְּלֵיל שִׁמּוּר פֶּסַח.
כַּבִּיר עַל בֵּן בְּכוֹר פָּסַחְתָּ בְּדַם פֶּסַח.
לְבִלְתִּי תֵּת מַשְׁחִית לָבֹא בִּפְתָחַי בַּפֶּסַח.
וַאֲמַרְתֶּם זֶבַח פֶּסַח.
מְסֻגֶּרֶת סֻגָּרָה בְּעִתּוֹתֵי פֶּסַח.
נִשְׁמְדָה מִדְיָן בִּצְלִיל שְׂעוֹרֵי עֹמֶר פֶּסַח.
שׂוֹרְפוּ מִשְׁמַנֵּי פּוּל וְלוּד בִּיקַד יְקוֹד פֶּסַח.
וַאֲמַרְתֶּם זֶבַח פֶּסַח.
עוֹד הַיּוֹם בְּנֹב לַעֲמוֹד עַד גָּעָה עוֹנַת פֶּסַח.
פַּס יַד כָּתְבָה לְקַעֲקֵעַ צוּל בַּפֶּסַח.
צָפֹה הַצָּפִית עָרוֹךְ הַשֻּׁלְחָן בַּפֶּסַח.
וַאֲמַרְתֶּם זֶבַח פֶּסַח.
קָהָל כִּנְּסָה הֲדַסָּה צוֹם לְשַׁלֵּשׁ בַּפֶּסַח.
רֹאשׁ מִבֵּית רָשָׁע מָחַצְתָּ בְּעֵץ חֲמִשִּׁים בַּפֶּסַח.
שְׁתֵּי אֵלֶּה רֶגַע תָּבִיא לְעוּצִית בַּפֶּסַח.
תָּעֹז יָדְךָ וְתָרוּם יְמִינְךָ כְּלֵיל הִתְקַדֵּשׁ חַג פֶּסַח.
וַאֲמַרְתֶּם זֶבַח פֶּסַח.

On both nights continue here:

כִּי לוֹ נָאֶה, כִּי לוֹ יָאֶה:

אַדִּיר בִּמְלוּכָה, **בָּ**חוּר כַּהֲלָכָה, **גְּ**דוּדָיו יֹאמְרוּ לוֹ, לְךָ וּלְךָ, לְךָ כִּי לְךָ, לְךָ אַף לְךָ, לְךָ יהוה הַמַּמְלָכָה, כִּי לוֹ נָאֶה, כִּי לוֹ יָאֶה.

דָּגוּל בִּמְלוּכָה, **הָ**דוּר כַּהֲלָכָה, **וָ**תִיקָיו יֹאמְרוּ לוֹ, לְךָ וּלְךָ, לְךָ כִּי לְךָ, לְךָ אַף לְךָ, לְךָ יהוה הַמַּמְלָכָה, כִּי לוֹ נָאֶה, כִּי לוֹ יָאֶה.

זַכַּאי בִּמְלוּכָה, **חָ**סִין כַּהֲלָכָה, **טַ**פְסְרָיו יֹאמְרוּ לוֹ, לְךָ וּלְךָ, לְךָ כִּי לְךָ, לְךָ אַף לְךָ, לְךָ יהוה הַמַּמְלָכָה, כִּי לוֹ נָאֶה, כִּי לוֹ יָאֶה.

יָחִיד בִּמְלוּכָה, **כַּ**בִּיר כַּהֲלָכָה, **לִ**מּוּדָיו יֹאמְרוּ לוֹ, לְךָ וּלְךָ, לְךָ כִּי לְךָ, לְךָ אַף לְךָ, לְךָ יהוה הַמַּמְלָכָה, כִּי לוֹ נָאֶה, כִּי לוֹ יָאֶה.

מוֹשֵׁל בִּמְלוּכָה, **נ**וֹרָא כַּהֲלָכָה, **סְ**בִיבָיו יֹאמְרוּ לוֹ, לְךָ וּלְךָ, לְךָ כִּי לְךָ, לְךָ אַף לְךָ, לְךָ יהוה הַמַּמְלָכָה, כִּי לוֹ נָאֶה, כִּי לוֹ יָאֶה.

עָנָיו בִּמְלוּכָה, **פּ**וֹדֶה כַּהֲלָכָה, **צַ**דִּיקָיו יֹאמְרוּ לוֹ, לְךָ וּלְךָ, לְךָ כִּי לְךָ, לְךָ אַף לְךָ, לְךָ יהוה הַמַּמְלָכָה, כִּי לוֹ נָאֶה, כִּי לוֹ יָאֶה.

קָדוֹשׁ בִּמְלוּכָה, **רַ**חוּם כַּהֲלָכָה, **שִׁ**נְאַנָּיו יֹאמְרוּ לוֹ, לְךָ וּלְךָ, לְךָ כִּי לְךָ, לְךָ אַף לְךָ, לְךָ יהוה הַמַּמְלָכָה, כִּי לוֹ נָאֶה, כִּי לוֹ יָאֶה.

תַּקִּיף בִּמְלוּכָה, **תּ**וֹמֵךְ כַּהֲלָכָה, **תְּ**מִימָיו יֹאמְרוּ לוֹ, לְךָ וּלְךָ, לְךָ כִּי לְךָ, לְךָ אַף לְךָ, לְךָ יהוה הַמַּמְלָכָה, כִּי לוֹ נָאֶה, כִּי לוֹ יָאֶה.

You swept clean the soil of Moph and Noph (in Egypt) when You passed through — *on Passover.*
And you shall say: This is the feast of Passover.

God, You crushed every firstborn of On (in Egypt) on the watchful night — *of Passover.*
But Master — Your own firstborn, You skipped by merit of the blood — *of Passover,*
Not to allow the Destroyer to enter my doors — *on Passover.*
And you shall say: This is the feast of Passover.

The beleaguered (Jericho) was besieged — *on Passover.*
Midian was destroyed with a barley cake, from the Omer — *of Passover.*
The mighty nobles of Pul and Lud (Assyria) were consumed in a great conflagration — *on Passover.*
And you shall say: This is the feast of Passover.

He (Sennacherib) would have stood that day at Nob, but for the advent of Passover.
A hand inscribed the destruction of Zul (Babylon) — *on Passover.*
As the watch was set, and the royal table decked — *on Passover.*
And you shall say: This is the feast of Passover.

Hadassah (Esther) gathered a congregation for a three-day fast — *on Passover.*
You caused the head of the evil clan (Haman) to be hanged on a fifty-cubit gallows — *on Passover.*
Doubly, will You bring in an instant upon Utsis (Edom) — *on Passover.*
Let Your hand be strong, and Your right arm exalted, as on that night when You hallowed the festival — *of Passover.*
And you shall say: This is the feast of Passover.

On both nights continue here:

To Him praise is due! To Him praise is fitting!

Powerful in majesty, perfectly distinguished, His companies of angels say to Him: Yours and only Yours; Yours, yes Yours; Yours, surely Yours; Yours, HASHEM, *is the sovereignty. To Him praise is due! To Him praise is fitting!*

Supreme in kingship, perfectly glorious, His faithful say to Him: Yours and only Yours; Yours, yes Yours; Yours, surely Yours; Yours, HASHEM, *is the sovereignty. To Him praise is due! To Him praise is fitting!*

Pure in kingship, perfectly mighty, His angels say to Him: Yours and only Yours; Yours, yes Yours; Yours, surely Yours; Yours, HASHEM, *is the sovereignty. To Him praise is due! To Him praise is fitting!*

Alone in kingship, perfectly omnipotent, His scholars say to Him: Yours and only Yours; Yours, yes Yours; Yours, surely Yours; Yours, HASHEM, *is the sovereignty. To Him praise is due! To Him praise is fitting!*

Commanding in kingship, perfectly wondrous, His surrounding (angels) say to Him: Yours and only Yours; Yours, yes Yours; Yours, surely Yours; Yours, HASHEM, *is the sovereignty. To Him praise is due! To Him praise is fitting!*

Gentle in Kingship, perfectly the Redeemer, His righteous say to Him: Yours and only Yours; Yours, yes Yours; Yours, surely Yours; Yours, HASHEM, *is the sovereignty. To Him praise is due! To Him praise is fitting!*

Holy in kingship, perfectly merciful, His troops of angels say to Him: Yours and only Yours; Yours, yes Yours; Yours, surely Yours; Yours, HASHEM, *is the sovereignty. To Him praise is due! To Him praise is fitting.*

Almighty in kingship, perfectly sustaining, His perfect ones say to Him: Yours and only Yours; Yours, yes Yours; Yours, surely Yours; Yours, HASHEM, *is the sovereignty. To Him praise is due! To Him praise is fitting!*

אַדִּיר הוּא יִבְנֶה בֵיתוֹ בְּקָרוֹב, בִּמְהֵרָה, בִּמְהֵרָה, בְּיָמֵינוּ בְּקָרוֹב. אֵל בְּנֵה, אֵל בְּנֵה, בְּנֵה בֵיתְךָ בְּקָרוֹב.

בָּחוּר הוּא. **גָּ**דוֹל הוּא. **דָּ**גוּל הוּא. יִבְנֶה בֵיתוֹ בְּקָרוֹב, בִּמְהֵרָה, בִּמְהֵרָה, בְּיָמֵינוּ בְּקָרוֹב. אֵל בְּנֵה, אֵל בְּנֵה, בְּנֵה בֵיתְךָ בְּקָרוֹב.

הָדוּר הוּא. **וָ**תִיק הוּא. **זַ**כַּאי הוּא. **חָ**סִיד הוּא. יִבְנֶה בֵיתוֹ בְּקָרוֹב, בִּמְהֵרָה, בִּמְהֵרָה, בְּיָמֵינוּ בְּקָרוֹב. אֵל בְּנֵה, אֵל בְּנֵה, בְּנֵה בֵיתְךָ בְּקָרוֹב.

טָהוֹר הוּא. **יָ**חִיד הוּא. **כַּ**בִּיר הוּא. **לָ**מוּד הוּא. **מֶ**לֶךְ הוּא. **נוֹ**רָא הוּא. **סַ**גִּיב הוּא. **עִ**זּוּז הוּא. **פּוֹ**דֶה הוּא. **צַ**דִּיק הוּא. יִבְנֶה בֵיתוֹ בְּקָרוֹב, בִּמְהֵרָה, בִּמְהֵרָה, בְּיָמֵינוּ בְּקָרוֹב. אֵל בְּנֵה, אֵל בְּנֵה, בְּנֵה בֵיתְךָ בְּקָרוֹב.

קָדוֹשׁ הוּא. **רַ**חוּם הוּא. **שַׁ**דַּי הוּא. **תַּ**קִּיף הוּא. יִבְנֶה בֵיתוֹ בְּקָרוֹב, בִּמְהֵרָה, בִּמְהֵרָה, בְּיָמֵינוּ בְּקָרוֹב. אֵל בְּנֵה, אֵל בְּנֵה, בְּנֵה בֵיתְךָ בְּקָרוֹב.

אֶחָד מִי יוֹדֵעַ? אֶחָד אֲנִי יוֹדֵעַ. אֶחָד אֱלֹהֵינוּ שֶׁבַּשָּׁמַיִם וּבָאָרֶץ.

שְׁנַיִם מִי יוֹדֵעַ? שְׁנַיִם אֲנִי יוֹדֵעַ. שְׁנֵי לֻחוֹת הַבְּרִית, אֶחָד אֱלֹהֵינוּ שֶׁבַּשָּׁמַיִם וּבָאָרֶץ.

שְׁלֹשָׁה מִי יוֹדֵעַ? שְׁלֹשָׁה אֲנִי יוֹדֵעַ. שְׁלֹשָׁה אָבוֹת, שְׁנֵי לֻחוֹת הַבְּרִית, אֶחָד אֱלֹהֵינוּ שֶׁבַּשָּׁמַיִם וּבָאָרֶץ.

אַרְבַּע מִי יוֹדֵעַ? אַרְבַּע אֲנִי יוֹדֵעַ. אַרְבַּע אִמָּהוֹת, שְׁלֹשָׁה אָבוֹת, שְׁנֵי לֻחוֹת הַבְּרִית, אֶחָד אֱלֹהֵינוּ שֶׁבַּשָּׁמַיִם וּבָאָרֶץ.

חֲמִשָּׁה מִי יוֹדֵעַ? חֲמִשָּׁה אֲנִי יוֹדֵעַ. חֲמִשָּׁה חֻמְשֵׁי תוֹרָה, אַרְבַּע אִמָּהוֹת, שְׁלֹשָׁה אָבוֹת, שְׁנֵי לֻחוֹת הַבְּרִית, אֶחָד אֱלֹהֵינוּ שֶׁבַּשָּׁמַיִם וּבָאָרֶץ.

שִׁשָּׁה מִי יוֹדֵעַ? שִׁשָּׁה אֲנִי יוֹדֵעַ. שִׁשָּׁה סִדְרֵי מִשְׁנָה, חֲמִשָּׁה חֻמְשֵׁי תוֹרָה, אַרְבַּע אִמָּהוֹת, שְׁלֹשָׁה אָבוֹת, שְׁנֵי לֻחוֹת הַבְּרִית, אֶחָד אֱלֹהֵינוּ שֶׁבַּשָּׁמַיִם וּבָאָרֶץ.

שִׁבְעָה מִי יוֹדֵעַ? שִׁבְעָה אֲנִי יוֹדֵעַ. שִׁבְעָה יְמֵי שַׁבַּתָּא, שִׁשָּׁה סִדְרֵי מִשְׁנָה, חֲמִשָּׁה חֻמְשֵׁי תוֹרָה, אַרְבַּע אִמָּהוֹת, שְׁלֹשָׁה אָבוֹת, שְׁנֵי לֻחוֹת הַבְּרִית, אֶחָד אֱלֹהֵינוּ שֶׁבַּשָּׁמַיִם וּבָאָרֶץ.

שְׁמוֹנָה מִי יוֹדֵעַ? שְׁמוֹנָה אֲנִי יוֹדֵעַ. שְׁמוֹנָה יְמֵי מִילָה, שִׁבְעָה יְמֵי שַׁבַּתָּא, שִׁשָּׁה סִדְרֵי מִשְׁנָה, חֲמִשָּׁה חֻמְשֵׁי תוֹרָה, אַרְבַּע אִמָּהוֹת, שְׁלֹשָׁה אָבוֹת, שְׁנֵי לֻחוֹת הַבְּרִית, אֶחָד אֱלֹהֵינוּ שֶׁבַּשָּׁמַיִם וּבָאָרֶץ.

תִּשְׁעָה מִי יוֹדֵעַ? תִּשְׁעָה אֲנִי יוֹדֵעַ. תִּשְׁעָה יַרְחֵי לֵדָה, שְׁמוֹנָה יְמֵי מִילָה, שִׁבְעָה יְמֵי שַׁבַּתָּא, שִׁשָּׁה סִדְרֵי מִשְׁנָה, חֲמִשָּׁה חֻמְשֵׁי תוֹרָה, אַרְבַּע אִמָּהוֹת, שְׁלֹשָׁה אָבוֹת, שְׁנֵי לֻחוֹת הַבְּרִית, אֶחָד אֱלֹהֵינוּ שֶׁבַּשָּׁמַיִם וּבָאָרֶץ.

עֲשָׂרָה מִי יוֹדֵעַ? עֲשָׂרָה אֲנִי יוֹדֵעַ. עֲשָׂרָה דִבְּרַיָּא, תִּשְׁעָה יַרְחֵי לֵדָה, שְׁמוֹנָה יְמֵי מִילָה, שִׁבְעָה יְמֵי שַׁבַּתָּא, שִׁשָּׁה סִדְרֵי מִשְׁנָה, חֲמִשָּׁה חֻמְשֵׁי תוֹרָה, אַרְבַּע אִמָּהוֹת, שְׁלֹשָׁה אָבוֹת, שְׁנֵי לֻחוֹת הַבְּרִית, אֶחָד אֱלֹהֵינוּ שֶׁבַּשָּׁמַיִם וּבָאָרֶץ.

אַחַד עָשָׂר מִי יוֹדֵעַ? אַחַד עָשָׂר אֲנִי יוֹדֵעַ. אַחַד עָשָׂר כּוֹכְבַיָּא,

אַדִּיר הוּא *He is most mighty. May He soon rebuild His House, speedily, yes speedily, in our days, soon. God, rebuild, God, rebuild, rebuild Your House soon!*

He is distinguished, He is great, He is exalted. May He soon rebuild His House, speedily, yes speedily, in our days, soon. God, rebuild, God, rebuild, rebuild Your House soon!

He is all glorious, He is faithful, He is faultless, He is righteous. May He soon rebuild His House, speedily, yes speedily, in our days, soon. God, rebuild, God, rebuild, rebuild Your House soon!

He is pure, He is unique, He is powerful, He is all-wise, He is King, He is awesome, He is sublime, He is all-powerful, He is the Redeemer, He is the all-righteous. May He soon rebuild His House, speedily, yes speedily, in our days, soon. God, rebuild, God, rebuild, rebuild Your House soon!

He is holy, He is compassionate, He is Almighty, He is omnipotent. May He soon rebuild His House, speedily, yes speedily, in our days, soon. God, rebuild, God, rebuild, rebuild Your House soon!

אֶחָד מִי יוֹדֵעַ? *Who knows one? I know one: One is our God, in heaven and on earth.*

Who knows two? I know two: two are the Tablets of the Covenant; One is our God, in heaven and on earth.

Who knows three? I know three: three are the Patriarchs; two are the Tablets of the Covenant; One is our God, in heaven and on earth.

Who knows four? I know four: four are the Matriarchs; three are the Patriarchs; two are the Tablets of the Covenant; One is our God, in heaven and on earth.

Who knows five? I know five: five are the Books of Torah; four are the Matriarchs; three are the Patriarchs; two are the Tablets of the Covenant; One is our God, in heaven and on earth.

Who knows six? I know six: six are the Orders of the Mishnah; five are the Books of the Torah; four are the Matriarchs; three are the Patriarchs; two are the Tablets of the Covenant; One is our God, in heaven and on earth.

Who knows seven? I know seven: seven are the days of the week; six are the Orders of the Mishnah; five are the Books of the Torah; four are the Matriarchs; three are the Patriarchs; two are the Tablets of the Covenant; One is our God, in heaven and on earth.

Who knows eight? I know eight: eight are the days of circumcision; seven are the days of the week; six are the Orders of the Mishnah; five are the Books of the Torah; four are the Matriarchs; three are the Patriarchs; two are the Tablets of the Covenant; One is our God, in heaven and on earth.

Who knows nine? I know nine: nine are the months of pregnancy; eight are the days of circumcision; seven are the days of the week; six are the Orders of the Mishnah; five are the Books of the Torah; four are the Matriarchs; three are the Patriarchs; two are the Tablets of the Covenant; One is our God, in heaven and on earth.

Who knows ten? I know ten: ten are the Ten Commandments; nine are the months of pregnancy; eight are the days of circumcision; seven are the days of the week; six are the Orders of the Mishnah; five are the Books of the Torah; four are the Matriarchs; three are the Patriarchs; two are the Tablets of the Covenant; One is our God, in heaven and on earth.

Who knows eleven? I know eleven: eleven are the stars (in Yosef's

עֲשָׂרָה דִבְּרַיָּא, תִּשְׁעָה יַרְחֵי לֵדָה, שְׁמוֹנָה יְמֵי מִילָה, שִׁבְעָה יְמֵי שַׁבַּתָּא, שִׁשָּׁה סִדְרֵי מִשְׁנָה, חֲמִשָּׁה חֻמְשֵׁי תוֹרָה, אַרְבַּע אִמָּהוֹת, שְׁלֹשָׁה אָבוֹת, שְׁנֵי לֻחוֹת הַבְּרִית, אֶחָד אֱלֹהֵינוּ שֶׁבַּשָּׁמַיִם וּבָאָרֶץ.

שְׁנֵים עָשָׂר מִי יוֹדֵעַ? שְׁנֵים עָשָׂר אֲנִי יוֹדֵעַ. שְׁנֵים עָשָׂר שִׁבְטַיָּא, אַחַד עָשָׂר כּוֹכְבַיָּא, עֲשָׂרָה דִבְּרַיָּא, תִּשְׁעָה יַרְחֵי לֵדָה, שְׁמוֹנָה יְמֵי מִילָה, שִׁבְעָה יְמֵי שַׁבַּתָּא, שִׁשָּׁה סִדְרֵי מִשְׁנָה, חֲמִשָּׁה חֻמְשֵׁי תוֹרָה, אַרְבַּע אִמָּהוֹת, שְׁלֹשָׁה אָבוֹת, שְׁנֵי לֻחוֹת הַבְּרִית, אֶחָד אֱלֹהֵינוּ שֶׁבַּשָּׁמַיִם וּבָאָרֶץ.

שְׁלֹשָׁה עָשָׂר מִי יוֹדֵעַ? שְׁלֹשָׁה עָשָׂר אֲנִי יוֹדֵעַ. שְׁלֹשָׁה עָשָׂר מִדַּיָּא, שְׁנֵים עָשָׂר שִׁבְטַיָּא, אַחַד עָשָׂר כּוֹכְבַיָּא, עֲשָׂרָה דִבְּרַיָּא, תִּשְׁעָה יַרְחֵי לֵדָה, שְׁמוֹנָה יְמֵי מִילָה, שִׁבְעָה יְמֵי שַׁבַּתָּא, שִׁשָּׁה סִדְרֵי מִשְׁנָה, חֲמִשָּׁה חֻמְשֵׁי תוֹרָה, אַרְבַּע אִמָּהוֹת, שְׁלֹשָׁה אָבוֹת, שְׁנֵי לֻחוֹת הַבְּרִית, אֶחָד אֱלֹהֵינוּ שֶׁבַּשָּׁמַיִם וּבָאָרֶץ.

חַד גַּדְיָא, חַד גַּדְיָא, דְּזַבִּין אַבָּא בִּתְרֵי זוּזֵי, חַד גַּדְיָא חַד גַּדְיָא.

וְאָתָא **שׁוּנְרָא** וְאָכְלָה לְגַדְיָא, דְּזַבִּין אַבָּא בִּתְרֵי זוּזֵי, חַד גַּדְיָא חַד גַּדְיָא.

וְאָתָא **כַלְבָּא** וְנָשַׁךְ לְשׁוּנְרָא, דְּאָכְלָה לְגַדְיָא, דְּזַבִּין אַבָּא בִּתְרֵי זוּזֵי, חַד גַּדְיָא חַד גַּדְיָא.

וְאָתָא **חוּטְרָא** וְהִכָּה לְכַלְבָּא, דְּנָשַׁךְ לְשׁוּנְרָא, דְּאָכְלָה לְגַדְיָא, דְּזַבִּין אַבָּא בִּתְרֵי זוּזֵי, חַד גַּדְיָא חַד גַּדְיָא.

וְאָתָא **נוּרָא** וְשָׂרַף לְחוּטְרָא, דְּהִכָּה לְכַלְבָּא, דְּנָשַׁךְ לְשׁוּנְרָא, דְּאָכְלָה לְגַדְיָא, דְּזַבִּין אַבָּא בִּתְרֵי זוּזֵי, חַד גַּדְיָא חַד גַּדְיָא.

וְאָתָא **מַיָּא** וְכָבָה לְנוּרָא, דְּשָׂרַף לְחוּטְרָא, דְּהִכָּה לְכַלְבָּא, דְּנָשַׁךְ לְשׁוּנְרָא, דְּאָכְלָה לְגַדְיָא, דְּזַבִּין אַבָּא בִּתְרֵי זוּזֵי, חַד גַּדְיָא חַד גַּדְיָא.

וְאָתָא **תוֹרָא** וְשָׁתָה לְמַיָּא, דְּכָבָה לְנוּרָא, דְּשָׂרַף לְחוּטְרָא, דְּהִכָּה לְכַלְבָּא, דְּנָשַׁךְ לְשׁוּנְרָא, דְּאָכְלָה לְגַדְיָא, דְּזַבִּין אַבָּא בִּתְרֵי זוּזֵי, חַד גַּדְיָא חַד גַּדְיָא.

וְאָתָא **הַשּׁוֹחֵט** וְשָׁחַט לְתוֹרָא, דְּשָׁתָא לְמַיָּא, דְּכָבָה לְנוּרָא, דְּשָׂרַף לְחוּטְרָא, דְּהִכָּה לְכַלְבָּא, דְּנָשַׁךְ לְשׁוּנְרָא, דְּאָכְלָה לְגַדְיָא, דְּזַבִּין אַבָּא בִּתְרֵי זוּזֵי, חַד גַּדְיָא חַד גַּדְיָא.

וְאָתָא **מַלְאַךְ הַמָּוֶת** וְשָׁחַט לְשׁוֹחֵט, דְּשָׁחַט לְתוֹרָא, דְּשָׁתָה לְמַיָּא, דְּכָבָה לְנוּרָא, דְּשָׂרַף לְחוּטְרָא, דְּהִכָּה לְכַלְבָּא, דְּנָשַׁךְ לְשׁוּנְרָא, דְּאָכְלָה לְגַדְיָא, דְּזַבִּין אַבָּא בִּתְרֵי זוּזֵי, חַד גַּדְיָא חַד גַּדְיָא.

וְאָתָא **הַקָּדוֹשׁ בָּרוּךְ הוּא** וְשָׁחַט לְמַלְאַךְ הַמָּוֶת, דְּשָׁחַט לְשׁוֹחֵט, דְּשָׁחַט לְתוֹרָא, דְּשָׁתָה לְמַיָּא, דְּכָבָה לְנוּרָא, דְּשָׂרַף לְחוּטְרָא, דְּהִכָּה לְכַלְבָּא, דְּנָשַׁךְ לְשׁוּנְרָא, דְּאָכְלָה לְגַדְיָא, דְּזַבִּין אַבָּא בִּתְרֵי זוּזֵי, חַד גַּדְיָא חַד גַּדְיָא.

Although the *Haggadah* formally ends at this point, many recite שִׁיר הַשִּׁירִים, *Song of Songs* (p. 566), after the *Haggadah*. Moreover, one should continue to occupy himself with the story of the Exodus, and the laws of Pesach, until sleep overtakes him.

dream); ten are the Ten Commandments; nine are the months of pregnancy; eight are the days of circumcision; seven are the days of the week; six are the Orders of the Mishnah; five are the Books of the Torah; four are the Matriarchs; three are the Patriarchs; two are the Tablets of the Covenant; One is our God, in heaven and on earth.

Who knows twelve? I know twelve: twelve are the tribes; eleven are the stars (in Yosef's dream); ten are the Ten Commandments; nine are the months of pregnancy; eight are the days of circumcision; seven are the days of the week; six are the Orders of the Mishnah; five are the Books of the Torah; four are the Matriarchs; three are the Patriarchs; two are the Tablets of the Covenant; One is our God, in heaven and on earth.

Who knows thirteen? I know thirteen: thirteen are the attributes of God; twelve are the tribes; eleven are the stars (in Yosef's dream); ten are the Ten Commandments; nine are the months of pregnancy; eight are the days of circumcision; seven are the days of the week; six are the Orders of the Mishnah; five are the Books of the Torah; four are the Matriarchs; three are the Patriarchs; two are the Tablets of the Covenant; One is our God, in heaven and on earth.

חַד גַּדְיָא *A kid, a kid, that father bought for two zuzim, a kid, a kid.*

A cat then came and devoured the kid, that father bought for two zuzim, a kid, a kid.

A dog then came and bit the cat, that devoured the kid, that father bought for two zuzim, a kid, a kid.

A stick then came and beat the dog, that bit the cat, that devoured the kid, that father bought for two zuzim, a kid, a kid.

A fire then came and burnt the stick, that beat the dog, that bit the cat, that devoured the kid, that father bought for two zuzim, a kid, a kid.

Water then came and quenched the fire, that burnt the stick, that beat the dog, that bit the cat, that devoured the kid, that father bought for two zuzim, a kid, a kid.

An ox then came and drank the water, that quenched the fire, that burnt the stick, that beat the dog, that bit the cat, that devoured the kid, that father bought for two zuzim, a kid, a kid.

A slaughterer then came and slaughtered the ox, that drank the water, that quenched the fire, that burnt the stick, that beat the dog, that bit the cat, that devoured the kid, that father bought for two zuzim, a kid, a kid.

The angel of death then came and killed the slaughterer, who slaughtered the ox, that drank the water, that quenched the fire, that burnt the stick, that beat the dog, that bit the cat, that devoured the kid, that father bought for two zuzim, a kid, a kid.

The Holy One, Blessed is He, then came and slew the angel of death, who killed the slaughterer, who slaughtered the ox, that drank the water, that quenched the fire, that burnt the stick, that beat the dog, that bit the cat, that devoured the kid, that father bought for two zuzim, a kid, a kid.

Although the *Haggadah* formally ends at this point, many recite שִׁיר הַשִּׁירִים, *Song of Songs* (p. 566), after the *Haggadah*. Moreover, one should continue to occupy himself with the story of the Exodus, and the laws of Pesach, until sleep overtakes him.

משניות פסחים

It is customary to study the *mishnah* of Tractate *Pesachim* during Pesach.

פרק ראשון

[א] **אוֹר** לְאַרְבָּעָה עָשָׂר בּוֹדְקִים אֶת הֶחָמֵץ לְאוֹר הַנֵּר. כָּל מָקוֹם שֶׁאֵין מַכְנִיסִין בּוֹ חָמֵץ אֵין צָרִיךְ בְּדִיקָה.

וְלָמָה אָמְרוּ: „שְׁתֵּי שׁוּרוֹת בְּמַרְתֵּף״? מָקוֹם שֶׁמַּכְנִיסִין בּוֹ חָמֵץ. בֵּית שַׁמַּאי אוֹמְרִים: שְׁתֵּי שׁוּרוֹת עַל פְּנֵי כָל הַמַּרְתֵּף. וּבֵית הִלֵּל אוֹמְרִים: שְׁתֵּי שׁוּרוֹת הַחִיצוֹנוֹת שֶׁהֵן הָעֶלְיוֹנוֹת.

[ב] אֵין חוֹשְׁשִׁין שֶׁמָּא גֵרְרָה חֻלְדָּה מִבַּיִת לְבַיִת, וּמִמָּקוֹם לְמָקוֹם; דְּאִם כֵּן, מֵחָצֵר לְחָצֵר וּמֵעִיר לְעִיר – אֵין לַדָּבָר סוֹף.

[ג] רַבִּי יְהוּדָה אוֹמֵר: בּוֹדְקִין אוֹר אַרְבָּעָה עָשָׂר, וּבְאַרְבָּעָה עָשָׂר שַׁחֲרִית, וּבִשְׁעַת הַבִּעוּר.

וַחֲכָמִים אוֹמְרִים: לֹא בָדַק אוֹר אַרְבָּעָה עָשָׂר, יִבְדֹּק בְּאַרְבָּעָה עָשָׂר; לֹא בָדַק בְּאַרְבָּעָה עָשָׂר, יִבְדֹּק בְּתוֹךְ הַמּוֹעֵד; לֹא בָדַק בְּתוֹךְ הַמּוֹעֵד, יִבְדֹּק לְאַחַר הַמּוֹעֵד.

וּמַה שֶּׁמְּשַׁיֵּר, יַנִּיחֶנּוּ בְּצִנְעָא, כְּדֵי שֶׁלֹּא יְהֵא צָרִיךְ בְּדִיקָה אַחֲרָיו.

[ד] רַבִּי מֵאִיר אוֹמֵר: אוֹכְלִין כָּל חָמֵשׁ, וְשׂוֹרְפִין בִּתְחִלַּת שֵׁשׁ. וְרַבִּי

יד אברהם

[A full treatment of these mishnayos may be found in the ArtScroll Mishnah with the *Yad Avraham* commentary, from which the following commentary has been adapted.]

⊷§ Tractate Pesachim

Tractate *Pesachim* deals with the many *mitzvos* relevant to the festival of Pesach. It is divided into two basic parts [and is for this reason named in the plural, *Pesachim*]. Chapters 1-4 and 10 deal with all the laws unrelated to the *pesach* offering, such as the prohibition to eat or even possess *chametz* during Pesach, the requirement to eat matzah on the *Seder* night, and the *mitzvah* to relate the story of the redemption from Egypt. Chapters 5-9 deal with the laws of the *pesach* offering made in Temple times on the fourteenth of Nissan.

CHAPTER ONE

1. This tractate begins with the law of בְּדִיקַת חָמֵץ, *the search for chametz.* This is predicated upon the dual *mitzvos* of: (1) eliminating *chametz* from Jewish possession; and (2) the prohibition of having *chametz* during Pesach.

אוֹר לְאַרְבָּעָה עָשָׂר — *The evening of the fourteenth* was fixed as the time for the search (rather than the day) because people are home then and a search by candlelight in the darkness is especially effective [making the illuminated area stand out]. The requirement to use a candle for the search is derived by the *Gemara* exegetically (7b; see *O. Ch.* 433:1).

בּוֹדְקִים אֶת הֶחָמֵץ — *One must search for the chametz* and eliminate it so as not to transgress the prohibition against keeping *chametz* on Pesach (*Rashi*). *Tosafos*, however, state that the purpose of the search is to prevent its inadvertent consumption on Pesach. [The Scriptural requirement not to possess *chametz*, however, could be met by בִּטּוּל, *nullifying* the *chametz*.]

מָקוֹם שֶׁמַּכְנִיסִין בּוֹ חָמֵץ — *A place into which chametz is [customarily] brought*. Thus a cellar used to store wine for sale does not need to be searched. Only a domestic wine cellar must be searched because servants fetching wine from there occasionally enter carrying a piece of bread.

שְׁתֵּי שׁוּרוֹת . . . — *Two rows* . . . It was the practice to arrange the barrels so that each one rested upon the two barrels under it, very much as bricks are laid. Beis Shammai require that the entire wall of barrels facing the front of the cellar be searched from floor to ceiling, as well as the entire top layer of barrels from front to back [i.e. the layer facing the ceiling]. But Beis Hillel equate

MISHNAYOS PESACHIM

It is customary to study the *mishnah* of Tractate *Pesachim* during Pesach.

CHAPTER ONE

[1] **אוֹר** *On the evening of the fourteenth [of Nissan] one must search for chametz by the light of a candle. Any place into which chametz is not [customarily] brought does not require a search. In regard to what [have the Sages] said, 'Two rows of a [wine] cellar [must be searched]'? For a place into which chametz is [customarily] brought. Beis Shammai say: Two rows over the entire front of the [wine] cellar [must be searched]. But Beis Hillel say: The two outer rows which are the uppermost.*

[2] *We need not be concerned that a weasel dragged [chametz] from one house to another, or from one place to another; for if so, [we would have to be concerned] from one courtyard to another and from one town to another — [and] there is no end to the matter.*

[3] *R' Yehudah says: One must search on the evening of the fourteenth, or on the morning of the fourteenth, or at the time of removal. But the Sages say: [If] one did not search on the evening of the fourteenth, he must search on the [day of the] fourteenth; [if] he did not search on the fourteenth, he must search during the festival; [if] he did not search during the festival, he must search after the festival.*

That which he leaves over [to eat in the morning], he should put in a safe place, so that it will not be necessary to search for it [again].

[4] *R' Meir says: One may eat [chametz] the entire fifth [hour], and he must burn [it] at the onset of the sixth [hour]. But R' Yehudah says: One*

YAD AVRAHAM

row with layers, of which only the two uppermost layers of the front row of barrels must be searched (*Rav*).

2. **וּמִמָּקוֹם לְמָקוֹם** — *Or from one place to another,* i.e. from an unsearched corner of the house to one that has been searched (*Rav*).

דְּאִם כֵּן — *For if* we have to concern ourselves that a weasel brought *chametz* from one house to another after the search had been completed, we would also have to be concerned that *chametz* had been dragged in from another courtyard or town which had not yet been searched (*Rav*).

3. **וּבְאַרְבָּעָה עָשָׂר שַׁחֲרִית** — *Or on the morning of the fourteenth,* if one forgot or was unable to search at night (*Rav*).

וּבִשְׁעַת הַבִּעוּר — *Or at the time of removal,* when the left-over *chametz* must be destroyed. This is at the beginning of the sixth hour (approximately the hour before noon). R' Yehudah contends that the search may not be performed after midday, because one might inadvertently eat the *chametz* he finds and transgress a Scriptural prohibition [see m. 4] (*Rav*). The prohibition to eat *chametz* before then, however, is only Rabbinic in origin, and the search is not waived because of it.

וַחֲכָמִים אוֹמְרִים — *But the Sages* are not concerned that the searcher may eat the *chametz* he finds, because his purpose for searching is to destroy the *chametz*. Thus, he may search even on the festival.

יִבְדֹּק לְאַחַר הַמּוֹעֵד — *He must search after the festival,* since *chametz* left in a Jew's possession over Pesach is forbidden (2:5).

בְּצִנְעָא — *In a safe place,* so that it does not scatter (*Rambam*), for if one does not find the *chametz* he put aside, or if he put aside ten pieces and found only nine, it is necessary to search again. However, if he put it in a secure spot, he may assume that it was eaten by a person and another search is unnecessary (*O. Ch.* 434:1).

4. The *Gemara* deduces from our mishnah that there is a Biblical ban on possessing *chametz* from midday of the fourteenth forward. Because many people cannot accurately estimate midday, the Sages decreed that the prohibition be observed even before noon.

רַבִּי מֵאִיר אוֹמֵר — *R' Meir says:* Hours throughout the Mishnah are **שָׁעוֹת זְמַנִּיּוֹת**, *seasonal hours*, in which daylight is divided into twelve equal parts; accordingly, an 'hour' may be longer or shorter than the traditional 60 minutes, depending on the season. R' Meir permits eating *chametz* on

יְהוּדָה אוֹמֵר: אוֹכְלִין כָּל אַרְבַּע, וְתוֹלִין כָּל חָמֵשׁ, וְשׂוֹרְפִין בִּתְחִלַּת שֵׁשׁ.

[ה] וְעוֹד אָמַר רַבִּי יְהוּדָה: שְׁתֵּי חַלּוֹת שֶׁל תּוֹדָה פְּסוּלוֹת מֻנָּחוֹת עַל גַּג הָאִצְטְבָא. כָּל זְמַן שֶׁמֻּנָּחוֹת, כָּל הָעָם אוֹכְלִים. נִטְּלָה אַחַת, תּוֹלִין – לֹא אוֹכְלִין וְלֹא שׂוֹרְפִין. נִטְּלוּ שְׁתֵּיהֶן, הִתְחִילוּ כָּל הָעָם שׂוֹרְפִין.

רַבָּן גַּמְלִיאֵל אוֹמֵר: חֻלִּין נֶאֱכָלִים כָּל אַרְבַּע; וּתְרוּמָה כָּל חָמֵשׁ; וְשׂוֹרְפִין בִּתְחִלַּת שֵׁשׁ.

[ו] רַבִּי חֲנִינָא, סְגַן הַכֹּהֲנִים, אוֹמֵר: מִימֵיהֶם שֶׁל כֹּהֲנִים, לֹא נִמְנְעוּ מִלִּשְׂרֹף אֶת הַבָּשָׂר שֶׁנִּטְמָא בִּוְלַד הַטֻּמְאָה עִם הַבָּשָׂר שֶׁנִּטְמָא בְּאַב הַטֻּמְאָה, אַף עַל פִּי שֶׁמּוֹסִיפִין טֻמְאָה עַל טֻמְאָתוֹ.

הוֹסִיף רַבִּי עֲקִיבָא וְאָמַר: מִימֵיהֶם שֶׁל כֹּהֲנִים, לֹא נִמְנְעוּ מִלְּהַדְלִיק אֶת הַשֶּׁמֶן שֶׁנִּפְסַל בִּטְבוּל יוֹם בְּנֵר שֶׁנִּטְמָא בִּטְמֵא מֵת, אַף עַל פִּי שֶׁמּוֹסִיפִין טֻמְאָה עַל טֻמְאָתוֹ.

יד אברהם

Erev Pesach until the end of the fifth hour. [For example, if the length of the day is twelve hours, from 6 a.m. to 6 p.m., one may eat *chametz* until 11 a.m.] One must then burn it at the onset of the sixth [hour], and no benefit may be derived from it. Although the *chametz* is Biblically permitted in the sixth hour, the Sages forbade its use then because one might miscalculate the end of the sixth hour (*Rav*).

וְרַבִּי יְהוּדָה אוֹמֵר — *But R' Yehudah says* that in the fifth hour we neither eat *chametz* nor destroy it, but we may derive other benefit from it, such as by feeding it to our animals (*Rav*). In his view, the Sages restricted the consumption of *chametz* two hours before the Biblical prohibition, to allow more of a margin of error for a cloudy day (*Gem.*). However, because this is not a common problem, the Sages did not prohibit all benefit in the fifth hour (*Pnei Yehoshua*).

The custom is to burn *chametz* before the fifth hour, in order to be able to nullify the *chametz* again after burning it, as stated by *Rama* (434:2). *Chametz* in the sixth hour is forbidden for any benefit and therefore worthless; thus it can no longer be nullified because it can no longer be considered the property of its owner.

5. [R' Yehudah now relates how the times of the prohibitions of *chametz* were made known in Jerusalem during the Temple era.]

שֶׁל תּוֹדָה — *Of a thanksgiving offering.* This is an offering brought by a person who has been delivered from misfortune, such as a dangerous sickness or sea voyage. Accompanying the animal offering are forty loaves, ten of which are *chametz* while the rest are matzah. Since a thanksgiving offering may be eaten the night after its sacrifice, it was forbidden to bring one on Erev Pesach, when the *chametz* loaves could be eaten only till midday. Therefore, numerous offerings were brought on the day before by festival pilgrims, and those that could not be finished on time became unfit at daybreak of the fourteenth. Two of these unfit loaves were used to signify the various stages of the status of *chametz* (*Gem.*).

נִטְּלָה אַחַת — *[When] one [loaf] was removed* by a messenger of the Court at the beginning of the fifth hour (approximately 10 a.m.), people stopped using *chametz*.

וּתְרוּמָה כָּל חָמֵשׁ — *Terumah [which is chametz may be eaten] the entire fifth [hour].* Because it possesses sanctity and should not be destroyed unless absolutely necessary, Rabban Gamliel allows its consumption for an additional hour (*Rav*).

6. *Terumah* [the tithe given to the *Kohen*] must be safeguarded against *tumah*-contamination and destruction. However, on Erev Pesach, *terumah*, too, must be destroyed if it is *chametz*. The question arises whether care must be taken even during the burning to safeguard it from contamination. If so, two pyres would be required, one for uncontaminated *terumah*, and a second for all other *chametz*, so that the *terumah* not come in contact with contaminated *chametz*. It might be, however, that since destruction of the *terumah* is imminent, the mandate to safeguard it against *tumah* no longer applies. In order to resolve this question, mishnah 6 introduces a parallel situation regarding the destruction of

may eat [it] the entire fourth [hour], but we suspend [it] the entire fifth [hour], and one must burn it at the onset of the sixth [hour].

[5] *R' Yehudah also said: Two loaves of a thanksgiving offering [which had become] unfit were placed on the roof of the [Temple] portico. As long as they lay [there], the people would eat [chametz]. [When] one [loaf] was removed, they suspended [it] — neither eating nor burning [the chametz]. When both were removed, the people would begin burning [the chametz].*

Rabban Gamliel says: Non-consecrated [chametz] may be eaten the entire fourth [hour]; terumah [which is chametz may be eaten] the entire fifth [hour]; and we must burn [all chametz] at the onset of the sixth [hour].

[6] *R' Chanina, the administrator of the Kohanim, says: In all the days of the Kohanim, never did they refrain from burning [sacrificial] meat that had been contaminated by a secondary tumah together with [sacrificial] meat that had been contaminated by a primary tumah, although [by so doing] they added tumah to its tumah. R' Akiva added, saying: In all the days of the Kohanim, never did they refrain from lighting oil that had become unfit [through contact] with a tevul yom in a lamp that had been contaminated by one contaminated by a corpse, although [by so doing] they added tumah to its tumah.*

YAD AVRAHAM

contaminated sacrificial parts, followed by a dispute (mishnah 7) between R' Meir and R' Yose whether this situation is analogous to burning *terumah* that is *chametz*.

Tumah is a legally defined state of impurity which the Torah attaches to people or objects in certain conditions. It can be transmitted to other persons or objects, but the recipient's level of *tumah* is generally one degree lower than the transmitter's. The greatest degree of *tumah* is that of a human corpse, which is classified as אֲבִי אֲבוֹת הַטֻּמְאָה, *avi avos hatumah* [lit. *grandfather of all tumos*]. All other *sources* of *tumah* [e.g. a *zav, niddah, sheretz;* see 8:5] are classified one level lower as *av hatumah*, or primary *tumah*. A person, utensil or food that is contaminated by an *av hatumah* becomes a *rishon*, or first degree of acquired *tumah*. A *rishon* can pass *tumah* only to a food or beverage, which then becomes a *sheni*, or second degree of acquired *tumah*. In the case of unsanctified food, *tumah* can go no further. However, due to its greater sanctity, *terumah* can become *tamei* to a third degree [*shlishi*] by touching a *sheni*, while sacrifices have still one more level of possible *tumah* and can become a *revi'i*, fourth degree of *tumah*.

מִימֵיהֶם שֶׁל כֹּהֲנִים — *In all the days of the Kohanim* who oversaw the disposal of disqualified and contaminated offerings, i.e., as long as the Temple stood.

אֶת הַבָּשָׂר שֶׁנִּטְמָא בִּוְלַד הַטֻּמְאָה — *[Sacrificial] meat that had been contaminated by a secondary tumah*, i.e. a second degree of acquired *tumah* [*sheni*]. The contaminated meat was thus a *shlishi* (*Rav*).

עִם הַבָּשָׂר שֶׁנִּטְמָא בְּאַב הַטֻּמְאָה — *Together with [sacrificial] meat that had been contaminated by a primary tumah*. By coming in contact with an *av hatumah*, this meat became a *rishon*, i.e. *tamei* in the first degree. Burning it together with meat possessing only a third-degree *tumah* imparts to the latter a greater degree of *tumah*. Nevertheless, since both are being burned in any case, we are unconcerned with the increase in *tumah* (*Rav*).

לֹא נִמְנְעוּ מִלְהַדְלִיק . . . — *Never did they refrain from lighting oil* . . . A *tevul yom* is any person who has immersed in a *mikveh* to purify himself of *tumah*. Such a person does not regain his purity in regard to *terumah* until nightfall. In the interim his status is equivalent to a *sheni* [second degree], and any *terumah* he touches becomes *tamei* in the third degree. Contaminated *terumah* must be burned, though the oil may be used to kindle a lamp in the process. If the lamp had been contaminated by someone who had touched a human corpse, it is *tamei* in the degree of *av* [primary]. This is due to the rule [exclusive to human-corpse *tumah*] that חֶרֶב הֲרֵי הוּא כְּחָלָל, *the sword has the same status as the corpse;* i.e. that any utensil (except one made of earthenware) which touches an *avi avos hatumah* (the corpse itself) or an *av hatumah* (whatever touched the corpse) receives the *same* degree of *tumah* as the object it touched (*Rambam;* according to some, this stringency applies only to metal utensils). Thus, the oil burned in this metal lamp will become a *rishon* (*tamei* in the first degree), whereas the unfit *terumah* oil had previously only possessed a third degree of *tumah*. Nevertheless, the Sages permitted doing this.

[ז] אָמַר רַבִּי מֵאִיר: מִדִּבְרֵיהֶם לָמַדְנוּ שֶׁשּׂוֹרְפִין תְּרוּמָה טְהוֹרָה עִם הַטְּמֵאָה בַּפֶּסַח.

אָמַר לוֹ רַבִּי יוֹסֵי: אֵינָהּ הִיא הַמִּדָּה. וּמוֹדִים רַבִּי אֱלִיעֶזֶר וְרַבִּי יְהוֹשֻׁעַ שֶׁשּׂוֹרְפִין זוֹ לְעַצְמָהּ וְזוֹ לְעַצְמָהּ. עַל מַה נֶּחֱלָקוּ? עַל הַתְּלוּיָה וְעַל הַטְּמֵאָה. שֶׁרַבִּי אֱלִיעֶזֶר אוֹמֵר תִּשָּׂרֵף זוֹ לְעַצְמָהּ וְזוֹ לְעַצְמָהּ, וְרַבִּי יְהוֹשֻׁעַ אוֹמֵר שְׁתֵּיהֶן כְּאַחַת.

פרק שני

[א] **כָּל** שָׁעָה שֶׁמֻּתָּר לֶאֱכוֹל, מַאֲכִיל לִבְהֵמָה, לְחַיָּה וּלְעוֹפוֹת, וּמוֹכְרוֹ לְנָכְרִי, וּמֻתָּר בַּהֲנָאָתוֹ. עָבַר זְמַנּוֹ, אָסוּר בַּהֲנָאָתוֹ, וְלֹא יַסִּיק בּוֹ תַּנּוּר וְכִירַיִם.

רַבִּי יְהוּדָה אוֹמֵר: אֵין בִּעוּר חָמֵץ אֶלָּא שְׂרֵפָה.

וַחֲכָמִים אוֹמְרִים: אַף מְפָרֵר וְזוֹרֶה לָרוּחַ אוֹ מַטִּיל לַיָּם.

[ב] חָמֵץ שֶׁל נָכְרִי שֶׁעָבַר עָלָיו הַפֶּסַח, מֻתָּר בַּהֲנָאָה; וְשֶׁל יִשְׂרָאֵל, אָסוּר בַּהֲנָאָה — שֶׁנֶּאֱמַר: „וְלֹא יֵרָאֶה לְךָ שְׂאֹר.״

[ג] נָכְרִי שֶׁהִלְוָה אֶת יִשְׂרָאֵל עַל חֲמֵצוֹ, אַחַר הַפֶּסַח מֻתָּר בַּהֲנָאָה; וְיִשְׂרָאֵל שֶׁהִלְוָה אֶת הַנָּכְרִי עַל חֲמֵצוֹ, אַחַר הַפֶּסַח אָסוּר בַּהֲנָאָה.

יד אברהם

7. מִדִּבְרֵיהֶם לָמַדְנוּ — *From their words* [R' Chanina's and R' Akiva's in the previous mishnah] *we may infer* that the *Kohanim* burned flesh that was a third-degree *tumah* together with flesh that was a first-degree *tumah*; we may infer that we may burn uncontaminated *terumah* with contaminated *terumah* on Erev Pesach, although this contaminates the former while burning it (*Rav*). Since the uncontaminated *terumah* must be burned, it need not be safeguarded against *tumah*. The second-degree *tumah* mentioned by R' Chanina as the contaminator of the meat refers even to liquids. However, R' Meir holds that according to Biblical law, liquids cannot transmit *tumah*. Consequently, the meat touched by the liquid is *tamei* only according to Rabbinic decree, but is *tahor* on the Biblical level. Since the Sages nevertheless permitted burning it with meat that is a *rishon*, which renders it Biblically *tamei*, it is evident that even uncontaminated sacrificial parts being burned need not be protected against *tumah*.

אָמַר לוֹ רַבִּי יוֹסֵי — *R' Yose said to him* that the cases are not analogous. In his view the power of liquids to contaminate is Biblical. Accordingly, R' Chanina's precedent demonstrates only that meat which was *tamei* at least to some degree Biblically may be further contaminated while being burned. But the *terumah* of mishnah 6 is not *tamei* at all, merely *chametz*. Thus, we may not contaminate it while burning it in the sixth hour (*Rav*). [However, even R' Yose agrees that once the Biblical requirement to destroy *chametz* takes effect at noon, the *terumah* may be allowed to become *tamei* in the process (*Gem.*).]

וּמוֹדִים רַבִּי אֱלִיעֶזֶר וְרַבִּי יְהוֹשֻׁעַ. . . — *[Furthermore, even] R' Eliezer and R' Yehoshua concur* . . . R' Eliezer and R' Yehoshua disagree whether there is a prohibition to burn *terumah* whose *tumah* is in doubt together with *terumah* that is definitely *tamei*. R' Eliezer rules that it may not be burned because there is an obligation to safeguard even doubtfully contaminated *terumah* from becoming definitely *tamei*. R' Yehoshua, however, rules that once its purity is in question and it can no longer be used, the Torah no longer requires us to safeguard it from *tumah*. [The dispute is based on different exegetical interpretations of the relevant verse.] Nevertheless, R' Yose states, they both concur that clearly uncontaminated *terumah* may not be burned with contaminated *terumah*, even in the sixth hour when it is already Rabbinically prohibited (*Rav*).

CHAPTER TWO

1. The mishnah now returns to the topic of the time limits for eating and benefiting from *chametz* on Erev Pesach.

כָּל שָׁעָה שֶׁמֻּתָּר לֶאֱכוֹל — *As long as it is permitted to eat [chametz]*, one may feed it to his animals. But once the prohibition to eat *chametz* takes effect, it is forbidden for all benefit. Thus according to Rabban Gamliel (1:5)

[7] *R' Meir said: From their words we may infer that we may burn uncontaminated terumah [that is chametz] with contaminated terumah on Pesach. R' Yose said to him: This is not analogous. [Furthermore, even] R' Eliezer and R' Yehoshua concur that each is burned separately. Concerning what did they differ? Concerning questionably contaminated [terumah] and definitely contaminated [terumah]. R' Eliezer says that each must be burned separately, but R' Yehoshua says that both [may be burned] together.*

CHAPTER TWO

[1] **כָּל** *As long as it is permitted to eat [chametz], one may feed [it] to livestock, beasts and birds, and sell it to a non-Jew, and one is permitted to derive benefit from it. Once its period has passed, it is forbidden to derive benefit from it, and one may not fire an oven or a stove with it.*

R' Yehudah says: Chametz may be removed only by burning. But the Sages say: He may also crumble [it] and throw [it] to the wind or cast [it] into the sea.

[2] *The chametz of a non-Jew over which Pesach has passed is permitted for benefit, but [the chametz] of a Jew is forbidden for benefit — since it is said: Nor shall leaven be seen with you (Ex. 13:7).*

[3] *[If] a non-Jew lent [money] to a Jew with his chametz [as collateral], it is permitted to benefit from it after Pesach; but if a Jew lent [money] to a non-Jew with his chametz [as collateral], it is forbidden to benefit from it after Pesach.*

YAD AVRAHAM

who gives *Kohanim* an extra hour for eating *terumah*, even an Israelite who must stop eating *chametz* at the beginning of the fifth hour may continue to feed *chametz* to his livestock until the onset of the sixth hour. [This is indeed the *halachah;* see O. Ch. 443:1.]

וּמֻתָּר בַּהֲנָאָתוֹ — *And one is permitted to derive benefit from it.* The *Gemara* concludes that this [seemingly redundant] clause alludes to the rule that if *chametz* is charred before it becomes forbidden to such an extent that it is inedible even to dogs, he is permitted to derive benefit from it even after the *chametz* prohibition takes effect (*Rav*).

עָבַר זְמַנּוֹ, אָסוּר בַּהֲנָאָתוֹ — *Once its period has passed* [i.e., the fifth hour], *it is forbidden to derive benefit from it.* During the sixth hour, *chametz* is forbidden by Rabbinic injunction, and after noon, by Biblical law. Even while burning it he may not benefit from it [by using it to fire an oven] (*Rav*).

רַבִּי יְהוּדָה אוֹמֵר — *R' Yehudah* derives his rule from a comparison of *chametz* to נוֹתָר, *leftover* sacrificial meat. Since *leftover* offerings must be burned (*Ex.* 12:10), *chametz* too must be burned (*Rav*).

וַחֲכָמִים אוֹמְרִים — *The Sages* reject R' Yehudah's analogy because not all forbidden substances share the requirement of burning. Although the *halachah* follows the Sages, it is customary to burn the *chametz* (*Rama, O. Ch.* 445:1).

אוֹ מֵטִיל לַיָּם — *Or cast [it] into the sea.* Hard *chametz* or grain, which does not disintegrate rapidly, must first be crumbled; other kinds may simply be cast into the sea.

2. חָמֵץ שֶׁל נָכְרִי — The *chametz* kept by a non-Jew until the end of Pesach is permitted for a Jew's benefit, and may even be eaten.

וְשֶׁל יִשְׂרָאֵל — *But [the chametz]* kept by a Jew over Pesach is forbidden after Pesach for consumption and even benefit. According to the *Gemara's* conclusion, the post-festival prohibition is a Rabbinically imposed penalty. The mishnah quotes this verse because it is the verse upon which the Sages based their decree. *Chametz* left in a Jew's possession over Pesach is forbidden forever even if it was left over *accidentally* (*O. Ch.* 448:3).

3. נָכְרִי שֶׁהִלְוָה אֶת יִשְׂרָאֵל . . . — *[If] a non-Jew lent [money] to a Jew* before Pesach, with the Jew pledging his *chametz* as collateral, and the Jew then defaulted on the loan, the *chametz* does not become prohibited because it belonged to the gentile over Pesach. This is true only if their agreement stipulated that in case of default the collateral would become the lender's retroactive to the time of the loan. Also, the collateral must have been held in the lender's premises during Pesach, so that he need not take any action to collect his debt (*Rav*). A Jew is permitted to purchase this *chametz* after Pesach and eat it.

וְיִשְׂרָאֵל שֶׁהִלְוָה אֶת הַנָּכְרִי — *But if a Jew lent [money] to a non-Jew,* i.e., if the situation was reversed and the non-Jew defaulted on the debt,

חָמֵץ שֶׁנָּפְלָה עָלָיו מַפֹּלֶת, הֲרֵי הוּא כִּמְבֹעָר. רַבָּן שִׁמְעוֹן בֶּן גַּמְלִיאֵל אוֹמֵר: כָּל שֶׁאֵין הַכֶּלֶב יָכוֹל לְחַפֵּשׂ אַחֲרָיו.

[ד] הָאוֹכֵל תְּרוּמַת חָמֵץ בַּפֶּסַח בְּשׁוֹגֵג, מְשַׁלֵּם קֶרֶן וָחֹמֶשׁ. בְּמֵזִיד, פָּטוּר מִתַּשְׁלוּמִים וּמִדְּמֵי עֵצִים.

[ה] אֵלּוּ דְבָרִים שֶׁאָדָם יוֹצֵא בָהֶן יְדֵי חוֹבָתוֹ בַּפֶּסַח: בְּחִטִּים, בִּשְׂעוֹרִים, בְּכֻסְּמִין, וּבְשִׁיפוֹן וּבְשִׁבֹּלֶת שׁוּעָל. וְיוֹצְאִין בִּדְמַאי, וּבְמַעֲשֵׂר רִאשׁוֹן שֶׁנִּטְּלָה תְרוּמָתוֹ, וּבְמַעֲשֵׂר שֵׁנִי וְהֶקְדֵּשׁ שֶׁנִּפְדּוּ; וְהַכֹּהֲנִים בְּחַלָּה וּבִתְרוּמָה; אֲבָל לֹא בְטֶבֶל, וְלֹא בְמַעֲשֵׂר רִאשׁוֹן שֶׁלֹּא נִטְּלָה תְרוּמָתוֹ, וְלֹא בְמַעֲשֵׂר שֵׁנִי וְהֶקְדֵּשׁ שֶׁלֹּא נִפְדּוּ.

חַלּוֹת תּוֹדָה וּרְקִיקֵי נָזִיר — עֲשָׂאָן לְעַצְמוֹ, אֵין יוֹצְאִין בָּהֶן; עֲשָׂאָן לִמְכֹּר בַּשּׁוּק, יוֹצְאִין בָּהֶן.

יד אברהם

the *chametz* is considered the lender's and consequently forbidden since it had been 'kept' by a Jew over Pesach.

חָמֵץ שֶׁנָּפְלָה עָלָיו מַפֹּלֶת — *If a ruin collapsed over chametz,* it is not necessary to remove the debris in order to find and destroy the *chametz* (*Tif. Yis.*). However, the owner must nullify it in his heart (בִּטּוּל), because it is conceivable that the debris will be removed during Pesach (*Rav*).

כָּל שֶׁאֵין הַכֶּלֶב ... — *Provided a dog cannot search it out*; i.e., it is under at least three handbreadths of debris.

4. *Terumah* [the portion separated from produce and given a *Kohen*] may not be eaten by anyone except *Kohanim* and members of their households. If *terumah* is mistakenly [בְּשׁוֹגֵג] eaten by a non-*Kohen* (e.g. he was unaware that it was *terumah*), he must atone by repaying the principal and adding a fifth. The payment must be made in produce (not money), which is then rendered *terumah*. If he knowingly eats *terumah*, he is liable to the punishment of premature 'death at the hands of Heaven' [מִיתָה בִידֵי שָׁמַיִם]; if he had been forewarned by two witnesses, he is liable to lashes. His only financial liability, however, is to pay damages; this can be done with money, and even if it is with produce, it does not become *terumah*.

מְשַׁלֵּם קֶרֶן וָחֹמֶשׁ — *Must repay the principal plus a fifth.* Although *chametz* on Pesach becomes forbidden forever and the *terumah* he ate was thus worthless, *terumah* is unique in that the amount repaid for eating it mistakenly does not depend on its value, but on the volume consumed. A pound of fruit must be replaced with a pound of the same kind of fruit regardless of the price at the time of repayment. Thus, the original value of the *terumah* is irrelevant.

בְּמֵזִיד ... — *[If he eats it] deliberately,* knowing that it was *terumah* and forbidden to him, he does not pay anything. In this case the obligation to pay is not determined by quantity but by the value of the damage. *Chametz* on Pesach, however, has no value (*Rav*).

וּמִדְּמֵי עֵצִים — *And from [liability for] its value as fuel,* because *chametz* on Pesach may not even be burned as a fuel.

5. There is a Biblical obligation to eat matzah on the first night of Pesach. The mishnah delineates the products that may be used to fulfill this *mitzvah.* [Many of the other items mentioned here may be eaten on Pesach but they cannot be used to fulfill the first night's obligation.]

בְּחִטִּים ... — *With wheat* ... However, one does not discharge his obligation with millet, rice, or matzah made from any other grain but these five. It is customary to use only wheat (*O. Ch.* 453:1), because it is the tastiest.

בִּדְמַאי — *With demai,* i.e. produce purchased from a common person. The Sages decreed that such produce may not be eaten until it has been tithed, because they observed that many common people had become lax in separating tithes other than *terumah.* However, they did not impose this burden upon poor people, in view of the compliance of *most* ignorant people with the laws of tithes. Technically, anyone can avail himself of the right to eat *demai* by declaring his property *hefker* (ownerless) and becoming poor. Consequently, fulfilling the matzah obligation with *demai* is not per se disqualified as a *mitzvah* that comes about through a transgression (*Gem.*).

וּבְמַעֲשֵׂר רִאשׁוֹן שֶׁנִּטְּלָה תְרוּמָתוֹ — *[And] with maaser rishon whose terumah has been separated.* The produce of *Eretz Yisrael* may not be

If a ruin collapsed over chametz, it is regarded as removed. Rabban Shimon ben Gamliel says: Provided a dog cannot search it out.

[4] *One who eats terumah of chametz on Pesach mistakenly, must repay the principal plus a fifth. [If he eats it] deliberately, he is exempt from payment and from [liability for] its value as fuel.*

[5] *These are the species [of grain] with which a man fulfills his [matzah] obligation on Pesach: with wheat, barley, spelt, rye and oats. One can discharge [his obligation to eat matzah] with demai, with maaser rishon whose terumah has been separated, with maaser sheni or consecrated produce that were redeemed; and Kohanim with challah and terumah; but not with untithed produce, nor with maaser rishon whose terumah has not been separated, nor with maaser sheni or consecrated produce that were not redeemed.*

The [unleavened] loaves of the thanksgiving offering, and the nazir's wafers — [if] he made them for himself, he cannot fulfill his obligation with them; [but if] he made them to sell in the market, he can fulfill his obligation with them.

YAD AVRAHAM

eaten until various tithes have been separated from it. These are: *terumah* (about 2% of the crop) which is given a *Kohen*, and *maaser rishon* (10% of the remainder), which goes to a Levite. *Maaser*, however, may not be eaten until the Levite tithes it by separating a tenth to give to a *Kohen*. This is called the *terumah* of the *maaser* and has all the laws of *terumah*. Obviously, one may use such tithed *maaser* for matzah. The mishnah's point is that there are circumstances in which it may be used even if *only* the Levite's *terumah* had been separated but not the general *terumah* which should have come first. This occurs when the *maaser* was separated before the *terumah* obligation took effect at threshing (*Gem.*).

וּבְמַעֲשֵׂר שֵׁנִי וְהֶקְדֵּשׁ שֶׁנִּפְדּוּ — *With maaser sheni or consecrated produce that were redeemed.* There is yet another tithe required. In the first, second, fourth and fifth years of the Sabbatical cycle, *maaser sheni* is separated (also 10%). This belongs to the owner but it must be eaten in Jerusalem. However, the owner may redeem the *maaser sheni* [which then loses its sanctity] and take the money to Jerusalem in place of the produce. This he uses to buy food which then assumes the *maaser sheni* sanctity. When redeeming his own *maaser*, the owner must add an extra fifth to the price. The same is true when one redeems items he has consecrated to the Temple treasury. Thus, he may fulfill his matzah obligation with redeemed *maaser sheni* and consecrated produce. In stating the obvious, the mishnah also teaches that even if the fifth has not yet been paid the redemption has already taken effect and the matzah obligation is fulfilled (*Gem.*).

וְהַכֹּהֲנִים בְּחַלָּה — *And Kohanim with challah.* Dough requires an additional *terumah*, called *challah*. Since *challah* and *terumah* are forbidden to non-*Kohanim*, only *Kohanim* fulfill their obligation with them.

אֲבָל לֹא בְטֶבֶל — *But not with untithed produce,* because it is prohibited and thus obviously unfit for matzah. Our mishnah means to include even Rabbinically forbidden *tevel*, i.e., grain not subject to tithing under Biblical law, but for which the Sages imposed an obligation. All the substances disqualified here are because of the principle invalidating a מִצְוָה הַבָּאָה בַּעֲבֵירָה, *mitzvah brought about by means of a transgression.*

חַלּוֹת תּוֹדָה — *Loaves of the thanksgiving offering;* see 1:5.

וּרְקִיקֵי נָזִיר — *Nazir's wafers.* When the term of a *nazir's* vow ends, he brings a set of offerings which include *a basket of unleavened bread, loaves of fine flour mixed with oil, and unleavened wafers smeared with oil* (*Num.* 6:15).

עֲשָׂאָן לְעַצְמוֹ . . . — *[If] he made them for himself,* to use for his own *nazir* offering, he cannot fulfill his matzah obligation with them, because the Torah states: *you shall guard the matzos* (*Ex.* 12:17), which the Sages understand to teach that the matzah must be guarded during its preparation for the sake of the *mitzvah* of eating matzah; not for any other purpose, such as a sacrifice (*Rav*).

עֲשָׂאָן לִמְכֹּר . . . — *[But if] he made them to sell* to other nazirites, he may fulfill his first-night obligation with them. Anyone making loaves for sale stipulates beforehand: 'If it is sold, well and good; if not, I will fulfill the obligation of matzah with it' (*Gem.*).

[ו] וְאֵלּוּ יְרָקוֹת שֶׁאָדָם יוֹצֵא בָהֶן יְדֵי חוֹבָתוֹ בַּפֶּסַח: בְּחֲזֶרֶת, וּבְעֻלְשִׁין, וּבְתַמְכָא, וּבְחַרְחֲבִינָה, וּבְמָרוֹר. יוֹצְאִין בָּהֶן בֵּין לַחִין בֵּין יְבֵשִׁין, אֲבָל לֹא כְבוּשִׁין, וְלֹא שְׁלוּקִין, וְלֹא מְבֻשָּׁלִין. וּמִצְטָרְפִין לִכְזַיִת. וְיוֹצְאִין בְּקֶלַח שֶׁלָּהֶן; וּבִדְמַאי; וּבְמַעֲשֵׂר רִאשׁוֹן שֶׁנִּטְּלָה תְרוּמָתוֹ; וּבְמַעֲשֵׂר שֵׁנִי וְהֶקְדֵּשׁ שֶׁנִּפְדּוּ.

[ז] אֵין שׁוֹרִין אֶת הַמֻּרְסָן לְתַרְנְגוֹלִים, אֲבָל חוֹלְטִין.
הָאִשָּׁה לֹא תִשְׁרֶה אֶת הַמֻּרְסָן שֶׁתּוֹלִיךְ בְּיָדָהּ לַמֶּרְחָץ, אֲבָל שָׁפָה הִיא בִּבְשָׂרָהּ יָבֵשׁ. לֹא יִלְעֹס אָדָם חִטִּין וְיַנִּיחַ עַל מַכָּתוֹ בַּפֶּסַח, מִפְּנֵי שֶׁהֵן מַחְמִיצוֹת.

[ח] אֵין נוֹתְנִין קֶמַח לְתוֹךְ הַחֲרֹסֶת אוֹ לְתוֹךְ הַחַרְדָּל. וְאִם נָתַן, יֹאכַל מִיָּד. וְרַבִּי מֵאִיר אוֹסֵר. אֵין מְבַשְּׁלִין אֶת הַפֶּסַח לֹא בְמַשְׁקִין וְלֹא בְמֵי פֵרוֹת. אֲבָל סָכִין וּמַטְבִּילִין אוֹתוֹ בָּהֶן.
מֵי תַשְׁמִישׁוֹ שֶׁל נַחְתּוֹם יִשָּׁפְכוּ, מִפְּנֵי שֶׁהֵן מַחְמִיצִין.

פרק שלישי

[א] **אֵלּוּ** עוֹבְרִין בַּפֶּסַח: כֻּתָּח הַבַּבְלִי, וְשֵׁכָר הַמָּדִי, וְחֹמֶץ הָאֲדוֹמִי, וְזִיתוֹם הַמִּצְרִי, וְזוֹמָן שֶׁל צַבָּעִים, וַעֲמִילָן שֶׁל טַבָּחִים,

---

יד אברהם

6. חַרְחֲבִינָה — *Charchavinah.* The *Gemara* identifies this as a type of vine growing around palms. *Rambam* identifies it as a type of thistle, while *R' Hai Gaon* considers it a type of acacia.

וּבְמָרוֹר — *And [with] maror.* According to *Rashi*, this is wormwood (cf. *Rama O. Ch.* 473:5 and *Beur Halachah* there). *Rambam* and *Aruch* identify it as a wild lettuce.

יְבֵשִׁין — *Dry*, i.e., the stalks; the leaves, however, must be fresh (*Gem.*).

אֲבָל לֹא כְבוּשִׁין — *But not soaked* in vinegar (*Rashi*), or in water (*Mag. Av.* 473:14). Vinegar disqualifies the herbs after 18 minutes of soaking; water after 24 hours (*Tif. Yis.*).

שְׁלוּקִין — *Stewed*, i.e., cooked until they are reduced to a mush (*Rashi*). Boiling, stewing and soaking remove the herbs' bitter taste.

7. אֵין שׁוֹרִין אֶת הַמֻּרְסָן ... — *One may not soak bran* even in cold water, and even for less than eighteen minutes, because soaking causes the leavening process to begin. *But one may scald it*, because scalded grain will not leaven (just as baked matzah will not leaven). However, the *Geonim* and *Rambam* prohibited scalding grain on Pesach, for fear that people will not make the water hot enough.

אֲבָל שָׁפָה — *But she may rub* her skin with dry bran although she is sweating because sweat is not a leavening agent. Nevertheless, it is advisable not to rub grain on the skin in any case, because one may forget to remove it before washing (*O.Ch.* 465:2). Saliva, however, causes leavening.

8. לְתוֹךְ הַחֲרֹסֶת ... הַחַרְדָּל — *Into charoses ... mustard*, which in Mishnaic times, contained water in addition to vinegar.

יֹאכַל מִיָּד — *It must be eaten immediately.* This applies *only* to mustard, because its pungency delays the flour's leavening. *Charoses*, however, begins leavening immediately, and it should therefore be burned without delay (*Gem.*). R' Meir, however, maintains that even the sharpness of mustard will not retard the leavening process. *Rama* (*O. Ch.* 464) remarks that it is customary (among Ashkenazim) to refrain from eating mustard on Pesach altogether.

אֵין מְבַשְּׁלִין אֶת הַפֶּסַח ... — *We may not cook the Pesach offering* ... The term *liquids* refers specifically to seven liquids: wine, honey, oil, milk, dew, blood, and water (*Machshirin* 6:4). *Fruit juices* includes any other fruit juice. In prohibiting the consumption of a cooked Pesach offering, the Torah mentions only cooking in water (*Ex.* 12:9); nevertheless the Sages found an allusion in this verse to prohibit cooking in any liquid.

מֵי תַשְׁמִישׁוֹ ... — *The water used* by a baker to cool his hands retains some of the dough which becomes *chametz*.

CHAPTER THREE

1. There are three categories of *chametz*, each with a different degree of stringency: (1) Pure,

[6] *These are the [bitter] herbs with which one fulfills his [maror] obligation on Pesach: with lettuce, endives, horseradish, charchavinah, and [with] maror. One fulfills his obligation with them whether they are fresh or dry, but not soaked, nor stewed, nor boiled. These [may be] combined to [form] the olive-sized [minimum]. One can fulfill his obligation with their stalk; with demai; with maaser rishon whose terumah has been separated; and with consecrated property and maaser sheni which were redeemed.*

[7] *One may not soak bran for chickens, but one may scald it. A woman may not soak bran to take with her to the baths, but she may rub it on her skin dry. A person may not chew wheat and place it on his wound on Pesach, because it becomes chametz.*

[8] *One may not put flour into charoses nor into mustard. If one did so, it must be eaten immediately. But R' Meir forbids [it]. We may not cook the Pesach offering either in liquids or in fruit juices. But we may baste it and dip it in them. The water used by a baker must be poured out, because they have become chametz.*

CHAPTER THREE

[1] **אֵלּוּ** *The following must be removed on Pesach: Babylonian dairy condiment, Median beer, Idumean vinegar, Egyptian zisom, dyers' broth,*

YAD AVRAHAM

unadulterated *chametz;* (2) *chametz* mixed with other substances; (3) *chametz nuksheh*. Consumption of unadulterated *chametz* on Pesach is punishable by *kares*. Consumption of a mixture containing *chametz* is Biblically prohibited, but the severity of the prohibition is subject to dispute. If the percentage of *chametz* in the mixture is such that a person eating an amount equal to three (*Rambam*) or four (*Rashi*) eggs consumes an olive's volume of *chametz* [כְּזַיִת בִּכְדֵי אֲכִילַת פְּרַס], it is subject to a negative commandment [לֹא תַעֲשֶׂה] but not *kares* (*Rambam*). [According to *Ramban* it is even subject to *kares*.] If the proportion of *chametz* is less than this, it is certainly not subject to *kares*, but there is a Tannaitic dispute whether it is included in the negative commandment against consumption of *chametz*. R' Eliezer maintains that it is, whereas the Sages hold that it is Biblically prohibited, but by less than a negative commandment. *Chametz nuksheh* (lit. *hardened chametz*) is incomplete *chametz*, either dough whose leavening was never completed (see 3:5), or *chametz* that was never fit for consumption. Some *Tannaim* hold *chametz nuksheh* to be Biblically prohibited by a negative commandment, while others contend that it is only Rabbinically prohibited (*Gem.*).

אֵלּוּ עוֹבְרִין בְּפֶסַח — *The following must be removed* from the world, i.e., destroyed, because one is not permitted to possess them on Pesach (*Tos.*). This requirement is Rabbinic, to prevent anyone from eating them by mistake (*Ran*). The Torah prohibition to own *chametz* applies only to completed *chametz* that is unmixed.

כָּתָח הַבַּבְלִי . . . — *Babylonian dairy condiment* consisted of sour milk, moldy bread crusts and salt (*Gem.*). *Median beer* was brewed from dates and barley, making it mixed *chametz*. By contrast, most beers in Talmudic times were brewed from dates alone. [However, contemporary beer, prepared exclusively from barley, is subject to *kares*.] *Idumean vinegar* was made from wine fermented with barley soaked in water (*Tos.*). *Egyptian zisom* was made from equal quantities of barley, saffron (or safflower) and salt, kneaded with water and used for medicinal purposes (*Rambam*). Though these four substances contain amounts of complete *chametz*, there is no *kares* for their consumption because they also contain large amounts of other ingredients. The next three listed are pure *chametz* with no admixture of foreign ingredients. However, because they are not meant for consumption (though theoretically they can be eaten), they are considered *chametz nuksheh* and therefore exempted from *kares*.

וְזוֹמָן שֶׁל צַבָּעִים . . . — *Dyers' broth* was made of bran mixed with water and used in the preparation of certain red dyes. *Cooks' dough* was made of flour from grain less than one-third ripe. The dough was fashioned into a pot cover which, when placed over a pot of cooking meat, drew out the muck and bad smell (*Gem.*). *Scribes' paste* was made of rye flour; it was used by tanners to paste layers of leather together and by scribes to prepare paper (*Gem.*).

וְקוֹלָן שֶׁל סוֹפְרִים. רַבִּי אֱלִיעֶזֶר אוֹמֵר: אַף תַּכְשִׁיטֵי נָשִׁים. זֶה הַכְּלָל: כָּל שֶׁהוּא מִמִּין דָּגָן, הֲרֵי זֶה עוֹבֵר בַּפֶּסַח. הֲרֵי אֵלּוּ בְּאַזְהָרָה, וְאֵין בָּהֶן מִשּׁוּם כָּרֵת.

[ב] בָּצֵק שֶׁבְּסִדְקֵי עֲרֵבָה, אִם יֵשׁ כְּזַיִת בְּמָקוֹם אֶחָד, חַיָּב לְבָעֵר; וְאִם לֹא, בָּטֵל בְּמִעוּטוֹ. וְכֵן לְעִנְיַן הַטֻּמְאָה. אִם מַקְפִּיד עָלָיו, חוֹצֵץ; וְאִם רוֹצֶה בְקִיּוּמוֹ, הֲרֵי הוּא כָעֲרֵבָה. בָּצֵק הַחֵרֵשׁ, אִם יֵשׁ כַּיּוֹצֵא בוֹ שֶׁהֶחְמִיץ, הֲרֵי זֶה אָסוּר.

[ג] כֵּיצַד מַפְרִישִׁין חַלָּה בְטֻמְאָה בְּיוֹם טוֹב? רַבִּי אֱלִיעֶזֶר אוֹמֵר: לֹא תִקְרָא לָהּ שֵׁם עַד שֶׁתֵּאָפֶה.

רַבִּי יְהוּדָה בֶּן בְּתֵירָא אוֹמֵר: תַּטִּיל בְּצוֹנֵן. אָמַר רַבִּי יְהוֹשֻׁעַ: לֹא זֶה הוּא חָמֵץ שֶׁמֻּזְהָרִים עָלָיו „בְּבַל יֵרָאֶה" וּ„בְבַל יִמָּצֵא." אֶלָּא מַפְרַשְׁתָּהּ וּמַנִּחַתָּהּ עַד הָעֶרֶב; וְאִם הֶחֱמִיצָה, הֶחֱמִיצָה.

[ד] רַבָּן גַּמְלִיאֵל אוֹמֵר: שָׁלֹשׁ נָשִׁים לָשׁוֹת כְּאַחַת וְאוֹפוֹת בְּתַנּוּר אֶחָד, זוֹ אַחַר זוֹ. וַחֲכָמִים אוֹמְרִים: שָׁלֹשׁ נָשִׁים עוֹסְקוֹת בְּבָצֵק — אַחַת לָשָׁה, וְאַחַת עוֹרֶכֶת, וְאַחַת אוֹפָה. רַבִּי עֲקִיבָא אוֹמֵר: לֹא כָל הַנָּשִׁים וְלֹא כָל הָעֵצִים וְלֹא כָל הַתַּנּוּרִים שָׁוִין. זֶה הַכְּלָל: תָּפַח, תִּלְטוֹשׁ בְּצוֹנֵן.

יד אברהם

רַבִּי אֱלִיעֶזֶר אוֹמֵר — *R' Eliezer says:* The *Tanna Kamma* forbade only a mixture containing complete *chametz* or pure *chametz nuksheh*, but he permitted the possession of *chametz nuksheh* as part of a mixture. R' Eliezer disagrees and rules that even a mixture containing *chametz nuksheh* is forbidden. The cosmetics specified by him are such a mixture.

מִמִּין דָּגָן — *[Made] of* one of the five species of grain (wheat, barley, spelt, rye and oats) and mixed with water (*Rashi*).

הֲרֵי אֵלּוּ בְּאַזְהָרָה . . . — *These* [substances listed above] *are prohibited by a negative commandment*, but he is not subject to *kares* for eating them. Our mishnah represents a minority opinion. The (*Gem.*) consensus of *Tannaim* is that mixtures containing pure *chametz*, as well as *chametz nuksheh*, are not included in the negative commandment prohibiting consumption of *chametz*, though they are Biblically forbidden and may not be kept on Pesach; see preface.

2. כְּזַיִת בְּמָקוֹם אֶחָד — *An olive's [volume] in one place* is too significant an amount to be nullified and considered part of the trough. However, less than an olive's volume in any *one* part of the trough is no longer considered a foodstuff but an integral part of the utensil, because it serves to seal the cracks and holes. However, if the dough does not serve as a seal, even the smaller amount must be removed before Pesach, because the owner may decide to detach it and it is thus not subsidiary to the trough.

וְכֵן לְעִנְיַן הַטֻּמְאָה — *And likewise regarding [the laws of] tumah-contamination.* Should a source of *tumah* touch an olive-sized piece of dough in the crack of a trough, its size gives it an identity independent of the trough. The dough thus intervenes between the contaminating agent and the trough, and only the dough becomes *tamei*, not the trough. [The dough cannot in turn pass its *tumah* to the utensil, for it is a cardinal rule that foodstuffs cannot pass *tumah* to people and utensils, only to other food or liquids.] If the amount of dough was less than an olive's size, it is considered part of the utensil (if the owner intends to leave it in the cracks), and any *tumah* touching it contaminates the entire utensil (*Rav*).

אִם מַקְפִּיד עָלָיו חוֹצֵץ — *If he objects to it*, and plans to remove it eventually, *it interposes*. The previous ruling that an olive-sized piece is never considered part of the trough is true only on Pesach, when the laws of *chametz* make the size of an olive a key factor in whether *chametz* may be retained. The mishnah now teaches that during the rest of the year the size of the dough is of no concern and the only consideration is whether the owner plans to leave it attached to the vessel.

בָּצֵק הַחֵרֵשׁ — *'Deaf' dough*, i.e., a dough which there is reason to suspect has leavened, but exhibits none of the symptoms of leavening outlined in mishnah 5. The dough as yet emits no *cooks' dough and scribes' paste. R' Eliezer says: Also women's cosmetics. This is the rule: Whatever is of a species of grain must be removed on Pesach. These are prohibited by a negative commandment but they are not subject to kares.*

[2] *When dough remains in the grooves of a kneading trough, if there is as much as an olive's [volume] in one place, he must remove [it]; but if not, it is null because of its insignificant amount. And likewise regarding the [laws of] tumah-contamination. If he objects to it, it interposes; but if he desires it to remain, it is as the trough. 'Deaf' dough — if there is [dough] similar to it that has already leavened, it is forbidden.*

[3] *How does one separate challah from contaminated dough on the festival? R' Eliezer says: She should not designate it with the name [challah] until it is baked. R' Yehudah ben Beseira says: She should cast into cold water. Said R' Yehoshua: This is not the leaven concerning which we are warned, it shall not be seen (Exodus 13:7) and it shall not be found (Exodus 12:19). Rather, he separates it and leaves it until the evening; and if it leavens, it leavens.*

[4] *Rabban Gamliel says: Three women may knead at the same time and bake in the same oven, one after the other. But the Sages say: Three women may be occupied with dough [simultaneously] — one kneading, another shaping, and a third baking. R' Akiva says: Not all women and not all kinds of wood and not all ovens are alike. This is the rule: [If the dough] rises, let her wet it with cold water.*

YAD AVRAHAM

sound when struck, like a deaf person who, when addressed, shows no reaction. [Emitting such a sound is considered a sign of leavening.] If there is another dough that was kneaded at the same time that has become leavened, the 'deaf' dough is also forbidden. In the absence of another dough, the dough is considered *chametz* if it has been left without being kneaded for 18 minutes. As long as it is constantly being worked upon, however, the process of leavening does not take place (*O. Ch.* 459:2).

3. כֵּיצַד מַפְרִישִׁין חַלָּה בְּטֻמְאָה בְּיוֹם טוֹב? — *How does one separate challah from contaminated dough on the festival? Challah* is the portion separated from dough and given to a *Kohen*. When dough is *tamei* the *challah* is separated (to permit the remainder of the dough) and then burned, because *challah*, like *terumah*, may be eaten only *tahor*. This presents a problem on Pesach since one cannot lay the *challah* aside until evening when it can be burned because the dough will leaven, causing the owner to be in possession of *chametz*. Nor can one follow the normal Pesach procedure for *challah* of separating and baking it immediately, because cooking and baking on *Yom Tov* are permitted only for the purpose of אוֹכֶל נֶפֶשׁ, *human consumption*, which is impossible here. R' Eliezer therefore suggests that the housewife bake her dough into matzah before separating *challah*, separate some of the matzah as *challah*, and burn it after *Yom Tov*. R' Yehudah ben Beseirah advises her to separate *challah* from the dough and put it into frigid water (which prevents leavening) and leave it until nightfall for burning. [R' Eliezer rejects this option, because the water may not be cold enough to retard leavening in every case.]

אָמַר רַבִּי יְהוֹשֻׁעַ — *R' Yehoshua* rejects the need for any precaution because once dough is designated *challah* it becomes the collective property of all *Kohanim* and does not belong to the original owner any longer. Thus the *challah* dough need not be destroyed because it is the property of neither the original owner nor of any specific *Kohen* (*Rav*). [However, R' Eliezer and Ben Beseira maintain that since the original owner still retains the power to give the *challah* to the *Kohen* of his choice, this constitutes a certain degree of ownership (טוֹבַת הֲנָאָה מָמוֹן). R' Yehoshua considers this right inconsequential (*Gem.*).]

4. שָׁלֹשׁ נָשִׁים לָשׁוֹת כְּאַחַת — *Three women may knead at the same time* although they are using an oven large enough for only one dough. Although the third dough will be left standing until the other two bake, R' Gamliel maintains that dough does not leaven in so short a time. However, the Sages fear that the time lapse may be too long. Thus, they rule that they must stagger their work so that one kneads while the second shapes or rolls the dough and bastes it with cold water, and a third bakes, with the cycle repeating itself, so that no dough is left unattended. R' Akiva disputes R' Gamliel and concurs with the Sages because one cannot generalize about the pace at which different women work, ovens heat, or wood burns (*Rav*).

זֶה הַכְּלָל: — *This is the rule:* [This phrase is not part of R' Akiva's statement but a unanimous

[ה] שְׂאוֹר יִשָּׂרֵף, וְהָאוֹכְלוֹ פָּטוּר. סִדּוּק יִשָּׂרֵף, וְהָאוֹכְלוֹ חַיָּב כָּרֵת. אֵיזֶהוּ שְׂאוֹר? כְּקַרְנֵי חֲגָבִים. סִדּוּק? שֶׁנִּתְעָרְבוּ סְדָקָיו זֶה בָזֶה; דִּבְרֵי רַבִּי יְהוּדָה. וַחֲכָמִים אוֹמְרִים: זֶה וָזֶה הָאוֹכְלוֹ חַיָּב כָּרֵת. וְאֵיזֶהוּ שְׂאוֹר? כָּל שֶׁהִכְסִיפוּ פָנָיו, כְּאָדָם שֶׁעָמְדוּ שַׂעֲרוֹתָיו.

[ו] אַרְבָּעָה עָשָׂר שֶׁחָל לִהְיוֹת בַּשַּׁבָּת, מְבַעֲרִין אֶת הַכֹּל מִלִּפְנֵי הַשַּׁבָּת; דִּבְרֵי רַבִּי מֵאִיר. וַחֲכָמִים אוֹמְרִים: בִּזְמַנָּן.

רַבִּי אֶלְעָזָר בַּר צָדוֹק אוֹמֵר: תְּרוּמָה מִלִּפְנֵי הַשַּׁבָּת וְחוּלִין בִּזְמַנָּן.

[ז] הַהוֹלֵךְ לִשְׁחֹט אֶת פִּסְחוֹ, וְלָמוּל אֶת בְּנוֹ, וְלֶאֱכוֹל סְעוּדַת אֵרוּסִין בְּבֵית חָמִיו, וְנִזְכַּר שֶׁיֵּשׁ לוֹ חָמֵץ בְּתוֹךְ בֵּיתוֹ – אִם יָכוֹל לַחֲזוֹר, וּלְבַעֵר, וְלַחֲזוֹר לְמִצְוָתוֹ, יַחֲזוֹר וִיבַעֵר; וְאִם לָאו, מְבַטְּלוֹ בְּלִבּוֹ. לְהַצִּיל מִן הַגַּיִס, וּמִן הַנָּהָר, וּמִן הַלִּסְטִים, וּמִן הַדְּלֵקָה, וּמִן הַמַּפֹּלֶת, יְבַטֵּל בְּלִבּוֹ. וְלִשְׁבּוֹת שְׁבִיתַת הָרְשׁוּת, יַחֲזוֹר מִיָּד.

[ח] וְכֵן מִי שֶׁיָּצָא מִירוּשָׁלַיִם וְנִזְכַּר שֶׁיֵּשׁ בְּיָדוֹ בְּשַׂר קֹדֶשׁ – אִם עָבַר צוֹפִים, שׂוֹרְפוֹ בִּמְקוֹמוֹ; וְאִם לָאו, חוֹזֵר וְשׂוֹרְפוֹ לִפְנֵי הַבִּירָה מֵעֲצֵי הַמַּעֲרָכָה.

וְעַד כַּמָּה הֵן חוֹזְרִין? רַבִּי מֵאִיר אוֹמֵר: זֶה וָזֶה בִּכְבֵיצָה. רַבִּי יְהוּדָה אוֹמֵר: זֶה וָזֶה בִּכְזַיִת. וַחֲכָמִים אוֹמְרִים: בְּשַׂר קֹדֶשׁ בִּכְזַיִת, וְחָמֵץ בִּכְבֵיצָה.

יד אברהם

statement of the mishnah.] When a woman notices that dough is about to rise, she should baste it with cold water. This retards the leavening process (*Rav*).

5. שְׂאוֹר יִשָּׂרֵף — *Partly leavened dough* is classified as *chametz nuksheh* (mishnah 1) and must be burned. Nevertheless, one who eats it on Pesach is exempt from both *malkos* [lashes] and *kares*.

סִדּוּק יִשָּׂרֵף — *Furrowed dough must be burned.* The appearance of furrows on dough is a symptom of fermentation, indicating that the leavening process has been completed.

כְּקַרְנֵי חֲגָבִים — *Like locusts' horns.* When there are so few furrows on the dough's surface that they do not meet (*Rashi*), and they are very thin (*Rambam*). The Sages, however, maintain that furrows in any form, even if they do not run into each other, are an indication of complete leavening. Consequently, the dough classified as 'partly leavened' by R' Yehudah is categorized by the Sages as finished *chametz*, subject to *kares*. [Conversely, what the Sages classify as partly leavened is, according to R' Yehudah, matzah (albeit Rabbinically prohibited).]

6. וַחֲכָמִים אוֹמְרִים — *But the Sages say* that one may leave as much *chametz* as he likes for the Sabbath on the assumption that there will be enough people to eat it. Should any *chametz* remain, it can be eliminated when the proper time comes in those manners permissible on the Sabbath; see *O. Ch.* 444:4-5 with *Mishnah Berurah*.

רַבִּי אֶלְעָזָר בַּר צָדוֹק אוֹמֵר — *R' Elazar bar Tzadok* differentiates between *terumah*, which is forbidden to non-*Kohanim* and their animals and is therefore more likely to remain uneaten, and non-*terumah*, which can easily be disposed of by human and animal consumption before the time of removal (*Rashi*).

7. ... הַהוֹלֵךְ — *[If] someone is going* ... All the actions enumerated here are *mitzvos*. Therefore, if one realizes on Erev Pesach that if he goes ahead to perform the *mitzvah* upon which he embarked, he will not have time to return home and eliminate his *chametz* before it is too late, he should nullify the *chametz* in his mind and proceed to his *mitzvah*. The Scriptural requirement of removal is fulfilled by בִּטּוּל בְּלֵב, *conscious nullification*. [According to many, this is because nullification removes the person's ownership of the *chametz*.] With that accomplished, the remaining requirement to physically remove the *chametz* is only Rabbinic, which the Rabbis waived for the sake of these *mitzvos* (*Rav*).

[5] *Partly leavened dough must be burned, but one who eats it is exempt [from punishment]. Furrowed dough must be burned and one who eats it is liable to kares. Which [dough] is partly leavened? [When the furrows are] like locusts' horns. [Which is] furrowed? When the furrows run into each other; [these are] the words of R' Yehudah. But the Sages say: If one eats either of these he is liable to kares. Which [then] is partly leavened dough [which is exempted]? Any [dough] whose surface has blanched, like a man whose hairs stand on end [out of fright].*

[6] *[If] the fourteenth [of Nissan] falls on the Sabbath, one must remove all chametz before the Sabbath; [these are] the words of R' Meir. But the Sages say: At its [usual] time. R' Elazar bar Tzadok says: Terumah [must be removed] before the Sabbath and chullin at its [usual] time.*

[7] *[If] someone is going to slaughter his Pesach-offering, to circumcise his son, or to dine at a betrothal feast at the house of his [future] father-in-law, and he remembers that he has chametz in his home — if he is able to return, remove [it], and [then] return to his mitzvah, he must go back and remove [it]; but if not, he nullifies it in his heart. [If he is on his way] to save [people] from a [marauding] troop, from a river, from bandits, from a fire, or from a collapsed building, he nullifies it in his heart. If it was but to establish a voluntary resting place, he must return at once.*

[8] *Similarly, [if] someone left Jerusalem and remembered that he had sacrificial meat in his hand — if he has passed Tzofim, he burns it where he is; but if not, he [must] return and burn it before the Temple with the wood of the [Altar] pyre. For how much [chametz or meat] must one return? R' Meir says: In both cases for [the equivalent of] an egg. R' Yehudah says: In both cases for [the equivalent of] an olive. But the Sages say: [For] sacrificial meat, [the equivalent of] an olive, but [for] chametz, [the equivalent of] an egg.*

YAD AVRAHAM

לְהַצִּיל מִן הַגַּיִס ... — *To save [people] from a [marauding] troop* ... Because human life is endangered in this group of cases, he should fulfill his Scriptural obligation through nullification and not delay his mission by going back even if there is time to do so and still save them.

וְלִשְׁבֹּת שְׁבִיתַת הָרְשׁוּת — *If it was but to establish a voluntary resting place.* On the Sabbath and festivals, one may not go beyond 2000 cubits (3000-4000 ft.) from the area of his domicile. [This is the law of *techum Shabbos;* see *Eruvin* ch. 5-6.] The Rabbis created a device for extending this range another 2000 cubits (in one direction). This is by designating a spot within 2000 cubits of his abode as his 'home' for the Sabbath [קוֹנֶה שְׁבִיתָה], so that his 2000 cubits will be measured from there. To do so one must place food sufficient for two meals at that spot before the Sabbath [*eruvei techumin*]. If his need for establishing this place is for personal rather than *mitzvah* reasons, he may not rely upon nullification, but must return home to dispose of his *chametz*.

8. בְּשַׂר קֹדֶשׁ — *Sacrificial meat* is rendered unfit by being removed from Jerusalem and must then be burned (*Rav*).

אִם עָבַר צוֹפִים — *If he has passed Tzofim* [Scopus, in Latin], from which the Temple first becomes visible (*Rashi*).

וְאִם לָאו ... — *But if not*, he is still close enough to return without major inconvenience and the Sages therefore required him to do so *and burn it before the Temple*; i.e., on the Temple Mount, in the place designated for burning disqualified offerings, as derived from *Lev.* 6:23 (*Rav*; see further 7:8). Since he burns it at the Temple, he uses wood consecrated for use upon the Altar (see 8:2).

וַחֲכָמִים אוֹמְרִים — *But the Sages say* that because of the stringency attached by the Torah to leftover sacred meat, we also take a stringent attitude and demand a return for an amount as small as an olive. In the case of *chametz*, however, where nullification satisfies the Scriptural requirement, we are more lenient and do not require the owner's return for any amount smaller than an egg (*Rav*).

פרק רביעי

[א] **מְקוֹם** שֶׁנָּהֲגוּ לַעֲשׂוֹת מְלָאכָה בְּעַרְבֵי פְסָחִים עַד חֲצוֹת, עוֹשִׂין; מְקוֹם שֶׁנָּהֲגוּ שֶׁלֹּא לַעֲשׂוֹת, אֵין עוֹשִׂין. הַהוֹלֵךְ מִמְּקוֹם שֶׁעוֹשִׂין לִמְקוֹם שֶׁאֵין עוֹשִׂין, אוֹ מִמְּקוֹם שֶׁאֵין עוֹשִׂין לִמְקוֹם שֶׁעוֹשִׂין, נוֹתְנִין עָלָיו חֻמְרֵי מָקוֹם שֶׁיָּצָא מִשָּׁם וְחֻמְרֵי מָקוֹם שֶׁהָלַךְ לְשָׁם. וְאַל יְשַׁנֶּה אָדָם, מִפְּנֵי הַמַּחֲלֹקֶת.

[ב] כַּיּוֹצֵא בוֹ, הַמּוֹלִיךְ פֵּרוֹת שְׁבִיעִית מִמְּקוֹם שֶׁכָּלוּ לִמְקוֹם שֶׁלֹּא כָלוּ, אוֹ מִמְּקוֹם שֶׁלֹּא כָלוּ לִמְקוֹם שֶׁכָּלוּ, חַיָּב לְבָעֵר. רַבִּי יְהוּדָה אוֹמֵר: אוֹמְרִים לוֹ: „צֵא וְהָבֵא לָךְ אַף אַתָּה.״

[ג] מְקוֹם שֶׁנָּהֲגוּ לִמְכֹּר בְּהֵמָה דַקָּה לְעוֹבֵד כּוֹכָבִים, מוֹכְרִין; מְקוֹם שֶׁלֹּא נָהֲגוּ לִמְכּוֹר, אֵין מוֹכְרִין; וּבְכָל מָקוֹם אֵין מוֹכְרִין לָהֶם בְּהֵמָה גַסָּה, עֲגָלִים וּסְיָחִים, שְׁלֵמִין וּשְׁבוּרִין. רַבִּי יְהוּדָה מַתִּיר בִּשְׁבוּרָה. בֶּן בְּתֵירָא מַתִּיר בְּסוּס.

[ד] מְקוֹם שֶׁנָּהֲגוּ לֶאֱכוֹל צָלִי בְּלֵילֵי פְסָחִים, אוֹכְלִין; מְקוֹם שֶׁנָּהֲגוּ שֶׁלֹּא לֶאֱכוֹל, אֵין אוֹכְלִין.

יד אברהם

CHAPTER FOUR

Chapter Four discusses the rule obligating people to follow the customs of their native towns, for a generally adopted custom has the force of halachah.

1. מְלָאכָה בְּעַרְבֵי פְסָחִים — Abstention from *work on Erev Pesach* before noon is only a custom, and is permitted where this custom was not adopted; after midday, however, labor is prohibited everywhere because it is not proper that a person go about his work while his Pesach offering is being sacrificed (*Yerushalmi*). [This prohibition remains in effect even today (*O. Ch.* 468:1) because there is still much to do to prepare for Pesach.] This prohibition, however, is no more stringent than that in effect on *Chol HaMoed*, and is milder in some respects (*M.B.* 468:7).

מְקוֹם שֶׁנָּהֲגוּ שֶׁלֹּא לַעֲשׂוֹת — *Where it is customary not to work*, even before midday, it was as a precaution against forgetting to remove the *chametz*, sacrifice the Pesach offering, and bake the matzah (*Rashi*). [In ancient days, it was a universal custom to bake the Seder matzos on Erev Pesach. This time-honored custom persists today in many (especially Chassidic) communities.]

נוֹתְנִין עָלָיו חֻמְרֵי ... — *We lay upon him the stringencies* ... If a person grew up with one custom and finds himself in a place that observes a different custom, he must keep whichever custom is stricter in the particular instance. [However, if he has no intention of returning to his home town, its customs are no longer binding upon him (*O. Ch.* 574:1; *M.B.* 468:19).]

וְאַל יְשַׁנֶּה אָדָם, מִפְּנֵי הַמַּחֲלֹקֶת — *And let no man deviate [from local custom], because it arouses conflict.* One must follow the stricter local custom because persisting in one's more lenient native custom would arouse conflict in this place. But for a non-working visitor to remain idle while his neighbors are working would antagonize no one — observers would assume that he simply has nothing to do.

2. The Torah decrees that a Sabbatical year [known as *Sheviis*] be observed every seventh year by abstaining from cultivating and harvesting the fields, vineyards and orchards of *Eretz Yisrael* (*Lev.* 25:1-7). With certain exceptions, produce growing during *Sheviis* without cultivation is permitted for consumption, provided it is left accessible to all who wish to take it. [See Gen. Intro. to ArtScroll *Sheviis*.] The Torah states about such produce: *And the Sabbath [produce] of the land shall be food for you ... and for your animals and for the beasts that are in your land* (*Lev.* 25:6,7). This teaches that the food gathered from the field is permitted for consumption only as long as there remains something for the beasts to eat in the field; once the fields are bare of a particular species, we are obligated to remove what remains in our houses. This is called בִּעוּר, *removal*, and its time differs from place to place.

CHAPTER FOUR

[1] **מְקוֹם** *Where it is customary to work on Erev Pesach until midday, one may do so; [but] where it is customary not to work, one may not do so. [If] one goes from where they work to where they do not, or from where they do not to where they do, we lay upon him the stringencies of the place which he has left and the stringencies of the place to which he has gone. And let no man deviate [from local custom], because it arouses conflict.*

[2] *Similarly, one who transports Sabbatical-year crops from a place where they have been exhausted to a place where they have not been exhausted, or from a place where they have not been exhausted to a place where they have been exhausted, is required to remove [them]. R' Yehudah says: We say to him, 'Go out and bring for yourself.'*

[3] *Where it is customary to sell small livestock to non-Jews, we may sell; where it is customary not to sell, we may not sell; but in all places we may not sell them large livestock, calves or foals, healthy or maimed. R' Yehudah permits [selling] in the case of a maimed one. Ben Beseira permits [selling] in the case of a horse.*

[4] *Where it is customary to eat roast [meat] on the night of Pesach, we may eat [it]; where it is customary not to eat [roast], we may not eat [it].*

YAD AVRAHAM

הַמּוֹלִיךְ פֵּרוֹת שְׁבִיעִית ... — *One who transports Sabbatical-year crops* ... If a traveler brings produce from a place where they have been exhausted from the fields [and are thus forbidden] to a place where some still remains of this species in the fields, and the inhabitants of the new place still eat the produce in their houses — or vice versa — he is required to remove them so as to comply with the restrictions of both the place he left and the place to which he has come. By his use of the plural '*they* have been exhausted,' the first *Tanna* indicates that if there are several species marinated together [so that each has absorbed some of the other's flavor], the 'removal' need not be made unless *all* of them have reached the stage of removal. In this, he follows the view of R' Yehoshua (*Sheviis* 9:5) who derives exegetically that a food need not be removed until *no part* of it is left in the fields. R' Yehudah disputes this and says that we tell him to go out and either find supplies of the species in question or remove it. This ruling follows the view of Rabban Gamliel (ibid.) (*Gem.*).

3. ... לִמְכֹּר בְּהֵמָה — *To sell livestock* ... Small livestock are sheep and goats; large livestock are oxen, donkeys, and horses. Some places instituted the practice of not selling even small livestock to non-Jews to prevent the sale of large animals. The latter was decreed because of the possibility that a Jew might also rent or lend his ox or donkey to a non-Jew who will work the animal on the Sabbath. The Torah, however, forbids allowing an animal owned by a Jew to be worked on the Sabbath (*Ex.* 23:12), even if it has been leased or loaned. The Rabbis were also concerned that a Jew might sell an ox on Friday just before sundown and the buyer might then ask him to get the laden animal to move. In doing so, the Jew violates the prohibition of causing an animal, even one which is not his, to work on the Sabbath [מְחַמֵּר] (*Rav*).

עֲגָלִים וּסְיָחִים, שְׁלֵמִין וּשְׁבוּרִין — *Calves or foals, healthy or maimed.* Although young animals are not fit to work and should not fall under the prohibition of selling large livestock, allowing their sale could lead to the sale of large ones as well. The same is true of maimed animals. R' Yehudah, however, permits selling maimed animals because, in contrast to calves and foals, these will never be able to work.

בֶּן בְּתֵירָא ... — *Ben Beseira* permits selling a horse used exclusively for riding. Carrying a human being on the Sabbath [who can move on his own] is only Rabbinically forbidden because of the principle of חַי נוֹשֵׂא אֶת עַצְמוֹ, *a living person [partially] carries himself* (*Shabbos* 94a). Accordingly, the Rabbis did not enact any further safeguards to prevent the inadvertent violation of the Rabbinic prohibition. The custom nowadays is to sell all kinds of animals to non-Jews. Various reasons for this are given by the *Poskim*. See *Y. D.* 151:4.

4. מְקוֹם שֶׁנָּהֲגוּ שֶׁלֹּא לֶאֱכוֹל — *Where it is customary not to eat* roast meat on the night of Pesach, to avoid the impression that one is eating a Pesach offering [which must be eaten roasted] outside Jerusalem. This indeed is the custom in Ashkenazic communities (*M.B.* 476:1).

מְקוֹם שֶׁנָּהֲגוּ לְהַדְלִיק אֶת הַנֵּר בְּלֵילֵי יוֹם הַכִּפּוּרִים, מַדְלִיקִין; מְקוֹם שֶׁנָּהֲגוּ שֶׁלֹּא לְהַדְלִיק, אֵין מַדְלִיקִין. וּמַדְלִיקִין בְּבָתֵּי כְנֵסִיּוֹת, וּבְבָתֵּי מִדְרָשׁוֹת, וּבִמְבוֹאוֹת הָאֲפֵלִים, וְעַל גַּבֵּי הַחוֹלִים.

[ה] מְקוֹם שֶׁנָּהֲגוּ לַעֲשׂוֹת מְלָאכָה בְּתִשְׁעָה בְּאָב, עוֹשִׂין; מְקוֹם שֶׁנָּהֲגוּ שֶׁלֹּא לַעֲשׂוֹת מְלָאכָה, אֵין עוֹשִׂין; וּבְכָל מָקוֹם תַּלְמִידֵי חֲכָמִים בְּטֵלִים. רַבָּן שִׁמְעוֹן בֶּן גַּמְלִיאֵל אוֹמֵר: לְעוֹלָם יַעֲשֶׂה אָדָם עַצְמוֹ תַּלְמִיד חָכָם.

וַחֲכָמִים אוֹמְרִים: בִּיהוּדָה הָיוּ עוֹשִׂין מְלָאכָה בְּעַרְבֵי פְסָחִים עַד חֲצוֹת, וּבַגָּלִיל לֹא הָיוּ עוֹשִׂין כָּל עִקָּר. וְהַלַּיְלָה — בֵּית שַׁמַּאי אוֹסְרִין, וּבֵית הִלֵּל מַתִּירִין עַד הָנֵץ הַחַמָּה.

[ו] רַבִּי מֵאִיר אוֹמֵר: כָּל מְלָאכָה שֶׁהִתְחִיל בָּהּ קֹדֶם לְאַרְבָּעָה עָשָׂר, גּוֹמְרָהּ בְּאַרְבָּעָה עָשָׂר; אֲבָל לֹא יַתְחִיל בָּהּ בַּתְּחִלָּה בְּאַרְבָּעָה עָשָׂר, אַף עַל פִּי שֶׁיָּכוֹל לְגוֹמְרָהּ. וַחֲכָמִים אוֹמְרִים: שָׁלֹשׁ אֻמָּנִיּוֹת עוֹשִׂין מְלָאכָה בְּעַרְבֵי פְסָחִים עַד חֲצוֹת; וְאֵלּוּ הֵן: הַחַיָּטִים, הַסַּפָּרִים וְהַכּוֹבְסִין. רַבִּי יוֹסֵי בַּר יְהוּדָה אוֹמֵר: אַף הָרַצְעָנִים.

[ז] מוֹשִׁיבִין שׁוֹבָכִין לְתַרְנְגוֹלִים בְּאַרְבָּעָה עָשָׂר. וְתַרְנְגֹלֶת שֶׁבָּרְחָה, מַחֲזִירִין אוֹתָהּ לִמְקוֹמָהּ; וְאִם מֵתָה, מוֹשִׁיבִין אַחֶרֶת תַּחְתֶּיהָ. גּוֹרְפִין מִתַּחַת רַגְלֵי בְהֵמָה בְּאַרְבָּעָה עָשָׂר, וּבַמּוֹעֵד מְסַלְּקִין לַצְּדָדִין. מוֹלִיכִין וּמְבִיאִין כֵּלִים מִבֵּית הָאֻמָּן, אַף עַל פִּי שֶׁאֵינָם לְצֹרֶךְ הַמּוֹעֵד.

[ח] שִׁשָּׁה דְבָרִים עָשׂוּ אַנְשֵׁי יְרִיחוֹ; עַל שְׁלֹשָׁה מִחוּ בְיָדָם, וְעַל

יד אברהם

לְהַדְלִיק אֶת הַנֵּר בְּלֵילֵי יוֹם הַכִּפּוּרִים — *To light [lamps] on the night of Yom Kippur* was forbidden in some communities [despite the festival status of Yom Kippur] because it was feared that if a husband and wife could see one another they might feel a desire to cohabit, which is prohibited on Yom Kippur. Other communities adopted a different safeguard against this, *requiring* that lamps be lit in the homes and bedrooms, on the assumption that people would thereby be discouraged from cohabitation, which is forbidden in an illuminated place [see *Niddah* 17a]. This is the custom of Ashkenazic communities (*O. Ch.* 610:2).

The *Gemara* praises both customs (each intended to preserve the sanctity of the holy day) with the verse *Your people are all righteous, they shall inherit the land forever* (*Isaiah* 60:21).

וּמַדְלִיקִין בְּבָתֵּי כְנֵסִיּוֹת . . . — *But [in all places] we light [lamps] in the synagogues* and wherever illumination is needed, for it is a *mitzvah* to light lamps in honor of the festival.

5. מְלָאכָה בְּתִשְׁעָה בְּאָב — *Work on the Ninth of Av* is avoided because *Tishah B'Av* should evoke a sense of mourning for the Temple, and work distracts a person from his mourning. The communities which permitted work reasoned that an ancient sorrow does not carry with it the extreme restrictions of a recent loss (*Meiri*). However, *talmidei chachamim* should abstain in all places because they should feel the loss of the Temple more keenly than others. Also, their abstention is not so noticeable for they refrain from work on many occasions. Rabban Shimon ben Gamliel says that even a layman may refrain from work without fear of appearing to assume the rank of scholar, because people will assume that he simply has no work to do. *Rama* states that the Ashkenazic custom is to refrain from work until noon on *Tishah B'Av*.

וַחֲכָמִים אוֹמְרִים: בִּיהוּדָה . . . עַד חֲצוֹת — *The Sages say: In Judea . . . until midday*. The mishnah now refers back to the ruling of mishnah 1 that abstaining from work on Erev Pesach morning is a matter of custom, not halachah. Our mishnah now informs us that the Sages disagree and consider its status a matter of halachic dispute, not popular custom. The Sages of Judea permitted work while those in Galilee prohibited it (*Gem.*). According to Beis Shammai, the

Where it is customary to light [lamps] on the night of Yom Kippur, we may light [them]; where it is customary not to light [them], we may not light [them]. But [in all places] we light [lamps] in the synagogues, houses of study, dark alleys, and for the sick.

[5] *Where it is customary to do work on the Ninth of Av, we may do [it]; where it is customary not to do work, we may not do [it]; but in all places Torah scholars abstain. Rabban Shimon ben Gamliel says: A man should always adopt the behavior of a Torah scholar.*

The Sages say: In Judea they used to work on Erev Pesach until midday, while in Galilee they did not [work] at all. [As for] the night, Beis Shammai forbid [work], while Beis Hillel permit it until sunrise.

[6] *R' Meir says: Any work which one began before the fourteenth, he may finish on the fourteenth; but he may not begin it initially on the fourteenth, even if he can finish it [before midday]. But the Sages say: [Practitioners of] three crafts may work on Erev Pesach until midday; they are: tailors, barbers and launderers. R' Yose bar Yehudah says: Also shoemakers.*

[7] *We may set up coops for chickens on the fourteenth. If a [brooding] hen escaped, we may return her to her place; if she died, we may set another in her stead. One may sweep away [dung] from under an animal's feet on the fourteenth, but on the [Intermediate Days of the] festival he may [only] clear it away to the sides [of the stall]. One may take utensils to, and bring them back from, the house of a craftsman, even though they are not needed for the festival.*

[8] *The citizens of Jericho did six things; for three the Sages reproved them, and*

YAD AVRAHAM

Galileans prohibited work even on the night before, treating the fourteenth like a festival, when work is restricted from evening. Beis Hillel, however, permit it until sunrise, comparing the work prohibition to eating on fast days, when only the day is included.

6. רַבִּי מֵאִיר אוֹמֵר — *R' Meir says* that even in places where it is customary not to work before midday, it is still permitted to complete tasks begun earlier, provided the work is being done for the sake of the festival (*Rav*). Similarly, the exemptions assigned by the Sages and R' Yose bar Yehudah to certain crafts are only for work needed for the festival.

7. בְּאַרְבָּעָה עָשָׂר — [All day] *on the fourteenth,* because this is not considered forbidden labor.

וְתַרְנְגֹלֶת שֶׁבָּרְחָה — *If a [brooding] hen escaped.* This refers to *Chol HaMoed*. If a hen left her fertilized eggs after sitting on them for three days, the embryo has started to form and the eggs are now fit only for hatching. The hen may therefore be returned to her place because the eggs would be a total loss [דְּבַר הָאָבֵד] otherwise. This is certainly permitted on the fourteenth as well, inasmuch as one may then even *set* the fowl to brood.

וְאִם מֵתָה — *If she died.* There is a question whether this too refers to *Chol HaMoed* or only to the fourteenth. It is much harder to set a hen on a brood that is not hers, and the extra effort may be prohibited on *Chol HaMoed* (see *O. Ch.* 536).

מוֹלִיכִין . . . כֵּלִים — *One may take utensils* to a craftsman on the fourteenth even if they are not needed for the festival. On *Chol HaMoed*, however, one may bring home only utensils needed for the festival.

8. שִׁשָּׁה דְבָרִים עָשׂוּ אַנְשֵׁי יְרִיחוֹ . . . — *The citizens of Jericho did six things* ... Although the Sages found all six objectionable, they reproved them for only three. The following they did not reprove them for: (1) They would graft fruit-bearing branches of a (male) palm tree onto a barren (female) palm. Grafting within the same species is permitted, but they would graft even on the afternoon of Erev Pesach. (2) They would also recite the *Shema* without the appropriate pauses, e.g. without drawing out the word אֶחָד to allow a moment for meditating upon and accepting God's sovereignty. (3) They also reaped and stacked new grain prior to the *Omer*, although the Sages had forbidden this as a safeguard against eating some while working with it (*Menachos* 10:5; see page 184).

The Sages reproved them for the following: (4) They permitted branches of sacred property for personal use. Although the Biblical prohibition

שְׁלֹשָׁה לֹא מִחוּ בְיָדָם. וְאֵלּוּ הֵן שֶׁלֹּא מִחוּ בְיָדָם: מַרְכִּיבִין דְּקָלִים כָּל הַיּוֹם; וְכוֹרְכִין אֶת שְׁמַע; וְקוֹצְרִין וְגוֹדְשִׁין לִפְנֵי הָעֹמֶר, וְלֹא מִחוּ בְיָדָם. וְאֵלּוּ שֶׁמִּחוּ בְיָדָם: מַתִּירִין גַּמְזִיּוֹת שֶׁל הֶקְדֵּשׁ; וְאוֹכְלִין מִתַּחַת הַנְּשָׁרִים בַּשַּׁבָּת; וְנוֹתְנִין פֵּאָה לְיָרָק, וּמִחוּ בְיָדָם חֲכָמִים.

[ט] שִׁשָּׁה דְבָרִים עָשָׂה חִזְקִיָּה הַמֶּלֶךְ, עַל שְׁלֹשָׁה הוֹדוּ לוֹ, וְעַל שְׁלֹשָׁה לֹא הוֹדוּ לוֹ. גֵּרַר עַצְמוֹת אָבִיו עַל מִטָּה שֶׁל חֲבָלִים, וְהוֹדוּ לוֹ. כִּתַּת נְחַשׁ הַנְּחֹשֶׁת, וְהוֹדוּ לוֹ. גָּנַז סֵפֶר רְפוּאוֹת, וְהוֹדוּ לוֹ. עַל שְׁלֹשָׁה לֹא הוֹדוּ לוֹ. קִצֵּץ דַּלְתוֹת שֶׁל הֵיכָל וְשִׁגְּרָן לְמֶלֶךְ אַשּׁוּר, וְלֹא הוֹדוּ לוֹ. סָתַם מֵי גִיחוֹן הָעֶלְיוֹן, וְלֹא הוֹדוּ לוֹ. עִבֵּר נִיסָן בְּנִיסָן, וְלֹא הוֹדוּ לוֹ.

פרק חמישי

[א] **תָּמִיד** נִשְׁחָט בִּשְׁמוֹנֶה וּמֶחֱצָה וְקָרֵב בְּתֵשַׁע וּמֶחֱצָה. בְּעַרְבֵי פְסָחִים נִשְׁחָט בְּשֶׁבַע וּמֶחֱצָה וְקָרֵב בִּשְׁמוֹנֶה וּמֶחֱצָה, בֵּין בַּחוֹל בֵּין בַּשַּׁבָּת. חָל עֶרֶב פֶּסַח לִהְיוֹת בְּעֶרֶב שַׁבָּת, נִשְׁחָט בְּשֵׁשׁ וּמֶחֱצָה, וְקָרֵב בְּשֶׁבַע וּמֶחֱצָה, וְהַפֶּסַח אַחֲרָיו.

[ב] הַפֶּסַח שֶׁשְּׁחָטוֹ שֶׁלֹּא לִשְׁמוֹ, וְקִבֵּל וְהִלֵּךְ וְזָרַק שֶׁלֹּא לִשְׁמוֹ, אוֹ לִשְׁמוֹ וְשֶׁלֹּא לִשְׁמוֹ, אוֹ שֶׁלֹּא לִשְׁמוֹ וְלִשְׁמוֹ, פָּסוּל.

יד אברהם

of *me'ilah* for making personal use of *hekdesh* applies only to objects that had *themselves* been consecrated, not to branches that grew later, their use is nevertheless Rabbinically prohibited (*Gem.*). (5) Fruit that falls from a tree on the Sabbath is Rabbinically forbidden that day. The people of Jericho ate fallen fruit as long as it was not clear that it had fallen that day because they invoked the rule that Rabbinic prohibitions do not apply in doubtful cases. The Sages held this particular prohibition to apply even in doubtful cases (*Rambam*). (6) They also left *pe'ah* [a corner of the field for the poor] for certain kinds of vegetables. Vegetables are exempt from *pe'ah*. The Sages objected to their unwarranted designation as *pe'ah* because the poor, thinking that they were *pe'ah*, ate them untithed. [*Pe'ah* is exempt from tithes.] (*Rav*)

9. עַל שְׁלֹשָׁה הוֹדוּ לוֹ . . . — *Concerning three [the Sages] agreed with him:* (1) *He dragged the bones of his father* Achaz, a wicked king, in order to expiate his sins and sanctify God's Name by demonstrating the repulsiveness of his evil. Instead of a royal bier, a lowly bed of ropes was used, and it was dragged to its place of interment rather than carried. Chizkiah was not obliged to honor his father since he was a wicked person (*Rashi*). (2) *He crushed the brazen serpent* which Moses had fashioned as an antidote to the plague of poisonous snakes that God had sent against the Israelites (*Num.* 21:4-9). This brazen serpent was brought to *Eretz Yisrael* where it eventually became an object of worship. (3) *He hid the Book of Remedies* which contained directions for curing all illnesses. He did so because people were cured so easily that illness failed to promote the desired spirit of contrition and humility (*Rashi*). However, *Rambam* explains that it contained either prohibited remedies (such as magical formulae) or instructions for preparing toxic substances to remedy certain sicknesses. When Chizkiah saw that people began to use it as a primer for preparing poisons, he hid it.

עַל שְׁלֹשָׁה לֹא הוֹדוּ לוֹ — *Concerning three they did not agree with him:* (4) When Sennacherib, king of Assyria, levied a heavy tribute upon Chizkiah in return for removing his armies from Judea, Chizkiah's resources were strained and he removed the gold of the Temple's doors to meet the levy (*II Kings* 18:16). The Sages did not approve, contending that he should have had faith that God would save him. (5) *He blocked the upper waters of the Gichon* to deny the water to the enemy besieging Jerusalem (*II Chronicles* 32:30). But the Sages did not approve, for God had promised (*II Kings* 20:6, *Isaiah* 37:35), *I will protect this city.* (6) *He intercalated* [made a leap year] *in Nissan*. In ancient times the calendar was not fixed and a decision was made each year whether to declare a leap year. The leap month of the Jewish calendar is always Adar, and once Nissan begins, a second Adar can no longer be added. Chizkiah declared the extra month on the thirtieth of Adar (*Gem.*), but since the thirtieth of *for three they did not reprove them. These are the things for which they did not reprove them: They grafted palms all day [of the fourteenth]; they ran together the Shema; and they reaped and stacked prior to the Omer, but they did not reprove them. These are the things for which they did reprove them: They permitted the branches of sacred property [for personal use]; they ate the fallen fruit from beneath [the trees] on the Sabbath; and they gave pe'ah from vegetables, and the Sages reproved them.*

[9] *King Chizkiah did six things. Concerning three [the Sages] agreed with him, and concerning three they did not agree with him. He dragged the bones of his father on a bier of ropes, and they agreed with him. He crushed the brazen serpent, and they agreed with him. He hid the Book of Remedies, and they agreed with him. Concerning three they did not agree with him: He cut off the doors of the Temple and sent them to the king of Assyria, but they did not agree with him. He blocked the upper waters of the Gichon, but they did not agree with him. He intercalated Nissan in Nissan, but they did not agree with him.*

CHAPTER FIVE

[1] **תָּמִיד** *The [afternoon] daily offering is [ordinarily] slaughtered at eight and a half [hours] and offered [on the Altar] at nine and a half [hours]. On Erev Pesach it is slaughtered at seven and a half [hours] and offered at eight and a half [hours], whether it is a weekday or the Sabbath. [If] Erev Pesach falls on Friday, it is slaughtered at six and a half [hours], offered at seven and a half [hours], and the pesach [is offered] after it.*

[2] *[If] the pesach offering was slaughtered for some other designation, or [the Kohen] received, transported, or threw [its blood] for some other designation, or for its own designation and [then] for some other designation, or for some other designation and [then] for its own designation — it is invalid.*

YAD AVRAHAM

any month is fit to be designated the first of the following month (a lunar month has either twenty-nine or thirty days), the Sages ruled that intercalation on the thirtieth is tantamount to declaring a leap year in Nissan.

CHAPTER FIVE

The next four chapters discuss the laws of the *pesach* offering made on the afternoon of the fourteenth and eaten that night at the Seder.

1. תָּמִיד — *The [afternoon] daily offering*. As part of the regular Temple service, two lambs were offered as *olah* (burnt) offerings each day [the *tamid* offering], one in the morning and one in the afternoon. On a normal afternoon, the *tamid* was slaughtered at approximately 2:30 p.m. [eight and a half hours after a typical sunrise; see comm. to 1:4] to allow more time for private offerings. With the exception of the *pesach* and some unusual instances, no offering could be made after the afternoon *tamid*. Slaughtering the *tamid*, performing its blood service, cutting it up, and placing it on the Altar consumed an hour.

בְּעַרְבֵי פְסָחִים . . . — *On Erev Pesach* the *tamid* is slaughtered an hour earlier, because the *pesach* must be slaughtered after the *tamid* and we must allow enough time for a multitude of *pesach* offerings to be offered before sunset. When Erev Pesach falls on Friday, more time is needed to allow the participants to roast their offerings before the beginning of the Sabbath. Roasting does not supersede the Sabbath (*Rav*).

2. The essential part of any offering is its עֲבוֹדַת הַדָּם, *blood service*, which is divided into four parts: שְׁחִיטָה, *slaughtering* the offering; קַבָּלָה, *receiving* the gushing blood in a special vessel; הוֹלָכָה, *transporting* the blood to the Altar; and זְרִיקָה, *throwing* the blood against the Altar wall. If the blood service is properly done, the offering is valid and the owner has discharged his obligation, even though the fats and meat were neither burned on the Altar nor eaten. Should any of these four *avodos* be done with the intention that it serve for another type of offering, or for a person other than its owner, the offering — in the case of a *pesach* — is invalidated. [The rule for most other types of offerings is somewhat different; see comm. end of mishnah 4.] The following mishnah focuses on disqualifications caused by improper intentions.

שֶׁלֹּא לִשְׁמוֹ — *For some other designation*, e.g. with the intention that it be a *shelamim* (peace

כֵּיצַד לִשְׁמוֹ וְשֶׁלֹּא לִשְׁמוֹ? לְשֵׁם פֶּסַח וּלְשֵׁם שְׁלָמִים. שֶׁלֹּא לִשְׁמוֹ וְלִשְׁמוֹ? לְשֵׁם שְׁלָמִים וּלְשֵׁם פֶּסַח.

[ג] שְׁחָטוֹ שֶׁלֹּא לְאוֹכְלָיו, וְשֶׁלֹּא לִמְנוּיָו, לַעֲרֵלִים, וְלִטְמֵאִים — פָּסוּל. לְאוֹכְלָיו וְשֶׁלֹּא לְאוֹכְלָיו, לִמְנוּיָו וְשֶׁלֹּא לִמְנוּיָו, לְמוּלִים וְלַעֲרֵלִים, לִטְמֵאִים וְלִטְהוֹרִים — כָּשֵׁר.

שְׁחָטוֹ קֹדֶם חֲצוֹת, פָּסוּל — מִשּׁוּם שֶׁנֶּאֱמַר: „בֵּין הָעַרְבָּיִם.״ שְׁחָטוֹ קֹדֶם לַתָּמִיד, כָּשֵׁר, וּבִלְבַד שֶׁיְּהֵא אֶחָד מְמָרֵס בְּדָמוֹ, עַד שֶׁיִּזָּרֵק דַּם הַתָּמִיד; וְאִם נִזְרַק, כָּשֵׁר.

[ד] הַשּׁוֹחֵט אֶת הַפֶּסַח עַל הֶחָמֵץ עוֹבֵר בְּלֹא תַעֲשֶׂה. רַבִּי יְהוּדָה אוֹמֵר: אַף הַתָּמִיד.

רַבִּי שִׁמְעוֹן אוֹמֵר: הַפֶּסַח בְּאַרְבָּעָה עָשָׂר לִשְׁמוֹ חַיָּב; וְשֶׁלֹּא לִשְׁמוֹ פָּטוּר. וּשְׁאָר כָּל הַזְּבָחִים בֵּין לִשְׁמָן וּבֵין שֶׁלֹּא לִשְׁמָן, פָּטוּר. וּבַמּוֹעֵד לִשְׁמוֹ פָּטוּר; שֶׁלֹּא לִשְׁמוֹ חַיָּב. וּשְׁאָר כָּל הַזְּבָחִים, בֵּין לִשְׁמָן בֵּין שֶׁלֹּא לִשְׁמָן, חַיָּב; חוּץ מִן הַחַטָּאת שֶׁשְּׁחָטָהּ שֶׁלֹּא לִשְׁמָהּ.

[ה] הַפֶּסַח נִשְׁחָט בְּשָׁלֹשׁ כִּתּוֹת, שֶׁנֶּאֱמַר: „וְשָׁחֲטוּ אֹתוֹ כֹּל קְהַל עֲדַת יִשְׂרָאֵל,״ קָהָל, וְעֵדָה, וְיִשְׂרָאֵל. נִכְנְסָה כַּת הָרִאשׁוֹנָה; נִתְמַלֵּאת הָעֲזָרָה, נָעֲלוּ דַּלְתוֹת הָעֲזָרָה. תָּקְעוּ הֵרִיעוּ וְתָקְעוּ. הַכֹּהֲנִים עוֹמְדִים

יד אברהם

offering). If the wrong intention was explicitly stated during this or *any* of the other three essential *avodos*, the offering is disqualified, even if the remaining *avodos* were performed properly. The mishnah states that the same is true even if he began the *avodah* with the proper intention and then completed it with an improper one, or vice versa. Any improper intention, whether indicated first or second, is sufficient to invalidate the offering when stated during any one of the four blood *avodos*.

3. שֶׁלֹּא לְאוֹכְלָיו — *For those who cannot eat it*, i.e. for someone too old, young or sick to eat at least a *kezayis* (the volume of an olive) of *pesach* meat. [This disqualification is unique to the *pesach* offering.]

וְשֶׁלֹּא לִמְנוּיָו ... — *For those not registered on it*. Several people may share a *pesach* offering but it may be eaten only by those who have registered to eat from that particular offering prior to its slaughter. A *pesach* slaughtered for unregistered people is thus equivalent to one slaughtered for people who cannot eat it. For this reason slaughtering it for uncircumcised men or people contaminated with *tumah* invalidates it, since these too are ineligible to eat from a *pesach* offering.

לְאוֹכְלָיו וְשֶׁלֹּא לְאוֹכְלָיו ... כָּשֵׁר — *[If he slaughtered it] both for those who can and those who cannot eat it . . . it is valid* because the verse indicates that intent for people who cannot eat the *pesach* disqualifies it only if it is entirely for the wrong people. [This is in contrast to offering it for a different designation, where even a mixed intent invalidates.]

קֹדֶם לַתָּמִיד ... — *Before the [afternoon] daily offering*... If the rule requiring the *pesach's* slaughter to follow the *tamid's* (5:1) was violated, the offering is nevertheless valid. Throwing the *pesach's* blood should be delayed until the *tamid's* blood is thrown. This requires that someone keep stirring the *pesach's* blood to prevent it from congealing and thereby becoming unfit for throwing. If, however, the *pesach* offering's blood was thrown before that of the *tamid*, it is still valid.

4. The verse *You shall not slaughter with chametz the blood of My offering* (Ex. 34:25) teaches that one is forbidden to have *chametz* in his possession at the time his *pesach* is slaughtered.

אַף הַתָּמִיד — *The daily offering as well*. If the afternoon *tamid* of the fourteenth is slaughtered by someone still in possession of *chametz*, he violates this commandment.

רַבִּי שִׁמְעוֹן אוֹמֵר — *R' Shimon says* that one transgresses this prohibition only if his *pesach* offering is valid. Therefore, if one slaughtered his *pesach* for the wrong designation while in possession of *chametz*, he does not transgress this prohibition, since the *pesach* is then invalid (5:2).

What is an example of 'for its own designation and [then] for some other designation'? For the designation of a pesach offering and [then] for the designation of a peace offering. [What is an example of] 'for some other designation and [then] for its own designation?' For the designation of a peace offering and [then] for the designation of a pesach offering.

[3] *[If] he slaughtered it for those who cannot eat it, for those not registered on it, [or] for uncircumcised or contaminated persons — it is invalid. [If he slaughtered it] both for those who can and those who cannot eat it, for both its registrants and those not registered for it, for both circumcised and uncircumcised persons, [or] for both contaminated and for uncontaminated [persons] — it is valid.*

[If] he slaughtered it before noon, it is invalid — because it says: In the afternoon (Ex. 12:6). [If] he slaughtered it before the [afternoon] daily offering, it is valid, provided someone stirs its blood until the blood of the daily offering is thrown; but if it was thrown [earlier], it is [also] valid.

[4] *One who slaughters the pesach offering with chametz [in his possession] is in violation of a negative command. R' Yehudah says: The daily offering as well. R' Shimon says: [If he slaughters] the pesach offering on the fourteenth under its own designation, he is liable; but [if] under some other designation, he is exempt. [With] all other offerings whether [he slaughters them] under their own designation or under some other designation, he is exempt.*

However, during a festival, [if he slaughters a pesach offering] under its own designation, he is exempt; [but] under some other designation, he is liable. [With] all other offerings, whether [he slaughters them] under their own designations or under some other designations, he is liable; except for a sin offering which he slaughtered under some other designation.

[5] *The pesach offering is slaughtered in three groups, for it is written (Ex. 12:6): "And the whole assembly of the congregation of Israel shall slaughter it" — 'assembly,' 'congregation' and 'Israel.' The first group entered; when the [Temple] Courtyard was filled, they closed the gates of the Courtyard. They sounded a tekiah, a teruah, and again a tekiah. The Kohanim stood*

YAD AVRAHAM

Moreover, R' Shimon disagrees with limiting the prohibition of slaughtering with *chametz* to the *pesach* and *tamid* offerings. R' Shimon deduces by Biblical exegesis that it applies to all sacrifices during the period when *chametz* is forbidden. However, the same exegesis teaches that the prohibition does not apply to other offerings when it is in effect for the *pesach*. Thus, from noon till nightfall of Erev *pesach* one transgresses the *chametz* prohibition only if he slaughters a *pesach*. However, during the seven days of the festival, one does not transgress this prohibition by making a *pesach* offering, according to R' Shimon, because a *pesach* offering is then invalid. Thus, during these seven days the prohibition to slaughter with *chametz* applies to all other offerings.

The above is true, however, only for a *pesach* slaughtered as a *pesach* offering. But there is a rule that if a *pesach* is slaughtered for another designation [during a time inappropriate for a *pesach* offering], it becomes valid as a *shelamim* offering. It is therefore included in the category of other valid offerings, which, if slaughtered with *chametz* during the festival, are in violation of the Torah commandment (*Rav*).

וּשְׁאָר כָּל הַזְּבָחִים — However, during the festival *all other offerings* are subject to this prohibition whether they are slaughtered under their own designation or another. This is because other sacrifices are valid even when slaughtered for the wrong designation (*Zevachim* 1:1). The only other exception to this rule is the *chatas* (sin offering) which, like the *pesach*, is invalid when offered for the wrong designation. Therefore, a person offering a *chatas* in this manner during the festival has not violated the prohibition of slaughtering with *chametz*.

5. . . . תָּקְעוּ — *They sounded a tekiah* . . . Communal sacrifices are accompanied by the sounding of trumpets, like the shofar blasts of Rosh Hashanah. The sounding preceded the recitation of the *Hallel* which accompanied the *pesach's* offering (*Rambam*).

שׁוּרוֹת שׁוּרוֹת, וּבִידֵיהֶם בָּזִיכֵי כֶסֶף וּבָזִיכֵי זָהָב. שׁוּרָה שֶׁכֻּלָּהּ כֶּסֶף כֶּסֶף, וְשׁוּרָה שֶׁכֻּלָּהּ זָהָב זָהָב; לֹא הָיוּ מְעֹרָבִין. וְלֹא הָיוּ לַבָּזִיכִין שׁוּלַיִם, שֶׁמָּא יַנִּיחוּם וְיִקָּרֵשׁ הַדָּם.

[ו] שָׁחַט יִשְׂרָאֵל וְקִבֵּל הַכֹּהֵן; נוֹתְנוֹ לַחֲבֵרוֹ וַחֲבֵרוֹ לַחֲבֵרוֹ. וּמְקַבֵּל אֶת הַמָּלֵא וּמַחֲזִיר אֶת הָרֵיקָן. כֹּהֵן הַקָּרוֹב אֵצֶל הַמִּזְבֵּחַ זוֹרְקוֹ זְרִיקָה אַחַת כְּנֶגֶד הַיְסוֹד.

[ז] יָצְתָה כַת רִאשׁוֹנָה וְנִכְנְסָה כַת שְׁנִיָּה. יָצְתָה שְׁנִיָּה, נִכְנְסָה שְׁלִישִׁית. כְּמַעֲשֵׂה הָרִאשׁוֹנָה כָּךְ מַעֲשֵׂה הַשְּׁנִיָּה וְהַשְּׁלִישִׁית.
קָרְאוּ אֶת הַהַלֵּל. אִם גָּמְרוּ שָׁנוּ, וְאִם שָׁנוּ שִׁלֵּשׁוּ, אַף עַל פִּי שֶׁלֹּא שִׁלְּשׁוּ מִימֵיהֶם. רַבִּי יְהוּדָה אוֹמֵר: מִימֵיהֶם שֶׁל כַּת הַשְּׁלִישִׁית לֹא הִגִּיעוּ לְ„אָהַבְתִּי כִּי יִשְׁמַע ה׳," מִפְּנֵי שֶׁעַמָּהּ מֻעָטִין.

[ח] כְּמַעֲשֵׂהוּ בְּחוֹל כָּךְ מַעֲשֵׂהוּ בְּשַׁבָּת, אֶלָּא שֶׁהַכֹּהֲנִים מְדִיחִים אֶת הָעֲזָרָה שֶׁלֹּא בִרְצוֹן חֲכָמִים.
רַבִּי יְהוּדָה אוֹמֵר: כּוֹס הָיָה מְמַלֵּא מִדַּם הַתַּעֲרֹבוֹת, זְרָקוֹ זְרִיקָה אַחַת עַל גַּבֵּי הַמִּזְבֵּחַ. וְלֹא הוֹדוּ לוֹ חֲכָמִים.

[ט] כֵּיצַד תּוֹלִין וּמַפְשִׁיטִין? אֻנְקְלָיוֹת שֶׁל בַּרְזֶל הָיוּ קְבוּעִים בַּכְּתָלִים וּבָעַמּוּדִים, שֶׁבָּהֶן תּוֹלִין וּמַפְשִׁיטִין. וְכָל מִי שֶׁאֵין לוֹ מָקוֹם לִתְלוֹת וּלְהַפְשִׁיט, מַקְלוֹת דַּקִּים חֲלָקִים הָיוּ שָׁם, וּמַנִּיחַ עַל כְּתֵפוֹ וְעַל כֶּתֶף חֲבֵרוֹ, וְתוֹלֶה וּמַפְשִׁיט. רַבִּי אֱלִיעֶזֶר אוֹמֵר: אַרְבָּעָה עָשָׂר שֶׁחָל לִהְיוֹת בַּשַּׁבָּת, מַנִּיחַ יָדוֹ עַל כֶּתֶף חֲבֵרוֹ, וְיַד חֲבֵרוֹ עַל כְּתֵפוֹ, וְתוֹלֶה וּמַפְשִׁיט.

[י] קְרָעוֹ וְהוֹצִיא אֵמוּרָיו, נְתָנוֹ בְּמָגֵיס וְהִקְטִירָן עַל גַּבֵּי הַמִּזְבֵּחַ.

יד אברהם

הַכֹּהֲנִים עוֹמְדִים שׁוּרוֹת שׁוּרוֹת — *The Kohanim stood row upon row* forming lines across the Courtyard from the place of slaughter to the Altar. Each row had its own type of consecrated vessel — either silver or gold. The uniform appearance of the rows enhanced their festive spectacle and was a נוֹי מִצְוָה, *beautification of the mitzvah (Gem.)*.

וְלֹא הָיוּ לַבָּזִיכִין שׁוּלַיִם — *Nor did the bowls have bases*, being wide at the top and pointed at the bottom, so that the *Kohanim* would not be able to set the bowls down and in their preoccupation with the many offerings, forget to throw the blood immediately. Congealed blood is unfit for the Altar (*Rav*).

6. שָׁחַט יִשְׂרָאֵל — *An Israelite* [was permitted to] *slaughter it*. Slaughtering is the only blood *avodah* that need not be performed by a *Kohen;* receiving, transporting, and throwing the blood *must* be done by a *Kohen*.

וַחֲבֵרוֹ לַחֲבֵרוֹ — *And he to his fellow*, passing it up the line of *Kohanim* to the Altar. At the same time the *Kohen* would take an empty one from up the line and return it down the line for reuse.

וּזְרִיקָה אַחַת כְּנֶגֶד הַיְסוֹד — *Once, opposite the base.* The blood was thrown upon the lower half of the Altar wall, on any section that stood above the Altar's base. The one-cubit-high base jutted out beyond the wall, but did *not* extend along most of the eastern and southern walls of the Altar.

7. קָרְאוּ אֶת הַהַלֵּל — *They* [the Levites] *recited the Hallel* during the slaughter and blood service of the multitude of *pesach* offerings. If they finished the *Hallel* before all the offerings in that group had been completed, they started the *Hallel* over again.

שֶׁעַמָּהּ מֻעָטִין — *Its people were few* because most Jews were eager to perform the *mitzvah* as early as possible.

row upon row, and in their hands were silver bowls and golden bowls. One row was altogether of silver, the other row was altogether of gold; and they were not mixed. Nor did the bowls have bases, lest they set them down and the blood congeal.

[6] *An Israelite slaughtered it, and a Kohen received its [blood]; he would hand it to his fellow and he to his fellow. He would accept the full one and return the empty one. The Kohen nearest the Altar would throw it once, opposite the base.*

[7] *When the first group [concluded and] left, the second group entered. When the second left, the third entered. The procedure followed for the first [group] was repeated for the second and third [groups].*

They recited the Hallel. If they finish it, they repeat it, and if they complete the repetition they recite it a third time, although it never happened that they should recite it a third time. R' Yehudah says: The third group never reached as far as 'I love, for HASHEM hears' (Psalms 116:1), because its people were few.

[8] *The procedure on weekdays was followed on the Sabbath as well, except that the Kohanim rinsed the Temple Courtyard without the consent of the Sages.*

R' Yehudah says: He would fill a cup with the mixed blood [and] throw it once upon the Altar [wall]. But the Sages did not agree with him.

[9] *How did they suspend and flay [them]? Iron hooks were affixed to [the Courtyard's] walls and pillars, from which they suspended [the Pesach offering] and flayed [it]. Anyone who had not place to suspend and flay [his offering, would use a] thin smooth stave kept there, which he placed upon his shoulder and upon the shoulder of his fellow and so suspended and flayed [it]. R' Eliezer says: [If] the fourteenth fell on the Sabbath, he placed his hand on his fellow's shoulder, and the hand of his fellow upon his shoulder, and [thus] suspended and flayed [it].*

[10] *He cut it open and removed its sacrificial parts, put them on a plate and burned them on the Altar.*

YAD AVRAHAM

8. כָּךְ מַעֲשֵׂהוּ בְּשַׁבָּת — *Was followed* [when Erev Pesach fell] *on the Sabbath,* because the slaughter and offering of the *pesach* supersedes the Sabbath prohibitions. The *Kohanim* even rinsed the floor of the Temple Courtyard, but this latter activity did not meet with the Rabbis' approval because of the Rabbinic prohibition of washing floors on the Sabbath. Since rinsing the Courtyard is not essential to the Temple service, they did not relax the prohibition (*Gem.*).

מִדַּם הַתַּעֲרֹבוֹת — *With the mixed blood*, i.e., the accumulated blood on the floor, which was a mixture of the blood of all the sacrifices offered that day. By applying it once to the Altar, he insured that even if the blood of a sacrifice had spilled before reaching the Altar, a drop of it would now reach via the cup of mixed blood and render the offering valid. The Sages, however, disagree because most of the blood on the Courtyard floor would be of the kind which is not valid for throwing, having drained from the animal after the initial gush, and the acceptable blood would thus have lost its legal identity in the majority. R' Yehudah's view is that a minority component does not become nullified in a majority of the same type of substance.

9. וּמַפְשִׁיטִין — *Flay*. The *pesach,* like other offerings, had to have its hide removed prior to placing its sacrificial parts on the Altar. To facilitate this, the carcass was suspended by its hind legs and skinned. R' Eliezer forbids using staves for this on the Sabbath because they are *muktzeh*. The Sages permit the use of staves because of the principle that 'Rabbinic [Sabbath] restrictions do not [usually] apply in the Temple' (*Rav*).

10. אֵמוּרָיו — *Its sacrificial parts,* certain of its fats and internal organs (*Lev.* 3:9-10, 14-15).

יָצְתָה כַת רִאשׁוֹנָה וְיָשְׁבָה לָהּ בְּהַר הַבַּיִת, שְׁנִיָּה בַּחֵיל, וְהַשְּׁלִישִׁית בִּמְקוֹמָהּ עוֹמֶדֶת. חָשֵׁכָה, יָצְאוּ וְצָלוּ אֶת פִּסְחֵיהֶן.

פרק ששי

[א] **אֵלּוּ** דְבָרִים בַּפֶּסַח דּוֹחִין אֶת הַשַּׁבָּת: שְׁחִיטָתוֹ; וּזְרִיקַת דָּמוֹ; וּמִחוּי קְרָבָיו; וְהֶקְטֵר חֲלָבָיו. אֲבָל צְלִיָּתוֹ וַהֲדָחַת קְרָבָיו אֵינָן דּוֹחִין אֶת הַשַּׁבָּת. הַרְכָּבָתוֹ, וַהֲבָאָתוֹ מִחוּץ לַתְּחוּם, וַחֲתִיכַת יַבַּלְתּוֹ אֵין דּוֹחִין אֶת הַשַּׁבָּת. רַבִּי אֱלִיעֶזֶר אוֹמֵר: דּוֹחִין.

[ב] אָמַר רַבִּי אֱלִיעֶזֶר: "וַהֲלֹא דִין הוּא! מָה אִם שְׁחִיטָה, שֶׁהִיא מִשּׁוּם מְלָאכָה, דּוֹחָה אֶת הַשַּׁבָּת, אֵלּוּ שֶׁהֵן מִשּׁוּם שְׁבוּת, לֹא יִדְחוּ אֶת הַשַּׁבָּת?"

אָמַר לוֹ רַבִּי יְהוֹשֻׁעַ: "יוֹם טוֹב יוֹכִיחַ, שֶׁהִתִּירוּ בוֹ מִשּׁוּם מְלָאכָה, וְאָסוּר בּוֹ מִשּׁוּם שְׁבוּת."

אָמַר לוֹ רַבִּי אֱלִיעֶזֶר: "מַה זֶּה, יְהוֹשֻׁעַ? מָה רְאָיָה רְשׁוּת לְמִצְוָה?"

הֵשִׁיב רַבִּי עֲקִיבָא וְאָמַר: "הַזָּאָה תוֹכִיחַ, שֶׁהִיא מִצְוָה, וְהִיא מִשּׁוּם שְׁבוּת, וְאֵינָהּ דּוֹחָה אֶת הַשַּׁבָּת. אַף אַתָּה אַל תִּתְמַהּ עַל אֵלּוּ, שֶׁאַף עַל פִּי שֶׁהֵן מִצְוָה, וְהֵן מִשּׁוּם שְׁבוּת, לֹא יִדְחוּ אֶת הַשַּׁבָּת."

אָמַר לוֹ רַבִּי אֱלִיעֶזֶר: "וְעָלֶיהָ אֲנִי דָן. וּמָה אִם שְׁחִיטָה שֶׁהִיא מִשּׁוּם מְלָאכָה דּוֹחָה אֶת הַשַּׁבָּת, הַזָּאָה שֶׁהִיא מִשּׁוּם שְׁבוּת אֵינוֹ דִין שֶׁדּוֹחָה אֶת הַשַּׁבָּת?"

אָמַר לוֹ רַבִּי עֲקִיבָא: "אוֹ חִלּוּף! מָה אִם הַזָּאָה שֶׁהִיא מִשּׁוּם שְׁבוּת אֵינָהּ דּוֹחָה אֶת הַשַּׁבָּת, שְׁחִיטָה שֶׁהִיא מִשּׁוּם מְלָאכָה אֵינוֹ דִין שֶׁלֹּא תִדְחֶה אֶת הַשַּׁבָּת?"

יד אברהם

וְיָשְׁבָה לָהּ ... — *And remained...* When Erev Pesach fell on the Sabbath, the first group carried out its sacrifices no further than the Temple Mount, because carrying was forbidden in the streets of Jerusalem. The second group stayed in the *Chel*, a ten-cubit-wide section of the Temple Mount between the outer Courtyard wall to the low wooden partition called the סוֹרֵג, *soreg* (see *Middos* 2:3). The third group remained in the Courtyard. After dark, they went to their residences and roasted their *pesachim*; roasting the *pesach* does not override the Sabbath (*Rav*).

CHAPTER SIX

1. דוֹחִין אֶת הַשַּׁבָּת — *Override the Sabbath.* The *pesach* is offered on the Sabbath even though this involves acts which violate the Sabbath laws, as derived from the Torah's statement that the *pesach* be brought בְּמוֹעֲדוֹ, *in its appointed time* (Num. 9:2). *Slaughter* is one of the thirty-nine primary labors prohibited on the Sabbath; it must be done on the fourteenth of Nissan and cannot be postponed until nightfall. The same is true of

throwing the blood [which is in any case not a forbidden labor]. Cleaning the entrails is permitted to prevent putrefaction. Burning the sacrificial parts is an integral part of the offering which should properly be performed by day.

אֵינָן דּוֹחִין אֶת הַשַּׁבָּת — *Do not override the Sabbath*, the first two because they can wait until nightfall, and the last three because they could have been done before the Sabbath. Roasting is classified as *cooking*, and is Biblically forbidden. Rinsing the entrails would be Rabbinically prohibited as excessive bother (טִרְחָה), and once the offal has been removed, rinsing can be deferred until nightfall without risk of putrefaction. Carrying the lamb through the public domain to the Temple, or bringing it from outside the *techum* (see 3:7), could have been done before the Sabbath (*Rav*). A wart is a disqualifying blemish for a sacrifice until it is removed. However, removal is included in the labor of גּוֹזֵז, *shearing*, and could have been done before the Sabbath. These may not be done on the Sabbath even if it means that the sacrifice will

The first group went out and remained on the Temple Mount, the second [group] in the Chel, and the third [group] remained where they were [inside the Courtyard]. After dark, they went out and roasted their pesach offerings.

CHAPTER SIX

[1] **אֵלּוּ** *The following aspects of the pesach offering override the Sabbath: Its slaughter; throwing its blood; cleaning its entrails; and burning its fats. But roasting it and rinsing its entrails do not override the Sabbath. Nor do carrying it, bringing it from outside the Sabbath limit, and cutting off its wart override the Sabbath. R' Eliezer says: These do override [it].*

[2] *Said R' Eliezer: But does not logic dictate this? If slaughtering [the pesach], which is a [Biblically prohibited] labor, overrides the Sabbath, [then] these, which are forbidden [merely] because of a Rabbinic prohibition, should certainly override the Sabbath!*

R' Yehoshua said to him: Let [the] festival [laws] demonstrate [this], for they permitted [Biblical] labor on it, but forbade on it [what is] Rabbinically proscribed.

R' Eliezer replied: What is this, Yehoshua? What proof [can be adduced from] an act [which is merely] permissible to one that is a mitzvah?

R' Akiva responded and said: Let 'sprinkling' demonstrate [this], for it is a mitzvah, and it is [forbidden] by a Rabbinic prohibition, and it does not override the Sabbath. So you should not wonder about these, that even though they are a mitzvah, and are [forbidden only] by a Rabbinic prohibition, they do not override the Sabbath.

R' Eliezer replied: I apply my logic to this too. If slaughter, which is [Biblically forbidden] labor, overrides the Sabbath, [then] sprinkling, which is [forbidden only] by Rabbinic prohibition, should surely override the Sabbath!

R' Akiva said to him: Perhaps [the argument should be] reversed? If sprinkling, which is [forbidden] by Rabbinic prohibition, does not override the Sabbath, [then] slaughtering which is a [Biblically forbidden] labor, should [surely] not override the Sabbath!

YAD AVRAHAM

not be brought (*Rav*). However, R' Eliezer's opinion is that if they are necessary, even the preliminaries (מַכְשִׁירִין) override the Sabbath.

2. אָמַר רַבִּי אֱלִיעֶזֶר — *R' Eliezer* presented the following argument to support his position that one may violate the Sabbath even for the preliminaries of the *pesach*. Although R' Eliezer permitted overriding even Biblical prohibitions, his argument here is to force the first *Tanna* to concede that at least Rabbinic prohibitions should be waived.

אֵלּוּ — *[Then] these.* As noted above, some of the forbidden preliminaries involve only Rabbinic prohibitions.

אָמַר לוֹ רַבִּי יְהוֹשֻׁעַ — *R' Yehoshua said to him:* The festival laws prove otherwise, since it is permissible to cook and bake on a festival, though these are labors Biblically prohibited on the Sabbath and even on festivals when not needed for the festival. Yet it is prohibited to bring food for the festival from outside the 2000-cubit *techum* — something proscribed only by Rabbinic decree (*Rav*). Thus we see that a valid basis for overriding a Biblical prohibition does not necessarily justify waiving a Rabbinic one. R' Eliezer rejected this argument because bringing food on the festival is not required for the fulfillment of a *mitzvah*; while one honors the festival by dining well, he is not *required* to do so. However, since the Torah does require one to make a *pesach* offering on the Sabbath, Rabbinic prohibitions should be waived no less than Biblical ones.

הַזָּאָה תוֹכִיחַ — *Let sprinkling demonstrate [this].* A person *tamei* by contact with a corpse must be sprinkled with water containing the ashes of the *parah adumah* to become *tahor*.

Sprinkling is Rabbinically prohibited on the Sabbath because it is akin to מְתַקֵּן, *repairing* [the person], by permitting him to partake from offerings. Even so, if the final day of purification falls on Erev Pesach which is also the Sabbath, we do not permit sprinkling even to enable him to perform the *mitzvah* of eating the *pesach* offering. To this, R' Eliezer replied that he extends the same reasoning to permit sprinkling as well. R' Eliezer had forgotten his own teaching that sprinkling was indeed forbidden and R' Akiva tried to remind him respectfully of it by reversing the argument. For if sprinkling would

אָמַר לוֹ רַבִּי אֱלִיעֶזֶר: „עֲקִיבָא! עָקַרְתָּ מַה שֶּׁכָּתוּב בַּתּוֹרָה: ,בֵּין הָעַרְבַּיִם . . . בְּמֹעֲדוֹ,' בֵּין בְּחוֹל בֵּין בְּשַׁבָּת."

אָמַר לוֹ: „רַבִּי, הָבֵא לִי מוֹעֵד לְאֵלּוּ כְּמוֹעֵד לִשְׁחִיטָה."

כְּלָל אָמַר רַבִּי עֲקִיבָא: כָּל מְלָאכָה שֶׁאֶפְשָׁר לַעֲשׂוֹתָהּ מֵעֶרֶב שַׁבָּת אֵינָהּ דּוֹחָה אֶת הַשַּׁבָּת. שְׁחִיטָה שֶׁאִי אֶפְשָׁר לַעֲשׂוֹתָהּ מֵעֶרֶב שַׁבָּת דּוֹחָה אֶת הַשַּׁבָּת.

[ג] אֵימָתַי מֵבִיא חֲגִיגָה עִמּוֹ? בִּזְמַן שֶׁהוּא בָא בְחוֹל בְּטָהֳרָה וּבְמֻעָט. וּבִזְמַן שֶׁהוּא בָא בַּשַּׁבָּת בִּמְרֻבֶּה וּבְטֻמְאָה, אֵין מְבִיאִין עִמּוֹ חֲגִיגָה.

[ד] חֲגִיגָה הָיְתָה בָאָה מִן הַצֹּאן, מִן הַבָּקָר, מִן הַכְּבָשִׂים, וּמִן הָעִזִּים; מִן הַזְּכָרִים וּמִן הַנְּקֵבוֹת. וְנֶאֱכֶלֶת לִשְׁנֵי יָמִים וְלַיְלָה אֶחָד.

[ה] הַפֶּסַח שֶׁשְּׁחָטוֹ שֶׁלֹּא לִשְׁמוֹ בַּשַּׁבָּת, חַיָּב עָלָיו חַטָּאת. וּשְׁאָר כָּל הַזְּבָחִים שֶׁשְּׁחָטָן לְשׁוּם פֶּסַח: אִם אֵינָן רְאוּיִין, חַיָּב; וְאִם רְאוּיִין הֵן – רַבִּי אֱלִיעֶזֶר מְחַיֵּב חַטָּאת, וְרַבִּי יְהוֹשֻׁעַ פּוֹטֵר.

אָמַר רַבִּי אֱלִיעֶזֶר: מָה אִם הַפֶּסַח, שֶׁהוּא מֻתָּר לִשְׁמוֹ, כְּשֶׁשִּׁנָּה אֶת שְׁמוֹ חַיָּב, זְבָחִים שֶׁהֵן אֲסוּרִין לִשְׁמָן, כְּשֶׁשִּׁנָּה אֶת שְׁמָן, אֵינוֹ דִין שֶׁיְּהֵא חַיָּב? אָמַר לוֹ רַבִּי יְהוֹשֻׁעַ: לֹא! אִם אָמַרְתָּ בְּפֶסַח, שֶׁשִּׁנָּהוּ לְדָבָר אָסוּר; תֹּאמַר בִּזְבָחִים שֶׁשִּׁנָּן לְדָבָר מֻתָּר?

אָמַר לוֹ רַבִּי אֱלִיעֶזֶר: אֵמוּרֵי צִבּוּר יוֹכִיחוּ, שֶׁהֵן מֻתָּרִין לִשְׁמָן, וְהַשּׁוֹחֵט לִשְׁמָן חַיָּב.

יד אברהם

indeed override the Sabbath, logic would require the untenable conclusion that even slaughter is forbidden (*Gem.*). Prior to this exchange, R' Akiva had studied under R' Eliezer for thirteen years without ever speaking up to contradict his mentor (*Yerushalmi*).

אָמַר לוֹ — *He [R' Akiva]* suggested to his teacher R' Eliezer that it is incorrect to compare the Biblical prohibition against slaughter with the Rabbinic prohibitions under discussion in this and the previous mishnah. Since the source for the permission to override the Sabbath is the Biblical phrase *appointed time*, this precludes any analogy to the Rabbinically prohibited acts, since their performance is not mandated for a specific time. Even the act of sprinkling, which must be performed at a specific time, is also prohibited because, unlike the other Rabbinic prohibitions under discussion, it is not intrinsically related to the *pesach* offering itself, and is therefore not included in the Biblical dispensation that requires overriding the Sabbath (*Rav*).

3. Along with the *pesach* sacrifice, an additional offering is brought on the fourteenth of Nissan, known as the *chagigah*. This is apart from the *chagigah* offering required for each of the three festivals [Pesach, Shavuos, and Succos]. The purpose of this *chagigah* is to enable one to satisfy his hunger and eat the *pesach* עַל הַשּׂבַע, *sated*. However, since the Torah does not *require* that *chagigah* meat be eaten at the Seder, its slaughter does not override the Sabbath nor the prohibition of making an offering in a state of *tumah,* and is therefore not brought when the fourteenth occurs on the Sabbath. [This stands in contrast to the *pesach* offering which may sometimes be sacrificed and eaten by people who are *tamei*; see 7:4,5.] It is also only necessary when there are many people registered on the *pesach*. However, when the registrants are few, they may satisfy themselves from the *pesach* offering itself before eating a final *kezayis*.

4. מִן הַצֹּאן — *From the flock*. The term צֹאן denotes both sheep and goats, as elaborated by the mishnah in the next phrase.

וְנֶאֱכֶלֶת . . . — *It may be eaten* on the fourteenth and fifteenth of Nissan, as well as the intervening night. Nevertheless, once the *chagigah* is put on the table with the *pesach,* it must be consumed before midnight, exactly like the *pesach*, lest its meat become mixed with the *pesach's* (*Rambam*).

5. The prohibition to slaughter on the Sabbath is superseded by the obligation to offer a *pesach*. If the sacrifice is invalidated, however, the slaughter is considered a desecration of the Sabbath.

R' Eliezer replied: Akiva! You have uprooted [with your argument] what is written in the Torah: 'In the afternoon ... in its appointed time' (Numbers 9:3), [which implies] both on weekdays and on the Sabbath.

He [R' Akiva] said to him: My master! Give me an appointed time for these which is like the appointed time for slaughter.

A general rule was stated by R' Akiva: Any labor that can be performed on the eve of the Sabbath does not override the Sabbath. Slaughtering which cannot be performed on the eve of the Sabbath does override the Sabbath.

[3] *When does one bring a chagigah with [the pesach]? When it is offered on a weekday, in purity, and [the pesach] is insufficient. But when [the pesach] is offered on the Sabbath, or is abundant, or in tumah-contamination, one does not bring a chagigah with [the pesach].*

[4] *A chagigah may be brought from the flock, from cattle, from sheep, or from goats; either male or female. It may be eaten for two days and one night.*

[5] *[If] one slaughtered the pesach offering for some other designation on the Sabbath, he is liable thereby for a sin offering. As for any other sacrifices that he slaughtered with the designation of a pesach offering: if they are not suitable, he is liable [for a sin offering]; but if they are suitable — R' Eliezer obligates him to bring a sin offering, while R' Yehoshua absolves [him].*

Said R' Eliezer: If the pesach offering, which is permitted [on the Sabbath] for its own designation, makes him liable [for a sin offering] if he changed its designation, [then] other sacrifices, which are forbidden [on the Sabbath even] for their own designations, should surely make him liable [for a sin offering] when he changed their designations. R' Yehoshua replied: Not so! If you say [this] of the pesach, [it is because] he altered it to a forbidden matter; will you [therefore] say the same of [other] sacrifices, when he altered them to a permitted matter?

R' Eliezer responded: Let communal offerings prove it, for they are permitted [to be offered] for their own designation, yet one who slaughters [other sacrifices] for their designations is liable.

YAD AVRAHAM

Ordinarily one is obliged to atone for a non-intentional [שוֹגֵג] desecration of the Sabbath by bringing a *chatas* (sin) offering. In the view of some, however, desecration of the Sabbath caused by slaughtering an invalid offering is exempt from this obligation, because it was committed in the course of an intended *mitzvah*.

שֶׁלֹּא לִשְׁמוֹ — *For some other designation*, e.g., as an *olah;* this invalidates the *pesach* (5:2).

... וּשְׁאָר כָּל הַזְּבָחִים שֶׁשְּׁחָטָן — *Any other sacrifices that he slaughtered* on the fourteenth which falls on the Sabbath with the mistaken intention of using it as a *pesach* offering is not valid as a *pesach* and he has desecrated the Sabbath. Nonetheless, this was an attempt to perform the *mitzvah*. His liability for a *chatas* depends on the following: If the animal he used was unsuitable for a *pesach* offering (i.e., anything other than a male sheep or goat, less than a year old), his error is too obvious to rank as an instance of טוֹעֶה בִּדְבַר מִצְוָה, *erring in the commission of a mitzvah*. But if it was of the proper age, gender, and species for a *pesach* but had been sanctified for a different offering, R' Eliezer obligates him to bring a *chatas* because he does not consider the intention to perform a *mitzvah* a mitigating factor. R' Yehoshua, however, rules that his action does not require the atonement of a *chatas* offering since it resulted from an intention to perform a *mitzvah*.

... אָמַר רַבִּי אֱלִיעֶזֶר — *R' Eliezer* argued that if slaughtering a *pesach* offering invalidly on the Sabbath requires the atonement of a *chatas*, then slaughtering a totally unauthorized offering [even as a *pesach*] should certainly require one. R' Yehoshua replied that this argument is not convincing. In slaughtering a *pesach* for another designation the intention is to do something forbidden on the Sabbath; therefore he is liable for a *chatas*. By contrast, slaughtering another sacrifice as *pesach* expresses an intention to do something permissible on the Sabbath; therefore, it does not incur a *chatas*.

... אָמַר לוֹ רַבִּי אֱלִיעֶזֶר — *R' Eliezer responded* that the case of *communal offerings* [such as the daily *tamid* and festival *mussaf* offerings] proves that

אָמַר לוֹ רַבִּי יְהוֹשֻׁעַ: „לֹא! אִם אָמַרְתָּ בְּאֵמוּרֵי צִבּוּר שֶׁיֵּשׁ לָהֶן קִצְבָּה, תֹּאמַר בְּפֶסַח שֶׁאֵין לוֹ קִצְבָה?״

רַבִּי מֵאִיר אוֹמֵר: אַף הַשּׁוֹחֵט לְשֵׁם אֵמוּרֵי צִבּוּר, פָּטוּר.

[ו] שְׁחָטוֹ שֶׁלֹּא לְאוֹכְלָיו וְשֶׁלֹּא לִמְנוּיָו, לַעֲרֵלִין וְלִטְמֵאִין, חַיָּב. לְאוֹכְלָיו וְשֶׁלֹּא לְאוֹכְלָיו, לִמְנוּיָו וְשֶׁלֹּא לִמְנוּיָו, לַמּוּלִין וְלַעֲרֵלִין, לִטְהוֹרִים וְלִטְמֵאִים, פָּטוּר.

שְׁחָטוֹ וְנִמְצָא בַעַל מוּם, חַיָּב. שְׁחָטוֹ וְנִמְצָא טְרֵפָה בַסֵּתֶר, פָּטוּר. שְׁחָטוֹ וְנוֹדַע שֶׁמָּשְׁכוּ הַבְּעָלִים אֶת יָדָם, אוֹ שֶׁמֵּתוּ, אוֹ שֶׁנִּטְמְאוּ, פָּטוּר, מִפְּנֵי שֶׁשָּׁחַט בִּרְשׁוּת.

פרק שביעי

[א] **כֵּיצַד** צוֹלִין אֶת הַפֶּסַח? מְבִיאִין שְׁפוֹד שֶׁל רִמּוֹן תּוֹחֲבוֹ מִתּוֹךְ פִּיו עַד בֵּית נְקוּבָתוֹ, וְנוֹתֵן אֶת כְּרָעָיו וְאֶת בְּנֵי מֵעָיו לְתוֹכוֹ; דִּבְרֵי רַבִּי יוֹסֵי הַגְּלִילִי. רַבִּי עֲקִיבָא אוֹמֵר: כְּמִין בִּשּׁוּל הוּא זֶה; אֶלָּא תּוֹלִין חוּצָה לוֹ.

[ב] אֵין צוֹלִין אֶת הַפֶּסַח לֹא עַל הַשְּׁפוֹד וְלֹא עַל הָאַסְכְּלָא. אָמַר רַבִּי צָדוֹק: מַעֲשֶׂה בְּרַבָּן גַּמְלִיאֵל שֶׁאָמַר לְטָבִי עַבְדּוֹ: „צֵא וּצְלֵה לָנוּ אֶת הַפֶּסַח עַל הָאַסְכְּלָא.״ נָגַע בְּחַרְסוֹ שֶׁל תַּנּוּר, יִקְלוֹף אֶת מְקוֹמוֹ. נָטַף מֵרַטְבּוֹ עַל הַחֶרֶס וְחָזַר עָלָיו, יִטּוֹל אֶת מְקוֹמוֹ. נָטַף מֵרַטְבּוֹ עַל הַסֹּלֶת, יִקְמוֹץ אֶת מְקוֹמוֹ.

יד אברהם

one who intends to perform a *mitzvah* which is permissible on the Sabbath but fails to execute it properly incurs a *chatas*. These communal sacrifices are required on the Sabbath, yet one who slaughters a personal offering for the communal one is liable for a *chatas*. To this R' Yehoshua replied that the analogy is inaccurate. Communal offerings on the Sabbath consist of only two *tamid* offerings and two *mussaf* offerings, and it is therefore easy to avoid a mistake. Thus, a mistake is not regarded as having *erred* in the commission of a *mitzvah*, but as having desecrated the Sabbath through negligence. In the case of the *pesach*, however, since an enormous number of animals were slaughtered that day, it is quite possible for someone to err, and he is regarded as having erred in the commission of a *mitzvah* (*Rav*).

רַבִּי מֵאִיר אוֹמֵר — *R' Meir* disagrees with both R' Eliezer and R' Yehoshua and absolves him from a *chatas* even in the case of a personal sacrifice slaughtered for the sake of a communal offering.

6. . . . שְׁחָטוֹ שֶׁלֹּא לְאוֹכְלָיו — *[If] he slaughtered it* [exclusively] *for those who cannot eat it*, the *pesach* is invalid (5:3), and if it is a Sabbath, he has thus desecrated the Sabbath. [Since he intended it for something unacceptable as a *pesach*, he is liable for a *chatas* according to all opinions.] The same is true for the other cases mentioned here.

. . . לְאוֹכְלָיו וְשֶׁלֹּא לְאוֹכְלָיו — *[However, if he slaughtered it both] for those who can eat it and those who cannot*, the offering is valid (5:3) and the Sabbath has not been desecrated.

בַעַל מוּם . . . טְרֵפָה בַסֵּתֶר — *A blemish* invalidates an offering. Since an external blemish could have been discovered prior to the slaughter, the desecration of the Sabbath is not classified as unavoidable [אונס] but as negligence [שוגג], and therefore requires a *chatas* to atone for the desecration of the Sabbath (*Rav*). However, if after slaughtering the *pesach*, one of its internal organs was found to be defective in a way that renders it *tereifah* [unkosher], the offering is invalid, but there is no *chatas* obligation. The internal status of the animal is not something that could have been detected in advance, and the resulting Sabbath desecration is therefore considered to have occurred in the commission of a *mitzvah* [see mishnah 5] (*Tos.*).

. . . שֶׁמָּשְׁכוּ הַבְּעָלִים אֶת יָדָם — *That the owners had withdrawn from it* [before its slaughter] and registered on another *pesach*, leaving this offering without owners and thus invalid. The same applies if all the registrants died or became *tamei* and thus unfit to eat.

R' Yehoshua replied: Not so! If you say this of public offerings which are [brought in] limited numbers [on the Sabbath], will you say the same of the pesach offering which is [brought in] unlimited numbers?

R' Meir says: Even one who slaughters [other sacrifices] for the designation of public offerings is not liable.

[6] *[If] he slaughtered it for those who cannot eat it or for those not registered on it, [or] for uncircumcised or tumah-contaminated [people], he is liable. [However, if he slaughtered it both] for those who can eat it and those who cannot, for those registered and those unregistered, for the circumcised and uncircumcised, [or] for those who are not contaminated and those who are contaminated, he is not liable.*

[If] he slaughtered it and it was found to have a blemish, he is liable. [If] he slaughtered it and it was found to be a tereifah internally, he is not liable. [If] he slaughtered it and then it became known that the owners had withdrawn from it, or had died, or had become contaminated, he is not liable, because he slaughtered with permission.

CHAPTER SEVEN

[1] **כֵּיצַד** *How does one roast the pesach? He brings a spit of pomegranate wood and thrusts it through its mouth to its anus, and places its knees and its entrails inside it; [these are] the words of R' Yose HaGlili. R' Akiva says: This is [considered] a form of cooking; rather they are hung outside it.*

[2] *One may not roast the pesach offering on a [metal] spit or roasting tray. R' Tzadok said: It once happened that Rabban Gamliel said to Tavi, his slave, 'Go out and roast for us the pesach offering on the roasting tray.' [If the offering] made contact with the earthen sides of the oven, he must slice off that part. [If] some of its juices dripped onto the earthen sides and spattered back onto it, he must remove that part. [If] some of its juices dripped onto flour, he must remove a handful from that place.*

YAD AVRAHAM

מִפְּנֵי שֶׁשָּׁחַט בִּרְשׁוּת — *Because he slaughtered with permission,* i.e., he had no way of knowing about the changed circumstances nor any reason to inquire about them.

CHAPTER SEVEN

1. כֵּיצַד צוֹלִין אֶת הַפֶּסַח — *How does one roast the pesach?* The Torah requires the *pesach* to be eaten roasted over a fire and not cooked (*Ex.* 12:9). A metal spit is unacceptable because the metal becomes hot and part of the *pesach* becomes roasted from the heat of the spit rather than the fire. Likewise, woods other than pomegranate are forbidden because they exude moisture, thereby causing the *pesach* to be partially cooked rather than completely roasted (*Rav*).

תּוֹחֲבוֹ מִתּוֹךְ פִּיו — *And thrusts it through its mouth* ... so that the carcass may be suspended head down, allowing the blood to drain freely from the cut in the neck.

כְּמִין בִּשּׁוּל הוּא זֶה — *This is [considered] a form of cooking,* because the entrails become cooked in the body cavity, as if in a pot (*Rav*).

2. ... מַעֲשֶׂה בְּרַבָּן גַּמְלִיאֵל — *It once happened that Rabban Gamliel* ... The *Gemara* explains that R' Gamliel referred to a grill-like tray, in which the spaces between the bars are big enough for the entire carcass to fit between them. The bars of the grill are used only to support the spit holding the offering (*Rashi*), and the spit is not of metal.

נָגַע בְּחַרְסוֹ שֶׁל תַּנּוּר — *[If the offering] made contact with the earthen sides of the oven,* the part of the meat that touched is not fire roasted, but roasted through an intermediary substance (*Rav*). This, however, disqualifies only the meat at the point of contact with the hot oven, which must therefore be sliced off.

... נָטַף מֵרָטְבּוֹ — *[If] some of its juices dripped* onto the walls of the oven, they become heated by the hot earthenware and thereby disqualified. When these are reabsorbed by the meat of the *pesach,* they disqualify it to the extent of their spread. [A forbidden (hot) liquid is assumed to penetrate a (permitted hot) solid to some depth.] Therefore, he must *remove* an appropriate thickness of meat, and not just *slice off* a thin sliver [as in the previous case] (*Rashi*).

נָטַף מֵרָטְבּוֹ עַל הַסֹּלֶת — *[If] some of its juices dripped onto flour* already seething from the fire, the drippings become cooked by the heat of the flour, thus disqualifying them. Since they become

[ג] סָכוֹ בְּשֶׁמֶן תְּרוּמָה, אִם חֲבוּרַת כֹּהֲנִים, יֹאכֵלוּ. אִם יִשְׂרָאֵל: אִם חַי הוּא, יְדִיחֶנּוּ; וְאִם צָלִי הוּא, יִקְלוֹף אֶת הַחִיצוֹן.

סָכוֹ בְּשֶׁמֶן שֶׁל מַעֲשֵׂר שֵׁנִי, לֹא יַעֲשֶׂנּוּ דָמִים עַל בְּנֵי חֲבוּרָה, שֶׁאֵין פּוֹדִין מַעֲשֵׂר שֵׁנִי בִּירוּשָׁלָיִם.

[ד] חֲמִשָּׁה דְבָרִים בָּאִין בְּטֻמְאָה, וְאֵינָן נֶאֱכָלִין בְּטֻמְאָה: הָעֹמֶר, וּשְׁתֵּי הַלֶּחֶם, וְלֶחֶם הַפָּנִים, וְזִבְחֵי שַׁלְמֵי צִבּוּר, וּשְׂעִירֵי רָאשֵׁי חֳדָשִׁים. הַפֶּסַח שֶׁבָּא בְטֻמְאָה נֶאֱכָל בְּטֻמְאָה, שֶׁלֹּא בָא מִתְּחִלָּתוֹ אֶלָּא לַאֲכִילָה.

[ה] נִטְמָא הַבָּשָׂר וְהַחֵלֶב קַיָּם, אֵינוֹ זוֹרֵק אֶת הַדָּם. נִטְמָא הַחֵלֶב וְהַבָּשָׂר קַיָּם, זוֹרֵק אֶת הַדָּם. וּבַמֻּקְדָּשִׁין אֵינוֹ כֵן. אֶלָּא אַף עַל פִּי שֶׁנִּטְמָא הַבָּשָׂר וְהַחֵלֶב קַיָּם, זוֹרֵק אֶת הַדָּם.

[ו] נִטְמָא הַקָּהָל אוֹ רֻבּוֹ, אוֹ שֶׁהָיוּ הַכֹּהֲנִים טְמֵאִים וְהַקָּהָל טְהוֹרִים, יֵעָשֶׂה בְטֻמְאָה. נִטְמָא מִעוּט הַקָּהָל, הַטְּהוֹרִין עוֹשִׂין אֶת הָרִאשׁוֹן, וְהַטְּמֵאִין עוֹשִׂין אֶת הַשֵּׁנִי.

[ז] הַפֶּסַח שֶׁנִּזְרַק דָּמוֹ וְאַחַר כָּךְ נוֹדַע שֶׁהוּא טָמֵא, הַצִּיץ מְרַצֶּה. נִטְמָא הַגּוּף, אֵין הַצִּיץ מְרַצֶּה. מִפְּנֵי שֶׁאָמְרוּ: הַנָּזִיר וְעוֹשֶׂה פֶסַח, הַצִּיץ מְרַצֶּה עַל טֻמְאַת הַדָּם, וְאֵין הַצִּיץ מְרַצֶּה עַל טֻמְאַת הַגּוּף.

יד אברהם

absorbed by the flour, he must remove a complete handful of flour and burn it (*Rav*).

3. סָכוֹ בְּשֶׁמֶן תְּרוּמָה — *Basting the pesach with* a small amount of oil during the roasting does not constitute cooking and is permitted (*Rav*; see 2:8). However, his use of *terumah* oil bars consumption of the offering by non-*Kohanim*, to whom *terumah* is forbidden. Once the meat has been roasted, it absorbs the liquids smeared on it and he must therefore remove a thin section of the outer layer. However, since basting involves only a minute amount of liquid, it does not result in a deep penetration of the meat and it therefore suffices to slice off a thin outer layer of the offering rather than the finger-thick layer required in the previous case of the drippings (*Gem.*).

מַעֲשֵׂר שֵׁנִי — *Maaser sheni* (see 2:5) must be eaten in Jerusalem. If the *pesach* was basted with such oil, the members of the group may not be charged for it, because *maaser sheni* may not be redeemed or sold in Jerusalem (*Rav*).

4. Although a person contaminated with *tumah* may not offer a sacrifice and invalidates it if he does, an exception is made for the regular communal sacrifices and the *pesach* offering. If the majority of the *Kohanim* in Jerusalem, or in the case of the *pesach*, the majority of the assembled people, are *tamei*, the sacrifices may be offered despite the *tumah* of the participants. [This exception is only for *tumah* arising from human corpses, not for any other kind of *tumah*.] This dispensation, however, extends only to offering the sacrifice, not to eating its meat portions. These must be burned like any sacrificial meat that has become *tamei*. The only exception to this rule is the *pesach* offering, which is eaten even if offered in *tumah*, and even by those who are *tamei*, because its purpose is not to atone but to provide the meat to be eaten at the Seder.

הָעֹמֶר — *The Omer* is an offering of barley flour made on the sixteenth of Nissan. After a *kometz* (handful) is removed from it and burnt on the Altar, the rest is eaten by the *Kohanim*.

וּשְׁתֵּי הַלֶּחֶם — *Two Loaves* of leavened breads are brought on Shavuos together with a complement of animal sacrifices. The loaves are 'waved' [תְּנוּפָה] together with the two *shelamim* lambs, the lambs are offered, and the Loaves are eaten by the *Kohanim*. These lambs are known as שַׁלְמֵי צִבּוּר, *the communal peace offerings*, and their meat is eaten by the *Kohanim*.

וְלֶחֶם הַפָּנִים — Twelve *Panim Breads* were arranged each week on the *Shulchan* (golden table) inside the Temple, together with two spoonfuls of *levonah* (frankincense). These were replaced each Sabbath, and the old *levonah* was burned on the Altar, while the breads were eaten by the *Kohanim*.

5. אֵינוֹ זוֹרֵק אֶת הַדָּם — *One may not throw the blood*. The essential sacrificial procedure is to slaughter the animal, catch the blood spurting from its neck in a bowl, and throw the blood against the Altar wall. Throwing the blood is what renders the offering valid, not burning the fats or eating the meat. Nevertheless, the mishnah indicates that at least one of the other components

[3] *[If] he basted [the pesach] with oil of terumah, if the group is composed of Kohanim, they may eat it. If they are Israelites: if it is raw, he must rinse it; but if it is roasted, he must slice off the outer layer. [If] he basted it with oil of maaser sheni, its value may not be charged to the members of the company, since maaser sheni may not be redeemed in Jerusalem.*

[4] *Five things may be offered in a state of tumah-contamination, but may not be eaten in a state of tumah-contamination: the Omer, the Two Loaves, the Panim Breads, the communal peace offerings, and the he-goats of Rosh Chodesh. [But] the pesach offering that is offered in tumah may be eaten in tumah, because its very purpose is for eating.*

[5] *[If] the meat [of the pesach offering] became contaminated with tumah but the fat remained [uncontaminated], one may not throw the blood. [If] the fat became contaminated with tumah but the meat remained [uncontaminated], he throws the blood. But in the case of [other] consecrated animals it is not so. Rather, even when the meat became contaminated and the fat remained [uncontaminated], one throws the blood.*

[6] *[If] the entire community, or a majority of it, became contaminated with tumah, or if the Kohanim were contaminated while the community was uncontaminated, [the pesach] is offered in tumah-contamination. [If only] a minority of the community became contaminated, those uncontaminated observe the first [pesach offering], while the contaminated observe the second [pesach offering].*

[7] *[For] any pesach offering whose blood had been thrown and it was learned afterwards that it had been contaminated, the tzitz effects acceptance. [But if it was later learned that] if the person had been contaminated, the tzitz does not effect acceptance. For they have said [concerning] the nazir and one making the pesach offering, that the tzitz effects acceptance for contamination of the blood, but the tzitz does not effect acceptance for the contamination of the person.*

YAD AVRAHAM

must remain fit in order for the blood to be thrown. In the case of the *pesach*, it must be the meat that remains fit, because the main purpose of the *pesach* is for its meat to be eaten at the Seder. [Our mishnah discusses a situation where the community was not in a state of *tumah* but a particular *pesach* became *tamei*.]

6. נִטְמָא — *Became contaminated with the tumah* of human corpses — the only *tumah* for which an exception is made in regard to sacrifices.

הָרִאשׁוֹן ... הַשֵּׁנִי — *The first pesach offering* is Nissan 14, while *the second pesach offering* [known as the *pesach sheni*] is Iyar 14. This date is reserved for those unable to perform the regular offering because of *tumah* or other reasons (see 9:1-2). The dispensation for offering the *pesach* in *tumah* on Nissan 14 is only if the majority of the populace is *tamei*.

7. The following three mishnayos discuss cases in which the meat of the offering became *tamei* (but not the people). The Sages expound that where such contamination would result in the entire offering being disqualified, the צִיץ, *tzitz* [gold plate worn by the *Kohen Gadol* on his forehead], propitiates the sin of *tumah* and lifts the disqualification (*Gem.*). This atonement not only renders valid sacrifices already offered, releasing the participants from the obligation of a second offering, but even permits the completion of those still in progress. The Sages decreed, however, that if the *tumah* becomes known prior to the blood service, the blood should not be thrown.

וְאַחַר כָּךְ נוֹדַע שֶׁהוּא טָמֵא — *It was learned afterwards that it* [the blood or the meat] *had been contaminated*, the offering is valid. If the blood alone became *tamei*, the meat is eaten. If the meat has become *tamei*, however, it cannot be eaten because the acceptance effected by the *tzitz* does not extend to lifting the prohibition against eating *tumah*-contaminated meat (*Rav*).

נִטְמָא הַגּוּף — *[But if it was later learned that] the person had been contaminated* — either the participants or the *Kohen* making the offering — the *tzitz* does not effect acceptance and the participants must bring another offering, the *pesach sheni*.

הַנָּזִיר וְעוֹשֵׂה פֶּסַח — *The nazir and one making the Pesach offering*. A *nazir* is one who has taken upon himself a vow that bars him from drinking

נִטְמָא טֻמְאַת הַתְּהוֹם, הַצִּיץ מְרַצֶּה.

[ח] נִטְמָא שָׁלֵם אוֹ רֻבּוֹ, שׂוֹרְפִין אוֹתוֹ לִפְנֵי הַבִּירָה מֵעֲצֵי הַמַּעֲרָכָה. נִטְמָא מִעוּטוֹ, וְהַנּוֹתָר, שׂוֹרְפִין אוֹתוֹ בְּחַצְרוֹתֵיהֶן אוֹ עַל גַּגּוֹתֵיהֶן מֵעֲצֵי עַצְמָן. הַצַּיְקָנִין שׂוֹרְפִין אוֹתוֹ לִפְנֵי הַבִּירָה, בִּשְׁבִיל לֵהָנוֹת מֵעֲצֵי הַמַּעֲרָכָה.

[ט] הַפֶּסַח שֶׁיָּצָא אוֹ שֶׁנִּטְמָא יִשָּׂרֵף מִיָּד. נִטְמְאוּ הַבְּעָלִים אוֹ שֶׁמֵּתוּ תְּעֻבַּר צוּרָתוֹ, וְיִשָּׂרֵף בְּשִׁשָּׁה עָשָׂר. רַבִּי יוֹחָנָן בֶּן בְּרוֹקָה אוֹמֵר: אַף זֶה יִשָּׂרֵף מִיָּד, לְפִי שֶׁאֵין לוֹ אוֹכְלִין.

[י] הָעֲצָמוֹת וְהַגִּידִין וְהַנּוֹתָר יִשָּׂרְפוּ בְּשִׁשָּׁה עָשָׂר. חָל שִׁשָּׁה עָשָׂר לִהְיוֹת בַּשַּׁבָּת, יִשָּׂרְפוּ בְּשִׁבְעָה עָשָׂר, לְפִי שֶׁאֵינָן דּוֹחִין לֹא אֶת הַשַּׁבָּת וְלֹא אֶת יוֹם טוֹב.

[יא] כָּל הַנֶּאֱכָל בְּשׁוֹר הַגָּדוֹל יֵאָכֵל בִּגְדִי הָרַךְ, וְרָאשֵׁי כְנָפַיִם וְהַסְּחוּסִים. הַשּׁוֹבֵר אֶת הָעֶצֶם בְּפֶסַח הַטָּהוֹר, הֲרֵי זֶה לוֹקֶה אַרְבָּעִים. אֲבָל הַמּוֹתִיר בַּטָּהוֹר וְהַשּׁוֹבֵר בַּטָּמֵא, אֵינוֹ לוֹקֶה אֶת הָאַרְבָּעִים.

יד אברהם

wine, cutting his hair, and contaminating himself with the *tumah* of a human corpse for a certain period of time. The term of *nezirus* cannot conclude, however, until the *nazir* brings certain offerings. By the *tzitz* effecting atonement for the contaminated offering, it permits the *nazir* to perform those acts that had been previously forbidden him (*Rav*).

טֻמְאַת הַתְּהוֹם — *Tumah-contamination of the deep* is a technical term denoting a human-corpse *tumah* that was previously unrecognized, e.g. a corpse discovered buried beneath a house. If this *tumah* was discovered after the *nazir* offered his sacrifices, or after the *pesach* service had been completed, the *tzitz* atones for the *tumah* of the person who became *tamei* by it even though it concerns a contamination of the person.

8. נִטְמָא שָׁלֵם אוֹ רֻבּוֹ — *[If] the whole or the greater part of* [the *pesach* offering] *became contaminated*, the meat must be burned like that of any contaminated offering. Although the *pesach* sacrifice may be burned throughout Jerusalem (3:8), the Sages made an exception here [where most or all of the sacrifice is affected and it can be presumed that it happened due to gross negligence] in order to embarrass them so that they and the onlookers be more careful in the future (*Gem.*).

וְהַנּוֹתָר — Sacrificial *meat that was left past the time* prescribed for eating it must be burned even if not contaminated.

9. הַפֶּסַח שֶׁיָּצָא — *Any pesach offering taken out* of Jerusalem becomes disqualified, because it has left the area within which it may be eaten. The mishnah speaks of a case in which it was removed on the fourteenth after its service, but before sundown (*Rav*).

יִשָּׂרֵף — *Must be burned.* The Torah requires that disqualified sacrificial parts be burned. Those that have been disqualified directly, e.g., by becoming *tamei* or by leaving the area permitted for them, are burned immediately. Thus, in the case of the *pesach*, they should be burned before sunset of the fourteenth. Once night falls, however, they cannot be burned because disqualified sacrifices may not be burned at night, nor on a festival (*Gem.*).

נִטְמְאוּ הַבְּעָלִים אוֹ שֶׁמֵּתוּ — *[If] the owners became contaminated or died*, the offering has only been indirectly disqualified because there is no one to eat it. Consequently, it may not be burned until it becomes 'disfigured,' [meaning its state was changed] i.e., נוֹתָר, *leftover* past the time allowed for its consumption. This occurs for a *pesach* on the morning of the fifteenth, but the disqualified parts may not be burned then because it is the festival. Thus, it must wait for the sixteenth.

רַבִּי יוֹחָנָן בֶּן בְּרוֹקָה — *R' Yochanan ben Berokah* maintains that the disqualification resulting from the *tumah* of the owners is treated the same as the disqualification of the sacrifice itself.

10. הָעֲצָמוֹת — *The bones* of the *pesach* may not be broken (*Ex.* 12:46). As a result, their edible marrow, which cannot be removed, becomes

[If] one became contaminated from a tumah-contamination of the deep, the tzitz effects acceptance.

[8] *[If] the whole or the greater part of [the pesach offering] became contaminated, it must be burned before the Temple complex with wood [set aside] for the [Altar] pyre. [However, if] the lesser part became contaminated, or [if the meat] was left past its time, they burn it in their courtyards or on their rooftops with their own wood. The misers would burn it before the Temple complex, in order to make use of the wood of the pyre.*

[9] *Any pesach offering taken out [of Jerusalem] or which became contaminated with tumah must be burned immediately. [If] the owners became contaminated or died, it must become disfigured and be burned on the sixteenth. R' Yochanan ben Berokah says: This too must be burned immediately, because there are none to eat it.*

[10] *The bones, the sinews, and the leftover [meat] must be burned on the sixteenth. [If] the sixteenth falls on the Sabbath, they must be burned on the seventeenth, because [the mitzvah to burn] them does not override the Sabbath or the festival.*

[11] *Any parts edible in a full-grown ox must be eaten in a tender kid, including the ends of the shoulder blades and the cartilage. [If] one breaks the bone of an uncontaminated pesach offering, he incurs the [penalty of] forty lashes. But one who leaves over [meat] of an uncontaminated one, or who breaks [the bone] of a contaminated one, does not incur the [penalty of] forty lashes.*

YAD AVRAHAM

leftover and must be burned [together with the bones].

וְהַגִּידִין — The term *sinews* in this context includes such soft tissue as tendons, sinews, and nerves. Since the mishnah considers sinews distinct from meat, it is evident that it does not refer to ordinarily edible sinews. On the other hand, sinews too tough to be eaten do not become disqualified and need not be burned. The *Gemara* concludes that it refers to the fat of the thigh sinew, or the outer sinew of the thigh. The thigh sinew itself [גִּיד הַנָּשֶׁה] is Scripturally forbidden, but its fat is technically permitted, although it is not customarily eaten. The outer sinew is forbidden only by Rabbinic law, and therefore Biblically requires burning like edible meat.

11. כָּל הַנֶּאֱכָל... — *Any parts edible*... When a group registers on a *pesach* offering, there must be sufficient meat for each one to receive an *edible* portion the size of an olive (כְּזַיִת). Inedible parts do not count towards this amount, nor does the prohibition against leaving over offering meat. The mishnah now defines what is considered edible.

יֵאָכֵל בִּגְדִי הָרַךְ — *Must be eaten in a tender kid*, i.e., the *pesach* offering. However, parts of the *pesach* that will harden and be inedible in an adult goat or sheep (as in a grown ox) are not included even though they are still soft in the young kid. The ends of the shoulder blades and the cartilage are considered edible, though they become so (in an adult ox) only after being boiled for a long period of time (*Rav*).

הַשּׁוֹבֵר אֶת הָעֶצֶם — *Breaking the bone of* a *pesach* offering is forbidden by the Torah (*Ex*. 12:10). *Chinuch* (*Mitzvah* 16) offers a reason for this. Breaking and gnawing at bones is the practice of the poor, who lack sufficient food. We, who proclaim that on this day we became *a kingdom of priests and a sanctified people* (*Ex*. 19:6), should deport ourselves in a manner befitting princes.

In general, the prohibition does not apply to a *pesach* that has become *tamei*. However, even breaking the bones of a contaminated *pesach* incurs punishment if the contamination occurred after the offering had already been permitted for consumption, i.e., after the 'throwing' of the blood.

אֲבָל הַמּוֹתִיר בְּטָהוֹר — *But one who leaves over [meat] of an uncontaminated pesach* is not liable to lashes, although he is forbidden to do so. This is because the Torah follows the prohibition with a compensatory commandment to burn the leftover, and whenever an affirmative command follows a negative command (לָאו הַנִּתָּק לַעֲשֵׂה), it is regarded as the remedy for the transgression, replacing punishment. Also, leaving over violates the prohibition passively rather than actively [לָאו שֶׁאֵין בּוֹ מַעֲשֶׂה], for which there is no penalty of lashes (*Gem.*).

[יב] אֵבֶר שֶׁיָּצָא מִקְצָתוֹ, חוֹתֵךְ עַד שֶׁמַּגִּיעַ לָעֶצֶם, וְקוֹלֵף עַד שֶׁמַּגִּיעַ לַפֶּרֶק, וְחוֹתֵךְ. וּבַמֻּקְדָּשִׁין קוֹצֵץ בְּקוֹפִיץ, שֶׁאֵין בּוֹ מִשּׁוּם שְׁבִירַת הָעֶצֶם. מִן הָאֲגַף וְלִפְנִים, כְּלִפְנִים; מִן הָאֲגַף וְלַחוּץ, כְּלַחוּץ. הַחַלּוֹנוֹת וְעֹבִי הַחוֹמָה, כְּלִפְנִים.

[יג] שְׁתֵּי חֲבוּרוֹת שֶׁהָיוּ אוֹכְלוֹת בְּבַיִת אֶחָד, אֵלּוּ הוֹפְכִין אֶת פְּנֵיהֶם הֵילָךְ וְאוֹכְלִין, וְאֵלּוּ הוֹפְכִין אֶת פְּנֵיהֶם הֵילָךְ וְאוֹכְלִין, וְהַמֵּחַם בָּאֶמְצַע. וּכְשֶׁהַשַּׁמָּשׁ עוֹמֵד לִמְזוֹג, קוֹפֵץ אֶת פִּיו וּמַחֲזִיר אֶת פָּנָיו עַד שֶׁמַּגִּיעַ אֵצֶל חֲבוּרָתוֹ, וְאוֹכֵל. וְהַכַּלָּה הוֹפֶכֶת אֶת פָּנֶיהָ וְאוֹכֶלֶת.

פרק שמיני

[א] **הָאִשָּׁה** בִּזְמַן שֶׁהִיא בְּבֵית בַּעְלָהּ, שָׁחַט עָלֶיהָ בַּעְלָהּ וְשָׁחַט עָלֶיהָ אָבִיהָ, תֹּאכַל מִשֶּׁל בַּעְלָהּ. הָלְכָה רֶגֶל רִאשׁוֹן לַעֲשׂוֹת בְּבֵית אָבִיהָ, שָׁחַט עָלֶיהָ אָבִיהָ וְשָׁחַט עָלֶיהָ בַּעְלָהּ, תֹּאכַל בִּמְקוֹם שֶׁהִיא רוֹצָה. יָתוֹם שֶׁשָּׁחֲטוּ עָלָיו אַפִּטְרוֹפְּסִין יֹאכַל בִּמְקוֹם שֶׁהוּא רוֹצֶה. עֶבֶד שֶׁל שְׁנֵי שֻׁתָּפִין לֹא יֹאכַל מִשֶּׁל שְׁנֵיהֶן. מִי שֶׁחֶצְיוֹ עֶבֶד וְחֶצְיוֹ בֶּן חוֹרִין לֹא יֹאכַל מִשֶּׁל רַבּוֹ.

[ב] הָאוֹמֵר לְעַבְדּוֹ: „צֵא וּשְׁחֹט עָלַי אֶת הַפֶּסַח," שָׁחַט גְּדִי יֹאכַל, שָׁחַט טָלֶה יֹאכַל. שָׁחַט גְּדִי וְטָלֶה, יֹאכַל מִן הָרִאשׁוֹן. שָׁכַח מָה

יד אברהם

12. אֵבֶר שֶׁיָּצָא מִקְצָתוֹ — *[If] part of a limb*... The Torah restricts an offering to certain areas and any offering that exits its permitted area is disqualified. If part of a limb of an offering extrudes beyond the permitted boundary, only that part becomes disqualified. Removing that part from a *pesach* offering must be done without breaking any bone. Thus, he must first cut around the bone to separate the meat that has become forbidden from the remainder that must be eaten. He then removes all the permissible meat from that bone as far back as the joint and cuts through the tendons, which are not considered bone, to separate the bone from the rest of the carcass. He then burns the disqualified meat and disposes of the bone. The boundaries for *pesach* offerings are the walls of Jerusalem and the group in which it is designated to be eaten (see m. 13).

13. שְׁתֵּי חֲבוּרוֹת — *Two groups* may eat from the same offering in the same house without any necessity of appearing like one group by facing each other. However, each individual is limited to eating with one company (*Rav*).

וְהַמֵּחַם בָּאֶמְצַע — *With the kettle between them.* In Talmudic times it was customary to dilute wine with warm water. The heater upon which the water kettle stands may be placed between the two groups for the waiter's convenience, even though it appears to divide the two groups, because a *pesach* may be eaten in two separate companies. However, since the waiter is a registered participant in this *pesach* and a member of one of these groups, he must close his mouth and turn his face when he stands up to mix the wine for the other group, to remove any suspicion that he is eating with the other group.

וְהַכַּלָּה הוֹפֶכֶת אֶת פָּנֶיהָ — *A bride may turn her face away* [out of modesty and shyness] when eating, because a *pesach* may be eaten in two companies.

CHAPTER EIGHT

1. To partake of a *pesach* offering, a person must register on it before its slaughter. However, he need not purchase a portion but may have it assigned to him by a second party. Thus it may happen that an individual is registered for more than one *pesach* without his knowledge. But since one person may not bring more than one *pesach* offering, a determination must be made as to which of the two registrations is valid.

בִּזְמַן שֶׁהִיא בְּבֵית בַּעְלָהּ — *While a woman resides in her husband's house,* i.e., she is fully married, not merely betrothed. Also, she plans to spend the festival in her husband's house rather than with her parents. Accordingly, she eats from her husband's *pesach* because it is assumed that she prefers to join her husband's offering. [A woman

[12] [If] part of a limb left the area [permitted for it], he cuts [it] until he reaches the bone, and pares [the meat] away until he reaches the joint and severs [the limb]. But with other offerings he may chop with a cleaver, for they are not subject to the [prohibition of] breaking a bone.

From the jamb [of the city's gates] is considered within [the city]; from the jamb outward is considered outside [the city]. The windows and the thickness [atop] the walls are treated as within [the city].

[13] [If] two groups were eating in the same house, one group may turn in one direction and eat, and the other group may turn in another direction and eat, with the kettle between them. When the waiter stands up to mix the wine, he must close his mouth and turn his face until he gets back to his own group, [when] he may [resume] eating. A bride may turn her face away and eat.

CHAPTER EIGHT

[1] **הָאִשָּׁה** *While a woman resides in her husband's house, [if] her husband slaughtered [a pesach] on her behalf and her father slaughtered on her behalf, she eats from [the pesach] of her husband. [If] she went to spend the first festival in her father's house, [and] both her father and husband slaughtered on her behalf, she may eat in whichever place she desires. An orphan whose guardians slaughtered for him may eat in whichever place he desires. A slave belonging to two partners may not eat from either one's [pesach]. One who is half slave and half free may not eat from his master's.*

[2] *One who instructed his slave, 'Go out and have a pesach offering slaughtered for me,' [whether] he [arranged for] a kid to be slaughtered or a lamb [to be] slaughtered, he may eat [of it]. [If] he arranged for [both] a kid and a lamb to be slaughtered, he must eat of the first. [If] he forgot which his*

YAD AVRAHAM

is obligated in the *mitzvah* of eating the *pesach* offering.]

רֶגֶל ראשון — *The first festival* after marriage was customary for a woman to spend at her father's house. Thus, it is not self-evident that she intends to eat from her husband's *pesach* rather than her father's. Accordingly, though she may eat whichever she desires, she must state her preference by the time of slaughter in order to be able to eat from either one (*Gem.*). [Stating her preference at the *Seder*, however, cannot retroactively register her on one *pesach* or the other.]

יָתוֹם שֶׁשָּׁחֲטוּ עָלָיו — *An orphan* who had more than one guardian and each slaughtered a *pesach* on his behalf, may choose the *pesach* in which he will participate even after the slaughter. The problem of retroactive choice does not apply here because the Torah says (*Ex.* 12:3): *And they shall take ... a kid for a household,* implying that the head of the household [the guardian in this case] has the power to purchase a *pesach* for his minor children without their acquiescence (*Gem.*). Thus, the subsequent choice made by the orphan does not have to be effective retroactively.

עֶבֶד שֶׁל שְׁנֵי שֻׁתָּפִין — *A* [gentile] *slave belonging to two* [Jewish] *partners* is obligated to eat the *pesach,* but may not do so unless both owners agree on which *pesach* to register him. Otherwise, since half of him belongs to each partner, neither one's registration is valid without permission from the other owner.

מִי שֶׁחֶצְיוֹ עֶבֶד — *One who is half slave* and half free, having been freed by one of his two owners, may not eat from his master's offering because it is assumed that the master of half of him did not intend to register the free half upon his offering (*Rashi*).

2. ... הָאוֹמֵר לְעַבְדּוֹ — *One who instructed his slave* to arrange a *pesach* offering for him, without specifying whether he wanted a lamb or a kid. Since he did not specify, we assume that he depends completely on the slave's discretion (*Gem.*).

If the slave had one of each slaughtered, the master is considered registered on the one slaughtered first, and the second offering is burned (*Rashi*). The *Gemara* explains that this last case refers specifically to a king who, because of the abundance of food available to him, is assumed not to have any fixed preferences about the kind of meat he wants for the *pesach.* Ordinary people, who are assumed to

אָמַר לוֹ רַבּוֹ, כֵּיצַד יַעֲשֶׂה? יִשְׁחֹט טָלֶה וּגְדִי וְיֹאמַר: „אִם גְּדִי אָמַר לִי רַבִּי, גְּדִי שֶׁלּוֹ וְטָלֶה שֶׁלִּי; וְאִם טָלֶה אָמַר לִי רַבִּי, טָלֶה שֶׁלּוֹ וּגְדִי שֶׁלִּי." שָׁכַח רַבּוֹ מָה אָמַר לוֹ, שְׁנֵיהֶם יֵצְאוּ לְבֵית הַשְּׂרֵפָה, וּפְטוּרִין מִלַּעֲשׂוֹת פֶּסַח שֵׁנִי.

[ג] הָאוֹמֵר לְבָנָיו: „הֲרֵינִי שׁוֹחֵט אֶת הַפֶּסַח עַל מִי שֶׁיַּעֲלֶה מִכֶּם לִירוּשָׁלַיִם," כֵּיוָן שֶׁהִכְנִיס הָרִאשׁוֹן רֹאשׁוֹ וְרֻבּוֹ, זָכָה בְחֶלְקוֹ, וּמְזַכֶּה אֶת אֶחָיו עִמּוֹ. לְעוֹלָם נִמְנִין עָלָיו עַד שֶׁיְּהֵא בוֹ כְּזַיִת לְכָל אֶחָד וְאֶחָד. נִמְנִין וּמוֹשְׁכִין אֶת יְדֵיהֶן מִמֶּנּוּ עַד שֶׁיִּשָּׁחֵט. רַבִּי שִׁמְעוֹן אוֹמֵר: עַד שֶׁיִּזָּרֵק עָלָיו אֶת הַדָּם.

[ד] הַמְּמַנֶּה עִמּוֹ אֲחֵרִים בְּחֶלְקוֹ, רַשָּׁאִין בְּנֵי חֲבוּרָה לִתֵּן לוֹ אֶת שֶׁלּוֹ, וְהוּא אוֹכֵל מִשֶּׁלּוֹ וְהֵן אוֹכְלִין מִשֶּׁלָּהֶן.

[ה] זָב שֶׁרָאָה שְׁתֵּי רְאִיּוֹת, שׁוֹחֲטִין עָלָיו בַּשְּׁבִיעִי. רָאָה שָׁלֹשׁ, שׁוֹחֲטִין עָלָיו בַּשְּׁמִינִי שֶׁלּוֹ.

שׁוֹמֶרֶת יוֹם כְּנֶגֶד יוֹם, שׁוֹחֲטִין עָלֶיהָ בַּשֵּׁנִי שֶׁלָּהּ. רָאֲתָה שְׁנֵי יָמִים, שׁוֹחֲטִין עָלֶיהָ בַּשְּׁלִישִׁי.

וְהַזָּבָה, שׁוֹחֲטִין עָלֶיהָ בַּשְּׁמִינִי.

יד אברהם

have preferences, would have both offerings judged invalid, since a person cannot be registered on two offerings, nor can he designate his choice retroactively [אֵין בְּרֵירָה].

יִשְׁחֹט טָלֶה וּגְדִי וְיֹאמַר — *Let him slaughter a lamb and a kid and stipulate* that whichever his master had previously ordered be for him and the remaining one for the slave. Retroactive selection [בְּרֵירָה] is of no concern here, because no new choice will be made by anyone after the slaughter. The master has *already* made his choice; it is merely the slave who does not know. [This course, however, is not as simple as it seems because it involves the problem of a slave owning property independently of his master. See the full *Yad Avraham* comm. p. 159.]

שָׁכַח רַבּוֹ ... — *[If]* [by the time the slave returns] *his master* also cannot recall his instructions, both offerings are dispensed to the 'place of burning' to be destroyed, because it cannot be determined which offering is the master's and which the slave's. Eating of either offering, therefore, runs the risk of transgressing the prohibition against eating of a *pesach* without registration. However, if the master still remembered his instructions at the time these offerings were made [and only forgot them later], each was *offered* as a valid *pesach,* and both master and slave are exempt from participating in the *pesach sheni* [for those who did not offer a *pesach* on Nissan 14] (*Gem.*).

3. הָאוֹמֵר לְבָנָיו — *[If] one says to his sons.* The father leaves for Jerusalem to perform the sacrifice in the afternoon and allows the children to arrive after the service, in time to eat from the offering at night. To speed them on their way he offers to slaughter the *pesach for* the one to reach Jerusalem first; he will be given a single large portion [and the other brothers will have to receive their portions from him]. However, the father had actually registered all his sons on this offering. The mishnah teaches that this statement is meant merely as a spur and not to void the original registration (*Gem.*).

רַבִּי שִׁמְעוֹן אוֹמֵר — *R' Shimon* permits withdrawal even after the slaughter, as long as the offering's blood has not been thrown [which renders the offering valid]. He concurs, however, that registration must take place before the slaughter.

4. הַמְּמַנֶּה עִמּוֹ אֲחֵרִים בְּחֶלְקוֹ — *[If] one registers others upon his portion* of the *pesach* without consulting the rest of the group, the original members may claim that they do not wish to spend their meal with strangers (*Gem.*). They may therefore give him his portion (e.g., his tenth) and tell him to eat separately with those he registered. Separating presents no problems, because the *pesach* may be eaten in two groups [see 7:13] (*Rav*).

5. זָב — *A zav.* A man who experiences

master had specified, what should he do? Let him slaughter a lamb and a kid and stipulate: 'If my master specified a kid, let the kid be his and the lamb mine; and if my master specified a lamb, let the lamb be his and the kid mine. [If] his master [also] forgot what he had specified, both are dispensed to the place of burning, and both are exempt from participating in [the] pesach sheni.

[3] *[If] one says to his sons: 'I will slaughter the pesach for the first among you to reach Jerusalem,' as soon as the first one enters [the city] with his head and the greater part of his body, he acquires his portion and acquires his brothers' [portions] for them.*

Registration for a [pesach offering] may continue for as long as there is [at least] an olive's volume for each [registrant]. People may register or withdraw from it until it is slaughtered. R' Shimon says: Until the blood is thrown for it.

[4] *[If] one registers others upon his portion [of the pesach], the [other] members of the company are permitted to [separate and] give him his [portion], and he eats his and they eat theirs.*

[5] *A zav who experienced two discharges may have his [pesach] offering slaughtered on the seventh [day]. [If] he experienced three, they may slaughter for him on his eighth [day].*

A woman who observes a day against a day may have her offering slaughtered on her second [day]. [If] she experienced discharges for two days, they may slaughter for her on the third [day]. A zavah may have her offering slaughtered on the eighth [day].

YAD AVRAHAM

spontaneous seminal emissions (differing somewhat from ordinary seminal emissions in their texture and color) is rendered *tamei*. If he experiences one discharge, he may immerse in a *mikveh* immediately and be rid of his *tumah* at nightfall. If he experiences two discharges in one day or on two consecutive days, he is classified a *zav* and must observe seven consecutive 'clean' days (i.e. free of discharges) and immerse himself in a spring of running water [מַעְיָן] on the seventh day before becoming *tahor* on the evening of the eighth. Thus, if his seventh day falls on Erev Pesach, and he has already immersed himself, they may offer his *pesach* in the Temple, because he will be fit to eat it that night (*Rav*).

However, a man who experienced three discharges on one, two, or three consecutive days does not become *tahor* until he offers a pair of bird sacrifices on the eighth day, after completing the previous procedure. Thus, only if his *eighth* day is on Erev Pesach may they offer the *pesach* sacrifice for him, provided the *zav* offerings have already been brought to the Temple.

שׁוֹמֶרֶת יוֹם כְּנֶגֶד יוֹם — *A woman who observes a day against a day*. When a woman menstruates she becomes a *niddah* for seven days. This is followed by an eleven-day period during which she may become a *zavah* by menstruating again, as follows: If she menstruates on one day during these eleven, she must make sure that the next day is free from discharge and immerse herself before sundown; she is then totally *tahor* (purified) at nightfall. She is known as *one who observes a day* [free from discharge] *against a day* [of discharge]. Similarly, if she experiences two discharges on two consecutive days, she observes the third day free of discharge, then immerses and is *tahor* by evening. Therefore, should this second or third day fall on Erev Pesach and she has already immersed herself in a *mikveh*, they may slaughter a *pesach* for her since she will be fit to eat it that night (*Rav*).

If, however, she menstruates on three consecutive days in this eleven-day period, she is a זָבָה גְדוֹלָה, *major zavah* [in contrast to the previous cases of a *minor zavah*]. She must now observe seven consecutive days free from discharge and may immerse herself in a *mikveh* on the seventh day. However, she must also offer sacrifices on the eighth day. Thus her *pesach* sacrifice may be offered only on her eighth clean day, provided she has brought her *zavah* sacrifices. [The above is the Scriptural law. Rabbinically, a woman who menstruates even one day requires seven clean days before she may purify herself in a *mikveh* and resume marital relations with her husband.]

[ו] הָאוֹנֵן, וְהַמְפַקֵּחַ אֶת הַגַּל; וְכֵן מִי שֶׁהִבְטִיחוּהוּ לְהוֹצִיאוֹ מִבֵּית הָאֲסוּרִים, וְהַחוֹלֶה וְהַזָּקֵן שֶׁהֵן יְכוֹלִין לֶאֱכוֹל כְּזַיִת, שׁוֹחֲטִין עֲלֵיהֶן. עַל כֻּלָּן אֵין שׁוֹחֲטִין עֲלֵיהֶן בִּפְנֵי עַצְמָן, שֶׁמָּא יָבִיאוּ אֶת הַפֶּסַח לִידֵי פְסוּל. לְפִיכָךְ, אִם אֵרַע בָּהֶן פְּסוּל, פְּטוּרִין מִלַּעֲשׂוֹת פֶּסַח שֵׁנִי; חוּץ מִן הַמְפַקֵּחַ בַּגַּל, שֶׁהוּא טָמֵא מִתְּחִלָּתוֹ.

[ז] אֵין שׁוֹחֲטִין אֶת הַפֶּסַח עַל הַיָּחִיד: דִּבְרֵי רַבִּי יְהוּדָה. וְרַבִּי יוֹסֵי מַתִּיר. אֲפִלּוּ חֲבוּרָה שֶׁל מֵאָה שֶׁאֵין יְכוֹלִין לֶאֱכוֹל כְּזַיִת, אֵין שׁוֹחֲטִין עֲלֵיהֶן.

וְאֵין עוֹשִׂין חֲבוּרַת נָשִׁים, וַעֲבָדִים, וּקְטַנִּים.

[ח] אוֹנֵן טוֹבֵל וְאוֹכֵל אֶת פִּסְחוֹ לָעֶרֶב, אֲבָל לֹא בְקָדָשִׁים. הַשּׁוֹמֵעַ עַל מֵתוֹ, וְהַמְלַקֵּט לוֹ עֲצָמוֹת, טוֹבֵל וְאוֹכֵל בְּקָדָשִׁים.

גֵּר שֶׁנִּתְגַּיֵּר בְּעֶרֶב פֶּסַח — בֵּית שַׁמַּאי אוֹמְרִים: טוֹבֵל וְאוֹכֵל אֶת פִּסְחוֹ לָעֶרֶב. וּבֵית הִלֵּל אוֹמְרִים: הַפּוֹרֵשׁ מִן הָעָרְלָה כְּפוֹרֵשׁ מִן הַקֶּבֶר.

פרק תשיעי

[א] **מִי** שֶׁהָיָה טָמֵא אוֹ בְדֶרֶךְ רְחוֹקָה, וְלֹא עָשָׂה אֶת הָרִאשׁוֹן, יַעֲשֶׂה אֶת הַשֵּׁנִי. שָׁגַג אוֹ נֶאֱנַס, וְלֹא עָשָׂה אֶת הָרִאשׁוֹן, יַעֲשֶׂה אֶת

יד אברהם

6. הָאוֹנֵן — *An onain* is a person newly in mourning for the death of his father, mother, brother, sister, son, daughter, or spouse, on the day of their death. The Torah prohibits him from partaking of sacrifices until nightfall of that day. Thus, his *pesach* may be slaughtered that afternoon.

וְהַמְפַקֵּחַ אֶת הַגַּל — *[A rescuer] who clears a pile of rubble* from a collapsed building to see if anyone is trapped inside. Although he may find the victim dead and be contaminated by the body and thus forbidden to eat the *pesach* offering, the offering is slaughtered on his behalf. Since the victim's fate is not known, the searcher must be assumed to retain his uncontaminated status [חֲזָקַת טָהֳרָה] (*Rav*).

אֵין שׁוֹחֲטִין עֲלֵיהֶן בִּפְנֵי עַצְמָן — *They may not slaughter for any of these alone*, because they may in the end not be able to partake of the *pesach* and cause it to be invalidated for lack of anyone to eat it. The grief-stricken mourners may touch the corpse and become *tamei*, the rescuer may find the victim dead and become *tamei*, the prisoner may remain incarcerated, and the sick or elderly may find it difficult to consume an adequate portion of meat. Thus, they must also register on this offering people not burdened with these problems, so that even if these prove unable to eat, the offering will not be disqualified. [A *pesach* is valid if it was slaughtered both for those fit to eat and those unable to do so (5:3).]

לְפִיכָךְ . . . פְּטוּרִין מִלַּעֲשׂוֹת פֶּסַח שֵׁנִי — *Therefore . . . they are exempt from participating in the pesach sheni.* Since they were considered fit to eat the offering at the time it was slaughtered and its blood was thrown, the sacrificial service was valid and they have discharged their obligation even if they are not in the end able to eat (see 7:4). The exception to this is the one clearing rubble, if a corpse was, in fact, discovered. In this case he became *tamei* when he started to clear the ruin, before the service took place, because a corpse contaminates even one who passes over it without touching it (*Rav*).

7. וְאֵין עוֹשִׂין חֲבוּרַת . . . . — *A group may not be formed* [solely] of women, slaves and minors because heathen slaves generally had low morals and this could lead to licentiousness. However, a group may be comprised exclusively of women or of slaves.

8. אוֹנֵן טוֹבֵל וְאוֹכֵל — *An onain immerses* [himself in a *mikveh*] *and eats* his *pesach* offering in the evening because Biblical law forbids mourners to eat offerings only on the day of death. The Rabbinic law prohibiting the following night was lifted for the sake of the *pesach*. However, he must first immerse himself

[6] *They may slaughter [the pesach] for an onain, and [a rescuer] who clears a pile of rubble; likewise for one who they have promised to release from prison, and a sick or aged person able to eat the volume of an olive. [However,] they may not slaughter for any of these alone, because they cause the pesach offering to become invalid. Therefore, if any disqualification befalls them, they are exempt from participating in the pesach sheni; except for the rescuer clearing rubble, for he was [found to be] contaminated retroactively.*

[7] *A pesach offering may not be slaughtered for an individual; [these are] the words of R' Yehudah. R' Yose permits [this]. [However,] we may not slaughter even for a group [consisting of] a hundred if they are unable to eat the volume of an olive. A group may not be formed [solely] of women, slaves and minors.*

[8] *An onain immerses and eats his pesach offering in the evening, but not [the other] offerings. One who hears about the death of his relative, or one who has arranged for the bones [of a close relative] to be gathered on his behalf, immerses [himself] and may eat offerings.*

[If] someone converted on Erev Pesach — Beis Shammai say: He immerses [himself] and eats his pesach offering in the evening. But Beis Hillel say: One who separates [himself] from an uncircumcised state is like one who separates himself from the grave.

CHAPTER NINE

[1] **מִי** *One who was contaminated with tumah or was on a distant journey, and [therefore] had not made [his offering] on the First [Pesach], makes [it] on the Second [Pesach]. [If] he erred or was prevented [by circumstances], and did not make [his offering] on the First [Pesach], he makes [his offering] on the*

YAD AVRAHAM

in a *mikveh* because of a Rabbinic rule requiring immersion for anyone who has been prohibited to partake of offerings (*Rashi*). He may not, however, eat the other offerings that night, because that is a *mitzvah* not subject to *kares* and it does not merit a waiver of a Rabbinic prohibition (*Rambam*).

הַשּׁוֹמֵעַ עַל מֵתוֹ ... — *One who hears about the death of his relative* after the day of death is an *onain* only by Rabbinic decree. Similarly, one who has arranged for the bones of a close relative to be exhumed from a temporary grave (e.g., one belonging to someone else) or for reburial near his parents or in *Eretz Yisrael* (see *Y.D.* 363:1), is Rabbinically obliged to observe a period of mourning until nightfall on the day of the reburial. The night after these mourning periods is not under this ban, and he may thus eat even from the other offerings as well.

בֵּית שַׁמַּאי אוֹמְרִים — *Beis Shammai say* that he may offer his *pesach* on the very day of his conversion as long as he undergoes an additional immersion (similar to the immersion required of a mourner), and eat the *pesach* that night.

וּבֵית הִלֵּל אוֹמְרִים — *But Beis Hillel* liken a convert to one who has been contaminated by a grave, requiring a seven-day purification process, including sprinkling with the water containing the ashes of the *parah adumah*. While Beis Hillel agree that the proselyte does not truly have corpse *tumah*, because the Torah subjects only Jews to such *tumah*, they maintain, however, that the Rabbis decreed a seven-day purification for the newly converted [and thus unlearned] proselyte, to forestall the possibility of his assuming that contact with corpses does not prevent someone from offering the *pesach* [not realizing that this was only because he was still a gentile at the time].

CHAPTER NINE

1. Although the time for the *pesach's* offering is the fourteenth of Nissan, the Torah provided a make-up date on the fourteenth of Iyar (a month after the first Pesach) for those who missed the primary date. The alternate date is called *Pesach Sheni*, the Second Pesach.

שָׁגַג — *[If] he erred* and forgot that it was Erev Pesach or that one is obligated to bring a *pesach* offering at that time.

הַשֵּׁנִי. אִם כֵּן, לָמָּה נֶאֱמַר „טָמֵא" אוֹ שֶׁהָיָה „בְדֶרֶךְ רְחֹקָה"? — שֶׁאֵלּוּ פְּטוּרִין מֵהִכָּרֵת, וְאֵלּוּ חַיָּבִין בְּהִכָּרֵת.

[ב] אֵיזוֹ הִיא „דֶּרֶךְ רְחוֹקָה"? מִן הַמּוֹדִיעִים וְלַחוּץ, וּכְמִדָּתָהּ לְכָל רוּחַ; דִּבְרֵי רַבִּי עֲקִיבָא. רַבִּי אֱלִיעֶזֶר אוֹמֵר: מֵאִסְקֻפַּת הָעֲזָרָה וְלַחוּץ. אָמַר רַבִּי יוֹסֵי: לְפִיכָךְ נָקוּד עַל 'ה' — לוֹמַר, לֹא מִפְּנֵי שֶׁרְחוֹקָה וַדַּאי, אֶלָּא מֵאִסְקֻפַּת הָעֲזָרָה וְלַחוּץ.

[ג] מַה בֵּין פֶּסַח הָרִאשׁוֹן לַשֵּׁנִי? הָרִאשׁוֹן אָסוּר בְּבַל יֵרָאֶה וּבַל יִמָּצֵא, וְהַשֵּׁנִי, מַצָּה וְחָמֵץ עִמּוֹ בַּבַּיִת; הָרִאשׁוֹן טָעוּן הַלֵּל בַּאֲכִילָתוֹ, וְהַשֵּׁנִי אֵינוֹ טָעוּן הַלֵּל בַּאֲכִילָתוֹ.
זֶה וָזֶה טְעוּנִין הַלֵּל בַּעֲשִׂיָּתָן; וְנֶאֱכָלִין צָלִי, עַל מַצָּה וּמְרוֹרִים; וְדוֹחִין אֶת הַשַּׁבָּת.

[ד] הַפֶּסַח שֶׁבָּא בְטֻמְאָה, לֹא יֹאכְלוּ מִמֶּנּוּ זָבִין וְזָבוֹת נִדּוֹת וְיוֹלְדוֹת; וְאִם אָכְלוּ, פְּטוּרִים מִכָּרֵת.
רַבִּי אֱלִיעֶזֶר פּוֹטֵר אַף עַל בִּיאַת מִקְדָּשׁ.

[ה] מַה בֵּין פֶּסַח מִצְרַיִם לְפֶסַח דּוֹרוֹת? פֶּסַח מִצְרַיִם מִקָּחוֹ מִבֶּעָשׂוֹר, וְטָעוּן הַזָּאָה בַּאֲגֻדַּת אֵזוֹב עַל הַמַּשְׁקוֹף וְעַל שְׁתֵּי הַמְּזוּזוֹת, וְנֶאֱכָל בְּחִפָּזוֹן, בְּלַיְלָה אֶחָד. וּפֶסַח דּוֹרוֹת נוֹהֵג כָּל שִׁבְעָה.

[ו] אָמַר רַבִּי יְהוֹשֻׁעַ: „שָׁמַעְתִּי שֶׁתְּמוּרַת הַפֶּסַח קְרֵבָה, וּתְמוּרַת הַפֶּסַח אֵינָהּ קְרֵבָה, וְאֵין לִי לְפָרֵשׁ." אָמַר רַבִּי עֲקִיבָא: „אֲנִי

יד אברהם

יַעֲשֶׂה אֶת הַשֵּׁנִי — *He makes [his offering] on the Second.* The provision for offering on the Second Pesach is for anyone who neglected to bring his *pesach* offering on the first, for whatever reason, even one who willfully neglected to offer on the First Pesach (*Gem.*).

שֶׁאֵלּוּ פְּטוּרִין מֵהִכָּרֵת — *Because these* [two cases] *are exempt from* [the punishment of] *kares*, even if they willfully (בְּמֵזִיד) neglect to offer their offering on the Second Pesach. Since the Torah *exempts* them from making an offering on the First Pesach, their obligation to make one on the Second Pesach is a new one, for which the Torah nowhere assigns a penalty of *kares*. However, those who omit the offering on the First Pesach for other reasons have violated a *kares*-bearing requirement and merely have an opportunity of making it up on the Second Pesach. If they willfully ignore this obligation, the *kares* penalty takes effect (*Gem.*).

2. מִן הַמּוֹדִיעִים — *From Modi'in*, which was about fifteen *mil* from Jerusalem (a *mil* is 2000 cubits). This is the distance one can walk at a normal pace from noontime to sunset on Erev Pesach. This is regarded as far away because had he left at noon when the *pesach* service was about to begin, he would not have reached Jerusalem in time to offer a *pesach* (*Rashi*).

רַבִּי אֱלִיעֶזֶר אוֹמֵר — *R' Eliezer says* that even if he was in Jerusalem, but was prevented by uncontrollable circumstances (e.g. illness) from reaching the Temple Courtyard in time, he is considered to have been far away. R' Akiva, however, classifies this as אוֹנֶס, *accidental delay* (*Rav*).

לְפִיכָךְ נָקוּד עַל ה' — *Therefore, there is a dot over the letter 'hei'* of the word רְחוֹקָה, *distant*. In the Torah scroll a dot is placed above certain letters indicating a hidden meaning. R' Yose expounds that the significance of this is to teach that *distant* refers to anyone who is removed from the Temple, no matter what the distance.

3. . . . וְהַשֵּׁנִי — *At the Second [Pesach]* there is no prohibition to possess *chametz*, even at the time of the *pesach*'s offering.

הָרִאשׁוֹן טָעוּן הַלֵּל — *The First* [Pesach] *requires the recitation of Hallel* at the Seder, but the Second does not. Nor is the *Haggadah* recited at the Second Pesach (*Sfas Emes*).

4. הַפֶּסַח שֶׁבָּא בְטֻמְאָה — *A pesach offered in a state of tumah-contamination* occurs when the

Second. If so, why does [the verse] say: 'One who was contaminated or was on a distant journey' (Num. 9:10)? Because these are exempt from kares, but those are liable to kares.

[2] *What is [considered] a 'distant journey'? From Modi'in and beyond, or a like distance in any direction; [these are] the words of R' Akiva. R' Eliezer says: From the threshold of the Temple Courtyard and beyond. Said R' Yose: Therefore, there is a dot over the letter* ה *— as if to say, not because it is literally distant, but rather from the threshold of the Temple Courtyard and beyond.*

[3] *What are the differences between the First Pesach and the Second? The First [Pesach] is subject to the prohibition of 'It shall not be seen and it shall not be found' (Ex. 12:19), whereas at the Second [Pesach both] matzah and chametz [may be] with him in the house; the First requires the recitation of Hallel at [the pesach's] eating, but the Second does not require Hallel at its eating. Both [however] require the recitation of Hallel when they are offered; [both] are eaten roasted, together with matzah and bitter herbs; and [both] override the Sabbath.*

[4] *A pesach offered in a state of tumah-contamination may not be eaten by zavin, zavos, niddos, or women who have just given birth; but if they did eat, they are exempt from [the penalty of] kares. R' Eliezer exempts [them] even [from the kares due] for entering the Temple.*

[5] *What are the differences between the pesach in Egypt and the pesach of [succeeding] generations? The purchase of the Egyptian pesach [offering] was on the tenth [of Nissan], it required the sprinkling [of its blood] with a bundle of hyssop upon the lintel and upon the two doorposts, and it was eaten in haste during one night. The pesach of [succeeding] generations is observed all seven days.*

[6] *Said R' Yehoshua: I have heard that the substitute of a pesach is offered, and that the substitute of a pesach is not offered, but I cannot explain [it]. Said*

YAD AVRAHAM

majority of the nation is *tamei* on Nissan 14 (see 7:4). This dispensation is granted by the Torah only for corpse-related *tumah*. Other forms of *tumah* require the affected person or community to wait for the Second Pesach (*Gem.*). Thus, even when it is offered in *tumah*, it may not be eaten by other classes of contaminated people such as *zavim, zavos* [plural of *zav, zavah* (see 8:5)], *niddos* and women who have just given birth. [Such a woman has the status of a *niddah* for a period of one week after the birth of a son and two weeks for a daughter, after which she can purify herself through immersion in a *mikveh*. However, she may not eat the offerings until she brings her birth offerings, which she cannot do before forty days after the birth of a son, or eighty days after a daughter.] Moreover, people *tamei* for these reasons are not counted towards the majority necessary to permit this offering. If they do eat, though, they are exempt from *kares*, because this penalty applies only to offerings meant to be eaten by those who are *tahor*.

5. פֶּסַח מִצְרַיִם — *The Pesach* [celebrated] *in Egypt* on the eve of the Exodus was subject to special rules that applied only that year. Conversely, *chametz* was forbidden that first year for only one day (Nissan 15) rather than the usual seven.

6. The Torah prohibits substituting for a sacrifice, even a choicer animal (*Lev.* 27:10). Should a person designate a substitute, it does not remove the sanctity of the first animal, but it *does* serve to consecrate the second animal, with the result that both animals are sacred. This substitute is called a *temurah*.

שָׁמַעְתִּי .. וְאֵין לִי לְפָרֵשׁ — *I have heard ... but I cannot explain [it].* R' Yehoshua had heard two seemingly contradictory traditions regarding the *temurah*-substitute of a *pesach*, and was at a loss to resolve it. Generally, a *pesach* offering that went unused is transformed into a *shelamim* (5:4). Since the *temurah* of any offering assumes the status of that sacrifice, the *temurah* of an unused *pesach* should also be offered as a *shelamim*. One tradition indeed said that this was so, but a second tradition said that it could not be offered but must be left until it develops a blemish, when it is sold, and a *shelamim* is bought with the money (*Rav*).

אֲפָרֵשׁ״: הַפֶּסַח שֶׁנִּמְצָא קֹדֶם שְׁחִיטַת הַפֶּסַח, יִרְעֶה עַד שֶׁיִּסְתָּאֵב, וְיִמָּכֵר, וְיִקַּח בְּדָמָיו שְׁלָמִים. וְכֵן תְּמוּרָתוֹ. אַחַר שְׁחִיטַת הַפֶּסַח, קָרֵב שְׁלָמִים, וְכֵן תְּמוּרָתוֹ.

[ז] הַמַּפְרִישׁ נְקֵבָה לְפִסְחוֹ, אוֹ זָכָר בֶּן שְׁתֵּי שָׁנִים, יִרְעֶה עַד שֶׁיִּסְתָּאֵב, וְיִמָּכֵר, וְיִפְּלוּ דָמָיו לִנְדָבָה.

הַמַּפְרִישׁ פִּסְחוֹ וָמֵת, לֹא יְבִיאֶנּוּ בְנוֹ אַחֲרָיו לְשֵׁם פֶּסַח, אֶלָּא לְשֵׁם שְׁלָמִים.

[ח] הַפֶּסַח שֶׁנִּתְעָרֵב בִּזְבָחִים, כֻּלָּן יִרְעוּ עַד שֶׁיִּסְתָּאֲבוּ, וְיִמָּכְרוּ; וְהָבִיא בִדְמֵי הַיָּפֶה שֶׁבָּהֶן מִמִּין זֶה, וּבִדְמֵי הַיָּפֶה שֶׁבָּהֶן מִמִּין זֶה, וְיַפְסִיד הַמּוֹתָר מִבֵּיתוֹ. נִתְעָרֵב בִּבְכוֹרוֹת — רַבִּי שִׁמְעוֹן אוֹמֵר: אִם חֲבוּרַת כֹּהֲנִים, יֵאָכֵלוּ.

[ט] חֲבוּרָה שֶׁאָבְדָה פִּסְחָהּ, וְאָמְרָה לְאֶחָד: „צֵא וּבַקֵּשׁ וּשְׁחוֹט עָלֵינוּ,״ וְהָלַךְ וּמָצָא וְשָׁחַט, וְהֵם לָקְחוּ וְשָׁחֲטוּ — אִם שֶׁלּוֹ נִשְׁחַט רִאשׁוֹן, הוּא אוֹכֵל מִשֶּׁלּוֹ, וְהֵם אוֹכְלִים עִמּוֹ מִשֶּׁלּוֹ; וְאִם שֶׁלָּהֶן נִשְׁחַט רִאשׁוֹן, הֵם אוֹכְלִין מִשֶּׁלָּהֶן, וְהוּא אוֹכֵל מִשֶּׁלּוֹ. וְאִם אֵינוֹ יָדוּעַ אֵיזֶה מֵהֶן נִשְׁחַט רִאשׁוֹן, אוֹ שֶׁשָּׁחֲטוּ שְׁנֵיהֶן כְּאֶחָד — הוּא אוֹכֵל מִשֶּׁלּוֹ, וְהֵם אֵינָם אוֹכְלִים עִמּוֹ, וְשֶׁלָּהֶן יֵצֵא לְבֵית הַשְּׂרֵפָה; וּפְטוּרִין מִלַּעֲשׂוֹת פֶּסַח שֵׁנִי.

יד אברהם

הַפֶּסַח שֶׁנִּמְצָא — *[If] the [original] pesach* offering was lost and another one was designated, but the original was then found before the time of slaughter, two animals are now available for sacrifice as a *pesach*. If the original *pesach* is bypassed in favor of the replacement, the original can no longer be offered as a *shelamim* because it had been explicitly rejected [נִדְחָה], and a rejected sacrifice cannot become qualified again. Thus, it must be left to develop a blemish that disqualifies it as an offering, after which it may be redeemed. The money from the sale assumes the *shelamim* sanctity and is used to purchase a replacement. This animal assumes the money's sanctity and is then offered as a *shelamim*.

וְכֵן תְּמוּרָתוֹ — *The same is for its substitute.* If the owner made a *temurah* substitution for the 'rejected' original *pesach* while it was awaiting a blemish and redemption, the *temurah*-substitute assumes the same level of holiness. Thus, it too must be put out to pasture, etc., and its redemption funds used to purchase a *shelamim* (*Rav*).

אַחַר שְׁחִיטַת הַפֶּסַח — *[If]* the lost *pesach [was found] after a [replacement] pesach was slaughtered*, then it was not rejected, but merely unavailable. Thus, the recovered *pesach* itself may be offered as a *shelamim* and there is no need to wait for a blemish and sell it. In this case, its *temurah* is also slaughtered as a *shelamim*. Since the original *pesach* is acceptable as a *shelamim*, so is its *temurah*-substitute.

7. . . . הַמַּפְרִישׁ נְקֵבָה — *[If] someone designates a female [animal]* ... Neither a female nor a second-year lamb are fit for a *pesach* offering, which must be a male in its first year.

לִנְדָבָה — *In* one of the six chests in the Temple marked נְדָבָה, *donative offering* (*Shekalim* 6:5). These are used for extra communal *olah* offerings (*Rav*). [This is the reading of our editions of the Mishnah. However, most *Rishonim* had the reading *he brings from its money shelamim-offerings.* Thus the rule here is the same as in mishnah 6, which states that a substitute of a *pesach* that cannot itself be offered becomes a *shelamim-offering*.]

הַמַּפְרִישׁ פִּסְחוֹ וָמֵת — *[If] a person designated a pesach offering* for himself, with no partners, *and [then] died*, so that it is left without anyone registered to eat it, it is invalid (5:3). His heir may therefore not use it as his *pesach*. [Although people may register on an offering until its slaughter (8:3), this is so only if there is no instant when the *pesach* is completely ownerless.] It is thus like an unused *pesach*, which becomes a *shelamim* (m. 6).

8. הַפֶּסַח שֶׁנִּתְעָרֵב — *[If] a pesach offering became mixed* with other types of offerings (e.g. a *shelamim* and an *olah*) and it is not known which is which, none of them can be offered,

R' Akiva: I will explain: [If] the [original] pesach offering was [lost and then] found before a [replacement] pesach was slaughtered, it must be left to pasture until it develops a blemish, after which it is sold, and a shelamim offering is bought with its proceeds. The same is for its substitute. [But if it was found] after a [replacement] pesach was slaughtered, it is offered as a shelamim offering, as is its substitute.

[7] *[If] someone designates a female [animal] for his pesach offering, or a male in its second year, it must be left to pasture until it develops a blemish, [then] be sold, and its money [placed] in a donative offering [chest].*

[If] a person designated his pesach offering and [then] died, his son who inherits it may not bring it as a pesach offering, but rather as a peace offering.

[8] *[If] a pesach offering became mixed with [other] offerings [and it cannot be identified], they must all be left to pasture until they develop blemishes, after which they are sold; he must then bring one of each type of offering equal in value to the most expensive of them, and bear the added cost from his own purse. [If] the pesach became confused with firstborn offerings — R' Shimon says: If the group is composed of Kohanim, they may be eaten.*

[9] *A group that lost its pesach offering and said to one [of their company], 'Go out, seek [it] and slaughter [it] for us,' and he went, found [it] and slaughtered [it], while they bought and slaughtered [another] — if his was slaughtered first, he eats of his and they eat of his with him; but if theirs was slaughtered first, they eat of theirs and he eats of his. If it is not known which was slaughtered first, or if both were slaughtered at the same time — he eats of his, but they do not eat with him, and theirs must be burned; nevertheless, they are exempt from offering the pesach sheni.*

YAD AVRAHAM

since they are each governed by different rules. They must be left to become disqualified by a blemish, after which they are redeemed and their money is used to purchase replacements. If each of these animals fetches a different price, however, the money from the redemption sale is also subject to uncertainty, because each animal's money must be used to purchase its type of offering. Since it is not known which type of offering was the most expensive, the only way to remove all the doubts is to buy three replacements *each* worth as much as the most expensive of the original three offerings. For example, if one lamb was worth a *sela* and the other two half a *sela* each, three lambs worth at least a *sela* each must be purchased, one for each of the three types of offerings (*Rav*). The additional expense this involves must be borne by the owner.

בִּבְכוֹרוֹת — *With firstborn offerings.* The blood *avodah* is the same for both types of sacrifices (*Zevachim* 5:8), and the confusion thus poses no problems regarding the service. However, there are differences regarding their consumption: *Bechoros* may be eaten only by *Kohanim* and members of their households, for up to two days and a night. The *pesach* may be eaten by any registrants, but only till midnight following the sacrifice. Accordingly, if the *pesach* was owned by a group of *Kohanim*, R' Shimon permits both animals to be slaughtered and eaten on *pesach* night, since regardless of which animal is which, they may be eaten by these people on this night. The Sages, however, disagree because they contend that it is forbidden to create a condition that will require an offering to be consumed in a period of time shorter than that allowed by the Torah, since that may unnecessarily result in the meat becoming *nosar* (leftover) and forbidden (*Gem.*).

9. אִם שֶׁלּוֹ נִשְׁחַט רִאשׁוֹן . . . — *If his* [i.e. the lost and recovered *pesach] was slaughtered first,* they all eat from that offering. Since they appointed him to act as their agent to slaughter the first animal, they were all registered on his offering at the time of its slaughter, and could not be numbered on another *pesach.* Accordingly, the second animal was slaughtered with no one eligible to eat it and it must therefore be burned. However, if theirs was slaughtered first, they have, in effect, withdrawn their registration from the first (lost) offering prior to its slaughter (8:4) and transferred it to the second one. Therefore, they eat of the second offering, while he alone eats from the original offering, since he never registered for the second one.

אָמַר לָהֶן: „אִם אֵחַרְתִּי, צְאוּ וְשַׁחֲטוּ עָלַי," הָלַךְ וּמָצָא וְשָׁחַט, וְהֵן לָקְחוּ וְשָׁחֲטוּ — אִם שֶׁלָּהֶן נִשְׁחַט רִאשׁוֹן, הֵן אוֹכְלִין מִשֶּׁלָּהֶן, וְהוּא אוֹכֵל עִמָּהֶן; וְאִם שֶׁלּוֹ נִשְׁחַט רִאשׁוֹן, הוּא אוֹכֵל מִשֶּׁלּוֹ, וְהֵן אוֹכְלִין מִשֶּׁלָּהֶן. וְאִם אֵינוֹ יָדוּעַ אֵיזֶה מֵהֶם נִשְׁחַט רִאשׁוֹן, אוֹ שֶׁשָּׁחֲטוּ שְׁנֵיהֶם כְּאֶחָד — הֵן אוֹכְלִין מִשֶּׁלָּהֶן, וְהוּא אֵינוֹ אוֹכֵל עִמָּהֶן, וְשֶׁלּוֹ יֵצֵא לְבֵית הַשְּׂרֵפָה; וּפָטוּר מִלַּעֲשׂוֹת פֶּסַח שֵׁנִי.

אָמַר לָהֶן וְאָמְרוּ לוֹ, אוֹכְלִין כֻּלָּם מִן הָרִאשׁוֹן. וְאִם אֵין יָדוּעַ אֵיזֶה מֵהֶן נִשְׁחַט רִאשׁוֹן, שְׁנֵיהֶן יוֹצְאִין לְבֵית הַשְּׂרֵפָה. לֹא אָמַר לָהֶן וְלֹא אָמְרוּ לוֹ, אֵינָן אַחֲרָאִין זֶה לָזֶה.

[י] שְׁתֵּי חֲבוּרוֹת שֶׁנִּתְעָרְבוּ פִּסְחֵיהֶן, אֵלּוּ מוֹשְׁכִין לָהֶן אֶחָד, וְאֵלּוּ מוֹשְׁכִין לָהֶן אֶחָד, אֶחָד מֵאֵלּוּ בָּא לוֹ אֵצֶל אֵלּוּ, וְאֶחָד מֵאֵלּוּ בָּא לוֹ אֵצֶל אֵלּוּ, וְכָךְ הֵם אוֹמְרִים: „אִם שֶׁלָּנוּ הוּא הַפֶּסַח הַזֶּה, יָדֶיךָ מְשׁוּכוֹת מִשֶּׁלְּךָ וְנִמְנֵיתָ עַל שֶׁלָּנוּ. וְאִם שֶׁלְּךָ הוּא הַפֶּסַח הַזֶּה, יָדֵינוּ מְשׁוּכוֹת מִשֶּׁלָּנוּ וְנִמְנֵינוּ עַל שֶׁלָּךְ." וְכֵן, חָמֵשׁ חֲבוּרוֹת שֶׁל חֲמִשָּׁה חֲמִשָּׁה וְשֶׁל עֲשָׂרָה עֲשָׂרָה, מוֹשְׁכִין לָהֶן אֶחָד מִכָּל חֲבוּרָה וַחֲבוּרָה, וְכֵן הֵם אוֹמְרִים.

[יא] שְׁנַיִם שֶׁנִּתְעָרְבוּ פִּסְחֵיהֶם, זֶה מוֹשֵׁךְ לוֹ אֶחָד וְזֶה מוֹשֵׁךְ לוֹ אֶחָד; זֶה מְמַנֶּה עִמּוֹ אֶחָד מִן הַשּׁוּק, וְזֶה מְמַנֶּה עִמּוֹ אֶחָד מִן הַשּׁוּק. זֶה בָּא אֵצֶל זֶה, וְזֶה בָּא אֵצֶל זֶה, וְכָךְ הֵם אוֹמְרִים: „אִם שֶׁלִּי הוּא פֶּסַח זֶה, יָדֶיךָ מְשׁוּכוֹת מִשֶּׁלְּךָ וְנִמְנֵיתָ עַל שֶׁלִּי; וְאִם שֶׁלְּךָ הוּא פֶּסַח זֶה, יָדַי מְשׁוּכוֹת מִשֶּׁלִּי וְנִמְנֵיתִי עַל שֶׁלָּךְ."

יד אברהם

If it is not known which was slaughtered first, he eats from the original offering [since this is what he does regardless], while they may not eat from either one since it cannot be determined which is theirs. The second offering is therefore burned. Nevertheless, they are exempt from offering on the Second Pesach because that is only for those who had not offered on the First Pesach. In our situation, however, they *did* offer one of the two sacrifices; it is only their inability to identity which Pesach is theirs that bars them from eating, and this does not nullify their fulfillment of the *mitzvah* [אֲכִילָה לֹא מְעַכְּבָא] (*Rav*).

אָמַר לָהֶן — *[If] he said to them.* This case is the reverse of the previous one. The searcher told the others to slaughter for him if he did not return on time; they, however, did not instruct him to slaughter for them. Thus, he is registered on their *pesach* as well as the lost one. However, when they purchased the second offering, they effectively withdrew from the first offering. [In the absence of any instruction to their agent to the contrary, purchase alone effects withdrawal.]

אָמַר לָהֶן וְאָמְרוּ לוֹ — *[If] he said to them,* 'If I am delayed, slaughter for me,' *and they said to him,* 'Go out, seek, and slaughter for us,' they must all eat from the first *pesach* slaughtered, since each is an agent for the other (*Rav*). Therefore, if it is not known which offering was slaughtered first, none of them may eat from either of them. Nevertheless, they are all exempt from offering on the Second Pesach (*Rav*).

10. . . . **שְׁתֵּי חֲבוּרוֹת שֶׁנִּתְעָרְבוּ פִּסְחֵיהֶן** — *[If] the pesach offerings of two groups were confused* before their slaughter, when people may still withdraw and re-register on another *pesach* (8:3). Thus, it is possible to rectify the situation by having each group take one of the offerings, withdraw from the other [in case it was theirs], and register on the one they have now taken. However, this course may not be taken by *all* members of the group because this would leave the *pesach* momentarily ownerless, which would invalidate it (see comm. m. 7). Thus, we must insure that at least one of the original members remains registered on each offering, which is accomplished by removing one member of each group and joining him to the other. Using the mishnah's stipulation, it emerges that if each group actually receives its original lamb, only the new member has withdrawn from his

[If] he said to them, 'If I am delayed, go and slaughter for me,' and he went, found [it] and slaughtered [it], while they bought and slaughtered [another] — if theirs was slaughtered first, they eat of theirs and he eats with them; but if his was slaughtered first, he eats of his and they eat of theirs. If it is not known which was slaughtered first, or if both were slaughtered at the same time — they eat of theirs, but he does not eat with them, and his is burned; nevertheless, he is exempt from offering the pesach sheni.

[If] he said to them and they said to him, all [of them] eat of the first. But if it is not known which was slaughtered first, both are burned. [If] he said nothing to them and they said nothing to him, they are not responsible for each other.

[10] *[If] the pesach offering of two groups were confused, each take one for themselves, [then] a member of each group comes to the other group, and they declare the following: 'If this pesach is ours, [then] you are withdrawn from your own [pesach] and are registered on ours. But if this pesach is yours, then we withdraw from ours and register on yours.' Similarly, if there were five groups [whose offerings were confused], each comprising five or ten [members], they take to themselves one person from each group and declare the same.*

[11] *[If] the pesach offerings of two [individuals] were confused, each takes one [of them] for himself, and each registers some stranger with him. [Then] each goes to the other's [pesach] and says thus: 'If this pesach offering is mine, [then] you are withdrawn from yours and are registered upon mine; and if that pesach offering is yours, I am withdrawn from mine and am registered upon yours.'*

YAD AVRAHAM

lamb and re-registered on the other. If the lamb they now receive should turn out not to be their original lamb, that lamb has not been left ownerless because the one member of the original company who transferred to the other group is still with it (*Rav*).

מוּשְׁכִין לָהֶן אֶחָד מִכָּל חֲבוּרָה וַחֲבוּרָה ... — *They take to themselves one person from each group.* For example, if there were five groups of five members each, five new groups are formed, each comprised of one member from each of the original groups, thereby ensuring that at least one of the original owners retained his original registration. Four of the new group say to the fifth member: If the *pesach* we have chosen was originally yours, the four of us have withdrawn from our four respective offerings and register upon yours. Then the fifth member [to whom this declaration had been directed] joins with three of the other members and forms a new foursome (e.g., members 1, 2, 3, 5) who will now direct this formula to another member (e.g., member 4). So they continue until each member has had this declaration made to himself by the other four. This must be repeated in all the groups (*Rav*).

11. שְׁנַיִם שֶׁנִּתְעָרְבוּ פִּסְחֵיהֶם — *[If] the pesach offerings of two [individuals] were confused.* Reuven and Shimon had each designated an animal for his *pesach*, and had not yet registered a group upon it. The animals' identity then became confused before the slaughter. To rectify the situation [and keep each one valid as a *pesach*], each must register another person on his original *pesach*, whichever it happens to be, and take one animal [e.g. Reuven, A; Shimon, B]. In this manner they will be able to switch registrations without leaving either offering ownerless even momentarily. For example, Reuven added Levi to his original *pesach*, while Shimon added Yehudah. Reuven then goes to the animal B, now held by Shimon and Yehudah, and tells Yehudah, 'If this *pesach* taken by Shimon is actually mine, then Shimon had no power to register you on *this* animal, and you are [really] registered on the other one. Therefore, I ask you to withdraw from that animal and register with me on this one. On the other hand, if this is truly Shimon's animal, you [Yehudah] *are* registered on it, and I [Reuven] withdraw from my original animal and register on this one with you.' Shimon then makes the same declaration to Levi in regard to the animal A. Accordingly, regardless of which animal originally belonged to whom, Reuven is now a partner with Yehudah in animal B, while Shimon and Levi are partners in A.

פרק עשירי

[א] **עַרְבֵי** פְסָחִים סָמוּךְ לַמִּנְחָה, לֹא יֹאכַל אָדָם עַד שֶׁתֶּחְשַׁךְ. וַאֲפִלּוּ עָנִי שֶׁבְּיִשְׂרָאֵל לֹא יֹאכַל עַד שֶׁיָּסֵב. וְלֹא יִפְחֲתוּ לוֹ מֵאַרְבָּעָה כוֹסוֹת שֶׁל יַיִן, וַאֲפִלּוּ מִן הַתַּמְחוּי.

[ב] מָזְגוּ לוֹ כוֹס רִאשׁוֹן. בֵּית שַׁמַּאי אוֹמְרִים: מְבָרֵךְ עַל הַיּוֹם, וְאַחַר כָּךְ מְבָרֵךְ עַל הַיַּיִן. וּבֵית הִלֵּל אוֹמְרִים: מְבָרֵךְ עַל הַיַּיִן, וְאַחַר כָּךְ מְבָרֵךְ עַל הַיּוֹם.

[ג] הֵבִיאוּ לְפָנָיו; מְטַבֵּל בְּחַזֶּרֶת עַד שֶׁמַּגִּיעַ לְפַרְפֶּרֶת הַפַּת. הֵבִיאוּ לְפָנָיו מַצָּה וְחַזֶּרֶת וַחֲרֹסֶת וּשְׁנֵי תַבְשִׁילִין, אַף עַל פִּי שֶׁאֵין חֲרֹסֶת מִצְוָה. רַבִּי אֱלִיעֶזֶר בְּרַבִּי צָדוֹק אוֹמֵר: מִצְוָה. וּבַמִּקְדָּשׁ הָיוּ מְבִיאִין לְפָנָיו גּוּפוֹ שֶׁל פֶּסַח.

[ד] מָזְגוּ לוֹ כוֹס שֵׁנִי; וְכָאן הַבֵּן שׁוֹאֵל אָבִיו. וְאִם אֵין דַּעַת בַּבֵּן, אָבִיו מְלַמְּדוֹ: „מַה נִּשְׁתַּנָּה הַלַּיְלָה הַזֶּה מִכָּל הַלֵּילוֹת? שֶׁבְּכָל הַלֵּילוֹת אָנוּ אוֹכְלִין חָמֵץ וּמַצָּה, הַלַּיְלָה הַזֶּה כֻּלּוֹ מַצָּה. שֶׁבְּכָל הַלֵּילוֹת אָנוּ אוֹכְלִין שְׁאָר יְרָקוֹת, הַלַּיְלָה הַזֶּה מָרוֹר. שֶׁבְּכָל הַלֵּילוֹת אָנוּ אוֹכְלִין בָּשָׂר צָלִי שָׁלוּק וּמְבֻשָּׁל, הַלַּיְלָה הַזֶּה כֻּלּוֹ צָלִי. שֶׁבְּכָל הַלֵּילוֹת אָנוּ מַטְבִּילִין פַּעַם אַחַת, הַלַּיְלָה הַזֶּה שְׁתֵּי פְעָמִים."

יד אברהם

CHAPTER TEN

1. This final chapter of *Pesachim* deals with the Seder ritual. In the Temple era this included eating the *pesach* offering at the end of the meal. The Seder [literally *order*] assures the fulfillment of the many Biblical and Rabbinical *mitzvos* of the evening.

סָמוּךְ לַמִּנְחָה — *Close to the Minchah [period],* from approximately 3 P.M. until it becomes dark one may not eat so that he will have a good appetite for the matzah. It is a הִדּוּר מִצְוָה, *enhancement of the mitzvah*, that it be done with gusto (*Gem.*). [However, one may eat small amounts of vegetables and fruits if he does not gorge himself (ibid.).]

עַד שֶׁיָּסֵב — *Unless he reclines.* Reclining during a meal was regarded as the mark of a free man, and the Seder celebration requires that one's action conform to the habits of the liberated. Therefore, even a person who does not customarily recline must do so while eating the matzah and drinking the four cups at the Seder, even if he must recline on a hard bench (see *O. Ch.* 472:2).

מֵאַרְבָּעָה כוֹסוֹת שֶׁל יַיִן — *Than four cups of wine*, although this is a Rabbinic *mitzvah*. It goes without saying that the charities must provide the poor with matzah and food.

וַאֲפִלּוּ מִן הַתַּמְחוּי — *Even though he is* [from among the poorest of the poor, who are] *supported from the [charity] plate*, i.e., the food collected every day to be distributed that evening to the neediest.

2. כוֹס רִאשׁוֹן — *The first cup* over which *Kiddush* is said. This contains two blessings, one for the wine [בּוֹרֵא פְּרִי הַגָּפֶן], and a second for the festival day: מְקַדֵּשׁ יִשְׂרָאֵל וְהַזְּמַנִּים. Beis Shammai reason that the benediction regarding the day be said first because the holiness of the festival began at nightfall, long before the wine is brought for *Kiddush*. In addition, the sanctity of the day is the reason that *Kiddush* is recited over wine. However, Beis Hillel reason the reverse, because if one has no wine (or bread), *Kiddush* is not recited. Moreover, the benediction over wine is more frequently used than *Kiddush*, which gives it precedence (*Gem.*).

3. מְטַבֵּל בְּחַזֶּרֶת — *He eats dipped lettuce*, i.e., the *karpas* dipped in salt water (*Rashbam*). The vegetable need not be lettuce; the mishnah states lettuce to teach that if he uses lettuce, he has not fulfilled his obligation to eat *maror* (see 2:6). Why is it necessary to eat vegetables at this point? So that the children will [be provoked to] ask (*Gem.*).

עַד שֶׁמַּגִּיעַ לְפַרְפֶּרֶת הַפַּת — *Before he reaches the course secondary to the matzah*, i.e., the part of the meal not eaten with the matzah, but after it; in this case, *maror*. Thus, the mishnah teaches that eating dipped lettuce takes place before the eating of *maror*.

CHAPTER TEN

[1] **עַרְבֵי** *On the eve of Passover close to the Minchah [period], a person may not eat until it becomes dark. Even the poorest man in Israel may not eat unless he reclines. And they [the administrators of the charities] must provide him with not less than four cups of wine, even though he is supported from the [charity] plate.*

[2] *They pour the first cup [of wine] for him. Beis Shammai say: He recites the benediction regarding the day and then the benediction over the wine. But Beis Hillel say: He [first] recites the benediction over the wine and then the benediction regarding the day.*

[3] *They [then] bring [vegetables] before him; he eats dipped lettuce before he reaches the course secondary to the matzah. They bring matzah, lettuce, charoses, and two cooked dishes before him; although the charoses is not a mitzvah. R' Eliezer bar R' Tzadok says: [The dipping is] a mitzvah. In the Temple they would [also] bring the body of the pesach [offering] before him.*

[4] *They pour a second cup [of wine] for him; and at this point the son asks of his father. If the son lacks [sufficient] understanding, his father instructs him [to ask]: 'Why is this night different from all [other] nights? On all [other] nights we may eat either chametz or matzah, but on this night only matzah. On all [other] nights we eat other greens, but on this night [we eat] bitter herbs. On all [other] nights we eat meat roasted, stewed, or cooked, but on this night [we eat the meat] only roasted. On all [other] nights we might eat dipped vegetables once, but on this night [we must do so] twice.'*

YAD AVRAHAM

... הֵבִיאוּ לְפָנָיו — *They bring ... before him ...* The entire table, ostensibly containing all the essentials of the meal, had been before him previously (with the lettuce). *Tosafos* explain that after the dipped lettuce had been eaten, the table with the foodstuffs on it was removed in order to draw the children's attention and cause them to ask why. The matzah and bitter herbs must now be returned so that the *Haggadah* may be said over them (see mishnah 5).

וַחֲזֶרֶת — *Lettuce*, for the *mitzvah* of *maror*, bitter herbs. This is the first choice among the five vegetables mentioned as valid (2:6).

וַחֲרֹסֶת — *And charoses* as a dipping sauce for the *maror*, although it is not a required *mitzvah*. *Rav* describes *charoses* as made from figs, nuts, and many types of fruit, especially apples. These ingredients are pounded to a pulp, and [fruit] vinegar is added. Thin spice fibers, e.g., cinnamon, are placed upon it, to resemble the straw which was mixed into the mortar in Egypt. The *charoses* should have a thick texture as a remembrance of the טִיט, *mortar*, made by the Jews in Egypt (*Gem.*). See *Rama, O. Ch.* 473:6. R' Eliezer bar R' Tzadok maintains that using *charoses* is a *mitzvah* because of its symbolism. The apple tree was instrumental in the Jewish nation's fertility in Egypt (*Shir HaShirim* 8:5, *Sotah* 11b), and the *charoses* also symbolizes the mortar produced by the slave labor of the Jews in Egypt (*Gem.*). The halachah follows this view (*O. Ch.* 475:1).

וּשְׁנֵי תַבְשִׁילִין — *And two cooked dishes*, to commemorate the *pesach* and *chagigah* sacrifices (6:3-4) (*Gem.*). It is customary nowadays to take a roasted shank bone and a boiled egg (*O. Ch.* 473:4). The roasted shank bone may not be eaten, for it is forbidden to eat roasted meat at the Seder in the absence of a *pesach* offering (4:4).

4. מָזְגוּ לוֹ כוֹס שֵׁנִי — *They pour a second cup [of wine] for him* prior to beginning the *Haggadah*, to arouse the child's curiosity (*Rashi*).

וְכָאן הַבֵּן שׁוֹאֵל אָבִיו — *And at this point the son asks of his father* the Four Questions. Even if the son is intelligent enough to formulate his own questions, there is an obligation to ask the four listed here.

הַלַּיְלָה הַזֶּה מָרוֹר — *But on this night [we eat] bitter herbs;* but we do not say כֻּלּוֹ מָרוֹר, only *bitter herbs*, for we *do* eat other vegetables, e.g., *karpas* for the first dipping.

הַלַּיְלָה הַזֶּה כֻּלּוֹ צָלִי — *But on this night [we eat the meat] only roasted.* This question was posed only when the Temple stood. In our days the question about reclining is substituted for it. The mishnah follows the view that the *chagigah* eaten with the Pesach must also be roasted. Therefore, it is correct to say *only* (כֻּלּוֹ) roasted.

אָנוּ מַטְבִּילִין פַּעַם אַחַת — *We might eat dipped vegetables once.* The *Gemara* emends the text to

וּלְפִי דַעְתּוֹ שֶׁל בֵּן אָבִיו מְלַמְּדוֹ. מַתְחִיל בִּגְנוּת וּמְסַיֵּם בְּשֶׁבַח. וְדוֹרֵשׁ מֵ„אֲרַמִּי אוֹבֵד אָבִי” עַד שֶׁיִּגְמֹר כָּל הַפָּרָשָׁה כֻּלָּהּ.

[ה] רַבָּן גַּמְלִיאֵל הָיָה אוֹמֵר: כָּל שֶׁלֹּא אָמַר שְׁלֹשָׁה דְבָרִים אֵלּוּ בַּפֶּסַח, לֹא יָצָא יְדֵי חוֹבָתוֹ. וְאֵלּוּ הֵן: פֶּסַח, מַצָּה, וּמָרוֹר. פֶּסַח — עַל שׁוּם שֶׁפָּסַח הַמָּקוֹם עַל בָּתֵּי אֲבוֹתֵינוּ בְּמִצְרָיִם. מַצָּה — עַל שׁוּם שֶׁנִּגְאֲלוּ אֲבוֹתֵינוּ בְּמִצְרָיִם. מָרוֹר — עַל שׁוּם שֶׁמֵּרְרוּ הַמִּצְרִיִּים אֶת חַיֵּי אֲבוֹתֵינוּ בְּמִצְרָיִם.

בְּכָל דּוֹר וָדוֹר חַיָּב אָדָם לִרְאוֹת אֶת עַצְמוֹ כְּאִלּוּ הוּא יָצָא מִמִּצְרַיִם — שֶׁנֶּאֱמַר: „וְהִגַּדְתָּ לְבִנְךָ בַּיּוֹם הַהוּא לֵאמֹר, בַּעֲבוּר זֶה עָשָׂה ה׳ לִי בְּצֵאתִי מִמִּצְרָיִם.” לְפִיכָךְ אֲנַחְנוּ חַיָּבִין לְהוֹדוֹת, לְהַלֵּל, לְשַׁבֵּחַ, לְפָאֵר, לְרוֹמֵם, לְהַדֵּר, לְבָרֵךְ, לְעַלֵּה, וּלְקַלֵּס לְמִי שֶׁעָשָׂה לַאֲבוֹתֵינוּ וְלָנוּ אֶת כָּל הַנִּסִּים הָאֵלּוּ: הוֹצִיאָנוּ מֵעַבְדוּת לְחֵרוּת, מִיָּגוֹן לְשִׂמְחָה, וּמֵאֵבֶל לְיוֹם טוֹב, וּמֵאֲפֵלָה לְאוֹר גָּדוֹל, וּמִשִּׁעְבּוּד לִגְאֻלָּה! וְנֹאמַר לְפָנָיו: „הַלְלוּיָהּ!”

[ו] עַד הֵיכָן הוּא אוֹמֵר? בֵּית שַׁמַּאי אוֹמְרִים: עַד „אֵם הַבָּנִים שְׂמֵחָה.” וּבֵית הִלֵּל אוֹמְרִים: עַד „חַלָּמִישׁ לְמַעְיְנוֹ מָיִם.” וְחוֹתֵם בִּגְאֻלָּה. רַבִּי טַרְפוֹן אוֹמֵר: „אֲשֶׁר גְּאָלָנוּ וְגָאַל אֶת אֲבוֹתֵינוּ מִמִּצְרַיִם,” וְלֹא הָיָה חוֹתֵם. רַבִּי עֲקִיבָא אוֹמֵר: „כֵּן ה׳ אֱלֹהֵינוּ וֵאלֹהֵי אֲבוֹתֵינוּ יַגִּיעֵנוּ לְמוֹעֲדִים וְלִרְגָלִים אֲחֵרִים, הַבָּאִים לִקְרָאתֵנוּ לְשָׁלוֹם, שְׂמֵחִים בְּבִנְיַן עִירֶךָ וְשָׂשִׂים בַּעֲבוֹדָתֶךָ. וְנֹאכַל שָׁם מִן הַזְּבָחִים וּמִן הַפְּסָחִים,” כו׳ עַד „בָּרוּךְ אַתָּה ה׳ גָּאַל יִשְׂרָאֵל.”

יד אברהם

read, אֵין אָנוּ מַטְבִּילִין אֲפִלּוּ פַּעַם אַחַת, *We do not dip [greens] even one time*, i.e., it is not customary to eat even one course of greens before the meal.

דַּעְתּוֹ שֶׁל בֵּן — *The son's [level of] intelligence of the son*. The father's response should be geared to the mental level of the child.

מַתְחִיל בִּגְנוּת . . . — *He begins [the Haggadah]* with a narrative of Israel's shameful origins. The *Gemara* presents two views about this: Rav says it refers to the passage עֲבָדִים הָיִינוּ, *We were slaves to Pharaoh in Egypt;* Shmuel says it is מִתְּחִלָּה עוֹבְדֵי עֲבוֹדָה זָרָה הָיוּ אֲבוֹתֵינוּ, *In the beginning our ancestors were idol worshipers* . . . Our version of the *Haggadah* includes both views.

וּמְסַיֵּם בְּשֶׁבַח — *And concludes with* a recital of the *glory* with which God has blessed us; for He brought us close to His service, and took our ancestors from Egypt.

וְדוֹרֵשׁ . . . — *And he expounds* . . . The *Haggadah*'s method takes the form of citing one complete verse from this passage and then giving the midrashic exposition of it phrase by phrase. The next verse is then recited and expounded phrase by phrase, and so on until the portion is concluded.

5. לֹא יָצָא יְדֵי חוֹבָתוֹ — *Has not fulfilled his obligation* of *Haggadah* in an ideal manner; however, the basic obligation has been discharged without the explanation (*Ran*). Others suggest that without the explanation, one has not [fully] fulfilled even his obligation to eat them.

מַצָּה — עַל שׁוּם שֶׁנִּגְאֲלוּ אֲבוֹתֵינוּ בְּמִצְרָיִם — *Matzah [is eaten] — because our ancestors were redeemed in Egypt* and our ancestors had no time to leaven their dough before they left Egypt (*Haggadah*).

כְּאִלּוּ הוּא יָצָא מִמִּצְרַיִם — *As if he himself had gone out of Egypt*, i.e., as if he was redeemed this very night (*Rambam*).

וְנֹאמַר לְפָנָיו: „הַלְלוּיָהּ” — *So let us say before Him: 'Halleluyah!'* 'Who instituted this

The father instructs the son according to [the] son's [level of] intelligence. He begins [the Haggadah] with [a recitation of our national] disgrace and concludes with the glory; and he expounds [the passage of], 'The Aramean sought to destroy my father,' until he concludes the entire passage [relating to the Exodus] (Deut. 26:5-8).

[5] *Rabban Gamliel used to say: Whoever has not explained [the reasons for] these three things at the Pesach [Seder] has not fulfilled his obligation. They are: the pesach [offering], the matzah, and the maror. The pesach [is offered] — because the Omnipresent One passed over the houses of our ancestors in Egypt. Matzah [is eaten] — because our ancestors were redeemed in Egypt. Maror [is eaten] — because the Egyptians embittered the lives of our ancestors in Egypt.*

In every generation a man must regard himself as if he himself had gone out of Egypt — for it is said (Ex. 13:8): 'And you shall tell your son on that day saying, for the sake of this Hashem did for me when I went out of Egypt.' Therefore we are obliged to give thanks, praise, laud, glorify, exalt, honor, bless, extol, and shower acclaim upon Him Who performed all these miracles for our ancestors and for us: He brought us forth from slavery to freedom, from sorrow to joy, from mourning to festivity, from darkness to great light, and from servitude to redemption! So let us say before Him: Halleluyah!

[6] *How far does one recite [the Hallel]? Beis Shammai say: Until [the verse], 'A joyful mother of children' (Psalms 113:8). But Beis Hillel say: Until [the verse], 'The flint into a spring of water' (Psalms 114:8). He concludes [the Haggadah recital] with [a blessing about] redemption. R' Tarfon says [its text is]: 'Who redeemed us and redeemed our ancestors from Egypt,' and he does not conclude [with a final blessing]. R' Akiva says [its text is]: '. . . so may* HASHEM *our God, and God of our ancestors, bring us to future festivals and pilgrimages, which approach us, in peace, gladdened in the rebuilding of Your city and joyful at Your service. May we eat there of the offerings and Pesach sacrifices. . .' until [the blessing], 'Blessed are You* HASHEM *Who has redeemed Israel.'*

YAD AVRAHAM

Hallel? The prophets among them [i.e., the Jews departing from Egypt] instituted that Israel should recite *Hallel* for every festival and at every misfortune — may it not come upon them! — from which they are redeemed, as thanks for their redemption' (*Gem.*).

6. עַד הֵיכָן הוּא אוֹמֵר — *How far does one recite [the Hallel]* before the meal? *Hallel* is cut short before the meal to help finish the *Haggadah* quicker, so that the children will not fall asleep before eating matzah (*Gem.*). Thus, only the section alluding to the Exodus is attached to the *Haggadah;* the rest, which alludes to the future redemption, is left for after the meal (*Tos. Yom Tov*). *Maharal* explains that the purpose of dividing the *Hallel* is to demonstrate that the praises are being said in conjunction with the feast of redemption. Indeed, by this insertion the Sages symbolized that the very feast of Pesach is a form of praise. Beis Shammai break the recitation of the *Hallel* before the second paragraph because the redemption described in it did not occur until midnight — when the firstborns died — and it behooves us to recite this as near to midnight as possible, i.e., after the meal. Beis Hillel include the second paragraph because this section of the Seder concludes by blessing God for redeeming Israel, and it would be incongruous to say this without mentioning its climactic event, the portion of *Hallel* that speaks of the Splitting of the Sea and the drowning of the Egyptian army.

רַבִּי טַרְפוֹן אוֹמֵר . . . — *R' Tarfon* gives an abbreviated text for this blessing and therefore rules there is no need to summarize it with a final blessing [as one would a lengthy blessing]. R' Akiva adopts R' Tarfon's text for the beginning of the blessing, but adds to it. Since this makes for a lengthy blessing, it requires a brief concluding blessing to summarize its major point (*Rav*).

[ז] מָזְגוּ לוֹ כוֹס שְׁלִישִׁי, מְבָרֵךְ עַל מְזוֹנוֹ; רְבִיעִי, גּוֹמֵר עָלָיו אֶת הַהַלֵּל, וְאוֹמֵר עָלָיו בִּרְכַּת הַשִּׁיר. בֵּין הַכּוֹסוֹת הַלָּלוּ, אִם רוֹצֶה לִשְׁתּוֹת יִשְׁתֶּה; בֵּין שְׁלִישִׁי לִרְבִיעִי לֹא יִשְׁתֶּה.

[ח] וְאֵין מַפְטִירִין אַחַר הַפֶּסַח אֲפִיקוֹמָן. יָשְׁנוּ מִקְצָתָן, יֹאכֵלוּ; כֻּלָּן, לֹא יֹאכְלוּ. רַבִּי יוֹסֵי אוֹמֵר: נִתְנַמְנְמוּ, יֹאכֵלוּ; נִרְדְּמוּ, לֹא יֹאכֵלוּ.

[ט] הַפֶּסַח אַחַר חֲצוֹת מְטַמֵּא אֶת הַיָּדַיִם. הַפִּגּוּל וְהַנּוֹתָר מְטַמְּאִין אֶת הַיָּדַיִם.

בֵּרֵךְ בִּרְכַּת הַפֶּסַח, פָּטַר אֶת שֶׁל זֶבַח; בֵּרֵךְ אֶת שֶׁל זֶבַח, לֹא פָּטַר אֶת שֶׁל פֶּסַח; דִּבְרֵי רַבִּי יִשְׁמָעֵאל. רַבִּי עֲקִיבָא אוֹמֵר: לֹא זוֹ פוֹטֶרֶת זוֹ, וְלֹא זוֹ פוֹטֶרֶת זוֹ.

יד אברהם

7. מְבָרֵךְ עַל מְזוֹנוֹ — *He recites the benediction for his food*, i.e., the *Bircas HaMazon* that is recited after meals.

גּוֹמֵר עָלָיו אֶת הַהַלֵּל — *He completes the Hallel over* the fourth cup, having already recited one or two chapters of it before the meal (mishnah 6). After the completion of the regular *Hallel*, one should recite the הַלֵּל הַגָּדוֹל, *Great Hallel*, the title given to *Psalm* 136. That psalm is composed of twenty-six verses describing God's goodness, each of which ends with the refrain כִּי לְעוֹלָם חַסְדּוֹ, *for His kindness endures forever*.

בִּרְכַּת הַשִּׁיר — *The 'Blessing of the Song.'* R' Yehudah says it is יְהַלְלוּךָ, the blessing with which *Hallel* always concludes. R' Yochanan says it is נִשְׁמַת כָּל חַי, the long and beautiful song of praise — concluding with the blessing יִשְׁתַּבַּח, with which the first section of the morning service is concluded on the Sabbath and festivals. There are three customs regarding the exact order of the praises and the concluding blessing; see *O. Ch.* 480.

... בֵּין הַכּוֹסוֹת הַלָּלוּ — *Between these cups*, i.e., between the first two cups and the last two cups, one may drink additional wine, if he wishes, but not between the third and fourth [cups], because he might become drunk and be unable to finish the *Haggadah*. However, we do not fear that drunkenness will result from drinking during the feast because wine does not have so intoxicating an effect when it is taken with food (*Rav*). However, there is a difference of opinion whether drinking is permitted between the first two cups as well (see *O. Ch.* 473:3).

8. וְאֵין מַפְטִירִין — *One may not conclude*. After eating the *pesach*, one may not conclude the meal by having dessert. This is a Rabbinical decree enacted so that 'the taste of the *pesach* and matzah remain in his mouth' (*Rambam*). As used in our mishnah, the word *afikoman* refers to desserts. Today it is applied to the final portion of matzah eaten in place of the *pesach* offering. The reason for this is that just as one does not eat an [*afikoman*] dessert after the meat of the *pesach*, so too, in the absence of the sacrifice, one does not conclude the Seder with desert. Since the Sages ordained that the Seder meal must be concluded with the final portion of matzah, it came to be called *afikoman*, dessert.

יָשְׁנוּ מִקְצָתָן — *If some of the [party] fell asleep* ... The mishnah (7:13) taught earlier that is forbidden for members of a group to eat their *pesach* offering in one location and finish it in another. Our mishnah teaches that under certain circumstances, the Rabbis decreed that the group is considered to have ceased to exist as a unit. For its members to reconstitute themselves even in the same place is forbidden Rabbinically, because it appears similar to a case of the same group moving elsewhere to continue its eating. The Rabbis considered sleep equivalent to having concluded the meal and left the place, because when someone sleeps he cannot be considered as yet intending to resume the meal. If the meal is subsequently resumed, it is viewed as a different meal, and it is thus akin to a *pesach* eaten in two places. However, as long as at least some members of the group remained awake, the group is not viewed as having dissolved, and they may *all* still eat the *pesach*, even those who slept (*Rav*). This rule applies today to the *afikoman* matzah, which may not be eaten if the entire group has fallen asleep (*O.Ch.* 478:2), nor in two places (*Rama*).

נִתְנַמְנְמוּ, יֹאכֵלוּ — *If they* [merely] *dozed, they may eat*. The *Gemara* defines dozing as 'sleeping yet not sleeping, awake yet not awake, e.g., if someone calls him he answers, yet he cannot respond coherently;

[7] *They pour a third cup [of wine] for him, [and] he recites the benediction for his food; a fourth [cup, and] he completes the Hallel over it, and recites the 'Blessing of the Song' over it. Between these cups, one may drink if he wishes; [but] one may not drink between the third and fourth cups.*

[8] *One may not conclude after the pesach with dessert. If some of the [party] fell asleep, they may [still] eat [the pesach]; if all [of them fell asleep], they may not eat. R' Yose says: If they dozed, they may eat; [but] if they fell into a deep sleep, they may not eat.*

[9] *After midnight, the pesach offering contaminates the hands. Piggul and leftover [sacrificial meat] contaminate the hands.*

Reciting the benediction over the pesach offering exempts the [chagigah] offering [as well; but] reciting the [chagigah] offering's [benediction] does not exempt that of the pesach offering; [these are] the words of R' Yishmael. R' Akiva says: Neither one exempts the other.

YAD AVRAHAM

however, if he is reminded [of something] he recalls.'

9. הַפֶּסַח אַחַר חֲצוֹת — *After midnight, the pesach offering* ... Like all other offerings on the last night allotted for their consumption, the *pesach* offering may be eaten only until midnight. However, our mishnah follows the view of R' Elazar ben Azaryah, that *the pesach* differs from other offerings. While they are prohibited only Rabbinically in the second half of the night — 'to keep a man distant from transgression' (*Berachos* 1:1) — the *pesach's* permissible term of eating expires at midnight by *Biblical* law. Consequently, at midnight, it is not only forbidden for consumption, it becomes נוֹתָר, *leftover*. The Rabbis decreed *tumah*-contamination upon the hands of anyone touching leftover sacrificial meat. For other offerings this contamination applies only in the morning, when they become leftover.

However, in R' Akiva's view the *pesach* does not differ from other offerings; it, too, may be eaten until dawn under Biblical law, and is prohibited at midnight only Rabbinically. *Rambam* rules according to R' Akiva, while *Tosafos* adopt R' Elazar ben Azaryah's view. This disagreement has implications for current practice because the *afikoman* commemorates the *pesach* and is subject to the same laws. Similarly, the *mitzvah* of matzah is subject to the same time limitations (*Gem.*). Furthermore, even in R' Akiva's view one should ideally eat the matzah before midnight 'in order to keep distance from a transgression' (*Rosh*). *Shulchan Aruch* (477:1) rules that even the *afikoman* should be eaten before midnight. If one did not eat even the first portion of matzah before midnight, there is a question whether he may recite the blessing for the *mitzvah* of matzah (see *Mishnah Berurah*).

הַפִּגּוּל — *Piggul* is a term denoting a sacrifice disqualified during the performance of the blood service by the offerer's intent for the meat to be eaten or for the sacrificial parts to be burned on the Altar after the time allotted by the Torah. Consumption of *piggul* meat is forbidden under penalty of *kares* and the Rabbis decreed *tumah* of the hands for touching it, as they did for leftover.

בֵּרַךְ בִּרְכַּת הַפֶּסַח ... — *Reciting the benediction over the pesach offering* ... Before partaking of the *pesach*, one recites a blessing, as for most *mitzvos*. This blessing also exempts the blessing that would otherwise be said for the *chagigah* brought in conjunction with the *pesach* (6:4). [Although nothing may be eaten after the *pesach* at the conclusion of the meal (m. 8), *Tzlach* demonstrates from *Rambam* that the *pesach* was eaten twice, once at the *beginning* of the meal immediately after matzah and *maror* (when the blessing was recited over it), and at least an olive's volume of *pesach* meat again at the end of the meal.]

However, reciting the *chagigah's* benediction does not exempt the *pesach*, because *the pesach* is not included in the term *offering* used in that blessing. R' Yishmael's view is that unlike other offerings, the *pesach* has its blood poured onto the wall of the Altar rather than thrown against it. Therefore, it is not included under the term זֶבַח, *offering*, and the blessing, *to eat the offering*, cannot exempt it. The term *pesach* can include the *chagigah*, however, because in R' Yishmael's view, even offerings whose blood should be thrown are valid if their blood was poured in the fashion of the *pesach*. R' Akiva holds that other offerings are *not* valid if their blood is poured upon the Altar and they therefore cannot be included in the term *pesach*, just as the *pesach* cannot be included under the term 'offering' (*Gem.*).

משניות מנחות

פרק עשירי

[א] **רַבִּי יִשְׁמָעֵאל** אוֹמֵר: הָעֹמֶר הָיָה בָא בְּשַׁבָּת מִשָּׁלֹשׁ סְאִין, וּבְחֹל מֵחָמֵשׁ. וַחֲכָמִים אוֹמְרִים: אֶחָד בְּשַׁבָּת וְאֶחָד בְּחֹל, מִשָּׁלֹשׁ הָיָה בָא. רַבִּי חֲנִינָא סְגַן הַכֹּהֲנִים אוֹמֵר: בְּשַׁבָּת הָיָה נִקְצָר בְּיָחִיד, וּבְמַגָּל אַחַת, וּבְקֻפָּה אַחַת; וּבְחֹל בִּשְׁלֹשָׁה, וּבְשָׁלֹשׁ קֻפּוֹת, וּבְשָׁלֹשׁ מַגָּלוֹת. וַחֲכָמִים אוֹמְרִים: אֶחָד בְּשַׁבָּת וְאֶחָד בְּחֹל, בִּשְׁלֹשָׁה, וּבְשָׁלֹשׁ קֻפּוֹת, וּבְשָׁלֹשׁ מַגָּלוֹת.

[ב] מִצְוַת הָעֹמֶר לָבֹא מִן הַקָּרוֹב. לֹא בִכֵּר הַקָּרוֹב לִירוּשָׁלַיִם, מְבִיאִים אוֹתוֹ מִכָּל מָקוֹם. מַעֲשֶׂה שֶׁבָּא מִגַּגּוֹת צְרִיפִין, וּשְׁתֵּי הַלֶּחֶם מִבִּקְעַת עֵין סוֹכֵר.

[ג] כֵּיצַד הָיוּ עוֹשִׂים? שְׁלוּחֵי בֵית דִּין יוֹצְאִים מֵעֶרֶב יוֹם טוֹב וְעוֹשִׂים אוֹתוֹ כְּרִיכוֹת בִּמְחֻבָּר לַקַּרְקַע, כְּדֵי שֶׁיְּהֵא נוֹחַ לִקְצוֹר. וְכָל הָעֲיָרוֹת הַסְּמוּכוֹת לְשָׁם מִתְכַּנְּסוֹת לְשָׁם כְּדֵי שֶׁיְּהֵא נִקְצָר בְּעֵסֶק גָּדוֹל. כֵּיוָן שֶׁחֲשֵׁכָה, אוֹמֵר לָהֶם: בָּא הַשֶּׁמֶשׁ? אוֹמְרִים: הֵין. בָּא הַשֶּׁמֶשׁ? אוֹמְרִים: הֵין. מַגָּל זוֹ? אוֹמְרִים: הֵין. מַגָּל זוֹ? אוֹמְרִים: הֵין. קֻפָּה זוֹ? אוֹמְרִים: הֵין. קֻפָּה זוֹ? אוֹמְרִים: הֵין. בְּשַׁבָּת, אוֹמֵר לָהֶם: שַׁבָּת זוֹ? אוֹמְרִים: הֵין. שַׁבָּת זוֹ? אוֹמְרִים: הֵין. אֶקְצֹר? וְהֵם אוֹמְרִים לוֹ: קְצֹר! אֶקְצֹר? וְהֵם אוֹמְרִים לוֹ: קְצֹר! שְׁלֹשָׁה פְעָמִים עַל כָּל דָּבָר וְדָבָר, וְהֵם אוֹמְרִים לוֹ: הֵין, הֵין, הֵין. כָּל כָּךְ לָמָּה? מִפְּנֵי הַבַּיְתוֹסִים, שֶׁהָיוּ אוֹמְרִים אֵין קְצִירַת הָעֹמֶר בְּמוֹצָאֵי יוֹם טוֹב.

יד אברהם

⋄§ Tractate Menachos — Ch. 10

The following selection deals with the *Omer* offering brought in the Temple. The *Omer* was a *minchah*-offering brought from barley. The Torah (*Lev.* 23:9ff) states: ... וַהֲבֵאתֶם אֶת עֹמֶר רֵאשִׁית קְצִירְכֶם אֶל הַכֹּהֵן. וְהֵנִיף אֶת הָעֹמֶר לִפְנֵי ה׳ לִרְצֹנְכֶם; מִמָּחֳרַת הַשַּׁבָּת יְנִיפֶנּוּ הַכֹּהֵן..., *and you are to bring an Omer of the first of your reaping to the Kohen. And he shall wave the Omer before* HASHEM *to your satisfaction; on the morrow of the Sabbath shall the Kohen wave it.*

The Torah sets the date of the *Omer* as *the morrow of the Sabbath.* According to the Oral Law, this refers to the second day of Pesach, which is the morrow of [the first day of] the Pesach festival (see mishnah 3). There was, however, a group of Jews called *Baytusim* [Boethusians], who insisted that the date of the *Omer* was literally *the morrow of the Sabbath,* i.e., Sunday, the first Sunday after Pesach. In order to reinforce the truth of the received tradition, the Sages ordained that the reaping of the *Omer* on its proper date be accompanied with fanfare and ceremony, which will be discussed below.

Associated with the *Omer*-offering is a Biblical prohibition forbidding the use of the new crop of grain [viz. wheat, barley, rye, spelt, oats] before the offering of the *Omer.* Thus, a function of the *Omer* offering was to allow the use of the new crop of grain. Any grain that took root after the *Omer's* offering could not be eaten until the following year's *Omer* was offered. This prohibition is called חָדָשׁ, *chadash,* lit. *the new [grain].*

1. This mishnah deals with the procedure for bringing the *Omer* when the second day of Pesach falls on the Sabbath.

הָעֹמֶר הָיָה בָא בְּשַׁבָּת — *The Omer was brought on the Sabbath,* like any other offering for which the Torah set a specific time. Even reaping the grain overrides the Sabbath. However, only the minimum necessary for the offering to be brought may be done. Thus, when the second day of Pesach fell on the Sabbath, only three *seah* of barley were cut, the minimum amount from which [with sufficient sifting] the required tenth of an *ephah* of fine flour can be extracted. On a weekday, when there is no *melachah* restriction involved, five *seah* were cut, from

MISHNAYOS MENACHOS

CHAPTER 10

[1] רַבִּי יִשְׁמָעֵאל R' Yishmael says: The Omer offering was brought on the Sabbath from three seah [of barley], and on a weekday from five. But the Sages say: Whether on the Sabbath or on a weekday, it came from three. R' Chanina, the administrator of the Kohanim, says: On the Sabbath it was reaped by an individual, with one sickle, and in one basket; on a weekday by three [people], in three baskets, with three sickles. But the Sages say: Whether on the Sabbath or on weekdays, [it was done] by three [people], with three baskets, and three sickles.

[2] The preferred [procedure for the] Omer is that [the grain] come from [fields] close [to Jerusalem]. If that which is close to Jerusalem did not ripen [early enough], we may bring it from any place. It once occurred that [the barley] came from Gaggoth Tzerifin, and the [wheat for the] shtei halechem from the valley of Ein Socher.

[3] How did they do it? Agents of Beis Din would go out on the eve of the Festival and tie [the grain] into bundles while it was still attached to the ground, so that it would be easier to reap. All of the towns nearby would gather there so that it should be reaped with great ceremony. As soon as it became dark, he would say to the [assembled crowd], 'Has the sun set?' and they would say, 'Yes.' 'Has the sun set?' and they would say, 'Yes.' '[Shall I use] this sickle?' and they would say, 'Yes.' 'This sickle?' and they would say, 'Yes.' 'This basket?' and they would say, 'Yes.' 'This basket?' and they would say, 'Yes.' On the Sabbath, he would say to them, '[Shall I cut on] this Sabbath?' and they would say, 'Yes.' 'This Sabbath?' and they would say, 'Yes.' 'Shall I [begin to] reap?' and they would say to him, 'Reap!' 'Shall I reap?' and they would say to him, 'Reap!' Three times for each item, and they would say to him, 'Yes, yes, yes.' Why was all this necessary? Because of the Baytusim, who said that the Omer is not reaped on the night after Yom Tov.

YAD AVRAHAM

which an *ephah* of even finer quality can be more readily extracted (*Gem.*).

:וַחֲכָמִים אוֹמְרִים — *But the Sages say* that even on weekdays no more than three *seah* were cut, to minimize the burden upon the multitudes who stood and observed the reaping (mishnah 3).

:רַבִּי חֲנִינָא סְגַן הַכֹּהֲנִים אוֹמֵר — *R' Chanina, the administrator of the Kohanim, says:* As mentioned in the prefatory remarks, the Baytusim maintained that the *Omer* was not offered on the second day of Pesach but on the Sunday following the first day of Pesach. To demonstrate the error of this view, the proceedings surrounding the *Omer* were done on the proper date with great fanfare. Therefore, the barley was reaped by three people, each using a separate sickle, and each placed his barley in a separate basket (*Rav*). However, on the Sabbath, the work was limited to the minimum necessary for the offering.

:וַחֲכָמִים אוֹמְרִים — *But the Sages* contend that since any labor necessary for the *Omer* offering is permitted on the Sabbath, demonstrating the error of the Baytusian view takes precedence over limiting the work on the Sabbath.

2. לָבֹא מִן הַקָּרוֹב — *That it come from the [fields] close [to Jerusalem],* because of the principle אֵין מַעֲבִירִין עַל הַמִּצְוֹת, *we do not pass over mitzvos,* i.e., a *mitzvah* should be performed as soon as the opportunity presents itself (*Gem.*)

מְבִיאִים אוֹתוֹ מִכָּל מָקוֹם — *We may bring it from any place* in *Eretz Yisrael.*

וּשְׁתֵּי הַלֶּחֶם — *Shtei halechem,* an offering of Two Loaves of bread brought on Shavuos.

3. וְכָל הָעֲיָרוֹת הַסְּמוּכוֹת — [*The inhabitants of*] *all of the towns nearby* would gather at the close of the first day of Pesach at the harvest site. This, too, was done to publicize that the *Omer* is cut on the second night of Pesach (*Rav*). Reaping took place at night, to coincide with the counting of the *Omer*, as derived by the *Gem.*

הַבַּיְתוּסִים — *The Baytusim* were a sect similar to the Sadducees [צְדוֹקִים], who rejected the interpretations of the Oral Torah and chose to accept only the apparent literal meaning of Scripture. Since the Torah (*Lev.* 23:15) states, *and you shall count for yourselves from the morrow of the Sabbath,* they mistakenly assumed that the *Omer* period

[ד] קְצָרוּהוּ וּנְתָנוּהוּ בַּקֻּפּוֹת, הֱבִיאוּהוּ לָעֲזָרָה. הָיוּ מְהַבְהֲבִין אוֹתוֹ בָּאוּר כְּדֵי לְקַיֵּם בּוֹ מִצְוַת קָלִי; דִּבְרֵי רַבִּי מֵאִיר. וַחֲכָמִים אוֹמְרִים: בְּקָנִים וּבְקְלִיחוֹת חוֹבְטִים אוֹתוֹ כְּדֵי שֶׁלֹּא יִתְמָעֵךְ. נְתָנוּהוּ לָאַבּוּב, וְאַבּוּב הָיָה מְנֻקָּב כְּדֵי שֶׁיְּהֵא הָאוּר שׁוֹלֵט בְּכֻלּוֹ. שְׁטָחוּהוּ בָּעֲזָרָה וְהָרוּחַ מְנַשֶּׁבֶת בּוֹ. נְתָנוּהוּ בְּרֵחַיִם שֶׁל גָּרוֹסוֹת וְהוֹצִיאוּ מִמֶּנּוּ עִשָּׂרוֹן, שֶׁהוּא מְנֻפֶּה מִשְּׁלֹשׁ עֶשְׂרֵה נָפָה. וְהַשְּׁאָר נִפְדֶּה וְנֶאֱכָל לְכָל אָדָם. וְחַיָּב בַּחַלָּה וּפָטוּר מִן הַמַּעַשְׂרוֹת. רַבִּי עֲקִיבָא מְחַיֵּב בַּחַלָּה וּבַמַּעַשְׂרוֹת.

בָּא לוֹ לָעִשָּׂרוֹן, וְנָתַן שַׁמְנוֹ וּלְבוֹנָתוֹ, יָצַק וּבָלַל, הֵנִיף וְהִגִּישׁ, וְקָמַץ וְהִקְטִיר; וְהַשְּׁאָר נֶאֱכָל לַכֹּהֲנִים.

[ה] מִשֶּׁקָּרַב הָעֹמֶר, יוֹצְאִין וּמוֹצְאִין שׁוּק יְרוּשָׁלַיִם שֶׁהוּא מָלֵא קֶמַח וְקָלִי, שֶׁלֹּא בִרְצוֹן חֲכָמִים; דִּבְרֵי רַבִּי מֵאִיר. רַבִּי יְהוּדָה אוֹמֵר: בִּרְצוֹן חֲכָמִים הָיוּ עוֹשִׂים. מִשֶּׁקָּרַב הָעֹמֶר, הֻתַּר הֶחָדָשׁ מִיָּד. וְהָרְחוֹקִים מֻתָּרִים מֵחֲצוֹת הַיּוֹם וּלְהַלָּן. מִשֶּׁחָרַב בֵּית הַמִּקְדָּשׁ, הִתְקִין רַבָּן יוֹחָנָן בֶּן זַכַּאי שֶׁיְּהֵא יוֹם הָנֵף כֻּלּוֹ אָסוּר. אָמַר רַבִּי יְהוּדָה: וַהֲלֹא מִן הַתּוֹרָה הוּא אָסוּר, שֶׁנֶּאֱמַר: „עַד עֶצֶם הַיּוֹם הַזֶּה"? מִפְּנֵי מָה הָרְחוֹקִים מֻתָּרִים מֵחֲצוֹת הַיּוֹם וּלְהַלָּן? מִפְּנֵי שֶׁהֵן יוֹדְעִין שֶׁאֵין בֵּית דִּין מִתְעַצְּלִין בּוֹ.

יד אברהם

must begin on a Sunday. However, the Oral Tradition transmitted from generation to generation in an unbroken chain streching back to Sinai explains the word Sabbath to mean the first day of Pesach, regardless of which day of the week it falls. [The term Sabbath is used because of the obligation to cease from labor on that day] (*Rav*).

4. הָיוּ מְהַבְהֲבִין אוֹתוֹ בָּאוּר — *They [then] toasted it in fire* to fulfill the Torah's requirement (*Lev.* 2:14) that the *Omer* be brought אָבִיב קָלוּי בָּאֵשׁ, *when it is first ripe, toasted in fire.* R' Meir holds that 'toasting' requires that it be roasted directly in the fire without a utensil intervening, i.e., while still in its stalks (*Rambam*).

וַחֲכָמִים אוֹמְרִים — *But the Sages say* that the kernels should be removed from the husks prior to toasting because removing them later may damage the toasted kernels. To avoid crushing the soft, fresh kernels while separating them from their husks, they beat them with soft reeds and stalks rather than with sticks. The kernels were then removed and placed in a copper pipe perforated with numerous holes, and toasted over a fire. The Sages maintain that the term קָלִי does not mean toasted directly over a fire, but rather toasted through a medium (*Rav*).

בְּרֵחַיִם שֶׁל גָּרוֹסוֹת — *A grist-mill* (which grinds coarsely) leaves pieces of shell large enough to be held back by the sieve while the flour passes through. Hence, the Torah refers to the *Omer* as גֶּרֶשׂ כַּרְמֶל, *'coarsely ground* out of full ears of grain' (*Rav*).

מְנֻפֶּה מִשְּׁלֹשׁ עֶשְׂרֵה נָפָה — *Sifted with thirteen sieves,* to produce the desired grade of flour.

וְהַשְּׁאָר נִפְדֶּה — *The remainder* [*of the grain* from which the *issaron* was extracted] *is redeemed,* thereby permitting it for general use.

וְחַיָּב בַּחַלָּה וּפָטוּר מִן הַמַּעַשְׂרוֹת — *It is subject to challah but exempt from maaser.* [As a rule, *hekdesh* property is exempt from tithes such as *terumah* (given to a *Kohen*), *maaser* (a pair of tithes, one given to a Levite and the other eaten by the owner in Jerusalem, or given to the poor), and from *challah* (a tithe of dough given to a *Kohen*). Nevertheless, the dough made from the remainder of the grain is subject to *challah,* because this obligation takes effect at the time of גִּלְגּוּל עִיסָה, *the making of the dough,* at which time the flour has already been redeemed and is *chullin.*

The [*terumah* and] *maaser* obligations, however, take effect when the threshed grain is made into a pile. Since in our case this occurred while the barley was still *hekdesh,* the grain never became subject to these obligations (*Rav*).

רַבִּי עֲקִיבָא מְחַיֵּב — *R' Akiva declares it subject* to both *challah* and *maaser,* maintaining that the remaining grain was never *hekdesh* in the first place. Since the payment made by the Temple treasury for this grain was intended solely for the *issaron* of the *Omer,* the remaining grain never became consecrated by this purchase, and thus became subject to *maaser* obligations.

בָּא לוֹ לָעִשָּׂרוֹן . . . — *He* [*the Kohen*] *approached the issaron* . . . The mishnah now moves on to the offering of the *Omer* on the second day of Pesach. Oil and frankincense are required components of most *minchah* offerings. The oil is mixed with the flour, and the frankincense is placed on top of it.

[4] *They would reap it and place it in baskets [and] bring it to the [Temple] Courtyard. They [then] toasted [the grain] in fire in order to fulfill the mitzvah of toasting; [these are] the words of R' Meir. But the Sages say: They beat [the grain] with reeds and stalks so that [the kernels] should not be crushed. They [then] placed [the kernels] in a perforated pipe so that the fire should reach all of them. They spread out [the toasted kernels] in the [Temple] Courtyard, where the wind would blow on them [and dry them out]. They then placed them in a grist-mill and extracted from them an issaron [of flour], which was sifted with thirteen sieves. The remainder [of the grain] is redeemed and may be eaten by anyone. It is subject to challah but exempt from maaser. R' Akiva declares it subject to challah and to maaser.*

He [the Kohen] approached the issaron [of barley flour], and put in its oil and frankincense; he poured and mixed, waved and brought [it] near [to the Altar], performed kemitzah and burnt [it] on the Altar; the remainder [of the Omer offering] is eaten by the Kohanim.

[5] *After the Omer was offered, they would go out and find the market place of Jerusalem full of flour and the toasted flour, against the will of the Sages; [these are] the words of R' Meir. R' Yehudah says: They did it in accordance with the will of the Sages.*

After the Omer was offered, the new grain was permitted immediately. Those who were distant were permitted from midday and onward. After the Temple was destroyed, Rabban Yochanan ben Zakkai instituted that the day of the Omer's offering should be forbidden. Said R' Yehudah: Is it not Biblically forbidden [this entire day], as it is stated (Lev. 23:14): Until this very day? Why are those who are distant permitted from midday and onward? Because they know that the Beis Din does not procrastinate with it.

YAD AVRAHAM

In common with most *minchah* offerings, the *Omer* must be brought and touched to the southwest corner of the Altar before being offered (see *Menachos* 5:5). Prior to this, the *Omer* is waved to and fro in a ritual known as *tenufah*, waving.

The offering of a *minchah* such as the *Omer* begins with the act of *kemitzah*, in which a *Kohen* removes a portion of the flour with the three middle fingers of his right hand. This he places in another sacred vessel and carries to the Altar, where the *kometz*-flour is placed on the fires.

5. . . . מִשֶּׁקָּרַב הָעֹמֶר — *After the Omer was offered,* the markets of Jerusalem would be immediately filled with the new grain, which had been rendered permissible by that offering. Since processing grain into flour takes time, the new grain had clearly been harvested before the *Omer* was brought. The Rabbis disapproved of this for fear that a person might inadvertently eat some of it. R' Yehudah, however, does not consider this concern significant and therefore permits harvesting grain before the *Omer* [subject to the conditions set in mishnah 7 and 8] (*Rav*).

וְהָרְחוֹקִים מֻתָּרִים מֵחֲצוֹת — *Those who were distant* [and unable to ascertain the time that the *Omer* was offered] *were permitted* [to eat new grain] *from midday* Jerusalem time, when it could be safely assumed that it had already been offered.

. . . הִתְקִין רַבָּן יוֹחָנָן בֶּן זַכַּאי — *Rabban Yochanan ben Zakkai instituted*, following the destruction of the Temple and consequent cessation of the *Omer*-offering, that new grain should be prohibited until after the sixteenth of Nissan (on which the *Omer* would have been offered).

אָמַר רַבִּי יְהוּדָה — *Said R' Yehudah:* The Torah (*Lev.* 23:14) states: וְלֶחֶם וְקָלִי וְכַרְמֶל לֹא תֹאכְלוּ עַד עֶצֶם הַיּוֹם הַזֶּה, *the bread and flour [from new grain] you shall not eat 'until this very day.'* R' Yehudah interprets the word עַד, *until*, as *through* [i.e., *until and including*]. The Torah follows this by adding עַד הֲבִיאֲכֶם אֶת־קָרְבַּן אֱלֹהֵיכֶם, *until you bring the offering of your God*, which clearly permits the new grain upon the offering of the *Omer*. R' Yehudah explains that both statements are true: When the *Omer* is offered, the offering permits new grain; when an offering is not possible, new grain may not be eaten until the entire day has passed. R' Yochanan ben Zakkai, however, interprets the phrase עַד, *until*, to mean *until but not including*. Thus, when there is no Temple the new grain is Biblically permitted at daybreak. Nevertheless, Rabban Yochanan ben Zakkai feared that people accustomed to eating the new grain on the morning of the sixteenth in non-Temple times would continue doing so even after the Temple is rebuilt, not realizing that one must then wait until the *Omer* is brought (*Gem.*).

[ו] הָעֹמֶר הָיָה מַתִּיר בַּמְּדִינָה, וּשְׁתֵּי הַלֶּחֶם בַּמִּקְדָּשׁ. אֵין מְבִיאִין מְנָחוֹת, וּבִכּוּרִים, וּמִנְחַת בְּהֵמָה קֹדֶם לָעֹמֶר; וְאִם הֵבִיא, פָּסוּל. קֹדֶם לִשְׁתֵּי הַלֶּחֶם לֹא יָבִיא; וְאִם הֵבִיא, כָּשֵׁר.

[ז] הַחִטִּים, וְהַשְּׂעֹרִים, וְהַכֻּסְּמִין, וְשִׁבֹּלֶת שׁוּעָל, וְהַשִּׁיפוֹן חַיָּבִין בְּחַלָּה וּמִצְטָרְפִים זֶה עִם זֶה. וַאֲסוּרִים בֶּחָדָשׁ מִלִּפְנֵי הַפֶּסַח וּמִלִּקְצֹר מִלִּפְנֵי הָעֹמֶר. וְאִם הִשְׁרִישׁוּ קֹדֶם לָעֹמֶר, הָעֹמֶר מַתִּירָן; וְאִם לָאו, אֲסוּרִים, עַד שֶׁיָּבֹא עֹמֶר הַבָּא.

[ח] קוֹצְרִים בֵּית הַשְּׁלָחִים שֶׁבָּעֲמָקִים, אֲבָל לֹא גוֹדְשִׁין. אַנְשֵׁי יְרִיחוֹ קוֹצְרִין בִּרְצוֹן חֲכָמִים וְגוֹדְשִׁין שֶׁלֹּא בִרְצוֹן חֲכָמִים, וְלֹא מִחוּ בְיָדָם חֲכָמִים. קוֹצֵר לַשַּׁחַת וּמַאֲכִיל לַבְּהֵמָה. אָמַר רַבִּי יְהוּדָה: אֵימָתַי? בִּזְמַן שֶׁהִתְחִיל עַד שֶׁלֹּא הֵבִיאָה שְׁלִישׁ. רַבִּי שִׁמְעוֹן אוֹמֵר: אַף יִקְצֹר וְיַאֲכִיל אַף מִשֶּׁהֵבִיאָה שְׁלִישׁ.

[ט] קוֹצְרִין מִפְּנֵי הַנְּטִיעוֹת, מִפְּנֵי בֵית הָאֵבֶל, מִפְּנֵי בִטּוּל בֵּית הַמִּדְרָשׁ. לֹא יַעֲשֶׂה אוֹתָן כְּרִיכוֹת; אֲבָל מַנִּיחָן צְבָתִים. מִצְוַת הָעֹמֶר לָבֹא מִן הַקָּמָה; לֹא מָצָא, יָבִיא מִן הָעֳמָרִים. מִצְוָתוֹ לָבֹא מִן הַלַּח; לֹא מָצָא, יָבִיא מִן הַיָּבֵשׁ. מִצְוָתוֹ לִקְצוֹר בַּלַּיְלָה; נִקְצַר בַּיּוֹם, כָּשֵׁר. וְדוֹחֶה אֶת הַשַּׁבָּת.

יד אברהם

6. The *minchas haOmer* on the second day of Pesach permits ordinary consumption of new grain. However, before new grain may be used for a Temple offering, yet another offering — the *Shtei Halechem*, the Two Loaves of Shavuos — must be brought. The Torah (*Num.* 28:26) refers to the *Shtei Halechem* as מִנְחָה חֲדָשָׁה, *the new minchah,* indicating that it is to be the first *minchah* brought from the new grain (*Gem*).

וּבִכּוּרִים — *Or bikkurim.* These are the first fruits of the seven species [wheat, barley, grapes, figs, pomegranates, olives and dates (*Deut.* 8:8)]; these are separated and brought to the Temple (see *Deut.* 26:1-11).

וּמִנְחַת בְּהֵמָה — *Or the minchah-offering of an animal*; i.e., the *minchah* which accompanies animal offerings.

וְאִם הֵבִיא פָּסוּל — *And if one brought* [*them*], *they are invalid.* Temple sacrifices must come מִמַּשְׁקֵה יִשְׂרָאֵל, *from foods permitted for a Jew's consumption* (Ez. 45:15). Since new grain prior to the *Omer* is prohibited, offerings brought from them are invalid.

וְאִם הֵבִיא, כָּשֵׁר — *But if he did bring* [any of these from new grain between the *Omer* and the *Shtei Halechem*], *they are valid,* because the grain is at least fit for ordinary consumption (*Gem*).

7. **בְּחַלָּה** — *Challah.* When one kneads a dough from one of these five species of grain, a portion of the dough [called *challah*] must be separated and given to the *Kohen* [see *Num.* 15:17-21].

וּמִצְטָרְפִים זֶה עִם זֶה — *And combine with one another* to complete the minimum quantity of flour needed before the obligation of *challah* takes effect — the volume of 43 1/5 eggs. However, only those that are similar combine. Thus, spelt is similar to and combines with either wheat or barley; oats and rye are similar to and combine with barley only.

חָדָשׁ — *Chadash,* the prohibition of new grain prior to the *Omer* offering of the second day of Pesach, applies only to those five grains. In addition, there is a prohibition against reaping the new grain before the *Omer* is cut, but only to reaping with a sickle; to pluck by hand is permitted.

8. The next two mishnayos delineate exceptions to the prohibition against reaping new grain before the *Omer.*

קוֹצְרִים בֵּית הַשְּׁלָחִים שֶׁבָּעֲמָקִים — *We may reap the irrigated fields in the valleys,* because the prohibition against reaping does not apply to areas that produce grain of inferior quality which is not used for the *Omer*-offering.

Nevertheless, the Sages prohibited this grain to

[6] The Omer-offering rendered [the new grain] permissible in the Provinces, and the Shtei Halechem [did so] in the Temple. We do not bring minchah-offerings, or bikkurim, or the minchah-offering of an animal prior to the Omer-offering; and if one brought [them], they are invalid. Prior to the Shtei Halechem one may not bring [them]; but if he did bring [them], they are valid.

[7] Wheat, barley, spelt, oats, and rye are subject to challah and combine with one another. They are forbidden [to be eaten] as chadash before Pesach and from being reaped before the Omer. If they took root before the Omer, the Omer renders them permissible; if not, they are forbidden until the following Omer.

[8] We may reap the irrigated fields in the valleys, but we may not stack [the harvest prior to the Omer]. The people of Jericho reaped with the approval of the Sages and stacked against the Sages' wishes, but the Sages did not issue a protest against them. One may reap unripe grain [before the Omer] and feed it to animals. Said R' Yehudah: When? When he began before it reached a third. R' Shimon says: He may reap and feed [it] even after it has reached a third.

[9] We may reap to benefit the saplings, [to make room] for a place of mourning, [and] in order to [avoid] a cessation of study. [Even when one may cut,] he may not make them into bundles; rather, he leaves them in heaps. The commandment of the Omer is that it should come from standing grain; if he did not find, he may bring from the [previously harvested] sheaves. The commandment is that it come from fresh [grain]; if he did not find, he may bring from dry [grain]. The commandment is that it be reaped on the night [of the sixteenth] however, if it is reaped by day it is valid. It overrides the Sabbath.

YAD AVRAHAM

be stacked in organized piles prior to the reaping of the *Omer*, because the stacking is not necessary to forestall damage to the grain. The Sages prohibited unnecessary involvement with the grain so that one should not come to eat it before the *Omer* is offered (*Rashi*).

[However, the Sages made a special exception to their ban in order to provide for the needs of the people who traveled to Jerusalem for the Festivals (see mishnah 5).]

עַד שֶׁלֹּא הֵבִיאָה שְׁלִישׁ — *Before it reached a third,* when it becomes minimally fit for human consumption.

9. מִפְּנֵי הַנְּטִיעוֹת — *To benefit the saplings,* it is permitted to reap prior to the *Omer*, grain which grows between them in order to prevent damage to the saplings. Since this grain is inferior and not preferred for the *Omer*, there is no Biblical prohibition against harvesting it before the *Omer* [mishnah 8].

מִפְּנֵי בֵית הָאֵבֶל — *For a place of mourning.* The first meal served to a mourner was arranged in a broad, open area. If there is no area with enough space to accommodate the number of people in attendance, it is permitted to clear grain from a field to make room, even before the *Omer*.

מִפְּנֵי בִטּוּל בֵּית הַמִּדְרָשׁ — [*And*] *in order to* [*avoid*] *a cessation of study,* when there is not sufficient place for those who are studying Torah to sit.

The reason for these last two exceptions is that the prohibition is only for harvesting for private benefit, but not for the sake of a *mitzvah* (*Gem.*).

אֲבָל מְנִיחָן צְבָתִים — *Rather, he leaves them* [*the cut stalks*] *in heaps,* to minimize his involvement with the harvesting process prior to the *Omer* offering (*Gem.*).

מִן הַקָּמָה — *From standing grain,* i.e., grain still growing from the ground, not from previously cut grain.

וְדוֹחָה אֶת הַשַּׁבָּת — [Offering the *Omer*] *overrides the Sabbath,* i.e., is performed even if the second day of Pesach is the Sabbath. [The *Omer* is in this respect like any other communal sacrifice that must be brought on a fixed day.] However, the reaping, which according to our mishnah is valid even when done before Pesach, does not have this dispensation and it may not be done on the Sabbath. The statement in mishnah 1 that the *Omer* is reaped on the Sabbath is in accord only with the opinion of R' Eliezer ben R' Shimon who holds that the *Omer* is invalid if not reaped on the night of the sixteenth. Thus reaping the *Omer* has a specific time mandated by the Torah, (*Gem.*).

השכמת הבוקר

A Jew should wake up with gratitude to God for having restored his faculties and with a lionlike resolve to serve his Creator. Before getting off the bed or commencing any other conversation or activity, he declares his gratitude:

מוֹדֶה אֲנִי לְפָנֶיךָ,* מֶלֶךְ חַי וְקַיָּם, שֶׁהֶחֱזַרְתָּ בִּי נִשְׁמָתִי בְּחֶמְלָה — רַבָּה אֱמוּנָתֶךָ.

Wash the hands according to the ritual procedure: pick up the vessel of water with the right hand, pass it to the left, and pour water over the right. Then with the right hand pour over the left. Follow this procedure until water has been poured over each hand three times. Then, recite:

רֵאשִׁית חָכְמָה יִרְאַת יהוה, שֵׂכֶל טוֹב לְכָל עֹשֵׂיהֶם, תְּהִלָּתוֹ עֹמֶדֶת לָעַד.[1] בָּרוּךְ שֵׁם כְּבוֹד מַלְכוּתוֹ לְעוֹלָם וָעֶד.

לבישת ציצית

Hold the *tallis kattan* in readiness to put on, inspect the *tzitzis* (see commentary) and recite the following blessing. Then don the *tallis kattan* and kiss the *tzitzis*. One who wears a *tallis* for *Shacharis* does not recite this blessing (see commentary).

בָּרוּךְ אַתָּה יהוה אֱלֹהֵינוּ מֶלֶךְ הָעוֹלָם, אֲשֶׁר קִדְּשָׁנוּ בְּמִצְוֹתָיו, וְצִוָּנוּ עַל מִצְוַת צִיצִת.

יְהִי רָצוֹן מִלְּפָנֶיךָ, יהוה אֱלֹהַי וֵאלֹהֵי אֲבוֹתַי, שֶׁתְּהֵא חֲשׁוּבָה מִצְוַת צִיצִת לְפָנֶיךָ, כְּאִלּוּ קִיַּמְתִּיהָ בְּכָל פְּרָטֶיהָ וְדִקְדּוּקֶיהָ וְכַוָּנוֹתֶיהָ, וְתַרְיַ״ג מִצְוֹת הַתְּלוּיִם בָּהּ. אָמֵן סֶלָה.

עטיפת טלית

Before donning the *tallis*, inspect the *tzitzis* (see commentary) while reciting these verses:

בָּרְכִי נַפְשִׁי* אֶת יהוה, יהוה אֱלֹהַי גָּדַלְתָּ מְּאֹד, הוֹד וְהָדָר לָבָשְׁתָּ. עֹטֶה אוֹר כַּשַּׂלְמָה, נוֹטֶה שָׁמַיִם כַּיְרִיעָה.[2]

Many recite the following declaration of intent before donning the *tallis:*

לְשֵׁם יִחוּד* קֻדְשָׁא בְּרִיךְ הוּא וּשְׁכִינְתֵּהּ, בִּדְחִילוּ וּרְחִימוּ לְיַחֵד שֵׁם י״ה בְּו״ה בְּיִחוּדָא שְׁלִים, בְּשֵׁם כָּל יִשְׂרָאֵל.

הַשְׁכָּמַת הַבּוֹקֶר / UPON ARISING

מוֹדֶה אֲנִי לְפָנֶיךָ — *I gratefully thank You.* A Jew opens his eyes and thanks God for restoring his faculties to him in the morning. Then, he acknowledges that God did so in the expectation that he will serve Him, and that He is abundantly faithful to reward those who do.

לְבִישַׁת צִיצִית / DONNING THE TZITZIS

Since *tzitzis* need not be worn at night, the commandment of *tzitzis [Numbers* 15:38] is classified as a time-related *mitzvah*, and as such, is not required of women. It may be fulfilled in two ways: the *tallis kattan* (lit., small garment), worn all day, usually under the shirt; and the large *tallis*, worn during the morning prayers. Among Sephardic and German Jews, the large *tallis* is worn even by young boys, but in most Ashkenazic congregations it is worn only by one who is or has been married. Although, strictly speaking, one should recite the appropriate blessing over each garment, the custom is that one who wears a *tallis* at *Shacharis* does not recite a blessing over the *tallis kattan*. Instead, before donning the large *tallis*, he has in mind that its blessing apply to both garments.

Before donning his *tallis* or *tallis kattan*, one

UPON ARISING

A Jew should wake up with gratitude to God for having restored his faculties and with a lionlike resolve to serve his Creator. Before getting off the bed or commencing any other conversation or activity, he declares his gratitude:

מוֹדֶה אֲנִי *I gratefully thank You,* O living and eternal King, for You have returned my soul within me with compassion — abundant is Your faithfulness!*

Wash the hands according to the ritual procedure: pick up the vessel of water with the right hand, pass it to the left, and pour water over the right. Then with the right hand pour over the left. Follow this procedure until water has been poured over each hand three times. Then, recite:

רֵאשִׁית חָכְמָה *The beginning of wisdom is the fear of HASHEM — good understanding to all their practitioners; His praise endures forever.[1] Blessed is the Name of His glorious kingdom for all eternity.*

DONNING THE TZITZIS

Hold the *tallis kattan* in readiness to put on, inspect the *tzitzis* (see commentary) and recite the following blessing. Then don the *tallis kattan* and kiss the *tzitzis*. One who wears a *tallis* for *Shacharis* does not recite this blessing (see commentary).

בָּרוּךְ *Blessed are You, HASHEM, our God, King of the universe, Who has sanctified us with His commandments, and has commanded us regarding the commandment of tzitzis.*

יְהִי רָצוֹן *May it be Your will, HASHEM, my God and the God of my forefathers, that the commandment of tzitzis be as worthy before You as if I had fulfilled it in all its details, implications, and intentions, as well as the six hundred thirteen commandments that are dependent upon it. Amen, Selah!*

DONNING THE TALLIS

Before donning the *tallis*, inspect the *tzitzis* (see commentary) while reciting these verses:

בָּרְכִי נַפְשִׁי *Bless HASHEM, O my soul;* HASHEM, my God, You are very great; You have donned majesty and splendor; cloaked in light as with a garment, stretching out the heavens like a curtain.[2]*

Many recite the following declaration of intent before donning the *tallis:*

לְשֵׁם יִחוּד *For the sake of the unification* of the Holy One, Blessed is He, and His Presence, in fear and love to unify the Name* — yud-kei with vav-kei — in perfect unity, in the name of all Israel.*

(1) *Psalms* 111:10. (2) 104:1-2.

---

must examine the fringes carefully, especially at the point where the strings are looped through the holes in the corners of the garment, for if one of the strings is torn there, the *tzitzis* are invalid and the garment may not be worn.

עֲטִיפַת טַלִּית / DONNING THE TALLIS

בָּרְכִי נַפְשִׁי — *Bless ... O my soul.* Because the *tallis* symbolizes the splendor of God's commandments, we liken our wearing of it to wrapping ourselves in God's glory and brilliance.

לְשֵׁם יִחוּד — *For the sake of the unification.* This preliminary formulation serves two purposes: a statement of intent that the act about to be performed fulfills the Torah's commandment; and a prayer that the spiritual qualities of the commandment be realized. Some omit the sentence beginning לְשֵׁם יִחוּד and start from הֲרֵינִי. Others omit the entire prayer, but all agree that one should have intent to fulfill the *mitzvah*.

לְיַחֵד שֵׁם ... — *To unify the Name ...* The first half of the Divine Name, formed of the letters *yud* and *hei*, symbolizes the Attribute of Judgment, while the second half, formed of the

הֲרֵינִי מִתְעַטֵּף גּוּפִי בַּצִּיצִת, כֵּן תִּתְעַטֵּף נִשְׁמָתִי וּרְמַ״ח אֵבָרַי וּשְׁסָ״ה גִידַי* בְּאוֹר הַצִּיצִת הָעוֹלֶה תַּרְיַ״ג. וּכְשֵׁם שֶׁאֲנִי מִתְכַּסֶּה בְּטַלִּית בָּעוֹלָם הַזֶּה, כַּךְ אֶזְכֶּה לַחֲלוּקָא דְרַבָּנָן וּלְטַלִּית נָאָה לָעוֹלָם הַבָּא בְּגַן עֵדֶן. וְעַל יְדֵי מִצְוַת צִיצִת תִּנָּצֵל נַפְשִׁי וְרוּחִי וְנִשְׁמָתִי וּתְפִלָּתִי מִן הַחִיצוֹנִים. וְהַטַּלִּית יִפְרוֹשׂ כְּנָפָיו עֲלֵיהֶם וְיַצִּילֵם כְּנֶשֶׁר יָעִיר קִנּוֹ, עַל גּוֹזָלָיו יְרַחֵף.[1] וּתְהֵא חֲשׁוּבָה מִצְוַת צִיצִת לִפְנֵי הַקָּדוֹשׁ בָּרוּךְ הוּא כְּאִלּוּ קִיַּמְתִּיהָ בְּכָל פְּרָטֶיהָ וְדִקְדּוּקֶיהָ וְכַוָּנוֹתֶיהָ וְתַרְיַ״ג מִצְוֹת הַתְּלוּיִם בָּהּ. אָמֵן סֶלָה.

Unfold the *tallis*, hold it in readiness to wrap around yourself, and recite the following blessing:

בָּרוּךְ אַתָּה יהוה אֱלֹהֵינוּ מֶלֶךְ הָעוֹלָם, אֲשֶׁר קִדְּשָׁנוּ בְּמִצְוֹתָיו, וְצִוָּנוּ לְהִתְעַטֵּף בַּצִּיצִת.

Wrap the *tallis* around your head and body, then recite:

מַה יָּקָר חַסְדְּךָ אֱלֹהִים, וּבְנֵי אָדָם בְּצֵל כְּנָפֶיךָ יֶחֱסָיוּן. יִרְוְיֻן מִדֶּשֶׁן בֵּיתֶךָ, וְנַחַל עֲדָנֶיךָ תַשְׁקֵם. כִּי עִמְּךָ מְקוֹר חַיִּים, בְּאוֹרְךָ נִרְאֶה אוֹר. מְשֹׁךְ חַסְדְּךָ לְיֹדְעֶיךָ, וְצִדְקָתְךָ לְיִשְׁרֵי לֵב.[2]

Recite the following collection of verses upon entering the synagogue:

מַה טֹּבוּ אֹהָלֶיךָ* יַעֲקֹב, מִשְׁכְּנֹתֶיךָ יִשְׂרָאֵל.[3] וַאֲנִי בְּרֹב חַסְדְּךָ אָבוֹא בֵיתֶךָ, אֶשְׁתַּחֲוֶה אֶל הֵיכַל קָדְשְׁךָ בְּיִרְאָתֶךָ.[4] יהוה אָהַבְתִּי מְעוֹן בֵּיתֶךָ, וּמְקוֹם מִשְׁכַּן כְּבוֹדֶךָ.[5] וַאֲנִי אֶשְׁתַּחֲוֶה וְאֶכְרָעָה, אֶבְרְכָה לִפְנֵי יהוה עֹשִׂי.[6] וַאֲנִי, תְפִלָּתִי לְךָ יהוה, עֵת רָצוֹן, אֱלֹהִים בְּרָב חַסְדֶּךָ, עֲנֵנִי בֶּאֱמֶת יִשְׁעֶךָ.[7]

⤛ Tefillin on Chol HaMoed

There are three different customs (all halachically valid) regarding the wearing of *tefillin* on Chol HaMoed:

a) *Tefillin* are worn but the blessings usually recited upon donning them are omitted (*Taz* to *O.C.* 31:2).

b) *Tefillin* are worn and the blessings recited, but silently *(Rama)*.

c) *Tefillin* should not be worn (*Orach Chaim* 31:2 and *Vilna Gaon)*.

Mishnah Berurah advises that before putting on the *tefillin* one should stipulate mentally the following: 'If I am obligated to wear *tefillin* today, then I am donning them in fulfillment of my obligation; but if I am not obligated to wear *tefillin* today, then I do not intend to fulfill any *mitzvah* by donning them;' and that the blessing not be recited.

It is not proper for a congregation to follow contradictory customs. Thus, if one whose custom is not to wear *tefillin* during Chol HaMoed prays with a *tefillin*-wearing *minyan,* he should don *tefillin* without a blessing. Conversely, if one whose custom is to wear *tefillin* prays with a non-*tefillin*-wearing *minyan,* he should not wear his *tefillin* while praying but may don them at home before going to the synagogue (*M.B.*).

Those who wear *tefillin* customarily remove them before *Hallel.* (However, since the Torah reading of the first day Chaol HaMoed Pesach mentions the *mitzvah* of *tefillin,* on that day many people do not remove their *tefillin* until after the Torah reading.

הֲרֵינִי *I am ready to wrap my body in tzitzis, so may my soul, my two hundred forty-eight organs and my three hundred sixty-five sinews* be wrapped in the illumination of tzitzis which has the numerical value of six hundred thirteen. Just as I cover myself with a tallis in This World, so may I merit the rabbinical garb and a beautiful cloak in the World to Come in the Garden of Eden. Through the commandment of tzitzis may my life-force, spirit, soul, and prayer be rescued from the external forces. May the tallis spread its wings over them and rescue them like an eagle rousing his nest, fluttering over his eaglets.*[1] *May the commandment of tzitzis be worthy before the Holy One, Blessed is He, as if I had fulfilled it in all its details, implications, and intentions, as well as the six hundred thirteen commandments that are dependent upon it. Amen, Selah!*

Unfold the *tallis*, hold it in readiness to wrap around yourself, and recite the following blessing:

בָּרוּךְ *Blessed are You, HASHEM, our God, King of the universe, Who has sanctified us with His commandments and has commanded us to wrap ourselves in tzitzis.*

Wrap the *tallis* around your head and body, then recite:

מַה יָּקָר *How precious is Your kindness, O God! The sons of man take refuge in the shadows of Your wings. May they be sated from the abundance of Your house; and may You give them to drink from the stream of Your delights. For with You is the source of life — by Your light we shall see light. Extend Your kindness to those who know You, and Your charity to the upright of heart.*[2]

Recite the following collection of verses upon entering the synagogue:

מַה טֹּבוּ *How goodly are your tents,* O Jacob, your dwelling places, O Israel.*[3] *As for me, through Your abundant kindness I will enter Your House; I will prostrate myself toward Your Holy Sanctuary in awe of You.*[4] *O HASHEM, I love the House where You dwell, and the place where Your glory resides.*[5] *I shall prostrate myself and bow, I shall kneel before HASHEM my Maker.*[6] *As for me, may my prayer to You, HASHEM, be at an opportune time; O God, in Your abundant kindness, answer me with the truth of Your salvation.*[7]

(1) *Deuteronomy* 32:11. (2) *Psalms* 36:8-11. (3) *Numbers* 24:5.
(4) *Psalms* 5:8. (5) 26:8. (6) Cf. 95:6. (7) 69:14.

---

letters *vav* and *hei*, symbolizes the Attribute of Mercy. The blend of both attributes leads to His desired goal for Creation. Since these letters form the sacred Four-Letter Name that is not to be uttered as it is spelled, and since many authorities maintain that this prohibition extends even to uttering the four letters of the Name, the commonly used pronunciation of these letters in the לְשֵׁם יִחוּד prayer is *yud-kei b'vav kei.*

רְמַ״ח אֵבָרַי וּשְׁסָ״ה גִידַי — *My two hundred forty-eight organs and my three hundred sixty-five sinews.* The Sages' computation of the important organs, two hundred forty-eight, is equal to the number of positive commandments, while the three hundred sixty-five sinews equal the number of negative commandments. This symbolizes the principle that man was created to perform God's will. The total number of sinews and organs in man, and the total of Divine commandments, are each six hundred thirteen.

☙ מַה טֹּבוּ אֹהָלֶיךָ — *How goodly are your tents.* The Sages interpret this praise of Israel as a reference to its 'tents of learning and prayer.' In a deeper sense, the Jewish home achieves its highest level when it incorporates the values of the synagogue and study hall. This collection of verses expresses love and reverence for the synagogue that, in the absence of the Holy Temple, is *the place where God's glory resides* among Israel.

אֲדוֹן עוֹלָם* אֲשֶׁר מָלַךְ, בְּטֶרֶם כָּל יְצִיר נִבְרָא.
לְעֵת נַעֲשָׂה בְחֶפְצוֹ כֹּל, אֲזַי מֶלֶךְ שְׁמוֹ נִקְרָא.
וְאַחֲרֵי כִּכְלוֹת הַכֹּל, לְבַדּוֹ יִמְלוֹךְ נוֹרָא.
וְהוּא הָיָה וְהוּא הֹוֶה, וְהוּא יִהְיֶה בְּתִפְאָרָה.
וְהוּא אֶחָד וְאֵין שֵׁנִי, לְהַמְשִׁיל לוֹ לְהַחְבִּירָה.
בְּלִי רֵאשִׁית בְּלִי תַכְלִית, וְלוֹ הָעֹז וְהַמִּשְׂרָה.
וְהוּא אֵלִי וְחַי גֹּאֲלִי, וְצוּר חֶבְלִי בְּעֵת צָרָה.
וְהוּא נִסִּי וּמָנוֹס לִי, מְנָת כּוֹסִי בְּיוֹם אֶקְרָא.
בְּיָדוֹ אַפְקִיד רוּחִי, בְּעֵת אִישַׁן וְאָעִירָה.
וְעִם רוּחִי גְּוִיָּתִי, יהוה לִי וְלֹא אִירָא.

יִגְדַּל אֱלֹהִים חַי* וְיִשְׁתַּבַּח, נִמְצָא וְאֵין עֵת אֶל מְצִיאוּתוֹ.*
אֶחָד וְאֵין יָחִיד כְּיִחוּדוֹ, נֶעְלָם וְגַם אֵין סוֹף לְאַחְדּוּתוֹ.
אֵין לוֹ דְּמוּת הַגּוּף וְאֵינוֹ גוּף,* לֹא נַעֲרוֹךְ אֵלָיו קְדֻשָּׁתוֹ.
קַדְמוֹן לְכָל דָּבָר אֲשֶׁר נִבְרָא, רִאשׁוֹן וְאֵין רֵאשִׁית לְרֵאשִׁיתוֹ.
הִנּוֹ אֲדוֹן עוֹלָם* לְכָל נוֹצָר, יוֹרֶה גְדֻלָּתוֹ וּמַלְכוּתוֹ.
שֶׁפַע נְבוּאָתוֹ* נְתָנוֹ, אֶל אַנְשֵׁי סְגֻלָּתוֹ וְתִפְאַרְתּוֹ.
לֹא קָם בְּיִשְׂרָאֵל כְּמֹשֶׁה* עוֹד, נָבִיא וּמַבִּיט אֶת תְּמוּנָתוֹ.
תּוֹרַת אֱמֶת* נָתַן לְעַמּוֹ אֵל, עַל יַד נְבִיאוֹ נֶאֱמַן בֵּיתוֹ.
לֹא יַחֲלִיף הָאֵל וְלֹא יָמִיר דָּתוֹ, לְעוֹלָמִים לְזוּלָתוֹ.
צוֹפֶה וְיוֹדֵעַ סְתָרֵינוּ, מַבִּיט לְסוֹף דָּבָר בְּקַדְמָתוֹ.
גּוֹמֵל לְאִישׁ חֶסֶד כְּמִפְעָלוֹ, נוֹתֵן לְרָשָׁע רָע כְּרִשְׁעָתוֹ.
יִשְׁלַח לְקֵץ הַיָּמִין מְשִׁיחֵנוּ, לִפְדּוֹת מְחַכֵּי קֵץ יְשׁוּעָתוֹ.
מֵתִים יְחַיֶּה אֵל בְּרֹב חַסְדּוֹ, בָּרוּךְ עֲדֵי עַד שֵׁם תְּהִלָּתוֹ.

אֲדוֹן עוֹלָם — *Master of the universe.* This inspiring song of praise is attributed to R' Shlomo ibn Gabirol, one of the greatest early *paytanim* [liturgical poets], who flourished in the eleventh century. The daily prayer service is inaugurated with the Name אָדוֹן to recall the merit of Abraham, the first one to address God with this title [*Genesis* 15:2] (*Etz Yosef*), and the one who instituted the morning prayers [*Berachos* 26b] (*Vilna Gaon*).

The song emphasizes that God is timeless, infinite and omnipotent. Mankind can offer Him only one thing: to proclaim Him as King, by doing His will and praising Him. Despite God's greatness, however, He involves Himself with man's personal needs in time of pain and distress. The prayer concludes on the inspiring note that, lofty though He is, *HASHEM is with me, I shall not fear.*

יִגְדַּל אֱלֹהִים חַי — *Exalted be the Living God.* This song of uncertain authorship summarizes the 'Thirteen Principles of Faith' expounded by *Rambam* in his *Commentary to Mishnah*, ch. 10, and stated succinctly in the famous *Ani Maamin* prayer. They comprise the basic principles that every Jew is required to believe. In *Rambam's* view, to deny any of them constitutes heresy.

וְאֵין עֵת אֶל מְצִיאוּתוֹ — *Unbounded by time is His existence.* If God's existence were timebound, it would be no different in kind from that of any living, but not eternal, being. *Rambam* comments that the principle of God's timelessness, with neither beginning or end, implies that

אֲדוֹן עוֹלָם *Master of the universe,* Who reigned*
before any form was created,
At the time when His will brought all into being —
then as 'King' was His Name proclaimed.
After all has ceased to be, He, the Awesome One, will reign alone.
It is He Who was, He Who is, and He Who shall remain, in splendor.
He is One — there is no second to compare to Him, to declare as His equal.
Without beginning, without conclusion — His is the power and dominion.
He is my God, my living Redeemer, Rock of my pain in time of distress.
He is my banner, a refuge for me, the portion in my cup on the day I call.
Into His hand I shall entrust my spirit when I go to sleep — and I shall awaken!
With my spirit shall my body remain. HASHEM *is with me, I shall not fear.*

יִגְדַּל *Exalted be the Living God* and praised,*
*He exists — unbounded by time is His existence.**
He is One — and there is no unity like His Oneness.
Inscrutable and infinite is His Oneness.
*He has no semblance of a body nor is He corporeal;**
nor has His holiness any comparison.
He preceded every being that was created —
the First, and nothing precedes His precedence.
Behold! He is Master of the universe to every creature,*
He demonstrates His greatness and His sovereignty.
*He granted His flow of prophecy**
to His treasured splendrous people.
In Israel none like Moses arose again —*
a prophet who perceived His vision clearly.
*God gave His people a Torah of truth,**
by means of His prophet, the most trusted of His household.
God will never amend nor exchange His law
for any other one, for all eternity.
He scrutinizes and knows our hiddenmost secrets;
He perceives a matter's outcome at its inception.
He recompenses man with kindness according to his deed;
He places evil on the wicked according to his wickedness.
By the End of Days He will send our Messiah,
to redeem those longing for His final salvation.
God will revive the dead in His abundant kindness —
Blessed forever is His praised Name.

He cannot be dependent in any way on any other being: the timebound is inherently inferior to the timeless. Nothing can exist without God, but He depends on no one and on nothing.

וְאֵינוֹ גוּף — *Nor is He corporeal.* God has no physicality, not even that of invisible, intangible angels.

הִנּוֹ אֲדוֹן עוֹלָם — *Behold! He is Master of the universe.* Because He is absolute Master, there is nothing else to which prayers may be directed.

שֶׁפַע נְבוּאָתוֹ — *His flow of prophecy.* Judaism depends on the principle that God, through His prophets, revealed His will to Israel.

כְּמֹשֶׁה — *Like Moses.* It is necessary to acknowledge that Moses' prophecy is unparalleled; otherwise another 'prophet' could conceivably challenge or amend it, thus challenging the authenticity of the Torah.

תּוֹרַת אֱמֶת — *A Torah of truth.* God gave Moses not only the Written Law, but the Oral Law as well. Neither can be complete without the other, and *Torah of truth* is a term that includes both.

ברכות השחר

Although many hold that the blessing עַל נְטִילַת יָדָיִם should be recited immediately after the ritual washing of the hands upon arising, others customarily recite it at this point. Similarly, some recite אֲשֶׁר יָצַר immediately after relieving themselves in the morning, while others recite it here.

בָּרוּךְ אַתָּה יהוה אֱלֹהֵינוּ מֶלֶךְ הָעוֹלָם, אֲשֶׁר קִדְּשָׁנוּ בְּמִצְוֹתָיו, וְצִוָּנוּ עַל נְטִילַת יָדָיִם.*

בָּרוּךְ אַתָּה יהוה אֱלֹהֵינוּ מֶלֶךְ הָעוֹלָם, אֲשֶׁר יָצַר אֶת הָאָדָם בְּחָכְמָה,* וּבָרָא בוֹ נְקָבִים נְקָבִים, חֲלוּלִים* חֲלוּלִים. גָּלוּי וְיָדוּעַ לִפְנֵי כִסֵּא כְבוֹדֶךָ, שֶׁאִם יִפָּתֵחַ אֶחָד מֵהֶם, אוֹ יִסָּתֵם אֶחָד מֵהֶם, אִי אֶפְשַׁר לְהִתְקַיֵּם וְלַעֲמוֹד לְפָנֶיךָ. בָּרוּךְ אַתָּה יהוה, רוֹפֵא כָל בָּשָׂר וּמַפְלִיא לַעֲשׂוֹת.*

At this point, some recite אֱלֹהַי נְשָׁמָה (p. 196).

ברכות התורה

It is forbidden to study or recite Torah passages before reciting the following blessings. Since the commandment to study Torah is in effect all day long, these blessings need not be repeated if one studies at various times of the day. Although many *siddurim* begin a new paragraph at וְהַעֲרֶב נָא, according to the vast majority of commentators the first blessing does not end until לְעַמּוֹ יִשְׂרָאֵל.

בָּרוּךְ אַתָּה יהוה אֱלֹהֵינוּ מֶלֶךְ הָעוֹלָם, אֲשֶׁר קִדְּשָׁנוּ בְּמִצְוֹתָיו, וְצִוָּנוּ לַעֲסוֹק בְּדִבְרֵי תוֹרָה. וְהַעֲרֶב נָא יהוה אֱלֹהֵינוּ אֶת דִּבְרֵי תוֹרָתְךָ בְּפִינוּ וּבְפִי עַמְּךָ בֵּית יִשְׂרָאֵל. וְנִהְיֶה אֲנַחְנוּ וְצֶאֱצָאֵינוּ וְצֶאֱצָאֵי עַמְּךָ בֵּית יִשְׂרָאֵל, כֻּלָּנוּ יוֹדְעֵי שְׁמֶךָ וְלוֹמְדֵי תוֹרָתֶךָ לִשְׁמָהּ.* בָּרוּךְ אַתָּה יהוה, הַמְלַמֵּד תּוֹרָה לְעַמּוֹ יִשְׂרָאֵל.

בָּרוּךְ אַתָּה יהוה אֱלֹהֵינוּ מֶלֶךְ הָעוֹלָם, אֲשֶׁר בָּחַר בָּנוּ מִכָּל הָעַמִּים וְנָתַן לָנוּ אֶת תּוֹרָתוֹ. בָּרוּךְ אַתָּה יהוה, נוֹתֵן הַתּוֹרָה.

במדבר ו:כד-כו

יְבָרֶכְךָ יהוה וְיִשְׁמְרֶךָ. יָאֵר יהוה פָּנָיו אֵלֶיךָ וִיחֻנֶּךָּ. יִשָּׂא יהוה פָּנָיו אֵלֶיךָ, וְיָשֵׂם לְךָ שָׁלוֹם.

ברכות השחר / MORNING BLESSINGS

עַל נְטִילַת יָדָיִם — *Regarding washing the hands.* In the case of blessings, the general rule is that they should be recited in conjunction with the acts to which they apply. Nevertheless, some postpone the blessings עַל נְטִילַת יָדָיִם for washing the hands and אֲשֶׁר יָצַר for relieving oneself so that they will be recited as part of *Shacharis* (see *Mishnah Berurah* 4:4 and 6:9).

אֲשֶׁר יָצַר אֶת הָאָדָם בְּחָכְמָה — *Who fashioned man with wisdom.* This phrase has two meanings: (a) When God created man, He gave him the gift of wisdom; and (b) God used wisdom when He created man, as is demonstrated in the precise balance of his organs and functions.

נְקָבִים, חֲלוּלִים — *Openings and . . . cavities.* The mouth, nostrils, and other orifices are the *openings* that lead in and out of the body. The *cavities* are the inner hollows that contain such organs as the lungs, heart, stomach, and brain.

וּמַפְלִיא לַעֲשׂוֹת — *And acts wondrously.* The delicate balance of the organs is a wonder of wonders *(Beis Yosef);* alternatively, it is

MORNING BLESSINGS

Although many hold that the blessing עַל נְטִילַת יָדָיִם, '*. . .regarding washing the hands,*' should be recited immediately after the ritual washing of the hands upon arising, others customarily recite it at this point. Similarly, some recite אֲשֶׁר יָצַר, *'Who fashioned . . .,'* immediately after relieving themselves in the morning, while others recite it here.

בָּרוּךְ *Blessed are You, HASHEM, our God, King of the universe, Who has sanctified us with His commandments and has commanded us regarding washing the hands.**

בָּרוּךְ *Blessed are You, HASHEM, our God, King of the universe, Who fashioned man with wisdom* and created within him many openings and many cavities.* It is obvious and known before Your Throne of Glory that if but one of them were to be ruptured or but one of them were to be blocked it would be impossible to survive and to stand before You. Blessed are You, HASHEM, Who heals all flesh and acts wondrously.**

At this point, some recite אֱלֹהַי נְשָׁמָה, *'My God, the soul . . .'* (p. 196).

BLESSINGS OF THE TORAH

It is forbidden to study or recite Torah passages before reciting the following blessings. Since the commandment to study Torah is in effect all day long, these blessings need not be repeated if one studies at various times of the day. Although many *siddurim* begin a new paragraph at וְהַעֲרֶב נָא, *'Please, HASHEM,'* according to the vast majority of commentators the first blessing does not end until לְעַמּוֹ יִשְׂרָאֵל, *'. . . His people Israel.'*

בָּרוּךְ *Blessed are You, HASHEM, our God, King of the universe, Who has sanctified us with His commandments and has commanded us to engross ourselves in the words of Torah. Please, HASHEM, our God, sweeten the words of Your Torah in our mouth and in the mouth of Your people, the family of Israel. May we and our offspring and the offspring of Your people, the House of Israel — all of us — know Your Name and study Your Torah for its own sake.* Blessed are You, HASHEM, Who teaches Torah to His people Israel.*

בָּרוּךְ *Blessed are You, HASHEM, our God, King of the universe, Who selected us from all the peoples and gave us His Torah. Blessed are You, HASHEM, Giver of the Torah.*

Numbers 6:24-26

יְבָרֶכְךָ *May HASHEM bless you and safeguard you. May HASHEM illuminate His countenance for you and be gracious to you. May HASHEM turn His countenance to you and establish peace for you.*

---

wondrous that the spiritual soul fuses with the physical body to create a human being *(Rama)*.

בִּרְכוֹת הַתּוֹרָה / Blessings of the Torah

As stated explicitly in the Talmudic selection[אֵלּוּ דְבָרִים] at the conclusion of these blessings, the study of Torah is the paramount commandment. Without it, man cannot know God's will; with it, he can penetrate the wisdom of the Creator Himself. Each part of the blessings expresses a different idea. The first, אֲשֶׁר קִדְּשָׁנוּ, *Who has sanctified us,* applies to the commandments; the second, וְהַעֲרֶב נָא, *Please . . . sweeten,* is a prayer; the third, אֲשֶׁר בָּחַר בָּנוּ, *Who selected us,* is an expression of thanks for the gift of the Torah.

לִשְׁמָהּ — *For its own sake.* May we study Torah for no other reason than to know it and become imbued with its wisdom.

Selections from the Written and Oral Torah

Whenever a blessing is recited for a *mitzvah,* the *mitzvah* must be performed immediately. Having recited the blessings for the study of Torah, we immediately recite selections from

משנה, פאה א:א

אֵלּוּ דְבָרִים שֶׁאֵין לָהֶם שִׁעוּר:* הַפֵּאָה וְהַבִּכּוּרִים וְהָרֵאָיוֹן* וּגְמִילוּת חֲסָדִים וְתַלְמוּד תּוֹרָה.

שבת קכז.

אֵלּוּ דְבָרִים שֶׁאָדָם אוֹכֵל פֵּרוֹתֵיהֶם בָּעוֹלָם הַזֶּה וְהַקֶּרֶן קַיֶּמֶת לוֹ* לָעוֹלָם הַבָּא. וְאֵלּוּ הֵן: כִּבּוּד אָב וָאֵם, וּגְמִילוּת חֲסָדִים, וְהַשְׁכָּמַת בֵּית הַמִּדְרָשׁ שַׁחֲרִית וְעַרְבִית, וְהַכְנָסַת אוֹרְחִים, וּבִקּוּר חוֹלִים, וְהַכְנָסַת כַּלָּה, וּלְוָיַת הַמֵּת, וְעִיּוּן תְּפִלָּה, וַהֲבָאַת שָׁלוֹם בֵּין אָדָם לַחֲבֵרוֹ – וְתַלְמוּד תּוֹרָה כְּנֶגֶד כֻּלָּם.

אֱלֹהַי, נְשָׁמָה* שֶׁנָּתַתָּ בִּי טְהוֹרָה הִיא. אַתָּה בְרָאתָהּ אַתָּה יְצַרְתָּהּ, אַתָּה נְפַחְתָּהּ בִּי, וְאַתָּה מְשַׁמְּרָהּ בְּקִרְבִּי, וְאַתָּה עָתִיד לִטְּלָהּ מִמֶּנִּי, וּלְהַחֲזִירָהּ בִּי לֶעָתִיד לָבֹא. כָּל זְמַן שֶׁהַנְּשָׁמָה בְקִרְבִּי, מוֹדֶה אֲנִי לְפָנֶיךָ, יהוה אֱלֹהַי וֵאלֹהֵי אֲבוֹתַי, רִבּוֹן כָּל הַמַּעֲשִׂים, אֲדוֹן כָּל הַנְּשָׁמוֹת. בָּרוּךְ אַתָּה יהוה, הַמַּחֲזִיר נְשָׁמוֹת לִפְגָרִים מֵתִים.

The *chazzan* recites the following blessings aloud, and the congregation responds אָמֵן to each blessing. Nevertheless, each person must recite these blessings for himself. Some people recite the blessings aloud for one another so that each one can have the merit of responding אָמֵן many times (see commentary).

בָּרוּךְ אַתָּה יהוה אֱלֹהֵינוּ מֶלֶךְ הָעוֹלָם, אֲשֶׁר נָתַן לַשֶּׂכְוִי בִינָה[1]* לְהַבְחִין בֵּין יוֹם וּבֵין לָיְלָה.

בָּרוּךְ אַתָּה יהוה אֱלֹהֵינוּ מֶלֶךְ הָעוֹלָם, שֶׁלֹּא עָשַׂנִי גּוֹי.*

בָּרוּךְ אַתָּה יהוה אֱלֹהֵינוּ מֶלֶךְ הָעוֹלָם, שֶׁלֹּא עָשַׂנִי עָבֶד.*

Men say:

בָּרוּךְ אַתָּה יהוה אֱלֹהֵינוּ מֶלֶךְ הָעוֹלָם, שֶׁלֹּא עָשַׂנִי אִשָּׁה.*

Women say:

בָּרוּךְ אַתָּה יהוה אֱלֹהֵינוּ מֶלֶךְ הָעוֹלָם, שֶׁעָשַׂנִי כִּרְצוֹנוֹ.

---

both the Written and Oral Torah. First we recite the Scriptural verses of the Priestly Blessings, then a Talmudic selection from the *Mishnah* [אֵלּוּ דְבָרִים שֶׁאֵין] (*Peah* 1:1) and *Gemara* [אֵלּוּ דְבָרִים שֶׁאָדָם] (*Shabbos* 127a). The Talmudic selection discusses the reward for various commandments and concludes with the declaration that Torah study is equivalent to them all, an appropriate addendum to the Blessings of the Torah.

אֵלּוּ דְבָרִים שֶׁאֵין לָהֶם שִׁעוּר ☙ — *These are the precepts that have no prescribed measure.* The Torah does not prescribe how much is involved in the performance of the following commandments *(Rav).*

וְהָרֵאָיוֹן — *The pilgrimage.* Though the Torah ordains that a Jew visit the Temple on each of the three festivals (Pesach, Shavuos, and Succos), one may visit as often as he wishes. Alternatively, there is no set amount for the value of the elevation-offering [עוֹלַת רְאִיָּה] that one must bring at such times.

וְהַקֶּרֶן קַיֶּמֶת לוֹ — *But whose principal remains intact for him.* Though one is rewarded for these *mitzvos* in This World, his reward in the World to Come is not diminished.

Mishnah, *Peah* 1:1

אֵלּוּ דְבָרִים *These are the precepts that have no prescribed measure:* the corner of a field [which must be left for the poor], the first-fruit offering, the pilgrimage,* acts of kindness, and Torah study.*

Talmud, *Shabbos* 127a

אֵלּוּ דְבָרִים *These are the precepts whose fruits a person enjoys in This World but whose principal remains intact for him* in the World to Come. They are: the honor due to father and mother, acts of kindness, early attendance at the house of study morning and evening, hospitality to guests, visiting the sick, providing for a bride, escorting the dead, absorption in prayer, bringing peace between man and his fellow — and the study of Torah is equivalent to them all.*

אֱלֹהַי *My God, the soul* You placed within me is pure. You created it, You fashioned it, You breathed it into me, You safeguard it within me, and eventually You will take it from me, and restore it to me in Time to Come. As long as the soul is within me, I gratefully thank You, HASHEM, my God and the God of my forefathers, Master of all works, Lord of all souls. Blessed are You, HASHEM, Who restores souls to dead bodies.*

The *chazzan* recites the following blessings aloud, and the congregation responds *'Amen'* to each blessing. Nevertheless, each person must recite these blessings for himself. Some people recite the blessings aloud for one another so that each one can have the merit of responding *Amen* many times (see commentary).

בָּרוּךְ *Blessed are You, HASHEM, our God, King of the universe, Who gave the heart understanding*[1] to distinguish between day and night.*

*Blessed are You, HASHEM, our God, King of the universe, for not having made me a gentile.**

*Blessed are You, HASHEM, our God, King of the universe, for not having made me a slave.**

Men say:	Women say:
*Blessed are You, HASHEM, our God, King of the universe, for not having made me a woman.**	*Blessed are You, HASHEM, our God, King of the universe, for having made me according to His will.*

(1) Cf. *Job* 38:36.

אֱלֹהַי, נְשָׁמָה — *My God, the soul* ... This prayerful blessing is an expression of gratitude to God for restoring our vitality in the morning with a soul of pure, celestial origin, and for maintaining us in life and health.

בָּרוּךְ ... אֲשֶׁר נָתַן לַשֶּׂכְוִי בִינָה — *Blessed ... Who gave the heart understanding.* The word שֶׂכְוִי means both *heart* and *rooster.* In the context of this blessing, both meanings are implied: the rooster crows, but man's heart reacts and understands how to deal with new situations *(Rosh).*

שֶׁלֹּא עָשַׂנִי גּוֹי ... עָבֶד ... אִשָּׁה — *For not having made me a gentile ... a slave ... a woman.* The Torah assigns missions to respective groups of people. Within Israel, for example, the Davidic family, *Kohanim,* and Levites are set apart by virtue of their particular callings, in addition to their shared mission as Jews. All such missions carry extra responsibilities and call for the performance of the *mitzvos* associated with them. We thank God, therefore, for the challenge of improving His universe in accordance with

בָּרוּךְ אַתָּה יהוה אֱלֹהֵינוּ מֶלֶךְ הָעוֹלָם, פּוֹקֵחַ עִוְרִים.[1]
בָּרוּךְ אַתָּה יהוה אֱלֹהֵינוּ מֶלֶךְ הָעוֹלָם, מַלְבִּישׁ עֲרֻמִּים.
בָּרוּךְ אַתָּה יהוה אֱלֹהֵינוּ מֶלֶךְ הָעוֹלָם, מַתִּיר אֲסוּרִים.[2]
בָּרוּךְ אַתָּה יהוה אֱלֹהֵינוּ מֶלֶךְ הָעוֹלָם, זוֹקֵף כְּפוּפִים.[1]
בָּרוּךְ אַתָּה יהוה אֱלֹהֵינוּ מֶלֶךְ הָעוֹלָם, רוֹקַע הָאָרֶץ עַל הַמָּיִם.*[3]
בָּרוּךְ אַתָּה יהוה אֱלֹהֵינוּ מֶלֶךְ הָעוֹלָם, שֶׁעָשָׂה לִי כָּל צָרְכִּי.
בָּרוּךְ אַתָּה יהוה אֱלֹהֵינוּ מֶלֶךְ הָעוֹלָם, הַמֵּכִין מִצְעֲדֵי גָבֶר.[4]
בָּרוּךְ אַתָּה יהוה אֱלֹהֵינוּ מֶלֶךְ הָעוֹלָם, אוֹזֵר יִשְׂרָאֵל בִּגְבוּרָה.
בָּרוּךְ אַתָּה יהוה אֱלֹהֵינוּ מֶלֶךְ הָעוֹלָם, עוֹטֵר יִשְׂרָאֵל בְּתִפְאָרָה.
בָּרוּךְ אַתָּה יהוה אֱלֹהֵינוּ מֶלֶךְ הָעוֹלָם, הַנּוֹתֵן לַיָּעֵף כֹּחַ.[5]

Although many *siddurim* begin a new paragraph at וִיהִי רָצוֹן, the following is one long blessing that ends at לְעַמּוֹ יִשְׂרָאֵל.

בָּרוּךְ אַתָּה יהוה אֱלֹהֵינוּ מֶלֶךְ הָעוֹלָם, הַמַּעֲבִיר שֵׁנָה מֵעֵינָי וּתְנוּמָה מֵעַפְעַפָּי. וִיהִי רָצוֹן* מִלְּפָנֶיךָ, יהוה אֱלֹהֵינוּ וֵאלֹהֵי אֲבוֹתֵינוּ,* שֶׁתַּרְגִּילֵנוּ בְּתוֹרָתֶךָ וְדַבְּקֵנוּ בְּמִצְוֹתֶיךָ, וְאַל תְּבִיאֵנוּ לֹא לִידֵי חֵטְא, וְלֹא לִידֵי עֲבֵרָה וְעָוֹן, וְלֹא לִידֵי נִסָּיוֹן, וְלֹא לִידֵי בִזָּיוֹן, וְאַל תַּשְׁלֶט בָּנוּ יֵצֶר הָרָע. וְהַרְחִיקֵנוּ מֵאָדָם רָע וּמֵחָבֵר רָע. וְדַבְּקֵנוּ בְּיֵצֶר הַטּוֹב וּבְמַעֲשִׂים טוֹבִים, וְכוֹף אֶת יִצְרֵנוּ לְהִשְׁתַּעְבֶּד לָךְ. וּתְנֵנוּ הַיּוֹם וּבְכָל יוֹם לְחֵן וּלְחֶסֶד וּלְרַחֲמִים בְּעֵינֶיךָ, וּבְעֵינֵי כָל רוֹאֵינוּ, וְתִגְמְלֵנוּ חֲסָדִים טוֹבִים. בָּרוּךְ אַתָּה יהוה, גּוֹמֵל חֲסָדִים טוֹבִים לְעַמּוֹ יִשְׂרָאֵל.

His will. Male, free Jews have responsibilities and duties not shared by others. For this, they express gratitude that, unlike women, they were *not* freed from the obligation to perform the time-related commandments. This follows the Talmudic dictum that an obligatory performance of a *mitzvah* is superior to a voluntary one, because it is human nature to resist obligations [גָּדוֹל הַמְצֻוֶּה וְעוֹשֶׂה מִמִּי שֶׁאֵינוֹ מְצֻוֶּה וְעוֹשֶׂה]. Women, on the other hand, both historically and because of their nature, are the guardians of tradition, the molders of character, children, and family. Furthermore, women have often been the protectors of Judaism when the impetuosity and aggressiveness of the male nature led the men astray. The classic precedent was in the Wilderness when men — not women — worshiped the Golden Calf. Thus, though women were not given the privilege of the challenge assigned to men, they are created closer to God's ideal of satisfaction. They express their gratitude in the blessing שֶׁעָשַׂנִי כִּרְצוֹנוֹ, *for having made me according to His will* (*R' Munk*).

רוֹקַע הָאָרֶץ עַל הַמָּיִם — *Who spreads out the earth upon the water.* By nature, water spreads and floods everything in its path, while earth tends to sink beneath the surface of the water. God formed the earth so that it remains always in place (*Radak*).

וִיהִי רָצוֹן — *And may it be Your will.* When a person starts off well, his chances for future success are enhanced immeasurably. Having thanked God for giving us new life, health, and vigor at the start of a new day, we pray that He provide us the conditions to serve Him and that He remove impediments to His service (*Siach Yitzchak*).

וֵאלֹהֵי אֲבוֹתֵינוּ — *And the God of our forefathers.* As is common in prayers, we call upon God as *the God of our forefathers,* because we wish to identify with the merit of our righteous forebears (*Etz Yosef*).

The above series of fifteen blessings is based on *Berachos* 60b, where the Sages teach that as one experiences the phenomena of the new day,

Blessed are You, HASHEM, our God, King of the universe, Who gives sight to the blind.[1]

Blessed are You, HASHEM, our God, King of the universe, Who clothes the naked.

Blessed are You, HASHEM, our God, King of the universe, Who releases the bound.[2]

Blessed are You, HASHEM, our God, King of the universe, Who straightens the bent.[1]

*Blessed are You, HASHEM, our God, King of the universe, Who spreads out the earth upon the waters.**[3]

Blessed are You, HASHEM, our God, King of the universe, Who has provided me my every need.

Blessed are You, HASHEM, our God, King of the universe, Who firms man's footsteps.[4]

Blessed are You, HASHEM, our God, King of the universe, Who girds Israel with strength.

Blessed are You, HASHEM, our God, King of the universe, Who crowns Israel with splendor.

Blessed are You, HASHEM, our God, King of the universe, Who gives strength to the weary.[5]

Although many *siddurim* begin a new paragraph at וִיהִי רָצוֹן, *'And may it be Your will,'* the following is one long blessing that ends at לְעַמּוֹ יִשְׂרָאֵל, *'. . . His people Israel.'*

בָּרוּךְ *Blessed are You, HASHEM, our God, King of the universe, Who removes sleep from my eyes and slumber from my eyelids. And may it be Your will,* HASHEM, our God, and the God of our forefathers,* that You accustom us to [study] Your Torah and attach us to Your commandments. Do not bring us into the power of error, nor into the power of transgression and sin, nor into the power of challenge, nor into the power of scorn. Let not the Evil Inclination dominate us. Distance us from an evil person and an evil companion. Attach us to the Good Inclination and to good deeds and compel our Evil Inclination to be subservient to You. Grant us today and every day grace, kindness, and mercy in Your eyes and in the eyes of all who see us, and bestow beneficent kindnesses upon us. Blessed are You, HASHEM, Who bestows beneficent kindnesses upon His people Israel.*

(1) *Psalms* 146:8. (2) v. 7. (3) Cf. 136:6. (4) Cf. 37:23. (5) *Isaiah* 40:29.

---

he should bless God for providing them. For example, one thanks God for giving man the crucial ability to make distinctions in life, such as that between day and night; when he rubs his eyes and sees; when he gets dressed, and so on. Some of these phenomena are not so obvious from the text of the blessing. Among them are: sitting up and stretching *[releases the bound]*; getting out of bed *[straightens the bent]*; standing on the floor *[spreads out the earth . . .]*; donning shoes which symbolizes man's ability to go on his way comfortably *[provided me my every need]*; setting out on one's destination *[firms . . . footsteps]*; fastening one's clothing *[girds Israel . . .]*; putting on a hat, which symbolizes the Jew's reminder that Someone is above him *[crowns Israel . . .]*; feeling the passing of nighttime exhaustion *[gives strength . . .* and *removes sleep . . .]*.

Arizal teaches that each day a righteous person should endeavor to respond to a minimum of ninety blessings, four times *Kedushah* (i.e., the verse קָדוֹשׁ קָדוֹשׁ קָדוֹשׁ, *Holy, Holy, Holy . . .*), ten times *Kaddish*, and to recite no less than one hundred blessings. These figures are alluded to by the letters of the word

יְהִי רָצוֹן* מִלְּפָנֶיךָ, יהוה אֱלֹהַי וֵאלֹהֵי אֲבוֹתַי, שֶׁתַּצִּילֵנִי הַיּוֹם וּבְכָל יוֹם מֵעַזֵּי פָנִים וּמֵעַזּוּת פָּנִים, מֵאָדָם רָע, וּמֵחָבֵר רָע, וּמִשָּׁכֵן רָע, וּמִפֶּגַע רָע, וּמִשָּׂטָן הַמַּשְׁחִית, מִדִּין קָשֶׁה וּמִבַּעַל דִּין קָשֶׁה, בֵּין שֶׁהוּא בֶן בְּרִית,* וּבֵין שֶׁאֵינוֹ בֶן בְּרִית.

עקדה

Some omit the following paragraph on the Sabbath and Yom Tov.

אֱלֹהֵינוּ* וֵאלֹהֵי אֲבוֹתֵינוּ, זָכְרֵנוּ בְּזִכָּרוֹן טוֹב לְפָנֶיךָ, וּפָקְדֵנוּ בִּפְקֻדַּת יְשׁוּעָה וְרַחֲמִים מִשְּׁמֵי שְׁמֵי קֶדֶם. וּזְכָר לָנוּ יהוה אֱלֹהֵינוּ אַהֲבַת הַקַּדְמוֹנִים אַבְרָהָם יִצְחָק וְיִשְׂרָאֵל עֲבָדֶיךָ, אֶת הַבְּרִית וְאֶת הַחֶסֶד וְאֶת הַשְּׁבוּעָה שֶׁנִּשְׁבַּעְתָּ לְאַבְרָהָם אָבִינוּ בְּהַר הַמּוֹרִיָּה, וְאֶת הָעֲקֵדָה שֶׁעָקַד אֶת יִצְחָק בְּנוֹ עַל גַּבֵּי הַמִּזְבֵּחַ, כַּכָּתוּב בְּתוֹרָתֶךָ:

בראשית כב:א-יט

וַיְהִי אַחַר הַדְּבָרִים הָאֵלֶּה, וְהָאֱלֹהִים נִסָּה אֶת אַבְרָהָם, וַיֹּאמֶר אֵלָיו, אַבְרָהָם, וַיֹּאמֶר, הִנֵּנִי. וַיֹּאמֶר, קַח נָא אֶת בִּנְךָ, אֶת יְחִידְךָ, אֲשֶׁר אָהַבְתָּ, אֶת יִצְחָק, וְלֶךְ לְךָ אֶל אֶרֶץ הַמֹּרִיָּה, וְהַעֲלֵהוּ שָׁם לְעֹלָה עַל אַחַד הֶהָרִים אֲשֶׁר אֹמַר אֵלֶיךָ. וַיַּשְׁכֵּם אַבְרָהָם בַּבֹּקֶר,* וַיַּחֲבֹשׁ אֶת חֲמֹרוֹ, וַיִּקַּח אֶת שְׁנֵי נְעָרָיו* אִתּוֹ, וְאֵת יִצְחָק בְּנוֹ, וַיְבַקַּע עֲצֵי עֹלָה, וַיָּקָם וַיֵּלֶךְ אֶל הַמָּקוֹם אֲשֶׁר אָמַר לוֹ הָאֱלֹהִים. בַּיּוֹם הַשְּׁלִישִׁי, וַיִּשָּׂא אַבְרָהָם אֶת עֵינָיו, וַיַּרְא אֶת הַמָּקוֹם מֵרָחֹק. וַיֹּאמֶר אַבְרָהָם אֶל נְעָרָיו, שְׁבוּ לָכֶם פֹּה עִם הַחֲמוֹר, וַאֲנִי וְהַנַּעַר נֵלְכָה עַד כֹּה, וְנִשְׁתַּחֲוֶה וְנָשׁוּבָה* אֲלֵיכֶם. וַיִּקַּח אַבְרָהָם אֶת עֲצֵי הָעֹלָה, וַיָּשֶׂם עַל יִצְחָק בְּנוֹ, וַיִּקַּח בְּיָדוֹ אֶת הָאֵשׁ וְאֶת הַמַּאֲכֶלֶת, וַיֵּלְכוּ שְׁנֵיהֶם יַחְדָּו. וַיֹּאמֶר יִצְחָק אֶל אַבְרָהָם אָבִיו, וַיֹּאמֶר, אָבִי, וַיֹּאמֶר, הִנֶּנִּי בְנִי, וַיֹּאמֶר, הִנֵּה הָאֵשׁ

צַדִּיק, *righteous one*, which have the numerical equivalents of 90, 4, 10, and 100 respectively. To assure ninety *Amen* responses, some people recite these fifteen blessings aloud for one another.

יְהִי רָצוֹן — *May it be Your will.* This personal prayer was recited by Rabbi Yehudah HaNassi every day after *Shacharis (Berachos* 16b). It is a prayer for protection in day-to-day dealings with one's fellow men. During the recitation, one may add his personal requests for God's help during the day *(Tur)*.

בֶּן בְּרִית — *A member of the covenant*, i.e., Abraham's covenant of circumcision, the emblem of Israel's bond with God.

עֲקֵדָה / THE AKEIDAH

The *Akeidah* is the story of the most difficult challenge to Abraham's faith in God. He was commanded to sacrifice Isaac, his beloved son and sole heir, to God. Father and son jointly demonstrated their total devotion, upon which God ordered Abraham to release Isaac. The Kabbalistic masters, from *Zohar* to *Arizal*, have stressed the great importance of the daily recitation of the *Akeidah*. In response to their writings, the *Akeidah* has been incorporated into the great majority of *siddurim*, although it is not recited in all congregations. In some congregations, it is recited individually rather than as part of the public morning service. The *Zohar* records that this recitation of Abraham and Isaac's readiness to put love of God ahead of life itself is a source of heavenly mercy whenever Jewish lives are threatened. *Avodas HaKodesh* comments that the *Akeidah* should inspire us

יְהִי רָצוֹן *May it be Your will,* HASHEM, my God, and the God of my forefathers, that You rescue me today and every day from brazen men and from brazenness, from an evil man, an evil companion, an evil neighbor, an evil mishap, the destructive spiritual impediment, a harsh trial and a harsh opponent, whether he is a member of the covenant* or whether he is not a member of the covenant.*

THE AKEIDAH

Some omit the following paragraph on the Sabbath and Yom Tov.

אֱלֹהֵינוּ *Our God* and the God of our forefathers, remember us with a favorable memory before You, and recall us with a recollection of salvation and mercy from the primeval loftiest heavens. Remember on our behalf — O HASHEM, our God — the love of the Patriarchs, Abraham, Isaac and Israel, Your servants; the covenant, the kindness, and the oath that You swore to our father Abraham at Mount Moriah, and the Akeidah, when he bound his son Isaac atop the altar, as it is written in Your Torah:*

Genesis 22:1-19

וַיְהִי *And it happened after these things that God tested Abraham and said to him, 'Abraham.'*

And he replied, 'Here I am.'

And He said, 'Please take your son, your only one, whom you love — Isaac — and get yourself to the Land of Moriah; bring him up there as an offering, upon one of the mountains which I shall indicate to you.'

So Abraham awoke early in the morning and he saddled his donkey; he took his two young men* with him, and Isaac, his son. He split the wood for the offering, and rose and went toward the place which God had indicated to him.*

On the third day, Abraham looked up, and perceived the place from afar. And Abraham said to his young men, 'Stay here by yourselves with the donkey, while I and the lad will go yonder; we will prostrate ourselves and we will return to you.'*

And Abraham took the wood for the offering, and placed it on Isaac, his son. He took in his hand the fire and the knife, and the two of them went together. Then Isaac spoke to Abraham his father and said, 'Father — '

And he said, 'Here I am, my son.'

---

toward greater love of God, by following the example of Abraham and Isaac. *Arizal* teaches that the recitation brings atonement to someone who repents sincerely, for he identifies himself with the two Patriarchs who placed loyalty to God above all other considerations.

אֱלֹהֵינוּ — *Our God.* This preliminary supplication is one of the highlights of the Rosh Hashanah *Mussaf.*

וַיַּשְׁכֵּם אַבְרָהָם בַּבֹּקֶר — *So Abraham awoke early in the morning.* He began early, with alacrity, to do God's will, even though he had been commanded to slaughter his beloved Isaac. From this verse the Sages derive that one should perform his religious obligations (e.g., circumcision) as early in the day as possible (*Pesachim* 4a).

שְׁנֵי נְעָרָיו — *His two young men.* Ishmael, his older son, and Eliezer, his trusted servant.

וְנִשְׁתַּחֲוֶה וְנָשׁוּבָה — *We will prostrate ourselves and we will return.* An unintended prophecy came from Abraham's lips. Instead of saying 'I will return,' — without Isaac — he said 'we,' for

וְהָעֵצִים, וְאַיֵּה הַשֶּׂה לְעֹלָה. וַיֹּאמֶר אַבְרָהָם, אֱלֹהִים יִרְאֶה לּוֹ הַשֶּׂה* לְעֹלָה, בְּנִי, וַיֵּלְכוּ שְׁנֵיהֶם יַחְדָּו. וַיָּבֹאוּ אֶל הַמָּקוֹם אֲשֶׁר אָמַר לוֹ הָאֱלֹהִים, וַיִּבֶן שָׁם אַבְרָהָם אֶת הַמִּזְבֵּחַ, וַיַּעֲרֹךְ אֶת הָעֵצִים, וַיַּעֲקֹד אֶת יִצְחָק בְּנוֹ, וַיָּשֶׂם אֹתוֹ עַל הַמִּזְבֵּחַ מִמַּעַל לָעֵצִים. וַיִּשְׁלַח אַבְרָהָם אֶת יָדוֹ, וַיִּקַּח אֶת הַמַּאֲכֶלֶת לִשְׁחֹט אֶת בְּנוֹ. וַיִּקְרָא אֵלָיו מַלְאַךְ יהוה מִן הַשָּׁמַיִם, וַיֹּאמֶר, אַבְרָהָם, אַבְרָהָם, וַיֹּאמֶר, הִנֵּנִי. וַיֹּאמֶר, אַל תִּשְׁלַח יָדְךָ אֶל הַנַּעַר, וְאַל תַּעַשׂ לוֹ מְאוּמָה, כִּי עַתָּה יָדַעְתִּי כִּי יְרֵא אֱלֹהִים אַתָּה, וְלֹא חָשַׂכְתָּ אֶת בִּנְךָ אֶת יְחִידְךָ מִמֶּנִּי. וַיִּשָּׂא אַבְרָהָם אֶת עֵינָיו וַיַּרְא, וְהִנֵּה אַיִל, אַחַר, נֶאֱחַז בַּסְּבַךְ בְּקַרְנָיו, וַיֵּלֶךְ אַבְרָהָם וַיִּקַּח אֶת הָאַיִל, וַיַּעֲלֵהוּ לְעֹלָה תַּחַת בְּנוֹ. וַיִּקְרָא אַבְרָהָם שֵׁם הַמָּקוֹם הַהוּא יהוה יִרְאֶה,* אֲשֶׁר יֵאָמֵר הַיּוֹם, בְּהַר יהוה יֵרָאֶה. וַיִּקְרָא מַלְאַךְ יהוה אֶל אַבְרָהָם, שֵׁנִית מִן הַשָּׁמָיִם. וַיֹּאמֶר, בִּי נִשְׁבַּעְתִּי נְאֻם יהוה, כִּי יַעַן אֲשֶׁר עָשִׂיתָ אֶת הַדָּבָר הַזֶּה, וְלֹא חָשַׂכְתָּ אֶת בִּנְךָ אֶת יְחִידֶךָ. כִּי בָרֵךְ אֲבָרֶכְךָ, וְהַרְבָּה אַרְבֶּה אֶת זַרְעֲךָ כְּכוֹכְבֵי הַשָּׁמַיִם, וְכַחוֹל אֲשֶׁר עַל שְׂפַת הַיָּם, וְיִרַשׁ זַרְעֲךָ אֵת שַׁעַר אֹיְבָיו. וְהִתְבָּרְכוּ בְזַרְעֲךָ כֹּל גּוֹיֵי הָאָרֶץ, עֵקֶב אֲשֶׁר שָׁמַעְתָּ בְּקֹלִי. וַיָּשָׁב אַבְרָהָם אֶל נְעָרָיו, וַיָּקֻמוּ וַיֵּלְכוּ יַחְדָּו אֶל בְּאֵר שָׁבַע, וַיֵּשֶׁב אַבְרָהָם בִּבְאֵר שָׁבַע.

Some omit the following paragraph on the Sabbath and Yom Tov.

רִבּוֹנוֹ שֶׁל עוֹלָם, יְהִי רָצוֹן מִלְּפָנֶיךָ, יהוה אֱלֹהֵינוּ וֵאלֹהֵי אֲבוֹתֵינוּ, שֶׁתִּזְכָּר לָנוּ בְּרִית אֲבוֹתֵינוּ. כְּמוֹ שֶׁכָּבַשׁ אַבְרָהָם אָבִינוּ אֶת רַחֲמָיו מִבֶּן יְחִידוֹ, וְרָצָה לִשְׁחוֹט אוֹתוֹ כְּדֵי לַעֲשׂוֹת רְצוֹנֶךָ, כֵּן יִכְבְּשׁוּ רַחֲמֶיךָ אֶת כַּעַסְךָ מֵעָלֵינוּ, וְיָגֹלּוּ רַחֲמֶיךָ עַל מִדּוֹתֶיךָ, וְתִכָּנֵס אִתָּנוּ לִפְנִים מִשּׁוּרַת דִּינֶךָ, וְתִתְנַהֵג עִמָּנוּ, יהוה אֱלֹהֵינוּ, בְּמִדַּת הַחֶסֶד וּבְמִדַּת הָרַחֲמִים. וּבְטוּבְךָ הַגָּדוֹל, יָשׁוּב חֲרוֹן אַפְּךָ מֵעַמְּךָ וּמֵעִירְךָ וּמֵאַרְצְךָ וּמִנַּחֲלָתֶךָ. וְקַיֶּם לָנוּ, יהוה אֱלֹהֵינוּ, אֶת הַדָּבָר שֶׁהִבְטַחְתָּנוּ עַל יְדֵי מֹשֶׁה עַבְדֶּךָ, כָּאָמוּר: וְזָכַרְתִּי אֶת בְּרִיתִי יַעֲקוֹב, וְאַף אֶת בְּרִיתִי יִצְחָק, וְאַף אֶת בְּרִיתִי אַבְרָהָם אֶזְכֹּר, וְהָאָרֶץ אֶזְכֹּר.[1]

---

such, indeed, was God's intention.

אֱלֹהִים יִרְאֶה לוֹ הַשֶּׂה — *God will seek out for Himself the lamb.* The Midrash teaches that Isaac understood from this reply that he would be the sacrificial 'lamb.' Nevertheless, though Isaac was in the prime of life at the age of 37 and Abraham was a century his senior, *the two of them went together,* united in their dedication.

ה' יִרְאֶה — HASHEM *Yireh,* literally, HASHEM *will see,* i.e., God will see the mountain where the *Akeidah* took place as the appropriate site for His Temple. Indeed, the *Akeidah* took place on the future Temple Mount *(Onkelos).* Alternatively, God will eternally 'see' the *Akeidah* as a source of merit for the offspring of Abraham and Isaac *(R' Bachya).*

And he said, 'Here are the fire and the wood, but where is the lamb for the offering?'

And Abraham said, 'God will seek out for Himself the lamb for the offering, my son.' And the two of them went together.*

They arrived at the place which God indicated to him. Abraham built the altar there, and arranged the wood; he bound Isaac, his son, and he placed him on the altar atop the wood. Abraham stretched out his hand, and took the knife to slaughter his son.

And an angel of HASHEM *called to him from heaven, and said, 'Abraham! Abraham!'*

And he said, 'Here I am.'

And he [the angel quoting HASHEM*] said, 'Do not stretch out your hand against the lad nor do anything to him, for now I know that you are a God-fearing man, since you have not withheld your son, your only one, from Me.'*

*And Abraham looked up and saw — behold a ram! — after it had been caught in the thicket by its horns. So Abraham went and took the ram and brought it as an offering instead of his son. And Abraham named that site '*HASHEM *Yireh,'* as it is said this day: On the mountain* HASHEM *is seen.*

The angel of HASHEM *called to Abraham, a second time from heaven, and said, " 'By Myself I swear,' declared* HASHEM*, 'that since you have done this thing, and have not withheld your son, your only one, I shall surely bless you and greatly increase your offspring like the stars of the heavens and like the sand on the seashore; and your offspring shall inherit the gate of its enemy; and all the nations of the earth shall bless themselves by your offspring, because you have listened to My voice.' "*

Abraham returned to his young men, and they rose and went together to Beer Sheba, and Abraham stayed at Beer Sheba.

Some omit the following paragraph on the Sabbath and Yom Tov.

רִבּוֹנוֹ שֶׁל עוֹלָם *Master of the universe! May it be Your will,* HASHEM*, our God, and the God of our forefathers, that You remember for our sake the covenant of our forefathers. Just as Abraham our forefather suppressed his mercy for his only son and wished to slaughter him in order to do Your will, so may Your mercy suppress Your anger from upon us and may Your mercy overwhelm Your attributes. May You overstep with us the line of Your law and deal with us — O* HASHEM*, our God — with the attribute of kindness and the attribute of mercy. In Your great goodness may You turn aside Your burning wrath from Your people, Your city, Your land, and Your heritage. Fulfill for us,* HASHEM*, our God, the word You pledged through Moses, Your servant, as it is said: 'I shall remember My covenant with Jacob; also My covenant with Isaac, and also My covenant with Abraham shall I remember; and the land shall I remember.'*[1]

(1) *Leviticus* 26:42.

לְעוֹלָם* יְהֵא אָדָם יְרֵא שָׁמַיִם בְּסֵתֶר וּבַגָּלוּי,* וּמוֹדֶה עַל הָאֱמֶת,* וְדוֹבֵר אֱמֶת בִּלְבָבוֹ,* וְיַשְׁכֵּם וְיֹאמַר:

רִבּוֹן כָּל הָעוֹלָמִים,* לֹא עַל צִדְקוֹתֵינוּ אֲנַחְנוּ מַפִּילִים תַּחֲנוּנֵינוּ לְפָנֶיךָ, כִּי עַל רַחֲמֶיךָ הָרַבִּים. מָה אֲנַחְנוּ, מֶה חַיֵּינוּ, מֶה חַסְדֵּנוּ, מַה צִּדְקוֹתֵינוּ, מַה יְּשׁוּעָתֵנוּ, מַה כֹּחֵנוּ, מַה גְּבוּרָתֵנוּ. מַה נֹּאמַר לְפָנֶיךָ, יהוה אֱלֹהֵינוּ וֵאלֹהֵי אֲבוֹתֵינוּ, הֲלֹא כָּל הַגִּבּוֹרִים כְּאַיִן לְפָנֶיךָ, וְאַנְשֵׁי הַשֵּׁם כְּלֹא הָיוּ, וַחֲכָמִים כִּבְלִי מַדָּע, וּנְבוֹנִים כִּבְלִי הַשְׂכֵּל. כִּי רוֹב מַעֲשֵׂיהֶם תֹּהוּ, וִימֵי חַיֵּיהֶם הֶבֶל לְפָנֶיךָ, וּמוֹתַר הָאָדָם מִן הַבְּהֵמָה אָיִן, כִּי הַכֹּל הָבֶל.[1]

אֲבָל אֲנַחְנוּ* עַמְּךָ, בְּנֵי בְרִיתֶךָ, בְּנֵי אַבְרָהָם אֹהַבְךָ שֶׁנִּשְׁבַּעְתָּ לּוֹ בְּהַר הַמּוֹרִיָּה, זֶרַע יִצְחָק יְחִידוֹ שֶׁנֶּעֱקַד עַל גַּב הַמִּזְבֵּחַ, עֲדַת יַעֲקֹב בִּנְךָ בְּכוֹרֶךָ, שֶׁמֵּאַהֲבָתְךָ שֶׁאָהַבְתָּ אוֹתוֹ וּמִשִּׂמְחָתְךָ שֶׁשָּׂמַחְתָּ בּוֹ, קָרָאתָ אֶת שְׁמוֹ יִשְׂרָאֵל וִישֻׁרוּן.*

לְפִיכָךְ אֲנַחְנוּ חַיָּבִים לְהוֹדוֹת לְךָ, וּלְשַׁבֵּחֲךָ, וּלְפָאֶרְךָ, וּלְבָרֵךְ וּלְקַדֵּשׁ וְלָתֵת שֶׁבַח וְהוֹדָיָה לִשְׁמֶךָ. אַשְׁרֵינוּ,* מַה טּוֹב חֶלְקֵנוּ, וּמַה נָּעִים גּוֹרָלֵנוּ, וּמַה יָּפָה יְרֻשָּׁתֵנוּ. ❖ אַשְׁרֵינוּ, שֶׁאֲנַחְנוּ מַשְׁכִּימִים וּמַעֲרִיבִים, עֶרֶב וָבֹקֶר וְאוֹמְרִים פַּעֲמַיִם בְּכָל יוֹם:

שְׁמַע יִשְׂרָאֵל,* יהוה אֱלֹהֵינוּ, יהוה אֶחָד.[2]

—In an undertone בָּרוּךְ שֵׁם כְּבוֹד מַלְכוּתוֹ לְעוֹלָם וָעֶד.

✤ לְעוֹלָם — *Always.* The section beginning with לְעוֹלָם and extending until קָרְבָּנוֹת/*Offerings* is in its totality a profound and succinct summation of basic Jewish faith and loyalty to God. What is more, it is a ringing declaration of joyous pride in our Jewishness, a pride that overcomes all persecutions and that moves us to pray for the time when all will recognize the truth of the Torah's message, and we will proudly proclaim the message that the anti-Semites of the world attempt to still.

Furthermore, the declarations contained in this section represent the manner in which a Jew should conduct himself *always,* not merely on ceremonial occasions.

יְרֵא שָׁמַיִם בְּסֵתֶר וּבַגָּלוּי — *God-fearing privately and publicly.* Some people behave piously when in the view of others, but not when their behavior goes unseen. Others are God-fearing in private but are ashamed to do so in public for fear of being labeled as non-conformists. But the Jew must strive to be consistently God-fearing, whatever his surroundings.

וּמוֹדֶה עַל הָאֱמֶת — *[Let him] acknowledge the truth.* One who seeks the truth is not ashamed to concede his errors. But if he cares more about his reputation than the truth, he will stubbornly persist in falsehood and sin.

וְדוֹבֵר אֱמֶת בִּלְבָבוֹ — *[Let him] speak the truth within his heart.* The Sages cite Rav Safra as the prototype of inner honesty (*Chullin* 94b and *Rashi* to *Makkos* 24a). Once, while he was praying and therefore not permitted to speak, Rav Safra was offered a satisfactory price for something he wished to sell. The buyer did not realize why Rav Safra did not respond, so he kept raising his bid. When Rav Safra finished his prayers, he insisted on accepting no more than the first offer, because in his heart he had intended to sell for that price.

רִבּוֹן כָּל הָעוֹלָמִים — *Master of all worlds!* We now begin leading up to *Shema,* the affirmation of the Oneness of God and acknowledgment of His absolute mastery. We declare that, given the inherent powerlessness and inadequacy of man,

לְעוֹלָם *Always* let a person be God-fearing privately and publicly,* acknowledge the truth,* speak the truth within his heart,* and arise early and proclaim:*

Master of all worlds! Not in the merit of our righteousness do we cast our supplications before You, but in the merit of Your abundant mercy. What are we? What is our life? What is our kindness? What is our righteousness? What is our salvation? What is our strength? What is our might? What can we say before You,* HASHEM, *our God, and the God of our forefathers — are not all the heroes like nothing before You, the famous as if they had never existed, the wise as if devoid of wisdom and the perceptive as if devoid of intelligence? For most of their deeds are desolate and the days of their lives are empty before You. The pre-eminence of man over beast is non-existent for all is vain.*[1]

But we are Your people, members of Your covenant, children of Abraham, Your beloved, to whom You took an oath at Mount Moriah; the offspring of Isaac, his only son, who was bound atop the altar; the community of Jacob, Your firstborn son, whom — because of the love with which You adored him and the joy with which You delighted in him — You named Israel and Jeshurun.**

לְפִיכָךְ *Therefore, we are obliged to thank You, praise You, glorify You, bless, sanctify, and offer praise and thanks to Your Name. We are fortunate* — how good is our portion, how pleasant our lot, and how beautiful our heritage!* Chazzan— *We are fortunate for we come early and stay late, evening and morning, and proclaim twice each day:*

Hear, O Israel:* HASHEM is our God, HASHEM, the One and Only.[2]

In an undertone— *Blessed is the Name of His glorious kingdom for all eternity.*

(1) *Ecclesiastes* 3:19. (2) *Deuteronomy* 6:4.

Israel is enormously privileged in having been selected as God's Chosen People. Therefore, we dedicate ourselves to proclaim His Oneness through the *Shema.* After the blessing that follows the *Shema* we pray for Israel's salvation so that we may be able to sanctify His Name without hindrance. This prayer was composed by the Talmudic sage Rabbi Yochanan *(Yoma* 87b) for use in the Yom Kippur *vidui* (confession) service.

אֲבָל אֲנַחְנוּ — *But we are.* In contrast to the above-described futility of man, we Jews are privileged to carry on the legacy and mission of our forefathers. Abraham is described as God's beloved, which, our Sages explain, means that he sought always to make God beloved in the eyes of his fellow human beings. God made an oath to him at Mount Moriah where the *Akeidah* took place and where Isaac demonstrated his own devotion to God. Jacob is called God's firstborn because the Jewish nation, which bears his name, was given that title by God Himself *(Exodus* 4:22) and to ratify the fact that God considered Jacob, not Esau, to be the legitimate firstborn.

יִשְׂרָאֵל וִישֻׁרוּן — *Israel and Jeshurun.* These two names describe Jacob's stature. יִשְׂרָאֵל (from שְׂרָרָה, *mastery)* means that Jacob *triumphed* over an angel (see *Genesis* 35:10) and יְשֻׁרוּן (from יָשָׁר, *upright, fair)* refers to *dedication to justice* in accordance with God's will.

אַשְׁרֵינוּ — *We are fortunate.* Although, as noted in *Tikkun Tefillah,* this section of the service was compiled during a period of intense persecution, we do not feel downtrodden. To the contrary, we are fortunate to be God's Chosen People and proud to proclaim His Oneness.

שְׁמַע יִשְׂרָאֵל — *Hear, O Israel.* During the

Some congregations complete the first chapter of the *Shema* (following paragraph) at this point, although most omit it. However if you fear that you will not recite the full *Shema* later in *Shacharis* before the prescribed time has elapsed, recite all three chapters of *Shema* (p. 306-308) here.

דברים ו:ה-ט

וְאָהַבְתָּ אֵת יהוה אֱלֹהֶיךָ, בְּכָל לְבָבְךָ, וּבְכָל נַפְשְׁךָ, וּבְכָל מְאֹדֶךָ. וְהָיוּ הַדְּבָרִים הָאֵלֶּה, אֲשֶׁר אָנֹכִי מְצַוְּךָ הַיּוֹם, עַל לְבָבֶךָ. וְשִׁנַּנְתָּם לְבָנֶיךָ, וְדִבַּרְתָּ בָּם, בְּשִׁבְתְּךָ בְּבֵיתֶךָ, וּבְלֶכְתְּךָ בַדֶּרֶךְ, וּבְשָׁכְבְּךָ וּבְקוּמֶךָ. וּקְשַׁרְתָּם לְאוֹת עַל יָדֶךָ, וְהָיוּ לְטֹטָפֹת בֵּין עֵינֶיךָ. וּכְתַבְתָּם עַל מְזֻזוֹת בֵּיתֶךָ וּבִשְׁעָרֶיךָ.

אַתָּה הוּא* עַד שֶׁלֹּא נִבְרָא הָעוֹלָם, אַתָּה הוּא מִשֶּׁנִּבְרָא הָעוֹלָם, אַתָּה הוּא בָּעוֹלָם הַזֶּה, וְאַתָּה הוּא לָעוֹלָם הַבָּא. ❖ קַדֵּשׁ אֶת שִׁמְךָ עַל מַקְדִּישֵׁי שְׁמֶךָ,* וְקַדֵּשׁ אֶת שִׁמְךָ בְּעוֹלָמֶךָ. וּבִישׁוּעָתְךָ תָּרִים וְתַגְבִּיהַּ קַרְנֵנוּ. בָּרוּךְ אַתָּה יהוה, מְקַדֵּשׁ אֶת שִׁמְךָ בָּרַבִּים.* (.Cong. – אָמֵן)

אַתָּה הוּא יהוה אֱלֹהֵינוּ, בַּשָּׁמַיִם וּבָאָרֶץ וּבִשְׁמֵי הַשָּׁמַיִם הָעֶלְיוֹנִים. אֱמֶת, אַתָּה הוּא רִאשׁוֹן, וְאַתָּה הוּא אַחֲרוֹן,* וּמִבַּלְעָדֶיךָ אֵין אֱלֹהִים.[1] קַבֵּץ קֹוֶיךָ מֵאַרְבַּע כַּנְפוֹת הָאָרֶץ. יַכִּירוּ וְיֵדְעוּ כָּל בָּאֵי עוֹלָם כִּי אַתָּה הוּא הָאֱלֹהִים לְבַדְּךָ לְכֹל מַמְלְכוֹת הָאָרֶץ. אַתָּה עָשִׂיתָ אֶת הַשָּׁמַיִם וְאֶת הָאָרֶץ,[2] אֶת הַיָּם, וְאֶת כָּל אֲשֶׁר בָּם. וּמִי בְּכָל מַעֲשֵׂה יָדֶיךָ בָּעֶלְיוֹנִים אוֹ בַתַּחְתּוֹנִים שֶׁיֹּאמַר לְךָ, מַה תַּעֲשֶׂה. אָבִינוּ שֶׁבַּשָּׁמַיִם, עֲשֵׂה עִמָּנוּ חֶסֶד בַּעֲבוּר שִׁמְךָ הַגָּדוֹל שֶׁנִּקְרָא עָלֵינוּ, וְקַיֶּם לָנוּ יהוה אֱלֹהֵינוּ מַה שֶּׁכָּתוּב: בָּעֵת הַהִיא אָבִיא אֶתְכֶם, וּבָעֵת קַבְּצִי אֶתְכֶם, כִּי אֶתֵּן אֶתְכֶם לְשֵׁם וְלִתְהִלָּה בְּכֹל עַמֵּי הָאָרֶץ, בְּשׁוּבִי אֶת שְׁבוּתֵיכֶם לְעֵינֵיכֶם, אָמַר יהוה.[3]

---

middle of the fifth century the Persian king, Yezdegerd II, forbade the Jews to observe the Sabbath and to recite the *Shema*. His purpose was to eradicate belief in Hashem as the Creator (which is symbolized by the Sabbath) and in His Oneness, as it is proclaimed in the *Shema*. To insure that the *Shema* would not be read in defiance of his decree, the king stationed guards in the synagogue for the first quarter of the day, when the *Shema* must be read. To counteract his design, the Sages instituted two recitations of the first verse of *Shema:* the one here, which was to be recited at home, and another one as part of *Kedushah* of *Mussaf* (see p. 404). Although these services contain only the first verse of the *Shema,* this is sufficient to fulfill the *Shema* obligation in cases of extreme emergency (*Berachos* 13b). Even when Yezdegerd was killed in response to the prayers of the Sages and his decree was lifted, the two *Shema* recitations remained part of the regular ritual, and the one that had been recited at home was moved to this part of the synagogue service.

אַתָּה הוּא ☙ — *It was You.* The first four phrases of this prayer express the idea that God is eternal and unchanging, unaffected by time or place.

Some congregations complete the first chapter of the *Shema* (following paragraph) at this point, although most omit it. However if you fear that you will not recite the full *Shema* later in *Shacharis* before the prescribed time has elapsed, recite all three chapters of *Shema* (p. 306-308) here.

Deuteronomy 6:5-9

וְאָהַבְתָּ *You shall love* HASHEM, *your God, with all your heart, with all your soul and with all your resources. Let these matters, which I command you today, be upon your heart. Teach them thoroughly to your children and speak of them while you sit in your home, while you walk on the way, when you retire and when you arise. Bind them as a sign upon your arm and let them be tefillin between your eyes. And write them on the doorposts of your house and upon your gates.*

אַתָּה *It was You* before the world was created, it is You since the world was created, it is You in This World, and it is You in the World to Come.* Chazzan– *Sanctify Your Name through those who sanctify Your Name,* and sanctify Your Name in Your universe. Through Your salvation may You exalt and raise our pride. Blessed are You,* HASHEM, *Who sanctifies Your Name among the multitudes.**

(Cong.– *Amen.*)

אַתָּה *It is You Who are* HASHEM, *our God, in heaven and on earth and in the loftiest heavens. True — You are the First and You are the Last,* and other than You there is no God.*[1] *Gather in those who yearn for You, from the four corners of the earth. Let all who walk the earth recognize and know that You alone are the God over all the kingdoms of the earth. You have made the heavens, the earth,*[2] *the sea, and all that is in them. Who among all Your handiwork, those above and those below, can say to You, 'What are You doing?' Our Father in Heaven, do kindness with us for the sake of Your great Name that has been proclaimed upon us. Fulfill for us,* HASHEM, *our God, what is written: 'At that time I will bring you and at that time I will gather you in, for I will set you up for renown and praise among all the peoples of the earth, when I bring back your captivity, before your own eyes,' said* HASHEM.[3]

(1) Cf. *Isaiah* 44:6. (2) *II Kings* 19:15. (3) *Zephaniah* 3:20.

קַדֵּשׁ אֶת שִׁמְךָ עַל מַקְדִּישֵׁי שְׁמֶךָ — *Sanctify Your Name through those who sanctify Your Name.* When originally composed, this referred to the Jewish martyrs who had sanctified the Name through unyielding loyalty. In later times, it came to refer also to those who cling to the commandments despite hardship and temptation.

מְקַדֵּשׁ אֶת שִׁמְךָ בָּרַבִּים — *Who sanctifies Your Name* [some versions read שְׁמוֹ, *His Name]* *among the multitudes.* May the time come when no Jew need ever fear to express his Jewishness openly.

רִאשׁוֹן ... אַחֲרוֹן — *The First ... the Last.* We mean only to say that God pre-existed everything and will survive everything — not that He had a beginning or will have an end, for God is infinite and timeless.

❧ קרבנות ❧

הכיור

שמות ל:יז-כא

וַיְדַבֵּר יהוה אֶל מֹשֶׁה לֵּאמֹר. וְעָשִׂיתָ כִּיּוֹר נְחֹשֶׁת, וְכַנּוֹ נְחֹשֶׁת, לְרָחְצָה, וְנָתַתָּ אֹתוֹ בֵּין אֹהֶל מוֹעֵד וּבֵין הַמִּזְבֵּחַ, וְנָתַתָּ שָׁמָּה מָיִם. וְרָחֲצוּ אַהֲרֹן וּבָנָיו מִמֶּנּוּ, אֶת יְדֵיהֶם וְאֶת רַגְלֵיהֶם. בְּבֹאָם אֶל אֹהֶל מוֹעֵד יִרְחֲצוּ מַיִם וְלֹא יָמֻתוּ,* אוֹ בְגִשְׁתָּם אֶל הַמִּזְבֵּחַ לְשָׁרֵת לְהַקְטִיר אִשֶּׁה לַיהוה. וְרָחֲצוּ יְדֵיהֶם וְרַגְלֵיהֶם וְלֹא יָמֻתוּ, וְהָיְתָה לָהֶם חָק עוֹלָם, לוֹ וּלְזַרְעוֹ לְדֹרֹתָם.

תרומת הדשן

ויקרא ו:א-ו

וַיְדַבֵּר יהוה אֶל מֹשֶׁה לֵּאמֹר. צַו אֶת אַהֲרֹן וְאֶת בָּנָיו לֵאמֹר, זֹאת תּוֹרַת הָעֹלָה, הִוא הָעֹלָה עַל מוֹקְדָה עַל הַמִּזְבֵּחַ כָּל הַלַּיְלָה* עַד הַבֹּקֶר, וְאֵשׁ הַמִּזְבֵּחַ תּוּקַד בּוֹ. וְלָבַשׁ הַכֹּהֵן מִדּוֹ בַד,* וּמִכְנְסֵי בַד יִלְבַּשׁ עַל בְּשָׂרוֹ, וְהֵרִים אֶת הַדֶּשֶׁן* אֲשֶׁר תֹּאכַל הָאֵשׁ אֶת הָעֹלָה עַל הַמִּזְבֵּחַ, וְשָׂמוֹ אֵצֶל הַמִּזְבֵּחַ. וּפָשַׁט אֶת בְּגָדָיו,* וְלָבַשׁ בְּגָדִים אֲחֵרִים, וְהוֹצִיא אֶת הַדֶּשֶׁן אֶל מִחוּץ לַמַּחֲנֶה, אֶל מָקוֹם טָהוֹר. וְהָאֵשׁ עַל הַמִּזְבֵּחַ תּוּקַד בּוֹ, לֹא

❧ קָרְבָּנוֹת / OFFERINGS ❧

From the beginning of its existence as a nation, Israel *saw* — whether or not it understood why or how — that the sacrificial service brought it a closeness to God and the manifestation of His Presence. The offerings represented the Jew's submission to God of his self and his resources.

Abraham asked God how Israel would achieve forgiveness when the Temple would lie in ruins and they could no longer offer sacrifices.

God replied, 'When Israel recites the Scriptural order of the offerings, I will consider it as if they had brought the sacrifices and I will forgive their sins' (*Megillah* 31a; *Taanis* 27b).

Rav Yitzchak said: The Torah writes זֹאת תּוֹרַת הַחַטָּאת, *this is the Torah* [i.e., teaching] *of the sin-offering* (*Leviticus* 6:18), to imply that whoever involves himself in the study of the sin-offering is regarded as if he had actually brought a sin-offering (*Menachos* 110a).

In the inspiring words of *R' Hirsch* (*Horeb* 624): 'The Temple has fallen, the Altar has disappeared, the harps of the singers are heard no more, but their spirit has become the heritage of Israel; it still infuses the word which alone survives as an expression of the inward Divine service.'

The section dealing with the קָרְבָּנוֹת, *offerings,* logically follows the previous prayer, אַתָּה הוּא, which longs for Israel's redemption. Given the fact that the offerings require the existence of the Holy Temple as the spiritual center of the nation, we pray that God gather us in from our dispersion. Then, our message will become a truly universal one, for God will have set us up *'for renown and praise among all the peoples of the earth.'*

The offerings whose laws are about to be recited are all communal ones; the Sages chose them because they illustrate our wish that Israel become united as a single nation in God's service.

❧ הַכִּיּוֹר / The Laver

Before the *Kohanim* could begin the Temple service, they had to take sanctified water and pour it over their hands and feet. This water was drawn from the כִּיּוֹר, *laver,* a large copper basin in the Temple Courtyard. In preparation for our 'verbal sacrificial service,' therefore, we 'wash' ourselves with water from the laver, as it were.

וְלֹא יָמֻתוּ — *So that they not die.* The offense of performing the service without washing does *not* incur a court-imposed death penalty, but the violator makes himself liable to a Heavenly

OFFERINGS

THE LAVER

Exodus 30:17-21

וַיְדַבֵּר *HASHEM spoke to Moses, saying: Make a laver of copper, and its base of copper, for washing; and place it between the Tent of Appointment and the Altar and put water there. Aaron and his sons are to wash their hands and feet from it. When they arrive at the Tent of Appointment they are to wash with water so that they not die,* or when they approach the Altar to serve, to burn a fire-offering to HASHEM. They are to wash their hands and feet so that they not die; and this shall be an eternal decree for them — for him and for his offspring — throughout their generations.*

THE TAKING OF ASHES

Leviticus 6:1-6

וַיְדַבֵּר *HASHEM spoke to Moses saying: Instruct Aaron and his sons saying: This is the teaching of the elevation-offering, it is the elevation-offering that stays on the pyre on the Altar all night* until morning, and the fire of the Altar should be kept burning on it. The Kohen should don his linen garment,* and he is to don linen breeches upon his flesh; he is to pick up the ashes* of what the fire consumed of the elevation-offering upon the Altar and place it next to the Altar. Then he should remove his garments* and don other garments; then he should remove the ashes to the outside of the camp to a pure place. The fire on the Altar shall be kept burning on it, it may not be*

---

punishment for his display of contempt.

תְּרוּמַת הַדֶּשֶׁן / The Taking of Ashes

These verses are recited here because they concern the first service of the day: to remove a small portion of the ashes from the previous day's offerings. It was done first thing in the morning, before the *tamid*, daily continual offering, was brought. In addition, the passage contains three references to fire on the Altar: (a) עַל מוֹקְדָה, *on the pyre;* (b) וְאֵשׁ הַמִּזְבֵּחַ, *the fire of the Altar;* (c) וְהָאֵשׁ עַל הַמִּזְבֵּחַ, *the fire on the Altar.* This teaches that three fires were kept burning on the Altar (*Yoma* 45a). They were: מַעֲרָכָה גְדוֹלָה, *the large pyre,* upon which the offerings were burned; מַעֲרָכָה שְׁנִיָּה שֶׁל קְטֹרֶת, *the second pyre for the incense,* from which burning coals were taken and brought into the Sanctuary for the morning and afternoon incense service; and מַעֲרָכָה לְקִיּוּם הָאֵשׁ, *the pyre for perpetuation of the flame,* which was kept burning at all times in case either of the other fires became extinguished.

הִוא הָעֹלָה . . . כָּל הַלַּיְלָה — *It is the elevation-offering . . . all night.* Although it was preferable to burn a day's offerings during the day, it was permitted to place them on the fires all night, provided the service of the blood was completed during the day.

מִדּוֹ בַד — *His linen garment.* The *Kohen* must wear his full priestly raiment; like all Temple services, this one may not be performed if the *Kohen* is lacking even one of the prescribed garments (described in *Exodus* 28).

וְהֵרִים אֶת הַדֶּשֶׁן — *He is to pick up the ashes.* He is to take glowing ashes from the burnt flesh of offerings, not from wood ashes. The portion taken for this service need be no larger than a handful and it is placed on the floor of the Courtyard, to the east of the ramp leading up to the Altar (the ramp is on the south side of the Altar). This removal of ashes is a required part of the daily morning service, whether or not the Altar had to be cleaned of excess ashes.

וּפָשַׁט אֶת בְּגָדָיו — *Then he should remove his garments.* Unlike the previous verse that discusses a daily *mitzvah,* this verse discusses the cleaning of the Altar, which was done whenever the accumulation of ashes atop the Altar interfered with the service, but was not done daily. The ashes were removed and taken to a designated place outside of Jerusalem; in the Wilderness, they were taken to a place outside of the Israelite camp. In speaking of 'removal' of the priestly garments the verse advises that the *Kohen* should wear less expensive or well-worn priestly garments when performing this service because the ashes would

תִכְבֶּה, וּבִעֵר עָלֶיהָ הַכֹּהֵן עֵצִים בַּבֹּקֶר בַּבֹּקֶר,* וְעָרַךְ עָלֶיהָ הָעֹלָה, וְהִקְטִיר עָלֶיהָ חֶלְבֵי הַשְּׁלָמִים.* אֵשׁ תָּמִיד תּוּקַד עַל הַמִּזְבֵּחַ, לֹא תִכְבֶּה.

קרבן התמיד

Some authorities hold that the following (until קְטֹרֶת) should be recited standing.
Some omit the following paragraph on the Sabbath and *Yom Tov*.

יְהִי רָצוֹן מִלְּפָנֶיךָ,* יהוה אֱלֹהֵינוּ וֵאלֹהֵי אֲבוֹתֵינוּ, שֶׁתְּרַחֵם עָלֵינוּ וְתִמְחָל לָנוּ עַל כָּל חַטֹּאתֵינוּ, וּתְכַפֵּר לָנוּ אֶת כָּל עֲוֹנוֹתֵינוּ, וְתִסְלַח לְכָל פְּשָׁעֵינוּ, וְתִבְנֶה בֵּית הַמִּקְדָּשׁ בִּמְהֵרָה בְיָמֵינוּ, וְנַקְרִיב לְפָנֶיךָ קָרְבַּן הַתָּמִיד שֶׁיְּכַפֵּר בַּעֲדֵנוּ, כְּמוֹ שֶׁכָּתַבְתָּ עָלֵינוּ בְּתוֹרָתֶךָ עַל יְדֵי מֹשֶׁה עַבְדֶּךָ, מִפִּי כְבוֹדֶךָ, כָּאָמוּר:

במדבר כח:א־ח

וַיְדַבֵּר יהוה אֶל מֹשֶׁה לֵּאמֹר. צַו אֶת בְּנֵי יִשְׂרָאֵל וְאָמַרְתָּ אֲלֵהֶם, אֶת קָרְבָּנִי לַחְמִי* לְאִשַּׁי, רֵיחַ נִיחֹחִי, תִּשְׁמְרוּ לְהַקְרִיב לִי בְּמוֹעֲדוֹ. וְאָמַרְתָּ לָהֶם, זֶה הָאִשֶּׁה אֲשֶׁר תַּקְרִיבוּ לַיהוה, כְּבָשִׂים בְּנֵי שָׁנָה תְמִימִם, שְׁנַיִם לַיּוֹם, עֹלָה תָמִיד. אֶת הַכֶּבֶשׂ אֶחָד תַּעֲשֶׂה בַבֹּקֶר, וְאֵת הַכֶּבֶשׂ הַשֵּׁנִי תַּעֲשֶׂה בֵּין הָעַרְבָּיִם. וַעֲשִׂירִית הָאֵיפָה סֹלֶת לְמִנְחָה,* בְּלוּלָה בְּשֶׁמֶן כָּתִית רְבִיעִת הַהִין. עֹלַת תָּמִיד, הָעֲשֻׂיָה בְּהַר סִינַי, לְרֵיחַ נִיחֹחַ, אִשֶּׁה לַיהוה. וְנִסְכּוֹ רְבִיעִת הַהִין לַכֶּבֶשׂ הָאֶחָד, בַּקֹּדֶשׁ הַסֵּךְ נֶסֶךְ שֵׁכָר לַיהוה. וְאֵת הַכֶּבֶשׂ הַשֵּׁנִי תַּעֲשֶׂה בֵּין הָעַרְבָּיִם, כְּמִנְחַת הַבֹּקֶר וּכְנִסְכּוֹ תַּעֲשֶׂה, אִשֵּׁה רֵיחַ נִיחֹחַ לַיהוה.

וְשָׁחַט אֹתוֹ עַל יֶרֶךְ הַמִּזְבֵּחַ צָפֹנָה לִפְנֵי יהוה, וְזָרְקוּ בְּנֵי אַהֲרֹן הַכֹּהֲנִים אֶת דָּמוֹ עַל הַמִּזְבֵּחַ סָבִיב.*[1]

---

tend to soil his clothing: 'The outfit one wears while cooking his master's meal, one should not wear while filling his master's goblet' (*Yoma* 23a).

עֵצִים בַּבֹּקֶר בַּבֹּקֶר — *Wood ... every morning.* Wood must be placed on the Altar fire every morning.

הָעֹלָה ... הַשְּׁלָמִים — *The elevation-offering ... the peace-offerings.* The morning continual elevation-offering had to go on the Altar before any other offerings; similarly, the last offering of the day was the afternoon continual offering.

⧼ הַתָּמִיד / The Tamid (Continual) Offering

⧼ **יְהִי רָצוֹן מִלְּפָנֶיךָ** — *May it be Your will.* We are about to begin 'offering' our communal sacrifices, as it were. Before doing so, we recite a brief prayer that God end the exile and make it possible for us to offer the true offerings, not just the recitations that take their place.

⧼ **וַיְדַבֵּר ה' . . . קָרְבָּנִי לַחְמִי** — *HASHEM spoke ... My offering, My food.* The offering referred to here is the עֹלַת תָּמִיד, *continual elevation-offering* or *tamid.* The offering is called תָּמִיד, *continual,* because it is brought regularly, day in and day out; it is a communal offering purchased with the annual half-*shekel* contributions, collected especially for this purpose. The offering is called *food* in the figurative sense, referring to the parts that are burned on the Altar. The *satisfying odor* does not refer to the odor *per se*, for just as God does not require our 'food,' He does not benefit from the aroma of burning flesh. Rather, the aroma of the burning offering is pleasing to God because it represents the culmination of our performance *extinguished, and the Kohen shall burn wood upon it every morning.* He is to prepare the elevation-offering upon it and burn upon it the fats of the peace-offerings.* A permanent fire should remain burning on the Altar; it may not be extinguished.*

THE TAMID OFFERING

Some authorities hold that the following (until קְטֹרֶת /Incense) should be recited standing. Some omit the following paragraph on the Sabbath and *Yom Tov*.

יְהִי רָצוֹן *May it be Your will,* HASHEM, our God, and the God of our forefathers, that You have mercy on us and pardon us for all our errors, atone for us all our iniquities, forgive all our willful sins; and that You rebuild the Holy Temple speedily, in our days, so that we may offer to You the continual offering that it may atone for us, as You have prescribed for us in Your Torah through Moses, Your servant, from Your glorious mouth, as it is said:*

Numbers 28:1-8

וַיְדַבֵּר *HASHEM spoke to Moses, saying: Command the Children of Israel and tell them: My offering, My food* for My fires, My satisfying aroma, you are to be scrupulous to offer Me in its appointed time. And you are to tell them: 'This is the fire-offering that you are to bring to HASHEM: [male] first-year lambs, unblemished, two a day, as a continual elevation-offering. One lamb-service you are to perform in the morning and the second lamb-service you are to perform in the afternoon; with a tenth-ephah of fine flour as a meal-offering,* mixed with a quarter-hin of crushed olive oil. It is the continual elevation-offering that was done at Mount Sinai, for a satisfying aroma, a fire-offering to HASHEM. And its libation is a quarter-hin for each lamb, to be poured on the Holy [Altar], a fermented libation to HASHEM. And the second lamb-service you are to perform in the afternoon, like the meal-offering of the morning and its libation are you to make, a fire-offering for a satisfying aroma to HASHEM.'*

*He is to slaughter it on the north side of the Altar before HASHEM, and Aaron's sons the Kohanim are to dash its blood upon the Altar, all around.**[1]

(1) *Leviticus* 1:11.

of His will. In the words of the Sages, God is pleased, שֶׁאָמַרְתִּי וְנַעֲשָׂה רְצוֹנִי, *for I have spoken, and My will has been done.*

סֹלֶת לְמִנְחָה — *Fine flour as a meal-offering.* Every elevation- and peace-offering, whether communal or private, is accompanied by a meal-offering, which is burned completely on the Altar, and a libation of wine, which is poured onto the Altar. The wine is called נְסָכִים and the meal-offering, which consists of fine flour mixed with olive oil, is called מִנְחַת נְסָכִים. The amount of flour, oil and wine depends on the species of the animal. For sheep — the animal used for the *tamid* — the amounts are a tenth-*ephah* (approximately 4½ lbs.) of flour, and a quarter-*hin* (approx. 30 fl. oz.) each of oil and wine. The amounts needed for other species may be found on page 408.

סָבִיב — *All around.* Immediately after slaughter, the blood of the *tamid* was caught by a *Kohen* in a sacred utensil and dashed on the northeast and southwest corners of the Altar. This is called 'all around' because blood thrown at a corner would spread out to the two adjacent

Some omit the following paragraph on the Sabbath and *Yom Tov.*

יְהִי רָצוֹן מִלְּפָנֶיךָ, יהוה אֱלֹהֵינוּ וֵאלֹהֵי אֲבוֹתֵינוּ, שֶׁתְּהֵא אֲמִירָה זוּ חֲשׁוּבָה וּמְקֻבֶּלֶת וּמְרֻצָּה לְפָנֶיךָ כְּאִלּוּ הִקְרַבְנוּ קָרְבַּן הַתָּמִיד בְּמוֹעֲדוֹ וּבִמְקוֹמוֹ וּכְהִלְכָתוֹ.

קטרת

אַתָּה הוּא יהוה אֱלֹהֵינוּ שֶׁהִקְטִירוּ אֲבוֹתֵינוּ לְפָנֶיךָ אֶת קְטֹרֶת הַסַּמִּים בִּזְמַן שֶׁבֵּית הַמִּקְדָּשׁ קַיָּם, כַּאֲשֶׁר צִוִּיתָ אוֹתָם עַל יְדֵי מֹשֶׁה נְבִיאֶךָ, כַּכָּתוּב בְּתוֹרָתֶךָ:

שמות ל:לד-לו, ז-ח

וַיֹּאמֶר יהוה אֶל מֹשֶׁה, קַח לְךָ סַמִּים, נָטָף וּשְׁחֵלֶת וְחֶלְבְּנָה, סַמִּים וּלְבֹנָה זַכָּה, בַּד בְּבַד יִהְיֶה.* וְעָשִׂיתָ אֹתָהּ קְטֹרֶת, רֹקַח, מַעֲשֵׂה רוֹקֵחַ, מְמֻלָּח, טָהוֹר, קֹדֶשׁ. וְשָׁחַקְתָּ* מִמֶּנָּה הָדֵק, וְנָתַתָּה מִמֶּנָּה* לִפְנֵי הָעֵדֻת בְּאֹהֶל מוֹעֵד אֲשֶׁר אִוָּעֵד לְךָ שָׁמָּה, קֹדֶשׁ קָדָשִׁים תִּהְיֶה לָכֶם.

וְנֶאֱמַר: וְהִקְטִיר עָלָיו אַהֲרֹן קְטֹרֶת סַמִּים, בַּבֹּקֶר בַּבֹּקֶר, בְּהֵיטִיבוֹ אֶת הַנֵּרֹת* יַקְטִירֶנָּה. וּבְהַעֲלֹת אַהֲרֹן אֶת הַנֵּרֹת בֵּין הָעַרְבַּיִם, יַקְטִירֶנָּה, קְטֹרֶת תָּמִיד לִפְנֵי יהוה לְדֹרֹתֵיכֶם.

כריתות ו., ירושלמי יומא ד:ה

תָּנוּ רַבָּנָן, פִּטּוּם הַקְּטֹרֶת כֵּיצַד.* שְׁלֹשׁ מֵאוֹת וְשִׁשִּׁים וּשְׁמוֹנָה מָנִים* הָיוּ בָהּ. שְׁלֹשׁ מֵאוֹת וְשִׁשִּׁים וַחֲמִשָּׁה כְּמִנְיַן יְמוֹת הַחַמָּה — מָנֶה לְכָל יוֹם, פְּרַס בְּשַׁחֲרִית וּפְרַס בֵּין הָעַרְבַּיִם; וּשְׁלֹשָׁה מָנִים יְתֵרִים,* שֶׁמֵּהֶם מַכְנִיס כֹּהֵן גָּדוֹל מְלֹא חָפְנָיו בְּיוֹם הַכִּפֻּרִים. וּמַחֲזִירָם לְמַכְתֶּשֶׁת בְּעֶרֶב יוֹם הַכִּפֻּרִים, וְשׁוֹחֲקָן יָפֶה יָפֶה כְּדֵי שֶׁתְּהֵא דַקָּה מִן הַדַּקָּה. וְאַחַד עָשָׂר סַמָּנִים*

---

sides, so there would be some blood on each of the Altar's four sides.

קְטֹרֶת / INCENSE

Incense, blended according to a strictly prescribed formula, was burned in the Temple on the Golden Altar, morning and evening. The Golden Altar was located inside the Temple building. It was much smaller than the Altar used for offerings, which was covered with copper plates and was located in the Courtyard. *Arizal* writes that the careful recitation of this section helps bring one to repentance. *R' Hirsch* comments that the incense symbolized Israel's duty to make all its actions pleasing to God.

According to *Zohar*, the chapter and laws of קְטֹרֶת should be recited here 'in order to remove impurity from the world prior to the prayers [i.e., the complete *Shacharis* service] that take the place of offerings.' In response to the *Zohar's* dictum, it has become customary to include קְטֹרֶת in this part of the service. *Rama* notes that it is important to pronounce each of the ingredients and measurements carefully and clearly, because the recitation takes the place of the actual mixture which, as we shall see below, had to be exact (*Orach Chaim* 132:2).

בַּד בְּבַד יִהְיֶה — *They are all to be of equal weight.* The four spices given by name are of equal weight. The other seven, however, were different from these four, as will be seen from the Talmudic passage that follows.

וְשָׁחַקְתָּ — *You are to grind.* The incense must

Some omit the following paragraph on the Sabbath and *Yom Tov.*

יְהִי רָצוֹן *May it be Your will, HASHEM, our God and the God of our forefathers, that this recital be worthy and acceptable, and favorable before You as if we had offered the continual offering in its set time, in its place, and according to its requirement.*

INCENSE

אַתָּה *It is You, HASHEM, our God, before Whom our forefathers burned the incense-spices in the time when the Holy Temple stood, as You commanded them through Moses Your prophet, as is written in Your Torah:*

Exodus 30:34-36, 7-8

וַיֹּאמֶר *HASHEM said to Moses: Take yourself spices — stacte, onycha, and galbanum — spices and pure frankincense; they are all to be of equal weight.* You are to make it into incense, a spice-compound, the handiwork of an expert spice-compounder, thoroughly mixed, pure and holy. You are to grind* some of it finely and place some of it* before the Testimony in the Tent of Appointment, where I shall designate a time to meet you; it shall be a holy of holies for you.*

It is also written: Aaron shall burn upon it the incense-spices every morning; when he cleans the lamps he is to burn it. And when Aaron ignites the lamps in the afternoon, he is to burn it, as continual incense before HASHEM throughout your generations.*

Talmud, *Kereisos* 6a, *Yerushalmi Yoma* 4:5

תָּנוּ רַבָּנָן *The Rabbis taught: How is the incense mixture formulated?* Three hundred sixty-eight maneh* were in it: three hundred sixty-five corresponding to the days of the solar year — a maneh for each day, half in the morning and half in the afternoon; and three extra maneh,* from which the Kohen Gadol would bring both his handfuls [into the Holy of Holies] on Yom Kippur. He would return them to the mortar on the day before Yom Kippur, and grind them very thoroughly so that it would be exceptionally fine. Eleven kinds of spices**

---

be pulverized into a fine powder.

מִמֶּנָּה ... מִמֶּנָּה — *Some of it ... some of it.* The repetition alludes to the special Yom Kippur incense service, when the incense is reground and the *Kohen Gadol* [High Priest] takes it into the Holy of Holies, the only time of the year when a human being enters that most sacred place. On all other days, incense is burned twice a day in the Sanctuary.

בְּהֵיטִיבוֹ אֶת הַנֵּרֹת — *When he cleans the lamps.* The *Kohen* cleans the lamps of the Menorah every morning, after which the incense is burned.

תָּנוּ רַבָּנָן פִּטּוּם הַקְּטֹרֶת כֵּיצַד — *The Rabbis taught: How is the incense mixture formulated?* This passage explains how the incense mixture was prepared and it gives the names and amounts that are not specified in Scriptures.

מָנִים — *Maneh.* A *maneh* is equal to approximately twenty ounces.

וּשְׁלֹשָׁה מָנִים יְתֵרִים — *And three extra maneh.* In addition to the regular incense service on Yom Kippur, there was a special service that was performed in the Holy of Holies. Three *maneh* were taken before Yom Kippur and ground again to make them extra fine. From that incense, the *Kohen Gadol* filled both hands, which he used for the special Yom Kippur service.

וְאַחַד עָשָׂר סַמָּנִים — *Eleven kinds of spices.* Eleven different spices were used in the incense mixture, but only four of them — stacte, onycha, galbanum, and frankincense — are named in the Scriptural verse, above. The identity of the other spices is part of the Oral Law. That there are a total of eleven spices is derived from this verse in the following manner:

הָיוּ בָהּ, וְאֵלּוּ הֵן: (א) הַצֳּרִי, (ב) וְהַצִּפֹּרֶן, (ג) הַחֶלְבְּנָה, (ד) וְהַלְּבוֹנָה, מִשְׁקַל שִׁבְעִים שִׁבְעִים מָנֶה; (ה) מוֹר, (ו) וּקְצִיעָה, (ז) שִׁבֹּלֶת נֵרְדְּ, (ח) וְכַרְכֹּם, מִשְׁקַל שִׁשָּׁה עָשָׂר שִׁשָּׁה עָשָׂר מָנֶה; (ט) הַקֹּשְׁטְ שְׁנֵים עָשָׂר, (י) וְקִלּוּפָה שְׁלֹשָׁה, (יא) וְקִנָּמוֹן תִּשְׁעָה. בֹּרִית כַּרְשִׁינָה תִּשְׁעָה קַבִּין, יֵין קַפְרִיסִין סְאִין* תְּלָתָא וְקַבִּין תְּלָתָא, וְאִם אֵין לוֹ יֵין קַפְרִיסִין, מֵבִיא חֲמַר חִוַּרְיָן עַתִּיק, מֶלַח סְדוֹמִית רֹבַע הַקָּב; מַעֲלֶה עָשָׁן* כָּל שֶׁהוּא. רַבִּי נָתָן הַבַּבְלִי אוֹמֵר: אַף כִּפַּת הַיַּרְדֵּן כָּל שֶׁהוּא. וְאִם נָתַן בָּהּ דְּבַשׁ, פְּסָלָהּ. וְאִם חִסַּר* אַחַת מִכָּל סַמָּנֶיהָ, חַיָּב מִיתָה.

רַבָּן שִׁמְעוֹן בֶּן גַּמְלִיאֵל אוֹמֵר: הַצֳּרִי אֵינוֹ אֶלָּא שְׂרָף הַנּוֹטֵף מֵעֲצֵי הַקְּטָף. בֹּרִית כַּרְשִׁינָה לָמָּה הִיא בָאָה, כְּדֵי לְיַפּוֹת בָּהּ אֶת הַצִּפֹּרֶן, כְּדֵי שֶׁתְּהֵא נָאָה. יֵין קַפְרִיסִין לָמָּה הוּא בָא, כְּדֵי לִשְׁרוֹת בּוֹ אֶת הַצִּפֹּרֶן, כְּדֵי שֶׁתְּהֵא עַזָּה. וַהֲלֹא מֵי רַגְלַיִם יָפִין לָהּ, אֶלָּא שֶׁאֵין מַכְנִיסִין מֵי רַגְלַיִם בַּמִּקְדָּשׁ מִפְּנֵי הַכָּבוֹד.

תַּנְיָא, רַבִּי נָתָן אוֹמֵר: כְּשֶׁהוּא שׁוֹחֵק, אוֹמֵר הָדֵק הֵיטֵב, הֵיטֵב הָדֵק, מִפְּנֵי שֶׁהַקּוֹל יָפֶה לַבְּשָׂמִים. פִּטְּמָהּ לַחֲצָאִין,* כְּשֵׁרָה; לִשְׁלִישׁ וְלִרְבִיעַ, לֹא שָׁמַעְנוּ. אָמַר רַבִּי יְהוּדָה: זֶה הַכְּלָל – אִם כְּמִדָּתָהּ, כְּשֵׁרָה לַחֲצָאִין; וְאִם חִסַּר אַחַת מִכָּל סַמָּנֶיהָ, חַיָּב מִיתָה.

תַּנְיָא, בַּר קַפָּרָא אוֹמֵר: אַחַת לְשִׁשִּׁים אוֹ לְשִׁבְעִים שָׁנָה* הָיְתָה בָאָה שֶׁל שִׁירַיִם לַחֲצָאִין. וְעוֹד תָּנֵי בַּר קַפָּרָא: אִלּוּ הָיָה נוֹתֵן בָּהּ קוֹרְטוֹב שֶׁל דְּבַשׁ,* אֵין אָדָם יָכוֹל לַעֲמֹד מִפְּנֵי רֵיחָהּ. וְלָמָּה אֵין מְעָרְבִין בָּהּ דְּבַשׁ, מִפְּנֵי שֶׁהַתּוֹרָה אָמְרָה: כִּי כָל שְׂאֹר וְכָל דְּבַשׁ לֹא תַקְטִירוּ מִמֶּנּוּ אִשֶּׁה לַיהוה.[1]

סַמִּים, *spices,* is plural, yielding two kinds; then three spices are named, for a total of five; the word סַמִּים appears again implying the addition of another group of five (equivalent to the five given above). Finally *frankincense* is added, for a total of eleven.

It should be noted that the exact translations of the spices are not known with absolute certainty.

קַבִּין ... סְאִין — *Kab ... se'ah.* A *kab* contains a volume of approximately forty fluid ounces. A *se'ah* is equal to six *kab.*

מַעֲלֶה עָשָׁן — *A smoke-raising herb.* The addition of this herb, which is not identified by name, caused the smoke of the incense to ascend straight as a pillar.

וְאִם חִסַּר — *But if he left out,* i.e., if he used either more or less than the prescribed amount of any ingredient, he is liable to the heavenly death penalty *(Etz Yosef).* According to *Rashi (Kereisos* 6b), this liability applies only to the annual Yom Kippur service performed in the Holy of Holies, because the *Kohen Gadol* is considered to have made a בִּיאָה רֵיקָנִית, *an empty-handed coming,* since he did not have the proper mixture. *Rambam,* however, applies this *were in it, as follows: (1) stacte, (2) onycha, (3) galbanum, (4) frankincense — each weighing seventy maneh; (5) myrrh, (6) cassia, (7) spikenard, (8) saffron — each weighing sixteen maneh; (9) costus — twelve maneh; (10) aromatic bark — three; and (11) cinnamon — nine. [Additionally] Carshina lye, nine kab; Cyprus wine, three se'ah* and three kab — if he has no Cyprus wine, he brings old white wine; Sodom salt, a quarter-kab; and a minute amount of a smoke-raising herb.* Rabbi Nassan the Babylonian says: Also a minute amount of Jordan amber. If he placed fruit-honey into it, he invalidated it. But if he left out* any of its spices, he is liable to the death penalty.*

רַבָּן שִׁמְעוֹן *Rabban Shimon ben Gamliel says: The stacte is simply the sap that drips from balsam trees. Why is Carshina lye used? To bleach the onycha, to make it pleasing. Why is Cyprus wine used? So that the onycha could be soaked in it, to make it pungent. Even though urine is more suitable for that, nevertheless they do not bring urine into the Temple out of respect.*

תַּנְיָא *It is taught, Rabbi Nassan says: As one would grind [the incense] another would say, 'Grind thoroughly, thoroughly grind,' because the sound is beneficial for the spices. If one mixed it in half-quantities,* it was fit for use, but as to a third or a quarter — we have not heard the law. Rabbi Yehudah said: This is the general rule — In its proper proportion, it is fit for use in half the full amount; but if he left out any one of its spices, he is liable to the death penalty.*

תַּנְיָא *It is taught, Bar Kappara says: Once every sixty or seventy years,* the accumulated leftovers reached half the yearly quantity. Bar Kappara taught further: Had one put a kortov of fruit-honey* into it, no person could have resisted its scent. Why did they not mix fruit-honey into it? — because the Torah says: 'For any leaven or any fruit-honey, you are not to burn from them a fire-offering to HASHEM.'*[1]

(1) *Leviticus* 2:11.

ruling to the whole year (*Hil. Klei HaMikdash* 2:8) because it is regarded as קְטֹרֶת זָרָה, *strange* [i.e., unauthorized] *incense.*

פִּטְּמָהּ לַחֲצָאִין — *If one mixed it in half-quantities.* Instead of mixing 368 *maneh* as was customarily done, someone mixed only 184 *maneh.* Since the manner of compounding was transmitted orally, the question arose whether it was forbidden to prepare spice-mixtures totaling *less* than the usual 368 *maneh.* Rabbi Nassan stated that he had learned that it *was* permitted to make mixtures containing exactly half the normal amount, but he did not know whether smaller mixtures, too, were permitted. To this Rabbi Yehudah replied that any amount, even a one-day supply, was acceptable, provided the ingredients were in the correct proportion.

אַחַת לְשִׁשִּׁים אוֹ לְשִׁבְעִים שָׁנָה — *Once every sixty or seventy years.* We learned earlier that three *maneh* were set aside from which the *Kohen Gadol* filled his hands on Yom Kippur. A quantity (depending on the size of the *Kohen Gadol's* hands) of this mixture was unused, and was set aside. Over many years, enough of this leftover incense had accumulated to provide 184 *maneh,* or a half-year supply of incense. When that happened, only half the normal mixture had to be made for the coming year.

קוֹרְטוֹב שֶׁל דְּבַשׁ — *A kortov of fruit-honey.* Honey or any other fruit juice or product would have made the scent irresistible, but the Torah

The next three verses, each beginning ה׳, are recited three times each.

יהוה צְבָאוֹת עִמָּנוּ,* מִשְׂגָּב לָנוּ אֱלֹהֵי יַעֲקֹב, סֶלָה.[1]
יהוה צְבָאוֹת, אַשְׁרֵי אָדָם בֹּטֵחַ בָּךְ.[2]
יהוה הוֹשִׁיעָה, הַמֶּלֶךְ יַעֲנֵנוּ בְיוֹם קָרְאֵנוּ.[3]

אַתָּה סֵתֶר לִי, מִצַּר תִּצְּרֵנִי, רָנֵּי פַלֵּט, תְּסוֹבְבֵנִי, סֶלָה.[4] וְעָרְבָה לַיהוה מִנְחַת יְהוּדָה וִירוּשָׁלָיִם, כִּימֵי עוֹלָם וּכְשָׁנִים קַדְמֹנִיּוֹת.[5]

יומא לג.

אַבַּיֵי הֲוָה מְסַדֵּר* סֵדֶר הַמַּעֲרָכָה מִשְּׁמָא דִגְמָרָא וְאַלִּבָּא דְאַבָּא שָׁאוּל: מַעֲרָכָה גְדוֹלָה* קוֹדֶמֶת לְמַעֲרָכָה שְׁנִיָּה* שֶׁל קְטֹרֶת; וּמַעֲרָכָה שְׁנִיָּה שֶׁל קְטֹרֶת קוֹדֶמֶת לְסִדּוּר שְׁנֵי גִזְרֵי עֵצִים;* וְסִדּוּר שְׁנֵי גִזְרֵי עֵצִים קוֹדֵם לְדִשּׁוּן מִזְבֵּחַ הַפְּנִימִי; וְדִשּׁוּן מִזְבֵּחַ הַפְּנִימִי קוֹדֵם לַהֲטָבַת חָמֵשׁ נֵרוֹת;* וַהֲטָבַת חָמֵשׁ נֵרוֹת קוֹדֶמֶת לְדַם הַתָּמִיד; וְדַם הַתָּמִיד קוֹדֵם לַהֲטָבַת שְׁתֵּי נֵרוֹת; וַהֲטָבַת שְׁתֵּי נֵרוֹת קוֹדֶמֶת לִקְטֹרֶת; וּקְטֹרֶת קוֹדֶמֶת לְאֵבָרִים; וְאֵבָרִים לְמִנְחָה; וּמִנְחָה לַחֲבִתִּין;* וַחֲבִתִּין לִנְסָכִין; וּנְסָכִין לְמוּסָפִין;* וּמוּסָפִין לְבָזִיכִין;* וּבָזִיכִין קוֹדְמִין לְתָמִיד שֶׁל בֵּין הָעַרְבָּיִם, שֶׁנֶּאֱמַר: וְעָרַךְ עָלֶיהָ הָעֹלָה, וְהִקְטִיר עָלֶיהָ חֶלְבֵי הַשְּׁלָמִים.[6] עָלֶיהָ הַשְׁלֵם* כָּל הַקָּרְבָּנוֹת כֻּלָּם.

---

forbids the use of fruit products in the incense (*Rashi* to *Leviticus* 2:11; see *Mishnah L'Melech* to *Hil. Issurei Mizbe'ach* 5:1).

A *kortov* equals 1/256 of a *kab*. Here it is used to mean a minimal amount, a touch.

ה׳ צְבָאוֹת עִמָּנוּ — *HASHEM, Master of Legions, is with us. Yerushalmi Berachos* 5:1 cites Rabbi Yochanan who says of the first two verses, 'One should never let them depart from his mouth.' Therefore, they have been introduced into the daily prayers at several points. *Arizal* teaches that they should be repeated three times after each mention of קְטֹרֶת, *incense*, which is why they are inserted here.

The first verse proclaims the principle of הַשְׁגָּחָה פְּרָטִית, *individual Providence*, while the second declares the praise of one who trusts in God. *Iyun Tefillah* points to two events that show how הַשְׁגָּחָה פְּרָטִית and total trust in God played important roles in shaping Rabbi Yochanan's life and lifestyle:

Once, Rabbi Yochanan and his colleague Ilfa were so poverty stricken that they had no choice but to leave the study hall to seek their fortune. On the way, Rabbi Yochanan — but not Ilfa — heard one angel say to another that the two former students deserve to die because 'they forsake the eternal life and go to engage in a temporary life.' Since Ilfa did not hear the message, Rabbi Yochanan understood that it was directed not at Ilfa but at himself. He returned to the yeshivah and became the outstanding sage of his time (*Taanis* 21a). Thus, Rabbi Yochanan's life was changed by a particular incident of individual Providence.

As an elderly man, Rabbi Yochanan, who had become wealthy despite his Torah study, pointed out to Rabbi Chiya bar Abba many valuable properties that he had sold in order to enable him not to interrupt his Torah study. Rabbi Chiya wept at the thought that Rabbi Yochanan had left nothing for his own old age. Rabbi Yochanan replied, 'Chiya, my son, do you think so little of what I have done? I have sold a material thing, that was presented after six days, as it says (*Exodus* 20:11): *For in six days HASHEM made heaven and earth.* But the Torah was given after forty days [of God's instruction to Moses] as it says (ibid. 34:28): *And* [Moses] *was there with HASHEM for forty days.*' It was because of such commitment that Rabbi Yochanan was regarded by his generation as the very symbol of dedication to Torah study and faith that God would provide for his material

The next three verses, each beginning *'HASHEM,'* are recited three times each.

*HASHEM, Master of Legions, is with us,**
a stronghold for us is the God of Jacob, Selah![1]
HASHEM, Master of Legions,
praiseworthy is the person who trusts in You.[2]
HASHEM, save! May the King answer us on the day we call![3]

You are a shelter for me; from distress You preserve me; with glad song of rescue, You envelop me, Selah![4] *May the offering of Judah and Jerusalem be pleasing to HASHEM, as in days of old and in former years.*[5]

Talmud, *Yoma* 33a

אַבַּיֵי *Abaye listed* the order of the Altar service based on the tradition and according to Abba Shaul: The arrangement of the large pyre* precedes that of the secondary pyre* for the incense-offering; the secondary pyre for the incense-offering precedes the placement of two logs;* the placement of two logs precedes the removal of ashes from the Inner Altar; the removal of ashes from the Inner Altar precedes the cleaning of five lamps [of the Menorah];* the cleaning of the five lamps precedes the [dashing of the] blood of the continual offering; the blood of the continual offering precedes the cleaning of the [other] two lamps; the cleaning of the two lamps precedes the incense; the incense precedes the [burning of the] limbs; the [burning of the] limbs [precedes] the meal-offering; the meal-offering [precedes] the pancakes;* the pancakes [precede] the wine-libations; the wine-libations [precede] the mussaf-offering;* the mussaf-offering [precedes] the bowls [of frankincense];* the bowls [precede] the afternoon continual offering, for it is said: 'And he is to arrange the elevation-offering upon it and burn the fats of the peace-offerings upon it,'*[6] *— 'upon it' [the elevation-offering] you are to complete* all the [day's] offerings.*

(1) *Psalms* 46:8. (2) 84:13. (3) 20:10. (4) 32:7. (5) *Malachi* 3:4. (6) *Leviticus* 6:5.

---

needs (*Shir HaShirim Rabbah* to 8:7). As a man of such faith, Rabbi Yochanan personifies the verse ... *praiseworthy is the person who trusts in You.*

◆§ **אַבַּיֵי הֲוָה מְסַדֵּר** — *Abaye listed.* To conclude the description of the daily service, we recite the full order of the morning service as transmitted by Abaye. Although he lived several generations after the Destruction, he taught the order, as it had been transmitted orally, in the name of Abba Shaul, a Mishnaic sage (*Tanna*).

מַעֲרָכָה גְדוֹלָה — *The large pyre* at the center of the Altar, upon which the offerings were burned.

מַעֲרָכָה שְׁנִיָּה — *The secondary pyre* near the southwest corner of the Altar, from which glowing coals were taken into the Sanctuary for the burning of the daily incense.

סִדּוּר שְׁנֵי גִּזְרֵי עֵצִים — *The placement of two logs.* Two large sections of wood were placed on the large pyre every morning. More wood could be added during the day, as needed.

הֲטָבַת חָמֵשׁ נֵרוֹת — *The cleaning of five lamps [of the Menorah].* The Temple Menorah had seven lamps. Scriptural exegesis teaches that the lamps, which had burned all night, are cleaned in two steps, first five and then two.

חֲבִתִּין — *The pancakes.* The *Kohen Gadol* was required to bring a meal-offering every day, half in the morning and half in the afternoon. It was baked in a low, flat pan called a מַחֲבַת, hence the name מִנְחַת חֲבִתִּין.

מוּסָפִין — *The mussaf-offering,* on the Sabbath, Festivals, and Rosh Chodesh.

בָּזִיכִין — *The bowls [of frankincense].* These two bowls were placed with the showbread every week. The bread was eaten by the *Kohanim* and the incense was burned on the Altar after the showbread was removed from the Table.

הַשְּׁלָמִים עָלֶיהָ הַשְׁלֵם — *Of the peace-offerings ... upon it you are to complete.* The Sages expound the word הַשְּׁלָמִים, *the peace-offerings.* It is

אָנָּא בְּכֹחַ* גְּדֻלַּת יְמִינְךָ תַּתִּיר צְרוּרָה.* אב״ג ית״ץ
קַבֵּל רִנַּת עַמְּךָ שַׂגְּבֵנוּ טַהֲרֵנוּ נוֹרָא. קר״ע שט״ן
נָא גִבּוֹר דּוֹרְשֵׁי יִחוּדְךָ* כְּבָבַת שָׁמְרֵם. נג״ד יכ״ש
בָּרְכֵם טַהֲרֵם רַחֲמֵם* צִדְקָתְךָ תָּמִיד גָּמְלֵם. בט״ר צת״ג
חֲסִין קָדוֹשׁ בְּרוֹב טוּבְךָ נַהֵל עֲדָתֶךָ. חק״ב טנ״ע
יָחִיד גֵּאֶה לְעַמְּךָ פְּנֵה זוֹכְרֵי קְדֻשָּׁתֶךָ. יג״ל פז״ק
שַׁוְעָתֵנוּ קַבֵּל וּשְׁמַע צַעֲקָתֵנוּ יוֹדֵעַ תַּעֲלֻמוֹת. שק״ו צי״ת
בָּרוּךְ שֵׁם כְּבוֹד מַלְכוּתוֹ לְעוֹלָם וָעֶד.

Some omit the following paragraph on the Sabbath and *Yom Tov.*

רִבּוֹן הָעוֹלָמִים,* אַתָּה צִוִּיתָנוּ לְהַקְרִיב קָרְבַּן הַתָּמִיד בְּמוֹעֲדוֹ, וְלִהְיוֹת כֹּהֲנִים בַּעֲבוֹדָתָם, וּלְוִיִּם בְּדוּכָנָם, וְיִשְׂרָאֵל בְּמַעֲמָדָם. וְעַתָּה בַּעֲוֹנוֹתֵינוּ חָרַב בֵּית הַמִּקְדָּשׁ וּבָטֵל הַתָּמִיד, וְאֵין לָנוּ לֹא כֹהֵן בַּעֲבוֹדָתוֹ, וְלֹא לֵוִי בְּדוּכָנוֹ, וְלֹא יִשְׂרָאֵל בְּמַעֲמָדוֹ.* וְאַתָּה אָמַרְתָּ: וּנְשַׁלְּמָה פָרִים שְׂפָתֵינוּ.[1] לָכֵן יְהִי רָצוֹן מִלְּפָנֶיךָ, יהוה אֱלֹהֵינוּ וֵאלֹהֵי אֲבוֹתֵינוּ, שֶׁיְּהֵא שִׂיחַ שִׂפְתוֹתֵינוּ חָשׁוּב וּמְקֻבָּל וּמְרֻצֶּה לְפָנֶיךָ, כְּאִלּוּ הִקְרַבְנוּ קָרְבַּן הַתָּמִיד בְּמוֹעֲדוֹ, וְעָמַדְנוּ עַל מַעֲמָדוֹ.

On the Sabbath add (במדבר כח:ט-י):

וּבְיוֹם הַשַּׁבָּת* שְׁנֵי כְבָשִׂים בְּנֵי שָׁנָה תְּמִימִם, וּשְׁנֵי עֶשְׂרֹנִים סֹלֶת מִנְחָה בְּלוּלָה בַשֶּׁמֶן, וְנִסְכּוֹ. עֹלַת שַׁבַּת בְּשַׁבַּתּוֹ, עַל עֹלַת הַתָּמִיד וְנִסְכָּהּ.

interpreted as if pronounced הַשְׁלָמִים, *the completions,* meaning that all the services of the day should be completed after the morning *tamid,* and before the afternoon *tamid.*

אָנָּא בְּכֹחַ — *We beg You! With the strength ...* Tradition ascribes this mystic prayer to the *tanna* R' Nechuniah ben Hakanah. It contains forty-two words, the initials of which form the secret forty-two letter Name of God. Moreover, the six initials of each of its seven verses form Divine Names. The Kabbalists teach that it should be divided into phrases of two words each, but our translation follows the division indicated by a simple reading of the phrases.

תַּתִּיר צְרוּרָה — *Untie the bundled sins.* The accumulated sins of Israel are bound together like a barrier that prevents our prayers from ascending to the Heavenly Throne. We ask God to remove this impediment *(Iyun Tefillah).*

דּוֹרְשֵׁי יִחוּדְךָ — *Those who foster Your Oneness.* The acknowledgment of God's Oneness is paramount (see commentary to שְׁמַע יִשְׂרָאֵל, p. 46). As the nation that accepts this obligation upon itself, Israel pleads for God's protection *(Iyun Tefillah).*

רַחֲמֵם — *Show them pity.* According to some versions, this phrase reads רַחֲמֵי צִדְקָתְךָ, *the mercy of Your righteousness.*

רִבּוֹן הָעוֹלָמִים — *Master of the worlds.* We pray that our recitation of the morning service be accepted in place of the Temple service that we cannot perform. As we say later in this prayer, *'Let our lips compensate for the bulls,'* meaning that our recitation must take the place of the actual offerings.

לֹא כֹהֵן בַּעֲבוֹדָתוֹ, וְלֹא לֵוִי בְּדוּכָנוֹ, וְלֹא יִשְׂרָאֵל בְּמַעֲמָדוֹ — *Neither Kohen at his service, nor Levite on his platform, nor Israelite at his station.* All three categories of Jews were

אָנָּא בְּכֹחַ *We beg You! With the strength* of Your right hand's greatness, untie the bundled sins.* Accept the prayer of Your nation; strengthen us, purify us, O Awesome One. Please, O Strong One — those who foster Your Oneness,* guard them like the pupil of an eye. Bless them, purify them, show them pity,* may Your righteousness always recompense them. Powerful Holy One, with Your abundant goodness guide Your congregation. One and only Exalted One, turn to Your nation, which proclaims Your holiness. Accept our entreaty and hear our cry, O Knower of mysteries.*

Blessed is the Name of His glorious Kingdom for all eternity.

Some omit the following paragraph on the Sabbath and *Yom Tov*.

רִבּוֹן הָעוֹלָמִים *Master of the worlds,* You commanded us to bring the continual offering at its set time, and that the Kohanim be at their assigned service, the Levites on their platform, and the Israelites at their station. But now, through our sins, the Holy Temple is destroyed, the continual offering is discontinued, and we have neither Kohen at his service, nor Levite on his platform, nor Israelite at his station.* But You said: 'Let our lips compensate for the bulls'[1] — therefore may it be Your will, HASHEM, our God and the God of our forefathers, that the prayer of our lips be worthy, acceptable and favorable before You, as if we had brought the continual offering at its set time and we had stood at its station.*

On the Sabbath add (*Numbers* 28:9-10):

וּבְיוֹם *And on the Sabbath day* [the mussaf-offering is]: two [male] first-year lambs, unblemished; two tenth-ephah of fine flour for a meal-offering, mixed with olive oil, and its wine-libation. The elevation-offering of the Sabbath must be on its particular Sabbath, in addition to the continual elevation-offering and its wine-libation.*

(1) *Hoshea* 14:3.

represented in the daily communal service. The *Kohanim* performed the service, Levites stood on a platform to sing the Song of the Day, and the rest of the nation had delegates who recited special prayers and Scriptural passages.

וּבְיוֹם הַשַּׁבָּת – *And on the Sabbath day.* The verses of the Sabbath additional offerings are recited at this point because they will not be read from the Torah. It is never necessary to recite the verses of the Pesach or other Festival offerings because they will be read as the *Maftir* of the day. Although the portion of Rosh Chodesh is read from the Torah on all new moons (with the exception of Rosh Hashanah), the Rosh Chodesh verses are recited here (again with the exception of Rosh Hashanah) for a different reason: since the *Maariv Shemoneh Esrei* is essentially unchanged from that of other days (with the minor exception of יַעֲלֶה וְיָבֹא), the verses of Rosh Chodesh at this point serve as a reminder of the day to the congregants (*Orach Chaim* 48:1).

אֵיזֶהוּ מְקוֹמָן / What is the Location?

The Talmud (*Kiddushin* 30a) teaches that one should study Scripture, *Mishnah* [i.e., the compilation of laws], and *Gemara* [i.e., the explanation of the laws] every day. In fulfillment of that injunction, the Sages instituted that appropriate passages from each of these three categories be included in this section of *Shacharis*. Since Scriptural passages regarding the Temple offerings are part of the service in any case, the Sages chose a chapter of the Mishnah on the same subject. Chapter 5 of *Zevachim*, which begins אֵיזֶהוּ מְקוֹמָן, *What is the location*, was chosen for three reasons: (a) It discusses all the sacrifices; (b) it is the only chapter in the Mishnah in which there is no halachic dispute; and (c) its text is of very ancient origin, possibly even from the days of Moses.

משנה, זבחים פרק ה

[א] **אֵיזֶהוּ** מְקוֹמָן* שֶׁל זְבָחִים. קָדְשֵׁי קָדָשִׁים* שְׁחִיטָתָן בַּצָּפוֹן.* פַּר וְשָׂעִיר שֶׁל יוֹם הַכִּפּוּרִים שְׁחִיטָתָן בַּצָּפוֹן, וְקִבּוּל דָּמָן בִּכְלִי שָׁרֵת* בַּצָּפוֹן. וְדָמָן טָעוּן הַזָּיָה עַל בֵּין הַבַּדִּים,* וְעַל הַפָּרֹכֶת,* וְעַל מִזְבַּח הַזָּהָב.* מַתָּנָה אַחַת מֵהֶן מְעַכָּבֶת.* שְׁיָרֵי הַדָּם הָיָה שׁוֹפֵךְ עַל יְסוֹד מַעֲרָבִי שֶׁל מִזְבֵּחַ הַחִיצוֹן; אִם לֹא נָתַן, לֹא עִכֵּב.

[ב] **פָּרִים** הַנִּשְׂרָפִים* וּשְׂעִירִים הַנִּשְׂרָפִים* שְׁחִיטָתָן בַּצָּפוֹן, וְקִבּוּל דָּמָן בִּכְלִי שָׁרֵת בַּצָּפוֹן. וְדָמָן טָעוּן הַזָּיָה עַל הַפָּרֹכֶת וְעַל מִזְבַּח הַזָּהָב. מַתָּנָה אַחַת מֵהֶן מְעַכָּבֶת. שְׁיָרֵי הַדָּם הָיָה שׁוֹפֵךְ עַל יְסוֹד מַעֲרָבִי שֶׁל מִזְבֵּחַ הַחִיצוֹן; אִם לֹא נָתַן, לֹא עִכֵּב. אֵלּוּ וָאֵלּוּ נִשְׂרָפִין בְּבֵית הַדָּשֶׁן.*

[ג] **חַטֹּאת** הַצִּבּוּר וְהַיָּחִיד* – אֵלּוּ הֵן חַטֹּאת הַצִּבּוּר, שְׂעִירֵי רָאשֵׁי חֳדָשִׁים וְשֶׁל מוֹעֲדוֹת – שְׁחִיטָתָן בַּצָּפוֹן, וְקִבּוּל דָּמָן בִּכְלִי שָׁרֵת בַּצָּפוֹן. וְדָמָן טָעוּן אַרְבַּע מַתָּנוֹת עַל אַרְבַּע קְרָנוֹת. כֵּיצַד, עָלָה בַכֶּבֶשׁ, וּפָנָה לַסּוֹבֵב* וּבָא לוֹ לְקֶרֶן

---

1. אֵיזֶהוּ מְקוֹמָן — *What is the location?* In discussing the various categories of animal offerings, this chapter focuses on the location in the Courtyard where they were slaughtered and the part of the Altar upon which their blood was placed.

קָדְשֵׁי קָדָשִׁים — *The most holy offerings.* Sin- [חַטָּאוֹת], guilt- [אֲשָׁמוֹת], elevation- [עוֹלוֹת], and communal peace- [זִבְחֵי שַׁלְמֵי צִבּוּר] offerings are called 'most holy offerings' because they have stricter laws than individual peace- [שְׁלָמִים] and thanksgiving- [תּוֹדָה] offerings [see below, 6-8], which are called 'offerings of lesser holiness' [קָדָשִׁים קַלִּים]. Among the stricter laws that typify the most holy offerings are that they must be eaten in, and may not be removed from, the Temple Courtyard; and that anyone who makes personal use of them, even before their blood is sprinkled [מוֹעֵל בְּהֶקְדֵּשׁ], must undergo a procedure of atonement. Offerings of lesser holiness, on the other hand, may be eaten and taken anywhere within the walls of Jerusalem, and one who makes personal use of them requires atonement only if he does so after the blood has been sprinkled.

בַּצָּפוֹן — *In the north,* i.e., in the Courtyard to the north of the Altar.

בִּכְלִי שָׁרֵת — *In a service-vessel.* Special vessels were set aside in the Sanctuary for the purpose of receiving blood from the animal's neck after slaughter.

עַל בֵּין הַבַּדִּים — *Between the poles [of the Holy Ark].* On Yom Kippur, the *Kohen Gadol* brought blood into the Holy of Holies and sprinkled part of it toward the Holy Ark, between the two poles of the Ark that extended from either side of it toward the Sanctuary.

וְעַל הַפָּרֹכֶת — *And toward the Curtain,* that separated the Holy of Holies from the Sanctuary. Toward this Curtain, too, the *Kohen Gadol* sprinkled blood.

מִזְבַּח הַזָּהָב — *The Golden Altar.* This Altar, also referred to as מִזְבַּח הַפְּנִימִי, *the Inner Altar,* was actually made of wood and was plated with gold.

מַתָּנָה אַחַת מֵהֶן מְעַכָּבֶת — *Every one of these applications [of blood] is essential* [lit. *prevents*], i.e., atonement has not been achieved if even one of the above blood applications was omitted.

2. פָּרִים הַנִּשְׂרָפִים — *The bulls that are completely burned.* Certain parts (see *Leviticus* 4:8-12) of the animal are placed upon the Altar-pyre to be consumed by the fire. The remainder of the animal is burned outside of Jerusalem (see below).

With the exception of the Yom Kippur sacrifices, only two kinds of bull offerings are completely burned, no part of them being eaten by the *Kohanim.* They are (a) פַּר הֶעְלֵם דָּבָר שֶׁל

Mishnah, *Zevachim* Chapter 5

[1] **אֵיזֶהוּ** *What is the location* of the offerings? [Regarding] the most holy offerings,* their slaughter is in the north.* The slaughter of the bull and the he-goat of Yom Kippur is in the north and the reception of their blood in a service-vessel* is in the north. Their blood requires sprinkling between the poles [of the Holy Ark],* and toward the Curtain* [of the Holy of Holies] and upon the Golden Altar.* Every one of these applications [of blood] is essential.* The leftover blood he would pour onto the western base of the Outer Altar; but if he failed to apply it [the leftover blood on the base], he has not prevented [atonement].*

[2] **פָּרִים** *[Regarding] the bulls that are completely burned* and he-goats that are completely burned,* their slaughter is in the north, and the reception of their blood in a service-vessel is in the north. Their blood requires sprinkling toward the Curtain and upon the Golden Altar. Every one of these applications is essential. The leftover blood he would pour onto the western base of the Outer Altar; but if he failed to apply it [the leftover blood on the base], he has not prevented [atonement]. Both these and those [the Yom Kippur offerings] are burned in the place where the [Altar] ashes are deposited.**

[3] **חַטֹּאת** *[Regarding] sin-offerings of the community and of the individual* — the communal sin-offerings are the following: the he-goats of Rosh Chodesh and festivals — their slaughter [of all sin-offerings] is in the north and the reception of their blood in a service-vessel is in the north. Their blood requires four applications, [one] on [each of] the four corners [of the Altar]. How is it done? He [the Kohen] ascended the [Altar] ramp, turned to the surrounding ledge* and*

צִבּוּר, the bull brought if the *Sanhedrin* erred in a halachic ruling, and, as a result of following that ruling, most of the people violated a commandment for which, if the sin had been committed intentionally, the penalty would be כָּרֵת, *spiritual excision;* (b) פַּר כֹּהֵן מָשִׁיחַ, the bull brought by the *Kohen Gadol* if he made an erroneous halachic decision regarding the above type of sin and himself acted on this ruling.

שְׂעִירִים הַנִּשְׂרָפִים — *He-goats that are completely burned.* If the *Sanhedrin* (highest court) erroneously permitted an act that was a violation of the laws against idol worship, and a majority of the community followed their ruling, their atonement consists of a communal sin-offering — a he-goat that is completely burned.

נִשְׂרָפִין בְּבֵית הַדֶּשֶׁן — *Are burned in the place where the [Altar] ashes are deposited.* The excess ashes from the Altar were removed daily (or as needed) to a ritually clean place outside of Jerusalem. The offerings mentioned in this mishnah and also the offerings of Yom Kippur were burned in that place.

3. חַטֹּאת הַצִּבּוּר וְהַיָּחִיד — *Sin-offerings of the community and of the individual.* Before giving the laws of sin-offerings, the mishnah lists the kinds of communal sin-offerings that fall under this category. The listing is necessary, because the earlier mishnayos, too, have discussed communal sin-offerings, but they fell under the special category of offerings that were completely burned.

וּפָנָה לַסּוֹבֵב — *Turned to the surrounding ledge.* The Altar was ten cubits high. Six cubits above the ground, a one-cubit-wide ledge went completely around the Altar. The walls ascended another three cubits to the Altar top upon which the pyres (see p. 209) burned. In the square cubit located at each corner of the Altar top, the walls rose an additional cubit. These four protrusions were called קַרְנוֹת הַמִּזְבֵּחַ, *the 'corners' of the Altar,* and it was on these 'corners' that the blood of the sin-offerings was placed. In order to reach these ten-cubit-high 'corners,' the *Kohen* walked around the Altar on the surrounding ledge, with the utensil containing the blood. He stopped at each 'corner' of

דְּרוֹמִית מִזְרָחִית, מִזְרָחִית צְפוֹנִית, צְפוֹנִית מַעֲרָבִית, מַעֲרָבִית דְּרוֹמִית. שְׁיָרֵי הַדָּם הָיָה שׁוֹפֵךְ עַל יְסוֹד דְּרוֹמִי. וְנֶאֱכָלִין לִפְנִים מִן הַקְּלָעִים,* לְזִכְרֵי כְהֻנָּה, בְּכָל מַאֲכָל, לְיוֹם וָלַיְלָה, עַד חֲצוֹת.*

[ד] **הָעוֹלָה** קֹדֶשׁ קָדָשִׁים. שְׁחִיטָתָהּ בַּצָּפוֹן, וְקִבּוּל דָּמָהּ בִּכְלִי שָׁרֵת בַּצָּפוֹן. וְדָמָהּ טָעוּן שְׁתֵּי מַתָּנוֹת שֶׁהֵן אַרְבַּע;* וּטְעוּנָה הַפְשֵׁט* וְנִתּוּחַ,* וְכָלִיל לָאִשִּׁים.

[ה] **זִבְחֵי** שַׁלְמֵי צִבּוּר* וַאֲשָׁמוֹת,* אֵלּוּ הֵן אֲשָׁמוֹת: אֲשַׁם גְּזֵלוֹת,* אֲשַׁם מְעִילוֹת,* אֲשַׁם שִׁפְחָה חֲרוּפָה,* אֲשַׁם נָזִיר,* אֲשַׁם מְצוֹרָע,* אָשָׁם תָּלוּי.* שְׁחִיטָתָן בַּצָּפוֹן, וְקִבּוּל דָּמָן בִּכְלִי שָׁרֵת בַּצָּפוֹן, וְדָמָן טָעוּן שְׁתֵּי מַתָּנוֹת שֶׁהֵן אַרְבַּע. וְנֶאֱכָלִין לִפְנִים מִן הַקְּלָעִים לְזִכְרֵי כְהֻנָּה, בְּכָל מַאֲכָל, לְיוֹם וָלַיְלָה, עַד חֲצוֹת.

[ו] **הַתּוֹדָה*** וְאֵיל נָזִיר* קָדָשִׁים קַלִּים.* שְׁחִיטָתָן בְּכָל מָקוֹם בָּעֲזָרָה, וְדָמָן טָעוּן שְׁתֵּי מַתָּנוֹת שֶׁהֵן אַרְבַּע. וְנֶאֱכָלִין בְּכָל הָעִיר, לְכָל אָדָם, בְּכָל מַאֲכָל, לְיוֹם וָלַיְלָה, עַד חֲצוֹת. הַמּוּרָם מֵהֶם כַּיּוֹצֵא בָהֶם, אֶלָּא שֶׁהַמּוּרָם נֶאֱכָל לַכֹּהֲנִים, לִנְשֵׁיהֶם וְלִבְנֵיהֶם וּלְעַבְדֵיהֶם.

---

the Altar, dipped his right index finger into the utensil containing the blood, and deposited the blood upon the 'corner.' Then he would go on to the next 'corner.'

וְנֶאֱכָלִין לִפְנִים מִן הַקְּלָעִים — *They are eaten within the [Courtyard] curtains.* After the specified fats are removed to be burned on the Altar, the flesh of the sin-offerings is distributed to be eaten by male *Kohanim.* It is prepared and eaten only within the Temple Courtyard. The term 'curtains' is borrowed from the period in the Wilderness, when the Tabernacle Courtyard was enclosed not by walls, but by curtains.

עַד חֲצוֹת — *Until midnight.* A sin-offering could be eaten for the remainder of the day on which it was sacrificed and for the following evening. Under Scriptural law it could be eaten until dawn, but the Sages imposed a deadline of midnight to prevent mishaps.

4. שְׁתֵּי מַתָּנוֹת שֶׁהֵן אַרְבַּע — *Two applications that are equivalent to four.* As explained above in the chapter of the *tamid*, p. 211, blood was thrown from the service-vessel at two corners of the Altar walls: the northeast and southwest. The blood would spread out to the two adjacent walls. Thus, the two applications of blood would put blood on all four walls of the Altar.

הַפְשֵׁט — *Flaying.* The hide of all offerings of greater holiness (other than those discussed in mishnah 2) was given to the *Kohanim.*

וְנִתּוּחַ — *And dismemberment.* The elevation offering was cut up in a prescribed way; only then was it completely burned.

5. זִבְחֵי שַׁלְמֵי צִבּוּר — *Communal peace-offerings.* The only such offerings are the two sheep that are brought in addition to the Shavuos *mussaf*-offering [*Leviticus* 23:19]. The other communal offerings are either sin- or elevation-offerings.

אֲשָׁמוֹת — *Guilt-offerings.* There are six kinds of guilt-offerings, all of which are listed in this mishnah. They are:

(a) אֲשַׁם גְּזֵלוֹת — *... for thefts.* If someone owed money — whether a loan, a theft, an article held in safekeeping, or whatever — and intentionally swore falsely that he did not owe it, he is required to bring a guilt-offering as an atonement. See *Leviticus* 5:20-26.

(b) אֲשַׁם מְעִילוֹת — *... for misuse of sacred objects.* If someone unintentionally used objects belonging to the Sanctuary for his personal benefit he must atone by bringing a guilt-offering. See ibid. 5:14-16.

(c) אֲשַׁם שִׁפְחָה חֲרוּפָה — *... [for violating] a*

arrived at the southeast [corner], the northeast, the northwest, and the southwest. The leftover blood he would pour out on the southern base. They are eaten within the [Courtyard] curtains, by males of the priesthood, prepared in any manner, on the same day and that night until midnight.**

[4] **הָעוֹלָה** *The elevation-offering is among the most holy offerings. Its slaughter is in the north and the reception of its blood in a service-vessel is in the north. Its blood requires two applications that are equivalent to four.* It requires flaying* and dismemberment,* and it is entirely consumed by the fire.*

[5] **זִבְחֵי** *[Regarding] communal peace-offerings* and [personal] guilt-offerings* — the guilt-offerings are as follows: the guilt-offering for thefts,* the guilt-offering for misuse of sacred objects,* the guilt-offering [for violating] a betrothed maidservant,* the guilt-offering of a Nazirite,* the guilt-offering of a metzora,* and a guilt-offering in case of doubt* — their slaughter is in the north and the reception of their blood in a service-vessel is in the north. Their blood requires two applications that are equivalent to four. They are eaten within the [Courtyard] curtains, by males of the priesthood, prepared in any manner, on the same day and that night until midnight.*

[6] **הַתּוֹדָה** *The thanksgiving-offering* and the ram of a Nazirite* are offerings of lesser holiness.* Their slaughter is anywhere in the Courtyard, and their blood requires two applications that are equivalent to four. They are eaten throughout the City [of Jerusalem] by anyone, prepared in any manner, on the same day and that night until midnight. The [priestly] portion separated from them is treated like them, except that that portion may be eaten only by the Kohanim, their wives, children and slaves.*

---

betrothed maidservant. The woman involved was a non-Jewish slave who had been owned by two Jewish partners. One of the partners freed her, thus making her half-free and half-slave. But since a freed non-Jewish slave has the same status as a proselyte, this half-free maidservant is half Jewish and half non-Jewish and is forbidden to marry either a non-Jew or a Jew. She is, however, permitted to a Jewish indentured servant [עֶבֶד עִבְרִי], who is permitted to both a Jewish woman and a non-Jewish maidservant. If she became betrothed to a Jewish indentured servant and subsequently had relations with another man, the adulterer must bring a guilt-offering in atonement.

(d) אֲשַׁם נָזִיר — *... of a Nazirite,* who became טָמֵא, *ritually contaminated,* through contact with a corpse. See *Numbers* 6:9-12.

(e) אֲשַׁם מְצוֹרָע — *... of a metzora.* One afflicted by the leprous disease described in *Leviticus* (ch. 13) regains his complete ritual purity upon bringing a series of offerings after he is cured. The guilt-offering is brought on the eighth day after he is pronounced cured. See *Leviticus* 14:10-12.

(f) אֲשַׁם תָּלוּי — *... in case of doubt.* This is the only guilt-offering not prescribed for a specific offense or phenomenon. It is required whenever there is a question of whether one has become liable to bring a חַטָּאת, *sin-offering.* As long as such a doubt exists, the possible transgressor can protect himself from punishment through a guilt-offering. However, if and when it becomes established that the offense was indeed committed, the person must bring his sin-offering. See *Leviticus* 5:17-19.

6. הַתּוֹדָה — *The thanksgiving-offering.* This offering is brought by someone who survives serious danger or illness. See ibid. 7:12.

אֵיל נָזִיר — *Ram of a Nazirite,* which is brought when a Nazirite completes the period of abstinence he has accepted upon himself. See *Numbers* 6:13-21.

קָדָשִׁים קַלִּים — *Offerings of lesser holiness.* Their greater leniency is obvious from a comparison of

[ז] **שְׁלָמִים*** קָדָשִׁים קַלִּים. שְׁחִיטָתָן בְּכָל מָקוֹם בָּעֲזָרָה, וְדָמָן טָעוּן שְׁתֵּי מַתָּנוֹת שֶׁהֵן אַרְבַּע. וְנֶאֱכָלִין בְּכָל הָעִיר, לְכָל אָדָם, בְּכָל מַאֲכָל, לִשְׁנֵי יָמִים וְלַיְלָה אֶחָד. הַמּוּרָם מֵהֶם כַּיּוֹצֵא בָהֶם, אֶלָּא שֶׁהַמּוּרָם נֶאֱכָל לַכֹּהֲנִים, לִנְשֵׁיהֶם וְלִבְנֵיהֶם וּלְעַבְדֵיהֶם.

[ח] **הַבְּכוֹר** וְהַמַּעֲשֵׂר וְהַפֶּסַח קָדָשִׁים קַלִּים. שְׁחִיטָתָן בְּכָל מָקוֹם בָּעֲזָרָה, וְדָמָן טָעוּן מַתָּנָה אֶחָת,* וּבִלְבָד שֶׁיִּתֵּן כְּנֶגֶד הַיְסוֹד. שִׁנָּה בַאֲכִילָתָן: הַבְּכוֹר נֶאֱכָל לַכֹּהֲנִים, וְהַמַּעֲשֵׂר לְכָל אָדָם. וְנֶאֱכָלִין בְּכָל הָעִיר, בְּכָל מַאֲכָל, לִשְׁנֵי יָמִים וְלַיְלָה אֶחָד. הַפֶּסַח אֵינוֹ נֶאֱכָל אֶלָּא בַלַּיְלָה, וְאֵינוֹ נֶאֱכָל אֶלָּא עַד חֲצוֹת, וְאֵינוֹ נֶאֱכָל אֶלָּא לִמְנוּיָו,* וְאֵינוֹ נֶאֱכָל אֶלָּא צָלִי.

ברייתא דר' ישמעאל – ספרא, פתיחה

רַבִּי יִשְׁמָעֵאל אוֹמֵר: בִּשְׁלשׁ עֶשְׂרֵה מִדּוֹת הַתּוֹרָה נִדְרֶשֶׁת בָּהֵן. (א) מִקַּל וָחֹמֶר; (ב) וּמִגְּזֵרָה שָׁוָה; (ג) מִבִּנְיַן אָב מִכָּתוּב אֶחָד, וּמִבִּנְיַן אָב מִשְּׁנֵי כְתוּבִים; (ד) מִכְּלָל

---

the laws in this mishnah with those above.

7. שְׁלָמִים — *Peace-offerings.* The peace-offerings may be eaten for *two* days and the night between them, while thanksgiving-offerings (mishnah 6) are eaten for only *one* day and a night.

8. וְדָמָן טָעוּן מַתָּנָה אֶחָת — *Their blood requires a single application.* Unlike all the offerings mentioned above, the offerings mentioned in this mishnah do not require multiple applications of blood. The יְסוֹד, *base,* is a part of the Altar, one cubit high and one cubit wide, that juts out along the entire lengths of the west and north walls, but only one cubit along the south and east walls. The blood may be applied only to a part of the Altar wall that is directly above the base.

הַפֶּסַח ... לִמְנוּיָו — *The pesach-offering ... by those registered for it.* Those who eat from a particular *pesach*-offering must reserve their share in it before the slaughter. [See *Exodus* 12:4.] In the case of all other offerings, any qualified person may partake of the flesh.

☙ רַבִּי יִשְׁמָעֵאל / Rabbi Yishmael

As noted above, the Sages prefaced *Shacharis* with selections from Scripture, *Mishnah,* and *Gemara.* As used in the Talmud, *Mishnah* means a listing of laws and *Gemara* means the logic behind and the application of the laws. As a selection from *Gemara,* the Sages chose one that gives the thirteen methods used in Scriptural interpretation. This passage is a *baraisa* [literally, *outside*], meaning that it is one of the countless Talmudic teachings that was 'left out' of the *Mishnah* when that basic compendium of laws was formulated. Though not part of the *Mishnah,* the *baraisos* are authoritative and are cited by the *Gemara* constantly. Unlike most *baraisos* which are statements of law, this one is a basic introduction to an understanding of the derivation of the laws. It shows us how the very brief statements of the Torah can be 'mined' to reveal a host of principles and teachings. This is why such use of these thirteen rules is called דְּרַשׁ, which implies *investigation* and *seeking out;* we seek to elicit principles and laws from the sometimes cryptic words of the Torah.

This particular *baraisa* is the introduction to *Sifra,* a midrashic work that exhaustively interprets the Book of *Leviticus.* Since most of *Sifra* is of a halachic nature, it was natural that it be introduced with a listing of the principles of halachic interpretation. And since *Sifra* deals mainly with the Temple service, this *baraisa* is particularly apt for this section of *Shacharis.*

☙ The Oral Law

The Torah was composed by God according to the rules of logic and textual analysis contained in Rabbi Yishmael's *baraisa.* (These rules are also known as hermeneutic principles.) The oral tradition governs the way in which these rules are applied and we have no authority to use them in a manner that contradicts or is not sanctioned by the Oral Law. Thus, when

[7] **שְׁלָמִים** *The peace-offerings* are offerings of lesser holiness. Their slaughter is anywhere in the Courtyard, and their blood requires two applications that are equivalent to four. They are eaten throughout the City [of Jerusalem] by anyone, prepared in any manner, for two days and one night. The [priestly] portion separated from them is treated like them, except that that portion may be eaten only by the Kohanim, their wives, children and slaves.*

[8] **הַבְּכוֹר** *The firstborn and tithe of animals and the pesach-offering are offerings of lesser holiness. Their slaughter is anywhere in the Courtyard, and their blood requires a single application,* provided he applies it above the base. They differ in their consumption: The firstborn is eaten by Kohanim, and the tithe by anyone. They are eaten throughout the City [of Jerusalem], prepared in any manner, for two days and one night. The pesach-offering is eaten only at night and it may be eaten only until midnight; it may be eaten only by those registered for it;* and it may be eaten only if roasted.*

Introduction to *Sifra*

רַבִּי יִשְׁמָעֵאל *Rabbi Yishmael says: Through thirteen rules is the Torah elucidated: (1) Through a conclusion inferred from a lenient law to a strict one, and vice versa; (2) through tradition that similar words in different contexts are meant to clarify one another; (3) through a general principle derived from one verse, and a general principle derived from two verses; (4) through a general*

---

we speak of Rabbinic exegesis, or the way in which the Torah is expounded, we do not speak of the invention of new laws, but of the means by which the Oral Law was implied in the Torah itself. It should also be noted that the great majority of the laws were handed down for many centuries from teacher to student, and they were well known without a need to search for their Scriptural sources. Consequently, in the Talmud era when the Sages attempted to set forth the Scriptural derivation of such well-known laws as the use of an *esrog* or the law that an eye for an eye refers to monetary compensation, there were disputes concerning the exact Scriptural interpretations although the laws were familiar.

☙ The Thirteen Rules

The following is a brief explanation with illustrations of the Thirteen Rules by means of which the Torah is expounded:

(1) קַל וָחֹמֶר. Logic dictates that if a lenient case has a stringency, the same stringency applies to a stricter case. Another way of putting it is that laws can be derived from less obvious situations and applied to more obvious ones. For example, if it is forbidden to pluck an apple from a tree on Festivals (when food may be prepared by cooking and other means that may be prohibited on the Sabbath), surely plucking is forbidden on the Sabbath. Conversely, if it is permitted to slice vegetables on the Sabbath, it is surely permitted on Festivals.

(2) גְּזֵרָה שָׁוָה. In strictly limited cases, the Sinaitic tradition teaches that two independent laws or cases are meant to shed light upon one another. The indication that the two laws are complementary can be seen in two ways: (a) The same or similar words appear in both cases, e.g., the word בְּמוֹעֲדוֹ, *in its proper time* (*Numbers* 28:2), is understood to indicate that the daily offering must be brought even on the Sabbath. Similarly, the same word in the context of the *pesach*-offering (*Numbers* 9:2) should be interpreted to mean that it is offered even if its appointed day, too, falls on the Sabbath (*Pesachim* 66a); (b) When two different topics are placed next to one another (this is also called הֶיקֵּשׁ, *comparison*), e.g., many laws regarding the technical processes of divorce and betrothal are derived from one another because Scripture (*Deuteronomy* 24:2) mentions divorce and betrothal in the same phrase by saying ... וְיָצְאָה וְהָיְתָה לְאִישׁ אַחֵר, *she shall depart* [through divorce] ... *and become betrothed to another man*. This juxtaposition implies that the two changes of marital status are accomplished through similar legal processes (*Kiddushin* 5a).

(3) ... בִּנְיַן אָב. A general principle derived from one verse is applied to all cases that

וּפְרָט; (ה) וּמִפְּרָט וּכְלָל; (ו) כְּלָל וּפְרָט וּכְלָל, אִי אַתָּה דָן אֶלָּא כְּעֵין הַפְּרָט; (ז) מִכְּלָל שֶׁהוּא צָרִיךְ לִפְרָט, וּמִפְּרָט שֶׁהוּא צָרִיךְ לִכְלָל; (ח) כָּל דָּבָר שֶׁהָיָה בִּכְלָל וְיָצָא מִן הַכְּלָל לְלַמֵּד, לֹא לְלַמֵּד עַל עַצְמוֹ יָצָא, אֶלָּא לְלַמֵּד עַל הַכְּלָל כֻּלּוֹ יָצָא; (ט) כָּל דָּבָר שֶׁהָיָה בִּכְלָל וְיָצָא לִטְעוֹן טוֹעַן אֶחָד שֶׁהוּא כְעִנְיָנוֹ, יָצָא לְהָקֵל וְלֹא לְהַחֲמִיר; (י) כָּל דָּבָר שֶׁהָיָה בִּכְלָל וְיָצָא לִטְעוֹן טֹעַן אַחֵר שֶׁלֹּא כְעִנְיָנוֹ, יָצָא לְהָקֵל וּלְהַחֲמִיר; (יא) כָּל דָּבָר שֶׁהָיָה בִּכְלָל וְיָצָא לִדּוֹן בַּדָּבָר הֶחָדָשׁ, אִי אַתָּה יָכוֹל לְהַחֲזִירוֹ לִכְלָלוֹ, עַד שֶׁיַּחֲזִירֶנּוּ הַכָּתוּב לִכְלָלוֹ בְּפֵרוּשׁ; (יב) דָּבָר הַלָּמֵד מֵעִנְיָנוֹ, וְדָבָר הַלָּמֵד מִסּוֹפוֹ; (יג) וְכֵן שְׁנֵי כְתוּבִים הַמַּכְחִישִׁים זֶה אֶת זֶה, עַד שֶׁיָּבוֹא הַכָּתוּב הַשְּׁלִישִׁי וְיַכְרִיעַ בֵּינֵיהֶם.

---

logically appear to be similar. This rule is also known as a מָה מָצִינוּ, lit., *'what do we find?'* For example, since the Torah specifies that one may not marry even his maternal half sister, this בִּנְיַן אָב, *general principle*, dictates that the prohibition against marrying one's father's sister applies equally to his father's maternal half sister (*Yevamos* 54b). The same rule applies when two different verses shed light on one another. Similar situations may be derived from the combination of the two verses.

(4) כְּלָל וּפְרָט. When a generality is followed by a specific, the law is applied only to the specific. For example, in listing the animals from which sacrificial offerings may be brought, the Torah says: *From the [domestic] animals, from the cattle and sheep/goats* (*Leviticus* 1:2). This rule teaches that no animals but cattle and sheep/goats may be used. In such cases the generality [i.e., domestic animals] is mentioned only to teach that no part of the species is included in the law except for the specified items.

(5) פְּרָט וּכְלָל. This is the reverse of the above case. In describing the obligation to return lost objects, the Torah says that one should return: *His donkey ... his garment ... any lost object* (*Deuteronomy* 22:3). The concluding generality teaches that there are *no* exceptions to this rule.

(6) ...כְּלָל וּפְרָט וּכְלָל. The difference between this rule and כְּלָל וּפְרָט (rule 4) is that here the Scriptural phrase is concluded by a general statement. The two general statements imply that everything is included while the specific items in the middle imply that only they are meant. The apparent contradiction is resolved this way: Everything *is* included, provided it is essentially similar to the items specified. For example, in the verse imposing a fine on a thief, there are two general terms — *for any matter of dishonesty* and *for any lost item* — implying that the thief is liable no matter what he has taken. However, sandwiched between these general terms, a number of specific items are mentioned: *an ox ... or a garment* (*Exodus* 22:8). This teaches that the fine applies to any movable object that has intrinsic value, but *not* to real estate, which is not movable, or to contracts, which testify to a debt, but have no intrinsic value (*Bava Metzia* 57b).

(7) ... כְּלָל שֶׁהוּא צָרִיךְ לִפְרָט. This rule tells us that the principles of כְּלָל וּפְרָט and פְּרָט וּכְלָל (numbers 4 and 5 above) do not apply in cases where the introductory general statement or specification requires further clarification for its meaning to be clear. For example, the Torah commands that after slaughtering fowl or non-domesticated kosher animals, וְכִסָּהוּ בֶּעָפָר, *he is to cover [its blood] with dirt* (*Leviticus* 17:13). The generalization *to cover* requires clarification because it could be taken to mean that it can be poured into an enclosed pot or covered with wood or some other solid. Therefore, *with dirt* is needed to indicate that the covering must be a soft substance that can easily mix with the blood. Accordingly, it is not a 'specification' in the sense of principle 4, but a clarification (*Chullin* 88b).

(8) ... כָּל דָּבָר שֶׁהָיָה בִּכְלָל וְיָצָא ... לְלַמֵּד. This principle is best explained by an example. The Torah (*Leviticus* 7:19) forbids the eating of sacrificial meat by anyone who is טָמֵא, *ritually contaminated*. The very next verse singles out the שְׁלָמִים, *peace-offering*, and states that a contaminated person who eats of it is liable to כָּרֵת, *spiritual excision*. This principle teaches that the peace-offering is not an exception to the general rule; rather, that the punishment specified for the peace-offering applies to all offerings.

(9) ... וְיָצָא לִטְעוֹן ... כְעִנְיָנוֹ ... Again, this principle requires an example. In imposing the death penalty on a murderer (*Leviticus* 24:21),

statement limited by a specification; (5) through a specification broadened by a general statement; (6) through a general statement followed by a specification followed, in turn, by another general statement — you may only infer whatever is similar to the specification; (7) when a general statement requires a specification or a specification requires a general statement to clarify its meaning; (8) anything that was included in a general statement, but was then singled out from the general statement in order to teach something, was not singled out to teach only about itself, but to apply its teaching to the entire generality; (9) anything that was included in a general statement, but was then singled out to discuss a provision similar to the general category, has been singled out to be more lenient rather than more severe; (10) anything that was included in a general statement, but was then singled out to discuss a provision not similar to the general category, has been singled out both to be more lenient and more severe; (11) anything that was included in a general statement, but was then singled out to be treated as a new case, cannot be returned to its general statement unless Scripture returns it explicitly to its general statement; (12) a matter elucidated from its context, or from the following passage; (13) similarly, two passages that contradict one another — until a third passage comes to reconcile them.

---

the Torah does not differentiate between premeditated and careless murders. Then the Torah describes a person who chops wood carelessly with the result that someone is killed by a flying piece of wood. Although this case would seem to require the death penalty discussed earlier, the Torah requires such a murderer to go into exile. This principle teaches that he has been singled out for *lenient* treatment, meaning that his exile is *instead* of the death penalty, not in *addition* to it.

(10) ... שֶׁלֹּא כְעִנְיָנוֹ ... וְיָצָא לִטְעוֹן ... After describing the laws regulating a Jewish indentured servant (עֶבֶד עִבְרִי) who goes free after six years of service *(Exodus* 21:1-6), the Torah turns to a Jewish indentured maidservant — who should have been included with her male counterpart. Instead, the Torah says of her that her avenues of going free are entirely unlike those of the male. This has lenient applications, for she may go free even before six years of service (upon the onset of puberty or the death of her master) and it also has a stringent application, for her master can betroth her against her will to himself or to his son (see *Exodus* 21:7-11).

(11) ... וְיָצָא לִדּוֹן ... A *Kohen's* entire family is permitted to eat *terumah* [the priestly tithe], but if his daughter marries a non-*Kohen*, she is no longer permitted to eat *terumah (Leviticus* 22:11,12). What if she is widowed or divorced and returns to her father's household? Since marriage had removed her from the permitted status of the rest of the family, she would not have been permitted to eat *terumah* again unless the Torah had specifically returned her to the family group (which it did, ibid. 22:13).

(12) דָּבָר הַלָּמֵד מֵעִנְיָנוֹ. In the Ten Commandments, the Torah commands, *'You shall not steal.'* The Sages derive from the context that the theft in question must be a capital offense since the injunction against stealing is preceded by the commandments not to kill and not to commit adultery with a married woman which are both capital offenses. The only theft for which someone can receive the death penalty is kidnaping a fellow Jew and treating him as a slave. Thus, *You shall not steal* refers to kidnaping.

דָּבָר הַלָּמֵד מִסּוֹפוֹ. Another form of contextual clarification is that which is found in *Leviticus* 14:34,35. First the Torah teaches that a house with a 'leprous' spot must be torn down. From the end of the passage — which describes the cleansing of the stone, wood and mortar of the house — we derive that this law applies only to houses made of stone, wood, and mortar.

(13) ... שְׁנֵי כְתוּבִים. Two verses may seem to be contradictory, until a third verse explains that each of the two has its own application. After being commanded to remove Isaac from the altar, Abraham asked God to explain two contradictory verses. First God said that Isaac would be the forefather of Israel *(Genesis* 21:12) and then He commanded that Abraham slaughter him (ibid. 22:2). God explained that the wording of the command was to *place Isaac on the altar,* but not to *slaughter* him on it *(Midrash* to *Genesis* 22:12). Thus, there is no contradiction.

יְהִי רָצוֹן מִלְּפָנֶיךָ, יהוה אֱלֹהֵינוּ וֵאלֹהֵי אֲבוֹתֵינוּ, שֶׁיִּבָּנֶה בֵּית הַמִּקְדָּשׁ* בִּמְהֵרָה בְיָמֵינוּ, וְתֵן חֶלְקֵנוּ בְּתוֹרָתֶךָ. וְשָׁם נַעֲבָדְךָ בְּיִרְאָה כִּימֵי עוֹלָם וּכְשָׁנִים קַדְמוֹנִיּוֹת.

קדיש דרבנן

Mourners recite קַדִּישׁ דְּרַבָּנָן. See *Laws* §84-85.

יִתְגַּדַּל וְיִתְקַדַּשׁ שְׁמֵהּ רַבָּא. (.Cong – אָמֵן.) בְּעָלְמָא דִּי בְרָא כִרְעוּתֵהּ. וְיַמְלִיךְ מַלְכוּתֵהּ, בְּחַיֵּיכוֹן וּבְיוֹמֵיכוֹן וּבְחַיֵּי דְכָל בֵּית יִשְׂרָאֵל, בַּעֲגָלָא וּבִזְמַן קָרִיב. וְאִמְרוּ: אָמֵן.

(.Cong – אָמֵן. יְהֵא שְׁמֵהּ רַבָּא מְבָרַךְ לְעָלַם וּלְעָלְמֵי עָלְמַיָּא.)

יְהֵא שְׁמֵהּ רַבָּא מְבָרַךְ לְעָלַם וּלְעָלְמֵי עָלְמַיָּא.

יִתְבָּרַךְ וְיִשְׁתַּבַּח וְיִתְפָּאַר וְיִתְרוֹמַם וְיִתְנַשֵּׂא וְיִתְהַדָּר וְיִתְעַלֶּה וְיִתְהַלָּל שְׁמֵהּ דְּקֻדְשָׁא בְּרִיךְ הוּא (.Cong – בְּרִיךְ הוּא) לְעֵלָּא מִן כָּל בִּרְכָתָא וְשִׁירָתָא תֻּשְׁבְּחָתָא וְנֶחֱמָתָא, דַּאֲמִירָן בְּעָלְמָא. וְאִמְרוּ: אָמֵן. (.Cong – אָמֵן.)

עַל יִשְׂרָאֵל וְעַל רַבָּנָן,* וְעַל תַּלְמִידֵיהוֹן וְעַל כָּל תַּלְמִידֵי תַלְמִידֵיהוֹן, וְעַל כָּל מָאן דְּעָסְקִין בְּאוֹרַיְתָא, דִּי בְאַתְרָא הָדֵין וְדִי בְכָל אֲתַר וַאֲתַר.* יְהֵא לְהוֹן וּלְכוֹן* שְׁלָמָא רַבָּא, חִנָּא וְחִסְדָּא וְרַחֲמִין,* וְחַיִּין אֲרִיכִין, וּמְזוֹנֵי רְוִיחֵי, וּפֻרְקָנָא מִן קֳדָם אֲבוּהוֹן דִּי בִשְׁמַיָּא* (וְאַרְעָא). וְאִמְרוּ: אָמֵן. (.Cong – אָמֵן.)

יְהֵא שְׁלָמָא רַבָּא מִן שְׁמַיָּא, וְחַיִּים (טוֹבִים) עָלֵינוּ וְעַל כָּל יִשְׂרָאֵל. וְאִמְרוּ: אָמֵן. (.Cong – אָמֵן.)

Take three steps back. Bow left and say . . . עֹשֶׂה; bow right and say . . . הוּא; bow forward and say וְעַל כָּל . . . אָמֵן. Remain standing in place for a few moments, then take three steps forward.

עֹשֶׂה שָׁלוֹם בִּמְרוֹמָיו, הוּא בְּרַחֲמָיו יַעֲשֶׂה שָׁלוֹם עָלֵינוּ, וְעַל כָּל יִשְׂרָאֵל. וְאִמְרוּ: אָמֵן. (.Cong – אָמֵן.)

☙ יְהִי רָצוֹן . . . שֶׁיִּבָּנֶה בֵּית הַמִּקְדָּשׁ — *May it be Your will . . . that the Holy Temple be rebuilt.* Having substituted the laws of the offerings for the actual Temple service, we pray that we may soon be able to offer them in the rebuilt Temple.

☙ **קַדִּישׁ דְּרַבָּנָן / The Rabbis' Kaddish**

'Whenever ten or more Israelites engage in the study of the Oral Law — for example, *Mishnah, Halachah,* and even *Midrash* or *Aggadah* — one of them recites the Rabbis' *Kaddish* [upon conclusion of the study]' *(Rambam, Nusach HaKaddish).* Although the implication from *Rambam* is that this *Kaddish* is recited primarily after the study of halachic portions of the Oral Law, many other authorities maintain that it is recited only after Midrashic material or Scriptural exegesis. *Magen Avraham,* therefore, rules that unless Scriptural verses have been expounded upon, as in the above section of *Shacharis,* a brief Aggadic passage should be taught after halachic study in order that this *Kaddish* may be recited according to all opinions. It has become customary in most communities for this *Kaddish* to be recited by mourners.

עַל יִשְׂרָאֵל וְעַל רַבָּנָן — *Upon Israel, (and) upon the teachers.* The distinctive feature of the Rabbis' *Kaddish* is the paragraph containing a prayer for the welfare of the rabbis, students, and the people who support their study. In the text of the prayer, Israel is named first, out of respect for the nation and because Moses, too, gave first mention to those who provide the necessary support for Torah study. In *Deuteronomy* 33:18, where Moses referred to the partnership of Zevulun, the supporter of scholars, and Issachar, the scholarly tribe, he blessed Zevulun first.

Any prayer for Torah scholars is indeed a

יְהִי רָצוֹן *May it be Your will,* H*ASHEM*, *our God and the God of our forefathers, that the Holy Temple be rebuilt,* speedily in our days, and grant us our share in Your Torah, and may we serve You there with reverence as in days of old and in former years.*

THE RABBIS' KADDISH

Mourners recite the Rabbis' *Kaddish*. See *Laws* §84-85.
[A transliteration of this *Kaddish* appears on page 1146.]

יִתְגַּדַּל *May His great Name grow exalted and sanctified* (Cong.– *Amen.*) *in the world that He created as He willed. May He give reign to His kingship in your lifetimes and in your days, and in the lifetimes of the entire Family of Israel, swiftly and soon. Now respond: Amen.*

(Cong.– *Amen. May His great Name be blessed forever and ever.*)

May His great Name be blessed forever and ever.

Blessed, praised, glorified, exalted, extolled, mighty, upraised, and lauded be the Name of the Holy One, Blessed is He (Cong.– *Blessed is He*) — *beyond any blessing and song, praise and consolation that are uttered in the world. Now respond: Amen.* (Cong.– *Amen.*)

Upon Israel, upon the teachers, their disciples and all of their disciples and upon all those who engage in the study of Torah, who are here or anywhere else;* may they and you have* abundant peace, grace, kindness, and mercy,* long life, ample nourishment, and salvation from before their Father Who is in Heaven* (and on earth). Now respond: Amen.* (Cong. – *Amen.*)

May there be abundant peace from Heaven, and (good) life, upon us and upon all Israel. Now respond: Amen. (Cong.– *Amen.*)

Take three steps back. Bow left and say, *'He Who makes peace . . .'*; bow right and say, *'may He . . .'*; bow forward and say, *'and upon all Israel . . .'* Remain standing in place for a few moments, then take three steps forward.

He Who makes peace in His heights, may He, in His compassion, make peace upon us, and upon all Israel. Now respond: Amen. (Cong.– *Amen.*)

---

prayer for the entire nation, because Israel's welfare is directly dependent on Torah study *(R' Hirsch)*.

This special prayer for members of the Torah community was appended only to the study of the Oral — but not the Written — Law, because that part of the Torah, in particular, was left for the Sages to teach, expound, and study. Historically, the transmission of the Oral Law depended on the teacher-student relationship and tradition, hence the prayer for their welfare.

See commentary to the beginning of *Kaddish* on pages 30-31. [A full commentary and Overview appear in the ArtScroll *Kaddish*.]

דִּי בְאַתְרָא הָדֵין וְדִי בְכָל אֲתַר וַאֲתַר — *Who are here or anywhere else.* The references to all the various places are meant to imply that every town and neighborhood, individually, benefits from those who study Torah within it.

יְהֵא לְהוֹן וּלְכוֹן — *May they and you have.* The blessing is extended not only to the Torah teachers and their students, but to all the people present in the congregation.

חִנָּא וְחִסְדָּא וְרַחֲמִין — *Grace, kindness, and mercy.* [These terms are often used synonymously, but when they are used together we must assume that they have distinct meanings. Some interpretations are as follows:]

— These characteristics refer to how God views us: The most deserving people are nourished through God's חִנָּא, *grace*, while at the other extreme, even the least worthy are recipients of רַחֲמִין, *mercy*, because He displays compassion to every living thing. Those in between are provided for through חִסְדָּא, *kindness (R' Hirsch)*.

— Or, these are characteristics that *we* hope to have: חִנָּא, *grace*, is the quality that makes a person beloved by others; חִסְדָּא, *kindness*, refers to a generous, considerate human being who is kind to others, even the undeserving; רַחֲמִין, *mercy*, is the quality of compassion by which one withholds punishment even when a wrongdoer has earned it *(Siach Yitzchak)*.

אֲבוּהוֹן דִּי בִשְׁמַיָּא — *Their Father Who is in Heaven.* Some *siddurim* add the word וְאַרְעָא, *and on earth*, an addition which, although rejected by some commentators, is used in many congregations.

ON CHOL HAMOED WEEKDAYS CONTINUE ON PAGE 688.
ON ALL OTHER DAYS CONTINUE BELOW.

INTRODUCTORY PSALM TO PESUKEI D'ZIMRAH

תהלים ל

מִזְמוֹר שִׁיר חֲנֻכַּת הַבַּיִת* לְדָוִד. אֲרוֹמִמְךָ יהוה כִּי דִלִּיתָנִי, וְלֹא שִׂמַּחְתָּ אֹיְבַי לִי. יהוה אֱלֹהָי, שִׁוַּעְתִּי אֵלֶיךָ וַתִּרְפָּאֵנִי. יהוה הֶעֱלִיתָ מִן שְׁאוֹל נַפְשִׁי,* חִיִּיתַנִי מִיָּרְדִי בוֹר. זַמְּרוּ לַיהוה חֲסִידָיו, וְהוֹדוּ לְזֵכֶר קָדְשׁוֹ. כִּי רֶגַע בְּאַפּוֹ, חַיִּים בִּרְצוֹנוֹ, בָּעֶרֶב יָלִין בֶּכִי וְלַבֹּקֶר רִנָּה. וַאֲנִי אָמַרְתִּי בְשַׁלְוִי, בַּל אֶמּוֹט לְעוֹלָם. יהוה בִּרְצוֹנְךָ הֶעֱמַדְתָּה לְהַרְרִי עֹז, הִסְתַּרְתָּ פָנֶיךָ הָיִיתִי נִבְהָל. אֵלֶיךָ יהוה אֶקְרָא, וְאֶל אֲדֹנָי אֶתְחַנָּן. מַה בֶּצַע בְּדָמִי, בְּרִדְתִּי אֶל שָׁחַת, הֲיוֹדְךָ עָפָר, הֲיַגִּיד אֲמִתֶּךָ. שְׁמַע יהוה וְחָנֵּנִי, יהוה הֱיֵה עֹזֵר לִי. ❖ הָפַכְתָּ מִסְפְּדִי לְמָחוֹל לִי, פִּתַּחְתָּ שַׂקִּי, וַתְּאַזְּרֵנִי שִׂמְחָה. לְמַעַן יְזַמֶּרְךָ כָבוֹד וְלֹא יִדֹּם, יהוה אֱלֹהַי לְעוֹלָם אוֹדֶךָּ.

Mourners recite קַדִּישׁ יָתוֹם. See *Laws* §81-83.

יִתְגַּדַּל וְיִתְקַדַּשׁ שְׁמֵהּ רַבָּא. (.Cong – אָמֵן.) בְּעָלְמָא דִּי בְרָא כִרְעוּתֵהּ. וְיַמְלִיךְ מַלְכוּתֵהּ, בְּחַיֵּיכוֹן וּבְיוֹמֵיכוֹן וּבְחַיֵּי דְכָל בֵּית יִשְׂרָאֵל, בַּעֲגָלָא וּבִזְמַן קָרִיב. וְאִמְרוּ: אָמֵן.

(.Cong – אָמֵן. יְהֵא שְׁמֵהּ רַבָּא מְבָרַךְ לְעָלַם וּלְעָלְמֵי עָלְמַיָּא.)

יְהֵא שְׁמֵהּ רַבָּא מְבָרַךְ לְעָלַם וּלְעָלְמֵי עָלְמַיָּא.

יִתְבָּרַךְ וְיִשְׁתַּבַּח וְיִתְפָּאַר וְיִתְרוֹמַם וְיִתְנַשֵּׂא וְיִתְהַדָּר וְיִתְעַלֶּה וְיִתְהַלָּל שְׁמֵהּ דְּקֻדְשָׁא בְּרִיךְ הוּא (.Cong – בְּרִיךְ הוּא) – לְעֵלָּא מִן כָּל בִּרְכָתָא וְשִׁירָתָא תֻּשְׁבְּחָתָא וְנֶחֱמָתָא, דַּאֲמִירָן בְּעָלְמָא. וְאִמְרוּ: אָמֵן. (.Cong – אָמֵן.)

יְהֵא שְׁלָמָא רַבָּא מִן שְׁמַיָּא, וְחַיִּים עָלֵינוּ וְעַל כָּל יִשְׂרָאֵל. וְאִמְרוּ: אָמֵן. (.Cong – אָמֵן.)

Take three steps back. Bow left and say . . . עֹשֶׂה; bow right and say . . . הוּא; bow forward and say וְעַל כָּל . . . אָמֵן. Remain standing in place for a few moments, then take three steps forward.

עֹשֶׂה שָׁלוֹם בִּמְרוֹמָיו, הוּא יַעֲשֶׂה שָׁלוֹם עָלֵינוּ, וְעַל כָּל יִשְׂרָאֵל. וְאִמְרוּ: אָמֵן. (.Cong – אָמֵן.)

מִזְמוֹר שִׁיר / Psalm 30 ◆§

This psalm is not part of *Pesukei D'zimrah* (see below) and it did not become customary to include it in the morning prayers until the seventeenth century. Apparently, it was decided to include it in *Shacharis* because it was sung to inaugurate the morning Temple service, and thus is an appropriate prelude to the prayers that take the place of that service *(Tikun Tefillah)*. It is also a fitting conclusion to the Scriptural and Talmudical passages regarding the offerings. Additionally, מִזְמוֹר שִׁיר is an appropriate introduction to the morning psalms of praise because of its emphasis in the faith that God rescues from even the most hopeless situations *(R' Munk)*.

חֲנֻכַּת הַבַּיִת — *The inauguration of the Temple.* How is this psalm, which deals only with David's illness, related to the dedication of the Temple? *Radak* explains that Solomon's eventual inauguration of the Temple represented

ON CHOL HAMOED WEEKDAYS CONTINUE ON PAGE 688.
ON ALL OTHER DAYS CONTINUE BELOW.

INTRODUCTORY PSALM TO PESUKEI D'ZIMRAH

Psalm 30

מִזְמוֹר *A psalm — a song for the inauguration of the Temple*— by David. I will exalt You, HASHEM, for You have drawn me up and not let my foes rejoice over me. HASHEM, my God, I cried out to You and You healed me. HASHEM, You have raised my soul from the lower world,* You have preserved me from my descent to the Pit. Make music to HASHEM, His devout ones, and give thanks to His Holy Name. For His anger endures but a moment; life results from His favor. In the evening one lies down weeping, but with dawn — a cry of joy! I had said in my serenity, 'I will never falter.' But, HASHEM, all is through Your favor — You supported my greatness with might; should You but conceal Your face, I would be confounded. To You, HASHEM, I would call and to my Lord I would appeal. What gain is there in my death, when I descend to the Pit? Will the dust acknowledge You? Will it declare Your truth? Hear, HASHEM, and favor me; HASHEM, be my Helper!* Chazzan– *You have changed for me my lament into dancing; You undid my sackcloth and girded me with gladness. So that my soul might make music to You and not be stilled, HASHEM my God, forever will I thank You.*

Mourners recite the Mourners' *Kaddish*. See *Laws* §81-83.
[A transliteration of this *Kaddish* appears on page 1147.]

יִתְגַּדַּל *May His great Name grow exalted and sanctified* (Cong.– *Amen.*) *in the world that He created as He willed. May He give reign to His kingship in your lifetimes and in your days, and in the lifetimes of the entire Family of Israel, swiftly and soon. Now respond: Amen.*

(Cong.– *Amen. May His great Name be blessed forever and ever.*)
May His great Name be blessed forever and ever.

Blessed, praised, glorified, exalted, extolled, mighty, upraised, and lauded be the Name of the Holy One, Blessed is He (Cong.– *Blessed is He*) *— beyond any blessing and song, praise and consolation that are uttered in the world. Now respond: Amen.* (Cong.– *Amen.*)

May there be abundant peace from Heaven, and life, upon us and upon all Israel. Now respond: Amen. (Cong.– *Amen.*)

Take three steps back. Bow left and say, *'He Who makes peace . . .'*; bow right and say, *'may He . . .'*; bow forward and say, *'and upon all Israel . . .'* Remain standing in place for a few moments, then take three steps forward.

He Who makes peace in His heights, may He make peace upon us, and upon all Israel. Now respond: Amen. (Cong.– *Amen.*)

David's vindication against the taunts and charges of his enemies. His offspring could not have gained the privilege of building the Temple if David had been a sinner.

Another explanation is that the Temple's purpose is best achieved when each individual Jew recognizes God's presence and help in his personal life. Accordingly, by never losing his faith in God, and by finally being vindicated through God's deliverance, David is the perfect embodiment of the Temple's role in the life of the nation (*R' Hirsch*).

ה' הֶעֱלִיתָ מִן שְׁאוֹל נַפְשִׁי — *HASHEM, You have raised my soul from the lower world. R' Yerucham Levovitz* notes that David speaks as if he had already died and descended to the 'lower world,' where sinners are punished after death. From this we learn that one can suffer the anguish of purgatory even while alive! As the Talmud (*Nedarim* 22a) teaches: 'Whoever be-

פסוקי דזמרה ליום טוב ולשבת חול המועד

(Some recite this short Kabbalistic declaration of intent before beginning *Pesukei D'zimrah:)*

(הֲרֵינִי מְזַמֵּן אֶת פִּי לְהוֹדוֹת וּלְהַלֵּל וּלְשַׁבֵּחַ אֶת בּוֹרְאִי. לְשֵׁם יִחוּד קֻדְשָׁא בְּרִיךְ הוּא וּשְׁכִינְתֵּיהּ עַל יְדֵי הַהוּא טָמִיר וְנֶעְלָם, בְּשֵׁם כָּל יִשְׂרָאֵל.)

Pesukei D'zimrah begins with the recital of בָּרוּךְ שֶׁאָמַר. Stand while reciting בָּרוּךְ שֶׁאָמַר. During its recitation, hold the two front *tzitzis* of the *tallis* (or *tallis kattan)* in the right hand, and at its conclusion kiss the *tzitzis* and release them. Conversation is forbidden from this point until after *Shemoneh Esrei,* except for certain prayer responses (see box below).

בָּרוּךְ שֶׁאָמַר וְהָיָה הָעוֹלָם,* בָּרוּךְ הוּא. בָּרוּךְ עוֹשֶׂה בְרֵאשִׁית, בָּרוּךְ אוֹמֵר וְעוֹשֶׂה,* בָּרוּךְ גּוֹזֵר וּמְקַיֵּם, בָּרוּךְ מְרַחֵם עַל הָאָרֶץ,* בָּרוּךְ מְרַחֵם עַל הַבְּרִיּוֹת, בָּרוּךְ מְשַׁלֵּם שָׂכָר טוֹב לִירֵאָיו,* בָּרוּךְ חַי לָעַד וְקַיָּם לָנֶצַח,* בָּרוּךְ פּוֹדֶה וּמַצִּיל,* בָּרוּךְ שְׁמוֹ.* בָּרוּךְ אַתָּה יהוה אֱלֹהֵינוּ מֶלֶךְ הָעוֹלָם, הָאֵל הָאָב הָרַחֲמָן* הַמְּהֻלָּל בְּפֶה עַמּוֹ,* מְשֻׁבָּח וּמְפֹאָר בִּלְשׁוֹן חֲסִידָיו

---

comes angry is subjected to all types of *Gehinnom.'* The flames of frustration, anguish, and melancholy are the equivalent of the fires of *Gehinnom.* Throughout the Book of *Psalms,* most references to 'falling into the lower world' refer to this type of emotional inferno.

פְּסוּקֵי דְזִמְרָה / PESUKEI D'ZIMRAH

The Sages taught that one should set forth the praises of God before making requests of Him *(Berachos* 32a). In this section of *Shacharis,* we concentrate on God's revelation in nature and history — on how His glory can be seen in creation and in the unfolding of events. Accordingly פְּסוּקֵי דְזִמְרָה means *Verses of Praise.* However, many commentators relate the word דְּזִמְרָה to the verb תִזְמֹר, *prune (Leviticus* 25:4). In this view, we now recite 'Verses of Pruning,' which are designed to 'cut away' the mental and spiritual hindrances to proper prayer. Thus, by focusing on God's glory all around us, we prepare ourselves for the *Shema* and *Shemoneh Esrei,* when we accept Him as our King and pray for the needs of the Jewish people.

Because it is a separate section of *Shacharis* with a purpose all its own, *Pesukei D'zimrah* is introduced with a blessing [בָּרוּךְ שֶׁאָמַר] and concluded with a blessing [יִשְׁתַּבַּח]. In this way, it is similar to *Hallel,* which is a complete unit and is therefore introduced by, and concluded with, a blessing.

בָּרוּךְ שֶׁאָמַר / Baruch She'amar

The commentators record an ancient tradition that this prayer was transcribed by the Men of the Great Assembly approximately 2400 years ago from a script that fell from heaven. The prayer contains 87 words, equal to the numerical value of פָּז, *finest gold.* This alludes to the verse *(Song of Songs* 5:11): רֹאשׁוֹ כֶּתֶם פָּז, *His opening words* [i.e., the introductory words of *Pesukei D'zimrah] were finest gold.*

In recognition of its lofty status, one must stand when reciting *Baruch She'amar.* Kabbalists teach that one should hold his two front *tzitzis* during *Baruch She'amar* and kiss them upon concluding the prayer. Mystically, this signifies that *Baruch She'amar* has an effect on 'the higher regions.'

Baruch She'amar begins with a series of phrases in which we bless seven aspects of God. *Rabbi David Hoffmann,* cited and explained in *World of Prayer,* asserts that these seven ideas are all implied by the Four-Letter Name, י־ה־ו־ה. That Name contains the letters of הָיָה הֹוֶה יִהְיֶה, *He was, He is, He will be.* It is the Name that symbolizes God's eternity, mastery of all conditions, and the fact that He brought everything into being and will carry out His will and word. The seven ideas expressed by this Name are:

(1) שֶׁאָמַר וְהָיָה הָעוֹלָם — *Who spoke, and the world came into being.* God is the Creator Who brought all of creation into being and maintains it [עוֹשֶׂה בְרֵאשִׁית] with no more than His word.

(2) אוֹמֵר וְעוֹשֶׂה — *Who speaks and does.* God brings His promise into being even when people no longer seem to deserve His generosity. Conversely, גּוֹזֵר וּמְקַיֵּם, He *decrees and fulfills;* when He warns of punishment, the sinner cannot escape unless he repents sincerely.

(3) מְרַחֵם עַל הָאָרֶץ — *Who has mercy on the earth.* The Four-Letter Name also refers to Him as the merciful God, Who has compassion on the *earth* and all its בְּרִיּוֹת, *creatures,* human or otherwise.

(4) מְשַׁלֵּם שָׂכָר טוֹב לִירֵאָיו — *Who gives goodly reward to those who fear Him.* His reward may not be dispensed in This World, but it will surely be dispensed in the World to Come. Whatever the case, no good deed goes unrewarded.

(5) חַי לָעַד וְקַיָּם לָנֶצַח — *Who lives forever*

PESUKEI D'ZIMRAH FOR YOM TOV AND SHABBOS CHOL HAMOED

(Some recite this short Kabbalistic declaration of intent before beginning *Pesukei D'zimrah:)*

(I now prepare my mouth to thank, laud, and praise my Creator. For the sake of the unification of the Holy One, Blessed is He, and His Presence, through Him Who is hidden and inscrutable — [I pray] in the name of all Israel.)

Pesukei D'zimrah begins with the recital of בָּרוּךְ שֶׁאָמַר, *Blessed is He Who spoke* . . . Stand while reciting בָּרוּךְ שֶׁאָמַר. During its recitation, hold the two front *tzitzis* of the *tallis* (or *tallis kattan)* in the right hand, and at its conclusion kiss the *tzitzis* and release them. Conversation is forbidden from this point until after *Shemoneh Esrei,* except for certain prayer responses (see box below).

בָּרוּךְ שֶׁאָמַר *Blessed is He Who spoke, and the world came into being* — blessed is He. Blessed is He Who maintains creation; blessed is He Who speaks and does;* blessed is He Who decrees and fulfills; blessed is He Who has mercy on the earth;* blessed is He Who has mercy on the creatures; blessed is He Who gives goodly reward to those who fear Him;* blessed is He Who lives forever and endures to eternity;* blessed is He Who redeems and rescues* — blessed is His Name!* Blessed are You,* HASHEM, *our God, King of the universe, the God, the merciful Father,* Who is lauded by the mouth of His people,* praised and glorified by the tongue of His devout ones*

---

and endures to eternity. Not only is God's existence infinite and eternal, He *endures forever,* in the sense that He continues to involve Himself in the affairs of the universe.

(6) פּוֹדֶה וּמַצִּיל — *Who redeems* people from moral decline *and rescues* them from physical danger. The classic example is the Redemption from Egypt, when God took a degraded, powerless rabble and made it a great nation.

(7) בָּרוּךְ שְׁמוֹ — *Blessed is His Name!* The Name by which we call God can in no way express His true essence. Nevertheless, in His kindness to man, He allows us to glimpse some of His properties and express them in a Name.

הָאֵל הָאָב הָרַחֲמָן — *The God, the merciful Father.* We bless God with awareness that He is both all-powerful [אֵל] and filled with mercy, like a father whose behavior is a constant expression of mercy, even when he must be harsh *(Siach Yitzchak).*

בְּפֶה עַמּוֹ — *By the mouth of His people.* The Kabbalists comment that בְּפֶה has the numerical value of 87, and alludes to the number of words

Permitted responses during Pesukei D'zimrah

From this point until after *Shemoneh Esrei* conversation is forbidden. During *Pesukei D'zimrah* [from בָּרוּךְ שֶׁאָמַר until יִשְׁתַּבַּח, p. 272] certain congregational and individual responses [e.g., בָּרוּךְ הוּא וּבָרוּךְ שְׁמוֹ] are omitted. The following responses, however, should be made: אָמֵן, *Amen,* after any blessing; *Kaddish; Borchu; Kedushah;* and the Rabbis' *Modim.* Additionally, one should join the congregation in reciting the first verse of the *Shema,* and may recite the אֲשֶׁר יָצַר blessing if he had to relieve himself during *Pesukei D'zimrah.*

If one is in the middle of *Pesukei D'zimrah* and the congregation has already reached the Torah reading, it is preferable that he not be called to the Torah. However, if (a) one is the only *Kohen* or Levite present, or (b) the *gabbai* inadvertently called him to the Torah, then he may recite the blessings and even read the portion softly along with the Torah reader.

If after beginning *Pesukei D'zimrah* one realizes that he has forgotten to recite the morning Blessings of the Torah (p. 194), he should pause to recite them and their accompanying verses. Likewise, if he fears that he will not reach the *Shema* before the prescribed time (see *Laws* §55), he should recite all three paragraphs of *Shema.*

In all cases of permitted responses it is preferable to respond between psalms, whenever possible. Thus, for example, if one realizes that the congregation is approaching *Kedushah,* he should not begin a new psalm, but should wait for the congregation to recite *Kedushah,* then continue his prayers.

The responses permitted above do not apply during the 'blessing' portions of בָּרוּךְ שֶׁאָמַר and יִשְׁתַּבַּח [i.e., from the words בָּרוּךְ אַתָּה ה׳, *Blessed are You,* HASHEM, until the blessing's conclusion] where no interruptions are permitted.

וַעֲבָדָיו,* וּבְשִׁירֵי דָוִד עַבְדֶּךָ. נְהַלֶּלְךָ יהוה אֱלֹהֵינוּ, בִּשְׁבָחוֹת
וּבִזְמִרוֹת. נְגַדֶּלְךָ וּנְשַׁבֵּחֲךָ וּנְפָאֶרְךָ וְנַזְכִּיר שִׁמְךָ וְנַמְלִיכְךָ, מַלְכֵּנוּ
אֱלֹהֵינוּ. ❖ יָחִיד, חֵי הָעוֹלָמִים, מֶלֶךְ מְשֻׁבָּח וּמְפֹאָר עֲדֵי עַד שְׁמוֹ
הַגָּדוֹל. בָּרוּךְ אַתָּה יהוה, מֶלֶךְ מְהֻלָּל בַּתִּשְׁבָּחוֹת. (Cong. – אָמֵן.)

דברי הימים א טז:ח-לו

הוֹדוּ לַיהוה* קִרְאוּ בִשְׁמוֹ,* הוֹדִיעוּ בָעַמִּים עֲלִילֹתָיו. שִׁירוּ לוֹ,
זַמְּרוּ לוֹ, שִׂיחוּ בְּכָל נִפְלְאֹתָיו. הִתְהַלְלוּ בְּשֵׁם קָדְשׁוֹ,
יִשְׂמַח לֵב מְבַקְשֵׁי יהוה. דִּרְשׁוּ יהוה וְעֻזּוֹ, בַּקְּשׁוּ פָנָיו תָּמִיד. זִכְרוּ
נִפְלְאֹתָיו אֲשֶׁר עָשָׂה, מֹפְתָיו וּמִשְׁפְּטֵי פִיהוּ. זֶרַע יִשְׂרָאֵל עַבְדּוֹ, בְּנֵי
יַעֲקֹב בְּחִירָיו. הוּא יהוה אֱלֹהֵינוּ, בְּכָל הָאָרֶץ מִשְׁפָּטָיו. זִכְרוּ
לְעוֹלָם בְּרִיתוֹ, דָּבָר צִוָּה לְאֶלֶף דּוֹר.* אֲשֶׁר כָּרַת אֶת אַבְרָהָם,
וּשְׁבוּעָתוֹ לְיִצְחָק. וַיַּעֲמִידֶהָ לְיַעֲקֹב לְחֹק, לְיִשְׂרָאֵל בְּרִית עוֹלָם.
לֵאמֹר, לְךָ אֶתֵּן אֶרֶץ כְּנָעַן, חֶבֶל נַחֲלַתְכֶם. בִּהְיוֹתְכֶם מְתֵי מִסְפָּר,
כִּמְעַט וְגָרִים בָּהּ. וַיִּתְהַלְּכוּ מִגּוֹי אֶל גּוֹי, וּמִמַּמְלָכָה אֶל עַם אַחֵר.
לֹא הִנִּיחַ לְאִישׁ לְעָשְׁקָם, וַיּוֹכַח עֲלֵיהֶם מְלָכִים. אַל תִּגְּעוּ
בִּמְשִׁיחָי, וּבִנְבִיאַי אַל תָּרֵעוּ. שִׁירוּ לַיהוה* כָּל הָאָרֶץ, בַּשְּׂרוּ מִיּוֹם
אֶל יוֹם יְשׁוּעָתוֹ. סַפְּרוּ בַגּוֹיִם אֶת כְּבוֹדוֹ, בְּכָל הָעַמִּים נִפְלְאֹתָיו.
כִּי גָדוֹל יהוה וּמְהֻלָּל מְאֹד, וְנוֹרָא הוּא עַל כָּל אֱלֹהִים. ❖ כִּי כָּל
אֱלֹהֵי הָעַמִּים אֱלִילִים, (pause) וַיהוה שָׁמַיִם עָשָׂה.*

---

in this prayer. *Magen Avraham* and *Mishnah Berurah* (51:1) favor the usage of this word. Nevertheless, some authorities feel that the word בְּפִי, which has the same meaning, is the preferred grammatical form.

חֲסִידָיו וַעֲבָדָיו — *His devout ones and His servants.* We would not dare to compose praises on our own, for we are totally inadequate to evaluate God. We praise Him with the words of the great and holy people of the past and with the psalms of David, which are the backbone of *Pesukei D'zimrah* (*Etz Yosef*).

הודו / Give Thanks

הודו לַה׳ — *Give thanks to* HASHEM. The first twenty-nine verses of this lengthy prayer form a jubilant song that David taught Assaf and his colleagues. Assaf and his family were musicians and psalmists whose own compositions are included in the *Book of Psalms.* This song was intended by David to be sung when the Holy Ark was brought to Jerusalem.

According to *Seder Olam,* during the last forty-three years before Solomon inaugurated the Temple, the first fifteen of these verses were sung in the Tabernacle every day during the morning *tamid*-offering service, and the last fourteen were sung during the afternoon *tamid* service. With very minor changes, these verses are also found in *Psalms* 105:1-15, 96:2-13, and 106:47-48. [Incidentally, it is because these verses were recited during the sacrificial service that the *Nusach Sefard* ritual places הודו before *Pesukei D'zimrah.* Given the fact that these verses relate to the offerings, they should be recited immediately after the *Korbanos* section of *Shacharis. Nusach Ashkenaz,* however, does not make this change, because the verses are in *general* praise, and thus similar to the rest of *Pesukei D'zimrah.*]

In its entirety this song calls upon Israel to maintain its faith in God and its confidence that He will bring it salvation from exile and persecution. The first fifteen verses refer to the miracles of past salvations and how our Patriarchs had complete faith in God even though they had nothing to go by but His covenant and oath. The second group of fourteen verses begins שירו לַה׳ כָּל הָאָרֶץ, *Sing to* HASHEM, *everyone on earth.* It refers to the song of gratitude that everyone will sing in Messianic times. Thus, this section parallels the *and His servants* and through the psalms of David Your servant. We shall laud You, HASHEM, our God, with praises and songs. We shall exalt You, praise You, glorify You, mention Your Name and proclaim Your reign, our King, our God.* Chazzan– *O Unique One, Life-giver of the worlds, King Whose great Name is eternally praised and glorified. Blessed are You, HASHEM, the King Who is lauded with praises.*

(Cong.– *Amen.*)

I Chronicles 16:8-36

הוֹדוּ *Give thanks to HASHEM,* declare His Name,* make His acts known among the peoples. Sing to Him, make music to Him, speak of all His wonders. Glory in His holy Name, be glad of heart, you who seek HASHEM. Search out HASHEM and His might, seek His Presence always. Remember His wonders that He wrought, His marvels and the judgments of His mouth. O seed of Israel, His servant, O children of Jacob, His chosen ones — He is HASHEM, our God, over all the earth are His judgments. Remember His covenant forever — the word He commanded for a thousand generations* — that He made with Abraham and His vow to Isaac. Then He established it for Jacob as a statute, for Israel as an everlasting covenant; saying, 'To you I shall give the Land of Canaan, the lot of your heritage.' When you were but few in number, hardly dwelling there, and they wandered from nation to nation, from one kingdom to another people. He let no man rob them, and He rebuked kings for their sake: 'Dare not touch My anointed ones, and to My prophets do no harm.' Sing to HASHEM,* everyone on earth, announce His salvation daily. Relate His glory among the nations, among all the peoples His wonders. That HASHEM is great and exceedingly lauded, and awesome is He above all heavenly powers.* Chazzan– *For all the gods of the peoples are nothings — but HASHEM made heaven!**

---

theme of the morning *Shema* blessings in which we emphasize the redemption of the past, while the second section parallels the evening *Shema* blessings in which we stress the redemption of the future.

The third section of this prayer continues with a collection of verses. It is discussed on the next page, s.v. רוֹמְמוּ.

קִרְאוּ בִשְׁמוֹ — *Declare His Name.* Whatever you accomplish, ascribe it to God's help, and let even the gentile nations know that God's guiding hand is everywhere *(Vilna Gaon).*

לְאֶלֶף דּוֹר — *For a thousand generations.* God's *word,* i.e., His covenant with Israel lasts for a *thousand generations,* a poetic expression meaning forever. He sealed His covenant with Abraham, designated Isaac as Abraham's successor, and then chose Jacob over Esau, thus making Israel His chosen people everlastingly *(Tzilosa D'Avraham).*

שִׁירוּ לַה׳ — *Sing to HASHEM.* As we find repeatedly in the Prophets, in Messianic times all nations will follow Israel's lead in recognizing and serving God. The fourteen verses beginning here allude to those days. However, David also referred to a salvation that occurred in his own lifetime. The Philistines had captured the Holy Ark and destroyed the Tabernacle at Shiloh. But the presence of the Ark in the Philistine cities brought plagues upon them. Recognizing the hand of God in their suffering, the Philistines returned the Ark with a gift of tribute to God. The same will happen in future times when Israel's oppressors will recognize God's mastery.

וַה׳ שָׁמַיִם עָשָׂה — *But HASHEM made heaven.* After having proclaimed that the gods of the nations are vain and useless *nothings,* David made this logical argument: the most prominent and seemingly powerful idols were the heavenly

הוֹד וְהָדָר לְפָנָיו, עֹז וְחֶדְוָה בִּמְקֹמוֹ. הָבוּ לַיהוה מִשְׁפְּחוֹת עַמִּים, הָבוּ לַיהוה כָּבוֹד וָעֹז. הָבוּ לַיהוה כְּבוֹד שְׁמוֹ, שְׂאוּ מִנְחָה וּבֹאוּ לְפָנָיו, הִשְׁתַּחֲווּ לַיהוה בְּהַדְרַת קֹדֶשׁ. חִילוּ מִלְּפָנָיו כָּל הָאָרֶץ, אַף תִּכּוֹן תֵּבֵל בַּל תִּמּוֹט.* יִשְׂמְחוּ הַשָּׁמַיִם וְתָגֵל הָאָרֶץ, וְיֹאמְרוּ בַגּוֹיִם, יהוה מָלָךְ. יִרְעַם הַיָּם וּמְלוֹאוֹ, יַעֲלֹץ הַשָּׂדֶה וְכָל אֲשֶׁר בּוֹ. אָז יְרַנְּנוּ עֲצֵי הַיָּעַר, מִלִּפְנֵי יהוה, כִּי בָא לִשְׁפּוֹט אֶת הָאָרֶץ. הוֹדוּ לַיהוה כִּי טוֹב, כִּי לְעוֹלָם חַסְדּוֹ. וְאִמְרוּ הוֹשִׁיעֵנוּ אֱלֹהֵי יִשְׁעֵנוּ, וְקַבְּצֵנוּ וְהַצִּילֵנוּ מִן הַגּוֹיִם, לְהֹדוֹת לְשֵׁם קָדְשֶׁךָ, לְהִשְׁתַּבֵּחַ בִּתְהִלָּתֶךָ. בָּרוּךְ יהוה אֱלֹהֵי יִשְׂרָאֵל מִן הָעוֹלָם וְעַד הָעֹלָם, וַיֹּאמְרוּ כָל הָעָם, אָמֵן, וְהַלֵּל לַיהוה.

❖ רוֹמְמוּ יהוה אֱלֹהֵינוּ* וְהִשְׁתַּחֲווּ לַהֲדֹם רַגְלָיו, קָדוֹשׁ הוּא.[1]
רוֹמְמוּ יהוה אֱלֹהֵינוּ וְהִשְׁתַּחֲווּ לְהַר קָדְשׁוֹ, כִּי קָדוֹשׁ יהוה אֱלֹהֵינוּ.[2]

וְהוּא רַחוּם יְכַפֵּר עָוֹן וְלֹא יַשְׁחִית, וְהִרְבָּה לְהָשִׁיב אַפּוֹ, וְלֹא
יָעִיר כָּל חֲמָתוֹ.[3] אַתָּה יהוה, לֹא תִכְלָא רַחֲמֶיךָ מִמֶּנִּי, חַסְדְּךָ
וַאֲמִתְּךָ תָּמִיד יִצְּרוּנִי.[4] זְכֹר רַחֲמֶיךָ יהוה וַחֲסָדֶיךָ, כִּי מֵעוֹלָם
הֵמָּה.[5] תְּנוּ עֹז לֵאלֹהִים, עַל יִשְׂרָאֵל גַּאֲוָתוֹ, וְעֻזּוֹ בַּשְּׁחָקִים. נוֹרָא
אֱלֹהִים מִמִּקְדָּשֶׁיךָ, אֵל יִשְׂרָאֵל הוּא נֹתֵן עֹז וְתַעֲצֻמוֹת לָעָם, בָּרוּךְ
אֱלֹהִים.[6] אֵל נְקָמוֹת יהוה, אֵל נְקָמוֹת הוֹפִיעַ. הִנָּשֵׂא שֹׁפֵט הָאָרֶץ,
הָשֵׁב גְּמוּל עַל גֵּאִים.[7] לַיהוה הַיְשׁוּעָה, עַל עַמְּךָ בִרְכָתֶךָ סֶּלָה.[8]
❖ יהוה צְבָאוֹת עִמָּנוּ, מִשְׂגָּב לָנוּ אֱלֹהֵי יַעֲקֹב סֶלָה.[9] יהוה צְבָאוֹת,
אַשְׁרֵי אָדָם בֹּטֵחַ בָּךְ.[10] יהוה הוֹשִׁיעָה, הַמֶּלֶךְ יַעֲנֵנוּ בְיוֹם קָרְאֵנוּ.[11]
הוֹשִׁיעָה אֶת עַמֶּךָ, וּבָרֵךְ אֶת נַחֲלָתֶךָ, וּרְעֵם וְנַשְּׂאֵם עַד
הָעוֹלָם.[12] נַפְשֵׁנוּ חִכְּתָה לַיהוה, עֶזְרֵנוּ וּמָגִנֵּנוּ הוּא. כִּי בוֹ יִשְׂמַח
לִבֵּנוּ, כִּי בְשֵׁם קָדְשׁוֹ בָטָחְנוּ. יְהִי חַסְדְּךָ יהוה עָלֵינוּ, כַּאֲשֶׁר
יִחַלְנוּ לָךְ.[13] הַרְאֵנוּ יהוה חַסְדֶּךָ, וְיֶשְׁעֲךָ תִּתֶּן לָנוּ.[14] קוּמָה

---

bodies — but since *HASHEM made heaven*, how can anyone justify worshiping His creatures in preference to Him? *(Radak)*.

It is important to pause between אֱלִילִים, *nothings* [i.e., the idols] and וַה׳, *but* [lit. *and*] HASHEM. If the two words are read together, it could be understood to mean ח״ו, *all of the gods . . . are nothings and* HASHEM, as if to say that He is like them.

תֵּבֵל בַּל תִּמּוֹט — *The world . . . it cannot falter.* Though the turbulent history of war and conflict often makes it seem as though man will destroy his planet, the climax of history will be the peace and fulfillment of Messianic times. The world cannot be totally destroyed for God has ordained that it will survive *(Radak)*.

רוֹמְמוּ ה׳ אֱלֹהֵינוּ — *Exalt* HASHEM, *our God . . .* From this point until its end, the prayer contains a collection of verses from throughout *Psalms*. *Tzilosa D'Avraham* cites Rabbi Profiat Duran, a refugee from the Spanish massacres of 1391, that these verses collectively were known as פְּסוּקֵי דְרַחְמֵי, *Verses of Mercy*, because they are effective in pleading for God's mercy. Accord-

Glory and majesty are before Him, might and delight are in His place. Render to HASHEM, *O families of the peoples, render to* HASHEM *honor and might. Render to* HASHEM *honor worthy of His Name, take an offering and come before Him, prostrate yourselves before* HASHEM *in His intensely holy place. Tremble before Him, everyone on earth, indeed, the world is fixed so that it cannot falter.* The heavens will be glad and the earth will rejoice and say among the nations, '*HASHEM *has reigned!' The sea and its fullness will roar, the field and everything in it will exult. Then the trees of the forest will sing with joy before* HASHEM, *for He will have arrived to judge the earth. Give thanks to* HASHEM, *for He is good, for His kindness endures forever. And say, 'Save us, O God of our salvation, gather us and rescue us from the nations, to thank Your Holy Name and to glory in Your praise!' Blessed is* HASHEM, *the God of Israel, from This World to the World to Come — and let the entire people say, 'Amen and praise to God!'*

Chazzan– *Exalt* HASHEM, *our God,* and bow at His footstool; He is holy!*[1] *Exalt* HASHEM, *our God, and bow at His holy mountain; for holy is* HASHEM, *our God.*[2]

He, the Merciful One, is forgiving of iniquity and does not destroy; frequently, He withdraws His anger, not arousing His entire rage.[3] *You,* HASHEM *— withhold not Your mercy from me; may Your kindness and Your truth always protect me.*[4] *Remember Your mercies,* HASHEM, *and Your kindnesses, for they are from the beginning of the world.*[5] *Render might to God, Whose majesty hovers over Israel and Whose might is in the clouds. You are awesome, O God, from Your sanctuaries, O God of Israel — it is He Who grants might and power to the people, blessed is God.*[6] *O God of vengeance,* HASHEM, *O God of vengeance, appear! Arise, O Judge of the earth, render recompense to the haughty.*[7] *Salvation is* HASHEM'*s, upon Your people is Your blessing, Selah.*[8] Chazzan– HASHEM, *Master of Legions, is with us, a stronghold for us is the God of Jacob, Selah.*[9] HASHEM, *Master of Legions, praiseworthy is the person who trusts in You.*[10] HASHEM, *save! May the King answer us on the day we call.*[11]

Save Your people and bless Your heritage, tend them and elevate them forever.[12] *Our soul longed for* HASHEM *— our help and our shield is He. For in Him will our hearts be glad, for in His Holy Name we trusted. May Your kindness,* HASHEM, *be upon us, just as we awaited You.*[13] *Show us Your kindness,* HASHEM, *and grant us Your salvation.*[14] *Arise —*

(1) *Psalms* 99:5. (2) 99:9. (3) 78:38. (4) 40:12. (5) 25:6. (6) 68:35-36. (7) 94:1-2. (8) 3:9. (9) 46:8. (10) 84:13. (11) 20:10. (12) 28:9. (13) 33:20-22. (14) 85:8.

ingly, they were adopted in the prayers for an end to exile and dispersion.

From *Etz Yosef, World of Prayer* and others, the following progression of thought emerges from these verses. Even if הֲדֹם רַגְלָיו, *His footstool,* i.e., the Temple, has been destroyed, God heeds our prayers at הַר קָדְשׁוֹ, *His holy mountain.* But the millions of Jews who cannot come to the Temple Mount need not fear that their prayers are in vain because God is always merciful and ready to withdraw His anger in the face of sincere prayer. Though Israel may have suffered grievously in the many places of its dispersion, God avenges it and helps those who

עֶזְרָתָה לָּנוּ, וּפְדֵנוּ לְמַעַן חַסְדֶּךָ.[1] אָנֹכִי יהוה אֱלֹהֶיךָ הַמַּעַלְךָ מֵאֶרֶץ מִצְרָיִם, הַרְחֶב פִּיךָ וַאֲמַלְאֵהוּ.[2] אַשְׁרֵי הָעָם שֶׁכָּכָה לּוֹ, אַשְׁרֵי הָעָם שֶׁיהוה אֱלֹהָיו.[3] ❖ וַאֲנִי בְּחַסְדְּךָ בָטַחְתִּי, יָגֵל לִבִּי בִּישׁוּעָתֶךָ, אָשִׁירָה לַיהוה, כִּי גָמַל עָלָי.[4]

תהלים יט

לַמְנַצֵּחַ מִזְמוֹר לְדָוִד. הַשָּׁמַיִם מְסַפְּרִים כְּבוֹד אֵל, וּמַעֲשֵׂה יָדָיו מַגִּיד הָרָקִיעַ.* יוֹם לְיוֹם יַבִּיעַ אֹמֶר,* וְלַיְלָה לְּלַיְלָה יְחַוֶּה דָּעַת. אֵין אֹמֶר וְאֵין דְּבָרִים,* בְּלִי נִשְׁמָע קוֹלָם. בְּכָל הָאָרֶץ יָצָא קַוָּם,* וּבִקְצֵה תֵבֵל מִלֵּיהֶם,* לַשֶּׁמֶשׁ שָׂם אֹהֶל* בָּהֶם. וְהוּא כְּחָתָן יֹצֵא מֵחֻפָּתוֹ, יָשִׂישׂ כְּגִבּוֹר לָרוּץ אֹרַח.* מִקְצֵה הַשָּׁמַיִם מוֹצָאוֹ, וּתְקוּפָתוֹ עַל קְצוֹתָם, וְאֵין נִסְתָּר מֵחַמָּתוֹ. תּוֹרַת יהוה תְּמִימָה, מְשִׁיבַת נָפֶשׁ, עֵדוּת יהוה נֶאֱמָנָה,* מַחְכִּימַת פֶּתִי. פִּקּוּדֵי יהוה יְשָׁרִים, מְשַׂמְּחֵי לֵב,* מִצְוַת יהוה בָּרָה, מְאִירַת עֵינָיִם. יִרְאַת יהוה טְהוֹרָה,* עוֹמֶדֶת לָעַד, מִשְׁפְּטֵי יהוה אֱמֶת, צָדְקוּ יַחְדָּו.* הַנֶּחֱמָדִים מִזָּהָב וּמִפַּז רָב, וּמְתוּקִים מִדְּבַשׁ וְנֹפֶת צוּפִים. גַּם עַבְדְּךָ נִזְהָר בָּהֶם, בְּשָׁמְרָם עֵקֶב רָב. שְׁגִיאוֹת מִי יָבִין,* מִנִּסְתָּרוֹת נַקֵּנִי. גַּם מִזֵּדִים חֲשֹׂךְ עַבְדֶּךָ, אַל יִמְשְׁלוּ בִי,* אָז אֵיתָם, וְנִקֵּיתִי מִפֶּשַׁע רָב. ❖ יִהְיוּ לְרָצוֹן אִמְרֵי פִי, וְהֶגְיוֹן לִבִּי* לְפָנֶיךָ, יהוה צוּרִי וְגֹאֲלִי.

---

call upon Him.

The term God's 'footstool' refers to the place on earth where He rests His glory, as we find in *Isaiah* 66:1: *So says* HASHEM, *'The heaven is My throne and the earth is My footstool.'*

⊰ לַמְנַצֵּחַ / Psalm 19

This psalm describes how the wonders of creation are a testimony to the glory of God Who made them. Nature sings to God in the sense that each part of the universe acts as God wanted it to and in harmony with all other parts. Seen this way, the universe is like a symphony orchestra playing a continuous song of praise. But after lyrically recounting the wonders of creation, the Psalmist says that all of this is merely an example of the greatness of the Torah — the blueprint that enables man to understand and fulfill God's will.

הַשָּׁמַיִם . . . הָרָקִיעַ — *The heavens . . . the expanse of the sky.* The upper reaches where the planets and stars orbit are called שָׁמַיִם, *the heavens.* The רָקִיעַ, *expanse of the sky,* contains the atmosphere and evaporated moisture that forms clouds and becomes precipitation *(Malbim).*

יוֹם לְיוֹם יַבִּיעַ אֹמֶר — *Day following day brings expressions [of praise].* The daily renewed works of creation, such as the rising and setting of the sun, stir mankind to speak and express God's praises *(Rashi).*

אֵין אֹמֶר וְאֵין דְּבָרִים — *There is no speech and there are no words.* The heavens do not speak, yet the inner soul of man can discern their message clearly *(Radak).*

קַוָּם — *Their line.* The precision of the universe is likened metaphorically to a surveyor's tape stretched out to the ends of the earth. This means that the precision of the cosmos is evident all over the earth to any observer.

מִלֵּיהֶם — *Their words.* The performance of the heavenly bodies speaks of God's wisdom with greater eloquence than the spoken word *(Radak).*

אֹהֶל — *A tent.* The sky is likened to a tent with the sun affixed in its roof *(Ibn Ezra).*

יָשִׂישׂ כְּגִבּוֹר לָרוּץ אֹרַח — *Rejoicing like a warrior to run the course.* The warrior rejoices at the opportunity to go out to war, for he has confidence in his strength. So too, the sun is confident that it will run its course with no interference *(Metzudos).*

עֵדוּת ה׳ נֶאֱמָנָה — *The testimony of* HASHEM *is*

assist us, and redeem us by virtue of Your kindness.[1] *I am* HASHEM, *your God, Who raised you from the land of Egypt, open wide your mouth and I will fill it.*[2] *Praiseworthy is the people for whom this is so, praiseworthy is the people whose God is* HASHEM.[3] Chazzan– *As for me, I trust in Your kindness; my heart will rejoice in Your salvation. I will sing to* HASHEM, *for He dealt kindly with me.*[4]

Psalm 19

לַמְנַצֵּחַ *For the Conductor; a song of David. The heavens declare the glory of God, and the expanse of the sky* tells of His handiwork. Day following day brings expressions of praise,* and night following night bespeaks wisdom. There is no speech and there are no words;* their sound is unheard. Their line* goes forth throughout the earth, and their words* reach the farthest ends of the land; He has set up a tent* for the sun in their midst. And it is like a groom coming forth from his bridal chamber, rejoicing like a warrior to run the course.* The end of the heavens is its source, and its circuit is to their other end; nothing is hidden from its heat. The Torah of* HASHEM *is perfect, restoring the soul; the testimony of* HASHEM *is trustworthy,* making the simple one wise. The orders of* HASHEM *are upright, gladdening the heart;* the command of* HASHEM *is clear, enlightening the eyes. The fear of* HASHEM *is pure,* enduring forever; the judgments of* HASHEM *are true, altogether righteous.* They are more desirable than gold, than even much fine gold; sweeter than honey and drippings from the combs. Even Your servant is careful of them, for in observing them there is great reward. Yet, who can discern mistakes?* From unperceived faults cleanse me. Also from intentional sins, restrain Your servant; let them not rule me;* then I shall be perfect and cleansed of great transgression.* Chazzan– *May the expressions of my mouth and the thoughts of my heart* find favor before You,* HASHEM, *my Rock and my Redeemer.*

(1) *Psalms* 44:27. (2) 81:11. (3) 144:15. (4) 13:6.

---

trustworthy. The *mitzvos* of the Torah are called *testimony*, because they attest to the *faith* of the people who fulfill them *(Metzudos)*.

מְשַׂמְּחֵי לֵב — *Gladdening the heart*. The wise man will rejoice when his intellect will dominate the passions of his body *(Radak)*.

יִרְאַת ה׳ טְהוֹרָה — *The fear of* HASHEM *is pure*. This refers to the negative commandments. The person who is careful not to transgress them is pure, for he has not sullied himself with sin *(Ibn Ezra)*.

צָדְקוּ יַחְדָּו — *Altogether righteous*. There is no contradiction between one law of the Torah and another, whereas in civil law one will very often find inconsistencies and conflicts between different statutes *(Ibn Ezra)*.

שְׁגִיאוֹת מִי יָבִין — *Yet, who can discern mistakes?* Though I try to keep Your commands, who can be so careful that he never errs unintentionally? *(Rashi; Radak)*. שְׁגִיאָה, *mistake*, denotes an error due to imperfect understanding and reasoning from which no man is immune and of which he is unaware. Only Divine assistance can protect a person from these inborn human flaws *(R' Hirsch)*.

אַל יִמְשְׁלוּ בִי — *Let them not rule me*. Do not let my evil inclination overpower me. For, God helps those whose hearts yearn to do what is right and proper [cf. *Yoma* 38b].

וְהֶגְיוֹן לִבִּי — *And the thoughts of my heart*. Please do not limit Your attention to the requests which I express orally. Be aware of the many inner thoughts that I am incapable of expressing *(Radak)*.

תהלים לד

לְדָוִד, בְּשַׁנּוֹתוֹ אֶת טַעְמוֹ לִפְנֵי אֲבִימֶלֶךְ, וַיְגָרְשֵׁהוּ וַיֵּלַךְ.
אֲבָרְכָה* אֶת יהוה בְּכָל עֵת, תָּמִיד תְּהִלָּתוֹ בְּפִי.
בַּיהוה תִּתְהַלֵּל נַפְשִׁי, יִשְׁמְעוּ עֲנָוִים וְיִשְׂמָחוּ.
גַּדְּלוּ לַיהוה אִתִּי,* וּנְרוֹמְמָה שְׁמוֹ יַחְדָּו.
דָּרַשְׁתִּי אֶת יהוה וְעָנָנִי, וּמִכָּל מְגוּרוֹתַי הִצִּילָנִי.
הִבִּיטוּ אֵלָיו וְנָהָרוּ,
וּפְנֵיהֶם אַל יֶחְפָּרוּ.
זֶה עָנִי* קָרָא וַיהוה שָׁמֵעַ,* וּמִכָּל צָרוֹתָיו הוֹשִׁיעוֹ.
חֹנֶה מַלְאַךְ יהוה סָבִיב לִירֵאָיו, וַיְחַלְּצֵם.
טַעֲמוּ וּרְאוּ* כִּי טוֹב יהוה, אַשְׁרֵי הַגֶּבֶר יֶחֱסֶה בּוֹ.
יְראוּ אֶת יהוה קְדֹשָׁיו,* כִּי אֵין מַחְסוֹר לִירֵאָיו.
כְּפִירִים רָשׁוּ* וְרָעֵבוּ, וְדֹרְשֵׁי יהוה לֹא יַחְסְרוּ כָל טוֹב.*
לְכוּ בָנִים* שִׁמְעוּ לִי, יִרְאַת יהוה אֲלַמֶּדְכֶם.
מִי הָאִישׁ הֶחָפֵץ חַיִּים,* אֹהֵב יָמִים לִרְאוֹת טוֹב.
נְצֹר לְשׁוֹנְךָ מֵרָע, וּשְׂפָתֶיךָ מִדַּבֵּר מִרְמָה.*
סוּר מֵרָע וַעֲשֵׂה טוֹב, בַּקֵּשׁ שָׁלוֹם וְרָדְפֵהוּ.
עֵינֵי יהוה אֶל צַדִּיקִים, וְאָזְנָיו אֶל שַׁוְעָתָם.
פְּנֵי יהוה בְּעֹשֵׂי רָע, לְהַכְרִית מֵאֶרֶץ זִכְרָם.

לְדָוִד בְּשַׁנּוֹתוֹ ❧ / Psalm 34

Everything in creation has its place. The previous psalm spoke of the loftiest physical and spiritual forces in creation and how they sing to God. Here we see how His greatness can be perceived even in the most painful depths. David once said to God, 'All that You created is beautiful, and wisdom is the most beautiful of all. However, I fail to understand or to appreciate the value of madness. What satisfaction can You derive from having created a lunatic who walks about ripping his clothing, is chased by little children and is mocked by all?'

God replied, 'David, you will some day need this madness which you now criticize. Furthermore, you will even pray that I give this madness to you.'

A short time later, David was forced to flee for his life from King Saul. Only among the Philistines, Israel's sworn enemies, did he find safety. But even there he was recognized as Israel's greatest warrior and threatened with death. He pretended to be insane and King Abimelech — disgusted by David's lunatic behavior — drove him out. [See *I Samuel* 21:11-16.] Instead of feeling despair, David composed this beautiful and profound hymn. Its verses begin according to the letters of the *Aleph-Beis,* to show that we are to praise God with our every faculty, and to acknowledge that whatever He created — from *aleph* to *tav* — is for the good.

אֲבָרְכָה — *I shall bless.* David's frightening experiences and his miraculous escape inspired him to understand that God's ways are merciful. Hence, he responds with a blessing *(Sforno).*

גַּדְּלוּ לַה' אִתִּי — *Declare the greatness of HASHEM with me.* Not content merely to have been saved, he wants his salvation to be a lesson to others. Let everyone declare God's greatness.

זֶה עָנִי — *This poor man.* In his humility, David looks upon himself as poor and undeserving *(Radak).*

וַה' שָׁמֵעַ — *And HASHEM hears.* He hears and responds even before the supplicant has completed his prayer *(R' Chaim Vital).*

טַעֲמוּ וּרְאוּ — *Contemplate and see. Contemplate* intellectually, by analyzing events, and *see,* by noticing God's deeds — and you will realize *that HASHEM is good (Radak).*

Psalm 34

לְדָוִד *Of David: When he disguised his sanity before Abimelech who drove him out and he left.*

א *I shall bless* HASHEM at all times,*
always shall His praise be in my mouth.

ב *In HASHEM does my soul glory,*
may humble ones hear and be glad.

ג *Declare the greatness of HASHEM with me,**
and let us exalt His Name together.

ד *I sought out HASHEM and He answered me,*
and from all my terror He delivered me.

ה *They look to Him and become radiant,*
ו *and their faces were not shamed.*

ז *This poor man* calls and HASHEM hears* —*
and from all his troubles He saved him.

ח *The angel of HASHEM encamps around His reverent ones*
and releases them.

ט *Contemplate and see* that HASHEM is good —*
praiseworthy is the man who takes refuge in Him.

י *Fear HASHEM, you — His holy ones* —*
for there is no deprivation for His reverent ones.

כ *Young lions may want* and hunger,*
*but those who seek HASHEM will not lack any good.**

ל *Go, O sons,* heed me,*
the fear of HASHEM will I teach you.

מ *Which man desires life,**
who loves days of seeing good?

נ *Guard your tongue from evil,*
*and your lips from speaking deceit.**

ס *Turn from evil and do good,*
seek peace and pursue it.

ע *The eyes of HASHEM are toward the righteous,*
and His ears to their cry.

פ *The face of HASHEM is against evildoers,*
to cut off their memory from earth.

קְדשָׁיו — *His holy ones.* Holy people are those who control their lusts, even the permitted ones (*Ramban*).

כְּפִירִים רָשׁוּ — *Young lions may want.* Strong, vigorous people — like lions in the prime of life — become helpless and destitute, but God will provide for those who trust in Him.

לֹא יַחְסְרוּ כָל טוֹב — *Will not lack any good.* They may not have all the luxuries enjoyed by their neighbors, but they feel no lack of anything because they are content with their lot (*Sh'lah*).

לְכוּ בָנִים — *Go, O sons.* In this sense, go is an exhortation to accomplish a goal (*Radak*).

מִי הָאִישׁ הֶחָפֵץ חַיִּים — *Which man desires life,* i.e., in the World to Come (*Sforno*). In another vein, however, the Psalmist urged people to better their lives in This World by avoiding gossip and slander. David was the victim of constant slander and his generation suffered defeats in battle because they were not careful in their speech [*Yerushalmi Peah* 1:1] (*R' A. Ch. Feuer*).

The *Baal Shem Tov* taught that every person is allotted a given number of words during his life. When he has used up his quota, he dies. Thus, by guarding his tongue, one assures himself of greater longevity.

מֵרָע . . . מִרְמָה — *From evil . . . deceit,* i.e., slander, false testimony, and cursing. *Deceit* refers to

צָעֲקוּ וַיהוה שָׁמֵעַ, וּמִכָּל צָרוֹתָם הִצִּילָם.
קָרוֹב יהוה לְנִשְׁבְּרֵי לֵב, וְאֶת דַּכְּאֵי רוּחַ יוֹשִׁיעַ.
רַבּוֹת רָעוֹת צַדִּיק,* וּמִכֻּלָּם יַצִּילֶנּוּ יהוה.
שֹׁמֵר כָּל עַצְמוֹתָיו, אַחַת מֵהֵנָּה לֹא נִשְׁבָּרָה.
תְּמוֹתֵת רָשָׁע רָעָה,* וְשֹׂנְאֵי צַדִּיק יֶאְשָׁמוּ.
❖ פּוֹדֶה יהוה נֶפֶשׁ עֲבָדָיו, וְלֹא יֶאְשְׁמוּ כָּל הַחֹסִים בּוֹ.

תהלים צ

תְּפִלָּה לְמֹשֶׁה אִישׁ הָאֱלֹהִים,* אֲדֹנָי מָעוֹן אַתָּה הָיִיתָ לָּנוּ בְּדֹר וָדֹר. בְּטֶרֶם הָרִים יֻלָּדוּ וַתְּחוֹלֵל אֶרֶץ וְתֵבֵל, וּמֵעוֹלָם עַד עוֹלָם אַתָּה אֵל. תָּשֵׁב אֱנוֹשׁ* עַד דַּכָּא, וַתֹּאמֶר שׁוּבוּ* בְנֵי אָדָם. כִּי אֶלֶף שָׁנִים בְּעֵינֶיךָ כְּיוֹם אֶתְמוֹל כִּי יַעֲבֹר, וְאַשְׁמוּרָה בַלָּיְלָה. זְרַמְתָּם, שֵׁנָה יִהְיוּ,* בַּבֹּקֶר כֶּחָצִיר יַחֲלֹף. בַּבֹּקֶר יָצִיץ וְחָלָף, לָעֶרֶב יְמוֹלֵל וְיָבֵשׁ. כִּי כָלִינוּ בְאַפֶּךָ, וּבַחֲמָתְךָ נִבְהָלְנוּ. שַׁתָּ עֲוֹנֹתֵינוּ לְנֶגְדֶּךָ,* עֲלֻמֵנוּ לִמְאוֹר פָּנֶיךָ. כִּי כָל יָמֵינוּ פָּנוּ* בְעֶבְרָתֶךָ, כִּלִּינוּ שָׁנֵינוּ כְמוֹ הֶגֶה. יְמֵי שְׁנוֹתֵינוּ בָהֶם* שִׁבְעִים שָׁנָה, וְאִם בִּגְבוּרֹת שְׁמוֹנִים* שָׁנָה, וְרָהְבָּם עָמָל וָאָוֶן, כִּי גָז חִישׁ וַנָּעֻפָה.* מִי יוֹדֵעַ עֹז אַפֶּךָ,* וּכְיִרְאָתְךָ עֶבְרָתֶךָ. לִמְנוֹת יָמֵינוּ* כֵּן הוֹדַע, וְנָבִא לְבַב חָכְמָה. שׁוּבָה יהוה עַד מָתָי,* וְהִנָּחֵם עַל עֲבָדֶיךָ. שַׂבְּעֵנוּ בַבֹּקֶר חַסְדֶּךָ, וּנְרַנְּנָה וְנִשְׂמְחָה בְּכָל יָמֵינוּ. שַׂמְּחֵנוּ כִּימוֹת עִנִּיתָנוּ,* שְׁנוֹת רָאִינוּ רָעָה. יֵרָאֶה אֶל עֲבָדֶיךָ פָעֳלֶךָ, וַהֲדָרְךָ

---

insincere friendship that masks evil designs (*Radak*). It also includes exaggerated praise that lays the groundwork for discussing vices. 'He is a wonderful person, *but* . . .' (*Chazeh Zion*).

רַבּוֹת רָעוֹת צַדִּיק — *Many are the mishaps of the righteous.* Greatness is a product of challenges, brave attempts, and many mistakes. No one becomes truly *righteous* without his share of *mishaps* (*Sfas Emes*).

תְּמוֹתֵת רָשָׁע רָעָה — *The death blow of the wicked is evil.* Wicked people will be destroyed by the very evil they set in motion (*Radak; Rashi*).

תְּפִלָּה לְמֹשֶׁה / Psalm 90

In composing *Psalms,* David drew upon the works of ten psalmists — including Moses — in addition to his own (*Bava Basra* 14b). According to *Radak,* David found an ancient scroll written by Moses. It contained eleven psalms (90-100), which David adapted for incorporation in the Book of *Psalms.* The Talmud (*Nedarim* 39b) teaches that repentance was a prerequisite to creation, for man is the centerpoint of the universe, and unless he can free himself of sin, he will neither fulfill his purpose nor survive. Therefore, this psalm is appended to those that recall the Sabbath, the day dedicated as the memorial of creation.

אִישׁ הָאֱלֹהִים — *The man of God.* Though Moses was a flesh-and-blood man, he elevated himself to the level of a Godly being (*Devarim Rabbah* 11:4).

תָּשֵׁב אֱנוֹשׁ — *You reduce* [lit., *return*] *man.* God crushes the pride of arrogant people (*Rashi*).

וַתֹּאמֶר שׁוּבוּ — *And You say, 'Repent.'* By showing vulnerable man that he is powerless, God 'tells' him to *repent.*

זְרַמְתָּם שֵׁנָה יִהְיוּ — *You flood them away, they become sleeplike.* The Psalmist continues to describe man's transitory nature. His life is like a dream that vanishes without a trace (*Radak*).

שַׁתָּ עֲוֹנֹתֵינוּ לְנֶגְדֶּךָ — *You have set our iniquities before Yourself.* Man may forget his sins, but God's memory is eternal (*Radak*).

יָמֵינוּ פָּנוּ — *Our days passed by.* Because we

צ *They cried out and* HASHEM *heeds,*
and from all their troubles He rescues them.
ק HASHEM *is close to the brokenhearted;*
and those crushed in spirit, He saves.
ר *Many are the mishaps of the righteous,**
but from them all HASHEM *rescues him.*
ש *He guards all his bones,*
even one of them was not broken.
ת *The death blow of the wicked is evil,**
and the haters of the righteous will be condemned.
Chazzan– HASHEM *redeems the soul of His servants,*
and all those who take refuge in Him will not be condemned.

Psalm 90

תְּפִלָּה *A prayer by Moses, the man of God:* My Lord, an abode have You been for us in all generations; before the mountains were born and You had not yet fashioned the earth and the inhabited land, and from This World to the World to Come You are God. You reduce man* to pulp and You say, 'Repent,* O sons of man.' For a thousand years in Your eyes are but a bygone yesterday, and like a watch in the night. You flood them away, they become sleeplike,* by morning they are like grass that withers. In the morning it blossoms and is rejuvenated, by evening it is cut down and brittle. For we are consumed by Your fury; and we are confounded by Your wrath. You have set our iniquities before Yourself,* our immaturity before the light of Your countenance. For all our days passed by* because of Your anger, we consumed our years like a fleeting thought. The days of our years among them* are seventy years, and if with strength, eighty* years; their proudest success is but toil and pain, for it is cut off swiftly and we fly away.* Who knows the power of Your fury?* As You are feared, so is Your anger. According to the count of our days,* so may You teach us; then we shall acquire a heart of wisdom. Return, HASHEM, how long?* Relent concerning Your servants. Satisfy us in the morning with Your kindness, then we shall sing out and rejoice throughout our days. Gladden us according to the days You afflicted us,* the years when we saw evil. May Your works be visible to Your servants, and Your majesty*

---

incurred God's wrath, our days passed by unproductively *(Rashi).*

יְמֵי שְׁנוֹתֵינוּ בָהֶם — *The days of our years among them.* Our time on earth surrounded by the sins and immaturity mentioned above consists of seventy years, on average *(Rashi).*

שִׁבְעִים ... שְׁמוֹנִים — *Seventy ... eighty.* Although Moses, who composed this psalm, lived to one hundred twenty years, this verse speaks of average people *(Radak);* or it was inserted by David [who lived seventy years], since life spans were shorter in his time *(Tosafos).*

כִּי גָז חִישׁ וַנָּעֻפָה — *For it is cut off swiftly and we fly away.* Man's success is fleeting. When our souls fly away, life and accomplishment go with it.

מִי יוֹדֵעַ עֹז אַפֶּךָ — *Who knows the power of Your fury?* Once God's wrath is unleashed, who can guard against it? *(Radak).*

לִמְנוֹת יָמֵינוּ — *According to the count of our days.* Since our lives are so short, make the truth known to us so that we may comprehend it *(Sforno).*

שׁוּבָה ה' עַד מָתָי — *Return,* HASHEM, *how long?* Come back to us — how long will You abandon us? *(Radak).*

שַׂמְּחֵנוּ כִּימוֹת עִנִּיתָנוּ — *Gladden us according to*

עַל בְּנֵיהֶם. ❖ וִיהִי נֹעַם* אֲדֹנָי אֱלֹהֵינוּ עָלֵינוּ, וּמַעֲשֵׂה יָדֵינוּ כּוֹנְנָה עָלֵינוּ, וּמַעֲשֵׂה יָדֵינוּ* כּוֹנְנֵהוּ.

תהלים צא

יֹשֵׁב בְּסֵתֶר עֶלְיוֹן,* בְּצֵל שַׁדַּי יִתְלוֹנָן. אֹמַר לַיהוה מַחְסִי וּמְצוּדָתִי, אֱלֹהַי אֶבְטַח בּוֹ. כִּי הוּא יַצִּילְךָ מִפַּח יָקוּשׁ, מִדֶּבֶר הַוּוֹת. בְּאֶבְרָתוֹ יָסֶךְ לָךְ, וְתַחַת כְּנָפָיו תֶּחְסֶה, צִנָּה וְסֹחֵרָה אֲמִתּוֹ. לֹא תִירָא מִפַּחַד לָיְלָה,* מֵחֵץ יָעוּף יוֹמָם. מִדֶּבֶר בָּאֹפֶל יַהֲלֹךְ, מִקֶּטֶב יָשׁוּד צָהֳרָיִם. יִפֹּל מִצִּדְּךָ אֶלֶף, וּרְבָבָה מִימִינֶךָ,* אֵלֶיךָ לֹא יִגָּשׁ. רַק בְּעֵינֶיךָ תַבִּיט, וְשִׁלֻּמַת רְשָׁעִים תִּרְאֶה. כִּי אַתָּה יהוה מַחְסִי, עֶלְיוֹן שַׂמְתָּ מְעוֹנֶךָ. לֹא תְאֻנֶּה אֵלֶיךָ רָעָה, וְנֶגַע לֹא יִקְרַב בְּאָהֳלֶךָ.* כִּי מַלְאָכָיו יְצַוֶּה לָּךְ, לִשְׁמָרְךָ בְּכָל דְּרָכֶיךָ. עַל כַּפַּיִם יִשָּׂאוּנְךָ,* פֶּן תִּגֹּף בָּאֶבֶן רַגְלֶךָ. עַל שַׁחַל וָפֶתֶן* תִּדְרֹךְ, תִּרְמֹס כְּפִיר וְתַנִּין. כִּי בִי חָשַׁק* וַאֲפַלְּטֵהוּ, אֲשַׂגְּבֵהוּ כִּי יָדַע שְׁמִי. יִקְרָאֵנִי וְאֶעֱנֵהוּ, עִמּוֹ אָנֹכִי בְצָרָה, אֲחַלְּצֵהוּ וַאֲכַבְּדֵהוּ. ❖ אֹרֶךְ יָמִים אַשְׂבִּיעֵהוּ, וְאַרְאֵהוּ בִּישׁוּעָתִי.* אֹרֶךְ יָמִים אַשְׂבִּיעֵהוּ, וְאַרְאֵהוּ בִּישׁוּעָתִי.

תהלים קלה

הַלְלוּיָהּ הַלְלוּ אֶת שֵׁם יהוה, הַלְלוּ עַבְדֵי יהוה.* שֶׁעֹמְדִים בְּבֵית יהוה,* בְּחַצְרוֹת בֵּית אֱלֹהֵינוּ. הַלְלוּיָהּ כִּי טוֹב

---

the days You afflicted us. May our joy in the future be equal in intensity to our past suffering.

וִיהִי נֹעַם — *May the pleasantness.* When the Tabernacle was built, Moses uttered this prayer that it might endure and be blessed by God *(Midrash).* The term נֹעַם, *pleasantness,* refers to the bliss one feels when he has done something that achieved its purpose. When man has this feeling of accomplishment, God, too, feels satisfaction that His will has been done *(Malbim).*

וּמַעֲשֵׂה יָדֵינוּ — *Our handiwork.* Moses repeated the prayer for the success of *our handiwork,* once referring to the newly built Tabernacle and once referring to man's general activities *(Rashi).* This is a plea that we be independent of human pressures that interfere with our service of God *(R' Hirsch).*

⁂ יֹשֵׁב בְּסֵתֶר / Psalm 91

Moses continues his theme that man achieves fulfillment only through closeness to God. Moreover, God will rescue him from all danger. The Talmud *(Shavuos* 15b) calls this hymn *Song of Plagues,* [שִׁיר שֶׁל פְּגָעִים או שֶׁל נְגָעִים] because one who recites it with faith in God will be helped by Him in time of danger. In this psalm, Moses speaks of the faithful believer who finds refuge in *the shadow of the Almighty.* This is the true hero whom God promises long life and salvation.

According to the Midrash, Moses composed this work on the day he completed construction of the מִשְׁכָּן *[Mishkan], Tabernacle,* and these verses describe Moses himself, who entered the Divine clouds and was enveloped *in the shadow of the Almighty.* At that moment, a great question arose: How could a Tabernacle with walls and curtains contain the Presence of the Almighty? The Master of the Universe Himself explained, 'The entire world cannot contain My glory, yet when I wish, I can concentrate My entire essence into one small spot. Indeed, I am Most High, yet I sit in a [limited, constricted] refuge — in the shadow of the Tabernacle.' God's intention in removing the nation from the Egyptian slavery was, *'You shall serve God upon this mountain' (Exodus* 3:12). And it was to this service that the *Mishkan* was dedicated.

יֹשֵׁב בְּסֵתֶר עֶלְיוֹן — *Whoever sits in the refuge of the Most High.* The person who scorns conventional forms of protection and seeks only the refuge provided by the Most High will find his faith rewarded. He will be enveloped by God's *upon their children.* Chazzan– *May the pleasantness* of my Lord, our God, be upon us — our handiwork, may He establish for us; our handiwork,* may He establish.*

Psalm 91

יֹשֵׁב *Whoever sits in the refuge of the Most High,* he shall dwell in the shadow of the Almighty. I will say of* HASHEM, *'He is my refuge and my fortress, my God, I will trust in Him.' For He will deliver you from the ensnaring trap, from devastating pestilence. With His pinion He will cover you, and beneath His wings you will be protected; shield and armor is His truth. You shall not fear the terror of night;* nor of the arrow that flies by day; nor the pestilence that walks in gloom; nor the destroyer who lays waste at noon. Let a thousand encamp at your side and a myriad at your right hand,* but to you they shall not approach. You will merely peer with your eyes and you will see the retribution of the wicked. Because [you said] 'You,* HASHEM, *are my refuge,' you have made the Most High your dwelling place. No evil will befall you, nor will any plague come near your tent.* He will charge His angels for you, to protect you in all your ways. On your palms they will carry you,* lest you strike your foot against a stone. Upon the lion and the viper* you will tread; you will trample the young lion and the serpent. For he has yearned for Me* and I will deliver him; I will elevate him because he knows My Name. He will call upon Me and I will answer him, I am with him in distress, I will release him and I will honor him.* Chazzan– *With long life will I satisfy him, and I will show him My salvation.* With long life will I satisfy him, and I will show him My salvation.*

Psalm 135

הַלְלוּיָהּ *Halleluyah! Praise the Name of* HASHEM! *Praise — you servants of* HASHEM;* *you who stand in the House of* HASHEM,* *in the courtyards of the House of our God — praise God, for*

---

providence so that he can continue to seek holiness and wisdom without fear of those who would seek to do him harm: *He shall dwell in the shadow of the Almighty (Rashi).*

לֹא תִירָא מִפַּחַד לָיְלָה — *You shall not fear the terror of night.* If you put your faith in God, fear will be banished from your heart *(Rashi).*

יִפֹּל מִצִּדְּךָ אֶלֶף וּרְבָבָה מִימִינֶךָ — *Let a thousand encamp at your side and a myriad at your right hand.* Thousands and myriads of demons may encamp around the man who is shielded by God's truth, but they will not be able to come near to harm him *(Rashi).*

וְנֶגַע לֹא יִקְרַב בְּאָהֳלֶךָ — *Nor will any plague come near your tent.* The Talmud *(Sanhedrin* 103a) perceives this as a blessing for domestic tranquillity and that one will have worthy children and students, who will not shame him.

עַל כַּפַּיִם יִשָּׂאוּנְךָ — *On [your] palms they will carry you.* The angels created by the *mitzvos* you perform with your *palms* [i.e., charity and other acts of kindness] will raise you above all dangers that lurk in your path *(Zera Yaakov).*

עַל שַׁחַל וָפֶתֶן — *Upon the lion and the viper.* Even when confronted by ferocious beasts and poisonous reptiles, you will simply tread on them and remain unharmed.

כִּי בִי חָשַׁק — *For he has yearned for Me.* From here to the end of the psalm, God praises and assures the person who has faith in Him.

וְאַרְאֵהוּ בִּישׁוּעָתִי — *And I will show him My salvation.* He will witness the salvation I will bring about at the advent of the Messiah, at the time of the revival of the dead, and at the salvation of the World to Come *(Radak).*

Indeed, it is not God who needs salvation, but Israel; yet God calls Israel's victory, 'My salvation,' to emphasize that Israel's salvation is His as well *(Midrash Shocher Tov).*

⁂ הַלְלוּיָהּ / Psalm 135

The Exodus from Egypt complements the Sabbath. While the Sabbath testifies that God created the universe, the miracles of the Exodus testify that He continues to supervise and guide history. This psalm recounts the miracles of the Exodus and Israel's trek through the Wilderness

יְהוָה, זַמְּרוּ לִשְׁמוֹ כִּי נָעִים. כִּי יַעֲקֹב בָּחַר לוֹ יָהּ, יִשְׂרָאֵל* לִסְגֻלָּתוֹ.
כִּי אֲנִי יָדַעְתִּי כִּי גָדוֹל יְהוָה, וַאֲדֹנֵינוּ מִכָּל אֱלֹהִים. כֹּל אֲשֶׁר חָפֵץ
יְהוָה עָשָׂה, בַּשָּׁמַיִם וּבָאָרֶץ, בַּיַּמִּים וְכָל תְּהֹמוֹת. מַעֲלֶה נְשִׂאִים
מִקְצֵה הָאָרֶץ, בְּרָקִים לַמָּטָר עָשָׂה, מוֹצֵא רוּחַ מֵאוֹצְרוֹתָיו. שֶׁהִכָּה
בְּכוֹרֵי מִצְרָיִם, מֵאָדָם עַד בְּהֵמָה. שָׁלַח אוֹתֹת וּמֹפְתִים בְּתוֹכֵכִי
מִצְרָיִם, בְּפַרְעֹה וּבְכָל עֲבָדָיו. שֶׁהִכָּה גּוֹיִם רַבִּים, וְהָרַג מְלָכִים
עֲצוּמִים. לְסִיחוֹן מֶלֶךְ הָאֱמֹרִי, וּלְעוֹג* מֶלֶךְ הַבָּשָׁן, וּלְכֹל מַמְלְכוֹת
כְּנָעַן. וְנָתַן אַרְצָם נַחֲלָה, נַחֲלָה לְיִשְׂרָאֵל עַמּוֹ. יְהוָה שִׁמְךָ לְעוֹלָם,*
יְהוָה זִכְרְךָ לְדֹר וָדֹר. כִּי יָדִין יְהוָה* עַמּוֹ, וְעַל עֲבָדָיו יִתְנֶחָם. עֲצַבֵּי
הַגּוֹיִם כֶּסֶף וְזָהָב, מַעֲשֵׂה יְדֵי אָדָם. פֶּה לָהֶם וְלֹא יְדַבֵּרוּ,* עֵינַיִם
לָהֶם וְלֹא יִרְאוּ. אָזְנַיִם לָהֶם וְלֹא יַאֲזִינוּ, אַף אֵין יֶשׁ רוּחַ בְּפִיהֶם.
כְּמוֹהֶם יִהְיוּ עֹשֵׂיהֶם,* כֹּל אֲשֶׁר בֹּטֵחַ בָּהֶם. ❖ בֵּית יִשְׂרָאֵל בָּרְכוּ
אֶת יְהוָה, בֵּית אַהֲרֹן בָּרְכוּ אֶת יְהוָה. בֵּית הַלֵּוִי* בָּרְכוּ אֶת יְהוָה,
יִרְאֵי יְהוָה בָּרְכוּ אֶת יְהוָה. בָּרוּךְ יְהוָה מִצִּיּוֹן* שֹׁכֵן יְרוּשָׁלָיִם,
הַלְלוּיָהּ.

Most congregations recite the following psalm while standing.

תהלים קלו

הוֹדוּ לַיהוָה כִּי טוֹב,*   כִּי לְעוֹלָם חַסְדּוֹ.*

הוֹדוּ לֵאלֹהֵי הָאֱלֹהִים,*   כִּי לְעוֹלָם חַסְדּוֹ.

הוֹדוּ לַאֲדֹנֵי הָאֲדֹנִים,*   כִּי לְעוֹלָם חַסְדּוֹ.

---

to *Eretz Yisrael.* It ends with the conclusion that it is worthless to worship anything except HASHEM.

הַלְלוּ עַבְדֵי ה' — *Praise — you servants of* HASHEM. You are free from the bonds of Pharaoh or any other human ruler — you owe allegiance only to God (*Sforno*).

שֶׁעֹמְדִים בְּבֵית ה' — *You who stand in the House of* HASHEM. The prime responsibility to lead Israel in God's praise falls upon the scholars and teachers in the synagogues and study halls (*Sforno*).

יַעֲקֹב ... יִשְׂרָאֵל — *Jacob ... Israel.* 'Jacob' represents the multitude of Jews while 'Israel' represents the great people among them. God chooses even ordinary Jews for His Own, but 'Israel' is His *treasure* (*Siach Yitzchak*).

לְסִיחוֹן ... וּלְעוֹג — *Sichon ... Og.* Upon coming to the part of *Eretz Yisrael* that lay east of the Jordan, the Jewish people encountered and defeated these two kings [*Numbers* 21:21-35].

Thus, they are symbolic of all the rulers whom Israel defeated. Also, they are singled out because of their unusual might (*Radak*).

ה' שִׁמְךָ לְעוֹלָם — HASHEM *is Your Name forever.* This Name symbolizes God's eternity. Just as He controlled history in the past, He continues to do so always (*Rashi*).

כִּי יָדִין ה' — *When* HASHEM *will judge.* Eventually, God will consider the plight of oppressed Israel, and then He will show mercy to His people.

פֶּה לָהֶם וְלֹא יְדַבֵּרוּ — *They have mouths, but they speak not.* Intelligent speech is man's greatest distinction, yet idolaters are foolish enough to worship mute idols! (*Ibn Ezra*).

כְּמוֹהֶם יִהְיוּ עֹשֵׂיהֶם — *Like them shall their makers become.* This can be taken as a prayer, or as a statement of fact that eventually idol worshipers will perish and be as lifeless as the clods they worship (*Radak*).

בֵּית יִשְׂרָאֵל ... בֵּית אַהֲרֹן ... בֵּית הַלֵּוִי — *House of*

HASHEM is good. Sing to His Name, for It is pleasant. For God selected Jacob for His own, Israel as His treasure. For I know that HASHEM is greater — our Lord — than all heavenly powers. Whatever HASHEM wished, He did, in heaven and on earth; in the seas and all the depths. He raises clouds from the end of the earth; He made lightning bolts for the rain; He brings forth wind from His treasuries. It was He who smote the firstborn of Egypt, from man to beast. He sent signs and wonders into your midst, O Egypt, upon Pharaoh and upon all of his servants. It was He who smote many nations, and slew mighty kings — Sichon, King of the Emorites, Og,* King of Bashan, and all the kingdoms of Canaan — and presented their land as a heritage, a heritage for Israel, His people. HASHEM is Your Name forever,* HASHEM is Your memorial throughout the generations. When HASHEM will judge* His people, He will relent concerning His servants. The idols of the nations are silver and gold, human handiwork. They have mouths, but they speak not;* they have eyes, but they see not; they have ears, but they heed not; neither is there any breath in their mouths. Like them shall their makers become,* everyone who trusts in them.* Chazzan– *O House of Israel, bless HASHEM; O House of Aaron, bless HASHEM. O House of Levi,* bless HASHEM; O those who fear HASHEM, bless HASHEM. Blessed is HASHEM from Zion,* He Who dwells in Jerusalem. Halleluyah!*

Most congregations recite the following psalm while standing.

Psalm 136

הוֹדוּ *Give thanks to HASHEM for He is good,**
*for His kindness endures forever.**
*Give thanks to the God of the heavenly powers,**
for His kindness endures forever.
*Give thanks to the Lord of the lords,**
for His kindness endures forever.

Israel . . . House of Aaron . . . House of Levi. First comes the general call to all Jews, then the *Kohanim* [House of Aaron], who are privileged to perform the Temple service; the Levites, who sing and play the Temple songs; and finally the righteous people *who fear HASHEM.*

בָּרוּךְ ה׳ מִצִּיּוֹן — *Blessed is HASHEM from Zion.* May the end of the exile come soon — when we will be able to bless God from Zion, His holy mountain *(Sforno).*

הוֹדוּ לַה׳ / Psalm 136

The Talmud *(Pesachim* 118a) calls this psalm הַלֵּל הַגָּדוֹל, *the Great Song of Praise,* because it lauds God for giving sustenance to every living being. Thus, although it speaks of a multitude of mighty miracles, including the Creation of the universe and the Exodus from Egypt, the psalm concludes by saying נֹתֵן לֶחֶם לְכָל בָּשָׂר, *He gives nourishment* [lit., *bread*] *to all flesh,* because God's mercy upon every creature is equal to all the 'great' miracles. The twenty-six verses of the psalm are another allusion to God's mercy, for all twenty-six generations before the Torah was given, God provided for all living things out of His mercy. Once the Torah was given, man can *earn* his keep by performing the commandments.

כִּי טוֹב — *For He is good.* An aspect of His goodness is that He punishes man for his sins each according to his own level of prosperity. The rich man may lose an expensive bull while the pauper will be deprived of a crust of bread *(Pesachim* 118a).

כִּי לְעוֹלָם חַסְדּוֹ — *For His kindness endures forever.* Homiletically, this can be rendered: His kindness is for the *world.* Man's kindnesses can be prompted by selfish motives, but God acts for the sake of the *world,* not Himself *(Alshich).*

הָאֱלֹהִים — *The heavenly powers,* i.e., the angels *(Radak).*

הָאֲדֹנִים — *The lords,* i.e., the heavenly bodies *(Radak).*

לְעֹשֵׂה נִפְלָאוֹת גְּדֹלוֹת לְבַדּוֹ, כִּי לְעוֹלָם חַסְדּוֹ.
לְעֹשֵׂה הַשָּׁמַיִם בִּתְבוּנָה,* כִּי לְעוֹלָם חַסְדּוֹ.
לְרוֹקַע הָאָרֶץ עַל הַמָּיִם, כִּי לְעוֹלָם חַסְדּוֹ.
לְעֹשֵׂה אוֹרִים גְּדֹלִים, כִּי לְעוֹלָם חַסְדּוֹ.
אֶת הַשֶּׁמֶשׁ לְמֶמְשֶׁלֶת בַּיּוֹם, כִּי לְעוֹלָם חַסְדּוֹ.
אֶת הַיָּרֵחַ וְכוֹכָבִים לְמֶמְשְׁלוֹת בַּלָּיְלָה, כִּי לְעוֹלָם חַסְדּוֹ.
לְמַכֵּה מִצְרַיִם בִּבְכוֹרֵיהֶם,* כִּי לְעוֹלָם חַסְדּוֹ.
וַיּוֹצֵא יִשְׂרָאֵל מִתּוֹכָם, כִּי לְעוֹלָם חַסְדּוֹ.
בְּיָד חֲזָקָה וּבִזְרוֹעַ נְטוּיָה, כִּי לְעוֹלָם חַסְדּוֹ.
לְגֹזֵר יַם סוּף לִגְזָרִים,* כִּי לְעוֹלָם חַסְדּוֹ.
וְהֶעֱבִיר יִשְׂרָאֵל בְּתוֹכוֹ, כִּי לְעוֹלָם חַסְדּוֹ.
וְנִעֵר פַּרְעֹה וְחֵילוֹ בְיַם סוּף, כִּי לְעוֹלָם חַסְדּוֹ.
לְמוֹלִיךְ עַמּוֹ בַּמִּדְבָּר, כִּי לְעוֹלָם חַסְדּוֹ.
לְמַכֵּה מְלָכִים גְּדֹלִים,* כִּי לְעוֹלָם חַסְדּוֹ.
וַיַּהֲרֹג מְלָכִים אַדִּירִים,* כִּי לְעוֹלָם חַסְדּוֹ.
לְסִיחוֹן מֶלֶךְ הָאֱמֹרִי, כִּי לְעוֹלָם חַסְדּוֹ.
וּלְעוֹג מֶלֶךְ הַבָּשָׁן, כִּי לְעוֹלָם חַסְדּוֹ.
וְנָתַן אַרְצָם לְנַחֲלָה, כִּי לְעוֹלָם חַסְדּוֹ.
נַחֲלָה לְיִשְׂרָאֵל עַבְדּוֹ, כִּי לְעוֹלָם חַסְדּוֹ.
שֶׁבְּשִׁפְלֵנוּ* זָכַר לָנוּ, כִּי לְעוֹלָם חַסְדּוֹ.
וַיִּפְרְקֵנוּ מִצָּרֵינוּ, כִּי לְעוֹלָם חַסְדּוֹ.
❖ נֹתֵן לֶחֶם לְכָל בָּשָׂר, כִּי לְעוֹלָם חַסְדּוֹ.
הוֹדוּ לְאֵל הַשָּׁמָיִם, כִּי לְעוֹלָם חַסְדּוֹ.

בִּתְבוּנָה — *With understanding.* The solar system and the countless galaxies function with a complexity that is beyond human comprehension *(R' Hirsch).*

לְמַכֵּה מִצְרַיִם בִּבְכוֹרֵיהֶם — *Who smote Egypt through their firstborn.* Upon hearing that they would soon die, the firstborn Egyptians insisted that the Jews be set free. When their countrymen refused, the firstborn attacked and killed many of their fellow Egyptians. Thus, the plague of the firstborn was a double blow *(Midrash).*

יַם סוּף לִגְזָרִים — *The Sea of Reeds into parts.* The Midrash teaches that the sea was divided into twelve parts, one for each tribe. This shows that each tribe has its own mission and deserved the miracle for its own sake *(Sfas Emes).*

מְלָכִים גְּדֹלִים — *Great kings,* i.e., the thirty-one Canaanite kings *(Rashi).*

מְלָכִים אַדִּירִים — *Mighty kings,* i.e. Pharaoh and his legion, who were even mightier than the combined Canaanite nations *(Rashi).*

שֶׁבְּשִׁפְלֵנוּ — *In our lowliness,* i.e., during our Egyptian enslavement *(Rashi);* or this is a prophetic reference to Israel's downtrodden condition during the periods when the Temples were destroyed *(Radak).*

To Him Who alone performs great wonders,
for His kindness endures forever.
*To Him Who made the heavens with understanding,**
for His kindness endures forever.
To Him Who spread out the earth upon the waters,
for His kindness endures forever.
To Him Who made great lights,
for His kindness endures forever.
The sun for the reign of the day,
for His kindness endures forever.
The moon and the stars for the reign of the night,
for His kindness endures forever.
*To Him Who smote Egypt through their firstborn,**
for His kindness endures forever.
And brought Israel forth from their midst,
for His kindness endures forever.
With strong hand and outstretched arm,
for His kindness endures forever.
*To Him Who divided the Sea of Reeds into parts,**
for His kindness endures forever.
And caused Israel to pass through it,
for His kindness endures forever.
And threw Pharaoh and his army into the Sea of Reeds,
for His kindness endures forever.
To Him Who led His people through the wilderness,
for His kindness endures forever.
*To Him Who smote great kings,**
for His kindness endures forever.
*And slew mighty kings,**
for His kindness endures forever.
Sichon, king of the Emorites,
for His kindness endures forever.
And Og, king of Bashan,
for His kindness endures forever.
And presented their land as a heritage,
for His kindness endures forever.
A heritage for Israel, His servant,
for His kindness endures forever.
In our lowliness He remembered us,*
for His kindness endures forever.
And released us from our tormentors,
for His kindness endures forever.
Chazzan– *He gives nourishment to all flesh,*
for His kindness endures forever.
Give thanks to God of the heavens,
for His kindness endures forever.

תהלים לג

רַנְּנוּ צַדִּיקִים בַּיהוה, לַיְשָׁרִים נָאוָה תְהִלָּה. הוֹדוּ לַיהוה בְּכִנּוֹר, בְּנֵבֶל עָשׂוֹר זַמְּרוּ לוֹ. שִׁירוּ לוֹ שִׁיר חָדָשׁ, הֵיטִיבוּ נַגֵּן בִּתְרוּעָה. כִּי יָשָׁר דְּבַר יהוה, וְכָל מַעֲשֵׂהוּ בֶּאֱמוּנָה.* אֹהֵב צְדָקָה וּמִשְׁפָּט, חֶסֶד יהוה מָלְאָה הָאָרֶץ. בִּדְבַר יהוה שָׁמַיִם נַעֲשׂוּ, וּבְרוּחַ פִּיו כָּל צְבָאָם. כֹּנֵס כַּנֵּד מֵי הַיָּם, נֹתֵן בְּאוֹצָרוֹת תְּהוֹמוֹת. יִירְאוּ מֵיהוה כָּל הָאָרֶץ, מִמֶּנּוּ יָגוּרוּ כָּל יֹשְׁבֵי תֵבֵל. כִּי הוּא אָמַר וַיֶּהִי, הוּא צִוָּה וַיַּעֲמֹד.* יהוה הֵפִיר עֲצַת גּוֹיִם, הֵנִיא מַחְשְׁבוֹת עַמִּים. עֲצַת יהוה לְעוֹלָם תַּעֲמֹד, מַחְשְׁבוֹת לִבּוֹ לְדֹר וָדֹר. אַשְׁרֵי הַגּוֹי אֲשֶׁר יהוה אֱלֹהָיו, הָעָם בָּחַר לְנַחֲלָה לוֹ. מִשָּׁמַיִם הִבִּיט יהוה, רָאָה אֶת כָּל בְּנֵי הָאָדָם. מִמְּכוֹן שִׁבְתּוֹ הִשְׁגִּיחַ,* אֶל כָּל יֹשְׁבֵי הָאָרֶץ. הַיֹּצֵר יַחַד לִבָּם, הַמֵּבִין אֶל כָּל מַעֲשֵׂיהֶם. אֵין הַמֶּלֶךְ נוֹשָׁע בְּרָב חָיִל, גִּבּוֹר לֹא יִנָּצֵל בְּרָב כֹּחַ. שֶׁקֶר הַסּוּס לִתְשׁוּעָה, וּבְרֹב חֵילוֹ לֹא יְמַלֵּט. הִנֵּה עֵין יהוה אֶל יְרֵאָיו, לַמְיַחֲלִים לְחַסְדּוֹ. לְהַצִּיל מִמָּוֶת נַפְשָׁם, וּלְחַיּוֹתָם בָּרָעָב. ❖ נַפְשֵׁנוּ חִכְּתָה לַיהוה, עֶזְרֵנוּ וּמָגִנֵּנוּ הוּא. כִּי בוֹ יִשְׂמַח לִבֵּנוּ, כִּי בְשֵׁם קָדְשׁוֹ בָטָחְנוּ. יְהִי חַסְדְּךָ יהוה עָלֵינוּ, כַּאֲשֶׁר יִחַלְנוּ לָךְ.

תהלים צב

מִזְמוֹר שִׁיר לְיוֹם הַשַּׁבָּת.* טוֹב לְהֹדוֹת לַיהוה, וּלְזַמֵּר לְשִׁמְךָ עֶלְיוֹן. לְהַגִּיד בַּבֹּקֶר חַסְדֶּךָ, וֶאֱמוּנָתְךָ בַּלֵּילוֹת. עֲלֵי עָשׂוֹר וַעֲלֵי נָבֶל, עֲלֵי הִגָּיוֹן בְּכִנּוֹר. כִּי שִׂמַּחְתַּנִי יהוה בְּפָעֳלֶךָ, בְּמַעֲשֵׂי יָדֶיךָ אֲרַנֵּן. מַה גָּדְלוּ מַעֲשֶׂיךָ יהוה, מְאֹד עָמְקוּ מַחְשְׁבֹתֶיךָ. אִישׁ בַּעַר לֹא יֵדָע, וּכְסִיל לֹא יָבִין אֶת זֹאת. בִּפְרֹחַ רְשָׁעִים כְּמוֹ עֵשֶׂב, וַיָּצִיצוּ כָּל פֹּעֲלֵי אָוֶן, לְהִשָּׁמְדָם עֲדֵי עַד. וְאַתָּה מָרוֹם לְעֹלָם יהוה. כִּי הִנֵּה אֹיְבֶיךָ יהוה, כִּי הִנֵּה אֹיְבֶיךָ יֹאבֵדוּ, יִתְפָּרְדוּ כָּל פֹּעֲלֵי אָוֶן. וַתָּרֶם כִּרְאֵים קַרְנִי, בַּלֹּתִי בְּשֶׁמֶן רַעֲנָן. וַתַּבֵּט עֵינִי בְּשׁוּרָי, בַּקָּמִים עָלַי מְרֵעִים, תִּשְׁמַעְנָה אָזְנָי. ❖ צַדִּיק כַּתָּמָר יִפְרָח, כְּאֶרֶז

רַנְּנוּ צַדִּיקִים / Psalm 33

We turn now to the celebration of the World to Come when all will recognize that God controls events. The Sabbath represents awareness of this truth, and it calls upon us to *sing Him a new song.*

וְכָל מַעֲשֵׂהוּ בֶּאֱמוּנָה — *And all His deeds are done with faithfulness.* The natural forces are reliable and consistent. Otherwise we would be in constant fear of upheaval (*Malbim*).

הוּא צִוָּה וַיַּעֲמֹד — *He commanded and it stood firm.* When God ordered the world to come into being, it kept expanding until it reached the size He desired; then He commanded it to stand firm (*Chagigah* 12a).

הִבִּיט ה׳ ... הִשְׁגִּיחַ — HASHEM *looks down ... He oversees.* These expressions imply the two differing forms of God's הַשְׁגָּחָה, *supervision.*

Psalm 33

רַנְּנוּ *Sing joyfully, O righteous, before HASHEM; for the upright, praise is fitting. Give thanks to HASHEM with the harp, with the ten-stringed lyre make music to Him. Sing Him a new song, play well with sounds of deepest feeling. For upright is the word of HASHEM, and all His deeds are done with faithfulness.* He loves charity and justice, the kindness of HASHEM fills the earth. By the word of HASHEM the heavens were made, and by the breath of His mouth all their host. He assembles like a wall the waters of the sea, He places the deep waters in vaults. Fear HASHEM, all the earth; of Him be in dread, all inhabitants of the world. For He spoke and it came to be, He commanded and it stood firm.* HASHEM annuls the counsel of nations, He balks the designs of peoples. The counsel of HASHEM will endure forever, the designs of His heart throughout the generations. Praiseworthy is the nation whose God is HASHEM, the people He chose for His own heritage. From heaven HASHEM looks down, He sees all mankind. From His dwelling place He oversees* all inhabitants of earth. He fashions their hearts all together, He comprehends all their deeds. A king is not saved by a great army, nor is a hero rescued by great strength; sham is the horse for salvation; despite its great strength it provides no escape. Behold, the eye of HASHEM is on those who fear Him, upon those who await His kindness. To rescue their soul from death, and to sustain them in famine.* Chazzan– *Our soul longed for HASHEM — our help and our shield is He. For in Him will our hearts be glad, for in His Holy Name we trusted. May Your kindness, HASHEM, be upon us, just as we awaited You.*

Psalm 92

מִזְמוֹר שִׁיר *A psalm, a song for the Sabbath day.* It is good to thank HASHEM and to sing praise to Your Name, O Exalted One; to relate Your kindness in the dawn and Your faith in the nights. Upon ten-stringed instrument and lyre, with singing accompanied by a harp. For You have gladdened me, HASHEM, with Your deeds; at the works of Your Hands I sing glad song. How great are Your deeds, HASHEM; exceedingly profound are Your thoughts. A boor cannot know, nor can a fool understand this: when the wicked bloom like grass and all the doers of iniquity blossom — it is to destroy them till eternity. But You remain exalted forever, HASHEM. For behold! — Your enemies, HASHEM, for behold! — Your enemies shall perish, dispersed shall be all doers of iniquity. As exalted as a re'eim's shall be my pride, I will be saturated with ever-fresh oil. My eyes have seen my vigilant foes; when those who would harm me rise up against me, my ears have heard their doom.* Chazzan– *A righteous man will flourish like a date palm, like a cedar*

There is the general supervision [הַשְׁגָּחָה כְּלָלִית] of the laws of nature; in that sense, God seems to *look down* from a distance. But God also exercises close supervision [הַשְׁגָּחָה פְּרָטִית] — *He oversees* — over each person according to his own deeds *(Malbim)*.

⁂ מִזְמוֹר שִׁיר לְיוֹם הַשַּׁבָּת / Psalm 92

מִזְמוֹר שִׁיר לְיוֹם הַשַּׁבָּת — *A psalm, a song for the Sabbath day*. This psalm is recited on Festivals as well as the Sabbath because they, too, are referred to as 'Sabbath' in the Torah. Although this psalm is identified as belonging particularly

בַּלְּבָנוֹן יִשְׂגֶּה. שְׁתוּלִים בְּבֵית יהוה, בְּחַצְרוֹת אֱלֹהֵינוּ יַפְרִיחוּ. עוֹד יְנוּבוּן בְּשֵׂיבָה, דְּשֵׁנִים וְרַעֲנַנִּים יִהְיוּ. לְהַגִּיד כִּי יָשָׁר יהוה, צוּרִי וְלֹא עַוְלָתָה בּוֹ.

תהלים צג

יהוה מָלָךְ גֵּאוּת לָבֵשׁ, לָבֵשׁ יהוה עֹז הִתְאַזָּר, אַף תִּכּוֹן תֵּבֵל בַּל תִּמּוֹט. נָכוֹן כִּסְאֲךָ מֵאָז, מֵעוֹלָם אָתָּה. נָשְׂאוּ נְהָרוֹת יהוה, נָשְׂאוּ נְהָרוֹת קוֹלָם, יִשְׂאוּ נְהָרוֹת דָּכְיָם. ❖ מִקֹּלוֹת מַיִם רַבִּים אַדִּירִים מִשְׁבְּרֵי יָם, אַדִּיר בַּמָּרוֹם יהוה. עֵדֹתֶיךָ נֶאֶמְנוּ מְאֹד לְבֵיתְךָ נַאֲוָה קֹּדֶשׁ, יהוה לְאֹרֶךְ יָמִים.

The following prayer should be recited with special intensity.

יְהִי כְבוֹד יהוה* לְעוֹלָם, יִשְׂמַח יהוה בְּמַעֲשָׂיו.[1] יְהִי שֵׁם יהוה מְבֹרָךְ, מֵעַתָּה וְעַד עוֹלָם. מִמִּזְרַח שֶׁמֶשׁ עַד מְבוֹאוֹ, מְהֻלָּל שֵׁם יהוה. רָם עַל כָּל גּוֹיִם יהוה, עַל הַשָּׁמַיִם כְּבוֹדוֹ.[2] יהוה שִׁמְךָ לְעוֹלָם, יהוה זִכְרְךָ* לְדֹר וָדֹר.[3] יהוה בַּשָּׁמַיִם הֵכִין כִּסְאוֹ, וּמַלְכוּתוֹ בַּכֹּל מָשָׁלָה.[4] יִשְׂמְחוּ הַשָּׁמַיִם וְתָגֵל הָאָרֶץ,* וְיֹאמְרוּ בַגּוֹיִם יהוה מָלָךְ.[5] יהוה מֶלֶךְ,*[6] יהוה מָלָךְ,[7] יהוה יִמְלֹךְ לְעֹלָם וָעֶד.[8] יהוה מֶלֶךְ עוֹלָם וָעֶד, אָבְדוּ גוֹיִם* מֵאַרְצוֹ.[9] יהוה הֵפִיר עֲצַת גּוֹיִם, הֵנִיא מַחְשְׁבוֹת עַמִּים.[10] רַבּוֹת מַחֲשָׁבוֹת בְּלֶב אִישׁ, וַעֲצַת יהוה הִיא תָקוּם.[11] עֲצַת יהוה לְעוֹלָם תַּעֲמֹד, מַחְשְׁבוֹת לִבּוֹ לְדֹר וָדֹר.[12] כִּי הוּא אָמַר וַיֶּהִי, הוּא צִוָּה וַיַּעֲמֹד.[13] כִּי בָחַר יהוה בְּצִיּוֹן, אִוָּהּ לְמוֹשָׁב לוֹ.[14] כִּי יַעֲקֹב בָּחַר לוֹ יָהּ, יִשְׂרָאֵל לִסְגֻלָּתוֹ.[15] כִּי

---

to the theme of the Sabbath — indeed, it was the Levites' song for the Sabbath Temple service *(Rashi)* — the text contains not a single direct reference to the Sabbath. One explanation is that it refers not to the weekly Sabbath, but to the World to Come, when man will achieve the spiritual perfection we only glimpse during the Sabbath. The psalm is thus well suited to the Sabbath which is a semblance of that future spiritual perfection *(Rashi)*. Additional commentary to this psalm appears on p. 38.

⧼ ה׳ מָלָךְ / Psalm 93

This psalm is a direct continuation of the previous theme that God's greatness will be recognized by all in the Messianic era. It describes God in His full grandeur and power as He was when He completed the six days of Creation, and as 'donning' grandeur and 'girding' Himself like one dressing in his Sabbath finery. Additional commentary to this psalm appears on p. 40.

⧼ **יְהִי כְבוֹד ה׳** — *May the glory of* HASHEM. This collection of verses, primarily from *Psalms*, revolves around two themes: the sovereignty of God and the role of Israel. Central to *tefillah* and to the purpose of creation is מַלְכוּת שָׁמַיִם, *Kingship of Heaven*, which means that every being exists as part of God's plan and is dedicated to His service. This idea is found in nature itself, for, as David says lyrically, man attains awareness of God when he contemplates the beauty and perfection of the universe. The Sages chose *Psalms* 104:31 to begin this prayer because it was the praise proclaimed by an angel when the newly created plant world developed according to God's wishes (*Chullin* 60a). In other words, the 'glory' of God is revealed on earth when His will is done. Most of this prayer deals with this idea of God's glory and Kingship. The last five verses speak of God's selection of the Jewish people and pleads for His mercy and attentiveness to their prayers (see *World of Prayer*).

in the Lebanon he will grow tall. Planted in the house of HASHEM, *in the courtyards of our God they will flourish. They will still be fruitful in old age, vigorous and fresh they will be — to declare that* HASHEM *is just, my Rock in Whom there is no wrong.*

Psalm 93

יהוה מָלָךְ HASHEM *will have reigned, He will have donned grandeur; He will have donned might and girded Himself; even firmed the world that it should not falter. Your throne was established from of old; eternal are You. Like rivers they raised, O* HASHEM, *like rivers they raised their voice; like rivers they shall raise their destructiveness.* Chazzan— *More than the roars of many waters, mightier than the waves of the sea — You are mighty on high,* HASHEM. *Your testimonies are exceedingly trustworthy about Your House, the Sacred Dwelling — O* HASHEM, *may it be for long days.*

The following prayer should be recited with special intensity.

יְהִי כְבוֹד *May the glory of* HASHEM* *endure forever, let* HASHEM *rejoice in His works.*[1] *Blessed be the Name of* HASHEM, *from this time and forever. From the rising of the sun to its setting,* HASHEM'*s Name is praised. High above all nations is* HASHEM, *above the heavens is His glory.*[2] *'*HASHEM*' is Your Name forever, '*HASHEM*' is Your memorial* throughout the generations.*[3] HASHEM *has established His throne in the heavens, and His kingdom reigns over all.*[4] *The heavens will be glad and the earth will rejoice,* they will proclaim among the nations, '*HASHEM *has reigned!'*[5] HASHEM *reigns,**[6] HASHEM *has reigned,*[7] HASHEM *shall reign for all eternity.*[8] HASHEM *reigns forever and ever, even when the nations will have perished* from His earth.*[9] HASHEM *annuls the counsel of nations, He balks the designs of peoples.*[10] *Many designs are in man's heart, but the counsel of* HASHEM *— only it will prevail.*[11] *The counsel of* HASHEM *will endure forever, the designs of His heart throughout the generations.*[12] *For He spoke and it came to be; He commanded and it stood firm.*[13] *For God selected Zion, He desired it for His dwelling place.*[14] *For God selected Jacob as His own, Israel as His treasure.*[15] *For*

(1) *Psalms* 104:31. (2) 113:2-4. (3) 135:13. (4) 103:19. (5) *I Chronicles* 16:31.
(6) *Psalms* 10:16. (7) 93:1 et al. (8) *Exodus* 15:18. (9) *Psalms* 10:16.
(10) 33:10. (11) *Proverbs* 19:21. (12) *Psalms* 33:11. (13) 33:9. (14) 132:13. (15) 135:4.

ה׳ שִׁמְךָ . . . זִכְרְךָ — *'*HASHEM*' is Your Name . . . Your memorial.* The *Name* of God represents what He truly is and implies a thorough understanding of His actions and the reasons for them. But because man's limited intelligence cannot reach this level of understanding, we do not pronounce the Name י־ה־ו־ה as it is spelled; thereby we symbolize our inability to know God as He truly is. In this sense, the pronunciation HASHEM is God's *memorial* (see *Pesachim* 50a).

יִשְׂמְחוּ הַשָּׁמַיִם וְתָגֵל הָאָרֶץ — *The heavens will be glad and the earth will rejoice.* The celestial and terrestrial parts of creation serve God. They will truly rejoice when all nations, too, acknowledge that *HASHEM has reigned.*

ה׳ מֶלֶךְ . . . — *HASHEM reigns . . .* — This is one of the most familiar verses in the entire liturgy, but, surprisingly enough, it is not found in Scripture. Rather, each phrase comes from a different part of Scripture. In combination, the three phrases express the eternity of God's reign.

אָבְדוּ גוֹיִם — *Even when the nations will have perished.* The verse refers only to the *evil* people among the nations, for their deeds prevent others from acknowledging God *(Rashi, Radak).*

לֹא יִטֹּשׁ יהוה עַמּוֹ, וְנַחֲלָתוֹ לֹא יַעֲזֹב.[1] ❖ וְהוּא רַחוּם יְכַפֵּר עָוֹן וְלֹא יַשְׁחִית, וְהִרְבָּה לְהָשִׁיב אַפּוֹ, וְלֹא יָעִיר כָּל חֲמָתוֹ.[2] יהוה הוֹשִׁיעָה, הַמֶּלֶךְ יַעֲנֵנוּ בְיוֹם קָרְאֵנוּ.[3]

אַשְׁרֵי יוֹשְׁבֵי בֵיתֶךָ, עוֹד יְהַלְלוּךָ סֶּלָה.[4] אַשְׁרֵי הָעָם שֶׁכָּכָה לּוֹ, אַשְׁרֵי הָעָם שֶׁיהוה אֱלֹהָיו.[5]

תהלים קמה

תְּהִלָּה לְדָוִד,
אֲרוֹמִמְךָ אֱלוֹהַי הַמֶּלֶךְ, וַאֲבָרְכָה שִׁמְךָ לְעוֹלָם וָעֶד.
בְּכָל יוֹם אֲבָרְכֶךָּ, וַאֲהַלְלָה שִׁמְךָ לְעוֹלָם וָעֶד.
גָּדוֹל יהוה וּמְהֻלָּל מְאֹד, וְלִגְדֻלָּתוֹ אֵין חֵקֶר.
דּוֹר לְדוֹר יְשַׁבַּח מַעֲשֶׂיךָ, וּגְבוּרֹתֶיךָ יַגִּידוּ.
הֲדַר כְּבוֹד הוֹדֶךָ, וְדִבְרֵי נִפְלְאוֹתֶיךָ אָשִׂיחָה.
וֶעֱזוּז נוֹרְאוֹתֶיךָ יֹאמֵרוּ, וּגְדוּלָּתְךָ אֲסַפְּרֶנָּה.
זֵכֶר רַב טוּבְךָ יַבִּיעוּ, וְצִדְקָתְךָ יְרַנֵּנוּ.
חַנּוּן וְרַחוּם יהוה, אֶרֶךְ אַפַּיִם וּגְדָל חָסֶד.
טוֹב יהוה לַכֹּל, וְרַחֲמָיו עַל כָּל מַעֲשָׂיו.
יוֹדוּךָ יהוה כָּל מַעֲשֶׂיךָ, וַחֲסִידֶיךָ יְבָרְכוּכָה.
כְּבוֹד מַלְכוּתְךָ יֹאמֵרוּ, וּגְבוּרָתְךָ יְדַבֵּרוּ.
לְהוֹדִיעַ לִבְנֵי הָאָדָם גְּבוּרֹתָיו, וּכְבוֹד הֲדַר מַלְכוּתוֹ.
מַלְכוּתְךָ מַלְכוּת כָּל עֹלָמִים, וּמֶמְשַׁלְתְּךָ בְּכָל דּוֹר וָדֹר.
סוֹמֵךְ יהוה לְכָל הַנֹּפְלִים, וְזוֹקֵף לְכָל הַכְּפוּפִים.
עֵינֵי כֹל אֵלֶיךָ יְשַׂבֵּרוּ, וְאַתָּה נוֹתֵן לָהֶם אֶת אָכְלָם בְּעִתּוֹ.
פּוֹתֵחַ אֶת יָדֶךָ,
וּמַשְׂבִּיעַ לְכָל חַי רָצוֹן.
צַדִּיק יהוה בְּכָל דְּרָכָיו, וְחָסִיד בְּכָל מַעֲשָׂיו.

While reciting the verse פּוֹתֵחַ, concentrate intently on its meaning.

◆§ אַשְׁרֵי / Ashrei

Rambam writes: The Sages praised anyone who recites hymns from the Book of Psalms every day, from תְּהִלָּה לְדָוִד, *A psalm of praise by David* [145:1; the third verse of *Ashrei*] to the end of the Book [i.e., the six psalms including *Ashrei*, and the five familiarly known as the *Halleluyahs*]. It has become customary to recite other verses before and after these, and [the Sages] instituted a blessing, *Baruch She'amar*, before these psalms and a blessing, *Yishtabach*, after them (*Hil. Tefillah* 7:12).

From *Rambam's* formulation, it is clear that the six psalms beginning with *Ashrei* are the very essence of *Pesukei D'zimrah*. This is based on the Talmud (*Shabbos* 118b) which cites Rabbi Yose: 'May my share be with those who complete *Hallel* every day.' The Talmud explains that, in Rabbi Yose's context, *Hallel* means the six concluding chapters of *Psalms*

HASHEM will not cast off His people, nor will He forsake His heritage.[1] Chazzan– *He, the Merciful One, is forgiving of iniquity and does not destroy; frequently He withdraws His anger, not arousing His entire rage.*[2] *HASHEM, save! May the King answer us on the day we call.*[3]

אַשְׁרֵי *Praiseworthy are those who dwell in Your house; may they always praise You, Selah!*[4] *Praiseworthy is the people for whom this is so, praiseworthy is the people whose God is HASHEM.*[5]

Psalm 145 *A psalm of praise by David:*

א *I will exalt You, my God the King,*
and I will bless Your Name forever and ever.

ב *Every day I will bless You,*
and I will laud Your Name forever and ever.

ג *HASHEM is great and exceedingly lauded,*
and His greatness is beyond investigation.

ד *Each generation will praise Your deeds to the next*
and of Your mighty deeds they will tell.

ה *The splendrous glory of Your power*
and Your wondrous deeds I shall discuss.

ו *And of Your awesome power they will speak,*
and Your greatness I shall relate.

ז *A recollection of Your abundant goodness they will utter*
and of Your righteousness they will sing exultantly.

ח *Gracious and merciful is HASHEM,*
slow to anger, and great in [bestowing] kindness.

ט *HASHEM is good to all; His mercies are on all His works.*

י *All Your works shall thank You, HASHEM,*
and Your devout ones will bless You.

כ *Of the glory of Your kingdom they will speak,*
and of Your power they will tell;

ל *To inform human beings of His mighty deeds,*
and the glorious splendor of His kingdom.

מ *Your kingdom is a kingdom spanning all eternities,*
and Your dominion is throughout every generation.

ס *HASHEM supports all the fallen ones and straightens all the bent.*

ע *The eyes of all look to You with hope*
and You give them their food in its proper time;

פ *You open Your hand,*
and satisfy the desire
of every living thing.

While reciting the verse, *'You open . . .'* concentrate intently on its meaning.

צ *Righteous is HASHEM in all His ways*
and magnanimous in all His deeds.

(1) *Psalms* 94:14. (29 78:38. (3) 20:10. (4) 84:5. (5) 144:15.

that we are about to recite. [However, see *Rashi.*]
Ashrei has a special significance of its own, because the Talmud (*Berachos* 4b) teaches that the Sages assured a share in the World to Come

קָרוֹב יהוה לְכָל קֹרְאָיו, לְכֹל אֲשֶׁר יִקְרָאֻהוּ בֶאֱמֶת.
רְצוֹן יְרֵאָיו יַעֲשֶׂה, וְאֶת שַׁוְעָתָם יִשְׁמַע וְיוֹשִׁיעֵם.
שׁוֹמֵר יהוה אֶת כָּל אֹהֲבָיו, וְאֵת כָּל הָרְשָׁעִים יַשְׁמִיד.
❖ תְּהִלַּת יהוה יְדַבֶּר פִּי, וִיבָרֵךְ כָּל בָּשָׂר שֵׁם קָדְשׁוֹ לְעוֹלָם וָעֶד.
וַאֲנַחְנוּ נְבָרֵךְ יָהּ, מֵעַתָּה וְעַד עוֹלָם, הַלְלוּיָהּ.[1]

תהלים קמו

הַלְלוּיָהּ, הַלְלִי נַפְשִׁי אֶת יהוה.* אֲהַלְלָה יהוה בְּחַיָּי, אֲזַמְּרָה לֵאלֹהַי בְּעוֹדִי. אַל תִּבְטְחוּ בִנְדִיבִים, בְּבֶן אָדָם* שֶׁאֵין לוֹ תְשׁוּעָה. תֵּצֵא רוּחוֹ, יָשֻׁב לְאַדְמָתוֹ, בַּיּוֹם הַהוּא אָבְדוּ עֶשְׁתֹּנֹתָיו. אַשְׁרֵי שֶׁאֵל יַעֲקֹב בְּעֶזְרוֹ, שִׂבְרוֹ עַל יהוה אֱלֹהָיו. עֹשֶׂה שָׁמַיִם וָאָרֶץ,* אֶת הַיָּם וְאֶת כָּל אֲשֶׁר בָּם, הַשֹּׁמֵר אֱמֶת לְעוֹלָם. עֹשֶׂה מִשְׁפָּט לַעֲשׁוּקִים, נֹתֵן לֶחֶם לָרְעֵבִים, יהוה מַתִּיר אֲסוּרִים. יהוה פֹּקֵחַ עִוְרִים, יהוה זֹקֵף כְּפוּפִים, יהוה אֹהֵב צַדִּיקִים. יהוה שֹׁמֵר אֶת גֵּרִים,* יָתוֹם וְאַלְמָנָה יְעוֹדֵד, וְדֶרֶךְ רְשָׁעִים יְעַוֵּת.
❖ יִמְלֹךְ יהוה לְעוֹלָם, אֱלֹהַיִךְ צִיּוֹן, לְדֹר וָדֹר, הַלְלוּיָהּ.

תהלים קמז

הַלְלוּיָהּ, כִּי טוֹב* זַמְּרָה אֱלֹהֵינוּ, כִּי נָעִים נָאוָה תְהִלָּה. בּוֹנֵה יְרוּשָׁלַיִם יהוה, נִדְחֵי יִשְׂרָאֵל יְכַנֵּס. הָרוֹפֵא לִשְׁבוּרֵי לֵב, וּמְחַבֵּשׁ לְעַצְּבוֹתָם. מוֹנֶה מִסְפָּר לַכּוֹכָבִים,* לְכֻלָּם שֵׁמוֹת יִקְרָא. גָּדוֹל אֲדוֹנֵינוּ וְרַב כֹּחַ, לִתְבוּנָתוֹ אֵין מִסְפָּר. מְעוֹדֵד עֲנָוִים יהוה, מַשְׁפִּיל רְשָׁעִים עֲדֵי אָרֶץ. עֱנוּ לַיהוה בְּתוֹדָה, זַמְּרוּ לֵאלֹהֵינוּ בְכִנּוֹר. הַמְּכַסֶּה שָׁמַיִם בְּעָבִים, הַמֵּכִין לָאָרֶץ מָטָר,

---

to anyone who recites it properly three times a day. It has this special status because no other psalm possesses both of its two virtues: (a) Beginning with the word אֲרוֹמִמְךָ (the first substantive word of the psalm), the initials of the psalm's respective verses follow the order of the *Aleph-Beis;* and (b) it contains inspiring and reassuring testimony to God's mercy, . . . פּוֹתֵחַ אֶת יָדֶךָ, *You open Your hand* . . . As *Zohar* teaches, the recitation of this verse in *Pesukei D'zimrah* is not considered a *request* that God open His hand for us; rather it is purely a recitation of praise. Similarly, the five psalms that follow are expressions of sublime ecstatic praise.

Commentary to *Ashrei* begins on page 9.

⊱ **הַלְלוּיָהּ הַלְלִי נַפְשִׁי אֶת ה׳** — *Halleluyah! Praise* HASHEM, *O my soul! Radak* interprets this psalm as a hymn of encouragement for Jews in exile. It begins with the Psalmist insisting that he will praise God as long as he lives and warning his fellow Jews not to rely on human beings. After praising God as the One Who cares for the underprivileged and oppressed, the Psalmist concludes that God will reign forever — despite the current ascendancy of our enemies.

בְּבֶן אָדָם — *Nor on a human being.* Even when rulers help Israel, it is because God has influenced them to do so. So it will be when the nations seem to have a hand in the Messianic redemption *(Radak).*

עֹשֶׂה שָׁמַיִם וָאָרֶץ — *Maker of heaven and earth.* Unlike kings and rulers whose power is limited

ק *HASHEM is close to all who call upon Him —*
to all who call upon Him sincerely.
ר *The will of those who fear Him He will do;*
and their cry He will hear, and save them.
ש *HASHEM protects all who love Him;*
but all the wicked He will destroy.
ת Chazzan– *May my mouth declare the praise of HASHEM*
and may all flesh bless His Holy Name forever and ever.
We will bless God from this time and forever, Halleluyah![1]

Psalm 146

הַלְלוּיָהּ *Halleluyah! Praise HASHEM, O my Soul!* I will praise HASHEM while I live, I will make music to my God while I exist. Do not rely on nobles, nor on a human being* for he holds no salvation. When his spirit departs he returns to his earth, on that day his plans all perish. Praiseworthy is one whose help is Jacob's God, whose hope is in HASHEM, his God. He is the Maker of heaven and earth,* the sea and all that is in them, Who safeguards truth forever. He does justice for the exploited; He gives bread to the hungry; HASHEM releases the bound. HASHEM gives sight to the blind; HASHEM straightens the bent; HASHEM loves the righteous. HASHEM protects strangers;* orphan and widow He encourages; but the way of the wicked He contorts.* Chazzan– *HASHEM shall reign forever — your God, O Zion — from generation to generation. Halleluyah!*

Psalm 147

הַלְלוּיָהּ *Halleluyah! For it is good* to make music to our God, for praise is pleasant and befitting. The Builder of Jerusalem is HASHEM, the outcast of Israel He will gather in. He is the Healer of the broken-hearted, and the One Who binds up their sorrows. He counts the number of the stars,* to all of them He assigns names. Great is our Lord and abundant in strength, His understanding is beyond calculation. HASHEM encourages the humble, He lowers the wicked down to the ground. Call out to HASHEM with thanks, with the harp sing to our God — Who covers the heavens with clouds, Who prepares rain for the earth,*

(1) *Psalms* 115:18.

in both time and space, God is everywhere and all-powerful (*Yerushalmi Berachos* 9:1).

ה׳ שֹׁמֵר אֶת גֵּרִים — *HASHEM protects strangers.* God is the Protector of all weak and defenseless strangers, whether uprooted Jews or gentile converts (*Radak*).

הַלְלוּיָהּ כִּי טוֹב — *Halleluyah! For it is good . . .* Continuing the theme of redemption, this psalm places its primary focus on Jerusalem, the center from which holiness, redemption, and Torah will emanate. In this sense, Jerusalem cannot be considered rebuilt until the Redemption, because the city's spiritual grandeur cannot be recaptured by mere architecture and growing numbers of people.

מוֹנֶה מִסְפָּר לַכּוֹכָבִים — *He counts the number of the stars.* Having given the assurance that God will rebuild Jerusalem and gather in Israel in joy, the Psalmist goes on to illustrate God's ability to do so. The next series of verses catalogue His might, compassion and attention to individual needs.

The stars number in the billions, but God is aware of each one and gives it a 'name' that denotes its purpose in the universe. Thus, nothing goes unnoticed or unprovided for.

הַמַּצְמִיחַ הָרִים חָצִיר. נוֹתֵן לִבְהֵמָה לַחְמָהּ, לִבְנֵי עֹרֵב אֲשֶׁר יִקְרָאוּ. לֹא בִגְבוּרַת הַסּוּס יֶחְפָּץ, לֹא בְשׁוֹקֵי הָאִישׁ* יִרְצֶה. רוֹצֶה יהוה אֶת יְרֵאָיו, אֶת הַמְיַחֲלִים לְחַסְדּוֹ. שַׁבְּחִי יְרוּשָׁלַיִם אֶת יהוה, הַלְלִי אֱלֹהַיִךְ צִיּוֹן. כִּי חִזַּק בְּרִיחֵי* שְׁעָרָיִךְ, בֵּרַךְ בָּנַיִךְ בְּקִרְבֵּךְ. הַשָּׂם גְּבוּלֵךְ שָׁלוֹם, חֵלֶב חִטִּים* יַשְׂבִּיעֵךְ. הַשֹּׁלֵחַ אִמְרָתוֹ אָרֶץ, עַד מְהֵרָה יָרוּץ דְּבָרוֹ. הַנֹּתֵן שֶׁלֶג כַּצָּמֶר, כְּפוֹר כָּאֵפֶר יְפַזֵּר. מַשְׁלִיךְ קַרְחוֹ כְפִתִּים, לִפְנֵי קָרָתוֹ מִי יַעֲמֹד. יִשְׁלַח דְּבָרוֹ וְיַמְסֵם,* יַשֵּׁב רוּחוֹ יִזְּלוּ מָיִם. ❖ מַגִּיד דְּבָרָיו לְיַעֲקֹב,* חֻקָּיו וּמִשְׁפָּטָיו לְיִשְׂרָאֵל. לֹא עָשָׂה כֵן לְכָל גּוֹי, וּמִשְׁפָּטִים בַּל יְדָעוּם, הַלְלוּיָהּ.

תהלים קמח

הַלְלוּיָהּ, הַלְלוּ אֶת יהוה* מִן הַשָּׁמַיִם,* הַלְלוּהוּ בַּמְּרוֹמִים. הַלְלוּהוּ כָל מַלְאָכָיו, הַלְלוּהוּ כָּל צְבָאָיו.* הַלְלוּהוּ שֶׁמֶשׁ וְיָרֵחַ, הַלְלוּהוּ כָּל כּוֹכְבֵי אוֹר. הַלְלוּהוּ שְׁמֵי הַשָּׁמָיִם, וְהַמַּיִם אֲשֶׁר מֵעַל הַשָּׁמָיִם. יְהַלְלוּ אֶת שֵׁם יהוה, כִּי הוּא צִוָּה וְנִבְרָאוּ. וַיַּעֲמִידֵם לָעַד לְעוֹלָם, חָק נָתַן* וְלֹא יַעֲבוֹר. הַלְלוּ אֶת יהוה מִן הָאָרֶץ, תַּנִּינִים וְכָל תְּהֹמוֹת. אֵשׁ וּבָרָד, שֶׁלֶג וְקִיטוֹר, רוּחַ סְעָרָה עֹשָׂה דְבָרוֹ. הֶהָרִים וְכָל גְּבָעוֹת, עֵץ פְּרִי וְכָל אֲרָזִים. הַחַיָּה וְכָל בְּהֵמָה, רֶמֶשׂ וְצִפּוֹר כָּנָף. מַלְכֵי אֶרֶץ וְכָל לְאֻמִּים, שָׂרִים וְכָל שֹׁפְטֵי אָרֶץ. בַּחוּרִים וְגַם בְּתוּלוֹת,* זְקֵנִים עִם נְעָרִים. ❖ יְהַלְלוּ אֶת שֵׁם יהוה, כִּי נִשְׂגָּב שְׁמוֹ לְבַדּוֹ, הוֹדוֹ עַל אֶרֶץ וְשָׁמָיִם. וַיָּרֶם קֶרֶן לְעַמּוֹ, תְּהִלָּה לְכָל חֲסִידָיו, לִבְנֵי יִשְׂרָאֵל עַם קְרֹבוֹ, הַלְלוּיָהּ.

בִּגְבוּרַת הַסּוּס . . . בְּשׁוֹקֵי הָאִישׁ — *In the strength of the horse . . . the legs of man.* The earlier verses spoke of God's compassion for helpless creatures. Now the Psalmist says in contrast, God is unimpressed with powerful battle horses or with the skill of the rider who controls the horse with his legs *(Radak; Ibn Ezra).*

כִּי חִזַּק בְּרִיחֵי — *For He has strengthened the bars.* The verse is figurative. The Jerusalem of the future will need no bars on its gates. The people will feel secure because God will protect their city *(Radak).*

חֵלֶב חִטִּים — *The cream of the wheat.* Wheat is a symbol of prosperity and, therefore, it is an omen of peace, because prosperous people are less contentious *(Berachos 57a).*

יִשְׁלַח דְּבָרוֹ וְיַמְסֵם — *He issues His command and it melts them.* The Psalmist had spoken of the many solid forms of moisture: snow, frost, ice — but at God's command, everything melts and flows like water. The Jew should emulate nature by conforming to the will of God *(R' Hirsch).*

מַגִּיד דְּבָרָיו לְיַעֲקֹב — *He relates His Word to Jacob.* God gave *His word,* the Torah, to *Jacob,* i.e., the entire Jewish nation, even those who are not capable of understanding its intricacies and mysteries. But to *Israel,* i.e., the greatest members of the nation, He made known the many variations and shadings of wisdom to be found within His statutes and judgments *(Zohar).*

Lest you wonder at the many centuries that have gone by without the redemption of Jerusalem and Israel, do not forget that the Torah itself — the very purpose of creation — was not given to man until 2448 years after Creation. That God sees fit to delay is no cause for despair *(Siach Yitzchak).*

Who makes mountains sprout with grass. He gives to an animal its food, to young ravens that cry out. Not in the strength of the horse does He desire, and not in the legs of man does He favor. HASHEM favors those who fear Him, those who hope for His kindness. Praise HASHEM, O Jerusalem, laud your God, O Zion. For He has strengthened the bars* of your gates, and blessed your children in your midst; He Who makes your borders peaceful, and with the cream of the wheat* He sates you; He Who dispatches His utterance earthward; how swiftly His commandment runs! He Who gives snow like fleece, He scatters frost like ashes. He hurls His ice like crumbs — before His cold, who can stand? He issues His command and it melts them,* He blows His wind — the waters flow.* Chazzan– *He relates His Word to Jacob,* His statutes and judgments to Israel. He did not do so for any other nation, such judgments — they know them not. Halleluyah!*

Psalm 148

הַלְלוּיָהּ *Halleluyah! Praise HASHEM* from the heavens;* praise Him in the heights. Praise Him, all His angels; praise Him, all His legions.* Praise Him, sun and moon; praise Him, all bright stars. Praise Him, the most exalted of the heavens and the waters that are above the heavens. Let them praise the Name of HASHEM, for He commanded and they were created. And He established them forever and ever, He issued a decree* that will not change. Praise HASHEM from the earth, sea giants and all watery depths. Fire and hail, snow and vapor, stormy wind fulfilling His word. Mountains and all hills, fruitful trees and all cedars. Beasts and all cattle, crawling things and winged fowl. Kings of the earth and all governments, princes and all judges on earth. Young men and also maidens,* old men together with youths.* Chazzan– *Let them praise the Name of HASHEM, for His Name alone will have been exalted; His glory is above earth and heaven. And He will have exalted the pride of His nation, causing praise for all His devout ones, for the Children of Israel, His intimate people. Halleluyah!*

הַלְלוּיָהּ הַלְלוּ אֶת ה׳ — *Halleluyah! Praise HASHEM.* Only after the Temple and Jerusalem are rebuilt will all the universe join in joyous songs of praise to God. Zion is the meeting point of heaven and earth, as it were, because it is from there that God's heavenly blessings emanate to the rest of the universe.

הַלְלוּ . . . מִן הַשָּׁמַיִם — *Praise . . . from the heavens.* The Psalmist begins by calling upon the heavenly beings to praise God, and then he directs his call to earthly beings. God's praises echo from the heavens and descend to earth, where the devout echo the heavenly songs with their own praises (*Sforno*).

מַלְאָכָיו . . . צְבָאָיו — *His angels . . . His legions.* The *angels* are spiritual beings without physical form while the *legions* are the heavenly bodies, which are so numerous that they are likened to legions (*Radak*).

חָק נָתַן — *He issued a decree.* God ordained that the sun shine by day and the moon by night, and this *decree* can never be violated (*Rashi*).

בַּחוּרִים וְגַם בְּתוּלוֹת — *Young men and also maidens.* The use here of the word וְגַם, *and also,* is noteworthy. The Psalmist does not say that young men *and* women will be together, because such mingling would be immodest. Only later, when he speaks of old men and youths, does the Psalmist say עִם, *with* — that they will be *together* (*Sefer Chassidim*).

תהלים קמט

הַלְלוּיָהּ, שִׁירוּ לַיהוה* שִׁיר חָדָשׁ, תְּהִלָּתוֹ בִּקְהַל חֲסִידִים. יִשְׂמַח יִשְׂרָאֵל בְּעֹשָׂיו,* בְּנֵי צִיּוֹן* יָגִילוּ בְמַלְכָּם. יְהַלְּלוּ שְׁמוֹ בְמָחוֹל, בְּתֹף וְכִנּוֹר יְזַמְּרוּ לוֹ. כִּי רוֹצֶה יהוה בְּעַמּוֹ,* יְפָאֵר עֲנָוִים בִּישׁוּעָה. יַעְלְזוּ חֲסִידִים בְּכָבוֹד, יְרַנְּנוּ עַל מִשְׁכְּבוֹתָם.* רוֹמְמוֹת אֵל בִּגְרוֹנָם,* וְחֶרֶב פִּיפִיּוֹת בְּיָדָם. לַעֲשׂוֹת נְקָמָה בַּגּוֹיִם, תּוֹכֵחוֹת* בַּלְאֻמִּים. ❖ לֶאְסֹר מַלְכֵיהֶם בְּזִקִּים, וְנִכְבְּדֵיהֶם בְּכַבְלֵי בַרְזֶל. לַעֲשׂוֹת בָּהֶם מִשְׁפָּט כָּתוּב,* הָדָר הוּא לְכָל חֲסִידָיו, הַלְלוּיָהּ.

תהלים קנ

הַלְלוּיָהּ, הַלְלוּ אֵל* בְּקָדְשׁוֹ, הַלְלוּהוּ בִּרְקִיעַ עֻזּוֹ. הַלְלוּהוּ בִגְבוּרֹתָיו, הַלְלוּהוּ כְּרֹב גֻּדְלוֹ. הַלְלוּהוּ בְּתֵקַע שׁוֹפָר, הַלְלוּהוּ בְּנֵבֶל וְכִנּוֹר. הַלְלוּהוּ בְתֹף וּמָחוֹל, הַלְלוּהוּ בְּמִנִּים וְעוּגָב. הַלְלוּהוּ בְצִלְצְלֵי שָׁמַע, הַלְלוּהוּ בְּצִלְצְלֵי תְרוּעָה. ❖ כֹּל הַנְּשָׁמָה תְּהַלֵּל* יָהּ, הַלְלוּיָהּ. כֹּל הַנְּשָׁמָה תְּהַלֵּל יָהּ, הַלְלוּיָהּ.

בָּרוּךְ יהוה לְעוֹלָם,* אָמֵן וְאָמֵן.*[1] בָּרוּךְ יהוה מִצִּיּוֹן, שֹׁכֵן יְרוּשָׁלָיִם, הַלְלוּיָהּ.[2] בָּרוּךְ יהוה אֱלֹהִים אֱלֹהֵי יִשְׂרָאֵל, עֹשֵׂה נִפְלָאוֹת לְבַדּוֹ. ❖ וּבָרוּךְ שֵׁם כְּבוֹדוֹ לְעוֹלָם, וְיִמָּלֵא כְבוֹדוֹ אֶת כָּל הָאָרֶץ, אָמֵן וְאָמֵן.[3]

☙ הַלְלוּיָהּ שִׁירוּ לַה׳ — *Halleluyah! Sing to* HASHEM. In every generation, God confronts us with new challenges and problems, yet He provides us with the opportunity to solve them. For this, our songs of praise never grow stale, because they are always infused with new meaning. But the greatest, newest song of all will spring from Israel's lips when history reaches its climax with the coming of the Messiah.

בְּעֹשָׂיו — *In its Maker.* Although God made *all* nations, only Israel is His Chosen People *(Sforno).*

בְּנֵי צִיּוֹן — *The Children of Zion.* The future holiness of Zion — the place from which the Torah's teachings will emanate — will be of a higher order than anything we now know. The Jews who benefit from this spiritual aura will be called *the Children of Zion.*

כִּי רוֹצֶה ה׳ בְּעַמּוֹ — *For* HASHEM *favors His nation.* God looks forward to Israel's praises *(Radak).*

עַל מִשְׁכְּבוֹתָם — *Upon their beds.* The righteous will thank God for allowing them to go to bed without fear of danger and attack *(Etz Yosef).*

רוֹמְמוֹת אֵל בִּגְרוֹנָם — *The lofty praises of God are in their throats.* Though Israel goes into battle holding its *double-edged sword,* it knows that its victory depends on the help of God to Whom it sings praises *(Rashi; Radak).* The expression *in their throats* symbolizes that the prayers are not merely mouthed, but are deeply felt internally *(Radak).*

תּוֹכֵחוֹת — *Rebukes.* Though Israel is forced to wage battle against its enemies, its primary goal is that they accept moral rebuke and mend their ways.

לַעֲשׂוֹת בָּהֶם מִשְׁפָּט כָּתוּב — *To execute upon them written judgment.* The future judgment upon the nations has been written in the Prophets. The execution of that judgment will bring the reign of justice to earth, and that will be the *splendor* — the pride and vindication — of the righteous who have always lived that way.

☙ הַלְלוּיָהּ הַלְלוּ אֵל — *Halleluyah! Praise God.* In

Psalm 149

הַלְלוּיָהּ *Halleluyah! Sing to* HASHEM* *a new song, let His praise be in the congregation of the devout. Let Israel exult in its Maker,* let the Children of Zion* rejoice in their King. Let them praise His Name with dancing, with drums and harp let them make music to Him. For* HASHEM *favors His nation,* He adorns the humble with salvation. Let the devout exult in glory, let them sing joyously upon their beds.* The lofty praises of God are in their throats,* and a double-edged sword is in their hand — to execute vengeance among the nations, rebukes* among the governments.* Chazzan– *To bind their kings with chains, and their nobles with fetters of iron. To execute upon them written judgment* — that will be the splendor of all His devout ones. Halleluyah!*

Psalm 150

הַלְלוּיָהּ *Halleluyah! Praise God* in His Sanctuary; praise Him in the firmament of His power. Praise Him for His mighty acts; praise Him as befits His abundant greatness. Praise Him with the blast of the shofar; praise Him with lyre and harp. Praise Him with drum and dance; praise Him with organ and flute. Praise Him with clanging cymbals; praise Him with resonant trumpets.* Chazzan– *Let all souls praise* God, Halleluyah!* Let all souls praise God, Halleluyah!*

בָּרוּךְ *Blessed is* HASHEM *forever,* Amen and Amen.**[1] *Blessed is* HASHEM *from Zion, Who dwells in Jerusalem, Halleluyah.*[2] *Blessed is* HASHEM, *God, the God of Israel, Who alone does wonders.* Chazzan– *Blessed is His glorious Name forever, and may all the earth be filled with His glory, Amen and Amen.*[3]

(1) *Psalms* 89:53. (2) 135:21. (3) 72:18-19.

---

this, the final psalm in the Book of *Psalms*, the Psalmist sums up his task by saying that man must enrich his spiritual self by recognizing God's greatness and kindness and by praising Him. The Psalmist's long list of musical instruments reflects the full spectrum of human emotions and spiritual potential, all of which can be aroused by music.

[A series of musical instruments is mentioned here. In many cases, we do not know the exact translations; those given here are based on the interpretations of various major commentators. A full exposition can be found in the ArtScroll *Tehillim/Psalms.*]

כֹּל הַנְּשָׁמָה תְּהַלֵּל — *Let all souls praise.* Far greater than the most sublime instrumental songs of praise is the song of the human soul. God's greatest praise is the soul that utilizes its full potential in His service *(Radak).*

Having now concluded the six psalms that are the main part of *Pesukei D'zimrah,* we repeat the last verse to signify that this section has come to an end *(Avudraham).*

הַלְלוּיָהּ — *Halleluyah.* The root הלל, *praise,* appears thirteen times in this psalm, an allusion to God's Thirteen Attributes of Mercy. [In counting the thirteen times, the repetition of the last verse is not included, since it appears only one time in *Psalms.*] *(Radak)*

בָּרוּךְ ה' לְעוֹלָם — *Blessed is* HASHEM *forever.* This collection of verses, each of which begins with the word בָּרוּךְ, is in the nature of a blessing after the six psalms that, as noted above, are the very essence of *Pesukei D'zimrah (Etz Yosef).* The term בָּרוּךְ, which refers to God as the Source of all blessing, is particularly relevant to the just concluded psalms, since they describe God's kindness, power, and future redemption *(R' Munk).*

אָמֵן וְאָמֵן — *Amen and Amen.* The repetition is meant to re-emphasize the statement. A listener's *Amen* can have three connotations *(Shevuos* 29b): (a) to accept a vow upon oneself, (b) to acknowledge the truth of a statement, and (c) to express the hope that a statement come true. In our prayers, any or all are expressed by *Amen,* depending on the context *(Iyun Tefillah).*

One must stand from וַיְבָרֶךְ דָּוִיד, until after the phrase אַתָּה הוּא ה׳ הָאֱלֹהִים; however, there is a generally accepted custom to remain standing until after completing אָז יָשִׁיר (p. 266).

דברי הימים א כט:י-יג

וַיְבָרֶךְ דָּוִיד* אֶת יהוה לְעֵינֵי כָּל הַקָּהָל, וַיֹּאמֶר דָּוִיד: בָּרוּךְ אַתָּה יהוה, אֱלֹהֵי יִשְׂרָאֵל אָבִינוּ,* מֵעוֹלָם וְעַד עוֹלָם. לְךָ יהוה הַגְּדֻלָּה* וְהַגְּבוּרָה וְהַתִּפְאֶרֶת וְהַנֵּצַח וְהַהוֹד, כִּי כֹל בַּשָּׁמַיִם וּבָאָרֶץ; לְךָ יהוה הַמַּמְלָכָה וְהַמִּתְנַשֵּׂא לְכֹל לְרֹאשׁ. וְהָעֹשֶׁר וְהַכָּבוֹד מִלְּפָנֶיךָ, וְאַתָּה מוֹשֵׁל בַּכֹּל, וּבְיָדְךָ כֹּחַ וּגְבוּרָה, וּבְיָדְךָ לְגַדֵּל וּלְחַזֵּק לַכֹּל. וְעַתָּה אֱלֹהֵינוּ מוֹדִים אֲנַחְנוּ לָךְ, וּמְהַלְּלִים לְשֵׁם תִּפְאַרְתֶּךָ.

נחמיה ט:ו-יא

אַתָּה הוּא יהוה* לְבַדֶּךָ, אַתָּה עָשִׂיתָ אֶת הַשָּׁמַיִם, שְׁמֵי הַשָּׁמַיִם* וְכָל צְבָאָם, הָאָרֶץ וְכָל אֲשֶׁר עָלֶיהָ, הַיַּמִּים וְכָל אֲשֶׁר בָּהֶם, וְאַתָּה מְחַיֶּה אֶת כֻּלָּם,* וּצְבָא הַשָּׁמַיִם לְךָ מִשְׁתַּחֲוִים.* ❖ אַתָּה הוּא יהוה הָאֱלֹהִים אֲשֶׁר בָּחַרְתָּ בְּאַבְרָם,* וְהוֹצֵאתוֹ מֵאוּר כַּשְׂדִּים, וְשַׂמְתָּ שְׁמוֹ אַבְרָהָם.* וּמָצָאתָ אֶת לְבָבוֹ נֶאֱמָן לְפָנֶיךָ — — וְכָרוֹת* עִמּוֹ הַבְּרִית לָתֵת אֶת אֶרֶץ הַכְּנַעֲנִי הַחִתִּי הָאֱמֹרִי וְהַפְּרִזִּי וְהַיְבוּסִי וְהַגִּרְגָּשִׁי, לָתֵת* לְזַרְעוֹ, וַתָּקֶם אֶת דְּבָרֶיךָ, כִּי צַדִּיק אָתָּה.* וַתֵּרֶא אֶת עֳנִי אֲבֹתֵינוּ בְּמִצְרָיִם, וְאֶת זַעֲקָתָם שָׁמַעְתָּ עַל יַם סוּף. וַתִּתֵּן אֹתֹת וּמֹפְתִים* בְּפַרְעֹה וּבְכָל

☙ **וַיְבָרֶךְ דָּוִיד** — *And David blessed.* The following selections from the praises of David, Nehemiah, and Moses, in that order, were appended to *Pesukei D'zimrah* because the fifteen terms of praise used in *Yishtabach* are based on these selections *(Avudraham).*

The first four verses of this prayer were uttered by David at one of the supreme moments of his life: although he had been denied Divine permission to build the Holy Temple, he had assembled the necessary contributions and materials so that his heir, Solomon, could be ready to build immediately upon assuming the throne. In the presence of the assembled congregation, he thanked and blessed God for having allowed him to set aside resources for the Divine service (*I Chronicles* 29:10-13).

יִשְׂרָאֵל אָבִינוּ — *Israel our forefather.* David mentioned only Israel/Jacob, because he was the first to make a vow to contribute tithes for a holy cause as a source of merit in a time of distress (*Genesis* 28:20), an example followed by David (*Bereishis Rabbah* 70:1); and also because it was Jacob who first spoke of the Holy Temple (*Radak*) and designated Mount Moriah as its site [see ArtScroll *Bereishis* 28:16-19].

לְךָ ה׳ הַגְּדֻלָּה — *Yours, HASHEM, is the greatness.* In his moment of public glory, David scrupulously made clear that his every achievement was made possible by God and that it was meant to be utilized in His service. Lest anyone think that his attainments are to his *own* credit, David proclaims that God is Master of everything in heaven and earth and — because He has *sovereignty over every leader* — He decrees who shall gain high positions and who shall be toppled.

אַתָּה הוּא ה׳ — *It is You alone, HASHEM.* The next six verses were recited by the people, led by Ezra, Nehemiah, and the most distinguished Levites the day after Shemini Atzeres, when the newly returned Jews had completed their first festival season in Jerusalem after returning from their Babylonian exile. They gathered in devotion and repentance and echoed the resolve voiced by David nearly five hundred years earlier.

שְׁמֵי הַשָּׁמַיִם — *The most exalted heaven.* This refers either to the highest spiritual spheres or to the furthest reaches of space.

וְאַתָּה מְחַיֶּה אֶת כֻּלָּם — *And You give them all life.* Even inanimate objects have 'life' in the sense that they have whatever conditions are

One must stand from here until after the phrase *'It is You, HASHEM the God'*; however, there is a generally accepted custom to remain standing until after completing the Song at the Sea (p. 266).

I Chronicles 29:10-13

וַיְבָרֶךְ *And David blessed* HASHEM in the presence of the entire congregation; David said, 'Blessed are You, HASHEM, the God of Israel our forefather* from This World to the World to Come. Yours, HASHEM, is the greatness,* the strength, the splendor, the triumph, and the glory, even everything in heaven and earth; Yours, HASHEM, is the kingdom, and the sovereignty over every leader. Wealth and honor come from You and You rule everything — in Your hand is power and strength and it is in Your hand to make anyone great or strong. So now, our God, we thank You and praise Your splendrous Name.'*

Nehemiah 9:6-11

It is You alone, HASHEM, You have made the heaven, the most exalted heaven* and all their legions, the earth and everything upon it, the seas and everything in them and You give them all life;* the heavenly legions bow to You.** Chazzan– *It is You, HASHEM the God, Who selected Abram,* brought him out of Ur Kasdim and made his name Abraham.* You found his heart faithful before You —*

— and You established the covenant with him to give the land of the Canaanite, Hittite, Emorite, Perizzite, Jebusite, and Girgashite, to give* it to his offspring; and You affirmed Your word, for You are righteous.* You observed the suffering of our forefathers in Egypt, and their outcry You heard at the Sea of Reeds. You imposed signs and wonders**

---

necessary for their continued existence *(Iyun Tefillah).*

לְךָ מִשְׁתַּחֲוִים — *Bow to You.* Despite their awesome size and power over other parts of the universe, the heavenly bodies *bow* in the sense that they exist totally to serve God *(Iyun Tefillah).*

אֲשֶׁר בָּחַרְתָּ בְּאַבְרָם — *Who selected Abram.* After cataloguing the endless array of creation and its components, we acknowledge that from them all, God chose Abraham and his offspring as His chosen ones — an astonishing testimony to the Patriarch and the nation he founded *(Siach Yitzchak).*

וְשַׂמְתָּ שְׁמוֹ אַבְרָהָם — *And made his name Abraham.* The change of name signified that Abram's mission had been changed and elevated. His original name was a contracted version of אַב אֲרָם, *father of Aram,* because he had been a spiritual father of his native Aram. The additional ה implies that he had become אַב הֲמוֹן גּוֹיִם, *father of a multitude of nations,* marking him as the spiritual mentor of all mankind (see *Genesis* 17:4-5).

וְכָרוֹת — *And You established* ... We have followed the virtually universal practice that *siddurim* begin a paragraph with וְכָרוֹת; however in the Book of *Nehemiah,* this is not the beginning of a new verse, but a continuation of the above; namely, that in reward for Abraham's faithfulness, God made a covenant with him.

In many congregations, the section beginning with וְכָרוֹת is chanted aloud when a circumcision is to be performed in the synagogue, because the circumcision sealed the covenant of which Abraham's new name was part. There are varying customs regarding reciting this section at a circumcision. In most of these congregations it is said by the *mohel,* in some by the rabbi. In some, all the verses from וְכָרוֹת until (but not including) יִשְׁתַּבַּח are recited responsively, with the *mohel* reciting the first aloud, the congregation the next, and so on. However, no verses are actually *omitted* by anyone; those not said aloud are said quietly. In some congregations, the *mohel* recites aloud only the verses from וְכָרוֹת until בְּמַיִם עַזִּים.

לָתֵת ... לָתֵת — *To give ... to give.* In effect, the Land was given twice: once it was pledged to Abraham, and centuries later it was ceded to his offspring *(Iyun Tefillah).*

כִּי צַדִּיק אָתָּה — *For You are righteous.* God keeps His word even when Israel, on its own merits, would have been unworthy *(Iyun Tefillah).*

אֹתֹת וּמֹפְתִים — *Signs and wonders. Signs* are miracles that were foretold by a prophet; *won-*

עֲבָדָיו וּבְכָל עַם אַרְצוֹ, כִּי יָדַעְתָּ כִּי הֵזִידוּ* עֲלֵיהֶם, וַתַּעַשׂ לְךָ שֵׁם
כְּהַיּוֹם הַזֶּה.* ❖ וְהַיָּם בָּקַעְתָּ לִפְנֵיהֶם, וַיַּעַבְרוּ בְתוֹךְ הַיָּם בַּיַּבָּשָׁה,
וְאֶת רֹדְפֵיהֶם הִשְׁלַכְתָּ בִמְצוֹלֹת, כְּמוֹ אֶבֶן בְּמַיִם עַזִּים.

שירת הים

On the seventh day of Pesach, many congregations recite the Song of the Sea responsively. Each verse is recited by the *chazzan* and repeated by the congregation.

שמות יד:ל-טו:יט

וַיּוֹשַׁע יהוה* בַּיּוֹם הַהוּא אֶת־יִשְׂרָאֵל מִיַּד מִצְרָיִם, וַיַּרְא
יִשְׂרָאֵל אֶת־מִצְרַיִם מֵת עַל־שְׂפַת הַיָּם: ❖ וַיַּרְא יִשְׂרָאֵל
אֶת־הַיָּד הַגְּדֹלָה אֲשֶׁר עָשָׂה יהוה בְּמִצְרַיִם, וַיִּירְאוּ הָעָם
אֶת־יהוה, וַיַּאֲמִינוּ* בַּיהוה וּבְמֹשֶׁה עַבְדּוֹ:

אָז יָשִׁיר־מֹשֶׁה וּבְנֵי יִשְׂרָאֵל אֶת־הַשִּׁירָה הַזֹּאת לַיהוה, וַיֹּאמְרוּ
לֵאמֹר, אָשִׁירָה לַּיהוה כִּי־גָאֹה גָּאָה, סוּס
וְרֹכְבוֹ רָמָה בַיָּם: עָזִּי וְזִמְרָת יָהּ* וַיְהִי־לִי
לִישׁוּעָה, זֶה אֵלִי* וְאַנְוֵהוּ,* אֱלֹהֵי
אָבִי וַאֲרֹמְמֶנְהוּ: יהוה אִישׁ מִלְחָמָה, יהוה
שְׁמוֹ:* מַרְכְּבֹת פַּרְעֹה וְחֵילוֹ יָרָה בַיָּם, וּמִבְחַר
שָׁלִשָׁיו טֻבְּעוּ בְיַם־סוּף: תְּהֹמֹת יְכַסְיֻמוּ, יָרְדוּ בִמְצוֹלֹת כְּמוֹ־
אָבֶן: יְמִינְךָ* יהוה נֶאְדָּרִי בַּכֹּחַ, יְמִינְךָ
יהוה תִּרְעַץ אוֹיֵב: וּבְרֹב גְּאוֹנְךָ תַּהֲרֹס
קָמֶיךָ, תְּשַׁלַּח חֲרֹנְךָ יֹאכְלֵמוֹ כַּקַּשׁ: וּבְרוּחַ

---

ders take place without prior announcement *(Rambam).*

כִּי הֵזִידוּ — *That they sinned flagrantly* [lit., *willfully*]. The Egyptians sinned against the Jews by mistreating and enslaving them. Had the servitude not been so harsh and hatefully cruel, the Egyptians would not have suffered such devastation.

כְּהַיּוֹם הַזֶּה — *As [clear as] this very day.* The miracles of the Exodus were public and indisputable *(Etz Yosef).*

☙ שִׁירַת הַיָּם / The Song at the Sea

The early commentators note that the miracles of the Exodus, beginning with the Ten Plagues, illustrated that God controls every facet of nature at will. Thus, they remained the testimony to God as the all-powerful Creator: no human being saw the creation of the universe, but millions of Jews witnessed the Exodus. The climax of those miraculous events was the splitting of the sea; as the Passover *Haggadah* relates, the miracles at the sea were five times as great as those that took place in Egypt itself. That event was celebrated by Moses and the entire nation in the glorious Song of the Sea, a combination of praise and faith that fits in with the theme of *Pesukei D'zimrah.*

We have included the cantillation symbols *[trop]* for the convenience of those who recite the Song in the manner it is read from the Torah. Nevertheless, we have inserted commas for those unfamiliar with this notation. The basis for reciting the Song with this cantillation is found in Kabbalistic literature, which attaches great importance to the joyful, musical recitation of the Song, as if one were standing at the seashore witnessing the miracle. The *Zohar* states that one who recites the Song with the proper intent will merit to sing the praises of future miracles.

☙ וַיּוֹשַׁע ה׳ — *HASHEM saved.* The Torah sums up the miracle at the sea as a prelude to Moses' song.

וַיִּירְאוּ... וַיַּאֲמִינוּ — *(They) feared... and they had faith.* The fact that God has the power to perform miracles is unimportant; the Creator of the universe has no difficulty in stopping the flow of a sea. What *did* matter was the effect the miracle had on Israel. The people felt a new and higher *upon Pharaoh and upon all his servants, and upon all the people of his land. For You knew that they sinned flagrantly* against them, and You brought Yourself renown as [clear as] this very day.** Chazzan– *You split the Sea before them and they crossed in the midst of the Sea on dry land; but their pursuers You hurled into the depths, like a stone into turbulent waters.*

THE SONG AT THE SEA

On the seventh day of Pesach, many congregations recite the Song of the Sea responsively. Each verse is recited by the *chazzan* and repeated by the congregation.

Exodus 14:30-15:19

וַיּוֹשַׁע *HASHEM saved* — on that day — Israel from the hand of Egypt, and Israel saw the Egyptians dead on the seashore.* Chazzan– *Israel saw the great hand that HASHEM inflicted upon Egypt and the people feared HASHEM, and they had faith* in HASHEM and in Moses, His servant.*

Then Moses and the Children of Israel chose to sing this song to HASHEM, and they said the following:*

I shall sing to HASHEM for He is exalted above the arrogant, having hurled horse with its rider into the sea.

God is my might and my praise, and He was a salvation for me. This is my God,* and I will build Him a Sanctuary;* the God of my father, and I will exalt Him.*

*HASHEM is Master of war, through His Name HASHEM.**

Pharaoh's chariots and army He threw into the sea; and the pick of his officers were mired in the Sea of Reeds.

Deep waters covered them; they descended in the depths like stone.

Your right hand, HASHEM, is adorned with strength; Your right hand, HASHEM, smashes the enemy.*

In Your abundant grandeur You shatter Your opponents; You dispatch Your wrath, it consumes them like straw.

---

degree of *fear*, in the sense of awe and reverence. And their *faith* increased immeasurably, for they had seen that, through His prophet, God promised salvation from danger and had indeed saved them.

אָז יָשִׁיר מֹשֶׁה — *Then Moses . . . chose to sing.* Rather than שָׁר, *sang*, the Torah uses the verb יָשִׁיר, literally, *will sing*. In the simple sense, the verse means that upon seeing the miracle the people decided that they *would* sing. Midrashically, the verb implies the principle that God will bring the dead back to life in Messianic times — and then they *will* sing God's praises once again (*Rashi*).

עָזִּי וְזִמְרָת יָהּ — *God is my might and my praise.* The translation follows *Targum Onkelos*. According to *Rashi* the phrase is translated: *God's might and His cutting away [of the enemy] was a salvation for me.*

זֶה אֵלִי — *This is my God.* So obvious was God's Presence, that the Jews could point to it, as it were, and say 'This is my God.' As the Sages put it: 'A maidservant at the sea saw more than the prophet Yechezkel [saw in his heavenly prophecy]' (*Rashi*).

וְאַנְוֵהוּ — *And I will build Him a Sanctuary.* The root of the word is נָוֶה, *abode*. An alternative interpretation based on the same root: I will make myself into a Godly sanctuary (*Rashi*) — to remake oneself in God's image is to build the greatest of all sanctuaries.

Another translation is *I will beautify* or *glorify Him* [based on the root נאה, *fitting, beautiful*]. The Sages teach that this is done by performing the commandments in a beautiful manner, by having beautiful *tefillin*, a beautiful *succah*, a beautiful *esrog* and so on (*Shabbos* 133b).

ה׳ שְׁמוֹ — *Through His Name HASHEM.* Mortal kings require legions and armaments, but God overcomes His enemies with nothing more than His Name. Moreover, this Name of mercy applies to Him even when He is forced to vanquish the wicked (*Rashi*).

יְמִינְךָ — *Your right hand.* Of course God has no

אַפֶּיךָ נֶעֶרְמוּ מַיִם, נִצְּבוּ כְמוֹ־נֵד
נֹזְלִים, קָפְאוּ תְהֹמֹת בְּלֶב־יָם: אָמַר
אוֹיֵב,* אֶרְדֹּף אַשִּׂיג אֲחַלֵּק שָׁלָל, תִּמְלָאֵמוֹ
נַפְשִׁי, אָרִיק חַרְבִּי, תּוֹרִישֵׁמוֹ יָדִי: נָשַׁפְתָּ
בְרוּחֲךָ כִּסָּמוֹ יָם, צָלְלוּ כַּעוֹפֶרֶת בְּמַיִם,
אַדִּירִים: מִי־כָמֹכָה בָּאֵלִם יהוה, מִי
כָּמֹכָה נֶאְדָּר בַּקֹּדֶשׁ, נוֹרָא תְהִלֹּת עֹשֵׂה
פֶלֶא: נָטִיתָ יְמִינְךָ, תִּבְלָעֵמוֹ אָרֶץ: נָחִיתָ
בְחַסְדְּךָ עַם־זוּ גָּאָלְתָּ, נֵהַלְתָּ בְעָזְּךָ אֶל־נְוֵה
קָדְשֶׁךָ:* שָׁמְעוּ עַמִּים יִרְגָּזוּן, חִיל
אָחַז יֹשְׁבֵי פְּלָשֶׁת: אָז נִבְהֲלוּ אַלּוּפֵי
אֱדוֹם,* אֵילֵי מוֹאָב יֹאחֲזֵמוֹ רָעַד, נָמֹגוּ
כֹּל יֹשְׁבֵי כְנָעַן: תִּפֹּל עֲלֵיהֶם אֵימָתָה
וָפַחַד, בִּגְדֹל זְרוֹעֲךָ יִדְּמוּ כָּאָבֶן, עַד־
יַעֲבֹר עַמְּךָ* יהוה, עַד־יַעֲבֹר עַם־זוּ
קָנִיתָ: תְּבִאֵמוֹ* וְתִטָּעֵמוֹ בְּהַר נַחֲלָתְךָ, מָכוֹן
לְשִׁבְתְּךָ פָּעַלְתָּ יהוה, מִקְּדָשׁ אֲדֹנָי כּוֹנְנוּ
יָדֶיךָ: יהוה ׀ יִמְלֹךְ* לְעֹלָם וָעֶד:

יהוה יִמְלֹךְ לְעֹלָם וָעֶד. (יהוה מַלְכוּתֵהּ קָאֵם, לְעָלַם וּלְעָלְמֵי עָלְמַיָּא.) כִּי בָא סוּס פַּרְעֹה בְּרִכְבּוֹ וּבְפָרָשָׁיו בַּיָּם, וַיָּשֶׁב יהוה עֲלֵהֶם אֶת מֵי הַיָּם, וּבְנֵי יִשְׂרָאֵל הָלְכוּ בַיַּבָּשָׁה בְּתוֹךְ הַיָּם. ❖ כִּי לַיהוה הַמְּלוּכָה,* וּמֹשֵׁל בַּגּוֹיִם.[1] וְעָלוּ מוֹשִׁעִים* בְּהַר צִיּוֹן, לִשְׁפֹּט אֶת הַר עֵשָׂו, וְהָיְתָה לַיהוה הַמְּלוּכָה.[2] וְהָיָה יהוה לְמֶלֶךְ* עַל כָּל הָאָרֶץ, בַּיּוֹם הַהוּא יִהְיֶה יהוה אֶחָד וּשְׁמוֹ אֶחָד.*[3] (וּבְתוֹרָתְךָ כָּתוּב לֵאמֹר: שְׁמַע יִשְׂרָאֵל יהוה אֱלֹהֵינוּ יהוה אֶחָד.[4])

---

physical characteristics. All the many Scriptural references to physicality are allegorical.

אָמַר אוֹיֵב — *The enemy declared.* In order to coax his people to join him in pursuit of the Jews, Pharaoh *(the enemy)* spoke confidently of his ability to overtake and plunder them.

אֶל נְוֵה קָדְשֶׁךָ — *To Your holy abode,* i.e., the Holy Temple. Although the Temple would not be built for over four hundred years, prophetic song typically combines past with future, because in the Divine perception they are interrelated.

פְּלָשֶׁת . . . אֱדוֹם — *Philistia . . . Edom . . .* Not all the nations were of equal status. Philistia and Canaan rightly feared conquest because their lands comprised *Eretz Yisrael.* Edom and Moab did not fear losing their land, but rather feared retribution because they did not and would not show compassion for Jewish suffering *(Rashi).*

עַד יַעֲבֹר עַמְּךָ — *Until Your people passes through.* This continues the previous thought; the terror of the nations would continue until Israel crossed into *Eretz Yisrael.* The term *passes through* is used twice: once in reference to the crossing of the Jordan and once in reference to the waters of the Arnon, on the border of Israel and Moab [see *Numbers* 21:13-20] *(Rashi).*

תְּבִאֵמוֹ — *You shall bring them.* Moses unconsciously prophesied that he would not enter the

At a blast from Your nostrils the waters were heaped up; straight as a wall stood the running water, the deep waters congealed in the heart of the sea.

The enemy declared: 'I will pursue, I will overtake, I will divide plunder; I will satisfy my lust with them; I will unsheathe my sword, my hand will impoverish them.'*

You blew with Your wind — the sea enshrouded them; the mighty ones sank like lead in the waters.

Who is like You among the heavenly powers, HASHEM! Who is like You, mighty in holiness, too awesome for praise, doing wonders!

You stretched out Your right hand — the earth swallowed them.

*You guided in Your kindness this people that You redeemed; You led with Your might to Your holy abode.**

Peoples heard — they were agitated; convulsive terror gripped the dwellers of Philistia.

Then the chieftains of Edom were confounded, trembling gripped the powers of Moab, all the dwellers of Canaan dissolved.*

May fear and terror befall them, at the greatness of Your arm may they be still as stone; until Your people passes through, HASHEM, until this people You have acquired passes through.*

You shall bring them and implant them on the mount of Your heritage, the foundation of Your dwelling-place, which You, HASHEM, have made: the Sanctuary, my Lord, that Your hands established.*

HASHEM shall reign for all eternity.*

HASHEM shall reign for all eternity. (HASHEM — His kingdom is established forever and ever.) When Pharaoh's cavalry came — with his chariots and horsemen — into the sea and HASHEM turned back the waters of the sea upon them, the Children of Israel walked on the dry bed amid the sea. Chazzan– *For the sovereignty is HASHEM's* and He rules over nations.*[1] *The saviors* will ascend Mount Zion to judge Esau's mountain, and the kingdom will be HASHEM's.*[2] *Then HASHEM will be King* over all the world, on that day HASHEM will be One and His Name will be One.**[3] *(And in Your Torah it is written: Hear O Israel: HASHEM is our God, HASHEM, the One and Only.*[4]*)*

(1) *Psalms* 22:29. (2) *Ovadiah* 1:21. (3) *Zechariah* 14:9. (4) *Deuteronomy* 6:4.

Land, for he said, 'You shall bring *them*,' and not 'You shall bring *us*' *(Rashi)*.

ה׳ יִמְלֹךְ — *HASHEM shall reign.* We repeat this verse to signify the climax of the Song — that God's sovereignty shall be recognized forever. Because this is so important, most congregations follow the *Arizal*, who taught that the Aramaic Targum of this verse also be recited.

כִּי לַה׳ הַמְּלוּכָה — *For the sovereignty is HASHEM's.* The collected verses attached to the Song are appropriate to the climactic verse that God will reign forever.

מוֹשִׁעִים — *The saviors.* Those who will in the future lead Israel out of exile will come to Mount Zion from which they will complete the conquest of the archenemy, Esau, whose descendants are responsible for our exile *(Rashi)*.

וּמֹשֵׁל ... לְמֶלֶךְ — *He rules ... be King.* The term מוֹשֵׁל, *ruler*, refers to one who forces his subjects to obey him, while מֶלֶךְ, *king*, is one who is willingly accepted. Now God is *King* over Israel alone because only Israel acknowledges His sovereignty with love, but He *rules* the nations despite their unwillingness to accept Him as their God. In the future, however, all nations will proclaim Him as their King *(Vilna Gaon)*.

ה׳ אֶחָד וּשְׁמוֹ אֶחָד — *HASHEM will be One and His Name will be One.* But does He not have One

לשני ימים הראשונים של פסח

ON THE FIRST TWO DAYS OF PESACH CONTINUE HERE.
ON THE SABBATH OF CHOL HAMOED CONTINUE ON PAGE 520;
ON THE LAST TWO DAYS CONTINUE ON PAGE 840.

נִשְׁמַת כָּל חַי תְּבָרֵךְ אֶת שִׁמְךָ יהוה אֱלֹהֵינוּ, וְרוּחַ* כָּל בָּשָׂר תְּפָאֵר וּתְרוֹמֵם זִכְרְךָ מַלְכֵּנוּ תָּמִיד. מִן הָעוֹלָם וְעַד הָעוֹלָם אַתָּה אֵל,[1] וּמִבַּלְעָדֶיךָ אֵין לָנוּ מֶלֶךְ[2] גּוֹאֵל וּמוֹשִׁיעַ. פּוֹדֶה וּמַצִּיל וּמְפַרְנֵס וּמְרַחֵם בְּכָל עֵת צָרָה וְצוּקָה,* אֵין לָנוּ מֶלֶךְ אֶלָּא אָתָּה. אֱלֹהֵי הָרִאשׁוֹנִים וְהָאַחֲרוֹנִים,* אֱלוֹהַּ כָּל בְּרִיּוֹת, אֲדוֹן כָּל תּוֹלָדוֹת, הַמְּהֻלָּל בְּרֹב הַתִּשְׁבָּחוֹת, הַמְּנַהֵג עוֹלָמוֹ בְּחֶסֶד וּבְרִיּוֹתָיו בְּרַחֲמִים. וַיהוה לֹא יָנוּם וְלֹא יִישָׁן.[3] הַמְּעוֹרֵר יְשֵׁנִים, וְהַמֵּקִיץ נִרְדָּמִים, וְהַמֵּשִׂיחַ אִלְּמִים, וְהַמַּתִּיר אֲסוּרִים,[4] וְהַסּוֹמֵךְ נוֹפְלִים, וְהַזּוֹקֵף כְּפוּפִים.[5] לְךָ לְבַדְּךָ אֲנַחְנוּ מוֹדִים. אִלּוּ פִינוּ* מָלֵא שִׁירָה כַּיָּם, וּלְשׁוֹנֵנוּ רִנָּה כַּהֲמוֹן גַּלָּיו, וְשִׂפְתוֹתֵינוּ שֶׁבַח כְּמֶרְחֲבֵי רָקִיעַ, וְעֵינֵינוּ מְאִירוֹת כַּשֶּׁמֶשׁ וְכַיָּרֵחַ,* וְיָדֵינוּ פְרוּשׂוֹת כְּנִשְׁרֵי שָׁמָיִם, וְרַגְלֵינוּ קַלּוֹת כָּאַיָּלוֹת, אֵין אֲנַחְנוּ מַסְפִּיקִים לְהוֹדוֹת לְךָ, יהוה אֱלֹהֵינוּ וֵאלֹהֵי אֲבוֹתֵינוּ, וּלְבָרֵךְ אֶת שְׁמֶךָ עַל אַחַת מֵאָלֶף אֶלֶף אַלְפֵי אֲלָפִים וְרִבֵּי רְבָבוֹת פְּעָמִים הַטּוֹבוֹת שֶׁעָשִׂיתָ עִם אֲבוֹתֵינוּ וְעִמָּנוּ.* מִמִּצְרַיִם גְּאַלְתָּנוּ יהוה אֱלֹהֵינוּ, וּמִבֵּית עֲבָדִים פְּדִיתָנוּ. בְּרָעָב זַנְתָּנוּ, וּבְשָׂבָע כִּלְכַּלְתָּנוּ, מֵחֶרֶב הִצַּלְתָּנוּ, וּמִדֶּבֶר מִלַּטְתָּנוּ, וּמֵחֳלָיִם רָעִים וְנֶאֱמָנִים דִּלִּיתָנוּ. עַד הֵנָּה עֲזָרוּנוּ רַחֲמֶיךָ, וְלֹא עֲזָבוּנוּ חֲסָדֶיךָ. וְאַל תִּטְּשֵׁנוּ יהוה אֱלֹהֵינוּ לָנֶצַח. עַל כֵּן אֵבָרִים שֶׁפִּלַּגְתָּ בָּנוּ, וְרוּחַ וּנְשָׁמָה שֶׁנָּפַחְתָּ בְּאַפֵּינוּ, וְלָשׁוֹן אֲשֶׁר

Name today? Rabbi Nachman bar Yitzchak taught: The world of the future will be unlike the world of today. In the world of today God's Name is spelled one way and pronounced differently, whereas in the world of the future all will be One — the spelling and pronunciation will both be י־ה־ו־ה (*Pesachim* 50a). Since we fail to perceive God's nature as it is expressed in the true pronunciation of His Name, we may not utter it. But in time to come, there will be no contradiction between perception and reality.

נִשְׁמַת / Nishmas

This beautiful and moving prayer is an outpouring of praise and gratitude to God. Lyrically, it depicts our utter dependency on God's mercy, our total inadequacy to laud Him properly, and our enthusiastic resolve to dedicate ourselves to His service. It is especially appropriate for recitation on the Sabbath and Festivals — although it contains no mention of the day — because the additional holiness of the Sabbath and the time it affords for extra contemplation make man better able to understand and express the message of the *Nishmas* prayer.

The Talmud (*Pesachim* 118a) calls this prayer בִּרְכַּת הַשִּׁיר, *the Blessing of the Song,* because it concludes the psalms and songs of *Pesukei D'zimrah,* and because it continues the theme of the Song of the Sea. In the Sabbath and Festival service as in the Passover *Haggadah, Nishmas* introduces the series of praises that culminate with יִשְׁתַּבַּח, *Yishtabach.* There, too, it climaxes the grateful narrative of the Exodus with an outpouring of dedication.

So highly was this prayer regarded that such great commentators as *Rabbi Yehudah HaLevi* and *Ibn Ezra* composed poetic introductions to *Nishmas.* That of *Ibn Ezra,* incidentally, צָמְאָה

THE FIRST TWO DAYS OF PESACH

ON THE FIRST TWO DAYS OF PESACH CONTINUE HERE.
ON THE SABBATH OF CHOL HAMOED CONTINUE ON PAGE 520;
ON THE LAST TWO DAYS CONTINUE ON PAGE 840.

נִשְׁמַת *The soul of every living being shall bless Your Name, HASHEM, our God; the spirit* of all flesh shall always glorify and exalt Your remembrance, our King. From This World to the World to Come, You are God,[1] and other than You we have no king,[2] redeemer or savior. Liberator, Rescuer, Sustainer and Merciful One in every time of distress and anguish,* we have no king but You! — God of the first and of the last,* God of all creatures, Master of all generations, Who is extolled through a multitude of praises, Who guides His world with kindness and His creatures with mercy. HASHEM neither slumbers nor sleeps.[3] He Who rouses the sleepers and awakens the slumberers, Who makes the mute speak and releases the bound;[4] Who supports the fallen and straightens the bent.[5] To You alone we give thanks. Were our mouth* as full of song as the sea, and our tongue as full of joyous song as its multitude of waves, and our lips as full of praise as the breadth of the heavens, and our eyes as brilliant as the sun and the moon,* and our hands as outspread as eagles of the sky and our feet as swift as hinds — we still could not thank You sufficiently, HASHEM, our God and God of our forefathers, and to bless Your Name for even one of the thousand thousand, thousands of thousands and myriad myriads of favors that You performed for our ancestors and for us.* You redeemed us from Egypt, HASHEM, our God, and liberated us from the house of bondage. In famine You nourished us and in plenty You sustained us. From sword You saved us; from plague You let us escape; and from severe and enduring diseases You spared us. Until now Your mercy has helped us, and Your kindness has not forsaken us. Do not abandon us, HASHEM, our God, forever. Therefore, the organs that You set within us, and the spirit and soul that You breathed into our nostrils, and the tongue that*

(1) Cf. *Psalms* 90:2. (2) Cf. *Isaiah* 44:6. (3) Cf. *Psalms* 121:4. (4) Cf. 146:7. (5) Cf. 145:14.

נַפְשִׁי לֵאלֹהִים, *My soul thirsts for God,* is sung by many in the Sabbath Eve Zemiros (see Artscroll *Zemiroth,* p. 118).

נִשְׁמַת ... רוּחַ — *The soul ... the spirit.* Essentially, these two concepts are similar, but נְשָׁמָה represents a higher degree of spiritual awareness than רוּחַ. Thus, on the Sabbath and Festivals when Jews are invested with a נְשָׁמָה יְתֵרָה, a higher degree of spiritual awareness, we dedicate that, too, to bless God.

בְּכָל עֵת צָרָה וְצוּקָה — *In every time of distress and anguish.* Commonly, people express gratitude in happy times and pray for salvation in hard times. We go further, however — even in times of distress and anguish, we express our gratitude to God for allowing us to survive the suffering.

אֱלֹהֵי הָרִאשׁוֹנִים וְהָאַחֲרוֹנִים — *God of the first and of the last.* When God initiates a course of action, He takes into account the results it will bring about centuries into the future. Thus He is the Master of the *first* set of events as well as of the *last (R' Moshe Cordevero).*

אִלּוּ פִינוּ — *Were our mouth ...* Having stated that God is All-powerful and All-merciful, and thus worthy of our grateful thanks, the liturgist now begins to explain that no creature could do justice to this task — even if he were endowed with superhuman qualities.

מְאִירוֹת כַּשֶּׁמֶשׁ וְכַיָּרֵחַ — *As brilliant as the sun and the moon,* which see everything on earth.

עִם אֲבוֹתֵינוּ וְעִמָּנוּ — *For our ancestors and for us.* Man does not live in a vacuum. The favors done for previous generations have lasting effects that benefit us as well.

שַׂמְתָּ בְּפִינוּ, הֵן הֵם יוֹדוּ וִיבָרְכוּ וִישַׁבְּחוּ וִיפָאֲרוּ וִירוֹמְמוּ וְיַעֲרִיצוּ וְיַקְדִּישׁוּ וְיַמְלִיכוּ אֶת שִׁמְךָ מַלְכֵּנוּ. כִּי כָל פֶּה לְךָ יוֹדֶה, וְכָל לָשׁוֹן לְךָ תִשָּׁבַע, וְכָל בֶּרֶךְ לְךָ תִכְרַע,[1] וְכָל קוֹמָה לְפָנֶיךָ תִשְׁתַּחֲוֶה,* וְכָל לְבָבוֹת יִירָאוּךָ, וְכָל קֶרֶב וּכְלָיוֹת יְזַמְּרוּ לִשְׁמֶךָ, כַּדָּבָר שֶׁכָּתוּב: כָּל עַצְמֹתַי תֹּאמַרְנָה,* יהוה מִי כָמוֹךָ, מַצִּיל עָנִי מֵחָזָק מִמֶּנּוּ, וְעָנִי וְאֶבְיוֹן מִגֹּזְלוֹ.[2] מִי יִדְמֶה לָּךְ, וּמִי יִשְׁוֶה לָּךְ, וּמִי יַעֲרָךְ לָךְ.[3] הָאֵל הַגָּדוֹל הַגִּבּוֹר וְהַנּוֹרָא, אֵל עֶלְיוֹן, קֹנֵה שָׁמַיִם וָאָרֶץ. ❖ נְהַלֶּלְךָ וּנְשַׁבֵּחֲךָ וּנְפָאֶרְךָ וּנְבָרֵךְ אֶת שֵׁם קָדְשֶׁךָ, כָּאָמוּר: לְדָוִד, בָּרְכִי נַפְשִׁי אֶת יהוה, וְכָל קְרָבַי אֶת שֵׁם קָדְשׁוֹ.[4]

The *chazzan* of *Shacharis* begins here:

הָאֵל* בְּתַעֲצֻמוֹת עֻזֶּךָ,* הַגָּדוֹל בִּכְבוֹד שְׁמֶךָ, הַגִּבּוֹר לָנֶצַח וְהַנּוֹרָא בְּנוֹרְאוֹתֶיךָ. הַמֶּלֶךְ הַיּוֹשֵׁב עַל כִּסֵּא רָם וְנִשָּׂא.[5]

שׁוֹכֵן עַד* מָרוֹם וְקָדוֹשׁ שְׁמוֹ.[6] וְכָתוּב: רַנְּנוּ צַדִּיקִים בַּיהוה לַיְשָׁרִים נָאוָה תְהִלָּה.[7]

❖ בְּפִי **יְ**שָׁרִים* תִּתְהַלָּל.
וּבְדִבְרֵי **צַ**דִּיקִים תִּתְבָּרַךְ.
וּבִלְשׁוֹן **חֲ**סִידִים תִּתְרוֹמָם.
וּבְקֶרֶב **קְ**דוֹשִׁים תִּתְקַדָּשׁ.

וְכָל קוֹמָה לְפָנֶיךָ תִשְׁתַּחֲוֶה — *Every erect spine shall prostrate itself before You.* One must bow to God even while he is standing erect. 'Bowing' is not only a physical action; it must also be done in the heart and mind *(R' Baruch of Mezhibozh).*

כָּל עַצְמֹתַי תֹּאמַרְנָה — *All my bones shall say.* Having just described how each limb and organ will offer praise to God, we cite the Scriptural source for this obligation. The verse concludes with the inspiring praise that God's greatness is manifested in His rescue of the powerless from their oppressors. This is meant both literally and figuratively, for, as *Radak* explains, God rescues the seemingly overmatched good inclination from the seductions of the evil inclination.

☙ הָאֵל — *O God.* It is customary to divide the Sabbath and *Yom Tov* services among several *chazzanim:* one for *Pesukei D'zimrah;* another for *Shacharis;* and a third for *Mussaf.* On the Sabbath, the *chazzan* of *Shacharis* begins שׁוֹכֵן עַד, *He Who abides forever,* because the Sabbath was the climax of creation, when God had all of creation, including man, to acknowledge and praise Him.

On Pesach, Shavuos, and Succos, the *chazzan* of *Shacharis* begins הָאֵל בְּתַעֲצֻמוֹת, *O God, in the omnipotence,* because those three festivals testify to the Exodus, the great event when God revealed 'the omnipotence of His strength.' Thus the characteristics spoken of in this paragraph are fitting for the way in which God revealed Himself in bringing Israel to freedom and its new status as His people. However, on Rosh Hashanah and Yom Kippur when God is the 'King sitting in judgment,' the *chazzan* begins הַמֶּלֶךְ, *the King.*

הָאֵל בְּתַעֲצֻמוֹת עֻזֶּךָ — *O God, in the omnipotence of Your strength.* This and the following verses elaborate upon the themes of *Nishmas.* The last sentence of *Nishmas* contains the four terms הָאֵל הַגָּדוֹל הַגִּבּוֹר וְהַנּוֹרָא, *O great, mighty, and awesome God.* Now, each of those terms is used and elaborated upon in a phrase lauding God:

1. הָאֵל — *O God.* This Name refers to God as the All-Powerful. Thus, God's power is expressed by the idea that He does not depend on servants, armies, or the consent of His subjects. He is omnipotent in His strength without

You placed in our mouth — all of them shall thank and bless, praise and glorify, exalt and revere, sanctify and declare the sovereignty of Your Name, our King. For every mouth shall offer thanks to You; every tongue shall vow allegiance to You; every knee shall bend to You;[1] every erect spine shall prostrate itself before You; all hearts shall fear You, and all innermost feelings and thoughts shall sing praises to Your name, as it is written: "All my bones shall say:* 'HASHEM, who is like You?' You save the poor man from one stronger than he, the poor and destitute from one who would rob him."[2] Who is like unto You? Who is equal to You? Who can be compared to You?[3] O great, mighty, and awesome God, the supreme God, Creator of heaven and earth.* Chazzan– *We shall laud, praise, and glorify You and bless Your holy Name, as it is said 'Of David: Bless HASHEM, O my soul, and let all my innermost being bless His holy Name!'[4]*

The *chazzan* of *Shacharis* begins here:

הָאֵל *O God,* in the omnipotence of Your strength,* great in the glory of Your Name, mighty forever and awesome through Your awesome deeds. O King enthroned upon a high and lofty throne![5]*

שׁוֹכֵן עַד *He Who abides forever,* exalted and holy is His Name.[6] And it is written: 'Sing joyfully, O righteous, before HASHEM; for the upright, praise is fitting.'[7]*

Chazzan: *By the mouth of the upright* shall You be lauded;*
by the words of the righteous shall You be blessed;
by the tongue of the devout shall You be exalted;
and amid the holy shall You be sanctified.

(1) Cf. *Isaiah* 45:23. (2) *Psalms* 35:10. (3) Cf. 89:7; cf. *Isaiah* 40:25. (4) *Psalms* 103:1. (5) Cf. *Isaiah* 6:1. (6) Cf. 57:15. (7) *Psalms* 33:1.

---

reliance on anything else.

2. הַגָּדוֹל — *Great.* His greatness is signified by the fact that all creatures give honor to His Name.

3. הַגִּבּוֹר — *Mighty.* Unlike mighty human rulers, whose powers ebb as they grow old, God's majesty and strength are eternal and undiminished.

4. וְהַנּוֹרָא — *Awesome.* Unlike human kings who are held in awe only because they have the power to punish their detractors, God's awesomeness is obvious because the entire universe testifies to His greatness.

⊲§ שׁוֹכֵן עַד — *He Who abides forever.* Although God is *exalted and holy,* He nevertheless makes His abode on earth, for it is only here — through the deeds of the righteous — that His commandments can be carried out. Therefore, this paragraph goes on to say that the primary praise of God comes from such people. The key, however, is not in their rhetoric but in the 'song' of their good deeds.

בְּפִי יְשָׁרִים — *By the mouth of the upright.* Four categories of people are listed as praising God: יְשָׁרִים צַדִּיקִים חֲסִידִים קְדוֹשִׁים, *upright, righteous, devout,* and *holy.* The initials of these four words spell יִצְחָק, leading some to speculate that it is the signature of the unknown author of *Nishmas.*

Rabbi Shraga Feivel Mendlowitz noted that these four categories seem to be listed in ascending order of their spiritual accomplishment, the lowest being the upright, fair-minded people and the highest being the holy ones. The higher the level of the person, the more meaningful the manner in which he praises God. While the *upright* praises God with his *mouth,* the *righteous* uses articulated *words.* The *devout* uses his *tongue,* implying that the praise comes from deeper within himself. The *holy* person, however, praises God with his very *essence* [קֶרֶב, literally, *inner being*].

וּבְמַקְהֲלוֹת רִבְבוֹת* עַמְּךָ בֵּית יִשְׂרָאֵל, בְּרִנָּה יִתְפָּאַר שִׁמְךָ מַלְכֵּנוּ בְּכָל דּוֹר וָדוֹר. ❖ שֶׁכֵּן חוֹבַת כָּל הַיְּצוּרִים,* לְפָנֶיךָ יהוה אֱלֹהֵינוּ וֵאלֹהֵי אֲבוֹתֵינוּ, לְהוֹדוֹת לְהַלֵּל לְשַׁבֵּחַ לְפָאֵר לְרוֹמֵם לְהַדֵּר לְבָרֵךְ לְעַלֵּה וּלְקַלֵּס, עַל כָּל דִּבְרֵי שִׁירוֹת וְתִשְׁבְּחוֹת דָּוִד* בֶּן יִשַׁי עַבְדְּךָ מְשִׁיחֶךָ.

Stand while reciting יִשְׁתַּבַּח . . . The fifteen expressions of praise — שִׁיר וּשְׁבָחָה . . . בְּרָכוֹת וְהוֹדָאוֹת — should be recited without pause, preferably in one breath.

יִשְׁתַּבַּח שִׁמְךָ לָעַד מַלְכֵּנוּ, הָאֵל הַמֶּלֶךְ הַגָּדוֹל וְהַקָּדוֹשׁ, בַּשָּׁמַיִם וּבָאָרֶץ. כִּי לְךָ נָאֶה יהוה אֱלֹהֵינוּ וֵאלֹהֵי אֲבוֹתֵינוּ, שִׁיר וּשְׁבָחָה, הַלֵּל וְזִמְרָה, עֹז וּמֶמְשָׁלָה, נֶצַח* גְּדֻלָּה וּגְבוּרָה, תְּהִלָּה וְתִפְאֶרֶת, קְדֻשָּׁה וּמַלְכוּת, בְּרָכוֹת וְהוֹדָאוֹת מֵעַתָּה וְעַד עוֹלָם. ❖ בָּרוּךְ אַתָּה יהוה, אֵל מֶלֶךְ גָּדוֹל בַּתִּשְׁבָּחוֹת,* אֵל הַהוֹדָאוֹת, אֲדוֹן הַנִּפְלָאוֹת, הַבּוֹחֵר בְּשִׁירֵי זִמְרָה,* מֶלֶךְ אֵל חֵי הָעוֹלָמִים.* (.Cong.— אָמֵן)

The *chazzan* recites חֲצִי קַדִּישׁ.

יִתְגַּדַּל וְיִתְקַדַּשׁ שְׁמֵהּ רַבָּא. (.Cong.— אָמֵן) בְּעָלְמָא דִּי בְרָא כִרְעוּתֵהּ. וְיַמְלִיךְ מַלְכוּתֵהּ, בְּחַיֵּיכוֹן וּבְיוֹמֵיכוֹן וּבְחַיֵּי דְכָל בֵּית יִשְׂרָאֵל, בַּעֲגָלָא וּבִזְמַן קָרִיב. וְאִמְרוּ: אָמֵן.

(.Cong.— אָמֵן. יְהֵא שְׁמֵהּ רַבָּא מְבָרַךְ לְעָלַם וּלְעָלְמֵי עָלְמַיָּא.)

יְהֵא שְׁמֵהּ רַבָּא מְבָרַךְ לְעָלַם וּלְעָלְמֵי עָלְמַיָּא.

יִתְבָּרַךְ וְיִשְׁתַּבַּח וְיִתְפָּאַר וְיִתְרוֹמַם וְיִתְנַשֵּׂא וְיִתְהַדָּר וְיִתְעַלֶּה וְיִתְהַלָּל שְׁמֵהּ דְּקֻדְשָׁא בְּרִיךְ הוּא (.Cong.— בְּרִיךְ הוּא) — לְעֵלָּא מִן כָּל בִּרְכָתָא וְשִׁירָתָא תֻּשְׁבְּחָתָא וְנֶחֱמָתָא, דַּאֲמִירָן בְּעָלְמָא. וְאִמְרוּ: אָמֵן. (.Cong.— אָמֵן)

⊰ וּבְמַקְהֲלוֹת רִבְבוֹת — *And in the assemblies of the myriads.* In future times, Jews will gather in their tens of thousands to glorify God.

שֶׁכֵּן חוֹבַת כָּל הַיְצוּרִים — *For such is the duty of all creatures.* It is their duty because of the simple fact that they are God's creatures; since He fashioned them, they must feel obligated to pay Him homage.

עַל כָּל דִּבְרֵי . . . דָּוִד — *Even beyond all expressions . . . of David.* Although David, the נְעִים זְמִרוֹת יִשְׂרָאֵל, *sweet singer of Israel (II Samuel* 23:1), is the quintessential composer of God's praises, even he could not nearly do justice to God's greatness. Therefore we now say that we are obligated to praise Him limitlessly — even beyond the songs of David.

⊰ **יִשְׁתַּבַּח / Yishtabach**

As noted in the commentary to בָּרוּךְ שֶׁאָמַר (p. 232), the יִשְׁתַּבַּח prayer ends the *Pesukei D'zimrah* section of *Shacharis.* The theme of fifteen is repeated twice in this prayer: there are fifteen expressions of praise in the first half of the paragraph, and after בָּרוּךְ אַתָּה ה׳, there are fifteen words. This number alludes to the fifteen שִׁיר הַמַּעֲלוֹת, *Songs of Ascents* [*Psalms* 120-134], composed by David. Also, fifteen is the numerical value of the Divine Name יָהּ, the letters of which were used by God to create heaven and earth; therefore, it alludes to the idea that everything is God's and He is its Creator. *Yishtabach* makes repeated use of this number to remind us to carry its message into our daily lives.

וּבְמַקְהֲלוֹת *And in the assemblies of the myriads* of Your people, the House of Israel, with joyous song shall Your Name be glorified, our King, throughout every generation.* Chazzan– *For such is the duty of all creatures* — before You, HASHEM, our God, God of our forefathers, to thank, laud, praise, glorify, exalt, adore, bless, raise high, and sing praises — even beyond all expressions of the songs and praises of David* the son of Jesse, Your servant, Your anointed.*

Stand while reciting *'May Your Name be praised . . .'*
The fifteen expressions of praise — *'song and praise. . .blessings and thanksgivings'* — should be recited without pause, preferably in one breath.

יִשְׁתַּבַּח *May Your Name be praised forever — our King, the God, the great and holy King — in heaven and on earth. Because for You is fitting — O HASHEM, our God, and the God of our forefathers — song and praise, lauding and hymns, power and dominion, triumph,* greatness and strength, praise and splendor, holiness and sovereignty, blessings and thanksgivings from this time and forever.* Chazzan– *Blessed are You, HASHEM, God, King exalted through praises,* God of thanksgivings, Master of wonders, Who chooses musical songs of praise* — King, God, Life-giver of the world.** (Cong.– *Amen.)*

The *chazzan* recites Half-*Kaddish*.

יִתְגַּדַּל *May His great Name grow exalted and sanctified* (Cong.– *Amen.) in the world that He created as He willed. May He give reign to His kingship in your lifetimes and in your days, and in the lifetimes of the entire Family of Israel, swiftly and soon. Now respond: Amen.*

(Cong.– *Amen. May His great Name be blessed forever and ever.)*

May His great Name be blessed forever and ever.

Blessed, praised, glorified, exalted, extolled, mighty, upraised, and lauded be the Name of the Holy One, Blessed is He (Cong.– *Blessed is He*) — *beyond any blessing and song, praise and consolation that are uttered in the world. Now respond: Amen.* (Cong.– *Amen*.)

עֹז וּמֶמְשָׁלָה נֶצַח ... — *Power and dominion, triumph* ... Although these qualities are attributed to God, we find them in people as well. When man uses them to further God's goals, they are praiseworthy. But if people seek power and pursue triumph for their own selfish ends, they bring destruction upon the world *(R' Gedaliah Schorr).*

גָּדוֹל בַּתִּשְׁבָּחוֹת — *Exalted through praises.* The implication is not that God requires our praises in order to become exalted; for His infinite greatness is beyond our capacity to comprehend, much less express. Rather, it is His will that we have the privilege of exalting Him, despite our inability to do so adequately. This is the implication of *Who chooses musical songs,* i.e., we praise Him because He wishes us to.

הַבּוֹחֵר בְּשִׁירֵי זִמְרָה — *Who chooses musical songs of praise. Rabbi Bunam of P'shis'cha* interpreted homiletically that the word שִׁירֵי can be translated *remnants* (from שִׁירַיִם*, leftovers).* God wishes to see how much of the lofty sentiments of our prayers remain with us after we close our *siddur.* Thus, He *chooses what is left over* after the Songs of Praise have been uttered.

חֵי הָעוֹלָמִים — *Life-giver of the world.* This essential principle of Jewish belief reiterates that creation is an ongoing process — God created and continues to create. Because He gives life constantly, our thanks and praise are likewise constant *(R' Munk).*

In some congregations the *chazzan* chants a melody during his recitation of בָּרְכוּ, so that the congregation can then recite יִתְבָּרַךְ.

Chazzan bows at בָּרְכוּ and straightens up at 'ה.

בָּרְכוּ* אֶת יהוה הַמְּבֹרָךְ.

Congregation, followed by *chazzan*, responds, bowing at בָּרוּךְ and straightening up at 'ה.

בָּרוּךְ יהוה הַמְּבֹרָךְ לְעוֹלָם וָעֶד.

יִתְבָּרַךְ וְיִשְׁתַּבַּח וְיִתְפָּאַר וְיִתְרוֹמַם וְיִתְנַשֵּׂא שְׁמוֹ שֶׁל מֶלֶךְ מַלְכֵי הַמְּלָכִים, הַקָּדוֹשׁ בָּרוּךְ הוּא. שֶׁהוּא רִאשׁוֹן וְהוּא אַחֲרוֹן, וּמִבַּלְעָדָיו אֵין אֱלֹהִים.[1] סֹלּוּ, לָרֹכֵב בָּעֲרָבוֹת, בְּיָהּ שְׁמוֹ, וְעִלְזוּ לְפָנָיו.[2] וּשְׁמוֹ מְרוֹמַם עַל כָּל בְּרָכָה וּתְהִלָּה.[3] בָּרוּךְ שֵׁם כְּבוֹד מַלְכוּתוֹ לְעוֹלָם וָעֶד. יְהִי שֵׁם יהוה מְבֹרָךְ, מֵעַתָּה וְעַד עוֹלָם.[4]

ברכות קריאת שמע

It is preferable that one sit while reciting the following series of prayers — particularly the *Kedushah* verses, קָדוֹשׁ קָדוֹשׁ קָדוֹשׁ and בָּרוּךְ כְּבוֹד — until *Shemoneh Esrei.*

The following paragraph is recited aloud by the *chazzan*, then repeated by the congregation.

בָּרוּךְ אַתָּה יהוה אֱלֹהֵינוּ מֶלֶךְ הָעוֹלָם, יוֹצֵר אוֹר וּבוֹרֵא חֹשֶׁךְ,* עֹשֶׂה שָׁלוֹם וּבוֹרֵא אֶת הַכֹּל.[5]

Congregations that do not recite *Yotzros* continue on page 292.

Congregations that recite *Yotzros* continue:

אוֹר עוֹלָם בְּאוֹצַר חַיִּים, אוֹרוֹת מֵאֹפֶל אָמַר וַיֶּהִי.

❧ בִּרְכוֹת קְרִיאַת שְׁמַע / BLESSINGS OF THE SHEMA ❧

❧ בָּרְכוּ — *Bless.* Commentary to *Borchu* appears on page 42.

The third section of *Shacharis* is about to begin. Its central feature is the *Shema,* whose recitation is required by the Torah and which is the basic acknowledgment of God's sovereignty and Oneness. The *Shema* is accompanied by three blessings (two before it and one after it), which express God's mastery over nature, pray for intellectual and moral attainment through the study of Torah, and describe God's role in the flow of history *(R' Munk).*

❧ יוֹצֵר אוֹר וּבוֹרֵא חֹשֶׁךְ — *Who forms light and creates darkness.* Since the beginning of time, the term 'light' has symbolized new life, wisdom, happiness — all the things associated with goodness. 'Darkness,' however, is associated with suffering, failure and death. The philosophers of idolatry claimed that the 'good' god who creates light cannot be the 'bad' one who creates darkness. Therefore, they reasoned, there must be at least two gods. To the contrary, we believe unequivocally that God is One; what appears to our limited human intelligence to be contradictory or evil is really part of the plan of the One Merciful God, despite our failure to understand it.

The 'light' of this blessing refers not merely to the newly dawned day, but to the physical forces of creation itself. Light is the energy-giving, life-giving force of the universe, and, in the

❧ Interruptions During the Blessings of the Shema

As a general rule, no אָמֵן or other prayer response may be recited between בָּרְכוּ and *Shemoneh Esrei,* but there are exceptions. The main exception is 'between chapters' [בֵּין הַפְּרָקִים] of the *Shema* Blessings — i.e., after יוֹצֵר הַמְּאוֹרוֹת and הַבּוֹחֵר ... בְּאַהֲבָה, and between the three chapters of *Shema.* At those points, אָמֵן (but not בָּרוּךְ הוּא וּבָרוּךְ שְׁמוֹ) may be responded to any blessing. Some responses, however, are so important that they are permitted at any point in the *Shema* blessings. They are:

(a) In Kaddish, אָמֵן יְהֵא שְׁמֵהּ רַבָּא ... עָלְמַיָּא, and the אָמֵן after דַּאֲמִירָן בְּעָלְמָא; (b) the response to בָּרְכוּ (even of one called to the Torah); and (c) during the *chazzan's* repetition of *Shemoneh Esrei* — 1) in *Kedushah,* the verses קָדוֹשׁ קָדוֹשׁ קָדוֹשׁ ... כְּבוֹדוֹ and בָּרוּךְ כְּבוֹד ה' מִמְּקוֹמוֹ; 2) the אָמֵן after הָאֵל הַקָּדוֹשׁ; 3) the three words מוֹדִים אֲנַחְנוּ לָךְ.

During the recital of the two verses שְׁמַע and בָּרוּךְ שֵׁם, absolutely no interruptions are permitted.

In some congregations the *chazzan* chants a melody during his recitation of *Borchu*, so that the congregation can then recite *'Blessed, praised . . .'*

Chazzan bows at *'Bless,'* and straightens up at *'HASHEM.'*

Bless* HASHEM, the blessed One.

Congregation, followed by *chazzan*, responds, bowing at *'Blessed'* and straightening up at *'HASHEM.'*

Blessed is HASHEM, the blessed One, for all eternity.

Blessed, praised, glorified, exalted and upraised is the Name of the King Who rules over kings — the Holy One, Blessed is He. For He is the First and He is the Last and aside from Him there is no god.[1] *Extol Him — Who rides the highest heavens — with His Name, YAH, and exult before Him.*[2] *His Name is exalted beyond every blessing and praise.*[3] *Blessed is the Name of His glorious kingdom for all eternity. Blessed be the Name of HASHEM from this time and forever.*[4]

BLESSINGS OF THE SHEMA

It is preferable that one sit while reciting the following series of prayers — particularly the *Kedushah* verses, *'Holy, holy, holy . . .'* and *'Blessed is the glory . . .'* — until *Shemoneh Esrei.*

The following paragraph is recited aloud by the *chazzan*, then repeated by the congregation.

בָּרוּךְ *Blessed are You, HASHEM, our God, King of the universe, Who forms light and creates darkness,* makes peace and creates all.*[5]

Congregations that do not recite *Yotzros* continue on page 292.

Congregations that recite *Yotzros* continue:

The primeval light is in the treasury of eternal life;
'Let there be lights from the darkness,' He declared — and so it was!

(1) Cf. *Isaiah* 44:6. (2) *Psalms* 68:5. (3) Cf. *Nehemiah* 9:5.
(4) *Psalms* 113:2. (5) Cf. *Isaiah* 45:7.

words of the Psalmist (19:2): *The heavens declare the glory of God,* by functioning harmoniously and efficiently in accordance with His will (*R' Munk*).

Yotzros

Piyutim (liturgical poems) are inserted at various points in the synagogue service on the Festivals and on certain Sabbaths during the year. These prayers, which date back to ancient times (see page 43), are commonly known as *yotzer* or *yotzros*, but this is a misnomer. Depending upon the point at which it is recited, a *piyut* may be properly classified as an *ofan, me'orah, ahavah, zulas,* etc. Those *piyutim* recited at this point are correctly called *yotzros*, because they appear after the passage that begins יוֹצֵר *[yotzer], Who forms. Piyutim* inserted during the *chazzan's Amidah* repetition are collectively called קְרוּבוֹת, *kerovos* [from קרב, *to draw near*], an allusion to 'the *chazzan* who presents the prayers.' These *piyutim* are sometimes called קְרוֹבָץ, *krovetz*, the acronym of קוֹל רִנָּה וִישׁוּעָה בְּאָהֳלֵי צַדִּיקִים, *The sound of rejoicing and salvation in the tents of the righteous* (*Psalms* 118:15), a verse that aptly describes these compositions. Again, the location of the *piyut* determines its proper name: *reshus, magen, mechayeh, meshalesh,* etc. Nevertheless, in common practice, all of the morning *piyutim* are known as *yotzros*.

The *yotzros* of the first and second days of Pesach are based on שִׁיר הַשִּׁירִים, *Song of Songs.* Each stanza (or verse) of the *piyut* contains the opening phrase of its respective corresponding verse in *Song of Songs.* The major portion of the first day's *piyut* is attributed to R' Shlomo bar Yehudah HaBavli (d. 990), a contemporary of R' Sherira Gaon and his son R' Hai Gaon. One of Rashi's mentors, R' Yitzchak ben Yehudah, ranks R' Shlomo HaBavli — together with R' Elazar HaKalir (see p. 43) — among the קְדוֹשֵׁי עֶלְיוֹן, *exalted, holy ones.* His *piyutim* are cited by various *Rishonim*. Two stiches of the *yotzer* before us are quoted by *Rashi* (*Exodus* 26:15).

In the manner of most *paytanim*, R' Shlomo affixed his signature to his composition as an acrostic forming his name and a prayer for his spiritual well being. Thus his name appears at least five times in the first day's *yotzros*, as indicated by bold print and as noted in the commentary.

Two sections of the first day's *yotzros* bear a different signature, מָרְדְּכַי הַקָּטָן, *Mordechai the Lesser,* who is otherwise unidentified.

The second day's *yotzros* were composed by R' Meshullam (Lucca, Italy, c. 950 — Mainz, Germany, c. 1020) a disciple of R' Shlomo HaBavli, and the son of R' Klonimos of Lucca, also a well-know *paytan*. *Rashi* (*Zevachim* 45b) refers to R' Meshullam with the title *Gaon.* Many of his compositions appear in the Yom Kippur *machzor*.

FIRST DAY

אוֹר יֶשַׁע* מְאֻשָּׁרִים,
שִׁמּוּר זֶה מְכֻשָּׁרִים,
אֲהוֹדֶנּוּ בִּידִידָיו כְּשָׁרִים,
שִׁיר הַשִּׁירִים.[1]*
אַיֶּלֶת אִוּוּי תְּשׁוּקוֹת,*
לְחָלוּחַ עִיּוּף שׁוֹקְקוֹת,
אֲסָמֵי שֹׂבַע לְהַשְׁקוֹת,
יִשָּׁקֵנִי מִנְּשִׁיקוֹת.[2]
בְּרוּכֵי מֵעֲלָמוֹת מִשְׁמַנֶּיךָ,
מוֹשְׁלֵי גִּנְזָכֵי מִכְמַנֶּיךָ,
בְּשַׂמְתָּם תַּמְרוּק סַמְּמָנֶיךָ,
לְרֵיחַ שְׁמָנֶיךָ.[3]
בְּנֵי בֵיתְךָ וְחוֹרֶיךָ,
הִנָּם חָזַר סְחוֹרֶיךָ,
בֵּית מִדִּין צְחוֹרֶיךָ,
מָשְׁכֵנִי אַחֲרֶיךָ.[4]
גֵּאֶה וְרַב עֲנָוָה,
הוֹדִי מִבָּנוֹת נָוָה,
גַּם כִּי דָוָה,
שְׁחוֹרָה אֲנִי וְנָאוָה.[5]
גַּחַל בִּי מְחָרְחֶרֶת,
קָרַב רַגָּז סְחַרְחֹרֶת,
גַּחַן קְדוֹרַנִּית כַּהֶרֶת,
אַל תִּרְאֻנִי שֶׁאֲנִי שְׁחַרְחֹרֶת.[6]
דּוֹלִי וּכְמַר מִדְּלִי בְּדָלִי,[7]
טוֹטֶפֶת כְּלִילוֹ גְּדָלִי,*
דִּגְלִי עֹז מִגְדָּלִי, הִגִּידָה לִּי.[8]

SECOND DAY

אָפִיק* רֶנֶן וְשִׁירִים,
לְנוֹשְׂאֵי עַל נְשָׁרִים,[9]
אֲשׁוֹרֵר כְּעָזֵּי* שָׂרִים,
שִׁיר הַשִּׁירִים.[1]
אָיוֹם שְׂבַע שׁוֹקְקוֹת,
נָחֲנִי עֲסִיסוֹ לְהַשְׁקוֹת,
אִלְּפַנִי דָת בִּנְשִׁיקוֹת,
יִשָּׁקֵנִי מִנְּשִׁיקוֹת.[2]
בַּטְּחָה לְאוֹת מַאֲמִינֶיךָ,
הִמְטַרְתָּ לָמוֹ מַנֶּיךָ,
בְּחַרְתָּם הִשְׁתַּעְשֵׁעַ בְּאָמְנֶיךָ,
לְרֵיחַ שְׁמָנֶיךָ.[3]
בְּהָקְקָתָּ אוֹר שְׁחָרֶיךָ,
זָרוּעַ לְאוֹם מְשַׁחֲרֶיךָ,
בּוֹאִי בְּנִצּוּחַ לְשַׁחֲרֶיךָ,
מָשְׁכֵנִי אַחֲרֶיךָ.[4]
גֵּאֶה עֲדוּי גַּאֲוָה,
עֲבוּר בְּרָאשֵׁי הִתְאַוָּה,
גּוֹרָלִי הִשְׁפִּיר וְהִנְוָה,
שְׁחוֹרָה אֲנִי וְנָאוָה.[5]
גְּלֵף לְחוּת חָרֶת,
יְקָרָה מִדַּר וְסֹחֶרֶת,
גֵּאַנִי וְלֹא לְאַחֶרֶת,
אַל תִּרְאֻנִי שֶׁאֲנִי שְׁחַרְחֹרֶת.[6]
דֶּלֶג קֵץ* לְהַבְדִּילִי,
מִמְּשׁוּלֵי מַר מִדְּלִי,[7]
דִּגְּלַנִי וְשָׂח לְגַדְּלִי, הַגִּידָה לִּי.[8]

אוֹר יֶשַׁע — *Light of Salvation.* The first and third stiches of the respective stanzas form a quadruple *aleph-beis* acrostic, and the fourth stich is the opening phrase of a verse in *Song of Songs.* The initial letters of the second stiches form the sentence שְׁלֹמֹה הַקָּטָן בְּרַבִּי יְהוּדָה יִחְיֶה וְיִגְדַּל בְּתוֹרָה וּמַעֲשִׂים טוֹבִים אָמֵן, *Shlomo the Lesser, son of R' Yehudah, may he live and become great in Torah and good deeds, Amen.*

אֲהוֹדֶנּוּ בִּידִידָיו כְּשָׁרִים שִׁיר הַשִּׁירִים — *I shall thank Him, as did His beloved, when they sang the song that excels all songs.* Most of the lines in the *piyut* can be understood in more than one way. Using this verse as an example, we will cite three interpretations: (a) 'His beloved' refers to Israel (see *Jeremiah* 12:7); 'the song' is the Song at the Sea (*Exodus* 15:1-19) which excels other songs since it is the first song recorded in the Torah; (b) 'His beloved' is King Solomon [whom the prophet called יְדִידְיָה, Beloved of God (*II Samuel* 12:25)], composer of *Song of Songs;* 'the song' is *Song of Songs* upon which the *paytan* based this *piyut*; and (c) 'His beloved' is the Holy Temple (see *Psalms* 84:2), 'they' are the Levites who sang psalms while the offerings were being brought; 'the song' is the Song of the Day (see p. 448) 'that excels all song' because of the circumstances under which it was sung.

An exhaustive exposition of each line of this *piyut* would require volumes. Therefore, we will limit our comments to short explanations of the more difficult passages.

תְּשׁוּקוֹת — *Desire.* Israel's longing to learn the Torah is compared to a thirsty man's desire for water, to coveted hidden treasures, and to the enticement of perfumed spices and oils.

טוֹטֶפֶת כְּלִילוֹ גְּדָלִי — *He Whose tefillin-crown*

FIRST DAY	SECOND DAY
א *Light of Salvation* for the praiseworthy,*	א *I shall bring forth* joyous songs, for Him who bore me on eagles' wings.*[9]
ש *those prepared for this [night of] watching,*	א *I shall sing — as they sang the Song at the Sea —* the Song of Songs.*[1]
א *I shall thank Him, as did His beloved, when they sang the song that excels all songs.**[1]	א *The Awesome One Who satiates those who thirst, led me to drink the wine [of His Torah].*
א *[Israel, the] morningstar, longing with desire,**	א *He taught me the law that is more [sweet] than kisses, O may He again kiss me with those kisses.*[2]
ל *[provide] moisture for the weary who thirst;*	ב *You observed the weariness of Your faithful,*
א *fill my cisterns to provide drink, O, may He kiss me with the kisses of old.*[2]	*You rained upon them Your manna,*
ב *Most blessed of the maiden [nations] with Your richness,*	ב *You chose them to delight in Your nurturing Torah,*
מ *controllers of Your hidden treasures,*	*[to endear them] with the scent of Your oils.*[3]
ב *when You placed the perfume of Your spices upon them, [to endow them] with the scent of Your oils.*[3]	ב *You made Your morningstar's light shine,*
ב *Members of Your household, Your princes,*	*planted for the nation that seeks You.*
ה *behold, may they return to Your environs,*	ב *She comes with paeans of supplication, [saying], 'O draw me after You!'*[4]
ב *to the Temple of Your whitened law, [as they pray,] 'O draw me after You!'*[4]	ג *O Exalted One, bedecked in grandeur, May You desire to pass before me and lead me.*
ג *O, You Who are grand yet filled with humility,*	ג *Beautify and adorn my fate,*
ה *find me more beautiful than the attractive daughters.*	*for [although] I am black, I am [potentially] comely.*[5]
ג *Although I am sickly [with exile], [although] I am black, I am [potentially] comely.*[5]	ג *He carved and engraved on His Tablets, [the Torah,] more valuable than coral and gemstones.*
ג *The [wicked] coals have charred me,*	ג *He exalted me and no other,*
ק *raging battle all around,*	*not viewing me as if I were swarthy.*[6]
ג *I am forced to crawl, black as dye, but do not view me as naturally swarthy.*[6]	ד *He hastened the end one hundred ninety years* to separate me,*
ד *O, He Who draws me up, set me aside as a drop from the bucket,*[7]	*from those compared to a drop from a bucket.*[7]
ט *He Whose tefillin-crown exalts me,**	ד *He raised me high as a banner, declaring He would exalt me,*
ד *my Banner, Tower of my strength, Tell me [when redemption will come].*[8]	*[and He commanded,] 'Tell [others] about Me.'*[8]

(1) *Song of Songs* 1:1. (2) 1:2. (3) 1:3. (4) 1:4. (5) 1:5. (6) 1:6. (7) Cf. *Isaiah* 40:15. (8) 1:7. (9) Cf. *Exodus* 19:14.

exalts me. The Talmud teaches that just as Israel wears *tefillin*, so does God wear *tefillin*. Israel's *tefillin* exalt God and declare His Oneness with the verse, *Hear, O Israel; Hashem is our God, Hashem is One and Only* (*Deuteronomy* 6:4), so God's *tefillin* exalt Israel and declare its uniqueness with the verse, *And who is like Your people Israel, one nation on the earth* (*II Samuel* 7:23).

☙ **אָפִיק** — *I shall bring forth.* Modeled after the first day's *yotzer*, אוֹר יֶשַׁע, *Light of Salvation*, this *piyut* begins with a quadruple *aleph-beis* scheme. Each fourth stich consists of the opening words of its corresponding verse in *Song of Songs*. The remaining verses contain the acrostic מְשֻׁלָּם בִּירַבִּי קְלוֹנִימוּס חֲזַק, *Meshullam son of R' Klonimos, may he be strong.*

כְּעֻזִּי — *As ... the Song at the Sea.* After its introductory verse (which begins אָז יָשִׁיר), the Song at the Sea [*Exodus* 15:1-19] continues עָזִּי וְזִמְרָת, *my might and praise.*

דִּלַּג קֵץ — *He hastened the end one hundred ninety years.* There is a play on words here. The

FIRST DAY

דָּרְבוֹנִי מְלַמֵּד מַרְדָּעִי,
נָתוּן רוֹעֶה דַּרְדַּעִי,
דָּן וְהוֹכִיחַ פִּדְעִי, אִם לֹא תֵדְעִי.[1]
הִדְרִיךְ סוּס לִמְנוּסָתִי,
בַּיָּם בָּקַע לִבְסִיסָתִי,
הֶמִירוֹ וּמָלֵא בְּפִיסָתִי,
לְסֻסָתִי.[2]*
הִתְרַנִּי מִלֵּי חַיָּיךְ,
רְטִיַּת נוּמֵי מְחָיֶיךָ,
הַזֶּה וְהַבָּא לִתְחִיָּיךְ,
נָאווּ לְחָיַיִךְ.[3]
וְחַנְּנִי חֵן מֻצְהָב,
בְּנִצּוּל צוּל רַהַב,
וְכַבִּיר הִצְבִּיר יַהַב, תּוֹרֵי זָהָב.[4]
וְלִבִּי גַּס בּוֹ,
יִדַּע סִיג סִבּוֹ,
וְסָר בְּאוֹכֵל עֶשְׂבּוֹ,*
עַד שֶׁהַמֶּלֶךְ בִּמְסִבּוֹ.[5]
זְמַן זְמַן מִזְמוֹר,
יְחוּר עָרִיצִים לִזְמוֹר,
זִבְּלַנִי בַּצַּר לִכְמוֹר, צְרוֹר הַמּוֹר.[6]
זִלְזוּל כְּרוּם כֹּפֶר,
הִזּוּל כַּרְכּוּם חֵפֶר,
זִיף חוֹב מִסֵּפֶר, אֶשְׁכֹּל הַכֹּפֶר.[7]
חָשַׁק חִבַּת רְעוּתִי,
וְחָפֵץ חֶלְבֵּי רַעֲוָתִי,

SECOND DAY

דְּרוֹר קָרָא לְפָדְעִי,
כְּאָב מְיַסְּרִי וּמְיַדְּעִי,
דָּרְבָן כַּבָּקָר רִדְּעִי, אִם לֹא תֵדְעִי.[1]
הֵנִיס יָם וּקְרָעוֹ,
וְצָר בְּסַאסְּאָה פְרָעוֹ,
הִקְדִּים פָּנָיו וְהִכְרִיעוֹ,
לְסֻסָתִי* בְּרִכְבֵי פַרְעֹה.[2]
הֱבִינַנִי סוֹדֵי סְתָרִים,
עִנְּדַנִי שִׁלּוּשׁ כְּתָרִים,*
הִשְׁמִיעַ לִמְנַחֲחַת תּוֹרִים,
נָאווּ לְחָיַיִךְ בַּתּוֹרִים.[3]
וְתֵר דֵּי זָהָב,
אוֹיְבַי זִקֵּר טָהַב,
וְהֶעֱנִיק לְזֶרַע אָהַב, תּוֹרֵי זָהָב.[4]
וְזָכַר בְּרִית סָבוֹ,[8]
וּמִפְּלֶשֶׁת עַם הֱסִבּוֹ,[9]
וְנֹכַח סִין סִבְּבוֹ,
עַד שֶׁהַמֶּלֶךְ בִּמְסִבּוֹ.[5]
זְכוּת עָקוּד מוֹר,
אָץ רַחֲמִים לִכְמוֹר,
זִלְעֵף בְּשַׂר חֲמוֹר,[10] צְרוֹר הַמֹּר.[6]
זִכְרוֹן מִשְׁלֵי אֵפֶר,*
חַק בְּגִינָם בַּסֵּפֶר,
זָרִים תֵּת כֹּפֶר, אֶשְׁכּוֹל הַכֹּפֶר.[7]
חָבַשׁ מַחַץ טְרִיָּתִי,[11]
כִּסָּה עֵרוֹם עֶרְיָתִי,[12]

(1) *Song of Songs* 1:8. (2) 1:9. (3) 1:10. (4) 1:11. (5) 1:12. (6) 1:13. (7) 1:14. (8) See *Genesis* 21:22-32. (9) See *Exodus* 13:17. (10) See *Ezekiel* 23:20. (11) Cf. *Isaiah* 1:6. (12) Cf. *Ezekiel* 16:7-8.

numerical value of the word קֵץ, *end*, is one hundred ninety [ק=100 צ=90]. Although God had told Abraham, '*Your offspring will be aliens in a land not their own ... four hundred years*' (*Genesis* 15:13), He, nevertheless, ended this period one hundred and ninety years earlier.

לְסֻסָתִי — *My mare [in Pharaoh's chariot]*. Pharaoh prided himself as the greatest breeder of horses. His cavalry boasted the finest horses in the world. Certainly, his personal battle horse was the cream of them all. As Pharaoh rode his stallion in the vanguard of his armies, God (so to speak) appeared riding an even finer stallion. Not to be outdone Pharaoh changed horses for a beautiful mare. God did the same. And as God's mare raced before them, all the Egyptian stallions stampeded after it into the sea (*Shir Hashirim Rabbah* 1:9, as interpreted by *Ma'aseh Oreig*).

בְּאוֹכֵל עֶשְׂבּוֹ — *To one that eats grass*. The Golden Calf is described as 'a grass-eating ox' (*Psalms* 106:20).

שִׁלּוּשׁ כְּתָרִים — *A triad of crowns*. He made me understand the tri-partite Scriptures: תּוֹרָה, *Pentateuch*; נְבִיאִים, *Prophets*; and כְּתוּבִים, *Hagiographa*. Alternatively: the three parts are מִקְרָא, *Scriptures*, מִשְׁנָה, *Mishnah*, and גְּמָרָא, *Gemara*.

According to some commentaries, this refers to the three crowns enumerated in *Avos* (4:17) — the crowns of תּוֹרָה, *Torah scholarship*, כְּהֻנָּה, *Priesthood*, and מַלְכוּת, *Kingship*. [This interpretation is difficult, however. Firstly, the word שִׁלּוּשׁ, which means *a set of three* or *a linked chain*, indicates a

FIRST DAY

ד *[Moses,] my prod,*
who taught me to pull the yoke,
נ *who was appointed shepherd*
to the 'generation of knowledge,'
ד *may he admonish and rebuke my iniquities,*
[saying,] 'If you do not know . . .'[1]
ה *He [God] rode a stallion to allow my escape,*
ב *in the sea which He split and paved for me,*
ה *then changed [mounts],*
as the verse at hand,
'My mare [in Pharaoh's chariot] . . .'*[2]
ה *He has warned me,*
'My words are your life,
ר *swathe and bandage for your wounds,*
ה *to enliven you in this world and the next, [if] your cheeks will be beautiful [by uttering My words].'*[3]
ו *He favored me with golden grace,*
ב *when He rescued [me] from the snares of the arrogant [Egyptians].*
ו *And the Mighty One assembled booty,*
circlets of gold . . .[4]
ו *My heart gloated over it.*
י *Then the impure*
made their cause known,
ו *and turned to one that eats His grass,**
while the king was yet at His table [Sinai].[5]
ז *He [God] set a time of cutting [them] down,*
י *to trim the branches of the wicked.*
ז *In my troubles,*
He ordained a Sanctuary, to pity me,
[and to cleanse me as] with a bundle of myrrh.[6]
ז *When baseness was exalted*
with heresy [of the Calf],
ה *He poured crimson shame upon us;*
ז *Yet He erased [our] guilt*
from [His] ledger,
He, to Whom all belongs, forgave us.[7]
ח *He yearned for my loving companionship,*
ו *and desired the choicest of my offerings.*

SECOND DAY

ד *He announced freedom*
from my wounds,
like a Father Who admonishes
and teaches me.
ד *With a prod as for cattle at the yoke,*
[saying,] 'Since you do not know . . .'[1]
ה *He made the Sea flee and He split it,*
and repaid the oppressor
measure for measure.
ה *He [God] advanced before him*
and drowned his cavalry,
My mare in Pharaoh's chariot.[2]*
ה *He made me understand [the Torah's]*
hidden secrets, and adorned me
*with a triad of crowns.**
ה *He let the bringers of dove-offerings hear,*
'You cheeks will be beautiful
with words of Torah.'[3]
ו *He vouchsafed me*
abundant gold [booty],
when He threw my enemies
to the floor of the sea.
ו *And He bestowed upon the*
beloved [Abraham's] offspring,
circlets of gold . . .[4]
ו *He recalled the treaty of His elder*
[Abraham with Abimelech],[8]
and caused the people to detour
around Philistia.[9]
ו *He stood them in a circle around Sinai,*
until the King arrived at His table.[5]
ז *In the merit of Isaac, bound at Moriah,*
he hastened to kindle His pity.
ז *He made the donkey-fleshed*
[Egyptians] tremble,[10]
[He Who is compared to]
a bundle of myrrh.[6]
ז *The remembrance of*
*those compared to ashes,**
for their sake
He inscribed in Scriptures,
ז *'The strangers shall give*
redemption money,
[for Israel], the cluster of henna.'[7]
ח *He healed the fresh wounds*
of my oppression.[11]
He covered my naked shame.[12]

close relationship between the crowns. But the crowns of Torah, *Kehunah* and Kingship are independent of each other. Secondly, since the previous stich speaks of the Torah's hidden secrets, this stich assumedly also refers to the Torah.]

מְשֻׁלֵי אֵפֶר — *Those compared to ashes.* An allusion to the Patriarchs: Abraham said, *'I am but dust and ashes'* (*Genesis* 18:27); Isaac is considered as if he had been burnt to ashes on the altar (see *Genesis* 22); and about Jacob it is written, *'Who can count Jacob's dust?'* (*Numbers* 23:10).

FIRST DAY

חִוָּה לְחֻפַּת יְרִיעָתִי,
הִנָּךְ יָפָה רַעְיָתִי,[1]
חָשׁ חַפְשִׁי מִדּוֹדִי,
דָּץ בְּרִוּוּי דּוֹדִי,
חִנַּנְתִּיו חֲתָנִי יְדִידִי, הִנְּךָ יָפֶה דוֹדִי.[2]
טִלְטֵל פַּנִיקְטֵי נִתְרָזִים,
הָרִים עוֹקֵר וּתְרָזִים,
טָם מַטַּע מְזֹרָזִים,
קוֹרוֹת בָּתֵּינוּ אֲרָזִים.[3]
טִירַת בֵּיתוֹ נֶאֱצֶלֶת,
יִתְּנֵנִי רוֹן מְצַהֶלֶת,
טַכְסִיס חֲתֻנָּה מְצַלְצֶלֶת,
אֲנִי חֲבַצֶּלֶת.[4]
יַעֲלוּ רוֹם מְתוּחִים,
חֲרוּשִׁים דּוּשִׁים תְּחוּחִים,
יָאִים עֲרֵבֵי נִיחוֹחִים,
כְּשׁוֹשַׁנָּה בֵּין הַחוֹחִים.[5]
יָצִיץ וְלֹא לְמִצְעָר,
יֶתֶר שְׁאָר מִזְעָר,
יִפְרַח לִוּוּי מַעַר,
כְּתַפּוּחַ בַּעֲצֵי הַיַּעַר.[6]
כִּתְּרַנִי מֵהַכְשֵׁר זַיִן,
הִרְבַּנִי מְלֹא עַיִן,
כְּתָב רְאָיָה וּמִנְיַן,*
הֱבִיאַנִי אֶל בֵּית הַיָּיִן.[7]
כִּלְכֵּל עֶדְנִי מִתְּשִׁישׁוּת,
יִסְּרַנִי קָשׁוֹת מְקֻשָּׁשׁוֹת,
כִּוַּנְתִּי חוֹלַת חֲשָׁשׁוֹת,
סַמְּכוּנִי בָּאֲשִׁישׁוֹת.[8]
לֹא דֶרֶךְ כְּהִפְלִישִׁי,
גַּם צִיָּה כְּהִפְרִישִׁי,
לְמָסָךְ וּפִנּוּי טְרָשִׁי,
שְׂמֹאלוֹ תַּחַת לְרֹאשִׁי.[9]
לֵב אֶחָד וּשְׁכֶם,

SECOND DAY

חִבְּבַנִי כְּשָׁע גַּעְיָתִי,
הִנָּךְ יָפָה רַעְיָתִי.[1]
חִבֵּל עֹל רוֹדִי,
נָגַף שׁוֹלְלֵי רְדִידִי,
חִדַּשְׁתִּי שִׁיר לִידִידִי, הִנְּךָ יָפֶה דוֹדִי.[2]
טָהוֹר פֵּעֲנַח רָזִים,
חֲכָמַי מִדּוֹת מַפְרִיזִים,
טַעֲמֵי תוֹרוֹת חוֹרְזִים,
קֹרוֹת בָּתֵּינוּ אֲרָזִים.[3]
טוֹב עֵרָה מְנֻצֶּלֶת,
עֶגְלָה[10] גֵּוִי מְפַצֶּלֶת,
טְלָאָיו סָךְ כִּבְחוֹצֶלֶת,
אֲנִי חֲבַצֶּלֶת.[4]
יִשְּׁרַנִי מֵעִקּוּשׁ זְחִיחִים,
חֲשָׂכַנִי מִבּוּל שׁוֹחֲחִים,
יִקְּרַנִי בְּגֵיא צְחִיחִים,
כְּשׁוֹשַׁנָּה בֵּין הַחוֹחִים.[5]
יוֹשְׁבֵי נוֹף כְּגָעַר,
חַיַּת קָנֶה* יִגְעַר,[11]
יְחַלְּצֵנִי מִמְּכַרְסֵם מִיַּעַר,[12]
כְּתַפּוּחַ בַּעֲצֵי הַיַּעַר.[6]
כְּגִבּוֹר מִתְרוֹנֵן מִיַּיִן,[13]
יָקַץ וְהֵרִיק זַיִן,
כֹּהֲנַי לְנַסֵּךְ יַיִן,
הֱבִיאַנִי אֶל בֵּית הַיָּיִן.[7]
כַּפּוֹת מְשִׁיחֲכֶם בּוֹשְׁשׁוֹת,
חֵרְפוּנִי טוּחֵי עֲשָׁשׁוֹת,
כְּלַפִּיד אֵשׁ בַּחֲשָׁשׁוֹת,
סַמְּכוּנִי בָּאֲשִׁישׁוֹת.[8]
לִי יִשְׁקֹד לְדָרְשִׁי,
מִכַּף מְשַׁדְּדִי וְחֹרְשִׁי,
לְהַרְבִּיצֵנִי בִּנְוֵה מִדְרָשִׁי,
שְׂמֹאלוֹ תַּחַת לְרֹאשִׁי.[9]
לִסְבֹּל עֹל גָּלוּתְכֶם,

(1) *Song of Songs* 1:15. (2) 1:16. (3) 1:17. (4) 2:1 (5) 2:2. (6) 2:3. (7) 2:4. (8) 2:5 (9) 2:6.
(10) See *Jeremiah* 46:20. (11) Cf. *Psalms* 68:31. (12) Cf. 80:14. (13) 78:65.

כְּתָב רְאָיָה וּמִנְיַן — *With written proof and census.* When Moses took a census of the Jews in the wilderness, each person had to bring a written record of his lineage in order to be counted as a member of one of the tribes (*Rashi* to *Numbers* 1:18; *Yalkut Shimoni* I, 284).

חַיַּת קָנֶה — *The beast of the reeds.* This transla-

FIRST DAY

ח *He said of my curtains' canopy, 'Behold, you[r works] are beautiful, My companion.'[1]*
ח *Hasten, free me from my menial cauldron,*
ד *and rejoice, satiating me with joy, my Beloved.*
ח *I will return His favor, my Groom, my Beloved. 'Behold, You are beautiful, my Companion.'[2]*
ט *[His voice at Sinai] traveled to palaces, frightening [their inhabitants],*
ה *uprooting mountains and trees.*
ט *It flew to the [Sanctuary, the] planting of the alacritous [Israel], the cedar beams of our Temple.[3]*
ט *His palatial Temple was set apart,*
י *He placed me within it with glad song and rejoicing.*
ט *Arrayed as at a wedding, resonant with music, I was [before Him as] a rose.[4]*
י *May they be elevated to the heavens,*
ח *those who are plowed under, downtrodden and crumbled.*
י *May the sweetness of their offerings be satisfying, like a rose among the thorns.[5]*
י *May they sprout and never decrease,*
י *their remnant that remains is so small.*
י *May the [Temple of] camaraderie and fellowship blossom, like the apple among the forest's trees.[6]*
כ *He has crowned me with a jeweled crown;*
ה *He has sated me with my eyes' desire,*
כ *with written proof and census,* He brought me into the [Tabernacle's] wine chamber.[7]*
כ *He fed me luscious fruits that I not become weak,*
י *He admonished me with and adorned me strict moral laws.*
כ *I concentrated until my head ached with sickness, He sustained me, among the flaming fires.[8]*
ל *He opened a never-trodden path for me,*
ג *and set me apart in a barren waste.*
ל *[He sent clouds] to shield and to clear the rocky path, His left hand protecting my head.[9]*
ל *With one heart and shoulder [to bear the Torah's yoke],*

SECOND DAY

ח *He cherished me when He heard my cry, [and said,] 'Behold, you are beautiful, My companion.'[1]*
ח *He destroyed my oppressor's yoke. He plagued those who looted my wealth.*
ח *I composed a new song to my Beloved, 'Behold, You are beautiful, my Companion.'[2]*
ט *The Pure One revealed the [Torah's] secrets, to the Sages who increase the measure [of their knowledge],*
ט *And to those who compose explanations of the Torah [verses], they are the cedar beams of our house [of study].[3]*
ט *The Good One poured out and emptied, the [Egyptian] calf[10] that tore at my flesh.*
ט *His lambs He protected with cloud-mats, [for they stood loyal to Him] like a rose.[4]*
י *He led me on the straight path, away from the crookedness of the haughty. He kept me from those who bow to idols.*
י *He honored me in the arid valley, like a rose among the thorns.[5]*
י *As He destroyed the inhabitants of Nof [Egypt], so may He destroy the beast of the reeds.*[11]*
י *May He extricate me from [Edom,] the ravaging boar of the forest,[12] [that I might praise Him,] 'Like the apple among the forest's trees.'[6]*
כ *Like a warrior rousing from wine-induced sleep,[13] He awoke and armed Himself with weaponry.*
כ *That my Kohanim may pour wine libations, He brought me to the wine chamber.[7]*
כ *By [saying], 'The footsteps of your Messiah are late!' those of black thoughts shame me.*
כ *[Their words scorch me] like the fire's flame consuming the straw heaps; O, sustain me among the flaming fires.[8]*
ל *Ah me! May He hasten to seek me, from those who plow me under as a field.*
ל *To give me rest in my sought-after city, with His left hand protecting my head.[9]*
ל *[But He replies,] 'Endure the yoke of your Exile;*

FIRST DAY

דָּאִים כָּעָב לְמָשְׁכָם,
לַאֲסִירִים יַחְפֹּץ בְּסֶכֶם,
הִשְׁבַּעְתִּי אֶתְכֶם.[1]
מִבּוֹר תַּחְתִּיּוֹת רְדוּדִי,
לַחַץ עַקְרַבֵּי גְדוּדִי,
מִהֵר וְקִדֵּר מְדַדִּי, קוֹל דּוֹדִי.[2]
מִבֵּית חֹמֶר קִצְבִי,
בֵּית חַיִּים נְצִיבִי,
מְצַפִּי מְצִיפִי מַצָּבִי,
דּוֹמֶה דוֹדִי לִצְבִי.[3]
נַחֲלָה שָׁפְרָה לִי,[4]
תִּקְוַת שְׁלוֹשׁ* גּוֹרָלִי,
נְעִימוֹת בְּמַר לִי,
עָנָה דוֹדִי וְאָמַר לִי.[5]
נָם תִּתִּי סְבַר,
וְרַק אֵין דָּבָר,[6]
נוֹסוּ נוֹדוּ כְּבָר,
כִּי הִנֵּה הַסְּתָו עָבָר.[7]
סַרְסוּר זֵרוּז מֶרֶץ,
רֹאשׁ פֵּרוּז הֶרֶץ,
סְלוֹל שָׁלוֹם וָתֶרֶץ,
הַנִּצָּנִים נִרְאוּ בָאָרֶץ.[8]
סִפֵּק עַתִּיק מְפִיגֶיהָ,*
הָפֵק מַמְתִּיק פַּגֶּיהָ,
סַלֵּת סֹלֶת סְפוּגֶיהָ,
הַתְּאֵנָה חָנְטָה פַגֶּיהָ.[9]
עֲקַלָּתוֹן נוֹשֵׁף קֶלַע,
וּפִיתוֹם מְכַשֵּׁף נִצְלַע,
עָרֵב שִׁלְשׁוּל בְּהַקְלַע,
יוֹנָתִי בְּחַגְוֵי הַסֶּלַע.*[10]

SECOND DAY

בְּלִי לִדְחֹק גְּאֻלַּתְכֶם,
לְהָחִישׁ יֶשַׁע בְּעִתְּכֶם,[11]
הִשְׁבַּעְתִּי אֶתְכֶם.[1]
מֵרִים רֹאשִׁי וּכְבוֹדִי,[12]
לֶקַח טוֹב הִזְבִּידִי,
מַלְאָכָיו צָו לְדַדִּי, קוֹל דּוֹדִי.[2]
מִגֵּר בְּאַף מַעֲצִיבִי,
נִחֲלַנִי חֶמְדַּת צְבִי,
מְדַמֶּה לְעֹפֶר נְצִיבִי,
דּוֹמֶה דוֹדִי לִצְבִי.[3]
נִעֵר מֵצֵר לִי,
עָנֵנִי בַּצָּר לִי,
נִינַי חֲסוּ בְצִלִּי,
עָנָה דוֹדִי וְאָמַר לִי.[5]
נְגִידִים לִי דִבֵּר,
שִׁבְעָה קוֹלוֹת* כִּמְדַבֵּר,
נִטְפֵי מוֹר הֶעֱבַר,
כִּי הִנֵּה הַסְּתָו עָבָר.[7]
סָכַת שַׁוְעִי וַיִּרֶץ,
שָׁלַח גּוֹדְרֵי פֶרֶץ,
סְוֵנִים חִבֵּל בְּמֶרֶץ,
הַנִּצָּנִים נִרְאוּ בָאָרֶץ.[8]
סוּגָה עִוְעֵו מוֹגֶיהָ,
מוֹף כַּדּוֹנַג לְמוֹגְגֶיהָ,
סְעָרָה מֵאֲנָחָה לַהֲפִיגֶהָ,
הַתְּאֵנָה חָנְטָה פַגֶּיהָ.[9]
עַזִּים שָׁת כַּסֶּלַע,
רָאשֵׁי תַנִּינִים[13] לְקַלַּע,
עָלוֹת פְּדוּיָה לְצֶלַע,
יוֹנָתִי בְּחַגְוֵי הַסֶּלַע.[10]

(1) *Song of Songs* 2:7. (2) 2:8. (3) 2:9. (4) Cf. *Psalms* 16:6. (5) *Song of Songs* 2:10. (6) Cf. *Deuteronomy* 32:47. (7) *Song of Songs* 2:11. (8) 2:12. (9) 2:13. (10) 2:14. (11) Cf. *Isaiah* 60:22. (12) Cf. *Psalms* 3:4. (13) See *Ezekiel* 29:3.

tion follows *Rashi* (*Psalms* 68:31). *Ibn Ezra* and *Meiri* translate *the army of sword-bearers.* According to some editions of *Rashi*, it alludes to Amalek; according to other editions, Ishmael.

תִּקְוַת שְׁלוֹשׁ — *The hope of the three.* The Land of Israel is called 'the hope of the three' because it was the desired and promised heritage, of the Patriarchs — Abraham, Isaac, and Jacob (*Matteh Levi*). Alternatively, Moses, Aaron and Miriam all longed to enter the Land, but their hopes were not fulfilled (*Ma'aseh Oreig*).

סִפֵּק עַתִּיק מְפִיגֶיהָ — *He supplied aged [wine] to relax her.* עַתִּיק refers to חֲמַת עַתִּיק, *aged wine,* which brings relaxation. Another interpretation views עַתִּיק as an appellation of God Who is called עַתִּיק יוֹמִין, *the Ancient of Days* (*Daniel* 7:9). thus the stich reads, *The Ancient One supplied her relaxant [wine].*

FIRST DAY	SECOND DAY
ד *they flew like a cloud to where they were drawn.* ל *Those who had been captives, He desired approvingly, [and said,] 'I adjure you [to remain loyal to Me].'*[1] מ *[I called] from the nethermost pit of my persecution,* ל *the oppressive scorpions at my sides,* מ *He hastened, He Who measured and shortened [my exile], [and I heard] the voice of my Beloved.*[2] מ *From the house of accounted mortar [Egypt],* ב *He stood me in the house of life [the Land of Israel].* מ *My longed-for One saw my position, like a deer, my Beloved [raced to save me].*[3] נ *A heritage befitting me,*[4] ת *the hope of the three* was my lot.* נ *Sweet words, when things were bitter for me, my Beloved called out to me and said.*[5] נ *He said, 'I have given [you the Torah of] hope,* ו *[in it] there is no empty word.'*[6] נ *[The exile period] has already expired and moved on, behold, the winter has passed.*[7] ס *The intermediary [Moses] was strengthened with alacrity,* ר *to smash the head of the land,* ס *to provide smooth, straight paths of peace, the blossoms [Moses and Aaron] are seen in the land.*[8] ס *He supplied aged [wine] to relax her,** ה *the sweet trees brought forth her fruits,* ס *the wheat gave fine flour for her loaves, the fig tree put forth its fruits.*[9] ע *The twisting puffing adder [Pharaoh] went down as if shot from a sling,* ו *and the sorcerers of Pisom were crippled.* ע *[At the Sea, Israel was] entwined with the braided chain, like a dove in the clefts of the rock.**[10]	*do not force your redemption,* ל *by rushing your time for salvation;*[11] *thus do I adjure you.'*[1] מ *He Who raised my head and my soul,*[12] *Who presented me with a goodly portion [the Torah].* מ *He commanded His angels to support me, [when I heeded] the voice of my Beloved.*[2] מ *He threw down my oppressors [Egypt] with anger. He granted me a heritage in the desirous Land.* מ *My Commander was [swift] like a gazelle [to redeem me], my Beloved was like a deer.*[3] נ *He spilled [into the sea] those who opposed me, He answered me, when I was in dire straits.* נ *'My offspring, take shelter in My protective shade,' my Beloved called out to me and said.*[5] נ *He spoke to me lofty words [of the Torah], seven voices,* as it is stated.* נ *He made [the Torah's sweet secrets] pass before me like drops of myrrh, for, behold, the winter [of our servitude] has passed.*[7] ס *He hearkened to my cries and found favor, and sent menders of the breach;* ס *they destroyed Aswan [Egypt] with dispatch, they are the blossoms [Moses and Aaron] seen in the land.*[8] ס *They tried to drive [Israel] the [nation] encircled [with roses] mad; Moph tried to melt them like wax;* ס *so to relieve the storm-tossed from groaning, [He made] the fig tree [Yocheved] issue its fruits [Moses and Aaron].*[9] ע *He turned the rushing waters to rock, to enchain the great sea-serpent [Pharaoh].*[13] ע *To raise the redeemed to the sea bank, my dove, [protected] in the cleft of the rock.*[10]

יוֹנָתִי בְּחַגְוֵי הַסֶּלַע — *Like a dove in the clefts of the rock.* This refers to the Jews being trapped between the pursuing Egyptian army and the Sea. Their situation resembled that of a dove being chased by a hawk. It flew into the cleft of a boulder, and found a serpent lurking there. It could not take shelter there, because of the snake, nor could it leave, because of the hawk (*Rashi* to *Song of Songs* 2:14).

שִׁבְעָה קוֹלוֹת — *Seven voices.* The phrase קוֹל ה׳, *the voice of* HASHEM, appears seven times in Psalm 29. According to the Midrash (*Yalkut*

FIRST DAY

עֲרוֹדִים* עִם עִלִּים,
מָרוּ זָדוּ שְׁעוּלִים,
עִנְיָן לֹא מַעֲלִים,
אֶחֱזוּ לָנוּ שֻׁעָלִים.[1]
פְּתִיגִיל וְעָגִיל בְּדָלִי,
עִנּוּק פִּנּוּק קְדָלִי,
פָּנִים בְּפָנִים הִשְׁדִּילִי, דּוֹדִי לִי.[2]
פֹּעַל בָּם תָּפוּחַ,
שָׂכָר לֹא קָפוּחַ,
פְּקֹד דַּר טָפוּחַ,
עַד שֶׁיָּפוּחַ.[3]
צִמְצֵם שִׁכְנוֹ מֶרְכָּבִי,
יוֹם חִנּוּךְ כַּרְכּוּבִי,
צִפִּיתִי פֹּה עִכּוּבִי, עַל מִשְׁכָּבִי.[4]
צְבִי קֹדֶשׁ מִנָּה,
מְקוֹם מִבְחַר מָנָה,
צִיּוֹן קִרְיָה נֶאֱמָנָה,[5] אָקוּמָה נָּא.[6]
קָרַצְתִּי דַּצְתִּי בְּאוֹמְרִים,
טַפְתִּי נַפְתִּי בְּמוֹרִים,
קִלְקַלְתִּי שְׁמָנִים שְׁמָרִים,
מְצָאוּנִי הַשֹּׁמְרִים.[7]
קִנְיָן כִּי שָׁבַרְתִּי,
וְטוֹב לֹא סִבַּרְתִּי,
קָדְשׁוֹ לוּלֵא חִבַּרְתִּי,
כִּמְעַט שֶׁעָבַרְתִּי.[8]
רָשַׁם אִסָּר בְּצִבְאוֹתֵיכֶם,
בְּזַעֲזוּעַ חִיל אֱיָלוּתְכֶם,
רִחוּק דִּחוּק אֶתְכֶם,
הִשְׁבַּעְתִּי אֶתְכֶם.[9]
רֵישׁ גְּלִי כְּהֶעֱלָה,
יוֹנָה תַּמָּה עִלָּה,

SECOND DAY

עִזּוּז הִדְרִיךְ בַּנְּעָלִים,
יְפִי פַעֲמֵי נְעָלִים.[10]
עָרַף קָמַי בַּשְּׁעָלִים,
אֶחֱזוּ לָנוּ שֻׁעָלִים.[1]
פָּץ לִי מַחֲשִׁילִי,
מַה דּוֹדֵךְ מִשֶּׁלִּי,[11]
פּוֹצִי מֵרֶפֶשׁ וּמִדְּלִי, דּוֹדִי לִי.[2]
פִּלַּלְתִּי לְנוֹרָא וְאָיוֹם,
רְאוֹת כָּמוּס יוֹם,
פְּקַח קוֹחַ אֲסִירֶיךָ[12] לְפִדְיוֹם,
עַד שֶׁיָּפוּחַ הַיּוֹם.[3]
צָעַקְתִּי לַצּוּר מִכְּאֵבִי,
מָתַי חִתּוּל מַכְאוּבִי,
צְפוֹת בְּאָבְדַן מֶרְכָּבִי, עַל מִשְׁכָּבִי.[5]
צַחֲנָתִי הָתֵם נָא,
שׁוּר מֵרֹאשׁ אֲמָנָה,[13]
צִיּוֹן קִרְיָה נֶאֱמָנָה,[5] אָקוּמָה נָּא.[6]
קִוִּיתִי לְמַשְׁפִּיל וּמֵרִים,
לְחַפְּשִׂי כְּאָז מֵחֲמוֹרִים,[14]
קוֹבֶלֶת מֵאֲרָיוֹת וּנְמֵרִים,*
מְצָאוּנִי הַשֹּׁמְרִים.[7]
קְרָנוֹת עֶשֶׂר* שִׁבַּרְתִּי,
לְאֻמִּים תַּחְתֶּיךָ הִדְבַּרְתִּי,[15]
קוֹלוֹ שִׁמַּעֲנִי וְהִגְבַּרְתִּי,
כִּמְעַט שֶׁעָבַרְתִּי.[8]
רוֹמַמְתִּי קֶרֶן נְגִידְּכֶם,
יֶשַׁע אָשִׁית מַדֵּיכֶם,
רוֹגְנִים מִלְּגַלּוֹת סוֹדְכֶם,
הִשְׁבַּעְתִּי אֶתְכֶם.[9]
רַבָּתִי אָשִׁים בְּעוּלָה,
מִכָּל עֲלָמוֹת לְעַלָּה,

Shimoni), these allude to the seven times the word קול, *voice*, is mentioned in the portions describing the giving of the Torah at Sinai (see *Exodus* 19:16-20:15; 24:3).

ערודים — *The wild donkeys.* The prophet describes the Egyptians as *'those whose flesh is the flesh of donkeys'* (*Ezekiel* 23:20).

מֵאֲרָיוֹת וּנְמֵרִים . . . קְרָנוֹת עֶשֶׂר — *From lions and leopards . . . the ten-horned beast.* Daniel (chapter 7) records his prophetic vision of four immense beasts which represented the four kingdoms that successively would rule the world, and to whom Israel would be subjugated in four periods of exile. The first beast, a lion with eagle's wings, represented Babylon. The second, a bear, symbolized Persia. The third, a four-headed, four-winged leopard, stood for Greece, which — after the death of Alexander the Great — was split up among four of his generals.

The fourth beast, unnamed in Daniel's vision, is described (*Daniel* 7:7) as *'excessively terrifying, awesome and strong; with immense iron teeth, eating and crumbling, trampling the rest*

FIRST DAY

ע *The wild donkeys* and their young,*
מ *purposefully measured their evil acts against the downtrodden [Israel].*
ע *[Wicked] acts that no one could ever imagine, 'Seize for us the [young Jewish] foxes [to drown in the Nile].'*[1]
פ *[With Torah and mitzvos He adorned me, as] with silken sashes, rings for my ears,*
ע *and necklace to delight my throat;*
פ *face to face He enticed me [with them], [and showed me] that He is my Beloved.*[2]
פ *May the one who toils in them until he is weary,*
ש *never be denied his just reward;*
פ *O Dweller of heaven, remember [his merits], when the winds [of retribution] will blow.*[3]
צ *He condensed His residence to my chariot,*
י *on the day my Altar was dedicated.*
צ *I looked forward to remaining here, upon my couch [in the Wilderness].*[4]
צ *But He assigned a land of holiness and delight,*
מ *the site of the chosen portion.*
צ *Zion, the city of faithfulness,*[5] *O, may I arise now [to ascend there].*[6]
ק *But, I winked and smiled at what they [the false prophets] said,*
ט *while I railed and ranted against the [true] teachers.*
ק *I spoiled the pure oil [of the Torah's words], treating them as dregs, and then the sentinels found me.*[7]
ק *When I broke the [mitzvos of His] possession [the Torah],*
ו *for goodness I no longer had any hope.*
ק *Had I not had assembled His Sanctuary, I would have almost passed away.*[8]
ר *He has inscribed a limitation for your armies,*
ב *despite the trembling trepidation before your might.*
ר *He shall distance you, He shall push you, so I adjure you [to remember this warning].*[9]
ר *When He uplifts with head held high,*
י *when He elevates the dove, the perfect one,*

SECOND DAY

ע *The Mighty One made a path for the foot travelers, those who shod themselves beautifully in pilgrims' sandals.*[10]
ע *He broke my opponent's neck in the waters, [saying to the waters,] 'Seize for us the [sly Egyptian] foxes.'*[1]
פ *He who wished to weaken me asked, 'How does your Beloved differ from mine?'*[11]
פ *[I replied,] 'He released me from the mud and mire, [proving that] He is my Beloved.'*[2]
פ *I prayed to the Awesome, Fearful One, to show me the day held in store [for the wicked].*
פ *O, open the jail to redeem your prisoners,*[12] *before the winds [of retribution] will blow.*[3]
צ *I cried to the Rock, from my pain, 'When will my wounds be healed?*
צ *May I see the destruction of those who ride upon me, while I lie on my bed [during the exile night].'*[4]
צ *Please, bring my filth[y sinfulness] to an end, contemplate the onset of [my] faith.*[13]
צ *Zion, the city of faithfulness,*[5] *O, may I arise now [to ascend there].*[6]
ק *I hope to Him Who humbles and exalts, to free me [today], as [He freed me] then from the donkey[-like Egyptians].*[14]
ק *I cry, [for I suffer] from lions and leopards,* they are the sentinels who found [and beat] me.*[7]
ק *[Let me hear You say,] 'I have broken the ten-horned beast;* I have brought the nations under your reign.'*[15]
ק *If He would only let me hear His voice, I will be reassured, for I have almost passed away.*[8]
ר *[Let me hear You say,] 'I have raised the horn of your king [Messiah], I have clad you in your garb of salvation.*
ר *From mentioning and revealing the secret [of your redemption date], I have adjured you [to refrain].*[9]
ר *I shall repopulate [Jerusalem,] once filled with masses, to exalt her above all nations.*

---

(1) *Song of Songs* 2:15. (2) 2:16. (3) 2:17. (4) 3:1. (5) *Isaiah* 1:21. (6) *Song of Songs* 3:2. (7) 3:3. (8) 3:4. (9) 3:5. (10) Cf. 7:2. (11) Cf. 5:9. (12) Cf. *Isaiah* 61:1. (13) Cf. *Song of Songs* 4:8. (14) See *Ezekiel* 23:20. (15) Cf. *Psalms* 47:4.

FIRST DAY

רָגְשׁוּ בְּנֵי עַוְלָה, מִי זֹאת עוֹלָה.[1]
שֵׁרוּת שַׁפְרִיר שִׁטָּתוֹ,
מַטּוֹת וְרִבּוֹא חִטָּתוֹ,
שַׁעַר צֵא וְשִׁטָּתוֹ, הִנֵּה מִטָּתוֹ.[2]
שִׁירַת עִרְבּוּב* מִלְּעָרֵב,
אֻמָּנוּת אַבּוּב עָרֵב,
שִׁירוֹת נִבּוּב הֶרֶב,
כֻּלָּם אֲחֻזֵי חֶרֶב.[3]
תָּאָיו פָּסַק לוֹ,
מַלֹּאת כַּנֵּי טְרַסְקֵלוֹ,*
תַּטְלִיל חָסָה לוֹ,
אַפִּרְיוֹן עָשָׂה לוֹ.[4]
❖ תֹּאַר פָּנִים מֵהִכָּסֵף,
נָעֳמוֹ יְדִידוּת כֹּסֶף,
תַּבְנִית אוֹת יוֹסֵף,*
עַמּוּדָיו עָשָׂה כֶסֶף.[5]

Responsively:

❖ צְאֶינָה וּרְאֶינָה,*[6]
All – מַשְׂכִּיל שִׁיר יְדִידִים,[7]
רִנַּת חֲתֻנַּת דּוֹדִים.
❖ הִנָּךְ יָפָה,[8]
All – דָּת דִּין וּפִקּוּדִים,
כָּפַל יָחִיד לִפְקוּדִים.
❖ שִׁנַּיִךְ,[9]
All – הַרְחֵק כִּעוּר חֲמוּדִים,
קְשׁוּט לְשׁוֹן לִמּוּדִים.
❖ כְּחוּט הַשָּׁנִי,[10]
All – טַעַם זַיִן יְלִידִים,

SECOND DAY

רְצוּיָה כְּרֵיחַ עוֹלָה, מִי זֹאת עֹלָה.[1]
שָׁרֵת בְּבֵית אוּלָמוֹ,
אִפְּדַנֵי שִׁבּוּץ יַהֲלוֹמוֹ,
שְׁתִיָּה מִכְלַל עוֹלָמוֹ,
הִנֵּה מִטָּתוֹ שֶׁלִּשְׁלֹמֹה.[2]
שׁוֹאֲגֵי בְּקוֹל עָרֵב,
יִחוּד בְּבֹקֶר וָעֶרֶב,
שִׁנּוּן שְׁחוֹרוֹת כָּעוֹרֵב,
כֻּלָּם אֲחֻזֵי חֶרֶב.[3]
תַּלְפִּיּוֹת* דְּבִיר הֵיכָלוֹ,
כָּבוֹד אוֹמֵר כֻּלּוֹ,[11]
תַּעַף רְאֵם[12] הִכְלִילוֹ,
אַפִּרְיוֹן עָשָׂה לוֹ.[4]
❖ תַּחֲנָתוֹ אִוָּה וְכִסֵּף,
לוֹ הַזָּהָב וְהַכֶּסֶף,[13]
תָּאָיו רִצֵּף בְּכֹסֶף,
עַמּוּדָיו עָשָׂה כֶסֶף.[5]

Responsively:

❖ צְאֶינָה וּרְאֶינָה,[6]
All – מֶלֶךְ בְּיָפְיוֹ[14] מֻכְלָל.
❖ הִנָּךְ יָפָה,[8]
All – שְׁוּבָה מְחַלֶּקֶת שָׁלָל.
❖ שִׁנַּיִךְ,[9]
All – לְחַתֵּךְ פְּרָט וּכְלָל.
❖ כְּחוּט הַשָּׁנִי,[10]
All – מְשׁוֹרֶשֶׁת לוֹ מַהֲלָל.

(1) *Song of Songs* 3:6. (2) 3:7. (3) 3:8. (4) 3:9. (5) 3:10. (6) 3:11. (7) Cf. *Psalms* 45:1.
(8) *Song of Songs* 4:1. (9) 4:2. (10) 4:3. (11) Cf. *Psalms* 29:9. (12) See commentary, p. 39
(13) Cf. *Haggai* 2:8. (14) Cf. *Isaiah* 33:17.

with its feet; it was different from all the beasts that preceded it, and it had ten horns.' This beast represented the present exile, considered to have begun with Julius Caesar's ascension to the Roman Empirate.

שִׁירַת עִרְבּוּב . . . — *The dulcet song . . .* The *paytan* now describes the Levite choir and orchestra that accompanied the Temple offering.

טְרַסְקֵלוֹ — *His three-legged stool.* An allusion to the world, as the Mishnah teaches, 'The world stands upon three things: upon Torah study, upon the Temple service, and upon kind deeds' (*Avos* 1:2).

אות יוסף — *Joseph's symbol.* When blessing the Tribe of Joseph, Moses called it *'the first born bull'* (*Deuteronomy* 33:17). Thus, the idolatrous Golden Calf was in 'the form that was Joseph's symbol.'

צְאֶינָה וּרְאֶינָה — *Go forth and see!* This begins the first section of the *yotzer* that bears a second signature. The verses of *Song of Songs* alternate with rhymed couplets that form the acrostic מָרְדְּכַי הַקָּטָן יִגְדַּל יִצְלַח בְּתוֹרָה אָמֵן וְאָמֵן סֶלָה — *Mordechai the Lesser, may he become great and successful in Torah, Amen and Amen, Selah.*

FIRST DAY

ר *the children of iniquity [Egypt] will gather,*
[and ask], 'Who is this on the ascent?'[1]
ש *The service of His beautiful shittim-wood Tabernacle,*
מ *[built by] the wheaten tribes and their myriads,*
ש *the measured orderliness of its activity,*
behold, [all this in the Tabernacle that is] His couch.[2]
ש *The dulcet song* of blended [voices],*
א *the musicians, masters of the sweet flute,*
ש *abounding with songs of the hollow reed,* *all [the players] holding sword-like instruments.*[3]
ת *He ordained for Himself [the Tabernacle] chambers,*
מ *to fulfill the purpose of His three-legged stool.**
ת *A protective shade for those who take refuge in Him,* *He has made a crowned canopy for Himself.*[4]
ת Chazzan — *He brightened their faces that they be not embarrassed [by the sin of the Golden Calf],*
נ *[by commanding the erection of] His sweet, beloved, desirous [Tabernacle].*
ת *The form that was Joseph's symbol,**
[was atoned for with] its pillars made of silver.[5]

Responsively:

Chazzan — *Go forth and see!*[6]*
מ All — *Become wise through the song of the beloved ones,*[7]
ר *with the glad song of the dear ones' marriage.*
Chazzan — *You are beautiful!*[8]
ד All — *The Written Torah's laws and the Oral Torah's decrees,*
כי *thus the One doubled [His words] to the counted ones [by twice saying, 'You are beautiful'].*
Chazzan — *Your teeth!*[9]
ה All — *They are far from desiring ugly speech,*
ק *they are adorned with the language of [Torah] learning.*
Chazzan — *Like a scarlet thread!*[10]
ט All — *[Your lips have] educated [your] offspring,*

SECOND DAY

ר *She will be favorable as the aroma of an offering;*
she who is on the ascent.'[1]
ש *O, to serve in the Hall of His Temple, I will don the Ephod set with jewels.*
ש *The foundation, the center of His world,*
behold, the couch of the King to whom peace belongs.[2]
ש *Those who cry with sweet voice, reciting the Shema morning and night,*
ש *they study the raven-black [letters of the Torah],*
all of them gripping the sword [of tradition].[3]
ת *Talpios,* Sanctuary of His Temple, its every part bespeaking honor.*[11]
ת *He has adorned it like the towering re'eim,*[12]
He has made a crowned canopy for himself.[4]
ת Chazzan — *His admired and desired dwelling, Him to Whom the gold and silver belong,*[13]
ת *He decked its chambers with delight,*
He made its pillars of silver.[5]

Responsively:

Chazzan — *Go forth and see . . .*[6]
מ All — *. . . the King in His consummate beauty.*[14]
Chazzan — *You are beautiful . . .*[8]
ש All — *. . . when you return to divide the spoils.*
Chazzan — *Your teeth. . .*[9]
ל All — *. . . utter [the Torah's] general principles and particulars.*
Chazzan — *Like a scarlet thread. . .*[10]
ם All — *. . . [your lips] sing to Him in praise.*

תַּלְפִּיּוֹת — *Talpios.* The Temple was called *Talpios* (*Song of Songs* 4:4), an adornment, because everyone gazed upon it to study its forms and the beautiful masterwork of its design (*Rashi*).

SECOND DAY	FIRST DAY

SECOND DAY

נֶגְדּוֹ שֶׁלֶם לַיְּלָדִים.
❖ כְּמִגְדַּל דָּוִיד,[1]
All – יִקְרַת פִּנַּת יְסוֹדִים,
גְּבוּל הוֹרָיוֹת יְסוּדִים.[2]
All continue:
שְׁנֵי שָׁדַיִךְ,[3]
דִּבּוּק אַחִים חֲסִידִים,
לְרוֹעִים תַּיָּרִים חֲסוּדִים,
עַד שֶׁיָּפְוּחַ הַיּוֹם.[4]
יוֹם צְדָקָה לַחֲרֵדִים,
חִבּוּל זֵדִים זְרָדִים, כֻּלָּךְ יָפָה.[5]
בְּלִי מוּם מְכֻבָּדִים,
תָּם וְחֶלְקוֹ מְזֻבָּדִים,
אִתִּי מִלְּבָנוֹן כַּלָּה.[6]
וְעוֹד שְׁכִינָה בְּשִׁעְבּוּדִים,
רָצוּף בְּבֹאוֹ מֵאִבּוּדִים,
לִבַּבְתִּנִי אֲחוֹתִי כַלָּה.[7]
הַבַּת בַּת נְגִידִים,
אַהֲבָה וְחִבָּה אֲגוּדִים,
מַה יָּפוּ דֹדַיִךְ אֲחוֹתִי כַלָּה.[8]
מְנוּחָה וּשְׁאָר וְעוֹדִים,
וּשְׁמָנַיִךְ קִרְיַת מוֹעֲדִים,[9]
נֹפֶת תִּטֹּפְנָה שִׂפְתוֹתַיִךְ כַּלָּה.[10]
אַחֲוַת מְשִׁיחִים עוֹמְדִים,
מִבְּלִי קִנְאָה מְצֻמָּדִים, גַּן נָעוּל.[11]
נָקָם וְאֵין מַגִּידִים,
סָתוּם לְתִלְבֹּשֶׁת הַבְּגָדִים.
שְׁלָחַיִךְ פַּרְדֵּס,*[12]
שְׁפַר נָאִים וְהֲדוּרִים,
לְטַכְסִיס מְלָכִים אֲדוּרִים.
נֵרְדְּ וְכַרְכֹּם,[13]
מִזֶּה וּמִזֶּה סְדוּרִים,
הַחוּט הַמְּשֻׁלָּשׁ גְּדוּרִים.
מַעְיַן גַּנִּים,[14]

FIRST DAY

❖ כְּמִגְדַּל דָּוִיד,[1]
All – בְּרוּם אָשְׁיוֹתָיו מִתְלָל.
All continue:
שְׁנֵי שָׁדַיִךְ,[3]
יָכִילוּ מְלֹא כָל הֶחָלָל.
עַד שֶׁיָּפְוּחַ,[4]
רֵיחַ נִדְבָּכִין מְגֻלָּל.
כֻּלָּךְ,[5]
בָּרָה כְּנוֹצְצִים כְּעֵין קָלָל.[15]
אִתִּי,[6]
יָפָתִי קִשּׁוּרַיִךְ לְהִתְכַּלָּל.
לִבַּבְתִּנִי,[7]
וְאֵרַשְׂתִּיךְ נוֹגְשַׂיִךְ יִתְעוֹלָל.
מַה יָּפוּ,[8]
מַעְגְּלוֹתַיִךְ וְאָרְחֵךְ סוֹלָל.
נֹפֶת,[10]
חִכֵּךְ זֵכֶר קְדֻשָּׁה לִכְלָל.
לְרוֹמֵם לְגָדוֹל וּמְהֻלָּל,
הַמֵּאִיר גֵּיא וְחָלָל.

The service continues on page 292.

(1) *Song of Songs* 4:4. (2) Cf. *Isaiah* 28:16. (3) *Song of Songs* 4:5. (4) 4:6. (5) 4:7. (6) 4:8. (7) 4:9. (8) 4:10. (9) Cf. *Isaiah* 33:20. (10) *Song of Songs* 4:11. (11) 4:12. (12) 4:13. (13) 4:14. (14) 4:15. (15) Cf. *Ezekiel* 1:7.

Other interpretations of *Talpios* include: landmark (*Ibn Yanach*); a place to hang swords (לִתְלוֹת פִּיוֹת) [i.e., a fortress (*Ibn Ezra*); teaching, training ... to guide the traveler, for its height made it visible from afar (*Metzudos*); and a hill (תֵּל) to which all mouth (פִּיוֹת) turn in prayer (*Berachos* 30a).

שְׁלָחַיִךְ פַּרְדֵּס — *Your sprouts are an orchard.*

FIRST DAY

נ *in return, He has rewarded [your] children.*
Chazzan — Like the Tower of David![1]
י All — *Valuable cornerstone of foundation,*[2]
ג *site of basic halachic decisions.*
All continue:
Your two nurturers [Moses and Aaron]![3]
ד *Two pious brothers joined as one,*
ל *to shepherd and guide the gracious nation, when the winds [of retribution] will blow.*[4]
יצל *A day of righteousness for the alacritous ones,*
ח *of destruction for the wicked, the evil branches, then you will be completely beautiful.*[5]
ב *The honorable, flawless ones,*
ת *[Children of] Jacob, His assigned portion, with Me [you were exiled] from the Temple, O bride.*[6]
ו *My Shechinah is with you in your oppression,*
ר *It shall be joined to you when you return from the Diaspora, for you have captured My heart, My sister, My bride.*[7]
ה *The maiden [Israel] is the daughter of princes [the Patriarchs],*
א *bound [to God] with love and endearment; How beautiful is My love for you, My sister, My bride.*[8]
מנ *At the serenity [of Shiloh] and other appointed places,*
ו *and in [Jerusalem, the] choicest city of the [pilgrimage] festivals,*[9] *the sweetness of honey are [the prayers of] your lips, My bride.*[10]
א *In brotherhood the Saviors are standing,*
מ *bound together without any jealousy; but the garden [gate] is sealed.*[11]
נ *The day of vengeance [is sealed], there are no prophets [to apprise us],*
סלה *it is closed until He dons the uniform [of vengeance].*
Your sprouts are an orchard,[12]*
ש *beautiful and comely,*
ל *like the armies of crowned kings.*
Nard and Saffron,[13]
מ *aligned on all sides [of the orchard],*
ה *the three-ply [Patriarchal] thread encircling you.*
A garden spring,[14]

SECOND DAY

Chazzan — Like the Tower of David . . .[1]
ב All — *. . . whose foundation raises it high; so are you tall [with fulfillment of mitzvos].*

All continue:
The two poles of Your Ark,[3]
י *[will be able to] enclose the entire world.*
When it [the Temple] will be revitalized,[4]
ר *with marble walls absorbing the offerings' aromas.*
While you are all[5]
ב *pure as [the angels] who glitter like burnished bronze.*[15]
[You will be] With Me,[6]
יקל *My beautiful one, encrowned with your wreaths.*
You have captured My heart.;[7]
וני *when I betroth you, your oppressors will be shamed.*
How beautiful are[8]
מוס *your curved and your straight paths.*
The sweetness of honey[10]
חזק *is on your palate, when you recite the Kedushah portion, to exalt He Who is great and praised, He Who illuminates the earth and its atmosphere.*

The service continues on page 292.

FIRST DAY

הַדָּחַת קָלִים וַחֲמוּרִים, טְבִילוֹת נְקִיּוֹת שְׁמוּרִים.
עוּרִי צָפוֹן וּבוֹאִי תֵימָן,[1]
יַחַד לְכַנֵּס נִסְעָרִים, גָּלוּת כָּל שְׁעָרִים.
בָּאתִי לְגַנִּי אֲחֹתִי כַלָּה,[2]
דְּגִמַת מִלּוּאִים גְּמוּרִים, לְקַבֵּל אֵבָרִים וְאֵמוּרִים.
אֲנִי יְשֵׁנָה,[3]
בִּיאַת עִיר מִשְּׂעִירִים, תּוֹחֶלֶת יִסְחָבוּם צְעִירִים.[4]
פָּשַׁטְתִּי אֶת כֻּתָּנְתִּי,[5]
רַבָּתִי וּשְׁנֵי כְתָרִים, הָאוּרִים וְתֻמֵּי סְתָרִים.
דּוֹדִי שָׁלַח יָדוֹ,[6]
אָז לִסְעֹד הוֹרִים, מְזֻמָּן עוֹד לְנִמְהָרִים.
קַמְתִּי,[7]
נִצַּבְתִּי בְּחֶמֶד הָרִים, וְדַצְתִּי אַצְתִּי בַּזְּהָרִים.
פָּתַחְתִּי,[8]
מֵאֵלַי כְּנָטוּף מוֹרִים, נַעֲשֶׂה וְנִשְׁמַע אֲמָרִים.[9]
מְצָאוּנִי,[10]
לִגְיוֹנוֹת סְבָבוּנִי כַּנְּהָרִים, עוֹמֵד כַּהֲדַסִּים בֶּהָרִים.[11]
הִשְׁבַּעְתִּי אֶתְכֶם,[12]
דְּרֹשׁ דּוֹד מֵישָׁרִים, סוּר מֶרְכְּסֵי קְשָׁרִים.
מַה דּוֹדֵךְ מִדּוֹד,[13]
לֶעָתִיד שְׁאוֹל נִפְשָׁרִים, הֵם בָּאֻמּוֹת הַכְּשֵׁרִים.
מַה דּוֹדֵךְ מִדּוֹד,[13]
נוֹאֲמִים בְּזֶה הַקּוֹשְׁרִים, נֶגְדוֹ נֶהֱרָגִים כַּשְּׁוָרִים,
נֵזֶר יִחוּדוֹ קוֹשְׁרִים, נֵצַח מַלְכוּתוֹ שָׁרִים.
דּוֹדִי,[14]
נָעֳמוֹ עִמּוֹ מְיַשְּׁרִים, נִכְתָּב וְנִקְרָא בַּשִּׁירִים,
צִדְקוֹתָיו לְרֵקִים מְחַזְּרִים, צִבְיוֹנוֹ עֲשׂוֹת מִתְאַזְּרִים,
צְפוּתֵנוּ צְפוּת מְשַׁחֲרִים, צִיּוֹן עַמּוּד שְׁחָרִים,
צוּר קוֹנֵנוּ מַכְתִּירִים, צָרְכֵּנוּ בְּפֶלֶל מַעְתִּירִים,
חָזֹה נֶחֱזֶה בְּבֵאוּרִים, חָשְׁבֵּנוּ לָעַד לְאוֹרִים.
❖ חַי זַכֵּנוּ בְּמִתְפָּאֲרִים, קַיָּם לְדוֹר דּוֹרִים,
הַמֵּאִיר לָאָרֶץ וְלַדָּרִים.

(1) *Song of Songs* 4:16. (2) 5:1. (3) 5:2. (4) Cf. *Jeremiah* 49:20.
(5) *Song of Songs* 5:3. (6) 5:4. (7) 5:5. (8) 5:6. (9) Cf. *Exodus* 24:7.
(10) *Song of Songs* 5:7. (11) Cf. *Zechariah* 1:8. (12) *Song of Songs* 5:8. (13) 5:9. (14) 5:10.

FIRST DAY

הק *which cleanses the light and the heavy stains [of defilement],*
טנ *from those who maintain the purifying immersions.*
Awaken, O north wind, and come, O south wind;[1]
י *together to gather those dispersed by the storm,*
ג *those exiled at every gate.*
I came to My [Temple] Garden, My sister, My bride,[2]
ד *the picture of total perfection,*
ל *to accept the fats of the assigned offerings.*
But I am asleep,[3]
ב *until You come to the city [Jerusalem], from [venting Your anger upon] Seir,*
תו *hopefully, the young ones will drag them.*[4]
I have doffed my robe —[5]
ר *my great One [the protective Shechinah] — and my two crowns,*
ה *the Urim Vesumim that reveal the hidden.*
My Beloved offered His hand,[6]
א *to assist [Ezra and his court] the decisors of the law, at that time;*
מ *and He is again prepared to help the alacritous ones.*
I arose,[7]
נ *I stood on the most desirous of mountains,*
וא *I rejoiced, I hastened, to heed His admonitions.*
I began [speaking][8]
מ *of my own accord, [at Sinai,] dripping with myrrh,*
נ *saying, 'We shall do, and we shall listen.'*[9]
They found me,[10]
ל *angelic legions surrounded me like rivers,*
ע *while He stood like myrtles on the mountains.*[11]
[Then God said:] 'I adjure you,[12]
ד *to seek Me, dear ones, that I might lead you on the straight path;*
ס *turn away from the company of the wicked.'*
[The nations will ask:] 'How does your Beloved [God] differ from our idols?[13]
ל *that, in the future, [our reward will be] the Pit, and [yours will be] cool waters?'*
ה *[We will reply to] them: 'Among the nations, [we are] the worthy ones.'*
'How does your Beloved [God] differ from our idols?'[13]
נ *Thus speak the wicked,*
נ *'That you are slaughtered for His sake like cattle;*
נ *that you bind Him a crown of Oneness;*
נ *that you sing of His kingdom's eternality?'*
[Israel responds,] 'My Beloved![14]
נ *His people study His sweet Torah in a straightforward manner;*
נ *His Torah, written and read in sing-song.*
צ *They review His righteousness with those barren [of mitzvos],*
צ *that they should strengthen themselves by doing His will.'*
צ *We yearn and plead that our hopes be fulfilled,*
צ *the sign of our morningstar's appearance.*
צ *We crown the Protector of our nest;*
צ *for our needs we pray in supplication.*
ח *May we clearly see,*
ח *our darkness turn to eternal light.*
חזו *O Living One, find us worthy, as we take pride [in proclaiming],*
ק *'He endures through all generations;*
He illuminates the world and those who dwell upon it.'

From this point onward, the acrostic reads, שְׁלֹמֹה הַקָּטָן יִגְדַּל בְּתוֹרָה אָמֵן וְאָמֵן לָעַד סֶלָה נֶצַח חֲזַק, ***Shlomo the Lesser, may he become great in Torah,*** *Amen and Amen, forever, Selah, eternally, may he be strong.*

ON A WEEKDAY CONTINUE HERE:

הַמֵּאִיר לָאָרֶץ וְלַדָּרִים* עָלֶיהָ בְּרַחֲמִים, וּבְטוּבוֹ מְחַדֵּשׁ בְּכָל יוֹם תָּמִיד מַעֲשֵׂה בְרֵאשִׁית. מָה רַבּוּ מַעֲשֶׂיךָ* יהוה,

⁂ הַמֵּאִיר לָאָרֶץ וְלַדָּרִים — *He Who illuminates the earth and those who dwell.* The earth's dwellers enjoy the light, but so does the earth itself, because sunlight makes vegetation possible.

ON THE SABBATH CONTINUE HERE:

הַכֹּל יוֹדוּךָ,* וְהַכֹּל יְשַׁבְּחוּךָ, וְהַכֹּל יֹאמְרוּ אֵין קָדוֹשׁ כַּיהוה.[1] הַכֹּל יְרוֹמְמוּךָ סֶּלָה, יוֹצֵר הַכֹּל. הָאֵל הַפּוֹתֵחַ בְּכָל יוֹם דַּלְתוֹת שַׁעֲרֵי מִזְרָח, וּבוֹקֵעַ חַלּוֹנֵי רָקִיעַ,* מוֹצִיא חַמָּה מִמְּקוֹמָהּ וּלְבָנָה מִמְּכוֹן שִׁבְתָּהּ, וּמֵאִיר לָעוֹלָם כֻּלּוֹ וּלְיוֹשְׁבָיו, שֶׁבָּרָא בְּמִדַּת רַחֲמִים. הַמֵּאִיר לָאָרֶץ וְלַדָּרִים עָלֶיהָ בְּרַחֲמִים, וּבְטוּבוֹ מְחַדֵּשׁ בְּכָל יוֹם תָּמִיד מַעֲשֵׂה בְרֵאשִׁית. הַמֶּלֶךְ הַמְּרוֹמָם לְבַדּוֹ מֵאָז, הַמְּשֻׁבָּח וְהַמְּפֹאָר וְהַמִּתְנַשֵּׂא מִימוֹת עוֹלָם. אֱלֹהֵי עוֹלָם בְּרַחֲמֶיךָ הָרַבִּים, רַחֵם עָלֵינוּ, אֲדוֹן עֻזֵּנוּ, צוּר מִשְׂגַּבֵּנוּ, מָגֵן יִשְׁעֵנוּ, מִשְׂגָּב בַּעֲדֵנוּ. אֵין כְּעֶרְכֶּךָ,* וְאֵין זוּלָתֶךָ, אֶפֶס בִּלְתֶּךָ, וּמִי דּוֹמֶה לָּךְ. אֵין כְּעֶרְכְּךָ יהוה אֱלֹהֵינוּ בָּעוֹלָם הַזֶּה, וְאֵין זוּלָתְךָ מַלְכֵּנוּ לְחַיֵּי הָעוֹלָם הַבָּא. אֶפֶס בִּלְתְּךָ גּוֹאֲלֵנוּ לִימוֹת הַמָּשִׁיחַ, וְאֵין דּוֹמֶה לְּךָ מוֹשִׁיעֵנוּ לִתְחִיַּת הַמֵּתִים.

⁂ **The Sabbath Additions**

Since the Sabbath is the weekly testimony to the fact that God created the world, the first blessing of the Shema, which deals with creation, is augmented on the Sabbath with three apt passages:

1. הַכֹּל יוֹדוּךָ, *All will thank You,* speaks of the Creator Who renews creation daily;

2. אֵל אָדוֹן, *God — The Master,* praises the glory of creation itself;

3. לָאֵל אֲשֶׁר שָׁבַת, *To the God Who rested,* celebrates the Sabbath. Thus, these three passages are appropriate only on the Sabbath, and are omitted on all weekday Festivals *(World of Prayer).*

⁂ הַכֹּל יוֹדוּךָ — *All will thank You.* The word 'all' refers to the previous blessing, which ends וּבוֹרֵא אֶת הַכֹּל, *and creates all.* Thus, every facet of the universe will join in thanking and lauding God. Only man and the angels do this verbally; the rest of creation does so by carrying out its assigned tasks and inspiring man to recognize the Guiding Hand that created and orders everything.

דַּלְתוֹת שַׁעֲרֵי מִזְרָח ... חַלּוֹנֵי רָקִיעַ — *Doors of the gateways of the East ... windows of the firmament.* These expressions are given various interpretations. On the simple level, they refer poetically to the rising sun breaking through the portals of darkness. Alternatively, the phrase *doors of the gateways* refers to daybreak, which illuminates the sky long before sunrise. The *windows* are different points in the sky at which the sun rises as the seasons move to the longer days of summer and then back again to the shorter days of winter *(R' Hirsch; Iyun Tefillah).*

אֵין כְּעֶרְכֶּךָ — *There is no comparison to You.* This verse makes four statements about God that are explained in the next verse. Thus the two verses should be seen as a unit. As explained by *R'*

ON A WEEKDAY CONTINUE HERE:

הַמֵּאִיר *He Who illuminates the earth and those who dwell* upon it, with compassion; and in His goodness renews daily, perpetually, the work of Creation. How great are Your works,* Hashem,*

מָה רַבּוּ מַעֲשֶׂיךָ — *How great are Your works.* This refers to the heavenly bodies and other major forces in creation. Homiletically, the Talmud (*Chullin* 127a) interprets, *how diverse are Your works;* some can live only on land, others only in the sea, and so on.

ON THE SABBATH CONTINUE HERE:

הַכֹּל יוֹדְוּךָ *All will thank You* and all will praise You — and all will declare: 'Nothing is as holy as Hashem!'[1] All will exalt You, Selah! — You Who forms everything. The God Who opens daily the doors of the gateways of the East, and splits the windows of the firmament,* Who removes the sun from its place and the moon from the site of its dwelling, and Who illuminates all the world and its inhabitants, which He created with the attribute of mercy. He Who illuminates the earth and those who dwell upon it, with compassion; and in His goodness renews daily, perpetually, the work of creation. The King Who was exalted in solitude from before creation, Who is praised, glorified, and extolled since days of old. Eternal God, with Your abundant compassion be compassionate to us — O Master of our power, our rocklike stronghold; O Shield of our salvation, be a stronghold for us. There is no comparison to You,* there is nothing except for You, there is nothing without You, for who is like You? There is no comparison to You, Hashem, our God, in this world; and there will be nothing except for You, our King, in the life of the World to Come; there will be nothing without You, our Redeemer, in Messianic days; and there will be none like You, our Savior; at the Resuscitation of the Dead.*

(1) *I Samuel* 2:2.

Hirsch, the four statements are:

(a) אֵין כְּעֶרְכֶּךָ — *There is no comparison to You.* Although we have expressed our gratitude for the heavenly bodies and the various forces of the universe, we hasten to affirm that none of them can even be compared to God's power on earth.

(b) וְאֵין זוּלָתֶךָ — *There is nothing except for You.* In the World to Come, even the most beneficial aspects of life in this material world will not exist. In the blissful state of that world, nothing will exist except for God and those whose lives on earth have made them worthy of His spiritual grandeur.

(c) אֶפֶס בִּלְתֶּךָ — *There is nothing without You.* On earth, too, there will be a state of bliss with the coming of the Messiah — but that redemption is impossible without God, despite the earthly factors that will seem to contribute to it.

(d) וּמִי דּוֹמֶה לָּךְ — *For who is like You?* Nothing will so clearly reveal God's absolute mastery as the Resuscitation of the Dead. That is the ultimate redemption, for it will demonstrate that not only slavery and freedom, but even life and death, depend on Him.

ON A WEEKDAY

כֻּלָּם בְּחָכְמָה עָשִׂיתָ, מָלְאָה הָאָרֶץ קִנְיָנֶךָ. הַמֶּלֶךְ הַמְּרוֹמָם לְבַדּוֹ* מֵאָז, הַמְּשֻׁבָּח וְהַמְּפֹאָר וְהַמִּתְנַשֵּׂא מִימוֹת עוֹלָם. אֱלֹהֵי עוֹלָם, בְּרַחֲמֶיךָ הָרַבִּים רַחֵם עָלֵינוּ, אֲדוֹן עֻזֵּנוּ, צוּר מִשְׂגַּבֵּנוּ, מָגֵן יִשְׁעֵנוּ, מִשְׂגָּב בַּעֲדֵנוּ. אֵל בָּרוּךְ* גְּדוֹל דֵּעָה, הֵכִין וּפָעַל

הַמֶּלֶךְ הַמְּרוֹמָם לְבַדּוֹ — *The King Who was exalted in solitude.* Before Creation, God was *exalted in solitude,* because there were no creatures to praise Him *(Etz Yosef).*

אֵל בָּרוּךְ — *The blessed God.* This begins a lyric praise consisting of twenty-two words following the order of the *Aleph-Beis.* As noted at the bottom of the page in the commentary to אֵל

ON THE SABBATH

The following liturgical song is recited responsively in most congregations.
In some congregations, the *chazzan* and congregation sing the stanzas together.

אֵל אָדוֹן* עַל כָּל הַמַּעֲשִׂים, בָּרוּךְ וּמְבֹרָךְ* בְּפִי כָּל נְשָׁמָה,
גָּדְלוֹ וְטוּבוֹ מָלֵא עוֹלָם, דַּעַת וּתְבוּנָה סוֹבְבִים אֹתוֹ.
הַמִּתְגָּאֶה* עַל חַיּוֹת הַקֹּדֶשׁ, וְנֶהְדָּר בְּכָבוֹד עַל הַמֶּרְכָּבָה,
זְכוּת וּמִישׁוֹר לִפְנֵי כִסְאוֹ, חֶסֶד וְרַחֲמִים לִפְנֵי כְבוֹדוֹ.
טוֹבִים מְאוֹרוֹת שֶׁבָּרָא אֱלֹהֵינוּ, יְצָרָם בְּדַעַת בְּבִינָה וּבְהַשְׂכֵּל,
כֹּחַ וּגְבוּרָה נָתַן בָּהֶם, לִהְיוֹת מוֹשְׁלִים בְּקֶרֶב תֵּבֵל.
מְלֵאִים זִיו וּמְפִיקִים נֹגַהּ, נָאֶה זִיוָם בְּכָל הָעוֹלָם,
שְׂמֵחִים בְּצֵאתָם* וְשָׂשִׂים בְּבוֹאָם, עוֹשִׂים בְּאֵימָה רְצוֹן קוֹנָם.
פְּאֵר וְכָבוֹד* נוֹתְנִים לִשְׁמוֹ, צָהֳלָה וְרִנָּה לְזֵכֶר מַלְכוּתוֹ,
קָרָא לַשֶּׁמֶשׁ וַיִּזְרַח אוֹר, רָאָה וְהִתְקִין צוּרַת הַלְּבָנָה.*
שֶׁבַח נוֹתְנִים לוֹ כָּל צְבָא מָרוֹם,
תִּפְאֶרֶת וּגְדֻלָּה, שְׂרָפִים וְאוֹפַנִּים וְחַיּוֹת הַקֹּדֶשׁ—

⋄§ אֵל אָדוֹן — *God — the Master.* This poetic prayer comprises twenty-two phrases, the initial letters of which form the *Aleph-Beis.* It is parallel to the alphabetical prayer אֵל בָּרוּךְ גְּדוֹל דֵּעָה of the weekday *Shacharis;* but the weekday prayer contains only twenty-two words. The *Vilna Gaon* explains that the lesser holiness of the weekdays is expressed not only in the shorter version, but in the content. There, the praise concentrates on God's greatness as we perceive it in the form of the heavenly bodies. Here, the greater holiness of the Sabbath enables us to perceive more — though clearly not all — of His greatness.

בָּרוּךְ וּמְבֹרָךְ — *The Blessed One — and He is blessed,* i.e., God is the source of all blessing. In addition, His creatures bless Him in their prayers and through their obedience to His will *(Vilna Gaon).*

הַמִּתְגָּאֶה — *He Who exalts Himself.* The *Chayos* are the highest category of angels, and the Chariot [מֶרְכָּבָה] refers to the order of angelic praises of God. Both were seen by Ezekiel (ch. 1) in his *Ma'aseh Merkavah* prophecy. Thus, they represent the highest degree of holiness accessible to human understanding. Nevertheless, God is exalted far above even this.

שְׂמֵחִים בְּצֵאתָם — *Glad as they go forth.* The heavenly bodies are likened to a loyal servant

ON A WEEKDAY

You make them all with wisdom, the world is full of Your possessions.[1] *The King Who was exalted in solitude* before Creation, Who is praised, glorified, and upraised since days of old. Eternal God, with Your abundant compassion be compassionate to us — O Master of our power, our rocklike stronghold, O Shield of our salvation, be a stronghold for us. The blessed God,* Who is great in knowledge, prepared and worked on*

(1) *Psalms* 104:24.

אֲדוֹן, *God — the Master,* which is recited on the Sabbath, this formula of an *Aleph-Beis* acrostic is followed on the Sabbath as well, except that on the Sabbath each letter introduces an entire

ON THE SABBATH

The following liturgical song is recited responsively in most congregations. In some congregations, the *chazzan* and congregation sing the stanzas together.

אֵל אָדוֹן *God — the Master* over all works;* ב *the Blessed One — and He is blessed* by the mouth of every soul;*
ג *His greatness and goodness fill the world,*
ד *wisdom and insight surround Him.*
ה *He Who exalts Himself* over the holy Chayos*
ו *and is splendrous in glory above the Chariot;*
ז *Merit and fairness are before His throne,*
ח *kindness and mercy are before His glory.*
ט *Good are the luminaries that our God has created,*
י *He has fashioned them with wisdom,*
with insight and discernment;
כ *Strength and power has He granted them,*
ל *to be dominant within the world.*
מ *Filled with luster and radiating brightness,*
נ *their luster is beautiful throughout the world;*
ס *Glad as they go forth* and exultant as they return,*
ע *they do with awe their Creator's will.*
פ *Splendor and glory* they bestow upon His Name,*
צ *jubilation and glad song upon the mention of His reign —*
ק *He called out to the sun and it glowed with light,*
ר *He saw and fashioned the form of the moon.**
ש *All the host above bestows praise on Him,*
ת *splendor and greatness — the Seraphim, Ophanim,*
and holy Chayos —

entrusted with an important mission. He is proud and happy when he sets out, but is even more joyous when he returns to his master.

פְּאֵר וְכָבוֹד — *Splendor and glory.* The exact movements of the heavenly bodies inspire people to praise the One Who created them.

צוּרַת הַלְּבָנָה — *The form of the moon.* With insight, God shaped the phases of the moon so

ON A WEEKDAY

זָהֳרֵי חַמָּה, טוֹב יָצַר כָּבוֹד לִשְׁמוֹ,* מְאוֹרוֹת נָתַן סְבִיבוֹת עֻזּוֹ, פִּנּוֹת צְבָאָיו קְדוֹשִׁים רוֹמְמֵי שַׁדַּי, תָּמִיד מְסַפְּרִים כְּבוֹד אֵל וּקְדֻשָּׁתוֹ. תִּתְבָּרַךְ יהוה אֱלֹהֵינוּ עַל שֶׁבַח מַעֲשֵׂה יָדֶיךָ, וְעַל מְאוֹרֵי אוֹר שֶׁעָשִׂיתָ, יְפָאֲרוּךָ, סֶּלָה.

phrase. See commentary below for the significance of this difference.

As a general rule, the use of the *Aleph-Beis* acrostic in the prayers conveys the idea that we praise God with every available sound and that His greatness is absolutely complete and harmonious. Furthermore, the emphasis on the letters implies our acknowledgment that the Torah, whose words and thoughts are formed with the letters of the *Aleph-Beis,* is the very basis of the continued existence of heaven and earth. In the familiar teaching of the Sages *(Pesachim* 68b), R' Elazar explains: Were it not for the [constant study of] Torah, heaven and earth would not exist, as it is said, *Were it not for My covenant* [i.e., the Torah] *day and night, I would not have established the systematic function of heaven and earth (Jeremiah* 33:25). This concept of the letters of the Torah is further alluded to in the verse from *Song of Songs* (1:4) in which Israel allegorically says to God: נָגִילָה וְנִשְׂמְחָה בָּךְ, *we will rejoice and be glad in You.* The word בָּךְ has the numerical value of twenty-two, an allusion to the twenty-two letters of the *Aleph-Beis*, as if

ON THE SABBATH

לָאֵל אֲשֶׁר שָׁבַת* מִכָּל הַמַּעֲשִׂים, בַּיּוֹם הַשְּׁבִיעִי הִתְעַלָּה וְיָשַׁב עַל כִּסֵּא כְבוֹדוֹ, תִּפְאֶרֶת עָטָה לְיוֹם הַמְּנוּחָה, עֹנֶג קָרָא לְיוֹם הַשַּׁבָּת. זֶה שֶׁבַח שֶׁל יוֹם הַשְּׁבִיעִי,* שֶׁבּוֹ שָׁבַת אֵל מִכָּל מְלַאכְתּוֹ. וְיוֹם הַשְּׁבִיעִי מְשַׁבֵּחַ וְאוֹמֵר: מִזְמוֹר שִׁיר לְיוֹם הַשַּׁבָּת, טוֹב לְהוֹדוֹת לַיהוה.[1] לְפִיכָךְ יְפָאֲרוּ* וִיבָרְכוּ לָאֵל כָּל יְצוּרָיו. שֶׁבַח יְקָר וּגְדֻלָּה יִתְּנוּ לְאֵל מֶלֶךְ יוֹצֵר כֹּל, הַמַּנְחִיל מְנוּחָה לְעַמּוֹ יִשְׂרָאֵל בִּקְדֻשָּׁתוֹ בְּיוֹם שַׁבַּת קֹדֶשׁ. שִׁמְךָ יהוה אֱלֹהֵינוּ יִתְקַדַּשׁ, וְזִכְרְךָ מַלְכֵּנוּ יִתְפָּאַר, בַּשָּׁמַיִם מִמַּעַל וְעַל הָאָרֶץ מִתָּחַת. תִּתְבָּרַךְ מוֹשִׁיעֵנוּ עַל שֶׁבַח מַעֲשֵׂה יָדֶיךָ, וְעַל מְאוֹרֵי אוֹר שֶׁעָשִׂיתָ, יְפָאֲרוּךָ, סֶּלָה.

that they would enable Israel to order the calendar as commanded by the Torah.

⚜ **לָאֵל אֲשֶׁר שָׁבַת** — *To the God Who rested.* To Whom are directed the praises mentioned above? — to the God Who rested on the Sabbath from His six days of creation. We say that He 'ascended on the Seventh Day' in the sense that His Presence is no longer obvious on earth. Nevertheless, He left us with the Sabbath as an eternal testimony to His six days of activity and the Sabbath of His rest.

זֶה שֶׁבַח שֶׁל יוֹם הַשְּׁבִיעִי — *This is the praise of the Sabbath Day.* The glory of the Sabbath is not in the leisure it offers, but in its witness to the Creator and its stimulus to man to join it in praising God. In this sense, the very existence of

ON A WEEKDAY

the rays of the sun; the Beneficent One fashioned honor for His Name, emplaced luminaries all around His power; the leaders of His legions, holy ones, exalt the Almighty, constantly relate the honor of God and His sanctity. May You be blessed, HASHEM, our God, beyond the praises of Your handiwork and beyond the bright luminaries that You have made — may they glorify You — Selah!*

to say that we declare our joy in having been worthy to receive the Torah that is formed with the sacred letters (*Abudraham*). Since this portion of the liturgy focuses on the creation and functioning of heaven and earth, it is especially appropriate to insert this allusion to the primacy of Torah study.

According to a tradition cited by *Etz Yosef*, R' Elazar HaKalir, composer of this prayer, communicated with the angel Michael and asked him how the angels formulated their songs of praise. Michael told him that they based their praises on the *Aleph-Beis*. Accordingly, R' Elazar used that formulation in this and his many other *piyutim*. He alluded to the source of this knowledge, Michael, by inserting his name acrostically immediately after these twenty-two words: מְסַפְּרִים כְּבוֹד אֵל, *relate the honor of God.*

יָצַר כָּבוֹד לִשְׁמוֹ — *Fashioned honor for His Name.* The complexity and perfection of creation testifies to the fact that there must be a Creator. Consequently, by creating and emplacing the heavenly bodies, God fashioned the instruments that would bring honor to His Name.

ON THE SABBATH

לָאֵל *To the God Who rested* from all works, Who ascended on the Seventh Day and sat on the Throne of His Glory. With splendor He enwrapped the Day of Contentment — He declared the Sabbath day a delight! This is the praise of the Sabbath Day:* that on it God rested from all His work. And the Seventh Day gives praise saying: 'A psalm, a song for the Sabbath Day. It is good to thank HASHEM . . .'[1] Therefore let all that He has fashioned glorify* and bless God. Praise, honor, and greatness let them render to God, the King Who fashioned everything, Who gives a heritage of contentment to His People, Israel, in His holiness on the holy Sabbath Day. May Your Name, HASHEM, our God, be sanctified and may Your remembrance, Our King, be glorified in the heaven above and upon the earth below. May You be blessed, our Savior, beyond the praises of Your handiwork and beyond the brilliant luminaries that You have made — may they glorify You — Selah.*

(1) *Psalms* 92:1-2.

the Sabbath is a praise to God; alternatively, the 'praise' can be understood as the Song of the Day for the Sabbath.

לְפִיכָךְ יְפָאֲרוּ — *Therefore let all . . . glorify.* As the prayer goes on to say, the reason that Creation glorifies God is that He has given the Sabbath to Israel. By observing the Sabbath and absorbing its holiness, Israel brings a higher degree of fulfillment and holiness to the entire universe.

ON ALL DAYS CONTINUE HERE:

תִּתְבָּרַךְ צוּרֵנוּ* מַלְכֵּנוּ וְגֹאֲלֵנוּ,* בּוֹרֵא קְדוֹשִׁים. יִשְׁתַּבַּח שִׁמְךָ לָעַד מַלְכֵּנוּ, יוֹצֵר מְשָׁרְתִים,* וַאֲשֶׁר מְשָׁרְתָיו כֻּלָּם עוֹמְדִים בְּרוּם עוֹלָם, וּמַשְׁמִיעִים בְּיִרְאָה יַחַד בְּקוֹל דִּבְרֵי אֱלֹהִים חַיִּים וּמֶלֶךְ עוֹלָם.[1] כֻּלָּם אֲהוּבִים, כֻּלָּם בְּרוּרִים, כֻּלָּם גִּבּוֹרִים, וְכֻלָּם עֹשִׂים בְּאֵימָה וּבְיִרְאָה רְצוֹן קוֹנָם. ❖ וְכֻלָּם פּוֹתְחִים אֶת פִּיהֶם בִּקְדֻשָּׁה וּבְטָהֳרָה, בְּשִׁירָה וּבְזִמְרָה, וּמְבָרְכִים וּמְשַׁבְּחִים וּמְפָאֲרִים וּמַעֲרִיצִים וּמַקְדִּישִׁים וּמַמְלִיכִים —

אֶת שֵׁם הָאֵל הַמֶּלֶךְ הַגָּדוֹל הַגִּבּוֹר וְהַנּוֹרָא קָדוֹשׁ הוּא.[2] ❖ וְכֻלָּם מְקַבְּלִים עֲלֵיהֶם עֹל מַלְכוּת שָׁמַיִם זֶה מִזֶּה,* וְנוֹתְנִים רְשׁוּת זֶה לָזֶה, לְהַקְדִּישׁ לְיוֹצְרָם, בְּנַחַת רוּחַ בְּשָׂפָה בְרוּרָה וּבִנְעִימָה. קְדֻשָּׁה כֻּלָּם כְּאֶחָד עוֹנִים וְאוֹמְרִים בְּיִרְאָה:

Congregation recites aloud:

קָדוֹשׁ קָדוֹשׁ קָדוֹשׁ* יהוה צְבָאוֹת,*
מְלֹא כָל הָאָרֶץ כְּבוֹדוֹ.[3]

⊲§ **תִּתְבָּרַךְ צוּרֵנוּ** — *May You be blessed, our Rock.* The previous paragraph expressed man's praise of God for having created the heavenly bodies. They are indeed outstanding manifestations of God's greatness, as the prophet Isaiah put it, *Raise your eyes up high and see Who created these (Isaiah* 40:26). The heavenly bodies, like the angels, are agents of God that carry out His will in conducting the universe. Thus, the sun's role in giving light, heat, and energy and the moon's role in causing the tides are in reality not demonstrations of their own power, but of the means God utilizes to carry out those functions of nature according to His will. If perceived accurately, such aspects of creation bear testimony to the existence of an omniscient, omnipotent Creator.

However, they can be understood perversely as well. *Rambam (Hil. Avodah Zarah* 1:1-2) notes that man began to view the heavenly bodies first as servants of God that should be honored and glorified for the sake of their Maker. Eventually they went further and built temples and brought offerings to them. All of this is forbidden idolatry, but at least the people guilty of these practices acknowledged that the objects of their homage were creatures of God. In time, the practice deteriorated to the point where false prophets and their followers went so far as to say that such objects and graven images of them and other creatures were actually gods with independent powers.

In contrast to such perversity and heresy, we now proclaim that the very bodies that man perceives as being so mighty — the sun and other heavenly bodies — are but part of the heavenly forces that themselves stand in awe before God and are privileged to proclaim His praises *(Kol Bo).*

צוּרֵנוּ מַלְכֵּנוּ וְגֹאֲלֵנוּ — *Our Rock, our King, and our Redeemer.* These three appellations for God allude to the three broad stages of creation as described by the Talmud *(Avodah Zarah* 9a): The world in its present form will endure for six thousand years including two thousand years of emptiness, two thousand years of Torah, and two thousand years of the days of Messiah. The first period continued until Abraham was fifty-two years old. In those days, the Torah had not yet been given nor were its teachings widespread. Those were days of emptiness, when God was צוּרֵנוּ, *our Rock,* in the sense that He was the Creator and Stronghold of the universe, but was not acknowledged. Then Abraham began to remake man's understanding of the world. Thus began the era of Torah and its teachings, a time during which the Jewish nation came into being to teach that God was מַלְכֵּנוּ, *our King,* to Whom we owe total allegiance. The final period of two

ON ALL DAYS CONTINUE HERE:

תִּתְבָּרַךְ *May You be blessed, our Rock,* our King and our Redeemer,* Creator of holy ones; may Your Name be praised forever, our King, O Fashioner of ministering angels;* all of Whose ministering angels stand at the summit of the universe and proclaim — with awe, together, loudly — the words of the living God and King of the universe.*[1] *They are all beloved; they are all flawless; they are all mighty; they all do the will of their Maker with dread and reverence.* Chazzan– *And they all open their mouth in holiness and purity, in song and hymn — and bless, praise, glorify, revere, sanctify and declare the kingship of —*

אֶת שֵׁם *The Name of God, the great, mighty, and awesome King; holy is He.*[2] Chazzan– *Then they all accept upon themselves the yoke of heavenly sovereignty from one another,* and grant permission to one another to sanctify the One Who formed them, with tranquillity, with clear articulation, and with sweetness. All of them as one proclaim His holiness and say with awe:*

Congregation recites aloud:

'Holy, holy, holy* is HASHEM, Master of Legions,* the whole world is filled with His glory.'[3]

(1) Cf. *Jeremiah* 10:10. (2) Cf. *Deuteronomy* 10:17; *Psalms* 99:3. (3) *Isaiah* 6:3.

thousand years began after the destruction of the Temple. Despite the chaos, hardship, persecution, and slaughters of these dark years of exile, it is a time when the conditions for the ultimate and final Redemption are being formed. Hard though it is to understand, these are the centuries when God will eventually come to be recognized as גֹּאֲלֵנוּ, *our Redeemer* (*Siddur Sha'ar HaRachamim*).

קְדוֹשִׁים ... מְשָׁרְתִים — *Holy ones ... ministering angels.* Generally speaking, there are two forms of angels. The first and holier kind never take physical form and have no part in controlling material existence. These *holy ones* are spiritual beings whose closeness to God is most intense. Below them are the *ministering angels,* who are charged with tasks relating to the universe and man. They 'minister' to such matters as health, rain, prosperity, punishment, and so on. These angels sometimes take human form as found in the narratives of Scriptures (*Iyun Tefillah*).

The creation of these heavenly beings is expressed in the present tense, because God constantly creates new angels as He desires and as they are needed to serve Him (*Etz Yosef*).

וְכֻלָּם מְקַבְּלִים ... זֶה מִזֶּה — *Then they all accept ... from one another. Tanna d'Bei Eliyahu* contrasts the behavior of the angels with that of human beings. Unlike people whose competitive jealousies cause them to thwart and outdo one another, the angels urge one another to take the initiative in serving and praising God. Conflict is the foe of perfection, harmony is its ally.

⁂ קָדוֹשׁ קָדוֹשׁ קָדוֹשׁ — *Holy, holy, holy. Targum Yonasan* (*Isaiah* 6:3) renders: *Holy* in the most exalted heaven, the abode of His Presence; *holy* on earth, product of His strength; *holy* forever and ever is HASHEM, Master of Legions ...

כָּבוֹד, *glory,* refers to the glory of God that is present *within* the material world; it is the degree of Godliness that man is capable of perceiving even within creation. קָדוֹשׁ, *holy,* on the other hand, refers to God's essence, which is beyond all comprehension.

צְבָאוֹת — *Master of Legions.* Although it is commonly translated simply as *hosts* or *legions,* the word צְבָאוֹת is a Name of God (see *Shevuos* 35a), which means that He is the *Master* of all the heavenly hosts. The word צָבָא is used to refer to an organized, disciplined group. Thus, an army is commonly called צָבָא. In the context of this Divine Name, it refers to the idea that the infinite heavenly bodies are organized according to God's will to do His service.

FIRST DAY

רֹאשׁוֹ* כֶּתֶם פָּז,[1]
תָּג עִטּוּר כֶּתֶר,
תַּחַן יוֹחַן עֶתֶר,*
שִׁכְנוֹ בְּיוֹשֵׁב סֵתֶר,
שָׁלִיחַ מְפֹרָשׁ פּוֹתֵר,
רָם וְנִשָּׂא בְּיוֹתֵר,
רַב בִּנְיָן וְסוֹתֵר,
קוֹרְאָיו פֶּתַח חוֹתֵר,
קַבֵּל כְּנִתּוּחַ בָּתֶר.[2]

עֵינָיו כְּיוֹנִים,[2]
צַד רִבּוּעַ דְּפַנִּים,
צוֹפוֹת צְפוֹת צְפוּנִים,
פְּתוּחוֹת שִׂיחַ סְפוּנִים,
פּוֹנוֹת לְאֵלָיו פּוֹנִים,
עָתִיד וְגָנוּז פְּנִינִים,
עָרוּךְ נֶגְדּוֹ מִלְּפָנִים,
סְכִיוֹנוֹ אֵין לְפָנִים,
שְׂרָפִים וְחַיּוֹת וְאוֹפַנִּים.

לְחָיָו,[3]
נְטוּף מוֹר לְקָחִים,
נְעִימִים אֲמָרִים מַלְקוֹחִים,
מִגְדְּלוֹת מֶרְקַח רִקּוּחִים,
מַתַּן לְנֶפֶשׁ פִּקּוּחִים,
לוּחוֹת חֲרוּת* מְשִׂיחִים,
לֵב עָלוּב מְשַׂמְּחִים,
כְּאֵב מַמְרִיחִים וּמוֹשְׁחִים,
כַּעֲרוּגוֹת עֲרֵבִים שִׂיחִים.

יָדָיו[4]
יְדֵי אָדָם[5] פְּשׁוּטוֹת,
יְצוּרָיו לְקַבֵּל מִלְּשְׁטוֹת,

SECOND DAY

גַּן נָעוּל,[6]
אִוָּה שׁוֹכֵן תַּרְשִׁישִׁים.
שְׁלָחַיִךְ,[7]
בָּחַר כְּעִירִין וְקַדִּישִׁין.
נֵרְדְּ וְכַרְכֹּם,[8]
גֹּמֶר תִּמְרוֹתַיִךְ לְהַעֲשִׁין.
מַעְיַן,[9]
דָּלוּחַ גָּעַל וְהֶאֱשִׁים.
עוּרִי,[10]
הַמַּצֶּבֶת רַהַב לְגָזִים.[11]
בָּאתִי,[12]
וְהוּשַׁת לִי דֶּרֶךְ בְּעַזִּים.
אֲנִי יְשֵׁנָה,[13]
זָךְ הִנְנִי בַּחֲרוּזִים.
פָּשַׁטְתִּי,[14]
חֶלְיָתִי בִּבְרָעִי לִתְרָזִים.

דּוֹדִי,[15]
טִכְּסַנִי תַּבְנִית מֶרְכָּבוֹ.*
קַמְתִּי,[16]
יִחַדְתִּיו כַּחֲצוּבֵי שַׁלְהָבוֹ.
פָּתַחְתִּי,[17]
כְּבוֹדוֹ חָמַק מִלָּבֹא.
מְצָאֻנִי,[18]
לוֹחֲמֵי פְּצָעֻנִי בְּנָווֹ.
הִשְׁבַּעְתִּי,[19]
מַחֲלָתִי לְדוֹדִי לְחַוּוֹת.
מַה דּוֹדֵךְ,[20]
נָמוּ אֲלָתִי קְשָׁבוֹת.
דּוֹדִי,[21]
סִלְסוּלוֹ בְּרִבֵּי רְבָבוֹת.

⋄ **רֹאשׁוֹ** — *His head.* This *piyut*, following the pattern of the previous one, begins each stanza with a verse from *Song of Songs*. The remaining stiches of the respective stanzas form a doubled, reverse alphabetic acrostic (תשר״ק) followed by the author's signature שְׁלֹמֹה חֲזַק, *Shlomo, may he be strong.*

תָּג עִטּוּר כֶּתֶר תַּחַן יוֹחַן עֶתֶר — *A triple crown of tripled prayer.* The three words תָּג עִטּוּר כֶּתֶר all mean *crown*; and the words תַּחַן יוֹחַן עֶתֶר all mean *prayer*. The tripled prayer alludes to the just concluded verse, קָדוֹשׁ קָדוֹשׁ קָדוֹשׁ, *Holy, holy, holy* ... The triple crown refers to talmudic teaching: There is an angel ... named Sandalfon ... who stands behind the Divine Chariot wearing crowns for his Creator (*Chagigah* 13b). These crowns are woven from the prayers of the righteous (*Tosafos*). This is the meaning of the *Kedushah* recited at *Mussaf* [according to *Nusach Sefard*] which begins: כֶּתֶר יִתְּנוּ לְךָ׳, *A crown will they give You, O HASHEM, our God — the angels of the multitude above, together with Your people Israel who are assembled below'* (*Rabbeinu Chananel*).

FIRST DAY	SECOND DAY
His head encircled with the finest gold[1] —* ת *a triple crown,* ת *of tripled prayer* —* ש *for Him Whose Presence dwells in the Hidden place.* ש *His angel interprets and explains,* ר *[the prayers that crown] the One Who is extremely high and exalted,* ר *the Great One Who builds and destroys [at His will].* ק *He opens a passageway for those who call to Him,* ק *to receive [their prayers] as if they were [offerings] cut into portions.* *His eyes are like doves [seeking water],[2]* צ *gazing in all four directions,* צ *watching those engrossed in the [Torah's] secrets,* פ *opening major wellsprings [of knowledge] for them,* פ *turning to those who turn to Him.* ע *[Their] future [reward] stored in inner sanctums,* ע *have been arranged before Him from earliest times,* ס *visions of it never before seen,* ס *[even by] Seraphim, Chayos and Ofanim.* *His cheeks,[3]* נ *dripping with the myrrh of the Torah,* נ *the sweet sayings of His palate,* מ *like incense and blended spices,* מ *a present to the soul of the wise,* ל *the Tablets that bespeak freedom,** ל *that gladden the saddened heart,* כ *that anoint and bandage aching wounds,* כ *that are like rows of luscious fruit trees.* *His hands are[4]* י *like a man's hands[5] outstretched,* י *to receive His creatures that they not go astray.*	*[O Israel, chaste as] a locked garden,[6]* א *He Who dwells among marble-like angels longs . . .* *For your offspring,[7]* ב *whom He has chosen to serve Him as do the angelic Irin and Kaddishin.* *Nard and Saffron[8]* ג *has He censed, to raise a column of smoke [at Sinai].* *While the [Egyptian] wellspring[9]* ד *turned stagnant, disgusting and guilt-ridden.* *Awaken[10]* ה *[O hand] that hacked Rahab [Egypt] to pieces,[11]* *That I may pass;[12]* ו *and set a road for me through the raging waters.* *I had been sleeping [in the Egyptian exile],[13]* ז *and the Pure One beautified me with jeweled bands.* *But I removed from myself[14]* ח *my jewels, when I kneeled to idols.* *My Beloved[15]* ט *arranged my camp in the form of His Chariot.** *[When] I arose [in the morning],"[16]* י *I declared His Oneness as do the fiery angels,* *[But then,] I opened [my heart to idolatry],[17]* כ *and His honor went into hiding.* *They [the Babylonians] found me,[18]* ל *my enemy beat me in His Temple.* *I adjured [the nations][19]* מ *to tell my Beloved of my [love] sickness.* *'What is [so special about] your Beloved?'[20]* נ *said those who heard my oath.* *'My Beloved,[21]* ס *His praise is extolled by myriad myriads;*

(1) *Song of Songs* 5:11. (2) 5:12. (3) 5:13. (4) 5:14. (5) See *Ezekiel* 1:8. (6) *Song of Songs* 4:12. (7) 4:13. (8) 4:14. (9) 4:15. (10) 4:16. (11) Cf. *Isaiah* 51:9. (12) *Song* 5:1. (13) 5:2. (14) 5:3. (15) 5:4. (16) 5:5. (17) 5:6. (18) 5:7. (19) 5:8. (20) 5:9. (21) 5:10.

לוּחוֹת חֵרוּת מְשִׂיחִים — *The Tablets that bespeak freedom.* The Mishnah expounds on the verse חָרוּת עַל הַלֻּחֹת, *engraved on the Tablets* (*Exodus* 32:16): Since the Torah is written without vowel-points we may read חֵרוּת, *freedom* in place of חָרוּת, *engraved*, for you can have no freer man than one who engages in Torah study (*Avos* 6:2).

טִכְּסַנִי תַּבְנִית מֶרְכָּבוֹ — *Arranged my camp in the form of His Chariot.* The Divine Chariot is described in the first chapter of *Ezekiel*. It is borne by four *Chayos*, each with a four-faced head — a man's face, a lion's, a bull's, and an eagle's. The Israelite encampment is described in *Numbers* (ch. 2). The camp was laid out in a square with

FIRST DAY

טוֹעִים הֶֽרֶךְ קוֹשְׁטוֹת,
טֶֽרֶף לַכֹּל מוֹשִׁיטוֹת,
חֲזָקוֹת וּמַחֲזִיקוֹת מָטוֹת,
חִישׁ מְדֶֽחִי מִלְּקְטוֹת,
זְכוּת מְגַלְגְּלוֹת וּמַטּוֹת,
זַֽעַם הַדִּין מִלְּנְטוֹת.
שׁוֹקָיו[1]
וַֽעַד כָּתְלֵֽנוּ מְצָרֵף,*
וְתַֽחַת רַגְלָיו שְׁרַפְרֵף,
הֲדוֹמוֹ[2] מַרְעִיד וּמְרַפְרֵף,
הַיָּם מַלְחִיךְ וּמְשָׂרֵף.
חִכּוֹ מַמְתַקִּים,[3]
דַּת מְשָׁלִים עַתִּיקִים,
גּוֹזֵר אֹמֶר וּמֵקִים,
בִּדְבָרוֹ שִׁפַּר שְׁחָקִים,
אָמַר וַיִּקְרָא אֲרָקִים.
שְׁבָחוֹ לִגְיוֹנָיו מְפִיקִים,
הֲמוּלַּת הֲמוֹן אֲפִיקִים,
חָלִים זָעִים
קְרִיאַת שִׁלּוּשׁ קְדֻשָּׁה מַסְפִּיקִים.

SECOND DAY

רֹאשׁוֹ,[4]
עָטוּר רְכוּבוֹ בָּעֲרָבוֹת.[5]
עֵינָיו כְּיוֹנִים,[6]
פּוֹנוֹת בְּכָל חֶבְיוֹנִים.
לְחָיָו כַּעֲרוּגוֹת,[7]
צוֹמְחוֹת בֹּשֶׂם רִגְיוֹנִים.*
יָדָיו,[8]
קְשׁוּטוֹת מְקַבְּלוֹת הֶגְיוֹנִים.
שׁוֹקָיו,[9]
רָמוּ לַהֲדֹךְ גֵּאוֹנִים.
חִכּוֹ מַמְתַקִּים,[10]
שַׁעֲשׁוּעַ מִדְרָשׁ וְחֻקִּים.
אָנָה הָלַךְ,[11]
שֶׁרַעְיָתוֹ מַדְּקִים וְשׁוֹחֲקִים.
דּוֹדִי,[12]
תְּפוּצוֹתַי יְכַנֵּס מִמֶּרְחַקִּים.
אֲנִי,[13]
תִּפְאַרְתּוֹ אֲשַׁנֵּן
כְּלוֹהֲטִים הַמִּתְלַהֲקִים.

Congregation, followed by the *chazzan,* recites one of these versions, according to its tradition.

וְהָאוֹפַנִּים* וְחַיּוֹת הַקֹּֽדֶשׁ בְּרַֽעַשׁ גָּדוֹל מִתְנַשְּׂאִים לְעֻמַּת שְׂרָפִים. לְעֻמָּתָם מְשַׁבְּחִים וְאוֹמְרִים:

וְהַחַיּוֹת יְשׁוֹרֵֽרוּ,* וּכְרוּבִים יְפָאֵֽרוּ, וּשְׂרָפִים יָרֹֽנּוּ, וְאֶרְאֶלִּים יְבָרֵֽכוּ. פְּנֵי כָּל חַיָּה וְאוֹפָן וּכְרוּב לְעֻמַּת שְׂרָפִים. לְעֻמָּתָם מְשַׁבְּחִים וְאוֹמְרִים:

Congregation recites aloud:

בָּרוּךְ כְּבוֹד יהוה מִמְּקוֹמוֹ.[14]*

three tribes on each side, one of the three being appointed as the chief tribe for the side. Each group of three tribes was named for its chief tribe. Thus, for example, the eastern three tribes were called collectively דֶּגֶל מַחֲנֵה יְהוּדָה, *the Banner of Judah's camp.* According to a Midrash cited by *Matteh Levi*, each of the four banners bore a likeness of one of the faces of the celestial *Chayos*.

וַעַד כָּתְלֵנוּ מְצָרֵף — *Eternally bound to our wall.* The שְׁכִינָה, *Divine Presence*, has never left the כּוֹתֶל הַמַּעֲרָבִי, *Western Wall (Tanchuma,* ed. Buber, *Shemos* 10).

רִגְיוֹנִים — *Desirous.* This translation is based on the *Targum's* rendering of וְלֹא תִתְאַוֶּה, *You shall not desire* (*Deuteronomy* 5:18), as וְלָא תַרוֹג. Alternatively, רִגְיוֹן, *Rigyon*, is another name for נְהַר דִּי־נוּר, *the River of Fire* (*Daniel* 7:10). This river serves many functions: angels who have completed their missions have become superfluous and are destroyed in it; new angels are created from it; the angels preparing to recite *Kedushah* immerse in it; as in a *mikveh*. Accordingly, בּוֹשֶׂם רִגְיוֹנִים would mean 'spices that grow alongside the River Rigyon,' thus, heavenly or angelic spices.

קְשׁוּטוֹת — *Aligned.* Although many *machzorim* read פְּשׁוּטוֹת, *outstretched,* we have followed *Ra'avan* who reads קְשׁוּטוֹת, *trued,* or *aligned.* The reading פְּשׁוּטוֹת is puzzling since the *piyut* follows an *aleph-beis* scheme, a word beginning

FIRST DAY

ט *even those who have wandered from the true way.*
ט *They extend sustenance to all,*
ח *they are strong, they support the fallen,*
ח *they hasten to protect from stumbling,*
ז *they tilt the scales toward merit,*
ז *and replace anger [with kindness] in time of judgment.*

His legs[1]
ו *eternally bound to our wall,**
ו *under His feet a low bench,*
ה *His footstool*[2] *trembles with weakness,*
ה *He evaporates and scorches the sea.*

His palate is sweet,[3]
ד *with ancient law and parable,*
ג *He decrees, says and fulfills.*
ב *He shaped the heavens with His words,*
א *He spoke and summoned forth the earth.*
שלם *His legions bring forth His praise,*
ה *the roar of the powerful multitudes,*
חזק *trembling, shaking, as they clap [their wings] and recite the trebled Kedushah.*

SECOND DAY

His head[4]
ע *is crowned [with prayers]; His chariot is in the heavens.*[5]

His eyes are like doves[6]
פ *peering into hidden places.*
[The words of] His cheeks are like rows[7]
צ *sprouting desirous* spices.*
His hands[8]
ק *are aligned* to receive heartfelt prayers.*
His legs[9]
ר *are tall to trample the haughty.*

[The words of] His palate are sweet,[10]
ש *delightful with exegesis and laws.*
Where has He gone,[11]
ש *that His companion has been ground into dust?*

My Beloved[12]
ת *will gather my dispersed from afar.*
And I will[13]
ת *relate His glory as do the massing fiery angels.*

Congregation, followed by the *chazzan,* recites one of these versions, according to its tradition.

Then the Ofanim and the holy Chayos, with great noise, raise themselves towards the Seraphim. Facing them they give praise saying:*

Then the Chayos sing, the Cherubim glorify, the Seraphim rejoice, and the Erelim bless, in the presence of every Chayah, Ofan, and Cherub towards the Seraphim. Facing them they give praise saying:*

Congregation recites aloud:

'Blessed is the glory of HASHEM from His place.'*[14]

(1) *Song of Songs* 5:15. (2) See *Isaiah* 66:1. (3) *Song of Songs* 5:16. (4) 5:11. (5) Cf. *Psalms* 68:5. (6) *Song of Songs* 5:12. (7) 5:13. (8) 5:14. (9) 5:15. (10) 5:16. (11) 6:1. (12) 6:2. (13) 6:3. (14) *Ezekiel* 3:12.

with ק is expected here. Moreover, *R' Wolf Heidenheim* states that קְשׁוּטוֹת is the version he found in all the manuscript *machzorim* to which he had access (*Maaseh Oreig*).

◆§ וְהָאוֹפַנִּים — *Then the Ofanim.* The varieties of angels are not translated since we lack the vocabulary to define them. *Rambam (Yesodei HaTorah* 2:7) notes that there are ten levels of angels. Their names are *Chayos, Ofanim, Erelim, Chashmalim, Seraphim, Malachim, Elohim, Bnai Elohim, Cherubim,* and *Ishim.*

◆§ וְהַחַיּוֹת יְשׁוֹרֵרוּ – *Then the Chayos sing.* In keeping with the expanded liturgy of Rosh Hashanah, some congregations set forth lyrically how the various categories of angels render praise, each in its own way. Other congregations do not deviate from the text recited every day of the year.

◆§ בָּרוּךְ . . . מִמְּקוֹמוֹ — *Blessed . . . from His place.* 'Place' refers to a particular position or level of eminence. For example, we say that a person 'takes his father's place.' But in the case of God — all we can do is bless His eminence as *we* perceive it coming to us *from* His place. In other words, we see Him acting as Sustainer, Healer, Judge, Life-giver and so on, but we don't know what He really is. Though the angels have a better knowledge of God than people, they too have no comprehension of His true essence *(Nefesh HaChaim).*

לְאֵל בָּרוּךְ* נְעִימוֹת יִתֵּנוּ. לְמֶלֶךְ* אֵל חַי וְקַיָּם, זְמִרוֹת יֹאמֵרוּ, וְתִשְׁבָּחוֹת יַשְׁמִיעוּ. כִּי הוּא לְבַדּוֹ פּוֹעֵל גְּבוּרוֹת, עֹשֶׂה חֲדָשׁוֹת, בַּעַל מִלְחָמוֹת, זוֹרֵעַ צְדָקוֹת,* מַצְמִיחַ יְשׁוּעוֹת, בּוֹרֵא רְפוּאוֹת, נוֹרָא תְהִלּוֹת, אֲדוֹן הַנִּפְלָאוֹת. הַמְּחַדֵּשׁ בְּטוּבוֹ בְּכָל יוֹם תָּמִיד מַעֲשֵׂה בְרֵאשִׁית. כָּאָמוּר: לְעֹשֵׂה אוֹרִים גְּדֹלִים, כִּי לְעוֹלָם חַסְדּוֹ.[1] ❖ אוֹר חָדָשׁ* עַל צִיּוֹן תָּאִיר, וְנִזְכֶּה כֻלָּנוּ מְהֵרָה לְאוֹרוֹ. בָּרוּךְ אַתָּה יהוה, יוֹצֵר הַמְּאוֹרוֹת. (Cong.– אָמֵן.)

אַהֲבָה רַבָּה* אֲהַבְתָּנוּ יהוה אֱלֹהֵינוּ, חֶמְלָה גְדוֹלָה וִיתֵרָה חָמַלְתָּ עָלֵינוּ. אָבִינוּ מַלְכֵּנוּ, בַּעֲבוּר אֲבוֹתֵינוּ שֶׁבָּטְחוּ בְךָ, וַתְּלַמְּדֵם חֻקֵּי חַיִּים, כֵּן תְּחָנֵּנוּ וּתְלַמְּדֵנוּ. אָבִינוּ הָאָב הָרַחֲמָן הַמְּרַחֵם, רַחֵם עָלֵינוּ, וְתֵן בְּלִבֵּנוּ לְהָבִין וּלְהַשְׂכִּיל, לִשְׁמֹעַ לִלְמוֹד וּלְלַמֵּד, לִשְׁמֹר וְלַעֲשׂוֹת וּלְקַיֵּם אֶת כָּל דִּבְרֵי תַלְמוּד תּוֹרָתֶךָ בְּאַהֲבָה. וְהָאֵר עֵינֵינוּ* בְּתוֹרָתֶךָ,* וְדַבֵּק לִבֵּנוּ בְּמִצְוֹתֶיךָ, וְיַחֵד לְבָבֵנוּ* לְאַהֲבָה וּלְיִרְאָה אֶת שְׁמֶךָ,[2] וְלֹא נֵבוֹשׁ לְעוֹלָם וָעֶד.* כִּי בְשֵׁם קָדְשְׁךָ הַגָּדוֹל וְהַנּוֹרָא בָּטָחְנוּ, נָגִילָה וְנִשְׂמְחָה בִּישׁוּעָתֶךָ.

At this point, gather the four *tzitzis* between the fourth and fifth fingers of the left hand. Hold *tzitzis* in this manner throughout the *Shema*.

וַהֲבִיאֵנוּ לְשָׁלוֹם מֵאַרְבַּע כַּנְפוֹת הָאָרֶץ, וְתוֹלִיכֵנוּ קוֹמְמִיּוּת לְאַרְצֵנוּ. כִּי אֵל פּוֹעֵל יְשׁוּעוֹת אָתָּה, וּבָנוּ בָחַרְתָּ מִכָּל עַם וְלָשׁוֹן. ❖ וְקֵרַבְתָּנוּ לְשִׁמְךָ הַגָּדוֹל סֶלָה בֶּאֱמֶת, לְהוֹדוֹת לְךָ וּלְיַחֶדְךָ בְּאַהֲבָה. בָּרוּךְ אַתָּה יהוה, הַבּוֹחֵר בְּעַמּוֹ יִשְׂרָאֵל בְּאַהֲבָה. (Cong.– אָמֵן.)

⊲§ לְאֵל בָּרוּךְ — *To the blessed God.* Earlier in this *Shema* blessing (p. 294), we recited a twenty-two word *Aleph-Beis* acrostic that began with this same expression: אֵל בָּרוּךְ, *the blessed God.* Now, in keeping with the general principle regarding a long blessing, we conclude it by returning to the theme with which the blessing began. Thus, we return to the theme of *the blessed God,* Whom we gratefully praise for His works of creation in general and the heavenly luminaries in particular — upon which we will conclude by blessing Him as יוֹצֵר הַמְּאוֹרוֹת, *[God] Who fashions the luminaries.*

לְאֵל ... לְמֶלֶךְ — *To the ... God ... to the King.* The commentators differ regarding the vocalization of these two words. Many hold that they are read לָאֵל and לַמֶּלֶךְ. We have followed the version of most *siddurim,* but every congregation should maintain its custom.

זוֹרֵעַ צְדָקוֹת — *Sows kindnesses.* God does not merely reward man for his good deeds; He rewards him even for the chain reaction that results from human kindness. Thus, an act of kindness is like a seed that can produce luxuriant vegetation *(Etz Yosef).*

אוֹר חָדָשׁ — *A new light.* The *new* light is actually a return of the original brilliance of creation. That light was concealed for the enjoyment of the righteous in the Messianic era. May it soon shine upon Zion *(Yaavetz).*

⊲§ אַהֲבָה רַבָּה — *With an abundant love.* Up to now, we have blessed God for having created the luminaries, but there is a light even greater than that of the brightest stars and the sun — the light of the Torah. Now, in this second blessing before *Shema,* we thank God for the Torah and pray that He grant us the wisdom to understand it properly *(Yaavetz; R' Munk).*

וְהָאֵר עֵינֵינוּ — *Enlighten our eyes.* This begins a series of brief supplications with one general

לְאֵל *To the blessed God* they shall offer sweet melodies; to the King,* the living and enduring God, they shall sing hymns and proclaim praises. For He alone effects mighty deeds, makes new things, is Master of wars, sows kindnesses,* makes salvations flourish, creates cures, is too awesome for praise, is Lord of wonders. In His goodness He renews daily, perpetually, the work of creation. As it is said: '[Give thanks] to Him Who makes the great luminaries, for His kindness endures forever.'*[1] Chazzan– *May You shine a new light* on Zion, and may we all speedily merit its light. Blessed are You,* HASHEM, *Who fashions the luminaries.* (Cong.– *Amen.)*

אַהֲבָה *With an abundant love* have You loved us,* HASHEM, *our God; with exceedingly great pity have You pitied us. Our Father, our King, for the sake of our forefathers who trusted in You and whom You taught the decrees of life, may You be equally gracious to us and teach us. Our Father, the merciful Father, Who acts mercifully, have mercy upon us, instill in our hearts to understand and elucidate, to listen, learn, teach, safeguard, perform, and fulfill all the words of Your Torah's teaching with love. Enlighten our eyes* in Your Torah,* attach our hearts to Your commandments, and unify our hearts* to love and fear Your Name,*[2] *and may we not feel inner shame for all eternity.* Because we have trusted in Your great and awesome holy Name, may we exult and rejoice in Your salvation.*

At this point, gather the four *tzitzis* between the fourth and fifth fingers of the left hand. Hold *tzitzis* in this manner throughout the *Shema.*

Bring us in peacefulness from the four corners of the earth and lead us with upright pride to our land. For You effect salvations, O God; You have chosen us from among every people and tongue. Chazzan– *And You have brought us close to Your great Name forever in truth, to offer praiseful thanks to You, and proclaim Your Oneness with love. Blessed are You,* HASHEM, *Who chooses His people Israel with love.* (Cong.– *Amen.)*

(1) *Psalms* 136:7. (2) Cf. 86:11.

purpose: A Jew's involvement with Torah study and observance must saturate all his activities, even his business, leisure, and social life.

בְּתוֹרָתֶךָ — *In Your Torah.* Enlighten us so that we may understand all aspects of Your Torah.

וְיַחֵד לְבָבֵנוּ — *And unify our hearts.* Man's likes and needs propel him in many directions. We ask God to unify our emotions and wishes to serve Him in love and fear.

וְלֹא נֵבוֹשׁ לְעוֹלָם וָעֶד — *And may we not feel inner shame for all eternity.* Inner shame is the humiliation one feels deep within himself when he knows he has done wrong — even though the people around him may sing his praises. The cost of such shame is borne primarily in the World to Come, where it can diminish one's eternal bliss or even destroy it entirely. Therefore we pray that our eternity not be marred by inner shame.

שְׁמַע / THE SHEMA

The recitation of *Shema* is required by the Torah, and one must have in mind that he is about to fulfill this commandment. Although one should try to concentrate on the meaning of all three paragraphs, one must concentrate at least on the meaning of the first verse (שְׁמַע) and the second verse (בָּרוּךְ שֵׁם) because this represents fulfillment of the paramount *mitzvah* of acceptance of God's absolute sovereignty (קַבָּלַת עוֹל מַלְכוּת שָׁמַיִם). By declaring that God is One, Unique, and Indivisible, we subordinate every facet of our personalities, possessions — our very lives — to His will.

In the שְׁמַע we have included the cantillation symbols *(trop)* for the convenience of those who recite שְׁמַע in the manner it is read from the Torah. Nevertheless, to enable those unfamiliar with this notation to group the words properly,

שמע

Immediately before its recitation concentrate on fulfilling the positive commandment of reciting the *Shema* twice daily. It is important to enunciate each word clearly and not to run words together. For this reason, vertical lines have been placed between two words that are prone to be slurred into one and are not separated by a comma or a hyphen. See *Laws* §40-55.

When praying without a *minyan,* begin with the following three-word formula:

אֵל מֶלֶךְ נֶאֱמָן.

Recite the first verse aloud, with the right hand covering the eyes, and concentrate intently upon accepting God's absolute sovereignty.

שְׁמַע | יִשְׂרָאֵל, יְהוָה | אֱלֹהֵינוּ, יְהוָה | אֶחָד:

In an undertone – בָּרוּךְ שֵׁם כְּבוֹד מַלְכוּתוֹ לְעוֹלָם וָעֶד.

While reciting the first paragraph (דברים ו:ה-ט), concentrate on accepting the commandment to love God.

וְאָהַבְתָּ אֵת | יְהוָה | אֱלֹהֶיךָ, בְּכָל־לְבָבְךָ, וּבְכָל־נַפְשְׁךָ, וּבְכָל־
מְאֹדֶךָ: וְהָיוּ הַדְּבָרִים הָאֵלֶּה, אֲשֶׁר | אָנֹכִי מְצַוְּךָ הַיּוֹם,
עַל־לְבָבֶךָ: וְשִׁנַּנְתָּם לְבָנֶיךָ, וְדִבַּרְתָּ בָּם, בְּשִׁבְתְּךָ בְּבֵיתֶךָ, וּבְלֶכְתְּךָ
בַדֶּרֶךְ, וּבְשָׁכְבְּךָ וּבְקוּמֶךָ: וּקְשַׁרְתָּם לְאוֹת | עַל־יָדֶךָ, וְהָיוּ לְטֹטָפֹת
בֵּין | עֵינֶיךָ: וּכְתַבְתָּם | עַל־מְזֻזוֹת בֵּיתֶךָ, וּבִשְׁעָרֶיךָ:

While reciting the second paragraph (דברים יא:יג-כא), concentrate on accepting all the commandments and the concept of reward and punishment.

וְהָיָה, אִם־שָׁמֹעַ תִּשְׁמְעוּ אֶל־מִצְוֹתַי, אֲשֶׁר | אָנֹכִי מְצַוֶּה |
אֶתְכֶם הַיּוֹם, לְאַהֲבָה אֶת־יְהוָה | אֱלֹהֵיכֶם וּלְעָבְדוֹ,
בְּכָל־לְבַבְכֶם, וּבְכָל־נַפְשְׁכֶם: וְנָתַתִּי מְטַר־אַרְצְכֶם בְּעִתּוֹ, יוֹרֶה
וּמַלְקוֹשׁ, וְאָסַפְתָּ דְגָנֶךָ וְתִירֹשְׁךָ וְיִצְהָרֶךָ: וְנָתַתִּי | עֵשֶׂב | בְּשָׂדְךָ
לִבְהֶמְתֶּךָ, וְאָכַלְתָּ וְשָׂבָעְתָּ: הִשָּׁמְרוּ לָכֶם, פֶּן־יִפְתֶּה לְבַבְכֶם,
וְסַרְתֶּם וַעֲבַדְתֶּם | אֱלֹהִים | אֲחֵרִים, וְהִשְׁתַּחֲוִיתֶם לָהֶם: וְחָרָה |
אַף־יְהוָה בָּכֶם, וְעָצַר | אֶת־הַשָּׁמַיִם, וְלֹא־יִהְיֶה מָטָר, וְהָאֲדָמָה
לֹא תִתֵּן אֶת־יְבוּלָהּ, וַאֲבַדְתֶּם | מְהֵרָה מֵעַל הָאָרֶץ הַטֹּבָה | אֲשֶׁר
| יְהוָה נֹתֵן לָכֶם: וְשַׂמְתֶּם | אֶת־דְּבָרַי | אֵלֶּה, עַל־לְבַבְכֶם וְעַל־
נַפְשְׁכֶם, וּקְשַׁרְתֶּם | אֹתָם לְאוֹת | עַל־יֶדְכֶם, וְהָיוּ לְטוֹטָפֹת בֵּין |
עֵינֵיכֶם: וְלִמַּדְתֶּם | אֹתָם | אֶת־בְּנֵיכֶם, לְדַבֵּר בָּם, בְּשִׁבְתְּךָ
בְּבֵיתֶךָ, וּבְלֶכְתְּךָ בַדֶּרֶךְ, וּבְשָׁכְבְּךָ וּבְקוּמֶךָ: וּכְתַבְתָּם | עַל־מְזוּזוֹת
בֵּיתֶךָ, וּבִשְׁעָרֶיךָ: לְמַעַן | יִרְבּוּ | יְמֵיכֶם וִימֵי בְנֵיכֶם, עַל הָאֲדָמָה
| אֲשֶׁר נִשְׁבַּע | יְהוָה לַאֲבֹתֵיכֶם לָתֵת לָהֶם, כִּימֵי הַשָּׁמַיִם |
עַל־הָאָרֶץ:

THE SHEMA

Immediately before its recitation concentrate on fulfilling the positive commandment of reciting the *Shema* twice daily. It is important to enunciate each word clearly and not to run words together. See *Laws* §40-55.

When praying without a *minyan,* begin with the following three-word formula:
God, trustworthy King.

Recite the first verse aloud, with the right hand covering the eyes, and concentrate intently upon accepting God's absolute sovereignty.

Hear, O Israel: HASHEM is our God, HASHEM, the One and Only.[1]

In an undertone— *Blessed is the Name of His glorious kingdom for all eternity.*

While reciting the first paragraph (*Deuteronomy* 6:5-9), concentrate on accepting the commandment to love God.

וְאָהַבְתָּ *You shall love HASHEM, your God, with all your heart, with all your soul and with all your resources. Let these matters that I command you today be upon your heart. Teach them thoroughly to your children and speak of them while you sit in your home, while you walk on the way, when you retire and when you arise. Bind them as a sign upon your arm and let them be tefillin between your eyes. And write them on the doorposts of your house and upon your gates.*

While reciting the second paragraph (*Deuteronomy* 11:13-21), concentrate on accepting all the commandments and the concept of reward and punishment.

וְהָיָה *And it will come to pass that if you continually hearken to My commandments that I command you today, to love HASHEM, your God, and to serve Him, with all your heart and with all your soul — then I will provide rain for your land in its proper time, the early and late rains, that you may gather in your grain, your wine, and your oil. I will provide grass in your field for your cattle and you will eat and be satisfied. Beware lest your heart be seduced and you turn astray and serve gods of others and bow to them. Then the wrath of HASHEM will blaze against you. He will restrain the heaven so there will be no rain and the ground will not yield its produce. And you will swiftly be banished from the goodly land which HASHEM gives you. Place these words of Mine upon your heart and upon your soul; bind them for a sign upon your arm and let them be tefillin between your eyes. Teach them to your children, to discuss them, while you sit in your home, while you walk on the way, when you retire and when you arise. And write them on the doorposts of your house and upon your gates. In order to prolong your days and the days of your children upon the ground that HASHEM has sworn to your ancestors to give them, like the days of the heaven on the earth.*

(1) *Deuteronomy* 6:4.

commas have been inserted. Additionally, vertical lines have been placed between any two words that are prone to be slurred into one and are not separated by a comma or hyphen.

Before reciting the third paragraph (במדבר טו:לז-מא), the *tzitzis,* which have been held in the left hand, are taken in the right hand also. The *tzitzis* are kissed at each mention of the word and at the end of the paragraph, and are passed before the eyes at וּרְאִיתֶם אֹתוֹ.

וַיֹּאמֶר | יְהוָה | אֶל־מֹשֶׁה לֵּאמֹר: דַּבֵּר | אֶל־בְּנֵי | יִשְׂרָאֵל, וְאָמַרְתָּ אֲלֵהֶם, וְעָשׂוּ לָהֶם צִיצִת, עַל־כַּנְפֵי בִגְדֵיהֶם לְדֹרֹתָם, וְנָתְנוּ | עַל־צִיצִת הַכָּנָף, פְּתִיל תְּכֵלֶת: וְהָיָה לָכֶם לְצִיצִת, וּרְאִיתֶם | אֹתוֹ, וּזְכַרְתֶּם | אֶת־כָּל־מִצְוֹת | יְהוָה, וַעֲשִׂיתֶם | אֹתָם, וְלֹא תָתֻרוּ | אַחֲרֵי לְבַבְכֶם וְאַחֲרֵי | עֵינֵיכֶם, אֲשֶׁר־אַתֶּם זֹנִים | אַחֲרֵיהֶם: לְמַעַן תִּזְכְּרוּ, וַעֲשִׂיתֶם | אֶת־כָּל־מִצְוֹתָי, וִהְיִיתֶם קְדֹשִׁים לֵאלֹהֵיכֶם: אֲנִי יְהוָה | אֱלֹהֵיכֶם, אֲשֶׁר הוֹצֵאתִי | אֶתְכֶם | מֵאֶרֶץ מִצְרַיִם, לִהְיוֹת לָכֶם לֵאלֹהִים, אֲנִי | יְהוָה | אֱלֹהֵיכֶם: אֱמֶת —

Concentrate on fulfilling the commandment of remembering the Exodus from Egypt.

Although the word אֱמֶת belongs to the next paragraph, it is appended to the conclusion of the previous one, as explained in the commentary.

Chazzan repeats— **יְהוָה אֱלֹהֵיכֶם אֱמֶת.***

וְיַצִּיב* וְנָכוֹן וְקַיָּם וְיָשָׁר וְנֶאֱמָן וְאָהוּב וְחָבִיב וְנֶחְמָד וְנָעִים וְנוֹרָא וְאַדִּיר וּמְתֻקָּן וּמְקֻבָּל וְטוֹב וְיָפֶה הַדָּבָר הַזֶּה עָלֵינוּ לְעוֹלָם וָעֶד. אֱמֶת אֱלֹהֵי עוֹלָם מַלְכֵּנוּ צוּר יַעֲקֹב, מָגֵן יִשְׁעֵנוּ, לְדֹר וָדֹר הוּא קַיָּם, וּשְׁמוֹ קַיָּם, וְכִסְאוֹ נָכוֹן, וּמַלְכוּתוֹ וֶאֱמוּנָתוֹ לָעַד קַיָּמֶת. וּדְבָרָיו חָיִים וְקַיָּמִים, נֶאֱמָנִים וְנֶחֱמָדִים לָעַד (kiss the *tzitzis* and release them) וּלְעוֹלְמֵי עוֹלָמִים. ❖ עַל אֲבוֹתֵינוּ וְעָלֵינוּ, עַל בָּנֵינוּ וְעַל דּוֹרוֹתֵינוּ, וְעַל כָּל דּוֹרוֹת זֶרַע יִשְׂרָאֵל עֲבָדֶיךָ.

עַל הָרִאשׁוֹנִים וְעַל הָאַחֲרוֹנִים, דָּבָר טוֹב וְקַיָּם לְעוֹלָם וָעֶד, אֱמֶת וֶאֱמוּנָה חֹק וְלֹא יַעֲבֹר. אֱמֶת שָׁאַתָּה הוּא יְהוָה אֱלֹהֵינוּ וֵאלֹהֵי אֲבוֹתֵינוּ, ❖ מַלְכֵּנוּ מֶלֶךְ אֲבוֹתֵינוּ, גֹּאֲלֵנוּ גֹּאֵל אֲבוֹתֵינוּ, יוֹצְרֵנוּ צוּר יְשׁוּעָתֵנוּ, פּוֹדֵנוּ וּמַצִּילֵנוּ מֵעוֹלָם שְׁמֶךָ, אֵין אֱלֹהִים זוּלָתֶךָ.

אֱמֶת — *True.* The law that one may not interrupt between the last words of the *Shema* and אֱמֶת is of ancient origin. The reason for it is so that we may declare as did the prophet [*Jeremiah* 10:10], וַה׳ אֱלֹהִים אֱמֶת, HASHEM, *God, is true* (*Berachos* 14a).

אֱמֶת וְיַצִּיב — *True and certain.* This paragraph begins the third and final blessing of the *Shema,* which ends with גָּאַל יִשְׂרָאֵל, *Who redeemed Israel.* Like אֱמֶת וֶאֱמוּנָה, *True and faithful,* its counterpart in the Evening Service, this blessing continues our fulfillment of the requirement to recall the Exodus, morning and evening.

As the Sages teach (*Berachos* 12a), whoever omits either the morning or evening blessing has not properly discharged his obligation of reciting the *Shema* and its attendant prayers. Although both the morning and evening blessings of redemption refer to the Exodus, there is a basic difference between them. The Talmud (ibid.) teaches that the formulation of these blessings is based on the verse לְהַגִּיד בַּבֹּקֶר חַסְדֶּךָ וֶאֱמוּנָתְךָ

Before reciting the third paragraph (*Numbers* 15:37-41), the *tzitzis,* which have been held in the left hand, are taken in the right hand also. The *tzitzis* are kissed at each mention of the word and at the end of the paragraph, and are passed before the eyes at *'that you may see it.'*

וַיֹּאמֶר *And HASHEM said to Moses saying: Speak to the Children of Israel and say to them that they are to make themselves tzitzis on the corners of their garments, throughout their generations. And they are to place upon the tzitzis of each corner a thread of techeiles. And it shall constitute tzitzis for you, that you may see it and remember all the commandments of HASHEM and perform them; and not explore after your heart and after your eyes after which you stray. So that you may remember and perform all My commandments; and be holy to your God. I am HASHEM, your God, Who has removed you from the land of Egypt to be a God to you; I am HASHEM your God — it is true* —*

Concentrate on fulfilling the commandment of remembering the Exodus from Egypt.

Although the word אֱמֶת, *'it is true,'* belongs to the next paragraph, it is appended to the conclusion of the previous one, as explained in the commentary.

Chazzan repeats: **HASHEM, your God, is true.***

וְיַצִּיב *And certain,* established and enduring, fair and faithful, beloved and cherished, delightful and pleasant, awesome and powerful, correct and accepted, good and beautiful is this affirmation to us forever and ever. True — the God of the universe is our King; the Rock of Jacob is the Shield of our salvation. From generation to generation He endures and His Name endures and His throne is well established; His sovereignty and faithfulness endure forever. His words are living and enduring, faithful and delightful forever* (kiss the *tzitzis* and release them) *and to all eternity;* Chazzan– *for our forefathers and for us, for our children and for our generations, and for all the generations of Your servant Israel's offspring.*

עַל הָרִאשׁוֹנִים *Upon the earlier and upon the later generations, this affirmation is good and enduring forever. True and faithful, it is an unbreachable decree. It is true that You are HASHEM, our God and the God of our forefathers,* Chazzan– *our King and the King of our forefathers, our Redeemer, the Redeemer of our forefathers; our Molder, the Rock of our salvation; our Liberator and our Rescuer — this has ever been Your Name. There is no God but You.*

בַּלֵּילוֹת, *to relate Your kindness in the dawn and Your faithfulness in the nights* (*Psalms* 92:3). This implies that in the morning we express gratitude for already existing *kindness,* while in the evening we express our *faith* in something that has not yet taken place.

As *Rashi* and *Tosafos* explain, the morning blessing of אֱמֶת וְיַצִּיב, which is recited after *dawn,* concentrates on God's *kindness* in having redeemed us from Egypt, while אֱמֶת וֶאֱמוּנָה, which is recited at *night,* is based on the theme of our *faith* that God will redeem us in the future, just as He did at the time of Exodus.

Including the word אֱמֶת, *true,* there are sixteen adjectives describing הַדָּבָר הַזֶּה, *this affirmation* [lit., *this thing*]. What is this 'thing'? It is the total message contained in the sixteen verses of the first two paragraphs of the *Shema* (including בָּרוּךְ שֵׁם). Thus, it is as if we affirm each verse with an adjective acknowledging its truth. *Etz Yosef* and others show how each adjective is suited to the verse it affirms.

FIRST DAY

אֲהֵבוּךָ* נֶפֶשׁ לְהָדֵךְ,
מוֹנִים בּוֹטֵחַ וְשׁוֹדֵךְ, אָנָה הָלַךְ דּוֹדֵךְ.[1]
בְּשׁוּב נוֹחֵךְ גִּנּוּנוֹ,
רְבָבָה תְּרַנֵּן בְּגִינוֹ, דּוֹדִי יָרַד לְגַנּוֹ.[2]
גָּשִׁים* נִבְנֶה[3] כְּהַחֲדִילִי,
דּוֹבְבִים נֵלְכָה לְהַבְדִּילִי,
אֲנִי לְדוֹדִי וְדוֹדִי לִי.[4]
דִּמַּנִי נָאוָה וּתְרוּצָה,
כִּנַּנִי* בְּלֹא פִרְצָה, יָפָה אַתְּ רַעְיָתִי כְּתִרְצָה.[6]
הִזְהִירַנִי מִמַּעַשׂ מְעַנַּיִךְ,
הַתְעֵב גֵּיא כְּנַעֲנַיִךְ,[7] הָסֵבִּי עֵינַיִךְ.[8]
וְעַמֵּךְ כֻּלָּם הִלּוּלִים,[9]
קֹדֶשׁ וְלֹא חוּלִים, שִׁנַּיִךְ* כְּעֵדֶר הָרְחֵלִים.[10]*
זְבָדַנִי זְבוּל אַרְמוֹן,
טִיֵּב יוֹשְׁבֵי אָמוֹן, כְּפֶלַח הָרִמּוֹן.[11]
חַכְמֵי מַלְאֲכוֹת מְלָאכוֹת,
נֶצַח עוֹלָם הֲלִיכוֹת,[12]
שִׁשִּׁים הֵמָּה מְלָכוֹת.[13]

SECOND DAY

אוֹדְךָ* כִּי עֲנִיתָנִי,[14]
מוֹעֵד מִפֶּרֶךְ הִדְרַכְתָּנִי,
לֹא יָדַעְתִּי נַפְשִׁי שָׂמַתְנִי.[15]
בְּחַרְתַּנִי סֶגֶל לְהַעֲמִית,
שַׁפֵּר נַחֲלָתְךָ עוֹלָמִית,
שׁוּבִי שׁוּבִי הַשּׁוּלַמִּית.[16]*
גְּאַלְתִּיךְ מִלַּחַץ מְזַעִימַיִךְ,
לָחֹג חַגֵּי מַנְעִימַיִךְ,
מַה יָּפוּ פְעָמַיִךְ.[17]
דִּמְיוֹן מַשְׂכִּילַיִךְ יִזְהַר,
מַרְאֵיהֶן כְּרָקִיעַ מֻנְהָר,[18]
שָׁרְרֵךְ אַגַּן הַסַּהַר.[19]
הִצְמַתִּי כָּל מַעֲבִידַיִךְ,
בְּהִתְלוֹנְנִי בֵּין בַּדַּיִךְ,
שְׁנֵי שָׁדַיִךְ.[20]*
וּכִּחַתִּי צָרַיִךְ לְעַשֵּׁן,
יְדַעְתִּיךְ לָאֵפוֹד וְלַחֹשֶׁן,*
צַוָּארֵךְ כְּמִגְדַּל הַשֵּׁן.[21]

⋄ **אֲהֵבוּךָ** — *Your beloved.* The next section of the *piyut* contains twenty-two triplets. The initial letters of the first stiches follow the *aleph-beis.* The second stiches bear the acrostic מָרְדְּכַי הַקָּטָן יִגְדַּל בְּתוֹרָה כְּהוֹגֶן וּכְשׁוּרָה, *Mordechai the Lesser, may he become great in Torah as is fitting and proper.*

גָּשִׁים — *They approached.* When Cyrus gave the small Jewish settlement in Jerusalem permission to rebuild the *Beis HaMikdash,* the enemies of the Jews — the Samaritans — sought every means at their disposal to prevent the Temple's completion. Their first move was to approach the Jewish leader Zerubavel with the request, *'Let us build with you, for like you, we seek your God . . .'* (*Ezra* 4:2). But the offer to help was a ruse. The Samaritans' true objective was to disrupt the reconstruction of the Temple. They meant to infiltrate the inner councils of the builders in order to discover their plans and frustrate them (*Rashi* and *Metzudos* based on *Arachin* 5b). Wise to their machinations, Zerubavel and the other communal leaders rejected their offer (*Ezra* 4:3). Upon seeing their ruse failed, the Samaritans openly *hindered the people of Judah and frightened them from building* (4:4).

כִּנַּנִי — *He called me.* The word is from the root כנה, *to nickname.* This spelling and translation is found in the *machzorim* and commentaries. [However, this presents a problem. The name מָרְדְּכַי in the *paytan's* signature is missing the letter י. It has been suggested that the proper reading is כִּינְנַנִי, *He has established me* (from the root כון). Thus, the first two letters of this word complete the name מָרְדְּכַי. In several other stiches the *paytan* also uses the first two letters of a word in his signature in several other stiches (e.g., the letters דל of יִגְדַּל are found in the word דַּלַּת; and תו of בְּתוֹרָה in the word תּוֹעֵה).]

שִׁנַּיִךְ — *Your leaders.* Although the word is usually translated *your teeth, Rashi* understands it as an allusion to the קְצִינִים וְגִבּוֹרִים, *leaders and warriors.* [Perhaps the words derives from the expression שֵׁן הַסֶּלַע, *jutting boulder* (*I Samuel* 14:4), thus, the most outstanding.]

כְּעֵדֶר הָרְחֵלִים — *Like a flock of ewes.* To show how the deeds of Israel are all 'sanctified and not mundane,' they are compared to a flock of sheep. Just as every part of the sheep may be used for the sacred service, so are all of Israel's actions sanctified. The sheep's wool is used for the *tzitzis* fringes [and for the garment of the *Kohen Gadol*]; its flesh [and blood] is offered on the Altar; its horn is used as a *shofar*; its leg-bone, sinews and skin are used for flutes, harpstrings and drums [among the instruments used by the Temple's Levite orchestra] (*Rashi*).

⋄ **אוֹדְךָ** — *I thank You.* This *piyut* consists of twenty-two triplets. The first stiches of the respective stanzas form an *aleph-beis* acrostic. The second stiches form the *paytan's* signature מְשֻׁלָּם בִּירַבִּי קְלוֹנִימוֹס חֲזַק, *Meshullam son of R' Klonimos, may he be strong.* The third stiches are from *Song of Songs.*

FIRST DAY

א *Your beloved* give themselves over*
to martyrdom,
מ *while the secure and serene [nations]*
torment them,
'Where has your Beloved gone?'[1]
ב *When He will return His dwelling*
to His canopied Temple,
ר *a myriad will sing glad song in his honor,*
'My Beloved has gone down to his garden.'[2]
ג *They approached* [saying],*
'Let us build together'[3] *in order to deter me,*
ד *they said, 'Let us go together,'*
in order to separate me [from God];
[but I would not listen, for]
I am my Beloved's and my Beloved is mine.[4]
ד *He considered me beautiful and desirable,*
כ *and He called me,* '[My perfect one,]*[5]
without blemish,'
[saying,] 'You are beautiful,
My companion, and desirable.'[6]
ה *He admonished me from [imitating]*
the acts of my [Egyptian] oppressors,
ה *and to abhor [the lifestyle of]*
the Land of Canaan,[7]
'Turn your eyes away [from them].'[8]
ו *Your entire nation is praiseworthy,*[9]
ק *[their deeds are] sanctified and not mundane,*
your leaders are like a flock of ewes.**[10]
ז *He apportioned me the palatial Temple,*
ט *benefitting the Sanhedrin who sit [and teach]*
the nurturing Torah,
while sitting in a semi-circle.[11]
ח *They are the Sages, whose labors are angelic,*
נ *whose paths are everlasting, eternal,*[12]
and whose regal tractates number sixty.[13]

SECOND DAY

א *I thank You,* for You*
have answered me,[14]
מ *at the time You freed me*
from backbreaking labor,
I know not myself
how my soul was set free.[15]
ב *You have chosen me*
as Your treasured nation,
ש *so beautify me,*
Your eternal heritage,
[and say,] 'Return, return
[to the city of] perfection.'[16]*
ג *I have redeemed you*
from the oppression of your foe,
ל *to enable you to celebrate*
your sweet festivals.
How lovely are your footsteps
[when you ascend
on the pilgrimages]![17]
ד *The form of your wise men*
shall shine brightly,
מ *their appearance like*
the brilliance of heaven,[18]
[in the Temple called]
'Your central nurturing basin.'[19]
ה *I have cut down all*
of your enslavers,
ב *when I lodged between*
your [Ark's] staves,
Your nurturing bosom.[20]*
ו *I have punished*
your oppressors
to dissipate them like smoke;
י *but I have chosen you to wear*
*the ephod and choshen,**
[around] the ivory tower
of your neck.[21]

(1) *Song of Songs* 6:1. (2) 6:2. (3) Cf. *Ezra* 4:2. (4) *Song of Songs* 6:3. (5) תַּמָּתִי, 5:2; 6:9. (6) 6:4. (7) Cf. *Leviticus* 18:3. (8) *Song of Songs* 6:5. (9) Cf. *Isaiah* 60:21. (10) *Song of Songs* 6:6. (11) 6:7 [lit., 'like a split pomegranate']. (12) Cf. *Habakkuk* 3:6. (13) *Song of Songs* 6:8. (14) *Psalms* 118:21. (15) *Song of Songs* 6:12. [The *paytan,* for unknown reasons, did not include passages from 6:4 through 6:11 in this *piyut.*] (16) 7:1. (17) 7:2. (18) Cf. *Daniel* 12:3. (19) *Song of Songs* 7:3. (20) 7:4. (21) 7:5.

הַשּׁוּלַמִּית — *[To the city of] perfection,* a reference to Jerusalem [note the similarity of **הַשּׁוּלַמִּית** and **יְרוּשָׁלַיִם**]. Alternatively, the word alludes to Israel (see *Song of Songs* 6:9, תַּמָּתִי, *My perfect one*), the perfect nation.

שְׁנֵי שָׁדַיִךְ — *Your nurturing bosom.* The staves on either side of the Ark were extremely long. When the Ark was placed in the inner sanctum of the Temple, the Holy of Holies, its staves stretched from one end of the chamber to the other — as Scripture describes: *'The staves extended until the tips of the staves could be seen from the Holy, the front of the Temple, yet they could not be seen outside'* (*I Kings* 8:8). The contradictory statements 'the staves could be seen' and 'they could not be seen' are reconciled by the Talmud. Because of their great length the twin poles pressed forth against the curtain that separated the Holy of Holies from the Holy. Thus, two bosom-like protrusions were visible from the outside, even though the staves themselves were not visible behind the curtain (*Yoma* 54a; *Menachos* 98a).

לְאֵפוֹד וְלַחשֶׁן — *The ephod and the choshen.* These are two of the *Kohen Gadol's* eight vestments. The *ephod* is an apron-like garment

FIRST DAY

טוֹעֲנִים אֲסֻפּוֹת גַּנָּתִי,*
יַחַד נוֹטְעִים כַּנָּתִי, אַחַת הִיא יוֹנָתִי.[1]
יָשְׁרָם לְהָלִיץ הִתְקְפָה,
גַּבְרוּת קֶרֶן זְקוּפָה, מִי זֹאת הַנִּשְׁקָפָה.[2]
כַּעַס וּשְׂחוֹק יָגוֹז,
דַּלַּת רֹאשׁ מִלָּגוֹז, אֶל גִּנַּת אֱגוֹז.[3]*
לְגוֹלֵל אֶבֶן צִמְתַּתְנִי,
בְּאֵר חַיַּי צִמַּתְנִי,[4]
לֹא יָדַעְתִּי נַפְשִׁי שָׂמַתְנִי.[5]
מָתַי לְחָצִיר נַעֲמִית,
תּוֹעָה וּמַתְעָה לְהַעֲמִית,
שׁוּבִי שׁוּבִי הַשּׁוּלַמִּית.[6]
נָאִים לְהִתְנַדֵּב מְעֻלִּים,
רְאוּת וּלְקַלֵּס מוֹעֲלִים,
מַה יָּפוּ פְעָמַיִךְ בַּנְּעָלִים.[7]
סֵדֶר עֲבוֹדָה מְהֻגָּן,
הָשֵׁב לְשִׁיתוֹ נֻגָּן, שָׁרְרֵךְ אַגַּן.[8]*
עֲרוֹךְ אֵילִים וּפָרִים,
כְּאָז בְּיַד סוֹפְרִים, שְׁנֵי שָׁדַיִךְ כִּשְׁנֵי עֳפָרִים.[9]
פֶּתַח שִׁיר מִלְּדַל,
הֲדַר זָקֵן[10] מְגֻדָּל, צַוָּארֵךְ כְּמִגְדַּל.[11]*
צַו חֶסֶד כְּגוֹמֵל,
וְנַשֵּׂא כָּאָמוּר[12] חוֹמֵל,
רֹאשֵׁךְ עָלַיִךְ כַּכַּרְמֶל.[13]

SECOND DAY

זַעֲכְתִּי קָמַיִךְ לְהַאֲמֵל,
רִצַּצְתִּים בְּקָנֶה קָמֵל,
רֹאשֵׁךְ עָלַיִךְ כַּכַּרְמֶל.[14]
חִשֶּׁר לַחְמִי הָטְעַמְתְּ,
בְּשֹׂבַע שְׂמָחוֹת הָנְעַמְתְּ,[15]
מַה יָּפִית וּמַה נָּעַמְתְּ.[16]
טִוּוּי יְרִיעוֹת רִקְמָתֵךְ,
יְדִידוּת שֶׁכֶן הֲקָמָתֵךְ,
זֹאת קוֹמָתֵךְ.[17]
יַחַד רֵיחֵךְ תְּמַר,
קֹדֶשׁ קָדָשִׁים לִתְמַר,
אָמַרְתִּי אֶעֱלֶה בְתָמָר.[18]
כִּנַּסְתִּיךְ לְהָהָר הַטּוֹב,
לִרְחֹשׁ דָּבָר טוֹב,[19]
וְחִכֵּךְ כְּיֵין הַטּוֹב.[20]
לֶאֱגוֹד נִדָּחַי וּלְוַעֲדִי,
וְלִרְאוֹת בְּקִרְיַת מוֹעֲדִי,[22]
אֲנִי לְדוֹדִי.[23]
מָעוֹן נֶחֱרַשׁ כַּשָּׂדֶה,[24]
נָאוֹר מִזִּיוְךְ תְּחַדֶּה,
לְכָה דוֹדִי נֵצֵא הַשָּׂדֶה.[25]
נָא שְׁאַג מִמְּרוֹמִים,

wrapped around the body from the waist down. Two cloth shoulder straps, each topped by a precious stone, support the *ephod* from behind; while the *choshen* served this function in the front. The *choshen* is a breastplate, suspended from the shoulder straps of the *ephod* on golden chains. Twelve precious gems, each engraved with the name of one of the tribes were set in four columns on the *choshen*. A series of rings and cloth bands connected the *choshen* to the waistband of the *ephod*. All in all, the two garments gave the *Kohen Gadol* a regal appearance.

טוֹעֲנִים אֲסֻפּוֹת גַּנָּתִי — *Those who gather in My garden[-like study hall] debate.* Most commentators understand טוֹעֲנִים as in the Talmudic expression טוֹעֵן וְנִטְעָן which means *claimant and respondent* or, loosely, *claim and counterclaimm*, and אֲסֻפּוֹת as a reference to the Sages *gathered* in the study hall (see *Ecclesiastes* 12:11).

[This interpretation presents two difficulties: (a) In *Ecclesiastes* 12:11 (upon which this stich is based), the Sages are called בַּעֲלֵי אֲסֻפּוֹת, *masters of collections;* thus, the word אֲסֻפּוֹת refers to the 'collected wisdom' and not to the 'wise.' (b) Since אֲסֻפּוֹת is the feminine gender, its verb should be טוֹעֲנוֹת.

Perhaps, the word טוֹעֲנִים derives from the Biblical טַעֲנוּ, *load* (*Genesis* 45:17), and means *those who bear.* Thus the stich would be translated, 'those who bear the gatherings (or, harvest) of My garden.']

The Sages' debates are not mere polemics in which each side seeks to prove its position. Rather, their debates are aimed at determining the true meaning of each Torah passage and law, and to establish their understanding and interpretation on a firm base. This is the single-minded goal of all the participants in the debates.

גִּנַּת אֱגוֹז — *[We whom You have called] a nut garden.* Just as a nut's shell conceals its nutritious kernel, so does Israel conceal its greatness. Its scholars are unpretentious and modest, yet full of wisdom. And just as when a nut falls into the mud, its contents are not defiled, so too Israel's essence is not defiled among the nations of its exile (*Rashi*).

FIRST DAY

ט *Those who gather in My garden[-like study hall] debate,**
י *together they plant My base,*
My dove, she is single[-minded].[1]
י *O may He speak of their uprightness to encourage them,*
ג *exalting their erect pride,* *[until all will wonder,] 'Who is this looking downward?'*[2]
כ *May anger and mocking pass away,*
לד *may our tresses no longer be plucked,*
[we whom You have called] a nut garden.[3]*
ל *[Hoping] to have rolled away the stone [Temple] for eternity,*
ב *they [try to] cut off my life in a pit,*[4]
placing unfamiliar [burdens] on my soul.[5]
מ *When will the brutal turn to withered grass,*
תו *the misled and the misleader become weakened,*
[those who cry,] 'Turn away, turn away [from God], O perfect ones.'[6]
נ *[O when will] the beautiful ones be able to offer the finest [sacrifices]?*
ר *That the usurpers may see and give praise,*
'How lovely are their footsteps in pilgrims' sandals!'[7]
ס *The order of [Temple] service will be performed properly,*
ה *when [the Levites] song is restored to the Altar,*
[in the Temple called] 'Your central nurturing basin.'[8]*
ע *Rams and bulls will be arranged [for the Altar],*
כ *as the Sages [taught their laws] in former times,*
[as they received them from] the two nurturers, the twins of the gazelle [Moses and Aaron].[9]
פ *The first to sing [Moses at the sea] will no longer be silent,*
ה *the flowing beard [of Aaron]*[10] *will return,*
[along with the Sanhedrin,] your towerlike throat.[11]*
צ *Command Your kindness as You have bestowed it in the past,*
ו *and exalt [us] as [the prophet Isaiah] said,*[12]
O Compassionate One,
[then the nations will say to us,] 'Your head is as lofty as Mount Carmel.'[13]

SECOND DAY

ז *I leaped to cut down your opponents,*
ר *I crushed them like dry reeds,*
but you are stately like Mount Carmel.[14]
ח *You tasted My manna that fell like rain,*
נ *You were sweetened with the fullness of joy,*[15]
You who are so beautiful and so pleasant.[16]
ט *Spun threads for the curtains of your weaving,*
י *for the beloved Tabernacle that you erected,*
this is your stature.[17]
י *When you are united, your fragrance rises like the column of incense smoke,*
ק *that fills the Holy of Holies [on Yom Kippur],*
I have said, 'I will be exalted through that palm-like pillar.'[18]
ב *I assembled you at the goodly mountain,*
ל *to bestir you with a good theme,*[19]
and your palate was like fine wine[20] *[when you said, 'We will do, and we will listen.'*[21]*]*
ל *[Israel replied,] Bind together my dispersed and meet with me,*
ו *to appear [in pilgrimage] in my city of Meeting,*[22]
for I am My Beloved's.[23]
מ *The Temple has been plowed over like a field,*[24]
נ *O Illuminated One, make it rejoice with Your sheen,*
Come my Beloved, let us leave [our exile] for the fields [of Jerusalem].[25]
נ *Please, issue a leonine roar from the heavens,*

(1) *Song of Songs* 6:9. (2) 6:10. (3) 6:11. (4) Cf. *Lamentations* 3:53. (5) *Song of Songs* 6:12. (6) 7:1. (7) 7:2. (8) 7:3. (9) 7:4. (10) Cf. *Psalms* 133:2. (11) *Song of Songs* 7:5. (12) See *Isaiah* 63:9. (13) *Song of Songs* 7:6. (14) 7:6. (15) Cf. *Psalms* 16:11. (16) *Song of Songs* 7:7. (17) 7:8. (18) 7:9. (19) Cf. *Psalms* 45:2. (20) *Song of Songs* 7:10. (21) *Exodus* 24:7. (22) Cf. *Isaiah* 33:20. (23) *Song of Songs* 7:11. (24) Cf. *Jeremiah* 26:18. (25) *Song of Songs* 7:12.

שָׁרְרֵךְ אַגַּן — *Your central nurturing basin* [lit., *your umbilicus is a basin*]. The *Beis HaMikdash* stands at the center of the world. It is the focal point from which heavenly blessing emanates to all parts of the globe, like the umbilicus through which flows sustenance for all of the embryo's limbs.

צַוָּארֵךְ כְּמִגְדַּל — *Your towerlike throat.* The

FIRST DAY

קֶלֶס תְּמוּר אֲשַׁמְתְּ,
גְּנַאי זִכְרוֹנֵךְ שַׁמְתְּ, מַה יָּפִית וּמַה נָּעַמְתְּ.[1]
רִיב לְטוֹב יוֹמָר,
וּלְשִׁפְלוּת עֵמֶק יְזַמָּר,
זֹאת קוֹמָתֵךְ דָּמְתָה לְתָמָר.[2]
שַׁתֵּף בְּכָל מִשְׁמָר,
כֻּלָּם צַדִּיקִים בְּמַאֲמָר,
אָמַרְתִּי אֶעֱלֶה בְתָמָר.[3]
תַּעַן דָּבָר טוֹב,
שׁוּרָה אַחַת לַחֲטוֹב, וְחִכֵּךְ כְּיֵין הַטּוֹב.[4]
שְׁחוֹרָה* וְנָאוָה[5]* תְּשׁוּקָתוֹ,
לֹא מֵרֹב* חֲשׁוּקָתוֹ,
אֲנִי לְדוֹדִי וְעָלַי תְּשׁוּקָתוֹ.[6]
מֵחֲפוּרִים שׁוּר שְׁפוּרִים,
הִסְתַּכֵּל בְּךָ כּוֹפְרִים,
לְכָה דוֹדִי נֵצֵא הַשָּׂדֶה נָלִינָה בַּכְּפָרִים.[7]
בֵּינָה רְצוּי תּוֹרְמִים,
בִּיסוּס עוֹלָם גּוֹרְמִים, נַשְׁכִּימָה לַכְּרָמִים.[8]
יִתַּן קוֹל צוֹרֵחַ,
הַטּוֹבוֹת וְהָרָעוֹת הַפְּרֵחַ,
הַדּוּדָאִים נָתְנוּ רֵיחַ.[9]*
דּוֹדִי נֹחַ לִי,
הַמְּנַחֲמִי וּמוֹחֵל לִי, מִי יִתֶּנְךָ כְּאָח* לִי.[10]
חֲזוּת כְּאָז צְבָאֲךָ,
וְהַר שְׁכִינַת מוֹרָאֲךָ, אֶנְהָגְךָ אֲבִיאֲךָ.[11]

SECOND DAY

יָרְדוּ לָטֶבַח רְאֵמִים,*
נַשְׁכִּימָה לַכְּרָמִים.[12]
סוּרָה בְּאוֹרְךָ תַזְרִיחַ,
מִנְחָתָהּ כְּקֶדֶם תָּרִיחַ,
הַדּוּדָאִים נָתְנוּ רֵיחַ.[13]
עֲלוֹז בְּשִׂמְחַת אַרְמוֹנְךָ,
וְלָדוּץ בְּיוֹם חֲתוּנָּתְךָ,*
מִי יִתֶּנְךָ.[14]
פְּרָזוֹת* מוֹשַׁב צְבָאֲךָ,
סַבֵּב כְּחָז נְבִיאֲךָ,
אֶנְהָגְךָ אֲבִיאֲךָ.[15]
צִפְצוּף נֹעַם בְּדָרְשִׁי,
חֲמוּדִים מִפָּז* בְּפָרְשִׁי,
שְׂמֹאלוֹ תַּחַת רֹאשִׁי.[16]
קֵץ אַהַב נִדְבַתְכֶם,
זְמַנּוֹ מִלְּעוֹרֵר מְתֵיכֶם,
הִשְׁבַּעְתִּי אֶתְכֶם.[17]
רְצוּצַת זָרִים וּרְעוּלָה,
קוֹמְמִיּוּת הוֹלֶכֶת וּמִתְעַלָּה,
מִי זֹאת עֹלָה.[18]
שְׁעֵה שִׁיר מִכְתָּם,*
חָשְׁכֵּנִי מְזֵידִים[19] וְאֵיתָם,
שִׂימֵנִי כַחוֹתָם.[20]

Sanhedrin is called this because it explains the words of Torah and issues their definitive interpretations.

שְׁחוֹרָה — *[Once] black*. This section bears the signature שְׁלֹמֹה בֵּירַבִּי יְהוּדָה חֲזַק וֶאֱמַץ מְאֹד בְּתוֹרָה אָמֵן וְאָמֵן, *Shlomo son of R' Yehudah, may he be strong and persevere very much in Torah, Amen and Amen.*

שְׁחוֹרָה וְנָאוָה — *[Once] black, [now] beautiful.* Though I was once blackened with sin, I have cleansed myself through repentance.

לֹא מֵרֹב — *Not for grandeur*. God's love for Israel is not due to Israel's pomp and grandeur. On the contrary, it is their humility and self-effacement that draws Him to them.

הַדּוּדָאִים נָתְנוּ רֵיחַ — *The baskets of both yield fragrance.* According to the Talmud, דּוּדָאִים are baskets of figs — some good, some spoiled. As the prophet states: *Behold, two baskets of figs are set . . . one basket of very good figs . . . and one basket of very bad figs . . .* (*Jeremiah* 24:1-2).

'Very good figs' allude to the extremely righteous; 'very bad figs,' to the extremely wicked. But do not imagine that they have no hope, for when they seek You through repentance, even the erstwhile wicked will emit a lovely fragrance (*Eruvin* 21a; *Rashi* to *Song* 7:14).

כְּאָח — *Like a brother*. Just as Joseph forgave his brothers who had sold him into slavery, and comforted them when they made atonement (see *Genesis* 50:21), so may God forgive our errant ways and comfort us in our remorse (see *Rashi* to *Song* 8:1).

רְאֵמִים — *Re'eimim*. See commentary, page 39.

כְּיוֹם חֲתוּנָּתְךָ — *As on Your wedding day*. The day on which God gave the Torah to the Jewish people is called יוֹם חֲתֻנָּתוֹ, *His wedding day* (*Song of Songs* 3:11).

פְּרָזוֹת — *Like the open cities.* Although the Holy City of Jerusalem is surrounded by a wall, we pray for the fulfillment of the prophecy: *Jerusalem shall sit like the open cities due to the*

FIRST DAY

ק *[I admonish myself,] 'You have become a laughingstock because you have sinned;*
גנ *you have placed your name in disgrace, you who had been so beautiful and so sweet.*[1]
ר *May your grievance be exchanged for beneficence,*
ו *and the valley of depression be removed, then your exaltedness will be like a palm tree.*[2]
ש *May You join in partnership with each guard [that prays for the redemption],*
כ *for they are all righteous — and as You have said, 'I have said that I shall ascend upon the righteous palm tree.'*[3]
ת *Reply to us with a beneficent answer,*
שורה *unite us in one row [and bring us our hoped-for redemption], [saying,] 'Your hopes are like fine wine.'*[4]
ש *[Once] black,* [now] beautiful,*[5]* *object of His longing,*
ל *not for grandeur* does His desire come, 'I am my Beloved's and He longs for me.'*[6]*
מ *From the abashedness [of exile], a wall of beautiful [deeds];*
ה *the heretics will look upon you with disbelief; "Come my Beloved, let us go forth to the field [Jerusalem], let us lodge among [those who eat] the frost[-like] manna]."*[7]
ביר *Understand the supplications of those who tithe;*
בי *they firm the world's foundation [by saying], 'Let us arise early and enter the vineyards [of Torah].'*[8]
י *Giving forth loud cries of prayer,*
הו *the good ones, even the bad, make [their prayers] sprout; the baskets of both yield fragrance.**[9]
ד *May my Beloved afford me contentment,*
ה *may He comfort and forgive me; if only He would treat me like a brother!*[10]*
ח *May [Israel] Your legion once again see,*
ז *the splendid sheen of Your Awesome Shechinah. [And say to them,] 'I will lead you, I will bring you [to My Temple].'*[11]

SECOND DAY

י *descend to slaughter the proud re'eimim,* allowing us to arise and build the Temple vineyard.*[12]
ס *Radiate Your light upon the displaced nation,*
מ *inhale as of old her aromatic offering, the baskets [of her prayer] yield fragrance.*[13]
ע *Exult in the rejoicing of Your Palace,*
ו *and celebrate as on Your wedding day,* if only You would!*[14]
פ *May Your legions' dwelling be like the open cities,**
ס *may You surround it, as the prophet spoke, O may I lead You, may I bring You there!*[15]
צ *Lips atwitter as I expound the sweet Torah,*
ח *as I interpret statements more desirable than fine gold,* may His left hand support my head.*[16]
ק *The End [of our exile], the generosity of Your love,*
ז *You have forbidden the populace from arousing it before its appointed time, [by saying,] 'I adjure you . . .'*[17]
ר *May those broken and oppressed by strangers,*
ק *walk erect, even higher, [until the erstwhile foe will wonder,] 'Who is that who ascends?'*[18]
ש *Turn to the crowning song,* restrain me from intentional sins,*[19] *that I may become wholesome, place me as a seal*[20] *[that You not forget me].*

(1) *Song of Songs* 7:7. (2) 7:8. (3) 7:9. (4) 7:10. (5) Cf. 1:5. (6) 7:11. (7) 7:12. (8) 7:13. (9) 7:14. (10) 8:1. (11) 8:2. (12) 7:13. (13) 7:14. (14) 8:1. (15) 8:2. (16) 8:3. (17) 8:4. (18) 8:5. (19) Cf. *Psalms* 19:14. (20) *Song of Songs* 8:6.

abundance of people and animals within her. And I shall be unto her — says HASHEM *— a surrounding wall of fire . . .* (Zechariah 2:8-9).

חֲמוּדִים מִפָּז — *More desirable than fine gold.* The phrase is borrowed from *Psalms* 19:11, which reads הַנֶּחֱמָדִים מִזָּהָב וּמִפָּז, *more desirable than gold, than even much fine gold.* Indeed, some *machzorim* read נֶחֱמָדִים here. However, we have followed the reading חֲמוּדִים, which bears the expected initial letter ח, to spell the word חָזָק of the *paytan's* signature.

שִׁיר מִכְתָּם — *Crowning song.* The word מִכְתָּם is

FIRST DAY	SECOND DAY

FIRST DAY

קְרוֹבְךָ עִם דַּבְּקֵנִי,
וְסֶת שִׁבְחֲךָ סַפְּקֵנִי,
שְׂמֹאלוֹ תַּחַת רֹאשִׁי וִימִינוֹ תְּחַבְּקֵנִי.[1]
אַחֲרִית לְטַהֵר שׁוּלַיִם,[2]
מַהֵר לְשַׁלֵּשׁ בְּכִפְלַיִם,
הִשְׁבַּעְתִּי אֶתְכֶם בְּנוֹת יְרוּשָׁלָיִם.[3]
צִיּוּן רְשָׁפִים מְלַבֶּיךָ,
מִי זֹאת[4] כְּלַבְּבֵךְ, שִׂימֵנוּ כַחוֹתָם עַל לִבֶּךָ.[5]
אוֹתוֹת רְאוֹת מְרֻבִּים,
דֶּרֶךְ לַעֲבֹר מְסֻבִּים, מַיִם רַבִּים.[6]
בִּיטָה עֲנִיָּה לְנַחֲמָה,[7]
תַּעֲרַת אֹם חוֹמָה, אֲנִי חוֹמָה.[8]
וִיהוּדָה כֶּרֶם גְּפָנִי,
רֶגֶל הַהֵיכָל לְפָנַי, כַּרְמִי שֶׁלִּי לְפָנָי.[9]
אֶלֶף* הַמָּגֵן מָגִנִּים,
אֶדֶר שָׂרִים סְגָנִים, הַיּוֹשֶׁבֶת בַּגַּנִּים.[10]*
מִסְּרִיּוֹת מַסְרִיחַ רְדִידִי,
נֵרְדְּ וֶרֶד יְדִידִי, בְּרַח דּוֹדִי.[11]
וּדְמֵה לְךָ בְּטִיּוּלִים,
אַמֵּץ כְּאָז חֲיָלִים,
לִצְבִי אוֹ לְעֹפֶר הָאַיָּלִים.[11]
מִשְׁקָל בְּמִשְׁקָל* שָׂמִים,
נִיחֹחַ מֹר סַמִּים, עַל הָרֵי בְשָׂמִים.[11]
עַל הָרֵי בְשָׂמִים, סֹב וּדְמֵה לְךָ דּוֹדִי.[12]
מַשְׁגִּיחַ וּמֵצִיץ מֵחֲרַכֵּי בֵּית וַעֲדִי,[13]
קוּמִי לָךְ רַעְיָתִי,[14] דְּפֹק לְעוֹדְדִי,
כִּי דַלֹּתִי מְאֹד מִמְּתֶנֶת מְעִידִי,
יוֹשֶׁבֶת עֲגוּמָה וַעֲגוּנָה וְאֵין מוֹעֲדִי,
וְאַתָּה יהוה מָגֵן בַּעֲדִי.[15]

SECOND DAY

תֹּקֶף עֹז אֲהָבִים,
כָּל יִשְׁטְפוּן רְהָבִים,
מַיִם רַבִּים.[16]

❖ מַיִם רַבִּים תִּלַּלְתָּ עֲרֵמוֹת,
אַדִּיר בִּמְרוֹמוֹת,[17]
תָּשִׁית יָם לַחֲרָמוֹת,[18]
וְנָפִיק לָךְ רוֹמֵמוֹת.

The service continues on page 318.

---

rendered עֲטָרָה, *crown*, by *Rashi* (*Psalms* 16:1). Other interpretations are: a special musical arrangement (*Rashi*); a particularly fine or significant hymn (*Ibn Ezra*); a musical instrument (*Radak*). Any of these meanings are apropos here.

The Talmud homiletically renders מִכְתָּם as two words: מָךְ, *humble*, and תָּם, *wholesome*, and applies it to King David the humble, wholesome author of *Psalms* (*Sotah* 10b). Accordingly, שִׁיר מִכְתָּם would be, *the song of the humble, wholesome* psalmist, which is recited in prayer by Israel (*Matteh Levi*), or *the song of humble, wholesome* Israel (*Machzor Shaar Ephraim*).

אֶלֶף — *A thousand.* The wording is based on *Song of Songs* 4:4. [Although the *machzorim* read אֶלֶף, *a thousand*, perhaps the definite article prefix הָ should be appended, thus completed the word בְּתוֹרָה of the *paytan's* signature. As it stands, this stich is anomalous for its initial letter does not fit the acrostic. (If the proper reading is אֶלֶף, the signature utilizes the initial ה of the word הַהֵיכָל to complete the acrostic.)]

אֶלֶף . . . בַּגַּנִּים — *A thousand . . . in the gardens.* The 'thousand shields' are the Torah scholars (see commentaries to *II Kings* 24:16); the 'princes and officials' are the members of the *Sanhedrin*; the 'gardens' are the synagogues and study halls.

מִשְׁקָל בְּמִשְׁקָל — *Equal measures.* See page 214 for the exact composition of the incense.

FIRST DAY	SECOND DAY

FIRST DAY

ק *Let me, the nation of You nearness, cleave to You,*
ו *may Your praiseworthy attributes sustain me, may Your left hand support my head and Your right hand embrace me.*[1]
א *The eventual cleansing of [the impurity of her] hems,*[2]
מ *hasten it, that which was repeated thrice, I adjure you, O daughters of Jerusalem.*[3]
צ *'[O Israel] symbolized by your flashing flames,*
מ *who else equals*[4] *your fiery zeal?'*
'[If so,] place me as a seal on Your heart.'[5]
א *[May I merit] to see an abundance of wondrous signs,*
ד *to travel the road while surrounded [by the Cloud of Glory], [as when you brought me through] the many waters.*[6]
ב *Look down upon the poor nation and comfort it,*[7]
ח *she who pours forth her soul with stonewall resoluteness, [proclaiming,] 'I am like a wall,'*[8]
ו *And Judah, vineyard of My grapevine,*
דה *will be the site of the inner chamber of the Temple, [when I gather] My vines before Me.*[9]
A thousand protective shields,*
א *the beauty of princes and officials, those who sit in the gardens.*[10]*
מ *[From] the disgusting filth [of sin] that has enwrapped me,*
נ *to the nard and roses of my Beloved [Temple], Flee, O my Beloved.*[11]
ו *Act to us as if You were strolling [with us],*
א *encouraging us as with the strength of old; [hasten to redeem us, with the speed] of a deer and a gazelle.*[11]
מ *Placing equal measures of incense,**
נ *the pleasantness of myrrh and herbs, [as] on [Sinai,] the mountain of spices.*[11]
Upon mountains of spices, turn about and act as my Beloved,[12] *observing and peering through the windows of my study hall,*[13]
[say to me,] 'Rise, O my companion!'[14]
Knock [on my door] to encourage me, for I have been brought very low while awaiting my Appointed Messiah, sitting bereaved and forsaken, with none to take me in; but You; HASHEM, are a shield for me.[15]

SECOND DAY

ת *The strength of our powerful love, cannot be drowned by the idolaters, even in the deepest waters.*[16]
Chazzan — *You heaped the many waters into piles, You Who are mighty in the heights,*[17] *may You again turn the sea to dry land,*[18] *and we will burst forth in exultation of You.*

The service continues on page 318.

(1) *Song of Songs* 8:3. (2) See *Lamentations* 1:9. (3) *Song of Songs* 8:4. (4) 8:5. (5) 8:6. (6) 8:7; see *Micah* 7:15. (7) Cf. *Isaiah* 54:11. (8) *Song of Songs* 8:10. [The *paytan,* for unknown reasons, did not include passages from 8:8,9 and 11 in this *piyut.*] (9) 8:12. (10) 8:13. (11) 8:14. (12) Cf. 2:17. (13) Cf. 2:9. (14) 2:10; 2:13. (15) *Psalms* 3:4. (16) *Song of Songs* 8:7. (17) Cf. *Psalms* 93:4. (18) Cf. *Isaiah* 11:15.

FIRST DAY

אֶל גִּבְעַת הָעֲרָלוֹת,[1]* מֹר וּלְבוֹנָה וַאֲהָלוֹת,[2]
הַבֵּט מִמַּעֲלוֹת, כִּי מַכּוֹת נַחְלוֹת. קוּמָה קַדְּמָה חוֹפֵשׂ עוֹלוֹת עֲלִילוֹת,
טֶנֶף וּגְעִילוֹת, יְחַלֵּל קֹדֶשׁ מְעִילוֹת, נָא שְׁבֹר זְרוֹעוֹ מִלְּהַעֲלוֹת תְּעָלוֹת,
וְעַם קְהִלּוֹת בְּמַקְהֵלוֹת, לְהוֹדוֹת הַלֵּלוֹת.
עַל הָרֵי בָתֶר,[3] עַל אַחַד הֶהָרִים,[4] יֵרָאֶה לִבְחִירִים, גְּמוּל פֹּעַל הוֹרִים,
דֻּבִּים נְמֵרִים, אֲרָיוֹת וַחֲזִירִים,* פָּרִים אַבִּירִים, לְפַסֵּג גִּזְרֵי גְזָרִים,
כִּיקַר כָּרִים, כָּלִים גְּמוּרִים, תֹּר וְגוֹזָל שְׁלֵמִים* וְלֹא חֲסֵרִים,
שְׁמוּרִים בְּלֵיל שִׁמֻּרִים, הַלֵּל גּוֹמְרִים, כְּעוֹבְרִים שָׁרִים זַמָּרִים,
אָשִׁירָה לַיהוה[5] אוֹמְרִים.

עֶזְרַת אֲבוֹתֵינוּ* אַתָּה הוּא מֵעוֹלָם, מָגֵן וּמוֹשִׁיעַ לִבְנֵיהֶם אַחֲרֵיהֶם בְּכָל דּוֹר וָדוֹר. בְּרוּם עוֹלָם מוֹשָׁבֶךָ, וּמִשְׁפָּטֶיךָ וְצִדְקָתְךָ עַד אַפְסֵי אָרֶץ. אַשְׁרֵי אִישׁ שֶׁיִּשְׁמַע לְמִצְוֹתֶיךָ, וְתוֹרָתְךָ וּדְבָרְךָ יָשִׂים עַל לִבּוֹ. אֱמֶת אַתָּה הוּא אָדוֹן לְעַמֶּךָ וּמֶלֶךְ גִּבּוֹר לָרִיב רִיבָם. אֱמֶת אַתָּה הוּא רִאשׁוֹן וְאַתָּה הוּא אַחֲרוֹן, וּמִבַּלְעָדֶיךָ אֵין לָנוּ מֶלֶךְ[6] גּוֹאֵל וּמוֹשִׁיעַ. מִמִּצְרַיִם גְּאַלְתָּנוּ יהוה אֱלֹהֵינוּ, וּמִבֵּית עֲבָדִים פְּדִיתָנוּ. כָּל בְּכוֹרֵיהֶם הָרָגְתָּ, וּבְכוֹרְךָ גָּאָלְתָּ, וְיַם סוּף בָּקַעְתָּ, וְזֵדִים טִבַּעְתָּ, וִידִידִים הֶעֱבַרְתָּ, וַיְכַסּוּ מַיִם צָרֵיהֶם, אֶחָד מֵהֶם לֹא נוֹתָר.[7] עַל זֹאת שִׁבְּחוּ אֲהוּבִים וְרוֹמְמוּ אֵל, וְנָתְנוּ יְדִידִים זְמִרוֹת שִׁירוֹת וְתִשְׁבָּחוֹת, בְּרָכוֹת וְהוֹדָאוֹת, לַמֶּלֶךְ אֵל חַי וְקַיָּם, רָם וְנִשָּׂא, גָּדוֹל וְנוֹרָא, מַשְׁפִּיל גֵּאִים, וּמַגְבִּיהַּ שְׁפָלִים, מוֹצִיא אֲסִירִים, וּפוֹדֶה עֲנָוִים, וְעוֹזֵר דַּלִּים, וְעוֹנֶה לְעַמּוֹ בְּעֵת שַׁוְּעָם אֵלָיו.

Rise for *Shemoneh Esrei.* Some take three steps backward at this point; others do so before צוּר יִשְׂרָאֵל.

❖ תְּהִלּוֹת לְאֵל עֶלְיוֹן, בָּרוּךְ הוּא וּמְבֹרָךְ. מֹשֶׁה וּבְנֵי יִשְׂרָאֵל לְךָ עָנוּ שִׁירָה בְּשִׂמְחָה רַבָּה וְאָמְרוּ כֻלָּם:

אֶל גִּבְעַת הָעֲרָלוֹת — *To the hill of foreskins.* Redeem us in the merit of Abraham who circumcised all of his household at one time, heaping their foreskins into a hill. This *mitzvah* is sweeter to You than the savory aroma of myrrh, frankincense and aloe.

דֻּבִּים נְמֵרִים אֲרָיוֹת וַחֲזִירִים — *Ursine Persia, leopard-like Greece, leonine Babylon, and boarish Edom.* In Daniel's vision of the four beasts that represented the four exiles, Babylon appeared as a lion, Persia as a bear, and Greece as a leopard. In *Psalms* (80:14), Edom is compared to a boar.

תֹּר וְגוֹזָל שְׁלֵמִים — *But the turtledove and the young pigeon shall remain whole.* At the Covenant Between the Parts, God instructed Abraham to take three calves, three goats, three rams, a turtledove and a young pigeon. The animals were to be slaughtered and cut in two, but the birds were to remain whole (*Genesis* 15:9-10).

According to *Rashi*, the severed animals

FIRST DAY

To the hill of foreskins,[1] myrrh, frankincense, and aloes,[2]*
look down from the heights, for the lashes sicken us.
Arise, [O God,] against him who seeks excuses to destroy us,
to vilify and abominate us, to desecrate and misappropriate the sacred.
Please, break his might that it not be healed.
Then the nation will congregate, to thank You and to recite Hallel at night.
Upon [Mount Moriah,] the mountain of [the Covenant Between] the Parts,[3]
upon the unique the mountains,[4] may You appear to the Chosen,
to reward the Patriarchs' labor.
*Ursine Persia, leopard-like Greece, leonine Babylon, and boarish Edom,**
the mighty oxen, cut them all to pieces,
as the valuable rams [that are butchered], to be totally consumed.
*But the turtledove and the young pigeon shall remain whole without imperfection,**
guarded on this guarded night, they complete the recitation of Hallel,
as those who crossed [the sea] sang and played music,
and they said, 'I shall sing to HASHEM . . .'[5]

עֶזְרַת *The Helper of our forefathers* are You alone, forever, Shield and Savior for their children after them in every generation. At the zenith of the universe is Your dwelling, and Your justice and Your righteousness extend to the ends of the earth. Praiseworthy is the person who obeys Your commandments and takes to his heart Your teaching and Your word. True — You are the Master for Your people and a mighty King to take up their grievance. True — You are the First and You are the Last, and other than You we have no king,[6] redeemer, or savior. From Egypt You redeemed us, HASHEM, our God, and from the house of slavery You liberated us. All their firstborn You slew, but Your firstborn You redeemed; the Sea of Reeds You split; the wanton sinners You drowned; the dear ones You brought across; and the water covered their foes — not one of them was left.[7] For this, the beloved praised and exalted God; the dear ones offered hymns, songs, praises, blessings, and thanksgivings to the King, the living and enduring God — exalted and uplifted, great and awesome, Who humbles the haughty and lifts the lowly; withdraws the captive, liberates the humble, and helps the poor; Who responds to His people upon their outcry to Him.*

Rise for *Shemoneh Esrei.* Some take three steps backward at this point; others do so before צוּר יִשְׂרָאֵל, *'Rock of Israel.'*

Chazzan– *Praises to the Supreme God, the blessed One Who is blessed. Moses and the Children of Israel exclaimed a song to You with great joy and they all said:*

(1) *Joshua* 5:3. (2) Cf. *Song of Songs* 4:14. (3) 2:17. (4). *Genesis* 22:2.
(5) *Exodus* 15:1. (6) Cf. *Isaiah* 44:6. (7) *Psalms* 106:11.

represent the nations of the world (see *Psalms* 22:13; *Daniel* 8:3,21) who will eventually be destroyed. The birds allude to Israel (see *Song of Songs* 2:14, et al.) who will endure eternally.

◆§ **עֶזְרַת אֲבוֹתֵינוּ** — *The Helper of our forefathers.* This passage elaborates upon the Exodus within the context of God's eternal supervision of Israel and mastery over its destiny.

מִי כָמְכָה בָּאֵלִם יהוה, מִי כָּמְכָה נֶאְדָּר בַּקֹּדֶשׁ, נוֹרָא
תְהִלֹּת עֹשֵׂה פֶלֶא.[1] ❖ שִׁירָה חֲדָשָׁה שִׁבְּחוּ גְאוּלִים לְשִׁמְךָ עַל
שְׂפַת הַיָּם, יַחַד כֻּלָּם הוֹדוּ וְהִמְלִיכוּ וְאָמְרוּ:

יהוה יִמְלֹךְ לְעֹלָם וָעֶד.[2]

It is forbidden to interrupt or pause between גָּאַל יִשְׂרָאֵל and *Shemoneh Esrei,* even for *Kaddish, Kedushah* or *Amen.*

❖ **צוּר** יִשְׂרָאֵל,* קוּמָה בְּעֶזְרַת יִשְׂרָאֵל, וּפְדֵה כִנְאֻמֶךָ יְהוּדָה
וְיִשְׂרָאֵל. גֹּאֲלֵנוּ יהוה צְבָאוֹת שְׁמוֹ, קְדוֹשׁ יִשְׂרָאֵל.[3]

FIRST DAY

בְּרַח דּוֹדִי[4] עַד* שֶׁתְּחְפָּץ
אַהֲבַת כְּלוּלֵינוּ,
שׁוּב לְרַחֵם כִּי כָלוּנוּ
מַלְכֵי זֵדִים, שׁוֹבֵינוּ תוֹלָלֵינוּ.*
הֲרוֹס וְקַעֲקֵעַ בִּצָּתָם מִתִּלֵּנוּ,
הָקֵם טוּרְךָ נַגֵּן שְׁתִילֵינוּ,*
הִנֵּה זֶה עוֹמֵד אַחַר כָּתְלֵנוּ.[5]
בְּרַח דּוֹדִי עַד שֶׁיָּפוּחַ קֵץ מַחֲזֶה,
חִישׁ וְנֵסוּ הַצְּלָלִים[6] מִזֶּה,
יָרוּם* וְנִשָּׂא וְגָבַהּ[7] נִבְזֶה,
יַשְׂכִּיל וְיוֹכִיחַ וְגוֹיִם רַבִּים יַזֶּה,[8]
חֲשׂוֹף זְרוֹעֲךָ[9] קְרוֹא כָזֶה,
קוֹל דּוֹדִי הִנֵּה זֶה.[10]

SECOND DAY

בְּרַח דּוֹדִי[4] אֶל* מָכוֹן
לְשִׁבְתָּךְ,*
וְאִם עָבַרְנוּ אֶת בְּרִיתָךְ,
אָנָּא זְכוֹר אִוּוּי חֶפְצָתָךְ,
הָקֵם קוֹשְׁטְ מִלָּתָךְ,
כּוֹנֵן מְשׂוֹשׂ קִרְיָתָךְ,
הַעֲלוֹתָהּ עַל רֹאשׁ שִׂמְחָתָךְ.[11]
בְּרַח דּוֹדִי אֶל שָׁלֵם סֻכָּךְ,[12]*
וְאִם תָּעִינוּ מִדַּרְכָּךְ,
אָנָּא הָצֵץ מֵחֲרַכָּךְ,[13]
וְתוֹשִׁיעַ עַם עָנִי וּמְתָכָּךְ,
חֲמָתְךָ מֵהֶם לְשַׁכָּךְ,
וּבְאֶבְרָתְךָ סֶלָה לְהִסְתּוֹכָךְ.

⚜ **צוּר יִשְׂרָאֵל** — *Rock of Israel.* Since the end of *Shema,* we have concentrated on an elaboration of the miracles of the Exodus. We do not lose sight, however, of our faith that there is another, greater redemption yet to come. Thus we conclude with a plea that God rise up again to redeem Israel from this exile as He did in ancient Egypt.

⚜ **בְּרַח דּוֹדִי עַד** — *Flee, my Beloved, while.* Based on the concluding verse of *Song of Songs,* this *piyut* pleads that God flee from His exile, taking Israel with Him, to renew their relationship of old in the *Beis HaMikdash.* The composer's signature reads: שְׁלֹמֹה הַקָּטָן חֲזַק יִגְדַּל לְתוֹרָה וְיֶחֱזַק, *Shlomo the Lesser, may he be strong, may he become great in Torah, and be strengthened.*

שׁוֹבֵינוּ תוֹלָלֵינוּ — *Our captors, our mockers.* The translation follows *Matteh Levi.* Accordingly, the root of **שׁוֹבֵינוּ** is שבה, *to capture,* and the root of **תוֹלָלֵינוּ** is הלל, *to jest.* Another interpretation derives **שׁוֹבֵינוּ** from ישב, *to dwell,* and **תוֹלָלֵינוּ** from תֵּל, *a hill.* Thus, the verse reads: *. . . for we are being destroyed by wanton kings; resettle us on our exalted Mount (Ma'aseh Oreig).*

שְׁתִילֵינוּ — *Our Levites* [lit., *our plantings*]. The translation follows *Ibn Ezra,* who explains the phrase, שְׁתוּלִים בְּבֵית ה׳, *they will be planted in the House of* HASHEM (*Psalms* 92:11), as an allusion to the *Kohanim* and to the Levite singers of the *Beis HaMikdash.*

Alternatively: שְׁתִילֵינוּ refers to *our children,* as in the verse (*Psalms* 128:3), בָּנֶיךָ כִּשְׁתִלֵי זֵיתִים, *your children shall be like olive shoots* (*Matteh Levi*).

יָרוּם — *May he be raised.* This stich and the next one are based on *Isaiah* 52:13, 15. According to *Rashi* and *Radak* those verses refer to presently downtrodden Israel which, through the reproach of its righteous leaders, will succeed in bettering itself and ridding itself of its oppressors.

Matteh Levi understands these stiches in light of the *Targum's* interpretation of these verses as a reference to the Messiah, who will succeed in reproving Israel and turning it to righteousness (see *Isaiah* 11:4).

'Who is like You among the heavenly powers, HASHEM! Who is like You, mighty in holiness, too awesome for praise, doing wonders.'[1] Chazzan– *With a new song the redeemed ones praised Your Name at the seashore, all of them in unison gave thanks, acknowledged [Your] sovereignty, and said:*

'HASHEM shall reign for all eternity.'[2]

It is forbidden to interrupt or pause between *'Who redeemed Israel'* and *Shemoneh Esrei,* even for *Kaddish, Kedushah* or *Amen.*

צוּר Chazzan– *Rock of Israel,* arise to the aid of Israel and liberate, as You pledged, Judah and Israel. Our Redeemer — HASHEM, Master of Legions, is His Name — the Holy One of Israel.*[3]

FIRST DAY	SECOND DAY
Flee, my Beloved[4] *[from Your estrangement], while* the love of our betrothal still gratifies;* **של** *return and be merciful for we are being destroyed* **מ** *by the wanton kings — our captors, our mockers;** **ה** *destroy and uproot their mire from our hill.* **הקטן** *Put up the walls of Your Temple and let our Levites* sing: 'Behold — He is standing behind our wall!'*[5] *Flee, my Beloved before the appointed deadline [for redemption] blows by, hurry and let the clouds [of exile] disperse*[6] *from here. May he be raised* and uplifted, and lofty,*[7] *he who is now debased; may he succeed through reproach; may he scatter the many [oppressor] nations.*[8] **חזק** *Bare Your arm*[9] *and proclaim the following: 'The voice of my Beloved, behold it [has come]!'*[10]	**מ** *Flee, my Beloved,*[4] *to* the foundation of Your dwelling.* Though we have violated Your covenant, please remember Your coveted canopy [the Temple], affirm the truth of Your word, establish the joy of Your city, elevate her above Your foremost joy.*[11] **ש** *Flee, my Beloved, to [Jeru]salem, Your Tabernacle.*[12]* *Though we have strayed from Your path, please peer [at us] through Your lattice,*[13] *and save the poor and bruised people. Calm your anger against them, and may Your wing always shelter them.*

(1) *Exodus* 15:11. (2) 15:18. (3) *Isaiah* 47:4. (4) *Song of Songs* 8:14. (5) 2:9. (6) 2:17; 4:6. (7) *Isaiah* 52:13. (8) Cf. 52:15. (9) Cf. 52:10. (10) *Song of Songs* 2:8. (11) Cf. *Psalms* 137:6. (12) Cf. 76:3. (13) Cf. *Song of Songs* 2:9.

⊲§ **בְּרַח דּוֹדִי אֶל** — *Flee, my Beloved, to.* Written in the style of the *piyut* for the first day, this prayer comprises four six-line stanzas. The first line of each stanza begins with בְּרַח דּוֹדִי אֶל, *Flee, my Beloved, to,* followed by a phrase descriptive of the *Beis HaMikdash.* These four phrases carry the *paytan's* signature, מְשֻׁלָּם, *Meshullam.*

מָכוֹן לְשִׁבְתְּךָ — *Foundation of Your dwelling.* Both Moses, in the Song at the Sea (*Exodus* 15:17), and Solomon, in his invocation at the Dedication of the Holy Temple (*I Kings* 8:13; *II Chronicles* 6:2), use this phrase to describe the Temple.

The word מָכוֹן may also be vocalized מְכֻוָּן, *corresponding,* thus offering an alternative interpretation. The Holy Temple on earth *corresponds* to the Throne of Glory in heaven (*Rashi* to *Exodus* 15:17). [See below, commentary to מָרוֹם מֵרִאשׁוֹן.]

שָׁלֵם סֻכָּךְ — *Salem, Your Tabernacle.* This refers to the *Beis HaMikdash* and is based on the verse,

SECOND DAY	FIRST DAY
בְּרַח דּוֹדִי אֶל לִבְּךָ וְעֵינֶיךָ שָׁם,[5]*	בְּרַח דּוֹדִי וּדְמֵה לְךָ לִצְבִי,[1]
וְאִם זָנַחְנוּ טוֹב[6] מְחֻדָּשָׁם,[7]	יְגַל יִגַּשׁ קֵץ קִצְבִּי,
אָנָּא שְׁמַע שַׁאֲגַת	דְּלוּתִי מִשְּׁבִי לַעֲטֶרֶת צְבִי,[2]
קוֹל צוֹרְרֶיךָ וְרִגְשָׁם,	תְּעוּבִים תְּאֵבִים הַר צְבִי,[3]
רַוֵּה מִדָּם גּוֹשָׁם,	וְאֵין מֵבִיא וְנָבִיא,
וַעֲפָרָם[8] מֵחֵלֶב יְדֻשַּׁן,	וְלֹא תִשְׁבִּי מְשַׁוֵּי מְשִׁיבִי,
וּפִגְרֵיהֶם יַעֲלֶה בָאְשָׁם.	רִיבָה רִיבִי,
בְּרַח דּוֹדִי אֶל מָרוֹם מֵרִאשׁוֹן,[9]*	הָסֵר חוֹבִי וּכְאֵבִי,
וְאִם בָּגַדְנוּ בְּכַחֲשׁוֹן,	וְיֵרָא וְיֵבוֹשׁ אוֹיְבִי,
אָנָּא סְכוּת צְקוֹן לַחֲשׁוֹן,[10]	וְאָשִׁיבָה חוֹרְפִי בְּנִיבִי,
דְּלֹתִי מִטְּבוֹעַ רִפְשׁוֹן,	זֶה דוֹדִי, גּוֹאֲלִי קְרוֹבִי,
גְּאַל נְצוּרֵי כְּאִישׁוֹן,	רֵעִי וַאֲהוּבִי, אֵל אֱלֹהֵי אָבִי.[4]
כְּאָז בַּחֹדֶשׁ הָרִאשׁוֹן.	

בִּגְלַל אָבוֹת תּוֹשִׁיעַ בָּנִים, וְתָבִיא גְאֻלָּה לִבְנֵי בְנֵיהֶם,

בָּרוּךְ אַתָּה יהוה, גָּאַל יִשְׂרָאֵל.*

שמונה עשרה – עמידה

Take three steps backward, then three steps forward. Remain standing with feet together while reciting *Shemoneh Esrei*. Recite it with quiet devotion and without interruption, verbal or otherwise. Although it should not be audible to others, one must pray loudly enough to hear himself.

אֲדֹנָי שְׂפָתַי תִּפְתָּח, וּפִי יַגִּיד תְּהִלָּתֶךָ.[11]

אבות

Bend the knees at בָּרוּךְ; bow at אַתָּה; straighten up at ה׳.

בָּרוּךְ אַתָּה יהוה אֱלֹהֵינוּ וֵאלֹהֵי אֲבוֹתֵינוּ, אֱלֹהֵי אַבְרָהָם, אֱלֹהֵי יִצְחָק, וֵאלֹהֵי יַעֲקֹב, הָאֵל הַגָּדוֹל הַגִּבּוֹר וְהַנּוֹרָא, אֵל עֶלְיוֹן, גּוֹמֵל חֲסָדִים טוֹבִים וְקוֹנֵה הַכֹּל, וְזוֹכֵר חַסְדֵי אָבוֹת, וּמֵבִיא גוֹאֵל לִבְנֵי בְנֵיהֶם, לְמַעַן שְׁמוֹ בְּאַהֲבָה. מֶלֶךְ עוֹזֵר וּמוֹשִׁיעַ וּמָגֵן.

Bend the knees at בָּרוּךְ; bow at אַתָּה; straighten up at ה׳.

בָּרוּךְ אַתָּה יהוה, מָגֵן אַבְרָהָם.

וַיְהִי בְשָׁלֵם סֻכּוֹ, *When His Tabernacle was in Salem* (*Psalms* 76:3).

Salem was an ancient name of Jerusalem. The *Midrash* teaches that Abraham called the city יִרְאֶה, *Yireh* [=Jeru], as is stated (*Genesis* 22:14): *Abraham named that site HASHEM Yireh.* Shem [son of Noah, also known as Malchi-zedek] called the place שָׁלֵם, *Shalem* [=Salem], as it is written (ibid. 14:18): *Malchi-zedek, king of Salem.*

Said God, 'If I call it Yireh [=Jeru] as Abraham did, then the righteous Shem will be distraught; but if I call it Shalem [=Salem], then the righteous Abraham will be distraught. Instead I will satisfy both of these righteous men by calling it *Yireh-Shalem* [=Jeru-Salem =Jerusalem] (*Bereishis Rabbah* 14:18).

לִבְּךָ וְעֵינֶיךָ שָׁם — *The site of Your Presence and Your will* [lit., *Your heart and eyes are there*]. After the dedication of the First Temple, God appeared to Solomon in a dream, and said, "*And now I have chosen and sanctified this Temple, that My Name shall be there externally;* וְהָיוּ עֵינַי וְלִבִּי שָׁם, *and My eyes and heart* [i.e., My Presence and My will (*Rashi*)] *shall be there all of the*

FIRST DAY	SECOND DAY
Flee, my Beloved, and be like a deer,[1] יג reveal and bring near my appointed time, דל draw me from captivity ל to be a crown of pride.[2] ת [Israel,] abominated [by the nations,] covet the cherished [Temple] Mount[3] — ו but there is neither leader nor prophet, nor [Elijah the] Tishbite to resolve [disputes] and reconcile [generations]. ר O take up my grievance, ה remove my guilt and my pain, יו let my enemy see and be shamed, ח may I answer my abusers by saying: זק This is my Beloved, my Redeemer, He is close to me, my Companion, and by Beloved, God, the God of my father!'[4]	ל Flee, my Beloved, to the site of Your Presence and Your will.[5]* Though we have forsaken the goodly Temple,[6] abundant [with offerings],[7] please listen to the roar of Your enemies' voice and their tumult; sate their earth with blood, and enrich their soil[8] with their fats; may their corpses raise a stench. מ Flee, my Beloved, to [Your] lofty [Throne] of old.[9]* Though we have rebelled treacherously, please hear the outpouring of whispered prayer,[10] draw me from sinking into the muck, redeem those who are protected like the pupil of the eye, as then [in Egypt] in the first month.

For the sake of the forefathers may You save the offspring,
and bring redemption to their children's children.

*Blessed are You, HASHEM, Who redeemed Israel.**

SHEMONEH ESREI — AMIDAH

Take three steps backward, then three steps forward. Remain standing with feet together while reciting *Shemoneh Esrei*. Recite it with quiet devotion and without interruption, verbal or otherwise. Although it should not be audible to others, one must pray loudly enough to hear himself.

My Lord, open my lips, that my mouth may declare Your praise.[11]

PATRIARCHS

Bend the knees at *'Blessed'*; bow at *'You'*; straighten up at *'HASHEM.'*

בָּרוּךְ *Blessed are You, HASHEM, our God and the God of our forefathers, God of Abraham, God of Isaac, and God of Jacob; the great, mighty, and awesome God, the supreme God, Who bestows beneficial kindnesses and creates everything, Who recalls the kindnesses of the Patriarchs and brings a Redeemer to their children's children, for His Name's sake, with love. O King, Helper, Savior, and Shield.*

Bend the knees at *'Blessed'*; bow at *'You'*; straighten up at 'HASHEM.'

Blessed are You, HASHEM, Shield of Abraham.

(1) *Song of Songs* 8:14. (2) See *Isaiah* 28:5. (3) See *Daniel* 11:45. (4) Cf. *Exodus* 15:2. (5)Cf. *II Chronicles* 7:16. (6) Cf. *Hoshea* 8:3. (7) An alternative reading is: טוב מֶרְשָׁם, *the good [words] inscribed [in the Torah]*. (8) Cf. *Job* 7:5. (9) *Jeremiah* 17:12. (10) Cf. *Isaiah* 26:16. (11) *Psalms* 51:17.

days" (II Chronicles 7:16).

מָרוֹם מֵרִאשׁוֹן — *[Your] lofty [throne] of old.* The prophet (*Jeremiah* 17:12) describes the correspondence of the celestial Throne of Glory with the terrestrial Holy Temple: כִּסֵּא כָבוֹד מָרוֹם מֵרִאשׁוֹן מְקוֹם מִקְדָּשֵׁנוּ, *The Throne of Glory, lofty of old, [it is] the site of our Sanctuary.*

גָּאַל יִשְׂרָאֵל — *Who redeemed Israel.* The text of the blessing is in keeping with the Talmudic dictum that prayer, i.e., *Shemoneh Esrei*, should follow mention of God's redemption of Israel. Only after we have set forth our faith in God as our Redeemer may we begin *Shemoneh Esrei*, in which we pray to Him for our personal and national needs (*R' Hirsch*).

גבורות

אַתָּה גִּבּוֹר לְעוֹלָם אֲדֹנָי, מְחַיֵּה מֵתִים אַתָּה, רַב לְהוֹשִׁיעַ.

[On the first day – מַשִּׁיב הָרְוּחַ וּמוֹרִיד הַגֶּשֶׁם.]

מְכַלְכֵּל חַיִּים בְּחֶסֶד, מְחַיֵּה מֵתִים בְּרַחֲמִים רַבִּים, סוֹמֵךְ נוֹפְלִים, וְרוֹפֵא חוֹלִים, וּמַתִּיר אֲסוּרִים, וּמְקַיֵּם אֱמוּנָתוֹ לִישֵׁנֵי עָפָר. מִי כָמְוֹךָ בַּעַל גְּבוּרוֹת, וּמִי דְּוֹמֶה לָּךְ, מֶלֶךְ מֵמִית וּמְחַיֶּה וּמַצְמִיחַ יְשׁוּעָה. וְנֶאֱמָן אַתָּה לְהַחֲיוֹת מֵתִים. בָּרוּךְ אַתָּה יהוה, מְחַיֵּה הַמֵּתִים.

During the *chazzan's* repetition, *Kedushah* (below) is recited at this point.

קדושת השם

INDIVIDUALS RECITE:

אַתָּה קָדוֹשׁ וְשִׁמְךָ קָדוֹשׁ, וּקְדוֹשִׁים בְּכָל יוֹם יְהַלְלְוּךָ סֶּלָה. בָּרוּךְ אַתָּה יהוה, הָאֵל הַקָּדוֹשׁ.

CHAZZAN RECITES DURING HIS REPETITION:

לְדוֹר וָדוֹר נַגִּיד גָּדְלֶךָ וּלְנֵצַח נְצָחִים קְדֻשָּׁתְךָ נַקְדִּישׁ, וְשִׁבְחֲךָ אֱלֹהֵינוּ מִפִּינוּ לֹא יָמוּשׁ לְעוֹלָם וָעֶד, כִּי אֵל מֶלֶךְ גָּדוֹל וְקָדוֹשׁ אָתָּה. בָּרוּךְ אַתָּה יהוה, הָאֵל הַקָּדוֹשׁ.

קדושה

When reciting *Kedushah,* one must stand with his feet together and avoid any interruptions. One should rise on his toes when saying the words קָדוֹשׁ, קָדוֹשׁ, קָדוֹשׁ; בָּרוּךְ (of בָּרוּךְ כְּבוֹד); and יִמְלֹךְ.

Cong. then *Chazzan* – **נְקַדֵּשׁ** אֶת שִׁמְךָ בָּעוֹלָם, כְּשֵׁם שֶׁמַּקְדִּישִׁים אוֹתוֹ בִּשְׁמֵי מָרוֹם, כַּכָּתוּב עַל יַד נְבִיאֶךָ, וְקָרָא זֶה אֶל זֶה וְאָמַר:

All – קָדוֹשׁ קָדוֹשׁ קָדוֹשׁ יהוה צְבָאוֹת, מְלֹא כָל הָאָרֶץ כְּבוֹדוֹ.[2] ❖ אָז בְּקוֹל רַעַשׁ גָּדוֹל אַדִּיר וְחָזָק מַשְׁמִיעִים קוֹל, מִתְנַשְּׂאִים לְעֻמַּת שְׂרָפִים, לְעֻמָּתָם בָּרוּךְ יֹאמֵרוּ:

All – בָּרוּךְ כְּבוֹד יהוה, מִמְּקוֹמוֹ.[3] ❖ מִמְּקוֹמְךָ מַלְכֵּנוּ תוֹפִיעַ, וְתִמְלֹךְ עָלֵינוּ, כִּי מְחַכִּים אֲנַחְנוּ לָךְ. מָתַי תִּמְלֹךְ בְּצִיּוֹן, בְּקָרוֹב בְּיָמֵינוּ, לְעוֹלָם וָעֶד תִּשְׁכּוֹן. תִּתְגַּדַּל וְתִתְקַדַּשׁ בְּתוֹךְ יְרוּשָׁלַיִם עִירְךָ, לְדוֹר וָדוֹר וּלְנֵצַח נְצָחִים. וְעֵינֵינוּ תִרְאֶינָה מַלְכוּתֶךָ, כַּדָּבָר הָאָמוּר בְּשִׁירֵי עֻזֶּךָ, עַל יְדֵי דָוִד מְשִׁיחַ צִדְקֶךָ:

All – יִמְלֹךְ יהוה לְעוֹלָם, אֱלֹהַיִךְ צִיּוֹן לְדֹר וָדֹר, הַלְלוּיָהּ.[4]

Chazzan continues . . . לְדוֹר וָדוֹר (above).

GOD'S MIGHT

אַתָּה *You are eternally mighty, my Lord, the Resuscitator of the dead are You; abundantly able to save.*

On the first day:

[He makes the wind blow and He makes the rain descend.]

He sustains the living with kindness, resuscitates the dead with abundant mercy, supports the fallen, heals the sick, releases the confined, and maintains His faith to those asleep in the dust. Who is like You, O Master of mighty deeds, and who is comparable to You, O King Who causes death and restores life and makes salvation sprout! And You are faithful to resuscitate the dead. Blessed are You, HASHEM, Who resuscitates the dead.

During the *chazzan's* repetition, *Kedushah* (below) is recited at this point.

HOLINESS OF GOD'S NAME

INDIVIDUALS RECITE:

אַתָּה *You are holy and Your Name is holy, and holy ones praise You every day, forever. Blessed are You, HASHEM, the holy God.*

CHAZZAN RECITES DURING HIS REPETITION:

לְדוֹר *From generation to generation we shall relate Your greatness and for infinite eternities we shall proclaim Your holiness. Your praise, our God, shall not leave our mouth forever and ever, for You, O God, are a great and holy King. Blessed are You, HASHEM, the holy God.*

KEDUSHAH

When reciting *Kedushah*, one must stand with his feet together and avoid any interruptions. One should rise on his toes when saying the words *Holy, holy, holy; Blessed is;* and *HASHEM shall reign.*

Cong. then Chazzan – **נְקַדֵּשׁ** *We shall sanctify Your Name in this world, just as they sanctify it in heaven above, as it is written by Your prophet, "And one [angel] will call another and say:*

All – *'Holy, holy, holy is HASHEM, Master of Legions, the whole world is filled with His glory.'"*[2] ❖ *Then, with a sound of great noise, mighty and powerful, they make heard a voice, raising themselves toward the seraphim; those facing them say 'Blessed ...':*

All – *'Blessed is the glory of HASHEM from His place.'*[3] ❖ *From Your place, our King, You will appear and reign over us, for we await You. When will You reign in Zion? Soon, in our days — forever and ever — may You dwell there. May You be exalted and sanctified within Jerusalem, Your city, from generation to generation and for all eternity. May our eyes see Your kingdom, as it is expressed in the songs of Your might, written by David, Your righteous anointed:*

All – *'HASHEM shall reign forever — your God, O Zion — from generation to generation, Halleluyah!'*[4]

Chazzan continues לְדוֹר וָדוֹר, *From generation ...* (above).

---

(1) *Psalms* 51:17. (2) *Isaiah* 6:3. (3) *Ezekiel* 3:12. (4) *Psalms* 146:10.

קדושת היום

אַתָּה בְחַרְתָּנוּ מִכָּל הָעַמִּים, אָהַבְתָּ אוֹתָנוּ, וְרָצִיתָ בָּנוּ, וְרוֹמַמְתָּנוּ מִכָּל הַלְּשׁוֹנוֹת, וְקִדַּשְׁתָּנוּ בְּמִצְוֹתֶיךָ, וְקֵרַבְתָּנוּ מַלְכֵּנוּ לַעֲבוֹדָתֶךָ, וְשִׁמְךָ הַגָּדוֹל וְהַקָּדוֹשׁ עָלֵינוּ קָרָאתָ.

On the Sabbath add the words in brackets. [If forgotten, see *Laws* §86-90.]

וַתִּתֶּן לָנוּ יהוה אֱלֹהֵינוּ בְּאַהֲבָה [שַׁבָּתוֹת לִמְנוּחָה וּ]מוֹעֲדִים לְשִׂמְחָה חַגִּים וּזְמַנִּים לְשָׂשׂוֹן, אֶת יוֹם [הַשַּׁבָּת הַזֶּה וְאֶת יוֹם] חַג הַמַּצּוֹת הַזֶּה, זְמַן חֵרוּתֵנוּ [בְּאַהֲבָה] מִקְרָא קֹדֶשׁ, זֵכֶר לִיצִיאַת מִצְרָיִם.

During the *chazzan's* repetition, congregation responds אָמֵן as indicated.

אֱלֹהֵינוּ וֵאלֹהֵי אֲבוֹתֵינוּ, יַעֲלֶה, וְיָבֹא, וְיַגִּיעַ, וְיֵרָאֶה, וְיֵרָצֶה, וְיִשָּׁמַע, וְיִפָּקֵד, וְיִזָּכֵר זִכְרוֹנֵנוּ וּפִקְדוֹנֵנוּ, וְזִכְרוֹן אֲבוֹתֵינוּ, וְזִכְרוֹן מָשִׁיחַ בֶּן דָּוִד עַבְדֶּךָ, וְזִכְרוֹן יְרוּשָׁלַיִם עִיר קָדְשֶׁךָ, וְזִכְרוֹן כָּל עַמְּךָ בֵּית יִשְׂרָאֵל לְפָנֶיךָ, לִפְלֵיטָה לְטוֹבָה לְחֵן וּלְחֶסֶד וּלְרַחֲמִים, לְחַיִּים וּלְשָׁלוֹם בְּיוֹם חַג הַמַּצּוֹת הַזֶּה. זָכְרֵנוּ יהוה אֱלֹהֵינוּ בּוֹ לְטוֹבָה (.Cong – אָמֵן), וּפָקְדֵנוּ בוֹ לִבְרָכָה (.Cong – אָמֵן), וְהוֹשִׁיעֵנוּ בוֹ לְחַיִּים (.Cong – אָמֵן). וּבִדְבַר יְשׁוּעָה וְרַחֲמִים, חוּס וְחָנֵּנוּ וְרַחֵם עָלֵינוּ וְהוֹשִׁיעֵנוּ, כִּי אֵלֶיךָ עֵינֵינוּ, כִּי אֵל מֶלֶךְ חַנּוּן וְרַחוּם אָתָּה.[1]

On the Sabbath add the words in brackets. [If forgotten, see *Laws* §86-90.]

וְהַשִּׂיאֵנוּ יהוה אֱלֹהֵינוּ אֶת בִּרְכַּת מוֹעֲדֶיךָ לְחַיִּים וּלְשָׁלוֹם, לְשִׂמְחָה וּלְשָׂשׂוֹן, כַּאֲשֶׁר רָצִיתָ וְאָמַרְתָּ לְבָרְכֵנוּ. [אֱלֹהֵינוּ וֵאלֹהֵי אֲבוֹתֵינוּ רְצֵה בִמְנוּחָתֵנוּ] קַדְּשֵׁנוּ בְּמִצְוֹתֶיךָ וְתֵן חֶלְקֵנוּ בְּתוֹרָתֶךָ, שַׂבְּעֵנוּ מִטּוּבֶךָ וְשַׂמְּחֵנוּ בִּישׁוּעָתֶךָ, וְטַהֵר לִבֵּנוּ לְעָבְדְּךָ בֶּאֱמֶת, וְהַנְחִילֵנוּ יהוה אֱלֹהֵינוּ [בְּאַהֲבָה וּבְרָצוֹן] בְּשִׂמְחָה וּבְשָׂשׂוֹן [שַׁבָּת וּ]מוֹעֲדֵי קָדְשֶׁךָ, וְיִשְׂמְחוּ בְךָ יִשְׂרָאֵל מְקַדְּשֵׁי שְׁמֶךָ. בָּרוּךְ אַתָּה יהוה, מְקַדֵּשׁ [הַשַּׁבָּת וְ]יִשְׂרָאֵל וְהַזְּמַנִּים.

SANCTIFICATION OF THE DAY

אַתָּה בְחַרְתָּנוּ *You have chosen us from all the peoples; You loved us and found favor in us; You exalted us above all the tongues and You sanctified us with Your commandments. You drew us close, our King, to Your service and proclaimed Your great and Holy Name upon us.*

On the Sabbath add the words in brackets. [If forgotten, see *Laws* §86-90.]

וַתִּתֶּן לָנוּ *And You gave us, HASHEM, our God, with love [Sabbaths for rest], appointed festivals for gladness, Festivals and times for joy, [this day of Sabbath and] this day of the Festival of Matzos, the time of our freedom [with love], a holy convocation, a memorial of the Exodus from Egypt.*

During the *chazzan's* repetition, congregation responds *Amen* as indicated.

אֱלֹהֵינוּ *Our God and God of our forefathers, may there rise, come, reach, be noted, be favored, be heard, be considered, and be remembered — the remembrance and consideration of ourselves; the remembrance of our forefathers; the remembrance of Messiah, son of David, Your servant; the remembrance of Jerusalem, the City of Your Holiness; the remembrance of Your entire people the Family of Israel — before You for deliverance, for goodness, for grace, for kindness, and for compassion, for life, and for peace on this day of the Festival of Matzos. Remember us on it, HASHEM, our God, for goodness (*Cong. – *Amen); consider us on it for blessing (*Cong. – *Amen); and help us on it for life (*Cong. – *Amen). In the matter of salvation and compassion, pity, be gracious and compassionate with us and help us, for our eyes are turned to You, because You are God, the gracious and compassionate King.*[1]

On the Sabbath add the words in brackets. [If forgotten, see *Laws* §86-90.]

וְהַשִּׂיאֵנוּ *Bestow upon us, O HASHEM, our God, the blessing of Your appointed Festivals for life and for peace, for gladness and for joy, as You desired and promised to bless us. [Our God and the God of our forefathers, may You be pleased with our rest.] Sanctify us with Your commandments and grant us our share in Your Torah; satisfy us from Your goodness and gladden us with Your salvation, and purify our heart to serve You sincerely. And grant us a heritage, O HASHEM, our God — [with love and with favor] with gladness and with joy — [the Sabbath and] the appointed festivals of Your holiness, and may Israel, the sanctifiers of Your Name, rejoice in You. Blessed are You, HASHEM, Who sanctifies [the Sabbath,] Israel and the festive seasons.*

(1) Cf. *Nehemiah* 9:31.

עבודה

רְצֵה יהוה אֱלֹהֵינוּ בְּעַמְּךָ יִשְׂרָאֵל וּבִתְפִלָּתָם, וְהָשֵׁב אֶת הָעֲבוֹדָה לִדְבִיר בֵּיתֶךָ. וְאִשֵּׁי יִשְׂרָאֵל וּתְפִלָּתָם בְּאַהֲבָה תְקַבֵּל בְּרָצוֹן, וּתְהִי לְרָצוֹן תָּמִיד עֲבוֹדַת יִשְׂרָאֵל עַמֶּךָ.

וְתֶחֱזֶינָה עֵינֵינוּ בְּשׁוּבְךָ לְצִיּוֹן בְּרַחֲמִים. בָּרוּךְ אַתָּה יהוה, הַמַּחֲזִיר שְׁכִינָתוֹ לְצִיּוֹן.

הודאה

Bow at מוֹדִים; straighten up at 'ה. In his repetition the *chazzan* should recite the entire מוֹדִים aloud, while the congregation recites מוֹדִים דְּרַבָּנָן softly.

מוֹדִים אֲנַחְנוּ לָךְ, שָׁאַתָּה הוּא יהוה אֱלֹהֵינוּ וֵאלֹהֵי אֲבוֹתֵינוּ לְעוֹלָם וָעֶד. צוּר חַיֵּינוּ, מָגֵן יִשְׁעֵנוּ אַתָּה הוּא לְדוֹר וָדוֹר. נוֹדֶה לְּךָ וּנְסַפֵּר תְּהִלָּתֶךָ[1] עַל חַיֵּינוּ הַמְּסוּרִים בְּיָדֶךָ, וְעַל נִשְׁמוֹתֵינוּ הַפְּקוּדוֹת לָךְ, וְעַל נִסֶּיךָ שֶׁבְּכָל יוֹם עִמָּנוּ, וְעַל נִפְלְאוֹתֶיךָ וְטוֹבוֹתֶיךָ שֶׁבְּכָל עֵת, עֶרֶב וָבֹקֶר וְצָהֳרָיִם. הַטּוֹב כִּי לֹא כָלוּ רַחֲמֶיךָ, וְהַמְּרַחֵם כִּי לֹא תַמּוּ חֲסָדֶיךָ,[2] מֵעוֹלָם קִוִּינוּ לָךְ.

מודים דרבנן

מוֹדִים אֲנַחְנוּ לָךְ, שָׁאַתָּה הוּא יהוה אֱלֹהֵינוּ וֵאלֹהֵי אֲבוֹתֵינוּ, אֱלֹהֵי כָל בָּשָׂר, יוֹצְרֵנוּ, יוֹצֵר בְּרֵאשִׁית. בְּרָכוֹת וְהוֹדָאוֹת לְשִׁמְךָ הַגָּדוֹל וְהַקָּדוֹשׁ, עַל שֶׁהֶחֱיִיתָנוּ וְקִיַּמְתָּנוּ. כֵּן תְּחַיֵּנוּ וּתְקַיְּמֵנוּ, וְתֶאֱסוֹף גָּלֻיּוֹתֵינוּ לְחַצְרוֹת קָדְשֶׁךָ, לִשְׁמוֹר חֻקֶּיךָ וְלַעֲשׂוֹת רְצוֹנֶךָ, וּלְעָבְדְּךָ בְּלֵבָב שָׁלֵם, עַל שֶׁאֲנַחְנוּ מוֹדִים לָךְ. בָּרוּךְ אֵל הַהוֹדָאוֹת.

וְעַל כֻּלָּם יִתְבָּרַךְ וְיִתְרוֹמַם שִׁמְךָ מַלְכֵּנוּ תָּמִיד לְעוֹלָם וָעֶד.

Bend the knees at בָּרוּךְ; bow at אַתָּה; straighten up at 'ה.

וְכֹל הַחַיִּים יוֹדוּךָ סֶּלָה, וִיהַלְלוּ אֶת שִׁמְךָ בֶּאֱמֶת, הָאֵל יְשׁוּעָתֵנוּ וְעֶזְרָתֵנוּ סֶלָה. בָּרוּךְ אַתָּה יהוה, הַטּוֹב שִׁמְךָ וּלְךָ נָאֶה לְהוֹדוֹת.

TEMPLE SERVICE

רְצֵה *Be favorable, HASHEM, our God, toward Your people Israel and their prayer and restore the service to the Holy of Holies of Your Temple. The fire-offerings of Israel and their prayer accept with love and favor, and may the service of Your people Israel always be favorable to You.*

וְתֶחֱזֶינָה *May our eyes behold Your return to Zion in compassion. Blessed are You, HASHEM, Who restores His Presence to Zion.*

THANKSGIVING [MODIM]

Bow at *'We gratefully thank You'*; straighten up at *'HASHEM.'* In his repetition the *chazzan* should recite the entire *Modim* aloud, while the congregation recites *Modim of the Rabbis* softly.

מוֹדִים *We gratefully thank You, for it is You Who are HASHEM, our God and the God of our forefathers for all eternity; Rock of our lives, Shield of our salvation are You from generation to generation. We shall thank You and relate Your praise[1] — for our lives, which are committed to Your power and for our souls that are entrusted to You; for Your miracles that are with us every day; and for Your wonders and favors in every season — evening, morning, and afternoon. The Beneficent One, for Your compassions were never exhausted, and the Compassionate One, for Your kindnesses never ended[2] — always have we put our hope in You.*

MODIM OF THE RABBIS

מוֹדִים *We gratefully thank You, for it is You Who are HASHEM, our God and the God of our forefathers, the God of all flesh, our Molder, the Molder of the universe. Blessings and thanks are due Your great and holy Name for You have given us life and sustained us. So may You continue to give us life and sustain us and gather our exiles to the Courtyards of Your Sanctuary, to observe Your decrees, to do Your will and to serve You wholeheartedly. [We thank You] for inspiring us to thank You. Blessed is the God of thanksgivings.*

For all these, may Your Name be blessed and exalted, our King, continually forever and ever.

Bend the knees at *'Blessed'*; bow at *'You'*; straighten up at *'HASHEM.'*

Everything alive will gratefully acknowledge You, Selah! and praise Your Name sincerely, O God of our salvation and help, Selah! Blessed are You, HASHEM, Your Name is 'The Beneficent One' and to You it is fitting to give thanks.

---

(1) Cf. *Psalms* 79:13. (2) Cf. *Lamentations* 3:22.

ברכת כהנים

The *chazzan* recites בִּרְכַּת כֹּהֲנִים during his repetition. He faces right at וְיִשְׁמְרֶךָ; faces left at אֵלֶיךָ וִיחֻנֶּךָּ; faces the Ark for the rest of the blessings.

אֱלֹהֵינוּ, וֵאלֹהֵי אֲבוֹתֵינוּ, בָּרְכֵנוּ בַבְּרָכָה הַמְּשֻׁלֶּשֶׁת בַּתּוֹרָה הַכְּתוּבָה עַל יְדֵי מֹשֶׁה עַבְדֶּךָ, הָאֲמוּרָה מִפִּי אַהֲרֹן וּבָנָיו, כֹּהֲנִים עַם קְדוֹשֶׁךָ, כָּאָמוּר:

יְבָרֶכְךָ יהוה, וְיִשְׁמְרֶךָ. (Cong. – כֵּן יְהִי רָצוֹן.)

יָאֵר יהוה פָּנָיו אֵלֶיךָ וִיחֻנֶּךָּ. (Cong. – כֵּן יְהִי רָצוֹן.)

יִשָּׂא יהוה פָּנָיו אֵלֶיךָ וְיָשֵׂם לְךָ שָׁלוֹם.[1] (Cong. – כֵּן יְהִי רָצוֹן.)

שלום

שִׂים שָׁלוֹם, טוֹבָה, וּבְרָכָה, חֵן, וָחֶסֶד וְרַחֲמִים עָלֵינוּ וְעַל כָּל יִשְׂרָאֵל עַמֶּךָ. בָּרְכֵנוּ אָבִינוּ, כֻּלָּנוּ כְּאֶחָד בְּאוֹר פָּנֶיךָ, כִּי בְאוֹר פָּנֶיךָ נָתַתָּ לָּנוּ, יהוה אֱלֹהֵינוּ, תּוֹרַת חַיִּים וְאַהֲבַת חֶסֶד, וּצְדָקָה, וּבְרָכָה, וְרַחֲמִים, וְחַיִּים, וְשָׁלוֹם. וְטוֹב בְּעֵינֶיךָ לְבָרֵךְ אֶת עַמְּךָ יִשְׂרָאֵל, בְּכָל עֵת וּבְכָל שָׁעָה בִּשְׁלוֹמֶךָ. בָּרוּךְ אַתָּה יהוה, הַמְּבָרֵךְ אֶת עַמּוֹ יִשְׂרָאֵל בַּשָּׁלוֹם.

יִהְיוּ לְרָצוֹן אִמְרֵי פִי וְהֶגְיוֹן לִבִּי לְפָנֶיךָ, יהוה צוּרִי וְגֹאֲלִי.[2]

THE *CHAZZAN'S* REPETITION ENDS HERE; TURN TO PAGE 348. INDIVIDUALS CONTINUE:

אֱלֹהַי, נְצוֹר לְשׁוֹנִי מֵרָע, וּשְׂפָתַי מִדַּבֵּר מִרְמָה,[3] וְלִמְקַלְלַי נַפְשִׁי תִדּוֹם, וְנַפְשִׁי כֶּעָפָר לַכֹּל תִּהְיֶה. פְּתַח לִבִּי בְּתוֹרָתֶךָ, וּבְמִצְוֹתֶיךָ תִּרְדּוֹף נַפְשִׁי. וְכֹל הַחוֹשְׁבִים עָלַי רָעָה, מְהֵרָה הָפֵר עֲצָתָם וְקַלְקֵל מַחֲשַׁבְתָּם. עֲשֵׂה לְמַעַן שְׁמֶךָ, עֲשֵׂה לְמַעַן יְמִינֶךָ, עֲשֵׂה לְמַעַן קְדֻשָּׁתֶךָ, עֲשֵׂה לְמַעַן תּוֹרָתֶךָ. לְמַעַן יֵחָלְצוּן יְדִידֶיךָ, הוֹשִׁיעָה יְמִינְךָ וַעֲנֵנִי.[4]

Some recite verses pertaining to their names here. See page 1143.

יִהְיוּ לְרָצוֹן אִמְרֵי פִי וְהֶגְיוֹן לִבִּי לְפָנֶיךָ, יהוה צוּרִי וְגֹאֲלִי.[2] עֹשֶׂה שָׁלוֹם בִּמְרוֹמָיו, הוּא יַעֲשֶׂה שָׁלוֹם עָלֵינוּ, וְעַל כָּל יִשְׂרָאֵל. וְאִמְרוּ: אָמֵן.

Bow and take three steps back. Bow left and say . . . עֹשֶׂה; bow right and say . . . הוּא יַעֲשֶׂה; bow forward and say וְעַל כָּל . . . אָמֵן.

יְהִי רָצוֹן מִלְּפָנֶיךָ יהוה אֱלֹהֵינוּ וֵאלֹהֵי אֲבוֹתֵינוּ, שֶׁיִּבָּנֶה בֵּית הַמִּקְדָּשׁ בִּמְהֵרָה בְיָמֵינוּ, וְתֵן חֶלְקֵנוּ בְּתוֹרָתֶךָ. וְשָׁם נַעֲבָדְךָ בְּיִרְאָה, כִּימֵי עוֹלָם וּכְשָׁנִים קַדְמוֹנִיּוֹת. וְעָרְבָה לַיהוה מִנְחַת יְהוּדָה וִירוּשָׁלָיִם, כִּימֵי עוֹלָם וּכְשָׁנִים קַדְמוֹנִיּוֹת.[5]

THE INDIVIDUAL'S RECITATION OF *SHEMONEH ESREI* ENDS HERE.

The individual remains standing in place until the *chazzan* reaches *Kedushah* — or at least until the *chazzan* begins his repetition — then he takes three steps forward.

FOR THOSE CONGREGATIONS THAT RECITE *PIYUTIM,* THE *CHAZZAN'S* REPETITION FOR THE SECOND DAY BEGINS ON PAGE 332. FOR THE FIRST DAY AND FOR CONGREGATIONS NOT RECITING *PIYUTIM,* THE REPETITION BEGINS ON PAGE 322.

THE PRIESTLY BLESSING

The *chazzan* recites the Priestly Blessing during his repetition.

אֱלֹהֵינוּ *Our God and the God of our forefathers, bless us with the three-verse blessing in the Torah that was written by the hand of Moses, Your servant, that was said by Aaron and his sons, the Kohanim, Your holy people, as it is said:*

May HASHEM bless you and safeguard you. (Cong.— *So may it be.*)

May HASHEM illuminate His countenance for you and be gracious to you. (Cong.— *So may it be.*)

May HASHEM turn His countenance to you and establish peace for you.[1] (Cong.— *So may it be.*)

PEACE

שִׂים *Establish peace, goodness, blessing, graciousness, kindness, and compassion upon us and upon all of Your people Israel. Bless us, our Father, all of us as one, with the light of Your countenance, for with the light of Your countenance You gave us, HASHEM, our God, the Torah of life and a love of kindness, righteousness, blessing, compassion, life, and peace. And may it be good in Your eyes to bless Your people Israel at every time and every hour with Your peace. Blessed are You, HASHEM, Who blesses His people Israel with peace.*

May the expressions of my mouth and the thoughts of my heart find favor before You, HASHEM, my Rock and my Redeemer.[2]

THE *CHAZZAN'S* REPETITION ENDS HERE; TURN TO PAGE 348. INDIVIDUALS CONTINUE:

אֱלֹהַי *My God, guard my tongue from evil and my lips from speaking deceitfully.*[3] *To those who curse me, let my soul be silent; and let my soul be like dust to everyone. Open my heart to Your Torah, then my soul will pursue Your commandments. As for all those who design evil against me, speedily nullify their counsel and disrupt their design. Act for Your Name's sake; act for Your right hand's sake; act for Your sanctity's sake; act for Your Torah's sake. That Your beloved ones may be given rest; let Your right hand save, and respond to me.*[4]

Some recite verses pertaining to their names at this point. See page 1143.

May the expressions of my mouth and the thoughts of my heart find favor before You, HASHEM, my Rock and my Redeemer.[2] *He Who makes peace in His heights, may He make peace upon us, and upon all Israel. Now respond: Amen.*

Bow and take three steps back. Bow left and say, *'He Who makes peace . . .'*; bow right and say, *'may He make peace . . .'*; bow forward and say, *'and upon . . . Amen.'*

יְהִי רָצוֹן *May it be Your will, HASHEM, our God and the God of our forefathers, that the Holy Temple be rebuilt, speedily in our days. Grant us our share in Your Torah, and may we serve You there with reverence, as in days of old and in former years. Then the offering of Judah and Jerusalem will be pleasing to HASHEM, as in days of old and in former years.*[5]

THE INDIVIDUAL'S RECITATION OF *SHEMONEH ESREI* ENDS HERE.

The individual remains standing in place until the *chazzan* reaches *Kedushah* — or at least until the *chazzan* begins his repetition — then he takes three steps forward. The *chazzan* himself, or one praying alone, should remain in place for a few moments before taking three steps forward.

FOR THOSE CONGREGATIONS THAT RECITE *PIYUTIM,* THE *CHAZZAN'S* REPETITION FOR THE SECOND DAY BEGINS ON PAGE 332. FOR THE FIRST DAY AND FOR CONGREGATIONS NOT RECITING *PIYUTIM,* THE REPETITION BEGINS ON PAGE 322.

(1) *Numbers* 6:24-26. (2) *Psalms* 19:15. (3) Cf. 34:14. (4) 60:7; 108:7. (5) *Malachi* 3:4.

חזרת הש״ץ ליום שני

אֲדֹנָי שְׂפָתַי תִּפְתָּח, וּפִי יַגִּיד תְּהִלָּתֶךָ.[1]

אבות

The *chazzan* bends his knees at בָּרוּךְ; bows at אַתָּה; straightens up at 'ה.

בָּרוּךְ אַתָּה יהוה אֱלֹהֵינוּ וֵאלֹהֵי אֲבוֹתֵינוּ, אֱלֹהֵי אַבְרָהָם, אֱלֹהֵי יִצְחָק, וֵאלֹהֵי יַעֲקֹב, הָאֵל הַגָּדוֹל הַגִּבּוֹר וְהַנּוֹרָא, אֵל עֶלְיוֹן, גּוֹמֵל חֲסָדִים טוֹבִים וְקוֹנֵה הַכֹּל, וְזוֹכֵר חַסְדֵי אָבוֹת, וּמֵבִיא גוֹאֵל לִבְנֵי בְנֵיהֶם, לְמַעַן שְׁמוֹ בְּאַהֲבָה. מֶלֶךְ עוֹזֵר וּמוֹשִׁיעַ וּמָגֵן.

מִסּוֹד* חֲכָמִים וּנְבוֹנִים, וּמִלֶּמֶד דַּעַת מְבִינִים, אֶפְתְּחָה פִּי בְּשִׁיר וּבִרְנָנִים, לְהוֹדוֹת וּלְהַלֵּל פְּנֵי שׁוֹכֵן מְעוֹנִים.

All:

אֲסִירִים* אֲשֶׁר בַּכֹּשֶׁר* שִׁעֲשַׁעְתָּ, בַּעֲנָם[2] שׁוּעַ צִקּוּנָם שַׁעְתָּ,
גּוֹי וֵאלֹהָיו* יַחַד הוֹשַׁעְתָּ, דִּלַּגְתָּ קֵץ וְאִתָּם נוֹשַׁעְתָּ.
הַמְּשָׁכוּ אַחֲרֶיךָ בַּמִּדְבָּר כִּבְהֵמָה,[3] וְצוֹרְרֵיהֶם הֲמַמְתָּ בְּשִׁלּוּשׁ מְהוּמָה,
זְעָמוּ בְּעֶשֶׂר מַכּוֹת בְּאַף וּבְחֵמָה,[4] חֲנוּנֶיךָ בְּפָסוֹחַ וְגָנוֹן[5] לְרַחֲמָה.
טֶרֶם חִמּוּצָה חֲרָרָה חִפְּזוּ לָצֵאת[6] בְּכִישׁוֹר,[7]
יָצְאוּ לְקֵץ רָץ דּוֹד רַךְ[8] לְתָשׁוֹר.
❖ כּוֹנַנְתָּ בְּכֵן חַג בַּעֲבוֹתוֹת קָשׁוֹר, לַהֲגוֹת בּוֹ בְּקֶקֶץ עֶרֶךְ עִנְיַן שׁוֹר.*
All – אֲהֵבוּךָ אוֹהֲבֶיךָ אוֹתָם חָנוֹן, בְּהַר הַלְּבָנוֹן.
❖ בְּפָסוֹחַ וְגָנוֹן,[5] בַּעֲדָם תִּגְנוֹן.

This *Machzor* includes those *piyutim* that are commonly recited. A few *piyutim* that are omitted by a vast majority of congregations have been included in an appendix beginning on page 1108. The text will indicate where they may be recited.

חֲזָרַת הַשַּׁ״ץ / CHAZZAN'S REPETITION

In ancient times, when *siddurim* were not available and many people did not know the text of *Shemoneh Esrei*, people could listen intently to the *chazzan's* repetition and respond *Amen* to the blessings, thereby fulfilling their own obligation to pray. Thus, the repetition has the status of a communal, rather than an individual, prayer.

On Rosh Hashanah and Yom Kippur — and, to a lesser extent, on other Festivals — *piyutim* are inserted in the *chazzan's* repetition. These *piyutim* [known as *kerovos*] express the mood and theme of the day, and many of them have become highlights of the day's service. Thus, the repetition is truly a communal prayer, for it involves the entire congregation.

מסוד – *Based on the tradition.* Many prominent halachic authorities from medieval times onward have opposed the insertion of *piyutim* into the prayer order, primarily on the grounds that they are an interference with and a change in the words of the prayers as they were set forth by the Sages. Most congregations, though by no means all, follow *Rama (Orach Chaim* 68 and 112) who permits the recitation of *piyutim.* To justify our recitation of *piyutim* during the *chazzan's Shemoneh Esrei,* they are prefaced with the formula, מִסּוֹד חֲכָמִים וּנְבוֹנִים, *Based on the tradition of our wise and discerning teachers,* meaning that we dare to interrupt the prayer service only because these *piyutim* were transmitted to us by the wise and discerning teachers of yore, based on the 'foundation' of their great wisdom and piety.

אֲסִירִים — *The prisoners.* This unsigned *piyut* was composed by R' Elazar HaKalir (see p. 43) as attested to by *Tosafos* (*Megillah* 25a). The first twelve stiches, recited at the end of the first blessing, begin with the letters א through ל. The next twelve, recited at the end of the second blessing, start with the letters מ through צ, each letter beginning two stiches. The final sixteen stiches bear the initials ק through ת, four times each, and are recited at the beginning of the third blessing.

❧ CHAZZAN'S REPETITION FOR THE SECOND DAY ❧

My Lord, open my lips, that my mouth may declare Your praise.[1]

PATRIARCHS

The *chazzan* bends his knees at *'Blessed'*; bows at *'You'*; straightens up at *'HASHEM.'*

בָּרוּךְ *Blessed are You, HASHEM, our God and the God of our forefathers, God of Abraham, God of Isaac, and God of Jacob; the great, mighty, and awesome God, the supreme God, Who bestows beneficial kindnesses and creates everything, Who recalls the kindnesses of the Patriarchs and brings a Redeemer to their children's children, for His Name's sake, with love. O King, Helper, Savior, and Shield.*

מִסּוֹד *Based on the tradition* of our wise and discerning teachers, and the teaching derived from the knowledge of the discerning, I open my mouth in song and joyful praise, to give thanks and to offer praise before Him Who dwells in the heavens.*

All:

א *The prisoners* whom You rejoiced at the suitable moment,**
ב *in Anam [Egypt],*[2] *You turned to their outpoured cry,*
ג *You saved a nation and its leaders* together,*
ד *You leaped over one hundred ninety years and were saved with them.*
ה *They drew themselves after You like a flock [following its Shepherd] in the desert,*[3]
ו *You terrified their enemies with a trebled panic,*
ז *You raged at them with ten plagues, in anger and fury,*[4]
ח *while You pitied Your gracious ones with compassion and protection.*[5]
ט *Before the dough could rise they were rushed to depart*[6] *at the suitable time,*[7]
י *they went forth on the day the beloved [Abraham] had run to serve tender meat.*[8]
כ Chazzan– *To commemorate this You ordained the festive offering be bound in braided rope,*
ל *and to discuss it at the time we read the portion, 'When a bull ....'**

All– *Be gracious to Your beloved who love You; On the cleansing Temple mount,*
Chazzan– *With compassion and protection*[5] *provide shelter for them.*

(1) *Psalms* 51:17. (2) See *Genesis* 10:13. (3) See *Psalms* 78:52. (4) Cf. 78:49. (5) Cf. *Isaiah* 31:5. (6) See *Exodus* 12:33-34. (7) Cf. *Psalms* 68:7. (8) See *Genesis* 18:7.

בְּכֹשֶׁר — *At the suitable moment.* According to the psalmist (68:7): *God . . . releases the prisoners* בַּכּוֹשָׁרוֹת, a word *Rashi* renders *at a suitable time* (akin to כָּשֵׁר, *kosher*). The spring month of Nissan boasts of the most suitable weather for traveling; it is neither too hot nor too cold.

Others render כּוֹשָׁרוֹת as *bonds* (קוֹשָׁרוֹת) with כ in place of ק. Such letter substitution is found elsewhere, for example, תִּכֵּן (*Isaiah* 40:13) and תִּקֵּן (*Ecclesiastes* 12:9) both mean *arranged* (*Radak*).

The Midrash (*Tanchuma* Bo 1) interprets בַּכּוֹשָׁרוֹת as בָּכוּ, *they cried,* and שָׁרוֹת, *they sang.* When Israel was released from slavery, the Egyptians wept while the Jews sang praise.

גוֹי וֵאלֹהָיו — *A nation and its leaders.* The translation follows *Rashi's* commentary to the phrase גוֹי וֵאלֹהִים in the *Hoshana* prayers of Succos. There *Rashi* cites the verse: *HASHEM said to Moses, 'See I have made you a lord* (אֱלֹהִים) *over Pharaoh'* (*Exodus* 7:1). Thus, the phrase refers to the leaders of Israel — Moses and Aaron.

Alternatively, the stich refers to God, and is an allusion to the שְׁכִינָה בְּגָלוּתָהּ, *Divine Presence in its exile,* together with the Jewish nation. This is based on the verses, *In all their troubles, He is troubled* (*Isaiah* 63:9), and, *I [God] am with him in distress* (*Psalms* 91:15). The Talmud comments: 'Come and observe how beloved Israel is before God, for wherever they are exiled, the *Shechinah* is with them . . . and when they will be redeemed, the *Shechinah* will be [redeemed] with them . . .' (*Taanis* 16a; *Megillah* 29a).

עִנְיַן שׁוֹר — *The portion, 'When a bull . . .'* This is a reference to the Torah reading of the day — *Leviticus* 22:26 to 23:44 — which begins: *HASHEM spoke to Moses saying: 'When a bull . . .'*

Chazzan bends his knees at בָּרוּךְ; bows at אַתָּה; straightens up at 'ה.

בָּרוּךְ אַתָּה יהוה, מָגֵן אַבְרָהָם. (.Cong. – אָמֵן)

גבורות

אַתָּה גִּבּוֹר לְעוֹלָם אֲדֹנָי, מְחַיֵּה מֵתִים אַתָּה, רַב לְהוֹשִׁיעַ. מְכַלְכֵּל חַיִּים בְּחֶסֶד, מְחַיֵּה מֵתִים בְּרַחֲמִים רַבִּים, סוֹמֵךְ נוֹפְלִים, וְרוֹפֵא חוֹלִים, וּמַתִּיר אֲסוּרִים, וּמְקַיֵּם אֱמוּנָתוֹ לִישֵׁנֵי עָפָר. מִי כָמוֹךָ בַּעַל גְּבוּרוֹת, וּמִי דּוֹמֶה לָּךְ, מֶלֶךְ מֵמִית וּמְחַיֶּה וּמַצְמִיחַ יְשׁוּעָה. וְנֶאֱמָן אַתָּה לְהַחֲיוֹת מֵתִים.

All:

מָה אֵילוּ פִּלְאֵי נִסֶּיךָ, מִתְנוֹסֵס בָּם אֶת מְנַסֶּיךָ,
נָאוֹר רַחֲמֶיךָ עַל כָּל מַעֲשֶׂיךָ, נִפְלָאִים וַתֵּר אֶת עֲמוּסֶיךָ.
סוֹךְ מֶסֶךְ רַעַל לְלוּדִים[1] מָסַכְתָּ, שִׂיחַ נוֹאֲקֶיךָ עֵת שָׁם הִסְכַּתָּ,
עִבְרִים* בְּאֶבְרָתְךָ סַכְתָּ, עִוְרִים בְּעֶבְרָתְךָ חָשַׂכְתָּ.
פַּצְתָּ תְנוּךְ הַטּוּ וְאַל תֶּחֱטָאוּ, פְּסִילֵי פוֹרְכִים* לְעֻמָּם לְהָטוּ.
❖ צֹאן לַפֶּסַח מִשְׁכוּ וְשַׁחֲטוּ,[2]
צַדְּקוּ אוֹתוֹ וְאֶת בְּנוֹ* בְּיוֹם אֶחָד בַּל תִּשְׁחֲטוּ.[3]
All – מַחְשְׁבוֹתֶיךָ לְרַחֲמֵנוּ, מִפְעֲלוֹתֶיךָ לְרוֹמְמֵנוּ.
❖ מְעוֹרֵר רְדוּמֵנוּ, מַרְעִיף מְרוֹמְמֵנוּ.

Chazzan:

בָּרוּךְ אַתָּה יהוה, מְחַיֵּה הַמֵּתִים. (.Cong. – אָמֵן)

All:

קָמֵי קְהָלָךְ, קִצַּצְתָּ בְּחֵילָךְ,
קָפַצְתָּ חֲמֵשׁ מֵאוֹת מַהֲלָךְ,* קְנוֹת לְךָ עַם מְיַחֲלָךְ.
רִשַּׁפְתָּ צָרִים, רִבּוּעַ מַכּוֹת* צוֹרְרִים,
רָאָה יִרְאוּ כֵּן יְצוּרִים,* רוֹמֵם צוּרִים בְּשִׁלּוּחַ צִירִים.*

עִבְרִים — *The Hebrews* . . . The *paytan* is playing on homophonous words. The Israelites are עִבְרִים, *Hebrews,* but the Egyptians are עִוְרִים, *blind men.* The Israelites are protected בְּאֶבְרָתְךָ, *with Your pinion,* while the Egyptians are punished בְּעֶבְרָתְךָ, *with Your fury.*

פְּסִילֵי פוֹרְכִים — *The taskmasters' idols.* The Egyptians worshiped the sheep, as the verse (*Genesis* 43:32) states: *the Egyptians could not eat a meal with the Hebrews for it was an abomination to the Egyptians.* The *Targum Onkelos* interprets: 'for the animals which the Egyptians worshiped, the Hebrews ate.'

אוֹתוֹ וְאֶת בְּנוֹ — *It and its offspring.* The Torah prohibits the slaughtering of an animal and its offspring on the same day. The *paytan* teaches that this prohibition supersedes the requirement to bring the *pesach* offering. Even though you have set aside a particular animal as the *pesach* offering, if you have slaughtered its mother on the fourteenth of Nissan, you may not slaughter it. [See *Tosafos* to *Megillah* 25a.]

חֲמֵשׁ מֵאוֹת מַהֲלָךְ — *A five-hundred[-year] journey.* The Talmud teaches that a five-hundred-year journey separates heaven from earth (*Chagigah* 13a). God leaped across this vast distance in an instant when He descended from his celestial Throne to Egypt to slay the

Chazzan bends his knees at *'Blessed'*; bows at *'You'*; straightens up at *'HASHEM.'*

Blessed are You, HASHEM, Shield of Abraham. (Cong.—*Amen.*)

GOD'S MIGHT

אַתָּה *You are eternally mighty, my Lord, the Resuscitator of the dead are You; abundantly able to save. He sustains the living with kindness, resuscitates the dead with abundant mercy, supports the fallen, heals the sick, releases the confined, and maintains His faith to those asleep in the dust. Who is like You, O Master of mighty deeds, and who is comparable to You, O King Who causes death and restores life and makes salvation sprout! And You are faithful to resuscitate the dead.*

All:

מ *How powerful are Your wondrous miracles,*
מ *through which You exalt Your proven ones,*
נ *O Illuminating One, Your compassion is upon all of Your works,*
נ *grant wonders to the nation You have borne.*
ס *You have poured the cup of retribution upon the Ludim [Egypt],*[1]
ס *when You hearkened to the prayer of those who cry to You;*
ע *The Hebrews* You protected with Your pinion,*
ע *while the unseeing [Egyptians] You restrained with Your fury.*
פ *You said, 'Incline your ear and sin not.'*
פ *You ordered the taskmasters' idols* to be burned before them,*
צ Chazzan — *[when You said,]*
'Take a sheep for the pesach offering and slaughter it.'[2]
צ *Yet You commanded them to fulfill righteously the mitzvah,*
'It and its offspring you shall not slaughter on the same day.'*[3]
All — *May Your thoughts be compassionate to us; may Your works exalt us;*
Chazzan— *may You awaken our slumberers,*
may You sprinkle the resuscitating dew, our Exalter.

Chazzan:

Blessed are You, HASHEM, Who resuscitates the dead. (Cong.—*Amen.*)

All:

ק *The opponents of Your congregation,*
ק *You cut down with Your might.*
ק *You leaped over a five-hundred[-year] journey,**
ק *to acquire for Yourself the people that awaits You.*
ר *You burned the enemy,*
ר *[sending] four-fold plagues* [against] the oppressors.*
ר *May all of Creation* be made to see,*
ר *as You exalt rock[-like Israel], by sending [Your] emissaries.**

(1) See *Genesis* 10:13. (2) Cf. *Exodus* 12:21. (3) Cf. *Leviticus* 22:28.

firstborns there, and to redeem Israel.

רִבּוּעַ מַכּוֹת — *Four-fold plagues.* The *Haggadah* (see page 96) records a dispute regarding the Ten Plagues. According to R' Eliezer each plague had four parts, while in R' Akiva's view each plague had five parts. The *paytan* here subscribes to R' Eliezer's view.

יְצוּרִים — *All of Creation* [lit., *the creatures*]. An alternate reading is צוּרִים, *Tyreans.* Accordingly, the stich is based on the verse in *Isaiah* (23:5): *As when they heard about Egypt, so shall they tremble when they hear about Tyre.* The Midrash explains that God will redeem Israel from its present exile through ten plagues that correspond to the Ten Plagues of Egypt (*Shemos Rabbah* 9:12; *Tanchuma Bo*).

צִירִים — *Emissaries,* i.e., Elijah the Prophet and the Messiah.

שַׁחַת מְשׁוּלֵי קַשׁ* בְּאֹסֶר, שְׁלוּם קְרָנוֹת עֶשֶׂר,[1]
שַׁלְהֲבָם כְּאֻכְּלוּ קַשׁ בְּחֹסֶר,* שְׁטַר תַּכְלִית מַכּוֹת עֶשֶׂר.
תַּמּוּ בְּרוּחַ זִלְעָפוֹת, תְּמִימִים כְּיָצְאוּ בְּתוֹעָפוֹת,
❖ תְּחַזֵּק יָדַיִם רָפוֹת,[2] תִּפְסַח עָלֵינוּ כְּצִפֳּרִים עָפוֹת.[3]

Congregation aloud, then *chazzan:*

יִמְלֹךְ יהוה* לְעוֹלָם, אֱלֹהַיִךְ צִיּוֹן לְדֹר וָדֹר, הַלְלוּיָהּ.[4]
וְאַתָּה קָדוֹשׁ, יוֹשֵׁב תְּהִלּוֹת יִשְׂרָאֵל,[5] אֵל נָא.

עֶרֶב אֲשֶׁר עָלָה אֶת עַם הִסְבַּבְתָּ,
בְּכָשְׁלוֹ נוֹקְשׁוּ עֲשׂוֹת זָרוֹת תִּעַבְתָּ,
וּמִכִּסְלֵי כוּר הֵם לְךָ חָצַבְתָּ,
וּכְתוֹעַ הָאֲסַפְסוּף בְּלִי לְתְעוֹת צִוִּיתָ,
וּמֵאָז מַכְאוֹב כְּדַעַת הִבְלַגְתָּ וְהִרְהַבְתָּ,
וּלְהַעֲלוֹת תַּעַל לְתַאַל תָּאַבְתָּ,
וּכְתַבְנִית אֲשֶׁר הֶמִירוּךְ לְעֵין כֹּל חִבַּבְתָּ,
שׁוֹר בְּעַד שׁוֹר לְתְשׁוּר הֵסַבְתָּ,
וְעַל כָּל תְּשׁוּרָה* תְּשׁוּרוֹ שִׂגַּבְתָּ,
שִׁמְצָם הֶעֱבַרְתָּ, דָּפְיָם הִצַלְלְתָּ, קִצְפָּם הִשְׁבַּתָּ,
לְהַתְּלָם חָשַׁבְתָּ, וְיֶשְׁעָם קֵרַבְתָּ, בְּוַעֲדָם נִצַּבְתָּ,
וּבְקִרְבָּם נִשְׂגַּבְתָּ וְנִתְקַדַּשְׁתָּ.

Chazzan, then congregation, aloud:

חַי וְקַיָּם, נוֹרָא וּמָרוֹם וְקָדוֹשׁ.

All:

אָז* עַל כָּל חַיְתוֹ יָעַר[6]* נִשֵּׂאתָ שׁוֹר,
וְעַל כָּל נִיחוֹחַ עִלִּיתָ תְּשׁוּרַת שׁוֹר,
לִיצִיר כַּף* רָצִיתָ בַּהֲטָבַת פַּר שׁוֹר,

מְשׁוּלֵי קַשׁ — *Those compared to straw.* This stich is based on the prophet's statement: *The House of Jacob shall be a fire, the House of Joseph a flame, and the House of Esau straw; and they will kindle them and consume them* (*Obadiah* 1:18).

בְּחֹסֶר — *Disintegrating.* An alternate reading is בְּאֹסֶר, *in bonds.* It alludes to the flame of Joseph (see above) who had been imprisoned in Egypt.

☙ יִמְלֹךְ ה׳ — HASHEM *shall reign.* The *piyutim* that stress pleas for Israel's redemption are now interrupted with this stirring verse that speaks of the power and sovereignty of God. This underscores that all our prayers for redemption and the Messiah are intended to enable us to serve Him better.

וְעַל כָּל תְּשׁוּרָה — *Above all other offerings.* There are various ways in which the bull offering is considered of greater sanctity than other animal offerings. Most obvious are the sizes of the flour-offering and libation that accompany every *olah* and *shelamim.* For a bull, three-tenths of an *ephah* of flour is mixed with half a *hin* oil for the flour-offering, and half a *hin* wine is used for the libation. The respective amounts for a ram are two-tenths of an *ephah* and one-third of a *hin;* for a lamb or kid even smaller measures are used, one-tenth *ephah* and one-quarter *hin.*

Another interpretation of this stich is that this alludes to the second day's Torah reading, which begins: שׁוֹר אוֹ כֶשֶׂב אוֹ עֵז, *a bull, a sheep, or a goat.* Scripture places the bull at the head of the list of animals which may be brought as Altar offerings.

☙ אָז — *Then.* The previous *piyut* had mentioned how God elevated the sacrificial bull over all other animal offerings. This would ensure atonement for the sin of the Golden Calf which the psalmist called, שׁוֹר אֹכֵל עֵשֶׂב, *a grass-eating bull* (*Psalms* 106:20). The *paytan* continues the same theme in this *piyut.*

ש *Destroy those compared to straw,* even those in hiding,*
ש *put an end to the ten-horned beast,*[1]
ש *consume them in flames like disintegrating* straw,*
ש *and fulfill totally the contract of ten plagues.*
ת *The [Egyptians'] end came in a spirit of panic,*
ת *when the wholesome [Israel] went powerfully forth.*
ת Chazzan — *[Now] strengthen the weakened hands,*[2]
ת *speed to us with compassion, as birds in flight.*[3]

Congregation aloud, then *Chazzan:*

HASHEM shall reign* forever — your God, O Zion — from generation to generation, Halleluyah![4] **You, O Holy One, are enthroned upon Israel's praises**[5] **— please, O God.**

The mixed multitude that ascended with the nation
You caused to go roundabout,
when they stumbled they took Israel along
into the idolatry that you abominated.
Yet You had separated them from the fools of the [Egyptian] cauldron.
When the mixed multitude went astray,
You commanded [Israel] not to be led astray.
Although You ached because You knew beforehand,
You strengthened Yourself and ignored [what You knew would happen].
You only sought to raise a cure for their spiritual malady.
When they exchanged You for an idolatrous form,
You publicly displayed Your love for them,
by causing the [idolatrous] bull to be replaced with the [sacrificial] bull,
*and by exalting the [bull] offering above all other offerings,**
You removed the stain [of their sins],
You threw their shamefulness into the depths,
You set aside the anger they had earned,
You planned methods of healing them,
You brought their redemption near,
You stood among their gatherings,
and You were exalted and sanctified among them.

Chazzan, then congregation, aloud:

Living and Enduring One, Awesome, Exalted and Holy.

All:

א *Then,* above all the land beasts,*[6]** You exalted the bull,*
and above all the sacrificial animals, You elevated the bull offering.
ל *With [Adam] the creation of Your hand* were You reconciled*
when he offered a bull,

(1) Cf. *Daniel* 7:7 [see commentary above, p. 61]. (2) Cf. *Isaiah* 35:3. (3) Cf. 31:5. (4) *Psalms* 146:10. (5) 22:4. (6) 50:10.

The *paytan's* signature, אֶלְעָזָר בִּירַבִּי קַלִּיר, *Elazar son of R' Kalir*, it appears in the acrostic of the first and third stich of each stanza.

אָז עַל כָּל חַיְתוֹ יַעַר — *Then, above all the land beasts.* 'Then' alludes to the period immediately following the idolatry of the Golden Calf.

לִיצִיר כַּף — *With [Adam] the creation* [lit., *the one formed*] *of Your hand.* Man's initial creation was through the direct hand of God, so to speak — as the Torah states: וַיִּיצֶר, *And HASHEM God formed Adam of dust from the ground (Genesis 2:7).*

The Talmud describes Adam's reaction to the

לְחַוּוֹת כִּי בְּהַרְרֵי אֶלֶף[1]* כְּנַן כֹּחַ שׁוֹר.
עֻלָּה וַיְּחַס שֵׁמוֹת חֲמִשָּׁה,
עֵגֶל פַּר אֶלֶף שׁוֹר בָּקָר כְּדַת חֲמִשָּׁה,
זְמַן כִּפּוּר בְּעַד נֶפֶשׁ נְקוּבַת חֲמִשָּׁה,
נֶפֶשׁ רוּחַ חַיָּה נְשָׁמָה יְחִידָה מֵחֲמִשָּׁה.
רָץ אֶל בָּקָר[2] אָב בְּזֶה מוֹעֵד,
עֵת אֲשֶׁר גְּדוּדִים לְהַזְמִין וָעֵד,
בְּכֵן זִכְרוֹן שׁוֹר אֶהֱג בְּזֶה מוֹעֵד,
שׁוֹר אוֹ כֶשֶׂב אוֹ עֵז[3] לִהְיוֹת לִי לְעֵד.
יוֹקְשִׁים כְּהִתְעוּ זוּ בְּמַעֲשֵׂה הָעֵגֶל,
רַבִּים עָלְצוּ וּפָצוּ אֵין יְשׁוּעָתָה לְסֶגֶל,
רָם כְּחָפֵץ לְהַצְדִּיק מְלֻמֶּדֶת עֵגֶל,
חַק בְּלֶדֶת שׁוֹר[4] בְּלִי לְהַזְכִּיר עֵגֶל.*
בִּטּוּי מָרֵי דְלִי[5] רוֹעַ דִּבָּה קֶשֶׁר,
בְּעַם הַמְּמִירִים כָּבוֹד בְּתַבְנִית שׁוֹר,[6]
יָהּ הוֹדִיעָמוֹ כִּי נָחָם בְּאֹרַח מִישׁוֹר,[7]
לְכָל עוֹרְכֵי שַׁי הִקְדִּים קָרְבַּן שׁוֹר.
קוֹל צִפְצְפָה יוֹנַת אֵלֶם[8] אֵיךְ בִּי יִבְחַר,
בְּקוֹל עֲנוֹת אֲשֶׁר שִׁמַּעְתִּי חַג לַיהוה מָחָר,[9]*
לְפִידָהּ נָתַן שׁוּעַ[10] בְּלִי עוֹד לְהִתְחַר,
כִּי תְּמוּר חַג מָחָר חֲגִיגַת שׁוֹר לְחַג בָּחָר.
יָקֵשׁ אֵלֶה* אֱלֹהֶיךָ[11] אֲשֶׁר תָּעוּ בִלְעָדַי,
יְכֻפַּר אֵלֶּה* בְּאֵלֶּה הֵם מוֹעֲדַי.[12]
❖ רְצוּי שְׁלֹשֶׁת אֵלֶּה* יַגִּישׁוּ עָדַי,
וְאֶזְכְּרָה לָמוֹ בְּרִית שְׁלֹשֶׁת עֵדַי.

---

world around him following his sin of eating from the Tree of Knowledge on the day he was created. Upon witnessing his first sunset, Adam thought, 'Because of my transgression the world is dimming. It will revert to its former state of nothingness. This is the death penalty of which God warned us.' Adam sat and cried all night ... until he saw the first rays of the morning sun come over the horizon. Seeing the light return, he said, 'This must be the normal way of the world.' Then he slaughtered a bull and offered it in atonement for his sin (*Avodah Zarah* 8a).

בְּהַרְרֵי אָלֶף — *With a thousand mountains.* According to various Midrashim, on the sixth day of creation, God brought forth from the earth the huge בְּהֵמוֹת, *Behemoth,* an ox so large that it stretched out over a thousand hills, each day grazing on their vegetation. Each night, God causes the vegetation to return as though the Behemoth had not touched it (*Pirkei D'R' Eliezer* 2). According to one view in *Rashi,* this is the meaning of the verse: כִּי לִי כָל חַיְתוֹ יָעַר בְּהֵמוֹת בְּהַרְרֵי אָלֶף, *For Mine are all land beasts, Behemoth of the thousand hills* (*Psalms* 50:10).

It seems that, in the *paytan's* view, Adam slaughtered the Behemoth as his atonement offering.

בְּלִי לְהַזְכִּיר עֵגֶל — *Without mentioning the word 'calf.'* Since the verse discusses the animal's birth, the expected form is עֵגֶל, *calf,* rather than שׁוֹר, *bull* or *ox,* an adult animal. Nevertheless, to avoid evoking memory of the Golden Calf, God inscribed the word 'bull' not 'calf.'

חַג לַה׳ מָחָר — *'A festival to* HASHEM *tomorrow.'* This is not the roseate statement that it seems to

to make known that with a thousand mountains,[1]*
the bull's strength is maintained.
ע *It was exalted and called with five names,*
'calf,' 'bull,' 'head,' 'ox,' and 'cattle,' corresponding to the Torah's five Books.
ז *He prepared the bull to atone for man's five-named soul,*
'nefesh,' 'ruach,' 'chayah,' 'neshamah,' and 'yechidah.'
ר *At this time of the year, the Patriarch [Abraham] ran to the cattle,*[2]
when he invited the angels to join him [at a meal].
ב *Therefore, to commemorate the bull, I shall read on this festival day,*
[the portion:] 'A bull, a sheep, or a goat,'[3] *as a testimony for me.*
י *When the stumblers went astray with the matter of the Calf,*
many nations exulted and said, 'There is no hope for the treasured [Israel]!'
ר *The Exalted One desired to indemnify [Israel] 'the trained calf,'*
by inscribing, 'When a bull . . . is born,'[4]* *without mentioning the word 'calf.'**
ב *The [nations who are like] drops from a bucket*[5] *speak and attach evil report,*
to the people who exchanged glory for the likeness of a bull.[6]
י *But God informed them, by leading the nation on a righteous path,*[7]
[that he forgave them,]
thus above all other offerings, He placed the bull offering.
ק *The twittering sound of the cooing dove,*[8] *'O, how He has chosen me!'*
Despite my letting Him hear the response,
'A festival to HASHEM tomorrow.'[9]*
ל *To their downfall, He sent salvation,*[10] *that the nations no longer taunt them,*
for in exchange for 'a festival tomorrow,'
He chose the bull as a festive offering.
י *The snare, 'This* is your god!'*[11] *that led them astray to idols,*
was atoned for through 'These are My festivals.'*[12]
ר Chazzan – *The propitiation of these three* will bring you closer to Me,*
and I shall remember the covenant of My three witnesses.

(1) *Psalms* 50:10. (2) Cf. *Genesis* 18:7. (3) *Leviticus* 22:27. (4) Cf. ibid.
(5) Cf. *Isaiah* 40:15. (6) Cf. *Psalms* 106:20. (7) Cf. 27:11. (8) See *Targum* to 56:1.
(9) *Exodus* 32:5. (10) Cf. *Job* 30:24. (11) *Exodus* 32:4. (12) *Leviticus* 23:2.

be. When the עֵרֶב רַב, *mixed multitude*, of converts who left Egypt with Israel fashioned the Golden Calf and seduced many Israelites to join them in its worship by proclaiming, 'This is your god, O Israel!,' Aaron tried to stall them off. Realizing that the forty-day period that Moses was to have been on the mountain had not yet expired, and knowing that Moses would descend on the morrow, Aaron cried out, 'A festival to HASHEM tomorrow!' He said 'to HASHEM,' but the idolaters applied his words to the Calf. Thus, as it is used here, the statement is a condemnation of Israel (see *Exodus* 32:1-6).

אֵלֶּה . . . אֵלֶּה — *This . . . These.* The demonstrative pronoun אֵלֶּה is used in reference to both the Golden Calf and the festivals. This indicates a relationship. Thus, the celebration of the festivals atones for the sin of the Calf.

שְׁלֹשֶׁת אֵלֶּה — *These three.* Three times in the Torah reading of the second day we find the word אֵלֶּה, *these.* Once, אֵלֶּה הֵם מוֹעֲדָי, *these are My festivals* (*Leviticus* 23:2), and twice, אֵלֶּה מוֹעֲדֵי ה׳, *these are the festivals of HASHEM* (ibid. vs. 4, 37). The fulfillment of the commandments regarding 'My festivals,' 'the festivals of HASHEM,' will draw Israel closer to God and reconcile them with Him (*Matteh Levi*).

Alternatively, 'these three' refers to the three species of animals valid for Temple offerings that are mentioned at the beginning of the day's Torah reading: *A bull, a sheep, or a goat* (*Leviticus* 22:27). These three correspond to the three Patriarchs. The bull alludes to the bulls Abraham slaughtered for his angelic guests (*Genesis* 18:7). The sheep stands for the ram that was slaughtered in lieu of Isaac (ibid. 22:13). And the goat corresponds to the two goats Jacob brought to his mother that she may prepare a meal for his father (ibid. 27:9; *Maaseh Oreig*).

Chazzan continues:

אֵל נָא לְעוֹלָם· תֻּעֲרָץ, וּלְעוֹלָם תֻּקְדָּשׁ,[1] וּלְעוֹלְמֵי עוֹלָמִים תִּמְלוֹךְ וְתִתְנַשֵּׂא, הָאֵל מֶלֶךְ נוֹרָא מָרוֹם וְקָדוֹשׁ, כִּי אַתָּה הוּא מֶלֶךְ מַלְכֵי הַמְּלָכִים, מַלְכוּתוֹ נֶצַח. נוֹרְאוֹתָיו שִׂיחוּ, סַפְּרוּ עֻזּוֹ, פָּאֲרוּהוּ צְבָאָיו, קַדְּשׁוּהוּ רוֹמְמוּהוּ, רוֹן שִׁיר וָשֶׁבַח, תּוֹקֶף תְּהִלּוֹת תִּפְאַרְתּוֹ.

Some congregations recite וּבְכֵן שׁוֹר (p. 1117) at this point.

וּבְכֵן וַאֲמַרְתֶּם· זֶבַח פֶּסַח.

אֹמֶץ גְּבוּרוֹתֶיךָ הִפְלֵאתָ בַּפֶּסַח,
בְּרֹאשׁ כָּל מוֹעֲדוֹת נִשֵּׂאתָ פֶּסַח,
גִּלִּיתָ לְאֶזְרָחִי חֲצוֹת לֵיל[2] פֶּסַח,
וַאֲמַרְתֶּם זֶבַח פֶּסַח.

דְּלָתָיו דָּפַקְתָּ כְּחוֹם הַיּוֹם בַּפֶּסַח,
הִסְעִיד נוֹצְצִים עֻגוֹת מַצּוֹת בַּפֶּסַח,
וְאֶל הַבָּקָר רָץ[3] זֵכֶר לְשׁוֹר עֵרֶךְ פֶּסַח,
וַאֲמַרְתֶּם זֶבַח פֶּסַח.

זוֹעֲמוּ סְדוֹמִים וְלֹהֲטוּ בָּאֵשׁ פֶּסַח,
חֻלַּץ לוֹט מֵהֶם וּמַצּוֹת אָפָה בְּקֵץ פֶּסַח,
טִאטֵאתָ אַדְמַת מוֹף וְנוֹף בְּעָבְרְךָ בַּפֶּסַח,
וַאֲמַרְתֶּם זֶבַח פֶּסַח.

יָהּ רֹאשׁ כָּל אוֹן מָחַצְתָּ בְּלֵיל שִׁמּוּר פֶּסַח,
כַּבִּיר עַל בֵּן בְּכוֹר פָּסַחְתָּ בְּדַם פֶּסַח,
לְבִלְתִּי תֵּת מַשְׁחִית לָבוֹא בִּפְתָחַי[4] בַּפֶּסַח,
וַאֲמַרְתֶּם זֶבַח פֶּסַח.

מְסֻגֶּרֶת סֻגָּרָה בְּעִתּוֹתֵי פֶּסַח,
נִשְׁמְדָה מִדְיָן בִּצְלִיל שְׂעוֹרֵי[5] עֹמֶר פֶּסַח,
שֹׂרְפוּ מִשְׁמַנֵּי פּוּל וְלוּד בִּיקַד יְקוֹד פֶּסַח,
וַאֲמַרְתֶּם זֶבַח פֶּסַח.

עוֹד הַיּוֹם בְּנֹב לַעֲמֹד עַד גָּעָה עוֹנַת פֶּסַח,
פַּס יָד[6] כָּתְבָה לְקַעֲקֵעַ צוּל בַּפֶּסַח,
צָפֹה הַצָּפִית עָרוֹךְ הַשֻּׁלְחָן בַּפֶּסַח,
וַאֲמַרְתֶּם זֶבַח פֶּסַח.

אֵל נָא לְעוֹלָם — *O God, may You always.* This ancient *piyut* of anonymous authorship seems to be a fragment of a longer composition, perhaps even the fragments of two *piyutim* that have been merged into one. The first half contains no apparent acrostic scheme. It praises God and prays that we may always praise Him. The second half follows a repetitive alphabetical acrostic, beginning with the letter מ — two word phrases, the first with the initial letters מ״נ, the next with נ״ס, then ס״ע, etc; but with some phrases missing. In this second part the *chazzan* calls upon the congregation to sing God's praises.

וּבְכֵן וַאֲמַרְתֶּם — *And so you shall say.* The *paytan* now offers an alphabetic listing of Scriptural events that happened, according to various Midrashim, on Pesach: the Covenant

Chazzan continues:

אֵל *O God, may You always* be lauded and always be sanctified,[1] and forever reign and be uplifted, the God, King, awesome, exalted, and holy, for You are the King Who reigns over kings, Whose sovereignty is eternal. Speak of His wonders, declare His stength, glorify Him, O His legions; sanctify Him, exalt Him. Sing song and praise, glorify Him with powerful psalms of praise.*

Some congregations recite וּבְכֵן שׁוֹר (p. 1117) at this point.

And so you shall say:* This is the pesach offering.

א *You displayed wondrously Your mighty powers* — *on Pesach.*
ב *Above all festivals You elevated* — *Pesach.*
ג *To the Easterner [Abraham] You revealed the future midnight[2]* — *of Pesach.*
And you shall say: This is the pesach offering.

ד *You knocked on his door in the heat of the day* — *on Pesach;*
ה *He satiated the angels with matzah-cakes* — *on Pesach.*
ו *And he ran to the herd[3], symbolic of the sacrificial beast* — *of Pesach.*
And you shall say: This is the pesach offering.

ז *The Sodomites provoked [God] and were devoured by fire* — *on Pesach;*
ח *Lot was withdrawn from them — he had baked matzos at the time* — *of Pesach.*
ט *You swept clean the soil of Mof and Nof [Egypt] when You passed through* — *on Pesach.*
And you shall say: This is the pesach offering.

י *God, You crushed every firstborn of On [Egypt] on the watchful night* — *of Pesach.*
כ *But Master, Your own firstborn, You skipped by merit of the blood* — *of Pesach,*
ל *Not to allow the Destroyer to enter my doors[4]* — *on Pesach.*
And you shall say: This is the pesach offering.

מ *The beleaguered [Jericho] was besieged* — *on Pesach.*
נ *Midian was destroyed with a barley cake,[5] from the Omer* — *of Pesach.*
ס *The mighty nobles of Pul and Lud [Assyria] were consumed in a great conflagration* — *on Pesach.*
And you shall say: This is the pesach offering.

ע *He [Sennacherib] would have stood that day at Nob, but for the advent* — *of Pesach.*
פ *A hand inscribed[6] the destruction of Tzul [Babylon]* — *on Pesach,*
צ *As the watch was set, and the royal table decked* — *on Pesach.*
And you shall say: This is the pesach offering.

(1) Cf. *Psalms* 89:8. (2) See commentary to עֲצוֹת מֵרָחוֹק, p. 45. (3) *Genesis* 18:7. (4) Cf. *Exodus* 12:23. (5) Cf. *Judges* 7:13 (see commentary, p. 56). (6) Cf. *Daniel* 5:5.

Between the Parts (*Genesis* ch. 15); the angels' visit to Abraham (ibid. 18:1-8); the destruction of Sodom and the rescue of Lot (ibid. 19:1-25); the plague of the firstborn (*Exodus* 11:4-8; 12:21-29); Joshua's capture of Jericho (*Joshua* ch. 6); Gideon's victory over Midian (*Judges* ch. 7); the defeat of Sennacherib's Assyrian hosts (*II Kings* 19:35); the handwriting on the wall predicting Babylon's downfall (*Daniel* ch. 5); and Esther's proclamation of the three-day fast which culminated in Haman being hanged (*Esther* 4:16; 7:10).

The last two verses plead for the fulfillment of the prophecy that Edom will be doubly punished with 'widowhood' and 'childlessness' (*Isaiah* 47:9), and pray that God reveal His might and bring the final redemption on Pesach.

קָהָל כִּנְּסָה הֲדַסָּה לְשַׁלֵּשׁ צוֹם בַּפֶּסַח,
רֹאשׁ מִבֵּית רָשָׁע מָחַצְתָּ בְּעֵץ חֲמִשִּׁים בַּפֶּסַח,
שְׁתֵּי אֵלֶּה רֶגַע[1] תָּבִיא לְעוּצִית בַּפֶּסַח,
תָּעֹז יָדְךָ תָּרוּם יְמִינְךָ כְּלֵיל הִתְקַדֵּשׁ חַג פֶּסַח,
וַאֲמַרְתֶּם זֶבַח פֶּסַח.

All:

וּבְכֵן וּלְךָ תַעֲלֶה קְדֻשָּׁה, כִּי אַתָּה קְדוֹשׁ יִשְׂרָאֵל וּמוֹשִׁיעַ.

Some congregations recite the prayer בְּעֶשֶׂר מַכּוֹת (p. 1118) before *Kedushah*.
Most congregations recite the standard *Yom Tov Kedushah* (below).
Those who recite בְּעֶשֶׂר מַכּוֹת omit the opening phrase in parentheses.

קדושה

When reciting *Kedushah,* one must stand with his feet together and avoid any interruptions. One should rise on his toes when saying the words קָדוֹשׁ, קָדוֹשׁ, קָדוֹשׁ; בָּרוּךְ כְּבוֹד (of בָּרוּךְ כְּבוֹד); and יִמְלֹךְ.

– Cong. then *Chazzan* (**נְקַדֵּשׁ** אֶת שִׁמְךָ בָּעוֹלָם, כְּשֵׁם שֶׁמַּקְדִּישִׁים אוֹתוֹ בִּשְׁמֵי מָרוֹם,) כַּכָּתוּב עַל יַד נְבִיאֶךָ, וְקָרָא זֶה אֶל זֶה וְאָמַר:

– All קָדוֹשׁ קָדוֹשׁ קָדוֹשׁ יהוה צְבָאוֹת, מְלֹא כָל הָאָרֶץ כְּבוֹדוֹ.[2] ❖ אָז בְּקוֹל* רַעַשׁ גָּדוֹל אַדִּיר וְחָזָק מַשְׁמִיעִים קוֹל, מִתְנַשְּׂאִים לְעֻמַּת שְׂרָפִים, לְעֻמָּתָם בָּרוּךְ יֹאמֵרוּ:

– All בָּרוּךְ כְּבוֹד יהוה, מִמְּקוֹמוֹ.[3] ❖ מִמְּקוֹמְךָ מַלְכֵּנוּ תוֹפִיעַ, וְתִמְלֹךְ עָלֵינוּ, כִּי מְחַכִּים אֲנַחְנוּ לָךְ. מָתַי תִּמְלֹךְ בְּצִיּוֹן, בְּקָרוֹב בְּיָמֵינוּ, לְעוֹלָם וָעֶד תִּשְׁכּוֹן. תִּתְגַּדַּל וְתִתְקַדַּשׁ בְּתוֹךְ יְרוּשָׁלַיִם עִירְךָ, לְדוֹר וָדוֹר וּלְנֵצַח נְצָחִים. וְעֵינֵינוּ תִרְאֶינָה מַלְכוּתֶךָ, כַּדָּבָר הָאָמוּר בְּשִׁירֵי עֻזֶּךָ, עַל יְדֵי דָוִד מְשִׁיחַ צִדְקֶךָ:

– All יִמְלֹךְ יהוה לְעוֹלָם, אֱלֹהַיִךְ צִיּוֹן לְדֹר וָדֹר, הַלְלוּיָהּ.[4]

קדושת השם

Chazzan continues:

לְדוֹר וָדוֹר נַגִּיד גָּדְלֶךָ וּלְנֵצַח נְצָחִים קְדֻשָּׁתְךָ נַקְדִּישׁ, וְשִׁבְחֲךָ אֱלֹהֵינוּ מִפִּינוּ לֹא יָמוּשׁ לְעוֹלָם וָעֶד, כִּי אֵל מֶלֶךְ גָּדוֹל וְקָדוֹשׁ אָתָּה. בָּרוּךְ אַתָּה יהוה, הָאֵל הַקָּדוֹשׁ. (.Cong – אָמֵן)

קדושת היום

אַתָּה בְחַרְתָּנוּ מִכָּל הָעַמִּים, אָהַבְתָּ אוֹתָנוּ, וְרָצִיתָ בָּנוּ, וְרוֹמַמְתָּנוּ מִכָּל הַלְּשׁוֹנוֹת, וְקִדַּשְׁתָּנוּ בְּמִצְוֹתֶיךָ,

(1) Cf. *Isaiah* 47:9. (2) 6:3. (3) *Ezekiel* 3:12. (4) *Psalms* 146:10.

ק *Hadassah [Esther] gathered a congregation for a three-day fast* *on Pesach.*
ר *You caused the head of the evil clan [Haman] to be hanged on a fifty-cubit gallows* *on Pesach.*
ש *May You bring double punishment in an instant*[1] *upon Utzis [Edom]* *on Pesach;*
ת *Let Your hand be strong, and Your right arm exalted, as on that night when You hallowed the festival* *of Pesach.*

And you shall say: This is the pesach offering.

All:

And so, the Kedushah prayer shall ascend to You, for You are the Holy One of Israel, and Savior.

Some congregations recite the prayer בְּעֶשֶׂר מַכּוֹת (p. 1118) before *Kedushah.*

Most congregations recite the standard *Yom Tov Kedushah* (below). Those who recite בְּעֶשֶׂר מַכּוֹת omit the opening phrase in parentheses.

KEDUSHAH

When reciting *Kedushah*, one must stand with his feet together and avoid any interruptions. One should rise on his toes when saying the words *Holy, holy, holy; Blessed is;* and *HASHEM shall reign.*

Cong. then Chazzan – **נְקַדֵּשׁ** *(We shall sanctify Your Name in this world, just as they sanctify it in heaven above,) as it is written by Your prophet, "And one [angel] will call another and say:*

All– *'Holy, holy, holy is HASHEM, Master of Legions, the whole world is filled with His glory.' "*[2] ❖ *Then, with a sound* of great noise, mighty and powerful, they make heard a voice, raising themselves toward the seraphim; those facing them say 'Blessed . . .':*

All– *'Blessed is the glory of HASHEM from His place.'*[3] ❖ *From Your place, our King, You will appear and reign over us, for we await You. When will You reign in Zion? Soon, in our days — forever and ever — may You dwell there. May You be exalted and sanctified within Jerusalem, Your city, from generation to generation and for all eternity. May our eyes see Your kingdom, as it is expressed in the songs of Your might, written by David, Your righteous anointed:*

All– *'HASHEM shall reign forever — your God, O Zion — from generation to generation, Halleluyah!'*[4]

HOLINESS OF GOD'S NAME

Chazzan continues:

לְדוֹר *From generation to generation we shall relate Your greatness and for infinite eternities we shall proclaim Your holiness. Your praise, our God, shall not leave our mouth forever and ever, for You, O God, are a great and holy King. Blessed are You, HASHEM, the holy God.* (Cong. – *Amen.*)

SANCTIFICATION OF THE DAY

אַתָּה בְחַרְתָּנוּ *You have chosen us from all the peoples; You loved us and found favor in us; You exalted us above all the tongues and You sanctified us with Your commandments.*

וְקֵרַבְתָּנוּ מַלְכֵּנוּ לַעֲבוֹדָתֶךָ, וְשִׁמְךָ הַגָּדוֹל וְהַקָּדוֹשׁ עָלֵינוּ קָרָאתָ.

וַתִּתֶּן לָנוּ יהוה אֱלֹהֵינוּ בְּאַהֲבָה מוֹעֲדִים לְשִׂמְחָה חַגִּים וּזְמַנִּים לְשָׂשׂוֹן, אֶת יוֹם חַג הַמַּצּוֹת הַזֶּה, זְמַן חֵרוּתֵנוּ מִקְרָא קֹדֶשׁ, זֵכֶר לִיצִיאַת מִצְרָיִם.

אֱלֹהֵינוּ וֵאלֹהֵי אֲבוֹתֵינוּ, יַעֲלֶה, וְיָבֹא, וְיַגִּיעַ, וְיֵרָאֶה, וְיֵרָצֶה, וְיִשָּׁמַע, וְיִפָּקֵד, וְיִזָּכֵר זִכְרוֹנֵנוּ וּפִקְדוֹנֵנוּ, וְזִכְרוֹן אֲבוֹתֵינוּ, וְזִכְרוֹן מָשִׁיחַ בֶּן דָּוִד עַבְדֶּךָ, וְזִכְרוֹן יְרוּשָׁלַיִם עִיר קָדְשֶׁךָ, וְזִכְרוֹן כָּל עַמְּךָ בֵּית יִשְׂרָאֵל לְפָנֶיךָ, לִפְלֵיטָה לְטוֹבָה לְחֵן וּלְחֶסֶד וּלְרַחֲמִים, לְחַיִּים וּלְשָׁלוֹם בְּיוֹם חַג הַמַּצּוֹת הַזֶּה. זָכְרֵנוּ יהוה אֱלֹהֵינוּ בּוֹ לְטוֹבָה (Cong. – אָמֵן), וּפָקְדֵנוּ בוֹ לִבְרָכָה (Cong. – אָמֵן), וְהוֹשִׁיעֵנוּ בוֹ לְחַיִּים (Cong. – אָמֵן). וּבִדְבַר יְשׁוּעָה וְרַחֲמִים, חוּס וְחָנֵּנוּ וְרַחֵם עָלֵינוּ וְהוֹשִׁיעֵנוּ, כִּי אֵלֶיךָ עֵינֵינוּ, כִּי אֵל מֶלֶךְ חַנּוּן וְרַחוּם אָתָּה.[1]

וְהַשִּׂיאֵנוּ יהוה אֱלֹהֵינוּ אֶת בִּרְכַּת מוֹעֲדֶיךָ לְחַיִּים וּלְשָׁלוֹם, לְשִׂמְחָה וּלְשָׂשׂוֹן, כַּאֲשֶׁר רָצִיתָ וְאָמַרְתָּ לְבָרְכֵנוּ. קַדְּשֵׁנוּ בְּמִצְוֹתֶיךָ וְתֵן חֶלְקֵנוּ בְּתוֹרָתֶךָ, שַׂבְּעֵנוּ מִטּוּבֶךָ וְשַׂמְּחֵנוּ בִּישׁוּעָתֶךָ, וְטַהֵר לִבֵּנוּ לְעָבְדְּךָ בֶּאֱמֶת, וְהַנְחִילֵנוּ יהוה אֱלֹהֵינוּ בְּשִׂמְחָה וּבְשָׂשׂוֹן מוֹעֲדֵי קָדְשֶׁךָ, וְיִשְׂמְחוּ בְךָ יִשְׂרָאֵל מְקַדְּשֵׁי שְׁמֶךָ. בָּרוּךְ אַתָּה יהוה, מְקַדֵּשׁ יִשְׂרָאֵל וְהַזְּמַנִּים. (Cong. – אָמֵן.)

עבודה

רְצֵה יהוה אֱלֹהֵינוּ בְּעַמְּךָ יִשְׂרָאֵל וּבִתְפִלָּתָם, וְהָשֵׁב אֶת הָעֲבוֹדָה לִדְבִיר בֵּיתֶךָ. וְאִשֵּׁי יִשְׂרָאֵל וּתְפִלָּתָם בְּאַהֲבָה תְקַבֵּל בְּרָצוֹן, וּתְהִי לְרָצוֹן תָּמִיד עֲבוֹדַת יִשְׂרָאֵל עַמֶּךָ.

וְתֶחֱזֶינָה עֵינֵינוּ בְּשׁוּבְךָ לְצִיּוֹן בְּרַחֲמִים. בָּרוּךְ אַתָּה יהוה, הַמַּחֲזִיר שְׁכִינָתוֹ לְצִיּוֹן. (Cong. – אָמֵן.)

You drew us close, our King, to Your service and proclaimed Your great and Holy Name upon us.

וַתִּתֶּן לָנוּ *And You gave us, HASHEM, our God, with love, appointed festivals for gladness, Festivals and times for joy, this day of the Festival of Matzos, the time of our freedom, a holy convocation, a memorial of the Exodus from Egypt.*

אֱלֹהֵינוּ *Our God and God of our forefathers, may there rise, come, reach, be noted, be favored, be heard, be considered, and be remembered — the remembrance and consideration of ourselves; the remembrance of our forefathers; the remembrance of Messiah, son of David, Your servant; the remembrance of Jerusalem, the City of Your Holiness; the remembrance of Your entire people the Family of Israel — before You for deliverance, for goodness, for grace, for kindness, and for compassion, for life, and for peace on this day of the Festival of Matzos. Remember us on it, HASHEM, our God, for goodness* (Cong. – *Amen); consider us on it for blessing* (Cong. – *Amen); and help us on it for life* (Cong. – *Amen). In the matter of salvation and compassion, pity, be gracious and compassionate with us and help us, for our eyes are turned to You, because You are God, the gracious and compassionate King.*[1]

וְהַשִּׂיאֵנוּ *Bestow upon us, O HASHEM, our God, the blessing of Your appointed Festivals for life and for peace, for gladness and for joy, as You desired and promised to bless us. Sanctify us with our commandments and grant us our share in Your Torah; satisfy us from Your goodness and gladden us with Your salvation, and purify our heart to serve You sincerely. And grant us a heritage, O HASHEM, our God — with gladness and with joy — the appointed festivals of Your holiness, and may Israel, the sanctifiers of Your Name, rejoice in You. Blessed are You, HASHEM, Who sanctifies Israel and the festive seasons.* (Cong. – *Amen.)*

TEMPLE SERVICE

רְצֵה *Be favorable, HASHEM, our God, toward Your people Israel and their prayer and restore the service to the Holy of Holies of Your Temple. The fire-offerings of Israel and their prayer accept with love and favor, and may the service of Your people Israel always be favorable to You.*

וְתֶחֱזֶינָה *May our eyes behold Your return to Zion in compassion. Blessed are You, HASHEM, Who restores His Presence to Zion.* (Cong. – *Amen.)*

(1) Cf. *Nehemiah* 9:31.

Bow at מודים; straighten up at 'ה. The *chazzan* should recite the entire מודים aloud, while the congregation recites מודים דְּרַבָּנָן softly.

מוֹדִים אֲנַחְנוּ לָךְ, שָׁאַתָּה הוּא יהוה אֱלֹהֵינוּ וֵאלֹהֵי אֲבוֹתֵינוּ לְעוֹלָם וָעֶד. צוּר חַיֵּינוּ, מָגֵן יִשְׁעֵנוּ אַתָּה הוּא לְדוֹר וָדוֹר. נוֹדֶה לְּךָ וּנְסַפֵּר תְּהִלָּתֶךָ[1] עַל חַיֵּינוּ הַמְּסוּרִים בְּיָדֶךָ, וְעַל נִשְׁמוֹתֵינוּ הַפְּקוּדוֹת לָךְ, וְעַל נִסֶּיךָ שֶׁבְּכָל יוֹם עִמָּנוּ, וְעַל נִפְלְאוֹתֶיךָ וְטוֹבוֹתֶיךָ שֶׁבְּכָל עֵת, עֶרֶב וָבֹקֶר וְצָהֳרָיִם. הַטּוֹב כִּי לֹא כָלוּ רַחֲמֶיךָ, וְהַמְּרַחֵם כִּי לֹא תַמּוּ חֲסָדֶיךָ,[2] מֵעוֹלָם קִוִּינוּ לָךְ.

מודים דרבנן

מוֹדִים אֲנַחְנוּ לָךְ, שָׁאַתָּה הוּא יהוה אֱלֹהֵינוּ וֵאלֹהֵי אֲבוֹתֵינוּ, אֱלֹהֵי כָל בָּשָׂר, יוֹצְרֵנוּ, יוֹצֵר בְּרֵאשִׁית. בְּרָכוֹת וְהוֹדָאוֹת לְשִׁמְךָ הַגָּדוֹל וְהַקָּדוֹשׁ, עַל שֶׁהֶחֱיִיתָנוּ וְקִיַּמְתָּנוּ. כֵּן תְּחַיֵּנוּ וּתְקַיְּמֵנוּ, וְתֶאֱסוֹף גָּלֻיּוֹתֵינוּ לְחַצְרוֹת קָדְשֶׁךָ, לִשְׁמוֹר חֻקֶּיךָ וְלַעֲשׂוֹת רְצוֹנֶךָ, וּלְעָבְדְּךָ בְּלֵבָב שָׁלֵם, עַל שֶׁאֲנַחְנוּ מוֹדִים לָךְ. בָּרוּךְ אֵל הַהוֹדָאוֹת.

וְעַל כֻּלָּם יִתְבָּרַךְ וְיִתְרוֹמַם שִׁמְךָ מַלְכֵּנוּ תָּמִיד לְעוֹלָם וָעֶד.

The *chazzan* bends his knees at בָּרוּךְ; bows at אַתָּה; straightens up at 'ה.

וְכֹל הַחַיִּים יוֹדוּךָ סֶּלָה, וִיהַלְלוּ אֶת שִׁמְךָ בֶּאֱמֶת, הָאֵל יְשׁוּעָתֵנוּ וְעֶזְרָתֵנוּ סֶלָה. בָּרוּךְ אַתָּה יהוה, הַטּוֹב שִׁמְךָ וּלְךָ נָאֶה לְהוֹדוֹת. (.Cong – אָמֵן)

The *chazzan* recites בִּרְכַּת כֹּהֲנִים during his repetition. He faces right at וְיִשְׁמְרֶךָ; faces left at אֵלֶיךָ וִיחֻנֶּךָּ; faces the Ark for the rest of the blessings.

אֱלֹהֵינוּ, וֵאלֹהֵי אֲבוֹתֵינוּ, בָּרְכֵנוּ בַבְּרָכָה הַמְּשֻׁלֶּשֶׁת בַּתּוֹרָה הַכְּתוּבָה עַל יְדֵי מֹשֶׁה עַבְדֶּךָ, הָאֲמוּרָה מִפִּי אַהֲרֹן וּבָנָיו, כֹּהֲנִים עַם קְדוֹשֶׁךָ, כָּאָמוּר: יְבָרֶכְךָ יהוה, וְיִשְׁמְרֶךָ. (.Cong – כֵּן יְהִי רָצוֹן)

יָאֵר יהוה פָּנָיו אֵלֶיךָ וִיחֻנֶּךָּ. (.Cong – כֵּן יְהִי רָצוֹן)

יִשָּׂא יהוה פָּנָיו אֵלֶיךָ וְיָשֵׂם לְךָ שָׁלוֹם.[3] (.Cong – כֵּן יְהִי רָצוֹן)

שִׂים שָׁלוֹם, טוֹבָה, וּבְרָכָה, חֵן, וָחֶסֶד וְרַחֲמִים עָלֵינוּ וְעַל כָּל יִשְׂרָאֵל עַמֶּךָ. בָּרְכֵנוּ אָבִינוּ, כֻּלָּנוּ כְּאֶחָד בְּאוֹר פָּנֶיךָ, כִּי בְאוֹר פָּנֶיךָ נָתַתָּ לָּנוּ, יהוה אֱלֹהֵינוּ, תּוֹרַת חַיִּים וְאַהֲבַת חֶסֶד, וּצְדָקָה, וּבְרָכָה, וְרַחֲמִים, וְחַיִּים, וְשָׁלוֹם. וְטוֹב בְּעֵינֶיךָ לְבָרֵךְ אֶת עַמְּךָ יִשְׂרָאֵל, בְּכָל עֵת וּבְכָל שָׁעָה בִּשְׁלוֹמֶךָ. בָּרוּךְ אַתָּה יהוה, הַמְּבָרֵךְ אֶת עַמּוֹ יִשְׂרָאֵל בַּשָּׁלוֹם. (.Cong– אָמֵן)

in an undertone– יִהְיוּ לְרָצוֹן אִמְרֵי פִי וְהֶגְיוֹן לִבִּי לְפָנֶיךָ, יהוה צוּרִי וְגֹאֲלִי.[4]

Bow at *'We gratefully thank You'*; straighten up at *'HASHEM.'* The *chazzan* should recite the entire *Modim* aloud, while congregation recites *Modim of the Rabbis* softly.

מוֹדִים *We gratefully thank You, for it is You Who are HASHEM, our God and the God of our forefathers for all eternity; Rock of our lives, Shield of our salvation are You from generation to generation. We shall thank You and relate Your praise[1] — for our lives, which are committed to Your power and for our souls that are entrusted to You; for Your miracles that are with us every day; and for Your wonders and favors in every season — evening, morning, and afternoon. The Beneficent One, for Your compassions were never exhausted, and the Compassionate One, for Your kindnesses never ended[2] — always have we put our hope in You.*

MODIM OF THE RABBIS

מוֹדִים *We gratefully thank You, for it is You Who are HASHEM, our God and the God of our forefathers, the God of all flesh, our Molder, the Molder of the universe. Blessings and thanks are due Your great and holy Name for You have given us life and sustained us. So may You continue to give us life and sustain us and gather our exiles to the Courtyards of Your Sanctuary, to observe Your decrees, to do Your will and to serve You wholeheartedly. [We thank You] for inspiring us to thank You. Blessed is the God of thanksgivings.*

For all these, may Your Name be blessed and exalted, our King, continually forever and ever.

The *chazzan* bends his knees at *'Blessed'*; bows at *'You'*; straightens up at *'HASHEM.'*

Everything alive will gratefully acknowledge You, Selah! and praise Your Name sincerely, O God of our salvation and help, Selah! Blessed are You, HASHEM, Your Name is 'The Beneficent One' and to You it is fitting to give thanks. (Cong.— *Amen.*)

THE PRIESTLY BLESSING

The *chazzan* recites the Priestly Blessing during his repetition.

אֱלֹהֵינוּ *Our God and the God of our forefathers, bless us with the three-verse blessing in the Torah that was written by the hand of Moses, Your servant, that was said by Aaron and his sons, the Kohanim, Your holy people, as it is said:*

May HASHEM bless you and safeguard you. (Cong.— *So may it be.*)

May HASHEM illuminate His countenance for you and be gracious to you. (Cong.— *So may it be.*)

May HASHEM turn His countenance to you and establish peace for you.[3] (Cong.— *So may it be.*)

שִׂים שָׁלוֹם *Establish peace, goodness, blessing, graciousness, kindness, and compassion upon us and upon all of Your people Israel. Bless us, our Father, all of us as one, with the light of Your countenance, for with the light of Your countenance You gave us, HASHEM, our God, the Torah of life and a love of kindness, righteousness, blessing, compassion, life, and peace. And may it be good in Your eyes to bless Your people Israel at every time and every hour with Your peace. Blessed are You, HASHEM, Who blesses His people Israel with peace.* (Cong.— *Amen.*)

May the expressions of my mouth and the thoughts of my heart find favor before You, HASHEM, my Rock and my Redeemer.[4]

---

(1) Cf. *Psalms* 79:13. (2) Cf. *Lamentations* 3:22. (3) *Numbers* 6:24-26. (4) *Psalms* 19:15.

❧ הלל ☙

The *chazzan* recites the blessing. The congregation, after responding אָמֵן, repeats it, and continues with the first psalm.

בָּרוּךְ אַתָּה יהוה אֱלֹהֵינוּ מֶלֶךְ הָעוֹלָם, אֲשֶׁר קִדְּשָׁנוּ בְּמִצְוֹתָיו, וְצִוָּנוּ לִקְרוֹא אֶת הַהַלֵּל. (Cong.– אָמֵן.)

תהלים קיג

הַלְלוּיָהּ הַלְּלוּ עַבְדֵי יהוה,* הַלְּלוּ אֶת שֵׁם יהוה. יְהִי שֵׁם יהוה מְבֹרָךְ, מֵעַתָּה וְעַד עוֹלָם. מִמִּזְרַח שֶׁמֶשׁ עַד מְבוֹאוֹ, מְהֻלָּל שֵׁם יהוה. רָם עַל כָּל גּוֹיִם יהוה, עַל הַשָּׁמַיִם כְּבוֹדוֹ. מִי כַּיהוה אֱלֹהֵינוּ, הַמַּגְבִּיהִי לָשָׁבֶת. הַמַּשְׁפִּילִי לִרְאוֹת, בַּשָּׁמַיִם וּבָאָרֶץ.* ❖ מְקִימִי מֵעָפָר דָּל, מֵאַשְׁפֹּת יָרִים אֶבְיוֹן. לְהוֹשִׁיבִי עִם נְדִיבִים,* עִם נְדִיבֵי עַמּוֹ. מוֹשִׁיבִי עֲקֶרֶת הַבַּיִת,* אֵם הַבָּנִים שְׂמֵחָה, הַלְלוּיָהּ.

תהלים קיד

בְּצֵאת יִשְׂרָאֵל מִמִּצְרָיִם,* בֵּית יַעֲקֹב מֵעַם לֹעֵז.* הָיְתָה יְהוּדָה לְקָדְשׁוֹ,* יִשְׂרָאֵל מַמְשְׁלוֹתָיו. הַיָּם רָאָה וַיָּנֹס, הַיַּרְדֵּן יִסֹּב לְאָחוֹר. הֶהָרִים רָקְדוּ כְאֵילִים,* גְּבָעוֹת כִּבְנֵי צֹאן. ❖ מַה לְּךָ הַיָּם כִּי תָנוּס, הַיַּרְדֵּן תִּסֹּב לְאָחוֹר.* הֶהָרִים תִּרְקְדוּ כְאֵילִים,

---

❧ הַלֵּל / HALLEL ☙

The prophets ordained that the six psalms of *Hallel* [literally, *praise*] be recited on each Festival, and to commemorate times of national deliverance from peril. Moreover, before David redacted and incorporated these psalms into the Book of Psalms, *Hallel* was already known to the nation: Moses and Israel recited it after being saved from the Egyptians at the sea; Joshua, after defeating the kings of Canaan; Deborah and Barak, after defeating Sisera. Later, Hezekiah recited it after defeating Sennacherib; Chananyah, Mishael and Azariah, after being saved from the wicked Nebuchadnezzar; and Mordechai and Esther, after the defeat of the wicked Haman (*Pesachim* 117a).

These psalms were singled out as the unit of praise because they contain five fundamental themes of Jewish faith: the Exodus, the Splitting of the Sea, the Giving of the Torah at Sinai, the future Resuscitation of the dead, and the coming of the Messiah (ibid. 118a).

☙ The Entire Hallel and 'Half Hallel'

On Pesach the entire *Hallel* (*Psalms* 113-118) is recited only on the first day (in the Diaspora on the first two days), in contrast to Succos, when the entire *Hallel* is recited on each of the seven days and on the concluding holiday, Shemini Atzeres. [see *Succah* 4:1,8]. The Talmud (*Arachin* 10a-b) explains that this distinction between Succos and Pesach is based on the difference between their respective *mussaf* offerings (*Numbers* 28:19-25; 29:13-34). During Pesach the *mussaf* offering consists of the same number of bulls, rams, sheep, and goats for each day. On Succos, although the numbers of rams, sheep, and goats are the same every day, the amount of bulls is diminished by one on each successive day. *Rashi* (*Taanis* 28b, s.v. יחיד) and *Tosafos* (loc. cit., s.v. ויום) explain that this changing number of bulls offered indicates that Succos should be considered a set of separate one-day festivals, each of which requires its own recitation of *Hallel*, whereas all of Pesach should be regarded as a single festival spread out over a seven-day period, for which a single full *Hallel* at the beginning is sufficient.

Although the entire *Hallel* is not recited on the last six days of Pesach, an abridged version which omits the first eleven verses of Psalms 115 and of 116 is recited on these days. The same verses are omitted on Rosh Chodesh. This abridged form is popularly known as 'half' *Hallel*.

Another interpretation of why only 'half' *Hallel* is said on the intermediate and final day(s) of Pesach is that since the Egyptians drowned on the seventh day of Pesach, it would be inappropriate to offer excessive praise to God on a day when so many people died — even though they were our enemies. As the Talmud [*Megillah* 10b] records, the angels wished to utter songs of praise to God upon the drowning of the Egyptians, but

HALLEL

The *chazzan* recites the blessing. The congregation, after responding *Amen,* repeats it, and continues with the first psalm.

בָּרוּךְ *Blessed are You, HASHEM, our God, King of the universe, Who has sanctified us with His commandments and has commanded us to read the Hallel.* (Cong.– *Amen.*)

Psalm 113

הַלְלוּיָהּ *Halleluyah! Give praise, you servants of HASHEM;* praise the Name of HASHEM! Blessed be the Name of HASHEM, from this time and forever. From the rising of the sun to its setting, HASHEM's Name is praised. High above all nations is HASHEM, above the heavens is His glory. Who is like HASHEM, our God, Who is enthroned on high — yet deigns to look upon the heaven and the earth?** Chazzan– *He raises the needy from the dust, from the trash heaps He lifts the destitute. To seat them with nobles,* with the nobles of His people. He transforms the barren wife* into a glad mother of children. Halleluyah!*

Psalm 114

בְּצֵאת *When Israel went out of Egypt,* Jacob's household from a people of alien tongue* — Judah became His sanctuary,* Israel His dominions. The sea saw and fled: the Jordan turned backward. The mountains skipped like rams,* the hills like young lambs.* Chazzan– *What ails you, O sea, that you flee? O Jordan, that you turn backward?* O mountains, that you skip like rams?*

He rebuked them saying: 'My handiwork [the Egyptians] are drowning in the sea and you utter praise!' Accordingly, so as not to make the Intermediate Days of Pesach appear more important than the final day(s), we recite only 'half' *Hallel* throughout the Intermediate Days of Pesach as well (*Turei Zahav, Orach Chaim* 490:3; see *Beis Yosef* there). It is true that the entire Jewish people *did* sing praises to God at the Sea of Reeds, despite the fate of the Egyptians, but God did not object, because people whose own lives were in danger praise God for helping them.

הַלְלוּיָהּ הַלְלוּ עַבְדֵי ה׳ — *Halleluyah! Give praise, you servants of HASHEM.* Only after their liberation from Pharaoh's bondage could the Jews be considered the *servants of HASHEM,* because they no longer vowed allegiance to any other ruler.

הַמַּשְׁפִּילִי לִרְאוֹת בַּשָּׁמַיִם וּבָאָרֶץ — *Yet deigns to look* [lit., *bends low to see*] *upon the heaven and the earth?* This is the challenging and exciting aspect of God's relationship to man: As we act towards God, so does He react to us. If we ignore Him, He withdraws above the heavens; but if we welcome Him, He lovingly involves Himself in every phase of our lives (*R' A.C. Feuer*).

לְהוֹשִׁיבִי עִם נְדִיבִים — *To seat them with nobles.* God does not merely lift the poor and needy out of degradation; He also elevates them to the highest ranks of nobility.

מוֹשִׁיבִי עֲקֶרֶת הַבַּיִת — *He transforms the barren wife.* The Creator exercises complete control over nature. This control is vividly demonstrated when God suddenly transforms a barren woman into a mother (*Radak*).

בְּצֵאת יִשְׂרָאֵל מִמִּצְרָיִם — *When Israel went out of Egypt.* This second chapter of Hallel continues the theme of the first chapter, which praises God for raising up the needy and destitute. Israel was thus elevated when they left Egypt and risked their lives by entering the sea at God's command.

בֵּית יַעֲקֹב מֵעַם לֹעֵז — *Jacob's household from a people of alien tongue.* Even the Jews who were forced to communicate with the Egyptians in the language of the land did so only under duress. Among themselves, however, they spoke only the Holy Tongue and regarded Egyptian as a foreign language.

הָיְתָה יְהוּדָה לְקָדְשׁוֹ — *Judah became His sanctuary.* God singled out the tribe of Judah to be the family of royalty, because they sanctified God's Name at the Sea of Reeds. Led by their prince, Nachshon ben Aminadav, this tribe was the first to jump into the threatening waters (*Rosh*).

הֶהָרִים רָקְדוּ כְאֵילִים — *The mountains skipped like rams.* When Israel received the Torah, Sinai and the neighboring mountains and hills trembled at the manifestation of God's Presence and the thunder and lightning that accompanied it.

מַה לְּךָ הַיָּם כִּי תָנוּס הַיַּרְדֵּן תִּסֹּב לְאָחוֹר — *What ails you, O sea, that you flee? O Jordan, that you turn

גְּבָעוֹת כִּבְנֵי צֹאן. מִלִּפְנֵי אָדוֹן חוּלִי אָרֶץ, מִלִּפְנֵי אֱלוֹהַּ יַעֲקֹב. הַהֹפְכִי הַצּוּר אֲגַם מָיִם,* חַלָּמִישׁ לְמַעְיְנוֹ מָיִם.

תהלים קטו:א-יא

לֹא לָנוּ* יהוה לֹא לָנוּ, כִּי לְשִׁמְךָ תֵּן כָּבוֹד,* עַל חַסְדְּךָ עַל אֲמִתֶּךָ. לָמָּה יֹאמְרוּ הַגּוֹיִם, אַיֵּה נָא אֱלֹהֵיהֶם. וֵאלֹהֵינוּ בַשָּׁמָיִם, כֹּל אֲשֶׁר חָפֵץ עָשָׂה. עֲצַבֵּיהֶם כֶּסֶף וְזָהָב, מַעֲשֵׂה יְדֵי אָדָם. פֶּה לָהֶם וְלֹא יְדַבֵּרוּ,* עֵינַיִם לָהֶם וְלֹא יִרְאוּ. אָזְנַיִם לָהֶם וְלֹא יִשְׁמָעוּ, אַף לָהֶם וְלֹא יְרִיחוּן. יְדֵיהֶם וְלֹא יְמִישׁוּן, רַגְלֵיהֶם וְלֹא יְהַלֵּכוּ, לֹא יֶהְגּוּ בִּגְרוֹנָם. כְּמוֹהֶם יִהְיוּ עֹשֵׂיהֶם, כֹּל אֲשֶׁר בֹּטֵחַ בָּהֶם. ❖ יִשְׂרָאֵל בְּטַח בַּיהוה,* עֶזְרָם וּמָגִנָּם הוּא.* בֵּית אַהֲרֹן בִּטְחוּ בַיהוה, עֶזְרָם וּמָגִנָּם הוּא. יִרְאֵי יהוה בִּטְחוּ בַיהוה, עֶזְרָם וּמָגִנָּם הוּא.

תהלים קטו:יב-יח

יהוה זְכָרָנוּ יְבָרֵךְ,* יְבָרֵךְ אֶת בֵּית יִשְׂרָאֵל, יְבָרֵךְ אֶת בֵּית אַהֲרֹן. יְבָרֵךְ יִרְאֵי יהוה, הַקְּטַנִּים עִם הַגְּדֹלִים. יֹסֵף יהוה עֲלֵיכֶם, עֲלֵיכֶם וְעַל בְּנֵיכֶם.* בְּרוּכִים אַתֶּם לַיהוה, עֹשֵׂה שָׁמַיִם וָאָרֶץ. ❖ הַשָּׁמַיִם שָׁמַיִם לַיהוה, וְהָאָרֶץ נָתַן לִבְנֵי אָדָם.* לֹא הַמֵּתִים יְהַלְלוּ יָהּ,* וְלֹא כָּל יֹרְדֵי דוּמָה. וַאֲנַחְנוּ נְבָרֵךְ יָהּ, מֵעַתָּה וְעַד עוֹלָם, הַלְלוּיָהּ.

---

backward? The Psalmist captures the sense of awe and bewilderment which then seized mankind.

הַהֹפְכִי הַצּוּר אֲגַם מָיִם — *Who turns the rock into a pond of water.* When the Jews thirsted for water in the wilderness, God instructed Moses (*Exodus* 17:6), '*You shall smite the rock and water shall come out of it, so that the people may drink.*'

☙ לֹא לָנוּ — *Not for our sake.* The preceding psalm depicts the awe inspired by God's miracles. Here the Psalmist describes the aftermath of that inspiration. Although Israel remained imbued with faith, our oppressors soon began to scoff, 'Where is their God?' We pray that God will intervene again in the affairs of man, not for our sake, but for His.

לֹא לָנוּ ה׳ . . . כִּי לְשִׁמְךָ תֵּן כָּבוֹד — *Not for our sake,* HASHEM *. . . but for Your Name's sake give glory.* We beg You to redeem us, but not because we are personally worthy, nor because of the merit of our forefathers (*Iyun Tefillah*). Rather we urgently strive to protect Your glorious Name, so that no one can deny Your mastery and dominion (*Radak*).

פֶּה לָהֶם וְלֹא יְדַבֵּרוּ — *They have a mouth, but cannot speak.* These illustrations emphasize the complete impotence of man-made idols, which even lack the senses that every ordinary man possesses.

יִשְׂרָאֵל בְּטַח בַּה׳ — *O Israel, trust in* HASHEM. The psalm now contrasts the Children of Israel, who trust in God alone, with those described in the previous verse, who trust in the lifeless and helpless idols (*Ibn Ezra*).

The Psalmist speaks of three kinds of Jews, each with a different motive for serving God. Some Jews cling to God simply because they feel that He is their Father, and they are His devoted sons. These are called יִשְׂרָאֵל, *Israel,* God's chosen, beloved nation. The second group serves God out of love. They resemble the *House of Aaron,* the *Kohanim*-priests who never betrayed God and were therefore designated to stand in

O hills, like young lambs? Before the Lord's Presence — did I, the earth, tremble — before the presence of the God of Jacob, Who turns the rock into a pond of water, the flint into a flowing fountain.*

Psalms 115:1-11

לֹא לָנוּ *Not for our sake,* HASHEM, not for our sake, but for Your Name's sake give glory,* for Your kindness and for Your truth! Why should the nations say, 'Where is their God now?' Our God is in the heavens; whatever He pleases, He does! Their idols are silver and gold, the handiwork of man. They have a mouth, but cannot speak;* they have eyes, but cannot see. They have ears, but cannot hear; they have a nose, but cannot smell. Their hands — they cannot feel; their feet — they cannot walk; they cannot utter a sound from their throat. Those who make them should become like them, whoever trusts in them!* Chazzan– *O Israel, trust in HASHEM;* — their help and their shield is He!* House of Aaron, trust in HASHEM; their help and their shield is He! You who fear HASHEM, trust in HASHEM; their help and their shield is He!*

Psalm 115:12-18

יהוה *HASHEM Who has remembered us will bless* — He will bless the House of Israel; He will bless the House of Aaron; He will bless those who fear HASHEM, the small as well as the great. May HASHEM increase upon you, upon you and upon your children!* You are blessed of HASHEM, maker of heaven and earth.* Chazzan– *As for the heavens — the heavens are HASHEM's, but the earth He has given to mankind.* Neither the dead can praise God,* nor any who descend into silence; but we will bless God from this time and forever. Halleluyah!*

His presence, in the Temple, for all time. Finally, *you who fear HASHEM* refers to a third group of Jews, who serve God out of fear and awe (*Maharal*).

עֶזְרָם וּמָגִנָּם הוּא — *Their help and their shield is He!* This is thrice repeated. Since each successive group possesses a different level of faith, it deserves a totally different degree of divine protection. Thus, God's reaction to each group is mentioned separately.

ה' זְכָרָנוּ יְבָרֵךְ — *HASHEM Who has remembered us will bless.* The Psalmist expresses confidence that just as God has blessed His people in the past, so He will bless them in the future.

יֹסֵף ה' עֲלֵיכֶם, עֲלֵיכֶם וְעַל בְּנֵיכֶם — *May HASHEM increase upon you, upon you and upon your children.* The true nature of **בְּרָכָה**, *blessing*, means increase and abundance (*Ibn Ezra*).

Abarbanel explains that the Psalmist foresaw that Israel would suffer from attrition in exile and they would fear eventual extinction. Therefore, he offers the assurance that, at the advent of the Messiah, they will increase dramatically.

הַשָּׁמַיִם שָׁמַיִם לַה', וְהָאָרֶץ נָתַן לִבְנֵי אָדָם — *As for the heavens — the heavens are HASHEM's, but the earth He has given to mankind.* Since the heavens remain under God's firm control, all celestial bodies are forced to act in accordance with His will without freedom of choice. aOn earth, however, man was granted the freedom to determine his own actions and beliefs (*Maharit*).

Many commentators explain this verse homiletically. Man need not perfect heaven because it is already dedicated to the holiness of God. But the earth is man's province. We are bidden to perfect it and transform its material nature into something spiritual. Indeed, we were created to make the earth heavenly.

לֹא הַמֵּתִים יְהַלְלוּ יָהּ — *Neither the dead can praise God.* The people who fail to recognize God's

תהלים קטז:א-יא

אָהַבְתִּי* כִּי יִשְׁמַע יהוה, אֶת קוֹלִי תַּחֲנוּנָי. כִּי הִטָּה אָזְנוֹ לִי, וּבְיָמַי אֶקְרָא.* אֲפָפוּנִי חֶבְלֵי מָוֶת,* וּמְצָרֵי שְׁאוֹל מְצָאוּנִי, צָרָה וְיָגוֹן אֶמְצָא. וּבְשֵׁם יהוה אֶקְרָא, אָנָּה יהוה מַלְּטָה נַפְשִׁי. חַנּוּן יהוה וְצַדִּיק, וֵאלֹהֵינוּ מְרַחֵם. שֹׁמֵר פְּתָאִים יהוה, דַּלּוֹתִי וְלִי יְהוֹשִׁיעַ. שׁוּבִי נַפְשִׁי לִמְנוּחָיְכִי,* כִּי יהוה גָּמַל עָלָיְכִי. כִּי חִלַּצְתָּ נַפְשִׁי מִמָּוֶת, אֶת עֵינִי מִן דִּמְעָה, אֶת רַגְלִי מִדֶּחִי. ❖ אֶתְהַלֵּךְ לִפְנֵי יהוה, בְּאַרְצוֹת הַחַיִּים.* הֶאֱמַנְתִּי כִּי אֲדַבֵּר, אֲנִי עָנִיתִי מְאֹד. אֲנִי אָמַרְתִּי בְחָפְזִי, כָּל הָאָדָם כֹּזֵב.*

תהלים קטז:יב-יט

מָה אָשִׁיב לַיהוה,* כָּל תַּגְמוּלוֹהִי עָלָי. כּוֹס יְשׁוּעוֹת אֶשָּׂא,* וּבְשֵׁם יהוה אֶקְרָא. נְדָרַי לַיהוה אֲשַׁלֵּם,* נֶגְדָה נָּא לְכָל עַמּוֹ. יָקָר בְּעֵינֵי יהוה, הַמָּוְתָה לַחֲסִידָיו. אָנָּה יהוה כִּי אֲנִי עַבְדֶּךָ, אֲנִי עַבְדְּךָ, בֶּן אֲמָתֶךָ,* פִּתַּחְתָּ לְמוֹסֵרָי. ❖ לְךָ אֶזְבַּח זֶבַח תּוֹדָה, וּבְשֵׁם יהוה אֶקְרָא. נְדָרַי לַיהוה אֲשַׁלֵּם, נֶגְדָה נָּא לְכָל עַמּוֹ. בְּחַצְרוֹת בֵּית יהוה, בְּתוֹכֵכִי יְרוּשָׁלָיִם הַלְלוּיָהּ.

---

omnipresence and influence over the world resemble the dead, who are insensitive to all external stimuli and who are oblivious to reality (*R' Azariah Figo*). However, the souls of the righteous continue to praise God even after they depart from their bodies (*Ibn Ezra*).

⊷ **אָהַבְתִּי** — *I love [Him].* The Psalmist foresaw that Israel would feel completely alone in exile. The nations would taunt them, 'Your prayers and pleas are worthless, because God has turned a deaf ear to you.' Therefore, he composed this psalm to encourage the downcast exiles with the assurance that indeed: *HASHEM hears my voice, my supplications.*

The Talmud (*Rosh Hashanah* 16b-17a) explains that this psalm describes the day of Final Judgment at the time of תְּחִיַּת הַמֵּתִים, *the Resurrection of the Dead.* The average people, who are neither completely righteous nor completely wicked, will be saved from Gehinnom because God will hear their cries, and He will forgive them. In gratitude, they will sing, *'I love Him, for HASHEM hears my voice, my supplications.'*

וּבְיָמַי אֶקְרָא — *So in my days shall I call. Arugas Habosem* cites this verse as the reason why *Hallel* is not recited on every Sabbath, despite its immense sanctity. The Sabbath was consecrated by God Himself during the first week of Creation, whereas the festivals have been sanctified by Jews throughout history. Moreover, it is the Jewish court on earth, rather than the Heavenly Tribunal, which determines the calendar and designates the dates of the festivals. Therefore, when the Psalmist declares וּבְיָמַי [lit., *in my days*], he is alluding to the festival days whose sanctity he and his fellow Jews have created. Only then, אֶקְרָא, *I will call* upon God with *Hallel.*

The recital of *Hallel* is restricted to special days. The *Talmud* (*Shabbos* 118b) rules that one who recites *Hallel* every day is blaspheming and insulting God because the prophets designated *Hallel* as the hallowed hymn to commemorate the most auspicious occasions in Jewish life. If one recites it daily, he lowers *Hallel* to the status of a common song and detracts from God's praise (*Rashi, Shabbos* 118b).

חֶבְלֵי מָוֶת — *The pains of death.* This is an apt description of the exile, when Israel is encircled by violent enemies who seek to kill them (*Abarbanel*).

Psalm 116:1-11

אָהַבְתִּי *I love Him,* for HASHEM hears my voice, my supplications. As He has inclined His ear to me, so in my days shall I call.* The pains of death* encircled me; the confines of the grave have found me; trouble and sorrow I would find. Then I would invoke the Name of HASHEM: 'Please, HASHEM, save my soul.' Gracious is HASHEM and righteous, our God is merciful. HASHEM protects the simple; I was brought low, but He saved me. Return, my soul, to your rest;* for HASHEM has been kind to you. For You have delivered my soul from death, my eyes from tears, my feet from stumbling.* Chazzan– *I shall walk before HASHEM in the lands of the living.* I have kept faith although I say: 'I suffer exceedingly.' I said in my haste: 'All mankind is deceitful.'**

Psalm 116:12-19

מָה אָשִׁיב *How can I repay HASHEM* for all His kindness to me? I will raise the cup of salvations* and the Name of HASHEM I will invoke. My vows to HASHEM I will pay,* in the presence, now, of His entire people. Difficult in the eyes of HASHEM is the death of His devout ones. Please, HASHEM — for I am Your servant, I am Your servant, son of Your handmaid* — You have released my bonds.* Chazzan– *To You I will sacrifice thanksgiving offerings, and the name of HASHEM I will invoke. My vows to HASHEM I will pay, in the presence, now, of His entire people. In the courtyards of the House of HASHEM, in your midst, O Jerusalem, Halleluyah!*

שׁוּבִי נַפְשִׁי לִמְנוּחָיְכִי — *Return, my soul, to your rest.* When misery and persecution upset me, I told my soul that it would find peace and comfort only if it would *return* to God *(Radak)*.

אֶתְהַלֵּךְ לִפְנֵי ה׳ בְּאַרְצוֹת הַחַיִּים — *I shall walk before HASHEM in the lands of the living.* How I yearn to return to *Eretz Yisrael* where the very air makes men healthy and robust and the holy atmosphere grants the mind renewed vitality and alertness! *(Radak). Eretz Yisrael* is identified as the *land of the living* because the dead are destined to be resurrected there. This is why the Patriarchs and the righteous of all generations yearned to be buried there.

אֲנִי אָמַרְתִּי בְחָפְזִי כָּל הָאָדָם כֹּזֵב — *I said in my haste: 'All mankind is deceitful.'* This bitter comment was originally uttered by David when the people of Zif betrayed his hiding place to King Saul [see *I Samuel* 23:19-29] *(Rashi)*. It is also a reference to the bleak, dismal exile [for the exile discourages the Jews and leads them to the hasty, premature conclusion that all the prophets' promises concerning redemption were *deceitful*] *(Abarbanel)*.

◆§ מָה אָשִׁיב לַה׳ — *How can I repay HASHEM?* What gift can I give to the King Who owns everything? *(Ibn Ezra)*. How can I possibly repay His acts of kindness, for they are too numerous to recount? *(Radak)*. How can I even approach Him? He is eternal and I am finite; He is the highest, and I am the lowest! *(Ibn Yachya)*.

כּוֹס יְשׁוּעוֹת אֶשָּׂא — *I will raise the cup of salvations.* This refers to the wine libations that will accompany the thanksgiving offerings of the returning exiles *(Rashi)*.

נְדָרַי לַה׳ אֲשַׁלֵּם — *My vows to HASHEM I will pay.* As I was fleeing and wandering in exile, I vowed that if God would return me safely to *Eretz Yisrael*, I would render thanksgiving offerings to His Name; now I will make good on my vows *(Radak)*.

אֲנִי עַבְדְּךָ בֶּן אֲמָתֶךָ — *I am Your servant, son of Your handmaid.* The slave who is born to a *handmaid* is far more submissive than a slave who was born free *(Rashi)*. The former serves his master naturally and instinctively, whereas the latter serves him only in response to external threats *(Sforno)*.

Congregation, then *chazzan:*

תהלים קיז

הַלְלוּ אֶת יהוה,* כָּל גּוֹיִם, שַׁבְּחוּהוּ כָּל הָאֻמִּים.* כִּי גָבַר עָלֵינוּ חַסְדּוֹ,* וֶאֱמֶת יהוה לְעוֹלָם, הַלְלוּיָהּ.

תהלים קיח

Chazzan – **הוֹדוּ** לַיהוה כִּי טוֹב,* כִּי לְעוֹלָם חַסְדּוֹ.

Cong. – הוֹדוּ לַיהוה כִּי טוֹב, כִּי לְעוֹלָם חַסְדּוֹ.

יֹאמַר נָא יִשְׂרָאֵל, כִּי לְעוֹלָם חַסְדּוֹ.

Chazzan – יֹאמַר נָא יִשְׂרָאֵל, כִּי לְעוֹלָם חַסְדּוֹ.

Cong. – הוֹדוּ לַיהוה כִּי טוֹב, כִּי לְעוֹלָם חַסְדּוֹ.

יֹאמְרוּ נָא בֵית אַהֲרֹן, כִּי לְעוֹלָם חַסְדּוֹ.

Chazzan – יֹאמְרוּ נָא בֵית אַהֲרֹן, כִּי לְעוֹלָם חַסְדּוֹ.

Cong. – הוֹדוּ לַיהוה כִּי טוֹב, כִּי לְעוֹלָם חַסְדּוֹ.

יֹאמְרוּ נָא יִרְאֵי יהוה, כִּי לְעוֹלָם חַסְדּוֹ.

Chazzan – יֹאמְרוּ נָא יִרְאֵי יהוה, כִּי לְעוֹלָם חַסְדּוֹ.

Cong. – הוֹדוּ לַיהוה כִּי טוֹב, כִּי לְעוֹלָם חַסְדּוֹ.

מִן הַמֵּצַר* קָרָאתִי יָּהּ, עָנָנִי בַמֶּרְחָב יָהּ. יהוה לִי לֹא אִירָא, מַה יַּעֲשֶׂה לִי אָדָם. יהוה לִי בְּעֹזְרָי,* וַאֲנִי אֶרְאֶה בְשֹׂנְאָי. טוֹב לַחֲסוֹת בַּיהוה, מִבְּטֹחַ בָּאָדָם.* טוֹב לַחֲסוֹת בַּיהוה, מִבְּטֹחַ בִּנְדִיבִים. כָּל גּוֹיִם סְבָבוּנִי, בְּשֵׁם יהוה כִּי אֲמִילַם. סַבּוּנִי גַם סְבָבוּנִי, בְּשֵׁם יהוה כִּי אֲמִילַם. סַבּוּנִי כִדְבֹרִים דֹּעֲכוּ כְּאֵשׁ קוֹצִים, בְּשֵׁם יהוה כִּי אֲמִילַם. דָּחֹה דְחִיתַנִי לִנְפֹּל, וַיהוה עֲזָרָנִי.*

⬥§ **הַלְלוּ אֶת ה׳** — *Praise HASHEM.* This psalm, containing only two verses, is the shortest chapter in all of Scripture. *Radak* explains that its brevity symbolizes the simplicity of the world order which will prevail after the advent of the Messiah.

גּוֹיִם . . . הָאֻמִּים — *Nations . . . the states.* הָאֻמִּים, *the states,* is written with the definite article, whereas גּוֹיִם, *nations,* is spelled without it. This teaches that הָאֻמִּים refers to large nations that are well known and powerful, whereas גּוֹיִם refers to small, backward nations that have no prominence *(Iyun Tefillah).*

כִּי גָבַר עָלֵינוּ חַסְדּוֹ — *For His kindness has overwhelmed us.* Why should non-Jewish peoples and nations praise God for overwhelming Israel with Divine kindness? Israel will merit God's kindness because of the extraordinary service they rendered to Him. Recognizing Israel's distinction, the nations will consider it a privilege to become subservient to God's chosen ones, and will praise Him for His kindness to the Jews *(Yaavetz Hadoresh).*

⬥§ **הוֹדוּ לַה׳ כִּי טוֹב** — *Give thanks to HASHEM, for He is good.* This is a general expression of thanks to God. No matter what occurs, God is always good and everything He does is for the best, even though this may not be immediately apparent to man *(Abarbanel).*

⬥§ **מִן הַמֵּצַר** — *From the straits.* This psalm expresses gratitude and confidence. Just as David himself was catapulted from his personal straits

Congregation, then *chazzan:*

Psalm 117

הַלְלוּ *Praise* HASHEM,* *all nations; praise Him, all the states!** *For His kindness has overwhelmed us,** *and the truth of* HASHEM *is eternal, Halleluyah!*

Psalm 118

Chazzan – *Give thanks to* HASHEM *for He is good;**
His kindness endures forever!

Cong. – *Give thanks to* HASHEM, *for He is good;*
His kindness endures forever!

Let Israel say now: *His kindness endures forever!*

Chazzan – *Let Israel say now:* *His kindness endures forever!*

Cong. – *Give thanks to* HASHEM, *for He is good;*
His kindness endures forever!

Let the House of Aaron say now:
His kindness endures forever!

Chazzan – *Let the House of Aaron say now:*
His kindness endures forever!

Cong. – *Give thanks to* HASHEM, *for He is good;*
His kindness endures forever!

Let those who fear HASHEM *say now:*
His kindness endures forever!

Chazzan – *Let those who fear* HASHEM *say now:*
His kindness endures forever!

Cong. – *Give thanks to* HASHEM, *for He is good;*
His kindness endures forever!

מִן הַמֵּצַר *From the straits** *did I call upon God; God answered me with expansiveness.* HASHEM *is with me, I have no fear; how can man affect me?* HASHEM *is with me through my helpers;** *therefore I can face my foes. It is better to take refuge in* HASHEM *than to rely on man.** *It is better to take refuge in* HASHEM *than to rely on nobles. All the nations surround me; in the Name of* HASHEM *I cut them down! They encircle me, they also surround me; in the Name of* HASHEM, *I cut them down! They encircle me like bees, but they are extinguished as a fire does thorns; in the Name of* HASHEM *I cut them down! You pushed me hard that I might fall, but* HASHEM *assisted me.**

---

to a reign marked by accomplishment and glory, so too Israel can look forward to Divine redemption from the straits of exile and oppression.

ה׳ לִי בְּעֹזְרָי — *HASHEM is with me through my helpers.* I have many helpers, but I place confidence in them only because HASHEM is with them. If my helpers were not granted strength by God, their assistance would be futile (*Ibn Ezra; Radak*).

טוֹב לַחֲסוֹת בַּה׳ מִבְּטֹחַ בָּאָדָם — *It is better to take refuge in HASHEM than to rely on man.* **חִסָּיוֹן**, here translated *taking refuge,* denotes absolute confidence even though no guarantees have been given; **בִּטָּחוֹן**, *reliance,* however, presupposes a promise of protection. The Psalmist says that it is far better to put one's trust in God's protection, even without a pledge from Him, than to rely on the most profuse assurances of human beings (*R' Bachya; Vilna Gaon*).

דַּחֹה דְחִיתַנִי לִנְפֹּל וַה׳ עֲזָרָנִי — *You pushed me hard that I might fall, but HASHEM assisted me.* In the preceding verses, the Psalmist speaks of his

עָזִּי וְזִמְרָת יָהּ, וַיְהִי לִי לִישׁוּעָה. קוֹל רִנָּה וִישׁוּעָה, בְּאָהֳלֵי צַדִּיקִים,* יְמִין יהוה עֹשָׂה חָיִל. יְמִין יהוה רוֹמֵמָה, יְמִין יהוה עֹשָׂה חָיִל. לֹא אָמוּת כִּי אֶחְיֶה, וַאֲסַפֵּר מַעֲשֵׂי יָהּ.* יַסֹּר יִסְּרַנִּי יָּהּ, וְלַמָּוֶת לֹא נְתָנָנִי.* ❖ פִּתְחוּ לִי שַׁעֲרֵי צֶדֶק, אָבֹא בָם אוֹדֶה יָהּ. זֶה הַשַּׁעַר לַיהוה, צַדִּיקִים יָבֹאוּ בוֹ.* אוֹדְךָ* כִּי עֲנִיתָנִי, וַתְּהִי לִי לִישׁוּעָה. אוֹדְךָ כִּי עֲנִיתָנִי, וַתְּהִי לִי לִישׁוּעָה. אֶבֶן מָאֲסוּ הַבּוֹנִים, הָיְתָה לְרֹאשׁ פִּנָּה.* אֶבֶן מָאֲסוּ הַבּוֹנִים, הָיְתָה לְרֹאשׁ פִּנָּה. מֵאֵת יהוה הָיְתָה זֹּאת, הִיא נִפְלָאת בְּעֵינֵינוּ.* מֵאֵת יהוה הָיְתָה זֹּאת, הִיא נִפְלָאת בְּעֵינֵינוּ. זֶה הַיּוֹם עָשָׂה יהוה, נָגִילָה וְנִשְׂמְחָה בוֹ. זֶה הַיּוֹם עָשָׂה יהוה, נָגִילָה וְנִשְׂמְחָה בוֹ.

אָנָּא יהוה הוֹשִׁיעָה נָּא.
אָנָּא יהוה הוֹשִׁיעָה נָּא.
אָנָּא יהוה הַצְלִיחָה נָא.
אָנָּא יהוה הַצְלִיחָה נָא.

בָּרוּךְ הַבָּא בְּשֵׁם יהוה,* בֵּרַכְנוּכֶם מִבֵּית יהוה. בָּרוּךְ הַבָּא בְּשֵׁם יהוה, בֵּרַכְנוּכֶם מִבֵּית יהוה. אֵל יהוה וַיָּאֶר לָנוּ, אִסְרוּ חַג בַּעֲבֹתִים, עַד קַרְנוֹת הַמִּזְבֵּחַ. אֵל יהוה וַיָּאֶר לָנוּ, אִסְרוּ חַג

---

enemy indirectly; now, however, he addresses the foe directly.

קוֹל רִנָּה וִישׁוּעָה בְּאָהֳלֵי צַדִּיקִים — *The sound of rejoicing and salvation is in the tents of the righteous.* When HASHEM's right hand does valiantly for the sake of His chosen people, then the righteous will respond by filling their tents with sounds of rejoicing over this salvation *(Radak).*

לֹא אָמוּת כִּי אֶחְיֶה וַאֲסַפֵּר מַעֲשֵׂי יָהּ — *I shall not die! But I shall live and relate the deeds of God.* I will survive the assassination attempts of my enemies and live to recount the deeds of God, Who saved me from my foes *(Radak).*

יַסֹּר יִסְּרַנִּי יָּהּ וְלַמָּוֶת לֹא נְתָנָנִי — *God has chastened me exceedingly, but He did not let me die.* Throughout the duration of the exile, I survived because whatever suffering God decreed was only to atone for my sins *(Rashi).*

זֶה הַשַּׁעַר לַה׳ צַדִּיקִים יָבֹאוּ בוֹ — *This is the gate of HASHEM; the righteous shall enter through it.* This refers to the gate of the Temple. When the exile is over, the righteous will enter through this gate, and they will thank God for answering their plea for redemption *(Targum; Rashi).*

☙ Repetition of Verses

אוֹדְךָ— *I thank You.* From this point until the end of the Scriptural part of *Hallel* — i.e., the nine verses until יְהַלְלוּךָ — each verse is recited twice.

This entire psalm, which begins with הוֹדוּ לַה׳, *Give thanks to HASHEM,* follows a pattern, namely, that each new theme is repeated in the next verse or two in the same or slightly different words. Therefore the custom was introduced to follow through on this repetition by repeating each of these verses as well *(Rashi* to *Succah* 38a).

Another reason for repeating each verse is based upon the Talmud *(Pesachim* 119a) which relates that these verses were recited in a responsive dialogue between Samuel, Jesse, David, and David's brothers when the prophet announced that the young shepherd would be the future king of Israel. To honor these distinguished personages, we repeat each one's statement, as if it were a full chapter.

אֶבֶן מָאֲסוּ הַבּוֹנִים הָיְתָה לְרֹאשׁ פִּנָּה — *The stone the*

God is my might and my praise, and He was a salvation for me. The sound of rejoicing and salvation is in the tents of the righteous: 'HASHEM's right hand does valiantly. HASHEM's right hand is raised triumphantly; HASHEM's right hand does valiantly!' I shall not die! But I shall live and relate the deeds of God.* God has chastened me exceedingly, but He did not let me die.* Chazzan– Open for me the gates of righteousness, I will enter them and thank God. This is the gate of HASHEM; the righteous shall enter through it.* I thank You* for You have answered me and become my salvation. I thank You for You have answered me and become my salvation. The stone the builders despised has become the cornerstone.* The stone the builders despised has become the cornerstone. This emanated from HASHEM; it is wondrous in our eyes.* This emanated from HASHEM; it is wondrous in our eyes. This is the day HASHEM has made; let us rejoice and be glad on it. This is the day HASHEM has made; let us rejoice and be glad on it.*

אָנָּא *Please, HASHEM, save now!*
Please, HASHEM, save now!
Please, HASHEM, bring success now!
Please, HASHEM, bring success now!

בָּרוּךְ *Blessed is he who comes in the Name of HASHEM;* we bless you from the House of HASHEM. Blessed is he who comes in the Name of HASHEM; we bless you from the House of HASHEM. HASHEM is God, He illuminated for us; bind the festival offering with cords until the corners of the Altar. HASHEM is God, He illuminated for us; bind the festival*

---

builders despised has become the cornerstone. This verse refers to David, who was rejected by his own father and brothers (*Targum*). When the prophet Samuel announced that one of Jesse's sons was to be anointed king, no one even thought of summoning David, who was out with the sheep [see *I Samuel* 16:4-13].

Israel too is called אֶבֶן, *stone* (*Genesis* 49:24), for Israel is the cornerstone of God's design for the world. The world endures only by virtue of Israel's observance of God's laws, a fact that has influenced all nations to appreciate and accept certain aspects of God's commands. If not for the order and meaning that Israel has brought to the world, it would long ago have sunk into chaos. But the builders, i.e., the rulers of the nations, despised the Jews, claiming that they were parasites who made no contribution to the common good. When the dawn of redemption arrives, however, all nations will realize that Israel is indeed the cornerstone of the world (*Radak*).

מֵאֵת ה׳ הָיְתָה זֹּאת הִיא נִפְלָאת בְּעֵינֵינוּ — *This emanated from HASHEM; it is wondrous in our eyes.* When David was crowned, all were amazed. But David said, 'This is even more surprising and wondrous to me than it is to anyone else!'

Similarly, when Israel is catapulted to glory and tranquillity in the future, the nations who persecuted the Jews will ask in surprise, 'Aren't these the very Jews who were once despised and afflicted?'

The Jews will respond, 'We are even more amazed than you are, for only we know the depths of degradation we suffered!'

Then a heavenly voice will proclaim, 'This has emanated from HASHEM!'

בָּרוּךְ הַבָּא בְּשֵׁם ה׳ — *Blessed is he who comes in the Name of HASHEM.* In the course of the long exile, many Jews unfortunately became estranged from their own tradition and no longer felt at home with their own heritage. In the future, however, righteous and congenial teachers will welcome back all those who strayed from the fold and will bless them *in the Name of HASHEM* (*R' A.C. Feuer*).

בַּעֲבֹתִים, עַד קַרְנוֹת הַמִּזְבֵּחַ. אֵלִי אַתָּה וְאוֹדֶךָּ, אֱלֹהַי אֲרוֹמְמֶךָּ.
אֵלִי אַתָּה וְאוֹדֶךָּ, אֱלֹהַי אֲרוֹמְמֶךָּ. הוֹדוּ לַיהוה כִּי טוֹב, כִּי לְעוֹלָם
חַסְדּוֹ. הוֹדוּ לַיהוה כִּי טוֹב, כִּי לְעוֹלָם חַסְדּוֹ.

יְהַלְלְוּךָ יהוה אֱלֹהֵינוּ כָּל מַעֲשֶׂיךָ,* וַחֲסִידֶיךָ צַדִּיקִים* עוֹשֵׂי רְצוֹנֶךָ,* וְכָל עַמְּךָ בֵּית יִשְׂרָאֵל בְּרִנָּה יוֹדוּ וִיבָרְכוּ וִישַׁבְּחוּ וִיפָאֲרוּ וִירוֹמְמוּ וְיַעֲרִיצוּ וְיַקְדִּישׁוּ וְיַמְלִיכוּ אֶת שִׁמְךָ מַלְכֵּנוּ. ❖ כִּי לְךָ טוֹב לְהוֹדוֹת וּלְשִׁמְךָ נָאֶה לְזַמֵּר, כִּי מֵעוֹלָם וְעַד עוֹלָם אַתָּה אֵל. בָּרוּךְ אַתָּה יהוה, מֶלֶךְ מְהֻלָּל בַּתִּשְׁבָּחוֹת.

(Cong. – אָמֵן.)

קדיש שלם

The *chazzan* recites *Kaddish:*

יִתְגַּדַּל וְיִתְקַדַּשׁ שְׁמֵהּ רַבָּא. (Cong. – אָמֵן.) בְּעָלְמָא דִּי בְרָא כִרְעוּתֵהּ. וְיַמְלִיךְ מַלְכוּתֵהּ, בְּחַיֵּיכוֹן וּבְיוֹמֵיכוֹן וּבְחַיֵּי דְכָל בֵּית יִשְׂרָאֵל, בַּעֲגָלָא וּבִזְמַן קָרִיב. וְאִמְרוּ: אָמֵן.

(Cong. – אָמֵן. יְהֵא שְׁמֵהּ רַבָּא מְבָרַךְ לְעָלַם וּלְעָלְמֵי עָלְמַיָּא.)

יְהֵא שְׁמֵהּ רַבָּא מְבָרַךְ לְעָלַם וּלְעָלְמֵי עָלְמַיָּא.

יִתְבָּרַךְ וְיִשְׁתַּבַּח וְיִתְפָּאַר וְיִתְרוֹמַם וְיִתְנַשֵּׂא וְיִתְהַדָּר וְיִתְעַלֶּה וְיִתְהַלָּל שְׁמֵהּ דְּקֻדְשָׁא בְּרִיךְ הוּא (Cong. – בְּרִיךְ הוּא) — לְעֵלָּא מִן כָּל בִּרְכָתָא וְשִׁירָתָא תֻּשְׁבְּחָתָא וְנֶחֱמָתָא, דַּאֲמִירָן בְּעָלְמָא. וְאִמְרוּ: אָמֵן. (Cong. – אָמֵן.)

(Cong. – קַבֵּל בְּרַחֲמִים וּבְרָצוֹן אֶת תְּפִלָּתֵנוּ.)

תִּתְקַבֵּל צְלוֹתְהוֹן וּבָעוּתְהוֹן דְּכָל בֵּית יִשְׂרָאֵל קֳדָם אֲבוּהוֹן דִּי בִשְׁמַיָּא. וְאִמְרוּ: אָמֵן. (Cong. – אָמֵן.)

(Cong. – יְהִי שֵׁם יהוה מְבֹרָךְ, מֵעַתָּה וְעַד עוֹלָם.[1])

יְהֵא שְׁלָמָא רַבָּא מִן שְׁמַיָּא, וְחַיִּים עָלֵינוּ וְעַל כָּל יִשְׂרָאֵל. וְאִמְרוּ: אָמֵן. (Cong. – אָמֵן.)

(Cong. – עֶזְרִי מֵעִם יהוה, עֹשֵׂה שָׁמַיִם וָאָרֶץ.[2])

Take three steps back. Bow left and say . . . עֹשֶׂה; bow right and say . . . הוּא; bow forward and say וְעַל כָּל . . . אָמֵן. Remain standing in place for a few moments, then take three steps forward.

עֹשֶׂה שָׁלוֹם בִּמְרוֹמָיו, הוּא יַעֲשֶׂה שָׁלוֹם עָלֵינוּ, וְעַל כָּל יִשְׂרָאֵל. וְאִמְרוּ: אָמֵן. (Cong. – אָמֵן.)

---

§► יְהַלְלוּךָ . . . כָּל מַעֲשֶׂיךָ — *All Your works shall praise You.* This paragraph is not part of Psalms, but is a concluding blessing that sums up the broad theme of *Hallel* — that Israel and the entire universe will join in praising God. *All Your works shall praise You* means that in the perfect world of the future, the entire universe, including the vast variety of human beings, will function harmoniously according to God's will. This is the highest form of praise, for without it all the beautiful spoken and sung words and songs of praise are insincere and meaningless.

וַחֲסִידֶיךָ צַדִּיקִים — *Your devout ones, the righ-*

offering with cords until the corners of the Altar. You are my God, and I will thank You; my God, I will exalt You. You are my God, and I will thank You; my God, I will exalt You. Give thanks to HASHEM, *for He is good; His kindness endures forever. Give thanks to* HASHEM, *for He is good; His kindness endures forever.*

יְהַלְלוּךָ *All Your works shall praise You,** HASHEM *our God. And Your devout ones, the righteous,* who do Your will,* and Your entire people, the House of Israel, with glad song will thank, bless, praise, glorify, exalt, extol, sanctify, and proclaim the sovereignty of Your Name, our King.* Chazzan— *For to You it is fitting to give thanks, and unto Your Name it is proper to sing praises, for from This World to the World to Come You are God. Blessed are You,* HASHEM, *the King Who is lauded with praises.* (Cong.— *Amen.)*

FULL KADDISH

The *chazzan* recites *Kaddish:*

יִתְגַּדַּל *May His great Name grow exalted and sanctified* (Cong.— *Amen.*) *in the world that He created as He willed. May He give reign to His kingship in your lifetimes and in your days, and in the lifetimes of the entire Family of Israel, swiftly and soon. Now respond: Amen.*

(Cong.— *Amen. May His great Name be blessed forever and ever.)*

May His great Name be blessed forever and ever.

Blessed, praised, glorified, exalted, extolled, mighty, upraised, and lauded be the Name of the Holy One, Blessed is He (Cong.— *Blessed is He*) — *beyond any blessing and song, praise and consolation that are uttered in the world. Now respond: Amen.* (Cong.— *Amen*).

(Cong.— *Accept our prayers with mercy and favor.*)

May the prayers and supplications of the entire Family of Israel be accepted before their Father Who is in Heaven. Now respond: Amen. (Cong.— *Amen.*)

(Cong.— *Blessed be the Name of* HASHEM, *from this time and forever.*[1])

May there be abundant peace from Heaven, and life, upon us and upon all Israel. Now respond: Amen. (Cong.— *Amen.*)

(Cong.— *My help is from* HASHEM, *Maker of heaven and earth.*[2])

Take three steps back. Bow left and say, *'He Who makes peace . . .'*; bow right and say, *'may He . . .'*; bow forward and say, *'and upon all Israel . . .'* Remain standing in place for a few moments, then take three steps forward.

He Who makes peace in His heights, may He make peace upon us, and upon all Israel. Now respond: Amen. (Cong.— *Amen.*)

(1) *Psalms* 113:2. (2) 121:2.

---

teous. The word חָסִיד, *devout one,* refers to one who serves God beyond the minimum requirement of the *Halachah.* The word is derived from חֶסֶד, *kindness,* as if to say that such people do acts of kindness for God's sake. They serve as an example for the *righteous* people, who fulfill all the requirements of the Law, and for the masses of Israel, whose goal is to serve God, even though they may not equal the spiritual accomplishments of the *devout* and the *righteous.*

עוֹשֵׂי רְצוֹנֶךָ — *Who do Your will.* In an inspiring homiletical interpretation, *Yismach Yisrael* interprets that the good deeds of the righteous can remake God's will, as it were. In other words, when Jews serve Him properly, God responds by lavishing kindness and a sense of fulfillment upon the world. Then, *Hallel* will become not only a song of praise for the miracles of the past, but also for the longed-for redemption.

הוצאת ספר תורה

From the moment the Ark is opened until the Torah is returned to it, one must conduct himself with the utmost respect, and avoid unnecessary conversation. It is commendable to kiss the Torah as it is carried to the *bimah* [reading table] and back to the Ark.

All rise and remain standing until the Torah is placed on the *bimah*. The congregation recites:

אֵין כָּמְוֹךָ* בָאֱלֹהִים אֲדֹנָי, וְאֵין כְּמַעֲשֶׂיךָ.*[1] מַלְכוּתְךָ מַלְכוּת כָּל עֹלָמִים, וּמֶמְשַׁלְתְּךָ בְּכָל דּוֹר וָדֹר.[2] יהוה מֶלֶךְ,[3] יהוה מָלָךְ,[4] יהוה יִמְלֹךְ לְעֹלָם וָעֶד.[5] יהוה עֹז לְעַמּוֹ יִתֵּן, יהוה יְבָרֵךְ אֶת עַמּוֹ בַשָּׁלוֹם.[6]

אַב הָרַחֲמִים, הֵיטִיבָה בִרְצוֹנְךָ אֶת צִיּוֹן,* תִּבְנֶה חוֹמוֹת יְרוּשָׁלָיִם.[7] כִּי בְךָ לְבַד בָּטָחְנוּ, מֶלֶךְ אֵל רָם וְנִשָּׂא, אֲדוֹן עוֹלָמִים.

THE ARK IS OPENED

Before the Torah is removed the congregation recites:

וַיְהִי בִּנְסֹעַ הָאָרֹן* וַיֹּאמֶר מֹשֶׁה, קוּמָה יהוה וְיָפֻצוּ אֹיְבֶיךָ וְיָנֻסוּ מְשַׂנְאֶיךָ מִפָּנֶיךָ.[8] כִּי מִצִּיּוֹן תֵּצֵא תוֹרָה, וּדְבַר יהוה מִירוּשָׁלָיִם.[9] בָּרוּךְ שֶׁנָּתַן תּוֹרָה לְעַמּוֹ יִשְׂרָאֵל בִּקְדֻשָּׁתוֹ.

ON THE SABBATH THE FOLLOWING PRAYERS ARE OMITTED
AND THE SERVICE CONTINUES WITH בְּרִיךְ שְׁמֵהּ (P. 362).

The following paragraph [the Thirteen Attributes of Mercy] is recited three times:

יהוה, יהוה, אֵל, רַחוּם, וְחַנּוּן, אֶרֶךְ אַפַּיִם, וְרַב חֶסֶד, וֶאֱמֶת, נֹצֵר חֶסֶד לָאֲלָפִים, נֹשֵׂא עָוֹן, וָפֶשַׁע, וְחַטָּאָה, וְנַקֵּה.[10]

הוֹצָאַת סֵפֶר תּוֹרָה / Removal of the Torah

אֵין כָּמְוֹךָ — *There is none like You.* On the Sabbath and Festivals, the service of removing the Torah from the Ark begins with an introductory series of verses that emphasize God's greatness and plead for the rebuilding of Zion and Jerusalem. Since we are about to read from God's word to Israel, it is fitting that we first call to mind that the One Who speaks to us is our All-powerful King.

וְאֵין כְּמַעֲשֶׂיךָ — *And there is nothing like Your works.* This refers to the work of creation. It follows, therefore, that since God is the Creator of the universe, He was and remains its King.

הֵיטִיבָה . . . אֶת צִיּוֹן — *Do good with Zion.* Only in God's chosen Sanctuary can His kingdom come to full flower among mankind. Only there can the Torah reading attain its greatest meaning.

וַיְהִי בִּנְסֹעַ הָאָרֹן — *When the Ark would travel.* When the Ark is opened we declare, as Moses did when the Ark traveled, that God's word is invincible. Having acknowledged this, we can read from the Torah with the proper awareness. We continue that it is God's will that the Torah's message go forth to the entire world, and by blessing Him for having given us the Torah, we accept our responsibility to carry out its commands and spread its message *(R' Hirsch).*

The Thirteen Attributes of Mercy

During Festivals a special prayer is inserted before בְּרִיךְ שְׁמֵהּ, *Blessed is the Name,* requesting God's help in attaining His goals for us. [Like all personal supplications, this is not recited on the Sabbath.] It is preceded by the י״ג מִדּוֹת הָרַחֲמִים, *Thirteen Attributes of Mercy,* the prayer that God Himself taught Moses after Israel worshiped the Golden Calf. Although Moses, quite understandably, thought that no prayers could help the nation that had bowed to and danced around an idol less than six weeks after hearing the Ten Commandments, God showed him that it was never too late for prayer and repentance. God made a Divine covenant with him that the prayerful, repentant recitation of the Thirteen Attributes of Mercy would never be turned back unanswered (*Rosh Hashanah* 17b).

There are various opinions among the com-

REMOVAL OF THE TORAH FROM THE ARK

From the moment the Ark is opened until the Torah is returned to it, one must conduct himself with the utmost respect, and avoid unnecessary conversation. It is commendable to kiss the Torah as it is carried to the *bimah* [reading table] and back to the Ark.

All rise and remain standing until the Torah is placed on the *bimah*. The congregation recites:

אֵין כָּמוֹךָ *There is none like You* among the gods, my Lord, and there is nothing like Your works.*[1] Your kingdom is a kingdom spanning all eternities, and Your dominion is throughout every generation.[2] HASHEM reigns,[3] HASHEM has reigned,[4] HASHEM shall reign for all eternity.[5] HASHEM will give might to His people; HASHEM will bless His people with peace.[6]*

אַב הָרַחֲמִים *Father of compassion, do good with Zion* according to Your will; rebuild the walls of Jerusalem.[7] For we trust in You alone, O King, God, exalted and uplifted, Master of worlds.*

THE ARK IS OPENED

Before the Torah is removed the congregation recites:

וַיְהִי בִּנְסֹעַ *When the Ark would travel,* Moses would say, 'Arise, HASHEM, and let Your foes be scattered, let those who hate You flee from You.'[8] For from Zion the Torah will come forth and the word of HASHEM from Jerusalem.[9] Blessed is He Who gave the Torah to His people Israel in His holiness.*

ON THE SABBATH THE FOLLOWING PRAYERS ARE OMITTED

AND THE SERVICE CONTINUES WITH בְּרִיךְ שְׁמֵהּ, *BLESSED IS THE NAME* (P. 362).

The following paragraph [the Thirteen Attributes of Mercy] is recited three times:

יהוה HASHEM, HASHEM, God, Compassionate and Gracious, Slow to anger, and Abundant in Kindness and Truth. Preserver of kindness for thousands of generations, Forgiver of iniquity, willful sin, and error, and Who cleanses.[10]

(1) *Psalms* 86:8. (2) 145:13. (3) 10:16. (4) 93:1 et al. (5) *Exodus* 15:18.
(6) *Psalms* 29:11. (7) 51:20. (8) *Numbers* 10:35. (9) *Isaiah* 2:3. (10) *Exodus* 34:6-7.

---

mentators regarding the precise enumeration of the Thirteen Attributes. The following is the opinion of *Rabbeinu Tam* (*Rosh Hashanah* 17b). For a fuller commentary, see the ArtScroll *Tashlich* and the *Yom Kippur Machzor*.

1. ה׳ — *HASHEM*. This Name denotes mercy. God is merciful before a person sins, though He knows that future evil lies dormant in him.

2. ה׳ — *HASHEM*. God is merciful after the sinner has gone astray.

3. אֵל — *God*. This Name denotes power: the force of God's mercy sometimes surpasses even that indicated by the Name *HASHEM*.

4. רַחוּם — *Compassionate*. God eases the punishment of the guilty; and He does not put people into extreme temptation.

5. וְחַנּוּן — *and Gracious*, even to the undeserving.

6. אֶרֶךְ אַפַּיִם — *Slow to anger*, so that the sinner can reconsider long before it is too late.

7. וְרַב חֶסֶד — *and Abundant in Kindness*, toward those who lack personal merits. Also, if the scales of good and evil are evenly balanced, He tips them to the good.

8. וֶאֱמֶת — *and Truth*. God never reneges on His word.

9. נֹצֵר חֶסֶד לָאֲלָפִים — *Preserver of kindness for thousands of generations*. The deeds of the righteous benefit their offspring far into the future.

10. נֹשֵׂא עָוֹן — *Forgiver of iniquity*. God forgives the intentional sinner, if he repents.

11. וָפֶשַׁע — *[Forgiver of] willful sin*. Even those who purposely anger God are allowed to repent.

12. וְחַטָּאָה — *and [Forgiver of] error*. This is a sin committed out of carelessness or apathy.

13. וְנַקֵּה — *and Who cleanses*. God wipes away the sins of those who repent.

רִבּוֹנוֹ שֶׁל עוֹלָם מַלֵּא מִשְׁאֲלוֹת לִבִּי לְטוֹבָה,* וְהָפֵק רְצוֹנִי, וְתֵן שְׁאֵלָתִי, לִי עַבְדְּךָ (name) בֶּן/בַּת (mother's name) אֲמָתֶךָ, וְזַכֵּנִי

Insert the appropriate phrase(s) — וְאֶת אִשְׁתִּי/בַּעְלִי, וּבְנִי/וּבָנַי, וּבִתִּי/וּבְנוֹתַי

וְכָל בְּנֵי בֵיתִי לַעֲשׂוֹת רְצוֹנְךָ בְּלֵבָב שָׁלֵם. וּמַלְּטֵנוּ מִיֵּצֶר הָרָע, וְתֵן חֶלְקֵנוּ בְּתוֹרָתֶךָ. וְזַכֵּנוּ שֶׁתִּשְׁרֶה שְׁכִינָתְךָ עָלֵינוּ, וְהוֹפַע עָלֵינוּ רוּחַ חָכְמָה וּבִינָה. וְיִתְקַיֵּם בָּנוּ מִקְרָא שֶׁכָּתוּב: וְנָחָה עָלָיו רוּחַ יהוה, רוּחַ חָכְמָה וּבִינָה, רוּחַ עֵצָה וּגְבוּרָה, רוּחַ דַּעַת וְיִרְאַת יהוה.[1] וְכֵן יְהִי רָצוֹן מִלְּפָנֶיךָ, יהוה אֱלֹהֵינוּ וֵאלֹהֵי אֲבוֹתֵינוּ, שֶׁתְּזַכֵּנוּ לַעֲשׂוֹת מַעֲשִׂים טוֹבִים בְּעֵינֶיךָ, וְלָלֶכֶת בְּדַרְכֵי יְשָׁרִים לְפָנֶיךָ. וְקַדְּשֵׁנוּ בְּמִצְוֹתֶיךָ כְּדֵי שֶׁנִּזְכֶּה לְחַיִּים טוֹבִים וַאֲרוּכִים לִימוֹת הַמָּשִׁיחַ וּלְחַיֵּי הָעוֹלָם הַבָּא. וְתִשְׁמְרֵנוּ מִמַּעֲשִׂים רָעִים, וּמִשָּׁעוֹת רָעוֹת הַמִּתְרַגְּשׁוֹת לָבֹא לָעוֹלָם. וְהַבּוֹטֵחַ בַּיהוה חֶסֶד יְסוֹבְבֶנְהוּ,[2] אָמֵן. יִהְיוּ לְרָצוֹן אִמְרֵי פִי וְהֶגְיוֹן לִבִּי לְפָנֶיךָ, יהוה צוּרִי וְגֹאֲלִי.[3]

Recite the following verse three times:

וַאֲנִי תְפִלָּתִי לְךָ* יהוה עֵת רָצוֹן, אֱלֹהִים בְּרָב חַסְדֶּךָ, עֲנֵנִי בֶּאֱמֶת יִשְׁעֶךָ.[4]

ON ALL DAYS CONTINUE:

זוהר ויקהל שסט:א

בְּרִיךְ שְׁמֵהּ* דְּמָרֵא עָלְמָא, בְּרִיךְ כִּתְרָךְ וְאַתְרָךְ. יְהֵא רְעוּתָךְ עִם עַמָּךְ יִשְׂרָאֵל לְעָלַם, וּפֻרְקַן יְמִינָךְ אַחֲזֵי לְעַמָּךְ בְּבֵית מַקְדְּשָׁךְ, וּלְאַמְטוּיֵי לָנָא מִטּוּב נְהוֹרָךְ, וּלְקַבֵּל צְלוֹתָנָא בְּרַחֲמִין. יְהֵא רַעֲוָא קֳדָמָךְ, דְּתוֹרִיךְ לָן חַיִּין בְּטִיבוּתָא, וְלֶהֱוֵי אֲנָא פְּקִידָא בְּגוֹ צַדִּיקַיָּא, לְמִרְחַם עָלַי וּלְמִנְטַר יָתִי וְיַת כָּל דִּי לִי, וְדִי לְעַמָּךְ יִשְׂרָאֵל. אַנְתְּ הוּא זָן לְכֹלָּא, וּמְפַרְנֵס לְכֹלָּא, אַנְתְּ הוּא שַׁלִּיט עַל כֹּלָּא. אַנְתְּ הוּא דְּשַׁלִּיט עַל מַלְכַיָּא, וּמַלְכוּתָא דִּילָךְ הִיא. אֲנָא עַבְדָּא דְקֻדְשָׁא בְּרִיךְ הוּא, דְּסָגִידְנָא קַמֵּהּ וּמִקַּמָּא דִּיקַר אוֹרַיְתֵהּ בְּכָל עִדָּן וְעִדָּן. לָא עַל אֱנָשׁ רָחִיצְנָא, וְלָא עַל בַּר אֱלָהִין סָמִיכְנָא, אֶלָּא בֶּאֱלָהָא דִשְׁמַיָּא, דְּהוּא אֱלָהָא קְשׁוֹט, וְאוֹרַיְתֵהּ קְשׁוֹט, וּנְבִיאוֹהִי קְשׁוֹט, וּמַסְגֵּא לְמֶעְבַּד טַבְוָן וּקְשׁוֹט. בֵּהּ אֲנָא

⊰ **רִבּוֹנוֹ שֶׁל עוֹלָם / Master of the Universe** ⊱ מַלֵּא מִשְׁאֲלוֹת לִבִּי לְטוֹבָה — *Fulfill my heartfelt requests for good.* Often man's personal goals are not to his real benefit. May my requests be filled in a way that will be truly good.

⊰ **וַאֲנִי תְפִלָּתִי לְךָ** — *As for me, may my prayer to You.* This verse makes three declarations: We pray to God alone; we hope that the time is proper in His eyes; and we know that only through His abundant kindness can we expect salvation.

רִבּוֹנוֹ *Master of the universe, fulfill my heartfelt requests for good,* satisfy my desire and grant my request, me—Your servant* (name) *son/daughter of* (mother's name) *Your maidservant—and privilege me*

Insert the appropriate phrase(s): *and my wife/husband, my son(s), my daughter(s)*

and everyone in my household to do Your will wholeheartedly. Rescue us from the Evil Inclination and grant our share in Your Torah. Privilege us that You may rest Your Presence upon us and radiate upon us a spirit of wisdom and insight. Let there be fulfilled in us the verse that is written: The spirit of HASHEM *shall rest upon him, the spirit of wisdom and insight, the spirit of counsel and strength, the spirit of knowledge and fear of* HASHEM.[1] *Similarly may it be Your will,* HASHEM, *our God and the God of our forefathers, that You privilege us to do deeds that are good in Your eyes and to walk before You in upright paths. Sanctify us with Your commandments so that we may be worthy of a good and long life, to the days of the Messiah and to the life of the World to Come. May You protect us against evil deeds and from bad times that surge upon the world. He who trusts in* HASHEM *— may kindness surround him.*[2] *Amen. May the expressions of my mouth and the thoughts of my heart find favor before You,* HASHEM, *my Rock and my Redeemer.*[3]

Recite the following verse three times:

וַאֲנִי תְפִלָּתִי *As for me, may my prayer to You,** HASHEM, *be at an opportune time; O God, in Your abundant kindness, answer me with the truth of Your salvation.*[4]

ON ALL DAYS CONTINUE:

Zohar, Vayakhel 369a

בְּרִיךְ שְׁמֵהּ *Blessed is the Name* of the Master of the universe, blessed is Your crown and Your place. May Your favor remain with Your people Israel forever; may You display the salvation of Your right hand to Your people in Your Holy Temple, to benefit us with the goodness of Your luminescence and to accept our prayers with mercy. May it be Your will that You extend our lives with goodness and that I be numbered among the righteous; that You have mercy on me and protect me, all that is mine and that is Your people Israel's. It is You Who nourishes all and sustains all; You control everything. It is You Who control kings, and kingship is Yours. I am a servant of the Holy One, Blessed is He, and I prostrate myself before Him and before the glory of His Torah at all times. Not in any man do I put trust, nor on any angel do I rely — only on the God of heaven Who is the God of truth, Whose Torah is truth and Whose prophets are true and Who acts liberally with kindness and truth. In Him do I*

(1) *Isaiah* 11:2. (2) Cf. *Psalms* 32:10. (3) 19:15. (4) 69:14.

בְּרִיךְ שְׁמֵהּ — *Blessed is the Name.* The *Zohar* declares that when the congregation prepares to read from the Torah, the heavenly gates of mercy are opened and God's love for Israel is aroused. Therefore, it is an auspicious occasion for the recital of this prayer which asks for God's compassion; pleads that He display His salvation in the finally rebuilt Holy Temple; declares our

רָחִיץ, וְלִשְׁמֵהּ קַדִּישָׁא יַקִּירָא אֲנָא אֵמַר תֻּשְׁבְּחָן. יְהֵא רַעֲוָא קֳדָמָךְ, דְּתִפְתַּח לִבָּאִי בְּאוֹרַיְתָא, וְתַשְׁלִים מִשְׁאֲלִין דְּלִבָּאִי, וְלִבָּא דְכָל עַמָּךְ יִשְׂרָאֵל, לְטַב וּלְחַיִּין וְלִשְׁלָם. (אָמֵן.)

Two Torah Scrolls are removed from the Ark; one for the main Torah reading and the second for *Maftir.* The first is presented to the *chazzan,* who accepts it in his right arm. Facing the congregation the *chazzan* raises the Torah and, followed by congregation, recites:

שְׁמַע יִשְׂרָאֵל* יהוה אֱלֹהֵינוּ יהוה אֶחָד.[1]

Still facing the congregation, the *chazzan* raises the Torah and, followed by congregation, recites:

אֶחָד (הוּא) אֱלֹהֵינוּ גָּדוֹל אֲדוֹנֵינוּ, קָדוֹשׁ שְׁמוֹ.

The *chazzan* turns to the Ark, bows while raising the Torah, and recites:

גַּדְּלוּ* לַיהוה אִתִּי וּנְרוֹמְמָה שְׁמוֹ יַחְדָּו.[2]

The *chazzan* turns to his right and carries the Torah to the *bimah,* as the congregation responds:

לְךָ יהוה הַגְּדֻלָּה* וְהַגְּבוּרָה וְהַתִּפְאֶרֶת וְהַנֵּצַח וְהַהוֹד כִּי כֹל בַּשָּׁמַיִם וּבָאָרֶץ, לְךָ יהוה הַמַּמְלָכָה וְהַמִּתְנַשֵּׂא לְכֹל לְרֹאשׁ.[3] רוֹמְמוּ יהוה אֱלֹהֵינוּ, וְהִשְׁתַּחֲווּ לַהֲדֹם רַגְלָיו,* קָדוֹשׁ הוּא. רוֹמְמוּ יהוה אֱלֹהֵינוּ, וְהִשְׁתַּחֲווּ לְהַר קָדְשׁוֹ, כִּי קָדוֹשׁ יהוה אֱלֹהֵינוּ.[4]

As the *chazzan* carries the Torah to the *bimah* the congregation recites:

עַל הַכֹּל,* יִתְגַּדַּל וְיִתְקַדַּשׁ וְיִשְׁתַּבַּח וְיִתְפָּאַר וְיִתְרוֹמַם וְיִתְנַשֵּׂא שְׁמוֹ שֶׁל מֶלֶךְ מַלְכֵי הַמְּלָכִים הַקָּדוֹשׁ בָּרוּךְ הוּא, בָּעוֹלָמוֹת שֶׁבָּרָא, הָעוֹלָם הַזֶּה וְהָעוֹלָם הַבָּא, כִּרְצוֹנוֹ,* וְכִרְצוֹן יְרֵאָיו, וְכִרְצוֹן כָּל בֵּית יִשְׂרָאֵל. צוּר הָעוֹלָמִים, אֲדוֹן כָּל הַבְּרִיּוֹת, אֱלוֹהַּ כָּל הַנְּפָשׁוֹת, הַיּוֹשֵׁב בְּמֶרְחֲבֵי מָרוֹם, הַשּׁוֹכֵן בִּשְׁמֵי שְׁמֵי קֶדֶם. קְדֻשָּׁתוֹ עַל הַחַיּוֹת, וּקְדֻשָּׁתוֹ עַל כִּסֵּא הַכָּבוֹד. וּבְכֵן יִתְקַדַּשׁ שִׁמְךָ בָּנוּ* יהוה אֱלֹהֵינוּ לְעֵינֵי כָּל חָי. וְנֹאמַר לְפָנָיו שִׁיר חָדָשׁ, כַּכָּתוּב: שִׁירוּ לֵאלֹהִים זַמְּרוּ שְׁמוֹ, סֹלּוּ

---

faith in Him and His Torah; and asks that He make us receptive to its wisdom.

⊰ שְׁמַע יִשְׂרָאֵל — *Hear, O Israel.* Holding the Torah Scroll, the *chazzan* leads the congregation in reciting three verses that help set the majestic tone of reading publicly from the word of God. The verses form a logical progression: God is One; He is great and holy; therefore we join in declaring His greatness.

⊰ גַּדְּלוּ — *Declare the greatness.* Our rejoicing in the Torah manifests itself in praise of its Giver. The *chazzan* calls upon the congregation to join him in praising God.

⊰ לְךָ ה׳ הַגְּדֻלָּה — *Yours, HASHEM, is the greatness.* This praise was first uttered by David in his ecstasy at seeing how wholeheartedly the people contributed their riches toward the eventual building of the Temple. He ascribed the greatness of that and every other achievement to God's graciousness.

⊰ לַהֲדֹם רַגְלָיו — *At His footstool,* i.e., the Temple, as if to say that God's Heavenly Presence extends earthward, like a footstool that helps support a monarch sitting on his throne. In a further sense, this represents our resolve to live in such a way that we are worthy of His Presence resting upon us (*R' Hirsch*).

⊰ עַל הַכֹּל — *For all this.* All the praises that we

trust, and to His glorious and holy Name do I declare praises. May it be Your will that You open my heart to the Torah and that You fulfill the wishes of my heart and the heart of Your entire people Israel for good, for life, and for peace. (Amen.)

Two Torah Scrolls are removed from the Ark; one for the main Torah reading and the second for *Maftir.* The first is presented to the *chazzan,* who accepts it in his right arm. Facing the congregation the *chazzan* raises the Torah and, followed by congregation, recites:

Hear, O Israel:* HASHEM is our God, HASHEM, the One and Only.[1]

Still facing the congregation, the *chazzan* raises the Torah and, followed by congregation, recites:

One is our God, great is our Master, Holy is His Name.

The *chazzan* turns to the Ark, bows while raising the Torah, and recites:

Declare the greatness* of HASHEM with me, and let us exalt His Name together.[2]

The *chazzan* turns to his right and carries the Torah to the *bimah,* as the congregation responds:

לְךָ *Yours, HASHEM, is the greatness,* the strength, the splendor, the triumph, and the glory; even everything in heaven and earth; Yours, HASHEM, is the kingdom, and the sovereignty over every leader.*[3] *Exalt HASHEM, our God, and bow at His footstool;* He is Holy! Exalt HASHEM, our God, and bow to His holy mountain; for holy is HASHEM, our God.*[4]

As the *chazzan* carries the Torah to the *bimah* the congregation recites:

עַל הַכֹּל *For all this,* let the Name of the King of kings, the Holy One, Blessed is He, grow exalted, sanctified, praised, glorified, exalted, and extolled in the worlds that He has created — This World and the World to Come — according to His will,* the will of those who fear Him, and the will of the entire House of Israel. Rock of the eternities, Master of all creatures, God of all souls, He Who sits in the expanses on high, Who rests in the loftiest primeval heavens. His holiness is upon the Chayos; His holiness is upon the Throne of Glory. Similarly, may Your Name be sanctified within us,* HASHEM, our God, in the sight of all the living. May we chant before Him a new song as it is written: 'Sing to God, make music for His Name, extol the One Who*

(1) *Deuteronomy* 6:4. (2) *Psalms* 34:4. (3) *I Chronicles* 29:11. (4) *Psalms* 99:5,9.

---

have uttered heretofore are inadequate to describe God's greatness. May His Name continue to grow exalted (*Kol Bo*).

This paragraph is intended to express the majesty of God especially now that we are about to read from the Torah. We say that although He is sanctified in the heavens and by the spiritual beings, we long to become worthy vehicles through which His greatness can be manifested on earth, as well.

כִּרְצוֹנוֹ — *According to His will.* May He be *exalted, sanctified, praised* ... as He wishes to be. God created the universe so that His glory could be appreciated and emulated by man (see *Isaiah* 43:7). We now pray that this will indeed take place.

וּבְכֵן יִתְקַדַּשׁ שִׁמְךָ בָּנוּ — *Similarly, may Your Name be sanctified within us.* The goal of people should be to demonstrate that God's greatness should not be reserved for the 'higher, spiritual' spheres. Rather, the most noble purpose of life is for mortal man to become a bearer of Godliness.

לָרֹכֵב בָּעֲרָבוֹת בְּיָהּ שְׁמוֹ, וְעִלְזוּ לְפָנָיו.[1] וְנִרְאֵהוּ עַיִן בְּעַיִן בְּשׁוּבוֹ אֶל נָוֵהוּ, כַּכָּתוּב: כִּי עַיִן בְּעַיִן יִרְאוּ בְּשׁוּב יהוה צִיּוֹן.[2] וְנֶאֱמַר: וְנִגְלָה כְּבוֹד יהוה, וְרָאוּ כָל בָּשָׂר יַחְדָּו כִּי פִּי יהוה דִּבֵּר.[3]

אַב הָרַחֲמִים הוּא יְרַחֵם עַם עֲמוּסִים, וְיִזְכֹּר בְּרִית אֵיתָנִים, וְיַצִּיל נַפְשׁוֹתֵינוּ מִן הַשָּׁעוֹת הָרָעוֹת, וְיִגְעַר בְּיֵצֶר הָרַע מִן הַנְּשׂוּאִים, וְיָחֹן אוֹתָנוּ לִפְלֵיטַת עוֹלָמִים, וִימַלֵּא מִשְׁאֲלוֹתֵינוּ בְּמִדָּה טוֹבָה יְשׁוּעָה וְרַחֲמִים.

The Torah is placed on the *bimah* and prepared for reading.

The *gabbai* uses the following formula to call a *Kohen* to the Torah:

וְיַעֲזוֹר וְיָגֵן וְיוֹשִׁיעַ לְכֹל הַחוֹסִים בּוֹ, וְנֹאמַר, אָמֵן. הַכֹּל הָבוּ גֹדֶל לֵאלֹהֵינוּ וּתְנוּ כָבוֹד לַתּוֹרָה, כֹּהֵן° קְרָב, יַעֲמֹד (name) בֶּן (father's name) הַכֹּהֵן.

°If no *Kohen* is present, the *gabbai* says:
„אֵין כָּאן כֹּהֵן, יַעֲמֹד (insert name) יִשְׂרָאֵל (לֵוִי) בִּמְקוֹם כֹּהֵן."

בָּרוּךְ שֶׁנָּתַן תּוֹרָה לְעַמּוֹ יִשְׂרָאֵל בִּקְדֻשָּׁתוֹ. (תּוֹרַת יהוה תְּמִימָה מְשִׁיבַת נָפֶשׁ, עֵדוּת יהוה נֶאֱמָנָה מַחְכִּימַת פֶּתִי. פִּקּוּדֵי יהוה יְשָׁרִים מְשַׂמְּחֵי לֵב, מִצְוַת יהוה בָּרָה מְאִירַת עֵינָיִם.[4] יהוה עֹז לְעַמּוֹ יִתֵּן, יהוה יְבָרֵךְ אֶת עַמּוֹ בַשָּׁלוֹם.[5] הָאֵל תָּמִים דַּרְכּוֹ, אִמְרַת יהוה צְרוּפָה, מָגֵן הוּא לְכֹל הַחוֹסִים בּוֹ.[6])

Congregation, then *gabbai:*

וְאַתֶּם הַדְּבֵקִים בַּיהוה אֱלֹהֵיכֶם, חַיִּים כֻּלְּכֶם הַיּוֹם.[7]

קריאת התורה

The reader shows the *oleh* (person called to the Torah) the place in the Torah. The *oleh* touches the Torah with a corner of his *tallis,* or the belt or mantle of the Torah, and kisses it. He then begins the blessing, bowing at בָּרְכוּ, and straightening up at 'ה.

בָּרְכוּ אֶת יהוה הַמְּבֹרָךְ.

Congregation, followed by *oleh,* responds, bowing at בָּרוּךְ, and straightening up at 'ה.

בָּרוּךְ יהוה הַמְּבֹרָךְ לְעוֹלָם וָעֶד.

Oleh continues:

בָּרוּךְ אַתָּה יהוה אֱלֹהֵינוּ מֶלֶךְ הָעוֹלָם, אֲשֶׁר בָּחַר בָּנוּ מִכָּל הָעַמִּים, וְנָתַן לָנוּ אֶת תּוֹרָתוֹ. בָּרוּךְ אַתָּה יהוה, נוֹתֵן הַתּוֹרָה. (Cong.– אָמֵן.)

⊰ קְרִיאַת הַתּוֹרָה / Reading of the Torah

There is a basic difference between the reading of the Torah and the prayers. When we pray, *we* call upon *God;* that is why the *chazzan* stands in front of the congregation as its representative. But the Torah reading is reminiscent of God's revelation to Israel, when the nation gathered around Mount Sinai to hear Him communicate His word to Israel. That is why the Torah is read from a *bimah,* platform, in the center of the congregation and usually elevated, like the mountain around which Israel gathered.

The number of people called to the Torah varies in accordance with the sanctity of the day. Thus, on Monday and Thursday, fast days, Purim and Chanukah, three people are called; on Rosh Chodesh and Chol HaMoed, four; on Festivals and Rosh Hashanah, five; on Yom Kippur, six; and on the Sabbath [whether an *rides in the highest heavens with His Name YAH, and exult before Him.'*[1] *May we see Him with a perceptive view upon His return to His Abode, as is written: 'For they shall see with a perceptive view as HASHEM returns to Zion.'*[2] *And it is said: 'The glory of HASHEM shall be revealed and all flesh together shall see that the mouth of HASHEM has spoken.'*[3]

אַב הָרַחֲמִים *May the Father of compassion have mercy on the nation that is borne by Him, and may He remember the covenant of the spiritually mighty. May He rescue our souls from the bad times, and upbraid the evil inclination to leave those borne by Him, graciously make us an eternal remnant, and fulfill our requests in good measure, for salvation and mercy.*

The Torah is placed on the *bimah* and prepared for reading.

The *gabbai* uses the following formula to call a *Kohen* to the Torah:

וְיַעֲזוֹר *May He help, shield, and save all who take refuge in Him — Now let us respond: Amen. All of you ascribe greatness to our God and give honor to the Torah. Kohen,° approach. Arise* (name) *son of* (father's name) *the Kohen*

°If no *Kohen* is present, the *gabbai* says: *'There is no Kohen present, stand* (name) *son of* (father's name) *an Israelite (Levite) in place of the Kohen.'*

Blessed is He Who gave the Torah to His people Israel in His holiness. (The Torah of HASHEM is perfect, restoring the soul; the testimony of HASHEM is trustworthy, making the simple one wise. The orders of HASHEM are upright, gladdening the heart; the command of HASHEM is clear, enlightening the eyes.[4] *HASHEM will give might to His nation; HASHEM will bless His nation with peace.*[5] *The God Whose way is perfect, the promise of HASHEM is flawless, He is a shield for all who take refuge in Him.*[6]*)*

Congregation, then *gabbai*:

You who cling to HASHEM, your God, you are all alive today.[7]

READING OF THE TORAH

The reader shows the *oleh* (person called to the Torah) the place in the Torah. The *oleh* touches the Torah with a corner of his *tallis,* or the belt or mantle of the Torah, and kisses it. He then begins the blessing, bowing at *'Bless,'* and straightening up at 'HASHEM.'

Bless HASHEM,* the blessed One.

Congregation, followed by *oleh,* responds, bowing at 'Blessed,' and straightening up at 'HASHEM.'

Blessed is HASHEM, the blessed One, for all eternity.

Oleh continues:

בָּרוּךְ *Blessed are You, HASHEM, our God, King of the universe, Who selected us from all the peoples and gave us His Torah. Blessed are You, HASHEM, Giver of the Torah.* (Cong.— *Amen.)*

(1) *Psalms* 68:5. (2) *Isaiah* 52:8. (3) 40:5. (4) *Psalms* 19:8-9. (4) 29:11. (6) 18:31. (7) *Deuteronomy* 4:4.

ordinary Sabbath or a Festival that falls on the Sabbath], seven. (It should be noted that *Maftir* is not included in the above number since *Maftir* is attached to the *Haftarah* reading.) Only three are called on Sabbath afternoons since the Torah has already been read in the morning.

On most Festivals the Torah reading is a selection on either the historical narrative of the day or the commandment to observe the Festivals.

בָּרְכוּ אֶת ה׳ — *Bless HASHEM.* This call to the congregation to bless God prior to the Torah reading is based on the practice of Ezra (*Nechemiah* 8:6). Before he read from the Torah to the multitude, he blessed God and they responded in kind. Similarly, the Sages (*Berachos* 21a) derive the Scriptural requirement to recite a blessing before Torah study from the verse, *When I proclaim the Name of HASHEM, ascribe greatness to our God* (*Deuteronomy* 32:3). The implication

After his Torah portion has been read, the *oleh* recites:

בָּרוּךְ אַתָּה יהוה אֱלֹהֵינוּ מֶלֶךְ הָעוֹלָם, אֲשֶׁר נָתַן לָנוּ תּוֹרַת אֱמֶת, וְחַיֵּי עוֹלָם* נָטַע בְּתוֹכֵנוּ. בָּרוּךְ אַתָּה יהוה, נוֹתֵן הַתּוֹרָה. (.Cong. – אָמֵן)

PRAYER FOR THE OLEH / מי שברך לעולה לתורה

After each *oleh* completes his concluding blessing, the *gabbai* calls the next *oleh* to the Torah, then blesses the one who has just concluded.

מִי שֶׁבֵּרַךְ אֲבוֹתֵינוּ אַבְרָהָם יִצְחָק וְיַעֲקֹב, הוּא יְבָרֵךְ אֶת (name) בֶּן (father's name) בַּעֲבוּר שֶׁעָלָה לִכְבוֹד הַמָּקוֹם, לִכְבוֹד הַתּוֹרָה, לִכְבוֹד הַשַּׁבָּת, לִכְבוֹד הָרֶגֶל. בִּשְׂכַר זֶה, הַקָּדוֹשׁ בָּרוּךְ הוּא יִשְׁמְּרֵהוּ וְיַצִּילֵהוּ מִכָּל צָרָה וְצוּקָה, וּמִכָּל נֶגַע וּמַחֲלָה, וְיִשְׁלַח בְּרָכָה וְהַצְלָחָה בְּכָל מַעֲשֵׂה יָדָיו, וְיִזְכֶּה לַעֲלוֹת לְרֶגֶל, עִם כָּל יִשְׂרָאֵל אֶחָיו. וְנֹאמַר: אָמֵן. (.Cong. – אָמֵן)

PRAYER FOR OTHERS / מי שברך לאחרים

It is customary that the following prayer be recited for the family members of the *oleh* and for anyone else that he may wish to include:

מִי שֶׁבֵּרַךְ אֲבוֹתֵינוּ אַבְרָהָם יִצְחָק וְיַעֲקֹב, הוּא יְבָרֵךְ אֶת (names of the recipients) בַּעֲבוּר שֶׁ(name of *oleh*) יִתֵּן לִצְדָקָה בַּעֲבוּרָם. בִּשְׂכַר זֶה, הַקָּדוֹשׁ בָּרוּךְ הוּא יִשְׁמְּרֵם וְיַצִּילֵם מִכָּל צָרָה וְצוּקָה, וּמִכָּל נֶגַע וּמַחֲלָה, וְיִשְׁלַח בְּרָכָה וְהַצְלָחָה בְּכָל מַעֲשֵׂה יְדֵיהֶם, וְיִזְכּוּ לַעֲלוֹת לְרֶגֶל, עִם כָּל יִשְׂרָאֵל אֲחֵיהֶם. וְנֹאמַר: אָמֵן. (.Cong. – אָמֵן)

PRAYER FOR A SICK PERSON / מי שברך לחולה

מִי שֶׁבֵּרַךְ אֲבוֹתֵינוּ אַבְרָהָם יִצְחָק וְיַעֲקֹב, מֹשֶׁה אַהֲרֹן דָּוִד וּשְׁלֹמֹה,

for a man

הוּא יְבָרֵךְ וִירַפֵּא אֶת הַחוֹלֶה (patient's name) בֶּן (mother's name) בַּעֲבוּר שֶׁ(supplicant's name) יִתֵּן לִצְדָקָה בַּעֲבוּרוֹ.°° בִּשְׂכַר זֶה, הַקָּדוֹשׁ בָּרוּךְ הוּא יִמָּלֵא רַחֲמִים עָלָיו, לְהַחֲלִימוֹ וּלְרַפְּאתוֹ לְהַחֲזִיקוֹ וּלְהַחֲיוֹתוֹ, וְיִשְׁלַח לוֹ מְהֵרָה רְפוּאָה שְׁלֵמָה מִן הַשָּׁמַיִם, לִרְמַ״ח אֵבָרָיו, וּשְׁסָ״ה גִּידָיו, בְּתוֹךְ

for a woman

הוּא יְבָרֵךְ וִירַפֵּא אֶת הַחוֹלָה (patient's name) בַּת (mother's name) בַּעֲבוּר שֶׁ(supplicant's name) יִתֵּן לִצְדָקָה בַּעֲבוּרָהּ.°° בִּשְׂכַר זֶה, הַקָּדוֹשׁ בָּרוּךְ הוּא יִמָּלֵא רַחֲמִים עָלֶיהָ, לְהַחֲלִימָהּ וּלְרַפְּאתָהּ וּלְהַחֲזִיקָהּ וּלְהַחֲיוֹתָהּ, וְיִשְׁלַח לָהּ מְהֵרָה רְפוּאָה שְׁלֵמָה מִן הַשָּׁמַיִם, לְכָל אֵבָרֶיהָ, וּלְכָל גִּידֶיהָ, בְּתוֹךְ

שְׁאָר חוֹלֵי יִשְׂרָאֵל, רְפוּאַת הַנֶּפֶשׁ, וּרְפוּאַת הַגּוּף, [On the Sabbath – שַׁבָּת הִיא מִלִּזְעֹק וּ] יוֹם טוֹב הוּא מִלִּזְעֹק, וּרְפוּאָה קְרוֹבָה לָבֹא, הַשְׁתָּא, בַּעֲגָלָא וּבִזְמַן קָרִיב. וְנֹאמַר: אָמֵן. (.Cong. – אָמֵן)

°°Many congregations substitute:

בַּעֲבוּר שֶׁכָּל הַקָּהָל מִתְפַּלְּלִים בַּעֲבוּרוֹ (בַּעֲבוּרָהּ)

After his Torah portion has been read, the *oleh* recites:

בָּרוּךְ *Blessed are You,* HASHEM, *our God, King of the universe, Who gave us the Torah of truth and implanted eternal life* within us. Blessed are You,* HASHEM, *Giver of the Torah.* (Cong.— *Amen.)*

PRAYER FOR THE OLEH

After each *oleh* completes his concluding blessing, the *gabbai* calls the next *oleh* to the Torah, then blesses the one who has just concluded.

מִי שֶׁבֵּרַךְ *He Who blessed our forefathers Abraham, Isaac, and Jacob — may He bless (* Hebrew name*) son of (* father's Hebrew name*) because he has come up to the Torah in honor of the Omnipresent, in honor of the Torah, in honor of the Sabbath, in honor of the pilgrimage festival. As reward for this, may the Holy One, Blessed is He, protect him and rescue him from every trouble and distress, from every plague and illness; may He send blessing and success in his every endeavor, and may he be privileged to ascend to Jerusalem for the pilgrimage, together with all Israel, his brethren. Now let us respond: Amen.*

(Cong.— *Amen.)*

PRAYER FOR OTHERS

It is customary that the following prayer be recited for the family members of the *oleh* and for anyone else that he may wish to include:

מִי שֶׁבֵּרַךְ *He Who blessed our forefathers Abraham, Isaac, and Jacob — may He bless (* names of recipients*) for (* name of *oleh) will contribute to charity on their behalf. As reward for this, may the Holy One, Blessed is He, protect them and rescue them from every trouble and distress, from every plague and illness; may He send blessing and success in their every endeavor and may they be privileged to ascend to Jerusalem for the pilgrimage, together with all Israel, their brethren. Now let us respond: Amen.* (Cong.— *Amen.)*

PRAYER FOR A SICK PERSON

מִי שֶׁבֵּרַךְ *He Who blessed our forefathers Abraham, Isaac and Jacob, Moses and Aaron, David and Solomon — may He bless and heal the sick person (* patient's Hebrew name*) son/daughter of (* patient's mother's Hebrew name*) because (* name of supplicant*) will contribute to charity on his/her behalf.°° In reward for this, may the Holy One, Blessed is He, be filled with*

for a man	for a woman
compassion for him to restore his health, to heal him, to strengthen him, and to revivify him. And may He send him speedily a complete recovery from heaven for his two hundred forty-eight organs and three hundred sixty-five blood vessels, among the other	*compassion for her to restore her health, to heal her, to strengthen her, and to revivify her. And may He send her speedily a complete recovery from heaven for all her organs and all her blood vessels, among the other*

sick people of Israel, a recovery of the body and a recovery of the spirit though the [on the Sabbath: *Sabbath and*] *Festival prohibit*[s] *us from crying out, may a recovery come speedily, swiftly and soon. Now let us respond: Amen.*

(Cong.—*Amen.)*

°°Many congregations substitute:
because the entire congregation prays for him (her)

---

is that public study of Torah requires a blessing.

תּוֹרַת אֱמֶת וְחַיֵּי עוֹלָם — *The Torah of truth . . . eternal life. Torah of Truth* refers to the Written Torah, and *eternal life* to the Oral Law. The Oral Law is described as *implanted within us,* because Jews constantly expand their Torah knowledge through their personal study and analysis (*Tur Orach Chaim* 139).

FIRST DAY

קריאת התורה ליום ראשון

שמות יב:כא-נא

כהן – וַיִּקְרָ֥א מֹשֶׁ֛ה לְכָל־זִקְנֵ֥י יִשְׂרָאֵ֖ל* וַיֹּ֣אמֶר אֲלֵהֶ֑ם מִֽשְׁכ֗וּ וּקְח֨וּ*
לָכֶ֥ם צֹ֛אן לְמִשְׁפְּחֹתֵיכֶ֖ם וְשַׁחֲט֥וּ הַפָּֽסַח׃ וּלְקַחְתֶּ֞ם אֲגֻדַּ֣ת אֵז֗וֹב
וּטְבַלְתֶּם֮ בַּדָּ֣ם אֲשֶׁר־בַּסַּף֒ וְהִגַּעְתֶּ֤ם אֶל־הַמַּשְׁקוֹף֙ וְאֶל־שְׁתֵּ֣י
הַמְּזוּזֹ֔ת מִן־הַדָּ֖ם אֲשֶׁ֣ר בַּסָּ֑ף וְאַתֶּ֗ם לֹ֥א תֵצְא֛וּ* אִ֥ישׁ מִפֶּֽתַח־בֵּית֖וֹ
עַד־בֹּֽקֶר׃ וְעָבַ֣ר יהוה֮ לִנְגֹּ֣ף אֶת־מִצְרַיִם֒ וְרָאָ֤ה אֶת־הַדָּם֙ עַל־
הַמַּשְׁק֔וֹף וְעַ֖ל שְׁתֵּ֣י הַמְּזוּזֹ֑ת וּפָסַ֤ח יהוה֙* עַל־הַפֶּ֔תַח וְלֹ֤א יִתֵּן֙
הַמַּשְׁחִ֔ית לָבֹ֥א אֶל־בָּתֵּיכֶ֖ם לִנְגֹּֽף׃ וּשְׁמַרְתֶּ֖ם אֶת־הַדָּבָ֣ר הַזֶּ֑ה
לְחָק־לְךָ֥ וּלְבָנֶ֖יךָ עַד־עוֹלָֽם׃

TORAH READING FOR THE FIRST DAY

The Torah reading of the first day is the history of the Exodus. It begins with the commandment to the Jewish people to select a lamb for the *pesach* offering, an act that was in itself a demonstration of courageous faith in God, because sheep were among the deities of Egypt, and the Egyptians could have been expected to react violently to the notion that the erstwhile slaves would actually slaughter an Egyptian god. Israel lacked a necessary prerequisite for redemption — they did not have the merit of commandments, because they had fallen precipitously from the spiritual level of the Patriarchs. Thus they were given two commandments, both involving blood: the sacrificial service of the *pesach* offering and the circumcision of all males (*Shemos Rabbah* 17:3) [since, as Moses informed them, no uncircumcised male was permitted to eat the flesh of the offering]. The people were commanded to place some of the *pesach's* blood on their lintels and doorposts as visible proof of their new status as servants of God, and this would save them from the Plague of the Firstborn, the last plague and the one that broke Pharaoh's resistance.

A major part of the reading deals with the laws of the *pesach* offering, which was to be offered by all Jews annually, native and proselyte alike. The laws of the actual service were given in greater detail earlier in chapter 12. The

SECOND DAY

קריאת התורה ליום שני

ויקרא כב:כו-כג:מד

כהן–וַיְדַבֵּ֥ר יהוה אֶל־מֹשֶׁ֥ה לֵּאמֹֽר׃ שׁ֣וֹר אוֹ־כֶ֤שֶׂב אוֹ־עֵז֙ כִּ֣י יִוָּלֵ֔ד
וְהָיָ֛ה שִׁבְעַ֥ת יָמִ֖ים תַּ֣חַת אִמּ֑וֹ וּמִיּ֤וֹם הַשְּׁמִינִי֙ וָהָ֔לְאָה יֵרָצֶ֕ה לְקָרְבַּ֥ן
אִשֶּׁ֖ה לַיהוָֽה׃ וְשׁ֖וֹר אוֹ־שֶׂ֑ה* אֹת֣וֹ וְאֶת־בְּנ֔וֹ לֹ֥א תִשְׁחֲט֖וּ בְּי֥וֹם אֶחָֽד׃
וְכִֽי־תִזְבְּח֥וּ זֶֽבַח־תּוֹדָ֖ה לַיהוָ֑ה לִֽרְצֹנְכֶ֖ם* תִּזְבָּֽחוּ׃ בַּיּ֤וֹם הַהוּא֙ יֵאָכֵ֔ל

TORAH READING FOR THE SECOND DAY

The Torah reading of the first day dealt with the historical background of the festival. On the second day, the reading is a chapter that discusses all the festivals in general. The chapter is prefaced with seven verses that seem to be unrelated to the festivals at hand. They are included for two reasons: Since Temple offerings are an integral part of every festival service, the eligibility requirements of these animals is logically appended to the festival reading. Secondly, these introductory verses conclude with an admonition not to desecrate the Name of Hashem Who liberated us from Egypt, and an exhortation to sanctify His Name through our deeds. Since all the festivals — and

FIRST DAY

TORAH READING FOR THE FIRST DAY

Exodus 12:21-51

Kohen – *Moses called to all the elders of Israel* and said to them: Draw forth and take* for yourselves lambs for your families, and slaughter the pesach offering. You shall take a bundle of hyssop and dip it in the blood that is in the basin, and touch the lintel and the two doorposts with some of the blood that is in the basin, and none of you shall leave* the entrance of his house until morning.* HASHEM *will pass through to smite Egypt, and He will see the blood that is on the lintel and on the two doorposts; and* HASHEM *will pass over* the entrance and He will not permit the destroyer to enter your homes, to smite. You shall observe this matter as a decree for you and for your children forever.*

offering would be brought every year the afternoon before Pesach and be eaten in the evening by family groups as the centerpiece of the Seder and the annual narrative, especially to children, of God's merciful elevation of Israel from the status of hapless slaves to the Chosen People that would receive the Torah at Sinai.

זִקְנֵי יִשְׂרָאֵל — *The elders of Israel.* Earlier in the same chapter (*Exodus 12:3*), God had commanded Moses to transmit the laws of the offering to *the entire assembly of Israel.* Either the elders were now instructed to assemble all of the people to Moses, or he spoke to them as representatives of the nation.

מִשְׁכוּ וּקְחוּ — *Draw forth and take.* Each family group was to designate a lamb or kid for its *pesach* offering. If the group owned such an animal, it would *draw forth* one of its own. Otherwise, it would *take,* i.e., buy one.

וְאַתֶּם לֹא תֵצְאוּ — *None of you shall leave.* Once permission has been given for a destroyer to kill, it does not differentiate between the righteous and the wicked (*Bava Kamma* 60a). Consequently, Jews were forbidden to circulate through the streets of Egypt at the time when the Plague of the Firstborn was taking place.

וּפָסַח ה׳ — HASHEM *will pass over.* This is the generally used translation of פָּסַח, and it is from this translation that the festival derives its English name, Passover. However, *Onkelos, Rashi* and *Ibn Ezra* render the word as *will have mercy,* i.e., God will mercifully prevent the destroyer from entering the homes of those who have carried out the *pesach* service as commanded.

SECOND DAY

TORAH READING FOR THE SECOND DAY

Leviticus 22:26-23:44

Kohen – HASHEM *spoke to Moses saying: When a bull, a sheep, or a goat is born, it shall remain under its mother for seven days; and from the eighth day on it is acceptable for a fiery offering to* HASHEM. *But a cow or a ewe* — you may not slaughter it and its offspring on the same day. And when you slaughter a thanksgiving offering to* HASHEM, *slaughter it to gain acceptance for yourselves*: it must be eaten on that same day,*

our very existence as a nation — flow from the Exodus, this section is used to introduce the reading.

וְשׁוֹר אוֹ שֶׂה – *But a cow or a ewe* [lit., a bull or a sheep]. According to the accepted Talmudic opinion, the prohibition applies only to the offspring (male or female) of the female, but not to the offspring of the male. However, if it is certain that a particular male is the sire of a calf or lamb, one should avoid slaughtering both on the same day (*Hil. Shechitah* 12:11).

לִרְצֹנְכֶם – *To gain acceptance for yourselves.* The one who slaughters an offering must have in mind that it will be eaten within the time frame the Torah prescribes. If his intention is that it will be eaten beyond the deadline, the offering becomes disqualified [פִּגּוּל] and does not *gain favor.*

FIRST DAY

לוי – וְהָיָ֞ה כִּֽי־תָבֹ֣אוּ אֶל־הָאָ֗רֶץ* אֲשֶׁ֨ר יִתֵּ֧ן יְהֹוָ֛ה לָכֶ֖ם כַּאֲשֶׁ֣ר דִּבֵּ֑ר וּשְׁמַרְתֶּ֖ם אֶת־הָעֲבֹדָ֥ה הַזֹּֽאת:* וְהָיָ֕ה כִּֽי־יֹאמְר֥וּ אֲלֵיכֶ֖ם בְּנֵיכֶ֑ם מָ֛ה הָעֲבֹדָ֥ה הַזֹּ֖את לָכֶֽם:* וַאֲמַרְתֶּ֡ם זֶֽבַח־פֶּ֨סַח ה֜וּא לַֽיהֹוָ֗ה אֲשֶׁ֣ר פָּ֠סַח עַל־בָּתֵּ֤י בְנֵֽי־יִשְׂרָאֵל֙ בְּמִצְרַ֔יִם בְּנׇגְפּ֥וֹ אֶת־מִצְרַ֖יִם וְאֶת־בָּתֵּ֣ינוּ הִצִּ֑יל וַיִּקֹּ֥ד* הָעָ֖ם וַיִּֽשְׁתַּחֲוֽוּ: וַיֵּלְכ֥וּ וַיַּֽעֲשׂ֖וּ בְּנֵ֣י יִשְׂרָאֵ֑ל כַּאֲשֶׁ֨ר צִוָּ֧ה יְהֹוָ֛ה אֶת־מֹשֶׁ֥ה וְאַהֲרֹ֖ן כֵּ֥ן עָשֽׂוּ:

וְהָיָה כִּי תָבֹאוּ אֶל הָאָרֶץ — *It shall be that when you come to the land.* According to the simple meaning of this verse, there would be no *pesach* offering in the Wilderness; the next *pesach* would be when the nation entered *Eretz Yisrael*. Indeed, had the people not sinned with the Golden Calf, they would have been there in time for the next Pesach festival. Thus, the one time when the people brought the *pesach* offering in the Wilderness, God specifically commanded them to do so (*Numbers 9:2*).

הָעֲבֹדָה הַזֹּאת — *This service.* Although the general rules of the service would be the same in all future years, there were differences. For example, in future years there would be no requirement to put blood on the doorposts and lintel.

מָה הָעֲבֹדָה הַזֹּאת לָכֶם — *What is this service to you?* In the 'Four Sons' section of the *Haggadah*, this verse is given as the question of the Wicked Son, who doubts the validity of the command-

SECOND DAY

לֹֽא־תוֹתִ֥ירוּ מִמֶּ֛נּוּ עַד־בֹּ֖קֶר אֲנִ֣י יְהֹוָֽה: וּשְׁמַרְתֶּם֙ מִצְוֺתַ֔י וַעֲשִׂיתֶ֖ם* אֹתָ֑ם אֲנִ֖י יְהֹוָֽה: וְלֹ֤א תְחַלְּלוּ֙* אֶת־שֵׁ֣ם קׇדְשִׁ֔י* וְנִ֨קְדַּשְׁתִּ֔י* בְּת֖וֹךְ בְּנֵ֣י יִשְׂרָאֵ֑ל אֲנִ֥י יְהֹוָ֖ה מְקַדִּשְׁכֶֽם: הַמּוֹצִ֤יא אֶתְכֶם֙ מֵאֶ֣רֶץ מִצְרַ֔יִם לִהְי֥וֹת לָכֶ֖ם לֵֽאלֹהִ֑ים אֲנִ֖י יְהֹוָֽה:* וַיְדַבֵּ֥ר יְהֹוָ֖ה אֶל־מֹשֶׁ֥ה לֵּאמֹֽר: דַּבֵּ֞ר אֶל־בְּנֵ֤י יִשְׂרָאֵל֙ וְאָמַרְתָּ֣ אֲלֵהֶ֔ם מוֹעֲדֵ֣י יְהֹוָ֔ה* אֲשֶׁר־תִּקְרְא֥וּ אֹתָ֖ם מִקְרָאֵ֣י קֹ֑דֶשׁ* אֵ֥לֶּה הֵ֖ם מוֹעֲדָֽי:* שֵׁ֣שֶׁת יָמִים֮ תֵּעָשֶׂ֣ה מְלָאכָה֒ וּבַיּ֣וֹם הַשְּׁבִיעִ֗י שַׁבַּ֤ת שַׁבָּתוֹן֙ מִקְרָא־קֹ֔דֶשׁ כׇּל־מְלָאכָ֖ה לֹ֣א תַעֲשׂ֑וּ שַׁבָּ֥ת הִוא֙ לַֽיהֹוָ֔ה בְּכֹ֖ל מֽוֹשְׁבֹתֵיכֶֽם:

לוי – אֵ֚לֶּה מֽוֹעֲדֵ֣י יְהֹוָ֔ה מִקְרָאֵ֖י קֹ֑דֶשׁ אֲשֶׁר־תִּקְרְא֥וּ* אֹתָ֖ם בְּמֽוֹעֲדָֽם: בַּחֹ֣דֶשׁ הָרִאשׁ֗וֹן בְּאַרְבָּעָ֥ה עָשָׂ֛ר לַחֹ֖דֶשׁ בֵּ֣ין הָעַרְבָּ֑יִם פֶּ֖סַח לַֽיהֹוָֽה: וּבַחֲמִשָּׁ֨ה עָשָׂ֥ר יוֹם֙ לַחֹ֣דֶשׁ הַזֶּ֔ה חַ֥ג הַמַּצּ֖וֹת לַֽיהֹוָ֑ה שִׁבְעַ֥ת יָמִ֖ים מַצּ֥וֹת תֹּאכֵֽלוּ:* בַּיּוֹם֙ הָרִאשׁ֔וֹן מִקְרָא־קֹ֖דֶשׁ יִהְיֶ֣ה לָכֶ֑ם כׇּל־מְלֶ֥אכֶת

וּשְׁמַרְתֶּם . . . וַעֲשִׂיתֶם — *You are to observe . . . and perform.* Study the laws [*observe*] so that you will be able to *perform* the *mitzvos* properly.

וְלֹא תְחַלְּלוּ — *You are not to desecrate.* If a Jew performs an act that the Torah forbids, he desecrates God's Name.

וְנִקְדַּשְׁתִּי — *Rather I should be sanctified.* There are times when one must be ready to give up his life rather than transgresss a commandment,

particularly in the presence of ten Jews [i.e., among the Children of Israel]. To do so is a sanctification of God's Name.

אֲנִי ה׳ — *I am Hashem.* I can be trusted to reward those who obey My commands.

מוֹעֲדֵי ה׳ — *Hashem's appointed festivals.* This term for the festivals has the connotation of "meeting," i.e., God has designated these times when Israel can greet His Presence.

FIRST DAY

Levi – *It shall be that when you come to the land* that HASHEM will give you, as He has spoken, you shall observe this service.* And it shall be that when your children say to you, 'What is this service to you?'* You shall say: 'It is a pesach feast-offering to HASHEM, Who passed over the houses of the Children of Israel in Egypt when He smote the Egyptians, but He rescued our houses;' and the people bowed their heads* and prostrated themselves. The Children of Israel went and did as HASHEM commanded Moses and Aaron, so did they do.*

ments. There, the answer is taken from *Exodus* 13:8, which is a sharp, blunt statement. The sense of our verse is to tell the sarcastic questioner that he has no share in the celebration, because, (a) this is an *offering to HASHEM*, so that only those who believe in Him and accept His commandments have the privilege of joining it, and (b) the offering reminds us that God saved the homes of those who obeyed Him.

וַיִּקֹּד — *Bowed their heads* . . . in gratitude for the impending redemption and for the news that they would have children. Even though the children of the previous verse are described in the *Haggadah* as wicked, the people were nevertheless grateful, because there is always the possibility that the wicked children would repent — and consequently their fellow Jews are obligated to work toward that end.

SECOND DAY

you may not leave any of it until morning; I am HASHEM. You are to observe My commandments and perform them; I am HASHEM. You are not to desecrate* My holy Name, rather I should be sanctified* among the Children of Israel; I am HASHEM Who sanctifies you; Who took you out of the land of Egypt to be your God; I am HASHEM.**

HASHEM spoke to Moses saying: Speak to the Children of Israel and say to them: HASHEM's appointed festivals that you are to proclaim as holy convocations* — these are My appointed festivals.* For six days labor may be done, and the seventh day is a day of complete rest,* a holy convocation, you may not do any work; it is a Sabbath for HASHEM in all your dwelling places.*

Levi – *These are the appointed festivals of HASHEM, the holy convocations, which you are to proclaim* in their appropriate time. In the first month on the fourteenth of the month in the afternoon is the time of the pesach offering to HASHEM. And on the fifteenth day of this month is the Festival of Matzos to HASHEM, you are to eat matzos* for seven days. On the first day is to be a holy convocation for you; you may do no laborious*

מִקְרָאֵי קֹדֶשׁ – *Holy convocations.* On these days, the nation is to gather for the pursuit of holiness, and to sanctify the festival through prayer and praise to God *(Ramban).*

מוֹעֲדָי – *My . . . festivals.* But holidays devoted to revelry, food, and pleasures are not My festivals (Sforno).

שַׁבַּת שַׁבָּתוֹן – *A day of complete rest.* This term differentiates the Sabbath, when all categories of work are forbidden, from the festivals, when certain kinds of work are permitted.

תִּקְרְאוּ – *You are to proclaim.* The nation, through its court, proclaims the New Moon, upon which the entire calendar — and, consequently, all the festivals — is based *(Ramban).*

מַצּוֹת תֹּאכֵלוּ – *You are to eat matzos.* Technically, the Scriptural requirement to eat matzah applies only to the Seder night. This verse means that whatever grain products one eats may not be leavened. Some hold that whenever one chooses to eat matzah during Pesach, it is a *mitzvah,* in the sense of a meritorious — but not required — deed.

FIRST DAY

שלישי – וַיְהִי ׀ בַּחֲצִי הַלַּיְלָה וַיהוה הִכָּה כָל־בְּכוֹר* בְּאֶרֶץ מִצְרַיִם
מִבְּכֹר פַּרְעֹה הַיֹּשֵׁב עַל־כִּסְאוֹ עַד בְּכוֹר הַשְּׁבִי אֲשֶׁר בְּבֵית הַבּוֹר
וְכֹל בְּכוֹר בְּהֵמָה: וַיָּקָם פַּרְעֹה לַיְלָה הוּא וְכָל־עֲבָדָיו וְכָל־מִצְרַיִם
וַתְּהִי צְעָקָה גְדֹלָה בְּמִצְרָיִם כִּי־אֵין בַּיִת אֲשֶׁר אֵין־שָׁם מֵת:
וַיִּקְרָא לְמֹשֶׁה וּלְאַהֲרֹן לַיְלָה* וַיֹּאמֶר קוּמוּ צְּאוּ מִתּוֹךְ עַמִּי גַּם־
אַתֶּם גַּם־בְּנֵי יִשְׂרָאֵל וּלְכוּ עִבְדוּ אֶת־יהוה כְּדַבֶּרְכֶם: גַּם־צֹאנְכֶם
גַּם־בְּקַרְכֶם קְחוּ כַּאֲשֶׁר דִּבַּרְתֶּם וָלֵכוּ וּבֵרַכְתֶּם גַּם־אֹתִי:*

כָּל־בְּכוֹר — *Every firstborn*. Even firstborn foreigners and prisoners died in the plague for two reasons. One, because they, too, had rejoiced in the suffering of the Jews. Two, so they should not be able to claim that their gods had saved them. As for Pharaoh, himself a firstborn, God had said that he would be spared in order that he should see all the miracles for himself and declare the praises of HASHEM (*Exodus* 9:16).

לַיְלָה — *At night*. In his panic and haste to rid himself and his land of the Jews, Pharaoh gave

SECOND DAY

עֲבֹדָה* לֹא תַעֲשׂוּ: וְהִקְרַבְתֶּם אִשֶּׁה* לַיהוה שִׁבְעַת יָמִים בַּיּוֹם
הַשְּׁבִיעִי מִקְרָא־קֹדֶשׁ כָּל־מְלֶאכֶת עֲבֹדָה לֹא תַעֲשׂוּ: וַיְדַבֵּר יהוה
אֶל־מֹשֶׁה לֵּאמֹר: דַּבֵּר אֶל־בְּנֵי יִשְׂרָאֵל וְאָמַרְתָּ אֲלֵהֶם כִּי־תָבֹאוּ
אֶל־הָאָרֶץ אֲשֶׁר אֲנִי נֹתֵן לָכֶם וּקְצַרְתֶּם אֶת־קְצִירָהּ וַהֲבֵאתֶם
אֶת־עֹמֶר* רֵאשִׁית קְצִירְכֶם אֶל־הַכֹּהֵן: וְהֵנִיף אֶת־הָעֹמֶר לִפְנֵי
יהוה לִרְצֹנְכֶם מִמָּחֳרַת הַשַּׁבָּת* יְנִיפֶנּוּ הַכֹּהֵן: וַעֲשִׂיתֶם בְּיוֹם
הֲנִיפְכֶם אֶת־הָעֹמֶר כֶּבֶשׂ תָּמִים בֶּן־שְׁנָתוֹ לְעֹלָה לַיהוה: וּמִנְחָתוֹ
שְׁנֵי עֶשְׂרֹנִים סֹלֶת בְּלוּלָה בַשֶּׁמֶן אִשֶּׁה לַיהוה רֵיחַ נִיחֹחַ וְנִסְכֹּה
יַיִן רְבִיעִת הַהִין: וְלֶחֶם וְקָלִי וְכַרְמֶל לֹא תֹאכְלוּ* עַד־עֶצֶם הַיּוֹם
הַזֶּה עַד הֲבִיאֲכֶם אֶת־קָרְבַּן אֱלֹהֵיכֶם חֻקַּת עוֹלָם לְדֹרֹתֵיכֶם
בְּכֹל מֹשְׁבֹתֵיכֶם:

שלישי – וּסְפַרְתֶּם לָכֶם מִמָּחֳרַת הַשַּׁבָּת מִיּוֹם הֲבִיאֲכֶם אֶת־עֹמֶר
הַתְּנוּפָה שֶׁבַע שַׁבָּתוֹת תְּמִימֹת תִּהְיֶינָה:* עַד מִמָּחֳרַת הַשַּׁבָּת
הַשְּׁבִיעִת תִּסְפְּרוּ חֲמִשִּׁים יוֹם* וְהִקְרַבְתֶּם מִנְחָה חֲדָשָׁה לַיהוה:
מִמּוֹשְׁבֹתֵיכֶם תָּבִיאוּ ׀ לֶחֶם תְּנוּפָה שְׁתַּיִם שְׁנֵי עֶשְׂרֹנִים סֹלֶת

מְלֶאכֶת עֲבֹדָה – *Laborious work*. But work performed for the preparation of food [except for certain restrictions] is permitted on the festivals, unlike the Sabbath (*Exodus* 12:16).

אִשֶּׁה – *Fire-offering*, i.e., the *Mussaf*, as described in *Numbers* 28:19-24. Similarly, the other *Mussaf* offerings mentioned in this chapter are described in *Numbers* 28 and 29.

עֹמֶר – *An Omer*. The word *omer* is a dry measurement, which is the volume of approximately 43.2 average eggs; by extension, however, the entire offering is called *Omer*. Unlike all other meal-offerings, it is barley instead of wheat. The grain used in this offering should be the very first

FIRST DAY

Third – *It happened at midnight that* HASHEM *smote every firstborn* in the land of Egypt, from the firstborn of Pharaoh sitting on his throne to the firstborn of the captive in the dungeon, and every firstborn animal. Pharaoh rose up at night, he and all his servants and all the Egyptians, and there was a great outcry in Egypt, for there was not a house where there was no corpse. He called to Moses and Aaron at night* and said: 'Rise up, go out from among my people, even you, even the Children of Israel; go and serve* HASHEM *as you have spoken! Take even your sheep and cattle, as you have spoken, and leave — and may you bless me, as well!'**

up all pretense at dignity. He ran through the unfamiliar streets in the dark of night, shouting the names of Moses and Aaron.

וּבֵרַכְתֶּם גַּם אֹתִי — *And may you bless me, as well.* Pharaoh had become utterly submissive. Not only had he surrendered to every request that he had previously refused, the once arrogant and haughty monarch was reduced to begging that Moses and Aaron should bless him so that he would suffer no further punishments. The blessing was either that they assure him that he would not die with the firstborn (*Rashi*); or that they include him in their prayers when they bring the offerings that are their official reason for leaving Egypt (*Ramban*).

SECOND DAY

work. You are to bring a fire-offering* to* HASHEM *for seven days; on the seventh day is to be a holy convocation, you may do no laborious work.*

HASHEM *spoke to Moses saying: Speak to the Children of Israel and say to them: When you arrive in the Land that I give you and you reap its harvest; you are to bring an Omer* from your first harvest to the Kohen. He is to wave the Omer before* HASHEM *to gain acceptance for you; on the morrow of the rest-day* the Kohen is to wave it. On the day when you wave the Omer you are to offer an unblemished lamb in its first year as an elevation-offering to* HASHEM. *And its meal-offering is to be two tenth-ephah of fine flour mixed with oil, a fire-offering to* HASHEM, *a satisfying aroma; and its wine-libation is to be a quarter-hin. You may not eat* bread nor roasted kernels, nor plump kernels until this very day, until you bring the offering of your God; it is an eternal decree for your generations in all your dwelling places.*

Third – *You are to count for yourselves — from the morrow of the rest-day, from the day when you bring the Omer of the waving — they are to be seven complete* weeks. Until the morrow of the seventh week you are to count, fifty days;* and then you are to offer a new meal-offering to* HASHEM. *From your dwelling places you are to bring bread which is to be waved, two loaves made from two tenth-ephah, they are to be fine flour,*

to be harvested. Indeed, it was cut the night before it was to be offered, and no species of grain products from the new crop may be eaten before the *Omer* is offered.

מִמָּחֳרַת הַשַּׁבָּת – *On the morrow of the rest-day.* The *rest-day* is the first day of Pesach. Thus, the *Omer* is offered on the morning of the second day of Pesach.

לֹא תֹאכְלוּ – *You may not eat.* The prohibition applies only to grain products from the new crop, but not to fruits and vegetables.

תְּמִימֹת תִּהְיֶינָה – *They are to be . . . complete.* The count must begin in the evening in order for it to be considered 'complete.'

חֲמִשִּׁים יוֹם – *Fifty days,* i.e., you are to count seven weeks until the fiftieth day, which is celebrated as Shavuos.

FIRST DAY

(בשבת רביעי) – וַתֶּחֱזַק מִצְרַיִם עַל־הָעָם לְמַהֵר לְשַׁלְּחָם מִן־הָאָרֶץ כִּי
אָמְרוּ כֻּלָּנוּ מֵתִים: וַיִּשָּׂא הָעָם אֶת־בְּצֵקוֹ טֶרֶם יֶחְמָץ* מִשְׁאֲרֹתָם
צְרֻרֹת בְּשִׂמְלֹתָם עַל־שִׁכְמָם: וּבְנֵי־יִשְׂרָאֵל עָשׂוּ כִּדְבַר מֹשֶׁה*
וַיִּשְׁאֲלוּ מִמִּצְרַיִם כְּלֵי־כֶסֶף וּכְלֵי זָהָב וּשְׂמָלֹת: וַיהוָה נָתַן אֶת־חֵן
הָעָם בְּעֵינֵי מִצְרַיִם וַיַּשְׁאִלוּם וַיְנַצְּלוּ אֶת־מִצְרָיִם:
רביעי (בשבת חמישי) – וַיִּסְעוּ בְנֵי־יִשְׂרָאֵל מֵרַעְמְסֵס סֻכֹּתָה כְּשֵׁשׁ־מֵאוֹת
אֶלֶף רַגְלִי הַגְּבָרִים לְבַד מִטָּף: וְגַם־עֵרֶב רַב* עָלָה אִתָּם וְצֹאן
וּבָקָר מִקְנֶה כָּבֵד מְאֹד: וַיֹּאפוּ אֶת־הַבָּצֵק אֲשֶׁר הוֹצִיאוּ מִמִּצְרַיִם

טֶרֶם יֶחְמָץ — *Before it could become leavened.* So urgently did the Egyptians insist that the Jews leave, that there was not even time for their dough to rise. The people took their *leftover* matzah and marror from the *Seder.* So beloved were these *mitzvah*-leftovers to them that they did not pack them with their belongings, but carried them on their shoulders.

עָשׂוּ כִּדְבַר מֹשֶׁה — *Carried out the word of Moses.* Had there not been a Divine order transmitted through a prophet, the people would not have

SECOND DAY

תִּהְיֶינָה חָמֵץ תֵּאָפֶינָה בִּכּוּרִים* לַיהוָה: וְהִקְרַבְתֶּם עַל־הַלֶּחֶם
שִׁבְעַת כְּבָשִׂים תְּמִימִם בְּנֵי שָׁנָה וּפַר בֶּן־בָּקָר אֶחָד וְאֵילִם שְׁנָיִם
יִהְיוּ עֹלָה לַיהוָה וּמִנְחָתָם וְנִסְכֵּיהֶם אִשֵּׁה רֵיחַ־נִיחֹחַ לַיהוָה:
וַעֲשִׂיתֶם שְׂעִיר־עִזִּים אֶחָד לְחַטָּאת וּשְׁנֵי כְבָשִׂים בְּנֵי שָׁנָה לְזֶבַח
שְׁלָמִים: וְהֵנִיף הַכֹּהֵן | אֹתָם* עַל לֶחֶם הַבִּכֻּרִים תְּנוּפָה לִפְנֵי יהוה
עַל־שְׁנֵי כְּבָשִׂים קֹדֶשׁ* יִהְיוּ לַיהוָה לַכֹּהֵן: וּקְרָאתֶם בְּעֶצֶם | הַיּוֹם
הַזֶּה מִקְרָא־קֹדֶשׁ יִהְיֶה לָכֶם כָּל־מְלֶאכֶת עֲבֹדָה לֹא תַעֲשׂוּ חֻקַּת
עוֹלָם בְּכָל־מוֹשְׁבֹתֵיכֶם לְדֹרֹתֵיכֶם: וּבְקֻצְרְכֶם* אֶת־קְצִיר
אַרְצְכֶם לֹא־תְכַלֶּה פְּאַת שָׂדְךָ בְּקֻצְרֶךָ וְלֶקֶט קְצִירְךָ לֹא תְלַקֵּט
לֶעָנִי וְלַגֵּר תַּעֲזֹב אֹתָם אֲנִי יהוה אֱלֹהֵיכֶם:
רביעי – וַיְדַבֵּר יהוה אֶל־מֹשֶׁה לֵּאמֹר: דַּבֵּר אֶל־בְּנֵי יִשְׂרָאֵל לֵאמֹר
בַּחֹדֶשׁ הַשְּׁבִיעִי בְּאֶחָד לַחֹדֶשׁ יִהְיֶה לָכֶם שַׁבָּתוֹן זִכְרוֹן תְּרוּעָה*
מִקְרָא־קֹדֶשׁ: כָּל־מְלֶאכֶת עֲבֹדָה לֹא תַעֲשׂוּ וְהִקְרַבְתֶּם אִשֶּׁה
לַיהוָה: וַיְדַבֵּר יהוה אֶל־מֹשֶׁה לֵּאמֹר: אַךְ* בֶּעָשׂוֹר לַחֹדֶשׁ

בִּכּוּרִים — *First-offerings.* Although the new grain was permitted after the *Omer*-offering, it could not be used as a Temple offering until this *new meal-offering* was brought on Shavuos.

אֹתָם — *Them.* The two peace-offering sheep are to be lifted up, while they are still alive, and waved together with the two breads.

קֹדֶשׁ — *Most holy.* This is the only case of *communal* peace-offerings. Therefore, they have the status of the holier offerings [קָדְשֵׁי קָדָשִׁים] and may be eaten only by *Kohanim,* unlike ordinary peace-offerings, which may be eaten by all Jews.

וּבְקֻצְרְכֶם — *When you reap.* The Jew harvesting his crop must leave a corner of his field for the

FIRST DAY

(On the Sabbath – Fourth) – *Egypt exerted itself upon the people to send them out of the land hurriedly, for they said, 'We are all dying!'*

The people picked up its dough before it could become leavened, their leftovers bound up in their garments on their shoulders. The Children of Israel carried out the word of Moses;* they borrowed from the Egyptians silver vessels, golden vessels, and garments. HASHEM gave the people favor in the eyes of the Egyptians, and they lent them, so they emptied out Egypt.*

Fourth (On the Sabbath – Fifth) – *The Children of Israel journeyed from Rameses to Succoth, about 600,000 men on foot, aside from children. Also a mixed multitude* went up with them, and sheep and cattle, a very large herd. They baked the dough that they took out of Egypt into*

been willing to deceive the Egyptians by "borrowing" things that they would not return. The Sages explain that the Jews were truly entitled to Egypt's wealth, because they had worked without payment for so many years.

עֵרֶב רַב — *A mixed multitude.* People from many nationalities converted and left Egypt with the Jews.

SECOND DAY

they are to be baked leavened; first-offerings to HASHEM. With the bread you are to offer seven unblemished lambs within their first year, one young bull, and two rams; they are to be an elevation-offering to HASHEM, with their meal-offering and libations — a fire-offering, a satisfying aroma to HASHEM. You are to offer one he-goat as a sin-offering; and two lambs within their first year for peace-offerings. The Kohen is to wave them* with the first-offering breads as a waving before HASHEM — with the two sheep — they shall be most holy,* for HASHEM and for the Kohen. You are to proclaim on this very day that it is to be a holy convocation for yourselves, you are to do no laborious work, it is an eternal decree in your dwelling places for your generations.*

When you reap the harvest of your land you are not to remove completely the corners of your field as you reap, and also do not gather the gleanings of your harvest; for the poor and the stranger are you to leave them, I am HASHEM your God.*

Fourth – *HASHEM spoke to Moses saying: Speak to the Children of Israel saying: in the seventh month on the first of the month, it shall be a rest-day for you, a remembrance with shofar blasts,* a holy convocation. You are to do no laborious work; and you are to offer a fire-offering to HASHEM.*

HASHEM spoke to Moses saying: However, the tenth day of this*

poor, and if he drops one or two stalks at a time he must leave them as well. These commandments are inserted among the festival laws to teach that one who shares his crop with the poor is regarded as if he had built the Temple and performed the festival service of the offerings.

זִכְרוֹן תְּרוּעָה – *A remembrance with shofar blasts.* By reciting verses describing God's remembrance and the events associated with blasts of the *shofar,* a ram's horn, you will cause God to remember the *Akeidah* of Isaac, who was replaced on the altar by a ram *(Rashi).*

אַךְ – *However.* Although people are judged on Rosh Hashanah, God has set aside Yom Kippur for atonement and forgiveness *(Ramban).* The word אַךְ, *however,* always implies a limitation:

FIRST DAY

עֻגֹת מַצּוֹת* כִּי לֹא חָמֵץ כִּי־גֹרְשׁוּ מִמִּצְרַיִם וְלֹא יָכְלוּ לְהִתְמַהְמֵהַּ
וְגַם־צֵדָה* לֹא־עָשׂוּ לָהֶם: וּמוֹשַׁב בְּנֵי יִשְׂרָאֵל אֲשֶׁר יָשְׁבוּ בְּמִצְרָיִם
שְׁלֹשִׁים שָׁנָה וְאַרְבַּע מֵאוֹת שָׁנָה: וַיְהִי מִקֵּץ* שְׁלֹשִׁים שָׁנָה וְאַרְבַּע
מֵאוֹת שָׁנָה* וַיְהִי בְּעֶצֶם הַיּוֹם הַזֶּה יָצְאוּ כָּל־צִבְאוֹת יהוה מֵאֶרֶץ
מִצְרָיִם: לֵיל שִׁמֻּרִים הוּא לַיהוה לְהוֹצִיאָם מֵאֶרֶץ מִצְרָיִם
הוּא־הַלַּיְלָה הַזֶּה לַיהוה שִׁמֻּרִים* לְכָל־בְּנֵי יִשְׂרָאֵל לְדֹרֹתָם:

עֻגֹת מַצּוֹת — *Unleavened cakes.* Since they had been forbidden to eat *chametz,* they baked the remaining dough as matzah. The baking had to be done on the road, since the Egyptians would not permit them to tarry.

צֵדָה — *Provisions.* The people had so much faith in God that they left Egypt for an unknown destination without even preparing food for the way.

מִקֵּץ — *At the end.* When the preordained time of redemption arrived, God did not delay for even an instant.

שְׁלֹשִׁים שָׁנָה וְאַרְבַּע מֵאוֹת שָׁנָה — *Four hundred thirty years.* The Jews were in Egypt for only

SECOND DAY

הַשְּׁבִיעִי הַזֶּה יוֹם הַכִּפֻּרִים הוּא מִקְרָא־קֹדֶשׁ יִהְיֶה לָכֶם וְעִנִּיתֶם*
אֶת־נַפְשֹׁתֵיכֶם וְהִקְרַבְתֶּם אִשֶּׁה לַיהוה: וְכָל־מְלָאכָה לֹא תַעֲשׂוּ*
בְּעֶצֶם הַיּוֹם הַזֶּה כִּי יוֹם כִּפֻּרִים הוּא לְכַפֵּר עֲלֵיכֶם לִפְנֵי יהוה
אֱלֹהֵיכֶם: כִּי כָל־הַנֶּפֶשׁ אֲשֶׁר לֹא־תְעֻנֶּה בְּעֶצֶם הַיּוֹם הַזֶּה וְנִכְרְתָה
מֵעַמֶּיהָ: וְכָל־הַנֶּפֶשׁ אֲשֶׁר תַּעֲשֶׂה כָּל־מְלָאכָה בְּעֶצֶם הַיּוֹם הַזֶּה
וְהַאֲבַדְתִּי אֶת־הַנֶּפֶשׁ הַהִוא מִקֶּרֶב עַמָּהּ: כָּל־מְלָאכָה לֹא תַעֲשׂוּ
חֻקַּת עוֹלָם לְדֹרֹתֵיכֶם בְּכֹל מֹשְׁבֹתֵיכֶם: שַׁבַּת שַׁבָּתוֹן הוּא לָכֶם
וְעִנִּיתֶם אֶת־נַפְשֹׁתֵיכֶם בְּתִשְׁעָה לַחֹדֶשׁ בָּעֶרֶב* מֵעֶרֶב עַד־עֶרֶב
תִּשְׁבְּתוּ שַׁבַּתְּכֶם:

חמישי — וַיְדַבֵּר יהוה אֶל־מֹשֶׁה לֵּאמֹר: דַּבֵּר אֶל־בְּנֵי יִשְׂרָאֵל לֵאמֹר
בַּחֲמִשָּׁה עָשָׂר יוֹם לַחֹדֶשׁ הַשְּׁבִיעִי הַזֶּה חַג הַסֻּכּוֹת שִׁבְעַת יָמִים
לַיהוה: בַּיּוֹם הָרִאשׁוֹן מִקְרָא־קֹדֶשׁ כָּל־מְלֶאכֶת עֲבֹדָה לֹא תַעֲשׂוּ:
שִׁבְעַת יָמִים תַּקְרִיבוּ אִשֶּׁה לַיהוה בַּיּוֹם הַשְּׁמִינִי מִקְרָא־קֹדֶשׁ
יִהְיֶה לָכֶם וְהִקְרַבְתֶּם אִשֶּׁה לַיהוה עֲצֶרֶת* הִוא כָּל־מְלֶאכֶת
עֲבֹדָה לֹא תַעֲשׂוּ: אֵלֶּה מוֹעֲדֵי יהוה אֲשֶׁר־תִּקְרְאוּ אֹתָם מִקְרָאֵי
קֹדֶשׁ לְהַקְרִיב אִשֶּׁה לַיהוה עֹלָה וּמִנְחָה זֶבַח וּנְסָכִים דְּבַר־יוֹם

the "atonement" is available only to those who repent, but not to those who ignore the opportunity to earn forgiveness through repentance.

וְעִנִּיתֶם — *You are to afflict,* i.e., fast.

וְכָל מְלָאכָה לֹא תַעֲשׂוּ — *You are not to do any work.* Unlike the other festivals, all work is forbidden on Yom Kippur, even food preparation.

בְּתִשְׁעָה לַחֹדֶשׁ בָּעֶרֶב — *On the ninth of the month in the evening.* The simple meaning is that the Yom Kippur fast begins in the evening after sunset of the ninth day. However, since the Torah specifies the ninth day, the Talmud finds support

FIRST DAY

unleavened cakes, for they could not be leavened, for they were driven from Egypt and they could not delay, nor had they made provisions* for themselves. The habitation of the Children of Israel during which they dwelled in Egypt was four hundred and thirty years. It was at the end* of four hundred and thirty years;* and it was on that very day that all the legions of HASHEM left the land of Egypt. It is a night of anticipation for HASHEM to take them out of the land of Egypt, it was this night for HASHEM, a protection* for all the Children of Israel for their generations.*

two hundred ten years, and the prophecy to Abraham that his offspring would suffer exile and bondage was for a total of four hundred years (*Genesis* 15:13). The four hundred years began with the birth of Isaac, who was treated as an alien by the inhabitants of Canaan, unlike Abraham who was held in very great respect. That prophecy was given to Abraham thirty years before Isaac's birth, thus the 'four hundred thirty years' of our verse alludes to the time of the prophecy, for it was from that time on that the future of the nation was clouded by the knowledge that there would be exile and suffering.

שִׁמֻּרִים ... שִׁמֻּרִים — *Of anticipation ... of protection.* The word has two different definitions. The first time in the verse, it means that from the time God told Abraham about the future enslavement, He kept this night in reserve for the promised redemption. The second use of the word promises us that the Seder night would always be a time when God protects Israel.

SECOND DAY

seventh month is a Day of Atonement, it shall be a holy convocation for you and you are to afflict yourselves; you are to offer a fire-offering to HASHEM. You are not to do any work* on this very day, for it is a Day of Atonement to atone for you before HASHEM your God. For any soul who will not be afflicted on this day will be excised from its people. And any soul who will perform work on this very day, I will destroy that soul from among its people. You are not to do any work; it is an eternal decree throughout your generations in all your dwelling places. It is a day of complete rest for you and you are to afflict yourselves; on the ninth of the month in the evening* — from evening to evening — you are to observe your rest day.*

Fifth – *HASHEM spoke to Moses saying: Speak to the Children of Israel saying: on the fifteenth day of this seventh month is the Succos festival, for seven days to HASHEM. On the first day is a holy convocation; you are to do no laborious work. For seven days you are to offer a fire-offering to HASHEM; the eighth day shall be a holy convocation for you, and you are to offer a fire-offering to HASHEM, it shall be an assembly,* you may not do any laborious work.*

These are the convocations of HASHEM that you are to proclaim as holy convocations; to offer a fire-offering to HASHEM: an elevation-offering and its meal-offering; an offering and its libation, each day

for the dictum that one who eats on the ninth day [to be strong for the fast] is reckoned as if he had fasted both days (*Yoma* 81b).

עֲצֶרֶת – *An assembly.* Known as Shemini Atzeres, the Eighth Day of Assembly, this day is treated as an independent festival, rather than part of Succos. On Shemini Atzeres, there is no requirement to eat in a *succah* or take the Four Species, and the *Mussaf* offering is of an entirely different nature from that of Succos.

Based on the *Midrash, Rashi* translates עֲצֶרֶת as *restraint.* God asks the Jewish people to restrain for one more day their desire to go back to their

FIRST DAY

חמישי (בשבת ששי) – וַיֹּאמֶר יהוה אֶל־מֹשֶׁה וְאַהֲרֹן זֹאת חֻקַּת הַפָּסַח
כָּל־בֶּן־נֵכָר* לֹא־יֹאכַל בּוֹ: וְכָל־עֶבֶד* אִישׁ מִקְנַת־כָּסֶף וּמַלְתָּה
אֹתוֹ אָז יֹאכַל בּוֹ: תּוֹשָׁב וְשָׂכִיר לֹא־יֹאכַל בּוֹ: בְּבַיִת אֶחָד יֵאָכֵל
לֹא־תוֹצִיא מִן־הַבַּיִת מִן־הַבָּשָׂר חוּצָה וְעֶצֶם לֹא תִשְׁבְּרוּ־בוֹ:
כָּל־עֲדַת יִשְׂרָאֵל* יַעֲשׂוּ אֹתוֹ:
(בשבת שביעי) – וְכִי־יָגוּר אִתְּךָ גֵּר* וְעָשָׂה פֶסַח לַיהוה הִמּוֹל לוֹ כָל־זָכָר
וְאָז יִקְרַב לַעֲשֹׂתוֹ וְהָיָה כְּאֶזְרַח הָאָרֶץ וְכָל־עָרֵל לֹא־יֹאכַל בּוֹ:
תּוֹרָה אַחַת יִהְיֶה לָאֶזְרָח וְלַגֵּר הַגָּר בְּתוֹכְכֶם: וַיַּעֲשׂוּ כָּל־בְּנֵי
יִשְׂרָאֵל כַּאֲשֶׁר צִוָּה יהוה אֶת־מֹשֶׁה וְאֶת־אַהֲרֹן כֵּן עָשׂוּ: וַיְהִי
בְּעֶצֶם הַיּוֹם הַזֶּה* הוֹצִיא יהוה אֶת־בְּנֵי יִשְׂרָאֵל מֵאֶרֶץ מִצְרַיִם
עַל־צִבְאֹתָם:

בֶּן נֵכָר — *Alien son.* Two kinds of aliens are forbidden to partake of the *pesach*: a gentile and a Jew whose deeds have become *alienated* from his Father in Heaven.

עֶבֶד — *Slave.* If a Jew purchases a non-Jewish slave, that slave must be circumcised, whereupon he may eat the *pesach* offering. There is a Talmudic dispute regarding the extent of this prohibition. According to R' Yehoshua, even the master is forbidden to eat of the offering if he owns uncircumcised servants; R' Eliezer disagrees, maintaining that only the servant is forbidden. The next verse states that a gentile

SECOND DAY

בְּיוֹמוֹ: מִלְּבַד* שַׁבְּתֹת יהוה וּמִלְּבַד מַתְּנוֹתֵיכֶם וּמִלְּבַד כָּל־
נִדְרֵיכֶם וּמִלְּבַד כָּל־נִדְבֹתֵיכֶם אֲשֶׁר תִּתְּנוּ לַיהוה: אַךְ בַּחֲמִשָּׁה
עָשָׂר יוֹם לַחֹדֶשׁ הַשְּׁבִיעִי בְּאָסְפְּכֶם אֶת־תְּבוּאַת הָאָרֶץ תָּחֹגּוּ*
אֶת־חַג־יהוה שִׁבְעַת יָמִים בַּיּוֹם הָרִאשׁוֹן שַׁבָּתוֹן וּבַיּוֹם הַשְּׁמִינִי
שַׁבָּתוֹן: וּלְקַחְתֶּם לָכֶם בַּיּוֹם הָרִאשׁוֹן* פְּרִי עֵץ הָדָר כַּפֹּת תְּמָרִים
וַעֲנַף עֵץ־עָבֹת וְעַרְבֵי־נָחַל וּשְׂמַחְתֶּם לִפְנֵי יהוה אֱלֹהֵיכֶם שִׁבְעַת
יָמִים: וְחַגֹּתֶם אֹתוֹ חַג לַיהוה שִׁבְעַת יָמִים בַּשָּׁנָה חֻקַּת עוֹלָם
לְדֹרֹתֵיכֶם בַּחֹדֶשׁ הַשְּׁבִיעִי תָּחֹגּוּ אֹתוֹ: בַּסֻּכֹּת* תֵּשְׁבוּ שִׁבְעַת
יָמִים כָּל־הָאֶזְרָח בְּיִשְׂרָאֵל יֵשְׁבוּ בַּסֻּכֹּת: לְמַעַן יֵדְעוּ דֹרֹתֵיכֶם כִּי
בַסֻּכּוֹת הוֹשַׁבְתִּי אֶת־בְּנֵי יִשְׂרָאֵל בְּהוֹצִיאִי אוֹתָם מֵאֶרֶץ מִצְרָיִם
אֲנִי יהוה אֱלֹהֵיכֶם: וַיְדַבֵּר מֹשֶׁה אֶת־מֹעֲדֵי יהוה אֶל־בְּנֵי יִשְׂרָאֵל:

homes. The *Midrash* gives the parable of a king who invited his children to a week-long celebration. When the time was over, he asked them to stay for an extra day before leaving him. So, too, after the joyous week of Succos, God asks Israel to stay behind for one more festive day.

מִלְּבַד – *Aside from.* The previous verse refers only to the festivals; this one refers to the *Mussaf* of the Sabbath and to personal offerings that may be brought on the Intermediate Days of Pesach and Succos *(Or HaChaim).*

בַּחֲמִשָּׁה עָשָׂר. . . תָּחֹגּוּ – *However, on the fifteenth . . . you are to celebrate.* This 'celebration' refers to the *Chagigah* offering, which is a peace-offering

FIRST DAY

Fifth (On the Sabbath – Sixth) – *HASHEM said to Moses and Aaron: This is the decree of the pesach: no alien son* may eat from it. But every slave* of a man, who was bought for money, you shall circumcise him, then he may eat it. A sojourner and a hired laborer may not eat it. In a single house shall it be eaten; you shall not remove any of the meat from the house to the outside, and you shall not break a bone in it. The entire assembly of Israel* shall perform it.*

(On the Sabbath – Seventh) – *When a proselyte* sojourns among you he shall perform the pesach for HASHEM, each of his males shall be circumcised, and then he may draw near to perform it, and he shall be like the native of the land; no uncircumcised male may eat of it. One law shall there be for the native and the proselyte who lives among you. All the Children of Israel as HASHEM had commanded Moses and Aaron, so did they do.*

It happened on that very day: HASHEM took out the Children of Israel from Egypt, in their legions.*

---

who merely *sojourns* in *Eretz Yisrael* or who has been hired, but not purchased, by a Jew may not eat from the offering.

כָּל עֲדַת יִשְׂרָאֵל — *The entire assembly of Israel.* The *pesach* offering in Egypt had to be eaten in family groups, but the offerings of later years had no such restriction.

גֵּר — *A proselyte.* Even though a proselyte's ancestors were not in Egypt, he brings the *pesach* offering as do all other Jews.

בְּעֶצֶם הַיּוֹם הַזֶּה — *On that very day.* This fact is repeated to emphasize that the *pesach* offering was responsible for the redemption, since, as noted above, Israel could not have merited such Divine intervention without the performance of commandments.

SECOND DAY

what is required for that day. Aside from HASHEM's Sabbaths, aside from your gifts, aside from your vows, and aside from your free-will offerings, which you will present to HASHEM.*

However, on the fifteenth day of the seventh month when you gather in the crop of the land you are to celebrate HASHEM's festival for seven days; the first day is a rest-day and the eighth day is a rest-day. On the first day* you are to take for yourselves the fruit of a citron tree, the branches of date palms, twigs of a plaited tree, brook willows; and you are to rejoice before HASHEM your God for seven days. You are to dwell in booths for seven days; every citizen of Israel is to dwell in booths. So that your generations will know that I caused the Children of Israel to dwell in booths* when I took them from the land of Egypt; I am HASHEM your God.*

And Moses declared the appointed festivals of HASHEM to the Children of Israel.

---

that is brought by everyone who comes to celebrate a pilgrimage festival. The word אַךְ, *however,* is a limitation, implying that the *Chagigah* offering may be brought only on a weekday. Were the festival to fall on the Sabbath, the offering would be deferred to a later day.

בַּיּוֹם הָרִאשׁוֹן – *On the first day.* Torah law requires that the Four Species be taken only on the first day. The commandment that they be taken all seven days is of Rabbinic origin.

בַּסֻּכֹּת – *In booths.* The Sages disagree. Some hold that the 'booths' of the wilderness were figurative; they were actually the Clouds of Glory that God provided for Israel's protection. The other opinion is that the people literally built booths for shelter (*Succah* 11b).

חצי קדיש

After the last *oleh* has completed his closing blessing, the second Torah Scroll is placed on the *bimah* alongside the first, and the reader recites Half-*Kaddish.*

יִתְגַּדַּל וְיִתְקַדַּשׁ שְׁמֵהּ רַבָּא. (.Cong. – אָמֵן.) בְּעָלְמָא דִּי בְרָא כִרְעוּתֵהּ. וְיַמְלִיךְ מַלְכוּתֵהּ, בְּחַיֵּיכוֹן וּבְיוֹמֵיכוֹן וּבְחַיֵּי דְכָל בֵּית יִשְׂרָאֵל, בַּעֲגָלָא וּבִזְמַן קָרִיב. וְאִמְרוּ: אָמֵן.

(.Cong. – אָמֵן. יְהֵא שְׁמֵהּ רַבָּא מְבָרַךְ לְעָלַם וּלְעָלְמֵי עָלְמַיָּא.)

יְהֵא שְׁמֵהּ רַבָּא מְבָרַךְ לְעָלַם וּלְעָלְמֵי עָלְמַיָּא.

יִתְבָּרַךְ וְיִשְׁתַּבַּח וְיִתְפָּאַר וְיִתְרוֹמַם וְיִתְנַשֵּׂא וְיִתְהַדָּר וְיִתְעַלֶּה וְיִתְהַלָּל שְׁמֵהּ דְּקֻדְשָׁא בְּרִיךְ הוּא (.Cong. – בְּרִיךְ הוּא) — לְעֵלָּא מִן כָּל בִּרְכָתָא וְשִׁירָתָא תֻּשְׁבְּחָתָא וְנֶחֱמָתָא, דַּאֲמִירָן בְּעָלְמָא. וְאִמְרוּ: אָמֵן. (.Cong. – אָמֵן.)

הגבהה וגלילה

The first Torah is raised for all to see. Each person looks at the Torah and recites aloud:

וְזֹאת הַתּוֹרָה• אֲשֶׁר שָׂם מֹשֶׁה לִפְנֵי בְּנֵי יִשְׂרָאֵל,[1] עַל פִּי יהוה בְּיַד מֹשֶׁה.[2]

Some add:

עֵץ חַיִּים הִיא לַמַּחֲזִיקִים בָּהּ, וְתֹמְכֶיהָ מְאֻשָּׁר.[3] דְּרָכֶיהָ דַרְכֵי נֹעַם, וְכָל נְתִיבוֹתֶיהָ שָׁלוֹם.[4] אֹרֶךְ יָמִים בִּימִינָהּ, בִּשְׂמֹאלָהּ עֹשֶׁר וְכָבוֹד.[5] יהוה חָפֵץ לְמַעַן צִדְקוֹ, יַגְדִּיל תּוֹרָה וְיַאְדִּיר.[6]

מפטיר

As the first Torah is wound, tied, and covered, the *oleh* for *Maftir* is called to the second Torah.

במדבר כח:טז-כה

וּבַחֹ֣דֶשׁ הָֽרִאשׁ֗וֹן בְּאַרְבָּעָ֥ה עָשָׂ֛ר י֖וֹם לַחֹ֑דֶשׁ פֶּ֖סַח לַֽיהוָֽה׃ וּבַחֲמִשָּׁ֨ה עָשָׂ֥ר י֛וֹם לַחֹ֥דֶשׁ הַזֶּ֖ה חָ֑ג שִׁבְעַ֣ת יָמִ֔ים מַצּ֖וֹת יֵאָכֵֽל׃ בַּיּ֥וֹם הָֽרִאשׁ֖וֹן מִקְרָא־קֹ֑דֶשׁ כָּל־מְלֶ֥אכֶת עֲבֹדָ֖ה לֹ֥א תַעֲשֽׂוּ׃ וְהִקְרַבְתֶּ֨ם אִשֶּׁ֤ה עֹלָה֙ לַֽיהוָ֔ה פָּרִ֧ים בְּנֵי־בָקָ֛ר שְׁנַ֖יִם וְאַ֣יִל אֶחָ֑ד וְשִׁבְעָ֤ה כְבָשִׂים֙ בְּנֵ֣י שָׁנָ֔ה תְּמִימִ֖ם יִהְי֥וּ לָכֶֽם׃

(1) *Deuteronomy* 4:44. (2) *Numbers* 9:23. (3) *Proverbs* 3:18. (4) 3:17. (5) 3:16. (6) *Isaiah* 42:21.

וְזֹאת הַתּוֹרָה — *This is the Torah.* As the congregation looks at the words and columns of the unrolled, upheld Torah Scroll, it declares the cardinal tenet of faith that the Torah now in our hands is the same one that God transmitted to Moses. Every word in the Torah was dictated to Moses by God. In *Rambam's* classic formulation — The Thirteen Principles of Faith — all the verses of the Torah have equal sanctity, and there is no difference between [the 'trivial' verses:] *and the children of Ham were Cush and Mitzrayim (Genesis* 10:6), or *his wife's name was Mehitabel* (ibid. 36:39), and [the 'important' verses:] *I am HASHEM, your God (Exodus* 20:2), or

HALF KADDISH

After the last *oleh* has completed his closing blessing, the second Torah Scroll is placed on the *bimah* alongside the first, and the reader recites Half-*Kaddish*.

יִתְגַּדַּל *May His great Name grow exalted and sanctified* (Cong.— *Amen.*) *in the world that He created as He willed. May He give reign to His kingship in your lifetimes and in your days, and in the lifetimes of the entire Family of Israel, swiftly and soon. Now respond: Amen.*

(Cong.— *Amen. May His great Name be blessed forever and ever.*)

May His great Name be blessed forever and ever.

Blessed, praised, glorified, exalted, extolled, mighty, upraised, and lauded be the Name of the Holy One, Blessed is He (Cong.— *Blessed is He*) *— beyond any blessing and song, praise and consolation that are uttered in the world. Now respond: Amen.* (Cong.— *Amen.*)

HAGBAHAH AND GELILAH

The first Torah is raised for all to see. Each person looks at the Torah and recites aloud:

This is the Torah* that Moses placed before the Children of Israel,[1] upon the command of HASHEM, through Moses' hand.[2]

Some add:

עֵץ *It is a tree of life for those who grasp it, and its supporters are praiseworthy.[3] Its ways are ways of pleasantness and all its paths are peace.[4] Lengthy days are at its right; at its left are wealth and honor.[5] HASHEM desired, for the sake of its [Israel's] righteousness, that the Torah be made great and glorious.[6]*

MAFTIR

As the first Torah is wound, tied, and covered, the *oleh* for *Maftir* is called to the second Torah.

Numbers 28:16-25

In the first month on the fourteenth day of the month is the pesach-offering for HASHEM. The fifteenth day of this month is a festival, matzos shall be eaten for seven days. The first day is a holy convocation, you shall do no laborious work. You shall offer a fire-offering, an elevation-offering to HASHEM, two young bulls, one ram, and seven lambs within their first year, unblemished shall they be for you.

Hear O Israel (*Deuteronomy* 6:4). Moreover the same applies to the Oral Law that explains the Torah. All was given by God to Moses.

⤚§ Maftir

On all festivals and Rosh Chodesh, the *Maftir* reading comes from the *Sidrah Pinchas* (*Numbers* ch. 28 and 29), which sets forth the *Mussaf* offerings of the respective days. Unlike Succos, which has a different *Mussaf* offering — and consequently a different *Maftir* reading — for each day of the festival, both the *Mussaf* offerings and the *Maftir* readings of Pesach are the same every day. However, since the first two verses of the *Maftir* speak specifically of the fourteenth and fifteenth days of Nissan, those two verses are omitted during *Chol HaMoed* and the last two days.

⤚§ The Haftarah

The practice of reading from the Prophets — today known as the *Haftarah* — was introduced during the reign of the infamous Syrian-Greek King Antiochus, who ruled and persecuted Israel prior to the time of the Chanukah miracle [165 B.C.E.]. In his attempts to rid the Jewish people of their religion, he forbade the public reading from the Torah. Unable to refresh their

וּמִנְחָתָם סֹלֶת בְּלוּלָה בַשָּׁמֶן שְׁלֹשָׁה עֶשְׂרֹנִים לַפָּר וּשְׁנֵי
עֶשְׂרֹנִים לָאַיִל תַּעֲשׂוּ: עִשָּׂרוֹן עִשָּׂרוֹן תַּעֲשֶׂה לַכֶּבֶשׂ הָאֶחָד
לְשִׁבְעַת הַכְּבָשִׂים: וּשְׂעִיר חַטָּאת אֶחָד לְכַפֵּר עֲלֵיכֶם: מִלְּבַד
עֹלַת הַבֹּקֶר אֲשֶׁר לְעֹלַת הַתָּמִיד תַּעֲשׂוּ אֶת־אֵלֶּה: כָּאֵלֶּה תַּעֲשׂוּ
לַיּוֹם שִׁבְעַת יָמִים לֶחֶם אִשֵּׁה רֵיחַ־נִיחֹחַ לַיהוָה עַל־עוֹלַת
הַתָּמִיד יֵעָשֶׂה וְנִסְכּוֹ: וּבַיּוֹם הַשְּׁבִיעִי מִקְרָא־קֹדֶשׁ יִהְיֶה לָכֶם
כָּל־מְלֶאכֶת עֲבֹדָה לֹא תַעֲשׂוּ:

הגבהה וגלילה

The *maftir* completes his closing blessing.
Then the second Torah Scroll is raised and each person looks at the Torah and recites aloud:

וְזֹאת הַתּוֹרָה אֲשֶׁר שָׂם מֹשֶׁה לִפְנֵי בְּנֵי יִשְׂרָאֵל,[1]
עַל פִּי יהוה בְּיַד מֹשֶׁה.[2]

Some add:

עֵץ חַיִּים הִיא לַמַּחֲזִיקִים בָּהּ, וְתֹמְכֶיהָ מְאֻשָּׁר.[3] דְּרָכֶיהָ דַרְכֵי נֹעַם, וְכָל
נְתִיבוֹתֶיהָ שָׁלוֹם.[4] אֹרֶךְ יָמִים בִּימִינָהּ, בִּשְׂמֹאלָהּ עֹשֶׁר וְכָבוֹד.[5]
יהוה חָפֵץ לְמַעַן צִדְקוֹ, יַגְדִּיל תּוֹרָה וְיַאְדִּיר.[6]

After the Torah Scroll has been wound, tied and covered,
the *maftir* recites the *Haftarah* blessings.

ברכה קודם ההפטרה

בָּרוּךְ אַתָּה יהוה אֱלֹהֵינוּ מֶלֶךְ הָעוֹלָם, אֲשֶׁר בָּחַר בִּנְבִיאִים
טוֹבִים,* וְרָצָה בְדִבְרֵיהֶם* הַנֶּאֱמָרִים בֶּאֱמֶת, בָּרוּךְ אַתָּה
יהוה,* הַבּוֹחֵר בַּתּוֹרָה וּבְמֹשֶׁה עַבְדּוֹ, וּבְיִשְׂרָאֵל עַמּוֹ, וּבִנְבִיאֵי
הָאֱמֶת וָצֶדֶק: (Cong. – אָמֵן.)

---

spiritual thirst from the Torah itself, the people resorted to readings from the Prophets, calling seven people to read at least three verses each. Later, when the ban was lifted, the people retained their custom of having someone read from the Prophets. However, in order not to let it seem as though the reading from the Prophets had equal standing with the reading from the Torah, the Sages decreed that the person reading the *Haftarah* must first read a portion from the Torah.

Generally, the last group of verses from the week's Torah reading is read as the *Maftir* portion, and the *Haftarah* is on a subject related to the Torah portion. On Festivals, including Rosh Hashanah, the *Maftir* portion is from the verses in *Numbers* that describe the day's *Mussaf* offerings, and is read from a second Torah Scroll.

The word *Haftarah* comes from פטר, to *dismiss*, to *complete*. The dessert of a meal is known in the Talmud as *haftarah* because it is the end of the meal, just as the Prophetic reading completes the Torah-reading part of the service. The person doing this 'completing,' therefore, is called the *maftir*.

⊲§ Blessing before the Haftarah

בִּנְבִיאִים טוֹבִים – *Good prophets.* The theme of the *Haftarah* blessings is the integrity of the

And their meal-offering shall be fine flour mixed with oil; you shall make it three tenth-ephah for each bull and two tenth-ephah for each ram. One tenth-ephah shall you make for each lamb, of the seven rams. And one he-goat for a sin-offering, to provide you atonement. Aside from the elevation-offering of the morning that is for the continual elevation-offering shall you offer these. Like these shall you offer each day of the seven days, food, a fire-offering, a satisfying aroma to HASHEM; *after the continual elevation-offering shall it be made, with its libation. The seventh day shall be a holy convocation for you, you shall not do any laborious work.*

HAGBAHAH AND GELILAH

The *maftir* completes his closing blessing.
Then the second Torah Scroll is raised and each person looks at the Torah and recites aloud:

This is the Torah that Moses placed before the Children of Israel,[1] upon the command of HASHEM, through Moses' hand.[2]

Some add:

עֵץ *It is a tree of life for those who grasp it, and its supporters are praiseworthy.[3] Its ways are ways of pleasantness and all its paths are peace.[4] Lengthy days are at its right; at its left are wealth and honor.[5]* HASHEM *desired, for the sake of its [Israel's] righteousness, that the Torah be made great and glorious.[6]*

After the Torah Scroll has been wound, tied and covered, the *maftir* recites the *Haftarah* blessings.

BLESSING BEFORE THE HAFTARAH

בָּרוּךְ *Blessed are You,* HASHEM, *our God, King of the universe, Who has chosen good prophets* and was pleased with their words* that were uttered with truth. Blessed are You,* HASHEM,* *Who chooses the Torah; Moses, His servant; Israel, His nation; and the prophets of truth and righteousness.* (Cong.— *Amen.*)

(1) *Deuteronomy* 4:44. (2) *Numbers* 9:23. (3) *Proverbs* 3:18. (4) 3:17. (5) 3:16. (6) *Isaiah* 42:21.

prophets and their teachings. They are good to the Jewish people, even when it is their mission to criticize and threaten. Also, they are chosen because they are good people: learned, righteous, impressive, and so on. Our tradition does not accept prophets who had been lacking in any of the attributes of Jewish greatness.

וְרָצָה בְדִבְרֵיהֶם — *And was pleased with their words.* There are a variety of interpretations:

— The words of the prophets are as authoritative to us as the Torah itself.

— God is especially pleased with the prophecies of Israel's future good.

— God is pleased even with what the prophets do on their own initiative.

— He is pleased that they adhere scrupulously to His mission.

בָּרוּךְ אַתָּה ה׳ — *Blessed are You,* HASHEM. Not a new blessing, this is a summing up of the previous points: God has chosen the Torah, which owes its authority to our absolute faith in the prophecy of Moses. The Torah was given to God's Chosen People, whom He instructs and chastises through His truthful and righteous prophets.

FIRST DAY

הפטרה ליום ראשון ﷯

יהושע ג:ה-ז; ה:ב-ו:א; ו:כז

וַיֹּ֤אמֶר יְהוֹשֻׁ֨עַ֙ אֶל־הָעָ֔ם הִתְקַדָּ֑שׁוּ כִּ֣י מָחָ֗ר יַעֲשֶׂ֧ה יהוֹה בְּקִרְבְּכֶ֖ם נִפְלָאֽוֹת:* וַיֹּ֤אמֶר יְהוֹשֻׁ֨עַ֙ אֶל־הַכֹּֽהֲנִים֙ לֵאמֹ֔ר שְׂא֖וּ אֶת־אֲר֣וֹן הַבְּרִ֔ית וְעִבְר֖וּ לִפְנֵ֣י הָעָ֑ם וַיִּשְׂאוּ֙ אֶת־אֲר֣וֹן הַבְּרִ֔ית וַיֵּֽלְכ֖וּ לִפְנֵ֥י הָעָֽם: וַיֹּ֨אמֶר יהוֹה אֶל־יְהוֹשֻׁ֔עַ הַיּ֣וֹם הַזֶּ֗ה אָחֵל֙ גַּדֶּלְךָ֔ בְּעֵינֵ֖י כָּל־ יִשְׂרָאֵ֑ל אֲשֶׁר֙ יֵֽדְע֔וּן כִּ֗י כַּֽאֲשֶׁ֤ר הָיִ֨יתִי֙ עִם־מֹשֶׁ֔ה אֶֽהְיֶ֖ה עִמָּֽךְ: בָּעֵ֣ת הַהִ֗יא אָמַ֤ר יהוֹה֙ אֶל־יְהוֹשֻׁ֔עַ עֲשֵׂ֥ה לְךָ֖ חַֽרְב֣וֹת צֻרִ֑ים וְשׁ֛וּב מֹ֥ל אֶת־בְּנֵֽי־יִשְׂרָאֵ֖ל שֵׁנִֽית:* וַיַּֽעַשׂ־ל֤וֹ יְהוֹשֻׁ֨עַ֙ חַֽרְב֣וֹת צֻרִ֔ים וַיָּ֨מָל֙ אֶת־בְּנֵ֣י יִשְׂרָאֵ֔ל אֶל־גִּבְעַ֖ת הָֽעֲרָלֽוֹת: וְזֶ֥ה הַדָּבָ֖ר אֲשֶׁר־מָ֣ל יְהוֹשֻׁ֑עַ כָּל־הָעָ֞ם הַיֹּצֵ֤א מִמִּצְרַ֨יִם֙ הַזְּכָרִ֔ים כֹּ֣ל | אַנְשֵׁ֣י הַמִּלְחָמָ֗ה מֵ֚תוּ בַמִּדְבָּ֔ר בַּדֶּ֖רֶךְ בְּצֵאתָ֥ם מִמִּצְרָֽיִם: כִּֽי־מֻלִ֣ים הָי֗וּ כָּל־הָעָם֙ הַיֹּֽצְאִ֔ים וְכָל־הָ֠עָ֠ם הַיִּלֹּדִ֧ים בַּמִּדְבָּ֛ר

◄ HAFTARAH FOR THE FIRST DAY ►

The narrative of the *Haftarah* parallels strikingly that of the Torah reading. In both cases, a long period of time had gone by during which the people had not been able to circumcise their young, and consequently they were not eligible

to bring the *pesach* offering. Joshua arranged for the entire nation to be circumcised in a massive demonstration of devotion to God and His covenant. After the offering was brought and the festival observed, Joshua turned his attention to the conquest of Jericho. The commandments

---

SECOND DAY

הפטרה ליום שני ﷯

מלכים ב כג:א-ט; כא-כה

וַיִּשְׁלַ֖ח הַמֶּ֑לֶךְ וַיַּֽאַסְפ֣וּ אֵלָ֔יו כָּל־זִקְנֵ֥י יְהוּדָ֖ה וִירֽוּשָׁלָֽ͏ִם: וַיַּ֣עַל הַמֶּ֣לֶךְ בֵּֽית־יהוֹה֩ וְכָל־אִ֨ישׁ יְהוּדָ֜ה וְכָל־יֹֽשְׁבֵ֤י יְרֽוּשָׁלַ֨͏ִם֙ אִתּ֔וֹ וְהַכֹּֽהֲנִ֖ים וְהַנְּבִיאִ֑ים וְכָל־הָעָ֖ם לְמִקָּטֹ֣ן וְעַד־גָּד֑וֹל וַיִּקְרָ֣א בְאָזְנֵיהֶ֗ם אֶת־כָּל־ דִּבְרֵי֙ סֵ֣פֶר הַבְּרִ֔ית הַנִּמְצָ֖א בְּבֵ֥ית יהוֹֽה: וַיַּֽעֲמֹ֣ד הַמֶּ֣לֶךְ עַל־הָֽעַמּ֗וּד וַיִּכְרֹ֣ת אֶֽת־הַבְּרִ֣ית | לִפְנֵ֣י יהוֹה֒ לָלֶ֜כֶת אַחַ֣ר יהוֹ֗ה וְלִשְׁמֹ֤ר מִצְוֺתָיו֙ וְאֶת־עֵֽדְוֺתָ֣יו וְאֶת־חֻקֹּתָ֔יו בְּכָל־לֵ֖ב וּבְכָל־נֶ֑פֶשׁ לְהָקִ֗ים אֶת־דִּבְרֵי֙ הַבְּרִ֣ית הַזֹּ֔את הַכְּתֻבִ֖ים עַל־הַסֵּ֣פֶר הַזֶּ֑ה וַיַּֽעֲמֹ֥ד כָּל־הָעָ֖ם בַּבְּרִֽית:

◄ HAFTARAH FOR THE SECOND DAY ►

The incident recorded in this *Haftarah* took place in the waning days of the First Temple era. It was a time when hope for a rejuvenation of the Jewish spirit seemed to be lost and when there was no way to avoid the impending destruction and exile. And then, an inspiring transformation

took place, one that the *Haftarah* describes as unprecedented.

The son of the great and righteous King Hezekiah was the diametrical opposite of his noble father. King Manassah was an idolater who zealously sought to uproot the service of Hashem from the Jewish people and replace it with the

FIRST DAY

HAFTARAH FOR THE FIRST DAY

Joshua 3:5-7; 5:2-6:1; 6:27

And Joshua said to the people, 'Prepare yourselves, for tomorrow HASHEM *will do wonders* in your midst.' And Joshua said to the Kohanim, 'Carry the Ark of the Covenant and advance to the head of the people.' And they carried the Ark of the Covenant, and they went to the head of the people.*

And HASHEM *said to Joshua, 'This day I will inaugurate your greatness in the sight of all Israel that they may know that as I was with Moses, so will I be with you.'*

At that time HASHEM *said to Joshua, 'Make sharp knives and return and circumcise the Children of Israel a second time.'* And Joshua made sharp knives and circumcised the Children of Israel at the Mound of Aralos.*

This is the reason why Joshua circumcised: the entire nation that left Egypt — the males, all the men of battle — had died in the wilderness on the way during their exodus from Egypt. All the people that left were circumcised, but all the people that were born in the wilderness

of *pesach* and circumcision once again provided the necessary merits for a great new chapter in Jewish history.

נִפְלָאוֹת — *Wonders.* This took place before Israel entered the Holy Land. The wonders of which Joshua spoke were the miraculous manner in which the Jordan split, to allow the nation to cross into *Eretz Yisrael.*

מֹל . . . שֵׁנִית — *Circumcise . . . a second time.* The first mass circumcision was in Egypt. During the years in the Wilderness, the people were not circumcised because the rigors of travel would

SECOND DAY

HAFTARAH FOR THE SECOND DAY

II Kings 23:1-9; 21-25

The king sent and all the elders of Judah and Jerusalem gathered before him. The king went up to the House of HASHEM, *and all the men of Judah and the inhabitants of Jerusalem were with him, and the Kohanim and the prophets and all the people, from young to old; he read in their ears all the words of the Book of the Covenant that had been found in the House of* HASHEM.

The king stood on the platform and sealed a covenant before HASHEM: *to follow* HASHEM *and to observe His commandments, His testimonies, and His decrees with a complete heart and a complete soul, to establish the words of this covenant that were written in this book — and the entire people accepted the covenant.*

vilest forms of idol worship. In his long reign he virtually succeeded and when his grandson Josiah succeeded to the throne as an eight year old, his education was so carefully controlled by the minions of the idols that he was not even aware that there was a Jewish Torah! Then, the Kohen Gadol Hilkiah found the Torah Scroll of Moses that had been hidden in the Temple to protect it from the destructive zeal of Manassah's cohorts. The king, then twenty-six, heard and asked to see it. It was read to him and caused a profound spiritual transformation. He repented and took the nation with him. He removed the idols and their priests, blew a fresh and wholesome spirit into a people grown decadent. The capstone of his return to the Torah was a joyous

FIRST DAY

בַּדֶּ֣רֶךְ בְּצֵאתָ֣ם מִמִּצְרַ֮יִם לֹא־מָֽלוּ׃ כִּ֣י ׀ אַרְבָּעִ֣ים שָׁנָ֗ה הָלְכ֣וּ בְנֵֽי־
יִשְׂרָאֵל֮ בַּמִּדְבָּר֒ עַד־תֹּ֨ם כָּל־הַגּ֜וֹי אַנְשֵׁ֤י הַמִּלְחָמָה֙ הַיֹּצְאִ֣ים
מִמִּצְרַ֔יִם אֲשֶׁ֥ר לֹֽא־שָׁמְע֖וּ בְּק֣וֹל יהו֑ה אֲשֶׁ֨ר נִשְׁבַּ֤ע יהוה֙ לָהֶ֔ם
לְבִלְתִּ֞י הַרְאוֹתָ֣ם אֶת־הָאָ֗רֶץ אֲשֶׁר֩ נִשְׁבַּ֨ע יהו֤ה לַאֲבוֹתָם֙ לָ֣תֶת לָ֔נוּ
אֶ֛רֶץ זָבַ֥ת חָלָ֖ב וּדְבָֽשׁ׃ וְאֶת־בְּנֵיהֶם֙ הֵקִ֣ים תַּחְתָּ֔ם אֹתָ֖ם מָ֣ל יְהוֹשֻׁ֑עַ
כִּֽי־עֲרֵלִ֣ים הָי֔וּ כִּ֛י לֹא־מָ֥לוּ אוֹתָ֖ם בַּדָּֽרֶךְ׃ וַיְהִ֛י כַּאֲשֶׁר־תַּ֥מּוּ כָל־
הַגּ֛וֹי לְהִמּ֖וֹל וַיֵּשְׁב֣וּ תַחְתָּ֑ם בַּֽמַּחֲנֶ֖ה עַ֥ד חֲיוֹתָֽם׃ וַיֹּ֤אמֶר יהוה֙ אֶל־
יְהוֹשֻׁ֔עַ הַיּ֗וֹם גַּלּ֛וֹתִי אֶת־חֶרְפַּ֥ת מִצְרַ֖יִם* מֵעֲלֵיכֶ֑ם וַיִּקְרָ֞א שֵׁ֣ם
הַמָּק֤וֹם הַהוּא֙ גִּלְגָּ֔ל עַ֖ד הַיּ֥וֹם הַזֶּֽה׃ וַיַּחֲנ֥וּ בְנֵֽי־יִשְׂרָאֵ֖ל בַּגִּלְגָּ֑ל
וַיַּעֲשׂ֣וּ אֶת־הַפֶּ֗סַח בְּאַרְבָּעָ֩ה עָשָׂ֨ר י֥וֹם לַחֹ֛דֶשׁ בָּעֶ֖רֶב בְּעַֽרְב֥וֹת
יְרִיחֽוֹ׃ וַיֹּ֨אכְל֜וּ מֵעֲב֤וּר הָאָ֙רֶץ֙* מִמָּֽחֳרַ֣ת הַפֶּ֔סַח מַצּ֖וֹת וְקָל֑וּי בְּעֶ֖צֶם
הַיּ֥וֹם הַזֶּֽה׃ וַיִּשְׁבֹּ֨ת הַמָּ֜ן* מִֽמָּחֳרָ֗ת בְּאָכְלָם֙ מֵעֲב֣וּר הָאָ֔רֶץ וְלֹא־הָ֥יָה
ע֛וֹד לִבְנֵ֥י יִשְׂרָאֵ֖ל מָ֑ן וַיֹּאכְל֗וּ מִתְּבוּאַת֙ אֶ֣רֶץ כְּנַ֔עַן בַּשָּׁנָ֖ה הַהִֽיא׃

have made it dangerous for newly circumcised infants, and because the climate in the Wilderness was not conducive to a proper recovery.

חֶרְפַּת מִצְרַיִם — *The reproach of Egypt.* Pharaoh's astrologers foretold that the Jews would encounter blood in the Wilderness, so the Egyptians taunted them that God was taking them to the Wilderness to annihilate them. Now it became obvious that this 'blood vision' referred to the blood of circumcision, Israel's covenant with God.

וַיֹּאכְלוּ מֵעֲבוּר הָאָרֶץ — *They ate from the aged grain of the Land.* Now that they were in *Eretz Yisrael,* they were not permitted to eat from the

SECOND DAY

וַיְצַ֣ו הַמֶּ֡לֶךְ אֶת־חִלְקִיָּהוּ֩ הַכֹּהֵ֨ן הַגָּד֜וֹל וְאֶת־כֹּהֲנֵ֣י הַמִּשְׁנֶה֮* וְאֶת־
שֹׁמְרֵ֣י הַסַּף֒ לְהוֹצִיא֙ מֵהֵיכַ֣ל יהו֔ה אֵ֣ת כָּל־הַכֵּלִ֗ים הָעֲשׂוּיִם֙ לַבַּ֔עַל
וְלָֽאֲשֵׁרָ֔ה וּלְכֹ֖ל צְבָ֣א הַשָּׁמָ֑יִם וַיִּשְׂרְפֵ֞ם מִח֤וּץ לִירֽוּשָׁלַ֙ם֙ בְּשַׁדְמ֣וֹת
קִדְר֔וֹן וְנָשָׂ֥א אֶת־עֲפָרָ֖ם בֵּֽית־אֵֽל׃ וְהִשְׁבִּ֣ית אֶת־הַכְּמָרִ֗ים אֲשֶׁ֤ר
נָֽתְנוּ֙ מַלְכֵ֣י יְהוּדָ֔ה וַיְקַטֵּ֖ר בַּבָּמ֑וֹת* בְּעָרֵ֣י יְהוּדָ֔ה וּמְסִבֵּ֖י יְרֽוּשָׁלָ֑͏ִם
וְאֶת־הַֽמְקַטְּרִ֣ים לַבַּ֗עַל לַשֶּׁ֤מֶשׁ וְלַיָּרֵ֙חַ֙ וְלַמַּזָּל֔וֹת וּלְכֹ֖ל צְבָ֥א
הַשָּׁמָֽיִם׃ וַיֹּצֵ֣א אֶת־הָאֲשֵׁרָ֩ה מִבֵּ֨ית יהו֜ה מִח֤וּץ לִירֽוּשָׁלַ֙͏ִם֙ אֶל־נַ֣חַל
קִדְר֗וֹן וַיִּשְׂרֹ֥ף אֹתָ֛הּ בְּנַ֥חַל קִדְר֖וֹן וַיָּ֣דֶק לְעָפָ֑ר וַיַּשְׁלֵךְ֙ אֶת־עֲפָרָ֔הּ
עַל־קֶ֖בֶר בְּנֵ֥י הָעָֽם׃* וַיִּתֹּ֗ץ אֶת־בָּתֵּ֤י הַקְּדֵשִׁים֙* אֲשֶׁ֣ר בְּבֵ֣ית יהו֔ה

and sincere celebration of Pesach, which was highlighted by the *pesach* offering in Jerusalem.

Aside from its relevance to the festival because of its story of the *pesach* offering, the *Haftarah* has another message that is appropriate to this time of the year. Both the first Pesach and the Pesach of Josiah represent times of renewal. In the time of Moses, Israel became a nation. In the time of Josiah, it renewed the soul of its nationhood. And if that could be done once, we can be confident that it will indeed be done again with the coming of the final redemption.

FIRST DAY

on the way during their exodus from Egypt were not circumcised. Because forty years the Children of Israel journeyed in the wilderness until the death of all the nation — the men of battle — who left Egypt and did not hearken to the voice of HASHEM, about whom HASHEM had sworn that He would not show them the Land which HASHEM had sworn to their forefathers to give us, a land flowing with milk and honey. But their children He raised in their stead — those Joshua circumcised since they were uncircumcised because they did not circumcise them on the way. It was when all the nation had finished being circumcised, they remained in their place in the camp until they recuperated.

And HASHEM said to Joshua, 'Today I have removed the reproach of Egypt from upon you.' He called the name of that place Gilgal until this day. And the Children of Israel encamped at Gilgal and made the pesach offering on the fourteenth day of the month at evening in the plains of Jericho. They ate from the aged grain of the Land on the day after the pesach offering, matzos and roasted grain, on this very day. When the manna was depleted the following day, they ate from the aged grain of the Land. The Children of Israel did not have manna anymore; they ate from the grain of the Land of Canaan that year.*

past year's grain crop until the second day of Pesach, when the *Omer* offering would be brought. That year was the first time they were able to bring it.

וַיִּשְׁבֹּת הַמָּן — *When the manna was depleted* [lit., *ceased*]. According to the Midrash (*Mechilta, Shemos* 16:35), the manna stopped falling on the seventh of Adar, when Moses died. At that time, the people stored enough manna to last for five weeks, a supply that lasted until the second day of Pesach.

SECOND DAY

The king instructed Hilkiyahu the Kohen Gadol, the Kohanim of the second rank, and the gate keepers to remove from the Temple of HASHEM all the vessels that had been made for the Baal, the Asherah, and all the heavenly hosts; they burned them outside of Jerusalem on the plains of Kidron, and they carried their ashes to Bethel. He dismissed the priests whom the kings of Judah had appointed to burn offerings on the high places* in the cities of Judah and the surroundings of Jerusalem, and also those who burned incense to the Baal, the sun, the moon, the constellations, and to all the heavenly hosts. He removed the Asherah from the House of HASHEM to the Kidron valley outside Jerusalem; he burned it and pounded it to dust, and he threw its dust upon the grave of the [idol-worshiping] common people.* He smashed the rooms of the idolaters* that were in the House of HASHEM,*

כֹּהֲנֵי הַמִּשְׁנֶה — *The Kohanim of the second rank.* These were the deputies to the Kohen Gadol who were in charge of various functions of the priesthood.

בַּבָּמוֹת — *On the high places*. The altars and shrines of the idols were generally set up on hills or other high places where they would appear to be prominent.

בְּנֵי הָעָם — *The [idol-worshiping] common people.* Josiah dumped the ashes of the idols on the graves of their worshipers as a symbol of contempt.

בָּתֵּי הַקְּדֵשִׁים — *The rooms of the idolaters*. The translation follows *Radak*, who explains that rooms were attached to the Temple, where

FIRST DAY

וַיְהִי בִּהְיוֹת יְהוֹשֻׁעַ בִּירִיחוֹ וַיִּשָּׂא עֵינָיו וַיַּרְא וְהִנֵּה־אִישׁ עֹמֵד
לְנֶגְדּוֹ וְחַרְבּוֹ שְׁלוּפָה בְּיָדוֹ וַיֵּלֶךְ יְהוֹשֻׁעַ אֵלָיו וַיֹּאמֶר לוֹ הֲלָנוּ
אַתָּה אִם־לְצָרֵינוּ: וַיֹּאמֶר | לֹא* כִּי אֲנִי שַׂר־צְבָא־יְהוָה עַתָּה
בָאתִי וַיִּפֹּל יְהוֹשֻׁעַ אֶל־פָּנָיו אַרְצָה וַיִּשְׁתָּחוּ וַיֹּאמֶר לוֹ מָה אֲדֹנִי
מְדַבֵּר אֶל־עַבְדּוֹ: וַיֹּאמֶר שַׂר־צְבָא יְהוָה אֶל־יְהוֹשֻׁעַ שַׁל־נַעַלְךָ
מֵעַל רַגְלֶךָ כִּי הַמָּקוֹם אֲשֶׁר אַתָּה עֹמֵד עָלָיו קֹדֶשׁ הוּא וַיַּעַשׂ
יְהוֹשֻׁעַ כֵּן: וִירִיחוֹ סֹגֶרֶת וּמְסֻגֶּרֶת מִפְּנֵי בְּנֵי יִשְׂרָאֵל אֵין יוֹצֵא
וְאֵין בָּא:
וַיְהִי יְהוָה אֶת־יְהוֹשֻׁעַ וַיְהִי שָׁמְעוֹ בְּכָל־הָאָרֶץ:

The Talmud (*Eruvin* 63b) comments that the drawn sworn sword indicates Divine displeasure. The angel reproached Joshua for having interrupted the Torah study of the people in order to prepare the siege of Jericho.

ויאמר לא . . . — *And he said, 'No . . .'* The angel said that it was not as Joshua feared, that the angel had come to oppose Israel, but to the contrary — he had come to lead them in battle.

SECOND DAY

אֲשֶׁר הַנָּשִׁים אֹרְגוֹת שָׁם בָּתִּים לָאֲשֵׁרָה: וַיָּבֵא אֶת־כָּל־הַכֹּהֲנִים
מֵעָרֵי יְהוּדָה וַיְטַמֵּא אֶת־הַבָּמוֹת אֲשֶׁר קִטְּרוּ־שָׁמָּה הַכֹּהֲנִים
מִגֶּבַע עַד־בְּאֵר שָׁבַע וְנָתַץ אֶת־בָּמוֹת הַשְּׁעָרִים אֲשֶׁר־פֶּתַח
שַׁעַר יְהוֹשֻׁעַ שַׂר־הָעִיר אֲשֶׁר־עַל־שְׂמֹאול אִישׁ בְּשַׁעַר הָעִיר:
אַךְ לֹא יַעֲלוּ כֹּהֲנֵי הַבָּמוֹת* אֶל־מִזְבַּח יְהוָה בִּירוּשָׁלָם כִּי
אִם־אָכְלוּ מַצּוֹת בְּתוֹךְ אֲחֵיהֶם:
וַיְצַו הַמֶּלֶךְ אֶת־כָּל־הָעָם לֵאמֹר עֲשׂוּ פֶסַח לַיהוָה אֱלֹהֵיכֶם
כַּכָּתוּב עַל סֵפֶר הַבְּרִית הַזֶּה: כִּי לֹא נַעֲשָׂה כַּפֶּסַח הַזֶּה מִימֵי
הַשֹּׁפְטִים אֲשֶׁר שָׁפְטוּ אֶת־יִשְׂרָאֵל וְכֹל יְמֵי מַלְכֵי יִשְׂרָאֵל וּמַלְכֵי
יְהוּדָה: כִּי אִם־בִּשְׁמֹנֶה עֶשְׂרֵה שָׁנָה לַמֶּלֶךְ יֹאשִׁיָּהוּ נַעֲשָׂה הַפֶּסַח
הַזֶּה לַיהוָה בִּירוּשָׁלָם: וְגַם אֶת־הָאֹבוֹת וְאֶת־הַיִּדְּעֹנִים וְאֶת־
הַתְּרָפִים וְאֶת־הַגִּלֻּלִים וְאֵת כָּל־הַשִּׁקֻּצִים אֲשֶׁר נִרְאוּ בְּאֶרֶץ
יְהוּדָה וּבִירוּשָׁלַם בִּעֵר יֹאשִׁיָּהוּ לְמַעַן הָקִים אֶת־דִּבְרֵי הַתּוֹרָה
הַכְּתֻבִים עַל־הַסֵּפֶר אֲשֶׁר מָצָא חִלְקִיָּהוּ הַכֹּהֵן בֵּית יְהוָה: וְכָמֹהוּ
לֹא־הָיָה לְפָנָיו מֶלֶךְ אֲשֶׁר־שָׁב אֶל־יְהוָה בְּכָל־לְבָבוֹ וּבְכָל־נַפְשׁוֹ
וּבְכָל־מְאֹדוֹ כְּכֹל תּוֹרַת מֹשֶׁה וְאַחֲרָיו לֹא־קָם כָּמֹהוּ:

FIRST DAY

It was when Joshua was in Jericho that he lifted up his eyes and saw, and behold! A man was standing opposite him with his sword drawn in his hand. Joshua went to him and said to him, 'Are you for us or for our enemies?'

And he said, 'No, I am the commander of the Host of HASHEM*; now I have come.'*

Joshua fell before him to the ground and prostrated himself and said to him, 'What does my lord say to his servant?'

And the commander of HASHEM*'s Host said to Joshua, 'Remove your shoe from your foot, for the place upon which you stand is holy.' And Joshua did so.*

Jericho had closed its gates and was barred because of the Children of Israel; no one could leave or enter.

And HASHEM *was with Joshua, and his renown traversed the land.*

SECOND DAY

where the women used to weave draperies for the Asherah.

He brought all the Kohanim from the cities of Judah and he defiled the high places where the priests used to burn offerings, from Geba to Beer Sheba, and he smashed the high places at the gates that were at the entrance of the gate of Joshua, the governor of the city, which were at a man's left at the gate of the city. But the priests of the high places were not permitted to ascend upon the Altar of* HASHEM *in Jerusalem, they were only permitted to eat matzos among their brethren.*

The king commanded the entire nation, saying: 'Bring the pesach-offering to HASHEM*, your God, as it is written in this Book of the Covenant.' For such a pesach offering had not been offered since the days of the Judges* who judged Israel, and all the days of the kings of Israel and the kings of Judah. But in the eighteenth year of King Josiah this pesach was offered to* HASHEM *in Jerusalem. Also Josiah removed the sorcery-objects of Ov, Yid'oni, and the teraphim, the filth-idols, and the abominations that had been seen in the land of Judah and Jerusalem, in order to establish the words of the Torah that were written in the Book that Hilkiah the Kohen found in the House of* HASHEM.

Before him there had never been a king who returned to HASHEM *with all his heart, with all his soul, and with all his resources, according to the entire Torah of Moses, and after him, no one arose like him.*

---

women would weave draperies and the like for use in the shrines of the idols. *Rashi*, however, renders *the rooms of the male prostitutes*.

כֹּהֲנֵי הַבָּמוֹת — *The priests of the high places.* There were priests of the idols who were Kohanim by birth. Josiah did not permit them to perform the Divine service in the Temple, even though they seemed to have repented. However, as the verse concludes, he did permit them to receive portions from the matzos of meal-offerings that were distributed to the Kohanim.

ברכות לאחר ההפטרה

After the *Haftarah* is read, the *oleh* recites the following blessings.

בָּרוּךְ אַתָּה יהוה אֱלֹהֵינוּ מֶלֶךְ הָעוֹלָם, צוּר כָּל הָעוֹלָמִים,* צַדִּיק בְּכָל הַדּוֹרוֹת,* הָאֵל הַנֶּאֱמָן הָאוֹמֵר וְעֹשֶׂה, הַמְּדַבֵּר וּמְקַיֵּם,* שֶׁכָּל דְּבָרָיו אֱמֶת וָצֶדֶק.* נֶאֱמָן* אַתָּה הוּא יהוה אֱלֹהֵינוּ, וְנֶאֱמָנִים דְּבָרֶיךָ, וְדָבָר אֶחָד מִדְּבָרֶיךָ אָחוֹר לֹא יָשׁוּב רֵיקָם, כִּי אֵל מֶלֶךְ נֶאֱמָן (וְרַחֲמָן) אָתָּה. בָּרוּךְ אַתָּה יהוה, הָאֵל הַנֶּאֱמָן בְּכָל דְּבָרָיו. (Cong.– אָמֵן.)

רַחֵם עַל צִיּוֹן כִּי הִיא בֵּית חַיֵּינוּ, וְלַעֲלוּבַת נֶפֶשׁ תּוֹשִׁיעַ בִּמְהֵרָה בְיָמֵינוּ. בָּרוּךְ אַתָּה יהוה, מְשַׂמֵּחַ צִיּוֹן בְּבָנֶיהָ. (Cong.– אָמֵן.)

שַׂמְּחֵנוּ יהוה אֱלֹהֵינוּ בְּאֵלִיָּהוּ הַנָּבִיא עַבְדֶּךָ, וּבְמַלְכוּת בֵּית דָּוִד* מְשִׁיחֶךָ, בִּמְהֵרָה יָבֹא וְיָגֵל לִבֵּנוּ, עַל כִּסְאוֹ לֹא יֵשֶׁב זָר וְלֹא יִנְחֲלוּ עוֹד אֲחֵרִים אֶת כְּבוֹדוֹ, כִּי בְשֵׁם קָדְשְׁךָ נִשְׁבַּעְתָּ לּוֹ, שֶׁלֹּא יִכְבֶּה נֵרוֹ לְעוֹלָם וָעֶד. בָּרוּךְ אַתָּה יהוה, מָגֵן דָּוִד.* (Cong.– אָמֵן.)

[On the Sabbath add the words in brackets.]

עַל הַתּוֹרָה,* וְעַל הָעֲבוֹדָה, וְעַל הַנְּבִיאִים, וְעַל יוֹם [הַשַּׁבָּת הַזֶּה, וְיוֹם] חַג הַמַּצּוֹת הַזֶּה שֶׁנָּתַתָּ לָּנוּ יהוה אֱלֹהֵינוּ, [לִקְדֻשָּׁה וְלִמְנוּחָה,] לְשָׂשׂוֹן וּלְשִׂמְחָה, לְכָבוֹד וּלְתִפְאָרֶת.* עַל הַכֹּל יהוה אֱלֹהֵינוּ, אֲנַחְנוּ מוֹדִים לָךְ, וּמְבָרְכִים אוֹתָךְ, יִתְבָּרַךְ שִׁמְךָ בְּפִי כָּל חַי תָּמִיד לְעוֹלָם וָעֶד. בָּרוּךְ אַתָּה יהוה, מְקַדֵּשׁ [הַשַּׁבָּת וְ]יִשְׂרָאֵל וְהַזְּמַנִּים. (Cong.– אָמֵן.)

ON WEEKDAYS THE SERVICE CONTINUES ON PAGE 394;
ON THE SABBATH, PAGE 392.

☙ Blessings after the Haftarah

צוּר כָּל הָעוֹלָמִים — *Rock of all eternities.* In its simple meaning this term describes God as all-powerful throughout the ages; therefore, only He is worthy of our trust. Nothing diminishes His power and nothing changes His sense of justice, fairness, and mercy. The *Zohar* interprets צוּר as צַיָּר, *Molder.* Thus, the term describes God as the One Who created and fashioned all the worlds and all ages. Both interpretations are especially apt with reference to the words of the prophets which we have read in the *Haftarah.* Because God is eternal, strong, and able to mold creation to suit His goal, we should have absolute faith in the prophecies He has communicated to us. This faith in the absolute truth and constancy of God's word is the theme of the first blessing.

צַדִּיק בְּכָל הַדּוֹרוֹת — *Righteous in all generations.* Whether a generation enjoys good fortune or suffers tragic oppression, God is righteous and His judgments are justified.

הַמְּדַבֵּר וּמְקַיֵּם — *Who speaks and fulfills.* The allusion of speaking is to prophecy, by means of which God speaks to the prophets.

אֱמֶת וָצֶדֶק — *True and righteous.* The universe was established on God's commitment to *truth*

BLESSINGS AFTER THE HAFTARAH

After the *Haftarah* is read, the *oleh* recites the following blessings.

בָּרוּךְ *Blessed are You, HASHEM, King of the universe, Rock of all eternities,* Righteous in all generations,* the trustworthy God, Who says and does, Who speaks and fulfills,* all of Whose words are true and righteous.* Trustworthy* are You, HASHEM, our God, and trustworthy are Your words, not one of Your words is turned back to its origin unfulfilled, for You are God, trustworthy (and compassionate) King. Blessed are You, HASHEM, the God Who is trustworthy in all His words.*

(Cong.– *Amen.*)

רַחֵם *Have mercy on Zion for it is the source of our life; to the one who is deeply humiliated bring salvation speedily, in our days. Blessed are You, HASHEM, Who gladdens Zion through her children.*

(Cong.– *Amen.*)

שַׂמְּחֵנוּ *Gladden us, HASHEM, our God, with Elijah the prophet, Your servant, and with the kingdom of the House of David,* Your anointed, may he come speedily and cause our heart to exult. On his throne let no stranger sit nor let others continue to inherit his honor, for by Your holy Name You swore to him that his heir will not be extinguished forever and ever. Blessed are You, HASHEM, Shield of David.**

(Cong.– *Amen.*)

[On the Sabbath add the words in brackets.]

עַל הַתּוֹרָה *For the Torah reading,* for the prayer service, for the reading from the Prophets [for this Sabbath day] and for this day of the Festival of Matzos that You, HASHEM, our God, have given us [for holiness and contentment,] for gladness and joy, for glory and splendor* — for all this, HASHEM, our God, we gratefully thank You and bless You. May Your Name be blessed by the mouth of all the living, always, for all eternity. Blessed are You, HASHEM, Who sanctifies [the Sabbath,] Israel and the festival seasons.* (Cong.– *Amen.*)

ON WEEKDAYS THE SERVICE CONTINUES ON PAGE 394;
ON THE SABBATH, PAGE 392.

---

and *righteousness.* Truth is the seal of God (*Shabbos* 55a), the theme underlying His guidance and control of the world. His truth endures because all those who violate it are brought to righteous judgment.

נֶאֱמָן – *Trustworthy.* Although in most *siddurim* this appears as a new paragraph, it does not begin a new blessing. Rather, in ancient times congregations would insert optional praises at this point (*Abudraham; Machzor Vitry*).

בְּאֵלִיָּהוּ ... בֵּית דָּוִד – *With Elijah ... the House of David.* The prophets teach that the prophet Elijah will appear to the Jewish people before the coming of the Messiah to announce that redemption is imminent. Since the Messiah will be descended from David and will restore the Davidic dynasty to the throne of the Jewish people — its first undisputed reign since the days of Solomon — this blessing relates Elijah with the House of David.

מָגֵן דָּוִד – *Shield of David.* In *II Samuel* (22:36) and *Psalms* (18:36), David praised God for shielding him against defeat.

עַל הַתּוֹרָה – *For the Torah [reading].* This final blessing sums up the entire service: not only the reading from the Prophets, but also the Torah reading, the prayers and the holiness of the Sabbath or Festival day.

וּלְתִפְאָרֶת – *And [for] splendor.* In Kabbalistic terminology, *splendor* refers to the perfect blend of truth and justice, kindness and strength.

יקום פרקן

On the Sabbath the following is recited. One praying alone omits the last two paragraphs.

יְקוּם פֻּרְקָן* מִן שְׁמַיָּא, חִנָּא וְחִסְדָּא וְרַחֲמֵי, וְחַיֵּי אֲרִיכֵי, וּמְזוֹנֵי רְוִיחֵי, וְסִיַּעְתָּא דִשְׁמַיָּא, וּבַרְיוּת גּוּפָא, וּנְהוֹרָא מַעַלְיָא, זַרְעָא חַיָּא וְקַיָּמָא, זַרְעָא דִּי לָא יִפְסוּק וְדִי לָא יִבְטוּל מִפִּתְגָּמֵי אוֹרַיְתָא. לְמָרָנָן וְרַבָּנָן חֲבוּרָתָא קַדִּישָׁתָא דִּי בְאַרְעָא דְיִשְׂרָאֵל וְדִי בְבָבֶל,* לְרֵישֵׁי כַלֵּי,* וּלְרֵישֵׁי גַלְוָתָא,* וּלְרֵישֵׁי מְתִיבָתָא, וּלְדַיָּנֵי דִי בָבָא, לְכָל תַּלְמִידֵיהוֹן, וּלְכָל תַּלְמִידֵי תַלְמִידֵיהוֹן, וּלְכָל מָן דְּעָסְקִין בְּאוֹרַיְתָא. מַלְכָּא דְעָלְמָא יְבָרֵךְ יַתְהוֹן, יַפִּישׁ חַיֵּיהוֹן, וְיַסְגֵּא יוֹמֵיהוֹן, וְיִתֵּן אַרְכָה לִשְׁנֵיהוֹן, וְיִתְפָּרְקוּן וְיִשְׁתֵּזְבוּן מִן כָּל עָקָא וּמִן כָּל מַרְעִין בִּישִׁין. מָרַן דִּי בִשְׁמַיָּא יְהֵא בְסַעְדְּהוֹן, כָּל זְמַן וְעִדָּן. וְנֹאמַר: אָמֵן.

(.אָמֵן –Cong.)

יְקוּם פֻּרְקָן* מִן שְׁמַיָּא, חִנָּא וְחִסְדָּא וְרַחֲמֵי, וְחַיֵּי אֲרִיכֵי, וּמְזוֹנֵי רְוִיחֵי, וְסִיַּעְתָּא דִשְׁמַיָּא, וּבַרְיוּת גּוּפָא, וּנְהוֹרָא מַעַלְיָא, זַרְעָא חַיָּא וְקַיָּמָא, זַרְעָא דִּי לָא יִפְסוּק וְדִי לָא יִבְטוּל מִפִּתְגָּמֵי אוֹרַיְתָא. לְכָל קְהָלָא קַדִּישָׁא הָדֵין, רַבְרְבַיָּא עִם זְעֵרַיָּא, טַפְלָא וּנְשַׁיָּא, מַלְכָּא דְעָלְמָא יְבָרֵךְ יַתְכוֹן, יַפִּישׁ חַיֵּיכוֹן, וְיַסְגֵּא יוֹמֵיכוֹן, וְיִתֵּן אַרְכָה לִשְׁנֵיכוֹן, וְתִתְפָּרְקוּן וְתִשְׁתֵּזְבוּן מִן כָּל עָקָא וּמִן כָּל מַרְעִין בִּישִׁין, מָרַן דִּי בִשְׁמַיָּא יְהֵא בְסַעְדְּכוֹן, כָּל זְמַן וְעִדָּן. וְנֹאמַר: אָמֵן. (.אָמֵן –Cong.)

מִי שֶׁבֵּרַךְ* אֲבוֹתֵינוּ אַבְרָהָם יִצְחָק וְיַעֲקֹב, הוּא יְבָרֵךְ אֶת כָּל הַקָּהָל הַקָּדוֹשׁ הַזֶּה, עִם כָּל קְהִלּוֹת הַקֹּדֶשׁ, הֵם, וּנְשֵׁיהֶם, וּבְנֵיהֶם, וּבְנוֹתֵיהֶם, וְכָל אֲשֶׁר לָהֶם. וּמִי שֶׁמְּיַחֲדִים בָּתֵּי כְנֵסִיּוֹת לִתְפִלָּה, וּמִי שֶׁבָּאִים בְּתוֹכָם לְהִתְפַּלֵּל, וּמִי שֶׁנּוֹתְנִים נֵר לַמָּאוֹר, וְיַיִן לְקִדּוּשׁ וּלְהַבְדָּלָה, וּפַת לָאוֹרְחִים, וּצְדָקָה לָעֲנִיִּים, וְכָל מִי שֶׁעוֹסְקִים בְּצָרְכֵי צִבּוּר בֶּאֱמוּנָה, הַקָּדוֹשׁ בָּרוּךְ הוּא יְשַׁלֵּם שְׂכָרָם, וְיָסִיר מֵהֶם כָּל מַחֲלָה, וְיִרְפָּא לְכָל גּוּפָם, וְיִסְלַח לְכָל עֲוֹנָם, וְיִשְׁלַח בְּרָכָה וְהַצְלָחָה בְּכָל מַעֲשֵׂה יְדֵיהֶם, עִם כָּל יִשְׂרָאֵל אֲחֵיהֶם. וְנֹאמַר: אָמֵן.

(.אָמֵן –Cong.)

In many congregations, a prayer for the welfare of the State is recited by the Rabbi, *chazzan*, or *gabbai* at this point.

יְקוּם פֻּרְקָן — *May salvation arise.* After reading from the Torah, a series of prayers is recited for those who teach, study, and support the Torah, and undertake the responsibilities of leadership. The first is a general prayer for all such people wherever they may be; consequently, it is recited even by people praying without a *minyan.* The second and third are prayers for the congregation with which one is praying; consequently, one praying alone omits them. The two יְקוּם פֻּרְקָן prayers were composed by the Babylonian *geonim* after the close of the Talmudic period, in Aramaic, the spoken language of that country. These prayers were instituted specifically for the Sabbath, not for Festivals, except those that fall on the Sabbath.

דִּי בְאַרְעָא דְיִשְׂרָאֵל וְדִי בְבָבֶל — *That are in Eretz Yisrael and that are in the Diaspora* [lit., *Babylonia].* Although the Jewish community in *Eretz Yisrael* at that time was comparatively insignificant, the *geonim* gave honor and precedence to the Holy Land. Although the great

YEKUM PURKAN

On the Sabbath the following is recited. One praying alone omits the last two paragraphs.

יְקוּם פֻּרְקָן *May salvation arise* from heaven — grace, kindness, compassion, long life, abundant sustenance, heavenly assistance, physical health, lofty vision, living and surviving offspring, offspring who will neither interrupt nor cease from words of the Torah — for our masters and sages, the holy fellowships that are in Eretz Yisrael and that are in the Diaspora*: for the leaders of the Torah assemblages,* the leaders of the exile communities,* the leaders of the academies, the judges at the gateways, and all their students and to all the students of their students, and to everyone who engages in Torah study. May the King of the universe bless them, make their lives fruitful, increase their days and grant length to their years. May He save them and rescue them from every distress and from all serious ailments. May the Master in heaven come to their assistance at every season and time. Now let us respond: Amen.* (Cong.—*Amen.*)

יְקוּם פֻּרְקָן *May salvation arise* from heaven — grace, kindness, compassion, long life, abundant sustenance, heavenly assistance, physical health, lofty vision, living and surviving offspring, offspring who will neither interrupt nor cease from the words of the Torah — to this entire holy congregation, adults along with children, infants and women. May the King of the universe bless you, make your lives fruitful, increase your days, and grant length to your years. May He save you and rescue you from every distress and from all serious ailments. May the Master in heaven come to your assistance at every season and time. Now let us respond: Amen.* (Cong.—*Amen.*)

מִי שֶׁבֵּרַךְ *He Who blessed* our forefathers, Abraham, Isaac, and Jacob — may He bless this entire holy congregation along with all the holy congregations; them, their wives, sons, and daughters and all that is theirs; and those who dedicate synagogues for prayer and those who enter them to pray, and those who give lamps for illumination and wine for Kiddush and Havdalah, bread for guests and charity for the poor; and all who are involved faithfully in the needs of the community — may the Holy One, Blessed is He, pay their reward and remove from them every affliction, heal their entire body and forgive their every iniquity, and send blessing and success to all their handiwork, along with all Israel, their brethren. And let us say: Amen.* (Cong.—*Amen.*)

In many congregations, a prayer for the welfare of the State is recited by the Rabbi, *chazzan,* or *gabbai* at this point.

---

masses of Jewry no longer live in Babylonia, this timeless prayer refers to all Jewish communities; the word Babylonia is used as a general term for all Jewish communities outside of *Eretz Yisrael.*

לְרֵישֵׁי כַלֵּי — *For the leaders of the Torah assemblages.* These were the scholars who deliver Torah lectures on the Sabbath and Festivals to mass gatherings of the people.

וּלְרֵישֵׁי גַלְוָתָא — *The leaders of the exile communities.* The רֵישׁ גָּלוּתָא, *Exilarch,* was the leader of the Jewish nation, equivalent to the *Nassi* in earlier times. His headquarters was in Babylonia.

יְקוּם פֻּרְקָן — *May salvation arise.* This prayer refers to the congregation with which one is praying. Thus it omits mention of national teachers and leaders. It includes the entire congregation, young and old, men and women, because it prays for the welfare of each one.

מִי שֶׁבֵּרַךְ — *He Who blessed.* This is a prayer for this and all other congregations, and singles out the people who provide the means and services for the general good. *Bais Yosef* (284) notes that these charitable causes are stressed so that the entire community will hear of the great reward of those who study and support Torah, and others will emulate their deeds.

יה אלי

Chazzan:

יָהּ אֵלִי* וְגוֹאֲלִי אֶתְיַצְּבָה לִקְרָאתֶךָ, הָיָה וְיִהְיֶה,* הָיָה וְהֹוֶה, כָּל גּוֹי אַדְמָתֶךָ.* וְתוֹדָה,* וְלָעוֹלָה, וְלַמִּנְחָה, וְלַחַטָּאת, וְלָאָשָׁם, וְלַשְּׁלָמִים, וְלַמִּלּוּאִים כָּל קָרְבָּנֶךָ. זְכוֹר נִלְאָה* אֲשֶׁר נָשְׂאָה וְהָשִׁיבָהּ לְאַדְמָתֶךָ. סֶלָה אֲהַלְלֶךָּ,* בְּאַשְׁרֵי יוֹשְׁבֵי בֵיתֶךָ.

דַּק עַל דַּק,* עַד אֵין נִבְדַּק, וְלִתְבוּנָתוֹ אֵין חֵקֶר. הָאֵל נוֹרָא, בְּאַחַת סְקִירָה,* בֵּין טוֹב לָרַע יְבַקֵּר. וְתוֹדָה, וְלָעוֹלָה, וְלַמִּנְחָה, וְלַחַטָּאת, וְלָאָשָׁם, וְלַשְּׁלָמִים, וְלַמִּלּוּאִים כָּל קָרְבָּנֶךָ. זְכוֹר נִלְאָה אֲשֶׁר נָשְׂאָה וְהָשִׁיבָהּ לְאַדְמָתֶךָ. סֶלָה אֲהַלְלֶךָּ, בְּאַשְׁרֵי יוֹשְׁבֵי בֵיתֶךָ.

אָדוֹן צְבָאוֹת,* בְּרוֹב פְּלָאוֹת, חִבֵּר כָּל אָהֳלוֹ. בִּנְתִיבוֹת לֵב לְבְלֵב, הַצּוּר תָּמִים פָּעֳלוֹ. וְתוֹדָה, וְלָעוֹלָה, וְלַמִּנְחָה, וְלַחַטָּאת, וְלָאָשָׁם, וְלַשְּׁלָמִים, וְלַמִּלּוּאִים כָּל קָרְבָּנֶךָ. זְכוֹר נִלְאָה אֲשֶׁר נָשְׂאָה וְהָשִׁיבָהּ לְאַדְמָתֶךָ. סֶלָה אֲהַלְלֶךָּ, בְּאַשְׁרֵי יוֹשְׁבֵי בֵיתֶךָ.

יָהּ אֵלִי — *O God, my God.* Since *Ashrei* is one of the most prominent of all the psalms (see p. 8), its recitation before the Festival *Mussaf* is introduced with a joyous prayer that longs for the opportunity to sing it before God in the rebuilt Temple, along with the order of sacrificial offerings. This is in keeping with the literal meaning of אַשְׁרֵי יוֹשְׁבֵי בֵיתֶךָ, *Praiseworthy are those who dwell in Your house.* Although, in the *Siddur*, God's 'house' has the broad meaning of the synagogue or any other place where one can serve God, it also refers specifically to the Temple, where the *Kohanim* and Levites have the good fortune to serve God (*Radak* and *Ibn Ezra* to *Psalms* 84:5). The spiritual elevation of the Festival, especially before *Mussaf* when we are about to cite the unique offering of the Festival, is a logical time for this prayer that combines joy in the Temple service and longing that we will soon be able to perform it in actuality as well as in aspiration. In view of the somber nature of *Yizkor*, this *piyut* is omitted on *Yizkor* days.

הָיָה וְיִהְיֶה — *Who was and Who will be.* God's Four-letter Name contains the letters that form the words indicating past, present, and future. Thus, this Name represents Him as the One Who creates and controls history — and Who will sooner or later return our service to the Temple.

כָּל גּוֹי אַדְמָתֶךָ — *With the entire nation on Your soil.* May all Israel be united in *Eretz Yisrael*, there to praise and thank God by offering all the prescribed offerings listed below.

וְתוֹדָה — *And the thanksgiving-offering.* We ask for the privilege of being in the Temple on God's soil so that we may bring Him all the offerings mentioned in the Torah.

The order of the offerings is difficult since the thanksgiving offering has less holiness than the next four on the list. Also, the meal offering consists of flour and oil, yet it is inserted between the animal offerings. Perhaps the order can be explained this way: first comes the thanksgiving offering because the very fact that we will have

PRE-MUSSAF PIYUT

Chazzan:

יָהּ אֵלִי *O God, my God* and Redeemer, I shall stand to greet You — Who was and Who will be,* Who was and Who is — with the entire nation on Your soil;* and the thanksgiving-,* elevation-, meal-, sin-, guilt-, peace-, and inauguration-offerings — Your every offering. Remember the exhausted [nation]* that won [Your favor], and return her to Your soil. Eternally will I laud You,* saying, 'Praiseworthy are those who dwell in Your House.'*

דַּק *Painstakingly exact,* beyond calculation — to His intelligence there is no limit. The awesome God — with a single stripe,* He differentiates the good from bad. And the thanksgiving-, elevation-, meal-, sin-, guilt-, peace-, and inauguration-offerings — Your every offering. Remember the exhausted [nation] that won [Your favor], and return her to Your soil. Eternally will I laud You, saying, 'Praiseworthy are those who dwell in Your House.'*

אֲדוֹן *The Lord of Legions,* with abundant miracles He connected His entire Tabernacle; in the paths of the heart may it blossom — the Rock, His work is perfect! And the thanksgiving-, elevation-, meal-, sin-, guilt-, peace-, and inauguration-offerings — Your every offering. Remember the exhausted [nation] that won [Your favor], and return her to Your soil. Eternally will I laud You, saying, 'Praiseworthy are those who dwell in Your House.'*

---

been returned to *Eretz Yisrael* and the rebuilt Temple will be cause for an enormous sense of thanksgiving. The elevation offering, which is consumed entirely on the altar, represents Israel's longing for elevation in God's service and dedication to Him; thus it takes precedence over offerings that come to atone for sin. Of the meal offering, the Sages derive from Scripture (see *Rashi, Leviticus* 2:1) that God heaps particular praise upon a poor man who can afford no more than a bit of flour and oil, yet wishes to bring an offering to express His dedication to God. The sin and guilt offerings are of greater holiness than the peace offering. The inauguration offerings are mentioned last because they will be offered only once — when the Temple is dedicated — and then will never be needed, because the Third Temple will be eternal.

זְכוֹר נִלְאָה — *Remember the exhausted [nation].* Israel has been exhausted by long exile and much travail, but she won God's favor long ago and therefore longs for her return from exile.

סֶלָה אֲהַלְלֶךָ — *Eternally will I laud You.* This verse is a rearrangement of the first verse of *Ashrei*. It expresses our resolve to praise God by declaring our pride at being able to serve Him.

דַּק עַל דַּק — *Painstakingly exact.* This verse and the next describe the inscrutable greatness of God's awesome judgment.

בְּאַחַת סְקִירָה — *With a single stripe.* This phrase is based on the Talmudic expression that on the Day of Judgment, 'All who walk the earth pass before Him כִּבְנֵי מָרוֹן, *like young sheep' (Rosh Hashanah* 16a, 18a). When sheep were tithed, they were released one by one through a small opening in a corral. Each tenth one was marked with a single stripe, identifying it as a tithe animal that would become an Altar offering. In the context of this prayer, it refers to God differentiating between the sinful and the righteous.

צְבָאוֹת — *Legions.* God's Legions are the entire host of the universe's components. He weaves them together to create the complex harmony of Creation. We pray that realization of His greatness will blossom in our hearts so that we will recognize His greatness and be worthy to serve Him in the rebuilt Temple.

אַשְׁרֵי יוֹשְׁבֵי בֵיתֶךָ, עוֹד יְהַלְּלְוּךָ סֶּלָה.[1] אַשְׁרֵי הָעָם שֶׁכָּכָה לּוֹ,
אַשְׁרֵי הָעָם שֶׁיהוה אֱלֹהָיו.[2]

תהלים קמה

תְּהִלָּה לְדָוִד,

אֲרוֹמִמְךָ אֱלוֹהַי הַמֶּלֶךְ, וַאֲבָרְכָה שִׁמְךָ לְעוֹלָם וָעֶד.
בְּכָל יוֹם אֲבָרְכֶךָּ, וַאֲהַלְלָה שִׁמְךָ לְעוֹלָם וָעֶד.
גָּדוֹל יהוה וּמְהֻלָּל מְאֹד, וְלִגְדֻלָּתוֹ אֵין חֵקֶר.
דּוֹר לְדוֹר יְשַׁבַּח מַעֲשֶׂיךָ, וּגְבוּרֹתֶיךָ יַגִּידוּ.
הֲדַר כְּבוֹד הוֹדֶךָ, וְדִבְרֵי נִפְלְאוֹתֶיךָ אָשִׂיחָה.
וֶעֱזוּז נוֹרְאוֹתֶיךָ יֹאמֵרוּ, וּגְדוּלָּתְךָ אֲסַפְּרֶנָּה.
זֵכֶר רַב טוּבְךָ יַבִּיעוּ, וְצִדְקָתְךָ יְרַנֵּנוּ.
חַנּוּן וְרַחוּם יהוה, אֶרֶךְ אַפַּיִם וּגְדָל חָסֶד.
טוֹב יהוה לַכֹּל, וְרַחֲמָיו עַל כָּל מַעֲשָׂיו.
יוֹדְוּךָ יהוה כָּל מַעֲשֶׂיךָ, וַחֲסִידֶיךָ יְבָרְכוּכָה.
כְּבוֹד מַלְכוּתְךָ יֹאמֵרוּ, וּגְבוּרָתְךָ יְדַבֵּרוּ.
לְהוֹדִיעַ לִבְנֵי הָאָדָם גְּבוּרֹתָיו, וּכְבוֹד הֲדַר מַלְכוּתוֹ.
מַלְכוּתְךָ מַלְכוּת כָּל עֹלָמִים, וּמֶמְשַׁלְתְּךָ בְּכָל דּוֹר וָדֹר.
סוֹמֵךְ יהוה לְכָל הַנֹּפְלִים, וְזוֹקֵף לְכָל הַכְּפוּפִים.
עֵינֵי כֹל אֵלֶיךָ יְשַׂבֵּרוּ, וְאַתָּה נוֹתֵן לָהֶם אֶת אָכְלָם בְּעִתּוֹ.
פּוֹתֵחַ אֶת יָדֶךָ,
וּמַשְׂבִּיעַ לְכָל חַי רָצוֹן.

While reciting the verse פּוֹתֵחַ, concentrate intently on its meaning.

צַדִּיק יהוה בְּכָל דְּרָכָיו, וְחָסִיד בְּכָל מַעֲשָׂיו.
קָרוֹב יהוה לְכָל קֹרְאָיו, לְכֹל אֲשֶׁר יִקְרָאֻהוּ בֶאֱמֶת.
רְצוֹן יְרֵאָיו יַעֲשֶׂה, וְאֶת שַׁוְעָתָם יִשְׁמַע וְיוֹשִׁיעֵם.
שׁוֹמֵר יהוה אֶת כָּל אֹהֲבָיו, וְאֵת כָּל הָרְשָׁעִים יַשְׁמִיד.
❖ תְּהִלַּת יהוה יְדַבֶּר פִּי,
וִיבָרֵךְ כָּל בָּשָׂר שֵׁם קָדְשׁוֹ לְעוֹלָם וָעֶד.
וַאֲנַחְנוּ נְבָרֵךְ יָהּ, מֵעַתָּה וְעַד עוֹלָם, הַלְלוּיָהּ.[3]

---

(1) ***Psalms*** **84:5. (2) 144:15. (3) 115:18.**

אַשְׁרֵי *Praiseworthy are those who dwell in Your house, may they always praise You, Selah![1] Praiseworthy is the people for whom this is so, praiseworthy is the people whose God is HASHEM.[2]*

Psalm 145

A psalm of praise by David:

א *I will exalt You, my God the King,*
and I will bless Your Name forever and ever.
ב *Every day I will bless You,*
and I will laud Your Name forever and ever.
ג *HASHEM is great and exceedingly lauded,*
and His greatness is beyond investigation.
ד *Each generation will praise Your deeds to the next*
and of Your mighty deeds they will tell;
ה *The splendrous glory of Your power*
and Your wondrous deeds I shall discuss.
ו *And of Your awesome power they will speak,*
and Your greatness I shall relate.
ז *A recollection of Your abundant goodness they will utter*
and of Your righteousness they will sing exultantly.
ח *Gracious and merciful is HASHEM,*
slow to anger, and great in [bestowing] kindness.
ט *HASHEM is good to all; His mercies are on all His works.*
י *All Your works shall thank You, HASHEM,*
and Your devout ones will bless You.
כ *Of the glory of Your kingdom they will speak,*
and of Your power they will tell;
ל *To inform human beings of His mighty deeds,*
and the glorious splendor of His kingdom.
מ *Your kingdom is a kingdom spanning all eternities,*
and Your dominion is throughout every generation.
ס *HASHEM supports all the fallen ones and straightens all the bent.*
ע *The eyes of all look to You with hope*
and You give them their food in its proper time;
פ *You open Your hand,* Concentrate intently while reciting the verse, *'You open...'*
and satisfy the desire of every living thing.
צ *Righteous is HASHEM in all His ways*
and magnanimous in all His deeds.
ק *HASHEM is close to all who call upon Him —*
to all who call upon Him sincerely.
ר *The will of those who fear Him He will do;*
and their cry He will hear, and save them.
ש *HASHEM protects all who love Him;*
but all the wicked He will destroy.
ת Chazzan– *May my mouth declare the praise of HASHEM*
and may all flesh bless His Holy Name forever and ever.

We will bless God from this time and forever, Halleluyah![3]

הכנסת ספר תורה

The *chazzan* takes the Torah in his right arm and recites:

יְהַלְּלוּ אֶת שֵׁם יהוה, כִּי נִשְׂגָּב שְׁמוֹ לְבַדּוֹ –

Congregation responds:

– הוֹדוֹ עַל אֶרֶץ וְשָׁמָיִם. וַיָּרֶם קֶרֶן לְעַמּוֹ, תְּהִלָּה לְכָל חֲסִידָיו, לִבְנֵי יִשְׂרָאֵל עַם קְרֹבוֹ, הַלְּלוּיָהּ.[1]

As the Torah is carried to the Ark the congregation recites the appropriate psalm.

ON A WEEKDAY:

תהלים כד

לְדָוִד מִזְמוֹר, לַיהוה הָאָרֶץ וּמְלוֹאָהּ, תֵּבֵל וְיֹשְׁבֵי בָהּ. כִּי הוּא עַל יַמִּים יְסָדָהּ, וְעַל נְהָרוֹת יְכוֹנְנֶהָ. מִי יַעֲלֶה בְהַר יהוה, וּמִי יָקוּם בִּמְקוֹם קָדְשׁוֹ. נְקִי כַפַּיִם וּבַר לֵבָב, אֲשֶׁר לֹא נָשָׂא לַשָּׁוְא נַפְשִׁי וְלֹא נִשְׁבַּע לְמִרְמָה. יִשָּׂא בְרָכָה מֵאֵת יהוה, וּצְדָקָה מֵאֱלֹהֵי יִשְׁעוֹ. זֶה דּוֹר דֹּרְשָׁיו, מְבַקְשֵׁי פָנֶיךָ, יַעֲקֹב, סֶלָה. שְׂאוּ שְׁעָרִים רָאשֵׁיכֶם, וְהִנָּשְׂאוּ פִּתְחֵי עוֹלָם, וְיָבוֹא מֶלֶךְ הַכָּבוֹד. מִי זֶה מֶלֶךְ הַכָּבוֹד, יהוה עִזּוּז וְגִבּוֹר, יהוה גִּבּוֹר מִלְחָמָה. שְׂאוּ שְׁעָרִים רָאשֵׁיכֶם, וּשְׂאוּ פִּתְחֵי עוֹלָם, וְיָבֹא מֶלֶךְ הַכָּבוֹד. מִי הוּא זֶה מֶלֶךְ הַכָּבוֹד, יהוה צְבָאוֹת הוּא מֶלֶךְ הַכָּבוֹד, סֶלָה.

ON THE SABBATH:

תהלים כט

מִזְמוֹר לְדָוִד, הָבוּ לַיהוה בְּנֵי אֵלִים, הָבוּ לַיהוה כָּבוֹד וָעֹז. הָבוּ לַיהוה כְּבוֹד שְׁמוֹ, הִשְׁתַּחֲווּ לַיהוה בְּהַדְרַת קֹדֶשׁ. קוֹל יהוה עַל הַמָּיִם, אֵל הַכָּבוֹד הִרְעִים, יהוה עַל מַיִם רַבִּים. קוֹל יהוה בַּכֹּחַ, קוֹל יהוה בֶּהָדָר. קוֹל יהוה שֹׁבֵר אֲרָזִים, וַיְשַׁבֵּר יהוה אֶת אַרְזֵי הַלְּבָנוֹן. וַיַּרְקִידֵם כְּמוֹ עֵגֶל, לְבָנוֹן וְשִׂרְיוֹן כְּמוֹ בֶן רְאֵמִים. קוֹל יהוה חֹצֵב לַהֲבוֹת אֵשׁ. קוֹל יהוה יָחִיל מִדְבָּר, יָחִיל יהוה מִדְבַּר קָדֵשׁ. קוֹל יהוה יְחוֹלֵל אַיָּלוֹת, וַיֶּחֱשֹׂף יְעָרוֹת, וּבְהֵיכָלוֹ, כֻּלּוֹ אֹמֵר כָּבוֹד. יהוה לַמַּבּוּל יָשָׁב, וַיֵּשֶׁב יהוה מֶלֶךְ לְעוֹלָם. יהוה עֹז לְעַמּוֹ יִתֵּן, יהוה יְבָרֵךְ אֶת עַמּוֹ בַשָּׁלוֹם.

לְדָוִד מִזְמוֹר / Psalm 24

This psalm is recited when the Torah is brought back to the Ark because its final verses: *Raise up your heads, O gates* ... were recited when King Solomon brought the Ark into the newly built Temple. Commentary to this psalm appears on pages 448-449.

מִזְמוֹר לְדָוִד / Psalm 29

Tur (284) points out that the phrase *the voice of* HASHEM appears seven times in Psalm 29. This seven-fold mention alludes to: (a) the heavenly voice heard at Mount Sinai during the Giving of the Torah; and (b) the seven blessings contained in the *[Mussaf] Shemoneh Esrei* of

RETURNING THE TORAH

The *chazzan* takes the Torah in his right arm and recites:

Let them praise the Name of HASHEM, for His Name alone will have been exalted —

Congregation responds:

— His glory is above earth and heaven. And He will have exalted the pride of His people, causing praise for all His devout ones, for the Children of Israel, His intimate people. Halleluyah![1]

As the Torah is carried to the Ark the congregation recites the appropriate psalm.

ON A WEEKDAY:

Psalm 24

לְדָוִד *Of David a psalm. HASHEM's is the earth and its fullness, the inhabited land and those who dwell in it. For He founded it upon seas, and established it upon rivers. Who may ascend the mountain of HASHEM, and who may stand in the place of His sanctity? One with clean hands and pure heart, who has not sworn in vain by My soul and has not sworn deceitfully. He will receive a blessing from HASHEM and just kindness from the God of his salvation. This is the generation of those who seek Him, those who strive for Your Presence — Jacob, Selah. Raise up your heads, O gates, and be uplifted, you everlasting entrances, so that the King of Glory may enter. Who is this King of Glory? — HASHEM, the mighty and strong, HASHEM, the strong in battle. Raise up your heads, O gates, and raise up, you everlasting entrances, so that the King of Glory may enter. Who then is the King of Glory? HASHEM, Master of Legions, He is the King of Glory. Selah!*

ON THE SABBATH:

Psalm 29

מִזְמוֹר *A psalm of David. Render unto HASHEM, you sons of the powerful; render unto HASHEM, honor and might. Render unto HASHEM the honor worthy of His Name, prostrate yourselves before HASHEM in His intensely holy place. The voice of HASHEM is upon the waters, the God of Glory thunders, HASHEM is upon vast waters. The voice of HASHEM is in power! The voice of HASHEM is in majesty! The voice of HASHEM breaks the cedars, HASHEM shatters the cedars of Lebanon! He makes them prance about like a calf; Lebanon and Siryon like young re'eimim. The voice of HASHEM carves with shafts of fire. The voice of HASHEM convulses the wilderness. HASHEM convulses the wilderness of Kadesh. The voice of HASHEM frightens the hinds, and strips the forests bare; while in His Temple all proclaim, 'Glory!' HASHEM sat enthroned at the Deluge; HASHEM sits enthroned as King forever. HASHEM will give might to His people, HASHEM will bless His people with peace.*

(1) 148:13-14.

---

the Sabbath. Thus, it is appropriate to recite this psalm at the time the Torah is returned to the Ark on the Sabbath just before the recitation of *Mussaf*.

As the Torah is placed into the Ark, the congregation recites the following verses:

וּבְנֻחֹה יֹאמַר,* שׁוּבָה יהוה רִבְבוֹת אַלְפֵי יִשְׂרָאֵל.[1] קוּמָה יהוה לִמְנוּחָתֶךָ, אַתָּה וַאֲרוֹן עֻזֶּךָ. כֹּהֲנֶיךָ יִלְבְּשׁוּ צֶדֶק, וַחֲסִידֶיךָ יְרַנֵּנוּ. בַּעֲבוּר דָּוִד עַבְדֶּךָ, אַל תָּשֵׁב פְּנֵי מְשִׁיחֶךָ.[2] כִּי לֶקַח טוֹב נָתַתִּי לָכֶם, תּוֹרָתִי אַל תַּעֲזֹבוּ.[3] ❖ עֵץ חַיִּים הִיא לַמַּחֲזִיקִים בָּהּ, וְתֹמְכֶיהָ מְאֻשָּׁר.[4] דְּרָכֶיהָ דַרְכֵי נֹעַם, וְכָל נְתִיבוֹתֶיהָ שָׁלוֹם.[5] הֲשִׁיבֵנוּ יהוה אֵלֶיךָ וְנָשׁוּבָה, חַדֵּשׁ יָמֵינוּ כְּקֶדֶם.[6]

The *chazzan* recites חֲצִי קַדִּישׁ.

יִתְגַּדַּל וְיִתְקַדַּשׁ שְׁמֵהּ רַבָּא. (.Cong – אָמֵן.) בְּעָלְמָא דִּי בְרָא כִרְעוּתֵהּ. וְיַמְלִיךְ מַלְכוּתֵהּ, בְּחַיֵּיכוֹן וּבְיוֹמֵיכוֹן וּבְחַיֵּי דְכָל בֵּית יִשְׂרָאֵל, בַּעֲגָלָא וּבִזְמַן קָרִיב. וְאִמְרוּ: אָמֵן.

(.Cong – אָמֵן. יְהֵא שְׁמֵהּ רַבָּא מְבָרַךְ לְעָלַם וּלְעָלְמֵי עָלְמַיָּא.)

יְהֵא שְׁמֵהּ רַבָּא מְבָרַךְ לְעָלַם וּלְעָלְמֵי עָלְמַיָּא.

יִתְבָּרַךְ וְיִשְׁתַּבַּח וְיִתְפָּאַר וְיִתְרוֹמַם וְיִתְנַשֵּׂא וְיִתְהַדָּר וְיִתְעַלֶּה וְיִתְהַלָּל שְׁמֵהּ דְּקֻדְשָׁא בְּרִיךְ הוּא (.Cong – בְּרִיךְ הוּא) – לְעֵלָּא מִן כָּל בִּרְכָתָא וְשִׁירָתָא תֻּשְׁבְּחָתָא וְנֶחֱמָתָא, דַּאֲמִירָן בְּעָלְמָא. וְאִמְרוּ: אָמֵן. (.Cong – אָמֵן.)

❦ מוסף לשני ימים הראשונים ❦

Take three steps backward, then three steps forward. Remain standing with the feet together while reciting *Shemoneh Esrei*. Recite it with quiet devotion and without interruption, verbal or otherwise. Although its recitation should not be audible to others, one must pray loudly enough to hear himself.

כִּי שֵׁם יהוה אֶקְרָא, הָבוּ גֹדֶל לֵאלֹהֵינוּ.[7]

אֲדֹנָי שְׂפָתַי תִּפְתָּח, וּפִי יַגִּיד תְּהִלָּתֶךָ.[8]

אבות

Bend the knees at בָּרוּךְ; bow at אַתָּה; straighten up at ה׳.

בָּרוּךְ אַתָּה יהוה אֱלֹהֵינוּ וֵאלֹהֵי אֲבוֹתֵינוּ, אֱלֹהֵי אַבְרָהָם, אֱלֹהֵי יִצְחָק, וֵאלֹהֵי יַעֲקֹב, הָאֵל הַגָּדוֹל הַגִּבּוֹר וְהַנּוֹרָא, אֵל עֶלְיוֹן, גּוֹמֵל חֲסָדִים טוֹבִים וְקוֹנֵה הַכֹּל, וְזוֹכֵר חַסְדֵי אָבוֹת, וּמֵבִיא גוֹאֵל לִבְנֵי בְנֵיהֶם, לְמַעַן שְׁמוֹ בְּאַהֲבָה. מֶלֶךְ עוֹזֵר וּמוֹשִׁיעַ וּמָגֵן.

Bend the knees at בָּרוּךְ; bow at אַתָּה; straighten up at ה׳.

בָּרוּךְ אַתָּה יהוה, מָגֵן אַבְרָהָם.

❧ **וּבְנֻחֹה יֹאמַר** — *And when it rested he would say*. This is the companion verse to וַיְהִי בִּנְסֹעַ הָאָרֹן, *When the Ark would travel*, above (p. 360), which Moses said when the Ark began to journey. When it came to rest, he expressed this hope that Israel should be worthy of being host to God's holiness.

❖ מוסף / MUSSAF ❖

Just as *Shacharis* and *Minchah* respectively correspond to the morning and afternoon continual offerings in the Temple, so does *Mussaf* correspond to the *mussaf*, or additional, offerings of the Festivals, Rosh Chodesh and the Sabbath. Thus, it is natural that these offerings be enumerated in the *Shemoneh Esrei* of *Mussaf*. This is especially true in view of the fact that the Festivals do not all have identical *mussaf* offerings. Moreover, the additional offerings of

As the Torah is placed into the Ark, the congregation recites the following verses:

ובנחה *And when it rested he would say,* 'Return, HASHEM, to the myriad thousands of Israel.'[1] Arise, HASHEM, to Your resting place, You and the Ark of Your strength. Let Your priests be clothed in righteousness, and Your devout ones will sing joyously. For the sake of David, Your servant, turn not away the face of Your anointed.[2] For I have given you a good teaching, do not forsake My Torah.[3]* Chazzan– *It is a tree of life for those who grasp it, and its supporters are praiseworthy.[4] Its ways are ways of pleasantness and all its paths are peace.[5] Bring us back to You, HASHEM, and we shall return, renew our days as of old.[6]*

The chazzan recites Half-*Kaddish:*

יִתְגַּדַּל *May His great Name grow exalted and sanctified* (Cong.– *Amen.*) *in the world that He created as He willed. May He give reign to His kingship in your lifetimes and in your days, and in the lifetimes of the entire Family of Israel, swiftly and soon. Now respond: Amen.*

(Cong.– *Amen. May His great Name be blessed forever and ever.*)

May His great Name be blessed forever and ever.

Blessed, praised, glorified, exalted, extolled, mighty, upraised, and lauded be the Name of the Holy One, Blessed is He (Cong.– *Blessed is He*) *— beyond any blessing and song, praise and consolation that are uttered in the world. Now respond: Amen.* (Cong.– *Amen.*)

MUSSAF FOR THE FIRST TWO DAYS

Take three steps backward, then three steps forward. Remain standing with the feet together while reciting *Shemoneh Esrei.* Recite it with quiet devotion and without interruption, verbal or otherwise. Although its recitation should not be audible to others, one must pray loudly enough to hear himself.

When I call out the Name of HASHEM, ascribe greatness to our God.[7]

My Lord, open my lips, that my mouth may declare Your praise.[8]

PATRIARCHS

Bend the knees at *'Blessed'*; bow at *'You'*; straighten up at *'HASHEM.'*

בָּרוּךְ *Blessed are You, HASHEM, our God and the God of our forefathers, God of Abraham, God of Isaac, and God of Jacob; the great, mighty, and awesome God, the supreme God, Who bestows beneficial kindnesses and creates everything, Who recalls the kindnesses of the Patriarchs and brings a Redeemer to their children's children, for His Name's sake, with love. O King, Helper, Savior, and Shield.*

Bend the knees at *'Blessed'*; bow at *'You'*; straighten up at *'HASHEM.'*

Blessed are You, HASHEM, Shield of Abraham.

(1) *Numbers* 10:36. (2) *Psalms* 132:8-10. (3) *Proverbs* 4:2. (4) 3:18. (5) 3:17. (6) *Lamentations* 5:21. (7) *Deuteronomy* 32:3. (8) *Psalms* 51:17.

Succos vary from day to day. This is because part of the Succos offerings symbolize the seventy primary nations of the world. Thus, thirteen bulls are offered on the first day of Succos; twelve on the second; and one less each day, until seven are offered on the last day, for a total of seventy bulls.

The necessity of enumerating the offerings of each day is the point of a halachic dispute between the *Rishonim* (medieval rabbinic authorities). In detailing the various offerings of each day, we follow the view of *Rabbeinu Tam* (*Rosh Hashanah* 35a). However, if one omitted the description of the offering, or recited the wrong day's offering, and has already completed the blessing . . . *Who sanctifies Israel and the seasons,* he may continue *Shemoneh Esrei* and is not required to rectify his error (*Mishnah Berurah* 488:13). This is in accord with *Rashi's* view that

גבורות

אַתָּה גִּבּוֹר לְעוֹלָם אֲדֹנָי, מְחַיֵּה מֵתִים אַתָּה, רַב לְהוֹשִׁיעַ.

[On the first day – מַשִּׁיב הָרְוּחַ וּמוֹרִיד הַגֶּשֶׁם.]

מְכַלְכֵּל חַיִּים בְּחֶסֶד, מְחַיֵּה מֵתִים בְּרַחֲמִים רַבִּים, סוֹמֵךְ נוֹפְלִים, וְרוֹפֵא חוֹלִים, וּמַתִּיר אֲסוּרִים, וּמְקַיֵּם אֱמוּנָתוֹ לִישֵׁנֵי עָפָר. מִי כָמְוֹךָ בַּעַל גְּבוּרוֹת, וּמִי דּוֹמֶה לָּךְ, מֶלֶךְ מֵמִית וּמְחַיֶּה וּמַצְמִיחַ יְשׁוּעָה. וְנֶאֱמָן אַתָּה לְהַחֲיוֹת מֵתִים. בָּרוּךְ אַתָּה יהוה, מְחַיֵּה הַמֵּתִים.

During the *chazzan's* repetition, *Kedushah* (below) is recited at this point.

קדושה

When reciting *Kedushah,* one must stand with his feet together, and avoid any interruptions. One should rise on his toes when saying the words קָדוֹשׁ, קָדוֹשׁ, קָדוֹשׁ; בָּרוּךְ (of בָּרוּךְ כְּבוֹד); and יִמְלֹךְ.

Cong. then *chazzan*:

נַעֲרִיצְךָ וְנַקְדִּישְׁךָ* כְּסוֹד שִׂיחַ שַׂרְפֵי קֹדֶשׁ, הַמַּקְדִּישִׁים שִׁמְךָ בַּקֹּדֶשׁ, כַּכָּתוּב עַל יַד נְבִיאֶךָ, וְקָרָא זֶה אֶל זֶה וְאָמַר:

All– קָדוֹשׁ קָדוֹשׁ קָדוֹשׁ יהוה צְבָאוֹת, מְלֹא כָל הָאָרֶץ כְּבוֹדוֹ.[1] ❖ כְּבוֹדוֹ מָלֵא עוֹלָם,* מְשָׁרְתָיו שׁוֹאֲלִים זֶה לָזֶה, אַיֵּה מְקוֹם כְּבוֹדוֹ, לְעֻמָּתָם בָּרוּךְ יֹאמֵרוּ:

All– בָּרוּךְ כְּבוֹד יהוה, מִמְּקוֹמוֹ.[2] ❖ מִמְּקוֹמוֹ הוּא יִפֶן בְּרַחֲמִים,* וְיָחוֹן עַם הַמְיַחֲדִים שְׁמוֹ, עֶרֶב וָבֹקֶר בְּכָל יוֹם תָּמִיד, פַּעֲמַיִם בְּאַהֲבָה שְׁמַע אוֹמְרִים.*

All– שְׁמַע יִשְׂרָאֵל, יהוה אֱלֹהֵינוּ, יהוה אֶחָד.[3] ❖ הוּא אֱלֹהֵינוּ,* הוּא אָבִינוּ, הוּא מַלְכֵּנוּ, הוּא מוֹשִׁיעֵנוּ, וְהוּא יַשְׁמִיעֵנוּ בְּרַחֲמָיו שֵׁנִית,* לְעֵינֵי כָּל חָי, לִהְיוֹת לָכֶם לֵאלֹהִים,* אֲנִי יהוה אֱלֹהֵיכֶם.[4]

All– אַדִּיר אַדִּירֵנוּ,* יהוה אֲדֹנֵינוּ, מָה אַדִּיר שִׁמְךָ בְּכָל הָאָרֶץ.[5] וְהָיָה יהוה לְמֶלֶךְ עַל כָּל הָאָרֶץ, בַּיּוֹם הַהוּא יִהְיֶה יהוה אֶחָד וּשְׁמוֹ אֶחָד.[6]

Chazzan– וּבְדִבְרֵי קָדְשְׁךָ כָּתוּב לֵאמֹר:

All– יִמְלֹךְ יהוה לְעוֹלָם, אֱלֹהַיִךְ צִיּוֹן, לְדֹר וָדֹר, הַלְלוּיָהּ.[7]

---

it is sufficient merely to recite the general statement, נַעֲשֶׂה וְנַקְרִיב ... בְּתוֹרָתֶךָ, *We will perform and bring near to You, according to the commandment of Your will, as You have written for us in Your Torah,'* and the offerings need not be enumerated.

☙ The commentary for the first section of *Shemoneh Esrei* and the shorter version of *Kedushah* may be found on pages 12- 14.

☙ **קְדוּשָׁה / Kedushah**

The *Kedushah* of *Mussaf* is based on *Pirkei D'Rabbi Eliezer's* narrative of the angelic praises. Indicative of the higher spirituality of *Mussaf,* Israel joins the angels by proclaiming שְׁמַע יִשְׂרָאֵל, our own declaration of God's greatness.

נַעֲרִיצְךָ וְנַקְדִּישְׁךָ — *We will revere You and sanctify You. Revere* refers to our recognition of God's outward greatness as displayed in His deeds. *Sanctify* refers to our attempt to express the idea that God's essence is elevated beyond man's capacity to comprehend.

כְּבוֹדוֹ מָלֵא עוֹלָם — *His glory fills the world.* The material nature of the earth is no barrier to His glory; it is everywhere.

הוּא יִפֶן בְּרַחֲמִים — *May He turn with compassion.* God's mercy causes Him to move from the throne of judgment to the throne of compassion.

עַם הַמְיַחֲדִים שְׁמוֹ ... שְׁמַע אוֹמְרִים — *The people who declare the Oneness of His Name ... they proclaim 'Shema.'* With its twice-a-day declaration of the *Shema,* Israel joins in the sacred chorus of the angels — and this is merit enough to win God's compassion.

As explained more fully in the commentary to קָרְבָּנוֹת (see p. 206), the fifth-century Persian

GOD'S MIGHT

אַתָּה *You are eternally mighty, my Lord, the Resuscitator of the dead are You; abundantly able to save.*

[On the first day – *He makes the wind blow and He makes the rain descend.*] *He sustains the living with kindness, resuscitates the dead with abundant mercy, supports the fallen, heals the sick, releases the confined, and maintains His faith to those asleep in the dust. Who is like You, O Master of mighty deeds, and who is comparable to You, O King Who causes death and restores life and makes salvation sprout! And You are faithful to resuscitate the dead. Blessed are You, HASHEM, Who resuscitates the dead.*

During the *chazzan's* repetition, *Kedushah* (below) is recited at this point.

KEDUSHAH

When reciting *Kedushah*, one must stand with his feet together and avoid any interruptions. One should rise on his toes when saying the words *'Holy, holy, holy; Blessed is; HASHEM shall reign.*

Cong. then *chazzan:*

נַעֲרִיצְךָ *We will revere You and sanctify You* according to the counsel of the holy Seraphim, who sanctify Your Name in the Sanctuary, as it is written by Your prophet: "And one [angel] will call another and say:*

All – *'Holy, holy, holy is HASHEM, Master of Legions, the whole world is filled with His glory.'"*[1] ∴*His glory fills the world.* His ministering angels ask one another, 'Where is the place of His glory?' Those facing them say 'Blessed':*

All – *'Blessed is the glory of HASHEM from His place.'*[2] ∴*From His place may He turn with compassion* and be gracious to the people who declare the Oneness of His Name; evening and morning, every day constantly, twice, with love, they proclaim 'Shema.'**

All – *'Hear O Israel: HASHEM is our God, HASHEM the One and Only.'*[3] ∴*He is our God;* He is our Father; He is our King; He is our Savior; and He will let us hear, in His compassion, for a second time* in the presence of all the living,' ... to be a God to you,* I am HASHEM, your God.'*[4]

All – *Mighty is our Mighty One,* HASHEM, our Master — how mighty is Your name throughout the earth!*[5] *HASHEM will be King over all the world — on that day HASHEM will be One and His Name will be One.*[6]

Chazzan – *And in Your holy Writings the following is written:*

All – *'HASHEM shall reign forever — your God, O Zion — from generation to generation, Halleluyah!'*[7]

(1) *Isaiah* 6:3. (2) *Ezekiel* 3:12. (3) *Deuteronomy* 6:4.
(4) *Numbers* 15:41. (5) *Psalms* 8:2. (6) *Zechariah* 14:9. (7) *Psalms* 146:10.

---

king Yezdegerd forbade the recitation of *Shema.* They had to comply during the morning when guards were present, but the Jews partially circumvented the decree by incorporating *Shema* into the *Mussaf Kedushah.*

הוּא אֱלֹהֵינוּ – *He is our God,* i.e., He controls nature; He is our merciful Father, the Ruler of all peoples, and our only hope for salvation.

שֵׁנִית – *For a second time.* The prophet *Isaiah* (11:11) foretold that God would redeem Israel from its final exile in as miraculous a manner as He did at the time of the Exodus from Egypt. Thus, the *second time* refers to the concept of a complete and total redemption, unlike the limited one that ended the Babylonian exile and led to the building of the Second Temple.

לִהְיוֹת לָכֶם לֵאלֹהִים – *To be a God to you.* When redeeming Israel from Egypt, God said that His purpose in doing so was to be a God to the Jewish people. The purpose of the *second* and ultimate redemption will be the same.

אַדִּיר אַדִּירֵנוּ – *Mighty is our Mighty One.* This brief selection is added to *Kedushah* only on Festivals, because, as discussed elsewhere,

קדושת השם

INDIVIDUALS RECITE:

אַתָּה קָדוֹשׁ וְשִׁמְךָ קָדוֹשׁ, וּקְדוֹשִׁים בְּכָל יוֹם יְהַלְלוּךָ סֶּלָה. בָּרוּךְ אַתָּה יהוה, הָאֵל הַקָּדוֹשׁ.

CHAZZAN RECITES DURING HIS REPETITION:

לְדוֹר וָדוֹר נַגִּיד גָּדְלֶךָ וּלְנֵצַח נְצָחִים קְדֻשָּׁתְךָ נַקְדִּישׁ, וְשִׁבְחֲךָ אֱלֹהֵינוּ מִפִּינוּ לֹא יָמוּשׁ לְעוֹלָם וָעֶד, כִּי אֵל מֶלֶךְ גָּדוֹל וְקָדוֹשׁ אָתָּה. בָּרוּךְ אַתָּה יהוה, הָאֵל הַקָּדוֹשׁ.

קדושת היום

אַתָּה בְחַרְתָּנוּ מִכָּל הָעַמִּים, אָהַבְתָּ אוֹתָנוּ, וְרָצִיתָ בָּנוּ, וְרוֹמַמְתָּנוּ מִכָּל הַלְּשׁוֹנוֹת, וְקִדַּשְׁתָּנוּ בְּמִצְוֹתֶיךָ, וְקֵרַבְתָּנוּ מַלְכֵּנוּ לַעֲבוֹדָתֶךָ, וְשִׁמְךָ הַגָּדוֹל וְהַקָּדוֹשׁ עָלֵינוּ קָרָאתָ.

On the Sabbath add the words in brackets. [If forgotten, see *Laws* §86-90.]

וַתִּתֶּן לָנוּ יהוה אֱלֹהֵינוּ בְּאַהֲבָה [שַׁבָּתוֹת לִמְנוּחָה וּ]מוֹעֲדִים לְשִׂמְחָה חַגִּים וּזְמַנִּים לְשָׂשׂוֹן, אֶת יוֹם [הַשַּׁבָּת הַזֶּה וְאֶת יוֹם] חַג הַמַּצּוֹת הַזֶּה, זְמַן חֵרוּתֵנוּ [בְּאַהֲבָה] מִקְרָא קֹדֶשׁ, זֵכֶר לִיצִיאַת מִצְרָיִם.

וּמִפְּנֵי חֲטָאֵינוּ* גָּלִינוּ מֵאַרְצֵנוּ, וְנִתְרַחַקְנוּ מֵעַל אַדְמָתֵנוּ.* וְאֵין אֲנַחְנוּ יְכוֹלִים לַעֲלוֹת וְלֵרָאוֹת וּלְהִשְׁתַּחֲוֹת לְפָנֶיךָ, וְלַעֲשׂוֹת חוֹבוֹתֵינוּ בְּבֵית בְּחִירָתֶךָ, בַּבַּיִת הַגָּדוֹל וְהַקָּדוֹשׁ שֶׁנִּקְרָא שִׁמְךָ עָלָיו, מִפְּנֵי הַיָּד שֶׁנִּשְׁתַּלְּחָה בְּמִקְדָּשֶׁךָ. יְהִי רָצוֹן מִלְּפָנֶיךָ יהוה אֱלֹהֵינוּ וֵאלֹהֵי אֲבוֹתֵינוּ, מֶלֶךְ רַחֲמָן, שֶׁתָּשׁוּב וּתְרַחֵם עָלֵינוּ וְעַל מִקְדָּשְׁךָ בְּרַחֲמֶיךָ הָרַבִּים, וְתִבְנֵהוּ מְהֵרָה וּתְגַדֵּל כְּבוֹדוֹ.* אָבִינוּ מַלְכֵּנוּ, גַּלֵּה כְּבוֹד מַלְכוּתְךָ

---

they are times of special closeness between God and Israel. In this brief prayer, we exclaim our confidence that God's absolute power will ultimately be recognized by the entire human race.

וּמִפְּנֵי חֲטָאֵינוּ — *But because of our sins.* This is a cardinal principle of Jewish faith. History is not haphazard; Israel's exile and centuries-long distress is a result of its sins. It is axiomatic, therefore, that only repentance can reverse this process.

מֵאַרְצֵנוּ . . . מֵעַל אַדְמָתֵנוּ — *From our land . . . from our soil.* The term **אֶרֶץ**, *land*, refers to the entire country from which the nation as a whole was exiled; **אֲדָמָה**, *soil*, refers to the individual parcels of land. These two conditions involve halachic differences. Some commandments, such as the laws of the Jubilee Year and the laws of Jewish indentured servants, cannot be observed unless the nation as a whole lives in *Eretz Yisrael*. Other

HOLINESS OF GOD'S NAME

INDIVIDUALS RECITE:

אַתָּה *You are holy and Your Name is holy, and holy ones praise You every day, forever. Blessed are You, HASHEM, the holy God.*

CHAZZAN RECITES DURING HIS REPETITION:

לְדוֹר *From generation to generation we shall relate Your greatness and for infinite eternities we shall proclaim Your holiness. Your praise, our God, shall not leave our mouth forever and ever, for You, O God, are a great and holy King. Blessed are You, HASHEM, the holy God.*

SANCTIFICATION OF THE DAY

אַתָּה בְחַרְתָּנוּ *You have chosen us from all the peoples; You loved us and found favor in us; You exalted us above all the tongues and You sanctified us with Your commandments. You drew us close, our King, to Your service and proclaimed Your great and Holy Name upon us.*

On the Sabbath add the words in brackets. [If forgotten, see *Laws* §86-90.]

וַתִּתֶּן לָנוּ *And You gave us, HASHEM, our God, with love [Sabbaths for rest], appointed festivals for gladness, Festivals and times for joy, [this day of Sabbath and] this day of the Festival of Matzos, the time of our freedom [with love], a holy convocation, a memorial of the Exodus from Egypt.*

וּמִפְּנֵי חֲטָאֵינוּ *But because of our sins* we have been exiled from our land and sent far from our soil.* We cannot ascend to appear and to prostrate ourselves before You, and to perform our obligations in the House of Your choice, in the great and holy House upon which Your Name was proclaimed, because of the hand that was dispatched against Your Sanctuary. May it be Your will, HASHEM, our God and the God of our forefathers, O merciful King, that You once more be compassionate upon us and upon Your Sanctuary in Your abundant mercy, and rebuild it soon and magnify its glory.* Our Father, our King, reveal the glory of Your Kingship*

---

commandments, such as those relating to tithes and the use of fruits during a tree's first four years, are observed by Jewish landowners in *Eretz Yisrael* even if the country is under foreign rule. We now say that the exile has deprived all or most of our people of these two categories of commandments. Then, we go on to mention a third category that we are deprived of in exile — the performance of the Temple service.

וְתִבְנֵהוּ מְהֵרָה וּתְגַדֵּל כְּבוֹדוֹ — *And rebuild it soon and magnify its glory. Eretz Yisrael* and the Temple are more than geographical or architectural concepts. There is a spiritual Presence that complements the material places on earth. When Israel sinned, the spiritual Presence withdrew because it could not tolerate the nearness of sinners. Consequently, the Jewish people were exiled from the land that they had spiritually contaminated. Conversely, Jewish return to the land is incomplete unless we can also bring about the return of the Divine holiness to the country and the Temple Mount. Thus we now pray that *God* rebuild the Temple in the sense that He return His Presence to the land, a condition that can come about only when God's sovereignty is accepted by all, and the Jews are returned to their land. Then will come the climax of our longing: that we will deserve to serve God in His Temple as He ordained in the Torah *(Sh'lah)*.

עָלֵינוּ מְהֵרָה, וְהוֹפַע וְהִנָּשֵׂא עָלֵינוּ לְעֵינֵי כָּל חָי. וְקָרֵב פְּזוּרֵינוּ* מִבֵּין הַגּוֹיִם, וּנְפוּצוֹתֵינוּ כַּנֵּס מִיַּרְכְּתֵי אָרֶץ. וַהֲבִיאֵנוּ לְצִיּוֹן עִירְךָ בְּרִנָּה, וְלִירוּשָׁלַיִם בֵּית מִקְדָּשְׁךָ בְּשִׂמְחַת עוֹלָם. וְשָׁם נַעֲשֶׂה לְפָנֶיךָ אֶת קָרְבְּנוֹת חוֹבוֹתֵינוּ, תְּמִידִים כְּסִדְרָם, וּמוּסָפִים כְּהִלְכָתָם. וְאֶת [Weekdays– וְיוֹם] [Sabbath– מוּסְפֵי יוֹם הַשַּׁבָּת הַזֶּה וְיוֹם] [מוּסַף יוֹם] חַג הַמַּצּוֹת הַזֶּה נַעֲשֶׂה וְנַקְרִיב לְפָנֶיךָ בְּאַהֲבָה כְּמִצְוַת רְצוֹנֶךָ, כְּמוֹ שֶׁכָּתַבְתָּ עָלֵינוּ בְּתוֹרָתֶךָ, עַל יְדֵי מֹשֶׁה עַבְדֶּךָ, מִפִּי כְבוֹדֶךָ כָּאָמוּר:

On the Sabbath add. [If forgotten, do not repeat *Shemoneh Esrei*. See *Laws* §86.]

וּבְיוֹם הַשַּׁבָּת שְׁנֵי כְבָשִׂים בְּנֵי שָׁנָה תְּמִימִם, וּשְׁנֵי עֶשְׂרֹנִים סֹלֶת מִנְחָה בְּלוּלָה בַשֶּׁמֶן, וְנִסְכּוֹ. עֹלַת שַׁבַּת בְּשַׁבַּתּוֹ, עַל עֹלַת הַתָּמִיד וְנִסְכָּהּ.[1] (זֶה קָרְבַּן שַׁבָּת. וְקָרְבַּן הַיּוֹם כָּאָמוּר:)

וּבַחֹדֶשׁ הָרִאשׁוֹן בְּאַרְבָּעָה עָשָׂר יוֹם לַחֹדֶשׁ, פֶּסַח לַיהוה. וּבַחֲמִשָּׁה עָשָׂר יוֹם לַחֹדֶשׁ הַזֶּה, חָג, שִׁבְעַת יָמִים מַצּוֹת יֵאָכֵל. בַּיּוֹם הָרִאשׁוֹן מִקְרָא קֹדֶשׁ, כָּל מְלֶאכֶת עֲבֹדָה לֹא תַעֲשׂוּ. וְהִקְרַבְתֶּם אִשֶּׁה עֹלָה לַיהוה, פָּרִים בְּנֵי בָקָר שְׁנַיִם, וְאַיִל אֶחָד, וְשִׁבְעָה כְבָשִׂים בְּנֵי שָׁנָה, תְּמִימִם יִהְיוּ לָכֶם.[2] וּמִנְחָתָם וְנִסְכֵּיהֶם כִּמְדֻבָּר, שְׁלֹשָׁה עֶשְׂרֹנִים לַפָּר, וּשְׁנֵי עֶשְׂרֹנִים לָאָיִל, וְעִשָּׂרוֹן לַכֶּבֶשׂ, וְיַיִן כְּנִסְכּוֹ. וְשָׂעִיר לְכַפֵּר, וּשְׁנֵי תְמִידִים כְּהִלְכָתָם.

On the Sabbath add. [If forgotten, do not repeat *Shemoneh Esrei*. See *Laws* §86.]

יִשְׂמְחוּ בְמַלְכוּתְךָ שׁוֹמְרֵי שַׁבָּת וְקוֹרְאֵי עֹנֶג, עַם מְקַדְּשֵׁי שְׁבִיעִי, כֻּלָּם יִשְׂבְּעוּ וְיִתְעַנְּגוּ מִטּוּבֶךָ, וּבַשְּׁבִיעִי רָצִיתָ בּוֹ וְקִדַּשְׁתּוֹ, חֶמְדַּת יָמִים אֹתוֹ קָרָאתָ, זֵכֶר לְמַעֲשֵׂה בְרֵאשִׁית.

On the Sabbath add the words in brackets. [If forgotten, see *Laws* §86-90.]

אֱלֹהֵינוּ וֵאלֹהֵי אֲבוֹתֵינוּ, [רְצֵה בִמְנוּחָתֵנוּ] מֶלֶךְ רַחֲמָן רַחֵם עָלֵינוּ, טוֹב וּמֵטִיב* הִדָּרֶשׁ לָנוּ, שׁוּבָה אֵלֵינוּ בַּהֲמוֹן רַחֲמֶיךָ, בִּגְלַל אָבוֹת שֶׁעָשׂוּ רְצוֹנֶךָ. בְּנֵה בֵיתְךָ כְּבַתְּחִלָּה, וְכוֹנֵן מִקְדָּשְׁךָ עַל מְכוֹנוֹ, וְהַרְאֵנוּ בְּבִנְיָנוֹ, וְשַׂמְּחֵנוּ בְּתִקּוּנוֹ.

וְקָרֵב פְּזוּרֵינוּ — *Draw our scattered ones near.* Israel's dispersion has created much dissension among Jews, because the communities in various lands have adopted different customs, languages, outlooks, etc. Sometimes it seems that unity could never be achieved. Therefore we pray not only for liberation, but that God bring us together in mutual understanding and a sharing of goals and aspirations *(Siach Yitzchak)*.

אֱלֹהֵינוּ . . . טוֹב וּמֵטִיב — *Our God . . . O good*

upon us, speedily; appear and be uplifted over us before the eyes of all the living. Draw our scattered ones near from among the nations, and bring in our dispersions from the ends of the earth. Bring us to Zion, Your City, in glad song, and to Jerusalem, home of Your Sanctuary, in eternal joy. There we will perform before You our obligatory offerings, the continual offerings according to their order and the additional offerings according to their law. And the additional offering[s of this day of Sabbath and] of this day of the Festival of Matzos, we will perform and bring near to You with love, according to the commandment of Your will, as You have written for us in Your Torah, through Moses, Your servant, from Your glorious expression, as it is said:*

On the Sabbath add. [If forgotten, do not repeat *Shemoneh Esrei.* See *Laws* §86.]

וּבְיוֹם הַשַּׁבָּת *On the Sabbath day: two [male] first-year lambs, unblemished; and two tenth-ephah of fine flour for a meal-offering, mixed with olive oil, and its wine-libation. The elevation-offering of the Sabbath must be on its particular Sabbath, in addition to the continual elevation-offering and its wine-libation.*[1] *(This is the offering of the Sabbath. And the offering of the day is as it is said:)*

וּבַחֹדֶשׁ הָרִאשׁוֹן *And in the first month on the fourteenth day of the month — the pesach offering to* HASHEM. *And on the fifteenth day of this month — a festival; for seven days, matzos are to be eaten. On the first day is a holy convocation, you may not do any laborious work. You are to bring a fire-offering, an elevation-offering to* HASHEM, *two young bulls, one ram and seven male lambs in their first year, they shall be unblemished for you.*[2] *And their meal-offerings and their wine-libations as mentioned: three tenth-ephah for each bull; two tenth-ephah for each ram; one tenth-ephah for each lamb; and wine for its libation. A he-goat for atonement, and two continual offerings according to their law.*

On the Sabbath add. [If forgotten, do not repeat *Shemoneh Esrei.* See *Laws* §86.]

יִשְׂמְחוּ *They shall rejoice in Your Kingship — those who observe the Sabbath and call it a delight. The people that sanctifies the Seventh — they will all be satisfied and delighted from Your goodness. And the Seventh — You found favor in it and sanctified it. 'Most coveted of days' You called it, a remembrance of creation.*

On the Sabbath add the words in brackets. [If forgotten, see *Laws* §86-90.]

אֱלֹהֵינוּ *Our God and the God of our forefathers, [may You be pleased with our rest] O merciful King, have mercy on us; O good and beneficent One,* let Yourself be sought out by us; return to us in Your yearning mercy for the sake of the forefathers who did Your will. Rebuild Your House as it was at first, and establish Your Sanctuary on its prepared site; show us its rebuilding and gladden us in its perfection.*

---

(1) *Numbers* 28:9-10. (2) 28:16-19.

וְהָשֵׁב כֹּהֲנִים לַעֲבוֹדָתָם, וּלְוִיִּם לְשִׁירָם וּלְזִמְרָם, וְהָשֵׁב יִשְׂרָאֵל לִנְוֵיהֶם. וְשָׁם נַעֲלֶה וְנֵרָאֶה* וְנִשְׁתַּחֲוֶה לְפָנֶיךָ, בְּשָׁלֹשׁ פַּעֲמֵי רְגָלֵינוּ, כַּכָּתוּב בְּתוֹרָתֶךָ: שָׁלוֹשׁ פְּעָמִים בַּשָּׁנָה, יֵרָאֶה כָל זְכוּרְךָ אֶת פְּנֵי יהוה אֱלֹהֶיךָ, בַּמָּקוֹם אֲשֶׁר יִבְחָר, בְּחַג הַמַּצּוֹת, וּבְחַג הַשָּׁבֻעוֹת, וּבְחַג הַסֻּכּוֹת, וְלֹא יֵרָאֶה אֶת פְּנֵי יהוה רֵיקָם.* אִישׁ כְּמַתְּנַת יָדוֹ, כְּבִרְכַּת יהוה אֱלֹהֶיךָ, אֲשֶׁר נָתַן לָךְ.¹

On the Sabbath add the words in brackets. [If forgotten, see *Laws* §86-90.]

וְהַשִּׂיאֵנוּ יהוה אֱלֹהֵינוּ אֶת בִּרְכַּת מוֹעֲדֶיךָ לְחַיִּים וּלְשָׁלוֹם, לְשִׂמְחָה וּלְשָׂשׂוֹן, כַּאֲשֶׁר רָצִיתָ וְאָמַרְתָּ לְבָרְכֵנוּ. [אֱלֹהֵינוּ וֵאלֹהֵי אֲבוֹתֵינוּ רְצֵה בִמְנוּחָתֵנוּ] קַדְּשֵׁנוּ בְּמִצְוֹתֶיךָ וְתֵן חֶלְקֵנוּ בְּתוֹרָתֶךָ, שַׂבְּעֵנוּ מִטּוּבֶךָ וְשַׂמְּחֵנוּ בִּישׁוּעָתֶךָ, וְטַהֵר לִבֵּנוּ לְעָבְדְּךָ בֶּאֱמֶת, וְהַנְחִילֵנוּ יהוה אֱלֹהֵינוּ [בְּאַהֲבָה וּבְרָצוֹן] בְּשִׂמְחָה וּבְשָׂשׂוֹן [שַׁבָּת וּ]מוֹעֲדֵי קָדְשֶׁךָ, וְיִשְׂמְחוּ בְךָ יִשְׂרָאֵל מְקַדְּשֵׁי שְׁמֶךָ. בָּרוּךְ אַתָּה יהוה, מְקַדֵּשׁ [הַשַּׁבָּת וְ]יִשְׂרָאֵל וְהַזְּמַנִּים.

עבודה

רְצֵה יהוה אֱלֹהֵינוּ בְּעַמְּךָ יִשְׂרָאֵל וּבִתְפִלָּתָם, וְהָשֵׁב אֶת הָעֲבוֹדָה לִדְבִיר בֵּיתֶךָ. וְאִשֵּׁי יִשְׂרָאֵל וּתְפִלָּתָם בְּאַהֲבָה תְקַבֵּל בְּרָצוֹן, וּתְהִי לְרָצוֹן תָּמִיד עֲבוֹדַת יִשְׂרָאֵל עַמֶּךָ.

WHEN THE *KOHANIM* ASCEND THE *DUCHAN*• TO PRONOUNCE *BIRCAS KOHANIM* [THE PRIESTLY BLESSING], THE *CHAZZAN'S* REPETITION CONTINUES ON PAGE 426.

If no *Kohen* is present, the *chazzan* continues here.

וְתֶחֱזֶינָה עֵינֵינוּ בְּשׁוּבְךָ לְצִיּוֹן בְּרַחֲמִים. בָּרוּךְ אַתָּה יהוה, הַמַּחֲזִיר שְׁכִינָתוֹ לְצִיּוֹן.

---

and beneficent One. In the case of human beings, one may be good, but not have the resources to benefit others. On the other hand, one may benefit others by helping them do good deeds, but for himself he may prefer to indulge his sinful nature. God, however, is perfect — He is both good and beneficent (*Iyun Tefillah*).

וְשָׁם נַעֲלֶה וְנֵרָאֶה — *And there we will ascend and appear.* Having been returned to *Eretz Yisrael,* we will be able to fulfill the commandment of going up to the Temple to appear before God.

רֵיקָם — *Empty-handed.* During the pilgrimages, each Jew must offer elevation-offerings and peace-offerings in honor of the Festivals. However, though no one may come emptyhanded — without offerings — he should give only as much as he can afford, but not more, *according to the gift of his hand,* i.e., depending on how much God has blessed him with (*Rashi*).

דּוּכָן — *Duchan.* The Priestly Blessing is often

Restore the Kohanim to their service and the Levites to their song and music; and restore Israel to their dwellings. And there we will ascend and appear and prostrate ourselves before You, during our three pilgrimage seasons, as it is written in Your Torah: Three times a year all your males are to appear before HASHEM, your God, in the place He shall choose, on the Festival of Matzos, on the Festival of Shavuos, and on the Festival of Succos, and they shall not appear before HASHEM empty-handed.* Every man according to the gift of his hand, according to the blessing of HASHEM, your God, that He gave you.*[1]

On the Sabbath add the words in brackets. [If forgotten, see *Laws* §86-90.]

וְהַשִּׂיאֵנוּ *Bestow upon us, O HASHEM, our God, the blessing of Your appointed Festivals for life and for peace, for gladness and for joy, as You desired and promised to bless us. [Our God and the God of our forefathers, may You be pleased with our rest.] Sanctify us with Your commandments and grant us our share in Your Torah; satisfy us from Your goodness and gladden us with Your salvation, and purify our heart to serve You sincerely. And grant us a heritage, O HASHEM, our God — [with love and with favor] with gladness and with joy — [the Sabbath and] the appointed festivals of Your holiness, and may Israel, the sanctifiers of Your Name, rejoice in You. Blessed are You, HASHEM, Who sanctifies [the Sabbath] Israel and the festive seasons.*

TEMPLE SERVICE

רְצֵה *Be favorable, HASHEM, our God, toward Your people Israel and their prayer and restore the service to the Holy of Holies of Your Temple. The fire-offerings of Israel and their prayer accept with love and favor, and may the service of Your people Israel always be favorable to You.*

WHEN THE *KOHANIM* ASCEND THE *DUCHAN** TO PRONOUNCE *BIRCAS KOHANIM* [THE PRIESTLY BLESSING], THE *CHAZZAN'S* REPETITION CONTINUES ON PAGE 426.

If no *Kohen* is present, the *chazzan* continues here.

וְתֶחֱזֶינָה *May our eyes behold Your return to Zion in compassion. Blessed are You, HASHEM, Who restores His Presence to Zion.*

(1) *Deuteronomy* 16:16-17.

---

referred to as עֲלִיָּה לְדוּכָן, *ascending the platform.* It refers to the location in the *Beis HaMikdash* from where the blessing was bestowed. The *Kohanim* stood on the stairs leading to the Temple proper as they raised their hands to pronounce *Bircas Kohanim* (*Tamid* 7:2). In most synagogues today the *Kohanim* stand on a *duchan,* or platform, in front of the Ark while they bestow the blessings on the congregation. Although the use of a *duchan* is not a necessary condition for *Bircas Kohanim,* use of a *duchan* is preferred.

הודאה

Bow at מוֹדִים; straighten up at 'ה. In his repetition the *chazzan* should recite the entire מוֹדִים aloud, while the congregation recites מוֹדִים דְּרַבָּנָן softly.

מוֹדִים אֲנַחְנוּ לָךְ, שָׁאַתָּה הוּא יהוה אֱלֹהֵינוּ וֵאלֹהֵי אֲבוֹתֵינוּ לְעוֹלָם וָעֶד. צוּר חַיֵּינוּ, מָגֵן יִשְׁעֵנוּ אַתָּה הוּא לְדוֹר וָדוֹר. נוֹדֶה לְּךָ וּנְסַפֵּר תְּהִלָּתֶךָ[1] עַל חַיֵּינוּ הַמְּסוּרִים בְּיָדֶךָ, וְעַל נִשְׁמוֹתֵינוּ הַפְּקוּדוֹת לָךְ, וְעַל נִסֶּיךָ שֶׁבְּכָל יוֹם עִמָּנוּ, וְעַל נִפְלְאוֹתֶיךָ וְטוֹבוֹתֶיךָ שֶׁבְּכָל עֵת, עֶרֶב וָבֹקֶר וְצָהֳרָיִם. הַטּוֹב כִּי לֹא כָלוּ רַחֲמֶיךָ, וְהַמְרַחֵם כִּי לֹא תַמּוּ חֲסָדֶיךָ,[2] מֵעוֹלָם קִוִּינוּ לָךְ.

מודים דרבנן

מוֹדִים אֲנַחְנוּ לָךְ, שָׁאַתָּה הוּא יהוה אֱלֹהֵינוּ וֵאלֹהֵי אֲבוֹתֵינוּ, אֱלֹהֵי כָל בָּשָׂר, יוֹצְרֵנוּ, יוֹצֵר בְּרֵאשִׁית. בְּרָכוֹת וְהוֹדָאוֹת לְשִׁמְךָ הַגָּדוֹל וְהַקָּדוֹשׁ, עַל שֶׁהֶחֱיִיתָנוּ וְקִיַּמְתָּנוּ. כֵּן תְּחַיֵּנוּ וּתְקַיְּמֵנוּ, וְתֶאֱסוֹף גָּלֻיּוֹתֵינוּ לְחַצְרוֹת קָדְשֶׁךָ, לִשְׁמוֹר חֻקֶּיךָ וְלַעֲשׂוֹת רְצוֹנֶךָ, וּלְעָבְדְּךָ בְּלֵבָב שָׁלֵם, עַל שֶׁאֲנַחְנוּ מוֹדִים לָךְ. בָּרוּךְ אֵל הַהוֹדָאוֹת.

וְעַל כֻּלָּם יִתְבָּרַךְ וְיִתְרוֹמַם שִׁמְךָ מַלְכֵּנוּ תָּמִיד לְעוֹלָם וָעֶד.

Bend the knees at בָּרוּךְ; bow at אַתָּה; straighten up at 'ה.

וְכֹל הַחַיִּים יוֹדוּךָ סֶּלָה, וִיהַלְלוּ אֶת שִׁמְךָ בֶּאֱמֶת, הָאֵל יְשׁוּעָתֵנוּ וְעֶזְרָתֵנוּ סֶלָה. בָּרוּךְ אַתָּה יהוה, הַטּוֹב שִׁמְךָ וּלְךָ נָאֶה לְהוֹדוֹת.

ברכת כהנים

If the *Kohanim* do not ascend the *duchan*, the *chazzan* recites the following during his repetition. He faces right at וְיִשְׁמְרֶךָ; faces left at אֵלֶיךָ וִיחֻנֶּךָּ; faces the Ark for the rest of the blessings.

אֱלֹהֵינוּ, וֵאלֹהֵי אֲבוֹתֵינוּ, בָּרְכֵנוּ בַבְּרָכָה הַמְּשֻׁלֶּשֶׁת בַּתּוֹרָה הַכְּתוּבָה עַל יְדֵי מֹשֶׁה עַבְדֶּךָ, הָאֲמוּרָה מִפִּי אַהֲרֹן וּבָנָיו, כֹּהֲנִים עַם קְדוֹשֶׁךָ, כָּאָמוּר:

יְבָרֶכְךָ יהוה, וְיִשְׁמְרֶךָ. (.Cong – כֵּן יְהִי רָצוֹן.)

יָאֵר יהוה פָּנָיו אֵלֶיךָ וִיחֻנֶּךָּ. (.Cong – כֵּן יְהִי רָצוֹן.)

יִשָּׂא יהוה פָּנָיו אֵלֶיךָ וְיָשֵׂם לְךָ שָׁלוֹם.[3] (.Cong – כֵּן יְהִי רָצוֹן.)

THANKSGIVING [MODIM]

Bow at *'We gratefully thank You'*; straighten up at *'HASHEM.'* In his repetition the *chazzan* should recite the entire *Modim* aloud, while the congregation recites *Modim of the Rabbis* softly.

מוֹדִים *We gratefully thank You, for it is You Who are HASHEM, our God and the God of our forefathers for all eternity; Rock of our lives, Shield of our salvation are You from generation to generation. We shall thank You and relate Your praise[1] — for our lives, which are committed to Your power and for our souls that are entrusted to You; for Your miracles that are with us every day; and for Your wonders and favors in every season — evening, morning, and afternoon. The Beneficent One, for Your compassions were never exhausted, and the Compassionate One, for Your kindnesses never ended[2] — always have we put our hope in You.*

MODIM OF THE RABBIS

מוֹדִים *We gratefully thank You, for it is You Who are HASHEM, our God and the God of our forefathers, the God of all flesh, our Molder, the Molder of the universe. Blessings and thanks are due Your great and holy Name for You have given us life and sustained us. So may You continue to give us life and sustain us and gather our exiles to the Courtyards of Your Sanctuary, to observe Your decrees, to do Your will and to serve You wholeheartedly. [We thank You] for inspiring us to thank You. Blessed is the God of thanksgivings.*

For all these, may Your Name be blessed and exalted, our King, continually forever and ever.

Bend the knees at *'Blessed'*; bow at *'You'*; straighten up at *'HASHEM.'*

Everything alive will gratefully acknowledge You, Selah! and praise Your Name sincerely, O God of our salvation and help, Selah! Blessed are You, HASHEM, Your Name is 'The Beneficent One' and to You it is fitting to give thanks.

THE PRIESTLY BLESSING

If the *Kohanim* do not ascend the *duchan*, the *chazzan* recites the following during his repetition.

אֱלֹהֵינוּ *Our God and the God of our forefathers, bless us with the three-verse blessing in the Torah that was written by the hand of Moses, Your servant, that was said by Aaron and his sons, the Kohanim, Your holy people, as it is said:*

May HASHEM bless you and safeguard you. (Cong.— *So may it be.*)

May HASHEM illuminate His countenance for you and be gracious to you. (Cong.— *So may it be.*)

May HASHEM turn His countenance to you and establish peace for you.[3] (Cong.— *So may it be.*)

---

(1) Cf. *Psalms* 79:13. (2) Cf. *Lamentations* 3:22. (3) *Numbers* 6:24-26.

שלום

שִׂים שָׁלוֹם, טוֹבָה, וּבְרָכָה, חֵן, וָחֶסֶד וְרַחֲמִים עָלֵינוּ וְעַל כָּל יִשְׂרָאֵל עַמֶּךָ. בָּרְכֵנוּ אָבִינוּ, כֻּלָּנוּ כְּאֶחָד בְּאוֹר פָּנֶיךָ, כִּי בְאוֹר פָּנֶיךָ נָתַתָּ לָּנוּ, יהוה אֱלֹהֵינוּ, תּוֹרַת חַיִּים וְאַהֲבַת חֶסֶד, וּצְדָקָה, וּבְרָכָה, וְרַחֲמִים, וְחַיִּים, וְשָׁלוֹם. וְטוֹב בְּעֵינֶיךָ לְבָרֵךְ אֶת עַמְּךָ יִשְׂרָאֵל, בְּכָל עֵת וּבְכָל שָׁעָה בִּשְׁלוֹמֶךָ. בָּרוּךְ אַתָּה יהוה, הַמְּבָרֵךְ אֶת עַמּוֹ יִשְׂרָאֵל בַּשָּׁלוֹם.

יִהְיוּ לְרָצוֹן אִמְרֵי פִי וְהֶגְיוֹן לִבִּי לְפָנֶיךָ, יהוה צוּרִי וְגֹאֲלִי.[1]

The *chazzan's* repetition of *Shemoneh Esrei* ends here.
Individuals continue below:

אֱלֹהַי, נְצוֹר לְשׁוֹנִי מֵרָע, וּשְׂפָתַי מִדַּבֵּר מִרְמָה,[2] וְלִמְקַלְלַי נַפְשִׁי תִדּוֹם, וְנַפְשִׁי כֶּעָפָר לַכֹּל תִּהְיֶה. פְּתַח לִבִּי בְּתוֹרָתֶךָ, וּבְמִצְוֹתֶיךָ תִּרְדּוֹף נַפְשִׁי. וְכֹל הַחוֹשְׁבִים עָלַי רָעָה, מְהֵרָה הָפֵר עֲצָתָם וְקַלְקֵל מַחֲשַׁבְתָּם. עֲשֵׂה לְמַעַן שְׁמֶךָ, עֲשֵׂה לְמַעַן יְמִינֶךָ, עֲשֵׂה לְמַעַן קְדֻשָּׁתֶךָ, עֲשֵׂה לְמַעַן תּוֹרָתֶךָ. לְמַעַן יֵחָלְצוּן יְדִידֶיךָ, הוֹשִׁיעָה יְמִינְךָ וַעֲנֵנִי.[3]

Some recite verses pertaining to their names here. See page 1143.

יִהְיוּ לְרָצוֹן אִמְרֵי פִי וְהֶגְיוֹן לִבִּי לְפָנֶיךָ, יהוה צוּרִי וְגֹאֲלִי.[1]

Bow and take three steps back. Bow left and say ... עֹשֶׂה; bow right and say ... הוּא יַעֲשֶׂה; bow forward and say וְעַל כָּל ... אָמֵן.

עֹשֶׂה שָׁלוֹם בִּמְרוֹמָיו, הוּא יַעֲשֶׂה שָׁלוֹם עָלֵינוּ, וְעַל כָּל יִשְׂרָאֵל. וְאִמְרוּ: אָמֵן.

יְהִי רָצוֹן מִלְּפָנֶיךָ יהוה אֱלֹהֵינוּ וֵאלֹהֵי אֲבוֹתֵינוּ, שֶׁיִּבָּנֶה בֵּית הַמִּקְדָּשׁ בִּמְהֵרָה בְיָמֵינוּ, וְתֵן חֶלְקֵנוּ בְּתוֹרָתֶךָ. וְשָׁם נַעֲבָדְךָ בְּיִרְאָה, כִּימֵי עוֹלָם וּכְשָׁנִים קַדְמוֹנִיּוֹת. וְעָרְבָה לַיהוה מִנְחַת יְהוּדָה וִירוּשָׁלָיִם, כִּימֵי עוֹלָם וּכְשָׁנִים קַדְמוֹנִיּוֹת.[4]

THE INDIVIDUAL'S RECITATION OF *SHEMONEH ESREI* ENDS HERE.

The individual remains standing in place until the *chazzan* reaches *Kedushah* — or at least until the *chazzan* begins his repetition — then he takes three steps forward. The *chazzan* himself, or one praying alone, should remain in place for at least a few moments before taking three steps forward.

ON THE FIRST DAY, THE *CHAZZAN' S* REPETITION BEGINS ON PAGE 416;
ON THE SECOND DAY, THE *CHAZZAN' S* REPETITION BEGINS ON PAGE 402

PEACE

שִׂים שָׁלוֹם *Establish peace, goodness, blessing, graciousness, kindness, and compassion upon us and upon all of Your people Israel. Bless us, our Father, all of us as one, with the light of Your countenance, for with the light of Your countenance You gave us,* HASHEM, *our God, the Torah of life and a love of kindness, righteousness, blessing, compassion, life, and peace. And may it be good in Your eyes to bless Your people Israel at every time and every hour with Your peace. Blessed are You,* HASHEM, *Who blesses His people Israel with peace.*

May the expressions of my mouth and the thoughts of my heart find favor before You, HASHEM, *my Rock and my Redeemer.*[1]

The *chazzan's* repetition of *Shemoneh Esrei* ends here.
Individuals continue below:

אֱלֹהַי *My God, guard my tongue from evil and my lips from speaking deceitfully.*[2] *To those who curse me, let my soul be silent; and let my soul be like dust to everyone. Open my heart to Your Torah, then my soul will pursue Your commandments. As for all those who design evil against me, speedily nullify their counsel and disrupt their design. Act for Your Name's sake; act for Your right hand's sake; act for Your sanctity's sake; act for Your Torah's sake. That Your beloved ones may be given rest; let Your right hand save, and respond to me.*[3]

Some recite verses pertaining to their names at this point. See page 1143.

May the expressions of my mouth and the thoughts of my heart find favor before You, HASHEM, *my Rock and my Redeemer.*[1] *He Who makes peace in His heights, may He make peace upon us, and upon all Israel. Now respond: Amen.*

Bow and take three steps back. Bow left and say, *'He Who makes peace . . .'*; bow right and say, *'may He make peace . . .'*; bow forward and say, *'and upon . . . Amen.'*

יְהִי רָצוֹן *May it be Your will,* HASHEM, *our God and the God of our forefathers, that the Holy Temple be rebuilt, speedily in our days. Grant us our share in Your Torah, and may we serve You there with reverence, as in days of old and in former years. Then the offering of Judah and Jerusalem will be pleasing to* HASHEM, *as in days of old and in former years.*[4]

THE INDIVIDUAL'S RECITATION OF *SHEMONEH ESREI* ENDS HERE.

The individual remains standing in place until the *chazzan* reaches *Kedushah* — or at least until the *chazzan* begins his repetition — then he takes three steps forward. The *chazzan* himself, or one praying alone, should remain in place for at least a few moments before taking three steps forward.

ON THE FIRST DAY, THE *CHAZZAN'S* REPETITION BEGINS ON PAGE 416;
ON THE SECOND DAY, THE *CHAZZAN'S* REPETITION BEGINS ON PAGE 402.

(1) *Psalms* 19:15. (2) Cf. 34:14. (3) 60:7; 108:7. (4) *Malachi* 3:4.

חזרת הש״ץ – תפלת טל

THE ARK IS OPENED AND THE CONGREGATION STANDS.

כִּי שֵׁם יהוה אֶקְרָא, הָבוּ גֹדֶל לֵאלֹהֵינוּ.[1]
אֲדֹנָי שְׂפָתַי תִּפְתָּח,* וּפִי יַגִּיד תְּהִלָּתֶךָ.[2]

אבות

Chazzan bends his knees at בָּרוּךְ; bows at אַתָּה; straightens up at ה׳.

בָּרוּךְ אַתָּה יהוה אֱלֹהֵינוּ וֵאלֹהֵי אֲבוֹתֵינוּ, אֱלֹהֵי אַבְרָהָם, אֱלֹהֵי יִצְחָק, וֵאלֹהֵי יַעֲקֹב, הָאֵל הַגָּדוֹל הַגִּבּוֹר וְהַנּוֹרָא, אֵל עֶלְיוֹן, גּוֹמֵל חֲסָדִים טוֹבִים וְקוֹנֵה הַכֹּל, וְזוֹכֵר חַסְדֵי אָבוֹת, וּמֵבִיא גוֹאֵל לִבְנֵי בְנֵיהֶם, לְמַעַן שְׁמוֹ בְּאַהֲבָה. מֶלֶךְ עוֹזֵר וּמוֹשִׁיעַ וּמָגֵן.

בְּדַעְתּוֹ אַבִּיעָה חִידוֹת,[3]* בְּעַם זוּ[4] בְּזוּ* בְּטַל לְהַחֲדוֹת.
טַל גַּיא וּדְשָׁאֶיהָ לַחֲדוֹת, דָּצִים בְּצִלּוֹ לְהֵחָדוֹת.
אוֹת יַלְדוּת* טַל[5] לְהָגֵן לְתוֹלָדוֹת.

Chazzan bends his knees at בָּרוּךְ; bows at אַתָּה; straightens up at ה׳.

בָּרוּךְ אַתָּה יהוה, מָגֵן אַבְרָהָם. (.Cong. – אָמֵן)

גבורות

אַתָּה גִּבּוֹר לְעוֹלָם אֲדֹנָי, מְחַיֵּה מֵתִים אַתָּה, רַב לְהוֹשִׁיעַ.

תְּהוֹמוֹת הֲדוֹם* לִרְסִיסוֹ כְּסוּפִים, וְכָל נְאוֹת דֶּשֶׁא לוֹ נִכְסָפִים.
טַל זִכְרוֹ גְּבוּרוֹת מוֹסִיפִים,* חָקוּק בְּגִישַׁת מוּסָפִים,
טַל לְהַחֲיוֹת בּוֹ נְקוּקֵי סְעִיפִים.*

[In some congregations the Ark is closed while additional prayers (p. 1112) are recited at this point.]

תְּפִלַּת טַל / PRAYER FOR DEW

When Isaac bestowed the Patriarchal blessing upon his son Jacob (*Genesis* ch. 27), he declared that Pesach, the time of redemption and of praise for God, is the time when the Heavenly chambers of dew and blessing are open (*Pirkei deR'Eliezer*, ch. 32). Thus, the first day of Pesach is an auspicious time to pray for dew (*Mateh Moshe* 662). Moreover, the prayer and the season suggest the principle that Creation was designed to accommodate the dictates of the Torah: Spring, the season of gentle dew and the rejuvenation of nature, is also the time when the Jewish nation was redeemed and began to blossom.

The prayer for dew was written by R' Elazar HaKalir (see p. 43) as is indicated by the acrostic of one of the prayers omitted by most congregations (see p. 114): אֶלְעָזָר בִּירַבִּי קַלִּיר מִקִּרְיַת סֵפֶר, *Elazar son of R' Kalir, from Kiryas Sefer.*

בְּדַעְתּוֹ אַבִּיעָה חִידוֹת — *With His consent I shall speak of mysteries.* The references to dew throughout this prayer have two meanings: (a) The moisture that makes plant growth possible; and (b) what the Sages call טַל שֶׁל תְּחִיָּה, *the dew of life*, i.e., the invigorating spiritual property that gives life to people and that can even resuscitate the dead (*Chagigah* 12b). Thus, the references to dew contain both simple meanings and deep mysteries.

בְּעַם זוּ בְּזוּ — *Among this people, through this [prayer],* i.e., may the Jewish people merit the

CHAZZAN'S REPETITION – PRAYER FOR DEW

THE ARK IS OPENED AND THE CONGREGATION STANDS.

When I call out the Name of HASHEM, ascribe greatness to our God.[1]
My Lord, open my lips, that my mouth may declare Your praise.[2]

PATRIARCHS

Chazzan bends his knees at *'Blessed'*; bows at *'You'*; straightens up at *'HASHEM.'*

בָּרוּךְ *Blessed are You, HASHEM, our God and the God of our forefathers, God of Abraham, God of Isaac, and God of Jacob; the great, mighty, and awesome God, the supreme God, Who bestows beneficial kindnesses and creates everything, Who recalls the kindnesses of the Patriarchs and brings a Redeemer to their children's children, for His Name's sake, with love. O King, Helper, Savior, and Shield.*

בְּדַעְתּוֹ *With His consent I shall speak of mysteries.*[3]*
Among this people,[4] *through this [prayer],**
may they be made exultant by the dew.
Dew — bringing joy to valley and its herbage;
taking pleasure in His shelter to be made exultant.
Dew is a symbol of youth[ful promise],[5]*
may it protect the generations.

Chazzan bends his knees at *'Blessed'*; bows at *'You'*; straightens up at *'HASHEM.'*

Blessed are You, HASHEM, Shield of Abraham. (Cong. – *Amen.)*

GOD'S MIGHT

אַתָּה *You are eternally mighty, my Lord, the Resuscitator of the dead are You; abundantly able to save.*

תְּהוֹמוֹת *The depths of the footstool* yearn for His droplet,*
and every lush meadow yearns for it.
*Dew — its mention enhances [His] powers,**
it is inscribed in the Mussaf prayer.
*Dew — to resuscitate with it those buried in the cleft of rocks.**

[In some congregations the Ark is closed while additional prayers (p. 1112) are recited at this point.]

(1) *Deuteronomy* 32:3. (2) *Psalms* 51:17. (3) *Psalms* 78:2. (4) *Exodus* 15:13, 16. (5) Cf. *Psalms* 110:3.

blessing of dew, for which we now pray in this *Mussaf* prayer.

אוֹת יַלְדוּת — *A symbol of youth[ful promise].* The Psalmist compares the sweet and gentle righteousness of Abraham's youth with the sweetness and gentleness of dew (*Rashi* to *Psalms* 110:3). The Patriarch's deeds serve to protect the generations of his offspring.

The allusion to Abraham at the end of this stanza returns us to the theme of the blessing into which it has been inserted.

תְּהוֹמוֹת הֲדוֹם — *The depths of the footstool.* The earth is referred to as God's footstool (*Isaiah* 66:1).

זִכְרוֹ גְבוּרוֹת מוֹסִיפִים — *Its mention enhances [His] powers.* The אַתָּה גִּבּוֹר verse in *Shemoneh Esrei* is called גְּבוּרוֹת גְּשָׁמִים, *the powers of rain,* because it describes God's mastery over precipitation. In a deeper sense, man's recognition of God's omnipotence increases holiness — hence, God's perceived power — on earth.

לְהַחֲיוֹת בּוֹ נְקוּקֵי סְעִיפִים — *To resuscitate with it those buried in the cleft of rocks.* As noted above, the dead will be resuscitated with a spiritual force referred to as 'dew.' In ancient *Eretz Yisrael* it was common to bury the dead in openings carved out of solid rock, thus the reference to clefts of rocks.

אֱלֹהֵינוּ וֵאלֹהֵי אֲבוֹתֵינוּ,

טַל תֵּן* לִרְצוֹת אַרְצָךְ,[1]
שִׁיתֵנוּ בְרָכָה בְּדִיצָךְ,
רֹב דָּגָן וְתִירוֹשׁ[2] בְּהַפְרִיצָךְ,[3]
קוֹמֵם עִיר בָּהּ חֶפְצָךְ,[4]* בְּטָל.

טַל צַוֵּה שָׁנָה טוֹבָה וּמְעֻטֶּרֶת,
פְּרִי הָאָרֶץ* לְגָאוֹן וּלְתִפְאֶרֶת,[5]
עִיר כַּסֻּכָּה נוֹתֶרֶת,[6]*
שִׂימָהּ בְּיָדְךָ עֲטֶרֶת,[7] בְּטָל.

טַל נוֹפֵף עֲלֵי אֶרֶץ בְּרוּכָה,
מִמֶּגֶד שָׁמַיִם שַׂבְּעֵנוּ בְרָכָה,[8]
לְהָאִיר מִתּוֹךְ חֲשֵׁכָה,[9]
כַּנָּה* אַחֲרֶיךָ מְשׁוּכָה, בְּטָל.

טַל יַעֲסִיס צוּף הָרִים,*
טְעֵם בִּמְאוֹדֶךָ מֻבְחָרִים,
חֲנוּנֶיךָ חַלֵּץ מִמַּסְגֵּרִים,
זִמְרָה נַנְעִים וְקוֹל נָרִים, בְּטָל.

טַל וָשׂוֹבַע מַלֵּא אֲסָמֵינוּ,[10]
הֲכָעֵת תְּחַדֵּשׁ יָמֵינוּ,[11]
דּוֹד כְּעֶרְכְּךָ הַעֲמֵד שְׁמֵנוּ,
גַּן רָוֶה[12] שִׂימֵנוּ, בְּטָל.

טַל בּוֹ תְבָרֵךְ מָזוֹן,
בְּמִשְׁמַנֵּינוּ אַל יְהִי רָזוֹן,[13]
אֲיֻמָּה אֲשֶׁר הִסַּעְתָּ כַּצֹּאן,[14]
אָנָּא תָּפֵק לָהּ רָצוֹן,[15] בְּטָל.

שָׁאַתָּה הוּא יהוה אֱלֹהֵינוּ, מַשִּׁיב הָרוּחַ וּמוֹרִיד הַטָּל.

Cong. then *chazzan* – **לִבְרָכָה וְלֹא לִקְלָלָה.** (Cong. – אָמֵן.)

Cong. then *chazzan* – **לְחַיִּים וְלֹא לְמָוֶת.** (Cong. – אָמֵן.)

Cong. then *chazzan* – **לְשׂוֹבַע וְלֹא לְרָזוֹן.** (Cong. – אָמֵן.)

THE ARK IS CLOSED.

Our God and the God of our forefathers:
Dew — **ת** *give it* to favor Your land;*[1]
ש *establish us for blessing in Your pleasure;*
ר *with abundant grain and wine*[2] *may You strengthen [us];*[3]
ק *establish the city of Your desire*[4]* — *with dew.*
Dew — **צ** *decree it for a year that is good and crowned;*
פ *may the fruit of the earth* become the pride and splendor;*[5]
ע *The city deserted like a booth*[6]* —
ס *let Your hand make it a crown*[7] — *with dew.*
Dew — **נ** *let it drop sweetly on the blessed land,*
מ *with the delicacies of heaven sate us with blessing,*[8]
ל *to enlighten from amid the darkness*
כ *the fundamental nation* that is drawn after You*[9] — *with dew.*
Dew — **י** *let it sweeten the honey of the mountains,**
ט *let the chosen [people] savor Your plenty.*
ח *Free Your favored ones from bondage;*
ז *sweetly we will sing and raise our voice!* — *with dew.*
Dew — **ו** *and plenty, may they fill our granaries,*[10]
ה *if only You would now rejuvenate our days!*[11]
ד *Beloved One, make our names enduring like Your own,*
ג *make us like a well-watered garden*[12] — *with dew.*
Dew — **ב** *may You bless [our] sustenance with it,*
ב *in our abundance may there be no scarcity.*[13]
א *This nation that You led like sheep*[14] —
א *please, fulfill her desire*[15] — *with dew.*

For You are HASHEM, our God,
Who makes the wind blow and makes the dew descend.

Cong. then *chazzan* — **For blessing and not for curse.** (Cong. — *Amen.)*
Cong. then *chazzan* — **For life and not for death.** (Cong. — *Amen.)*
Cong. then *chazzan* — **For plenty and not for scarcity.** (Cong. — *Amen.)*

THE ARK IS CLOSED.

(1) Cf. *Psalms* 85:2 [some *machzorim* read לִרְצוֹת]. (2) Cf. *Genesis* 27:28. (3) Cf. *Proverbs* 3:10. (4) Cf. *Isaiah* 62:4. (5) Cf. 4:2. (6) Cf. 1:8. (7) Cf. 62:3. (8) Cf. *Deuteronomy* 33:13. (9) Cf. *Song of Songs* 1:4. (10) Cf. *Proverbs* 3:10. (11) Cf. *Lamentations* 5:21. (12) Cf. *Isaiah* 58:11. (13) Cf. 10:16. (14) Cf. *Psalms* 78:52. (15) Cf. *Proverbs* 8:35.

טַל תֵּן — *Dew — give it.* The verses of this *piyut* follow a reverse *aleph-beis* acrostic (תשר״ק) as indicated by the bold print.

קוֹמֵם עִיר בָּהּ חֶפְצְךָ — *Establish the city of Your desire.* No prayer for success and prosperity is complete without a plea for the rebuilding of Jerusalem, the city of God's delight.

פְּרִי הָאָרֶץ — *The fruit of the earth. Isaiah* (4:2) likens the redeemed Jews of the future to the fruit of the earth.

עִיר כַּסֻּכָּה נוֹתֶרֶת — *The city deserted like a booth.* This refers to the booth put up by field hands for shade. Once the harvest is over, it has no utility and is deserted.

כַּנָּה — *The fundamental nation.* Since Israel is the nation charged with the mission of upholding the Torah and carrying out God's plan for creation, it is the 'foundation' of the universe.

צוּף הָרִים — *The honey of the mountains.* Alternatively, *sweeten the mountains' [crops] like honey (Matteh Levi).*

[The congregation may sit;] the *chazzan* continues:

מְכַלְכֵּל חַיִּים בְּחֶסֶד, מְחַיֵּה מֵתִים בְּרַחֲמִים רַבִּים, סוֹמֵךְ נוֹפְלִים, וְרוֹפֵא חוֹלִים, וּמַתִּיר אֲסוּרִים, וּמְקַיֵּם אֱמוּנָתוֹ לִישֵׁנֵי עָפָר. מִי כָמְוֹךָ בַּעַל גְּבוּרוֹת, וּמִי דּוֹמֶה לָּךְ, מֶלֶךְ מֵמִית וּמְחַיֶּה וּמַצְמִיחַ יְשׁוּעָה. וְנֶאֱמָן אַתָּה לְהַחֲיוֹת מֵתִים. בָּרוּךְ אַתָּה יהוה, מְחַיֵּה הַמֵּתִים. (Cong. – אָמֵן)

קדושה

When reciting *Kedushah,* one must stand with his feet together and avoid any interruptions. One should rise on his toes when saying the words קָדוֹשׁ, קָדוֹשׁ, קָדוֹשׁ; בָּרוּךְ (of בָּרוּךְ כְּבוֹד); and יִמְלֹךְ.

Cong. then *chazzan*:

נַעֲרִיצְךָ וְנַקְדִּישְׁךָ כְּסוֹד שִׂיחַ שַׂרְפֵי קֹדֶשׁ, הַמַּקְדִּישִׁים שִׁמְךָ בַּקֹּדֶשׁ, כַּכָּתוּב עַל יַד נְבִיאֶךָ, וְקָרָא זֶה אֶל זֶה וְאָמַר:

All – קָדוֹשׁ קָדוֹשׁ קָדוֹשׁ יהוה צְבָאוֹת, מְלֹא כָל הָאָרֶץ כְּבוֹדוֹ.[1] ❖ כְּבוֹדוֹ מָלֵא עוֹלָם, מְשָׁרְתָיו שׁוֹאֲלִים זֶה לָזֶה, אַיֵּה מְקוֹם כְּבוֹדוֹ, לְעֻמָּתָם בָּרוּךְ יֹאמֵרוּ:

All – בָּרוּךְ כְּבוֹד יהוה, מִמְּקוֹמוֹ.[2] ❖ מִמְּקוֹמוֹ הוּא יִפֶן בְּרַחֲמִים, וְיָחוֹן עַם הַמְּיַחֲדִים שְׁמוֹ, עֶרֶב וָבֹקֶר בְּכָל יוֹם תָּמִיד, פַּעֲמַיִם בְּאַהֲבָה שְׁמַע אוֹמְרִים.

All – שְׁמַע יִשְׂרָאֵל, יהוה אֱלֹהֵינוּ, יהוה אֶחָד.[3] ❖ הוּא אֱלֹהֵינוּ. הוּא אָבִינוּ, הוּא מַלְכֵּנוּ, הוּא מוֹשִׁיעֵנוּ, וְהוּא יַשְׁמִיעֵנוּ בְּרַחֲמָיו שֵׁנִית, לְעֵינֵי כָּל חָי, לִהְיוֹת לָכֶם לֵאלֹהִים, אֲנִי יהוה אֱלֹהֵיכֶם.[4]

All – אַדִּיר אַדִּירֵנוּ, יהוה אֲדֹנֵינוּ, מָה אַדִּיר שִׁמְךָ בְּכָל הָאָרֶץ.[5] וְהָיָה יהוה לְמֶלֶךְ עַל כָּל הָאָרֶץ, בַּיּוֹם הַהוּא יִהְיֶה יהוה אֶחָד וּשְׁמוֹ אֶחָד.[6]

Chazzan – וּבְדִבְרֵי קָדְשְׁךָ כָּתוּב לֵאמֹר:

All – יִמְלֹךְ יהוה לְעוֹלָם, אֱלֹהַיִךְ צִיּוֹן, לְדֹר וָדֹר, הַלְלוּיָהּ.[7]

קדושת השם

Chazzan continues:

לְדוֹר וָדוֹר נַגִּיד גָּדְלֶךָ וּלְנֵצַח נְצָחִים קְדֻשָּׁתְךָ נַקְדִּישׁ, וְשִׁבְחֲךָ אֱלֹהֵינוּ מִפִּינוּ לֹא יָמוּשׁ לְעוֹלָם וָעֶד, כִּי אֵל מֶלֶךְ גָּדוֹל וְקָדוֹשׁ אָתָּה. בָּרוּךְ אַתָּה יהוה, הָאֵל הַקָּדוֹשׁ. (Cong. – אָמֵן.)

קדושת היום

אַתָּה בְחַרְתָּנוּ מִכָּל הָעַמִּים, אָהַבְתָּ אוֹתָנוּ, וְרָצִיתָ בָּנוּ, וְרוֹמַמְתָּנוּ מִכָּל הַלְּשׁוֹנוֹת, וְקִדַּשְׁתָּנוּ בְּמִצְוֹתֶיךָ, וְקֵרַבְתָּנוּ מַלְכֵּנוּ לַעֲבוֹדָתֶךָ, וְשִׁמְךָ הַגָּדוֹל וְהַקָּדוֹשׁ עָלֵינוּ קָרָאתָ.

[The congregation may sit;] the *chazzan* continues:

He sustains the living with kindness, resuscitates the dead with abundant mercy, supports the fallen, heals the sick, releases the confined, and maintains His faith to those asleep in the dust. Who is like You, O Master of mighty deeds, and who is comparable to You, O King Who causes death and restores life and makes salvation sprout! And You are faithful to resuscitate the dead. Blessed are You, HASHEM, *Who resuscitates the dead.* (Cong.– *Amen.*)

KEDUSHAH

When reciting *Kedushah,* one must stand with his feet together and avoid any interruptions. One should rise on his toes when saying the words *Holy, holy, holy; Blessed is;* HASHEM *shall reign.*

Cong. then *chazzan:*

נַעֲרִיצְךָ *We will revere You and sanctify You according to the counsel of the holy Seraphim, who sanctify Your Name in the Sanctuary, as it is written by Your prophet: "And one [angel] will call another and say:*

All – *'Holy, holy, holy is* HASHEM, *Master of Legions, the whole world is filled with His glory.'"*[1] ❖*His glory fills the world. His ministering angels ask one another, 'Where is the place of His glory?' Those facing them say 'Blessed':*

All – *'Blessed is the glory of* HASHEM *from His place.'*[2] ❖*From His place may He turn with compassion and be gracious to the people who declare the Oneness of His Name; evening and morning, every day constantly, twice, with love, they proclaim 'Shema.'*

All – *'Hear O Israel:* HASHEM *is our God,* HASHEM *the One and Only.'*[3] ❖*He is our God; He is our Father; He is our King; He is our Savior; and He will let us hear, in His compassion, for a second time in the presence of all the living, '. . . to be a God to you, I am* HASHEM, *your God.'*[4]

All – *Mighty is our Mighty One,* HASHEM, *our Master — how mighty is Your name throughout the earth!*[5] HASHEM *will be King over all the world — on that day* HASHEM *will be One and His Name will be One.*[6]

Chazzan – *And in Your holy Writings the following is written:*

All – *'*HASHEM *shall reign forever — your God, O Zion — from generation to generation, Halleluyah!'*[7]

HOLINESS OF GOD'S NAME

Chazzan continues:

לְדוֹר *From generation to generation we shall relate Your greatness and for infinite eternities we shall proclaim Your holiness. Your praise, our God, shall not leave our mouth forever and ever, for You, O God, are a great and holy King. Blessed are You,* HASHEM, *the holy God.* (Cong.– *Amen.*)

SANCTIFICATION OF THE DAY

אַתָּה בְחַרְתָּנוּ *You have chosen us from all the peoples; You loved us and found favor in us; You exalted us above all the tongues and You sanctified us with Your commandments. You drew us close, our King, to Your service and proclaimed Your great and Holy Name upon us.*

---

(1) *Isaiah* 6:3. (2) *Ezekiel* 3:12. (3) *Deuteronomy* 6:4.
(4) *Numbers* 15:41. (5) *Psalms* 8:2. (6) *Zechariah* 14:9. (7) *Psalms* 146:10.

On the Sabbath add the words in brackets. [If forgotten, see *Laws* §86-90.]

וַתִּתֶּן לָנוּ יהוה אֱלֹהֵינוּ בְּאַהֲבָה [שַׁבָּתוֹת לִמְנוּחָה וּ]מוֹעֲדִים לְשִׂמְחָה חַגִּים וּזְמַנִּים לְשָׂשׂוֹן, אֶת יוֹם [הַשַּׁבָּת הַזֶּה וְאֶת יוֹם] חַג הַמַּצּוֹת הַזֶּה, זְמַן חֵרוּתֵנוּ [בְּאַהֲבָה] מִקְרָא קֹדֶשׁ, זֵכֶר לִיצִיאַת מִצְרָיִם.

וּמִפְּנֵי חֲטָאֵינוּ גָּלִינוּ מֵאַרְצֵנוּ, וְנִתְרַחַקְנוּ מֵעַל אַדְמָתֵנוּ. וְאֵין אֲנַחְנוּ יְכוֹלִים לַעֲלוֹת וְלֵרָאוֹת וּלְהִשְׁתַּחֲווֹת לְפָנֶיךָ, וְלַעֲשׂוֹת חוֹבוֹתֵינוּ בְּבֵית בְּחִירָתֶךָ, בַּבַּיִת הַגָּדוֹל וְהַקָּדוֹשׁ שֶׁנִּקְרָא שִׁמְךָ עָלָיו, מִפְּנֵי הַיָּד שֶׁנִּשְׁתַּלְּחָה בְּמִקְדָּשֶׁךָ. יְהִי רָצוֹן מִלְּפָנֶיךָ יהוה אֱלֹהֵינוּ וֵאלֹהֵי אֲבוֹתֵינוּ, מֶלֶךְ רַחֲמָן, שֶׁתָּשׁוּב וּתְרַחֵם עָלֵינוּ וְעַל מִקְדָּשְׁךָ בְּרַחֲמֶיךָ הָרַבִּים, וְתִבְנֵהוּ מְהֵרָה וּתְגַדֵּל כְּבוֹדוֹ. אָבִינוּ מַלְכֵּנוּ, גַּלֵּה כְּבוֹד מַלְכוּתְךָ עָלֵינוּ מְהֵרָה, וְהוֹפַע וְהִנָּשֵׂא עָלֵינוּ לְעֵינֵי כָּל חָי. וְקָרֵב פְּזוּרֵינוּ מִבֵּין הַגּוֹיִם, וּנְפוּצוֹתֵינוּ כַּנֵּס מִיַּרְכְּתֵי אָרֶץ. וַהֲבִיאֵנוּ לְצִיּוֹן עִירְךָ בְּרִנָּה, וְלִירוּשָׁלַיִם בֵּית מִקְדָּשְׁךָ בְּשִׂמְחַת עוֹלָם. וְשָׁם נַעֲשֶׂה לְפָנֶיךָ אֶת קָרְבְּנוֹת חוֹבוֹתֵינוּ, תְּמִידִים כְּסִדְרָם, וּמוּסָפִים כְּהִלְכָתָם. וְאֶת [Weekdays – מוּסַף יוֹם] [Sabbath – מוּסְפֵי יוֹם הַשַּׁבָּת הַזֶּה וְיוֹם] חַג הַמַּצּוֹת הַזֶּה נַעֲשֶׂה וְנַקְרִיב לְפָנֶיךָ בְּאַהֲבָה כְּמִצְוַת רְצוֹנֶךָ, כְּמוֹ שֶׁכָּתַבְתָּ עָלֵינוּ בְּתוֹרָתֶךָ, עַל יְדֵי מֹשֶׁה עַבְדֶּךָ, מִפִּי כְבוֹדֶךָ כָּאָמוּר:

On the Sabbath add. [If forgotten, do not repeat *Shemoneh Esrei*. See *Laws* §86.]

וּבְיוֹם הַשַּׁבָּת שְׁנֵי כְבָשִׂים בְּנֵי שָׁנָה תְּמִימִם, וּשְׁנֵי עֶשְׂרֹנִים סֹלֶת מִנְחָה בְּלוּלָה בַשֶּׁמֶן, וְנִסְכּוֹ. עֹלַת שַׁבַּת בְּשַׁבַּתּוֹ, עַל עֹלַת הַתָּמִיד וְנִסְכָּהּ.[1] (זֶה קָרְבַּן שַׁבָּת. וְקָרְבַּן הַיּוֹם כָּאָמוּר:)

וּבַחֹדֶשׁ הָרִאשׁוֹן בְּאַרְבָּעָה עָשָׂר יוֹם לַחֹדֶשׁ, פֶּסַח לַיהוה. וּבַחֲמִשָּׁה עָשָׂר יוֹם לַחֹדֶשׁ הַזֶּה, חָג, שִׁבְעַת יָמִים מַצּוֹת יֵאָכֵל. בַּיּוֹם הָרִאשׁוֹן מִקְרָא קֹדֶשׁ, כָּל מְלֶאכֶת עֲבֹדָה לֹא תַעֲשׂוּ. וְהִקְרַבְתֶּם אִשֶּׁה עֹלָה לַיהוה, פָּרִים בְּנֵי בָקָר שְׁנַיִם, וְאַיִל אֶחָד, וְשִׁבְעָה כְבָשִׂים בְּנֵי שָׁנָה, תְּמִימִם יִהְיוּ לָכֶם.[2] וּמִנְחָתָם וְנִסְכֵּיהֶם כִּמְדֻבָּר, שְׁלֹשָׁה עֶשְׂרֹנִים לַפָּר, וּשְׁנֵי עֶשְׂרֹנִים לָאָיִל, וְעִשָּׂרוֹן לַכֶּבֶשׂ, וְיַיִן כְּנִסְכּוֹ. וְשָׂעִיר לְכַפֵּר, וּשְׁנֵי תְמִידִים כְּהִלְכָתָם.

On the Sabbath add the words in brackets. [If forgotten, see *Laws* §86-90.]

וַתִּתֶּן לָנוּ *And You gave us,* HASHEM, *our God, with love [Sabbaths for rest], appointed festivals for gladness, Festivals and times for joy, [this day of Sabbath and] this day of the Festival of Matzos, the time of our freedom [with love], a holy convocation, a memorial of the Exodus from Egypt.*

וּמִפְּנֵי חֲטָאֵינוּ *But because of our sins we have been exiled from our land and sent far from our soil. We cannot ascend to appear and to prostrate ourselves before You, and to perform our obligations in the House of Your choice, in the great and holy House upon which Your Name was proclaimed, because of the hand that was dispatched against Your Sanctuary. May it be Your will,* HASHEM, *our God and the God of our forefathers, O merciful King, that You once more be compassionate upon us and upon Your Sanctuary in Your abundant mercy, and rebuild it soon and magnify its glory. Our Father, our King, reveal the glory of Your Kingship upon us, speedily; appear and be uplifted over us before the eyes of all the living. Draw our scattered ones near, from among the nations, and bring in our dispersions from the ends of the earth. Bring us to Zion, Your City, in glad song, and to Jerusalem, home of Your Sanctuary, in eternal joy. There we will perform before You our obligatory offerings, the continual offerings according to their order and the additional offerings according to their law. And the additional offering[s of this day of Sabbath and] of this day of the Festival of Matzos, we will perform and bring near to You with love, according to the commandment of Your will, as You have written for us in Your Torah, through Moses, Your servant, from Your glorious expression, as it is said:*

On the Sabbath add. [If forgotten, do not repeat *Shemoneh Esrei.* See *Laws* §86.]

וּבְיוֹם הַשַּׁבָּת *On the Sabbath day: two [male] first-year lambs, unblemished; and two tenth-ephah of fine flour for a meal-offering, mixed with olive oil, and its wine-libation. The elevation-offering of the Sabbath must be on its particular Sabbath, in addition to the continual elevation-offering and its wine-libation.*[1] *(This is the offering of the Sabbath. And the offering of the day is as it is said:)*

וּבַחֹדֶשׁ ***And in the first month on the fourteenth day of the month — the Pesach offering to* HASHEM. *And on the fifteenth day of this month — a festival; for seven days, matzos are to be eaten. On the first day is a holy convocation, you may not do any laborious work. You are to bring a fire-offering, an elevation-offering to* HASHEM, *two young bulls, one ram and seven male lambs in their first year, they shall be unblemished for you.*[2] *And their meal-offerings and their wine-libations as mentioned: three tenth-ephah for each bull; two tenth-ephah for each ram; one tenth-ephah for each lamb; and wine for its libation. A he-goat for atonement, and two continual offerings according to their law.***

(1) *Numbers* 28:9-10. (2) 28:16-19.

On the Sabbath add. [If forgotten, do not repeat *Shemoneh Esrei*. See *Laws* §86.]

יִשְׂמְחוּ בְמַלְכוּתְךָ שׁוֹמְרֵי שַׁבָּת וְקוֹרְאֵי עֹנֶג, עַם מְקַדְּשֵׁי שְׁבִיעִי, כֻּלָּם יִשְׂבְּעוּ וְיִתְעַנְּגוּ מִטּוּבֶךָ, וּבַשְּׁבִיעִי רָצִיתָ בּוֹ וְקִדַּשְׁתּוֹ, חֶמְדַּת יָמִים אוֹתוֹ קָרָאתָ, זֵכֶר לְמַעֲשֵׂה בְרֵאשִׁית.

On the Sabbath add the words in brackets. [If forgotten, see *Laws* §86-90.]

אֱלֹהֵינוּ וֵאלֹהֵי אֲבוֹתֵינוּ, [רְצֵה בִמְנוּחָתֵנוּ] מֶלֶךְ רַחֲמָן רַחֵם עָלֵינוּ, טוֹב וּמֵטִיב הִדָּרֶשׁ לָנוּ, שׁוּבָה אֵלֵינוּ בַּהֲמוֹן רַחֲמֶיךָ, בִּגְלַל אָבוֹת שֶׁעָשׂוּ רְצוֹנֶךָ. בְּנֵה בֵיתְךָ כְּבַתְּחִלָּה, וְכוֹנֵן מִקְדָּשְׁךָ עַל מְכוֹנוֹ, וְהַרְאֵנוּ בְּבִנְיָנוֹ, וְשַׂמְּחֵנוּ בְּתִקּוּנוֹ. וְהָשֵׁב כֹּהֲנִים לַעֲבוֹדָתָם, וּלְוִיִּם לְשִׁירָם וּלְזִמְרָם, וְהָשֵׁב יִשְׂרָאֵל לִנְוֵיהֶם. וְשָׁם נַעֲלֶה וְנֵרָאֶה וְנִשְׁתַּחֲוֶה לְפָנֶיךָ, בְּשָׁלֹשׁ פַּעֲמֵי רְגָלֵינוּ, כַּכָּתוּב בְּתוֹרָתֶךָ: שָׁלוֹשׁ פְּעָמִים בַּשָּׁנָה, יֵרָאֶה כָל זְכוּרְךָ אֶת פְּנֵי יהוה אֱלֹהֶיךָ, בַּמָּקוֹם אֲשֶׁר יִבְחָר, בְּחַג הַמַּצּוֹת, וּבְחַג הַשָּׁבֻעוֹת, וּבְחַג הַסֻּכּוֹת, וְלֹא יֵרָאֶה אֶת פְּנֵי יהוה רֵיקָם. אִישׁ כְּמַתְּנַת יָדוֹ, כְּבִרְכַּת יהוה אֱלֹהֶיךָ, אֲשֶׁר נָתַן לָךְ:[1]

וְהַשִּׂיאֵנוּ יהוה אֱלֹהֵינוּ אֶת בִּרְכַּת מוֹעֲדֶיךָ לְחַיִּים וּלְשָׁלוֹם, לְשִׂמְחָה וּלְשָׂשׂוֹן, כַּאֲשֶׁר רָצִיתָ וְאָמַרְתָּ לְבָרְכֵנוּ. [אֱלֹהֵינוּ וֵאלֹהֵי אֲבוֹתֵינוּ רְצֵה בִמְנוּחָתֵנוּ] קַדְּשֵׁנוּ בְּמִצְוֹתֶיךָ וְתֵן חֶלְקֵנוּ בְּתוֹרָתֶךָ, שַׂבְּעֵנוּ מִטּוּבֶךָ וְשַׂמְּחֵנוּ בִּישׁוּעָתֶךָ, וְטַהֵר לִבֵּנוּ לְעָבְדְּךָ בֶּאֱמֶת, וְהַנְחִילֵנוּ יהוה אֱלֹהֵינוּ [בְּאַהֲבָה וּבְרָצוֹן] בְּשִׂמְחָה וּבְשָׂשׂוֹן [שַׁבָּת וּ]מוֹעֲדֵי קָדְשֶׁךָ, וְיִשְׂמְחוּ בְךָ יִשְׂרָאֵל מְקַדְּשֵׁי שְׁמֶךָ. בָּרוּךְ אַתָּה יהוה, מְקַדֵּשׁ [הַשַּׁבָּת וְ]יִשְׂרָאֵל וְהַזְּמַנִּים. (Cong.– אָמֵן.)

עבודה

רְצֵה יהוה אֱלֹהֵינוּ בְּעַמְּךָ יִשְׂרָאֵל וּבִתְפִלָּתָם, וְהָשֵׁב אֶת הָעֲבוֹדָה לִדְבִיר בֵּיתֶךָ. וְאִשֵּׁי יִשְׂרָאֵל וּתְפִלָּתָם בְּאַהֲבָה תְקַבֵּל בְּרָצוֹן, וּתְהִי לְרָצוֹן תָּמִיד עֲבוֹדַת יִשְׂרָאֵל עַמֶּךָ.

On the Sabbath add. [If forgotten, do not repeat *Shemoneh Esrei*. See *Laws* §86.]

יִשְׂמְחוּ *They shall rejoice in Your Kingship — those who observe the Sabbath and call it a delight. The people that sanctifies the Seventh — they will all be satisfied and delighted from Your goodness. And the Seventh — You found favor in it and sanctified it. 'Most coveted of days' You called it, a remembrance of creation.*

On the Sabbath add the words in brackets. [If forgotten, see *Laws* §86-90.]

אֱלֹהֵינוּ *Our God and the God of our forefathers, [may You be pleased with our rest] O merciful King, have mercy on us; O good and beneficent One, let Yourself be sought out by us; return to us in Your yearning mercy for the sake of the forefathers who did Your will. Rebuild Your House as it was at first, and establish Your Sanctuary on its prepared site; show us its rebuilding and gladden us in its perfection. Restore the Kohanim to their service and the Levites to their song and music; and restore Israel to their dwellings. And there we will ascend and appear and prostrate ourselves before You, during our three pilgrimage seasons, as it is written in Your Torah: Three times a year all your males are to appear before HASHEM, your God, in the place He shall choose, on the Festival of Matzos, on the Festival of Shavuos, and on the Festival of Succos, and they shall not appear before HASHEM empty-handed. Every man according to the gift of his hand, according to the blessing of HASHEM, your God, that He gave you.*[1]

וְהַשִּׂיאֵנוּ *Bestow upon us, O HASHEM, our God, the blessing of Your appointed Festivals for life and for peace, for gladness and for joy, as You desired and promised to bless us. [Our God and the God of our forefathers, may You be pleased with our rest.] Sanctify us with Your commandments and grant us our share in Your Torah; satisfy us from Your goodness and gladden us with Your salvation, and purify our heart to serve You sincerely. And grant us a heritage, O HASHEM, our God — [with love and with favor] with gladness and with joy — [the Sabbath and] the appointed festivals of Your holiness, and may Israel, the sanctifiers of Your Name, rejoice in You. Blessed are You, HASHEM, Who sanctifies [the Sabbath] Israel and the festive seasons.*

(Cong.— *Amen.*)

TEMPLE SERVICE

רְצֵה *Be favorable, HASHEM, our God, toward Your people Israel and their prayer and restore the service to the Holy of Holies of Your Temple. The fire-offerings of Israel and their prayer accept with love and favor, and may the service of Your people Israel always be favorable to You.*

(1) *Deuteronomy* 16:16-17.

ברכת כהנים

When the *Kohanim* ascend the *duchan* to pronounce *Bircas Kohanim* [the Priestly Blessing], the *chazzan's* repetition of *Shemoneh Esrei* continues below.
If no *Kohanim* are present, *chazzan* continues with וְתֶחֱזֶינָה, below.
Congregation and *Kohanim,* then *chazzan.*

וְתֶעֱרַב לְפָנֶיךָ עֲתִירָתֵנוּ כְּעוֹלָה וּכְקָרְבָּן. אָנָּא, רַחוּם, בְּרַחֲמֶיךָ הָרַבִּים הָשֵׁב שְׁכִינָתְךָ לְצִיּוֹן עִירֶךָ, וְסֵדֶר הָעֲבוֹדָה לִירוּשָׁלָיִם. וְתֶחֱזֶינָה עֵינֵינוּ בְּשׁוּבְךָ לְצִיּוֹן בְּרַחֲמִים, וְשָׁם נַעֲבָדְךָ בְּיִרְאָה כִּימֵי עוֹלָם וּכְשָׁנִים קַדְמוֹנִיּוֹת.

Chazzan concludes when וְתֶעֱרַב is recited:

בָּרוּךְ אַתָּה יהוה, שֶׁאוֹתְךָ לְבַדְּךָ בְּיִרְאָה נַעֲבוֹד.

Chazzan concludes when וְתֶעֱרַב is not recited:

וְתֶחֱזֶינָה עֵינֵינוּ בְּשׁוּבְךָ לְצִיּוֹן בְּרַחֲמִים. בָּרוּךְ אַתָּה יהוה, הַמַּחֲזִיר שְׁכִינָתוֹ לְצִיּוֹן.

(—Cong. and *Kohanim* אָמֵן.)

הודאה

The *chazzan* recites the entire מוֹדִים aloud, while the congregation recites מוֹדִים דְּרַבָּנָן softly. Bow at מוֹדִים; straighten up at ה׳.

מוֹדִים אֲנַחְנוּ לָךְ, שָׁאַתָּה הוּא יהוה אֱלֹהֵינוּ וֵאלֹהֵי אֲבוֹתֵינוּ לְעוֹלָם וָעֶד. צוּר חַיֵּינוּ, מָגֵן יִשְׁעֵנוּ אַתָּה הוּא לְדוֹר וָדוֹר. נוֹדֶה לְּךָ וּנְסַפֵּר תְּהִלָּתֶךָ[1] עַל חַיֵּינוּ הַמְּסוּרִים בְּיָדֶךָ, וְעַל נִשְׁמוֹתֵינוּ הַפְּקוּדוֹת לָךְ, וְעַל נִסֶּיךָ שֶׁבְּכָל יוֹם עִמָּנוּ, וְעַל נִפְלְאוֹתֶיךָ וְטוֹבוֹתֶיךָ שֶׁבְּכָל עֵת, עֶרֶב וָבֹקֶר וְצָהֳרָיִם. הַטּוֹב כִּי לֹא כָלוּ רַחֲמֶיךָ, וְהַמְּרַחֵם כִּי לֹא תַמּוּ חֲסָדֶיךָ,[2] מֵעוֹלָם קִוִּינוּ לָךְ.

מודים דרבנן

מוֹדִים אֲנַחְנוּ לָךְ, שָׁאַתָּה הוּא יהוה אֱלֹהֵינוּ וֵאלֹהֵי אֲבוֹתֵינוּ, אֱלֹהֵי כָל בָּשָׂר, יוֹצְרֵנוּ, יוֹצֵר בְּרֵאשִׁית. בְּרָכוֹת וְהוֹדָאוֹת לְשִׁמְךָ הַגָּדוֹל וְהַקָּדוֹשׁ, עַל שֶׁהֶחֱיִיתָנוּ וְקִיַּמְתָּנוּ. כֵּן תְּחַיֵּנוּ וּתְקַיְּמֵנוּ, וְתֶאֱסוֹף גָּלֻיּוֹתֵינוּ לְחַצְרוֹת קָדְשֶׁךָ, לִשְׁמוֹר חֻקֶּיךָ וְלַעֲשׂוֹת רְצוֹנֶךָ, וּלְעָבְדְּךָ בְּלֵבָב שָׁלֵם, עַל שֶׁאֲנַחְנוּ מוֹדִים לָךְ. בָּרוּךְ אֵל הַהוֹדָאוֹת.

וְעַל כֻּלָּם יִתְבָּרַךְ וְיִתְרוֹמַם שִׁמְךָ מַלְכֵּנוּ תָּמִיד לְעוֹלָם וָעֶד.

The *chazzan* bends his knees at בָּרוּךְ; bows at אַתָּה; and straightens up at ה׳.
When the *chazzan* recites וְכֹל הַחַיִּים, the *Kohanim* recite יְהִי רָצוֹן.

וְכֹל הַחַיִּים יוֹדְוּךָ סֶּלָה, וִיהַלְלוּ אֶת שִׁמְךָ בֶּאֱמֶת, הָאֵל יְשׁוּעָתֵנוּ וְעֶזְרָתֵנוּ סֶלָה. בָּרוּךְ אַתָּה יהוה, הַטּוֹב שִׁמְךָ וּלְךָ נָאֶה לְהוֹדוֹת. (—Cong. and *Kohanim* אָמֵן.)

יְהִי רָצוֹן מִלְּפָנֶיךָ, יהוה אֱלֹהֵינוּ וֵאלֹהֵי אֲבוֹתֵינוּ, שֶׁתְּהֵא הַבְּרָכָה הַזֹּאת שֶׁצִּוִּיתָנוּ לְבָרֵךְ אֶת עַמְּךָ יִשְׂרָאֵל בְּרָכָה שְׁלֵמָה, וְלֹא יִהְיֶה בָּהּ שׁוּם מִכְשׁוֹל וְעָוֹן מֵעַתָּה וְעַד עוֹלָם.

THE PRIESTLY BLESSING

When the *Kohanim* ascend the *duchan* to pronounce *Bircas Kohanim* [the Priestly Blessing], the *chazzan's* repetition of *Shemoneh Esrei* continues below.
If no *Kohanim* are present, *chazzan* continues with וְתֶחֱזֶינָה, below.
Congregation and *Kohanim*, then *chazzan*.

וְתֶעֱרַב *May our entreaty be pleasing unto You as an elevation-offering and as a sacrifice. Please, O Merciful One, in Your abounding mercy return Your Shechinah to Zion, Your city, and the order of the Temple service to Jerusalem. And may our eyes behold when You return to Zion in mercy, that we may there serve You with awe as in days of old and as in earlier years.*

Chazzan concludes when וְתֶעֱרַב is recited:

בָּרוּךְ *Blessed are You,* H*ASHEM, for You alone do we serve, with awe.* (Cong. and *Kohanim*— *Amen.*)

Chazzan concludes when וְתֶעֱרַב is not recited:

וְתֶחֱזֶינָה *May our eyes behold Your return to Zion in compassion. Blessed are You,* H*ASHEM, Who restores His Presence to Zion.* (Cong.— *Amen.*)

THANKSGIVING [MODIM]

Chazzan recites the entire *Modim* aloud, while the congregation recites *Modim of the Rabbis* softly.
Bow at *'We gratefully thank You'*; straighten up at *'*H*ASHEM.'*

מוֹדִים *We gratefully thank You, for it is You Who are* H*ASHEM, our God and the God of our forefathers for all eternity; Rock of our lives, Shield of our salvation are You from generation to generation. We shall thank You and relate Your praise*[1] *— for our lives, which are committed to Your power and for our souls that are entrusted to You; for Your miracles that are with us every day; and for Your wonders and favors in every season — evening, morning, and afternoon. The Beneficent One, for Your compassions were never exhausted, and the Compassionate One, for Your kindnesses never ended*[2] *— always have we put our hope in You.*

MODIM OF THE RABBIS

מוֹדִים *We gratefully thank You, for it is You Who are* H*ASHEM, our God and the God of our forefathers, the God of all flesh, our Molder, the Molder of the universe. Blessings and thanks are due Your great and holy Name for You have given us life and sustained us. So may You continue to give us life and sustain us and gather our exiles to the Courtyards of Your Sanctuary, to observe Your decrees, to do Your will and to serve You wholeheartedly. [We thank You] for inspiring us to thank You. Blessed is the God of thanksgivings.*

For all these, may Your Name be blessed and exalted, our King, continually forever and ever.

When the *chazzan* recites וְכֹל הַחַיִּים, *Everything alive,* the *Kohanim* recite יְהִי רָצוֹן, *May it be Your will.*

וְכֹל *Everything alive will gratefully acknowledge You, Selah! and praise Your Name sincerely, O God of our salvation and help, Selah! Blessed are You,* H*ASHEM, Your Name is 'The Beneficent One' and to You it is fitting to give thanks.*
(Cong. and *Kohanim*— *Amen.*)

יְהִי רָצוֹן *May it be Your will,* H*ASHEM, our God and the God of our fathers, that this blessing which You have commanded us to bestow upon Your nation Israel be a full blessing, that there be in it neither stumbling block nor sin from now and forever.*

(1) Cf. *Psalms* 79:13. (2) Cf. *Lamentations* 3:22.

IF NO *KOHANIM* ARE PRESENT THE *CHAZZAN* CONTINUES WITH אֱלֹהֵינוּ ON PAGE 434.

The *chazzan* recites the following in an undertone but says the word כֹּהֲנִים aloud as a formal summons to the *Kohanim*• to bless the people. In some communities the congregation, but not the *Kohanim*, responds עַם קְדוֹשֶׁךָ כָּאָמוּר, aloud.

אֱלֹהֵינוּ וֵאלֹהֵי אֲבוֹתֵינוּ, בָּרְכֵנוּ בַבְּרָכָה* הַמְּשֻׁלֶּשֶׁת* בַּתּוֹרָה הַכְּתוּבָה עַל יְדֵי מֹשֶׁה עַבְדֶּךָ, הָאֲמוּרָה מִפִּי אַהֲרֹן וּבָנָיו,

כֹּהֲנִים

עַם קְדוֹשֶׁךָ* — כָּאָמוּר:

The *Kohanim* recite the following blessing aloud, in unison, and the congregation, but not the *chazzan*, responds אָמֵן.

בָּרוּךְ אַתָּה יהוה, אֱלֹהֵינוּ מֶלֶךְ הָעוֹלָם, אֲשֶׁר קִדְּשָׁנוּ בִּקְדֻשָּׁתוֹ שֶׁל אַהֲרֹן,* וְצִוָּנוּ לְבָרֵךְ אֶת עַמּוֹ יִשְׂרָאֵל בְּאַהֲבָה.*

(.Cong.– אָמֵן)

See commentary regarding the related verses• in small print that appear beside the words of the *Kohanim's* blessing.

יְבָרֶכְךָ יְבָרֶכְךָ יהוה מִצִּיּוֹן, עֹשֵׂה שָׁמַיִם וָאָרֶץ.[1]

יהוה* יהוה אֲדֹנֵינוּ, מָה אַדִּיר שִׁמְךָ בְּכָל הָאָרֶץ.[2]

וְיִשְׁמְרֶךָ.* שָׁמְרֵנִי, אֵל, כִּי חָסִיתִי בָךְ.[3]

בִּרְכַּת כֹּהֲנִים / THE PRIESTLY BLESSING

The Midrash (*Bamidbar Rabbah* 11:2) teaches that until the time of the Patriarchs, God Himself retained the power to bless people. With the advent of the Patriarchs, He gave this awesome power to them. After they died, God declared that henceforth the *Kohanim* would bless the Jewish people. Thus, the upraised hands of the *Kohanim* are the vehicle through which God's blessing flows upon His chosen people.

This section is abridged from ArtScroll's *Bircas Kohanim/The Priestly Blessings*, by Rabbi Avie Gold.

אֱלֹהֵינוּ . . . בָּרְכֵנוּ בַבְּרָכָה — *Our God . . . bless us with the ... blessing.* We ask God, not the *Kohanim*, to bless us, because, although the *Kohanim* pronounce the words, they are merely conduits through which the blessing descends from God to the nation below (*Chullin* 49a). This is made clear in the Scriptural commandment, which ends with God's pledge וַאֲנִי אֲבָרְכֵם, *and I will bless them* (*Numbers* 6:27).

הַמְּשֻׁלֶּשֶׁת — *Three-verse.* The Priestly Blessing contains three Torah verses: *Numbers* 6:24-26.

עַם קְדוֹשֶׁךָ — *Your holy people.* The *Kohanim* are so described (*I Chronicles* 23:13) because they were designated to serve God and bless Israel.

בָּרוּךְ . . . בִּקְדֻשָּׁתוֹ שֶׁל אַהֲרֹן — *Blessed . . . with the holiness of Aaron.* Just as the selection of Israel as the Holy Nation is not dependent solely upon the deeds of each individual member, but on the holiness of their forebears — indeed, it is the very sanctity of the Patriarchs which imbued their descendants with a capacity for holiness — so is the sanctity of the *Kehunah* [priesthood] unique among the descendants of Aaron.

בְּאַהֲבָה — *With love.* The *Kohanim* are to feel love for the congregation when they pronounce the blessing. The addition of this phrase is based upon *Zohar* (*Naso* 147b): 'Any *Kohen* who does not have love for the congregation or for whom the congregation has no love, may not raise his hands to bless the congregation . . .'

On his first day as *Kohen Gadol*, when he completed the service, *Aaron raised his hands toward the nation and blessed them* (*Leviticus* 9:22), but we are not told what he said (*Ramban*). This teaches that a person must rejoice in his fellow Jew's good fortune until his heart becomes filled with love, joy and blessing — a blessing so great that mere words cannot express it, so overflowing with love that the very movements of his hands express his joy and love.

Raising the hands is a symbol of a heart pouring forth blessing and joy from a treasure trove of happiness. Raising the hands is not a sterile act — it must be a wholehearted expression of the hope and blessing which are hidden in the soul. An ocean of inexpressible joy issues from a pure soul; and the purer the soul, the purer the blessing (*Ohr Chadash*).

יְבָרֶכְךָ ה׳ — *May HASHEM bless you*, with increasing wealth (*Rashi*) and long life (*Ibn Ezra*).

וְיִשְׁמְרֶךָ — *And safeguard you.* May the above blessings be preserved against loss or attack. Only God can guarantee that no one or nothing can

IF NO *KOHANIM* ARE PRESENT THE *CHAZZAN* CONTINUES WITH אֱלֹהֵינוּ ON PAGE 434.

The *chazzan* recites the following in an undertone but says the word *'Kohanim'* aloud as a formal summons to the *Kohanim*• to bless the people. In some communities the congregation, but not the *Kohanim*, responds, *'Your holy people — as it is said,'* aloud.

אֱלֹהֵינוּ *Our God and the God of our forefathers, bless us with the three-verse* blessing* in the Torah that was written by the hand of Moses, Your servant, that was said by Aaron and his sons, the*

Kohanim,

Your holy people — as it is said:*

The *Kohanim* recite the following blessing aloud, in unison, and the congregation, but not the *chazzan*, responds *Amen.*

בָּרוּךְ *Blessed are You, HASHEM, our God, King of the universe, Who has sanctified us with the holiness of Aaron,* and has commanded us to bless His people Israel with love.** (Cong.— *Amen.*)

See commentary regarding the related verses• in small print that appear beside the words of the *Kohanim's* blessing.

May [He] bless you	*May HASHEM bless you from Zion, Maker of heaven and earth.*[1]
— HASHEM• —	*HASHEM, our Master, how mighty is Your Name throughout the earth!*[2]
and safeguard you.•	*Safeguard me, O God, for in You have I taken refuge.*[3]

(1) *Psalms* 134:3. (2) 8:10. (3) 16:1.

tamper with the gifts He confers upon His loved ones (*Midrash Rabbah*).

Related verses appear alongside the fifteen words of *Bircas Kohanim* in most *Siddurim*. The

Laws of Bircas Kohanim

After *Kedushah,* a Levite pours water from a utensil over the *Kohen's* hands. When the *chazzan* begins רְצֵה the *Kohanim* slip off their shoes (the laces should be loosened before the hands are washed) and ascend the *duchan* [platform in front of the Ark] where they stand facing the Ark.

When the *chazzan* recites וְכֹל הַחַיִּים, the *Kohanim* quietly recite the יְהִי רָצוֹן supplication, concluding it to coincide with the ending of the *chazzan's* blessing, so that the congregational *Amen* will be in response to their prayer as well as the *chazzan's*.

In most congregations, the *chazzan* quietly recites, '. . . אֱלֹהֵינוּ וֵאלֹהֵי אֲבוֹתֵינוּ בָּרְכֵנוּ, *Our God . . . bless us . . .*' until the word כֹּהֲנִים, *Kohanim,* which he calls out in a loud voice. Then, resuming his undertone, he recites the next words, 'עַם קְדוֹשֶׁךָ כָּאָמוּר, *Your holy people, as it is said.*' Even if only one *Kohen* is present, the *chazzan* uses the word *Kohanim* in plural, since it is the established form of the prayer. In some congregations, however, the *chazzan* merely calls out, *'Kohanim,'* without reciting the introductory prayer. In these places the *chazzan* calls out the plural word *Kohanim,* only if two or more *Kohanim* ascend the *duchan*. If only one *Kohen* is present, however, that *Kohen* does not wait for a call, but raises his hands and begins his blessing immediately.

From this point until the *chazzan* begins שִׂים שָׁלוֹם, the congregation stands, facing the *Kohanim* attentively. No one may gaze at the *Kohanim's* raised hands.

Those standing behind the *Kohanim* do not receive the benefits of the blessing. Therefore, people behind them should move up during *Bircas Kohanim*.

The *chazzan* reads each word of *Bircas Kohanim* aloud and the *Kohanim* repeat it after him. The congregation may not respond אָמֵן until the *Kohanim* have completed the initial blessing; the *chazzan* may not call out יְבָרֶכְךָ until the congregation has finished its אָמֵן; the *Kohanim* may not repeat יְבָרֶכְךָ until the *chazzan* has read the full word; etc., etc.

When the *chazzan* begins שִׂים שָׁלוֹם, the *Kohanim,* with hands still raised, turn to the Ark, then lower their hands. While the *chazzan* recites שִׂים שָׁלוֹם, the *Kohanim* recite . . . רִבּוֹנוֹ שֶׁל עוֹלָם עָשִׂינוּ and the congregation recites אַדִּיר בַּמָּרוֹם. All should conclude their respective prayers simultaneously with the *chazzan's* conclusion of שִׂים שָׁלוֹם.

It is preferable that the *Kohanim* not return to their seats until after the *chazzan* completes *Kaddish* (except on Succos when the *Hoshana* prayers are recited before *Kaddish*).

The *Kohanim* sing an extended chant before saying וְיִשְׁמְרֶךָ, and the congregation recites the following supplication in an undertone. (On the Sabbath this supplication is omitted.) When the *Kohanim* conclude וְיִשְׁמְרֶךָ, the congregation and *chazzan* respond אָמֵן.

רִבּוֹנוֹ שֶׁל עוֹלָם,* אֲנִי שֶׁלָּךְ וַחֲלוֹמוֹתַי שֶׁלָּךְ. חֲלוֹם חָלַמְתִּי וְאֵינִי יוֹדֵעַ מַה הוּא.* יְהִי רָצוֹן מִלְּפָנֶיךָ, יהוה אֱלֹהַי וֵאלֹהֵי אֲבוֹתַי, שֶׁיִּהְיוּ כָּל חֲלוֹמוֹתַי עָלַי וְעַל כָּל יִשְׂרָאֵל לְטוֹבָה — בֵּין שֶׁחָלַמְתִּי עַל עַצְמִי, וּבֵין שֶׁחָלַמְתִּי עַל אֲחֵרִים, וּבֵין שֶׁחָלְמוּ אֲחֵרִים עָלָי. אִם טוֹבִים הֵם, חַזְּקֵם וְאַמְּצֵם, וְיִתְקַיְּמוּ בִי וּבָהֶם כַּחֲלוֹמוֹתָיו שֶׁל יוֹסֵף הַצַּדִּיק. וְאִם צְרִיכִים רְפוּאָה, רְפָאֵם כְּחִזְקִיָּהוּ מֶלֶךְ יְהוּדָה מֵחָלְיוֹ, וּכְמִרְיָם הַנְּבִיאָה מִצָּרַעְתָּהּ, וּכְנַעֲמָן מִצָּרַעְתּוֹ, וּכְמֵי מָרָה עַל יְדֵי מֹשֶׁה רַבֵּנוּ, וּכְמֵי יְרִיחוֹ עַל יְדֵי אֱלִישָׁע. וּכְשֵׁם שֶׁהָפַכְתָּ אֶת קִלְלַת בִּלְעָם הָרָשָׁע מִקְּלָלָה לִבְרָכָה, כֵּן תַּהֲפוֹךְ כָּל חֲלוֹמוֹתַי עָלַי וְעַל כָּל יִשְׂרָאֵל לְטוֹבָה, וְתִשְׁמְרֵנִי וּתְחָנֵּנִי וְתִרְצֵנִי. אָמֵן.

יָאֵר אֱלֹהִים יְחָנֵּנוּ וִיבָרְכֵנוּ, יָאֵר פָּנָיו אִתָּנוּ, סֶלָה.[1]

יהוה יהוה יהוה, אֵל רַחוּם וְחַנּוּן, אֶרֶךְ אַפַּיִם וְרַב חֶסֶד וֶאֱמֶת.[2]

פָּנָיו פְּנֵה אֵלַי וְחָנֵּנִי, כִּי יָחִיד וְעָנִי אָנִי.[3]

אֵלֶיךָ* אֵלֶיךָ יהוה נַפְשִׁי אֶשָּׂא.[4]

וִיחֻנֶּךָּ* הִנֵּה כְעֵינֵי עֲבָדִים אֶל יַד אֲדוֹנֵיהֶם, כְּעֵינֵי שִׁפְחָה אֶל יַד גְּבִרְתָּהּ, כֵּן עֵינֵינוּ אֶל יהוה אֱלֹהֵינוּ עַד שֶׁיְּחָנֵּנוּ.[5]

The *Kohanim* sing an extended chant before saying וִיחֻנֶּךָּ, and the congregation recites the supplication (above) in an undertone. (On the Sabbath this supplication is omitted.) When the *Kohanim* conclude וִיחֻנֶּךָּ, the congregation and *chazzan* respond אָמֵן.

יִשָּׂא יִשָּׂא בְרָכָה מֵאֵת יהוה, וּצְדָקָה מֵאֱלֹהֵי יִשְׁעוֹ.[6] וּמְצָא חֵן וְשֵׂכֶל טוֹב בְּעֵינֵי אֱלֹהִים וְאָדָם.[7]

יהוה יהוה, חָנֵּנוּ, לְךָ קִוִּינוּ, הֱיֵה זְרֹעָם לַבְּקָרִים, אַף יְשׁוּעָתֵנוּ בְּעֵת צָרָה.[8]

פָּנָיו אַל תַּסְתֵּר פָּנֶיךָ מִמֶּנִּי בְּיוֹם צַר לִי, הַטֵּה אֵלַי אָזְנֶךָ, בְּיוֹם אֶקְרָא מַהֵר עֲנֵנִי.[9]

אֵלֶיךָ* אֵלֶיךָ נָשָׂאתִי אֶת עֵינַי, הַיֹּשְׁבִי בַּשָּׁמָיִם.[10]

---

function of these verses and the propriety of reciting them presents a difficulty already dealt with in the Talmud (*Sotah* 39b,40a). Most authorities agree that no verses should be recited at all. Some permit the verses to be read in an undertone while the *chazzan* calls out the words of the blessing. In any case, the practice of the masses who read these verses aloud—and especially of those who repeat the words of *Bircas Kohanim* after the *chazzan* — is wrong and has no halachic basis (*Mishnah Berurah* 128:103).

יָאֵר ה' פָּנָיו אֵלֶיךָ — *May* HASHEM *illuminate His countenance for you.* This is the blessing of spiritual growth, the light of Torah, which is symbolized by God's 'countenance' (*Sifre*).

וִיחֻנֶּךָּ — *And be gracious to you.* May you find favor in God's eyes (*Ramban*); or, may you find favor in the eyes of others, for all a person's talents and qualities will avail him little if others dislike him (*Ohr HaChaim*).

יִשָּׂא ה' פָּנָיו אֵלֶיךָ — *May [He]* HASHEM *turn His countenance to you.* May He suppress His anger against you, even if you are sinful and deserve to be punished (*Rashi*). One's face is

The *Kohanim* sing an extended chant and the congregation recites the following supplication in an undertone. (On the Sabbath this supplication is omitted.) When the *Kohanim* conclude וְיִשְׁמְרֶךָ, *'and safeguard you,'* the congregation and *chazzan* respond *Amen.*

רִבּוֹנוֹ שֶׁל עוֹלָם *Master of the world,* I am Yours and my dreams are Yours. I have dreamed a dream but I do not know what it indicates.* May it be Your will,* HASHEM, *my God and the God of my fathers, that all my dreams regarding myself and regarding all of Israel be good ones — those I have dreamed about myself, those I have dreamed about others, and those that others dreamed about me. If they are good, strengthen them, fortify them, make them endure in me and in them like the dreams of the righteous Joseph. But if they require healing, heal them like Hezekiah, King of Judah, from his sickness; like Miriam the prophetess from her tzaraas; like Naaman from his tzaraas; like the waters of Marah through the hand of Moses our teacher; and like the waters of Jericho through the hand of Elisha. And just as You transformed the curse of the wicked Balaam from a curse to a blessing, so may You transform all of my dreams regarding myself and regarding all of Israel for goodness. May You protect me, may You be gracious to me, may You accept me. Amen.*

May [He] illuminate — *May God favor us and bless us, may He illuminate His countenance with us, Selah.*[1]

HASHEM — HASHEM, HASHEM, *God, Compassionate and Gracious, Slow to anger, and Abundant in Kindness and Truth.*[2]

His countenance — *Turn Your face to me and be gracious to me, for alone and afflicted am I.*[3]

for you• — *To You,* HASHEM, *I raise my soul.*[4]

and be gracious to you.• — *Behold! Like the eyes of servants unto their master's hand, like the eyes of a maid unto her mistress's hand, so are our eyes unto* HASHEM, *our God, until He will favor us.*[5]

The *Kohanim* sing an extended chant and the congregation recites the supplication (above) in an undertone. (On the Sabbath this supplication is omitted.) When the *Kohanim* conclude וִיחֻנֶּךָּ, *'and be gracious to you,'* the congregation and *chazzan* respond *Amen.*

May [He] turn — *May he receive a blessing from* HASHEM, *and just kindness from the God of his salvation.*[6] *And he will find favor and good understanding in the eyes of God and man.*[7]

— HASHEM — — HASHEM, *find favor with us, for You have we hoped! Be their power in the mornings, and our salvation in times of distress.*[8]

His countenance — *Do not hide Your countenance from me in a day that is distressing to me; lean Your ear toward me; in the day that I call, speedily answer me.*[9]

to you• — *To You I raised my eyes, O You Who dwells in the Heavens.*[10]

(1) *Psalms* 67:2. (2) *Exodus* 34:6. (3) *Psalms* 25:16. (4) 25:1. (5) 123:2. (6) 24:5. (7) *Proverbs* 3:4. (8) *Isaiah* 33:2. (9) *Psalms* 102:3. (10) 123:1.

indicative of his attitude toward someone else. If he is angry, he will turn away from the one he dislikes. God 'turns His face' *toward* Israel to show that He loves them (*Maharzu*).

וְיָשֵׂם וְשָׂמוּ אֶת שְׁמִי עַל בְּנֵי יִשְׂרָאֵל, וַאֲנִי אֲבָרְכֵם.[1]

לְךָ לְךָ יהוה, הַגְּדֻלָּה וְהַגְּבוּרָה וְהַתִּפְאֶרֶת וְהַנֵּצַח וְהַהוֹד, כִּי כֹל בַּשָּׁמַיִם וּבָאָרֶץ, לְךָ יהוה, הַמַּמְלָכָה וְהַמִּתְנַשֵּׂא לְכֹל לְרֹאשׁ.[2]

שָׁלוֹם.* שָׁלוֹם שָׁלוֹם לָרָחוֹק וְלַקָּרוֹב, אָמַר יהוה, וּרְפָאתִיו.[3]

The *Kohanim* sing an extended chant before saying שָׁלוֹם, and the congregation recites the following supplication in an undertone. [The twenty-two-letter Divine Name appears here in brackets and bold type. This Name should be scanned with the eyes but not spoken.]
(On the Sabbath this supplication is omitted.)
When the *Kohanim* conclude שָׁלוֹם, congregation and *chazzan* respond אָמֵן.

יְהִי רָצוֹן מִלְּפָנֶיךָ, יהוה אֱלֹהַי וֵאלֹהֵי אֲבוֹתַי, שֶׁתַּעֲשֶׂה לְמַעַן קְדֻשַּׁת חֲסָדֶיךָ וְגֹדֶל רַחֲמֶיךָ הַפְּשׁוּטִים, וּלְמַעַן טָהֳרַת שִׁמְךָ הַגָּדוֹל הַגִּבּוֹר וְהַנּוֹרָא, בֶּן עֶשְׂרִים וּשְׁתַּיִם אוֹתִיּוֹת* הַיּוֹצְאִים מִן הַפְּסוּקִים שֶׁל בִּרְכַּת כֹּהֲנִים **[אנקת״ם פסת״ם פספסי״ם דיונסי״ם]** הָאֲמוּרָה מִפִּי אַהֲרֹן וּבָנָיו עַם קְדוֹשֶׁךָ, שֶׁתִּהְיֶה קָרוֹב לִי בְּקָרְאִי לָךְ, וְתִשְׁמַע תְּפִלָּתִי נַאֲקָתִי וְאֶנְקָתִי תָּמִיד, כְּשֵׁם שֶׁשָּׁמַעְתָּ **אֶנְקַת** יַעֲקֹב תְּמִימֶךָ הַנִּקְרָא אִישׁ **תָּם**. וְתִתֶּן לִי וּלְכָל נַפְשׁוֹת בֵּיתִי מְזוֹנוֹתֵינוּ וּפַרְנָסָתֵנוּ — בְּרֶוַח וְלֹא בְצִמְצוּם, בְּהֶתֵּר וְלֹא בְאִסּוּר, בְּנַחַת וְלֹא בְצַעַר — מִתַּחַת יָדְךָ הָרְחָבָה, כְּשֵׁם שֶׁנָּתַתָּ **פַּת** לֶחֶם לֶאֱכוֹל וּבֶגֶד לִלְבּוֹשׁ לְיַעֲקֹב אָבִינוּ הַנִּקְרָא אִישׁ **תָּם**. וְתִתְּנֵנוּ לְאַהֲבָה, לְחֵן וּלְחֶסֶד וּלְרַחֲמִים בְּעֵינֶיךָ וּבְעֵינֵי כָל רוֹאֵינוּ, וְיִהְיוּ דְבָרַי נִשְׁמָעִים לַעֲבוֹדָתֶךָ, כְּשֵׁם שֶׁנָּתַתָּ אֶת יוֹסֵף צַדִּיקֶךָ — בְּשָׁעָה שֶׁהִלְבִּישׁוֹ אָבִיו כְּתֹנֶת **פַּסִּים** — לְחֵן וּלְחֶסֶד וּלְרַחֲמִים בְּעֵינֶיךָ וּבְעֵינֵי כָל רוֹאָיו. וְתַעֲשֶׂה עִמִּי נִפְלָאוֹת **וְנִסִּים**,* וּלְטוֹבָה אוֹת, וְתַצְלִיחֵנִי בִּדְרָכַי, וְתֵן בְּלִבִּי בִּינָה לְהָבִין וּלְהַשְׂכִּיל וּלְקַיֵּם אֶת כָּל דִּבְרֵי תַלְמוּד תּוֹרָתֶךָ וְסוֹדוֹתֶיהָ, וְתַצִּילֵנִי מִשְּׁגִיאוֹת, וּתְטַהֵר רַעְיוֹנַי וְלִבִּי לַעֲבוֹדָתֶךָ וּלְיִרְאָתֶךָ. וְתַאֲרִיךְ יָמַי (insert the appropriate words — וִימֵי אָבִי וְאִמִּי וְאִשְׁתִּי וּבָנַי וּבְנוֹתַי) בְּטוֹב וּבִנְעִימוֹת, בְּרֹב עֹז וְשָׁלוֹם, אָמֵן סֶלָה.

וְיָשֵׂם לְךָ שָׁלוֹם — *And establish for you peace.* Peace is the seal of all blessings, because without peace — prosperity, health, food, and drink are worthless (*Sifre*).

יְהִי רָצוֹן / May it be Your Will

שִׁמְךָ . . . בֶּן עֶשְׂרִים וּשְׁתַּיִם אוֹתִיּוֹת — *Your Name . . . composed of twenty-two letters.* Scripture uses many appellations for God. Each of these Divine Names represents an attribute by which God allows man to perceive Him. י־ה־ו־ה represents the attribute of Divine Kindness. Since this Name is composed of the letters of הָיָה הֹוֶה יִהְיֶה, *He was, He is, He will be,* it is also an indication of God's Eternality. אֱלֹהִים, *ELOHIM,* represents Divine Justice. This word can also mean *judge* and *power*. Similarly, each Name found in Scripture is but an allusion to a different Divine attribute. Kabbalah records many Divine Names which are not found explicitly in Scripture but may be derived through various Kabbalistic principles. One of the Names is described in Kabbalistic literature as the Twenty-two-letter Name, and the letters of *Bircas Kohanim* are said to allude to it.

The well-known Kabbalist Rabbi Moshe Cordovero *[Ramak]* explains that this Twenty-two-letter Name comprises four individual Names [אנקת״ם פסת״ם פספסי״ם דיונסי״ם], each capable of effecting the fulfillment of a particular human need. The first Name, אנקת״ם, — a contraction of אֶנְקַת תָּמִים, literally *the cry of the perfect ones* — is efficacious in making one's prayer accepted in Heaven; the second, פסת״ם,

and establish *And they shall place My Name upon the Children of Israel, and I shall bless them.*[1]

for you *Yours,* H*ASHEM*, *is the greatness, the strength, the splendor, the triumph, and the glory, even all that is in heaven and earth; Yours,* H*ASHEM*, *is the kingdom and the sovereignty over every leader.*[2]

peace.* *'Peace, peace, for far and near,' says* H*ASHEM*, *'and I shall heal him.'*[3]

The *Kohanim* sing an extended chant and the congregation recites the following supplication in an undertone. [The twenty-two-letter Divine Name appears here in brackets and bold type. This Name should be scanned with the eyes but not spoken.] (On the Sabbath this supplication is omitted.) When the *Kohanim* conclude שָׁלוֹם, *'peace,'* congregation and *chazzan* respond *Amen.*

יְהִי רָצוֹן *May it be Your will,* H*ASHEM*, *my God and the God of my forefathers, that You act for the sake of the holiness of Your kindness and the greatness of Your mercies which reach out, and for the sake of the sanctity of Your Name — the great, the mighty and the awesome; composed of twenty-two letters* which derive from the verses of Bircas Kohanim* **[אנקת״ם פסת״ם פספסי״ם דיונסי״ם]**; *spoken by Aaron and his sons, Your holy people — that You be near to me when I call to You; that You listen to my prayer, my plea and my cry at all times, just as You listened to the cry* **[אֶנְקַת]** *of Jacob, Your perfect one, who is called 'a wholesome man'* **[תָּם]**. *And may You bestow upon me and upon all the souls of my household, our food and our sustenance — generously and not sparsely, honestly and not in forbidden fashion, pleasurably and not in pain — from beneath Your generous hand, just as You gave a portion* **[פִּסַּת]** *of bread to eat and clothing to wear to our father Jacob who is called 'a wholesome man'* **[תָּם]**. *And may You grant that we find love, favor, kindness and mercy in Your eyes and in the eyes of all who behold us; and that my words in Your service be heard; just as You granted Joseph, Your righteous one — at the time that his father garbed him in a fine woolen tunic* **[פַּסִּים]** *— that he find favor, kindness and mercy in Your eyes and in the eyes of all who beheld him. May You perform wonders and miracles* **[וְנִסִּים]** *with me,* and a goodly sign; grant me success in my ways; place in my heart the power of understanding, to understand, to be wise, to fulfill all the words of Your Torah's teaching and its mysteries; save me from errors; and purify my thinking and my heart for Your service and Your awe. May You prolong my days [*insert the appropriate words— *and the days of my father, my mother, my wife, my son(s), my daughter(s)] with goodness, with sweetness, with an abundance of strength and peace. Amen: Selah.*

(1) *Numbers* 6:27. (2) *II Chronicles* 29:11. (3) *Isaiah* 57:19.

is the Name through which God distributes פִּסַּת בַּר, *portions of bread*, to the hungry; through the Name פספסי״ם — related to כְּתֹנֶת פַּסִּים, *woolen tunic*, that Jacob made for Joseph (*Genesis* 37:3) — He clothes the naked; and דיונסי״ם indicates that He performs נִסִּים, *miracles*, and wonders. These four Names were invoked by Jacob when he prayed (*Genesis* 28:21) that *God be with me and guard me on this way which I am going; and give me bread to eat and clothes to wear; and that I return in peace . . .* (*Pardes*, cited in *Siddur Amudei Shamayim*).

וְתַעֲשֶׂה עִמִּי נִפְלָאוֹת וְנִסִּים — *May You perform wonders and miracles with me.* It is unseemly for an individual to request miraculous intervention in his personal affairs, for what assurance does he have that he is deserving?

There are two classifications of miracle — overt [e.g., the splitting of the Sea; Joshua's stopping the sun] and covert [e.g., the seeming historic simplicity of the Purim story]. One should not request *obvious* miracles, but he may pray for covert miracles, because they are disguised as natural phenomena (*Bechor Shor*).

The *chazzan* immediately begins שִׂים שָׁלוֹם; the *Kohanim* turn back to the Ark, lower their hands and recite their concluding prayer רִבּוֹנוֹ שֶׁל עוֹלָם; and the congregation recites אַדִּיר בַּמָּרוֹם. All should conclude their respective prayers simultaneously with the *chazzan's* conclusion of שִׂים שָׁלוֹם.

Kohanim:

רִבּוֹנוֹ שֶׁל עוֹלָם, עָשִׂינוּ מַה שֶּׁגָּזַרְתָּ עָלֵינוּ, אַף אַתָּה עֲשֵׂה עִמָּנוּ כְּמָה שֶׁהִבְטַחְתָּנוּ: הַשְׁקִיפָה מִמְּעוֹן קָדְשְׁךָ, מִן הַשָּׁמַיִם, וּבָרֵךְ אֶת עַמְּךָ אֶת יִשְׂרָאֵל, וְאֵת הָאֲדָמָה אֲשֶׁר נָתַתָּה לָנוּ — כַּאֲשֶׁר נִשְׁבַּעְתָּ לַאֲבוֹתֵינוּ — אֶרֶץ זָבַת חָלָב וּדְבָשׁ.[1]

Congregation:

אַדִּיר בַּמָּרוֹם, שׁוֹכֵן בִּגְבוּרָה, אַתָּה שָׁלוֹם וְשִׁמְךָ שָׁלוֹם. יְהִי רָצוֹן שֶׁתָּשִׂים עָלֵינוּ וְעַל כָּל עַמְּךָ בֵּית יִשְׂרָאֵל חַיִּים וּבְרָכָה לְמִשְׁמֶרֶת שָׁלוֹם.

If the *Kohanim* do not ascend the *duchan,* the *chazzan* recites the following. He faces right at וְיִשְׁמְרֶךָ; faces left at אֵלֶיךָ וִיחֻנֶּךָּ; faces the Ark for the rest of the blessings.

אֱלֹהֵינוּ, וֵאלֹהֵי אֲבוֹתֵינוּ, בָּרְכֵנוּ בַבְּרָכָה הַמְּשֻׁלֶּשֶׁת בַּתּוֹרָה הַכְּתוּבָה עַל יְדֵי מֹשֶׁה עַבְדֶּךָ, הָאֲמוּרָה מִפִּי אַהֲרֹן וּבָנָיו, כֹּהֲנִים עַם קְדוֹשֶׁךָ, כָּאָמוּר:

יְבָרֶכְךָ יהוה, וְיִשְׁמְרֶךָ. (Cong.– כֵּן יְהִי רָצוֹן.)

יָאֵר יהוה פָּנָיו אֵלֶיךָ וִיחֻנֶּךָּ. (Cong.– כֵּן יְהִי רָצוֹן.)

יִשָּׂא יהוה פָּנָיו אֵלֶיךָ וְיָשֵׂם לְךָ שָׁלוֹם.[2] (Cong.– כֵּן יְהִי רָצוֹן.)

Chazzan:

שִׂים שָׁלוֹם, טוֹבָה וּבְרָכָה, חֵן, וָחֶסֶד וְרַחֲמִים עָלֵינוּ וְעַל כָּל יִשְׂרָאֵל עַמֶּךָ. בָּרְכֵנוּ אָבִינוּ, כֻּלָּנוּ כְּאֶחָד בְּאוֹר פָּנֶיךָ, כִּי בְאוֹר פָּנֶיךָ נָתַתָּ לָּנוּ, יהוה אֱלֹהֵינוּ, תּוֹרַת חַיִּים וְאַהֲבַת חֶסֶד, וּצְדָקָה, וּבְרָכָה, וְרַחֲמִים, וְחַיִּים, וְשָׁלוֹם. וְטוֹב בְּעֵינֶיךָ לְבָרֵךְ אֶת עַמְּךָ יִשְׂרָאֵל, בְּכָל עֵת וּבְכָל שָׁעָה בִּשְׁלוֹמֶךָ. בָּרוּךְ אַתָּה יהוה, הַמְּבָרֵךְ אֶת עַמּוֹ יִשְׂרָאֵל בַּשָּׁלוֹם.

(Cong. and *Kohanim*– אָמֵן.)

Chazzan, in an undertone:

יִהְיוּ לְרָצוֹן אִמְרֵי פִי וְהֶגְיוֹן לִבִּי לְפָנֶיךָ, יהוה צוּרִי וְגֹאֲלִי.[3]

קדיש שלם

The *chazzan* recites קַדִּישׁ שָׁלֵם.

יִתְגַּדַּל וְיִתְקַדַּשׁ שְׁמֵהּ רַבָּא. (Cong.– אָמֵן.) בְּעָלְמָא דִּי בְרָא כִרְעוּתֵהּ. וְיַמְלִיךְ מַלְכוּתֵהּ, בְּחַיֵּיכוֹן וּבְיוֹמֵיכוֹן וּבְחַיֵּי דְכָל בֵּית יִשְׂרָאֵל, בַּעֲגָלָא וּבִזְמַן קָרִיב. וְאִמְרוּ: אָמֵן.

(Cong.– אָמֵן. יְהֵא שְׁמֵהּ רַבָּא מְבָרַךְ לְעָלַם וּלְעָלְמֵי עָלְמַיָּא.)

יְהֵא שְׁמֵהּ רַבָּא מְבָרַךְ לְעָלַם וּלְעָלְמֵי עָלְמַיָּא.

The *chazzan* immediately begins שִׂים שָׁלוֹם, *Establish peace;* the *Kohanim* turn back to the Ark, lower their hands and recite their concluding prayer רִבּוֹנוֹ שֶׁל עוֹלָם, *Master of the World;* and the congregation recites אַדִּיר, *Mighty One.* All should conclude their respective prayers simultaneously with the *chazzan's* conclusion of שִׂים שָׁלוֹם.

Kohanim:

רִבּוֹנוֹ שֶׁל עוֹלָם *Master of the world, we have done what You have decreed upon us, now may You also do as You have promised us: Look down from Your sacred dwelling, from the heavens, and bless Your people, Israel, and the earth which You have given us — just as You have sworn to our fathers — a land that flows with milk and honey.*[1]

Congregation:

אַדִּיר *Mighty One on high, He Who dwells in power! You are Peace and Your Name is Peace! May it be acceptable that You grant us and all of Your people, the house of Israel, life and blessing for a safeguard of peace.*

If the *Kohanim* do not ascend the *duchan,* the *chazzan* recites the following:

אֱלֹהֵינוּ *Our God and the God of our forefathers, bless us with the three-verse blessing in the Torah that was written by the hand of Moses, Your servant, that was said by Aaron and his sons, the Kohanim, Your holy people, as it is said:*

May H*ASHEM* *bless you and safeguard you.* (Cong.— *So may it be.*)

May H*ASHEM* *illuminate His countenance for you and be gracious to you.* (Cong.— *So may it be.*)

May H*ASHEM* *turn His countenance to you and establish peace for you.*[2] (Cong.— *So may it be.*)

Chazzan:

שִׂים שָׁלוֹם *Establish peace, goodness, blessing, graciousness, kindness, and compassion upon us and upon all of Your people Israel. Bless us, our Father, all of us as one, with the light of Your countenance, for with the light of Your countenance You gave us,* H*ASHEM*, *our God, the Torah of life and a love of kindness, righteousness, blessing, compassion, life, and peace. And may it be good in Your eyes to bless Your people Israel, in every season and in every hour with Your Peace. Blessed are You,* H*ASHEM*, *Who blesses His people Israel with peace.* (Cong. and *Kohanim*— *Amen.*)

Chazzan, in an undertone:

May the expressions of my mouth and the thoughts of my heart find favor before You, H*ASHEM*, *my Rock and my Redeemer.*[3]

FULL KADDISH

The *chazzan* recites the Full *Kaddish.*

יִתְגַּדַּל *May His great Name grow exalted and sanctified* (Cong.— *Amen.*) *in the world that He created as He willed. May He give reign to His kingship in your lifetimes and in your days, and in the lifetimes of the entire Family of Israel, swiftly and soon. Now respond: Amen.*

(Cong.— *Amen. May His great Name be blessed forever and ever.*)
May His great Name be blessed forever and ever.

---

(1) *Deuteronomy* 26:15. (2) *Numbers* 6:24-26. (3) *Psalms* 19:15.

יִתְבָּרַךְ וְיִשְׁתַּבַּח וְיִתְפָּאַר וְיִתְרוֹמַם וְיִתְנַשֵּׂא וְיִתְהַדָּר וְיִתְעַלֶּה וְיִתְהַלָּל שְׁמֵהּ דְּקֻדְשָׁא בְּרִיךְ הוּא (.Cong – בְּרִיךְ הוּא) – לְעֵֽלָּא מִן כָּל בִּרְכָתָא וְשִׁירָתָא תֻּשְׁבְּחָתָא וְנֶחֱמָתָא, דַּאֲמִירָן בְּעָלְמָא. וְאִמְרוּ: אָמֵן. (.Cong – אָמֵן.)

(.Cong – קַבֵּל בְּרַחֲמִים וּבְרָצוֹן אֶת תְּפִלָּתֵנוּ.)

תִּתְקַבֵּל צְלוֹתְהוֹן וּבָעוּתְהוֹן דְּכָל בֵּית יִשְׂרָאֵל קֳדָם אֲבוּהוֹן דִּי בִשְׁמַיָּא. וְאִמְרוּ: אָמֵן. (.Cong – אָמֵן.)

(.Cong – יְהִי שֵׁם יהוה מְבֹרָךְ, מֵעַתָּה וְעַד עוֹלָם.[1])

יְהֵא שְׁלָמָא רַבָּא מִן שְׁמַיָּא, וְחַיִּים עָלֵינוּ וְעַל כָּל יִשְׂרָאֵל. וְאִמְרוּ: אָמֵן. (.Cong – אָמֵן.)

(.Cong – עֶזְרִי מֵעִם יהוה, עֹשֵׂה שָׁמַיִם וָאָרֶץ.[2])

Take three steps back. Bow left and say . . . עֹשֶׂה; bow right and say . . . הוּא; bow forward and say וְעַל כָּל . . . אָמֵן. Remain standing in place for a few moments, then take three steps forward.

עֹשֶׂה שָׁלוֹם בִּמְרוֹמָיו, הוּא יַעֲשֶׂה שָׁלוֹם עָלֵינוּ, וְעַל כָּל יִשְׂרָאֵל. וְאִמְרוּ: אָמֵן. (.Cong – אָמֵן.)

קַוֵּה אֶל יהוה, חֲזַק וְיַאֲמֵץ לִבֶּךָ, וְקַוֵּה אֶל יהוה.[3] אֵין קָדוֹשׁ כַּיהוה, כִּי אֵין בִּלְתֶּךָ, וְאֵין צוּר כֵּאלֹהֵינוּ.[4] כִּי מִי אֱלוֹהַּ מִבַּלְעֲדֵי יהוה, וּמִי צוּר זוּלָתִי אֱלֹהֵינוּ.[5]

אֵין כֵּאלֹהֵינוּ, אֵין כַּאדוֹנֵינוּ, אֵין כְּמַלְכֵּנוּ, אֵין כְּמוֹשִׁיעֵנוּ. מִי כֵאלֹהֵינוּ, מִי כַאדוֹנֵינוּ, מִי כְמַלְכֵּנוּ, מִי כְמוֹשִׁיעֵנוּ. נוֹדֶה לֵאלֹהֵינוּ, נוֹדֶה לַאדוֹנֵינוּ, נוֹדֶה לְמַלְכֵּנוּ, נוֹדֶה לְמוֹשִׁיעֵנוּ. בָּרוּךְ אֱלֹהֵינוּ, בָּרוּךְ אֲדוֹנֵינוּ, בָּרוּךְ מַלְכֵּנוּ, בָּרוּךְ מוֹשִׁיעֵנוּ. אַתָּה הוּא אֱלֹהֵינוּ, אַתָּה הוּא אֲדוֹנֵינוּ, אַתָּה הוּא מַלְכֵּנוּ, אַתָּה הוּא מוֹשִׁיעֵנוּ. אַתָּה הוּא שֶׁהִקְטִירוּ אֲבוֹתֵינוּ לְפָנֶיךָ אֶת קְטֹרֶת הַסַּמִּים.

כריתות ו.

פִּטּוּם הַקְּטֹרֶת: (א) הַצֳּרִי, (ב) וְהַצִּפֹּרֶן, (ג) הַחֶלְבְּנָה, (ד) וְהַלְּבוֹנָה, מִשְׁקַל שִׁבְעִים שִׁבְעִים מָנֶה; (ה) מוֹר, (ו) וּקְצִיעָה, (ז) שִׁבֹּלֶת נֵרְדְּ, (ח) וְכַרְכֹּם, מִשְׁקַל שִׁשָּׁה עָשָׂר שִׁשָּׁה עָשָׂר מָנֶה; (ט) הַקֹּשְׁטְ שְׁנֵים עָשָׂר, (י) וְקִלּוּפָה שְׁלשָׁה, (יא) וְקִנָּמוֹן תִּשְׁעָה. בֹּרִית כַּרְשִׁינָה תִּשְׁעָה קַבִּין, יֵין קַפְרִיסִין סְאִין תְּלָתָא וְקַבִּין תְּלָתָא; וְאִם אֵין לוֹ יֵין קַפְרִיסִין, מֵבִיא חֲמַר חִוַּרְיָן עַתִּיק; מֶלַח סְדוֹמִית רֹבַע הַקָּב; מַעֲלֶה עָשָׁן כָּל שֶׁהוּא. רַבִּי נָתָן הַבַּבְלִי אוֹמֵר: אַף כִּפַּת הַיַּרְדֵּן כָּל שֶׁהוּא. וְאִם נָתַן בָּהּ דְּבַשׁ פְּסָלָהּ. וְאִם חִסַּר אַחַת מִכָּל סַמָּנֶיהָ, חַיָּב מִיתָה.

Blessed, praised, glorified, exalted, extolled, mighty, upraised, and lauded be the Name of the Holy One, Blessed is He (Cong.– *Blessed is He*) *— beyond any blessing and song, praise and consolation that are uttered in the world. Now respond: Amen.* (Cong.– *Amen.*)

(Cong.– *Accept our prayers with mercy and favor.*)

May the prayers and supplications of the entire Family of Israel be accepted before their Father Who is in Heaven. Now respond: Amen. (Cong.– *Amen.*)

(Cong.– *Blessed be the Name of* HASHEM, *from this time and forever.*[1])

May there be abundant peace from Heaven, and life, upon us and upon all Israel. Now respond: Amen. (Cong.– *Amen.*)

(Cong.– *My help is from* HASHEM, *Maker of heaven and earth.*[2])

Take three steps back. Bow left and say, *'He Who makes peace . . .';* bow right and say, *'may He . . .';* bow forward and say, *'and upon all Israel . . .'* Remain standing in place for a few moments, then take three steps forward.

He Who makes peace in His heights, may He make peace upon us, and upon all Israel. Now respond: Amen. (Cong.– *Amen.*)

קַוֵּה *Hope to* HASHEM, *strengthen yourself and He will give you courage; and hope to* HASHEM.[3] *There is none holy as* HASHEM, *for there is none beside You, and there is no Rock like our God.*[4] *For who is a god beside* HASHEM, *and who is a Rock except for our God.*[5]

אֵין *There is none like our God; there is none like our Master;*
there is none like our King; there is none like our Savior.
Who is like our God? Who is like our Master?
Who is like our King? Who is like our Savior?
Let us thank our God; let us thank our Master;
let us thank our King; let us thank our Savior.
Blessed is our God; blessed is our Master;
blessed is our King; blessed is our Savior.
It is You Who is our God; it is You Who is our Master;
it is You Who is our King; it is You Who is our Savior.
It is You before Whom our forefathers burned the spice-incense.

Talmud, *Kereisos* 6a

פִּטּוּם הַקְּטֹרֶת *The incense mixture was formulated of [eleven spices]:* (1) *stacte,* (2) *onycha,* (3) *galbanum,* (4) *frankincense — each weighing seventy maneh;* (5) *myrrh,* (6) *cassia,* (7) *spikenard,* (8) *saffron — each weighing sixteen maneh;* (9) *costus — twelve [maneh];* (10) *aromatic bark — three; and* (11) *cinnamon — nine. [Additionally] Carshina lye — nine kab; Cyprus wine, three se'ah and three kab — if he has no Cyprus wine, he brings old white wine; Sodom salt, a quarter kab; and a minute amount of smoke-raising herb. Rabbi Nassan the Babylonian says: Also a minute amount of Jordan amber. If he placed fruit-honey into it, he invalidated it. And if he left out any of its spices, he is liable to the death penalty.*

(1) *Psalms* 113:2. (2) 121:2. (3) 27:14. (4) *I Samuel* 2:2. (5) *Psalms* 18:32.

רַבָּן שִׁמְעוֹן בֶּן גַּמְלִיאֵל אוֹמֵר: הַצֳּרִי אֵינוֹ אֶלָּא שְׂרָף הַנּוֹטֵף מֵעֲצֵי הַקְּטָף. בֹּרִית כַּרְשִׁינָה שֶׁשָּׁפִין בָּהּ אֶת הַצִּפֹּרֶן כְּדֵי שֶׁתְּהֵא נָאָה; יֵין קַפְרִיסִין שֶׁשּׁוֹרִין בּוֹ אֶת הַצִּפֹּרֶן כְּדֵי שֶׁתְּהֵא עַזָּה; וַהֲלֹא מֵי רַגְלַיִם יָפִין לָהּ, אֶלָּא שֶׁאֵין מַכְנִיסִין מֵי רַגְלַיִם בָּעֲזָרָה מִפְּנֵי הַכָּבוֹד.

משנה, תמיד ז:ד

הַשִּׁיר* שֶׁהַלְוִיִּם הָיוּ אוֹמְרִים בְּבֵית הַמִּקְדָּשׁ. בַּיּוֹם הָרִאשׁוֹן הָיוּ אוֹמְרִים: לַיהוה הָאָרֶץ וּמְלוֹאָהּ, תֵּבֵל וְיֹשְׁבֵי בָהּ.[1] בַּשֵּׁנִי הָיוּ אוֹמְרִים: גָּדוֹל יהוה וּמְהֻלָּל מְאֹד, בְּעִיר אֱלֹהֵינוּ הַר קָדְשׁוֹ.[2] בַּשְּׁלִישִׁי הָיוּ אוֹמְרִים: אֱלֹהִים נִצָּב בַּעֲדַת אֵל, בְּקֶרֶב אֱלֹהִים יִשְׁפֹּט.[3] בָּרְבִיעִי הָיוּ אוֹמְרִים: אֵל נְקָמוֹת יהוה, אֵל נְקָמוֹת הוֹפִיעַ.[4] בַּחֲמִישִׁי הָיוּ אוֹמְרִים: הַרְנִינוּ לֵאלֹהִים עוּזֵּנוּ, הָרִיעוּ לֵאלֹהֵי יַעֲקֹב.[5] בַּשִּׁשִּׁי הָיוּ אוֹמְרִים: יהוה מָלָךְ גֵּאוּת לָבֵשׁ, לָבֵשׁ יהוה עֹז הִתְאַזָּר, אַף תִּכּוֹן תֵּבֵל בַּל תִּמּוֹט.[6] בַּשַּׁבָּת הָיוּ אוֹמְרִים: מִזְמוֹר שִׁיר לְיוֹם הַשַּׁבָּת.[7] מִזְמוֹר שִׁיר לֶעָתִיד לָבֹא, לְיוֹם שֶׁכֻּלּוֹ שַׁבָּת וּמְנוּחָה לְחַיֵּי הָעוֹלָמִים.

מגילה כח:

תָּנָא דְבֵי אֵלִיָּהוּ:* כָּל הַשּׁוֹנֶה הֲלָכוֹת בְּכָל יוֹם, מֻבְטָח לוֹ שֶׁהוּא בֶּן עוֹלָם הַבָּא, שֶׁנֶּאֱמַר: הֲלִיכוֹת עוֹלָם לוֹ,[8] אַל תִּקְרֵי הֲלִיכוֹת, אֶלָּא הֲלָכוֹת.

ברכות סד.

אָמַר רַבִּי אֶלְעָזָר* אָמַר רַבִּי חֲנִינָא: תַּלְמִידֵי חֲכָמִים מַרְבִּים שָׁלוֹם בָּעוֹלָם, שֶׁנֶּאֱמַר: וְכָל בָּנַיִךְ לִמּוּדֵי יהוה, וְרַב שְׁלוֹם בָּנָיִךְ,[9] אַל תִּקְרֵי בָּנָיִךְ אֶלָּא בּוֹנָיִךְ. ❖ שָׁלוֹם רָב לְאֹהֲבֵי תוֹרָתֶךָ, וְאֵין לָמוֹ מִכְשׁוֹל.[10] יְהִי שָׁלוֹם בְּחֵילֵךְ, שַׁלְוָה בְּאַרְמְנוֹתָיִךְ. לְמַעַן אַחַי וְרֵעָי, אֲדַבְּרָה נָּא שָׁלוֹם בָּךְ. לְמַעַן בֵּית יהוה אֱלֹהֵינוּ, אֲבַקְשָׁה טוֹב לָךְ.[11] יהוה עֹז לְעַמּוֹ יִתֵּן, יהוה יְבָרֵךְ אֶת עַמּוֹ בַשָּׁלוֹם.[12]

הַשִּׁיר — *The [daily] song.* This *mishnah* (*Tamid* 7:4) is recited here because the daily song was chanted by the Levites at the conclusion of the incense service. [See pages 448-455.]

תָּנָא דְבֵי אֵלִיָּהוּ — *The Academy of Elijah taught.* This homiletical teaching likens the ways of the world to the laws that govern a Jew's life on earth. Only by studying, knowing and practicing the laws of the Torah can a Jew insure himself of ultimate success.

אָמַר רַבִּי אֶלְעָזָר — *Rabbi Elazar said.* This famous teaching is the concluding statement of tractate *Berachos.*

Maharsha there, in a comment that applies here as well, explains that the tractate dealt with prayers and blessings that had been instituted by

רַבָּן שִׁמְעוֹן *Rabban Shimon ben Gamliel says: The stacte is simply the sap that drips from balsam trees. Carshina lye is used to bleach the onycha to make it pleasing. Cyprus wine is used to soak the onycha to make it pungent. Even though urine is suitable for that, nevertheless they do not bring urine into the Temple out of respect.*

Mishnah, *Tamid* 7:4

הַשִּׁיר *The daily song* that the Levites would recite in the Temple was as follows: On the first day [of the week] they would say: 'HASHEM's is the earth and its fullness, the inhabited land and those who dwell in it.'[1] On the second day they would say: 'Great is HASHEM and much praised, in the city of our God, Mount of His Holiness.'[2] On the third day they would say: 'God stands in the Divine assembly, in the midst of judges shall He judge.'[3] On the fourth day they would say: 'O God of vengeance, HASHEM, O God of vengeance, appear.'[4] On the fifth day they would say: 'Sing joyously to the God of our might, call out to the God of Jacob.'[5] On the sixth day they would say: 'HASHEM will have reigned, He will have donned grandeur; He will have donned might and girded Himself; He even made the world firm so that it should not falter.'[6] On the Sabbath they would say: 'A psalm, a song for the Sabbath day.'[7] A psalm, a song for the time to come, to the day that will be entirely Sabbath and contentment for the eternal life.*

Talmud, *Megillah* 28b

תָּנָא *The Academy of Elijah taught:* He who studies Torah laws every day has the assurance that he will be in the World to Come, as it is said, 'The ways of the world are His'[8] — do not read* [הֲלִיכוֹת] *'ways,' but* [הֲלָכוֹת] *'laws.'*

Talmud, *Berachos* 64a

אָמַר *Rabbi Elazar said* on behalf of Rabbi Chanina: Torah scholars increase peace in the world, as it is said: 'And all your children will be students of HASHEM, and your children will have peace'[9] — do not read* [בָּנָיִךְ] *'your children,' but* [בּוֹנָיִךְ] *'your builders.'* Chazzan – ***There is abundant peace for the lovers of Your Torah, and there is no stumbling block for them.[10] May there be peace within your wall, serenity within your palaces. For the sake of my brethren and comrades I shall speak of peace in your midst. For the sake of the House of HASHEM, our God, I will request your good.[11] HASHEM will give might to His people, HASHEM will bless His people with peace.[12]***

(1) *Psalms* 24:1. (2) 48:2. (3) 82:1. (4) 94:1. (5) 81:2. (6) 93:1. (7) 92:1.
(8) *Habakkuk* 3:6. (9) *Isaiah* 54:13. (10) *Psalms* 119:165. (11) 122:7-9. (12) 29:11.

---

the Sages. The reason they promulgated these expressions of devotion was to increase the harmony in the universe between man and his Maker.

קדיש דרבנן

In the presence of a *minyan,* mourners recite קַדִּישׁ דְּרַבָּנָן (see *Laws* §84-85).

יִתְגַּדַּל וְיִתְקַדַּשׁ שְׁמֵהּ רַבָּא. (Cong.– אָמֵן.) בְּעָלְמָא דִּי בְרָא כִרְעוּתֵהּ. וְיַמְלִיךְ מַלְכוּתֵהּ, בְּחַיֵּיכוֹן וּבְיוֹמֵיכוֹן וּבְחַיֵּי דְכָל בֵּית יִשְׂרָאֵל, בַּעֲגָלָא וּבִזְמַן קָרִיב. וְאִמְרוּ: אָמֵן.

(Cong.– אָמֵן. יְהֵא שְׁמֵהּ רַבָּא מְבָרַךְ לְעָלַם וּלְעָלְמֵי עָלְמַיָּא.)

יְהֵא שְׁמֵהּ רַבָּא מְבָרַךְ לְעָלַם וּלְעָלְמֵי עָלְמַיָּא.

יִתְבָּרַךְ וְיִשְׁתַּבַּח וְיִתְפָּאַר וְיִתְרוֹמַם וְיִתְנַשֵּׂא וְיִתְהַדָּר וְיִתְעַלֶּה וְיִתְהַלָּל שְׁמֵהּ דְּקֻדְשָׁא בְּרִיךְ הוּא (Cong.– בְּרִיךְ הוּא) — לְעֵלָּא מִן כָּל בִּרְכָתָא וְשִׁירָתָא תֻּשְׁבְּחָתָא וְנֶחֱמָתָא, דַּאֲמִירָן בְּעָלְמָא. וְאִמְרוּ: אָמֵן. (Cong.– אָמֵן.)

עַל יִשְׂרָאֵל וְעַל רַבָּנָן, וְעַל תַּלְמִידֵיהוֹן וְעַל כָּל תַּלְמִידֵי תַלְמִידֵיהוֹן, וְעַל כָּל מָאן דְּעָסְקִין בְּאוֹרַיְתָא, דִּי בְאַתְרָא הָדֵין וְדִי בְכָל אֲתַר וַאֲתַר. יְהֵא לְהוֹן וּלְכוֹן שְׁלָמָא רַבָּא, חִנָּא וְחִסְדָּא וְרַחֲמִין, וְחַיִּין אֲרִיכִין, וּמְזוֹנֵי רְוִיחֵי, וּפֻרְקָנָא, מִן קֳדָם אֲבוּהוֹן דִּי בִשְׁמַיָּא (וְאַרְעָא). וְאִמְרוּ: אָמֵן. (Cong.– אָמֵן.)

יְהֵא שְׁלָמָא רַבָּא מִן שְׁמַיָּא, וְחַיִּים (טוֹבִים) עָלֵינוּ וְעַל כָּל יִשְׂרָאֵל. וְאִמְרוּ: אָמֵן. (Cong.– אָמֵן.)

Take three steps back. Bow left and say . . . עֹשֶׂה; bow right and say . . . הוּא; bow forward and say וְעַל כָּל . . . אָמֵן. Remain standing in place for a few moments, then take three steps forward.

עֹשֶׂה שָׁלוֹם בִּמְרוֹמָיו, הוּא בְּרַחֲמָיו יַעֲשֶׂה שָׁלוֹם עָלֵינוּ, וְעַל כָּל יִשְׂרָאֵל. וְאִמְרוּ: אָמֵן. (Cong.– אָמֵן.)

Stand while reciting עָלֵינוּ.

עָלֵינוּ לְשַׁבֵּחַ לַאֲדוֹן הַכֹּל, לָתֵת גְּדֻלָּה לְיוֹצֵר בְּרֵאשִׁית, שֶׁלֹּא עָשָׂנוּ כְּגוֹיֵי הָאֲרָצוֹת, וְלֹא שָׂמָנוּ כְּמִשְׁפְּחוֹת הָאֲדָמָה. שֶׁלֹּא שָׂם חֶלְקֵנוּ כָּהֶם, וְגוֹרָלֵנוּ כְּכָל הֲמוֹנָם. (שֶׁהֵם מִשְׁתַּחֲוִים לְהֶבֶל וָרִיק, וּמִתְפַּלְּלִים אֶל אֵל לֹא יוֹשִׁיעַ.[1]) וַאֲנַחְנוּ כּוֹרְעִים וּמִשְׁתַּחֲוִים וּמוֹדִים, לִפְנֵי מֶלֶךְ מַלְכֵי הַמְּלָכִים הַקָּדוֹשׁ בָּרוּךְ הוּא. שֶׁהוּא נוֹטֶה שָׁמַיִם וְיֹסֵד אָרֶץ,[2] וּמוֹשַׁב יְקָרוֹ בַּשָּׁמַיִם מִמַּעַל, וּשְׁכִינַת עֻזּוֹ בְּגָבְהֵי מְרוֹמִים. הוּא אֱלֹהֵינוּ, אֵין עוֹד. אֱמֶת מַלְכֵּנוּ, אֶפֶס זוּלָתוֹ, כַּכָּתוּב בְּתוֹרָתוֹ: וְיָדַעְתָּ הַיּוֹם וַהֲשֵׁבֹתָ אֶל לְבָבֶךָ, כִּי יהוה הוּא הָאֱלֹהִים בַּשָּׁמַיִם מִמַּעַל וְעַל הָאָרֶץ מִתָּחַת, אֵין עוֹד.[3]

Bow while reciting וַאֲנַחְנוּ כּוֹרְעִים וּמִשְׁתַּחֲוִים.

THE RABBIS' KADDISH

In the presence of a *minyan,* mourners recite the Rabbis' *Kaddish* (see *Laws* §84-85). [A transliteration of this *Kaddish* appears on p. 1146.]

יִתְגַּדַּל *May His great Name grow exalted and sanctified* (Cong.– *Amen.*) *in the world that He created as He willed. May He give reign to His kingship in your lifetimes and in your days, and in the lifetimes of the entire Family of Israel, swiftly and soon. Now respond: Amen.*

(Cong.– *Amen. May His great Name be blessed forever and ever.*)

May His great Name be blessed forever and ever.

Blessed, praised, glorified, exalted, extolled, mighty, upraised, and lauded be the Name of the Holy One, Blessed is He (Cong.– *Blessed is He*) — *beyond any blessing and song, praise and consolation that are uttered in the world. Now respond: Amen.* (Cong.– *Amen.*)

Upon Israel, upon the teachers, their disciples and all of their disciples and upon all those who engage in the study of Torah, who are here or anywhere else; may they and you have abundant peace, grace, kindness, and mercy, long life, ample nourishment, and salvation, from before their Father Who is in Heaven (and on earth). Now respond: Amen. (Cong. – *Amen.*)

May there be abundant peace from Heaven, and (good) life, upon us and upon all Israel. Now respond: Amen. (Cong.– *Amen.*)

Take three steps back. Bow left and say, *'He Who makes peace . . .';* bow right and say, *'may He . . .';* bow forward and say, *'and upon all Israel . . .'* Remain standing in place for a few moments, then take three steps forward.

He Who makes peace in His heights, may He, in His compassion, make peace upon us, and upon all Israel. Now respond: Amen. (Cong.– *Amen.*)

ALEINU

Stand while reciting עָלֵינוּ, *'It is our duty . . .'*

עָלֵינוּ *It is our duty to praise the Master of all, to ascribe greatness to the Molder of primeval creation, for He has not made us like the nations of the lands, and has not emplaced us like the families of the earth; for He has not assigned our portion like theirs nor our lot like all their multitudes. (For they bow to vanity and emptiness and pray to a god which helps not.[1]) But we bend our knees, bow, and acknowledge our thanks before the King Who reigns over kings, the Holy One, Blessed is He. He stretches out heaven and establishes earth's foundation,[2] the seat of His homage is in the heavens above and His powerful Presence is in the loftiest heights. He is our God and there is none other. True is our King, there is nothing beside Him, as it is written in His Torah: 'You are to know this day and take to your heart that* HASHEM *is the only God — in heaven above and on the earth below — there is none other.'[3]*

Bow while reciting *'But we bend our knees.'*

---

(1) *Isaiah* 45:20. (2) 51:13. (3) *Deuteronomy* 4:39.

עַל כֵּן נְקַוֶּה לְּךָ יהוה אֱלֹהֵינוּ לִרְאוֹת מְהֵרָה בְּתִפְאֶרֶת עֻזֶּךָ, לְהַעֲבִיר גִּלּוּלִים מִן הָאָרֶץ, וְהָאֱלִילִים כָּרוֹת יִכָּרֵתוּן, לְתַקֵּן עוֹלָם בְּמַלְכוּת שַׁדַּי. וְכָל בְּנֵי בָשָׂר יִקְרְאוּ בִשְׁמֶךָ, לְהַפְנוֹת אֵלֶיךָ כָּל רִשְׁעֵי אָרֶץ. יַכִּירוּ וְיֵדְעוּ כָּל יוֹשְׁבֵי תֵבֵל, כִּי לְךָ תִּכְרַע כָּל בֶּרֶךְ, תִּשָּׁבַע כָּל לָשׁוֹן.[1] לְפָנֶיךָ יהוה אֱלֹהֵינוּ יִכְרְעוּ וְיִפֹּלוּ, וְלִכְבוֹד שִׁמְךָ יְקָר יִתֵּנוּ. וִיקַבְּלוּ כֻלָּם אֶת עוֹל מַלְכוּתֶךָ, וְתִמְלֹךְ עֲלֵיהֶם מְהֵרָה לְעוֹלָם וָעֶד. כִּי הַמַּלְכוּת שֶׁלְּךָ הִיא וּלְעוֹלְמֵי עַד תִּמְלוֹךְ בְּכָבוֹד, כַּכָּתוּב בְּתוֹרָתֶךָ: יהוה יִמְלֹךְ לְעֹלָם וָעֶד.[2] ❖ וְנֶאֱמַר: וְהָיָה יהוה לְמֶלֶךְ עַל כָּל הָאָרֶץ, בַּיּוֹם הַהוּא יִהְיֶה יהוה אֶחָד וּשְׁמוֹ אֶחָד.[3]

Some congregations recite the following after עָלֵינוּ:

אַל תִּירָא מִפַּחַד פִּתְאֹם, וּמִשֹּׁאַת רְשָׁעִים כִּי תָבֹא.[4] עֻצוּ עֵצָה וְתֻפָר, דַּבְּרוּ דָבָר וְלֹא יָקוּם, כִּי עִמָּנוּ אֵל.[5] וְעַד זִקְנָה אֲנִי הוּא, וְעַד שֵׂיבָה אֲנִי אֶסְבֹּל, אֲנִי עָשִׂיתִי וַאֲנִי אֶשָּׂא, וַאֲנִי אֶסְבֹּל וַאֲמַלֵּט.[6]

קדיש יתום

In the presence of a *minyan*, mourners recite קַדִּישׁ יָתוֹם, the Mourner's *Kaddish* (see *Laws* §81-83).

יִתְגַּדַּל וְיִתְקַדַּשׁ שְׁמֵהּ רַבָּא. (.Cong – אָמֵן.) בְּעָלְמָא דִּי בְרָא כִרְעוּתֵהּ. וְיַמְלִיךְ מַלְכוּתֵהּ, בְּחַיֵּיכוֹן וּבְיוֹמֵיכוֹן וּבְחַיֵּי דְכָל בֵּית יִשְׂרָאֵל, בַּעֲגָלָא וּבִזְמַן קָרִיב. וְאִמְרוּ: אָמֵן.

(.Cong – אָמֵן. יְהֵא שְׁמֵהּ רַבָּא מְבָרַךְ לְעָלַם וּלְעָלְמֵי עָלְמַיָּא.)

יְהֵא שְׁמֵהּ רַבָּא מְבָרַךְ לְעָלַם וּלְעָלְמֵי עָלְמַיָּא.

יִתְבָּרַךְ וְיִשְׁתַּבַּח וְיִתְפָּאַר וְיִתְרוֹמַם וְיִתְנַשֵּׂא וְיִתְהַדָּר וְיִתְעַלֶּה וְיִתְהַלָּל שְׁמֵהּ דְּקֻדְשָׁא בְּרִיךְ הוּא (.Cong – בְּרִיךְ הוּא) — לְעֵלָּא מִן כָּל בִּרְכָתָא וְשִׁירָתָא תֻּשְׁבְּחָתָא וְנֶחֱמָתָא, דַּאֲמִירָן בְּעָלְמָא. וְאִמְרוּ: אָמֵן. (.Cong – אָמֵן.)

יְהֵא שְׁלָמָא רַבָּא מִן שְׁמַיָּא, וְחַיִּים עָלֵינוּ וְעַל כָּל יִשְׂרָאֵל. וְאִמְרוּ: אָמֵן. (.Cong – אָמֵן.)

Take three steps back. Bow left and say . . . עֹשֶׂה; bow right and say . . . הוּא; bow forward and say וְעַל כָּל . . . אָמֵן. Remain standing in place for a few moments, then take three steps forward.

עֹשֶׂה שָׁלוֹם בִּמְרוֹמָיו, הוּא יַעֲשֶׂה שָׁלוֹם עָלֵינוּ, וְעַל כָּל יִשְׂרָאֵל. וְאִמְרוּ: אָמֵן. (.Cong – אָמֵן.)

עַל כֵּן *Therefore we put our hope in You,* Hashem, *our God, that we may soon see Your mighty splendor, to remove detestable idolatry from the earth, and false gods will be utterly cut off, to perfect the universe through the Almighty's sovereignty. Then all humanity will call upon Your Name, to turn all the earth's wicked toward You. All the world's inhabitants will recognize and know that to You every knee should bend, every tongue should swear.*[1] *Before You,* Hashem, *our God, they will bend every knee and cast themselves down and to the glory of Your Name they will render homage, and they will all accept upon themselves the yoke of Your kingship that You may reign over them soon and eternally. For the kingdom is Yours and You will reign for all eternity in glory as it is written in Your Torah:* Hashem *shall reign for all eternity.*[2] Chazzan – *And it is said:* Hashem *will be King over all the world — on that day* Hashem *will be One and His Name will be One.*[3]

Some congregations recite the following after *Aleinu.*

אַל תִּירָא *Do not fear sudden terror, or the holocaust of the wicked when it comes.*[4] *Plan a conspiracy and it will be annulled; speak your piece and it shall not stand, for God is with us.*[5] *Even till your seniority, I remain unchanged; and even till your ripe old age, I shall endure. I created you and I shall bear you; I shall endure and rescue.*[6]

MOURNER'S KADDISH

In the presence of a *minyan,* mourners recite קַדִּישׁ יָתוֹם, the Mourner's *Kaddish* (see *Laws* 81-83).
[A transliteration of this *Kaddish* appears on page 1147.]

יִתְגַּדַּל *May His great Name grow exalted and sanctified* (Cong.– *Amen.*) *in the world that He created as He willed. May He give reign to His kingship in your lifetimes and in your days, and in the lifetimes of the entire Family of Israel, swiftly and soon. Now respond: Amen.*

(Cong.– *Amen. May His great Name be blessed forever and ever.*)

May His great Name be blessed forever and ever.

Blessed, praised, glorified, exalted, extolled, mighty, upraised, and lauded be the Name of the Holy One, Blessed is He (Cong.– *Blessed is He*) *— beyond any blessing and song, praise and consolation that are uttered in the world. Now respond: Amen.* (Cong.– *Amen*).

May there be abundant peace from Heaven, and life, upon us and upon all Israel. Now respond: Amen. (Cong.– *Amen.*)

Take three steps back. Bow left and say, *'He Who makes peace . . .';* bow right and say, *'may He . . .';* bow forward and say, *'and upon all Israel . . .'* Remain standing in place for a few moments, then take three steps forward.

He Who makes peace in His heights, may He make peace upon us, and upon all Israel. Now respond: Amen. (Cong.– *Amen.*)

---

(1) Cf. *Isaiah* 45:23. (2) *Exodus* 15:18. (3) *Zechariah* 14:9. (4) *Proverbs* 3:25. (5) *Isaiah* 8:10. (6) 46:4.

שיר הכבוד

The Ark is opened and שִׁיר הַכָּבוֹד, *The Song of Glory,* is recited responsively — the *chazzan* reciting the first verse, the congregation reciting the second and so on.

אַנְעִים זְמִירוֹת וְשִׁירִים אֶאֱרוֹג,*
כִּי אֵלֶיךָ נַפְשִׁי תַעֲרוֹג.
נַפְשִׁי חָמְדָה בְּצֵל יָדֶךָ, לָדַעַת כָּל רָז סוֹדֶךָ.
❖ מִדֵּי דַבְּרִי בִּכְבוֹדֶךָ, הוֹמֶה לִבִּי אֶל דּוֹדֶיךָ.
עַל כֵּן אֲדַבֵּר בְּךָ נִכְבָּדוֹת, וְשִׁמְךָ אֲכַבֵּד בְּשִׁירֵי יְדִידוֹת.
❖ אֲסַפְּרָה כְבוֹדְךָ וְלֹא רְאִיתִיךָ,* אֲדַמְּךָ אֲכַנְּךָ וְלֹא יְדַעְתִּיךָ.
בְּיַד נְבִיאֶיךָ* בְּסוֹד עֲבָדֶיךָ, דִּמִּיתָ הֲדַר כְּבוֹד הוֹדֶךָ.
❖ גְּדֻלָּתְךָ וּגְבוּרָתֶךָ, כִּנּוּ לְתֹקֶף פְּעֻלָּתֶךָ.
דִּמּוּ אוֹתְךָ וְלֹא כְּפִי יֶשְׁךָ, וַיְשַׁוּוּךָ לְפִי מַעֲשֶׂיךָ.*
❖ הִמְשִׁילוּךָ בְּרֹב חֶזְיוֹנוֹת, הִנְּךָ אֶחָד* בְּכָל דִּמְיוֹנוֹת.
וַיֶּחֱזוּ בְךָ זִקְנָה וּבַחֲרוּת, וּשְׂעַר רֹאשְׁךָ בְּשֵׂיבָה וְשַׁחֲרוּת.
❖ זִקְנָה* בְּיוֹם דִּין וּבַחֲרוּת בְּיוֹם קְרָב, כְּאִישׁ מִלְחָמוֹת יָדָיו לוֹ רָב.
חָבַשׁ כֹּבַע יְשׁוּעָה בְּרֹאשׁוֹ, הוֹשִׁיעָה לּוֹ יְמִינוֹ* וּזְרוֹעַ קָדְשׁוֹ.
❖ טַלְלֵי אוֹרוֹת* רֹאשׁוֹ נִמְלָא, קְוֻצּוֹתָיו רְסִיסֵי לָיְלָה.
יִתְפָּאֵר בִּי כִּי חָפֵץ בִּי. וְהוּא יִהְיֶה לִּי לַעֲטֶרֶת צְבִי.
❖ כֶּתֶם טָהוֹר פָּז דְּמוּת רֹאשׁוֹ, וְחַק עַל מֵצַח כְּבוֹד שֵׁם קָדְשׁוֹ.*
לְחֵן וּלְכָבוֹד* צְבִי תִפְאָרָה, אֻמָּתוֹ לוֹ עִטְּרָה עֲטָרָה.
❖ מַחְלְפוֹת רֹאשׁוֹ* כְּבִימֵי בְחֻרוֹת, קְוֻצּוֹתָיו תַּלְתַּלִּים שְׁחוֹרוֹת.
נְוֵה הַצֶּדֶק צְבִי תִפְאַרְתּוֹ, יַעֲלֶה נָּא עַל רֹאשׁ שִׂמְחָתוֹ.
❖ סְגֻלָּתוֹ תְּהִי בְיָדוֹ עֲטֶרֶת, וּצְנִיף מְלוּכָה צְבִי תִפְאֶרֶת.
עֲמוּסִים נְשָׂאָם עֲטֶרֶת עִנְּדָם, מֵאֲשֶׁר יָקְרוּ בְעֵינָיו כִּבְּדָם.

שִׁיר הַכָּבוֹד / Song of Glory

This beautiful sacred song has been ascribed to R' Yehudah HaChassid, the twelfth-century German scholar and Kabbalist. Due to the song's great holiness, the Ark is opened when it is recited, and it is not recited daily so that it not become too familiar *(Levush).* Most congregations recite it every Sabbath and on all Festivals. The *Vilna Gaon* held that it should be recited only on Festivals, and some congregations recite it only on Rosh Hashanah and Yom Kippur.

וְשִׁירִים אֶאֱרוֹג — *And weave hymns.* Just as a weaver unifies countless threads to make a finished garment, so does the *paytan* [liturgical poet] weave together words and phrases to compose beautiful songs of praise.

וְלֹא רְאִיתִיךָ — *Though I see You not.* This stich of the song introduces much of what comes later. We cannot see God, nor can we know His essence. The best we can do is to imagine and describe Him in human terms.

בְּיַד נְבִיאֶיךָ — *Through the hand of Your prophets.* The precedent for describing God in human, physical terminology comes from Him — for He described Himself to the prophets in such terms.

לְפִי מַעֲשֶׂיךָ — *According to Your deeds.* It is a familiar truth that we cannot conceive of what God *is;* we can only know something of Him through His deeds.

הִנְּךָ אֶחָד — *Yet You are a Unity.* God is One though He appears in many guises: merciful, judgmental, old, young, warrior and so on.

זִקְנָה — *Aged.* This stich expounds on the

SONG OF GLORY

The Ark is opened and the *Song of Glory* is recited responsively — the *chazzan* reciting the first verse, the congregation reciting the second and so on.

אַנְעִים זְמִירוֹת *I shall compose pleasant psalms and weave hymns,**
because for You shall my soul pine.

My soul desired the shelter of Your hand,
to know every mystery of Your secret.
∴ *As I speak of Your glory, my heart yearns for Your love.*
Therefore I shall speak of Your glories,
and Your Name I shall honor with loving songs.
∴ *I shall relate Your glory, though I see You not;**
I shall allegorize You, I shall describe You, though I know You not.
Through the hand of Your prophets, through the counsel of Your servants;*
You allegorized the splendrous glory of Your power.
∴ *Your greatness and Your strength,*
they described the might of Your works.
They allegorized You, but not according to Your reality,
*and they portrayed You according to Your deeds.**
∴ *They symbolized You in many varied visions;*
yet You are a Unity containing all the allegories.*
They envisioned in You agedness and virility,
and the hair of Your head as hoary and jet black.
∴ *Aged* on judgment day and virile on the day of battle,*
like a man of war whose powers are many.
The hat of salvation He put on His head;
salvation for Him, His right hand and His sacred arm.*
∴ *With illuminating dew drops* His head is filled,*
His locks are the rains of the night.
He shall glory in me for He desires me,
and He shall be for me a crown of pride.
∴ *A form of the very finest gold upon his head,*
*and carved on his forehead is His glorious, sacred Name.**
For grace and for glory the pride of His splendor;*
His nation crowns Him with its prayers.
∴ *The tresses of His head* are like His youthful days;*
His locks are jet-black ringlets.
The Abode of righteousness is the pride of His splendor;
may He elevate it to His foremost joy.
∴ *May His treasured nation be in His hand like a crown,*
and like a royal tiara the pride of His splendor.
From infancy He bore them and affixed them as a crown,
because they are precious in His eyes He honored them.

---

previous one. Since the song now begins an extensive discussion of God in human terms, it changes to third person out of respect.

הוֹשִׁיעָה לּוֹ יְמִינוֹ — *Salvation for Him, His right hand.* God was like a warrior winning victory through his powerful arm.

טַלְלֵי אוֹרוֹת — *[With] illuminating dew drops. Dew* refers to the illumination of the Torah and the life-giving dew that resuscitates the dead. *Rain* refers to the flow of heavenly blessings.

כֶּתֶם ... שֵׁם קָדְשׁוֹ — *A form ... sacred Name.* A reference to the headplate of the *Kohen Gadol* [High Priest], upon which was inscribed God's sacred Name.

לְחֵן וּלְכָבוֹד ... — *... For grace and for glory.* It is a mark of God's esteem for Israel that He desires its prayers and that He takes them, as it were, as a crown on His head.

מַחְלְפוֹת רֹאשׁוֹ — *The tresses of His head.* God does not change with the passage of time. His

❖ פְּאֵרוֹ* עָלַי וּפְאֵרִי עָלָיו, וְקָרוֹב אֵלַי בְּקָרְאִי אֵלָיו.
צַח וְאָדוֹם* לִלְבוּשׁוֹ אָדוֹם, פּוּרָה בְּדָרְכוֹ בְּבוֹאוֹ מֵאֱדוֹם.
❖ קֶשֶׁר תְּפִלִּין הֶרְאָה לֶעָנָו, תְּמוּנַת יהוה לְנֶגֶד עֵינָיו.
רוֹצֶה בְעַמּוֹ עֲנָוִים יְפָאֵר, יוֹשֵׁב תְּהִלּוֹת בָּם לְהִתְפָּאֵר.
❖ רֹאשׁ דְּבָרְךָ אֱמֶת קוֹרֵא מֵרֹאשׁ, דּוֹר וָדוֹר עַם דּוֹרֶשְׁךָ דְּרוֹשׁ.
שִׁית הֲמוֹן שִׁירַי נָא עָלֶיךָ, וְרִנָּתִי תִּקְרַב אֵלֶיךָ.
❖ תְּהִלָּתִי תְּהִי לְרֹאשְׁךָ עֲטֶרֶת, וּתְפִלָּתִי תִּכּוֹן קְטֹרֶת.
תִּיקַר שִׁירַת רָשׁ בְּעֵינֶיךָ, כַּשִּׁיר יוּשַׁר עַל קָרְבָּנֶיךָ.
❖ בִּרְכָתִי תַעֲלֶה לְרֹאשׁ מַשְׁבִּיר, מְחוֹלֵל וּמוֹלִיד צַדִּיק כַּבִּיר.
וּבְבִרְכָתִי תְנַעֲנַע לִי רֹאשׁ, וְאוֹתָהּ קַח לְךָ כִּבְשָׂמִים רֹאשׁ.
❖ יֶעֱרַב נָא שִׂיחִי עָלֶיךָ, כִּי נַפְשִׁי תַעֲרוֹג אֵלֶיךָ.

לְךָ יהוה הַגְּדֻלָּה וְהַגְּבוּרָה וְהַתִּפְאֶרֶת וְהַנֵּצַח וְהַהוֹד, כִּי כֹל בַּשָּׁמַיִם וּבָאָרֶץ; לְךָ יהוה הַמַּמְלָכָה וְהַמִּתְנַשֵּׂא לְכֹל לְרֹאשׁ.[1] מִי יְמַלֵּל גְּבוּרוֹת יהוה, יַשְׁמִיעַ כָּל תְּהִלָּתוֹ.[2]

קדיש יתום

In the presence of a *minyan*, mourners recite קַדִּישׁ יָתוֹם, the Mourner's *Kaddish* (see *Laws* §81-83):

יִתְגַּדַּל וְיִתְקַדַּשׁ שְׁמֵהּ רַבָּא. (Cong. – אָמֵן.) בְּעָלְמָא דִּי בְרָא כִרְעוּתֵהּ. וְיַמְלִיךְ מַלְכוּתֵהּ, בְּחַיֵּיכוֹן וּבְיוֹמֵיכוֹן וּבְחַיֵּי דְכָל בֵּית יִשְׂרָאֵל, בַּעֲגָלָא וּבִזְמַן קָרִיב. וְאִמְרוּ: אָמֵן.

(Cong. – אָמֵן. יְהֵא שְׁמֵהּ רַבָּא מְבָרַךְ לְעָלַם וּלְעָלְמֵי עָלְמַיָּא.)

יְהֵא שְׁמֵהּ רַבָּא מְבָרַךְ לְעָלַם וּלְעָלְמֵי עָלְמַיָּא.

יִתְבָּרַךְ וְיִשְׁתַּבַּח וְיִתְפָּאַר וְיִתְרוֹמַם וְיִתְנַשֵּׂא וְיִתְהַדָּר וְיִתְעַלֶּה וְיִתְהַלָּל שְׁמֵהּ דְּקֻדְשָׁא בְּרִיךְ הוּא (Cong. – בְּרִיךְ הוּא) – לְעֵלָּא מִן כָּל בִּרְכָתָא וְשִׁירָתָא תֻּשְׁבְּחָתָא וְנֶחֱמָתָא, דַּאֲמִירָן בְּעָלְמָא. וְאִמְרוּ: אָמֵן. (Cong. – אָמֵן.)

יְהֵא שְׁלָמָא רַבָּא מִן שְׁמַיָּא, וְחַיִּים עָלֵינוּ וְעַל כָּל יִשְׂרָאֵל. וְאִמְרוּ: אָמֵן. (Cong. – אָמֵן.)

Take three steps back. Bow left and say . . . עֹשֶׂה; bow right and say . . . הוּא; bow forward and say וְעַל כָּל . . . אָמֵן. Remain standing in place for a few moments, then take three steps forward.

עֹשֶׂה שָׁלוֹם בִּמְרוֹמָיו, הוּא יַעֲשֶׂה שָׁלוֹם עָלֵינוּ, וְעַל כָּל יִשְׂרָאֵל. וְאִמְרוּ: אָמֵן. (Cong. – אָמֵן.)

'youth' remains with Him, just as the 'maturity of age' was always with Him.

פְּאֵרוֹ – *His tefillin-splendor.* Just as Israel takes pride in God, so God takes pride in Israel. The Talmud (*Berachos* 6a) expresses this idea by saying that just as Israel wears *tefillin* in which are written the praises of God, so does God, as it were, wear *tefillin*, described as His *splendor*, which contain Scriptural verses that praise Israel.

צַח וְאָדוֹם – *He is white and crimson.* God is both

∴ His tefillin-splendor is upon me and my tefillin-splendor is upon Him,*
and He is near to me when I call to Him.
He is white and crimson; His garment will be bloody red,*
when He tramples as in a press on His coming from Edom.
∴ He showed the tefillin-knot to the humble [Moses],
the likeness of HASHEM before his eyes.
He desires His people, He will glorify the humble;
enthroned upon praises, He glories with them.
∴ The very beginning of Your word is truth — one reads it from the Torah's start; the people that seeks You expounds each generation's fate.
Place the multitude of my songs before You, please;
and my glad song bring near to You.
∴ May my praise be a crown for Your head,
and may my prayer be accepted like incense.
May the poor man's song be dear in Your eyes,
like the song that is sung over Your offerings.
∴ May my blessing rise up upon the head of the Sustainer —
Creator, Giver of life, mighty Righteous One.
And to my blessing, nod Your head to me,
and take it to Yourself like the finest incense.
∴ May my prayer be sweet to You, for my soul shall pine for You.

לְךָ *Yours, HASHEM, is the greatness, the strength, the splendor, the triumph, and the glory; even everything in heaven and earth; Yours, HASHEM, is the kingdom, and the sovereignty over every leader.[1] Who can express the mighty acts of HASHEM? Who can declare all His praise?[2]*

MOURNER'S KADDISH

In the presence of a *minyan,* mourners recite the Mourner's *Kaddish* (see *Laws* §81-83).

יִתְגַּדַּל *May His great Name grow exalted and sanctified* (Cong.– *Amen.*) *in the world that He created as He willed. May He give reign to His kingship in your lifetimes and in your days, and in the lifetimes of the entire Family of Israel, swiftly and soon. Now respond: Amen.*

(Cong.– *Amen. May His great Name be blessed forever and ever.*)
May His great Name be blessed forever and ever.

Blessed, praised, glorified, exalted, extolled, mighty, upraised, and lauded be the Name of the Holy One, Blessed is He (Cong.– *Blessed is He*) *— beyond any blessing and song, praise and consolation that are uttered in the world. Now respond: Amen.* (Cong.– *Amen.*)

May there be abundant peace from Heaven, and life, upon us and upon all Israel. Now respond: Amen. (Cong.– *Amen.*)

Take three steps back. Bow left and say, *'He Who makes peace . . .';* bow right and say, *'may He . . .';* bow forward and say, *'and upon all Israel . . .'* Remain standing in place for a few moments, then take three steps forward.

He Who makes peace in His heights, may He make peace upon us, and upon all Israel. Now respond: Amen. (Cong.– *Amen.*)

(1) *I Chronicles* 29:11. (2) *Psalms* 106:2.

compassionate, symbolized by white, and strict, symbolized by crimson. He is kind or harsh, depending on the need. When the final Redemption comes, God will execute judgment against Edom for that nation's outrages against Israel. God is metaphorically portrayed as a warrior whose clothing becomes soaked with blood as he kills his adversary. [See *Isaiah* 63:1, *Rashi.*]

שיר של יום

A different psalm is assigned as the שִׁיר שֶׁל יוֹם, *Song of the Day,* for each day of the week.

SUNDAY

הַיּוֹם יוֹם רִאשׁוֹן בַּשַּׁבָּת, שֶׁבּוֹ הָיוּ הַלְוִיִּם אוֹמְרִים בְּבֵית הַמִּקְדָּשׁ:

תהלים כד

לְדָוִד מִזְמוֹר, לַיהוה הָאָרֶץ* וּמְלוֹאָהּ, תֵּבֵל וְיֹשְׁבֵי בָהּ. כִּי הוּא עַל יַמִּים יְסָדָהּ,* וְעַל נְהָרוֹת יְכוֹנְנֶהָ. מִי יַעֲלֶה* בְהַר יהוה, וּמִי יָקוּם בִּמְקוֹם קָדְשׁוֹ. נְקִי כַפַּיִם* וּבַר לֵבָב, אֲשֶׁר לֹא נָשָׂא לַשָּׁוְא נַפְשִׁי,* וְלֹא נִשְׁבַּע לְמִרְמָה. יִשָּׂא בְרָכָה* מֵאֵת יהוה, וּצְדָקָה מֵאֱלֹהֵי יִשְׁעוֹ. זֶה דּוֹר דֹּרְשָׁיו, מְבַקְשֵׁי פָנֶיךָ יַעֲקֹב סֶלָה. שְׂאוּ שְׁעָרִים* רָאשֵׁיכֶם, וְהִנָּשְׂאוּ פִּתְחֵי עוֹלָם,* וְיָבוֹא מֶלֶךְ הַכָּבוֹד.* מִי זֶה מֶלֶךְ הַכָּבוֹד, יהוה עִזּוּז וְגִבּוֹר, יהוה גִּבּוֹר מִלְחָמָה. ❖ שְׂאוּ שְׁעָרִים רָאשֵׁיכֶם, וּשְׂאוּ פִּתְחֵי עוֹלָם, וְיָבֹא מֶלֶךְ הַכָּבוֹד. מִי הוּא זֶה מֶלֶךְ הַכָּבוֹד, יהוה צְבָאוֹת, הוּא מֶלֶךְ הַכָּבוֹד סֶלָה.

The service continues with קַדִּישׁ יָתוֹם, *the Mourner's Kaddish* (page 446).

MONDAY

הַיּוֹם יוֹם שֵׁנִי בַּשַּׁבָּת, שֶׁבּוֹ הָיוּ הַלְוִיִּם אוֹמְרִים בְּבֵית הַמִּקְדָּשׁ:

תהלים מח

שִׁיר מִזְמוֹר לִבְנֵי קֹרַח. גָּדוֹל יהוה וּמְהֻלָּל מְאֹד, בְּעִיר אֱלֹהֵינוּ, הַר קָדְשׁוֹ. יְפֵה נוֹף, מְשׂוֹשׂ כָּל הָאָרֶץ,* הַר צִיּוֹן* יַרְכְּתֵי צָפוֹן,* קִרְיַת מֶלֶךְ רָב. אֱלֹהִים בְּאַרְמְנוֹתֶיהָ נוֹדַע לְמִשְׂגָּב. כִּי הִנֵּה הַמְּלָכִים נוֹעֲדוּ,* עָבְרוּ יַחְדָּו. הֵמָּה רָאוּ כֵּן תָּמָהוּ, נִבְהֲלוּ נֶחְפָּזוּ. רְעָדָה אֲחָזָתַם שָׁם, חִיל כַּיּוֹלֵדָה. בְּרוּחַ קָדִים תְּשַׁבֵּר אֳנִיּוֹת

שִׁיר שֶׁל יוֹם / SONG OF THE DAY

As part of the morning Temple service, the Levites chanted a psalm that was suited to the significance of that particular day of the week (*Tamid* 7:4). As a memorial to the Temple, these psalms have been incorporated into daily *Shacharis.* The Talmud (*Rosh Hashanah* 31a) explains how each psalm was appropriate to its respective day; we will note the reasons in the commentary. The introductory sentence, *'Today is the first day of the Sabbath ...,'* helps fulfill the Torah's command to remember the Sabbath always. By counting the days of the week with reference to the forthcoming Sabbath we tie our existence to the Sabbath. This is in sharp contrast to the non-Jewish custom of assigning names to the days in commemoration of events or gods, such as Sunday for the sun, Monday for the moon and so on (*Ramban, Exodus* 20:8).

יוֹם רִאשׁוֹן / The First Day

The first day's psalm teaches that everything belongs to God, because on the first day of creation, God was the sole Power — even the angels had not yet been created. He took possession of His newly created world with the intention of ceding it to man (*Rosh Hashanah* 31a).

לַה׳ הָאָרֶץ — *HASHEM's is the earth.* Since the world belongs to God, anyone who derives pleasure from His world without reciting the proper blessing expressing thanks to the Owner is regarded as a thief (*Berachos* 35a).

כִּי הוּא עַל יַמִּים יְסָדָהּ — *For He founded it upon seas.* The entire planet was covered with water until God commanded it to gather in seas and rivers and to expose the dry land (*Ibn Ezra*).

מִי יַעֲלֶה ... — *Who may ascend ...* God's most intense Presence is in the Temple, so those who wish to draw near and to perceive His splendor must be especially worthy (*Rashi*). By extension, one who wishes to enjoy spiritual elevation must refine his behavior.

נְקִי כַפַּיִם — *One with clean hands.* This verse answers the previous questions. To 'ascend,' one's hands may not be soiled by dishonest gain. He must be honest in his dealings with man, and reverent in his attitude toward God.

נַפְשִׁי — *My soul.* God is the 'speaker.' He refers to

SONG OF THE DAY

A different psalm is assigned as the Song of the Day for each day of the week.

SUNDAY

Today is the first day of the Sabbath,
on which the Levites would recite in the Holy Temple:

Psalm 24

לְדָוִד *Of David a psalm. HASHEM's is the earth* and its fullness, the inhabited land and those who dwell in it. For He founded it upon seas,* and established it upon rivers. Who may ascend* the mountain of HASHEM, and who may stand in the place of His sanctity? One with clean hands* and pure heart, who has not sworn in vain by My soul* and has not sworn deceitfully. He will receive a blessing* from HASHEM and just kindness from the God of his salvation. This is the generation of those who seek Him, those who strive for Your Presence — Jacob, Selah. Raise up your heads, O gates,* and be uplifted, you everlasting entrances,* so that the King of Glory* may enter. Who is this King of Glory? — HASHEM, the mighty and strong, HASHEM, the strong in battle.* Chazzan— *Raise up your heads, O gates, and raise up, you everlasting entrances, so that the King of Glory may enter. Who then is the King of Glory? HASHEM, Master of Legions, He is the King of Glory. Selah!*

The service continues with קַדִּישׁ יָתוֹם, *the Mourner's Kaddish* (p. 446).

MONDAY

Today is the second day of the Sabbath,
on which the Levites would recite in the Holy Temple:

Psalm 48

שִׁיר מִזְמוֹר *A song, a psalm, by the sons of Korach. Great is HASHEM and much praised, in the city of our God, Mount of His Holiness. Fairest of sites, joy of all the earth* is Mount Zion,* by the northern sides* of the great king's city. In her palaces God is known as the Stronghold. For behold — the kings assembled,* they came together. They saw and they were astounded, they were confounded and hastily fled. Trembling gripped them there, convulsions like a woman in birth travail. With an east wind You smashed the ships*

---

one who swears falsely as having treated God's 'soul,' as it were, with disrespect.

יִשָּׂא בְרָכָה . . . — *He will receive a blessing.* Because he honors God's Name in heart and behavior, such a person earns God's *blessing, kindness,* and *salvation (R' Hirsch).*

שְׂאוּ שְׁעָרִים — *Raise up ... O gates.* When Solomon sought to bring the Ark into the Temple, the gates remained shut despite all his pleas, until he prayed that God open the gates in the merit of David, who made all the preparations to build the Temple. Thus, this verse alludes to Solomon's future prayer *(Shabbos* 30a). The plea to the gates is repeated later to allude to the Ark's re-entry when the Third Temple will be built *(Ibn Ezra).*

פִּתְחֵי עוֹלָם — *Everlasting entrances,* i.e. the holiness of the Temple gates is eternal.

מֶלֶךְ הַכָּבוֹד — *The King of Glory.* God is given this title because He gives glory to those who revere Him *(Midrash).*

יוֹם שֵׁנִי / The Second Day

On this day, God separated between the heavenly and earthly components of the universe and ruled over both. Nevertheless, the psalm specifies Jerusalem because the seat of His holiness is Jerusalem *(Rosh Hashanah* 31a). *Resisei Laylah* comments that this day's separation between heaven and earth initiated the eternal strife between the spiritual and the physical. This is why the Levites recited a psalm composed by the sons of Korach, the man who instigated a quarrel against Moses.

מְשׂוֹשׂ כָּל הָאָרֶץ — *Joy of all the earth.* Jerusalem was given this title because the Holy City gave joy to the troubled who were atoned through the Temple service, and because the spiritual uplift of its holiness eased troubles *(Rashi).*

הַר צִיּוֹן — *Mount Zion.* The word Zion comes from צִיּוּן, a *monument.* The site of God's Sanctuary remains an eternal memorial to truth and sanctity *(R' Hirsch).*

יַרְכְּתֵי צָפוֹן — *The northern sides.* Mount Zion was north of the City of David, the *great king (Radak).*

הַמְּלָכִים נוֹעֲדוּ — *The kings assembled.* When

תַּרְשִׁישׁ.* כַּאֲשֶׁר שָׁמַעְנוּ* כֵּן רָאִינוּ בְּעִיר יהוה צְבָאוֹת, בְּעִיר אֱלֹהֵינוּ, אֱלֹהִים יְכוֹנְנֶהָ עַד עוֹלָם סֶלָה. דִּמִּינוּ אֱלֹהִים חַסְדֶּךָ, בְּקֶרֶב הֵיכָלֶךָ. כְּשִׁמְךָ אֱלֹהִים* כֵּן תְּהִלָּתְךָ, עַל קַצְוֵי אֶרֶץ, צֶדֶק מָלְאָה יְמִינֶךָ. יִשְׂמַח הַר צִיּוֹן, תָּגֵלְנָה בְּנוֹת יְהוּדָה, לְמַעַן מִשְׁפָּטֶיךָ. סֹבּוּ צִיּוֹן וְהַקִּיפוּהָ, סִפְרוּ מִגְדָּלֶיהָ. ❖ שִׁיתוּ לִבְּכֶם לְחֵילָה, פַּסְּגוּ אַרְמְנוֹתֶיהָ, לְמַעַן תְּסַפְּרוּ לְדוֹר אַחֲרוֹן. כִּי זֶה אֱלֹהִים אֱלֹהֵינוּ עוֹלָם וָעֶד, הוּא יְנַהֲגֵנוּ עַל־מוּת.*

The service continues with קַדִּישׁ יָתוֹם, *the Mourner's Kaddish* (page 446).

TUESDAY

הַיּוֹם יוֹם שְׁלִישִׁי בַּשַּׁבָּת, שֶׁבּוֹ הָיוּ הַלְוִיִּם אוֹמְרִים בְּבֵית הַמִּקְדָּשׁ:

תהלים פב

מִזְמוֹר לְאָסָף,* אֱלֹהִים נִצָּב בַּעֲדַת אֵל,* בְּקֶרֶב אֱלֹהִים יִשְׁפֹּט. עַד מָתַי* תִּשְׁפְּטוּ עָוֶל, וּפְנֵי רְשָׁעִים תִּשְׂאוּ סֶלָה. שִׁפְטוּ דַל וְיָתוֹם, עָנִי וָרָשׁ הַצְדִּיקוּ. פַּלְּטוּ דַל וְאֶבְיוֹן, מִיַּד רְשָׁעִים הַצִּילוּ. לֹא יָדְעוּ וְלֹא יָבִינוּ, בַּחֲשֵׁכָה יִתְהַלָּכוּ, יִמּוֹטוּ כָּל מוֹסְדֵי אָרֶץ. אֲנִי אָמַרְתִּי אֱלֹהִים אַתֶּם, וּבְנֵי עֶלְיוֹן כֻּלְּכֶם. אָכֵן כְּאָדָם תְּמוּתוּן, וּכְאַחַד הַשָּׂרִים תִּפֹּלוּ. ❖ קוּמָה אֱלֹהִים שָׁפְטָה הָאָרֶץ, כִּי אַתָּה תִנְחַל בְּכָל הַגּוֹיִם.

The service continues with קַדִּישׁ יָתוֹם, *the Mourner's Kaddish* (page 446).

WEDNESDAY

הַיּוֹם יוֹם רְבִיעִי בַּשַּׁבָּת, שֶׁבּוֹ הָיוּ הַלְוִיִּם אוֹמְרִים בְּבֵית הַמִּקְדָּשׁ:

תהלים צד:א-צה:ג

אֵל נְקָמוֹת יהוה, אֵל נְקָמוֹת הוֹפִיעַ. הִנָּשֵׂא שֹׁפֵט הָאָרֶץ, הָשֵׁב גְּמוּל עַל גֵּאִים. עַד מָתַי רְשָׁעִים, יהוה, עַד מָתַי רְשָׁעִים יַעֲלֹזוּ. יַבִּיעוּ יְדַבְּרוּ עָתָק, יִתְאַמְּרוּ כָּל פֹּעֲלֵי אָוֶן. עַמְּךָ יהוה יְדַכְּאוּ, וְנַחֲלָתְךָ יְעַנּוּ. אַלְמָנָה וְגֵר יַהֲרֹגוּ, וִיתוֹמִים יְרַצֵּחוּ. וַיֹּאמְרוּ לֹא יִרְאֶה יָּהּ,* וְלֹא יָבִין אֱלֹהֵי יַעֲקֹב. בִּינוּ* בֹּעֲרִים בָּעָם, וּכְסִילִים מָתַי תַּשְׂכִּילוּ. הֲנֹטַע

---

kings assembled at various times to attack Jerusalem, they saw that God was its *stronghold*. Seeing His miracles (next verse), they were astounded and fled *(Radak)*.

אֳנִיּוֹת תַּרְשִׁישׁ — *The ships of Tarshish*. A sea near Africa, Tarshish represents invading fleets that were dispatched against *Eretz Yisrael*.

כַּאֲשֶׁר שָׁמַעְנוּ — *As we heard*. From our ancestors we heard of God's miraculous salvations — but we will see similar wonders as well *(Rashi)*.

כְּשִׁמְךָ אֱלֹהִים — *Like Your Name, O God*. The prophets gave You exalted Names, but we can testify that *Your praise*, given You for actual deeds, justifies those glorious titles *(Radak)*.

עַל־מוּת — *Like children*. The two words are rendered as one: עֲלָמוּת, *youth*. God will guide us like a father caring for his young *(Targum; Rashi)*; or He will preserve the enthusiasm and vigor of our youth *(Meiri)*. According to the Masoretic tradition that these are two words, they mean that God will continue to guide us *beyond death*, i.e., in the World to Come.

יוֹם שְׁלִישִׁי / The Third Day

On the third day, God caused the dry land to become visible and fit for habitation. He did so in order that man follow the Torah's laws and deal justly with other people. Therefore the psalm speaks of justice *(Rosh Hashanah* 31a). *Maharsha* explains that the theme of this psalm — the maintenance of equity and justice — is a prerequisite for the continued existence of the world that was revealed on the third day. But this message is not limited only to courts. In his own personal life, every Jew is a judge, for his opinions and decisions about people can affect their lives in a thousand different ways.

לְאָסָף — *Of Assaf*. A descendant of Korach, Assaf was one of the psalmists whose composi-

of Tarshish. As we heard,* so we saw in the city of* H*ASHEM*, *Master of Legions, in the city of our God — may God establish it to eternity, Selah! We hoped, O God, for Your kindness, in the midst of Your Sanctuary. Like Your Name, O God,* so is Your praise — to the ends of the earth; righteousness fills Your right hand. May Mount Zion be glad, may the daughters of Judah rejoice, because of Your judgments. Walk about Zion and encircle her, count her towers.* Chazzan— *Mark well in your hearts her ramparts, raise up her palaces, that you may recount it to the succeeding generation: that this is God, our God, forever and ever, He will guide us like children.**

The service continues with קַדִּישׁ יָתוֹם, *the Mourner's Kaddish* (p. 446).

TUESDAY

Today is the third day of the Sabbath,
on which the Levites would recite in the Holy Temple:

Psalm 82

מִזְמוֹר *A psalm of Assaf:* God stands in the Divine assembly,* in the midst of judges shall He judge. Until when* will you judge lawlessly and favor the presence of the wicked, Selah? Judge the needy and the orphan, vindicate the poor and impoverished. Rescue the needy and destitute, from the hand of the wicked deliver them. They do not know nor do they understand, in darkness they walk; all foundations of the earth collapse. I said, 'You are angelic, sons of the Most High are you all.' But like men you shall die, and like one of the princes you shall fall.* Chazzan— *Arise, O God, judge the earth, for You allot the heritage among all the nations.*

The service continues with קַדִּישׁ יָתוֹם, *the Mourner's Kaddish* (p. 446).

WEDNESDAY

Today is the fourth day of the Sabbath,
on which the Levites would recite in the Holy Temple:

Psalm 94:1-95:3

אֵל נְקָמוֹת *O God of vengeance,* H*ASHEM*; *O God of vengeance, appear! Arise, O Judge of the earth, render recompense to the haughty. How long shall the wicked — O* H*ASHEM* *— how long shall the wicked exult? They speak freely, they utter malicious falsehood, they glorify themselves, all workers of iniquity. Your nation,* H*ASHEM*, *they crush, and they afflict Your heritage. The widow and the stranger they slay, and the orphans they murder. And they say, 'God will not see,* nor will the God of Jacob understand.' Understand,* you boors among the people; and you fools, when will you gain wisdom? He Who implants*

---

tions David incorporated into the Book of Psalms.

בַּעֲדַת אֵל — *In the Divine assembly*. Judges who seek truth and justice are the *Divine assembly*, because they represent God's justice on earth. As a result of their sincerity, God Himself penetrates into their hearts — בְּקֶרֶב אֱלֹהִים, *in the midst of judges* — to assure them of reaching a just verdict (*Alshich*).

עַד מָתַי — *Until when . . .?* The next three verses address directly the judges who do not carry out their responsibilities. Included in this exhortation is the clear message for the judges to take the initiative in seeking out and correcting injustice.

יוֹם רְבִיעִי / The Fourth Day

On the fourth day, God created the sun, moon, and stars, but instead of recognizing them as God's servants, man eventually came to regard the luminaries as independent gods that should be worshiped. Because of this idolatry, God showed Himself to be, as this psalm describes Him, the *God of vengeance*, for despite His almost endless patience and mercy, He does not tolerate evil forever.

וַיֹּאמְרוּ לֹא יִרְאֶה יָּהּ — *And they say, 'God will not see . . .'* When the Temple was destroyed, it was as if God's power had been diminished and His Four-letter Name abbreviated to the two letters of יָהּ (*Eruvin* 18b). This gives evildoers the pretext to claim that God was detached from the world and unable to see the wickedness being done on earth (*Zera Yaakov*).

בִּינוּ — *Understand*. If only the boors would

אֹזֶן הֲלֹא יִשְׁמָע, אִם יֹצֵר עַיִן הֲלֹא יַבִּיט. הֲיֹסֵר גּוֹיִם הֲלֹא יוֹכִיחַ, הַמְלַמֵּד אָדָם דָּעַת. יהוה יֹדֵעַ מַחְשְׁבוֹת אָדָם, כִּי הֵמָּה הָבֶל. אַשְׁרֵי הַגֶּבֶר* אֲשֶׁר תְּיַסְּרֶנּוּ יָּהּ, וּמִתּוֹרָתְךָ תְלַמְּדֶנּוּ. לְהַשְׁקִיט לוֹ* מִימֵי רָע, עַד יִכָּרֶה לָרָשָׁע שָׁחַת. כִּי לֹא יִטֹּשׁ יהוה עַמּוֹ, וְנַחֲלָתוֹ* לֹא יַעֲזֹב. כִּי עַד צֶדֶק יָשׁוּב מִשְׁפָּט,* וְאַחֲרָיו כָּל יִשְׁרֵי לֵב. מִי יָקוּם לִי עִם מְרֵעִים, מִי יִתְיַצֵּב לִי עִם פֹּעֲלֵי אָוֶן. לוּלֵי יהוה עֶזְרָתָה לִּי, כִּמְעַט שָׁכְנָה דוּמָה נַפְשִׁי. אִם אָמַרְתִּי מָטָה רַגְלִי,* חַסְדְּךָ יהוה יִסְעָדֵנִי. בְּרֹב שַׂרְעַפַּי בְּקִרְבִּי, תַּנְחוּמֶיךָ יְשַׁעַשְׁעוּ נַפְשִׁי. הַיְחָבְרְךָ כִּסֵּא הַוּוֹת, יֹצֵר עָמָל* עֲלֵי חֹק. יָגוֹדּוּ עַל נֶפֶשׁ צַדִּיק, וְדָם נָקִי יַרְשִׁיעוּ. וַיְהִי יהוה לִי לְמִשְׂגָּב, וֵאלֹהַי לְצוּר מַחְסִי. וַיָּשֶׁב עֲלֵיהֶם אֶת אוֹנָם, וּבְרָעָתָם יַצְמִיתֵם, יַצְמִיתֵם יהוה אֱלֹהֵינוּ.

❖ לְכוּ נְרַנְּנָה* לַיהוה, נָרִיעָה לְצוּר יִשְׁעֵנוּ. נְקַדְּמָה פָנָיו בְּתוֹדָה, בִּזְמִרוֹת נָרִיעַ לוֹ. כִּי אֵל גָּדוֹל יהוה, וּמֶלֶךְ גָּדוֹל עַל כָּל אֱלֹהִים.

The service continues with קַדִּישׁ יָתוֹם, *the Mourner's Kaddish* (page 446).

THURSDAY

הַיּוֹם יוֹם חֲמִישִׁי בַּשַּׁבָּת, שֶׁבּוֹ הָיוּ הַלְוִיִּם אוֹמְרִים בְּבֵית הַמִּקְדָּשׁ:

תהלים פא

לַמְנַצֵּחַ עַל הַגִּתִּית* לְאָסָף. הַרְנִינוּ לֵאלֹהִים עוּזֵּנוּ, הָרִיעוּ לֵאלֹהֵי יַעֲקֹב.* שְׂאוּ זִמְרָה וּתְנוּ תֹף, כִּנּוֹר נָעִים עִם נָבֶל. תִּקְעוּ בַחֹדֶשׁ שׁוֹפָר,* בַּכֵּסֶה לְיוֹם חַגֵּנוּ. כִּי חֹק לְיִשְׂרָאֵל הוּא, מִשְׁפָּט* לֵאלֹהֵי יַעֲקֹב. עֵדוּת בִּיהוֹסֵף שָׂמוֹ,* בְּצֵאתוֹ עַל אֶרֶץ מִצְרָיִם, שְׂפַת לֹא יָדַעְתִּי אֶשְׁמָע. הֲסִירוֹתִי מִסֵּבֶל שִׁכְמוֹ, כַּפָּיו מִדּוּד תַּעֲבֹרְנָה. בַּצָּרָה קָרָאתָ, וָאֲחַלְּצֶךָּ, אֶעֶנְךָ בְּסֵתֶר רַעַם, אֶבְחָנְךָ עַל מֵי מְרִיבָה, סֶלָה. שְׁמַע עַמִּי וְאָעִידָה בָּךְ, יִשְׂרָאֵל אִם תִּשְׁמַע לִי. לֹא יִהְיֶה בְךָ אֵל זָר, וְלֹא תִשְׁתַּחֲוֶה לְאֵל נֵכָר.

---

realize that God cannot be fooled or ignored! *(Radak).*

אַשְׁרֵי הַגֶּבֶר — *Praiseworthy is the man.* The wicked ask why the righteous suffer, if God truly controls everything. The Psalmist answers that God afflicts the righteous only when it is to their benefit, to correct them, to make them realize the futility of physical pleasures, or to atone for their sins *(Radak; Meiri).*

לְהַשְׁקִיט לוֹ — *To give him rest.* The suffering of good people on earth spares them from the far worse *days of evil* in *Gehinnom,* but they will not suffer forever — only until evil is purged from the world and *a pit is dug for the wicked (Rashi).*

וְנַחֲלָתוֹ — *His heritage.* Even in exile, Israel knows it will survive, because it is God's *heritage (Radak).*

יָשׁוּב מִשְׁפָּט — *Shall revert to righteousness.* For the good person who has sinned, God's punishment will cause him to repent *(Rashi).*

מָטָה רַגְלִי — *'My foot falters.'* When Israel fears it will falter, God's goodness supports it *(Radak).*

יֹצֵר עָמָל . . . — *Those who fashion evil . . .* Would God associate with those who legitimize their evil by turning it into a code of law? *(Radak).*

לְכוּ נְרַנְּנָה — *Come — let us sing.* The next three verses are not part of the psalm of the day, and are not recited in all congregations. They are the beginning of the next psalm and are recited because of their inspiring message that is an apt climax to the song of the day.

יוֹם חֲמִישִׁי / The Fifth Day

On the fifth day of creation, God made the birds and the fish, which bring joy to the world. When people observe the vast variety of colorful birds and fish, they are awed by the tremendous scope of God's creative ability, and they are stirred to praise Him with song *(Rosh Hashanah* 31a).

הַגִּתִּית — *The gittis.* A musical instrument named after the town of Gath, where it was made *(Rashi).*

הָרִיעוּ לֵאלֹהֵי יַעֲקֹב — *Call out to the God of Jacob.*

the ear, shall He not hear? He Who fashions the eye, shall He not see? He Who chastises nations, shall He not rebuke? — He Who teaches man knowledge. HASHEM knows the thoughts of man, that they are futile. Praiseworthy is the man whom God disciplines, and whom You teach from Your Torah. To give him rest* from the days of evil, until a pit is dug for the wicked. For HASHEM will not cast off His people, nor will He forsake His heritage.* For justice shall revert to righteousness,* and following it will be all of upright heart. Who will rise up for me against evildoers? Who will stand up for me against the workers of iniquity? Had HASHEM not been a help to me, my soul would soon have dwelt in silence. If I said, 'My foot falters,'* Your kindness, HASHEM, supported me. When my forebodings were abundant within me, Your comforts cheered my soul. Can the throne of destruction be associated with You? — those who fashion evil* into a way of life. They join together against the soul of the righteous, and the blood of the innocent they condemn. Then HASHEM became a stronghold for me, and my God, the Rock of my refuge. He turned upon them their own violence, and with their own evil He will cut them off, HASHEM, our God, will cut them off.*

Chazzan— *Come — let us sing* to HASHEM, let us call out to the Rock of our salvation. Let us greet Him with thanksgiving, with praiseful songs let us call out to Him. For a great God is HASHEM, and a great King above all heavenly powers.*

The service continues with קַדִּישׁ יָתוֹם, *the Mourner's Kaddish* (p. 446).

THURSDAY

Today is the fifth day of the Sabbath,
on which the Levites would recite in the Holy Temple:

Psalm 81

לַמְנַצֵּחַ *For the Conductor, upon the gittis,* by Assaf. Sing joyously to the God of our might, call out to the God of Jacob.* Raise a song and sound the drum, the sweet harp with the lyre. Blow the shofar at the moon's renewal,* at the time appointed for our festive day. Because it is a decree for Israel, a judgment day* for the God of Jacob. He imposed it as a testimony for Joseph* when he went forth over the land of Egypt — 'I understood a language I never knew!' I removed his shoulder from the burden, his hands let go of the kettle. In distress you called out, and I released you, I answered you with thunder when you hid, I tested you at the Waters of Strife, Selah. Listen, My nation, and I will attest to you; O Israel, if you would but listen to Me. There shall be no strange god within you, nor shall you bow before an alien god.*

The Patriarch Jacob is singled out because he went down to Egypt with his sons and their families. The two hundred and ten years of bondage are counted from the moment Jacob arrived in Egypt. During this period the children of Jacob called out to God in their distress (*Radak*).

תִּקְעוּ בַחֹדֶשׁ שׁוֹפָר — *Blow the shofar at the moon's renewal.* The *moon's renewal* is a poetic term for the first day of the lunar month, when the moon becomes visible again. This refers to Rosh Hashanah, the only Festival that occurs on the first day of the month and when the *shofar* is blown.

Homiletically Rosh Hashanah is the time for חֹדֶשׁ, *renewal,* of one's dedication and שׁוֹפָר [cognate with שִׁפּוּר, *beautification*] *improvement,* of one's deeds (*Midrash Shocher Tov*).

חֹק . . . מִשְׁפָּט — *Decree . . . judgment [day].* It is a Divine decree that Israel blow the *shofar* on Rosh Hashanah, the day when God sits in judgment (*Rashi*).

The Talmud (*Beitzah* 16a) translates חֹק as a *fixed ration.* On Rosh Hashanah the heavenly tribunal fixes each person's sustenance for the coming year.

עֵדוּת בִּיהוֹסֵף שָׂמוֹ — *He imposed it as a testimony for Joseph.* This entire verse is based on the life of Joseph. The Talmud (*Rosh Hashanah* 10b) teaches that Joseph was released from prison and appointed viceroy of Egypt on Rosh Hashanah. In honor of that event, God ordained the *mitzvah* of *shofar* on Rosh Hashanah as a *testimony,* i.e.,

אָנֹכִי יהוה אֱלֹהֶיךָ, הַמַּעַלְךָ מֵאֶרֶץ מִצְרָיִם, הַרְחֶב פִּיךָ* וַאֲמַלְאֵהוּ. וְלֹא שָׁמַע עַמִּי לְקוֹלִי, וְיִשְׂרָאֵל לֹא אָבָה לִי. וָאֲשַׁלְּחֵהוּ בִּשְׁרִירוּת לִבָּם, יֵלְכוּ בְּמוֹעֲצוֹתֵיהֶם. לוּ עַמִּי שֹׁמֵעַ לִי, יִשְׂרָאֵל בִּדְרָכַי יְהַלֵּכוּ. כִּמְעַט אוֹיְבֵיהֶם אַכְנִיעַ, וְעַל צָרֵיהֶם אָשִׁיב יָדִי. מְשַׂנְאֵי יהוה יְכַחֲשׁוּ לוֹ,* וִיהִי עִתָּם לְעוֹלָם.* ❖ וַיַּאֲכִילֵהוּ* מֵחֵלֶב חִטָּה, וּמִצּוּר דְּבַשׁ אַשְׂבִּיעֶךָ.

The service continues with קַדִּישׁ יָתוֹם, *the Mourner's Kaddish* (page 446).

FRIDAY

הַיּוֹם יוֹם שִׁשִּׁי בַּשַּׁבָּת, שֶׁבּוֹ הָיוּ הַלְוִיִּם אוֹמְרִים בְּבֵית הַמִּקְדָּשׁ:

תהלים צג

יהוה מָלָךְ, גֵּאוּת לָבֵשׁ, לָבֵשׁ יהוה עֹז הִתְאַזָּר, אַף תִּכּוֹן תֵּבֵל בַּל תִּמּוֹט. נָכוֹן כִּסְאֲךָ מֵאָז, מֵעוֹלָם אָתָּה. נָשְׂאוּ נְהָרוֹת יהוה, נָשְׂאוּ נְהָרוֹת קוֹלָם, יִשְׂאוּ נְהָרוֹת דָּכְיָם. מִקֹּלוֹת מַיִם רַבִּים, אַדִּירִים מִשְׁבְּרֵי יָם, אַדִּיר בַּמָּרוֹם יהוה. ❖ עֵדֹתֶיךָ נֶאֶמְנוּ מְאֹד לְבֵיתְךָ נַאֲוָה קֹדֶשׁ, יהוה לְאֹרֶךְ יָמִים.

The service continues with קַדִּישׁ יָתוֹם, *the Mourner's Kaddish* (page 446).

THE SABBATH

הַיּוֹם יוֹם שַׁבַּת קֹדֶשׁ שֶׁבּוֹ הָיוּ הַלְוִיִּם אוֹמְרִים בְּבֵית הַמִּקְדָּשׁ:

תהלים צב

מִזְמוֹר שִׁיר לְיוֹם הַשַּׁבָּת. טוֹב לְהֹדוֹת לַיהוה, וּלְזַמֵּר לְשִׁמְךָ עֶלְיוֹן. לְהַגִּיד בַּבֹּקֶר חַסְדֶּךָ, וֶאֱמוּנָתְךָ בַּלֵּילוֹת. עֲלֵי עָשׂוֹר וַעֲלֵי נָבֶל, עֲלֵי הִגָּיוֹן בְּכִנּוֹר. כִּי שִׂמַּחְתַּנִי יהוה בְּפָעֳלֶךָ, בְּמַעֲשֵׂי יָדֶיךָ אֲרַנֵּן. מַה גָּדְלוּ מַעֲשֶׂיךָ יהוה, מְאֹד עָמְקוּ מַחְשְׁבֹתֶיךָ. אִישׁ בַּעַר לֹא יֵדָע, וּכְסִיל לֹא יָבִין אֶת זֹאת. בִּפְרֹחַ רְשָׁעִים כְּמוֹ עֵשֶׂב, וַיָּצִיצוּ כָּל פֹּעֲלֵי אָוֶן, לְהִשָּׁמְדָם עֲדֵי עַד. וְאַתָּה מָרוֹם לְעֹלָם יהוה. כִּי הִנֵּה אֹיְבֶיךָ יהוה, כִּי הִנֵּה אֹיְבֶיךָ יֹאבֵדוּ, יִתְפָּרְדוּ כָּל פֹּעֲלֵי אָוֶן. וַתָּרֶם כִּרְאֵים קַרְנִי, בַּלֹּתִי בְּשֶׁמֶן רַעֲנָן. וַתַּבֵּט עֵינִי בְּשׁוּרָי, בַּקָּמִים עָלַי מְרֵעִים, תִּשְׁמַעְנָה אָזְנָי. ❖ צַדִּיק כַּתָּמָר יִפְרָח, כְּאֶרֶז בַּלְּבָנוֹן יִשְׂגֶּה. שְׁתוּלִים בְּבֵית יהוה, בְּחַצְרוֹת אֱלֹהֵינוּ יַפְרִיחוּ. עוֹד יְנוּבוּן בְּשֵׂיבָה, דְּשֵׁנִים וְרַעֲנַנִּים יִהְיוּ. לְהַגִּיד כִּי יָשָׁר יהוה, צוּרִי וְלֹא עַוְלָתָה בּוֹ.

The service continues with קַדִּישׁ יָתוֹם, *the Mourner's Kaddish* (p. 446).

---

a reminder of Joseph's freedom. In order to qualify as a ruler under Egyptian law, Joseph had to know all the languages — a requirement that was fulfilled when the angel Gabriel taught them to him. Thus Joseph exclaimed, *'I understood a language I never knew' (Rashi).*

הַרְחֶב פִּיךָ — *Open wide your mouth,* with requests, and I will fulfill them. God urges Israel to ask all that its heart desires *(Ibn Ezra).* By asking God for *everything* that he needs, a person demonstrates his faith that God's power and generosity know no bounds *(Taanis 3:6).*

מְשַׂנְאֵי ה׳ יְכַחֲשׁוּ לוֹ — *Those who hate* HASHEM [i.e., because Israel's enemies are God's as well] *lie to Him.* They deny that they ever harmed Israel *(Rashi).*

וִיהִי עִתָּם לְעוֹלָם — *So their destiny is eternal.* Israel's tormentors will be condemned to eternal suffering. In contrast, concerning Israel, God promises that:

וַיַּאֲכִילֵהוּ — *But He would feed him.* In the Wilderness, God provided Israel with manna that

I am HASHEM, *your God, Who elevated you from the land of Egypt, open wide your mouth* and I will fill it. But My people did not heed My voice and Israel did not desire Me. So I let them follow their heart's fantasies, they follow their own counsels. If only My people would heed Me, if Israel would walk in My ways. In an instant I would subdue their foes, and against their tormentors turn My hand. Those who hate* HASHEM *lie to Him* — so their destiny is eternal.** Chazzan– *But He would feed him* with the cream of the wheat, and with honey from a rock sate you.*

The service continues with קַדִּישׁ יָתוֹם, *the Mourner's Kaddish* (p. 446).

FRIDAY

Today is the sixth day of the Sabbath,
on which the Levites would recite in the Holy Temple:

Psalm 93

יהוה מָלָךְ HASHEM *will have reigned, He will have donned grandeur; He will have donned might and girded Himself; He even made the world firm so that it should not falter. Your throne was established from of old, eternal are You. Like rivers they raised, O* HASHEM, *like rivers they raised their voice; like rivers they shall raise their destructiveness. More than the roars of many waters, mightier than the waves of the sea — You are mighty on high,* HASHEM. Chazzan– *Your testimonies are exceedingly trustworthy about Your House, the Sacred Dwelling — O* HASHEM, *may it be for long days.*

The service continues with קַדִּישׁ יָתוֹם, *the Mourner's Kaddish* (p. 446).

THE SABBATH

Today is the Holy Sabbath day,
on which the Levites would sing in the Holy Temple:

Psalm 92

מִזְמוֹר שִׁיר *A psalm, a song for the Sabbath day. It is good to thank* HASHEM *and to sing praise to Your Name, O Exalted One; to relate Your kindness in the dawn and Your faith in the nights. Upon ten-stringed instrument and lyre, with singing accompanied by a harp. For You have gladdened me,* HASHEM, *with Your deeds; at the works of Your Hands I sing glad song. How great are Your deeds,* HASHEM; *exceedingly profound are Your thoughts. A boor cannot know, nor can a fool understand this: when the wicked bloom like grass and all the doers of iniquity blossom — it is to destroy them till eternity. But You remain exalted forever,* HASHEM. *For behold! — Your enemies,* HASHEM, *for behold! — Your enemies shall perish, dispersed shall be all doers of iniquity. As exalted as a re'eim's shall be my pride, I will be saturated with ever-fresh oil. My eyes have seen my vigilant foes; when those who would harm me rise up against me, my ears have heard their doom.* Chazzan– *A righteous man will flourish like a date palm, like a cedar in the Lebanon he will grow tall. Planted in the house of* HASHEM, *in the courtyards of our God they will flourish. They will still be fruitful in old age, vigorous and fresh they will be — to declare that* HASHEM *is just, my Rock in Whom there is no wrong.*

The service continues with קַדִּישׁ יָתוֹם, *the Mourner's Kaddish* (p. 446).

---

was finer than *the cream of the wheat* and with honey-sweet water from a rock (*Ibn Ezra*).

⊷§ יוֹם שִׁשִּׁי / The Sixth Day

Because it describes God in His full grandeur and power as He was when He completed the six days of Creation, and because it describes Him as 'donning' grandeur and 'girding' Himself like one dressing in his Sabbath finery, this psalm was designated as the song of Friday, when the footsteps of the Sabbath begin to be heard. [Commentary appears on page 40.]

⊷§ שַׁבָּת / The Sabbath

Although this psalm is identified as belonging to the theme of the Sabbath and was the Levites'

קידושא רבא

ON THE SABBATH BEGIN HERE.

Many omit some or all of these verses and begin with עַל כֵּן.

אִם תָּשִׁיב* מִשַּׁבָּת רַגְלֶךָ, עֲשׂוֹת חֲפָצֶךָ בְּיוֹם קָדְשִׁי, וְקָרָאתָ לַשַּׁבָּת עֹנֶג, לִקְדוֹשׁ יהוה מְכֻבָּד, וְכִבַּדְתּוֹ מֵעֲשׂוֹת דְּרָכֶיךָ, מִמְּצוֹא חֶפְצְךָ וְדַבֵּר דָּבָר. אָז תִּתְעַנַּג עַל יהוה, וְהִרְכַּבְתִּיךָ עַל בָּמֳתֵי אָרֶץ, וְהַאֲכַלְתִּיךָ נַחֲלַת יַעֲקֹב אָבִיךָ,* כִּי פִּי יהוה דִּבֵּר.[1]

וְשָׁמְרוּ בְנֵי יִשְׂרָאֵל אֶת הַשַּׁבָּת, לַעֲשׂוֹת אֶת הַשַּׁבָּת לְדֹרֹתָם בְּרִית עוֹלָם. בֵּינִי וּבֵין בְּנֵי יִשְׂרָאֵל אוֹת הִיא לְעֹלָם, כִּי שֵׁשֶׁת יָמִים עָשָׂה יהוה אֶת הַשָּׁמַיִם וְאֶת הָאָרֶץ, וּבַיּוֹם הַשְּׁבִיעִי שָׁבַת וַיִּנָּפַשׁ.[2]

זָכוֹר* אֶת יוֹם הַשַּׁבָּת לְקַדְּשׁוֹ. שֵׁשֶׁת יָמִים תַּעֲבֹד וְעָשִׂיתָ כָּל מְלַאכְתֶּךָ. וְיוֹם הַשְּׁבִיעִי שַׁבָּת לַיהוה אֱלֹהֶיךָ, לֹא תַעֲשֶׂה כָל מְלָאכָה, אַתָּה וּבִנְךָ וּבִתֶּךָ עַבְדְּךָ וַאֲמָתְךָ וּבְהֶמְתֶּךָ, וְגֵרְךָ אֲשֶׁר בִּשְׁעָרֶיךָ. כִּי שֵׁשֶׁת יָמִים עָשָׂה יהוה אֶת הַשָּׁמַיִם וְאֶת הָאָרֶץ אֶת הַיָּם וְאֶת כָּל אֲשֶׁר בָּם, וַיָּנַח בַּיּוֹם הַשְּׁבִיעִי —

עַל כֵּן בֵּרַךְ יהוה אֶת יוֹם הַשַּׁבָּת וַיְקַדְּשֵׁהוּ.[3]

(אֵלֶּה מוֹעֲדֵי יהוה מִקְרָאֵי קֹדֶשׁ אֲשֶׁר תִּקְרְאוּ אֹתָם בְּמוֹעֲדָם.[4]

וַיְדַבֵּר מֹשֶׁה* אֶת מֹעֲדֵי יהוה, אֶל בְּנֵי יִשְׂרָאֵל.[5])

סַבְרִי מָרָנָן וְרַבָּנָן וְרַבּוֹתַי:

בָּרוּךְ אַתָּה יהוה אֱלֹהֵינוּ מֶלֶךְ הָעוֹלָם, בּוֹרֵא פְּרִי הַגָּפֶן.

(אָמֵן. – All present)

---

song for the Sabbath Temple service, the text contains not a single direct reference to the Sabbath. Among the explanations given are:

— The psalm refers not to the weekly Sabbath, but to the World to Come, when man will achieve the spiritual perfection we only glimpse during the Sabbath. The psalm is thus well suited to the Sabbath which is a semblance of that future spiritual perfection (*Rashi*).

— Praise of God is necessary, but difficult on weekdays when people must struggle for a livelihood. On the Sabbath, free from the strictures of the week, Jews can turn their minds to the perception of God's ways and His praise — which are the topics of this psalm (*Radak*).

Additional commentary to this psalm appears on page 38.

קִידּוּשָׁא רַבָּא / The Morning Kiddush

The morning *Kiddush* was introduced by the Sages, and its status is thus inferior to the evening *Kiddush* which is Scriptural in origin (*Pesachim* 106b). Therefore, it is euphemistically called קִידּוּשָׁא רַבָּא, the *Great Kiddush.* Originally, the *Kiddush* consisted only of the blessing over wine (*Pesachim* 106b), the Scriptural verses

KIDDUSHA RABBA

ON THE SABBATH BEGIN HERE.

Many omit some or all of these verses and begin with *'therefore HASHEM blessed.'*

אִם תָּשִׁיב *If you restrain,* because of the Sabbath, your feet, refrain from accomplishing your own needs on My holy day; if you proclaim the Sabbath 'a delight,' the holy one of HASHEM, 'honored one,' and you honor it by not doing your own ways, from seeking your needs or discussing the forbidden. Then you shall be granted pleasure with HASHEM and I shall mount you astride the heights of the world, and provide you the heritage of your forefather Jacob* — for the mouth of HASHEM has spoken.*[1]

וְשָׁמְרוּ *And the Children of Israel observed the Sabbath, to make the Sabbath for their generations an eternal covenant. Between Me and the Children of Israel it is a sign forever, that in six days did HASHEM make the heaven and the earth, and on the seventh day He rested and was refreshed.*[2]

זָכוֹר *Always remember* the Sabbath day to hallow it. For six days you may labor and do all your work. But the seventh day is the Sabbath for HASHEM, Your God; you may do no work — you, your son and your daughter, your slave and your maidservant, your animal, and the stranger who is in your gates. For in six days did HASHEM make the heaven and the earth, the sea and all that is in them and He rested on the seventh day;*

therefore HASHEM blessed the Sabbath day and sanctified it.[3]

(These are the appointed festivals of HASHEM, holy convocations, which you are to proclaim in their appointed times.[4]*)*

And Moses declared HASHEM's appointed festivals to the Children of Israel.*[5]

By your leave, my masters and teachers:

בָּרוּךְ *Blessed are You, HASHEM, our God, King of the universe, Who creates the fruit of the vine.* (All present — *Amen.)*

(1) *Isaiah* 58:13-14. (2) *Exodus* 31:16-17. (3) 20:8-11. (4) *Leviticus* 23:4. (5) 23:44.

having been added over the centuries. However, not everyone says all the verses.

אִם תָּשִׁיב — *If you restrain.* These verses from *Isaiah* conclude a chapter that urges a variety of good practices upon people and assures them of God's blessings in return for compliance.

נַחֲלַת יַעֲקֹב אָבִיךָ — *The heritage of your forefather Jacob.* The land promised Abraham and Isaac was delineated by borders, but Jacob's blessing had no limitation.

זָכוֹר — *Always remember.* The fourth of the Ten Commandments, this passage implies the positive commandments of the day.

אֵלֶּה מוֹעֲדֵי . . . וַיְדַבֵּר מֹשֶׁה — *These are the appointed festivals . . . And Moses declared.* These two verses bracket the Scriptural passage that delineates the laws pertaining to each Festival. Thus, they are an appropriate selection for the Festival *Kiddush.*

Laws of Kiddush

The laws for *Kiddush* on *Yom Tov* are the same as on Shabbos. It is essential that *Kiddush*

מעין שלש

The following blessing is recited after partaking of (a) grain products such as foods made with matzah meal (but not matzah itself which requires the full *Bircas HaMazon*); (b) grape wine or grape juice; (c) grapes, figs, pomegranates, olives, or dates. (If foods from two or three of these groups were consumed, then the insertions for each group are connected with the conjunctive ְו, thus וְעַל. The order of insertion in such a case is grain, wine, fruit.)

בָּרוּךְ אַתָּה יהוה אֱלֹהֵינוּ מֶלֶךְ הָעוֹלָם,

After fruits:	After wine:	After grain products:
עַל הָעֵץ	עַל הַגֶּפֶן	עַל הַמִּחְיָה
וְעַל פְּרִי הָעֵץ,	וְעַל פְּרִי הַגֶּפֶן,	וְעַל הַכַּלְכָּלָה,

וְעַל תְּנוּבַת הַשָּׂדֶה, וְעַל אֶרֶץ חֶמְדָּה טוֹבָה וּרְחָבָה, שֶׁרָצִיתָ וְהִנְחַלְתָּ לַאֲבוֹתֵינוּ, לֶאֱכוֹל מִפִּרְיָהּ וְלִשְׂבּוֹעַ מִטּוּבָהּ. רַחֵם יהוה אֱלֹהֵינוּ עַל יִשְׂרָאֵל עַמֶּךָ, וְעַל יְרוּשָׁלַיִם עִירֶךָ, וְעַל צִיּוֹן מִשְׁכַּן כְּבוֹדֶךָ, וְעַל מִזְבְּחֶךָ וְעַל הֵיכָלֶךָ. וּבְנֵה יְרוּשָׁלַיִם עִיר הַקֹּדֶשׁ בִּמְהֵרָה בְיָמֵינוּ, וְהַעֲלֵנוּ לְתוֹכָהּ, וְשַׂמְּחֵנוּ בְּבִנְיָנָהּ, וְנֹאכַל מִפִּרְיָהּ, וְנִשְׂבַּע מִטּוּבָהּ, וּנְבָרֶכְךָ עָלֶיהָ בִּקְדֻשָּׁה וּבְטָהֳרָה. [On the Sabbath – וּרְצֵה וְהַחֲלִיצֵנוּ בְּיוֹם הַשַּׁבָּת הַזֶּה.] וְשַׂמְּחֵנוּ בְּיוֹם חַג הַמַּצּוֹת הַזֶּה. כִּי אַתָּה יהוה טוֹב וּמֵטִיב לַכֹּל, וְנוֹדֶה לְּךָ עַל הָאָרֶץ

After fruit:	After wine:	After grain products
וְעַל הַפֵּרוֹת.°	וְעַל פְּרִי הַגֶּפֶן.	וְעַל הַמִּחְיָה.

בָּרוּךְ אַתָּה יהוה, עַל הָאָרֶץ

וְעַל הַפֵּרוֹת.°	וְעַל פְּרִי הַגֶּפֶן.	וְעַל הַמִּחְיָה.

°If the fruit grew in *Eretz Yisrael,* substitute פֵּירוֹתֶיהָ for הַפֵּרוֹת.

בורא נפשות

After eating or drinking any food for which neither *Bircas HaMazon* nor the Three-Faceted Blessing applies, such as fruits other than the above, vegetables or beverages other than wine, recite:

בָּרוּךְ אַתָּה יהוה אֱלֹהֵינוּ מֶלֶךְ הָעוֹלָם, בּוֹרֵא נְפָשׁוֹת רַבּוֹת וְחֶסְרוֹנָן, עַל כָּל מַה שֶּׁבָּרָא(תָ) לְהַחֲיוֹת בָּהֶם נֶפֶשׁ כָּל חָי. בָּרוּךְ חֵי הָעוֹלָמִים.

---

be followed by a meal at the site of the *Kiddush* (*Shulchan Aruch, Orach Chaim* 273:1). The Talmud (*Pesachim* 101a) states: אֵין קִידּוּשׁ אֶלָּא בִּמְקוֹם סְעוּדָה, *Kiddush is valid only at a meal.* It is also forbidden to eat or drink (even water) before one has recited *Kiddush* (O.C. 271:4). It follows from this that if one did say the *Kiddush,* but did not follow it with a meal, his *Kiddush* is not valid, and he may not eat or drink (see O.C. 269:1). These rules apply to the *Kiddush* recited at night and the one said in the morning as well (see O.C. 289:1).

Many *poskim* assert that a meal in this

THE THREE-FACETED BLESSING

The following blessing is recited after partaking of (a) grain products such as foods made with matzah meal (but not matzah itself which requires the full *Bircas HaMazon*); (b) grape wine or grape juice; (c) grapes, figs, pomegranates, olives, or dates. (If foods from two or three of these groups were consumed, then the insertions for each group are connected with the conjunctive וְ, thus וְעַל.
The order of insertion in such a case is grain, wine, fruit.)

בָּרוּךְ *Blessed are You, HASHEM, our God, King of the universe, for the*

After grain products:	After wine:	After fruits:
nourishment and the sustenance,	*vine and the fruit of the vine,*	*tree and the fruit of the tree,*

and for the produce of the field; for the desirable, good and spacious Land that You were pleased to give our forefathers as a heritage, to eat of its fruit and to be satisfied with its goodness. Have mercy, HASHEM, our God, on Israel, Your people; on Jerusalem, Your city; and on Zion, the resting place of Your glory; upon Your altar, and upon Your Temple. Rebuild Jerusalem, the city of holiness, speedily in our days. Bring us up into it and gladden us in its rebuilding and let us eat from its fruit and be satisfied with its goodness and bless You upon it in holiness and purity. [On the Sabbath— *And be pleased to let us rest on this Sabbath day.*] *And gladden us on this day of the Festival of Matzos. For You, HASHEM, are good and do good to all and we thank You for the land and for the*

After grain products:	After wine:	After fruit:
nourishment.	*fruit of the vine.*	*fruit.°*

Blessed are You, HASHEM, for the land and for the

nourishment.	*fruit of the vine.*	*fruit.°*

°If the fruit grew in *Eretz Yisrael,* substitute *'its fruit.'*

BOREI NEFASHOS

After eating or drinking any food for which neither *Bircas HaMazon* nor the Three-Faceted Blessing applies, such as fruits other than the above, vegetables or beverages other than wine, recite:

בָּרוּךְ *Blessed are You, HASHEM, our God, King of the universe, Who creates numerous living things with their deficiencies; for all that You have created with which to maintain the life of every being. Blessed is He, the life of the worlds.*

---

context need not consist of bread (i.e., matzah), but that it is sufficient to eat an olive's volume of cake made of one of the five grains (wheat, barley, oats, rye, and spelt), or to drink — besides the wine which is drunk for *Kiddush* — a *revi'is* of wine or grape juice. Other foods or drinks do not qualify as a meal in this regard (see O.C. 273:5 with *Mishnah Berurah*). Some *poskim* rule that one can be lenient in cases of emergency — e.g., a person feels faint but has no cake or extra wine/grape juice — and rely on the view of the *Shiltei HaGibborim* that fruit is also considered a meal concerning the morning *Kiddush*. Hence, if one goes to a *bris* or social function where *Kiddush* is made but no cake is served, he should drink an extra *revi'is* of wine or grape juice, otherwise he should not partake of any food, since he will, in essence, be eating before *Kiddush* (M.B. 273:26).

This law has special relevancy on Pesach, when the cake that is served at a *Kiddush* often will be made of potato flour. In case of emergency, however, one can follow the *Kiddush* with other foods, as stated above.

מנחה ליום ראשון ושני

אַשְׁרֵי יוֹשְׁבֵי בֵיתֶךָ, עוֹד יְהַלְלוּךָ סֶּלָה.[1] אַשְׁרֵי הָעָם שֶׁכָּכָה לּוֹ, אַשְׁרֵי הָעָם שֶׁיהוה אֱלֹהָיו.[2]

תהלים קמה

תְּהִלָּה לְדָוִד,
אֲרוֹמִמְךָ אֱלוֹהַי הַמֶּלֶךְ, וַאֲבָרְכָה שִׁמְךָ לְעוֹלָם וָעֶד.
בְּכָל יוֹם אֲבָרְכֶךָּ, וַאֲהַלְלָה שִׁמְךָ לְעוֹלָם וָעֶד.
גָּדוֹל יהוה וּמְהֻלָּל מְאֹד, וְלִגְדֻלָּתוֹ אֵין חֵקֶר.
דּוֹר לְדוֹר יְשַׁבַּח מַעֲשֶׂיךָ, וּגְבוּרֹתֶיךָ יַגִּידוּ.
הֲדַר כְּבוֹד הוֹדֶךָ, וְדִבְרֵי נִפְלְאֹתֶיךָ אָשִׂיחָה.
וֶעֱזוּז נוֹרְאוֹתֶיךָ יֹאמֵרוּ, וּגְדוּלָּתְךָ אֲסַפְּרֶנָּה.
זֵכֶר רַב טוּבְךָ יַבִּיעוּ, וְצִדְקָתְךָ יְרַנֵּנוּ.
חַנּוּן וְרַחוּם יהוה, אֶרֶךְ אַפַּיִם וּגְדָל חָסֶד.
טוֹב יהוה לַכֹּל, וְרַחֲמָיו עַל כָּל מַעֲשָׂיו.
יוֹדוּךָ יהוה כָּל מַעֲשֶׂיךָ, וַחֲסִידֶיךָ יְבָרְכוּכָה.
כְּבוֹד מַלְכוּתְךָ יֹאמֵרוּ, וּגְבוּרָתְךָ יְדַבֵּרוּ.
לְהוֹדִיעַ לִבְנֵי הָאָדָם גְּבוּרֹתָיו, וּכְבוֹד הֲדַר מַלְכוּתוֹ.
מַלְכוּתְךָ מַלְכוּת כָּל עֹלָמִים, וּמֶמְשַׁלְתְּךָ בְּכָל דּוֹר וָדֹר.
סוֹמֵךְ יהוה לְכָל הַנֹּפְלִים, וְזוֹקֵף לְכָל הַכְּפוּפִים.
עֵינֵי כֹל אֵלֶיךָ יְשַׂבֵּרוּ, וְאַתָּה נוֹתֵן לָהֶם אֶת אָכְלָם בְּעִתּוֹ.
פּוֹתֵחַ אֶת יָדֶךָ,
וּמַשְׂבִּיעַ לְכָל חַי רָצוֹן.

While reciting the verse פּוֹתֵחַ, concentrate intently on its meaning.

צַדִּיק יהוה בְּכָל דְּרָכָיו, וְחָסִיד בְּכָל מַעֲשָׂיו.
קָרוֹב יהוה לְכָל קֹרְאָיו, לְכֹל אֲשֶׁר יִקְרָאֻהוּ בֶאֱמֶת.
רְצוֹן יְרֵאָיו יַעֲשֶׂה, וְאֶת שַׁוְעָתָם יִשְׁמַע וְיוֹשִׁיעֵם.
שׁוֹמֵר יהוה אֶת כָּל אֹהֲבָיו, וְאֵת כָּל הָרְשָׁעִים יַשְׁמִיד.
❖ תְּהִלַּת יהוה יְדַבֶּר פִּי, וִיבָרֵךְ כָּל בָּשָׂר שֵׁם קָדְשׁוֹ לְעוֹלָם וָעֶד.
וַאֲנַחְנוּ נְבָרֵךְ יָהּ, מֵעַתָּה וְעַד עוֹלָם, הַלְלוּיָהּ.[3]

(1) *Psalms* 84:5. (2) 144:15. (3) 115:18.

MINCHAH / מִנְחָה

Minchah is usually recited in the late afternoon, a particularly apt time for prayer, for it is a time of Divine mercy. Thus, both Isaac (*Genesis* 24:63) and Elijah (*I Kings* 18:36) prayed in the afternoon. Prefatory remarks to *Minchah* and commentary to אַשְׁרֵי appear on page 8.

MINCHAH FOR THE FIRST TWO DAYS

אַשְׁרֵי *Praiseworthy are those who dwell in Your house; may they always praise You, Selah!*[1] *Praiseworthy is the people for whom this is so, praiseworthy is the people whose God is* HASHEM.[2]

Psalm 145 *A psalm of praise by David:*

א *I will exalt You, my God the King,*
and I will bless Your Name forever and ever.
ב *Every day I will bless You,*
and I will laud Your Name forever and ever.
ג HASHEM *is great and exceedingly lauded,*
and His greatness is beyond investigation.
ד *Each generation will praise Your deeds to the next*
and of Your mighty deeds they will tell.
ה *The splendrous glory of Your power*
and Your wondrous deeds I shall discuss.
ו *And of Your awesome power they will speak,*
and Your greatness I shall relate.
ז *A recollection of Your abundant goodness they will utter*
and of Your righteousness they will sing exultantly.
ח *Gracious and merciful is* HASHEM,
slow to anger, and great in [bestowing] kindness.
ט HASHEM *is good to all; His mercies are on all His works.*
י *All Your works shall thank You,* HASHEM,
and Your devout ones will bless You.
כ *Of the glory of Your kingdom they will speak,*
and of Your power they will tell;
ל *To inform human beings of His mighty deeds,*
and the glorious splendor of His kingdom.
מ *Your kingdom is a kingdom spanning all eternities,*
and Your dominion is throughout every generation.
ס HASHEM *supports all the fallen ones and straightens all the bent.*
ע *The eyes of all look to You with hope*
and You give them their food in its proper time;
פ *You open Your hand,*
and satisfy the desire of every living thing.

While reciting the verse, *'You open . . .'* concentrate intently on its meaning.

צ *Righteous is* HASHEM *in all His ways*
and magnanimous in all His deeds.
ק HASHEM *is close to all who call upon Him —*
to all who call upon Him sincerely.
ר *The will of those who fear Him He will do;*
and their cry He will hear, and save them.
ש HASHEM *protects all who love Him;*
but all the wicked He will destroy.
ת Chazzan– *May my mouth declare the praise of* HASHEM
and may all flesh bless His Holy Name forever and ever.
We will bless God from this time and forever, Halleluyah![3]

The primary part of וּבָא לְצִיּוֹן is the *Kedushah* recited by the angels. These verses are presented in bold type and it is preferable that the congregation recite them aloud and in unison. However, the interpretive translation in Aramaic (which follows the verses in bold type) should be recited softly.

וּבָא לְצִיּוֹן גּוֹאֵל,* וּלְשָׁבֵי פֶשַׁע בְּיַעֲקֹב, נְאֻם יהוה. וַאֲנִי, זֹאת בְּרִיתִי* אוֹתָם, אָמַר יהוה, רוּחִי אֲשֶׁר עָלֶיךָ, וּדְבָרַי אֲשֶׁר שַׂמְתִּי בְּפִיךָ, לֹא יָמְוּשׁוּ מִפִּיךָ וּמִפִּי זַרְעֲךָ* וּמִפִּי זֶרַע זַרְעֲךָ, אָמַר יהוה, מֵעַתָּה וְעַד עוֹלָם:[1] ❖ וְאַתָּה קָדוֹשׁ יוֹשֵׁב תְּהִלּוֹת יִשְׂרָאֵל.*[2] וְקָרָא זֶה אֶל זֶה וְאָמַר:

קָדוֹשׁ, קָדוֹשׁ, קָדוֹשׁ יהוה צְבָאוֹת, מְלֹא כָל הָאָרֶץ כְּבוֹדוֹ.[3]
וּמְקַבְּלִין דֵּין מִן דֵּין וְאָמְרִין:
קַדִּישׁ בִּשְׁמֵי מְרוֹמָא עִלָּאָה בֵּית שְׁכִינְתֵּהּ,
קַדִּישׁ עַל אַרְעָא עוֹבַד גְּבוּרְתֵּהּ,
קַדִּישׁ לְעָלַם וּלְעָלְמֵי עָלְמַיָּא, יהוה צְבָאוֹת,
מַלְיָא כָל אַרְעָא זִיו יְקָרֵהּ.[4]
❖ וַתִּשָּׂאֵנִי רוּחַ,* וָאֶשְׁמַע אַחֲרַי קוֹל רַעַשׁ גָּדוֹל:
בָּרוּךְ כְּבוֹד יהוה מִמְּקוֹמוֹ.[5]
וּנְטָלַתְנִי רוּחָא, וְשִׁמְעֵית בַּתְרַי קָל זִיעַ סַגִּיא
דִּמְשַׁבְּחִין וְאָמְרִין:
בְּרִיךְ יְקָרָא דַיהוה מֵאֲתַר בֵּית שְׁכִינְתֵּהּ.[6]
יהוה יִמְלֹךְ לְעֹלָם וָעֶד.[7]
יהוה מַלְכוּתֵהּ קָאֵם לְעָלַם וּלְעָלְמֵי עָלְמַיָּא.[8]

יהוה אֱלֹהֵי אַבְרָהָם יִצְחָק וְיִשְׂרָאֵל אֲבֹתֵינוּ, שָׁמְרָה זֹּאת* לְעוֹלָם, לְיֵצֶר מַחְשְׁבוֹת לְבַב עַמֶּךָ, וְהָכֵן לְבָבָם אֵלֶיךָ.[9] וְהוּא רַחוּם,

---

⁂ וּבָא לְצִיּוֹן / Uva Letzion

The most important part of the וּבָא לְצִיּוֹן prayer is the recitation of the angel's praises of God.

The Talmud (*Sotah* 49a) declares that since the destruction of the Temple, even the physical beauty and pleasures of the world began deteriorating. If so, by what merit does the world endure? Rava teaches: the *Kedushah* in the prayer *Uva Letzion,* and the recitation of *Kaddish* following the public study of Torah. *Rashi* explains that after the Destruction, the primary focus of holiness in the universe is Torah study. In *Uva Letzion,* the Sages combined the Scriptural verses containing the angel's praise of God with the interpretive translation of *Yonasan ben Uziel.* Thus, this prayer itself constitutes Torah study and its recitation involves the entire congregation in Torah study. This emphasis on Torah study is further stressed by the latter part of *Uva Letzion* which lauds the study and observance of the Torah. The *Kaddish* recited after public Torah study is a further affirmation of the Torah's central role in Jewish existence.

וּבָא לְצִיּוֹן גּוֹאֵל — *A redeemer shall come to Zion.* God pledges that the Messiah will come to redeem the city Zion and the people of Israel. Not only those who remained righteous throughout the ordeal of exile will be saved, but even those who had sinned will join in the glorious future, if they return to the ways of God (*Etz Yosef*).

בְּרִיתִי — *My covenant.* God affirms that His covenant, i.e., His *spirit* of prophecy and *words* of Torah, will remain with Israel forever (*Metzudos*).

מִפִּיךָ וּמִפִּי זַרְעֲךָ . . . — *From your mouth, nor from*

The primary part of וּבָא לְצִיּוֹן, *'A redeemer shall come . . .'*, is the *Kedushah* recited by the angels. These verses are presented in bold type and it is preferable that the congregation recite them aloud and in unison. However, the interpretive translation in Aramaic (which follows the verses in bold type) should be recited softly.

וּבָא לְצִיּוֹן *'A redeemer shall come to Zion* and to those of Jacob who repent from willful sin,' the words of* HASHEM. *'And as for Me, this is My covenant* with them,' said* HASHEM, *'My spirit that is upon you and My words that I have placed in your mouth shall not be withdrawn from your mouth, nor from the mouth of your offspring,* nor from the mouth of your offspring's offspring,' said* HASHEM, *'from this moment and forever.'*[1] Chazzan– *You are the Holy One, enthroned upon the praises of Israel.**[2] *And one [angel] will call another and say:*

'Holy, holy, holy is HASHEM, Master of Legions, the whole world is filled with His glory.'[3]

And they receive permission from one another and say:
'Holy in the most exalted heaven, the abode of His Presence;
holy on earth, product of His strength;
holy forever and ever is HASHEM, *Master of Legions —*
the entire world is filled with the radiance of His glory.'[4]
Chazzan– *And a wind lifted me;* and I heard behind me*
the sound of a great noise:

'Blessed is the glory of HASHEM from His place.'[5]

And a wind lifted me and I heard behind me the sound
of the powerful movement of those who praised saying:
'Blessed is the honor of HASHEM
from the place of the abode of His Presence.'[6]

HASHEM shall reign for all eternity.[7]

HASHEM *— His kingdom is established forever and ever.*[8]

HASHEM, *God of Abraham, Isaac, and Israel, our forefathers, may You preserve this* forever as the realization of the thoughts in Your people's heart, and may You direct their heart to You.*[9] *He, the Merciful One,*

(1) *Isaiah* 59:20-21. (2) *Psalms* 22:4. (3) *Isaiah* 6:3. (4) *Targum Yonasan.* (5) *Ezekiel* 3:12. (6) *Targum Yonasan.* (7) *Exodus* 15:18. (8) *Targum Onkelos.* (9) *I Chronicles* 29:18.

the mouth of your offspring . . . This is a Divine assurance that if a family produces three consecutive generations of profound Torah scholars, the blessing of Torah knowledge will not be withdrawn from its posterity (*Bava Metzia* 85a). In a broader sense, we see the fulfillment of this blessing in the miracle that Torah greatness has remained with Israel throughout centuries of exile and flight from country to country and from continent to continent (*Siach Yitzchak*).

יוֹשֵׁב תְּהִלּוֹת יִשְׂרָאֵל — *Enthroned upon the praises of Israel.* Although God is praised by myriad angels, He values the praises of Israel above all; as the Sages teach (*Chullin* 90b), the angels are not permitted to sing their praises above until the Jews sing theirs below (*Abudraham*).

וַתִּשָּׂאֵנִי רוּחַ — *And a wind lifted me.* This was uttered by the prophet Ezekiel, who had just been commanded to undertake a difficult mission on behalf of the exiled Jews. God sent a wind to transport him to Babylon, and as he was lifted, he heard the song of the angels. This suggests that the person who ignores his own convenience in order to serve God can expect to climb spiritual heights beyond his normal capacity.

שָׁמְרָה זֹּאת — *May You preserve this.* May God help us remain with the above fervent declaration of His holiness and kingship (*Abudraham*).

יְכַפֵּר עָוֹן וְלֹא יַשְׁחִית, וְהִרְבָּה לְהָשִׁיב אַפּוֹ, וְלֹא יָעִיר כָּל חֲמָתוֹ.[1] כִּי אַתָּה אֲדֹנָי טוֹב וְסַלָּח, וְרַב חֶסֶד לְכָל קֹרְאֶיךָ.[2] צִדְקָתְךָ צֶדֶק לְעוֹלָם, וְתוֹרָתְךָ אֱמֶת.[3] תִּתֵּן אֱמֶת לְיַעֲקֹב, חֶסֶד לְאַבְרָהָם, אֲשֶׁר נִשְׁבַּעְתָּ לַאֲבֹתֵינוּ מִימֵי קֶדֶם.[4] בָּרוּךְ אֲדֹנָי יוֹם יוֹם יַעֲמָס לָנוּ, הָאֵל יְשׁוּעָתֵנוּ סֶלָה.[5] יהוה צְבָאוֹת עִמָּנוּ, מִשְׂגָּב לָנוּ אֱלֹהֵי יַעֲקֹב סֶלָה.[6] יהוה צְבָאוֹת, אַשְׁרֵי אָדָם בֹּטֵחַ בָּךְ.[7] יהוה הוֹשִׁיעָה, הַמֶּלֶךְ יַעֲנֵנוּ בְיוֹם קָרְאֵנוּ.[8]

בָּרוּךְ הוּא אֱלֹהֵינוּ שֶׁבְּרָאָנוּ לִכְבוֹדוֹ, וְהִבְדִּילָנוּ מִן הַתּוֹעִים, וְנָתַן לָנוּ תּוֹרַת אֱמֶת, וְחַיֵּי עוֹלָם נָטַע בְּתוֹכֵנוּ. הוּא יִפְתַּח לִבֵּנוּ בְּתוֹרָתוֹ, וְיָשֵׂם בְּלִבֵּנוּ אַהֲבָתוֹ וְיִרְאָתוֹ וְלַעֲשׂוֹת רְצוֹנוֹ וּלְעָבְדוֹ בְּלֵבָב שָׁלֵם, לְמַעַן לֹא נִיגַע לָרִיק, וְלֹא נֵלֵד לַבֶּהָלָה.[9]

יְהִי רָצוֹן מִלְּפָנֶיךָ יהוה אֱלֹהֵינוּ וֵאלֹהֵי אֲבוֹתֵינוּ, שֶׁנִּשְׁמֹר חֻקֶּיךָ בָּעוֹלָם הַזֶּה, וְנִזְכֶּה וְנִחְיֶה וְנִרְאֶה וְנִירַשׁ טוֹבָה וּבְרָכָה לִשְׁנֵי יְמוֹת הַמָּשִׁיחַ וּלְחַיֵּי הָעוֹלָם הַבָּא. לְמַעַן יְזַמֶּרְךָ כָבוֹד וְלֹא יִדֹּם, יהוה אֱלֹהַי לְעוֹלָם אוֹדֶךָּ.[10] בָּרוּךְ הַגֶּבֶר אֲשֶׁר יִבְטַח בַּיהוה, וְהָיָה יהוה מִבְטַחוֹ.[11] בִּטְחוּ בַיהוה עֲדֵי עַד, כִּי בְּיָהּ יהוה צוּר עוֹלָמִים.[12] ❖ וְיִבְטְחוּ בְךָ יוֹדְעֵי שְׁמֶךָ, כִּי לֹא עָזַבְתָּ דֹּרְשֶׁיךָ, יהוה.[13] יהוה חָפֵץ לְמַעַן צִדְקוֹ, יַגְדִּיל תּוֹרָה וְיַאְדִּיר.[14]

חצי קדיש

Chazzan recites חֲצִי קַדִּישׁ.

יִתְגַּדַּל וְיִתְקַדַּשׁ שְׁמֵהּ רַבָּא. (.Cong – אָמֵן.) בְּעָלְמָא דִּי בְרָא כִרְעוּתֵהּ. וְיַמְלִיךְ מַלְכוּתֵהּ, בְּחַיֵּיכוֹן וּבְיוֹמֵיכוֹן וּבְחַיֵּי דְכָל בֵּית יִשְׂרָאֵל, בַּעֲגָלָא וּבִזְמַן קָרִיב. וְאִמְרוּ: אָמֵן.

(.Cong – אָמֵן. יְהֵא שְׁמֵהּ רַבָּא מְבָרַךְ לְעָלַם וּלְעָלְמֵי עָלְמַיָּא.)

יְהֵא שְׁמֵהּ רַבָּא מְבָרַךְ לְעָלַם וּלְעָלְמֵי עָלְמַיָּא.

יִתְבָּרַךְ וְיִשְׁתַּבַּח וְיִתְפָּאַר וְיִתְרוֹמַם וְיִתְנַשֵּׂא וְיִתְהַדָּר וְיִתְעַלֶּה וְיִתְהַלָּל שְׁמֵהּ דְּקֻדְשָׁא בְּרִיךְ הוּא (.Cong – בְּרִיךְ הוּא) — לְעֵלָּא מִן כָּל בִּרְכָתָא וְשִׁירָתָא תֻּשְׁבְּחָתָא וְנֶחֱמָתָא, דַּאֲמִירָן בְּעָלְמָא. וְאִמְרוּ: אָמֵן.

(.Cong – אָמֵן.)

ON WEEKDAYS CONTINUE WITH *SHEMONEH ESREI*, PAGE 478.
ON THE SABBATH THE TORAH IS READ, PAGE 466.

is forgiving of iniquity and does not destroy; frequently He withdraws His anger, not arousing His entire rage.[1] *For You, my Lord, are good and forgiving, and abundantly kind to all who call upon You.*[2] *Your righteousness remains righteous forever, and Your Torah is truth.*[3] *Grant truth to Jacob, kindness to Abraham, as You swore to our forefathers from ancient times.*[4] *Blessed is my Lord for every single day, He burdens us with blessings, the God of our salvation, Selah.*[5] *HASHEM, Master of Legions, is with us, a stronghold for us is the God of Jacob, Selah.*[6] *HASHEM, Master of Legions, praiseworthy is the man who trusts in You.*[7] *HASHEM, save! May the King answer us on the day we call.*[8]

Blessed is He, our God, Who created us for His glory, separated us from those who stray, gave us the Torah of truth and implanted eternal life within us. May He open our heart through His Torah and imbue our heart with love and awe of Him and that we may do His will and serve Him wholeheartedly, so that we do not struggle in vain nor produce for futility.[9]

May it be Your will, HASHEM, our God and the God of our forefathers, that we observe Your decrees in This World, and merit that we live and see and inherit goodness and blessing in the years of Messianic times and for the life of the World to Come. So that my soul might sing to You and not be stilled, HASHEM, my God, forever will I thank You.[10] *Blessed is the man who trusts in HASHEM, then HASHEM will be his security.*[11] *Trust in HASHEM forever, for in God, HASHEM, is the strength of the worlds.*[12] Chazzan– *Those knowing Your Name will trust in You, and You forsake not those Who seek You, HASHEM.*[13] *HASHEM desired, for the sake of its [Israel's] righteousness, that the Torah be made great and glorious.*[14]

HALF-KADDISH

Chazzan recites Half-*Kaddish.*

יִתְגַּדַּל *May His great Name grow exalted and sanctified* (Cong.– *Amen.*) *in the world that He created as He willed. May He give reign to His kingship in your lifetimes and in your days, and in the lifetimes of the entire Family of Israel, swiftly and soon. Now respond: Amen.*

(Cong.– *Amen. May His great Name be blessed forever and ever.*)

May His great Name be blessed forever and ever.

Blessed, praised, glorified, exalted, extolled, mighty, upraised, and lauded be the Name of the Holy One, Blessed is He (Cong.– *Blessed is He*) — *beyond any blessing and song, praise and consolation that are uttered in the world. Now respond: Amen.* (Cong.– *Amen.*)

ON WEEKDAYS CONTINUE WITH *SHEMONEH ESREI,* PAGE 478.

ON THE SABBATH THE TORAH IS READ, PAGE 466.

---

(1) *Psalms* 78:38. (2) 86:5. (3) 119:142. (4) *Micah* 7:20. (5) *Psalms* 68:20. (6) 46:8. (7) 84:13. (8) 20:10. (9) Cf. *Isaiah* 65:23. (10) *Psalms* 30:13. (11) *Jeremiah* 17:7. (12) *Isaiah* 26:4. (13) *Psalms* 9:11. (14) *Isaiah* 42:21.

Congregation, then *chazzan:*

וַאֲנִי תְפִלָּתִי לְךָ יהוה עֵת רָצוֹן, אֱלֹהִים בְּרָב חַסְדֶּךָ, עֲנֵנִי בֶּאֱמֶת יִשְׁעֶךָ.[1]

הוצאת ספר תורה

From the moment the Ark is opened until the Torah is returned to it, one must conduct himself with the utmost respect, and avoid unnecessary conversation. It is commendable to kiss the Torah as it is carried to the *bimah* [reading table] and back to the Ark.

All rise and remain standing until the Torah is placed on the *bimah.*
The Ark is opened; before the Torah is removed the congregation recites:

וַיְהִי בִּנְסֹעַ הָאָרֹן, וַיֹּאמֶר מֹשֶׁה, קוּמָה יהוה וְיָפֻצוּ אֹיְבֶיךָ, וְיָנֻסוּ מְשַׂנְאֶיךָ מִפָּנֶיךָ.[2] כִּי מִצִּיּוֹן תֵּצֵא תוֹרָה, וּדְבַר יהוה מִירוּשָׁלָיִם.[3] בָּרוּךְ שֶׁנָּתַן תּוֹרָה לְעַמּוֹ יִשְׂרָאֵל בִּקְדֻשָּׁתוֹ.

זוהר ויקהל שסט:א

בְּרִיךְ שְׁמֵהּ דְּמָרֵא עָלְמָא, בְּרִיךְ כִּתְרָךְ וְאַתְרָךְ. יְהֵא רְעוּתָךְ עִם עַמָּךְ יִשְׂרָאֵל לְעָלַם, וּפֻרְקַן יְמִינָךְ אַחֲזֵי לְעַמָּךְ בְּבֵית מַקְדְּשָׁךְ, וּלְאַמְטוּיֵי לָנָא מִטּוּב נְהוֹרָךְ, וּלְקַבֵּל צְלוֹתָנָא בְּרַחֲמִין. יְהֵא רַעֲוָא קֳדָמָךְ, דְּתוֹרִיךְ לָן חַיִּין בְּטִיבוּתָא, וְלֶהֱוֵי אֲנָא פְקִידָא בְּגוֹ צַדִּיקַיָּא, לְמִרְחַם עָלַי וּלְמִנְטַר יָתִי וְיַת כָּל דִּי לִי וְדִי לְעַמָּךְ יִשְׂרָאֵל. אַנְתְּ הוּא זָן לְכֹלָּא, וּמְפַרְנֵס לְכֹלָּא, אַנְתְּ הוּא שַׁלִּיט עַל כֹּלָּא. אַנְתְּ הוּא דְשַׁלִּיט עַל מַלְכַיָּא, וּמַלְכוּתָא דִילָךְ הִיא. אֲנָא עַבְדָּא דְקֻדְשָׁא בְּרִיךְ הוּא, דְּסָגִידְנָא קַמֵּהּ וּמִקַּמָּא דִיקַר אוֹרַיְתֵהּ בְּכָל עִדָּן וְעִדָּן. לָא עַל אֱנָשׁ רָחִיצְנָא, וְלָא עַל בַּר אֱלָהִין סָמִיכְנָא, אֶלָּא בֶּאֱלָהָא דִשְׁמַיָּא, דְּהוּא אֱלָהָא קְשׁוֹט, וְאוֹרַיְתֵהּ קְשׁוֹט, וּנְבִיאוֹהִי קְשׁוֹט, וּמַסְגֵּא לְמֶעְבַּד טַבְוָן וּקְשׁוֹט. בֵּהּ אֲנָא רָחִיץ, וְלִשְׁמֵהּ קַדִּישָׁא יַקִּירָא אֲנָא אֵמַר תֻּשְׁבְּחָן. יְהֵא רַעֲוָא קֳדָמָךְ, דְּתִפְתַּח לִבָּאִי בְּאוֹרַיְתָא, וְתַשְׁלִים מִשְׁאֲלִין דְּלִבָּאִי, וְלִבָּא דְכָל עַמָּךְ יִשְׂרָאֵל, לְטַב וּלְחַיִּין וְלִשְׁלָם. (אָמֵן.)

The Torah is removed from the Ark and presented to the *chazzan,* who accepts it in his right arm. He then turns to the Ark and raises the Torah slightly as he bows and recites:

גַּדְּלוּ לַיהוה אִתִּי, וּנְרוֹמְמָה שְׁמוֹ יַחְדָּו.[4]

The *chazzan* turns to his right and carries the Torah to the *bimah,* as the congregation responds:

לְךָ יהוה הַגְּדֻלָּה וְהַגְּבוּרָה וְהַתִּפְאֶרֶת וְהַנֵּצַח וְהַהוֹד, כִּי כֹל בַּשָּׁמַיִם וּבָאָרֶץ, לְךָ יהוה הַמַּמְלָכָה וְהַמִּתְנַשֵּׂא לְכֹל לְרֹאשׁ.[5] רוֹמְמוּ יהוה אֱלֹהֵינוּ וְהִשְׁתַּחֲווּ לַהֲדֹם רַגְלָיו, קָדוֹשׁ הוּא. רוֹמְמוּ יהוה אֱלֹהֵינוּ וְהִשְׁתַּחֲווּ לְהַר קָדְשׁוֹ, כִּי קָדוֹשׁ יהוה אֱלֹהֵינוּ.[6]

Congregation, then *chazzan:*

וַאֲנִי תְפִלָּתִי *As for me, may my prayer to You, HASHEM, be at an opportune time; O God, in Your abundant kindness, answer me with the truth of Your salvation.*[1]

REMOVAL OF THE TORAH FROM THE ARK

From the moment the Ark is opened until the Torah is returned to it, one must conduct himself with the utmost respect, and avoid unnecessary conversation. It is commendable to kiss the Torah as it is carried to the *bimah* [reading table] and back to the Ark.

All rise and remain standing until the Torah is placed on the *bimah.*
The Ark is opened; before the Torah is removed the congregation recites:

וַיְהִי בִּנְסֹעַ *When the Ark would travel, Moses would say, 'Arise, HASHEM, and let Your foes be scattered, let those who hate You flee from You.'*[2] *For from Zion will the Torah come forth and the word of HASHEM from Jerusalem.*[3] *Blessed is He Who gave the Torah to His people Israel in His holiness.*

Zohar, Vayakhel 369a

בְּרִיךְ שְׁמֵהּ *Blessed is the Name of the Master of the universe, blessed is Your crown and Your place. May Your favor remain with Your people Israel forever; may You display the salvation of Your right hand to Your people in Your Holy Temple, to benefit us with the goodness of Your luminescence and to accept our prayers with mercy. May it be Your will that You extend our lives with goodness and that I be numbered among the righteous; that You have mercy on me and protect me, all that is mine and that is Your people Israel's. It is You Who nourishes all and sustains all, You control everything. It is You Who control kings, and Kingship is Yours. I am a servant of the Holy One, Blessed is He, and I prostrate myself before Him and before the glory of His Torah at all times. Not in any man do I put trust, nor on any angel do I rely — only on the God of heaven Who is the God of truth, Whose Torah is truth and Whose prophets are true and Who acts liberally with kindness and truth. In Him do I trust, and to His glorious and Holy Name do I declare praises. May it be Your will that You open my heart to the Torah and that You fulfill the wishes of my heart and the heart of Your entire people Israel for good, for life, and for peace. (Amen.)*

The Torah is removed from the Ark and presented to the *chazzan,* who accepts it in his right arm He then turns to the Ark and raises the Torah slightly as he bows and recites:

Declare the greatness of HASHEM with me,
and let us exalt His Name together.[4]

The *chazzan* turns to his right and carries the Torah to the *bimah,* as the congregation responds:

לְךָ *Yours, HASHEM, is the greatness, the strength, the splendor, the triumph, and the glory; even everything in heaven and earth; Yours, HASHEM, is the kingdom, and the sovereignty over every leader.*[5] *Exalt HASHEM, our God, and bow at His footstool; He is Holy! Exalt HASHEM, our God, and bow at His holy mountain; for holy is HASHEM, our God.*[6]

(1) *Psalms* 69:14. (2) *Numbers* 10:35. (3) *Isaiah* 2:3.
(4) *Psalms* 34:4. (5) *I Chronicles* 29:11. (6) *Psalms* 99:5,9.

אַב הָרַחֲמִים הוּא יְרַחֵם עַם עֲמוּסִים, וְיִזְכֹּר בְּרִית אֵיתָנִים, וְיַצִּיל נַפְשׁוֹתֵינוּ מִן הַשָּׁעוֹת הָרָעוֹת, וְיִגְעַר בְּיֵצֶר הָרַע מִן הַנְּשׂוּאִים, וְיָחֹן אוֹתָנוּ לִפְלֵיטַת עוֹלָמִים, וִימַלֵּא מִשְׁאֲלוֹתֵינוּ בְּמִדָּה טוֹבָה יְשׁוּעָה וְרַחֲמִים.

The Torah is placed on the *bimah* and prepared for reading.

The *gabbai* uses the following formula to call a *Kohen* to the Torah:

וְתִגָּלֶה וְתֵרָאֶה מַלְכוּתוֹ עָלֵינוּ בִּזְמַן קָרוֹב, וְיָחֹן פְּלֵיטָתֵנוּ וּפְלֵיטַת עַמּוֹ בֵּית יִשְׂרָאֵל לְחֵן וּלְחֶסֶד וּלְרַחֲמִים וּלְרָצוֹן. וְנֹאמַר אָמֵן. הַכֹּל הָבוּ גֹדֶל לֵאלֹהֵינוּ וּתְנוּ כָבוֹד לַתּוֹרָה. כֹּהֵן° קְרָב, יַעֲמֹד (insert name) הַכֹּהֵן.

°If no *Kohen* is present, the *gabbai* says: "אֵין כָּאן כֹּהֵן, יַעֲמֹד (name) יִשְׂרָאֵל (לֵוִי) בִּמְקוֹם כֹּהֵן."

בָּרוּךְ שֶׁנָּתַן תּוֹרָה לְעַמּוֹ יִשְׂרָאֵל בִּקְדֻשָּׁתוֹ. (תּוֹרַת יהוה תְּמִימָה מְשִׁיבַת נָפֶשׁ, עֵדוּת יהוה נֶאֱמָנָה מַחְכִּימַת פֶּתִי. פִּקּוּדֵי יהוה יְשָׁרִים מְשַׂמְּחֵי לֵב, מִצְוַת יהוה בָּרָה מְאִירַת עֵינָיִם.[1] יהוה עֹז לְעַמּוֹ יִתֵּן, יהוה יְבָרֵךְ אֶת עַמּוֹ בַשָּׁלוֹם.[2] הָאֵל תָּמִים דַּרְכּוֹ, אִמְרַת יהוה צְרוּפָה, מָגֵן הוּא לְכֹל הַחֹסִים בּוֹ.[3])

Congregation, then *gabbai:*

וְאַתֶּם הַדְּבֵקִים בַּיהוה אֱלֹהֵיכֶם, חַיִּים כֻּלְּכֶם הַיּוֹם:[4]

קריאת התורה

The reader shows the *oleh* (person called to the Torah) the place in the Torah. The *oleh* touches the Torah with a corner of his *tallis,* or the belt or mantle of the Torah, and kisses it. He then begins the blessing, bowing at בָּרְכוּ, and straightening up at ה׳.

בָּרְכוּ אֶת יהוה הַמְּבֹרָךְ.

Congregation, followed by *oleh,* responds, bowing at בָּרוּךְ, and straightening up at ה׳:

בָּרוּךְ יהוה הַמְּבֹרָךְ לְעוֹלָם וָעֶד.

Oleh continues:

בָּרוּךְ אַתָּה יהוה אֱלֹהֵינוּ מֶלֶךְ הָעוֹלָם, אֲשֶׁר בָּחַר בָּנוּ מִכָּל הָעַמִּים, וְנָתַן לָנוּ אֶת תּוֹרָתוֹ. בָּרוּךְ אַתָּה יהוה, נוֹתֵן הַתּוֹרָה.

(.אָמֵן –Cong.)

After his Torah portion has been read, the *oleh* recites:

בָּרוּךְ אַתָּה יהוה אֱלֹהֵינוּ מֶלֶךְ הָעוֹלָם, אֲשֶׁר נָתַן לָנוּ תּוֹרַת אֱמֶת, וְחַיֵּי עוֹלָם נָטַע בְּתוֹכֵנוּ. בָּרוּךְ אַתָּה יהוה, נוֹתֵן הַתּוֹרָה.

(.אָמֵן –Cong.)

THE VARIOUS מִי שֶׁבֵּרַךְ PRAYERS APPEAR ON PAGE 368.

THE TORAH READING ON THE SABBATH

The Torah reading during the Sabbath *Minchah* includes the calling to the Torah of *Kohen,* Levite, and Israelite. The reading is the first section of the next *sidrah* in the regular order of weekly Torah reading. Since the Sabbath following Pesach can be either *Shemini, Acharei,* or *Kedoshim,* the first section from one of these *sidrahs* is read.

אַב הָרַחֲמִים *May the Father of mercy have mercy on the nation that is borne by Him, and may He remember the covenant of the spiritually mighty. May He rescue our souls from the bad times, and upbraid the evil inclination to leave those borne by Him, graciously make us an eternal remnant, and fulfill our requests in good measure, for salvation and mercy.*

The Torah is placed on the *bimah* and prepared for reading.

The *gabbai* uses the following formula to call a *Kohen* to the Torah:

וְתִגָּלֶה *And may His kingship over us be revealed and become visible soon, and may He be gracious to our remnant and the remnant of His people the Family of Israel, for graciousness, kindness, mercy, and favor. And let us respond, Amen. All of you ascribe greatness to our God and give honor to the Torah. Kohen,° approach. Stand* (name) *son of* (father's name) *the Kohen.*

°If no *Kohen* is present, the *gabbai* says: *'There is no Kohen present, stand* (name) *son of* (father's name) *an Israelite (Levite) in place of the Kohen.'*

Blessed is He Who gave the Torah to His people Israel in His holiness (The Torah of HASHEM is perfect, restoring the soul; the testimony of HASHEM is trustworthy, making the simple one wise. The orders of HASHEM are upright, gladdening the heart; the command of HASHEM is clear, enlightening the eyes.[1] HASHEM will give might to His people; HASHEM will bless His people with peace.[2] The God Whose way is perfect, the promise of HASHEM is flawless, He is a shield for all who take refuge in Him.[3])

Congregation, then *gabbai:*

You who cling to HASHEM your God—you are all alive today.[4]

READING OF THE TORAH

The reader shows the *oleh* (person called to the Torah) the place in the Torah. The *oleh* touches the Torah with a corner of his *tallis,* or the belt or mantle of the Torah, and kisses it. He then begins the blessing, bowing at *'Bless,'* and straightening up at 'HASHEM':

Bless HASHEM, the blessed One.

Congregation, followed by *oleh,* responds, bowing at 'Blessed,' and straightening up at 'HASHEM.'

Blessed is HASHEM, the blessed One, for all eternity.

Oleh continues:

בָּרוּךְ *Blessed are You, HASHEM, our God, King of the universe, Who selected us from all the peoples and gave us His Torah. Blessed are You, HASHEM, Giver of the Torah.* (Cong.— *Amen.*)

After his Torah portion has been read, the *oleh* recites:

בָּרוּךְ *Blessed are You, HASHEM, our God, King of the universe, Who gave us the Torah of truth and implanted eternal life within us. Blessed are You, HASHEM, Giver of the Torah.* (Cong.— *Amen.*)

THE VARIOUS *MI SHEBEIRACH* PRAYERS APPEAR ON PAGE 368.

(1) *Psalms* 19:8-9. (2) 29:11. (3) 18:31. (4) *Deuteronomy* 4:4.

The Torah reading just before the end of the Sabbath symbolizes that we will take the Torah-imbued spirit of the Sabbath with us into the next week.

The Torah reading at *Minchah* on *Shabbos* corresponds to the *sidrah* read on the *Shabbos* following Pesach. This reading is from *Shemini, Acharei Mos,* or *Kedoshim.*

פרשת שמיני

ויקרא ט:א-טז

כהן – וַיְהִי֙ בַּיּ֣וֹם הַשְּׁמִינִ֔י קָרָ֣א מֹשֶׁ֔ה לְאַהֲרֹ֖ן וּלְבָנָ֑יו וּלְזִקְנֵ֖י יִשְׂרָאֵֽל: וַיֹּ֣אמֶר אֶֽל־אַהֲרֹ֗ן קַח־לְ֠ךָ עֵ֣גֶל בֶּן־בָּקָ֥ר לְחַטָּ֛את וְאַ֥יִל לְעֹלָ֖ה תְּמִימִ֑ם וְהַקְרֵ֖ב לִפְנֵ֥י יְהֹוָֽה: וְאֶל־בְּנֵ֥י יִשְׂרָאֵ֖ל תְּדַבֵּ֣ר לֵאמֹ֑ר קְח֤וּ שְׂעִיר־עִזִּים֙ לְחַטָּ֔את וְעֵ֨גֶל וָכֶ֧בֶשׂ בְּנֵֽי־שָׁנָ֛ה תְּמִימִ֖ם לְעֹלָֽה: וְשׁ֤וֹר וָאַ֨יִל֙ לִשְׁלָמִ֔ים לִזְבֹּ֨חַ֙ לִפְנֵ֣י יְהֹוָ֔ה וּמִנְחָ֖ה בְּלוּלָ֣ה בַשָּׁ֑מֶן כִּ֣י הַיּ֔וֹם יְהֹוָ֖ה נִרְאָ֥ה אֲלֵיכֶֽם: וַיִּקְח֗וּ אֵ֚ת אֲשֶׁ֣ר צִוָּ֣ה מֹשֶׁ֔ה אֶל־פְּנֵ֖י אֹ֣הֶל מוֹעֵ֑ד וַיִּקְרְבוּ֙ כָּל־הָ֣עֵדָ֔ה וַיַּֽעַמְד֖וּ לִפְנֵ֥י יְהֹוָֽה: וַיֹּ֣אמֶר מֹשֶׁ֔ה זֶ֧ה הַדָּבָ֛ר אֲשֶׁר־צִוָּ֥ה יְהֹוָ֖ה תַּעֲשׂ֑וּ וְיֵרָ֥א אֲלֵיכֶ֖ם כְּב֥וֹד יְהֹוָֽה:

לוי – וַיֹּ֨אמֶר מֹשֶׁ֜ה אֶֽל־אַהֲרֹ֗ן קְרַ֤ב אֶל־הַמִּזְבֵּ֨חַ֙ וַעֲשֵׂ֞ה אֶת־חַטָּֽאתְךָ֙ וְאֶת־עֹ֣לָתֶ֔ךָ וְכַפֵּ֥ר בַּֽעַדְךָ֖ וּבְעַ֣ד הָעָ֑ם וַעֲשֵׂ֞ה אֶת־קָרְבַּ֤ן הָעָם֙ וְכַפֵּ֣ר בַּֽעֲדָ֔ם כַּאֲשֶׁ֖ר צִוָּ֥ה יְהֹוָֽה: וַיִּקְרַ֣ב אַהֲרֹן֘ אֶל־הַמִּזְבֵּ֒חַ֒ וַיִּשְׁחַ֛ט אֶת־עֵ֥גֶל הַֽחַטָּ֖את אֲשֶׁר־לֽוֹ: וַ֠יַּקְרִבוּ בְּנֵ֨י אַהֲרֹ֣ן אֶת־הַדָּם֘ אֵלָיו֒ וַיִּטְבֹּ֤ל אֶצְבָּעוֹ֙ בַּדָּ֔ם וַיִּתֵּ֖ן עַל־קַרְנ֣וֹת הַמִּזְבֵּ֑חַ וְאֶת־הַדָּ֣ם יָצַ֔ק אֶל־יְס֖וֹד הַמִּזְבֵּֽחַ: וְאֶת־הַחֵ֨לֶב וְאֶת־הַכְּלָיֹ֜ת וְאֶת־הַיֹּתֶ֤רֶת מִן־הַכָּבֵד֙ מִן־הַ֣חַטָּ֔את הִקְטִ֖יר הַמִּזְבֵּ֑חָה כַּאֲשֶׁ֛ר צִוָּ֥ה יְהֹוָ֖ה אֶת־מֹשֶֽׁה:

ישראל – וְאֶת־הַבָּשָׂ֖ר וְאֶת־הָע֑וֹר שָׂרַ֣ף בָּאֵ֔שׁ מִח֖וּץ לַֽמַּחֲנֶֽה: וַיִּשְׁחַ֖ט אֶת־הָעֹלָ֑ה וַ֠יַּמְצִאוּ בְּנֵ֨י אַהֲרֹ֤ן אֵלָיו֙ אֶת־הַדָּ֔ם וַיִּזְרְקֵ֥הוּ עַל־הַמִּזְבֵּ֖חַ סָבִֽיב: וְאֶת־הָ֨עֹלָ֔ה הִמְצִ֥יאוּ אֵלָ֖יו לִנְתָחֶ֑יהָ וְאֶת־הָרֹ֑אשׁ וַיַּקְטֵ֖ר עַל־הַמִּזְבֵּֽחַ: וַיִּרְחַ֥ץ אֶת־הַקֶּ֖רֶב וְאֶת־הַכְּרָעָ֑יִם וַיַּקְטֵ֥ר עַל־הָעֹלָ֖ה הַמִּזְבֵּֽחָה: וַיַּקְרֵ֕ב אֵ֖ת קָרְבַּ֣ן הָעָ֑ם וַיִּקַּ֞ח אֶת־שְׂעִ֤יר הַֽחַטָּאת֙ אֲשֶׁ֣ר לָעָ֔ם וַיִּשְׁחָטֵ֥הוּ וַֽיְחַטְּאֵ֖הוּ כָּרִאשֽׁוֹן: וַיַּקְרֵ֖ב אֶת־הָעֹלָ֑ה וַֽיַּעֲשֶׂ֖הָ כַּמִּשְׁפָּֽט:

The Torah reading at *Minchah* on *Shabbos* corresponds to the *sidrah* read on the *Shabbos* following Pesach. This reading is from *Shemini, Acharei Mos,* or *Kedoshim.*

PARASHAS SHEMINI

Leviticus 9:1-16

Kohen – *It was on the eighth day, Moses summoned Aaron and his sons, and the elders of Israel. He said to Aaron: Take yourself a young bull for a sin-offering and a ram for an elevation-offering — unblemished; and offer them before* HASHEM*. And to the Children of Israel speak as follows: Take a he-goat for a sin-offering, and a calf and a sheep in their first year — unblemished — for an elevation-offering. And a bull and a ram for a peace-offering to slaughter before* HASHEM*, and a meal-offering mixed with oil; for today* HASHEM *appears to you.*

They took what Moses had commanded to the front of the Tent of Meeting; the entire assembly approached and stood before HASHEM*. Moses said: This is the thing that* HASHEM *has commanded you to do; then the glory of* HASHEM *will appear to you.*

Levi – *Moses said to Aaron: Come near to the Altar and perform the service of your sin-offering and your elevation-offering and effect atonement for yourself and for the people; then perform the service of the people's offering and effect atonement for them, as* HASHEM *has commanded.*

Aaron came near to the Altar, and slaughtered the sin-offering calf that was his own. The sons of Aaron brought the blood to him. He dipped his finger into the blood and placed it upon the corners of the Altar, and he poured the blood upon the foundation of the Altar. The fats, the kidneys, and the diaphragm with the liver of the sin-offering, he caused to go up in smoke on the Altar, as HASHEM *had commanded Moses.*

Third – *The flesh and the hide he burned in fire outside the camp. He slaughtered the elevation- offering; the sons of Aaron presented the blood to him and he threw it upon the Altar, all around. They presented the elevation-offering to him in its pieces with the head; and he caused it to go up in smoke on the Altar. He washed the innards and the feet, and caused them to go up in smoke on the elevation-offering on the Altar.*

He brought near the offering of the people. He took the sin-offering goat that was for the people, and slaughtered it and performed the sin-offering service, as for the first one. He brought near the elevation-offering and performed its service as prescribed.

פרשת אחרי מות

ויקרא טז:א-יז

כהן – וַיְדַבֵּ֤ר יְהוָה֙ אֶל־מֹשֶׁ֔ה אַחֲרֵ֣י מ֔וֹת שְׁנֵ֖י בְּנֵ֣י אַהֲרֹ֑ן בְּקָרְבָתָ֥ם לִפְנֵי־יְהוָ֖ה וַיָּמֻֽתוּ׃ וַיֹּ֨אמֶר יְהוָ֜ה אֶל־מֹשֶׁ֗ה דַּבֵּר֮ אֶל־אַהֲרֹ֣ן אָחִ֒יךָ֒ וְאַל־יָבֹ֤א בְכָל־עֵת֙ אֶל־הַקֹּ֔דֶשׁ מִבֵּ֖ית לַפָּרֹ֑כֶת אֶל־פְּנֵ֨י הַכַּפֹּ֜רֶת אֲשֶׁ֤ר עַל־הָֽאָרֹן֙ וְלֹ֣א יָמ֔וּת כִּ֚י בֶּֽעָנָ֔ן אֵֽרָאֶ֖ה עַל־הַכַּפֹּֽרֶת׃ בְּזֹ֛את יָבֹ֥א אַהֲרֹ֖ן אֶל־הַקֹּ֑דֶשׁ בְּפַ֧ר בֶּן־בָּקָ֛ר לְחַטָּ֖את וְאַ֥יִל לְעֹלָֽה׃ כְּתֹֽנֶת־בַּ֨ד קֹ֜דֶשׁ יִלְבָּ֗שׁ וּמִכְנְסֵי־בַד֮ יִהְי֣וּ עַל־בְּשָׂרוֹ֒ וּבְאַבְנֵ֥ט בַּד֙ יַחְגֹּ֔ר וּבְמִצְנֶ֥פֶת בַּ֖ד יִצְנֹ֑ף בִּגְדֵי־קֹ֣דֶשׁ הֵ֔ם וְרָחַ֥ץ בַּמַּ֛יִם אֶת־בְּשָׂר֖וֹ וּלְבֵשָֽׁם׃ וּמֵאֵ֗ת עֲדַת֙ בְּנֵ֣י יִשְׂרָאֵ֔ל יִקַּ֛ח שְׁנֵֽי־שְׂעִירֵ֥י עִזִּ֖ים לְחַטָּ֑את וְאַ֥יִל אֶחָ֖ד לְעֹלָֽה׃ וְהִקְרִ֧יב אַהֲרֹ֛ן אֶת־פַּ֥ר הַחַטָּ֖את אֲשֶׁר־ל֑וֹ וְכִפֶּ֥ר בַּֽעֲד֖וֹ וּבְעַ֥ד בֵּיתֽוֹ׃

לוי – וְלָקַ֖ח אֶת־שְׁנֵ֣י הַשְּׂעִירִ֑ם וְהֶעֱמִ֤יד אֹתָם֙ לִפְנֵ֣י יְהוָ֔ה פֶּ֖תַח אֹ֥הֶל מוֹעֵֽד׃ וְנָתַ֧ן אַהֲרֹ֛ן עַל־שְׁנֵ֥י הַשְּׂעִירִ֖ם גֹּרָל֑וֹת גּוֹרָ֤ל אֶחָד֙ לַֽיהוָ֔ה וְגוֹרָ֥ל אֶחָ֖ד לַֽעֲזָאזֵֽל׃ וְהִקְרִ֤יב אַהֲרֹן֙ אֶת־הַשָּׂעִ֔יר אֲשֶׁ֨ר עָלָ֥ה עָלָ֛יו הַגּוֹרָ֖ל לַֽיהוָ֑ה וְעָשָׂ֖הוּ חַטָּֽאת׃ וְהַשָּׂעִ֗יר אֲשֶׁר֩ עָלָ֨ה עָלָ֤יו הַגּוֹרָל֙ לַֽעֲזָאזֵ֔ל יָֽעֳמַד־חַ֛י לִפְנֵ֥י יְהוָ֖ה לְכַפֵּ֣ר עָלָ֑יו לְשַׁלַּ֥ח אֹת֛וֹ לַֽעֲזָאזֵ֖ל הַמִּדְבָּֽרָה׃ וְהִקְרִ֨יב אַהֲרֹ֜ן אֶת־פַּ֣ר הַחַטָּאת֮ אֲשֶׁר־לוֹ֒ וְכִפֶּ֥ר בַּֽעֲד֖וֹ וּבְעַ֣ד בֵּית֑וֹ וְשָׁחַ֛ט אֶת־פַּ֥ר הַֽחַטָּ֖את אֲשֶׁר־לֽוֹ׃

ישראל – וְלָקַ֣ח מְלֹֽא־הַ֠מַּחְתָּ֠ה גַּֽחֲלֵי־אֵ֞שׁ מֵעַ֤ל הַמִּזְבֵּ֨חַ֙ מִלִּפְנֵ֣י יְהוָ֔ה וּמְלֹ֣א חָפְנָ֔יו קְטֹ֥רֶת סַמִּ֖ים דַּקָּ֑ה וְהֵבִ֖יא מִבֵּ֥ית לַפָּרֹֽכֶת׃ וְנָתַ֧ן אֶת־הַקְּטֹ֛רֶת עַל־הָאֵ֖שׁ לִפְנֵ֣י יְהוָ֑ה וְכִסָּ֣ה ׀ עֲנַ֣ן הַקְּטֹ֗רֶת אֶת־הַכַּפֹּ֛רֶת אֲשֶׁ֥ר עַל־הָֽעֵד֖וּת וְלֹ֥א יָמֽוּת׃ וְלָקַח֙ מִדַּ֣ם הַפָּ֔ר וְהִזָּ֧ה בְאֶצְבָּע֛וֹ עַל־פְּנֵ֥י הַכַּפֹּ֖רֶת קֵ֑דְמָה וְלִפְנֵ֣י הַכַּפֹּ֗רֶת יַזֶּ֧ה שֶֽׁבַע־פְּעָמִ֛ים מִן־הַדָּ֖ם בְּאֶצְבָּעֽוֹ׃ וְשָׁחַ֞ט אֶת־שְׂעִ֤יר הַֽחַטָּאת֙ אֲשֶׁ֣ר לָעָ֔ם וְהֵבִיא֙ אֶת־דָּמ֔וֹ אֶל־מִבֵּ֖ית לַפָּרֹ֑כֶת וְעָשָׂ֣ה אֶת־דָּמ֗וֹ כַּֽאֲשֶׁ֤ר עָשָׂה֙ לְדַ֣ם הַפָּ֔ר וְהִזָּ֥ה אֹת֛וֹ עַל־הַכַּפֹּ֖רֶת וְלִפְנֵ֥י הַכַּפֹּֽרֶת׃ וְכִפֶּ֣ר עַל־הַקֹּ֗דֶשׁ מִטֻּמְאֹת֙ בְּנֵ֣י יִשְׂרָאֵ֔ל וּמִפִּשְׁעֵיהֶ֖ם לְכָל־חַטֹּאתָ֑ם וְכֵ֤ן יַֽעֲשֶׂה֙ לְאֹ֣הֶל מוֹעֵ֔ד הַשֹּׁכֵ֣ן אִתָּ֔ם בְּת֖וֹךְ טֻמְאֹתָֽם׃ וְכָל־אָדָ֞ם לֹא־יִֽהְיֶ֣ה ׀ בְּאֹ֣הֶל מוֹעֵ֗ד ׀ בְּבֹא֛וֹ

PARASHAS ACHAREI MOS

Leviticus 16:1-17

Kohen – *HASHEM spoke to Moses after the death of Aaron's two sons, when they approached before HASHEM, and they died. And HASHEM said to Moses : Speak to Aaron, your brother — he may not come at any time into the Sanctuary, within the Curtain, in front of the cover that is upon the Ark, so that he should not die; for in a cloud will I appear upon the Ark-cover. With this shall Aaron come into the Sanctuary: with a young bull for a sin-offering and a ram for an elevation-offering. He shall don a sacred linen tunic; linen breeches shall be upon his flesh, he shall gird himself with a linen sash, and cover his head with a linen turban; they are sacred vestments — he shall immerse himself in water and then don them. From the assembly of the Children of Israel he shall take two he-goats for a sin-offering and one ram for an elevation-offering. Aaron shall bring near his own sin-offering bull, and atone for himself and for his household.*

Levi – *He shall take the two he-goats and stand them before HASHEM at the entrance of the Tent of Meeting. Aaron shall place lots upon the two he-goats: one lot "for HASHEM" and one lot "for Azazel". Aaron shall bring near the he-goat designated by lot for HASHEM, and which he was to declare as a sin-offering. And the he-goat designated by lot for Azazel shall be stood alive before HASHEM, to make atonement through it, to send it to Azazel to the Wilderness. Aaron shall have brought near his own sin-offering bull and he shall atone for himself and for his household; then he shall slaughter his own sin-offering bull.*

Third – *He shall take a shovelful of fiery coals from atop the Altar that is before HASHEM, and his cupped handsful of finely ground incense-spices, and bring it within the Curtain. He shall place the incense upon the fire before HASHEM; so that the cloud of the incense shall blanket the Ark-cover that is atop the [Tablets of the] Testimony — so that he shall not die.*

He shall take of the blood of the bull and sprinkle with his finger upon the eastern front of the Ark-cover; and in front of the Ark-cover he shall sprinkle seven times from the blood with his finger. He shall slaughter the sin-offering he-goat of the people, and bring its blood within the Curtain; he shall do with its blood as he had done with the blood of the bull, and sprinkle it upon the Ark-cover and in front of the Ark-cover. Thus shall he bring atonement upon the Sanctuary for the contaminations of the Children of Israel, even for their willful sins among all their sins; and so shall he do for the Tent of Meeting that dwells with them amid their contamination. Every person is forbidden to be in the Tent of Meeting when he comes

לְכַפֵּר בַּקֹּדֶשׁ עַד־צֵאתוֹ וְכִפֶּר בַּעֲדוֹ וּבְעַד בֵּיתוֹ וּבְעַד כָּל־קְהַל יִשְׂרָאֵל:

פרשת קדושים

ויקרא יט:א-יד

כֹּהֵן – וַיְדַבֵּר יהוה אֶל־מֹשֶׁה לֵּאמֹר: דַּבֵּר אֶל־כָּל־עֲדַת בְּנֵי־ יִשְׂרָאֵל וְאָמַרְתָּ אֲלֵהֶם קְדֹשִׁים תִּהְיוּ כִּי קָדוֹשׁ אֲנִי יהוה אֱלֹהֵיכֶם: אִישׁ אִמּוֹ וְאָבִיו תִּירָאוּ וְאֶת־שַׁבְּתֹתַי תִּשְׁמֹרוּ אֲנִי יהוה אֱלֹהֵיכֶם: אַל־תִּפְנוּ אֶל־הָאֱלִילִים וֵאלֹהֵי מַסֵּכָה לֹא תַעֲשׂוּ לָכֶם אֲנִי יהוה אֱלֹהֵיכֶם:

לֵוִי – וְכִי תִזְבְּחוּ זֶבַח שְׁלָמִים לַיהוה לִרְצֹנְכֶם תִּזְבָּחֻהוּ: בְּיוֹם זִבְחֲכֶם יֵאָכֵל וּמִמָּחֳרָת וְהַנּוֹתָר עַד־יוֹם הַשְּׁלִישִׁי בָּאֵשׁ יִשָּׂרֵף: וְאִם הֵאָכֹל יֵאָכֵל בַּיּוֹם הַשְּׁלִישִׁי פִּגּוּל הוּא לֹא יֵרָצֶה: וְאֹכְלָיו עֲוֹנוֹ יִשָּׂא כִּי־אֶת־קֹדֶשׁ יהוה חִלֵּל וְנִכְרְתָה הַנֶּפֶשׁ הַהִוא מֵעַמֶּיהָ: וּבְקֻצְרְכֶם אֶת־קְצִיר אַרְצְכֶם לֹא תְכַלֶּה פְּאַת שָׂדְךָ לִקְצֹר וְלֶקֶט קְצִירְךָ לֹא תְלַקֵּט: וְכַרְמְךָ לֹא תְעוֹלֵל וּפֶרֶט כַּרְמְךָ לֹא תְלַקֵּט לֶעָנִי וְלַגֵּר תַּעֲזֹב אֹתָם אֲנִי יהוה אֱלֹהֵיכֶם:

יִשְׂרָאֵל – לֹא תִּגְנֹבוּ וְלֹא־תְכַחֲשׁוּ וְלֹא־תְשַׁקְּרוּ אִישׁ בַּעֲמִיתוֹ: וְלֹא־תִשָּׁבְעוּ בִשְׁמִי לַשָּׁקֶר וְחִלַּלְתָּ אֶת־שֵׁם אֱלֹהֶיךָ אֲנִי יהוה: לֹא־תַעֲשֹׁק אֶת־רֵעֲךָ וְלֹא תִגְזֹל לֹא־תָלִין פְּעֻלַּת שָׂכִיר אִתְּךָ עַד־בֹּקֶר: לֹא־תְקַלֵּל חֵרֵשׁ וְלִפְנֵי עִוֵּר לֹא תִתֵּן מִכְשֹׁל וְיָרֵאתָ מֵּאֱלֹהֶיךָ אֲנִי יהוה:

When the Torah reading has been completed, the Torah is raised for all to see.
Each person looks at the Torah and recites aloud:

וְזֹאת הַתּוֹרָה אֲשֶׁר שָׂם מֹשֶׁה לִפְנֵי בְּנֵי יִשְׂרָאֵל,[1] עַל פִּי יהוה בְּיַד מֹשֶׁה.[2]

Some add the following verses:

עֵץ חַיִּים הִיא לַמַּחֲזִיקִים בָּהּ, וְתֹמְכֶיהָ מְאֻשָּׁר.[3] דְּרָכֶיהָ דַרְכֵי נֹעַם, וְכָל נְתִיבוֹתֶיהָ שָׁלוֹם.[4] אֹרֶךְ יָמִים בִּימִינָהּ, בִּשְׂמֹאלָהּ עֹשֶׁר וְכָבוֹד.[5] יהוה חָפֵץ לְמַעַן צִדְקוֹ, יַגְדִּיל תּוֹרָה וְיַאְדִּיר.[6]

to bring atonement in the Sanctuary until his departure; he shall atone for himself, for his household, and for the entire congregation of Israel.

PARASHAS KEDOSHIM

Leviticus 19:1-14

Kohen – *HASHEM spoke to Moses, saying: Speak to the entire assembly of the Children of Israel and say to them: Be holy, for I, HASHEM, your God, am holy.*

Every man: You shall revere your father and mother, and you shall observe My Sabbaths — I am HASHEM, your God. Do not turn to the idols and do not make molten gods for yourselves — I am HASHEM, your God.

Levi – *When you slaughter a feast peace-offering to HASHEM, you shall slaughter it to find favor for yourselves. It shall be eaten on the day you slaughter it and on the next day, and whatever remains until the third day shall be burned in fire. But if it was eaten on the third day, it is rejected — it does not find favor. Each of those who eat it will bear his iniquity, for he has desecrated what is sacred to HASHEM; and that soul will be cut off from its people.*

When you reap the harvest of your land, do not complete the reaping to the corner of your field, and do not take the gleanings of your harvest. Do not pick from the undeveloped twigs of your vineyard and do not gather the fallen fruit of your vineyard; for the poor and the proselyte shall you leave them — I am HASHEM, your God.

Third – *Do not steal, do not deny falsely, and do not lie to one another. Do not swear falsely by My Name, thereby desecrating the Name of your God — I am HASHEM. Do not cheat your fellow and do not rob; and do not withhold a worker's wage with you until morning. Do not curse a deaf person, do not place a stumbling-block before a blind person; you shall fear your God — I am HASHEM.*

When the Torah reading has been completed, the Torah is raised for all to see. Each person looks at the Torah and recites aloud:

This is the Torah that Moses placed before the Children of Israel,[1] upon the command of HASHEM, through Moses' hand.[2]

Some add the following verses:

עֵץ *It is a tree of life for those who grasp it, and its supporters are praiseworthy.[3] Its ways are ways of pleasantness and all its paths are peace.[4] Lengthy days are at its right; at its left are wealth and honor.[5] HASHEM desired, for the sake of its [Israel's] righteousness, that the Torah be made great and glorious.[6]*

(1) *Deuteronomy* 4:44. (2) *Numbers* 9:23. (3) *Proverbs* 3:18. (4) 3:17. (5) 3:16. (6) *Isaiah* 42:21.

Chazzan takes the Torah in his right arm and recites:

יְהַלְלוּ אֶת שֵׁם יהוה, כִּי נִשְׂגָּב שְׁמוֹ לְבַדּוֹ –

Congregation responds:

– הוֹדוֹ עַל אֶרֶץ וְשָׁמָיִם. וַיָּרֶם קֶרֶן לְעַמּוֹ, תְּהִלָּה לְכָל חֲסִידָיו, לִבְנֵי יִשְׂרָאֵל עַם קְרֹבוֹ, הַלְלוּיָהּ.[1]

As the Torah is carried to the Ark, congregation recites Psalm 24, לְדָוִד מִזְמוֹר.

לְדָוִד מִזְמוֹר, לַיהוה הָאָרֶץ וּמְלוֹאָהּ, תֵּבֵל וְיֹשְׁבֵי בָהּ. כִּי הוּא עַל יַמִּים יְסָדָהּ, וְעַל נְהָרוֹת יְכוֹנְנֶהָ. מִי יַעֲלֶה בְהַר יהוה, וּמִי יָקוּם בִּמְקוֹם קָדְשׁוֹ. נְקִי כַפַּיִם וּבַר לֵבָב, אֲשֶׁר לֹא נָשָׂא לַשָּׁוְא נַפְשִׁי וְלֹא נִשְׁבַּע לְמִרְמָה. יִשָּׂא בְרָכָה מֵאֵת יהוה, וּצְדָקָה מֵאֱלֹהֵי יִשְׁעוֹ. זֶה דּוֹר דֹּרְשָׁיו, מְבַקְשֵׁי פָנֶיךָ, יַעֲקֹב, סֶלָה. שְׂאוּ שְׁעָרִים רָאשֵׁיכֶם, וְהִנָּשְׂאוּ פִּתְחֵי עוֹלָם, וְיָבוֹא מֶלֶךְ הַכָּבוֹד. מִי זֶה מֶלֶךְ הַכָּבוֹד, יהוה עִזּוּז וְגִבּוֹר, יהוה גִּבּוֹר מִלְחָמָה. שְׂאוּ שְׁעָרִים רָאשֵׁיכֶם, וּשְׂאוּ פִּתְחֵי עוֹלָם, וְיָבֹא מֶלֶךְ הַכָּבוֹד. מִי הוּא זֶה מֶלֶךְ הַכָּבוֹד, יהוה צְבָאוֹת הוּא מֶלֶךְ הַכָּבוֹד, סֶלָה.

As the Torah is placed into the Ark, congregation recites the following verses:

וּבְנֻחֹה יֹאמַר, שׁוּבָה יהוה רִבְבוֹת אַלְפֵי יִשְׂרָאֵל.[2] קוּמָה יהוה לִמְנוּחָתֶךָ, אַתָּה וַאֲרוֹן עֻזֶּךָ. כֹּהֲנֶיךָ יִלְבְּשׁוּ צֶדֶק, וַחֲסִידֶיךָ יְרַנֵּנוּ. בַּעֲבוּר דָּוִד עַבְדֶּךָ אַל תָּשֵׁב פְּנֵי מְשִׁיחֶךָ.[3] כִּי לֶקַח טוֹב נָתַתִּי לָכֶם, תּוֹרָתִי אַל תַּעֲזֹבוּ.[4] ❖ עֵץ חַיִּים הִיא לַמַּחֲזִיקִים בָּהּ, וְתֹמְכֶיהָ מְאֻשָּׁר.[5] דְּרָכֶיהָ דַרְכֵי נֹעַם, וְכָל נְתִיבוֹתֶיהָ שָׁלוֹם.[6] הֲשִׁיבֵנוּ יהוה אֵלֶיךָ וְנָשׁוּבָה, חַדֵּשׁ יָמֵינוּ כְּקֶדֶם.[7]

חצי קדיש

The Ark is closed and the *chazzan* recites חֲצִי קַדִּישׁ.

יִתְגַּדַּל וְיִתְקַדַּשׁ שְׁמֵהּ רַבָּא. (.Cong – אָמֵן.) בְּעָלְמָא דִּי בְרָא כִרְעוּתֵהּ. וְיַמְלִיךְ מַלְכוּתֵהּ, בְּחַיֵּיכוֹן וּבְיוֹמֵיכוֹן וּבְחַיֵּי דְכָל בֵּית יִשְׂרָאֵל, בַּעֲגָלָא וּבִזְמַן קָרִיב. וְאִמְרוּ: אָמֵן.

(.Cong – אָמֵן. יְהֵא שְׁמֵהּ רַבָּא מְבָרַךְ לְעָלַם וּלְעָלְמֵי עָלְמַיָּא.)

יְהֵא שְׁמֵהּ רַבָּא מְבָרַךְ לְעָלַם וּלְעָלְמֵי עָלְמַיָּא.

יִתְבָּרַךְ וְיִשְׁתַּבַּח וְיִתְפָּאַר וְיִתְרוֹמַם וְיִתְנַשֵּׂא וְיִתְהַדָּר וְיִתְעַלֶּה וְיִתְהַלָּל שְׁמֵהּ דְּקֻדְשָׁא בְּרִיךְ הוּא (.Cong – בְּרִיךְ הוּא) – לְעֵלָּא מִן כָּל בִּרְכָתָא וְשִׁירָתָא תֻּשְׁבְּחָתָא וְנֶחֱמָתָא, דַּאֲמִירָן בְּעָלְמָא. וְאִמְרוּ: אָמֵן. (.Cong – אָמֵן.)

(1) *Psalms* 148:13-14. (2) *Numbers* 10:36. (3) *Psalms* 132:8-10.
(4) *Proverbs* 4:2. (5) 3:18. (6) 3:17. (7) *Lamentations* 5:21.

Chazzan takes the Torah in his right arm and recites:

Let them praise the Name of HASHEM, for His Name alone will have been exalted —

Congregation responds:

— His glory is above earth and heaven. And He will have exalted the pride of His people, causing praise for all His devout ones, for the Children of Israel, His intimate nation. Halleluyah![1]

As the Torah is carried to the Ark, congregation recites Psalm 24, *'Of David a psalm.'*

לְדָוִד *Of David a psalm. HASHEM's is the earth and its fullness, the inhabited land and those who dwell in it. For He founded it upon seas, and established it upon rivers. Who may ascend the mountain of HASHEM, and who may stand in the place of His sanctity? One with clean hands and pure heart, who has not sworn in vain by My soul and has not sworn deceitfully. He will receive a blessing from HASHEM and just kindness from the God of his salvation. This is the generation of those who seek Him, those who strive for Your Presence — Jacob, Selah. Raise up your heads, O gates, and be uplifted, you everlasting entrances, so that the King of Glory may enter. Who is this King of Glory? — HASHEM, the mighty and strong, HASHEM, the strong in battle. Raise up your heads, O gates, and raise up, you everlasting entrances, so that the King of Glory may enter. Who then is the King of Glory? HASHEM, Master of Legions, He is the King of Glory. Selah!*

As the Torah is placed into the Ark, congregation recites the following verses:

וּבְנֻחֹה *And when it rested he would say, 'Return, HASHEM, to the myriad thousands of Israel.'*[2] *Arise, HASHEM, to Your resting place, You and the Ark of Your strength. Let Your priests be clothed in righteousness, and Your devout ones will sing joyously. For the sake of David, Your servant, turn not away the face of Your anointed.*[3] *For I have given you a good teaching, do not forsake My Torah.*[4] Chazzan— *It is a tree of life for those who grasp it, and its supporters are praiseworthy.*[5] *Its ways are ways of pleasantness and all its paths are peace.*[6] *Bring us back to You, HASHEM, and we shall return, renew our days as of old.*[7]

HALF KADDISH

The Ark is closed and the *chazzan* recites Half-*Kaddish*.

יִתְגַּדַּל *May His great Name grow exalted and sanctified* (Cong.— *Amen.*) *in the world that He created as He willed. May He give reign to His kingship in your lifetimes and in your days, and in the lifetimes of the entire Family of Israel, swiftly and soon. Now respond: Amen.*

(Cong.— *Amen. May His great Name be blessed forever and ever.*)

May His great Name be blessed forever and ever.

Blessed, praised, glorified, exalted, extolled, mighty, upraised, and lauded be the Name of the Holy One, Blessed is He (Cong.— *Blessed is He*) *— beyond any blessing and song, praise and consolation that are uttered in the world. Now respond: Amen.* (Cong.— *Amen.*)

שמונה עשרה – עמידה

Take three steps backward, then three steps forward. Remain standing with feet together while reciting *Shemoneh Esrei.* Recite it with quiet devotion and without interruption, verbal or otherwise. Although it should not be audible to others, one must pray loudly enough to hear himself.

כִּי שֵׁם יהוה אֶקְרָא, הָבוּ גֹדֶל לֵאלֹהֵינוּ.[1]
אֲדֹנָי שְׂפָתַי תִּפְתָּח, וּפִי יַגִּיד תְּהִלָּתֶךָ.[2]

אבות

Bend the knees at בָּרוּךְ; bow at אַתָּה; straighten up at ה׳.

בָּרוּךְ אַתָּה יהוה אֱלֹהֵינוּ וֵאלֹהֵי אֲבוֹתֵינוּ, אֱלֹהֵי אַבְרָהָם, אֱלֹהֵי יִצְחָק, וֵאלֹהֵי יַעֲקֹב, הָאֵל הַגָּדוֹל הַגִּבּוֹר וְהַנּוֹרָא, אֵל עֶלְיוֹן, גּוֹמֵל חֲסָדִים טוֹבִים וְקוֹנֵה הַכֹּל, וְזוֹכֵר חַסְדֵי אָבוֹת, וּמֵבִיא גוֹאֵל לִבְנֵי בְנֵיהֶם, לְמַעַן שְׁמוֹ בְּאַהֲבָה. מֶלֶךְ עוֹזֵר וּמוֹשִׁיעַ וּמָגֵן.

Bend the knees at בָּרוּךְ; bow at אַתָּה; straighten up at ה׳.

בָּרוּךְ אַתָּה יהוה, מָגֵן אַבְרָהָם.

גבורות

אַתָּה גִּבּוֹר לְעוֹלָם אֲדֹנָי, מְחַיֵּה מֵתִים אַתָּה, רַב לְהוֹשִׁיעַ. מְכַלְכֵּל חַיִּים בְּחֶסֶד, מְחַיֵּה מֵתִים בְּרַחֲמִים רַבִּים, סוֹמֵךְ נוֹפְלִים, וְרוֹפֵא חוֹלִים, וּמַתִּיר אֲסוּרִים, וּמְקַיֵּם אֱמוּנָתוֹ לִישֵׁנֵי עָפָר. מִי כָמוֹךָ בַּעַל גְּבוּרוֹת, וּמִי דּוֹמֶה לָּךְ, מֶלֶךְ מֵמִית וּמְחַיֶּה וּמַצְמִיחַ יְשׁוּעָה. וְנֶאֱמָן אַתָּה לְהַחֲיוֹת מֵתִים. בָּרוּךְ אַתָּה יהוה, מְחַיֵּה הַמֵּתִים.

During the *chazzan's* repetition, *Kedushah* (below) is recited at this point.

קדושה

When reciting *Kedushah,* one must stand with his feet together and avoid any interruptions. One should rise on his toes when saying the words קָדוֹשׁ, קָדוֹשׁ, קָדוֹשׁ; בָּרוּךְ (of בָּרוּךְ כְּבוֹד); and יִמְלֹךְ.

Cong. then *Chazzan* – **נְקַדֵּשׁ** אֶת שִׁמְךָ בָּעוֹלָם, כְּשֵׁם שֶׁמַּקְדִּישִׁים אוֹתוֹ בִּשְׁמֵי מָרוֹם, כַּכָּתוּב עַל יַד נְבִיאֶךָ, וְקָרָא זֶה אֶל זֶה וְאָמַר:

All – קָדוֹשׁ קָדוֹשׁ קָדוֹשׁ יהוה צְבָאוֹת, מְלֹא כָל הָאָרֶץ כְּבוֹדוֹ.[3]

Chazzan – לְעֻמָּתָם בָּרוּךְ יֹאמֵרוּ:

All – בָּרוּךְ כְּבוֹד יהוה, מִמְּקוֹמוֹ.[4]

Chazzan – וּבְדִבְרֵי קָדְשְׁךָ כָּתוּב לֵאמֹר:

All – יִמְלֹךְ יהוה לְעוֹלָם, אֱלֹהַיִךְ צִיּוֹן לְדֹר וָדֹר, הַלְלוּיָהּ.[5]

Chazzan only concludes – לְדוֹר וָדוֹר נַגִּיד גָּדְלֶךָ וּלְנֵצַח נְצָחִים קְדֻשָּׁתְךָ נַקְדִּישׁ, וְשִׁבְחֲךָ אֱלֹהֵינוּ מִפִּינוּ לֹא יָמוּשׁ לְעוֹלָם וָעֶד, כִּי אֵל מֶלֶךְ גָּדוֹל וְקָדוֹשׁ אָתָּה. בָּרוּךְ אַתָּה יהוה, הָאֵל הַקָּדוֹשׁ.

Chazzan continues . . . אַתָּה בְחַרְתָּנוּ (page 480).

SHEMONEH ESREI — AMIDAH

Take three steps backward, then three steps forward. Remain standing with feet together while reciting *Shemoneh Esrei*. Recite it with quiet devotion and without interruption, verbal or otherwise. Although it should not be audible to others, one must pray loudly enough to hear himself.

When I call out the Name of HASHEM, ascribe greatness to our God.[1]
My Lord, open my lips, that my mouth may declare Your praise.[2]

PATRIARCHS

Bend the knees at *'Blessed'*; bow at *'You'*; straighten up at *'HASHEM.'*

בָּרוּךְ *Blessed are You, HASHEM, our God and the God of our forefathers, God of Abraham, God of Isaac, and God of Jacob; the great, mighty, and awesome God, the supreme God, Who bestows beneficial kindnesses and creates everything, Who recalls the kindnesses of the Patriarchs and brings a Redeemer to their children's children, for His Name's sake, with love. O King, Helper, Savior, and Shield.*

Bend the knees at *'Blessed'*; bow at *'You'*; straighten up at *'HASHEM.'*

Blessed are You, HASHEM, Shield of Abraham.

GOD'S MIGHT

אַתָּה *You are eternally mighty, my Lord, the Resuscitator of the dead are You; abundantly able to save. He sustains the living with kindness, resuscitates the dead with abundant mercy, supports the fallen, heals the sick, releases the confined, and maintains His faith to those asleep in the dust. Who is like You, O Master of mighty deeds, and who is comparable to You, O King Who causes death and restores life and makes salvation sprout! And You are faithful to resuscitate the dead. Blessed are You, HASHEM, Who resuscitates the dead.*

During the *chazzan's* repetition, *Kedushah* (below) is recited at this point.

KEDUSHAH

When reciting *Kedushah*, one must stand with his feet together and avoid any interruptions. One should rise on his toes when saying *Holy, holy, holy; Blessed is;* and *HASHEM shall reign.*

Cong. then Chazzan — **נְקַדֵּשׁ** *We shall sanctify Your Name in this world, just as they sanctify it in heaven above, as it is written by Your prophet, "And one [angel] will call another and say:*

All — *'Holy, holy, holy is HASHEM, Master of Legions, the whole world is filled with His glory.'"*[3]

Chazzan — *Those facing them say 'Blessed':*

All — *'Blessed is the glory of HASHEM from His place.'*[4]

Chazzan — *And in Your holy Writings the following is written:*

All — *'HASHEM shall reign forever — your God, O Zion — from generation to generation, Halleluyah!'*[5]

Chazzan only concludes — *From generation to generation we shall relate Your greatness and for infinite eternities we shall proclaim Your holiness. Your praise, our God, shall not leave our mouth forever and ever, for You, O God, are a great and holy King. Blessed are You, HASHEM, the holy God.*

Chazzan continues אַתָּה בְחַרְתָּנוּ, *You have chosen us . . .* (page 480).

---

(1) *Deuteronomy* 32:3. (2) *Psalms* 51:17. (3) *Isaiah* 6:3. (4) *Ezekiel* 3:12. (5) *Psalms* 146:10.

קדושת השם

אַתָּה קָדוֹשׁ וְשִׁמְךָ קָדוֹשׁ, וּקְדוֹשִׁים בְּכָל יוֹם יְהַלְּלוּךָ סֶּלָה. בָּרוּךְ אַתָּה יהוה, הָאֵל הַקָּדוֹשׁ.

קדושת היום

אַתָּה בְחַרְתָּנוּ מִכָּל הָעַמִּים, אָהַבְתָּ אוֹתָנוּ, וְרָצִיתָ בָּנוּ, וְרוֹמַמְתָּנוּ מִכָּל הַלְּשׁוֹנוֹת, וְקִדַּשְׁתָּנוּ בְּמִצְוֹתֶיךָ, וְקֵרַבְתָּנוּ מַלְכֵּנוּ לַעֲבוֹדָתֶךָ, וְשִׁמְךָ הַגָּדוֹל וְהַקָּדוֹשׁ עָלֵינוּ קָרָאתָ.

On the Sabbath add the words in brackets. [If forgotten, see *Laws* §86-90.]

וַתִּתֶּן לָנוּ יהוה אֱלֹהֵינוּ בְּאַהֲבָה [שַׁבָּתוֹת לִמְנוּחָה וּ]מוֹעֲדִים לְשִׂמְחָה חַגִּים וּזְמַנִּים לְשָׂשׂוֹן, אֶת יוֹם [הַשַּׁבָּת הַזֶּה וְאֶת יוֹם] חַג הַמַּצּוֹת הַזֶּה, זְמַן חֵרוּתֵנוּ [בְּאַהֲבָה] מִקְרָא קֹדֶשׁ, זֵכֶר לִיצִיאַת מִצְרָיִם.

During the *chazzan's* repetition, congregation responds אָמֵן as indicated.

אֱלֹהֵינוּ וֵאלֹהֵי אֲבוֹתֵינוּ, יַעֲלֶה, וְיָבֹא, וְיַגִּיעַ, וְיֵרָאֶה, וְיֵרָצֶה, וְיִשָּׁמַע, וְיִפָּקֵד, וְיִזָּכֵר זִכְרוֹנֵנוּ וּפִקְדוֹנֵנוּ, וְזִכְרוֹן אֲבוֹתֵינוּ, וְזִכְרוֹן מָשִׁיחַ בֶּן דָּוִד עַבְדֶּךָ, וְזִכְרוֹן יְרוּשָׁלַיִם עִיר קָדְשֶׁךָ, וְזִכְרוֹן כָּל עַמְּךָ בֵּית יִשְׂרָאֵל לְפָנֶיךָ, לִפְלֵיטָה לְטוֹבָה לְחֵן וּלְחֶסֶד וּלְרַחֲמִים, לְחַיִּים וּלְשָׁלוֹם בְּיוֹם חַג הַמַּצּוֹת הַזֶּה. זָכְרֵנוּ יהוה אֱלֹהֵינוּ בּוֹ לְטוֹבָה (.Cong – אָמֵן), וּפָקְדֵנוּ בוֹ לִבְרָכָה (.Cong – אָמֵן), וְהוֹשִׁיעֵנוּ בוֹ לְחַיִּים (.Cong – אָמֵן). וּבִדְבַר יְשׁוּעָה וְרַחֲמִים, חוּס וְחָנֵּנוּ וְרַחֵם עָלֵינוּ וְהוֹשִׁיעֵנוּ, כִּי אֵלֶיךָ עֵינֵינוּ, כִּי אֵל מֶלֶךְ חַנּוּן וְרַחוּם אָתָּה.[1]

On the Sabbath add the words in brackets. [If forgotten, see *Laws* §86-90.]

וְהַשִּׂיאֵנוּ יהוה אֱלֹהֵינוּ אֶת בִּרְכַּת מוֹעֲדֶיךָ לְחַיִּים וּלְשָׁלוֹם, לְשִׂמְחָה וּלְשָׂשׂוֹן, כַּאֲשֶׁר רָצִיתָ וְאָמַרְתָּ לְבָרְכֵנוּ. [אֱלֹהֵינוּ וֵאלֹהֵי אֲבוֹתֵינוּ רְצֵה בִמְנוּחָתֵנוּ] קַדְּשֵׁנוּ בְּמִצְוֹתֶיךָ וְתֵן חֶלְקֵנוּ בְּתוֹרָתֶךָ, שַׂבְּעֵנוּ מִטּוּבֶךָ וְשַׂמְּחֵנוּ בִּישׁוּעָתֶךָ, וְטַהֵר לִבֵּנוּ לְעָבְדְּךָ בֶּאֱמֶת, וְהַנְחִילֵנוּ יהוה אֱלֹהֵינוּ [בְּאַהֲבָה וּבְרָצוֹן] בְּשִׂמְחָה וּבְשָׂשׂוֹן [שַׁבַּת וּ]מוֹעֲדֵי קָדְשֶׁךָ, וְיִשְׂמְחוּ בְךָ יִשְׂרָאֵל מְקַדְּשֵׁי שְׁמֶךָ. בָּרוּךְ אַתָּה יהוה, מְקַדֵּשׁ [הַשַּׁבָּת וְ]יִשְׂרָאֵל וְהַזְּמַנִּים.

HOLINESS OF GOD'S NAME

אַתָּה *You are holy and Your Name is holy, and holy ones praise You every day, forever. Blessed are You,* H*ASHEM*, *the holy God.*

SANCTIFICATION OF THE DAY

אַתָּה בְחַרְתָּנוּ *You have chosen us from all the peoples; You loved us and found favor in us; You exalted us above all the tongues and You sanctified us with Your commandments. You drew us close, our King, to Your service and proclaimed Your great and Holy Name upon us.*

On the Sabbath add the words in brackets. [If forgotten, see *Laws* §86-90.]

וַתִּתֶּן לָנוּ *And You gave us,* H*ASHEM*, *our God, with love [Sabbaths for rest], appointed festivals for gladness, Festivals and times for joy, [this day of Sabbath and] this day of the Festival of Matzos, the time of our freedom [with love], a holy convocation, a memorial of the Exodus from Egypt.*

During the *chazzan's* repetition, congregation responds *Amen* as indicated.

אֱלֹהֵינוּ *Our God and God of our forefathers, may there rise, come, reach, be noted, be favored, be heard, be considered, and be remembered — the remembrance and consideration of ourselves; the remembrance of our forefathers; the remembrance of Messiah, son of David, Your servant; the remembrance of Jerusalem, the City of Your Holiness; the remembrance of Your entire people the Family of Israel — before You for deliverance, for goodness, for grace, for kindness, and for compassion, for life, and for peace on this day of the Festival of Matzos. Remember us on it,* H*ASHEM*, *our God, for goodness* (Cong. – *Amen*); *consider us on it for blessing* (Cong. – *Amen*); *and help us on it for life* (Cong. – *Amen*). *In the matter of salvation and compassion, pity, be gracious and compassionate with us and help us, for our eyes are turned to You, because You are God, the gracious and compassionate King.*[1]

On the Sabbath add the words in brackets. [If forgotten, see *Laws* §86-90.]

וְהַשִּׂיאֵנוּ *Bestow upon us, O* H*ASHEM*, *our God, the blessing of Your appointed Festivals for life and for peace, for gladness and for joy, as You desired and promised to bless us. [Our God and the God of our forefathers, may You be pleased with our rest.] Sanctify us with Your commandments and grant us our share in Your Torah; satisfy us from Your goodness and gladden us with Your salvation, and purify our heart to serve You sincerely. And grant us a heritage, O* H*ASHEM*, *our God — [with love and with favor] with gladness and with joy — [the Sabbath and] the appointed festivals of Your holiness, and may Israel, the sanctifiers of Your Name, rejoice in You. Blessed are You,* H*ASHEM*, *Who sanctifies [the Sabbath,] Israel and the festive seasons.*

---

(1) Cf. *Nechemiah* 9:31.

עבודה

רְצֵה יהוה אֱלֹהֵינוּ בְּעַמְּךָ יִשְׂרָאֵל וּבִתְפִלָּתָם, וְהָשֵׁב אֶת הָעֲבוֹדָה לִדְבִיר בֵּיתֶךָ. וְאִשֵּׁי יִשְׂרָאֵל וּתְפִלָּתָם בְּאַהֲבָה תְקַבֵּל בְּרָצוֹן, וּתְהִי לְרָצוֹן תָּמִיד עֲבוֹדַת יִשְׂרָאֵל עַמֶּךָ.

וְתֶחֱזֶינָה עֵינֵינוּ בְּשׁוּבְךָ לְצִיּוֹן בְּרַחֲמִים. בָּרוּךְ אַתָּה יהוה, הַמַּחֲזִיר שְׁכִינָתוֹ לְצִיּוֹן.

הודאה

Bow at מוֹדִים; straighten up at 'ה. In his repetition the *chazzan* should recite the entire מוֹדִים aloud, while the congregation recites מוֹדִים דְּרַבָּנָן softly.

מוֹדִים אֲנַחְנוּ לָךְ, שָׁאַתָּה הוּא יהוה אֱלֹהֵינוּ וֵאלֹהֵי אֲבוֹתֵינוּ לְעוֹלָם וָעֶד. צוּר חַיֵּינוּ, מָגֵן יִשְׁעֵנוּ אַתָּה הוּא לְדוֹר וָדוֹר. נוֹדֶה לְּךָ וּנְסַפֵּר תְּהִלָּתֶךָ[1] עַל חַיֵּינוּ הַמְּסוּרִים בְּיָדֶךָ, וְעַל נִשְׁמוֹתֵינוּ הַפְּקוּדוֹת לָךְ, וְעַל נִסֶּיךָ שֶׁבְּכָל יוֹם עִמָּנוּ, וְעַל נִפְלְאוֹתֶיךָ וְטוֹבוֹתֶיךָ שֶׁבְּכָל עֵת, עֶרֶב וָבֹקֶר וְצָהֳרָיִם. הַטּוֹב כִּי לֹא כָלוּ רַחֲמֶיךָ, וְהַמְּרַחֵם כִּי לֹא תַמּוּ חֲסָדֶיךָ,[2] מֵעוֹלָם קִוִּינוּ לָךְ.

מודים דרבנן

מוֹדִים אֲנַחְנוּ לָךְ, שָׁאַתָּה הוּא יהוה אֱלֹהֵינוּ וֵאלֹהֵי אֲבוֹתֵינוּ, אֱלֹהֵי כָל בָּשָׂר, יוֹצְרֵנוּ, יוֹצֵר בְּרֵאשִׁית. בְּרָכוֹת וְהוֹדָאוֹת לְשִׁמְךָ הַגָּדוֹל וְהַקָּדוֹשׁ, עַל שֶׁהֶחֱיִיתָנוּ וְקִיַּמְתָּנוּ. כֵּן תְּחַיֵּנוּ וּתְקַיְּמֵנוּ, וְתֶאֱסוֹף גָּלֻיּוֹתֵינוּ לְחַצְרוֹת קָדְשֶׁךָ, לִשְׁמוֹר חֻקֶּיךָ וְלַעֲשׂוֹת רְצוֹנֶךָ, וּלְעָבְדְּךָ בְּלֵבָב שָׁלֵם, עַל שֶׁאֲנַחְנוּ מוֹדִים לָךְ. בָּרוּךְ אֵל הַהוֹדָאוֹת.

וְעַל כֻּלָּם יִתְבָּרַךְ וְיִתְרוֹמַם שִׁמְךָ מַלְכֵּנוּ תָּמִיד לְעוֹלָם וָעֶד.

Bend the knees at בָּרוּךְ; bow at אַתָּה; straighten up at 'ה.

וְכֹל הַחַיִּים יוֹדוּךָ סֶּלָה, וִיהַלְלוּ אֶת שִׁמְךָ בֶּאֱמֶת, הָאֵל יְשׁוּעָתֵנוּ וְעֶזְרָתֵנוּ סֶלָה. בָּרוּךְ אַתָּה יהוה, הַטּוֹב שִׁמְךָ וּלְךָ נָאֶה לְהוֹדוֹת.

TEMPLE SERVICE

רְצֵה *Be favorable,* H*ASHEM*, *our God, toward Your people Israel and their prayer and restore the service to the Holy of Holies of Your Temple. The fire-offerings of Israel and their prayer accept with love and favor, and may the service of Your people Israel always be favorable to You.*

וְתֶחֱזֶינָה *May our eyes behold Your return to Zion in compassion. Blessed are You,* H*ASHEM*, *Who restores His Presence to Zion.*

THANKSGIVING [MODIM]

Bow at *'We gratefully thank You';* straighten up at *'HASHEM.'* In his repetition the *chazzan* should recite the entire *Modim* aloud, while the congregation recites *Modim of the Rabbis* softly.

מוֹדִים *We gratefully thank You, for it is You Who are* H*ASHEM*, *our God and the God of our forefathers for all eternity; Rock of our lives, Shield of our salvation are You from generation to generation. We shall thank You and relate Your praise*[1] *— for our lives, which are committed to Your power and for our souls that are entrusted to You; for Your miracles that are with us every day; and for Your wonders and favors in every season — evening, morning, and afternoon. The Beneficent One, for Your compassions were never exhausted, and the Compassionate One, for Your kindnesses never ended*[2] *— always have we put our hope in You.*

MODIM OF THE RABBIS

מוֹדִים *We gratefully thank You, for it is You Who are* H*ASHEM*, *our God and the God of our forefathers, the God of all flesh, our Molder, the Molder of the universe. Blessings and thanks are due Your great and holy Name for You have given us life and sustained us. So may You continue to give us life and sustain us and gather our exiles to the Courtyards of Your Sanctuary, to observe Your decrees, to do Your will and to serve You wholeheartedly. [We thank You] for inspiring us to thank You. Blessed is the God of thanksgivings.*

For all these, may Your Name be blessed and exalted, our King, continually forever and ever.

Bend the knees at *'Blessed'*; bow at *'You'*; straighten up at *'HASHEM.'*

Everything alive will gratefully acknowledge You, Selah! and praise Your Name sincerely, O God of our salvation and help, Selah! Blessed are You, H*ASHEM*, *Your Name is 'The Beneficent One' and to You it is fitting to give thanks.*

---

(1) Cf. *Psalms* 79:13. (2) Cf. *Lamentations* 3:22.

שלום

שָׁלוֹם רָב עַל יִשְׂרָאֵל עַמְּךָ תָּשִׂים לְעוֹלָם, כִּי אַתָּה הוּא מֶלֶךְ אָדוֹן לְכָל הַשָּׁלוֹם. וְטוֹב בְּעֵינֶיךָ לְבָרֵךְ אֶת עַמְּךָ יִשְׂרָאֵל בְּכָל עֵת וּבְכָל שָׁעָה בִּשְׁלוֹמֶךָ. בָּרוּךְ אַתָּה יהוה, הַמְּבָרֵךְ אֶת עַמּוֹ יִשְׂרָאֵל בַּשָּׁלוֹם.

יִהְיוּ לְרָצוֹן אִמְרֵי פִי וְהֶגְיוֹן לִבִּי לְפָנֶיךָ, יהוה צוּרִי וְגֹאֲלִי.[1]

The *chazzan's* repetition of *Shemoneh Esrei* ends here. Individuals continue below.

אֱלֹהַי, נְצוֹר לְשׁוֹנִי מֵרָע, וּשְׂפָתַי מִדַּבֵּר מִרְמָה,[2] וְלִמְקַלְלַי נַפְשִׁי תִדּוֹם, וְנַפְשִׁי כֶּעָפָר לַכֹּל תִּהְיֶה. פְּתַח לִבִּי בְּתוֹרָתֶךָ, וּבְמִצְוֹתֶיךָ תִּרְדּוֹף נַפְשִׁי. וְכֹל הַחוֹשְׁבִים עָלַי רָעָה, מְהֵרָה הָפֵר עֲצָתָם וְקַלְקֵל מַחֲשַׁבְתָּם. עֲשֵׂה לְמַעַן שְׁמֶךָ, עֲשֵׂה לְמַעַן יְמִינֶךָ, עֲשֵׂה לְמַעַן קְדֻשָּׁתֶךָ, עֲשֵׂה לְמַעַן תּוֹרָתֶךָ. לְמַעַן יֵחָלְצוּן יְדִידֶיךָ, הוֹשִׁיעָה יְמִינְךָ וַעֲנֵנִי.[3]

Some recite verses pertaining to their names at this point. See page 1143.

יִהְיוּ לְרָצוֹן אִמְרֵי פִי וְהֶגְיוֹן לִבִּי לְפָנֶיךָ, יהוה צוּרִי וְגֹאֲלִי.[1] עֹשֶׂה שָׁלוֹם בִּמְרוֹמָיו, הוּא יַעֲשֶׂה שָׁלוֹם עָלֵינוּ, וְעַל כָּל יִשְׂרָאֵל. וְאִמְרוּ: אָמֵן.

יְהִי רָצוֹן מִלְּפָנֶיךָ יהוה אֱלֹהֵינוּ וֵאלֹהֵי אֲבוֹתֵינוּ, שֶׁיִּבָּנֶה בֵּית הַמִּקְדָּשׁ בִּמְהֵרָה בְיָמֵינוּ, וְתֵן חֶלְקֵנוּ בְּתוֹרָתֶךָ. וְשָׁם נַעֲבָדְךָ בְּיִרְאָה, כִּימֵי עוֹלָם וּכְשָׁנִים קַדְמוֹנִיּוֹת. וְעָרְבָה לַיהוה מִנְחַת יְהוּדָה וִירוּשָׁלָיִם, כִּימֵי עוֹלָם וּכְשָׁנִים קַדְמוֹנִיּוֹת.[4]

THE INDIVIDUAL'S RECITATION OF שְׁמוֹנֶה עֶשְׂרֵה ENDS HERE.

The individual remains standing in place until the *chazzan* reaches *Kedushah* — or at least until the *chazzan* begins his repetition — then he takes three steps forward. The *chazzan* himself, or one praying alone, should remain in place for a few moments before taking three steps forward.

קדיש שלם

The *chazzan* recites קַדִּישׁ שָׁלֵם.

יִתְגַּדַּל וְיִתְקַדַּשׁ שְׁמֵהּ רַבָּא. (.Cong – אָמֵן.) בְּעָלְמָא דִּי בְרָא כִרְעוּתֵהּ. וְיַמְלִיךְ מַלְכוּתֵהּ, בְּחַיֵּיכוֹן וּבְיוֹמֵיכוֹן וּבְחַיֵּי דְכָל בֵּית יִשְׂרָאֵל, בַּעֲגָלָא וּבִזְמַן קָרִיב. וְאִמְרוּ: אָמֵן.

(.Cong – אָמֵן. יְהֵא שְׁמֵהּ רַבָּא מְבָרַךְ לְעָלַם וּלְעָלְמֵי עָלְמַיָּא.)

PEACE

שָׁלוֹם רָב *Establish abundant peace upon Your people Israel forever, for You are King, Master of all peace. May it be good in Your eyes to bless Your people Israel at every time and every hour with Your peace. Blessed are You, HASHEM, Who blesses His people Israel with peace.*

May the expressions of my mouth and the thoughts of my heart find favor before You, HASHEM, my Rock and my Redeemer.[1]

The *chazzan's* repetition of *Shemoneh Esrei* ends here. Individuals continue below.

אֱלֹהַי *My God, guard my tongue from evil and my lips from speaking deceitfully.*[2] *To those who curse me, let my soul be silent; and let my soul be like dust to everyone. Open my heart to Your Torah, then my soul will pursue Your commandments. As for all those who design evil against me, speedily nullify their counsel and disrupt their design. Act for Your Name's sake; act for Your right hand's sake; act for Your sanctity's sake; act for Your Torah's sake. That Your beloved ones may be given rest; let Your right hand save, and respond to me.*[3]

Some recite verses pertaining to their names at this point. See page 1143.

May the expressions of my mouth and the thoughts of my heart find favor before You, HASHEM, my Rock and my Redeemer.[1] *He Who makes peace in His heights, may He make peace upon us, and upon all Israel. Now respond: Amen.*

יְהִי רָצוֹן *May it be Your will, HASHEM, our God and the God of our forefathers, that the Holy Temple be rebuilt, speedily in our days. Grant us our share in Your Torah, and may we serve You there with reverence, as in days of old and in former years. Then the offering of Judah and Jerusalem will be pleasing to HASHEM, as in days of old and in former years.*[4]

THE INDIVIDUAL'S RECITATION OF *SHEMONEH ESREI* ENDS HERE.

The individual remains standing in place until the *chazzan* reaches *Kedushah* — or at least until the *chazzan* begins his repetition — then he takes three steps forward. The *chazzan* himself, or one praying alone, should remain in place for a few moments before taking three steps forward.

FULL KADDISH

The *chazzan* recites the Full *Kaddish.*

יִתְגַּדַּל *May His great Name grow exalted and sanctified* (Cong.— *Amen.*) *in the world that He created as He willed. May He give reign to His kingship in your lifetimes and in your days, and in the lifetimes of the entire Family of Israel, swiftly and soon. Now respond: Amen.*

(Cong.— *Amen. May His great Name be blessed forever and ever.*)

---

(1) *Psalms* 19:15. (2) Cf. 34:14. (3) 60:7; 108:7. (4) *Malachi* 3:4.

יְהֵא שְׁמֵהּ רַבָּא מְבָרַךְ לְעָלַם וּלְעָלְמֵי עָלְמַיָּא.

יִתְבָּרַךְ וְיִשְׁתַּבַּח וְיִתְפָּאַר וְיִתְרוֹמַם וְיִתְנַשֵּׂא וְיִתְהַדָּר וְיִתְעַלֶּה וְיִתְהַלָּל שְׁמֵהּ דְּקֻדְשָׁא בְּרִיךְ הוּא (.Cong – בְּרִיךְ הוּא) — לְעֵלָּא מִן כָּל בִּרְכָתָא וְשִׁירָתָא תֻּשְׁבְּחָתָא וְנֶחֱמָתָא, דַּאֲמִירָן בְּעָלְמָא. וְאִמְרוּ: אָמֵן. (.Cong – אָמֵן.)

(.Cong – קַבֵּל בְּרַחֲמִים וּבְרָצוֹן אֶת תְּפִלָּתֵנוּ.)

תִּתְקַבֵּל צְלוֹתְהוֹן וּבָעוּתְהוֹן דְּכָל בֵּית יִשְׂרָאֵל קֳדָם אֲבוּהוֹן דִּי בִשְׁמַיָּא. וְאִמְרוּ: אָמֵן. (.Cong – אָמֵן.)

(.Cong – יְהִי שֵׁם יהוה מְבֹרָךְ, מֵעַתָּה וְעַד עוֹלָם.[1])

יְהֵא שְׁלָמָא רַבָּא מִן שְׁמַיָּא, וְחַיִּים עָלֵינוּ וְעַל כָּל יִשְׂרָאֵל. וְאִמְרוּ: אָמֵן. (.Cong – אָמֵן.)

(.Cong – עֶזְרִי מֵעִם יהוה, עֹשֵׂה שָׁמַיִם וָאָרֶץ.[2])

Take three steps back. Bow left and say . . . עֹשֶׂה; bow right and say . . . הוּא; bow forward and sa' . . . וְעַל כָּל . . . אָמֵן. Remain standing in place for a few moments, then take three steps forward.

עֹשֶׂה שָׁלוֹם בִּמְרוֹמָיו, הוּא יַעֲשֶׂה שָׁלוֹם עָלֵינוּ, וְעַל כָּל יִשְׂרָאֵל. וְאִמְרוּ: אָמֵן. (.Cong – אָמֵן.)

עלינו

Stand while reciting עָלֵינוּ.

עָלֵינוּ לְשַׁבֵּחַ לַאֲדוֹן הַכֹּל, לָתֵת גְּדֻלָּה לְיוֹצֵר בְּרֵאשִׁית, שֶׁלֹּא עָשָׂנוּ כְּגוֹיֵי הָאֲרָצוֹת, וְלֹא שָׂמָנוּ כְּמִשְׁפְּחוֹת הָאֲדָמָה. שֶׁלֹּא שָׂם חֶלְקֵנוּ כָּהֶם, וְגוֹרָלֵנוּ כְּכָל הֲמוֹנָם. (שֶׁהֵם מִשְׁתַּחֲוִים לְהֶבֶל וָרִיק, וּמִתְפַּלְּלִים אֶל אֵל לֹא יוֹשִׁיעַ.[3]) וַאֲנַחְנוּ כּוֹרְעִים וּמִשְׁתַּחֲוִים וּמוֹדִים, לִפְנֵי מֶלֶךְ מַלְכֵי הַמְּלָכִים הַקָּדוֹשׁ בָּרוּךְ הוּא. שֶׁהוּא נוֹטֶה שָׁמַיִם וְיֹסֵד אָרֶץ,[4] וּמוֹשַׁב יְקָרוֹ בַּשָּׁמַיִם מִמַּעַל, וּשְׁכִינַת עֻזּוֹ בְּגָבְהֵי מְרוֹמִים. הוּא אֱלֹהֵינוּ, אֵין עוֹד. אֱמֶת מַלְכֵּנוּ, אֶפֶס זוּלָתוֹ, כַּכָּתוּב בְּתוֹרָתוֹ: וְיָדַעְתָּ הַיּוֹם וַהֲשֵׁבֹתָ אֶל לְבָבֶךָ, כִּי יהוה הוּא הָאֱלֹהִים בַּשָּׁמַיִם מִמַּעַל וְעַל הָאָרֶץ מִתָּחַת, אֵין עוֹד.[5]

Bow while reciting וַאֲנַחְנוּ כּוֹרְעִים וּמִשְׁתַּחֲוִים.

עַל כֵּן נְקַוֶּה לְּךָ יהוה אֱלֹהֵינוּ לִרְאוֹת מְהֵרָה בְּתִפְאֶרֶת עֻזֶּךָ, לְהַעֲבִיר גִּלּוּלִים מִן הָאָרֶץ, וְהָאֱלִילִים כָּרוֹת יִכָּרֵתוּן, לְתַקֵּן עוֹלָם בְּמַלְכוּת שַׁדַּי. וְכָל בְּנֵי בָשָׂר יִקְרְאוּ בִשְׁמֶךָ, לְהַפְנוֹת אֵלֶיךָ כָּל רִשְׁעֵי אָרֶץ. יַכִּירוּ וְיֵדְעוּ כָּל יוֹשְׁבֵי תֵבֵל, כִּי לְךָ

May His great Name be blessed forever and ever.

Blessed, praised, glorified, exalted, extolled, mighty, upraised, and lauded be the Name of the Holy One, Blessed is He (Cong.– *Blessed is He*) *— beyond any blessing and song, praise and consolation that are uttered in the world. Now respond: Amen.* (Cong.– *Amen.*)

(Cong.– *Accept our prayers with mercy and favor.*)

May the prayers and supplications of the entire Family of Israel be accepted before their Father Who is in Heaven. Now respond: Amen. (Cong.– *Amen.*)

(Cong.– *Blessed be the Name of* HASHEM, *from this time and forever.*[1])

May there be abundant peace from Heaven, and life, upon us and upon all Israel. Now respond: Amen. (Cong.– *Amen.*)

(Cong.– *My help is from* HASHEM, *Maker of heaven and earth.*[2])

Take three steps back. Bow left and say, *'He Who makes peace . . .';* bow right and say, *'may He . . .';* bow forward and say, *'and upon all Israel . . .'* Remain standing in place for a few moments, then take three steps forward.

He Who makes peace in His heights, may He make peace upon us, and upon all Israel. Now respond: Amen. (Cong.– *Amen.*)

ALEINU

Stand while reciting עָלֵינוּ, *'It is our duty . . .'*

עָלֵינוּ *It is our duty to praise the Master of all, to ascribe greatness to the Molder of primeval creation, for He has not made us like the nations of the lands, and has not emplaced us like the families of the earth; for He has not assigned our portion like theirs nor our lot like all their multitudes. (For they bow to vanity and emptiness and pray to a god which helps not.*[3]*) But we bend our knees, bow, and acknowledge our thanks before the King Who reigns over kings, the Holy One, Blessed is He. He stretches out heaven and establishes earth's foundation,*[4] *the seat of His homage is in the heavens above and His powerful Presence is in the loftiest heights. He is our God and there is none other. True is our King, there is nothing beside Him, as it is written in His Torah: 'You are to know this day and take to your heart that* HASHEM *is the only God — in heaven above and on the earth below — there is none other.'*[5]

Bow while reciting *'But we bend our knees.'*

עַל כֵּן *Therefore we put our hope in You,* HASHEM, *our God, that we may soon see Your mighty splendor, to remove detestable idolatry from the earth, and false gods will be utterly cut off, to perfect the universe through the Almighty's sovereignty. Then all humanity will call upon Your Name, to turn all the earth's wicked toward You. All the world's inhabitants will recognize and know that to You*

---

(1) *Psalms* 113:2. (2) 121:2. (3) *Isaiah* 45:20. (4) 51:13. (5) *Deuteronomy* 4:39.

תִּכְרַע כָּל בֶּרֶךְ, תִּשָּׁבַע כָּל לָשׁוֹן.[1] לְפָנֶיךָ יהוה אֱלֹהֵינוּ יִכְרְעוּ וְיִפֹּלוּ, וְלִכְבוֹד שִׁמְךָ יְקָר יִתֵּנוּ. וִיקַבְּלוּ כֻלָּם אֶת עוֹל מַלְכוּתֶךָ, וְתִמְלֹךְ עֲלֵיהֶם מְהֵרָה לְעוֹלָם וָעֶד. כִּי הַמַּלְכוּת שֶׁלְּךָ הִיא וּלְעוֹלְמֵי עַד תִּמְלוֹךְ בְּכָבוֹד, כַּכָּתוּב בְּתוֹרָתֶךָ: יהוה יִמְלֹךְ לְעֹלָם וָעֶד.[2] ❖ וְנֶאֱמַר: וְהָיָה יהוה לְמֶלֶךְ עַל כָּל הָאָרֶץ, בַּיּוֹם הַהוּא יִהְיֶה יהוה אֶחָד וּשְׁמוֹ אֶחָד.[3]

Some congregations recite the following after עָלֵינוּ:

אַל תִּירָא מִפַּחַד פִּתְאֹם, וּמִשֹּׁאַת רְשָׁעִים כִּי תָבֹא.[4] עֻצוּ עֵצָה וְתֻפָר, דַּבְּרוּ דָבָר וְלֹא יָקוּם, כִּי עִמָּנוּ אֵל.[5] וְעַד זִקְנָה אֲנִי הוּא, וְעַד שֵׂיבָה אֲנִי אֶסְבֹּל, אֲנִי עָשִׂיתִי וַאֲנִי אֶשָּׂא, וַאֲנִי אֶסְבֹּל וַאֲמַלֵּט.[6]

קדיש יתום

In the presence of a *minyan,* mourners recite קַדִּישׁ יָתוֹם, the Mourner's *Kaddish* (see *Laws* §81-83).

יִתְגַּדַּל וְיִתְקַדַּשׁ שְׁמֵהּ רַבָּא. (.Cong – אָמֵן.) בְּעָלְמָא דִּי בְרָא כִרְעוּתֵהּ. וְיַמְלִיךְ מַלְכוּתֵהּ, בְּחַיֵּיכוֹן וּבְיוֹמֵיכוֹן וּבְחַיֵּי דְכָל בֵּית יִשְׂרָאֵל, בַּעֲגָלָא וּבִזְמַן קָרִיב. וְאִמְרוּ: אָמֵן.

(.Cong – אָמֵן. יְהֵא שְׁמֵהּ רַבָּא מְבָרַךְ לְעָלַם וּלְעָלְמֵי עָלְמַיָּא.)

יְהֵא שְׁמֵהּ רַבָּא מְבָרַךְ לְעָלַם וּלְעָלְמֵי עָלְמַיָּא.

יִתְבָּרַךְ וְיִשְׁתַּבַּח וְיִתְפָּאַר וְיִתְרוֹמַם וְיִתְנַשֵּׂא וְיִתְהַדָּר וְיִתְעַלֶּה וְיִתְהַלָּל שְׁמֵהּ דְּקֻדְשָׁא בְּרִיךְ הוּא (.Cong – בְּרִיךְ הוּא) — לְעֵלָּא מִן כָּל בִּרְכָתָא וְשִׁירָתָא תֻּשְׁבְּחָתָא וְנֶחֱמָתָא, דַּאֲמִירָן בְּעָלְמָא. וְאִמְרוּ: אָמֵן. (.Cong – אָמֵן.)

יְהֵא שְׁלָמָא רַבָּא מִן שְׁמַיָּא, וְחַיִּים עָלֵינוּ וְעַל כָּל יִשְׂרָאֵל. וְאִמְרוּ: אָמֵן. (.Cong – אָמֵן.)

Take three steps back. Bow left and say . . . עֹשֶׂה; bow right and say . . . הוּא; bow forward and say וְעַל כָּל . . . אָמֵן. Remain standing in place for a few moments, then take three steps forward.

עֹשֶׂה שָׁלוֹם בִּמְרוֹמָיו, הוּא יַעֲשֶׂה שָׁלוֹם עָלֵינוּ, וְעַל כָּל יִשְׂרָאֵל. וְאִמְרוּ: אָמֵן. (.Cong – אָמֵן.)

MAARIV FOR THE SECOND NIGHT BEGINS ON PAGE 42.
KABBALAS SHABBOS FOR THE SABBATH OF *CHOL HAMOED* BEGINS ON PAGE 490.
MAARIV FOR THE WEEKDAYS OF *CHOL HAMOED* BEGINS ON PAGE 656.

every knee should bend, every tongue should swear.[1] *Before You, HASHEM, our God, they will bend every knee and cast themselves down and to the glory of Your Name they will render homage, and they will all accept upon themselves the yoke of Your kingship that You may reign over them soon and eternally. For the kingdom is Yours and You will reign for all eternity in glory as it is written in Your Torah: HASHEM shall reign for all eternity.*[2] Chazzan– *And it is said: HASHEM will be King over all the world — on that day HASHEM will be One and His Name will be One.*[3]

Some congregations recite the following after *Aleinu.*

אַל תִּירָא *Do not fear sudden terror, or the holocaust of the wicked when it comes.*[4] *Plan a conspiracy and it will be annulled; speak your piece and it shall not stand, for God is with us.*[5] *Even till your seniority, I remain unchanged; and even till your ripe old age, I shall endure. I created you and I shall bear you; I shall endure and rescue.*[6]

MOURNER'S KADDISH

In the presence of a *minyan,* mourners recite קַדִּישׁ יָתוֹם, the Mourner's *Kaddish* (see *Laws* 81-83).

[A transliteration of this *Kaddish* appears on page 1147.]

יִתְגַּדַּל *May His great Name grow exalted and sanctified* (Cong.– *Amen.*) *in the world that He created as He willed. May He give reign to His kingship in your lifetimes and in your days, and in the lifetimes of the entire Family of Israel, swiftly and soon. Now respond: Amen.*

(Cong.– *Amen. May His great Name be blessed forever and ever.*)

May His great Name be blessed forever and ever.

Blessed, praised, glorified, exalted, extolled, mighty, upraised, and lauded be the Name of the Holy One, Blessed is He (Cong.– *Blessed is He*) *— beyond any blessing and song, praise and consolation that are uttered in the world. Now respond: Amen.* (Cong.– *Amen*).

May there be abundant peace from Heaven, and life, upon us and upon all Israel. Now respond: Amen. (Cong.– *Amen.*)

Take three steps back. Bow left and say, *'He Who makes peace . . .';* bow right and say, *'may He . . .';* bow forward and say, *'and upon all Israel . . .'* Remain standing in place for a few moments, then take three steps forward.

He Who makes peace in His heights, may He make peace upon us, and upon all Israel. Now respond: Amen. (Cong.– *Amen.*)

MAARIV FOR THE SECOND NIGHT BEGINS ON PAGE 42.

KABBALAS SHABBOS FOR THE SABBATH OF *CHOL HAMOED* BEGINS ON PAGE 490.

MAARIV FOR THE WEEKDAYS OF *CHOL HAMOED* BEGINS ON PAGE 656.

(1) Cf. *Isaiah* 45:23. (2) *Exodus* 15:18. (3) *Zechariah* 14:9. (4) *Proverbs* 3:25. (5) *Isaiah* 8:10. (6) 46:4.

שבת חול המועד

Sabbath of Chol HaMoed

הדלקת הנרות לשבת חול המועד

[It is forbidden to create a new flame — for example, by striking a match — on *Yom Tov*. Therefore, since when the first day of Chol HaMoed falls on the Sabbath, the Sabbath candles will be kindled during *Yom Tov*, the candles must be lit from a previously existing flame that has been burning from before *Yom Tov*.]

Light the candles, then cover the eyes and recite the blessing. Uncover the eyes and gaze briefly at the candles.

בָּרוּךְ אַתָּה יהוה אֱלֹהֵינוּ מֶלֶךְ הָעוֹלָם, אֲשֶׁר קִדְּשָׁנוּ בְּמִצְוֹתָיו, וְצִוָּנוּ לְהַדְלִיק נֵר שֶׁל שַׁבָּת.

It is customary to recite the following prayer after the kindling. The words in brackets are included as they apply.

יְהִי רָצוֹן לְפָנֶיךָ, יהוה אֱלֹהַי וֵאלֹהֵי אֲבוֹתַי, שֶׁתְּחוֹנֵן אוֹתִי [וְאֶת אִישִׁי, וְאֶת בָּנַי, וְאֶת בְּנוֹתַי, וְאֶת אָבִי, וְאֶת אִמִּי] וְאֶת כָּל קְרוֹבַי; וְתִתֶּן לָנוּ וּלְכָל יִשְׂרָאֵל חַיִּים טוֹבִים וַאֲרוּכִים; וְתִזְכְּרֵנוּ בְּזִכְרוֹן טוֹבָה וּבְרָכָה; וְתִפְקְדֵנוּ בִּפְקֻדַּת יְשׁוּעָה וְרַחֲמִים; וּתְבָרְכֵנוּ בְּרָכוֹת גְּדוֹלוֹת; וְתַשְׁלִים בָּתֵּינוּ; וְתַשְׁכֵּן שְׁכִינָתְךָ בֵּינֵינוּ. וְזַכֵּנִי לְגַדֵּל בָּנִים וּבְנֵי בָנִים חֲכָמִים וּנְבוֹנִים, אוֹהֲבֵי יהוה, יִרְאֵי אֱלֹהִים, אַנְשֵׁי אֱמֶת, זֶרַע קֹדֶשׁ, בַּיהוה דְּבֵקִים, וּמְאִירִים אֶת הָעוֹלָם בַּתּוֹרָה וּבְמַעֲשִׂים טוֹבִים, וּבְכָל מְלֶאכֶת עֲבוֹדַת הַבּוֹרֵא. אָנָּא שְׁמַע אֶת תְּחִנָּתִי בָּעֵת הַזֹּאת, בִּזְכוּת שָׂרָה וְרִבְקָה וְרָחֵל וְלֵאָה אִמּוֹתֵינוּ, וְהָאֵר נֵרֵנוּ שֶׁלֹּא יִכְבֶּה לְעוֹלָם וָעֶד, וְהָאֵר פָּנֶיךָ וְנִוָּשֵׁעָה. אָמֵן.

קבלת שבת לשבת חול המועד

תהלים צב

מִזְמוֹר שִׁיר לְיוֹם הַשַּׁבָּת. טוֹב לְהֹדוֹת לַיהוה, וּלְזַמֵּר לְשִׁמְךָ עֶלְיוֹן. לְהַגִּיד בַּבֹּקֶר חַסְדֶּךָ, וֶאֱמוּנָתְךָ בַּלֵּילוֹת. עֲלֵי עָשׂוֹר וַעֲלֵי נָבֶל, עֲלֵי הִגָּיוֹן בְּכִנּוֹר. כִּי שִׂמַּחְתַּנִי יהוה בְּפָעֳלֶךָ, בְּמַעֲשֵׂי יָדֶיךָ אֲרַנֵּן. מַה גָּדְלוּ מַעֲשֶׂיךָ יהוה, מְאֹד עָמְקוּ מַחְשְׁבֹתֶיךָ. אִישׁ בַּעַר לֹא יֵדָע, וּכְסִיל לֹא יָבִין אֶת זֹאת. בִּפְרֹחַ רְשָׁעִים כְּמוֹ עֵשֶׂב, וַיָּצִיצוּ כָּל פֹּעֲלֵי אָוֶן, לְהִשָּׁמְדָם עֲדֵי עַד. וְאַתָּה מָרוֹם לְעֹלָם יהוה. כִּי הִנֵּה אֹיְבֶיךָ יהוה, כִּי הִנֵּה אֹיְבֶיךָ יֹאבֵדוּ, יִתְפָּרְדוּ כָּל פֹּעֲלֵי אָוֶן. וַתָּרֶם כִּרְאֵים קַרְנִי, בַּלֹּתִי בְּשֶׁמֶן רַעֲנָן. וַתַּבֵּט עֵינִי בְּשׁוּרָי, בַּקָּמִים עָלַי מְרֵעִים, תִּשְׁמַעְנָה אָזְנָי. ❖ צַדִּיק כַּתָּמָר יִפְרָח, כְּאֶרֶז בַּלְּבָנוֹן יִשְׂגֶּה. שְׁתוּלִים בְּבֵית יהוה, בְּחַצְרוֹת אֱלֹהֵינוּ יַפְרִיחוּ. עוֹד יְנוּבוּן בְּשֵׂיבָה, דְּשֵׁנִים וְרַעֲנַנִּים יִהְיוּ. לְהַגִּיד כִּי יָשָׁר יהוה, צוּרִי וְלֹא עַוְלָתָה בּוֹ.

KINDLING LIGHTS FOR THE SABBATH OF CHOL HAMOED

[It is forbidden to create a new flame – for example, by striking a match – on *Yom Tov*. Therefore, since when the first day of Chol HaMoed falls on the Sabbath, the Sabbath candles will be kindled during *Yom Tov*, the candles must be lit from a previously existing flame that has been burning from before *Yom Tov*.]

Light the candles, then cover the eyes and recite the blessing.
Uncover the eyes and gaze briefly at the candles.

בָּרוּךְ *Blessed are You,* HASHEM, *our God, King of the universe, Who has sanctified us with His commandments, and has commanded us to kindle the light of the Sabbath.*

It is customary to recite the following prayer after the kindling.
The words in brackets are included as they apply.

יְהִי רָצוֹן *May it be Your will,* HASHEM, *my God and God of my forefathers, that You show favor to me [my husband, my sons, my daughters, my father, my mother] and all my relatives; and that You grant us and all Israel a good and long life; that You remember us with a beneficent memory and blessing; that You consider us with a consideration of salvation and compassion; that You bless us with great blessings; that You make our households complete; that You cause Your Presence to dwell among us. Privilege me to raise children and grandchildren who are wise and understanding, who love* HASHEM *and fear God, people of truth, holy offspring, attached to* HASHEM, *who illuminate the world with Torah and good deeds and with every labor in the service of the Creator. Please, hear my supplication at this time, in the merit of Sarah, Rebecca, Rachel, and Leah, our mothers, and cause our light to illuminate that it be not extinguished forever, and let Your countenance shine so that we are saved. Amen.*

KABBALAS SHABBOS

Psalm 92

מִזְמוֹר שִׁיר *A psalm, a song for the Sabbath day. It is good to thank* HASHEM *and to sing praise to Your Name, O Exalted One; to relate Your kindness in the dawn and Your faith in the nights. Upon ten-stringed instrument and lyre, with singing accompanied by a harp. For You have gladdened me,* HASHEM, *with Your deeds; at the works of Your Hands I sing glad song. How great are Your deeds,* HASHEM; *exceedingly profound are Your thoughts. A boor cannot know, nor can a fool understand this: when the wicked bloom like grass and all the doers of iniquity blossom — it is to destroy them till eternity. But You remain exalted forever,* HASHEM. *For behold! — Your enemies,* HASHEM, *for behold! — Your enemies shall perish, dispersed shall be all doers of iniquity. As exalted as a re'eim's shall be my pride, I will be saturated with ever-fresh oil. My eyes have seen my vigilant foes; when those who would harm me rise up against me, my ears have heard their doom.* Chazzan– *A righteous man will flourish like a date palm, like a cedar in the Lebanon he will grow tall. Planted in the house of* HASHEM, *in the courtyards of our God they will flourish. They will still be fruitful in old age, vigorous and fresh they will be — to declare that* HASHEM *is just, my Rock in Whom there is no wrong.*

תהלים צג

יהוה מָלָךְ גֵּאוּת לָבֵשׁ, לָבֵשׁ יהוה עֹז הִתְאַזָּר, אַף תִּכּוֹן תֵּבֵל בַּל תִּמּוֹט. נָכוֹן כִּסְאֲךָ מֵאָז, מֵעוֹלָם אָתָּה. נָשְׂאוּ נְהָרוֹת, יהוה, נָשְׂאוּ נְהָרוֹת קוֹלָם, יִשְׂאוּ נְהָרוֹת דָּכְיָם. ❖ מִקֹּלוֹת מַיִם רַבִּים אַדִּירִים מִשְׁבְּרֵי יָם, אַדִּיר בַּמָּרוֹם יהוה. עֵדֹתֶיךָ נֶאֶמְנוּ מְאֹד לְבֵיתְךָ נַאֲוָה קֹּדֶשׁ, יהוה, לְאֹרֶךְ יָמִים.

קדיש יתום

Mourners recite קַדִּישׁ יָתוֹם, the Mourner's *Kaddish* (see *Laws* 81-83).

יִתְגַּדַּל וְיִתְקַדַּשׁ שְׁמֵהּ רַבָּא. (Cong. – אָמֵן.) בְּעָלְמָא דִּי בְרָא כִרְעוּתֵהּ. וְיַמְלִיךְ מַלְכוּתֵהּ, בְּחַיֵּיכוֹן וּבְיוֹמֵיכוֹן וּבְחַיֵּי דְכָל בֵּית יִשְׂרָאֵל, בַּעֲגָלָא וּבִזְמַן קָרִיב. וְאִמְרוּ: אָמֵן.

(Cong. – אָמֵן. יְהֵא שְׁמֵהּ רַבָּא מְבָרַךְ לְעָלַם וּלְעָלְמֵי עָלְמַיָּא.)

יְהֵא שְׁמֵהּ רַבָּא מְבָרַךְ לְעָלַם וּלְעָלְמֵי עָלְמַיָּא.

יִתְבָּרַךְ וְיִשְׁתַּבַּח וְיִתְפָּאַר וְיִתְרוֹמַם וְיִתְנַשֵּׂא וְיִתְהַדָּר וְיִתְעַלֶּה וְיִתְהַלָּל שְׁמֵהּ דְּקֻדְשָׁא בְּרִיךְ הוּא (Cong. – בְּרִיךְ הוּא) – לְעֵלָּא מִן כָּל בִּרְכָתָא וְשִׁירָתָא תֻּשְׁבְּחָתָא וְנֶחֱמָתָא, דַּאֲמִירָן בְּעָלְמָא. וְאִמְרוּ: אָמֵן. (Cong. – אָמֵן.)

יְהֵא שְׁלָמָא רַבָּא מִן שְׁמַיָּא, וְחַיִּים עָלֵינוּ וְעַל כָּל יִשְׂרָאֵל. וְאִמְרוּ: אָמֵן. (Cong. – אָמֵן.)

Take three steps back. Bow left and say . . . עֹשֶׂה; bow right and say . . . הוּא; bow forward and say וְעַל כָּל . . . אָמֵן. Remain standing in place for a few moments, then take three steps forward.

עֹשֶׂה שָׁלוֹם בִּמְרוֹמָיו, הוּא יַעֲשֶׂה שָׁלוֹם עָלֵינוּ, וְעַל כָּל יִשְׂרָאֵל. וְאִמְרוּ: אָמֵן. (Cong. – אָמֵן.)

❧ מעריב לשבת חול המועד ❧

In some congregations the *chazzan* chants a melody during his recitation of בָּרְכוּ, so that the congregation can then recite יִתְבָּרַךְ.

Chazzan bows at בָּרְכוּ and straightens up at ה׳.

בָּרְכוּ אֶת יהוה הַמְּבֹרָךְ.

Congregation, followed by *chazzan*, responds, bowing at בָּרוּךְ and straightening up at ה׳.

בָּרוּךְ יהוה הַמְּבֹרָךְ לְעוֹלָם וָעֶד.

יִתְבָּרַךְ וְיִשְׁתַּבַּח וְיִתְפָּאַר וְיִתְרוֹמַם וְיִתְנַשֵּׂא שְׁמוֹ שֶׁל מֶלֶךְ מַלְכֵי הַמְּלָכִים, הַקָּדוֹשׁ בָּרוּךְ הוּא. שֶׁהוּא רִאשׁוֹן וְהוּא אַחֲרוֹן, וּמִבַּלְעָדָיו אֵין אֱלֹהִים.[1] סֹלּוּ, לָרֹכֵב בָּעֲרָבוֹת, בְּיָהּ שְׁמוֹ, וְעִלְזוּ לְפָנָיו.[2] וּשְׁמוֹ מְרוֹמַם עַל כָּל בְּרָכָה וּתְהִלָּה.[3] בָּרוּךְ שֵׁם כְּבוֹד מַלְכוּתוֹ לְעוֹלָם וָעֶד. יְהִי שֵׁם יהוה מְבֹרָךְ, מֵעַתָּה וְעַד עוֹלָם.[4]

Psalm 93

יהוה מָלָךְ *HASHEM will have reigned, He will have donned grandeur; He will have donned might and girded Himself; even firmed the world that it should not falter. Your throne was established from of old; eternal are You. Like rivers they raised, O HASHEM, like rivers they raised their voice; like rivers they shall raise their destructiveness.* Chazzan– *More than the roars of many waters, mightier than the waves of the sea — You are mighty on high, HASHEM. Your testimonies are exceedingly trustworthy about Your House, the Sacred Dwelling — O HASHEM, may it be for long days.*

MOURNER'S KADDISH

Mourners recite the Mourner's *Kaddish* (see *Laws* §81-83).

יִתְגַּדַּל *May His great Name grow exalted and sanctified* (Cong.– *Amen.*) *in the world that He created as He willed. May He give reign to His kingship in your lifetimes and in your days, and in the lifetimes of the entire Family of Israel, swiftly and soon. Now respond: Amen.*

(Cong.– *Amen. May His great Name be blessed forever and ever.*)

May His great Name be blessed forever and ever.

Blessed, praised, glorified, exalted, extolled, mighty, upraised, and lauded be the Name of the Holy One, Blessed is He (Cong.– *Blessed is He*) *— beyond any blessing and song, praise and consolation that are uttered in the world. Now respond: Amen.* (Cong. – *Amen.*)

May there be abundant peace from Heaven, and life, upon us and upon all Israel. Now respond: Amen. (Cong.– *Amen.*)

Take three steps back. Bow left and say, *'He Who makes peace . . .';* bow right and say, *'may He . . .';* bow forward and say, *'and upon all Israel . . .'* Remain standing in place for a few moments, then take three steps forward.

He Who makes peace in His heights, may He make peace upon us, and upon all Israel. Now respond: Amen. (Cong.– *Amen.*)

MAARIV FOR THE SABBATH OF CHOL HAMOED

In some congregations the *chazzan* chants a melody during his recitation of *Borchu,* so that the congregation can then recite *'Blessed, praised . . .'*

Chazzan bows at *'Bless,'* and straightens up at *'HASHEM.'*

Bless HASHEM, the blessed One.

Congregation, followed by *chazzan,* responds, bowing at *'Blessed'* and straightening up at *'HASHEM.'*

Blessed is HASHEM, the blessed One, for all eternity.

Blessed, praised, glorified, exalted and upraised is the Name of the King Who rules over kings — the Holy One, Blessed is He. For He is the First and He is the Last and aside from Him there is no god.[1] *Extol Him — Who rides the highest heavens — with His Name, YAH, and exult before Him.*[2] *His Name is exalted beyond every blessing and praise.*[3] *Blessed is the Name of His glorious kingdom for all eternity. Blessed be the Name of HASHEM from this time and forever.*[4]

(1) Cf. *Isaiah* 44:6. (2) *Psalms* 68:5. (3) Cf. *Nechemiah* 9:5. (4) *Psalms* 113:2.

ברכות קריאת שמע

בָּרוּךְ אַתָּה יהוה אֱלֹהֵינוּ מֶלֶךְ הָעוֹלָם, אֲשֶׁר בִּדְבָרוֹ מַעֲרִיב עֲרָבִים, בְּחָכְמָה פּוֹתֵחַ שְׁעָרִים, וּבִתְבוּנָה מְשַׁנֶּה עִתִּים, וּמַחֲלִיף אֶת הַזְּמַנִּים, וּמְסַדֵּר אֶת הַכּוֹכָבִים בְּמִשְׁמְרוֹתֵיהֶם בָּרָקִיעַ כִּרְצוֹנוֹ. בּוֹרֵא יוֹם וָלָיְלָה, גּוֹלֵל אוֹר מִפְּנֵי חֹשֶׁךְ וְחֹשֶׁךְ מִפְּנֵי אוֹר. וּמַעֲבִיר יוֹם וּמֵבִיא לָיְלָה, וּמַבְדִּיל בֵּין יוֹם וּבֵין לָיְלָה, יהוה צְבָאוֹת שְׁמוֹ. ❖ אֵל חַי וְקַיָּם, תָּמִיד יִמְלוֹךְ עָלֵינוּ, לְעוֹלָם וָעֶד. בָּרוּךְ אַתָּה יהוה, הַמַּעֲרִיב עֲרָבִים. (Cong. – אָמֵן.)

אַהֲבַת עוֹלָם בֵּית יִשְׂרָאֵל עַמְּךָ אָהָבְתָּ. תּוֹרָה וּמִצְוֹת, חֻקִּים וּמִשְׁפָּטִים, אוֹתָנוּ לִמַּדְתָּ. עַל כֵּן יהוה אֱלֹהֵינוּ, בְּשָׁכְבֵנוּ וּבְקוּמֵנוּ נָשִׂיחַ בְּחֻקֶּיךָ, וְנִשְׂמַח בְּדִבְרֵי תוֹרָתֶךָ, וּבְמִצְוֹתֶיךָ לְעוֹלָם וָעֶד. ❖ כִּי הֵם חַיֵּינוּ, וְאֹרֶךְ יָמֵינוּ, וּבָהֶם נֶהְגֶּה יוֹמָם וָלָיְלָה. וְאַהֲבָתְךָ, אַל תָּסִיר מִמֶּנּוּ לְעוֹלָמִים. בָּרוּךְ אַתָּה יהוה, אוֹהֵב עַמּוֹ יִשְׂרָאֵל. (Cong. – אָמֵן.)

שמע

Immediately before its recitation concentrate on fulfilling the positive commandment of reciting the *Shema* twice daily. It is important to enunciate each word clearly and not to run words together. For this reason, vertical lines have been placed between two words that are prone to be slurred into one and are not separated by a comma or a hyphen. See *Laws* §40-52.

When praying without a *minyan*, begin with the following three-word formula:

אֵל מֶלֶךְ נֶאֱמָן.

Recite the first verse aloud, with the right hand covering the eyes, and concentrate intently upon accepting God's absolute sovereignty.

שְׁמַע | יִשְׂרָאֵל, יהוה | אֱלֹהֵינוּ, יהוה | אֶחָד:

In an undertone – בָּרוּךְ שֵׁם כְּבוֹד מַלְכוּתוֹ לְעוֹלָם וָעֶד.

While reciting the first paragraph (דברים ו:ה-ט), concentrate on accepting the commandment to love God.

וְאָהַבְתָּ אֵת | יהוה | אֱלֹהֶיךָ, בְּכָל־לְבָבְךָ, וּבְכָל־נַפְשְׁךָ, וּבְכָל־מְאֹדֶךָ: וְהָיוּ הַדְּבָרִים הָאֵלֶּה, אֲשֶׁר | אָנֹכִי מְצַוְּךָ הַיּוֹם, עַל־לְבָבֶךָ: וְשִׁנַּנְתָּם לְבָנֶיךָ, וְדִבַּרְתָּ בָּם, בְּשִׁבְתְּךָ בְּבֵיתֶךָ, וּבְלֶכְתְּךָ בַדֶּרֶךְ, וּבְשָׁכְבְּךָ וּבְקוּמֶךָ: וּקְשַׁרְתָּם לְאוֹת | עַל־יָדֶךָ, וְהָיוּ לְטֹטָפֹת בֵּין | עֵינֶיךָ: וּכְתַבְתָּם | עַל־מְזֻזוֹת בֵּיתֶךָ, וּבִשְׁעָרֶיךָ:

While reciting the second paragraph (דברים יא:יג-כא), concentrate on accepting all the commandments and the concept of reward and punishment.

וְהָיָה, אִם־שָׁמֹעַ תִּשְׁמְעוּ אֶל־מִצְוֹתַי, אֲשֶׁר | אָנֹכִי מְצַוֶּה | אֶתְכֶם הַיּוֹם, לְאַהֲבָה אֶת־יהוה | אֱלֹהֵיכֶם וּלְעָבְדוֹ, בְּכָל־לְבַבְכֶם, וּבְכָל־נַפְשְׁכֶם: וְנָתַתִּי מְטַר־אַרְצְכֶם בְּעִתּוֹ, יוֹרֶה

BLESSINGS OF THE SHEMA

בָּרוּךְ *Blessed are You, HASHEM, our God, King of the universe, Who by His word brings on evenings, with wisdom opens gates, with understanding alters periods, changes the seasons, and orders the stars in their heavenly constellations as He wills. He creates day and night, removing light before darkness and darkness before light. He causes day to pass and brings night, and separates between day and night — HASHEM, Master of Legions, is His Name.* Chazzan— *May the living and enduring God continuously reign over us, for all eternity. Blessed are You, HASHEM, Who brings on evenings.* (Cong.— *Amen.*)

אַהֲבַת *With an eternal love have You loved the House of Israel, Your nation. Torah and commandments, decrees and ordinances have You taught us. Therefore HASHEM, our God, upon our retiring and arising, we will discuss Your decrees and we will rejoice with the words of Your Torah and with Your commandments for all eternity.* Chazzan— *For they are our life and the length of our days and about them we will meditate day and night. May You not remove Your love from us forever. Blessed are You, HASHEM, Who loves His nation Israel.* (Cong.— *Amen.*)

THE SHEMA

Immediately before its recitation concentrate on fulfilling the positive commandment of reciting the *Shema* twice daily. It is important to enunciate each word clearly and not to run words together. See *Laws* §40-52.

When praying without a *minyan,* begin with the following three-word formula:

God, trustworthy King.

Recite the first verse aloud, with the right hand covering the eyes, and concentrate intently upon accepting God's absolute sovereignty.

Hear, O Israel: HASHEM is our God, HASHEM, the One and Only.[1]

In an undertone— *Blessed is the Name of His glorious kingdom for all eternity.*

While reciting the first paragraph (*Deuteronomy* 6:5-9), concentrate on accepting the commandment to love God.

וְאָהַבְתָּ *You shall love HASHEM, your God, with all your heart, with all your soul and with all your resources. Let these matters that I command you today be upon your heart. Teach them thoroughly to your children and speak of them while you sit in your home, while you walk on the way, when you retire and when you arise. Bind them as a sign upon your arm and let them be tefillin between your eyes. And write them on the doorposts of your house and upon your gates.*

While reciting the second paragraph (*Deuteronomy* 11:13-21), concentrate on accepting all the commandments and the concept of reward and punishment.

וְהָיָה *And it will come to pass that if you continually hearken to My commandments that I command you today, to love HASHEM, your God, and to serve Him, with all your heart and with all your soul — then I will provide rain for your land in its proper time, the early*

(1) *Deuteronomy* 6:4.

וּמַלְקוֹשׁ, וְאָסַפְתָּ דְגָנֶךָ וְתִירֹשְׁךָ וְיִצְהָרֶךָ: וְנָתַתִּי | עֵשֶׂב | בְּשָׂדְךָ לִבְהֶמְתֶּךָ, וְאָכַלְתָּ וְשָׂבָעְתָּ: הִשָּׁמְרוּ לָכֶם, פֶּן־יִפְתֶּה לְבַבְכֶם, וְסַרְתֶּם וַעֲבַדְתֶּם | אֱלֹהִים | אֲחֵרִים, וְהִשְׁתַּחֲוִיתֶם לָהֶם: וְחָרָה | אַף־יהוה בָּכֶם, וְעָצַר | אֶת־הַשָּׁמַיִם, וְלֹא־יִהְיֶה מָטָר, וְהָאֲדָמָה לֹא תִתֵּן אֶת־יְבוּלָהּ, וַאֲבַדְתֶּם | מְהֵרָה מֵעַל הָאָרֶץ הַטֹּבָה | אֲשֶׁר | יהוה נֹתֵן לָכֶם: וְשַׂמְתֶּם | אֶת־דְּבָרַי | אֵלֶּה, עַל־לְבַבְכֶם וְעַל־נַפְשְׁכֶם, וּקְשַׁרְתֶּם | אֹתָם לְאוֹת | עַל־יֶדְכֶם, וְהָיוּ לְטוֹטָפֹת בֵּין | עֵינֵיכֶם: וְלִמַּדְתֶּם | אֹתָם | אֶת־בְּנֵיכֶם, לְדַבֵּר בָּם, בְּשִׁבְתְּךָ בְּבֵיתֶךָ, וּבְלֶכְתְּךָ בַדֶּרֶךְ, וּבְשָׁכְבְּךָ וּבְקוּמֶךָ: וּכְתַבְתָּם | עַל־מְזוּזוֹת בֵּיתֶךָ, וּבִשְׁעָרֶיךָ: לְמַעַן | יִרְבּוּ | יְמֵיכֶם וִימֵי בְנֵיכֶם, עַל הָאֲדָמָה | אֲשֶׁר נִשְׁבַּע | יהוה לַאֲבֹתֵיכֶם לָתֵת לָהֶם, כִּימֵי הַשָּׁמַיִם | עַל־הָאָרֶץ:

במדבר טו:לז-מא

וַיֹּאמֶר | יהוה | אֶל־מֹשֶׁה לֵּאמֹר: דַּבֵּר | אֶל־בְּנֵי | יִשְׂרָאֵל, וְאָמַרְתָּ אֲלֵהֶם, וְעָשׂוּ לָהֶם צִיצִת, עַל־כַּנְפֵי בִגְדֵיהֶם לְדֹרֹתָם, וְנָתְנוּ | עַל־צִיצִת הַכָּנָף, פְּתִיל תְּכֵלֶת: וְהָיָה לָכֶם לְצִיצִת, וּרְאִיתֶם | אֹתוֹ, וּזְכַרְתֶּם | אֶת־כָּל־מִצְוֹת | יהוה, וַעֲשִׂיתֶם | אֹתָם, וְלֹא תָתוּרוּ | אַחֲרֵי לְבַבְכֶם וְאַחֲרֵי | עֵינֵיכֶם, אֲשֶׁר־אַתֶּם זֹנִים | אַחֲרֵיהֶם: לְמַעַן תִּזְכְּרוּ, וַעֲשִׂיתֶם | אֶת־כָּל־מִצְוֹתָי, וִהְיִיתֶם קְדֹשִׁים לֵאלֹהֵיכֶם: אֲנִי יהוה | אֱלֹהֵיכֶם, אֲשֶׁר הוֹצֵאתִי | אֶתְכֶם | מֵאֶרֶץ מִצְרַיִם, לִהְיוֹת לָכֶם לֵאלֹהִים, אֲנִי | יהוה | אֱלֹהֵיכֶם: אֱמֶת —

Concentrate on fulfilling the commandment of remembering the Exodus from Egypt.

Although the word אֱמֶת belongs to the next paragraph, it is appended to the conclusion of the previous one, as explained in the commentary on page 50.

יהוה אֱלֹהֵיכֶם אֱמֶת. – *Chazzan* repeats

וֶאֱמוּנָה כָּל זֹאת, וְקַיָּם עָלֵינוּ, כִּי הוּא יהוה אֱלֹהֵינוּ וְאֵין זוּלָתוֹ, וַאֲנַחְנוּ יִשְׂרָאֵל עַמּוֹ. הַפּוֹדֵנוּ מִיַּד מְלָכִים, מַלְכֵּנוּ הַגּוֹאֲלֵנוּ מִכַּף כָּל הֶעָרִיצִים. הָאֵל הַנִּפְרָע לָנוּ מִצָּרֵינוּ, וְהַמְשַׁלֵּם גְּמוּל לְכָל אֹיְבֵי נַפְשֵׁנוּ. הָעֹשֶׂה גְדֹלוֹת עַד אֵין חֵקֶר, וְנִפְלָאוֹת עַד אֵין מִסְפָּר.[1] הַשָּׂם נַפְשֵׁנוּ בַּחַיִּים, וְלֹא נָתַן לַמּוֹט רַגְלֵנוּ.[2] הַמַּדְרִיכֵנוּ עַל בָּמוֹת אוֹיְבֵינוּ, וַיָּרֶם קַרְנֵנוּ עַל כָּל שֹׂנְאֵינוּ. הָעֹשֶׂה לָּנוּ נִסִּים וּנְקָמָה בְּפַרְעֹה, אוֹתוֹת וּמוֹפְתִים בְּאַדְמַת בְּנֵי חָם. הַמַּכֶּה בְעֶבְרָתוֹ כָּל בְּכוֹרֵי מִצְרָיִם, וַיּוֹצֵא אֶת עַמּוֹ יִשְׂרָאֵל מִתּוֹכָם לְחֵרוּת עוֹלָם. הַמַּעֲבִיר בָּנָיו בֵּין גִּזְרֵי יַם סוּף, אֶת רוֹדְפֵיהֶם וְאֶת

and late rains, that you may gather in your grain, your wine, and your oil. I will provide grass in your field for your cattle and you will eat and be satisfied. Beware lest your heart be seduced and you turn astray and serve gods of others and bow to them. Then the wrath of HASHEM will blaze against you. He will restrain the heaven so there will be no rain and the ground will not yield its produce. And you will swiftly be banished from the goodly land which HASHEM gives you. Place these words of Mine upon your heart and upon your soul; bind them for a sign upon your arm and let them be tefillin between your eyes. Teach them to your children, to discuss them, while you sit in your home, while you walk on the way, when you retire and when you arise. And write them on the doorposts of your house and upon your gates. In order to prolong your days and the days of your children upon the ground that HASHEM has sworn to your ancestors to give them, like the days of the heaven on the earth.

Numbers 15:37-41

וַיֹּאמֶר *And HASHEM said to Moses saying: Speak to the Children of Israel and say to them that they are to make themselves tzitzis on the corners of their garments, throughout their generations. And they are to place upon the tzitzis of each corner a thread of techeiles. And it shall constitute tzitzis for you, that you may see it and remember all the commandments of HASHEM and perform them; and not explore after your heart and after your eyes after which you stray. So that you may remember and perform all My commandments; and be holy to your God. I am HASHEM, your God, Who has removed you from the land of Egypt to be a God to you; I am HASHEM your God — it is true —*

Concentrate on fulfilling the commandment of remembering the Exodus from Egypt.

Although the word אֱמֶת, *'it is true,'* belongs to the next paragraph, it is appended to the conclusion of the previous one, as explained in the commentary on page 50.

Chazzan repeats: **HASHEM, your God, is true.**

וֶאֱמוּנָה *And faithful is all this, and it is firmly established for us that He is HASHEM our God, and there is none but Him, and we are Israel, His nation. He redeems us from the power of kings, our King Who delivers us from the hand of all the cruel tyrants. He is the God Who exacts vengeance for us from our foes and Who brings just retribution upon all enemies of our soul; Who performs great deeds that are beyond comprehension, and wonders beyond number.*[1] *Who set our soul in life and did not allow our foot to falter.*[2] *Who led us upon the heights of our enemies and raised our pride above all who hate us; Who wrought for us miracles and vengeance upon Pharaoh; signs and wonders on the land of the offspring of Ham; Who struck with His anger all the firstborn of Egypt and removed His nation Israel from their midst to eternal freedom; Who brought His children through the split parts of the Sea of Reeds while those who pursued them and*

(1) *Job* 9:10. (2) *Psalms* 66:9.

שׂוֹנְאֵיהֶם בִּתְהוֹמוֹת טִבַּע. וְרָאוּ בָנָיו גְּבוּרָתוֹ, שִׁבְּחוּ וְהוֹדוּ לִשְׁמוֹ. ❖ וּמַלְכוּתוֹ בְּרָצוֹן קִבְּלוּ עֲלֵיהֶם. מֹשֶׁה וּבְנֵי יִשְׂרָאֵל לְךָ עָנוּ שִׁירָה, בְּשִׂמְחָה רַבָּה, וְאָמְרוּ כֻלָּם:

מִי כָמְכָה בָּאֵלִם יהוה, מִי כָּמְכָה נֶאְדָּר בַּקֹּדֶשׁ, נוֹרָא תְהִלֹּת, עֹשֵׂה פֶלֶא.[1] ❖ מַלְכוּתְךָ רָאוּ בָנֶיךָ בּוֹקֵעַ יָם לִפְנֵי מֹשֶׁה, זֶה אֵלִי[2] עָנוּ וְאָמְרוּ:

יהוה יִמְלֹךְ לְעֹלָם וָעֶד.[3] ❖ וְנֶאֱמַר: כִּי פָדָה יהוה אֶת יַעֲקֹב, וּגְאָלוֹ מִיַּד חָזָק מִמֶּנּוּ.[4] בָּרוּךְ אַתָּה יהוה, גָּאַל יִשְׂרָאֵל. (Cong.– אָמֵן.)

הַשְׁכִּיבֵנוּ יהוה אֱלֹהֵינוּ לְשָׁלוֹם, וְהַעֲמִידֵנוּ מַלְכֵּנוּ לְחַיִּים, וּפְרוֹשׂ עָלֵינוּ סֻכַּת שְׁלוֹמֶךָ, וְתַקְּנֵנוּ בְּעֵצָה טוֹבָה מִלְּפָנֶיךָ, וְהוֹשִׁיעֵנוּ לְמַעַן שְׁמֶךָ. וְהָגֵן בַּעֲדֵנוּ, וְהָסֵר מֵעָלֵינוּ אוֹיֵב, דֶּבֶר, וְחֶרֶב, וְרָעָב, וְיָגוֹן, וְהָסֵר שָׂטָן מִלְּפָנֵינוּ וּמֵאַחֲרֵינוּ, וּבְצֵל כְּנָפֶיךָ תַּסְתִּירֵנוּ,[5] כִּי אֵל שׁוֹמְרֵנוּ וּמַצִּילֵנוּ אָתָּה, כִּי אֵל מֶלֶךְ חַנּוּן וְרַחוּם אָתָּה.[6] ❖ וּשְׁמוֹר צֵאתֵנוּ וּבוֹאֵנוּ, לְחַיִּים וּלְשָׁלוֹם מֵעַתָּה וְעַד עוֹלָם.[7] וּפְרוֹשׂ עָלֵינוּ סֻכַּת שְׁלוֹמֶךָ. בָּרוּךְ אַתָּה יהוה, הַפּוֹרֵשׂ סֻכַּת שָׁלוֹם עָלֵינוּ וְעַל כָּל עַמּוֹ יִשְׂרָאֵל וְעַל יְרוּשָׁלָיִם. (Cong.– אָמֵן.)

Congregation rises and remains standing until after *Shemoneh Esrei.*
The congregation, followed by the *chazzan,* recites:

וְשָׁמְרוּ בְנֵי יִשְׂרָאֵל אֶת הַשַּׁבָּת, לַעֲשׂוֹת אֶת הַשַּׁבָּת לְדֹרֹתָם בְּרִית עוֹלָם. בֵּינִי וּבֵין בְּנֵי יִשְׂרָאֵל אוֹת הִיא לְעֹלָם, כִּי שֵׁשֶׁת יָמִים עָשָׂה יהוה אֶת הַשָּׁמַיִם וְאֶת הָאָרֶץ, וּבַיּוֹם הַשְּׁבִיעִי שָׁבַת וַיִּנָּפַשׁ.[8]

The *chazzan* recites חֲצִי קַדִּישׁ.

יִתְגַּדַּל וְיִתְקַדַּשׁ שְׁמֵהּ רַבָּא. (Cong.– אָמֵן.) בְּעָלְמָא דִּי בְרָא כִרְעוּתֵהּ, וְיַמְלִיךְ מַלְכוּתֵהּ, בְּחַיֵּיכוֹן וּבְיוֹמֵיכוֹן וּבְחַיֵּי דְכָל בֵּית יִשְׂרָאֵל, בַּעֲגָלָא וּבִזְמַן קָרִיב. וְאִמְרוּ: אָמֵן.

(Cong.– אָמֵן. יְהֵא שְׁמֵהּ רַבָּא מְבָרַךְ לְעָלַם וּלְעָלְמֵי עָלְמַיָּא.)

יְהֵא שְׁמֵהּ רַבָּא מְבָרַךְ לְעָלַם וּלְעָלְמֵי עָלְמַיָּא.

יִתְבָּרַךְ וְיִשְׁתַּבַּח וְיִתְפָּאַר וְיִתְרוֹמַם וְיִתְנַשֵּׂא וְיִתְהַדָּר וְיִתְעַלֶּה וְיִתְהַלָּל שְׁמֵהּ דְּקֻדְשָׁא בְּרִיךְ הוּא (Cong.– בְּרִיךְ הוּא) – לְעֵלָּא מִן כָּל בִּרְכָתָא וְשִׁירָתָא תֻּשְׁבְּחָתָא וְנֶחֱמָתָא, דַּאֲמִירָן בְּעָלְמָא. וְאִמְרוּ: אָמֵן. (Cong.– אָמֵן.)

hated them He caused to sink into the depths. When His children perceived His power, they lauded and gave grateful praise to His Name. Chazzan– *And His Kingship they accepted upon themselves willingly. Moses and the Children of Israel raised their voices to You in song with abundant gladness — and said unanimously:*

מִי כָמְכָה *Who is like You among the heavenly powers,* HASHEM! *Who is like You, mighty in holiness, too awesome for praise, doing wonders!*[1] Chazzan– *Your children beheld Your majesty, as You split the sea before Moses: 'This is my God!'*[2] *they exclaimed, then they said:*

יהוה *'*HASHEM *shall reign for all eternity!'*[3] Chazzan– *And it is further said: 'For* HASHEM *has redeemed Jacob and delivered him from a power mightier than he.'*[4] *Blessed are You,* HASHEM, *Who redeemed Israel.* (Cong.– *Amen.)*

הַשְׁכִּיבֵנוּ *Lay us down to sleep,* HASHEM *our God, in peace, raise us erect, our King, to life; and spread over us the shelter of Your peace. Set us aright with good counsel from before Your Presence, and save us for Your Name's sake. Shield us, remove from us foe, plague, sword, famine, and woe; and remove spiritual impediment from before us and behind us, and in the shadow of Your wings shelter us*[5] *— for God Who protects and rescues us are You; for God, the Gracious and Compassionate King, are You.*[6] Chazzan– *Safeguard our going and coming, for life and for peace from now to eternity.*[7] *And spread over us the shelter of Your peace. Blessed are You,* HASHEM, *Who spreads the shelter of peace upon us, upon all of His people Israel and upon Jerusalem.* (Cong.– *Amen.)*

Congregation rises and remains standing until after *Shemoneh Esrei.*

The congregation, followed by the *chazzan,* recites:

וְשָׁמְרוּ *And the Children of Israel shall keep the Sabbath, to make the Sabbath an eternal covenant for their generations. Between Me and the Children of Israel it is a sign forever that in six days* HASHEM *made heaven and earth, and on the seventh day He rested and was refreshed.*[8]

The *chazzan* recites Half-*Kaddish.*

יִתְגַּדַּל *May His great Name grow exalted and sanctified* (Cong.– *Amen.) in the world that He created as He willed. May He give reign to His kingship in your lifetimes and in your days, and in the lifetimes of the entire Family of Israel, swiftly and soon. Now respond: Amen.*

(Cong.– *Amen. May His great Name be blessed forever and ever.)*

May His great Name be blessed forever and ever.

Blessed, praised, glorified, exalted, extolled, mighty, upraised, and lauded be the Name of the Holy One, Blessed is He (Cong.– *Blessed is He) — beyond any blessing and song, praise and consolation that are uttered in the world. Now respond: Amen.* (Cong.– *Amen.)*

---

(1) *Exodus* 15:11. (2) 15:2. (3) 15:18. (4) *Jeremiah* 31:10. (5) Cf. *Psalms* 17:8.
(6) Cf. *Nechemiah* 9:31. (7) Cf. *Psalms* 121:8. (8) *Exodus* 31:16-17.

שמונה עשרה – עמידה

Take three steps backward, then three steps forward. Remain standing with the feet together while reciting *Shemoneh Esrei*. Recite it with quiet devotion and without interruption, verbal or otherwise. Although its recitation should not be audible to others, one must pray loudly enough to hear himself.

אֲדֹנָי שְׂפָתַי תִּפְתָּח, וּפִי יַגִּיד תְּהִלָּתֶךָ.[1]

אבות

Bend the knees at בָּרוּךְ; bow at אַתָּה; straighten up at ה׳.

בָּרוּךְ אַתָּה יהוה אֱלֹהֵינוּ וֵאלֹהֵי אֲבוֹתֵינוּ, אֱלֹהֵי אַבְרָהָם, אֱלֹהֵי יִצְחָק, וֵאלֹהֵי יַעֲקֹב, הָאֵל הַגָּדוֹל הַגִּבּוֹר וְהַנּוֹרָא, אֵל עֶלְיוֹן, גּוֹמֵל חֲסָדִים טוֹבִים וְקוֹנֵה הַכֹּל, וְזוֹכֵר חַסְדֵי אָבוֹת, וּמֵבִיא גוֹאֵל לִבְנֵי בְנֵיהֶם, לְמַעַן שְׁמוֹ בְּאַהֲבָה. מֶלֶךְ עוֹזֵר וּמוֹשִׁיעַ וּמָגֵן.

Bend the knees at בָּרוּךְ; bow at אַתָּה; straighten up at ה׳.

בָּרוּךְ אַתָּה יהוה, מָגֵן אַבְרָהָם.

גבורות

אַתָּה גִּבּוֹר לְעוֹלָם אֲדֹנָי, מְחַיֵּה מֵתִים אַתָּה, רַב לְהוֹשִׁיעַ. מְכַלְכֵּל חַיִּים בְּחֶסֶד, מְחַיֵּה מֵתִים בְּרַחֲמִים רַבִּים, סוֹמֵךְ נוֹפְלִים, וְרוֹפֵא חוֹלִים, וּמַתִּיר אֲסוּרִים, וּמְקַיֵּם אֱמוּנָתוֹ לִישֵׁנֵי עָפָר. מִי כָמוֹךָ בַּעַל גְּבוּרוֹת, וּמִי דּוֹמֶה לָּךְ, מֶלֶךְ מֵמִית וּמְחַיֶּה וּמַצְמִיחַ יְשׁוּעָה. וְנֶאֱמָן אַתָּה לְהַחֲיוֹת מֵתִים. בָּרוּךְ אַתָּה יהוה, מְחַיֵּה הַמֵּתִים.

קדושת השם

אַתָּה קָדוֹשׁ וְשִׁמְךָ קָדוֹשׁ, וּקְדוֹשִׁים בְּכָל יוֹם יְהַלְלוּךָ סֶּלָה. בָּרוּךְ אַתָּה יהוה, הָאֵל הַקָּדוֹשׁ.

קדושת היום

אַתָּה קִדַּשְׁתָּ אֶת יוֹם הַשְּׁבִיעִי לִשְׁמֶךָ,* תַּכְלִית מַעֲשֵׂה שָׁמַיִם וָאָרֶץ, וּבֵרַכְתּוֹ מִכָּל הַיָּמִים, וְקִדַּשְׁתּוֹ מִכָּל הַזְּמַנִּים, וְכֵן כָּתוּב בְּתוֹרָתֶךָ:

וַיְכֻלּוּ הַשָּׁמַיִם וְהָאָרֶץ* וְכָל צְבָאָם. וַיְכַל אֱלֹהִים בַּיּוֹם הַשְּׁבִיעִי מְלַאכְתּוֹ אֲשֶׁר עָשָׂה, וַיִּשְׁבֹּת בַּיּוֹם הַשְּׁבִיעִי מִכָּל

SHEMONEH ESREI OF SHABBOS / AMIDAH

The *Amidah* of the Sabbath and *Yom Tov* should have been identical to the weekday one, with the inclusion of an appropriate paragraph indicating the holiness of the day, as is done on Rosh Chodesh and *Chol HaMoed*. The Sages, however, wished to make the Sabbath Festival prayers simpler and less burdensome than they would be if we had to beseech God for the entire catalogue of our personal and national needs. Therefore they omitted the middle thirteen blessings, and replaced them with a single blessing known as קְדֻשַּׁת הַיּוֹם, *Sanctity of the Day* (*Berachos* 21a).

Because of the fact that the entire weekday *Shemoneh Esrei* would have been appropriate for the holy days as well, in the event someone erred in his prayers and began to recite the weekday

SHEMONEH ESREI – AMIDAH

Take three steps backward, then three steps forward. Remain standing with the feet together while reciting *Shemoneh Esrei*. Recite it with quiet devotion and without interruption, verbal or otherwise. Although its recitation should not be audible to others, one must pray loudly enough to hear himself.

My Lord, open my lips, that my mouth may declare Your praise.[1]

PATRIARCHS

Bend the knees at *'Blessed'*; bow at *'You'*; straighten up at *'HASHEM.'*

בָּרוּךְ *Blessed are You, HASHEM, our God and the God of our forefathers, God of Abraham, God of Isaac, and God of Jacob; the great, mighty, and awesome God, the supreme God, Who bestows beneficial kindnesses and creates everything, Who recalls the kindnesses of the Patriarchs and brings a Redeemer to their children's children, for His Name's sake, with love. O King, Helper, Savior, and Shield.*

Bend the knees at *'Blessed'*; bow at *'You'*; straighten up at 'HASHEM.'

Blessed are You, HASHEM, Shield of Abraham.

GOD'S MIGHT

אַתָּה *You are eternally mighty, my Lord, the Resuscitator of the dead are You; abundantly able to save. He sustains the living with kindness, resuscitates the dead with abundant mercy, supports the fallen, heals the sick, releases the confined, and maintains His faith to those asleep in the dust. Who is like You, O Master of mighty deeds, and who is comparable to You, O King Who causes death and restores life and makes salvation sprout! And You are faithful to resuscitate the dead. Blessed are You, HASHEM, Who resuscitates the dead.*

HOLINESS OF GOD'S NAME

אַתָּה *You are holy and Your Name is holy, and holy ones praise You every day, forever. Blessed are You, HASHEM, the holy God.*

SANCTIFICATION OF THE DAY

אַתָּה *You sanctified the seventh day for Your Name's sake,* the conclusion of the creation of heaven and earth. Of all days, You blessed it; and of all seasons, You sanctified it — and so it is written in Your Torah:*

וַיְכֻלּוּ *Thus the heaven and the earth were finished,* and all their legion. On the seventh day God completed His work which He had done, and He abstained on the seventh day from all His*

(1) *Psalms* 51:17.

blessings on the Sabbath or *Yom Tov*, he should complete whatever blessing he has begun and then begin the appropriate blessing of קְדוּשַּׁת הַיּוֹם, *Sanctity of the Day (Orach Chaim* 268:2). In the case of the Sabbath eve *Maariv* this would be אַתָּה קִדַּשְׁתָּ.

קְדוּשַּׁת הַיּוֹם / Sanctification of the Day

אַתָּה קִדַּשְׁתָּ... לִשְׁמֶךָ — *You sanctified... for Your Name's sake.* God sanctified the Sabbath as an eternal reminder that He rested on that day *(Abudraham);* and He made it clear that we are not to regard it as a humanly legislated day of rest for personal convenience, but are to dedicate it to His service, *for* [His] *Name's sake (R' Munk).*

וַיְכֻלּוּ הַשָּׁמַיִם וְהָאָרֶץ — *Thus the heaven and the earth were finished.* The Talmud *(Shabbos* 119b) derives homiletically from this verse that whoever recites this passage is regarded as God's partner in Creation, because the word וַיְכֻלּוּ homiletically can be vocalized וַיְכַלּוּ, *and* **they** [i.e., God and everyone who acknowledges His Creation] *finished.* God's Creation would have fallen

מְלַאכְתּוֹ אֲשֶׁר עָשָׂה. וַיְבָרֶךְ אֱלֹהִים אֶת יוֹם הַשְּׁבִיעִי, וַיְקַדֵּשׁ אֹתוֹ, כִּי בוֹ שָׁבַת מִכָּל מְלַאכְתּוֹ, אֲשֶׁר בָּרָא אֱלֹהִים לַעֲשׂוֹת.*[1]

אֱלֹהֵינוּ וֵאלֹהֵי אֲבוֹתֵינוּ רְצֵה בִמְנוּחָתֵנוּ.* קַדְּשֵׁנוּ בְּמִצְוֹתֶיךָ,* וְתֵן חֶלְקֵנוּ בְּתוֹרָתֶךָ. שַׂבְּעֵנוּ מִטּוּבֶךָ, וְשַׂמְּחֵנוּ בִּישׁוּעָתֶךָ, וְטַהֵר לִבֵּנוּ לְעָבְדְּךָ בֶּאֱמֶת. וְהַנְחִילֵנוּ יהוה אֱלֹהֵינוּ בְּאַהֲבָה וּבְרָצוֹן שַׁבַּת קָדְשֶׁךָ, וְיָנוּחוּ בָהּ יִשְׂרָאֵל מְקַדְּשֵׁי שְׁמֶךָ. בָּרוּךְ אַתָּה יהוה, מְקַדֵּשׁ הַשַּׁבָּת.

עבודה

רְצֵה יהוה אֱלֹהֵינוּ בְּעַמְּךָ יִשְׂרָאֵל וּבִתְפִלָּתָם, וְהָשֵׁב אֶת הָעֲבוֹדָה לִדְבִיר בֵּיתֶךָ. וְאִשֵּׁי יִשְׂרָאֵל וּתְפִלָּתָם בְּאַהֲבָה תְקַבֵּל בְּרָצוֹן, וּתְהִי לְרָצוֹן תָּמִיד עֲבוֹדַת יִשְׂרָאֵל עַמֶּךָ.

[If the following paragraph is forgotten, repeat *Shemoneh Esrei*. See *Laws* §56.]

אֱלֹהֵינוּ וֵאלֹהֵי אֲבוֹתֵינוּ, יַעֲלֶה, וְיָבֹא, וְיַגִּיעַ, וְיֵרָאֶה, וְיֵרָצֶה, וְיִשָּׁמַע, וְיִפָּקֵד, וְיִזָּכֵר זִכְרוֹנֵנוּ וּפִקְדוֹנֵנוּ, וְזִכְרוֹן אֲבוֹתֵינוּ, וְזִכְרוֹן מָשִׁיחַ בֶּן דָּוִד עַבְדֶּךָ, וְזִכְרוֹן יְרוּשָׁלַיִם עִיר קָדְשֶׁךָ, וְזִכְרוֹן כָּל עַמְּךָ בֵּית יִשְׂרָאֵל לְפָנֶיךָ, לִפְלֵיטָה לְטוֹבָה לְחֵן וּלְחֶסֶד וּלְרַחֲמִים, לְחַיִּים וּלְשָׁלוֹם בְּיוֹם חַג הַמַּצּוֹת הַזֶּה. זָכְרֵנוּ יהוה אֱלֹהֵינוּ בּוֹ לְטוֹבָה, וּפָקְדֵנוּ בוֹ לִבְרָכָה, וְהוֹשִׁיעֵנוּ בוֹ לְחַיִּים. וּבִדְבַר יְשׁוּעָה וְרַחֲמִים, חוּס וְחָנֵּנוּ וְרַחֵם עָלֵינוּ וְהוֹשִׁיעֵנוּ, כִּי אֵלֶיךָ עֵינֵינוּ, כִּי אֵל מֶלֶךְ חַנּוּן וְרַחוּם אָתָּה.[2]

וְתֶחֱזֶינָה עֵינֵינוּ בְּשׁוּבְךָ לְצִיּוֹן בְּרַחֲמִים. בָּרוּךְ אַתָּה יהוה, הַמַּחֲזִיר שְׁכִינָתוֹ לְצִיּוֹן.

הודאה

Bow at מוֹדִים; straighten up at ה׳.

מוֹדִים אֲנַחְנוּ לָךְ שָׁאַתָּה הוּא יהוה אֱלֹהֵינוּ וֵאלֹהֵי אֲבוֹתֵינוּ לְעוֹלָם וָעֶד. צוּר חַיֵּינוּ, מָגֵן יִשְׁעֵנוּ אַתָּה הוּא לְדוֹר

---

short of its purpose unless man acknowledged Him as the Creator (*Maharsha*).

אֲשֶׁר בָּרָא אֱלֹהִים לַעֲשׂוֹת — *Which God created to make.* People can labor long and hard to *create* something — whether it is a house, a tool, or a business. Then it is up to them to *use* it properly. God created the world for the use of humanity; the *completion* of Creation, however, He entrusted to mankind. Now it is up *to us* to *use it* as He intended (*Chasam Sofer*).

אֱלֹהֵינוּ . . . רְצֵה בִמְנוּחָתֵנוּ — *O God . . . may You be pleased with our rest.* Even though we may concentrate more on relaxation and good food than we will on spiritual growth, we ask *work which He had done. God blessed the seventh day and sanctified it, because on it He had abstained from all His work which God created to make.*[*1]

אֱלֹהֵינוּ *Our God and the God of our forefathers, may You be pleased with our rest.* Sanctify us with Your commandments* and grant our share in Your Torah; satisfy us from Your goodness and gladden us with Your salvation, and purify our heart to serve You sincerely. O* HASHEM, *our God, with love and favor grant us Your holy Sabbath as a heritage and may Israel, the sanctifiers of Your Name, rest on it. Blessed are You,* HASHEM, *Who sanctifies the Sabbath.*

TEMPLE SERVICE

רְצֵה *Be favorable,* HASHEM, *our God, toward Your people Israel and their prayer and restore the service to the Holy of Holies of Your Temple. The fire-offerings of Israel and their prayer accept with love and favor, and may the service of Your people Israel always be favorable to You.*

[If the following paragraph is forgotten, repeat *Shemoneh Esrei.* See *Laws* §56.]

אֱלֹהֵינוּ *Our God and God of our forefathers, may there rise, come, reach, be noted, be favored, be heard, be considered, and be remembered — the remembrance and consideration of ourselves; the remembrance of our forefathers; the remembrance of Messiah, son of David, Your servant; the remembrance of Jerusalem, the City of Your Holiness, the remembrance of Your entire people the Family of Israel — before You, for deliverance, for goodness, for grace, for kindness, and for compassion, for life, and for peace on this day of the Festival of Matzos. Remember us on it,* HASHEM, *our God, for goodness; consider us on it for blessing; and help us on it for life. In the matter of salvation and compassion, pity, be gracious and compassionate with us and help us, for our eyes are turned to You, because You are God, the gracious and compassionate King.*[2]

וְתֶחֱזֶינָה *May our eyes behold Your return to Zion in compassion. Blessed are You,* HASHEM, *Who restores His Presence to Zion.*

THANKSGIVING [MODIM]

Bow at *'We gratefully thank You'*; straighten up at *'HASHEM.'*

מוֹדִים *We gratefully thank You, for it is You Who are* HASHEM, *our God and the God of our forefathers for all eternity; Rock of our lives, Shield of our salvation are You from generation to generation.*

(1) *Genesis* 2:1-3. (2) Cf. *Nechemiah* 9:31.

that You not be displeased by our human frailty (*Etz Yosef*).

קַדְּשֵׁנוּ בְּמִצְוֹתֶיךָ — *Sanctify us with Your commandments.* The *performance* of *mitzvos* in itself elevates a person and makes him more prone to absorb sanctity. Alternatively, the word קַדְּשֵׁנוּ can be related to קִדּוּשִׁין, *betrothal.* God has *betrothed* Israel, as it were, by allowing us to perform His commandments (*Abudraham*).

וָדוֹר. נוֹדֶה לְּךָ וּנְסַפֵּר תְּהִלָּתֶךָ[1] עַל חַיֵּינוּ הַמְּסוּרִים בְּיָדֶךָ, וְעַל נִשְׁמוֹתֵינוּ הַפְּקוּדוֹת לָךְ, וְעַל נִסֶּיךָ שֶׁבְּכָל יוֹם עִמָּנוּ, וְעַל נִפְלְאוֹתֶיךָ וְטוֹבוֹתֶיךָ שֶׁבְּכָל עֵת, עֶרֶב וָבֹקֶר וְצָהֳרָיִם. הַטּוֹב כִּי לֹא כָלוּ רַחֲמֶיךָ, וְהַמְּרַחֵם כִּי לֹא תַמּוּ חֲסָדֶיךָ,[2] מֵעוֹלָם קִוִּינוּ לָךְ.

וְעַל כֻּלָּם יִתְבָּרַךְ וְיִתְרוֹמַם שִׁמְךָ מַלְכֵּנוּ תָּמִיד לְעוֹלָם וָעֶד.

Bend the knees at בָּרוּךְ; bow at אַתָּה; straighten up at ה׳.

וְכֹל הַחַיִּים יוֹדוּךָ סֶּלָה, וִיהַלְלוּ אֶת שִׁמְךָ בֶּאֱמֶת, הָאֵל יְשׁוּעָתֵנוּ וְעֶזְרָתֵנוּ סֶלָה. בָּרוּךְ אַתָּה יהוה, הַטּוֹב שִׁמְךָ וּלְךָ נָאֶה לְהוֹדוֹת.

שלום

שָׁלוֹם רָב עַל יִשְׂרָאֵל עַמְּךָ תָּשִׂים לְעוֹלָם, כִּי אַתָּה הוּא מֶלֶךְ אָדוֹן לְכָל הַשָּׁלוֹם. וְטוֹב בְּעֵינֶיךָ לְבָרֵךְ אֶת עַמְּךָ יִשְׂרָאֵל, בְּכָל עֵת וּבְכָל שָׁעָה בִּשְׁלוֹמֶךָ. בָּרוּךְ אַתָּה יהוה, הַמְּבָרֵךְ אֶת עַמּוֹ יִשְׂרָאֵל בַּשָּׁלוֹם.

יִהְיוּ לְרָצוֹן אִמְרֵי פִי וְהֶגְיוֹן לִבִּי לְפָנֶיךָ, יהוה צוּרִי וְגֹאֲלִי.[3]

אֱלֹהַי, נְצוֹר לְשׁוֹנִי מֵרָע, וּשְׂפָתַי מִדַּבֵּר מִרְמָה,[4] וְלִמְקַלְלַי נַפְשִׁי תִדּוֹם, וְנַפְשִׁי כֶּעָפָר לַכֹּל תִּהְיֶה. פְּתַח לִבִּי בְּתוֹרָתֶךָ, וּבְמִצְוֹתֶיךָ תִּרְדּוֹף נַפְשִׁי. וְכֹל הַחוֹשְׁבִים עָלַי רָעָה, מְהֵרָה הָפֵר עֲצָתָם וְקַלְקֵל מַחֲשַׁבְתָּם. עֲשֵׂה לְמַעַן שְׁמֶךָ, עֲשֵׂה לְמַעַן יְמִינֶךָ, עֲשֵׂה לְמַעַן קְדֻשָּׁתֶךָ, עֲשֵׂה לְמַעַן תּוֹרָתֶךָ. לְמַעַן יֵחָלְצוּן יְדִידֶיךָ, הוֹשִׁיעָה יְמִינְךָ וַעֲנֵנִי.[5]

Some recite verses pertaining to their names here. See page 1143.

יִהְיוּ לְרָצוֹן אִמְרֵי פִי וְהֶגְיוֹן לִבִּי לְפָנֶיךָ, יהוה צוּרִי וְגֹאֲלִי.[3]

Bow and take three steps back. Bow left and say . . . עֹשֶׂה; bow right and say . . . הוּא יַעֲשֶׂה; bow forward and say וְעַל כָּל . . . אָמֵן.

עֹשֶׂה שָׁלוֹם בִּמְרוֹמָיו, הוּא יַעֲשֶׂה שָׁלוֹם עָלֵינוּ, וְעַל כָּל יִשְׂרָאֵל. וְאִמְרוּ: אָמֵן.

יְהִי רָצוֹן מִלְּפָנֶיךָ יהוה אֱלֹהֵינוּ וֵאלֹהֵי אֲבוֹתֵינוּ, שֶׁיִּבָּנֶה בֵּית הַמִּקְדָּשׁ בִּמְהֵרָה בְיָמֵינוּ, וְתֵן חֶלְקֵנוּ בְּתוֹרָתֶךָ. וְשָׁם נַעֲבָדְךָ בְּיִרְאָה, כִּימֵי עוֹלָם וּכְשָׁנִים קַדְמוֹנִיּוֹת. וְעָרְבָה לַיהוה מִנְחַת יְהוּדָה וִירוּשָׁלָיִם, כִּימֵי עוֹלָם וּכְשָׁנִים קַדְמוֹנִיּוֹת.[6]

SHEMONEH ESREI ENDS HERE.

Remain standing in place for at least a few moments before taking three steps forward.

We shall thank You and relate Your praise[1] — *for our lives, which are committed to Your power and for our souls that are entrusted to You; for Your miracles that are with us every day; and for Your wonders and favors in every season — evening, morning, and afternoon. The Beneficent One, for Your compassions were never exhausted, and the Compassionate One, for Your kindnesses never ended*[2] — *always have we put our hope in You.*

For all these, may Your Name be blessed and exalted, our King, continually forever and ever.

Bend the knees at *'Blessed'*; bow at *'You'*; straighten up at *'HASHEM.'*

Everything alive will gratefully acknowledge You, Selah! and praise Your Name sincerely, O God of our salvation and help, Selah! Blessed are You, HASHEM, Your Name is 'The Beneficent One' and to You it is fitting to give thanks.

PEACE

שָׁלוֹם *Establish abundant peace upon Your people Israel forever, for You are King, Master of all peace. May it be good in Your eyes to bless Your people Israel at every time and every hour with Your peace. Blessed are You, HASHEM, Who blesses His people Israel with peace.*

May the expressions of my mouth and the thoughts of my heart find favor before You, HASHEM, my Rock and my Redeemer.[3]

אֱלֹהַי *My God, guard my tongue from evil and my lips from speaking deceitfully.*[4] *To those who curse me, let my soul be silent; and let my soul be like dust to everyone. Open my heart to Your Torah, then my soul will pursue Your commandments. As for all those who design evil against me, speedily nullify their counsel and disrupt their design. Act for Your Name's sake; act for Your right hand's sake; act for Your sanctity's sake; act for Your Torah's sake. That Your beloved ones may be given rest; let Your right hand save, and respond to me.*[5]

Some recite verses pertaining to their names at this point. See page 1143.

May the expressions of my mouth and the thoughts of my heart find favor before You, HASHEM, my Rock and my Redeemer.[3] *He Who makes peace in His heights, may He make peace upon us, and upon all Israel. Now respond: Amen.*

Bow and take three steps back. Bow left and say, *'He Who makes peace . . .'*; bow right and say, *'may He make peace . . .'*; bow forward and say, *'and upon . . . Amen.'*

יְהִי רָצוֹן *May it be Your will, HASHEM, our God and the God of our forefathers, that the Holy Temple be rebuilt, speedily in our days. Grant us our share in Your Torah, and may we serve You there with reverence, as in days of old and in former years. Then the offering of Judah and Jerusalem will be pleasing to HASHEM, as in days of old and in former years.*[6]

SHEMONEH ESREI ENDS HERE.

Remain standing in place for at least a few moments before taking three steps forward.

(1) Cf. *Psalms* 79:13. (2) Cf. *Lamentations* 3:22. (3) *Psalms* 19:15.
(4) Cf. 34:14. (5) 60:7; 108:7. (6) *Malachi* 3:4.

All present stand and recite וַיְכֻלּוּ aloud in unison.
Conversation is forbidden until after the אָמֵן response to the blessing מְקַדֵּשׁ הַשַּׁבָּת (below).

וַיְכֻלּוּ הַשָּׁמַיִם וְהָאָרֶץ וְכָל צְבָאָם. וַיְכַל אֱלֹהִים בַּיּוֹם הַשְּׁבִיעִי מְלַאכְתּוֹ אֲשֶׁר עָשָׂה, וַיִּשְׁבֹּת בַּיּוֹם הַשְּׁבִיעִי מִכָּל מְלַאכְתּוֹ אֲשֶׁר עָשָׂה. וַיְבָרֶךְ אֱלֹהִים אֶת יוֹם הַשְּׁבִיעִי, וַיְקַדֵּשׁ אֹתוֹ, כִּי בוֹ שָׁבַת מִכָּל מְלַאכְתּוֹ, אֲשֶׁר בָּרָא אֱלֹהִים לַעֲשׂוֹת.[1]

ברכה מעין שבע

Chazzan continues:

בָּרוּךְ אַתָּה יהוה אֱלֹהֵינוּ וֵאלֹהֵי אֲבוֹתֵינוּ, אֱלֹהֵי אַבְרָהָם, אֱלֹהֵי יִצְחָק, וֵאלֹהֵי יַעֲקֹב, הָאֵל הַגָּדוֹל הַגִּבּוֹר וְהַנּוֹרָא, אֵל עֶלְיוֹן, קוֹנֵה שָׁמַיִם וָאָרֶץ.

Congregation, then *chazzan:*

מָגֵן אָבוֹת בִּדְבָרוֹ, מְחַיֵּה מֵתִים בְּמַאֲמָרוֹ, הָאֵל הַקָּדוֹשׁ שֶׁאֵין כָּמוֹהוּ, הַמֵּנִיחַ לְעַמּוֹ בְּיוֹם שַׁבַּת קָדְשׁוֹ, כִּי בָם רָצָה לְהָנִיחַ לָהֶם. לְפָנָיו נַעֲבֹד בְּיִרְאָה וָפַחַד, וְנוֹדֶה לִשְׁמוֹ בְּכָל יוֹם תָּמִיד מֵעֵין הַבְּרָכוֹת. אֵל הַהוֹדָאוֹת, אֲדוֹן הַשָּׁלוֹם, מְקַדֵּשׁ הַשַּׁבָּת וּמְבָרֵךְ שְׁבִיעִי, וּמֵנִיחַ בִּקְדֻשָּׁה לְעַם מְדֻשְּׁנֵי עֹנֶג, זֵכֶר לְמַעֲשֵׂה בְרֵאשִׁית.

Chazzan continues:

אֱלֹהֵינוּ וֵאלֹהֵי אֲבוֹתֵינוּ רְצֵה בִמְנוּחָתֵנוּ. קַדְּשֵׁנוּ בְּמִצְוֹתֶיךָ, וְתֵן חֶלְקֵנוּ בְּתוֹרָתֶךָ. שַׂבְּעֵנוּ מִטּוּבֶךָ, וְשַׂמְּחֵנוּ בִּישׁוּעָתֶךָ, וְטַהֵר לִבֵּנוּ לְעָבְדְּךָ בֶּאֱמֶת. וְהַנְחִילֵנוּ יהוה אֱלֹהֵינוּ בְּאַהֲבָה וּבְרָצוֹן שַׁבַּת קָדְשֶׁךָ, וְיָנוּחוּ בָהּ יִשְׂרָאֵל מְקַדְּשֵׁי שְׁמֶךָ. בָּרוּךְ אַתָּה יהוה, מְקַדֵּשׁ הַשַּׁבָּת. (Cong. – אָמֵן.)

The *chazzan* recites קַדִּישׁ שָׁלֵם.

יִתְגַּדַּל וְיִתְקַדַּשׁ שְׁמֵהּ רַבָּא. (Cong. – אָמֵן.) בְּעָלְמָא דִּי בְרָא כִרְעוּתֵהּ. וְיַמְלִיךְ מַלְכוּתֵהּ, בְּחַיֵּיכוֹן וּבְיוֹמֵיכוֹן וּבְחַיֵּי דְכָל בֵּית יִשְׂרָאֵל, בַּעֲגָלָא וּבִזְמַן קָרִיב. וְאִמְרוּ: אָמֵן.

(Cong. – אָמֵן. יְהֵא שְׁמֵהּ רַבָּא מְבָרַךְ לְעָלַם וּלְעָלְמֵי עָלְמַיָּא.)

יְהֵא שְׁמֵהּ רַבָּא מְבָרַךְ לְעָלַם וּלְעָלְמֵי עָלְמַיָּא.

יִתְבָּרַךְ וְיִשְׁתַּבַּח וְיִתְפָּאַר וְיִתְרוֹמַם וְיִתְנַשֵּׂא וְיִתְהַדָּר וְיִתְעַלֶּה וְיִתְהַלָּל שְׁמֵהּ דְּקֻדְשָׁא בְּרִיךְ הוּא (Cong. – בְּרִיךְ הוּא) – לְעֵלָּא מִן כָּל בִּרְכָתָא וְשִׁירָתָא תֻּשְׁבְּחָתָא וְנֶחֱמָתָא, דַּאֲמִירָן בְּעָלְמָא. וְאִמְרוּ: אָמֵן. (Cong. – אָמֵן.)

(Cong. – קַבֵּל בְּרַחֲמִים וּבְרָצוֹן אֶת תְּפִלָּתֵנוּ.)

All present stand and recite וַיְכֻלּוּ, *'Thus the heavens . . .,'* aloud in unison. Conversation is forbidden until after the *'Amen'* response to the blessing, *'Who sanctifies the Sabbath'* (below).

וַיְכֻלּוּ *Thus the heavens and the earth were finished, and all their legion. On the seventh day God completed His work which He had done, and He abstained on the seventh day from all His work which He had done. God blessed the seventh day and sanctified it, because on it He had abstained from all His work which God created to make.*[1]

THE SEVEN-FACETED BLESSING

Chazzan continues:

בָּרוּךְ *Blessed are You,* H*ASHEM*, *our God and the God of our forefathers, God of Abraham, God of Isaac, and God of Jacob; the great, mighty, and awesome God, the supreme God, Creator of heaven and earth.*

Congregation, then *chazzan:*

מָגֵן *He Who was the shield of our forefathers with His word, Who resuscitates the dead with His utterance, the Holy God Who is unequaled, Who grants rest to His people on His holy Sabbath day, for He was pleased with them to grant them rest. Before Him we will serve with awe and dread and give thanks to His Name every day continually with appropriate blessings. God of grateful praise, Master of peace, Who sanctifies the Sabbath and blesses the seventh day, and gives rest with holiness to a people saturated with delight — in memory of the work of Creation.*

Chazzan continues:

אֱלֹהֵינוּ *Our God and the God of our forefathers, may You be pleased with our rest. Sanctify us with Your commandments and grant us our share in Your Torah; satisfy us from Your goodness and gladden us with Your salvation, and purify our heart to serve You sincerely. O* H*ASHEM*, *our God, with love and favor grant us Your holy Sabbath as a heritage and may Israel, the sanctifiers of Your Name, rest on it. Blessed are You,* H*ASHEM*, *Who sanctifies the Sabbath.*

(Cong.– *Amen.)*

The *chazzan* recites the Full *Kaddish.*

יִתְגַּדַּל *May His great Name grow exalted and sanctified* (Cong.– *Amen.*) *in the world that He created as He willed. May He give reign to His kingship in your lifetimes and in your days, and in the lifetimes of the entire Family of Israel, swiftly and soon. Now respond: Amen.*

(Cong.– *Amen. May His great Name be blessed forever and ever.)*

May His great Name be blessed forever and ever.

Blessed, praised, glorified, exalted, extolled, mighty, upraised, and lauded be the Name of the Holy One, Blessed is He (Cong.– *Blessed is He*) *— beyond any blessing and song, praise and consolation that are uttered in the world. Now respond: Amen.* (Cong.– *Amen*.)

(Cong.– *Accept our prayers with mercy and favor.)*

---

(1) *Genesis* 2:1-3.

תִּתְקַבֵּל צְלוֹתְהוֹן וּבָעוּתְהוֹן דְּכָל בֵּית יִשְׂרָאֵל קֳדָם אֲבוּהוֹן דִּי בִשְׁמַיָּא. וְאִמְרוּ: אָמֵן. (.Cong – אָמֵן.)

(.Cong – יְהִי שֵׁם יהוה מְבֹרָךְ, מֵעַתָּה וְעַד עוֹלָם.[1])

יְהֵא שְׁלָמָא רַבָּא מִן שְׁמַיָּא, וְחַיִּים עָלֵינוּ וְעַל כָּל יִשְׂרָאֵל. וְאִמְרוּ: אָמֵן. (.Cong – אָמֵן.)

(.Cong – עֶזְרִי מֵעִם יהוה, עֹשֵׂה שָׁמַיִם וָאָרֶץ.[2])

Take three steps back. Bow left and say ... עֹשֶׂה; bow right and say ... הוּא; bow forward and say וְעַל כָּל ... אָמֵן. Remain standing in place for a few moments, then take three steps forward.

עֹשֶׂה שָׁלוֹם בִּמְרוֹמָיו, הוּא יַעֲשֶׂה שָׁלוֹם עָלֵינוּ, וְעַל כָּל יִשְׂרָאֵל. וְאִמְרוּ: אָמֵן. (.Cong – אָמֵן.)

קידוש בבית הכנסת

In some congregations, the *chazzan* recites *Kiddush* [although he will repeat *Kiddush* at home].

סַבְרִי מָרָנָן וְרַבָּנָן וְרַבּוֹתַי:

בָּרוּךְ אַתָּה יהוה אֱלֹהֵינוּ מֶלֶךְ הָעוֹלָם, בּוֹרֵא פְּרִי הַגָּפֶן. (.Cong – אָמֵן.)

בָּרוּךְ אַתָּה יהוה אֱלֹהֵינוּ מֶלֶךְ הָעוֹלָם, אֲשֶׁר קִדְּשָׁנוּ בְּמִצְוֹתָיו, וְרָצָה בָנוּ, וְשַׁבַּת קָדְשׁוֹ בְּאַהֲבָה וּבְרָצוֹן הִנְחִילָנוּ, זִכָּרוֹן לְמַעֲשֵׂה בְרֵאשִׁית. כִּי הוּא יוֹם תְּחִלָּה לְמִקְרָאֵי קֹדֶשׁ, זֵכֶר לִיצִיאַת מִצְרָיִם. כִּי בָנוּ בָחַרְתָּ, וְאוֹתָנוּ קִדַּשְׁתָּ, מִכָּל הָעַמִּים. וְשַׁבַּת קָדְשְׁךָ בְּאַהֲבָה וּבְרָצוֹן הִנְחַלְתָּנוּ. בָּרוּךְ אַתָּה יהוה, מְקַדֵּשׁ הַשַּׁבָּת. (.Cong – אָמֵן.)

The *chazzan* should not drink the *Kiddush* wine, but should give some to a child who has listened to *Kiddush* and responded אָמֵן. If no child is present, the *chazzan* himself should drink the wine. In either case, he should recite *Kiddush* again at home for the benefit of his family.

ספירת העומר

The *Omer* is counted from the second night of Pesach until the night before Shavuos. Most congregations count the *Omer* at this point; some count after *Aleinu* (p. 512). See page 79 for pertinent laws.

In some congregations the following Kabbalistic prayer precedes the counting of the *Omer*.

לְשֵׁם יִחוּד קוּדְשָׁא בְּרִיךְ הוּא וּשְׁכִינְתֵּיהּ, בִּדְחִילוּ וּרְחִימוּ לְיַחֵד שֵׁם יוּ״ד הֵ״א בְּוָא״ו הֵ״א בְּיִחוּדָא שְׁלִים, בְּשֵׁם כָּל יִשְׂרָאֵל. הִנְּנִי מוּכָן וּמְזוּמָן לְקַיֵּם מִצְוַת עֲשֵׂה שֶׁל סְפִירַת הָעוֹמֶר, כְּמוֹ שֶׁכָּתוּב בַּתּוֹרָה: וּסְפַרְתֶּם לָכֶם מִמָּחֳרַת הַשַּׁבָּת, מִיּוֹם הֲבִיאֲכֶם אֶת עֹמֶר הַתְּנוּפָה, שֶׁבַע שַׁבָּתוֹת תְּמִימוֹת תִּהְיֶינָה. עַד מִמָּחֳרַת הַשַּׁבָּת הַשְּׁבִיעִית תִּסְפְּרוּ חֲמִשִּׁים יוֹם, וְהִקְרַבְתֶּם מִנְחָה חֲדָשָׁה לַיהוה.[3] וִיהִי נֹעַם אֲדֹנָי אֱלֹהֵינוּ עָלֵינוּ, וּמַעֲשֵׂה יָדֵינוּ כּוֹנְנָה עָלֵינוּ, וּמַעֲשֵׂה יָדֵינוּ כּוֹנְנֵהוּ.[4]

May the prayers and supplications of the entire Family of Israel be accepted before their Father Who is in Heaven. Now respond: Amen. (Cong.— *Amen.*)

(Cong.— *Blessed be the Name of* HASHEM, *from this time and forever.*[1])

May there be abundant peace from Heaven, and life, upon us and upon all Israel. Now respond: Amen. (Cong.— *Amen.*)

(Cong.— *My help is from* HASHEM, *Maker of heaven and earth.*[2])

Take three steps back. Bow left and say, *'He Who makes peace . . .'*; bow right and say, *'may He . . .'*; bow forward and say, *'and upon all Israel . . .'* Remain standing in place for a few moments, then take three steps forward.

He Who makes peace in His heights, may He make peace upon us, and upon all Israel. Now respond: Amen. (Cong.— *Amen.*)

KIDDUSH IN THE SYNAGOGUE

In some congregations, the *chazzan* recites *Kiddush* [although he will repeat *Kiddush* at home].

By your leave, my masters and teachers:

בָּרוּךְ *Blessed are You,* HASHEM, *our God, King of the universe, Who creates the fruit of the vine.* (Cong.— *Amen.*)

בָּרוּךְ *Blessed are You,* HASHEM, *our God, King of the universe, Who sanctified us with His commandments, took pleasure in us, and with love and favor gave us His holy Sabbath as a heritage, a remembrance of creation. For that day is the prologue to the holy convocations, a memorial of the Exodus from Egypt. For us did you choose and us did You sanctify from all the nations. And Your holy Sabbath, with love and favor did You give us as a heritage. Blessed are You,* HASHEM, *Who sanctifies the Sabbath.*

(Cong.— *Amen.*)

The *chazzan* should not drink the *Kiddush* wine, but should give some to a child who has listened to *Kiddush* and responded, *'Amen'*. If no child is present, the *chazzan* himself should drink the wine. In either case, he should recite *Kiddush* again at home for the benefit of his family.

COUNTING THE OMER

The *Omer* is counted from the second night of Pesach until the night before Shavuos. Most congregations count the *Omer* at this point; some count after *Aleinu* (p. 512).

See page 79 for pertinent laws.

In some congregations the following Kabbalistic prayer precedes the counting of the *Omer*.

לְשֵׁם *For the sake of the unification of the Holy One, Blessed is He, and His Presence, in fear and love to unify the Name Yud-Kei with Vav-Kei in perfect unity, in the name of all Israel. Behold I am prepared and ready to perform the commandment of counting the Omer, as it is written in the Torah: 'You are to count from the morrow of the rest day, from the day you brought the Omer-offering that is waved — they are to be seven complete weeks — until the morrow of the seventh week you are to count fifty days, and then offer a new meal-offering to* HASHEM.'[3] *May the pleasantness of my Lord, our God, be upon us — may He establish our handiwork for us; our handiwork, may He establish.*[4]

(1) *Psalms* 113:2. (2) 121:2. (3) *Leviticus* 23:15-16. (4) *Psalms* 90:17.

Chazzan, followed by congregation, recites the blessing and counts.
One praying without a *minyan* should, nevertheless, recite the entire Omer service.

בָּרוּךְ אַתָּה יהוה אֱלֹהֵינוּ מֶלֶךְ הָעוֹלָם, אֲשֶׁר קִדְּשָׁנוּ בְּמִצְוֹתָיו וְצִוָּנוּ עַל סְפִירַת הָעוֹמֶר.

On the first day *Chol HaMoed* – **הַיּוֹם שְׁנֵי יָמִים לָעוֹמֶר.**

On the third day *Chol HaMoed* – **הַיּוֹם אַרְבָּעָה יָמִים לָעוֹמֶר.**

הָרַחֲמָן הוּא יַחֲזִיר לָנוּ עֲבוֹדַת בֵּית הַמִּקְדָּשׁ לִמְקוֹמָהּ, בִּמְהֵרָה בְיָמֵינוּ. אָמֵן סֶלָה.

תהלים סז

לַמְנַצֵּחַ בִּנְגִינֹת מִזְמוֹר שִׁיר. אֱלֹהִים יְחָנֵּנוּ וִיבָרְכֵנוּ, יָאֵר פָּנָיו אִתָּנוּ סֶלָה. לָדַעַת בָּאָרֶץ דַּרְכֶּךָ, בְּכָל גּוֹיִם יְשׁוּעָתֶךָ. יוֹדוּךָ עַמִּים אֱלֹהִים, יוֹדוּךָ עַמִּים כֻּלָּם. יִשְׂמְחוּ וִירַנְּנוּ לְאֻמִּים, כִּי תִשְׁפֹּט עַמִּים מִישֹׁר, וּלְאֻמִּים בָּאָרֶץ תַּנְחֵם סֶלָה. יוֹדוּךָ עַמִּים, אֱלֹהִים, יוֹדוּךָ עַמִּים כֻּלָּם. אֶרֶץ נָתְנָה יְבוּלָהּ, יְבָרְכֵנוּ אֱלֹהִים אֱלֹהֵינוּ. יְבָרְכֵנוּ אֱלֹהִים, וְיִירְאוּ אוֹתוֹ כָּל אַפְסֵי אָרֶץ.

אָנָּא בְּכֹחַ גְּדֻלַּת יְמִינְךָ תַּתִּיר צְרוּרָה. — אב״ג ית״ץ
קַבֵּל רִנַּת עַמְּךָ שַׂגְּבֵנוּ טַהֲרֵנוּ נוֹרָא. — קר״ע שט״ן
נָא גִבּוֹר דּוֹרְשֵׁי יִחוּדְךָ כְּבָבַת שָׁמְרֵם. — נג״ד יכ״ש
בָּרְכֵם טַהֲרֵם רַחֲמֵם צִדְקָתְךָ תָּמִיד גָּמְלֵם. — בט״ר צת״ג
חֲסִין קָדוֹשׁ בְּרוֹב טוּבְךָ נַהֵל עֲדָתֶךָ. — חק״ב טנ״ע
יָחִיד גֵּאֶה לְעַמְּךָ פְּנֵה זוֹכְרֵי קְדֻשָּׁתֶךָ. — יג״ל פז״ק
שַׁוְעָתֵנוּ קַבֵּל וּשְׁמַע צַעֲקָתֵנוּ יוֹדֵעַ תַּעֲלֻמוֹת. — שק״ו צי״ת
בָּרוּךְ שֵׁם כְּבוֹד מַלְכוּתוֹ לְעוֹלָם וָעֶד.

רִבּוֹנוֹ שֶׁל עוֹלָם, אַתָּה צִוִּיתָנוּ עַל יְדֵי מֹשֶׁה עַבְדֶּךָ לִסְפּוֹר סְפִירַת הָעוֹמֶר, כְּדֵי לְטַהֲרֵנוּ מִקְּלִפּוֹתֵינוּ וּמִטֻּמְאוֹתֵינוּ, כְּמוֹ שֶׁכָּתַבְתָּ בְּתוֹרָתֶךָ: וּסְפַרְתֶּם לָכֶם מִמָּחֳרַת הַשַּׁבָּת מִיּוֹם הֲבִיאֲכֶם אֶת עֹמֶר הַתְּנוּפָה, שֶׁבַע שַׁבָּתוֹת תְּמִימֹת תִּהְיֶינָה. עַד מִמָּחֳרַת הַשַּׁבָּת הַשְּׁבִיעִית תִּסְפְּרוּ חֲמִשִּׁים יוֹם.[1] כְּדֵי שֶׁיִּטָּהֲרוּ נַפְשׁוֹת עַמְּךָ יִשְׂרָאֵל מִזֻּהֲמָתָם. וּבְכֵן יְהִי רָצוֹן מִלְּפָנֶיךָ יהוה אֱלֹהֵינוּ וֵאלֹהֵי אֲבוֹתֵינוּ, שֶׁבִּזְכוּת סְפִירַת הָעוֹמֶר שֶׁסָּפַרְתִּי הַיּוֹם, יְתֻקַּן מַה שֶּׁפָּגַמְתִּי בִּסְפִירָה [first day *Chol HaMoed* – גְּבוּרָה שֶׁבְּחֶסֶד.] [third day *Chol HaMoed* – נֶצַח שֶׁבְּחֶסֶד]. וְאֶטָּהֵר וְאֶתְקַדֵּשׁ בִּקְדֻשָּׁה שֶׁל מַעְלָה, וְעַל יְדֵי זֶה יֻשְׁפַּע שֶׁפַע רַב בְּכָל הָעוֹלָמוֹת. וּלְתַקֵּן אֶת נַפְשׁוֹתֵינוּ, וְרוּחוֹתֵינוּ, וְנִשְׁמוֹתֵינוּ, מִכָּל סִיג וּפְגַם, וּלְטַהֲרֵנוּ וּלְקַדְּשֵׁנוּ בִּקְדֻשָּׁתְךָ הָעֶלְיוֹנָה. אָמֵן סֶלָה.

In some congregations, if a mourner is present, the Mourner's *Kaddish* (p. 512) is recited, followed by *Aleinu*. In others, *Aleinu* is recited immediately.

Chazzan, followed by the congregation, recites the blessing and counts.
One praying without a *minyan* should, nevertheless, recite the entire Omer service.

בָּרוּךְ *Blessed are You, HASHEM, our God, King of the universe, Who has sanctified us with His commandments and has commanded us regarding the counting of the Omer.*

On the first day *Chol HaMoed:* **Today is two days of the Omer.**

On the third day *Chol HaMoed:* **Today is four days of the Omer.**

הָרַחֲמָן *The Compassionate One! May He return for us the service of the Temple to its place, speedily in our days. Amen, selah!*

Psalm 67

לַמְנַצֵּחַ *For the Conductor, upon Neginos, a psalm, a song. May God favor us and bless us, may He illuminate His countenance with us, Selah. To make known Your way on earth, among all the nations Your salvation. The peoples will acknowledge You, O God, the peoples will acknowledge You, all of them. Nations will be glad and sing for joy, because You will judge the peoples fairly and guide the nations on earth, Selah. The peoples will acknowledge You, O God, the peoples will acknowledge You, all of them. The earth has yielded its produce, may God, our own God, bless us. May God bless us and may all the ends of the earth fear him.*

אָנָּא *We beg You! With the strength of Your right hand's greatness, untie the bundled sins. Accept the prayer of Your nation; strengthen us, purify us, O Awesome One. Please, O Strong One — those who foster Your Oneness, guard them like the apple of an eye. Bless them, purify them, show them pity, may Your righteousness always recompense them. Powerful Holy One, with Your abundant goodness guide Your congregation. One and only Exalted One, turn to Your nation, which proclaims Your holiness. Accept our entreaty and hear our cry, O Knower of mysteries. Blessed is the Name of His glorious Kingdom for all eternity.*

רִבּוֹנוֹ שֶׁל עוֹלָם *Master of the universe, You commanded us through Moses, Your servant, to count the Omer Count in order to cleanse us from our encrustations of evil and from our contaminations, as You have written in Your Torah: You are to count from the morrow of the rest day, from the day you brought the Omer-offering that is waved — they are to be seven complete weeks. Until the morrow of the seventh week you are to count fifty days,*[1] *so that the souls of Your people Israel be cleansed from their contamination. Therefore, may it be You will, HASHEM, our God and the God of our forefathers, that in the merit of the Omer Count that I have counted today, may there be corrected whatever blemish I have caused in the sefirah*

first day *Chol HaMoed: gevurah shebechesed.*

third day *Chol HaMoed: netzach shebechesed.*

May I be cleansed and sanctified with the holiness of Above, and through this may abundant bounty flow in all the worlds. And may it correct our lives, spirits, and souls from all sediment and blemish; may it cleanse us and sanctify us with Your exalted holiness. Amen, Selah!

In some congregations, if a mourner is present, the Mourner's *Kaddish* (p. 512) is recited, followed by *Aleinu*. In others, *Aleinu* is recited immediately.

(1) *Leviticus* 23:15-16.

The congregation stands while reciting עָלֵינוּ.

עָלֵינוּ לְשַׁבֵּחַ לַאֲדוֹן הַכֹּל, לָתֵת גְּדֻלָּה לְיוֹצֵר בְּרֵאשִׁית, שֶׁלֹּא עָשָׂנוּ כְּגוֹיֵי הָאֲרָצוֹת, וְלֹא שָׂמָנוּ כְּמִשְׁפְּחוֹת הָאֲדָמָה. שֶׁלֹּא שָׂם חֶלְקֵנוּ כָּהֶם, וְגוֹרָלֵנוּ כְּכָל הֲמוֹנָם. (שֶׁהֵם מִשְׁתַּחֲוִים לְהֶבֶל וָרִיק, וּמִתְפַּלְּלִים אֶל אֵל לֹא יוֹשִׁיעַ.[1]) וַאֲנַחְנוּ כּוֹרְעִים וּמִשְׁתַּחֲוִים וּמוֹדִים, לִפְנֵי מֶלֶךְ מַלְכֵי הַמְּלָכִים הַקָּדוֹשׁ בָּרוּךְ הוּא. שֶׁהוּא נוֹטֶה שָׁמַיִם וְיֹסֵד אָרֶץ,[2] וּמוֹשַׁב יְקָרוֹ בַּשָּׁמַיִם מִמַּעַל, וּשְׁכִינַת עֻזּוֹ בְּגָבְהֵי מְרוֹמִים. הוּא אֱלֹהֵינוּ, אֵין עוֹד. אֱמֶת מַלְכֵּנוּ, אֶפֶס זוּלָתוֹ, כַּכָּתוּב בְּתוֹרָתוֹ: וְיָדַעְתָּ הַיּוֹם וַהֲשֵׁבֹתָ אֶל לְבָבֶךָ, כִּי יהוה הוּא הָאֱלֹהִים בַּשָּׁמַיִם מִמַּעַל וְעַל הָאָרֶץ מִתָּחַת, אֵין עוֹד.[3]

Bow while reciting וַאֲנַחְנוּ כּוֹרְעִים וּמִשְׁתַּחֲוִים.

עַל כֵּן נְקַוֶּה לְּךָ יהוה אֱלֹהֵינוּ לִרְאוֹת מְהֵרָה בְּתִפְאֶרֶת עֻזֶּךָ, לְהַעֲבִיר גִּלּוּלִים מִן הָאָרֶץ, וְהָאֱלִילִים כָּרוֹת יִכָּרֵתוּן, לְתַקֵּן עוֹלָם בְּמַלְכוּת שַׁדַּי. וְכָל בְּנֵי בָשָׂר יִקְרְאוּ בִשְׁמֶךָ, לְהַפְנוֹת אֵלֶיךָ כָּל רִשְׁעֵי אָרֶץ. יַכִּירוּ וְיֵדְעוּ כָּל יוֹשְׁבֵי תֵבֵל, כִּי לְךָ תִּכְרַע כָּל בֶּרֶךְ, תִּשָּׁבַע כָּל לָשׁוֹן.[4] לְפָנֶיךָ יהוה אֱלֹהֵינוּ יִכְרְעוּ וְיִפֹּלוּ, וְלִכְבוֹד שִׁמְךָ יְקָר יִתֵּנוּ. וִיקַבְּלוּ כֻלָּם אֶת עוֹל מַלְכוּתֶךָ, וְתִמְלֹךְ עֲלֵיהֶם מְהֵרָה לְעוֹלָם וָעֶד. כִּי הַמַּלְכוּת שֶׁלְּךָ הִיא וּלְעוֹלְמֵי עַד תִּמְלוֹךְ בְּכָבוֹד, כַּכָּתוּב בְּתוֹרָתֶךָ: יהוה יִמְלֹךְ לְעֹלָם וָעֶד.[5] ❖ וְנֶאֱמַר: וְהָיָה יהוה לְמֶלֶךְ עַל כָּל הָאָרֶץ, בַּיּוֹם הַהוּא יִהְיֶה יהוה אֶחָד וּשְׁמוֹ אֶחָד.[6]

Some recite the following after עָלֵינוּ:

אַל תִּירָא מִפַּחַד פִּתְאֹם, וּמִשֹּׁאַת רְשָׁעִים כִּי תָבֹא.[7] עֻצוּ עֵצָה וְתֻפָר, דַּבְּרוּ דָבָר וְלֹא יָקוּם, כִּי עִמָּנוּ אֵל.[8] וְעַד זִקְנָה אֲנִי הוּא, וְעַד שֵׂיבָה אֲנִי אֶסְבֹּל, אֲנִי עָשִׂיתִי וַאֲנִי אֶשָּׂא, וַאֲנִי אֶסְבֹּל וַאֲמַלֵּט.[9]

קדיש יתום

Mourners recite קַדִּישׁ יָתוֹם (see *Laws* §81-83.)

יִתְגַּדַּל וְיִתְקַדַּשׁ שְׁמֵהּ רַבָּא. (.Cong – אָמֵן.) בְּעָלְמָא דִּי בְרָא כִרְעוּתֵהּ. וְיַמְלִיךְ מַלְכוּתֵהּ, בְּחַיֵּיכוֹן וּבְיוֹמֵיכוֹן וּבְחַיֵּי דְכָל בֵּית יִשְׂרָאֵל, בַּעֲגָלָא וּבִזְמַן קָרִיב. וְאִמְרוּ: אָמֵן.

(.Cong – אָמֵן. יְהֵא שְׁמֵהּ רַבָּא מְבָרַךְ לְעָלַם וּלְעָלְמֵי עָלְמַיָּא.)

---

(1) *Isaiah* 45:20. (2) 51:13. (3) *Deuteronomy* 4:39. (4) Cf. *Isaiah* 45:23.
(5) *Exodus* 15:18. (6) *Zechariah* 14:9. (7) *Proverbs* 3:25. (8) *Isaiah* 8:10. (9) 46:4.

The congregation stands while reciting עָלֵינוּ, *'It is our duty . . .'*

עָלֵינוּ *It is our duty to praise the Master of all, to ascribe greatness to the Molder of primeval creation, for He has not made us like the nations of the lands, and has not emplaced us like the families of the earth; for He has not assigned our portion like theirs nor our lot like all their multitudes. (For they bow to vanity and emptiness and pray to a god which helps not.[1]) But we bend our knees, bow, and acknowledge our thanks before the King Who reigns over kings, the Holy One, Blessed is He. He stretches out heaven and establishes earth's foundation,[2] the seat of His homage is in the heavens above and His powerful Presence is in the loftiest heights. He is our God and there is none other. True is our King, there is nothing beside Him, as it is written in His Torah: 'You are to know this day and take to your heart that* HASHEM *is the only God — in heaven above and on the earth below — there is none other.'[3]*

Bow while reciting *'But we bend our knees.'*

עַל כֵּן *Therefore we put our hope in You,* HASHEM, *our God, that we may soon see Your mighty splendor, to remove detestable idolatry from the earth, and false gods will be utterly cut off, to perfect the universe through the Almighty's sovereignty. Then all humanity will call upon Your Name, to turn all the earth's wicked toward You. All the world's inhabitants will recognize and know that to You every knee should bend, every tongue should swear.[4] Before You,* HASHEM, *our God, they will bend every knee and cast themselves down and to the glory of Your Name they will render homage, and they will all accept upon themselves the yoke of Your kingship that You may reign over them soon and eternally. For the kingdom is Yours and You will reign for all eternity in glory as it is written in Your Torah:* HASHEM *shall reign for all eternity.[5]* Chazzan– *And it is said:* HASHEM *will be King over all the world — on that day* HASHEM *will be One and His Name will be One.[6]*

Some recite the following after *Aleinu:*

אַל תִּירָא *Do not fear sudden terror, or the holocaust of the wicked when it comes.[7] Plan a conspiracy and it will be annulled; speak your piece and it shall not stand, for God is with us.[8] Even till your seniority, I remain unchanged; and even till your ripe old age, I shall endure. I created you and I shall bear you; I shall endure and rescue.[9]*

MOURNER'S KADDISH

Mourners recite the Mourner's *Kaddish* (see *Laws* §81-83).
[A transliteration of this *Kaddish* appears on page 1147.]

יִתְגַּדַּל *May His great Name grow exalted and sanctified* (Cong.– *Amen.*) *in the world that He created as He willed. May He give reign to His kingship in your lifetimes and in your days, and in the lifetimes of the entire Family of Israel, swiftly and soon. Now respond: Amen.*

(Cong.– *Amen. May His great Name be blessed forever and ever.*)

יְהֵא שְׁמֵהּ רַבָּא מְבָרַךְ לְעָלַם וּלְעָלְמֵי עָלְמַיָּא.

יִתְבָּרַךְ וְיִשְׁתַּבַּח וְיִתְפָּאַר וְיִתְרוֹמַם וְיִתְנַשֵּׂא וְיִתְהַדָּר וְיִתְעַלֶּה וְיִתְהַלָּל שְׁמֵהּ דְּקֻדְשָׁא בְּרִיךְ הוּא (.Cong – בְּרִיךְ הוּא) – לְעֵלָּא מִן כָּל בִּרְכָתָא וְשִׁירָתָא תֻּשְׁבְּחָתָא וְנֶחֱמָתָא, דַּאֲמִירָן בְּעָלְמָא. וְאִמְרוּ: אָמֵן. (.Cong – אָמֵן.)

יְהֵא שְׁלָמָא רַבָּא מִן שְׁמַיָּא, וְחַיִּים עָלֵינוּ וְעַל כָּל יִשְׂרָאֵל. וְאִמְרוּ: אָמֵן. (.Cong – אָמֵן.)

Take three steps back. Bow left and say . . . עֹשֶׂה; bow right and say . . . הוּא; bow forward and say וְעַל כָּל . . . אָמֵן. Remain standing in place for a few moments, then take three steps forward.

עֹשֶׂה שָׁלוֹם בִּמְרוֹמָיו, הוּא יַעֲשֶׂה שָׁלוֹם עָלֵינוּ, וְעַל כָּל יִשְׂרָאֵל. וְאִמְרוּ: אָמֵן. (.Cong – אָמֵן.)

Many congregations recite either אֲדוֹן עוֹלָם or יִגְדַּל, or both, at this point.

אֲדוֹן עוֹלָם אֲשֶׁר מָלַךְ, בְּטֶרֶם כָּל יְצִיר נִבְרָא.
לְעֵת נַעֲשָׂה בְחֶפְצוֹ כֹּל, אֲזַי מֶלֶךְ שְׁמוֹ נִקְרָא.
וְאַחֲרֵי כִּכְלוֹת הַכֹּל, לְבַדּוֹ יִמְלוֹךְ נוֹרָא.
וְהוּא הָיָה וְהוּא הֹוֶה, וְהוּא יִהְיֶה בְּתִפְאָרָה.
וְהוּא אֶחָד וְאֵין שֵׁנִי, לְהַמְשִׁיל לוֹ לְהַחְבִּירָה.
בְּלִי רֵאשִׁית בְּלִי תַכְלִית, וְלוֹ הָעֹז וְהַמִּשְׂרָה.
וְהוּא אֵלִי וְחַי גֹּאֲלִי, וְצוּר חֶבְלִי בְּעֵת צָרָה.
וְהוּא נִסִּי וּמָנוֹס לִי, מְנָת כּוֹסִי בְּיוֹם אֶקְרָא.
בְּיָדוֹ אַפְקִיד רוּחִי, בְּעֵת אִישַׁן וְאָעִירָה.
וְעִם רוּחִי גְּוִיָּתִי, יהוה לִי וְלֹא אִירָא.

יִגְדַּל אֱלֹהִים חַי וְיִשְׁתַּבַּח, נִמְצָא וְאֵין עֵת אֶל מְצִיאוּתוֹ.
אֶחָד וְאֵין יָחִיד כְּיִחוּדוֹ, נֶעְלָם וְגַם אֵין סוֹף לְאַחְדוּתוֹ.
אֵין לוֹ דְּמוּת הַגּוּף וְאֵינוֹ גוּף, לֹא נַעֲרוֹךְ אֵלָיו קְדֻשָּׁתוֹ.
קַדְמוֹן לְכָל דָּבָר אֲשֶׁר נִבְרָא, רִאשׁוֹן וְאֵין רֵאשִׁית לְרֵאשִׁיתוֹ.
הִנּוֹ אֲדוֹן עוֹלָם לְכָל נוֹצָר, יוֹרֶה גְדֻלָּתוֹ וּמַלְכוּתוֹ.
שֶׁפַע נְבוּאָתוֹ נְתָנוֹ, אֶל אַנְשֵׁי סְגֻלָּתוֹ וְתִפְאַרְתּוֹ.
לֹא קָם בְּיִשְׂרָאֵל כְּמֹשֶׁה עוֹד, נָבִיא וּמַבִּיט אֶת תְּמוּנָתוֹ.
תּוֹרַת אֱמֶת נָתַן לְעַמּוֹ אֵל, עַל יַד נְבִיאוֹ נֶאֱמַן בֵּיתוֹ.
לֹא יַחֲלִיף הָאֵל וְלֹא יָמִיר דָּתוֹ, לְעוֹלָמִים לְזוּלָתוֹ.
צוֹפֶה וְיוֹדֵעַ סְתָרֵינוּ, מַבִּיט לְסוֹף דָּבָר בְּקַדְמָתוֹ.

May His great Name be blessed forever and ever.

Blessed, praised, glorified, exalted, extolled, mighty, upraised, and lauded be the Name of the Holy One, Blessed is He (Cong.– *Blessed is He*) *— beyond any blessing and song, praise and consolation that are uttered in the world. Now respond: Amen.* (Cong.– *Amen.*)

May there be abundant peace from Heaven, and life, upon us and upon all Israel. Now respond: Amen. (Cong.– *Amen.*)

Take three steps back. Bow left and say, *'He Who makes peace . . .';* bow right and say, *'may He . . .';* bow forward and say, *'and upon all Israel . . .'* Remain standing in place for a few moments, then take three steps forward.

He Who makes peace in His heights, may He make peace upon us, and upon all Israel. Now respond: Amen. (Cong.– *Amen.*)

Many congregations recite either אֲדוֹן עוֹלָם, *Master of the universe,* or יִגְדַּל, *Exalted be,* or both.

אֲדוֹן עוֹלָם *Master of the universe, Who reigned before any form was created,*
At the time when His will brought all into being —
then as 'King' was His Name proclaimed.
After all has ceased to be, He, the Awesome One, will reign alone.
It is He Who was, He Who is, and He Who shall remain, in splendor.
He is One — there is no second to compare to Him, to declare as His equal.
Without beginning, without conclusion — His is the power and dominion.
He is my God, my living Redeemer, Rock of my pain in time of distress.
He is my banner, a refuge for me, the portion in my cup on the day I call.
Into His hand I shall entrust my spirit when I go to sleep — and I shall awaken!
With my spirit shall my body remain. HASHEM *is with me, I shall not fear.*

יִגְדַּל *Exalted be the Living God and praised,*
He exists — unbounded by time is His existence.
He is One — and there is no unity like His Oneness.
Inscrutable and infinite is His Oneness.
He has no semblance of a body nor is He corporeal;
nor has His holiness any comparison.
He preceded every being that was created —
the First, and nothing precedes His precedence.
Behold! He is Master of the universe to every creature,
He demonstrates His greatness and His sovereignty.
He granted His flow of prophecy
to His treasured splendrous people.
In Israel none like Moses arose again —
a prophet who perceived His vision clearly.
God gave His people a Torah of truth,
by means of His prophet, the most trusted of His household.
God will never amend nor exchange His law
for any other one, for all eternity.
He scrutinizes and knows our hiddenmost secrets;
He perceives a matter's outcome at its inception.

גּוֹמֵל לְאִישׁ חֶסֶד כְּמִפְעָלוֹ, נוֹתֵן לְרָשָׁע רָע כְּרִשְׁעָתוֹ.
יִשְׁלַח לְקֵץ הַיָּמִין מְשִׁיחֵנוּ, לִפְדּוֹת מְחַכֵּי קֵץ יְשׁוּעָתוֹ.
מֵתִים יְחַיֶּה אֵל בְּרֹב חַסְדּוֹ, בָּרוּךְ עֲדֵי עַד שֵׁם תְּהִלָּתוֹ.

THE SYNAGOGUE SERVICE ENDS HERE.

Many recite the following before *Kiddush*. Each of the first four stanzas is recited three times.

שָׁלוֹם עֲלֵיכֶם, מַלְאֲכֵי הַשָּׁרֵת, מַלְאֲכֵי עֶלְיוֹן, מִמֶּלֶךְ מַלְכֵי הַמְּלָכִים הַקָּדוֹשׁ בָּרוּךְ הוּא.

בּוֹאֲכֶם לְשָׁלוֹם, מַלְאֲכֵי הַשָּׁלוֹם, מַלְאֲכֵי עֶלְיוֹן, מִמֶּלֶךְ מַלְכֵי הַמְּלָכִים הַקָּדוֹשׁ בָּרוּךְ הוּא.

בָּרְכוּנִי לְשָׁלוֹם, מַלְאֲכֵי הַשָּׁלוֹם, מַלְאֲכֵי עֶלְיוֹן, מִמֶּלֶךְ מַלְכֵי הַמְּלָכִים הַקָּדוֹשׁ בָּרוּךְ הוּא.

צֵאתְכֶם לְשָׁלוֹם, מַלְאֲכֵי הַשָּׁלוֹם, מַלְאֲכֵי עֶלְיוֹן, מִמֶּלֶךְ מַלְכֵי הַמְּלָכִים הַקָּדוֹשׁ בָּרוּךְ הוּא.

כִּי מַלְאָכָיו יְצַוֶּה לָּךְ, לִשְׁמָרְךָ בְּכָל דְּרָכֶיךָ.[1]
יהוה יִשְׁמָר צֵאתְךָ וּבוֹאֶךָ, מֵעַתָּה וְעַד עוֹלָם.[2]

(משלי לא:י־לא)

אֵשֶׁת חַיִל מִי יִמְצָא, וְרָחֹק מִפְּנִינִים מִכְרָהּ.
בָּטַח בָּהּ לֵב בַּעְלָהּ, וְשָׁלָל לֹא יֶחְסָר.
גְּמָלַתְהוּ טוֹב וְלֹא רָע, כֹּל יְמֵי חַיֶּיהָ.
דָּרְשָׁה צֶמֶר וּפִשְׁתִּים, וַתַּעַשׂ בְּחֵפֶץ כַּפֶּיהָ.
הָיְתָה כָּאֳנִיּוֹת סוֹחֵר, מִמֶּרְחָק תָּבִיא לַחְמָהּ.
וַתָּקָם בְּעוֹד לַיְלָה, וַתִּתֵּן טֶרֶף לְבֵיתָהּ, וְחֹק לְנַעֲרֹתֶיהָ.
זָמְמָה שָׂדֶה וַתִּקָּחֵהוּ, מִפְּרִי כַפֶּיהָ נָטְעָה כָּרֶם.
חָגְרָה בְעוֹז מָתְנֶיהָ, וַתְּאַמֵּץ זְרוֹעֹתֶיהָ.
טָעֲמָה כִּי טוֹב סַחְרָהּ, לֹא יִכְבֶּה בַלַּיְלָה נֵרָהּ.
יָדֶיהָ שִׁלְּחָה בַכִּישׁוֹר, וְכַפֶּיהָ תָּמְכוּ פָלֶךְ.
כַּפָּהּ פָּרְשָׂה לֶעָנִי, וְיָדֶיהָ שִׁלְּחָה לָאֶבְיוֹן.
לֹא תִירָא לְבֵיתָהּ מִשָּׁלֶג, כִּי כָל בֵּיתָהּ לָבֻשׁ שָׁנִים.
מַרְבַדִּים עָשְׂתָה לָּהּ, שֵׁשׁ וְאַרְגָּמָן לְבוּשָׁהּ.
נוֹדָע בַּשְּׁעָרִים בַּעְלָהּ, בְּשִׁבְתּוֹ עִם זִקְנֵי אָרֶץ.

---

(1) *Psalms* 91:11. (2) 121:8.

He recompenses man with kindness according to his deed;
He places evil on the wicked according to his wickedness.
By the End of Days He will send our Messiah,
to redeem those longing for His final salvation.
God will revive the dead in His abundant kindness —
Blessed forever is His praised Name.

THE SYNAGOGUE SERVICE ENDS HERE.

Many recite the following before *Kiddush*.
Each of the first four stanzas is recited three times.

שָׁלוֹם עֲלֵיכֶם *Peace upon you, O ministering angels, angels of the Exalted One — from the King Who reigns over kings, the Holy One, Blessed is He.*

בּוֹאֲכֶם לְשָׁלוֹם *May your coming be for peace, O angels of peace, angels of the Exalted One — from the King Who reigns over kings, the Holy One, Blessed is He.*

בָּרְכוּנִי לְשָׁלוֹם *Bless me for peace, O angels of peace, angels of the Exalted One — from the King Who reigns over kings, the Holy One, Blessed is He.*

צֵאתְכֶם לְשָׁלוֹם *May your departure be to peace, O angels of peace, angels of the Exalted One — from the King Who reigns over kings, the Holy One, Blessed is He.*

He will charge His angels for you, to protect you in all your ways.[1]
May HASHEM *protect your going and returning, from this time and forever.*[2]

(*Proverbs* 31:10-31)

אֵשֶׁת חַיִל *An accomplished woman, who can find? —*
Far beyond pearls is her value.
ב *Her husband's heart relies on her and he shall lack no fortune.*
ג *She repays his good, but never his harm, all the days of her life.*
ד *She seeks out wool and linen, and her hands work willingly.*
ה *She is like a merchant's ships, from afar she brings her sustenance.*
ו *She arises while it is yet nighttime,*
and gives food to her household and a ration to her maidens.
ז *She envisions a field and buys it,*
from the fruit of her handiwork she plants a vineyard.
ח *With strength she girds her loins, and invigorates her arms.*
ט *She discerns that her enterprise is good —*
so her lamp is not snuffed out by night.
י *Her hands she stretches out to the distaff, and her palms support the spindle.*
כ *She spreads out her palm to the poor, and extends her hands to the destitute.*
ל *She fears not snow for her household,*
for her entire household is clothed with scarlet wool.
מ *Luxurious bedspreads she made herself,*
linen and purple wool are her clothing.
נ *Distinctive in the councils is her husband,*
when he sits with the elders of the land.

סָדִין עָשְׂתָה וַתִּמְכֹּר, וַחֲגוֹר נָתְנָה לַכְּנַעֲנִי.
עֹז וְהָדָר לְבוּשָׁהּ, וַתִּשְׂחַק לְיוֹם אַחֲרוֹן.
פִּיהָ פָּתְחָה בְחָכְמָה, וְתוֹרַת חֶסֶד עַל לְשׁוֹנָהּ.
צוֹפִיָּה הֲלִיכוֹת בֵּיתָהּ, וְלֶחֶם עַצְלוּת לֹא תֹאכֵל.
קָמוּ בָנֶיהָ וַיְאַשְּׁרוּהָ, בַּעְלָהּ וַיְהַלְלָהּ.
רַבּוֹת בָּנוֹת עָשׂוּ חָיִל, וְאַתְּ עָלִית עַל כֻּלָּנָה.
שֶׁקֶר הַחֵן וְהֶבֶל הַיֹּפִי, אִשָּׁה יִרְאַת יהוה הִיא תִתְהַלָּל.
תְּנוּ לָהּ מִפְּרִי יָדֶיהָ, וִיהַלְלוּהָ בַשְּׁעָרִים מַעֲשֶׂיהָ.

קידוש לליל שבת חול המועד

(Recite silently — וַיְהִי עֶרֶב וַיְהִי בֹקֶר)

יוֹם הַשִּׁשִּׁי. וַיְכֻלּוּ הַשָּׁמַיִם וְהָאָרֶץ וְכָל צְבָאָם. וַיְכַל אֱלֹהִים בַּיּוֹם הַשְּׁבִיעִי מְלַאכְתּוֹ אֲשֶׁר עָשָׂה, וַיִּשְׁבֹּת בַּיּוֹם הַשְּׁבִיעִי מִכָּל מְלַאכְתּוֹ אֲשֶׁר עָשָׂה. וַיְבָרֶךְ אֱלֹהִים אֶת יוֹם הַשְּׁבִיעִי וַיְקַדֵּשׁ אֹתוֹ, כִּי בוֹ שָׁבַת מִכָּל מְלַאכְתּוֹ אֲשֶׁר בָּרָא אֱלֹהִים לַעֲשׂוֹת.[1]

סַבְרִי מָרָנָן וְרַבָּנָן וְרַבּוֹתַי:

בָּרוּךְ אַתָּה יהוה אֱלֹהֵינוּ מֶלֶךְ הָעוֹלָם, בּוֹרֵא פְּרִי הַגָּפֶן.

(All present respond — אָמֵן.)

בָּרוּךְ אַתָּה יהוה אֱלֹהֵינוּ מֶלֶךְ הָעוֹלָם, אֲשֶׁר קִדְּשָׁנוּ בְּמִצְוֹתָיו וְרָצָה בָנוּ, וְשַׁבַּת קָדְשׁוֹ בְּאַהֲבָה וּבְרָצוֹן הִנְחִילָנוּ, זִכָּרוֹן לְמַעֲשֵׂה בְרֵאשִׁית. כִּי הוּא יוֹם תְּחִלָּה לְמִקְרָאֵי קֹדֶשׁ,* זֵכֶר לִיצִיאַת מִצְרָיִם.* כִּי בָנוּ בָחַרְתָּ, וְאוֹתָנוּ קִדַּשְׁתָּ, מִכָּל הָעַמִּים. וְשַׁבַּת קָדְשְׁךָ בְּאַהֲבָה וּבְרָצוֹן הִנְחַלְתָּנוּ. בָּרוּךְ אַתָּה יהוה, מְקַדֵּשׁ הַשַּׁבָּת.*

(All present respond — אָמֵן.)

Bircas HaMazon appears on page 104.

תְּחִלָּה לְמִקְרָאֵי קֹדֶשׁ — *The prologue to the holy convocations.* The festivals are described as *holy convocations* because they come about as a result of the months which are proclaimed by the courts of Israel. The Sabbath, however, is independent of any proclamations of the court. As such it is not properly called a *holy convocation.* Nevertheless, *Leviticus* 23, which lists the festivals, begins by mentioning the Sabbath, thus making the Sabbath *the prologue to the holy convocations.*

זֵכֶר לִיצִיאַת מִצְרָיִם — *A memorial of the Exodus from Egypt. Ramban* explains that the Sabbath

ס *She makes a cloak to sell, and delivers a belt to the peddler.*
ע *Strength and majesty are her raiment, she joyfully awaits the last day.*
פ *She opens her mouth with wisdom,*
and a lesson of kindness is on her tongue.
צ *She anticipates the ways of her household,*
and partakes not of the bread of laziness.
ק *Her children arise and praise her, her husband, and he lauds her:*
ר *'Many daughters have amassed achievement,*
but you surpassed them all.'
ש *False is grace and vain is beauty,*
a God-fearing woman — she should be praised.
ת *Give her the fruits of her hand*
and let her be praised in the gates by her very own deeds.

KIDDUSH FOR THE SABBATH EVE OF CHOL HAMOED

(Recite silently— *And there was evening and there was morning)*

יוֹם הַשִּׁשִּׁי *The sixth day. Thus the heavens and earth were finished, and all their array. On the seventh day God completed His work which He had done, and He abstained on the seventh day from all His work which He had done. God blessed the seventh day and hallowed it, because on it He abstained from all His work which God created to make.*[1]

By your leave, my masters, rabbis and teachers,

בָּרוּךְ *Blessed are You,* H*ASHEM, our God, King of the universe, Who creates the fruit of the vine.* (All present respond— *Amen.)*

בָּרוּךְ *Blessed are You,* H*ASHEM, our God, King of the universe, Who has sanctified us with His commandments, took pleasure in us, and with love and favor gave us His holy Sabbath as a heritage, a remembrance of creation. For that day is the prologue to the holy convocations,* a memorial of the Exodus from Egypt.* For us did You choose and us did You sanctify from all the nations. And Your holy Sabbath, with love and favor did You give us as a heritage. Blessed are You,* H*ASHEM, Who sanctifies the Sabbath.**

(All present respond— *Amen.)*

Grace After Meals appears on page 104

(1) *Genesis* 2:1-3.

and the Exodus are intertwined. The Sabbath is symbolic of God's creation; the Exodus was His demonstration to humanity that He controls nature and manipulates it as His will sees fit. In turn, the events of the Exodus bear witness to God's creation — and, hence, His mastery — of the universe. The Sabbath on the other hand, is the backdrop of the Exodus, because the concept it represents explains how the events of the Exodus were possible.

מְקַדֵּשׁ הַשַּׁבָּת — *Who sanctifies the Sabbath.* Unlike the festivals whose sanctity is dependent upon the proclamation of the months by courts of Israel, the Sabbath owes its sanctity solely to God Who declared its holiness at the time of creation.

שחרית לשבת חול המועד

THE MORNING SERVICE BEGINS WITH PAGES 188-266, THEN CONTINUES HERE.

נִשְׁמַת כָּל חַי תְּבָרֵךְ אֶת שִׁמְךָ יהוה אֱלֹהֵינוּ, וְרוּחַ כָּל בָּשָׂר תְּפָאֵר וּתְרוֹמֵם זִכְרְךָ מַלְכֵּנוּ תָּמִיד. מִן הָעוֹלָם וְעַד הָעוֹלָם אַתָּה אֵל,[1] וּמִבַּלְעָדֶיךָ אֵין לָנוּ מֶלֶךְ[2] גּוֹאֵל וּמוֹשִׁיעַ. פּוֹדֶה וּמַצִּיל וּמְפַרְנֵס וּמְרַחֵם בְּכָל עֵת צָרָה וְצוּקָה, אֵין לָנוּ מֶלֶךְ אֶלָּא אָתָּה. אֱלֹהֵי הָרִאשׁוֹנִים וְהָאַחֲרוֹנִים, אֱלוֹהַּ כָּל בְּרִיּוֹת, אֲדוֹן כָּל תּוֹלָדוֹת, הַמְּהֻלָּל בְּרֹב הַתִּשְׁבָּחוֹת, הַמְנַהֵג עוֹלָמוֹ בְּחֶסֶד וּבְרִיּוֹתָיו בְּרַחֲמִים. וַיהוה לֹא יָנוּם וְלֹא יִישָׁן.[3] הַמְּעוֹרֵר יְשֵׁנִים, וְהַמֵּקִיץ נִרְדָּמִים, וְהַמֵּשִׂיחַ אִלְּמִים, וְהַמַּתִּיר אֲסוּרִים,[4] וְהַסּוֹמֵךְ נוֹפְלִים, וְהַזּוֹקֵף כְּפוּפִים.[5] לְךָ לְבַדְּךָ אֲנַחְנוּ מוֹדִים. אִלּוּ פִינוּ מָלֵא שִׁירָה כַּיָּם, וּלְשׁוֹנֵנוּ רִנָּה כַּהֲמוֹן גַּלָּיו, וְשִׂפְתוֹתֵינוּ שֶׁבַח כְּמֶרְחֲבֵי רָקִיעַ, וְעֵינֵינוּ מְאִירוֹת כַּשֶּׁמֶשׁ וְכַיָּרֵחַ, וְיָדֵינוּ פְרוּשׂוֹת כְּנִשְׁרֵי שָׁמָיִם, וְרַגְלֵינוּ קַלּוֹת כָּאַיָּלוֹת, אֵין אֲנַחְנוּ מַסְפִּיקִים לְהוֹדוֹת לְךָ, יהוה אֱלֹהֵינוּ וֵאלֹהֵי אֲבוֹתֵינוּ, וּלְבָרֵךְ אֶת שְׁמֶךָ עַל אַחַת מֵאָלֶף אֶלֶף אַלְפֵי אֲלָפִים וְרִבֵּי רְבָבוֹת פְּעָמִים הַטּוֹבוֹת שֶׁעָשִׂיתָ עִם אֲבוֹתֵינוּ וְעִמָּנוּ. מִמִּצְרַיִם גְּאַלְתָּנוּ יהוה אֱלֹהֵינוּ, וּמִבֵּית עֲבָדִים פְּדִיתָנוּ. בְּרָעָב זַנְתָּנוּ, וּבְשָׂבָע כִּלְכַּלְתָּנוּ, מֵחֶרֶב הִצַּלְתָּנוּ, וּמִדֶּבֶר מִלַּטְתָּנוּ, וּמֵחֳלָיִם רָעִים וְנֶאֱמָנִים דִּלִּיתָנוּ. עַד הֵנָּה עֲזָרוּנוּ רַחֲמֶיךָ, וְלֹא עֲזָבוּנוּ חֲסָדֶיךָ. וְאַל תִּטְּשֵׁנוּ יהוה אֱלֹהֵינוּ לָנֶצַח. עַל כֵּן אֵבָרִים שֶׁפִּלַּגְתָּ בָּנוּ, וְרוּחַ וּנְשָׁמָה שֶׁנָּפַחְתָּ בְּאַפֵּינוּ, וְלָשׁוֹן אֲשֶׁר שַׂמְתָּ בְּפִינוּ, הֵן הֵם יוֹדוּ וִיבָרְכוּ וִישַׁבְּחוּ וִיפָאֲרוּ וִירוֹמְמוּ וְיַעֲרִיצוּ וְיַקְדִּישׁוּ וְיַמְלִיכוּ אֶת שִׁמְךָ מַלְכֵּנוּ. כִּי כָל פֶּה לְךָ יוֹדֶה, וְכָל לָשׁוֹן לְךָ תִשָּׁבַע, וְכָל בֶּרֶךְ לְךָ תִכְרַע,[6] וְכָל קוֹמָה לְפָנֶיךָ תִשְׁתַּחֲוֶה, וְכָל לְבָבוֹת יִירָאוּךָ, וְכָל קֶרֶב וּכְלָיוֹת יְזַמְּרוּ לִשְׁמֶךָ, כַּדָּבָר שֶׁכָּתוּב: כָּל עַצְמֹתַי תֹּאמַרְנָה, יהוה מִי כָמוֹךָ, מַצִּיל עָנִי מֵחָזָק מִמֶּנּוּ, וְעָנִי וְאֶבְיוֹן מִגֹּזְלוֹ.[7] מִי יִדְמֶה לָּךְ, וּמִי יִשְׁוֶה לָּךְ, וּמִי יַעֲרָךְ לָךְ.[8] הָאֵל הַגָּדוֹל הַגִּבּוֹר וְהַנּוֹרָא, אֵל עֶלְיוֹן, קֹנֵה שָׁמַיִם וָאָרֶץ. ❖ נְהַלֶּלְךָ וּנְשַׁבֵּחֲךָ וּנְפָאֶרְךָ וּנְבָרֵךְ אֶת שֵׁם קָדְשֶׁךָ, כָּאָמוּר: לְדָוִד, בָּרְכִי נַפְשִׁי אֶת יהוה, וְכָל קְרָבַי אֶת שֵׁם קָדְשׁוֹ.[9] הָאֵל בְּתַעֲצֻמוֹת

(1) Cf. *Psalms* 90:2. (2) Cf. *Isaiah* 44:6. (3) Cf. *Psalms* 121:4. (4) Cf. 146:7. (5) Cf. 145:14. (6) Cf. *Isaiah* 45:23. (7) *Psalms* 35:10. (8) Cf. 89:7. (9) *Psalms* 103:1.

SHACHARIS FOR THE SABBATH OF CHOL HAMOED

THE MORNING SERVICE BEGINS WITH PAGES 188-266, THEN CONTINUES HERE.

נִשְׁמַת *The soul of every living being shall bless Your Name, HASHEM our God; the spirit of all flesh shall always glorify and exalt Your remembrance, our King. From This World to the World to Come, You are God,[1] and other than You we have no king,[2] redeemer or savior. Liberator, Rescuer, Sustainer and Merciful One in every time of distress and anguish, we have no king but You! — God of the first and of the last, God of all creatures, Master of all generations, Who is extolled through a multitude of praises, Who guides His world with kindness and His creatures with mercy. HASHEM neither slumbers nor sleeps.[3] He Who rouses the sleepers and awakens the slumberers, Who makes the mute speak and releases the bound;[4] Who supports the fallen and straightens the bent.[5] To You alone we give thanks. Were our mouth as full of song as the sea, and our tongue as full of joyous song as its multitude of waves, and our lips as full of praise as the breadth of the heavens, and our eyes as brilliant as the sun and the moon, and our hands as outspread as eagles of the sky and our feet as swift as hinds — we still could not thank You sufficiently, HASHEM our God and God of our forefathers, and to bless Your Name for even one of the thousand thousand, thousands of thousands and myriad myriads of favors that You performed for our ancestors and for us. You redeemed us from Egypt, HASHEM our God, and liberated us from the house of bondage. In famine You nourished us and in plenty You sustained us. From sword You saved us; from plague You let us escape; and from severe and enduring diseases You spared us. Until now Your mercy has helped us, and Your kindness has not forsaken us. Do not abandon us, HASHEM our God, forever. Therefore, the organs that You set within us, and the spirit and soul that You breathed into our nostrils, and the tongue that You placed in our mouth — all of them shall thank and bless, praise and glorify, exalt and revere, sanctify and declare the sovereignty of Your Name, our King. For every mouth shall offer thanks to You; every tongue shall vow allegiance to You; every knee shall bend to You;[6] every erect spine shall prostrate itself before You; all hearts shall fear You, and all innermost feelings and thoughts shall sing praises to Your name, as it is written: "All my bones shall say: 'HASHEM, who is like You?' You save the poor man from one stronger than he, the poor and destitute from one who would rob him."[7] Who is like unto You? Who is equal to You? Who can be compared to You?[8] O great, mighty, and awesome God, the supreme God, Creator of heaven and earth.*
Chazzan– *We shall laud, praise, and glorify You and bless Your holy Name, as it is said 'Of David: Bless HASHEM, O my soul, and let all my innermost being bless His holy Name!'[9] O God, in the omnipotence of*

עֻזֶּךָ, הַגָּדוֹל בִּכְבוֹד שְׁמֶךָ, הַגִּבּוֹר לָנֶצַח וְהַנּוֹרָא בְּנוֹרְאוֹתֶיךָ. הַמֶּלֶךְ הַיּוֹשֵׁב עַל כִּסֵּא רָם וְנִשָּׂא.[1]

The *chazzan* of *Shacharis* begins here.

שׁוֹכֵן עַד מָרוֹם וְקָדוֹשׁ שְׁמוֹ.[2] וְכָתוּב: רַנְּנוּ צַדִּיקִים בַּיהוה לַיְשָׁרִים נָאוָה תְהִלָּה.[3]

❖ בְּפִי **יְ**שָׁרִים תִּתְהַלָּל.
וּבְדִבְרֵי **צַ**דִּיקִים תִּתְבָּרַךְ.
וּבִלְשׁוֹן **חֲ**סִידִים תִּתְרוֹמָם.
וּבְקֶרֶב **קְ**דוֹשִׁים תִּתְקַדָּשׁ.

וּבְמַקְהֲלוֹת רִבְבוֹת עַמְּךָ בֵּית יִשְׂרָאֵל, בְּרִנָּה יִתְפָּאַר שִׁמְךָ מַלְכֵּנוּ בְּכָל דּוֹר וָדוֹר. ❖ שֶׁכֵּן חוֹבַת כָּל הַיְּצוּרִים, לְפָנֶיךָ יהוה אֱלֹהֵינוּ וֵאלֹהֵי אֲבוֹתֵינוּ, לְהוֹדוֹת לְהַלֵּל לְשַׁבֵּחַ לְפָאֵר לְרוֹמֵם לְהַדֵּר לְבָרֵךְ לְעַלֵּה וּלְקַלֵּס, עַל כָּל דִּבְרֵי שִׁירוֹת וְתִשְׁבְּחוֹת דָּוִד בֶּן יִשַׁי עַבְדְּךָ מְשִׁיחֶךָ.

Stand while reciting יִשְׁתַּבַּח . . .
The fifteen expressions of praise — שִׁיר וּשְׁבָחָה . . . בְּרָכוֹת וְהוֹדָאוֹת —
should be recited without pause, preferably in one breath.

יִשְׁתַּבַּח שִׁמְךָ לָעַד מַלְכֵּנוּ, הָאֵל הַמֶּלֶךְ הַגָּדוֹל וְהַקָּדוֹשׁ, בַּשָּׁמַיִם וּבָאָרֶץ. כִּי לְךָ נָאֶה יהוה אֱלֹהֵינוּ וֵאלֹהֵי אֲבוֹתֵינוּ, שִׁיר וּשְׁבָחָה, הַלֵּל וְזִמְרָה, עֹז וּמֶמְשָׁלָה, נֶצַח גְּדֻלָּה וּגְבוּרָה, תְּהִלָּה וְתִפְאֶרֶת, קְדֻשָּׁה וּמַלְכוּת, בְּרָכוֹת וְהוֹדָאוֹת מֵעַתָּה וְעַד עוֹלָם. ❖ בָּרוּךְ אַתָּה יהוה, אֵל מֶלֶךְ גָּדוֹל בַּתִּשְׁבָּחוֹת, אֵל הַהוֹדָאוֹת, אֲדוֹן הַנִּפְלָאוֹת, הַבּוֹחֵר בְּשִׁירֵי זִמְרָה, מֶלֶךְ אֵל חֵי הָעוֹלָמִים. (–Cong. אָמֵן.)

The *chazzan* recites חֲצִי קַדִּישׁ.

יִתְגַּדַּל וְיִתְקַדַּשׁ שְׁמֵהּ רַבָּא. (–Cong. אָמֵן.) בְּעָלְמָא דִּי בְרָא כִרְעוּתֵהּ. וְיַמְלִיךְ מַלְכוּתֵהּ, בְּחַיֵּיכוֹן וּבְיוֹמֵיכוֹן וּבְחַיֵּי דְכָל בֵּית יִשְׂרָאֵל, בַּעֲגָלָא וּבִזְמַן קָרִיב. וְאִמְרוּ: אָמֵן.

(–Cong. אָמֵן. יְהֵא שְׁמֵהּ רַבָּא מְבָרַךְ לְעָלַם וּלְעָלְמֵי עָלְמַיָּא.)

יְהֵא שְׁמֵהּ רַבָּא מְבָרַךְ לְעָלַם וּלְעָלְמֵי עָלְמַיָּא.

יִתְבָּרַךְ וְיִשְׁתַּבַּח וְיִתְפָּאַר וְיִתְרוֹמַם וְיִתְנַשֵּׂא וְיִתְהַדָּר וְיִתְעַלֶּה וְיִתְהַלָּל שְׁמֵהּ דְּקֻדְשָׁא בְּרִיךְ הוּא (–Cong. בְּרִיךְ הוּא) — לְעֵלָּא מִן כָּל בִּרְכָתָא וְשִׁירָתָא תֻּשְׁבְּחָתָא וְנֶחֱמָתָא, דַּאֲמִירָן בְּעָלְמָא. וְאִמְרוּ: אָמֵן. (–Cong. אָמֵן.)

Your strength, great in the glory of Your Name, mighty forever and awesome through Your awesome deeds. O King enthroned upon a high and lofty throne![1]

The chazzan of *Shacharis* begins here:

שׁוֹכֵן עַד *He Who abides forever, exalted and holy is His Name.*[2] *And it is written: 'Sing joyfully, O righteous, before* HASHEM; *for the upright, praise is fitting.'*[3]

Chazzan: *By the mouth of the upright shall You be lauded;*
by the words of the righteous shall You be blessed;
by the tongue of the devout shall You be exalted;
and amid the holy shall You be sanctified.

וּבְמַקְהֲלוֹת *And in the assemblies of the myriads of Your people, the House of Israel, with joyous song shall Your Name be glorified, our King, throughout every generation.* Chazzan– *For such is the duty of all creatures — before You,* HASHEM, *our God, God of our forefathers, to thank, laud, praise, glorify, exalt, adore, bless, raise high, and sing praises — even beyond all expressions of the songs and praises of David the son of Jesse, Your servant, Your anointed.*

Stand while reciting *'May Your Name be praised . . .'*
The fifteen expressions of praise — *'song and praise. . .blessings and thanksgivings'* — should be recited without pause, preferably in one breath.

יִשְׁתַּבַּח *May Your Name be praised forever — our King, the God, the great and holy King — in heaven and on earth. Because for You is fitting — O* HASHEM, *our God, and the God of our forefathers — song and praise, lauding and hymns, power and dominion, triumph, greatness and strength, praise and splendor, holiness and sovereignty, blessings and thanksgivings from this time and forever.* Chazzan– *Blessed are You,* HASHEM, *God, King exalted through praises, God of thanksgivings, Master of wonders, Who chooses musical songs of praise — King, God, Life-giver of the world.* (Cong.– *Amen.)*

The *chazzan* recites Half-*Kaddish*.

יִתְגַּדַּל *May His great Name grow exalted and sanctified* (Cong.– *Amen.) in the world that He created as He willed. May He give reign to His kingship in your lifetimes and in your days, and in the lifetimes of the entire Family of Israel, swiftly and soon. Now respond: Amen.*

(Cong.– *Amen. May His great Name be blessed forever and ever.)*
May His great Name be blessed forever and ever.

Blessed, praised, glorified, exalted, extolled, mighty, upraised, and lauded be the Name of the Holy One, Blessed is He (Cong.– *Blessed is He) — beyond any blessing and song, praise and consolation that are uttered in the world. Now respond: Amen.* (Cong.– *Amen.)*

---

(1) Cf. *Isaiah* 6:1. (2) Cf. 57:15. (3) *Psalms* 33:1.

In some congregations the *chazzan* chants a melody during his recitation of בָּרְכוּ, so that the congregation can then recite יִתְבָּרַךְ.

יִתְבָּרַךְ וְיִשְׁתַּבַּח וְיִתְפָּאַר וְיִתְרוֹמַם וְיִתְנַשֵּׂא שְׁמוֹ שֶׁל מֶלֶךְ מַלְכֵי הַמְּלָכִים, הַקָּדוֹשׁ בָּרוּךְ הוּא. שֶׁהוּא רִאשׁוֹן וְהוּא אַחֲרוֹן, וּמִבַּלְעָדָיו אֵין אֱלֹהִים.[1] סֹלּוּ, לָרֹכֵב בָּעֲרָבוֹת, בְּיָהּ שְׁמוֹ, וְעִלְזוּ לְפָנָיו.[2] וּשְׁמוֹ מְרוֹמַם עַל כָּל בְּרָכָה וּתְהִלָּה.[3] בָּרוּךְ שֵׁם כְּבוֹד מַלְכוּתוֹ לְעוֹלָם וָעֶד. יְהִי שֵׁם יהוה מְבֹרָךְ, מֵעַתָּה וְעַד עוֹלָם.[4]

Chazzan bows at בָּרְכוּ and straightens up at ה'.

בָּרְכוּ אֶת יהוה הַמְּבֹרָךְ.

Congregation, followed by *chazzan*, responds, bowing at בָּרוּךְ and straightening up at ה'.

בָּרוּךְ יהוה הַמְּבֹרָךְ לְעוֹלָם וָעֶד.

ברכות קריאת שמע

It is preferable that one sit while reciting the following series of prayers — particularly the *Kedushah* verses, קָדוֹשׁ קָדוֹשׁ קָדוֹשׁ and בָּרוּךְ כְּבוֹד — until *Shemoneh Esrei*.

The following paragraph is recited aloud by the *chazzan*, then repeated by the congregation.

בָּרוּךְ אַתָּה יהוה אֱלֹהֵינוּ מֶלֶךְ הָעוֹלָם, יוֹצֵר אוֹר וּבוֹרֵא חֹשֶׁךְ, עֹשֶׂה שָׁלוֹם וּבוֹרֵא אֶת הַכֹּל.[5]

Congregations that do not recite *Yotzros* continue on page 534.

Congregations that recite *Yotzros* continue:

אוֹר עוֹלָם בְּאוֹצַר חַיִּים, אוֹרוֹת מֵאֹפֶל אָמַר וַיֶּהִי.

All:

אֲהוּבֶיךָ* אֲהֵבוּךָ מֵישָׁרִים,[6] שִׁירָתְךָ נוֹגְנִים וְשׁוֹרְרִים,
אַחֲרֵימוֹ קִדְּמוּ שָׁרִים,*[7] שִׁיר הַשִּׁירִים.*[8]
אֱמוּנַת עִתַּי[9] חֻקּוֹת, מִפֶּה אֶל פֶּה נֶעְתָּקוֹת,
אִמְרוֹתָיו חֵךְ מַמְתִּיקוֹת, יִשָּׁקֵנִי מִנְּשִׁיקוֹת.[10]
בַּעֲשׂוֹתְךָ נוֹרָאוֹת לַהֲמוֹנֶיךָ, עַזִּים נָסוּ מִפָּנֶיךָ,
בָּאוּרִים כִּבְדוּךָ מְרַנְּנֶיךָ, לְרֵיחַ שְׁמָנֶיךָ.[11]
בְּחוּרֵי רַחַם[12] מְשַׁחֲרֶיךָ, וּוָעֲדוּ לִקְרַאת דְּבָרֶיךָ,
בְּאַהַב הֱבִיאַנִי חֲדָרֶיךָ, מָשְׁכֵנִי אַחֲרֶיךָ.[13]
גִּדַּלְנִי וְרוֹמַמְנִי לְתַאֲוָה,* נִנְעַמְתִּי בְּשִׁמּוּר מִצְוָה,
גָּדַר בְּשׁוּמִי עִוָּה, שְׁחוֹרָה אֲנִי וְנָאוָה.[14]

אֲהוּבֶיךָ ⧼ — *Your beloved*. The *piyutim* of the Sabbath of *Chol HaMoed* were written by R' Shimon HaGadol of Mainz, Germany (c. 950-1020). More than a dozen of his *piyutim* have entered the Rosh Hashanah, Yom Kippur and Festivals *machzorim*. The popular *zemer* of the Sabbath morning meal, *Baruch Hashem Yom Yom*, is his composition.

The present *piyut* follows the style of the *yotzros* for the first two days. In the first forty-four stanzas, the first and third lines form a four-fold *aleph-beis* acrostic. The fourth line is a verse fragment from *Song of Songs;* and the respective second verses form the signature, שִׁמְעוֹן בַּר יִצְחָק יִגְדַּל בְּתוֹרָה וּבְמִצְוֹת וּבְמַעֲשִׂים טוֹבִים אָמֵן סֶלָה, *Shimon son of Yitzchak, may he become great in Torah, in mitzvos, and in good deeds. Amen, Selah.*

אַחֲרֵימוֹ קִדְּמוּ שָׁרִים — *[The angels are] after them; for the singers are first.* When Israel crossed the Sea of Reeds, they vied with the ministering angels for the right to sing God's praises first. The debate continued until God intervened and said, 'Let My children praise Me before My servants do.' This is the Midrashic interpretation of the verse (*Psalms* 68:26): קִדְּמוּ שָׁרִים אַחַר נֹגְנִים, *First went singers, then musicians.* 'Singers' refers to Israel — as it is written, אָז יָשִׁיר, *Then Moses and the*

In some congregations the *chazzan* chants a melody during his recitation of *Borchu,* so that the congregation can then recite *'Blessed, praised . . .'*

Chazzan bows at *'Bless,'* and straightens up at *'HASHEM.'*

Bless HASHEM, the blessed One.

Congregation, followed by *chazzan,* responds, bowing at *'Blessed'* and straightening up at *'HASHEM.'*

Blessed is HASHEM, the blessed One, for all eternity.

Blessed, praised, glorified, exalted and upraised is the Name of the King Who rules over kings — the Holy One, Blessed is He. For He is the First and He is the Last and aside from Him there is no god.[1] *Extol Him — Who rides the highest heavens — with His Name, YAH, and exult before Him.*[2] *His Name is exalted beyond every blessing and praise.*[3] *Blessed is the Name of His glorious kingdom for all eternity. Blessed be the Name of HASHEM from this time and forever.*[4]

BLESSINGS OF THE SHEMA

It is preferable that one sit while reciting the following series of prayers — particularly the *Kedushah* verses, *'Holy, holy, holy . . .'* and *'Blessed is the glory . . .'* — until *Shemoneh Esrei.*

The following paragraph is recited aloud by the *chazzan,* then repeated by the congregation.

בָּרוּךְ *Blessed are You, HASHEM, our God, King of the universe, Who forms light and creates darkness, makes peace and creates all.*[5]

Congregations that do not recite *Yotzros* continue on page 534.

Congregations that recite *Yotzros* continue:

The primeval light is in the treasury of eternal life;
'Let there be lights from the darkness,' He declared — and so it was!

All:

א *Your beloved* [Israel] sincerely loves You.*[6]
ש *Your song by the [angelic] musicians and [Israelite] singers,*
א *[the angels are] after them; for the singers are first,*[7]*
*the song that excels all songs.**[8]
א *Your faithful Torah, [studied] at set times,*[9]
מ *transmitted from mouth to mouth,*
א *its sayings as sweet to the palate, as if He kissed me with kisses.*[10]
ב *When You performed wonders for Your multitudes,*
ע *strong [waters] fled from before You,*
ב *in the depths were You honored by those who sing Your praises,*
which are like the scent of fragrant oil.[11]
ב *[Israel] blessed of the womb,*[12] *who seek You,*
ו *gathered to greet Your appointed leader [Moses],*
ב *with love, You brought me into Your Sanctuary,*
O draw me after You [once again].[13]
ג *He exalted me and elevated me to the ends [of the world],**
נ *I was sweetened with mitzvah observance.*
ג *Even when I twisted the fence [with idolatry],*
and I was blackened; nevertheless, I was beautiful.[14]*

(1) Cf. *Isaiah* 44:6. (2) *Psalms* 68:5. (3) Cf. *Nehemiah* 9:5. (4) *Psalms* 113:2. (5) Cf. *Isaiah* 45:7. (6) Cf. *Song of Songs* 1:4. (7) Cf. *Psalms* 68:26. (8) *Song of Songs* 1:1. (9) Cf. *Isaiah* 33:6. (10) *Song of Songs* 1:2. (11) 1:3. (12) Cf. *Genesis* 49:25. (13) *Song of Songs* 1:4. (14) 1:5.

Children of Israel sang (Exodus 15:1); and 'musicians' refers to the angels (*Shemos Rabbah* 23:7).

שִׁיר הַשִּׁירִים — *The song that excels all songs.* See commentary on page 276.

לְתַאֲוָה — *To the ends [of the world].* The translation is based on the verses, עַד תַּאֲוַת גִּבְעֹת עוֹלָם (*Genesis* 49:26), which *Rashi* renders, *to the boundaries of the world's hills.* Alternatively, תַּאֲוָה means *desire,* and is an allusion to the desirable Torah.

גַּפַּי מְרוֹמֵי קֶרֶת,*[1] בְּרַדְתִּי מֵהֱיוֹת גְּבֶרֶת,
גֹּאֲלִי חַי אֲנִי[2] מַזְכֶּרֶת, אַל תִּרְאֻנִי שֶׁאֲנִי שְׁחַרְחֹרֶת.[3]
דִּבַּרְתִּי בְּפִי לִמְחוֹלְלִי, רִבְצוּ בְּצָהַר לְהַשְׂכִּילִי,
דּוֹדִי פּוֹדִי וְגוֹאֲלִי, הַגִּידָה לִּי.[4]
דַּרְכֵי הוֹרִים דְּעִי, יוֹנֶקֶת חֶמֶד מַטָּעִי,
דִּירַת מִשְׁכְּנוֹתָם תֵּדְעִי, אִם לֹא תֵדְעִי.[5]
הַפְלֵא וָפֶלֶא הִרְאֵיתִי, צֵאתִי לְיֵשַׁע רַעְיָתִי,
הֲמוֹן לְתוֹדָה הִתְעֵיתִי, לְסֻסָתִי.*[6]
הֶקְשַׁרְתִּי יְפִי כְּתָרִים, חֶמְדַּת נְצוּל מִצְרַיִם,
הֲקִימוֹתִי בְּרִית בְּתָרִים,[7] נָאווּ לְחָיַיִךְ בַּתֹּרִים.[8]
וְאֵלַי קֵרַבְתִּיךְ בְּאַהַב, קוֹל הִשְׁמַעְתִּיךְ מִלַּהַב,
וַתַּעְדִּי עֲדִי מֻצְהַב, תּוֹרֵי זָהָב.[9]
וְעַם בָּחַרְתִּי בוֹ, יָצָא שֶׁכֶל מִלִּבּוֹ,
וְהֵמִיר כְּבוֹד מִשְׂגַּבּוֹ, עַד שֶׁהַמֶּלֶךְ בִּמְסִבּוֹ.[10]
זָעַף אֶשָּׂא לִכְמֹר, גָּעַל פֶּשַׁע לִשְׁמֹר,
זִמַּת אִוֶּלֶת לִזְמֹר, צְרוֹר הַמֹּר.[11]
זָעַם עָצַר עֹפֶר, דְּפִי צַחַן כִּפֵּר,
זִכְרוֹן כָּתוּב בַּסֵּפֶר, אֶשְׁכֹּל הַכֹּפֶר.*[12]
חֹבֶשׁ חָשׁ וּתְרוּפָה, לְכַנְפֵי כֶסֶף נֶחְפָּה,*
חֵן וָחֶסֶד מְרְעָפָה, הִנָּךְ יָפָה.[13]
חַנּוּן מֵשִׂים פֶּה,[14] בְּרֹגֶז רַחֵם[15] מְצַפֶּה,
חַי סֵתֶר צוֹפֶה, הִנְּךָ יָפֶה.[16]
טִירַת מְצוּקֵי נֶעֱזָזִים, תְּאַר אֵיתָנֵי חֲרוּזִים,
טֶכֶס זְרוֹעֵי מְפֻזָּזִים, קֹרוֹת בָּתֵּינוּ אֲרָזִים.[17]
טֹרַח עֹל סוֹבֶלֶת, וְלֹא נִכְזָבָה תוֹחֶלֶת,
טָמוּן וְסָפוּן מְנַצֶּלֶת, אֲנִי חֲבַצֶּלֶת.*[18]

(1) *Proverbs* 9:3. (2) *Job* 19:25. (3) *Song of Songs* 1:6. (4) 1:7. (5) 1:8. (6) 1:9. (7) See *Genesis* ch. 15. (8) *Song of Songs* 1:10. (9) 1:11. (10) 1:12. (11) 1:13. (12) 1:14. (13) 1:15. (14) Cf. *Exodus* 4:11. (15) Cf. *Habakkuk* 3:2. (16) *Song of Songs* 1:16. (17) 1:17. (18) 2:1.

גַּפַּי מְרוֹמֵי קֶרֶת — *My wings had been spread to the highest heavens.* This stanza refers either to Israel, who were literally 'in the clouds,' for they were completely protected by the Clouds of Glory that surrounded them, and who had a great downfall when they sinned with the Golden Calf. Or it refers to Moses who was with God in the highest heaven during the incident of the Golden Calf, but was nevertheless lowered in stature when his nation sinned, even in his absence.

לְסֻסָתִי — *When [I rode] upon My mare.* See commentary, page 278.

אֶשְׁכֹּל הַכֹּפֶר — *To be clustered with every atoning visitation* [lit., *a cluster of henna*]. The *paytan* plays on the word הַכֹּפֶר, *henna,* treating it as כֹּפֶר, *atonement.* The verse is then an allusion to the limited forgiveness granted the nation after the sin of the Golden Calf. At that time God forgave the nation, in the sense that He withheld immediate retribution. Nevertheless, God declared, *'On the day that I visit punishment upon them [for some future sin], I shall visit upon them their [former] sin'* (*Exodus* 32:34).

לְכַנְפֵי כֶסֶף נֶחְפָּה — *To those covered with silver wings.* Part of the atonement for the Golden Calf included the contribution of silver for the construction of the Tabernacle.

אֲנִי חֲבַצֶּלֶת — *I am sheltered by God's shadow*

*ג My wings had been spread to the highest heavens,[1]**
ב when I was demoted from being the mistress;
ג I recall my Living Redeemer,[2]
O do not look upon me, for I have been sullied.[3]
ד I spoke with my mouth to Him Who bore me,
ר 'Teach me how to endure the sundown [of exile].
ד O my Beloved, my Liberator, my Redeemer, tell me how.'[4]
ד [He answered,] 'You must know the ways of Your parents,
י nurtured by [the Torah,] my desirous planting,
ד accustom yourselves to dwell in their synagogues and study halls,
as if you did not know!'[5]
ה 'Wonder of wonders have I shown you,
צ when I went forth to save you, My companion,
*ה the multitudes of Lud [Egypt] I led astray, when [I rode] upon My mare.'[6]**
ה I adorned [you] with beautiful crowns,
ח the coveted [booty] of which Egypt was emptied,
ה I fulfilled the Covenant Between the Parts,[7]
and your cheeks are comely with circlets.'[8]
ו 'I drew you near Me with love,
ק I made My voice heard among flames,
ו I adorned you with golden jewelry, circlets of gold.'[9]
ו 'But the people whom I have chosen,
י understanding departed from their hearts,
ו when they exchanged the glory of their Stronghold,
while the king was yet at His table [Sinai].'[10]
ז 'I shall forgo My anger, replacing it with pity,
ג protecting against [the results of] abominable sin,
ז to excise foolish, sinful thoughts,
[exchanging your offensive smelling sin for] a bundle of myrrh.'[11]
ז [Moses,] the gazelle restrained fury [with his prayers],
ר he atoned for the falsehood and impurity,
ז yet its remembrance is written in the Torah,
*to be clustered with every atoning visitation.[12]**
ח He hurried remedy and cure,
*ל to those covered with silver wings,**
ח He rained grace and kindness upon them,
[saying,] 'Behold, you are beautiful.'[13]
ח O Gracious One, Who gave man the ability to speak,[14]
ב Who seeks pity, even in time of anger,[15]
ח O Living One, Who searches the hidden [crevices of our hearts],
it is You Who are beautiful.[16]
ט The Temple of the firmly based and powerful [righteous],
ת formed with strong rows [of building stone],
ט like an arm arrayed with [bracelets of] the finest gold,
the beams of our Temple are cedar.[17]
ט Bearing the oppressive yoke [of exile],
ו yet never forsaking hope [of salvation],
ט although the time of emptying [the exile] is hidden and concealed,
*I am sheltered by God's shadow.[18]**

יְקָר נֶעֱרַב כְּנִיחוֹחִים, רַחֲשׁ תְּחַן נֶאֱנָחִים,
יְדָעָם בְּגֵיא כַּסְלְחִים, כְּשׁוֹשַׁנָּה בֵּין הַחוֹחִים.[1]
יוֹרְשֵׁי הַר לְמִצְעָר, הִכִּיר וְאָהַב מִנֹּעַר,[2]
יְחַדְּוּהוּ זָקֵן וָנַעַר, כְּתַפּוּחַ בַּעֲצֵי הַיָּעַר.[3]
כִּלְכְּלַנִי בְּצִיָּה מְסֻבֶּבֶת, וְנִפְרַע נִשְׁיוֹן מַגְבֶּבֶת,*
כִּנְּסַנִי לְאֶרֶץ נוֹשֶׁבֶת, הֱבִיאַנִי אֶל בֵּית.[4]
כִּלְלַנִי בְּעֹז מִדְרָשׁוֹת, בְּשִׁבְעִים פָּנִים נִדְרָשׁוֹת,
כְּבוֹדָם חֲקוֹר מִלַּחֲשׁוֹת, סַמְּכוּנִי בָּאֲשִׁישׁוֹת.[5]
לֹא עֲזָבַנִי לְנַטְּשִׁי, מָגִנִּי וּמֵרִים רֹאשִׁי,[6]
לוּדִים מֵרְרוּ בְּקָשִׁי, שְׂמֹאלוֹ תַּחַת לְרֹאשִׁי.[7]
לְנַחֵץ קֵץ* יִשְׁעֲכֶם, צֵאת מֵאֹסֶר כִּבְלֵיהֶם,
לְהַמְתִּין בֹּא עִתְּכֶם, הִשְׁבַּעְתִּי אֶתְכֶם.[8]
מְסַבֵּל עֹל רוֹדִי, וַעֲדַנִי צוּר פּוֹדִי,
מְמַהֵר יֶשַׁע בַּעֲדִי, קוֹל דּוֹדִי.[9]
מְקַצֵּר זְמַן אָבִי, תֵּת צֳרִי לְמַכְאוֹבִי,
מְדַלֵּג מְקַפֵּץ לְהַאֲהִיבִי, דּוֹמֶה דוֹדִי לִצְבִי.[10]
נִגְדְּשָׁה סְאַת שׁוֹדְדִי, וְהִגִּיעַ עֵת מוֹעֲדִי,
נִסְעִי נָא וְהִכָּבְדִי, עָנָה דוֹדִי.[11]
נִגְדַּע עֹל וְנִשְׁבָּר, בְּאֵין מַחְסוֹר דָּבָר,
נֶאֱמָן רוֹעֶה גָבָר, כִּי הִנֵּה הַסְּתָו עָבָר.[12]
שָׂרֵי מוֹפֵת נִבְרָאוּ, מְלִיצֵי יֹשֶׁר נִקְרָאוּ,
סוֹרְרִים תְּמָהוּ כְּרָאוּ, הַנִּצָּנִים נִרְאוּ.[13]
סִבּוּ עֶגְלָה וַהֲרוּגֶיהָ, עֲבוֹתֶיהָ לְקַצֵּץ וְעוּגֶיהָ,
סוּף לְהַשְׁבִּית סִיגֶיהָ, הַתְּאֵנָה חָנְטָה פַגֶּיהָ.[14]
עֹז תּוּשִׁיָּה מִלְּגַלֵּעַ,[15] סָבִיב הֻגְבְּלוּ בְצֶלַע,
עָמְדָה בְּמִישׁוֹר מִלְּקַלַּע,* יוֹנָתִי בְּחַגְוֵי הַסֶּלַע.[16]
עֲוִילִים הֻצְּעוּ חֲלָלִים, יְצִיאֵי עַקְרַבֵּי אֻמְלָלִים,

(1) *Song of Songs* 2:2. (2) Cf. *Hoshea* 11:1. (3) *Song of Songs* 2:3. (4) 2:4. (5) 2:5. (6) Cf. *Psalms* 3:4. (7) *Song of Songs* 2:6. (8) 2:7. (9) 2:8. (10) 2:9. (11) 2:10. (12) 2:11. (13) 2:12. (14) 2:13. (15) Cf. *Proverbs* 18:1. (16) *Song of Songs* 2:14.

[lit., *I am a rose*]. The *paytan* treats חֲבַצֶּלֶת as if it were a contraction of the root חבא, *to hide* or *take shelter*, and צל, *shadow*.

וְנִפְרַע נִשְׁיוֹן מַגְבֶּבֶת — *And when the due debt was collected.* As atonement for believing the spies' evil report about the Land of Canaan, the nation was told they would have to sojourn forty years in the wilderness before they would be allowed to enter the Land. When the time was up, their debt was paid in full. [See *Numbers* 14:34.]

קֵץ — *One hundred ninety years.* See commentary, page 277.

מִלְּקַלַּע — *Not to be stoned.* God ordered Moses to set a boundary around Mount Sinai. If anyone would cross that boundary the nation was to pelt him with stones (see *Exodus* 19:12-13). Thus by standing on level ground at the foot of the mountain, one would protect himself from being stoned.

י *Precious one, sweet and satisfying as the offerings,*
ר *when their lips moved in supplication and groaning,*
י *He heard them in the Valley of the Kasluchim [Egypt],*
they were like a rose among the thorns.[1]
י *[Israel,] inheritors of the [Temple] Mount for a brief span,*
ה *He recognized and loved them from their childhood,*[2]
י *when elder and youth proclaimed His uniqueness,*
'He is like an apple among the forest's trees.'[3]
כ *He sustained me when I wandered in the parched desert,*
ו *and when the due debt was collected,**
כ *He brought me into an inhabited land, He brought me to the Temple.*[4]
כ *He encrowned me with Torah's exegesis,*
ב *expounded in seventy facets,*
כ *their glory is in delving deep — not in silent accession,*
they sustain me among flaming fires.[5]
ל *He did not forsake me or abandon me,*
מ *He is my shield, He raises my head.*[6]
ל *The Ludim [Egyptians] embittered me with heavy labor,*
but his left hand [gave support] under my head.[7]
ל *[In Egypt,] I advanced your salvation one hundred ninety years,**
צ *to remove you from the chain of your captivity.*
ל *[But in your present exile,] you must await the proper time,*
for thus have I adjured you.[8]
מ *[For freeing me] from bearing the yoke of my oppressors,*
ו *set a time, O my Rock, my Liberator,*
מ *hasten salvation for my sake, [let me hear] the voice of my Beloved.*[9]
מ *O He Who shortened my ancestor's time [of exile],*
ת *give balm to my pains,*
מ *leap, jump, to show Your love for me, for my Beloved is like a deer.*[10]
נ *When my looters' measure [of evil] will be filled,*
ו *and my time [for freedom] will have arrived,*
נ *'Travel forth and be glorified,' my Beloved will have called out.*[11]
נ *[In Egypt,] He cut and broke the yoke,*
ב *[He brought us out,] there was nothing lacking,*
נ *[Moses] the faithful shepherd overpowered [Pharaoh],*
for the wintertide [of exile] had passed.[12]
ס *When [Moses and Aaron] the masters of wonder were born,*
מ *those who were called speakers of righteousness,*
ס *the rebellious [Egyptians] wondered at what they saw,*
'The blossoms are seen [in the land].'[13]
ס *[God commanded the destructive angels:]*
Bring the [Egyptian] calf to its murderers,
ע *cut off her ropes and her anchors,*
ס *to destroy her evildoers in the Sea of Reeds.*
For the fig tree [Israel] has formed its fruits [of redemption].[14]
ע *Not revealing to them [the Torah,] the stronghold of wisdom,*[15]
ש *until a boundary was placed around the mountainside,*
ע *they stood on level land not to be stoned,**
[Israel,] My dove, in the clefts of the rock.[16]
ע *The sinful [Amalekites] were laid out like corpses,*
י *they are the issue of accursed scorpions,*

עוֹמְדִים לְזַנֵּב נֶחֱשָׁלִים,[1] אֶחֱזוּ לָנוּ שֻׁעָלִים.[2]
פָּרַשׂ עָנָן לְהַאֲהִילִי, מַגִּיהַּ בְּלֵיל הִלִּי,
פְּנוּקִים שָׁלֹשׁ* הֶאֱכִילִי, דּוֹדִי לִי.[3]
פְּעֻלַּת שָׂכָר קָפוּחַ, טָפַלְתִּי כְּנֹאד נָפוּחַ,
פֻּלַּצְתִּי בִּשְׂאֵת וְסַפּוּחַ, עַד שֶׁיָּפוּחַ.[4]
צִפִּיתִי עֹצֶב בִּי, וָתִיק רָחַק מִקִּרְבִּי,
צַגְתִּי לְבַקֵּשׁ אוֹהֲבִי, עַל מִשְׁכָּבִי.[5]
צִיר עֲלוֹת בִּתְחִנָּה, בַּקֵּשׁ כִּפּוּר לְמִי מָנָה,[6]
צְעוֹק וְחַלּוֹת אָנָּא,[7] אָקוּמָה נָּא.[8]
קֻשְּׁרוּ לְוִיִּם קְשׁוּרִים, יְפִי תֻמִּים וְאוּרִים,
קוֹמָם לְהַכּוֹת בּוֹעֲרִים, מְצָאוּנִי הַשּׁוֹמְרִים.[9]
קַבֵּל מָרוֹם תְּפִלָּתִי, מָחֹל פֶּשַׁע חַטָּאתִי,
קִרְבָתוֹ שָׁת בַּעֲדָתִי, כִּמְעַט שֶׁעָבַרְתִּי.[10]
רְאוּ בָּחַרְתִּי בָכֶם,[11] אַל תְּנַחֲצוּ יְצִיאַתְכֶם,
רְאוּת בְּצִיָּה עִתּוֹתֵיכֶם, הִשְׁבַּעְתִּי אֶתְכֶם.[12]
רָמָה קֶרֶן סְגֻלָּה, מִמִּדְבָּר יָצְאָה נִדְגָּלָה,
רוֹזְנִים נוֹסְדוּ[13] לְמַלְּלָה, מִי זֹאת עֹלָה.[14]
שִׁכֵּן בָּאָדָם שְׁכִינָתוֹ,[15] נִכְלְלָה מִצִּיּוֹן יִפְעָתוֹ,[16]
שִׁתֵּת אֶבֶן שְׁתִיָּתוֹ, הִנֵּה מִטָּתוֹ.[17]
שְׁלָמִים וְעוֹלוֹת לְקָרֵב, סֵדֶר בֹּקֶר וָעֶרֶב,
שָׁת כֹּהֲנֵי לְהִתְקָרֵב, כֻּלָּם אֲחֻזֵי חֶרֶב.*[18]
תִּכֵּן אֲרוֹן מִכְלוּלוֹ, לוּחוֹת מֻנָּחוֹת בְּצִלּוֹ,
תַּבְנִית כְּרוּבִים לְהַאֲהִילוֹ, אַפִּרְיוֹן עָשָׂה לוֹ.[19]
❖ תְּעוּדָה נְתוּנָה בְּחֹסֶף, הֲמוֹן עָם בְּהִתְאַסֵּף,
תֹּאַר סִפְּרָה בְּכֹסֶף, עַמּוּדָיו עָשָׂה כֶסֶף.[20]

Responsively:

❖ צְאֶינָה וּרְאֶינָה.[21] All– שׁוּר* בַּעֲטָרָה הַמְעֻטֶּרֶת.
❖ הִנָּךְ יָפָה.[22] All– מוֹר וּלְבוֹנָה מְקֻטֶּרֶת.[23]

(1) Cf. *Deuteronomy* 25:18. (2) *Song of Songs* 2:15. (3) 2:16. (4) 2:17. (5) 3:1. (6) Cf. *Numbers* 23:10. (7) See *Exodus* 32:31. (8) *Song of Songs* 3:2. (9) 3:3. (10) 3:4. (11) Cf. *Isaiah* 44:1-2. (12) *Song of Songs* 3:5. (13) Cf. *Psalms* 2:2. (14) *Song of Songs* 3:6. (15) Cf. *Psalms* 78:60. (16) Cf. 50:2. (17) *Song of Songs* 3:7. (18) 3:8. (19) 3:9. (20) 3:10. (21) 3:11. (22) 4:1. (23) Cf. 3:6.

פְּנוּקִים שָׁלֹשׁ — *Three types of delicacy.* This is a reference to the manna, the quails, and the well. [See *Exodus* 16:31; 17:6; *Numbers* 11:7-8, 31-32; 20:7-11.]

כֻּלָּם אֲחֻזֵי חֶרֶב — *All of them gripping the sword [of the Priestly Blessing].* This verse is connected to the preceding one in *Song of Songs* (3:7): *Behold the couch of the King of peace, sixty warriors surround it . . . all of them gripping the sword.* The Midrash interprets the 'sixty warriors' as an allusion to the sixty letters contained in the three verses of the Priestly Blessing (*Numbers* 6:24-26). And the Sages teach that every prayer which includes the Name of HASHEM is like a sword that pierces all obstacles.

שׁוּר — *To see.* From this point the acrostic reads: שִׁמְעוֹן בַּר יִצְחָק חֲזַק בְּתוֹרָה אָמֵן סֶלָה, *Shimon son of Yitzchak, may he be strong in Torah, Amen, Selah.*

ע *when they stood to encounter the weary stragglers [of Israel],*[1]
[God said to the angels:]
'Let us seize for ourselves the [Amalekite] foxes.'[2]
פ *He spread a cloud to tent over me,*
מ *He illuminated the night with a [pillar of] fire,*
פ *He fed me three types of delicacy,** *[proving that] my Beloved is for me.*[3]
פ *The earned reward [for accepting the Torah] was forfeited,*
ט *I became degraded, like an air-filled canteen,*
פ *I was awestruck, as if I had leprous scabs,*
until it [the flaming anger] blew by.[4]
צ *I beheld sadness within me,*
ו *when God distanced Himself from me,*
צ *I arose to seek my Beloved,* *from upon my bed [of sorrow].*[5]
צ *The emissary [Moses] raised supplications,*
ב *to seek atonement for the uncountable nation,*[6]
צ *to cry and to plead, 'I beg of You . . .*[7] *let me arise please.'*[8]
ק *The Levites adorned themselves with jewelry,*
י *as beautiful as the Kohen Gadol's breastplate,*
ק *when they stood up to beat the boorish sinners,*
[and the iniquitous ones cried,]
'The guardians [Levites] have found me . . .'[9]
ק *The Exalted One accepted my prayer,*
מ *and forgave my willful and erroneous sins,*
ק *the nearness of His Presence He placed among my flock [in the Tabernacle],* *[otherwise,] I almost would have passed away.*[10]
ר *[But now He has said:] See that I have chosen you,*[11]
א *but do not hasten your departure,*
ר *by seeing — while still in the arid wilderness [of your exile] — your time [for redemption],* *so have I adjured you.*[12]
ר *The pride of the treasured [Israel] was elevated,*
מ *and from the wilderness they went forth in bannered encampments;*
ר *the princes took counsel*[13] *to discuss it,* *'Who is this on the ascent?'*[14]
ש *He made His Presence dwell among man,*[15]
נ *He appeared among Zion's consummate beauty,*[16]
ש *He placed His foundation stone [there],* *behold, there is His couch.*[17]
ש *There to bring peace- and elevation-offerings,*
ס *to arrange every morning and evening,*
ש *He appointed my Kohanim to bring the offerings,*
all of them gripping the sword [of the Priestly Blessing].[18]*
ת *He prepared an Ark in its full beauty,*
ל *the Tablets lying in its shelter,*
ת *the forms of Cherubim tenting over it,*
thus He made for Himself a crowned canopy.[19]
ת Chazzan— *The testimony [Torah] was given openly,*
when the nation's multitude assembled,
the [Torah's] words illuminated with desirousness,
[Torah,] the world's pillar is made of [material more valuable than] silver.[20]

Responsively:

Chazzan— *Go forth and see!*[21] ש All— *To see** *the crown that crowns Him.*
Chazzan— *You are beautiful!*[22] מ All— *Censed with myrrh and frankincense.*[23]

❖ שִׁנַּיִךְ.[1] All— עוֹרְכֵי טַעֲמֵי מַסֹּרֶת.
❖ כְּחוּט הַשָּׁנִי.[2] All— וָתֵק שִׂפְתוֹתַיִךְ מְדַבֶּרֶת.
❖ כְּמִגְדַּל דָּוִיד.[3] All— נוֹשְׁקֵי הַגִּבּוֹרִים נֶאֱזֶרֶת.

All continue:

שְׁנֵי שָׁדַיִךְ,[4] בְּמַלְכוּת וּכְהֻנָּה מֻכְתֶּרֶת.
עַד שֶׁיָּפוּחַ,[5] רֶגֶשׁ הֱמוּלָּה עוֹבֶרֶת.
כֻּלָּךְ יָפָה,[6] יָפְיָפִית לִהְיוֹת גְּבֶרֶת.
אִתִּי מִלְּבָנוֹן כַּלָּה,[7] צַעֲדֵי טוֹטֶפֶת מְקֻשֶּׁרֶת.
לִבַּבְתִּנִי,[8] חֹסֶן יְקָרֵי מַזְכֶּרֶת.
מַה יָּפוּ,[9] קִשּׁוּטַיִךְ בְּעֹז וְתִפְאֶרֶת.
נֹפֶת,[10] חִכֵּךְ הָרִים עוֹקֶרֶת.
גַּן נָעוּל,[11] זוֹרַעַת חֶסֶד וְקוֹצֶרֶת.[12]
שְׁלָחַיִךְ,[13] קְבוּצֵי סִלְסוּל מַגְבֶּרֶת.
נֵרְדְּ וְכַרְכֹּם,[14] בְּשׁוּמֵךְ בְּאַפִּי קְטֹרֶת.
מַעְיַן גַּנִּים,[15] תְּעוּדָה דוֹרֶשֶׁת וְגוֹמֶרֶת.
עוּרִי צָפוֹן,[16] וּבוֹאִי לְהַעֲלוֹת תְּמוּרֶת.
בָּאתִי לְגַנִּי,[17] רְאוֹת גֻּלַּת הַכֹּתֶרֶת.[18]
אֲנִי יְשֵׁנָה,[19] הַלֵּב עֵר בְּמִשְׁמֶרֶת.
פָּשַׁטְתִּי,[20] אֶדֶר כְּתֹנֶת מְשֻׁזֶּרֶת.
דּוֹדִי,[21] מוֹשִׁיעַ פְּלֵיטָה הַנִּשְׁאֶרֶת.
קַמְתִּי,[22] נִצּוּחַ קְדֻשָּׁתוֹ מְסַפֶּרֶת.
פָּתַחְתִּי,[23] סִגּוּב תְּהִלָּתוֹ מְזַמֶּרֶת.
מְצָאֻנִי,[24] לִישְׁעוֹ מְקַוָּה וּמְסַבֶּרֶת.[25]
הִשְׁבַּעְתִּי,[26] הֲמוֹן מַלְאֲכֵי הַשָּׁרֵת.
מַה דּוֹדֵךְ,[27] שְׁאָלוּנִי תָּמִיד מַחֲשֶׁבֶת וּמַאֲמֶרֶת.
נַעֲרָץ וְנִשְׂגָּב תִּכֵּן שְׁחָקִים בַּזֶּרֶת.[28]
הַנַּעֲרָץ בְּשִׁלּוּשׁ קְדֻשָּׁה הַמְאֻשֶּׁרֶת.

(1) *Song of Songs* 4:2. (2) 4:3. (3) 4:4. (4) 4:5. (5) 4:6. (6) 4:7. (7) 4:8. (8) 4:9. (9) 4:10. (10) 4:11. (11) 4:12. (12) Cf. *Hoshea* 10:12. (13) *Song of Songs* 4:13. (14) 4:14. (15) 4:15. (16) 4:16. (17) 5:1. (18) Cf. *I Kings* 7:41. (19) *Song of Songs* 5:2. (20) 5:3. (21) 5:4. (22) 5:5. (23) 5:6. (24) 5:7. (25) Cf. *Genesis* 49:18 with *Targum Onkelos*. (26) *Song of Songs* 5:8. (27) 5:9. (28) Cf. *Isaiah* 40:12.

Chazzan— *Your teeth!*[1] ע All— *[Their speech is of] the orderly reasoning of the tradition.*

Chazzan— *Like a scarlet thread!*[2]
ו All— *Is the power of speech in your lips.*

Chazzan— *Like the Tower of David!*[3]
נ All— *Fortified with the weapons of the warriors.*

All continue:

[Then,] Your two nurturers [Moses and Aaron],[4]
ב *with kingship and priesthood were crowned.*
Soon there will blow [the winds of retribution],[5]
ר *the excited tumultuous gathering shall pass.*
Then you will be completely beautiful,[6]
י *beautiful enough to become the mistress.*
When you left the Temple with Me,[7]
צ *you were ornamented and bound in Tefillin.*
You captured My heart,[8]
ח *when you proclaimed My powerful glory [in the Shema].*
How beautiful you are,[9]
ק *when you are adorned with [Torah's] might and splendor.*
How sweet[10] ה *is your palate, uprooting mountains [with your Torah logic].*
[Your wives are modest] like a sealed garden,[11]
ז *sowing kindness and harvesting.*[12]
Your offspring[13] ק *gathering with powerful praise.*
Like nard and saffron,[14]
ב *[are the prayers] you place in My nostrils, like incense.*
Like a garden spring[15]
ת *they are everfresh in studying and expounding the [Torah's] testimony.*
Awaken from the north,[16]
ו *and come to bring up smoke-raising offerings.*
I came to My garden[-like Temple],[17]
ר *to see the capitals crowning the columns.*[18]
I am asleep,[19] ה *but my heart is awake with anticipation.*

Amen.

Although I have doffed[20]
א *the priestly tunic of braided linen;*
[nevertheless, I am assuaged, for] my Beloved[21]
מ *will save the remnant that has escaped.*
[Therefore] I have arisen[22]
נ *to sing and tell of His greatness.*
I began[23] ס *to sing His powerful praise.*
[Although] they have found me [wanting],[24]
ל *for His salvation I, nevertheless, long and pine.*[25]
I adjured[26] ה *the multitude of ministering angels,*

Chazzan— *'How does your Beloved differ from others,'*[27]
they ask, 'that you always proclaim His Oneness and exalt Him?'
[I reply,] 'He is mighty and powerful,
He measured the heavens with His little finger,[28]
He is exalted through the three-fold praises of Kedushah.

הַכֹּל יוֹדוּךָ, וְהַכֹּל יְשַׁבְּחוּךָ, וְהַכֹּל יֹאמְרוּ אֵין קָדוֹשׁ כַּיהוה.[1] הַכֹּל יְרוֹמְמְוּךָ סֶּלָה, יוֹצֵר הַכֹּל. הָאֵל הַפּוֹתֵחַ בְּכָל יוֹם דַּלְתוֹת שַׁעֲרֵי מִזְרָח, וּבוֹקֵעַ חַלּוֹנֵי רָקִיעַ, מוֹצִיא חַמָּה מִמְּקוֹמָהּ וּלְבָנָה מִמְּכוֹן שִׁבְתָּהּ, וּמֵאִיר לָעוֹלָם כֻּלּוֹ וּלְיוֹשְׁבָיו, שֶׁבָּרָא בְּמִדַּת רַחֲמִים. הַמֵּאִיר לָאָרֶץ וְלַדָּרִים עָלֶיהָ בְּרַחֲמִים, וּבְטוּבוֹ מְחַדֵּשׁ בְּכָל יוֹם תָּמִיד מַעֲשֵׂה בְרֵאשִׁית. הַמֶּלֶךְ הַמְּרוֹמָם לְבַדּוֹ מֵאָז, הַמְּשֻׁבָּח וְהַמְּפֹאָר וְהַמִּתְנַשֵּׂא מִימוֹת עוֹלָם. אֱלֹהֵי עוֹלָם בְּרַחֲמֶיךָ הָרַבִּים, רַחֵם עָלֵינוּ, אֲדוֹן עֻזֵּנוּ, צוּר מִשְׂגַּבֵּנוּ, מָגֵן יִשְׁעֵנוּ, מִשְׂגָּב בַּעֲדֵנוּ. אֵין כְּעֶרְכֶּךָ, וְאֵין זוּלָתֶךָ, אֶפֶס בִּלְתֶּךָ, וּמִי דּוֹמֶה לָּךְ. אֵין כְּעֶרְכְּךָ יהוה אֱלֹהֵינוּ בָּעוֹלָם הַזֶּה, וְאֵין זוּלָתְךָ מַלְכֵּנוּ לְחַיֵּי הָעוֹלָם הַבָּא. אֶפֶס בִּלְתְּךָ גּוֹאֲלֵנוּ לִימוֹת הַמָּשִׁיחַ, וְאֵין דּוֹמֶה לְּךָ מוֹשִׁיעֵנוּ לִתְחִיַּת הַמֵּתִים.

The following liturgical song is recited responsively in most congregations. In some congregations, the *chazzan* and congregation sing the stanzas together.

אֵל אָדוֹן עַל כָּל הַמַּעֲשִׂים, בָּרוּךְ וּמְבֹרָךְ בְּפִי כָּל נְשָׁמָה,
גָּדְלוֹ וְטוּבוֹ מָלֵא עוֹלָם, דַּעַת וּתְבוּנָה סוֹבְבִים אֹתוֹ.

הַמִּתְגָּאֶה עַל חַיּוֹת הַקֹּדֶשׁ, וְנֶהְדָּר בְּכָבוֹד עַל הַמֶּרְכָּבָה,
זְכוּת וּמִישׁוֹר לִפְנֵי כִסְאוֹ, חֶסֶד וְרַחֲמִים לִפְנֵי כְבוֹדוֹ.

טוֹבִים מְאוֹרוֹת שֶׁבָּרָא אֱלֹהֵינוּ, יְצָרָם בְּדַעַת בְּבִינָה וּבְהַשְׂכֵּל,
כֹּחַ וּגְבוּרָה נָתַן בָּהֶם, לִהְיוֹת מוֹשְׁלִים בְּקֶרֶב תֵּבֵל.

מְלֵאִים זִיו וּמְפִיקִים נֹגַהּ, נָאֶה זִיוָם בְּכָל הָעוֹלָם,
שְׂמֵחִים בְּצֵאתָם וְשָׂשִׂים בְּבוֹאָם, עוֹשִׂים בְּאֵימָה רְצוֹן קוֹנָם.

פְּאֵר וְכָבוֹד נוֹתְנִים לִשְׁמוֹ, צָהֳלָה וְרִנָּה לְזֵכֶר מַלְכוּתוֹ,
קָרָא לַשֶּׁמֶשׁ וַיִּזְרַח אוֹר, רָאָה וְהִתְקִין צוּרַת הַלְּבָנָה.

שֶׁבַח נוֹתְנִים לוֹ כָּל צְבָא מָרוֹם.
תִּפְאֶרֶת וּגְדֻלָּה, שְׂרָפִים וְאוֹפַנִּים וְחַיּוֹת הַקֹּדֶשׁ—

(1) *I Samuel* 2:2.

הַכֹּל יוֹדְוּךָ *All will thank You and all will praise You — and all will declare: 'Nothing is as holy as HASHEM!'[1] All will exalt You, Selah! — You Who forms everything. The God Who opens daily the doors of the gateways of the East, and splits the windows of the firmament, Who removes the sun from its place and the moon from the site of its dwelling, and Who illuminates all the world and its inhabitants, which He created with the attribute of mercy. He Who illuminates the earth and those who dwell upon it, with compassion; and in His goodness renews daily, perpetually, the work of creation. The King Who was exalted in solitude from before creation, Who is praised, glorified, and extolled since days of old. Eternal God, with Your abundant compassion be compassionate to us — O Master of our power, our rocklike stronghold; O Shield of our salvation, be a stronghold for us. There is no comparison to You, there is nothing except for You, there is nothing without You, for who is like You? There is no comparison to You, HASHEM, our God, in this world; and there will be nothing except for You, our King, in the life of the World to Come; there will be nothing without You, our Redeemer, in Messianic days; and there will be none like You, our Savior; at the Resuscitation of the Dead.*

The following liturgical song is recited responsively in most congregations.
In some congregations, the *chazzan* and congregation sing the stanzas together.

אֵל אָדוֹן *God — the Master over all works; the Blessed One —*
ב *and He is blessed by the mouth of every soul;*
ג *His greatness and goodness fill the world,*
ד *wisdom and insight surround Him.*
ה *He Who exalts Himself over the holy Chayos*
ו *and is splendrous in glory above the Chariot;*
ז *Merit and fairness are before His throne,*
ח *kindness and mercy are before His glory.*
ט *Good are the luminaries that our God has created,*
י *He has fashioned them with wisdom,*
with insight and discernment;
כ *Strength and power has He granted them,*
ל *to be dominant within the world.*
מ *Filled with luster and radiating brightness,*
נ *their luster is beautiful throughout the world;*
ס *Glad as they go forth and exultant as they return,*
ע *they do with awe their Creator's will.*
פ *Splendor and glory they bestow upon His Name,*
צ *jubilation and glad song upon the mention of His reign —*
ק *He called out to the sun and it glowed with light,*
ר *He saw and fashioned the form of the moon.*
ש *All the host above bestows praise on Him,*
ת *splendor and greatness — the Seraphim, Ophanim,*
and holy Chayos —

לָאֵל אֲשֶׁר שָׁבַת מִכָּל הַמַּעֲשִׂים, בַּיּוֹם הַשְּׁבִיעִי הִתְעַלָּה וְיָשַׁב עַל כִּסֵּא כְבוֹדוֹ, תִּפְאֶרֶת עָטָה לְיוֹם הַמְּנוּחָה, עֹנֶג קָרָא לְיוֹם הַשַּׁבָּת. זֶה שֶׁבַח שֶׁל יוֹם הַשְּׁבִיעִי, שֶׁבּוֹ שָׁבַת אֵל מִכָּל מְלַאכְתּוֹ. וְיוֹם הַשְּׁבִיעִי מְשַׁבֵּחַ וְאוֹמֵר: מִזְמוֹר שִׁיר לְיוֹם הַשַּׁבָּת, טוֹב לְהוֹדוֹת לַיהוה.[1] לְפִיכָךְ יְפָאֲרוּ וִיבָרְכוּ לָאֵל כָּל יְצוּרָיו. שֶׁבַח יְקָר וּגְדֻלָּה יִתְּנוּ לָאֵל מֶלֶךְ יוֹצֵר כֹּל, הַמַּנְחִיל מְנוּחָה לְעַמּוֹ יִשְׂרָאֵל בִּקְדֻשָּׁתוֹ בְּיוֹם שַׁבַּת קֹדֶשׁ. שִׁמְךָ יהוה אֱלֹהֵינוּ יִתְקַדַּשׁ, וְזִכְרְךָ מַלְכֵּנוּ יִתְפָּאַר, בַּשָּׁמַיִם מִמַּעַל וְעַל הָאָרֶץ מִתָּחַת. תִּתְבָּרַךְ מוֹשִׁיעֵנוּ עַל שֶׁבַח מַעֲשֵׂה יָדֶיךָ, וְעַל מְאוֹרֵי אוֹר שֶׁעָשִׂיתָ, יְפָאֲרוּךָ, סֶּלָה.

תִּתְבָּרַךְ צוּרֵנוּ מַלְכֵּנוּ וְגֹאֲלֵנוּ, בּוֹרֵא קְדוֹשִׁים. יִשְׁתַּבַּח שִׁמְךָ לָעַד מַלְכֵּנוּ, יוֹצֵר מְשָׁרְתִים, וַאֲשֶׁר מְשָׁרְתָיו כֻּלָּם עוֹמְדִים בְּרוּם עוֹלָם, וּמַשְׁמִיעִים בְּיִרְאָה יַחַד בְּקוֹל דִּבְרֵי אֱלֹהִים חַיִּים וּמֶלֶךְ עוֹלָם.[2] כֻּלָּם אֲהוּבִים, כֻּלָּם בְּרוּרִים, כֻּלָּם גִּבּוֹרִים, וְכֻלָּם עֹשִׂים בְּאֵימָה וּבְיִרְאָה רְצוֹן קוֹנָם. ❖ וְכֻלָּם פּוֹתְחִים אֶת פִּיהֶם בִּקְדֻשָּׁה וּבְטָהֳרָה, בְּשִׁירָה וּבְזִמְרָה, וּמְבָרְכִים וּמְשַׁבְּחִים וּמְפָאֲרִים וּמַעֲרִיצִים וּמַקְדִּישִׁים וּמַמְלִיכִים –

אֶת שֵׁם הָאֵל הַמֶּלֶךְ הַגָּדוֹל הַגִּבּוֹר וְהַנּוֹרָא קָדוֹשׁ הוּא.[3] ❖ וְכֻלָּם מְקַבְּלִים עֲלֵיהֶם עֹל מַלְכוּת שָׁמַיִם זֶה מִזֶּה, וְנוֹתְנִים רְשׁוּת זֶה לָזֶה, לְהַקְדִּישׁ לְיוֹצְרָם, בְּנַחַת רוּחַ בְּשָׂפָה בְרוּרָה וּבִנְעִימָה. קְדֻשָּׁה כֻּלָּם כְּאֶחָד עוֹנִים וְאוֹמְרִים בְּיִרְאָה:

Congregation recites aloud:

קָדוֹשׁ קָדוֹשׁ קָדוֹשׁ יהוה צְבָאוֹת,
מְלֹא כָל הָאָרֶץ כְּבוֹדוֹ.[4]

דּוֹדִי,[5] שַׁלִּיט* בְּכָל מִפְעָל, הַכֹּל לְמַעֲנֵהוּ פָּעַל,[6]
מְרֻבָּבָה דָּגוּל[7] וּמוּעָל, קָדוֹשׁ בְּמַטָּה וּבְמָעַל.
רֹאשׁוֹ עָטוּר פָּז[8] כֶּתֶר, טָהוֹר צוֹפֶה כָּל סֵתֶר,
וּמַאֲזִין לְקוֹל עֶתֶר, נַעֲרָץ בִּשְׂפַת יֶתֶר.

(1) *Psalms* 92:1-2. (2) Cf. *Jeremiah* 10:10. (3) Cf. *Deuteronomy* 10:17; *Psalms* 99:3. (4) *Isaiah* 6:3. (5) *Song of Songs* 5:10. (6) Cf. *Proverbs* 16:4. (7) Cf. *Song of Songs* 5:10. (8) 5:11.

לָאֵל *To the God Who rested from all works, Who ascended on the Seventh Day and sat on the Throne of His Glory. With splendor He enwrapped the Day of Contentment — He declared the Sabbath day a delight! This is the praise of the Sabbath Day: that on it God rested from all His work. And the Seventh Day gives praise saying: 'A psalm, a song for the Sabbath Day. It is good to thank* HASHEM *. . .'*[1] *Therefore let all that He has fashioned glorify and bless God. Praise, honor, and greatness let them render to God, the King Who fashioned everything, Who gives a heritage of contentment to His People, Israel, in His holiness on the holy Sabbath Day. May Your Name,* HASHEM, *our God, be sanctified and may Your remembrance, our King, be glorified in the heaven above and upon the earth below. May You be blessed, our Savior, beyond the praises of Your handiwork and beyond the brilliant luminaries that You have made — may they glorify You — Selah.*

תִּתְבָּרַךְ *May You be blessed, our Rock, our King and our Redeemer, Creator of holy ones; may Your Name be praised forever, our King, O Fashioner of ministering angels; all of Whose ministering angels stand at the summit of the universe and proclaim — with awe, together, loudly — the words of the living God and King of the universe.*[2] *They are all beloved; they are all flawless; they are all mighty; they all do the will of their Maker with dread and reverence.* Chazzan– *And they all open their mouth in holiness and purity, in song and hymn — and bless, praise, glorify, revere, sanctify and declare the kingship of —*

אֶת שֵׁם *The Name of God, the great, mighty, and awesome King; holy is He.*[3] Chazzan– *Then they all accept upon themselves the yoke of heavenly sovereignty from one another, and grant permission to one another to sanctify the One Who formed them, with tranquillity, with clear articulation, and with sweetness. All of them as one proclaim His holiness and say with awe:*

Congregation recites aloud:

'Holy, holy, holy is HASHEM, Master of Legions, the whole world is filled with His glory.'[4]

My beloved,[5] ש *Ruler* over all works,*
ה *He made everything for His glory,*[6]
מ *He is surrounded and exalted by myriads,*[7]
ק *holy on the earth below and in the heavens above.*
His head ע *is adorned with a crown of the finest gold,*[8]
ט *He is pure and sees all that is hidden,*
ו *He listens to the voice of prayer,*
נ *He is more powerful than even the most exaggerated praise.*

☙ דודי שליט — *My Beloved, Ruler.* This *piyut* continues citing the verses of *Song of Songs,* beginning where the previous one ended. It contains nine quatrains. Except for the first word of each stanza which is from *Song of Songs,* the odd-numbered lines form the acrostic שִׁמְעוֹן בַּר יִצְחָק בַּר אֲבוּנָא, *Shimon son of Yitzchak son of Avuna.* The even-numbered lines spell the remainder of the signature, הַקָּטָן יִזְכֶּה לְחַיֵּי עַד אָמֵן, *the Lesser, may he merit eternal life, Amen.*

עֵינָיו,[1] נֶגְדּוֹ יְיַשִּׁירוּ חוֹזִים, יָהּ חֲכַם הָרָזִים,
בָּחוּר נָעִים כָּאֲרָזִים,[2] זָךְ עוֹשֶׂה חֲזִיזִים.[3]
לְחָיָו רֶקַח מִגְדְּלוֹת בְּשָׂמִים,[4] כַּבִּיר מֵשִׁיב טְעָמִים,
יֹשֶׁר אֲמָרָיו נְעִימִים, הֶגְיוֹנָיו בֵּין מְחֻכָּמִים.
יָדָיו,[5] צֶדֶק וּמִשְׁפָּט מְפְלָאִים, לִגְלִילֵי תַרְשִׁישׁ מְמֻלָּאִים,[5]
חֲיָלֵי צְבָאָיו נוֹרָאִים, חַתִּים וּמִפָּנָיו יְרֵאִים.
שׁוֹקָיו,* קוֹמַת עַמּוּדֵי שֵׁשׁ,[6] יְסוֹד עוֹלָם[7] לְהִתְאַשֵּׁשׁ,
בַּשְּׁבִיעִי* לְמַעְלָה מִשֵּׁשׁ, יָפֶה כִסְאוֹ לְיַשֵּׁשׁ.
חִכּוֹ,[8] רִבֵּי תוֹרוֹת וְחֻקִּים, יִחוּדוֹ בְּתֵבֵל וּבִשְׁחָקִים,
אַדִּירֵי חַשְׁמַלֵּי* בְרָקִים, עֹצֶם קְדֻשָּׁתוֹ מְפִיקִים.
אָנָה[9] בָּרוּךְ וּמְבֹרָךְ שְׁמוֹ, דּוֹרְשִׁים אֶרְאֶלֵּי מְרוֹמוֹ,
וְזֶה אֶל זֶה קוֹרֵא נְאָמוֹ, אֹמֵר קָדוֹשׁ בְּשִׁלְּשׁוֹמוֹ.[10]
דּוֹדִי,[11] נוֹתֵן לְעַמּוֹ עֹז,[12] מִפִּימוֹ יִתְבָּרֵךְ בְּמָעוֹז,
אֲנִי, אֲחַזֵּק תְּהִלָּה וָעֹז, נֹעַם לְשֵׁם מִגְדַּל עֹז.[13]

Congregation, followed by the *chazzan,* recites one of these versions, according to its tradition.

וְהָאוֹפַנִּים וְחַיּוֹת הַקֹּדֶשׁ בְּרַעַשׁ גָּדוֹל מִתְנַשְּׂאִים לְעֻמַּת שְׂרָפִים. לְעֻמָּתָם מְשַׁבְּחִים וְאוֹמְרִים:

וְהַחַיּוֹת יְשׁוֹרֵרוּ, וּכְרוּבִים יְפָאֵרוּ, וּשְׂרָפִים יָרֹנּוּ, וְאֶרְאֶלִּים יְבָרֵכוּ. פְּנֵי כָל חַיָּה וְאוֹפָן וּכְרוּב לְעֻמַּת שְׂרָפִים. לְעֻמָּתָם מְשַׁבְּחִים וְאוֹמְרִים:

Congregation recites aloud:

בָּרוּךְ כְּבוֹד יהוה מִמְּקוֹמוֹ.[14]

לְאֵל בָּרוּךְ נְעִימוֹת יִתֵּנוּ. לְמֶלֶךְ אֵל חַי וְקַיָּם, זְמִרוֹת יֹאמֵרוּ, וְתִשְׁבָּחוֹת יַשְׁמִיעוּ. כִּי הוּא לְבַדּוֹ פּוֹעֵל גְּבוּרוֹת, עֹשֶׂה חֲדָשׁוֹת, בַּעַל מִלְחָמוֹת, זוֹרֵעַ צְדָקוֹת, מַצְמִיחַ יְשׁוּעוֹת, בּוֹרֵא רְפוּאוֹת, נוֹרָא תְהִלּוֹת, אֲדוֹן הַנִּפְלָאוֹת. הַמְּחַדֵּשׁ בְּטוּבוֹ בְּכָל יוֹם תָּמִיד מַעֲשֵׂה בְרֵאשִׁית. כָּאָמוּר: לְעֹשֵׂה אוֹרִים גְּדֹלִים,

(1) *Song of Songs* 5:12. (2) Cf. 5:15. (3) *Zechariah* 10:1. (4) *Song of Songs* 5:13. (5) 5:14. (6) 5:15. (7) Cf. *Proverbs* 10:25. (8) *Song of Songs* 5:16. (9) 6:1. (10) Cf. *Isaiah* 6:3. (11) *Song of Songs* 6:2. (12) Cf. *Psalms* 29:11. (13) Cf. *Proverbs* 18:10. (14) *Ezekiel* 3:12.

שׁוֹקָיו — *His legs.* This is an allusion to the righteous people, for just as the legs support the body, so does the righteous one support the world — as King Solomon wrote: **וְצַדִּיק יְסוֹד עוֹלָם**, *and the righteous one is the foundation of the world (Proverbs 10:25).*

בַּשְּׁבִיעִי — *In the seventh [heaven].* The Talmud (*Chagigah* 12b) names the seven heavens and describes the function of each. The seven, in ascending order, are: *Vilon, Rakiya, Shechakim, Zevul, Ma'on, Machon,* and *Aravos.*

חַשְׁמַלֵּי — *Chashmalim.* According to *Rambam* (*Yesodei HaTorah* 2:7) there are ten levels of angels: *Chayos, Ofanim, Erelim, Chashmalim, Seraphim, Malachim, Elohim, Bnei Elohim, Cheruvim* and *Ishim.*

His eyes[1] נ *observe how Israel aligns itself towards Him,*
י *He is God, the knower of secrets,*
ב *the choicest sweetness, [yet strong] like the cedars,*[2]
ז *He is the Pure One, Maker of the rain clouds.*[3]
His cheeks' [words at Sinai]
ר *were like a blend of sprouted spices.*[4]
כ *He is the Mighty One, Who replies with logic,*
י *the righteousness of His words are sweet,*
ה *His thoughts are understood by the Sages.*
His handiwork[5] *[the Tablets]*
צ *are marvels of righteousness and justice,*
ל *like [silver] rods set with blue crystal.*[5]
ח *The awesome armies of His [angelic] hosts,*
ח *shudder in fear before Him.*
*His legs** ק *erect as marble pillars,*[6]
י *to strengthen the world's foundation.*[7]
ב *In the seventh [heaven],* above the other six,*
י *it is fitting for His Throne to be placed forever.*
His palate[8] *[speaks]*
ר *abundant laws and decrees.*
י *He is unique on earth and in the heavens.*
א *The powerful flashing Chashmalim,**
ע *relate His mighty Holiness.*
'Where is[9] ב *the Blessed One, Whose Name is Blessed?'*
ד *inquire the Erelim of His heights.*
ו *And one to another calls out his words,*
א *as they thrice recite 'Holy.'*[10]
My Beloved,[11] נ *gives [the Torah's] strength to His people,*[12]
מ *from their mouth is He praised as the Fortress.*
א *I shall utter powerful praise*
נ *in sweetness, to Him Whose Name is a Tower of strength.*[13]

Congregation, followed by the *chazzan,* recites one of these versions, according to its tradition.

Then the Ofanim and the holy Chayos, with great noise raise themselves towards the Seraphim. Facing them they give praise saying:

Then the Chayos sing, the Cherubim glorify, the Seraphim rejoice, and the Erelim bless, in the presence of every Chayah, Ofan, and Cherub towards the Seraphim. Facing them they give praise saying:

Congregation recites aloud:

'Blessed is the glory of HASHEM from His place.'[14]

לְאֵל *To the blessed God they shall offer sweet melodies; to the King, the living and enduring God, they shall sing hymns and proclaim praises. For He alone effects mighty deeds, makes new things, is Master of wars, sows kindnesses, makes salvations flourish, creates cures, is too awesome for praise, is Lord of wonders. In His goodness He renews daily, perpetually, the work of creation. As it is said: '[Give thanks] to Him Who makes the great luminaries,*

כִּי לְעוֹלָם חַסְדּוֹ.[1] ❖ אוֹר חָדָשׁ עַל צִיּוֹן תָּאִיר, וְנִזְכֶּה כֻלָּנוּ מְהֵרָה לְאוֹרוֹ. בָּרוּךְ אַתָּה יהוה, יוֹצֵר הַמְּאוֹרוֹת. (Cong. – אָמֵן.)

אַהֲבָה רַבָּה אֲהַבְתָּנוּ יהוה אֱלֹהֵינוּ, חֶמְלָה גְדוֹלָה וִיתֵרָה חָמַלְתָּ עָלֵינוּ. אָבִינוּ מַלְכֵּנוּ, בַּעֲבוּר אֲבוֹתֵינוּ שֶׁבָּטְחוּ בְךָ, וַתְּלַמְּדֵם חֻקֵּי חַיִּים, כֵּן תְּחָנֵּנוּ וּתְלַמְּדֵנוּ. אָבִינוּ הָאָב הָרַחֲמָן הַמְּרַחֵם, רַחֵם עָלֵינוּ, וְתֵן בְּלִבֵּנוּ לְהָבִין וּלְהַשְׂכִּיל, לִשְׁמֹעַ לִלְמוֹד וּלְלַמֵּד, לִשְׁמֹר וְלַעֲשׂוֹת וּלְקַיֵּם אֶת כָּל דִּבְרֵי תַלְמוּד תּוֹרָתֶךָ בְּאַהֲבָה. וְהָאֵר עֵינֵינוּ בְּתוֹרָתֶךָ, וְדַבֵּק לִבֵּנוּ בְּמִצְוֹתֶיךָ, וְיַחֵד לְבָבֵנוּ לְאַהֲבָה וּלְיִרְאָה אֶת שְׁמֶךָ,[2] וְלֹא נֵבוֹשׁ לְעוֹלָם וָעֶד. כִּי בְשֵׁם קָדְשְׁךָ הַגָּדוֹל וְהַנּוֹרָא בָּטָחְנוּ, נָגִילָה וְנִשְׂמְחָה בִּישׁוּעָתֶךָ. וַהֲבִיאֵנוּ לְשָׁלוֹם מֵאַרְבַּע כַּנְפוֹת הָאָרֶץ, וְתוֹלִיכֵנוּ קוֹמְמִיּוּת לְאַרְצֵנוּ. כִּי אֵל פּוֹעֵל יְשׁוּעוֹת אָתָּה, וּבָנוּ בָחַרְתָּ מִכָּל עַם וְלָשׁוֹן. ❖ וְקֵרַבְתָּנוּ לְשִׁמְךָ הַגָּדוֹל סֶלָה בֶּאֱמֶת, לְהוֹדוֹת לְךָ וּלְיַחֶדְךָ בְּאַהֲבָה. בָּרוּךְ אַתָּה יהוה, הַבּוֹחֵר בְּעַמּוֹ יִשְׂרָאֵל בְּאַהֲבָה. (Cong. – אָמֵן.)

At this point, gather the four *tzitzis* between the fourth and fifth fingers of the left hand. Hold *tzitzis* in this manner throughout the *Shema*.

שמע

Immediately before its recitation, concentrate on fulfilling the positive commandment of reciting the *Shema* twice daily. It is important to enunciate each word clearly and not to run words together. For this reason, vertical lines have been placed between two words that are prone to be slurred into one and are not separated by a comma or a hyphen. See *Laws* §40-55.

When praying without a *minyan,* begin with the following three-word formula:

אֵל מֶלֶךְ נֶאֱמָן.

Recite the first verse aloud, with the right hand covering the eyes, and concentrate intently upon accepting God's absolute sovereignty.

שְׁמַע ׀ יִשְׂרָאֵל, יהוה ׀ אֱלֹהֵינוּ, יהוה ׀ אֶחָד:[3]

In an undertone – בָּרוּךְ שֵׁם כְּבוֹד מַלְכוּתוֹ לְעוֹלָם וָעֶד.

While reciting the first paragraph (דברים ו:ה־ט), concentrate on accepting the commandment to love God.

וְאָהַבְתָּ אֵת ׀ יהוה ׀ אֱלֹהֶיךָ, בְּכָל־לְבָבְךָ, וּבְכָל־נַפְשְׁךָ, וּבְכָל־מְאֹדֶךָ: וְהָיוּ הַדְּבָרִים הָאֵלֶּה, אֲשֶׁר ׀ אָנֹכִי מְצַוְּךָ הַיּוֹם, עַל־לְבָבֶךָ: וְשִׁנַּנְתָּם לְבָנֶיךָ, וְדִבַּרְתָּ בָּם, בְּשִׁבְתְּךָ בְּבֵיתֶךָ, וּבְלֶכְתְּךָ בַדֶּרֶךְ, וּבְשָׁכְבְּךָ וּבְקוּמֶךָ: וּקְשַׁרְתָּם לְאוֹת ׀ עַל־יָדֶךָ, וְהָיוּ לְטֹטָפֹת בֵּין ׀ עֵינֶיךָ: וּכְתַבְתָּם ׀ עַל־מְזֻזוֹת בֵּיתֶךָ, וּבִשְׁעָרֶיךָ:

for His kindness endures forever.'[1] Chazzan– *May You shine a new light on Zion, and may we all speedily merit its light. Blessed are You,* HASHEM, *Who fashions the luminaries.* (Cong.– *Amen*)

אַהֲבָה *With an abundant love have You loved us,* HASHEM, *our God; with exceedingly great pity have You pitied us. Our Father, our King, for the sake of our forefathers who trusted in You and whom You taught the decrees of life, may You be equally gracious to us and teach us. Our Father, the merciful Father, Who acts mercifully, have mercy upon us, instill in our hearts to understand and elucidate, to listen, learn, teach, safeguard, perform, and fulfill all the words of Your Torah's teaching with love. Enlighten our eyes in Your Torah, attach our hearts to Your commandments, and unify our hearts to love and fear Your Name,*[2] *and may we not feel inner shame for all eternity. Because we have trusted in Your great and awesome holy Name, may we exult and rejoice in Your salvation. Bring us in peacefulness from the four corners of the earth and lead us with upright pride to our land. For You effect salvations O God; You have chosen us from among every people and tongue.* Chazzan– *And You have brought us close to Your great Name forever in truth, to offer praiseful thanks to You, and proclaim Your Oneness with love. Blessed are You,* HASHEM, *Who chooses His people Israel with love.* (Cong.– *Amen.*)

At this point, gather the four *tzitzis* between the fourth and fifth fingers of the left hand. Hold *tzitzis* in this manner throughout the *Shema.*

THE SHEMA

Immediately before its recitation, concentrate on fulfilling the positive commandment of reciting the *Shema* twice daily. It is important to enunciate each word clearly and not to run words together. See *Laws* §40-55.

When praying without a *minyan,* begin with the following three-word formula:
God, trustworthy King.

Recite the first verse aloud, with the right hand covering the eyes, and concentrate intently upon accepting God's absolute sovereignty.

Hear, O Israel: HASHEM is our God, HASHEM, the One and Only.[3]

In an undertone– *Blessed is the Name of His glorious kingdom for all eternity.*

While reciting the first paragraph (*Deuteronomy* 6:5-9), concentrate on accepting the commandment to love God.

וְאָהַבְתָּ *You shall love* HASHEM, *your God, with all your heart, with all your soul and with all your resources. Let these matters that I command you today be upon your heart. Teach them thoroughly to your children and speak of them while you sit in your home, while you walk on the way, when you retire and when you arise. Bind them as a sign upon your arm and let them be tefillin between your eyes. And write them on the doorposts of your house and upon your gates.*

(1) *Psalms* 136:7. (2) Cf. 86:11. (3) *Deuteronomy* 6:4.

While reciting the second paragraph (דברים יא:יג-כא), concentrate on accepting all the commandments and the concept of reward and punishment.

וְהָיָה, אִם־שָׁמֹעַ תִּשְׁמְעוּ אֶל־מִצְוֹתַי, אֲשֶׁר | אָנֹכִי מְצַוֶּה | אֶתְכֶם הַיּוֹם, לְאַהֲבָה אֶת־יהוה | אֱלֹהֵיכֶם וּלְעָבְדוֹ, בְּכָל־לְבַבְכֶם, וּבְכָל־נַפְשְׁכֶם: וְנָתַתִּי מְטַר־אַרְצְכֶם בְּעִתּוֹ, יוֹרֶה וּמַלְקוֹשׁ, וְאָסַפְתָּ דְגָנֶךָ וְתִירֹשְׁךָ וְיִצְהָרֶךָ: וְנָתַתִּי | עֵשֶׂב | בְּשָׂדְךָ לִבְהֶמְתֶּךָ, וְאָכַלְתָּ וְשָׂבָעְתָּ: הִשָּׁמְרוּ לָכֶם, פֶּן־יִפְתֶּה לְבַבְכֶם, וְסַרְתֶּם וַעֲבַדְתֶּם | אֱלֹהִים | אֲחֵרִים, וְהִשְׁתַּחֲוִיתֶם לָהֶם: וְחָרָה | אַף־יהוה בָּכֶם, וְעָצַר | אֶת־הַשָּׁמַיִם, וְלֹא־יִהְיֶה מָטָר, וְהָאֲדָמָה לֹא תִתֵּן אֶת־יְבוּלָהּ, וַאֲבַדְתֶּם | מְהֵרָה מֵעַל הָאָרֶץ הַטֹּבָה | אֲשֶׁר | יהוה נֹתֵן לָכֶם: וְשַׂמְתֶּם | אֶת־דְּבָרַי | אֵלֶּה, עַל־לְבַבְכֶם וְעַל־נַפְשְׁכֶם, וּקְשַׁרְתֶּם | אֹתָם לְאוֹת | עַל־יֶדְכֶם, וְהָיוּ לְטוֹטָפֹת בֵּין | עֵינֵיכֶם: וְלִמַּדְתֶּם | אֹתָם | אֶת־בְּנֵיכֶם, לְדַבֵּר בָּם, בְּשִׁבְתְּךָ בְּבֵיתֶךָ, וּבְלֶכְתְּךָ בַדֶּרֶךְ, וּבְשָׁכְבְּךָ וּבְקוּמֶךָ: וּכְתַבְתָּם | עַל־מְזוּזוֹת בֵּיתֶךָ, וּבִשְׁעָרֶיךָ: לְמַעַן | יִרְבּוּ | יְמֵיכֶם וִימֵי בְנֵיכֶם, עַל הָאֲדָמָה | אֲשֶׁר נִשְׁבַּע | יהוה לַאֲבֹתֵיכֶם לָתֵת לָהֶם, כִּימֵי הַשָּׁמַיִם | עַל־הָאָרֶץ:

Before reciting the third paragraph (במדבר טו:לז-מא), the *tzitzis*, which have been held in the left hand, are taken in the right hand also. The *tzitzis* are kissed at each mention of the word and at the end of the paragraph, and are passed before the eyes at וּרְאִיתֶם אֹתוֹ.

וַיֹּאמֶר | יהוה | אֶל־מֹשֶׁה לֵּאמֹר: דַּבֵּר | אֶל־בְּנֵי | יִשְׂרָאֵל, וְאָמַרְתָּ אֲלֵהֶם, וְעָשׂוּ לָהֶם צִיצִת, עַל־כַּנְפֵי בִגְדֵיהֶם לְדֹרֹתָם, וְנָתְנוּ | עַל־צִיצִת הַכָּנָף, פְּתִיל תְּכֵלֶת: וְהָיָה לָכֶם לְצִיצִת, וּרְאִיתֶם | אֹתוֹ, וּזְכַרְתֶּם | אֶת־כָּל־מִצְוֹת | יהוה, וַעֲשִׂיתֶם | אֹתָם, וְלֹא תָתוּרוּ | אַחֲרֵי לְבַבְכֶם וְאַחֲרֵי | עֵינֵיכֶם, אֲשֶׁר־אַתֶּם זֹנִים | אַחֲרֵיהֶם: לְמַעַן תִּזְכְּרוּ, וַעֲשִׂיתֶם | אֶת־כָּל־מִצְוֹתָי, וִהְיִיתֶם קְדֹשִׁים לֵאלֹהֵיכֶם: אֲנִי יהוה | אֱלֹהֵיכֶם, אֲשֶׁר הוֹצֵאתִי | אֶתְכֶם | מֵאֶרֶץ מִצְרַיִם, לִהְיוֹת לָכֶם לֵאלֹהִים, אֲנִי | יהוה | אֱלֹהֵיכֶם: אֱמֶת –

Concentrate on fulfilling the commandment of remembering the Exodus from Egypt.

Although the word אֱמֶת belongs to the next paragraph, it is appended to the conclusion of the previous one, as explained in the commentary on page 50.

Chazzan repeats – **יהוה אֱלֹהֵיכֶם אֱמֶת.**

וְיַצִּיב וְנָכוֹן וְקַיָּם וְיָשָׁר וְנֶאֱמָן וְאָהוּב וְחָבִיב וְנֶחְמָד וְנָעִים וְנוֹרָא וְאַדִּיר וּמְתֻקָּן וּמְקֻבָּל וְטוֹב וְיָפֶה הַדָּבָר הַזֶּה עָלֵינוּ לְעוֹלָם וָעֶד. אֱמֶת אֱלֹהֵי עוֹלָם מַלְכֵּנוּ צוּר יַעֲקֹב, מָגֵן יִשְׁעֵנוּ, לְדֹר וָדֹר הוּא קַיָּם, וּשְׁמוֹ קַיָּם, וְכִסְאוֹ נָכוֹן, וּמַלְכוּתוֹ וֶאֱמוּנָתוֹ לָעַד קַיָּמֶת.

While reciting the second paragraph (*Deuteronomy* 11:13-21), concentrate on accepting all the commandments and the concept of reward and punishment.

וְהָיָה *And it will come to pass that if you continually hearken to My commandments that I command you today, to love HASHEM, your God, and to serve Him, with all your heart and with all your soul — then I will provide rain for your land in its proper time, the early and late rains, that you may gather in your grain, your wine, and your oil. I will provide grass in your field for your cattle and you will eat and be satisfied. Beware lest your heart be seduced and you turn astray and serve gods of others and bow to them. Then the wrath of HASHEM will blaze against you. He will restrain the heaven so there will be no rain and the ground will not yield its produce. And you will swiftly be banished from the goodly land which HASHEM gives you. Place these words of Mine upon your heart and upon your soul; bind them for a sign upon your arm and let them be tefillin between your eyes. Teach them to your children, to discuss them, while you sit in your home, while you walk on the way, when you retire and when you arise. And write them on the doorposts of your house and upon your gates. In order to prolong your days and the days of your children upon the ground that HASHEM has sworn to your ancestors to give them, like the days of the heaven on the earth.*

Before reciting the third paragraph (*Numbers* 15:37-41), the *tzitzis,* which have been held in the left hand, are taken in the right hand also. The *tzitzis* are kissed at each mention of the word and at the end of the paragraph, and are passed before the eyes at *'that you may see it.'*

וַיֹּאמֶר *And HASHEM said to Moses saying: Speak to the Children of Israel and say to them that they are to make themselves tzitzis on the corners of their garments, throughout their generations. And they are to place upon the tzitzis of each corner a thread of techeiles. And it shall constitute tzitzis for you, that you may see it and remember all the commandments of HASHEM and perform them; and not explore after your heart and after your eyes after which you stray. So that you may remember and perform all My commandments; and be holy to your God. I am HASHEM, your God, Who has removed you from the land of Egypt to be a God to you; I am HASHEM your God — it is true —*

Concentrate on fulfilling the commandment of remembering the Exodus from Egypt.

Although the word אֱמֶת, *'it is true,'* belongs to the next paragraph, it is appended to the conclusion of the previous one, as explained in the commentary on page 50.

Chazzan repeats: **HASHEM, your God, is true.**

וְיַצִּיב *And certain, established and enduring, fair and faithful, beloved and cherished, delightful and pleasant, awesome and powerful, correct and accepted, good and beautiful is this affirmation to us forever and ever. True — the God of the universe is our King; the Rock of Jacob is the Shield of our salvation. From generation to generation He endures and His Name endures and His throne is well established; His sovereignty and faithfulness endure forever.*

וּדְבָרָיו חָיִים וְקַיָּמִים, נֶאֱמָנִים וְנֶחֱמָדִים לָעַד (kiss the *tzitzis* and release them) וּלְעוֹלְמֵי עוֹלָמִים. ❖ עַל אֲבוֹתֵינוּ וְעָלֵינוּ, עַל בָּנֵינוּ וְעַל דּוֹרוֹתֵינוּ, וְעַל כָּל דּוֹרוֹת זֶרַע יִשְׂרָאֵל עֲבָדֶיךָ.

עַל הָרִאשׁוֹנִים וְעַל הָאַחֲרוֹנִים, דָּבָר טוֹב וְקַיָּם לְעוֹלָם וָעֶד, אֱמֶת וֶאֱמוּנָה חֹק וְלֹא יַעֲבֹר. אֱמֶת שָׁאַתָּה הוּא יהוה אֱלֹהֵינוּ וֵאלֹהֵי אֲבוֹתֵינוּ, ❖ מַלְכֵּנוּ מֶלֶךְ אֲבוֹתֵינוּ, גֹּאֲלֵנוּ גֹּאֵל אֲבוֹתֵינוּ, יוֹצְרֵנוּ צוּר יְשׁוּעָתֵנוּ, פּוֹדֵנוּ וּמַצִּילֵנוּ מֵעוֹלָם שְׁמֶךָ, אֵין אֱלֹהִים זוּלָתֶךָ.

All:

אֵלֶּה* וְכָאֵלֶּה* הֶרְאִיתַנִי, שָׁמְעָה אָזְנִי וְהֵבַנְתִּי,
לֹא יָדַעְתִּי נַפְשִׁי שָׂמַתְנִי.[1]
בְּבוֹאֲךָ לְהָדִיץ דְּאֵבִי,[2] מֶלֶל פַּצְתָּ לְהֵיטִיבִי, שׁוּבִי, שׁוּבִי.[3]*
גֵּיא חִזָּיוֹן[4] תְּחוּמַיִךְ, עֲלוֹתֵךְ לְהַגִּישׁ שְׁלָמַיִךְ, מַה יָּפוּ פְעָמַיִךְ.[5]
דְּגָלַיִךְ יַזְהִירוּ כְּזֹהַר,[6] וּכְעֶצֶם הַשָּׁמַיִם לָטֹהַר,[7]
שָׁרְרֵךְ אַגַּן הַסַּהַר.[8]
הֲדַר כִּהוּן אִפּוּדַיִךְ, נֹעַם מַלְכוּת כִּבּוּדַיִךְ, שְׁנֵי שָׁדַיִךְ.[9]
וְנַחַת שֻׁלְחָן דֶּשֶׁן,*[10] בְּנֹכַח מְנוֹרָה לְדַשֵּׁן,
צַוָּארֵךְ כְּמִגְדַּל הַשֵּׁן.[11]
זְבוּל קֹדֶשׁ הִלּוּלַיִךְ, רֶפֶד יְפִי מִכְלוּלַיִךְ, רֹאשֵׁךְ עָלַיִךְ.[12]
חַיִל לִמְאֹד עָצַמְתְּ, בְּרִבֵּי תוֹרוֹת נִתְחַכַּמְתְּ,
מַה יָּפִית וּמַה נָּעַמְתְּ.[13]
טַכְסִיס נוֹי תְּהִלָּתֵךְ, יִתְאַוּוּ לְאֻמִּים לִרְאוּתֵךְ, זֹאת קוֹמָתֵךְ.[14]
יְדוּעַיִךְ נְטוּעִים כְּמַשְׁמָר,*[15] צְנוּעִים בְּכָל מִשְׁמָר,
אָמַרְתִּי אֶעֱלֶה בְתָמָר.[16]

אֵלֶּה — *These.* The *paytan* now presents us with twenty-two triplets. The first two lines of the respective stanzas follow the *aleph-beis;* the third lines are from the verses of *Song of Songs* (although, for reasons unknown, the *paytan* omitted most of the verses of chapter six); and the composer's signature is formed by the initial letters of the second lines — שִׁמְעוֹן בְּרַב יִצְחָק חֲזַק וֶאֱמָץ אָמֵן, *Shimon son of R' Yitzchak, may he be strong and persevere, Amen.*

אֵלֶּה וְכָאֵלֶּה — *These and like these.* אֵלֶּה, *these,* alludes to the *mitzvos* in general — as it is written: אֵלֶּה הַמִּצְוֹת, *these are the mitzvos* (*Numbers* 36:13). כָאֵלֶּה, *like these,* refers to the laws peculiar to the festivals — as it is written: כָּאֵלֶּה תַּעֲשׂוּ לַיּוֹם שִׁבְעַת יָמִים, *like this shall you do each day for a seven-day period* (ibid. 28:24). Thus, although You taught me 'these' *mitzvos* and the *mitzvos* 'like these,' nevertheless, I went astray after the Golden Calf, about which the mixed multitude had declared, אֵלֶּה, when they said: אֵלֶּה אֱלֹהֶיךָ יִשְׂרָאֵל, *This is your god, O Israel!* (*Exodus* 32:4).

שׁוּבִי שׁוּבִי — *Return, [and] you shall return.* If you 'return' to Me in repentance, then you will 'return' to Jerusalem.

וְנַחַת שֻׁלְחָן דֶּשֶׁן — *The stationary Table with its abundant bread.* This stich is based on the verse: וְנַחַת שֻׁלְחָנְךָ מָלֵא דָשֶׁן, *and that which is placed on your table will be oily* [i.e., rich and filling] (*Job* 36:16). And the commentaries so treat the stich here: 'the *Lechem HaPanim* placed upon the Table shall be full of fat and oil.' We have rejected this translation because the *Lechem*

His words are living and enduring, faithful and delightful forever (kiss the *tzitzis* and release them) *and to all eternity;* Chazzan– *for our forefathers and for us, for our children and for our generations, and for all the generations of Your servant Israel's offspring.*

עַל הָרִאשׁוֹנִים *Upon the earlier and upon the later generations, this affirmation is good and enduring forever. True and faithful, it is an unbreachable decree. It is true that You are* HASHEM, *our God and the God of our forefathers,* Chazzan– *our King and the King of our forefathers, our Redeemer, the Redeemer of our forefathers; our Molder, the Rock of our salvation; our Liberator and our Rescuer — this has ever been Your Name. There is no God but You.*

All:

א *These* and like these* have You shown me,*
ש *my ears heard and You made me understand,*
yet I did not know, for my soul misled me [after the Golden Calf].[1]
ב *When You came to assuage my sadness,*[2]
מ *You spoke words [of admonition and love] for my benefit:*
'Return, [and] you shall return . . .[3]*
ג *'To [Jerusalem,] Valley of Visions,*[4] *your estate,*
ע *there you shall ascend to bring your peace-offerings.*
How lovely you will be there during the pilgrimage festivals![5]
ד *'Your noted Sages [of the Sanhedrin] shine brightly,*[6]
ו *like the brilliant purity of the heavens,*[7]
[sitting] in a crescent at the center of the world.[8]
ה *'The splendor of [Aaron] the Kohen Gadol wearing your ephod,*
ו *The serene majesty [of Moses] is your glory,*
[they are] your two nurturers.[9]
ו *'The stationary Table with its abundant bread,*[10]*
כ *opposite the Menorah of the charred wicks,*
[in] your Temple, [stately] as an ivory tower.[11]
ז *'The Temple of your sanctified praise,*
ר *your couch of consummate beauty,* *your King is upon it.*[12]
ח *'You have strengthened yourself with abundant wealth,*
ב *you have become wise in many facets of Torah knowledge.*
How beautiful you are! How pleasant you are![13]
ט *'Your praises form a comely array,*
י *nations desire to see you.* *That is your stature!*[14]
י *'Your knowledgeable ones are planted like a nail,*[15]*
צ *modestly observing all mitzvos,*
I have said, "I shall be exalted through the palm-like [righteous ones]."[16]

(1) *Song of Songs* 6:12. (2) Cf. *Job* 41:14. (3) *Song of Songs* 7:1. (4) *Isaiah* 22:1 [see commentary, p. 64]. (5) *Song of Songs* 7:2. (6) *Daniel* 12:3. (7) *Exodus* 24:10. (8) *Song of Songs* 7:3. (9) 7:4. (10) Cf. *Job* 36:16. (11) *Song of Songs* 7:5. (12) 7:6. (13) 7:7. (14) 7:8. (15) Cf. *Ecclesiastes* 12:11. (16) *Song of Songs* 7:9 [see also *Psalms* 92:13].

HaPanim did not contain oil — as is evident from the Mishnah (*Menachos* 5:3). The translation *stationary* for נַחַת is based on the Talmud's description of the Table (*Chagigah* 26b) as: כְּלִי עֵץ הֶעָשׂוּי לְנַחַת, *a wooden vessel made to be used as a stationary fixture.*

נְטוּעִים כְּמַשְׂמָר— *Planted like a nail.* Just as a well-driven nail is permanent, so are the word

כְּתוּרָה בְּשֵׂכֶל טוֹב, חֲמוּדָה מִזָּהָב טוֹב,[1] וְחִכֵּךְ כְּיֵין הַטּוֹב.[2]
לָאֵל אֲקַוֶּה לְסַעֲדִי, קְדוֹשִׁי פּוֹדִי וּכְבוֹדִי, אֲנִי לְדוֹדִי.[3]
מְפֻזֶּרֶת מִקָּצֶה לְקָצֶה, חַנּוּן סְגוּרֶיהָ הַיְצֵא, לְכָה דוֹדִי נֵצֵא.[4]
נַהֵל מְעוּטֵי עַמִּים,[5] זָרַח אוֹרֵךְ לַעֲמוּמִים, נַשְׁכִּימָה לַכְּרָמִים.[6]
שׁוֹשׁ מְסִבָּה לְהַאֲרִיחַ, קוֹל קוֹרֵא לְהַצְרִיחַ,
הַדּוּדָאִים נָתְנוּ רֵיחַ.[7]
עִמְּךָ בְּנוֹעַד לְהַאֲהִילִי, וְלָבֹא בְּשִׂמְחַת גִּילִי,[8] מִי יִתֶּנְךָ כְּאָח לִי.[9]
פְּנוֹת דֶּרֶךְ בְּבוֹאֶךָ, אֶל מְכוֹנָךְ וּמִקְרָאֶךָ, אֶנְהָגֲךָ אֲבִיאֲךָ.[10]
צֵאת מִמַּסְגֵּר נַפְשִׁי,[11] מֵבִין מַעֲבִידֵי בְּקָשִׁי,
שְׂמֹאלוֹ תַּחַת רֹאשִׁי.[12]
קַוּוֹת מוֹעֵד עִתְּכֶם, צִיּוֹן עֲלוֹת קִרְיַתְכֶם, הִשְׁבַּעְתִּי אֶתְכֶם.[13]
רוֹאֵי מוֹפְתֵי הַגְּאֻלָּה, אֹמֶר יַעֲנוּ בְמִלָּה, מִי זֹאת עוֹלָה.[14]
שׁוֹכְנֵי בְּגֵיא גָלוּתָם, מַהֵר מֵאִתְּךָ תְּהִלָּתָם, שִׂימֵנִי כַחוֹתָם.[15]
תְּקֶף עֹז אֲהָבִים, נַגֵּן שִׁירִים עֲרֵבִים, כְּעַל מַיִם רַבִּים.[16]

מַיִם רַבִּים,[16] שַׂמְתָּ נְתִיבָה.*[17]
אָחוֹת,[18] מָשַׁכְתָּ לְךָ בְּאַהֲבָה.
אִם,[19] עֻנֵּתִי וְנַפְשִׁי תְאֵבָה.
אֲנִי חוֹמָה[20] וְשָׁדַי לְאֵין קִצְבָה.
כֶּרֶם,[21] נָעִים וְנַחֲלָה חֲשׁוּבָה.
כַּרְמִי,[22] בָּזְזוּ וְשָׁמוּנִי חֳרֵבָה.
הַיּוֹשֶׁבֶת,[23] רְבוּצָה וְיֶשַׁע מְקַוָּה.[24]
בְּרַח,[25] יֶשַׁע הַפְלֵא דָּגוּל מֵרְבָבָה,[26]
דּוֹדִי,[25] צוּר נַעֲרָץ בְּאַלְפֵי רְבָבָה.
וּדְמֵה לְךָ,[25] חַי כְּעַל מֵי תְהוֹם רַבָּה.
קְדוֹשִׁים שִׁבְּחוּךָ שִׁירָה עֲרֵבָה.
בְּגִילָה בְּרִנָּה בְּשִׂמְחָה רַבָּה.

On *Chol HaMoed* continue on page 548.
On the seventh and eighth days continue עֶזְרַת on page 868.

(1) Cf. *Psalms* 19:11. (2) *Song of Songs* 7:10. (3) 7:11. (4) 7:12. (5) Cf. *Deuteronomy* 7:7. (6) *Song of Songs* 7:13. (7) 7:14 [see commentary, p. 314]. (8) Cf. *Psalms* 43:4. (9) *Song of Songs* 8:1. (10) 8:2. (11) Cf. *Psalms* 142:8. (12) *Song* 8:3. (13) 8:4. (14) 8:5. (15) 8:6. (16) 8:7. (17) Cf. *Isaiah* 43:16. (18) *Song of Songs* 8:8. (19) 8:9. (20) 8:10. (21) 8:11. (22) 8:12. (23) 8:13. (24) Cf. *Genesis* 49:18. (25) *Song of Songs* 8:14. (26) 5:10.

of the Sages permanent. Just as a planting sprouts, blossoms and bears fruit, so do the words of the Sages sprout, blossom and bear fruit (*Rashi* to *Ecclesiastes* 12:11).

(מַיִם רַבִּים) שַׂמְתָּ נְתִיבָה — *(Through the many waters,) You placed a road.* The acrostic of this section of the *piyut* spells שִׁמְעוֹן בַּר יִצְחָק, *Shimon son of Yitzchak.*

כ *'[You are] crowned with [the Torah's] good understanding,*
ח *more desirous than fine gold,*[1]
[the words of] your palate like the best wine.'[2]
ל *[Israel responds] 'To God do I hope for my support,*
ק *He is my Holy One, my Liberator, my Glory, I am my Beloved's.'*[3]
מ *She is dispersed from one end of the earth to the other,*
ח *O Gracious One, liberate her incarcerated ones.*
Come, my Beloved, let us go out.[4]
נ *Lead [Israel] the smallest of nations,*[5]
ז *shine forth Your light to those in the darkness [of exile],*
let us awake and head for the [Temple's] vineyards.[6]
ס *Rejoice, prepare a feast,*
ק *may a voice call, to cry out [the news of the Messiah's arrival],*
for the two baskets emit a fragrance.[7]
ע *To join with You in the Tent of Meeting,*
ו *to come to my joyous celebration,*[8]
if only You would be like a brother to me![9]
פ *Clear the way for your arrival,*
א *at your Temple, your convocation.*
I shall lead you; I shall bring you![10]
צ *Release my soul from confinement,*[11]
מ *from among those who enclosed me with hard labor,*
with Your left hand under my head,[12]
ק *[God replies:] To hope for the time I have set for you,*
צ *to ascend to Zion, your city, so have I adjured you.*[13]
ר *Those who see the wonders of the Redemption,*
א *will say, will speak these words, 'Who is this who is ascending?'*[14]
ש *Those who dwell in the valley of their exile,*
מ *hasten [to allow them] to praise You [by saying],*
'From You [has redemption come]!
O place me as a seal [on Your heart]!'[15]
ת *[Arouse] powerfully strong love,*
נ *so that we will sing sweet songs,*
as [we sang] upon the many waters [of the Sea of Reeds].[16]

Through the many waters,[16] ש *You placed a road;*[17]*
Your 'sister' [Israel],[18] מ *You drew to Yourself with love.*
Although[19] ע *I am pained, I long for You.*
My faith is a solid wall,[20] ו *and my nurturing [Sages expound the Torah] without end.*
I am a vineyard[21] נ *sweet — and a valuable heritage.*
My vineyard[22] ב *have they despoiled and me have they laid waste.*
She sits[23] ר *stooped over, hoping for salvation.*[24]
Run![25] י *Bring wondrous salvation, O You Who are surrounded by myriads [of angels].*[26]
My Beloved,[25] צ *Rock, revered by thousands of myriads.*
Do comparably[25] *—* ח *O Living One — to what You did to the waters of the great depths.*
ק *Then the holy ones will praise You with sweet song,*
with mirth, with glad song, with abundant gladness.

עֶזְרַת אֲבוֹתֵינוּ אַתָּה הוּא מֵעוֹלָם, מָגֵן וּמוֹשִׁיעַ לִבְנֵיהֶם אַחֲרֵיהֶם בְּכָל דּוֹר וָדוֹר. בְּרוּם עוֹלָם מוֹשָׁבֶךָ, וּמִשְׁפָּטֶיךָ וְצִדְקָתְךָ עַד אַפְסֵי אָרֶץ. אַשְׁרֵי אִישׁ שֶׁיִּשְׁמַע לְמִצְוֹתֶיךָ, וְתוֹרָתְךָ וּדְבָרְךָ יָשִׂים עַל לִבּוֹ. אֱמֶת אַתָּה הוּא אָדוֹן לְעַמֶּךָ וּמֶלֶךְ גִּבּוֹר לָרִיב רִיבָם. אֱמֶת אַתָּה הוּא רִאשׁוֹן וְאַתָּה הוּא אַחֲרוֹן, וּמִבַּלְעָדֶיךָ אֵין לָנוּ מֶלֶךְ[1] גּוֹאֵל וּמוֹשִׁיעַ. מִמִּצְרַיִם גְּאַלְתָּנוּ יהוה אֱלֹהֵינוּ, וּמִבֵּית עֲבָדִים פְּדִיתָנוּ. כָּל בְּכוֹרֵיהֶם הָרָגְתָּ, וּבְכוֹרְךָ גָּאָלְתָּ, וְיַם סוּף בָּקַעְתָּ, וְזֵדִים טִבַּעְתָּ, וִידִידִים הֶעֱבַרְתָּ, וַיְכַסּוּ מַיִם צָרֵיהֶם, אֶחָד מֵהֶם לֹא נוֹתָר.[2] עַל זֹאת שִׁבְּחוּ אֲהוּבִים וְרוֹמְמוּ אֵל, וְנָתְנוּ יְדִידִים זְמִרוֹת שִׁירוֹת וְתִשְׁבָּחוֹת, בְּרָכוֹת וְהוֹדָאוֹת, לְמֶלֶךְ אֵל חַי וְקַיָּם, רָם וְנִשָּׂא, גָּדוֹל וְנוֹרָא, מַשְׁפִּיל גֵּאִים, וּמַגְבִּיהַּ שְׁפָלִים, מוֹצִיא אֲסִירִים, וּפוֹדֶה עֲנָוִים, וְעוֹזֵר דַּלִּים, וְעוֹנֶה לְעַמּוֹ בְּעֵת שַׁוְּעָם אֵלָיו.

Rise for *Shemoneh Esrei.* Some take three steps backward at this point; others do so before צוּר יִשְׂרָאֵל.

❖ תְּהִלּוֹת לְאֵל עֶלְיוֹן, בָּרוּךְ הוּא וּמְבֹרָךְ. מֹשֶׁה וּבְנֵי יִשְׂרָאֵל לְךָ עָנוּ שִׁירָה בְּשִׂמְחָה רַבָּה וְאָמְרוּ כֻלָּם:

מִי כָמֹכָה בָּאֵלִם יהוה, מִי כָּמֹכָה נֶאְדָּר בַּקֹּדֶשׁ, נוֹרָא תְהִלֹּת עֹשֵׂה פֶלֶא.[3] ❖ שִׁירָה חֲדָשָׁה שִׁבְּחוּ גְאוּלִים לְשִׁמְךָ עַל שְׂפַת הַיָּם, יַחַד כֻּלָּם הוֹדוּ וְהִמְלִיכוּ וְאָמְרוּ:

יהוה יִמְלֹךְ לְעֹלָם וָעֶד.[4]

It is forbidden to interrupt or pause between גָּאַל יִשְׂרָאֵל and *Shemoneh Esrei,* even for *Kaddish, Kedushah* or *Borchu.*

❖ **צוּר** יִשְׂרָאֵל, קוּמָה בְּעֶזְרַת יִשְׂרָאֵל, וּפְדֵה כִנְאֻמֶךָ יְהוּדָה וְיִשְׂרָאֵל. גֹּאֲלֵנוּ יהוה צְבָאוֹת שְׁמוֹ, קְדוֹשׁ יִשְׂרָאֵל.[5]

בְּרַח דּוֹדִי[6] אֶל שֶׁאֲנַן נָוֶה,[7] וְאִם הֶלְאֵינוּ דֶּרֶךְ הָעֲוֶה,[8]
הִנֵּה לָקִינוּ בְּכָל מַדְוֶה,[9] וְאַתָּה יהוה מָעוֹז וּמִקְוֶה,
עָלֶיךָ כָּל הַיּוֹם נְקַוֶּה,[10] לְגָאֳלֵינוּ וּלְשִׁיתֵינוּ כְּגַן רָוֶה.[11]

בְּרַח דּוֹדִי אֶל מְקוֹם מִקְדָּשֵׁנוּ,[12] וְאִם עֲוֹנוֹת עָבְרוּ רֹאשֵׁנוּ,[13]
הִנֵּה בָאָה בְּבַרְזֶל נַפְשֵׁנוּ,[14] וְאַתָּה יהוה גֹּאֲלֵנוּ קְדוֹשֵׁנוּ,[15]
עָלֶיךָ נִשְׁפֹּךְ שִׂיחַ[16] רַחֲשֵׁנוּ, לְגָאֳלֵנוּ מִמְּעוֹן קָדְשֶׁךָ[17] לְהַחְפִּישֵׁנוּ.

(1) Cf. *Isaiah* 44:6. (2) *Psalms* 106:11. (3) *Exodus* 15:11. (4) 15:18. (5) *Isaiah* 47:4. (6) *Song of Songs* 8:14. (7) Cf. *Isaiah* 33:20. (8) Cf. *Jeremiah* 3:21. (9) Cf. *Deuteronomy* 7:15; 28:60. (10) Cf. *Psalms* 25:5. (11) Cf. *Isaiah* 58:11; *Jeremiah* 31:11. (12) *Jeremiah* 17:12. (13) Cf. *Psalms* 38:5. (14) Cf. 105:18. (15) Cf. *Isaiah* 47:4; 48:17. (16) Cf. *Psalms* 102:1; 142:3. (17) Cf. *Jeremiah* 25:30.

עֶזְרַת *The Helper of our forefathers are You alone, forever, Shield and Savior for their children after them in every generation. At the zenith of the universe is Your dwelling, and Your justice and Your righteousness extend to the ends of the earth. Praiseworthy is the person who obeys Your commandments and takes to his heart Your teaching and Your word. True — You are the Master for Your people and a mighty King to take up their grievance. True — You are the First and You are the Last, and other than You we have no king,*[1] *redeemer, or savior. From Egypt You redeemed us,* HASHEM, *our God, and from the house of slavery You liberated us. All their firstborn You slew, but Your firstborn You redeemed; the Sea of Reeds You split; the wanton sinners You drowned; the dear ones You brought across; and the water covered their foes — not one of them was left.*[2] *For this, the beloved praised and exalted God; the dear ones offered hymns, songs, praises, blessings, and thanksgivings to the King, the living and enduring God — exalted and uplifted, great and awesome, Who humbles the haughty and lifts the lowly; withdraws the captive, liberates the humble, and helps the poor; Who responds to His people upon their outcry to Him.*

Rise for *Shemoneh Esrei.* Some take three steps backward at this point; others do so before צוּר יִשְׂרָאֵל, *'Rock of Israel.'*

Chazzan– *Praises to the Supreme God, the blessed One Who is blessed. Moses and the Children of Israel exclaimed a song to You with great joy and they all said:*

'Who is like You among the heavenly powers, HASHEM*! Who is like You, mighty in holiness, too awesome for praise, doing wonders.'*[3]

Chazzan– *With a new song the redeemed ones praised Your Name at the seashore, all of them in unison gave thanks, acknowledged [Your] sovereignty, and said:*

'HASHEM shall reign for all eternity.'[4]

It is forbidden to interrupt or pause between *'Who redeemed Israel'* and *Shemoneh Esrei,* even for *Kaddish, Kedushah* or *Borchu.*

צוּר Chazzan– *Rock of Israel, arise to the aid of Israel and liberate, as You pledged, Judah and Israel. Our Redeemer —* HASHEM, *Master of Legions, is His Name — the Holy One of Israel.*[5]

ש *Flee, my Beloved,*[6] *to the tranquil abode.*[7]
Though we have grown weary on a perverted path,[8]
behold we have been afflicted with every sort of pain.[9]
You, HASHEM, *are power and hope;*
for You we hope all the day,[10]
to redeem us and to make us a fertile garden.[11]

מ *Flee, my Beloved, to the site of our Sanctuary.*[12]
Though sins have overflowed our head,[13]
behold our lives are fettered in an iron exile.[14]
You, HASHEM, *our Redeemer, our Holy One,*[15]
to You we pour out the words[16] *of our prayer,*
to redeem us — from Your holy abode[17] *— and to set us free.*

בְּרַח דּוֹדִי אֶל עִיר צִדְקֵנוּ,[1] וְאִם לֹא שָׁמַעְנוּ לְקוֹל מַצְדִּיקֵנוּ,
הִנֵּה אֲכָלוּנוּ בְּכָל פֶּה מַדִּיקֵינוּ,[2] וְאַתָּה יהוה שׁוֹפְטֵנוּ מְחֹקְקֵנוּ,[3]
עָלֶיךָ נַשְׁלִיךְ יְהַב חֶלְקֵנוּ,[4] לְגָאֳלֵנוּ בְּהַשְׁקֵט וּבְבִטְחָה לְהַחֲזִיקֵנוּ.[5]

בְּרַח דּוֹדִי אֶל וְעַד הַזְּבוּל, וְאִם עֻלָּךְ שָׁבַרְנוּ בְּלִי סָבוֹל,[6]
הִנֵּה לָקִינוּ בְּכָל מִינֵי חִבּוּל, וְאַתָּה יהוה מְשַׂמֵּחַ אָבוּל,[7]
עָלֶיךָ נַסְבִּיר לְהַתִּיר כָּבוּל, לְגָאֳלֵנוּ לְהִתְגַּדֵּל מֵעַל לִגְבוּל.[8]

בְּרַח דּוֹדִי אֶל נִשָּׂא מִגְּבָעוֹת,[9] וְאִם זַדְנוּ בִּפְרֹעַ פְּרָעוֹת,[10]
הִנֵּה הִשִּׂיגוּנוּ צָרוֹת רַבּוֹת וְרָעוֹת,[11] וְאַתָּה יהוה אֵל לְמוֹשָׁעוֹת,[12]
עָלֶיךָ נִשְׁפֹּךְ שִׂיחַ[13] שְׁוָעוֹת, לְגָאֳלֵנוּ וּלְעַתְּרֵנוּ כְּוֹבַע יְשׁוּעוֹת.[14]
בִּגְלַל אָבוֹת תּוֹשִׁיעַ בָּנִים, וְתָבִיא גְאֻלָּה לִבְנֵי בְנֵיהֶם.

בָּרוּךְ אַתָּה יהוה, גָּאַל יִשְׂרָאֵל.

❧ שמונה עשרה – עמידה ❧

Take three steps backward, then three steps forward. Remain standing with feet together while reciting *Shemoneh Esrei*. Recite it with quiet devotion and without interruption, verbal or otherwise. Although it should not be audible to others, one must pray loudly enough to hear himself.

אֲדֹנָי שְׂפָתַי תִּפְתָּח, וּפִי יַגִּיד תְּהִלָּתֶךָ.[15]

אבות

Bend the knees at בָּרוּךְ; bow at אַתָּה; straighten up at ה׳.

בָּרוּךְ אַתָּה יהוה אֱלֹהֵינוּ וֵאלֹהֵי אֲבוֹתֵינוּ, אֱלֹהֵי אַבְרָהָם, אֱלֹהֵי יִצְחָק, וֵאלֹהֵי יַעֲקֹב, הָאֵל הַגָּדוֹל הַגִּבּוֹר וְהַנּוֹרָא, אֵל עֶלְיוֹן, גּוֹמֵל חֲסָדִים טוֹבִים וְקוֹנֵה הַכֹּל, וְזוֹכֵר חַסְדֵי אָבוֹת, וּמֵבִיא גוֹאֵל לִבְנֵי בְנֵיהֶם, לְמַעַן שְׁמוֹ בְּאַהֲבָה. מֶלֶךְ עוֹזֵר וּמוֹשִׁיעַ וּמָגֵן.

Bend the knees at בָּרוּךְ; bow at אַתָּה; straighten up at ה׳.

בָּרוּךְ אַתָּה יהוה, מָגֵן אַבְרָהָם.

גבורות

אַתָּה גִּבּוֹר לְעוֹלָם אֲדֹנָי, מְחַיֵּה מֵתִים אַתָּה, רַב לְהוֹשִׁיעַ. מְכַלְכֵּל חַיִּים בְּחֶסֶד, מְחַיֵּה מֵתִים בְּרַחֲמִים רַבִּים, סוֹמֵךְ נוֹפְלִים, וְרוֹפֵא חוֹלִים, וּמַתִּיר אֲסוּרִים, וּמְקַיֵּם אֱמוּנָתוֹ לִישֵׁנֵי עָפָר. מִי כָמוֹךָ בַּעַל גְּבוּרוֹת, וּמִי דּוֹמֶה לָּךְ, מֶלֶךְ מֵמִית וּמְחַיֶּה וּמַצְמִיחַ יְשׁוּעָה. וְנֶאֱמָן אַתָּה לְהַחֲיוֹת מֵתִים. בָּרוּךְ אַתָּה יהוה, מְחַיֵּה הַמֵּתִים.

During the *chazzan's* repetition, *Kedushah* (page 552) is recited at this point.

(1) Cf. *Isaiah* 1:21,26. (2) Cf. *Daniel* 7:19. (3) Cf. *Isaiah* 33:22. (4) Cf. *Psalms* 55:23. (5) Cf. *Isaiah* 30:15. (6) Cf. *Jeremiah* 5:5; *Isaiah* 9:3. (7) Cf. *Esther* 9:22. (8) Cf. *Malachi* 1:5. (9) Cf. *Isaiah* 2:2. (10) *Judges* 5:2. (11) *Psalms* 71:20. (12) 68:21. (13) Cf. 102:1. (14) Cf. *Isaiah* 59:17. (15) *Psalms* 51:17.

ע *Flee, my Beloved, to our righteous City.*[1]
Though we have not listened to the voice of those [the prophets] who would make us righteous,
behold our foes have devoured and ground us down.[2]
You, HASHEM, our Judge and Lawgiver,[3]
upon You we cast our granted portion,[4]
to redeem us quietly and to strengthen us in security.[5]
ו *Flee, my Beloved, to the appointed abode.*
Though we have broken Your yoke unwilling to endure it,[6]
behold we have been struck with every manner of assault.
You, HASHEM, gladden the aggrieved;[7]
upon You is our hope to release the chained,
to redeem us and make us unboundedly great.[8]
נ *Flee, my Beloved, to the most exalted mountain.*[9]
Though we have sinned wantonly in breaching [the faith],[10]
behold we have been overtaken by abundant and evil travails.[11]
You, HASHEM, God of salvations,[12]
upon You we pour our prayerful cries,[13]
to redeem us and crown us with the cap of salvations.[14]
For the sake of the forefathers may You save the offspring and bring the redemption to their children's children.

Blessed are You, HASHEM, Who redeemed Israel.

SHEMONEH ESREI – AMIDAH

Take three steps backward, then three steps forward. Remain standing with feet together while reciting *Shemoneh Esrei*. Recite it with quiet devotion and without interruption, verbal or otherwise. Although it should not be audible to others, one must pray loudly enough to hear himself.

My Lord, open my lips, that my mouth may declare Your praise.[15]

PATRIARCHS

Bend the knees at *'Blessed'*; bow at *'You'*; straighten up at *'HASHEM.'*

בָּרוּךְ *Blessed are You, HASHEM, our God and the God of our forefathers, God of Abraham, God of Isaac, and God of Jacob; the great, mighty, and awesome God, the supreme God, Who bestows beneficial kindnesses and creates everything, Who recalls the kindnesses of the Patriarchs and brings a Redeemer to their children's children, for His Name's sake, with love. O King, Helper, Savior, and Shield.*

Bend the knees at *'Blessed'*; bow at *'You'*; straighten up at *'HASHEM.'*

Blessed are You, HASHEM, Shield of Abraham.

GOD'S MIGHT

אַתָּה *You are eternally mighty, my Lord, the Resuscitator of the dead are You; abundantly able to save. He sustains the living with kindness, resuscitates the dead with abundant mercy, supports the fallen, heals the sick, releases the confined, and maintains His faith to those asleep in the dust. Who is like You, O Master of mighty deeds, and who is comparable to You, O King Who causes death and restores life and makes salvation sprout! And You are faithful to resuscitate the dead. Blessed are You, HASHEM, Who resuscitates the dead.*

During the *chazzan's* repetition, *Kedushah* (page 552) is recited at this point.

קדושת השם

INDIVIDUALS RECITE:

אַתָּה קָדוֹשׁ וְשִׁמְךָ קָדוֹשׁ, וּקְדוֹשִׁים בְּכָל יוֹם יְהַלְלוּךָ סֶּלָה. בָּרוּךְ אַתָּה יהוה, הָאֵל הַקָּדוֹשׁ.

CHAZZAN RECITES DURING HIS REPETITION:

לְדוֹר וָדוֹר נַגִּיד גָּדְלֶךָ וּלְנֵצַח נְצָחִים קְדֻשָּׁתְךָ נַקְדִּישׁ, וְשִׁבְחֲךָ אֱלֹהֵינוּ מִפִּינוּ לֹא יָמוּשׁ לְעוֹלָם וָעֶד, כִּי אֵל מֶלֶךְ גָּדוֹל וְקָדוֹשׁ אָתָּה. בָּרוּךְ אַתָּה יהוה, הָאֵל הַקָּדוֹשׁ.

קדושת היום

יִשְׂמַח מֹשֶׁה* בְּמַתְּנַת חֶלְקוֹ, כִּי עֶבֶד נֶאֱמָן קָרָאתָ לּוֹ. כְּלִיל תִּפְאֶרֶת* בְּרֹאשׁוֹ נָתַתָּ (לוֹ), בְּעָמְדוֹ לְפָנֶיךָ עַל הַר סִינָי. וּשְׁנֵי לוּחוֹת אֲבָנִים הוֹרִיד בְּיָדוֹ,[1] וְכָתוּב בָּהֶם שְׁמִירַת שַׁבָּת. וְכֵן כָּתוּב בְּתוֹרָתֶךָ:

וְשָׁמְרוּ בְנֵי יִשְׂרָאֵל אֶת הַשַּׁבָּת, לַעֲשׂוֹת אֶת הַשַּׁבָּת לְדֹרֹתָם בְּרִית עוֹלָם. בֵּינִי וּבֵין בְּנֵי יִשְׂרָאֵל אוֹת הִיא לְעֹלָם, כִּי שֵׁשֶׁת יָמִים עָשָׂה יהוה אֶת הַשָּׁמַיִם וְאֶת הָאָרֶץ, וּבַיּוֹם הַשְּׁבִיעִי שָׁבַת וַיִּנָּפַשׁ.[2]

קדושה

When reciting *Kedushah,* one must stand with his feet together and avoid any interruptions. One should rise on his toes when saying the words קָדוֹשׁ, קָדוֹשׁ, קָדוֹשׁ; בָּרוּךְ (of בָּרוּךְ כְּבוֹד); and יִמְלֹךְ.

Cong. then *Chazzan* – **נְקַדֵּשׁ** אֶת שִׁמְךָ בָּעוֹלָם, כְּשֵׁם שֶׁמַּקְדִּישִׁים אוֹתוֹ בִּשְׁמֵי מָרוֹם, כַּכָּתוּב עַל יַד נְבִיאֶךָ, וְקָרָא זֶה אֶל זֶה וְאָמַר:

All – קָדוֹשׁ קָדוֹשׁ קָדוֹשׁ יהוה צְבָאוֹת, מְלֹא כָל הָאָרֶץ כְּבוֹדוֹ.[3] ❖ אָז בְּקוֹל רַעַשׁ גָּדוֹל אַדִּיר וְחָזָק מַשְׁמִיעִים קוֹל, מִתְנַשְּׂאִים לְעֻמַּת שְׂרָפִים, לְעֻמָּתָם בָּרוּךְ יֹאמֵרוּ:

All – בָּרוּךְ כְּבוֹד יהוה, מִמְּקוֹמוֹ.[4] ❖ מִמְּקוֹמְךָ מַלְכֵּנוּ תוֹפִיעַ, וְתִמְלֹךְ עָלֵינוּ, כִּי מְחַכִּים אֲנַחְנוּ לָךְ. מָתַי תִּמְלֹךְ בְּצִיּוֹן, בְּקָרוֹב בְּיָמֵינוּ, לְעוֹלָם וָעֶד תִּשְׁכּוֹן. תִּתְגַּדַּל וְתִתְקַדַּשׁ בְּתוֹךְ יְרוּשָׁלַיִם עִירְךָ, לְדוֹר וָדוֹר וּלְנֵצַח נְצָחִים. וְעֵינֵינוּ תִרְאֶינָה מַלְכוּתֶךָ, כַּדָּבָר הָאָמוּר בְּשִׁירֵי עֻזֶּךָ, עַל יְדֵי דָוִד מְשִׁיחַ צִדְקֶךָ:

All – יִמְלֹךְ יהוה לְעוֹלָם, אֱלֹהַיִךְ צִיּוֹן לְדֹר וָדֹר, הַלְלוּיָהּ.[5]

Chazzan continues . . . לְדוֹר וָדוֹר (above).

⁂ **יִשְׂמַח מֹשֶׁה** — *Moses rejoiced* that God considered him a faithful servant *[Numbers* 12:7] and that, in reward for Moses' dedication, God chose him to receive the tablets of the Ten Commandments, which included the *mitzvah* of the Sabbath.

Why is Moses singled out for mention in connection with the Sabbath and why only in the morning *Amidah?* Among the reasons are: — The Ten Commandments were given to

HOLINESS OF GOD'S NAME

INDIVIDUALS RECITE:

אַתָּה *You are holy and Your Name is holy, and holy ones praise You every day, forever. Blessed are You,* HASHEM, *the holy God.*

CHAZZAN RECITES DURING HIS REPETITION:

לְדוֹר *From generation to generation we shall relate Your greatness and for infinite eternities we shall proclaim Your holiness. Your praise, our God, shall not leave our mouth forever and ever, for You, O God, are a great and holy King. Blessed are You,* HASHEM, *the holy God.*

SANCTIFICATION OF THE DAY

יִשְׂמַח *Moses rejoiced* in the gift of his portion: that You called him a faithful servant. A crown of splendor* You placed on his head when he stood before You on Mount Sinai. He brought down two stone tablets in his hand,*[1] *on which is inscribed the observance of the Sabbath. So it is written in Your Torah:*

וְשָׁמְרוּ *And the Children of Israel shall keep the Sabbath, to make the Sabbath an eternal covenant for their generations. Between Me and the Children of Israel it is a sign forever that in six days* HASHEM *made heaven and earth, and on the seventh day He rested and was refreshed.*[2]

KEDUSHAH

When reciting *Kedushah*, one must stand with his feet together and avoid any interruptions. One should rise on his toes when saying the words *Holy, holy, holy; Blessed is;* and *HASHEM shall reign.*

Cong. then Chazzan — **נְקַדֵּשׁ** *We shall sanctify Your Name in this world, just as they sanctify it in heaven above, as it is written by Your prophet, "And one [angel] will call another and say:*

All — *'Holy, holy, holy is* HASHEM, *Master of Legions, the whole world is filled with His glory.'"*[3] ❖ *Then, with a sound of great noise, mighty and powerful, they make heard a voice, raising themselves toward the seraphim; those facing them say 'Blessed . . .':*

All — *'Blessed is the glory of* HASHEM *from His place.'*[4] ❖ *From Your place, our King, You will appear and reign over us, for we await You. When will You reign in Zion? Soon, in our days — forever and ever — may You dwell there. May You be exalted and sanctified within Jerusalem, Your city, from generation to generation and for all eternity. May our eyes see Your kingdom, as it is expressed in the songs of Your might, written by David, Your righteous anointed:*

All — *'*HASHEM *shall reign forever — your God, O Zion — from generation to generation, Halleluyah!'*[5]

Chazzan continues לְדוֹר וָדוֹר, *From generation . . .* (above).

---

(1) Cf. *Exodus* 32:15. (2) 31:16-17. (3) *Isaiah* 6:3. (4) *Ezekiel* 3:12. (5) *Psalms* 146:10.

Moses on the morning of the Sabbath.
— When he was still a child growing up in Pharaoh's palace, Moses asked the king to proclaim the Sabbath as a day of rest for the enslaved Jews.
— God told Moses in Marah, before Israel came to Mount Sinai, 'I have a precious gift called Sabbath. Teach the Jews about it.'

כְּלִיל תִּפְאֶרֶת — *A crown of splendor.* When Moses descended from Sinai, his face glowed with a Divine radiance, signifying that he was worthy to be a bearer of God's splendor. [See *Exodus* 34:29.]

וְלֹא נְתַתּוֹ* יהוה אֱלֹהֵינוּ לְגוֹיֵי הָאֲרָצוֹת, וְלֹא הִנְחַלְתּוֹ מַלְכֵּנוּ לְעוֹבְדֵי פְסִילִים, וְגַם בִּמְנוּחָתוֹ לֹא יִשְׁכְּנוּ עֲרֵלִים. כִּי לְיִשְׂרָאֵל עַמְּךָ נְתַתּוֹ בְּאַהֲבָה, לְזֶרַע יַעֲקֹב אֲשֶׁר בָּם בָּחָרְתָּ. עַם מְקַדְּשֵׁי שְׁבִיעִי, כֻּלָּם יִשְׂבְּעוּ וְיִתְעַנְּגוּ מִטּוּבֶךָ. וּבַשְּׁבִיעִי רָצִיתָ בּוֹ וְקִדַּשְׁתּוֹ חֶמְדַּת יָמִים אוֹתוֹ קָרָאתָ, זֵכֶר לְמַעֲשֵׂה בְרֵאשִׁית.

אֱלֹהֵינוּ וֵאלֹהֵי אֲבוֹתֵינוּ, רְצֵה בִמְנוּחָתֵנוּ, קַדְּשֵׁנוּ בְּמִצְוֹתֶיךָ, וְתֵן חֶלְקֵנוּ בְּתוֹרָתֶךָ, שַׂבְּעֵנוּ מִטּוּבֶךָ, וְשַׂמְּחֵנוּ בִּישׁוּעָתֶךָ, וְטַהֵר לִבֵּנוּ לְעָבְדְּךָ בֶּאֱמֶת. וְהַנְחִילֵנוּ יהוה אֱלֹהֵינוּ בְּאַהֲבָה וּבְרָצוֹן שַׁבַּת קָדְשֶׁךָ, וְיָנוּחוּ בוֹ יִשְׂרָאֵל מְקַדְּשֵׁי שְׁמֶךָ. בָּרוּךְ אַתָּה יהוה, מְקַדֵּשׁ הַשַּׁבָּת.

עבודה

רְצֵה יהוה אֱלֹהֵינוּ בְּעַמְּךָ יִשְׂרָאֵל וּבִתְפִלָּתָם, וְהָשֵׁב אֶת הָעֲבוֹדָה לִדְבִיר בֵּיתֶךָ. וְאִשֵּׁי יִשְׂרָאֵל וּתְפִלָּתָם בְּאַהֲבָה תְקַבֵּל בְּרָצוֹן, וּתְהִי לְרָצוֹן תָּמִיד עֲבוֹדַת יִשְׂרָאֵל עַמֶּךָ.

During the *chazzan's* repetition, congregation responds אָמֵן as indicated.
[If the following paragraph is forgotten, repeat *Shemoneh Esrei*. See *Laws* §56.]

אֱלֹהֵינוּ וֵאלֹהֵי אֲבוֹתֵינוּ, יַעֲלֶה, וְיָבֹא, וְיַגִּיעַ, וְיֵרָאֶה, וְיֵרָצֶה, וְיִשָּׁמַע, וְיִפָּקֵד, וְיִזָּכֵר זִכְרוֹנֵנוּ וּפִקְדוֹנֵנוּ, וְזִכְרוֹן אֲבוֹתֵינוּ, וְזִכְרוֹן מָשִׁיחַ בֶּן דָּוִד עַבְדֶּךָ, וְזִכְרוֹן יְרוּשָׁלַיִם עִיר קָדְשֶׁךָ, וְזִכְרוֹן כָּל עַמְּךָ בֵּית יִשְׂרָאֵל לְפָנֶיךָ, לִפְלֵיטָה לְטוֹבָה לְחֵן וּלְחֶסֶד וּלְרַחֲמִים, לְחַיִּים וּלְשָׁלוֹם בְּיוֹם חַג הַמַּצּוֹת הַזֶּה. זָכְרֵנוּ יהוה אֱלֹהֵינוּ בּוֹ לְטוֹבָה (Cong.–אָמֵן), וּפָקְדֵנוּ בוֹ לִבְרָכָה (Cong.–אָמֵן), וְהוֹשִׁיעֵנוּ בוֹ לְחַיִּים (Cong.–אָמֵן). וּבִדְבַר יְשׁוּעָה וְרַחֲמִים, חוּס וְחָנֵּנוּ וְרַחֵם עָלֵינוּ וְהוֹשִׁיעֵנוּ, כִּי אֵלֶיךָ עֵינֵינוּ, כִּי אֵל מֶלֶךְ חַנּוּן וְרַחוּם אָתָּה.[1]

וְתֶחֱזֶינָה עֵינֵינוּ בְּשׁוּבְךָ לְצִיּוֹן בְּרַחֲמִים. בָּרוּךְ אַתָּה יהוה, הַמַּחֲזִיר שְׁכִינָתוֹ לְצִיּוֹן.

⊲§ **וְלֹא נְתַתּוֹ** — *You did not give it.* If the Sabbath were nothing more than a day of rest, it could be the equal property of all nations. But the Sabbath is a day of holiness and, as such, it could be given only to the nation that accepts the mission of sanctity. God did not give the Sabbath to such unworthy nations as גּוֹיֵי הָאֲרָצוֹת, *nations of the lands,* who worship the 'land' and the power its possession implies; nor to עוֹבְדֵי פְסִילִים, *the worshipers of graven idols,* who ascribe mastery of the world to such natural forces as the heavenly bodies, fertility,

וְלֹא נְתַתּוֹ *You did not give it,* HASHEM, our God, to the nations of the lands, nor did You make it the inheritance, our King, of the worshipers of graven idols. And in its contentment the uncircumcised shall not abide — for to Israel, Your people, have You given it in love, to the seed of Jacob, whom You have chosen. The people that sanctifies the Seventh — they will all be satisfied and delighted from Your goodness. And the Seventh — You found favor in it and sanctified it! 'Most coveted of days,' You called it, a remembrance of the act of creation.*

אֱלֹהֵינוּ *Our God and the God of our fathers, may You be pleased with our rest. Sanctify us with Your commandments and grant our share in Your Torah; satisfy us from Your goodness and gladden us with Your salvation, and purify our heart to serve You sincerely. O* HASHEM, *our God, with love and favor grant us Your holy Sabbath as a heritage, and may Israel, the sanctifiers of Your Name, rest on it. Blessed are You,* HASHEM, *Who sanctifies the Sabbath.*

TEMPLE SERVICE

רְצֵה *Be favorable,* HASHEM, *our God, toward Your people Israel and their prayer and restore the service to the Holy of Holies of Your Temple. The fire-offerings of Israel and their prayer accept with love and favor, and may the service of Your people Israel always be favorable to You.*

During the *chazzan's* repetition, congregation responds *Amen* as indicated.
[If the following paragraph is forgotten, repeat *Shemoneh Esrei.* See *Laws* §56.]

אֱלֹהֵינוּ *Our God and God of our forefathers, may there rise, come, reach, be noted, be favored, be heard, be considered, and be remembered — the remembrance and consideration of ourselves; the remembrance of our forefathers; the remembrance of Messiah, son of David, Your servant; the remembrance of Jerusalem, the City of Your Holiness; the remembrance of Your entire people the Family of Israel — before You for deliverance, for goodness, for grace, for kindness, and for compassion, for life, and for peace on this day of the Festival of Matzos. Remember us on it,* HASHEM, *our God, for goodness (*Cong.*–Amen); consider us on it for blessing (*Cong.*–Amen); and help us on it for life (*Cong.*–Amen). In the matter of salvation and compassion, pity, be gracious and compassionate with us and help us, for our eyes are turned to You, because You are God, the gracious and compassionate King.*[1]

וְתֶחֱזֶינָה *May our eyes behold Your return to Zion in compassion. Blessed are You,* HASHEM, *Who restores His Presence to Zion.*

(1) Cf. *Nehemiah* 9:31.

nature and so on that they symbolize by means of idols; nor to עֲרֵלִים, *uncircumcised people,* who are unwilling to curb their lusts for the sake of a higher goal (*R' Hirsch*).

הודאה

Bow at מודים; straighten up at ה׳. In his repetition the *chazzan* should recite the entire מודים aloud, while the congregation recites מודים דְּרַבָּנָן softly.

מוֹדִים אֲנַחְנוּ לָךְ שָׁאַתָּה הוּא יהוה אֱלֹהֵינוּ וֵאלֹהֵי אֲבוֹתֵינוּ לְעוֹלָם וָעֶד. צוּר חַיֵּינוּ, מָגֵן יִשְׁעֵנוּ אַתָּה הוּא לְדוֹר וָדוֹר. נוֹדֶה לְּךָ וּנְסַפֵּר תְּהִלָּתֶךָ[1] עַל חַיֵּינוּ הַמְּסוּרִים בְּיָדֶךָ, וְעַל נִשְׁמוֹתֵינוּ הַפְּקוּדוֹת לָךְ, וְעַל נִסֶּיךָ שֶׁבְּכָל יוֹם עִמָּנוּ, וְעַל נִפְלְאוֹתֶיךָ וְטוֹבוֹתֶיךָ שֶׁבְּכָל עֵת, עֶרֶב וָבֹקֶר וְצָהֳרָיִם. הַטּוֹב כִּי לֹא כָלוּ רַחֲמֶיךָ, וְהַמְּרַחֵם כִּי לֹא תַמּוּ חֲסָדֶיךָ,[2] מֵעוֹלָם קִוִּינוּ לָךְ.

מודים דרבנן

מוֹדִים אֲנַחְנוּ לָךְ, שָׁאַתָּה הוּא יהוה אֱלֹהֵינוּ וֵאלֹהֵי אֲבוֹתֵינוּ, אֱלֹהֵי כָל בָּשָׂר, יוֹצְרֵנוּ, יוֹצֵר בְּרֵאשִׁית. בְּרָכוֹת וְהוֹדָאוֹת לְשִׁמְךָ הַגָּדוֹל וְהַקָּדוֹשׁ, עַל שֶׁהֶחֱיִיתָנוּ וְקִיַּמְתָּנוּ. כֵּן תְּחַיֵּנוּ וּתְקַיְּמֵנוּ, וְתֶאֱסוֹף גָּלֻיּוֹתֵינוּ לְחַצְרוֹת קָדְשֶׁךָ, לִשְׁמוֹר חֻקֶּיךָ וְלַעֲשׂוֹת רְצוֹנֶךָ, וּלְעָבְדְּךָ בְּלֵבָב שָׁלֵם, עַל שֶׁאֲנַחְנוּ מוֹדִים לָךְ. בָּרוּךְ אֵל הַהוֹדָאוֹת.

וְעַל כֻּלָּם יִתְבָּרַךְ וְיִתְרוֹמַם שִׁמְךָ מַלְכֵּנוּ תָּמִיד לְעוֹלָם וָעֶד.

Bend the knees at בָּרוּךְ; bow at אַתָּה; straighten up at ה׳.

וְכֹל הַחַיִּים יוֹדוּךָ סֶּלָה, וִיהַלְלוּ אֶת שִׁמְךָ בֶּאֱמֶת, הָאֵל יְשׁוּעָתֵנוּ וְעֶזְרָתֵנוּ סֶלָה. בָּרוּךְ אַתָּה יהוה, הַטּוֹב שִׁמְךָ וּלְךָ נָאֶה לְהוֹדוֹת.

ברכת כהנים

The *chazzan* recites בִּרְכַּת כֹּהֲנִים during his repetition. He faces right at וְיִשְׁמְרֶךָ; faces left at אֵלֶיךָ וִיחֻנֶּךָּ; faces the Ark for the rest of the blessings.

אֱלֹהֵינוּ, וֵאלֹהֵי אֲבוֹתֵינוּ, בָּרְכֵנוּ בַבְּרָכָה הַמְּשֻׁלֶּשֶׁת בַּתּוֹרָה הַכְּתוּבָה עַל יְדֵי מֹשֶׁה עַבְדֶּךָ, הָאֲמוּרָה מִפִּי אַהֲרֹן וּבָנָיו, כֹּהֲנִים עַם קְדוֹשֶׁךָ, כָּאָמוּר:

יְבָרֶכְךָ יהוה, וְיִשְׁמְרֶךָ. (Cong. – כֵּן יְהִי רָצוֹן.)

יָאֵר יהוה פָּנָיו אֵלֶיךָ וִיחֻנֶּךָּ. (Cong. – כֵּן יְהִי רָצוֹן.)

יִשָּׂא יהוה פָּנָיו אֵלֶיךָ וְיָשֵׂם לְךָ שָׁלוֹם.[3] (Cong. – כֵּן יְהִי רָצוֹן.)

שלום

שִׂים שָׁלוֹם, טוֹבָה, וּבְרָכָה, חֵן, וָחֶסֶד וְרַחֲמִים עָלֵינוּ וְעַל כָּל יִשְׂרָאֵל עַמֶּךָ. בָּרְכֵנוּ אָבִינוּ, כֻּלָּנוּ כְּאֶחָד בְּאוֹר פָּנֶיךָ, כִּי בְאוֹר פָּנֶיךָ נָתַתָּ לָּנוּ, יהוה אֱלֹהֵינוּ, תּוֹרַת חַיִּים וְאַהֲבַת חֶסֶד, וּצְדָקָה, וּבְרָכָה, וְרַחֲמִים, וְחַיִּים, וְשָׁלוֹם. וְטוֹב בְּעֵינֶיךָ לְבָרֵךְ

THANKSGIVING [MODIM]

Bow at *'We gratefully thank You'*; straighten up at *'HASHEM.'* In his repetition the *chazzan* should recite the entire *Modim* aloud, while the congregation recites *Modim of the Rabbis* softly.

מוֹדִים *We gratefully thank You, for it is You Who are HASHEM, our God and the God of our forefathers for all eternity; Rock of our lives, Shield of our salvation are You from generation to generation. We shall thank You and relate Your praise*[1] *— for our lives, which are committed to Your power and for our souls that are entrusted to You; for Your miracles that are with us every day; and for Your wonders and favors in every season — evening, morning, and afternoon. The Beneficent One, for Your compassions were never exhausted, and the Compassionate One, for Your kindnesses never ended*[2] *— always have we put our hope in You.*

MODIM OF THE RABBIS

מוֹדִים *We gratefully thank You, for it is You Who are HASHEM, our God and the God of our forefathers, the God of all flesh, our Molder, the Molder of the universe. Blessings and thanks are due Your great and holy Name for You have given us life and sustained us. So may You continue to give us life and sustain us and gather our exiles to the Courtyards of Your Sanctuary, to observe Your decrees, to do Your will and to serve You wholeheartedly. [We thank You] for inspiring us to thank You. Blessed is the God of thanksgivings.*

For all these, may Your Name be blessed and exalted, our King, continually forever and ever.

Bend the knees at *'Blessed'*; bow at *'You'*; straighten up at *'HASHEM.'*

Everything alive will gratefully acknowledge You, Selah! and praise Your Name sincerely, O God of our salvation and help, Selah! Blessed are You, HASHEM, Your Name is 'The Beneficent One' and to You it is fitting to give thanks.

THE PRIESTLY BLESSING

The *chazzan* recites the Priestly Blessing during his repetition.

אֱלֹהֵינוּ *Our God and the God of our forefathers, bless us with the three-verse blessing in the Torah that was written by the hand of Moses, Your servant, that was said by Aaron and his sons, the Kohanim, Your holy people, as it is said:*

May HASHEM bless you and safeguard you. (Cong.– *So may it be.*)

May HASHEM illuminate His countenance for you and be gracious to you. (Cong.– *So may it be.*)

May HASHEM turn His countenance to you and establish peace for you.[3] (Cong.– *So may it be.*)

PEACE

שִׂים *Establish peace, goodness, blessing, graciousness, kindness, and compassion upon us and upon all of Your people Israel. Bless us, our Father, all of us as one, with the light of Your countenance, for with the light of Your countenance You gave us, HASHEM, our God, the Torah of life and a love of kindness, righteousness, blessing, compassion, life, and peace. And may it be good in Your eyes to bless*

(1) Cf. *Psalms* 79:13. (2) Cf. *Lamentations* 3:22. (3) *Numbers* 6:24-26.

אֶת עַמְּךָ יִשְׂרָאֵל, בְּכָל עֵת וּבְכָל שָׁעָה בִּשְׁלוֹמֶךָ. בָּרוּךְ אַתָּה יהוה, הַמְּבָרֵךְ אֶת עַמּוֹ יִשְׂרָאֵל בַּשָּׁלוֹם.

יִהְיוּ לְרָצוֹן אִמְרֵי פִי וְהֶגְיוֹן לִבִּי לְפָנֶיךָ, יהוה צוּרִי וְגֹאֲלִי.[1]

Chazzan's repetition of *Shemoneh Esrei* ends here. Individuals continue:

אֱלֹהַי, נְצוֹר לְשׁוֹנִי מֵרָע, וּשְׂפָתַי מִדַּבֵּר מִרְמָה,[2] וְלִמְקַלְלַי נַפְשִׁי תִדּוֹם, וְנַפְשִׁי כֶּעָפָר לַכֹּל תִּהְיֶה. פְּתַח לִבִּי בְּתוֹרָתֶךָ, וּבְמִצְוֹתֶיךָ תִּרְדּוֹף נַפְשִׁי. וְכֹל הַחוֹשְׁבִים עָלַי רָעָה, מְהֵרָה הָפֵר עֲצָתָם וְקַלְקֵל מַחֲשַׁבְתָּם. עֲשֵׂה לְמַעַן שְׁמֶךָ, עֲשֵׂה לְמַעַן יְמִינֶךָ, עֲשֵׂה לְמַעַן קְדֻשָּׁתֶךָ, עֲשֵׂה לְמַעַן תּוֹרָתֶךָ. לְמַעַן יֵחָלְצוּן יְדִידֶיךָ, הוֹשִׁיעָה יְמִינְךָ וַעֲנֵנִי.[3]

Some recite verses pertaining to their names here. See page 1143.

יִהְיוּ לְרָצוֹן אִמְרֵי פִי וְהֶגְיוֹן לִבִּי לְפָנֶיךָ, יהוה צוּרִי וְגֹאֲלִי.[1]

Bow and take three steps back. Bow left and say . . . עֹשֶׂה; bow right and say . . . הוּא יַעֲשֶׂה; bow forward and say וְעַל כָּל . . . אָמֵן.

עֹשֶׂה שָׁלוֹם בִּמְרוֹמָיו, הוּא יַעֲשֶׂה שָׁלוֹם עָלֵינוּ, וְעַל כָּל יִשְׂרָאֵל. וְאִמְרוּ: אָמֵן.

יְהִי רָצוֹן מִלְּפָנֶיךָ יהוה אֱלֹהֵינוּ וֵאלֹהֵי אֲבוֹתֵינוּ, שֶׁיִּבָּנֶה בֵּית הַמִּקְדָּשׁ בִּמְהֵרָה בְיָמֵינוּ, וְתֵן חֶלְקֵנוּ בְּתוֹרָתֶךָ. וְשָׁם נַעֲבָדְךָ בְּיִרְאָה, כִּימֵי עוֹלָם וּכְשָׁנִים קַדְמוֹנִיּוֹת. וְעָרְבָה לַיהוה מִנְחַת יְהוּדָה וִירוּשָׁלָיִם, כִּימֵי עוֹלָם וּכְשָׁנִים קַדְמוֹנִיּוֹת.[4]

THE INDIVIDUAL'S RECITATION OF *SHEMONEH ESREI* ENDS HERE.

The individual remains standing in place until the *chazzan* reaches *Kedushah* — or at least until the *chazzan* begins his repetition — then he takes three steps forward. The *chazzan* himself, or one praying alone, should remain in place for a few moments before taking three steps forward.

הלל

The *chazzan* recites the blessing. The congregation, after responding אָמֵן, repeats it, and continues with the first psalm.

בָּרוּךְ אַתָּה יהוה אֱלֹהֵינוּ מֶלֶךְ הָעוֹלָם, אֲשֶׁר קִדְּשָׁנוּ בְּמִצְוֹתָיו, וְצִוָּנוּ לִקְרוֹא אֶת הַהַלֵּל. (Cong.— אָמֵן.)

תהלים קיג

הַלְלוּיָהּ הַלְלוּ עַבְדֵי יהוה, הַלְלוּ אֶת שֵׁם יהוה. יְהִי שֵׁם יהוה מְבֹרָךְ, מֵעַתָּה וְעַד עוֹלָם. מִמִּזְרַח שֶׁמֶשׁ עַד מְבוֹאוֹ, מְהֻלָּל שֵׁם יהוה. רָם עַל כָּל גּוֹיִם יהוה, עַל הַשָּׁמַיִם כְּבוֹדוֹ. מִי כַּיהוה אֱלֹהֵינוּ, הַמַּגְבִּיהִי לָשָׁבֶת. הַמַּשְׁפִּילִי לִרְאוֹת, בַּשָּׁמַיִם וּבָאָרֶץ. ❖ מְקִימִי מֵעָפָר דָּל, מֵאַשְׁפֹּת יָרִים אֶבְיוֹן. לְהוֹשִׁיבִי עִם נְדִיבִים, עִם נְדִיבֵי עַמּוֹ. מוֹשִׁיבִי עֲקֶרֶת הַבַּיִת, אֵם הַבָּנִים שְׂמֵחָה, הַלְלוּיָהּ.

Your people Israel at every time and every hour with Your peace. Blessed are You, HASHEM, Who blesses His people Israel with peace.

May the expressions of my mouth and the thoughts of my heart find favor before You, HASHEM, my Rock and my Redeemer.[1]

Chazzan's repetition of *Shemoneh Esrei* ends here. Individuals continue:

אֱלֹהַי *My God, guard my tongue from evil and my lips from speaking deceitfully.*[2] *To those who curse me, let my soul be silent; and let my soul be like dust to everyone. Open my heart to Your Torah, then my soul will pursue Your commandments. As for all those who design evil against me, speedily nullify their counsel and disrupt their design. Act for Your Name's sake; act for Your right hand's sake; act for Your sanctity's sake; act for Your Torah's sake. That Your beloved ones may be given rest; let Your right hand save, and respond to me.*[3]

Some recite verses pertaining to their names at this point. See page 1143.

May the expressions of my mouth and the thoughts of my heart find favor before You, HASHEM, my Rock and my Redeemer.[1] *He Who makes peace in His heights, may He make peace upon us, and upon all Israel. Now respond: Amen.*

Bow and take three steps back. Bow left and say, *'He Who makes peace . . .'*; bow right and say, *'may He make peace . . .'*; bow forward and say, *'and upon . . . Amen.'*

יְהִי רָצוֹן *May it be Your will, HASHEM, our God and the God of our forefathers, that the Holy Temple be rebuilt, speedily in our days. Grant us our share in Your Torah, and may we serve You there with reverence, as in days of old and in former years. Then the offering of Judah and Jerusalem will be pleasing to HASHEM, as in days of old and in former years.*[4]

THE INDIVIDUAL'S RECITATION OF *SHEMONEH ESREI* ENDS HERE.

The individual remains standing in place until the *chazzan* reaches *Kedushah* or at least until the *chazzan* begins his repetition — then he takes three steps forward. The *chazzan* himself, or one praying alone, should remain in place for a few moments before taking three steps forward.

HALLEL

The *chazzan* recites the blessing. The congregation, after responding *Amen,* repeats it, and continues with the first psalm.

בָּרוּךְ *Blessed are You, HASHEM, our God, King of the universe, Who has sanctified us with His commandments and has commanded us to read the Hallel.* (Cong.– *Amen.)*

Psalm 113

הַלְלוּיָהּ *Halleluyah! Give praise, you servants of HASHEM; praise the Name of HASHEM! Blessed be the Name of HASHEM, from this time and forever. From the rising of the sun to its setting, HASHEM's Name is praised. High above all nations is HASHEM, above the heavens is His glory. Who is like HASHEM, our God, Who is enthroned on high — yet deigns to look upon the heaven and the earth?* Chazzan– *He raises the needy from the dust, from the trash heaps He lifts the destitute. To seat them with nobles, with the nobles of His people. He transforms the barren wife into a glad mother of children. Halleluyah!*

(1) *Psalms* 19:15. (2) Cf. 34:14. (3) 60:7; 108:7. (4) *Malachi* 3:4.

תהלים קיד

בְּצֵאת יִשְׂרָאֵל מִמִּצְרָיִם, בֵּית יַעֲקֹב מֵעַם לֹעֵז. הָיְתָה יְהוּדָה לְקָדְשׁוֹ, יִשְׂרָאֵל מַמְשְׁלוֹתָיו. הַיָּם רָאָה וַיָּנֹס, הַיַּרְדֵּן יִסֹּב לְאָחוֹר. הֶהָרִים רָקְדוּ כְאֵילִים, גְּבָעוֹת כִּבְנֵי צֹאן. ❖ מַה לְּךָ הַיָּם כִּי תָנוּס, הַיַּרְדֵּן תִּסֹּב לְאָחוֹר. הֶהָרִים תִּרְקְדוּ כְאֵילִים, גְּבָעוֹת כִּבְנֵי צֹאן. מִלִּפְנֵי אָדוֹן חוּלִי אָרֶץ, מִלִּפְנֵי אֱלוֹהַּ יַעֲקֹב. הַהֹפְכִי הַצּוּר אֲגַם מָיִם, חַלָּמִישׁ לְמַעְיְנוֹ מָיִם.

תהלים קטו:יב-יח

יהוה זְכָרָנוּ יְבָרֵךְ, יְבָרֵךְ אֶת בֵּית יִשְׂרָאֵל, יְבָרֵךְ אֶת בֵּית אַהֲרֹן. יְבָרֵךְ יִרְאֵי יהוה, הַקְּטַנִּים עִם הַגְּדֹלִים. יֹסֵף יהוה עֲלֵיכֶם, עֲלֵיכֶם וְעַל בְּנֵיכֶם. בְּרוּכִים אַתֶּם לַיהוה, עֹשֵׂה שָׁמַיִם וָאָרֶץ. ❖ הַשָּׁמַיִם שָׁמַיִם לַיהוה, וְהָאָרֶץ נָתַן לִבְנֵי אָדָם. לֹא הַמֵּתִים יְהַלְלוּ יָהּ, וְלֹא כָּל יֹרְדֵי דוּמָה. וַאֲנַחְנוּ נְבָרֵךְ יָהּ, מֵעַתָּה וְעַד עוֹלָם, הַלְלוּיָהּ.

תהלים קטז:יב-יט

מָה אָשִׁיב לַיהוה, כָּל תַּגְמוּלוֹהִי עָלָי. כּוֹס יְשׁוּעוֹת אֶשָּׂא, וּבְשֵׁם יהוה אֶקְרָא. נְדָרַי לַיהוה אֲשַׁלֵּם, נֶגְדָה נָּא לְכָל עַמּוֹ. יָקָר בְּעֵינֵי יהוה, הַמָּוְתָה לַחֲסִידָיו. אָנָּה יהוה כִּי אֲנִי עַבְדֶּךָ, אֲנִי עַבְדְּךָ, בֶּן אֲמָתֶךָ, פִּתַּחְתָּ לְמוֹסֵרָי. ❖ לְךָ אֶזְבַּח זֶבַח תּוֹדָה, וּבְשֵׁם יהוה אֶקְרָא. נְדָרַי לַיהוה אֲשַׁלֵּם, נֶגְדָה נָּא לְכָל עַמּוֹ. בְּחַצְרוֹת בֵּית יהוה, בְּתוֹכֵכִי יְרוּשָׁלָיִם הַלְלוּיָהּ.

Congregation, then *chazzan:*

תהלים קיז

הַלְלוּ אֶת יהוה, כָּל גּוֹיִם, שַׁבְּחוּהוּ כָּל הָאֻמִּים. כִּי גָבַר עָלֵינוּ חַסְדּוֹ, וֶאֱמֶת יהוה לְעוֹלָם, הַלְלוּיָהּ.

תהלים קיח

Chazzan – **הוֹדוּ** לַיהוה כִּי טוֹב, כִּי לְעוֹלָם חַסְדּוֹ.

Cong. – הוֹדוּ לַיהוה כִּי טוֹב, כִּי לְעוֹלָם חַסְדּוֹ.

יֹאמַר נָא יִשְׂרָאֵל, כִּי לְעוֹלָם חַסְדּוֹ.

Chazzan – יֹאמַר נָא יִשְׂרָאֵל, כִּי לְעוֹלָם חַסְדּוֹ.

Psalm 114

בְּצֵאת *When Israel went out of Egypt, Jacob's household from a people of alien tongue — Judah became His sanctuary, Israel His dominions. The sea saw and fled: the Jordan turned backward. The mountains skipped like rams, the hills like young lambs.* Chazzan– *What ails you, O sea, that you flee? O Jordan, that you turn backward? O mountains, that you skip like rams? O hills, like young lambs? Before the Lord's Presence — did I, the earth, tremble — before the presence of the God of Jacob, Who turns the rock into a pond of water, the flint into a flowing fountain.*

Psalm 115:12-18

יהוה *HASHEM Who has remembered us will bless — He will bless the House of Israel; He will bless the House of Aaron; He will bless those who fear HASHEM, the small as well as the great. May HASHEM increase upon you, upon you and upon your children! You are blessed of HASHEM, Maker of heaven and earth.* Chazzan– *As for the heavens — the heavens are HASHEM's, but the earth He has given to mankind. Neither the dead can praise God, nor any who descend into silence; but we will bless God from this time and forever. Halleluyah!*

Psalm 116:12-19

מָה אָשִׁיב *How can I repay HASHEM for all His kindness to me? I will raise the cup of salvations and the Name of HASHEM I will invoke. My vows to HASHEM I will pay, in the presence, now, of His entire people. Difficult in the eyes of HASHEM is the death of His devout ones. Please, HASHEM — for I am Your servant, I am Your servant, son of Your handmaid — You have released my bonds.* Chazzan– *To You I will sacrifice thanksgiving offerings, and the name of HASHEM I will invoke. My vows to HASHEM I will pay, in the presence, now, of His entire people. In the courtyards of the House of HASHEM, in your midst, O Jerusalem, Halleluyah!*

Congregation, then *chazzan:*

Psalm 117

הַלְלוּ *Praise HASHEM, all nations; praise Him, all the states! For His kindness has overwhelmed us, and the truth of HASHEM is eternal, Halleluyah!*

Psalm 118

Chazzan – **הוֹדוּ** *Give thanks to HASHEM for He is good; His kindness endures forever!*

Cong. – *Give thanks to HASHEM, for He is good; His kindness endures forever!*

Let Israel say now: His kindness endures forever!

Chazzan – *Let Israel say now: His kindness endures forever!*

Cong. – הוֹדוּ לַיהוה כִּי טוֹב, כִּי לְעוֹלָם חַסְדּוֹ.
יֹאמְרוּ נָא בֵית אַהֲרֹן, כִּי לְעוֹלָם חַסְדּוֹ.
Chazzan – יֹאמְרוּ נָא בֵית אַהֲרֹן, כִּי לְעוֹלָם חַסְדּוֹ.
Cong. – הוֹדוּ לַיהוה כִּי טוֹב, כִּי לְעוֹלָם חַסְדּוֹ.
יֹאמְרוּ נָא יִרְאֵי יהוה, כִּי לְעוֹלָם חַסְדּוֹ.
Chazzan – יֹאמְרוּ נָא יִרְאֵי יהוה, כִּי לְעוֹלָם חַסְדּוֹ.
Cong. – הוֹדוּ לַיהוה כִּי טוֹב, כִּי לְעוֹלָם חַסְדּוֹ.

מִן הַמֵּצַר קָרָאתִי יָּהּ, עָנָנִי בַמֶּרְחָב יָהּ. יהוה לִי לֹא אִירָא, מַה יַּעֲשֶׂה לִי אָדָם. יהוה לִי בְּעֹזְרָי, וַאֲנִי אֶרְאֶה בְשֹׂנְאָי. טוֹב לַחֲסוֹת בַּיהוה, מִבְּטֹחַ בָּאָדָם. טוֹב לַחֲסוֹת בַּיהוה, מִבְּטֹחַ בִּנְדִיבִים. כָּל גּוֹיִם סְבָבוּנִי, בְּשֵׁם יהוה כִּי אֲמִילַם. סַבּוּנִי גַם סְבָבוּנִי, בְּשֵׁם יהוה כִּי אֲמִילַם. סַבּוּנִי כִדְבֹרִים דֹּעֲכוּ כְּאֵשׁ קוֹצִים, בְּשֵׁם יהוה כִּי אֲמִילַם. דָּחֹה דְחִיתַנִי לִנְפֹּל, וַיהוה עֲזָרָנִי. עָזִּי וְזִמְרָת יָהּ, וַיְהִי לִי לִישׁוּעָה. קוֹל רִנָּה וִישׁוּעָה, בְּאָהֳלֵי צַדִּיקִים, יְמִין יהוה עֹשָׂה חָיִל. יְמִין יהוה רוֹמֵמָה, יְמִין יהוה עֹשָׂה חָיִל. לֹא אָמוּת כִּי אֶחְיֶה, וַאֲסַפֵּר מַעֲשֵׂי יָהּ. יַסֹּר יִסְּרַנִּי יָּהּ, וְלַמָּוֶת לֹא נְתָנָנִי. ❖ פִּתְחוּ לִי שַׁעֲרֵי צֶדֶק, אָבֹא בָם אוֹדֶה יָהּ. זֶה הַשַּׁעַר לַיהוה, צַדִּיקִים יָבֹאוּ בוֹ. אוֹדְךָ כִּי עֲנִיתָנִי, וַתְּהִי לִי לִישׁוּעָה. אוֹדְךָ כִּי עֲנִיתָנִי, וַתְּהִי לִי לִישׁוּעָה. אֶבֶן מָאֲסוּ הַבּוֹנִים, הָיְתָה לְרֹאשׁ פִּנָּה. אֶבֶן מָאֲסוּ הַבּוֹנִים, הָיְתָה לְרֹאשׁ פִּנָּה. מֵאֵת יהוה הָיְתָה זֹּאת, הִיא נִפְלָאת בְּעֵינֵינוּ. מֵאֵת יהוה הָיְתָה זֹּאת, הִיא נִפְלָאת בְּעֵינֵינוּ. זֶה הַיּוֹם עָשָׂה יהוה, נָגִילָה וְנִשְׂמְחָה בוֹ. זֶה הַיּוֹם עָשָׂה יהוה, נָגִילָה וְנִשְׂמְחָה בוֹ.

The next four lines are recited responsively — *chazzan,* then congregation.

אָנָּא יהוה הוֹשִׁיעָה נָּא.
אָנָּא יהוה הוֹשִׁיעָה נָּא.
אָנָּא יהוה הַצְלִיחָה נָא.
אָנָּא יהוה הַצְלִיחָה נָא.

Cong. – *Give thanks to HASHEM, for He is good;*
His kindness endures forever!
Let the House of Aaron say now: His kindness endures forever!
Chazzan – *Let the House of Aaron say now: His kindness endures forever!*
Cong. – *Give thanks to HASHEM, for He is good;*
His kindness endures forever!
Let those who fear HASHEM say now:
His kindness endures forever!
Chazzan – *Let those who fear HASHEM say now:*
His kindness endures forever!
Cong. – *Give thanks to HASHEM, for He is good;*
His kindness endures forever!

מִן הַמֵּצַר *From the straits did I call upon God; God answered me with expansiveness. HASHEM is with me, I have no fear; how can man affect me? HASHEM is with me through my helpers; therefore I can face my foes. It is better to take refuge in HASHEM than to rely on man. It is better to take refuge in HASHEM than to rely on nobles. All the nations surround me; in the Name of HASHEM I cut them down! They encircle me, they also surround me; in the Name of HASHEM, I cut them down! They encircle me like bees, but they are extinguished as a fire does thorns; in the Name of HASHEM I cut them down! You pushed me hard that I might fall, but HASHEM assisted me. God is my might and my praise, and He was a salvation for me. The sound of rejoicing and salvation is in the tents of the righteous: 'HASHEM's right hand does valiantly. HASHEM's right hand is raised triumphantly; HASHEM's right hand does valiantly!' I shall not die! But I shall live and relate the deeds of God. God has chastened me exceedingly, but He did not let me die.* Chazzan– *Open for me the gates of righteousness, I will enter them and thank God. This is the gate of HASHEM; the righteous shall enter through it. I thank You for You have answered me and become my salvation. I thank You for You have answered me and become my salvation. The stone the builders despised has become the cornerstone. The stone the builders despised has become the cornerstone. This emanated from HASHEM; it is wondrous in our eyes. This emanated from HASHEM; it is wondrous in our eyes. This is the day HASHEM has made; let us rejoice and be glad on it. This is the day HASHEM has made; let us rejoice and be glad on it.*

The next four lines are recited responsively – *chazzan,* then congregation.

אָנָּא *Please, HASHEM, save now!*
Please, HASHEM, save now!
Please, HASHEM, bring success now!
Please, HASHEM, bring success now!

בָּרוּךְ הַבָּא בְּשֵׁם יהוה, בֵּרַכְנוּכֶם מִבֵּית יהוה. בָּרוּךְ הַבָּא בְּשֵׁם יהוה, בֵּרַכְנוּכֶם מִבֵּית יהוה. אֵל יהוה וַיָּאֶר לָנוּ, אִסְרוּ חַג בַּעֲבֹתִים, עַד קַרְנוֹת הַמִּזְבֵּחַ. אֵל יהוה וַיָּאֶר לָנוּ, אִסְרוּ חַג בַּעֲבֹתִים, עַד קַרְנוֹת הַמִּזְבֵּחַ. אֵלִי אַתָּה וְאוֹדֶךָּ, אֱלֹהַי אֲרוֹמְמֶךָּ. אֵלִי אַתָּה וְאוֹדֶךָּ, אֱלֹהַי אֲרוֹמְמֶךָּ. הוֹדוּ לַיהוה כִּי טוֹב, כִּי לְעוֹלָם חַסְדּוֹ. הוֹדוּ לַיהוה כִּי טוֹב, כִּי לְעוֹלָם חַסְדּוֹ.

יְהַלְלוּךָ יהוה אֱלֹהֵינוּ כָּל מַעֲשֶׂיךָ, וַחֲסִידֶיךָ צַדִּיקִים עוֹשֵׂי רְצוֹנֶךָ, וְכָל עַמְּךָ בֵּית יִשְׂרָאֵל בְּרִנָּה יוֹדוּ וִיבָרְכוּ וִישַׁבְּחוּ וִיפָאֲרוּ וִירוֹמְמוּ וְיַעֲרִיצוּ וְיַקְדִּישׁוּ וְיַמְלִיכוּ אֶת שִׁמְךָ מַלְכֵּנוּ. ❖ כִּי לְךָ טוֹב לְהוֹדוֹת וּלְשִׁמְךָ נָאֶה לְזַמֵּר, כִּי מֵעוֹלָם וְעַד עוֹלָם אַתָּה אֵל. בָּרוּךְ אַתָּה יהוה, מֶלֶךְ מְהֻלָּל בַּתִּשְׁבָּחוֹת.
(.Cong. – אָמֵן)

קדיש שלם

The *chazzan* recites *Kaddish:*

יִתְגַּדַּל וְיִתְקַדַּשׁ שְׁמֵהּ רַבָּא. (.Cong. – אָמֵן.) בְּעָלְמָא דִּי בְרָא כִרְעוּתֵהּ. וְיַמְלִיךְ מַלְכוּתֵהּ, בְּחַיֵּיכוֹן וּבְיוֹמֵיכוֹן וּבְחַיֵּי דְכָל בֵּית יִשְׂרָאֵל, בַּעֲגָלָא וּבִזְמַן קָרִיב. וְאִמְרוּ: אָמֵן.

(.Cong. – אָמֵן. יְהֵא שְׁמֵהּ רַבָּא מְבָרַךְ לְעָלַם וּלְעָלְמֵי עָלְמַיָּא.)

יְהֵא שְׁמֵהּ רַבָּא מְבָרַךְ לְעָלַם וּלְעָלְמֵי עָלְמַיָּא.

יִתְבָּרַךְ וְיִשְׁתַּבַּח וְיִתְפָּאַר וְיִתְרוֹמַם וְיִתְנַשֵּׂא וְיִתְהַדָּר וְיִתְעַלֶּה וְיִתְהַלָּל שְׁמֵהּ דְּקֻדְשָׁא בְּרִיךְ הוּא (.Cong. – בְּרִיךְ הוּא) — לְעֵלָּא מִן כָּל בִּרְכָתָא וְשִׁירָתָא תֻּשְׁבְּחָתָא וְנֶחֱמָתָא, דַּאֲמִירָן בְּעָלְמָא. וְאִמְרוּ: אָמֵן. (.Cong. – אָמֵן.)

(.Cong. – קַבֵּל בְּרַחֲמִים וּבְרָצוֹן אֶת תְּפִלָּתֵנוּ.)

תִּתְקַבֵּל צְלוֹתְהוֹן וּבָעוּתְהוֹן דְּכָל בֵּית יִשְׂרָאֵל קֳדָם אֲבוּהוֹן דִּי בִשְׁמַיָּא. וְאִמְרוּ: אָמֵן. (.Cong. – אָמֵן.)

(.Cong. – יְהִי שֵׁם יהוה מְבֹרָךְ, מֵעַתָּה וְעַד עוֹלָם.[1])

יְהֵא שְׁלָמָא רַבָּא מִן שְׁמַיָּא, וְחַיִּים עָלֵינוּ וְעַל כָּל יִשְׂרָאֵל. וְאִמְרוּ: אָמֵן. (.Cong. – אָמֵן.)

(.Cong. – עֶזְרִי מֵעִם יהוה, עֹשֵׂה שָׁמַיִם וָאָרֶץ.[2])

Take three steps back. Bow left and say . . . עֹשֶׂה; bow right and say . . . הוּא; bow forward and say וְעַל כָּל . . . אָמֵן. Remain standing in place for a few moments, then take three steps forward.

עֹשֶׂה שָׁלוֹם בִּמְרוֹמָיו, הוּא יַעֲשֶׂה שָׁלוֹם עָלֵינוּ, וְעַל כָּל יִשְׂרָאֵל. וְאִמְרוּ: אָמֵן. (.Cong. – אָמֵן.)

בָּרוּךְ *Blessed is he who comes in the Name of* HASHEM*; we bless you from the House of* HASHEM*. Blessed is he who comes in the Name of* HASHEM*; we bless you from the House of* HASHEM*.* HASHEM *is God, He illuminated for us; bind the festival offering with cords until the corners of the Altar.* HASHEM *is God, He illuminated for us; bind the festival offering with cords until the corners of the Altar. You are my God, and I will thank You; my God, I will exalt You. You are my God, and I will thank You; my God, I will exalt You. Give thanks to* HASHEM*, for He is good; His kindness endures forever. Give thanks to* HASHEM*, for He is good; His kindness endures forever.*

יְהַלְלוּךָ *All Your works shall praise You,* HASHEM *our God. And Your devout ones, the righteous, who do Your will, and Your entire people, the House of Israel, with glad song will thank, bless, praise, glorify, exalt, extol, sanctify, and proclaim the sovereignty of Your Name, our King.* Chazzan– *For to You it is fitting to give thanks, and unto Your Name it is proper to sing praises, for from This World to the World to Come You are God. Blessed are You,* HASHEM*, the King Who is lauded with praises.* (Cong.– *Amen.)*

FULL KADDISH

The *chazzan* recites *Kaddish:*

יִתְגַּדַּל *May His great Name grow exalted and sanctified* (Cong.– *Amen.*) *in the world that He created as He willed. May He give reign to His kingship in your lifetimes and in your days, and in the lifetimes of the entire Family of Israel, swiftly and soon. Now respond: Amen.*

(Cong.– *Amen. May His great Name be blessed forever and ever.)*

May His great Name be blessed forever and ever.

Blessed, praised, glorified, exalted, extolled, mighty, upraised, and lauded be the Name of the Holy One, Blessed is He (Cong.– *Blessed is He*) *— beyond any blessing and song, praise and consolation that are uttered in the world. Now respond: Amen.* (Cong.– *Amen*).

(Cong.– *Accept our prayers with mercy and favor.)*

May the prayers and supplications of the entire Family of Israel be accepted before their Father Who is in Heaven. Now respond: Amen. (Cong.– *Amen.)*

(Cong.– *Blessed be the Name of* HASHEM*, from this time and forever.*[1])

May there be abundant peace from Heaven, and life, upon us and upon all Israel. Now respond: Amen. (Cong.– *Amen.)*

(Cong.– *My help is from* HASHEM*, Maker of heaven and earth.*[2])

Take three steps back. Bow left and say, *'He Who makes peace . . .';* bow right and say, *'may He . . .';* bow forward and say, *'and upon all Israel . . .'* Remain standing in place for a few moments, then take three steps forward.

He Who makes peace in His heights, may He make peace upon us, and upon all Israel. Now respond: Amen. (Cong.– *Amen.)*

(1) *Psalms* 113:2. (2) 121:2.

❧ שיר השירים ❧

Song of Songs is read before the Torah reading on the Sabbath of *Chol HaMoed.* In the event there is no Sabbath of *Chol HaMoed,* it is read on either the seventh or eighth day, whichever falls on the Sabbath.

פרק א

א שִׁ֥יר הַשִּׁירִ֖ים אֲשֶׁ֥ר לִשְׁלֹמֹֽה׃ ב יִשָּׁקֵ֙נִי֙ מִנְּשִׁיק֣וֹת פִּ֔יהוּ כִּֽי־טוֹבִ֥ים דֹּדֶ֖יךָ
מִיָּֽיִן׃ ג לְרֵ֙יחַ֙ שְׁמָנֶ֣יךָ טוֹבִ֔ים שֶׁ֖מֶן תּוּרַ֣ק שְׁמֶ֑ךָ עַל־כֵּ֖ן עֲלָמ֥וֹת אֲהֵבֽוּךָ׃
ד מָשְׁכֵ֖נִי אַחֲרֶ֣יךָ נָּר֑וּצָה הֱבִיאַ֨נִי הַמֶּ֜לֶךְ חֲדָרָ֗יו נָגִ֤ילָה וְנִשְׂמְחָה֙ בָּ֔ךְ
נַזְכִּ֤ירָה דֹדֶ֙יךָ֙ מִיַּ֔יִן מֵישָׁרִ֖ים אֲהֵבֽוּךָ׃ ה שְׁחוֹרָ֤ה אֲנִי֙ וְֽנָאוָ֔ה בְּנ֖וֹת
יְרֽוּשָׁלִָ֑ם כְּאָהֳלֵ֣י קֵדָ֔ר כִּירִיע֖וֹת שְׁלֹמֹֽה׃ ו אַל־תִּרְא֙וּנִי֙ שֶׁאֲנִ֣י שְׁחַרְחֹ֔רֶת
שֶׁשֱּׁזָפַ֖תְנִי הַשָּׁ֑מֶשׁ בְּנֵ֧י אִמִּ֣י נִֽחֲרוּ־בִ֗י שָׂמֻ֙נִי֙ נֹטֵרָ֣ה אֶת־הַכְּרָמִ֔ים
כַּרְמִ֥י שֶׁלִּ֖י לֹ֥א נָטָֽרְתִּי׃ ז הַגִּ֣ידָה לִּ֗י שֶׁאָהֲבָה֙ נַפְשִׁ֔י אֵיכָ֣ה תִרְעֶ֔ה
אֵיכָ֖ה תַּרְבִּ֣יץ בַּֽצָּהֳרָ֑יִם שַׁלָּמָ֤ה אֶֽהְיֶה֙ כְּעֹ֣טְיָ֔ה עַ֖ל עֶדְרֵ֥י חֲבֵרֶֽיךָ׃

❧ שִׁיר הַשִּׁירִים / SONG OF SONGS ❧

Without question, King Solomon's Song of Songs, *Shir HaShirim,* is one of the most difficult books of Scripture — not because it is so hard to understand but because it is so easy to misunderstand. Not only is it a love song, it is a love song of uncommon passion. No other book seems to be so out of place among the twenty-four books of prophecy and sacred spirit. Nevertheless, one of the greatest and holiest of all the Sages of the Talmud, Rabbi Akiva, said, 'All of the songs [of Scripture] are holy, but *Shir HaShirim* is holy of holies.' How is a 'love song' holy?

This question is perplexing only if *Shir HaShirim* is taken literally, but neither the Sages nor the commentators take it so. The Song is an allegory. It is the duet of love between God and Israel. Its verses are so saturated with meaning that nearly every one of the major commentators finds new themes in its beautiful but cryptic words. All agree, however, that the true and simple meaning of *Shir HaShirim* is the allegorical meaning. The literal meaning of the words is so far from their meaning that it is false.

That is why ArtScroll's translation of *Shir HaShirim* is completely different from any other ArtScroll translation. We translate it according to *Rashi's* allegorical interpretation. As he writes in his own introduction:

Solomon foresaw through רוּחַ הַקֹּדֶשׁ, *the Holy Spirit,* that Israel is destined to suffer a series of exiles and will lament, nostalgically recalling her former status as God's chosen beloved. She will say, *'I shall return to my first husband* [i.e., to God] *for it was better with me then than now' (Hoshea* 2:9). The Children of Israel will recall His beneficence and *'the trespasses which they trespassed' (Leviticus* 26:40). And they will recall the goodness which He promised for the End of Days.

The prophets frequently likened the relationship between God and Israel to that of a loving husband angered by a straying wife who betrayed him. Solomon composed *Shir HaShirim* in the form of that same allegory. It is a passionate dialogue between the husband [God] who still loves his exiled wife [Israel], and a 'veritable widow of a living husband' *(II Samuel* 20:3) who longs for her husband and seeks to endear herself to him once more, as she recalls her youthful love for him and admits her guilt.

God, too, is *'afflicted by her afflictions' (Isaiah* 63:9), and He recalls the kindness of her youth, her beauty, and her skillful deeds for which He loved her [Israel] so. He proclaimed that He has *'not afflicted her capriciously' (Lamentations* 3:33), nor is she cast away permanently. For she is still His 'wife' and He her 'husband,' and He will yet return to her.

During the mid-nineteenth-century period of the most vicious Czarist persecutions of Jews, it was common for the leading rabbis to visit St. Petersburg to plead the case of their people with the Czar's ministers. During one of these visits a Russian official asked one of the rabbis how he could account for the many Aggadic tales in the Talmud which were patently 'inconceivable.'

The rabbi answered, 'You know very well that the Czar and his advisors have often planned decrees that would order the expulsion of the Jews. If God had not thwarted your plans, the decree would have been written and placed before the Czar for his signature. He would have dipped his pen into the inkwell and signed. His signature would have made final the greatest Jewish catastrophe in centuries. A poet might write that a drop of ink drowned three million people. All of us would have understood what he meant. But a hundred years later, someone

SHIR HASHIRIM / SONG OF SONGS

Song of Songs is read before the Torah reading on the Sabbath of *Chol HaMoed*. In the event there is no Sabbath of *Chol HaMoed,* it is read on either the seventh or eighth day, whichever falls on the Sabbath.

CHAPTER ONE

1 *The song that excels all songs dedicated to God, Him to Whom peace belongs.*

2 *Communicate Your innermost wisdom to me again in loving closeness, for Your friendship is dearer than all earthly delights.* 3 *Like the scent of goodly oils is the spreading fame of Your great deeds; Your very name is Flowing Oil, therefore have nations loved You.*

[Israel in Exile to God:] 4 *Upon perceiving a mere hint that You wished to draw me, we rushed with perfect faith after You into the wilderness. The King brought me into His cloud-pillared chamber; whatever our travail we shall always be glad and rejoice in Your Torah. We recall Your love more than earthly delights, unrestrainedly do they love You.*

[Israel to the nations:] 5 *Though I am black with sin, I am comely with virtue, O nations who are destined to ascend to Jerusalem; though sullied as the tents of Kedar, I will be immaculate as the draperies of Him to Whom peace belongs.* 6 *Do not view me with contempt despite my swarthiness, for it is but the sun which has glared upon me. The alien children of my mother were incensed with me and made me a keeper of the vineyards of idols, but the vineyard of my own true God I did not keep.*

[Israel to God:] 7 *Tell me, You Whom my soul loves: Where will You graze Your flock? Where will You rest them under the fiercest sun of harshest Exile? Why shall I be like one veiled in mourning among the flocks of Your fellow shepherds?*

---

might read it and consider it nonsense. Could a small drop of ink drown people? In truth, the expression is apt and pithy; it is only a lack of knowledge that could lead a reader to dismiss it out of hand. So it is with many parables of our Sages. They were written in the form of far-fetched stories to conceal their meaning from those unqualified to understand. Those same unqualified people laugh at the stories, instead of lamenting their own puny stature. (See also *Maamar al HaAggados* by *Rabbi Moshe Chaim Luzzatto.)*

In general history as well, many figures of speech have an obvious meaning to those familiar with them, but would be incomprehensible to the uninitiated. Everyone knows that a shot cannot be heard more than several hundred yards away. But every American knows that 'a shot heard round the world' began the American Revolution.

Shir HaShirim is read on Pesach because the Sages interpret it as the story of Israel after the Exodus, a time of such great spiritual passion, that God said many centuries later: *I remember for your sake the kindness of your youth, the love of your bridal days, how you followed Me in the Wilderness in an unsown land (Jeremiah* 2:2).

The message of *Shir HaShirim* is so lofty, so exalted, so spiritual, so holy that God in His infinite wisdom knew that it could be presented to us only in its present form. Only in this manner could it engender the passionate love for God which is Israel's highest mission.

Has it been misinterpreted by fools and twisted by scoundrels? Most assuredly yes! But: לֹא חָשׁ הקב״ה לְהָאִיר הַחַמָּה מִפְּנֵי עוֹבְדֶיהָ, *God did not refrain from creating the sun because it would have worshipers.*

Let us, therefore, read and understand *Shir HaShirim* with the ecstasy of love between God and Israel, for it is this intimacy that it expresses more than any other Song in Scripture.

CHAPTER ONE

1. *God, Him to Whom peace belongs.* Throughout this Book the word שְׁלֹמֹה standing by itself refers not to Solomon but to שֶׁהַשָּׁלוֹם שֶׁלּוֹ, *Him to Whom peace belongs* [שָׁלוֹם לוֹ = שְׁלֹמֹה]; i.e., God, the Source of all peace *(Talmud).*

5-6. Jerusalem will one day become the metropolis of all countries and will draw people to her in streams to honor her. Thus the nations of the world are figuratively referred to as 'daughters' of the great metropolis Jerusalem *(Midrash).*

7. Israel, allegorized here as a sheep beloved by its shepherd, addresses God directly as a woman addressing her husband, and remonstrates with Him that the exile is too difficult for her and too unbecoming to Him.

ח אִם־לֹא תֵדְעִי לָךְ הַיָּפָה בַּנָּשִׁים צְאִי־לָךְ בְּעִקְבֵי הַצֹּאן וּרְעִי
אֶת־גְּדִיֹּתַיִךְ עַל מִשְׁכְּנוֹת הָרֹעִים: ט לְסֻסָתִי בְּרִכְבֵי פַרְעֹה דִּמִּיתִיךְ
רַעְיָתִי: י נָאווּ לְחָיַיִךְ בַּתֹּרִים צַוָּארֵךְ בַּחֲרוּזִים: יא תּוֹרֵי זָהָב נַעֲשֶׂה־
לָּךְ עִם נְקֻדּוֹת הַכָּסֶף: יב עַד־שֶׁהַמֶּלֶךְ בִּמְסִבּוֹ נִרְדִּי נָתַן רֵיחוֹ:
יג צְרוֹר הַמֹּר ׀ דּוֹדִי לִי בֵּין שָׁדַי יָלִין: יד אֶשְׁכֹּל הַכֹּפֶר ׀ דּוֹדִי לִי
בְּכַרְמֵי עֵין גֶּדִי: טו הִנָּךְ יָפָה רַעְיָתִי הִנָּךְ יָפָה עֵינַיִךְ יוֹנִים: טז הִנְּךָ יָפֶה
דוֹדִי אַף נָעִים אַף־עַרְשֵׂנוּ רַעֲנָנָה: יז קֹרוֹת בָּתֵּינוּ אֲרָזִים רַהִיטֵנוּ
בְּרוֹתִים:

פרק ב

א אֲנִי חֲבַצֶּלֶת הַשָּׁרוֹן שׁוֹשַׁנַּת הָעֲמָקִים: ב כְּשׁוֹשַׁנָּה בֵּין הַחוֹחִים כֵּן
רַעְיָתִי בֵּין הַבָּנוֹת: ג כְּתַפּוּחַ בַּעֲצֵי הַיַּעַר כֵּן דּוֹדִי בֵּין הַבָּנִים בְּצִלּוֹ
חִמַּדְתִּי וְיָשַׁבְתִּי וּפִרְיוֹ מָתוֹק לְחִכִּי: ד הֱבִיאַנִי אֶל־בֵּית הַיָּיִן וְדִגְלוֹ עָלַי
אַהֲבָה: ה סַמְּכוּנִי בָּאֲשִׁישׁוֹת רַפְּדוּנִי בַּתַּפּוּחִים כִּי־חוֹלַת אַהֲבָה אָנִי:
ו שְׂמֹאלוֹ תַּחַת לְרֹאשִׁי וִימִינוֹ תְּחַבְּקֵנִי: ז הִשְׁבַּעְתִּי אֶתְכֶם בְּנוֹת
יְרוּשָׁלִַם בִּצְבָאוֹת אוֹ בְּאַיְלוֹת הַשָּׂדֶה אִם־תָּעִירוּ ׀ וְאִם־תְּעוֹרְרוּ
אֶת־הָאַהֲבָה עַד שֶׁתֶּחְפָּץ: ח קוֹל דּוֹדִי הִנֵּה־זֶה בָּא מְדַלֵּג עַל־הֶהָרִים
מְקַפֵּץ עַל־הַגְּבָעוֹת: ט דּוֹמֶה דוֹדִי לִצְבִי אוֹ לְעֹפֶר הָאַיָּלִים הִנֵּה־זֶה
עוֹמֵד אַחַר כָּתְלֵנוּ מַשְׁגִּיחַ מִן־הַחַלֹּנוֹת מֵצִיץ מִן־הַחֲרַכִּים: י עָנָה דוֹדִי
וְאָמַר לִי קוּמִי לָךְ רַעְיָתִי יָפָתִי וּלְכִי־לָךְ: יא כִּי־הִנֵּה הַסְּתָו עָבָר הַגֶּשֶׁם
חָלַף הָלַךְ לוֹ: יב הַנִּצָּנִים נִרְאוּ בָאָרֶץ עֵת הַזָּמִיר הִגִּיעַ וְקוֹל הַתּוֹר נִשְׁמַע
בְּאַרְצֵנוּ: יג הַתְּאֵנָה חָנְטָה פַגֶּיהָ וְהַגְּפָנִים ׀ סְמָדַר נָתְנוּ רֵיחַ קוּמִי לָךְ
רַעְיָתִי יָפָתִי וּלְכִי־לָךְ: יד יוֹנָתִי בְּחַגְוֵי הַסֶּלַע בְּסֵתֶר הַמַּדְרֵגָה הַרְאִינִי
אֶת־מַרְאַיִךְ הַשְׁמִיעִינִי אֶת־קוֹלֵךְ כִּי־קוֹלֵךְ עָרֵב וּמַרְאֵיךְ נָאוֶה:
טו אֶחֱזוּ־לָנוּ שֻׁעָלִים קְטַנִּים מְחַבְּלִים כְּרָמִים וּכְרָמֵינוּ סְמָדַר:

8-11. In these verses God continues recounting His beneficence to the Jews while, at the same time, implying their ingratitude.

CHAPTER TWO

The chapter division of Scripture is of non-Jewish origin, introduced by Christian Bible printers. We follow these divisions for convenience of identification only. Accordingly verse 2:1 does not begin a new thought, but is a continuation of the previous verses.

5. Proper love for God is to be constantly enraptured by Him like a love-sick individual whose mind is never free from the passion that fills his heart at all times *(Rambam)*.

8-17 The community of Israel reminisces how God, rushing to deliver her from Egyptian bondage, called upon her to bestir her to carry out His precepts and become worthy of deliverance.

11-13. These verses paint a beautiful picture describing the propitiousness of the season of Redemption. They conjure up an image of the worst being over — Delivery at hand.

13. *The K'siv* [Masoretic written form] of the word לָךְ, spelled לכי in this verse, has a superfluous י, *yud*, the numerical equivalent of ten. This suggests that the intent of the verse is: 'Arise to receive the *Ten* Commandments, My love, My fair one' *(Rashi)*.

[God responds to Israel:] 8 *If you know not where to graze, O fairest of nations, follow the footsteps of the sheep — your forefathers who traced a straight, unswerving path after My Torah. Then you can graze your tender kids even among the dwellings of foreign shepherds.*

9 *With My mighty steeds who battled Pharaoh's riders I revealed that you are My beloved.* 10 *Your cheeks are lovely with rows of gems, your neck with necklaces — My gifts to you from the splitting sea,* 11 *by inducing Pharaoh to engage in pursuit, to add circlets of gold to your spangles of silver.*

[Israel about God:] 12 *While the King was yet at Sinai my malodorous deed gave forth its scent as my Golden Calf defiled the covenant.* 13 *But my Beloved responded with a bundle of myrrh — the fragrant atonement of erecting a Tabernacle where His Presence would dwell amid the Holy Ark's staves.* 14 *Like a cluster of henna in Ein Gedi vineyards has my Beloved multiplied his forgiveness to me.*

15 *He said, 'I forgive you, My friend, for you are lovely in deed and lovely in resolve. The righteous among you are loyal as a dove.'*

[Israel to God:] 16 *It is You Who are lovely, my Beloved, so pleasant that You pardoned my sin enabling our Temple to make me ever fresh.* 17 *The beams of our House are cedar, our panels are cypress.*

CHAPTER TWO

1 *I am but a rose of Sharon, even an ever-fresh rose of the valleys.*

[God to Israel:] 2 *Like the rose maintaining its beauty among the thorns, so is My faithful beloved among the nations.*

[Israel reminisces . . .:] 3 *Like the fruitful, fragrant apple tree among the barren trees of the forest, so is my Beloved among the gods. In His shade I delighted and there I sat, and the fruit of His Torah was sweet to my palate.* 4 *He brought me to the chamber of Torah delights and clustered my encampments about Him in love.* 5 *I say to Him, 'Sustain me in exile with dainty cakes, spread fragrant apples about me to comfort my dispersion — for, bereft of Your Presence, I am sick with love.'* 6 *With memories of His loving support in the desert, of His left hand under my head, of His right hand enveloping me.*

[Turns to the nations:] 7 *I adjure you, O nations who are destined to ascend to Jerusalem — for if you violate your oath you will become as defenseless as gazelles or hinds of the field — if you dare provoke God to hate me or disturb His love for me while He still desires it.*

[Then reminisces further:] 8 *The voice of my Beloved! Behold — it came suddenly to redeem me, as if leaping over mountains, skipping over hills.* 9 *In His swiftness to redeem me, my Beloved is like a gazelle or a young hart. I thought I would be forever alone, but behold! He was standing behind our wall, observing through the windows, peering through the lattices.*

10 *When He redeemed me from Egypt, my Beloved called out and said to me, 'Arise My love, My fair one, and go forth.* 11 *For the winter of bondage has passed, the deluge of suffering is over and gone.* 12 *The righteous blossoms are seen in the land, the time of your song has arrived, and the voice of your guide is heard in the land.* 13 *The fig tree has formed its first small figs, ready for ascent to the Temple. The vines are in blossom, their fragrance declaring they are ready for libation. Arise, My love, My fair one, and go forth!'*

14 *At the sea, He said to me, 'O My dove, trapped at the sea as if in the clefts of the rock, the concealment of the terrace. Show Me your prayerful gaze, let Me hear your supplicating voice, for your voice is sweet and your countenance comely.'* 15 *Then He told the sea, 'Seize for us the Egyptian foxes, even the small foxes who spoiled Israel's vineyards while our vineyards had just begun to blossom.'*

טז דּוֹדִי לִי֙ וַאֲנִי ל֔וֹ הָרֹעֶ֖ה בַּשּֽׁוֹשַׁנִּֽים: יז עַ֤ד שֶׁיָּפ֙וּחַ֙ הַיּ֔וֹם וְנָ֖סוּ הַצְּלָלִ֑ים סֹב֩ דְּמֵה־לְךָ֨ דוֹדִ֜י לִצְבִ֗י א֛וֹ לְעֹ֥פֶר הָאַיָּלִ֖ים עַל־הָ֥רֵי בָֽתֶר:

<h3 style="text-align:center">פרק ג</h3>

א עַל־מִשְׁכָּבִי֙ בַּלֵּיל֔וֹת בִּקַּ֕שְׁתִּי אֵ֥ת שֶׁאָהֲבָ֖ה נַפְשִׁ֑י בִּקַּשְׁתִּ֖יו וְלֹ֥א מְצָאתִֽיו: ב אָק֨וּמָה נָּ֜א וַאֲסוֹבְבָ֣ה בָעִ֗יר בַּשְּׁוָקִים֙ וּבָ֣רְחֹב֔וֹת אֲבַקְשָׁ֕ה אֵ֥ת שֶׁאָהֲבָ֖ה נַפְשִׁ֑י בִּקַּשְׁתִּ֖יו וְלֹ֥א מְצָאתִֽיו: ג מְצָא֙וּנִי֙ הַשֹּׁ֣מְרִ֔ים הַסֹּבְבִ֖ים בָּעִ֑יר אֵ֛ת שֶׁאָהֲבָ֥ה נַפְשִׁ֖י רְאִיתֶֽם: ד כִּמְעַט֙ שֶׁעָבַ֣רְתִּי מֵהֶ֔ם עַ֣ד שֶֽׁמָּצָ֔אתִי אֵ֥ת שֶׁאָהֲבָ֖ה נַפְשִׁ֑י אֲחַזְתִּיו֙ וְלֹ֣א אַרְפֶּ֔נּוּ עַד־שֶׁהֲבֵיאתִיו֙ אֶל־בֵּ֣ית אִמִּ֔י וְאֶל־חֶ֖דֶר הֽוֹרָתִֽי: ה הִשְׁבַּ֨עְתִּי אֶתְכֶ֜ם בְּנ֤וֹת יְרוּשָׁלִַ֙ם֙ בִּצְבָא֔וֹת א֖וֹ בְּאַיְל֣וֹת הַשָּׂדֶ֑ה אִם־תָּעִ֧ירוּ ׀ וְֽאִם־תְּעֽוֹרְר֛וּ אֶת־הָאַהֲבָ֖ה עַ֥ד שֶׁתֶּחְפָּֽץ: ו מִ֣י זֹ֗את עֹלָה֙ מִן־הַמִּדְבָּ֔ר כְּתִֽימְר֖וֹת עָשָׁ֑ן מְקֻטֶּ֤רֶת מֹר֙ וּלְבוֹנָ֔ה מִכֹּ֖ל אַבְקַ֥ת רוֹכֵֽל: ז הִנֵּ֗ה מִטָּתוֹ֙ שֶׁלִּשְׁלֹמֹ֔ה שִׁשִּׁ֥ים גִּבֹּרִ֖ים סָבִ֣יב לָ֑הּ מִגִּבֹּרֵ֖י יִשְׂרָאֵֽל: ח כֻּלָּם֙ אֲחֻ֣זֵי חֶ֔רֶב מְלֻמְּדֵ֖י מִלְחָמָ֑ה אִ֤ישׁ חַרְבּוֹ֙ עַל־יְרֵכ֔וֹ מִפַּ֖חַד בַּלֵּילֽוֹת: ט אַפִּרְי֗וֹן עָ֤שָׂה לוֹ֙ הַמֶּ֣לֶךְ שְׁלֹמֹ֔ה מֵעֲצֵ֖י הַלְּבָנֽוֹן: י עַמּוּדָיו֙ עָ֣שָׂה כֶ֔סֶף רְפִֽידָת֣וֹ זָהָ֔ב מֶרְכָּב֖וֹ אַרְגָּמָ֑ן תּוֹכוֹ֙ רָצ֣וּף אַהֲבָ֔ה מִבְּנ֖וֹת יְרוּשָׁלִָֽם: יא צְאֶ֧ינָה ׀ וּֽרְאֶ֛ינָה בְּנ֥וֹת צִיּ֖וֹן בַּמֶּ֣לֶךְ שְׁלֹמֹ֑ה בָּֽעֲטָרָ֗ה שֶׁעִטְּרָה־לּ֤וֹ אִמּוֹ֙ בְּי֣וֹם חֲתֻנָּת֔וֹ וּבְי֖וֹם שִׂמְחַ֥ת לִבּֽוֹ:

<h3 style="text-align:center">פרק ד</h3>

א הִנָּ֨ךְ יָפָ֤ה רַעְיָתִי֙ הִנָּ֣ךְ יָפָ֔ה עֵינַ֣יִךְ יוֹנִ֔ים מִבַּ֖עַד לְצַמָּתֵ֑ךְ שַׂעְרֵךְ֙ כְּעֵ֣דֶר הָֽעִזִּ֔ים שֶׁגָּֽלְשׁ֖וּ מֵהַ֥ר גִּלְעָֽד: ב שִׁנַּ֙יִךְ֙ כְּעֵ֣דֶר הַקְּצוּב֔וֹת שֶׁעָל֖וּ מִן־הָרַחְצָ֑ה שֶׁכֻּלָּם֙ מַתְאִימ֔וֹת וְשַׁכֻּלָ֖ה אֵ֥ין בָּהֶֽם: ג כְּח֤וּט הַשָּׁנִי֙ שִׂפְתֹתַ֔יִךְ וּמִדְבָּרֵ֖ךְ נָאוֶ֑ה כְּפֶ֤לַח הָֽרִמּוֹן֙ רַקָּתֵ֔ךְ מִבַּ֖עַד לְצַמָּתֵֽךְ: ד כְּמִגְדַּ֤ל דָּוִיד֙ צַוָּארֵ֔ךְ בָּנ֖וּי לְתַלְפִּיּ֑וֹת אֶ֤לֶף הַמָּגֵן֙ תָּל֣וּי עָלָ֔יו כֹּ֖ל שִׁלְטֵ֥י הַגִּבֹּרִֽים: ה שְׁנֵ֥י שָׁדַ֛יִךְ כִּשְׁנֵ֥י עֳפָרִ֖ים תְּאוֹמֵ֣י צְבִיָּ֑ה הָֽרוֹעִ֖ים בַּשּֽׁוֹשַׁנִּֽים:

CHAPTER THREE

1. In context with the previous verse, *Rashi* explains *'night'* as referring to the torment of Israel's thirty-eight-year sojourn in the desert in spiritual darkness when they were under the 'Ban' [incurred because of the sin of the Spies who turned the people against the land. During this period, the *Midrash* (2:11) explains, God did not speak with Moses (see *Deut.* 2:14-17). This verse metaphorically describes Israel's quest for God, *'Whom my soul loves,'* during these years of silence].

6-11. These verses follow Israel's adjuration to the nations of the world, as if to say, 'Do not attempt to disturb God's love for us. It was *we* who

followed Him into the desert; it was *us* whom He engulfed in His cloud; *we* accepted His Torah; *we* built the Tabernacle as He commanded; *we* crowned Him as our God. He will, therefore, surely resume His love for us, and we adjure you not to attempt to interfere with our love' (*Metzudas David*).

CHAPTER FOUR

1-16. *Dovelike constancy.* Your quality and actions are like the dove which is loyal to its mate; and which, when it is to be slaughtered, does not fidget, but [willingly] stretches forth its neck. So have you bent your shoulders to endure My yoke and My awe (*Rashi*).

4. An erect posture in a woman is beautiful, and

16 My Beloved is mine, He fills all my needs and I seek from Him and none other. He grazes me in roselike bounty. 17 Until my sin blows His friendship away and sears me like the midday sun and His protection departs, my sin caused Him to turn away.

I say to him, 'My Beloved, You became like a gazelle or a young hart on the distant mountains.'

CHAPTER THREE

[Israel to the nations:] 1 As I lay on my bed in the night of my desert travail, I sought Him Whom my soul loves. I sought Him but I found Him not, for He maintained His aloofness. 2 I resolved to arise then, and roam through the city, in the streets and squares; that through Moses I would seek Him Whom my soul loved. I sought Him, but I found Him not. 3 They found me, Moses and Aaron, the watchmen patrolling the city. 'You have seen Him Whom my soul loves — what has He said?' 4 Scarcely had I departed from them when, in the days of Joshua, I found Him Whom my soul loves. I grasped Him, determined that my deeds would never again cause me to lose hold of Him, until I brought His Presence to the Tabernacle of my mother and to the chamber of the one who conceived me. 5 I adjure you, O nations who are destined to ascend to Jerusalem — for if you violate your oath you will become as defenseless as gazelles or hinds of the field — if you dare provoke God to hate me or disturb His love for me while He still desires it.

6 You nations have asked, 'Who is this ascending from the desert, its way secured and smoothed by palmlike pillars of smoke, burning fragrant myrrh and frankincense, of all the perfumer's powders?' 7 Behold the resting place of Him to Whom peace belongs, with sixty myriads of Israel's mighty encircling it. 8 All of them gripping the sword of tradition, skilled in the battle of Torah, each with his sword ready at his side, lest he succumb in the nights of exile. 9 A Tabernacle for His presence has the King to Whom peace belongs made of the wood of Lebanon. 10 Its pillars He made of silver, His resting place was gold, its suspended curtain was purple wool, its midst was decked with implements bespeaking love by the daughters of Jerusalem. 11 Go forth and gaze, O daughters distinguished by loyalty to God, upon the King to Whom peace belongs adorned with the crown His nation made for Him, on the day His Law was given and He became one with Israel, and on the day His heart was gladdened by His Tabernacle's consecration.

CHAPTER FOUR

[God to Israel:] 1 Behold, you are lovely, My friend, behold you are lovely, your very appearance radiates dovelike constancy. The most common sons within your encampments are as dearly beloved as the children of Jacob in the goatlike procession descending the slopes of Mount Gilead. 2 Accountable in deed are your fiercest warriors like a well-numbered flock come up from the washing, all of them unblemished with no miscarriage of action in them.

3 Like the scarlet thread, guarantor of Rachav's safety, is the sincerity of your lips, and your word is unfeigned. As many as a pomegranate's seeds are the merits of your unworthiest within your modest veil. 4 As stately as the Tower of David is the site of your Sanhedrin built as a model to emulate, with a thousand shields of Torah armor hung upon it, all the disciple-filled quivers of the mighty. 5 Moses and Aaron, your two sustainers, are like two fawns, twins of the gazelle, who graze their sheep in roselike bounty.

ו עַד שֶׁיָּפוּחַ הַיּוֹם וְנָסוּ הַצְּלָלִים אֵלֶךְ לִי אֶל־הַר הַמּוֹר וְאֶל־גִּבְעַת
הַלְּבוֹנָה: ז כֻּלָּךְ יָפָה רַעְיָתִי וּמוּם אֵין בָּךְ: ח אִתִּי מִלְּבָנוֹן כַּלָּה אִתִּי
מִלְּבָנוֹן תָּבוֹאִי תָּשׁוּרִי ׀ מֵרֹאשׁ אֲמָנָה מֵרֹאשׁ שְׂנִיר וְחֶרְמוֹן מִמְּעֹנוֹת
אֲרָיוֹת מֵהַרְרֵי נְמֵרִים: ט לִבַּבְתִּנִי אֲחֹתִי כַלָּה לִבַּבְתִּנִי בְּאַחַד מֵעֵינַיִךְ
בְּאַחַד עֲנָק מִצַּוְּרֹנָיִךְ: י מַה־יָּפוּ דֹדַיִךְ אֲחֹתִי כַלָּה מַה־טֹּבוּ דֹדַיִךְ מִיַּיִן
וְרֵיחַ שְׁמָנַיִךְ מִכָּל־בְּשָׂמִים: יא נֹפֶת תִּטֹּפְנָה שִׂפְתוֹתַיִךְ כַּלָּה דְּבַשׁ וְחָלָב
תַּחַת לְשׁוֹנֵךְ וְרֵיחַ שַׂלְמֹתַיִךְ כְּרֵיחַ לְבָנוֹן: יב גַּן ׀ נָעוּל אֲחֹתִי כַלָּה גַּל
נָעוּל מַעְיָן חָתוּם: יג שְׁלָחַיִךְ פַּרְדֵּס רִמּוֹנִים עִם פְּרִי מְגָדִים כְּפָרִים
עִם־נְרָדִים: יד נֵרְדְּ ׀ וְכַרְכֹּם קָנֶה וְקִנָּמוֹן עִם כָּל־עֲצֵי לְבוֹנָה מֹר וַאֲהָלוֹת
עִם כָּל־רָאשֵׁי בְשָׂמִים: טו מַעְיַן גַּנִּים בְּאֵר מַיִם חַיִּים וְנֹזְלִים מִן־לְבָנוֹן:
טז עוּרִי צָפוֹן וּבוֹאִי תֵימָן הָפִיחִי גַנִּי יִזְּלוּ בְשָׂמָיו יָבֹא דוֹדִי לְגַנּוֹ וְיֹאכַל
פְּרִי מְגָדָיו:

פרק ה

א בָּאתִי לְגַנִּי אֲחֹתִי כַלָּה אָרִיתִי מוֹרִי עִם־בְּשָׂמִי אָכַלְתִּי יַעְרִי
עִם־דִּבְשִׁי שָׁתִיתִי יֵינִי עִם־חֲלָבִי אִכְלוּ רֵעִים שְׁתוּ וְשִׁכְרוּ דּוֹדִים:
ב אֲנִי יְשֵׁנָה וְלִבִּי עֵר קוֹל ׀ דּוֹדִי דוֹפֵק פִּתְחִי־לִי אֲחֹתִי רַעְיָתִי
יוֹנָתִי תַמָּתִי שֶׁרֹּאשִׁי נִמְלָא־טָל קְוֻצּוֹתַי רְסִיסֵי לָיְלָה: ג פָּשַׁטְתִּי
אֶת־כֻּתָּנְתִּי אֵיכָכָה אֶלְבָּשֶׁנָּה רָחַצְתִּי אֶת־רַגְלַי אֵיכָכָה אֲטַנְּפֵם: ד דּוֹדִי
שָׁלַח יָדוֹ מִן־הַחוֹר וּמֵעַי הָמוּ עָלָיו: ה קַמְתִּי אֲנִי לִפְתֹּחַ לְדוֹדִי וְיָדַי
נָטְפוּ־מוֹר וְאֶצְבְּעֹתַי מוֹר עֹבֵר עַל כַּפּוֹת הַמַּנְעוּל: ו פָּתַחְתִּי אֲנִי
לְדוֹדִי וְדוֹדִי חָמַק עָבָר נַפְשִׁי יָצְאָה בְדַבְּרוֹ בִּקַּשְׁתִּיהוּ וְלֹא מְצָאתִיהוּ
קְרָאתִיו וְלֹא עָנָנִי: ז מְצָאֻנִי הַשֹּׁמְרִים הַסֹּבְבִים בָּעִיר הִכּוּנִי פְצָעוּנִי
נָשְׂאוּ אֶת־רְדִידִי מֵעָלַי שֹׁמְרֵי הַחֹמוֹת: ח הִשְׁבַּעְתִּי אֶתְכֶם בְּנוֹת
יְרוּשָׁלִָם אִם־תִּמְצְאוּ אֶת־דּוֹדִי מַה־תַּגִּידוּ לוֹ שֶׁחוֹלַת אַהֲבָה אָנִי:

---

the simile to *Tower of David* refers to מְצוּדַת צִיּוֹן, *the Stronghold of Zion*, a beautiful, stately tower and fortification. So is your *'neck'* — i.e., the לִשְׁכַּת הַגָּזִית, *the Chamber of Hewn Stone* [the seat of the Sanhedrin], which was the spiritual stronghold of Israel *(Rashi)*.

9. Precepts of the Torah are allegorized as beads (see *Proverbs* 1:9).

11. *Kol Bo* cites *'honey and milk under your tongue'* as a reason for the custom of eating dairy foods and honey on Shavuos, the holiday commemorating the giving of the Torah, which is symbolized by honey and milk.

CHAPTER FIVE

2-7. *My Beloved knocks!* [throughout all my slumbering.] God caused His *Shechinah* to dwell upon the prophets, issuing daily warnings through them [see *Jeremiah* 7:25]. Now Israel remorsefully recalls how, secure in the peaceful period of the First Temple, she neglected the call of the prophets to return to the service of God, as if she slumbered and slept; but God nevertheless was wakeful to guard her and grant her goodness *(Rashi)*.

9. The nations ask Israel: 'Why are you so loyal to a God Who has forsaken you? Let us become one nation, and together serve our god!' *(Metzudas David)*.

16. *This is my Beloved* — and it is for all these virtues that 'I am sick for His love' *(Rashi)*.

6 *Until My sunny benevolence was withdrawn from Shiloh and the protective shadows were dispersed by your sin. I will go to Mount Moriah and the hill of frankincense —* 7 *where you will be completely fair, My beloved, and no blemish will be in you.*

8 *With Me will you be exiled from the Temple, O bride, with Me from the Temple until you return; then to contemplate the fruits of your faith from its earliest beginnings from your first arrival at the summits of Snir and of Hermon, the lands of mighty Sichon and Og, as impregnable as dens of lions, and as mountains of leopards.*

9 *You captured My heart, My sister, O bride; you captured My heart with but one of your virtues, with but one of the precepts that adorn you like beads of a necklace resplendent.* 10 *How fair was your love in so many settings, My sister, O bride; so superior is your love to wine and your spreading fame to all perfumes.*

11 *The sweetness of Torah drops from your lips, like honey and milk it lies under your tongue; your very garments are scented with precepts like the scent of Lebanon.* 12 *As chaste as a garden locked, My sister, O bride; a spring locked up, a fountain sealed.* 13 *Your least gifted ones are a pomegranate orchard with luscious fruit; henna with nard;* 14 *nard and saffron, calamus and cinnamon, with all trees of frankincense, myrrh and aloes with all the chief spices;* 15 *purified in a garden spring, a well of waters alive and flowing clean from Lebanon.*

16 *Awake from the north and come from the south! Like the winds let My exiles return to My garden, let their fragrant goodness flow in Jerusalem.*

[Israel responds:] *Let but my Beloved come to His garden and enjoy His precious people.*

CHAPTER FIVE

[God replies:] 1 *To your Tabernacle Dedication, My sister, O bride, I came as if to My garden. I gathered My myrrh with My spice from your princely incense; I accepted your unbidden as well as your bidden offerings to Me; I drank your libations pure as milk. Eat, My beloved priests! Drink and become God-intoxicated, O friends!*

[Israel reminisces regretfully:] 2 *I let my devotion slumber, but the God of my heart was awake! A sound! My Beloved knocks!*

He said, 'Open your heart to Me, My sister, My love, My dove, My perfection; admit Me and My head is filled with dewlike memories of Abraham; spurn Me and I bear collections of punishing rains in exile-nights.'

3 *And I responded, 'I have doffed my robe of devotion; how can I don it? I have washed my feet that trod Your path; how can I soil them?'*

4 *In anger at my recalcitrance, my Beloved sent forth His Hand from the portal in wrath, and my intestines churned with longing for Him.* 5 *I arose to open for my Beloved and my hands dripped myrrh of repentant devotion to Torah and God, and my fingers flowing with myrrh to remove the traces of my foolish rebuke from the handles of the lock.* 6 *I opened for my Beloved; but, alas, my Beloved had turned His back on my plea and was gone. My soul departed at His decree! I sought His closeness but could not find it; I beseeched Him but He would not answer.*

7 *They found me, the enemy watchmen patrolling the city; they struck me, they bloodied me wreaking God's revenge on me. They stripped my mantle of holiness from me, the angelic watchmen of the wall.*

[Israel to the nations:] 8 *I adjure you, O nations who are destined to ascend to Jerusalem, when you see my Beloved on the future Day of Judgment, won't you tell Him that I bore all travails for love of Him?*

ט מַה־דּוֹדֵךְ מִדּוֹד הַיָּפָה בַּנָּשִׁים מַה־דּוֹדֵךְ מִדּוֹד שֶׁכָּכָה הִשְׁבַּעְתָּנוּ:
י דּוֹדִי צַח וְאָדוֹם דָּגוּל מֵרְבָבָה: יא רֹאשׁוֹ כֶּתֶם פָּז קְוֻצּוֹתָיו תַּלְתַּלִּים
שְׁחֹרוֹת כָּעוֹרֵב: יב עֵינָיו כְּיוֹנִים עַל־אֲפִיקֵי מָיִם רֹחֲצוֹת בֶּחָלָב יֹשְׁבוֹת
עַל־מִלֵּאת: יג לְחָיָו כַּעֲרוּגַת הַבֹּשֶׂם מִגְדְּלוֹת מֶרְקָחִים שִׂפְתוֹתָיו
שׁוֹשַׁנִּים נֹטְפוֹת מוֹר עֹבֵר: יד יָדָיו גְּלִילֵי זָהָב מְמֻלָּאִים בַּתַּרְשִׁישׁ מֵעָיו
עֶשֶׁת שֵׁן מְעֻלֶּפֶת סַפִּירִים: טו שׁוֹקָיו עַמּוּדֵי שֵׁשׁ מְיֻסָּדִים עַל־אַדְנֵי־פָז
מַרְאֵהוּ כַּלְּבָנוֹן בָּחוּר כָּאֲרָזִים: טז חִכּוֹ מַמְתַקִּים וְכֻלּוֹ מַחֲמַדִּים זֶה דוֹדִי
וְזֶה רֵעִי בְּנוֹת יְרוּשָׁלִָם:

פרק ו

א אָנָה הָלַךְ דּוֹדֵךְ הַיָּפָה בַּנָּשִׁים אָנָה פָּנָה דוֹדֵךְ וּנְבַקְשֶׁנּוּ עִמָּךְ:
ב דּוֹדִי יָרַד לְגַנּוֹ לַעֲרוּגוֹת הַבֹּשֶׂם לִרְעוֹת בַּגַּנִּים וְלִלְקֹט שׁוֹשַׁנִּים:
ג אֲנִי לְדוֹדִי וְדוֹדִי לִי הָרֹעֶה בַּשּׁוֹשַׁנִּים: ד יָפָה אַתְּ רַעְיָתִי כְּתִרְצָה נָאוָה
כִּירוּשָׁלִָם אֲיֻמָּה כַּנִּדְגָּלוֹת: ה הָסֵבִּי עֵינַיִךְ מִנֶּגְדִּי שֶׁהֵם הִרְהִיבֻנִי שַׂעְרֵךְ
כְּעֵדֶר הָעִזִּים שֶׁגָּלְשׁוּ מִן־הַגִּלְעָד: ו שִׁנַּיִךְ כְּעֵדֶר הָרְחֵלִים שֶׁעָלוּ
מִן־הָרַחְצָה שֶׁכֻּלָּם מַתְאִימוֹת וְשַׁכֻּלָה אֵין בָּהֶם: ז כְּפֶלַח הָרִמּוֹן רַקָּתֵךְ
מִבַּעַד לְצַמָּתֵךְ: ח שִׁשִּׁים הֵמָּה מְלָכוֹת וּשְׁמֹנִים פִּילַגְשִׁים וַעֲלָמוֹת אֵין
מִסְפָּר: ט אַחַת הִיא יוֹנָתִי תַמָּתִי אַחַת הִיא לְאִמָּהּ בָּרָה הִיא לְיוֹלַדְתָּהּ
רָאוּהָ בָנוֹת וַיְאַשְּׁרוּהָ מְלָכוֹת וּפִילַגְשִׁים וַיְהַלְלוּהָ: י מִי־זֹאת הַנִּשְׁקָפָה
כְּמוֹ־שָׁחַר יָפָה כַלְּבָנָה בָּרָה כַּחַמָּה אֲיֻמָּה כַּנִּדְגָּלוֹת: יא אֶל־גִּנַּת אֱגוֹז
יָרַדְתִּי לִרְאוֹת בְּאִבֵּי הַנָּחַל לִרְאוֹת הֲפָרְחָה הַגֶּפֶן הֵנֵצוּ הָרִמֹּנִים: יב לֹא
יָדַעְתִּי נַפְשִׁי שָׂמַתְנִי מַרְכְּבוֹת עַמִּי נָדִיב:

פרק ז

א שׁוּבִי שׁוּבִי הַשּׁוּלַמִּית שׁוּבִי שׁוּבִי וְנֶחֱזֶה־בָּךְ מַה־תֶּחֱזוּ בַּשּׁוּלַמִּית
כִּמְחֹלַת הַמַּחֲנָיִם: ב מַה־יָּפוּ פְעָמַיִךְ בַּנְּעָלִים בַּת־נָדִיב חַמּוּקֵי יְרֵכַיִךְ

CHAPTER SIX

1. Why has your Beloved left you alone, widowed? *(Rashi)*.

3. I, alone, am My Beloved's. You are not His, and you will not assist us in constructing our new Temple [see *Ezra* 4:3] *(Rashi)*.

5. Another interpretaion: 'Turn your pleading eyes from Me,' says God. 'Endure your Exile, and do not anticipate the End — because there is an appointed time for every event. Your eyes overwhelm Me and fill Me with compassion — but the Edict has already been proclaimed: until the pre-established time, you must faithfully bear the yoke. Rather, turn away your eyes, and if you repent, I will respond accordingly by redeeming you sooner' *(Midrash Lekach Tov; Vilna Gaon)*.

12. Hearing God's praise of her glorious past, Israel reflects on her current plight and responds sadly.

CHAPTER SEVEN

1. Israel is still the speaker, recalling how the heathens tried to entice her to join with them.

[The nations ask Israel:] [9] *With what does your beloved God excel all others that you suffer for His Name, O fairest of nations? With what does your beloved God excel all others that you dare to adjure us?*

[Israel responds:] [10] *My Beloved is pure and purifies sin, and ruddy with vengeance to punish betrayers, surrounded with myriad angels.* [11] *His opening words were finest gold, His crowns hold mounds of statutes written in raven-black flame.* [12] *Like the gaze of doves toward their cotes, His eyes are fixed on the waters of Torah, bathing all things in clarity, established upon creation's fullness.* [13] *Like a bed of spices are His words at Sinai, like towers of perfume. His comforting words from the Tabernacle are roses dripping flowing myrrh.* [14] *The Tablets, His handiwork, are desirable above even rolls of gold; they are studded with commandments precious as gems, the Torah's innards are sparkling as ivory intricately overlaid with precious stone.* [15] *The Torah's columns are marble set in contexts of finest gold, its contemplation flowers like Lebanon, it is sturdy as cedars.* [16] *The words of His palate are sweet and He is all delight.*

This is my Beloved and this is my Friend, O nations who are destined to ascend to Jerusalem.

CHAPTER SIX

[The nations derisively, to Israel:] [1] *Where has your Beloved gone, O forsaken fairest among women? Where has your Beloved turned to rejoin you? Let us seek Him with you and build His Temple with you.*

[Israel responds:] [2] *My Beloved has descended to His Temple garden, to His incense altar, yet still He grazes my brethren remaining in gardens of exile to gather the roseate fragrance of their words of Torah.* [3] *I alone am my Beloved's and my Beloved is mine, He Who grazes His sheep in roselike pastures.*

[God to Israel:] [4] *You are beautiful, My love, when your deeds are pleasing, as comely now as once you were in Jerusalem of old, hosts of angels stand in awe of you.* [5] *Turn your pleading eyes from Me lest I be tempted to bestow upon you holiness more than you can bear. But with all your flaws, your most common sons are as dearly beloved as the children of Jacob in the goatlike procession descending the slopes of Mount Gilead.* [6] *Your mighty leaders are perfect, as a flock of ewes come up from the washing, all of them unblemished with no miscarriage of action in them.* [7] *As many as a pomegranate's seeds are the merits of your unworthiest within your modest veil.* [8] *The queenly offspring of Abraham are sixty, compared to whom the eighty Noachides and all their countless nations are like mere concubines.*

[9] *Unique is she, My constant dove, My perfect one. Unique is she, this nation striving for the truth; pure is she to Jacob who begot her. Nations saw her and acclaimed her; queens and concubines, and they praised her:* [10] *'Who is this that gazes down from atop the Temple Mount, brightening like the dawn, beautiful as the moon, brilliant as the sun, awesome as the bannered hosts of kings?'*

[11] *I descended upon the deceptively simple holiness of the Second Temple to see your moisture-laden deeds in valleys. Had your Torah scholars budded on the vine, had your merit-laden righteous flowered like the pomegranates filled with seeds?*

[Israel responds:] [12] *Alas, I knew not how to guard myself from sin! My own devices harnessed me, like chariots subject to a foreign nation's mercies.*

CHAPTER SEVEN

[1] *The nations have said to me, 'Turn away, turn away from God, O nation whose faith in Him is perfect, turn away, turn away, and we shall choose nobility from you.'*

But I replied to them, 'What can you bestow upon a nation whole in faith to Him commensurate even with the desert camps encircling?'

[The nations to Israel:] [2] *But your footsteps were so lovely when shod in pilgrim's*

כְּמוֹ חֲלָאִים מַעֲשֵׂה יְדֵי אָמָּן: ג שָׁרְרֵךְ אַגַּן הַסַּהַר אַל־יֶחְסַר הַמָּזֶג בִּטְנֵךְ
עֲרֵמַת חִטִּים סוּגָה בַּשּׁוֹשַׁנִּים: ד שְׁנֵי שָׁדַיִךְ כִּשְׁנֵי עֳפָרִים תָּאֳמֵי צְבִיָּה:
ה צַוָּארֵךְ כְּמִגְדַּל הַשֵּׁן עֵינַיִךְ בְּרֵכוֹת בְּחֶשְׁבּוֹן עַל־שַׁעַר בַּת־רַבִּים
אַפֵּךְ כְּמִגְדַּל הַלְּבָנוֹן צוֹפֶה פְּנֵי דַמָּשֶׂק: ו רֹאשֵׁךְ עָלַיִךְ כַּכַּרְמֶל וְדַלַּת
רֹאשֵׁךְ כָּאַרְגָּמָן מֶלֶךְ אָסוּר בָּרְהָטִים: ז מַה־יָּפִית וּמַה־נָּעַמְתְּ
אַהֲבָה בַּתַּעֲנוּגִים: ח זֹאת קוֹמָתֵךְ דָּמְתָה לְתָמָר וְשָׁדַיִךְ לְאַשְׁכֹּלוֹת:
ט אָמַרְתִּי אֶעֱלֶה בְתָמָר אֹחֲזָה בְּסַנְסִנָּיו וְיִהְיוּ־נָא שָׁדַיִךְ כְּאֶשְׁכְּלוֹת
הַגֶּפֶן וְרֵיחַ אַפֵּךְ כַּתַּפּוּחִים: י וְחִכֵּךְ כְּיֵין הַטּוֹב הוֹלֵךְ לְדוֹדִי לְמֵישָׁרִים
דּוֹבֵב שִׂפְתֵי יְשֵׁנִים: יא אֲנִי לְדוֹדִי וְעָלַי תְּשׁוּקָתוֹ: יב לְכָה דוֹדִי
נֵצֵא הַשָּׂדֶה נָלִינָה בַּכְּפָרִים: יג נַשְׁכִּימָה לַכְּרָמִים נִרְאֶה אִם פָּרְחָה
הַגֶּפֶן פִּתַּח הַסְּמָדַר הֵנֵצוּ הָרִמּוֹנִים שָׁם אֶתֵּן אֶת־דֹּדַי לָךְ:
יד הַדּוּדָאִים נָתְנוּ־רֵיחַ וְעַל־פְּתָחֵינוּ כָּל־מְגָדִים חֲדָשִׁים גַּם־יְשָׁנִים דּוֹדִי
צָפַנְתִּי לָךְ:

פרק ח

א מִי יִתֶּנְךָ כְּאָח לִי יוֹנֵק שְׁדֵי אִמִּי אֶמְצָאֲךָ בַחוּץ אֶשָּׁקְךָ גַּם לֹא־יָבֻזוּ
לִי: ב אֶנְהָגֲךָ אֲבִיאֲךָ אֶל־בֵּית אִמִּי תְּלַמְּדֵנִי אַשְׁקְךָ מִיַּיִן הָרֶקַח מֵעֲסִיס
רִמֹּנִי: ג שְׂמֹאלוֹ תַּחַת רֹאשִׁי וִימִינוֹ תְּחַבְּקֵנִי: ד הִשְׁבַּעְתִּי אֶתְכֶם בְּנוֹת
יְרוּשָׁלָםִ מַה־תָּעִירוּ ׀ וּמַה־תְּעֹרְרוּ אֶת־הָאַהֲבָה עַד שֶׁתֶּחְפָּץ: ה מִי זֹאת
עֹלָה מִן־הַמִּדְבָּר מִתְרַפֶּקֶת עַל־דּוֹדָהּ תַּחַת הַתַּפּוּחַ עוֹרַרְתִּיךָ שָׁמָּה
חִבְּלַתְךָ אִמֶּךָ שָׁמָּה חִבְּלָה יְלָדַתְךָ: ו שִׂימֵנִי כַחוֹתָם עַל־לִבֶּךָ כַּחוֹתָם
עַל־זְרוֹעֶךָ כִּי־עַזָּה כַמָּוֶת אַהֲבָה קָשָׁה כִשְׁאוֹל קִנְאָה, רְשָׁפֶיהָ רִשְׁפֵּי
אֵשׁ, שַׁלְהֶבֶתְיָה. ז מַיִם רַבִּים לֹא יוּכְלוּ לְכַבּוֹת אֶת־הָאַהֲבָה, וּנְהָרוֹת לֹא
יִשְׁטְפוּהָ, אִם יִתֵּן אִישׁ אֶת כָּל־הוֹן בֵּיתוֹ בָּאַהֲבָה, בּוֹז יָבוּזוּ לוֹ.

---

3. A rose hedge is hardly an imposing barrier. Despite its thorns it can be trampled easily. Its true effectiveness is in its beauty; only a callous person would trample a rose bush. Thus it can only deter those who appreciate its beauty; for the esthetically blind, it is no barrier at all. Similarly, the sanctions of Torah and Rabbinic ordinances are gentle reminders to refrain from trespass against the handiwork of God and are effective only for those who understand the greatness and majesty of Torah *(Harav Mordechai Gifter)*.

10. *In love so upright*, i.e., a love so intense that even my departed ancestors will rejoice in me and be thankful for their lot *(Rashi)*.

13. Israel invites God to observe the fine conduct of her children.

CHAPTER EIGHT

God had earlier expressed His desire to rest His *Shechinah* upon His people once again. They now continue their response with a longing plea for His aid and comfort.

3-4. Know, you nations: Although I complain and lament, my Beloved holds my hand and is my support throughout my Exile *(Rashi)*.

5-7. It was I and no other who sought out Your shade under the apple tree to which You are compared [see 2:3], and I jumped at the opportunity to cry out נַעֲשֶׂה וְנִשְׁמָע, '*we will do and we*

*sandals, O daughter of nobles. The rounded shafts for your libations' abysslike
trenches, handiwork of the Master Craftsman. 3 At earth's very center your
Sanhedrin site is an ivory basin of ceaseless, flowing teaching; your national center
an indispensable heap of nourishing knowledge hedged about with roses. 4 Your twin
sustainers, the Tablets of the Law, are like two fawns, twins of the gazelle. 5 Your altar
and Temple, erect and stately as an ivory tower; your wise men aflow with springs
of complex wisdom at the gate of the many-peopled city; your face, like a Lebanese
tower, looks to your future boundary as far as Damascus.*

*6 The Godly name on your head is as mighty as Carmel; your crowning braid is
royal purple, your King is bound in nazaritic tresses. 7 How beautiful and pleasant are
you, befitting the pleasures of spiritual love. 8 Such is your stature, likened to a
towering palm tree, from your teachers flow sustenance like wine-filled clusters.*

[God to Israel:] *9 I boast on High that your deeds cause Me to ascend on your palm
tree, I grasp onto your branches. I beg now your teachers that they may remain like
clusters of grapes from which flow strength to your weakest ones, and the fragrance
of your face like apples.* **[Israel interjects:]** *10 and may your utterance be like finest
wine.*

*I shall heed Your plea to uphold my faith before my Beloved in love so upright and
honest that my slumbering fathers will move their lips in approval.*

11 I say to the nations, 'I am my Beloved's and He longs for my perfection.'

*12 Come, my Beloved, let us go to the fields where Your children serve You in want,
there let us lodge with Esau's children who are blessed with plenty yet still deny.*

*13 Let us wake at dawn in vineyards of prayer and study. Let us see if students of
Writ have budded, if students of Oral Law have blossomed, if ripened scholars have
bloomed — there I will display my finest products to You.*

*14 All my baskets, good and bad, emit a fragrance, all at our doors have the precious
fruits of comely deeds — those the Scribes have newly ordained and Your Torah's
timeless wisdom, for You, Beloved, has my heart stored them.*

CHAPTER EIGHT

*1 If only, despite my wrongs, You could comfort me as Joseph did, like a
brother nurtured at the bosom of my mother, if in the streets I found Your prophets
I would kiss You and embrace You through them, nor could anyone despise me for it.
2 I would lead You, I would bring You to my mother's Temple for You to teach me as
You did in Moses' Tent; to drink I'd give You spiced libations, wines like pomegranate
nectar.*

[Israel to the nations:] *3 Despite my laments in Exile, His left hand supports my
head and His right hand embraces me in support. 4 I adjure you, O nations destined
to ascend to Jerusalem — for if you violate your oath you will become defenseless —
if you dare provoke God to hate me or disturb His love for me while He still desires
it.*

[God and the Heavenly Tribunal:] *5 How worthy she is who rises from the desert
bearing Torah and His Presence, clinging to her Beloved!*

[Israel interjects:] *Under Sinai suspended above me, there I roused Your love, there
was Your people born; a mother to other nations, there she endured the travail of her
birth. 6 For the sake of my love, place me like a seal on Your heart, like a seal to dedicate
Your strength for me, for strong till the death is my love; though their zeal for
vengeance is hard as the grave, its flashes are flashes of fire from the flame of God.
7 Many waters of heathen tribulation cannot extinguish the fire of this love, nor rivers
of royal seduction or torture wash it away.*

[God replies to Israel:] *Were any man to offer all the treasure of his home to entice
you away from your love, they would scorn him to extreme.*

ח אָחוֹת לָנוּ קְטַנָּה, וְשָׁדַיִם אֵין לָהּ, מַה־נַּעֲשֶׂה לַאֲחוֹתֵנוּ בַּיּוֹם
שֶׁיְּדֻבַּר־בָּהּ. ט אִם־חוֹמָה הִיא, נִבְנֶה עָלֶיהָ טִירַת כָּסֶף, וְאִם־דֶּלֶת הִיא,
נָצוּר עָלֶיהָ לוּחַ אָרֶז. י אֲנִי חוֹמָה, וְשָׁדַי כַּמִּגְדָּלוֹת, אָז הָיִיתִי בְעֵינָיו
כְּמוֹצְאֵת שָׁלוֹם. יא כֶּרֶם הָיָה לִשְׁלֹמֹה בְּבַעַל הָמוֹן, נָתַן אֶת הַכֶּרֶם
לַנֹּטְרִים, אִישׁ יָבִא בְּפִרְיוֹ אֶלֶף כָּסֶף. יב כַּרְמִי שֶׁלִּי לְפָנָי, הָאֶלֶף לְךָ
שְׁלֹמֹה, וּמָאתַיִם לְנֹטְרִים אֶת־פִּרְיוֹ. יג הַיּוֹשֶׁבֶת בַּגַּנִּים, חֲבֵרִים
מַקְשִׁיבִים לְקוֹלֵךְ, הַשְׁמִיעִנִי. יד בְּרַח דּוֹדִי, וּדְמֵה לְךָ לִצְבִי, אוֹ לְעֹפֶר
הָאַיָּלִים, עַל הָרֵי בְשָׂמִים.

קדיש יתום

יִתְגַּדַּל וְיִתְקַדַּשׁ שְׁמֵהּ רַבָּא. (Cong. – אָמֵן.) בְּעָלְמָא דִּי בְרָא כִרְעוּתֵהּ. וְיַמְלִיךְ מַלְכוּתֵהּ, בְּחַיֵּיכוֹן וּבְיוֹמֵיכוֹן וּבְחַיֵּי דְכָל בֵּית יִשְׂרָאֵל, בַּעֲגָלָא וּבִזְמַן קָרִיב. וְאִמְרוּ: אָמֵן.

(Cong. – אָמֵן. יְהֵא שְׁמֵהּ רַבָּא מְבָרַךְ לְעָלַם וּלְעָלְמֵי עָלְמַיָּא.)

יְהֵא שְׁמֵהּ רַבָּא מְבָרַךְ לְעָלַם וּלְעָלְמֵי עָלְמַיָּא.

יִתְבָּרַךְ וְיִשְׁתַּבַּח וְיִתְפָּאַר וְיִתְרוֹמַם וְיִתְנַשֵּׂא וְיִתְהַדָּר וְיִתְעַלֶּה וְיִתְהַלָּל שְׁמֵהּ דְּקוּדְשָׁא בְּרִיךְ הוּא (Cong. – בְּרִיךְ הוּא) – לְעֵלָּא מִן כָּל בִּרְכָתָא וְשִׁירָתָא תֻּשְׁבְּחָתָא וְנֶחֱמָתָא, דַּאֲמִירָן בְּעָלְמָא. וְאִמְרוּ: אָמֵן. (Cong. – אָמֵן.)

יְהֵא שְׁלָמָא רַבָּא מִן שְׁמַיָּא, וְחַיִּים עָלֵינוּ וְעַל כָּל יִשְׂרָאֵל. וְאִמְרוּ: אָמֵן. (Cong. – אָמֵן.)

Take three steps back. Bow left and say . . . עֹשֶׂה; bow right and say . . . הוּא; bow forward and say וְעַל כָּל . . . אָמֵן. Remain standing in place for a few moments, then take three steps forward.

עֹשֶׂה שָׁלוֹם בִּמְרוֹמָיו, הוּא יַעֲשֶׂה שָׁלוֹם עָלֵינוּ, וְעַל כָּל יִשְׂרָאֵל. וְאִמְרוּ: אָמֵן. (Cong. – אָמֵן.)

On the Sabbath of *Chol HaMoed* continue on page 580.
On the seventh day and eighth day of Pesach continue on page 944.

---

will obey!' (Alshich).

9. The Tribunal's response depends upon how she conducts herself in the interim while in Exile.

10. Israel replies proudly: 'Your fear is unjustified!'

12. The nations will reply: Whatever, we filched from Israel [verses] will be returned to You, for the vineyard is Yours *(Rashi)*.

[The Heavenly Tribunal reflects:] [8] *Israel desires to cleave to us, the small and humble one, but her time of spiritual maturity has not come. What shall we do for our cleaving one on the day the nations plot against her?*

[9] *If her faith and belief are strong as a wall withstanding incursions from without, we shall become her fortress and beauty; building her City and Holy Temple; but if she wavers like a door, succumbing to every alien knock, with fragile cedar panels shall we then enclose her.*

[Israel replies proudly:] [10] *My faith is firm as a wall, and my nourishing synagogues and study halls are strong as towers! Then, having said so, I become in His eyes like a bride found perfect.*

[. . . and reminisces:] [11] *Israel was vineyard of Him to Whom peace belongs in populous Jerusalem. He gave His vineyard to harsh, cruel guardians; each one came to extort his fruit, even a thousand silver pieces.*

[God to the nations, on the Day of Judgment:] [12] *The vineyard is Mine! Your iniquities are before Me!*

[The nations will reply:] *The thousand silver pieces are Yours, You to Whom peace belongs, and two hundred more to the Sages who guarded the fruit of Torah from our designs.*

[God to Israel:] [13] *O My beloved, dwelling in far-flung gardens, your fellows, the angels hearken to your voice of Torah and prayer. Let Me hear it that they may then sanctify Me.*

[Israel to God:] [14] *Flee, my Beloved, from our common Exile and be like a gazelle or a young hart in Your swiftness to redeem and rest your Presence among us on the fragrant Mount Moriah, site of Your Temple.*

MOURNER'S KADDISH

יִתְגַּדַּל *May His great Name grow exalted and sanctified* (Cong.– *Amen.*) *in the world that He created as He willed. May He give reign to His kingship in your lifetimes and in your days, and in the lifetimes of the entire Family of Israel, swiftly and soon. Now respond: Amen.*

(Cong.– *Amen. May His great Name be blessed forever and ever.*)

May His great Name be blessed forever and ever.

Blessed, praised, glorified, exalted, extolled, mighty, upraised, and lauded be the Name of the Holy One, Blessed is He (Cong.– *Blessed is He*) *— beyond any blessing and song, praise and consolation that are uttered in the world. Now respond: Amen.* (Cong.– *Amen*).

May there be abundant peace from Heaven, and life, upon us and upon all Israel. Now respond: Amen. (Cong.– *Amen.*)

Take three steps back. Bow left and say, *'He Who makes peace . . .'*; bow right and say, *'may He . . .'*; bow forward and say, *'and upon all Israel . . .'* Remain standing in place for a few moments, then take three steps forward.

He Who makes peace in His heights, may He make peace upon us, and upon all Israel. Now respond: Amen. (Cong.– *Amen.*)

On the Sabbath of *Chol HaMoed* continue on page 580.
On the seventh day and eighth day of Pesach continue on page 944.

הוצאת ספר תורה לשבת חול המועד

From the moment the Ark is opened until the Torah is returned to it, one must conduct himself with the utmost respect, and avoid unnecessary conversation. It is commendable to kiss the Torah as it is carried to the *bimah* [reading table] and back to the Ark.

All rise and remain standing until the Torah is placed on the *bimah*. The congregation recites:

אֵין כָּמְוֹךָ בָאֱלֹהִים אֲדֹנָי, וְאֵין כְּמַעֲשֶׂיךָ.[1] מַלְכוּתְךָ מַלְכוּת כָּל עֹלָמִים, וּמֶמְשַׁלְתְּךָ בְּכָל דּוֹר וָדֹר.[2] יהוה מֶלֶךְ,[3] יהוה מָלָךְ,[4] יהוה יִמְלֹךְ לְעֹלָם וָעֶד.[5] יהוה עֹז לְעַמּוֹ יִתֵּן, יהוה יְבָרֵךְ אֶת עַמּוֹ בַשָּׁלוֹם.[6]

אַב הָרַחֲמִים, הֵיטִיבָה בִרְצוֹנְךָ אֶת צִיּוֹן, תִּבְנֶה חוֹמוֹת יְרוּשָׁלָיִם.[7] כִּי בְךָ לְבַד בָּטָחְנוּ, מֶלֶךְ אֵל רָם וְנִשָּׂא, אֲדוֹן עוֹלָמִים.

THE ARK IS OPENED

Before the Torah is removed the congregation recites:

וַיְהִי בִּנְסֹעַ הָאָרֹן וַיְּאמֶר מֹשֶׁה, קוּמָה יהוה וְיָפֻצוּ אֹיְבֶיךָ וְיָנֻסוּ מְשַׂנְאֶיךָ מִפָּנֶיךָ.[8] כִּי מִצִּיּוֹן תֵּצֵא תוֹרָה, וּדְבַר יהוה מִירוּשָׁלָיִם.[9] בָּרוּךְ שֶׁנָּתַן תּוֹרָה לְעַמּוֹ יִשְׂרָאֵל בִּקְדֻשָּׁתוֹ.

זוהר ויקהל שסט:א

בְּרִיךְ שְׁמֵהּ דְּמָרֵא עָלְמָא, בְּרִיךְ כִּתְרָךְ וְאַתְרָךְ. יְהֵא רְעוּתָךְ עִם עַמָּךְ יִשְׂרָאֵל לְעָלַם, וּפֻרְקַן יְמִינָךְ אַחֲזֵי לְעַמָּךְ בְּבֵית מַקְדְּשָׁךְ, וּלְאַמְטְוּיֵי לָנָא מִטּוּב נְהוֹרָךְ, וּלְקַבֵּל צְלוֹתָנָא בְּרַחֲמִין. יְהֵא רַעֲוָא קֳדָמָךְ, דְּתוֹרִיךְ לָן חַיִּין בְּטִיבוּתָא, וְלֶהֱוֵי אֲנָא פְקִידָא בְּגוֹ צַדִּיקַיָּא, לְמִרְחַם עָלַי וּלְמִנְטַר יָתִי וְיַת כָּל דִּי לִי, וְדִי לְעַמָּךְ יִשְׂרָאֵל. אַנְתְּ הוּא זָן לְכֹלָּא, וּמְפַרְנֵס לְכֹלָּא, אַנְתְּ הוּא שַׁלִּיט עַל כֹּלָּא. אַנְתְּ הוּא דְשַׁלִּיט עַל מַלְכַיָּא, וּמַלְכוּתָא דִּילָךְ הִיא. אֲנָא עַבְדָּא דְקֻדְשָׁא בְּרִיךְ הוּא, דְּסָגִידְנָא קַמֵּהּ וּמִקַּמָּא דִּיקַר אוֹרַיְתֵהּ בְּכָל עִדָּן וְעִדָּן. לָא עַל אֱנָשׁ רָחִיצְנָא, וְלָא עַל בַּר אֱלָהִין סָמִיכְנָא, אֶלָּא בֶּאֱלָהָא דִשְׁמַיָּא, דְּהוּא אֱלָהָא קְשׁוֹט, וְאוֹרַיְתֵהּ קְשׁוֹט, וּנְבִיאוֹהִי קְשׁוֹט, וּמַסְגֵּא לְמֶעְבַּד טַבְוָן וּקְשׁוֹט. בֵּהּ אֲנָא רָחִיץ, וְלִשְׁמֵהּ קַדִּישָׁא יַקִּירָא אֲנָא אֵמַר תֻּשְׁבְּחָן. יְהֵא רַעֲוָא קֳדָמָךְ, דְּתִפְתַּח לִבָּאִי בְּאוֹרַיְתָא, וְתַשְׁלִים מִשְׁאֲלִין דְּלִבָּאִי, וְלִבָּא דְכָל עַמָּךְ יִשְׂרָאֵל, לְטַב וּלְחַיִּין וְלִשְׁלָם. (אָמֵן.)

REMOVAL OF THE TORAH FROM THE ARK
FOR SABBATH CHOL HAMOED

From the moment the Ark is opened until the Torah is returned to it, one must conduct himself with the utmost respect, and avoid unnecessary conversation. It is commendable to kiss the Torah as it is carried to the *bimah* [reading table] and back to the Ark.

All rise and remain standing until the Torah is placed on the *bimah*. The congregation recites:

אֵין כָּמְוֹךָ *There is none like You among the gods, my Lord, and there is nothing like Your works.[1] Your kingdom is a kingdom spanning all eternities, and Your dominion is throughout every generation.[2] HASHEM reigns,[3] HASHEM has reigned,[4] HASHEM shall reign for all eternity.[5] HASHEM will give might to His people; HASHEM will bless His people with peace.[6]*

אַב הָרַחֲמִים *Father of compassion, do good with Zion according to Your will; rebuild the walls of Jerusalem.[7] For we trust in You alone, O King, God, exalted and uplifted, Master of worlds.*

THE ARK IS OPENED

Before the Torah is removed the congregation recites:

וַיְהִי בִּנְסֹעַ *When the Ark would travel, Moses would say, 'Arise, HASHEM, and let Your foes be scattered, let those who hate You flee from You.'[8] For from Zion the Torah will come forth and the word of HASHEM from Jerusalem.[9] Blessed is He Who gave the Torah to His people Israel in His holiness.*

Zohar, Vayakhel 369a

בְּרִיךְ שְׁמֵהּ *Blessed is the Name of the Master of the universe, blessed is Your crown and Your place. May Your favor remain with Your people Israel forever; may You display the salvation of Your right hand to Your people in Your Holy Temple, to benefit us with the goodness of Your luminescence and to accept our prayers with mercy. May it be Your will that You extend our lives with goodness and that I be numbered among the righteous; that You have mercy on me and protect me, all that is mine and that is Your people Israel's. It is You Who nourishes all and sustains all; You control everything. It is You Who control kings, and kingship is Yours. I am a servant of the Holy One, Blessed is He, and I prostrate myself before Him and before the glory of His Torah at all times. Not in any man do I put trust, nor on any angel do I rely — only on the God of heaven Who is the God of truth, Whose Torah is truth and Whose prophets are true and Who acts liberally with kindness and truth. In Him do I trust, and to His glorious and holy Name do I declare praises. May it be Your will that You open my heart to the Torah and that You fulfill the wishes of my heart and the heart of Your entire people Israel for good, for life, and for peace. (Amen.)*

(1) *Psalms* 86:8. (2) 145:13. (3) 10:16. (4) 93:1 et al. (5) *Exodus* 15:18.
(6) *Psalms* 29:11. (7) 51:20. (8) *Numbers* 10:35. (9) *Isaiah* 2:3.

Two Torah Scrolls are removed from the Ark; the first for the main Torah reading and the second for *Maftir.* The first is presented to the *chazzan,* who accepts it in his right arm. Facing the congregation, the *chazzan* raises the Torah and, followed by congregation, recites:

שְׁמַע יִשְׂרָאֵל• יהוה אֱלֹהֵינוּ יהוה אֶחָד.[1]

Still facing the congregation, the *chazzan* raises the Torah and, followed by congregation, recites:

אֶחָד (הוּא) אֱלֹהֵינוּ גָּדוֹל אֲדוֹנֵינוּ, קָדוֹשׁ שְׁמוֹ.

The *chazzan* turns to the Ark, bows while raising the Torah, and recites:

גַּדְּלוּ• לַיהוה אִתִּי וּנְרוֹמְמָה שְׁמוֹ יַחְדָּו.[2]

The *chazzan* turns to his right and carries the Torah to the *bimah,* as the congregation responds:

לְךָ יהוה הַגְּדֻלָּה• וְהַגְּבוּרָה וְהַתִּפְאֶרֶת וְהַנֵּצַח וְהַהוֹד כִּי כֹל בַּשָּׁמַיִם וּבָאָרֶץ, לְךָ יהוה הַמַּמְלָכָה וְהַמִּתְנַשֵּׂא לְכֹל לְרֹאשׁ.[3] רוֹמְמוּ יהוה אֱלֹהֵינוּ, וְהִשְׁתַּחֲווּ לַהֲדֹם רַגְלָיו,• קָדוֹשׁ הוּא. רוֹמְמוּ יהוה אֱלֹהֵינוּ, וְהִשְׁתַּחֲווּ לְהַר קָדְשׁוֹ, כִּי קָדוֹשׁ יהוה אֱלֹהֵינוּ.[4]

As the *chazzan* carries the Torah to the *bimah,* the congregation recites:

עַל הַכֹּל,• יִתְגַּדַּל וְיִתְקַדַּשׁ וְיִשְׁתַּבַּח וְיִתְפָּאַר וְיִתְרוֹמַם וְיִתְנַשֵּׂא שְׁמוֹ שֶׁל מֶלֶךְ מַלְכֵי הַמְּלָכִים הַקָּדוֹשׁ בָּרוּךְ הוּא, בָּעוֹלָמוֹת שֶׁבָּרָא, הָעוֹלָם הַזֶּה וְהָעוֹלָם הַבָּא, כִּרְצוֹנוֹ,• וְכִרְצוֹן יְרֵאָיו, וְכִרְצוֹן כָּל בֵּית יִשְׂרָאֵל. צוּר הָעוֹלָמִים, אֲדוֹן כָּל הַבְּרִיּוֹת, אֱלוֹהַּ כָּל הַנְּפָשׁוֹת, הַיּוֹשֵׁב בְּמֶרְחֲבֵי מָרוֹם, הַשּׁוֹכֵן בִּשְׁמֵי שְׁמֵי קֶדֶם. קְדֻשָּׁתוֹ עַל הַחַיּוֹת, וּקְדֻשָּׁתוֹ עַל כִּסֵּא הַכָּבוֹד. וּבְכֵן יִתְקַדַּשׁ שִׁמְךָ בָּנוּ יהוה אֱלֹהֵינוּ לְעֵינֵי כָּל חָי. וְנֹאמַר לְפָנָיו שִׁיר חָדָשׁ, כַּכָּתוּב: שִׁירוּ לֵאלֹהִים זַמְּרוּ שְׁמוֹ, סֹלּוּ לָרֹכֵב בָּעֲרָבוֹת בְּיָהּ שְׁמוֹ, וְעִלְזוּ לְפָנָיו.[5] וְנִרְאֵהוּ עַיִן בְּעַיִן בְּשׁוּבוֹ אֶל נָוֵהוּ, כַּכָּתוּב: כִּי עַיִן בְּעַיִן יִרְאוּ בְּשׁוּב יהוה צִיּוֹן.[6] וְנֶאֱמַר: וְנִגְלָה כְּבוֹד יהוה, וְרָאוּ כָל בָּשָׂר יַחְדָּו כִּי פִּי יהוה דִּבֵּר.[7]

◆§ **שְׁמַע יִשְׂרָאֵל** — *Hear, O Israel.* Holding the Torah Scroll, the *chazzan* leads the congregation in reciting three verses that help set the majestic tone of reading publicly from the word of God. The verses form a logical progression: God is One; He is great and holy; therefore we join in declaring His greatness.

◆§ **גַּדְּלוּ** — *Declare the greatness.* Our rejoicing in the Torah manifests itself in praise of its Giver. The *chazzan* calls upon the congregation to join him in praising God.

◆§ **לְךָ ה׳ הַגְּדֻלָּה** — *Yours, HASHEM, is the greatness.* This praise was first uttered by David in his ecstasy at seeing how wholeheartedly the people contributed their riches toward the eventual building of the Temple. He ascribed the greatness of that and every other achievement to God's graciousness.

לַהֲדֹם רַגְלָיו — *At His footstool,* i.e., the Temple, as if to say that God's Heavenly Presence extends earthward, like a footstool that helps support a monarch sitting on his throne. In a further sense, this represents our resolve to live in such a way that we are worthy of His Presence resting upon us *(R' Hirsch).*

◆§ **עַל הַכֹּל** — *For all this.* All the praises that we

Two Torah Scrolls are removed from the Ark; the first for the main Torah reading and the second for *Maftir.* The first is presented to the *chazzan,* who accepts it in his right arm. Facing the congregation, the *chazzan* raises the Torah and, followed by congregation, recites:

Hear, O Israel:* HASHEM is our God, HASHEM, the One and Only.[1]

Still facing the congregation, the *chazzan* raises the Torah and, followed by congregation, recites:

One is our God, great is our Master, Holy is His Name.

The *chazzan* turns to the Ark, bows while raising the Torah, and recites:

Declare the greatness* of HASHEM with me, and let us exalt His Name together.[2]

The *chazzan* turns to his right and carries the Torah to the *bimah,* as the congregation responds:

לְךָ *Yours, HASHEM, is the greatness,* the strength, the splendor, the triumph, and the glory; even everything in heaven and earth; Yours, HASHEM, is the kingdom, and the sovereignty over every leader.*[3] *Exalt HASHEM, our God, and bow at His footstool;* He is Holy! Exalt HASHEM, our God, and bow to His holy mountain; for holy is HASHEM, our God.*[4]

As the *chazzan* carries the Torah to the *bimah,* the congregation recites:

עַל הַכֹּל *For all this,* let the Name of the King of kings, the Holy One, Blessed is He, grow exalted, sanctified, praised, glorified, exalted, and extolled in the worlds that He has created — This World and the World to Come — according to His will,* the will of those who fear Him, and the will of the entire House of Israel. Rock of the eternities, Master of all creatures, God of all souls, He Who sits in the expanses on high, Who rests in the loftiest primeval heavens. His holiness is upon the Chayos; His holiness is upon the Throne of Glory. Similarly, may Your Name be sanctified within us, HASHEM, our God, in the sight of all the living. May we chant before Him a new song as it is written: 'Sing to God, make music for His Name, extol the One Who rides in the highest heavens with His Name YAH, and exult before Him.'*[5] *May we see Him with a perceptive view upon His return to His Abode, as is written: 'For they shall see with a perceptive view as HASHEM returns to Zion.'*[6] *And it is said: 'The glory of HASHEM shall be revealed and all flesh together shall see that the mouth of HASHEM has spoken.'*[7]

(1) *Deuteronomy* 6:4. (2) *Psalms* 34:4. (3) *I Chronicles* 29:11.
(4) *Psalms* 99:5,9. (5) 68:5. (6) *Isaiah* 52:8. (7) 40:5.

---

have uttered heretofore are inadequate to describe God's greatness. May His Name continue to grow exalted (*Kol Bo*).

This paragraph is intended to express the majesty of God especially now that we are about to read from the Torah. We say that although He is sanctified in the heavens and by the spiritual beings, we long to become worthy vehicles through which His greatness can be manifested on earth, as well.

כִּרְצוֹנוֹ — *According to His will.* May He be *exalted, sanctified, praised* . . . as He wishes to be. God created the universe so that His glory could be appreciated and emulated by man (see *Isaiah* 43:7). We now pray that this will indeed take place.

אַב הָרַחֲמִים הוּא יְרַחֵם עַם עֲמוּסִים, וְיִזְכֹּר בְּרִית אֵיתָנִים, וְיַצִּיל נַפְשׁוֹתֵינוּ מִן הַשָּׁעוֹת הָרָעוֹת, וְיִגְעַר בְּיֵצֶר הָרַע מִן הַנְּשׂוּאִים, וְיָחֹן אוֹתָנוּ לִפְלֵיטַת עוֹלָמִים, וִימַלֵּא מִשְׁאֲלוֹתֵינוּ בְּמִדָּה טוֹבָה יְשׁוּעָה וְרַחֲמִים.

The Torah is placed on the *bimah* and prepared for reading.

The *gabbai* uses the following formula to call a *Kohen* to the Torah:

וְיַעֲזוֹר וְיָגֵן וְיוֹשִׁיעַ לְכֹל הַחוֹסִים בּוֹ, וְנֹאמַר, אָמֵן. הַכֹּל הָבוּ גֹדֶל לֵאלֹהֵינוּ וּתְנוּ כָבוֹד לַתּוֹרָה, כֹּהֵן° קְרָב, יַעֲמֹד (name) בֶּן (father's name) הַכֹּהֵן.

°If no *Kohen* is present, the *gabbai* says:
„אֵין כָּאן כֹּהֵן, יַעֲמֹד (insert name) יִשְׂרָאֵל (לֵוִי) בִּמְקוֹם כֹּהֵן.“

בָּרוּךְ שֶׁנָּתַן תּוֹרָה לְעַמּוֹ יִשְׂרָאֵל בִּקְדֻשָּׁתוֹ. (תּוֹרַת יהוה תְּמִימָה מְשִׁיבַת נָפֶשׁ, עֵדוּת יהוה נֶאֱמָנָה מַחְכִּימַת פֶּתִי. פִּקּוּדֵי יהוה יְשָׁרִים מְשַׂמְּחֵי לֵב, מִצְוַת יהוה בָּרָה מְאִירַת עֵינָיִם.[1] יהוה עֹז לְעַמּוֹ יִתֵּן, יהוה יְבָרֵךְ אֶת עַמּוֹ בַשָּׁלוֹם.[2] הָאֵל תָּמִים דַּרְכּוֹ, אִמְרַת יהוה צְרוּפָה, מָגֵן הוּא לְכֹל הַחוֹסִים בּוֹ.[3])

Congregation, then *gabbai*:

וְאַתֶּם הַדְּבֵקִים בַּיהוה אֱלֹהֵיכֶם, חַיִּים כֻּלְּכֶם הַיּוֹם.[4]

קריאת התורה

The reader shows the *oleh* (person called to the Torah) the place in the Torah. The *oleh* touches the Torah with a corner of his *tallis,* or the belt or mantle of the Torah, and kisses it. He then begins the blessing, bowing at בָּרְכוּ, and straightening up at 'ה.

בָּרְכוּ אֶת יהוה* הַמְּבֹרָךְ.

Congregation, followed by *oleh,* responds, bowing at בָּרוּךְ, and straightening up at 'ה.

בָּרוּךְ יהוה הַמְּבֹרָךְ לְעוֹלָם וָעֶד.

Oleh continues:

בָּרוּךְ אַתָּה יהוה אֱלֹהֵינוּ מֶלֶךְ הָעוֹלָם, אֲשֶׁר בָּחַר בָּנוּ מִכָּל הָעַמִּים, וְנָתַן לָנוּ אֶת תּוֹרָתוֹ. בָּרוּךְ אַתָּה יהוה, נוֹתֵן הַתּוֹרָה. (Cong. – אָמֵן.)

After his Torah portion has been read, the *oleh* recites:

בָּרוּךְ אַתָּה יהוה אֱלֹהֵינוּ מֶלֶךְ הָעוֹלָם, אֲשֶׁר נָתַן לָנוּ תּוֹרַת אֱמֶת, וְחַיֵּי עוֹלָם נָטַע בְּתוֹכֵנוּ. בָּרוּךְ אַתָּה יהוה, נוֹתֵן הַתּוֹרָה. (Cong. – אָמֵן.)

קְרִיאַת הַתּוֹרָה / Reading of the Torah

There is a basic difference between the reading of the Torah and the prayers. When we pray, *we* call upon *God;* that is why the *chazzan* stands in front of the congregation as its representative. But the Torah reading is reminiscent of God's revelation to Israel, when the nation gathered around Mount Sinai to hear Him communicate His word to Israel. That is why the Torah is read from a *bimah,* platform, in the center of the congregation and usually elevated, like the mountain around which Israel gathered.

The number of people called to the Torah varies in accordance with the sanctity of the day.

אַב הָרַחֲמִים *May the Father of compassion have mercy on the nation that is borne by Him, and may He remember the covenant of the spiritually mighty. May He rescue our souls from the bad times, and upbraid the evil inclination to leave those borne by Him, graciously make us an eternal remnant, and fulfill our requests in good measure, for salvation and mercy.*

The Torah is placed on the *bimah* and prepared for reading.

The *gabbai* uses the following formula to call a *Kohen* to the Torah:

וְיַעֲזוֹר *May He help, shield, and save all who take refuge in Him — Now let us respond: Amen. All of you ascribe greatness to our God and give honor to the Torah. Kohen,*° *approach. Arise* (name) *son of* (father's name) *the Kohen.*

°If no *Kohen* is present, the *gabbai* says: *'There is no Kohen present, stand* (name) *son of* (father's name) *an Israelite (Levite) in place of the Kohen.'*

Blessed is He Who gave the Torah to His people Israel in His holiness. (The Torah of HASHEM is perfect, restoring the soul; the testimony of HASHEM is trustworthy, making the simple one wise. The orders of HASHEM are upright, gladdening the heart; the command of HASHEM is clear, enlightening the eyes.[1] *HASHEM will give might to His nation; HASHEM will bless His nation with peace.*[2] *The God Whose way is perfect, the promise of HASHEM is flawless, He is a shield for all who take refuge in Him.*[3]*)*

Congregation, then *gabbai:*

You who cling to HASHEM, your God, you are all alive today.[4]

READING OF THE TORAH

The reader shows the *oleh* (person called to the Torah) the place in the Torah. The *oleh* touches the Torah with a corner of his *tallis,* or the belt or mantle of the Torah, and kisses it. He then begins the blessing, bowing at *'Bless,'* and straightening up at 'HASHEM.'

Bless HASHEM,* the blessed One.

Congregation, followed by *oleh,* responds, bowing at 'Blessed,' and straightening up at 'HASHEM.'

Blessed is HASHEM, the blessed One, for all eternity.

Oleh continues:

בָּרוּךְ *Blessed are You, HASHEM, our God, King of the universe, Who selected us from all the peoples and gave us His Torah. Blessed are You, HASHEM, Giver of the Torah.* (Cong.– *Amen.*)

After his Torah portion has been read, the *oleh* recites:

בָּרוּךְ *Blessed are You, HASHEM, our God, King of the universe, Who gave us the Torah of truth and implanted eternal life within us. Blessed are You, HASHEM, Giver of the Torah.* (Cong.– *Amen.*)

(1) *Psalms* 19:8-9. (2) 29:11. (3) 18:31. (4) *Deuteronomy* 4:4.

Thus, on Monday and Thursday, fast days, Purim and Chanukah, three people are called; on Rosh Chodesh and Chol HaMoed, four; on Festivals and Rosh Hashanah, five; on Yom Kippur, six; and on the Sabbath [whether an ordinary Sabbath or a Festival that falls on the Sabbath], seven. (It should be noted that *Maftir* is not included in the above number since *Maftir* is attached to the *Haftarah* reading.) Only three are called on Sabbath afternoons since the Torah has already been read in the morning.

On most Festivals the Torah reading is a selection on either the historical narrative of the day or the commandment to observe the Festivals.

בָּרְכוּ אֶת ה׳ — *Bless HASHEM.* This call to the congregation to bless God prior to the Torah reading is based on the practice of Ezra (*Nehemiah* 8:6). Before he read from the Torah to the multitude, he blessed God and they responded in kind. Similarly, the Sages (*Berachos* 21a) derive the Scriptural requirement to recite a

PRAYER FOR THE OLEH / מי שברך לעולה לתורה

After each *oleh* completes his concluding blessing, the *gabbai* calls the next *oleh* to the Torah, then blesses the one who has just concluded.

מִי שֶׁבֵּרַךְ אֲבוֹתֵינוּ אַבְרָהָם יִצְחָק וְיַעֲקֹב, הוּא יְבָרֵךְ אֶת (name) בֶּן (father's name) בַּעֲבוּר שֶׁעָלָה לִכְבוֹד הַמָּקוֹם, לִכְבוֹד הַתּוֹרָה, לִכְבוֹד הַשַּׁבָּת, לִכְבוֹד הָרֶגֶל. בִּשְׂכַר זֶה, הַקָּדוֹשׁ בָּרוּךְ הוּא יִשְׁמְּרֵהוּ וְיַצִּילֵהוּ מִכָּל צָרָה וְצוּקָה, וּמִכָּל נֶגַע וּמַחֲלָה, וְיִשְׁלַח בְּרָכָה וְהַצְלָחָה בְּכָל מַעֲשֵׂה יָדָיו, וְיִזְכֶּה לַעֲלוֹת לְרֶגֶל, עִם כָּל יִשְׂרָאֵל אֶחָיו. וְנֹאמַר: אָמֵן.

(–Cong. אָמֵן.)

PRAYER FOR OTHERS / מי שברך לאחרים

It is customary that the following prayer be recited for the family members of the *oleh* and for anyone else that he may wish to include:

מִי שֶׁבֵּרַךְ אֲבוֹתֵינוּ אַבְרָהָם יִצְחָק וְיַעֲקֹב, הוּא יְבָרֵךְ אֶת (names of the recipients) בַּעֲבוּר שֶׁ(name of *oleh*) יִתֵּן לִצְדָקָה* בַּעֲבוּרָם. בִּשְׂכַר זֶה, הַקָּדוֹשׁ בָּרוּךְ הוּא יִשְׁמְּרֵם וְיַצִּילֵם מִכָּל צָרָה וְצוּקָה, וּמִכָּל נֶגַע וּמַחֲלָה, וְיִשְׁלַח בְּרָכָה וְהַצְלָחָה בְּכָל מַעֲשֵׂה יְדֵיהֶם, וְיִזְכּוּ לַעֲלוֹת לְרֶגֶל, עִם כָּל יִשְׂרָאֵל אֲחֵיהֶם. וְנֹאמַר: אָמֵן.

(–Cong. אָמֵן.)

PRAYER FOR A SICK PERSON / מי שברך לחולה

מִי שֶׁבֵּרַךְ אֲבוֹתֵינוּ אַבְרָהָם יִצְחָק וְיַעֲקֹב, מֹשֶׁה אַהֲרֹן דָּוִד וּשְׁלֹמֹה,

for a man

הוּא יְבָרֵךְ וִירַפֵּא אֶת הַחוֹלֶה (patient's name) בֶּן (mother's name) בַּעֲבוּר שֶׁ(supplicant's name) יִתֵּן לִצְדָקָה בַּעֲבוּרוֹ.°° בִּשְׂכַר זֶה, הַקָּדוֹשׁ בָּרוּךְ הוּא יִמָּלֵא רַחֲמִים עָלָיו, לְהַחֲלִימוֹ וּלְרַפְּאתוֹ לְהַחֲזִיקוֹ וּלְהַחֲיוֹתוֹ, וְיִשְׁלַח לוֹ מְהֵרָה רְפוּאָה שְׁלֵמָה מִן הַשָּׁמַיִם, לִרְמַ״ח אֵבָרָיו, וּשְׁסָ״ה גִּידָיו, בְּתוֹךְ

for a woman

הוּא יְבָרֵךְ וִירַפֵּא אֶת הַחוֹלָה (patient's name) בַּת (mother's name) בַּעֲבוּר שֶׁ(supplicant's name) יִתֵּן לִצְדָקָה בַּעֲבוּרָהּ.°° בִּשְׂכַר זֶה, הַקָּדוֹשׁ בָּרוּךְ הוּא יִמָּלֵא רַחֲמִים עָלֶיהָ, לְהַחֲלִימָהּ וּלְרַפְּאתָהּ וּלְהַחֲזִיקָהּ וּלְהַחֲיוֹתָהּ, וְיִשְׁלַח לָהּ מְהֵרָה רְפוּאָה שְׁלֵמָה מִן הַשָּׁמַיִם, לְכָל אֵבָרֶיהָ, וּלְכָל גִּידֶיהָ, בְּתוֹךְ

שְׁאָר חוֹלֵי יִשְׂרָאֵל, רְפוּאַת הַנֶּפֶשׁ, וּרְפוּאַת הַגּוּף, שַׁבָּת הִיא מִלִּזְעֹק, וּרְפוּאָה קְרוֹבָה לָבֹא, הַשְׁתָּא, בַּעֲגָלָא וּבִזְמַן קָרִיב. וְנֹאמַר: אָמֵן.

(–Cong. אָמֵן.)

°°Many congregations substitute:

בַּעֲבוּר שֶׁכָּל הַקָּהָל מִתְפַּלְּלִים בַּעֲבוּרוֹ (בַּעֲבוּרָהּ)

---

blessing before Torah study from the verse, *When I proclaim the Name of HASHEM, ascribe greatness to our God* (*Deuteronomy* 32:3). The implication is that the public study of Torah requires a blessing.

§ מִי שֶׁבֵּרַךְ / He Who blessed

בַּעֲבוּר שֶׁיִּתֵּן לִצְדָקָה — *For . . . will contribute to charity.* The custom of blessing those called to the Torah is centuries old, and it has become

PRAYER FOR THE OLEH

After each *oleh* completes his concluding blessing, the *gabbai* calls the next *oleh* to the Torah, then blesses the one who has just concluded.

מִי שֶׁבֵּרַךְ *He Who blessed our forefathers Abraham, Isaac, and Jacob — may He bless (* Hebrew name*) son of (* father's Hebrew name*) because he has come up to the Torah in honor of the Omnipresent, in honor of the Torah, in honor of the Sabbath, in honor of the pilgrimage festival. As reward for this, may the Holy One, Blessed is He, protect him and rescue him from every trouble and distress, from every plague and illness; may He send blessing and success in his every endeavor, and may he be privileged to ascend to Jerusalem for the pilgrimage, together with all Israel, his brethren. Now let us respond: Amen.* (Cong.— *Amen.*)

PRAYER FOR OTHERS

It is customary that the following prayer be recited for the family members of the *oleh* and for anyone else that he may wish to include:

מִי שֶׁבֵּרַךְ *He Who blessed our forefathers Abraham, Isaac, and Jacob — may He bless (* names of recipients*) for (* name of *oleh) will contribute to charity* on their behalf. As reward for this, may the Holy One, Blessed is He, protect them and rescue them from every trouble and distress, from every plague and illness; may He send blessing and success in their every endeavor and may they be privileged to ascend to Jerusalem for the pilgrimage, together with all Israel, their brethren. Now let us respond: Amen.* (Cong.— *Amen.*)

PRAYER FOR A SICK PERSON

מִי שֶׁבֵּרַךְ *He Who blessed our forefathers Abraham, Isaac and Jacob, Moses and Aaron, David and Solomon — may He bless and heal the sick person (* patient's Hebrew name*) son/daughter of (* patient's mother's Hebrew name*) because (* name of supplicant*) will contribute to charity on his/her behalf.°° In reward for this, may the Holy One, Blessed is He, be filled with*

for a man

compassion for him to restore his health, to heal him, to strengthen him, and to revivify him. And may He send him speedily a complete recovery from heaven for his two hundred forty-eight organs and three hundred sixty-five blood vessels,

for a woman

compassion for her to restore her health, to heal her, to strengthen her, and to revivify her. And may He send her speedily a complete recovery from heaven for all her organs and all her blood vessels,

among the other sick people of Israel, a recovery of the body and a recovery of the spirit though the Sabbath prohibits us from crying out, may a recovery come speedily, swiftly and soon. Now let us respond: Amen. (Cong.—*Amen.*)

°°Many congregations substitute:
because the entire congregation prays for him (her)

customary for these blessings to include pledges to charitable causes. Although the formula most often used is בַּעֲבוּר שֶׁנָּדַר, *for he has pledged,* it is preferable to use the formula בַּעֲבוּר שֶׁיִּתֵּן, *for he will contribute.* This is based on the Talmudic teaching (*Beitzah* 36b) that it is improper to make certain types of monetary pledges on the Sabbath and Festivals, and this latter formula does not have the status of a vow. Variations of the מִי שֶׁבֵּרַךְ blessing express prayers for the congregation as a whole or individual members of it, sick people, or new mothers and their infants. In all cases, the concept behind the prayer is that the merit of the Torah reading and of the person who has read from it is a source of blessing.

קריאת התורה לשבת חול המועד

שמות לג:יב-לד:כו

כהן – וַיֹּאמֶר מֹשֶׁה* אֶל־יהוה רְאֵה אַתָּה אֹמֵר אֵלַי הַעַל אֶת־הָעָם
הַזֶּה וְאַתָּה לֹא הוֹדַעְתַּנִי אֵת אֲשֶׁר־תִּשְׁלַח עִמִּי וְאַתָּה אָמַרְתָּ
יְדַעְתִּיךָ בְשֵׁם* וְגַם־מָצָאתָ חֵן בְּעֵינָי: וְעַתָּה אִם־נָא מָצָאתִי חֵן
בְּעֵינֶיךָ הוֹדִעֵנִי נָא אֶת־דְּרָכֶךָ וְאֵדָעֲךָ לְמַעַן אֶמְצָא־חֵן* בְּעֵינֶיךָ
וּרְאֵה כִּי עַמְּךָ הַגּוֹי הַזֶּה: וַיֹּאמַר פָּנַי יֵלֵכוּ וַהֲנִחֹתִי לָךְ: וַיֹּאמֶר אֵלָיו
אִם־אֵין פָּנֶיךָ הֹלְכִים* אַל־תַּעֲלֵנוּ מִזֶּה: וּבַמֶּה | יִוָּדַע אֵפוֹא כִּי־
מָצָאתִי חֵן בְּעֵינֶיךָ אֲנִי וְעַמֶּךָ הֲלוֹא בְּלֶכְתְּךָ עִמָּנוּ וְנִפְלֵינוּ אֲנִי
וְעַמְּךָ מִכָּל־הָעָם אֲשֶׁר עַל־פְּנֵי הָאֲדָמָה:

לוי – וַיֹּאמֶר יהוה אֶל־מֹשֶׁה גַּם אֶת־הַדָּבָר הַזֶּה* אֲשֶׁר דִּבַּרְתָּ
אֶעֱשֶׂה כִּי־מָצָאתָ חֵן בְּעֵינַי וָאֵדָעֲךָ בְּשֵׁם: וַיֹּאמַר הַרְאֵנִי נָא*
אֶת־כְּבֹדֶךָ: וַיֹּאמֶר אֲנִי אַעֲבִיר כָּל־טוּבִי* עַל־פָּנֶיךָ וְקָרָאתִי בְשֵׁם
יהוה* לְפָנֶיךָ וְחַנֹּתִי אֶת־אֲשֶׁר אָחֹן וְרִחַמְתִּי אֶת־אֲשֶׁר אֲרַחֵם:

שלישי – וַיֹּאמֶר לֹא תוּכַל לִרְאֹת* אֶת־פָּנָי כִּי לֹא־יִרְאַנִי הָאָדָם וָחָי:
וַיֹּאמֶר יהוה הִנֵּה מָקוֹם אִתִּי* וְנִצַּבְתָּ עַל־הַצּוּר: וְהָיָה בַּעֲבֹר כְּבֹדִי
וְשַׂמְתִּיךָ בְּנִקְרַת הַצּוּר וְשַׂכֹּתִי כַפִּי עָלֶיךָ עַד־עָבְרִי: וַהֲסִרֹתִי
אֶת־כַּפִּי וְרָאִיתָ אֶת־אֲחֹרָי וּפָנַי לֹא יֵרָאוּ:

רביעי – וַיֹּאמֶר יהוה אֶל־מֹשֶׁה פְּסָל־לְךָ* שְׁנֵי־לֻחֹת אֲבָנִים
כָּרִאשֹׁנִים וְכָתַבְתִּי עַל־הַלֻּחֹת אֶת־הַדְּבָרִים אֲשֶׁר הָיוּ עַל־

Torah Reading for the Sabbath of Chol HaMoed

וַיֹּאמֶר מֹשֶׁה – *Moses said.* After the sin of the Golden Calf, God commanded Moses to lead the Jews into *Eretz Yisrael,* but said that they would be accompanied by an angel, rather than by Hashem's Presence (*Exodus* 32:34). Now Moses came before God with three requests: (1) Moses could not accept the substitution of an angel for God Himself; he wanted God to promise that His own Divine Presence would accompany the people; (2) Moses wanted to understand God's ways of reward and punishment; (3) and he wanted to be sure that Israel would always remain God's people.

יְדַעְתִּיךָ בְשֵׁם – *I have distinguished you with high repute.* Prior to the Revelation at Sinai, God promised to appear personally to Moses and that the entire nation would always trust him.

לְמַעַן אֶמְצָא חֵן – *That I may find favor.* I wish to understand the rewards awaiting one who finds favor in Your eyes.

אִם אֵין פָּנֶיךָ הֹלְכִים – *If Your Presence does not go along.* Although God had already agreed to accompany Israel, Moses repeated this to stress how important it was to him and his people. In the next verse, Moses goes on to say that only if God does so will he and Israel know that God indeed loves them.

הַדָּבָר הַזֶּה – *This thing,* i.e., that Moses and Israel be distinguished from all other peoples in that God's Presence will rest on them alone.

הַרְאֵנִי נָא – *Show me now.* Seeing that God was receptive, Moses asked that he be permitted to perceive a deeper insight into God's glory than ever before *(Or HaChaim).*

כָּל טוּבִי – *All of My goodness.* The time had come when God would reveal to Moses the formula of prayer that Israel should employ whenever it is faced with impending catastrophe, as had now happened in the wake of the worship of the Golden Calf. Even if the merit of the Patriarchs can no longer suffice, this prayer would always awaken God's mercy.

וְקָרָאתִי בְשֵׁם ה׳ – *I will call out with the Name*

TORAH READING FOR THE SABBATH OF CHOL HAMOED

Exodus 33:12-34:26

Kohen – *Moses said* to* HASHEM: *"Look — You say to me, 'Take this people onward,' but You did not inform me whom You will send with me; and You had said, 'I have distinguished you with high repute* and you have also found favor in My eyes.' And now, if I have indeed found favor in Your eyes, let me know Your ways — that I may know You — in order that I may find favor* in Your eyes; but see to it that this nation remains Your people.'*

He said, 'My Own Presence will go along and provide you rest.'

He said to Him, 'If Your Presence does not go along, do not bring us onward from here. How, then will it be known that I have found favor in Your eyes — I and Your people — unless You accompany us, and thereby distinguish me and Your people from every people that is on the face of the earth?'*

Levi – HASHEM *said to Moses, 'I will even do this thing* of which you have spoken; for you have found favor in My eyes, and I have distinguished you with high repute.'*

He said, 'Show me now Your glory.'*

He said, 'I will cause all of My goodness to pass before you, and I will call out with the Name '*HASHEM*'* before you; I will be gracious when I wish to be gracious, and I will be merciful when I wish to show mercy.'*

Third – *He said, 'You cannot see* My face; for no human can see My face and live.' Then* HASHEM *said, 'Behold there is a place near Me;* you may stand on the rock. And when My Glory passes by, I shall place you in a cleft of the rock; I shall shield you with My hand until I have passed. Then I shall remove My hand, and you will see My back; but My face will not be seen.'*

Fourth – HASHEM *said to Moses, 'Carve yourself* two stone tablets, like the first ones; and I will inscribe upon the tablets the words that were on*

'*HASHEM.*' The prayer that God was about to teach Moses, the Thirteen Attributes of Mercy, begins with the word *HASHEM.*

לֹא תוּכַל לִרְאֹת – *You cannot see.* Although I am ready to reveal all of My glory, the flesh and blood nature of man makes it impossible for him to assimilate such holiness completely (*Sforno*).

הִנֵּה מָקוֹם אִתִּי – *Behold there is a place near Me.* In the next three verses, God speaks to Moses in figurative terms, telling him that a place has been prepared where he will be able to receive the new and higher degree of revelation, but that God would protect him from receiving a degree of prophecy that would be beyond human capacity. Thus, Moses would *see God's back,* i.e., a lower degree of revelation, but not His essence, for man cannot fully understand God's way, just as someone may recognize a person from behind, but, because he cannot see his eyes and expression, cannot be certain of his identity or mood.

פְּסָל לְךָ – *Carve yourself.* Moses' forty days of prayer have achieved their goal. God has consented to give the Ten Commandments once again to the Jewish people. This time, however, the stone tablets are to be carved by Moses, unlike the first tablets, which were hewn by God. The commandments, however, will be inscribed by God Himself. The fact that these tablets were not of Divine origin was proof that, despite Israel's repentance and Moses' prayers, the nation had not regained the spiritual pinnacle it had attained prior to the sin.

הַלֻּחֹת הָרִאשֹׁנִים אֲשֶׁר שִׁבַּרְתָּ: וֶהְיֵה נָכוֹן לַבֹּקֶר וְעָלִיתָ בַבֹּקֶר
אֶל־הַר סִינַי וְנִצַּבְתָּ לִי שָׁם עַל־רֹאשׁ הָהָר: וְאִישׁ לֹא־יַעֲלֶה עִמָּךְ*
וְגַם־אִישׁ אַל־יֵרָא בְּכָל־הָהָר גַּם־הַצֹּאן וְהַבָּקָר אַל־יִרְעוּ אֶל־מוּל
הָהָר הַהוּא:

חמישי – וַיִּפְסֹל שְׁנֵי־לֻחֹת אֲבָנִים כָּרִאשֹׁנִים וַיַּשְׁכֵּם מֹשֶׁה בַבֹּקֶר וַיַּעַל
אֶל־הַר סִינַי כַּאֲשֶׁר צִוָּה יהוה אֹתוֹ וַיִּקַּח בְּיָדוֹ שְׁנֵי לֻחֹת אֲבָנִים:
וַיֵּרֶד יהוה בֶּעָנָן וַיִּתְיַצֵּב עִמּוֹ שָׁם וַיִּקְרָא* בְשֵׁם יהוה: וַיַּעֲבֹר יהוה
| עַל־פָּנָיו וַיִּקְרָא יהוה | יהוה* אֵל רַחוּם וְחַנּוּן אֶרֶךְ אַפַּיִם
וְרַב־חֶסֶד וֶאֱמֶת: נֹצֵר חֶסֶד לָאֲלָפִים נֹשֵׂא עָוֹן וָפֶשַׁע וְחַטָּאָה וְנַקֵּה
לֹא יְנַקֶּה פֹּקֵד | עֲוֹן אָבוֹת עַל־בָּנִים* וְעַל־בְּנֵי בָנִים עַל־שִׁלֵּשִׁים
וְעַל־רִבֵּעִים: וַיְמַהֵר מֹשֶׁה וַיִּקֹּד אַרְצָה וַיִּשְׁתָּחוּ: וַיֹּאמֶר אִם־נָא
מָצָאתִי חֵן בְּעֵינֶיךָ אֲדֹנָי יֵלֶךְ־נָא אֲדֹנָי* בְּקִרְבֵּנוּ כִּי עַם־קְשֵׁה־עֹרֶף
הוּא וְסָלַחְתָּ לַעֲוֹנֵנוּ וּלְחַטָּאתֵנוּ וּנְחַלְתָּנוּ: וַיֹּאמֶר הִנֵּה אָנֹכִי כֹּרֵת
בְּרִית נֶגֶד כָּל־עַמְּךָ אֶעֱשֶׂה נִפְלָאֹת אֲשֶׁר לֹא־נִבְרְאוּ בְכָל־הָאָרֶץ
וּבְכָל־הַגּוֹיִם וְרָאָה כָל־הָעָם אֲשֶׁר־אַתָּה בְקִרְבּוֹ אֶת־מַעֲשֵׂה יהוה
כִּי־נוֹרָא הוּא אֲשֶׁר אֲנִי עֹשֶׂה עִמָּךְ:

וְאִישׁ לֹא יַעֲלֶה עִמָּךְ – *No man is to climb up with you.* There is nothing better than modesty. Moses' ascent for the first tablets was made with great pomp and in the presence of the entire nation. Those tablets were smashed. The ascent for the second tablets was made in complete privacy. Those tablets remained (*Tanchuma, Ki Sissa* 1:31).

וַיִּקְרָא – *And he called out.* According to *Rashi*, it was Moses who called out. Most other commentators, however, hold that God proclaimed His Own Name, meaning that He taught Moses His Attributes, as given in the next two verses.

י״ג מִדּוֹת / The Thirteen Attributes

R' Yehudah taught that God sealed a covenant with Moses and Israel that in any time of crisis or danger, they should pray for God's mercy by reciting these attributes, and God sealed a covenant that such a prayer would never be in vain (*Rosh Hashanah* 17b).

ה׳ ה׳ – HASHEM, HASHEM. There are various opinions regarding how to enumerate the Thirteen Attributes. We follow the view of *Rabbeinu Tam* (*Rosh Hashanah* 17b), which is generally accepted:

(1) ה׳ – HASHEM. This Name [containing the letters of הָיָה הֹוֶה יִהְיֶה, *He was, He is, He will be*] designates God as the מְהַוֶּה, *Prime Cause*, of everything. It is only natural that He wishes to assure the survival of all that He brought into being. Consequently, this Name represents the Attribute of Mercy. In addition, the Name's spelling implies God's timelessness. Though man may sin, he can repent and call upon the timeless God to restore him to his original innocent state. As the Talmud states: אֲנִי הוּא קוֹדֶם שֶׁיֶּחֱטָא הָאָדָם, וַאֲנִי הוּא לְאַחַר שֶׁיֶּחֱטָא הָאָדָם, וְיַעֲשֶׂה תְּשׁוּבָה, *I am He* [i.e., the God of Mercy] *before a person sins, and I am He after a person sins and repents* (*Rosh Hashanah* 17b). Based on this dictum, *Rabbeinu Tam* counts the twin use of the Name HASHEM as two attributes. The first is that God is merciful before a person sins, even though He knows that the sin will be committed.

(2) ה׳ – HASHEM. God is merciful after the sin has been committed, by allowing the sinner time to repent, and by accepting his repentance, though it may be imperfect.

(3) אֵל – *God.* This Name denotes the power of God's mercy, which sometimes surpasses even the compassion indicated by the Name HASHEM. He displays this higher degree of mercy to genuinely righteous people who sin, but repent. In return for their previous behavior, God exerts Himself, as it were, to ensure their survival.

(4) רַחוּם – *Compassionate.* In response to pleas for mercy, God eases the suffering of those being punished for their sins. Another manifestation of compassion is that God does not confront deserving people with overpowering temptation.

(5) וְחַנּוּן – *And Gracious.* God is gracious even to those unworthy of His kindness. Also, if someone lacks the willpower to avoid sin, and he

the first tablets which you shattered. Be prepared in the morning; climb up Mount Sinai in the morning and stand by Me on the mountain top. No man is to climb up with you nor should anyone be seen on the entire mountain; even the sheep and cattle are not to graze facing that mountain.'*

Fifth – *So he carved two stone tablets like the first ones. Moses arose in the morning and climbed up Mount Sinai as HASHEM had commanded him; and he took the two stone tablets in his hand. HASHEM descended in a cloud and stood with him there, and he called out* with the Name — HASHEM.*

And HASHEM passed before him and proclaimed: HASHEM, HASHEM, God, Compassionate and Gracious, Slow to anger, and Abundant in Kindness and truth. Preserver of kindness for thousands of generations, Forgiver of iniquity, willful sin, and error — and who cleanses but does not cleanse completely — He recalls the sin of parents upon children* and grandchildren, for the third and fourth generations.'*

Moses hastened to kneel upon the ground and prostrate himself. He said, 'If I have found favor in Your eyes, my Lord, may my Lord go among us, for it is a stiff-necked people; so may You forgive our iniquity and our sin, and make us Your heritage.'*

He said, 'Behold, I seal a covenant; before your entire nation I will make distinctions such as have never been created in the entire world and among all the nations; and the entire people among whom you are will see the work of HASHEM — which is awesome — that I am about to do with you.'*

---

seeks God's help, he will get it.

(6) **אֶרֶךְ אַפַּיִם** – *Slow to anger.* So that the sinner will have time to repent.

(7) **וְרַב חֶסֶד** – *And Abundant in Kindness.* God shows great kindness to those who lack personal merits. The Talmud teaches, as described above, that God exercises this attribute by removing sins from the scale of justice, thus tilting the scales in favor of merit.

(8) **וֶאֱמֶת** – *And Truth.* God never reneges; His promise to reward the deserving will be carried out unequivocally.

(9) **נֹצֵר חֶסֶד לָאֲלָפִים** – *Preserver of kindness for thousands [of generations].* The deeds of the righteous — especially those who serve Him out of intense love — bring benefits to their offspring far into the future.

(10) **נֹשֵׂא עָוֹן** – *Forgiver of iniquity.* God forgives the intentional sinner, if he repents.

(11) **וָפֶשַׁע** – *[Forgiver of] willful sin.* Even those who rebel against God and purposely seek to anger Him are given an opportunity to repent.

(12) **וְחַטָּאָה** – *And [Forgiver of] error.* God forgives those who repent of sins that are committed out of carelessness or apathy. Having already praised God as the forgiver of intentional sin and rebelliousness, why do we revert to praising Him for this seemingly lesser level of mercy? Because if someone repents out of fear rather than love, his intentional sins are reduced in severity and are treated by God as if they had been done in error. Thus, even after having partially forgiven the intentional sins by reducing their severity, God further forgives those who continue to repent for these lesser sins.

(13) **וְנַקֵּה** – *And Who cleanses.* God wipes away the sins of those who repent sincerely, as if they had never existed.

In the Torah the verse continues **לֹא יְנַקֶּה**, *He does not cleanse.* The simple interpretation of the verse is that God does not completely erase the sin, but He exacts retribution in minute stages. The Talmud (*Yoma* 86a), however, explains that *He cleanses* the sins of those who truly repent; but *He does not cleanse* the sins of those who do not repent.

פֹּקֵד עֲוֹן אָבוֹת עַל בָּנִים – *He recalls the sin of parents upon children.* As the Ten Commandments in *Exodus* 20:5,6 indicate, children may suffer for the sins of their elders only if the children consciously and willingly copy those sins. On the other hand, God spreads out reward for two thousand generations. The extent of His reward is five hundred times greater than the extent of His punishment.

יֵלֶךְ נָא אֲדֹנָי – *May my Lord go.* Having been taught God's attributes of Mercy, Moses reiterated his earlier plea that HASHEM Himself guide

ששי – שְׁמָר־לְךָ אֵת אֲשֶׁר אָנֹכִי מְצַוְּךָ הַיּוֹם הִנְנִי גֹרֵשׁ מִפָּנֶיךָ אֶת־הָאֱמֹרִי וְהַכְּנַעֲנִי וְהַחִתִּי וְהַפְּרִזִּי וְהַחִוִּי וְהַיְבוּסִי: הִשָּׁמֶר לְךָ פֶּן־תִּכְרֹת בְּרִית לְיוֹשֵׁב הָאָרֶץ אֲשֶׁר אַתָּה בָּא עָלֶיהָ פֶּן־יִהְיֶה לְמוֹקֵשׁ* בְּקִרְבֶּךָ: כִּי אֶת־מִזְבְּחֹתָם תִּתֹּצוּן וְאֶת־מַצֵּבֹתָם תְּשַׁבֵּרוּן וְאֶת־אֲשֵׁרָיו תִּכְרֹתוּן: כִּי לֹא תִשְׁתַּחֲוֶה לְאֵל אַחֵר כִּי יהוה קַנָּא* שְׁמוֹ אֵל קַנָּא הוּא: פֶּן־*תִּכְרֹת בְּרִית לְיוֹשֵׁב הָאָרֶץ וְזָנוּ | אַחֲרֵי אֱלֹהֵיהֶם וְזָבְחוּ לֵאלֹהֵיהֶם וְקָרָא לְךָ וְאָכַלְתָּ מִזִּבְחוֹ: וְלָקַחְתָּ מִבְּנֹתָיו לְבָנֶיךָ וְזָנוּ בְנֹתָיו אַחֲרֵי אֱלֹהֵיהֶן וְהִזְנוּ אֶת־בָּנֶיךָ אַחֲרֵי אֱלֹהֵיהֶן: אֱלֹהֵי מַסֵּכָה לֹא תַעֲשֶׂה־לָּךְ:

שביעי – אֶת־חַג הַמַּצּוֹת תִּשְׁמֹר שִׁבְעַת יָמִים תֹּאכַל מַצּוֹת אֲשֶׁר צִוִּיתִךָ לְמוֹעֵד חֹדֶשׁ הָאָבִיב* כִּי בְּחֹדֶשׁ הָאָבִיב יָצָאתָ מִמִּצְרָיִם: כָּל־פֶּטֶר רֶחֶם* לִי וְכָל־מִקְנְךָ תִּזָּכָר פֶּטֶר שׁוֹר וָשֶׂה: וּפֶטֶר חֲמוֹר תִּפְדֶּה בְשֶׂה* וְאִם־לֹא תִפְדֶּה וַעֲרַפְתּוֹ כֹּל בְּכוֹר בָּנֶיךָ תִּפְדֶּה וְלֹא־יֵרָאוּ פָנַי רֵיקָם:* שֵׁשֶׁת יָמִים תַּעֲבֹד וּבַיּוֹם הַשְּׁבִיעִי תִּשְׁבֹּת בֶּחָרִישׁ וּבַקָּצִיר* תִּשְׁבֹּת: וְחַג שָׁבֻעֹת תַּעֲשֶׂה לְךָ בִּכּוּרֵי קְצִיר חִטִּים* וְחַג הָאָסִיף תְּקוּפַת הַשָּׁנָה:* שָׁלֹשׁ פְּעָמִים בַּשָּׁנָה יֵרָאֶה כָּל־זְכוּרְךָ אֶת־פְּנֵי הָאָדֹן | יהוה אֱלֹהֵי יִשְׂרָאֵל: כִּי־אוֹרִישׁ גּוֹיִם מִפָּנֶיךָ וְהִרְחַבְתִּי אֶת־גְּבֻלֶךָ וְלֹא־יַחְמֹד אִישׁ* אֶת־אַרְצְךָ בַּעֲלֹתְךָ לֵרָאוֹת אֶת־פְּנֵי יהוה אֱלֹהֶיךָ שָׁלֹשׁ פְּעָמִים בַּשָּׁנָה: לֹא־תִשְׁחַט עַל־חָמֵץ* דַּם־זִבְחִי וְלֹא־יָלִין לַבֹּקֶר זֶבַח חַג הַפָּסַח: רֵאשִׁית בִּכּוּרֵי אַדְמָתְךָ תָּבִיא בֵּית יהוה אֱלֹהֶיךָ לֹא־תְבַשֵּׁל גְּדִי* בַּחֲלֵב אִמּוֹ:

---

the people. Precisely because Israel is *stiff-necked* and prone to sin, it must have God's ever-present mercy to preserve it.

לְמוֹקֵשׁ – *Be a snare.* Israel's fraternization with gentile nations, in *Eretz Yisrael* or elsewhere, results in calamity.

קַנָּא – *'Jealous One.'* A jealous person does not permit another to take what is rightfully his. Similarly, God will not tolerate those who extend their reverence and worship to idols instead of (or in addition) to Him.

פֶּן – *Lest.* This verse and the next give a list of idolatrous practices that the Jewish people are warned not to do. The term *lest* implies that something dire will befall them if they do these things, but the punishment is not specified. It is similar, in the vernacular, to saying, 'Do not do this — or else!'

חֹדֶשׁ הָאָבִיב – *The month of spring.* The requirement that Pesach be in the springtime is the basis for the addition (seven times every nineteen years) of a thirteenth month in the Jewish calendar. Only thereby can it be assured that the month of Passover will be in the spring.

פֶּטֶר רֶחֶם – *Opening issue of a womb.* The first male born normally from the womb must be redeemed, but not one born by Caesarian section (*Bechoros* 19a).

תִּפְדֶּה בְשֶׂה – *You are to redeem with a lamb or kid.* The donkey then loses its sanctity and the lamb or kid becomes the personal property of the *Kohen;* it is not an offering.

רֵיקָם – *Empty-handed.* This does not refer to the firstborn. It is a general commandment that people who come to Jerusalem for the three pilgrimage festivals should bring offerings.

בֶּחָרִישׁ וּבַקָּצִיר – *Plowing and harvest.* These are singled out because they are labors upon which

Sixth – *Be careful of what I command you today: behold I drive out before you the Emorite, the Canaanite, the Hittite, the Perizite, the Hivvite, and the Jebusite. Beware lest you seal a covenant with the inhabitants of the Land to which you come; lest it be a snare* among you. Rather you are to break apart their altars, smash their pillars and cut down their sacred trees. For you are not to prostrate yourselves to an alien god, for the very name of* HASHEM *is 'Jealous One,'* He is a jealous God. Lest* you seal a covenant with the inhabitants of the land and you stray after their gods, sacrifice to their gods, and they invite you and you eat from their offering! And you select their daughters for your sons; and their daughters stray after their gods and entice your sons to stray after their gods!*

Do not make yourselves molten gods.

Seventh – *You are to observe the Festival of Matzos: For seven days you are to eat matzos as I commanded you, at the appointed time in the month of spring;* for in the month of spring you went out of Egypt.*

Every opening issue of a womb is Mine; and all your flock that produces a male, the opening issue of cattle or sheep. The first issue of a donkey you are to redeem with a lamb or kid,* and if you do not redeem it, you are to axe the back of its neck; you are to redeem every firstborn of your sons; they may not appear before Me empty-handed.* Six days you are to work and on the seventh day you are to refrain from work; you are to refrain from plowing and harvest.* You are to mark the Festival of Shavuos with the first fruits of your wheat harvest;* and the Festival of the Harvest at the year's change of seasons.* Three times a year all your males are to appear before the Lord* HASHEM, *the God of Israel. For I shall banish nations before you and broaden your boundary; no man will covet* your land when you go up to appear before* HASHEM, *your God, three times a year.*

You may not slaughter My blood-offering while in possession of leavened food; nor may the offering of the Pesach festival be left overnight until morning. The first of your land's early produce you are to bring to the Temple of* HASHEM, *your God; do not cook a kid* in its mother's milk.*

---

human life depends; even such necessary work is forbidden on the Sabbath *(Ramban). Rashi* cites the Sages' halachic interpretations.

בִּכּוּרֵי קְצִיר חִטִּים – *The first fruits of your wheat harvest.* I.e., the two loaves of Shavuos, which are the first meal-offerings that may be offered from the new crop.

תְּקוּפַת הַשָּׁנָה – *At the year's change of seasons.* Succos is the time when the agricultural year is over and the new plowing season begins.

לֹא יַחְמֹד אִישׁ – *No man will covet.* God promised a miracle: Multitudes of Jews would leave their homes and boundaries undefended to go to Jerusalem, but no enemy would seize the opportunity to attack.

עַל חָמֵץ – *While in possession of leavened food.* All *chametz* must have been removed before the time when the Pesach offering may be brought.

לֹא תְבַשֵּׁל גְּדִי – *Do not cook a kid.* This is the general prohibition to cook meat in milk. It is included in the context of the first fruits because the Canaanites thought that cooking a kid in its mother's milk would result in bountiful crops *(Sforno).*

חצי קדיש

After the last *oleh* has completed his closing blessing, the second Torah Scroll is placed on the *bimah* alongside the first, and the reader recites Half *Kaddish*.

יִתְגַּדַּל וְיִתְקַדַּשׁ שְׁמֵהּ רַבָּא. (.Cong. – אָמֵן.) בְּעָלְמָא דִּי בְרָא כִרְעוּתֵהּ. וְיַמְלִיךְ מַלְכוּתֵהּ, בְּחַיֵּיכוֹן וּבְיוֹמֵיכוֹן וּבְחַיֵּי דְכָל בֵּית יִשְׂרָאֵל, בַּעֲגָלָא וּבִזְמַן קָרִיב. וְאִמְרוּ: אָמֵן.

(.Cong. – אָמֵן. יְהֵא שְׁמֵהּ רַבָּא מְבָרַךְ לְעָלַם וּלְעָלְמֵי עָלְמַיָּא.)

יְהֵא שְׁמֵהּ רַבָּא מְבָרַךְ לְעָלַם וּלְעָלְמֵי עָלְמַיָּא.

יִתְבָּרַךְ וְיִשְׁתַּבַּח וְיִתְפָּאַר וְיִתְרוֹמַם וְיִתְנַשֵּׂא וְיִתְהַדָּר וְיִתְעַלֶּה וְיִתְהַלָּל שְׁמֵהּ דְּקֻדְשָׁא בְּרִיךְ הוּא (.Cong. – בְּרִיךְ הוּא) — לְעֵלָּא מִן כָּל בִּרְכָתָא וְשִׁירָתָא תֻּשְׁבְּחָתָא וְנֶחֱמָתָא, דַּאֲמִירָן בְּעָלְמָא. וְאִמְרוּ: אָמֵן. (.Cong. – אָמֵן.)

הגבהה וגלילה

The first Torah is raised for all to see. Each person looks at the Torah and recites aloud:

וְזֹאת הַתּוֹרָה אֲשֶׁר שָׂם מֹשֶׁה לִפְנֵי בְּנֵי יִשְׂרָאֵל,[1] עַל פִּי יהוה בְּיַד מֹשֶׁה.[2]

Some add:

עֵץ חַיִּים הִיא לַמַּחֲזִיקִים בָּהּ, וְתֹמְכֶיהָ מְאֻשָּׁר.[3] דְּרָכֶיהָ דַרְכֵי נֹעַם, וְכָל נְתִיבוֹתֶיהָ שָׁלוֹם.[4] אֹרֶךְ יָמִים בִּימִינָהּ, בִּשְׂמֹאלָהּ עֹשֶׁר וְכָבוֹד.[5] יהוה חָפֵץ לְמַעַן צִדְקוֹ, יַגְדִּיל תּוֹרָה וְיַאְדִּיר.[6]

מפטיר

As the first Torah is wound, tied, and covered, the *oleh* for *Maftir* is called to the second Torah.

במדבר כח:יט-כה

וְהִקְרַבְתֶּ֨ם אִשֶּׁ֤ה עֹלָה֙ לַיהוָ֔ה פָּרִ֧ים בְּנֵֽי־בָקָ֛ר שְׁנַ֖יִם וְאַ֣יִל אֶחָ֑ד וְשִׁבְעָ֤ה כְבָשִׂים֙ בְּנֵ֣י שָׁנָ֔ה תְּמִימִ֖ם יִהְי֥וּ לָכֶֽם׃ וּמִ֨נְחָתָ֔ם סֹ֖לֶת בְּלוּלָ֣ה בַשָּׁ֑מֶן שְׁלֹשָׁ֨ה עֶשְׂרֹנִ֜ים לַפָּ֗ר וּשְׁנֵ֧י עֶשְׂרֹנִ֛ים לָאַ֖יִל תַּעֲשֽׂוּ׃ עִשָּׂר֤וֹן עִשָּׂרוֹן֙ תַּעֲשֶׂ֔ה לַכֶּ֖בֶשׂ הָאֶחָ֑ד לְשִׁבְעַ֖ת הַכְּבָשִֽׂים׃ וּשְׂעִ֥יר חַטָּ֖את אֶחָ֑ד לְכַפֵּ֖ר עֲלֵיכֶֽם׃ מִלְּבַד֙ עֹלַ֣ת הַבֹּ֔קֶר אֲשֶׁ֖ר לְעֹלַ֣ת הַתָּמִ֑יד תַּעֲשׂ֖וּ אֶת־אֵֽלֶּה׃ כָּאֵ֜לֶּה תַּעֲשׂ֤וּ לַיּוֹם֙ שִׁבְעַ֣ת יָמִ֔ים לֶ֛חֶם אִשֵּׁ֥ה רֵֽיחַ־נִיחֹ֖חַ לַיהוָ֑ה עַל־עוֹלַ֧ת הַתָּמִ֛יד יֵעָשֶׂ֖ה וְנִסְכּֽוֹ׃ וּבַיּוֹם֙ הַשְּׁבִיעִ֔י מִקְרָא־קֹ֖דֶשׁ יִהְיֶ֣ה לָכֶ֑ם כָּל־מְלֶ֥אכֶת עֲבֹדָ֖ה לֹ֥א תַעֲשֽׂוּ׃

HALF KADDISH

After the last *oleh* has completed his closing blessing, the second Torah Scroll is placed on the *bimah* alongside the first, and the reader recites Half *Kaddish:*

יִתְגַּדַּל *May His great Name grow exalted and sanctified* (Cong.– *Amen.*) *in the world that He created as He willed. May He give reign to His kingship in your lifetimes and in your days, and in the lifetimes of the entire Family of Israel, swiftly and soon. Now respond: Amen.*

(Cong.– *Amen. May His great Name be blessed forever and ever.*)

May His great Name be blessed forever and ever.

Blessed, praised, glorified, exalted, extolled, mighty, upraised, and lauded be the Name of the Holy One, Blessed is He (Cong.– *Blessed is He*) *— beyond any blessing and song, praise and consolation that are uttered in the world. Now respond: Amen.* (Cong.– *Amen.*)

HAGBAHAH AND GELILAH

The first Torah is raised for all to see. Each person looks at the Torah and recites aloud:

This is the Torah that Moses placed before the Children of Israel,[1] upon the command of HASHEM, through Moses' hand.[2]

Some add:

עֵץ *It is a tree of life for those who grasp it, and its supporters are praiseworthy.[3] Its ways are ways of pleasantness and all its paths are peace.[4] Lengthy days are at its right; at its left are wealth and honor.[5] HASHEM desired, for the sake of its [Israel's] righteousness, that the Torah be made great and glorious.[6]*

MAFTIR

As the first Torah is wound, tied, and covered, the *oleh* for *Maftir* is called to the second Torah.

Numbers 28:19-25

You shall offer a fire-offering, an elevation-offering to HASHEM, two young bulls, one ram, and seven lambs within their first year, unblemished shall they be for you. And their meal-offering shall be fine flour mixed with oil; you shall make it three tenth-ephah for each bull and two tenth-ephah for each ram. One tenth-ephah shall you make for each lamb, of the seven rams. And one he-goat for a sin-offering, to provide you atonement. Aside from the elevation-offering of the morning that is for the continual elevation-offering shall you offer these. Like these shall you offer each day of the seven days, food, a fire-offering, a satisfying aroma to HASHEM; after the continual elevation-offering shall it be made, with its libation. The seventh day shall be a holy convocation for you, you shall not do any laborious work.

---

(1) *Deuteronomy* 4:44. (2) *Numbers* 9:23. (3) *Proverbs* 3:18. (4) 3:17. (5) 3:16. (6) *Isaiah* 42:21.

הגבהה וגלילה

The *maftir* completes his closing blessing.
Then the second Torah Scroll is raised and each person looks at the Torah and recites aloud:

וְזֹאת הַתּוֹרָה אֲשֶׁר שָׂם מֹשֶׁה לִפְנֵי בְּנֵי יִשְׂרָאֵל,[1] עַל פִּי יהוה בְּיַד מֹשֶׁה.[2]

Some add:

עֵץ חַיִּים הִיא לַמַּחֲזִיקִים בָּהּ, וְתֹמְכֶיהָ מְאֻשָּׁר.[3] דְּרָכֶיהָ דַרְכֵי נֹעַם, וְכָל נְתִיבוֹתֶיהָ שָׁלוֹם.[4] אֹרֶךְ יָמִים בִּימִינָהּ, בִּשְׂמֹאלָהּ עֹשֶׁר וְכָבוֹד.[5] יהוה חָפֵץ לְמַעַן צִדְקוֹ, יַגְדִּיל תּוֹרָה וְיַאְדִּיר.[6]

After the Torah Scroll has been wound, tied and covered, the *maftir* recites the *Haftarah* blessings.

ברכה קודם ההפטרה

בָּרוּךְ אַתָּה יהוה אֱלֹהֵינוּ מֶלֶךְ הָעוֹלָם, אֲשֶׁר בָּחַר בִּנְבִיאִים טוֹבִים, וְרָצָה בְדִבְרֵיהֶם הַנֶּאֱמָרִים בֶּאֱמֶת, בָּרוּךְ אַתָּה יהוה, הַבּוֹחֵר בַּתּוֹרָה וּבְמֹשֶׁה עַבְדּוֹ, וּבְיִשְׂרָאֵל עַמּוֹ, וּבִנְבִיאֵי הָאֱמֶת וָצֶדֶק: (Cong. – אָמֵן.)

הפטרה לשבת חול המועד

[Although the Divine Name יהוה is pronounced as if it were spelled אֲדֹנָי, when it is vowelized יֱהֹוִה it is pronounced as if it were spelled אֱלֹהִים.]

יחזקאל לז:א-יד

הָיְתָה עָלַי יַד־יהוה וַיּוֹצִאֵנִי בְרוּחַ יהוה וַיְנִיחֵנִי בְּתוֹךְ הַבִּקְעָה וְהִיא מְלֵאָה עֲצָמוֹת: וְהֶעֱבִירַנִי עֲלֵיהֶם סָבִיב ׀ סָבִיב וְהִנֵּה רַבּוֹת מְאֹד עַל־פְּנֵי הַבִּקְעָה וְהִנֵּה יְבֵשׁוֹת מְאֹד: וַיֹּאמֶר אֵלַי בֶּן־אָדָם הֲתִחְיֶינָה הָעֲצָמוֹת הָאֵלֶּה וָאֹמַר אֲדֹנָי יֱהֹוִה אַתָּה יָדָעְתָּ: וַיֹּאמֶר אֵלַי הִנָּבֵא עַל־הָעֲצָמוֹת הָאֵלֶּה וְאָמַרְתָּ אֲלֵיהֶם הָעֲצָמוֹת הַיְבֵשׁוֹת שִׁמְעוּ דְּבַר־יהוה: כֹּה אָמַר אֲדֹנָי יֱהֹוִה לָעֲצָמוֹת הָאֵלֶּה הִנֵּה אֲנִי מֵבִיא בָכֶם רוּחַ וִחְיִיתֶם: וְנָתַתִּי עֲלֵיכֶם גִּידִים וְהַעֲלֵתִי עֲלֵיכֶם בָּשָׂר וְקָרַמְתִּי עֲלֵיכֶם עוֹר וְנָתַתִּי בָכֶם רוּחַ וִחְיִיתֶם וִידַעְתֶּם כִּי־אֲנִי יהוה: וְנִבֵּאתִי כַּאֲשֶׁר צֻוֵּיתִי וַיְהִי־קוֹל כְּהִנָּבְאִי וְהִנֵּה־רַעַשׁ וַתִּקְרְבוּ עֲצָמוֹת עֶצֶם אֶל־עַצְמוֹ: וְרָאִיתִי וְהִנֵּה־עֲלֵיהֶם גִּדִים וּבָשָׂר עָלָה וַיִּקְרַם עֲלֵיהֶם עוֹר מִלְמָעְלָה

☙ The Haftarah

This *Haftarah* is the story of Ezekiel's revival of the 'dry bones' that lay lifeless in a valley. Although there is one opinion in the Talmud (*Sanhedrin* 92b) that this was a parable that Ezekiel was shown in a prophetic vision, the general thrust of the Talmud (ibid.) and several *Midrashim* is that the miracle actually took place. The commentators give various reasons why it was chosen for a *Haftarah* during Pesach:

The bones were those of 200,000 members of

HAGBAHAH AND GELILAH

The *maftir* completes his closing blessing.
Then the second Torah Scroll is raised and each person looks at the Torah and recites aloud:

This is the Torah that Moses placed before the Children of Israel,[1] upon the command of HASHEM, through Moses' hand.[2]

Some add:

עֵץ *It is a tree of life for those who grasp it, and its supporters are praiseworthy.[3] Its ways are ways of pleasantness and all its paths are peace.[4] Lengthy days are at its right; at its left are wealth and honor.[5] HASHEM desired, for the sake of its [Israel's] righteousness, that the Torah be made great and glorious.[6]*

After the Torah Scroll has been wound, tied and covered, the *maftir* recites the *Haftarah* blessings.

BLESSING BEFORE THE HAFTARAH

בָּרוּךְ *Blessed are You, HASHEM, our God, King of the universe, Who has chosen good prophets and was pleased with their words that were uttered with truth. Blessed are You, HASHEM, Who chooses the Torah; Moses, His servant; Israel, His nation; and the prophets of truth and righteousness.* (Cong.— *Amen.)*

HAFTARAH READING FOR THE SABBATH OF CHOL HAMOED

Ezekiel 37:1-14

The hand of HASHEM was upon me; it took me out, by the spirit of HASHEM, and set me down in the valley, which was full of bones. He led me around and around them, and behold! — they were very abundant upon the surface of the valley, and behold! — they were very dry. Then He said to me, 'Ben Adam, can these bones live?' And I said, 'My Lord HASHEM / ELOHIM, You know.'

He said to me, "Prophesy over these bones and say to them: 'O dry bones, hear the words of HASHEM. Thus says my Lord HASHEM / ELOHIM to these bones: Behold! — I bring spirit into you and you shall live. I shall put sinews upon you and bring flesh upon you and draw skin over you. Then I shall put spirit into you and you shall live; and you shall know that I am HASHEM.' "

And I prophesied as I had been commanded, and there was a noise while I prophesied, and behold! — a rattling and the bones drew near, bone to matching bone. Then I looked and behold! — sinews were upon them and flesh had come up and skin had been drawn over them;

(1) *Deuteronomy* 4:44. (2) *Numbers* 9:23. (3) *Proverbs* 3:18. (4) 3:17. (5) 3:16. (6) *Isaiah* 42:21.

the tribe of Ephraim who left Egypt prematurely under the leadership of a false messiah. They were slain by the Philistines. Thus, their resurrection was a culmination of the Pesach exodus (*Rashi*).

There is a tradition that תְּחִיַּת הַמֵּתִים, *the Resuscitation of the Dead*, will take place on Pesach, so that this early occurrence of the same miracle is appropriate for the festival (*R' Hai Gaon*).

The reason God performed this miracle through Ezekiel was to give strength and en-

וְר֖וּחַ אֵ֥ין בָּהֶֽם׃ וַיֹּ֣אמֶר אֵלַ֔י הִנָּבֵ֖א אֶל־הָר֑וּחַ הִנָּבֵ֣א בֶן־אָדָ֠ם וְאָמַרְתָּ֨ אֶל־הָר֜וּחַ כֹּה־אָמַ֣ר ׀ אֲדֹנָ֣י יֱהֹוִ֗ה מֵאַרְבַּ֤ע רוּחוֹת֙ בֹּ֣אִי הָר֔וּחַ וּפְחִ֛י בַּהֲרוּגִ֥ים הָאֵ֖לֶּה וְיִחְיֽוּ׃ וְהִנַּבֵּ֖אתִי כַּאֲשֶׁ֣ר צִוָּ֑נִי וַתָּב֨וֹא בָהֶ֜ם הָר֗וּחַ וַיִּֽחְי֙וּ֙ וַיַּֽעַמְד֣וּ֙ עַל־רַגְלֵיהֶ֔ם חַ֖יִל גָּד֥וֹל מְאֹד־מְאֹֽד׃ וַיֹּאמֶר֮ אֵלַי֒ בֶּן־אָדָ֗ם הָעֲצָמ֣וֹת הָאֵ֔לֶּה כָּל־בֵּ֥ית יִשְׂרָאֵ֖ל הֵ֑מָּה הִנֵּ֣ה אֹמְרִ֗ים יָבְשׁ֧וּ עַצְמוֹתֵ֛ינוּ וְאָבְדָ֥ה תִקְוָתֵ֖נוּ נִגְזַ֥רְנוּ לָֽנוּ׃ לָכֵ֡ן הִנָּבֵא֩ וְאָמַרְתָּ֨ אֲלֵיהֶ֜ם כֹּֽה־אָמַר֮ אֲדֹנָ֣י יֱהֹוִה֒ הִנֵּ֨ה אֲנִ֜י פֹתֵ֣חַ אֶת־קִבְרוֹתֵיכֶ֗ם וְהַעֲלֵיתִ֥י אֶתְכֶ֛ם מִקִּבְרוֹתֵיכֶ֖ם עַמִּ֑י וְהֵבֵאתִ֥י אֶתְכֶ֖ם אֶל־אַדְמַ֥ת יִשְׂרָאֵֽל׃ וִֽידַעְתֶּ֖ם כִּֽי־אֲנִ֣י יְהֹוָ֑ה בְּפִתְחִ֣י אֶת־קִבְרֽוֹתֵיכֶ֗ם וּבְהַעֲלוֹתִ֥י אֶתְכֶ֛ם מִקִּבְרוֹתֵיכֶ֖ם עַמִּֽי׃ וְנָתַתִּ֨י רוּחִ֤י בָכֶם֙ וִחְיִיתֶ֔ם וְהִנַּחְתִּ֥י אֶתְכֶ֖ם עַל־אַדְמַתְכֶ֑ם וִֽידַעְתֶּ֞ם כִּֽי־אֲנִ֧י יְהֹוָ֛ה דִּבַּ֥רְתִּי וְעָשִׂ֖יתִי נְאֻם־יְהֹוָֽה׃

ברכות לאחר ההפטרה

After the *Haftarah* is read, the *oleh* recites the following blessings.

בָּרוּךְ אַתָּה יהוה אֱלֹהֵינוּ מֶלֶךְ הָעוֹלָם, צוּר כָּל הָעוֹלָמִים, צַדִּיק בְּכָל הַדּוֹרוֹת, הָאֵל הַנֶּאֱמָן הָאוֹמֵר וְעֹשֶׂה, הַמְּדַבֵּר וּמְקַיֵּם, שֶׁכָּל דְּבָרָיו אֱמֶת וָצֶדֶק. נֶאֱמָן אַתָּה הוּא יהוה אֱלֹהֵינוּ, וְנֶאֱמָנִים דְּבָרֶיךָ, וְדָבָר אֶחָד מִדְּבָרֶיךָ אָחוֹר לֹא יָשׁוּב רֵיקָם, כִּי אֵל מֶלֶךְ נֶאֱמָן (וְרַחֲמָן) אָתָּה. בָּרוּךְ אַתָּה יהוה, הָאֵל הַנֶּאֱמָן בְּכָל דְּבָרָיו.
(.אָמֵן –Cong)

רַחֵם עַל צִיּוֹן כִּי הִיא בֵּית חַיֵּינוּ, וְלַעֲלוּבַת נֶפֶשׁ תּוֹשִׁיעַ בִּמְהֵרָה בְיָמֵינוּ. בָּרוּךְ אַתָּה יהוה, מְשַׂמֵּחַ צִיּוֹן בְּבָנֶיהָ.
(.אָמֵן –Cong)

שַׂמְּחֵנוּ יהוה אֱלֹהֵינוּ בְּאֵלִיָּהוּ הַנָּבִיא עַבְדֶּךָ, וּבְמַלְכוּת בֵּית דָּוִד מְשִׁיחֶךָ, בִּמְהֵרָה יָבֹא וְיָגֵל לִבֵּנוּ, עַל כִּסְאוֹ לֹא יֵשֵׁב זָר וְלֹא יִנְחֲלוּ עוֹד אֲחֵרִים אֶת כְּבוֹדוֹ, כִּי בְשֵׁם קָדְשְׁךָ נִשְׁבַּעְתָּ לּוֹ, שֶׁלֹּא יִכְבֶּה נֵרוֹ לְעוֹלָם וָעֶד. בָּרוּךְ אַתָּה יהוה, מָגֵן דָּוִד.
(.אָמֵן –Cong)

---

couragement to Israel, which had just endured a bitter exile and the destruction of the Temple. By seeing how the dry bones came to life, the people would realize that they, too, should not lose hope for their eventual redemption and 'new life' (*Kuzari*).

but the spirit was not in them. Then He said to me, "Prophesy to the spirit, prophesy, Ben Adam, and say to the spirit, 'Thus says my Lord HASHEM / ELOHIM: *From the four directions come, O spirit, and blow into these slain ones that they may live.' "*

I prophesied as I had been commanded; the spirit entered them and they lived and they stood upon their feet — a very, very vast multitude.

And he said to me, "Ben Adam, these bones — they are the whole family of Israel; behold! — they say, 'Our bones have dried and our hope is lost. We are doomed.' Therefore, prophesy and say to them, 'Thus says my Lord HASHEM / ELOHIM: *Behold! — I open your graves and I raise you from your graves, O My people, and I shall bring you to the Land of Israel. Then you shall know that I am* HASHEM, *when I open your graves and when I raise you from your graves, O My people. I shall put My spirit into you and you shall live, and I shall set you on your soil, and you shall know that I,* HASHEM, *have spoken and done — the words of* HASHEM.' "

BLESSINGS AFTER THE HAFTARAH

After the *Haftarah* is read, the *oleh* recites the following blessings.

בָּרוּךְ *Blessed are You,* HASHEM, *our God, King of the universe, Rock of all eternities, Righteous in all generations, the trustworthy God, Who says and does, Who speaks and fulfills, all of Whose words are true and righteous. Trustworthy are You,* HASHEM, *our God, and trustworthy are Your words, not one of Your words is turned back to its origin unfulfilled, for You are God, trustworthy (and compassionate) King. Blessed are You,* HASHEM, *the God Who is trustworthy in all His words.* (Cong.– *Amen.*)

רַחֵם *Have mercy on Zion for it is the source of our life; to the one who is deeply humiliated bring salvation speedily, in our days. Blessed are You,* HASHEM, *Who gladdens Zion through her children.* (Cong.– *Amen.*)

שַׂמְּחֵנוּ *Gladden us,* HASHEM, *our God, with Elijah the prophet, Your servant, and with the kingdom of the House of David, Your anointed, may he come speedily and cause our heart to exult. On his throne let no stranger sit nor let others continue to inherit his honor, for by Your holy Name You swore to him that his heir will not be extinguished forever and ever. Blessed are You,* HASHEM, *Shield of David.* (Cong.– *Amen.*)

עַל הַתּוֹרָה, וְעַל הָעֲבוֹדָה, וְעַל הַנְּבִיאִים, וְעַל יוֹם הַשַּׁבָּת הַזֶּה שֶׁנָּתַתָּ לָּנוּ יהוה אֱלֹהֵינוּ, לִקְדֻשָּׁה וְלִמְנוּחָה, לְכָבוֹד וּלְתִפְאָרֶת. עַל הַכֹּל יהוה אֱלֹהֵינוּ, אֲנַחְנוּ מוֹדִים לָךְ, וּמְבָרְכִים אוֹתָךְ, יִתְבָּרַךְ שִׁמְךָ בְּפִי כָּל חַי תָּמִיד לְעוֹלָם וָעֶד. בָּרוּךְ אַתָּה יהוה, מְקַדֵּשׁ הַשַּׁבָּת. (Cong. – אָמֵן.)

יקום פרקן

One praying alone recites only the first paragraph and omits the following two paragraphs.

יְקוּם פֻּרְקָן מִן שְׁמַיָּא, חִנָּא וְחִסְדָּא וְרַחֲמֵי, וְחַיֵּי אֲרִיכֵי, וּמְזוֹנֵי רְוִיחֵי, וְסִיַּעְתָּא דִשְׁמַיָּא, וּבַרְיוּת גּוּפָא, וּנְהוֹרָא מַעַלְיָא, זַרְעָא חַיָּא וְקַיָּמָא, זַרְעָא דִּי לָא יִפְסוּק וְדִי לָא יִבְטוּל מִפִּתְגָּמֵי אוֹרַיְתָא. לְמָרָנָן וְרַבָּנָן חֲבוּרָתָא קַדִּישָׁתָא דִּי בְאַרְעָא דְיִשְׂרָאֵל וְדִי בְּבָבֶל, לְרֵישֵׁי כַלֵּי, וּלְרֵישֵׁי גַלְוָתָא, וּלְרֵישֵׁי מְתִיבָתָא, וּלְדַיָּנֵי דִי בָבָא, לְכָל תַּלְמִידֵיהוֹן, וּלְכָל תַּלְמִידֵי תַלְמִידֵיהוֹן, וּלְכָל מָן דְּעָסְקִין בְּאוֹרַיְתָא. מַלְכָּא דְעָלְמָא יְבָרֵךְ יַתְהוֹן, יַפִּישׁ חַיֵּיהוֹן, וְיַסְגֵּא יוֹמֵיהוֹן, וְיִתֵּן אַרְכָה לִשְׁנֵיהוֹן, וְיִתְפָּרְקוּן וְיִשְׁתֵּזְבוּן מִן כָּל עָקָא וּמִן כָּל מַרְעִין בִּישִׁין. מָרָן דִּי בִשְׁמַיָּא יְהֵא בְסַעְדְּהוֹן, כָּל זְמַן וְעִדָּן. וְנֹאמַר: אָמֵן. (Cong. – אָמֵן.)

יְקוּם פֻּרְקָן מִן שְׁמַיָּא, חִנָּא וְחִסְדָּא וְרַחֲמֵי, וְחַיֵּי אֲרִיכֵי, וּמְזוֹנֵי רְוִיחֵי, וְסִיַּעְתָּא דִשְׁמַיָּא, וּבַרְיוּת גּוּפָא, וּנְהוֹרָא מַעַלְיָא, זַרְעָא חַיָּא וְקַיָּמָא, זַרְעָא דִּי לָא יִפְסוּק וְדִי לָא יִבְטוּל מִפִּתְגָּמֵי אוֹרַיְתָא. לְכָל קְהָלָא קַדִּישָׁא הָדֵין, רַבְרְבַיָּא עִם זְעֵרַיָּא, טַפְלָא וּנְשַׁיָּא, מַלְכָּא דְעָלְמָא יְבָרֵךְ יַתְכוֹן, יַפִּישׁ חַיֵּיכוֹן, וְיַסְגֵּא יוֹמֵיכוֹן, וְיִתֵּן אַרְכָה לִשְׁנֵיכוֹן, וְתִתְפָּרְקוּן וְתִשְׁתֵּזְבוּן מִן כָּל עָקָא וּמִן כָּל מַרְעִין בִּישִׁין, מָרָן דִּי בִשְׁמַיָּא יְהֵא בְסַעְדְּכוֹן, כָּל זְמַן וְעִדָּן. וְנֹאמַר: אָמֵן. (Cong. – אָמֵן.)

מִי שֶׁבֵּרַךְ אֲבוֹתֵינוּ אַבְרָהָם יִצְחָק וְיַעֲקֹב, הוּא יְבָרֵךְ אֶת כָּל הַקָּהָל הַקָּדוֹשׁ הַזֶּה, עִם כָּל קְהִלּוֹת הַקֹּדֶשׁ, הֵם, וּנְשֵׁיהֶם, וּבְנֵיהֶם, וּבְנוֹתֵיהֶם, וְכָל אֲשֶׁר לָהֶם. וּמִי שֶׁמְּיַחֲדִים בָּתֵּי כְנֵסִיּוֹת לִתְפִלָּה, וּמִי שֶׁבָּאִים בְּתוֹכָם לְהִתְפַּלֵּל, וּמִי שֶׁנּוֹתְנִים נֵר

עַל הַתּוֹרָה *For the Torah reading, for the prayer service, for the reading from the Prophets for this Sabbath day that You, HASHEM, our God, have given us for holiness and contentment, for glory and splendor — for all this, HASHEM, our God, we gratefully thank You and bless You. May Your Name be blessed by the mouth of all the living, always, for all eternity. Blessed are You, HASHEM, Who sanctifies the Sabbath.* (Cong.— *Amen.)*

⁂ YEKUM PURKAN ⁂

One praying alone recites only the first paragraph and omits the following two paragraphs.

יְקוּם פֻּרְקָן *May salvation arise from heaven — grace, kindness, compassion, long life, abundant sustenance, heavenly assistance, physical health, lofty vision, living and surviving off-spring, offspring who will neither interrupt nor cease from words of the Torah — for our masters and sages, the holy fellowships that are in Eretz Yisrael and that are in the Diaspora: for the leaders of the Torah assemblages, the leaders of the exile communities, the leaders of the academies, the judges at the gateways, and all their students and to all the students of their students, and to everyone who engages in Torah study. May the King of the universe bless them, make their lives fruitful, increase their days and grant length to their years. May He save them and rescue them from every distress and from all serious ailments. May the Master in heaven come to their assistance at every season and time. Now let us respond: Amen.* (Cong.—*Amen.)*

יְקוּם פֻּרְקָן *May salvation arise from heaven — grace, kindness, compassion, long life, abundant sustenance, heavenly assistance, physical health, lofty vision, living and surviving offspring, offspring who will neither interrupt nor cease from the words of the Torah — to this entire holy congregation, adults along with children, infants and women. May the King of the universe bless you, make your lives fruitful, increase your days, and grant length to your years. May He save you and rescue you from every distress and from all serious ailments. May the Master in heaven come to your assistance at every season and time. Now let us respond: Amen.* (Cong.—*Amen.)*

מִי שֶׁבֵּרַךְ *He Who blessed our forefathers, Abraham, Isaac, and Jacob — may He bless this entire holy congregation along with all the holy congregations; them, their wives, sons, and daughters and all that is theirs; and those who dedicate synagogues for prayer and those who enter them to pray, and those who give lamps*

לַמָּאוֹר, וְיַֽיִן לְקִדּוּשׁ וּלְהַבְדָּלָה, וּפַת לְאוֹרְחִים, וּצְדָקָה לַעֲנִיִּים, וְכָל מִי שֶׁעוֹסְקִים בְּצָרְכֵי צִבּוּר בֶּאֱמוּנָה, הַקָּדוֹשׁ בָּרוּךְ הוּא יְשַׁלֵּם שְׂכָרָם, וְיָסִיר מֵהֶם כָּל מַחֲלָה, וְיִרְפָּא לְכָל גּוּפָם, וְיִסְלַח לְכָל עֲוֹנָם, וְיִשְׁלַח בְּרָכָה וְהַצְלָחָה בְּכָל מַעֲשֵׂה יְדֵיהֶם, עִם כָּל יִשְׂרָאֵל אֲחֵיהֶם. וְנֹאמַר: אָמֵן. (.אָמֵן —Cong.)

In many congregations, a prayer for the welfare of the State is recited by the Rabbi, chazzan, or gabbai at this point.

אַשְׁרֵי יוֹשְׁבֵי בֵיתֶֽךָ, עוֹד יְהַלְלֽוּךָ סֶּֽלָה.[1] אַשְׁרֵי הָעָם שֶׁכָּֽכָה לּוֹ, אַשְׁרֵי הָעָם שֶׁיהוה אֱלֹהָיו.[2]

תהלים קמה

תְּהִלָּה לְדָוִד,

אֲרוֹמִמְךָ אֱלוֹהַי הַמֶּֽלֶךְ, וַאֲבָרְכָה שִׁמְךָ לְעוֹלָם וָעֶד.
בְּכָל יוֹם אֲבָרְכֶֽךָּ, וַאֲהַלְלָה שִׁמְךָ לְעוֹלָם וָעֶד.
גָּדוֹל יהוה וּמְהֻלָּל מְאֹד, וְלִגְדֻלָּתוֹ אֵין חֵֽקֶר.
דּוֹר לְדוֹר יְשַׁבַּח מַעֲשֶֽׂיךָ, וּגְבוּרֹתֶֽיךָ יַגִּֽידוּ.
הֲדַר כְּבוֹד הוֹדֶֽךָ, וְדִבְרֵי נִפְלְאֹתֶֽיךָ אָשִֽׂיחָה.
וֶעֱזוּז נוֹרְאֹתֶֽיךָ יֹאמֵֽרוּ, וּגְדוּלָּתְךָ אֲסַפְּרֶֽנָּה.
זֵֽכֶר רַב טוּבְךָ יַבִּֽיעוּ, וְצִדְקָתְךָ יְרַנֵּֽנוּ.
חַנּוּן וְרַחוּם יהוה, אֶֽרֶךְ אַפַּֽיִם וּגְדָל חָֽסֶד.
טוֹב יהוה לַכֹּל, וְרַחֲמָיו עַל כָּל מַעֲשָׂיו.
יוֹדֽוּךָ יהוה כָּל מַעֲשֶֽׂיךָ, וַחֲסִידֶֽיךָ יְבָרְכֽוּכָה.
כְּבוֹד מַלְכוּתְךָ יֹאמֵֽרוּ, וּגְבוּרָתְךָ יְדַבֵּֽרוּ.
לְהוֹדִֽיעַ לִבְנֵי הָאָדָם גְּבוּרֹתָיו, וּכְבוֹד הֲדַר מַלְכוּתוֹ.
מַלְכוּתְךָ מַלְכוּת כָּל עֹלָמִים, וּמֶמְשַׁלְתְּךָ בְּכָל דּוֹר וָדֹר.
סוֹמֵךְ יהוה לְכָל הַנֹּפְלִים, וְזוֹקֵף לְכָל הַכְּפוּפִים.
עֵינֵי כֹל אֵלֶֽיךָ יְשַׂבֵּֽרוּ, וְאַתָּה נוֹתֵן לָהֶם אֶת אָכְלָם בְּעִתּוֹ.
פּוֹתֵֽחַ אֶת יָדֶֽךָ,

While reciting the verse פּוֹתֵחַ, *concentrate intently on its meaning.*

וּמַשְׂבִּֽיעַ לְכָל חַי רָצוֹן.
צַדִּיק יהוה בְּכָל דְּרָכָיו, וְחָסִיד בְּכָל מַעֲשָׂיו.

(1) *Psalms* 84:5. (2) 144:15.

for illumination and wine for Kiddush and Havdalah, bread for guests and charity for the poor; and all who are involved faithfully in the needs of the community — may the Holy One, Blessed is He, pay their reward and remove from them every affliction, heal their entire body and forgive their every iniquity, and send blessing and success to all their handiwork, along with all Israel, their brethren. And let us say: Amen.

(Cong.—*Amen.*)

In many congregations, a prayer for the welfare of the State is recited by the Rabbi, *chazzan,* or *gabbai* at this point.

אַשְׁרֵי *Praiseworthy are those who dwell in Your house; may they always praise You, Selah!*[1] *Praiseworthy is the people for whom this is so, praiseworthy is the people whose God is* HASHEM.[2]

Psalm 145 *A psalm of praise by David:*

א *I will exalt You, my God the King,*
and I will bless Your Name forever and ever.
ב *Every day I will bless You,*
and I will laud Your Name forever and ever.
ג HASHEM *is great and exceedingly lauded,*
and His greatness is beyond investigation.
ד *Each generation will praise Your deeds to the next*
and of Your mighty deeds they will tell;
ה *The splendrous glory of Your power*
and Your wondrous deeds I shall discuss.
ו *And of Your awesome power they will speak,*
and Your greatness I shall relate.
ז *A recollection of Your abundant goodness they will utter*
and of Your righteousness they will sing exultantly.
ח *Gracious and merciful is* HASHEM,
slow to anger, and great in [bestowing] kindness.
ט HASHEM *is good to all; His mercies are on all His works.*
י *All Your works shall thank You,* HASHEM,
and Your devout ones will bless You.
כ *Of the glory of Your kingdom they will speak,*
and of Your power they will tell;
ל *To inform human beings of His mighty deeds,*
and the glorious splendor of His kingdom.
מ *Your kingdom is a kingdom spanning all eternities,*
and Your dominion is throughout every generation.
ס HASHEM *supports all the fallen ones and straightens all the bent.*
ע *The eyes of all look to You with hope*
and You give them their food in its proper time;
פ *You open Your hand,* Concentrate intently while reciting the verse, *'You open. . .'*
and satisfy the desire of every living thing.
צ *Righteous is* HASHEM *in all His ways*
and magnanimous in all His deeds.

קָרוֹב יהוה לְכָל קֹרְאָיו, לְכֹל אֲשֶׁר יִקְרָאֻהוּ בֶאֱמֶת.
רְצוֹן יְרֵאָיו יַעֲשֶׂה, וְאֶת שַׁוְעָתָם יִשְׁמַע וְיוֹשִׁיעֵם.
שׁוֹמֵר יהוה אֶת כָּל אֹהֲבָיו, וְאֵת כָּל הָרְשָׁעִים יַשְׁמִיד.
❖ תְּהִלַּת יהוה יְדַבֶּר פִּי, וִיבָרֵךְ כָּל בָּשָׂר שֵׁם קָדְשׁוֹ לְעוֹלָם וָעֶד.
וַאֲנַחְנוּ נְבָרֵךְ יָהּ, מֵעַתָּה וְעַד עוֹלָם, הַלְלוּיָהּ.[1]

הכנסת ספר תורה

The *chazzan* takes the Torah from which *Maftir* was read in his right arm and recites:

יְהַלְלוּ אֶת שֵׁם יהוה, כִּי נִשְׂגָּב שְׁמוֹ לְבַדּוֹ –

Congregation responds:

– הוֹדוֹ עַל אֶרֶץ וְשָׁמָיִם. וַיָּרֶם קֶרֶן לְעַמּוֹ, תְּהִלָּה לְכָל חֲסִידָיו, לִבְנֵי יִשְׂרָאֵל עַם קְרֹבוֹ, הַלְלוּיָהּ.[2]

As the Torah Scrolls are carried to the Ark the following psalm is recited.

תהלים כט

מִזְמוֹר לְדָוִד, הָבוּ לַיהוה בְּנֵי אֵלִים, הָבוּ לַיהוה כָּבוֹד וָעֹז. הָבוּ לַיהוה כְּבוֹד שְׁמוֹ, הִשְׁתַּחֲווּ לַיהוה בְּהַדְרַת קֹדֶשׁ. קוֹל יהוה עַל הַמָּיִם, אֵל הַכָּבוֹד הִרְעִים, יהוה עַל מַיִם רַבִּים. קוֹל יהוה בַּכֹּחַ, קוֹל יהוה בֶּהָדָר. קוֹל יהוה שֹׁבֵר אֲרָזִים, וַיְשַׁבֵּר יהוה אֶת אַרְזֵי הַלְּבָנוֹן. וַיַּרְקִידֵם כְּמוֹ עֵגֶל, לְבָנוֹן וְשִׂרְיוֹן כְּמוֹ בֶן רְאֵמִים. קוֹל יהוה חֹצֵב לַהֲבוֹת אֵשׁ. קוֹל יהוה יָחִיל מִדְבָּר, יָחִיל יהוה מִדְבַּר קָדֵשׁ. קוֹל יהוה יְחוֹלֵל אַיָּלוֹת, וַיֶּחֱשֹׂף יְעָרוֹת, וּבְהֵיכָלוֹ, כֻּלּוֹ אֹמֵר כָּבוֹד. יהוה לַמַּבּוּל יָשָׁב, וַיֵּשֶׁב יהוה מֶלֶךְ לְעוֹלָם. יהוה עֹז לְעַמּוֹ יִתֵּן, יהוה יְבָרֵךְ אֶת עַמּוֹ בַשָּׁלוֹם.

As the Torah Scrolls are placed into the Ark, the congregation recites the following verses:

וּבְנֻחֹה יֹאמַר, שׁוּבָה יהוה רִבְבוֹת אַלְפֵי יִשְׂרָאֵל.[3] קוּמָה יהוה לִמְנוּחָתֶךָ, אַתָּה וַאֲרוֹן עֻזֶּךָ. כֹּהֲנֶיךָ יִלְבְּשׁוּ צֶדֶק, וַחֲסִידֶיךָ יְרַנֵּנוּ. בַּעֲבוּר דָּוִד עַבְדֶּךָ, אַל תָּשֵׁב פְּנֵי מְשִׁיחֶךָ.[4] כִּי לֶקַח טוֹב נָתַתִּי לָכֶם, תּוֹרָתִי אַל תַּעֲזֹבוּ.[5] ❖ עֵץ חַיִּים הִיא לַמַּחֲזִיקִים בָּהּ, וְתֹמְכֶיהָ מְאֻשָּׁר.[6] דְּרָכֶיהָ דַרְכֵי נֹעַם, וְכָל נְתִיבֹתֶיהָ שָׁלוֹם.[7] הֲשִׁיבֵנוּ יהוה אֵלֶיךָ וְנָשׁוּבָה, חַדֵּשׁ יָמֵינוּ כְּקֶדֶם.[8]

---

(1) *Psalms* 115:18. (2) 148:13-14. (3) *Numbers* 10:36. (4) *Psalms* 132:8-10.
(5) *Proverbs* 4:2. (6) 3:18. (7) 3:17. (8) *Lamentations* 5:21.

ק *HASHEM is close to all who call upon Him —*
to all who call upon Him sincerely.
ר *The will of those who fear Him He will do;*
and their cry He will hear, and save them.
ש *HASHEM protects all who love Him;*
but all the wicked He will destroy.
ת Chazzan– *May my mouth declare the praise of HASHEM*
and may all flesh bless His Holy Name forever and ever.
We will bless God from this time and forever, Halleluyah![1]

RETURNING THE TORAH

The *chazzan* takes the Torah from which *Maftir* was read in his right arm and recites:

Let them praise the Name of HASHEM,
for His Name alone will have been exalted –

Congregation responds:

— His glory is above earth and heaven. And He will have exalted the pride of His people, causing praise for all His devout ones, for the Children of Israel, His intimate people. Halleluyah![2]

As the Torah Scrolls are carried to the Ark the following psalm is recited:

Psalm 29

מִזְמוֹר *A psalm of David. Render unto HASHEM, you sons of the powerful; render unto HASHEM, honor and might. Render unto HASHEM the honor worthy of His Name, prostrate yourselves before HASHEM in His intensely holy place. The voice of HASHEM is upon the waters, the God of Glory thunders, HASHEM is upon vast waters. The voice of HASHEM is in power! The voice of HASHEM is in majesty! The voice of HASHEM breaks the cedars, HASHEM shatters the cedars of Lebanon! He makes them prance about like a calf; Lebanon and Siryon like young re'eimim. The voice of HASHEM carves with shafts of fire. The voice of HASHEM convulses the wilderness. HASHEM convulses the wilderness of Kadesh. The voice of HASHEM frightens the hinds, and strips the forests bare; while in His Temple all proclaim, 'Glory!' HASHEM sat enthroned at the Deluge; HASHEM sits enthroned as King forever. HASHEM will give might to His people, HASHEM will bless His people with peace.*

As the Torah Scrolls are placed into the Ark, the congregation recites the following verses:

וּבְנֻחֹה *And when it rested he would say, 'Return, HASHEM to the myriad thousands of Israel.'*[3] *Arise, HASHEM, to Your resting place, You and the Ark of Your strength. Let Your priests be clothed in righteousness, and Your devout ones will sing joyously. For the sake of David, Your servant, turn not away the face of Your anointed.*[4] *For I have given you a good teaching, do not forsake My Torah.*[5] Chazzan– *It is a tree of life for those who grasp it, and its supporters are praiseworthy.*[6] *Its ways are ways of pleasantness and all its paths are peace.*[7] *Bring us back to You, HASHEM, and we shall return, renew our days as of old.*[8]

חצי קדיש

The *chazzan* recites חֲצִי קַדִּישׁ.

יִתְגַּדַּל וְיִתְקַדַּשׁ שְׁמֵהּ רַבָּא. (.Cong – אָמֵן.) בְּעָלְמָא דִּי בְרָא כִרְעוּתֵהּ. וְיַמְלִיךְ מַלְכוּתֵהּ, בְּחַיֵּיכוֹן וּבְיוֹמֵיכוֹן וּבְחַיֵּי דְכָל בֵּית יִשְׂרָאֵל, בַּעֲגָלָא וּבִזְמַן קָרִיב. וְאִמְרוּ: אָמֵן.

(.Cong – אָמֵן. יְהֵא שְׁמֵהּ רַבָּא מְבָרַךְ לְעָלַם וּלְעָלְמֵי עָלְמַיָּא.)

יְהֵא שְׁמֵהּ רַבָּא מְבָרַךְ לְעָלַם וּלְעָלְמֵי עָלְמַיָּא.

יִתְבָּרַךְ וְיִשְׁתַּבַּח וְיִתְפָּאַר וְיִתְרוֹמַם וְיִתְנַשֵּׂא וְיִתְהַדָּר וְיִתְעַלֶּה וְיִתְהַלָּל שְׁמֵהּ דְּקֻדְשָׁא בְּרִיךְ הוּא (.Cong – בְּרִיךְ הוּא) – לְעֵלָּא מִן כָּל בִּרְכָתָא וְשִׁירָתָא תֻּשְׁבְּחָתָא וְנֶחֱמָתָא, דַּאֲמִירָן בְּעָלְמָא. וְאִמְרוּ: אָמֵן. (.Cong – אָמֵן.)

מוסף לשבת חול המועד

Take three steps backward, then three steps forward. Remain standing with the feet together while reciting *Shemoneh Esrei*. Recite it with quiet devotion and without interruption, verbal or otherwise. Although its recitation should not be audible to others, one must pray loudly enough to hear himself.

כִּי שֵׁם יהוה אֶקְרָא, הָבוּ גֹדֶל לֵאלֹהֵינוּ.[1]

אֲדֹנָי שְׂפָתַי תִּפְתָּח, וּפִי יַגִּיד תְּהִלָּתֶךָ.[2]

אבות

Bend the knees at בָּרוּךְ; bow at אַתָּה; straighten up at ה׳.

בָּרוּךְ אַתָּה יהוה אֱלֹהֵינוּ וֵאלֹהֵי אֲבוֹתֵינוּ, אֱלֹהֵי אַבְרָהָם, אֱלֹהֵי יִצְחָק, וֵאלֹהֵי יַעֲקֹב, הָאֵל הַגָּדוֹל הַגִּבּוֹר וְהַנּוֹרָא, אֵל עֶלְיוֹן, גּוֹמֵל חֲסָדִים טוֹבִים וְקוֹנֵה הַכֹּל, וְזוֹכֵר חַסְדֵי אָבוֹת, וּמֵבִיא גוֹאֵל לִבְנֵי בְנֵיהֶם, לְמַעַן שְׁמוֹ בְּאַהֲבָה. מֶלֶךְ עוֹזֵר וּמוֹשִׁיעַ וּמָגֵן.

Bend the knees at בָּרוּךְ; bow at אַתָּה; straighten up at ה׳.

בָּרוּךְ אַתָּה יהוה, מָגֵן אַבְרָהָם.

גבורות

אַתָּה גִּבּוֹר לְעוֹלָם אֲדֹנָי, מְחַיֵּה מֵתִים אַתָּה, רַב לְהוֹשִׁיעַ. מְכַלְכֵּל חַיִּים בְּחֶסֶד, מְחַיֵּה מֵתִים בְּרַחֲמִים רַבִּים, סוֹמֵךְ נוֹפְלִים, וְרוֹפֵא חוֹלִים, וּמַתִּיר אֲסוּרִים, וּמְקַיֵּם אֱמוּנָתוֹ לִישֵׁנֵי עָפָר. מִי כָמוֹךָ בַּעַל גְּבוּרוֹת, וּמִי דּוֹמֶה לָּךְ, מֶלֶךְ מֵמִית וּמְחַיֶּה וּמַצְמִיחַ יְשׁוּעָה. וְנֶאֱמָן אַתָּה לְהַחֲיוֹת מֵתִים. בָּרוּךְ אַתָּה יהוה, מְחַיֵּה הַמֵּתִים.

During the *chazzan's* repetition, *Kedushah* (page 608) is recited at this point.

HALF KADDISH

The *chazzan* recites Half *Kaddish:*

יִתְגַּדַּל *May His great Name grow exalted and sanctified* (Cong.– *Amen.*) *in the world that He created as He willed. May He give reign to His kingship in your lifetimes and in your days, and in the lifetimes of the entire Family of Israel, swiftly and soon. Now respond: Amen.*

(Cong.– *Amen. May His great Name be blessed forever and ever.*)

May His great Name be blessed forever and ever.

Blessed, praised, glorified, exalted, extolled, mighty, upraised, and lauded be the Name of the Holy One, Blessed is He (Cong.– *Blessed is He*) *— beyond any blessing and song, praise and consolation that are uttered in the world. Now respond: Amen.* (Cong.– *Amen.*)

MUSSAF FOR THE SABBATH OF CHOL HAMOED

Take three steps backward, then three steps forward. Remain standing with the feet together while reciting *Shemoneh Esrei.* Recite it with quiet devotion and without interruption, verbal or otherwise. Although its recitation should not be audible to others, one must pray loudly enough to hear himself.

When I call out the Name of HASHEM*, ascribe greatness to our God.*[1]

My Lord, open my lips, that my mouth may declare Your praise.[2]

PATRIARCHS

Bend the knees at *'Blessed'*; bow at *'You'*; straighten up at *'*HASHEM.*'*

בָּרוּךְ *Blessed are You,* HASHEM*, our God and the God of our forefathers, God of Abraham, God of Isaac, and God of Jacob; the great, mighty, and awesome God, the supreme God, Who bestows beneficial kindnesses and creates everything, Who recalls the kindnesses of the Patriarchs and brings a Redeemer to their children's children, for His Name's sake, with love. O King, Helper, Savior, and Shield.*

Bend the knees at *'Blessed'*; bow at *'You'*; straighten up at *'*HASHEM.*'*

Blessed are You, HASHEM*, Shield of Abraham.*

GOD'S MIGHT

אַתָּה *You are eternally mighty, my Lord, the Resuscitator of the dead are You; abundantly able to save. He sustains the living with kindness, resuscitates the dead with abundant mercy, supports the fallen, heals the sick, releases the confined, and maintains His faith to those asleep in the dust. Who is like You, O Master of mighty deeds, and who is comparable to You, O King Who causes death and restores life and makes salvation sprout! And You are faithful to resuscitate the dead. Blessed are You,* HASHEM*, Who resuscitates the dead.*

During the *chazzan's* repetition, *Kedushah* (page 608) is recited at this point.

---

(1) *Deuteronomy* 32:3. (2) *Psalms* 51:17.

קדושת השם

INDIVIDUALS RECITE:

אַתָּה קָדוֹשׁ וְשִׁמְךָ קָדוֹשׁ, וּקְדוֹשִׁים בְּכָל יוֹם יְהַלְּלְוּךָ סֶּלָה. בָּרוּךְ אַתָּה יהוה, הָאֵל הַקָּדוֹשׁ.

CHAZZAN RECITES DURING HIS REPETITION:

לְדוֹר וָדוֹר נַגִּיד גָּדְלֶךָ וּלְנֵצַח נְצָחִים קְדֻשָּׁתְךָ נַקְדִּישׁ, וְשִׁבְחֲךָ אֱלֹהֵינוּ מִפִּינוּ לֹא יָמוּשׁ לְעוֹלָם וָעֶד, כִּי אֵל מֶלֶךְ גָּדוֹל וְקָדוֹשׁ אָתָּה. בָּרוּךְ אַתָּה יהוה, הָאֵל הַקָּדוֹשׁ.

קדושת היום

אַתָּה בְחַרְתָּנוּ מִכָּל הָעַמִּים, אָהַבְתָּ אוֹתָנוּ, וְרָצִיתָ בָּנוּ, וְרוֹמַמְתָּנוּ מִכָּל הַלְּשׁוֹנוֹת, וְקִדַּשְׁתָּנוּ בְּמִצְוֹתֶיךָ, וְקֵרַבְתָּנוּ מַלְכֵּנוּ לַעֲבוֹדָתֶךָ, וְשִׁמְךָ הַגָּדוֹל וְהַקָּדוֹשׁ עָלֵינוּ קָרָאתָ.

וַתִּתֶּן לָנוּ יהוה אֱלֹהֵינוּ בְּאַהֲבָה שַׁבָּתוֹת לִמְנוּחָה וּמוֹעֲדִים לְשִׂמְחָה חַגִּים וּזְמַנִּים לְשָׂשׂוֹן, אֶת יוֹם הַשַּׁבָּת הַזֶּה וְאֶת יוֹם חַג הַמַּצּוֹת הַזֶּה, זְמַן חֵרוּתֵנוּ בְּאַהֲבָה מִקְרָא קֹדֶשׁ, זֵכֶר לִיצִיאַת מִצְרָיִם.

קדושה

When reciting *Kedushah,* one must stand with his feet together, and avoid any interruptions. One should rise on his toes when saying the words קָדוֹשׁ, קָדוֹשׁ, קָדוֹשׁ; בָּרוּךְ (of בָּרוּךְ כְּבוֹד); and יִמְלֹךְ.

Cong. then *chazzan*:

נַעֲרִיצְךָ וְנַקְדִּישְׁךָ כְּסוֹד שִׂיחַ שַׂרְפֵי קֹדֶשׁ, הַמַּקְדִּישִׁים שִׁמְךָ בַּקֹּדֶשׁ, כַּכָּתוּב עַל יַד נְבִיאֶךָ, וְקָרָא זֶה אֶל זֶה וְאָמַר:

All– קָדוֹשׁ קָדוֹשׁ קָדוֹשׁ יהוה צְבָאוֹת, מְלֹא כָל הָאָרֶץ כְּבוֹדוֹ.[1] ❖ כְּבוֹדוֹ מָלֵא עוֹלָם, מְשָׁרְתָיו שׁוֹאֲלִים זֶה לָזֶה, אַיֵּה מְקוֹם כְּבוֹדוֹ, לְעֻמָּתָם בָּרוּךְ יֹאמֵרוּ:

All– בָּרוּךְ כְּבוֹד יהוה, מִמְּקוֹמוֹ.[2] ❖ מִמְּקוֹמוֹ הוּא יִפֶן בְּרַחֲמִים, וְיָחוֹן עַם הַמְיַחֲדִים שְׁמוֹ, עֶרֶב וָבֹקֶר בְּכָל יוֹם תָּמִיד, פַּעֲמַיִם בְּאַהֲבָה שְׁמַע אוֹמְרִים.

All– שְׁמַע יִשְׂרָאֵל, יהוה אֱלֹהֵינוּ, יהוה אֶחָד.[3] ❖ הוּא אֱלֹהֵינוּ, הוּא אָבִינוּ, הוּא מַלְכֵּנוּ, הוּא מוֹשִׁיעֵנוּ, וְהוּא יַשְׁמִיעֵנוּ בְּרַחֲמָיו שֵׁנִית, לְעֵינֵי כָּל חָי, לִהְיוֹת לָכֶם לֵאלֹהִים, אֲנִי יהוה אֱלֹהֵיכֶם.[4]

In some congregations the following is added:

All– אַדִּיר אַדִּירֵנוּ, יהוה אֲדֹנֵינוּ, מָה אַדִּיר שִׁמְךָ בְּכָל הָאָרֶץ.[5] וְהָיָה יהוה לְמֶלֶךְ עַל כָּל הָאָרֶץ, בַּיּוֹם הַהוּא יִהְיֶה יהוה אֶחָד וּשְׁמוֹ אֶחָד.[6]

Chazzan– וּבְדִבְרֵי קָדְשְׁךָ כָּתוּב לֵאמֹר:

All– יִמְלֹךְ יהוה לְעוֹלָם, אֱלֹהַיִךְ צִיּוֹן, לְדֹר וָדֹר, הַלְלוּיָהּ.[7]

Chazzan continues לְדוֹר וָדוֹר (above).

HOLINESS OF GOD'S NAME

INDIVIDUALS RECITE:

אַתָּה *You are holy and Your Name is holy, and holy ones praise You every day, forever. Blessed are You,* HASHEM, *the holy God.*

CHAZZAN RECITES DURING HIS REPETITION:

לְדוֹר *From generation to generation we shall relate Your greatness and for infinite eternities we shall proclaim Your holiness. Your praise, our God, shall not leave our mouth forever and ever, for You, O God, are a great and holy King. Blessed are You,* HASHEM, *the holy God.*

SANCTIFICATION OF THE DAY

אַתָּה בְחַרְתָּנוּ *You have chosen us from all the peoples; You loved us and found favor in us; You exalted us above all the tongues and You sanctified us with Your commandments. You drew us close, our King, to Your service and proclaimed Your great and Holy Name upon us.*

וַתִּתֶּן לָנוּ *And You gave us,* HASHEM, *our God, with love Sabbaths for rest, appointed festivals for gladness, Festivals and times for joy, this day of Sabbath and this day of the Festival of Matzos, the time of our freedom with love, a holy convocation, a memorial of the Exodus from Egypt.*

KEDUSHAH

When reciting *Kedushah*, one must stand with his feet together and avoid any interruptions. One should rise on his toes when saying the words *Holy, holy, holy; Blessed is;* HASHEM *shall reign.*

Cong. then *chazzan:*

נַעֲרִיצְךָ *We will revere You and sanctify You according to the counsel of the holy Seraphim, who sanctify Your Name in the Sanctuary, as it is written by Your prophet: "And one [angel] will call another and say:*

All – *'Holy, holy, holy is* HASHEM, *Master of Legions, the whole world is filled with His glory.'"*[1] ❖*His glory fills the world. His ministering angels ask one another, 'Where is the place of His glory?' Those facing them say 'Blessed':*

All – *'Blessed is the glory of* HASHEM *from His place.'*[2] ❖*From His place may He turn with compassion and be gracious to the people who declare the Oneness of His Name; evening and morning, every day constantly, twice, with love, they proclaim 'Shema.'*

All – *'Hear O Israel:* HASHEM *is our God,* HASHEM *the One and Only.'*[3] ❖*He is our God; He is our Father; He is our King; He is our Savior; and He will let us hear, in His compassion, for a second time in the presence of all the living,' . . . to be a God to you, I am* HASHEM, *your God.'*[4]

In some congregations the following is added:

All – *Mighty is our Mighty One,* HASHEM, *our Master — how mighty is Your name throughout the earth!*[5] HASHEM *will be King over all the world — on that day* HASHEM *will be One and His Name will be One.*[6]

Chazzan – *And in Your holy Writings the following is written:*

All – *'*HASHEM *shall reign forever — your God, O Zion — from generation to generation, Halleluyah!'*[7]

Chazzan continues לְדוֹר וָדוֹר, *From generation* . . . (above).

(1) *Isaiah* 6:3. (2) *Ezekiel* 3:12. (3) *Deuteronomy* 6:4.
(4) *Numbers* 15:41. (5) *Psalms* 8:2. (6) *Zechariah* 14:9. (7) *Psalms* 146:10.

וּמִפְּנֵי חֲטָאֵינוּ גָּלִינוּ מֵאַרְצֵנוּ, וְנִתְרַחַקְנוּ מֵעַל אַדְמָתֵנוּ. וְאֵין אֲנַחְנוּ יְכוֹלִים לַעֲלוֹת וְלֵרָאוֹת וּלְהִשְׁתַּחֲוֹת לְפָנֶיךָ, וְלַעֲשׂוֹת חוֹבוֹתֵינוּ בְּבֵית בְּחִירָתֶךָ, בַּבַּיִת הַגָּדוֹל וְהַקָּדוֹשׁ שֶׁנִּקְרָא שִׁמְךָ עָלָיו, מִפְּנֵי הַיָּד שֶׁנִּשְׁתַּלְּחָה בְּמִקְדָּשֶׁךָ. יְהִי רָצוֹן מִלְּפָנֶיךָ יהוה אֱלֹהֵינוּ וֵאלֹהֵי אֲבוֹתֵינוּ, מֶלֶךְ רַחֲמָן, שֶׁתָּשׁוּב וּתְרַחֵם עָלֵינוּ וְעַל מִקְדָּשְׁךָ בְּרַחֲמֶיךָ הָרַבִּים, וְתִבְנֵהוּ מְהֵרָה וּתְגַדֵּל כְּבוֹדוֹ. אָבִינוּ מַלְכֵּנוּ, גַּלֵּה כְּבוֹד מַלְכוּתְךָ עָלֵינוּ מְהֵרָה, וְהוֹפַע וְהִנָּשֵׂא עָלֵינוּ לְעֵינֵי כָּל חָי. וְקָרֵב פְּזוּרֵינוּ מִבֵּין הַגּוֹיִם, וּנְפוּצוֹתֵינוּ כַּנֵּס מִיַּרְכְּתֵי אָרֶץ. וַהֲבִיאֵנוּ לְצִיּוֹן עִירְךָ בְּרִנָּה, וְלִירוּשָׁלַיִם בֵּית מִקְדָּשְׁךָ בְּשִׂמְחַת עוֹלָם. וְשָׁם נַעֲשֶׂה לְפָנֶיךָ אֶת קָרְבְּנוֹת חוֹבוֹתֵינוּ, תְּמִידִים כְּסִדְרָם, וּמוּסָפִים כְּהִלְכָתָם. וְאֶת מוּסְפֵי יוֹם הַשַּׁבָּת הַזֶּה וְיוֹם חַג הַמַּצּוֹת הַזֶּה נַעֲשֶׂה וְנַקְרִיב לְפָנֶיךָ בְּאַהֲבָה כְּמִצְוַת רְצוֹנֶךָ, כְּמוֹ שֶׁכָּתַבְתָּ עָלֵינוּ בְּתוֹרָתֶךָ, עַל יְדֵי מֹשֶׁה עַבְדֶּךָ, מִפִּי כְבוֹדֶךָ כָּאָמוּר:

וּבְיוֹם הַשַּׁבָּת שְׁנֵי כְבָשִׂים בְּנֵי שָׁנָה תְּמִימִם, וּשְׁנֵי עֶשְׂרֹנִים סֹלֶת מִנְחָה בְּלוּלָה בַשֶּׁמֶן, וְנִסְכּוֹ. עֹלַת שַׁבַּת בְּשַׁבַּתּוֹ, עַל עֹלַת הַתָּמִיד וְנִסְכָּהּ.[1] (זֶה קָרְבַּן שַׁבָּת. וְקָרְבַּן הַיּוֹם כָּאָמוּר:)

וְהִקְרַבְתֶּם אִשֶּׁה עֹלָה לַיהוה, פָּרִים בְּנֵי בָקָר שְׁנַיִם, וְאַיִל אֶחָד, וְשִׁבְעָה כְבָשִׂים בְּנֵי שָׁנָה, תְּמִימִים יִהְיוּ לָכֶם.[2] וּמִנְחָתָם וְנִסְכֵּיהֶם כִּמְדֻבָּר, שְׁלֹשָׁה עֶשְׂרֹנִים לַפָּר, וּשְׁנֵי עֶשְׂרֹנִים לָאָיִל, וְעִשָּׂרוֹן לַכֶּבֶשׂ, וְיַיִן כְּנִסְכּוֹ. וְשָׂעִיר לְכַפֵּר, וּשְׁנֵי תְמִידִים כְּהִלְכָתָם.

יִשְׂמְחוּ בְמַלְכוּתְךָ שׁוֹמְרֵי שַׁבָּת וְקוֹרְאֵי עֹנֶג, עַם מְקַדְּשֵׁי שְׁבִיעִי, כֻּלָּם יִשְׂבְּעוּ וְיִתְעַנְּגוּ מִטּוּבֶךָ, וּבַשְּׁבִיעִי רָצִיתָ בּוֹ וְקִדַּשְׁתּוֹ, חֶמְדַּת יָמִים אוֹתוֹ קָרָאתָ, זֵכֶר לְמַעֲשֵׂה בְרֵאשִׁית.

אֱלֹהֵינוּ וֵאלֹהֵי אֲבוֹתֵינוּ, רְצֵה בִמְנוּחָתֵנוּ, מֶלֶךְ רַחֲמָן רַחֵם עָלֵינוּ, טוֹב וּמֵטִיב הִדָּרֶשׁ לָנוּ, שׁוּבָה אֵלֵינוּ בַּהֲמוֹן רַחֲמֶיךָ, בִּגְלַל אָבוֹת שֶׁעָשׂוּ רְצוֹנֶךָ. בְּנֵה בֵיתְךָ כְּבַתְּחִלָּה, וְכוֹנֵן מִקְדָּשְׁךָ עַל מְכוֹנוֹ, וְהַרְאֵנוּ בְּבִנְיָנוֹ, וְשַׂמְּחֵנוּ בְּתִקּוּנוֹ. וְהָשֵׁב כֹּהֲנִים לַעֲבוֹדָתָם, וּלְוִיִּם לְשִׁירָם וּלְזִמְרָם, וְהָשֵׁב יִשְׂרָאֵל לִנְוֵיהֶם. וְשָׁם נַעֲלֶה וְנֵרָאֶה וְנִשְׁתַּחֲוֶה לְפָנֶיךָ, בְּשָׁלֹשׁ פַּעֲמֵי רְגָלֵינוּ,

(1) *Numbers* 28:9-10. (2) 28:19.

וּמִפְּנֵי *But because of our sins we have been exiled from our land and sent far from our soil. We cannot ascend to appear and to prostrate ourselves before You, and to perform our obligations in the House of Your choice, in the great and holy House upon which Your Name was proclaimed, because of the hand that was dispatched against Your Sanctuary. May it be Your will, HASHEM, our God and the God of our forefathers, O merciful King, that You once more be compassionate upon us and upon Your Sanctuary in Your abundant mercy, and rebuild it soon and magnify its glory. Our Father, our King, reveal the glory of Your Kingship upon us, speedily; appear and be uplifted over us before the eyes of all the living. Draw our scattered ones near from among the nations, and bring in our dispersions from the ends of the earth. Bring us to Zion, Your City, in glad song, and to Jerusalem, home of Your Sanctuary, in eternal joy. There we will perform before You our obligatory offerings, the continual offerings according to their order and the additional offerings according to their law. And the additional offerings of this day of Sabbath and of this day of the Festival of Matzos, we will perform and bring near to You with love, according to the commandment of Your will, as You have written for us in Your Torah, through Moses, Your servant, from Your glorious expression, as it is said:*

וּבְיוֹם *On the Sabbath day: two [male] first-year unblemished; and two tenth-ephah of fine flour for a meal-offering, mixed with olive oil, and its wine-libation. The elevation-offering of the Sabbath must be on its particular Sabbath, in addition to the continual elevation-offering and its wine-libation.*[1] *(This is the offering of the Sabbath. And the offering of the day is as it is said:)*

וְהִקְרַבְתֶּם *You are to bring a fire-offering, an elevation-offering to HASHEM, two young bulls, one ram and seven male lambs in their first year, they shall be unblemished for you.*[2] *And their meal-offerings and their wine-libations as mentioned: three tenth-ephah for each bull; two tenth-ephah for each ram; one tenth-ephah for each lamb; and wine for its libation. A he-goat for atonement, and two continual offerings according to their law.*

יִשְׂמְחוּ *They shall rejoice in Your Kingship — those who observe the Sabbath and call it a delight. The people that sanctifies the Seventh — they will all be satisfied and delighted from Your goodness. And the Seventh — You found favor in it and sanctified it. 'Most coveted of days' You called it, a remembrance of creation.*

אֱלֹהֵינוּ *Our God and the God of our forefathers, may You be pleased with our rest, O merciful King, have mercy on us; O good and beneficent One, let Yourself be sought out by us; return to us in Your yearning mercy for the sake of the forefathers who did Your will. Rebuild Your House as it was at first, and establish Your Sanctuary on its prepared site; show us its rebuilding and gladden us in its perfection. Restore the Kohanim to their service and the Levites to their song and music; and restore Israel to their dwellings. And there we will ascend and appear and prostrate ourselves before You, during our three pilgrimage seasons,*

כַּכָּתוּב בְּתוֹרָתֶךָ: שָׁלוֹשׁ פְּעָמִים בַּשָּׁנָה, יֵרָאֶה כָל זְכוּרְךָ אֶת פְּנֵי יהוה אֱלֹהֶיךָ, בַּמָּקוֹם אֲשֶׁר יִבְחָר, בְּחַג הַמַּצּוֹת, וּבְחַג הַשָּׁבֻעוֹת, וּבְחַג הַסֻּכּוֹת, וְלֹא יֵרָאֶה אֶת פְּנֵי יהוה רֵיקָם. אִישׁ כְּמַתְּנַת יָדוֹ, כְּבִרְכַּת יהוה אֱלֹהֶיךָ, אֲשֶׁר נָתַן לָךְ.[1]

וְהַשִּׂיאֵנוּ יהוה אֱלֹהֵינוּ אֶת בִּרְכַּת מוֹעֲדֶיךָ לְחַיִּים וּלְשָׁלוֹם, לְשִׂמְחָה וּלְשָׂשׂוֹן, כַּאֲשֶׁר רָצִיתָ וְאָמַרְתָּ לְבָרְכֵנוּ. אֱלֹהֵינוּ וֵאלֹהֵי אֲבוֹתֵינוּ רְצֵה בִמְנוּחָתֵנוּ קַדְּשֵׁנוּ בְּמִצְוֹתֶיךָ וְתֵן חֶלְקֵנוּ בְּתוֹרָתֶךָ, שַׂבְּעֵנוּ מִטּוּבֶךָ וְשַׂמְּחֵנוּ בִּישׁוּעָתֶךָ, וְטַהֵר לִבֵּנוּ לְעָבְדְּךָ בֶּאֱמֶת, וְהַנְחִילֵנוּ יהוה אֱלֹהֵינוּ בְּאַהֲבָה וּבְרָצוֹן בְּשִׂמְחָה וּבְשָׂשׂוֹן שַׁבָּת וּמוֹעֲדֵי קָדְשֶׁךָ, וְיִשְׂמְחוּ בְךָ יִשְׂרָאֵל מְקַדְּשֵׁי שְׁמֶךָ. בָּרוּךְ אַתָּה יהוה, מְקַדֵּשׁ הַשַּׁבָּת וְיִשְׂרָאֵל וְהַזְּמַנִּים.

עבודה

רְצֵה יהוה אֱלֹהֵינוּ בְּעַמְּךָ יִשְׂרָאֵל וּבִתְפִלָּתָם, וְהָשֵׁב אֶת הָעֲבוֹדָה לִדְבִיר בֵּיתֶךָ. וְאִשֵּׁי יִשְׂרָאֵל וּתְפִלָּתָם בְּאַהֲבָה תְקַבֵּל בְּרָצוֹן, וּתְהִי לְרָצוֹן תָּמִיד עֲבוֹדַת יִשְׂרָאֵל עַמֶּךָ.

וְתֶחֱזֶינָה עֵינֵינוּ בְּשׁוּבְךָ לְצִיּוֹן בְּרַחֲמִים. בָּרוּךְ אַתָּה יהוה, הַמַּחֲזִיר שְׁכִינָתוֹ לְצִיּוֹן.

הודאה

Bow at מוֹדִים; straighten up at 'ה. In his repetition the *chazzan* should recite the entire מוֹדִים aloud, while the congregation recites מוֹדִים דְּרַבָּנָן softly.

מוֹדִים אֲנַחְנוּ לָךְ, שָׁאַתָּה הוּא יהוה אֱלֹהֵינוּ וֵאלֹהֵי אֲבוֹתֵינוּ לְעוֹלָם וָעֶד. צוּר חַיֵּינוּ, מָגֵן יִשְׁעֵנוּ אַתָּה הוּא לְדוֹר וָדוֹר. נוֹדֶה לְּךָ וּנְסַפֵּר תְּהִלָּתֶךָ[2] עַל חַיֵּינוּ הַמְּסוּרִים בְּיָדֶךָ, וְעַל נִשְׁמוֹתֵינוּ הַפְּקוּדוֹת לָךְ, וְעַל נִסֶּיךָ שֶׁבְּכָל יוֹם עִמָּנוּ, וְעַל נִפְלְאוֹתֶיךָ וְטוֹבוֹתֶיךָ שֶׁבְּכָל עֵת, עֶרֶב וָבֹקֶר וְצָהֳרָיִם. הַטּוֹב כִּי לֹא כָלוּ רַחֲמֶיךָ, וְהַמְרַחֵם כִּי לֹא תַמּוּ חֲסָדֶיךָ,[3] מֵעוֹלָם קִוִּינוּ לָךְ.

מודים דרבנן

מוֹדִים אֲנַחְנוּ לָךְ, שָׁאַתָּה הוּא יהוה אֱלֹהֵינוּ וֵאלֹהֵי אֲבוֹתֵינוּ, אֱלֹהֵי כָל בָּשָׂר, יוֹצְרֵנוּ, יוֹצֵר בְּרֵאשִׁית. בְּרָכוֹת וְהוֹדָאוֹת לְשִׁמְךָ הַגָּדוֹל וְהַקָּדוֹשׁ, עַל שֶׁהֶחֱיִיתָנוּ וְקִיַּמְתָּנוּ. כֵּן תְּחַיֵּנוּ וּתְקַיְּמֵנוּ, וְתֶאֱסוֹף גָּלֻיּוֹתֵינוּ לְחַצְרוֹת קָדְשֶׁךָ, לִשְׁמוֹר חֻקֶּיךָ וְלַעֲשׂוֹת רְצוֹנֶךָ, וּלְעָבְדְּךָ בְּלֵבָב שָׁלֵם, עַל שֶׁאֲנַחְנוּ מוֹדִים לָךְ. בָּרוּךְ אֵל הַהוֹדָאוֹת.

---

(1) *Deuteronomy* 16:16-17. (2) Cf. *Psalms* 79:13. (3) Cf. *Lamentations* 3:22.

as it is written in Your Torah: Three times a year all your males are to appear before HASHEM, *your God, in the place He shall choose, on the Festival of Matzos, on the Festival of Shavuos, and on the Festival of Succos, and they shall not appear before* HASHEM *empty-handed. Every man according to the gift of his hand, according to the blessing of* HASHEM, *your God, that He gave you.*[1]

וְהַשִּׂיאֵנוּ *Bestow upon us, O* HASHEM, *our God, the blessing of Your appointed Festivals for life and for peace, for gladness and for joy, as You desired and promised to bless us. Our God and the God of our forefathers, may You be pleased with our rest. Sanctify us with Your commandments and grant us our share in Your Torah; satisfy us from Your goodness and gladden us with Your salvation, and purify our heart to serve You sincerely. And grant us a heritage, O* HASHEM, *our God — with love and with favor, with gladness and with joy — the Sabbath and the appointed festivals of Your holiness, and may Israel, the sanctifiers of Your Name, rejoice in You. Blessed are You,* HASHEM, *Who sanctifies the Sabbath, Israel and the festive seasons.*

TEMPLE SERVICE

רְצֵה *Be favorable,* HASHEM, *our God, toward Your people Israel and their prayer and restore the service to the Holy of Holies of Your Temple. The fire-offerings of Israel and their prayer accept with love and favor, and may the service of Your people Israel always be favorable to You.*

וְתֶחֱזֶינָה *May our eyes behold Your return to Zion in compassion. Blessed are You,* HASHEM, *Who restores His Presence to Zion.*

THANKSGIVING [MODIM]

Bow at *'We gratefully thank You'*; straighten up at *'*HASHEM.*'* In his repetition the *chazzan* should recite the entire *Modim* aloud, while the congregation recites *Modim of the Rabbis* softly.

מוֹדִים *We gratefully thank You, for it is You Who are* HASHEM, *our God and the God of our forefathers for all eternity; Rock of our lives, Shield of our salvation are You from generation to generation. We shall thank You and relate Your praise*[2] *— for our lives, which are committed to Your power and for our souls that are entrusted to You; for Your miracles that are with us every day; and for Your wonders and favors in every season — evening, morning, and afternoon. The Beneficent One, for Your compassions were never exhausted, and the Compassionate One, for Your kindnesses never ended*[3] *— always have we put our hope in You.*

MODIM OF THE RABBIS

מוֹדִים *We gratefully thank You, for it is You Who are* HASHEM, *our God and the God of our forefathers, the God of all flesh, our Molder, the Molder of the universe. Blessings and thanks are due Your great and holy Name for You have given us life and sustained us. So may You continue to give us life and sustain us and gather our exiles to the Courtyards of Your Sanctuary, to observe Your decrees, to do Your will and to serve You wholeheartedly. [We thank You] for inspiring us to thank You. Blessed is the God of thanksgivings.*

וְעַל כֻּלָּם יִתְבָּרַךְ וְיִתְרוֹמַם שִׁמְךָ מַלְכֵּנוּ תָּמִיד לְעוֹלָם וָעֶד.

Bend the knees at בָּרוּךְ; bow at אַתָּה; straighten up at ה׳.

וְכֹל הַחַיִּים יוֹדוּךָ סֶּלָה, וִיהַלְלוּ אֶת שִׁמְךָ בֶּאֱמֶת, הָאֵל יְשׁוּעָתֵנוּ וְעֶזְרָתֵנוּ סֶלָה. בָּרוּךְ אַתָּה יהוה, הַטּוֹב שִׁמְךָ וּלְךָ נָאֶה לְהוֹדוֹת.

ברכת כהנים

The *chazzan* recites the following during his repetition.
He faces right at וְיִשְׁמְרֶךָ; faces left at אֵלֶיךָ וִיחֻנֶּךָּ; faces the Ark for the rest of the blessings.

אֱלֹהֵינוּ, וֵאלֹהֵי אֲבוֹתֵינוּ, בָּרְכֵנוּ בַבְּרָכָה הַמְּשֻׁלֶּשֶׁת בַּתּוֹרָה הַכְּתוּבָה עַל יְדֵי מֹשֶׁה עַבְדֶּךָ, הָאֲמוּרָה מִפִּי אַהֲרֹן וּבָנָיו, כֹּהֲנִים עַם קְדוֹשֶׁךָ, כָּאָמוּר:

יְבָרֶכְךָ יהוה, וְיִשְׁמְרֶךָ. (Cong. – כֵּן יְהִי רָצוֹן.)

יָאֵר יהוה פָּנָיו אֵלֶיךָ וִיחֻנֶּךָּ. (Cong. – כֵּן יְהִי רָצוֹן.)

יִשָּׂא יהוה פָּנָיו אֵלֶיךָ וְיָשֵׂם לְךָ שָׁלוֹם.[1] (Cong. – כֵּן יְהִי רָצוֹן.)

שלום

שִׂים שָׁלוֹם, טוֹבָה, וּבְרָכָה, חֵן, וָחֶסֶד וְרַחֲמִים עָלֵינוּ וְעַל כָּל יִשְׂרָאֵל עַמֶּךָ. בָּרְכֵנוּ אָבִינוּ, כֻּלָּנוּ כְּאֶחָד בְּאוֹר פָּנֶיךָ, כִּי בְאוֹר פָּנֶיךָ נָתַתָּ לָּנוּ, יהוה אֱלֹהֵינוּ, תּוֹרַת חַיִּים וְאַהֲבַת חֶסֶד, וּצְדָקָה, וּבְרָכָה, וְרַחֲמִים, וְחַיִּים, וְשָׁלוֹם. וְטוֹב בְּעֵינֶיךָ לְבָרֵךְ אֶת עַמְּךָ יִשְׂרָאֵל, בְּכָל עֵת וּבְכָל שָׁעָה בִּשְׁלוֹמֶךָ. בָּרוּךְ אַתָּה יהוה, הַמְּבָרֵךְ אֶת עַמּוֹ יִשְׂרָאֵל בַּשָּׁלוֹם.

יִהְיוּ לְרָצוֹן אִמְרֵי פִי וְהֶגְיוֹן לִבִּי לְפָנֶיךָ, יהוה צוּרִי וְגֹאֲלִי.[2]

The *chazzan's* repetition of *Shemoneh Esrei* ends here. The individual continues below:

אֱלֹהַי, נְצוֹר לְשׁוֹנִי מֵרָע, וּשְׂפָתַי מִדַּבֵּר מִרְמָה,[3] וְלִמְקַלְלַי נַפְשִׁי תִדּוֹם, וְנַפְשִׁי כֶּעָפָר לַכֹּל תִּהְיֶה. פְּתַח לִבִּי בְּתוֹרָתֶךָ, וּבְמִצְוֹתֶיךָ תִּרְדּוֹף נַפְשִׁי. וְכֹל הַחוֹשְׁבִים עָלַי רָעָה, מְהֵרָה הָפֵר עֲצָתָם וְקַלְקֵל מַחֲשַׁבְתָּם. עֲשֵׂה לְמַעַן שְׁמֶךָ, עֲשֵׂה לְמַעַן יְמִינֶךָ, עֲשֵׂה לְמַעַן קְדֻשָּׁתֶךָ, עֲשֵׂה לְמַעַן תּוֹרָתֶךָ. לְמַעַן יֵחָלְצוּן יְדִידֶיךָ, הוֹשִׁיעָה יְמִינְךָ וַעֲנֵנִי.[4]

Some recite verses pertaining to their names here. See page 1143.

יִהְיוּ לְרָצוֹן אִמְרֵי פִי וְהֶגְיוֹן לִבִּי לְפָנֶיךָ, יהוה צוּרִי וְגֹאֲלִי.[2]

Bow and take three steps back. Bow left and say . . . עֹשֶׂה; bow right and say . . . הוּא יַעֲשֶׂה; bow forward and say וְעַל כָּל . . . אָמֵן.

עֹשֶׂה שָׁלוֹם בִּמְרוֹמָיו, הוּא יַעֲשֶׂה שָׁלוֹם עָלֵינוּ, וְעַל כָּל יִשְׂרָאֵל. וְאִמְרוּ: אָמֵן.

For all these, may Your Name be blessed and exalted, our King, continually forever and ever.

Bend the knees at *'Blessed'*; bow at *'You'*; straighten up at *'HASHEM.'*

Everything alive will gratefully acknowledge You, Selah! and praise Your Name sincerely, O God of our salvation and help, Selah! Blessed are You, HASHEM, Your Name is 'The Beneficent One' and to You it is fitting to give thanks.

THE PRIESTLY BLESSING

The *chazzan* recites the following during his repetition.

אֱלֹהֵינוּ *Our God and the God of our forefathers, bless us with the three-verse blessing in the Torah that was written by the hand of Moses, Your servant, that was said by Aaron and his sons, the Kohanim, Your holy people, as it is said:*

May HASHEM bless you and safeguard you. (Cong.— *So may it be.*)

May HASHEM illuminate His countenance for you and be gracious to you. (Cong.— *So may it be.*)

May HASHEM turn His countenance to you and establish peace for you.[1] (Cong.— *So may it be.*)

PEACE

שִׂים שָׁלוֹם *Establish peace, goodness, blessing, graciousness, kindness, and compassion upon us and upon all of Your people Israel. Bless us, our Father, all of us as one, with the light of Your countenance, for with the light of Your countenance You gave us, HASHEM, our God, the Torah of life and a love of kindness, righteousness, blessing, compassion, life, and peace. And may it be good in Your eyes to bless Your people Israel at every time and every hour with Your peace. Blessed are You, HASHEM, Who blesses His people Israel with peace.*

May the expressions of my mouth and the thoughts of my heart find favor before You, HASHEM, my Rock and my Redeemer.[2]

Chazzan's repetition of *Shemoneh Esrei* ends here. Individuals continue:

אֱלֹהַי *My God, guard my tongue from evil and my lips from speaking deceitfully.*[3] *To those who curse me, let my soul be silent; and let my soul be like dust to everyone. Open my heart to Your Torah, then my soul will pursue Your commandments. As for all those who design evil against me, speedily nullify their counsel and disrupt their design. Act for Your Name's sake; act for Your right hand's sake; act for Your sanctity's sake; act for Your Torah's sake. That Your beloved ones may be given rest; let Your right hand save, and respond to me.*[4] *May the expressions of my mouth and the thoughts of my heart find favor before You, HASHEM, my Rock and my Redeemer.*[2] *He Who makes peace in His heights, may He make peace upon us, and upon all Israel. Now respond: Amen.*

Some recite verses pertaining to their names at this point. See page 1143.

Bow and take three steps back. Bow left and say, *'He Who makes peace . . .'*; bow right and say, *'may He make peace . . .'*; bow forward and say, *'and upon . . . Amen.'*

(1) *Numbers* 6:24-26. (2) *Psalms* 19:15. (3) Cf. 34:14. (4) 60:7; 108:7.

יְהִי רָצוֹן מִלְּפָנֶיךָ יהוה אֱלֹהֵינוּ וֵאלֹהֵי אֲבוֹתֵינוּ, שֶׁיִּבָּנֶה בֵּית הַמִּקְדָּשׁ בִּמְהֵרָה בְיָמֵינוּ, וְתֵן חֶלְקֵנוּ בְּתוֹרָתֶךָ. וְשָׁם נַעֲבָדְךָ בְּיִרְאָה, כִּימֵי עוֹלָם וּכְשָׁנִים קַדְמוֹנִיּוֹת. וְעָרְבָה לַיהוה מִנְחַת יְהוּדָה וִירוּשָׁלָיִם, כִּימֵי עוֹלָם וּכְשָׁנִים קַדְמוֹנִיּוֹת.[1]

THE INDIVIDUAL'S RECITATION OF *SHEMONEH ESREI* ENDS HERE.

The individual remains standing in place until the *chazzan* reaches *Kedushah* — or at least until the *chazzan* begins his repetition — then he takes three steps forward. The *chazzan* himself, or one praying alone, should remain in place for a few moments before taking three steps forward.

קדיש שלם

The *chazzan* recites קַדִּישׁ שָׁלֵם.

יִתְגַּדַּל וְיִתְקַדַּשׁ שְׁמֵהּ רַבָּא. (Cong. — אָמֵן.) בְּעָלְמָא דִּי בְרָא כִרְעוּתֵהּ. וְיַמְלִיךְ מַלְכוּתֵהּ, בְּחַיֵּיכוֹן וּבְיוֹמֵיכוֹן וּבְחַיֵּי דְכָל בֵּית יִשְׂרָאֵל, בַּעֲגָלָא וּבִזְמַן קָרִיב. וְאִמְרוּ: אָמֵן.

(Cong. — אָמֵן. יְהֵא שְׁמֵהּ רַבָּא מְבָרַךְ לְעָלַם וּלְעָלְמֵי עָלְמַיָּא.)

יְהֵא שְׁמֵהּ רַבָּא מְבָרַךְ לְעָלַם וּלְעָלְמֵי עָלְמַיָּא.

יִתְבָּרַךְ וְיִשְׁתַּבַּח וְיִתְפָּאַר וְיִתְרוֹמַם וְיִתְנַשֵּׂא וְיִתְהַדָּר וְיִתְעַלֶּה וְיִתְהַלָּל שְׁמֵהּ דְּקֻדְשָׁא בְּרִיךְ הוּא (Cong. — בְּרִיךְ הוּא) — לְעֵלָּא מִן כָּל בִּרְכָתָא וְשִׁירָתָא תֻּשְׁבְּחָתָא וְנֶחֱמָתָא, דַּאֲמִירָן בְּעָלְמָא. וְאִמְרוּ: אָמֵן. (Cong. — אָמֵן.)

(Cong. — קַבֵּל בְּרַחֲמִים וּבְרָצוֹן אֶת תְּפִלָּתֵנוּ.)

תִּתְקַבֵּל צְלוֹתְהוֹן וּבָעוּתְהוֹן דְּכָל בֵּית יִשְׂרָאֵל קֳדָם אֲבוּהוֹן דִּי בִשְׁמַיָּא. וְאִמְרוּ: אָמֵן. (Cong. — אָמֵן.)

(Cong. — יְהִי שֵׁם יהוה מְבֹרָךְ, מֵעַתָּה וְעַד עוֹלָם.[2])

יְהֵא שְׁלָמָא רַבָּא מִן שְׁמַיָּא, וְחַיִּים עָלֵינוּ וְעַל כָּל יִשְׂרָאֵל. וְאִמְרוּ: אָמֵן. (Cong. — אָמֵן.)

(Cong. — עֶזְרִי מֵעִם יהוה, עֹשֵׂה שָׁמַיִם וָאָרֶץ.[3])

Take three steps back. Bow left and say . . . עֹשֶׂה; bow right and say . . . הוּא; bow forward and say וְעַל כָּל . . . אָמֵן. Remain standing in place for a few moments, then take three steps forward.

עֹשֶׂה שָׁלוֹם בִּמְרוֹמָיו, הוּא יַעֲשֶׂה שָׁלוֹם עָלֵינוּ, וְעַל כָּל יִשְׂרָאֵל. וְאִמְרוּ: אָמֵן. (Cong. — אָמֵן.)

קַוֵּה אֶל יהוה, חֲזַק וְיַאֲמֵץ לִבֶּךָ, וְקַוֵּה אֶל יהוה.[4] אֵין קָדוֹשׁ כַּיהוה, כִּי אֵין בִּלְתֶּךָ, וְאֵין צוּר כֵּאלֹהֵינוּ.[5] כִּי מִי אֱלוֹהַּ מִבַּלְעֲדֵי יהוה, וּמִי צוּר זוּלָתִי אֱלֹהֵינוּ.[6]

אֵין כֵּאלֹהֵינוּ, אֵין כַּאדוֹנֵינוּ, אֵין כְּמַלְכֵּנוּ, אֵין כְּמוֹשִׁיעֵנוּ. מִי כֵאלֹהֵינוּ, מִי כַאדוֹנֵינוּ, מִי כְמַלְכֵּנוּ, מִי כְמוֹשִׁיעֵנוּ. נוֹדֶה לֵאלֹהֵינוּ, נוֹדֶה לַאדוֹנֵינוּ, נוֹדֶה לְמַלְכֵּנוּ, נוֹדֶה לְמוֹשִׁיעֵנוּ. בָּרוּךְ אֱלֹהֵינוּ, בָּרוּךְ אֲדוֹנֵינוּ, בָּרוּךְ מַלְכֵּנוּ, בָּרוּךְ מוֹשִׁיעֵנוּ.

יְהִי רָצוֹן *May it be Your will,* H*ASHEM, our God and the God of our forefathers, that the Holy Temple be rebuilt, speedily in our days. Grant us our share in Your Torah, and may we serve You there with reverence, as in days of old and in former years. Then the offering of Judah and Jerusalem will be pleasing to* H*ASHEM, as in days of old and in former years.*[1]

THE INDIVIDUAL'S RECITATION OF *SHEMONEH ESREI* ENDS HERE.

The individual remains standing in place until the *chazzan* reaches *Kedushah* — or at least until the *chazzan* begins his repetition — then he takes three steps forward. The *chazzan* himself, or one praying alone, should remain in place for a few moments before taking three steps forward.

FULL KADDISH

The chazzan recites the Full *Kaddish.*

יִתְגַּדַּל *May His great Name grow exalted and sanctified* (Cong.— *Amen.*) *in the world that He created as He willed. May He give reign to His kingship in your lifetimes and in your days, and in the lifetimes of the entire Family of Israel, swiftly and soon. Now respond: Amen.*

(Cong.— *Amen. May His great Name be blessed forever and ever.*)

May His great Name be blessed forever and ever.

Blessed, praised, glorified, exalted, extolled, mighty, upraised, and lauded be the Name of the Holy One, Blessed is He (Cong.— *Blessed is He*) *— beyond any blessing and song, praise and consolation that are uttered in the world. Now respond: Amen.* (Cong.— *Amen.*)

(Cong.— *Accept our prayers with mercy and favor.*)

May the prayers and supplications of the entire Family of Israel be accepted before their Father Who is in Heaven. Now respond: Amen. (Cong.— *Amen.*)

(Cong.— *Blessed be the Name of* H*ASHEM, from this time and forever.*[2])

May there be abundant peace from Heaven, and life, upon us and upon all Israel. Now respond: Amen. (Cong.— *Amen.*)

(Cong.— *My help is from* H*ASHEM, Maker of heaven and earth.*[3])

Take three steps back. Bow left and say, *'He Who makes peace . . .';* bow right and say, *'may He . . .';* bow forward and say, *'and upon all Israel . . .'* Remain standing in place for a few moments, then take three steps forward.

He Who makes peace in His heights, may He make peace upon us, and upon all Israel. Now respond: Amen. (Cong.— *Amen.*)

קַוֵּה *Hope to* H*ASHEM, strengthen yourself and He will give you courage; and hope to* H*ASHEM.*[4] *There is none holy as* H*ASHEM, for there is none beside You, and there is no Rock like our God.*[5] *For who is a god beside* H*ASHEM, and who is a Rock except for our God.*[6]

אֵין *There is none like our God; there is none like our Master;*
there is none like our King; there is none like our Savior.
Who is like our God? Who is like our Master?
Who is like our King? Who is like our Savior?
Let us thank our God; let us thank our Master;
let us thank our King; let us thank our Savior.
Blessed is our God; blessed is our Master;
blessed is our King; blessed is our Savior.

(1) *Malachi* 3:4. (2) *Psalms* 113:2. (3) 121:2. (4) 27:14. (5) *I Samuel* 2:2. (6) *Psalms* 18:32.

אַתָּה הוּא אֱלֹהֵינוּ, אַתָּה הוּא אֲדוֹנֵינוּ, אַתָּה הוּא מַלְכֵּנוּ, אַתָּה הוּא מוֹשִׁיעֵנוּ. אַתָּה הוּא שֶׁהִקְטִירוּ אֲבוֹתֵינוּ לְפָנֶיךָ אֶת קְטֹרֶת הַסַּמִּים.

כריתות ו.

פִּטּוּם הַקְּטֹרֶת: (א) הַצֳּרִי, (ב) וְהַצִּפֹּרֶן, (ג) הַחֶלְבְּנָה, (ד) וְהַלְּבוֹנָה, מִשְׁקַל שִׁבְעִים שִׁבְעִים מָנֶה; (ה) מוֹר, (ו) וּקְצִיעָה, (ז) שִׁבֹּלֶת נֵרְדְּ, (ח) וְכַרְכֹּם, מִשְׁקַל שִׁשָּׁה עָשָׂר שִׁשָּׁה עָשָׂר מָנֶה; (ט) הַקֹּשְׁטְ שְׁנֵים עָשָׂר, (י) וְקִלּוּפָה שְׁלֹשָׁה, (יא) וְקִנָּמוֹן תִּשְׁעָה. בֹּרִית כַּרְשִׁינָה תִּשְׁעָה קַבִּין, יֵין קַפְרִיסִין סְאִין תְּלָתָא וְקַבִּין תְּלָתָא; וְאִם אֵין לוֹ יֵין קַפְרִיסִין, מֵבִיא חֲמַר חִוַּרְיָן עַתִּיק; מֶלַח סְדוֹמִית רֹבַע הַקָּב; מַעֲלֶה עָשָׁן כָּל שֶׁהוּא. רַבִּי נָתָן הַבַּבְלִי אוֹמֵר: אַף כִּפַּת הַיַּרְדֵּן כָּל שֶׁהוּא. וְאִם נָתַן בָּהּ דְּבַשׁ פְּסָלָהּ. וְאִם חִסַּר אַחַת מִכָּל סַמָּנֶיהָ, חַיָּב מִיתָה.

רַבָּן שִׁמְעוֹן בֶּן גַּמְלִיאֵל אוֹמֵר: הַצֳּרִי אֵינוֹ אֶלָּא שְׂרָף הַנּוֹטֵף מֵעֲצֵי הַקְּטָף. בֹּרִית כַּרְשִׁינָה שֶׁשָּׁפִין בָּהּ אֶת הַצִּפֹּרֶן כְּדֵי שֶׁתְּהֵא נָאָה; יֵין קַפְרִיסִין שֶׁשּׁוֹרִין בּוֹ אֶת הַצִּפֹּרֶן כְּדֵי שֶׁתְּהֵא עַזָּה; וַהֲלֹא מֵי רַגְלַיִם יָפִין לָהּ, אֶלָּא שֶׁאֵין מַכְנִיסִין מֵי רַגְלַיִם בָּעֲזָרָה מִפְּנֵי הַכָּבוֹד.

משנה, תמיד ז:ד

הַשִּׁיר שֶׁהַלְוִיִּם הָיוּ אוֹמְרִים בְּבֵית הַמִּקְדָּשׁ. בַּיּוֹם הָרִאשׁוֹן הָיוּ אוֹמְרִים: לַיהוה הָאָרֶץ וּמְלוֹאָהּ, תֵּבֵל וְיֹשְׁבֵי בָהּ.[1] בַּשֵּׁנִי הָיוּ אוֹמְרִים: גָּדוֹל יהוה וּמְהֻלָּל מְאֹד, בְּעִיר אֱלֹהֵינוּ הַר קָדְשׁוֹ.[2] בַּשְּׁלִישִׁי הָיוּ אוֹמְרִים: אֱלֹהִים נִצָּב בַּעֲדַת אֵל, בְּקֶרֶב אֱלֹהִים יִשְׁפֹּט.[3] בָּרְבִיעִי הָיוּ אוֹמְרִים: אֵל נְקָמוֹת יהוה, אֵל נְקָמוֹת הוֹפִיעַ.[4] בַּחֲמִישִׁי הָיוּ אוֹמְרִים: הַרְנִינוּ לֵאלֹהִים עוּזֵּנוּ, הָרִיעוּ לֵאלֹהֵי יַעֲקֹב.[5] בַּשִּׁשִּׁי הָיוּ אוֹמְרִים: יהוה מָלָךְ גֵּאוּת לָבֵשׁ, לָבֵשׁ יהוה עֹז הִתְאַזָּר, אַף תִּכּוֹן תֵּבֵל בַּל תִּמּוֹט.[6] בַּשַּׁבָּת הָיוּ אוֹמְרִים: מִזְמוֹר שִׁיר לְיוֹם הַשַּׁבָּת.[7] מִזְמוֹר שִׁיר לֶעָתִיד לָבֹא, לְיוֹם שֶׁכֻּלּוֹ שַׁבָּת וּמְנוּחָה לְחַיֵּי הָעוֹלָמִים.

מגילה כח:

תָּנָא דְבֵי אֵלִיָּהוּ: כָּל הַשּׁוֹנֶה הֲלָכוֹת בְּכָל יוֹם, מֻבְטָח לוֹ שֶׁהוּא בֶּן עוֹלָם הַבָּא, שֶׁנֶּאֱמַר: הֲלִיכוֹת עוֹלָם לוֹ,[8] אַל תִּקְרֵי הֲלִיכוֹת, אֶלָּא הֲלָכוֹת.

It is You Who is our God; it is You Who is our Master;
it is You Who is our King; it is You Who is our Savior.
It is You before Whom our forefathers burned the spice-incense.

Talmud, *Kereisos* 6a

פִּטּוּם הַקְּטֹרֶת *The incense mixture was formulated of [eleven spices]: (1) stacte, (2) onycha, (3) galbanum, (4) frankincense — each weighing seventy maneh; (5) myrrh, (6) cassia, (7) spikenard, (8) saffron — each weighing sixteen maneh; (9) costus — twelve [maneh]; (10) aromatic bark — three; and (11) cinnamon — nine. [Additionally] Carshina lye — nine kab; Cyprus wine, three se'ah and three kab — if he has no Cyprus wine, he brings old white wine; Sodom salt, a quarter kab; and a minute amount of smoke-raising herb. Rabbi Nassan the Babylonian says: Also a minute amount of Jordan amber. If he placed fruit-honey into it, he invalidated it. And if he left out any of its spices, he is liable to the death penalty.*

רַבָּן שִׁמְעוֹן *Rabban Shimon ben Gamliel says: The stacte is simply the sap that drips from balsam trees. Carshina lye is used to bleach the onycha to make it pleasing. Cyprus wine is used to soak the onycha to make it pungent. Even though urine is suitable for that, nevertheless they do not bring urine into the Temple out of respect.*

Mishnah, *Tamid* 7:4

הַשִּׁיר *The daily song that the Levites would recite in the Temple was as follows: On the first day [of the week] they would say: 'HASHEM's is the earth and its fullness, the inhabited land and those who dwell in it.'[1] On the second day they would say: 'Great is HASHEM and much praised, in the city of our God, Mount of His Holiness.'[2] On the third day they would say: 'God stands in the Divine assembly, in the midst of judges shall He judge.'[3] On the fourth day they would say: 'O God of vengeance, HASHEM, O God of vengeance, appear.'[4] On the fifth day they would say: 'Sing joyously to the God of our might, call out to the God of Jacob.'[5] On the sixth day they would say: 'HASHEM will have reigned, He will have donned grandeur; He will have donned might and girded Himself; He even made the world firm so that it should not falter.'[6] On the Sabbath they would say: 'A psalm, a song for the Sabbath day.'[7] A psalm, a song for the time to come, to the day that will be entirely Sabbath and contentment for the eternal life.*

Talmud, *Megillah* 28b

תָּנָא *The Academy of Elijah taught: He who studies Torah laws every day has the assurance that he will be in the World to Come, as it is said, 'The ways of the world are His'[8] — do not read* [הֲלִיכוֹת] *'ways,' but* [הֲלָכוֹת] *'laws.'*

(1) *Psalms* 24:1. (2) 48:2. (3) 82:1. (4) 94:1. (5) 81:2. (6) 93:1. (7) 92:1. (8) *Habakkuk* 3:6.

ברכות סד.

אָמַר רַבִּי אֶלְעָזָר אָמַר רַבִּי חֲנִינָא: תַּלְמִידֵי חֲכָמִים מַרְבִּים שָׁלוֹם בָּעוֹלָם, שֶׁנֶּאֱמַר: וְכָל בָּנַיִךְ לִמּוּדֵי יהוה, וְרַב שְׁלוֹם בָּנָיִךְ,[1] אַל תִּקְרֵי בָּנָיִךְ אֶלָּא בּוֹנָיִךְ. ❖ שָׁלוֹם רָב לְאֹהֲבֵי תוֹרָתֶךָ, וְאֵין לָמוֹ מִכְשׁוֹל.[2] יְהִי שָׁלוֹם בְּחֵילֵךְ, שַׁלְוָה בְּאַרְמְנוֹתָיִךְ. לְמַעַן אַחַי וְרֵעָי, אֲדַבְּרָה נָּא שָׁלוֹם בָּךְ. לְמַעַן בֵּית יהוה אֱלֹהֵינוּ, אֲבַקְשָׁה טוֹב לָךְ.[3] יהוה עֹז לְעַמּוֹ יִתֵּן, יהוה יְבָרֵךְ אֶת עַמּוֹ בַשָּׁלוֹם.[4]

קדיש דרבנן

In the presence of a *minyan*, mourners recite קַדִּישׁ דְּרַבָּנָן (see *Laws* §84-85).

יִתְגַּדַּל וְיִתְקַדַּשׁ שְׁמֵהּ רַבָּא. (.Cong – אָמֵן.) בְּעָלְמָא דִּי בְרָא כִרְעוּתֵהּ. וְיַמְלִיךְ מַלְכוּתֵהּ, בְּחַיֵּיכוֹן וּבְיוֹמֵיכוֹן וּבְחַיֵּי דְכָל בֵּית יִשְׂרָאֵל, בַּעֲגָלָא וּבִזְמַן קָרִיב. וְאִמְרוּ: אָמֵן.

(.Cong – אָמֵן. יְהֵא שְׁמֵהּ רַבָּא מְבָרַךְ לְעָלַם וּלְעָלְמֵי עָלְמַיָּא.)

יְהֵא שְׁמֵהּ רַבָּא מְבָרַךְ לְעָלַם וּלְעָלְמֵי עָלְמַיָּא.

יִתְבָּרַךְ וְיִשְׁתַּבַּח וְיִתְפָּאַר וְיִתְרוֹמַם וְיִתְנַשֵּׂא וְיִתְהַדָּר וְיִתְעַלֶּה וְיִתְהַלָּל שְׁמֵהּ דְּקֻדְשָׁא בְּרִיךְ הוּא (.Cong – בְּרִיךְ הוּא) — לְעֵלָּא מִן כָּל בִּרְכָתָא וְשִׁירָתָא תֻּשְׁבְּחָתָא וְנֶחֱמָתָא, דַּאֲמִירָן בְּעָלְמָא. וְאִמְרוּ: אָמֵן. (.Cong – אָמֵן.)

עַל יִשְׂרָאֵל וְעַל רַבָּנָן, וְעַל תַּלְמִידֵיהוֹן וְעַל כָּל תַּלְמִידֵי תַלְמִידֵיהוֹן, וְעַל כָּל מָאן דְּעָסְקִין בְּאוֹרַיְתָא, דִּי בְאַתְרָא הָדֵין וְדִי בְכָל אֲתַר וַאֲתַר. יְהֵא לְהוֹן וּלְכוֹן שְׁלָמָא רַבָּא, חִנָּא וְחִסְדָּא וְרַחֲמִין, וְחַיִּין אֲרִיכִין, וּמְזוֹנֵי רְוִיחֵי, וּפֻרְקָנָא, מִן קֳדָם אֲבוּהוֹן דִּי בִשְׁמַיָּא (וְאַרְעָא). וְאִמְרוּ: אָמֵן. (.Cong – אָמֵן.)

יְהֵא שְׁלָמָא רַבָּא מִן שְׁמַיָּא, וְחַיִּים (טוֹבִים) עָלֵינוּ וְעַל כָּל יִשְׂרָאֵל. וְאִמְרוּ: אָמֵן. (.Cong – אָמֵן.)

Take three steps back. Bow left and say . . . עֹשֶׂה; bow right and say . . . הוּא; bow forward and say וְעַל כָּל . . . אָמֵן. Remain standing in place for a few moments, then take three steps forward.

עֹשֶׂה שָׁלוֹם בִּמְרוֹמָיו, הוּא בְּרַחֲמָיו יַעֲשֶׂה שָׁלוֹם עָלֵינוּ, וְעַל כָּל יִשְׂרָאֵל. וְאִמְרוּ: אָמֵן. (.Cong – אָמֵן.)

Stand while reciting עָלֵינוּ.

עָלֵינוּ לְשַׁבֵּחַ לַאֲדוֹן הַכֹּל, לָתֵת גְּדֻלָּה לְיוֹצֵר בְּרֵאשִׁית, שֶׁלֹּא עָשָׂנוּ כְּגוֹיֵי הָאֲרָצוֹת, וְלֹא שָׂמָנוּ כְּמִשְׁפְּחוֹת הָאֲדָמָה. שֶׁלֹּא שָׂם חֶלְקֵנוּ כָּהֶם, וְגוֹרָלֵנוּ כְּכָל הֲמוֹנָם. (שֶׁהֵם מִשְׁתַּחֲוִים לְהֶבֶל וָרִיק, וּמִתְפַּלְּלִים אֶל אֵל לֹא יוֹשִׁיעַ.[5]) וַאֲנַחְנוּ כּוֹרְעִים וּמִשְׁתַּחֲוִים וּמוֹדִים, לִפְנֵי מֶלֶךְ מַלְכֵי הַמְּלָכִים הַקָּדוֹשׁ בָּרוּךְ הוּא. שֶׁהוּא נוֹטֶה שָׁמַיִם וְיֹסֵד אָרֶץ,[6] וּמוֹשַׁב יְקָרוֹ

Bow while reciting וַאֲנַחְנוּ כּוֹרְעִים וּמִשְׁתַּחֲוִים.

Talmud, *Berachos* 64a

אָמַר *Rabbi Elazar said on behalf of Rabbi Chanina: Torah scholars increase peace in the world, as it is said: 'And all your children will be students of* H*ASHEM, and your children will have peace'*[1] *— do not read** [בָּנָיִךְ] *'your children,' but* [בּוֹנָיִךְ] *'your builders.'* Chazzan– *There is abundant peace for the lovers of Your Torah, and there is no stumbling block for them.*[2] *May there be peace within your wall, serenity within your palaces. For the sake of my brethren and comrades I shall speak of peace in your midst. For the sake of the House of* H*ASHEM, our God, I will request your good.*[3] H*ASHEM will give might to His people,* H*ASHEM will bless His people with peace.*[4]

THE RABBIS' KADDISH

In the presence of a *minyan,* mourners recite the Rabbis' *Kaddish* (see *Laws* §84-85).
[A transliteration of this *Kaddish* appears on p. 1146.]

יִתְגַּדַּל *May His great Name grow exalted and sanctified* (Cong.– *Amen.*) *in the world that He created as He willed. May He give reign to His kingship in your lifetimes and in your days, and in the lifetimes of the entire Family of Israel, swiftly and soon. Now respond: Amen.*

(Cong.– *Amen. May His great Name be blessed forever and ever.*)
May His great Name be blessed forever and ever.

Blessed, praised, glorified, exalted, extolled, mighty, upraised, and lauded be the Name of the Holy One, Blessed is He (Cong.– *Blessed is He*) *— beyond any blessing and song, praise and consolation that are uttered in the world. Now respond: Amen.* (Cong.– *Amen.*)

Upon Israel, upon the teachers, their disciples and all of their disciples and upon all those who engage in the study of Torah, who are here or anywhere else; may they and you have abundant peace, grace, kindness, and mercy, long life, ample nourishment, and salvation, from before their Father Who is in Heaven (and on earth). Now respond: Amen. (Cong. – *Amen.*)

May there be abundant peace from Heaven, and (good) life, upon us and upon all Israel. Now respond: Amen. (Cong.– *Amen.*)

Take three steps back. Bow left and say, *'He Who makes peace . . .';* bow right and say, *'may He . . .';* bow forward and say, *'and upon all Israel . . .'* Remain standing in place for a few moments, then take three steps forward.

He Who makes peace in His heights, may He, in His compassion, make peace upon us, and upon all Israel. Now respond: Amen. (Cong.– *Amen.*)

Stand while reciting עָלֵינוּ, *'It is our duty . . .'*

עָלֵינוּ *It is our duty to praise the Master of all, to ascribe greatness to the Molder of primeval creation, for He has not made us like the nations of the lands, and has not emplaced us like the families of the earth; for He has not assigned our portion like theirs nor our lot like all their multitudes. (For they bow to vanity and emptiness and pray to a god which helps not.*[5]*) But we bend our knees, bow, and acknowledge our thanks before the King Who reigns over kings, the Holy One, Blessed is He. He stretches out heaven and establishes earth's foundation,*[6] *the seat of His homage*

Bow while reciting *'But we bend our knees.'*

(1) *Isaiah* 54:13. (2) *Psalms* 119:165. (3) 122:7-9. (4) 29:11. (5) *Isaiah* 45:20. (6) 51:13.

בַּשָּׁמַיִם מִמַּעַל, וּשְׁכִינַת עֻזּוֹ בְּגָבְהֵי מְרוֹמִים. הוּא אֱלֹהֵינוּ, אֵין עוֹד.
אֱמֶת מַלְכֵּנוּ, אֶפֶס זוּלָתוֹ, כַּכָּתוּב בְּתוֹרָתוֹ: וְיָדַעְתָּ הַיּוֹם וַהֲשֵׁבֹתָ אֶל
לְבָבֶךָ, כִּי יהוה הוּא הָאֱלֹהִים בַּשָּׁמַיִם מִמַּעַל וְעַל הָאָרֶץ מִתָּחַת,
אֵין עוֹד.[1]

עַל כֵּן נְקַוֶּה לְּךָ יהוה אֱלֹהֵינוּ לִרְאוֹת מְהֵרָה בְּתִפְאֶרֶת עֻזֶּךָ,
לְהַעֲבִיר גִּלּוּלִים מִן הָאָרֶץ, וְהָאֱלִילִים כָּרוֹת יִכָּרֵתוּן,
לְתַקֵּן עוֹלָם בְּמַלְכוּת שַׁדַּי. וְכָל בְּנֵי בָשָׂר יִקְרְאוּ בִשְׁמֶךָ, לְהַפְנוֹת
אֵלֶיךָ כָּל רִשְׁעֵי אָרֶץ. יַכִּירוּ וְיֵדְעוּ כָּל יוֹשְׁבֵי תֵבֵל, כִּי לְךָ תִּכְרַע כָּל
בֶּרֶךְ, תִּשָּׁבַע כָּל לָשׁוֹן.[2] לְפָנֶיךָ יהוה אֱלֹהֵינוּ יִכְרְעוּ וְיִפֹּלוּ, וְלִכְבוֹד
שִׁמְךָ יְקָר יִתֵּנוּ. וִיקַבְּלוּ כֻלָּם אֶת עוֹל מַלְכוּתֶךָ, וְתִמְלֹךְ עֲלֵיהֶם
מְהֵרָה לְעוֹלָם וָעֶד. כִּי הַמַּלְכוּת שֶׁלְּךָ הִיא וּלְעוֹלְמֵי עַד תִּמְלוֹךְ
בְּכָבוֹד, כַּכָּתוּב בְּתוֹרָתֶךָ: יהוה יִמְלֹךְ לְעֹלָם וָעֶד.[3] ❖ וְנֶאֱמַר: וְהָיָה
יהוה לְמֶלֶךְ עַל כָּל הָאָרֶץ, בַּיּוֹם הַהוּא יִהְיֶה יהוה אֶחָד וּשְׁמוֹ אֶחָד.[4]

Some congregations recite the following after עָלֵינוּ:

אַל תִּירָא מִפַּחַד פִּתְאֹם, וּמִשֹּׁאַת רְשָׁעִים כִּי תָבֹא.[5] עֻצוּ עֵצָה וְתֻפָר,
דַּבְּרוּ דָבָר וְלֹא יָקוּם, כִּי עִמָּנוּ אֵל.[6] וְעַד זִקְנָה אֲנִי הוּא, וְעַד
שֵׂיבָה אֲנִי אֶסְבֹּל, אֲנִי עָשִׂיתִי וַאֲנִי אֶשָּׂא, וַאֲנִי אֶסְבֹּל וַאֲמַלֵּט.[7]

קדיש יתום

In the presence of a *minyan,* mourners recite קַדִּישׁ יָתוֹם, the Mourner's *Kaddish* (see *Laws* §81-83):

יִתְגַּדַּל וְיִתְקַדַּשׁ שְׁמֵהּ רַבָּא. (.Cong. – אָמֵן) בְּעָלְמָא דִּי בְרָא כִרְעוּתֵהּ.
וְיַמְלִיךְ מַלְכוּתֵהּ, בְּחַיֵּיכוֹן וּבְיוֹמֵיכוֹן וּבְחַיֵּי דְכָל בֵּית יִשְׂרָאֵל,
בַּעֲגָלָא וּבִזְמַן קָרִיב. וְאִמְרוּ: אָמֵן.

(.Cong. – אָמֵן. יְהֵא שְׁמֵהּ רַבָּא מְבָרַךְ לְעָלַם וּלְעָלְמֵי עָלְמַיָּא.)

יְהֵא שְׁמֵהּ רַבָּא מְבָרַךְ לְעָלַם וּלְעָלְמֵי עָלְמַיָּא.

יִתְבָּרַךְ וְיִשְׁתַּבַּח וְיִתְפָּאַר וְיִתְרוֹמַם וְיִתְנַשֵּׂא וְיִתְהַדָּר וְיִתְעַלֶּה
וְיִתְהַלָּל שְׁמֵהּ דְּקֻדְשָׁא בְּרִיךְ הוּא (.Cong. – בְּרִיךְ הוּא) — לְעֵלָּא מִן כָּל
בִּרְכָתָא וְשִׁירָתָא תֻּשְׁבְּחָתָא וְנֶחֱמָתָא, דַּאֲמִירָן בְּעָלְמָא. וְאִמְרוּ: אָמֵן.
(.Cong. – אָמֵן.)

יְהֵא שְׁלָמָא רַבָּא מִן שְׁמַיָּא, וְחַיִּים עָלֵינוּ וְעַל כָּל יִשְׂרָאֵל. וְאִמְרוּ:
אָמֵן. (.Cong. – אָמֵן.)

Take three steps back. Bow left and say . . . עֹשֶׂה; bow right and say . . . הוּא; bow forward and say וְעַל כָּל . . . אָמֵן. Remain standing in place for a few moments, then take three steps forward.

עֹשֶׂה שָׁלוֹם בִּמְרוֹמָיו, הוּא יַעֲשֶׂה שָׁלוֹם עָלֵינוּ, וְעַל כָּל יִשְׂרָאֵל.
וְאִמְרוּ: אָמֵן. (.Cong. – אָמֵן.)

is in the heavens above and His powerful Presence is in the loftiest heights. He is our God and there is none other. True is our King, there is nothing beside Him, as it is written in His Torah: 'You are to know this day and take to your heart that HASHEM *is the only God — in heaven above and on the earth below — there is none other.'*[1]

עַל כֵּן *Therefore we put our hope in You,* HASHEM, *our God, that we may soon see Your mighty splendor, to remove detestable idolatry from the earth, and false gods will be utterly cut off, to perfect the universe through the Almighty's sovereignty. Then all humanity will call upon Your Name, to turn all the earth's wicked toward You. All the world's inhabitants will recognize and know that to You every knee should bend, every tongue should swear.*[2] *Before You,* HASHEM, *our God, they will bend every knee and cast themselves down and to the glory of Your Name they will render homage, and they will all accept upon themselves the yoke of Your kingship that You may reign over them soon and eternally. For the kingdom is Yours and You will reign for all eternity in glory as it is written in Your Torah:* HASHEM *shall reign for all eternity.*[3] Chazzan– *And it is said:* HASHEM *will be King over all the world — on that day* HASHEM *will be One and His Name will be One.*[4]

Some congregations recite the following after *Aleinu.*

אַל תִּירָא *Do not fear sudden terror, or the holocaust of the wicked when it comes.*[5] *Plan a conspiracy and it will be annulled; speak your piece and it shall not stand, for God is with us.*[6] *Even till your seniority, I remain unchanged; and even till your ripe old age, I shall endure. I created you and I shall bear you; I shall endure and rescue.*[7]

MOURNER'S KADDISH

In the presence of a *minyan,* mourners recite קַדִּישׁ יָתוֹם, the Mourner's *Kaddish* (see *Laws* §81-83).
[A transliteration of this *Kaddish* appears on p. 1147.]

יִתְגַּדַּל *May His great Name grow exalted and sanctified* (Cong.– *Amen.*) *in the world that He created as He willed. May He give reign to His kingship in your lifetimes and in your days, and in the lifetimes of the entire Family of Israel, swiftly and soon. Now respond: Amen.*

(Cong.– *Amen. May His great Name be blessed forever and ever.*)

May His great Name be blessed forever and ever.

Blessed, praised, glorified, exalted, extolled, mighty, upraised, and lauded be the Name of the Holy One, Blessed is He (Cong.– *Blessed is He*) *— beyond any blessing and song, praise and consolation that are uttered in the world. Now respond: Amen.* (Cong.– *Amen*).

May there be abundant peace from Heaven, and life, upon us and upon all Israel. Now respond: Amen. (Cong.– *Amen.*)

Take three steps back. Bow left and say, *'He Who makes peace . . .';* bow right and say, *'may He . . .';* bow forward and say, *'and upon all Israel . . .'* Remain standing in place for a few moments, then take three steps forward.

He Who makes peace in His heights, may He make peace upon us, and upon all Israel. Now respond: Amen. (Cong.– *Amen.*)

---

(1) *Deuteronomy* 4:39. (2) Cf. *Isaiah* 45:23. (3) *Exodus* 15:18.
(4) *Zechariah* 14:9. (5) *Proverbs* 3:25. (6) *Isaiah* 8:10. (7) 46:4.

שיר הכבוד

The Ark is opened and שִׁיר הַכָּבוֹד, *The Song of Glory,* is recited responsively – the *chazzan* reciting the first verse, the congregation reciting the second and so on.

אַנְעִים זְמִירוֹת וְשִׁירִים אֶאֱרוֹג, כִּי אֵלֶיךָ נַפְשִׁי תַעֲרוֹג.
נַפְשִׁי חָמְדָה בְּצֵל יָדֶךָ, לָדַעַת כָּל רָז סוֹדֶךָ.
❖ מִדֵּי דַבְּרִי בִּכְבוֹדֶךָ, הוֹמֶה לִבִּי אֶל דּוֹדֶיךָ.
עַל כֵּן אֲדַבֵּר בְּךָ נִכְבָּדוֹת, וְשִׁמְךָ אֲכַבֵּד בְּשִׁירֵי יְדִידוֹת.
❖ אֲסַפְּרָה כְבוֹדְךָ וְלֹא רְאִיתִיךָ, אֲדַמְּךָ אֲכַנְּךָ וְלֹא יְדַעְתִּיךָ.
בְּיַד נְבִיאֶיךָ בְּסוֹד עֲבָדֶיךָ, דִּמִּיתָ הֲדַר כְּבוֹד הוֹדֶךָ.
❖ גְּדֻלָּתְךָ וּגְבוּרָתֶךָ, כִּנּוּ לְתֹקֶף פְּעֻלָּתֶךָ.
דִּמּוּ אוֹתְךָ וְלֹא כְפִי יֶשְׁךָ, וַיְשַׁוּוּךָ לְפִי מַעֲשֶׂיךָ.
❖ הִמְשִׁילוּךָ בְּרֹב חֶזְיוֹנוֹת, הִנְּךָ אֶחָד בְּכָל דִּמְיוֹנוֹת.
וַיֶּחֱזוּ בְךָ זִקְנָה וּבַחֲרוּת, וּשְׂעַר רֹאשְׁךָ בְּשֵׂיבָה וְשַׁחֲרוּת.
❖ זִקְנָה בְּיוֹם דִּין וּבַחֲרוּת בְּיוֹם קְרָב, כְּאִישׁ מִלְחָמוֹת יָדָיו לוֹ רָב.
חָבַשׁ כּוֹבַע יְשׁוּעָה בְּרֹאשׁוֹ, הוֹשִׁיעָה לּוֹ יְמִינוֹ וּזְרוֹעַ קָדְשׁוֹ.
❖ טַלְלֵי אוֹרוֹת רֹאשׁוֹ נִמְלָא, קְוֻצּוֹתָיו רְסִיסֵי לָיְלָה.
יִתְפָּאֵר בִּי כִּי חָפֵץ בִּי. וְהוּא יִהְיֶה לִּי לַעֲטֶרֶת צְבִי.
❖ כֶּתֶם טָהוֹר פָּז דְּמוּת רֹאשׁוֹ, וְחַק עַל מֵצַח כְּבוֹד שֵׁם קָדְשׁוֹ.
לְחֵן וּלְכָבוֹד צְבִי תִפְאָרָה, אֻמָּתוֹ לוֹ עִטְּרָה עֲטָרָה.
❖ מַחְלְפוֹת רֹאשׁוֹ כְּבִימֵי בְחֻרוֹת, קְוֻצּוֹתָיו תַּלְתַּלִּים שְׁחוֹרוֹת.
נְוֵה הַצֶּדֶק צְבִי תִפְאַרְתּוֹ, יַעֲלֶה נָּא עַל רֹאשׁ שִׂמְחָתוֹ.
❖ סְגֻלָּתוֹ תְּהִי בְיָדוֹ עֲטֶרֶת, וּצְנִיף מְלוּכָה צְבִי תִפְאֶרֶת.
עֲמוּסִים נְשָׂאָם עֲטֶרֶת עִנְּדָם, מֵאֲשֶׁר יָקְרוּ בְעֵינָיו כִּבְּדָם.
❖ פְּאֵרוֹ עָלַי וּפְאֵרִי עָלָיו, וְקָרוֹב אֵלַי בְּקָרְאִי אֵלָיו.
צַח וְאָדוֹם לִלְבוּשׁוֹ אָדוֹם, פּוּרָה בְּדָרְכוֹ בְּבוֹאוֹ מֵאֱדוֹם.
❖ קֶשֶׁר תְּפִלִּין הֶרְאָה לֶעָנָו, תְּמוּנַת יהוה לְנֶגֶד עֵינָיו.
רוֹצֶה בְעַמּוֹ עֲנָוִים יְפָאֵר, יוֹשֵׁב תְּהִלּוֹת בָּם לְהִתְפָּאֵר.
❖ רֹאשׁ דְּבָרְךָ אֱמֶת קוֹרֵא מֵרֹאשׁ, דּוֹר וָדוֹר עַם דּוֹרֶשְׁךָ דְּרוֹשׁ.

SONG OF GLORY

The Ark is opened and the *Song of Glory* is recited responsively — the *chazzan* reciting the first verse, the congregation reciting the second and so on.

אַנְעִים זְמִירוֹת *I shall compose pleasant psalms and weave hymns,*
because for You shall my soul pine.

My soul desired the shelter of Your hand,
to know every mystery of Your secret.

❖ *As I speak of Your glory, my heart yearns for Your love.*

Therefore I shall speak of Your glories,
and Your Name I shall honor with loving songs.

❖ *I shall relate Your glory, though I see You not;*
I shall allegorize You, I shall describe You, though I know You not.

Through the hand of Your prophets, through the counsel of Your servants;
You allegorized the splendrous glory of Your power.

❖ *Your greatness and Your strength,*
they described the might of Your works.

They allegorized You, but not according to Your reality,
and they portrayed You according to Your deeds.

❖ *They symbolized You in many varied visions;*
yet You are a Unity containing all the allegories.

They envisioned in You agedness and virility,
and the hair of Your head as hoary and jet black.

❖ *Aged on judgment day and virile on the day of battle,*
like a man of war whose powers are many.

The hat of salvation He put on His head;
salvation for Him, His right hand and His sacred arm.

❖ *With illuminating dew drops His head is filled,*
His locks are the rains of the night.

He shall glory in me for He desires me,
and He shall be for me a crown of pride.

❖ *A form of the very finest gold upon his head,*
and carved on his forehead is His glorious, sacred Name.

For grace and for glory the pride of His splendor;
His nation crowns Him with its prayers.

❖ *The tresses of His head are like His youthful days;*
His locks are jet-black ringlets.

The Abode of righteousness is the pride of His splendor;
may He elevate it to His foremost joy.

❖ *May His treasured nation be in His hand like a crown,*
and like a royal tiara the pride of His splendor.

From infancy He bore them and affixed them as a crown,
because they are precious in His eyes He honored them.

❖ *His tefillin-splendor is upon me and my tefillin-splendor is upon Him,*
and He is near to me when I call to Him.

He is white and crimson; His garment will be bloody red,
when He tramples as in a press on His coming from Edom.

❖ *He showed the tefillin-knot to the humble [Moses],*
the likeness of HASHEM *before his eyes.*

He desires His people, He will glorify the humble;
enthroned upon praises, He glories with them.

❖ *The very beginning of Your word is truth — one reads it from the*
Torah's start; the people that seeks You expounds each generation's fate.

שִׂית הֲמוֹן שִׁירַי נָא עָלֶיךָ, וְרִנָּתִי תִּקְרַב אֵלֶיךָ.
❖ תְּהִלָּתִי תְּהִי לְרֹאשְׁךָ עֲטֶרֶת, וּתְפִלָּתִי תִּכּוֹן קְטֹרֶת.
תִּיקַר שִׁירַת רָשׁ בְּעֵינֶיךָ, כַּשִּׁיר יוּשַׁר עַל קָרְבָּנֶיךָ.
❖ בִּרְכָתִי תַעֲלֶה לְרֹאשׁ מַשְׁבִּיר, מְחוֹלֵל וּמוֹלִיד צַדִּיק כַּבִּיר.
וּבְבִרְכָתִי תְנַעֲנַע לִי רֹאשׁ, וְאוֹתָהּ קַח לְךָ כִּבְשָׂמִים רֹאשׁ.
❖ יֶעֱרַב נָא שִׂיחִי עָלֶיךָ, כִּי נַפְשִׁי תַעֲרוֹג אֵלֶיךָ.

לְךָ יהוה הַגְּדֻלָּה וְהַגְּבוּרָה וְהַתִּפְאֶרֶת וְהַנֵּצַח וְהַהוֹד, כִּי כֹל בַּשָּׁמַיִם וּבָאָרֶץ; לְךָ יהוה הַמַּמְלָכָה וְהַמִּתְנַשֵּׂא לְכֹל לְרֹאשׁ.[1] מִי יְמַלֵּל גְּבוּרוֹת יהוה, יַשְׁמִיעַ כָּל תְּהִלָּתוֹ.[2]

קדיש יתום

In the presence of a *minyan,* mourners recite קַדִּישׁ יָתוֹם, the Mourner's *Kaddish* (see *Laws* §81-83):

יִתְגַּדַּל וְיִתְקַדַּשׁ שְׁמֵהּ רַבָּא. (.Cong – אָמֵן.) בְּעָלְמָא דִּי בְרָא כִרְעוּתֵהּ. וְיַמְלִיךְ מַלְכוּתֵהּ, בְּחַיֵּיכוֹן וּבְיוֹמֵיכוֹן וּבְחַיֵּי דְכָל בֵּית יִשְׂרָאֵל, בַּעֲגָלָא וּבִזְמַן קָרִיב. וְאִמְרוּ: אָמֵן.

(.Cong – אָמֵן. יְהֵא שְׁמֵהּ רַבָּא מְבָרַךְ לְעָלַם וּלְעָלְמֵי עָלְמַיָּא.)

יְהֵא שְׁמֵהּ רַבָּא מְבָרַךְ לְעָלַם וּלְעָלְמֵי עָלְמַיָּא.

יִתְבָּרַךְ וְיִשְׁתַּבַּח וְיִתְפָּאַר וְיִתְרוֹמַם וְיִתְנַשֵּׂא וְיִתְהַדָּר וְיִתְעַלֶּה וְיִתְהַלָּל שְׁמֵהּ דְּקֻדְשָׁא בְּרִיךְ הוּא (.Cong – בְּרִיךְ הוּא) — לְעֵלָּא מִן כָּל בִּרְכָתָא וְשִׁירָתָא תֻּשְׁבְּחָתָא וְנֶחֱמָתָא, דַּאֲמִירָן בְּעָלְמָא. וְאִמְרוּ: אָמֵן. (.Cong – אָמֵן.)

יְהֵא שְׁלָמָא רַבָּא מִן שְׁמַיָּא, וְחַיִּים עָלֵינוּ וְעַל כָּל יִשְׂרָאֵל. וְאִמְרוּ: אָמֵן. (.Cong – אָמֵן.)

Take three steps back. Bow left and say . . . עֹשֶׂה; bow right and say . . . הוּא; bow forward and say וְעַל כָּל . . . אָמֵן. Remain standing in place for a few moments, then take three steps forward.

עֹשֶׂה שָׁלוֹם בִּמְרוֹמָיו, הוּא יַעֲשֶׂה שָׁלוֹם עָלֵינוּ, וְעַל כָּל יִשְׂרָאֵל. וְאִמְרוּ: אָמֵן. (.Cong – אָמֵן.)

שיר של יום

הַיּוֹם יוֹם שַׁבַּת קֹדֶשׁ שֶׁבּוֹ הָיוּ הַלְוִיִּם אוֹמְרִים בְּבֵית הַמִּקְדָּשׁ:

תהלים צב

מִזְמוֹר שִׁיר לְיוֹם הַשַּׁבָּת. טוֹב לְהֹדוֹת לַיהוה, וּלְזַמֵּר לְשִׁמְךָ עֶלְיוֹן. לְהַגִּיד בַּבֹּקֶר חַסְדֶּךָ, וֶאֱמוּנָתְךָ בַּלֵּילוֹת. עֲלֵי עָשׂוֹר וַעֲלֵי נָבֶל, עֲלֵי הִגָּיוֹן בְּכִנּוֹר. כִּי שִׂמַּחְתַּנִי יהוה בְּפָעֳלֶךָ, בְּמַעֲשֵׂי יָדֶיךָ אֲרַנֵּן. מַה גָּדְלוּ מַעֲשֶׂיךָ יהוה, מְאֹד עָמְקוּ מַחְשְׁבֹתֶיךָ. אִישׁ בַּעַר לֹא יֵדָע, וּכְסִיל לֹא יָבִין אֶת זֹאת. בִּפְרֹחַ רְשָׁעִים כְּמוֹ

Place the multitude of my songs before You, please;
and my glad song bring near to You.
∴ *May my praise be a crown for Your head,*
and may my prayer be accepted like incense.
May the poor man's song be dear in Your eyes,
like the song that is sung over Your offerings.
∴ *May my blessing rise up upon the head of the Sustainer —*
Creator, Giver of life, mighty Righteous One.
And to my blessing, nod Your head to me,
and take it to Yourself like the finest incense.
∴ *May my prayer be sweet to You, for my soul shall pine for You.*

לְךָ *Yours, HASHEM, is the greatness, the strength, the splendor, the triumph, and the glory; even everything in heaven and earth; Yours, HASHEM, is the kingdom, and the sovereignty over every leader.[1] Who can express the mighty acts of HASHEM? Who can declare all His praise?[2]*

MOURNER'S KADDISH

In the presence of a *minyan,* mourners recite קַדִּישׁ יָתוֹם, the Mourner's *Kaddish* (see *Laws* §81-83). [A transliteration of this *Kaddish* appears on p. 1147.]

יִתְגַּדַּל *May His great Name grow exalted and sanctified* (Cong.– *Amen.*) *in the world that He created as He willed. May He give reign to His kingship in your lifetimes and in your days, and in the lifetimes of the entire Family of Israel, swiftly and soon. Now respond: Amen.*

(Cong.– *Amen. May His great Name be blessed forever and ever.*)

May His great Name be blessed forever and ever.

Blessed, praised, glorified, exalted, extolled, mighty, upraised, and lauded be the Name of the Holy One, Blessed is He (Cong.– *Blessed is He*) *— beyond any blessing and song, praise and consolation that are uttered in the world. Now respond: Amen.* (Cong.– *Amen*).

May there be abundant peace from Heaven, and life, upon us and upon all Israel. Now respond: Amen. (Cong.– *Amen.*)

Take three steps back. Bow left and say, *'He Who makes peace . . .';* bow right and say, *'may He . . .';* bow forward and say, *'and upon all Israel . . .'* Remain standing in place for a few moments, then take three steps forward.

He Who makes peace in His heights, may He make peace upon us, and upon all Israel. Now respond: Amen. (Cong.– *Amen.*)

SONG OF THE DAY

Today is the Holy Sabbath day,
on which the Levites would sing in the Holy Temple:

Psalm 92

מִזְמוֹר שִׁיר *A psalm, a song for the Sabbath day. It is good to thank HASHEM and to sing praise to Your Name, O Exalted One; to relate Your kindness in the dawn and Your faith in the nights. Upon ten-stringed instrument and lyre, with singing accompanied by a harp. For You have gladdened me, HASHEM, with Your deeds; at the works of Your Hands I sing glad song. How great are Your deeds, HASHEM; exceedingly profound are Your thoughts. A boor cannot know, nor can a fool understand this: when the wicked bloom like*

(1) *I Chronicles* 29:11. (2) *Psalms* 106:2.

עֵשֶׂב, וַיָּצִיצוּ כָּל פֹּעֲלֵי אָוֶן, לְהִשָּׁמְדָם עֲדֵי עַד. וְאַתָּה מָרוֹם לְעֹלָם יהוה. כִּי הִנֵּה אֹיְבֶיךָ יהוה, כִּי הִנֵּה אֹיְבֶיךָ יֹאבֵדוּ, יִתְפָּרְדוּ כָּל פֹּעֲלֵי אָוֶן. וַתָּרֶם כִּרְאֵים קַרְנִי, בַּלֹּתִי בְּשֶׁמֶן רַעֲנָן. וַתַּבֵּט עֵינִי בְּשׁוּרָי בַּקָּמִים עָלַי מְרֵעִים, תִּשְׁמַעְנָה אָזְנָי. ❖ צַדִּיק כַּתָּמָר יִפְרָח, כְּאֶרֶז בַּלְּבָנוֹן יִשְׂגֶּה. שְׁתוּלִים בְּבֵית יהוה, בְּחַצְרוֹת אֱלֹהֵינוּ יַפְרִיחוּ. עוֹד יְנוּבוּן בְּשֵׂיבָה, דְּשֵׁנִים וְרַעֲנַנִּים יִהְיוּ. לְהַגִּיד כִּי יָשָׁר יהוה, צוּרִי וְלֹא עַוְלָֽתָה בּוֹ.

In the presence of a *minyan,* mourners recite קַדִּישׁ יָתוֹם, the Mourner's *Kaddish* (page 626).

קידושא רבא

The laws governing this *Kiddush* appear on page 455.

Many omit some or all of these verses and begin with עַל כֵּן.

אִם תָּשִׁיב מִשַּׁבָּת רַגְלֶךָ, עֲשׂוֹת חֲפָצֶךָ בְּיוֹם קָדְשִׁי, וְקָרָֽאתָ לַשַּׁבָּת עֹנֶג, לִקְדוֹשׁ יהוה מְכֻבָּד, וְכִבַּדְתּוֹ מֵעֲשׂוֹת דְּרָכֶיךָ, מִמְּצוֹא חֶפְצְךָ וְדַבֵּר דָּבָר. אָז תִּתְעַנַּג עַל יהוה, וְהִרְכַּבְתִּיךָ עַל בָּֽמֳתֵי אָֽרֶץ, וְהַאֲכַלְתִּיךָ נַחֲלַת יַעֲקֹב אָבִיךָ, כִּי פִּי יהוה דִּבֵּר.[1]

וְשָׁמְרוּ בְנֵי יִשְׂרָאֵל אֶת הַשַּׁבָּת, לַעֲשׂוֹת אֶת הַשַּׁבָּת לְדֹרֹתָם בְּרִית עוֹלָם. בֵּינִי וּבֵין בְּנֵי יִשְׂרָאֵל אוֹת הִיא לְעֹלָם, כִּי שֵׁשֶׁת יָמִים עָשָׂה יהוה אֶת הַשָּׁמַיִם וְאֶת הָאָֽרֶץ, וּבַיּוֹם הַשְּׁבִיעִי שָׁבַת וַיִּנָּפַשׁ.[2]

זָכוֹר אֶת יוֹם הַשַּׁבָּת לְקַדְּשׁוֹ. שֵׁשֶׁת יָמִים תַּעֲבֹד וְעָשִׂיתָ כָּל מְלַאכְתֶּךָ. וְיוֹם הַשְּׁבִיעִי שַׁבָּת לַיהוה אֱלֹהֶיךָ, לֹא תַעֲשֶׂה כָל מְלָאכָה, אַתָּה וּבִנְךָ וּבִתֶּךָ עַבְדְּךָ וַאֲמָתְךָ וּבְהֶמְתֶּךָ, וְגֵרְךָ אֲשֶׁר בִּשְׁעָרֶיךָ. כִּי שֵׁשֶׁת יָמִים עָשָׂה יהוה אֶת הַשָּׁמַיִם וְאֶת הָאָֽרֶץ אֶת הַיָּם וְאֶת כָּל אֲשֶׁר בָּם, וַיָּֽנַח בַּיּוֹם הַשְּׁבִיעִי –

עַל כֵּן בֵּרַךְ יהוה אֶת יוֹם הַשַּׁבָּת וַיְקַדְּשֵׁהוּ.[3]

סַבְרִי מָרָנָן וְרַבָּנָן וְרַבּוֹתַי:

בָּרוּךְ אַתָּה יהוה אֱלֹהֵינוּ מֶלֶךְ הָעוֹלָם, בּוֹרֵא פְּרִי הַגָּֽפֶן.

(All present – אָמֵן.)

עַל הַמִּחְיָה appears on page 458; בִּרְכַּת הַמָּזוֹן, on page 104.

grass and all the doers of iniquity blossom — it is to destroy them till eternity. But You remain exalted forever, HASHEM. For behold! — Your enemies, HASHEM, for behold! — Your enemies shall perish, dispersed shall be all doers of iniquity. As exalted as a re'eim's shall be my pride, I will be saturated with ever-fresh oil. My eyes have seen my vigilant foes; when those who would harm me rise up against me, my ears have heard their doom. Chazzan– *A righteous man will flourish like a date palm, like a cedar in the Lebanon he will grow tall. Planted in the house of HASHEM, in the courtyards of our God they will flourish. They will still be fruitful in old age, vigorous and fresh they will be — to declare that HASHEM is just, my Rock in Whom there is no wrong.*

In the presence of a *minyan*, mourners recite קַדִּישׁ יָתוֹם, the Mourner's *Kaddish* (page 626).

KIDDUSHA RABBA

The laws governing this *Kiddush* appear on page 455.

Many omit some or all of these verses and begin with *'therefore HASHEM blessed.'*

אִם תָּשִׁיב *If you restrain, because of the Sabbath, your feet, refrain from accomplishing your own needs on My holy day; if you proclaim the Sabbath 'a delight,' the holy one of HASHEM, 'honored one,' and you honor it by not doing your own ways, from seeking your needs or discussing the forbidden. Then you shall be granted pleasure with HASHEM and I shall mount you astride the heights of the world, and provide you the heritage of your forefather Jacob — for the mouth of HASHEM has spoken.*[1]

וְשָׁמְרוּ *And the Children of Israel observed the Sabbath, to make the Sabbath for their generations an eternal covenant. Between Me and the Children of Israel it is a sign forever, that in six days did HASHEM make the heaven and the earth, and on the seventh day He rested and was refreshed.*[2]

זָכוֹר *Always remember the Sabbath day to hallow it. For six days you may labor and do all your work. But the seventh day is the Sabbath for HASHEM, Your God; you may do no work — you, your son and your daughter, your slave and your maidservant, your animal, and the stranger who is in your gates. For in six days did HASHEM make the heaven and the earth, the sea and all that is in them and He rested on the seventh day;*

therefore HASHEM blessed the Sabbath day and sanctified it.[3]

By your leave, my masters and teachers:

בָּרוּךְ *Blessed are You, HASHEM, our God, King of the universe, Who creates the fruit of the vine.* (All present – *Amen.*)

The blessing after cake and wine appears on page 458; Grace after Meals, on page 104.

---

(1) *Isaiah* 58:13-14. (2) *Exodus* 31:16-17. (3) 20:8-11.

מנחה לשבת חול המועד

אַשְׁרֵי יוֹשְׁבֵי בֵיתֶךָ, עוֹד יְהַלְלְוּךָ סֶּלָה.[1] אַשְׁרֵי הָעָם שֶׁכָּכָה לּוֹ, אַשְׁרֵי הָעָם שֶׁיהוה אֱלֹהָיו.[2]

תהלים קמה

תְּהִלָּה לְדָוִד,

אֲרוֹמִמְךָ אֱלוֹהַי הַמֶּלֶךְ, וַאֲבָרְכָה שִׁמְךָ לְעוֹלָם וָעֶד.
בְּכָל יוֹם אֲבָרְכֶךָּ, וַאֲהַלְלָה שִׁמְךָ לְעוֹלָם וָעֶד.
גָּדוֹל יהוה וּמְהֻלָּל מְאֹד, וְלִגְדֻלָּתוֹ אֵין חֵקֶר.
דּוֹר לְדוֹר יְשַׁבַּח מַעֲשֶׂיךָ, וּגְבוּרֹתֶיךָ יַגִּידוּ.
הֲדַר כְּבוֹד הוֹדֶךָ, וְדִבְרֵי נִפְלְאֹתֶיךָ אָשִׂיחָה.
וֶעֱזוּז נוֹרְאוֹתֶיךָ יֹאמֵרוּ, וּגְדוּלָּתְךָ אֲסַפְּרֶנָּה.
זֵכֶר רַב טוּבְךָ יַבִּיעוּ, וְצִדְקָתְךָ יְרַנֵּנוּ.
חַנּוּן וְרַחוּם יהוה, אֶרֶךְ אַפַּיִם וּגְדָל חָסֶד.
טוֹב יהוה לַכֹּל, וְרַחֲמָיו עַל כָּל מַעֲשָׂיו.
יוֹדְוּךָ יהוה כָּל מַעֲשֶׂיךָ, וַחֲסִידֶיךָ יְבָרְכוּכָה.
כְּבוֹד מַלְכוּתְךָ יֹאמֵרוּ, וּגְבוּרָתְךָ יְדַבֵּרוּ.
לְהוֹדִיעַ לִבְנֵי הָאָדָם גְּבוּרֹתָיו, וּכְבוֹד הֲדַר מַלְכוּתוֹ.
מַלְכוּתְךָ מַלְכוּת כָּל עֹלָמִים, וּמֶמְשַׁלְתְּךָ בְּכָל דּוֹר וָדֹר.
סוֹמֵךְ יהוה לְכָל הַנֹּפְלִים, וְזוֹקֵף לְכָל הַכְּפוּפִים.
עֵינֵי כֹל אֵלֶיךָ יְשַׂבֵּרוּ, וְאַתָּה נוֹתֵן לָהֶם אֶת אָכְלָם בְּעִתּוֹ.

While reciting the verse פּוֹתֵחַ, concentrate intently on its meaning.

פּוֹתֵחַ אֶת יָדֶךָ,
וּמַשְׂבִּיעַ לְכָל חַי רָצוֹן.
צַדִּיק יהוה בְּכָל דְּרָכָיו, וְחָסִיד בְּכָל מַעֲשָׂיו.
קָרוֹב יהוה לְכָל קֹרְאָיו, לְכֹל אֲשֶׁר יִקְרָאֻהוּ בֶאֱמֶת.
רְצוֹן יְרֵאָיו יַעֲשֶׂה, וְאֶת שַׁוְעָתָם יִשְׁמַע וְיוֹשִׁיעֵם.
שׁוֹמֵר יהוה אֶת כָּל אֹהֲבָיו, וְאֵת כָּל הָרְשָׁעִים יַשְׁמִיד.
❖ תְּהִלַּת יהוה יְדַבֶּר פִּי,
וִיבָרֵךְ כָּל בָּשָׂר שֵׁם קָדְשׁוֹ לְעוֹלָם וָעֶד.
וַאֲנַחְנוּ נְבָרֵךְ יָהּ, מֵעַתָּה וְעַד עוֹלָם, הַלְלוּיָהּ.[3]

(1) *Psalms* 84:5. (2) 144:15. (3) 115:18.

MINCHAH FOR THE SABBATH OF CHOL HAMOED

אַשְׁרֵי *Praiseworthy are those who dwell in Your house; may they always praise You, Selah![1] Praiseworthy is the people for whom this is so, praiseworthy is the people whose God is HASHEM.[2]*

Psalm 145 *A psalm of praise by David:*

א *I will exalt You, my God the King,*
and I will bless Your Name forever and ever.
ב *Every day I will bless You,*
and I will laud Your Name forever and ever.
ג *HASHEM is great and exceedingly lauded,*
and His greatness is beyond investigation.
ד *Each generation will praise Your deeds to the next*
and of Your mighty deeds they will tell.
ה *The splendrous glory of Your power*
and Your wondrous deeds I shall discuss.
ו *And of Your awesome power they will speak,*
and Your greatness I shall relate.
ז *A recollection of Your abundant goodness they will utter*
and of Your righteousness they will sing exultantly.
ח *Gracious and merciful is HASHEM,*
slow to anger, and great in [bestowing] kindness.
ט *HASHEM is good to all; His mercies are on all His works.*
י *All Your works shall thank You, HASHEM,*
and Your devout ones will bless You.
כ *Of the glory of Your kingdom they will speak,*
and of Your power they will tell;
ל *To inform human beings of His mighty deeds,*
and the glorious splendor of His kingdom.
מ *Your kingdom is a kingdom spanning all eternities,*
and Your dominion is throughout every generation.
ס *HASHEM supports all the fallen ones and straightens all the bent.*
ע *The eyes of all look to You with hope*
and You give them their food in its proper time;
פ *You open Your hand,*
and satisfy the desire of every living thing.

While reciting the verse, *'You open . . .'* concentrate intently on its meaning

צ *Righteous is HASHEM in all His ways*
and magnanimous in all His deeds.
ק *HASHEM is close to all who call upon Him —*
to all who call upon Him sincerely.
ר *The will of those who fear Him He will do;*
and their cry He will hear, and save them.
ש *HASHEM protects all who love Him;*
but all the wicked He will destroy.
ת Chazzan– *May my mouth declare the praise of HASHEM*
and may all flesh bless His Holy Name forever and ever.
We will bless God from this time and forever, Halleluyah![3]

The primary part of וּבָא לְצִיּוֹן is the *Kedushah* recited by the angels. These verses are presented in bold type and it is preferable that the congregation recite them aloud and in unison. However, the interpretive translation in Aramaic (which follows the verses in bold type) should be recited softly.

וּבָא לְצִיּוֹן גּוֹאֵל, וּלְשָׁבֵי פֶשַׁע בְּיַעֲקֹב, נְאֻם יהוה. וַאֲנִי, זֹאת בְּרִיתִי אוֹתָם, אָמַר יהוה, רוּחִי אֲשֶׁר עָלֶיךָ, וּדְבָרַי אֲשֶׁר שַׂמְתִּי בְּפִיךָ, לֹא יָמוּשׁוּ מִפִּיךָ וּמִפִּי זַרְעֲךָ וּמִפִּי זֶרַע זַרְעֲךָ, אָמַר יהוה, מֵעַתָּה וְעַד עוֹלָם:[1] ❖ וְאַתָּה קָדוֹשׁ יוֹשֵׁב תְּהִלּוֹת יִשְׂרָאֵל.[2] וְקָרָא זֶה אֶל זֶה וְאָמַר:

קָדוֹשׁ, קָדוֹשׁ, קָדוֹשׁ יהוה צְבָאוֹת, מְלֹא כָל הָאָרֶץ כְּבוֹדוֹ.[3]

וּמְקַבְּלִין דֵּין מִן דֵּין וְאָמְרִין:
קַדִּישׁ בִּשְׁמֵי מְרוֹמָא עִלָּאָה בֵּית שְׁכִינְתֵּהּ,
קַדִּישׁ עַל אַרְעָא עוֹבַד גְּבוּרְתֵּהּ,
קַדִּישׁ לְעָלַם וּלְעָלְמֵי עָלְמַיָּא, יהוה צְבָאוֹת,
מַלְיָא כָל אַרְעָא זִיו יְקָרֵהּ.[4]

❖ וַתִּשָּׂאֵנִי רוּחַ, וָאֶשְׁמַע אַחֲרַי קוֹל רַעַשׁ גָּדוֹל:

בָּרוּךְ כְּבוֹד יהוה מִמְּקוֹמוֹ.[5]

וּנְטָלַתְנִי רוּחָא, וּשְׁמָעִית בַּתְרַי קָל זִיעַ סַגִּיא דִּמְשַׁבְּחִין וְאָמְרִין:
בְּרִיךְ יְקָרָא דַיהוה מֵאֲתַר בֵּית שְׁכִינְתֵּהּ.[6]

יהוה יִמְלֹךְ לְעֹלָם וָעֶד.[7]

יהוה מַלְכוּתֵהּ קָאֵם לְעָלַם וּלְעָלְמֵי עָלְמַיָּא.[8]

יהוה אֱלֹהֵי אַבְרָהָם יִצְחָק וְיִשְׂרָאֵל אֲבֹתֵינוּ, שָׁמְרָה זֹּאת לְעוֹלָם, לְיֵצֶר מַחְשְׁבוֹת לְבַב עַמֶּךָ, וְהָכֵן לְבָבָם אֵלֶיךָ.[9] וְהוּא רַחוּם, יְכַפֵּר עָוֹן וְלֹא יַשְׁחִית, וְהִרְבָּה לְהָשִׁיב אַפּוֹ, וְלֹא יָעִיר כָּל חֲמָתוֹ.[10] כִּי אַתָּה אֲדֹנָי טוֹב וְסַלָּח, וְרַב חֶסֶד לְכָל קֹרְאֶיךָ.[11] צִדְקָתְךָ צֶדֶק לְעוֹלָם, וְתוֹרָתְךָ אֱמֶת.[12] תִּתֵּן אֱמֶת לְיַעֲקֹב, חֶסֶד לְאַבְרָהָם, אֲשֶׁר נִשְׁבַּעְתָּ לַאֲבֹתֵינוּ מִימֵי קֶדֶם.[13] בָּרוּךְ אֲדֹנָי יוֹם יוֹם יַעֲמָס לָנוּ, הָאֵל יְשׁוּעָתֵנוּ סֶלָה.[14] יהוה צְבָאוֹת עִמָּנוּ, מִשְׂגָּב לָנוּ אֱלֹהֵי יַעֲקֹב סֶלָה.[15] יהוה צְבָאוֹת, אַשְׁרֵי אָדָם בֹּטֵחַ בָּךְ.[16] יהוה הוֹשִׁיעָה, הַמֶּלֶךְ יַעֲנֵנוּ בְיוֹם קָרְאֵנוּ.[17]

בָּרוּךְ הוּא אֱלֹהֵינוּ שֶׁבְּרָאָנוּ לִכְבוֹדוֹ, וְהִבְדִּילָנוּ מִן הַתּוֹעִים, וְנָתַן לָנוּ תּוֹרַת אֱמֶת, וְחַיֵּי עוֹלָם נָטַע בְּתוֹכֵנוּ. הוּא יִפְתַּח לִבֵּנוּ

(1) *Isaiah* 59:20-21. (2) *Psalms* 22:4. (3) *Isaiah* 6:3. (4) *Targum Yonasan.* (5) *Ezekiel* 3:12. (6) *Targum Yonasan.* (7) *Exodus* 15:18. (8) *Targum Onkelos.* (9) *I Chronicles* 29:18. (10) *Psalms* 78:38. (11) 86:5. (12) 119:142. (13) *Micah* 7:20. (14) *Psalms* 68:20. (15) 46:8. (16) 84:13. (17) 20:10.

The primary part of וּבָא לְצִיּוֹן, *'A redeemer shall come . . .'*, is the *Kedushah* recited by the angels. These verses are presented in bold type and it is preferable that the congregation recite them aloud and in unison. However, the interpretive translation in Aramaic (which follows the verses in bold type) should be recited softly.

וּבָא לְצִיּוֹן *'A redeemer shall come to Zion and to those of Jacob who repent from willful sin,' the words of HASHEM. 'And as for Me, this is My covenant with them,' said HASHEM, 'My spirit that is upon you and My words that I have placed in your mouth shall not be withdrawn from your mouth, nor from the mouth of your offspring, nor from the mouth of your offspring's offspring,' said HASHEM, 'from this moment and forever.'*[1] Chazzan– *You are the Holy One, enthroned upon the praises of Israel.*[2] *And one [angel] will call another and say:*

'Holy, holy, holy is HASHEM, Master of Legions,
the whole world is filled with His glory.'[3]

And they receive permission from one another and say:
'Holy in the most exalted heaven, the abode of His Presence;
holy on earth, product of His strength;
holy forever and ever is HASHEM, Master of Legions —
the entire world is filled with the radiance of His glory.'[4]

Chazzan– *And a wind lifted me; and I heard behind me*
the sound of a great noise:

'Blessed is the glory of HASHEM from His place.'[5]

And a wind lifted me and I heard behind me the sound
of the powerful movement of those who praised saying:
'Blessed is the honor of HASHEM
from the place of the abode of His Presence.'[6]

HASHEM shall reign for all eternity.[7]

HASHEM — His kingdom is established forever and ever.[8]

HASHEM, God of Abraham, Isaac, and Israel, our forefathers, may You preserve this forever as the realization of the thoughts in Your people's heart, and may You direct their heart to You.[9] *He, the Merciful One, is forgiving of iniquity and does not destroy; frequently He withdraws His anger, not arousing His entire rage.*[10] *For You, my Lord, are good and forgiving, and abundantly kind to all who call upon You.*[11] *Your righteousness remains righteous forever, and Your Torah is truth.*[12] *Grant truth to Jacob, kindness to Abraham, as You swore to our forefathers from ancient times.*[13] *Blessed is my Lord for every single day, He burdens us with blessings, the God of our salvation, Selah.*[14] *HASHEM, Master of Legions, is with us, a stronghold for us is the God of Jacob, Selah.*[15] *HASHEM, Master of Legions, praiseworthy is the man who trusts in You.*[16] *HASHEM, save! May the King answer us on the day we call.*[17]

Blessed is He, our God, Who created us for His glory, separated us from those who stray, gave us the Torah of truth and implanted eternal life within us. May He open our heart through His Torah and imbue our

בְּתוֹרָתוֹ, וְיָשֵׂם בְּלִבֵּנוּ אַהֲבָתוֹ וְיִרְאָתוֹ וְלַעֲשׂוֹת רְצוֹנוֹ וּלְעָבְדוֹ בְּלֵבָב שָׁלֵם, לְמַעַן לֹא נִיגַע לָרִיק, וְלֹא נֵלֵד לַבֶּהָלָה.[1]

יְהִי רָצוֹן מִלְּפָנֶיךָ יהוה אֱלֹהֵינוּ וֵאלֹהֵי אֲבוֹתֵינוּ, שֶׁנִּשְׁמֹר חֻקֶּיךָ בָּעוֹלָם הַזֶּה, וְנִזְכֶּה וְנִחְיֶה וְנִרְאֶה וְנִירַשׁ טוֹבָה וּבְרָכָה לִשְׁנֵי יְמוֹת הַמָּשִׁיחַ וּלְחַיֵּי הָעוֹלָם הַבָּא. לְמַעַן יְזַמֶּרְךָ כָבוֹד וְלֹא יִדֹּם, יהוה אֱלֹהַי לְעוֹלָם אוֹדֶךָּ.[2] בָּרוּךְ הַגֶּבֶר אֲשֶׁר יִבְטַח בַּיהוה, וְהָיָה יהוה מִבְטַחוֹ.[3] בִּטְחוּ בַיהוה עֲדֵי עַד, כִּי בְּיָהּ יהוה צוּר עוֹלָמִים.[4] ❖ וְיִבְטְחוּ בְךָ יוֹדְעֵי שְׁמֶךָ, כִּי לֹא עָזַבְתָּ דֹּרְשֶׁיךָ, יהוה.[5] יהוה חָפֵץ לְמַעַן צִדְקוֹ, יַגְדִּיל תּוֹרָה וְיַאְדִּיר.[6]

Chazzan recites חֲצִי קַדִּישׁ.

יִתְגַּדַּל וְיִתְקַדַּשׁ שְׁמֵהּ רַבָּא. (.Cong – אָמֵן.) בְּעָלְמָא דִּי בְרָא כִרְעוּתֵהּ. וְיַמְלִיךְ מַלְכוּתֵהּ, בְּחַיֵּיכוֹן וּבְיוֹמֵיכוֹן וּבְחַיֵּי דְכָל בֵּית יִשְׂרָאֵל, בַּעֲגָלָא וּבִזְמַן קָרִיב. וְאִמְרוּ: אָמֵן.

(.Cong – אָמֵן. יְהֵא שְׁמֵהּ רַבָּא מְבָרַךְ לְעָלַם וּלְעָלְמֵי עָלְמַיָּא.)

יְהֵא שְׁמֵהּ רַבָּא מְבָרַךְ לְעָלַם וּלְעָלְמֵי עָלְמַיָּא.

יִתְבָּרַךְ וְיִשְׁתַּבַּח וְיִתְפָּאַר וְיִתְרוֹמַם וְיִתְנַשֵּׂא וְיִתְהַדָּר וְיִתְעַלֶּה וְיִתְהַלָּל שְׁמֵהּ דְּקֻדְשָׁא בְּרִיךְ הוּא (.Cong – בְּרִיךְ הוּא) – לְעֵֽלָּא מִן כָּל בִּרְכָתָא וְשִׁירָתָא תֻּשְׁבְּחָתָא וְנֶחֱמָתָא, דַּאֲמִירָן בְּעָלְמָא. וְאִמְרוּ: אָמֵן. (.Cong – אָמֵן.)

Congregation, then *chazzan:*

וַאֲנִי תְפִלָּתִי לְךָ יהוה עֵת רָצוֹן, אֱלֹהִים בְּרָב חַסְדֶּךָ, עֲנֵנִי בֶּאֱמֶת יִשְׁעֶךָ.[7]

הוצאת ספר תורה

From the moment the Ark is opened until the Torah is returned to it, one must conduct himself with the utmost respect, and avoid unnecessary conversation. It is commendable to kiss the Torah as it is carried to the *bimah* [reading table] and back to the Ark.

All rise and remain standing until the Torah is placed on the *bimah*.
The Ark is opened; before the Torah is removed, the congregation recites:

וַיְהִי בִּנְסֹעַ הָאָרֹן, וַיֹּאמֶר מֹשֶׁה, קוּמָה יהוה וְיָפֻצוּ אֹיְבֶיךָ, וְיָנֻסוּ מְשַׂנְאֶיךָ מִפָּנֶיךָ.[8] כִּי מִצִּיּוֹן תֵּצֵא תוֹרָה, וּדְבַר יהוה מִירוּשָׁלָיִם.[9] בָּרוּךְ שֶׁנָּתַן תּוֹרָה לְעַמּוֹ יִשְׂרָאֵל בִּקְדֻשָּׁתוֹ.

זוהר ויקהל שסט:א

בְּרִיךְ שְׁמֵהּ דְּמָרֵא עָלְמָא, בְּרִיךְ כִּתְרָךְ וְאַתְרָךְ. יְהֵא רְעוּתָךְ עִם עַמָּךְ יִשְׂרָאֵל לְעָלַם, וּפֻרְקַן יְמִינָךְ אַחֲזֵי לְעַמָּךְ בְּבֵית מַקְדְּשָׁךְ, וּלְאַמְטוּיֵי לָנָא מִטּוּב נְהוֹרָךְ, וּלְקַבֵּל צְלוֹתָנָא בְּרַחֲמִין. יְהֵא רַעֲוָא קֳדָמָךְ, דְּתוֹרִיךְ לָן חַיִּין בְּטִיבוּתָא, וְלֶהֱוֵי אֲנָא פְקִידָא בְּגוֹ צַדִּיקַיָּא,

heart with love and awe of Him and that we may do His will and serve Him wholeheartedly, so that we do not struggle in vain nor produce for futility.[1]

May it be Your will, HASHEM, our God and the God of our forefathers, that we observe Your decrees in This World, and merit that we live and see and inherit goodness and blessing in the years of Messianic times and for the life of the World to Come. So that my soul might sing to You and not be stilled, HASHEM, my God, forever will I thank You.[2] *Blessed is the man who trusts in HASHEM, then HASHEM will be his security.*[3] *Trust in HASHEM forever, for in God, HASHEM, is the strength of the worlds.*[4] Chazzan– *Those knowing Your Name will trust in You, and You forsake not those Who seek You, HASHEM.*[5] *HASHEM desired, for the sake of its [Israel's] righteousness, that the Torah be made great and glorious.*[6]

Chazzan recites Half-*Kaddish.*

יִתְגַּדַּל *May His great Name grow exalted and sanctified* (Cong.– *Amen.*) *in the world that He created as He willed. May He give reign to His kingship in your lifetimes and in your days, and in the lifetimes of the entire Family of Israel, swiftly and soon. Now respond: Amen.*

(Cong.– *Amen. May His great Name be blessed forever and ever.*)

May His great Name be blessed forever and ever.

Blessed, praised, glorified, exalted, extolled, mighty, upraised, and lauded be the Name of the Holy One, Blessed is He (Cong.– *Blessed is He*) — *beyond any blessing and song, praise and consolation that are uttered in the world. Now respond: Amen.* (Cong.– *Amen.*)

Congregation, then *chazzan:*

וַאֲנִי תְפִלָּתִי *As for me, may my prayer to You, HASHEM, be at an opportune time; O God, in Your abundant kindness, answer me with the truth of Your salvation.*[7]

REMOVAL OF THE TORAH FROM THE ARK

From the moment the Ark is opened until the Torah is returned to it, one must conduct himself with the utmost respect, and avoid unnecessary conversation. It is commendable to kiss the Torah as it is carried to the *bimah* [reading table] and back to the Ark.

All rise and remain standing until the Torah is placed on the *bimah.*
The Ark is opened; before the Torah is removed, the congregation recites:

וַיְהִי בִּנְסֹעַ *When the Ark would travel, Moses would say, 'Arise, HASHEM, and let Your foes be scattered, let those who hate You flee from You.'*[8] *For from Zion will the Torah come forth and the word of HASHEM from Jerusalem.*[9] *Blessed is He Who gave the Torah to His people Israel in His holiness.*

Zohar, Vayakhel 369a

בְּרִיךְ שְׁמֵהּ *Blessed is the Name of the Master of the universe, blessed is Your crown and Your place. May Your favor remain with Your people Israel forever; may You display the salvation of Your right hand to Your people in Your Holy Temple, to benefit us with the goodness of Your luminescence and to accept our prayers with mercy. May it be Your will that You extend our lives with goodness and that I be numbered among the righteous; that*

(1) Cf. *Isaiah* 65:23. (2) *Psalms* 30:13. (3) *Jeremiah* 17:7. (4) *Isaiah* 26:4.
(5) *Psalms* 9:11. (6) *Isaiah* 42:21. (7) *Psalms* 69:14. (8) *Numbers* 10:35. (9) *Isaiah* 2:3.

לְמִרְחַם עֲלַי וּלְמִנְטַר יָתִי וְיַת כָּל דִּי לִי וְדִי לְעַמָּךְ יִשְׂרָאֵל. אַנְתְּ הוּא זָן לְכֹלָּא, וּמְפַרְנֵס לְכֹלָּא, אַנְתְּ הוּא שַׁלִּיט עַל כֹּלָּא. אַנְתְּ הוּא דְּשַׁלִּיט עַל מַלְכַיָּא, וּמַלְכוּתָא דִּילָךְ הִיא. אֲנָא עַבְדָּא דְקֻדְשָׁא בְּרִיךְ הוּא, דְּסָגִידְנָא קַמֵּהּ וּמִקַּמָּא דִּיקַר אוֹרַיְתֵהּ בְּכָל עִדָּן וְעִדָּן. לָא עַל אֱנָשׁ רָחִיצְנָא, וְלָא עַל בַּר אֱלָהִין סָמֵיכְנָא, אֶלָּא בֶּאֱלָהָא דִשְׁמַיָּא, דְּהוּא אֱלָהָא קְשׁוֹט, וְאוֹרַיְתֵהּ קְשׁוֹט, וּנְבִיאוֹהִי קְשׁוֹט, וּמַסְגֵּא לְמֶעְבַּד טַבְוָן וּקְשׁוֹט. בֵּהּ אֲנָא רָחִיץ, וְלִשְׁמֵהּ קַדִּישָׁא יַקִּירָא אֲנָא אֵמַר תֻּשְׁבְּחָן. יְהֵא רַעֲוָא קֳדָמָךְ, דְּתִפְתַּח לִבָּאִי בְּאוֹרַיְתָא, וְתַשְׁלִים מִשְׁאֲלִין דְּלִבָּאִי, וְלִבָּא דְכָל עַמָּךְ יִשְׂרָאֵל, לְטַב וּלְחַיִּין וְלִשְׁלָם. (אָמֵן.)

The Torah is removed from the Ark and presented to the *chazzan,* who accepts it in his right arm. He then turns to the Ark and raises the Torah slightly as he bows and recites:

גַּדְּלוּ לַיהוה אִתִּי, וּנְרוֹמְמָה שְׁמוֹ יַחְדָּו.[1]

The *chazzan* turns to his right and carries the Torah to the *bimah,* as the congregation responds:

לְךָ יהוה הַגְּדֻלָּה וְהַגְּבוּרָה וְהַתִּפְאֶרֶת וְהַנֵּצַח וְהַהוֹד, כִּי כֹל בַּשָּׁמַיִם וּבָאָרֶץ, לְךָ יהוה הַמַּמְלָכָה וְהַמִּתְנַשֵּׂא לְכֹל לְרֹאשׁ.[2] רוֹמְמוּ יהוה אֱלֹהֵינוּ וְהִשְׁתַּחֲווּ לַהֲדֹם רַגְלָיו, קָדוֹשׁ הוּא. רוֹמְמוּ יהוה אֱלֹהֵינוּ וְהִשְׁתַּחֲווּ לְהַר קָדְשׁוֹ, כִּי קָדוֹשׁ יהוה אֱלֹהֵינוּ.[3]

אַב הָרַחֲמִים הוּא יְרַחֵם עַם עֲמוּסִים, וְיִזְכֹּר בְּרִית אֵיתָנִים, וְיַצִּיל נַפְשׁוֹתֵינוּ מִן הַשָּׁעוֹת הָרָעוֹת, וְיִגְעַר בְּיֵצֶר הָרָע מִן הַנְּשׂוּאִים, וְיָחֹן אוֹתָנוּ לִפְלֵיטַת עוֹלָמִים, וִימַלֵּא מִשְׁאֲלוֹתֵינוּ בְּמִדָּה טוֹבָה יְשׁוּעָה וְרַחֲמִים.

The Torah is placed on the *bimah* and prepared for reading.

The *gabbai* uses the following formula to call a *Kohen* to the Torah:

וְתִגָּלֶה וְתֵרָאֶה מַלְכוּתוֹ עָלֵינוּ בִּזְמַן קָרוֹב, וְיָחֹן פְּלֵיטָתֵנוּ וּפְלֵיטַת עַמּוֹ בֵּית יִשְׂרָאֵל לְחֵן וּלְחֶסֶד וּלְרַחֲמִים וּלְרָצוֹן. וְנֹאמַר אָמֵן. הַכֹּל הָבוּ גֹדֶל לֵאלֹהֵינוּ וּתְנוּ כָבוֹד לַתּוֹרָה. כֹּהֵן° קְרָב, יַעֲמֹד (insert name) הַכֹּהֵן.

°If no *Kohen* is present, the *gabbai* says: "אֵין כַּאן כֹּהֵן, יַעֲמֹד (name) יִשְׂרָאֵל (לֵוִי) בִּמְקוֹם כֹּהֵן."

בָּרוּךְ שֶׁנָּתַן תּוֹרָה לְעַמּוֹ יִשְׂרָאֵל בִּקְדֻשָּׁתוֹ. (תּוֹרַת יהוה תְּמִימָה מְשִׁיבַת נָפֶשׁ, עֵדוּת יהוה נֶאֱמָנָה מַחְכִּימַת פֶּתִי. פִּקּוּדֵי יהוה יְשָׁרִים מְשַׂמְּחֵי לֵב, מִצְוַת יהוה בָּרָה מְאִירַת עֵינָיִם.[4] יהוה עֹז לְעַמּוֹ יִתֵּן, יהוה יְבָרֵךְ אֶת עַמּוֹ בַשָּׁלוֹם.[5] הָאֵל תָּמִים דַּרְכּוֹ, אִמְרַת יהוה צְרוּפָה, מָגֵן הוּא לְכֹל הַחֹסִים בּוֹ.[6])

Congregation, then *gabbai*:

וְאַתֶּם הַדְּבֵקִים בַּיהוה אֱלֹהֵיכֶם, חַיִּים כֻּלְּכֶם הַיּוֹם:[7]

You have mercy on me and protect me, all that is mine and that is Your people Israel's. It is You Who nourishes all and sustains all, You control everything. It is You Who control kings, and Kingship is Yours. I am a servant of the Holy One, Blessed is He, and I prostrate myself before Him and before the glory of His Torah at all times. Not in any man do I put trust, nor on any angel do I rely — only on the God of heaven Who is the God of truth, Whose Torah is truth and Whose prophets are true and Who acts liberally with kindness and truth. In Him do I trust, and to His glorious and Holy Name do I declare praises. May it be Your will that You open my heart to the Torah and that You fulfill the wishes of my heart and the heart of Your entire people Israel for good, for life, and for peace. (Amen.)

The Torah is removed from the Ark and presented to the *chazzan,* who accepts it in his right arm. He then turns to the Ark and raises the Torah slightly as he bows and recites:

Declare the greatness of HASHEM with me, and let us exalt His Name together.[1]

The *chazzan* turns to his right and carries the Torah to the *bimah,* as the congregation responds:

לְךָ *Yours, HASHEM, is the greatness, the strength, the splendor, the triumph, and the glory; even everything in heaven and earth; Yours, HASHEM, is the kingdom, and the sovereignty over every leader.*[2] *Exalt HASHEM, our God, and bow at His footstool; He is Holy! Exalt HASHEM, our God, and bow at His holy mountain; for holy is HASHEM, our God.*[3]

אַב הָרַחֲמִים *May the Father of mercy have mercy on the nation that is borne by Him, and may He remember the covenant of the spiritually mighty. May He rescue our souls from the bad times, and upbraid the evil inclination to leave those borne by Him, graciously make us an eternal remnant, and fulfill our requests in good measure, for salvation and mercy.*

The Torah is placed on the *bimah* and prepared for reading.
The *gabbai* uses the following formula to call a *Kohen* to the Torah:

וְתִגָּלֶה *And may His kingship over us be revealed and become visible soon, and may He be gracious to our remnant and the remnant of His people the Family of Israel, for graciousness, kindness, mercy, and favor. And let us respond, Amen. All of you ascribe greatness to our God and give honor to the Torah. Kohen,*° *approach. Stand* (name) *son of* (father's name) *the Kohen.*

°If no *Kohen* is present, the *gabbai* says: *'There is no Kohen present, stand* (name) *son of* (father's name) *an Israelite (Levite) in place of the Kohen.'*

Blessed is He Who gave the Torah to His people Israel in His holiness (The Torah of HASHEM is perfect, restoring the soul; the testimony of HASHEM is trustworthy, making the simple one wise. The orders of HASHEM are upright, gladdening the heart; the command of HASHEM is clear, enlightening the eyes.[4] *HASHEM will give might to His people; HASHEM will bless His people with peace.*[5] *The God Whose way is perfect, the promise of HASHEM is flawless, He is a shield for all who take refuge in Him.*[6]*)*

Congregation, then *gabbai:*

You who cling to HASHEM your God—you are all alive today.[7]

---

(1) *Psalms* 34:4. (2) *I Chronicles* 29:11. (3) *Psalms* 99:5,9.
(4) 19:8-9. (5) 29:11. (6) 18:31. (7) *Deuteronomy* 4:4.

קריאת התורה

The reader shows the *oleh* (person called to the Torah) the place in the Torah. The *oleh* touches the Torah with a corner of his *tallis,* or the belt or mantle of the Torah, and kisses it. He then begins the blessing, bowing at בָּרְכוּ, and straightening up at 'ה.

בָּרְכוּ אֶת יהוה הַמְּבֹרָךְ.

Congregation, followed by *oleh,* responds, bowing at בָּרוּךְ, and straightening up at 'ה.

בָּרוּךְ יהוה הַמְּבֹרָךְ לְעוֹלָם וָעֶד.

***Oleh* continues:**

בָּרוּךְ אַתָּה יהוה אֱלֹהֵינוּ מֶלֶךְ הָעוֹלָם, אֲשֶׁר בָּחַר בָּנוּ מִכָּל הָעַמִּים, וְנָתַן לָנוּ אֶת תּוֹרָתוֹ. בָּרוּךְ אַתָּה יהוה, נוֹתֵן הַתּוֹרָה.

(–Cong. אָמֵן.)

After his Torah portion has been read, the *oleh* recites:

בָּרוּךְ אַתָּה יהוה אֱלֹהֵינוּ מֶלֶךְ הָעוֹלָם, אֲשֶׁר נָתַן לָנוּ תּוֹרַת אֱמֶת, וְחַיֵּי עוֹלָם נָטַע בְּתוֹכֵנוּ. בָּרוּךְ אַתָּה יהוה, נוֹתֵן הַתּוֹרָה.

(–Cong. אָמֵן.)

THE VARIOUS מִי שֶׁבֵּרַךְ PRAYERS APPEAR ON PAGE 368.

The Torah reading at *Minchah* on *Shabbos* corresponds to the *sidrah* read on the *Shabbos* following Pesach. This reading is from *Shemini, Acharei Mos,* or *Kedoshim*.

פרשת שמיני

ויקרא ט:א-טז

כהן – וַיְהִי֙ בַּיּ֣וֹם הַשְּׁמִינִ֔י קָרָ֣א מֹשֶׁ֔ה לְאַהֲרֹ֖ן וּלְבָנָ֑יו וּלְזִקְנֵ֖י יִשְׂרָאֵֽל: וַיֹּ֣אמֶר אֶֽל־אַהֲרֹ֗ן קַח־לְךָ֞ עֵ֧גֶל בֶּן־בָּקָ֛ר לְחַטָּ֖את וְאַ֣יִל לְעֹלָ֑ה תְּמִימִ֕ם וְהַקְרֵ֖ב לִפְנֵ֥י יהוה: וְאֶל־בְּנֵ֥י יִשְׂרָאֵ֖ל תְּדַבֵּ֣ר לֵאמֹ֑ר קְח֤וּ שְׂעִיר־עִזִּים֙ לְחַטָּ֔את וְעֵ֨גֶל וָכֶ֧בֶשׂ בְּנֵֽי־שָׁנָ֛ה תְּמִימִ֖ם לְעֹלָֽה: וְשׁ֨וֹר וָאַ֜יִל לִשְׁלָמִ֗ים לִזְבֹּ֙חַ֙ לִפְנֵ֣י יהוה וּמִנְחָ֖ה בְּלוּלָ֣ה בַשָּׁ֑מֶן כִּ֣י הַיּ֔וֹם יהוה נִרְאָ֥ה אֲלֵיכֶֽם: וַיִּקְח֗וּ אֵ֚ת אֲשֶׁ֣ר צִוָּ֣ה מֹשֶׁ֔ה אֶל־פְּנֵ֖י אֹ֣הֶל מוֹעֵ֑ד וַיִּקְרְבוּ֙ כָּל־הָ֣עֵדָ֔ה וַיַּֽעַמְד֖וּ לִפְנֵ֥י יהוה: וַיֹּ֣אמֶר מֹשֶׁ֔ה זֶ֧ה הַדָּבָ֛ר אֲשֶׁר־צִוָּ֥ה יהוה תַּעֲשׂ֑וּ וְיֵרָ֥א אֲלֵיכֶ֖ם כְּב֥וֹד יהוה:

לוי – וַיֹּ֨אמֶר מֹשֶׁ֜ה אֶֽל־אַהֲרֹ֗ן קְרַ֤ב אֶל־הַמִּזְבֵּ֙חַ֙ וַעֲשֵׂ֞ה אֶת־חַטָּֽאתְךָ֙ וְאֶת־עֹ֣לָתֶ֔ךָ וְכַפֵּ֥ר בַּֽעַדְךָ֖ וּבְעַ֣ד הָעָ֑ם וַעֲשֵׂ֞ה אֶת־קָרְבַּ֤ן הָעָם֙ וְכַפֵּ֣ר בַּעֲדָ֔ם כַּאֲשֶׁ֖ר צִוָּ֥ה יהוה: וַיִּקְרַ֥ב אַהֲרֹ֖ן אֶל־הַמִּזְבֵּ֑חַ וַיִּשְׁחַ֛ט אֶת־עֵ֥גֶל הַֽחַטָּ֖את אֲשֶׁר־לֽוֹ: וַ֠יַּקְרִבוּ בְּנֵ֨י אַהֲרֹ֥ן אֶת־הַדָּם֮ אֵלָיו֒ וַיִּטְבֹּ֤ל אֶצְבָּעוֹ֙ בַּדָּ֔ם וַיִּתֵּ֖ן עַל־קַרְנ֣וֹת הַמִּזְבֵּ֑חַ וְאֶת־הַדָּ֣ם יָצַ֔ק אֶל־יְס֖וֹד הַמִּזְבֵּֽחַ: וְאֶת־הַחֵ֨לֶב וְאֶת־הַכְּלָיֹ֜ת וְאֶת־הַיֹּתֶ֤רֶת מִן־הַכָּבֵד֙ מִן־הַ֣חַטָּ֔את הִקְטִ֖יר הַמִּזְבֵּ֑חָה כַּאֲשֶׁ֛ר צִוָּ֥ה יהוה אֶת־מֹשֶֽׁה:

ישראל – וְאֶת־הַבָּשָׂ֖ר וְאֶת־הָע֑וֹר שָׂרַ֣ף בָּאֵ֔שׁ מִח֖וּץ לַֽמַּחֲנֶֽה: וַיִּשְׁחַ֖ט אֶת־הָֽעֹלָ֑ה וַ֠יַּמְצִאוּ בְּנֵ֨י אַהֲרֹ֤ן אֵלָיו֙ אֶת־הַדָּ֔ם וַיִּזְרְקֵ֥הוּ עַל־הַמִּזְבֵּ֖חַ סָבִֽיב: וְאֶת־הָעֹלָ֗ה הִמְצִ֧יאוּ אֵלָ֛יו לִנְתָחֶ֖יהָ וְאֶת־הָרֹ֑אשׁ וַיַּקְטֵ֖ר

READING OF THE TORAH

The reader shows the *oleh* (person called to the Torah) the place in the Torah. The *oleh* touches the Torah with a corner of his *tallis,* or the belt or mantle of the Torah, and kisses it. He then begins the blessing, bowing at *'Bless,'* and straightening up at 'HASHEM':

Bless HASHEM, the blessed One.

Congregation, followed by *oleh,* responds, bowing at 'Blessed,' and straightening up at 'HASHEM.'

Blessed is HASHEM, the blessed One, for all eternity.

Oleh continues:

בָּרוּךְ *Blessed are You, HASHEM, our God, King of the universe, Who selected us from all the peoples and gave us His Torah. Blessed are You, HASHEM, Giver of the Torah.* (Cong.— *Amen.)*

After his Torah portion has been read, the *oleh* recites:

בָּרוּךְ *Blessed are You, HASHEM, our God, King of the universe, Who gave us the Torah of truth and implanted eternal life within us. Blessed are You, HASHEM, Giver of the Torah.* (Cong.— *Amen.)*

THE VARIOUS *MI SHEBEIRACH* PRAYERS APPEAR ON PAGE 368.

The Torah reading at *Minchah* on *Shabbos* corresponds to the *sidrah* read on the *Shabbos* following Pesach. This reading is from *Shemini, Acharei Mos,* or *Kedoshim.*

PARASHAS SHEMINI

Leviticus 9:1-16

Kohen – *It was on the eighth day, Moses summoned Aaron and his sons, and the elders of Israel. He said to Aaron: Take yourself a young bull for a sin-offering and a ram for an elevation-offering — unblemished; and offer them before HASHEM. And to the Children of Israel speak as follows: Take a he-goat for a sin-offering, and a calf and a sheep in their first year — unblemished — for an elevation-offering. And a bull and a ram for a peace-offering to slaughter before HASHEM, and a meal-offering mixed with oil; for today HASHEM appears to you.*

They took what Moses had commanded to the front of the Tent of Meeting; the entire assembly approached and stood before HASHEM. Moses said: This is the thing that HASHEM has commanded you to do; then the glory of HASHEM will appear to you.

Levi – *Moses said to Aaron: Come near to the Altar and perform the service of your sin-offering and your elevation-offering and effect atonement for yourself and for the people; then perform the service of the people's offering and effect atonement for them, as HASHEM has commanded.*

Aaron came near to the Altar, and slaughtered the sin-offering calf that was his own. The sons of Aaron brought the blood to him. He dipped his finger into the blood and placed it upon the corners of the Altar, and he poured the blood upon the foundation of the Altar. The fats, the kidneys, and the diaphragm with the liver of the sin-offering, he caused to go up in smoke on the Altar, as HASHEM had commanded Moses.

Third – *The flesh and the hide he burned in fire outside the camp. He slaughtered the elevation-offering; the sons of Aaron presented the blood to him and he threw it upon the Altar, all around. They presented the elevation-offering to him in its pieces with the head; and he caused it to go up in smoke*

עַל־הַמִּזְבֵּחַ: וַיִּרְחַ֣ץ אֶת־הַקֶּ֗רֶב וְאֶת־הַכְּרָעַ֑יִם וַיַּקְטֵ֥ר עַל־הָעֹלָ֖ה
הַמִּזְבֵּ֑חָה: וַיַּקְרֵ֖ב אֵ֣ת קָרְבַּ֣ן הָעָ֑ם וַיִּקַּ֞ח אֶת־שְׂעִ֤יר הַֽחַטָּאת֙ אֲשֶׁ֣ר
לָעָ֔ם וַיִּשְׁחָטֵ֥הוּ וַֽיְחַטְּאֵ֖הוּ כָּרִאשֽׁוֹן: וַיַּקְרֵ֖ב אֶת־הָעֹלָ֑ה וַיַּֽעֲשֶׂ֖הָ
כַּמִּשְׁפָּֽט:

פרשת אחרי מות

ויקרא טז:א-יז

כהן – וַיְדַבֵּ֤ר יְהוָה֙ אֶל־מֹשֶׁ֔ה אַֽחֲרֵ֣י מ֔וֹת שְׁנֵ֖י בְּנֵ֣י אַֽהֲרֹ֑ן בְּקָרְבָתָ֥ם
לִפְנֵֽי־יְהוָ֖ה וַיָּמֻֽתוּ: וַיֹּ֨אמֶר יְהוָ֜ה אֶל־מֹשֶׁ֗ה דַּבֵּר֮ אֶל־אַֽהֲרֹ֣ן אָחִיךָ֒
וְאַל־יָבֹ֤א בְכָל־עֵת֙ אֶל־הַקֹּ֔דֶשׁ מִבֵּ֖ית לַפָּרֹ֑כֶת אֶל־פְּנֵ֨י הַכַּפֹּ֜רֶת אֲשֶׁ֤ר
עַל־הָֽאָרֹן֙ וְלֹ֣א יָמ֔וּת כִּ֚י בֶּֽעָנָ֔ן אֵֽרָאֶ֖ה עַל־הַכַּפֹּֽרֶת: בְּזֹ֛את יָבֹ֥א אַֽהֲרֹ֖ן
אֶל־הַקֹּ֑דֶשׁ בְּפַ֧ר בֶּן־בָּקָ֛ר לְחַטָּ֖את וְאַ֥יִל לְעֹלָֽה: כְּתֹֽנֶת־בַּ֨ד קֹ֜דֶשׁ יִלְבָּ֗שׁ
וּמִכְנְסֵי־בַד֮ יִהְי֣וּ עַל־בְּשָׂרוֹ֒ וּבְאַבְנֵ֥ט בַּד֙ יַחְגֹּ֔ר וּבְמִצְנֶ֥פֶת בַּ֖ד יִצְנֹ֑ף
בִּגְדֵי־קֹ֣דֶשׁ הֵ֔ם וְרָחַ֥ץ בַּמַּ֛יִם אֶת־בְּשָׂר֖וֹ וּלְבֵשָֽׁם: וּמֵאֵ֗ת עֲדַ֨ת בְּנֵ֤י
יִשְׂרָאֵל֙ יִקַּ֗ח שְׁנֵֽי־שְׂעִירֵ֥י עִזִּ֛ים לְחַטָּ֖את וְאַ֥יִל אֶחָ֖ד לְעֹלָֽה: וְהִקְרִ֧יב
אַֽהֲרֹ֛ן אֶת־פַּ֥ר הַֽחַטָּ֖את אֲשֶׁר־ל֑וֹ וְכִפֶּ֥ר בַּֽעֲד֖וֹ וּבְעַ֥ד בֵּיתֽוֹ:

לוי – וְלָקַ֖ח אֶת־שְׁנֵ֣י הַשְּׂעִירִ֑ם וְהֶֽעֱמִ֤יד אֹתָם֙ לִפְנֵ֣י יְהוָ֔ה פֶּ֖תַח אֹ֥הֶל
מוֹעֵֽד: וְנָתַ֧ן אַֽהֲרֹ֛ן עַל־שְׁנֵ֥י הַשְּׂעִירִ֖ם גֹּֽרָל֑וֹת גּוֹרָ֤ל אֶחָד֙ לַֽיהוָ֔ה וְגוֹרָ֥ל
אֶחָ֖ד לַֽעֲזָאזֵֽל: וְהִקְרִ֤יב אַֽהֲרֹן֙ אֶת־הַשָּׂעִ֔יר אֲשֶׁ֨ר עָלָ֥ה עָלָ֛יו הַגּוֹרָ֖ל
לַֽיהוָ֑ה וְעָשָׂ֖הוּ חַטָּֽאת: וְהַשָּׂעִ֗יר אֲשֶׁר֩ עָלָ֨ה עָלָ֤יו הַגּוֹרָל֙ לַֽעֲזָאזֵ֔ל
יָֽעֳמַד־חַ֛י לִפְנֵ֥י יְהוָ֖ה לְכַפֵּ֣ר עָלָ֑יו לְשַׁלַּ֥ח אֹת֛וֹ לַֽעֲזָאזֵ֖ל הַמִּדְבָּֽרָה:
וְהִקְרִ֨יב אַֽהֲרֹ֜ן אֶת־פַּ֣ר הַֽחַטָּאת֮ אֲשֶׁר־לוֹ֒ וְכִפֶּ֥ר בַּֽעֲד֖וֹ וּבְעַ֣ד בֵּית֑וֹ וְשָׁחַ֛ט
אֶת־פַּ֥ר הַֽחַטָּ֖את אֲשֶׁר־לֽוֹ:

ישראל – וְלָקַ֣ח מְלֹֽא־הַ֠מַּחְתָּ֠ה גַּֽחֲלֵי־אֵ֞שׁ מֵעַ֤ל הַמִּזְבֵּ֨חַ֙ מִלִּפְנֵ֣י יְהוָ֔ה וּמְלֹ֣א
חָפְנָ֔יו קְטֹ֥רֶת סַמִּ֖ים דַּקָּ֑ה וְהֵבִ֖יא מִבֵּ֥ית לַפָּרֹֽכֶת: וְנָתַ֧ן אֶת־הַקְּטֹ֛רֶת
עַל־הָאֵ֖שׁ לִפְנֵ֣י יְהוָ֑ה וְכִסָּ֣ה ׀ עֲנַ֣ן הַקְּטֹ֗רֶת אֶת־הַכַּפֹּ֛רֶת אֲשֶׁ֥ר
עַל־הָֽעֵד֖וּת וְלֹ֥א יָמֽוּת: וְלָקַח֙ מִדַּ֣ם הַפָּ֔ר וְהִזָּ֧ה בְאֶצְבָּע֛וֹ עַל־פְּנֵ֥י הַכַּפֹּ֖רֶת
קֵ֑דְמָה וְלִפְנֵ֣י הַכַּפֹּ֗רֶת יַזֶּ֧ה שֶֽׁבַע־פְּעָמִ֛ים מִן־הַדָּ֖ם בְּאֶצְבָּעֽוֹ: וְשָׁחַ֞ט
אֶת־שְׂעִ֤יר הַֽחַטָּאת֙ אֲשֶׁ֣ר לָעָ֔ם וְהֵבִיא֙ אֶת־דָּמ֔וֹ אֶל־מִבֵּ֖ית לַפָּרֹ֑כֶת
וְעָשָׂ֣ה אֶת־דָּמ֗וֹ כַּֽאֲשֶׁ֤ר עָשָׂה֙ לְדַ֣ם הַפָּ֔ר וְהִזָּ֥ה אֹת֛וֹ עַל־הַכַּפֹּ֖רֶת וְלִפְנֵ֥י
הַכַּפֹּֽרֶת: וְכִפֶּ֣ר עַל־הַקֹּ֗דֶשׁ מִטֻּמְאֹת֙ בְּנֵ֣י יִשְׂרָאֵ֔ל וּמִפִּשְׁעֵיהֶ֖ם לְכָל־
חַטֹּאתָ֑ם וְכֵ֤ן יַֽעֲשֶׂה֙ לְאֹ֣הֶל מוֹעֵ֔ד הַשֹּׁכֵ֣ן אִתָּ֔ם בְּת֖וֹךְ טֻמְאֹתָֽם: וְכָל־אָדָ֞ם
לֹֽא־יִֽהְיֶ֣ה ׀ בְּאֹ֣הֶל מוֹעֵ֗ד בְּבֹא֛וֹ לְכַפֵּ֥ר בַּקֹּ֖דֶשׁ עַד־צֵאת֑וֹ וְכִפֶּ֤ר בַּֽעֲדוֹ֙
וּבְעַ֣ד בֵּית֔וֹ וּבְעַ֖ד כָּל־קְהַ֥ל יִשְׂרָאֵֽל:

on the Altar. He washed the innards and the feet, and caused them to go up in smoke on the elevation-offering on the Altar.

He brought near the offering of the people. He took the sin-offering goat that was for the people, and slaughtered it and performed the sin-offering service, as for the first one. He brought near the elevation-offering and performed its service as prescribed.

PARASHAS ACHAREI MOS

Leviticus 16:1-17

Kohen – *HASHEM spoke to Moses after the death of Aaron's two sons, when they approached before HASHEM, and they died. And HASHEM said to Moses: Speak to Aaron, your brother — he may not come at any time into the Sanctuary, within the Curtain, in front of the cover that is upon the Ark, so that he should not die; for in a cloud will I appear upon the Ark-cover. With this shall Aaron come into the Sanctuary: with a young bull for a sin-offering and a ram for an elevation-offering. He shall don a sacred linen tunic; linen breeches shall be upon his flesh, he shall gird himself with a linen sash, and cover his head with a linen turban; they are sacred vestments — he shall immerse himself in water and then don them. From the assembly of the Children of Israel he shall take two he-goats for a sin-offering and one ram for an elevation-offering. Aaron shall bring near his own sin-offering bull, and atone for himself and for his household.*

Levi – *He shall take the two he-goats and stand them before HASHEM at the entrance of the Tent of Meeting. Aaron shall place lots upon the two he-goats: one lot "for HASHEM" and one lot "for Azazel". Aaron shall bring near the he-goat designated by lot for HASHEM, and which he was to declare as a sin-offering. And the he-goat designated by lot for Azazel shall be stood alive before HASHEM, to make atonement through it, to send it to Azazel to the Wilderness. Aaron shall have brought near his own sin-offering bull and he shall atone for himself and for his household; then he shall slaughter his own sin-offering bull.*

Third – *He shall take a shovelful of fiery coals from atop the Altar that is before HASHEM, and his cupped handsful of finely ground incense-spices, and bring it within the Curtain. He shall place the incense upon the fire before HASHEM; so that the cloud of the incense shall blanket the Ark-cover that is atop the [Tablets of the] Testimony — so that he shall not die.*

He shall take of the blood of the bull and sprinkle with his finger upon the eastern front of the Ark-cover; and in front of the Ark-cover he shall sprinkle seven times from the blood with his finger. He shall slaughter the sin-offering he-goat of the people, and bring its blood within the Curtain; he shall do with its blood as he had done with the blood of the bull, and sprinkle it upon the Ark-cover and in front of the Ark-cover. Thus shall he bring atonement upon the Sanctuary for the contaminations of the Children of Israel, even for their willful sins among all their sins; and so shall he do for the Tent of Meeting that dwells with them amid their contamination. Every person is forbidden to be in the Tent of Meeting when he comes to bring atonement in the Sanctuary until his departure; he shall atone for himself, for his household, and for the entire congregation of Israel.

פרשת קדושים

ויקרא יט:א־יד

כהן – וַיְדַבֵּ֥ר יהוָ֖ה אֶל־מֹשֶׁ֥ה לֵּאמֹֽר׃ דַּבֵּ֞ר אֶל־כָּל־עֲדַ֧ת בְּנֵֽי־יִשְׂרָאֵ֛ל
וְאָמַרְתָּ֥ אֲלֵהֶ֖ם קְדֹשִׁ֣ים תִּהְי֑וּ כִּ֣י קָד֔וֹשׁ אֲנִ֖י יהוָ֥ה אֱלֹהֵיכֶֽם׃ אִ֣ישׁ אִמּ֤וֹ
וְאָבִיו֙ תִּירָ֔אוּ וְאֶת־שַׁבְּתֹתַ֖י תִּשְׁמֹ֑רוּ אֲנִ֖י יהוָ֥ה אֱלֹהֵיכֶֽם׃ אַל־תִּפְנוּ֙
אֶל־הָ֣אֱלִילִ֔ם וֵֽאלֹהֵי֙ מַסֵּכָ֔ה לֹ֥א תַעֲשׂ֖וּ לָכֶ֑ם אֲנִ֖י יהוָ֥ה אֱלֹהֵיכֶֽם׃
לוי – וְכִ֧י תִזְבְּח֛וּ זֶ֥בַח שְׁלָמִ֖ים לַֽיהוָ֑ה לִֽרְצֹנְכֶ֖ם תִּזְבָּחֻֽהוּ׃ בְּי֧וֹם זִבְחֲכֶ֛ם
יֵאָכֵ֖ל וּמִֽמָּחֳרָ֑ת וְהַנּוֹתָר֙ עַד־י֣וֹם הַשְּׁלִישִׁ֔י בָּאֵ֖שׁ יִשָּׂרֵֽף׃ וְאִ֛ם הֵאָכֹ֥ל
יֵאָכֵ֖ל בַּיּ֣וֹם הַשְּׁלִישִׁ֑י פִּגּ֥וּל ה֖וּא לֹ֥א יֵרָצֶֽה׃ וְאֹֽכְלָיו֙ עֲוֺנ֣וֹ יִשָּׂ֔א
כִּֽי־אֶת־קֹ֥דֶשׁ יהוָ֖ה חִלֵּ֑ל וְנִכְרְתָ֛ה הַנֶּ֥פֶשׁ הַהִ֖וא מֵעַמֶּֽיהָ׃ וּֽבְקֻצְרְכֶם֙
אֶת־קְצִ֣יר אַרְצְכֶ֔ם לֹ֧א תְכַלֶּ֛ה פְּאַ֥ת שָׂדְךָ֖ לִקְצֹ֑ר וְלֶ֥קֶט קְצִֽירְךָ֖ לֹ֥א
תְלַקֵּֽט׃ וְכַרְמְךָ֙ לֹ֣א תְעוֹלֵ֔ל וּפֶ֥רֶט כַּרְמְךָ֖ לֹ֣א תְלַקֵּ֑ט לֶֽעָנִ֤י וְלַגֵּר֙ תַּעֲזֹ֣ב
אֹתָ֔ם אֲנִ֖י יהוָ֥ה אֱלֹהֵיכֶֽם׃
ישראל – לֹ֖א תִּגְנֹ֑בוּ וְלֹא־תְכַחֲשׁ֥וּ וְלֹֽא־תְשַׁקְּר֖וּ אִ֥ישׁ בַּעֲמִיתֽוֹ׃ וְלֹֽא־
תִשָּׁבְע֥וּ בִשְׁמִ֖י לַשָּׁ֑קֶר וְחִלַּלְתָּ֛ אֶת־שֵׁ֥ם אֱלֹהֶ֖יךָ אֲנִ֥י יהוָֽה׃ לֹֽא־תַעֲשֹׁ֥ק
אֶת־רֵֽעֲךָ֖ וְלֹ֣א תִגְזֹ֑ל לֹֽא־תָלִ֞ין פְּעֻלַּ֥ת שָׂכִ֛יר אִתְּךָ֖ עַד־בֹּֽקֶר׃ לֹא־תְקַלֵּ֣ל
חֵרֵ֔שׁ וְלִפְנֵ֣י עִוֵּ֔ר לֹ֥א תִתֵּ֖ן מִכְשֹׁ֑ל וְיָרֵ֥אתָ מֵּאֱלֹהֶ֖יךָ אֲנִ֥י יהוָֽה׃

When the Torah reading has been completed, the Torah is raised for all to see. Each person looks at the Torah and recites aloud:

וְזֹאת הַתּוֹרָה אֲשֶׁר שָׂם מֹשֶׁה לִפְנֵי בְּנֵי יִשְׂרָאֵל,[1] עַל פִּי יהוה בְּיַד מֹשֶׁה.[2]

Some add the following verses:

עֵץ חַיִּים הִיא לַמַּחֲזִיקִים בָּהּ, וְתֹמְכֶיהָ מְאֻשָּׁר.[3] דְּרָכֶיהָ דַרְכֵי נֹעַם, וְכָל נְתִיבוֹתֶיהָ שָׁלוֹם.[4] אֹרֶךְ יָמִים בִּימִינָהּ, בִּשְׂמֹאלָהּ עֹשֶׁר וְכָבוֹד.[5] יהוה חָפֵץ לְמַעַן צִדְקוֹ, יַגְדִּיל תּוֹרָה וְיַאְדִּיר.[6]

Chazzan takes the Torah in his right arm and recites:

יְהַלְלוּ אֶת שֵׁם יהוה, כִּי נִשְׂגָּב שְׁמוֹ לְבַדּוֹ –

Congregation responds:

– הוֹדוֹ עַל אֶרֶץ וְשָׁמָיִם. וַיָּרֶם קֶרֶן לְעַמּוֹ, תְּהִלָּה לְכָל חֲסִידָיו, לִבְנֵי יִשְׂרָאֵל עַם קְרֹבוֹ, הַלְלוּיָהּ.[7]

As the Torah is carried to the Ark, congregation recites Psalm 24, לְדָוִד מִזְמוֹר.

לְדָוִד מִזְמוֹר, לַיהוה הָאָרֶץ וּמְלוֹאָהּ, תֵּבֵל וְיֹשְׁבֵי בָהּ. כִּי הוּא עַל יַמִּים יְסָדָהּ, וְעַל נְהָרוֹת יְכוֹנְנֶהָ. מִי יַעֲלֶה בְהַר יהוה, וּמִי יָקוּם בִּמְקוֹם קָדְשׁוֹ. נְקִי כַפַּיִם וּבַר לֵבָב, אֲשֶׁר לֹא נָשָׂא לַשָּׁוְא נַפְשִׁי וְלֹא נִשְׁבַּע לְמִרְמָה. יִשָּׂא בְרָכָה מֵאֵת יהוה, וּצְדָקָה מֵאֱלֹהֵי יִשְׁעוֹ. זֶה דּוֹר דֹּרְשָׁיו, מְבַקְשֵׁי פָנֶיךָ,

PARASHAS KEDOSHIM

Leviticus 19:1-14

Kohen – *HASHEM spoke to Moses, saying: Speak to the entire assembly of the Children of Israel and say to them: Be holy, for I, HASHEM, your God, am holy.*

Every man: You shall revere your father and mother, and you shall observe My Sabbaths — I am HASHEM, your God. Do not turn to the idols and do not make molten gods for yourselves — I am HASHEM, your God.

Levi – *When you slaughter a feast peace-offering to HASHEM, you shall slaughter it to find favor for yourselves. It shall be eaten on the day you slaughter it and on the next day, and whatever remains until the third day shall be burned in fire. But if it was eaten on the third day, it is rejected — it does not find favor. Each of those who eat it will bear his iniquity, for he has desecrated what is sacred to HASHEM; and that soul will be cut off from its people.*

When you reap the harvest of your land, do not complete the reaping to the corner of your field, and do not take the gleanings of your harvest. Do not pick from the undeveloped twigs of your vineyard and do not gather the fallen fruit of your vineyard; for the poor and the proselyte shall you leave them — I am HASHEM, your God.

Third – *Do not steal, do not deny falsely, and do not lie to one another. Do not swear falsely by My Name, thereby desecrating the Name of your God — I am HASHEM. Do not cheat your fellow and do not rob; and do not withhold a worker's wage with you until morning. Do not curse a deaf person, do not place a stumbling-block before a blind person; you shall fear your God — I am HASHEM.*

When the Torah reading has been completed, the Torah is raised for all to see. Each person looks at the Torah and recites aloud:

This is the Torah that Moses placed before the Children of Israel,[1] upon the command of HASHEM, through Moses' hand.[2]

Some add the following verses:

עֵץ *It is a tree of life for those who grasp it, and its supporters are praiseworthy.[3] Its ways are ways of pleasantness and all its paths are peace.[4] Lengthy days are at its right; at its left are wealth and honor.[5] HASHEM desired, for the sake of its [Israel's] righteousness, that the Torah be made great and glorious.[6]*

Chazzan takes the Torah in his right arm and recites:

Let them praise the Name of HASHEM, for His Name alone will have been exalted —

Congregation responds:

— His glory is above earth and heaven. And He will have exalted the pride of His people, causing praise for all His devout ones, for the Children of Israel, His intimate nation. Halleluyah![7]

As the Torah is carried to the Ark, congregation recites Psalm 24, *'Of David a psalm.'*

לְדָוִד *Of David a psalm. HASHEM's is the earth and its fullness, the inhabited land and those who dwell in it. For He founded it upon seas, and established it upon rivers. Who may ascend the mountain of HASHEM, and who may stand in the place of His sanctity? One with clean hands and pure heart, who has not sworn in vain by My soul and has not sworn deceitfully. He will receive a blessing from HASHEM and just kindness from the God of his salvation. This is the generation of those who seek Him, those who strive for Your Presence*

---

(1) *Deuteronomy* 4:44. (2) *Numbers* 9:23. (3) *Proverbs* 3:18.
(4) 3:17.(5) 3:16. (6) *Isaiah* 42:21. (7) *Psalms* 148:13-14.

יַעֲקֹב, סֶלָה. שְׂאוּ שְׁעָרִים רָאשֵׁיכֶם, וְהִנָּשְׂאוּ פִּתְחֵי עוֹלָם, וְיָבוֹא מֶלֶךְ הַכָּבוֹד. מִי זֶה מֶלֶךְ הַכָּבוֹד, יהוה עִזּוּז וְגִבּוֹר, יהוה גִּבּוֹר מִלְחָמָה. שְׂאוּ שְׁעָרִים רָאשֵׁיכֶם, וּשְׂאוּ פִּתְחֵי עוֹלָם, וְיָבֹא מֶלֶךְ הַכָּבוֹד. מִי הוּא זֶה מֶלֶךְ הַכָּבוֹד, יהוה צְבָאוֹת הוּא מֶלֶךְ הַכָּבוֹד, סֶלָה.

As the Torah is placed into the Ark, congregation recites the following verses:

וּבְנֻחֹה יֹאמַר, שׁוּבָה יהוה רִבְבוֹת אַלְפֵי יִשְׂרָאֵל.[1] קוּמָה יהוה לִמְנוּחָתֶךָ, אַתָּה וַאֲרוֹן עֻזֶּךָ. כֹּהֲנֶיךָ יִלְבְּשׁוּ צֶדֶק, וַחֲסִידֶיךָ יְרַנֵּנוּ. בַּעֲבוּר דָּוִד עַבְדֶּךָ, אַל תָּשֵׁב פְּנֵי מְשִׁיחֶךָ.[2] כִּי לֶקַח טוֹב נָתַתִּי לָכֶם, תּוֹרָתִי אַל תַּעֲזֹבוּ.[3] ❖ עֵץ חַיִּים הִיא לַמַּחֲזִיקִים בָּהּ, וְתֹמְכֶיהָ מְאֻשָּׁר.[4] דְּרָכֶיהָ דַרְכֵי נֹעַם, וְכָל נְתִיבֹתֶיהָ שָׁלוֹם.[5] הֲשִׁיבֵנוּ יהוה אֵלֶיךָ וְנָשׁוּבָה, חַדֵּשׁ יָמֵינוּ כְּקֶדֶם.[6]

The Ark is closed and the chazzan recites חֲצִי קַדִּישׁ.

יִתְגַּדַּל וְיִתְקַדַּשׁ שְׁמֵהּ רַבָּא. (Cong.– אָמֵן.) בְּעָלְמָא דִּי בְרָא כִרְעוּתֵהּ, וְיַמְלִיךְ מַלְכוּתֵהּ, בְּחַיֵּיכוֹן וּבְיוֹמֵיכוֹן וּבְחַיֵּי דְכָל בֵּית יִשְׂרָאֵל, בַּעֲגָלָא וּבִזְמַן קָרִיב. וְאִמְרוּ: אָמֵן.

(Cong.– אָמֵן. יְהֵא שְׁמֵהּ רַבָּא מְבָרַךְ לְעָלַם וּלְעָלְמֵי עָלְמַיָּא.)

יְהֵא שְׁמֵהּ רַבָּא מְבָרַךְ לְעָלַם וּלְעָלְמֵי עָלְמַיָּא.

יִתְבָּרַךְ וְיִשְׁתַּבַּח וְיִתְפָּאַר וְיִתְרוֹמַם וְיִתְנַשֵּׂא וְיִתְהַדָּר וְיִתְעַלֶּה וְיִתְהַלָּל שְׁמֵהּ דְּקֻדְשָׁא בְּרִיךְ הוּא (Cong.– בְּרִיךְ הוּא) – לְעֵלָּא מִן כָּל בִּרְכָתָא וְשִׁירָתָא תֻּשְׁבְּחָתָא וְנֶחֱמָתָא, דַּאֲמִירָן בְּעָלְמָא. וְאִמְרוּ: אָמֵן. (Cong.– אָמֵן.)

❧ שְׁמוֹנֶה עֶשְׂרֵה ❧

Take three steps backward, then three steps forward. Remain standing with the feet together while reciting *Shemoneh Esrei*. Recite it with quiet devotion and without interruption, verbal or otherwise. Although its recitation should not be audible to others, one must pray loudly enough to hear himself.

כִּי שֵׁם יהוה אֶקְרָא, הָבוּ גֹדֶל לֵאלֹהֵינוּ.[7]
אֲדֹנָי שְׂפָתַי תִּפְתָּח, וּפִי יַגִּיד תְּהִלָּתֶךָ.[8]

אבות

Bend the knees at בָּרוּךְ; bow at אַתָּה; straighten up at ה'.

בָּרוּךְ אַתָּה יהוה אֱלֹהֵינוּ וֵאלֹהֵי אֲבוֹתֵינוּ, אֱלֹהֵי אַבְרָהָם, אֱלֹהֵי יִצְחָק, וֵאלֹהֵי יַעֲקֹב, הָאֵל הַגָּדוֹל הַגִּבּוֹר וְהַנּוֹרָא, אֵל עֶלְיוֹן, גּוֹמֵל חֲסָדִים טוֹבִים וְקוֹנֵה הַכֹּל, וְזוֹכֵר חַסְדֵי אָבוֹת, וּמֵבִיא גוֹאֵל לִבְנֵי בְנֵיהֶם, לְמַעַן שְׁמוֹ בְּאַהֲבָה. מֶלֶךְ עוֹזֵר וּמוֹשִׁיעַ וּמָגֵן.

Bend the knees at בָּרוּךְ; bow at אַתָּה; straighten up at ה'.

בָּרוּךְ אַתָּה יהוה, מָגֵן אַבְרָהָם.

גבורות

אַתָּה גִּבּוֹר לְעוֹלָם אֲדֹנָי, מְחַיֵּה מֵתִים אַתָּה, רַב לְהוֹשִׁיעַ. מְכַלְכֵּל חַיִּים בְּחֶסֶד, מְחַיֵּה מֵתִים בְּרַחֲמִים רַבִּים, סוֹמֵךְ

— Jacob, Selah. Raise up your heads, O gates, and be uplifted, you everlasting entrances, so that the King of Glory may enter. Who is this King of Glory? — HASHEM, the mighty and strong, HASHEM, the strong in battle. Raise up your heads, O gates, and raise up, you everlasting entrances, so that the King of Glory may enter. Who then is the King of Glory? HASHEM, Master of Legions, He is the King of Glory. Selah!

As the Torah is placed into the Ark, the congregation recites the following verses:

וּבְנֻחֹה *And when it rested he would say, 'Return, HASHEM, to the myriad thousands of Israel.'*[1] *Arise, HASHEM, to Your resting place, You and the Ark of Your strength. Let Your priests be clothed in righteousness, and Your devout ones will sing joyously. For the sake of David, Your servant, turn not away the face of Your anointed.*[2] *For I have given you a good teaching, do not forsake My Torah.*[3] Chazzan— *It is a tree of life for those who grasp it, and its supporters are praiseworthy.*[4] *Its ways are ways of pleasantness and all its paths are peace.*[5] *Bring us back to You, HASHEM, and we shall return, renew our days as of old.*[6]

The Ark is closed and the *chazzan* recites Half *Kaddish*.

יִתְגַּדַּל *May His great Name grow exalted and sanctified* (Cong.— *Amen.*) *in the world that He created as He willed. May He give reign to His kingship in your lifetimes and in your days, and in the lifetimes of the entire Family of Israel, swiftly and soon. Now respond: Amen.*

(Cong.— *Amen. May His great Name be blessed forever and ever.*)

May His great Name be blessed forever and ever.

Blessed, praised, glorified, exalted, extolled, mighty, upraised, and lauded be the Name of the Holy One, Blessed is He (Cong.— *Blessed is He*) *— beyond any blessing and song, praise and consolation that are uttered in the world. Now respond: Amen.* (Cong.— *Amen.*)

SHEMONEH ESREI – AMIDAH

Take three steps backward, then three steps forward. Remain standing with the feet together while reciting *Shemoneh Esrei*. Recite it with quiet devotion and without interruption, verbal or otherwise. Although its recitation should not be audible to others, one must pray loudly enough to hear himself.

When I call out the Name of HASHEM, ascribe greatness to our God.[7]

My Lord, open my lips, that my mouth may declare Your praise.[8]

PATRIARCHS

Bend the knees at *'Blessed'*; bow at *'You'*; straighten up at *'HASHEM.'*

בָּרוּךְ *Blessed are You, HASHEM, our God and the God of our forefathers, God of Abraham, God of Isaac, and God of Jacob; the great, mighty, and awesome God, the supreme God, Who bestows beneficial kindnesses and creates everything, Who recalls the kindnesses of the Patriarchs and brings a Redeemer to their children's children, for His Name's sake, with love. O King, Helper, Savior, and Shield.*

Bend the knees at *'Blessed'*; bow at *'You'*; straighten up at *'HASHEM.'*

Blessed are You, HASHEM, Shield of Abraham.

GOD'S MIGHT

אַתָּה *You are eternally mighty, my Lord, the Resuscitator of the dead are You; abundantly able to save. He sustains the living with kindness, resuscitates the dead with abundant mercy, supports the fallen, heals the sick, releases the confined, and maintains His faith*

---

(1) *Numbers* 10:36. (2) *Psalms* 132:8-10. (3) *Proverbs* 4:2. (4) 3:18. (5) 3:17.
(6) *Lamentations* 5:21. (7) *Deuteronomy* 32:3. (8) *Psalms* 51:17.

נוֹפְלִים, וְרוֹפֵא חוֹלִים, וּמַתִּיר אֲסוּרִים, וּמְקַיֵּם אֱמוּנָתוֹ לִישֵׁנֵי עָפָר. מִי כָמְוֹךָ בַּעַל גְּבוּרוֹת, וּמִי דּוֹמֶה לָּךְ, מֶלֶךְ מֵמִית וּמְחַיֶּה וּמַצְמִיחַ יְשׁוּעָה. וְנֶאֱמָן אַתָּה לְהַחֲיוֹת מֵתִים. בָּרוּךְ אַתָּה יהוה, מְחַיֵּה הַמֵּתִים.

During the *chazzan's* repetition, *Kedushah* (below) is recited at this point.

קדושת השם

אַתָּה קָדוֹשׁ וְשִׁמְךָ קָדוֹשׁ, וּקְדוֹשִׁים בְּכָל יוֹם יְהַלְלְוּךָ סֶּלָה.
בָּרוּךְ אַתָּה יהוה, הָאֵל הַקָּדוֹשׁ.

קדושת היום

אַתָּה אֶחָד* וְשִׁמְךָ אֶחָד, וּמִי כְּעַמְּךָ יִשְׂרָאֵל* גּוֹי אֶחָד בָּאָרֶץ, תִּפְאֶרֶת גְּדֻלָּה,* וַעֲטֶרֶת יְשׁוּעָה, יוֹם מְנוּחָה וּקְדֻשָּׁה לְעַמְּךָ נָתָתָּ, אַבְרָהָם יָגֵל, יִצְחָק יְרַנֵּן, יַעֲקֹב וּבָנָיו יָנוּחוּ בוֹ, מְנוּחַת אַהֲבָה וּנְדָבָה, מְנוּחַת אֱמֶת וֶאֱמוּנָה, מְנוּחַת שָׁלוֹם וְשַׁלְוָה וְהַשְׁקֵט וָבֶטַח, מְנוּחָה שְׁלֵמָה שֶׁאַתָּה רוֹצֶה בָּהּ, יַכִּירוּ בָנֶיךָ וְיֵדְעוּ כִּי מֵאִתְּךָ הִיא מְנוּחָתָם, וְעַל מְנוּחָתָם יַקְדִּישׁוּ אֶת שְׁמֶךָ.

אֱלֹהֵינוּ וֵאלֹהֵי אֲבוֹתֵינוּ, רְצֵה בִמְנוּחָתֵנוּ, קַדְּשֵׁנוּ בְּמִצְוֹתֶיךָ, וְתֵן חֶלְקֵנוּ בְּתוֹרָתֶךָ, שַׂבְּעֵנוּ מִטּוּבֶךָ, וְשַׂמְּחֵנוּ בִּישׁוּעָתֶךָ, וְטַהֵר לִבֵּנוּ לְעָבְדְּךָ בֶּאֱמֶת. וְהַנְחִילֵנוּ יהוה אֱלֹהֵינוּ

קדושה

When reciting *Kedushah,* one must stand with his feet together and avoid any interruptions. One should rise on his toes when saying the words קָדוֹשׁ, קָדוֹשׁ, קָדוֹשׁ; בָּרוּךְ (of בָּרוּךְ כְּבוֹד); and יִמְלֹךְ.

Cong. then *Chazzan* – **נְקַדֵּשׁ** אֶת שִׁמְךָ בָּעוֹלָם, כְּשֵׁם שֶׁמַּקְדִּישִׁים אוֹתוֹ בִּשְׁמֵי מָרוֹם, כַּכָּתוּב עַל יַד נְבִיאֶךָ, וְקָרָא זֶה אֶל זֶה וְאָמַר:

All – קָדוֹשׁ קָדוֹשׁ קָדוֹשׁ יהוה צְבָאוֹת, מְלֹא כָל הָאָרֶץ כְּבוֹדוֹ.[1]

Chazzan – לְעֻמָּתָם בָּרוּךְ יֹאמֵרוּ:

All – בָּרוּךְ כְּבוֹד יהוה, מִמְּקוֹמוֹ.[2]

Chazzan – וּבְדִבְרֵי קָדְשְׁךָ כָּתוּב לֵאמֹר:

All – יִמְלֹךְ יהוה לְעוֹלָם, אֱלֹהַיִךְ צִיּוֹן לְדֹר וָדֹר, הַלְלוּיָהּ.[3]

Chazzan only concludes – לְדוֹר וָדוֹר נַגִּיד גָּדְלֶךָ וּלְנֵצַח נְצָחִים קְדֻשָּׁתְךָ נַקְדִּישׁ, וְשִׁבְחֲךָ אֱלֹהֵינוּ מִפִּינוּ לֹא יָמוּשׁ לְעוֹלָם וָעֶד, כִּי אֵל מֶלֶךְ גָּדוֹל וְקָדוֹשׁ אָתָּה. בָּרוּךְ אַתָּה יהוה, הָאֵל הַקָּדוֹשׁ.

Chazzan continues . . . אַתָּה אֶחָד (above).

אַתָּה אֶחָד — *You are One.* The opening verse is a clear reference to the verse (*Zechariah* 14:9) stating that when the final redemption comes, all the world will recognize the Oneness of God, meaning that there are no contradictions in His behavior. As noted above, the Sabbath *Minchah* alludes to the long-awaited day when history will attain God's goal of perfection. Thus the *to those asleep in the dust. Who is like You, O Master of mighty deeds, and who is comparable to You, O King Who causes death and restores life and makes salvation sprout! And You are faithful to resuscitate the dead. Blessed are You, HASHEM, Who resuscitates the dead.*

During the *chazzan's* repetition, *Kedushah* (below) is recited at this point.

HOLINESS OF GOD'S NAME

אַתָּה *You are holy and Your Name is holy, and holy ones praise You every day, forever. Blessed are You, HASHEM, the holy God.*

SANCTIFICATION OF THE DAY

אַתָּה אֶחָד *You are One* and Your Name is One; and who is like Your people Israel,* one nation on earth. The splendor of greatness* and the crown of salvation, the day of contentment and holiness have You given to Your people. Abraham would rejoice, Isaac would exult, Jacob and his children would rest on it, a rest of love and magnanimity, a rest of truth and faith, a rest of peace and serenity and tranquility and security, a perfect rest in which You find favor. May Your children recognize and know that from You comes their rest, and through their rest, they will sanctify Your Name.*

אֱלֹהֵינוּ *Our God and the God of our fathers, may You be pleased with our rest. Sanctify us with Your commandments and grant our share in Your Torah; satisfy us from Your goodness and gladden us with Your salvation, and purify our heart to serve You sincerely. O HASHEM, our God, with love and favor grant us Your holy*

KEDUSHAH

When reciting *Kedushah*, one must stand with his feet together and avoid any interruptions. One should rise on his toes when saying *Holy, holy, holy; Blessed is;* and *HASHEM shall reign.*

Cong. then Chazzan – **נְקַדֵּשׁ** *We shall sanctify Your Name in this world, just as they sanctify it in heaven above, as it is written by Your prophet, "And one [angel] will call another and say:*

All – *'Holy, holy, holy is HASHEM, Master of Legions, the whole world is filled with His glory.' "*[1]

Chazzan – *Those facing them say 'Blessed':*

All – *'Blessed is the glory of HASHEM from His place.'*[2]

Chazzan – *And in Your holy Writings the following is written:*

All – *'HASHEM shall reign forever — your God, O Zion — from generation to generation, Halleluyah!'*[3]

Chazzan only concludes – *From generation to generation we shall relate Your greatness and for infinite eternities we shall proclaim Your holiness. Your praise, our God, shall not leave our mouth forever and ever, for You, O God, are a great and holy King. Blessed are You, HASHEM, the holy God.*

Chazzan continues אַתָּה אֶחָד, *You are One . . .* (above).

(1) *Isaiah* 6:3. (2) *Ezekiel* 3:12. (3) *Psalms* 146:10.

Minchah Shemoneh Esrei directs our focus not only to the holiness of the Sabbath day, but to the spiritual bliss of the future.

וּמִי כְּעַמְּךָ יִשְׂרָאֵל — *And who is like Your people Israel.* Israel is unique because it alone accepted the Torah and dedicated itself to God's service. Consequently, God awarded Israel the spiritual gifts cited in the next verse.

תִּפְאֶרֶת גְּדֻלָּה — *The splendor of greatness.* Some interpret this to mean the Temple. Others interpret this phrase and the others in this verse as references to various aspects of Messianic times.

בְּאַהֲבָה וּבְרָצוֹן שַׁבַּת קָדְשֶׁךָ, וְיָנְוּחוּ בָם יִשְׂרָאֵל מְקַדְּשֵׁי שְׁמֶךָ. בָּרוּךְ אַתָּה יהוה, מְקַדֵּשׁ הַשַּׁבָּת.

עבודה

רְצֵה יהוה אֱלֹהֵינוּ בְּעַמְּךָ יִשְׂרָאֵל וּבִתְפִלָּתָם, וְהָשֵׁב אֶת הָעֲבוֹדָה לִדְבִיר בֵּיתֶךָ. וְאִשֵּׁי יִשְׂרָאֵל וּתְפִלָּתָם בְּאַהֲבָה תְקַבֵּל בְּרָצוֹן, וּתְהִי לְרָצוֹן תָּמִיד עֲבוֹדַת יִשְׂרָאֵל עַמֶּךָ.

During the *chazzan's* repetition, congregation responds אָמֵן as indicated.
[If the following paragraph is forgotten, repeat *Shemoneh Esrei*. See *Laws* §56.]

אֱלֹהֵינוּ וֵאלֹהֵי אֲבוֹתֵינוּ, יַעֲלֶה, וְיָבֹא, וְיַגִּיעַ, וְיֵרָאֶה, וְיֵרָצֶה, וְיִשָּׁמַע, וְיִפָּקֵד, וְיִזָּכֵר זִכְרוֹנֵנוּ וּפִקְדוֹנֵנוּ, וְזִכְרוֹן אֲבוֹתֵינוּ, וְזִכְרוֹן מָשִׁיחַ בֶּן דָּוִד עַבְדֶּךָ, וְזִכְרוֹן יְרוּשָׁלַיִם עִיר קָדְשֶׁךָ, וְזִכְרוֹן כָּל עַמְּךָ בֵּית יִשְׂרָאֵל לְפָנֶיךָ, לִפְלֵיטָה לְטוֹבָה לְחֵן וּלְחֶסֶד וּלְרַחֲמִים, לְחַיִּים וּלְשָׁלוֹם בְּיוֹם חַג הַמַּצּוֹת הַזֶּה. זָכְרֵנוּ יהוה אֱלֹהֵינוּ בּוֹ לְטוֹבָה (Cong.–אָמֵן), וּפָקְדֵנוּ בוֹ לִבְרָכָה (Cong.–אָמֵן), וְהוֹשִׁיעֵנוּ בוֹ לְחַיִּים (Cong.–אָמֵן). וּבִדְבַר יְשׁוּעָה וְרַחֲמִים, חוּס וְחָנֵּנוּ וְרַחֵם עָלֵינוּ וְהוֹשִׁיעֵנוּ, כִּי אֵלֶיךָ עֵינֵינוּ, כִּי אֵל מֶלֶךְ חַנּוּן וְרַחוּם אָתָּה.[1]

וְתֶחֱזֶינָה עֵינֵינוּ בְּשׁוּבְךָ לְצִיּוֹן בְּרַחֲמִים. בָּרוּךְ אַתָּה יהוה, הַמַּחֲזִיר שְׁכִינָתוֹ לְצִיּוֹן.

הודאה

Bow at מוֹדִים; straighten up at 'ה. In his repetition the *chazzan* should recite the entire מוֹדִים aloud, while the congregation recites מוֹדִים דְּרַבָּנָן softly.

מוֹדִים אֲנַחְנוּ לָךְ שָׁאַתָּה הוּא יהוה אֱלֹהֵינוּ וֵאלֹהֵי אֲבוֹתֵינוּ לְעוֹלָם וָעֶד. צוּר חַיֵּינוּ, מָגֵן יִשְׁעֵנוּ אַתָּה הוּא לְדוֹר וָדוֹר. נוֹדֶה לְּךָ וּנְסַפֵּר תְּהִלָּתֶךָ[2] עַל חַיֵּינוּ הַמְּסוּרִים בְּיָדֶךָ, וְעַל נִשְׁמוֹתֵינוּ הַפְּקוּדוֹת לָךְ, וְעַל נִסֶּיךָ שֶׁבְּכָל יוֹם עִמָּנוּ, וְעַל נִפְלְאוֹתֶיךָ וְטוֹבוֹתֶיךָ שֶׁבְּכָל עֵת, עֶרֶב וָבֹקֶר וְצָהֳרָיִם. הַטּוֹב כִּי לֹא כָלוּ רַחֲמֶיךָ, וְהַמְרַחֵם כִּי לֹא תַמּוּ חֲסָדֶיךָ,[3] מֵעוֹלָם קִוִּינוּ לָךְ.

מודים דרבנן

מוֹדִים אֲנַחְנוּ לָךְ, שָׁאַתָּה הוּא יהוה אֱלֹהֵינוּ וֵאלֹהֵי אֲבוֹתֵינוּ, אֱלֹהֵי כָל בָּשָׂר, יוֹצְרֵנוּ, יוֹצֵר בְּרֵאשִׁית. בְּרָכוֹת וְהוֹדָאוֹת לְשִׁמְךָ הַגָּדוֹל וְהַקָּדוֹשׁ, עַל שֶׁהֶחֱיִיתָנוּ וְקִיַּמְתָּנוּ. כֵּן תְּחַיֵּנוּ וּתְקַיְּמֵנוּ, וְתֶאֱסוֹף גָּלֻיּוֹתֵינוּ לְחַצְרוֹת קָדְשֶׁךָ, לִשְׁמוֹר חֻקֶּיךָ וְלַעֲשׂוֹת רְצוֹנֶךָ, וּלְעָבְדְּךָ בְּלֵבָב שָׁלֵם, עַל שֶׁאֲנַחְנוּ מוֹדִים לָךְ. בָּרוּךְ אֵל הַהוֹדָאוֹת.

Sabbath as a heritage, and may Israel, the sanctifiers of Your Name, rest on them. Blessed are You, HASHEM, Who sanctifies the Sabbath.

TEMPLE SERVICE

רְצֵה *Be favorable, HASHEM, our God, toward Your people Israel and their prayer and restore the service to the Holy of Holies of Your Temple. The fire-offerings of Israel and their prayer accept with love and favor, and may the service of Your people Israel always be favorable to You.*

During the *chazzan's* repetition, congregation responds *Amen* as indicated.
[If the following paragraph is forgotten, repeat *Shemoneh Esrei*. See *Laws* §56.]

אֱלֹהֵינוּ *Our God and God of our forefathers, may there rise, come, reach, be noted, be favored, be heard, be considered, and be remembered — the remembrance and consideration of ourselves; the remembrance of our forefathers; the remembrance of Messiah, son of David, Your servant; the remembrance of Jerusalem, the City of Your Holiness; the remembrance of Your entire people the Family of Israel — before You for deliverance, for goodness, for grace, for kindness, and for compassion, for life, and for peace on this day of the Festival of Matzos. Remember us on it, HASHEM, our God, for goodness* (Cong.–*Amen*)*; consider us on it for blessing* (Cong.–*Amen*)*; and help us on it for life* (Cong.–*Amen*)*. In the matter of salvation and compassion, pity, be gracious and compassionate with us and help us, for our eyes are turned to You, because You are God, the gracious and compassionate King.*[1]

וְתֶחֱזֶינָה *May our eyes behold Your return to Zion in compassion. Blessed are You, HASHEM, Who restores His Presence to Zion.*

THANKSGIVING [MODIM]

Bow at *'We gratefully thank You'*; straighten up at *'HASHEM.'* In his repetition the *chazzan* should recite the entire *Modim* aloud, while the congregation recites *Modim of the Rabbis* softly.

מוֹדִים *We gratefully thank You, for it is You Who are HASHEM, our God and the God of our forefathers for all eternity; Rock of our lives, Shield of our salvation are You from generation to generation. We shall thank You and relate Your praise*[2] *— for our lives, which are committed to Your power and for our souls that are entrusted to You; for Your miracles that are with us every day; and for Your wonders and favors in every season — evening, morning, and afternoon. The Beneficent One, for Your compassions were never exhausted, and the Compassionate One, for Your kindnesses never ended*[3] *— always have we put our hope in You.*

MODIM OF THE RABBIS

מוֹדִים *We gratefully thank You, for it is You Who are HASHEM, our God and the God of our forefathers, the God of all flesh, our Molder, the Molder of the universe. Blessings and thanks are due Your great and holy Name for You have given us life and sustained us. So may You continue to give us life and sustain us and gather our exiles to the Courtyards of Your Sanctuary, to observe Your decrees, to do Your will and to serve You wholeheartedly. [We thank You] for inspiring us to thank You. Blessed is the God of thanksgivings.*

---

(1) Cf. *Nehemiah* 9:31. (2) Cf. *Psalms* 79:13. (3) Cf. *Lamentations* 3:22.

וְעַל כֻּלָּם יִתְבָּרַךְ וְיִתְרוֹמַם שִׁמְךָ מַלְכֵּנוּ תָּמִיד לְעוֹלָם וָעֶד.

Bend the knees at בָּרוּךְ; bow at אַתָּה; straighten up at ה׳.

וְכֹל הַחַיִּים יוֹדְוּךָ סֶּלָה, וִיהַלְּלוּ אֶת שִׁמְךָ בֶּאֱמֶת, הָאֵל יְשׁוּעָתֵנוּ וְעֶזְרָתֵנוּ סֶלָה. בָּרוּךְ אַתָּה יהוה, הַטּוֹב שִׁמְךָ וּלְךָ נָאֶה לְהוֹדוֹת.

שלום

שָׁלוֹם רָב עַל יִשְׂרָאֵל עַמְּךָ תָּשִׂים לְעוֹלָם, כִּי אַתָּה הוּא מֶלֶךְ אָדוֹן לְכָל הַשָּׁלוֹם. וְטוֹב בְּעֵינֶיךָ לְבָרֵךְ אֶת עַמְּךָ יִשְׂרָאֵל, בְּכָל עֵת וּבְכָל שָׁעָה בִּשְׁלוֹמֶךָ. בָּרוּךְ אַתָּה יהוה, הַמְּבָרֵךְ אֶת עַמּוֹ יִשְׂרָאֵל בַּשָּׁלוֹם.

יִהְיוּ לְרָצוֹן אִמְרֵי פִי וְהֶגְיוֹן לִבִּי לְפָנֶיךָ, יהוה צוּרִי וְגֹאֲלִי.[1]

Chazzan's **repetition of** ***Shemoneh Esrei*** **ends here. Individuals continue below.**

אֱלֹהַי, נְצוֹר לְשׁוֹנִי מֵרָע, וּשְׂפָתַי מִדַּבֵּר מִרְמָה,[2] וְלִמְקַלְלַי נַפְשִׁי תִדּוֹם, וְנַפְשִׁי כֶּעָפָר לַכֹּל תִּהְיֶה. פְּתַח לִבִּי בְּתוֹרָתֶךָ, וּבְמִצְוֹתֶיךָ תִּרְדּוֹף נַפְשִׁי. וְכֹל הַחוֹשְׁבִים עָלַי רָעָה, מְהֵרָה הָפֵר עֲצָתָם וְקַלְקֵל מַחֲשַׁבְתָּם. עֲשֵׂה לְמַעַן שְׁמֶךָ, עֲשֵׂה לְמַעַן יְמִינֶךָ, עֲשֵׂה לְמַעַן קְדֻשָּׁתֶךָ, עֲשֵׂה לְמַעַן תּוֹרָתֶךָ. לְמַעַן יֵחָלְצוּן יְדִידֶיךָ, הוֹשִׁיעָה יְמִינְךָ וַעֲנֵנִי.[3]

Some recite verses pertaining to their names. See page 1143.

יִהְיוּ לְרָצוֹן אִמְרֵי פִי וְהֶגְיוֹן לִבִּי לְפָנֶיךָ, יהוה צוּרִי וְגֹאֲלִי:

Bow and take three steps back. Bow left and say . . . עֹשֶׂה; bow right and say . . . הוּא יַעֲשֶׂה; bow forward and say וְעַל כָּל . . . אָמֵן.

עֹשֶׂה שָׁלוֹם בִּמְרוֹמָיו, הוּא יַעֲשֶׂה שָׁלוֹם עָלֵינוּ, וְעַל כָּל יִשְׂרָאֵל. וְאִמְרוּ: אָמֵן.

יְהִי רָצוֹן מִלְּפָנֶיךָ יהוה אֱלֹהֵינוּ וֵאלֹהֵי אֲבוֹתֵינוּ, שֶׁיִּבָּנֶה בֵּית הַמִּקְדָּשׁ בִּמְהֵרָה בְיָמֵינוּ, וְתֵן חֶלְקֵנוּ בְּתוֹרָתֶךָ. וְשָׁם נַעֲבָדְךָ בְּיִרְאָה, כִּימֵי עוֹלָם וּכְשָׁנִים קַדְמוֹנִיּוֹת. וְעָרְבָה לַיהוה מִנְחַת יְהוּדָה וִירוּשָׁלָיִם, כִּימֵי עוֹלָם וּכְשָׁנִים קַדְמוֹנִיּוֹת.[4]

THE INDIVIDUAL'S RECITATION OF שְׁמוֹנֶה עֶשְׂרֵה ENDS HERE.

The individual remains standing in place until the chazzan reaches ***Kedushah*** **— or at least until the chazzan begins his repetition — then he takes three steps forward. The chazzan himself, or one praying alone, should remain in place for a few moments before taking three steps forward.**

For all these, may Your Name be blessed and exalted, our King, continually forever and ever.

Bend the knees at *'Blessed'*; bow at *'You'*; straighten up at *'HASHEM.'*

Everything alive will gratefully acknowledge You, Selah! and praise Your Name sincerely, O God of our salvation and help, Selah! Blessed are You, HASHEM, Your Name is 'The Beneficent One' and to You it is fitting to give thanks.

PEACE

שָׁלוֹם *Establish abundant peace upon Your people Israel forever, for You are King, Master of all peace. May it be good in Your eyes to bless Your people Israel at every time and every hour with Your peace. Blessed are You, HASHEM, Who blesses His people Israel with peace.*

May the expressions of my mouth and the thoughts of my heart find favor before You, HASHEM, my Rock and my Redeemer.[1]

Chazzan's repetition of *Shemoneh Esrei* ends here. Individuals continue below:

אֱלֹהַי ***My God, guard my tongue from evil and my lips from speaking deceitfully.[2] To those who curse me, let my soul be silent; and let my soul be like dust to everyone. Open my heart to Your Torah, then my soul will pursue Your commandments. As for all those who design evil against me, speedily nullify their counsel and disrupt their design. Act for Your Name's sake; act for Your right hand's sake; act for Your sanctity's sake; act for Your Torah's sake. That Your beloved ones may be given rest; let Your right hand save, and respond to me.[3]***

Some recite verses pertaining to their names at this point. See page 1143.

Bow and take three steps back. Bow left and say, *'He Who makes peace . . .'*; bow right and say, *'may He make peace . . .'*; bow forward and say, *'and upon . . . Amen.'*

May the expressions of my mouth and the thoughts of my heart find favor before You, HASHEM, my Rock and my Redeemer.[1] He Who makes peace in His heights, may He make peace upon us, and upon all Israel. Now respond: Amen.

יְהִי רָצוֹן ***May it be Your will, HASHEM, our God and the God of our forefathers, that the Holy Temple be rebuilt, speedily in our days. Grant us our share in Your Torah, and may we serve You there with reverence, as in days of old and in former years. Then the offering of Judah and Jerusalem will be pleasing to HASHEM, as in days of old and in former years.[4]***

THE INDIVIDUAL'S RECITATION OF *SHEMONEH ESREI* ENDS HERE.

The individual remains standing in place until the chazzan reaches *Kedushah* — or at least until the chazzan begins his repetition — then he takes three steps forward. The chazzan himself, or one praying alone, should remain in place for a few moments before taking three steps forward.

---

(1) *Psalms* 19:15. (2) Cf. 34:14. (3) 60:7; 108:7. (4) *Malachi* 3:4.

קדיש שלם

The *chazzan* recites קַדִּישׁ שָׁלֵם.

יִתְגַּדַּל וְיִתְקַדַּשׁ שְׁמֵהּ רַבָּא. (.Cong – אָמֵן.) בְּעָלְמָא דִּי בְרָא כִרְעוּתֵהּ. וְיַמְלִיךְ מַלְכוּתֵהּ, בְּחַיֵּיכוֹן וּבְיוֹמֵיכוֹן וּבְחַיֵּי דְכָל בֵּית יִשְׂרָאֵל, בַּעֲגָלָא וּבִזְמַן קָרִיב. וְאִמְרוּ: אָמֵן.

(.Cong – אָמֵן. יְהֵא שְׁמֵהּ רַבָּא מְבָרַךְ לְעָלַם וּלְעָלְמֵי עָלְמַיָּא.)

יְהֵא שְׁמֵהּ רַבָּא מְבָרַךְ לְעָלַם וּלְעָלְמֵי עָלְמַיָּא.

יִתְבָּרַךְ וְיִשְׁתַּבַּח וְיִתְפָּאַר וְיִתְרוֹמַם וְיִתְנַשֵּׂא וְיִתְהַדָּר וְיִתְעַלֶּה וְיִתְהַלָּל שְׁמֵהּ דְּקֻדְשָׁא בְּרִיךְ הוּא (.Cong – בְּרִיךְ הוּא) – לְעֵלָּא מִן כָּל בִּרְכָתָא וְשִׁירָתָא תֻּשְׁבְּחָתָא וְנֶחֱמָתָא, דַּאֲמִירָן בְּעָלְמָא. וְאִמְרוּ: אָמֵן. (.Cong – אָמֵן.)

(.Cong – קַבֵּל בְּרַחֲמִים וּבְרָצוֹן אֶת תְּפִלָּתֵנוּ.)

תִּתְקַבֵּל צְלוֹתְהוֹן וּבָעוּתְהוֹן דְּכָל בֵּית יִשְׂרָאֵל קֳדָם אֲבוּהוֹן דִּי בִשְׁמַיָּא. וְאִמְרוּ: אָמֵן. (.Cong – אָמֵן.)

(.Cong – יְהִי שֵׁם יהוה מְבֹרָךְ, מֵעַתָּה וְעַד עוֹלָם.[1])

יְהֵא שְׁלָמָא רַבָּא מִן שְׁמַיָּא, וְחַיִּים עָלֵינוּ וְעַל כָּל יִשְׂרָאֵל. וְאִמְרוּ: אָמֵן. (.Cong – אָמֵן.)

(.Cong – עֶזְרִי מֵעִם יהוה, עֹשֵׂה שָׁמַיִם וָאָרֶץ.[2])

Take three steps back. Bow left and say . . . עֹשֶׂה; bow right and say . . . הוּא; bow forward and say וְעַל כָּל . . . אָמֵן. Remain standing in place for a few moments, then take three steps forward.

עֹשֶׂה שָׁלוֹם בִּמְרוֹמָיו, הוּא יַעֲשֶׂה שָׁלוֹם עָלֵינוּ, וְעַל כָּל יִשְׂרָאֵל. וְאִמְרוּ: אָמֵן. (.Cong – אָמֵן.)

עלינו

Stand while reciting עָלֵינוּ.

עָלֵינוּ לְשַׁבֵּחַ לַאֲדוֹן הַכֹּל, לָתֵת גְּדֻלָּה לְיוֹצֵר בְּרֵאשִׁית, שֶׁלֹּא עָשָׂנוּ כְּגוֹיֵי הָאֲרָצוֹת, וְלֹא שָׂמָנוּ כְּמִשְׁפְּחוֹת הָאֲדָמָה. שֶׁלֹּא שָׂם חֶלְקֵנוּ כָּהֶם, וְגוֹרָלֵנוּ כְּכָל הֲמוֹנָם. (שֶׁהֵם מִשְׁתַּחֲוִים לְהֶבֶל וָרִיק, וּמִתְפַּלְּלִים אֶל אֵל לֹא יוֹשִׁיעַ.[3]) וַאֲנַחְנוּ כּוֹרְעִים וּמִשְׁתַּחֲוִים וּמוֹדִים, לִפְנֵי מֶלֶךְ מַלְכֵי הַמְּלָכִים הַקָּדוֹשׁ בָּרוּךְ הוּא. שֶׁהוּא נוֹטֶה שָׁמַיִם וְיֹסֵד אָרֶץ,[4] וּמוֹשַׁב יְקָרוֹ בַּשָּׁמַיִם מִמַּעַל, וּשְׁכִינַת עֻזּוֹ בְּגָבְהֵי מְרוֹמִים. הוּא אֱלֹהֵינוּ, אֵין עוֹד. אֱמֶת מַלְכֵּנוּ, אֶפֶס זוּלָתוֹ, כַּכָּתוּב בְּתוֹרָתוֹ: וְיָדַעְתָּ הַיּוֹם וַהֲשֵׁבֹתָ אֶל לְבָבֶךָ, כִּי יהוה הוּא הָאֱלֹהִים בַּשָּׁמַיִם מִמַּעַל וְעַל הָאָרֶץ מִתָּחַת, אֵין עוֹד.[5]

Bow while reciting וַאֲנַחְנוּ כּוֹרְעִים וּמִשְׁתַּחֲוִים.

FULL KADDISH

The *chazzan* recites the Full *Kaddish.*

יִתְגַּדַּל *May His great Name grow exalted and sanctified* (Cong.– *Amen.*) *in the world that He created as He willed. May He give reign to His kingship in your lifetimes and in your days, and in the lifetimes of the entire Family of Israel, swiftly and soon. Now respond: Amen.*

(Cong.– *Amen. May His great Name be blessed forever and ever.*)

May His great Name be blessed forever and ever.

Blessed, praised, glorified, exalted, extolled, mighty, upraised, and lauded be the Name of the Holy One, Blessed is He (Cong.– *Blessed is He*) *— beyond any blessing and song, praise and consolation that are uttered in the world. Now respond: Amen.* (Cong.– *Amen.*)

(Cong.– *Accept our prayers with mercy and favor.*)

May the prayers and supplications of the entire Family of Israel be accepted before their Father Who is in Heaven. Now respond: Amen. (Cong.– *Amen.*)

(Cong.– *Blessed be the Name of* HASHEM, *from this time and forever.*[1])

May there be abundant peace from Heaven, and life, upon us and upon all Israel. Now respond: Amen. (Cong.– *Amen.*)

(Cong.– *My help is from* HASHEM, *Maker of heaven and earth.*[2])

Take three steps back. Bow left and say, *'He Who makes peace . . .';* bow right and say, *'may He . . .';* bow forward and say, *'and upon all Israel . . .'* Remain standing in place for a few moments, then take three steps forward.

He Who makes peace in His heights, may He make peace upon us, and upon all Israel. Now respond: Amen. (Cong.– *Amen.*)

ALEINU

Stand while reciting עָלֵינוּ, *'It is our duty . . .'*

עָלֵינוּ *It is our duty to praise the Master of all, to ascribe greatness to the Molder of primeval creation, for He has not made us like the nations of the lands, and has not emplaced us like the families of the earth; for He has not assigned our portion like theirs nor our lot like all their multitudes. (For they bow to vanity and emptiness and pray to a god which helps not.*[3]*) But we bend our knees, bow, and acknowledge our thanks before the King Who reigns over kings, the Holy One, Blessed is He. He stretches out heaven and establishes earth's foundation,*[4] *the seat of His homage is in the heavens above and His powerful Presence is in the loftiest heights. He is our God and there is none other. True is our King, there is nothing beside Him, as it is written in His Torah: 'You are to know this day and take to your heart that* HASHEM *is the only God — in heaven above and on the earth below — there is none other.'*[5]

Bow while reciting *'But we bend our knees.'*

(1) *Psalms* 113:2. (2) 121:2. (3) *Isaiah* 45:20. (4) 51:13. (5) *Deuteronomy* 4:39.

עַל כֵּן נְקַוֶּה לְּךָ יהוה אֱלֹהֵינוּ לִרְאוֹת מְהֵרָה בְּתִפְאֶרֶת עֻזֶּךָ, לְהַעֲבִיר גִּלּוּלִים מִן הָאָרֶץ, וְהָאֱלִילִים כָּרוֹת יִכָּרֵתוּן, לְתַקֵּן עוֹלָם בְּמַלְכוּת שַׁדַּי. וְכָל בְּנֵי בָשָׂר יִקְרְאוּ בִשְׁמֶךָ, לְהַפְנוֹת אֵלֶיךָ כָּל רִשְׁעֵי אָרֶץ. יַכִּירוּ וְיֵדְעוּ כָּל יוֹשְׁבֵי תֵבֵל, כִּי לְךָ תִּכְרַע כָּל בֶּרֶךְ, תִּשָּׁבַע כָּל לָשׁוֹן.[1] לְפָנֶיךָ יהוה אֱלֹהֵינוּ יִכְרְעוּ וְיִפֹּלוּ, וְלִכְבוֹד שִׁמְךָ יְקָר יִתֵּנוּ. וִיקַבְּלוּ כֻלָּם אֶת עוֹל מַלְכוּתֶךָ, וְתִמְלֹךְ עֲלֵיהֶם מְהֵרָה לְעוֹלָם וָעֶד. כִּי הַמַּלְכוּת שֶׁלְּךָ הִיא וּלְעוֹלְמֵי עַד תִּמְלוֹךְ בְּכָבוֹד, כַּכָּתוּב בְּתוֹרָתֶךָ: יהוה יִמְלֹךְ לְעֹלָם וָעֶד.[2] ❖ וְנֶאֱמַר: וְהָיָה יהוה לְמֶלֶךְ עַל כָּל הָאָרֶץ, בַּיּוֹם הַהוּא יִהְיֶה יהוה אֶחָד וּשְׁמוֹ אֶחָד.[3]

Some congregations recite the following after עָלֵינוּ:

אַל תִּירָא מִפַּחַד פִּתְאֹם, וּמִשֹּׁאַת רְשָׁעִים כִּי תָבֹא.[4] עֻצוּ עֵצָה וְתֻפָר, דַּבְּרוּ דָבָר וְלֹא יָקוּם, כִּי עִמָּנוּ אֵל.[5] וְעַד זִקְנָה אֲנִי הוּא, וְעַד שֵׂיבָה אֲנִי אֶסְבֹּל, אֲנִי עָשִׂיתִי וַאֲנִי אֶשָּׂא, וַאֲנִי אֶסְבֹּל וַאֲמַלֵּט.[5]

קדיש יתום

In the presence of a *minyan,* mourners recite קַדִּישׁ יָתוֹם, the Mourner's *Kaddish* (see *Laws* §81-83).

יִתְגַּדַּל וְיִתְקַדַּשׁ שְׁמֵהּ רַבָּא. (.Cong – אָמֵן.) בְּעָלְמָא דִּי בְרָא כִרְעוּתֵהּ. וְיַמְלִיךְ מַלְכוּתֵהּ, בְּחַיֵּיכוֹן וּבְיוֹמֵיכוֹן וּבְחַיֵּי דְכָל בֵּית יִשְׂרָאֵל, בַּעֲגָלָא וּבִזְמַן קָרִיב. וְאִמְרוּ: אָמֵן.

(.Cong – אָמֵן. יְהֵא שְׁמֵהּ רַבָּא מְבָרַךְ לְעָלַם וּלְעָלְמֵי עָלְמַיָּא.)

יְהֵא שְׁמֵהּ רַבָּא מְבָרַךְ לְעָלַם וּלְעָלְמֵי עָלְמַיָּא.

יִתְבָּרַךְ וְיִשְׁתַּבַּח וְיִתְפָּאַר וְיִתְרוֹמַם וְיִתְנַשֵּׂא וְיִתְהַדָּר וְיִתְעַלֶּה וְיִתְהַלָּל שְׁמֵהּ דְּקֻדְשָׁא בְּרִיךְ הוּא (.Cong – בְּרִיךְ הוּא) — לְעֵלָּא מִן כָּל בִּרְכָתָא וְשִׁירָתָא תֻּשְׁבְּחָתָא וְנֶחֱמָתָא, דַּאֲמִירָן בְּעָלְמָא. וְאִמְרוּ: אָמֵן. (.Cong – אָמֵן.)

יְהֵא שְׁלָמָא רַבָּא מִן שְׁמַיָּא, וְחַיִּים עָלֵינוּ וְעַל כָּל יִשְׂרָאֵל. וְאִמְרוּ: אָמֵן. (.Cong – אָמֵן.)

Take three steps back. Bow left and say . . . עֹשֶׂה; bow right and say . . . הוּא; bow forward and say וְעַל כָּל . . . אָמֵן. Remain standing in place for a few moments, then take three steps forward.

עֹשֶׂה שָׁלוֹם בִּמְרוֹמָיו, הוּא יַעֲשֶׂה שָׁלוֹם עָלֵינוּ, וְעַל כָּל יִשְׂרָאֵל. וְאִמְרוּ: אָמֵן. (.Cong – אָמֵן.)

עַל כֵּן *Therefore we put our hope in You, HASHEM, our God, that we may soon see Your mighty splendor, to remove detestable idolatry from the earth, and false gods will be utterly cut off, to perfect the universe through the Almighty's sovereignty. Then all humanity will call upon Your Name, to turn all the earth's wicked toward You. All the world's inhabitants will recognize and know that to You every knee should bend, every tongue should swear.*[1] *Before You, HASHEM, our God, they will bend every knee and cast themselves down and to the glory of Your Name they will render homage, and they will all accept upon themselves the yoke of Your kingship that You may reign over them soon and eternally. For the kingdom is Yours and You will reign for all eternity in glory as it is written in Your Torah: HASHEM shall reign for all eternity.*[2] Chazzan– *And it is said: HASHEM will be King over all the world — on that day HASHEM will be One and His Name will be One.*[3]

Some congregations recite the following after *Aleinu*.

אַל תִּירָא *Do not fear sudden terror, or the holocaust of the wicked when it comes.*[4] *Plan a conspiracy and it will be annulled; speak your piece and it shall not stand, for God is with us.*[5] *Even till your seniority, I remain unchanged; and even till your ripe old age, I shall endure. I created you and I shall bear you; I shall endure and rescue.*[6]

MOURNER'S KADDISH

In the presence of a *minyan*, mourners recite קַדִּישׁ יָתוֹם, the Mourner's *Kaddish* (see *Laws* 81-83).
[A transliteration of this *Kaddish* appears on page 1147.]

יִתְגַּדַּל *May His great Name grow exalted and sanctified* (Cong.– *Amen.*) *in the world that He created as He willed. May He give reign to His kingship in your lifetimes and in your days, and in the lifetimes of the entire Family of Israel, swiftly and soon. Now respond: Amen.*

(Cong.– *Amen. May His great Name be blessed forever and ever.*)

May His great Name be blessed forever and ever.

Blessed, praised, glorified, exalted, extolled, mighty, upraised, and lauded be the Name of the Holy One, Blessed is He (Cong.– *Blessed is He*) *— beyond any blessing and song, praise and consolation that are uttered in the world. Now respond: Amen.* (Cong.– *Amen*).

May there be abundant peace from Heaven, and life, upon us and upon all Israel. Now respond: Amen. (Cong.– *Amen.*)

Take three steps back. Bow left and say, *'He Who makes peace . . .'*; bow right and say, *'may He . . .'*; bow forward and say, *'and upon all Israel . . .'* Remain standing in place for a few moments, then take three steps forward.

He Who makes peace in His heights, may He make peace upon us, and upon all Israel. Now respond: Amen. (Cong.– *Amen.*)

---

(1) Cf. *Isaiah* 45:23. (2) *Exodus* 15:18. (3) *Zechariah* 14:9. (4) *Proverbs* 3:25. (5) *Isaiah* 8:10. (6) 46:4.

חול המועד

Chol HaMoed

❧ מעריב לחול המועד ולמוצאי שבת ❧

ON ALL CHOL HAMOED NIGHTS OTHER THAN FRIDAY NIGHT BEGIN HERE

ON FRIDAY NIGHT, TURN TO PAGE 490.

Congregation, then *chazzan:*

וְהוּא רַחוּם יְכַפֵּר עָוֹן וְלֹא יַשְׁחִית, וְהִרְבָּה לְהָשִׁיב אַפּוֹ, וְלֹא יָעִיר כָּל חֲמָתוֹ.[1] יהוה הוֹשִׁיעָה, הַמֶּלֶךְ יַעֲנֵנוּ בְיוֹם קָרְאֵנוּ.[2]

In some congregations the *chazzan* chants a melody during his recitation of בָּרְכוּ, so that the congregation can then recite יִתְבָּרַךְ.

Chazzan bows at בָּרְכוּ and straightens up at ה׳.

בָּרְכוּ אֶת יהוה הַמְּבֹרָךְ.

Congregation, followed by *chazzan,* responds, bowing at בָּרוּךְ and straightening up at ה׳.

בָּרוּךְ יהוה הַמְּבֹרָךְ לְעוֹלָם וָעֶד.

יִתְבָּרַךְ וְיִשְׁתַּבַּח וְיִתְפָּאַר וְיִתְרוֹמַם וְיִתְנַשֵּׂא שְׁמוֹ שֶׁל מֶלֶךְ מַלְכֵי הַמְּלָכִים, הַקָּדוֹשׁ בָּרוּךְ הוּא. שֶׁהוּא רִאשׁוֹן וְהוּא אַחֲרוֹן, וּמִבַּלְעָדָיו אֵין אֱלֹהִים.[3] סֹלּוּ, לָרֹכֵב בָּעֲרָבוֹת, בְּיָהּ שְׁמוֹ, וְעִלְזוּ לְפָנָיו.[4] וּשְׁמוֹ מְרוֹמָם עַל כָּל בְּרָכָה וּתְהִלָּה.[5] בָּרוּךְ שֵׁם כְּבוֹד מַלְכוּתוֹ לְעוֹלָם וָעֶד. יְהִי שֵׁם יהוה מְבֹרָךְ, מֵעַתָּה וְעַד עוֹלָם.[6]

ברכות קריאת שמע

בָּרוּךְ אַתָּה יהוה אֱלֹהֵינוּ מֶלֶךְ הָעוֹלָם, אֲשֶׁר בִּדְבָרוֹ מַעֲרִיב עֲרָבִים, בְּחָכְמָה פּוֹתֵחַ שְׁעָרִים, וּבִתְבוּנָה מְשַׁנֶּה עִתִּים, וּמַחֲלִיף אֶת הַזְּמַנִּים, וּמְסַדֵּר אֶת הַכּוֹכָבִים בְּמִשְׁמְרוֹתֵיהֶם בָּרָקִיעַ כִּרְצוֹנוֹ. בּוֹרֵא יוֹם וָלָיְלָה, גּוֹלֵל אוֹר מִפְּנֵי חֹשֶׁךְ וְחֹשֶׁךְ מִפְּנֵי אוֹר. וּמַעֲבִיר יוֹם וּמֵבִיא לָיְלָה, וּמַבְדִּיל בֵּין יוֹם וּבֵין לָיְלָה, יהוה צְבָאוֹת שְׁמוֹ. ❖ אֵל חַי וְקַיָּם, תָּמִיד יִמְלוֹךְ עָלֵינוּ, לְעוֹלָם וָעֶד. בָּרוּךְ אַתָּה יהוה, הַמַּעֲרִיב עֲרָבִים.

(Cong. – אָמֵן.)

אַהֲבַת עוֹלָם בֵּית יִשְׂרָאֵל עַמְּךָ אָהָבְתָּ. תּוֹרָה וּמִצְוֹת, חֻקִּים וּמִשְׁפָּטִים, אוֹתָנוּ לִמַּדְתָּ. עַל כֵּן יהוה אֱלֹהֵינוּ, בְּשָׁכְבֵנוּ וּבְקוּמֵנוּ נָשִׂיחַ בְּחֻקֶּיךָ, וְנִשְׂמַח בְּדִבְרֵי תוֹרָתֶךָ, וּבְמִצְוֹתֶיךָ לְעוֹלָם וָעֶד. ❖ כִּי הֵם חַיֵּינוּ, וְאֹרֶךְ יָמֵינוּ, וּבָהֶם נֶהְגֶּה יוֹמָם וָלָיְלָה. וְאַהֲבָתְךָ, אַל תָּסִיר מִמֶּנּוּ לְעוֹלָמִים. בָּרוּךְ אַתָּה יהוה, אוֹהֵב עַמּוֹ יִשְׂרָאֵל.

(Cong. – אָמֵן.)

MAARIV FOR CHOL HAMOED & CONCLUSION OF SABBATH

ON ALL CHOL HAMOED NIGHTS OTHER THAN FRIDAY NIGHT BEGIN HERE.
ON FRIDAY NIGHT, TURN TO PAGE 490.

Congregation, then *chazzan:*

וְהוּא רַחוּם *He, the Merciful One, is forgiving of iniquity and does not destroy. Frequently He withdraws His anger, not arousing His entire rage.[1] HASHEM, save! May the King answer us on the day we call.[2]*

In some congregations the *chazzan* chants a melody during his recitation of *Borchu,* so that the congregation can then recite *'Blessed, praised . . .'*

Chazzan bows at *'Bless,'* and straightens up at *'HASHEM.'*

Bless HASHEM, the blessed One.

Congregation, followed by *chazzan,* responds, bowing at *'Blessed'* and straightening up at *'HASHEM.'*

Blessed is HASHEM, the blessed One, for all eternity.

Blessed, praised, glorified, exalted and upraised is the Name of the King Who rules over kings — the Holy One, Blessed is He. For He is the First and He is the Last and aside from Him there is no god.[3] Extol Him — Who rides the highest heavens — with His Name, YAH, and exult before Him.[4] His Name is exalted beyond every blessing and praise.[5] Blessed is the Name of His glorious kingdom for all eternity. Blessed be the Name of HASHEM from this time and forever.[6]

BLESSINGS OF THE SHEMA

בָּרוּךְ *Blessed are You, HASHEM, our God, King of the universe, Who by His word brings on evenings, with wisdom opens gates, with understanding alters periods, changes the seasons, and orders the stars in their heavenly constellations as He wills. He creates day and night, removing light before darkness and darkness before light. He causes day to pass and brings night, and separates between day and night — HASHEM, Master of Legions, is His Name.* Chazzan– *May the living and enduring God continuously reign over us, for all eternity. Blessed are You, HASHEM, Who brings on evenings.* (Cong.– *Amen.)*

אַהֲבַת *With an eternal love have You loved the House of Israel, Your nation. Torah and commandments, decrees and ordinances have You taught us. Therefore HASHEM, our God, upon our retiring and arising, we will discuss Your decrees and we will rejoice with the words of Your Torah and with Your commandments for all eternity.* Chazzan– *For they are our life and the length of our days and about them we will meditate day and night. May You not remove Your love from us forever. Blessed are You, HASHEM, Who loves His nation Israel.* (Cong.– *Amen.)*

---

(1) *Psalms* 78:38. (2) 20:10. (3) Cf. *Isaiah* 44:6. (4) *Psalms* 68:5.
(5) Cf. *Nehemiah* 9:5. (6) *Psalms* 113.2.

שמע

Immediately before its recitation, concentrate on fulfilling the positive commandment of reciting the *Shema* twice daily. It is important to enunciate each word clearly and not to run words together. For this reason, vertical lines have been placed between two words that are prone to be slurred into one and are not separated by a comma or a hyphen. See *Laws* §40-52.

When praying without a *minyan,* begin with the following three-word formula:

אֵל מֶלֶךְ נֶאֱמָן.

Recite the first verse aloud, with the right hand covering the eyes, and concentrate intently upon accepting God's absolute sovereignty.

שְׁמַע ׀ יִשְׂרָאֵל, יְהֹוָה ׀ אֱלֹהֵינוּ, יְהֹוָה ׀ אֶחָד:

– In an undertone בָּרוּךְ שֵׁם כְּבוֹד מַלְכוּתוֹ לְעוֹלָם וָעֶד.

While reciting the first paragraph (דברים ו:ה-ט), concentrate on accepting the commandment to love God.

וְאָהַבְתָּ אֵת ׀ יְהֹוָה ׀ אֱלֹהֶיךָ, בְּכָל־לְבָבְךָ, וּבְכָל־נַפְשְׁךָ, וּבְכָל־מְאֹדֶךָ: וְהָיוּ הַדְּבָרִים הָאֵלֶּה, אֲשֶׁר ׀ אָנֹכִי מְצַוְּךָ הַיּוֹם, עַל־לְבָבֶךָ: וְשִׁנַּנְתָּם לְבָנֶיךָ, וְדִבַּרְתָּ בָּם, בְּשִׁבְתְּךָ בְּבֵיתֶךָ, וּבְלֶכְתְּךָ בַדֶּרֶךְ, וּבְשָׁכְבְּךָ וּבְקוּמֶךָ: וּקְשַׁרְתָּם לְאוֹת ׀ עַל־יָדֶךָ, וְהָיוּ לְטֹטָפֹת בֵּין ׀ עֵינֶיךָ: וּכְתַבְתָּם ׀ עַל־מְזֻזוֹת בֵּיתֶךָ, וּבִשְׁעָרֶיךָ:

While reciting the second paragraph (דברים יא:יג-כא), concentrate on accepting all the commandments and the concept of reward and punishment.

וְהָיָה, אִם־שָׁמֹעַ תִּשְׁמְעוּ אֶל־מִצְוֹתַי, אֲשֶׁר ׀ אָנֹכִי מְצַוֶּה ׀ אֶתְכֶם הַיּוֹם, לְאַהֲבָה אֶת־יְהֹוָה ׀ אֱלֹהֵיכֶם וּלְעָבְדוֹ, בְּכָל־לְבַבְכֶם, וּבְכָל־נַפְשְׁכֶם: וְנָתַתִּי מְטַר־אַרְצְכֶם בְּעִתּוֹ, יוֹרֶה וּמַלְקוֹשׁ, וְאָסַפְתָּ דְגָנֶךָ וְתִירֹשְׁךָ וְיִצְהָרֶךָ: וְנָתַתִּי ׀ עֵשֶׂב ׀ בְּשָׂדְךָ לִבְהֶמְתֶּךָ, וְאָכַלְתָּ וְשָׂבָעְתָּ: הִשָּׁמְרוּ לָכֶם, פֶּן־יִפְתֶּה לְבַבְכֶם, וְסַרְתֶּם וַעֲבַדְתֶּם ׀ אֱלֹהִים ׀ אֲחֵרִים, וְהִשְׁתַּחֲוִיתֶם לָהֶם: וְחָרָה ׀ אַף־יְהֹוָה בָּכֶם, וְעָצַר ׀ אֶת־הַשָּׁמַיִם, וְלֹא־יִהְיֶה מָטָר, וְהָאֲדָמָה לֹא תִתֵּן אֶת־יְבוּלָהּ, וַאֲבַדְתֶּם ׀ מְהֵרָה ׀ מֵעַל הָאָרֶץ הַטֹּבָה ׀ אֲשֶׁר ׀ יְהֹוָה נֹתֵן לָכֶם: וְשַׂמְתֶּם ׀ אֶת־דְּבָרַי ׀ אֵלֶּה, עַל־לְבַבְכֶם וְעַל־נַפְשְׁכֶם, וּקְשַׁרְתֶּם ׀ אֹתָם לְאוֹת ׀ עַל־יֶדְכֶם, וְהָיוּ לְטוֹטָפֹת בֵּין ׀ עֵינֵיכֶם: וְלִמַּדְתֶּם ׀ אֹתָם ׀ אֶת־בְּנֵיכֶם, לְדַבֵּר בָּם, בְּשִׁבְתְּךָ בְּבֵיתֶךָ, וּבְלֶכְתְּךָ בַדֶּרֶךְ, וּבְשָׁכְבְּךָ וּבְקוּמֶךָ: וּכְתַבְתָּם ׀ עַל־מְזוּזוֹת בֵּיתֶךָ, וּבִשְׁעָרֶיךָ: לְמַעַן ׀ יִרְבּוּ ׀ יְמֵיכֶם וִימֵי בְנֵיכֶם, עַל הָאֲדָמָה ׀ אֲשֶׁר נִשְׁבַּע ׀ יְהֹוָה לַאֲבֹתֵיכֶם לָתֵת לָהֶם, כִּימֵי הַשָּׁמַיִם ׀ עַל־הָאָרֶץ:

THE SHEMA

Immediately before its recitation, concentrate on fulfilling the positive commandment of reciting the *Shema* twice daily. It is important to enunciate each word clearly and not to run words together. See *Laws* §40-52.

When praying without a *minyan,* begin with the following three-word formula:

God, trustworthy King.

Recite the first verse aloud, with the right hand covering the eyes, and concentrate intently upon accepting God's absolute sovereignty.

Hear, O Israel: HASHEM is our God, HASHEM, the One and Only.[1]

In an undertone— *Blessed is the Name of His glorious kingdom for all eternity.*

While reciting the first paragraph (*Deuteronomy* 6:5-9), concentrate on accepting the commandment to love God.

וְאָהַבְתָּ *You shall love HASHEM, your God, with all your heart, with all your soul and with all your resources. Let these matters that I command you today be upon your heart. Teach them thoroughly to your children and speak of them while you sit in your home, while you walk on the way, when you retire and when you arise. Bind them as a sign upon your arm and let them be tefillin between your eyes. And write them on the doorposts of your house and upon your gates.*

While reciting the second paragraph (*Deuteronomy* 11:13-21), concentrate on accepting all the commandments and the concept of reward and punishment.

וְהָיָה *And it will come to pass that if you continually hearken to My commandments that I command you today, to love HASHEM, your God, and to serve Him, with all your heart and with all your soul — then I will provide rain for your land in its proper time, the early and late rains, that you may gather in your grain, your wine, and your oil. I will provide grass in your field for your cattle and you will eat and be satisfied. Beware lest your heart be seduced and you turn astray and serve gods of others and bow to them. Then the wrath of HASHEM will blaze against you. He will restrain the heaven so there will be no rain and the ground will not yield its produce. And you will swiftly be banished from the goodly land which HASHEM gives you. Place these words of Mine upon your heart and upon your soul; bind them for a sign upon your arm and let them be tefillin between your eyes. Teach them to your children, to discuss them, while you sit in your home, while you walk on the way, when you retire and when you arise. And write them on the doorposts of your house and upon your gates. In order to prolong your days and the days of your children upon the ground that HASHEM has sworn to your ancestors to give them, like the days of the heaven on the earth.*

---

(1) *Deuteronomy* 6:4.

במדבר טו:לז-מא

וַיֹּ֣אמֶר ׀ יהוה ׀ אֶל־מֹשֶׁ֥ה לֵּאמֹֽר׃ דַּבֵּ֞ר ׀ אֶל־בְּנֵ֤י ׀ יִשְׂרָאֵל֙, וְאָמַרְתָּ֣ אֲלֵהֶ֔ם, וְעָשׂ֨וּ לָהֶ֥ם צִיצִ֛ת, עַל־כַּנְפֵ֥י בִגְדֵיהֶ֖ם לְדֹרֹתָ֑ם, וְנָ֥תְנ֛וּ ׀ עַל־צִיצִ֥ת הַכָּנָ֖ף, פְּתִ֥יל תְּכֵֽלֶת׃ וְהָיָ֣ה לָכֶם֮ לְצִיצִת֒, וּרְאִיתֶ֣ם ׀ אֹת֗וֹ, וּזְכַרְתֶּם֙ ׀ אֶת־כָּל־מִצְוֺ֣ת ׀ יהוה, וַעֲשִׂיתֶ֖ם ׀ אֹתָ֑ם, וְלֹֽא־תָת֜וּרוּ ׀ אַחֲרֵ֤י לְבַבְכֶם֙ וְאַחֲרֵ֣י ׀ עֵֽינֵיכֶ֔ם, אֲשֶׁר־אַתֶּ֥ם זֹנִ֖ים ׀ אַחֲרֵיהֶֽם׃ לְמַ֣עַן תִּזְכְּר֔וּ, וַעֲשִׂיתֶ֖ם ׀ אֶת־כָּל־מִצְוֺתָ֑י, וִהְיִיתֶ֥ם קְדֹשִׁ֖ים לֵאלֹהֵיכֶֽם׃ אֲנִ֞י יהוה ׀ אֱלֹהֵיכֶ֗ם, אֲשֶׁ֨ר הוֹצֵ֤אתִי ׀ אֶתְכֶם֙ ׀ מֵאֶ֣רֶץ מִצְרַ֔יִם, לִהְי֥וֹת לָכֶ֖ם לֵאלֹהִ֑ים, אֲנִ֖י ׀ יהוה ׀ אֱלֹהֵיכֶֽם׃ אֱמֶת —

Concentrate on fulfilling the commandment of remembering the Exodus from Egypt.

Although the word אֱמֶת belongs to the next paragraph, it is appended to the conclusion of the previous one, as explained in the commentary on page 50.

Chazzan repeats – **יהוה אֱלֹהֵיכֶם אֱמֶת.**

וֶאֱמוּנָה כָּל זֹאת, וְקַיָּם עָלֵינוּ, כִּי הוּא יהוה אֱלֹהֵינוּ וְאֵין זוּלָתוֹ, וַאֲנַחְנוּ יִשְׂרָאֵל עַמּוֹ. הַפּוֹדֵנוּ מִיַּד מְלָכִים, מַלְכֵּנוּ הַגּוֹאֲלֵנוּ מִכַּף כָּל הֶעָרִיצִים. הָאֵל הַנִּפְרָע לָנוּ מִצָּרֵינוּ, וְהַמְשַׁלֵּם גְּמוּל לְכָל אֹיְבֵי נַפְשֵׁנוּ. הָעֹשֶׂה גְדֹלוֹת עַד אֵין חֵקֶר, וְנִפְלָאוֹת עַד אֵין מִסְפָּר.[1] הַשָּׂם נַפְשֵׁנוּ בַּחַיִּים, וְלֹא נָתַן לַמּוֹט רַגְלֵנוּ.[2] הַמַּדְרִיכֵנוּ עַל בָּמוֹת אוֹיְבֵינוּ, וַיָּרֶם קַרְנֵנוּ עַל כָּל שׂנְאֵינוּ. הָעֹשֶׂה לָּנוּ נִסִּים וּנְקָמָה בְּפַרְעֹה, אוֹתוֹת וּמוֹפְתִים בְּאַדְמַת בְּנֵי חָם. הַמַּכֶּה בְעֶבְרָתוֹ כָּל בְּכוֹרֵי מִצְרָיִם, וַיּוֹצֵא אֶת עַמּוֹ יִשְׂרָאֵל מִתּוֹכָם לְחֵרוּת עוֹלָם. הַמַּעֲבִיר בָּנָיו בֵּין גִּזְרֵי יַם סוּף, אֶת רוֹדְפֵיהֶם וְאֶת שׂוֹנְאֵיהֶם בִּתְהוֹמוֹת טִבַּע. וְרָאוּ בָנָיו גְּבוּרָתוֹ, שִׁבְּחוּ וְהוֹדוּ לִשְׁמוֹ. ❖ וּמַלְכוּתוֹ בְּרָצוֹן קִבְּלוּ עֲלֵיהֶם. מֹשֶׁה וּבְנֵי יִשְׂרָאֵל לְךָ עָנוּ שִׁירָה, בְּשִׂמְחָה רַבָּה, וְאָמְרוּ כֻלָּם:

מִי כָמֹכָה בָּאֵלִים יהוה, מִי כָּמֹכָה נֶאְדָּר בַּקֹּדֶשׁ, נוֹרָא תְהִלֹּת, עֹשֵׂה פֶלֶא.[3] ❖ מַלְכוּתְךָ רָאוּ בָנֶיךָ בּוֹקֵעַ יָם לִפְנֵי מֹשֶׁה, זֶה אֵלִי[4] עָנוּ וְאָמְרוּ:

יהוה יִמְלֹךְ לְעֹלָם וָעֶד.[5] ❖ וְנֶאֱמַר: כִּי פָדָה יהוה אֶת יַעֲקֹב, וּגְאָלוֹ מִיַּד חָזָק מִמֶּנּוּ.[6] בָּרוּךְ אַתָּה יהוה, גָּאַל יִשְׂרָאֵל.

(Cong. – אָמֵן.)

(1) *Job* 9:10. (2) *Psalms* 66:9. (3) *Exodus* 15:11. (4) 15:2. (5) 15:18. (6) *Jeremiah* 31:10.

Numbers 15:37-41

וַיֹּאמֶר *And HASHEM said to Moses saying: Speak to the Children of Israel and say to them that they are to make themselves tzitzis on the corners of their garments, throughout their generations. And they are to place upon the tzitzis of each corner a thread of techeiles. And it shall constitute tzitzis for you, that you may see it and remember all the commandments of HASHEM and perform them; and not explore after your heart and after your eyes after which you stray. So that you may remember and perform all My commandments; and be holy to your God. I am HASHEM, your God, Who has removed you from the land of Egypt to be a God to you; I am HASHEM your God — it is true —*

Concentrate on fulfilling the commandment of remembering the Exodus from Egypt.

Although the word אֱמֶת, *'it is true,'* belongs to the next paragraph, it is appended to the conclusion of the previous one, as explained in the commentary on page 50.

Chazzan repeats: **HASHEM, your God, is true.**

וֶאֱמוּנָה *And faithful is all this, and it is firmly established for us that He is HASHEM our God, and there is none but Him, and we are Israel, His nation. He redeems us from the power of kings, our King Who delivers us from the hand of all the cruel tyrants. He is the God Who exacts vengeance for us from our foes and Who brings just retribution upon all enemies of our soul; Who performs great deeds that are beyond comprehension, and wonders beyond number.*[1] *Who set our soul in life and did not allow our foot to falter.*[2] *Who led us upon the heights of our enemies and raised our pride above all who hate us; Who wrought for us miracles and vengeance upon Pharaoh; signs and wonders on the land of the offspring of Ham; Who struck with His anger all the firstborn of Egypt and removed His nation Israel from their midst to eternal freedom; Who brought His children through the split parts of the Sea of Reeds while those who pursued them and hated them He caused to sink into the depths. When His children perceived His power, they lauded and gave grateful praise to His Name.* Chazzan— *And His Kingship they accepted upon themselves willingly. Moses and the Children of Israel raised their voices to You in song with abundant gladness — and said unanimously:*

מִי כָמֹכָה *Who is like You among the heavenly powers, HASHEM! Who is like You, mighty in holiness, too awesome for praise, doing wonders!*[3] Chazzan— *Your children beheld Your majesty, as You split the sea before Moses: 'This is my God!'*[4] *they exclaimed, then they said:*

יהוה *'HASHEM shall reign for all eternity!'*[5] Chazzan— *And it is further said: 'For HASHEM has redeemed Jacob and delivered him from a power mightier than he.'*[6] *Blessed are You, HASHEM, Who redeemed Israel.*

(Cong.— *Amen.*)

הַשְׁכִּיבֵנוּ יהוה אֱלֹהֵינוּ לְשָׁלוֹם, וְהַעֲמִידֵנוּ מַלְכֵּנוּ לְחַיִּים, וּפְרוֹשׂ עָלֵינוּ סֻכַּת שְׁלוֹמֶךָ, וְתַקְּנֵנוּ בְּעֵצָה טוֹבָה מִלְּפָנֶיךָ, וְהוֹשִׁיעֵנוּ לְמַעַן שְׁמֶךָ. וְהָגֵן בַּעֲדֵנוּ, וְהָסֵר מֵעָלֵינוּ אוֹיֵב, דֶּבֶר, וְחֶרֶב, וְרָעָב, וְיָגוֹן, וְהָסֵר שָׂטָן מִלְּפָנֵינוּ וּמֵאַחֲרֵינוּ, וּבְצֵל כְּנָפֶיךָ תַּסְתִּירֵנוּ,[1] כִּי אֵל שׁוֹמְרֵנוּ וּמַצִּילֵנוּ אָתָּה, כִּי אֵל מֶלֶךְ חַנּוּן וְרַחוּם אָתָּה.[2] ❖ וּשְׁמוֹר צֵאתֵנוּ וּבוֹאֵנוּ, לְחַיִּים וּלְשָׁלוֹם מֵעַתָּה וְעַד עוֹלָם.[3] בָּרוּךְ אַתָּה יהוה, שׁוֹמֵר עַמּוֹ יִשְׂרָאֵל לָעַד.

(.אָמֵן –Cong.)

Some congregations omit the following prayers and continue with Half-*Kaddish* (p. 664).

בָּרוּךְ יהוה לְעוֹלָם, אָמֵן וְאָמֵן.[4] בָּרוּךְ יהוה מִצִּיּוֹן, שֹׁכֵן יְרוּשָׁלָיִם, הַלְּלוּיָהּ.[5] בָּרוּךְ יהוה אֱלֹהִים אֱלֹהֵי יִשְׂרָאֵל, עֹשֵׂה נִפְלָאוֹת לְבַדּוֹ. וּבָרוּךְ שֵׁם כְּבוֹדוֹ לְעוֹלָם, וְיִמָּלֵא כְבוֹדוֹ אֶת כָּל הָאָרֶץ, אָמֵן וְאָמֵן.[6] יְהִי כְבוֹד יהוה לְעוֹלָם, יִשְׂמַח יהוה בְּמַעֲשָׂיו.[7] יְהִי שֵׁם יהוה מְבֹרָךְ, מֵעַתָּה וְעַד עוֹלָם.[8] כִּי לֹא יִטֹּשׁ יהוה אֶת עַמּוֹ בַּעֲבוּר שְׁמוֹ הַגָּדוֹל, כִּי הוֹאִיל יהוה לַעֲשׂוֹת אֶתְכֶם לוֹ לְעָם.[9] וַיַּרְא כָּל הָעָם וַיִּפְּלוּ עַל פְּנֵיהֶם, וַיֹּאמְרוּ, יהוה הוּא הָאֱלֹהִים, יהוה הוּא הָאֱלֹהִים.[10] וְהָיָה יהוה לְמֶלֶךְ עַל כָּל הָאָרֶץ, בַּיּוֹם הַהוּא יִהְיֶה יהוה אֶחָד וּשְׁמוֹ אֶחָד.[11] יְהִי חַסְדְּךָ יהוה עָלֵינוּ, כַּאֲשֶׁר יִחַלְנוּ לָךְ.[12] הוֹשִׁיעֵנוּ יהוה אֱלֹהֵינוּ, וְקַבְּצֵנוּ מִן הַגּוֹיִם, לְהוֹדוֹת לְשֵׁם קָדְשֶׁךָ, לְהִשְׁתַּבֵּחַ בִּתְהִלָּתֶךָ.[13] כָּל גּוֹיִם אֲשֶׁר עָשִׂיתָ יָבוֹאוּ וְיִשְׁתַּחֲווּ לְפָנֶיךָ אֲדֹנָי, וִיכַבְּדוּ לִשְׁמֶךָ. כִּי גָדוֹל אַתָּה וְעֹשֵׂה נִפְלָאוֹת, אַתָּה אֱלֹהִים לְבַדֶּךָ.[14] וַאֲנַחְנוּ עַמְּךָ וְצֹאן מַרְעִיתֶךָ, נוֹדֶה לְּךָ לְעוֹלָם, לְדוֹר וָדֹר נְסַפֵּר תְּהִלָּתֶךָ.[15] בָּרוּךְ יהוה בַּיּוֹם. בָּרוּךְ יהוה בַּלָּיְלָה. בָּרוּךְ יהוה בְּשָׁכְבֵנוּ. בָּרוּךְ יהוה בְּקוּמֵנוּ. כִּי בְיָדְךָ נַפְשׁוֹת הַחַיִּים וְהַמֵּתִים. אֲשֶׁר בְּיָדוֹ נֶפֶשׁ כָּל חָי, וְרוּחַ כָּל בְּשַׂר אִישׁ.[16] בְּיָדְךָ אַפְקִיד רוּחִי, פָּדִיתָה אוֹתִי, יהוה אֵל אֱמֶת.[17] אֱלֹהֵינוּ שֶׁבַּשָּׁמַיִם יַחֵד שִׁמְךָ, וְקַיֵּם מַלְכוּתְךָ תָּמִיד, וּמְלוֹךְ עָלֵינוּ לְעוֹלָם וָעֶד.

יִרְאוּ עֵינֵינוּ וְיִשְׂמַח לִבֵּנוּ וְתָגֵל נַפְשֵׁנוּ בִּישׁוּעָתְךָ בֶּאֱמֶת, בֶּאֱמֹר לְצִיּוֹן מָלַךְ אֱלֹהָיִךְ.[18] יהוה מֶלֶךְ,[19] יהוה מָלָךְ,[20] יהוה יִמְלֹךְ לְעֹלָם וָעֶד.[21] כִּי הַמַּלְכוּת שֶׁלְּךָ הִיא, וּלְעוֹלְמֵי עַד

הַשְׁכִּיבֵנוּ *Lay us down to sleep,* H*ASHEM* *our God, in peace, raise us erect, our King, to life; and spread over us the shelter of Your peace. Set us aright with good counsel from before Your Presence, and save us for Your Name's sake. Shield us, remove from us foe, plague, sword, famine, and woe; and remove spiritual impediment from before us and behind us, and in the shadow of Your wings shelter us*[1] *— for God Who protects and rescues us are You; for God, the Gracious and Compassionate King, are You.*[2] Chazzan– *Safeguard our going and coming, for life and for peace from now to eternity.*[3] *Blessed are You,* H*ASHEM*, *Who protects His people Israel forever.* (Cong.– *Amen.*)

Some congregations omit the following prayers and continue with Half-*Kaddish* (p. 664).

בָּרוּךְ *Blessed is* H*ASHEM* *forever, Amen and Amen.*[4] *Blessed is* H*ASHEM* *from Zion, Who dwells in Jerusalem, Halleluyah!*[5] *Blessed is* H*ASHEM*, *God, the God of Israel, Who alone does wondrous things. Blessed is His glorious Name forever, and may all the earth be filled with His glory, Amen and Amen.*[6] *May the glory of* H*ASHEM* *endure forever, let* H*ASHEM* *rejoice in His works.*[7] *Blessed be the Name of* H*ASHEM* *from this time and forever.*[8] *For* H*ASHEM* *will not cast off His nation for the sake of His Great Name, for* H*ASHEM* *has vowed to make you His own people.*[9] *Then the entire nation saw and fell on their faces and said, '*H*ASHEM* *— only He is God!* H*ASHEM* *— only He is God!'*[10] *Then* H*ASHEM* *will be King over all the world, on that day* H*ASHEM* *will be One and His Name will be One.*[11] *May Your kindness,* H*ASHEM*, *be upon us, just as we awaited You.*[12] *Save us,* H*ASHEM*, *our God, gather us from the nations, to thank Your Holy Name and to glory in Your praise!*[13] *All the nations that You made will come and bow before You, My Lord, and shall glorify Your Name. For You are great and work wonders; You alone, O God.*[14] *Then we, Your nation and the sheep of Your pasture, shall thank You forever; for generation after generation we will relate Your praise.*[15] *Blessed is* H*ASHEM* *by day; Blessed is* H*ASHEM* *by night; Blessed is* H*ASHEM* *when we retire; Blessed is* H*ASHEM* *when we arise. For in Your hand are the souls of the living and the dead. He in Whose hand is the soul of all the living and the spirit of every human being.*[16] *In Your hand I shall entrust my spirit, You redeemed me,* H*ASHEM*, *God of truth.*[17] *Our God, Who is in heaven, bring unity to Your Name; establish Your kingdom forever and reign over us for all eternity.*

יִרְאוּ *May our eyes see, our heart rejoice and our soul exult in Your salvation in truth, when Zion is told, 'Your God has reigned!'*[18] H*ASHEM* *reigns,*[19] H*ASHEM* *has reigned,*[20] H*ASHEM* *will reign for all eternity.*[21] Chazzan– *For the kingdom is Yours and for all eternity*

(1) Cf. *Psalms* 17:8. (2) Cf. *Nehemiah* 9:31. (3) Cf. *Psalms* 121:8. (4) *Psalms* 89:53. (5) 135:21. (6) 72:18-19. (7) 104:31. (8) 113:2. (9) *I Samuel* 12:22. (10) *I Kings* 18:39. (11) *Zechariah* 14:9. (12) *Psalms* 33:22. (13) 106:47. (14) 86:9-10. (15) 79:13. (16) *Job* 12:10. (17) *Psalms* 31:6. (18) Cf. *Isaiah* 52:7. (19) *Psalms* 10:16. (20) 93:1 et al. (21) *Exodus* 15:18.

תִּמְלוֹךְ בְּכָבוֹד, כִּי אֵין לָנוּ מֶלֶךְ אֶלָּא אָתָּה. בָּרוּךְ אַתָּה יהוה, הַמֶּלֶךְ בִּכְבוֹדוֹ תָּמִיד יִמְלוֹךְ עָלֵינוּ לְעוֹלָם וָעֶד, וְעַל כָּל מַעֲשָׂיו.

(Cong. – אָמֵן.)

The *chazzan* recites חֲצִי קַדִּישׁ.

יִתְגַּדַּל וְיִתְקַדַּשׁ שְׁמֵהּ רַבָּא. (Cong. – אָמֵן.) בְּעָלְמָא דִּי בְרָא כִרְעוּתֵהּ, וְיַמְלִיךְ מַלְכוּתֵהּ, בְּחַיֵּיכוֹן וּבְיוֹמֵיכוֹן וּבְחַיֵּי דְכָל בֵּית יִשְׂרָאֵל, בַּעֲגָלָא וּבִזְמַן קָרִיב. וְאִמְרוּ: אָמֵן.

(Cong. – אָמֵן. יְהֵא שְׁמֵהּ רַבָּא מְבָרַךְ לְעָלַם וּלְעָלְמֵי עָלְמַיָּא.)

יְהֵא שְׁמֵהּ רַבָּא מְבָרַךְ לְעָלַם וּלְעָלְמֵי עָלְמַיָּא.

יִתְבָּרַךְ וְיִשְׁתַּבַּח וְיִתְפָּאַר וְיִתְרוֹמַם וְיִתְנַשֵּׂא וְיִתְהַדָּר וְיִתְעַלֶּה וְיִתְהַלָּל שְׁמֵהּ דְּקֻדְשָׁא בְּרִיךְ הוּא (Cong. – בְּרִיךְ הוּא) — לְעֵלָּא מִן כָּל בִּרְכָתָא וְשִׁירָתָא תֻּשְׁבְּחָתָא וְנֶחֱמָתָא, דַּאֲמִירָן בְּעָלְמָא. וְאִמְרוּ: אָמֵן.

(Cong. – אָמֵן.)

❧ שמונה עשרה – עמידה ❧

Take three steps backward, then three steps forward. Remain standing with the feet together while reciting *Shemoneh Esrei*. Recite it with quiet devotion and without interruption, verbal or otherwise. Although its recitation should not be audible to others, one must pray loudly enough to hear himself.

אֲדֹנָי שְׂפָתַי תִּפְתָּח, וּפִי יַגִּיד תְּהִלָּתֶךָ.[1]

אבות

Bend the knees at בָּרוּךְ; bow at אַתָּה; straighten up at 'ה.

בָּרוּךְ אַתָּה יהוה אֱלֹהֵינוּ וֵאלֹהֵי אֲבוֹתֵינוּ, אֱלֹהֵי אַבְרָהָם, אֱלֹהֵי יִצְחָק, וֵאלֹהֵי יַעֲקֹב, הָאֵל הַגָּדוֹל הַגִּבּוֹר וְהַנּוֹרָא, אֵל עֶלְיוֹן, גּוֹמֵל חֲסָדִים טוֹבִים וְקוֹנֵה הַכֹּל, וְזוֹכֵר חַסְדֵי אָבוֹת, וּמֵבִיא גוֹאֵל לִבְנֵי בְנֵיהֶם, לְמַעַן שְׁמוֹ בְּאַהֲבָה. מֶלֶךְ עוֹזֵר וּמוֹשִׁיעַ וּמָגֵן.

Bend the knees at בָּרוּךְ; bow at אַתָּה; straighten up at 'ה.

בָּרוּךְ אַתָּה יהוה, מָגֵן אַבְרָהָם.

גבורות

אַתָּה גִּבּוֹר לְעוֹלָם אֲדֹנָי, מְחַיֵּה מֵתִים אַתָּה, רַב לְהוֹשִׁיעַ. מְכַלְכֵּל חַיִּים בְּחֶסֶד, מְחַיֵּה מֵתִים בְּרַחֲמִים רַבִּים, סוֹמֵךְ נוֹפְלִים, וְרוֹפֵא חוֹלִים, וּמַתִּיר אֲסוּרִים, וּמְקַיֵּם אֱמוּנָתוֹ לִישֵׁנֵי עָפָר. מִי כָמוֹךָ בַּעַל גְּבוּרוֹת, וּמִי דּוֹמֶה לָּךְ, מֶלֶךְ מֵמִית וּמְחַיֶּה וּמַצְמִיחַ יְשׁוּעָה. וְנֶאֱמָן אַתָּה לְהַחֲיוֹת מֵתִים. בָּרוּךְ אַתָּה יהוה, מְחַיֵּה הַמֵּתִים.

קדושת השם

[illegible]ה קָדוֹשׁ וְ[illegible]דוֹשׁ, וּ[illegible]ם בְּכָל יוֹם יְהַלְלוּךָ סֶּלָה. בָּרוּךְ אַתָּה יהוה, הָאֵל הַקָּדוֹשׁ.

You will reign in glory, for we have no King but You. Blessed are You, HASHEM, the King in His glory — He shall constantly reign over us forever and ever, and over all His creatures. (Cong.– *Amen.*)

The *chazzan* recites Half-*Kaddish*.

יִתְגַּדַּל *May His great Name grow exalted and sanctified* (Cong.– *Amen.*) *in the world that He created as He willed. May He give reign to His kingship in your lifetimes and in your days, and in the lifetimes of the entire Family of Israel, swiftly and soon. Now respond: Amen.*

(Cong.– *Amen. May His great Name be blessed forever and ever.*)

May His great Name be blessed forever and ever.

Blessed, praised, glorified, exalted, extolled, mighty, upraised, and lauded be the Name of the Holy One, Blessed is He (Cong.– *Blessed is He*) *— beyond any blessing and song, praise and consolation that are uttered in the world. Now respond: Amen.* (Cong.– *Amen.*)

SHEMONEH ESREI – AMIDAH

Take three steps backward, then three steps forward. Remain standing with the feet together while reciting *Shemoneh Esrei*. Recite it with quiet devotion and without interruption, verbal or otherwise. Although its recitation should not be audible to others, one must pray loudly enough to hear himself.

My Lord, open my lips, that my mouth may declare Your praise.[1]

PATRIARCHS

Bend the knees at *'Blessed'*; bow at *'You'*; straighten up at *'HASHEM.'*

בָּרוּךְ ***Blessed are You, HASHEM, our God and the God of our forefathers, God of Abraham, God of Isaac, and God of Jacob; the great, mighty, and awesome God, the supreme God, Who bestows beneficial kindnesses and creates everything, Who recalls the kindnesses of the Patriarchs and brings a Redeemer to their children's children, for His Name's sake, with love.***

Bend the knees at *'Blessed'*; bow at *'You'*; straighten up at *'HASHEM.'*

O King, Helper, Savior, and Shield. Blessed are You, HASHEM, Shield of Abraham.

GOD'S MIGHT

אַתָּה ***You are eternally mighty, my Lord, the Resuscitator of the dead are You; abundantly able to save. He sustains the living with kindness, resuscitates the dead with abundant mercy, supports the fallen, heals the sick, releases the confined, and maintains His faith to those asleep in the dust. Who is like You, O Master of mighty deeds, and who is comparable to You, O King Who causes death and restores life and makes salvation sprout! And You are faithful to resuscitate the dead. Blessed are You, HASHEM, Who resuscitates the dead.***

HOLINESS OF GOD'S NAME

אַתָּה ***You are holy and Your Name is holy, and holy ones praise You every day, forever. Blessed are You, HASHEM, the holy God.***

(1) Psalms 51:17.

בינה

אַתָּה חוֹנֵן לְאָדָם דַּעַת, וּמְלַמֵּד לֶאֱנוֹשׁ בִּינָה.

After the Sabbath or *Yom Tov*, add [if forgotten do not repeat *Shemoneh Esrei; see Laws* §93]:

אַתָּה חוֹנַנְתָּנוּ לְמַדַּע תּוֹרָתֶךָ, וַתְּלַמְּדֵנוּ לַעֲשׂוֹת חֻקֵּי רְצוֹנֶךָ וַתַּבְדֵּל יהוה אֱלֹהֵינוּ בֵּין קֹדֶשׁ לְחוֹל בֵּין אוֹר לְחוֹשֶׁךְ, בֵּין יִשְׂרָאֵל לָעַמִּים בֵּין יוֹם הַשְּׁבִיעִי לְשֵׁשֶׁת יְמֵי הַמַּעֲשֶׂה. אָבִינוּ מַלְכֵּנוּ הָחֵל עָלֵינוּ הַיָּמִים הַבָּאִים לִקְרָאתֵנוּ לְשָׁלוֹם חֲשׂוּכִים מִכָּל חֵטְא וּמְנֻקִּים מִכָּל עָוֹן וּמְדֻבָּקִים בְּיִרְאָתֶךָ. וְ...

חָנֵּנוּ מֵאִתְּךָ דֵּעָה בִּינָה וְהַשְׂכֵּל. בָּרוּךְ אַתָּה יהוה, חוֹנֵן הַדָּעַת.

תשובה

הֲשִׁיבֵנוּ אָבִינוּ לְתוֹרָתֶךָ, וְקָרְבֵנוּ מַלְכֵּנוּ לַעֲבוֹדָתֶךָ, וְהַחֲזִירֵנוּ בִּתְשׁוּבָה שְׁלֵמָה לְפָנֶיךָ. בָּרוּךְ אַתָּה יהוה, הָרוֹצֶה בִּתְשׁוּבָה.

סליחה

Strike the left side of the chest with the right fist while reciting the words חָטָאנוּ and פָּשָׁעְנוּ.

סְלַח לָנוּ אָבִינוּ כִּי חָטָאנוּ, מְחַל לָנוּ מַלְכֵּנוּ כִּי פָשָׁעְנוּ, כִּי מוֹחֵל וְסוֹלֵחַ אָתָּה. בָּרוּךְ אַתָּה יהוה, חַנּוּן הַמַּרְבֶּה לִסְלֹחַ.

גאולה

רְאֵה בְעָנְיֵנוּ, וְרִיבָה רִיבֵנוּ, וּגְאָלֵנוּ[1] מְהֵרָה לְמַעַן שְׁמֶךָ, כִּי גוֹאֵל חָזָק אָתָּה. בָּרוּךְ אַתָּה יהוה, גּוֹאֵל יִשְׂרָאֵל.

רפואה

רְפָאֵנוּ יהוה וְנֵרָפֵא, הוֹשִׁיעֵנוּ וְנִוָּשֵׁעָה, כִּי תְהִלָּתֵנוּ אָתָּה,[2] וְהַעֲלֵה רְפוּאָה שְׁלֵמָה לְכָל מַכּוֹתֵינוּ, °°כִּי אֵל מֶלֶךְ רוֹפֵא נֶאֱמָן וְרַחֲמָן אָתָּה. בָּרוּךְ אַתָּה יהוה, רוֹפֵא חוֹלֵי עַמּוֹ יִשְׂרָאֵל.

ברכת השנים

בָּרֵךְ עָלֵינוּ יהוה אֱלֹהֵינוּ אֶת הַשָּׁנָה הַזֹּאת וְאֶת כָּל מִינֵי תְבוּאָתָהּ לְטוֹבָה, וְתֵן בְּרָכָה עַל פְּנֵי הָאֲדָמָה, וְשַׂבְּעֵנוּ מִטּוּבֶךָ, וּבָרֵךְ שְׁנָתֵנוּ כַּשָּׁנִים הַטּוֹבוֹת. בָּרוּךְ אַתָּה יהוה, מְבָרֵךְ הַשָּׁנִים.

°°At this point one may interject a prayer for one who is ill:

יְהִי רָצוֹן מִלְּפָנֶיךָ יהוה אֱלֹהַי וֵאלֹהֵי אֲבוֹתַי, שֶׁתִּשְׁלַח מְהֵרָה רְפוּאָה שְׁלֵמָה מִן הַשָּׁמַיִם, רְפוּאַת הַנֶּפֶשׁ וּרְפוּאַת הַגּוּף

for a male—לַחוֹלֶה (patient's name) בֶּן (mother's name) בְּתוֹךְ שְׁאָר חוֹלֵי יִשְׂרָאֵל.

for a female—לַחוֹלָה (patient's name) בַּת (mother's name) בְּתוֹךְ שְׁאָר חוֹלֵי יִשְׂרָאֵל.

continue—כִּי אֵל . . .

INSIGHT

אַתָּה *You graciously endow man with wisdom and teach insight to a frail mortal.*

After the Sabbath or *Yom Tov*, add [if forgotten do not repeat *Shemoneh Esrei;* see *Laws* §93]:

אַתָּה *You have graced us with intelligence to study Your Torah and You have taught us to perform the decrees You have willed. HASHEM, our God, You have distinguished between the sacred and the secular, between light and darkness, between Israel and the peoples, between the seventh day and the six days of labor. Our Father, our King, begin for us the days approaching us for peace, free from all sin, cleansed from all iniquity and attached to fear of You. And ...*

Endow us graciously from Yourself with wisdom, insight, and discernment. Blessed are You, HASHEM, gracious Giver of wisdom.

REPENTANCE

הֲשִׁיבֵנוּ *Bring us back, our Father, to Your Torah, and bring us near, our King, to Your service, and influence us to return in perfect repentance before You. Blessed are You, HASHEM, Who desires repentance.*

FORGIVENESS

Strike the left side of the chest with the right fist while reciting the words *'erred'* and *'sinned.'*

סְלַח *Forgive us, our Father, for we have erred; pardon us, our King, for we have willfully sinned; for You pardon and forgive. Blessed are You, HASHEM, the gracious One Who pardons abundantly.*

REDEMPTION

רְאֵה *Behold our affliction, take up our grievance, and redeem us*[1] *speedily for Your Name's sake, for You are a powerful Redeemer. Blessed are You, HASHEM, Redeemer of Israel.*

HEALTH AND HEALING

רְפָאֵנוּ *Heal us, HASHEM — then we will be healed; save us — then we will be saved, for You are our praise.*[2] *Bring complete recovery for all our ailments,* °°*for You are God, King, the faithful and compassionate Healer. Blessed are You, HASHEM, Who heals the sick of His people Israel.*

YEAR OF PROSPERITY

בָּרֵךְ *Bless on our behalf — O HASHEM, our God — this year and all its kinds of crops for the best, and give a blessing on the face of the earth, and satisfy us from Your bounty, and bless our year like the best years. Blessed are You, HASHEM, Who blesses the years.*

°°At this point one may interject a prayer for one who is ill:

May it be Your will, HASHEM, my God, and the God of my forefathers, that You quickly send a complete recovery from heaven, spiritual healing and physical healing to the patient (name) *son/daughter of* (mother's name) *among the other patients of Israel.* Continue: *For You are God ...*

(1) Cf. *Psalms* 119:153-154. (2) Cf. *Jeremiah* 17:14.

קיבוץ גליות

תְּקַע בְּשׁוֹפָר גָּדוֹל לְחֵרוּתֵנוּ, וְשָׂא נֵס לְקַבֵּץ גָּלֻיּוֹתֵינוּ, וְקַבְּצֵנוּ יַחַד מֵאַרְבַּע כַּנְפוֹת הָאָרֶץ.[1] בָּרוּךְ אַתָּה יהוה, מְקַבֵּץ נִדְחֵי עַמּוֹ יִשְׂרָאֵל.

דין

הָשִׁיבָה שׁוֹפְטֵינוּ כְּבָרִאשׁוֹנָה, וְיוֹעֲצֵינוּ כְּבַתְּחִלָּה,[2] וְהָסֵר מִמֶּנּוּ יָגוֹן וַאֲנָחָה, וּמְלוֹךְ עָלֵינוּ אַתָּה יהוה לְבַדְּךָ בְּחֶסֶד וּבְרַחֲמִים, וְצַדְּקֵנוּ בַּמִּשְׁפָּט. בָּרוּךְ אַתָּה יהוה, מֶלֶךְ אוֹהֵב צְדָקָה וּמִשְׁפָּט.

ברכת המינים

וְלַמַּלְשִׁינִים אַל תְּהִי תִקְוָה, וְכָל הָרִשְׁעָה כְּרֶגַע תֹּאבֵד, וְכָל אֹיְבֶיךָ מְהֵרָה יִכָּרֵתוּ, וְהַזֵּדִים מְהֵרָה תְעַקֵּר וּתְשַׁבֵּר וּתְמַגֵּר וְתַכְנִיעַ בִּמְהֵרָה בְיָמֵינוּ. בָּרוּךְ אַתָּה יהוה, שׁוֹבֵר אֹיְבִים וּמַכְנִיעַ זֵדִים.

צדיקים

עַל הַצַּדִּיקִים וְעַל הַחֲסִידִים, וְעַל זִקְנֵי עַמְּךָ בֵּית יִשְׂרָאֵל, וְעַל פְּלֵיטַת סוֹפְרֵיהֶם, וְעַל גֵּרֵי הַצֶּדֶק וְעָלֵינוּ, יֶהֱמוּ רַחֲמֶיךָ יהוה אֱלֹהֵינוּ, וְתֵן שָׂכָר טוֹב לְכָל הַבּוֹטְחִים בְּשִׁמְךָ בֶּאֱמֶת, וְשִׂים חֶלְקֵנוּ עִמָּהֶם לְעוֹלָם, וְלֹא נֵבוֹשׁ כִּי בְךָ בָּטָחְנוּ. בָּרוּךְ אַתָּה יהוה, מִשְׁעָן וּמִבְטָח לַצַּדִּיקִים.

בנין ירושלים

וְלִירוּשָׁלַיִם עִירְךָ בְּרַחֲמִים תָּשׁוּב, וְתִשְׁכּוֹן בְּתוֹכָהּ כַּאֲשֶׁר דִּבַּרְתָּ, וּבְנֵה אוֹתָהּ בְּקָרוֹב בְּיָמֵינוּ בִּנְיַן עוֹלָם, וְכִסֵּא דָוִד מְהֵרָה לְתוֹכָהּ תָּכִין. בָּרוּךְ אַתָּה יהוה, בּוֹנֵה יְרוּשָׁלָיִם.

מלכות בית דוד

אֶת צֶמַח דָּוִד עַבְדְּךָ מְהֵרָה תַצְמִיחַ, וְקַרְנוֹ תָּרוּם בִּישׁוּעָתֶךָ, כִּי לִישׁוּעָתְךָ קִוִּינוּ כָּל הַיּוֹם. בָּרוּךְ אַתָּה יהוה, מַצְמִיחַ קֶרֶן יְשׁוּעָה.

קבלת תפלה

שְׁמַע קוֹלֵנוּ יהוה אֱלֹהֵינוּ, חוּס וְרַחֵם עָלֵינוּ, וְקַבֵּל בְּרַחֲמִים וּבְרָצוֹן אֶת תְּפִלָּתֵנוּ, כִּי אֵל שׁוֹמֵעַ תְּפִלּוֹת וְתַחֲנוּנִים אָתָּה. וּמִלְּפָנֶיךָ מַלְכֵּנוּ רֵיקָם אַל תְּשִׁיבֵנוּ,

INGATHERING OF EXILES

תְּקַע *Sound the great shofar for our freedom, raise the banner to gather our exiles and gather us together from the four corners of the earth.*[1] *Blessed are You,* HASHEM, *Who gathers in the dispersed of His people Israel.*

RESTORATION OF JUSTICE

הָשִׁיבָה *Restore our judges as in earliest times and our counselors as at first;*[2] *remove from us sorrow and groan; and reign over us — You,* HASHEM, *alone — with kindness and compassion, and justify us through judgment. Blessed are You,* HASHEM, *the King Who loves righteousness and judgment.*

AGAINST HERETICS

וְלַמַּלְשִׁינִים *And for slanderers let there be no hope; and may all wickedness perish in an instant; and may all Your enemies be cut down speedily. May You speedily uproot, smash, cast down, and humble the wanton sinners — speedily in our days. Blessed are You,* HASHEM, *Who breaks enemies and humbles wanton sinners.*

THE RIGHTEOUS

עַל הַצַּדִּיקִים *On the righteous, on the devout, on the elders of Your people the Family of Israel, on the remnant of their scholars, on the righteous converts and on ourselves — may Your compassion be aroused,* HASHEM, *our God, and give goodly reward to all who sincerely believe in Your Name. Put our lot with them forever, and we will not feel ashamed, for we trust in You. Blessed are You,* HASHEM, *Mainstay and Assurance of the righteous.*

REBUILDING JERUSALEM

וְלִירוּשָׁלַיִם *And to Jerusalem, Your city, may You return in compassion, and may You rest within it, as You have spoken. May You rebuild it soon in our days as an eternal structure, and may You speedily establish the throne of David within it. Blessed are You,* HASHEM, *the Builder of Jerusalem.*

DAVIDIC REIGN

אֶת צֶמַח *The offspring of Your servant David may You speedily cause to flourish, and enhance his pride through Your salvation, for we hope for Your salvation all day long. Blessed are You,* HASHEM, *Who causes the pride of salvation to flourish.*

ACCEPTANCE OF PRAYER

שְׁמַע *Hear our voice,* HASHEM *our God, pity and be compassionate to us, and accept — with compassion and favor — our prayer, for God Who hears prayers and supplications are You. From before Yourself, our King, turn us not away empty-handed,*

(1) Cf. *Isaiah* 11:12. (2) Cf. 1:26.

°°כִּי אַתָּה שׁוֹמֵעַ תְּפִלַּת עַמְּךָ יִשְׂרָאֵל בְּרַחֲמִים. בָּרוּךְ אַתָּה יהוה, שׁוֹמֵעַ תְּפִלָּה.

עבודה

רְצֵה יהוה אֱלֹהֵינוּ בְּעַמְּךָ יִשְׂרָאֵל וּבִתְפִלָּתָם, וְהָשֵׁב אֶת הָעֲבוֹדָה לִדְבִיר בֵּיתֶךָ. וְאִשֵּׁי יִשְׂרָאֵל וּתְפִלָּתָם בְּאַהֲבָה תְקַבֵּל בְּרָצוֹן, וּתְהִי לְרָצוֹן תָּמִיד עֲבוֹדַת יִשְׂרָאֵל עַמֶּךָ.

[If the following paragraph is forgotten, repeat *Shemoneh Esrei*. See *Laws* §56.]

אֱלֹהֵינוּ וֵאלֹהֵי אֲבוֹתֵינוּ, יַעֲלֶה, וְיָבֹא, וְיַגִּיעַ, וְיֵרָאֶה, וְיֵרָצֶה, וְיִשָּׁמַע, וְיִפָּקֵד, וְיִזָּכֵר זִכְרוֹנֵנוּ וּפִקְדוֹנֵנוּ, וְזִכְרוֹן אֲבוֹתֵינוּ, וְזִכְרוֹן מָשִׁיחַ בֶּן דָּוִד עַבְדֶּךָ, וְזִכְרוֹן יְרוּשָׁלַיִם עִיר קָדְשֶׁךָ, וְזִכְרוֹן כָּל עַמְּךָ בֵּית יִשְׂרָאֵל לְפָנֶיךָ, לִפְלֵיטָה לְטוֹבָה לְחֵן וּלְחֶסֶד וּלְרַחֲמִים, לְחַיִּים וּלְשָׁלוֹם בְּיוֹם חַג הַמַּצּוֹת הַזֶּה. זָכְרֵנוּ יהוה אֱלֹהֵינוּ בּוֹ לְטוֹבָה, וּפָקְדֵנוּ בוֹ לִבְרָכָה, וְהוֹשִׁיעֵנוּ בוֹ לְחַיִּים. וּבִדְבַר יְשׁוּעָה וְרַחֲמִים, חוּס וְחָנֵּנוּ וְרַחֵם עָלֵינוּ וְהוֹשִׁיעֵנוּ, כִּי אֵלֶיךָ עֵינֵינוּ, כִּי אֵל מֶלֶךְ חַנּוּן וְרַחוּם אָתָּה.[1]

וְתֶחֱזֶינָה עֵינֵינוּ בְּשׁוּבְךָ לְצִיּוֹן בְּרַחֲמִים. בָּרוּךְ אַתָּה יהוה, הַמַּחֲזִיר שְׁכִינָתוֹ לְצִיּוֹן.

°°During the silent *Shemoneh Esrei* one may insert either or both of these personal prayers.

For forgiveness:

אָנָּא יהוה, חָטָאתִי עָוִיתִי וּפָשַׁעְתִּי לְפָנֶיךָ, מִיּוֹם הֱיוֹתִי עַל הָאֲדָמָה עַד הַיּוֹם הַזֶּה (וּבִפְרַט בַּחֵטְא ....). אָנָּא יהוה, עֲשֵׂה לְמַעַן שִׁמְךָ הַגָּדוֹל, וּתְכַפֶּר לִי עַל עֲוֹנַי וַחֲטָאַי וּפְשָׁעַי שֶׁחָטָאתִי וְשֶׁעָוִיתִי וְשֶׁפָּשַׁעְתִּי לְפָנֶיךָ, מִנְּעוּרַי עַד הַיּוֹם הַזֶּה. וּתְמַלֵּא כָּל הַשֵּׁמוֹת שֶׁפָּגַמְתִּי בְּשִׁמְךָ הַגָּדוֹל.

For livelihood:

אַתָּה הוּא יהוה הָאֱלֹהִים, הַזָּן וּמְפַרְנֵס וּמְכַלְכֵּל מִקַּרְנֵי רְאֵמִים עַד בֵּיצֵי כִנִּים. הַטְרִיפֵנִי לֶחֶם חֻקִּי, וְהַמְצֵא לִי וּלְכָל בְּנֵי בֵיתִי מְזוֹנוֹתַי קוֹדֶם שֶׁאֶצְטָרֵךְ לָהֶם, בְּנַחַת וְלֹא בְצַעַר, בְּהֶתֵּר וְלֹא בְאִסּוּר, בְּכָבוֹד וְלֹא בְבִזָּיוֹן, לְחַיִּים וּלְשָׁלוֹם, מִשֶּׁפַע בְּרָכָה וְהַצְלָחָה, וּמִשֶּׁפַע בְּרֵכָה עֶלְיוֹנָה, כְּדֵי שֶׁאוּכַל לַעֲשׂוֹת רְצוֹנֶךָ וְלַעֲסוֹק בְּתוֹרָתֶךָ וּלְקַיֵּם מִצְוֹתֶיךָ. וְאַל תַּצְרִיכֵנִי לִידֵי מַתְּנַת בָּשָׂר וָדָם. וִיקֻיַּם בִּי מִקְרָא שֶׁכָּתוּב: פּוֹתֵחַ אֶת יָדֶךָ, וּמַשְׂבִּיעַ לְכָל חַי רָצוֹן.[2] וְכָתוּב: הַשְׁלֵךְ עַל יהוה יְהָבְךָ וְהוּא יְכַלְכְּלֶךָ.[3]

Continue— כִּי אַתָּה . . .

°° *for You hear the prayer of Your people Israel with compassion. Blessed are You, HASHEM, Who hears prayer.*

TEMPLE SERVICE

רְצֵה *Be favorable, HASHEM, our God, toward Your people Israel and their prayer and restore the service to the Holy of Holies of Your Temple. The fire-offerings of Israel and their prayer accept with love and favor, and may the service of Your people Israel always be favorable to You.*

[If the following paragraph is forgotten, repeat *Shemoneh Esrei*. See *Laws* §56.]

אֱלֹהֵינוּ *Our God and God of our forefathers, may there rise, come, reach, be noted, be favored, be heard, be considered, and be remembered — the remembrance and consideration of ourselves; the remembrance of our forefathers; the remembrance of Messiah, son of David, Your servant; the remembrance of Jerusalem, the City of Your Holiness; the remembrance of Your entire people the Family of Israel — before You for deliverance, for goodness, for grace, for kindness, and for compassion, for life, and for peace on this day of the Festival of Matzos. Remember us on it, HASHEM, our God, for goodness, consider us on it for blessing, and help us on it for life. In the matter of salvation and compassion, pity, be gracious and compassionate with us and help us, for our eyes are turned to You, because You are God, the gracious and compassionate King.*[1]

וְתֶחֱזֶינָה *May our eyes behold Your return to Zion in compassion. Blessed are You, HASHEM, Who restores His Presence to Zion.*

°°During the silent *Shemoneh Esrei* one may insert either or both of these personal prayers.

For forgiveness:

אָנָּא *Please, O HASHEM, I have erred, been iniquitous, and willfully sinned before You, from the day I have existed on earth until this very day (and especially with the sin of . . .). Please, HASHEM, act for the sake of Your Great Name and grant me atonement for my iniquities, my errors, and my willful sins through which I have erred, been iniquitous, and willfully sinned before You, from my youth until this day. And make whole all the Names that I have blemished in Your Great Name.*

For livelihood:

אַתָּה *It is You, HASHEM the God, Who nourishes, sustains, and supports, from the horns of re'eimim to the eggs of lice. Provide me with my allotment of bread; and bring forth for me and all members of my household, my food, before I have need for it; in contentment but not in pain, in a permissible but not a forbidden manner, in honor but not in disgrace, for life and for peace; from the flow of blessing and success and from the flow of the Heavenly spring, so that I be enabled to do Your will and engage in Your Torah and fulfill Your commandments. Make me not needful of people's largesse; and may there be fulfilled in me the verse that states, 'You open Your hand and satisfy the desire of every living thing'*[2] *and that states, 'Cast Your burden upon HASHEM and He will support you.'*[3]

Continue: *For You hear the prayer . . .*

(1) Cf. *Nehemiah* 9:31. (2) *Psalms* 145:16. (3) 55:23.

הודאה

Bow at מוֹדִים; straighten up at 'ה.

מוֹדִים אֲנַחְנוּ לָךְ שָׁאַתָּה הוּא יהוה אֱלֹהֵינוּ וֵאלֹהֵי אֲבוֹתֵינוּ לְעוֹלָם וָעֶד. צוּר חַיֵּינוּ, מָגֵן יִשְׁעֵנוּ אַתָּה הוּא לְדוֹר וָדוֹר. נוֹדֶה לְּךָ וּנְסַפֵּר תְּהִלָּתֶךָ[1] עַל חַיֵּינוּ הַמְּסוּרִים בְּיָדֶךָ, וְעַל נִשְׁמוֹתֵינוּ הַפְּקוּדוֹת לָךְ, וְעַל נִסֶּיךָ שֶׁבְּכָל יוֹם עִמָּנוּ, וְעַל נִפְלְאוֹתֶיךָ וְטוֹבוֹתֶיךָ שֶׁבְּכָל עֵת, עֶרֶב וָבֹקֶר וְצָהֳרָיִם. הַטּוֹב כִּי לֹא כָלוּ רַחֲמֶיךָ, וְהַמְּרַחֵם כִּי לֹא תַמּוּ חֲסָדֶיךָ,[2] מֵעוֹלָם קִוִּינוּ לָךְ.

וְעַל כֻּלָּם יִתְבָּרַךְ וְיִתְרוֹמַם שִׁמְךָ מַלְכֵּנוּ תָּמִיד לְעוֹלָם וָעֶד.

Bend the knees at בָּרוּךְ; bow at אַתָּה; straighten up at 'ה.

וְכֹל הַחַיִּים יוֹדוּךָ סֶּלָה, וִיהַלְלוּ אֶת שִׁמְךָ בֶּאֱמֶת, הָאֵל יְשׁוּעָתֵנוּ וְעֶזְרָתֵנוּ סֶלָה. בָּרוּךְ אַתָּה יהוה, הַטּוֹב שִׁמְךָ וּלְךָ נָאֶה לְהוֹדוֹת.

שלום

שָׁלוֹם רָב עַל יִשְׂרָאֵל עַמְּךָ תָּשִׂים לְעוֹלָם, כִּי אַתָּה הוּא מֶלֶךְ אָדוֹן לְכָל הַשָּׁלוֹם. וְטוֹב בְּעֵינֶיךָ לְבָרֵךְ אֶת עַמְּךָ יִשְׂרָאֵל, בְּכָל עֵת וּבְכָל שָׁעָה בִּשְׁלוֹמֶךָ. בָּרוּךְ אַתָּה יהוה, הַמְּבָרֵךְ אֶת עַמּוֹ יִשְׂרָאֵל בַּשָּׁלוֹם.

יִהְיוּ לְרָצוֹן אִמְרֵי פִי וְהֶגְיוֹן לִבִּי לְפָנֶיךָ, יהוה צוּרִי וְגֹאֲלִי.[3]

אֱלֹהַי, נְצוֹר לְשׁוֹנִי מֵרָע, וּשְׂפָתַי מִדַּבֵּר מִרְמָה,[4] וְלִמְקַלְלַי נַפְשִׁי תִדּוֹם, וְנַפְשִׁי כֶּעָפָר לַכֹּל תִּהְיֶה. פְּתַח לִבִּי בְּתוֹרָתֶךָ, וּבְמִצְוֹתֶיךָ תִּרְדּוֹף נַפְשִׁי. וְכֹל הַחוֹשְׁבִים עָלַי רָעָה, מְהֵרָה הָפֵר עֲצָתָם וְקַלְקֵל מַחֲשַׁבְתָּם. עֲשֵׂה לְמַעַן שְׁמֶךָ, עֲשֵׂה לְמַעַן יְמִינֶךָ, עֲשֵׂה לְמַעַן קְדֻשָּׁתֶךָ, עֲשֵׂה לְמַעַן תּוֹרָתֶךָ. לְמַעַן יֵחָלְצוּן יְדִידֶיךָ, הוֹשִׁיעָה יְמִינְךָ וַעֲנֵנִי.[5] Some recite verses pertaining to their names here. See page 1143.

יִהְיוּ לְרָצוֹן אִמְרֵי פִי וְהֶגְיוֹן לִבִּי לְפָנֶיךָ, יהוה צוּרִי וְגֹאֲלִי.[3]

Bow and take three steps back. Bow left and say . . . עֹשֶׂה; bow right and say . . . הוּא יַעֲשֶׂה; bow forward and say וְעַל כָּל . . . אָמֵן.

עֹשֶׂה שָׁלוֹם בִּמְרוֹמָיו, הוּא יַעֲשֶׂה שָׁלוֹם עָלֵינוּ, וְעַל כָּל יִשְׂרָאֵל. וְאִמְרוּ: אָמֵן.

יְהִי רָצוֹן מִלְּפָנֶיךָ יהוה אֱלֹהֵינוּ וֵאלֹהֵי אֲבוֹתֵינוּ, שֶׁיִּבָּנֶה בֵּית הַמִּקְדָּשׁ בִּמְהֵרָה בְיָמֵינוּ, וְתֵן חֶלְקֵנוּ בְּתוֹרָתֶךָ. וְשָׁם נַעֲבָדְךָ בְּיִרְאָה, כִּימֵי עוֹלָם וּכְשָׁנִים קַדְמוֹנִיּוֹת. וְעָרְבָה לַיהוה מִנְחַת יְהוּדָה וִירוּשָׁלָיִם, כִּימֵי עוֹלָם וּכְשָׁנִים קַדְמוֹנִיּוֹת.[6]

***SHEMONEH ESREI* ENDS HERE.**

Remain standing in place for at least a few moments before taking three steps forward.

(1) Cf. *Psalms* 79:13. (2) Cf. *Lam.* 3:22. (3) *Psalms* 19:15. (4) Cf. 34:14. (5) 60:7;108:7. (6) *Malachi* 3:4.

THANKSGIVING [MODIM]

Bow at *'We gratefully thank You'*; straighten up at *'HASHEM.'*

מוֹדִים *We gratefully thank You, for it is You Who are HASHEM, our God and the God of our forefathers for all eternity; Rock of our lives, Shield of our salvation are You from generation to generation. We shall thank You and relate Your praise[1] — for our lives, which are committed to Your power and for our souls that are entrusted to You; for Your miracles that are with us every day; and for Your wonders and favors in every season — evening, morning, and afternoon. The Beneficent One, for Your compassions were never exhausted, and the Compassionate One, for Your kindnesses never ended[2] — always have we put our hope in You.*

For all these, may Your Name be blessed and exalted, our King, continually forever and ever.

Bend the knees at *'Blessed'*; bow at *'You'*; straighten up at *'HASHEM.'*

Everything alive will gratefully acknowledge You, Selah! and praise Your Name sincerely, O God of our salvation and help, Selah! Blessed are You, HASHEM, Your Name is 'The Beneficent One' and to You it is fitting to give thanks.

PEACE

שָׁלוֹם *Establish abundant peace upon Your people Israel forever, for You are King, Master of all peace. May it be good in Your eyes to bless Your people Israel at every time and every hour with Your peace. Blessed are You, HASHEM, Who blesses His people Israel with peace.*

May the expressions of my mouth and the thoughts of my heart find favor before You, HASHEM, my Rock and my Redeemer.[3]

אֱלֹהַי *My God, guard my tongue from evil and my lips from speaking deceitfully.[4] To those who curse me, let my soul be silent; and let my soul be like dust to everyone. Open my heart to Your Torah, then my soul will pursue Your commandments. As for all those who design evil against me, speedily nullify their counsel and disrupt their design. Act for Your Name's sake; act for Your right hand's sake; act for Your sanctity's sake; act for Your Torah's sake. That Your beloved ones may be given rest; let Your right hand save, and respond to me.[5]*

Some recite verses pertaining to their names at this point. See page 1143.

May the expressions of my mouth and the thoughts of my heart find favor before You, HASHEM, my Rock and my Redeemer.[3] He Who makes peace in His heights, may He make peace upon us, and upon all Israel. Now respond: Amen.

Bow and take three steps back. Bow left and say, *'He Who makes peace . . .'*; bow right and say, *'may He make peace . . .'*; bow forward and say, *'and upon . . . Amen.'*

יְהִי רָצוֹן *May it be Your will, HASHEM, our God and the God of our forefathers, that the Holy Temple be rebuilt, speedily in our days. Grant us our share in Your Torah, and may we serve You there with reverence, as in days of old and in former years. Then the offering of Judah and Jerusalem will be pleasing to HASHEM, as in days of old and in former years.[6]*

SHEMONEH ESREI ENDS HERE.

Remain standing in place for at least a few moments before taking three steps forward

The *chazzan* recites קַדִּישׁ שָׁלֵם.

יִתְגַּדַּל וְיִתְקַדַּשׁ שְׁמֵהּ רַבָּא. (.Cong – אָמֵן.) בְּעָלְמָא דִּי בְרָא כִרְעוּתֵהּ. וְיַמְלִיךְ מַלְכוּתֵהּ, בְּחַיֵּיכוֹן וּבְיוֹמֵיכוֹן וּבְחַיֵּי דְכָל בֵּית יִשְׂרָאֵל, בַּעֲגָלָא וּבִזְמַן קָרִיב. וְאִמְרוּ: אָמֵן.

(.Cong – אָמֵן. יְהֵא שְׁמֵהּ רַבָּא מְבָרַךְ לְעָלַם וּלְעָלְמֵי עָלְמַיָּא.)

יְהֵא שְׁמֵהּ רַבָּא מְבָרַךְ לְעָלַם וּלְעָלְמֵי עָלְמַיָּא.

יִתְבָּרַךְ וְיִשְׁתַּבַּח וְיִתְפָּאַר וְיִתְרוֹמַם וְיִתְנַשֵּׂא וְיִתְהַדָּר וְיִתְעַלֶּה וְיִתְהַלָּל שְׁמֵהּ דְּקֻדְשָׁא בְּרִיךְ הוּא (.Cong – בְּרִיךְ הוּא) – לְעֵלָּא מִן כָּל בִּרְכָתָא וְשִׁירָתָא תֻּשְׁבְּחָתָא וְנֶחֱמָתָא, דַּאֲמִירָן בְּעָלְמָא. וְאִמְרוּ: אָמֵן. (.Cong – אָמֵן.)

(.Cong – קַבֵּל בְּרַחֲמִים וּבְרָצוֹן אֶת תְּפִלָּתֵנוּ.)

תִּתְקַבֵּל צְלוֹתְהוֹן וּבָעוּתְהוֹן דְּכָל בֵּית יִשְׂרָאֵל קֳדָם אֲבוּהוֹן דִּי בִשְׁמַיָּא. וְאִמְרוּ: אָמֵן. (.Cong – אָמֵן.)

(.Cong – יְהִי שֵׁם יהוה מְבֹרָךְ, מֵעַתָּה וְעַד עוֹלָם.[1])

יְהֵא שְׁלָמָא רַבָּא מִן שְׁמַיָּא, וְחַיִּים עָלֵינוּ וְעַל כָּל יִשְׂרָאֵל. וְאִמְרוּ: אָמֵן. (.Cong – אָמֵן.)

(.Cong – עֶזְרִי מֵעִם יהוה, עֹשֵׂה שָׁמַיִם וָאָרֶץ.[2])

Take three steps back. Bow left and say . . . עֹשֶׂה; bow right and say . . . הוּא; bow forward and say וְעַל כָּל . . . אָמֵן. Remain standing in place for a few moments, then take three steps forward.

עֹשֶׂה שָׁלוֹם בִּמְרוֹמָיו, הוּא יַעֲשֶׂה שָׁלוֹם עָלֵינוּ, וְעַל כָּל יִשְׂרָאֵל. וְאִמְרוּ: אָמֵן. (.Cong – אָמֵן.)

ספירת העומר

Most congregations count the *Omer* at this point; some count after *Aleinu* (p. 684).
See page 79 for pertinent laws.
In some congregations the following Kabbalistic prayer precedes the counting of the *Omer*.

לְשֵׁם יִחוּד קוּדְשָׁא בְּרִיךְ הוּא וּשְׁכִינְתֵּיהּ, בִּדְחִילוּ וּרְחִימוּ לְיַחֵד שֵׁם יו״ד הֵ״א בְּוָא״ו הֵ״א בְּיִחוּדָא שְׁלִים, בְּשֵׁם כָּל יִשְׂרָאֵל. הִנְנִי מוּכָן וּמְזוּמָן לְקַיֵּם מִצְוַת עֲשֵׂה שֶׁל סְפִירַת הָעְוֹמֶר, כְּמוֹ שֶׁכָּתוּב בַּתּוֹרָה: וּסְפַרְתֶּם לָכֶם מִמָּחֳרַת הַשַּׁבָּת, מִיּוֹם הֲבִיאֲכֶם אֶת עֹמֶר הַתְּנוּפָה, שֶׁבַע שַׁבָּתוֹת תְּמִימֹת תִּהְיֶינָה. עַד מִמָּחֳרַת הַשַּׁבָּת הַשְּׁבִיעִת תִּסְפְּרוּ חֲמִשִּׁים יוֹם, וְהִקְרַבְתֶּם מִנְחָה חֲדָשָׁה לַיהוה.[3] וִיהִי נֹעַם אֲדֹנָי אֱלֹהֵינוּ עָלֵינוּ, וּמַעֲשֵׂה יָדֵינוּ כּוֹנְנָה עָלֵינוּ, וּמַעֲשֵׂה יָדֵינוּ כּוֹנְנֵהוּ.[4]

Chazzan, followed by congregation, recites the blessing and counts.
One praying without a *minyan* should, nevertheless, recite the entire *Omer* service.

בָּרוּךְ אַתָּה יהוה אֱלֹהֵינוּ מֶלֶךְ הָעוֹלָם, אֲשֶׁר קִדְּשָׁנוּ בְּמִצְוֹתָיו וְצִוָּנוּ עַל סְפִירַת הָעְוֹמֶר.

הַיּוֹם שְׁנֵי יָמִים לָעְוֹמֶר. – On the first day *Chol HaMoed*

הַיּוֹם שְׁלֹשָׁה יָמִים לָעְוֹמֶר. – On the second day *Chol HaMoed*

הַיּוֹם אַרְבָּעָה יָמִים לָעְוֹמֶר. – On the third day *Chol HaMoed*

הַיּוֹם חֲמִשָּׁה יָמִים לָעְוֹמֶר. – On the fourth day *Chol HaMoed*

The *chazzan* recites the Full *Kaddish*.

יִתְגַּדַּל *May His great Name grow exalted and sanctified* (Cong.— *Amen.*) *in the world that He created as He willed. May He give reign to His kingship in your lifetimes and in your days, and in the lifetimes of the entire Family of Israel, swiftly and soon. Now respond: Amen.*

(Cong.— *Amen. May His great Name be blessed forever and ever.*)

May His great Name be blessed forever and ever.

Blessed, praised, glorified, exalted, extolled, mighty, upraised, and lauded be the Name of the Holy One, Blessed is He (Cong.— *Blessed is He*) — *beyond any blessing and song, praise and consolation that are uttered in the world. Now respond: Amen.* (Cong.— *Amen.*)

(Cong.— *Accept our prayers with mercy and favor.*)

May the prayers and supplications of the entire Family of Israel be accepted before their Father Who is in Heaven. Now respond: Amen. (Cong.— *Amen.*)

(Cong.— *Blessed be the Name of* HASHEM, *from this time and forever.*[1])

May there be abundant peace from Heaven, and life, upon us and upon all Israel. Now respond: Amen. (Cong.— *Amen.*)

(Cong.— *My help is from* HASHEM, *Maker of heaven and earth.*[2])

Take three steps back. Bow left and say, *'He Who makes peace . . .'*; bow right and say, *'may He . . .'*; bow forward and say, *'and upon all Israel . . .'* Remain standing in place for a few moments, then take three steps forward.

He Who makes peace in His heights, may He make peace upon us, and upon all Israel. Now respond: Amen. (Cong.— *Amen.*)

COUNTING THE OMER

Most congregations count the *Omer* at this point; some count after *Aleinu* (p. 684). See page 79 for pertinent laws.

In some congregations the following Kabbalistic prayer precedes the counting of the *Omer*.

לְשֵׁם *For the sake of the unification of the Holy One, Blessed is He, and His Presence, in fear and love to unify the Name Yud-Kei with Vav-Kei in perfect unity, in the name of all Israel. Behold I am prepared and ready to perform the commandment of counting the Omer, as it is written in the Torah: 'You are to count from the morrow of the rest day, from the day you brought the Omer-offering that is waved — they are to be seven complete weeks — until the morrow of the seventh week you are to count fifty days, and then offer a new meal-offering to* HASHEM.'[3] *May the pleasantness of my Lord, our God, be upon us — may He establish our handiwork for us; our handiwork, may He establish.*[4]

Chazzan, followed by congregation, recites the blessing and counts. One praying without a *minyan* should, nevertheless, recite the entire *Omer* service.

בָּרוּךְ *Blessed are You,* HASHEM, *our God, King of the universe, Who has sanctified us with His commandments and has commanded us regarding the counting of the Omer.*

On the first day *Chol HaMoed:* **Today is two days of the Omer.**

On the second day *Chol HaMoed:* **Today is three days of the Omer.**

On the third day *Chol HaMoed:* **Today is four days of the Omer.**

On the fourth day *Chol HaMoed:* **Today is five days of the Omer.**

---

(1) *Psalms* 113:2. (2) 121:2. (3) *Leviticus* 23:15. (4) *Psalms* 90:17.

הָרַחֲמָן הוּא יַחֲזִיר לָנוּ עֲבוֹדַת בֵּית הַמִּקְדָּשׁ לִמְקוֹמָהּ, בִּמְהֵרָה בְיָמֵינוּ. אָמֵן סֶלָה.

תהלים סז

לַמְנַצֵּחַ בִּנְגִינֹת מִזְמוֹר שִׁיר. אֱלֹהִים יְחָנֵּנוּ וִיבָרְכֵנוּ, יָאֵר פָּנָיו אִתָּנוּ סֶלָה. לָדַעַת בָּאָרֶץ דַּרְכֶּךָ, בְּכָל גּוֹיִם יְשׁוּעָתֶךָ. יוֹדוּךָ עַמִּים אֱלֹהִים, יוֹדוּךָ עַמִּים כֻּלָּם. יִשְׂמְחוּ וִירַנְּנוּ לְאֻמִּים, כִּי תִשְׁפֹּט עַמִּים מִישֹׁר, וּלְאֻמִּים בָּאָרֶץ תַּנְחֵם סֶלָה. יוֹדוּךָ עַמִּים, אֱלֹהִים, יוֹדוּךָ עַמִּים כֻּלָּם. אֶרֶץ נָתְנָה יְבוּלָהּ, יְבָרְכֵנוּ אֱלֹהִים אֱלֹהֵינוּ. יְבָרְכֵנוּ אֱלֹהִים, וְיִירְאוּ אוֹתוֹ כָּל אַפְסֵי אָרֶץ.

אָנָּא בְּכֹחַ גְּדֻלַּת יְמִינְךָ תַּתִּיר צְרוּרָה. אב״ג ית״ץ
קַבֵּל רִנַּת עַמְּךָ שַׂגְּבֵנוּ טַהֲרֵנוּ נוֹרָא. קר״ע שט״ן
נָא גִבּוֹר דּוֹרְשֵׁי יִחוּדְךָ כְּבָבַת שָׁמְרֵם. נג״ד יכ״ש
בָּרְכֵם טַהֲרֵם רַחֲמֵם צִדְקָתְךָ תָּמִיד גָּמְלֵם. בט״ר צת״ג
חֲסִין קָדוֹשׁ בְּרוֹב טוּבְךָ נַהֵל עֲדָתֶךָ. חק״ב טנ״ע
יָחִיד גֵּאֶה לְעַמְּךָ פְּנֵה זוֹכְרֵי קְדֻשָּׁתֶךָ. יג״ל פז״ק
שַׁוְעָתֵנוּ קַבֵּל וּשְׁמַע צַעֲקָתֵנוּ יוֹדֵעַ תַּעֲלֻמוֹת. שק״ו צי״ת
בָּרוּךְ שֵׁם כְּבוֹד מַלְכוּתוֹ לְעוֹלָם וָעֶד.

רִבּוֹנוֹ שֶׁל עוֹלָם, אַתָּה צִוִּיתָנוּ עַל יְדֵי מֹשֶׁה עַבְדֶּךָ לִסְפּוֹר סְפִירַת הָעֹמֶר, כְּדֵי לְטַהֲרֵנוּ מִקְּלִפּוֹתֵינוּ וּמִטֻּמְאוֹתֵינוּ, כְּמוֹ שֶׁכָּתַבְתָּ בְּתוֹרָתֶךָ: וּסְפַרְתֶּם לָכֶם מִמָּחֳרַת הַשַּׁבָּת מִיּוֹם הֲבִיאֲכֶם אֶת עֹמֶר הַתְּנוּפָה, שֶׁבַע שַׁבָּתוֹת תְּמִימֹת תִּהְיֶינָה. עַד מִמָּחֳרַת הַשַּׁבָּת הַשְּׁבִיעִת תִּסְפְּרוּ חֲמִשִּׁים יוֹם.[1] כְּדֵי שֶׁיִּטָּהֲרוּ נַפְשׁוֹת עַמְּךָ יִשְׂרָאֵל מִזֻּהֲמָתָם. וּבְכֵן יְהִי רָצוֹן מִלְּפָנֶיךָ יהוה אֱלֹהֵינוּ וֵאלֹהֵי אֲבוֹתֵינוּ, שֶׁבִּזְכוּת סְפִירַת הָעֹמֶר שֶׁסָּפַרְתִּי הַיּוֹם, יְתֻקַּן מַה שֶׁפָּגַמְתִּי בִּסְפִירָה

1st day *Chol HaMoed* – גְּבוּרָה שֶׁבְּחֶסֶד. 2nd day *Chol HaMoed* – תִּפְאֶרֶת שֶׁבְּחֶסֶד.
3rd day *Chol HaMoed* – נֶצַח שֶׁבְּחֶסֶד. 4th day *Chol HaMoed* – הוֹד שֶׁבְּחֶסֶד.

וְאֶטָּהֵר וְאֶתְקַדֵּשׁ בִּקְדֻשָּׁה שֶׁל מַעְלָה, וְעַל יְדֵי זֶה יֻשְׁפַּע שֶׁפַע רַב בְּכָל הָעוֹלָמוֹת. וּלְתַקֵּן אֶת נַפְשׁוֹתֵינוּ, וְרוּחוֹתֵינוּ, וְנִשְׁמוֹתֵינוּ, מִכָּל סִיג וּפְגַם, וּלְטַהֲרֵנוּ וּלְקַדְּשֵׁנוּ בִּקְדֻשָּׁתְךָ הָעֶלְיוֹנָה. אָמֵן סֶלָה.

In some congregations, if a mourner is present, the Mourner's *Kaddish* (p. 684) is recited, followed by *Aleinu*. In others, *Aleinu* is recited immediately.

AT THE CONCLUSION OF THE SABBATH THE SERVICE CONTINUES BELOW.

פסוקי ברכה

וְיִתֶּן לְךָ הָאֱלֹהִים מִטַּל הַשָּׁמַיִם וּמִשְׁמַנֵּי הָאָרֶץ, וְרֹב דָּגָן וְתִירֹשׁ. יַעַבְדוּךָ עַמִּים, וְיִשְׁתַּחֲווּ לְךָ לְאֻמִּים, הֱוֵה גְבִיר לְאַחֶיךָ, וְיִשְׁתַּחֲווּ לְךָ בְּנֵי אִמֶּךָ, אֹרְרֶיךָ אָרוּר, וּמְבָרְכֶיךָ בָּרוּךְ.[1] וְאֵל שַׁדַּי

הָרַחֲמָן *The Compassionate One! May He return for us the service of the Temple to its place, speedily in our days. Amen, selah!*

Psalm 67

לַמְנַצֵּחַ *For the Conductor, upon Neginos, a psalm, a song. May God favor us and bless us, may He illuminate His countenance with us, Selah. To make known Your way on earth, among all the nations Your salvation. The peoples will acknowledge You, O God, the peoples will acknowledge You, all of them. Nations will be glad and sing for joy, because You will judge the peoples fairly and guide the nations on earth, Selah. The peoples will acknowledge You, O God, the peoples will acknowledge You, all of them. The earth has yielded its produce, may God, our own God, bless us. May God bless us and may all the ends of the earth fear him.*

אָנָּא *We beg You! With the strength of Your right hand's greatness, untie the bundled sins. Accept the prayer of Your nation; strengthen us, purify us, O Awesome One. Please, O Strong One — those who foster Your Oneness, guard them like the apple of an eye. Bless them, purify them, show them pity, may Your righteousness always recompense them. Powerful Holy One, with Your abundant goodness guide Your congregation. One and only Exalted One, turn to Your nation, which proclaims Your holiness. Accept our entreaty and hear our cry, O Knower of mysteries. Blessed is the Name of His glorious Kingdom for all eternity.*

רִבּוֹנוֹ שֶׁל עוֹלָם *Master of the universe, You commanded us through Moses, Your servant, to count the Omer Count in order to cleanse us from our encrustations of evil and from our contaminations, as You have written in Your Torah: You are to count from the morrow of the rest day, from the day you brought the Omer-offering that is waved — they are to be seven complete weeks. Until the morrow of the seventh week you are to count fifty days,[1] so that the souls of Your people Israel be cleansed from their contamination. Therefore, may it be Your will, HASHEM, our God and the God of our forefathers, that in the merit of the Omer Count that I have counted today, may there be corrected whatever blemish I have caused in the sefirah*

first day *Chol HaMoed:* *gevurah shebechesed.*
second day *Chol HaMoed:* *tiferes shebechesed.*
third day *Chol HaMoed:* *netzach shebechesed.*
fourth day *Chol HaMoed:* *hod shebechesed.*

May I be cleansed and sanctified with the holiness of Above, and through this may abundant bounty flow in all the worlds. And may it correct our lives, spirits, and souls from all sediment and blemish; may it cleanse us and sanctify us with Your exalted holiness. Amen, Selah!

In some congregations, if a mourner is present, the Mourner's *Kaddish* (p. 684) is recited, followed by *Aleinu*. In others, *Aleinu* is recited immediately.

AT THE CONCLUSION OF THE SABBATH THE SERVICE CONTINUES BELOW.

VERSES OF BLESSING

וְיִתֶּן *And may God give you of the dew of the heavens and of the fatness of the earth, and abundant grain and wine. Peoples will serve you, and regimes will prostrate themselves to you; be a lord to your kinsmen, and your mother's sons will prostrate themselves to you; they who curse you are cursed, and they who bless you are blessed.[2] And may El Shaddai*

(1) *Leviticus* 23:15-16. (2) *Genesis* 27:28-29.

יְבָרֵךְ אֹתְךָ וְיַפְרְךָ וְיַרְבֶּךָ, וְהָיִיתָ לִקְהַל עַמִּים. וְיִתֶּן לְךָ אֶת בִּרְכַּת אַבְרָהָם, לְךָ וּלְזַרְעֲךָ אִתָּךְ, לְרִשְׁתְּךָ אֶת אֶרֶץ מְגֻרֶיךָ, אֲשֶׁר נָתַן אֱלֹהִים לְאַבְרָהָם.[1] מֵאֵל אָבִיךָ וְיַעְזְרֶךָּ, וְאֵת שַׁדַּי וִיבָרְכֶךָּ, בִּרְכֹת שָׁמַיִם מֵעָל, בִּרְכֹת תְּהוֹם רֹבֶצֶת תָּחַת, בִּרְכֹת שָׁדַיִם וָרָחַם. בִּרְכֹת אָבִיךָ גָּבְרוּ עַל בִּרְכֹת הוֹרַי, עַד תַּאֲוַת גִּבְעֹת עוֹלָם, תִּהְיֶיןָ לְרֹאשׁ יוֹסֵף, וּלְקָדְקֹד נְזִיר אֶחָיו.[2] וַאֲהֵבְךָ וּבֵרַכְךָ וְהִרְבֶּךָ, וּבֵרַךְ פְּרִי בִטְנְךָ וּפְרִי אַדְמָתֶךָ, דְּגָנְךָ וְתִירֹשְׁךָ וְיִצְהָרֶךָ, שְׁגַר אֲלָפֶיךָ וְעַשְׁתְּרֹת צֹאנֶךָ, עַל הָאֲדָמָה אֲשֶׁר נִשְׁבַּע לַאֲבֹתֶיךָ לָתֶת לָךְ. בָּרוּךְ תִּהְיֶה מִכָּל הָעַמִּים, לֹא יִהְיֶה בְךָ עָקָר וַעֲקָרָה, וּבִבְהֶמְתֶּךָ. וְהֵסִיר יהוה מִמְּךָ כָּל חֹלִי, וְכָל מַדְוֵי מִצְרַיִם הָרָעִים אֲשֶׁר יָדַעְתָּ, לֹא יְשִׂימָם בָּךְ, וּנְתָנָם בְּכָל שֹׂנְאֶיךָ.[3]

הַמַּלְאָךְ הַגֹּאֵל אֹתִי מִכָּל רָע יְבָרֵךְ אֶת הַנְּעָרִים וְיִקָּרֵא בָהֶם שְׁמִי, וְשֵׁם אֲבֹתַי אַבְרָהָם וְיִצְחָק, וְיִדְגּוּ לָרֹב בְּקֶרֶב הָאָרֶץ.[4] יהוה אֱלֹהֵיכֶם הִרְבָּה אֶתְכֶם, וְהִנְּכֶם הַיּוֹם כְּכוֹכְבֵי הַשָּׁמַיִם לָרֹב. יהוה אֱלֹהֵי אֲבוֹתֵכֶם יֹסֵף עֲלֵיכֶם כָּכֶם אֶלֶף פְּעָמִים, וִיבָרֵךְ אֶתְכֶם כַּאֲשֶׁר דִּבֶּר לָכֶם.[5]

בָּרוּךְ אַתָּה בָּעִיר, וּבָרוּךְ אַתָּה בַּשָּׂדֶה. בָּרוּךְ אַתָּה בְּבֹאֶךָ, וּבָרוּךְ אַתָּה בְּצֵאתֶךָ. בָּרוּךְ טַנְאֲךָ וּמִשְׁאַרְתֶּךָ. בָּרוּךְ פְּרִי בִטְנְךָ וּפְרִי אַדְמָתְךָ וּפְרִי בְהֶמְתֶּךָ, שְׁגַר אֲלָפֶיךָ וְעַשְׁתְּרוֹת צֹאנֶךָ.[6] יְצַו יהוה אִתְּךָ אֶת הַבְּרָכָה בַּאֲסָמֶיךָ וּבְכֹל מִשְׁלַח יָדֶךָ, וּבֵרַכְךָ בָּאָרֶץ אֲשֶׁר יהוה אֱלֹהֶיךָ נֹתֵן לָךְ. יִפְתַּח יהוה לְךָ אֶת אוֹצָרוֹ הַטּוֹב, אֶת הַשָּׁמַיִם, לָתֵת מְטַר אַרְצְךָ בְּעִתּוֹ, וּלְבָרֵךְ אֵת כָּל מַעֲשֵׂה יָדֶךָ, וְהִלְוִיתָ גּוֹיִם רַבִּים, וְאַתָּה לֹא תִלְוֶה.[7] כִּי יהוה אֱלֹהֶיךָ בֵּרַכְךָ כַּאֲשֶׁר דִּבֶּר לָךְ, וְהַעֲבַטְתָּ גּוֹיִם רַבִּים, וְאַתָּה לֹא תַעֲבֹט, וּמָשַׁלְתָּ בְּגוֹיִם רַבִּים, וּבְךָ לֹא יִמְשֹׁלוּ.[8] אַשְׁרֶיךָ יִשְׂרָאֵל, מִי כָמוֹךָ, עַם נוֹשַׁע בַּיהוה, מָגֵן עֶזְרֶךָ, וַאֲשֶׁר חֶרֶב גַּאֲוָתֶךָ, וְיִכָּחֲשׁוּ אֹיְבֶיךָ לָךְ, וְאַתָּה עַל בָּמוֹתֵימוֹ תִדְרֹךְ.[9]

גאולה

מָחִיתִי כָעָב פְּשָׁעֶיךָ וְכֶעָנָן חַטֹּאתֶיךָ, שׁוּבָה אֵלַי כִּי גְאַלְתִּיךָ. רָנּוּ שָׁמַיִם, כִּי עָשָׂה יהוה, הָרִיעוּ תַּחְתִּיּוֹת אָרֶץ, פִּצְחוּ הָרִים רִנָּה, יַעַר וְכָל עֵץ בּוֹ, כִּי גָאַל יהוה יַעֲקֹב וּבְיִשְׂרָאֵל יִתְפָּאָר.[10] גֹּאֲלֵנוּ יהוה צְבָאוֹת שְׁמוֹ, קְדוֹשׁ יִשְׂרָאֵל.[11]

ישועה

יִשְׂרָאֵל נוֹשַׁע בַּיהוה תְּשׁוּעַת עוֹלָמִים, לֹא תֵבֹשׁוּ וְלֹא תִכָּלְמוּ עַד עוֹלְמֵי עַד.[12] וַאֲכַלְתֶּם אָכוֹל וְשָׂבוֹעַ, וְהִלַּלְתֶּם אֶת שֵׁם יהוה אֱלֹהֵיכֶם אֲשֶׁר עָשָׂה עִמָּכֶם לְהַפְלִיא, וְלֹא יֵבֹשׁוּ עַמִּי לְעוֹלָם.

(1) *Genesis* 28:3-4. (2) 49:25-26. (3) *Deuteronomy* 7:13-15. (4) *Genesis* 48:16. (5) *Deuteronomy* 1:10-11. (6) 28:3,6,5,4. (7) 28:8,12. (8) 15:6. (9) 33:29. (10) *Isaiah* 44:22-23. (11) 47:4. (12) 45:17.

bless you, make you fruitful and make you numerous, and may you be a congregation of peoples. May He grant you the blessing of Abraham, to you and to your offspring with you, that you may possess the land of your sojourns which God gave to Abraham.[1] *It is from the God of your father and He will help you, and with Shaddai and He will bless you — blessings of heaven from above, blessings of the deep crouching below, blessings of the bosom and womb. The blessings of your father surpassed the blessings of my fathers, to the endless bounds of the world's hills; let them be upon Joseph's head and upon the head of the one separated from his brothers.*[2] *And He shall love you, and He shall bless you, and He shall make you numerous; may He bless the fruit of your womb and the fruit of your land, your grain, your wine and your oil, the offspring of your cattle and the flocks of your sheep, on the land that He swore to your forefathers to give to you. Blessed shall you be above all peoples; there shall not be among you a barren man or woman, nor among your cattle.* HASHEM *shall remove from you all illness; and all the evil sufferings of Egypt that you knew, He will not place upon you, but He will set them upon all your enemies.*[3]

הַמַּלְאָךְ *May the angel who redeems me from all evil bless the lads, and may my name be declared upon them — and the names of my forefathers Abraham and Isaac — and may they proliferate abundantly like fish within the land.*[4] HASHEM, *your God, has made you numerous, and behold! you are today like the stars of heaven in abundance. May* HASHEM, *the God of your forefathers, increase you a thousandfold and bless you as He spoke to you.*[5]

בָּרוּךְ *Blessed are you in the city; blessed are you in the field. Blessed are you upon your arrival; blessed are you upon your departure. Blessed is your fruit basket and your kneading trough. Blessed is the fruit of your womb, the fruit of your land and the fruit of your animal, the offspring of your cattle and the flocks of your sheep.*[6] *May* HASHEM *command that the blessing accompany you in your storehouse and wherever you set your hand, and may He bless you in the land that* HASHEM, *your God, gives you. May* HASHEM *open for you His good treasury, the heaven, to give you rain for your land in its time and to bless your every handiwork; and may you lend many nations, but may you not borrow.*[7] *For* HASHEM, *your God, will have blessed you as He spoke to you; and may you make many nations indebted to you, but may you not become indebted; and you will dominate many nations, but they will not dominate you.*[8] *Praiseworthy are you, O Israel, who is like you! — a people saved by God, Who is the Shield of your help, and Who is the Sword of your majesty. Your enemies will be false with you, but you will tread upon their heights.*[9]

REDEMPTION

מָחִיתִי *I have blotted out your willful sins like a thick mist and your errors like a cloud — return to Me for I have redeemed you. Sing gladly, O heaven, for* HASHEM *has done so; exult O depths of the earth; break out, O mountains, in glad song, forest and every tree within it, for* HASHEM *has redeemed Jacob and will take pride in Israel.*[10] *Our Redeemer —* HASHEM, *Master of Legions, is His Name — is the Holy One of Israel.*[11]

SALVATION

יִשְׂרָאֵל *Israel is saved by God in an everlasting salvation; they will not be shamed nor humiliated forever and ever.*[12] *You shall eat food and be satisfied, and you shall praise the Name of* HASHEM, *your God, Who has done wondrously with you, and My people shall not be shamed forever.*

וִידַעְתֶּם כִּי בְקֶרֶב יִשְׂרָאֵל אָנִי, וַאֲנִי יהוה אֱלֹהֵיכֶם, וְאֵין עוֹד, וְלֹא יֵבֹשׁוּ עַמִּי לְעוֹלָם.[1] כִּי בְשִׂמְחָה תֵצֵאוּ וּבְשָׁלוֹם תּוּבָלוּן, הֶהָרִים וְהַגְּבָעוֹת יִפְצְחוּ לִפְנֵיכֶם רִנָּה, וְכָל עֲצֵי הַשָּׂדֶה יִמְחֲאוּ כָף.[2] הִנֵּה אֵל יְשׁוּעָתִי, אֶבְטַח וְלֹא אֶפְחָד, כִּי עָזִּי וְזִמְרָת יָהּ יהוה וַיְהִי לִי לִישׁוּעָה. וּשְׁאַבְתֶּם מַיִם בְּשָׂשׂוֹן, מִמַּעַיְנֵי הַיְשׁוּעָה. וַאֲמַרְתֶּם בַּיּוֹם הַהוּא, הוֹדוּ לַיהוה קִרְאוּ בִשְׁמוֹ, הוֹדִיעוּ בָעַמִּים עֲלִילֹתָיו, הַזְכִּירוּ כִּי נִשְׂגָּב שְׁמוֹ. זַמְּרוּ יהוה כִּי גֵאוּת עָשָׂה, מוּדַעַת זֹאת בְּכָל הָאָרֶץ. צַהֲלִי וָרֹנִּי יוֹשֶׁבֶת צִיּוֹן, כִּי גָדוֹל בְּקִרְבֵּךְ קְדוֹשׁ יִשְׂרָאֵל.[3] וְאָמַר בַּיּוֹם הַהוּא, הִנֵּה אֱלֹהֵינוּ זֶה, קִוִּינוּ לוֹ וְיוֹשִׁיעֵנוּ, זֶה יהוה קִוִּינוּ לוֹ, נָגִילָה וְנִשְׂמְחָה בִּישׁוּעָתוֹ.[4]

דעת ה'

בֵּית יַעֲקֹב, לְכוּ וְנֵלְכָה בְּאוֹר יהוה.[5] וְהָיָה אֱמוּנַת עִתֶּיךָ חֹסֶן יְשׁוּעֹת חָכְמַת וָדָעַת, יִרְאַת יהוה הִיא אוֹצָרוֹ.[6] וַיְהִי דָוִד לְכָל דְּרָכָיו מַשְׂכִּיל, וַיהוה עִמּוֹ.[7]

פדיום

פָּדָה בְשָׁלוֹם נַפְשִׁי מִקְּרָב לִי, כִּי בְרַבִּים הָיוּ עִמָּדִי.[8] וַיֹּאמֶר הָעָם אֶל שָׁאוּל, הֲיוֹנָתָן יָמוּת אֲשֶׁר עָשָׂה הַיְשׁוּעָה הַגְּדוֹלָה הַזֹּאת בְּיִשְׂרָאֵל, חָלִילָה, חַי יהוה, אִם יִפֹּל מִשַּׂעֲרַת רֹאשׁוֹ אַרְצָה, כִּי עִם אֱלֹהִים עָשָׂה הַיּוֹם הַזֶּה, וַיִּפְדּוּ הָעָם אֶת יוֹנָתָן וְלֹא מֵת.[9] וּפְדוּיֵי יהוה יְשֻׁבוּן, וּבָאוּ צִיּוֹן בְּרִנָּה, וְשִׂמְחַת עוֹלָם עַל רֹאשָׁם, שָׂשׂוֹן וְשִׂמְחָה יַשִּׂיגוּ וְנָסוּ יָגוֹן וַאֲנָחָה.[10]

הפוך צרה

הָפַכְתָּ מִסְפְּדִי לְמָחוֹל לִי, פִּתַּחְתָּ שַׂקִּי, וַתְּאַזְּרֵנִי שִׂמְחָה.[11] וְלֹא אָבָה יהוה אֱלֹהֶיךָ לִשְׁמֹעַ אֶל בִּלְעָם, וַיַּהֲפֹךְ יהוה אֱלֹהֶיךָ לְּךָ אֶת הַקְּלָלָה לִבְרָכָה, כִּי אֲהֵבְךָ יהוה אֱלֹהֶיךָ.[12] אָז תִּשְׂמַח בְּתוּלָה בְּמָחוֹל, וּבַחֻרִים וּזְקֵנִים יַחְדָּו, וְהָפַכְתִּי אֶבְלָם לְשָׂשׂוֹן, וְנִחַמְתִּים וְשִׂמַּחְתִּים מִיגוֹנָם.[13]

שלום

בּוֹרֵא נִיב שְׂפָתָיִם, שָׁלוֹם שָׁלוֹם לָרָחוֹק וְלַקָּרוֹב, אָמַר יהוה וּרְפָאתִיו.[14] וְרוּחַ לָבְשָׁה אֶת עֲמָשַׂי, רֹאשׁ הַשָּׁלִישִׁים, לְךָ דָוִיד וְעִמְּךָ בֶן יִשַׁי שָׁלוֹם, שָׁלוֹם לְךָ, וְשָׁלוֹם לְעֹזְרֶךָ כִּי עֲזָרְךָ אֱלֹהֶיךָ וַיְקַבְּלֵם דָּוִיד וַיִּתְּנֵם בְּרָאשֵׁי הַגְּדוּד.[15] וַאֲמַרְתֶּם, כֹּה לֶחָי, וְאַתָּה שָׁלוֹם וּבֵיתְךָ שָׁלוֹם וְכֹל אֲשֶׁר לְךָ שָׁלוֹם.[16] יהוה עֹז לְעַמּוֹ יִתֵּן יהוה יְבָרֵךְ אֶת עַמּוֹ בַשָּׁלוֹם.[17]

מסכת מגילה לא.

אָמַר רַבִּי יוֹחָנָן: בְּכָל מָקוֹם שֶׁאַתָּה מוֹצֵא גְּדֻלָּתוֹ שֶׁל הַקָּדוֹשׁ בָּרוּךְ הוּא, שָׁם אַתָּה מוֹצֵא עַנְוְתָנוּתוֹ. דָּבָר זֶה כָּתוּב בַּתּוֹרָה, וְשָׁנוּי

(1) *Joel* 2:26-27. (2) *Isaiah* 55:12. (3) 12:2-6. (4) 25:9. (5) *Isaiah* 2:5. (6) 33:6. (7) *I Samuel* 18:14. (8) *Psalms* 55:19. (9) *I Samuel* 14:45. (10) *Isaiah* 35:10. (11) *Psalms* 30:12. (12) *Deuteronomy* 23:6. (13) *Jeremiah* 31:12. (14) *Isaiah* 57:19. (15) *I Chronicles* 12:19. (16) *I Samuel* 25:6. (17) *Psalms* 29:11.

And you shall know that in the midst of Israel am I, and I am HASHEM, *your God — there is none other; and My people shall not be shamed forever.*[1] *For in gladness shall you go out and in peace shall you arrive; the mountains and the hills will break out before you in glad song and all the trees of the field will clap hands.*[2] *Behold! God is my help, I shall trust and not fear — for God is my might and my praise —* HASHEM *— and He was a salvation to me. You can draw water in joy, from the springs of salvation. And you shall say on that day, 'Give thanks to* HASHEM, *declare His name, make His acts known among the peoples;' remind one another, for His Name is powerful. Make music to* HASHEM *for He has established grandeur — this is known throughout the earth. Exult and sing for joy, O inhabitant of Zion, for the Holy One of Israel has done greatly among you.*[3] *And he shall say on that day, 'Behold! this is our God, we have hoped for Him, that He would save us — this is* HASHEM, *we have hoped for Him, we shall rejoice and be glad at His salvation.*[4]

KNOWLEDGE OF GOD

בֵּית *O House of Jacob — come let us go by the light of* HASHEM.[5] *The stability of your times, the strength of your salvations shall be through knowledge and wisdom, fear of God — that is one's treasure.*[6] *And David was successful in all his ways, and* HASHEM *was with him.*[7]

RESCUE

פָּדָה *He redeemed my soul in peace from the battles that were upon me, for the sake of the multitudes who were with me.*[8] *And the people said to Saul, 'Shall Jonathan die, who performed this great salvation for Israel? A sacrilege! — as* HASHEM *lives, if a hair of his head falls to the ground, for with* HASHEM *has he acted this day!' And the people redeemed Jonathan and he did not die.*[9] *Those redeemed by God will return and arrive at Zion with glad song and eternal gladness on their heads; joy and gladness shall they attain, and sorrow and groan shall flee.*[10]

TRANSFORMATION OF DISTRESS TO RELIEF

הָפַכְתָּ *You have changed for me my lament into dancing; You undid my sackcloth and girded me with gladness.*[11] HASHEM, *your God, did not wish to pay heed to Balaam, and* HASHEM, *your God, transformed for you the curse to blessing, for* HASHEM, *your God, loves you.*[12] *Then the maiden shall rejoice in a dance, and lads and elders together; and I shall change their mourning to joy, and I shall console them and gladden them from their sorrow.*[13]

PEACE

בּוֹרֵא *I create fruit of the lips: 'Peace, peace, for far and near,' says* HASHEM, *'and I shall heal him.'*[14] *A spirit clothed Amasai, head of the officers, 'For your sake, David, and to be with you, son of Jesse; peace, peace to you, and peace to him who helps you, for your God has helped you.' David accepted them and appointed them heads of the band.*[15] *And you shall say: 'So may it be as long as you live; peace for you, peace for your household and peace for all that is with you.'*[16] HASHEM *will give might to His people,* HASHEM *will bless His people with peace.*[17]

Talmud, Tractate *Megillah* 31a

אָמַר *Rabbi Yochanan said: Wherever you find the greatness of the Holy One, Blessed is He, there you find His humility. This phenomenon is written in the Torah, repeated in the Prophets and stated a third time in the*

בַּנְּבִיאִים, וּמְשֻׁלָּשׁ בַּכְּתוּבִים. כָּתוּב בַּתּוֹרָה: כִּי יהוה אֱלֹהֵיכֶם הוּא אֱלֹהֵי הָאֱלֹהִים וַאֲדֹנֵי הָאֲדֹנִים, הָאֵל הַגָּדֹל הַגִּבֹּר וְהַנּוֹרָא אֲשֶׁר לֹא יִשָּׂא פָנִים וְלֹא יִקַּח שֹׁחַד.[1] וּכְתִיב בַּתְרֵהּ: עֹשֶׂה מִשְׁפַּט יָתוֹם וְאַלְמָנָה, וְאֹהֵב גֵּר לָתֶת לוֹ לֶחֶם וְשִׂמְלָה.[2] שָׁנוּי בַּנְּבִיאִים, דִּכְתִיב: כִּי כֹה אָמַר רָם וְנִשָּׂא שֹׁכֵן עַד וְקָדוֹשׁ שְׁמוֹ, מָרוֹם וְקָדוֹשׁ אֶשְׁכּוֹן, וְאֶת דַּכָּא וּשְׁפַל רוּחַ, לְהַחֲיוֹת רוּחַ שְׁפָלִים וּלְהַחֲיוֹת לֵב נִדְכָּאִים.[3] מְשֻׁלָּשׁ בַּכְּתוּבִים, דִּכְתִיב: שִׁירוּ לֵאלֹהִים, זַמְּרוּ שְׁמוֹ, סֹלּוּ לָרֹכֵב בָּעֲרָבוֹת, בְּיָהּ שְׁמוֹ, וְעִלְזוּ לְפָנָיו.[4] וּכְתִיב בַּתְרֵהּ: אֲבִי יְתוֹמִים וְדַיַּן אַלְמָנוֹת, אֱלֹהִים בִּמְעוֹן קָדְשׁוֹ.[5]

יְהִי יהוה אֱלֹהֵינוּ עִמָּנוּ כַּאֲשֶׁר הָיָה עִם אֲבֹתֵינוּ, אַל יַעַזְבֵנוּ וְאַל יִטְּשֵׁנוּ.[6] וְאַתֶּם הַדְּבֵקִים בַּיהוה אֱלֹהֵיכֶם חַיִּים כֻּלְּכֶם הַיּוֹם.[7] כִּי נִחַם יהוה צִיּוֹן, נִחַם כָּל חָרְבֹתֶיהָ, וַיָּשֶׂם מִדְבָּרָהּ כְּעֵדֶן וְעַרְבָתָהּ כְּגַן יהוה, שָׂשׂוֹן וְשִׂמְחָה יִמָּצֵא בָהּ, תּוֹדָה וְקוֹל זִמְרָה.[8] יהוה חָפֵץ לְמַעַן צִדְקוֹ, יַגְדִּיל תּוֹרָה וְיַאְדִּיר.[9]

תהלים קכח

שִׁיר הַמַּעֲלוֹת אַשְׁרֵי כָּל יְרֵא יהוה, הַהֹלֵךְ בִּדְרָכָיו. יְגִיעַ כַּפֶּיךָ כִּי תֹאכֵל, אַשְׁרֶיךָ וְטוֹב לָךְ. אֶשְׁתְּךָ כְּגֶפֶן פֹּרִיָּה בְּיַרְכְּתֵי בֵיתֶךָ, בָּנֶיךָ כִּשְׁתִלֵי זֵיתִים, סָבִיב לְשֻׁלְחָנֶךָ. הִנֵּה כִי כֵן יְבֹרַךְ גָּבֶר יְרֵא יהוה. יְבָרֶכְךָ יהוה מִצִּיּוֹן וּרְאֵה בְּטוּב יְרוּשָׁלָיִם, כֹּל יְמֵי חַיֶּיךָ. וּרְאֵה בָנִים לְבָנֶיךָ, שָׁלוֹם עַל יִשְׂרָאֵל.

In some congregations mourners recite קַדִּישׁ יָתוֹם (p. 684) at this point.

הבדלה בבית הכנסת

סַבְרִי מָרָנָן וְרַבָּנָן וְרַבּוֹתַי:

בָּרוּךְ אַתָּה יהוה אֱלֹהֵינוּ מֶלֶךְ הָעוֹלָם, בּוֹרֵא פְּרִי הַגָּפֶן.

(.Cong. – אָמֵן)

At the departure of the Sabbath the following two blessings are recited.

After the following blessing smell the spices.

בָּרוּךְ אַתָּה יהוה אֱלֹהֵינוּ מֶלֶךְ הָעוֹלָם, בּוֹרֵא מִינֵי בְשָׂמִים.

(.Cong. – אָמֵן)

After the following blessing hold fingers up to the flame to see the reflected light:

בָּרוּךְ אַתָּה יהוה אֱלֹהֵינוּ מֶלֶךְ הָעוֹלָם, בּוֹרֵא מְאוֹרֵי הָאֵשׁ.

(.Cong. – אָמֵן)

בָּרוּךְ אַתָּה יהוה אֱלֹהֵינוּ מֶלֶךְ הָעוֹלָם, הַמַּבְדִּיל בֵּין קֹדֶשׁ לְחוֹל, בֵּין אוֹר לְחֹשֶׁךְ, בֵּין יִשְׂרָאֵל לָעַמִּים, בֵּין יוֹם הַשְּׁבִיעִי לְשֵׁשֶׁת יְמֵי הַמַּעֲשֶׂה. בָּרוּךְ אַתָּה יהוה, הַמַּבְדִּיל בֵּין קֹדֶשׁ לְחוֹל.

(.Cong. – אָמֵן)

The *chazzan,* or someone else present for *Havdalah,* should drink most of the cup.

Writings. It is written in the Torah: 'For HASHEM*, your God, He is the God of heavenly forces and the Master of masters, the great, mighty and awesome God, Who shows no favoritism and accepts no bribe.'*[1] *Afterwards it is written: 'He performs justice for orphan and widow, and loves the stranger, to give him food and clothing.'*[2] *It is repeated in the Prophets, as it is written: "For so says the exalted and uplifted One, Who abides forever, and Whose Name is holy, 'I abide in exaltedness and holiness — but am with the contrite and lowly of spirit, to revive the spirit of the lowly and to revive the heart of the contrite.' "*[3] *And it is stated a third time in the Writings, as it is written: 'Sing to God, make music for His Name, extol Him Who rides in the highest heaven, with His Name — God — and exult before Him.'*[4] *Afterwards it is written: 'Father of orphans and Judge of widows, God in the habitation of His holiness.'*[5]

May HASHEM*, our God, be with us as He was with our forefathers, may He not forsake us nor cast us off.*[6] *You who cling to* HASHEM*, our God, are all alive today.*[7] *For* HASHEM *comforts Zion, He comforts all her ruins, He will make her wilderness like Eden and her wastes like a garden of* HASHEM *— joy and gladness will be found there, thanksgiving and the sound of music.*[8] HASHEM *desired, for the sake of its [Israel's] righteousness, that the Torah be made great and glorious.*[9]

Psalm 128

שִׁיר הַמַּעֲלוֹת *A song of ascents. Praiseworthy is each person who fears* HASHEM*, who walks in His paths. When you eat the labor of your hands, you are praiseworthy, and it is well with you. Your wife shall be like a fruitful vine in the inner chambers of your home; your children shall be like olive shoots surrounding your table. Behold! For so is blessed the man who fears* HASHEM*. May* HASHEM *bless you from Zion, and may you gaze upon the goodness of Jerusalem, all the days of your life. And may you see children born to children, peace upon Israel.*

In some congregations mourners recite the Mourner's *Kaddish* (page 684) at this point.

HAVDALAH IN THE SYNAGOGUE

By your leave, my masters and teachers:

בָּרוּךְ *Blessed are You,* HASHEM*, our God, King of the universe, Who creates the fruit of the vine.* (Cong. – *Amen.*)

At the departure of the Sabbath the following two blessings are recited.

After the following blessing smell the spices.

בָּרוּךְ *Blessed are You,* HASHEM*, our God, King of the universe, Who creates species of fragrance.* (Cong. – *Amen.*)

After the following blessing hold fingers up to the flame to see the reflected light:.

בָּרוּךְ *Blessed are You,* HASHEM*, our God, King of the universe, Who creates the illuminations of the fire.* (Cong.– *Amen.*)

בָּרוּךְ *Blessed are You,* HASHEM *our God, King of the universe, Who separates between holy and secular, between light and darkness, between Israel and the nations, between the seventh day and the six days of labor. Blessed are You,* HASHEM*, Who separates between holy and secular.* (Cong. – *Amen.*)

The *chazzan* or someone else present for *Havdalah,* should drink most of the cup.

(1) *Deut.* 10:17. (2) 10:18. (3) *Isaiah* 57:15. (4) *Psalms* 68:5. (5) 68:6.
(6) *I Kings* 8:57. (7) *Deut.* 4:4. (8) *Isaiah* 51:3. (9) 42:21.

The congregation stands while reciting עָלֵינוּ.

עָלֵינוּ לְשַׁבֵּחַ לַאֲדוֹן הַכֹּל, לָתֵת גְּדֻלָּה לְיוֹצֵר בְּרֵאשִׁית, שֶׁלֹּא עָשָׂנוּ כְּגוֹיֵי הָאֲרָצוֹת, וְלֹא שָׂמָנוּ כְּמִשְׁפְּחוֹת הָאֲדָמָה. שֶׁלֹּא שָׂם חֶלְקֵנוּ כָּהֶם, וְגוֹרָלֵנוּ כְּכָל הֲמוֹנָם. (שֶׁהֵם מִשְׁתַּחֲוִים לְהֶבֶל וָרִיק, וּמִתְפַּלְּלִים אֶל אֵל לֹא יוֹשִׁיעַ.[1]) וַאֲנַחְנוּ כּוֹרְעִים וּמִשְׁתַּחֲוִים וּמוֹדִים, לִפְנֵי מֶלֶךְ מַלְכֵי הַמְּלָכִים הַקָּדוֹשׁ בָּרוּךְ הוּא. שֶׁהוּא נוֹטֶה שָׁמַיִם וְיֹסֵד אָרֶץ,[2] וּמוֹשַׁב יְקָרוֹ בַּשָּׁמַיִם מִמַּעַל, וּשְׁכִינַת עֻזּוֹ בְּגָבְהֵי מְרוֹמִים. הוּא אֱלֹהֵינוּ, אֵין עוֹד. אֱמֶת מַלְכֵּנוּ, אֶפֶס זוּלָתוֹ, כַּכָּתוּב בְּתוֹרָתוֹ: וְיָדַעְתָּ הַיּוֹם וַהֲשֵׁבֹתָ אֶל לְבָבֶךָ, כִּי יהוה הוּא הָאֱלֹהִים בַּשָּׁמַיִם מִמַּעַל וְעַל הָאָרֶץ מִתָּחַת, אֵין עוֹד.[3]

Bow while reciting וַאֲנַחְנוּ כּוֹרְעִים וּמִשְׁתַּחֲוִים.

עַל כֵּן נְקַוֶּה לְּךָ יהוה אֱלֹהֵינוּ לִרְאוֹת מְהֵרָה בְּתִפְאֶרֶת עֻזֶּךָ, לְהַעֲבִיר גִּלּוּלִים מִן הָאָרֶץ, וְהָאֱלִילִים כָּרוֹת יִכָּרֵתוּן, לְתַקֵּן עוֹלָם בְּמַלְכוּת שַׁדַּי. וְכָל בְּנֵי בָשָׂר יִקְרְאוּ בִשְׁמֶךָ, לְהַפְנוֹת אֵלֶיךָ כָּל רִשְׁעֵי אָרֶץ. יַכִּירוּ וְיֵדְעוּ כָּל יוֹשְׁבֵי תֵבֵל, כִּי לְךָ תִּכְרַע כָּל בֶּרֶךְ, תִּשָּׁבַע כָּל לָשׁוֹן.[4] לְפָנֶיךָ יהוה אֱלֹהֵינוּ יִכְרְעוּ וְיִפֹּלוּ, וְלִכְבוֹד שִׁמְךָ יְקָר יִתֵּנוּ. וִיקַבְּלוּ כֻלָּם אֶת עוֹל מַלְכוּתֶךָ, וְתִמְלוֹךְ עֲלֵיהֶם מְהֵרָה לְעוֹלָם וָעֶד. כִּי הַמַּלְכוּת שֶׁלְּךָ הִיא וּלְעוֹלְמֵי עַד תִּמְלוֹךְ בְּכָבוֹד, כַּכָּתוּב בְּתוֹרָתֶךָ: יהוה יִמְלֹךְ לְעֹלָם וָעֶד.[5] ❖ וְנֶאֱמַר: וְהָיָה יהוה לְמֶלֶךְ עַל כָּל הָאָרֶץ, בַּיּוֹם הַהוּא יִהְיֶה יהוה אֶחָד וּשְׁמוֹ אֶחָד.[6]

אַל תִּירָא מִפַּחַד פִּתְאֹם, וּמִשֹּׁאַת רְשָׁעִים כִּי תָבֹא.[7] עֻצוּ עֵצָה וְתֻפָר, דַּבְּרוּ דָבָר וְלֹא יָקוּם, כִּי עִמָּנוּ אֵל.[8] וְעַד זִקְנָה אֲנִי הוּא, וְעַד שֵׂיבָה אֲנִי אֶסְבֹּל, אֲנִי עָשִׂיתִי וַאֲנִי אֶשָּׂא, וַאֲנִי אֶסְבֹּל וַאֲמַלֵּט.[9]

קדיש יתום

Mourners recite קַדִּישׁ יָתוֹם.

יִתְגַּדַּל וְיִתְקַדַּשׁ שְׁמֵהּ רַבָּא. (.Cong – אָמֵן.) בְּעָלְמָא דִּי בְרָא כִרְעוּתֵהּ. וְיַמְלִיךְ מַלְכוּתֵהּ, בְּחַיֵּיכוֹן וּבְיוֹמֵיכוֹן וּבְחַיֵּי דְכָל בֵּית יִשְׂרָאֵל, בַּעֲגָלָא וּבִזְמַן קָרִיב. וְאִמְרוּ: אָמֵן.

(.Cong – אָמֵן. יְהֵא שְׁמֵהּ רַבָּא מְבָרַךְ לְעָלַם וּלְעָלְמֵי עָלְמַיָּא.)

יְהֵא שְׁמֵהּ רַבָּא מְבָרַךְ לְעָלַם וּלְעָלְמֵי עָלְמַיָּא.

---

(1) *Isaiah* 45:20. (2) 51:13. (3) *Deuteronomy* 4:39. (4) Cf. *Isaiah* 45:23.
(5) *Exodus* 15:18. (6) *Zechariah* 14:9. (7) *Proverbs* 3:25. (8) *Isaiah* 8:10. (9) 46:4.

The congregation stands while reciting עָלֵינוּ, *'It is our duty . . .'*

עָלֵינוּ *It is our duty to praise the Master of all, to ascribe greatness to the Molder of primeval creation, for He has not made us like the nations of the lands, and has not emplaced us like the families of the earth; for He has not assigned our portion like theirs nor our lot like all their multitudes. (For they bow to vanity and emptiness and pray to a god which helps not.*[1]*) But we bend our knees, bow, and acknowledge our thanks before the King Who reigns over kings, the Holy One, Blessed is He. He stretches out heaven and establishes earth's foundation,*[2] *the seat of His homage is in the heavens above and His powerful Presence is in the loftiest heights. He is our God and there is none other. True is our King, there is nothing beside Him, as it is written in His Torah: 'You are to know this day and take to your heart that* HASHEM *is the only God — in heaven above and on the earth below — there is none other.'*[3]

Bow while reciting *'But we bend our knees.'*

עַל כֵּן *Therefore we put our hope in You,* HASHEM, *our God, that we may soon see Your mighty splendor, to remove detestable idolatry from the earth, and false gods will be utterly cut off, to perfect the universe through the Almighty's sovereignty. Then all humanity will call upon Your Name, to turn all the earth's wicked toward You. All the world's inhabitants will recognize and know that to You every knee should bend, every tongue should swear.*[4] *Before You,* HASHEM, *our God, they will bend every knee and cast themselves down and to the glory of Your Name they will render homage, and they will all accept upon themselves the yoke of Your kingship that You may reign over them soon and eternally. For the kingdom is Yours and You will reign for all eternity in glory as it is written in Your Torah:* HASHEM *shall reign for all eternity.*[5] Chazzan– *And it is said:* HASHEM *will be King over all the world — on that day* HASHEM *will be One and His Name will be One.*[6]

אַל תִּירָא *Do not fear sudden terror, or the holocaust of the wicked when it comes.*[7] *Plan a conspiracy and it will be annulled; speak your piece and it shall not stand, for God is with us.*[8] *Even till your seniority, I remain unchanged; and even till your ripe old age, I shall endure. I created you and I shall bear you; I shall endure and rescue.*[9]

MOURNER'S KADDISH

Mourners recite the Mourners' *Kaddish*. See Laws §81-83.

[A transliteration of this *Kaddish* appears on page 1147.]

יִתְגַּדַּל *May His great Name grow exalted and sanctified* (Cong.– *Amen.*) *in the world that He created as He willed. May He give reign to His kingship in your lifetimes and in your days, and in the lifetimes of the entire Family of Israel, swiftly and soon. Now respond: Amen.*

(Cong.– ***Amen. May His great Name be blessed forever and ever.***)

May His great Name be blessed forever and ever.

יִתְבָּרַךְ וְיִשְׁתַּבַּח וְיִתְפָּאַר וְיִתְרוֹמַם וְיִתְנַשֵּׂא וְיִתְהַדָּר וְיִתְעַלֶּה וְיִתְהַלָּל שְׁמֵהּ דְּקֻדְשָׁא בְּרִיךְ הוּא (.Cong – בְּרִיךְ הוּא) – לְעֵֽלָּא מִן כָּל בִּרְכָתָא וְשִׁירָתָא תֻּשְׁבְּחָתָא וְנֶחֱמָתָא, דַּאֲמִירָן בְּעָלְמָא. וְאִמְרוּ: אָמֵן. (.Cong – אָמֵן.)

יְהֵא שְׁלָמָא רַבָּא מִן שְׁמַיָּא, וְחַיִּים עָלֵינוּ וְעַל כָּל יִשְׂרָאֵל. וְאִמְרוּ: אָמֵן. (.Cong – אָמֵן.)

Take three steps back. Bow left and say . . . עֹשֶׂה; bow right and say . . . הוּא; bow forward and say וְעַל כָּל . . . אָמֵן. Remain standing in place for a few moments, then take three steps forward.

עֹשֶׂה שָׁלוֹם בִּמְרוֹמָיו, הוּא יַעֲשֶׂה שָׁלוֹם עָלֵינוּ, וְעַל כָּל יִשְׂרָאֵל. וְאִמְרוּ: אָמֵן. (.Cong – אָמֵן.)

הבדלה

At the departure of the Sabbath begin here.

הִנֵּה אֵל יְשׁוּעָתִי אֶבְטַח וְלֹא אֶפְחָד, כִּי עָזִּי וְזִמְרָת יָהּ יהוה, וַיְהִי לִי לִישׁוּעָה. וּשְׁאַבְתֶּם מַיִם בְּשָׂשׂוֹן, מִמַּעַיְנֵי הַיְשׁוּעָה.[1] לַיהוה הַיְשׁוּעָה, עַל עַמְּךָ בִרְכָתֶךָ סֶּלָה.[2] יהוה צְבָאוֹת עִמָּנוּ, מִשְׂגָּב לָנוּ אֱלֹהֵי יַעֲקֹב סֶלָה.[3] יהוה צְבָאוֹת, אַשְׁרֵי אָדָם בֹּטֵחַ בָּךְ.[4] יהוה הוֹשִׁיעָה, הַמֶּלֶךְ יַעֲנֵנוּ בְיוֹם קָרְאֵנוּ.[5] לַיְּהוּדִים הָיְתָה אוֹרָה וְשִׂמְחָה, וְשָׂשֹׂן וִיקָר,[6] כֵּן תִּהְיֶה לָּנוּ. כּוֹס יְשׁוּעוֹת אֶשָּׂא, וּבְשֵׁם יהוה אֶקְרָא.[7]

סַבְרִי מָרָנָן וְרַבָּנָן וְרַבּוֹתַי:

בָּרוּךְ אַתָּה יהוה אֱלֹהֵינוּ מֶלֶךְ הָעוֹלָם, בּוֹרֵא פְּרִי הַגָּפֶן.

(all present respond – אָמֵן.)

At the departure of the Sabbath the following two blessings are recited.
After the following blessing smell the spices.

בָּרוּךְ אַתָּה יהוה אֱלֹהֵינוּ מֶלֶךְ הָעוֹלָם, בּוֹרֵא מִינֵי בְשָׂמִים.

(all present respond – אָמֵן.)

After the following blessing hold fingers up to the flame to see the reflected light.

בָּרוּךְ אַתָּה יהוה אֱלֹהֵינוּ מֶלֶךְ הָעוֹלָם, בּוֹרֵא מְאוֹרֵי הָאֵשׁ.

(all present respond – אָמֵן.)

בָּרוּךְ אַתָּה יהוה אֱלֹהֵינוּ מֶלֶךְ הָעוֹלָם, הַמַּבְדִּיל בֵּין קֹדֶשׁ לְחוֹל, בֵּין אוֹר לְחֹשֶׁךְ, בֵּין יִשְׂרָאֵל לָעַמִּים, בֵּין יוֹם הַשְּׁבִיעִי לְשֵׁשֶׁת יְמֵי הַמַּעֲשֶׂה. בָּרוּךְ אַתָּה יהוה, הַמַּבְדִּיל בֵּין קֹדֶשׁ לְחוֹל.

(all present respond – אָמֵן.)

The one who recited *Havdalah,* or someone else present for *Havdalah,* should drink most of the wine from the cup.

At the departure of the Sabbath extinguish the flame by pouring leftover wine over it into a dish. It is customary to dip the fingers into the wine-dish and touch the eyelids and inner pockets with them. This symbolizes that the 'light of the *mitzvah'* will guide us and it invokes blessing for the week.

The blessing after wine appears on page 458.

Blessed, praised, glorified, exalted, extolled, mighty, upraised, and lauded be the Name of the Holy One, Blessed is He (Cong.— *Blessed is He*) — *beyond any blessing and song, praise and consolation that are uttered in the world. Now respond: Amen.* (Cong.— *Amen.*)

May there be abundant peace from Heaven, and life, upon us and upon all Israel. Now respond: Amen. (Cong.— *Amen.*)

Take three steps back. Bow left and say, *'He Who makes peace . . .'*; bow right and say, *'may He . . .'*; bow forward and say, *'and upon all Israel . . .'* Remain standing in place for a few moments, then take three steps forward.

He Who makes peace in His heights, may He make peace upon us, and upon all Israel. Now respond: Amen. (Cong.— *Amen.*)

HAVDALAH

At the departure of the Sabbath begin here.

הִנֵּה *Behold! God is my salvation, I shall trust and not fear — for God is my might and my praise — HASHEM — and He was a salvation for me. You can draw water with joy, from the springs of salvation.*[1] *Salvation is HASHEM's, upon Your people is Your blessing, Selah.*[2] *HASHEM, Master of legions, is with us, a stronghold for us is the God of Jacob, Selah.*[3] *HASHEM, Master of legions, praised is the man who trusts in You.*[4] *HASHEM save! May the King answer us on the day we call.*[5] *For the Jews there was light, gladness, joy, and honor*[6] *— so may it be for us. I will raise the cup of salvations, and I shall invoke the Name of HASHEM.*[7]

By your leave, my masters and teachers:

בָּרוּךְ *Blessed are You, HASHEM, our God, King of the universe, Who creates the fruit of the vine.* (All present respond— *Amen.*)

At the departure of the Sabbath the following two blessings are recited. After the following blessing smell the spices.

בָּרוּךְ *Blessed are You, HASHEM, our God, King of the universe, Who creates species of fragrance.* (All present respond— *Amen.*)

After the following blessing hold fingers up to the flame to see the reflected light.

בָּרוּךְ *Blessed are You, HASHEM, our God, King of the universe, Who creates the illuminations of the fire.* (All present respond— *Amen.*)

בָּרוּךְ *Blessed are You, HASHEM our God, King of the universe, Who separates between holy and secular, between light and darkness, between Israel and the nations, between the seventh day and the six days of labor. Blessed are You, HASHEM, Who separates between holy and secular.* (All present respond— *Amen.*)

The one who recited *Havdalah,* or someone else present for *Havdalah,* should drink most of the wine from the cup.

At the departure of the Sabbath extinguish the flame by pouring leftover wine over it into a dish. It is customary to dip the fingers into the wine-dish and touch the eyelids and inner pockets with them. This symbolizes that the 'light of the *mitzvah'* will guide us and it invokes blessing for the week. The blessing after wine appears on page 458.

(1) *Isaiah* 12:2-3. (2) *Psalms* 3:9. (3) 46:12. (4) 84:13. (5) 20:10. (6) *Esther* 8:16. (7) *Psalms* 116:13.

פסוקי דזמרה לחול המועד

THE MORNING SERVICE BEGINS WITH PAGES 188-228, THEN CONTINUES HERE.

INTRODUCTORY PSALM TO PESUKEI D'ZIMRAH

תהלים ל

מִזְמוֹר שִׁיר חֲנֻכַּת הַבַּיִת לְדָוִד. אֲרוֹמִמְךָ יהוה כִּי דִלִּיתָנִי, וְלֹא שִׂמַּחְתָּ אֹיְבַי לִי. יהוה אֱלֹהָי, שִׁוַּעְתִּי אֵלֶיךָ וַתִּרְפָּאֵנִי. יהוה הֶעֱלִיתָ מִן שְׁאוֹל נַפְשִׁי, חִיִּיתַנִי מִיָּרְדִי בוֹר. זַמְּרוּ לַיהוה חֲסִידָיו, וְהוֹדוּ לְזֵכֶר קָדְשׁוֹ. כִּי רֶגַע בְּאַפּוֹ, חַיִּים בִּרְצוֹנוֹ, בָּעֶרֶב יָלִין בֶּכִי וְלַבֹּקֶר רִנָּה. וַאֲנִי אָמַרְתִּי בְשַׁלְוִי, בַּל אֶמּוֹט לְעוֹלָם. יהוה בִּרְצוֹנְךָ הֶעֱמַדְתָּה לְהַרְרִי עֹז, הִסְתַּרְתָּ פָנֶיךָ הָיִיתִי נִבְהָל. אֵלֶיךָ יהוה אֶקְרָא, וְאֶל אֲדֹנָי אֶתְחַנָּן. מַה בֶּצַע בְּדָמִי, בְּרִדְתִּי אֶל שָׁחַת, הֲיוֹדְךָ עָפָר, הֲיַגִּיד אֲמִתֶּךָ. שְׁמַע יהוה וְחָנֵּנִי, יהוה הֱיֵה עֹזֵר לִי. ❖ הָפַכְתָּ מִסְפְּדִי לְמָחוֹל לִי, פִּתַּחְתָּ שַׂקִּי, וַתְּאַזְּרֵנִי שִׂמְחָה. לְמַעַן יְזַמֶּרְךָ כָבוֹד וְלֹא יִדֹּם, יהוה אֱלֹהַי לְעוֹלָם אוֹדֶךָּ.

קדיש יתום

Mourners recite קַדִּישׁ יָתוֹם. See *Laws* §81-83.

יִתְגַּדַּל וְיִתְקַדַּשׁ שְׁמֵהּ רַבָּא. (.Cong – אָמֵן.) בְּעָלְמָא דִּי בְרָא כִרְעוּתֵהּ. וְיַמְלִיךְ מַלְכוּתֵהּ, בְּחַיֵּיכוֹן וּבְיוֹמֵיכוֹן וּבְחַיֵּי דְכָל בֵּית יִשְׂרָאֵל, בַּעֲגָלָא וּבִזְמַן קָרִיב. וְאִמְרוּ: אָמֵן.

(.Cong – אָמֵן. יְהֵא שְׁמֵהּ רַבָּא מְבָרַךְ לְעָלַם וּלְעָלְמֵי עָלְמַיָּא.)

יְהֵא שְׁמֵהּ רַבָּא מְבָרַךְ לְעָלַם וּלְעָלְמֵי עָלְמַיָּא.

יִתְבָּרַךְ וְיִשְׁתַּבַּח וְיִתְפָּאַר וְיִתְרוֹמַם וְיִתְנַשֵּׂא וְיִתְהַדָּר וְיִתְעַלֶּה וְיִתְהַלָּל שְׁמֵהּ דְּקֻדְשָׁא בְּרִיךְ הוּא (.Cong – בְּרִיךְ הוּא) — לְעֵלָּא מִן כָּל בִּרְכָתָא וְשִׁירָתָא תֻּשְׁבְּחָתָא וְנֶחֱמָתָא, דַּאֲמִירָן בְּעָלְמָא. וְאִמְרוּ: אָמֵן. (.Cong – אָמֵן.)

יְהֵא שְׁלָמָא רַבָּא מִן שְׁמַיָּא, וְחַיִּים עָלֵינוּ וְעַל כָּל יִשְׂרָאֵל. וְאִמְרוּ: אָמֵן. (.Cong – אָמֵן.)

Take three steps back. Bow left and say . . . עֹשֶׂה; bow right and say . . . הוּא; bow forward and say וְעַל כָּל . . . אָמֵן. Remain standing in place for a few moments, then take three steps forward.

עֹשֶׂה שָׁלוֹם בִּמְרוֹמָיו, הוּא יַעֲשֶׂה שָׁלוֹם עָלֵינוּ, וְעַל כָּל יִשְׂרָאֵל. וְאִמְרוּ: אָמֵן. (.Cong – אָמֵן.)

(Some recite this short Kabbalistic declaration of intent before beginning *Pesukei D'zimrah:*)

(הֲרֵינִי מְזַמֵּן אֶת פִּי לְהוֹדוֹת וּלְהַלֵּל וּלְשַׁבֵּחַ אֶת בּוֹרְאִי. לְשֵׁם יִחוּד קוּדְשָׁא בְּרִיךְ הוּא וּשְׁכִינְתֵּיהּ עַל יְדֵי הַהוּא טָמִיר וְנֶעְלָם, בְּשֵׁם כָּל יִשְׂרָאֵל.)

PESUKEI D'ZIMRAH FOR CHOL HAMOED

THE MORNING SERVICE BEGINS WITH PAGES 188-228, THEN CONTINUES HERE.

INTRODUCTORY PSALM TO PESUKEI D'ZIMRAH

Psalm 30

מִזְמוֹר *A psalm — a song for the inauguration of the Temple— by David. I will exalt You,* HASHEM, *for You have drawn me up and not let my foes rejoice over me.* HASHEM, *my God, I cried out to You and You healed me.* HASHEM, *You have raised my soul from the lower world, You have preserved me from my descent to the Pit. Make music to* HASHEM, *His devout ones, and give thanks to His Holy Name. For His anger endures but a moment; life results from His favor. In the evening one lies down weeping, but with dawn — a cry of joy! I had said in my serenity, 'I will never falter.' But,* HASHEM, *all is through Your favor — You supported my greatness with might; should You but conceal Your face, I would be confounded. To You,* HASHEM, *I would call and to my Lord I would appeal. What gain is there in my death, when I descend to the Pit? Will the dust acknowledge You? Will it declare Your truth? Hear,* HASHEM, *and favor me;* HASHEM, *be my Helper!* Chazzan– *You have changed for me my lament into dancing; You undid my sackcloth and girded me with gladness. So that my soul might make music to You and not be stilled,* HASHEM *my God, forever will I thank You.*

MOURNER'S KADDISH

Mourners recite the Mourners' *Kaddish. See Laws* §81-83.
[A transliteration of this *Kaddish* appears on page 1147.]

יִתְגַּדַּל *May His great Name grow exalted and sanctified* (Cong.– *Amen.*) *in the world that He created as He willed. May He give reign to His kingship in your lifetimes and in your days, and in the lifetimes of the entire Family of Israel, swiftly and soon. Now respond: Amen.*

(Cong.– *Amen. May His great Name be blessed forever and ever.*)

May His great Name be blessed forever and ever.

Blessed, praised, glorified, exalted, extolled, mighty, upraised, and lauded be the Name of the Holy One, Blessed is He (Cong.– *Blessed is He*) *— beyond any blessing and song, praise and consolation that are uttered in the world. Now respond: Amen.* (Cong.– *Amen.*)

May there be abundant peace from Heaven, and life, upon us and upon all Israel. Now respond: Amen. (Cong.– *Amen.*)

Take three steps back. Bow left and say, *'He Who makes peace . . .';* bow right and say, *'may He . . .';* bow forward and say, *'and upon all Israel . . .'* Remain standing in place for a few moments, then take three steps forward.

He Who makes peace in His heights, may He make peace upon us, and upon all Israel. Now respond: Amen. (Cong.– *Amen.*)

(Some recite this short Kabbalistic declaration of intent before beginning *Pesukei D'zimrah:*)

(I now prepare my mouth to thank, laud, and praise my Creator. For the sake of the unification of the Holy One, Blessed is He, and His Presence, through Him Who is hidden and inscrutable — [I pray] in the name of all Israel.)

Pesukei D'zimrah begins with the recital of בָּרוּךְ שֶׁאָמַר. Stand while reciting בָּרוּךְ שֶׁאָמַר. During its recitation, hold the two front *tzitzis* of the *tallis* (or *tallis kattan)* in the right hand, and at its conclusion kiss the *tzitzis* and release them. Conversation is forbidden from this point until after *Shemoneh Esrei,* except for certain prayer responses (see p. 233).

בָּרוּךְ שֶׁאָמַר וְהָיָה הָעוֹלָם, בָּרוּךְ הוּא. בָּרוּךְ עוֹשֶׂה בְרֵאשִׁית, בָּרוּךְ אוֹמֵר וְעוֹשֶׂה, בָּרוּךְ גּוֹזֵר וּמְקַיֵּם, בָּרוּךְ מְרַחֵם עַל הָאָרֶץ, בָּרוּךְ מְרַחֵם עַל הַבְּרִיּוֹת, בָּרוּךְ מְשַׁלֵּם שָׂכָר טוֹב לִירֵאָיו, בָּרוּךְ חַי לָעַד וְקַיָּם לָנֶצַח, בָּרוּךְ פּוֹדֶה וּמַצִּיל, בָּרוּךְ שְׁמוֹ. בָּרוּךְ אַתָּה יהוה אֱלֹהֵינוּ מֶלֶךְ הָעוֹלָם, הָאֵל הָאָב הָרַחֲמָן הַמְּהֻלָּל בְּפֶה עַמּוֹ, מְשֻׁבָּח וּמְפֹאָר בִּלְשׁוֹן חֲסִידָיו וַעֲבָדָיו, וּבְשִׁירֵי דָוִד עַבְדֶּךָ. נְהַלֶּלְךָ יהוה אֱלֹהֵינוּ, בִּשְׁבָחוֹת וּבִזְמִרוֹת. נְגַדֶּלְךָ וּנְשַׁבֵּחֲךָ וּנְפָאֶרְךָ וְנַזְכִּיר שִׁמְךָ וְנַמְלִיכְךָ, מַלְכֵּנוּ אֱלֹהֵינוּ. ❖ יָחִיד, חֵי הָעוֹלָמִים, מֶלֶךְ מְשֻׁבָּח וּמְפֹאָר עֲדֵי עַד שְׁמוֹ הַגָּדוֹל. בָּרוּךְ אַתָּה יהוה, מֶלֶךְ מְהֻלָּל בַּתִּשְׁבָּחוֹת. (Cong.– אָמֵן.)

דברי הימים א טז:ח-לו

הוֹדוּ לַיהוה קִרְאוּ בִשְׁמוֹ, הוֹדִיעוּ בָעַמִּים עֲלִילֹתָיו. שִׁירוּ לוֹ, זַמְּרוּ לוֹ, שִׂיחוּ בְּכָל נִפְלְאֹתָיו. הִתְהַלְּלוּ בְּשֵׁם קָדְשׁוֹ, יִשְׂמַח לֵב מְבַקְשֵׁי יהוה. דִּרְשׁוּ יהוה וְעֻזּוֹ, בַּקְּשׁוּ פָנָיו תָּמִיד. זִכְרוּ נִפְלְאֹתָיו אֲשֶׁר עָשָׂה, מֹפְתָיו וּמִשְׁפְּטֵי פִיהוּ. זֶרַע יִשְׂרָאֵל עַבְדּוֹ, בְּנֵי יַעֲקֹב בְּחִירָיו. הוּא יהוה אֱלֹהֵינוּ, בְּכָל הָאָרֶץ מִשְׁפָּטָיו. זִכְרוּ לְעוֹלָם בְּרִיתוֹ, דָּבָר צִוָּה לְאֶלֶף דּוֹר. אֲשֶׁר כָּרַת אֶת אַבְרָהָם, וּשְׁבוּעָתוֹ לְיִצְחָק. וַיַּעֲמִידֶהָ לְיַעֲקֹב לְחֹק, לְיִשְׂרָאֵל בְּרִית עוֹלָם. לֵאמֹר, לְךָ אֶתֵּן אֶרֶץ כְּנָעַן, חֶבֶל נַחֲלַתְכֶם. בִּהְיוֹתְכֶם מְתֵי מִסְפָּר, כִּמְעַט וְגָרִים בָּהּ. וַיִּתְהַלְּכוּ מִגּוֹי אֶל גּוֹי, וּמִמַּמְלָכָה אֶל עַם אַחֵר. לֹא הִנִּיחַ לְאִישׁ לְעָשְׁקָם, וַיּוֹכַח עֲלֵיהֶם מְלָכִים. אַל תִּגְּעוּ בִּמְשִׁיחָי, וּבִנְבִיאַי אַל תָּרֵעוּ. שִׁירוּ לַיהוה כָּל הָאָרֶץ, בַּשְּׂרוּ מִיּוֹם אֶל יוֹם יְשׁוּעָתוֹ. סַפְּרוּ בַגּוֹיִם אֶת כְּבוֹדוֹ, בְּכָל הָעַמִּים נִפְלְאוֹתָיו. כִּי גָדוֹל יהוה וּמְהֻלָּל מְאֹד, וְנוֹרָא הוּא עַל כָּל אֱלֹהִים. ❖ כִּי כָּל אֱלֹהֵי הָעַמִּים אֱלִילִים, (pause) וַיהוה שָׁמַיִם עָשָׂה.

הוֹד וְהָדָר לְפָנָיו, עֹז וְחֶדְוָה בִּמְקֹמוֹ. הָבוּ לַיהוה מִשְׁפְּחוֹת עַמִּים, הָבוּ לַיהוה כָּבוֹד וָעֹז. הָבוּ לַיהוה כְּבוֹד שְׁמוֹ, שְׂאוּ מִנְחָה וּבֹאוּ לְפָנָיו, הִשְׁתַּחֲווּ לַיהוה בְּהַדְרַת קֹדֶשׁ. חִילוּ מִלְּפָנָיו כָּל הָאָרֶץ, אַף תִּכּוֹן תֵּבֵל בַּל תִּמּוֹט. יִשְׂמְחוּ הַשָּׁמַיִם וְתָגֵל

Pesukei D'zimrah begins with the recital of בָּרוּךְ שֶׁאָמַר, *Blessed is He Who spoke* . . . Stand while reciting בָּרוּךְ שֶׁאָמַר. During its recitation, hold the two front *tzitzis* of the *tallis* (or *tallis kattan)* in the right hand, and at its conclusion kiss the *tzitzis* and release them. Conversation is forbidden from this point until after *Shemoneh Esrei,* except for certain prayer responses (see p. 233).

בָּרוּךְ שֶׁאָמַר *Blessed is He Who spoke, and the world came into being — blessed is He. Blessed is He Who maintains Creation; blessed is He Who speaks and does; blessed is He Who decrees and fulfills; blessed is He Who has mercy on the earth; blessed is He Who has mercy on the creatures; blessed is He Who gives goodly reward to those who fear Him; blessed is He Who lives forever and endures to eternity; blessed is He Who redeems and rescues — blessed is His Name! Blessed are You, HASHEM, our God, King of the universe, the God, the merciful Father, Who is lauded by the mouth of His people, praised and glorified by the tongue of His devout ones and His servants and through the psalms of David Your servant. We shall laud You, HASHEM, our God, with praises and songs. We shall exalt You, praise You, glorify You, mention Your Name and proclaim Your reign, our King, our God.* Chazzan– *O Unique One, Life-giver of the worlds, King Whose great Name is eternally praised and glorified. Blessed are You, HASHEM, the King Who is lauded with praises.* (Cong.– *Amen.)*

I Chronicles 16:8-36

הוֹדוּ *Give thanks to HASHEM, declare His Name, make His acts known among the peoples. Sing to Him, make music to Him, speak of all His wonders. Glory in His holy Name, be glad of heart, you who seek HASHEM. Search out HASHEM and His might, seek His Presence always. Remember His wonders that He wrought, His marvels and the judgments of His mouth. O seed of Israel, His servant, O children of Jacob, His chosen ones — He is HASHEM, our God, over all the earth are His judgments. Remember His covenant forever — the word He commanded for a thousand generations — that He made with Abraham and His vow to Isaac. Then He established it for Jacob as a statute, for Israel as an everlasting covenant; saying, 'To you I shall give the Land of Canaan, the lot of your heritage.' When you were but few in number, hardly dwelling there, and they wandered from nation to nation, from one kingdom to another people. He let no man rob them, and He rebuked kings for their sake: 'Dare not touch My anointed ones, and to My prophets do no harm.' Sing to HASHEM, everyone on earth, announce His salvation daily. Relate His glory among the nations, among all the peoples His wonders. That HASHEM is great and exceedingly lauded, and awesome is He above all heavenly powers.* Chazzan– *For all the gods of the peoples are nothings — but HASHEM made heaven!*

Glory and majesty are before Him, might and delight are in His place. Render to HASHEM, O families of the peoples, render to HASHEM honor and might. Render to HASHEM honor worthy of His Name, take an offering and come before Him, prostrate yourselves before HASHEM in His intensely holy place. Tremble before Him, everyone on earth, indeed, the world is fixed so that it cannot falter. The heavens will be glad and

הָאָרֶץ, וְיֹאמְרוּ בַגּוֹיִם, יהוה מָלָךְ. יִרְעַם הַיָּם וּמְלוֹאוֹ, יַעֲלֹץ הַשָּׂדֶה
וְכָל אֲשֶׁר בּוֹ. אָז יְרַנְּנוּ עֲצֵי הַיָּעַר, מִלִּפְנֵי יהוה, כִּי בָא לִשְׁפּוֹט אֶת
הָאָרֶץ. הוֹדוּ לַיהוה כִּי טוֹב, כִּי לְעוֹלָם חַסְדּוֹ. וְאִמְרוּ הוֹשִׁיעֵנוּ
אֱלֹהֵי יִשְׁעֵנוּ, וְקַבְּצֵנוּ וְהַצִּילֵנוּ מִן הַגּוֹיִם, לְהֹדוֹת לְשֵׁם קָדְשֶׁךָ,
לְהִשְׁתַּבֵּחַ בִּתְהִלָּתֶךָ. בָּרוּךְ יהוה אֱלֹהֵי יִשְׂרָאֵל מִן הָעוֹלָם וְעַד
הָעֹלָם, וַיֹּאמְרוּ כָל הָעָם, אָמֵן, וְהַלֵּל לַיהוה.

❖ רוֹמְמוּ יהוה אֱלֹהֵינוּ וְהִשְׁתַּחֲווּ לַהֲדֹם רַגְלָיו, קָדוֹשׁ הוּא.[1]
רוֹמְמוּ יהוה אֱלֹהֵינוּ וְהִשְׁתַּחֲווּ לְהַר קָדְשׁוֹ, כִּי קָדוֹשׁ יהוה אֱלֹהֵינוּ.[2]

וְהוּא רַחוּם יְכַפֵּר עָוֹן וְלֹא יַשְׁחִית, וְהִרְבָּה לְהָשִׁיב אַפּוֹ, וְלֹא
יָעִיר כָּל חֲמָתוֹ.[3] אַתָּה יהוה, לֹא תִכְלָא רַחֲמֶיךָ מִמֶּנִּי, חַסְדְּךָ
וַאֲמִתְּךָ תָּמִיד יִצְּרוּנִי.[4] זְכֹר רַחֲמֶיךָ יהוה וַחֲסָדֶיךָ, כִּי מֵעוֹלָם
הֵמָּה.[5] תְּנוּ עֹז לֵאלֹהִים, עַל יִשְׂרָאֵל גַּאֲוָתוֹ, וְעֻזּוֹ בַּשְּׁחָקִים. נוֹרָא
אֱלֹהִים מִמִּקְדָּשֶׁיךָ, אֵל יִשְׂרָאֵל הוּא נֹתֵן עֹז וְתַעֲצֻמוֹת לָעָם, בָּרוּךְ
אֱלֹהִים.[6] אֵל נְקָמוֹת יהוה, אֵל נְקָמוֹת הוֹפִיעַ. הִנָּשֵׂא שֹׁפֵט הָאָרֶץ,
הָשֵׁב גְּמוּל עַל גֵּאִים.[7] לַיהוה הַיְשׁוּעָה, עַל עַמְּךָ בִרְכָתֶךָ סֶּלָה.[8]
❖ יהוה צְבָאוֹת עִמָּנוּ, מִשְׂגָּב לָנוּ אֱלֹהֵי יַעֲקֹב סֶלָה.[9] יהוה צְבָאוֹת,
אַשְׁרֵי אָדָם בֹּטֵחַ בָּךְ.[10] יהוה הוֹשִׁיעָה, הַמֶּלֶךְ יַעֲנֵנוּ בְיוֹם קָרְאֵנוּ.[11]

הוֹשִׁיעָה אֶת עַמֶּךָ, וּבָרֵךְ אֶת נַחֲלָתֶךָ, וּרְעֵם וְנַשְּׂאֵם עַד
הָעוֹלָם.[12] נַפְשֵׁנוּ חִכְּתָה לַיהוה, עֶזְרֵנוּ וּמָגִנֵּנוּ הוּא. כִּי בוֹ יִשְׂמַח
לִבֵּנוּ, כִּי בְשֵׁם קָדְשׁוֹ בָטָחְנוּ. יְהִי חַסְדְּךָ יהוה עָלֵינוּ, כַּאֲשֶׁר יִחַלְנוּ
לָךְ.[13] הַרְאֵנוּ יהוה חַסְדֶּךָ, וְיֶשְׁעֲךָ תִּתֶּן לָנוּ.[14] קוּמָה עֶזְרָתָה לָּנוּ,
וּפְדֵנוּ לְמַעַן חַסְדֶּךָ.[15] אָנֹכִי יהוה אֱלֹהֶיךָ הַמַּעַלְךָ מֵאֶרֶץ מִצְרָיִם,
הַרְחֶב פִּיךָ וַאֲמַלְאֵהוּ.[16] אַשְׁרֵי הָעָם שֶׁכָּכָה לּוֹ, אַשְׁרֵי הָעָם שֶׁיהוה
אֱלֹהָיו.[17] ❖ וַאֲנִי בְּחַסְדְּךָ בָטַחְתִּי, יָגֵל לִבִּי בִּישׁוּעָתֶךָ, אָשִׁירָה
לַיהוה, כִּי גָמַל עָלָי.[18]

The following prayer should be recited with special intensity.

יְהִי כְבוֹד יהוה לְעוֹלָם, יִשְׂמַח יהוה בְּמַעֲשָׂיו.[19] יְהִי שֵׁם יהוה
מְבֹרָךְ, מֵעַתָּה וְעַד עוֹלָם. מִמִּזְרַח שֶׁמֶשׁ עַד מְבוֹאוֹ, מְהֻלָּל
שֵׁם יהוה. רָם עַל כָּל גּוֹיִם יהוה, עַל הַשָּׁמַיִם כְּבוֹדוֹ.[20] יהוה
שִׁמְךָ לְעוֹלָם, יהוה זִכְרְךָ לְדֹר וָדֹר.[21] יהוה בַּשָּׁמַיִם הֵכִין כִּסְאוֹ,

(1) *Psalms* 99:5. (2) 99:9. (3) 78:38. (4) 40:12. (5) 25:6. (6) 68:35-36. (7) 94:1-2. (8) 3:9. (9) 46:8. (10) 84:13. (11) 20:10. (12) 28:9. (13) 33:20-22. (14) 85:8. (15) 44:27. (16) 81:11. (17) 144:15. (18) 13:6. (19) 104:31. (20) 113:2-4. (21) 135:13.

the earth will rejoice and say among the nations, 'HASHEM has reigned!' The sea and its fullness will roar, the field and everything in it will exult. Then the trees of the forest will sing with joy before HASHEM, for He will have arrived to judge the earth. Give thanks to HASHEM, for He is good, for His kindness endures forever. And say, 'Save us, O God of our salvation, gather us and rescue us from the nations, to thank Your Holy Name and to glory in Your praise!' Blessed is HASHEM, the God of Israel, from This World to the World to Come — and let the entire people say, 'Amen and praise to God!'

Chazzan– *Exalt HASHEM, our God, and bow at His footstool; He is holy![1] Exalt HASHEM, our God, and bow at His holy mountain; for holy is HASHEM, our God.[2]*

He, the Merciful One, is forgiving of iniquity and does not destroy; frequently, He withdraws His anger, not arousing His entire rage.[3] You, HASHEM — withhold not Your mercy from me; may Your kindness and Your truth always protect me.[4] Remember Your mercies, HASHEM, and Your kindnesses, for they are from the beginning of the world.[5] Render might to God, Whose majesty hovers over Israel and Whose might is in the clouds. You are awesome, O God, from Your sanctuaries, O God of Israel — it is He Who grants might and power to the people, blessed is God.[6] O God of vengeance, HASHEM, O God of vengeance, appear! Arise, O Judge of the earth, render recompense to the haughty.[7] Salvation is HASHEM's, upon Your people is Your blessing, Selah.[8] Chazzan– *HASHEM, Master of Legions, is with us, a stronghold for us is the God of Jacob, Selah.[9] HASHEM, Master of Legions, praiseworthy is the person who trusts in You.[10] HASHEM, save! May the King answer us on the day we call.[11]*

Save Your people and bless Your heritage, tend them and elevate them forever.[12] Our soul longed for HASHEM — our help and our shield is He. For in Him will our hearts be glad, for in His Holy Name we trusted. May Your kindness, HASHEM, be upon us, just as we awaited You.[13] Show us Your kindness, HASHEM, and grant us Your salvation.[14] Arise — assist us, and redeem us by virtue of Your kindness.[15] I am HASHEM, your God, Who raised you from the land of Egypt, open wide your mouth and I will fill it.[16] Praiseworthy is the people for whom this is so, praiseworthy is the people whose God is HASHEM.[17] Chazzan– *As for me, I trust in Your kindness; my heart will rejoice in Your salvation. I will sing to HASHEM, for He dealt kindly with me.[18]*

The following prayer should be recited with special intensity.

יְהִי *May the glory of HASHEM endure forever, let HASHEM rejoice in His works.[19] Blessed be the Name of HASHEM, from this time and forever. From the rising of the sun to its setting, HASHEM's Name is praised. High above all nations is HASHEM, above the heavens is His glory.[20] 'HASHEM' is Your Name forever, 'HASHEM' is Your memorial throughout the generations.[21] HASHEM has established His throne in the heavens,*

וּמַלְכוּתוֹ בַּכֹּל מָשָׁלָה.[1] יִשְׂמְחוּ הַשָּׁמַיִם וְתָגֵל הָאָרֶץ, וְיֹאמְרוּ
בַגּוֹיִם יהוה מָלָךְ.[2] יהוה מֶלֶךְ,[3] יהוה מָלָךְ,[4] יהוה יִמְלֹךְ לְעֹלָם
וָעֶד.[5] יהוה מֶלֶךְ עוֹלָם וָעֶד, אָבְדוּ גוֹיִם מֵאַרְצוֹ.[6] יהוה הֵפִיר עֲצַת
גּוֹיִם, הֵנִיא מַחְשְׁבוֹת עַמִּים.[7] רַבּוֹת מַחֲשָׁבוֹת בְּלֶב אִישׁ, וַעֲצַת
יהוה הִיא תָקוּם.[8] עֲצַת יהוה לְעוֹלָם תַּעֲמֹד, מַחְשְׁבוֹת לִבּוֹ לְדֹר
וָדֹר.[9] כִּי הוּא אָמַר וַיֶּהִי, הוּא צִוָּה וַיַּעֲמֹד.[10] כִּי בָחַר יהוה בְּצִיּוֹן,
אִוָּהּ לְמוֹשָׁב לוֹ.[11] כִּי יַעֲקֹב בָּחַר לוֹ יָהּ, יִשְׂרָאֵל לִסְגֻלָּתוֹ.[12] כִּי לֹא
יִטֹּשׁ יהוה עַמּוֹ, וְנַחֲלָתוֹ לֹא יַעֲזֹב.[13] ❖ וְהוּא רַחוּם יְכַפֵּר עָוֹן וְלֹא
יַשְׁחִית, וְהִרְבָּה לְהָשִׁיב אַפּוֹ, וְלֹא יָעִיר כָּל חֲמָתוֹ.[14] יהוה
הוֹשִׁיעָה, הַמֶּלֶךְ יַעֲנֵנוּ בְיוֹם קָרְאֵנוּ.[15]

אַשְׁרֵי יוֹשְׁבֵי בֵיתֶךָ, עוֹד יְהַלְלוּךָ סֶּלָה.[16] אַשְׁרֵי הָעָם שֶׁכָּכָה לּוֹ,
אַשְׁרֵי הָעָם שֶׁיהוה אֱלֹהָיו.[17]

תהלים קמה

תְּהִלָּה לְדָוִד,

אֲרוֹמִמְךָ אֱלוֹהַי הַמֶּלֶךְ, וַאֲבָרְכָה שִׁמְךָ לְעוֹלָם וָעֶד.
בְּכָל יוֹם אֲבָרְכֶךָּ, וַאֲהַלְלָה שִׁמְךָ לְעוֹלָם וָעֶד.
גָּדוֹל יהוה וּמְהֻלָּל מְאֹד, וְלִגְדֻלָּתוֹ אֵין חֵקֶר.
דּוֹר לְדוֹר יְשַׁבַּח מַעֲשֶׂיךָ, וּגְבוּרֹתֶיךָ יַגִּידוּ.
הֲדַר כְּבוֹד הוֹדֶךָ, וְדִבְרֵי נִפְלְאֹתֶיךָ אָשִׂיחָה.
וֶעֱזוּז נוֹרְאוֹתֶיךָ יֹאמֵרוּ, וּגְדוּלָּתְךָ אֲסַפְּרֶנָּה.
זֵכֶר רַב טוּבְךָ יַבִּיעוּ, וְצִדְקָתְךָ יְרַנֵּנוּ.
חַנּוּן וְרַחוּם יהוה, אֶרֶךְ אַפַּיִם וּגְדָל חָסֶד.
טוֹב יהוה לַכֹּל, וְרַחֲמָיו עַל כָּל מַעֲשָׂיו.
יוֹדוּךָ יהוה כָּל מַעֲשֶׂיךָ, וַחֲסִידֶיךָ יְבָרְכוּכָה.
כְּבוֹד מַלְכוּתְךָ יֹאמֵרוּ, וּגְבוּרָתְךָ יְדַבֵּרוּ.
לְהוֹדִיעַ לִבְנֵי הָאָדָם גְּבוּרֹתָיו, וּכְבוֹד הֲדַר מַלְכוּתוֹ.
מַלְכוּתְךָ מַלְכוּת כָּל עֹלָמִים, וּמֶמְשַׁלְתְּךָ בְּכָל דּוֹר וָדֹר.
סוֹמֵךְ יהוה לְכָל הַנֹּפְלִים, וְזוֹקֵף לְכָל הַכְּפוּפִים.

(1) *Psalms* 103:19. (2) *I Chronicles* 16:31. (3) *Psalms* 10:16. (4) 93:1 et al. (5) *Exodus* 15:18. (6) *Psalms* 10:16. (7) 33:10. (8) *Proverbs* 19:21. (9) *Psalms* 33:11. (10) 33:9. (11) 132:13. (12) 135:4. (13) 94:14. (14) 78:38. (15) 20:10. (16) 84:5. (17) 144:15.

and His kingdom reigns over all.[1] The heavens will be glad and the earth will rejoice, they will proclaim among the nations, 'HASHEM has reigned!'[2] HASHEM reigns,[3] HASHEM has reigned,[4] HASHEM shall reign for all eternity.[5] HASHEM reigns forever and ever, even when the nations will have perished from His earth.[6] HASHEM annuls the counsel of nations, He balks the designs of peoples.[7] Many designs are in man's heart, but the counsel of HASHEM — only it will prevail.[8] The counsel of HASHEM will endure forever, the designs of His heart throughout the generations.[9] For He spoke and it came to be; He commanded and it stood firm.[10] For God selected Zion, He desired it for His dwelling place.[11] For God selected Jacob as His own, Israel as His treasure.[12] For HASHEM will not cast off His people, nor will He forsake His heritage.[13] Chazzan– *He, the Merciful One, is forgiving of iniquity and does not destroy; frequently He withdraws His anger, not arousing His entire rage.[14] HASHEM, save! May the King answer us on the day we call.[15]*

אַשְׁרֵי *Praiseworthy are those who dwell in Your house; may they always praise You, Selah![16] Praiseworthy is the people for whom this is so, praiseworthy is the people whose God is HASHEM.[17]*

Psalm 145 *A psalm of praise by David:*

א *I will exalt You, my God the King,*
and I will bless Your Name forever and ever.
ב *Every day I will bless You,*
and I will laud Your Name forever and ever.
ג *HASHEM is great and exceedingly lauded,*
and His greatness is beyond investigation.
ד *Each generation will praise Your deeds to the next*
and of Your mighty deeds they will tell.
ה *The splendrous glory of Your power*
and Your wondrous deeds I shall discuss.
ו *And of Your awesome power they will speak,*
and Your greatness I shall relate.
ז *A recollection of Your abundant goodness they will utter*
and of Your righteousness they will sing exultantly.
ח *Gracious and merciful is HASHEM,*
slow to anger, and great in [bestowing] kindness.
ט *HASHEM is good to all; His mercies are on all His works.*
י *All Your works shall thank You, HASHEM,*
and Your devout ones will bless You.
כ *Of the glory of Your kingdom they will speak,*
and of Your power they will tell;
ל *To inform human beings of His mighty deeds,*
and the glorious splendor of His kingdom.
מ *Your kingdom is a kingdom spanning all eternities,*
and Your dominion is throughout every generation.
ס *HASHEM supports all the fallen ones and straightens all the bent.*

עֵינֵי כֹל אֵלֶיךָ יְשַׂבֵּרוּ, וְאַתָּה נוֹתֵן לָהֶם אֶת אָכְלָם בְּעִתּוֹ.

While reciting the verse פּוֹתֵחַ, concentrate intently on its meaning.

פּוֹתֵחַ אֶת יָדֶךָ,
וּמַשְׂבִּיעַ לְכָל חַי רָצוֹן.
צַדִּיק יהוה בְּכָל דְּרָכָיו, וְחָסִיד בְּכָל מַעֲשָׂיו.
קָרוֹב יהוה לְכָל קֹרְאָיו, לְכֹל אֲשֶׁר יִקְרָאֻהוּ בֶאֱמֶת.
רְצוֹן יְרֵאָיו יַעֲשֶׂה, וְאֶת שַׁוְעָתָם יִשְׁמַע וְיוֹשִׁיעֵם.
שׁוֹמֵר יהוה אֶת כָּל אֹהֲבָיו, וְאֵת כָּל הָרְשָׁעִים יַשְׁמִיד.
❖ תְּהִלַּת יהוה יְדַבֶּר פִּי, וִיבָרֵךְ כָּל בָּשָׂר שֵׁם קָדְשׁוֹ לְעוֹלָם וָעֶד.
וַאֲנַחְנוּ נְבָרֵךְ יָהּ, מֵעַתָּה וְעַד עוֹלָם, הַלְלוּיָהּ.[1]

תהלים קמו

הַלְלוּיָהּ, הַלְלִי נַפְשִׁי אֶת יהוה. אֲהַלְלָה יהוה בְּחַיָּי, אֲזַמְּרָה לֵאלֹהַי בְּעוֹדִי. אַל תִּבְטְחוּ בִנְדִיבִים, בְּבֶן אָדָם שֶׁאֵין לוֹ תְשׁוּעָה. תֵּצֵא רוּחוֹ, יָשֻׁב לְאַדְמָתוֹ, בַּיּוֹם הַהוּא אָבְדוּ עֶשְׁתֹּנֹתָיו. אַשְׁרֵי שֶׁאֵל יַעֲקֹב בְּעֶזְרוֹ, שִׂבְרוֹ עַל יהוה אֱלֹהָיו. עֹשֶׂה שָׁמַיִם וָאָרֶץ, אֶת הַיָּם וְאֶת כָּל אֲשֶׁר בָּם, הַשֹּׁמֵר אֱמֶת לְעוֹלָם. עֹשֶׂה מִשְׁפָּט לָעֲשׁוּקִים, נֹתֵן לֶחֶם לָרְעֵבִים, יהוה מַתִּיר אֲסוּרִים. יהוה פֹּקֵחַ עִוְרִים, יהוה זֹקֵף כְּפוּפִים, יהוה אֹהֵב צַדִּיקִים. יהוה שֹׁמֵר אֶת גֵּרִים, יָתוֹם וְאַלְמָנָה יְעוֹדֵד, וְדֶרֶךְ רְשָׁעִים יְעַוֵּת. ❖ יִמְלֹךְ יהוה לְעוֹלָם, אֱלֹהַיִךְ צִיּוֹן, לְדֹר וָדֹר, הַלְלוּיָהּ.

תהלים קמז

הַלְלוּיָהּ, כִּי טוֹב זַמְּרָה אֱלֹהֵינוּ, כִּי נָעִים נָאוָה תְהִלָּה. בּוֹנֵה יְרוּשָׁלַיִם יהוה, נִדְחֵי יִשְׂרָאֵל יְכַנֵּס. הָרוֹפֵא לִשְׁבוּרֵי לֵב, וּמְחַבֵּשׁ לְעַצְּבוֹתָם. מוֹנֶה מִסְפָּר לַכּוֹכָבִים, לְכֻלָּם שֵׁמוֹת יִקְרָא. גָּדוֹל אֲדוֹנֵינוּ וְרַב כֹּחַ, לִתְבוּנָתוֹ אֵין מִסְפָּר. מְעוֹדֵד עֲנָוִים יהוה, מַשְׁפִּיל רְשָׁעִים עֲדֵי אָרֶץ. עֱנוּ לַיהוה בְּתוֹדָה, זַמְּרוּ לֵאלֹהֵינוּ בְכִנּוֹר. הַמְּכַסֶּה שָׁמַיִם בְּעָבִים, הַמֵּכִין לָאָרֶץ מָטָר, הַמַּצְמִיחַ הָרִים חָצִיר. נוֹתֵן לִבְהֵמָה לַחְמָהּ, לִבְנֵי עֹרֵב אֲשֶׁר יִקְרָאוּ. לֹא בִגְבוּרַת הַסּוּס יֶחְפָּץ, לֹא בְשׁוֹקֵי הָאִישׁ יִרְצֶה. רוֹצֶה יהוה אֶת יְרֵאָיו, אֶת הַמְּיַחֲלִים לְחַסְדּוֹ. שַׁבְּחִי יְרוּשָׁלַיִם אֶת יהוה, הַלְלִי אֱלֹהַיִךְ צִיּוֹן. כִּי חִזַּק בְּרִיחֵי שְׁעָרָיִךְ, בֵּרַךְ בָּנַיִךְ בְּקִרְבֵּךְ. הַשָּׂם גְּבוּלֵךְ שָׁלוֹם, חֵלֶב חִטִּים יַשְׂבִּיעֵךְ.

(1) *Psalms* 115:8.

ע *The eyes of all look to You with hope*
and You give them their food in its proper time;
פ *You open Your hand, and satisfy*
the desire of every living thing.

While reciting the verse, *'You open . . .'* concentrate intently on its meaning.

צ *Righteous is HASHEM in all His ways*
and magnanimous in all His deeds.
ק *HASHEM is close to all who call upon Him —*
to all who call upon Him sincerely.
ר *The will of those who fear Him He will do;*
and their cry He will hear, and save them.
ש *HASHEM protects all who love Him;*
but all the wicked He will destroy.
ת Chazzan– *May my mouth declare the praise of HASHEM*
and may all flesh bless His Holy Name forever and ever.
We will bless God from this time and forever, Halleluyah![1]

Psalm 146

הַלְלוּיָהּ *Halleluyah! Praise HASHEM, O my Soul! I will praise HASHEM while I live, I will make music to my God while I exist. Do not rely on nobles, nor on a human being for he holds no salvation. When his spirit departs he returns to his earth, on that day his plans all perish. Praiseworthy is one whose help is Jacob's God, whose hope is in HASHEM, his God. He is the Maker of heaven and earth, the sea and all that is in them, Who safeguards truth forever. He does justice for the exploited; He gives bread to the hungry; HASHEM releases the bound. HASHEM gives sight to the blind; HASHEM straightens the bent; HASHEM loves the righteous. HASHEM protects strangers; orphan and widow He encourages; but the way of the wicked He contorts.* Chazzan– *HASHEM shall reign forever — your God, O Zion — from generation to generation. Halleluyah!*

Psalm 147

הַלְלוּיָהּ *Halleluyah! For it is good to make music to our God, for praise is pleasant and befitting. The Builder of Jerusalem is HASHEM, the outcast of Israel He will gather in. He is the Healer of the broken-hearted, and the One Who binds up their sorrows. He counts the number of the stars, to all of them He assigns names. Great is our Lord and abundant in strength, His understanding is beyond calculation. HASHEM encourages the humble, He lowers the wicked down to the ground. Call out to HASHEM with thanks, with the harp sing to our God — Who covers the heavens with clouds, Who prepares rain for the earth, Who makes mountains sprout with grass. He gives to an animal its food, to young ravens that cry out. Not in the strength of the horse does He desire, and not in the legs of man does He favor. HASHEM favors those who fear Him, those who hope for His kindness. Praise HASHEM, O Jerusalem, laud your God, O Zion. For He has strengthened the bars of your gates, and blessed your children in your midst; He Who makes your borders peaceful, and with the cream of the wheat He sates you;*

הַשֹּׁלֵחַ אִמְרָתוֹ אָרֶץ, עַד מְהֵרָה יָרוּץ דְּבָרוֹ. הַנֹּתֵן שֶׁלֶג כַּצָּמֶר, כְּפוֹר כָּאֵפֶר יְפַזֵּר. מַשְׁלִיךְ קַרְחוֹ כְפִתִּים, לִפְנֵי קָרָתוֹ מִי יַעֲמֹד. יִשְׁלַח דְּבָרוֹ וְיַמְסֵם, יַשֵּׁב רוּחוֹ יִזְּלוּ מָיִם. ❖ מַגִּיד דְּבָרָיו לְיַעֲקֹב, חֻקָּיו וּמִשְׁפָּטָיו לְיִשְׂרָאֵל. לֹא עָשָׂה כֵן לְכָל גּוֹי, וּמִשְׁפָּטִים בַּל יְדָעוּם, הַלְלוּיָהּ.

תהלים קמח

הַלְלוּיָהּ, הַלְלוּ אֶת יהוה מִן הַשָּׁמַיִם, הַלְלוּהוּ בַּמְּרוֹמִים. הַלְלוּהוּ כָל מַלְאָכָיו, הַלְלוּהוּ כָּל צְבָאָיו. הַלְלוּהוּ שֶׁמֶשׁ וְיָרֵחַ, הַלְלוּהוּ כָּל כּוֹכְבֵי אוֹר. הַלְלוּהוּ שְׁמֵי הַשָּׁמָיִם, וְהַמַּיִם אֲשֶׁר מֵעַל הַשָּׁמָיִם. יְהַלְלוּ אֶת שֵׁם יהוה, כִּי הוּא צִוָּה וְנִבְרָאוּ. וַיַּעֲמִידֵם לָעַד לְעוֹלָם, חָק נָתַן וְלֹא יַעֲבוֹר. הַלְלוּ אֶת יהוה מִן הָאָרֶץ, תַּנִּינִים וְכָל תְּהֹמוֹת. אֵשׁ וּבָרָד, שֶׁלֶג וְקִיטוֹר, רוּחַ סְעָרָה עֹשָׂה דְבָרוֹ. הֶהָרִים וְכָל גְּבָעוֹת, עֵץ פְּרִי וְכָל אֲרָזִים. הַחַיָּה וְכָל בְּהֵמָה, רֶמֶשׂ וְצִפּוֹר כָּנָף. מַלְכֵי אֶרֶץ וְכָל לְאֻמִּים, שָׂרִים וְכָל שֹׁפְטֵי אָרֶץ. בַּחוּרִים וְגַם בְּתוּלוֹת, זְקֵנִים עִם נְעָרִים. ❖ יְהַלְלוּ אֶת שֵׁם יהוה, כִּי נִשְׂגָּב שְׁמוֹ לְבַדּוֹ, הוֹדוֹ עַל אֶרֶץ וְשָׁמָיִם. וַיָּרֶם קֶרֶן לְעַמּוֹ, תְּהִלָּה לְכָל חֲסִידָיו, לִבְנֵי יִשְׂרָאֵל עַם קְרֹבוֹ, הַלְלוּיָהּ.

תהלים קמט

הַלְלוּיָהּ, שִׁירוּ לַיהוה שִׁיר חָדָשׁ, תְּהִלָּתוֹ בִּקְהַל חֲסִידִים. יִשְׂמַח יִשְׂרָאֵל בְּעֹשָׂיו, בְּנֵי צִיּוֹן יָגִילוּ בְמַלְכָּם. יְהַלְלוּ שְׁמוֹ בְמָחוֹל, בְּתֹף וְכִנּוֹר יְזַמְּרוּ לוֹ. כִּי רוֹצֶה יהוה בְּעַמּוֹ, יְפָאֵר עֲנָוִים בִּישׁוּעָה. יַעְלְזוּ חֲסִידִים בְּכָבוֹד, יְרַנְּנוּ עַל מִשְׁכְּבוֹתָם. רוֹמְמוֹת אֵל בִּגְרוֹנָם, וְחֶרֶב פִּיפִיּוֹת בְּיָדָם. לַעֲשׂוֹת נְקָמָה בַּגּוֹיִם, תּוֹכֵחוֹת בַּלְאֻמִּים. ❖ לֶאְסֹר מַלְכֵיהֶם בְּזִקִּים, וְנִכְבְּדֵיהֶם בְּכַבְלֵי בַרְזֶל. לַעֲשׂוֹת בָּהֶם מִשְׁפָּט כָּתוּב, הָדָר הוּא לְכָל חֲסִידָיו, הַלְלוּיָהּ.

תהלים קנ

הַלְלוּיָהּ, הַלְלוּ אֵל בְּקָדְשׁוֹ, הַלְלוּהוּ בִּרְקִיעַ עֻזּוֹ. הַלְלוּהוּ בִגְבוּרֹתָיו, הַלְלוּהוּ כְּרֹב גֻּדְלוֹ. הַלְלוּהוּ בְּתֵקַע שׁוֹפָר, הַלְלוּהוּ בְּנֵבֶל וְכִנּוֹר. הַלְלוּהוּ בְתֹף וּמָחוֹל, הַלְלוּהוּ בְּמִנִּים וְעֻגָב. הַלְלוּהוּ בְצִלְצְלֵי שָׁמַע, הַלְלוּהוּ בְּצִלְצְלֵי תְרוּעָה. ❖ כֹּל הַנְּשָׁמָה תְּהַלֵּל יָהּ, הַלְלוּיָהּ. כֹּל הַנְּשָׁמָה תְּהַלֵּל יָהּ, הַלְלוּיָהּ.

He Who dispatches His utterance earthward; how swiftly His commandment runs! He Who gives snow like fleece, He scatters frost like ashes. He hurls His ice like crumbs — before His cold, who can stand? He issues His command and it melts them, He blows His wind — the waters flow. Chazzan– *He relates His Word to Jacob, His statutes and judgments to Israel. He did not do so for any other nation, such judgments — they know them not. Halleluyah!*

Psalm 148

הַלְלוּיָהּ *Halleluyah! Praise* HASHEM *from the heavens; praise Him in the heights. Praise Him, all His angels; praise Him, all His legions. Praise Him, sun and moon; praise Him, all bright stars. Praise Him, the most exalted of the heavens and the waters that are above the heavens. Let them praise the Name of* HASHEM, *for He commanded and they were created. And He established them forever and ever, He issued a decree that will not change. Praise* HASHEM *from the earth, sea giants and all watery depths. Fire and hail, snow and vapor, stormy wind fulfilling His word. Mountains and all hills, fruitful trees and all cedars. Beasts and all cattle, crawling things and winged fowl. Kings of the earth and all governments, princes and all judges on earth. Young men and also maidens, old men together with youths.* Chazzan– *Let them praise the Name of* HASHEM, *for His Name alone will have been exalted; His glory is above earth and heaven. And He will have exalted the pride of His nation, causing praise for all His devout ones, for the Children of Israel, His intimate people. Halleluyah!*

Psalm 149

הַלְלוּיָהּ *Halleluyah! Sing to* HASHEM *a new song, let His praise be in the congregation of the devout. Let Israel exult in its Maker, let the Children of Zion rejoice in their King. Let them praise His Name with dancing, with drums and harp let them make music to Him. For* HASHEM *favors His nation, He adorns the humble with salvation. Let the devout exult in glory, let them sing joyously upon their beds. The lofty praises of God are in their throats, and a double-edged sword is in their hand — to execute vengeance among the nations, rebukes among the governments.* Chazzan– *To bind their kings with chains, and their nobles with fetters of iron. To execute upon them written judgment — that will be the splendor of all His devout ones. Halleluyah!*

Psalm 150

הַלְלוּיָהּ *Halleluyah! Praise God in His Sanctuary; praise Him in the firmament of His power. Praise Him for His mighty acts; praise Him as befits His abundant greatness. Praise Him with the blast of the shofar; praise Him with lyre and harp. Praise Him with drum and dance; praise Him with organ and flute. Praise Him with clanging cymbals; praise Him with resonant trumpets.* Chazzan– *Let all souls praise God, Halleluyah! Let all souls praise God, Halleluyah!*

בָּרוּךְ יהוה לְעוֹלָם, אָמֵן וְאָמֵן.[1] בָּרוּךְ יהוה מִצִּיּוֹן, שֹׁכֵן יְרוּשָׁלָיִם, הַלְלוּיָהּ.[2] בָּרוּךְ יהוה אֱלֹהִים אֱלֹהֵי יִשְׂרָאֵל, עֹשֵׂה נִפְלָאוֹת לְבַדּוֹ. ❖ וּבָרוּךְ שֵׁם כְּבוֹדוֹ לְעוֹלָם, וְיִמָּלֵא כְבוֹדוֹ אֶת כָּל הָאָרֶץ, אָמֵן וְאָמֵן.[3]

One must stand from וַיְבָרֶךְ דָּוִיד, until after the phrase אַתָּה הוּא ה׳ הָאֱלֹהִים; however, there is a generally accepted custom to remain standing until after completing אָז יָשִׁיר (below).

דברי הימים א כט:י-יג

וַיְבָרֶךְ דָּוִיד אֶת יהוה לְעֵינֵי כָּל הַקָּהָל, וַיֹּאמֶר דָּוִיד: בָּרוּךְ אַתָּה יהוה, אֱלֹהֵי יִשְׂרָאֵל אָבִינוּ, מֵעוֹלָם וְעַד עוֹלָם. לְךָ יהוה הַגְּדֻלָּה וְהַגְּבוּרָה וְהַתִּפְאֶרֶת וְהַנֵּצַח וְהַהוֹד, כִּי כֹל בַּשָּׁמַיִם וּבָאָרֶץ; לְךָ יהוה הַמַּמְלָכָה וְהַמִּתְנַשֵּׂא לְכֹל לְרֹאשׁ. וְהָעֹשֶׁר וְהַכָּבוֹד מִלְּפָנֶיךָ, וְאַתָּה מוֹשֵׁל בַּכֹּל, וּבְיָדְךָ כֹּחַ וּגְבוּרָה, וּבְיָדְךָ לְגַדֵּל וּלְחַזֵּק לַכֹּל. וְעַתָּה אֱלֹהֵינוּ מוֹדִים אֲנַחְנוּ לָךְ, וּמְהַלְלִים לְשֵׁם תִּפְאַרְתֶּךָ.

It is customary to set aside something for charity at this point.

נחמיה ט:ו-יא

אַתָּה הוּא יהוה לְבַדֶּךָ, אַתָּה עָשִׂיתָ אֶת הַשָּׁמַיִם, שְׁמֵי הַשָּׁמַיִם וְכָל צְבָאָם, הָאָרֶץ וְכָל אֲשֶׁר עָלֶיהָ, הַיַּמִּים וְכָל אֲשֶׁר בָּהֶם, וְאַתָּה מְחַיֶּה אֶת כֻּלָּם, וּצְבָא הַשָּׁמַיִם לְךָ מִשְׁתַּחֲוִים. ❖ אַתָּה הוּא יהוה הָאֱלֹהִים אֲשֶׁר בָּחַרְתָּ בְּאַבְרָם, וְהוֹצֵאתוֹ מֵאוּר כַּשְׂדִּים, וְשַׂמְתָּ שְׁמוֹ אַבְרָהָם. וּמָצָאתָ אֶת לְבָבוֹ נֶאֱמָן לְפָנֶיךָ – – וְכָרוֹת עִמּוֹ הַבְּרִית לָתֵת אֶת אֶרֶץ הַכְּנַעֲנִי הַחִתִּי הָאֱמֹרִי וְהַפְּרִזִּי וְהַיְבוּסִי וְהַגִּרְגָּשִׁי, לָתֵת לְזַרְעוֹ, וַתָּקֶם אֶת דְּבָרֶיךָ, כִּי צַדִּיק אָתָּה. וַתֵּרֶא אֶת עֳנִי אֲבֹתֵינוּ בְּמִצְרָיִם, וְאֶת זַעֲקָתָם שָׁמַעְתָּ עַל יַם סוּף. וַתִּתֵּן אֹתֹת וּמֹפְתִים בְּפַרְעֹה וּבְכָל עֲבָדָיו וּבְכָל עַם אַרְצוֹ, כִּי יָדַעְתָּ כִּי הֵזִידוּ עֲלֵיהֶם, וַתַּעַשׂ לְךָ שֵׁם כְּהַיּוֹם הַזֶּה. ❖ וְהַיָּם בָּקַעְתָּ לִפְנֵיהֶם, וַיַּעַבְרוּ בְתוֹךְ הַיָּם בַּיַּבָּשָׁה, וְאֶת רֹדְפֵיהֶם הִשְׁלַכְתָּ בִמְצוֹלֹת, כְּמוֹ אֶבֶן בְּמַיִם עַזִּים.

שירת הים

שמות יד:ל-טו:יט

וַיּוֹשַׁע יהוה בַּיּוֹם הַהוּא אֶת־יִשְׂרָאֵל מִיַּד מִצְרָיִם, וַיַּרְא יִשְׂרָאֵל אֶת־מִצְרַיִם מֵת עַל־שְׂפַת הַיָּם: ❖ וַיַּרְא יִשְׂרָאֵל אֶת־הַיָּד הַגְּדֹלָה אֲשֶׁר עָשָׂה יהוה בְּמִצְרַיִם, וַיִּירְאוּ הָעָם אֶת־יהוה, וַיַּאֲמִינוּ בַּיהוה וּבְמֹשֶׁה עַבְדּוֹ:

בָּרוּךְ *Blessed is HASHEM forever, Amen and Amen.*[1] *Blessed is HASHEM from Zion, Who dwells in Jerusalem, Halleluyah.*[2] *Blessed is HASHEM, God, the God of Israel, Who alone does wonders.* Chazzan– *Blessed is His glorious Name forever, and may all the earth be filled with His glory, Amen and Amen.*

One must stand from here until after the phrase *'It is You, HASHEM the God'*; however, there is a generally accepted custom to remain standing until after completing the Song at the Sea (below).

I Chronicles 29:10-13

וַיְבָרֶךְ *And David blessed HASHEM in the presence of the entire congregation; David said, 'Blessed are You, HASHEM, the God of Israel our forefather from This World to the World to Come. Yours, HASHEM, is the greatness, the strength, the splendor, the triumph, and the glory, even everything in heaven and earth; Yours, HASHEM, is the kingdom, and the sovereignty over every leader.* It is customary to set aside something for charity at this point. *Wealth and honor come from You and You rule everything — in Your hand is power and strength and it is in Your hand to make anyone great or strong. So now, our God, we thank You and praise Your splendrous Name.'*

Nehemiah 9:6-11

It is You alone, HASHEM, You have made the heaven, the most exalted heaven and all their legions, the earth and everything upon it, the seas and everything in them and You give them all life; the heavenly legions bow to You. Chazzan– *It is You, HASHEM the God, Who selected Abram, brought him out of Ur Kasdim and made his name Abraham. You found his heart faithful before You —*

— and You established the covenant with him to give the land of the Canaanite, Hittite, Emorite, Perizzite, Jebusite, and Girgashite, to give it to his offspring; and You affirmed Your word, for You are righteous. You observed the suffering of our forefathers in Egypt, and their outcry You heard at the Sea of Reeds. You imposed signs and wonders upon Pharaoh and upon all his servants, and upon all the people of his land. For You knew that they sinned flagrantly against them, and You brought Yourself renown as [clear as] this very day. Chazzan– *You split the Sea before them and they crossed in the midst of the Sea on dry land; but their pursuers You hurled into the depths, like a stone into turbulent waters.*

THE SONG AT THE SEA

Exodus 14:30-15:19

וַיּוֹשַׁע *HASHEM saved — on that day — Israel from the hand of Egypt, and Israel saw the Egyptians dead on the seashore.* Chazzan– *Israel saw the great hand that HASHEM inflicted upon Egypt and the people feared HASHEM, and they had faith in HASHEM and in Moses, His servant.*

---

(1) *Psalms* 89:53. (2) 135:21. (3) 72:18-19.

אָז יָשִׁיר־מֹשֶׁה וּבְנֵי יִשְׂרָאֵל אֶת־הַשִּׁירָה הַזֹּאת לַיהוָה, וַיֹּאמְרוּ
לֵאמֹר, אָשִׁירָה לַיהוָה כִּי־גָאֹה גָּאָה, סוּס
וְרֹכְבוֹ רָמָה בַיָּם: עָזִּי וְזִמְרָת יָהּ וַיְהִי־לִי
לִישׁוּעָה, זֶה אֵלִי וְאַנְוֵהוּ, אֱלֹהֵי
אָבִי וַאֲרֹמְמֶנְהוּ: יהוה אִישׁ מִלְחָמָה, יהוה
שְׁמוֹ: מַרְכְּבֹת פַּרְעֹה וְחֵילוֹ יָרָה בַיָּם, וּמִבְחַר
שָׁלִשָׁיו טֻבְּעוּ בְיַם־סוּף: תְּהֹמֹת יְכַסְיֻמוּ, יָרְדוּ בִמְצוֹלֹת כְּמוֹ־
אָבֶן: יְמִינְךָ יהוה נֶאְדָּרִי בַּכֹּחַ, יְמִינְךָ
יהוה תִּרְעַץ אוֹיֵב: וּבְרֹב גְּאוֹנְךָ תַּהֲרֹס
קָמֶיךָ, תְּשַׁלַּח חֲרֹנְךָ יֹאכְלֵמוֹ כַּקַּשׁ: וּבְרוּחַ
אַפֶּיךָ נֶעֶרְמוּ מַיִם, נִצְּבוּ כְמוֹ־נֵד
נֹזְלִים, קָפְאוּ תְהֹמֹת בְּלֶב־יָם: אָמַר
אוֹיֵב, אֶרְדֹּף אַשִּׂיג אֲחַלֵּק שָׁלָל, תִּמְלָאֵמוֹ
נַפְשִׁי, אָרִיק חַרְבִּי, תּוֹרִישֵׁמוֹ יָדִי: נָשַׁפְתָּ
בְרוּחֲךָ כִּסָּמוֹ יָם, צָלְלוּ כַּעוֹפֶרֶת בְּמַיִם,
אַדִּירִים: מִי־כָמֹכָה בָּאֵלִם יהוה, מִי
כָּמֹכָה נֶאְדָּר בַּקֹּדֶשׁ, נוֹרָא תְהִלֹּת עֹשֵׂה
פֶלֶא: נָטִיתָ יְמִינְךָ, תִּבְלָעֵמוֹ אָרֶץ: נָחִיתָ
בְחַסְדְּךָ עַם־זוּ גָּאָלְתָּ, נֵהַלְתָּ בְעָזְּךָ אֶל־נְוֵה
קָדְשֶׁךָ: שָׁמְעוּ עַמִּים יִרְגָּזוּן, חִיל
אָחַז יֹשְׁבֵי פְּלָשֶׁת: אָז נִבְהֲלוּ אַלּוּפֵי
אֱדוֹם, אֵילֵי מוֹאָב יֹאחֲזֵמוֹ רָעַד, נָמֹגוּ
כֹּל יֹשְׁבֵי כְנָעַן: תִּפֹּל עֲלֵיהֶם אֵימָתָה
וָפַחַד, בִּגְדֹל זְרוֹעֲךָ יִדְּמוּ כָּאָבֶן, עַד־
יַעֲבֹר עַמְּךָ יהוה, עַד־יַעֲבֹר עַם־זוּ
קָנִיתָ: תְּבִאֵמוֹ וְתִטָּעֵמוֹ בְּהַר נַחֲלָתְךָ, מָכוֹן
לְשִׁבְתְּךָ פָּעַלְתָּ יהוה, מִקְּדָשׁ אֲדֹנָי כּוֹנְנוּ
יָדֶיךָ: יהוה | יִמְלֹךְ לְעֹלָם וָעֶד:

יהוה יִמְלֹךְ לְעֹלָם וָעֶד. (יהוה מַלְכוּתֵהּ קָאֵם, לְעָלַם וּלְעָלְמֵי עָלְמַיָּא.) כִּי בָא סוּס פַּרְעֹה בְּרִכְבּוֹ וּבְפָרָשָׁיו בַּיָּם, וַיָּשֶׁב יהוה עֲלֵהֶם אֶת מֵי הַיָּם, וּבְנֵי יִשְׂרָאֵל הָלְכוּ בַיַּבָּשָׁה בְּתוֹךְ הַיָּם. ❖ כִּי לַיהוה הַמְּלוּכָה, וּמֹשֵׁל בַּגּוֹיִם.[1] וְעָלוּ מוֹשִׁעִים בְּהַר צִיּוֹן, לִשְׁפֹּט

Then Moses and the Children of Israel chose to sing this song to HASHEM, *and they said the following:*

I shall sing to HASHEM *for He is exalted above the arrogant, having hurled horse with its rider into the sea.*

God is my might and my praise, and He was a salvation for me. This is my God, and I will build Him a Sanctuary; the God of my father, and I will exalt Him.

HASHEM *is Master of war, through His Name* HASHEM.

Pharaoh's chariots and army He threw into the sea; and the pick of his officers were mired in the Sea of Reeds.

Deep waters covered them; they descended in the depths like stone.

Your right hand, HASHEM, *is adorned with strength; Your right hand,* HASHEM, *smashes the enemy.*

In Your abundant grandeur You shatter Your opponents; You dispatch Your wrath, it consumes them like straw.

At a blast from Your nostrils the waters were heaped up; straight as a wall stood the running water, the deep waters congealed in the heart of the sea.

The enemy declared: 'I will pursue, I will overtake, I will divide plunder; I will satisfy my lust with them; I will unsheathe my sword, my hand will impoverish them.'

You blew with Your wind — the sea enshrouded them; the mighty ones sank like lead in the waters.

Who is like You among the heavenly powers, HASHEM! *Who is like You, mighty in holiness, too awesome for praise, doing wonders!*

You stretched out Your right hand — the earth swallowed them.

You guided in Your kindness this people that You redeemed; You led with Your might to Your holy abode.

Peoples heard — they were agitated; convulsive terror gripped the dwellers of Philistia.

Then the chieftains of Edom were confounded, trembling gripped the powers of Moab, all the dwellers of Canaan dissolved.

May fear and terror befall them, at the greatness of Your arm may they be still as stone; until Your people passes through, HASHEM, *until this people You have acquired passes through.*

You shall bring them and implant them on the mount of Your heritage, the foundation of Your dwelling-place, which You, HASHEM, *have made: the Sanctuary, my Lord, that Your hands established.*

HASHEM *shall reign for all eternity.*

HASHEM *shall reign for all eternity. (*HASHEM *— His kingdom is established forever and ever.) When Pharaoh's cavalry came — with his chariots and horsemen — into the sea and* HASHEM *turned back the waters of the sea upon them, the Children of Israel walked on the dry bed amid the sea.* Chazzan— *For the sovereignty is* HASHEM*'s and He rules over nations.*[1] *The saviors will ascend Mount Zion to judge*

(1) *Psalms* 22:29.

אֶת הַר עֵשָׂו, וְהָיְתָה לַיהוה הַמְּלוּכָה.[1] וְהָיָה יהוה לְמֶלֶךְ עַל כָּל הָאָרֶץ, בַּיּוֹם הַהוּא יִהְיֶה יהוה אֶחָד וּשְׁמוֹ אֶחָד.[2] (וּבְתוֹרָתְךָ כָּתוּב לֵאמֹר: שְׁמַע יִשְׂרָאֵל יהוה אֱלֹהֵינוּ יהוה אֶחָד.[3])

Stand while reciting יִשְׁתַּבַּח . . . The fifteen expressions of praise — שִׁיר וּשְׁבָחָה . . . בְּרָכוֹת וְהוֹדָאוֹת — should be recited without pause, preferably in one breath.

יִשְׁתַּבַּח שִׁמְךָ לָעַד מַלְכֵּנוּ, הָאֵל הַמֶּלֶךְ הַגָּדוֹל וְהַקָּדוֹשׁ, בַּשָּׁמַיִם וּבָאָרֶץ. כִּי לְךָ נָאֶה יהוה אֱלֹהֵינוּ וֵאלֹהֵי אֲבוֹתֵינוּ, שִׁיר וּשְׁבָחָה, הַלֵּל וְזִמְרָה, עֹז וּמֶמְשָׁלָה, נֶצַח גְּדֻלָּה וּגְבוּרָה, תְּהִלָּה וְתִפְאֶרֶת, קְדֻשָּׁה וּמַלְכוּת, בְּרָכוֹת וְהוֹדָאוֹת מֵעַתָּה וְעַד עוֹלָם. ❖ בָּרוּךְ אַתָּה יהוה, אֵל מֶלֶךְ גָּדוֹל בַּתִּשְׁבָּחוֹת, אֵל הַהוֹדָאוֹת, אֲדוֹן הַנִּפְלָאוֹת, הַבּוֹחֵר בְּשִׁירֵי זִמְרָה, מֶלֶךְ אֵל חֵי הָעוֹלָמִים. (Cong. – אָמֵן.)

The *chazzan* recites חֲצִי קַדִּישׁ.

יִתְגַּדַּל וְיִתְקַדַּשׁ שְׁמֵהּ רַבָּא. (Cong. – אָמֵן.) בְּעָלְמָא דִּי בְרָא כִרְעוּתֵהּ. וְיַמְלִיךְ מַלְכוּתֵהּ, בְּחַיֵּיכוֹן וּבְיוֹמֵיכוֹן וּבְחַיֵּי דְכָל בֵּית יִשְׂרָאֵל, בַּעֲגָלָא וּבִזְמַן קָרִיב. וְאִמְרוּ: אָמֵן.

(Cong. – אָמֵן. יְהֵא שְׁמֵהּ רַבָּא מְבָרַךְ לְעָלַם וּלְעָלְמֵי עָלְמַיָּא.)

יְהֵא שְׁמֵהּ רַבָּא מְבָרַךְ לְעָלַם וּלְעָלְמֵי עָלְמַיָּא.

יִתְבָּרַךְ וְיִשְׁתַּבַּח וְיִתְפָּאַר וְיִתְרוֹמַם וְיִתְנַשֵּׂא וְיִתְהַדָּר וְיִתְעַלֶּה וְיִתְהַלָּל שְׁמֵהּ דְּקֻדְשָׁא בְּרִיךְ הוּא (Cong. – בְּרִיךְ הוּא) — לְעֵלָּא מִן כָּל בִּרְכָתָא וְשִׁירָתָא תֻּשְׁבְּחָתָא וְנֶחֱמָתָא, דַּאֲמִירָן בְּעָלְמָא. וְאִמְרוּ: אָמֵן. (Cong. – אָמֵן.)

In some congregations the *chazzan* chants a melody during his recitation of בָּרְכוּ, so that the congregation can then recite יִתְבָּרַךְ.

Chazzan bows at בָּרְכוּ and straightens up at ה׳.

בָּרְכוּ אֶת יהוה הַמְּבֹרָךְ.

Congregation, followed by *chazzan*, responds, bowing at בָּרוּךְ and straightening up at ה׳.

בָּרוּךְ יהוה הַמְּבֹרָךְ לְעוֹלָם וָעֶד.

יִתְבָּרַךְ וְיִשְׁתַּבַּח וְיִתְפָּאַר וְיִתְרוֹמַם וְיִתְנַשֵּׂא שְׁמוֹ שֶׁל מֶלֶךְ מַלְכֵי הַמְּלָכִים, הַקָּדוֹשׁ בָּרוּךְ הוּא. שֶׁהוּא רִאשׁוֹן וְהוּא אַחֲרוֹן, וּמִבַּלְעָדָיו אֵין אֱלֹהִים.[4] סֹלּוּ, לָרֹכֵב בָּעֲרָבוֹת, בְּיָהּ שְׁמוֹ, וְעִלְזוּ לְפָנָיו.[5] וּשְׁמוֹ מְרוֹמָם עַל כָּל בְּרָכָה וּתְהִלָּה.[6] בָּרוּךְ שֵׁם כְּבוֹד מַלְכוּתוֹ לְעוֹלָם וָעֶד. יְהִי שֵׁם יהוה מְבֹרָךְ, מֵעַתָּה וְעַד עוֹלָם.[7]

ברכות קריאת שמע

It is preferable that one sit while reciting the following series of prayers — particularly the *Kedushah* verses, קָדוֹשׁ קָדוֹשׁ קָדוֹשׁ and בָּרוּךְ כְּבוֹד — until *Shemoneh Esrei*.

בָּרוּךְ אַתָּה יהוה אֱלֹהֵינוּ מֶלֶךְ הָעוֹלָם, יוֹצֵר אוֹר וּבוֹרֵא חֹשֶׁךְ, עֹשֶׂה שָׁלוֹם וּבוֹרֵא אֶת הַכֹּל.[8]

Esau's mountain, and the kingdom will be H*ASHEM's.*[1] *Then* H*ASHEM will be King over all the world, on that day* H*ASHEM will be One and His Name will be One.*[2] *(And in Your Torah it is written: Hear O Israel:* H*ASHEM is our God,* H*ASHEM, the One and Only.*[3]*)*

Stand while reciting *'May Your Name be praised . . .'*
The fifteen expressions of praise — *'song and praise. . .blessings and thanksgivings'* — should be recited without pause, preferably in one breath.

יִשְׁתַּבַּח *May Your Name be praised forever — our King, the God, the great and holy King — in heaven and on earth. Because for You is fitting — O* H*ASHEM, our God, and the God of our forefathers — song and praise, lauding and hymns, power and dominion, triumph, greatness and strength, praise and splendor, holiness and sovereignty, blessings and thanksgivings from this time and forever.* Chazzan– *Blessed are You,* H*ASHEM, God, King exalted through praises, God of thanksgivings, Master of wonders, Who chooses musical songs of praise — King, God, Life-giver of the world.* (Cong.– *Amen.)*

The *chazzan* recites Half-*Kaddish.*

יִתְגַּדַּל *May His great Name grow exalted and sanctified* (Cong.– *Amen.) in the world that He created as He willed. May He give reign to His kingship in your lifetimes and in your days, and in the lifetimes of the entire Family of Israel, swiftly and soon. Now respond: Amen.*

(Cong.– *Amen. May His great Name be blessed forever and ever.)*
May His great Name be blessed forever and ever.

Blessed, praised, glorified, exalted, extolled, mighty, upraised, and lauded be the Name of the Holy One, Blessed is He (Cong.– *Blessed is He) — beyond any blessing and song, praise and consolation that are uttered in the world. Now respond: Amen.* (Cong.– *Amen.)*

In some congregations the *chazzan* chants a melody during his recitation of *Borchu,* so that the congregation can then recite *'Blessed, praised . . .'*

Chazzan bows at *'Bless,'* and straightens up at *'*H*ASHEM.'*

Bless HASHEM, the blessed One.

Congregation, followed by *chazzan,* responds, bowing at *'Blessed'* and straightening up at *'*H*ASHEM.'*

Blessed is HASHEM, the blessed One, for all eternity.

Blessed, praised, glorified, exalted and upraised is the Name of the King Who rules over kings — the Holy One, Blessed is He. For He is the First and He is the Last and aside from Him there is no god.[4] *Extol Him — Who rides the highest heavens — with His Name,* Y*AH, and exult before Him.*[5] *His Name is exalted beyond every blessing and praise.*[6] *Blessed is the Name of His glorious kingdom for all eternity. Blessed be the Name of* H*ASHEM from this time and forever.*[7]

BLESSINGS OF THE SHEMA

It is preferable that one sit while reciting the following series of prayers — particularly the *Kedushah* verses, *'Holy, holy, holy . . .'* and *'Blessed is the glory . . .'* — until *Shemoneh Esrei.*

בָּרוּךְ *Blessed are You,* H*ASHEM, our God, King of the universe, Who forms light and creates darkness, makes peace and creates all.*[8]

(1) *Ovadiah* 1:21. (2) *Zechariah* 14:9. (3) *Deuteronomy* 6:4. (4) Cf. *Isaiah* 44:6. (5) *Psalms* 68:5. (6) Cf. *Nehemiah* 9:5. (7) *Psalms* 113:2. (8) Cf. *Isaiah* 45:7.

הַמֵּאִיר לָאָרֶץ וְלַדָּרִים עָלֶיהָ בְּרַחֲמִים, וּבְטוּבוֹ מְחַדֵּשׁ בְּכָל יוֹם תָּמִיד מַעֲשֵׂה בְרֵאשִׁית. מָה רַבּוּ מַעֲשֶׂיךָ יהוה, כֻּלָּם בְּחָכְמָה עָשִׂיתָ, מָלְאָה הָאָרֶץ קִנְיָנֶךָ.[1] הַמֶּלֶךְ הַמְּרוֹמָם לְבַדּוֹ מֵאָז, הַמְּשֻׁבָּח וְהַמְּפֹאָר וְהַמִּתְנַשֵּׂא מִימוֹת עוֹלָם. אֱלֹהֵי עוֹלָם, בְּרַחֲמֶיךָ הָרַבִּים רַחֵם עָלֵינוּ, אֲדוֹן עֻזֵּנוּ, צוּר מִשְׂגַּבֵּנוּ, מָגֵן יִשְׁעֵנוּ, מִשְׂגָּב בַּעֲדֵנוּ. אֵל בָּרוּךְ גְּדוֹל דֵּעָה, הֵכִין וּפָעַל זָהֳרֵי חַמָּה, טוֹב יָצַר כָּבוֹד לִשְׁמוֹ, מְאוֹרוֹת נָתַן סְבִיבוֹת עֻזּוֹ, פִּנּוֹת צְבָאָיו קְדוֹשִׁים רוֹמְמֵי שַׁדַּי, תָּמִיד מְסַפְּרִים כְּבוֹד אֵל וּקְדֻשָּׁתוֹ. תִּתְבָּרַךְ יהוה אֱלֹהֵינוּ עַל שֶׁבַח מַעֲשֵׂה יָדֶיךָ, וְעַל מְאוֹרֵי אוֹר שֶׁעָשִׂיתָ, יְפָאֲרוּךָ, סֶּלָה.

תִּתְבָּרַךְ צוּרֵנוּ מַלְכֵּנוּ וְגֹאֲלֵנוּ, בּוֹרֵא קְדוֹשִׁים. יִשְׁתַּבַּח שִׁמְךָ לָעַד מַלְכֵּנוּ, יוֹצֵר מְשָׁרְתִים, וַאֲשֶׁר מְשָׁרְתָיו כֻּלָּם עוֹמְדִים בְּרוּם עוֹלָם, וּמַשְׁמִיעִים בְּיִרְאָה יַחַד בְּקוֹל דִּבְרֵי אֱלֹהִים חַיִּים וּמֶלֶךְ עוֹלָם.[2] כֻּלָּם אֲהוּבִים, כֻּלָּם בְּרוּרִים, כֻּלָּם גִּבּוֹרִים, וְכֻלָּם עֹשִׂים בְּאֵימָה וּבְיִרְאָה רְצוֹן קוֹנָם. ❖ וְכֻלָּם פּוֹתְחִים אֶת פִּיהֶם בִּקְדֻשָּׁה וּבְטָהֳרָה, בְּשִׁירָה וּבְזִמְרָה, וּמְבָרְכִים וּמְשַׁבְּחִים וּמְפָאֲרִים וּמַעֲרִיצִים וּמַקְדִּישִׁים וּמַמְלִיכִים —

אֶת שֵׁם הָאֵל הַמֶּלֶךְ הַגָּדוֹל הַגִּבּוֹר וְהַנּוֹרָא קָדוֹשׁ הוּא.[3] ❖ וְכֻלָּם מְקַבְּלִים עֲלֵיהֶם עֹל מַלְכוּת שָׁמַיִם זֶה מִזֶּה, וְנוֹתְנִים רְשׁוּת זֶה לָזֶה, לְהַקְדִּישׁ לְיוֹצְרָם, בְּנַחַת רוּחַ בְּשָׂפָה בְרוּרָה וּבִנְעִימָה. קְדֻשָּׁה כֻּלָּם כְּאֶחָד עוֹנִים וְאוֹמְרִים בְּיִרְאָה:

Congregation recites aloud:

קָדוֹשׁ קָדוֹשׁ קָדוֹשׁ יהוה צְבָאוֹת,
מְלֹא כָל הָאָרֶץ כְּבוֹדוֹ.[4]

וְהָאוֹפַנִּים וְחַיּוֹת הַקֹּדֶשׁ בְּרַעַשׁ גָּדוֹל מִתְנַשְּׂאִים לְעֻמַּת שְׂרָפִים. לְעֻמָּתָם מְשַׁבְּחִים וְאוֹמְרִים:

Congregation recites aloud:

בָּרוּךְ כְּבוֹד יהוה מִמְּקוֹמוֹ.[5]

לְאֵל בָּרוּךְ נְעִימוֹת יִתֵּנוּ. לַמֶּלֶךְ אֵל חַי וְקַיָּם, זְמִרוֹת יֹאמֵרוּ, וְתִשְׁבָּחוֹת יַשְׁמִיעוּ. כִּי הוּא לְבַדּוֹ פּוֹעֵל גְּבוּרוֹת, עֹשֶׂה חֲדָשׁוֹת, בַּעַל מִלְחָמוֹת, זוֹרֵעַ צְדָקוֹת, מַצְמִיחַ יְשׁוּעוֹת, בּוֹרֵא

הַמֵּאִיר *He Who illuminates the earth and those who dwell upon it, with compassion; and in His goodness renews daily, perpetually, the work of Creation. How great are Your works, HASHEM, You make them all with wisdom, the world is full of Your possessions.*[1] *The King Who was exalted in solitude before Creation, Who is praised, glorified, and upraised since days of old. Eternal God, with Your abundant compassion be compassionate to us — O Master of our power, our rocklike stronghold, O Shield of our salvation, be a stronghold for us. The blessed God, Who is great in knowledge, prepared and worked on the rays of the sun; the Beneficent One fashioned honor for His Name, emplaced luminaries all around His power; the leaders of His legions, holy ones, exalt the Almighty, constantly relate the honor of God and His sanctity. May You be blessed, HASHEM, our God, beyond the praises of Your handiwork and beyond the bright luminaries that You have made — may they glorify You — Selah!*

תִּתְבָּרַךְ *May You be blessed, our Rock, our King and our Redeemer, Creator of holy ones; may Your Name be praised forever, our King, O Fashioner of ministering angels; all of Whose ministering angels stand at the summit of the universe and proclaim — with awe, together, loudly — the words of the living God and King of the universe.*[2] *They are all beloved; they are all flawless; they are all mighty; they all do the will of their Maker with dread and reverence.* Chazzan– *And they all open their mouth in holiness and purity, in song and hymn — and bless, praise, glorify, revere, sanctify and declare the kingship of —*

אֶת שֵׁם *The Name of God, the great, mighty, and awesome King; holy is He.*[3] Chazzan– *Then they all accept upon themselves the yoke of heavenly sovereignty from one another, and grant permission to one another to sanctify the One Who formed them, with tranquillity, with clear articulation, and with sweetness. All of them as one proclaim His holiness and say with awe:*

Congregation recites aloud:

'Holy, holy, holy is HASHEM, Master of Legions, the whole world is filled with His glory.'[4]

וְהָאוֹפַנִּים *Then the Ofanim and the holy Chayos, with great noise, raise themselves towards the Seraphim. Facing them they give praise saying:*

Congregation recites aloud:

'Blessed is the glory of HASHEM from His place.'[5]

לְאֵל *To the blessed God they shall offer sweet melodies; to the King, the living and enduring God, they shall sing hymns and proclaim praises. For He alone effects mighty deeds, makes new things, is Master of wars, sows kindnesses, makes salvations flourish, creates*

---

(1) *Psalms* 104:24. (2) Cf. *Jeremiah* 10:10. (3) Cf. *Deuteronomy* 10:17; *Psalms* 99:3.
(4) *Isaiah* 6:3. (5) *Ezekiel* 3:12.

רְפוּאוֹת, נוֹרָא תְהִלּוֹת, אֲדוֹן הַנִּפְלָאוֹת. הַמְּחַדֵּשׁ בְּטוּבוֹ בְּכָל יוֹם תָּמִיד מַעֲשֵׂה בְרֵאשִׁית. כָּאָמוּר: לְעֹשֵׂה אוֹרִים גְּדֹלִים, כִּי לְעוֹלָם חַסְדּוֹ.[1] ❖ אוֹר חָדָשׁ עַל צִיּוֹן תָּאִיר, וְנִזְכֶּה כֻלָּנוּ מְהֵרָה לְאוֹרוֹ. בָּרוּךְ אַתָּה יהוה, יוֹצֵר הַמְּאוֹרוֹת. (Cong. – אָמֵן.)

אַהֲבָה רַבָּה אֲהַבְתָּנוּ יהוה אֱלֹהֵינוּ, חֶמְלָה גְדוֹלָה וִיתֵרָה חָמַלְתָּ עָלֵינוּ. אָבִינוּ מַלְכֵּנוּ, בַּעֲבוּר אֲבוֹתֵינוּ שֶׁבָּטְחוּ בְךָ, וַתְּלַמְּדֵם חֻקֵּי חַיִּים, כֵּן תְּחָנֵּנוּ וּתְלַמְּדֵנוּ. אָבִינוּ הָאָב הָרַחֲמָן הַמְּרַחֵם, רַחֵם עָלֵינוּ, וְתֵן בְּלִבֵּנוּ לְהָבִין וּלְהַשְׂכִּיל, לִשְׁמֹעַ לִלְמֹד וּלְלַמֵּד, לִשְׁמֹר וְלַעֲשׂוֹת וּלְקַיֵּם אֶת כָּל דִּבְרֵי תַלְמוּד תּוֹרָתֶךָ בְּאַהֲבָה. וְהָאֵר עֵינֵינוּ בְּתוֹרָתֶךָ, וְדַבֵּק לִבֵּנוּ בְּמִצְוֹתֶיךָ, וְיַחֵד לְבָבֵנוּ לְאַהֲבָה וּלְיִרְאָה אֶת שְׁמֶךָ,[2] וְלֹא נֵבוֹשׁ לְעוֹלָם וָעֶד. כִּי בְשֵׁם קָדְשְׁךָ הַגָּדוֹל וְהַנּוֹרָא בָּטָחְנוּ, נָגִילָה וְנִשְׂמְחָה בִּישׁוּעָתֶךָ.

At this point, gather the four *tzitzis* between the fourth and fifth fingers of the left hand. Hold *tzitzis* in this manner throughout the *Shema*.

וַהֲבִיאֵנוּ לְשָׁלוֹם מֵאַרְבַּע כַּנְפוֹת הָאָרֶץ, וְתוֹלִיכֵנוּ קוֹמְמִיּוּת לְאַרְצֵנוּ. כִּי אֵל פּוֹעֵל יְשׁוּעוֹת אָתָּה, וּבָנוּ בָחַרְתָּ מִכָּל עַם וְלָשׁוֹן. ❖ וְקֵרַבְתָּנוּ לְשִׁמְךָ הַגָּדוֹל סֶלָה בֶּאֱמֶת, לְהוֹדוֹת לְךָ וּלְיַחֶדְךָ בְּאַהֲבָה. בָּרוּךְ אַתָּה יהוה, הַבּוֹחֵר בְּעַמּוֹ יִשְׂרָאֵל בְּאַהֲבָה. (Cong. – אָמֵן.)

שמע

Immediately before its recitation concentrate on fulfilling the positive commandment of reciting the *Shema* twice daily. It is important to enunciate each word clearly and not to run words together. For this reason, vertical lines have been placed between two words that are prone to be slurred into one and are not separated by a comma or a hyphen. See *Laws* §40-55.

When praying without a *minyan,* begin with the following three-word formula:

אֵל מֶלֶךְ נֶאֱמָן.

Recite the first verse aloud, with the right hand covering the eyes, and concentrate intently upon accepting God's absolute sovereignty.

שְׁמַע | יִשְׂרָאֵל, יהוה | אֱלֹהֵינוּ, יהוה | אֶחָד:[3]

In an undertone – בָּרוּךְ שֵׁם כְּבוֹד מַלְכוּתוֹ לְעוֹלָם וָעֶד.

While reciting the first paragraph (דברים ו:ה-ט), concentrate on accepting the commandment to love God.

וְאָהַבְתָּ אֵת | יהוה | אֱלֹהֶיךָ, בְּכָל־לְבָבְךָ, וּבְכָל־נַפְשְׁךָ, וּבְכָל־מְאֹדֶךָ: וְהָיוּ הַדְּבָרִים הָאֵלֶּה, אֲשֶׁר | אָנֹכִי מְצַוְּךָ הַיּוֹם, עַל־לְבָבֶךָ: וְשִׁנַּנְתָּם לְבָנֶיךָ, וְדִבַּרְתָּ בָּם, בְּשִׁבְתְּךָ בְּבֵיתֶךָ, וּבְלֶכְתְּךָ בַדֶּרֶךְ, וּבְשָׁכְבְּךָ וּבְקוּמֶךָ: וּקְשַׁרְתָּם לְאוֹת | עַל־יָדֶךָ, וְהָיוּ לְטֹטָפֹת בֵּין | עֵינֶיךָ: וּכְתַבְתָּם | עַל־מְזֻזוֹת בֵּיתֶךָ, וּבִשְׁעָרֶיךָ:

cures, is too awesome for praise, is Lord of wonders. In His goodness He renews daily, perpetually, the work of creation. As it is said: '[Give thanks] to Him Who makes the great luminaries, for His kindness endures forever.'[1] Chazzan– *May You shine a new light on Zion, and may we all speedily merit its light. Blessed are You, HASHEM, Who fashions the luminaries.* (Cong.– *Amen.*)

אַהֲבָה *With an abundant love have You loved us, HASHEM, our God; with exceedingly great pity have You pitied us. Our Father, our King, for the sake of our forefathers who trusted in You and whom You taught the decrees of life, may You be equally gracious to us and teach us. Our Father, the merciful Father, Who acts mercifully, have mercy upon us, instill in our hearts to understand and elucidate, to listen, learn, teach, safeguard, perform, and fulfill all the words of Your Torah's teaching with love. Enlighten our eyes in Your Torah, attach our hearts to Your commandments, and unify our hearts to love and fear Your Name,*[2] *and may we not feel inner shame for all eternity. Because we have trusted in Your great and awesome holy Name, may we exult and rejoice in Your salvation. Bring us in peacefulness from the four corners of the earth and lead us with upright pride to our land. For You effect salvations, O God; You have chosen us from among every people and tongue.* Chazzan– *And You have brought us close to Your great Name forever in truth, to offer praiseful thanks to You, and proclaim Your Oneness with love. Blessed are You, HASHEM, Who chooses His people Israel with love.* (Cong.– *Amen.*)

At this point, gather the four *tzitzis* between the fourth and fifth fingers of the left hand. Hold *tzitzis* in this manner throughout the *Shema*.

THE SHEMA

Immediately before its recitation concentrate on fulfilling the positive commandment of reciting the *Shema* twice daily. It is important to enunciate each word clearly and not to run words together. See *Laws* §40-55.

When praying without a *minyan,* begin with the following three-word formula:

God, trustworthy King.

Recite the first verse aloud, with the right hand covering the eyes, and concentrate intently upon accepting God's absolute sovereignty.

Hear, O Israel: HASHEM is our God, HASHEM, the One and Only.[3]

In an undertone– *Blessed is the Name of His glorious kingdom for all eternity.*

While reciting the first paragraph (*Deuteronomy* 6:5-9), concentrate on accepting the commandment to love God.

וְאָהַבְתָּ *You shall love HASHEM, your God, with all your heart, with all your soul and with all your resources. Let these matters that I command you today be upon your heart. Teach them thoroughly to your children and speak of them while you sit in your home, while you walk on the way, when you retire and when you arise. Bind them as a sign upon your arm and let them be tefillin between your eyes. And write them on the doorposts of your house and upon your gates.*

---

(1) *Psalms* 136:7. (2) Cf. 86:11. (3) *Deuteronomy* 6:4.

While reciting the second paragraph (דברים יא:יג-כא), concentrate on accepting all the commandments and the concept of reward and punishment.

וְהָיָה, אִם־שָׁמֹעַ תִּשְׁמְעוּ אֶל־מִצְוֹתַי, אֲשֶׁר | אָנֹכִי מְצַוֶּה | אֶתְכֶם הַיּוֹם, לְאַהֲבָה אֶת־יהוה | אֱלֹהֵיכֶם וּלְעָבְדוֹ, בְּכָל־לְבַבְכֶם, וּבְכָל־נַפְשְׁכֶם: וְנָתַתִּי מְטַר־אַרְצְכֶם בְּעִתּוֹ, יוֹרֶה וּמַלְקוֹשׁ, וְאָסַפְתָּ דְגָנֶךָ וְתִירֹשְׁךָ וְיִצְהָרֶךָ: וְנָתַתִּי | עֵשֶׂב | בְּשָׂדְךָ לִבְהֶמְתֶּךָ, וְאָכַלְתָּ וְשָׂבָעְתָּ: הִשָּׁמְרוּ לָכֶם, פֶּן־יִפְתֶּה לְבַבְכֶם, וְסַרְתֶּם וַעֲבַדְתֶּם | אֱלֹהִים | אֲחֵרִים, וְהִשְׁתַּחֲוִיתֶם לָהֶם: וְחָרָה | אַף־יהוה בָּכֶם, וְעָצַר | אֶת־הַשָּׁמַיִם, וְלֹא־יִהְיֶה מָטָר, וְהָאֲדָמָה לֹא תִתֵּן אֶת־יְבוּלָהּ, וַאֲבַדְתֶּם | מְהֵרָה מֵעַל הָאָרֶץ הַטֹּבָה | אֲשֶׁר | יהוה נֹתֵן לָכֶם: וְשַׂמְתֶּם | אֶת־דְּבָרַי | אֵלֶּה, עַל־לְבַבְכֶם וְעַל־נַפְשְׁכֶם, וּקְשַׁרְתֶּם | אֹתָם | לְאוֹת | עַל־יֶדְכֶם, וְהָיוּ לְטוֹטָפֹת בֵּין | עֵינֵיכֶם: וְלִמַּדְתֶּם | אֹתָם | אֶת־בְּנֵיכֶם, לְדַבֵּר בָּם, בְּשִׁבְתְּךָ בְּבֵיתֶךָ, וּבְלֶכְתְּךָ בַדֶּרֶךְ, וּבְשָׁכְבְּךָ וּבְקוּמֶךָ: וּכְתַבְתָּם | עַל־מְזוּזוֹת בֵּיתֶךָ, וּבִשְׁעָרֶיךָ: לְמַעַן | יִרְבּוּ | יְמֵיכֶם וִימֵי בְנֵיכֶם, עַל הָאֲדָמָה | אֲשֶׁר נִשְׁבַּע | יהוה לַאֲבֹתֵיכֶם לָתֵת לָהֶם, כִּימֵי הַשָּׁמַיִם | עַל־הָאָרֶץ:

Before reciting the third paragraph (במדבר טו:לז-מא) the *tzitzis*, which have been held in the left hand, are taken in the right hand also. The *tzitzis* are kissed at each mention of the word and at the end of the paragraph, and are passed before the eyes at וּרְאִיתֶם אֹתוֹ.

וַיֹּאמֶר | יהוה | אֶל־מֹשֶׁה לֵּאמֹר: דַּבֵּר | אֶל־בְּנֵי | יִשְׂרָאֵל, וְאָמַרְתָּ אֲלֵהֶם, וְעָשׂוּ לָהֶם צִיצִת, עַל־כַּנְפֵי בִגְדֵיהֶם לְדֹרֹתָם, וְנָתְנוּ | עַל־צִיצִת הַכָּנָף, פְּתִיל תְּכֵלֶת: וְהָיָה לָכֶם לְצִיצִת, וּרְאִיתֶם | אֹתוֹ, וּזְכַרְתֶּם | אֶת־כָּל־מִצְוֹת | יהוה, וַעֲשִׂיתֶם | אֹתָם, וְלֹא תָתֻרוּ | אַחֲרֵי לְבַבְכֶם וְאַחֲרֵי | עֵינֵיכֶם, אֲשֶׁר־אַתֶּם זֹנִים | אַחֲרֵיהֶם: לְמַעַן תִּזְכְּרוּ, וַעֲשִׂיתֶם | אֶת־כָּל־מִצְוֹתָי, וִהְיִיתֶם קְדֹשִׁים לֵאלֹהֵיכֶם: אֲנִי יהוה | אֱלֹהֵיכֶם, אֲשֶׁר הוֹצֵאתִי | אֶתְכֶם | מֵאֶרֶץ מִצְרַיִם, לִהְיוֹת לָכֶם לֵאלֹהִים, אֲנִי | יהוה | אֱלֹהֵיכֶם: אֱמֶת —

Concentrate on fulfilling the commandment of remembering the Exodus from Egypt.

Although the word אֱמֶת belongs to the next paragraph, it is appended to the conclusion of the previous one, as explained in the commentary (page 50).

–*Chazzan* repeats **יהוה אֱלֹהֵיכֶם אֱמֶת.**

וְיַצִּיב וְנָכוֹן וְקַיָּם וְיָשָׁר וְנֶאֱמָן וְאָהוּב וְחָבִיב וְנֶחְמָד וְנָעִים וְנוֹרָא וְאַדִּיר וּמְתֻקָּן וּמְקֻבָּל וְטוֹב וְיָפֶה הַדָּבָר הַזֶּה עָלֵינוּ לְעוֹלָם וָעֶד. אֱמֶת אֱלֹהֵי עוֹלָם מַלְכֵּנוּ צוּר יַעֲקֹב, מָגֵן יִשְׁעֵנוּ, לְדֹר וָדֹר הוּא קַיָּם, וּשְׁמוֹ קַיָּם, וְכִסְאוֹ נָכוֹן, וּמַלְכוּתוֹ וֶאֱמוּנָתוֹ לָעַד קַיֶּמֶת.

While reciting the second paragraph (*Deuteronomy* 11:13-21), concentrate on accepting all the commandments and the concept of reward and punishment.

וְהָיָה *And it will come to pass that if you continually hearken to My commandments that I command you today, to love HASHEM, your God, and to serve Him, with all your heart and with all your soul — then I will provide rain for your land in its proper time, the early and late rains, that you may gather in your grain, your wine, and your oil. I will provide grass in your field for your cattle and you will eat and be satisfied. Beware lest your heart be seduced and you turn astray and serve gods of others and bow to them. Then the wrath of HASHEM will blaze against you. He will restrain the heaven so there will be no rain and the ground will not yield its produce. And you will swiftly be banished from the goodly land which HASHEM gives you. Place these words of Mine upon your heart and upon your soul; bind them for a sign upon your arm and let them be tefillin between your eyes. Teach them to your children, to discuss them, while you sit in your home, while you walk on the way, when you retire and when you arise. And write them on the doorposts of your house and upon your gates. In order to prolong your days and the days of your children upon the ground that HASHEM has sworn to your ancestors to give them, like the days of the heaven on the earth.*

Before reciting the third paragraph (*Numbers* 15:37-41) the *tzitzis*, which have been held in the left hand, are taken in the right hand also. The *tzitzis* are kissed at each mention of the word and at the end of the paragraph, and are passed before the eyes at *'that you may see it.'*

וַיֹּאמֶר *And HASHEM said to Moses saying: Speak to the Children of Israel and say to them that they are to make themselves tzitzis on the corners of their garments, throughout their generations. And they are to place upon the tzitzis of each corner a thread of techeiles. And it shall constitute tzitzis for you, that you may see it and remember all the commandments of HASHEM and perform them; and not explore after your heart and after your eyes after which you stray. So that you may remember and perform all My commandments; and be holy to your God. I am HASHEM, your God, Who has removed you from the land of Egypt to be a God to You; I am HASHEM your God — it is true —*

Concentrate on fulfilling the commandment of remembering the Exodus from Egypt.

Although the word אֱמֶת, *'it is true,'* belongs to the next paragraph, it is appended to the conclusion of the previous one, as explained in the commentary (page 50).

Chazzan repeats: **HASHEM, your God, is true.**

וְיַצִּיב *And certain, established and enduring, fair and faithful, beloved and cherished, delightful and pleasant, awesome and powerful, correct and accepted, good and beautiful is this affirmation to us forever and ever. True — the God of the universe is our King; the Rock of Jacob is the Shield of our salvation. From generation to generation He endures and His Name endures and His throne is well established; His sovereignty and faithfulness endure forever.*

וּדְבָרָיו חָיִים וְקַיָּמִים, נֶאֱמָנִים וְנֶחֱמָדִים לָעַד (kiss the *tzitzis* and release them) וּלְעוֹלְמֵי עוֹלָמִים. ❖ עַל אֲבוֹתֵינוּ וְעָלֵינוּ, עַל בָּנֵינוּ וְעַל דּוֹרוֹתֵינוּ, וְעַל כָּל דּוֹרוֹת זֶרַע יִשְׂרָאֵל עֲבָדֶיךָ.

עַל הָרִאשׁוֹנִים וְעַל הָאַחֲרוֹנִים, דָּבָר טוֹב וְקַיָּם לְעוֹלָם וָעֶד, אֱמֶת וֶאֱמוּנָה חֹק וְלֹא יַעֲבֹר. אֱמֶת שָׁאַתָּה הוּא יהוה אֱלֹהֵינוּ וֵאלֹהֵי אֲבוֹתֵינוּ, ❖ מַלְכֵּנוּ מֶלֶךְ אֲבוֹתֵינוּ, גֹּאֲלֵנוּ גֹּאֵל אֲבוֹתֵינוּ, יוֹצְרֵנוּ צוּר יְשׁוּעָתֵנוּ, פּוֹדֵנוּ וּמַצִּילֵנוּ מֵעוֹלָם שְׁמֶךָ, אֵין אֱלֹהִים זוּלָתֶךָ.

עֶזְרַת אֲבוֹתֵינוּ אַתָּה הוּא מֵעוֹלָם, מָגֵן וּמוֹשִׁיעַ לִבְנֵיהֶם אַחֲרֵיהֶם בְּכָל דּוֹר וָדוֹר. בְּרוּם עוֹלָם מוֹשָׁבֶךָ, וּמִשְׁפָּטֶיךָ וְצִדְקָתְךָ עַד אַפְסֵי אָרֶץ. אַשְׁרֵי אִישׁ שֶׁיִּשְׁמַע לְמִצְוֹתֶיךָ, וְתוֹרָתְךָ וּדְבָרְךָ יָשִׂים עַל לִבּוֹ. אֱמֶת אַתָּה הוּא אָדוֹן לְעַמֶּךָ וּמֶלֶךְ גִּבּוֹר לָרִיב רִיבָם. אֱמֶת אַתָּה הוּא רִאשׁוֹן וְאַתָּה הוּא אַחֲרוֹן, וּמִבַּלְעָדֶיךָ אֵין לָנוּ מֶלֶךְ[1] גּוֹאֵל וּמוֹשִׁיעַ. מִמִּצְרַיִם גְּאַלְתָּנוּ יהוה אֱלֹהֵינוּ, וּמִבֵּית עֲבָדִים פְּדִיתָנוּ. כָּל בְּכוֹרֵיהֶם הָרָגְתָּ, וּבְכוֹרְךָ גָּאָלְתָּ, וְיַם סוּף בָּקַעְתָּ, וְזֵדִים טִבַּעְתָּ, וִידִידִים הֶעֱבַרְתָּ, וַיְכַסּוּ מַיִם צָרֵיהֶם, אֶחָד מֵהֶם לֹא נוֹתָר.[2] עַל זֹאת שִׁבְּחוּ אֲהוּבִים וְרוֹמְמוּ אֵל, וְנָתְנוּ יְדִידִים זְמִרוֹת שִׁירוֹת וְתִשְׁבָּחוֹת, בְּרָכוֹת וְהוֹדָאוֹת, לְמֶלֶךְ אֵל חַי וְקַיָּם, רָם וְנִשָּׂא, גָּדוֹל וְנוֹרָא, מַשְׁפִּיל גֵּאִים, וּמַגְבִּיהַּ שְׁפָלִים, מוֹצִיא אֲסִירִים, וּפוֹדֶה עֲנָוִים, וְעוֹזֵר דַּלִּים, וְעוֹנֶה לְעַמּוֹ בְּעֵת שַׁוְּעָם אֵלָיו.

Rise for *Shemoneh Esrei.* Some take three steps backward at this point; others do so before צוּר יִשְׂרָאֵל.

❖ תְּהִלּוֹת לְאֵל עֶלְיוֹן, בָּרוּךְ הוּא וּמְבֹרָךְ. מֹשֶׁה וּבְנֵי יִשְׂרָאֵל לְךָ עָנוּ שִׁירָה בְּשִׂמְחָה רַבָּה וְאָמְרוּ כֻלָּם:

מִי כָמֹכָה בָּאֵלִם יהוה, מִי כָּמֹכָה נֶאְדָּר בַּקֹּדֶשׁ, נוֹרָא תְהִלֹּת עֹשֵׂה פֶלֶא.[3] ❖ שִׁירָה חֲדָשָׁה שִׁבְּחוּ גְאוּלִים לְשִׁמְךָ עַל שְׂפַת הַיָּם, יַחַד כֻּלָּם הוֹדוּ וְהִמְלִיכוּ וְאָמְרוּ:

יהוה יִמְלֹךְ לְעֹלָם וָעֶד.[4]

It is forbidden to interrupt or pause between גָּאַל יִשְׂרָאֵל and *Shemoneh Esrei,* even for *Kaddish, Kedushah* or *Borchu.*

❖ **צוּר יִשְׂרָאֵל,** קוּמָה בְּעֶזְרַת יִשְׂרָאֵל, וּפְדֵה כִנְאֻמֶךָ יְהוּדָה וְיִשְׂרָאֵל. גֹּאֲלֵנוּ יהוה צְבָאוֹת שְׁמוֹ, קְדוֹשׁ יִשְׂרָאֵל.[5] בָּרוּךְ אַתָּה יהוה, גָּאַל יִשְׂרָאֵל.

(1) Cf. *Isaiah* 44:6. (2) *Psalms* 106:11. (3) *Exodus* 15:11. (4) 15:18. (5) *Isaiah* 47:4.

His words are living and enduring, faithful and delightful forever (kiss the *tzitzis* and release them) *and to all eternity;* Chazzan– *for our forefathers and for us, for our children and for our generations, and for all the generations of Your servant Israel's offspring.*

עַל *Upon the earlier and upon the later generations, this affirmation is good and enduring forever. True and faithful, it is an unbreachable decree. It is true that You are* HASHEM, *our God and the God of our forefathers,* Chazzan– *our King and the King of our forefathers, our Redeemer, the Redeemer of our forefathers; our Molder, the Rock of our salvation; our Liberator and our Rescuer — this has ever been Your Name. There is no God but You.*

עֶזְרַת *The Helper of our forefathers are You alone, forever, Shield and Savior for their children after them in every generation. At the zenith of the universe is Your dwelling, and Your justice and Your righteousness extend to the ends of the earth. Praiseworthy is the person who obeys Your commandments and takes to his heart Your teaching and Your word. True — You are the Master for Your people and a mighty King to take up their grievance. True — You are the First and You are the Last, and other than You we have no king,*[1] *redeemer, or savior. From Egypt You redeemed us,* HASHEM, *our God, and from the house of slavery You liberated us. All their firstborn You slew, but Your firstborn You redeemed; the Sea of Reeds You split; the wanton sinners You drowned; the dear ones You brought across; and the water covered their foes — not one of them was left.*[2] *For this, the beloved praised and exalted God; the dear ones offered hymns, songs, praises, blessings, and thanksgivings to the King, the living and enduring God — exalted and uplifted, great and awesome, Who humbles the haughty and lifts the lowly; withdraws the captive, liberates the humble, and helps the poor; Who responds to His people upon their outcry to Him.*

Rise for *Shemoneh Esrei.* Some take three steps backward at this point; others do so before צוּר יִשְׂרָאֵל, *'Rock of Israel.'*

Chazzan– *Praises to the Supreme God, the blessed One Who is blessed. Moses and the Children of Israel exclaimed a song to You with great joy and they all said:*

'Who is like You among the heavenly powers, HASHEM! *Who is like You, mighty in holiness, too awesome for praise, doing wonders.'*[3]

Chazzan– *With a new song the redeemed ones praised Your Name at the seashore, all of them in unison gave thanks, acknowledged [Your] sovereignty, and said:*

'HASHEM shall reign for all eternity.'[4]

It is forbidden to interrupt or pause between *'Who redeemed Israel'* and *Shemoneh Esrei,* even for *Kaddish, Kedushah* or *Borchu*.

צוּר יִשְׂרָאֵל Chazzan– *Rock of Israel, arise to the aid of Israel and liberate, as You pledged, Judah and Israel. Our Redeemer — HASHEM, Master of Legions, is His Name — the Holy One of Israel.*[5] *Blessed are You,* HASHEM, *Who redeemed Israel.*

שמונה עשרה – עמידה

Take three steps backward, then three steps forward. Remain standing with feet together while reciting *Shemoneh Esrei.* Recite it with quiet devotion and without interruption, verbal or otherwise. Although it should not be audible to others, one must pray loudly enough to hear himself.

אֲדֹנָי שְׂפָתַי תִּפְתָּח, וּפִי יַגִּיד תְּהִלָּתֶךָ.[1]

אבות

Bend the knees at בָּרוּךְ; bow at אַתָּה; straighten up at ה׳.

בָּרוּךְ אַתָּה יהוה אֱלֹהֵינוּ וֵאלֹהֵי אֲבוֹתֵינוּ, אֱלֹהֵי אַבְרָהָם, אֱלֹהֵי יִצְחָק, וֵאלֹהֵי יַעֲקֹב, הָאֵל הַגָּדוֹל הַגִּבּוֹר וְהַנּוֹרָא, אֵל עֶלְיוֹן, גּוֹמֵל חֲסָדִים טוֹבִים וְקוֹנֵה הַכֹּל, וְזוֹכֵר חַסְדֵי אָבוֹת, וּמֵבִיא גוֹאֵל לִבְנֵי בְנֵיהֶם, לְמַעַן שְׁמוֹ בְּאַהֲבָה. מֶלֶךְ עוֹזֵר וּמוֹשִׁיעַ וּמָגֵן.

Bend the knees at בָּרוּךְ; bow at אַתָּה; straighten up at ה׳.

בָּרוּךְ אַתָּה יהוה, מָגֵן אַבְרָהָם.

גבורות

אַתָּה גִּבּוֹר לְעוֹלָם אֲדֹנָי, מְחַיֵּה מֵתִים אַתָּה, רַב לְהוֹשִׁיעַ. מְכַלְכֵּל חַיִּים בְּחֶסֶד, מְחַיֵּה מֵתִים בְּרַחֲמִים רַבִּים, סוֹמֵךְ נוֹפְלִים, וְרוֹפֵא חוֹלִים, וּמַתִּיר אֲסוּרִים, וּמְקַיֵּם אֱמוּנָתוֹ לִישֵׁנֵי עָפָר. מִי כָמוֹךָ בַּעַל גְּבוּרוֹת, וּמִי דּוֹמֶה לָּךְ, מֶלֶךְ מֵמִית וּמְחַיֶּה וּמַצְמִיחַ יְשׁוּעָה. וְנֶאֱמָן אַתָּה לְהַחֲיוֹת מֵתִים. בָּרוּךְ אַתָּה יהוה, מְחַיֵּה הַמֵּתִים.

During the *chazzan's* repetition, *Kedushah* (below) is recited at this point.

קדושה

When reciting *Kedushah,* one must stand with his feet together and avoid any interruptions. One should rise on his toes when saying the words קָדוֹשׁ, קָדוֹשׁ, קָדוֹשׁ; בָּרוּךְ (of בָּרוּךְ כְּבוֹד); and יִמְלֹךְ.

Cong. then *Chazzan* – **נְקַדֵּשׁ** אֶת שִׁמְךָ בָּעוֹלָם, כְּשֵׁם שֶׁמַּקְדִּישִׁים אוֹתוֹ בִּשְׁמֵי מָרוֹם, כַּכָּתוּב עַל יַד נְבִיאֶךָ, וְקָרָא זֶה אֶל זֶה וְאָמַר:

All – קָדוֹשׁ קָדוֹשׁ קָדוֹשׁ יהוה צְבָאוֹת, מְלֹא כָל הָאָרֶץ כְּבוֹדוֹ.[2]

Chazzan – לְעֻמָּתָם בָּרוּךְ יֹאמֵרוּ:

All – בָּרוּךְ כְּבוֹד יהוה, מִמְּקוֹמוֹ.[3]

Chazzan – וּבְדִבְרֵי קָדְשְׁךָ כָּתוּב לֵאמֹר:

All – יִמְלֹךְ יהוה לְעוֹלָם, אֱלֹהַיִךְ צִיּוֹן לְדֹר וָדֹר, הַלְלוּיָהּ.[4]

Chazzan only concludes – לְדוֹר וָדוֹר נַגִּיד גָּדְלֶךָ וּלְנֵצַח נְצָחִים קְדֻשָּׁתְךָ נַקְדִּישׁ, וְשִׁבְחֲךָ אֱלֹהֵינוּ מִפִּינוּ לֹא יָמוּשׁ לְעוֹלָם וָעֶד, כִּי אֵל מֶלֶךְ גָּדוֹל וְקָדוֹשׁ אָתָּה. בָּרוּךְ אַתָּה יהוה, הָאֵל הַקָּדוֹשׁ.

Chazzan continues ... אַתָּה חוֹנֵן (p. 716).

SHEMONEH ESREI — AMIDAH

Take three steps backward, then three steps forward. Remain standing with feet together while reciting *Shemoneh Esrei*. Recite it with quiet devotion and without interruption, verbal or otherwise. Although it should not be audible to others, one must pray loudly enough to hear himself.

My Lord, open my lips, that my mouth may declare Your praise.[1]

PATRIARCHS

Bend the knees at *'Blessed'*; bow at *'You'*; straighten up at *'HASHEM.'*

בָּרוּךְ *Blessed are You, HASHEM, our God and the God of our forefathers, God of Abraham, God of Isaac, and God of Jacob; the great, mighty, and awesome God, the supreme God, Who bestows beneficial kindnesses and creates everything, Who recalls the kindnesses of the Patriarchs and brings a Redeemer to their children's children, for His Name's sake, with love.*

Bend the knees at *'Blessed'*; bow at *'You'*; straighten up at *'HASHEM.'*

O King, Helper, Savior, and Shield. Blessed are You, HASHEM, Shield of Abraham.

GOD'S MIGHT

אַתָּה *You are eternally mighty, my Lord, the Resuscitator of the dead are You; abundantly able to save. He sustains the living with kindness, resuscitates the dead with abundant mercy, supports the fallen, heals the sick, releases the confined, and maintains His faith to those asleep in the dust. Who is like You, O Master of mighty deeds, and who is comparable to You, O King Who causes death and restores life and makes salvation sprout! And You are faithful to resuscitate the dead. Blessed are You, HASHEM, Who resuscitates the dead.*

During the *chazzan's* repetition, *Kedushah* (below) is recited at this point.

KEDUSHAH

When reciting *Kedushah*, one must stand with his feet together and avoid any interruptions. One should rise on his toes when saying the words *Holy, holy, holy; Blessed is;* and *HASHEM shall reign.*

Cong. then *Chazzan* — **נְקַדֵּשׁ** *We shall sanctify Your Name in this world, just as they sanctify it in heaven above, as it is written by Your prophet, "And one [angel] will call another and say:*

All—*'Holy, holy, holy is HASHEM, Master of Legions, the whole world is filled with His glory.' "*[2]

Chazzan—*Those facing them say 'Blessed':*

All—*'Blessed is the glory of HASHEM from His place.'*[3]

Chazzan—*And in Your holy Writings the following is written:*

All—*'HASHEM shall reign forever — your God, O Zion — from generation to generation, Halleluyah!'*[4]

Chazzan only concludes— *From generation to generation we shall relate Your greatness and for infinite eternities we shall proclaim Your holiness. Your praise, our God, shall not leave our mouth forever and ever, for You, O God, are a great and holy King. Blessed are You, HASHEM, the holy God.*

Chazzan continues אַתָּה חוֹנֵן, *You graciously endow . . .* (p. 716).

---

(1) *Psalms* 51:17. (2) *Isaiah* 6:3. (3) *Ezekiel* 3:12. (4) *Psalms* 146:10.

קדושת השם

אַתָּה קָדוֹשׁ וְשִׁמְךָ קָדוֹשׁ, וּקְדוֹשִׁים בְּכָל יוֹם יְהַלְּלוּךָ סֶּלָה. בָּרוּךְ אַתָּה יהוה, הָאֵל הַקָּדוֹשׁ.

בינה

אַתָּה חוֹנֵן לְאָדָם דַּעַת, וּמְלַמֵּד לֶאֱנוֹשׁ בִּינָה. חָנֵּנוּ מֵאִתְּךָ דֵּעָה בִּינָה וְהַשְׂכֵּל. בָּרוּךְ אַתָּה יהוה, חוֹנֵן הַדָּעַת.

תשובה

הֲשִׁיבֵנוּ אָבִינוּ לְתוֹרָתֶךָ, וְקָרְבֵנוּ מַלְכֵּנוּ לַעֲבוֹדָתֶךָ, וְהַחֲזִירֵנוּ בִּתְשׁוּבָה שְׁלֵמָה לְפָנֶיךָ. בָּרוּךְ אַתָּה יהוה, הָרוֹצֶה בִּתְשׁוּבָה.

סליחה

Strike the left side of the chest with the right fist while reciting the words חָטָאנוּ and פָּשָׁעְנוּ.

סְלַח לָנוּ אָבִינוּ כִּי חָטָאנוּ, מְחַל לָנוּ מַלְכֵּנוּ כִּי פָשָׁעְנוּ, כִּי מוֹחֵל וְסוֹלֵחַ אָתָּה. בָּרוּךְ אַתָּה יהוה, חַנּוּן הַמַּרְבֶּה לִסְלוֹחַ.

גאולה

רְאֵה בְעָנְיֵנוּ, וְרִיבָה רִיבֵנוּ, וּגְאָלֵנוּ[1] מְהֵרָה לְמַעַן שְׁמֶךָ, כִּי גוֹאֵל חָזָק אָתָּה. בָּרוּךְ אַתָּה יהוה, גּוֹאֵל יִשְׂרָאֵל.

רפואה

רְפָאֵנוּ יהוה וְנֵרָפֵא, הוֹשִׁיעֵנוּ וְנִוָּשֵׁעָה, כִּי תְהִלָּתֵנוּ אָתָּה,[2] וְהַעֲלֵה רְפוּאָה שְׁלֵמָה לְכָל מַכּוֹתֵינוּ, °°כִּי אֵל מֶלֶךְ רוֹפֵא נֶאֱמָן וְרַחֲמָן אָתָּה. בָּרוּךְ אַתָּה יהוה, רוֹפֵא חוֹלֵי עַמּוֹ יִשְׂרָאֵל.

ברכת השנים

בָּרֵךְ עָלֵינוּ יהוה אֱלֹהֵינוּ אֶת הַשָּׁנָה הַזֹּאת וְאֶת כָּל מִינֵי תְבוּאָתָהּ לְטוֹבָה, וְתֵן בְּרָכָה עַל פְּנֵי הָאֲדָמָה, וְשַׂבְּעֵנוּ מִטּוּבֶךָ, וּבָרֵךְ שְׁנָתֵנוּ כַּשָּׁנִים הַטּוֹבוֹת. בָּרוּךְ אַתָּה יהוה, מְבָרֵךְ הַשָּׁנִים.

°°At this point one may interject a prayer for one who is ill:

יְהִי רָצוֹן מִלְּפָנֶיךָ יהוה אֱלֹהַי וֵאלֹהֵי אֲבוֹתַי, שֶׁתִּשְׁלַח מְהֵרָה רְפוּאָה שְׁלֵמָה מִן הַשָּׁמַיִם, רְפוּאַת הַנֶּפֶשׁ וּרְפוּאַת הַגּוּף

for a male—לַחוֹלֶה (patient's name) בֶּן (mother's name) בְּתוֹךְ שְׁאָר חוֹלֵי יִשְׂרָאֵל.

for a female—לַחוֹלָה (patient's name) בַּת (mother's name) בְּתוֹךְ שְׁאָר חוֹלֵי יִשְׂרָאֵל.

Continue—כִּי אֵל . . .

HOLINESS OF GOD'S NAME

אַתָּה *You are holy and Your Name is holy, and holy ones praise You every day, forever. Blessed are You, HASHEM, the holy God.*

INSIGHT

אַתָּה *You graciously endow man with wisdom and teach insight to a frail mortal. Endow us graciously from Yourself with wisdom, insight, and discernment. Blessed are You, HASHEM, gracious Giver of wisdom.*

REPENTANCE

הֲשִׁיבֵנוּ *Bring us back, our Father, to Your Torah, and bring us near, our King, to Your service, and influence us to return in perfect repentance before You. Blessed are You, HASHEM, Who desires repentance.*

FORGIVENESS

Strike the left side of the chest with the right fist while reciting the words *'erred'* and *'sinned.'*

סְלַח *Forgive us, our Father, for we have erred; pardon us, our King, for we have willfully sinned; for You pardon and forgive. Blessed are You, HASHEM, the gracious One Who pardons abundantly.*

REDEMPTION

רְאֵה *Behold our affliction, take up our grievance, and redeem us*[1] *speedily for Your Name's sake, for You are a powerful Redeemer. Blessed are You, HASHEM, Redeemer of Israel.*

HEALTH AND HEALING

רְפָאֵנוּ *Heal us, HASHEM — then we will be healed; save us — then we will be saved, for You are our praise.*[2] *Bring complete recovery for all our ailments,* °°*for You are God, King, the faithful and compassionate Healer. Blessed are You, HASHEM, Who heals the sick of His people Israel.*

YEAR OF PROSPERITY

בָּרֵךְ *Bless on our behalf — O HASHEM, our God — this year and all its kinds of crops for the best, and give a blessing on the face of the earth, and satisfy us from Your bounty, and bless our year like the best years. Blessed are You, HASHEM, Who blesses the years.*

°°At this point one may interject a prayer for one who is ill:

May it be Your will, HASHEM, my God, and the God of my forefathers, that You quickly send a complete recovery from heaven, spiritual healing and physical healing to the patient (name) *son/daughter of* (mother's name) *among the other patients of Israel.*

Continue: *For You are God ...*

(1) Cf. *Psalms* 119:153-154. (2) Cf. *Jeremiah* 17:14.

קיבוץ גליות

תְּקַע בְּשׁוֹפָר גָּדוֹל לְחֵרוּתֵנוּ, וְשָׂא נֵס לְקַבֵּץ גָּלֻיּוֹתֵינוּ, וְקַבְּצֵנוּ יַחַד מֵאַרְבַּע כַּנְפוֹת הָאָרֶץ.[1] בָּרוּךְ אַתָּה יהוה, מְקַבֵּץ נִדְחֵי עַמּוֹ יִשְׂרָאֵל.

דין

הָשִׁיבָה שׁוֹפְטֵינוּ כְּבָרִאשׁוֹנָה, וְיוֹעֲצֵינוּ כְּבַתְּחִלָּה,[2] וְהָסֵר מִמֶּנּוּ יָגוֹן וַאֲנָחָה, וּמְלוֹךְ עָלֵינוּ אַתָּה יהוה לְבַדְּךָ בְּחֶסֶד וּבְרַחֲמִים, וְצַדְּקֵנוּ בַּמִּשְׁפָּט. בָּרוּךְ אַתָּה יהוה, מֶלֶךְ אוֹהֵב צְדָקָה וּמִשְׁפָּט.

ברכת המינים

וְלַמַּלְשִׁינִים אַל תְּהִי תִקְוָה, וְכָל הָרִשְׁעָה כְּרֶגַע תֹּאבֵד, וְכָל אֹיְבֶיךָ מְהֵרָה יִכָּרֵתוּ, וְהַזֵּדִים מְהֵרָה תְעַקֵּר וּתְשַׁבֵּר וּתְמַגֵּר וְתַכְנִיעַ בִּמְהֵרָה בְיָמֵינוּ. בָּרוּךְ אַתָּה יהוה, שׁוֹבֵר אֹיְבִים וּמַכְנִיעַ זֵדִים.

צדיקים

עַל הַצַּדִּיקִים וְעַל הַחֲסִידִים, וְעַל זִקְנֵי עַמְּךָ בֵּית יִשְׂרָאֵל, וְעַל פְּלֵיטַת סוֹפְרֵיהֶם, וְעַל גֵּרֵי הַצֶּדֶק וְעָלֵינוּ, יֶהֱמוּ רַחֲמֶיךָ יהוה אֱלֹהֵינוּ, וְתֵן שָׂכָר טוֹב לְכָל הַבּוֹטְחִים בְּשִׁמְךָ בֶּאֱמֶת, וְשִׂים חֶלְקֵנוּ עִמָּהֶם לְעוֹלָם, וְלֹא נֵבוֹשׁ כִּי בְךָ בָּטָחְנוּ. בָּרוּךְ אַתָּה יהוה, מִשְׁעָן וּמִבְטָח לַצַּדִּיקִים.

בנין ירושלים

וְלִירוּשָׁלַיִם עִירְךָ בְּרַחֲמִים תָּשׁוּב, וְתִשְׁכּוֹן בְּתוֹכָהּ כַּאֲשֶׁר דִּבַּרְתָּ, וּבְנֵה אוֹתָהּ בְּקָרוֹב בְּיָמֵינוּ בִּנְיַן עוֹלָם, וְכִסֵּא דָוִד מְהֵרָה לְתוֹכָהּ תָּכִין. בָּרוּךְ אַתָּה יהוה, בּוֹנֵה יְרוּשָׁלָיִם.

מלכות בית דוד

אֶת צֶמַח דָּוִד עַבְדְּךָ מְהֵרָה תַצְמִיחַ, וְקַרְנוֹ תָּרוּם בִּישׁוּעָתֶךָ, כִּי לִישׁוּעָתְךָ קִוִּינוּ כָּל הַיּוֹם. בָּרוּךְ אַתָּה יהוה, מַצְמִיחַ קֶרֶן יְשׁוּעָה.

קבלת תפלה

שְׁמַע קוֹלֵנוּ יהוה אֱלֹהֵינוּ, חוּס וְרַחֵם עָלֵינוּ, וְקַבֵּל בְּרַחֲמִים וּבְרָצוֹן אֶת תְּפִלָּתֵנוּ, כִּי אֵל שׁוֹמֵעַ תְּפִלּוֹת וְתַחֲנוּנִים אָתָּה. וּמִלְּפָנֶיךָ מַלְכֵּנוּ רֵיקָם אַל תְּשִׁיבֵנוּ,

INGATHERING OF EXILES

תְּקַע *Sound the great shofar for our freedom, raise the banner to gather our exiles and gather us together from the four corners of the earth.*[1] *Blessed are You, HASHEM, Who gathers in the dispersed of His people Israel.*

RESTORATION OF JUSTICE

הָשִׁיבָה *Restore our judges as in earliest times and our counselors as at first;*[2] *remove from us sorrow and groan; and reign over us — You, HASHEM, alone — with kindness and compassion, and justify us through judgment. Blessed are You, HASHEM, the King Who loves righteousness and judgment.*

AGAINST HERETICS

וְלַמַּלְשִׁינִים *And for slanderers let there be no hope; and may all wickedness perish in an instant; and may all Your enemies be cut down speedily. May You speedily uproot, smash, cast down, and humble the wanton sinners — speedily in our days. Blessed are You, HASHEM, Who breaks enemies and humbles wanton sinners.*

THE RIGHTEOUS

עַל הַצַּדִּיקִים *On the righteous, on the devout, on the elders of Your people the Family of Israel, on the remnant of their scholars, on the righteous converts and on ourselves — may Your compassion be aroused, HASHEM, our God, and give goodly reward to all who sincerely believe in Your Name. Put our lot with them forever, and we will not feel ashamed, for we trust in You. Blessed are You, HASHEM, Mainstay and Assurance of the righteous.*

REBUILDING JERUSALEM

וְלִירוּשָׁלַיִם *And to Jerusalem, Your city, may You return in compassion, and may You rest within it, as You have spoken. May You rebuild it soon in our days as an eternal structure, and may You speedily establish the throne of David within it. Blessed are You, HASHEM, the Builder of Jerusalem.*

DAVIDIC REIGN

אֶת צֶמַח *The offspring of Your servant David may You speedily cause to flourish, and enhance his pride through Your salvation, for we hope for Your salvation all day long. Blessed are You, HASHEM, Who causes the pride of salvation to flourish.*

ACCEPTANCE OF PRAYER

שְׁמַע *Hear our voice, HASHEM our God, pity and be compassionate to us, and accept — with compassion and favor — our prayer, for God Who hears prayers and supplications are You. From before Yourself, our King, turn us not away empty-handed,*

(1) Cf. *Isaiah* 11:12. (2) Cf. 1:26.

°° כִּי אַתָּה שׁוֹמֵעַ תְּפִלַּת עַמְּךָ יִשְׂרָאֵל בְּרַחֲמִים. בָּרוּךְ אַתָּה יהוה, שׁוֹמֵעַ תְּפִלָּה.

עבודה

רְצֵה יהוה אֱלֹהֵינוּ בְּעַמְּךָ יִשְׂרָאֵל וּבִתְפִלָּתָם, וְהָשֵׁב אֶת הָעֲבוֹדָה לִדְבִיר בֵּיתֶךָ. וְאִשֵּׁי יִשְׂרָאֵל וּתְפִלָּתָם בְּאַהֲבָה תְקַבֵּל בְּרָצוֹן, וּתְהִי לְרָצוֹן תָּמִיד עֲבוֹדַת יִשְׂרָאֵל עַמֶּךָ.

During the *chazzan's* repetition, congregation responds אָמֵן as indicated.
[If paragraph is forgotten, repeat *Shemoneh Esrei*. See *Laws* §56.]

אֱלֹהֵינוּ וֵאלֹהֵי אֲבוֹתֵינוּ, יַעֲלֶה, וְיָבֹא, וְיַגִּיעַ, וְיֵרָאֶה, וְיֵרָצֶה, וְיִשָּׁמַע, וְיִפָּקֵד, וְיִזָּכֵר זִכְרוֹנֵנוּ וּפִקְדוֹנֵנוּ, וְזִכְרוֹן אֲבוֹתֵינוּ, וְזִכְרוֹן מָשִׁיחַ בֶּן דָּוִד עַבְדֶּךָ, וְזִכְרוֹן יְרוּשָׁלַיִם עִיר קָדְשֶׁךָ, וְזִכְרוֹן כָּל עַמְּךָ בֵּית יִשְׂרָאֵל לְפָנֶיךָ, לִפְלֵיטָה לְטוֹבָה לְחֵן וּלְחֶסֶד וּלְרַחֲמִים, לְחַיִּים וּלְשָׁלוֹם בְּיוֹם חַג הַמַּצּוֹת הַזֶּה. זָכְרֵנוּ יהוה אֱלֹהֵינוּ בּוֹ לְטוֹבָה (.Cong – אָמֵן), וּפָקְדֵנוּ בוֹ לִבְרָכָה (.Cong – אָמֵן), וְהוֹשִׁיעֵנוּ בוֹ לְחַיִּים (.Cong – אָמֵן). וּבִדְבַר יְשׁוּעָה וְרַחֲמִים, חוּס וְחָנֵּנוּ וְרַחֵם עָלֵינוּ וְהוֹשִׁיעֵנוּ, כִּי אֵלֶיךָ עֵינֵינוּ, כִּי אֵל מֶלֶךְ חַנּוּן וְרַחוּם אָתָּה.[1]

וְתֶחֱזֶינָה עֵינֵינוּ בְּשׁוּבְךָ לְצִיּוֹן בְּרַחֲמִים. בָּרוּךְ אַתָּה יהוה, הַמַּחֲזִיר שְׁכִינָתוֹ לְצִיּוֹן.

°°During the silent *Shemoneh Esrei* one may insert either or both of these personal prayers.

For forgiveness:

אָנָּא יהוה, חָטָאתִי עָוִיתִי וּפָשַׁעְתִּי לְפָנֶיךָ, מִיּוֹם הֱיוֹתִי עַל הָאֲדָמָה עַד הַיּוֹם הַזֶּה (וּבִפְרַט בַּחֵטְא ....). אָנָּא יהוה, עֲשֵׂה לְמַעַן שִׁמְךָ הַגָּדוֹל, וּתְכַפֶּר לִי עַל עֲוֹנַי וַחֲטָאַי וּפְשָׁעַי שֶׁחָטָאתִי וְשֶׁעָוִיתִי וְשֶׁפָּשַׁעְתִּי לְפָנֶיךָ, מִנְּעוּרַי עַד הַיּוֹם הַזֶּה. וּתְמַלֵּא כָּל הַשֵּׁמוֹת שֶׁפָּגַמְתִּי בְּשִׁמְךָ הַגָּדוֹל.

For livelihood:

אַתָּה הוּא יהוה הָאֱלֹהִים, הַזָּן וּמְפַרְנֵס וּמְכַלְכֵּל מִקַּרְנֵי רְאֵמִים עַד בֵּיצֵי כִנִּים. הַטְרִיפֵנִי לֶחֶם חֻקִּי, וְהַמְצֵא לִי וּלְכָל בְּנֵי בֵיתִי מְזוֹנוֹתַי קוֹדֶם שֶׁאֶצְטָרֵךְ לָהֶם, בְּנַחַת וְלֹא בְצַעַר, בְּהֶתֵּר וְלֹא בְאִסּוּר, בְּכָבוֹד וְלֹא בְּבִזָּיוֹן, לְחַיִּים וּלְשָׁלוֹם, מִשֶּׁפַע בְּרָכָה וְהַצְלָחָה, וּמִשֶּׁפַע בְּרֵכָה עֶלְיוֹנָה, כְּדֵי שֶׁאוּכַל לַעֲשׂוֹת רְצוֹנֶךָ וְלַעֲסוֹק בְּתוֹרָתֶךָ וּלְקַיֵּם מִצְוֹתֶיךָ. וְאַל תַּצְרִיכֵנִי לִידֵי מַתְּנַת בָּשָׂר וָדָם. וִיקֻיַּם בִּי מִקְרָא שֶׁכָּתוּב: פּוֹתֵחַ אֶת יָדֶךָ, וּמַשְׂבִּיעַ לְכָל חַי רָצוֹן.[2] וְכָתוּב: הַשְׁלֵךְ עַל יהוה יְהָבְךָ וְהוּא יְכַלְכְּלֶךָ.[3]

Continue – כִּי אַתָּה ...

°° *for You hear the prayer of Your people Israel with compassion. Blessed are You, HASHEM, Who hears prayer.*

TEMPLE SERVICE

רְצֵה *Be favorable, HASHEM, our God, toward Your people Israel and their prayer and restore the service to the Holy of Holies of Your Temple. The fire-offerings of Israel and their prayer accept with love and favor, and may the service of Your people Israel always be favorable to You.*

During the *chazzan's* repetition, congregation responds *Amen* as indicated.
[If paragraph is forgotten, repeat *Shemoneh Esrei*. See *Laws* §56.]

אֱלֹהֵינוּ *Our God and God of our forefathers, may there rise, come, reach, be noted, be favored, be heard, be considered, and be remembered — the remembrance and consideration of ourselves; the remembrance of our forefathers; the remembrance of Messiah, son of David, Your servant; the remembrance of Jerusalem, the City of Your Holiness; the remembrance of Your entire people the Family of Israel — before You for deliverance, for goodness, for grace, for kindness, and for compassion, for life, and for peace on this day of the Festival of Matzos. Remember us on it, HASHEM, our God, for goodness* (Cong.–*Amen*)*; consider us on it for blessing* (Cong.–*Amen*)*; and help us on it for life* (Cong.–*Amen*)*. In the matter of salvation and compassion, pity, be gracious and compassionate with us and help us, for our eyes are turned to You, because You are God, the gracious and compassionate King.*[1]

וְתֶחֱזֶינָה *May our eyes behold Your return to Zion in compassion. Blessed are You, HASHEM, Who restores His Presence to Zion.*

°°During the silent *Shemoneh Esrei* one may insert either or both of these personal prayers.

For forgiveness:

אָנָּא *Please, O HASHEM, I have erred, been iniquitous, and willfully sinned before You, from the day I have existed on earth until this very day (and especially with the sin of . . .). Please, HASHEM, act for the sake of Your Great Name and grant me atonement for my iniquities, my errors, and my willful sins through which I have erred, been iniquitous, and willfully sinned before You, from my youth until this day. And make whole all the Names that I have blemished in Your Great Name.*

For livelihood:

אַתָּה *It is You, HASHEM the God, Who nourishes, sustains, and supports, from the horns of re'eimim to the eggs of lice. Provide me with my allotment of bread; and bring forth for me and all members of my household, my food, before I have need for it; in contentment but not in pain, in a permissible but not a forbidden manner, in honor but not in disgrace, for life and for peace; from the flow of blessing and success and from the flow of the Heavenly spring, so that I be enabled to do Your will and engage in Your Torah and fulfill Your commandments. Make me not needful of people's largesse; and may there be fulfilled in me the verse that states, 'You open Your hand and satisfy the desire of every living thing'*[2] *and that states, 'Cast Your burden upon HASHEM and He will support you.'*[3]

Continue: *For You hear the prayer . . .*

(1) Cf. *Nehemiah* 9:31. (2) *Psalms* 145:16. (3) 55:23.

הודאה

Bow at מוֹדִים; straighten up at 'ה. In his repetition the *chazzan* should recite the entire מוֹדִים aloud, while the congregation recites מוֹדִים דְּרַבָּנָן softly.

מוֹדִים אֲנַחְנוּ לָךְ, שָׁאַתָּה הוּא יהוה אֱלֹהֵינוּ וֵאלֹהֵי אֲבוֹתֵינוּ לְעוֹלָם וָעֶד. צוּר חַיֵּינוּ, מָגֵן יִשְׁעֵנוּ אַתָּה הוּא לְדוֹר וָדוֹר. נוֹדֶה לְּךָ וּנְסַפֵּר תְּהִלָּתֶךָ[1] עַל חַיֵּינוּ הַמְּסוּרִים בְּיָדֶךָ, וְעַל נִשְׁמוֹתֵינוּ הַפְּקוּדוֹת לָךְ, וְעַל נִסֶּיךָ שֶׁבְּכָל יוֹם עִמָּנוּ, וְעַל נִפְלְאוֹתֶיךָ וְטוֹבוֹתֶיךָ שֶׁבְּכָל עֵת, עֶרֶב וָבֹקֶר וְצָהֳרָיִם. הַטּוֹב כִּי לֹא כָלוּ רַחֲמֶיךָ, וְהַמְּרַחֵם כִּי לֹא תַמּוּ חֲסָדֶיךָ,[2] מֵעוֹלָם קִוִּינוּ לָךְ.

מוֹדִים דְּרַבָּנָן

מוֹדִים אֲנַחְנוּ לָךְ, שָׁאַתָּה הוּא יהוה אֱלֹהֵינוּ וֵאלֹהֵי אֲבוֹתֵינוּ, אֱלֹהֵי כָל בָּשָׂר, יוֹצְרֵנוּ, יוֹצֵר בְּרֵאשִׁית. בְּרָכוֹת וְהוֹדָאוֹת לְשִׁמְךָ הַגָּדוֹל וְהַקָּדוֹשׁ, עַל שֶׁהֶחֱיִיתָנוּ וְקִיַּמְתָּנוּ. כֵּן תְּחַיֵּנוּ וּתְקַיְּמֵנוּ, וְתֶאֱסוֹף גָּלֻיּוֹתֵינוּ לְחַצְרוֹת קָדְשֶׁךָ, לִשְׁמוֹר חֻקֶּיךָ וְלַעֲשׂוֹת רְצוֹנֶךָ, וּלְעָבְדְּךָ בְּלֵבָב שָׁלֵם, עַל שֶׁאֲנַחְנוּ מוֹדִים לָךְ. בָּרוּךְ אֵל הַהוֹדָאוֹת.

וְעַל כֻּלָּם יִתְבָּרַךְ וְיִתְרוֹמַם שִׁמְךָ מַלְכֵּנוּ תָּמִיד לְעוֹלָם וָעֶד.

Bend the knees at בָּרוּךְ; bow at אַתָּה; straighten up at 'ה.

וְכֹל הַחַיִּים יוֹדְוּךָ סֶּלָה, וִיהַלְלוּ אֶת שִׁמְךָ בֶּאֱמֶת, הָאֵל יְשׁוּעָתֵנוּ וְעֶזְרָתֵנוּ סֶלָה. בָּרוּךְ אַתָּה יהוה, הַטּוֹב שִׁמְךָ וּלְךָ נָאֶה לְהוֹדוֹת.

ברכת כהנים

The *chazzan* recites בִּרְכַּת כֹּהֲנִים during his repetition. He faces right at וְיִשְׁמְרֶךָ; faces left at אֵלֶיךָ וִיחֻנֶּךָּ; faces the Ark for the rest of the blessings.

אֱלֹהֵינוּ, וֵאלֹהֵי אֲבוֹתֵינוּ, בָּרְכֵנוּ בַבְּרָכָה הַמְּשֻׁלֶּשֶׁת בַּתּוֹרָה הַכְּתוּבָה עַל יְדֵי מֹשֶׁה עַבְדֶּךָ, הָאֲמוּרָה מִפִּי אַהֲרֹן וּבָנָיו, כֹּהֲנִים עַם קְדוֹשֶׁךָ, כָּאָמוּר:

יְבָרֶכְךָ יהוה, וְיִשְׁמְרֶךָ. (.Cong–כֵּן יְהִי רָצוֹן.)

יָאֵר יהוה פָּנָיו אֵלֶיךָ וִיחֻנֶּךָּ. (.Cong–כֵּן יְהִי רָצוֹן.)

יִשָּׂא יהוה פָּנָיו אֵלֶיךָ וְיָשֵׂם לְךָ שָׁלוֹם.[3] (.Cong–כֵּן יְהִי רָצוֹן.)

שִׂים שָׁלוֹם, טוֹבָה, וּבְרָכָה, חֵן, וָחֶסֶד וְרַחֲמִים עָלֵינוּ וְעַל כָּל יִשְׂרָאֵל עַמֶּךָ. בָּרְכֵנוּ אָבִינוּ, כֻּלָּנוּ כְּאֶחָד בְּאוֹר פָּנֶיךָ, כִּי בְאוֹר פָּנֶיךָ נָתַתָּ לָּנוּ, יהוה אֱלֹהֵינוּ, תּוֹרַת חַיִּים וְאַהֲבַת חֶסֶד, וּצְדָקָה, וּבְרָכָה, וְרַחֲמִים, וְחַיִּים, וְשָׁלוֹם. וְטוֹב

THANKSGIVING [MODIM]

Bow at *'We gratefully thank You'*; straighten up at *'HASHEM.'* In his repetition the *chazzan* should recite the entire *Modim* aloud, while the congregation recites *Modim of the Rabbis* softly.

מוֹדִים *We gratefully thank You, for it is You Who are HASHEM, our God and the God of our forefathers for all eternity; Rock of our lives, Shield of our salvation are You from generation to generation. We shall thank You and relate Your praise[1] — for our lives, which are committed to Your power and for our souls that are entrusted to You; for Your miracles that are with us every day; and for Your wonders and favors in every season — evening, morning, and afternoon. The Beneficent One, for Your compassions were never exhausted, and the Compassionate One, for Your kindnesses never ended[2] — always have we put our hope in You.*

MODIM OF THE RABBIS

מוֹדִים *We gratefully thank You, for it is You Who are HASHEM, our God and the God of our forefathers, the God of all flesh, our Molder, the Molder of the universe. Blessings and thanks are due Your great and holy Name for You have given us life and sustained us. So may You continue to give us life and sustain us and gather our exiles to the Courtyards of Your Sanctuary, to observe Your decrees, to do Your will and to serve You wholeheartedly. [We thank You] for inspiring us to thank You. Blessed is the God of thanksgivings.*

For all these, may Your Name be blessed and exalted, our King, continually forever and ever.

Bend the knees at *'Blessed'*; bow at *'You'*; straighten up at *'HASHEM.'*

Everything alive will gratefully acknowledge You, Selah! and praise Your Name sincerely, O God of our salvation and help, Selah! Blessed are You, HASHEM, Your Name is 'The Beneficent One' and to You it is fitting to give thanks.

THE PRIESTLY BLESSING

The *chazzan* recites the Priestly Blessing during his repetition.

אֱלֹהֵינוּ *Our God and the God of our forefathers, bless us with the three-verse blessing in the Torah that was written by the hand of Moses, Your servant, that was said by Aaron and his sons, the Kohanim, Your holy people, as it is said:*

May HASHEM bless you and safeguard you. (Cong.— *So may it be.*)

May HASHEM illuminate His countenance for you and be gracious to you. (Cong.— *So may it be.*)

May HASHEM turn His countenance to you and establish peace for you.[3] (Cong.— *So may it be.*)

PEACE

שִׂים שָׁלוֹם *Establish peace, goodness, blessing, graciousness, kindness, and compassion upon us and upon all of Your people Israel. Bless us, our Father, all of us as one, with the light of Your countenance, for with the light of Your countenance You gave us, HASHEM, our God, the Torah of life and a love of kindness, righteousness, blessing, compassion, life, and peace. And may it be good*

(1) Cf. *Psalms* 79:13. (2) Cf. *Lamentations* 3:22. (3) *Numbers* 6:24-26.

בְּעֵינֶיךָ לְבָרֵךְ אֶת עַמְּךָ יִשְׂרָאֵל, בְּכָל עֵת וּבְכָל שָׁעָה בִּשְׁלוֹמֶךָ. בָּרוּךְ אַתָּה יהוה, הַמְבָרֵךְ אֶת עַמּוֹ יִשְׂרָאֵל בַּשָּׁלוֹם.

יִהְיוּ לְרָצוֹן אִמְרֵי פִי וְהֶגְיוֹן לִבִּי לְפָנֶיךָ, יהוה צוּרִי וְגֹאֲלִי.[1]

Chazzan's repetition of *Shemoneh Esrei* ends here. Individuals continue below:

אֱלֹהַי, נְצוֹר לְשׁוֹנִי מֵרָע, וּשְׂפָתַי מִדַּבֵּר מִרְמָה,[2] וְלִמְקַלְלַי נַפְשִׁי תִדּוֹם, וְנַפְשִׁי כֶּעָפָר לַכֹּל תִּהְיֶה. פְּתַח לִבִּי בְּתוֹרָתֶךָ, וּבְמִצְוֹתֶיךָ תִּרְדּוֹף נַפְשִׁי. וְכֹל הַחוֹשְׁבִים עָלַי רָעָה, מְהֵרָה הָפֵר עֲצָתָם וְקַלְקֵל מַחֲשַׁבְתָּם. עֲשֵׂה לְמַעַן שְׁמֶךָ, עֲשֵׂה לְמַעַן יְמִינֶךָ, עֲשֵׂה לְמַעַן קְדֻשָּׁתֶךָ, עֲשֵׂה לְמַעַן תּוֹרָתֶךָ. לְמַעַן יֵחָלְצוּן יְדִידֶיךָ, הוֹשִׁיעָה יְמִינְךָ וַעֲנֵנִי.[3]

Some recite verses pertaining to their names here. See page 1143.

יִהְיוּ לְרָצוֹן אִמְרֵי פִי וְהֶגְיוֹן לִבִּי לְפָנֶיךָ, יהוה צוּרִי וְגֹאֲלִי.[1]

Bow and take three steps back. Bow left and say ... עֹשֶׂה; bow right and say ... הוּא יַעֲשֶׂה; bow forward and say וְעַל כָּל ... אָמֵן.

עֹשֶׂה שָׁלוֹם בִּמְרוֹמָיו, הוּא יַעֲשֶׂה שָׁלוֹם עָלֵינוּ, וְעַל כָּל יִשְׂרָאֵל. וְאִמְרוּ: אָמֵן.

יְהִי רָצוֹן מִלְּפָנֶיךָ יהוה אֱלֹהֵינוּ וֵאלֹהֵי אֲבוֹתֵינוּ, שֶׁיִּבָּנֶה בֵּית הַמִּקְדָּשׁ בִּמְהֵרָה בְיָמֵינוּ, וְתֵן חֶלְקֵנוּ בְּתוֹרָתֶךָ. וְשָׁם נַעֲבָדְךָ בְּיִרְאָה, כִּימֵי עוֹלָם וּכְשָׁנִים קַדְמוֹנִיּוֹת. וְעָרְבָה לַיהוה מִנְחַת יְהוּדָה וִירוּשָׁלָיִם, כִּימֵי עוֹלָם וּכְשָׁנִים קַדְמוֹנִיּוֹת.[4]

THE INDIVIDUAL'S RECITATION OF *SHEMONEH ESREI* ENDS HERE.

Remain standing in place for at least a few moments before taking three steps forward.

הלל

The *chazzan* recites the blessing. The congregation, after responding אָמֵן, repeats it, and continues with the first psalm.

בָּרוּךְ אַתָּה יהוה אֱלֹהֵינוּ מֶלֶךְ הָעוֹלָם, אֲשֶׁר קִדְּשָׁנוּ בְּמִצְוֹתָיו, וְצִוָּנוּ לִקְרוֹא אֶת הַהַלֵּל. (—Cong. אָמֵן.)

תהלים קיג

הַלְלוּיָהּ הַלְלוּ עַבְדֵי יהוה, הַלְלוּ אֶת שֵׁם יהוה. יְהִי שֵׁם יהוה מְבֹרָךְ, מֵעַתָּה וְעַד עוֹלָם. מִמִּזְרַח שֶׁמֶשׁ עַד מְבוֹאוֹ, מְהֻלָּל שֵׁם יהוה. רָם עַל כָּל גּוֹיִם יהוה, עַל הַשָּׁמַיִם כְּבוֹדוֹ. מִי כַּיהוה אֱלֹהֵינוּ, הַמַּגְבִּיהִי לָשָׁבֶת. הַמַּשְׁפִּילִי לִרְאוֹת, בַּשָּׁמַיִם וּבָאָרֶץ. ❖ מְקִימִי מֵעָפָר דָּל, מֵאַשְׁפֹּת יָרִים אֶבְיוֹן. לְהוֹשִׁיבִי עִם נְדִיבִים, עִם נְדִיבֵי עַמּוֹ. מוֹשִׁיבִי עֲקֶרֶת הַבַּיִת, אֵם הַבָּנִים שְׂמֵחָה, הַלְלוּיָהּ.

in Your eyes to bless Your people Israel at every time and every hour with Your peace. Blessed are You, HASHEM, Who blesses His people Israel with peace.

Chazzan's repetition of *Shemoneh Esrei* ends here. Individuals continue below:

May the expressions of my mouth and the thoughts of my heart find favor before You, HASHEM, my Rock and my Redeemer.[1]

אֱלֹהַי *My God, guard my tongue from evil and my lips from speaking deceitfully.*[2] *To those who curse me, let my soul be silent; and let my soul be like dust to everyone. Open my heart to Your Torah, then my soul will pursue Your commandments. As for all those who design evil against me, speedily nullify their counsel and disrupt their design. Act for Your Name's sake; act for Your right hand's sake; act for Your sanctity's sake; act for Your Torah's sake. That Your beloved ones may be given rest; let Your right hand save, and respond to me.*[3]

Some recite verses pertaining to their names at this point. See page 1143.

May the expressions of my mouth and the thoughts of my heart find favor before You, HASHEM, my Rock and my Redeemer.[1] °°*He Who makes peace in His heights, may He make peace upon us, and upon all Israel. Now respond: Amen.*

Bow and take three steps back. Bow left and say, *'He Who makes peace . . .'*; bow right and say, *'may He make peace . . .'*; bow forward and say, *'and upon . . . Amen.'*

יְהִי רָצוֹן *May it be Your will, HASHEM, our God and the God of our forefathers, that the Holy Temple be rebuilt, speedily in our days. Grant us our share in Your Torah, and may we serve You there with reverence, as in days of old and in former years. Then the offering of Judah and Jerusalem will be pleasing to HASHEM, as in days of old and in former years.*[4]

THE INDIVIDUAL'S RECITATION OF *SHEMONEH ESREI* ENDS HERE.

Remain standing in place for at least a few moments before taking three steps forward.

HALLEL

The *chazzan* recites the blessing. The congregation, after responding *Amen*, repeats it, and continues with the first psalm.

בָּרוּךְ *Blessed are You, HASHEM, our God, King of the universe, Who has sanctified us with His commandments and has commanded us to read the Hallel.* (Cong.— *Amen.*)

Psalm 113

הַלְלוּיָהּ *Halleluyah! Give praise, you servants of HASHEM; praise the Name of HASHEM! Blessed be the Name of HASHEM, from this time and forever. From the rising of the sun to its setting, HASHEM's Name is praised. High above all nations is HASHEM, above the heavens is His glory. Who is like HASHEM, our God, Who is enthroned on high — yet deigns to look upon the heaven and the earth?* Chazzan— *He raises the needy from the dust, from the trash heaps He lifts the destitute. To seat them with nobles, with the nobles of His people. He transforms the barren wife into a glad mother of children. Halleluyah!*

---

(1) *Psalms* 19:15. (2) Cf. 34:14. (3) 60:7; 108:7. (4) *Malachi* 3:4.

תהלים קיד

בְּצֵאת יִשְׂרָאֵל מִמִּצְרָיִם, בֵּית יַעֲקֹב מֵעַם לֹעֵז. הָיְתָה יְהוּדָה לְקָדְשׁוֹ, יִשְׂרָאֵל מַמְשְׁלוֹתָיו. הַיָּם רָאָה וַיָּנֹס, הַיַּרְדֵּן יִסֹּב לְאָחוֹר. הֶהָרִים רָקְדוּ כְאֵילִים, גְּבָעוֹת כִּבְנֵי צֹאן. ❖ מַה לְּךָ הַיָּם כִּי תָנוּס, הַיַּרְדֵּן תִּסֹּב לְאָחוֹר. הֶהָרִים תִּרְקְדוּ כְאֵילִים, גְּבָעוֹת כִּבְנֵי צֹאן. מִלִּפְנֵי אָדוֹן חוּלִי אָרֶץ, מִלִּפְנֵי אֱלוֹהַּ יַעֲקֹב. הַהֹפְכִי הַצּוּר אֲגַם מָיִם, חַלָּמִישׁ לְמַעְיְנוֹ מָיִם.

תהלים קטו:יב-יח

יהוה זְכָרָנוּ יְבָרֵךְ, יְבָרֵךְ אֶת בֵּית יִשְׂרָאֵל, יְבָרֵךְ אֶת בֵּית אַהֲרֹן. יְבָרֵךְ יִרְאֵי יהוה, הַקְּטַנִּים עִם הַגְּדֹלִים. יֹסֵף יהוה עֲלֵיכֶם, עֲלֵיכֶם וְעַל בְּנֵיכֶם. בְּרוּכִים אַתֶּם לַיהוה, עֹשֵׂה שָׁמַיִם וָאָרֶץ. ❖ הַשָּׁמַיִם שָׁמַיִם לַיהוה, וְהָאָרֶץ נָתַן לִבְנֵי אָדָם. לֹא הַמֵּתִים יְהַלְּלוּ יָהּ, וְלֹא כָּל יֹרְדֵי דוּמָה. וַאֲנַחְנוּ נְבָרֵךְ יָהּ, מֵעַתָּה וְעַד עוֹלָם, הַלְלוּיָהּ.

תהלים קטז:יב-יט

מָה אָשִׁיב לַיהוה, כָּל תַּגְמוּלוֹהִי עָלָי. כּוֹס יְשׁוּעוֹת אֶשָּׂא, וּבְשֵׁם יהוה אֶקְרָא. נְדָרַי לַיהוה אֲשַׁלֵּם, נֶגְדָה נָּא לְכָל עַמּוֹ. יָקָר בְּעֵינֵי יהוה, הַמָּוְתָה לַחֲסִידָיו. אָנָּה יהוה כִּי אֲנִי עַבְדֶּךָ, אֲנִי עַבְדְּךָ, בֶּן אֲמָתֶךָ, פִּתַּחְתָּ לְמוֹסֵרָי. ❖ לְךָ אֶזְבַּח זֶבַח תּוֹדָה, וּבְשֵׁם יהוה אֶקְרָא. נְדָרַי לַיהוה אֲשַׁלֵּם, נֶגְדָה נָּא לְכָל עַמּוֹ. בְּחַצְרוֹת בֵּית יהוה, בְּתוֹכֵכִי יְרוּשָׁלָיִם הַלְלוּיָהּ.

Congregation, then *chazzan:*

תהלים קיז

הַלְלוּ אֶת יהוה, כָּל גּוֹיִם, שַׁבְּחוּהוּ כָּל הָאֻמִּים. כִּי גָבַר עָלֵינוּ חַסְדּוֹ, וֶאֱמֶת יהוה לְעוֹלָם, הַלְלוּיָהּ.

תהלים קיח

Chazzan – **הוֹדוּ** לַיהוה כִּי טוֹב, כִּי לְעוֹלָם חַסְדּוֹ.

Cong. – הוֹדוּ לַיהוה כִּי טוֹב, כִּי לְעוֹלָם חַסְדּוֹ.

יֹאמַר נָא יִשְׂרָאֵל, כִּי לְעוֹלָם חַסְדּוֹ.

Chazzan – יֹאמַר נָא יִשְׂרָאֵל, כִּי לְעוֹלָם חַסְדּוֹ

Cong. – הוֹדוּ לַיהוה כִּי טוֹב, כִּי לְעוֹלָם חַסְדּוֹ.

יֹאמְרוּ נָא בֵית אַהֲרֹן, כִּי לְעוֹלָם חַסְדּוֹ.

Psalm 114

בְּצֵאת *When Israel went out of Egypt, Jacob's household from a people of alien tongue — Judah became His sanctuary, Israel His dominions. The sea saw and fled: the Jordan turned backward. The mountains skipped like rams, the hills like young lambs.* Chazzan– *What ails you, O sea, that you flee? O Jordan, that you turn backward? O mountains, that you skip like rams? O hills, like young lambs? Before the Lord's Presence — did I, the earth, tremble — before the presence of the God of Jacob, Who turns the rock into a pond of water, the flint into a flowing fountain.*

Psalm 115:12-18

יהוה *HASHEM Who has remembered us will bless — He will bless the House of Israel; He will bless the House of Aaron; He will bless those who fear HASHEM, the small as well as the great. May HASHEM increase upon you, upon you and upon your children! You are blessed of HASHEM, maker of heaven and earth.* Chazzan– *As for the heavens — the heavens are HASHEM's, but the earth He has given to mankind. Neither the dead can praise God, nor any who descend into silence; but we will bless God from this time and forever. Halleluyah!*

Psalm 116:12-19

מָה אָשִׁיב *How can I repay HASHEM for all His kindness to me? I will raise the cup of salvations and the Name of HASHEM I will invoke. My vows to HASHEM I will pay, in the presence, now, of His entire people. Difficult in the eyes of HASHEM is the death of His devout ones. Please, HASHEM — for I am Your servant, I am Your servant, son of Your handmaid — You have released my bonds.* Chazzan– *To You I will sacrifice thanksgiving offerings, and the name of HASHEM I will invoke. My vows to HASHEM I will pay, in the presence, now, of His entire people. In the courtyards of the House of HASHEM, in your midst, O Jerusalem, Halleluyah!*

Congregation, then *chazzan:*

Psalm 117

הַלְלוּ *Praise HASHEM, all nations; praise Him, all the states! For His kindness has overwhelmed us, and the truth of HASHEM is eternal, Halleluyah!*

Psalm 118

Chazzan – *Give thanks to HASHEM for He is good;*
His kindness endures forever!
Cong. – *Give thanks to HASHEM, for He is good;*
His kindness endures forever!
Let Israel say now: *His kindness endures forever!*
Chazzan – *Let Israel say now:* *His kindness endures forever!*
Cong. – *Give thanks to HASHEM, for He is good;*
His kindness endures forever!
Let the House of Aaron say now:
His kindness endures forever!

Chazzan – יֹאמְרוּ נָא בֵית אַהֲרֹן, כִּי לְעוֹלָם חַסְדּוֹ.
Cong. – הוֹדוּ לַיהוה כִּי טוֹב, כִּי לְעוֹלָם חַסְדּוֹ.
יֹאמְרוּ נָא יִרְאֵי יהוה, כִּי לְעוֹלָם חַסְדּוֹ.
Chazzan – יֹאמְרוּ נָא יִרְאֵי יהוה, כִּי לְעוֹלָם חַסְדּוֹ.
Cong. – הוֹדוּ לַיהוה כִּי טוֹב, כִּי לְעוֹלָם חַסְדּוֹ.

מִן הַמֵּצַר קָרָאתִי יָּהּ, עָנָנִי בַמֶּרְחָב יָהּ. יהוה לִי לֹא אִירָא, מַה יַּעֲשֶׂה לִי אָדָם. יהוה לִי בְּעֹזְרָי, וַאֲנִי אֶרְאֶה בְשֹׂנְאָי. טוֹב לַחֲסוֹת בַּיהוה, מִבְּטֹחַ בָּאָדָם. טוֹב לַחֲסוֹת בַּיהוה, מִבְּטֹחַ בִּנְדִיבִים. כָּל גּוֹיִם סְבָבוּנִי, בְּשֵׁם יהוה כִּי אֲמִילַם. סַבּוּנִי גַם סְבָבוּנִי, בְּשֵׁם יהוה כִּי אֲמִילַם. סַבּוּנִי כִדְבֹרִים דֹּעֲכוּ כְּאֵשׁ קוֹצִים, בְּשֵׁם יהוה כִּי אֲמִילַם. דָּחֹה דְחִיתַנִי לִנְפֹּל, וַיהוה עֲזָרָנִי. עָזִּי וְזִמְרָת יָהּ, וַיְהִי לִי לִישׁוּעָה. קוֹל רִנָּה וִישׁוּעָה, בְּאָהֳלֵי צַדִּיקִים, יְמִין יהוה עֹשָׂה חָיִל. יְמִין יהוה רוֹמֵמָה, יְמִין יהוה עֹשָׂה חָיִל. לֹא אָמוּת כִּי אֶחְיֶה, וַאֲסַפֵּר מַעֲשֵׂי יָהּ. יַסֹּר יִסְּרַנִּי יָּהּ, וְלַמָּוֶת לֹא נְתָנָנִי. ❖ פִּתְחוּ לִי שַׁעֲרֵי צֶדֶק, אָבֹא בָם אוֹדֶה יָהּ. זֶה הַשַּׁעַר לַיהוה, צַדִּיקִים יָבֹאוּ בוֹ. אוֹדְךָ כִּי עֲנִיתָנִי, וַתְּהִי לִי לִישׁוּעָה. אוֹדְךָ כִּי עֲנִיתָנִי, וַתְּהִי לִי לִישׁוּעָה. אֶבֶן מָאֲסוּ הַבּוֹנִים, הָיְתָה לְרֹאשׁ פִּנָּה. אֶבֶן מָאֲסוּ הַבּוֹנִים, הָיְתָה לְרֹאשׁ פִּנָּה. מֵאֵת יהוה הָיְתָה זֹּאת, הִיא נִפְלָאת בְּעֵינֵינוּ. מֵאֵת יהוה הָיְתָה זֹּאת, הִיא נִפְלָאת בְּעֵינֵינוּ. זֶה הַיּוֹם עָשָׂה יהוה, נָגִילָה וְנִשְׂמְחָה בוֹ. זֶה הַיּוֹם עָשָׂה יהוה, נָגִילָה וְנִשְׂמְחָה בוֹ.

אָנָּא יהוה הוֹשִׁיעָה נָּא.
אָנָּא יהוה הוֹשִׁיעָה נָּא.
אָנָּא יהוה הַצְלִיחָה נָא.
אָנָּא יהוה הַצְלִיחָה נָא.

בָּרוּךְ הַבָּא בְּשֵׁם יהוה, בֵּרַכְנוּכֶם מִבֵּית יהוה. בָּרוּךְ הַבָּא בְּשֵׁם יהוה, בֵּרַכְנוּכֶם מִבֵּית יהוה. אֵל יהוה

Chazzan – *Let the House of Aaron say now:*
His kindness endures forever!
Cong. – *Give thanks to HASHEM, for He is good;*
His kindness endures forever!
Let those who fear HASHEM say now:
His kindness endures forever!
Chazzan – *Let those who fear HASHEM say now:*
His kindness endures forever!
Cong. – *Give thanks to HASHEM, for He is good;*
His kindness endures forever!

מִן הַמֵּצַר *From the straits did I call upon God; God answered me with expansiveness. HASHEM is with me, I have no fear; how can man affect me? HASHEM is with me through my helpers; therefore I can face my foes. It is better to take refuge in HASHEM than to rely on man. It is better to take refuge in HASHEM than to rely on nobles. All the nations surround me; in the Name of HASHEM I cut them down! They encircle me, they also surround me; in the Name of HASHEM, I cut them down! They encircle me like bees, but they are extinguished as a fire does thorns; in the Name of HASHEM I cut them down! You pushed me hard that I might fall, but HASHEM assisted me. God is my might and my praise, and He was a salvation for me. The sound of rejoicing and salvation is in the tents of the righteous: 'HASHEM's right hand does valiantly. HASHEM's right hand is raised triumphantly; HASHEM's right hand does valiantly!' I shall not die! But I shall live and relate the deeds of God. God has chastened me exceedingly, but He did not let me die.* Chazzan – *Open for me the gates of righteousness, I will enter them and thank God. This is the gate of HASHEM; the righteous shall enter through it. I thank You for You have answered me and become my salvation. I thank You for You have answered me and become my salvation. The stone the builders despised has become the cornerstone. The stone the builders despised has become the cornerstone. This emanated from HASHEM; it is wondrous in our eyes. This emanated from HASHEM; it is wondrous in our eyes. This is the day HASHEM has made; let us rejoice and be glad on it. This is the day HASHEM has made; let us rejoice and be glad on it.*

אָנָּא *Please, HASHEM, save now!*
Please, HASHEM, save now!
Please, HASHEM, bring success now!
Please, HASHEM, bring success now!

בָּרוּךְ *Blessed is he who comes in the Name of HASHEM; we bless you from the House of HASHEM. Blessed is he who comes in the Name of HASHEM; we bless you from the House of HASHEM. HASHEM is God,*

וַיָּאֶר לָנוּ, אִסְרוּ חַג בַּעֲבֹתִים, עַד קַרְנוֹת הַמִּזְבֵּחַ. אֵל יהוה וַיָּאֶר לָנוּ, אִסְרוּ חַג בַּעֲבֹתִים, עַד קַרְנוֹת הַמִּזְבֵּחַ. אֵלִי אַתָּה וְאוֹדֶךָּ, אֱלֹהַי אֲרוֹמְמֶךָּ. אֵלִי אַתָּה וְאוֹדֶךָּ, אֱלֹהַי אֲרוֹמְמֶךָּ. הוֹדוּ לַיהוה כִּי טוֹב, כִּי לְעוֹלָם חַסְדּוֹ. הוֹדוּ לַיהוה כִּי טוֹב, כִּי לְעוֹלָם חַסְדּוֹ.

יְהַלְלוּךָ יהוה אֱלֹהֵינוּ כָּל מַעֲשֶׂיךָ, וַחֲסִידֶיךָ צַדִּיקִים עוֹשֵׂי רְצוֹנֶךָ, וְכָל עַמְּךָ בֵּית יִשְׂרָאֵל בְּרִנָּה יוֹדוּ וִיבָרְכוּ וִישַׁבְּחוּ וִיפָאֲרוּ וִירוֹמְמוּ וְיַעֲרִיצוּ וְיַקְדִּישׁוּ וְיַמְלִיכוּ אֶת שִׁמְךָ מַלְכֵּנוּ. ❖ כִּי לְךָ טוֹב לְהוֹדוֹת וּלְשִׁמְךָ נָאֶה לְזַמֵּר, כִּי מֵעוֹלָם וְעַד עוֹלָם אַתָּה אֵל. בָּרוּךְ אַתָּה יהוה, מֶלֶךְ מְהֻלָּל בַּתִּשְׁבָּחוֹת. (.Cong – אָמֵן.)

קדיש שלם

The *chazzan* recites *Kaddish:*

יִתְגַּדַּל וְיִתְקַדַּשׁ שְׁמֵהּ רַבָּא. (.Cong – אָמֵן.) בְּעָלְמָא דִּי בְרָא כִרְעוּתֵהּ. וְיַמְלִיךְ מַלְכוּתֵהּ, בְּחַיֵּיכוֹן וּבְיוֹמֵיכוֹן וּבְחַיֵּי דְכָל בֵּית יִשְׂרָאֵל, בַּעֲגָלָא וּבִזְמַן קָרִיב. וְאִמְרוּ: אָמֵן.

(.Cong – אָמֵן. יְהֵא שְׁמֵהּ רַבָּא מְבָרַךְ לְעָלַם וּלְעָלְמֵי עָלְמַיָּא.)

יְהֵא שְׁמֵהּ רַבָּא מְבָרַךְ לְעָלַם וּלְעָלְמֵי עָלְמַיָּא.

יִתְבָּרַךְ וְיִשְׁתַּבַּח וְיִתְפָּאַר וְיִתְרוֹמַם וְיִתְנַשֵּׂא וְיִתְהַדָּר וְיִתְעַלֶּה וְיִתְהַלָּל שְׁמֵהּ דְּקֻדְשָׁא בְּרִיךְ הוּא (.Cong – בְּרִיךְ הוּא) – לְעֵלָּא מִן כָּל בִּרְכָתָא וְשִׁירָתָא תֻּשְׁבְּחָתָא וְנֶחֱמָתָא, דַּאֲמִירָן בְּעָלְמָא. וְאִמְרוּ: אָמֵן. (.Cong – אָמֵן.)

(.Cong – קַבֵּל בְּרַחֲמִים וּבְרָצוֹן אֶת תְּפִלָּתֵנוּ.)

תִּתְקַבֵּל צְלוֹתְהוֹן וּבָעוּתְהוֹן דְּכָל בֵּית יִשְׂרָאֵל קֳדָם אֲבוּהוֹן דִּי בִשְׁמַיָּא. וְאִמְרוּ: אָמֵן. (.Cong – אָמֵן.)

(.Cong – יְהִי שֵׁם יהוה מְבֹרָךְ, מֵעַתָּה וְעַד עוֹלָם.[1])

יְהֵא שְׁלָמָא רַבָּא מִן שְׁמַיָּא, וְחַיִּים עָלֵינוּ וְעַל כָּל יִשְׂרָאֵל. וְאִמְרוּ: אָמֵן. (.Cong – אָמֵן.)

(.Cong – עֶזְרִי מֵעִם יהוה, עֹשֵׂה שָׁמַיִם וָאָרֶץ.[2])

Take three steps back. Bow left and say . . . עֹשֶׂה; bow right and say . . . הוּא; bow forward and say וְעַל כָּל . . . אָמֵן. Remain standing in place for a few moments, then take three steps forward.

עֹשֶׂה שָׁלוֹם בִּמְרוֹמָיו, הוּא יַעֲשֶׂה שָׁלוֹם עָלֵינוּ, וְעַל כָּל יִשְׂרָאֵל. וְאִמְרוּ: אָמֵן. (.Cong – אָמֵן.)

He illuminated for us; bind the festival offering with cords until the corners of the Altar. HASHEM *is God, He illuminated for us; bind the festival offering with cords until the corners of the Altar. You are my God, and I will thank You; my God, I will exalt You. You are my God, and I will thank You; my God, I will exalt You. Give thanks to* HASHEM, *for He is good; His kindness endures forever. Give thanks to* HASHEM, *for He is good; His kindness endures forever.*

יְהַלְלוּךָ *All Your works shall praise You,* HASHEM *our God. And Your devout ones, the righteous, who do Your will, and Your entire people, the House of Israel, with glad song will thank, bless, praise, glorify, exalt, extol, sanctify, and proclaim the sovereignty of Your Name, our King.* Chazzan– *For to You it is fitting to give thanks, and unto Your Name it is proper to sing praises, for from This World to the World to Come You are God. Blessed are You,* HASHEM, *the King Who is lauded with praises.* (Cong.– *Amen.*)

FULL KADDISH

The *chazzan* recites *Kaddish:*

יִתְגַּדַּל *May His great Name grow exalted and sanctified* (Cong.– *Amen.*) *in the world that He created as He willed. May He give reign to His kingship in your lifetimes and in your days, and in the lifetimes of the entire Family of Israel, swiftly and soon. Now respond: Amen.*

(Cong.– *Amen. May His great Name be blessed forever and ever.*)

May His great Name be blessed forever and ever.

Blessed, praised, glorified, exalted, extolled, mighty, upraised, and lauded be the Name of the Holy One, Blessed is He (Cong.– *Blessed is He*) — *beyond any blessing and song, praise and consolation that are uttered in the world. Now respond: Amen.* (Cong.– *Amen.*)

(Cong.– *Accept our prayers with mercy and favor.*)

May the prayers and supplications of the entire Family of Israel be accepted before their Father Who is in Heaven. Now respond: Amen. (Cong.– *Amen.*)

(Cong.– *Blessed be the Name of* HASHEM, *from this time and forever.*[1])

May there be abundant peace from Heaven, and life, upon us and upon all Israel. Now respond: Amen. (Cong.– *Amen.*)

(Cong.– *My help is from* HASHEM, *Maker of heaven and earth.*[2])

Take three steps back. Bow left and say, *'He Who makes peace . . .';* bow right and say, *'may He . . .';* bow forward and say, *'and upon all Israel . . .'* Remain standing in place for a few moments, then take three steps forward.

He Who makes peace in His heights, may He make peace upon us, and upon all Israel. Now respond: Amen. (Cong.– *Amen.*)

(1) *Psalms* 113:2. (2) 121:2.

הוצאת ספר תורה לחול המועד

From the moment the Ark is opened until the Torah is returned to it, one must conduct himself with the utmost respect, and avoid unnecessary conversation. It is commendable to kiss the Torah as it is carried to the *bimah* [reading table] and back to the Ark.

All rise and remain standing until the Torah is placed on the *bimah*.

THE ARK IS OPENED

On each day of *Chol HaMoed* Pesach two Torah scrolls are removed from the Ark. Before the Torahs are removed the congregation recites:

וַיְהִי בִּנְסֹעַ הָאָרֹן וַיֹּאמֶר מֹשֶׁה, קוּמָה יהוה וְיָפֻצוּ אֹיְבֶיךָ וְיָנֻסוּ מְשַׂנְאֶיךָ מִפָּנֶיךָ.[1] כִּי מִצִּיּוֹן תֵּצֵא תוֹרָה, וּדְבַר יהוה מִירוּשָׁלָיִם.[2] בָּרוּךְ שֶׁנָּתַן תּוֹרָה לְעַמּוֹ יִשְׂרָאֵל בִּקְדֻשָּׁתוֹ.

זוהר ויקהל שסט:א

בְּרִיךְ שְׁמֵהּ דְּמָרֵא עָלְמָא, בְּרִיךְ כִּתְרָךְ וְאַתְרָךְ. יְהֵא רְעוּתָךְ עִם עַמָּךְ יִשְׂרָאֵל לְעָלַם, וּפֻרְקַן יְמִינָךְ אַחֲזֵי לְעַמָּךְ בְּבֵית מַקְדְּשָׁךְ, וּלְאַמְטוּיֵי לָנָא מִטּוּב נְהוֹרָךְ, וּלְקַבֵּל צְלוֹתָנָא בְּרַחֲמִין. יְהֵא רַעֲוָא קֳדָמָךְ, דְּתוֹרִיךְ לָן חַיִּין בְּטִיבוּתָא, וְלֶהֱוֵי אֲנָא פְקִידָא בְּגוֹ צַדִּיקַיָּא, לְמִרְחַם עָלַי וּלְמִנְטַר יָתִי וְיַת כָּל דִּי לִי, וְדִי לְעַמָּךְ יִשְׂרָאֵל. אַנְתְּ הוּא זָן לְכֹלָּא, וּמְפַרְנֵס לְכֹלָּא, אַנְתְּ הוּא שַׁלִּיט עַל כֹּלָּא. אַנְתְּ הוּא דְשַׁלִּיט עַל מַלְכַיָּא, וּמַלְכוּתָא דִּילָךְ הִיא. אֲנָא עַבְדָּא דְקֻדְשָׁא בְּרִיךְ הוּא, דְּסָגִידְנָא קַמֵּהּ וּמִקַּמָּא דִּיקַר אוֹרַיְתֵהּ בְּכָל עִדָּן וְעִדָּן. לָא עַל אֱנָשׁ רָחִיצְנָא, וְלָא עַל בַּר אֱלָהִין סָמִיכְנָא, אֶלָּא בֶּאֱלָהָא דִשְׁמַיָּא, דְּהוּא אֱלָהָא קְשׁוֹט, וְאוֹרַיְתֵהּ קְשׁוֹט, וּנְבִיאוֹהִי קְשׁוֹט, וּמַסְגֵּא לְמֶעְבַּד טַבְוָן וּקְשׁוֹט. בֵּהּ אֲנָא רָחִיץ, וְלִשְׁמֵהּ קַדִּישָׁא יַקִּירָא אֲנָא אֵמַר תֻּשְׁבְּחָן. יְהֵא רַעֲוָא קֳדָמָךְ, דְּתִפְתַּח לִבָּאִי בְּאוֹרַיְתָא, וְתַשְׁלִים מִשְׁאֲלִין דְּלִבָּאִי, וְלִבָּא דְכָל עַמָּךְ יִשְׂרָאֵל, לְטַב וּלְחַיִּין וְלִשְׁלָם. (אָמֵן.)

The Torah is removed from the Ark and presented to the *chazzan,* who accepts it in his right arm. He then turns to the Ark, bows while raising the Torah, and recites:

גַּדְּלוּ לַיהוה אִתִּי וּנְרוֹמְמָה שְׁמוֹ יַחְדָּו.[3]

The *chazzan* turns to his right and carries the Torah to the *bimah,* as the congregation responds:

לְךָ יהוה הַגְּדֻלָּה וְהַגְּבוּרָה וְהַתִּפְאֶרֶת וְהַנֵּצַח וְהַהוֹד כִּי כֹל בַּשָּׁמַיִם וּבָאָרֶץ, לְךָ יהוה הַמַּמְלָכָה וְהַמִּתְנַשֵּׂא לְכֹל לְרֹאשׁ.[4] רוֹמְמוּ יהוה אֱלֹהֵינוּ, וְהִשְׁתַּחֲווּ לַהֲדֹם רַגְלָיו, קָדוֹשׁ הוּא. רוֹמְמוּ יהוה אֱלֹהֵינוּ, וְהִשְׁתַּחֲווּ לְהַר קָדְשׁוֹ, כִּי קָדוֹשׁ יהוה אֱלֹהֵינוּ.[5]

REMOVAL OF THE TORAH FROM THE ARK

From the moment the Ark is opened until the Torah is returned to it, one must conduct himself with the utmost respect, and avoid unnecessary conversation. It is commendable to kiss the Torah as it is carried to the *bimah* [reading table] and back to the Ark.

All rise and remain standing until the Torah is placed on the *bimah.*

THE ARK IS OPENED

On each day of *Chol HaMoed* Pesach two Torah scrolls are removed from the Ark. Before the Torahs are removed the congregation recites:

וַיְהִי בִּנְסֹעַ *When the Ark would travel, Moses would say, 'Arise, HASHEM, and let Your foes be scattered, let those who hate You flee from You.'[1] For from Zion the Torah will come forth and the word of HASHEM from Jerusalem.[2] Blessed is He Who gave the Torah to His people Israel in His holiness.*

Zohar, Vayakhel 369a

בְּרִיךְ שְׁמֵהּ *Blessed is the Name of the Master of the universe, blessed is Your crown and Your place. May Your favor remain with Your people Israel forever; may You display the salvation of Your right hand to Your people in Your Holy Temple, to benefit us with the goodness of Your luminescence and to accept our prayers with mercy. May it be Your will that You extend our lives with goodness and that I be numbered among the righteous; that You have mercy on me and protect me, all that is mine and that is Your people Israel's. It is You Who nourishes all and sustains all; You control everything. It is You Who control kings, and kingship is Yours. I am a servant of the Holy One, Blessed is He, and I prostrate myself before Him and before the glory of His Torah at all times. Not in any man do I put trust, nor on any angel do I rely — only on the God of heaven Who is the God of truth, Whose Torah is truth and Whose prophets are true and Who acts liberally with kindness and truth. In Him do I trust, and to His glorious and holy Name do I declare praises. May it be Your will that You open my heart to the Torah and that You fulfill the wishes of my heart and the heart of Your entire people Israel for good, for life, and for peace. (Amen.)*

The Torah is removed from the Ark and presented to the *chazzan,* who accepts it in his right arm. He turns to the Ark, bows while raising the Torah, and recites:

Declare the greatness of HASHEM with me, and let us exalt His Name together.[3]

The *chazzan* turns to his right and carries the Torah to the *bimah,* as the congregation responds:

לְךָ *Yours, HASHEM, is the greatness, the strength, the splendor, the triumph, and the glory; even everything in heaven and earth; Yours, HASHEM, is the kingdom, and the sovereignty over every leader.[4] Exalt HASHEM, our God, and bow at His footstool; He is Holy! Exalt HASHEM, our God, and bow to His holy mountain; for holy is HASHEM, our God.[5]*

---

(1) *Numbers* 10:35. (2) *Isaiah* 2:3. (3) *Psalms* 34:4. (4) *I Chronicles* 29:11. (5) *Psalms* 99:5,9.

אַב הָרַחֲמִים הוּא יְרַחֵם עַם עֲמוּסִים, וְיִזְכֹּר בְּרִית אֵיתָנִים, וְיַצִּיל נַפְשׁוֹתֵינוּ מִן הַשָּׁעוֹת הָרָעוֹת, וְיִגְעַר בְּיֵצֶר הָרָע מִן הַנְּשׂוּאִים, וְיָחֹן אוֹתָנוּ לִפְלֵיטַת עוֹלָמִים, וִימַלֵּא מִשְׁאֲלוֹתֵינוּ בְּמִדָּה טוֹבָה יְשׁוּעָה וְרַחֲמִים.

The Torah is placed on the *bimah* and prepared for reading.
The *gabbai* uses the following formula to call a *Kohen* to the Torah:

וְתִגָּלֶה וְתֵרָאֶה מַלְכוּתוֹ עָלֵינוּ בִּזְמַן קָרוֹב, וְיָחֹן פְּלֵיטָתֵנוּ וּפְלֵיטַת עַמּוֹ בֵּית יִשְׂרָאֵל לְחֵן וּלְחֶסֶד וּלְרַחֲמִים וּלְרָצוֹן. וְנֹאמַר אָמֵן. הַכֹּל הָבוּ גֹדֶל לֵאלֹהֵינוּ וּתְנוּ כָבוֹד לַתּוֹרָה. כֹּהֵן° קְרָב, יַעֲמֹד (insert name) הַכֹּהֵן.

°If no *Kohen* is present, the *gabbai* says: "אֵין כַּאן כֹּהֵן, יַעֲמֹד (name) יִשְׂרָאֵל (לֵוִי) בִּמְקוֹם כֹּהֵן".

בָּרוּךְ שֶׁנָּתַן תּוֹרָה לְעַמּוֹ יִשְׂרָאֵל בִּקְדֻשָּׁתוֹ. (תּוֹרַת יהוה תְּמִימָה מְשִׁיבַת נָפֶשׁ, עֵדוּת יהוה נֶאֱמָנָה מַחְכִּימַת פֶּתִי. פִּקּוּדֵי יהוה יְשָׁרִים מְשַׂמְּחֵי לֵב, מִצְוַת יהוה בָּרָה מְאִירַת עֵינָיִם.[1] יהוה עֹז לְעַמּוֹ יִתֵּן, יהוה יְבָרֵךְ אֶת עַמּוֹ בַשָּׁלוֹם.[2] הָאֵל תָּמִים דַּרְכּוֹ, אִמְרַת יהוה צְרוּפָה, מָגֵן הוּא לְכֹל הַחוֹסִים בּוֹ.[3])

Congregation, then *gabbai:*

וְאַתֶּם הַדְּבֵקִים בַּיהוה אֱלֹהֵיכֶם, חַיִּים כֻּלְּכֶם הַיּוֹם.[4]

The reader shows the *oleh* (person called to the Torah) the place in the Torah. The *oleh* touches the Torah with a corner of his *tallis,* or the belt or mantle of the Torah, and kisses it. He then begins the blessing, bowing at בָּרְכוּ, and straightening up at ה׳.

בָּרְכוּ אֶת יהוה הַמְּבֹרָךְ.

Congregation, followed by *oleh,* responds, bowing at בָּרוּךְ, and straightening up at ה׳.

בָּרוּךְ יהוה הַמְּבֹרָךְ לְעוֹלָם וָעֶד.

Oleh continues:

בָּרוּךְ אַתָּה יהוה אֱלֹהֵינוּ מֶלֶךְ הָעוֹלָם, אֲשֶׁר בָּחַר בָּנוּ מִכָּל הָעַמִּים, וְנָתַן לָנוּ אֶת תּוֹרָתוֹ. בָּרוּךְ אַתָּה יהוה, נוֹתֵן הַתּוֹרָה. (Cong. – אָמֵן.)

After his Torah portion has been read, the *oleh* recites:

בָּרוּךְ אַתָּה יהוה אֱלֹהֵינוּ מֶלֶךְ הָעוֹלָם, אֲשֶׁר נָתַן לָנוּ תּוֹרַת אֱמֶת, וְחַיֵּי עוֹלָם נָטַע בְּתוֹכֵנוּ. בָּרוּךְ אַתָּה יהוה, נוֹתֵן הַתּוֹרָה. (Cong. – אָמֵן.)

THE VARIOUS *MI SHEBERACH* PRAYERS APPEAR ON PAGE 368.

אַב הָרַחֲמִים *May the Father of compassion have mercy on the nation that is borne by Him, and may He remember the covenant of the spiritually mighty. May He rescue our souls from the bad times, and upbraid the evil inclination to leave those borne by Him, graciously make us an eternal remnant, and fulfill our requests in good measure, for salvation and mercy.*

The Torah is placed on the *bimah* and prepared for reading.

The *gabbai* uses the following formula to call a *Kohen* to the Torah:

וְתִגָּלֶה *And may His kingship over us be revealed and become visible soon, and may He be gracious to our remnant and the remnant of His people the Family of Israel, for graciousness, kindness, mercy, and favor. And let us respond, Amen. All of you ascribe greatness to our God and give honor to the Torah. Kohen,° approach. Stand* (name) *son of* (father's name) *the Kohen.*

°If no *Kohen* is present, the *gabbai* says: *'There is no Kohen present, stand* (name) *son of* (father's name) *an Israelite (Levite) in place of the Kohen.'*

Blessed is He Who gave the Torah to His people Israel in His holiness. (The Torah of HASHEM is perfect, restoring the soul; the testimony of HASHEM is trustworthy, making the simple one wise. The orders of HASHEM are upright, gladdening the heart; the command of HASHEM is clear, enlightening the eyes.[1] HASHEM will give might to His nation; HASHEM will bless His nation with peace.[2] The God Whose way is perfect, the promise of HASHEM is flawless, He is a shield for all who take refuge in Him.[3])

Congregation, then *gabbai:*

You who cling to HASHEM, your God, you are all alive today.[4]

The reader shows the *oleh* (person called to the Torah) the place in the Torah. The *oleh* touches the Torah with a corner of his *tallis,* or the belt or mantle of the Torah, and kisses it. He then begins the blessing, bowing at *'Bless,'* and straightening up at 'HASHEM.'

Bless HASHEM, the blessed One.

Congregation, followed by *oleh,* responds, bowing at 'Blessed,' and straightening up at 'HASHEM.'

Blessed is HASHEM, the blessed One, for all eternity.

Oleh continues:

בָּרוּךְ *Blessed are You, HASHEM, our God, King of the universe, Who selected us from all the peoples and gave us His Torah. Blessed are You, HASHEM, Giver of the Torah.* (Cong.— *Amen.)*

After his Torah portion has been read, the *oleh* recites:

בָּרוּךְ *Blessed are You, HASHEM, our God, King of the universe, Who gave us the Torah of truth and implanted eternal life within us. Blessed are You, HASHEM, Giver of the Torah.* (Cong.— *Amen.)*

THE VARIOUS *MI SHEBERACH* PRAYERS APPEAR ON PAGE 368.

---

(1) *Psalms* 19:8-9. (2) 29:11. (3) 18:31. (4) *Deuteronomy* 4:4.

Each day of Chol HaMoed, two scrolls are removed from the Ark. Three people are called to read from the first scroll and one from the second. The reading from the first scroll varies from day to day, as given below. From the second one, the reading is that of the Pesach *Mussaf* offering, and is the same each day. Half-Kaddish is recited after the final reading.

FIRST DAY CHOL HAMOED ON MONDAY, TUESDAY OR THURSDAY.
SECOND DAY CHOL HAMOED ON SUNDAY.

שמות יג:א-טז

כהן – וַיְדַבֵּ֥ר יהוה֖* אֶל־מֹשֶׁ֥ה לֵּאמֹֽר: קַדֶּשׁ־לִ֨י כָל־בְּכ֜וֹר* פֶּ֤טֶר כָּל־רֶ֨חֶם֙ בִּבְנֵ֣י יִשְׂרָאֵ֔ל בָּאָדָ֖ם וּבַבְּהֵמָ֑ה* לִ֖י הֽוּא: וַיֹּ֨אמֶר מֹשֶׁ֜ה אֶל־הָעָ֗ם זָכ֞וֹר אֶת־הַיּ֤וֹם הַזֶּה֙ אֲשֶׁ֨ר יְצָאתֶ֤ם מִמִּצְרַ֨יִם֙ מִבֵּ֣ית עֲבָדִ֔ים כִּ֚י בְּחֹ֣זֶק יָ֔ד הוֹצִ֧יא יהו֛ה אֶתְכֶ֖ם מִזֶּ֑ה וְלֹ֥א יֵאָכֵ֖ל חָמֵֽץ: הַיּ֖וֹם אַתֶּ֣ם יֹצְאִ֑ים בְּחֹ֖דֶשׁ הָאָבִֽיב:*

לוי – וְהָיָ֣ה כִֽי־יְבִיאֲךָ֣ יהו֡ה אֶל־אֶ֣רֶץ הַֽכְּנַעֲנִ֣י וְהַֽחִתִּ֣י וְהָֽאֱמֹרִ֣י וְהַֽחִוִּ֣י וְהַיְבוּסִ֗י אֲשֶׁ֨ר נִשְׁבַּ֤ע לַֽאֲבֹתֶ֨יךָ֙ לָ֣תֶת לָ֔ךְ אֶ֛רֶץ זָבַ֥ת חָלָ֖ב וּדְבָ֑שׁ וְעָֽבַדְתָּ֛ אֶת־הָֽעֲבֹדָ֥ה הַזֹּ֖את בַּחֹ֥דֶשׁ הַזֶּֽה: שִׁבְעַ֥ת יָמִ֖ים תֹּאכַ֣ל מַצֹּ֑ת* וּבַיּוֹם֙ הַשְּׁבִיעִ֔י חַ֖ג* לַֽיהוֹה: מַצּוֹת֙ יֵֽאָכֵ֔ל אֵ֖ת שִׁבְעַ֣ת הַיָּמִ֑ים וְלֹֽא־יֵֽרָאֶ֨ה לְךָ֜ חָמֵ֗ץ* וְלֹֽא־יֵֽרָאֶ֥ה לְךָ֛ שְׂאֹ֖ר בְּכָל־גְּבֻלֶֽךָ: וְהִגַּדְתָּ֣ לְבִנְךָ֔ בַּיּ֥וֹם הַה֖וּא לֵאמֹ֑ר בַּֽעֲב֣וּר זֶ֗ה* עָשָׂ֤ה יהוה֙ לִ֔י בְּצֵאתִ֖י מִמִּצְרָֽיִם: וְהָיָה֩ לְךָ֨ לְא֜וֹת עַל־יָֽדְךָ֗ וּלְזִכָּרוֹן֙ בֵּ֣ין עֵינֶ֔יךָ לְמַ֗עַן תִּֽהְיֶ֛ה תּוֹרַ֥ת יהו֖ה בְּפִ֑יךָ כִּ֚י בְּיָ֣ד חֲזָקָ֔ה הֽוֹצִֽאֲךָ֥ יהו֖ה מִמִּצְרָֽיִם: וְשָֽׁמַרְתָּ֛ אֶת־הַֽחֻקָּ֥ה הַזֹּ֖את לְמֽוֹעֲדָ֑הּ מִיָּמִ֖ים יָמִֽימָה:

שלישי – וְהָיָ֞ה כִּֽי־יְבִֽאֲךָ֤ יהוה֙* אֶל־אֶ֣רֶץ הַֽכְּנַעֲנִ֔י כַּֽאֲשֶׁ֛ר נִשְׁבַּ֥ע לְךָ֖ וְלַֽאֲבֹתֶ֑יךָ וּנְתָנָ֖הּ לָֽךְ: וְהַֽעֲבַרְתָּ֥ כָל־פֶּֽטֶר־רֶ֖חֶם לַֽיהוֹה וְכָל־פֶּ֣טֶר | שֶׁ֤גֶר בְּהֵמָה֙ אֲשֶׁ֨ר יִֽהְיֶ֥ה לְךָ֛ הַזְּכָרִ֖ים לַֽיהוֹה: וְכָל־פֶּ֤טֶר

⧬§ First Day of Chol HaMoed

וַיְדַבֵּ֥ר ה׳ — *Hashem spoke.* God spoke these words to Moses immediately after the death of the Egyptian firstborns and the Exodus of the Jewish people from Egypt. The portion commands Israel forever to commemorate the Exodus in the form of specific commandments.

קַדֶּשׁ לִי כָל בְּכוֹר — *Sanctify to Me every firstborn.* In the most obvious sense, the sanctification of firstborn Jews is in commemoration of the fact that when God slew the Egyptian firstborn, He spared those of Israel. Although these firstborn are redeemed at the age of thirty days (*Numbers* 18:16), this commandment always keeps fresh in the Jewish mind that God has first claim, as it were, on its firstborn. In another sense, this unique sanctity of the first involves not only people, but firstborn domestic animals, first fruits, first crops and the various tithes. All of them are dedicated in one way or another to God's service. This particular chapter discusses human and animal firstborn; the others are discussed elsewhere in the Torah.

וּבַבְּהֵמָה — *And of beast.* Firstborn male cattle, sheep and goats are given to the *Kohen* to be offered on the Altar. But if the firstborn animal has a physical blemish that renders it invalid as an offering, it becomes the personal property of the *Kohen* to use as he wishes.

בְּחֹדֶשׁ הָאָבִיב — *In the month of springtime.* This phrase is a key element in the Hebrew calendar because it ordains that Pesach, the festival of the Exodus, always occur in springtime. Since twelve ordinary lunar months have only 354 days, a thirteenth month is added to the Hebrew calendar seven times every nineteen years in order that Pesach will indeed fall in the spring. [The workings of the calendar are discussed at length

Each day of Chol HaMoed, two scrolls are removed from the Ark. Three people are called to read from the first scroll and one from the second. The reading from the first scroll varies from day to day, as given below. From the second one, the reading is that of the Pesach *Mussaf* offering, and is the same each day. Half-Kaddish is recited after the final reading.

FIRST DAY CHOL HAMOED ON MONDAY, TUESDAY OR THURSDAY.
SECOND DAY CHOL HAMOED ON SUNDAY.

Exodus 13:1-16

Kohen– *HASHEM spoke* to Moses, saying: Sanctify to Me every firstborn,* the first issue of every womb among the Children of Israel, both of man and of beast,* is Mine. Moses said to the people: Remember this day on which you departed from Egypt, from the house of bondage, for with a strong hand HASHEM removed you from here, and therefore no chametz may be eaten. Today you are leaving in the month of springtime.**

Levi– *And it will come to pass, when HASHEM shall bring you to the land of the Canaanites, Hittites, Emorites, Hivvites, and Jebusites, which He swore to your forefathers to give you — a land flowing with milk and honey — you shall perform this service in this month. Seven days you shall eat matzos,* and on the seventh day there shall be a festival* to HASHEM. Matzos shall be eaten throughout the seven days; no chametz may be seen in your possession,* nor may leaven be seen in your possession in all your borders. And you shall tell your son on that day, saying: 'It is because of this* that HASHEM acted on my behalf when I left Egypt.' And it shall serve you as a sign on your arm* and as a reminder between your eyes — so that HASHEM's Torah may be in your mouth; for with a strong hand HASHEM removed you from Egypt. And you shall observe this ordinance at its designated time from year to year.*

Third– *And it shall come to pass, when HASHEM will bring you* to the land of the Canaanites as He swore to you and your forefathers, and will have given it to you. Then you shall set apart every first issue of the womb to HASHEM, and every first issue that is dropped by cattle that belong to you, the males shall belong to HASHEM. Every first issue*

---

in ArtScroll *Bircas HaChammah* and *Mishnah Rosh Hashanah.]* The relationship between spring and the Exodus symbolizes the idea that the Jewish people always remain fresh and filled with the potential for growth.

שִׁבְעַת יָמִים תֹּאכַל מַצֹּת — *Seven days you shall eat matzos.* The absolute requirement that one eat *matzah* applies only to the Seder night. This verse means that if one wishes to eat 'bread' at any time during Pesach, it must be *matzah*. The prohibition of *chametz,* however, applies throughout the festival.

וּבַיּוֹם הַשְּׁבִיעִי חַג — *And on the seventh day there shall be a festival.* The seventh day is a *Yom Tov* on which labor is forbidden. Outside of *Eretz Yisrael,* an eighth day is added to Pesach.

וְלֹא יֵרָאֶה לְךָ חָמֵץ — *No chametz may be seen in your possession.* This verse is the basis for the prohibition against keeping or owning *chametz* during Pesach. Among the familiar observances resulting from this commandment is the search for *chametz* the night before Pesach and the selling of *chametz* to a non-Jew.

בַּעֲבוּר זֶה — *It is because of this.* Tell your children that we were redeemed from Egypt because we were ready to observe God's commandments. In the Haggadah this verse is the answer to the wicked son who questions the purpose of fulfilling the commandments. He is told, *'It is because of this that HASHEM acted on* my *behalf* . . . i.e., He acted to remove me from Egypt, but had you, the wicked son, been there, you would not have been redeemed.'

לְאוֹת עַל יָדְךָ — *As a sign on your arm.* As expressed in the לְשֵׁם יִחוּד prayer, the placement of *tefillin* symbolizes that we subjugate our physical strength, the arm, and our soul and intellect, the head, to the service of God.

וְהָיָה כִּי יְבִאֲךָ ה׳ — *And it shall come to pass, when HASHEM will bring you.* The Talmud (*Bechoros* 4b-5a) offers two versions: Either the consecration of the firstborn would affect only those

חֲמֹר תִּפְדֶּה בְשֶׂה* וְאִם־לֹא תִפְדֶּה וַעֲרַפְתּוֹ וְכֹל בְּכוֹר אָדָם
בְּבָנֶיךָ תִּפְדֶּה: וְהָיָה כִּי־יִשְׁאָלְךָ בִנְךָ מָחָר לֵאמֹר מַה־זֹּאת*
וְאָמַרְתָּ אֵלָיו בְּחֹזֶק יָד הוֹצִיאָנוּ יהוה מִמִּצְרַיִם מִבֵּית עֲבָדִים: וַיְהִי
כִּי־הִקְשָׁה פַרְעֹה לְשַׁלְּחֵנוּ וַיַּהֲרֹג יהוה כָּל־בְּכוֹר בְּאֶרֶץ מִצְרַיִם
מִבְּכֹר אָדָם וְעַד־בְּכוֹר בְּהֵמָה עַל־כֵּן אֲנִי זֹבֵחַ לַיהוה כָּל־פֶּטֶר
רֶחֶם הַזְּכָרִים וְכָל־בְּכוֹר בָּנַי אֶפְדֶּה: וְהָיָה לְאוֹת עַל־יָדְכָה
וּלְטוֹטָפֹת* בֵּין עֵינֶיךָ כִּי בְּחֹזֶק יָד הוֹצִיאָנוּ יהוה מִמִּצְרָיִם:

The service continues with Hagbahah and Gelilah, page 748.

SECOND DAY OF CHOL HAMOED ON TUESDAY, WEDNESDAY OR FRIDAY.
THIRD DAY OF CHOL HAMOED ON MONDAY.

שמות כב:כד-כג:יט

כהן – אִם־כֶּסֶף ׀ תַּלְוֶה* אֶת־עַמִּי אֶת־הֶעָנִי עִמָּךְ לֹא־תִהְיֶה לוֹ
כְּנֹשֶׁה* לֹא־תְשִׂימוּן עָלָיו נֶשֶׁךְ: אִם־חָבֹל תַּחְבֹּל* שַׂלְמַת רֵעֶךָ
עַד־בֹּא הַשֶּׁמֶשׁ תְּשִׁיבֶנּוּ לוֹ: כִּי הִוא כְסוּתֹה לְבַדָּהּ הִוא שִׂמְלָתוֹ
לְעֹרוֹ בַּמֶּה יִשְׁכָּב וְהָיָה כִּי־יִצְעַק אֵלַי וְשָׁמַעְתִּי כִּי־חַנּוּן אָנִי:
לוי – אֱלֹהִים לֹא תְקַלֵּל וְנָשִׂיא בְעַמְּךָ לֹא תָאֹר: מְלֵאָתְךָ*
וְדִמְעֲךָ לֹא תְאַחֵר בְּכוֹר בָּנֶיךָ* תִּתֶּן־לִּי: כֵּן־תַּעֲשֶׂה לְשֹׁרְךָ
לְצֹאנֶךָ שִׁבְעַת יָמִים יִהְיֶה עִם־אִמּוֹ בַּיּוֹם הַשְּׁמִינִי תִּתְּנוֹ־
לִי: וְאַנְשֵׁי־קֹדֶשׁ* תִּהְיוּן לִי וּבָשָׂר בַּשָּׂדֶה טְרֵפָה לֹא תֹאכֵלוּ
לַכֶּלֶב* תַּשְׁלִכוּן אֹתוֹ: לֹא תִשָּׂא שֵׁמַע שָׁוְא* אַל־תָּשֶׁת יָדְךָ עִם־

---

born after the Jewish nation was brought into *Eretz Yisrael;* or the nation would earn its right to the Holy Land in the merit of sanctifying the firstborn.

וְכָל פֶּטֶר חֲמֹר תִּפְדֶּה בְשֶׂה — *Every first issue donkey you shall redeem with a lamb or kid.* In Hebrew, the word שֶׂה refers to the young of both sheep and goats (as, for example, in *Genesis* 30:32, *Numbers* 15:11, and *Deuteronomy* 14:4). There is no equivalent word in English, therefore we are forced to translate שֶׂה as *lamb or kid.*

The donkey is the only non-kosher animal that has the privileged status of the firstborn. Although the Talmud *(Bechoros* 5b) refers to this as a decree, it also offers the reason that this commandment is a memorial of the Exodus when the Jews left Egypt with countless donkeys laden with the riches of the land. *Rashi* suggests also that the donkey recalls the plague on the Egyptians who were likened to donkeys *(Ezekiel* 23:20).

Since a donkey cannot be consecrated as an offering, it is redeemed with a lamb or kid, which becomes the private property of a *Kohen* while the donkey may be used unrestrictedly by its owner. Should the Israelite owner refuse to redeem his donkey, he is denied its use; he must put it to death instantly by administering a blow with an axe to the back of the neck.

מַה זֹּאת — *What is this?* In the Haggadah, this question is ascribed to the simple child, who wishes to learn but cannot analyze the Seder service very well.

טוֹטָפֹת — *Totafos.* Many interpretations are given for this untranslatable word; all agree, however, that it refers to the *tefillin* on the head.

◆§ Second Day of Chol HaMoed

אִם כֶּסֶף תַּלְוֶה — *If you lend money.* R' Yishmael teaches that although the verse begins with the word *if*, this is a positive commandment that Jews are required to lend money to one another (*Mechilta*). From the progression of terms in the verse — *My people, the poor man, with you* — the Sages derive a system of priorities in deciding to whom to lend. Fellow Jews (*My people*) come before non-Jews; the poor come before the rich;

donkey you shall redeem with a lamb or kid; if you do not redeem it, then you must axe the back of its neck. And you must redeem every human firstborn among your sons. And it shall be when your son asks you at some future time, 'What is this?'* you shall answer him, 'With a strong hand* HASHEM *removed us from Egypt, from the house of bondage. And it happened, when Pharaoh stubbornly refused to let us go, that* HASHEM *killed all the firstborn in the land of Egypt, from the firstborn of man to the firstborn of beast. Therefore, I sacrifice to* HASHEM *all first male issue of the womb, and redeem all the firstborn of my sons.' And it shall be a sign upon your arm and totafos* between your eyes, for with a strong hand* HASHEM *removed us from Egypt.*

The service continues with Hagbahah and Gelilah, page 748.

SECOND DAY OF CHOL HAMOED ON TUESDAY, WEDNESDAY OR FRIDAY.
THIRD DAY OF CHOL HAMOED ON MONDAY.

Exodus 22:24-23:19

Kohen — *If you lend money* to My people, to the poor man who is with you, do not be like a creditor* toward him; do not place interest upon him. If you take your neighbor's garment as security,* return it to him before sunset. For it alone is his clothing, it is his garment for his skin — in what should he sleep? — so it will be that if he cries out to Me, I will listen, for I am compassionate.*

Levi — *You shall not curse God, nor shall you curse a leader among your people. Your fully grown offering* and your terumah you shall not delay; the firstborn of your sons* shall you present to Me. So shall you do to your ox and your sheep; seven days shall it be with its mother, on the eighth day you may present it to Me. Holy people* shall you be to Me; you shall not eat flesh of an animal that was torn in the field, to the dog* shall you throw it.*

Do not accept a false report, and do not extend your hand with the*

---

and those who are closer to you (*with you*) — such as neighbors or relatives — come before others.

כְּנֹשֶׁה — *Like a creditor.* If the money is not yet due, the lender should not make the borrower feel beholden to him. Even if the money is due, but the borrower cannot pay as yet, the lender should avoid any word or act that could cause embarrassment.

אִם חָבֹל תַּחְבֹּל — *If you take . . . as security.* The subject of the verse is a security pledge that was taken upon the ruling of the court after non-payment of a legally due obligation. If the borrower is so poor that he has no other garment — or no replacement for whatever else was used as security — it must be returned to him when he needs it, after which the creditor may have it back.

מְלֵאָתְךָ — *Your fully grown offering.* The reference is to *bikkurim,* or first fruits, which are brought to the *Kohen* from the first fully grown produce.

בְּכוֹר בָּנֶיךָ — *Firstborn of your sons.* By redeeming your firstborn, you signify that the first of your sons is devoted to God's service. Originally, the firstborn had the role later assigned to *Kohanim.* In this sense, the redemption of the firstborn signifies that they were truly intended for the Divine service, and for that reason had to be redeemed.

וְאַנְשֵׁי קֹדֶשׁ — *Holy people.* By juxtaposing holiness with the prohibition against eating flesh of an animal that was not killed through kosher slaughter, the Torah teaches that only a Jew who avoids non-kosher food belongs to God.

לַכֶּלֶב — *To the dog.* The verse teaches the lesson of gratitude. Because dogs did not bark at Jews in Egypt (*Exodus 11:7*), they are rewarded by the preference (though not requirement) that such non-kosher meat be given to them.

שֵׁמַע שָׁוְא — *A false report.* This is the commandment not to accept gossip [לְשׁוֹן הָרַע].

רָשָׁע לִהְיֹת עֵד חָמָס:* לֹא־תִהְיֶה אַחֲרֵי־רַבִּים* לְרָעֹת וְלֹא־תַעֲנֶה
עַל־רִב לִנְטֹת אַחֲרֵי רַבִּים לְהַטֹּת: וְדָל* לֹא תֶהְדַּר בְּרִיבוֹ: כִּי תִפְגַּע
שׁוֹר אֹיִבְךָ אוֹ חֲמֹרוֹ תֹּעֶה הָשֵׁב תְּשִׁיבֶנּוּ לוֹ:* כִּי־תִרְאֶה חֲמוֹר
שֹׂנַאֲךָ* רֹבֵץ תַּחַת מַשָּׂאוֹ וְחָדַלְתָּ מֵעֲזֹב לוֹ עָזֹב תַּעֲזֹב עִמּוֹ:*
שלישי – לֹא תַטֶּה מִשְׁפַּט אֶבְיֹנְךָ בְּרִיבוֹ: מִדְּבַר־שֶׁקֶר תִּרְחָק* וְנָקִי
וְצַדִּיק* אַל־תַּהֲרֹג כִּי לֹא־אַצְדִּיק* רָשָׁע: וְשֹׁחַד לֹא תִקָּח כִּי
הַשֹּׁחַד יְעַוֵּר* פִּקְחִים וִיסַלֵּף דִּבְרֵי צַדִּיקִים: וְגֵר לֹא תִלְחָץ וְאַתֶּם
יְדַעְתֶּם אֶת־נֶפֶשׁ הַגֵּר כִּי־גֵרִים הֱיִיתֶם בְּאֶרֶץ מִצְרָיִם: וְשֵׁשׁ שָׁנִים*
תִּזְרַע אֶת־אַרְצֶךָ וְאָסַפְתָּ אֶת־תְּבוּאָתָהּ: וְהַשְּׁבִיעִת תִּשְׁמְטֶנָּה
וּנְטַשְׁתָּהּ* וְאָכְלוּ אֶבְיֹנֵי עַמֶּךָ וְיִתְרָם תֹּאכַל חַיַּת הַשָּׂדֶה כֵּן־תַּעֲשֶׂה
לְכַרְמְךָ לְזֵיתֶךָ: שֵׁשֶׁת יָמִים תַּעֲשֶׂה מַעֲשֶׂיךָ וּבַיּוֹם הַשְּׁבִיעִי תִּשְׁבֹּת
לְמַעַן יָנוּחַ שׁוֹרְךָ וַחֲמֹרֶךָ וְיִנָּפֵשׁ בֶּן־אֲמָתְךָ וְהַגֵּר:* וּבְכֹל
אֲשֶׁר־אָמַרְתִּי אֲלֵיכֶם תִּשָּׁמֵרוּ וְשֵׁם אֱלֹהִים אֲחֵרִים לֹא תַזְכִּירוּ*
לֹא יִשָּׁמַע עַל־פִּיךָ:* שָׁלֹשׁ רְגָלִים תָּחֹג לִי בַּשָּׁנָה: אֶת־חַג
הַמַּצּוֹת תִּשְׁמֹר שִׁבְעַת יָמִים תֹּאכַל מַצּוֹת כַּאֲשֶׁר צִוִּיתִךָ לְמוֹעֵד
חֹדֶשׁ הָאָבִיב כִּי־בוֹ יָצָאתָ מִמִּצְרָיִם וְלֹא־יֵרָאוּ פָנַי רֵיקָם: וְחַג
הַקָּצִיר* בִּכּוּרֵי מַעֲשֶׂיךָ אֲשֶׁר תִּזְרַע בַּשָּׂדֶה וְחַג הָאָסִף* בְּצֵאת
הַשָּׁנָה בְּאָסְפְּךָ אֶת־מַעֲשֶׂיךָ מִן־הַשָּׂדֶה: שָׁלֹשׁ פְּעָמִים בַּשָּׁנָה

עֵד חָמָס — *A mercenary witness.* Someone who is willing to testify to something that he has not actually seen — even if he believes it to be true — brands himself as a *mercenary witness.*

לֹא תִהְיֶה אַחֲרֵי רַבִּים — *Do not follow the majority.* The verse cautions us not to give in to a majority whom we know to be wrong.

וְדָל — *A poor man.* Despite everyone's obligation to help the poor, a judge may not pervert the law to declare the poor man the winner who is entitled to payment. The law must be upheld; charity does not override justice.

הָשֵׁב תְּשִׁיבֶנּוּ לוֹ — *You shall return it to him continually.* The commandment to return lost property does not end after it has been returned one time. No matter how often it is lost, one is responsible to retrieve and return it.

שֹׂנַאֲךָ — *Of your enemy.* Again, the Torah stresses that the commandments to help fellow Jews apply as much to enemies as to friends. One must divorce his personal feelings from his obligation to someone as a fellow Jew. In fact, the Sages derive that if both an enemy and a friend need help, one should first help his enemy, as a way of suppressing his evil inclination.

עִמּוֹ — *With him.* If the owner helps to carry the load and right his fallen animal, there is an obligation to help *with him,* but one is not required to help someone who refuses to participate.

תִּרְחָק — *Distance yourself.* R' Bunam of P'shis'cha noted that the only sin from which the Torah commands us to *distance* ourselves is falsehood. One must exert himself to stay away from even the *appearance* of falsehood.

וְנָקִי וְצַדִּיק — *The innocent or the righteous.* Even if the court has convicted him and sentenced him to death, you must be ready to reopen the case if there is a possibility that he is *innocent* by virtue of new evidence. However, if the court has declared someone to be *righteous*, his case is not reopened, even if the claim is made that there is new proof against him.

לֹא אַצְדִּיק — *I will not exonerate.* Do not be concerned that the guilty party will go free if you cannot consider new evidence against him, for I, God, will not allow him to escape punishment.

יְעַוֵּר — *Will blind.* Even someone who is wise and is convinced that he can retain his objectiv-

wicked to be a mercenary witness. Do not follow the majority* for wrong judgments, and do not respond to a dispute by yielding to the majority to pervert. Do not glorify a poor man* in his dispute.*

*If you encounter the ox of your foe or his donkey wandering, you shall return it to him continually.**

If you see the donkey of your enemy crouching under its load, would you refrain from helping him? — you shall help continually with him.**

Third – *Do not pervert the judgment of the indigent in his dispute. Distance yourself* from a false word; do not execute the innocent or the righteous,* for I will not exonerate* a wicked person. Do not accept a bribe, for a bribe will blind* the wise and corrupt just words. Do not oppress a stranger; you know the feelings of the stranger, for you were strangers in the land of Egypt. Six years* shall you sow your land and gather in its produce. In the seventh, you shall leave it untended and unharvested,* and the destitute of your people shall eat, and the wildlife of the field shall eat their leftovers; so shall you do to your vineyard and your olive grove. For six days you shall do your work and on the seventh day you shall desist, so that your ox and your donkey can rest, and your maidservant's son and the sojourner* may be refreshed. You shall beware of everything that I have commanded you; the names of strange gods you shall not mention,* they shall not be heard through your mouth.* Three times shall you celebrate for Me during the year: You shall observe the Festival of Matzos, seven days shall you eat matzos as I have commanded you, at the appointed time of the month of springtime, for in it did you go out of Egypt; you shall not be seen before Me empty-handed. And the Festival of the Harvest* of the first fruits of your work that you sow in the field; and the Festival of the Ingathering* at the close of the year, when you gather in your work from the field. Three times during the year*

---

ity will become blinded to the truth if he accepts a bribe.

וְשֵׁשׁ שָׁנִים — *Six years.* By juxtaposing the commandment of the seventh year with that of concern for strangers, the Torah implies that neglect of *Shemittah* will cause Israel to be exiled and become strangers. Indeed, one of the reasons for the destruction of the First Temple was Jewish violation of the laws of *Shemittah.*

תִּשְׁמְטֶנָּה וּנְטַשְׁתָּהּ — *You shall leave it untended and unharvested.* During the seventh year, the field must be left untended, without plowing or other agricultural work. What grows wild must be left unharvested, so that poor people and even animals are free to take what they like without interference by the owner of the property.

בֶּן אֲמָתְךָ וְהַגֵּר — *And your maidservant's son and the sojourner.* The *maidservant* of the verse is a non-Jewish slave, so that her son, too, is a slave. He is not permitted to work on the Sabbath even for himself, because he is required to observe most commandments. The *sojourner* is a non-Jew who is permitted to reside in *Eretz Yisrael* because he renounces idolatry. He may work on the Sabbath for himself, since he is not Jewish, but not for his Jewish employer.

לֹא תַזְכִּירוּ — *You shall not mention.* A Jew may not use the name of an idol to indicate a place or day, by saying, for example, we will meet in front of the temple of such-and-such idol.

עַל פִּיךָ — *Through your mouth.* Do not cause a non-Jew to take an oath in the name of his idol, for if you do so it is *your mouth* that causes the name to be spoken.

וְחַג הַקָּצִיר — *And the Festival of the Harvest,* i.e., Shavuos, the time when the harvest begins and when the first fruits may be brought to the Temple.

וְחַג הָאָסִף — *And the Festival of the Ingathering,* i.e., Succos. During the summer, the grain crops would be left in the fields to dry in the sun. With the coming of Succos, and the expected advent of the rainy season, the crops would be gathered in, and the agricultural year was over.

יֵרָאֶה֙ כָּל־זְכֽוּרְךָ֔ אֶל־פְּנֵ֖י הָאָדֹ֣ן ׀ יְהֹוָֽה: לֹֽא־תִזְבַּ֤ח* עַל־חָמֵץ֙ דַּם־זִבְחִ֔י וְלֹֽא־יָלִ֣ין חֵ֧לֶב־חַגִּ֛י* עַד־בֹּֽקֶר: רֵאשִׁ֗ית בִּכּוּרֵי֙ אַדְמָ֣תְךָ֔ תָּבִ֕יא בֵּ֖ית יְהֹוָ֣ה אֱלֹהֶ֑יךָ לֹֽא־תְבַשֵּׁ֥ל גְּדִ֖י* בַּחֲלֵ֥ב אִמּֽוֹ:

The service continues with Hagbahah and Gelilah, page 748.

THIRD DAY OF CHOL HAMOED ON WEDNESDAY OR THURSDAY.

שמות לד:א-כו

כהן – וַיֹּ֤אמֶר יְהֹוָה֙ אֶל־מֹשֶׁ֔ה פְּסָל־לְךָ֛* שְׁנֵֽי־לֻחֹ֥ת אֲבָנִ֖ים כָּרִֽאשֹׁנִ֑ים וְכָתַבְתִּי֙ עַל־הַלֻּחֹ֔ת אֶת־הַדְּבָרִ֔ים אֲשֶׁ֥ר הָי֖וּ עַל־הַלֻּחֹ֥ת הָרִֽאשֹׁנִ֖ים אֲשֶׁ֥ר שִׁבַּֽרְתָּ: וֶהְיֵ֥ה נָכ֖וֹן לַבֹּ֑קֶר וְעָלִ֤יתָ בַבֹּ֨קֶר֙ אֶל־הַ֣ר סִינַ֔י וְנִצַּבְתָּ֥ לִ֛י שָׁ֖ם עַל־רֹ֥אשׁ הָהָֽר: וְאִישׁ֙ לֹֽא־יַעֲלֶ֣ה עִמָּ֔ךְ* וְגַם־אִ֥ישׁ אַל־יֵרָ֖א בְּכָל־הָהָ֑ר גַּם־הַצֹּ֤אן וְהַבָּקָר֙ אַל־יִרְע֔וּ אֶל־מ֖וּל הָהָ֥ר הַהֽוּא:

לוי – וַיִּפְסֹ֡ל שְׁנֵֽי־לֻחֹ֨ת אֲבָנִ֜ים כָּרִֽאשֹׁנִ֗ים וַיַּשְׁכֵּ֨ם מֹשֶׁ֤ה בַבֹּ֨קֶר֙ וַיַּ֨עַל֙ אֶל־הַ֣ר סִינַ֔י כַּאֲשֶׁ֛ר צִוָּ֥ה יְהֹוָ֖ה אֹת֑וֹ וַיִּקַּ֣ח בְּיָד֔וֹ שְׁנֵ֖י לֻחֹ֥ת אֲבָנִֽים: וַיֵּ֤רֶד יְהֹוָה֙ בֶּֽעָנָ֔ן וַיִּתְיַצֵּ֥ב עִמּ֖וֹ שָׁ֑ם וַיִּקְרָ֥א* בְשֵׁ֖ם יְהֹוָֽה: וַיַּעֲבֹ֨ר יְהֹוָ֥ה ׀ עַל־פָּנָיו֮ וַיִּקְרָא֒* יְהֹוָ֣ה ׀ יְהֹוָ֔ה* אֵ֥ל רַח֖וּם וְחַנּ֑וּן אֶ֥רֶךְ אַפַּ֖יִם וְרַב־חֶ֥סֶד וֶאֱמֶֽת: נֹצֵ֥ר חֶ֨סֶד֙ לָאֲלָפִ֔ים נֹשֵׂ֥א

לֹא תִזְבַּח — *You shall not slaughter.* The reference is to the *pesach*-offering, which may not be slaughtered, nor may its blood be placed on the Altar wall, until all *chametz*, or leavened food, has been removed from the possession of the people bringing the offering.

חֵלֶב חַגִּי — *The fat of My festival-offering.* Specifically, the verse refers to the *chagigah*, the peace-offering that is brought by individuals in honor of each of the three pilgrimage festivals. This law, which applies to all offerings, provides that, while the sacrificial parts may be placed on the Altar throughout the night after the slaughter, these parts become disqualified if they are not yet on the Altar by daybreak.

לֹא תְבַשֵּׁל גְּדִי — *You shall not cook a kid.* The law is expressed in terms of a kid and its mother's milk because it was common in ancient times to prepare meat in this manner, but it refers to all kinds of animal meat and all kinds of milk. The Torah repeats this commandment three times to teach that there are three aspects to the prohibition: It is forbidden to cook meat with milk, to eat it, or to benefit from it commercially or any other way.

◈§ Third Day of Chol HaMoed

פְּסָל לְךָ — *Carve yourself.* Moses' forty days of prayer have achieved their goal. God has con-

sented to give the Ten Commandments once again to the Jewish people. This time, however, the stone tablets are to be carved by Moses, unlike the first tablets, which were hewn by God. The commandments, however, will be inscribed by God Himself. The fact that these tablets were not of Divine origin was proof that, despite Israel's repentance and Moses' prayers, the nation had not regained the spiritual pinnacle it had attained prior to the sin.

וְאִישׁ לֹא יַעֲלֶה עִמָּךְ — *No man is to climb up with you.* There is nothing better than modesty. Moses' ascent for the first tablets was made with great pomp and in the presence of the entire nation. Those tablets were smashed. The ascent for the second tablets was made in complete privacy. Those tablets remained (*Tanchuma, Ki Sissa* 1:31).

וַיִּקְרָא — *And he called out.* According to *Rashi*, it was Moses who called out. Most other commentators, however, hold that God proclaimed His Own Name, meaning that He taught Moses His Attributes, as given in the next two verses.

◈§ י"ג מדות / The Thirteen Attributes

R' Yehudah taught that God sealed a covenant with Moses and Israel that in any time of crisis or danger, they should pray for God's mercy by reciting these attributes, and God sealed a *shall all your menfolk appear before the Lord, HASHEM. You shall not slaughter* the blood of My feast-offering upon leavened food; nor may the fat of My festival-offering* remain overnight until morning. The choicest first fruit of your land shall you bring to the House of HASHEM, your God; you shall not cook a kid* in the milk of its mother.*

The service continues with Hagbahah and Gelilah, page 748.

THIRD DAY OF CHOL HAMOED ON WEDNESDAY OR THURSDAY.

Exodus 34:1-26

Kohen – *HASHEM said to Moses, 'Carve yourself* two stone tablets, like the first ones; and I will inscribe upon the tablets the words that were on the first tablets which you shattered. Be prepared in the morning; climb up Mount Sinai in the morning and stand by Me on the mountain top. No man is to climb up with you* nor should anyone be seen on the entire mountain; even the sheep and cattle are not to graze facing that mountain.'*

Levi – *So he carved two stone tablets like the first ones. Moses arose in the morning and climbed up Mount Sinai as HASHEM had commanded him; and he took the two stone tablets in his hand. HASHEM descended in a cloud and stood with him there, and he called out* with the Name — HASHEM.*

And HASHEM passed before him and proclaimed: HASHEM, HASHEM, God, Compassionate and Gracious, Slow to anger, and Abundant in Kindness and truth. Preserver of kindness for thousands of generations,*

---

covenant that such a prayer would never be in vain (*Rosh Hashanah* 17b).

ה׳ ה׳ – *HASHEM, HASHEM.* There are various opinions regarding how to enumerate the Thirteen Attributes. We follow the view of *Rabbeinu Tam (Rosh Hashanah* 17b), which is generally accepted:

(1) ה׳ – *HASHEM.* This Name [containing the letters of הָיָה הֹוֶה יִהְיֶה, *He was, He is, He will be*] designates God as the מְהַוֶּה, *Prime Cause,* of everything. It is only natural that He wishes to assure the survival of all that He brought into being. Consequently, this Name represents the Attribute of Mercy. In addition, the Name's spelling implies God's timelessness. Though man may sin, he can repent and call upon the timeless God to restore him to his original innocent state. As the Talmud states: אֲנִי הוּא קוֹדֶם שֶׁיֶּחֱטָא הָאָדָם וַאֲנִי הוּא לְאַחַר שֶׁיֶּחֱטָא הָאָדָם, וְיַעֲשֶׂה תְּשׁוּבָה, *I am He* [i.e., the God of Mercy] *before a person sins, and I am He after a person sins and repents (Rosh Hashanah* 17b). Based on this dictum, *Rabbeinu Tam* counts the twin use of the Name *HASHEM* as two attributes. The first is that God is merciful before a person sins, even though He knows that the sin will be committed.

(2) ה׳ – *HASHEM.* God is merciful after the sin has been committed, by allowing the sinner time to repent, and by accepting his repentance, though it may be imperfect.

(3) אֵל – *God.* This Name denotes the power of God's mercy, which sometimes surpasses even the compassion indicated by the Name *HASHEM.* He displays this higher degree of mercy to genuinely righteous people who sin, but repent. In return for their previous behavior, God exerts Himself, as it were, to ensure their survival.

(4) רַחוּם – *Compassionate.* In response to pleas for mercy, God eases the suffering of those being punished for their sins. Another manifestation of compassion is that God does not confront deserving people with overpowering temptation.

(5) וְחַנּוּן – *And Gracious.* God is gracious even to those unworthy of His kindness. Also, if someone lacks the willpower to avoid sin, and he seeks God's help, he will get it.

(6) אֶרֶךְ אַפַּיִם – *Slow to anger.* So that the sinner will have time to repent.

(7) וְרַב חֶסֶד – *And Abundant in Kindness.* God shows great kindness to those who lack personal merits. The Talmud teaches, as described above, that God exercises this attribute by removing sins from the scale of justice, thus tilting the scales in favor of merit.

(8) וֶאֱמֶת – *And Truth.* God never reneges; His promise to reward the deserving will be carried out unequivocally.

(9) נֹצֵר חֶסֶד לָאֲלָפִים – *Preserver of kindness for thousands [of generations].* The deeds of the righteous — especially those who serve Him out of intense love — bring benefits to their offspring far into the future.

עָוֹן וָפֶשַׁע וְחַטָּאָה וְנַקֵּה לֹא יְנַקֶּה פֹּקֵד ׀ עֲוֹן אָבוֹת עַל־בָּנִים*
וְעַל־בְּנֵי בָנִים עַל־שִׁלֵּשִׁים וְעַל־רִבֵּעִים: וַיְמַהֵר מֹשֶׁה וַיִּקֹּד אַרְצָה
וַיִּשְׁתָּחוּ: וַיֹּאמֶר אִם־נָא מָצָאתִי חֵן בְּעֵינֶיךָ אֲדֹנָי יֵלֶךְ־נָא אֲדֹנָי*
בְּקִרְבֵּנוּ כִּי עַם־קְשֵׁה־עֹרֶף הוּא וְסָלַחְתָּ לַעֲוֹנֵנוּ וּלְחַטָּאתֵנוּ
וּנְחַלְתָּנוּ: וַיֹּאמֶר הִנֵּה אָנֹכִי כֹּרֵת בְּרִית נֶגֶד כָּל־עַמְּךָ אֶעֱשֶׂה
נִפְלָאֹת אֲשֶׁר לֹא־נִבְרְאוּ בְכָל־הָאָרֶץ וּבְכָל־הַגּוֹיִם וְרָאָה כָל־
הָעָם אֲשֶׁר־אַתָּה בְקִרְבּוֹ אֶת־מַעֲשֵׂה יהוה כִּי־נוֹרָא הוּא אֲשֶׁר
אֲנִי עֹשֶׂה עִמָּךְ: שְׁמָר־לְךָ אֵת אֲשֶׁר אָנֹכִי מְצַוְּךָ הַיּוֹם הִנְנִי גֹרֵשׁ
מִפָּנֶיךָ אֶת־הָאֱמֹרִי וְהַכְּנַעֲנִי וְהַחִתִּי וְהַפְּרִזִּי וְהַחִוִּי וְהַיְבוּסִי:
הִשָּׁמֶר לְךָ פֶּן־תִּכְרֹת בְּרִית לְיוֹשֵׁב הָאָרֶץ אֲשֶׁר אַתָּה בָּא עָלֶיהָ
פֶּן־יִהְיֶה לְמוֹקֵשׁ* בְּקִרְבֶּךָ: כִּי אֶת־מִזְבְּחֹתָם תִּתֹּצוּן וְאֶת־מַצֵּבֹתָם
תְּשַׁבֵּרוּן וְאֶת־אֲשֵׁרָיו תִּכְרֹתוּן: כִּי לֹא תִשְׁתַּחֲוֶה לְאֵל אַחֵר כִּי
יהוה קַנָּא* שְׁמוֹ אֵל קַנָּא הוּא: פֶּן*־תִּכְרֹת בְּרִית לְיוֹשֵׁב הָאָרֶץ וְזָנוּ
׀ אַחֲרֵי אֱלֹהֵיהֶם וְזָבְחוּ לֵאלֹהֵיהֶם וְקָרָא לְךָ וְאָכַלְתָּ מִזִּבְחוֹ:
וְלָקַחְתָּ מִבְּנֹתָיו לְבָנֶיךָ וְזָנוּ בְנֹתָיו אַחֲרֵי אֱלֹהֵיהֶן וְהִזְנוּ אֶת־בָּנֶיךָ
אַחֲרֵי אֱלֹהֵיהֶן: אֱלֹהֵי מַסֵּכָה לֹא תַעֲשֶׂה־לָּךְ:
שלישי – אֶת־חַג הַמַּצּוֹת תִּשְׁמֹר שִׁבְעַת יָמִים תֹּאכַל מַצּוֹת אֲשֶׁר
צִוִּיתִךָ לְמוֹעֵד חֹדֶשׁ הָאָבִיב* כִּי בְּחֹדֶשׁ הָאָבִיב יָצָאתָ מִמִּצְרָיִם:
כָּל־פֶּטֶר רֶחֶם* לִי וְכָל־מִקְנְךָ תִּזָּכָר פֶּטֶר שׁוֹר וָשֶׂה: וּפֶטֶר חֲמוֹר
תִּפְדֶּה בְשֶׂה* וְאִם־לֹא תִפְדֶּה וַעֲרַפְתּוֹ כֹּל בְּכוֹר בָּנֶיךָ תִּפְדֶּה
וְלֹא־יֵרָאוּ פָנַי רֵיקָם:* שֵׁשֶׁת יָמִים תַּעֲבֹד וּבַיּוֹם הַשְּׁבִיעִי תִּשְׁבֹּת

---

(10) נֹשֵׂא עָוֹן – *Forgiver of iniquity.* God forgives the intentional sinner, if he repents.

(11) וָפֶשַׁע – *[Forgiver of] willful sin.* Even those who rebel against God and purposely seek to anger Him are given an opportunity to repent.

(12) וְחַטָּאָה – *And [Forgiver of] error.* God forgives those who repent of sins that are committed out of carelessness or apathy. Having already praised God as the forgiver of intentional sin and rebelliousness, why do we revert to praising Him for this seemingly lesser level of mercy? Because if someone repents out of fear rather than love, his intentional sins are reduced in severity and are treated by God as if they had been done in error. Thus, even after having partially forgiven the intentional sins by reducing their severity, God further forgives those who continue to repent for these lesser sins.

(13) וְנַקֵּה – *And Who cleanses.* God wipes away the sins of those who repent sincerely, as if they had never existed.

In the Torah the verse continues לֹא יְנַקֶּה, *He does not cleanse.* The simple interpretation of the verse is that God does not completely erase the sin, but He exacts retribution in minute stages. The Talmud (*Yoma* 86a), however, explains that *He cleanses* the sins of those who truly repent; but *He does not cleanse* the sins of those who do not repent.

פֹּקֵד עֲוֹן אָבוֹת עַל בָּנִים – *He recalls the sin of parents upon children.* As the Ten Commandments in *Exodus* 20:5,6 indicate, children may suffer for the sins of their elders only if the children consciously and willingly copy those sins. On the other hand, God spreads out reward for two thousand generations. The extent of His reward is five hundred times greater than the extent of His punishment.

יֵלֶךְ נָא אֲדֹנָי – *May my Lord go.* Having been taught God's attributes of Mercy, Moses reiterated his earlier plea that HASHEM Himself guide

Forgiver of iniquity, willful sin, and error — and who cleanses but does not cleanse completely — He recalls the sin of parents upon children and grandchildren, for the third and fourth generations.'*

Moses hastened to kneel upon the ground and prostrate himself. He said, 'If I have found favor in Your eyes, my Lord, may my Lord go among us, for it is a stiff-necked people; so may You forgive our iniquity and our sin, and make us Your heritage.'*

He said, 'Behold, I seal a covenant; before your entire nation I will make distinctions such as have never been created in the entire world and among all the nations; and the entire people among whom you are will see the work of HASHEM — which is awesome — that I am about to do with you.'*

Be careful of what I command you today: behold I drive out before you the Emorite, the Canaanite, the Hittite, the Perizite, the Hivvite, and the Jebusite. Beware lest you seal a covenant with the inhabitants of the Land to which you come; lest it be a snare among you. Rather you are to break apart their altars, smash their pillars and cut down their sacred trees. For you are not to prostrate yourselves to an alien god, for the very name of HASHEM is 'Jealous One,'* He is a jealous God. Lest* you seal a covenant with the inhabitants of the land and you stray after their gods, sacrifice to their gods, and they invite you and you eat from their offering! And you select their daughters for your sons; and their daughters stray after their gods and entice your sons to stray after their gods!*

Do not make yourselves molten gods.

Third – *You are to observe the Festival of Matzos: For seven days you are to eat matzos as I commanded you, at the appointed time in the month of spring;* for in the month of spring you went out of Egypt.*

Every opening issue of a womb is Mine; and all your flock that produces a male, the opening issue of cattle or sheep. The first issue of a donkey you are to redeem with a lamb or kid,* and if you do not redeem it, you are to axe the back of its neck; you are to redeem every firstborn of your sons; they may not appear before Me empty-handed.* Six days you are to work and on the seventh day you are to refrain from work;*

---

the people. Precisely because Israel is *stiff-necked* and prone to sin, it must have God's ever-present mercy to preserve it.

לְמוֹקֵשׁ – *Be a snare.* Israel's fraternization with gentile nations, in *Eretz Yisrael* or elsewhere, results in calamity.

קַנָּא – *'Jealous One.'* A jealous person does not permit another to take what is rightfully his. Similarly, God will not tolerate those who extend their reverence and worship to idols instead of (or in addition) to Him.

פֶּן – *Lest.* This verse and the next give a list of idolatrous practices that the Jewish people are warned not to do. The term *lest* implies that something dire will befall them if they do these things, but the punishment is not specified. It is similar, in the vernacular, to saying, 'Do not do this — or else!'

חֹדֶשׁ הָאָבִיב – *The month of spring.* The requirement that Pesach be in the springtime is the basis for the addition (seven times every nineteen years) of a thirteenth month in the Jewish calendar. Only thereby can it be assured that the month of Passover will be in the spring.

פֶּטֶר רֶחֶם – *Opening issue of a womb.* The first male born normally from the womb must be redeemed, but not one born by Caesarian section (*Bechoros* 19a).

תִּפְדֶּה בְשֶׂה – *You are to redeem with a lamb or kid.* The donkey then loses its sanctity and the lamb or kid becomes the personal property of the *Kohen;* it is not an offering.

רֵיקָם – *Empty-handed.* This does not refer to the firstborn. It is a general commandment that

בֶּחָרִישׁ וּבַקָּצִיר* תִּשְׁבֹּת: וְחַג שָׁבֻעֹת תַּעֲשֶׂה לְךָ בִּכּוּרֵי קְצִיר חִטִּים* וְחַג הָאָסִיף תְּקוּפַת הַשָּׁנָה:* שָׁלֹשׁ פְּעָמִים בַּשָּׁנָה יֵרָאֶה כָּל־זְכוּרְךָ אֶת־פְּנֵי הָאָדֹן | יהוה אֱלֹהֵי יִשְׂרָאֵל: כִּי־אוֹרִישׁ גּוֹיִם מִפָּנֶיךָ וְהִרְחַבְתִּי אֶת־גְּבֻלֶךָ וְלֹא־יַחְמֹד אִישׁ אֶת־אַרְצְךָ בַּעֲלֹתְךָ לֵרָאוֹת אֶת־פְּנֵי יהוה אֱלֹהֶיךָ שָׁלֹשׁ פְּעָמִים בַּשָּׁנָה: לֹא־תִשְׁחַט עַל־חָמֵץ דַּם־זִבְחִי וְלֹא־יָלִין לַבֹּקֶר זֶבַח חַג הַפָּסַח: רֵאשִׁית בִּכּוּרֵי אַדְמָתְךָ תָּבִיא בֵּית יהוה אֱלֹהֶיךָ לֹא־תְבַשֵּׁל גְּדִי בַּחֲלֵב אִמּוֹ:

The service continues with Hagbahah and Gelilah, page 748.

FOURTH DAY OF CHOL HAMOED

במדבר ט:א־יד

כהן – וַיְדַבֵּר יהוה אֶל־מֹשֶׁה בְמִדְבַּר־סִינַי בַּשָּׁנָה הַשֵּׁנִית לְצֵאתָם מֵאֶרֶץ מִצְרַיִם בַּחֹדֶשׁ הָרִאשׁוֹן לֵאמֹר: וְיַעֲשׂוּ בְנֵי־יִשְׂרָאֵל אֶת־הַפָּסַח* בְּמוֹעֲדוֹ: בְּאַרְבָּעָה עָשָׂר־יוֹם בַּחֹדֶשׁ הַזֶּה בֵּין הָעַרְבַּיִם תַּעֲשׂוּ אֹתוֹ בְּמֹעֲדוֹ כְּכָל־חֻקֹּתָיו וּכְכָל־מִשְׁפָּטָיו תַּעֲשׂוּ אֹתוֹ: וַיְדַבֵּר מֹשֶׁה אֶל־בְּנֵי יִשְׂרָאֵל לַעֲשֹׂת הַפָּסַח: וַיַּעֲשׂוּ אֶת־הַפֶּסַח בָּרִאשׁוֹן בְּאַרְבָּעָה עָשָׂר יוֹם לַחֹדֶשׁ בֵּין הָעַרְבַּיִם בְּמִדְבַּר סִינָי כְּכֹל אֲשֶׁר צִוָּה יהוה אֶת־מֹשֶׁה כֵּן עָשׂוּ בְּנֵי יִשְׂרָאֵל:

לוי – וַיְהִי אֲנָשִׁים אֲשֶׁר הָיוּ טְמֵאִים לְנֶפֶשׁ אָדָם* וְלֹא־יָכְלוּ לַעֲשֹׂת־הַפֶּסַח בַּיּוֹם הַהוּא וַיִּקְרְבוּ לִפְנֵי מֹשֶׁה וְלִפְנֵי אַהֲרֹן בַּיּוֹם הַהוּא: וַיֹּאמְרוּ הָאֲנָשִׁים הָהֵמָּה אֵלָיו אֲנַחְנוּ טְמֵאִים לְנֶפֶשׁ אָדָם לָמָּה נִגָּרַע לְבִלְתִּי הַקְרִיב אֶת־קָרְבַּן יהוה בְּמֹעֲדוֹ בְּתוֹךְ בְּנֵי יִשְׂרָאֵל: וַיֹּאמֶר אֲלֵהֶם מֹשֶׁה עִמְדוּ וְאֶשְׁמְעָה מַה־יְצַוֶּה יהוה לָכֶם:

שלישי – וַיְדַבֵּר יהוה אֶל־מֹשֶׁה לֵּאמֹר: דַּבֵּר אֶל־בְּנֵי יִשְׂרָאֵל

---

people who come to Jerusalem for the three pilgrimage festivals should bring offerings.

בֶּחָרִישׁ וּבַקָּצִיר – *Plowing and harvest.* These are singled out because they are labors upon which human life depends; even such necessary work is forbidden on the Sabbath *(Ramban). Rashi* cites the Sages' halachic interpretations.

בִּכּוּרֵי קְצִיר חִטִּים – *The first fruits of your wheat harvest.* I.e., the two loaves of Shavuos, which are the first meal-offerings that may be offered from the new crop.

תְּקוּפַת הַשָּׁנָה – *At the year's change of seasons.* Succos is the time when the agricultural year is over and the new plowing season begins.

◆§ Fourth Day of Chol HaMoed

וְיַעֲשׂוּ . . . אֶת הַפָּסַח — *Shall perform the pesach-offering.* The original commandment in Egypt to perform the *pesach*-offering specified that, after the first offering in Egypt, the commandment would apply annually only when Israel entered its land (*Exodus* 12:25). Consequently, a new commandment was required in order that it be brought in the Wilderness, and, indeed, this was the only *pesach*-offering that was brought *you are to refrain from plowing and harvest.* You are to mark the Festival of Shavuos with the first fruits of your wheat harvest;* and the Festival of the Harvest at the year's change of seasons.* Three times a year all your males are to appear before the Lord* HASHEM, *the God of Israel. For I shall banish nations before you and broaden your boundary; no man will covet your land when you go up to appear before* HASHEM, *your God, three times a year.*

You may not slaughter My blood-offering while in possession of leavened food; nor may the offering of the Pesach festival be left overnight until morning. The first of your land's early produce you are to bring to the Temple of HASHEM, *your God; do not cook a kid in its mother's milk.*

The service continues with Hagbahah and Gelilah, page 748.

FOURTH DAY OF CHOL HAMOED

Numbers 9:1-14

Kohen — HASHEM *spoke to Moses in the Wilderness of Sinai, in the second year from their exodus from the land of Egypt, in the first month, saying: The Children of Israel shall perform the pesach-offering* in its appointed time. On the fourteenth day in this month in the afternoon shall you perform it, in its appointed time, according to all its decrees and according to all its ordinances shall you perform it. Moses spoke to the Children of Israel, that they should perform the pesach-offering. They performed the pesach-offering in the first [month] on the fourteenth day of the month, in the afternoon, in the Wilderness of Sinai; in accord with everything that* HASHEM *commanded Moses, so the Children of Israel did.*

Levi — *There were people who had been contaminated through a human [corpse],* and were not permitted to perform the pesach-offering on that day; they came before Moses and Aaron on that day. Those people said to him, 'We are contaminated through a human corpse — why should we be deprived, not to offer the offering of* HASHEM *in its appointed time, among the Children of Israel?' Moses said, 'Stand here, and I will hear what* HASHEM *will command about you.'*

Third — HASHEM *spoke to Moses, saying: Speak to the Children of Israel,*

---

during the entire forty-year period of wandering. The Sages explain that it could not be brought during those years because it was unhealthy to circumcise children in the Wilderness, and the Torah requires that all male members of the family be circumcised. But the Sages reproach Israel for this condition. Had the people not sinned, they would have entered *Eretz Yisrael* a few months after the Exodus, thus the people were responsible for their own physical inability to bring the *pesach*-offering. The other laws of Pesach, such as the commandment to eat matzah and the prohibition against *chametz,* however, did apply in the Wilderness, since they are not conditional on circumcision.

טְמֵאִים לְנֶפֶשׁ אָדָם — *Contaminated through a human [corpse].* How had they become contaminated? The Sages offer two versions. They were Mishael and Elizaphan, who removed the bodies of Nadav and Avihu from the Tabernacle (*Leviticus* 10:3), or they were the people who were caring for the remains of Joseph, which were being taken to *Eretz Yisrael.* This explains why they felt that they were entitled to bring the *pesach*-offering. Since they had become contaminated because of the unselfish performance of a *mitzvah,* it was not fair in their judgment that they be deprived of the opportunity to participate in the offering.

לֵאמֹ֑ר אִ֣ישׁ אִ֣ישׁ כִּֽי־יִהְיֶֽה־טָמֵ֣א ׀ לָנֶ֡פֶשׁ אוֹ֩ בְדֶ֨רֶךְ רְחֹקָ֜ה* לָכֶ֗ם אֽוֹ לְדֹרֹֽתֵיכֶ֔ם וְעָ֥שָׂה פֶ֖סַח לַֽיהוָֽה׃ בַּחֹ֨דֶשׁ הַשֵּׁנִ֜י בְּאַרְבָּעָ֨ה עָשָׂ֥ר י֛וֹם בֵּ֥ין הָעַרְבַּ֖יִם יַעֲשׂ֣וּ אֹת֑וֹ עַל־מַצּ֥וֹת* וּמְרֹרִ֖ים יֹאכְלֻֽהוּ׃ לֹֽא־יַשְׁאִ֤ירוּ מִמֶּ֙נּוּ֙ עַד־בֹּ֔קֶר וְעֶ֖צֶם לֹ֣א יִשְׁבְּרוּ־ב֑וֹ כְּכָל־חֻקַּ֥ת הַפֶּ֖סַח יַעֲשׂ֥וּ אֹתֽוֹ׃ וְהָאִ֡ישׁ אֲשֶׁר־הוּא֩ טָה֨וֹר וּבְדֶ֜רֶךְ לֹא־הָיָ֗ה וְחָדַל֙ לַעֲשׂ֣וֹת הַפֶּ֔סַח וְנִכְרְתָ֛ה הַנֶּ֥פֶשׁ הַהִ֖וא מֵעַמֶּ֑יהָ כִּ֣י ׀ קָרְבַּ֣ן יהוה לֹ֤א הִקְרִיב֙ בְּמֹ֣עֲד֔וֹ חֶטְא֥וֹ יִשָּׂ֖א הָאִ֥ישׁ הַהֽוּא׃ וְכִֽי־יָג֨וּר אִתְּכֶ֜ם גֵּ֗ר וְעָ֤שָׂה* פֶ֙סַח֙ לַיהוה כְּחֻקַּ֥ת הַפֶּ֛סַח וּכְמִשְׁפָּט֖וֹ כֵּ֣ן יַעֲשֶׂ֑ה חֻקָּ֤ה אַחַת֙ יִהְיֶ֣ה לָכֶ֔ם וְלַגֵּ֖ר וּלְאֶזְרַ֥ח הָאָֽרֶץ׃

The service continues with Hagbahah and Gelilah, below.

ON ALL DAYS CONTINUE HERE:

הגבהה וגלילה

The first Torah is raised for all to see. Each person looks at the Torah and recites aloud:

וְזֹאת הַתּוֹרָה אֲשֶׁר שָׂם מֹשֶׁה לִפְנֵי בְּנֵי יִשְׂרָאֵל,[1] עַל פִּי יהוה בְּיַד מֹשֶׁה.[2]

Some add:

עֵץ חַיִּים הִיא לַמַּחֲזִיקִים בָּהּ, וְתֹמְּכֶיהָ מְאֻשָּׁר.[3] דְּרָכֶיהָ דַרְכֵי נֹעַם, וְכָל נְתִיבוֹתֶיהָ שָׁלוֹם.[4] אֹרֶךְ יָמִים בִּימִינָהּ, בִּשְׂמֹאלָהּ עֹשֶׁר וְכָבוֹד.[5] יהוה חָפֵץ לְמַעַן צִדְקוֹ, יַגְדִּיל תּוֹרָה וְיַאְדִּיר.[6]

After the first Torah is wound, tied, and covered, an *oleh* is called to the second Torah.

במדבר כח:יט-כה

וְהִקְרַבְתֶּ֨ם אִשֶּׁ֤ה עֹלָה֙ לַיהוה פָּרִ֧ים בְּנֵי־בָקָ֛ר שְׁנַ֖יִם וְאַ֣יִל אֶחָ֑ד וְשִׁבְעָ֤ה כְבָשִׂים֙ בְּנֵ֣י שָׁנָ֔ה תְּמִימִ֖ם יִהְי֥וּ לָכֶֽם׃ וּמִ֨נְחָתָ֔ם סֹ֖לֶת בְּלוּלָ֣ה בַשָּׁ֑מֶן שְׁלֹשָׁ֨ה עֶשְׂרֹנִ֜ים לַפָּ֗ר וּשְׁנֵ֧י עֶשְׂרֹנִ֛ים לָאַ֖יִל תַּעֲשֽׂוּ׃ עִשָּׂר֤וֹן עִשָּׂרוֹן֙ תַּעֲשֶׂ֔ה לַכֶּ֖בֶשׂ הָאֶחָ֑ד לְשִׁבְעַ֖ת הַכְּבָשִֽׂים׃ וּשְׂעִ֥יר חַטָּ֖את אֶחָ֑ד לְכַפֵּ֖ר עֲלֵיכֶֽם׃ מִלְּבַד֙ עֹלַ֣ת הַבֹּ֔קֶר אֲשֶׁ֖ר לְעֹלַ֣ת הַתָּמִ֑יד תַּעֲשׂ֖וּ אֶת־אֵֽלֶּה׃ כָּאֵ֜לֶּה תַּעֲשׂ֤וּ לַיּוֹם֙ שִׁבְעַ֣ת יָמִ֔ים לֶ֛חֶם אִשֵּׁ֥ה רֵֽיחַ־נִיחֹ֖חַ לַֽיהוה עַל־עוֹלַ֧ת הַתָּמִ֛יד יֵעָשֶׂ֖ה וְנִסְכּֽוֹ׃ וּבַיּוֹם֙ הַשְּׁבִיעִ֔י מִקְרָא־קֹ֖דֶשׁ יִהְיֶ֣ה לָכֶ֑ם כָּל־מְלֶ֥אכֶת עֲבֹדָ֖ה לֹ֥א תַעֲשֽׂוּ׃

בְּדֶרֶךְ רְחֹקָה — *A distant road.* The Sages derive that one need not be far away to qualify for the second *pesach*-offering; it is sufficient for him to be outside of the Temple Courtyard at the time when the first offering was to be brought.

עַל מַצּוֹת ... — *Upon matzos ...* This is the only Pesach law that applies to the second *pesach*-offering. Although matzah and bitter herbs must *saying: Any man among you or your generations, who will be contaminated through a corpse or shall be on a distant road,* shall perform the pesach-offering for HASHEM. In the second month on the fourteenth day in the afternoon shall they perform it; upon matzos* and bitter herbs shall they eat it. They shall not leave of it until morning, nor may they break a bone of it; like the entire decree of the pesach-offering shall they perform it. But the man who was pure and was not on a distant journey and refrained from performing the pesach-offering, that soul shall be cut off from its people, for he had not brought the offering of HASHEM in its appointed time — that man will bear his sin. When a proselyte sojourns among you, he shall perform* a pesach-offering for HASHEM, like the decree of the pesach-offering and its ordinances, so shall he do; the same decree shall apply to you, to the proselyte and to the citizen of the land.*

The service continues with Hagbahah and Gelilah, below.

ON ALL DAYS CONTINUE HERE:

HAGBAHAH AND GELILAH

The first Torah is raised for all to see. Each person looks at the Torah and recites aloud:

This is the Torah that Moses placed before the Children of Israel,[1] upon the command of HASHEM, through Moses' hand.[2]

Some add:

עֵץ *It is a tree of life for those who grasp it, and its supporters are praiseworthy.[3] Its ways are ways of pleasantness and all its paths are peace.[4] Lengthy days are at its right; at its left are wealth and honor.[5] HASHEM desired, for the sake of its [Israel's] righteousness, that the Torah be made great and glorious.[6]*

After the first Torah is wound, tied, and covered, an *oleh* is called to the second Torah.

Numbers 28:19-25

You shall offer a fire-offering, an elevation-offering to HASHEM, two young bulls, one ram, and seven lambs within their first year, unblemished shall they be for you. And their meal-offering shall be fine flour mixed with oil; you shall make it three tenth-ephah for each bull and two tenth-ephah for each ram. One tenth-ephah shall you make for each lamb, of the seven rams. And one he-goat for a sin-offering, to provide you atonement. Aside from the elevation-offering of the morning that is for the continual elevation-offering shall you offer these. Like these shall you offer each day of the seven days, food, a fire-offering, a satisfying aroma to HASHEM; after the continual elevation-offering shall it be made, with its libation. The seventh day shall be a holy convocation for you, you shall not do any laborious work.

(1) *Deuteronomy* 4:44. (2) *Numbers* 9:23. (3) *Proverbs* 3:18. (4) 3:17. (5) 3:16. (6) *Isaiah* 42:21.

be eaten with it, there is no prohibition against labor, and one may have *chametz* in his home, provided he does not eat it with the offering.

וְעָשָׂה — *He shall perform.* A proselyte brings the *pesach*-offering on the day before Pesach, like all other Jews.

חצי קדיש

After the second Torah has been read from, the reader recites Half *Kaddish*.
[The first Torah need not be placed on the *bimah* during *Kaddish.*]

יִתְגַּדַּל וְיִתְקַדַּשׁ שְׁמֵהּ רַבָּא. (.Cong – אָמֵן.) בְּעָלְמָא דִּי בְרָא כִרְעוּתֵהּ. וְיַמְלִיךְ מַלְכוּתֵהּ, בְּחַיֵּיכוֹן וּבְיוֹמֵיכוֹן וּבְחַיֵּי דְכָל בֵּית יִשְׂרָאֵל, בַּעֲגָלָא וּבִזְמַן קָרִיב. וְאִמְרוּ: אָמֵן.

(.Cong – אָמֵן. יְהֵא שְׁמֵהּ רַבָּא מְבָרַךְ לְעָלַם וּלְעָלְמֵי עָלְמַיָּא.)

יְהֵא שְׁמֵהּ רַבָּא מְבָרַךְ לְעָלַם וּלְעָלְמֵי עָלְמַיָּא.

יִתְבָּרַךְ וְיִשְׁתַּבַּח וְיִתְפָּאַר וְיִתְרוֹמַם וְיִתְנַשֵּׂא וְיִתְהַדָּר וְיִתְעַלֶּה וְיִתְהַלָּל שְׁמֵהּ דְּקֻדְשָׁא בְּרִיךְ הוּא (.Cong – בְּרִיךְ הוּא) – לְעֵלָּא מִן כָּל בִּרְכָתָא וְשִׁירָתָא תֻּשְׁבְּחָתָא וְנֶחֱמָתָא, דַּאֲמִירָן בְּעָלְמָא. וְאִמְרוּ: אָמֵן. (.Cong – אָמֵן.)

הגבהה וגלילה

The second Torah Scroll is raised and each person looks at the Torah and recites aloud:

וְזֹאת הַתּוֹרָה אֲשֶׁר שָׂם מֹשֶׁה לִפְנֵי בְּנֵי יִשְׂרָאֵל,[1] עַל פִּי יהוה בְּיַד מֹשֶׁה.[2]

Some add:

עֵץ חַיִּים הִיא לַמַּחֲזִיקִים בָּהּ, וְתֹמְכֶיהָ מְאֻשָּׁר.[3] דְּרָכֶיהָ דַרְכֵי נֹעַם, וְכָל נְתִיבוֹתֶיהָ שָׁלוֹם.[4] אֹרֶךְ יָמִים בִּימִינָהּ, בִּשְׂמֹאלָהּ עֹשֶׁר וְכָבוֹד.[5] יהוה חָפֵץ לְמַעַן צִדְקוֹ, יַגְדִּיל תּוֹרָה וְיַאְדִּיר.[6]

הכנסת ספר תורה

The *chazzan* takes the Torah in his right arm and recites:

יְהַלְלוּ אֶת שֵׁם יהוה, כִּי נִשְׂגָּב שְׁמוֹ לְבַדּוֹ –

Congregation responds:

– הוֹדוֹ עַל אֶרֶץ וְשָׁמָיִם. וַיָּרֶם קֶרֶן לְעַמּוֹ, תְּהִלָּה לְכָל חֲסִידָיו, לִבְנֵי יִשְׂרָאֵל עַם קְרֹבוֹ, הַלְלוּיָהּ.[7]

As the Torah is carried to the Ark, the congregation recites the following psalm.

תהלים כד

לְדָוִד מִזְמוֹר, לַיהוה הָאָרֶץ וּמְלוֹאָהּ, תֵּבֵל וְיֹשְׁבֵי בָהּ. כִּי הוּא עַל יַמִּים יְסָדָהּ, וְעַל נְהָרוֹת יְכוֹנְנֶהָ. מִי יַעֲלֶה בְהַר יהוה, וּמִי יָקוּם בִּמְקוֹם קָדְשׁוֹ. נְקִי כַפַּיִם וּבַר לֵבָב, אֲשֶׁר לֹא נָשָׂא לַשָּׁוְא נַפְשִׁי וְלֹא נִשְׁבַּע לְמִרְמָה. יִשָּׂא בְרָכָה מֵאֵת יהוה, וּצְדָקָה מֵאֱלֹהֵי יִשְׁעוֹ. זֶה דּוֹר דֹּרְשָׁיו, מְבַקְשֵׁי פָנֶיךָ, יַעֲקֹב, סֶלָה. שְׂאוּ שְׁעָרִים רָאשֵׁיכֶם, וְהִנָּשְׂאוּ פִּתְחֵי עוֹלָם, וְיָבוֹא מֶלֶךְ הַכָּבוֹד. מִי זֶה מֶלֶךְ הַכָּבוֹד, יהוה עִזּוּז וְגִבּוֹר, יהוה גִּבּוֹר מִלְחָמָה. שְׂאוּ שְׁעָרִים רָאשֵׁיכֶם, וּשְׂאוּ פִּתְחֵי עוֹלָם, וְיָבֹא מֶלֶךְ הַכָּבוֹד. מִי הוּא זֶה מֶלֶךְ הַכָּבוֹד, יהוה צְבָאוֹת הוּא מֶלֶךְ הַכָּבוֹד, סֶלָה.

HALF KADDISH

After the second Torah has been read from, the reader recites Half *Kaddish.*
[The first Torah need not be placed on the *bimah* during *Kaddish.*]

יִתְגַּדַּל *May His great Name grow exalted and sanctified* (Cong.– *Amen.*) *in the world that He created as He willed. May He give reign to His kingship in your lifetimes and in your days, and in the lifetimes of the entire Family of Israel, swiftly and soon. Now respond: Amen.*

(Cong.– *Amen. May His great Name be blessed forever and ever.*)
May His great Name be blessed forever and ever.

Blessed, praised, glorified, exalted, extolled, mighty, upraised, and lauded be the Name of the Holy One, Blessed is He (Cong.– *Blessed is He*) — *beyond any blessing and song, praise and consolation that are uttered in the world. Now respond: Amen.* (Cong.– *Amen.*)

HAGBAHAH AND GELILAH

The second Torah Scroll is raised and each person looks at the Torah and recites aloud:

This is the Torah that Moses placed before the Children of Israel,[1] upon the command of HASHEM, through Moses' hand.[2]

Some add:

עֵץ *It is a tree of life for those who grasp it, and its supporters are praiseworthy.[3] Its ways are ways of pleasantness and all its paths are peace.[4] Lengthy days are at its right; at its left are wealth and honor.[5] HASHEM desired, for the sake of its [Israel's] righteousness, that the Torah be made great and glorious.[6]*

RETURNING THE TORAH

The *chazzan* takes the Torah in his right arm and recites:

**Let them praise the Name of HASHEM,
for His Name alone will have been exalted —**

Congregation responds:

— His glory is above earth and heaven. And He will have exalted the pride of His people, causing praise for all His devout ones, for the Children of Israel, His intimate people. Halleluyah![7]

As the Torah is carried to the Ark, the congregation recites the following (*Psalm* 24).

לְדָוִד *Of David a psalm. HASHEM's is the earth and its fullness, the inhabited land and those who dwell in it. For He founded it upon seas, and established it upon rivers. Who may ascend the mountain of HASHEM, and who may stand in the place of His sanctity? One with clean hands and pure heart, who has not sworn in vain by My soul and has not sworn deceitfully. He will receive a blessing from HASHEM and just kindness from the God of his salvation. This is the generation of those who seek Him, those who strive for Your Presence — Jacob, Selah. Raise up your heads, O gates, and be uplifted, you everlasting entrances, so that the King of Glory may enter. Who is this King of Glory? — HASHEM, the mighty and strong, HASHEM, the strong in battle. Raise up your heads, O gates, and raise up, you everlasting entrances, so that the King of Glory may enter. Who then is the King of Glory? HASHEM, Master of Legions, He is the King of Glory. Selah!*

---

(1) *Deut.* 4:44. (2) *Num.* 9:23. (3) *Prov.* 3:18. (4) 3:17. (5) 3:16. (6) *Isaiah* 42:21. (7) *Psalms* 148:13-14.

As the Torah is placed into the Ark, the congregation recites the following verses:

וּבְנֻחֹה יֹאמַר, שׁוּבָה יהוה רִבְבוֹת אַלְפֵי יִשְׂרָאֵל.[1] קוּמָה יהוה לִמְנוּחָתֶךָ, אַתָּה וַאֲרוֹן עֻזֶּךָ. כֹּהֲנֶיךָ יִלְבְּשׁוּ צֶדֶק, וַחֲסִידֶיךָ יְרַנֵּנוּ. בַּעֲבוּר דָּוִד עַבְדֶּךָ, אַל תָּשֵׁב פְּנֵי מְשִׁיחֶךָ.[2] כִּי לֶקַח טוֹב נָתַתִּי לָכֶם, תּוֹרָתִי אַל תַּעֲזֹבוּ.[3] ❖ עֵץ חַיִּים הִיא לַמַּחֲזִיקִים בָּהּ, וְתֹמְכֶיהָ מְאֻשָּׁר.[4] דְּרָכֶיהָ דַרְכֵי נֹעַם, וְכָל נְתִיבוֹתֶיהָ שָׁלוֹם.[5] הֲשִׁיבֵנוּ יהוה אֵלֶיךָ וְנָשׁוּבָה, חַדֵּשׁ יָמֵינוּ כְּקֶדֶם.[6]

אַשְׁרֵי יוֹשְׁבֵי בֵיתֶךָ, עוֹד יְהַלְלוּךָ סֶּלָה.[7] אַשְׁרֵי הָעָם שֶׁכָּכָה לּוֹ, אַשְׁרֵי הָעָם שֶׁיהוה אֱלֹהָיו.[8]

תהלים קמה

תְּהִלָּה לְדָוִד,

אֲרוֹמִמְךָ אֱלוֹהַי הַמֶּלֶךְ, וַאֲבָרְכָה שִׁמְךָ לְעוֹלָם וָעֶד.
בְּכָל יוֹם אֲבָרְכֶךָּ, וַאֲהַלְלָה שִׁמְךָ לְעוֹלָם וָעֶד.
גָּדוֹל יהוה וּמְהֻלָּל מְאֹד, וְלִגְדֻלָּתוֹ אֵין חֵקֶר.
דּוֹר לְדוֹר יְשַׁבַּח מַעֲשֶׂיךָ, וּגְבוּרֹתֶיךָ יַגִּידוּ.
הֲדַר כְּבוֹד הוֹדֶךָ, וְדִבְרֵי נִפְלְאֹתֶיךָ אָשִׂיחָה.
וֶעֱזוּז נוֹרְאוֹתֶיךָ יֹאמֵרוּ, וּגְדוּלָּתְךָ אֲסַפְּרֶנָּה.
זֵכֶר רַב טוּבְךָ יַבִּיעוּ, וְצִדְקָתְךָ יְרַנֵּנוּ.
חַנּוּן וְרַחוּם יהוה, אֶרֶךְ אַפַּיִם וּגְדָל חָסֶד.
טוֹב יהוה לַכֹּל, וְרַחֲמָיו עַל כָּל מַעֲשָׂיו.
יוֹדוּךָ יהוה כָּל מַעֲשֶׂיךָ, וַחֲסִידֶיךָ יְבָרְכוּכָה.
כְּבוֹד מַלְכוּתְךָ יֹאמֵרוּ, וּגְבוּרָתְךָ יְדַבֵּרוּ.
לְהוֹדִיעַ לִבְנֵי הָאָדָם גְּבוּרֹתָיו, וּכְבוֹד הֲדַר מַלְכוּתוֹ.
מַלְכוּתְךָ מַלְכוּת כָּל עֹלָמִים, וּמֶמְשַׁלְתְּךָ בְּכָל דּוֹר וָדֹר.
סוֹמֵךְ יהוה לְכָל הַנֹּפְלִים, וְזוֹקֵף לְכָל הַכְּפוּפִים.
עֵינֵי כֹל אֵלֶיךָ יְשַׂבֵּרוּ, וְאַתָּה נוֹתֵן לָהֶם אֶת אָכְלָם בְּעִתּוֹ.

While reciting the verse פּוֹתֵחַ, concentrate intently on its meaning.

פּוֹתֵחַ אֶת יָדֶךָ,
וּמַשְׂבִּיעַ לְכָל חַי רָצוֹן.
צַדִּיק יהוה בְּכָל דְּרָכָיו, וְחָסִיד בְּכָל מַעֲשָׂיו.

(1) *Numbers* 10:36. (2) *Psalms* 132:8-10. (3) *Proverbs* 4:2. (4) 3:18.
(5) 3:17. (6) *Lamentations* 5:21. (7) *Psalms* 84:5. (8) 144:15.

As the Torah is placed into the Ark, the congregation recites the following verses:

וּבְנֻחֹה *And when it rested he would say, 'Return,* HASHEM, *to the myriad thousands of Israel.'*[1] *Arise,* HASHEM, *to Your resting place, You and the Ark of Your strength. Let Your priests be clothed in righteousness, and Your devout ones will sing joyously. For the sake of David, Your servant, turn not away the face of Your anointed.*[2] *For I have given you a good teaching, do not forsake My Torah.*[3] Chazzan– *It is a tree of life for those who grasp it, and its supporters are praiseworthy.*[4] *Its ways are ways of pleasantness and all its paths are peace.*[5] *Bring us back to You,* HASHEM, *and we shall return, renew our days as of old.*[6]

אַשְׁרֵי *Praiseworthy are those who dwell in Your house; may they always praise You, Selah!*[7] *Praiseworthy is the people for whom this is so, praiseworthy is the people whose God is* HASHEM.[8]

Psalm 145 *A psalm of praise by David:*

א *I will exalt You, my God the King,*
and I will bless Your Name forever and ever.
ב *Every day I will bless You,*
and I will laud Your Name forever and ever.
ג HASHEM *is great and exceedingly lauded,*
and His greatness is beyond investigation.
ד *Each generation will praise Your deeds to the next*
and of Your mighty deeds they will tell.
ה *The splendrous glory of Your power*
and Your wondrous deeds I shall discuss.
ו *And of Your awesome power they will speak,*
and Your greatness I shall relate.
ז *A recollection of Your abundant goodness they will utter*
and of Your righteousness they will sing exultantly.
ח *Gracious and merciful is* HASHEM,
slow to anger, and great in [bestowing] kindness.
ט HASHEM *is good to all; His mercies are on all His works.*
י *All Your works shall thank You,* HASHEM,
and Your devout ones will bless You.
כ *Of the glory of Your kingdom they will speak,*
and of Your power they will tell;
ל *To inform human beings of His mighty deeds,*
and the glorious splendor of His kingdom.
מ *Your kingdom is a kingdom spanning all eternities,*
and Your dominion is throughout every generation.
ס HASHEM *supports all the fallen ones and straightens all the bent.*
ע *The eyes of all look to You with hope*
and You give them their food in its proper time;
פ *You open Your hand,*
and satisfy the desire of every living thing.

While reciting the verse, 'You open . . .' concentrate intently on its meaning.

צ *Righteous is* HASHEM *in all His ways*
and magnanimous in all His deeds.

קָרוֹב יהוה לְכָל קֹרְאָיו, לְכֹל אֲשֶׁר יִקְרָאֻהוּ בֶאֱמֶת.
רְצוֹן יְרֵאָיו יַעֲשֶׂה, וְאֶת שַׁוְעָתָם יִשְׁמַע וְיוֹשִׁיעֵם.
שׁוֹמֵר יהוה אֶת כָּל אֹהֲבָיו, וְאֵת כָּל הָרְשָׁעִים יַשְׁמִיד.
❖ תְּהִלַּת יהוה יְדַבֶּר פִּי, וִיבָרֵךְ כָּל בָּשָׂר שֵׁם קָדְשׁוֹ לְעוֹלָם וָעֶד.
וַאֲנַחְנוּ נְבָרֵךְ יָהּ, מֵעַתָּה וְעַד עוֹלָם, הַלְלוּיָהּ.[1]

The primary part of וּבָא לְצִיּוֹן is the *Kedushah* recited by the angels. These verses are presented in bold type and it is preferable that the congregation recite them aloud and in unison. However, the interpretive translation in Aramaic (which follows the verses in bold type) should be recited softly.

וּבָא לְצִיּוֹן גּוֹאֵל, וּלְשָׁבֵי פֶשַׁע בְּיַעֲקֹב, נְאֻם יהוה. וַאֲנִי, זֹאת בְּרִיתִי אוֹתָם, אָמַר יהוה, רוּחִי אֲשֶׁר עָלֶיךָ, וּדְבָרַי אֲשֶׁר שַׂמְתִּי בְּפִיךָ, לֹא יָמוּשׁוּ מִפִּיךָ וּמִפִּי זַרְעֲךָ וּמִפִּי זֶרַע זַרְעֲךָ, אָמַר יהוה, מֵעַתָּה וְעַד עוֹלָם:[2] ❖ וְאַתָּה קָדוֹשׁ יוֹשֵׁב תְּהִלּוֹת יִשְׂרָאֵל.[3]

וְקָרָא זֶה אֶל זֶה וְאָמַר:

קָדוֹשׁ, קָדוֹשׁ, קָדוֹשׁ יהוה צְבָאוֹת, מְלֹא כָל הָאָרֶץ כְּבוֹדוֹ.[4]

וּמְקַבְּלִין דֵּין מִן דֵּין וְאָמְרִין:
קַדִּישׁ בִּשְׁמֵי מְרוֹמָא עִלָּאָה בֵּית שְׁכִינְתֵּהּ,
קַדִּישׁ עַל אַרְעָא עוֹבַד גְּבוּרְתֵּהּ,
קַדִּישׁ לְעָלַם וּלְעָלְמֵי עָלְמַיָּא, יהוה צְבָאוֹת,
מַלְיָא כָל אַרְעָא זִיו יְקָרֵהּ.[5]

❖ וַתִּשָּׂאֵנִי רוּחַ, וָאֶשְׁמַע אַחֲרַי קוֹל רַעַשׁ גָּדוֹל:

בָּרוּךְ כְּבוֹד יהוה מִמְּקוֹמוֹ.[6]

וּנְטָלַתְנִי רוּחָא, וְשִׁמְעֵת בַּתְרַי קָל זִיעַ סַגִּיא
דִּמְשַׁבְּחִין וְאָמְרִין:
בְּרִיךְ יְקָרָא דַיהוה מֵאֲתַר בֵּית שְׁכִינְתֵּהּ.[7]

יהוה יִמְלֹךְ לְעֹלָם וָעֶד.[8]

יהוה מַלְכוּתֵהּ קָאֵם לְעָלַם וּלְעָלְמֵי עָלְמַיָּא.[9]

יהוה אֱלֹהֵי אַבְרָהָם יִצְחָק וְיִשְׂרָאֵל אֲבֹתֵינוּ, שָׁמְרָה זֹּאת לְעוֹלָם, לְיֵצֶר מַחְשְׁבוֹת לְבַב עַמֶּךָ, וְהָכֵן לְבָבָם אֵלֶיךָ.[10] וְהוּא רַחוּם, יְכַפֵּר עָוֹן וְלֹא יַשְׁחִית, וְהִרְבָּה לְהָשִׁיב אַפּוֹ, וְלֹא יָעִיר כָּל חֲמָתוֹ.[11] כִּי אַתָּה אֲדֹנָי טוֹב וְסַלָּח, וְרַב חֶסֶד לְכָל קֹרְאֶיךָ.[12] צִדְקָתְךָ צֶדֶק לְעוֹלָם, וְתוֹרָתְךָ אֱמֶת.[13] תִּתֵּן אֱמֶת לְיַעֲקֹב, חֶסֶד לְאַבְרָהָם, אֲשֶׁר נִשְׁבַּעְתָּ לַאֲבֹתֵינוּ מִימֵי קֶדֶם.[14] בָּרוּךְ אֲדֹנָי יוֹם יוֹם יַעֲמָס לָנוּ, הָאֵל יְשׁוּעָתֵנוּ סֶלָה.[15]

---

(1) *Psalms* 115:18. (2) *Isaiah* 59:20-21. (3) *Psalms* 22:4. (4) *Isaiah* 6:3. (5) *Targum Yonasan.* (6) *Ezekiel* 3:12. (7) *Targum Yonasan.* (8) *Exodus* 15:18. (9) *Targum Onkelos.* (10) *I Chronicles* 29:18. (11) *Psalms* 78:38. (12) 86:5. (13) 119:142. (14) *Micah* 7:20. (15) *Psalms* 68:20.

ק *HASHEM is close to all who call upon Him —*
to all who call upon Him sincerely.
ר *The will of those who fear Him He will do;*
and their cry He will hear, and save them.
ש *HASHEM protects all who love Him;*
but all the wicked He will destroy.
ת Chazzan– *May my mouth declare the praise of HASHEM*
and may all flesh bless His Holy Name forever and ever.
We will bless God from this time and forever, Halleluyah![1]

The primary part of וּבָא לְצִיּוֹן, *'A redeemer shall come . . .',* is the *Kedushah* recited by the angels. These verses are presented in bold type and it is preferable that the congregation recite them aloud and in unison. However, the interpretive translation in Aramaic (which follows the verses in bold type) should be recited softly.

וּבָא לְצִיּוֹן *'A redeemer shall come to Zion and to those of Jacob who repent from willful sin,' the words of HASHEM. 'And as for Me, this is My covenant with them,' said HASHEM, 'My spirit that is upon you and My words that I have placed in your mouth shall not be withdrawn from your mouth, nor from the mouth of your offspring, nor from the mouth of your offspring's offspring,' said HASHEM, 'from this moment and forever.'*[2] Chazzan– *You are the Holy One, enthroned upon the praises of Israel.*[3] *And one [angel] will call another and say:*

'Holy, holy, holy is HASHEM, Master of Legions,
the whole world is filled with His glory.'[4]

And they receive permission from one another and say:
'Holy in the most exalted heaven, the abode of His Presence;
holy on earth, product of His strength;
holy forever and ever is HASHEM, Master of Legions —
the entire world is filled with the radiance of His glory.'[5]
Chazzan– *And a wind lifted me; and I heard behind me*
the sound of a great noise:

'Blessed is the glory of HASHEM from His place.'[6]

And a wind lifted me and I heard behind me the sound
of the powerful movement of those who praised saying:
'Blessed is the honor of HASHEM
from the place of the abode of His Presence.'[7]

HASHEM shall reign for all eternity.[8]

HASHEM — His kingdom is established forever and ever.[9]

HASHEM, God of Abraham, Isaac, and Israel, our forefathers, may You preserve this forever as the realization of the thoughts in Your people's heart, and may You direct their heart to You.[10] *He, the Merciful One, is forgiving of iniquity and does not destroy; frequently He withdraws His anger, not arousing His entire rage.*[11] *For You, my Lord, are good and forgiving, and abundantly kind to all who call upon You.*[12] *Your righteousness remains righteous forever, and Your Torah is truth.*[13] *Grant truth to Jacob, kindness to Abraham, as You swore to our forefathers from ancient times.*[14] *Blessed is my Lord for every single day, He burdens us with blessings, the God of our salvation, Selah.*[15]

יהוה צְבָאוֹת עִמָּנוּ, מִשְׂגָּב לָנוּ אֱלֹהֵי יַעֲקֹב סֶלָה.[1] יהוה צְבָאוֹת, אַשְׁרֵי אָדָם בֹּטֵחַ בָּךְ.[2] יהוה הוֹשִׁיעָה, הַמֶּלֶךְ יַעֲנֵנוּ בְיוֹם קָרְאֵנוּ.[3]

בָּרוּךְ הוּא אֱלֹהֵינוּ שֶׁבְּרָאָנוּ לִכְבוֹדוֹ, וְהִבְדִּילָנוּ מִן הַתּוֹעִים, וְנָתַן לָנוּ תּוֹרַת אֱמֶת, וְחַיֵּי עוֹלָם נָטַע בְּתוֹכֵנוּ. הוּא יִפְתַּח לִבֵּנוּ בְּתוֹרָתוֹ, וְיָשֵׂם בְּלִבֵּנוּ אַהֲבָתוֹ וְיִרְאָתוֹ וְלַעֲשׂוֹת רְצוֹנוֹ וּלְעָבְדוֹ בְּלֵבָב שָׁלֵם, לְמַעַן לֹא נִיגַע לָרִיק, וְלֹא נֵלֵד לַבֶּהָלָה.[4]

יְהִי רָצוֹן מִלְּפָנֶיךָ יהוה אֱלֹהֵינוּ וֵאלֹהֵי אֲבוֹתֵינוּ, שֶׁנִּשְׁמֹר חֻקֶּיךָ בָּעוֹלָם הַזֶּה, וְנִזְכֶּה וְנִחְיֶה וְנִרְאֶה וְנִירַשׁ טוֹבָה וּבְרָכָה לִשְׁנֵי יְמוֹת הַמָּשִׁיחַ וּלְחַיֵּי הָעוֹלָם הַבָּא. לְמַעַן יְזַמֶּרְךָ כָבוֹד וְלֹא יִדֹּם, יהוה אֱלֹהַי לְעוֹלָם אוֹדֶךָּ.[5] בָּרוּךְ הַגֶּבֶר אֲשֶׁר יִבְטַח בַּיהוה, וְהָיָה יהוה מִבְטַחוֹ.[6] בִּטְחוּ בַיהוה עֲדֵי עַד, כִּי בְּיָהּ יהוה צוּר עוֹלָמִים.[7] ❖ וְיִבְטְחוּ בְךָ יוֹדְעֵי שְׁמֶךָ, כִּי לֹא עָזַבְתָּ דֹּרְשֶׁיךָ, יהוה.[8] יהוה חָפֵץ לְמַעַן צִדְקוֹ, יַגְדִּיל תּוֹרָה וְיַאְדִּיר.[9]

Chazzan recites חֲצִי קַדִּישׁ.

יִתְגַּדַּל וְיִתְקַדַּשׁ שְׁמֵהּ רַבָּא. (.Cong – אָמֵן.) בְּעָלְמָא דִּי בְרָא כִרְעוּתֵהּ. וְיַמְלִיךְ מַלְכוּתֵהּ, בְּחַיֵּיכוֹן וּבְיוֹמֵיכוֹן וּבְחַיֵּי דְכָל בֵּית יִשְׂרָאֵל, בַּעֲגָלָא וּבִזְמַן קָרִיב. וְאִמְרוּ: אָמֵן.

(.Cong – אָמֵן. יְהֵא שְׁמֵהּ רַבָּא מְבָרַךְ לְעָלַם וּלְעָלְמֵי עָלְמַיָּא.)

יְהֵא שְׁמֵהּ רַבָּא מְבָרַךְ לְעָלַם וּלְעָלְמֵי עָלְמַיָּא.

יִתְבָּרַךְ וְיִשְׁתַּבַּח וְיִתְפָּאַר וְיִתְרוֹמַם וְיִתְנַשֵּׂא וְיִתְהַדָּר וְיִתְעַלֶּה וְיִתְהַלָּל שְׁמֵהּ דְּקֻדְשָׁא בְּרִיךְ הוּא (.Cong – בְּרִיךְ הוּא) – לְעֵלָּא מִן כָּל בִּרְכָתָא וְשִׁירָתָא תֻּשְׁבְּחָתָא וְנֶחֱמָתָא, דַּאֲמִירָן בְּעָלְמָא. וְאִמְרוּ: אָמֵן. (.Cong – אָמֵן.)

מוסף לחול המועד

Take three steps backward, then three steps forward. Remain standing with the feet together while reciting *Shemoneh Esrei*. Recite it with quiet devotion and without interruption, verbal or otherwise. Although its recitation should not be audible to others, one must pray loudly enough to hear himself.

כִּי שֵׁם יהוה אֶקְרָא, הָבוּ גֹדֶל לֵאלֹהֵינוּ.[10]

אֲדֹנָי שְׂפָתַי תִּפְתָּח, וּפִי יַגִּיד תְּהִלָּתֶךָ.[11]

אבות

Bend the knees at בָּרוּךְ; bow at אַתָּה; straighten up at 'ה.

בָּרוּךְ אַתָּה יהוה אֱלֹהֵינוּ וֵאלֹהֵי אֲבוֹתֵינוּ, אֱלֹהֵי אַבְרָהָם, אֱלֹהֵי יִצְחָק, וֵאלֹהֵי יַעֲקֹב, הָאֵל הַגָּדוֹל הַגִּבּוֹר וְהַנּוֹרָא, אֵל עֶלְיוֹן, גּוֹמֵל חֲסָדִים טוֹבִים וְקוֹנֵה הַכֹּל, וְזוֹכֵר חַסְדֵי אָבוֹת, וּמֵבִיא גוֹאֵל לִבְנֵי בְנֵיהֶם, לְמַעַן שְׁמוֹ בְּאַהֲבָה. מֶלֶךְ עוֹזֵר וּמוֹשִׁיעַ וּמָגֵן.

Bend the knees at בָּרוּךְ; bow at אַתָּה; straighten up at 'ה.

בָּרוּךְ אַתָּה יהוה, מָגֵן אַבְרָהָם.

HASHEM, Master of Legions, is with us, a stronghold for us is the God of Jacob, Selah.[1] *HASHEM, Master of Legions, praiseworthy is the man who trusts in You.*[2] *HASHEM, save! May the King answer us on the day we call.*[3]

Blessed is He, our God, Who created us for His glory, separated us from those who stray, gave us the Torah of truth and implanted eternal life within us. May He open our heart through His Torah and imbue our heart with love and awe of Him and that we may do His will and serve Him wholeheartedly, so that we do not struggle in vain nor produce for futility.[4]

May it be Your will, HASHEM, our God and the God of our forefathers, that we observe Your decrees in This World, and merit that we live and see and inherit goodness and blessing in the years of Messianic times and for the life of the World to Come. So that my soul might sing to You and not be stilled, HASHEM, my God, forever will I thank You.[5] *Blessed is the man who trusts in HASHEM, then HASHEM will be his security.*[6] *Trust in HASHEM forever, for in God, HASHEM, is the strength of the worlds.*[7] Chazzan– *Those knowing Your Name will trust in You, and You forsake not those Who seek You, HASHEM.*[8] *HASHEM desired, for the sake of its [Israel's] righteousness, that the Torah be made great and glorious.*[9]

Chazzan recites Half-*Kaddish.*

יִתְגַּדַּל *May His great Name grow exalted and sanctified* (Cong.– *Amen.*) *in the world that He created as He willed. May He give reign to His kingship in your lifetimes and in your days, and in the lifetimes of the entire Family of Israel, swiftly and soon. Now respond: Amen.*

(Cong.– *Amen. May His great Name be blessed forever and ever.*)

May His great Name be blessed forever and ever.

Blessed, praised, glorified, exalted, extolled, mighty, upraised, and lauded be the Name of the Holy One, Blessed is He (Cong.– *Blessed is He*) — *beyond any blessing and song, praise and consolation that are uttered in the world. Now respond: Amen.* (Cong.– *Amen.*)

MUSSAF FOR CHOL HAMOED

Take three steps backward, then three steps forward. Remain standing with the feet together while reciting *Shemoneh Esrei.* Recite it with quiet devotion and without interruption, verbal or otherwise. Although its recitation should not be audible to others, one must pray loudly enough to hear himself.

When I call out the Name of HASHEM, ascribe greatness to our God.[10]

My Lord, open my lips, that my mouth may declare Your praise.[11]

PATRIARCHS

Bend the knees at *'Blessed'*; bow at *'You'*; straighten up at *'HASHEM.'*

בָּרוּךְ *Blessed are You, HASHEM, our God and the God of our forefathers, God of Abraham, God of Isaac, and God of Jacob; the great, mighty, and awesome God, the supreme God, Who bestows beneficial kindnesses and creates everything, Who recalls the kindnesses of the Patriarchs and brings a Redeemer to their children's children, for His Name's sake, with love. O King, Helper, Savior, and Shield.*

Bend the knees at *'Blessed'*; bow at *'You'*; straighten up at *'HASHEM.'*

Blessed are You, HASHEM, Shield of Abraham.

---

(1) *Psalms* 46:8. (2) 84:13. (3) 20:10. (4) Cf. *Isaiah* 65:23. (5) *Psalms* 30:13. (6) *Jeremiah* 17:7. (7) *Isaiah* 26:4. (8) *Psalms* 9:11. (9) *Isaiah* 42:21. (10) *Deuteronomy* 32:3. (11) *Psalms* 51:17.

גבורות

אַתָּה גִּבּוֹר לְעוֹלָם אֲדֹנָי, מְחַיֵּה מֵתִים אַתָּה, רַב לְהוֹשִׁיעַ. מְכַלְכֵּל חַיִּים בְּחֶסֶד, מְחַיֵּה מֵתִים בְּרַחֲמִים רַבִּים, סוֹמֵךְ נוֹפְלִים, וְרוֹפֵא חוֹלִים, וּמַתִּיר אֲסוּרִים, וּמְקַיֵּם אֱמוּנָתוֹ לִישֵׁנֵי עָפָר. מִי כָמוֹךָ בַּעַל גְּבוּרוֹת, וּמִי דּוֹמֶה לָּךְ, מֶלֶךְ מֵמִית וּמְחַיֶּה וּמַצְמִיחַ יְשׁוּעָה. וְנֶאֱמָן אַתָּה לְהַחֲיוֹת מֵתִים. בָּרוּךְ אַתָּה יהוה, מְחַיֵּה הַמֵּתִים.

During the *chazzan's* repetition, *Kedushah* (below) is recited at this point.

קדושת השם

INDIVIDUALS RECITE:

אַתָּה קָדוֹשׁ וְשִׁמְךָ קָדוֹשׁ, וּקְדוֹשִׁים בְּכָל יוֹם יְהַלְלוּךָ סֶּלָה. בָּרוּךְ אַתָּה יהוה, הָאֵל הַקָּדוֹשׁ.

CHAZZAN RECITES DURING HIS REPETITION:

לְדוֹר וָדוֹר נַגִּיד גָּדְלֶךָ וּלְנֵצַח נְצָחִים קְדֻשָּׁתְךָ נַקְדִּישׁ, וְשִׁבְחֲךָ אֱלֹהֵינוּ מִפִּינוּ לֹא יָמוּשׁ לְעוֹלָם וָעֶד, כִּי אֵל מֶלֶךְ גָּדוֹל וְקָדוֹשׁ אָתָּה. בָּרוּךְ אַתָּה יהוה, הָאֵל הַקָּדוֹשׁ.

קדושת היום

אַתָּה בְחַרְתָּנוּ מִכָּל הָעַמִּים, אָהַבְתָּ אוֹתָנוּ, וְרָצִיתָ בָּנוּ, וְרוֹמַמְתָּנוּ מִכָּל הַלְּשׁוֹנוֹת, וְקִדַּשְׁתָּנוּ בְּמִצְוֹתֶיךָ, וְקֵרַבְתָּנוּ מַלְכֵּנוּ לַעֲבוֹדָתֶךָ, וְשִׁמְךָ הַגָּדוֹל וְהַקָּדוֹשׁ עָלֵינוּ קָרָאתָ.

וַתִּתֶּן לָנוּ יהוה אֱלֹהֵינוּ בְּאַהֲבָה מוֹעֲדִים לְשִׂמְחָה חַגִּים וּזְמַנִּים לְשָׂשׂוֹן, אֶת יוֹם חַג הַמַּצּוֹת הַזֶּה, זְמַן חֵרוּתֵנוּ מִקְרָא קֹדֶשׁ, זֵכֶר לִיצִיאַת מִצְרָיִם.

קדושה

When reciting *Kedushah,* one must stand with his feet together and avoid any interruptions. One should rise on his toes when saying the words קָדוֹשׁ, קָדוֹשׁ, קָדוֹשׁ; בָּרוּךְ (of בָּרוּךְ כְּבוֹד); and יִמְלֹךְ.

Cong. then *Chazzan* – **נְקַדֵּשׁ** אֶת שִׁמְךָ בָּעוֹלָם, כְּשֵׁם שֶׁמַּקְדִּישִׁים אוֹתוֹ בִּשְׁמֵי מָרוֹם, כַּכָּתוּב עַל יַד נְבִיאֶךָ, וְקָרָא זֶה אֶל זֶה וְאָמַר:

All – קָדוֹשׁ קָדוֹשׁ קָדוֹשׁ יהוה צְבָאוֹת, מְלֹא כָל הָאָרֶץ כְּבוֹדוֹ.[1]

Chazzan – לְעֻמָּתָם בָּרוּךְ יֹאמֵרוּ:

All – בָּרוּךְ כְּבוֹד יהוה, מִמְּקוֹמוֹ.[2]

Chazzan – וּבְדִבְרֵי קָדְשְׁךָ כָּתוּב לֵאמֹר:

All – יִמְלֹךְ יהוה לְעוֹלָם, אֱלֹהַיִךְ צִיּוֹן לְדֹר וָדֹר, הַלְלוּיָהּ.[3]

Chazzan continues לְדוֹר וָדוֹר (above).

GOD'S MIGHT

אַתָּה *You are eternally mighty, my Lord, the Resuscitator of the dead are You; abundantly able to save. He sustains the living with kindness, resuscitates the dead with abundant mercy, supports the fallen, heals the sick, releases the confined, and maintains His faith to those asleep in the dust. Who is like You, O Master of mighty deeds, and who is comparable to You, O King Who causes death and restores life and makes salvation sprout! And You are faithful to resuscitate the dead. Blessed are You,* HASHEM, *Who resuscitates the dead.*

During the *chazzan's* repetition, *Kedushah* (below) is recited at this point.

HOLINESS OF GOD'S NAME

INDIVIDUALS RECITE:

אַתָּה *You are holy and Your Name is holy, and holy ones praise You every day, forever. Blessed are You,* HASHEM, *the holy God.*

CHAZZAN RECITES DURING HIS REPETITION:

לְדוֹר *From generation to generation we shall relate Your greatness and for infinite eternities we shall proclaim Your holiness. Your praise, our God, shall not leave our mouth forever and ever, for You, O God, are a great and holy King. Blessed are You,* HASHEM, *the holy God.*

SANCTIFICATION OF THE DAY

אַתָּה בְחַרְתָּנוּ *You have chosen us from all the peoples; You loved us and found favor in us; You exalted us above all the tongues and You sanctified us with Your commandments. You drew us close, our King, to Your service and proclaimed Your great and Holy Name upon us.*

וַתִּתֶּן לָנוּ *And You gave us,* HASHEM, *our God, with love, appointed festivals for gladness, Festivals and times for joy, this day of the Festival of Matzos, the time of our freedom, a holy convocation, a memorial of the Exodus from Egypt.*

KEDUSHAH

When reciting *Kedushah*, one must stand with his feet together and avoid any interruptions. One should rise on his toes when saying the words *Holy, holy, holy; Blessed is;* and *HASHEM shall reign.*

Cong. then Chazzan – **נְקַדֵּשׁ** *We shall sanctify Your Name in this world, just as they sanctify it in heaven above, as it is written by Your prophet, "And one [angel] will call another and say:*

All – *'Holy, holy, holy is* HASHEM, *Master of Legions, the whole world is filled with His glory.'"*[1]

Chazzan – *Those facing them say 'Blessed':*

All – *'Blessed is the glory of* HASHEM *from His place.'*[2]

Chazzan – *And in Your holy Writings the following is written:*

All – *'*HASHEM *shall reign forever — your God, O Zion — from generation to generation, Halleluyah!'*[3]

Chazzan continues לְדוֹר וָדוֹר, *From generation to generation . . .* (above).

---

(1) *Isaiah* 6:3. (2) *Ezekiel* 3:12. (3) *Psalms* 146:10.

וּמִפְּנֵי חֲטָאֵינוּ גָּלִינוּ מֵאַרְצֵנוּ, וְנִתְרַחַקְנוּ מֵעַל אַדְמָתֵנוּ. וְאֵין אֲנַחְנוּ יְכוֹלִים לַעֲלוֹת וְלֵרָאוֹת וּלְהִשְׁתַּחֲווֹת לְפָנֶיךָ, וְלַעֲשׂוֹת חוֹבוֹתֵינוּ בְּבֵית בְּחִירָתֶךָ, בַּבַּיִת הַגָּדוֹל וְהַקָּדוֹשׁ שֶׁנִּקְרָא שִׁמְךָ עָלָיו, מִפְּנֵי הַיָּד שֶׁנִּשְׁתַּלְּחָה בְּמִקְדָּשֶׁךָ. יְהִי רָצוֹן מִלְּפָנֶיךָ יהוה אֱלֹהֵינוּ וֵאלֹהֵי אֲבוֹתֵינוּ, מֶלֶךְ רַחֲמָן, שֶׁתָּשׁוּב וּתְרַחֵם עָלֵינוּ וְעַל מִקְדָּשְׁךָ בְּרַחֲמֶיךָ הָרַבִּים, וְתִבְנֵהוּ מְהֵרָה וּתְגַדֵּל כְּבוֹדוֹ. אָבִינוּ מַלְכֵּנוּ, גַּלֵּה כְּבוֹד מַלְכוּתְךָ עָלֵינוּ מְהֵרָה, וְהוֹפַע וְהִנָּשֵׂא עָלֵינוּ לְעֵינֵי כָּל חָי. וְקָרֵב פְּזוּרֵינוּ מִבֵּין הַגּוֹיִם, וּנְפוּצוֹתֵינוּ כַּנֵּס מִיַּרְכְּתֵי אָרֶץ. וַהֲבִיאֵנוּ לְצִיּוֹן עִירְךָ בְּרִנָּה, וְלִירוּשָׁלַיִם בֵּית מִקְדָּשְׁךָ בְּשִׂמְחַת עוֹלָם. וְשָׁם נַעֲשֶׂה לְפָנֶיךָ אֶת קָרְבְּנוֹת חוֹבוֹתֵינוּ, תְּמִידִים כְּסִדְרָם, וּמוּסָפִים כְּהִלְכָתָם. וְאֶת מוּסַף יוֹם חַג הַמַּצּוֹת הַזֶּה נַעֲשֶׂה וְנַקְרִיב לְפָנֶיךָ בְּאַהֲבָה כְּמִצְוַת רְצוֹנֶךָ, כְּמוֹ שֶׁכָּתַבְתָּ עָלֵינוּ בְּתוֹרָתֶךָ, עַל יְדֵי מֹשֶׁה עַבְדֶּךָ, מִפִּי כְבוֹדֶךָ כָּאָמוּר:

וְהִקְרַבְתֶּם אִשֶּׁה עֹלָה לַיהוה, פָּרִים בְּנֵי בָקָר שְׁנַיִם, וְאַיִל אֶחָד, וְשִׁבְעָה כְבָשִׂים בְּנֵי שָׁנָה, תְּמִימִים יִהְיוּ לָכֶם.[1] וּמִנְחָתָם וְנִסְכֵּיהֶם כִּמְדֻבָּר, שְׁלֹשָׁה עֶשְׂרֹנִים לַפָּר, וּשְׁנֵי עֶשְׂרֹנִים לָאָיִל, וְעִשָּׂרוֹן לַכֶּבֶשׂ, וְיַיִן כְּנִסְכּוֹ. וְשָׂעִיר לְכַפֵּר, וּשְׁנֵי תְמִידִים כְּהִלְכָתָם.

אֱלֹהֵינוּ וֵאלֹהֵי אֲבוֹתֵינוּ, מֶלֶךְ רַחֲמָן רַחֵם עָלֵינוּ, טוֹב וּמֵטִיב הִדָּרֶשׁ לָנוּ, שׁוּבָה אֵלֵינוּ בַּהֲמוֹן רַחֲמֶיךָ, בִּגְלַל אָבוֹת שֶׁעָשׂוּ רְצוֹנֶךָ. בְּנֵה בֵיתְךָ כְּבַתְּחִלָּה, וְכוֹנֵן מִקְדָּשְׁךָ עַל מְכוֹנוֹ, וְהַרְאֵנוּ בְּבִנְיָנוֹ, וְשַׂמְּחֵנוּ בְּתִקּוּנוֹ. וְהָשֵׁב כֹּהֲנִים לַעֲבוֹדָתָם, וּלְוִיִּם לְשִׁירָם וּלְזִמְרָם, וְהָשֵׁב יִשְׂרָאֵל לִנְוֵיהֶם. וְשָׁם נַעֲלֶה וְנֵרָאֶה וְנִשְׁתַּחֲוֶה לְפָנֶיךָ, בְּשָׁלֹשׁ פַּעֲמֵי רְגָלֵינוּ, כַּכָּתוּב בְּתוֹרָתֶךָ: שָׁלוֹשׁ פְּעָמִים בַּשָּׁנָה, יֵרָאֶה כָל זְכוּרְךָ אֶת פְּנֵי יהוה אֱלֹהֶיךָ, בַּמָּקוֹם אֲשֶׁר יִבְחָר, בְּחַג הַמַּצּוֹת, וּבְחַג

וּמִפְּנֵי חֲטָאֵינוּ *But because of our sins we have been exiled from our land and sent far from our soil. We cannot ascend to appear and to prostrate ourselves before You, and to perform our obligations in the House of Your choice, in the great and holy House upon which Your Name was proclaimed, because of the hand that was dispatched against Your Sanctuary. May it be Your will,* HASHEM, *our God and the God of our forefathers, O merciful King, that You once more be compassionate upon us and upon Your Sanctuary in Your abundant mercy, and rebuild it soon and magnify its glory. Our Father, our King, reveal the glory of Your Kingship upon us, speedily; appear and be uplifted over us before the eyes of all the living. Draw our scattered ones near from among the nations, and bring in our dispersions from the ends of the earth. Bring us to Zion, Your City, in glad song, and to Jerusalem, home of Your Sanctuary, in eternal joy. There we will perform before You our obligatory offerings, the continual offerings according to their order and the additional offerings according to their law. And the additional offering of this day of the Festival of Matzos, we will perform and bring near to You with love, according to the commandment of Your will, as You have written for us in Your Torah, through Moses, Your servant, from Your glorious expression, as it is said:*

וְהִקְרַבְתֶּם *You are to bring a fire-offering, an elevation-offering to* HASHEM, *two young bulls, one ram and seven male lambs in their first year, they shall be unblemished for you.*[1] *And their meal-offerings and their wine-libations as mentioned: three tenth-ephah for each bull; two tenth-ephah for each ram; one tenth-ephah for each lamb; and wine for its libation. A he-goat for atonement, and two continual offerings according to their law.*

אֱלֹהֵינוּ *Our God and the God of our forefathers, O merciful King, have mercy on us; O good and beneficent One, let Yourself be sought out by us; return to us in Your yearning mercy for the sake of the forefathers who did Your will. Rebuild Your House as it was at first, and establish Your Sanctuary on its prepared site; show us its rebuilding and gladden us in its perfection. Restore the Kohanim to their service and the Levites to their song and music; and restore Israel to their dwellings. And there we will ascend and appear and prostrate ourselves before You, during our three pilgrimage seasons, as it is written in Your Torah: Three times a year all your males are to appear before* HASHEM, *your God, in the place He shall choose, on the Festival of Matzos, on the Festival*

(1) *Numbers* 28:19.

וּבְחַג הַשָּׁבֻעוֹת, וּבְחַג הַסֻּכּוֹת, וְלֹא יֵרָאֶה אֶת פְּנֵי יהוה רֵיקָם.
אִישׁ כְּמַתְּנַת יָדוֹ, כְּבִרְכַּת יהוה אֱלֹהֶיךָ, אֲשֶׁר נָתַן לָךְ.[1]

וְהַשִּׂיאֵנוּ יהוה אֱלֹהֵינוּ אֶת בִּרְכַּת מוֹעֲדֶיךָ לְחַיִּים וּלְשָׁלוֹם,
לְשִׂמְחָה וּלְשָׂשׂוֹן, כַּאֲשֶׁר רָצִיתָ וְאָמַרְתָּ לְבָרְכֵנוּ.
קַדְּשֵׁנוּ בְּמִצְוֹתֶיךָ וְתֵן חֶלְקֵנוּ בְּתוֹרָתֶךָ, שַׂבְּעֵנוּ מִטּוּבֶךָ וְשַׂמְּחֵנוּ
בִּישׁוּעָתֶךָ, וְטַהֵר לִבֵּנוּ לְעָבְדְּךָ בֶּאֱמֶת, וְהַנְחִילֵנוּ יהוה אֱלֹהֵינוּ
בְּשִׂמְחָה וּבְשָׂשׂוֹן מוֹעֲדֵי קָדְשֶׁךָ, וְיִשְׂמְחוּ בְךָ יִשְׂרָאֵל מְקַדְּשֵׁי
שְׁמֶךָ. בָּרוּךְ אַתָּה יהוה, מְקַדֵּשׁ יִשְׂרָאֵל וְהַזְּמַנִּים.

עבודה

רְצֵה יהוה אֱלֹהֵינוּ בְּעַמְּךָ יִשְׂרָאֵל וּבִתְפִלָּתָם, וְהָשֵׁב אֶת
הָעֲבוֹדָה לִדְבִיר בֵּיתֶךָ. וְאִשֵּׁי יִשְׂרָאֵל וּתְפִלָּתָם בְּאַהֲבָה
תְקַבֵּל בְּרָצוֹן, וּתְהִי לְרָצוֹן תָּמִיד עֲבוֹדַת יִשְׂרָאֵל עַמֶּךָ.

וְתֶחֱזֶינָה עֵינֵינוּ בְּשׁוּבְךָ לְצִיּוֹן בְּרַחֲמִים. בָּרוּךְ אַתָּה יהוה,
הַמַּחֲזִיר שְׁכִינָתוֹ לְצִיּוֹן.

הודאה

Bow at מוֹדִים; straighten up at ה'. In his repetition the *chazzan* should recite
the entire מוֹדִים aloud, while the congregation recites מוֹדִים דְּרַבָּנָן softly.

מוֹדִים אֲנַחְנוּ לָךְ, שָׁאַתָּה הוּא
יהוה אֱלֹהֵינוּ וֵאלֹהֵי
אֲבוֹתֵינוּ לְעוֹלָם וָעֶד. צוּר חַיֵּינוּ,
מָגֵן יִשְׁעֵנוּ אַתָּה הוּא לְדוֹר וָדוֹר.
נוֹדֶה לְּךָ וּנְסַפֵּר תְּהִלָּתֶךָ[2] עַל
חַיֵּינוּ הַמְּסוּרִים בְּיָדֶךָ, וְעַל
נִשְׁמוֹתֵינוּ הַפְּקוּדוֹת לָךְ, וְעַל
נִסֶּיךָ שֶׁבְּכָל יוֹם עִמָּנוּ, וְעַל
נִפְלְאוֹתֶיךָ וְטוֹבוֹתֶיךָ שֶׁבְּכָל עֵת,
עֶרֶב וָבֹקֶר וְצָהֳרָיִם. הַטּוֹב כִּי לֹא
כָלוּ רַחֲמֶיךָ, וְהַמְרַחֵם כִּי לֹא
תַמּוּ חֲסָדֶיךָ,[3] מֵעוֹלָם קִוִּינוּ לָךְ.

מוֹדִים דְּרַבָּנָן

מוֹדִים אֲנַחְנוּ לָךְ, שָׁאַתָּה
הוּא יהוה אֱלֹהֵינוּ
וֵאלֹהֵי אֲבוֹתֵינוּ, אֱלֹהֵי כָל
בָּשָׂר, יוֹצְרֵנוּ, יוֹצֵר בְּרֵאשִׁית.
בְּרָכוֹת וְהוֹדָאוֹת לְשִׁמְךָ הַגָּדוֹל
וְהַקָּדוֹשׁ, עַל שֶׁהֶחֱיִיתָנוּ
וְקִיַּמְתָּנוּ. כֵּן תְּחַיֵּנוּ וּתְקַיְּמֵנוּ,
וְתֶאֱסוֹף גָּלֻיּוֹתֵינוּ לְחַצְרוֹת
קָדְשֶׁךָ, לִשְׁמוֹר חֻקֶּיךָ וְלַעֲשׂוֹת
רְצוֹנֶךָ, וּלְעָבְדְּךָ בְּלֵבָב שָׁלֵם,
עַל שֶׁאֲנַחְנוּ מוֹדִים לָךְ. בָּרוּךְ
אֵל הַהוֹדָאוֹת.

---

(1) *Deuteronomy* 16:16-17. (2) Cf. *Psalms* 79:13. (3) Cf. *Lamentations* 3:22.

of Shavuos, and on the Festival of Succos, and they shall not appear before HASHEM empty-handed. Every man according to the gift of his hand, according to the blessing of HASHEM, your God, that He gave you.[1]

וְהַשִּׂיאֵנוּ *Bestow upon us, O HASHEM, our God, the blessing of Your appointed Festivals for life and for peace, for gladness and for joy, as You desired and promised to bless us. Sanctify us with Your commandments and grant us our share in Your Torah; satisfy us from Your goodness and gladden us with Your salvation, and purify our heart to serve You sincerely. And grant us a heritage, O HASHEM, our God — with gladness and with joy — the appointed festivals of Your holiness, and may Israel, the sanctifiers of Your Name, rejoice in You. Blessed are You, HASHEM, Who sanctifies Israel and the festive seasons.*

TEMPLE SERVICE

רְצֵה *Be favorable, HASHEM, our God, toward Your people Israel and their prayer and restore the service to the Holy of Holies of Your Temple. The fire-offerings of Israel and their prayer accept with love and favor, and may the service of Your people Israel always be favorable to You.*

וְתֶחֱזֶינָה *May our eyes behold Your return to Zion in compassion. Blessed are You, HASHEM, Who restores His Presence to Zion.*

THANKSGIVING [MODIM]

Bow at *'We gratefully thank You'*; straighten up at *'HASHEM.'* In his repetition the *chazzan* should recite the entire *Modim* aloud, while the congregation recites *Modim of the Rabbis* softly.

מוֹדִים *We gratefully thank You, for it is You Who are HASHEM, our God and the God of our forefathers for all eternity; Rock of our lives, Shield of our salvation are You from generation to generation. We shall thank You and relate Your praise*[2] *— for our lives, which are committed to Your power and for our souls that are entrusted to You; for Your miracles that are with us every day; and for Your wonders and favors in every season — evening, morning, and afternoon. The Beneficent One, for Your compassions were never exhausted, and the Compassionate One, for Your kindnesses never ended*[3] *— always have we put our hope in You.*

MODIM OF THE RABBIS

מוֹדִים *We gratefully thank You, for it is You Who are HASHEM, our God and the God of our forefathers, the God of all flesh, our Molder, the Molder of the universe. Blessings and thanks are due Your great and holy Name for You have given us life and sustained us. So may You continue to give us life and sustain us and gather our exiles to the Courtyards of Your Sanctuary, to observe Your decrees, to do Your will and to serve You wholeheartedly. [We thank You] for inspiring us to thank You. Blessed is the God of thanksgivings.*

וְעַל כֻּלָּם יִתְבָּרַךְ וְיִתְרוֹמַם שִׁמְךָ מַלְכֵּנוּ תָּמִיד לְעוֹלָם וָעֶד.

Bend the knees at בָּרוּךְ; bow at אַתָּה; straighten up at ה׳.

וְכֹל הַחַיִּים יוֹדְוּךָ סֶּלָה, וִיהַלְלוּ אֶת שִׁמְךָ בֶּאֱמֶת, הָאֵל יְשׁוּעָתֵנוּ וְעֶזְרָתֵנוּ סֶלָה. בָּרוּךְ אַתָּה יהוה, הַטּוֹב שִׁמְךָ וּלְךָ נָאֶה לְהוֹדוֹת.

ברכת כהנים

The *chazzan* recites the following during his repetition.
He faces right at וְיִשְׁמְרֶךָ; faces left at אֵלֶיךָ וִיחֻנֶּךָּ; faces the Ark for the rest of the blessings.

אֱלֹהֵינוּ, וֵאלֹהֵי אֲבוֹתֵינוּ, בָּרְּכֵנוּ בַבְּּרָכָה הַמְּשֻׁלֶּשֶׁת בַּתּוֹרָה הַכְּּתוּבָה עַל יְדֵי מֹשֶׁה עַבְדֶּךָ, הָאֲמוּרָה מִפִּי אַהֲרֹן וּבָנָיו, כֹּהֲנִים עַם קְדוֹשֶׁךָ, כָּאָמוּר:

יְבָרֶכְךָ יהוה, וְיִשְׁמְרֶךָ. (Cong. – כֵּן יְהִי רָצוֹן.)

יָאֵר יהוה פָּנָיו אֵלֶיךָ וִיחֻנֶּךָּ. (Cong. – כֵּן יְהִי רָצוֹן.)

יִשָּׂא יהוה פָּנָיו אֵלֶיךָ וְיָשֵׂם לְךָ שָׁלוֹם.[1] (Cong. – כֵּן יְהִי רָצוֹן.)

שלום

שִׂים שָׁלוֹם, טוֹבָה, וּבְרָכָה, חֵן, וָחֶסֶד וְרַחֲמִים עָלֵינוּ וְעַל כָּל יִשְׂרָאֵל עַמֶּךָ. בָּרְּכֵנוּ אָבִינוּ, כֻּלָּנוּ כְּאֶחָד בְּאוֹר פָּנֶיךָ, כִּי בְאוֹר פָּנֶיךָ נָתַתָּ לָּנוּ, יהוה אֱלֹהֵינוּ, תּוֹרַת חַיִּים וְאַהֲבַת חֶסֶד, וּצְדָקָה, וּבְרָכָה, וְרַחֲמִים, וְחַיִּים, וְשָׁלוֹם. וְטוֹב בְּעֵינֶיךָ לְבָרֵךְ אֶת עַמְּךָ יִשְׂרָאֵל, בְּכָל עֵת וּבְכָל שָׁעָה בִּשְׁלוֹמֶךָ. בָּרוּךְ אַתָּה יהוה, הַמְּבָרֵךְ אֶת עַמּוֹ יִשְׂרָאֵל בַּשָּׁלוֹם.

יִהְיוּ לְרָצוֹן אִמְרֵי פִי וְהֶגְיוֹן לִבִּי לְפָנֶיךָ, יהוה צוּרִי וְגֹאֲלִי.[2]

The *chazzan's* repetiiton of *Shemoneh Esrei* ends here. The individual continues below:

אֱלֹהַי, נְצוֹר לְשׁוֹנִי מֵרָע, וּשְׂפָתַי מִדַּבֵּר מִרְמָה,[3] וְלִמְקַלְלַי נַפְשִׁי תִדּוֹם, וְנַפְשִׁי כֶּעָפָר לַכֹּל תִּהְיֶה. פְּתַח לִבִּי בְּתוֹרָתֶךָ, וּבְמִצְוֹתֶיךָ תִּרְדּוֹף נַפְשִׁי. וְכֹל הַחוֹשְׁבִים עָלַי רָעָה, מְהֵרָה הָפֵר עֲצָתָם וְקַלְקֵל מַחֲשַׁבְתָּם. עֲשֵׂה לְמַעַן שְׁמֶךָ, עֲשֵׂה לְמַעַן יְמִינֶךָ, עֲשֵׂה לְמַעַן קְדֻשָּׁתֶךָ, עֲשֵׂה לְמַעַן תּוֹרָתֶךָ. לְמַעַן יֵחָלְצוּן יְדִידֶיךָ, הוֹשִׁיעָה יְמִינְךָ וַעֲנֵנִי.[4]

Some recite verses pertaining to their names here. See page 1143.

יִהְיוּ לְרָצוֹן אִמְרֵי פִי וְהֶגְיוֹן לִבִּי לְפָנֶיךָ, יהוה צוּרִי וְגֹאֲלִי.[2]

Bow and take three steps back. Bow left and say . . . עֹשֶׂה; bow right and say . . . הוּא יַעֲשֶׂה; bow forward and say וְעַל כָּל . . . אָמֵן.

עֹשֶׂה שָׁלוֹם בִּמְרוֹמָיו, הוּא יַעֲשֶׂה שָׁלוֹם עָלֵינוּ, וְעַל כָּל יִשְׂרָאֵל. וְאִמְרוּ: אָמֵן.

For all these, may Your Name be blessed and exalted, our King, continually forever and ever.

Bend the knees at *'Blessed'*; bow at *'You'*; straighten up at *'HASHEM.'*

Everything alive will gratefully acknowledge You, Selah! and praise Your Name sincerely, O God of our salvation and help, Selah! Blessed are You, HASHEM, Your Name is 'The Beneficent One' and to You it is fitting to give thanks.

THE PRIESTLY BLESSING

The *chazzan* recites the following during his repetition.

אֱלֹהֵינוּ *Our God and the God of our forefathers, bless us with the three-verse blessing in the Torah that was written by the hand of Moses, Your servant, that was said by Aaron and his sons, the Kohanim, Your holy people, as it is said:*

May HASHEM bless you and safeguard you. (Cong.— *So may it be.*)

May HASHEM illuminate His countenance for you and be gracious to you. (Cong.— *So may it be.*)

May HASHEM turn His countenance to you and establish peace for you.[1] (Cong.— *So may it be.*)

PEACE

שִׂים שָׁלוֹם *Establish peace, goodness, blessing, graciousness, kindness, and compassion upon us and upon all of Your people Israel. Bless us, our Father, all of us as one, with the light of Your countenance, for with the light of Your countenance You gave us, HASHEM, our God, the Torah of life and a love of kindness, righteousness, blessing, compassion, life, and peace. And may it be good in Your eyes to bless Your people Israel at every time and every hour with Your peace. Blessed are You, HASHEM, Who blesses His people Israel with peace.*

May the expressions of my mouth and the thoughts of my heart find favor before You, HASHEM, my Rock and my Redeemer.[2]

Chazzan's repetition of *Shemoneh Esrei* ends here. Individuals continue:

אֱלֹהַי *My God, guard my tongue from evil and my lips from speaking deceitfully.*[3] *To those who curse me, let my soul be silent; and let my soul be like dust to everyone. Open my heart to Your Torah, then my soul will pursue Your commandments. As for all those who design evil against me, speedily nullify their counsel and disrupt their design. Act for Your Name's sake; act for Your right hand's sake; act for Your sanctity's sake; act for Your Torah's sake. That Your beloved ones may be given rest; let Your right hand save, and respond to me.*[4]

Some recite verses pertaining to their names at this point. See page 1143.

May the expressions of my mouth and the thoughts of my heart find favor before You, HASHEM, my Rock and my Redeemer.[2] *He Who makes peace in His heights, may He make peace upon us, and upon all Israel. Now respond: Amen.*

Bow and take three steps back. Bow left and say, *'He Who makes peace . . .'*; bow right and say, *'may He make peace . . .'*; bow forward and say, *'and upon . . . Amen.'*

---

(1) *Numbers* 6:24-26. (2) *Psalms* 19:15. (3) Cf. 34:14. (4) 60:7; 108:7.

יְהִי רָצוֹן מִלְּפָנֶיךָ יהוה אֱלֹהֵינוּ וֵאלֹהֵי אֲבוֹתֵינוּ, שֶׁיִּבָּנֶה בֵּית הַמִּקְדָּשׁ בִּמְהֵרָה בְיָמֵינוּ, וְתֵן חֶלְקֵנוּ בְּתוֹרָתֶךָ. וְשָׁם נַעֲבָדְךָ בְּיִרְאָה, כִּימֵי עוֹלָם וּכְשָׁנִים קַדְמוֹנִיּוֹת. וְעָרְבָה לַיהוה מִנְחַת יְהוּדָה וִירוּשָׁלָיִם, כִּימֵי עוֹלָם וּכְשָׁנִים קַדְמוֹנִיּוֹת.[1]

THE INDIVIDUAL'S RECITATION OF *SHEMONEH ESREI* ENDS HERE.

The individual remains standing in place until the *chazzan* reaches *Kedushah* — or at least until the *chazzan* begins his repetition — then he takes three steps forward. The *chazzan* himself, or one praying alone, should remain in place for a few moments before taking three steps forward.

קדיש שלם

The *chazzan* recites קַדִּישׁ שָׁלֵם.

יִתְגַּדַּל וְיִתְקַדַּשׁ שְׁמֵהּ רַבָּא. (.Cong — אָמֵן.) בְּעָלְמָא דִּי בְרָא כִרְעוּתֵהּ. וְיַמְלִיךְ מַלְכוּתֵהּ, בְּחַיֵּיכוֹן וּבְיוֹמֵיכוֹן וּבְחַיֵּי דְכָל בֵּית יִשְׂרָאֵל, בַּעֲגָלָא וּבִזְמַן קָרִיב. וְאִמְרוּ: אָמֵן.

(.Cong — אָמֵן. יְהֵא שְׁמֵהּ רַבָּא מְבָרַךְ לְעָלַם וּלְעָלְמֵי עָלְמַיָּא.)

יְהֵא שְׁמֵהּ רַבָּא מְבָרַךְ לְעָלַם וּלְעָלְמֵי עָלְמַיָּא.

יִתְבָּרַךְ וְיִשְׁתַּבַּח וְיִתְפָּאַר וְיִתְרוֹמַם וְיִתְנַשֵּׂא וְיִתְהַדָּר וְיִתְעַלֶּה וְיִתְהַלָּל שְׁמֵהּ דְּקֻדְשָׁא בְּרִיךְ הוּא (.Cong — בְּרִיךְ הוּא) — לְעֵלָּא מִן כָּל בִּרְכָתָא וְשִׁירָתָא תֻּשְׁבְּחָתָא וְנֶחֱמָתָא, דַּאֲמִירָן בְּעָלְמָא. וְאִמְרוּ: אָמֵן. (.Cong — אָמֵן.)

(.Cong — קַבֵּל בְּרַחֲמִים וּבְרָצוֹן אֶת תְּפִלָּתֵנוּ.)

תִּתְקַבֵּל צְלוֹתְהוֹן וּבָעוּתְהוֹן דְּכָל בֵּית יִשְׂרָאֵל קֳדָם אֲבוּהוֹן דִּי בִשְׁמַיָּא. וְאִמְרוּ: אָמֵן. (.Cong — אָמֵן.)

(.Cong — יְהִי שֵׁם יהוה מְבֹרָךְ, מֵעַתָּה וְעַד עוֹלָם.[2])

יְהֵא שְׁלָמָא רַבָּא מִן שְׁמַיָּא, וְחַיִּים עָלֵינוּ וְעַל כָּל יִשְׂרָאֵל. וְאִמְרוּ: אָמֵן. (.Cong — אָמֵן.)

(.Cong — עֶזְרִי מֵעִם יהוה, עֹשֵׂה שָׁמַיִם וָאָרֶץ.[3])

Take three steps back. Bow left and say . . . עֹשֶׂה; bow right and say . . . הוּא; bow forward and say וְעַל כָּל . . . אָמֵן. Remain standing in place for a few moments, then take three steps forward.

עֹשֶׂה שָׁלוֹם בִּמְרוֹמָיו, הוּא יַעֲשֶׂה שָׁלוֹם עָלֵינוּ, וְעַל כָּל יִשְׂרָאֵל. וְאִמְרוּ: אָמֵן. (.Cong — אָמֵן.)

Stand while reciting עָלֵינוּ.

עָלֵינוּ לְשַׁבֵּחַ לַאֲדוֹן הַכֹּל, לָתֵת גְּדֻלָּה לְיוֹצֵר בְּרֵאשִׁית, שֶׁלֹּא עָשָׂנוּ כְּגוֹיֵי הָאֲרָצוֹת, וְלֹא שָׂמָנוּ כְּמִשְׁפְּחוֹת הָאֲדָמָה. שֶׁלֹּא שָׂם חֶלְקֵנוּ כָּהֶם, וְגוֹרָלֵנוּ כְּכָל הֲמוֹנָם. (שֶׁהֵם מִשְׁתַּחֲוִים לְהֶבֶל וָרִיק, וּמִתְפַּלְּלִים אֶל אֵל לֹא יוֹשִׁיעַ.[4]) וַאֲנַחְנוּ כּוֹרְעִים וּמִשְׁתַּחֲוִים וּמוֹדִים, לִפְנֵי מֶלֶךְ מַלְכֵי הַמְּלָכִים הַקָּדוֹשׁ בָּרוּךְ הוּא. שֶׁהוּא נוֹטֶה שָׁמַיִם וְיֹסֵד אָרֶץ,[5] וּמוֹשַׁב יְקָרוֹ בַּשָּׁמַיִם מִמַּעַל, וּשְׁכִינַת עֻזּוֹ בְּגָבְהֵי מְרוֹמִים.

Bow while reciting וַאֲנַחְנוּ כּוֹרְעִים וּמִשְׁתַּחֲוִים.

יְהִי רָצוֹן *May it be Your will,* H*ASHEM*, *our God and the God of our forefathers, that the Holy Temple be rebuilt, speedily in our days. Grant us our share in Your Torah, and may we serve You there with reverence, as in days of old and in former years. Then the offering of Judah and Jerusalem will be pleasing to* H*ASHEM*, *as in days of old and in former years.*[1]

THE INDIVIDUAL'S RECITATION OF *SHEMONEH ESREI* ENDS HERE.

The individual remains standing in place until the *chazzan* reaches *Kedushah* — or at least until the *chazzan* begins his repetition — then he takes three steps forward. The *chazzan* himself, or one praying alone, should remain in place for a few moments before taking three steps forward.

FULL KADDISH

The *chazzan* recites the Full *Kaddish.*

יִתְגַּדַּל *May His great Name grow exalted and sanctified* (Cong.— *Amen.*) *in the world that He created as He willed. May He give reign to His kingship in your lifetimes and in your days, and in the lifetimes of the entire Family of Israel, swiftly and soon. Now respond: Amen.*

(Cong.— *Amen. May His great Name be blessed forever and ever.*)

May His great Name be blessed forever and ever.

Blessed, praised, glorified, exalted, extolled, mighty, upraised, and lauded be the Name of the Holy One, Blessed is He (Cong.— *Blessed is He*) — *beyond any blessing and song, praise and consolation that are uttered in the world. Now respond: Amen.* (Cong.— *Amen.*)

(Cong.— *Accept our prayers with mercy and favor.*)

May the prayers and supplications of the entire Family of Israel be accepted before their Father Who is in Heaven. Now respond: Amen. (Cong.— *Amen.*)

(Cong.— *Blessed be the Name of* H*ASHEM*, *from this time and forever.*[2])

May there be abundant peace from Heaven, and life, upon us and upon all Israel. Now respond: Amen. (Cong.— *Amen.*)

(Cong.— *My help is from* H*ASHEM*, *Maker of heaven and earth.*[3])

Take three steps back. Bow left and say, *'He Who makes peace . . .'*; bow right and say, *'may He . . .'*; bow forward and say, *'and upon all Israel . . .'* Remain standing in place for a few moments, then take three steps forward.

He Who makes peace in His heights, may He make peace upon us, and upon all Israel. Now respond: Amen. (Cong.— *Amen.*)

Stand while reciting עָלֵינוּ, *'It is our duty . . .'*

עָלֵינוּ *It is our duty to praise the Master of all, to ascribe greatness to the Molder of primeval creation, for He has not made us like the nations of the lands, and has not emplaced us like the families of the earth; for He has not assigned our portion like theirs nor our lot like all their multitudes. (For they bow to vanity and emptiness and pray to a god which helps not.*[4]*) But we bend our knees, bow, and acknowledge our thanks before the King Who reigns over kings, the Holy One, Blessed is He. He stretches out heaven and establishes earth's foundation,*[5] *the seat of His homage is in the heavens above and His powerful Presence is in the loftiest heights.*

Bow while reciting *'But we bend our knees.'*

(1) *Malachi* 3:4. (2) *Psalms* 113:2. (3) 121:2. (4) *Isaiah* 45:20. (5) 51:13.

הוּא אֱלֹהֵינוּ, אֵין עוֹד. אֱמֶת מַלְכֵּנוּ, אֶפֶס זוּלָתוֹ, כַּכָּתוּב בְּתוֹרָתוֹ: וְיָדַעְתָּ הַיּוֹם וַהֲשֵׁבֹתָ אֶל לְבָבֶךָ, כִּי יהוה הוּא הָאֱלֹהִים בַּשָּׁמַיִם מִמַּעַל וְעַל הָאָרֶץ מִתָּחַת, אֵין עוֹד.[1]

עַל כֵּן נְקַוֶּה לְּךָ יהוה אֱלֹהֵינוּ לִרְאוֹת מְהֵרָה בְּתִפְאֶרֶת עֻזֶּךָ, לְהַעֲבִיר גִּלּוּלִים מִן הָאָרֶץ, וְהָאֱלִילִים כָּרוֹת יִכָּרֵתוּן, לְתַקֵּן עוֹלָם בְּמַלְכוּת שַׁדַּי. וְכָל בְּנֵי בָשָׂר יִקְרְאוּ בִשְׁמֶךָ, לְהַפְנוֹת אֵלֶיךָ כָּל רִשְׁעֵי אָרֶץ. יַכִּירוּ וְיֵדְעוּ כָּל יוֹשְׁבֵי תֵבֵל, כִּי לְךָ תִּכְרַע כָּל בֶּרֶךְ, תִּשָּׁבַע כָּל לָשׁוֹן.[2] לְפָנֶיךָ יהוה אֱלֹהֵינוּ יִכְרְעוּ וְיִפֹּלוּ, וְלִכְבוֹד שִׁמְךָ יְקָר יִתֵּנוּ. וִיקַבְּלוּ כֻלָּם אֶת עוֹל מַלְכוּתֶךָ, וְתִמְלֹךְ עֲלֵיהֶם מְהֵרָה לְעוֹלָם וָעֶד. כִּי הַמַּלְכוּת שֶׁלְּךָ הִיא וּלְעוֹלְמֵי עַד תִּמְלוֹךְ בְּכָבוֹד, כַּכָּתוּב בְּתוֹרָתֶךָ: יהוה יִמְלֹךְ לְעֹלָם וָעֶד.[3] ❖ וְנֶאֱמַר: וְהָיָה יהוה לְמֶלֶךְ עַל כָּל הָאָרֶץ, בַּיּוֹם הַהוּא יִהְיֶה יהוה אֶחָד וּשְׁמוֹ אֶחָד.[4]

Some congregations recite the following after עָלֵינוּ:

אַל תִּירָא מִפַּחַד פִּתְאֹם, וּמִשֹּׁאַת רְשָׁעִים כִּי תָבֹא.[5] עֻצוּ עֵצָה וְתֻפָר, דַּבְּרוּ דָבָר וְלֹא יָקוּם, כִּי עִמָּנוּ אֵל.[6] וְעַד זִקְנָה אֲנִי הוּא, וְעַד שֵׂיבָה אֲנִי אֶסְבֹּל, אֲנִי עָשִׂיתִי וַאֲנִי אֶשָּׂא, וַאֲנִי אֶסְבֹּל וַאֲמַלֵּט.[7]

קדיש יתום

In the presence of a *minyan,* mourners recite קַדִּישׁ יָתוֹם, the Mourner's *Kaddish* (see *Laws* §81-83):

יִתְגַּדַּל וְיִתְקַדַּשׁ שְׁמֵהּ רַבָּא. (.Cong – אָמֵן.) בְּעָלְמָא דִּי בְרָא כִרְעוּתֵהּ. וְיַמְלִיךְ מַלְכוּתֵהּ, בְּחַיֵּיכוֹן וּבְיוֹמֵיכוֹן וּבְחַיֵּי דְכָל בֵּית יִשְׂרָאֵל, בַּעֲגָלָא וּבִזְמַן קָרִיב. וְאִמְרוּ: אָמֵן.

(.Cong – אָמֵן. יְהֵא שְׁמֵהּ רַבָּא מְבָרַךְ לְעָלַם וּלְעָלְמֵי עָלְמַיָּא.)

יְהֵא שְׁמֵהּ רַבָּא מְבָרַךְ לְעָלַם וּלְעָלְמֵי עָלְמַיָּא.

יִתְבָּרַךְ וְיִשְׁתַּבַּח וְיִתְפָּאַר וְיִתְרוֹמַם וְיִתְנַשֵּׂא וְיִתְהַדָּר וְיִתְעַלֶּה וְיִתְהַלָּל שְׁמֵהּ דְּקֻדְשָׁא בְּרִיךְ הוּא (.Cong – בְּרִיךְ הוּא) — לְעֵלָּא מִן כָּל בִּרְכָתָא וְשִׁירָתָא תֻּשְׁבְּחָתָא וְנֶחֱמָתָא, דַּאֲמִירָן בְּעָלְמָא. וְאִמְרוּ: אָמֵן. (.Cong – אָמֵן.)

יְהֵא שְׁלָמָא רַבָּא מִן שְׁמַיָּא, וְחַיִּים עָלֵינוּ וְעַל כָּל יִשְׂרָאֵל. וְאִמְרוּ: אָמֵן. (.Cong – אָמֵן.)

Take three steps back. Bow left and say . . . עֹשֶׂה; bow right and say . . . הוּא; bow forward and say וְעַל כָּל . . . אָמֵן. Remain standing in place for a few moments, then take three steps forward.

עֹשֶׂה שָׁלוֹם בִּמְרוֹמָיו, הוּא יַעֲשֶׂה שָׁלוֹם עָלֵינוּ, וְעַל כָּל יִשְׂרָאֵל. וְאִמְרוּ: אָמֵן. (.Cong – אָמֵן.)

He is our God and there is none other. True is our King, there is nothing beside Him, as it is written in His Torah: 'You are to know this day and take to your heart that HASHEM is the only God — in heaven above and on the earth below — there is none other.'[1]

עַל כֵּן *Therefore we put our hope in You, HASHEM, our God, that we may soon see Your mighty splendor, to remove detestable idolatry from the earth, and false gods will be utterly cut off, to perfect the universe through the Almighty's sovereignty. Then all humanity will call upon Your Name, to turn all the earth's wicked toward You. All the world's inhabitants will recognize and know that to You every knee should bend, every tongue should swear.*[2] *Before You, HASHEM, our God, they will bend every knee and cast themselves down and to the glory of Your Name they will render homage, and they will all accept upon themselves the yoke of Your kingship that You may reign over them soon and eternally. For the kingdom is Yours and You will reign for all eternity in glory as it is written in Your Torah: HASHEM shall reign for all eternity.*[3] Chazzan– *And it is said: HASHEM will be King over all the world — on that day HASHEM will be One and His Name will be One.*[4]

Some congregations recite the following after *Aleinu.*

אַל תִּירָא *Do not fear sudden terror, or the holocaust of the wicked when it comes.*[5] *Plan a conspiracy and it will be annulled; speak your piece and it shall not stand, for God is with us.*[6] *Even till your seniority, I remain unchanged; and even till your ripe old age, I shall endure. I created you and I shall bear you; I shall endure and rescue.*[7]

MOURNER'S KADDISH

In the presence of a *minyan,* mourners recite קַדִּישׁ יָתוֹם, the Mourner's *Kaddish* (see *Laws* §81-83).

[A transliteration of this *Kaddish* appears on p. 1147.]

יִתְגַּדַּל *May His great Name grow exalted and sanctified* (Cong.– *Amen.*) *in the world that He created as He willed. May He give reign to His kingship in your lifetimes and in your days, and in the lifetimes of the entire Family of Israel, swiftly and soon. Now respond: Amen.*

(Cong.– *Amen. May His great Name be blessed forever and ever.*)

May His great Name be blessed forever and ever.

Blessed, praised, glorified, exalted, extolled, mighty, upraised, and lauded be the Name of the Holy One, Blessed is He (Cong.– *Blessed is He*) *— beyond any blessing and song, praise and consolation that are uttered in the world. Now respond: Amen.* (Cong.– *Amen*).

May there be abundant peace from Heaven, and life, upon us and upon all Israel. Now respond: Amen. (Cong.– *Amen.*)

Take three steps back. Bow left and say, *'He Who makes peace . . .';*
bow right and say, *'may He . . .';* bow forward and say, *'and upon all Israel . . .'*
Remain standing in place for a few moments, then take three steps forward.

He Who makes peace in His heights, may He make peace upon us, and upon all Israel. Now respond: Amen. (Cong.– *Amen.*)

---

(1) *Deuteronomy* 4:39. (2) Cf. *Isaiah* 45:23. (3) *Exodus* 15:18.
(4) *Zechariah* 14:9. (5) *Proverbs* 3:25. (6) *Isaiah* 8:10. (7) 46:4.

שיר של יום

A different apsalm is assigned as the Song of the Day for each day of the week (see p. 448).

SUNDAY

הַיּוֹם יוֹם רִאשׁוֹן בַּשַּׁבָּת, שֶׁבּוֹ הָיוּ הַלְוִיִּם אוֹמְרִים בְּבֵית הַמִּקְדָּשׁ:

תהלים כד

לְדָוִד מִזְמוֹר, לַיהוה הָאָרֶץ וּמְלוֹאָהּ, תֵּבֵל וְיֹשְׁבֵי בָהּ. כִּי הוּא עַל יַמִּים יְסָדָהּ, וְעַל נְהָרוֹת יְכוֹנְנֶהָ. מִי יַעֲלֶה בְהַר יהוה, וּמִי יָקוּם בִּמְקוֹם קָדְשׁוֹ. נְקִי כַפַּיִם וּבַר לֵבָב, אֲשֶׁר לֹא נָשָׂא לַשָּׁוְא נַפְשִׁי, וְלֹא נִשְׁבַּע לְמִרְמָה. יִשָּׂא בְרָכָה מֵאֵת יהוה, וּצְדָקָה מֵאֱלֹהֵי יִשְׁעוֹ. זֶה דּוֹר דֹּרְשָׁיו, מְבַקְשֵׁי פָנֶיךָ יַעֲקֹב סֶלָה. שְׂאוּ שְׁעָרִים רָאשֵׁיכֶם, וְהִנָּשְׂאוּ פִּתְחֵי עוֹלָם, וְיָבוֹא מֶלֶךְ הַכָּבוֹד. מִי זֶה מֶלֶךְ הַכָּבוֹד, יהוה עִזּוּז וְגִבּוֹר, יהוה גִּבּוֹר מִלְחָמָה. ❖ שְׂאוּ שְׁעָרִים רָאשֵׁיכֶם, וּשְׂאוּ פִּתְחֵי עוֹלָם, וְיָבֹא מֶלֶךְ הַכָּבוֹד. מִי הוּא זֶה מֶלֶךְ הַכָּבוֹד, יהוה צְבָאוֹת, הוּא מֶלֶךְ הַכָּבוֹד סֶלָה.

The service continues with קַדִּישׁ יָתוֹם, *the Mourner's Kaddish* (page 774).

MONDAY

הַיּוֹם יוֹם שֵׁנִי בַּשַּׁבָּת, שֶׁבּוֹ הָיוּ הַלְוִיִּם אוֹמְרִים בְּבֵית הַמִּקְדָּשׁ:

תהלים מח

שִׁיר מִזְמוֹר לִבְנֵי קֹרַח. גָּדוֹל יהוה וּמְהֻלָּל מְאֹד, בְּעִיר אֱלֹהֵינוּ, הַר קָדְשׁוֹ. יְפֵה נוֹף, מְשׂוֹשׂ כָּל הָאָרֶץ, הַר צִיּוֹן יַרְכְּתֵי צָפוֹן, קִרְיַת מֶלֶךְ רָב. אֱלֹהִים בְּאַרְמְנוֹתֶיהָ נוֹדַע לְמִשְׂגָּב. כִּי הִנֵּה הַמְּלָכִים נוֹעֲדוּ, עָבְרוּ יַחְדָּו. הֵמָּה רָאוּ כֵּן תָּמָהוּ, נִבְהֲלוּ נֶחְפָּזוּ. רְעָדָה אֲחָזָתַם שָׁם, חִיל כַּיּוֹלֵדָה. בְּרוּחַ קָדִים תְּשַׁבֵּר אֳנִיּוֹת תַּרְשִׁישׁ. כַּאֲשֶׁר שָׁמַעְנוּ כֵּן רָאִינוּ בְּעִיר יהוה צְבָאוֹת, בְּעִיר אֱלֹהֵינוּ, אֱלֹהִים יְכוֹנְנֶהָ עַד עוֹלָם סֶלָה. דִּמִּינוּ אֱלֹהִים חַסְדֶּךָ, בְּקֶרֶב הֵיכָלֶךָ. כְּשִׁמְךָ אֱלֹהִים כֵּן תְּהִלָּתְךָ, עַל קַצְוֵי אֶרֶץ, צֶדֶק מָלְאָה יְמִינֶךָ. יִשְׂמַח הַר צִיּוֹן, תָּגֵלְנָה בְּנוֹת יְהוּדָה, לְמַעַן מִשְׁפָּטֶיךָ. סֹבּוּ צִיּוֹן וְהַקִּיפוּהָ, סִפְרוּ מִגְדָּלֶיהָ. ❖ שִׁיתוּ לִבְּכֶם לְחֵילָה, פַּסְּגוּ אַרְמְנוֹתֶיהָ, לְמַעַן תְּסַפְּרוּ לְדוֹר אַחֲרוֹן. כִּי זֶה אֱלֹהִים אֱלֹהֵינוּ עוֹלָם וָעֶד, הוּא יְנַהֲגֵנוּ עַל־מוּת.

The service continues with קַדִּישׁ יָתוֹם, *the Mourner's Kaddish* (page 774).

TUESDAY

הַיּוֹם יוֹם שְׁלִישִׁי בַּשַּׁבָּת, שֶׁבּוֹ הָיוּ הַלְוִיִּם אוֹמְרִים בְּבֵית הַמִּקְדָּשׁ:

תהלים פב

מִזְמוֹר לְאָסָף, אֱלֹהִים נִצָּב בַּעֲדַת אֵל, בְּקֶרֶב אֱלֹהִים יִשְׁפֹּט. עַד מָתַי תִּשְׁפְּטוּ עָוֶל, וּפְנֵי רְשָׁעִים תִּשְׂאוּ סֶלָה. שִׁפְטוּ דַל וְיָתוֹם, עָנִי וָרָשׁ הַצְדִּיקוּ. פַּלְּטוּ דַל וְאֶבְיוֹן, מִיַּד רְשָׁעִים הַצִּילוּ. לֹא יָדְעוּ וְלֹא יָבִינוּ, בַּחֲשֵׁכָה יִתְהַלָּכוּ, יִמּוֹטוּ כָּל מוֹסְדֵי אָרֶץ. אֲנִי אָמַרְתִּי אֱלֹהִים אַתֶּם,

SONG OF THE DAY

A different psalm is assigned as the Song of the Day for each day of the week (see p. 448).

SUNDAY

Today is the first day of the Sabbath,
on which the Levites would recite in the Holy Temple:

Psalm 24

לְדָוִד *Of David a psalm. HASHEM's is the earth and its fullness, the inhabited land and those who dwell in it. For He founded it upon seas, and established it upon rivers. Who may ascend the mountain of HASHEM, and who may stand in the place of His sanctity? One with clean hands and pure heart, who has not sworn in vain by My soul and has not sworn deceitfully. He will receive a blessing from HASHEM and just kindness from the God of his salvation. This is the generation of those who seek Him, those who strive for Your Presence — Jacob, Selah. Raise up your heads, O gates, and be uplifted, you everlasting entrances, so that the King of Glory may enter. Who is this King of Glory? — HASHEM, the mighty and strong, HASHEM, the strong in battle.* Chazzan— *Raise up your heads, O gates, and raise up, you everlasting entrances, so that the King of Glory may enter. Who then is the King of Glory? HASHEM, Master of Legions, He is the King of Glory. Selah!*

The service continues with קַדִּישׁ יָתוֹם, *the Mourner's Kaddish* (p. 774).

MONDAY

Today is the second day of the Sabbath,
on which the Levites would recite in the Holy Temple:

Psalm 48

שִׁיר מִזְמוֹר *A song, a psalm, by the sons of Korach. Great is HASHEM and much praised, in the city of our God, Mount of His Holiness. Fairest of sites, joy of all the earth is Mount Zion, by the northern sides of the great king's city. In her palaces God is known as the Stronghold. For behold — the kings assembled, they came together. They saw and they were astounded, they were confounded and hastily fled. Trembling gripped them there, convulsions like a woman in birth travail. With an east wind You smashed the ships of Tarshish. As we heard, so we saw in the city of HASHEM, Master of Legions, in the city of our God — may God establish it to eternity, Selah! We hoped, O God, for Your kindness, in the midst of Your Sanctuary. Like Your Name, O God, so is Your praise — to the ends of the earth; righteousness fills Your right hand. May Mount Zion be glad, may the daughters of Judah rejoice, because of Your judgments. Walk about Zion and encircle her, count her towers.* Chazzan— *Mark well in your hearts her ramparts, raise up her palaces, that you may recount it to the succeeding generation: that this is God, our God, forever and ever, He will guide us like children.*

The service continues with קַדִּישׁ יָתוֹם, *the Mourner's Kaddish* (p. 774).

TUESDAY

Today is the third day of the Sabbath,
on which the Levites would recite in the Holy Temple:

Psalm 82

מִזְמוֹר *A psalm of Assaf: God stands in the Divine assembly, in the midst of judges shall He judge. Until when will you judge lawlessly and favor the presence of the wicked, Selah? Judge the needy and the orphan, vindicate the poor and impoverished. Rescue the needy and destitute, from the hand of the wicked deliver them. They do not know nor do they understand, in darkness they walk; all foundations of the earth collapse. I said, 'You are angelic,*

וּבְנֵי עֶלְיוֹן כֻּלְּכֶם. אָכֵן כְּאָדָם תְּמוּתוּן, וּכְאַחַד הַשָּׂרִים תִּפֹּלוּ. ❖ קוּמָה אֱלֹהִים שָׁפְטָה הָאָרֶץ, כִּי אַתָּה תִנְחַל בְּכָל הַגּוֹיִם.

The service continues with קַדִּישׁ יָתוֹם, *the Mourner's Kaddish* (page 774).

WEDNESDAY

הַיּוֹם יוֹם רְבִיעִי בְּשַׁבָּת, שֶׁבּוֹ הָיוּ הַלְוִיִּם אוֹמְרִים בְּבֵית הַמִּקְדָּשׁ:

תהלים צד:א-צה:ג

אֵל נְקָמוֹת יהוה, אֵל נְקָמוֹת הוֹפִיעַ. הִנָּשֵׂא שֹׁפֵט הָאָרֶץ, הָשֵׁב גְּמוּל עַל גֵּאִים. עַד מָתַי רְשָׁעִים, יהוה, עַד מָתַי רְשָׁעִים יַעֲלֹזוּ. יַבִּיעוּ יְדַבְּרוּ עָתָק, יִתְאַמְּרוּ כָּל פֹּעֲלֵי אָוֶן. עַמְּךָ יהוה יְדַכְּאוּ, וְנַחֲלָתְךָ יְעַנּוּ. אַלְמָנָה וְגֵר יַהֲרֹגוּ, וִיתוֹמִים יְרַצֵּחוּ. וַיֹּאמְרוּ לֹא יִרְאֶה יָּהּ, וְלֹא יָבִין אֱלֹהֵי יַעֲקֹב. בִּינוּ בֹּעֲרִים בָּעָם, וּכְסִילִים מָתַי תַּשְׂכִּילוּ. הֲנֹטַע אֹזֶן הֲלֹא יִשְׁמָע, אִם יֹצֵר עַיִן הֲלֹא יַבִּיט. הֲיֹסֵר גּוֹיִם הֲלֹא יוֹכִיחַ, הַמְלַמֵּד אָדָם דָּעַת. יהוה יֹדֵעַ מַחְשְׁבוֹת אָדָם, כִּי הֵמָּה הָבֶל. אַשְׁרֵי הַגֶּבֶר אֲשֶׁר תְּיַסְּרֶנּוּ יָּהּ, וּמִתּוֹרָתְךָ תְלַמְּדֶנּוּ. לְהַשְׁקִיט לוֹ מִימֵי רָע, עַד יִכָּרֶה לָרָשָׁע שָׁחַת. כִּי לֹא יִטֹּשׁ יהוה עַמּוֹ, וְנַחֲלָתוֹ לֹא יַעֲזֹב. כִּי עַד צֶדֶק יָשׁוּב מִשְׁפָּט, וְאַחֲרָיו כָּל יִשְׁרֵי לֵב. מִי יָקוּם לִי עִם מְרֵעִים, מִי יִתְיַצֵּב לִי עִם פֹּעֲלֵי אָוֶן. לוּלֵי יהוה עֶזְרָתָה לִּי, כִּמְעַט שָׁכְנָה דוּמָה נַפְשִׁי. אִם אָמַרְתִּי מָטָה רַגְלִי, חַסְדְּךָ יהוה יִסְעָדֵנִי. בְּרֹב שַׂרְעַפַּי בְּקִרְבִּי, תַּנְחוּמֶיךָ יְשַׁעַשְׁעוּ נַפְשִׁי. הַיְחָבְרְךָ כִּסֵּא הַוּוֹת, יֹצֵר עָמָל עֲלֵי חֹק. יָגוֹדּוּ עַל נֶפֶשׁ צַדִּיק, וְדָם נָקִי יַרְשִׁיעוּ. וַיְהִי יהוה לִי לְמִשְׂגָּב, וֵאלֹהַי לְצוּר מַחְסִי. וַיָּשֶׁב עֲלֵיהֶם אֶת אוֹנָם, וּבְרָעָתָם יַצְמִיתֵם, יַצְמִיתֵם יהוה אֱלֹהֵינוּ.

❖ לְכוּ נְרַנְּנָה לַיהוה, נָרִיעָה לְצוּר יִשְׁעֵנוּ. נְקַדְּמָה פָנָיו בְּתוֹדָה, בִּזְמִרוֹת נָרִיעַ לוֹ. כִּי אֵל גָּדוֹל יהוה, וּמֶלֶךְ גָּדוֹל עַל כָּל אֱלֹהִים.

The service continues with קַדִּישׁ יָתוֹם, *the Mourner's Kaddish* (page 774).

THURSDAY

הַיּוֹם יוֹם חֲמִישִׁי בְּשַׁבָּת, שֶׁבּוֹ הָיוּ הַלְוִיִּם אוֹמְרִים בְּבֵית הַמִּקְדָּשׁ:

תהלים פא

לַמְנַצֵּחַ עַל הַגִּתִּית לְאָסָף. הַרְנִינוּ לֵאלֹהִים עוּזֵּנוּ, הָרִיעוּ לֵאלֹהֵי יַעֲקֹב. שְׂאוּ זִמְרָה וּתְנוּ תֹף, כִּנּוֹר נָעִים עִם נָבֶל. תִּקְעוּ בַחֹדֶשׁ שׁוֹפָר, בַּכֶּסֶה לְיוֹם חַגֵּנוּ. כִּי חֹק לְיִשְׂרָאֵל הוּא, מִשְׁפָּט לֵאלֹהֵי יַעֲקֹב. עֵדוּת בִּיהוֹסֵף שָׂמוֹ, בְּצֵאתוֹ עַל אֶרֶץ מִצְרָיִם, שְׂפַת לֹא יָדַעְתִּי אֶשְׁמָע. הֲסִירוֹתִי מִסֵּבֶל שִׁכְמוֹ, כַּפָּיו מִדּוּד תַּעֲבֹרְנָה. בַּצָּרָה קָרָאתָ, וָאֲחַלְּצֶךָּ, אֶעֶנְךָ בְּסֵתֶר רַעַם, אֶבְחָנְךָ עַל מֵי מְרִיבָה, סֶלָה. שְׁמַע עַמִּי וְאָעִידָה בָּךְ,

sons of the Most High are you all.' But like men you shall die, and like one of the princes you shall fall. Chazzan– *Arise, O God, judge the earth, for You allot the heritage among all the nations.*

The service continues with קדיש יתום, *the Mourner's Kaddish* (p. 774).

WEDNESDAY

Today is the fourth day of the Sabbath,
on which the Levites would recite in the Holy Temple:

Psalm 94:1-95:3

אֵל נְקָמוֹת *O God of vengeance, HASHEM; O God of vengeance, appear! Arise, O Judge of the earth, render recompense to the haughty. How long shall the wicked — O HASHEM — how long shall the wicked exult? They speak freely, they utter malicious falsehood, they glorify themselves, all workers of iniquity. Your nation, HASHEM, they crush, and they afflict Your heritage. The widow and the stranger they slay, and the orphans they murder. And they say, 'God will not see, nor will the God of Jacob understand.' Understand, you boors among the people; and you fools, when will you gain wisdom? He Who implants the ear, shall He not hear? He Who fashions the eye, shall He not see? He Who chastises nations, shall He not rebuke? — He Who teaches man knowledge. HASHEM knows the thoughts of man, that they are futile. Praiseworthy is the man whom God disciplines, and whom You teach from Your Torah. To give him rest from the days of evil, until a pit is dug for the wicked. For HASHEM will not cast off His people, nor will He forsake His heritage. For justice shall revert to righteousness, and following it will be all of upright heart. Who will rise up for me against evildoers? Who will stand up for me against the workers of iniquity? Had HASHEM not been a help to me, my soul would soon have dwelt in silence. If I said, 'My foot falters,' Your kindness, HASHEM, supported me. When my forebodings were abundant within me, Your comforts cheered my soul. Can the throne of destruction be associated with You? — those who fashion evil into a way of life. They join together against the soul of the righteous, and the blood of the innocent they condemn. Then HASHEM became a stronghold for me, and my God, the Rock of my refuge. He turned upon them their own violence, and with their own evil He will cut them off, HASHEM, our God, will cut them off.*

Chazzan– *Come — let us sing to HASHEM, let us call out to the Rock of our salvation. Let us greet Him with thanksgiving, with praiseful songs let us call out to Him. For a great God is HASHEM, and a great King above all heavenly powers.*

The service continues with קדיש יתום, *the Mourner's Kaddish* (p. 774).

THURSDAY

Today is the fifth day of the Sabbath,
on which the Levites would recite in the Holy Temple:

Psalm 81

לַמְנַצֵּחַ *For the Conductor, upon the gittis, by Assaf. Sing joyously to the God of our might, call out to the God of Jacob. Raise a song and sound the drum, the sweet harp with the lyre. Blow the shofar at the moon's renewal, at the time appointed for our festive day. Because it is a decree for Israel, a judgment day for the God of Jacob. He imposed it as a testimony for Joseph when he went forth over the land of Egypt — 'I understood a language I never knew!' I removed his shoulder from the burden, his hands let go of the kettle. In distress you called out, and I released you, I answered you with thunder when you hid, I tested you at the Waters of Strife, Selah. Listen,*

יִשְׂרָאֵל אִם תִּשְׁמַע לִי. לֹא יִהְיֶה בְךָ אֵל זָר, וְלֹא תִשְׁתַּחֲוֶה לְאֵל נֵכָר. אָנֹכִי יהוה אֱלֹהֶיךָ, הַמַּעַלְךָ מֵאֶרֶץ מִצְרָיִם, הַרְחֶב פִּיךָ וַאֲמַלְאֵהוּ. וְלֹא שָׁמַע עַמִּי לְקוֹלִי, וְיִשְׂרָאֵל לֹא אָבָה לִי. וָאֲשַׁלְּחֵהוּ בִּשְׁרִירוּת לִבָּם, יֵלְכוּ בְּמוֹעֲצוֹתֵיהֶם. לוּ עַמִּי שֹׁמֵעַ לִי, יִשְׂרָאֵל בִּדְרָכַי יְהַלֵּכוּ. כִּמְעַט אוֹיְבֵיהֶם אַכְנִיעַ, וְעַל צָרֵיהֶם אָשִׁיב יָדִי. מְשַׂנְאֵי יהוה יְכַחֲשׁוּ לוֹ, וִיהִי עִתָּם לְעוֹלָם. ❖ וַיַּאֲכִילֵהוּ מֵחֵלֶב חִטָּה, וּמִצּוּר דְּבַשׁ אַשְׂבִּיעֶךָ.

The service continues with קַדִּישׁ יָתוֹם, *the Mourner's Kaddish* (below).

FRIDAY

הַיּוֹם יוֹם שִׁשִּׁי בַּשַּׁבָּת, שֶׁבּוֹ הָיוּ הַלְוִיִּם אוֹמְרִים בְּבֵית הַמִּקְדָּשׁ:

תהלים צג

יהוה מָלָךְ, גֵּאוּת לָבֵשׁ, לָבֵשׁ יהוה עֹז הִתְאַזָּר, אַף תִּכּוֹן תֵּבֵל בַּל תִּמּוֹט. נָכוֹן כִּסְאֲךָ מֵאָז, מֵעוֹלָם אָתָּה. נָשְׂאוּ נְהָרוֹת יהוה, נָשְׂאוּ נְהָרוֹת קוֹלָם, יִשְׂאוּ נְהָרוֹת דָּכְיָם. מִקֹּלוֹת מַיִם רַבִּים, אַדִּירִים מִשְׁבְּרֵי יָם, אַדִּיר בַּמָּרוֹם יהוה. ❖ עֵדֹתֶיךָ נֶאֶמְנוּ מְאֹד לְבֵיתְךָ נַאֲוָה קֹדֶשׁ, יהוה לְאֹרֶךְ יָמִים.

The service continues with קַדִּישׁ יָתוֹם, *the Mourner's Kaddish* (below).

קדיש יתום

In the presence of a *minyan,* mourners recite קַדִּישׁ יָתוֹם, the Mourner's *Kaddish* (see *Laws* §81-83):

יִתְגַּדַּל וְיִתְקַדַּשׁ שְׁמֵהּ רַבָּא. (.Cong – אָמֵן.) בְּעָלְמָא דִּי בְרָא כִרְעוּתֵהּ. וְיַמְלִיךְ מַלְכוּתֵהּ, בְּחַיֵּיכוֹן וּבְיוֹמֵיכוֹן וּבְחַיֵּי דְכָל בֵּית יִשְׂרָאֵל, בַּעֲגָלָא וּבִזְמַן קָרִיב. וְאִמְרוּ: אָמֵן.

(.Cong – אָמֵן. יְהֵא שְׁמֵהּ רַבָּא מְבָרַךְ לְעָלַם וּלְעָלְמֵי עָלְמַיָּא.)

יְהֵא שְׁמֵהּ רַבָּא מְבָרַךְ לְעָלַם וּלְעָלְמֵי עָלְמַיָּא.

יִתְבָּרַךְ וְיִשְׁתַּבַּח וְיִתְפָּאַר וְיִתְרוֹמַם וְיִתְנַשֵּׂא וְיִתְהַדָּר וְיִתְעַלֶּה וְיִתְהַלָּל שְׁמֵהּ דְּקֻדְשָׁא בְּרִיךְ הוּא (.Cong – בְּרִיךְ הוּא) – לְעֵלָּא מִן כָּל בִּרְכָתָא וְשִׁירָתָא תֻּשְׁבְּחָתָא וְנֶחֱמָתָא, דַּאֲמִירָן בְּעָלְמָא. וְאִמְרוּ: אָמֵן. (.Cong – אָמֵן.)

יְהֵא שְׁלָמָא רַבָּא מִן שְׁמַיָּא, וְחַיִּים עָלֵינוּ וְעַל כָּל יִשְׂרָאֵל. וְאִמְרוּ: אָמֵן. (.Cong – אָמֵן.)

Take three steps back. Bow left and say . . . עֹשֶׂה; bow right and say . . . הוּא; bow forward and say וְעַל כָּל . . . אָמֵן. Remain standing in place for a few moments, then take three steps forward.

עֹשֶׂה שָׁלוֹם בִּמְרוֹמָיו, הוּא יַעֲשֶׂה שָׁלוֹם עָלֵינוּ, וְעַל כָּל יִשְׂרָאֵל. וְאִמְרוּ: אָמֵן. (.Cong – אָמֵן.)

My nation, and I will attest to you; O Israel, if you would but listen to Me. There shall be no strange god within you, nor shall you bow before an alien god. I am HASHEM, *your God, who elevated you from the land of Egypt, open wide your mouth and I will fill it. But My people did not heed My voice and Israel did not desire Me. So I let them follow their heart's fantasies, they follow their own counsels. If only My people would heed Me, if Israel would walk in My ways. In an instant I would subdue their foes, and against their tormentors turn My hand. Those who hate* HASHEM *lie to Him — so their destiny is eternal.* Chazzan— *But He would feed him with the cream of the wheat, and with honey from a rock sate you.*

The service continues with קַדִּישׁ יָתוֹם, *the Mourner's Kaddish* (below).

FRIDAY

Today is the sixth day of the Sabbath,
on which the Levites would recite in the Holy Temple:

Psalm 93

יהוה מָלָךְ HASHEM *will have reigned, He will have donned grandeur; He will have donned might and girded Himself; He even made the world firm so that it should not falter. Your throne was established from of old, eternal are You. Like rivers they raised, O* HASHEM, *like rivers they raised their voice; like rivers they shall raise their destructiveness. More than the roars of many waters, mightier than the waves of the sea — You are mighty on high,* HASHEM. Chazzan— *Your testimonies are exceedingly trustworthy about Your House, the Sacred Dwelling — O* HASHEM, *may it be for long days.*

The service continues with קַדִּישׁ יָתוֹם, *the Mourner's Kaddish* (below).

MOURNER'S KADDISH

In the presence of a *minyan,* mourners recite קַדִּישׁ יָתוֹם, the Mourner's *Kaddish* (see *Laws* §81-83):
[A transliteration of this *Kaddish* appears on p. 1147.]

יִתְגַּדַּל *May His great Name grow exalted and sanctified* (Cong.— *Amen.*) *in the world that He created as He willed. May He give reign to His kingship in your lifetimes and in your days, and in the lifetimes of the entire Family of Israel, swiftly and soon. Now respond: Amen.*

(Cong.— *Amen. May His great Name be blessed forever and ever.*)
May His great Name be blessed forever and ever.

Blessed, praised, glorified, exalted, extolled, mighty, upraised, and lauded be the Name of the Holy One, Blessed is He (Cong.— *Blessed is He*) *— beyond any blessing and song, praise and consolation that are uttered in the world. Now respond: Amen.* (Cong.— *Amen*).

May there be abundant peace from Heaven, and life, upon us and upon all Israel. Now respond: Amen. (Cong.— *Amen.*)

Take three steps back. Bow left and say, *'He Who makes peace . . .';* bow right and say, *'may He . . .';* bow forward and say, *'and upon all Israel . . .'* Remain standing in place for a few moments, then take three steps forward.

He Who makes peace in His heights, may He make peace upon us, and upon all Israel. Now respond: Amen. (Cong.— *Amen.*)

❧ מנחה לחול המועד ☙

אַשְׁרֵי יוֹשְׁבֵי בֵיתֶךָ, עוֹד יְהַלְלְוּךָ סֶּלָה.[1] אַשְׁרֵי הָעָם שֶׁכָּכָה לּוֹ, אַשְׁרֵי הָעָם שֶׁיהוה אֱלֹהָיו.[2]

תהלים קמה

תְּהִלָּה לְדָוִד,
אֲרוֹמִמְךָ אֱלוֹהַי הַמֶּלֶךְ, וַאֲבָרְכָה שִׁמְךָ לְעוֹלָם וָעֶד.
בְּכָל יוֹם אֲבָרְכֶךָּ, וַאֲהַלְלָה שִׁמְךָ לְעוֹלָם וָעֶד.
גָּדוֹל יהוה וּמְהֻלָּל מְאֹד, וְלִגְדֻלָּתוֹ אֵין חֵקֶר.
דּוֹר לְדוֹר יְשַׁבַּח מַעֲשֶׂיךָ, וּגְבוּרֹתֶיךָ יַגִּידוּ.
הֲדַר כְּבוֹד הוֹדֶךָ, וְדִבְרֵי נִפְלְאֹתֶיךָ אָשִׂיחָה.
וֶעֱזוּז נוֹרְאוֹתֶיךָ יֹאמֵרוּ, וּגְדוּלָּתְךָ אֲסַפְּרֶנָּה.
זֵכֶר רַב טוּבְךָ יַבִּיעוּ, וְצִדְקָתְךָ יְרַנֵּנוּ.
חַנּוּן וְרַחוּם יהוה, אֶרֶךְ אַפַּיִם וּגְדָל חָסֶד.
טוֹב יהוה לַכֹּל, וְרַחֲמָיו עַל כָּל מַעֲשָׂיו.
יוֹדְוּךָ יהוה כָּל מַעֲשֶׂיךָ, וַחֲסִידֶיךָ יְבָרְכוּכָה.
כְּבוֹד מַלְכוּתְךָ יֹאמֵרוּ, וּגְבוּרָתְךָ יְדַבֵּרוּ.
לְהוֹדִיעַ לִבְנֵי הָאָדָם גְּבוּרֹתָיו, וּכְבוֹד הֲדַר מַלְכוּתוֹ.
מַלְכוּתְךָ מַלְכוּת כָּל עֹלָמִים, וּמֶמְשַׁלְתְּךָ בְּכָל דּוֹר וָדֹר.
סוֹמֵךְ יהוה לְכָל הַנֹּפְלִים, וְזוֹקֵף לְכָל הַכְּפוּפִים.
עֵינֵי כֹל אֵלֶיךָ יְשַׂבֵּרוּ, וְאַתָּה נוֹתֵן לָהֶם אֶת אָכְלָם בְּעִתּוֹ.
פּוֹתֵחַ אֶת יָדֶךָ,
וּמַשְׂבִּיעַ לְכָל חַי רָצוֹן.

While reciting the verse פּוֹתֵחַ, concentrate intently on its meaning.

צַדִּיק יהוה בְּכָל דְּרָכָיו, וְחָסִיד בְּכָל מַעֲשָׂיו.
קָרוֹב יהוה לְכָל קֹרְאָיו, לְכֹל אֲשֶׁר יִקְרָאֻהוּ בֶאֱמֶת.
רְצוֹן יְרֵאָיו יַעֲשֶׂה, וְאֶת שַׁוְעָתָם יִשְׁמַע וְיוֹשִׁיעֵם.
שׁוֹמֵר יהוה אֶת כָּל אֹהֲבָיו, וְאֵת כָּל הָרְשָׁעִים יַשְׁמִיד.
❖ תְּהִלַּת יהוה יְדַבֶּר פִּי, וִיבָרֵךְ כָּל בָּשָׂר שֵׁם קָדְשׁוֹ לְעוֹלָם וָעֶד.
וַאֲנַחְנוּ נְבָרֵךְ יָהּ, מֵעַתָּה וְעַד עוֹלָם, הַלְלוּיָהּ.[3]

---

(1) *Psalms* 84:5. (2) 144:15. (3) 115:18.

MINCHAH FOR CHOL HAMOED

אַשְׁרֵי *Praiseworthy are those who dwell in Your house; may they always praise You, Selah!*[1] *Praiseworthy is the people for whom this is so, praiseworthy is the people whose God is* HASHEM.[2]

Psalm 145 *A psalm of praise by David:*

א *I will exalt You, my God the King,*
and I will bless Your Name forever and ever.
ב *Every day I will bless You,*
and I will laud Your Name forever and ever.
ג HASHEM *is great and exceedingly lauded,*
and His greatness is beyond investigation.
ד *Each generation will praise Your deeds to the next*
and of Your mighty deeds they will tell.
ה *The splendrous glory of Your power*
and Your wondrous deeds I shall discuss.
ו *And of Your awesome power they will speak,*
and Your greatness I shall relate.
ז *A recollection of Your abundant goodness they will utter*
and of Your righteousness they will sing exultantly.
ח *Gracious and merciful is* HASHEM,
slow to anger, and great in [bestowing] kindness.
ט HASHEM *is good to all; His mercies are on all His works.*
י *All Your works shall thank You,* HASHEM,
and Your devout ones will bless You.
כ *Of the glory of Your kingdom they will speak,*
and of Your power they will tell;
ל *To inform human beings of His mighty deeds,*
and the glorious splendor of His kingdom.
מ *Your kingdom is a kingdom spanning all eternities,*
and Your dominion is throughout every generation.
ס HASHEM *supports all the fallen ones and straightens all the bent.*
ע *The eyes of all look to You with hope*
and You give them their food in its proper time;
פ *You open Your hand,*
and satisfy the desire of every living thing.

While reciting the verse *'You open . . .,'* concentrate intently on its meaning.

צ *Righteous is* HASHEM *in all His ways*
and magnanimous in all His deeds.
ק HASHEM *is close to all who call upon Him —*
to all who call upon Him sincerely.
ר *The will of those who fear Him He will do;*
and their cry He will hear, and save them.
ש HASHEM *protects all who love Him;*
but all the wicked He will destroy.
ת Chazzan— *May my mouth declare the praise of* HASHEM
and may all flesh bless His Holy Name forever and ever.
We will bless God from this time and forever, Halleluyah![3]

חצי קדיש

The *chazzan* recites חֲצִי קַדִּישׁ.

יִתְגַּדַּל וְיִתְקַדַּשׁ שְׁמֵהּ רַבָּא. (.Cong – אָמֵן.) בְּעָלְמָא דִּי בְרָא כִרְעוּתֵהּ. וְיַמְלִיךְ מַלְכוּתֵהּ, בְּחַיֵּיכוֹן וּבְיוֹמֵיכוֹן וּבְחַיֵּי דְכָל בֵּית יִשְׂרָאֵל, בַּעֲגָלָא וּבִזְמַן קָרִיב. וְאִמְרוּ: אָמֵן.

(.Cong – אָמֵן. יְהֵא שְׁמֵהּ רַבָּא מְבָרַךְ לְעָלַם וּלְעָלְמֵי עָלְמַיָּא.)

יְהֵא שְׁמֵהּ רַבָּא מְבָרַךְ לְעָלַם וּלְעָלְמֵי עָלְמַיָּא.

יִתְבָּרַךְ וְיִשְׁתַּבַּח וְיִתְפָּאַר וְיִתְרוֹמַם וְיִתְנַשֵּׂא וְיִתְהַדָּר וְיִתְעַלֶּה וְיִתְהַלָּל שְׁמֵהּ דְּקֻדְשָׁא בְּרִיךְ הוּא (.Cong – בְּרִיךְ הוּא) – לְעֵלָּא מִן כָּל בִּרְכָתָא וְשִׁירָתָא תֻּשְׁבְּחָתָא וְנֶחֱמָתָא, דַּאֲמִירָן בְּעָלְמָא. וְאִמְרוּ: אָמֵן. (.Cong – אָמֵן.)

שמונה עשרה – עמידה

Take three steps backward, then three steps forward. Remain standing with the feet together while reciting *Shemoneh Esrei*. Recite it with quiet devotion and without interruption, verbal or otherwise. Although its recitation should not be audible to others, one must pray loudly enough to hear himself.

כִּי שֵׁם יהוה אֶקְרָא, הָבוּ גֹדֶל לֵאלֹהֵינוּ.[1]

אֲדֹנָי שְׂפָתַי תִּפְתָּח, וּפִי יַגִּיד תְּהִלָּתֶךָ.[2]

אבות

Bend the knees at בָּרוּךְ; bow at אַתָּה; straighten up at ה'.

בָּרוּךְ אַתָּה יהוה אֱלֹהֵינוּ וֵאלֹהֵי אֲבוֹתֵינוּ, אֱלֹהֵי אַבְרָהָם, אֱלֹהֵי יִצְחָק, וֵאלֹהֵי יַעֲקֹב, הָאֵל הַגָּדוֹל הַגִּבּוֹר וְהַנּוֹרָא, אֵל עֶלְיוֹן, גּוֹמֵל חֲסָדִים טוֹבִים וְקוֹנֵה הַכֹּל, וְזוֹכֵר חַסְדֵי אָבוֹת, וּמֵבִיא גוֹאֵל לִבְנֵי בְנֵיהֶם, לְמַעַן שְׁמוֹ בְּאַהֲבָה. מֶלֶךְ עוֹזֵר וּמוֹשִׁיעַ וּמָגֵן.

Bend the knees at בָּרוּךְ; bow at אַתָּה; straighten up at ה'.

בָּרוּךְ אַתָּה יהוה, מָגֵן אַבְרָהָם.

גבורות

אַתָּה גִּבּוֹר לְעוֹלָם אֲדֹנָי, מְחַיֵּה מֵתִים אַתָּה, רַב לְהוֹשִׁיעַ. מְכַלְכֵּל חַיִּים בְּחֶסֶד, מְחַיֵּה מֵתִים בְּרַחֲמִים רַבִּים, סוֹמֵךְ נוֹפְלִים, וְרוֹפֵא חוֹלִים, וּמַתִּיר אֲסוּרִים, וּמְקַיֵּם אֱמוּנָתוֹ לִישֵׁנֵי עָפָר. מִי כָמוֹךָ בַּעַל גְּבוּרוֹת, וּמִי דּוֹמֶה לָּךְ, מֶלֶךְ מֵמִית וּמְחַיֶּה וּמַצְמִיחַ יְשׁוּעָה. וְנֶאֱמָן אַתָּה לְהַחֲיוֹת מֵתִים. בָּרוּךְ אַתָּה יהוה, מְחַיֵּה הַמֵּתִים.

During the *chazzan's* repetition, *Kedushah* (page 780) is recited at this point.

HALF KADDISH

The *chazzan* recites Half *Kaddish:*

יִתְגַּדַּל *May His great Name grow exalted and sanctified* (Cong.– *Amen.*) *in the world that He created as He willed. May He give reign to His kingship in your lifetimes and in your days, and in the lifetimes of the entire Family of Israel, swiftly and soon. Now respond: Amen.*

(Cong.– *Amen. May His great Name be blessed forever and ever.*)

May His great Name be blessed forever and ever.

Blessed, praised, glorified, exalted, extolled, mighty, upraised, and lauded be the Name of the Holy One, Blessed is He (Cong.– *Blessed is He*) *— beyond any blessing and song, praise and consolation that are uttered in the world. Now respond: Amen.* (Cong.– *Amen.*)

SHEMONEH ESREI – AMIDAH

Take three steps backward, then three steps forward. Remain standing with the feet together while reciting *Shemoneh Esrei.* Recite it with quiet devotion and without interruption, verbal or otherwise. Although its recitation should not be audible to others, one must pray loudly enough to hear himself.

When I call out the Name of HASHEM, ascribe greatness to our God.[1]

My Lord, open my lips, that my mouth may declare Your praise.[2]

PATRIARCHS

Bend the knees at *'Blessed'*; bow at *'You'*; straighten up at *'HASHEM.'*

בָּרוּךְ *Blessed are You, HASHEM, our God and the God of our forefathers, God of Abraham, God of Isaac, and God of Jacob; the great, mighty, and awesome God, the supreme God, Who bestows beneficial kindnesses and creates everything, Who recalls the kindnesses of the Patriarchs and brings a Redeemer to their children's children, for His Name's sake, with love. O King, Helper, Savior, and Shield.*

Bend the knees at *'Blessed'*; bow at *'You'*; straighten up at *'HASHEM.'*

Blessed are You, HASHEM, Shield of Abraham.

GOD'S MIGHT

אַתָּה *You are eternally mighty, my Lord, the Resuscitator of the dead are You; abundantly able to save. He sustains the living with kindness, resuscitates the dead with abundant mercy, supports the fallen, heals the sick, releases the confined, and maintains His faith to those asleep in the dust. Who is like You, O Master of mighty deeds, and who is comparable to You, O King Who causes death and restores life and makes salvation sprout! And You are faithful to resuscitate the dead. Blessed are You, HASHEM, Who resuscitates the dead.*

During the *chazzan's* repetition, *Kedushah* (page 780) is recited at this point.

---

(1) *Deuteronomy* 32:3. (2) *Psalms* 51:17.

קדושת השם

אַתָּה קָדוֹשׁ וְשִׁמְךָ קָדוֹשׁ, וּקְדוֹשִׁים בְּכָל יוֹם יְהַלְלְוּךָ סֶּלָה. בָּרוּךְ אַתָּה יהוה, הָאֵל הַקָּדוֹשׁ.

בינה

אַתָּה חוֹנֵן לְאָדָם דַּעַת, וּמְלַמֵּד לֶאֱנוֹשׁ בִּינָה. חָנֵּנוּ מֵאִתְּךָ דֵּעָה בִּינָה וְהַשְׂכֵּל. בָּרוּךְ אַתָּה יהוה, חוֹנֵן הַדָּעַת.

תשובה

הֲשִׁיבֵנוּ אָבִינוּ לְתוֹרָתֶךָ, וְקָרְבֵנוּ מַלְכֵּנוּ לַעֲבוֹדָתֶךָ, וְהַחֲזִירֵנוּ בִּתְשׁוּבָה שְׁלֵמָה לְפָנֶיךָ. בָּרוּךְ אַתָּה יהוה, הָרוֹצֶה בִּתְשׁוּבָה.

סליחה

Strike the left side of the chest with the right fist while reciting the words חָטָאנוּ and פָּשָׁעְנוּ.

סְלַח לָנוּ אָבִינוּ כִּי חָטָאנוּ, מְחַל לָנוּ מַלְכֵּנוּ כִּי פָשָׁעְנוּ, כִּי מוֹחֵל וְסוֹלֵחַ אָתָּה. בָּרוּךְ אַתָּה יהוה, חַנּוּן הַמַּרְבֶּה לִסְלוֹחַ.

גאולה

רְאֵה בְעָנְיֵנוּ, וְרִיבָה רִיבֵנוּ, וּגְאָלֵנוּ[1] מְהֵרָה לְמַעַן שְׁמֶךָ, כִּי גוֹאֵל חָזָק אָתָּה. בָּרוּךְ אַתָּה יהוה, גּוֹאֵל יִשְׂרָאֵל.

קדושה

When reciting *Kedushah,* one must stand with his feet together and avoid any interruptions. One should rise on his toes when saying the words קָדוֹשׁ, קָדוֹשׁ, קָדוֹשׁ; בָּרוּךְ (of בָּרוּךְ כְּבוֹד); and יִמְלֹךְ.

Cong. then *Chazzan* – **נְקַדֵּשׁ** אֶת שִׁמְךָ בָּעוֹלָם, כְּשֵׁם שֶׁמַּקְדִּישִׁים אוֹתוֹ בִּשְׁמֵי מָרוֹם, כַּכָּתוּב עַל יַד נְבִיאֶךָ, וְקָרָא זֶה אֶל זֶה וְאָמַר:

All – קָדוֹשׁ קָדוֹשׁ קָדוֹשׁ יהוה צְבָאוֹת, מְלֹא כָל הָאָרֶץ כְּבוֹדוֹ.[2]

Chazzan – לְעֻמָּתָם בָּרוּךְ יֹאמֵרוּ:

All – בָּרוּךְ כְּבוֹד יהוה, מִמְּקוֹמוֹ.[3]

Chazzan – וּבְדִבְרֵי קָדְשְׁךָ כָּתוּב לֵאמֹר:

All – יִמְלֹךְ יהוה לְעוֹלָם, אֱלֹהַיִךְ צִיּוֹן לְדֹר וָדֹר, הַלְלוּיָהּ.[4]

– *Chazzan* only concludes – לְדוֹר וָדוֹר נַגִּיד גָּדְלֶךָ וּלְנֵצַח נְצָחִים קְדֻשָּׁתְךָ נַקְדִּישׁ, וְשִׁבְחֲךָ אֱלֹהֵינוּ מִפִּינוּ לֹא יָמוּשׁ לְעוֹלָם וָעֶד, כִּי אֵל מֶלֶךְ גָּדוֹל וְקָדוֹשׁ אָתָּה. בָּרוּךְ אַתָּה יהוה, הָאֵל הַקָּדוֹשׁ.

Chazzan continues . . . אַתָּה חוֹנֵן (above).

HOLINESS OF GOD'S NAME

אַתָּה *You are holy and Your Name is holy, and holy ones praise You every day, forever. Blessed are You, HASHEM, the holy God.*

INSIGHT

אַתָּה *You graciously endow man with wisdom and teach insight to a frail mortal. Endow us graciously from Yourself with wisdom, insight, and discernment. Blessed are You, HASHEM, gracious Giver of wisdom.*

REPENTANCE

הֲשִׁיבֵנוּ *Bring us back, our Father, to Your Torah, and bring us near, our King, to Your service, and influence us to return in perfect repentance before You. Blessed are You, HASHEM, Who desires repentance.*

FORGIVENESS

Strike the left side of the chest with the right fist while reciting the words *'erred'* and *'sinned.'*

סְלַח *Forgive us, our Father, for we have erred; pardon us, our King, for we have willfully sinned; for You pardon and forgive. Blessed are You, HASHEM, the gracious One Who pardons abundantly.*

REDEMPTION

רְאֵה *Behold our affliction, take up our grievance, and redeem us*[1] *speedily for Your Name's sake, for You are a powerful Redeemer. Blessed are You, HASHEM, Redeemer of Israel.*

KEDUSHAH

When reciting *Kedushah*, one must stand with his feet together and avoid any interruptions. One should rise on his toes when saying the words *Holy, holy, holy; Blessed is;* and *HASHEM shall reign.*

Cong. then Chazzan – **נְקַדֵּשׁ** *We shall sanctify Your Name in this world, just as they sanctify it in heaven above, as it is written by Your prophet, "And one [angel] will call another and say:*

All – *'Holy, holy, holy is HASHEM, Master of Legions, the whole world is filled with His glory.'"*[2]

Chazzan – *Those facing them say 'Blessed':*

All – *'Blessed is the glory of HASHEM from His place.'*[3]

Chazzan – *And in Your holy Writings the following is written:*

All – *'HASHEM shall reign forever — your God, O Zion — from generation to generation, Halleluyah!'*[4]

Chazzan only concludes – *From generation to generation we shall relate Your greatness and for infinite eternities we shall proclaim Your holiness. Your praise, our God, shall not leave our mouth forever and ever, for You, O God, are a great and holy King. Blessed are You, HASHEM, the holy God.*

Chazzan continues אַתָּה חוֹנֵן, *You graciously endow . . .* (above).

---

(1) Cf. *Psalms* 119:153-154. (2) *Isaiah* 6:3. (3) *Ezekiel* 3:12. (4) *Psalms* 146:10.

רפואה

רְפָאֵנוּ יהוה וְנֵרָפֵא, הוֹשִׁיעֵנוּ וְנִוָּשֵׁעָה, כִּי תְהִלָּתֵנוּ אָתָּה,[1] וְהַעֲלֵה רְפוּאָה שְׁלֵמָה לְכָל מַכּוֹתֵינוּ, °°כִּי אֵל מֶלֶךְ רוֹפֵא נֶאֱמָן וְרַחֲמָן אָתָּה. בָּרוּךְ אַתָּה יהוה, רוֹפֵא חוֹלֵי עַמּוֹ יִשְׂרָאֵל.

ברכת השנים

בָּרֵךְ עָלֵינוּ יהוה אֱלֹהֵינוּ אֶת הַשָּׁנָה הַזֹּאת וְאֶת כָּל מִינֵי תְבוּאָתָהּ לְטוֹבָה, וְתֵן בְּרָכָה עַל פְּנֵי הָאֲדָמָה, וְשַׂבְּעֵנוּ מִטּוּבֶךָ, וּבָרֵךְ שְׁנָתֵנוּ כַּשָּׁנִים הַטּוֹבוֹת. בָּרוּךְ אַתָּה יהוה, מְבָרֵךְ הַשָּׁנִים.

קיבוץ גליות

תְּקַע בְּשׁוֹפָר גָּדוֹל לְחֵרוּתֵנוּ, וְשָׂא נֵס לְקַבֵּץ גָּלֻיּוֹתֵינוּ, וְקַבְּצֵנוּ יַחַד מֵאַרְבַּע כַּנְפוֹת הָאָרֶץ.[2] בָּרוּךְ אַתָּה יהוה, מְקַבֵּץ נִדְחֵי עַמּוֹ יִשְׂרָאֵל.

דין

הָשִׁיבָה שׁוֹפְטֵינוּ כְּבָרִאשׁוֹנָה, וְיוֹעֲצֵינוּ כְּבַתְּחִלָּה,[3] וְהָסֵר מִמֶּנּוּ יָגוֹן וַאֲנָחָה, וּמְלוֹךְ עָלֵינוּ אַתָּה יהוה לְבַדְּךָ בְּחֶסֶד וּבְרַחֲמִים, וְצַדְּקֵנוּ בַּמִּשְׁפָּט. בָּרוּךְ אַתָּה יהוה, מֶלֶךְ אוֹהֵב צְדָקָה וּמִשְׁפָּט.

ברכת המינים

וְלַמַּלְשִׁינִים אַל תְּהִי תִקְוָה, וְכָל הָרִשְׁעָה כְּרֶגַע תֹּאבֵד, וְכָל אֹיְבֶיךָ מְהֵרָה יִכָּרֵתוּ, וְהַזֵּדִים מְהֵרָה תְעַקֵּר וּתְשַׁבֵּר וּתְמַגֵּר וְתַכְנִיעַ בִּמְהֵרָה בְיָמֵינוּ. בָּרוּךְ אַתָּה יהוה, שׁוֹבֵר אֹיְבִים וּמַכְנִיעַ זֵדִים.

צדיקים

עַל הַצַּדִּיקִים וְעַל הַחֲסִידִים, וְעַל זִקְנֵי עַמְּךָ בֵּית יִשְׂרָאֵל, וְעַל פְּלֵיטַת סוֹפְרֵיהֶם, וְעַל גֵּרֵי הַצֶּדֶק וְעָלֵינוּ, יֶהֱמוּ רַחֲמֶיךָ יהוה אֱלֹהֵינוּ, וְתֵן שָׂכָר טוֹב לְכָל

°°At this point one may interject a prayer for one who is ill:

יְהִי רָצוֹן מִלְּפָנֶיךָ יהוה אֱלֹהַי וֵאלֹהֵי אֲבוֹתַי, שֶׁתִּשְׁלַח מְהֵרָה רְפוּאָה שְׁלֵמָה מִן הַשָּׁמַיִם, רְפוּאַת הַנֶּפֶשׁ וּרְפוּאַת הַגּוּף

for a male—לַחוֹלֶה (patient's name) בֶּן (mother's name) בְּתוֹךְ שְׁאָר חוֹלֵי יִשְׂרָאֵל.

for a female—לַחוֹלָה (patient's name) בַּת (mother's name) בְּתוֹךְ שְׁאָר חוֹלֵי יִשְׂרָאֵל.

Continue—כִּי אֵל . . .

HEALTH AND HEALING

רְפָאֵנוּ *Heal us,* HASHEM *— then we will be healed; save us — then we will be saved, for You are our praise.*[1] *Bring complete recovery for all our ailments,* °°*for You are God, King, the faithful and compassionate Healer. Blessed are You,* HASHEM, *Who heals the sick of His people Israel.*

YEAR OF PROSPERITY

בָּרֵךְ *Bless on our behalf — O* HASHEM, *our God — this year and all its kinds of crops for the best, and give a blessing on the face of the earth, and satisfy us from Your bounty, and bless our year like the best years. Blessed are You,* HASHEM, *Who blesses the years.*

INGATHERING OF EXILES

תְּקַע *Sound the great shofar for our freedom, raise the banner to gather our exiles and gather us together from the four corners of the earth.*[2] *Blessed are You,* HASHEM, *Who gathers in the dispersed of His people Israel.*

RESTORATION OF JUSTICE

הָשִׁיבָה *Restore our judges as in earliest times and our counselors as at first;*[3] *remove from us sorrow and groan; and reign over us — You,* HASHEM, *alone — with kindness and compassion, and justify us through judgment. Blessed are You,* HASHEM, *the King Who loves righteousness and judgment.*

AGAINST HERETICS

וְלַמַּלְשִׁינִים *And for slanderers let there be no hope; and may all wickedness perish in an instant; and may all Your enemies be cut down speedily. May You speedily uproot, smash, cast down, and humble the wanton sinners — speedily in our days. Blessed are You,* HASHEM, *Who breaks enemies and humbles wanton sinners.*

THE RIGHTEOUS

עַל הַצַּדִּיקִים *On the righteous, on the devout, on the elders of Your people the Family of Israel, on the remnant of their scholars, on the righteous converts and on ourselves — may Your compassion be aroused,* HASHEM, *our God, and give goodly reward to all*

°°At this point one may interject a prayer for one who is ill:

May it be Your will, HASHEM, *my God, and the God of my forefathers, that You quickly send a complete recovery from heaven, spiritual healing and physical healing to the patient* (name) *son/daughter of* (mother's name) *among the other patients of Israel.* Continue: *For You are God . . .*

(1) Cf. *Jeremiah* 17:14. (2) Cf. *Isaiah* 11:12. (3) Cf. 1:26.

הַבּוֹטְחִים בְּשִׁמְךָ בֶּאֱמֶת, וְשִׂים חֶלְקֵנוּ עִמָּהֶם לְעוֹלָם, וְלֹא נֵבוֹשׁ כִּי בְךָ בָּטָחְנוּ. בָּרוּךְ אַתָּה יהוה, מִשְׁעָן וּמִבְטָח לַצַּדִּיקִים.

בנין ירושלים

וְלִירוּשָׁלַיִם עִירְךָ בְּרַחֲמִים תָּשׁוּב, וְתִשְׁכּוֹן בְּתוֹכָהּ כַּאֲשֶׁר דִּבַּרְתָּ, וּבְנֵה אוֹתָהּ בְּקָרוֹב בְּיָמֵינוּ בִּנְיַן עוֹלָם, וְכִסֵּא דָוִד מְהֵרָה לְתוֹכָהּ תָּכִין. בָּרוּךְ אַתָּה יהוה, בּוֹנֵה יְרוּשָׁלָיִם.

מלכות בית דוד

אֶת צֶמַח דָּוִד עַבְדְּךָ מְהֵרָה תַצְמִיחַ, וְקַרְנוֹ תָּרוּם בִּישׁוּעָתֶךָ, כִּי לִישׁוּעָתְךָ קִוִּינוּ כָּל הַיּוֹם. בָּרוּךְ אַתָּה יהוה, מַצְמִיחַ קֶרֶן יְשׁוּעָה.

קבלת תפלה

שְׁמַע קוֹלֵנוּ יהוה אֱלֹהֵינוּ, חוּס וְרַחֵם עָלֵינוּ, וְקַבֵּל בְּרַחֲמִים וּבְרָצוֹן אֶת תְּפִלָּתֵנוּ, כִּי אֵל שׁוֹמֵעַ תְּפִלּוֹת וְתַחֲנוּנִים אָתָּה. וּמִלְּפָנֶיךָ מַלְכֵּנוּ רֵיקָם אַל תְּשִׁיבֵנוּ, °° כִּי אַתָּה שׁוֹמֵעַ תְּפִלַּת עַמְּךָ יִשְׂרָאֵל בְּרַחֲמִים. בָּרוּךְ אַתָּה יהוה, שׁוֹמֵעַ תְּפִלָּה.

עבודה

רְצֵה יהוה אֱלֹהֵינוּ בְּעַמְּךָ יִשְׂרָאֵל וּבִתְפִלָּתָם, וְהָשֵׁב אֶת הָעֲבוֹדָה לִדְבִיר בֵּיתֶךָ. וְאִשֵּׁי יִשְׂרָאֵל וּתְפִלָּתָם בְּאַהֲבָה תְקַבֵּל בְּרָצוֹן, וּתְהִי לְרָצוֹן תָּמִיד עֲבוֹדַת יִשְׂרָאֵל עַמֶּךָ.

°°During the silent *Shemoneh Esrei* one may insert either or both of these personal prayers.

For forgiveness:

אָנָּא יהוה, חָטָאתִי עָוִיתִי וּפָשַׁעְתִּי לְפָנֶיךָ, מִיּוֹם הֱיוֹתִי עַל הָאֲדָמָה עַד הַיּוֹם הַזֶּה (וּבִפְרַט בַּחֵטְא ....). אָנָּא יהוה, עֲשֵׂה לְמַעַן שִׁמְךָ הַגָּדוֹל, וּתְכַפֶּר לִי עַל עֲוֹנַי וַחֲטָאַי וּפְשָׁעַי שֶׁחָטָאתִי וְשֶׁעָוִיתִי וְשֶׁפָּשַׁעְתִּי לְפָנֶיךָ, מִנְּעוּרַי עַד הַיּוֹם הַזֶּה. וּתְמַלֵּא כָּל הַשֵּׁמוֹת שֶׁפָּגַמְתִּי בְּשִׁמְךָ הַגָּדוֹל.

For livelihood:

אַתָּה הוּא יהוה הָאֱלֹהִים, הַזָּן וּמְפַרְנֵס וּמְכַלְכֵּל מִקַּרְנֵי רְאֵמִים עַד בֵּיצֵי כִנִּים. הַטְרִיפֵנִי לֶחֶם חֻקִּי, וְהַמְצֵא לִי וּלְכָל בְּנֵי בֵיתִי מְזוֹנוֹתַי קוֹדֶם שֶׁאֶצְטָרֵךְ לָהֶם, בְּנַחַת וְלֹא בְצַעַר, בְּהֶתֵּר וְלֹא בְאִסּוּר, בְּכָבוֹד וְלֹא בְבִזָּיוֹן, לְחַיִּים וּלְשָׁלוֹם, מִשֶּׁפַע בְּרָכָה וְהַצְלָחָה, וּמִשֶּׁפַע בְּרֵכָה עֶלְיוֹנָה, כְּדֵי שֶׁאוּכַל לַעֲשׂוֹת רְצוֹנֶךָ וְלַעֲסוֹק בְּתוֹרָתֶךָ וּלְקַיֵּם מִצְוֹתֶיךָ. וְאַל תַּצְרִיכֵנִי לִידֵי מַתְּנַת בָּשָׂר וָדָם. וִיקֻיַּם בִּי מִקְרָא שֶׁכָּתוּב: פּוֹתֵחַ אֶת יָדֶךָ, וּמַשְׂבִּיעַ לְכָל חַי רָצוֹן.[1] וְכָתוּב: הַשְׁלֵךְ עַל יהוה יְהָבְךָ וְהוּא יְכַלְכְּלֶךָ.[2]

Continue — כִּי אַתָּה . . .

who sincerely believe in Your Name. Put our lot with them forever, and we will not feel ashamed, for we trust in You. Blessed are You, HASHEM, Mainstay and Assurance of the righteous.

REBUILDING JERUSALEM

וְלִירוּשָׁלַיִם *And to Jerusalem, Your city, may You return in compassion, and may You rest within it, as You have spoken. May You rebuild it soon in our days as an eternal structure, and may You speedily establish the throne of David within it. Blessed are You, HASHEM, the Builder of Jerusalem.*

DAVIDIC REIGN

אֶת צֶמַח *The offspring of Your servant David may You speedily cause to flourish, and enhance his pride through Your salvation, for we hope for Your salvation all day long. Blessed are You, HASHEM, Who causes the pride of salvation to flourish.*

ACCEPTANCE OF PRAYER

שְׁמַע *Hear our voice, HASHEM our God, pity and be compassionate to us, and accept — with compassion and favor — our prayer, for God Who hears prayers and supplications are You. From before Yourself, our King, turn us not away empty-handed,* °° *for You hear the prayer of Your people Israel with compassion. Blessed are You, HASHEM, Who hears prayer.*

TEMPLE SERVICE

רְצֵה *Be favorable, HASHEM, our God, toward Your people Israel and their prayer and restore the service to the Holy of Holies of Your Temple. The fire-offerings of Israel and their prayer accept with love and favor, and may the service of Your people Israel always be favorable to You.*

°°During the silent *Shemoneh Esrei* one may insert either or both of these personal prayers.

For forgiveness:

אָנָּא *Please, O HASHEM, I have erred, been iniquitous, and willfully sinned before You, from the day I have existed on earth until this very day (and especially with the sin of . . .). Please, HASHEM, act for the sake of Your Great Name and grant me atonement for my iniquities, my errors, and my willful sins through which I have erred, been iniquitous, and willfully sinned before You, from my youth until this day. And make whole all the Names that I have blemished in Your Great Name.*

For livelihood:

אַתָּה *It is You, HASHEM the God, Who nourishes, sustains, and supports, from the horns of re'eimim to the eggs of lice. Provide me with my allotment of bread; and bring forth for me and all members of my household, my food, before I have need for it; in contentment but not in pain, in a permissible but not a forbidden manner, in honor but not in disgrace, for life and for peace; from the flow of blessing and success and from the flow of the Heavenly spring, so that I be enabled to do Your will and engage in Your Torah and fulfill Your commandments. Make me not needful of people's largesse; and may there be fulfilled in me the verse that states, 'You open Your hand and satisfy the desire of every living thing'[1] and that states, 'Cast Your burden upon HASHEM and He will support you.'[2]*

Continue: *For You hear the prayer . . .*

---

(1) *Psalms* 145:16. (2) 55:23.

During the *chazzan's* repetition, congregation responds אָמֵן as indicated.
[If paragraph is forgotten, repeat *Shemoneh Esrei.* See *Laws* §56.]

אֱלֹהֵינוּ וֵאלֹהֵי אֲבוֹתֵינוּ, יַעֲלֶה, וְיָבֹא, וְיַגִּיעַ, וְיֵרָאֶה, וְיֵרָצֶה, וְיִשָּׁמַע, וְיִפָּקֵד, וְיִזָּכֵר זִכְרוֹנֵנוּ וּפִקְדוֹנֵנוּ, וְזִכְרוֹן אֲבוֹתֵינוּ, וְזִכְרוֹן מָשִׁיחַ בֶּן דָּוִד עַבְדֶּךָ, וְזִכְרוֹן יְרוּשָׁלַיִם עִיר קָדְשֶׁךָ, וְזִכְרוֹן כָּל עַמְּךָ בֵּית יִשְׂרָאֵל לְפָנֶיךָ, לִפְלֵיטָה לְטוֹבָה לְחֵן וּלְחֶסֶד וּלְרַחֲמִים, לְחַיִּים וּלְשָׁלוֹם בְּיוֹם חַג הַמַּצּוֹת הַזֶּה. זָכְרֵנוּ יהוה אֱלֹהֵינוּ בּוֹ לְטוֹבָה (Cong.– אָמֵן), וּפָקְדֵנוּ בוֹ לִבְרָכָה (Cong.– אָמֵן), וְהוֹשִׁיעֵנוּ בוֹ לְחַיִּים (Cong.– אָמֵן). וּבִדְבַר יְשׁוּעָה וְרַחֲמִים, חוּס וְחָנֵּנוּ וְרַחֵם עָלֵינוּ וְהוֹשִׁיעֵנוּ, כִּי אֵלֶיךָ עֵינֵינוּ, כִּי אֵל מֶלֶךְ חַנּוּן וְרַחוּם אָתָּה.[1]

וְתֶחֱזֶינָה עֵינֵינוּ בְּשׁוּבְךָ לְצִיּוֹן בְּרַחֲמִים. בָּרוּךְ אַתָּה יהוה, הַמַּחֲזִיר שְׁכִינָתוֹ לְצִיּוֹן.

הודאה

Bow at מוֹדִים; straighten up at ה׳. In his repetition the *chazzan* should recite the entire מוֹדִים aloud, while the congregation recites מוֹדִים דְּרַבָּנָן softly.

מוֹדִים אֲנַחְנוּ לָךְ, שָׁאַתָּה הוּא יהוה אֱלֹהֵינוּ וֵאלֹהֵי אֲבוֹתֵינוּ לְעוֹלָם וָעֶד. צוּר חַיֵּינוּ, מָגֵן יִשְׁעֵנוּ אַתָּה הוּא לְדוֹר וָדוֹר. נוֹדֶה לְּךָ וּנְסַפֵּר תְּהִלָּתֶךָ[2] עַל חַיֵּינוּ הַמְּסוּרִים בְּיָדֶךָ, וְעַל נִשְׁמוֹתֵינוּ הַפְּקוּדוֹת לָךְ, וְעַל נִסֶּיךָ שֶׁבְּכָל יוֹם עִמָּנוּ, וְעַל נִפְלְאוֹתֶיךָ וְטוֹבוֹתֶיךָ שֶׁבְּכָל עֵת, עֶרֶב וָבֹקֶר וְצָהֳרָיִם. הַטּוֹב כִּי לֹא כָלוּ רַחֲמֶיךָ, וְהַמְרַחֵם כִּי לֹא תַמּוּ חֲסָדֶיךָ,[3] מֵעוֹלָם קִוִּינוּ לָךְ.

מודים דרבנן

מוֹדִים אֲנַחְנוּ לָךְ, שָׁאַתָּה הוּא יהוה אֱלֹהֵינוּ וֵאלֹהֵי אֲבוֹתֵינוּ, אֱלֹהֵי כָל בָּשָׂר, יוֹצְרֵנוּ, יוֹצֵר בְּרֵאשִׁית. בְּרָכוֹת וְהוֹדָאוֹת לְשִׁמְךָ הַגָּדוֹל וְהַקָּדוֹשׁ, עַל שֶׁהֶחֱיִיתָנוּ וְקִיַּמְתָּנוּ. כֵּן תְּחַיֵּנוּ וּתְקַיְּמֵנוּ, וְתֶאֱסוֹף גָּלֻיּוֹתֵינוּ לְחַצְרוֹת קָדְשֶׁךָ, לִשְׁמוֹר חֻקֶּיךָ וְלַעֲשׂוֹת רְצוֹנֶךָ, וּלְעָבְדְּךָ בְּלֵבָב שָׁלֵם, עַל שֶׁאֲנַחְנוּ מוֹדִים לָךְ. בָּרוּךְ אֵל הַהוֹדָאוֹת.

During the *chazzan's* repetition, congregation responds *Amen* as indicated.
[If paragraph is forgotten, repeat *Shemoneh Esrei*. See *Laws* §56.]

אֱלֹהֵינוּ *Our God and God of our forefathers, may there rise, come, reach, be noted, be favored, be heard, be considered, and be remembered — the remembrance and consideration of ourselves; the remembrance of our forefathers; the remembrance of Messiah, son of David, Your servant; the remembrance of Jerusalem, the City of Your Holiness; the remembrance of Your entire people the Family of Israel — before You for deliverance, for goodness, for grace, for kindness, and for compassion, for life, and for peace on this day of the Festival of Matzos. Remember us on it, HASHEM, our God, for goodness* (Cong.–*Amen*)*; consider us on it for blessing* (Cong.–*Amen*)*; and help us on it for life* (Cong.–*Amen*)*. In the matter of salvation and compassion, pity, be gracious and compassionate with us and help us, for our eyes are turned to You, because You are God, the gracious and compassionate King.*[1]

וְתֶחֱזֶינָה *May our eyes behold Your return to Zion in compassion. Blessed are You, HASHEM, Who restores His Presence unto Zion.*

THANKSGIVING [MODIM]

Bow at *'We gratefully thank You'*; straighten up at *'HASHEM.'* In his repetition the *chazzan* should recite the entire *Modim* aloud, while the congregation recites *Modim of the Rabbis* softly.

מוֹדִים *We gratefully thank You, for it is You Who are HASHEM, our God and the God of our forefathers for all eternity; Rock of our lives, Shield of our salvation are You from generation to generation. We shall thank You and relate Your praise*[2] *— for our lives, which are committed to Your power and for our souls that are entrusted to You; for Your miracles that are with us every day; and for Your wonders and favors in every season — evening, morning, and afternoon. The Beneficent One, for Your compassions were never exhausted, and the Compassionate One, for Your kindnesses never ended*[3] *— always have we put our hope in You.*

MODIM OF THE RABBIS

מוֹדִים *We gratefully thank You, for it is You Who are HASHEM, our God and the God of our forefathers, the God of all flesh, our Molder, the Molder of the universe. Blessings and thanks are due Your great and holy Name for You have given us life and sustained us. So may You continue to give us life and sustain us and gather our exiles to the Courtyards of Your Sanctuary, to observe Your decrees, to do Your will and to serve You wholeheartedly. [We thank You] for inspiring us to thank You. Blessed is the God of thanksgivings.*

(1) Cf. *Nehemiah* 9:31. (2) Cf. *Psalms* 79:13. (3) Cf. *Lamentations* 3:22.

וְעַל כֻּלָּם יִתְבָּרַךְ וְיִתְרוֹמַם שִׁמְךָ מַלְכֵּנוּ תָּמִיד לְעוֹלָם וָעֶד.

Bend the knees at בָּרוּךְ; bow at אַתָּה; straighten up at ה׳.

וְכֹל הַחַיִּים יוֹדְוּךָ סֶּלָה, וִיהַלְלוּ אֶת שִׁמְךָ בֶּאֱמֶת, הָאֵל יְשׁוּעָתֵנוּ וְעֶזְרָתֵנוּ סֶלָה. בָּרוּךְ אַתָּה יהוה, הַטּוֹב שִׁמְךָ וּלְךָ נָאֶה לְהוֹדוֹת.

שלום

שָׁלוֹם רָב עַל יִשְׂרָאֵל עַמְּךָ תָּשִׂים לְעוֹלָם, כִּי אַתָּה הוּא מֶלֶךְ אָדוֹן לְכָל הַשָּׁלוֹם. וְטוֹב בְּעֵינֶיךָ לְבָרֵךְ אֶת עַמְּךָ יִשְׂרָאֵל, בְּכָל עֵת וּבְכָל שָׁעָה בִּשְׁלוֹמֶךָ. בָּרוּךְ אַתָּה יהוה, הַמְּבָרֵךְ אֶת עַמּוֹ יִשְׂרָאֵל בַּשָּׁלוֹם.

יִהְיוּ לְרָצוֹן אִמְרֵי פִי וְהֶגְיוֹן לִבִּי לְפָנֶיךָ, יהוה צוּרִי וְגֹאֲלִי.[1]

Chazzan's repetition of *Shemoneh Esrei* ends here. Individuals continue below.

אֱלֹהַי, נְצוֹר לְשׁוֹנִי מֵרָע, וּשְׂפָתַי מִדַּבֵּר מִרְמָה,[2] וְלִמְקַלְּלַי נַפְשִׁי תִדּוֹם, וְנַפְשִׁי כֶּעָפָר לַכֹּל תִּהְיֶה. פְּתַח לִבִּי בְּתוֹרָתֶךָ, וּבְמִצְוֹתֶיךָ תִּרְדּוֹף נַפְשִׁי. וְכֹל הַחוֹשְׁבִים עָלַי רָעָה, מְהֵרָה הָפֵר עֲצָתָם וְקַלְקֵל מַחֲשַׁבְתָּם. עֲשֵׂה לְמַעַן שְׁמֶךָ, עֲשֵׂה לְמַעַן יְמִינֶךָ, עֲשֵׂה לְמַעַן קְדֻשָּׁתֶךָ, עֲשֵׂה לְמַעַן תּוֹרָתֶךָ. לְמַעַן יֵחָלְצוּן יְדִידֶיךָ, הוֹשִׁיעָה יְמִינְךָ וַעֲנֵנִי.[3]

Some recite verses pertaining to their names. See page 1143.

יִהְיוּ לְרָצוֹן אִמְרֵי פִי וְהֶגְיוֹן לִבִּי לְפָנֶיךָ, יהוה צוּרִי וְגֹאֲלִי.[1]

Bow and take three steps back. Bow left and say ... עֹשֶׂה; bow right and say ... הוּא יַעֲשֶׂה; bow forward and say וְעַל כָּל ... אָמֵן.

עֹשֶׂה שָׁלוֹם בִּמְרוֹמָיו, הוּא יַעֲשֶׂה שָׁלוֹם עָלֵינוּ, וְעַל כָּל יִשְׂרָאֵל. וְאִמְרוּ: אָמֵן.

יְהִי רָצוֹן מִלְּפָנֶיךָ יהוה אֱלֹהֵינוּ וֵאלֹהֵי אֲבוֹתֵינוּ, שֶׁיִּבָּנֶה בֵּית הַמִּקְדָּשׁ בִּמְהֵרָה בְיָמֵינוּ, וְתֵן חֶלְקֵנוּ בְּתוֹרָתֶךָ. וְשָׁם נַעֲבָדְךָ בְּיִרְאָה, כִּימֵי עוֹלָם וּכְשָׁנִים קַדְמוֹנִיּוֹת. וְעָרְבָה לַיהוה מִנְחַת יְהוּדָה וִירוּשָׁלָיִם, כִּימֵי עוֹלָם וּכְשָׁנִים קַדְמוֹנִיּוֹת.[4]

THE INDIVIDUAL'S RECITATION OF שְׁמוֹנֶה עֶשְׂרֵה ENDS HERE.

The individual remains standing in place until the *chazzan* reaches *Kedushah* — or at least until the *chazzan* begins his repetition — then he takes three steps forward. The *chazzan* himself, or one praying alone, should remain in place for a few moments before taking three steps forward.

For all these, may Your Name be blessed and exalted, our King, continually forever and ever.

Bend the knees at *'Blessed'*; bow at *'You'*; straighten up at *'HASHEM.'*

Everything alive will gratefully acknowledge You, Selah! and praise Your Name sincerely, O God of our salvation and help, Selah! Blessed are You, HASHEM, Your Name is 'The Beneficent One' and to You it is fitting to give thanks.

PEACE

שָׁלוֹם *Establish abundant peace upon Your people Israel forever, for You are King, Master of all peace. May it be good in Your eyes to bless Your people Israel at every time and every hour with Your peace. Blessed are You, HASHEM, Who blesses His people Israel with peace.*

May the expressions of my mouth and the thoughts of my heart find favor before You, HASHEM, my Rock and my Redeemer.[1]

Chazzan's repetition of *Shemoneh Esrei* ends here. Individuals continue below.

אֱלֹהַי *My God, guard my tongue from evil and my lips from speaking deceitfully.*[2] *To those who curse me, let my soul be silent; and let my soul be like dust to everyone. Open my heart to Your Torah, then my soul will pursue Your commandments. As for all those who design evil against me, speedily nullify their counsel and disrupt their design. Act for Your Name's sake; act for Your right hand's sake; act for Your sanctity's sake; act for Your Torah's sake. That Your beloved ones may be given rest; let Your right hand save, and respond to me.*[3]

Some recite verses pertaining to their names at this point. See page 1143.

May the expressions of my mouth and the thoughts of my heart find favor before You, HASHEM, my Rock and my Redeemer.[1] *He Who makes peace in His heights, may He make peace upon us, and upon all Israel. Now respond: Amen.*

Bow and take three steps back. Bow left and say, *'He Who makes peace . . .'*; bow right and say, *'may He make peace . . .'*; bow forward and say, *'and upon . . . Amen.'*

יְהִי רָצוֹן *May it be Your will, HASHEM, our God and the God of our forefathers, that the Holy Temple be rebuilt, speedily in our days. Grant us our share in Your Torah, and may we serve You there with reverence, as in days of old and in former years. Then the offering of Judah and Jerusalem will be pleasing to HASHEM, as in days of old and in former years.*[4]

THE INDIVIDUAL'S RECITATION OF *SHEMONEH ESREI* ENDS HERE.

The individual remains standing in place until the *chazzan* reaches *Kedushah* – or at least until the *chazzan* begins his repetition – then he takes three steps forward. The *chazzan* himself, or one praying alone, should remain in place for a few moments before taking three steps forward.

---

(1) *Psalms* 19:15. (2) Cf. 34:14. (3) 60:7;108:7. (4) *Malachi* 3:4.

קדיש שלם

The *chazzan* recites קַדִּישׁ שָׁלֵם.

יִתְגַּדַּל וְיִתְקַדַּשׁ שְׁמֵהּ רַבָּא. (.Cong – אָמֵן.) בְּעָלְמָא דִּי בְרָא כִרְעוּתֵהּ. וְיַמְלִיךְ מַלְכוּתֵהּ, בְּחַיֵּיכוֹן וּבְיוֹמֵיכוֹן וּבְחַיֵּי דְכָל בֵּית יִשְׂרָאֵל, בַּעֲגָלָא וּבִזְמַן קָרִיב. וְאִמְרוּ: אָמֵן.

(.Cong – אָמֵן. יְהֵא שְׁמֵהּ רַבָּא מְבָרַךְ לְעָלַם וּלְעָלְמֵי עָלְמַיָּא.)

יְהֵא שְׁמֵהּ רַבָּא מְבָרַךְ לְעָלַם וּלְעָלְמֵי עָלְמַיָּא.

יִתְבָּרַךְ וְיִשְׁתַּבַּח וְיִתְפָּאַר וְיִתְרוֹמַם וְיִתְנַשֵּׂא וְיִתְהַדָּר וְיִתְעַלֶּה וְיִתְהַלָּל שְׁמֵהּ דְּקֻדְשָׁא בְּרִיךְ הוּא (.Cong – בְּרִיךְ הוּא) – לְעֵלָּא מִן כָּל בִּרְכָתָא וְשִׁירָתָא תֻּשְׁבְּחָתָא וְנֶחֱמָתָא, דַּאֲמִירָן בְּעָלְמָא. וְאִמְרוּ: אָמֵן. (.Cong – אָמֵן.)

(.Cong – קַבֵּל בְּרַחֲמִים וּבְרָצוֹן אֶת תְּפִלָּתֵנוּ.)

תִּתְקַבֵּל צְלוֹתְהוֹן וּבָעוּתְהוֹן דְּכָל בֵּית יִשְׂרָאֵל קֳדָם אֲבוּהוֹן דִּי בִשְׁמַיָּא. וְאִמְרוּ: אָמֵן. (.Cong – אָמֵן.)

(.Cong – יְהִי שֵׁם יהוה מְבֹרָךְ, מֵעַתָּה וְעַד עוֹלָם.[1])

יְהֵא שְׁלָמָא רַבָּא מִן שְׁמַיָּא, וְחַיִּים עָלֵינוּ וְעַל כָּל יִשְׂרָאֵל. וְאִמְרוּ: אָמֵן. (.Cong – אָמֵן.)

(.Cong – עֶזְרִי מֵעִם יהוה, עֹשֵׂה שָׁמַיִם וָאָרֶץ.[2])

Take three steps back. Bow left and say . . . עֹשֶׂה; bow right and say . . . הוּא; bow forward and say וְעַל כָּל . . . אָמֵן. Remain standing in place for a few moments, then take three steps forward.

עֹשֶׂה שָׁלוֹם בִּמְרוֹמָיו, הוּא יַעֲשֶׂה שָׁלוֹם עָלֵינוּ, וְעַל כָּל יִשְׂרָאֵל. וְאִמְרוּ: אָמֵן. (.Cong – אָמֵן.)

עלינו

Stand while reciting עָלֵינוּ.

עָלֵינוּ לְשַׁבֵּחַ לַאֲדוֹן הַכֹּל, לָתֵת גְּדֻלָּה לְיוֹצֵר בְּרֵאשִׁית, שֶׁלֹּא עָשָׂנוּ כְּגוֹיֵי הָאֲרָצוֹת, וְלֹא שָׂמָנוּ כְּמִשְׁפְּחוֹת הָאֲדָמָה. שֶׁלֹּא שָׂם חֶלְקֵנוּ כָּהֶם, וְגוֹרָלֵנוּ כְּכָל הֲמוֹנָם. (שֶׁהֵם מִשְׁתַּחֲוִים לְהֶבֶל וָרִיק, וּמִתְפַּלְלִים אֶל אֵל לֹא יוֹשִׁיעַ.[3]) וַאֲנַחְנוּ כּוֹרְעִים וּמִשְׁתַּחֲוִים וּמוֹדִים, לִפְנֵי מֶלֶךְ מַלְכֵי הַמְּלָכִים הַקָּדוֹשׁ בָּרוּךְ הוּא. שֶׁהוּא נוֹטֶה שָׁמַיִם וְיֹסֵד אָרֶץ,[4] וּמוֹשַׁב יְקָרוֹ בַּשָּׁמַיִם מִמַּעַל, וּשְׁכִינַת עֻזּוֹ בְּגָבְהֵי מְרוֹמִים. הוּא אֱלֹהֵינוּ, אֵין עוֹד. אֱמֶת מַלְכֵּנוּ, אֶפֶס זוּלָתוֹ, כַּכָּתוּב בְּתוֹרָתוֹ: וְיָדַעְתָּ הַיּוֹם וַהֲשֵׁבֹתָ אֶל לְבָבֶךָ, כִּי יהוה הוּא הָאֱלֹהִים בַּשָּׁמַיִם מִמַּעַל וְעַל הָאָרֶץ מִתָּחַת, אֵין עוֹד.[5]

Bow while reciting וַאֲנַחְנוּ כּוֹרְעִים וּמִשְׁתַּחֲוִים.

FULL KADDISH

The *chazzan* recites the Full *Kaddish.*

יִתְגַּדַּל *May His great Name grow exalted and sanctified* (Cong.— *Amen.*) *in the world that He created as He willed. May He give reign to His kingship in your lifetimes and in your days, and in the lifetimes of the entire Family of Israel, swiftly and soon. Now respond: Amen.*

(Cong.— *Amen. May His great Name be blessed forever and ever.*)

May His great Name be blessed forever and ever.

Blessed, praised, glorified, exalted, extolled, mighty, upraised, and lauded be the Name of the Holy One, Blessed is He (Cong.— *Blessed is He*) — *beyond any blessing and song, praise and consolation that are uttered in the world. Now respond: Amen.* (Cong.— *Amen.*)

(Cong.— *Accept our prayers with mercy and favor.*)

May the prayers and supplications of the entire Family of Israel be accepted before their Father Who is in Heaven. Now respond: Amen. (Cong.— *Amen.*)

(Cong.— *Blessed be the Name of* HASHEM, *from this time and forever.*[1])

May there be abundant peace from Heaven, and life, upon us and upon all Israel. Now respond: Amen. (Cong.— *Amen.*)

(Cong.— *My help is from* HASHEM, *Maker of heaven and earth.*[2])

Take three steps back. Bow left and say, *'He Who makes peace . . .'*; bow right and say, *'may He . . .'*; bow forward and say, *'and upon all Israel . . .'* Remain standing in place for a few moments, then take three steps forward.

He Who makes peace in His heights, may He make peace upon us, and upon all Israel. Now respond: Amen. (Cong.— *Amen.*)

ALEINU

Stand while reciting עָלֵינוּ, *'It is our duty . . .'*

עָלֵינוּ *It is our duty to praise the Master of all, to ascribe greatness to the Molder of primeval creation, for He has not made us like the nations of the lands, and has not emplaced us like the families of the earth; for He has not assigned our portion like theirs nor our lot like all their multitudes. (For they bow to vanity and emptiness and pray to a god which helps not.*[3]*) But we bend our knees, bow, and acknowledge our thanks before the King Who reigns over kings, the Holy One, Blessed is He. He stretches out heaven and establishes earth's foundation,*[4] *the seat of His homage is in the heavens above and His powerful Presence is in the loftiest heights. He is our God and there is none other. True is our King, there is nothing beside Him, as it is written in His Torah: 'You are to know this day and take to your heart that* HASHEM *is the only God — in heaven above and on the earth below — there is none other.'*[5]

Bow while reciting *'But we bend our knees.'*

(1) *Psalms* 113:2. (2) 121:2. (3) *Isaiah* 45:20. (4) 51:13. (5) *Deuteronomy* 4:39.

עַל כֵּן נְקַוֶּה לְּךָ יהוה אֱלֹהֵינוּ לִרְאוֹת מְהֵרָה בְּתִפְאֶרֶת עֻזֶּךָ, לְהַעֲבִיר גִּלּוּלִים מִן הָאָרֶץ, וְהָאֱלִילִים כָּרוֹת יִכָּרֵתוּן, לְתַקֵּן עוֹלָם בְּמַלְכוּת שַׁדַּי. וְכָל בְּנֵי בָשָׂר יִקְרְאוּ בִשְׁמֶךָ, לְהַפְנוֹת אֵלֶיךָ כָּל רִשְׁעֵי אָרֶץ. יַכִּירוּ וְיֵדְעוּ כָּל יוֹשְׁבֵי תֵבֵל, כִּי לְךָ תִּכְרַע כָּל בֶּרֶךְ, תִּשָּׁבַע כָּל לָשׁוֹן.[1] לְפָנֶיךָ יהוה אֱלֹהֵינוּ יִכְרְעוּ וְיִפֹּלוּ, וְלִכְבוֹד שִׁמְךָ יְקָר יִתֵּנוּ. וִיקַבְּלוּ כֻלָּם אֶת עוֹל מַלְכוּתֶךָ, וְתִמְלֹךְ עֲלֵיהֶם מְהֵרָה לְעוֹלָם וָעֶד. כִּי הַמַּלְכוּת שֶׁלְּךָ הִיא וּלְעוֹלְמֵי עַד תִּמְלוֹךְ בְּכָבוֹד, כַּכָּתוּב בְּתוֹרָתֶךָ: יהוה יִמְלֹךְ לְעֹלָם וָעֶד.[2] ❖ וְנֶאֱמַר: וְהָיָה יהוה לְמֶלֶךְ עַל כָּל הָאָרֶץ, בַּיּוֹם הַהוּא יִהְיֶה יהוה אֶחָד וּשְׁמוֹ אֶחָד.[3]

Some congregations recite the following after עָלֵינוּ.

אַל תִּירָא מִפַּחַד פִּתְאֹם, וּמִשֹּׁאַת רְשָׁעִים כִּי תָבֹא.[4] עֻצוּ עֵצָה וְתֻפָר, דַּבְּרוּ דָבָר וְלֹא יָקוּם, כִּי עִמָּנוּ אֵל.[5] וְעַד זִקְנָה אֲנִי הוּא, וְעַד שֵׂיבָה אֲנִי אֶסְבֹּל, אֲנִי עָשִׂיתִי וַאֲנִי אֶשָּׂא, וַאֲנִי אֶסְבֹּל וַאֲמַלֵּט.[6]

קדיש יתום

In the presence of a *minyan,* mourners recite קַדִּישׁ יָתוֹם, the Mourner's *Kaddish* (see *Laws* §81-83).

יִתְגַּדַּל וְיִתְקַדַּשׁ שְׁמֵהּ רַבָּא. (.Cong – אָמֵן.) בְּעָלְמָא דִּי בְרָא כִרְעוּתֵהּ. וְיַמְלִיךְ מַלְכוּתֵהּ, בְּחַיֵּיכוֹן וּבְיוֹמֵיכוֹן וּבְחַיֵּי דְכָל בֵּית יִשְׂרָאֵל, בַּעֲגָלָא וּבִזְמַן קָרִיב. וְאִמְרוּ: אָמֵן.

(.Cong – אָמֵן. יְהֵא שְׁמֵהּ רַבָּא מְבָרַךְ לְעָלַם וּלְעָלְמֵי עָלְמַיָּא.)

יְהֵא שְׁמֵהּ רַבָּא מְבָרַךְ לְעָלַם וּלְעָלְמֵי עָלְמַיָּא.

יִתְבָּרַךְ וְיִשְׁתַּבַּח וְיִתְפָּאַר וְיִתְרוֹמַם וְיִתְנַשֵּׂא וְיִתְהַדָּר וְיִתְעַלֶּה וְיִתְהַלָּל שְׁמֵהּ דְּקֻדְשָׁא בְּרִיךְ הוּא (.Cong – בְּרִיךְ הוּא) — לְעֵלָּא מִן כָּל בִּרְכָתָא וְשִׁירָתָא תֻּשְׁבְּחָתָא וְנֶחֱמָתָא, דַּאֲמִירָן בְּעָלְמָא. וְאִמְרוּ: אָמֵן. (.Cong – אָמֵן.)

יְהֵא שְׁלָמָא רַבָּא מִן שְׁמַיָּא, וְחַיִּים עָלֵינוּ וְעַל כָּל יִשְׂרָאֵל. וְאִמְרוּ: אָמֵן. (.Cong – אָמֵן.)

Take three steps back. Bow left and say . . . עֹשֶׂה; bow right and say . . . הוּא; bow forward and say וְעַל כָּל . . . אָמֵן. Remain standing in place for a few moments, then take three steps forward.

עֹשֶׂה שָׁלוֹם בִּמְרוֹמָיו, הוּא יַעֲשֶׂה שָׁלוֹם עָלֵינוּ, וְעַל כָּל יִשְׂרָאֵל. וְאִמְרוּ: אָמֵן. (.Cong – אָמֵן.)

עַל כֵּן *Therefore we put our hope in You, HASHEM, our God, that we may soon see Your mighty splendor, to remove detestable idolatry from the earth, and false gods will be utterly cut off, to perfect the universe through the Almighty's sovereignty. Then all humanity will call upon Your Name, to turn all the earth's wicked toward You. All the world's inhabitants will recognize and know that to You every knee should bend, every tongue should swear.*[1] *Before You, HASHEM, our God, they will bend every knee and cast themselves down and to the glory of Your Name they will render homage, and they will all accept upon themselves the yoke of Your kingship that You may reign over them soon and eternally. For the kingdom is Yours and You will reign for all eternity in glory as it is written in Your Torah: HASHEM shall reign for all eternity.*[2] Chazzan– *And it is said: HASHEM will be King over all the world — on that day HASHEM will be One and His Name will be One.*[3]

Some congregations recite the following after *Aleinu*.

אַל תִּירָא *Do not fear sudden terror, or the holocaust of the wicked when it comes.*[4] *Plan a conspiracy and it will be annulled; speak your piece and it shall not stand, for God is with us.*[5] *Even till your seniority, I remain unchanged; and even till your ripe old age, I shall endure. I created you and I shall bear you; I shall endure and rescue.*[6]

MOURNER'S KADDISH

In the presence of a *minyan,* mourners recite קַדִּישׁ יָתוֹם, the Mourner's *Kaddish* (see *Laws* 81-83).

[A transliteration of this *Kaddish* appears on page 1147.]

יִתְגַּדַּל *May His great Name grow exalted and sanctified* (Cong.– *Amen.*) *in the world that He created as He willed. May He give reign to His kingship in your lifetimes and in your days, and in the lifetimes of the entire Family of Israel, swiftly and soon. Now respond: Amen.*

(Cong.– *Amen. May His great Name be blessed forever and ever.*)

May His great Name be blessed forever and ever.

Blessed, praised, glorified, exalted, extolled, mighty, upraised, and lauded be the Name of the Holy One, Blessed is He (Cong.– *Blessed is He*) *— beyond any blessing and song, praise and consolation that are uttered in the world. Now respond: Amen.* (Cong.– *Amen*).

May there be abundant peace from Heaven, and life, upon us and upon all Israel. Now respond: Amen. (Cong.– *Amen.*)

Take three steps back. Bow left and say, *'He Who makes peace . . .';* bow right and say, *'may He . . .';* bow forward and say, *'and upon all Israel . . .'* Remain standing in place for a few moments, then take three steps forward.

He Who makes peace in His heights, may He make peace upon us, and upon all Israel. Now respond: Amen. (Cong.– *Amen.*)

---

(1) Cf. *Isaiah* 45:23. (2) *Exodus* 15:18. (3) *Zechariah* 14:9.
(4) *Proverbs* 3:25. (5) *Isaiah* 8:10. (6) 46:4.

שני ימים האחרונים

Last Days

ערוב תבשילין

When the seventh day of Pesach falls on Friday, an *eruv tavshilin* is made on Thursday *Erev Yom Tov* [see commentary]. The *eruv*-foods are held while the following blessing and declaration are recited.

בָּרוּךְ אַתָּה יהוה אֱלֹהֵינוּ מֶלֶךְ הָעוֹלָם, אֲשֶׁר קִדְּשָׁנוּ בְּמִצְוֹתָיו, וְצִוָּנוּ עַל מִצְוַת עֵרוּב.

בַּהֲדֵין עֵרוּבָא יְהֵא שָׁרֵא לָנָא לַאֲפוּיֵי וּלְבַשּׁוּלֵי וּלְאַטְמוּנֵי וּלְאַדְלוּקֵי שְׁרָגָא וּלְתַקָּנָא וּלְמֶעְבַּד כָּל צָרְכָּנָא, מִיּוֹמָא טָבָא לְשַׁבְּתָא [לָנָא וּלְכָל יִשְׂרָאֵל* הַדָּרִים בָּעִיר הַזֹּאת].

ערובי תחומין

The *eruv*-food is put in a safe place [see commentary] and the following blessing and declaration are recited. The appropriate bracketed phrases should be added.

בָּרוּךְ אַתָּה יהוה אֱלֹהֵינוּ מֶלֶךְ הָעוֹלָם, אֲשֶׁר קִדְּשָׁנוּ בְּמִצְוֹתָיו, וְצִוָּנוּ עַל מִצְוַת עֵרוּב.

בְּזֶה הָעֵרוּב יְהֵא מֻתָּר [לִי/לָנוּ] לֵילֵךְ מִמָּקוֹם זֶה אַלְפַּיִם אַמָּה לְכָל רוּחַ בְּ[שַׁבָּת וּבְ]יוֹם טוֹב זֶה.

ערובי חצרות

This *eruv* is required for the Sabbath, but not for a weekday Festival [see commentary]. The *eruv*-foods are held while the following blessing and declaration are recited. [If the *eruv* is made for the entire year, the bracketed passage is added.]

בָּרוּךְ אַתָּה יהוה אֱלֹהֵינוּ מֶלֶךְ הָעוֹלָם, אֲשֶׁר קִדְּשָׁנוּ בְּמִצְוֹתָיו, וְצִוָּנוּ עַל מִצְוַת עֵרוּב.

בַּהֲדֵין עֵרוּבָא יְהֵא שָׁרֵא לָנָא לְאַפּוּקֵי וּלְעַיּוּלֵי מִן הַבָּתִּים לֶחָצֵר, וּמִן הֶחָצֵר לְבָתִּים, וּמִבַּיִת לְבַיִת, וּמֵחָצֵר לְחָצֵר, וּמִגַּג לְגַג, כָּל מַאי דִצְרִיךְ לָן, וּלְכָל יִשְׂרָאֵל הַדָּרִים בַּשְּׁכוּנָה זוּ [וּלְכָל מִי שֶׁיִּתּוֹסֵף בָּהּ, לְכָל שַׁבְּתוֹת הַשָּׁנָה, וּלְכָל יָמִים טוֹבִים].

עֵרוּב תַּבְשִׁילִין / ERUV TAVSHILIN

The Biblical prohibition against labor on the Festivals (*Exodus* 12:16) specifically excludes preparation of food. Still, it is forbidden to prepare food on a Festival for use on another day. When a Festival falls on Friday, however, it is permitted to prepare food needed for the Sabbath. But since this may lead people to think that they may even cook in preparation for a weekday, the Rabbis attached a condition to the preparation of Sabbath meals on a Festival — i.e., such preparations must be started before the Festival (*Pesachim* 46b). Thus, when Yom Tov falls on Friday and *Shabbos*, preparations for the Sabbath meal must begin on Thursday. This enactment is called *eruv tavshilin*, literally, *mingling of cooked foods*. It consists of a *matzah* along with any other cooked food (such as fish, meat or an egg), set aside on the day before the Festival to be eaten on the Sabbath. The *eruv*-foods are held in the hand (*Orach Chaim* 527:2) and a blessing is recited. Since the person setting the *eruv* must understand its purpose, the accompanying declaration [beginning בַּהֲדֵין, *'Through this . . .'*] must be said in

ERUV TAVSHILIN

When the seventh day of Pesach falls on Friday, an *eruv tavshilin* is made on Thursday *Erev Yom Tov* [see commentary]. The *eruv*-foods are held while the following blessing and declaration are recited.

בָּרוּךְ *Blessed are You, HASHEM, our God, King of the universe, Who has sanctified us with His commandments and has commanded us concerning the mitzvah of eruv.*

בַּהֲדֵין *Through this eruv may we be permitted to bake, cook, insulate, kindle flame, prepare, and do anything necessary on the Festival for the sake of the Sabbath [for ourselves and for all Jews* who live in this city].*

ERUVEI TECHUMIN

The *eruv*-food is put in a safe place [see commentary] and the following blessing and declaration are recited. The appropriate bracketed phrases should be added.

בָּרוּךְ *Blessed are You, HASHEM, our God, King of the universe, Who has sanctified us with His commandments and has commanded us concerning the mitzvah of eruv.*

בְּזֶה *Through this eruv may [I/we] be permitted to walk two thousand cubits in every direction from this place during this [Sabbath and] Festival.*

ERUVEI CHATZEIROS

This *eruv* is required for the Sabbath, but not for a weekday Festival [see commentary]. The *eruv*-foods are held while the following blessing and declaration are recited. [If the *eruv* is made for the entire year, the bracketed passage is added.]

בָּרוּךְ *Blessed are You, HASHEM, our God, King of the universe, Who has sanctified us with His commandments and has commanded us concerning the mitzvah of eruv.*

בַּהֲדֵין *Through this eruv may we be permitted to carry out or to carry in from the houses to the courtyard, and from the courtyard to the houses, from house to house, from courtyard to courtyard, and from roof to roof, all that we require, for ourselves and for all Jews who live in this area [and to all who will move into this area, for all the Sabbaths and Festivals of the year].*

---

a language he understands.

וּלְכָל יִשְׂרָאֵל — *And for all Jews.* The bracketed phrase is recited only if the maker of the *eruv* wishes to include those who may not have made an *eruv* for themselves. If so, a second person (not the minor child of the maker) must act as agent for the townspeople and take possession of the *eruv*-foods on their behalf.

עֵרוּבֵי תְּחוּמִין /MERGING OF BOUNDARIES

On the Sabbath and Festivals, one is forbidden to go more than 2,000 cubits from his halachically defined dwelling. This limit is called his תְּחוּם, *boundary*. Ordinarily, this 'dwelling' is the town in which one resides, but one has the option of establishing his dwelling elsewhere. By placing a sufficient amount of food for two Sabbath meals in a place as much as 2,000 cubits from his 'dwelling,' one establishes *that* place as his 'dwelling,' and his 2,000-cubit radius is reckoned from there. [For a full discussion of *eruvei chatzeiros* and *techumin*, see the Introduction to the ArtScroll Mishnah *Eruvin*.]

עֵרוּבֵי חֲצֵרוֹת / MERGING OF COURTYARDS

The Sages forbade carrying from the private domain of one person to that of another on the

הדלקת הנרות

On the seventh and eighth nights of Pesach one blessing is recited. When *Yom Tov* coincides with the Sabbath, light the candles, then cover the eyes and recite the blessings. Uncover the eyes and gaze briefly at the candles. When *Yom Tov* falls on a weekday, some follow the above procedure, while others recite the blessings before lighting the candles. When *Yom Tov* coincides with the Sabbath, the words in brackets are added.

[It is forbidden to create a new flame — for example, by striking a match — on *Yom Tov*. Therefore, on the eighth night the candles must be lit from a flame that has been burning from before *Yom Tov*.]

בָּרוּךְ אַתָּה יהוה אֱלֹהֵינוּ מֶלֶךְ הָעוֹלָם, אֲשֶׁר קִדְּשָׁנוּ בְּמִצְוֹתָיו, וְצִוָּנוּ לְהַדְלִיק נֵר* שֶׁל [שַׁבָּת וְשֶׁל] יוֹם טוֹב.*

It is customary to recite the following prayer after the kindling. The words in brackets are included as they apply.

יְהִי רָצוֹן* לְפָנֶיךָ, יהוה אֱלֹהַי וֵאלֹהֵי אֲבוֹתַי, שֶׁתְּחוֹנֵן אוֹתִי [וְאֶת אִישִׁי, וְאֶת בָּנַי, וְאֶת בְּנוֹתַי, וְאֶת אָבִי, וְאֶת אִמִּי] וְאֶת כָּל קְרוֹבַי; וְתִתֶּן לָנוּ וּלְכָל יִשְׂרָאֵל חַיִּים טוֹבִים וַאֲרוּכִים; וְתִזְכְּרֵנוּ בְּזִכְרוֹן טוֹבָה וּבְרָכָה; וְתִפְקְדֵנוּ בִּפְקֻדַּת יְשׁוּעָה וְרַחֲמִים; וּתְבָרְכֵנוּ בְּרָכוֹת גְּדוֹלוֹת; וְתַשְׁלִים בָּתֵּינוּ; וְתַשְׁכֵּן שְׁכִינָתְךָ בֵּינֵינוּ. וְזַכֵּנִי לְגַדֵּל בָּנִים וּבְנֵי בָנִים חֲכָמִים וּנְבוֹנִים, אוֹהֲבֵי יהוה, יִרְאֵי אֱלֹהִים, אַנְשֵׁי אֱמֶת, זֶרַע קֹדֶשׁ, בַּיהוה דְּבֵקִים, וּמְאִירִים אֶת הָעוֹלָם בַּתּוֹרָה וּבְמַעֲשִׂים טוֹבִים, וּבְכָל מְלֶאכֶת עֲבוֹדַת הַבּוֹרֵא. אָנָּא שְׁמַע אֶת תְּחִנָּתִי בָּעֵת הַזֹּאת, בִּזְכוּת שָׂרָה וְרִבְקָה וְרָחֵל וְלֵאָה אִמּוֹתֵינוּ, וְהָאֵר נֵרֵנוּ שֶׁלֹּא יִכְבֶּה לְעוֹלָם וָעֶד, וְהָאֵר פָּנֶיךָ וְנִוָּשֵׁעָה. אָמֵן.

Sabbath. Similarly a courtyard, hall, or staircase shared by the residents of houses or apartments is regarded as a separate domain, and it is forbidden to carry from the private dwellings into the shared area. The Sages also provided a procedure to remove this prohibition against carrying. Known as *eruvei chatzeiros,* or the 'merging of courtyards,' this procedure considers all houses opening into the shared area as owned by a single consortium. This is done by collecting *matzah* from each of the families and placing all the *matzah* in one of the dwelling units. [Even if only one person supplies the *matzah,* it is still possible to make an *eruv.* In this case, a second person (not the minor child of the donor) must act as agent for all those involved and take possession of the *matzah* on their behalf.] This symbolizes that all the contributors are legal residents of the unit where they have deposited their *matzah* and the entire area is regarded as a single dwelling. All the residents may carry in all its parts on the Sabbath, as long as the *matzos* were available and edible at the onset of the Sabbath. [The declaration as given here may not be used if the *eruv* area includes a public thoroughfare. Such an area requires complex additional procedures which should not be undertaken by a layman.]

The restrictions on carrying apply only to the Sabbath and not to the Festivals. Thus, *eruvei chatzeiros* is only necessary for *Yom Tov* that falls on the Sabbath but not for the other days of the Festival.

הַדְלָקַת הַנֵּרוֹת / KINDLING LIGHTS

Since women generally look after household matters, the *mitzvah* of kindling the lights has devolved upon the mistress of the house

KINDLING LIGHTS

On the seventh and eighth nights of Pesach one blessing is recited. When *Yom Tov* coincides with the Sabbath, light the candles, then cover the eyes and recite the blessings. Uncover the eyes and gaze briefly at the candles. When *Yom Tov* falls on a weekday, some follow the above procedure, while others recite the blessings before lighting the candles. When *Yom Tov* coincides with the Sabbath, the words in brackets are added.

[It is forbidden to create a new flame — for example, by striking a match — on *Yom Tov*. Therefore, on the eighth night the candles must be lit from a flame that has been burning from before *Yom Tov*.]

בָּרוּךְ *Blessed are You, HASHEM, our God, King of the universe, Who has sanctified us with His commandments, and has commanded us to kindle the light* of [the Sabbath and of] the Festival.**

It is customary to recite the following prayer after the kindling. The words in brackets are included as they apply.

יְהִי רָצוֹן *May it be Your will,* HASHEM, my God and God of my forefathers, that You show favor to me [my husband, my sons, my daughters, my father, my mother] and all my relatives; and that You grant us and all Israel a good and long life; that You remember us with a beneficent memory and blessing; that You consider us with a consideration of salvation and compassion; that You bless us with great blessings; that You make our households complete; that You cause Your Presence to dwell among us. Privilege me to raise children and grandchildren who are wise and understanding, who love HASHEM and fear God, people of truth, holy offspring, attached to HASHEM, who illuminate the world with Torah and good deeds and with every labor in the service of the Creator. Please, hear my supplication at this time, in the merit of Sarah, Rebecca, Rachel, and Leah, our mothers, and cause our light to illuminate that it be not extinguished forever, and let Your countenance shine so that we are saved. Amen.*

(Rambam). Nevertheless, a man living alone is required to kindle the lights and recite the proper blessing. Similarly, if a woman is too ill to light, her husband should light the candles and recite the blessing *(Magen Avraham)*.

There should be some light in every room where it will be needed—and indeed this is a halachic requirement—nevertheless, the blessing is recited upon the flames that are kindled in the dining room *(Mishnah Berurah)*. The lights honor the Sabbath and Festival by brightening and dignifying the festive meal *(Rashi)*.

נֵר — *The light*. Prevalent custom calls for at least two candles. According to *Eliyah Rabbah*, they symbolize man and wife. Nevertheless, since one can fulfill the *mitzvah* with a single candle [indeed, *Mishnah Berurah* advises one with extremely limited means to purchase one good candle rather than two inferior ones], the blessing is couched in the singular form, נֵר, *light*, and not נֵרוֹת, *lights*.

שֶׁל [שַׁבָּת וְשֶׁל] יוֹם טוֹב — *Of [the Sabbath and of] the Festival*. The Sabbath is mentioned first, following the Talmudic rule that a more frequently performed *mitzvah* takes precedence over a less frequent one.

יְהִי רָצוֹן — *May it be Your will*. It is customary to recite this prayer after the kindling. Because of the Talmudic declaration, 'One who is scrupulous in the kindling of lights will be blessed with children who are Torah scholars' *(Shabbos 23b)*, the prayer stresses the supplication that the children of the home grow up learned and righteous.

WHEN *YOM TOV* FALLS ON A WEEKDAY, TURN TO *MAARIV,* PAGE 802.

קבלת שבת

When *Yom Tov* coincides with the Sabbath, *Kabbalas Shabbos* [our acceptance upon ourselves of the holiness of the Sabbath] consists of Psalms 92 and 93.

תהלים צב

מִזְמוֹר שִׁיר לְיוֹם הַשַּׁבָּת.* טוֹב לְהֹדוֹת לַיהוה, וּלְזַמֵּר לְשִׁמְךָ עֶלְיוֹן. לְהַגִּיד בַּבֹּקֶר חַסְדֶּךָ, וֶאֱמוּנָתְךָ בַּלֵּילוֹת.* עֲלֵי עָשׂוֹר* וַעֲלֵי נָבֶל, עֲלֵי הִגָּיוֹן בְּכִנּוֹר. כִּי שִׂמַּחְתַּנִי יהוה בְּפָעֳלֶךָ, בְּמַעֲשֵׂי יָדֶיךָ אֲרַנֵּן. מַה גָּדְלוּ מַעֲשֶׂיךָ יהוה, מְאֹד עָמְקוּ מַחְשְׁבֹתֶיךָ.* אִישׁ בַּעַר לֹא יֵדָע, וּכְסִיל לֹא יָבִין אֶת זֹאת. בִּפְרֹחַ רְשָׁעִים* כְּמוֹ עֵשֶׂב, וַיָּצִיצוּ כָּל פֹּעֲלֵי אָוֶן, לְהִשָּׁמְדָם עֲדֵי עַד.* וְאַתָּה מָרוֹם לְעֹלָם יהוה. כִּי הִנֵּה אֹיְבֶיךָ יהוה, כִּי הִנֵּה אֹיְבֶיךָ יֹאבֵדוּ, יִתְפָּרְדוּ כָּל פֹּעֲלֵי אָוֶן. וַתָּרֶם כִּרְאֵים קַרְנִי,* בַּלֹּתִי בְּשֶׁמֶן רַעֲנָן.* וַתַּבֵּט עֵינִי בְּשׁוּרָי, בַּקָּמִים עָלַי מְרֵעִים, תִּשְׁמַעְנָה אָזְנָי. ❖ צַדִּיק כַּתָּמָר יִפְרָח, כְּאֶרֶז* בַּלְּבָנוֹן יִשְׂגֶּה. שְׁתוּלִים בְּבֵית יהוה,* בְּחַצְרוֹת אֱלֹהֵינוּ יַפְרִיחוּ. עוֹד יְנוּבוּן בְּשֵׂיבָה, דְּשֵׁנִים וְרַעֲנַנִּים יִהְיוּ. לְהַגִּיד כִּי יָשָׁר יהוה, צוּרִי וְלֹא עַוְלָתָה בּוֹ.

קַבָּלַת שַׁבָּת / KABBALAS SHABBOS

מִזְמוֹר שִׁיר לְיוֹם הַשַּׁבָּת / Psalm 92

The custom of reciting psalms ninety-two and ninety-three at the arrival of the Sabbath is ancient. In a responsa, *Rambam (Pe'er HaDor* 116) implies clearly that it predated him by many generations. With our recitation of this song of praise to the Sabbath, we accept its holiness upon ourselves together with all its positive and negative *mitzvos.*

מִזְמוֹר שִׁיר לְיוֹם הַשַּׁבָּת — *A psalm, a song for the Sabbath day.* Although this psalm is identified as belonging particularly to the theme of the Sabbath — indeed, it was the Levites' song for the Sabbath Temple service *(Rashi)* — the text contains not a single direct reference to the Sabbath. What is the connection? Many explanations are given. Among them are:

— The psalm refers not to the weekly Sabbath, but to the World to Come, when man will achieve the spiritual perfection we only glimpse during the Sabbath. The psalm is thus well suited to the Sabbath which is a semblance of that future spiritual perfection *(Rashi).*

— Praise of God is necessary, but difficult in the weekdays when people must struggle for a livelihood. On the Sabbath when Jews are free from the strictures of the week, they can turn their minds and hearts to the perception of God's ways and His praise — which are the topics of this psalm *(Radak).*

בַּבֹּקֶר . . . בַּלֵּילוֹת — *In the dawn . . . in the nights.* Dawn is an allusion to redemption, while night symbolizes exile. We express our faith that even when God made us suffer, that too was kindness, because He did it for our ultimate benefit. Thus we *relate* His *kindness,* whether it was as clear and pleasant as the bright *dawn* or whether it was as hard to accept as the dark *night.* During the harsh night of exile, we call it אֱמוּנָתְךָ, *Your faith,* because we have faith that God is good, even if we do not understand some of the things He does.

עֲלֵי עָשׂוֹר — *Upon ten-stringed instrument.* The Sages teach that the lyre of Messianic times will be ten-stringed, representing a beautiful enhancement of music, which is now limited to the octave of eight notes. Every period in life calls for its own unique expression of praise, just as each day has its own song of praise and each part of creation serves God in its own way. The

WHEN *YOM TOV* FALLS ON A WEEKDAY, TURN TO *MAARIV*, PAGE 802.

KABBALAS SHABBOS

When *Yom Tov* coincides with the Sabbath, *Kabbalas Shabbos* [our acceptance upon ourselves of the holiness of the Sabbath] consists of Psalms 92 and 93.

Psalm 92

מִזְמוֹר שִׁיר *A psalm, a song for the Sabbath day.* It is good to thank HASHEM and to sing praise to Your Name, O Exalted One; to relate Your kindness in the dawn and Your faith in the nights.* Upon ten-stringed instrument* and lyre, with singing accompanied by a harp. For You have gladdened me, HASHEM, with Your deeds; at the works of Your Hands I sing glad song. How great are Your deeds, HASHEM; exceedingly profound are Your thoughts.* A boor cannot know, nor can a fool understand this: when the wicked bloom* like grass and all the doers of iniquity blossom — it is to destroy them till eternity.* But You remain exalted forever, HASHEM. For behold! — Your enemies, HASHEM, for behold! — Your enemies shall perish, dispersed shall be all doers of iniquity. As exalted as a re'eim's shall be my pride,* I will be saturated with ever-fresh oil.* My eyes have seen my vigilant foes; when those who would harm me rise up against me, my ears have heard their doom.* Chazzan– *A righteous man will flourish like a date palm, like a cedar* in the Lebanon he will grow tall. Planted in the house of HASHEM,* in the courtyards of our God they will flourish. They will still be fruitful in old age, vigorous and fresh they will be — to declare that HASHEM is just, my Rock in Whom there is no wrong.*

---

enhanced spirituality of Messianic times will demand a heightened form of song (*Sfas Emes*; see *Overview*, ArtScroll *Tehillim*).

מַעֲשֶׂיךָ ... מַחְשְׁבֹתֶיךָ — *Your deeds ... Your thoughts.* God's *deeds* are the tangible parts of Creation and the events we perceive with our senses. His *thoughts* are His purposes and goals; they are profound beyond human comprehension (*Sfas Emes*).

בִּפְרֹחַ רְשָׁעִים — *When the wicked bloom.* Most people can find no answer to the eternal human dilemma: Why do the wicked prosper? If only these inquisitors could look beyond what their senses tell them, they would realize that ...

לְהִשָּׁמְדָם עֲדֵי עַד — *To destroy them till eternity.* God gives temporal success and happiness to the wicked as reward for whatever good deeds they may have done. Having been recompensed, they will sink to destruction, while the righteous gain eternal reward (*Rashi*).

וַתָּרֶם כִּרְאֵים קַרְנִי — *As exalted as a re'eim's shall be my pride* [lit. *my horn*]. The once-downtrodden pride of the righteous will rise and be as exalted as the upraised horns of the haughty *re'eim* [a beast of uncertain identity, variously translated as unicorn, rhinoceros, buffalo, antelope, and others]. In any case, its use in Scripture indicates that it has a long and powerful horn.

בְּשֶׁמֶן רַעֲנָן — *With ever-fresh oil.* Oil is a common Scriptural simile for blessing, prosperity, and supremacy (*Rashi*).

כַּתָּמָר ... כְּאֶרֶז — *Like a date palm, like a cedar.* The *tzaddik* will be as fruitful as a date palm, and as sturdy in health as a cedar (*Rashi*).

שְׁתוּלִים בְּבֵית ה׳ — *Planted in the house of* HASHEM. The quality of a tree — described in the previous verse — is only half the formula for success; for maximum benefit it must be planted in luxuriant soil. The righteous will be firmly rooted in the spiritual riches of God's House. There they will blossom without limit (*Radak*).

תהלים צג

יהוה מָלָךְ גֵּאוּת לָבֵשׁ,* לָבֵשׁ יהוה עֹז הִתְאַזָּר, אַף תִּכּוֹן תֵּבֵל בַּל תִּמּוֹט. נָכוֹן כִּסְאֲךָ מֵאָז, מֵעוֹלָם אָתָּה. נָשְׂאוּ נְהָרוֹת, יהוה, נָשְׂאוּ נְהָרוֹת קוֹלָם,* יִשְׂאוּ נְהָרוֹת דָּכְיָם. ❖ מִקֹּלוֹת מַיִם רַבִּים* אַדִּירִים מִשְׁבְּרֵי יָם, אַדִּיר בַּמָּרוֹם יהוה. עֵדֹתֶיךָ* נֶאֶמְנוּ מְאֹד לְבֵיתְךָ נַאֲוָה קֹדֶשׁ, יהוה, לְאֹרֶךְ יָמִים.*

קדיש יתום

Mourners recite קַדִּישׁ יָתוֹם, the Mourner's *Kaddish* (see *Laws* §81-83).

יִתְגַּדַּל וְיִתְקַדַּשׁ שְׁמֵהּ רַבָּא. (.Cong – אָמֵן.) בְּעָלְמָא דִּי בְרָא כִרְעוּתֵהּ. וְיַמְלִיךְ מַלְכוּתֵהּ, בְּחַיֵּיכוֹן וּבְיוֹמֵיכוֹן וּבְחַיֵּי דְכָל בֵּית יִשְׂרָאֵל, בַּעֲגָלָא וּבִזְמַן קָרִיב. וְאִמְרוּ: אָמֵן.

(.Cong – אָמֵן. יְהֵא שְׁמֵהּ רַבָּא מְבָרַךְ לְעָלַם וּלְעָלְמֵי עָלְמַיָּא.)

יְהֵא שְׁמֵהּ רַבָּא מְבָרַךְ לְעָלַם וּלְעָלְמֵי עָלְמַיָּא.

יִתְבָּרַךְ וְיִשְׁתַּבַּח וְיִתְפָּאַר וְיִתְרוֹמַם וְיִתְנַשֵּׂא וְיִתְהַדָּר וְיִתְעַלֶּה וְיִתְהַלָּל שְׁמֵהּ דְּקֻדְשָׁא בְּרִיךְ הוּא (.Cong – בְּרִיךְ הוּא) – לְעֵלָּא מִן כָּל בִּרְכָתָא וְשִׁירָתָא תֻּשְׁבְּחָתָא וְנֶחֱמָתָא, דַּאֲמִירָן בְּעָלְמָא. וְאִמְרוּ: אָמֵן. (.Cong – אָמֵן.)

יְהֵא שְׁלָמָא רַבָּא מִן שְׁמַיָּא, וְחַיִּים עָלֵינוּ וְעַל כָּל יִשְׂרָאֵל. וְאִמְרוּ: אָמֵן. (.Cong – אָמֵן.)

Take three steps back. Bow left and say . . . עֹשֶׂה; bow right and say . . . הוּא; bow forward and say וְעַל כָּל . . . אָמֵן. Remain standing in place for a few moments, then take three steps forward.

עֹשֶׂה שָׁלוֹם בִּמְרוֹמָיו, הוּא יַעֲשֶׂה שָׁלוֹם עָלֵינוּ, וְעַל כָּל יִשְׂרָאֵל. וְאִמְרוּ: אָמֵן. (.Cong – אָמֵן.)

ה׳ מָלָךְ / Psalm 93

This psalm is a direct continuation of the previous theme that God's greatness will be recognized by all in the Messianic era. Accordingly, the past-tense syntax of the psalm should be understood as uttered in retrospect. Because it describes God in His full grandeur and power as He was when He completed the six days of Creation, and because it describes Him as 'donning' grandeur and 'girding' Himself like one dressing in Sabbath finery, the psalm was designated as the Levite's 'Song of the Day' for Friday, when the footsteps of the Sabbath begin to be heard *(R' Yaakov Emden).*

An alternative interpretation of this psalm ascribes it to the beginning of Creation:

On the sixth day Adam was created. God blew a breath of life into his nostrils and invested him with a Divine soul. When Adam stood and scrutinized God's amazing creation, he realized how awesome and wonderful it was. As he sang God's praises, Adam truly looked Divine, because he was a reflection of God's image. The creatures of the earth were filled with awe, for they imagined that Adam was their creator. When they gathered to bow to him in submission, however, Adam was incredulous. 'Why do you bow to me?' he asked. 'Let us go together to pay homage to God, Who truly reigns. Let us robe the Creator in majesty.' Then Adam led all the creatures in this song, *HASHEM . . . reigned, He . . . donned grandeur (Pirkei deR' Eliezer* 11).

גֵּאוּת לָבֵשׁ — *He will have donned grandeur.* The concept of *grandeur* represents God's revelation as the dominant force before Whom yield the mightiest natural forces. In man, grandeur — or arrogance — is a contemptible trait, because man's power is limited at best. But to God, *grandeur* is becoming because all forces owe their existence to Him while He is dependent on nothing *(Midrash Shocher Tov).*

Iggeres HaRamban explains that the arrogant man is a rebel who defies the sovereignty of God. Such a person steals the royal vestments which belong to God alone, for, as our verse states, *HASHEM . . . reigned, He . . . donned grandeur.*

God 'dons' grandeur — it is similar to a person donning a garment; our comprehension of him is guided by the contours and quality of the garment, but the garment is hardly his essence.

Psalm 93

יהוה מָלָךְ *HASHEM will have reigned, He will have donned grandeur;* He will have donned might and girded Himself; even firmed the world that it should not falter. Your throne was established from of old; eternal are You. Like rivers they raised, O HASHEM, like rivers they raised their voice;* like rivers they shall raise their destructiveness.* Chazzan– *More than the roars of many waters,* mightier than the waves of the sea — You are mighty on high, HASHEM. Your testimonies* are exceedingly trustworthy about Your House, the Sacred Dwelling — O HASHEM, may it be for long days.**

MOURNER'S KADDISH

Mourners recite the Mourner's *Kaddish* (see *Laws* §81-83).

[A transliteration of this *Kaddish* appears on page 1147.]

יִתְגַּדַּל *May His great Name grow exalted and sanctified* (Cong.– *Amen.*) *in the world that He created as He willed. May He give reign to His kingship in your lifetimes and in your days, and in the lifetimes of the entire Family of Israel, swiftly and soon. Now respond: Amen.*

(Cong.– *Amen. May His great Name be blessed forever and ever.*)

May His great Name be blessed forever and ever.

Blessed, praised, glorified, exalted, extolled, mighty, upraised, and lauded be the Name of the Holy One, Blessed is He (Cong.– *Blessed is He*) — *beyond any blessing and song, praise and consolation that are uttered in the world. Now respond: Amen.* (Cong. – *Amen.*)

May there be abundant peace from Heaven, and life, upon us and upon all Israel. Now respond: Amen. (Cong.– *Amen.*)

Take three steps back. Bow left and say, *'He Who makes peace . . .';* bow right and say, *'may He . . .';* bow forward and say, *'and upon all Israel . . .'* Remain standing in place for a few moments, then take three steps forward.

He Who makes peace in His heights, may He make peace upon us, and upon all Israel. Now respond: Amen. (Cong.– *Amen.*)

No matter how much of God's greatness we think we understand, our puny intellect grasps but the minutest fraction of His infinite greatness. He does us the favor of allowing mankind this degree of perception so that we can aspire to the privilege of praising Him.

נָשְׂאוּ נְהָרוֹת קוֹלָם — *Like rivers they raised their voice.* The enemies of Israel will roar against Israel like raging rivers at flood stage (*Radak*).

The repetition of the phrase represents the destruction of the two Temples (*Etz Yosef*).

מִקֹּלוֹת מַיִם רַבִּים . . . — *More than the roars of many waters* . . . You, O God, are beyond the threatening roars of the hostile nations who wish to drown us. You are mightier than the powerful waves of the sea, i.e., the mighty forces of evil among those who wish to crush us.

עֵדֹתֶיךָ — *Your testimonies.* The assurances of Your prophets regarding the eventual rebuilding of the Temple (*Rashi*).

ה׳ לְאֹרֶךְ יָמִים — *O HASHEM, may it be for long days.* The psalm closes with a plea that when the *trustworthy* prophecies of the Third Temple are finally fulfilled, may it stand for *long days,* a Scriptural idiom meaning forever (*Radak*).

מַעֲרִיב / THE EVENING SERVICE

Like *Shacharis* and *Minchah* (see page 8), *Maariv* has its basis in the Temple service. In the Temple, no sacrifices were offered in the evening, but any sacrificial parts that had not been burned on the Altar during the day could be burned at night. Thus, although no sacrificial service was *required* during the night, the Altar was usually in use. This explains why *Maariv* began as a voluntary service; unlike *Shacharis* and *Minchah* that took the place of required offerings, *Maariv* corresponds to a service optional in the sense that it was unnecessary if all parts were burned during the day. During Talmudic times, Jewry universally adopted *Maariv* as an obligatory service, so it now has the status of *Shacharis* and *Minchah.* (It should be noted that the original optional status of *Maariv* applied only to *Shemoneh Esrei;* the *Shema* reading is Scripturally required.)

מעריב ללילי שביעי ואחרון של פסח

In some congregations the *chazzan* chants a melody during his recitation of בָּרְכוּ so that the congregation can then recite יִתְבָּרַךְ.

Chazzan bows at בָּרְכוּ and straightens up at ה׳.

בָּרְכוּ אֶת יהוה הַמְּבֹרָךְ.

Congregation, followed by *chazzan*, responds, bowing at בָּרוּךְ and straightening up at ה׳.

בָּרוּךְ יהוה הַמְּבֹרָךְ לְעוֹלָם וָעֶד.

יִתְבָּרַךְ[1] וְיִשְׁתַּבַּח וְיִתְפָּאַר וְיִתְרוֹמַם וְיִתְנַשֵּׂא שְׁמוֹ שֶׁל מֶלֶךְ מַלְכֵי הַמְּלָכִים, הַקָּדוֹשׁ בָּרוּךְ הוּא. שֶׁהוּא רִאשׁוֹן וְהוּא אַחֲרוֹן, וּמִבַּלְעָדָיו אֵין אֱלֹהִים.[2] סֹלּוּ, לָרֹכֵב בָּעֲרָבוֹת, בְּיָהּ שְׁמוֹ, וְעִלְזוּ לְפָנָיו.[3] וּשְׁמוֹ מְרוֹמָם עַל כָּל בְּרָכָה וּתְהִלָּה.[4] בָּרוּךְ שֵׁם כְּבוֹד מַלְכוּתוֹ לְעוֹלָם וָעֶד. יְהִי שֵׁם יהוה מְבֹרָךְ, מֵעַתָּה וְעַד עוֹלָם.[5]

ברכות קריאת שמע

בָּרוּךְ אַתָּה יהוה אֱלֹהֵינוּ מֶלֶךְ הָעוֹלָם, אֲשֶׁר בִּדְבָרוֹ מַעֲרִיב עֲרָבִים, בְּחָכְמָה פּוֹתֵחַ שְׁעָרִים, וּבִתְבוּנָה מְשַׁנֶּה עִתִּים, וּמַחֲלִיף אֶת הַזְּמַנִּים, וּמְסַדֵּר אֶת הַכּוֹכָבִים בְּמִשְׁמְרוֹתֵיהֶם בָּרָקִיעַ כִּרְצוֹנוֹ. בּוֹרֵא יוֹם וָלָיְלָה, גּוֹלֵל אוֹר מִפְּנֵי חֹשֶׁךְ וְחֹשֶׁךְ מִפְּנֵי אוֹר. וּמַעֲבִיר יוֹם וּמֵבִיא לָיְלָה, וּמַבְדִּיל בֵּין יוֹם וּבֵין לָיְלָה, יהוה צְבָאוֹת שְׁמוֹ. ❖ אֵל חַי וְקַיָּם, תָּמִיד יִמְלוֹךְ עָלֵינוּ, לְעוֹלָם וָעֶד.

ON THE SABBATH, NO PIYUTIM ARE RECITED AT MAARIV.

SEVENTH NIGHT	EIGHTH NIGHT
וַיּוֹשַׁע יהוה,[6]* אוֹם לְמוֹשָׁעוֹת. וַיַּרְא יִשְׂרָאֵל,[7] בִּפְרוֹעַ פְּרָעוֹת.[8] אָז יָשִׁיר,[9] גִּלָּה חֹסֶן יְשׁוּעוֹת.[10] עָזִּי,[11] דָּגוּל גִּיהַּ וְאִישׁוֹן לְהַשְׁעוֹת.	וַיּוֹשַׁע[6] אוֹמֶן אֶשְׁכְּלוֹת קֹדֶשׁ פֶּרַח תְּהִלָּה,[12] וַיַּרְא[7] בְּעִנּוּי וְקֹשִׁי נוֹרָא עֲלִילָה,[13] אָז[9] גְּדֻלָּתוֹ הִפְלִיא וְהֵאִיר אֲפֵלָה, אֱלוֹהַּ עֹשֶׂי נֹתֵן זְמִרוֹת בַּלָּיְלָה.[14]

בָּרוּךְ אַתָּה יהוה, הַמַּעֲרִיב עֲרָבִים. (.Cong.– אָמֵן)

Many congregations recite *piyutim* (liturgical poems) that are inserted at various points in the synagogue service, often in the middle of a paragraph. Those who do not recite *piyutim* should not assume their appearance to indicate a stop, but should continue until the next new paragraph as indicated by bold type for the first word. This *Machzor* includes those *piyutim* that are commonly recited. A few *piyutim* that are omitted by a vast majority of congregations have been included in an appendix beginning on page 1108. The text will indicate where they may be recited.

וַיּוֹשַׁע ה׳ — *HASHEM saved.* The *piyutim* for the seventh night were composed by *R' Yosef ben Yaakov,* and those of the eighth night by *R' Yekusiel ben Yosef.* Each of these *piyutim* follows an alphabetic acrostic and is based on the verses of the Song at the Sea (*Exodus* 14:30-15:19).

גִּיהַּ וְאִישׁוֹן לְהַשְׁעוֹת — *Who causes light and darkness to pass.* According to the translation both עָזִּי, *my Mighty One,* and דָּגוּל, *the Exalted One,* refer to God; the phrase 'light and darkness' alludes to the same attribute as the phrase וּמַעֲבִיר יוֹם וּמֵבִיא לָיְלָה, *He causes day to pass and brings night;* and the word לְהַשְׁעוֹת means *to cause to pass* (as in *Isaiah* 6:10). An alternative translation understands עָזִּי, *my might,* as an allusion to the Torah. If so, the *paytan* alludes to the *mitzvah* of studying Torah day and night,

MAARIV FOR THE LAST TWO NIGHTS OF PESACH

In some congregations the *chazzan* chants a melody during his recitation of *Borchu* so that the congregation can then recite *'Blessed, praised . . .'*

Chazzan bows at *'Bless'* and straightens up at *'HASHEM.'*

Bless HASHEM, the blessed One.

Congregation, followed by *chazzan*, responds, bowing at *'Blessed'* and straightening up at *'HASHEM.'*

Blessed is HASHEM, the blessed One, for all eternity.

Blessed,[1] praised, glorified, exalted and upraised is the Name of the King Who rules over kings — the Holy One, Blessed is He. For He is the First and He is the Last and aside from Him there is no god.[2] Extol Him — Who rides the highest heavens — with His Name, YAH, and exult before Him.[3] His Name is exalted beyond every blessing and praise.[4] Blessed is the Name of His glorious kingdom for all eternity. Blessed be the Name of HASHEM from this time and forever.[5]

BLESSINGS OF THE SHEMA

בָּרוּךְ *Blessed are You, HASHEM, our God, King of the universe, Who by His word brings on evenings, with wisdom opens gates, with understanding alters periods, changes the seasons, and orders the stars in their heavenly constellations as He wills. He creates day and night, removing light before darkness and darkness before light. He causes day to pass and brings night, and separates between day and night — HASHEM, Master of Legions, is His Name.* Chazzan— *May the living and enduring God continuously reign over us, for all eternity.*

ON THE SABBATH, NO PIYUTIM ARE RECITED AT MAARIV.

SEVENTH NIGHT	EIGHTH NIGHT
*HASHEM saved,[6]**	*He saved[6]* [his nation],*
א *the nation [worthy] of salvations,*	א *[He,] the nurturing Father, [they,] the holy clusters, the praiseworthy blossoms.[12]*
and Israel saw,[7]	*He saw,[7]*
ב *as He exacted retribution.[8]*	ב *[their] pain and suffering — He Who is awesome in deed.[13]*
Then [Moses] chose to sing,[9]	*Then,[9]*
ג *he who revealed the [Torah's] power of salvations.[10]*	גד *He displayed His wondrous greatness and lit up the darkness.*
My Mighty One,[11]	*God, my Maker, Who cuts down [evil]* at night.[14]*
ד *the Exalted One, Who causes light and darkness to pass.**	

Blessed are You, HASHEM, Who brings on evenings. (Cong.— *Amen.*)

(1) See *Orach Chaim* 57:1. (2) Cf. *Isaiah* 44:6. (3) *Psalms* 68:5. (4) Cf. *Nehemiah* 9:5. (5) *Psalms* 113:2. (6) *Exodus* 14:30. (7) 14:31. (8) *Judges* 5:2. (9) *Exodus* 15:1. (10) *Isaiah* 33:6. (11) *Exodus* 15:2. (12) [Some *machzorim* read: אֶשְׁכְּלוֹת פֶּרַח קֹדֶשׁ תְּהִלָּה, *clusters of blossoms, holy, praiseworthy.*] (13) *Psalms* 66:5. (14) *Job* 35:10.

as it is written: וְהָגִיתָ בּוֹ יוֹמָם וָלַיְלָה, *and you shall meditate upon it day and night* (*Joshua* 1:8).

נֹתֵן זְמִרוֹת — *Who cuts down [evil].* The translation follows *Rashi* (*Job* 35:10). The root זמר means *to prune*, as in: וְכַרְמְךָ לֹא תִזְמֹר, *You shall not cut down your vineyards* (*Leviticus* 25:4). According to *Targum* (*Job* 35:10) the word means *songs of praise*, and the stich is rendered *before Whom we sing praises in the night.*

אַהֲבַת עוֹלָם בֵּית יִשְׂרָאֵל עַמְּךָ אָהָבְתָּ. תּוֹרָה וּמִצְוֹת, חֻקִּים וּמִשְׁפָּטִים, אוֹתָנוּ לִמַּדְתָּ. עַל כֵּן יהוה אֱלֹהֵינוּ, בְּשָׁכְבֵנוּ וּבְקוּמֵנוּ נָשִׂיחַ בְּחֻקֶּיךָ, וְנִשְׂמַח בְּדִבְרֵי תוֹרָתֶךָ, וּבְמִצְוֹתֶיךָ לְעוֹלָם וָעֶד. ❖ כִּי הֵם חַיֵּינוּ, וְאֹרֶךְ יָמֵינוּ, וּבָהֶם נֶהְגֶּה יוֹמָם וָלָיְלָה. וְאַהֲבָתְךָ, אַל תָּסִיר מִמֶּנּוּ לְעוֹלָמִים.

SEVENTH NIGHT	EIGHTH NIGHT
יהוה,[1] הֵכִין כְּלֵי מִלְחָמָה. מַרְכְּבוֹת פַּרְעֹה, וְשָׁלִישָׁיו[2] נָהַג בִּמְהוּמָה. תְּהוֹמוֹת,[3] זִמְּנָם בְּאַף וּבְחֵמָה. יְמִינְךָ,[4] חֶבֶל נַחֲלָתְךָ[5] רִחֲמָה.	עָזִּי[6] הָרִים דִּלֵּג[7] כְּזָכַר בְּרִית אָבוֹת וָחֶסֶד, וּגְבָעוֹת קִפֵּץ[7] טָהוֹר כֹּל יִסֵּד, זֶרַע אַהֲבַת חוֹלַת[8] שְׁמַע לְהִוָּסֵד, וְאַהֲבַת עוֹלָם אֲהַבְתִּיךָ עַל כֵּן מְשַׁכְתִּיךָ חָסֶד.[9]

בָּרוּךְ אַתָּה יהוה, אוֹהֵב עַמּוֹ יִשְׂרָאֵל. (Cong. – אָמֵן.)

שמע

Immediately before its recitation concentrate on fulfilling the positive commandment of reciting the *Shema* twice daily. It is important to enunciate each word clearly and not to run words together. For this reason, vertical lines have been placed between two words that are prone to be slurred into one and are not separated by a comma or a hyphen. See *Laws* §40-52.

When praying without a *minyan*, begin with the following three-word formula:

אֵל מֶלֶךְ נֶאֱמָן.

Recite the first verse aloud, with the right hand covering the eyes, and concentrate intently upon accepting God's absolute sovereignty.

שְׁמַע | יִשְׂרָאֵל, יהוה | אֱלֹהֵינוּ, יהוה | אֶחָד:[10]

In an undertone– בָּרוּךְ שֵׁם כְּבוֹד מַלְכוּתוֹ לְעוֹלָם וָעֶד.

While reciting the first paragraph (דברים ו:ה-ט), concentrate on accepting the commandment to love God.

וְאָהַבְתָּ אֵת | יהוה | אֱלֹהֶיךָ, בְּכָל-לְבָבְךָ, וּבְכָל-נַפְשְׁךָ, וּבְכָל-מְאֹדֶךָ: וְהָיוּ הַדְּבָרִים הָאֵלֶּה, אֲשֶׁר | אָנֹכִי מְצַוְּךָ הַיּוֹם, עַל-לְבָבֶךָ: וְשִׁנַּנְתָּם לְבָנֶיךָ, וְדִבַּרְתָּ בָּם, בְּשִׁבְתְּךָ בְּבֵיתֶךָ, וּבְלֶכְתְּךָ בַדֶּרֶךְ, וּבְשָׁכְבְּךָ וּבְקוּמֶךָ: וּקְשַׁרְתָּם לְאוֹת | עַל-יָדֶךָ, וְהָיוּ לְטֹטָפֹת בֵּין | עֵינֶיךָ: וּכְתַבְתָּם | עַל-מְזֻזוֹת בֵּיתֶךָ, וּבִשְׁעָרֶיךָ:

While reciting the second paragraph (דברים יא:יג-כא), concentrate on accepting all the commandments and the concept of reward and punishment.

וְהָיָה, אִם-שָׁמֹעַ תִּשְׁמְעוּ אֶל-מִצְוֹתַי, אֲשֶׁר | אָנֹכִי מְצַוֶּה | אֶתְכֶם הַיּוֹם, לְאַהֲבָה אֶת-יהוה | אֱלֹהֵיכֶם וּלְעָבְדוֹ, בְּכָל-לְבַבְכֶם, וּבְכָל-נַפְשְׁכֶם: וְנָתַתִּי מְטַר-אַרְצְכֶם בְּעִתּוֹ, יוֹרֶה וּמַלְקוֹשׁ, וְאָסַפְתָּ דְגָנֶךָ וְתִירשְׁךָ וְיִצְהָרֶךָ: וְנָתַתִּי | עֵשֶׂב | בְּשָׂדְךָ לִבְהֶמְתֶּךָ,

(1) *Exodus* 15:3. (2) 15:4. (3) 15:5. (4) 15:6. (5) Cf. *Deuteronomy* 32:9. (6) *Exodus* 15:2. (7) Cf. *Song of Songs* 2:8. (8) Cf. 2:5. (9) *Jeremiah* 31:2. (10) *Deuteronomy* 6:4.

אַהֲבַת *With an eternal love have You loved the House of Israel, Your nation. Torah and commandments, decrees and ordinances have You taught us. Therefore* HASHEM, *our God, upon our retiring and arising, we will discuss Your decrees and we will rejoice with the words of Your Torah and with Your commandments for all eternity.* Chazzan– *For they are our life and the length of our days and about them we will meditate day and night. May You not remove Your love from us forever.*

SEVENTH NIGHT	EIGHTH NIGHT
HASHEM[1] ה *prepared the weapons of war.* *Pharaoh's chariots* ו *and his officers*[2] *He led in confusion.* *The deep waters*[3] ז *He prepared with anger and fury.* *Your right hand*[4] ח *showed compassion on [Israel,] the lot of Your heritage.*[5]	*My Mighty One*[6] ה *skipped over mountains*[7] *when He recalled the covenant and kindness of the Patriarchs.* ו *and over hills leaped*[7] *the Pure One, Who established everything.* זח *to firmly fix the offspring of those lovesick*[8] *to hear [You say]: 'I have loved you with an eternal love, therefore I have extended kindness to you.'*[9]

Blessed are You, HASHEM, *Who loves His nation Israel.* (Cong. – *Amen.*)

THE SHEMA

Immediately before its recitation concentrate on fulfilling the positive commandment of reciting the *Shema* twice daily. It is important to enunciate each word clearly and not to run words together. See *Laws* §40-52.

When praying without a *minyan,* begin with the following three-word formula:
God, trustworthy King.

Recite the first verse aloud, with the right hand covering the eyes, and concentrate intently upon accepting God's absolute sovereignty.

Hear, O Israel: HASHEM is our God, HASHEM, the One and Only.[10]

In an undertone– *Blessed is the Name of His glorious kingdom for all eternity.*

While reciting the first paragraph (*Deuteronomy* 6:5-9), concentrate on accepting the commandment to love God.

וְאָהַבְתָּ *You shall love* HASHEM, *your God, with all your heart, with all your soul and with all your resources. Let these matters that I command you today be upon your heart. Teach them thoroughly to your children and speak of them while you sit in your home, while you walk on the way, when you retire and when you arise. Bind them as a sign upon your arm and let them be tefillin between your eyes. And write them on the doorposts of your house and upon your gates.*

While reciting the second paragraph (*Deuteronomy* 11:13-21), concentrate on accepting all the commandments and the concept of reward and punishment.

וְהָיָה *And it will come to pass that if you continually hearken to My commandments that I command you today, to love* HASHEM, *your God, and to serve Him, with all your heart and with all your soul — then I will provide rain for your land in its proper time, the early and late rains, that you may gather in your grain, your wine, and your oil. I will provide grass in your field for your cattle and you*

וְאָכַלְתָּ וְשָׂבָֽעְתָּ: הִשָּֽׁמְרוּ לָכֶם, פֶּן־יִפְתֶּה לְבַבְכֶם, וְסַרְתֶּם וַעֲבַדְתֶּם | אֱלֹהִים | אֲחֵרִים, וְהִשְׁתַּחֲוִיתֶם לָהֶם: וְחָרָה | אַף־יהוה בָּכֶם, וְעָצַר | אֶת־הַשָּׁמַיִם, וְלֹא־יִהְיֶה מָטָר, וְהָאֲדָמָה לֹא תִתֵּן אֶת־יְבוּלָהּ, וַאֲבַדְתֶּם | מְהֵרָה מֵעַל הָאָרֶץ הַטֹּבָה | אֲשֶׁר | יהוה נֹתֵן לָכֶם: וְשַׂמְתֶּם | אֶת־דְּבָרַי | אֵלֶּה, עַל־לְבַבְכֶם וְעַל־נַפְשְׁכֶם, וּקְשַׁרְתֶּם | אֹתָם לְאוֹת | עַל־יֶדְכֶם, וְהָיוּ לְטוֹטָפֹת בֵּין | עֵינֵיכֶם: וְלִמַּדְתֶּם | אֹתָם | אֶת־בְּנֵיכֶם, לְדַבֵּר בָּם, בְּשִׁבְתְּךָ בְּבֵיתֶךָ, וּבְלֶכְתְּךָ בַדֶּרֶךְ, וּבְשָׁכְבְּךָ וּבְקוּמֶךָ: וּכְתַבְתָּם | עַל־מְזוּזוֹת בֵּיתֶךָ, וּבִשְׁעָרֶיךָ: לְמַעַן | יִרְבּוּ | יְמֵיכֶם וִימֵי בְנֵיכֶם, עַל הָאֲדָמָה | אֲשֶׁר נִשְׁבַּע | יהוה לַאֲבֹתֵיכֶם לָתֵת לָהֶם, כִּימֵי הַשָּׁמַיִם | עַל־הָאָרֶץ:

במדבר טו:לז-מא

וַיֹּאמֶר | יהוה | אֶל־מֹשֶׁה לֵּאמֹר: דַּבֵּר | אֶל־בְּנֵי | יִשְׂרָאֵל, וְאָמַרְתָּ אֲלֵהֶם, וְעָשׂוּ לָהֶם צִיצִת, עַל־כַּנְפֵי בִגְדֵיהֶם לְדֹרֹתָם, וְנָתְנוּ | עַל־צִיצִת הַכָּנָף, פְּתִיל תְּכֵלֶת: וְהָיָה לָכֶם לְצִיצִת, וּרְאִיתֶם | אֹתוֹ, וּזְכַרְתֶּם | אֶת־כָּל־מִצְוֹת | יהוה, וַעֲשִׂיתֶם | אֹתָם, וְלֹא תָתוּרוּ | אַחֲרֵי לְבַבְכֶם וְאַחֲרֵי | עֵינֵיכֶם, אֲשֶׁר־אַתֶּם זֹנִים | אַחֲרֵיהֶם: לְמַעַן תִּזְכְּרוּ, וַעֲשִׂיתֶם | אֶת־כָּל־מִצְוֹתָי, וִהְיִיתֶם קְדֹשִׁים לֵאלֹהֵיכֶם: אֲנִי יהוה | אֱלֹהֵיכֶם, אֲשֶׁר הוֹצֵאתִי | אֶתְכֶם | מֵאֶרֶץ מִצְרַיִם, לִהְיוֹת לָכֶם לֵאלֹהִים, אֲנִי | יהוה | אֱלֹהֵיכֶם: אֱמֶת —

Concentrate on fulfilling the commandment of remembering the Exodus from Egypt.

Although the word אֱמֶת belongs to the next paragraph, it is appended to the conclusion of the previous one, as explained in the commentary (page 50).

–*Chazzan* repeats **יהוה אֱלֹהֵיכֶם אֱמֶת.**

וֶאֱמוּנָה כָּל זֹאת, וְקַיָּם עָלֵינוּ, כִּי הוּא יהוה אֱלֹהֵינוּ וְאֵין זוּלָתוֹ, וַאֲנַחְנוּ יִשְׂרָאֵל עַמּוֹ. הַפּוֹדֵנוּ מִיַּד מְלָכִים, מַלְכֵּנוּ הַגּוֹאֲלֵנוּ מִכַּף כָּל הֶעָרִיצִים. הָאֵל הַנִּפְרָע לָנוּ מִצָּרֵינוּ, וְהַמְשַׁלֵּם גְּמוּל לְכָל אֹיְבֵי נַפְשֵׁנוּ. הָעֹשֶׂה גְדֹלוֹת עַד אֵין חֵקֶר, וְנִפְלָאוֹת עַד אֵין מִסְפָּר.[1] הַשָּׂם נַפְשֵׁנוּ בַּחַיִּים, וְלֹא נָתַן לַמּוֹט רַגְלֵנוּ.[2] הַמַּדְרִיכֵנוּ עַל בָּמוֹת אוֹיְבֵינוּ, וַיָּרֶם קַרְנֵנוּ עַל כָּל שׂוֹנְאֵינוּ. הָעֹשֶׂה לָּנוּ נִסִּים וּנְקָמָה בְּפַרְעֹה, אוֹתוֹת וּמוֹפְתִים בְּאַדְמַת בְּנֵי חָם. הַמַּכֶּה בְעֶבְרָתוֹ כָּל בְּכוֹרֵי מִצְרָיִם, וַיּוֹצֵא אֶת עַמּוֹ יִשְׂרָאֵל מִתּוֹכָם לְחֵרוּת עוֹלָם. הַמַּעֲבִיר בָּנָיו בֵּין גִּזְרֵי יַם סוּף, אֶת רוֹדְפֵיהֶם וְאֶת שׂוֹנְאֵיהֶם בִּתְהוֹמוֹת טִבַּע. וְרָאוּ בָנָיו גְּבוּרָתוֹ, שִׁבְּחוּ וְהוֹדוּ לִשְׁמוֹ. ❖ וּמַלְכוּתוֹ בְרָצוֹן קִבְּלוּ עֲלֵיהֶם. מֹשֶׁה וּבְנֵי יִשְׂרָאֵל לְךָ עָנוּ שִׁירָה,

will eat and be satisfied. Beware lest your heart be seduced and you turn astray and serve gods of others and bow to them. Then the wrath of HASHEM *will blaze against you. He will restrain the heaven so there will be no rain and the ground will not yield its produce. And you will swiftly be banished from the goodly land which* HASHEM *gives you. Place these words of Mine upon your heart and upon your soul; bind them for a sign upon your arm and let them be tefillin between your eyes. Teach them to your children, to discuss them, while you sit in your home, while you walk on the way, when you retire and when you arise. And write them on the doorposts of your house and upon your gates. In order to prolong your days and the days of your children upon the ground that* HASHEM *has sworn to your ancestors to give them, like the days of the heaven on the earth.*

Numbers 15:37-41

וַיֹּאמֶר *And* HASHEM *said to Moses saying: Speak to the Children of Israel and say to them that they are to make themselves tzitzis on the corners of their garments, throughout their generations. And they are to place upon the tzitzis of each corner a thread of techeiles. And it shall constitute tzitzis for you, that you may see it and remember all the commandments of* HASHEM *and perform them; and not explore after your heart and after your eyes after which you stray. So that you may remember and perform all My commandments; and be holy to your God.*

Concentrate on fulfilling the commandment of remembering the Exodus from Egypt.

I am HASHEM, *your God, Who has removed you from the land of Egypt to be a God to you; I am* HASHEM *your God — it is true —*

Although the word אֱמֶת, *'true,'* belongs to the next paragraph, it is appended to the conclusion of the previous one, as explained in the commentary (page 50).

Chazzan repeats: **HASHEM, your God, Is true.**

וֶאֱמוּנָה *And faithful is all this, and it is firmly established for us that He is* HASHEM *our God, and there is none but Him, and we are Israel, His nation. He redeems us from the power of kings, our King Who delivers us from the hand of all the cruel tyrants. He is the God Who exacts vengeance for us from our foes and Who brings just retribution upon all enemies of our soul; Who performs great deeds that are beyond comprehension, and wonders beyond number.*[1] *Who set our soul in life and did not allow our foot to falter.*[2] *Who led us upon the heights of our enemies and raised our pride above all who hate us; Who wrought for us miracles and vengeance upon Pharaoh; signs and wonders on the land of the offspring of Ham; Who struck with His anger all the firstborn of Egypt and removed His nation Israel from their midst to eternal freedom; Who brought His children through the split parts of the Sea of Reeds while those who pursued them and hated them He caused to sink into the depths. When His children perceived His power, they lauded and gave grateful praise to His Name.* Chazzan– *And His Kingship they accepted upon themselves willingly. Moses and the Children of Israel raised their voices to You in song,*

(1) *Job* 9:10. (2) *Psalms* 66:9.

SEVENTH NIGHT

פֶּסַח* אֱמוּנִים שִׁיר שׁוֹרְרוּהוּ,
וַיּוֹשַׁע יהוה
בַּיּוֹם הַהוּא,[1]
פֶּסַח מִצְרָיִם.
פֶּסַח בַּת קוֹל
יִשָּׁמַע מִמְּרוֹמִים,
יִשְׂרָאֵל נוֹשַׁע בַּיהוה
תְּשׁוּעַת עוֹלָמִים,[2]
פֶּסַח לֶעָתִיד.
פֶּסַח גְּאוּלִים עָבְרוּ
בְּמַשְׂאַת יָד,
וַיַּרְא יִשְׂרָאֵל אֶת הַיָּד,[3]
פֶּסַח מִצְרָיִם.
פֶּסַח דָּגוּל בְּעֹז כְּבוֹדוֹ,
יֹסִיף אֲדֹנָי, שֵׁנִית יָדוֹ,[4]
פֶּסַח לֶעָתִיד.
פֶּסַח הֲמוֹן חֲיָלָיו בְּטוּב דַּיָּם,
הָלְכוּ בַיַּבָּשָׁה
בְּתוֹךְ הַיָּם,[5] פֶּסַח מִצְרָיִם.
פֶּסַח וְהֵנִיף יָדוֹ בְּרוּחַ בַּעְיָם,
וְהֶחֱרִים יהוה
אֵת לְשׁוֹן יָם,[6]
פֶּסַח לֶעָתִיד.
פֶּסַח זִלְעַף בְּמִכְתָּב שֻׁנָּן,*
מַחֲנֵה מִצְרַיִם
בְּעַמּוּד אֵשׁ וְעָנָן,[7]
פֶּסַח מִצְרָיִם.
פֶּסַח חִדּוּשׁ מוֹפֵת עֲלֵי יָשָׁן,
דָּם וָאֵשׁ וְתִמְרוֹת עָשָׁן,[8]
פֶּסַח לֶעָתִיד.
פֶּסַח טִכֵּס בְּצָרָיו לַהַחֲרִימָה,
וּבְנֵי יִשְׂרָאֵל
יוֹצְאִים בְּיָד רָמָה,[9]
פֶּסַח מִצְרָיִם.

EIGHTH NIGHT

פֶּסַח* אִשְּׁרוּ בְּאוֹר הַחַיִּים לֵאוֹר,[10]
וּלְכָל בְּנֵי יִשְׂרָאֵל הָיָה אוֹר,[11]
פֶּסַח מִצְרָיִם.
פֶּסַח בְּאוֹת זֶה עוֹד לְהִתְבָּרֵךְ,
קוּמִי אוֹרִי כִּי בָא אוֹרֵךְ,[12]
פֶּסַח לֶעָתִיד.
פֶּסַח גְּאוּלִים אָז הִלְּלוּהוּ,
וַיּוֹשַׁע יהוה בַּיּוֹם הַהוּא,[13]
פֶּסַח מִצְרָיִם.
פֶּסַח דָּגוּל יָחִישׁ יִשְׁעֵנוּ,
יהוה מַלְכֵּנוּ הוּא יוֹשִׁיעֵנוּ,[14]
פֶּסַח לֶעָתִיד.
פֶּסַח הֻמְרְרוּ בְּקֹשִׁי וְנִלְאוּ,
מִמָּחֳרַת הַפֶּסַח יָצְאוּ,[15]
פֶּסַח מִצְרָיִם.
פֶּסַח וְיוֹם נָקָם תִּרְאוּ,
כִּי בְשִׂמְחָה תֵצֵאוּ,[16] פֶּסַח לֶעָתִיד.
פֶּסַח זַכִּים אִיְּמוּ לְעָצְמָה,
וְהַמַּיִם לָהֶם חוֹמָה,[17] פֶּסַח מִצְרָיִם.
פֶּסַח חוֹכָיו טוּבוֹ לְהַנְחִילָם,
וְעַל מַבּוּעֵי מַיִם יְנַהֲלֵם,[18]
פֶּסַח לֶעָתִיד.
פֶּסַח טָהוֹר עַנְוָתוֹ הִרְבָּה עֲלֵיהֶם,
וַיהוה הוֹלֵךְ לִפְנֵיהֶם,[19]
פֶּסַח מִצְרָיִם.
פֶּסַח יָעִיר נְאֻם חֶזְיוֹנָי,
כִּי הוֹלֵךְ לִפְנֵיכֶם יהוה,[20]
פֶּסַח לֶעָתִיד.
פֶּסַח כָּרָאוּי עָנְתָה נְבִיאָה,
שִׁירוּ לַיהוה כִּי גָאֹה גָּאָה,[21]
פֶּסַח מִצְרָיִם.
פֶּסַח לוֹעֲגָיו יִהְיוּ לִמְשִׁסָּה,
זַמְּרוּ יהוה כִּי גֵאוּת עָשָׂה,[22]
פֶּסַח לֶעָתִיד.

☙ פֶּסַח — *Pesach.* Descriptions of the Exodus alternate with prayers for the Final Redemption. Each stanza begins with the word 'Pesach' and ends with either 'the Pesach of Egypt' or 'the Pesach of the future.' The respective first lines form an alphabetical acrostic, while the second lines are Scriptural verses. In the seventh night's *piyut*, the last stanza contains the composer's signature, יוֹסֵף בַּר יַעֲקֹב, *Yosef son of Yaakov.* [He may have been R' Yosef ibn Sahal, a noted *paytan* who served on the *beis din* in Cordova, Spain, from 1113 until his death in 1124.] In the eighth night's *piyut*, the composer's signature — יְקוּתִיאֵל בַּר יוֹסֵף חֲזַק, *Yekusiel bar Yosef, may he be*

SEVENTH NIGHT

א *Pesach* — the faithful ones sang a song to Him, 'And HASHEM saved on that day'[1] — the Pesach of Egypt.*

ב *Pesach — may a heavenly voice be heard, 'Israel is saved by HASHEM, an eternal salvation'[2] the Pesach of the future.*

ג *Pesach — the redeemed ones crossed with an exalted hand, and Israel saw the [great] hand [of God][3] — the Pesach of Egypt.*

ד *Pesach — the Exalted One, with the might of His glory, once again may my Lord [redeem us] with His hand[4] — the Pesach of the future.*

ה *Pesach — the multitude of His armies with sufficient goodness, walked on the dry land in the middle of the sea[5] — the Pesach of Egypt.*

ו *Pesach — He shall have raised His hand with the power of His spirit, and HASHEM shall have dried up the tongue of the sea[6] — the Pesach of the future.*

ז *Pesach — He raged against them with the clearly inscribed [plagues],* the Egyptian camp, with pillar of fire and cloud[7] — the Pesach of Egypt.*

ח *Pesach — He shall create new wonders besides the old, blood, fire and columns of smoke[8] — the Pesach of the future.*

ט *Pesach — He planned strategies to destroy his enemies, and the children of Israel went forth with exalted hand[9] — the Pesach of Egypt.*

EIGHTH NIGHT

א *Pesach* — [Israel was] fortunate to shine with the light of life,[10] for all of the Children of Israel there was light[11] — the Pesach of Egypt.*

ב *Pesach — with this same sign [of light] they will again be blessed, rise up and shine for your light has come[12] — the Pesach of the future.*

ג *Pesach — the redeemed one praised you at that time, HASHEM saved on that day[13] — the Pesach of Egypt.*

ד *Pesach — O Exalted One, hurry our salvation, HASHEM is our King, He is our Savior[14] — the Pesach of the future.*

ה *Pesach — They embittered them with hardship and discouraged them, the day after the pesach offering, they went forth[15] — the Pesach of Egypt.*

ו *Pesach —and a day of vengeance shall you see, for in gladness shall you go forth[16] — the Pesach of the future.*

ז *Pesach — the pure ones were exceedingly awestruck, when the water became a wall for them[17] — the Pesach of Egypt.*

ח *Pesach — may He endow those who anticipate Him with His goodness, may He lead them beside flowing water[18] — the Pesach of the future.*

ט *Pesach — the Pure One multiplied His humility over them, and HASHEM went before them[19] — the Pesach of Egypt.*

י *Pesach — may He awaken the words of My prophetic vision, 'For HASHEM goes before you'[20] — the Pesach of the future.*

כ *Pesach — the prophetess [Miriam] responded properly, 'Sing to HASHEM for He is exalted above the arrogant'[21] — the Pesach of Egypt.*

ל *Pesach — may its scoffers be downtrodden, play music to HASHEM for He has established grandeur[22] — the Pesach of the future.*

(1) *Exodus* 14:30. (2) *Isaiah* 45:17. (3) *Exodus* 14:31. (4) *Isaiah* 11:11. (5) *Exodus* 15:19. (6) *Isaiah* 11:15. (7) *Exodus* 14:24. (8) *Joel* 3:3. (9) *Exodus* 14:8. (10) Cf. *Job* 33:30. (11) *Exodus* 10:23. (12) *Isaiah* 60:1. (13) *Exodus* 14:30. (14) *Isaiah* 33:22. (15) *Numbers* 33:3. (16) *Isaiah* 55:12. (17) *Exodus* 14:22; 29. (18) *Isaiah* 49:10. (19) *Exodus* 13:21. (20) *Isaiah* 52:12. (21) *Exodus* 15:21. (22) *Isaiah* 12:5.

strong — appears in the acrostic of the verses following the alphabetical verses.

בְּמִכְתָּב שְׁנָן — *The clearly inscribed [plagues].* The initial letters of the Ten Plagues, דצ״ך עד״ש

SEVENTH NIGHT

פֶּסַח יֶשַׁע וְתַעֲצוּם שָׁלוֹם,
בְּשִׂמְחָה תֵצֵאוּ וּבְשָׁלוֹם,[1]
פֶּסַח לֶעָתִיד.
פֶּסַח כָּלִיל עֲנָמִים לְהַצְמֵת,
כִּי אֵין בַּיִת
אֲשֶׁר אֵין שָׁם מֵת,[2]
פֶּסַח מִצְרָיִם.
פֶּסַח לְאֻמִּים יֶהְגּוּ רִיק[3]
לְנָגְפָה,
וְזֹאת תִּהְיֶה הַמַּגֵּפָה,[4]
פֶּסַח לֶעָתִיד.
פֶּסַח מִלּוּי שְׁעָרִים פֶּתַח,
וּפָסַח יהוה עַל הַפֶּתַח,[5]
פֶּסַח מִצְרָיִם.
פֶּסַח נוֹרָאוֹת עִזּוּז רַב וְשַׁלִּיט,
גָּנוֹן וְהִצִּיל
פָּסוֹחַ וְהִמְלִיט,[6]
פֶּסַח לֶעָתִיד.
פֶּסַח סְגוּלִים לְמַטַּע שְׂרִידִים,*
כִּי יהוה נִלְחָם
לָהֶם בְּמִצְרָיִם,[7]
פֶּסַח מִצְרָיִם.
פֶּסַח עָתִיד לְפִדְיוֹן שְׁבוּיִם,
וְיָצָא יהוה
וְנִלְחַם בַּגּוֹיִם,[8]
פֶּסַח לֶעָתִיד.
פֶּסַח פְּתִיחַת קוֹל
עָנְתָה נְבִיאָה,
שִׁירוּ לַיהוה
כִּי גָאֹה גָּאָה,[9]
פֶּסַח מִצְרָיִם.

EIGHTH NIGHT

פֶּסַח מְנֻעָם שִׁיר הוֹדָיָה,
עָזִּי וְזִמְרָת יָהּ,[10] פֶּסַח מִצְרָיִם.
פֶּסַח נַגֵּן שִׁיר הֲמוֹנַי,
כִּי עָזִּי וְזִמְרָת יָהּ יהוה,[11]
פֶּסַח לֶעָתִיד.
פֶּסַח סְגֻלִּים לָשׁוּב לְמַאֲוָיָם,
הָלְכוּ בַיַּבָּשָׁה בְּתוֹךְ הַיָּם,[12]
פֶּסַח מִצְרָיִם.
פֶּסַח עָתִיד לְהָשִׁיב שְׁבִיָּם,[13]
מֶחֱמַת וּמֵאִיֵּי הַיָּם,[14] פֶּסַח לֶעָתִיד.
פֶּסַח פּוֹרְכִים נָסוּ לִפְנֵיהֶם,
כִּי יהוה נִלְחָם לָהֶם,[15]
פֶּסַח מִצְרָיִם.
פֶּסַח צָרוֹת עִמּוֹ יָסִיר וְנִחַם,
וְיָצָא יהוה וְנִלְחַם,[16] פֶּסַח לֶעָתִיד.
פֶּסַח קֶרֶץ נָאוֹר הִרְעַם,
וַתֶּחֱזַק מִצְרַיִם עַל הָעָם,[17]
פֶּסַח מִצְרָיִם.
פֶּסַח רוּחַ עָרִיצִים לְהַנְשִׁים,
יַחֲזִיקוּ עֲשָׂרָה אֲנָשִׁים,*[18]
פֶּסַח לֶעָתִיד.
פֶּסַח שְׁאֵרָם נִמַּק וְנִכְחַד,
לֹא נִשְׁאַר בָּהֶם עַד אֶחָד,*[19]
פֶּסַח מִצְרָיִם.
פֶּסַח תִּתֵּן יְשׁוּעוֹת חוֹסָיו,
וְלֹא יִהְיֶה שָׂרִיד לְבֵית עֵשָׂו,[20]
פֶּסַח לֶעָתִיד.
פֶּסַח תּוֹפְפוּ יוֹנְקִים לְיַחֲדֵהוּ,
זֶה אֵלִי וְאַנְוֵהוּ,[21] פֶּסַח מִצְרָיִם.
פֶּסַח יְקָרִים יֹאמְרוּ כָּזֶה,
הִנֵּה אֱלֹהֵינוּ זֶה,*[22] פֶּסַח לֶעָתִיד.

באח״ב, were inscribed on the staff with which Moses brought the plagues.

שְׂרִידִים — *Those remaining.* Many Jews — those who did not believe Moses' message and chose not to follow him — died, and were buried, during the Plague of Darkness. Those remaining were loyal to *Hashem* and to His servant Moses (see *Rashi* to *Exodus* 10:22).

יַחֲזִיקוּ עֲשָׂרָה אֲנָשִׁים — *Ten men shall clasp them.* The prophet describes how many gentiles will attach themselves to each Jew in the future. *So says HASHEM, Master of Legions: In those days when ten men of all the tongues of the nations will clasp them; they will clasp a corner of the Jewish man's garment and say, 'Let us go with you, for we have heard that God is with you'* (*Zechariah* 8:23). According to the Talmud (*Shabbos* 32a) this verse alludes to the reward for wearing *tzitzis* — 2,800 angelic servants. *Rashi* explains that *'ten men of all the tongues'* means ten men from each of the seventy tongues of the world. Thus seven hundred will grasp at each corner. And for the four-cornered garment of the

SEVENTH NIGHT

י *Pesach — salvation*
and powerful peace,
in gladness shall you go out,
and in peace[1] *—*
the Pesach of the future.

כ *Pesach — the crowning glory*
of the Anamite [Egyptians,
their firstborn,] to slay,
for there is no home in which
there is no corpse[2] *—*
the Pesach of Egypt.

ל *Pesach — to push aside*
the nations that talk in vain,[3]
and thus shall be the plague[4] *—*
the Pesach of the future.

מ *Pesach — He opened the sealed*
[Egyptian] gates,
but HASHEM *passed over*
the [Jewish] doorway[5] *—*
the Pesach of Egypt.

נ *Pesach — the wondrous strength*
of the Master and Ruler,
protect and rescue, leap
and cause escape[6] *—*
the Pesach of the future.

ס *Pesach — those remaining**
became the treasured planting,
because HASHEM *did battle*
for them against Egypt[7] *—*
the Pesach of Egypt.

ע *Pesach — for the future ransom*
of captives,
HASHEM *shall go forth*
and battle those nations[8] *—*
the Pesach of the future.

פ *Pesach — the opening verse*
the prophetess [Miriam]
repeated,
'Sing to HASHEM *for He is exalted*
above the arrogant!'[9] *—*
the Pesach of Egypt.

EIGHTH NIGHT

מ *Pesach — a pleasant song of thanksgiving,*
'God is my might and praise'[10] *—*
the Pesach of Egypt.

נ *Pesach — my multitudes shall sing the song,*
'For HASHEM*, God, is my Might*
and my Praise'[11] *the Pesach of the future.*

ס *Pesach — to return the treasured ones*
to the longed-for Land,
they walked on the dry land amid the sea[12]
— the Pesach of Egypt.

ע *Pesach — in the future He shall return*
their captivity,[13]
from Chamas and from the isles of the sea[14]
— the Pesach of the future.

פ *Pesach — the taskmasters fled from before*
them, for HASHEM *did battle for them*[15] *—*
the Pesach of Egypt.

צ *Pesach — may He remove His people's*
troubles and assuage them,
when HASHEM *will go forth and do battle*[16]
— the Pesach of the future.

ק *the Illuminated One cut down and shattered,*
when the Egyptians forced the people
[to leave the land][17] *— the Pesach of Egypt.*

ר *Pesach — He shall blow away the spirit*
of the belligerent,
ten men shall clasp them[18]** —*
the Pesach of the future.

ש *Pesach — their flesh melted*
and was destroyed,
none remained of them save one[19]***
— the Pesach of Egypt.

ת *Pesach — may He grant salvation for those*
who rely on Him, and that there not remain
a remnant of the House of Esau[20] *—*
the Pesach of the future.

ת *Pesach — even the sucklings played*
on the drums to declare His Oneness,
'This is my God and I shall glorify Him'[21]
— the Pesach of Egypt.

י *Pesach — the treasured ones shall say thus,*
*'Behold, this is our God'**[22] *—*
the Pesach of the future.

(1) *Isaiah* 55:12. (2) *Exodus* 12:30. (3) *Psalms* 2:1. (4) *Zechariah* 14:12. (5) *Exodus* 12:23. (6) *Isaiah* 31:5. (7) *Exodus* 14:25. (8) *Zechariah* 14:3. (9) *Exodus* 15:21. (10) 15:2. (11) *Isaiah* 12:2. (12) *Exodus* 15:19. (13) Cf. *Psalms* 126:1. (14) *Isaiah* 11:11. (15) *Exodus* 14:25. (16) *Zechariah* 14:3. (17) *Exodus* 12:33. (18) *Zechariah* 8:23. (19) *Exodus* 14:28; cf. *Psalms* 106:11. (20) *Obadiah* 1:18. (21) *Exodus* 15:2. (22) *Isaiah* 25:9.

tzitzis there will be two thousand eight hundred.

עַד אֶחָד — *Save one.* When the Egyptians were drowned in the sea, God permitted Pharaoh to escape. Thus there will be at least one non-Jewish witness who could testify to the miracle at the sea (*Midrash Tehillim* 106).

הִנֵּה אֱלֹהֵינוּ זֶה — *Behold, this is our God.* In the world of the future, God will sit in the center of a circle of the righteous in *Gan Eden.* Each of the *tzaddikim* will point his finger and say: *Behold, this is our God, this is* HASHEM *to whom we have hoped, let us exult and be glad in His salvation* (*Isaiah* 25:9; *Taanis* 31a).

SEVENTH NIGHT

פֶּסַח צָפוּי בְּאוֹת אֲשֶׁר נַעֲשָׂה,
זַמְּרוּ יהוה
כִּי גֵאוּת עָשָׂה,[1]
פֶּסַח לֶעָתִיד.
פֶּסַח קֹדֶר לְצָרָיו מְאוֹרֵי אוֹר,
וּלְכָל בְּנֵי יִשְׂרָאֵל
הָיָה אוֹר,[2]
פֶּסַח מִצְרָיִם.
פֶּסַח רָצוּי בְּמַאֲמַר צוּרֵךְ,
קוּמִי אוֹרִי כִּי בָא אוֹרֵךְ,[3]
פֶּסַח לֶעָתִיד.
פֶּסַח שִׁבְּחוּהוּ בְּעֹז תַּעֲצוּמוֹ,
כִּי גָאַל יהוה אֶת עַמּוֹ,[4]
פֶּסַח מִצְרָיִם.
פֶּסַח תֹּקֶף תְּהִלּוֹת רִשּׁוּמוֹ,
גֹּאֲלֵנוּ יהוה צְבָאוֹת
שְׁמוֹ,[5]
פֶּסַח לֶעָתִיד.
פֶּסַח יוֹסֵף עַל יְשׁוּעוֹת יְשׁוּעָה,
בְּרִיתוֹ יִזְכֹּר לְהוֹשִׁיעָה,
עַם קְרוֹבוֹ בְּאַהַב לְהִוָּשֵׁעָה,
כַּאֲשֶׁר שֵׁמַע לְמִצְרַיִם
לְצוֹר נִשְׁמָעָה.[6]
בְּגִילָה בְּרִנָּה,

EIGHTH NIGHT

פֶּסַח קְדֻשָּׁה נְקֵבָה* בַּעֲלִיזוּת,
אֶת הַשִּׁירָה הַזֹּאת,[7] פֶּסַח מִצְרָיִם.
פֶּסַח וְגֶבֶר* יְסוֹבֵב וְיִתְקַדָּשׁ,
שִׁירוּ לַיהוה שִׁיר חָדָשׁ,[8]
פֶּסַח לֶעָתִיד.
פֶּסַח תְּבִיעַת עֲנוּי קְפַצְתָּ,
וּמִבֵּית כֶּלֶא עַם זוּ קָנִיתָ,[9]
פֶּסַח מִצְרָיִם.
פֶּסַח יַחֲשֹׂף זְרוֹעוֹ[10] וְתַעֲצוּמוֹ,
לִקְנוֹת אֶת שְׁאָר עַמּוֹ,[11]
פֶּסַח לֶעָתִיד.
פֶּסַח אוֹהֲבָיו הוֹצִיא צָהֳרָיִם,
וַיָּהָם אֶת מַחֲנֵה מִצְרָיִם,[12]
פֶּסַח מִצְרָיִם.
פֶּסַח לְהָשִׁיב לְקָמָיו גְּמוּלֵיהֶם,
מְהוּמַת יהוה רַבָּה בָּהֶם,[13]
פֶּסַח לֶעָתִיד.
פֶּסַח בִּרְאוֹתָם נָמוּ לְסַלְסְלָה,
אֶת הַיָּד הַגְּדוֹלָה,[14] פֶּסַח מִצְרָיִם.
פֶּסַח רָווּת בְּזִיז כְּבוֹדוֹ,[15]
יוֹסִיף אֲדֹנָי שֵׁנִית יָדוֹ,[16]
פֶּסַח לֶעָתִיד.
פֶּסַח חִזָּיוֹן שִׁירָה קִדְּמוּ לְנֶעְלָם,
יהוה יִמְלֹךְ לְעוֹלָם,[17]
פֶּסַח מִצְרָיִם.
פֶּסַח בְּצִיּוֹן יְשׁוֹרְרוּ לְגֹאֲלָם,
יִמְלֹךְ יהוה לְעוֹלָם,[18]
פֶּסַח לֶעָתִיד.
פֶּסַח טַכְסִיסֵי* הוֹד מְאֻשֶּׁרֶת לְהִגָּאֵל,
יְדִידֶיךָ הוֹשַׁעְתָּ שִׁעֲשַׁעְתָּ יִשְׁרֵי אֵל,
כְּשֵׁר לְקוֹחֶיךָ חָזוּ מִפְעֲלוֹת אֵל,
אָז יָשִׁיר מֹשֶׁה וּבְנֵי יִשְׂרָאֵל.[19]
בְּגִילָה בְּרִנָּה,

נְקֵבָה . . . וְגֶבֶר — *Feminine . . . masculine.* The word for song appears in Scripture in the masculine gender — שִׁיר — and in the feminine — שִׁירָה. In the feminine form, it refers to songs of joy in the world of the present. After every song of joy, a new tragedy is born, just as a female gives birth to one child after another. But the song of the World to Come is in the masculine form, because it is the song which will beget no further misfortunes (*Rashi* to *Arachin* 13b).

טַכְסִיסֵי הוֹד — *Regal strategies.* This stanza is not part of the long *piyut* that has been alternating between 'the Pesach of Egypt' and 'the Pesach of the future.' Rather, it is a continuation of the series of six four-line stanzas scattered throughout the *Maariv* service.

SEVENTH NIGHT

צ *Pesach — anticipating the sign*
that will have been fulfilled,
sing to HASHEM *for He will have*
established grandeur[1] *—*
the Pesach of the future.

ק *Pesach — He darkened*
the fire's light
for His [Egyptian] enemies,
but for all the Children of Israel
there was light[2] *—*
the Pesach of Egypt.

ר *Pesach — may Your Creator's*
utterance find favor,
'Rise up and shine,
for your light has come'[3] *—*
the Pesach of the future.

ש *Pesach — they praised Him with*
the full measure of His strength,
for HASHEM *redeemed*
His people[4]
— the Pesach of Egypt.

ת *Pesach — the powerful praise*
inherent in His Name,
our Redeemer, HASHEM,
Master of Legions, is His Name[5]
— the Pesach of the future.

יוסף *Pesach — may He increase*
salvation upon salvations,

ברי *remembering His covenant*
to save,

עקב *His close nation to save*
with love,
let the report regarding Egypt
be heard regarding Tyre.[6]
with mirth, with glad song,

EIGHTH NIGHT

ק *Pesach — the exultations of holiness*
*in the feminine gender,**
'This shirah-song,'[7] *— the Pesach of Egypt.*

ו *Pesach — but He shall sanctify it*
*and turn it to masculine,**
'Sing to HASHEM *a new shir-song'*[8]
— the Pesach of the future.

ת *Pesach — You leapt to exact retribution*
for [Israel's] pain,
from the dungeon,
You have acquired this people[9] *—*
the Pesach of Egypt.

י *Pesach — may He bare His arm*[10]
and His might,
to acquire the remnant of His people[11]
— the Pesach of the future.

א *Pesach — He brought out*
His loved ones in the afternoon,
when He bewildered the Egyptian camp[12]
— the Pesach of Egypt.

ל *Pesach — to return upon them*
their recompense,
HASHEM *will wreak great confusion*
upon them[13] *— the Pesach of the future.*

ב *Pesach — They decided to speak up*
and exalt when they saw,
the great hand [that God inflicted
upon Egypt][14] *— the Pesach of Egypt.*

ר *Pesach — may He satiate*
with the shine of His glory,[15]

יוסף *may my Lord increase His power*
a second time[16] *— the Pesach of the future.*

חזק *Pesach — a prophetic song they*
foresang to the Inscrutable One,
*'*HASHEM *shall reign forever'*[17] *—*
the Pesach of Egypt.

Pesach — in Zion they shall sing
to their Redeemer,
'May HASHEM *reign forever'*[18] *—*
the Pesach of the future.

ט *Pesach — Regal strategies** *by which*
to redeem the praiseworthy,

י *You save Your beloved, and You*
delighted God's upright nation,

כל *at the appropriate time, those whom*
You took to Yourself saw God's works,
then Moses and the Children of Israel
chose to sing,[19]
with mirth, with glad song,

---

(1) *Isaiah* 12:5. (2) *Exodus* 10:23. (3) *Isaiah* 60:1. (4) Cf. *Isaiah* 44:23 [some *machzorim* read כִּי פָקַד ה׳ אֶת עַמּוֹ, *for* HASHEM *remembered His people — Ruth* 1:6]. (5) *Isaiah* 47:4. (6) Cf. *Isaiah* 23:5. (7) *Exodus* 15:1. (8) *Psalms* 96:1. (9) *Exodus* 15:16. (10) Cf. *Isaiah* 52:10. (11) 11:11. (12) *Exodus* 14:24. (13) *Zechariah* 14:13. (14) *Exodus* 14:31. (15) Cf. *Isaiah* 66:11. (16) 11:11. (17) *Exodus* 15:18. (18) *Psalms* 146:10. (19) *Exodus* 15:1.

בְּשִׂמְחָה רַבָּה וְאָמְרוּ כֻלָּם:

מִי כָמֹכָה בָּאֵלִים יהוה, מִי כָּמֹכָה נֶאְדָּר בַּקֹּדֶשׁ, נוֹרָא תְהִלֹּת, עֹשֵׂה פֶלֶא.[1] ❖ מַלְכוּתְךָ רָאוּ בָנֶיךָ בּוֹקֵעַ יָם לִפְנֵי מֹשֶׁה,

SEVENTH NIGHT

וּבְרֹב[2] **טוּבְךָ*** נָחִיתָ יְדִידִים,
וּבְרוּחַ[3] יָם עָבְרוּ גְדוּדִים,
אָמַר[4] כּוֹשֵׁל לְהַצְלִיל
נְדוּדִים,
נָשַׁפְתָּ[5] לִהְיוֹת בְּסַאסְּאָה
נִמְדָּדִים.
זֶה צוּר יִשְׁעֵנוּ, פָּצוּ פֶה וְאָמְרוּ:

EIGHTH NIGHT

מִי[6] מְלֵּל נוֹי כֹּחַ סִפּוּר מְלַאכְתּוֹ,
סִלְסוּל תִּפְאַרְתּוֹ בְּעֻזִּים
הִדְרִיךְ הֲלִיכָתוֹ,
עוֹלְלִים וְיוֹנְקִים שִׁבְּחוּהוּ
וְצָפוּ מְסִלָּתוֹ,
גְּבוּרוֹתָיו וּכְבוֹד הֲדַר מַלְכוּתוֹ.[7]
Continue: ה' יִמְלֹךְ . . .

זֶה אֵלִי[8] עָנוּ וְאָמְרוּ:

יהוה יִמְלֹךְ לְעֹלָם וָעֶד.[9] ❖ וְנֶאֱמַר: כִּי פָדָה יהוה אֶת יַעֲקֹב, וּגְאָלוֹ מִיַּד חָזָק מִמֶּנּוּ.[10]

SEVENTH NIGHT

מִי כָמוֹכָה[11] מִשְׂגָּב לְעִתּוֹת
בַּצָּרָה,[12]
נָטִיתָ[13] נוֹאֲצֶיךָ בְּזַעַם וְעֶבְרָה,
נָחִיתָ[14] סְגֻלָּתְךָ בִּזְרוֹעַ גְּבוּרָה,
שָׁמְעוּ[15] עַמִּים גְּאֻלָּתְךָ
לְהַגְבִּירָה.

EIGHTH NIGHT

נָחִיתָ[14] פְּנִינֶיךָ בְּעֻזָּךְ
עַמְּךָ לְהִתְנָאוֹת,
צוֹרְרֵיהֶם הַמַּמְתָּ בְּמַכּוֹת לְהַלְאוֹת,
קְדוֹשׁ יִשְׂרָאֵל מְיַחֲדִים
מִסֵּבֶל וּתְלָאוֹת,
גֹּאֲלָם שְׁמוֹ יהוה צְבָאוֹת.[16]

[Some conclude the blessing as follows; others conclude with בָּרוּךְ . . . גָּאַל יִשְׂרָאֵל.]

בָּרוּךְ אַתָּה יהוה, מֶלֶךְ צוּר יִשְׂרָאֵל וְגוֹאֲלוֹ. (Cong. — אָמֵן.)

בָּרוּךְ אַתָּה יהוה, גָּאַל יִשְׂרָאֵל. (Cong. — אָמֵן.)

הַשְׁכִּיבֵנוּ יהוה אֱלֹהֵינוּ לְשָׁלוֹם, וְהַעֲמִידֵנוּ מַלְכֵּנוּ לְחַיִּים, וּפְרוֹשׂ עָלֵינוּ סֻכַּת שְׁלוֹמֶךָ, וְתַקְּנֵנוּ בְּעֵצָה טוֹבָה מִלְּפָנֶיךָ, וְהוֹשִׁיעֵנוּ לְמַעַן שְׁמֶךָ. וְהָגֵן בַּעֲדֵנוּ, וְהָסֵר מֵעָלֵינוּ אוֹיֵב, דֶּבֶר, וְחֶרֶב, וְרָעָב, וְיָגוֹן, וְהָסֵר שָׂטָן מִלְּפָנֵינוּ וּמֵאַחֲרֵינוּ, וּבְצֵל כְּנָפֶיךָ תַּסְתִּירֵנוּ,[17] כִּי אֵל שׁוֹמְרֵנוּ וּמַצִּילֵנוּ אָתָּה, כִּי אֵל מֶלֶךְ חַנּוּן

(1) *Exodus* 15:11. (2) 15:7. (3) 15:8. (4) 15:9. (5) 15:10. (6) 15:11. (7) *Psalms* 145:12. (8) *Exodus* 15:2. (9) 15:18. (10) *Jeremiah* 31:10. (11) *Exodus* 15:11. (12) *Psalms* 9:10. (13) *Exodus* 15:12. (14) 15:13. (15) 15:14. (16) Cf. *Jeremiah* 50:34; *Isaiah* 47:4. (17) Cf. *Psalms* 17:8.

וּבְרוֹב טוּבְךָ — *And with the abundance of Your goodness.* Some *machzorim* read וּבְרֹב גְּאוֹנְךָ, *And with the abundance of Your grandeur,* as the verse in *Exodus* (15:7) reads. However, that reading does not fit the *aleph-beis* scheme of the *piyut.*

with abundant gladness — and said unanimously:

מִי כָמֹכָה *Who is like You among the heavenly powers, HASHEM! Who is like You, mighty in holiness, too awesome for praise, doing wonders![1]* Chazzan– *Your children beheld Your majesty, as You split the sea before Moses,*

SEVENTH NIGHT	EIGHTH NIGHT
And with the abundance of[2] ט *Your goodness,** *You led the beloved ones.* *With the wind[3]* י *the hosts [of Israel] crossed the sea.* *He said[4] [— he is Pharaoh]* כ *the snarer — that he would drown the [Jewish] wanderers.* *But you blew[5]* *[the Egyptians into the sea],* ל *that they be punished measure for measure.*	*Who[6]* מנ *can recount the beauty and strength of the story of His work?* ס *The exaltation of His glory — in strong waters He made His path.* ע *Infants and sucklings praised Him and saw His way, His mighty deeds, and the glorious splendor of His kingdom.[7]*

'He is the Rock of our salvation!' they opened their mouths and said:

Continue: *'HASHEM shall reign . . .'*

'This is my God!'[8] they exclaimed, then they said:

יהוה *'HASHEM shall reign for all eternity!'[9]* Chazzan– *And it is further said: 'For HASHEM has redeemed Jacob and delivered him from a power mightier than he.'[10]*

SEVENTH NIGHT	EIGHTH NIGHT
Who is like You,[11] מ *a Fortress in times of distress?[12]* *You stretched out[13]* נ *fury and anger over those who scorn You.* *You led[14]* ס *Your treasured [nation] with a powerful arm.* ע *Peoples heard[15] about Your Powerful redemption.*	*You led[14]* פ *Your pearls — with Your [Torah's] strength to adorn Your people.* צ *You confounded their oppressors with plagues to tire them out.* ק *Holy One of Israel, they declare Your Oneness despite burdens and travail. Their Redeemer, 'HASHEM, Master of legions,' is His Name.[16]*

[Some conclude the blessing as follows; others conclude with *'Blessed . . . Who redeemed Israel'.*]

Blessed are You, HASHEM, King, Rock of Israel and its Redeemer.

Blessed are You, HASHEM, Who redeemed Israel. (Cong.– *Amen.)*

הַשְׁכִּיבֵנוּ *Lay us down to sleep, HASHEM, our God, in peace, raise us erect, our King, to life; and spread over us the shelter of Your peace. Set us aright with good counsel from before Your Presence, and save us for Your Name's sake. Shield us, remove from us foe, plague, sword, famine, and woe; and remove spiritual impediment from before us and behind us, and in the shadow of Your wings shelter us[17] — for God Who protects and rescues us are You; for God, the Gracious*

וְרַחוּם אָתָּה.[1] ❖ וּשְׁמוֹר צֵאתֵנוּ וּבוֹאֵנוּ, לְחַיִּים וּלְשָׁלוֹם מֵעַתָּה וְעַד עוֹלָם.[2] וּפְרוֹשׂ עָלֵינוּ סֻכַּת שְׁלוֹמֶךָ.

SEVENTH NIGHT	EIGHTH NIGHT
אָז נִבְהֲלוּ[3] פְּחוּזֵי דִינִים, תִּפֹּל עֲלֵיהֶם[4] צְוָחוֹת וּמְדָנִים, תְּבִאֵמוֹ[5] קְדוֹשֶׁיךָ רֶגֶשׁ מְעוֹנִים. יהוה יִמְלֹךְ[6] שׁוֹמֵר תְּשׁוּעַת אֱמוּנִים.	בְּחַסְדְּךָ רוֹמַמְתָּ קֶרֶן עַמְּךָ יָצְאוּ מְרֻוָחִים, שֶׁבַח וּרְנָנוֹת לְשִׁמְךָ מְסַלְּדִים וּמְשַׁבְּחִים, תְּבִאֵמוֹ וְתִטָּעֵמוֹ[5] עִיר מְנוּחִים, בִּנְוֵה שָׁלוֹם וּבְמִשְׁכְּנוֹת מִבְטָחִים[7]

בָּרוּךְ אַתָּה יהוה, הַפּוֹרֵשׂ סֻכַּת שָׁלוֹם עָלֵינוּ וְעַל כָּל עַמּוֹ יִשְׂרָאֵל וְעַל יְרוּשָׁלָיִם. (Cong. – אָמֵן.)

Congregation rises and remains standing until after *Shemoneh Esrei.*

On the Sabbath, the congregation, followed by the *chazzan,* recites:

וְשָׁמְרוּ בְנֵי יִשְׂרָאֵל אֶת הַשַּׁבָּת, לַעֲשׂוֹת אֶת הַשַּׁבָּת לְדֹרֹתָם בְּרִית עוֹלָם. בֵּינִי וּבֵין בְּנֵי יִשְׂרָאֵל אוֹת הִיא לְעֹלָם, כִּי שֵׁשֶׁת יָמִים עָשָׂה יהוה אֶת הַשָּׁמַיִם וְאֶת הָאָרֶץ, וּבַיּוֹם הַשְּׁבִיעִי שָׁבַת וַיִּנָּפַשׁ.[8]

Congregation, then *chazzan:*

וַיְדַבֵּר מֹשֶׁה אֶת מֹעֲדֵי יהוה, אֶל בְּנֵי יִשְׂרָאֵל.[9]

חצי קדיש

The *chazzan* recites חֲצִי קַדִּישׁ.

יִתְגַּדַּל וְיִתְקַדַּשׁ שְׁמֵהּ רַבָּא. (Cong. – אָמֵן.) בְּעָלְמָא דִּי בְרָא כִרְעוּתֵהּ, וְיַמְלִיךְ מַלְכוּתֵהּ, בְּחַיֵּיכוֹן וּבְיוֹמֵיכוֹן וּבְחַיֵּי דְכָל בֵּית יִשְׂרָאֵל, בַּעֲגָלָא וּבִזְמַן קָרִיב. וְאִמְרוּ: אָמֵן.

(Cong. – אָמֵן. יְהֵא שְׁמֵהּ רַבָּא מְבָרַךְ לְעָלַם וּלְעָלְמֵי עָלְמַיָּא.)

יְהֵא שְׁמֵהּ רַבָּא מְבָרַךְ לְעָלַם וּלְעָלְמֵי עָלְמַיָּא.

יִתְבָּרַךְ וְיִשְׁתַּבַּח וְיִתְפָּאַר וְיִתְרוֹמַם וְיִתְנַשֵּׂא וְיִתְהַדָּר וְיִתְעַלֶּה וְיִתְהַלָּל שְׁמֵהּ דְּקֻדְשָׁא בְּרִיךְ הוּא (Cong. – בְּרִיךְ הוּא) – לְעֵלָּא מִן כָּל בִּרְכָתָא וְשִׁירָתָא תֻּשְׁבְּחָתָא וְנֶחֱמָתָא, דַּאֲמִירָן בְּעָלְמָא. וְאִמְרוּ: אָמֵן. (Cong. – אָמֵן.)

and Compassionate King, are You.[1] Chazzan— *Safeguard our going and coming, for life and for peace from now to eternity.*[2] *And spread over us the shelter of Your peace.*

SEVENTH NIGHT	EIGHTH NIGHT
Then they were confounded[3] — פ *those hasty in judgment;* *make fall upon them*[4] צ *crying and punishments.* *May You bring them*[5] — קר *Your holy ones —* *speedily to the Temple.* *May* HASHEM *reign*[6] — שת *Guardian of the Salvations* *for the faithful.*	*With Your kindness* ר *You exalted Your people's pride* *when they went forth relieved.* ש *They sang and exulted to Your Name* *with praise and glad song.* ת *May You bring them* *and implant them*[5] *in the city of their contentment,* *in a Temple of peace* *and in secure dwellings.*[7]

Blessed are You, HASHEM, *Who spreads the shelter of peace upon us, upon all of His people Israel and upon Jerusalem.* (Cong.— *Amen.*)

Congregation rises and remains standing until after *Shemoneh Esrei.*

On the Sabbath, the congregation, followed by the *chazzan,* recites:

וְשָׁמְרוּ *And the Children of Israel shall keep the Sabbath, to make the Sabbath an eternal covenant for their generations. Between Me and the Children of Israel it is a sign forever that in six days* HASHEM *made heaven and earth, and on the seventh day He rested and was refreshed.*[8]

Congregation, then *chazzan:*

And Moses declared HASHEM's appointed festivals to the Children of Israel.[9]

HALF KADDISH

The *chazzan* recites Half-*Kaddish.*

יִתְגַּדַּל *May His great Name grow exalted and sanctified* (Cong.— *Amen.*) *in the world that He created as He willed. May He give reign to His kingship in your lifetimes and in your days, and in the lifetimes of the entire Family of Israel, swiftly and soon. Now respond: Amen.*

(Cong.— *Amen. May His great Name be blessed forever and ever.*)

May His great Name be blessed forever and ever.

Blessed, praised, glorified, exalted, extolled, mighty, upraised, and lauded be the Name of the Holy One, Blessed is He (Cong.— *Blessed is He*) — *beyond any blessing and song, praise and consolation that are uttered in the world. Now respond: Amen.* (Cong.— *Amen.*)

(1) Cf. *Nehemiah* 9:31. (2) Cf. *Psalms* 121:8. (3) *Exodus* 15:15. (4) 15:16. (5) 15:17. (6) 15:18. (7) *Isaiah* 32:18. (8) *Exodus* 31:16-17. (9) *Leviticus* 23:44.

❧ שמונה עשרה – עמידה ☙

Take three steps backward, then three steps forward. Remain standing with the feet together while reciting *Shemoneh Esrei*. Recite it with quiet devotion and without interruption, verbal or otherwise. Although its recitation should not be audible to others, one must pray loudly enough to hear himself.

אֲדֹנָי שְׂפָתַי תִּפְתָּח, וּפִי יַגִּיד תְּהִלָּתֶךָ.[1]

אבות

Bend the knees at בָּרוּךְ; bow at אַתָּה; straighten up at ה׳.

בָּרוּךְ אַתָּה יהוה אֱלֹהֵינוּ וֵאלֹהֵי אֲבוֹתֵינוּ, אֱלֹהֵי אַבְרָהָם, אֱלֹהֵי יִצְחָק, וֵאלֹהֵי יַעֲקֹב, הָאֵל הַגָּדוֹל הַגִּבּוֹר וְהַנּוֹרָא, אֵל עֶלְיוֹן, גּוֹמֵל חֲסָדִים טוֹבִים וְקוֹנֵה הַכֹּל, וְזוֹכֵר חַסְדֵי אָבוֹת, וּמֵבִיא גוֹאֵל לִבְנֵי בְנֵיהֶם, לְמַעַן שְׁמוֹ בְּאַהֲבָה. מֶלֶךְ עוֹזֵר וּמוֹשִׁיעַ וּמָגֵן.

Bend the knees at בָּרוּךְ; bow at אַתָּה; straighten up at ה׳.

בָּרוּךְ אַתָּה יהוה, מָגֵן אַבְרָהָם.

גבורות

אַתָּה גִּבּוֹר לְעוֹלָם אֲדֹנָי, מְחַיֵּה מֵתִים אַתָּה, רַב לְהוֹשִׁיעַ. מְכַלְכֵּל חַיִּים בְּחֶסֶד, מְחַיֵּה מֵתִים בְּרַחֲמִים רַבִּים, סוֹמֵךְ נוֹפְלִים, וְרוֹפֵא חוֹלִים, וּמַתִּיר אֲסוּרִים, וּמְקַיֵּם אֱמוּנָתוֹ לִישֵׁנֵי עָפָר. מִי כָמוֹךְ בַּעַל גְּבוּרוֹת, וּמִי דּוֹמֶה לָּךְ, מֶלֶךְ מֵמִית וּמְחַיֶּה וּמַצְמִיחַ יְשׁוּעָה. וְנֶאֱמָן אַתָּה לְהַחֲיוֹת מֵתִים. בָּרוּךְ אַתָּה יהוה, מְחַיֵּה הַמֵּתִים.

קדושת השם

אַתָּה קָדוֹשׁ וְשִׁמְךָ קָדוֹשׁ, וּקְדוֹשִׁים בְּכָל יוֹם יְהַלְלוּךָ סֶּלָה. בָּרוּךְ אַתָּה יהוה, הָאֵל הַקָּדוֹשׁ.

קדושת היום

אַתָּה בְחַרְתָּנוּ מִכָּל הָעַמִּים, אָהַבְתָּ אוֹתָנוּ, וְרָצִיתָ בָּנוּ, וְרוֹמַמְתָּנוּ מִכָּל הַלְּשׁוֹנוֹת, וְקִדַּשְׁתָּנוּ בְּמִצְוֹתֶיךָ, וְקֵרַבְתָּנוּ מַלְכֵּנוּ לַעֲבוֹדָתֶךָ, וְשִׁמְךָ הַגָּדוֹל וְהַקָּדוֹשׁ עָלֵינוּ קָרָאתָ.

On Saturday night add. [If forgotten, do not repeat *Shemoneh Esrei.* See *Laws* §91.]

וַתּוֹדִיעֵנוּ יהוה אֱלֹהֵינוּ אֶת מִשְׁפְּטֵי צִדְקֶךָ, וַתְּלַמְּדֵנוּ לַעֲשׂוֹת חֻקֵּי רְצוֹנֶךָ. וַתִּתֶּן לָנוּ יהוה אֱלֹהֵינוּ מִשְׁפָּטִים יְשָׁרִים וְתוֹרוֹת אֱמֶת חֻקִּים וּמִצְוֹת טוֹבִים. וַתַּנְחִילֵנוּ זְמַנֵּי שָׂשׂוֹן וּמוֹעֲדֵי קֹדֶשׁ וְחַגֵּי נְדָבָה. וַתּוֹרִישֵׁנוּ קְדֻשַּׁת שַׁבָּת וּכְבוֹד מוֹעֵד וַחֲגִיגַת הָרֶגֶל. וַתַּבְדֵּל יהוה אֱלֹהֵינוּ בֵּין קֹדֶשׁ לְחוֹל, בֵּין אוֹר לְחֹשֶׁךְ, בֵּין יִשְׂרָאֵל לָעַמִּים, בֵּין יוֹם הַשְּׁבִיעִי לְשֵׁשֶׁת יְמֵי הַמַּעֲשֶׂה. בֵּין קְדֻשַּׁת שַׁבָּת לִקְדֻשַּׁת יוֹם טוֹב הִבְדַּלְתָּ, וְאֶת יוֹם הַשְּׁבִיעִי מִשֵּׁשֶׁת יְמֵי הַמַּעֲשֶׂה קִדַּשְׁתָּ, הִבְדַּלְתָּ וְקִדַּשְׁתָּ אֶת עַמְּךָ יִשְׂרָאֵל בִּקְדֻשָּׁתֶךָ.

SHEMONEH ESREI — AMIDAH

Take three steps backward, then three steps forward. Remain standing with the feet together while reciting *Shemoneh Esrei.* Recite it with quiet devotion and without interruption, verbal or otherwise. Although its recitation should not be audible to others, one must pray loudly enough to hear himself.

My Lord, open my lips, that my mouth may declare Your praise.[1]

PATRIARCHS

Bend the knees at *'Blessed'*; bow at *'You'*; straighten up at *'HASHEM.'*

בָּרוּךְ *Blessed are You, HASHEM, our God and the God of our forefathers, God of Abraham, God of Isaac, and God of Jacob; the great, mighty, and awesome God, the supreme God, Who bestows beneficial kindnesses and creates everything, Who recalls the kindnesses of the Patriarchs and brings a Redeemer to their children's children, for His Name's sake, with love. O King, Helper, Savior, and Shield.*

Bend the knees at *'Blessed'*; bow at *'You'*; straighten up at 'HASHEM.'

Blessed are You, HASHEM, Shield of Abraham.

GOD'S MIGHT

אַתָּה *You are eternally mighty, my Lord, the Resuscitator of the dead are You; abundantly able to save. He sustains the living with kindness, resuscitates the dead with abundant mercy, supports the fallen, heals the sick, releases the confined, and maintains His faith to those asleep in the dust. Who is like You, O Master of mighty deeds, and who is comparable to You, O King Who causes death and restores life and makes salvation sprout! And You are faithful to resuscitate the dead. Blessed are You, HASHEM, Who resuscitates the dead.*

HOLINESS OF GOD'S NAME

אַתָּה *You are holy and Your Name is holy, and holy ones praise You every day, forever. Blessed are You, HASHEM, the holy God.*

SANCTIFICATION OF THE DAY

אַתָּה בְחַרְתָּנוּ *You have chosen us from all the peoples; You loved us and found favor in us; You exalted us above all the tongues and You sanctified us with Your commandments. You drew us close, our King, to Your service and proclaimed Your great and Holy Name upon us.*

On Saturday night add. [If forgotten, do not repeat *Shemoneh Esrei.* See Laws §91.]

וַתּוֹדִיעֵנוּ *You made known to us, HASHEM, our God, Your righteous ordinances, and You taught us to do the decrees of Your will. You gave us, HASHEM, our God, fair laws and true teachings, good decrees and commandments. As a heritage You gave us seasons of joy, appointed festivals of holiness, and free-willed festive offerings. You made us heir to the Sabbath holiness, the appointed festival glory, and festive offering of the pilgrimage. You distinguished, O HASHEM, our God, between the sacred and secular, between light and darkness, between Israel and the peoples, between the seventh day and the six days of labor. Between the sanctity of the Sabbath and the sanctity of the holiday You have distinguished, and the seventh day, from among the six days of labor You have sanctified. You have distinguished and You have sanctified Your people Israel with Your holiness.*

(1) *Psalms* 51:17.

On the Sabbath add the words in brackets. [If forgotten, see *Laws* §86-90.]

וַתִּתֶּן לָנוּ יהוה אֱלֹהֵינוּ בְּאַהֲבָה [שַׁבָּתוֹת לִמְנוּחָה וּ]מוֹעֲדִים לְשִׂמְחָה חַגִּים וּזְמַנִּים לְשָׂשׂוֹן, אֶת יוֹם [הַשַּׁבָּת הַזֶּה וְאֶת יוֹם] חַג הַמַּצּוֹת הַזֶּה, זְמַן חֵרוּתֵנוּ [בְּאַהֲבָה], מִקְרָא קֹדֶשׁ, זֵכֶר לִיצִיאַת מִצְרָיִם.

אֱלֹהֵינוּ וֵאלֹהֵי אֲבוֹתֵינוּ, יַעֲלֶה, וְיָבֹא, וְיַגִּיעַ, וְיֵרָאֶה, וְיֵרָצֶה, וְיִשָּׁמַע, וְיִפָּקֵד, וְיִזָּכֵר זִכְרוֹנֵנוּ וּפִקְדוֹנֵנוּ, וְזִכְרוֹן אֲבוֹתֵינוּ, וְזִכְרוֹן מָשִׁיחַ בֶּן דָּוִד עַבְדֶּךָ, וְזִכְרוֹן יְרוּשָׁלַיִם עִיר קָדְשֶׁךָ, וְזִכְרוֹן כָּל עַמְּךָ בֵּית יִשְׂרָאֵל לְפָנֶיךָ, לִפְלֵיטָה לְטוֹבָה לְחֵן וּלְחֶסֶד וּלְרַחֲמִים, לְחַיִּים וּלְשָׁלוֹם בְּיוֹם חַג הַמַּצּוֹת הַזֶּה. זָכְרֵנוּ יהוה אֱלֹהֵינוּ בּוֹ לְטוֹבָה, וּפָקְדֵנוּ בוֹ לִבְרָכָה, וְהוֹשִׁיעֵנוּ בוֹ לְחַיִּים. וּבִדְבַר יְשׁוּעָה וְרַחֲמִים, חוּס וְחָנֵּנוּ וְרַחֵם עָלֵינוּ וְהוֹשִׁיעֵנוּ, כִּי אֵלֶיךָ עֵינֵינוּ, כִּי אֵל מֶלֶךְ חַנּוּן וְרַחוּם אָתָּה.[1]

On the Sabbath add the words in brackets. [If forgotten, see *Laws* §86-90.]

וְהַשִּׂיאֵנוּ יהוה אֱלֹהֵינוּ אֶת בִּרְכַּת מוֹעֲדֶיךָ לְחַיִּים וּלְשָׁלוֹם, לְשִׂמְחָה וּלְשָׂשׂוֹן, כַּאֲשֶׁר רָצִיתָ וְאָמַרְתָּ לְבָרְכֵנוּ. [אֱלֹהֵינוּ וֵאלֹהֵי אֲבוֹתֵינוּ רְצֵה בִמְנוּחָתֵנוּ] קַדְּשֵׁנוּ בְּמִצְוֹתֶיךָ וְתֵן חֶלְקֵנוּ בְּתוֹרָתֶךָ, שַׂבְּעֵנוּ מִטּוּבֶךָ וְשַׂמְּחֵנוּ בִּישׁוּעָתֶךָ, וְטַהֵר לִבֵּנוּ לְעָבְדְּךָ בֶּאֱמֶת, וְהַנְחִילֵנוּ יהוה אֱלֹהֵינוּ [בְּאַהֲבָה וּבְרָצוֹן] בְּשִׂמְחָה וּבְשָׂשׂוֹן [שַׁבָּת וּ]מוֹעֲדֵי קָדְשֶׁךָ, וְיִשְׂמְחוּ בְךָ יִשְׂרָאֵל מְקַדְּשֵׁי שְׁמֶךָ. בָּרוּךְ אַתָּה יהוה, מְקַדֵּשׁ [הַשַּׁבָּת וְ]יִשְׂרָאֵל וְהַזְּמַנִּים.

עבודה

רְצֵה יהוה אֱלֹהֵינוּ בְּעַמְּךָ יִשְׂרָאֵל וּבִתְפִלָּתָם, וְהָשֵׁב אֶת הָעֲבוֹדָה לִדְבִיר בֵּיתֶךָ. וְאִשֵּׁי יִשְׂרָאֵל וּתְפִלָּתָם בְּאַהֲבָה תְקַבֵּל בְּרָצוֹן, וּתְהִי לְרָצוֹן תָּמִיד עֲבוֹדַת יִשְׂרָאֵל עַמֶּךָ.

וְתֶחֱזֶינָה עֵינֵינוּ בְּשׁוּבְךָ לְצִיּוֹן בְּרַחֲמִים. בָּרוּךְ אַתָּה יהוה, הַמַּחֲזִיר שְׁכִינָתוֹ לְצִיּוֹן.

הודאה

Bow at מוֹדִים; straighten up at 'ה.

מוֹדִים אֲנַחְנוּ לָךְ, שָׁאַתָּה הוּא יהוה אֱלֹהֵינוּ וֵאלֹהֵי אֲבוֹתֵינוּ לְעוֹלָם וָעֶד. צוּר חַיֵּינוּ, מָגֵן יִשְׁעֵנוּ אַתָּה הוּא לְדוֹר וָדוֹר.

(1) Cf. *Nehemiah* 9:31.

On the Sabbath add the words in brackets. [If forgotten, see *Laws* §86-90.]

וַתִּתֶּן לָנוּ *And You gave us, HASHEM, our God, with love [Sabbaths for rest], appointed festivals for gladness, Festivals and times for joy, [this day of Sabbath and] this day of the Festival of Matzos, the time of our freedom [with love], a holy convocation, a memorial of the Exodus from Egypt.*

אֱלֹהֵינוּ *Our God and God of our forefathers, may there rise, come, reach, be noted, be favored, be heard, be considered, and be remembered — the remembrance and consideration of ourselves; the remembrance of our forefathers; the remembrance of Messiah, son of David, Your servant; the remembrance of Jerusalem, the City of Your Holiness; the remembrance of Your entire people the Family of Israel — before You for deliverance, for goodness, for grace, for kindness, and for compassion, for life, and for peace on this day of the Festival of Matzos. Remember us on it, HASHEM, our God, for goodness, consider us on it for blessing, and help us on it for life. In the matter of salvation and compassion, pity, be gracious and compassionate with us and help us, for our eyes are turned to You, because You are God, the gracious and compassionate King.*[1]

On the Sabbath add the words in brackets. [If forgotten, see *Laws* §86-90.]

וְהַשִּׂיאֵנוּ *Bestow upon us, O HASHEM, our God, the blessing of Your appointed festivals for life and for peace, for gladness and for joy, as You desired and promised to bless us. [Our God and the God of our forefathers, may You be pleased with our rest.] Sanctify us withYour commandments and grant us our share in Your Torah; satisfy us from Your goodness and gladden us with Your salvation, and purify our heart to serve You sincerely. And grant us a heritage, O HASHEM, our God — [with love and with favor] with gladness and with joy — [the Sabbath and] the appointed festivals of Your holiness, and may Israel, the sanctifiers of Your Name, rejoice in You. Blessed are You, HASHEM, Who sanctifies [the Sabbath,] Israel and the festive seasons.*

TEMPLE SERVICE

רְצֵה *Be favorable, HASHEM, our God, toward Your people Israel and their prayer and restore the service to the Holy of Holies of Your Temple. The fire-offerings of Israel and their prayer accept with love and favor, and may the service of Your people Israel always be favorable to You.*

וְתֶחֱזֶינָה *May our eyes behold Your return to Zion in compassion. Blessed are You, HASHEM, Who restores His Presence to Zion.*

THANKSGIVING [MODIM]

Bow at *'We gratefully thank You'*; straighten up at *'HASHEM.'*

מוֹדִים *We gratefully thank You, for it is You Who are HASHEM, our God and the God of our forefathers for all eternity; Rock of our lives, Shield of our salvation are You from generation to generation.*

נוֹדֶה לְּךָ וּנְסַפֵּר תְּהִלָּתֶךָ[1] עַל חַיֵּינוּ הַמְּסוּרִים בְּיָדֶךָ, וְעַל נִשְׁמוֹתֵינוּ הַפְּקוּדוֹת לָךְ, וְעַל נִסֶּיךָ שֶׁבְּכָל יוֹם עִמָּנוּ, וְעַל נִפְלְאוֹתֶיךָ וְטוֹבוֹתֶיךָ שֶׁבְּכָל עֵת, עֶרֶב וָבֹקֶר וְצָהֳרָיִם. הַטּוֹב כִּי לֹא כָלוּ רַחֲמֶיךָ, וְהַמְּרַחֵם כִּי לֹא תַמּוּ חֲסָדֶיךָ,[2] מֵעוֹלָם קִוִּינוּ לָךְ.

וְעַל כֻּלָּם יִתְבָּרַךְ וְיִתְרוֹמַם שִׁמְךָ מַלְכֵּנוּ תָּמִיד לְעוֹלָם וָעֶד.

Bend the knees at בָּרוּךְ; bow at אַתָּה; straighten up at ה׳.

וְכֹל הַחַיִּים יוֹדוּךָ סֶּלָה, וִיהַלְלוּ אֶת שִׁמְךָ בֶּאֱמֶת, הָאֵל יְשׁוּעָתֵנוּ וְעֶזְרָתֵנוּ סֶלָה. בָּרוּךְ אַתָּה יהוה, הַטּוֹב שִׁמְךָ וּלְךָ נָאֶה לְהוֹדוֹת.

שלום

שָׁלוֹם רָב עַל יִשְׂרָאֵל עַמְּךָ תָּשִׂים לְעוֹלָם, כִּי אַתָּה הוּא מֶלֶךְ אָדוֹן לְכָל הַשָּׁלוֹם. וְטוֹב בְּעֵינֶיךָ לְבָרֵךְ אֶת עַמְּךָ יִשְׂרָאֵל, בְּכָל עֵת וּבְכָל שָׁעָה בִּשְׁלוֹמֶךָ. בָּרוּךְ אַתָּה יהוה, הַמְּבָרֵךְ אֶת עַמּוֹ יִשְׂרָאֵל בַּשָּׁלוֹם.

יִהְיוּ לְרָצוֹן אִמְרֵי פִי וְהֶגְיוֹן לִבִּי לְפָנֶיךָ, יהוה צוּרִי וְגֹאֲלִי.[3]

אֱלֹהַי, נְצוֹר לְשׁוֹנִי מֵרָע, וּשְׂפָתַי מִדַּבֵּר מִרְמָה,[4] וְלִמְקַלְּלַי נַפְשִׁי תִדּוֹם, וְנַפְשִׁי כֶּעָפָר לַכֹּל תִּהְיֶה. פְּתַח לִבִּי בְּתוֹרָתֶךָ, וּבְמִצְוֹתֶיךָ תִּרְדּוֹף נַפְשִׁי. וְכֹל הַחוֹשְׁבִים עָלַי רָעָה, מְהֵרָה הָפֵר עֲצָתָם וְקַלְקֵל מַחֲשַׁבְתָּם. עֲשֵׂה לְמַעַן שְׁמֶךָ, עֲשֵׂה לְמַעַן יְמִינֶךָ, עֲשֵׂה לְמַעַן קְדֻשָּׁתֶךָ, עֲשֵׂה לְמַעַן תּוֹרָתֶךָ. לְמַעַן יֵחָלְצוּן יְדִידֶיךָ, הוֹשִׁיעָה יְמִינְךָ וַעֲנֵנִי.[5]

Some recite verses pertaining to their names here. See p. 1143.

יִהְיוּ לְרָצוֹן אִמְרֵי פִי וְהֶגְיוֹן לִבִּי לְפָנֶיךָ, יהוה צוּרִי וְגֹאֲלִי.[3]

Bow and take three steps back. Bow left and say . . . עֹשֶׂה; bow right and say . . . הוּא יַעֲשֶׂה; bow forward and say וְעַל כָּל . . . אָמֵן.

עֹשֶׂה שָׁלוֹם בִּמְרוֹמָיו, הוּא יַעֲשֶׂה שָׁלוֹם עָלֵינוּ, וְעַל כָּל יִשְׂרָאֵל. וְאִמְרוּ: אָמֵן.

יְהִי רָצוֹן מִלְּפָנֶיךָ יהוה אֱלֹהֵינוּ וֵאלֹהֵי אֲבוֹתֵינוּ, שֶׁיִּבָּנֶה בֵּית הַמִּקְדָּשׁ בִּמְהֵרָה בְיָמֵינוּ, וְתֵן חֶלְקֵנוּ בְּתוֹרָתֶךָ. וְשָׁם נַעֲבָדְךָ בְּיִרְאָה, כִּימֵי עוֹלָם וּכְשָׁנִים קַדְמוֹנִיּוֹת. וְעָרְבָה לַיהוה מִנְחַת יְהוּדָה וִירוּשָׁלָיִם, כִּימֵי עוֹלָם וּכְשָׁנִים קַדְמוֹנִיּוֹת.[6]

SHEMONEH ESREI ENDS HERE.

Remain standing in place for at least a few moments before taking three steps forward.

We shall thank You and relate Your praise[1] — for our lives, which are committed to Your power and for our souls that are entrusted to You; for Your miracles that are with us every day; and for Your wonders and favors in every season — evening, morning, and afternoon. The Beneficent One, for Your compassions were never exhausted, and the Compassionate One, for Your kindnesses never ended[2] — always have we put our hope in You.

For all these, may Your Name be blessed and exalted, our King, continually forever and ever.

Bend the knees at *'Blessed'*; bow at *'You'*; straighten up at *'HASHEM.'*

Everything alive will gratefully acknowledge You, Selah! and praise Your Name sincerely, O God of our salvation and help, Selah! Blessed are You, HASHEM, Your Name is 'The Beneficent One' and to You it is fitting to give thanks.

PEACE

שָׁלוֹם *Establish abundant peace upon Your people Israel forever, for You are King, Master of all peace. May it be good in Your eyes to bless Your people Israel at every time and every hour with Your peace. Blessed are You, HASHEM, Who blesses His people Israel with peace.*

May the expressions of my mouth and the thoughts of my heart find favor before You, HASHEM, my Rock and my Redeemer.[3]

אֱלֹהַי *My God, guard my tongue from evil and my lips from speaking deceitfully.[4] To those who curse me, let my soul be silent; and let my soul be like dust to everyone. Open my heart to Your Torah, then my soul will pursue Your commandments. As for all those who design evil against me, speedily nullify their counsel and disrupt their design. Act for Your Name's sake; act for Your right hand's sake; act for Your sanctity's sake; act for Your Torah's sake. That Your beloved ones may be given rest; let Your right hand save, and respond to me.[5]*

Some recite verses pertaining to their names at this point. See page 1143.

May the expressions of my mouth and the thoughts of my heart find favor before You, HASHEM, my Rock and my Redeemer.[3] He Who makes peace in His heights, may He make peace upon us, and upon all Israel. Now respond: Amen.

Bow and take three steps back. Bow left and say, *'He Who makes peace . . .'*; bow right and say, *'may He make peace . . .'*; bow forward and say, *'and upon . . . Amen.'*

יְהִי רָצוֹן *May it be Your will, HASHEM, our God and the God of our forefathers, that the Holy Temple be rebuilt, speedily in our days. Grant us our share in Your Torah, and may we serve You there with reverence, as in days of old and in former years. Then the offering of Judah and Jerusalem will be pleasing to HASHEM, as in days of old and in former years.[6]*

SHEMONEH ESREI ENDS HERE.

Remain standing in place for at least a few moments before taking three steps forward.

(1) Cf. *Psalms* 79:13. (2) Cf. *Lamentations* 3:22. (3) *Psalms* 19:15.
(4) Cf. 34:14. (5) 60:7; 108:7. (6) *Malachi* 3:4.

On Friday night, all present stand and recite וַיְכֻלּוּ aloud in unison. Conversation is forbidden until after the אָמֵן response to the blessing מְקַדֵּשׁ הַשַּׁבָּת (below).

וַיְכֻלּוּ* הַשָּׁמַיִם וְהָאָרֶץ וְכָל צְבָאָם. וַיְכַל אֱלֹהִים בַּיּוֹם הַשְּׁבִיעִי מְלַאכְתּוֹ אֲשֶׁר עָשָׂה, וַיִּשְׁבֹּת בַּיּוֹם הַשְּׁבִיעִי מִכָּל מְלַאכְתּוֹ אֲשֶׁר עָשָׂה. וַיְבָרֶךְ אֱלֹהִים אֶת יוֹם הַשְּׁבִיעִי, וַיְקַדֵּשׁ אֹתוֹ, כִּי בוֹ שָׁבַת מִכָּל מְלַאכְתּוֹ, אֲשֶׁר בָּרָא אֱלֹהִים לַעֲשׂוֹת.[1]

ברכה מעין שבע

Chazzan continues:

בָּרוּךְ אַתָּה יהוה אֱלֹהֵינוּ וֵאלֹהֵי אֲבוֹתֵינוּ, אֱלֹהֵי אַבְרָהָם, אֱלֹהֵי יִצְחָק, וֵאלֹהֵי יַעֲקֹב, הָאֵל הַגָּדוֹל הַגִּבּוֹר וְהַנּוֹרָא, אֵל עֶלְיוֹן, קוֹנֵה שָׁמַיִם וָאָרֶץ.

Congregation, then *chazzan:*

מָגֵן אָבוֹת בִּדְבָרוֹ, מְחַיֵּה מֵתִים בְּמַאֲמָרוֹ, הָאֵל הַקָּדוֹשׁ שֶׁאֵין כָּמוֹהוּ, הַמֵּנִיחַ לְעַמּוֹ בְּיוֹם שַׁבַּת קָדְשׁוֹ, כִּי בָם רָצָה לְהָנִיחַ לָהֶם. לְפָנָיו נַעֲבֹד בְּיִרְאָה וָפַחַד, וְנוֹדֶה לִשְׁמוֹ בְּכָל יוֹם תָּמִיד מֵעֵין הַבְּרָכוֹת. אֵל הַהוֹדָאוֹת, אֲדוֹן הַשָּׁלוֹם, מְקַדֵּשׁ הַשַּׁבָּת וּמְבָרֵךְ שְׁבִיעִי, וּמֵנִיחַ בִּקְדֻשָּׁה לְעַם מְדֻשְּׁנֵי עֹנֶג, זֵכֶר לְמַעֲשֵׂה בְרֵאשִׁית.

Chazzan continues:

אֱלֹהֵינוּ וֵאלֹהֵי אֲבוֹתֵינוּ רְצֵה בִמְנוּחָתֵנוּ. קַדְּשֵׁנוּ בְּמִצְוֹתֶיךָ, וְתֵן חֶלְקֵנוּ בְּתוֹרָתֶךָ. שַׂבְּעֵנוּ מִטּוּבֶךָ, וְשַׂמְּחֵנוּ בִּישׁוּעָתֶךָ, וְטַהֵר לִבֵּנוּ לְעָבְדְּךָ בֶּאֱמֶת. וְהַנְחִילֵנוּ יהוה אֱלֹהֵינוּ בְּאַהֲבָה וּבְרָצוֹן שַׁבַּת קָדְשֶׁךָ, וְיָנוּחוּ בָהּ יִשְׂרָאֵל מְקַדְּשֵׁי שְׁמֶךָ. בָּרוּךְ אַתָּה יהוה, מְקַדֵּשׁ הַשַּׁבָּת.* (Cong. – אָמֵן.)

❧ וַיְכֻלּוּ — *... were finished.* We stand and recite this paragraph aloud because it is a form of testimony that God created heaven and earth — and witnesses must give their testimony while standing and in a loud, clear voice (*Ibn Yarchi*).

Because of this paragraph's status as a testimony, it should preferably be said with the congregation, or at least in the company of one other person. However, it may be recited by an individual as well (*Orach Chaim* 268).

Tur (ibid.) notes that it is especially important not to speak during וַיְכֻלּוּ or during the recitation of the seven-faceted blessing.

❧ בְּרָכָה מֵעֵין שֶׁבַע /

The Seven-faceted Blessing

In Talmudic times, the synagogues were generally located outside town limits, in open fields. Since it was dangerous to walk home alone in the dark after *Maariv*, the Sages instituted an extra prayer for the congregation so that everyone would stay a little longer, in case someone was slow in finishing his own *Maariv* (*Shabbos* 24b). On weekdays, the prayer בָּרוּךְ ה׳ לְעוֹלָם, *Blessed is HASHEM forever*, alludes to the number of blessings in the weekday *Shemoneh Esrei*. On the eve of the Sabbath, this extra prayer was formulated as a synopsis of the

On Friday night, all present stand and recite וַיְכֻלּוּ, *'Thus the heavens . . .,'* aloud in unison. Conversation is forbidden until after the *'Amen'* response to the blessing, *'Who sanctifies the Sabbath'* (below).

וַיְכֻלּוּ *Thus the heavens and the earth were finished,* and all their legion. On the seventh day God completed His work which He had done, and He abstained on the seventh day from all His work which He had done. God blessed the seventh day and sanctified it, because on it He had abstained from all His work which God created to make.*[1]

THE SEVEN-FACETED BLESSING

Chazzan continues:

בָּרוּךְ *Blessed are You, HASHEM, our God and the God of our forefathers, God of Abraham, God of Isaac, and God of Jacob; the great, mighty, and awesome God, the supreme God, Creator of heaven and earth.*

Congregation, then *chazzan:*

מָגֵן *He Who was the shield of our forefathers with His word, Who resuscitates the dead with His utterance, the Holy God Who is unequaled, Who grants rest to His people on His holy Sabbath day, for He was pleased with them to grant them rest. Before Him we will serve with awe and dread and give thanks to His Name every day continually with appropriate blessings. God of grateful praise, Master of peace, Who sanctifies the Sabbath and blesses the seventh day, and gives rest with holiness to a people saturated with delight — in memory of the work of Creation.*

Chazzan continues:

אֱלֹהֵינוּ *Our God and the God of our forefathers, may You be pleased with our rest. Sanctify us with Your commandments and grant us our share in Your Torah; satisfy us from Your goodness and gladden us with Your salvation, and purify our heart to serve You sincerely. O HASHEM, our God, with love and favor grant us Your holy Sabbath as a heritage and may Israel, the sanctifiers of Your Name, rest on it. Blessed are You, HASHEM, Who sanctifies the Sabbath.**

(Cong.— *Amen.)*

(1) *Genesis* 2:1-3.

---

seven blessings of the *Shemoneh Esrei.* It begins בָּרוּךְ אַתָּה ה׳, which is very similar to the beginning of *Shemoneh Esrei.* Then it continues with מָגֵן אָבוֹת, which has seven parts, as follows:

(1) מָגֵן אָבוֹת, *Shield of our forefathers* = the blessing of אָבוֹת, *forefathers;*

(2) מְחַיֵּה מֵתִים, *Who resuscitates the dead* = the blessing of resuscitation;

(3) הָאֵל הַקָּדוֹשׁ, *The Holy God* = the blessing of His holiness;

(4) הַמֵּנִיחַ לְעַמּוֹ, *Who grants rest to His people* = קְדוּשַּׁת הַיּוֹם, the intermediate blessing, which discusses the Sabbath;

(5) לְפָנָיו נַעֲבוֹד, *Before Him we serve* = רְצֵה, which appeals for acceptance of our service;

(6) וְנוֹדֶה לִשְׁמוֹ, *And give thanks to His Name* = the blessing of מוֹדִים, which thanks God for His many favors;

(7) אֲדוֹן הַשָּׁלוֹם, *Master of peace* = שָׁלוֹם רָב, the last blessing, which speaks of peace.

מְקַדֵּשׁ הַשַּׁבָּת — *Who sanctifies the Sabbath.* When a Festival falls on the Sabbath, this prayer is recited without any mention of the Festival, because the Sages did not compose a separate Seven-faceted Blessing for Festivals.

The *chazzan* recites קַדִּישׁ שָׁלֵם.

יִתְגַּדַּל וְיִתְקַדַּשׁ שְׁמֵהּ רַבָּא. (.Cong – אָמֵן.) בְּעָלְמָא דִּי בְרָא כִרְעוּתֵהּ. וְיַמְלִיךְ מַלְכוּתֵהּ, בְּחַיֵּיכוֹן וּבְיוֹמֵיכוֹן וּבְחַיֵּי דְכָל בֵּית יִשְׂרָאֵל, בַּעֲגָלָא וּבִזְמַן קָרִיב. וְאִמְרוּ: אָמֵן.

(.Cong – אָמֵן. יְהֵא שְׁמֵהּ רַבָּא מְבָרַךְ לְעָלַם וּלְעָלְמֵי עָלְמַיָּא.)

יְהֵא שְׁמֵהּ רַבָּא מְבָרַךְ לְעָלַם וּלְעָלְמֵי עָלְמַיָּא.

יִתְבָּרַךְ וְיִשְׁתַּבַּח וְיִתְפָּאַר וְיִתְרוֹמַם וְיִתְנַשֵּׂא וְיִתְהַדָּר וְיִתְעַלֶּה וְיִתְהַלָּל שְׁמֵהּ דְּקֻדְשָׁא בְּרִיךְ הוּא (.Cong – בְּרִיךְ הוּא) – לְעֵלָּא מִן כָּל בִּרְכָתָא וְשִׁירָתָא תֻּשְׁבְּחָתָא וְנֶחֱמָתָא, דַּאֲמִירָן בְּעָלְמָא. וְאִמְרוּ: אָמֵן. (.Cong – אָמֵן.)

(.Cong – קַבֵּל בְּרַחֲמִים וּבְרָצוֹן אֶת תְּפִלָּתֵנוּ.)

תִּתְקַבֵּל צְלוֹתְהוֹן וּבָעוּתְהוֹן דְּכָל בֵּית יִשְׂרָאֵל קֳדָם אֲבוּהוֹן דִּי בִשְׁמַיָּא. וְאִמְרוּ: אָמֵן. (.Cong – אָמֵן.)

(.Cong – יְהִי שֵׁם יהוה מְבֹרָךְ, מֵעַתָּה וְעַד עוֹלָם.[1])

יְהֵא שְׁלָמָא רַבָּא מִן שְׁמַיָּא, וְחַיִּים עָלֵינוּ וְעַל כָּל יִשְׂרָאֵל. וְאִמְרוּ: אָמֵן. (.Cong – אָמֵן.)

(.Cong – עֶזְרִי מֵעִם יהוה, עֹשֵׂה שָׁמַיִם וָאָרֶץ.[2])

Take three steps back. Bow left and say . . . עֹשֶׂה; bow right and say . . . הוּא; bow forward and say וְעַל כָּל . . . אָמֵן. Remain standing in place for a few moments, then take three steps forward.

עֹשֶׂה שָׁלוֹם בִּמְרוֹמָיו, הוּא יַעֲשֶׂה שָׁלוֹם עָלֵינוּ, וְעַל כָּל יִשְׂרָאֵל. וְאִמְרוּ: אָמֵן. (.Cong – אָמֵן.)

קידוש בבית הכנסת

In some congregations, the *chazzan* recites *Kiddush* [although he will repeat *Kiddush* at home]. The *chazzan's Kiddush* consists of the blessings over wine, the holiness of the day, and *Shehecheyanu*. On Saturday night, two *Havdalah* blessings are added.

סַבְרִי מָרָנָן וְרַבָּנָן וְרַבּוֹתַי:

בָּרוּךְ אַתָּה יהוה אֱלֹהֵינוּ מֶלֶךְ הָעוֹלָם, בּוֹרֵא פְּרִי הַגָּפֶן. (.Cong – אָמֵן.)

On Friday night, the words in brackets are included.

בָּרוּךְ אַתָּה יהוה אֱלֹהֵינוּ מֶלֶךְ הָעוֹלָם, אֲשֶׁר בָּחַר בָּנוּ מִכָּל עָם, וְרוֹמְמָנוּ מִכָּל לָשׁוֹן, וְקִדְּשָׁנוּ בְּמִצְוֹתָיו. וַתִּתֶּן לָנוּ יהוה אֱלֹהֵינוּ בְּאַהֲבָה [שַׁבָּתוֹת לִמְנוּחָה וּ]מוֹעֲדִים לְשִׂמְחָה חַגִּים וּזְמַנִּים לְשָׂשׂוֹן, אֶת יוֹם [הַשַּׁבָּת הַזֶּה וְאֶת יוֹם] חַג הַמַּצּוֹת הַזֶּה, זְמַן חֵרוּתֵנוּ [בְּאַהֲבָה] מִקְרָא קֹדֶשׁ, זֵכֶר לִיצִיאַת מִצְרָיִם. כִּי בָנוּ בָחַרְתָּ וְאוֹתָנוּ קִדַּשְׁתָּ מִכָּל הָעַמִּים, [וְשַׁבָּת] וּמוֹעֲדֵי קָדְשֶׁךָ [בְּאַהֲבָה וּבְרָצוֹן] בְּשִׂמְחָה וּבְשָׂשׂוֹן הִנְחַלְתָּנוּ. בָּרוּךְ אַתָּה יהוה, מְקַדֵּשׁ [הַשַּׁבָּת וְ]יִשְׂרָאֵל וְהַזְּמַנִּים. (.Cong – אָמֵן.)

KIDDUSH CONTINUES ON NEXT PAGE.

The *chazzan* recites the Full *Kaddish*.

יִתְגַּדַּל *May His great Name grow exalted and sanctified* (Cong.– *Amen.*) *in the world that He created as He willed. May He give reign to His kingship in your lifetimes and in your days, and in the lifetimes of the entire Family of Israel, swiftly and soon. Now respond: Amen.*

(Cong.– *Amen. May His great Name be blessed forever and ever.*)

May His great Name be blessed forever and ever.

Blessed, praised, glorified, exalted, extolled, mighty, upraised, and lauded be the Name of the Holy One, Blessed is He (Cong.– *Blessed is He*) *— beyond any blessing and song, praise and consolation that are uttered in the world. Now respond: Amen.* (Cong.– *Amen.*)

(Cong.– *Accept our prayers with mercy and favor.*)

May the prayers and supplications of the entire Family of Israel be accepted before their Father Who is in Heaven. Now respond: Amen. (Cong.– *Amen.*)

(Cong.– *Blessed be the Name of* H*ASHEM*, *from this time and forever.*[1])

May there be abundant peace from Heaven, and life, upon us and upon all Israel. Now respond: Amen. (Cong.– *Amen.*)

(Cong.– *My help is from* H*ASHEM*, *Maker of heaven and earth.*[2])

Take three steps back. Bow left and say, *'He Who makes peace . . .'*; bow right and say, *'may He . . .'*; bow forward and say, *'and upon all Israel . . .'* Remain standing in place for a few moments, then take three steps forward.

He Who makes peace in His heights, may He make peace upon us, and upon all Israel. Now respond: Amen. (Cong.– *Amen.*)

KIDDUSH IN THE SYNAGOGUE

In some congregations, the *chazzan* recites *Kiddush* [although he will repeat *Kiddush* at home]. The *chazzan's Kiddush* consists of the blessings over wine, the holiness of the day, and *Shehecheyanu*. On Saturday night, two *Havdalah* blessings are added.

By your leave, my masters and teachers:

בָּרוּךְ *Blessed are You,* H*ASHEM*, *our God, King of the universe, Who creates the fruit of the vine.* (Cong.– *Amen.*)

On Friday night, the words in brackets are included.

בָּרוּךְ *Blessed are You,* H*ASHEM*, *our God, King of the universe, Who has chosen us from every people, exalted us above every tongue, and sanctified us with His commandments. And You gave us,* H*ASHEM*, *our God, with love, [Sabbaths for rest] appointed festivals for gladness, festivals and times of joy, [this day of Sabbath and] this day of the Festival of Matzos, the time of our freedom [with love], a holy convocation, a memorial of the Exodus from Egypt. For You have chosen us and You have sanctified us above all the peoples, [and the Sabbath] and Your holy festivals [in love and in favor] in gladness and in joy have You granted us as a heritage. Blessed are You,* H*ASHEM*, *Who sanctifies [the Sabbath and] Israel and the seasons.* (Cong.– *Amen.*)

KIDDUSH CONTINUES ON NEXT PAGE.

(1) *Psalms* 113:2. (2) 121:2.

Kiddush in the Synagogue

The custom of reciting *Kiddush* in the synagogue dates back to very early times. It was instituted for the benefit of homeless people or travelers who often ate and slept in the synagogue. They were thus able to discharge their obligation of *Kiddush* by listening to the *chazzan's* recitation. Although the need for this *Kiddush* ceased to exist as even people without homes would be invited home by other congregants, the custom is maintained by

On Saturday night, add the following two paragraphs:

בָּרוּךְ אַתָּה יהוה אֱלֹהֵינוּ מֶלֶךְ הָעוֹלָם, בּוֹרֵא מְאוֹרֵי הָאֵשׁ.

בָּרוּךְ אַתָּה יהוה אֱלֹהֵינוּ מֶלֶךְ הָעוֹלָם, הַמַּבְדִּיל בֵּין קֹדֶשׁ לְחוֹל, בֵּין אוֹר לְחֹשֶׁךְ, בֵּין יִשְׂרָאֵל לָעַמִּים, בֵּין יוֹם הַשְּׁבִיעִי לְשֵׁשֶׁת יְמֵי הַמַּעֲשֶׂה. בֵּין קְדֻשַּׁת שַׁבָּת לִקְדֻשַּׁת יוֹם טוֹב הִבְדַּלְתָּ, וְאֶת יוֹם הַשְּׁבִיעִי מִשֵּׁשֶׁת יְמֵי הַמַּעֲשֶׂה קִדַּשְׁתָּ, הִבְדַּלְתָּ וְקִדַּשְׁתָּ אֶת עַמְּךָ יִשְׂרָאֵל בִּקְדֻשָּׁתֶךָ. בָּרוּךְ אַתָּה יהוה, הַמַּבְדִּיל בֵּין קֹדֶשׁ לְקֹדֶשׁ.

A child who listened to the *Kiddush* and responded *Amen* is given some of the wine. [If no child is present, the *chazzan* drinks the required amount; see commentary below.]

קדיש שלם

The *chazzan* recites קַדִּישׁ שָׁלֵם.

יִתְגַּדַּל וְיִתְקַדַּשׁ שְׁמֵהּ רַבָּא. (.Cong – אָמֵן.) בְּעָלְמָא דִּי בְרָא כִרְעוּתֵהּ. וְיַמְלִיךְ מַלְכוּתֵהּ, בְּחַיֵּיכוֹן וּבְיוֹמֵיכוֹן וּבְחַיֵּי דְכָל בֵּית יִשְׂרָאֵל, בַּעֲגָלָא וּבִזְמַן קָרִיב. וְאִמְרוּ: אָמֵן.

(.Cong – אָמֵן. יְהֵא שְׁמֵהּ רַבָּא מְבָרַךְ לְעָלַם וּלְעָלְמֵי עָלְמַיָּא.)

יְהֵא שְׁמֵהּ רַבָּא מְבָרַךְ לְעָלַם וּלְעָלְמֵי עָלְמַיָּא.

יִתְבָּרַךְ וְיִשְׁתַּבַּח וְיִתְפָּאַר וְיִתְרוֹמַם וְיִתְנַשֵּׂא וְיִתְהַדָּר וְיִתְעַלֶּה וְיִתְהַלָּל שְׁמֵהּ דְּקֻדְשָׁא בְּרִיךְ הוּא (.Cong – בְּרִיךְ הוּא) — לְעֵלָּא מִן כָּל בִּרְכָתָא וְשִׁירָתָא תֻּשְׁבְּחָתָא וְנֶחֱמָתָא, דַּאֲמִירָן בְּעָלְמָא. וְאִמְרוּ: אָמֵן. (.Cong – אָמֵן.)

(.Cong – קַבֵּל בְּרַחֲמִים וּבְרָצוֹן אֶת תְּפִלָּתֵנוּ.)

תִּתְקַבֵּל צְלוֹתְהוֹן וּבָעוּתְהוֹן דְּכָל בֵּית יִשְׂרָאֵל קֳדָם אֲבוּהוֹן דִּי בִשְׁמַיָּא. וְאִמְרוּ: אָמֵן. (.Cong – אָמֵן.)

(.Cong – יְהִי שֵׁם יהוה מְבֹרָךְ, מֵעַתָּה וְעַד עוֹלָם.[1])

יְהֵא שְׁלָמָא רַבָּא מִן שְׁמַיָּא, וְחַיִּים עָלֵינוּ וְעַל כָּל יִשְׂרָאֵל. וְאִמְרוּ: אָמֵן. (.Cong – אָמֵן.)

(.Cong – עֶזְרִי מֵעִם יהוה, עֹשֵׂה שָׁמַיִם וָאָרֶץ.[2])

Take three steps back. Bow left and say . . . עֹשֶׂה; bow right and say . . . הוּא; bow forward and say וְעַל כָּל . . . אָמֵן. Remain standing in place for a few moments, then take three steps forward.

עֹשֶׂה שָׁלוֹם בִּמְרוֹמָיו, הוּא יַעֲשֶׂה שָׁלוֹם עָלֵינוּ, וְעַל כָּל יִשְׂרָאֵל. וְאִמְרוּ: אָמֵן. (.Cong – אָמֵן.)

---

virtually all Ashkenaz synagogues. Since the person reciting the *Kiddush* will be reciting *Kiddush* at home for the benefit of his family — and for himself, as well, since that is where he will have his *Yom Tov* meal — he should have in mind that he will not discharge his own obligation in the synagogue. Therefore, he should not drink from the wine, but instead give some to one or more children who listened to the *Kiddush* and responded אָמֵן.

On Saturday night, add the following two paragraphs:

בָּרוּךְ *Blessed are You,* HASHEM, *our God, King of the universe, Who creates the illumination of the fire.*

בָּרוּךְ *Blessed are You,* HASHEM, *our God, King of the universe, Who distinguishes between sacred and secular, between light and darkness, between Israel and the nations, between the seventh day and the six days of activity. You have distinguished between the holiness of the Sabbath and the holiness of a Festival, and have sanctified the seventh day above the six days of activity. You distinguished and sanctified Your nation, Israel, with Your holiness. Blessed are You,* HASHEM, *who distinguishes between holiness and holiness.*

A child who listened to the *Kiddush* and responded *Amen* is given some of the wine. [If no child is present, the *chazzan* drinks the required amount; see commentary below.]

FULL KADDISH

The *chazzan* recites the Full *Kaddish.*

יִתְגַּדַּל *May His great Name grow exalted and sanctified* (Cong.– *Amen.*) *in the world that He created as He willed. May He give reign to His kingship in your lifetimes and in your days, and in the lifetimes of the entire Family of Israel, swiftly and soon. Now respond: Amen.*

(Cong.– *Amen. May His great Name be blessed forever and ever.*)

May His great Name be blessed forever and ever.

Blessed, praised, glorified, exalted, extolled, mighty, upraised, and lauded be the Name of the Holy One, Blessed is He (Cong.– *Blessed is He*) *— beyond any blessing and song, praise and consolation that are uttered in the world. Now respond: Amen.* (Cong.– *Amen.*)

(Cong.– *Accept our prayers with mercy and favor.*)

May the prayers and supplications of the entire Family of Israel be accepted before their Father Who is in Heaven. Now respond: Amen. (Cong.– *Amen.*)

(Cong.– *Blessed be the Name of* HASHEM, *from this time and forever.*[1])

May there be abundant peace from Heaven, and life, upon us and upon all Israel. Now respond: Amen. (Cong.– *Amen.*)

(Cong.– *My help is from* HASHEM, *Maker of heaven and earth.*[2])

Take three steps back. Bow left and say, *'He Who makes peace . . .';* bow right and say, *'may He . . .';* bow forward and say, *'and upon all Israel . . .'* Remain standing in place for a few moments, then take three steps forward.

He Who makes peace in His heights, may He make peace upon us, and upon all Israel. Now respond: Amen. (Cong.– *Amen.*)

(1) *Psalms* 113:2. (2) 121:2.

☙§ A Summary of Laws of Sefirah

The *Omer* is counted, standing, after nightfall. Before reciting the blessing, one should be careful *not* to say 'Today is the ———–th day.' If he did so, for example, in response to someone who asked which day it is, he may not recite the blessing, since he has already counted that day. Where there are days and weeks, this does not apply unless he also mentioned the week. In both cases, he may recite the blessing on succeeding nights.

If one forgets to count at night, he counts during the next day *without* a blessing, but may recite the blessing on succeeding nights. But if one forgot to count all day, he counts without a blessing on succeeding nights.

ספירת העומר

Most Congregations count the *Omer* at this point; some count after *Aleinu* (p. 832).
In some congregations the following Kabbalistic prayer precedes the counting of the *Omer*.

לְשֵׁם יִחוּד קוּדְשָׁא בְּרִיךְ הוּא וּשְׁכִינְתֵּיהּ, בִּדְחִילוּ וּרְחִימוּ לְיַחֵד שֵׁם יוּ״ד הֵ״א בְּוָא״ו הֵ״א בְּיִחוּדָא שְׁלִים, בְּשֵׁם כָּל יִשְׂרָאֵל. הִנְנִי מוּכָן וּמְזוּמָן לְקַיֵּם מִצְוַת עֲשֵׂה שֶׁל סְפִירַת הָעוֹמֶר, כְּמוֹ שֶׁכָּתוּב בַּתּוֹרָה: וּסְפַרְתֶּם לָכֶם מִמָּחֳרַת הַשַּׁבָּת, מִיּוֹם הֲבִיאֲכֶם אֶת עֹמֶר הַתְּנוּפָה, שֶׁבַע שַׁבָּתוֹת תְּמִימֹת תִּהְיֶינָה. עַד מִמָּחֳרַת הַשַּׁבָּת הַשְּׁבִיעִית תִּסְפְּרוּ חֲמִשִּׁים יוֹם, וְהִקְרַבְתֶּם מִנְחָה חֲדָשָׁה לַיהוה.[1] וִיהִי נֹעַם אֲדֹנָי אֱלֹהֵינוּ עָלֵינוּ, וּמַעֲשֵׂה יָדֵינוּ כּוֹנְנָה עָלֵינוּ, וּמַעֲשֵׂה יָדֵינוּ כּוֹנְנֵהוּ.[2]

Chazzan, followed by congregation, recites the blessing and counts.
One praying without a *minyan* should, nevertheless, recite the entire *Omer* service.

בָּרוּךְ אַתָּה יהוה אֱלֹהֵינוּ מֶלֶךְ הָעוֹלָם, אֲשֶׁר קִדְּשָׁנוּ בְּמִצְוֹתָיו וְצִוָּנוּ עַל סְפִירַת הָעוֹמֶר.

On the seventh night of Pesach – **הַיּוֹם שִׁשָּׁה יָמִים לָעוֹמֶר.**

On the eighth night of Pesach – **הַיּוֹם שִׁבְעָה יָמִים, שֶׁהֵם שָׁבוּעַ אֶחָד, לָעוֹמֶר.**

הָרַחֲמָן הוּא יַחֲזִיר לָנוּ עֲבוֹדַת בֵּית הַמִּקְדָּשׁ לִמְקוֹמָהּ, בִּמְהֵרָה בְיָמֵינוּ. אָמֵן סֶלָה.

תהלים סז

לַמְנַצֵּחַ בִּנְגִינֹת מִזְמוֹר שִׁיר. אֱלֹהִים יְחָנֵּנוּ וִיבָרְכֵנוּ, יָאֵר פָּנָיו אִתָּנוּ סֶלָה. לָדַעַת בָּאָרֶץ דַּרְכֶּךָ, בְּכָל גּוֹיִם יְשׁוּעָתֶךָ. יוֹדוּךָ עַמִּים אֱלֹהִים, יוֹדוּךָ עַמִּים כֻּלָּם. יִשְׂמְחוּ וִירַנְּנוּ לְאֻמִּים, כִּי תִשְׁפֹּט עַמִּים מִישֹׁר, וּלְאֻמִּים בָּאָרֶץ תַּנְחֵם סֶלָה. יוֹדוּךָ עַמִּים, אֱלֹהִים, יוֹדוּךָ עַמִּים כֻּלָּם. אֶרֶץ נָתְנָה יְבוּלָהּ, יְבָרְכֵנוּ אֱלֹהִים אֱלֹהֵינוּ. יְבָרְכֵנוּ אֱלֹהִים, וְיִירְאוּ אוֹתוֹ כָּל אַפְסֵי אָרֶץ.

אָנָּא בְּכֹחַ גְּדֻלַּת יְמִינְךָ תַּתִּיר צְרוּרָה. — אב״ג ית״ץ
קַבֵּל רִנַּת עַמְּךָ שַׂגְּבֵנוּ טַהֲרֵנוּ נוֹרָא. — קר״ע שט״ן
נָא גִבּוֹר דּוֹרְשֵׁי יִחוּדְךָ כְּבָבַת שָׁמְרֵם. — נג״ד יכ״ש
בָּרְכֵם טַהֲרֵם רַחֲמֵם צִדְקָתְךָ תָּמִיד גָּמְלֵם. — בט״ר צת״ג
חֲסִין קָדוֹשׁ בְּרוֹב טוּבְךָ נַהֵל עֲדָתֶךָ. — חק״ב טנ״ע
יָחִיד גֵּאֶה לְעַמְּךָ פְּנֵה זוֹכְרֵי קְדֻשָּׁתֶךָ. — יג״ל פז״ק
שַׁוְעָתֵנוּ קַבֵּל וּשְׁמַע צַעֲקָתֵנוּ יוֹדֵעַ תַּעֲלֻמוֹת. — שק״ו צי״ת
בָּרוּךְ שֵׁם כְּבוֹד מַלְכוּתוֹ לְעוֹלָם וָעֶד.

רִבּוֹנוֹ שֶׁל עוֹלָם, אַתָּה צִוִּיתָנוּ עַל יְדֵי מֹשֶׁה עַבְדֶּךָ לִסְפּוֹר סְפִירַת הָעוֹמֶר, כְּדֵי לְטַהֲרֵנוּ מִקְּלִפּוֹתֵינוּ וּמִטֻּמְאוֹתֵינוּ, כְּמוֹ שֶׁכָּתַבְתָּ בְּתוֹרָתֶךָ: וּסְפַרְתֶּם לָכֶם מִמָּחֳרַת הַשַּׁבָּת מִיּוֹם הֲבִיאֲכֶם אֶת עֹמֶר הַתְּנוּפָה, שֶׁבַע שַׁבָּתוֹת תְּמִימֹת תִּהְיֶינָה. עַד מִמָּחֳרַת

COUNTING THE OMER

Most Congregations count the *Omer* at this point; some count after *Aleinu* (p. 832).
In some congregations the following Kabbalistic prayer precedes the counting of the *Omer*.

לְשֵׁם *For the sake of the unification of the Holy One, Blessed is He, and His Presence, in fear and love to unify the Name Yud-Kei with Vav-Kei in perfect unity, in the name of all Israel. Behold I am prepared and ready to perform the commandment of counting the Omer, as it is written in the Torah: 'You are to count from the morrow of the rest day, from the day you brought the Omer-offering that is waved — they are to be seven complete weeks — until the morrow of the seventh week you are to count fifty days, and then offer a new meal-offering to* HASHEM.'[1] *May the pleasantness of my Lord, our God, be upon us — may He establish our handiwork for us; our handiwork, may He establish.*[2]

Chazzan, followed by the congregation, recites the blessing and counts.
One praying without a *minyan* should, nevertheless, recite the entire *Omer* service.

בָּרוּךְ *Blessed are You,* HASHEM, *our God, King of the universe, Who has sanctified us with His commandments and has commanded us regarding the counting of the Omer.*

On the seventh night of Pesach:

Today is six days of the Omer.

On the eighth night of Pesach:

Today is seven days, which are one week, of the Omer.

הָרַחֲמָן *The Compassionate One! May He return for us the service of the Temple to its place, speedily in our days. Amen, selah!*

Psalm 67

לַמְנַצֵּחַ *For the Conductor, upon Neginos, a psalm, a song. May God favor us and bless us, may He illuminate His countenance with us, Selah. To make known Your way on earth, among all the nations Your salvation. The peoples will acknowledge You, O God, the peoples will acknowledge You, all of them. Nations will be glad and sing for joy, because You will judge the peoples fairly and guide the nations on earth, Selah. The peoples will acknowledge You, O God, the peoples will acknowledge You, all of them. The earth has yielded its produce, may God, our own God, bless us. May God bless us and may all the ends of the earth fear Him.*

אָנָּא *We beg You! With the strength of Your right hand's greatness, untie the bundled sins. Accept the prayer of Your nation; strengthen us, purify us, O Awesome One. Please, O Strong One — those who foster Your Oneness, guard them like the apple of an eye. Bless them, purify them, show them pity, may Your righteousness always recompense them. Powerful Holy One, with Your abundant goodness guide Your congregation. One and only Exalted One, turn to Your nation, which proclaims Your holiness. Accept our entreaty and hear our cry, O Knower of mysteries. Blessed is the Name of His glorious Kingdom for all eternity.*

רִבּוֹנוֹ *Master of the universe, You commanded us through Moses, Your servant, to count the Omer Count in order to cleanse us from our encrustations of evil and from our contaminations, as You have written in Your Torah: You are to count from the morrow of the rest day, from the day you brought the Omer-offering that is waved—they are to be seven complete weeks. Until the morrow of*

(1) *Leviticus* 23:15. (2) *Psalms* 90:17.

הַשַּׁבָּת הַשְּׁבִיעִית תִּסְפְּרוּ חֲמִשִּׁים יוֹם.[1] כְּדֵי שֶׁיִּטָּהֲרוּ נַפְשׁוֹת עַמְּךָ יִשְׂרָאֵל מִזֻּהֲמָתָם. וּבְכֵן יְהִי רָצוֹן מִלְּפָנֶיךָ יהוה אֱלֹהֵינוּ וֵאלֹהֵי אֲבוֹתֵינוּ, שֶׁבִּזְכוּת סְפִירַת הָעֹמֶר שֶׁסָּפַרְתִּי הַיּוֹם, יְתֻקַּן מַה שֶּׁפָּגַמְתִּי בִּסְפִירָה – On the seventh night מַלְכוּת שֶׁבְּחֶסֶד. – On the eighth night יְסוֹד שֶׁבְּחֶסֶד. וְאֶטָּהֵר וְאֶתְקַדֵּשׁ בִּקְדֻשָּׁה שֶׁל מַעְלָה, וְעַל יְדֵי זֶה יֻשְׁפַּע שֶׁפַע רַב בְּכָל הָעוֹלָמוֹת. וּלְתַקֵּן אֶת נַפְשׁוֹתֵינוּ, וְרוּחוֹתֵינוּ, וְנִשְׁמוֹתֵינוּ, מִכָּל סִיג וּפְגַם, וּלְטַהֲרֵנוּ וּלְקַדְּשֵׁנוּ בִּקְדֻשָּׁתְךָ הָעֶלְיוֹנָה. אָמֵן סֶלָה.

In some congregations, if a mourner is present, the Mourner's *Kaddish* (p. 834) is recited, followed by *Aleinu*. In others, *Aleinu* is recited immediately.

The congregation stands while reciting עָלֵינוּ.

עָלֵינוּ לְשַׁבֵּחַ לַאֲדוֹן הַכֹּל, לָתֵת גְּדֻלָּה לְיוֹצֵר בְּרֵאשִׁית, שֶׁלֹּא עָשָׂנוּ כְּגוֹיֵי הָאֲרָצוֹת, וְלֹא שָׂמָנוּ כְּמִשְׁפְּחוֹת הָאֲדָמָה. שֶׁלֹּא שָׂם חֶלְקֵנוּ כָּהֶם, וְגוֹרָלֵנוּ כְּכָל הֲמוֹנָם. (שֶׁהֵם מִשְׁתַּחֲוִים לְהֶבֶל וָרִיק, וּמִתְפַּלְּלִים אֶל אֵל לֹא יוֹשִׁיעַ.[2]) וַאֲנַחְנוּ כּוֹרְעִים וּמִשְׁתַּחֲוִים וּמוֹדִים, לִפְנֵי מֶלֶךְ מַלְכֵי הַמְּלָכִים הַקָּדוֹשׁ בָּרוּךְ הוּא. שֶׁהוּא נוֹטֶה שָׁמַיִם וְיֹסֵד אָרֶץ,[3] וּמוֹשַׁב יְקָרוֹ בַּשָּׁמַיִם מִמַּעַל, וּשְׁכִינַת עֻזּוֹ בְּגָבְהֵי מְרוֹמִים. הוּא אֱלֹהֵינוּ, אֵין עוֹד. אֱמֶת מַלְכֵּנוּ, אֶפֶס זוּלָתוֹ, כַּכָּתוּב בְּתוֹרָתוֹ: וְיָדַעְתָּ הַיּוֹם וַהֲשֵׁבֹתָ אֶל לְבָבֶךָ, כִּי יהוה הוּא הָאֱלֹהִים בַּשָּׁמַיִם מִמַּעַל וְעַל הָאָרֶץ מִתָּחַת, אֵין עוֹד.[4]

Bow while reciting וַאֲנַחְנוּ כּוֹרְעִים וּמִשְׁתַּחֲוִים.

עַל כֵּן נְקַוֶּה לְךָ יהוה אֱלֹהֵינוּ לִרְאוֹת מְהֵרָה בְּתִפְאֶרֶת עֻזֶּךָ, לְהַעֲבִיר גִּלּוּלִים מִן הָאָרֶץ, וְהָאֱלִילִים כָּרוֹת יִכָּרֵתוּן, לְתַקֵּן עוֹלָם בְּמַלְכוּת שַׁדַּי. וְכָל בְּנֵי בָשָׂר יִקְרְאוּ בִשְׁמֶךָ, לְהַפְנוֹת אֵלֶיךָ כָּל רִשְׁעֵי אָרֶץ. יַכִּירוּ וְיֵדְעוּ כָּל יוֹשְׁבֵי תֵבֵל, כִּי לְךָ תִּכְרַע כָּל בֶּרֶךְ, תִּשָּׁבַע כָּל לָשׁוֹן.[5] לְפָנֶיךָ יהוה אֱלֹהֵינוּ יִכְרְעוּ וְיִפֹּלוּ, וְלִכְבוֹד שִׁמְךָ יְקָר יִתֵּנוּ. וִיקַבְּלוּ כֻלָּם אֶת עוֹל מַלְכוּתֶךָ, וְתִמְלֹךְ עֲלֵיהֶם מְהֵרָה לְעוֹלָם וָעֶד. כִּי הַמַּלְכוּת שֶׁלְּךָ הִיא וּלְעוֹלְמֵי עַד תִּמְלוֹךְ בְּכָבוֹד, כַּכָּתוּב בְּתוֹרָתֶךָ: יהוה יִמְלֹךְ לְעֹלָם וָעֶד.[6] ❖ וְנֶאֱמַר: וְהָיָה יהוה לְמֶלֶךְ עַל כָּל הָאָרֶץ, בַּיּוֹם הַהוּא יִהְיֶה יהוה אֶחָד וּשְׁמוֹ אֶחָד.[7]

אַל תִּירָא מִפַּחַד פִּתְאֹם, וּמִשֹּׁאַת רְשָׁעִים כִּי תָבֹא.[8] עֻצוּ עֵצָה וְתֻפָר, דַּבְּרוּ דָבָר וְלֹא יָקוּם, כִּי עִמָּנוּ אֵל.[9] וְעַד זִקְנָה אֲנִי הוּא, וְעַד שֵׂיבָה אֲנִי אֶסְבֹּל, אֲנִי עָשִׂיתִי וַאֲנִי אֶשָּׂא, וַאֲנִי אֶסְבֹּל וַאֲמַלֵּט.[10]

the seventh week you are to count fifty days,[1] *so that the souls of Your people Israel be cleansed from their contamination. Therefore, may it be Your will, HASHEM, our God and the God of our forefathers, that in the merit of the Omer Count that I have counted today, may there be corrected whatever blemish I have caused in the sefirah*

on the seventh night: *yesod shebechesed.* on the eighth night: *malchus shebechesed.*

May I be cleansed and sanctified with the holiness of Above, and through this may abundant bounty flow in all the worlds. And may it correct our lives, spirits, and souls from all sediment and blemish; may it cleanse us and sanctify us with Your exalted holiness. Amen, Selah!

In some congregations, if a mourner is present, the Mourner's *Kaddish* (p. 834) is recited, followed by *Aleinu*. In others, *Aleinu* is recited immediately.

The congregation stands while reciting עָלֵינוּ, *'It is our duty . . .'*

עָלֵינוּ *It is our duty to praise the Master of all, to ascribe greatness to the Molder of primeval creation, for He has not made us like the nations of the lands, and has not emplaced us like the families of the earth; for He has not assigned our portion like theirs nor our lot like all their multitudes. (For they bow to vanity and emptiness and pray to a god which helps not.*[2]*) But we bend our knees, bow, and acknowledge our thanks before the King Who reigns over kings, the Holy One, Blessed is He. He stretches out heaven and establishes earth's foundation,*[3] *the seat of His homage is in the heavens above and His powerful Presence is in the loftiest heights. He is our God and there is none other. True is our King, there is nothing beside Him, as it is written in His Torah: 'You are to know this day and take to your heart that HASHEM is the only God — in heaven above and on the earth below — there is none other.'*[4]

Bow while reciting 'But we bend our knees.'

עַל כֵּן *Therefore we put our hope in You, HASHEM our God, that we may soon see Your mighty splendor, to remove detestable idolatry from the earth, and false gods will be utterly cut off, to perfect the universe through the Almighty's sovereignty. Then all humanity will call upon Your Name, to turn all the earth's wicked toward You. All the world's inhabitants will recognize and know that to You every knee should bend, every tongue should swear.*[5] *Before You, HASHEM, our God, they will bend every knee and cast themselves down and to the glory of Your Name they will render homage, and they will all accept upon themselves the yoke of Your kingship that You may reign over them soon and eternally. For the kingdom is Yours and You will reign for all eternity in glory as it is written in Your Torah: HASHEM shall reign for all eternity.*[6] *And it is said: HASHEM will be King over all the world — on that day HASHEM will be One and His Name will be One.*[7]

אַל תִּירָא *Do not fear sudden terror, or the holocaust of the wicked when it comes.*[8] *Plan a conspiracy and it will be annulled; speak your piece and it shall not stand, for God is with us.*[9] *Even till your seniority, I remain unchanged; and even till your ripe old age, I shall endure. I created you and I shall bear you; I shall endure and rescue.*[10]

---

(1) *Leviticus* 23:15-16. (2) *Isaiah* 45:20. (3) 51:13. (4) *Deuteronomy* 4:39. (5) Cf. *Isaiah* 45:23. (6) *Exodus* 15:18. (7) *Zechariah* 14:9. (8) *Proverbs* 3:25. (9) *Isaiah* 8:10. (10) 46:4.

קדיש יתום

יִתְגַּדַּל וְיִתְקַדַּשׁ שְׁמֵהּ רַבָּא. (.Cong – אָמֵן.) בְּעָלְמָא דִּי בְרָא כִרְעוּתֵהּ. וְיַמְלִיךְ מַלְכוּתֵהּ, בְּחַיֵּיכוֹן וּבְיוֹמֵיכוֹן וּבְחַיֵּי דְכָל בֵּית יִשְׂרָאֵל, בַּעֲגָלָא וּבִזְמַן קָרִיב. וְאִמְרוּ: אָמֵן.

(.Cong – אָמֵן. יְהֵא שְׁמֵהּ רַבָּא מְבָרַךְ לְעָלַם וּלְעָלְמֵי עָלְמַיָּא.)

יְהֵא שְׁמֵהּ רַבָּא מְבָרַךְ לְעָלַם וּלְעָלְמֵי עָלְמַיָּא.

יִתְבָּרַךְ וְיִשְׁתַּבַּח וְיִתְפָּאַר וְיִתְרוֹמַם וְיִתְנַשֵּׂא וְיִתְהַדָּר וְיִתְעַלֶּה וְיִתְהַלָּל שְׁמֵהּ דְּקֻדְשָׁא בְּרִיךְ הוּא (.Cong – בְּרִיךְ הוּא) — לְעֵלָּא מִן כָּל בִּרְכָתָא וְשִׁירָתָא תֻּשְׁבְּחָתָא וְנֶחֱמָתָא, דַּאֲמִירָן בְּעָלְמָא. וְאִמְרוּ: אָמֵן. (.Cong – אָמֵן.)

יְהֵא שְׁלָמָא רַבָּא מִן שְׁמַיָּא, וְחַיִּים עָלֵינוּ וְעַל כָּל יִשְׂרָאֵל. וְאִמְרוּ: אָמֵן. (.Cong – אָמֵן.)

Take three steps back. Bow left and say . . . עֹשֶׂה; bow right and say . . . הוּא; bow forward and say וְעַל כָּל . . . אָמֵן. Remain standing in place for a few moments, then take three steps forward.

עֹשֶׂה שָׁלוֹם בִּמְרוֹמָיו, הוּא יַעֲשֶׂה שָׁלוֹם עָלֵינוּ, וְעַל כָּל יִשְׂרָאֵל. וְאִמְרוּ: אָמֵן. (.Cong – אָמֵן.)

אֲדוֹן עוֹלָם אֲשֶׁר מָלַךְ, בְּטֶרֶם כָּל יְצִיר נִבְרָא.
לְעֵת נַעֲשָׂה בְחֶפְצוֹ כֹּל, אֲזַי מֶלֶךְ שְׁמוֹ נִקְרָא.
וְאַחֲרֵי כִּכְלוֹת הַכֹּל, לְבַדּוֹ יִמְלוֹךְ נוֹרָא.
וְהוּא הָיָה וְהוּא הֹוֶה, וְהוּא יִהְיֶה בְּתִפְאָרָה.
וְהוּא אֶחָד וְאֵין שֵׁנִי, לְהַמְשִׁיל לוֹ לְהַחְבִּירָה.
בְּלִי רֵאשִׁית בְּלִי תַכְלִית, וְלוֹ הָעֹז וְהַמִּשְׂרָה.
וְהוּא אֵלִי וְחַי גֹּאֲלִי, וְצוּר חֶבְלִי בְּעֵת צָרָה.
וְהוּא נִסִּי וּמָנוֹס לִי, מְנָת כּוֹסִי בְּיוֹם אֶקְרָא.
בְּיָדוֹ אַפְקִיד רוּחִי, בְּעֵת אִישַׁן וְאָעִירָה.
וְעִם רוּחִי גְּוִיָּתִי, יהוה לִי וְלֹא אִירָא.

יִגְדַּל אֱלֹהִים חַי וְיִשְׁתַּבַּח, נִמְצָא וְאֵין עֵת אֶל מְצִיאוּתוֹ.
אֶחָד וְאֵין יָחִיד כְּיִחוּדוֹ, נֶעְלָם וְגַם אֵין סוֹף לְאַחְדוּתוֹ.
אֵין לוֹ דְּמוּת הַגּוּף וְאֵינוֹ גוּף, לֹא נַעֲרוֹךְ אֵלָיו קְדֻשָּׁתוֹ.
קַדְמוֹן לְכָל דָּבָר אֲשֶׁר נִבְרָא, רִאשׁוֹן וְאֵין רֵאשִׁית לְרֵאשִׁיתוֹ.
הִנּוֹ אֲדוֹן עוֹלָם לְכָל נוֹצָר, יוֹרֶה גְדֻלָּתוֹ וּמַלְכוּתוֹ.
שֶׁפַע נְבוּאָתוֹ נְתָנוֹ, אֶל אַנְשֵׁי סְגֻלָּתוֹ וְתִפְאַרְתּוֹ.
לֹא קָם בְּיִשְׂרָאֵל כְּמֹשֶׁה עוֹד, נָבִיא וּמַבִּיט אֶת תְּמוּנָתוֹ.
תּוֹרַת אֱמֶת נָתַן לְעַמּוֹ אֵל, עַל יַד נְבִיאוֹ נֶאֱמַן בֵּיתוֹ.
לֹא יַחֲלִיף הָאֵל וְלֹא יָמִיר דָּתוֹ, לְעוֹלָמִים לְזוּלָתוֹ.
צוֹפֶה וְיוֹדֵעַ סְתָרֵינוּ, מַבִּיט לְסוֹף דָּבָר בְּקַדְמָתוֹ.
גּוֹמֵל לְאִישׁ חֶסֶד כְּמִפְעָלוֹ, נוֹתֵן לְרָשָׁע רָע כְּרִשְׁעָתוֹ.
יִשְׁלַח לְקֵץ הַיָּמִין מְשִׁיחֵנוּ, לִפְדּוֹת מְחַכֵּי קֵץ יְשׁוּעָתוֹ.
מֵתִים יְחַיֶּה אֵל בְּרֹב חַסְדּוֹ, בָּרוּךְ עֲדֵי עַד שֵׁם תְּהִלָּתוֹ.

MOURNER'S KADDISH

Mourners recite the Mourner's *Kaddish* (see *Laws* §81-83).
[A transliteration of this *Kaddish* appears on page 1147.]

יִתְגַּדַּל *May His great Name grow exalted and sanctified* (Cong.— *Amen.*) *in the world that He created as He willed. May He give reign to His kingship in your lifetimes and in your days, and in the lifetimes of the entire Family of Israel, swiftly and soon. Now respond: Amen.*

(Cong.— *Amen. May His great Name be blessed forever and ever.*)
May His great Name be blessed forever and ever.

Blessed, praised, glorified, exalted, extolled, mighty, upraised, and lauded be the Name of the Holy One, Blessed is He (Cong.— *Blessed is He*) — *beyond any blessing and song, praise and consolation that are uttered in the world. Now respond: Amen.* (Cong.— *Amen.*)

May there be abundant peace from Heaven, and life, upon us and upon all Israel. Now respond: Amen. (Cong.— *Amen.*)

Take three steps back. Bow left and say, *'He Who makes peace . . .'*; bow right and say, *'may He . . .'*; bow forward and say, *'and upon all Israel . . .'* Remain standing in place for a few moments, then take three steps forward.

He Who makes peace in His heights, may He make peace upon us, and upon all Israel. Now respond: Amen. (Cong.— *Amen.*)

Many congregations recite either אֲדוֹן עוֹלָם, *Master of the universe,* or יִגְדַּל, *Exalted be,* or both.

אֲדוֹן עוֹלָם *Master of the universe, Who reigned before any form was created,*
At the time when His will brought all into being —
then as 'King' was His Name proclaimed.
After all has ceased to be, He, the Awesome One, will reign alone.
It is He Who was, He Who is, and He Who shall remain, in splendor.
He is One — there is no second to compare to Him, to declare as His equal.
Without beginning, without conclusion — His is the power and dominion.
He is my God, my living Redeemer, Rock of my pain in time of distress.
He is my banner, a refuge for me, the portion in my cup on the day I call.
Into His hand I shall entrust my spirit when I go to sleep — and I shall awaken!
With my spirit shall my body remain. HASHEM *is with me, I shall not fear.*

יִגְדַּל *Exalted be the Living God and praised,*
He exists — unbounded by time is His existence.
He is One — and there is no unity like His Oneness.
Inscrutable and infinite is His Oneness.
He has no semblance of a body nor is He corporeal; nor has His holiness any comparison.
He preceded every being that was created —
the First, and nothing precedes His precedence.
Behold! He is Master of the universe to every creature,
He demonstrates His greatness and His sovereignty.
He granted His flow of prophecy to His treasured splendrous people.
In Israel none like Moses arose again — a prophet who perceived His vision clearly.
God gave His people a Torah of truth,
by means of His prophet, the most trusted of His household.
God will never amend nor exchange His law for any other one, for all eternity.
He scrutinizes and knows our hiddenmost secrets;
He perceives a matter's outcome at its inception.
He recompenses man with kindness according to his deed;
He places evil on the wicked according to his wickedness.
By the End of Days He will send our Messiah,
to redeem those longing for His final salvation.
God will revive the dead in His abundant kindness — Blessed forever is His praised Name.

Many recite the following before *Kiddush*. Each of the first four stanzas is recited three times.

שָׁלוֹם עֲלֵיכֶם, מַלְאֲכֵי הַשָּׁרֵת, מַלְאֲכֵי עֶלְיוֹן, מִמֶּלֶךְ מַלְכֵי הַמְּלָכִים הַקָּדוֹשׁ בָּרוּךְ הוּא.

בּוֹאֲכֶם לְשָׁלוֹם, מַלְאֲכֵי הַשָּׁלוֹם, מַלְאֲכֵי עֶלְיוֹן, מִמֶּלֶךְ מַלְכֵי הַמְּלָכִים הַקָּדוֹשׁ בָּרוּךְ הוּא.

בָּרְכוּנִי לְשָׁלוֹם, מַלְאֲכֵי הַשָּׁלוֹם, מַלְאֲכֵי עֶלְיוֹן, מִמֶּלֶךְ מַלְכֵי הַמְּלָכִים הַקָּדוֹשׁ בָּרוּךְ הוּא.

צֵאתְכֶם לְשָׁלוֹם, מַלְאֲכֵי הַשָּׁלוֹם, מַלְאֲכֵי עֶלְיוֹן, מִמֶּלֶךְ מַלְכֵי הַמְּלָכִים הַקָּדוֹשׁ בָּרוּךְ הוּא.

כִּי מַלְאָכָיו יְצַוֶּה לָּךְ, לִשְׁמָרְךָ בְּכָל דְּרָכֶיךָ.[1]
יהוה יִשְׁמָר צֵאתְךָ וּבוֹאֶךָ, מֵעַתָּה וְעַד עוֹלָם.[2]

(משלי לא:י-לא)

אֵשֶׁת חַיִל מִי יִמְצָא, וְרָחֹק מִפְּנִינִים מִכְרָהּ.
בָּטַח בָּהּ לֵב בַּעְלָהּ, וְשָׁלָל לֹא יֶחְסָר.
גְּמָלַתְהוּ טוֹב וְלֹא רָע, כֹּל יְמֵי חַיֶּיהָ.
דָּרְשָׁה צֶמֶר וּפִשְׁתִּים, וַתַּעַשׂ בְּחֵפֶץ כַּפֶּיהָ.
הָיְתָה כָּאֳנִיּוֹת סוֹחֵר, מִמֶּרְחָק תָּבִיא לַחְמָהּ.
וַתָּקָם בְּעוֹד לַיְלָה, וַתִּתֵּן טֶרֶף לְבֵיתָהּ, וְחֹק לְנַעֲרֹתֶיהָ.
זָמְמָה שָׂדֶה וַתִּקָּחֵהוּ, מִפְּרִי כַפֶּיהָ נָטְעָה כָּרֶם.
חָגְרָה בְעוֹז מָתְנֶיהָ, וַתְּאַמֵּץ זְרוֹעֹתֶיהָ.
טָעֲמָה כִּי טוֹב סַחְרָהּ, לֹא יִכְבֶּה בַלַּיְלָה נֵרָהּ.
יָדֶיהָ שִׁלְּחָה בַכִּישׁוֹר, וְכַפֶּיהָ תָּמְכוּ פָלֶךְ.
כַּפָּהּ פָּרְשָׂה לֶעָנִי, וְיָדֶיהָ שִׁלְּחָה לָאֶבְיוֹן.
לֹא תִירָא לְבֵיתָהּ מִשָּׁלֶג, כִּי כָל בֵּיתָהּ לָבֻשׁ שָׁנִים.
מַרְבַדִּים עָשְׂתָה לָּהּ, שֵׁשׁ וְאַרְגָּמָן לְבוּשָׁהּ.
נוֹדָע בַּשְּׁעָרִים בַּעְלָהּ, בְּשִׁבְתּוֹ עִם זִקְנֵי אָרֶץ.
סָדִין עָשְׂתָה וַתִּמְכֹּר, וַחֲגוֹר נָתְנָה לַכְּנַעֲנִי.
עוֹז וְהָדָר לְבוּשָׁהּ, וַתִּשְׂחַק לְיוֹם אַחֲרוֹן.
פִּיהָ פָּתְחָה בְחָכְמָה, וְתוֹרַת חֶסֶד עַל לְשׁוֹנָהּ.
צוֹפִיָּה הֲלִיכוֹת בֵּיתָהּ, וְלֶחֶם עַצְלוּת לֹא תֹאכֵל.
קָמוּ בָנֶיהָ וַיְאַשְּׁרוּהָ, בַּעְלָהּ וַיְהַלְלָהּ.
רַבּוֹת בָּנוֹת עָשׂוּ חָיִל, וְאַתְּ עָלִית עַל כֻּלָּנָה.
שֶׁקֶר הַחֵן וְהֶבֶל הַיֹּפִי, אִשָּׁה יִרְאַת יהוה הִיא תִתְהַלָּל.
תְּנוּ לָהּ מִפְּרִי יָדֶיהָ, וִיהַלְלוּהָ בַשְּׁעָרִים מַעֲשֶׂיהָ.

(1) *Psalms* 91:11. (2) 121:8.

Many recite the following before *Kiddush*.
Each of the first four stanzas is recited three times.

שָׁלוֹם עֲלֵיכֶם *Peace upon you, O ministering angels, angels of the Exalted One — from the King Who reigns over kings, the Holy One, Blessed is He.*

בּוֹאֲכֶם לְשָׁלוֹם *May your coming be for peace, O angels of peace, angels of the Exalted One — from the King Who reigns over kings, the Holy One, Blessed is He.*

בָּרְכוּנִי לְשָׁלוֹם *Bless me for peace, O angels of peace, angels of the Exalted One — from the King Who reigns over kings, the Holy One, Blessed is He.*

צֵאתְכֶם לְשָׁלוֹם *May your departure be to peace, O angels of peace, angels of the Exalted One — from the King Who reigns over kings, the Holy One, Blessed is He.*

He will charge His angels for you, to protect you in all your ways.[1]
May HASHEM *protect your going and returning, from this time and forever.*[2]

(Proverbs 31:10-31)

אֵשֶׁת חַיִל *An accomplished woman, who can find? —*
Far beyond pearls is her value.
ב *Her husband's heart relies on her and he shall lack no fortune.*
ג *She repays his good, but never his harm, all the days of her life.*
ד *She seeks out wool and linen, and her hands work willingly.*
ה *She is like a merchant's ships, from afar she brings her sustenance.*
ו *She arises while it is yet nighttime,*
and gives food to her household and a ration to her maidens.
ז *She envisions a field and buys it,*
from the fruit of her handiwork she plants a vineyard.
ח *With strength she girds her loins, and invigorates her arms.*
ט *She discerns that her enterprise is good —*
so her lamp is not snuffed out by night.
י *Her hands she stretches out to the distaff, and her palms support the spindle.*
כ *She spreads out her palm to the poor, and extends her hands to the destitute.*
ל *She fears not snow for her household,*
for her entire household is clothed with scarlet wool.
מ *Luxurious bedspreads she made herself,*
linen and purple wool are her clothing.
נ *Distinctive in the councils is her husband,*
when he sits with the elders of the land.
ס *She makes a cloak to sell, and delivers a belt to the peddler.*
ע *Strength and majesty are her raiment, she joyfully awaits the last day.*
פ *She opens her mouth with wisdom, and a lesson of kindness is on her tongue.*
צ *She anticipates the ways of her household,*
and partakes not of the bread of laziness.
ק *Her children arise and praise her, her husband, and he lauds her:*
ר *'Many daughters have amassed achievement, but you surpassed them all.'*
ש *False is grace and vain is beauty,*
a God-fearing woman — she should be praised.
ת *Give her the fruits of her hand*
and let her be praised in the gates by her very own deeds.

קידוש ללילי שביעי ואחרון של פסח

On Friday night begin here:

(וַיְהִי עֶרֶב וַיְהִי בֹקֶר)

יוֹם הַשִּׁשִּׁי: וַיְכֻלּוּ הַשָּׁמַיִם וְהָאָרֶץ וְכָל צְבָאָם. וַיְכַל אֱלֹהִים בַּיּוֹם הַשְּׁבִיעִי מְלַאכְתּוֹ אֲשֶׁר עָשָׂה, וַיִּשְׁבֹּת בַּיּוֹם הַשְּׁבִיעִי מִכָּל מְלַאכְתּוֹ אֲשֶׁר עָשָׂה. וַיְבָרֶךְ אֱלֹהִים אֶת יוֹם הַשְּׁבִיעִי וַיְקַדֵּשׁ אֹתוֹ, כִּי בוֹ שָׁבַת מִכָּל מְלַאכְתּוֹ אֲשֶׁר בָּרָא אֱלֹהִים לַעֲשׂוֹת.[1]

On all nights other than Friday, begin here;
on Friday night include all passages in parentheses.

סַבְרִי מָרָנָן וְרַבָּנָן וְרַבּוֹתַי:

בָּרוּךְ אַתָּה יהוה אֱלֹהֵינוּ מֶלֶךְ הָעוֹלָם, בּוֹרֵא פְּרִי הַגָּפֶן.

בָּרוּךְ אַתָּה יהוה אֱלֹהֵינוּ מֶלֶךְ הָעוֹלָם, אֲשֶׁר בָּחַר בָּנוּ מִכָּל עָם, וְרוֹמְמָנוּ מִכָּל לָשׁוֹן, וְקִדְּשָׁנוּ בְּמִצְוֹתָיו. וַתִּתֶּן לָנוּ יהוה אֱלֹהֵינוּ בְּאַהֲבָה [שַׁבָּתוֹת לִמְנוּחָה וּ]מוֹעֲדִים לְשִׂמְחָה, חַגִּים וּזְמַנִּים לְשָׂשׂוֹן, אֶת יוֹם [הַשַּׁבָּת הַזֶּה וְאֶת יוֹם] חַג הַמַּצּוֹת הַזֶּה, זְמַן חֵרוּתֵנוּ [בְּאַהֲבָה] מִקְרָא קֹדֶשׁ, זֵכֶר לִיצִיאַת מִצְרָיִם, כִּי בָנוּ בָחַרְתָּ וְאוֹתָנוּ קִדַּשְׁתָּ מִכָּל הָעַמִּים, [וְשַׁבָּת] וּמוֹעֲדֵי קָדְשֶׁךָ [בְּאַהֲבָה וּבְרָצוֹן] בְּשִׂמְחָה וּבְשָׂשׂוֹן הִנְחַלְתָּנוּ. בָּרוּךְ אַתָּה יהוה, מְקַדֵּשׁ [הַשַּׁבָּת וְ]יִשְׂרָאֵל וְהַזְּמַנִּים.

ON SATURDAY NIGHT CONTINUE BELOW. ON ALL OTHER NIGHTS KIDDUSH ENDS HERE.

On Saturday night, add the following two *Havdalah* blessings. Two candles with flames touching each other should be held before the person reciting the *Havdalah*. After the first blessing, hold the fingers up to the flame to see the reflected light.

[It is forbidden to create a new flame — for example, by striking a match — on *Yom Tov*. Therefore, the *Havdalah* candles must be lit from a flame that has been burning from before the Sabbath. It is likewise forbidden to extinguish the flame.]

בָּרוּךְ אַתָּה יהוה אֱלֹהֵינוּ מֶלֶךְ הָעוֹלָם, בּוֹרֵא מְאוֹרֵי הָאֵשׁ.

בָּרוּךְ אַתָּה יהוה אֱלֹהֵינוּ מֶלֶךְ הָעוֹלָם, הַמַּבְדִּיל בֵּין קֹדֶשׁ לְחוֹל, בֵּין אוֹר לְחֹשֶׁךְ, בֵּין יִשְׂרָאֵל לָעַמִּים, בֵּין יוֹם הַשְּׁבִיעִי לְשֵׁשֶׁת יְמֵי הַמַּעֲשֶׂה. בֵּין קְדֻשַּׁת שַׁבָּת לִקְדֻשַּׁת יוֹם טוֹב הִבְדַּלְתָּ, וְאֶת יוֹם הַשְּׁבִיעִי מִשֵּׁשֶׁת יְמֵי הַמַּעֲשֶׂה קִדַּשְׁתָּ, הִבְדַּלְתָּ וְקִדַּשְׁתָּ אֶת עַמְּךָ יִשְׂרָאֵל בִּקְדֻשָּׁתֶךָ. בָּרוּךְ אַתָּה יהוה, הַמַּבְדִּיל בֵּין קֹדֶשׁ לְקֹדֶשׁ.

Bircas HaMazon appears on page 104.

KIDDUSH FOR THE LAST TWO NIGHTS OF PESACH

On Friday night begin here:

(And there was evening and there was morning)

יוֹם הַשִּׁשִּׁי: *The sixth day. Thus the heaven and the earth were finished, and all their array. On the seventh day God completed His work which He had done, and He abstained on the seventh day from all His work which He had done. God blessed the seventh day and hallowed it, because on it He abstained from all His work which God created to make.*[1]

On all nights other than Friday, begin here;
on Friday night include all passages in parentheses.

By your leave, my masters and teachers:

בָּרוּךְ *Blessed are You, HASHEM, our God, King of the universe, Who creates the fruit of the vine.*

בָּרוּךְ *Blessed are You, HASHEM, our God, King of the universe, Who has chosen us from all nations, exalted us above all tongues, and sanctified us with His commandments. And You, HASHEM, our God, have lovingly given us (Sabbaths for rest), appointed times for gladness, feasts and seasons for joy, (this Sabbath and) this Feast of Matzos, the season of our freedom (in love,) a holy convocation in memoriam of the Exodus from Egypt. For You have chosen and sanctified us above all peoples, (and the Sabbath) and Your holy festivals (in love and favor), in gladness and joy have You granted us as a heritage. Blessed are You, HASHEM, Who sanctifies (the Sabbath,) Israel, and the festive seasons.*

ON SATURDAY NIGHT CONTINUE BELOW. ON ALL OTHER NIGHTS KIDDUSH ENDS HERE.

On Saturday night, add the following two *Havdalah* blessings. Two candles with flames touching each other should be held before the person reciting the *Havdalah*.
After the first blessing, hold the fingers up to the flame to see the reflected light.

[It is forbidden to create a new flame — for example, by striking a match — on *Yom Tov*. Therefore, the *Havdalah* candles must be lit from a flame that has been burning from before the Sabbath. It is likewise forbidden to extinguish the flame.]

בָּרוּךְ *Blessed are You, HASHEM, our God, King of the universe, Who creates the illumination of the fire.*

בָּרוּךְ *Blessed are You, HASHEM, our God, King of the universe, Who distinguishes between sacred and secular, between light and darkness, between Israel and the nations, between the seventh day and the six days of activity. You have distinguished between the holiness of the Sabbath and the holiness of a Festival, and have sanctified the seventh day above the six days of activity. You distinguished and sanctified Your nation, Israel, with Your holiness. Blessed are You, HASHEM, who distinguishes between holiness and holiness.*

Bircas HaMazon appears on page 104.

(1) *Genesis* 1:31-2:3.

שחרית לשני ימים האחרונים של פסח

THE MORNING SERVICE BEGINS WITH PAGES 188-266, THEN CONTINUES HERE.

נִשְׁמַת כָּל חַי תְּבָרֵךְ אֶת שִׁמְךָ יהוה אֱלֹהֵינוּ, וְרְוּחַ כָּל בָּשָׂר תְּפָאֵר וּתְרוֹמֵם זִכְרְךָ מַלְכֵּנוּ תָּמִיד. מִן הָעוֹלָם וְעַד הָעוֹלָם אַתָּה אֵל,[1] וּמִבַּלְעָדֶיךָ אֵין לָנוּ מֶלֶךְ[2] גּוֹאֵל וּמוֹשִׁיעַ. פּוֹדֶה וּמַצִּיל וּמְפַרְנֵס וּמְרַחֵם בְּכָל עֵת צָרָה וְצוּקָה, אֵין לָנוּ מֶלֶךְ אֶלָּא אָתָּה. אֱלֹהֵי הָרִאשׁוֹנִים וְהָאַחֲרוֹנִים, אֱלוֹהַּ כָּל בְּרִיּוֹת, אֲדוֹן כָּל תּוֹלָדוֹת, הַמְּהֻלָּל בְּרֹב הַתִּשְׁבָּחוֹת, הַמְּנַהֵג עוֹלָמוֹ בְּחֶסֶד וּבְרִיּוֹתָיו בְּרַחֲמִים. וַיהוה לֹא יָנוּם וְלֹא יִישָׁן.[3] הַמְּעוֹרֵר יְשֵׁנִים, וְהַמֵּקִיץ נִרְדָּמִים, וְהַמֵּשִׂיחַ אִלְּמִים, וְהַמַּתִּיר אֲסוּרִים,[4] וְהַסּוֹמֵךְ נוֹפְלִים, וְהַזּוֹקֵף כְּפוּפִים.[5] לְךָ לְבַדְּךָ אֲנַחְנוּ מוֹדִים. אִלּוּ פִינוּ מָלֵא שִׁירָה כַּיָּם, וּלְשׁוֹנֵנוּ רִנָּה כַּהֲמוֹן גַּלָּיו, וְשִׂפְתוֹתֵינוּ שֶׁבַח כְּמֶרְחֲבֵי רָקִיעַ, וְעֵינֵינוּ מְאִירוֹת כַּשֶּׁמֶשׁ וְכַיָּרֵחַ, וְיָדֵינוּ פְרוּשׂוֹת כְּנִשְׁרֵי שָׁמָיִם, וְרַגְלֵינוּ קַלּוֹת כָּאַיָּלוֹת, אֵין אֲנַחְנוּ מַסְפִּיקִים לְהוֹדוֹת לְךָ, יהוה אֱלֹהֵינוּ וֵאלֹהֵי אֲבוֹתֵינוּ, וּלְבָרֵךְ אֶת שְׁמֶךָ עַל אַחַת מֵאָלֶף אֶלֶף אַלְפֵי אֲלָפִים וְרִבֵּי רְבָבוֹת פְּעָמִים הַטּוֹבוֹת שֶׁעָשִׂיתָ עִם אֲבוֹתֵינוּ וְעִמָּנוּ. מִמִּצְרַיִם גְּאַלְתָּנוּ יהוה אֱלֹהֵינוּ, וּמִבֵּית עֲבָדִים פְּדִיתָנוּ. בְּרָעָב זַנְתָּנוּ, וּבְשָׂבָע כִּלְכַּלְתָּנוּ, מֵחֶרֶב הִצַּלְתָּנוּ, וּמִדֶּבֶר מִלַּטְתָּנוּ, וּמֵחֳלָיִם רָעִים וְנֶאֱמָנִים דִּלִּיתָנוּ. עַד הֵנָּה עֲזָרוּנוּ רַחֲמֶיךָ, וְלֹא עֲזָבוּנוּ חֲסָדֶיךָ. וְאַל תִּטְּשֵׁנוּ יהוה אֱלֹהֵינוּ לָנֶצַח. עַל כֵּן אֵבָרִים שֶׁפִּלַּגְתָּ בָּנוּ, וְרְוּחַ וּנְשָׁמָה שֶׁנָּפַחְתָּ בְּאַפֵּינוּ, וְלָשׁוֹן אֲשֶׁר שַׂמְתָּ בְּפִינוּ, הֵן הֵם יוֹדוּ וִיבָרְכוּ וִישַׁבְּחוּ וִיפָאֲרוּ וִירוֹמְמוּ וְיַעֲרִיצוּ וְיַקְדִּישׁוּ וְיַמְלִיכוּ אֶת שִׁמְךָ מַלְכֵּנוּ. כִּי כָל פֶּה לְךָ יוֹדֶה, וְכָל לָשׁוֹן לְךָ תִשָּׁבַע, וְכָל בֶּרֶךְ לְךָ תִכְרַע,[6] וְכָל קוֹמָה לְפָנֶיךָ תִשְׁתַּחֲוֶה, וְכָל לְבָבוֹת יִירָאוּךָ, וְכָל קֶרֶב וּכְלָיוֹת יְזַמְּרוּ לִשְׁמֶךָ, כַּדָּבָר שֶׁכָּתוּב: כָּל עַצְמֹתַי תֹּאמַרְנָה, יהוה מִי כָמוֹךָ, מַצִּיל עָנִי מֵחָזָק מִמֶּנּוּ, וְעָנִי וְאֶבְיוֹן מִגֹּזְלוֹ.[7] מִי יִדְמֶה לָּךְ, וּמִי יִשְׁוֶה לָּךְ, וּמִי יַעֲרָךְ לָךְ.[8] הָאֵל הַגָּדוֹל הַגִּבּוֹר וְהַנּוֹרָא, אֵל עֶלְיוֹן, קֹנֵה שָׁמַיִם וָאָרֶץ. ❖ נְהַלֶּלְךָ וּנְשַׁבֵּחֲךָ וּנְפָאֶרְךָ וּנְבָרֵךְ אֶת שֵׁם קָדְשֶׁךָ, כָּאָמוּר: לְדָוִד, בָּרְכִי נַפְשִׁי אֶת יהוה, וְכָל קְרָבַי אֶת שֵׁם קָדְשׁוֹ.[9]

---

(1) Cf. *Psalms* 90:2. (2) Cf. *Isaiah* 44:6. (3) Cf. *Psalms* 121:4. (4) Cf. 146:7. (5) Cf. 145:14. (6) Cf. *Isaiah* 45:23. (7) *Psalms* 35:10. (8) Cf. 89:7. (9) *Psalms* 103:1.

SHACHARIS FOR THE LAST TWO DAYS OF PESACH

THE MORNING SERVICE BEGINS WITH PAGES 188-266, THEN CONTINUES HERE.

נִשְׁמַת *The soul of every living being shall bless Your Name,* HASHEM *our God; the spirit of all flesh shall always glorify and exalt Your remembrance, our King. From This World to the World to Come, You are God,*[1] *and other than You we have no king,*[2] *redeemer or savior. Liberator, Rescuer, Sustainer and Merciful One in every time of distress and anguish, we have no king but You! — God of the first and of the last, God of all creatures, Master of all generations, Who is extolled through a multitude of praises, Who guides His world with kindness and His creatures with mercy.* HASHEM *neither slumbers nor sleeps.*[3] *He Who rouses the sleepers and awakens the slumberers, Who makes the mute speak and releases the bound;*[4] *Who supports the fallen and straightens the bent.*[5] *To You alone we give thanks. Were our mouth as full of song as the sea, and our tongue as full of joyous song as its multitude of waves, and our lips as full of praise as the breadth of the heavens, and our eyes as brilliant as the sun and the moon, and our hands as outspread as eagles of the sky and our feet as swift as hinds — we still could not thank You sufficiently,* HASHEM *our God and God of our forefathers, and to bless Your Name for even one of the thousand thousand, thousands of thousands and myriad myriads of favors that You performed for our ancestors and for us. You redeemed us from Egypt,* HASHEM *our God, and liberated us from the house of bondage. In famine You nourished us and in plenty You sustained us. From sword You saved us; from plague You let us escape; and from severe and enduring diseases You spared us. Until now Your mercy has helped us, and Your kindness has not forsaken us. Do not abandon us,* HASHEM *our God, forever. Therefore, the organs that You set within us, and the spirit and soul that You breathed into our nostrils, and the tongue that You placed in our mouth — all of them shall thank and bless, praise and glorify, exalt and revere, sanctify and declare the sovereignty of Your Name, our King. For every mouth shall offer thanks to You; every tongue shall vow allegiance to You; every knee shall bend to You;*[6] *every erect spine shall prostrate itself before You; all hearts shall fear You, and all innermost feelings and thoughts shall sing praises to Your name, as it is written: "All my bones shall say: '*HASHEM*, who is like You?' You save the poor man from one stronger than he, the poor and destitute from one who would rob him."*[7] *Who is like unto You? Who is equal to You? Who can be compared to You?*[8] *O great, mighty, and awesome God, the supreme God, Creator of heaven and earth.* Chazzan– *We shall laud, praise, and glorify You and bless Your holy Name, as it is said 'Of David: Bless* HASHEM*, O my soul, and let all my innermost being bless His holy Name!'*[9]

The *chazzan* of *Shacharis* begins here.

הָאֵל בְּתַעֲצֻמוֹת עֻזֶּךָ, הַגָּדוֹל בִּכְבוֹד שְׁמֶךָ, הַגִּבּוֹר לָנֶצַח וְהַנּוֹרָא בְּנוֹרְאוֹתֶיךָ. הַמֶּלֶךְ הַיּוֹשֵׁב עַל כִּסֵּא רָם וְנִשָּׂא.[1]

שׁוֹכֵן עַד מָרוֹם וְקָדוֹשׁ שְׁמוֹ.[2] וְכָתוּב: רַנְּנוּ צַדִּיקִים בַּיהוה לַיְשָׁרִים נָאוָה תְהִלָּה.[3]

❖ בְּפִי **יְ**שָׁרִים תִּתְהַלָּל.
וּבְדִבְרֵי **צַ**דִּיקִים תִּתְבָּרַךְ.
וּבִלְשׁוֹן **חֲ**סִידִים תִּתְרוֹמָם.
וּבְקֶרֶב **קְ**דוֹשִׁים תִּתְקַדָּשׁ.

וּבְמַקְהֲלוֹת רִבְבוֹת עַמְּךָ בֵּית יִשְׂרָאֵל, בְּרִנָּה יִתְפָּאַר שִׁמְךָ מַלְכֵּנוּ בְּכָל דּוֹר וָדוֹר. ❖ שֶׁכֵּן חוֹבַת כָּל הַיְצוּרִים, לְפָנֶיךָ יהוה אֱלֹהֵינוּ וֵאלֹהֵי אֲבוֹתֵינוּ, לְהוֹדוֹת לְהַלֵּל לְשַׁבֵּחַ לְפָאֵר לְרוֹמֵם לְהַדֵּר לְבָרֵךְ לְעַלֵּה וּלְקַלֵּס, עַל כָּל דִּבְרֵי שִׁירוֹת וְתִשְׁבְּחוֹת דָּוִד בֶּן יִשַׁי עַבְדְּךָ מְשִׁיחֶךָ.

Stand while reciting יִשְׁתַּבַּח . . .
The fifteen expressions of praise — שִׁיר וּשְׁבָחָה . . . בְּרָכוֹת וְהוֹדָאוֹת — should be recited without pause, preferably in one breath.

יִשְׁתַּבַּח שִׁמְךָ לָעַד מַלְכֵּנוּ, הָאֵל הַמֶּלֶךְ הַגָּדוֹל וְהַקָּדוֹשׁ, בַּשָּׁמַיִם וּבָאָרֶץ. כִּי לְךָ נָאֶה יהוה אֱלֹהֵינוּ וֵאלֹהֵי אֲבוֹתֵינוּ, שִׁיר וּשְׁבָחָה, הַלֵּל וְזִמְרָה, עֹז וּמֶמְשָׁלָה, נֶצַח גְּדֻלָּה וּגְבוּרָה, תְּהִלָּה וְתִפְאֶרֶת, קְדֻשָּׁה וּמַלְכוּת, בְּרָכוֹת וְהוֹדָאוֹת מֵעַתָּה וְעַד עוֹלָם. ❖ בָּרוּךְ אַתָּה יהוה, אֵל מֶלֶךְ גָּדוֹל בַּתִּשְׁבָּחוֹת, אֵל הַהוֹדָאוֹת, אֲדוֹן הַנִּפְלָאוֹת, הַבּוֹחֵר בְּשִׁירֵי זִמְרָה, מֶלֶךְ אֵל חֵי הָעוֹלָמִים. (Cong. – אָמֵן.)

The *chazzan* recites חֲצִי קַדִּישׁ.

יִתְגַּדַּל וְיִתְקַדַּשׁ שְׁמֵהּ רַבָּא. (Cong. – אָמֵן.) בְּעָלְמָא דִּי בְרָא כִרְעוּתֵהּ. וְיַמְלִיךְ מַלְכוּתֵהּ, בְּחַיֵּיכוֹן וּבְיוֹמֵיכוֹן וּבְחַיֵּי דְכָל בֵּית יִשְׂרָאֵל, בַּעֲגָלָא וּבִזְמַן קָרִיב. וְאִמְרוּ: אָמֵן.

(Cong. – אָמֵן. יְהֵא שְׁמֵהּ רַבָּא מְבָרַךְ לְעָלַם וּלְעָלְמֵי עָלְמַיָּא.)

יְהֵא שְׁמֵהּ רַבָּא מְבָרַךְ לְעָלַם וּלְעָלְמֵי עָלְמַיָּא.

יִתְבָּרַךְ וְיִשְׁתַּבַּח וְיִתְפָּאַר וְיִתְרוֹמַם וְיִתְנַשֵּׂא וְיִתְהַדָּר וְיִתְעַלֶּה וְיִתְהַלָּל שְׁמֵהּ דְּקֻדְשָׁא בְּרִיךְ הוּא (Cong. – בְּרִיךְ הוּא) — לְעֵלָּא מִן כָּל בִּרְכָתָא וְשִׁירָתָא תֻּשְׁבְּחָתָא וְנֶחֱמָתָא, דַּאֲמִירָן בְּעָלְמָא. וְאִמְרוּ: אָמֵן. (Cong. – אָמֵן.)

The *chazzan* of *Shacharis* begins here:

הָאֵל *O God, in the omnipotence of Your strength, great in the glory of Your Name, mighty forever and awesome through Your awesome deeds. O King enthroned upon a high and lofty throne!*[1]

שׁוֹכֵן עַד *He Who abides forever, exalted and holy is His Name.*[2] *And it is written: 'Sing joyfully, O righteous, before* HASHEM; *for the upright, praise is fitting.'*[3]

Chazzan: *By the mouth of the upright shall You be lauded;*
by the words of the righteous shall You be blessed;
by the tongue of the devout shall You be exalted;
and amid the holy shall You be sanctified.

וּבְמַקְהֲלוֹת *And in the assemblies of the myriads of Your people, the House of Israel, with joyous song shall Your Name be glorified, our King, throughout every generation.* Chazzan– *For such is the duty of all creatures — before You,* HASHEM, *our God, God of our forefathers, to thank, laud, praise, glorify, exalt, adore, bless, raise high, and sing praises — even beyond all expressions of the songs and praises of David the son of Jesse, Your servant, Your anointed.*

Stand while reciting *'May Your Name be praised . . .'*
The fifteen expressions of praise — *'song and praise . . . blessings and thanksgivings'* — should be recited without pause, preferably in one breath.

יִשְׁתַּבַּח *May Your Name be praised forever — our King, the God, the great and holy King — in heaven and on earth. Because for You is fitting — O* HASHEM, *our God, and the God of our forefathers — song and praise, lauding and hymns, power and dominion, triumph, greatness and strength, praise and splendor, holiness and sovereignty, blessings and thanksgivings from this time and forever.* Chazzan– *Blessed are You,* HASHEM, *God, King exalted through praises, God of thanksgivings, Master of wonders, Who chooses musical songs of praise — King, God, Life-giver of the world.* (Cong.– *Amen.*)

The *chazzan* recites Half-*Kaddish*.

יִתְגַּדַּל *May His great Name grow exalted and sanctified* (Cong.– *Amen.*) *in the world that He created as He willed. May He give reign to His kingship in your lifetimes and in your days, and in the lifetimes of the entire Family of Israel, swiftly and soon. Now respond: Amen.*

(Cong.– *Amen. May His great Name be blessed forever and ever.*)
May His great Name be blessed forever and ever.

Blessed, praised, glorified, exalted, extolled, mighty, upraised, and lauded be the Name of the Holy One, Blessed is He (Cong.– *Blessed is He*) *— beyond any blessing and song, praise and consolation that are uttered in the world. Now respond: Amen.* (Cong.– *Amen.*)

---

(1) Cf. *Isaiah* 6:1. (2) Cf. 57:15. (3) *Psalms* 33:1.

In some congregations the *chazzan* chants a melody during his recitation of בָּרְכוּ, so that the congregation can then recite יִתְבָּרַךְ.

Chazzan bows at בָּרְכוּ and straightens up at 'ה.

בָּרְכוּ אֶת יהוה הַמְּבֹרָךְ.

יִתְבָּרַךְ וְיִשְׁתַּבַּח וְיִתְפָּאַר וְיִתְרוֹמַם וְיִתְנַשֵּׂא שְׁמוֹ שֶׁל מֶלֶךְ מַלְכֵי הַמְּלָכִים, הַקָּדוֹשׁ בָּרוּךְ הוּא. שֶׁהוּא רִאשׁוֹן וְהוּא אַחֲרוֹן, וּמִבַּלְעָדָיו אֵין אֱלֹהִים.[1] סֹלּוּ, לָרֹכֵב בָּעֲרָבוֹת, בְּיָהּ שְׁמוֹ, וְעִלְזוּ לְפָנָיו.[2] וּשְׁמוֹ מְרוֹמַם עַל כָּל בְּרָכָה וּתְהִלָּה.[3] בָּרוּךְ שֵׁם כְּבוֹד מַלְכוּתוֹ לְעוֹלָם וָעֶד. יְהִי שֵׁם יהוה מְבֹרָךְ, מֵעַתָּה וְעַד עוֹלָם.[4]

Congregation, followed by *chazzan*, responds, bowing at בָּרוּךְ and straightening up at 'ה.

בָּרוּךְ יהוה הַמְּבֹרָךְ לְעוֹלָם וָעֶד.

ברכות קריאת שמע

It is preferable that one sit while reciting the following series of prayers — particularly the *Kedushah* verses, קָדוֹשׁ קָדוֹשׁ קָדוֹשׁ and בָּרוּךְ כְּבוֹד — until *Shemoneh Esrei*.

The following paragraph is recited aloud by the *chazzan*, then repeated by the congregation.

בָּרוּךְ אַתָּה יהוה אֱלֹהֵינוּ מֶלֶךְ הָעוֹלָם, יוֹצֵר אוֹר וּבוֹרֵא חֹשֶׁךְ, עֹשֶׂה שָׁלוֹם וּבוֹרֵא אֶת הַכֹּל.[5]

Congregations that do not recite *Yotzros* continue on page 852.

Congregations that recite *Yotzros* continue:

אוֹר עוֹלָם בְּאוֹצַר חַיִּים אוֹרוֹת מֵאֹפֶל אָמַר וַיֶּהִי.

ON THE SABBATH, THE REGULAR *YOTZROS* ARE OMITTED AND THOSE OF *SABBATH CHOL HAMOED* (PAGES 524-546) ARE RECITED INSTEAD.

SEVENTH DAY

וַיּוֹשַׁע[6]*
שׁוֹשַׁנֵּי פֶּרַח[7] מַזְרִיחַ מְאוֹרִים,
שְׁמָרָם כְּאִישׁוֹן כִּרְדָפוּ אֲחוֹרַיִם,
בְּצֵאת יִשְׂרָאֵל מִמִּצְרָיִם.[8]
וַיַּרְא[9]
מְשִׁסַּת מְסֻתּוֹלֵל בּוֹ לְהַלְעֵז,
מְמֻשָּׁךְ מְפֻרָךְ בְּיָד רָמָה לְהָעֵז,
בֵּית יַעֲקֹב מֵעַם לֹעֵז.[8]
אָז יָשִׁיר[10]
עָנָיו וְסִיעָתוֹ לְהַקְדִּישׁוֹ,
עִזּוּז יְמִינוֹ וּזְרוֹעַ קָדְשׁוֹ,[11]
הָיְתָה יְהוּדָה לְקָדְשׁוֹ.[12]
שִׁמְךָ עַל כֹּל יִתְגַּדַּל וְיִתְקַדַּשׁ,
מוֹשָׁבְךָ בְּרוּם וְהִלּוּכְךָ בַּקֹּדֶשׁ,

EIGHTH DAY

אַתָּה הֵאַרְתָּ* יוֹמָם וָלַיְלָה
לִפְנֵי מַחֲנָי,
אַחֲרֵי רָדְּפוּ מַרְכְּבוֹת מְעַנָּי,
אֲבֵדַת גּוּפָם עַל שְׂפַת יָם רָאוּ עֵינָי,
אֱמוּנִים שׁוֹרְרוּ בַּיּוֹם הַהוּא
וַיּוֹשַׁע יהוה.[13]
בְּרִית בְּתָרִים הִזְהִיר דַּיָּן וְגוֹאֵל,
בִּנְטוֹתוֹ זְרוֹעוֹ וּגְדֻלַּת יַד כָּאֵל,
בְּכֵן עַם יְרֵאָיו הֶאֱמִינוּ בוֹ כִּי הוּא אֵל,
בְּלוֹעֵי גֵיא יַם סוּף
וַיַּרְא יִשְׂרָאֵל.[14]
גְּאוּלִים כְּיָצְאוּ מִכּוּר
לְחֵרוּת חֲפוּשָׁה,
גֹּשׁוּ לְיַם סוּף וְלַמָּוֶת אֲנוּשָׁה,

וַיּוֹשַׁע ◆ — *And He saved*. The first line of each stanza is the opening word or two from the respective verses of the Song at the Sea, followed by the composer's signature: שִׁמְעוֹן בַּר יִצְחָק חֲזַק וֶאֱמַץ אָמֵן, *Shimon son of Yitzchak, may he be strong and persevere, Amen*. The initial letters of the second lines repeat the signature. The third lines are verse fragments from psalm 114, which describes the crossing of the sea.

אַתָּה הֵאַרְתָּ ◆ — *You illuminated*. This unsigned *piyut* contains twenty-two quatrains and the acrostic forms a four-fold *aleph-beis*. The

In some congregations the *chazzan* chants a melody during his recitation of *Borchu,* so that the congregation can then recite *'Blessed, praised . . .'*

Chazzan bows at *'Bless,'* and straightens up at *'HASHEM.'*

Bless HASHEM, the blessed One.

Congregation, followed by *chazzan,* responds, bowing at *'Blessed'* and straightening up at *'HASHEM.'*

Blessed is HASHEM, the blessed One, for all eternity.

Blessed, praised, glorified, exalted and upraised is the Name of the King Who rules over kings — the Holy One, Blessed is He. For He is the First and He is the Last and aside from Him there is no god.[1] *Extol Him — Who rides the highest heavens — with His Name, YAH, and exult before Him.*[2] *His Name is exalted beyond every blessing and praise.*[3] *Blessed is the Name of His glorious kingdom for all eternity. Blessed be the Name of HASHEM from this time and forever.*[4]

BLESSINGS OF THE SHEMA

It is preferable that one sit while reciting the following series of prayers — particularly the *Kedushah* verses, *'Holy, holy, holy . . .'* and *'Blessed is the glory . . .'* — until *Shemoneh Esrei.*

The following paragraph is recited aloud by the *chazzan,* then repeated by the congregation.

בָּרוּךְ *Blessed are You, HASHEM, our God, King of the universe, Who forms light and creates darkness, makes peace and creates all.*[5]

Congregations that do not recite *Yotzros* continue on page 852.

Congregations that recite *Yotzros* continue:

The primeval light is in the treasury of eternal life;
'Let there be lights from the darkness,' He declared — and so it was!

ON THE SABBATH, THE REGULAR *YOTZROS* ARE OMITTED AND THOSE OF *SABBATH CHOL HAMOED* (PAGES 524-546) ARE RECITED INSTEAD.

SEVENTH DAY

And He saved,[6]*
ש *the rose blossoms [Israel]*[7] *— He Who makes the lightgivers shine,*
ש *He guarded them like a pupil of the eye*
when they were being chased after,
when Israel went out of Egypt.[8]
When He [God] saw[9]
מ *the oppressor's jibes and scorn*
מ *aimed at those drawn with heavy labor, He gathered them with an exalted hand,*
[and removed] Jacob's household
from a people of alien tongue.[8]
Then he chose to sing[10] *—*
ע *the humble one [Moses] and his company [Israel] — to sanctify Him,*
ע *of the strength of His right hand and His holy arm,*[11]
Judah then became His sanctuary.[12]
May Your Name be exalted and sanctified over all,
Your dwelling is on high and Your ways are in holiness,

EIGHTH DAY

א *You illuminated* day and night before my camp;*
א *the chariots of my oppressor chased after me.*
א *My eyes saw their destruction on the seashore;*
א *the faithful ones sang on that day, 'Hashem saved.'*[13]
ב *The Judge [of Egypt] and Redeemer [of Israel] alacritously fulfilled the Covenant of the Parts,*
ב *when He stretched forth His arm and His great hand, as befitting God.*
ב *Thus His fearful nation believed in Him that He is God.*
ב *[The Egyptians were] swallowed up by the earth, [after drowning in] the Sea of Reeds, while Israel watched.*[14]
ג *When the redeemed ones went forth from the [Egyptian] cauldron to freedom and liberty,*
ג *they approached the Sea of Reeds where they were threatened with the sickness of death.*

(1) Cf. *Isaiah* 44:6. (2) *Psalms* 68:5. (3) Cf. *Nehemiah* 9:5. (4) *Psalms* 113:2. (5) Cf. *Isaiah* 45:7. (6) *Exodus* 14:30. (7) Cf. *Hosea* 14:6. (8) *Psalms* 114:1. (9) *Exodus* 14:31. (10) 15:1. (11) *Psalms* 98:1. (12) 114:2. (13) *Exodus* 14:30. (14) 14:31.

SEVENTH DAY

עֵדֹתֶיךָ נֶאֶמְנוּ מְאֹד
לְבֵיתְךָ נַאֲוָה קֹדֶשׁ,[1] קָדוֹשׁ.
עָזִּי וְזִמְרָת יָהּ[2]
שׁוֹרְרוּ לוֹ מַקְהֵלוֹתָיו,
וְשִׁוּוּ הוֹד וְהָדָר בִּתְהִלּוֹתָיו,
יִשְׂרָאֵל מַמְשְׁלוֹתָיו.[3]
יהוה[4]
נִגְלָה לְעַמּוֹ הֱיוֹת מָנוֹס,
נוֹזְלִים צָגוּ כְּמוֹ נֵד לִכְנוֹס,
הַיָּם רָאָה וַיָּנֹס.[5]
מַרְכְּבֹת[6]
בּוֹגֵד בִּלְּעוּ בְּסוּף וְשִׁיחוֹר,*
בַּנְּהָרִים חָרָה אַפּוֹ[7]
וְנֶהֶפְכוּ סְחַרְחוֹר,
הַיַּרְדֵּן יִסֹּב לְאָחוֹר.[5]
תְּהוֹמֹת[8]
רָגְזוּ וַיֶּהֱמוּ גַּלִּים,
רָאוּךָ מַיִם מֵאֵימָתְךָ חָלִים,
הֶהָרִים רָקְדוּ כְאֵילִים.[9]
יְמִינְךָ[10]
יֶשַׁע הֵחִישָׁה בְּעֵת רָצוֹן,
יִרְעֲשׁוּ הֶהָרִים וְעַמּוּדֶיהָ יִתְפַּלָּצוּן,[11]
גְּבָעוֹת כִּבְנֵי צֹאן.[9]
וּבְרֹב[12]
צִדְקָתְךָ מַפַּלְתָּם תִּקְנֹס,
צוֹלָה חֳרָבִי וְנַהֲרוֹתֶיהָ תֶּאֱנֹס,
מַה לְּךָ הַיָּם כִּי תָנוּס.[13]
וּבְרוּחַ[14]
חֲזָקָה סְעַרְתָּם סְחַרְחוֹר,
חוֹמָה וּמְסִלָּה לְעַמְּךָ תִּבְחוֹר,
הַיַּרְדֵּן תִּסֹּב לְאָחוֹר.[13]
אָמַר,[15]
קִבֵּץ כְּעָמִיר שָׂרֵי אֱוִילִים,
קָלַע נַפְשׁוֹתָם חֶפְצוּ לְהַשְׁלִים,

EIGHTH DAY

גֵּאִים רָדְּפוּ וְאָבְדוּ בְּגַלֵּי יָם חֲלוּשָׁה,
גָּאֹה גָּאָה, שִׁיר יְשׁוּעָה,
אָז יָשִׁיר מֹשֶׁה.[16]
דָּפַק פִּתְחֵי יְשֵׁנָה בְּנֶפֶשׁ בְּזוּיָה,[17]
דְּרוֹר נָחַת מֵעַבְדוּת לְחֵרוּת עֲטוּיָה,
דָּדָהּ הוֹצִיאָהּ בִּזְרוֹעַ נְטוּיָה,
דּוֹבְבוּ יוֹנְקִים זֶה אֵלִי,
עָזִּי וְזִמְרָת יָהּ.[18]
הָלְּכוּ בְּתוֹךְ הַיָּם וְהַמַּיִם לָהֶם חוֹמָה,[19]
הוֹלִיכָם בַּתְּהוֹמוֹת כְּבַבִּקְעָה[20]
אָדָם וּבְהֵמָה,
הַבָּאִים אַחֲרֵיהֶם זוֹעֲמוּ בְּאַף וּבְחֵמָה,
הַדּוֹרִים שִׁבְּחוּ לִשְׁמוֹ וְנָמוּ,
יהוה אִישׁ מִלְחָמָה.[21]
וַיֶּחֱזַק לִבּוֹ לִרְדּוֹף עִם כָּל צְבָא קְהָלוֹ,
וְשֵׁשׁ מֵאוֹת רֶכֶב בָּחוּר לָקַח לוֹ,[22]
וַיּוֹרֵם בְּחִצֵּי אֵשׁ וְהָמָם וְהִבְהִילוֹ,
וְטֻבְּעוּ בְיַם סוּף,
מַרְכְּבֹת פַּרְעֹה וְחֵילוֹ.[23]
זָמְמוּ פֶּן יִרְבֶּה[24] יוֹעֲצֵי תוֹלָלֵימוֹ,
זָדוּ בְּפֶרֶךְ וְהִכְבִּידוּ עֻלֵּימוֹ,
זָדוֹן מַחְשְׁבוֹתָם נֶהְפַּךְ עֲלֵימוֹ,
זוֹרְקֵי יְלוּד בַּמַּיִם,
תְּהֹמֹת יְכַסְיֻמוּ.[25]
חָתַם עַל הָרֵי בֶתֶר נִקְמַת דִּינָי,
חִבֵּל נוֹגְשַׂי וְדָן דִּינָי,
חָלְקוּ בְּגַלֵּי יָם פִּגְרֵי מְדָנַי,
חִזַּקְתַּנִי בְּכֹחַ נֶאְדָּרִי,
יְמִינְךָ יהוה.[26]
טָמְנוּ בְּנֶגֶף בְּכוֹרֵי שׂוֹטְנֶיךָ,
טָרְפוּ פַּעֲמֵי רוֹדְפֵי הֲמוֹנֶיךָ,
טֻבְּעוּ בְּלִבּוֹתֵי יָם צוֹרְרֵי אֱמוּנֶיךָ,
טֵאטְאוּ קָמֶיךָ בַּחֲרוֹנְךָ,
וּבְרֹב גְּאוֹנְךָ.[27]

(1) *Psalms* 93:5. (2) *Exodus* 15:2. (3) *Psalms* 114:2. (4) *Exodus* 15:3. (5) *Psalms* 114:3. (6) *Exodus* 15:4. (7) Cf. *Habakkuk* 3:8. (8) *Exodus* 15:5. (9) *Psalms* 114:4. (10) *Exodus* 15:6. (11) Cf. *Job* 9:6. (12) *Exodus* 15:7. (13) *Psalms* 114:5. (14) *Exodus* 15:8. (15) 15:9. (16)15:1. (17) Cf. *Song of Songs* 5:2. (18) *Exodus* 15:2. (19) Cf. 14:29. (20) Cf. *Isaiah* 63:13-14. (21) *Exodus* 15:3. (22) Cf. 14:7. (23) 15:4. (24) See 1:10. (25) 15:5. (26) 15:6. (27) 15:7.

last phrase of each stanza is the opening phrase of a verse from the Song of the Sea.

וְשִׁיחוֹר — *And the Nile.* The *paytan* implies that even those Egyptians who did not chase after

SEVENTH DAY	EIGHTH DAY
Your testimonies about Your Temple, the Sacred dwelling, are exceedingly trustworthy,[1] *O Holy One.*	ג *The proud [Egyptians] pursued them but were destroyed when the waves of the sea tossed them about.*
'My might	ג *Then Moshe sang the song of salvation, 'He is exalted above the arrogant.'*[16]
ו *and my praise is God,'*[2] *His congregations sang to Him,*	ד *He knocked on the doors of those sleeping with degraded soul,*[17]
ו *and they rendered splendor and glory as His praises, [they,] Israel His dominions.*[3]	ד *to grant liberty, [to remove them] from slavery, to cloak them in freedom.*
HASHEM[4]	ד *Her Beloved brought her forth with outstretched arm.*
נ *revealed Himself as a refuge for His people,*	ד *And even the sucklings uttered, 'This is my God; God is my might and praise.'*[18]
נ *the running water stood gathered like a wall, the sea saw and fled.*[5]	ה *They went into the middle of the sea, and the water was a wall for them.*[19]
The chariots[6]	ה *He led them — man and animal — in the depths as if in a valley.*[20]
ב *of the rebel [Pharaoh] were swallowed up by the Sea of Reeds and the Nile,**	ה *Those who followed them were stricken with anger and fury.*
ב *He loosed his flaming anger on the rivers,*[7] *and they all reversed themselves, the Jordan turned backward.*[5]	ה *The splendid ones praised His Name and said, 'Hashem is Master of war.'*[21]
The deep waters[8]	ו *And he [Pharaoh] encouraged himself to pursue [Israel] with his entire army;*
ר *were agitated and the waves piled up [threatening to crash down on Israel also],*	ו *and he took six hundred chosen chariots with him.*[22]
ר *but when the waters saw You, they shuddered at Your awesomeness, the mountains jumped like rams.*[9]	ו *He shot flaming arrows at them; He confused and confounded them.*
Your right hand[10]	ו *And Pharaoh's chariots and his army drowned in the sea.*[23]
י *hastened salvation at the time of favor,*	ז *The mocking enemy's advisors planned, 'Lest they increase,'*[24]
י *the mountains stormed and the [earth's] pillars shook,*[11] *the hills [ran] like young lambs.*[9]	ז *so they wantonly forced backbreaking labor, and hardened their yoke.*
With Your abundant[12]	ז *The viciousness of their thoughts were turned back upon themselves;*
צ *righteousness You penalized [Egypt and brought about] their downfall,*	ז *those who threw their babies into the water were covered over by deep waters.*[25]
צ *[You told] the depths, 'Dry yourself out!' You coerced the rivers [by saying:] 'What is it to you if you flee [until Israel passes]?'*[13]	ח *The vengeance of My law was sealed on the Mount of the [Covenant Between the] Parts.*
With a strong wind,[14]	ח *He destroyed my oppressors and judged my grievance.*
ח *You stormed at them to turn them around,*	ח *With the waves of the sea, He split the corpses of my tormentors.*
ח *[making] a wall and a path for the people of Your choosing, the Jordan turned backwards.*[13]	ח *He fortified me with His right hand, adorned with strength.*[26]
He [Pharaoh] said[15]	ט *You buried Your enemies' firstborn in a plague.*
ק *that he would gather his foolish officers like sheaves of grain,*	ט *You ensnared the fee of Your multitude's pursuers.*
ק *they jeopardized their souls to fulfill his desire,*	ט *You drowned Your people's oppressors in the hearts of the sea.*
	ט *You swept away Your opponents with Your anger and with Your abundant grandeur.*[27]

SEVENTH DAY

הֶהָרִים תִּרְקְדוּ כְאֵילִים.[1]
נָשַׁפְתָּ[2]
חֲמָתְךָ תִּבְעַר פְּנִימִי וְחִיצוֹן,[3]
חֱלֶד הִתְפּוֹרְרָה תָּהֶךְ וְקִיצוֹן,
גְּבָעוֹת כִּבְנֵי צֹאן.[1]
מִי כָמֹכָה[4]
זְמִיר עָרִיצִים יַעֲנֶה בְּמֶרֶץ,
זְרוֹעֲךָ חָשַׂפְתָּ
וְהִתְמוֹטְטָה הָאָרֶץ,
מִלִּפְנֵי אָדוֹן חוּלִי אָרֶץ.[5]
נָטִיתָ[6]
קַשְׁתְּךָ רֹאשׁ פְּרָזָיו לִנְקֹב,[7]
קְרִיּוֹת וּמִבְצָרִים נֶחְשְׁבוּ לְרָקָב,
מִלִּפְנֵי אֱלוֹהַ יַעֲקֹב.[5]
נָחִיתָ
וְנֵהַלְתָּ[8] עַם עֲמוּסֵי מֵעַיִם,[9]
וְלֹא מָנַעְתָּ מִפִּיהֶם דְּגַן שָׁמַיִם,
הַהֹפְכִי הַצּוּר אֲגַם מָיִם.[10]
שָׁמְעוּ[11]
אָמְצְךָ כָּל אַפְסֵי תְחוּמַיִם,
אֶדֶר הוֹדְךָ עַל אֶרֶץ וְשָׁמַיִם,
בְּתִתְּךָ חַלָּמִישׁ לְמַעְיְנוֹ מָיִם.[10]
אָז[12] מָצְאוּ אָבוֹת חֵן וּבְצִלְּךָ לָנוּ,
אָנָּא הַבֵּט נָא עַמְּךָ כֻּלָּנוּ,
לֹא לָנוּ, יהוה, לֹא לָנוּ.[13]
תִּפֹּל[14]
צָרָה בַּעֲדִינָה מֵאֱנוֹשׁ לְאַבֵּד,
צַוֵּה יְשׁוּעוֹת יַעֲקֹב[15]
בְּיִרְאָה אוֹתְךָ לַעֲבֹד,
כִּי לְשִׁמְךָ תֵּן כָּבוֹד.[13]
תְּבִיאֵמוֹ
אֲגֻדִּים יַחַד לִמְכוֹן שִׁבְתֶּךָ,

EIGHTH DAY

יָרִיתָ בָּאֵשׁ וְעָנָן חִצֵּי רְשָׁפֶיךָ,
יָרְדוּ עַל מַחֲנוֹת צְבָא מְחָרְפֶיךָ,
יַעַן כִּי רָדְפוּ אַחַר עַם מְצַפֶּיךָ,
יַקְפְּתָּ תְּהוֹם כְּקֶרַח, וּבְרוּחַ אַפֶּיךָ.[16]
כִּנֵּס כָּל עַמּוֹ יָהִיר חֲסַר לֵב,
כַּעְסוֹ הֵעִיר לִרְדֹּף כְּדוֹב אוֹרֵב,
כְּחָפַר בּוֹר לִנְפֹּל בּוֹ חַיָּב,
כָּלָה לְהוֹרִישׁ שׁוֹר וָשֶׂה,
אָמַר אוֹיֵב.[17]
לִשְׁפֹּט זֵדִים לַמַּבּוּל יָשַׁבְתָּ,
לְאַדִּירֵי מַיִם כְּדָגִים לָרֶשֶׁת אָסַפְתָּ,
לְלוֹחֲצֵי עַמְּךָ
מַכּוֹת עַל מַכּוֹת הוֹסַפְתָּ,
לְכַסּוֹתָם מֵי יַם סוּף, בְּרוּחֲךָ נָשַׁפְתָּ.[18]
מוֹשָׁעֵי יַם סוּף בְּשִׁירָה קִדְּמוּךָ,
מְסַפְּרִים מַעֲשֶׂיךָ וְרֶנֶן הִנְעִימוּךָ,
מְנַשְּׂאִים כְּבוֹדְךָ בְּהִלּוּל רוֹמְמוּךָ,
מְשַׁבְּחִים לְשִׁמְךָ וְנָמוּ,
יהוה מִי כָמוֹךָ.[19]
נֶאֱנָחוּ מֵעַבְדוּת וְאֹזֶן הִטִּיתָ,
נָקְמָה לָבַשְׁתָּ וְקִנְאָה עָטִיתָ,
נוֹגְשֵׂימוֹ נִעַרְתָּ וְכֻלָּם טֵאטֵאתָ,
נִבְלָתָם לִבְלֹעַ גַּיְא,
יְמִינְךָ נָטִיתָ.[20]
סוֹבְלֵי עֹל כֹּבֶד לַחֲצָם רָאִיתָ,
סְגוּרֵי כּוּר בַּרְזֶל מִתּוֹכָם הוֹצֵאתָ,
סוֹטְנֵימוֹ נִעַרְתָּ וְלִתְהוֹם דָּחִיתָ,
סְמוּכִים עַל שֵׁם קָדְשֶׁךָ,
בְּחַסְדְּךָ נָחִיתָ.[21]
עוֹרֵר סְעָרָה בְּשַׁאֲגַת רְעָמִים,
עוֹכֵר זֵדִים בְּמִשְׁבְּרֵי יַמִּים,
עָרַץ גֵּאִים וְהִשְׁפִּיל רָמִים,

(1) *Psalms* 114:6. (2) *Exodus* 15:10. (3) See *Rashi* to 14:25. (4) 15:11. (5) *Psalms* 114:7. (6) *Exodus* 15:12. (7) Cf. *Habakkuk* 3:14. (8) *Exodus* 15:13. (9) Cf. *Isaiah* 46:3. (10) *Psalms* 114:8. (11) *Exodus* 15:14. (12) 15:15. (13) *Psalms* 115:1. (14) *Exodus* 15:16. (15) *Psalms* 44:5. (16) *Exodus* 15:8. (17) 15:9. (18) 15:10. (19) 15:11. (20) Cf. 15:12. (21) Cf. 15:13.

Israel also drowned — in the Nile. This is in accord with *Rashi's* interpretation of ה׳ נִלְחָם לָהֶם בְּמִצְרָיִם, *HASHEM is doing battle for them with* [literally, *in*] *Egypt* (*Exodus* 14:25). Although the verse is speaking of the Egyptians at the sea, it is also to be taken in its literal sense, namely, *HASHEM is doing battle for them in the Land of Egypt;* for just as these were stricken at the sea, so were those who remained behind also stricken.

SEVENTH DAY	EIGHTH DAY

SEVENTH DAY

and the mountain[-like officers] jumped like rams [into the sea].[1]
You blew[2]
ח Your flaming anger, and You burned those inside [Egypt] and outside [at the sea],[3]
ח the sea bottom crumbled, in the middle and at the edge, and the hills [ran] like young lambs.[1]
Who is like You[4]
ז who cuts down the mighty and speedily humbles them?
ז You have revealed Your arm and the earth fell down, before the Lord, the earth did tremble.[5]
You stretched out[6]
ק Your bow that Your arrow may penetrate the leader of the wanton ones;[7]
ק their fortified cities were considered as rotting, before the God of Jacob.[5]
You guided
ו and led[8] the nation borne from the womb,[9]
ו nor did You withhold from them Heavenly grain, and You turned the rock into a pond of water [for them].[10]
They heard[11]
א of Your might, those who dwell at Your borders,
א and Your powerful splendor that is on earth and heaven, when You made the flintstone into a flowing fountain.[10]
Then[12]
מ the forefathers found favor and rested in Your shade.
Please, see now that we are all Your people. [Redeem us,] not for our sake, HASHEM, not for our sake [but for Your Name's sake].[13]
Cause to fall on[14]
צ the pampered ones, troubles that will erase [their memory] from mankind,
צ command the salvation of Jacob,[15] for he shall serve You with awe. Thus, give glory for Your Name's sake.[13]
Bring them,
א bound together as one, to the foundation of Your dwelling place,

EIGHTH DAY

י You shot Your flashing arrows with fire and cloud.
י You descended upon Your blasphemer's army camps,
י because they pursued the people that look forward to You.
י You congealed the deep waters like ice with the winds of Your anger.[16]
כ The arrogant fool gathered all his people,
כ he kindled his anger to pursue like a lurking bear.
כ Since he dug a pit, he obligated himself to fall into it;
כ the enemy said,[17] 'We will destroy [Israel] completely to the last ox and sheep.'
ל You sat to judge and punish the wanton [Egyptians] with a flood.
ל You gathered them into the strong waters like fish into a net,
ל You increased blow upon blow for those who oppressed Your people.
ל To cover them with the Sea of Reed's water, You blew with Your wind.[18]
מ Those saved from the Sea of Reeds came to greet You with song.
מ They retell Your words and sweetly sing glad song to You.
מ They exalt Your glory; they elevate You with praise.
מ They give praise to Your Name and say, 'Hashem, who is like You?'[19]
נ When they groaned from slavery, You bent Your ear.
נ You donned vengeance and cloaked Yourself with jealousy,
נ You spilled their oppressors [into the sea], and swept them all away,
נ You stretched out Your right hand and their corpses were swallowed by the earth.[20]
ס You saw the oppression of those who bore the heavy yoke,
ס You brought forth those who were locked in the iron cauldron.
ס You spilled their enemies into the sea and pushed them into the depths.
ס But those who rely upon Your Holy Name, You guided with Your kindness.[21]
ע He arouses a stern wind with a roar of thunder.
ע He depresses the wanton ones in the waves of the seas.
ע He breaks the prideful, and humbles the haughty.

SEVENTH DAY

וְתִטָּעֵמוֹ בְּהַר[1]
צְבִי קֹדֶשׁ נַחֲלָתֶךָ,
עַל חַסְדְּךָ עַל אֲמִתֶּךָ.[2]*
יהוה,[3]
מְקַוֶּיךָ מְקַבְּלִים
עֹל מַלְכוּתְךָ עֲלֵיהֶם,
נָא הֱיֵה סֵתֶר לָמוֹ מִפְּנֵי שׁוֹדְדֵיהֶם,
לָמָּה יֹאמְרוּ הַגּוֹיִם
אַיֵּה נָא אֱלֹהֵיהֶם.[4]
כִּי בָא[5]
נוֹגֵשׂ וְכָל חֵילוֹ בַּמַּיִם,
נָא שִׂית אֹיְבֶיךָ לְמוֹרַשׁ קִפּוֹד*
וְאַגְמֵי מָיִם,[6]
וְיֵדְעוּ כִּי אֲנַחְנוּ עַמּוֹ
וֵאלֹהֵינוּ בַשָּׁמָיִם.[7]
כְּהִפְלֵאתָ לְדוֹר רִאשׁוֹן רֹב נִסֶּיךָ,
הַפְלֵא עִם אַחֲרוֹנִים
מְחַכֶּיךָ וְחוֹסֶיךָ,
וְכָל פֶּה יְהַלֶּלְךָ, מָה
רַבּוּ מַעֲשֶׂיךָ,[8] קָדוֹשׁ.

EIGHTH DAY

עֲלִילוֹת נִסֵּי נוֹרְאוֹתֶיךָ,
שָׁמְעוּ עַמִּים.[9]
פְּדוּיִם כְּיָצְאוּ לְחֵרוּת לְגָאֳלָם הִלְּלוּ,
פְּזוּרֵי כְנַעַן רָגְזוּ וְחָלוּ,
פַּאֲתֵי מוֹאָב רָעֲדוּ וְחִלְחֲלוּ,
פַּחֲתֵי אַלּוּפֵי אֱדוֹם,
אָז נִבְהֲלוּ.[10]
צִיר חִנֵּן לְהָנִיא עוֹבְדֵי פְּסִילֵיהֶם,
צְוָחוֹת פִּימוֹ לְדֹם כְּאַבְנֵי אֱלִילֵיהֶם,
צֹאנְךָ לְהַעֲבִיר עַד גְּבוּלֵיהֶם,
צוֹקַת אֵימָתָה וָפַחַד,
תִּפֹּל עֲלֵיהֶם.[11]
קְהִלּוֹת אִישׁ תָּם
בִּרְכַּת אָב תַּשְׂבִּיעֵמוֹ,
קָמֵיהֶם תַּפִּיל וּמִיָּדָם תּוֹשִׁיעֵמוֹ,
קַבֵּץ פְּזוּרִים וּבְמִרְעֶה טוֹב תַּרְעֵמוֹ,
קִרְיַת הַר נַחֲלָתְךָ
תְּבִיאֵמוֹ וְתִטָּעֵמוֹ.[12]
רַחֲבַת יָדַיִם גָּעַר וְהִרְעִד,
רָפוֹת יָדַיִם לְהַעֲבִיר בָּהּ צוּר וְעֵד,
רָז הַמְּלוּכָה יְשֻׁרוּן לְהָעֵד,
רֶנֶן וְשִׁירָה שׁוֹרְרוּ,
יהוה יִמְלֹךְ לְעוֹלָם וָעֶד.[13]
שָׁאַג אֵל כְּאַרְיֵה וְחָשַׂף זְרוֹעוֹ,
שִׁפְעַת יַם סוּף חָרַב וְהִבְקִיעוֹ,
שִׁדְּפוּ בְּרוּחַ קָדִים וְהִכְרִיעוֹ,
שָׁב וַיְכַס רִכְבּוֹ וְחֵילוֹ,
כִּי בָא סוּס פַּרְעֹה.[14]
תֹּקֶף בֵּית יַעֲקֹב אַדֶּרֶת עֲטָיִם,
תִּפְאֶרֶת בְּרֹאשָׁם וַעֲטֶרֶת עֲדָיִם,
תּוֹפְפוּ בִּמְחוֹלוֹת כְּיָצְאוּ מִן הַיָּם,
תְּעוּדָה שִׁירָה נָמָה,
וַתִּקַּח מִרְיָם.[15]

(1) *Exodus* 15:17. (2) *Psalms* 115:1. (3) *Exodus* 15:18. (4) *Psalms* 115:2. (5) *Exodus* 15:19. (6) *Isaiah* 14:23. (7) *Psalms* 115:3. (8) 104:24. (9) *Exodus* 15:14. (10) 15:15. (11) 15:16. (12) 15:17. (13) 15:18. (14) 15:19. (15) 15:20.

עַל חַסְדְּךָ עַל אֲמִתֶּךָ — *Through Your kindness, through Your truth.* That is, in the merit of Abraham and Jacob — as it is written: *Grant truth to Jacob, kindness to Abraham* (*Micah* 7:20).

קִפּוֹד — *Hedgehogs.* The translation follows *Rashi* (*Isaiah* 14:23) who renders הריצו״ן, *herisson,* the French word for 'hedgehog.' However, elsewhere (ibid. 34:11; see also *Zephaniah* 2:14), when the word appears among a

SEVENTH DAY

and plant them on Your desirous mountain,[1] Your holy heritage,
*through Your kindness, through Your truth.[2]**
HASHEM[3]
מ those who hope to You accept Your Kingship over themselves.
Please be a haven protecting them from their despoilers.
Why should the nations say, 'Where now is their God?'[4]
For as there came —[5]
נ the oppressor and all his armies — into the water,
so turn Your enemies' land into an estate for hedgehogs, into ponds of water.[6]*
Then they shall know that we are His people, and our God is in the heavens.[7]
As you worked wonders for the first generation, with the abundance of Your miracles,
So may You work wonders with the last generation, those who anticipate You and hope to You.
and then all mouths shall praise You, 'How great are Your works,'[8]
O Holy One.

EIGHTH DAY

ע The incidents of Your wondrous miracles, the nations heard.[9]
פ When the redeemed ones went out to freedom, they praised the Redeemer.
פ The nations spread throughout Canaan were agitated and trembled,
פ the princes of Moab shuddered with trepidation,
פ the rulers and chiefs of Edom were confounded.[10]
צ The emissary [Moses] prayed that idolaters be nullified,
צ that their mouths' cries be silenced like their stone idols.
צ Then Your flock will pass to their borders.
צ Cause the straits of their fear and awe to fall upon them.[11]
ק Satiate Jacob the wholesome one's flock with the blessing of the Patriarch Abraham.
ק Humble Your opponents, and save them [Israel] from their hands.
ק Gather the dispersed and graze them in [Eretz Yisrael] the goodly pasture.
ק To the city of Your heritage's mountain may You bring them and implant them.[12]
ר Scream at the broad handed and make them shudder.
ר To bring weakness to their hands, the Creator appointed a time,
ר that Jeshurun should bear testimony to the secret of the Kingdom,
ר when they sing glad song, 'Hashem shall reign for all eternity.'[13]
ש God roared like a lion and bared His arm,
ש He dried the flow of the Sea of Reeds and split it.
ש He blasted it with the east wind and humbled it.
ש It returned [to its strength] and covered his riders and his army, when Pharaoh's cavalry came.[14]
ת The strength of the House of Jacob and the mantle with which they are cloaked,
ת splendor on their heads and their crowned ornaments;
ת they drummed with circle dances when they left the sea,
ת Miriam recited testimonial song, as she took [the timbrel in hand].[15]

list of birds, *Rashi* renders צואיט״א, *civetta,* the Italian word for 'owl.' In all three verses, *Radak* translates טרטוג״א, *tortuga,* Spanish for 'turtle.'

ON A WEEKDAY CONTINUE HERE:

הַמֵּאִיר לָאָרֶץ וְלַדָּרִים* עָלֶיהָ בְּרַחֲמִים, וּבְטוּבוֹ מְחַדֵּשׁ בְּכָל יוֹם תָּמִיד מַעֲשֵׂה בְרֵאשִׁית. מָה רַבּוּ מַעֲשֶׂיךָ* יהוה,

הַמֵּאִיר לָאָרֶץ וְלַדָּרִים — *He Who illuminates the earth and those who dwell.* The earth's dwellers enjoy the light, but so does the earth itself, because sunlight makes vegetation possible.

ON THE SABBATH CONTINUE HERE:

הַכֹּל יוֹדוּךָ,* וְהַכֹּל יְשַׁבְּחוּךָ, וְהַכֹּל יֹאמְרוּ אֵין קָדוֹשׁ כַּיהוה.[1] הַכֹּל יְרוֹמְמוּךָ סֶּלָה, יוֹצֵר הַכֹּל. הָאֵל הַפּוֹתֵחַ בְּכָל יוֹם דַּלְתוֹת שַׁעֲרֵי מִזְרָח, וּבוֹקֵעַ חַלּוֹנֵי רָקִיעַ,* מוֹצִיא חַמָּה מִמְּקוֹמָהּ וּלְבָנָה מִמְּכוֹן שִׁבְתָּהּ, וּמֵאִיר לָעוֹלָם כֻּלּוֹ וּלְיוֹשְׁבָיו, שֶׁבָּרָא בְּמִדַּת רַחֲמִים. הַמֵּאִיר לָאָרֶץ וְלַדָּרִים עָלֶיהָ בְּרַחֲמִים, וּבְטוּבוֹ מְחַדֵּשׁ בְּכָל יוֹם תָּמִיד מַעֲשֵׂה בְרֵאשִׁית. הַמֶּלֶךְ הַמְּרוֹמָם לְבַדּוֹ מֵאָז, הַמְּשֻׁבָּח וְהַמְּפֹאָר וְהַמִּתְנַשֵּׂא מִימוֹת עוֹלָם. אֱלֹהֵי עוֹלָם בְּרַחֲמֶיךָ הָרַבִּים, רַחֵם עָלֵינוּ, אֲדוֹן עֻזֵּנוּ, צוּר מִשְׂגַּבֵּנוּ, מָגֵן יִשְׁעֵנוּ, מִשְׂגָּב בַּעֲדֵנוּ. אֵין כְּעֶרְכֶּךָ,* וְאֵין זוּלָתֶךָ, אֶפֶס בִּלְתֶּךָ, וּמִי דּוֹמֶה לָּךְ. אֵין כְּעֶרְכְּךָ יהוה אֱלֹהֵינוּ בָּעוֹלָם הַזֶּה, וְאֵין זוּלָתְךָ מַלְכֵּנוּ לְחַיֵּי הָעוֹלָם הַבָּא. אֶפֶס בִּלְתְּךָ גּוֹאֲלֵנוּ לִימוֹת הַמָּשִׁיחַ, וְאֵין דּוֹמֶה לְּךָ מוֹשִׁיעֵנוּ לִתְחִיַּת הַמֵּתִים.

The Sabbath Additions

Since the Sabbath is the weekly testimony to the fact that God created the world, the first blessing of the Shema, which deals with creation, is augmented on the Sabbath with three apt passages:

1. הַכֹּל יוֹדוּךָ, *All will thank You,* speaks of the Creator Who renews creation daily;

2. אֵל אָדוֹן, *God — The Master,* praises the glory of creation itself;

3. לָאֵל אֲשֶׁר שָׁבַת, *To the God Who rested,* celebrates the Sabbath. Thus, these three passages are appropriate only on the Sabbath, and are omitted on all weekday Festivals (*World of*).

הַכֹּל יוֹדוּךָ — *All will thank You.* The word 'all' refers to the previous blessing, which ends וּבוֹרֵא אֶת הַכֹּל, *and creates all.* Thus, every facet of the universe will join in thanking and lauding God. Only man and the angels do this verbally; the rest of creation does so by carrying out its assigned tasks and inspiring man to recognize the Guiding Hand that created and orders everything.

דַּלְתוֹת שַׁעֲרֵי מִזְרָח . . . חַלּוֹנֵי רָקִיעַ — *Doors of the gateways of the East ... windows of the firmament.* These expressions are given various interpretations. On the simple level, they refer poetically to the rising sun breaking through the portals of darkness. Alternatively, the phrase *doors of the gateways* refers to daybreak, which illuminates the sky long before sunrise. The *windows* are different points in the sky at which the sun rises as the seasons move to the longer days of summer and then back again to the shorter days of winter (*R' Hirsch; Iyun Tefillah*).

אֵין כְּעֶרְכֶּךָ — *There is no comparison to You.* This verse makes four statements about God that are explained in the next verse. Thus the two verses should be seen as a unit. As explained by *R'*

ON A WEEKDAY CONTINUE HERE:

הַמֵּאִיר *He Who illuminates the earth and those who dwell* upon it, with compassion; and in His goodness renews daily, perpetually, the work of Creation. How great are Your works,* HASHEM,*

מָה רַבּוּ מַעֲשֶׂיךָ — *How great are Your works.* This refers to the heavenly bodies and other major forces in creation. Homiletically, the Talmud (*Chullin* 127a) interprets, *how diverse are Your works;* some can live only on land, others only in the sea, and so on.

ON THE SABBATH CONTINUE HERE:

הַכֹּל יוֹדְוּךָ *All will thank You* and all will praise You — and all will declare: 'Nothing is as holy as HASHEM!'*[1] *All will exalt You, Selah! — You Who forms everything. The God Who opens daily the doors of the gateways of the East, and splits the windows of the firmament,* Who removes the sun from its place and the moon from the site of its dwelling, and Who illuminates all the world and its inhabitants, which He created with the attribute of mercy. He Who illuminates the earth and those who dwell upon it, with compassion; and in His goodness renews daily, perpetually, the work of creation. The King Who was exalted in solitude from before creation, Who is praised, glorified, and extolled since days of old. Eternal God, with Your abundant compassion be compassionate to us — O Master of our power, our rocklike stronghold; O Shield of our salvation, be a stronghold for us. There is no comparison to You,* there is nothing except for You, there is nothing without You, for who is like You? There is no comparison to You, HASHEM, our God, in this world; and there will be nothing except for You, our King, in the life of the World to Come; there will be nothing without You, our Redeemer, in Messianic days; and there will be none like You, our Savior; at the Resuscitation of the Dead.*

(1) *I Samuel* 2:2.

Hirsch, the four statements are:

(a) אֵין כְּעֶרְכֶּךָ — *There is no comparison to You.* Although we have expressed our gratitude for the heavenly bodies and the various forces of the universe, we hasten to affirm that none of them can even be compared to God's power on earth.

(b) וְאֵין זוּלָתֶךָ — *There is nothing except for You.* In the World to Come, even the most beneficial aspects of life in this material world will not exist. In the blissful state of that world, nothing will exist except for God and those whose lives on earth have made them worthy of His spiritual grandeur.

(c) אֶפֶס בִּלְתֶּךָ — *There is nothing without You.* On earth, too, there will be a state of bliss with the coming of the Messiah — but that redemption is impossible without God, despite the earthly factors that will seem to contribute to it.

(d) וּמִי דּוֹמֶה לָּךְ — *For who is like You?* Nothing will so clearly reveal God's absolute mastery as the Resuscitation of the Dead. That is the ultimate redemption, for it will demonstrate that not only slavery and freedom, but even life and death, depend on Him.

ON A WEEKDAY

כֻּלָּם בְּחָכְמָה עָשִׂיתָ, מָלְאָה הָאָרֶץ קִנְיָנֶךָ.[1] הַמֶּלֶךְ הַמְּרוֹמָם לְבַדּוֹ* מֵאָז, הַמְּשֻׁבָּח וְהַמְּפֹאָר וְהַמִּתְנַשֵּׂא מִימוֹת עוֹלָם. אֱלֹהֵי עוֹלָם, בְּרַחֲמֶיךָ הָרַבִּים רַחֵם עָלֵינוּ, אֲדוֹן עֻזֵּנוּ, צוּר מִשְׂגַּבֵּנוּ, מָגֵן יִשְׁעֵנוּ, מִשְׂגָּב בַּעֲדֵנוּ. אֵל בָּרוּךְ* גְּדוֹל דֵּעָה, הֵכִין וּפָעַל

הַמֶּלֶךְ הַמְּרוֹמָם לְבַדּוֹ — *The King Who was exalted in solitude.* Before Creation, God was *exalted in solitude,* because there were no creatures to praise Him *(Etz Yosef).*

אֵל בָּרוּךְ — *The blessed God.* This begins a lyric praise consisting of twenty-two words following the order of the *Aleph-Beis.* As noted at the bottom of the page in the commentary to אֵל

ON THE SABBATH

The following liturgical song is recited responsively in most congregations.
In some congregations, the *chazzan* and congregation sing the stanzas together.

אֵל אָדוֹן* עַל כָּל הַמַּעֲשִׂים, בָּרוּךְ וּמְבֹרָךְ* בְּפִי כָּל נְשָׁמָה,
גָּדְלוֹ וְטוּבוֹ מָלֵא עוֹלָם, דַּעַת וּתְבוּנָה סוֹבְבִים אֹתוֹ.
הַמִּתְגָּאֶה* עַל חַיּוֹת הַקֹּדֶשׁ, וְנֶהְדָּר בְּכָבוֹד עַל הַמֶּרְכָּבָה,
זְכוּת וּמִישׁוֹר לִפְנֵי כִסְאוֹ, חֶסֶד וְרַחֲמִים לִפְנֵי כְבוֹדוֹ.
טוֹבִים מְאוֹרוֹת שֶׁבָּרָא אֱלֹהֵינוּ, יְצָרָם בְּדַעַת בְּבִינָה וּבְהַשְׂכֵּל,
כֹּחַ וּגְבוּרָה נָתַן בָּהֶם, לִהְיוֹת מוֹשְׁלִים בְּקֶרֶב תֵּבֵל.
מְלֵאִים זִיו וּמְפִיקִים נֹגַהּ, נָאֶה זִיוָם בְּכָל הָעוֹלָם,
שְׂמֵחִים בְּצֵאתָם* וְשָׂשִׂים בְּבוֹאָם, עֹשִׂים בְּאֵימָה רְצוֹן קוֹנָם.
פְּאֵר וְכָבוֹד* נוֹתְנִים לִשְׁמוֹ, צָהֳלָה וְרִנָּה לְזֵכֶר מַלְכוּתוֹ,
קָרָא לַשֶּׁמֶשׁ וַיִּזְרַח אוֹר, רָאָה וְהִתְקִין צוּרַת הַלְּבָנָה.*
שֶׁבַח נוֹתְנִים לוֹ כָּל צְבָא מָרוֹם,
תִּפְאֶרֶת וּגְדֻלָּה, שְׂרָפִים וְאוֹפַנִּים וְחַיּוֹת הַקֹּדֶשׁ—

⇐ אֵל אָדוֹן — *God — the Master.* This poetic prayer comprises twenty-two phrases, the initial letters of which form the *Aleph-Beis.* It is parallel to the alphabetical prayer אֵל בָּרוּךְ גְּדוֹל דֵּעָה of the weekday *Shacharis;* but the weekday prayer contains only twenty-two words. The *Vilna Gaon* explains that the lesser holiness of the weekdays is expressed not only in the shorter version, but in the content. There, the praise concentrates on God's greatness as we perceive it in the form of the heavenly bodies. Here, the greater holiness of the Sabbath enables us to perceive more — though clearly not all — of His greatness.

בָּרוּךְ וּמְבֹרָךְ — *The Blessed One — and He is blessed,* i.e., God is the source of all blessing. In addition, His creatures bless Him in their prayers and through their obedience to His will *(Vilna Gaon).*

הַמִּתְגָּאֶה — *He Who exalts Himself.* The *Chayos* are the highest category of angels, and the Chariot [מֶרְכָּבָה] refers to the order of angelic praises of God. Both were seen by Ezekiel (ch. 1) in his *Ma'aseh Merkavah* prophecy. Thus, they represent the highest degree of holiness accessible to human understanding. Nevertheless, God is exalted far above even this.

שְׂמֵחִים בְּצֵאתָם — *Glad as they go forth.* The heavenly bodies are likened to a loyal servant

ON A WEEKDAY

You make them all with wisdom, the world is full of Your possessions.[1] *The King Who was exalted in solitude* before Creation, Who is praised, glorified, and upraised since days of old. Eternal God, with Your abundant compassion be compassionate to us — O Master of our power, our rocklike stronghold, O Shield of our salvation, be a stronghold for us. The blessed God,* Who is great in knowledge, prepared and worked on*

(1) *Psalms* 104:24.

אֲדוֹן, *God — the Master,* which is recited on the Sabbath, this formula of an *Aleph-Beis* acrostic is followed on the Sabbath as well, except that on the Sabbath each letter introduces an entire

ON THE SABBATH

The following liturgical song is recited responsively in most congregations.
In some congregations, the *chazzan* and congregation sing the stanzas together.

אֵל אָדוֹן *God — the Master* over all works;* ב *the Blessed One — and He is blessed* by the mouth of every soul;*
ג *His greatness and goodness fill the world,*
ד *wisdom and insight surround Him.*
ה *He Who exalts Himself* over the holy Chayos*
ו *and is splendrous in glory above the Chariot;*
ז *Merit and fairness are before His throne,*
ח *kindness and mercy are before His glory.*
ט *Good are the luminaries that our God has created,*
י *He has fashioned them with wisdom,*
with insight and discernment;
כ *Strength and power has He granted them,*
ל *to be dominant within the world.*
מ *Filled with luster and radiating brightness,*
נ *their luster is beautiful throughout the world;*
ס *Glad as they go forth* and exultant as they return,*
ע *they do with awe their Creator's will.*
פ *Splendor and glory* they bestow upon His Name,*
צ *jubilation and glad song upon the mention of His reign —*
ק *He called out to the sun and it glowed with light,*
ר *He saw and fashioned the form of the moon.**
ש *All the host above bestows praise on Him,*
ת *splendor and greatness — the Seraphim, Ophanim,*
and holy Chayos —

entrusted with an important mission. He is proud and happy when he sets out, but is even more joyous when he returns to his master.

פְּאֵר וְכָבוֹד — *Splendor and glory.* The exact movements of the heavenly bodies inspire people to praise the One Who created them.

צוּרַת הַלְּבָנָה — *The form of the moon.* With insight, God shaped the phases of the moon so

ON A WEEKDAY

זָהֳרֵי חַמָּה, טוֹב יָצַר כָּבוֹד לִשְׁמוֹ,* מְאוֹרוֹת נָתַן סְבִיבוֹת עֻזּוֹ, פִּנּוֹת צְבָאָיו קְדוֹשִׁים רוֹמְמֵי שַׁדַּי, תָּמִיד מְסַפְּרִים כְּבוֹד אֵל וּקְדֻשָּׁתוֹ. תִּתְבָּרַךְ יהוה אֱלֹהֵינוּ עַל שֶׁבַח מַעֲשֵׂה יָדֶיךָ, וְעַל מְאוֹרֵי אוֹר שֶׁעָשִׂיתָ, יְפָאֲרוּךָ, סֶּלָה.

phrase. See commentary below for the significance of this difference.

As a general rule, the use of the *Aleph-Beis* acrostic in the prayers conveys the idea that we praise God with every available sound and that His greatness is absolutely complete and harmonious. Furthermore, the emphasis on the letters implies our acknowledgment that the Torah, whose words and thoughts are formed with the letters of the *Aleph-Beis*, is the very basis of the continued existence of heaven and earth. In the familiar teaching of the Sages (*Pesachim* 68b) R' Elazar explains: Were it not for the [constant study of] Torah, heaven and earth would not exist, as it is said, *Were it not for My covenant* [i.e., the Torah] *day and night, I would not have established the systematic function of heaven and earth* (*Jeremiah* 33:25). This concept of the letters of the Torah is further alluded to in the verse from *Song of Songs* (1:4) in which Israel allegorically says to God: נָגִילָה וְנִשְׂמְחָה בָּךְ, *we will rejoice and be glad in You.* The word בָּךְ has the numerical value of twenty-two, an allusion to the twenty-two letters of the *Aleph-Beis*, as if

ON THE SABBATH

לָאֵל אֲשֶׁר שָׁבַת* מִכָּל הַמַּעֲשִׂים, בַּיּוֹם הַשְּׁבִיעִי הִתְעַלָּה וְיָשַׁב עַל כִּסֵּא כְבוֹדוֹ, תִּפְאֶרֶת עָטָה לְיוֹם הַמְּנוּחָה, עֹנֶג קָרָא לְיוֹם הַשַּׁבָּת. זֶה שֶׁבַח שֶׁל יוֹם הַשְּׁבִיעִי,* שֶׁבּוֹ שָׁבַת אֵל מִכָּל מְלַאכְתּוֹ. וְיוֹם הַשְּׁבִיעִי מְשַׁבֵּחַ וְאוֹמֵר: מִזְמוֹר שִׁיר לְיוֹם הַשַּׁבָּת, טוֹב לְהוֹדוֹת לַיהוה.[1] לְפִיכָךְ יְפָאֲרוּ* וִיבָרְכוּ לָאֵל כָּל יְצוּרָיו. שֶׁבַח יְקָר וּגְדֻלָּה יִתְּנוּ לָאֵל מֶלֶךְ יוֹצֵר כֹּל, הַמַּנְחִיל מְנוּחָה לְעַמּוֹ יִשְׂרָאֵל בִּקְדֻשָּׁתוֹ בְּיוֹם שַׁבַּת קֹדֶשׁ. שִׁמְךָ יהוה אֱלֹהֵינוּ יִתְקַדַּשׁ, וְזִכְרְךָ מַלְכֵּנוּ יִתְפָּאַר, בַּשָּׁמַיִם מִמַּעַל וְעַל הָאָרֶץ מִתָּחַת. תִּתְבָּרַךְ מוֹשִׁיעֵנוּ עַל שֶׁבַח מַעֲשֵׂה יָדֶיךָ, וְעַל מְאוֹרֵי אוֹר שֶׁעָשִׂיתָ, יְפָאֲרוּךָ, סֶּלָה.

that they would enable Israel to order the calendar as commanded by the Torah.

☙ לָאֵל אֲשֶׁר שָׁבַת — *To the God Who rested.* To Whom are directed the praises mentioned above? — to the God Who rested on the Sabbath from His six days of creation. We say that He 'ascended on the Seventh Day' in the sense that His Presence is no longer obvious on earth. Nevertheless, He left us with the Sabbath as an eternal testimony to His six days of activity and the Sabbath of His rest.

זֶה שֶׁבַח שֶׁל יוֹם הַשְּׁבִיעִי — *This is the praise of the Sabbath Day.* The glory of the Sabbath is not in the leisure it offers, but in its witness to the Creator and its stimulus to man to join it in praising God. In this sense, the very existence of

ON A WEEKDAY

the rays of the sun; the Beneficent One fashioned honor for His Name, emplaced luminaries all around His power; the leaders of His legions, holy ones, exalt the Almighty, constantly relate the honor of God and His sanctity. May You be blessed, HASHEM, our God, beyond the praises of Your handiwork and beyond the bright luminaries that You have made — may they glorify You — Selah!*

to say that we declare our joy in having been worthy to receive the Torah that is formed with the sacred letters (*Abudraham*). Since this portion of the liturgy focuses on the creation and functioning of heaven and earth, it is especially appropriate to insert this allusion to the primacy of Torah study.

According to a tradition cited by *Etz Yosef*, R' Elazar HaKalir, composer of this prayer, communicated with the angel Michael and asked him how the angels formulated their songs of praise. Michael told him that they based their praises on the *Aleph-Beis*. Accordingly, R' Elazar used that formulation in this and his many other *piyutim*. He alluded to the source of this knowledge, Michael, by inserting his name acrostically immediately after these twenty-two words: מְסַפְּרִים כְּבוֹד אֵל, *relate the honor of God.*

יָצַר כָּבוֹד לִשְׁמוֹ — *Fashioned honor for His Name.* The complexity and perfection of creation testifies to the fact that there must be a Creator. Consequently, by creating and emplacing the heavenly bodies, God fashioned the instruments that would bring honor to His Name.

ON THE SABBATH

לָאֵל *To the God Who rested* from all works, Who ascended on the Seventh Day and sat on the Throne of His Glory. With splendor He enwrapped the Day of Contentment — He declared the Sabbath day a delight! This is the praise of the Sabbath Day:* that on it God rested from all His work. And the Seventh Day gives praise saying: 'A psalm, a song for the Sabbath Day. It is good to thank HASHEM ...'[1] Therefore let all that He has fashioned glorify* and bless God. Praise, honor, and greatness let them render to God, the King Who fashioned everything, Who gives a heritage of contentment to His People, Israel, in His holiness on the holy Sabbath Day. May Your Name, HASHEM, our God, be sanctified and may Your remembrance, Our King, be glorified in the heaven above and upon the earth below. May You be blessed, our Savior, beyond the praises of Your handiwork and beyond the brilliant luminaries that You have made — may they glorify You — Selah.*

(1) *Psalms* 92:1-2.

the Sabbath is a praise to God; alternatively, the 'praise' can be understood as the Song of the Day for the Sabbath.

לְפִיכָךְ יְפָאֲרוּ — *Therefore let all ... glorify.* As the prayer goes on to say, the reason that Creation glorifies God is that He has given the Sabbath to Israel. By observing the Sabbath and absorbing its holiness, Israel brings a higher degree of fulfillment and holiness to the entire universe.

ON ALL DAYS CONTINUE HERE:

תִּתְבָּרַךְ צוּרֵנוּ מַלְכֵּנוּ וְגֹאֲלֵנוּ, בּוֹרֵא קְדוֹשִׁים. יִשְׁתַּבַּח שִׁמְךָ לָעַד מַלְכֵּנוּ, יוֹצֵר מְשָׁרְתִים, וַאֲשֶׁר מְשָׁרְתָיו כֻּלָּם עוֹמְדִים בְּרוּם עוֹלָם, וּמַשְׁמִיעִים בְּיִרְאָה יַחַד בְּקוֹל דִּבְרֵי אֱלֹהִים חַיִּים וּמֶלֶךְ עוֹלָם.[1] כֻּלָּם אֲהוּבִים, כֻּלָּם בְּרוּרִים, כֻּלָּם גִּבּוֹרִים, וְכֻלָּם עֹשִׂים בְּאֵימָה וּבְיִרְאָה רְצוֹן קוֹנָם. ❖ וְכֻלָּם פּוֹתְחִים אֶת פִּיהֶם בִּקְדֻשָּׁה וּבְטָהֳרָה, בְּשִׁירָה וּבְזִמְרָה, וּמְבָרְכִים וּמְשַׁבְּחִים וּמְפָאֲרִים וּמַעֲרִיצִים וּמַקְדִּישִׁים וּמַמְלִיכִים —

אֶת שֵׁם הָאֵל הַמֶּלֶךְ הַגָּדוֹל הַגִּבּוֹר וְהַנּוֹרָא קָדוֹשׁ הוּא.[2] ❖ וְכֻלָּם מְקַבְּלִים עֲלֵיהֶם עֹל מַלְכוּת שָׁמַיִם זֶה מִזֶּה, וְנוֹתְנִים רְשׁוּת זֶה לָזֶה, לְהַקְדִּישׁ לְיוֹצְרָם, בְּנַחַת רוּחַ בְּשָׂפָה בְרוּרָה וּבִנְעִימָה. קְדֻשָּׁה כֻּלָּם כְּאֶחָד עוֹנִים וְאוֹמְרִים בְּיִרְאָה:

Congregation recites aloud:

קָדוֹשׁ קָדוֹשׁ קָדוֹשׁ יהוה צְבָאוֹת,
מְלֹא כָל הָאָרֶץ כְּבוֹדוֹ.[3]

Some congregations recite different *piyutim* at this point:
יְדוּעֵי שֵׁם (p. 1120) on the seventh day and לְבַעַל הַתִּפְאֶרֶת (p. 1120) on the eighth day.

SEVENTH DAY

וַיּוֹשַׁע* אֵל אֱמוּנָה אֲיֻמָּה אַחַת,
וַיַּרְא בְּצָרָתָהּ וּמַפְרִיכָהּ יַחַת,
אָז גְּאָלָהּ מִפֶּרֶךְ וְרוּחָהּ נִחַת.
וְצַח נֶצַח נְצָחִים,
וְצַחֲצַח צַחֲצוּחַ מְצַחְצְחִים,
אֻצוּ פּוֹצְחִים וּמְנַצְּחִים
לְמָרוֹם וְקָדוֹשׁ.
עָזִּי דָּאָה כְּבָחוּר עַל יַמָּה,
יהוה הַמְּפֹאָר בְּפִי כָל הַנְּשָׁמָה,
מַרְכְּבוֹת פַּרְעֹה וַחֲיָלוֹתָיו
שִׁקַּע בִּתְהוֹמָה.

EIGHTH DAY

מְחוּלֶלֶת* מְהַלֶּלֶת,* נֶאְדָּרִי עַל מוּקְדָם.
שַׁלְהֶבֶת מְהַבְהֶבֶת מַחֲצֶבֶת כְּמוֹ נֶאְדָּם.
הֲמוֹן עָפִים מִתְרוֹפְפִים, מִכֹּחָהּ בְּמַעֲמָדָם.
רוֹם טִפְחָה וְאַף בְּשִׁיחָה נוֹטֵיהֶם וְתַפְקִידָם.[4]
תִּמְצָא שְׁנוּא טִבְעָה נוּא,* בְּעֵת רָפְתָה יָדָם.
בְּאֵימָה צְבָא רוּמָה, מְשַׁלְּשִׁים
קְדֻשָּׁה בְּמַעֲמָדָם.
יוֹדוּ לַיהוה חַסְדּוֹ וְנִפְלְאוֹתָיו לִבְנֵי אָדָם.[5]
וּמִתְחַדְּשִׁים,[6] וּמִתְאַשְּׁשִׁים,
שׂוֹרְפִים כֹּל בְּלַפִּידָם.
בִּרְעָדוֹת, וּבְקִדּוֹת, מִשְׁתַּחֲוִים לְצוּר הוֹדָם,

☙ וַיּוֹשַׁע — *And ... saved.* In this series of three-lined stanzas, the first word of each line is the first word of the respective verses in the Song at the Sea (*Exodus* 14:30-15:18; the commentaries differ regarding the inclusion of v. 19 as part of the Song or not; the *paytan* agrees with those who view verse 18 as the Song's end). The second words of the respective lines form an alphabetical acrostic. No composer's signature is apparent in this *piyut*.

☙ מְחוּלֶלֶת — *Creation's purpose.* This *piyut* was composed by the otherwise unknown R' Moshe bar Yitzchak, as indicated by the acrostic.

ON ALL DAYS CONTINUE HERE:

תִּתְבָּרַךְ *May You be blessed, our Rock, our King and our Redeemer, Creator of holy ones; may Your Name be praised forever, our King, O Fashioner of ministering angels; all of Whose ministering angels stand at the summit of the universe and proclaim — with awe, together, loudly — the words of the living God and King of the universe.*[1] *They are all beloved; they are all flawless; they are all mighty; they all do the will of their Maker with dread and reverence.* Chazzan– *And they all open their mouth in holiness and purity, in song and hymn — and bless, praise, glorify, revere, sanctify and declare the kingship of —*

אֶת שֵׁם *The Name of God, the great, mighty, and awesome King; holy is He.*[2] Chazzan– *Then they all accept upon themselves the yoke of heavenly sovereignty from one another, and grant permission to one another to sanctify the One Who formed them, with tranquillity, with clear articulation, and with sweetness. All of them as one proclaim His holiness and say with awe:*

Congregation recites aloud:

'Holy, holy, holy is HASHEM, Master of Legions, the whole world is filled with His glory.'[3]

Some congregations recite different *piyutim* at this point: יְדוּעֵי שֵׁם (p. 1120) on the seventh day and לְבַעַל הַתִּפְאֶרֶת (p. 1120) on the eighth day.

SEVENTH DAY	EIGHTH DAY
א *And the trustworthy God saved* the awesome unique nation,*	מ *Creation's purpose* [Israel] praises* the Adorned One['s right hand], even when they are immolated [in sanctification of His Name].*
ב *He saw her troubles and broke her taskmasters.*	ש *It is a searing flame that cleaves with [fiery] redness.*
ג *Then He redeemed her from backbreaking labor and gave her spiritual pleasure.*	ה *The winged [angelic] multitudes at their stations shudder because of its strength.*
The Pure One, He Who is eternally strong,	*It measured the heaven which, along with the heavenly bodies, were stretched out by [God's] word.*[4]
cleansed [Israel] with the cleansing of the clean [angels],	*It found the enemy, drowned the people of No,* when He weakened their hand.*
they [Israel] hied and began to sing to the Exalted and Holy One.	*With awe, the heavenly array recite the trebled Kedushah at their stations.*
ד *My Strong One flew like a youth at the sea,*	*Let them acknowledge to HASHEM His kindness, and His wonders to the children of man.*[5]
ה *He is Hashem, who is glorified by the mouth of all the living,*	*They [the angels] are renewed*[6] *and strengthened, burning everything with their flashes.*
ו *Pharaoh's chariots and his armies drowned in the depths.*	ב *With trembling and prostrations they bow to the glory of their Maker.*

(1) Cf. *Jeremiah* 10:10. (2) Cf. *Deuteronomy* 10:17; *Psalms* 99:3. (3) *Isaiah* 6:3. (4) Cf. *Psalms* 33:6; *Isaiah* 42:5. (5) *Psalms* 107:8,15,21,31. (6) Cf. *Lamentations* 3:23 [see commentary to רְגִיוֹנִים, p. 32].

מְחוּלֶּלֶת מְהַלֶּלֶת — *Creation's purpose [Israel] praises.* According to *Rashi* the first word in the Torah בְּרֵאשִׁית [usually translated *in the beginning*] is a contraction of two words, בִּשְׁבִיל

SEVENTH DAY

תְּהוֹמוֹת זָחֲלוּ וְחָלוּ מֵאֵימָתֶךָ,
יְמִינְךָ חֱיָּלָה בְּכֹחַ הַדְרָתֶךָ,
וּבְרֹב טוּבְךָ נִהַגְתָּ רַעְיָתֶךָ.
וּבְרוּחַ יָהִיר זְעַוְעְתָּ יַם סוּף,
אָמַר כַּבִּיר לְהָמָם בְּשִׁסּוּף,
נָשַׁפְתָּ לְמַעֲנִי בִּימִין חָשׂוּף.
מִי כָמֹכָה מִלְּלוּ בְּמֶלֶל,
נָטִיתָ נֶגְדָּם פִּגְרָם לְחַלֵּל,
נָחִיתָ סְגוּלִים עֻזְּךָ לְמַלֵּל.
שָׁמְעוּ עַמִּים וּבְרֶתֶת רוֹפָפוּ,
אָז פְּלִילֶמוֹ בְּרַעַד זָלְעָפוּ,
תִּפֹּל צְוָחָה עֲלֵיהֶם
וְיַחְדָּו יָסוּפוּ.
תְּבִאֵמוֹ קִרְיַת חָנָה דָוִד,[1]
אֵל רָם וְנִשָּׂא[2] תַּרְבִּיד,
יהוה יִמְלֹךְ שֵׁם תִּפְאַרְתֶּךָ
וְשֵׁם עֲדִינָה תְּאַבִּיד.

EIGHTH DAY

רוֹמְמוֹת אֵל יִשְׂרָאֵל מַעֲרִיבִים בְּסִלּוּדָם.
יוֹם שִׁירָה, וְלֵיל זִמְרָה, בְּגִילָה וּבְכָל מְאֹדָם.
יוֹדוּ לַיהוה חַסְדּוֹ
וְנִפְלְאוֹתָיו לִבְנֵי אָדָם.
צִבְאוֹת הֲדוֹם לְצַח וְאָדֹם,[3]
יַעֲלִיצוּ נִפְלָאִים.
חֵקֶר אַיִן,[4] סְאוֹן סוֹאֵן,[5] וְגַם מַעֲשָׂיו נוֹרָאִים.
קָרוֹב הוּא לְקוֹרְאֶיהוּ,[6] וּמוֹשִׁיעַ לְנִדְכָּאִים.
תּוֹעֵי הֲמוֹן בִּישִׁימוֹן,
עִיר מוֹשָׁב לֹא מוֹצְאִים.[7]
יוֹם שִׁירָה, וְלֵיל זִמְרָה,
בְּגִילָה וּבְכָל מְאֹדָם.
יוֹדוּ לַיהוה חַסְדּוֹ
וְנִפְלְאוֹתָיו לִבְנֵי אָדָם.
יָמִין וּשְׂמֹאל, לְהַלְאָה מוּל,
צַד הוֹלְכִים וּבָאִים.
לֹא יָדְעוּ, מַה יִּרְעוּ, וּרְעֵבִים וְגַם צְמֵאִים.
וּבְחָזְקָה מִמְּצוּקָה, קָרְאוּ לְשׁוֹנֵא גֵאִים.
וּבִמְהֵרָה, הֶעְתִּירָה, נִתְקַבְּלָה פְּרוֹס דָּאִים.
הִשְׂבִּיעָם כָּל יִנְעַם, חֵלֶף יְסַפְּרוּ בְּעוֹדָם.
יוֹדוּ לַיהוה חַסְדּוֹ
וְנִפְלְאוֹתָיו לִבְנֵי אָדָם.

Congregation, followed by the *chazzan,* recites one of these versions, according to its tradition.

וְהָאוֹפַנִּים וְחַיּוֹת הַקֹּדֶשׁ בְּרַעַשׁ גָּדוֹל מִתְנַשְּׂאִים לְעֻמַּת שְׂרָפִים. לְעֻמָּתָם מְשַׁבְּחִים וְאוֹמְרִים:

וְהַחַיּוֹת יְשׁוֹרֵרוּ, וּכְרוּבִים יְפָאֵרוּ, וּשְׂרָפִים יָרֹנּוּ, וְאֶרְאֶלִּים יְבָרֵכוּ. פְּנֵי כָּל חַיָּה וְאוֹפָן וּכְרוּב לְעֻמַּת שְׂרָפִים. לְעֻמָּתָם מְשַׁבְּחִים וְאוֹמְרִים:

Congregation recites aloud:

בָּרוּךְ כְּבוֹד יהוה מִמְּקוֹמוֹ.[8]

(1) *Isaiah* 29:1. (2) Cf. 57:15. (3) Cf. *Song of Songs* 5:10. (4) Cf. *Job* 9:10. (5) Cf. *Isaiah* 9:4 [and see *Rashi* there]. (6) Cf. *Psalms* 145:18. (7) Cf. 107:4. (8) *Ezekiel* 3:12.

רֵאשִׁית, *for the sake of* the things called רֵאשִׁית *beginning.* That is, the world was created for the sake of Israel — which is called רֵאשִׁית תְּבוּאָתֹה, *the beginning of His crops* (*Jeremiah* 2:3) — and Torah — which is called רֵאשִׁית דַּרְכּוֹ, *the beginning of His way* (*Proverbs* 8:22).

נוֹא — *No.* An Egyptian city, identified as Alexandria by Targum to *Ezekiel* 30:14.

SEVENTH DAY	EIGHTH DAY
ז *The depths trembled and feared Your awesomeness,* ח *Your right hand strengthened with the power of Your glory;* ט *and in Your abundant goodness You guided Your companion.* י *With a spirit of grandeur You shook the Sea of Reeds.* כ *The Mighty One said to confound them [the waters] by splitting them in parts.* ל *With Your exposed right hand You caused the wind to blow strongly for me.* מ *'Who is like You?' they verbalized and said.* נ *You stretched out [Your right hand] toward [Egypt] to turn them to corpses.* ס *While You lead Your treasured nation, that it may speak of Your strength.* ע *Peoples heard and weakened with fear.* פ *Then their judges shuddered with trepidation.* צ *Cause screaming to befall them, may they be destroyed as one.* רק *Bring [Israel] to the city where David rested,*[1] *O Exalted and Uplifted God,*[2] *bedeck [Jerusalem].* שת *May Your glorious Name, Hashem, reign; and may the name of the pampered [Edom] be lost.*	ר *The lofty praises of God, Israel sings sweetly with their exultations.* י *Song by day, music at night, in joy with all their strength.* *Let them acknowledge to* HASHEM *His kindness, and His wonders to the children of man.* צ *The armies of the [earth, His] footstool, rejoicingly praise the wonders of Him Who is pure yet ruddy [with vengeance].*[3] ח *[To His works] there is no limit;*[4] *He is always victorious in battle;*[5] *and His deeds are awesome.* ק *He is close to those who call Him;*[6] *and He saves the downtrodden.* *The multitude wandering in the desolate wilderness, finding no inhabited city.*[7] *Song by day, music at night, in joy with all their strength.* *Let them acknowledge to* HASHEM *His kindness, and His wonders to the children of man.* *Right and left, far and near, going and coming to every side.* *They did not know where to graze, and were hungry as well as thirsty.* *With strength [of prayer] from oppressive straits, they called to the One Who hates the arrogant.* *And with haste the prayer was accepted, and they were supplied with quail.* *He satiated them that they need not wander [to seek food], in exchange for their relating [His wonders] all their lives.* *Let them acknowledge to* HASHEM *His kindness, and His wonders to the children of man.*

Congregation, followed by the *chazzan,* recites one of these versions, according to its tradition.

Then the Ofanim and the holy Chayos, with great noise, raise themselves towards the Seraphim. Facing them they give praise saying:

Then the Chayos sing, the Cherubim glorify, the Seraphim rejoice, and the Erelim bless, in the presence of every Chayah, Ofan, and Cherub towards the Seraphim. Facing them they give praise saying:

Congregation recites aloud:

'Blessed is the glory of HASHEM from His place.'[8]

לָאֵל בָּרוּךְ נְעִימוֹת יִתֵּנוּ. לַמֶּלֶךְ אֵל חַי וְקַיָּם, זְמִרוֹת יֹאמֵרוּ, וְתִשְׁבָּחוֹת יַשְׁמִיעוּ. כִּי הוּא לְבַדּוֹ פּוֹעֵל גְּבוּרוֹת, עֹשֶׂה חֲדָשׁוֹת, בַּעַל מִלְחָמוֹת, זוֹרֵעַ צְדָקוֹת, מַצְמִיחַ יְשׁוּעוֹת, בּוֹרֵא רְפוּאוֹת, נוֹרָא תְהִלּוֹת, אֲדוֹן הַנִּפְלָאוֹת. הַמְּחַדֵּשׁ בְּטוּבוֹ בְּכָל יוֹם תָּמִיד מַעֲשֵׂה בְרֵאשִׁית. כָּאָמוּר: לְעֹשֵׂה אוֹרִים גְּדֹלִים, כִּי לְעוֹלָם חַסְדּוֹ.[1] ❖ אוֹר חָדָשׁ עַל צִיּוֹן תָּאִיר, וְנִזְכֶּה כֻלָּנוּ מְהֵרָה לְאוֹרוֹ. בָּרוּךְ אַתָּה יהוה, יוֹצֵר הַמְּאוֹרוֹת. (Cong. – אָמֵן.)

אַהֲבָה רַבָּה אֲהַבְתָּנוּ יהוה אֱלֹהֵינוּ, חֶמְלָה גְדוֹלָה וִיתֵרָה חָמַלְתָּ עָלֵינוּ. אָבִינוּ מַלְכֵּנוּ, בַּעֲבוּר אֲבוֹתֵינוּ שֶׁבָּטְחוּ בְךָ, וַתְּלַמְּדֵם חֻקֵּי חַיִּים, כֵּן תְּחָנֵּנוּ וּתְלַמְּדֵנוּ. אָבִינוּ הָאָב הָרַחֲמָן הַמְּרַחֵם, רַחֵם עָלֵינוּ, וְתֵן בְּלִבֵּנוּ לְהָבִין וּלְהַשְׂכִּיל, לִשְׁמֹעַ לִלְמֹד וּלְלַמֵּד, לִשְׁמֹר וְלַעֲשׂוֹת וּלְקַיֵּם אֶת כָּל דִּבְרֵי תַלְמוּד תּוֹרָתֶךָ בְּאַהֲבָה. וְהָאֵר עֵינֵינוּ בְּתוֹרָתֶךָ, וְדַבֵּק לִבֵּנוּ בְּמִצְוֹתֶיךָ, וְיַחֵד לְבָבֵנוּ לְאַהֲבָה וּלְיִרְאָה אֶת שְׁמֶךָ,[2] וְלֹא נֵבוֹשׁ לְעוֹלָם וָעֶד. כִּי בְשֵׁם קָדְשְׁךָ הַגָּדוֹל וְהַנּוֹרָא בָּטָחְנוּ, נָגִילָה וְנִשְׂמְחָה בִּישׁוּעָתֶךָ. וַהֲבִיאֵנוּ לְשָׁלוֹם מֵאַרְבַּע כַּנְפוֹת הָאָרֶץ, וְתוֹלִיכֵנוּ קוֹמְמִיּוּת לְאַרְצֵנוּ. כִּי אֵל פּוֹעֵל יְשׁוּעוֹת אָתָּה, וּבָנוּ בָחַרְתָּ מִכָּל עַם וְלָשׁוֹן. ❖ וְקֵרַבְתָּנוּ לְשִׁמְךָ הַגָּדוֹל סֶלָה בֶּאֱמֶת, לְהוֹדוֹת לְךָ וּלְיַחֶדְךָ בְּאַהֲבָה. בָּרוּךְ אַתָּה יהוה, הַבּוֹחֵר בְּעַמּוֹ יִשְׂרָאֵל בְּאַהֲבָה. (Cong. – אָמֵן.)

At this point, gather the four *tzitzis* between the fourth and fifth fingers of the left hand. Hold *tzitzis* in this manner throughout the *Shema*.

שמע

Immediately before its recitation concentrate on fulfilling the positive commandment of reciting the *Shema* twice daily. It is important to enunciate each word clearly and not to run words together. For this reason, vertical lines have been placed between two words that are prone to be slurred into one and are not separated by a comma or a hyphen. See *Laws* §40-55.

When praying without a *minyan,* begin with the following three-word formula:

אֵל מֶלֶךְ נֶאֱמָן.

Recite the first verse aloud, with the right hand covering the eyes, and concentrate intently upon accepting God's absolute sovereignty.

שְׁמַע ׀ יִשְׂרָאֵל, יהוה ׀ אֱלֹהֵינוּ, יהוה ׀ אֶחָד:[3]

In an undertone – בָּרוּךְ שֵׁם כְּבוֹד מַלְכוּתוֹ לְעוֹלָם וָעֶד.

While reciting the first paragraph (דברים ו:ה-ט), concentrate on accepting the commandment to love God.

וְאָהַבְתָּ אֵת ׀ יהוה ׀ אֱלֹהֶיךָ, בְּכָל־לְבָבְךָ, וּבְכָל־נַפְשְׁךָ, וּבְכָל־מְאֹדֶךָ: וְהָיוּ הַדְּבָרִים הָאֵלֶּה, אֲשֶׁר ׀ אָנֹכִי מְצַוְּךָ הַיּוֹם,

לָאֵל *To the blessed God they shall offer sweet melodies; to the King, the living and enduring God, they shall sing hymns and proclaim praises. For He alone effects mighty deeds, makes new things, is Master of wars, sows kindnesses, makes salvations flourish, creates cures, is too awesome for praise, is Lord of wonders. In His goodness He renews daily, perpetually, the work of creation. As it is said: '[Give thanks] to Him Who makes the great luminaries, for His kindness endures forever.'*[1] Chazzan— *May You shine a new light on Zion, and may we all speedily merit its light. Blessed are You,* HASHEM, *Who fashions the luminaries.* (Cong.— *Amen*)

אַהֲבָה *With an abundant love have You loved us,* HASHEM, *our God; with exceedingly great pity have You pitied us. Our Father, our King, for the sake of our forefathers who trusted in You and whom You taught the decrees of life, may You be equally gracious to us and teach us. Our Father, the merciful Father, Who acts mercifully, have mercy upon us, instill in our hearts to understand and elucidate, to listen, learn, teach, safeguard, perform, and fulfill all the words of Your Torah's teaching with love. Enlighten our eyes in Your Torah, attach our hearts to Your commandments, and unify our hearts to love and fear Your Name,*[2] *and may we not feel inner shame for all eternity. Because we have trusted in Your great and awesome holy Name, may we exult and rejoice in Your salvation. Bring us in peacefulness from the four corners of the earth and lead us with upright pride to our land. For You effect salvations O God; You have chosen us from among every people and tongue.* Chazzan— *And You have brought us close to Your great Name forever in truth, to offer praiseful thanks to You, and proclaim Your Oneness with love. Blessed are You,* HASHEM, *Who chooses His people Israel with love.* (Cong.— *Amen.*)

At this point, gather the four *tzitzis* between the fourth and fifth fingers of the left hand. Hold *tzitzis* in this manner throughout the *Shema.*

THE SHEMA

Immediately before its recitation, concentrate on fulfilling the positive commandment of reciting the *Shema* twice daily. It is important to enunciate each word clearly and not to run words together. See *Laws* §40-55.

When praying without a *minyan,* begin with the following three-word formula:

God, trustworthy King.

Recite the first verse aloud, with the right hand covering the eyes, and concentrate intently upon accepting God's absolute sovereignty.

Hear, O Israel: HASHEM is our God, HASHEM, the One and Only.[3]

In an undertone— *Blessed is the Name of His glorious kingdom for all eternity.*

While reciting the first paragraph (*Deuteronomy* 6:5-9), concentrate on accepting the commandment to love God.

וְאָהַבְתָּ *You shall love* HASHEM, *your God, with all your heart, with all your soul and with all your resources. Let these matters that*

(1) *Psalms* 136:7. (2) Cf. 86:11. (3) *Deuteronomy* 6:4.

עַל־לְבָבֶֽךָ: וְשִׁנַּנְתָּם לְבָנֶיךָ, וְדִבַּרְתָּ בָּם, בְּשִׁבְתְּךָ בְּבֵיתֶךָ,
וּבְלֶכְתְּךָ בַדֶּרֶךְ, וּֽבְשָׁכְבְּךָ וּבְקוּמֶֽךָ: וּקְשַׁרְתָּם לְאוֹת ׀ עַל־יָדֶךָ,
וְהָיוּ לְטֹטָפֹת בֵּין ׀ עֵינֶֽיךָ: וּכְתַבְתָּם ׀ עַל־מְזֻזוֹת בֵּיתֶךָ, וּבִשְׁעָרֶֽיךָ:

While reciting the second paragraph (דברים יא:יג־כא), concentrate on accepting all the commandments and the concept of reward and punishment.

וְהָיָה, אִם־שָׁמֹעַ תִּשְׁמְעוּ אֶל־מִצְוֹתַי, אֲשֶׁר ׀ אָנֹכִי מְצַוֶּה ׀ אֶתְכֶם
הַיּוֹם, לְאַהֲבָה אֶת־יהוה ׀ אֱלֹהֵיכֶם וּלְעָבְדוֹ, בְּכָל־לְבַבְכֶם,
וּבְכָל־נַפְשְׁכֶם: וְנָתַתִּי מְטַר־אַרְצְכֶם בְּעִתּוֹ, יוֹרֶה וּמַלְקוֹשׁ, וְאָסַפְתָּ
דְגָנֶךָ וְתִירֹשְׁךָ וְיִצְהָרֶךָ: וְנָתַתִּי ׀ עֵשֶׂב ׀ בְּשָׂדְךָ לִבְהֶמְתֶּךָ, וְאָכַלְתָּ
וְשָׂבָֽעְתָּ: הִשָּׁמְרוּ לָכֶם, פֶּן־יִפְתֶּה לְבַבְכֶם, וְסַרְתֶּם וַעֲבַדְתֶּם ׀
אֱלֹהִים ׀ אֲחֵרִים, וְהִשְׁתַּחֲוִיתֶם לָהֶם: וְחָרָה ׀ אַף־יהוה בָּכֶם, וְעָצַר
׀ אֶת־הַשָּׁמַיִם, וְלֹא־יִהְיֶה מָטָר, וְהָאֲדָמָה לֹא תִתֵּן אֶת־יְבוּלָהּ,
וַאֲבַדְתֶּם ׀ מְהֵרָה מֵעַל הָאָרֶץ הַטֹּבָה ׀ אֲשֶׁר ׀ יהוה נֹתֵן לָכֶם:
וְשַׂמְתֶּם ׀ אֶת־דְּבָרַי ׀ אֵלֶּה, עַל־לְבַבְכֶם וְעַל־נַפְשְׁכֶם, וּקְשַׁרְתֶּם ׀
אֹתָם לְאוֹת ׀ עַל־יֶדְכֶם, וְהָיוּ לְטוֹטָפֹת בֵּין ׀ עֵינֵיכֶם: וְלִמַּדְתֶּם ׀
אֹתָם ׀ אֶת־בְּנֵיכֶם, לְדַבֵּר בָּם, בְּשִׁבְתְּךָ בְּבֵיתֶךָ, וּבְלֶכְתְּךָ בַדֶּרֶךְ,
וּֽבְשָׁכְבְּךָ וּבְקוּמֶךָ: וּכְתַבְתָּם ׀ עַל־מְזוּזוֹת בֵּיתֶךָ, וּבִשְׁעָרֶיךָ: לְמַעַן ׀
יִרְבּוּ ׀ יְמֵיכֶם וִימֵי בְנֵיכֶם, עַל הָאֲדָמָה ׀ אֲשֶׁר נִשְׁבַּע ׀ יהוה
לַאֲבֹתֵיכֶם לָתֵת לָהֶם, כִּימֵי הַשָּׁמַיִם ׀ עַל־הָאָרֶץ:

Before reciting the third paragraph (במדבר טו:לז־מא), the *tzitzis,* which have been held in the left hand, are taken in the right hand also. The *tzitzis* are kissed at each mention of the word and at the end of the paragraph, and are passed before the eyes at וּרְאִיתֶם אֹתוֹ.

וַיֹּאמֶר ׀ יהוה ׀ אֶל־מֹשֶׁה לֵּאמֹר: דַּבֵּר ׀ אֶל־בְּנֵי ׀ יִשְׂרָאֵל,
וְאָמַרְתָּ אֲלֵהֶם, וְעָשׂוּ לָהֶם צִיצִת, עַל־כַּנְפֵי בִגְדֵיהֶם
לְדֹרֹתָם, וְנָתְנוּ ׀ עַל־צִיצִת הַכָּנָף, פְּתִיל תְּכֵלֶת: וְהָיָה לָכֶם לְצִיצִת,
וּרְאִיתֶם ׀ אֹתוֹ, וּזְכַרְתֶּם ׀ אֶת־כָּל־מִצְוֹת ׀ יהוה, וַעֲשִׂיתֶם ׀ אֹתָם,
וְלֹא תָתוּרוּ ׀ אַחֲרֵי לְבַבְכֶם וְאַחֲרֵי ׀ עֵינֵיכֶם, אֲשֶׁר־אַתֶּם זֹנִים ׀
אַחֲרֵיהֶם: לְמַעַן תִּזְכְּרוּ, וַעֲשִׂיתֶם ׀ אֶת־כָּל־מִצְוֹתָי, וִהְיִיתֶם קְדֹשִׁים
לֵאלֹהֵיכֶם: אֲנִי יהוה ׀ אֱלֹהֵיכֶם, אֲשֶׁר
הוֹצֵאתִי ׀ אֶתְכֶם ׀ מֵאֶרֶץ מִצְרַיִם, לִהְיוֹת
לָכֶם לֵאלֹהִים, אֲנִי ׀ יהוה ׀ אֱלֹהֵיכֶם: אֱמֶת –

Concentrate on fulfilling the commandment of remembering the Exodus from Egypt.

Although the word אֱמֶת belongs to the next paragraph, it is appended to the conclusion of the previous one, as explained in the commentary on page 50.

–*Chazzan* repeats **יהוה אֱלֹהֵיכֶם אֱמֶת.**

I command you today be upon your heart. Teach them thoroughly to your children and speak of them while you sit in your home, while you walk on the way, when you retire and when you arise. Bind them as a sign upon your arm and let them be tefillin between your eyes. And write them on the doorposts of your house and upon your gates.

While reciting the second paragraph (*Deuteronomy* 11:13-21), concentrate on accepting all the commandments and the concept of reward and punishment.

וְהָיָה *And it will come to pass that if you continually hearken to My commandments that I command you today, to love* HASHEM, *your God, and to serve Him, with all your heart and with all your soul — then I will provide rain for your land in its proper time, the early and late rains, that you may gather in your grain, your wine, and your oil. I will provide grass in your field for your cattle and you will eat and be satisfied. Beware lest your heart be seduced and you turn astray and serve gods of others and bow to them. Then the wrath of* HASHEM *will blaze against you. He will restrain the heaven so there will be no rain and the ground will not yield its produce. And you will swiftly be banished from the goodly land which* HASHEM *gives you. Place these words of Mine upon your heart and upon your soul; bind them for a sign upon your arm and let them be tefillin between your eyes. Teach them to your children, to discuss them, while you sit in your home, while you walk on the way, when you retire and when you arise. And write them on the doorposts of your house and upon your gates. In order to prolong your days and the days of your children upon the ground that* HASHEM *has sworn to your ancestors to give them, like the days of the heaven on the earth.*

Before reciting the third paragraph (*Numbers* 15:37-41), the *tzitzis,* which have been held in the left hand, are taken in the right hand also. The *tzitzis* are kissed at each mention of the word and at the end of the paragraph, and are passed before the eyes at *'that you may see it.'*

וַיֹּאמֶר *And* HASHEM *said to Moses saying: Speak to the Children of Israel and say to them that they are to make themselves tzitzis on the corners of their garments, throughout their generations. And they are to place upon the tzitzis of each corner a thread of techeiles. And it shall constitute tzitzis for you, that you may see it and remember all the commandments of* HASHEM *and perform them; and not explore after your heart and after your eyes after which you stray. So that you may remember and perform all My commandments; and be holy to your God. I am* HASHEM, *your God, Who has removed you from the land of Egypt to be a God to you; I am* HASHEM *your God — it is true —*

Concentrate on fulfilling the commandment of remembering the Exodus from Egypt.

Although the word אֱמֶת, *'it is true,'* belongs to the next paragraph, it is appended to the conclusion of the previous one, as explained in the commentary on page 50.

Chazzan repeats: **HASHEM, your God, is true.**

וְיַצִּיב וְנָכוֹן וְקַיָּם וְיָשָׁר וְנֶאֱמָן וְאָהוּב וְחָבִיב וְנֶחְמָד וְנָעִים וְנוֹרָא וְאַדִּיר וּמְתֻקָּן וּמְקֻבָּל וְטוֹב וְיָפֶה הַדָּבָר הַזֶּה עָלֵינוּ לְעוֹלָם וָעֶד. אֱמֶת אֱלֹהֵי עוֹלָם מַלְכֵּנוּ צוּר יַעֲקֹב, מָגֵן יִשְׁעֵנוּ, לְדֹר וָדֹר הוּא קַיָּם, וּשְׁמוֹ קַיָּם, וְכִסְאוֹ נָכוֹן, וּמַלְכוּתוֹ וֶאֱמוּנָתוֹ לָעַד קַיֶּמֶת. וּדְבָרָיו חָיִים וְקַיָּמִים, נֶאֱמָנִים וְנֶחֱמָדִים לָעַד (kiss the *tzitzis* and release them) וּלְעוֹלְמֵי עוֹלָמִים. ❖ עַל אֲבוֹתֵינוּ וְעָלֵינוּ, עַל בָּנֵינוּ וְעַל דּוֹרוֹתֵינוּ, וְעַל כָּל דּוֹרוֹת זֶרַע יִשְׂרָאֵל עֲבָדֶיךָ.

עַל הָרִאשׁוֹנִים וְעַל הָאַחֲרוֹנִים, דָּבָר טוֹב וְקַיָּם לְעוֹלָם וָעֶד, אֱמֶת וֶאֱמוּנָה חֹק וְלֹא יַעֲבֹר. אֱמֶת שָׁאַתָּה הוּא יהוה אֱלֹהֵינוּ וֵאלֹהֵי אֲבוֹתֵינוּ, ❖ מַלְכֵּנוּ מֶלֶךְ אֲבוֹתֵינוּ, גֹּאֲלֵנוּ גֹּאֵל אֲבוֹתֵינוּ, יוֹצְרֵנוּ צוּר יְשׁוּעָתֵנוּ, פּוֹדֵנוּ וּמַצִּילֵנוּ מֵעוֹלָם שְׁמֶךָ, אֵין אֱלֹהִים זוּלָתֶךָ.

ON BOTH DAYS:

אִי פַּתְרוֹס* בְּעָבְרְךָ רֹאשׁ תַּנִּין* לְהָדֵשׁ, בִּמְלֹאת סִפְּקוֹ שְׁאוֹנוֹ[1] מוֹד בְּגֹדֶשׁ,
בְּאוֹכְלֵי פְסָחִים נִתְקַדַּשְׁתָּ בְּשִׁיר לְחַדֵּשׁ, הַשִּׁיר יִהְיֶה לָכֶם כְּלֵיל הִתְקַדֶּשׁ חָג.[2]
גָּזוּ בְעַזִּים צִבְאוֹת יִשְׁרֵי אֵל, הִפְלֵאתָ לָמוֹ צְדָקָה כְּהַרְרֵי אֵל,[3]
דּוֹלְקֵימוֹ נִשְׁפַּטְתָּ תְּהוֹם רַבָּה לְהִתְאֵל, אָז יָשִׁיר מֹשֶׁה וּבְנֵי יִשְׂרָאֵל.[4]
הֵן עַל הַבְּאֵר* שׁוֹרְרוּ בַּעֲלִיזוֹת, בְּהַשָּׁקַת הָרִים אֶת וָהֵב לַחֲזוֹת,
וּבְסֵפֶר מִלְחֲמוֹת רְשׁוּמָה בְּשִׁטֵּי חֲרוּזוֹת, אָז יָשִׁיר יִשְׂרָאֵל אֶת הַשִּׁירָה הַזֹּאת.[5]
זֹהַר שֶׁמֶשׁ* הִדְמִים דּוֹדִי וּמַאֲמִירִי, וְיָרֵחַ הֶעֱמִיד כְּיוֹם תָּמִים תְּמוּרִי,
חֲקוּקָה בְּסֵפֶר הַיָּשָׁר שִׁירַת מִזְמוֹרִי,
אָז יְדַבֵּר יְהוֹשֻׁעַ לַיהוה בְּיוֹם תֵּת יהוה אֶת הָאֱמֹרִי.[6]
טָפְשׁוּ חָנֵף מָלְכוּ מִמּוֹקְשֵׁי עָם,[7] וְשָׁבוּ וְשִׁחֲרוּ אֵל וְצִוָּה לְהוֹשִׁיעָם,
יָבִין* וּנְגִיד חֲרֹשֶׁת לְמַפָּלָה הִכְנִיעָם, וַתָּשַׁר דְּבוֹרָה וּבָרָק בֶּן אֲבִינֹעַם.[8]

⊰ אִי פַּתְרוֹס — . . . *the Isle of Pasros.* Recited on both the seventh and eighth of Pesach, this *piyut* follows an *aleph-beis* acrostic. The composer's signature appears in the final stanza שִׁמְעוֹן בַּר יִצְחָק חֲזַק, *Shimon son of Yitzchak, may he be strong* (see p. 524). The last line of each stanza is a Scriptural verse that speaks of שִׁירָה, *song.*

רֹאשׁ תַּנִּין — *The sea serpent's head.* Pharaoh is described thus by the prophet (*Ezekiel* 29:3).

עַל הַבְּאֵר — *At the well.* When Israel traversed the Valley of Arnon, God performed a great miracle which saved them from a terrible ambush. The valley was extremely narrow. In fact, people on the cliffs of Moab on one side of Arnon could converse with those on the Emorite cliffs on the other side, as if they were standing next to each other. Moreover, the crags on one side of the rift corresponded exactly to the depressions on the other side, as if there was a single mountain that was ripped apart. Upon hearing of Israel's advance toward Canaan, the Emorites who lived there decided to ambush Israel as it passed through the Valley of Arnon. Unbeknown to Israel, the Emorites hid in the caves and behind the jutting rocks on the mountainside, ready to fire arrows and roll boulders on the unsuspecting nation below. Miraculously, God caused the clifftops to merge forming a tunnel through which Israel passed unharmed. The mountains fit together so exactly that the Emorites were literally crushed to death. When Israel had passed, the cliffs separated again. In order that Israel realize the great salvation that God had wrought for them, the blood and limbs of the Emorites flowed down the mountainside, mixing

וְיַצִּיב *And certain, established and enduring, fair and faithful, beloved and cherished, delightful and pleasant, awesome and powerful, correct and accepted, good and beautiful is this affirmation to us forever and ever. True — the God of the universe is our King; the Rock of Jacob is the Shield of our salvation. From generation to generation He endures and His Name endures and His throne is well established; His sovereignty and faithfulness endure forever. His words are living and enduring, faithful and delightful forever* (kiss the *tzitzis* and release them) *and to all eternity;* Chazzan– *for our forefathers and for us, for our children and for our generations, and for all the generations of Your servant Israel's offspring.*

עַל הָרִאשׁוֹנִים *Upon the earlier and upon the later generations, this affirmation is good and enduring forever. True and faithful, it is an unbreachable decree. It is true that You are HASHEM, our God and the God of our forefathers,* Chazzan– *our King and the King of our forefathers, our Redeemer, the Redeemer of our forefathers; our Molder, the Rock of our salvation; our Liberator and our Rescuer — this has ever been Your Name. There is no God but You.*

ON BOTH DAYS:

א *When You crossed the Isle of Pasros* [Egypt] to smite the sea serpent's head,**
according to his full lustfulness,[1] *You measured the heaping fullness of His sin.*
ב *Among the eaters of the pesach offerings, You were sanctified with a new song;*
May the song come to them [this Pesach]
as on the night they first sanctified the festival.[2]
ג *You cut through the mighty [waters] for the armies of God's upright nation,*
Your righteousness towards them is wondrous as the mighty mountains.[3]
ד *You judged their pursuers, tiring them in the great deeps;*
then Moses and the Children of Israel chose to sing.[4]
ה *At the well* they sang with joy,*
when the mountains kissed, to reveal what He gave them.
ו *And in the Book of Wars it is inscribed in lines of verse,*
'Then Israel chose to sing this song . . .'[5]
ז *My cherished Beloved silenced the sun's shine,**
and the moon stood still an entire day on my behalf.
ח *Etched in the Book of Rectitude is the song of my psalm,*
'Then Joshua decided to speak to HASHEM,
on the day when HASHEM delivered the Emorites.'[6]
ט *They foolishly sinned, so an evil king [Yavin of Canaan] ensnared the nation.*[7]
But they repented and sought God, Who commanded that they be saved.
י *Yavin* and his general [Sisera] from Charoshes were humbled.*
And Devorah sang, and Barak son of Avinoam.[8]

(1) Cf. *Job* 20:22. (2) Cf. *Isaiah* 30:29. (3) Cf. *Psalms* 36:7. (4) *Exodus* 15:1.
(5) *Numbers* 21:17. (6) *Joshua* 10:12. (7) Cf. *Job* 34:30. (8) *Judges* 5:1.

with the waters of the well that accompanied the nation in its journey through the desert. Seeing this, they sang the Song of the Well (see *Numbers* 21:13-20 with *Rashi*).

וְהַר שֶׁמֶשׁ — *The sun's shine.* The story of how Joshua caused the sun to stand still so that his army could defeat the Emorites before they could escape under cover of night is told in the Book of *Joshua* (10:8-14).

יָבִין — *Yavin.* For twenty years the Land was dominated by Yavin king of Canaan and his ruthless general Sisera. Then, after the people

כְּלַל וְהֻקַּם עָל[1] בַּמְּלָכִים לְהִתְאַשְּׁרָה, זְמִירוֹת הַנְּעִים וְהָלַךְ אֹרַח יְשָׁרָה,
לְעֵת זִקְנָתוֹ הוֹסִיף שֶׁבַח לְשׁוֹרְרָה, וַיְדַבֵּר דָּוִד לַיהוה אֶת דִּבְרֵי הַשִּׁירָה.[2]
מָסַר הָאָב לִבְנוֹ צָרְכֵי בִנְיָן לְהַזְבִּיד,[3] לִמְצֹא מָקוֹם נַפְשׁוֹ בְּנֶדֶר הֶעֱבִיד,[4]
נִקְרָא עַל שְׁמוֹ כִּי בְמַשָּׂאוֹ הִכְבִּיד, מִזְמוֹר שִׁיר חֲנֻכַּת הַבַּיִת לְדָוִד.[5]
שְׂמָחוֹת רַבּוּ וְהֻגַּהּ כָּל מַאֲפֵל, בִּיסוֹד הַבַּיִת נִבְצַר בְּחַן וָעֹפֶל,
עוֹלוֹת וּזְבָחִים לָרֹב וּשְׁלָמִים לְהִטָּפֵל,
אָז אָמַר שְׁלֹמֹה, יהוה אָמַר לִשְׁכֹּן בָּעֲרָפֶל.[6]
פֻּגְּרוּ שֵׂעִיר וְעַמּוֹן וּמוֹאָב חֵיל מְדָנַי, בְּמַעֲלֵה הַצִּיץ רְאוֹת יְשׁוּעַת יהוה,[7]
צֹרְבוּ לְמַשְׁחִית אִישׁ בְּרֵעֵהוּ לְעֵינָי,
נִקְהֲלוּ לְעֵמֶק בְּרָכָה, כִּי שָׁם בֵּרְכוּ אֶת יהוה.[8]
קוֹל שִׁירוֹת תֵּשַׁע* שָׁמַעְנוּ בְּמֶרֶץ, וְהָעֲשִׂירִית עוֹד נִשְׁמַע מִכְּנַף הָאָרֶץ,
רָנּוּ שָׁמַיִם וְהָרִיעוּ תַּחְתִּיּוֹת אָרֶץ,[9]
שִׁירוּ לַיהוה שִׁיר חָדָשׁ תְּהִלָּתוֹ מִקְצֵה הָאָרֶץ.[10]
שִׁירוֹת אֵלֶּה לְשׁוֹן שִׁירָה מְיֻסָּדִים,
כִּי תְשׁוּעָתָם כַּיּוֹלֵדָה לָבוֹא צָרוֹת וּמִסְפָּדִים,[11]
תֹּקֶף שִׁיר אַחֲרוֹן כִּזְכָרִים לֹא יוֹלְדִים,
שִׁירוּ לַיהוה שִׁיר חָדָשׁ תְּהִלָּתוֹ בִּקְהַל חֲסִידִים.[12]
שִׁעְבּוּד מַלְכֻיּוֹת* עִקָּר וְנִסִּים מְרֻבִּים, בִּרְאוֹת מַפַּלְתָּם יִשְׂמְחוּ אִיִּים רַבִּים,[13]*
יְצִיאַת חָנֵס קְרוֹא בְּטֶפֶל נֶאֱהָבִים, חַזֵּק קְדֻשָּׁתְךָ כְּעַל זֹאת שִׁבְּחוּ אֲהוּבִים.

עֶזְרַת אֲבוֹתֵינוּ אַתָּה הוּא מֵעוֹלָם, מָגֵן וּמוֹשִׁיעַ לִבְנֵיהֶם אַחֲרֵיהֶם בְּכָל דּוֹר וָדוֹר. בְּרוּם עוֹלָם מוֹשָׁבֶךָ, וּמִשְׁפָּטֶיךָ וְצִדְקָתְךָ עַד אַפְסֵי אָרֶץ. אַשְׁרֵי אִישׁ שֶׁיִּשְׁמַע לְמִצְוֹתֶיךָ, וְתוֹרָתְךָ וּדְבָרְךָ יָשִׂים עַל לִבּוֹ. אֱמֶת אַתָּה הוּא אָדוֹן לְעַמֶּךָ וּמֶלֶךְ גִּבּוֹר לָרִיב רִיבָם. אֱמֶת אַתָּה הוּא רִאשׁוֹן וְאַתָּה הוּא אַחֲרוֹן, וּמִבַּלְעָדֶיךָ אֵין לָנוּ מֶלֶךְ[14] גּוֹאֵל וּמוֹשִׁיעַ. מִמִּצְרַיִם גְּאַלְתָּנוּ יהוה אֱלֹהֵינוּ, וּמִבֵּית עֲבָדִים פְּדִיתָנוּ. כָּל בְּכוֹרֵיהֶם הָרָגְתָּ, וּבְכוֹרְךָ גָּאָלְתָּ, וְיַם סוּף בָּקַעְתָּ, וְזֵדִים טִבַּעְתָּ, וִידִידִים הֶעֱבַרְתָּ, וַיְכַסּוּ מַיִם צָרֵיהֶם, אֶחָד מֵהֶם לֹא נוֹתָר.[15] עַל זֹאת שִׁבְּחוּ אֲהוּבִים וְרוֹמְמוּ אֵל, וְנָתְנוּ יְדִידִים זְמִרוֹת שִׁירוֹת וְתִשְׁבָּחוֹת, בְּרָכוֹת

---

changed their ways and turned to God in prayer, Hashem sent Devorah the prophetess and her husband (see *Radak* to *Judges* 4:4) Barak to defeat the Canaanite oppressors. Their victory is described in *Judges* (chs. 4-5).

שִׁירוֹת תֵּשַׁע — *Nine songs.* The *Targum* at the beginning of *Song of Songs* (as well as various Midrashim) describes nine songs that are recorded in Scriptures and add: 'The tenth song will be sung by the dispersed when they will be removed from their exile.' The *paytan* here also enumerates nine Scriptural songs [although his count does not agree in all cases with *Targum's*]. The Songs: at the Sea, of the Well, of Joshua, of Deborah, of David, of the Inauguration, of Solomon, at Maaleh HaTzitz, and at the Valley of Blessings.

מַלְכֻיּוֹת — *Kingdoms.* Some *machzorim* read גָּלֻיּוֹת, *exiles.* Presumably this is the result of the censor's tampering, for the phrase שִׁעְבּוּד מַלְכוּת עִקָּר וְנִסִּים is part of the composer's signature.

אִיִּים רַבִּים — *The many islands [of civilization].* According to *Rashi* (*Isaiah* 20:6), the Land of

כ *Crowned and of exalted stature,*[1] *most praiseworthy among the kings,*
[David's] song was pleasant and he went on the straight path.
ל *In his senior years he added songs of praise,*
and David spoke to HASHEM *the words of the song.*[2]
מ *The father [David] gave his son [Solomon] all the necessary building materials,*[3]
and obligated himself with a vow to find a place [for the Temple].[4]
נ *It was called by his name for he bore the heavy burden —*
a psalm, a song, for the inauguration of the Temple of David.[5]
ס *Great joy that illuminated all the darkened places,*
accompanied the foundation of the Temple, its fortification and its towers.
ע *Elevation-offerings, other offerings and peace-offerings in abundance*
were brought at one time.
*Then Solomon said, '*HASHEM *said He would reside in the cloud.'*[6]
פ *The hordes of my opponents — Seir, Ammon and Moab — became corpses.*
HASHEM*'s salvation was seen at Maaleh HaTzitz.*[7]
צ *[My enemies were] burnt and destroyed by one another before my eyes.*
They [Israel] gathered in the Valley of Blessing,
[so named] because they blessed HASHEM *there.*[8]
ק *The sound of nine songs** *have we heard with pleasantness.*
The tenth will yet be heard from the ends of the earth.
ר *Sing joyously, O heaven, and shout, O center of the earth.*[9]
Sing to HASHEM *a new song, His praises from the ends of the earth.*[10]
ש *These [nine] songs are sent in the feminine form,*
for their salvations, like a woman in birth, harbinger renewed troubles and eulogies.[11]
ת *But the powerful final song is like males — non-bearing,*
sing to HASHEM *a new song, let His praise be in the congregation of the devout.*[12]
שמעון *[After the final Redemption, the release from] the servitude of the kingdoms**
and its abundant accompanying miracles will be the major theme.
בר *At the sight of their downfall the inhabitants of the many islands [of civilization]**
will be glad.[13]
יצחק *The Exodus from Chaneis [Egypt] will play a secondary role in the songs of the beloved [Israel].*
[Redeem us, thus] strengthening [the realization of] Your holiness, as when the beloved offered praise [at the Sea].

עֶזְרַת *The Helper of our forefathers are You alone, forever, Shield and Savior for their children after them in every generation. At the zenith of the universe is Your dwelling, and Your justice and Your righteousness extend to the ends of the earth. Praiseworthy is the person who obeys Your commandments and takes to his heart Your teaching and Your word. True — You are the Master for Your people and a mighty King to take up their grievance. True — You are the First and You are the Last, and other than You we have no king,*[14] *redeemer, or savior. From Egypt You redeemed us,* HASHEM, *our God, and from the house of slavery You liberated us. All their firstborn You slew, but Your firstborn You redeemed; the Sea of Reeds You split; the wanton sinners You drowned; the dear ones You brought across; and the water covered their foes — not one of them was left.*[15] *For this, the beloved praised and exalted God; the dear ones offered hymns, songs, praises, blessings,*

(1) Cf. *II Samuel* 23:1. (2) 22:1. (3) See *I Chronicles* 28:11-21. (4) See *Psalms* 132:2-5. (5) 30:1. (6) *I Kings* 8:12. (7) See *II Chronicles* 20:16. (8) 20:26. (9) Cf. *Isaiah* 44:23. (10) 42:10. (11) See commentary p. 812. (12) *Psalms* 149:1. (13) *Psalms* 97:1. (14) Cf. *Isaiah* 44:6. (15) *Psalms* 106:11.

וְהוֹדָאוֹת, לְמֶלֶךְ אֵל חַי וְקַיָּם, רָם וְנִשָּׂא, גָּדוֹל וְנוֹרָא, מַשְׁפִּיל גֵּאִים, וּמַגְבִּיהַּ שְׁפָלִים, מוֹצִיא אֲסִירִים, וּפוֹדֶה עֲנָוִים, וְעוֹזֵר דַּלִּים, וְעוֹנֶה לְעַמּוֹ בְּעֵת שַׁוְּעָם אֵלָיו.

Rise for *Shemoneh Esrei*. Some take three steps backward at this point; others do so before צוּר יִשְׂרָאֵל.

❖ תְּהִלּוֹת לְאֵל עֶלְיוֹן, בָּרוּךְ הוּא וּמְבֹרָךְ. מֹשֶׁה וּבְנֵי יִשְׂרָאֵל לְךָ עָנוּ שִׁירָה בְּשִׂמְחָה רַבָּה וְאָמְרוּ כֻלָּם:

מִי כָמֹכָה בָּאֵלִם יהוה, מִי כָּמֹכָה נֶאְדָּר בַּקֹּדֶשׁ, נוֹרָא תְהִלֹּת עֹשֵׂה פֶלֶא.[1]

When the seventh day falls on the Sabbath יוֹם לְיַבָּשָׁה (below) is recited at this point, but the last line (בְּגְלַל אָבוֹת . . .) is omitted.

❖ שִׁירָה חֲדָשָׁה שִׁבְּחוּ גְאוּלִים לְשִׁמְךָ עַל שְׂפַת הַיָּם, יַחַד כֻּלָּם הוֹדוּ וְהִמְלִיכוּ וְאָמְרוּ:

יהוה יִמְלֹךְ לְעֹלָם וָעֶד.[2]

It is forbidden to interrupt or pause between גָּאַל יִשְׂרָאֵל and *Shemoneh Esrei*, even for *Kaddish*, *Kedushah* or *Amen*.

❖ **צוּר** יִשְׂרָאֵל,* קוּמָה בְּעֶזְרַת יִשְׂרָאֵל, וּפְדֵה כִנְאֻמֶךָ יְהוּדָה וְיִשְׂרָאֵל. גֹּאֲלֵנוּ יהוה צְבָאוֹת שְׁמוֹ, קְדוֹשׁ יִשְׂרָאֵל.[3]

ON THE SEVENTH DAY:

יוֹם* לְיַבָּשָׁה* נֶהֶפְכוּ[4] מְצוּלִים,* שִׁירָה חֲדָשָׁה שִׁבְּחוּ גְאוּלִים.
הִטְבַּעְתָּ בְּתַרְמִית רַגְלֵי בַּת עֲנָמִית,* וּפַעֲמֵי שׁוּלַמִּית* יָפוּ בַּנְּעָלִים.[5]
שִׁירָה חֲדָשָׁה שִׁבְּחוּ גְאוּלִים.
וְכָל רוֹאַי יְשׁוּרוּן, בְּבֵית הוֹדִי יְשׁוֹרְרוּן, אֵין כָּאֵל יְשֻׁרוּן,[6]
וְאוֹיְבֵינוּ פְּלִילִים. שִׁירָה חֲדָשָׁה שִׁבְּחוּ גְאוּלִים.
דְּגָלַי כֵּן תָּרִים,* עַל הַנִּשְׁאָרִים, וּתְלַקֵּט נְפוּזָרִים, כִּמְלַקֵּט שִׁבֳּלִים.[7]
שִׁירָה חֲדָשָׁה שִׁבְּחוּ גְאוּלִים.

Israel is called אִי, *an island* [because it is situated on the sea (*Metzudos*)]. According to *Radak* (*Psalms* 97:1), *many islands* refers to the borders of the nations. Accordingly, any land delineated by boundaries may be called an island.

☙ יוֹם — *Today.* The *paytan's* signature in the acrostic reads יְהוּדָה הַלֵּוִי, *Yehudah HaLevi*. [His name is also alluded to in the word יַבָּשָׁה which is the acronym for יְהוּדָה בֶּן שְׁמוּאֵל הַלֵּוִי, *Yehudah son of Shmuel HaLevi*.] Born in Spain about 1080, his greatest contribution to Torah knowledge was *Kuzari*. This philosophical work tells of the King of the Khazars, who sought to determine the true religion by questioning a Christian, a Moslem and a Jewish scholar. In a deep and penetrating analysis, R' Yehudah describes the Jew's dialogue with the Khazar king. The king becomes convinced of the authenticity of Judaism, which he, together with his entire kingdom, embraces as the true religion.

To escape the Moslem persecution in southern Spain, R' Yehudah set out for the north, where he lived in various places until, later in his life, he decided to settle in *Eretz Yisrael*. He is known to have reached Damascus, Syria, but no further documentation of his journey has come down to us. Tradition has it that he finally reached Jerusalem where he fell to the ground in a state of ecstasy. As he was kissing the soil of the Holy City, he was trampled to death by an Arab horseman.

יוֹם לְיַבָּשָׁה — *Today . . . to dry land.* Redemption of Israel from exile is the major theme of this *piyut*. Among its minor themes are: (a) the Exodus, represented by the Splitting of the Sea —

and thanksgivings to the King, the living and enduring God — exalted and uplifted, great and awesome, Who humbles the haughty and lifts the lowly; withdraws the captive, liberates the humble, and helps the poor; Who responds to His people upon their outcry to Him.

Rise for *Shemoneh Esrei.* Some take three steps backward at this point; others do so before צוּר יִשְׂרָאֵל, *'Rock of Israel.'*

Chazzan– *Praises to the Supreme God, the blessed One Who is blessed. Moses and the children of Israel exclaimed a song to You with great joy and they all said:*

'Who is like You among the heavenly powers, HASHEM! Who is like You, mighty in holiness, too awesome for praise, doing wonders.'[1]

When the seventh day falls on the Sabbath יוֹם לְיַבָּשָׁה (below) is recited at this point, but the last line (. . . בְּגְלַל אָבוֹת) is omitted.

Chazzan– *With a new song the redeemed ones praised Your Name at the seashore, all of them in unison gave thanks, acknowledged [Your] sovereignty, and said:*

'HASHEM shall reign for all eternity.'[2]

It is forbidden to interrupt or pause between *'Who redeemed Israel'* and *Shemoneh Esrei,* even for *Kaddish, Kedushah* or *Amen.*

צוּר Chazzan– *Rock of Israel,* arise to the aid of Israel and liberate, as You pledged, Judah and Israel. Our Redeemer — HASHEM, Master of Legions, is His Name — the Holy One of Israel.*[3]

ON THE SEVENTH DAY:

י *Today* the depths* turned to dry land.*[4]* *the redeemed ones sang a new song.*

ה *Because of her deceitfulness, You caused the Anamite* daughter's feet to sink;*
but the footsteps of the wholesome one were beautiful in shoes*[5] —
the redeemed ones sang a new song.

ו *All who see Jeshurun will sing in My Majestic Home:*
'There is none like the God of Jeshurun,'[6] *and our enemies are judged —*
the redeemed ones sang a new song.

ד *May You raise my banners* over the survivors;*
and may You gather the scattered ones as one gathers sheaves[7] —
the redeemed ones sang a new song.

(1) *Exodus* 15:11. (2) 15:18. (3) *Isaiah* 47:4. (4) Cf. *Psalms* 66:6.
(5) Cf. *Song of Songs* 7:1-2. (6) *Deuteronomy* 33:26. (7) Cf. *Isaiah* 17:5.

thus making it appropriate for the seventh day of Pesach, the anniversary of that event; and (b) Israel's fulfillment of *mitzvos,* especially circumcision, which is mentioned in the fifth stanza and alluded to in the seventh. For this reason, some congregations recite this *piyut* every Sabbath (and *Yom Tov*) on which a *bris* is performed. The *piyut* is sung also at the festive meal served in honor of a *bris.*

The first word of this *piyut* is recorded in two versions, יוֹם as our text reads, and יָם, *sea* (based on *Psalms* 66:6), and the first stich is rendered, *[When] the sea [turned] into dry land.* According to *Pri Megadim,* both readings are correct. On the seventh day of Pesach, the anniversary of the Splitting of the Sea, the word יוֹם, *today,* is used; while on other occasions, the proper reading is יָם (*Aishel Avraham* 490:6; 584:7).

מְצוּלִים — *Depths.* Not only the Sea of Reeds, but all concentrations of water split; therefore, the *zemer* uses the plural מְצוּלִים, *depths.*

עֲנָמִית — *Anamite.* Egypt is entitled Anamite because Anamim was a son of Mitzrayim, the progenitor of Egypt (*Genesis* 10:13).

וּפְעָמֵי שׁוּלַמִּית — *But the footsteps of the wholesome one,* i.e., Israel. The beautifully shod footsteps of Israel refers to the loyalty of the Jewish people in going to Jerusalem three times a year for the pilgrimage festivals (*Sotah* 49b).

דְּגָלַי כֵּן תָּרִים — *May You raise my banners.* A prayer that God gather up our scattered survivors

הַבָּאִים עִמְּךָ,* בִּבְרִית חוֹתָמְךָ, וּמִבֶּטֶן לְשִׁמְךָ, הֵמָּה נִמּוֹלִים.[1]
שִׁירָה חֲדָשָׁה שִׁבְּחוּ גְאוּלִים.
הַרְאֵה אוֹתוֹתָם,* לְכָל רוֹאֵי אוֹתָם, וְעַל כַּנְפֵי כְסוּתָם, יַעֲשׂוּ גְּדִילִים.[2]*
שִׁירָה חֲדָשָׁה שִׁבְּחוּ גְאוּלִים.
לְמִי זֹאת* נִרְשֶׁמֶת, הַכֶּר נָא דְּבַר אֱמֶת, לְמִי הַחוֹתֶמֶת, וּלְמִי הַפְּתִילִים.[3]
שִׁירָה חֲדָשָׁה שִׁבְּחוּ גְאוּלִים.
וְשׁוּב שֵׁנִית לְקַדְּשָׁהּ,* וְאַל תּוֹסִיף לְגָרְשָׁהּ, וְהַעֲלֵה אוֹר שִׁמְשָׁהּ,
וְנָסוּ הַצְּלָלִים.[4] שִׁירָה חֲדָשָׁה שִׁבְּחוּ גְאוּלִים.
יְדִידִים רוֹמְמוּךָ, בְּשִׁירָה קִדְּמוּךָ, מִי כָמֹכָה, יהוה בָּאֵלִים.[5]
שִׁירָה חֲדָשָׁה שִׁבְּחוּ גְאוּלִים.

[When the Seventh Day falls on the Sabbath, continue with שִׁירָה חֲדָשָׁה (page 870).

בִּגְלַל אָבוֹת תּוֹשִׁיעַ בָּנִים, וְתָבִיא גְאוּלָה לִבְנֵי בְנֵיהֶם.

ON THE SABBATH

בְּרַח דּוֹדִי[6] אֶל שֶׁאַנָן נָוֶה,[7] וְאִם הֶלְאֵינוּ דֶּרֶךְ הָעֲוֶה,[8]
הִנֵּה לָקִינוּ בְּכָל מַדְוֶה,[9] וְאַתָּה יהוה מָעוֹז וּמִקְוֶה,
עָלֶיךָ כָּל הַיּוֹם נְקַוֶּה,[10] לְגָאֳלֵינוּ וּלְשִׁיתֵנוּ כְּגַן רָוֶה.[11]

בְּרַח דּוֹדִי אֶל מְקוֹם מִקְדָּשֵׁנוּ,[12] וְאִם עֲוֹנוֹת עָבְרוּ רֹאשֵׁנוּ,[13]
הִנֵּה בָאָה בַבַּרְזֶל נַפְשֵׁנוּ,[14] וְאַתָּה יהוה גֹּאֲלֵנוּ קְדוֹשֵׁנוּ,[15]
עָלֶיךָ נִשְׁפֹּךְ שִׂיחַ[16] רַחֲשֵׁנוּ, לְגָאֳלֵנוּ מִמְּעוֹן קָדְשְׁךָ[17] לְהַחְפִּישֵׁנוּ.

בְּרַח דּוֹדִי אֶל עִיר צִדְקֵנוּ,[18] וְאִם לֹא שָׁמַעְנוּ לְקוֹל מַצְדִּיקֵנוּ,
הִנֵּה אֲכָלוּנוּ בְּכָל פֶּה מַדִּיקֵינוּ,[19] וְאַתָּה יהוה שׁוֹפְטֵנוּ מְחֹקְקֵנוּ,[20]
עָלֶיךָ נַשְׁלִיךְ יַהַב חֶלְקֵנוּ,[21] לְגָאֳלֵנוּ בְּהַשְׁקֵט וּבְבִטְחָה לְהַחֲזִיקֵנוּ.[22]

בְּרַח דּוֹדִי אֶל וַעַד הַזְּבוּל, וְאִם עֻלְּךָ שָׁבַרְנוּ בְּלִי סָבוּל,[23]
הִנֵּה לָקִינוּ בְּכָל מִינֵי חִבּוּל, וְאַתָּה יהוה מְשַׂמֵּחַ אָבוּל,[24]
עָלֶיךָ נַסְבִּיר לְהַתִּיר כָּבוּל, לְגָאֳלֵנוּ לְהִתְגַּדֵּל מֵעַל לִגְבוּל.[25]

בְּרַח דּוֹדִי אֶל נִשָּׂא מִגְּבָעוֹת,[26] וְאִם זַדְנוּ בִּפְרֹעַ פְּרָעוֹת,[27]
הִנֵּה הִשִּׂיגוּנוּ צָרוֹת רַבּוֹת וְרָעוֹת,[28] וְאַתָּה יהוה אֵל לְמוֹשָׁעוֹת,[29]
עָלֶיךָ נִשְׁפֹּךְ שִׂיחַ[30] שְׁוָעוֹת, לְגָאֳלֵנוּ וּלְעַטְּרֵנוּ כּוֹבַע יְשׁוּעוֹת.[31]
בִּגְלַל אָבוֹת תּוֹשִׁיעַ בָּנִים, וְתָבִיא גְאֻלָּה לִבְנֵי בְנֵיהֶם.

בָּרוּךְ אַתָּה יהוה, גָּאַל יִשְׂרָאֵל.

(1) Cf. *Isaiah* 46:3. (2) Cf. *Deut.* 22:12. (3) Cf. *Genesis* 38:25. (4) *Song of Songs* 2:17; 4:6. (5) *Exodus* 15:11. (6) *Song of Songs* 8:14. (7) Cf. *Isaiah* 33:20. (8) Cf. *Jeremiah* 3:21. (9) Cf. *Deut.* 7:15; 28:60. (10) Cf. *Psalms* 25:5. (11) Cf. *Isaiah* 58:11; *Jeremiah* 31:11. (12) *Jeremiah* 17:12. (13) Cf. *Psalms* 38:5. (14) Cf. 105:18. (15) Cf. *Isaiah* 47:4; 48:17. (16) Cf. *Psalms* 102:1; 142:3. (17) Cf. *Jeremiah* 25:30. (18) Cf. *Isaiah* 1:21,26. (19) Cf. *Daniel* 7:19. (20) Cf. *Isaiah* 32:22. (21) Cf. *Psalms* 55:23. (22) Cf. *Isaiah* 30:15. (23) Cf. *Jeremiah* 5:5; *Isaiah* 9:3. (24) Cf. *Esther* 9:22. (25) Cf. *Malachi* 1:5. (26) Cf. *Isaiah* 2:2. (27) *Judges* 5:2. (28) *Psalms* 71:20. (29) 68:21. (30) Cf. 102:1. (31) Cf. *Isaiah* 59:17.

wherever they are and bring them together as a farmer collects stalks during the harvest.

הַבָּאִים עִמְּךָ — *Those who come with You.* We approach God with the mark of the covenant sealed into our flesh. From early infancy, almost as soon as he emerges from his mother's womb, a Jewish boy is circumcised. This stanza, which

ה *Those who come with You* into the covenant of Your seal,*
and from the womb they are circumcised[1] for Your Name's sake —
the redeemed ones sang a new song.

ה *Display their signs* to all who see them,*
and on the corners of their garments they will make fringes[2] —*
the redeemed ones sang a new song.

ל *Whose is this [Torah],* inscribed with commandments?*
— Please recognize the truth! Whose is the signet and Whose are the threads?[3] —
the redeemed ones sang a new song.

ו *Betroth her again* and drive her out no more;*
let her sunlight rise and let the shadows flee[4] — the redeemed ones sang a new song.

י *The beloved ones exalt You, with song they come to greet You;*
who is like You, HASHEM, *among the mighty ones[5] —*
the redeemed ones sang a new song.

[When the Seventh Day falls on the Sabbath, continue with *'With a new song . . .'* (page 871).

For the sake of the forefathers may You save the offspring,
and bring redemption to their children's children.

ON THE SABBATH

ש *Flee, my Beloved,[6] to the tranquil abode.[7]*
Though we have grown weary on a perverted path,[8]
behold we have been afflicted with every sort of pain.[9]
You, HASHEM, *are power and hope; for You we hope all the day,[10]*
to redeem us and to make us a fertile garden.[11]

מ *Flee, my Beloved, to the site of our Sanctuary.[12]*
Though sins have overflowed our head,[13]
behold our lives are fettered in an iron exile.[14]
You, HASHEM, *our Redeemer, our Holy One,[15]*
to You we pour out the words[16] of our prayer,
to redeem us — from Your holy abode[17] — and to set us free.

ע *Flee, my Beloved, to our righteous City.[18]*
Though we have not listened to the voice of those [the prophets] who would make us righteous,
behold our foes have devoured and ground us down.[19]
You, HASHEM, *our Judge and Lawgiver,[20] upon You we cast our granted portion,[21]*
to redeem us quietly and to strengthen us in security.[22]

ו *Flee, my Beloved, to the appointed abode.*
Though we have broken Your yoke unwilling to endure it,[23]
behold we have been struck with every manner of assault.
You, HASHEM, *gladden the aggrieved;[24] upon You is our hope to release the chained,*
to redeem us and make us unboundedly great.[25]

נ *Flee, my Beloved, to the most exalted mountain.[26]*
Though we have sinned wantonly in breaching [the faith],[27]
behold we have been overtaken by abundant and evil travails.[28]
You, HASHEM, *God of salvations,[29] upon You we pour our prayerful cries,[30]*
to redeem us and crown us with the cap of salvations.[31]

For the sake of the forefathers may You save the offspring
and bring the redemption to their children's children.

Blessed are You, HASHEM, *Who redeemed Israel.*

calls for God's mercy in the merit of *milah,* is the reason this *zemer* is sung at the circumcision feast.

אוֹתוֹתָם — *Their signs.* The Divine Presence resting upon the Jewish people is the *sign* that they are God's people (see *Deuteronomy* 28:10).

יַעֲשׂוּ גְּדִילִים — *They will make fringes. Tzitzis* are like the insignia of a royal servant.

לְמִי זֹאת — *Whose is this [Torah].* Israel's loyalty to God is plain to *all.* What other nation observes the Torah and has the signet, i.e., the seal of circumcision, and the threads of *tzitzis?*

וְשׁוּב שֵׁנִית לְקַדְּשָׁהּ — *Betroth her again.* May God

שמונה עשרה – עמידה

Take three steps backward, then three steps forward. Remain standing with feet together while reciting *Shemoneh Esrei*. Recite it with quiet devotion and without interruption, verbal or otherwise. Although it should not be audible to others, one must pray loudly enough to hear himself.

אֲדֹנָי שְׂפָתַי תִּפְתָּח, וּפִי יַגִּיד תְּהִלָּתֶךָ.[1]

אבות

Bend the knees at בָּרוּךְ; bow at אַתָּה; straighten up at ה׳.

בָּרוּךְ אַתָּה יהוה אֱלֹהֵינוּ וֵאלֹהֵי אֲבוֹתֵינוּ, אֱלֹהֵי אַבְרָהָם, אֱלֹהֵי יִצְחָק, וֵאלֹהֵי יַעֲקֹב, הָאֵל הַגָּדוֹל הַגִּבּוֹר וְהַנּוֹרָא, אֵל עֶלְיוֹן, גּוֹמֵל חֲסָדִים טוֹבִים וְקוֹנֵה הַכֹּל, וְזוֹכֵר חַסְדֵי אָבוֹת, וּמֵבִיא גוֹאֵל לִבְנֵי בְנֵיהֶם, לְמַעַן שְׁמוֹ בְּאַהֲבָה. מֶלֶךְ עוֹזֵר וּמוֹשִׁיעַ וּמָגֵן.

Bend the knees at בָּרוּךְ; bow at אַתָּה; straighten up at ה׳.

בָּרוּךְ אַתָּה יהוה, מָגֵן אַבְרָהָם.

גבורות

אַתָּה גִּבּוֹר לְעוֹלָם אֲדֹנָי, מְחַיֵּה מֵתִים אַתָּה, רַב לְהוֹשִׁיעַ. מְכַלְכֵּל חַיִּים בְּחֶסֶד, מְחַיֵּה מֵתִים בְּרַחֲמִים רַבִּים, סוֹמֵךְ נוֹפְלִים, וְרוֹפֵא חוֹלִים, וּמַתִּיר אֲסוּרִים, וּמְקַיֵּם אֱמוּנָתוֹ לִישֵׁנֵי עָפָר. מִי כָמוֹךָ בַּעַל גְּבוּרוֹת, וּמִי דּוֹמֶה לָּךְ, מֶלֶךְ מֵמִית וּמְחַיֶּה וּמַצְמִיחַ יְשׁוּעָה. וְנֶאֱמָן אַתָּה לְהַחֲיוֹת מֵתִים. בָּרוּךְ אַתָּה יהוה, מְחַיֵּה הַמֵּתִים.

During the *chazzan's* repetition, *Kedushah* (below) is recited at this point.

קדושה

When reciting *Kedushah,* one must stand with his feet together and avoid any interruptions. One should rise on his toes when saying the words קָדוֹשׁ, קָדוֹשׁ, קָדוֹשׁ; בָּרוּךְ (of בָּרוּךְ כְּבוֹד); and יִמְלֹךְ.

Cong. then *Chazzan* – **נְקַדֵּשׁ** אֶת שִׁמְךָ בָּעוֹלָם, כְּשֵׁם שֶׁמַּקְדִּישִׁים אוֹתוֹ בִּשְׁמֵי מָרוֹם, כַּכָּתוּב עַל יַד נְבִיאֶךָ, וְקָרָא זֶה אֶל זֶה וְאָמַר:

All – קָדוֹשׁ קָדוֹשׁ קָדוֹשׁ יהוה צְבָאוֹת, מְלֹא כָל הָאָרֶץ כְּבוֹדוֹ.[2]

❖ אָז בְּקוֹל רַעַשׁ גָּדוֹל אַדִּיר וְחָזָק מַשְׁמִיעִים קוֹל, מִתְנַשְּׂאִים לְעֻמַּת שְׂרָפִים, לְעֻמָּתָם בָּרוּךְ יֹאמֵרוּ:

All – בָּרוּךְ כְּבוֹד יהוה, מִמְּקוֹמוֹ.[3] ❖ מִמְּקוֹמְךָ מַלְכֵּנוּ תוֹפִיעַ, וְתִמְלֹךְ עָלֵינוּ, כִּי מְחַכִּים אֲנַחְנוּ לָךְ. מָתַי תִּמְלֹךְ בְּצִיּוֹן, בְּקָרוֹב בְּיָמֵינוּ, לְעוֹלָם וָעֶד תִּשְׁכּוֹן. תִּתְגַּדַּל וְתִתְקַדַּשׁ בְּתוֹךְ יְרוּשָׁלַיִם עִירְךָ, לְדוֹר וָדוֹר וּלְנֵצַח נְצָחִים. וְעֵינֵינוּ תִרְאֶינָה מַלְכוּתֶךָ, כַּדָּבָר הָאָמוּר בְּשִׁירֵי עֻזֶּךָ, עַל יְדֵי דָוִד מְשִׁיחַ צִדְקֶךָ:

All – יִמְלֹךְ יהוה לְעוֹלָם, אֱלֹהַיִךְ צִיּוֹן לְדֹר וָדֹר, הַלְלוּיָהּ.[4]

Chazzan continues . . . לְדוֹר וָדוֹר (page 876).

---

renew His ties to Israel by bringing her back to His 'home' and never again exiling her. May He show her the bright sun of redemption and banish the shadows of exile.

SHEMONEH ESREI — AMIDAH

Take three steps backward, then three steps forward. Remain standing with feet together while reciting *Shemoneh Esrei.* Recite it with quiet devotion and without interruption, verbal or otherwise. Although it should not be audible to others, one must pray loudly enough to hear himself.

My Lord, open my lips, that my mouth may declare Your praise.[1]

PATRIARCHS

Bend the knees at *'Blessed'*; bow at *'You'*; straighten up at *'HASHEM.'*

בָּרוּךְ *Blessed are You, HASHEM, our God and the God of our forefathers, God of Abraham, God of Isaac, and God of Jacob; the great, mighty, and awesome God, the supreme God, Who bestows beneficial kindnesses and creates everything, Who recalls the kindnesses of the Patriarchs and brings a Redeemer to their children's children, for His Name's sake, with love. O King, Helper, Savior, and Shield.*

Bend the knees at *'Blessed'*; bow at *'You'*; straighten up at 'HASHEM.'

Blessed are You, HASHEM, Shield of Abraham.

GOD'S MIGHT

אַתָּה *You are eternally mighty, my Lord, the Resuscitator of the dead are You; abundantly able to save. He sustains the living with kindness, resuscitates the dead with abundant mercy, supports the fallen, heals the sick, releases the confined, and maintains His faith to those asleep in the dust. Who is like You, O Master of mighty deeds, and who is comparable to You, O King Who causes death and restores life and makes salvation sprout! And You are faithful to resuscitate the dead. Blessed are You, HASHEM, Who resuscitates the dead.*

During the *chazzan's* repetition, *Kedushah* (below) is recited at this point.

KEDUSHAH

When reciting *Kedushah*, one must stand with his feet together and avoid any interruptions. One should rise on his toes when saying the words *Holy, holy, holy; Blessed is;* and *HASHEM shall reign.*

Cong. then *Chazzan* — **נְקַדֵּשׁ** *We shall sanctify Your Name in this world, just as they sanctify it in heaven above, as it is written by Your prophet, "And one [angel] will call another and say:*

All—*'Holy, holy, holy is HASHEM, Master of Legions, the whole world is filled with His glory.' "*[2] ❖ *Then, with a sound of great noise, mighty and powerful, they make heard a voice, raising themselves toward the seraphim; those facing them say 'Blessed . . .':*

All—*'Blessed is the glory of HASHEM from His place.'*[3] ❖ *From Your place, our King, You will appear and reign over us, for we await You. When will You reign in Zion? Soon, in our days — forever and ever — may You dwell there. May You be exalted and sanctified within Jerusalem, Your city, from generation to generation and for all eternity. May our eyes see Your kingdom, as it is expressed in the songs of Your might, written by David, Your righteous anointed:*

All—*'HASHEM shall reign forever — your God, O Zion — from generation to generation, Halleluyah!'*[4]

Chazzan continues לְדוֹר וָדוֹר, *From generation . . .* (page 876).

(1) *Psalms* 51:17. (2) *Isaiah* 6:3. (3) *Ezekiel* 3:12. (4) *Psalms* 146:10.

קדושת השם

INDIVIDUALS RECITE:

אַתָּה קָדוֹשׁ וְשִׁמְךָ קָדוֹשׁ, וּקְדוֹשִׁים בְּכָל יוֹם יְהַלְלְוּךָ סֶּלָה. בָּרוּךְ אַתָּה יהוה, הָאֵל הַקָּדוֹשׁ.

CHAZZAN RECITES DURING HIS REPETITION:

לְדוֹר וָדוֹר נַגִּיד גָּדְלֶךָ וּלְנֵצַח נְצָחִים קְדֻשָּׁתְךָ נַקְדִּישׁ, וְשִׁבְחֲךָ אֱלֹהֵינוּ מִפִּינוּ לֹא יָמוּשׁ לְעוֹלָם וָעֶד, כִּי אֵל מֶלֶךְ גָּדוֹל וְקָדוֹשׁ אָתָּה. בָּרוּךְ אַתָּה יהוה, הָאֵל הַקָּדוֹשׁ.

קדושת היום

אַתָּה בְחַרְתָּנוּ מִכָּל הָעַמִּים, אָהַבְתָּ אוֹתָנוּ, וְרָצִיתָ בָּנוּ, וְרוֹמַמְתָּנוּ מִכָּל הַלְּשׁוֹנוֹת, וְקִדַּשְׁתָּנוּ בְּמִצְוֹתֶיךָ, וְקֵרַבְתָּנוּ מַלְכֵּנוּ לַעֲבוֹדָתֶךָ, וְשִׁמְךָ הַגָּדוֹל וְהַקָּדוֹשׁ עָלֵינוּ קָרָאתָ.

On the Sabbath add the words in brackets. [If forgotten, see *Laws* §86-90.]

וַתִּתֶּן לָנוּ יהוה אֱלֹהֵינוּ בְּאַהֲבָה [שַׁבָּתוֹת לִמְנוּחָה וּ]מוֹעֲדִים לְשִׂמְחָה חַגִּים וּזְמַנִּים לְשָׂשׂוֹן, אֶת יוֹם [הַשַּׁבָּת הַזֶּה וְאֶת יוֹם] חַג הַמַּצּוֹת הַזֶּה, זְמַן חֵרוּתֵנוּ [בְּאַהֲבָה] מִקְרָא קֹדֶשׁ, זֵכֶר לִיצִיאַת מִצְרָיִם.

During the *chazzan's* repetition, congregation responds אָמֵן as indicated.

אֱלֹהֵינוּ וֵאלֹהֵי אֲבוֹתֵינוּ, יַעֲלֶה, וְיָבֹא, וְיַגִּיעַ, וְיֵרָאֶה, וְיֵרָצֶה, וְיִשָּׁמַע, וְיִפָּקֵד, וְיִזָּכֵר זִכְרוֹנֵנוּ וּפִקְדוֹנֵנוּ, וְזִכְרוֹן אֲבוֹתֵינוּ, וְזִכְרוֹן מָשִׁיחַ בֶּן דָּוִד עַבְדֶּךָ, וְזִכְרוֹן יְרוּשָׁלַיִם עִיר קָדְשֶׁךָ, וְזִכְרוֹן כָּל עַמְּךָ בֵּית יִשְׂרָאֵל לְפָנֶיךָ, לִפְלֵיטָה לְטוֹבָה לְחֵן וּלְחֶסֶד וּלְרַחֲמִים, לְחַיִּים וּלְשָׁלוֹם בְּיוֹם חַג הַמַּצּוֹת הַזֶּה. זָכְרֵנוּ יהוה אֱלֹהֵינוּ בּוֹ לְטוֹבָה (Cong. – אָמֵן), וּפָקְדֵנוּ בוֹ לִבְרָכָה (Cong. – אָמֵן), וְהוֹשִׁיעֵנוּ בוֹ לְחַיִּים (Cong. – אָמֵן). וּבִדְבַר יְשׁוּעָה וְרַחֲמִים, חוּס וְחָנֵּנוּ וְרַחֵם עָלֵינוּ וְהוֹשִׁיעֵנוּ, כִּי אֵלֶיךָ עֵינֵינוּ, כִּי אֵל מֶלֶךְ חַנּוּן וְרַחוּם אָתָּה.[1]

On the Sabbath add the words in brackets. [If forgotten, see *Laws* §86-90.]

וְהַשִּׂיאֵנוּ יהוה אֱלֹהֵינוּ אֶת בִּרְכַּת מוֹעֲדֶיךָ לְחַיִּים וּלְשָׁלוֹם, לְשִׂמְחָה וּלְשָׂשׂוֹן, כַּאֲשֶׁר רָצִיתָ וְאָמַרְתָּ לְבָרְכֵנוּ. [אֱלֹהֵינוּ וֵאלֹהֵי אֲבוֹתֵינוּ רְצֵה בִמְנוּחָתֵנוּ] קַדְּשֵׁנוּ בְּמִצְוֹתֶיךָ וְתֵן חֶלְקֵנוּ בְּתוֹרָתֶךָ, שַׂבְּעֵנוּ מִטּוּבֶךָ וְשַׂמְּחֵנוּ בִּישׁוּעָתֶךָ, וְטַהֵר לִבֵּנוּ לְעָבְדְּךָ בֶּאֱמֶת, וְהַנְחִילֵנוּ יהוה אֱלֹהֵינוּ [בְּאַהֲבָה וּבְרָצוֹן] בְּשִׂמְחָה וּבְשָׂשׂוֹן

(1) Cf. *Nehemiah* 9:31.

HOLINESS OF GOD'S NAME

INDIVIDUALS RECITE:

אַתָּה *You are holy and Your Name is holy, and holy ones praise You every day, forever. Blessed are You,* HASHEM, *the holy God.*

CHAZZAN RECITES DURING HIS REPETITION:

לְדוֹר *From generation to generation we shall relate Your greatness and for infinite eternities we shall proclaim Your holiness. Your praise, our God, shall not leave our mouth forever and ever, for You, O God, are a great and holy King. Blessed are You,* HASHEM, *the holy God.*

SANCTIFICATION OF THE DAY

אַתָּה בְחַרְתָּנוּ *You have chosen us from all the peoples; You loved us and found favor in us; You exalted us above all the tongues and You sanctified us with Your commandments. You drew us close, our King, to Your service and proclaimed Your great and Holy Name upon us.*

On the Sabbath add the words in brackets. [If forgotten, see *Laws* §86-90.]

וַתִּתֶּן לָנוּ *And You gave us,* HASHEM, *our God, with love [Sabbaths for rest], appointed festivals for gladness, Festivals and times for joy, [this day of Sabbath and] this day of the Festival of Matzos, the time of our freedom [with love], a holy convocation, a memorial of the Exodus from Egypt.*

During the *chazzan's* repetition, congregation responds *Amen* as indicated.

אֱלֹהֵינוּ *Our God and God of our forefathers, may there rise, come, reach, be noted, be favored, be heard, be considered, and be remembered — the remembrance and consideration of ourselves; the remembrance of our forefathers; the remembrance of Messiah, son of David, Your servant; the remembrance of Jerusalem, the City of Your Holiness; the remembrance of Your entire people the Family of Israel — before You for deliverance, for goodness, for grace, for kindness, and for compassion, for life, and for peace on this day of the Festival of Matzos. Remember us on it,* HASHEM, *our God, for goodness (*Cong. *– Amen); consider us on it for blessing (*Cong. *– Amen); and help us on it for life (*Cong. *– Amen). In the matter of salvation and compassion, pity, be gracious and compassionate with us and help us, for our eyes are turned to You, because You are God, the gracious and compassionate King.*[1]

On the Sabbath add the words in brackets. [If forgotten, see *Laws* §86-90.]

וְהַשִּׂיאֵנוּ *Bestow upon us, O* HASHEM, *our God, the blessing of Your appointed Festivals for life and for peace, for gladness and for joy, as You desired and promised to bless us. [Our God and the God of our forefathers, may You be pleased with our rest.] Sanctify us with Your commandments and grant us our share in Your Torah; satisfy us from Your goodness and gladden us with Your salvation, and purify our heart to serve You sincerely. And grant us a heritage, O* HASHEM, *our God — [with love and with favor] with gladness and with joy —*

[שַׁבָּת וּ]מוֹעֲדֵי קָדְשֶׁךָ, וְיִשְׂמְחוּ בְךָ יִשְׂרָאֵל מְקַדְּשֵׁי שְׁמֶךָ. בָּרוּךְ אַתָּה יהוה, מְקַדֵּשׁ [הַשַּׁבָּת וְ]יִשְׂרָאֵל וְהַזְּמַנִּים.

עבודה

רְצֵה יהוה אֱלֹהֵינוּ בְּעַמְּךָ יִשְׂרָאֵל וּבִתְפִלָּתָם, וְהָשֵׁב אֶת הָעֲבוֹדָה לִדְבִיר בֵּיתֶךָ. וְאִשֵּׁי יִשְׂרָאֵל וּתְפִלָּתָם בְּאַהֲבָה תְקַבֵּל בְּרָצוֹן, וּתְהִי לְרָצוֹן תָּמִיד עֲבוֹדַת יִשְׂרָאֵל עַמֶּךָ.

וְתֶחֱזֶינָה עֵינֵינוּ בְּשׁוּבְךָ לְצִיּוֹן בְּרַחֲמִים. בָּרוּךְ אַתָּה יהוה, הַמַּחֲזִיר שְׁכִינָתוֹ לְצִיּוֹן.

הודאה

Bow at מוֹדִים; straighten up at ה׳. In his repetition the *chazzan* should recite the entire מודים aloud, while the congregation recites מוֹדִים דְּרַבָּנָן softly.

מוֹדִים אֲנַחְנוּ לָךְ, שָׁאַתָּה הוּא יהוה אֱלֹהֵינוּ וֵאלֹהֵי אֲבוֹתֵינוּ לְעוֹלָם וָעֶד. צוּר חַיֵּינוּ, מָגֵן יִשְׁעֵנוּ אַתָּה הוּא לְדוֹר וָדוֹר. נוֹדֶה לְּךָ וּנְסַפֵּר תְּהִלָּתֶךָ[1] עַל חַיֵּינוּ הַמְּסוּרִים בְּיָדֶךָ, וְעַל נִשְׁמוֹתֵינוּ הַפְּקוּדוֹת לָךְ, וְעַל נִסֶּיךָ שֶׁבְּכָל יוֹם עִמָּנוּ, וְעַל נִפְלְאוֹתֶיךָ וְטוֹבוֹתֶיךָ שֶׁבְּכָל עֵת, עֶרֶב וָבֹקֶר וְצָהֳרָיִם. הַטּוֹב כִּי לֹא כָלוּ רַחֲמֶיךָ, וְהַמְּרַחֵם כִּי לֹא תַמּוּ חֲסָדֶיךָ,[2] מֵעוֹלָם קִוִּינוּ לָךְ.

מודים דרבנן

מוֹדִים אֲנַחְנוּ לָךְ, שָׁאַתָּה הוּא יהוה אֱלֹהֵינוּ וֵאלֹהֵי אֲבוֹתֵינוּ, אֱלֹהֵי כָל בָּשָׂר, יוֹצְרֵנוּ, יוֹצֵר בְּרֵאשִׁית. בְּרָכוֹת וְהוֹדָאוֹת לְשִׁמְךָ הַגָּדוֹל וְהַקָּדוֹשׁ, עַל שֶׁהֶחֱיִיתָנוּ וְקִיַּמְתָּנוּ. כֵּן תְּחַיֵּנוּ וּתְקַיְּמֵנוּ, וְתֶאֱסוֹף גָּלֻיּוֹתֵינוּ לְחַצְרוֹת קָדְשֶׁךָ, לִשְׁמוֹר חֻקֶּיךָ וְלַעֲשׂוֹת רְצוֹנֶךָ, וּלְעָבְדְּךָ בְּלֵבָב שָׁלֵם, עַל שֶׁאֲנַחְנוּ מוֹדִים לָךְ. בָּרוּךְ אֵל הַהוֹדָאוֹת.

וְעַל כֻּלָּם יִתְבָּרַךְ וְיִתְרוֹמַם שִׁמְךָ מַלְכֵּנוּ תָּמִיד לְעוֹלָם וָעֶד.

Bend the knees at בָּרוּךְ; bow at אַתָּה; straighten up at ה׳.

וְכֹל הַחַיִּים יוֹדוּךָ סֶּלָה, וִיהַלְלוּ אֶת שִׁמְךָ בֶּאֱמֶת, הָאֵל יְשׁוּעָתֵנוּ וְעֶזְרָתֵנוּ סֶלָה. בָּרוּךְ אַתָּה יהוה, הַטּוֹב שִׁמְךָ וּלְךָ נָאֶה לְהוֹדוֹת.

[the Sabbath and] the appointed festivals of Your holiness, and may Israel, the sanctifiers of Your Name, rejoice in You. Blessed are You, HASHEM, Who sanctifies [the Sabbath,] Israel and the festive seasons.

TEMPLE SERVICE

רְצֵה *Be favorable, HASHEM, our God, toward Your people Israel and their prayer and restore the service to the Holy of Holies of Your Temple. The fire-offerings of Israel and their prayer accept with love and favor, and may the service of Your people Israel always be favorable to You.*

וְתֶחֱזֶינָה *May our eyes behold Your return to Zion in compassion. Blessed are You, HASHEM, Who restores His Presence to Zion.*

THANKSGIVING [MODIM]

Bow at *'We gratefully thank You'*; straighten up at *'HASHEM.'* In his repetition the *chazzan* should recite the entire *Modim* aloud, while the congregation recites *Modim of the Rabbis* softly.

מוֹדִים *We gratefully thank You, for it is You Who are HASHEM, our God and the God of our forefathers for all eternity; Rock of our lives, Shield of our salvation are You from generation to generation. We shall thank You and relate Your praise[1] — for our lives, which are committed to Your power and for our souls that are entrusted to You; for Your miracles that are with us every day; and for Your wonders and favors in every season — evening, morning, and afternoon. The Beneficent One, for Your compassions were never exhausted, and the Compassionate One, for Your kindnesses never ended[2] — always have we put our hope in You.*

MODIM OF THE RABBIS

מוֹדִים *We gratefully thank You, for it is You Who are HASHEM, our God and the God of our forefathers, the God of all flesh, our Molder, the Molder of the universe. Blessings and thanks are due Your great and holy Name for You have given us life and sustained us. So may You continue to give us life and sustain us and gather our exiles to the Courtyards of Your Sanctuary, to observe Your decrees, to do Your will and to serve You wholeheartedly. [We thank You] for inspiring us to thank You. Blessed is the God of thanksgivings.*

For all these, may Your Name be blessed and exalted, our King, continually forever and ever.

Bend the knees at *'Blessed'*; bow at *'You'*; straighten up at *'HASHEM.'*

Everything alive will gratefully acknowledge You, Selah! and praise Your Name sincerely, O God of our salvation and help, Selah! Blessed are You, HASHEM, Your Name is 'The Beneficent One' and to You it is fitting to give thanks.

(1) Cf. *Psalms* 79:13. (2) Cf. *Lamentations* 3:22.

ברכת כהנים

The *chazzan* recites בִּרְכַּת כֹּהֲנִים during his repetition. He faces right at וְיִשְׁמְרֶךָ; faces left at אֵלֶיךָ וִיחֻנֶּךָּ; faces the Ark for the rest of the blessings.

אֱלֹהֵינוּ, וֵאלֹהֵי אֲבוֹתֵינוּ, בָּרְכֵנוּ בַבְּרָכָה הַמְּשֻׁלֶּשֶׁת בַּתּוֹרָה הַכְּתוּבָה עַל יְדֵי מֹשֶׁה עַבְדֶּךָ, הָאֲמוּרָה מִפִּי אַהֲרֹן וּבָנָיו, כֹּהֲנִים עַם קְדוֹשֶׁךָ, כָּאָמוּר:

יְבָרֶכְךָ יהוה, וְיִשְׁמְרֶךָ. (Cong. – כֵּן יְהִי רָצוֹן.)

יָאֵר יהוה פָּנָיו אֵלֶיךָ וִיחֻנֶּךָּ. (Cong. – כֵּן יְהִי רָצוֹן.)

יִשָּׂא יהוה פָּנָיו אֵלֶיךָ וְיָשֵׂם לְךָ שָׁלוֹם.[1] (Cong. – כֵּן יְהִי רָצוֹן.)

שלום

שִׂים שָׁלוֹם, טוֹבָה, וּבְרָכָה, חֵן, וָחֶסֶד וְרַחֲמִים עָלֵינוּ וְעַל כָּל יִשְׂרָאֵל עַמֶּךָ. בָּרְכֵנוּ אָבִינוּ, כֻּלָּנוּ כְּאֶחָד בְּאוֹר פָּנֶיךָ, כִּי בְאוֹר פָּנֶיךָ נָתַתָּ לָּנוּ, יהוה אֱלֹהֵינוּ, תּוֹרַת חַיִּים וְאַהֲבַת חֶסֶד, וּצְדָקָה, וּבְרָכָה, וְרַחֲמִים, וְחַיִּים, וְשָׁלוֹם. וְטוֹב בְּעֵינֶיךָ לְבָרֵךְ אֶת עַמְּךָ יִשְׂרָאֵל, בְּכָל עֵת וּבְכָל שָׁעָה בִּשְׁלוֹמֶךָ. בָּרוּךְ אַתָּה יהוה, הַמְּבָרֵךְ אֶת עַמּוֹ יִשְׂרָאֵל בַּשָּׁלוֹם.

יִהְיוּ לְרָצוֹן אִמְרֵי פִי וְהֶגְיוֹן לִבִּי לְפָנֶיךָ, יהוה צוּרִי וְגֹאֲלִי.[2]

THE *CHAZZAN'S* REPETITION ENDS HERE; TURN TO PAGE 938. INDIVIDUALS CONTINUE:

אֱלֹהַי, נְצוֹר לְשׁוֹנִי מֵרָע, וּשְׂפָתַי מִדַּבֵּר מִרְמָה,[3] וְלִמְקַלְלַי נַפְשִׁי תִדּוֹם, וְנַפְשִׁי כֶּעָפָר לַכֹּל תִּהְיֶה. פְּתַח לִבִּי בְּתוֹרָתֶךָ, וּבְמִצְוֹתֶיךָ תִּרְדּוֹף נַפְשִׁי. וְכֹל הַחוֹשְׁבִים עָלַי רָעָה, מְהֵרָה הָפֵר עֲצָתָם וְקַלְקֵל מַחֲשַׁבְתָּם. עֲשֵׂה לְמַעַן שְׁמֶךָ, עֲשֵׂה לְמַעַן יְמִינֶךָ, עֲשֵׂה לְמַעַן קְדֻשָּׁתֶךָ, עֲשֵׂה לְמַעַן תּוֹרָתֶךָ. לְמַעַן יֵחָלְצוּן יְדִידֶיךָ, הוֹשִׁיעָה יְמִינְךָ וַעֲנֵנִי.[4]

Some recite verses pertaining to their names here. See page 1143.

יִהְיוּ לְרָצוֹן אִמְרֵי פִי וְהֶגְיוֹן לִבִּי לְפָנֶיךָ, יהוה צוּרִי וְגֹאֲלִי.[2] עֹשֶׂה שָׁלוֹם בִּמְרוֹמָיו, הוּא יַעֲשֶׂה שָׁלוֹם עָלֵינוּ, וְעַל כָּל יִשְׂרָאֵל. וְאִמְרוּ: אָמֵן.

Bow and take three steps back. Bow left and say . . . עֹשֶׂה; bow right and say . . . הוּא יַעֲשֶׂה; bow forward and say . . . וְעַל כָּל אָמֵן.

יְהִי רָצוֹן מִלְּפָנֶיךָ יהוה אֱלֹהֵינוּ וֵאלֹהֵי אֲבוֹתֵינוּ, שֶׁיִּבָּנֶה בֵּית הַמִּקְדָּשׁ בִּמְהֵרָה בְיָמֵינוּ, וְתֵן חֶלְקֵנוּ בְּתוֹרָתֶךָ. וְשָׁם נַעֲבָדְךָ בְּיִרְאָה, כִּימֵי עוֹלָם וּכְשָׁנִים קַדְמוֹנִיּוֹת. וְעָרְבָה לַיהוה מִנְחַת יְהוּדָה וִירוּשָׁלָיִם, כִּימֵי עוֹלָם וּכְשָׁנִים קַדְמוֹנִיּוֹת.[5]

THE INDIVIDUAL'S RECITATION OF *SHEMONEH ESREI* ENDS HERE.

FOR THOSE CONGREGATIONS THAT RECITE *PIYUTIM*, THE *CHAZZAN'S* REPETITION BEGINS:
SEVENTH DAY ON MONDAY, WEDNESDAY, OR THE SABBATH — PAGE 882
SEVENTH DAY ON FRIDAY — PAGE 910
EIGHTH DAY ON SUNDAY, TUESDAY, OR THURSDAY — PAGE 910
EIGHTH DAY ON THE SABBATH — PAGE 882
FOR THOSE CONGREGATIONS THAT DO NOT RECITE *PIYUTIM*,
THE *CHAZZAN'S* REPETITION BEGINS ON PAGE 874

THE PRIESTLY BLESSING

The *chazzan* recites the Priestly Blessing during his repetition.

אֱלֹהֵינוּ *Our God and the God of our forefathers, bless us with the three-verse blessing in the Torah that was written by the hand of Moses, Your servant, that was said by Aaron and his sons, the Kohanim, Your holy people, as it is said:*

May HASHEM *bless you and safeguard you.* (Cong.— *So may it be.*)

May HASHEM *illuminate His countenance for you and be gracious to you.* (Cong.— *So may it be.*)

May HASHEM *turn His countenance to you and establish peace for you.*[1] (Cong.— *So may it be.*)

PEACE

שִׂים *Establish peace, goodness, blessing, graciousness, kindness, and compassion upon us and upon all of Your people Israel. Bless us, our Father, all of us as one, with the light of Your countenance, for with the light of Your countenance You gave us,* HASHEM, *our God, the Torah of life and a love of kindness, righteousness, blessing, compassion, life, and peace. And may it be good in Your eyes to bless Your people Israel at every time and every hour with Your peace. Blessed are You,* HASHEM, *Who blesses His people Israel with peace.*

May the expressions of my mouth and the thoughts of my heart find favor before You, HASHEM, *my Rock and my Redeemer.*[2]

THE *CHAZZAN'S* REPETITION ENDS HERE; TURN TO PAGE 938. INDIVIDUALS CONTINUE:

אֱלֹהַי *My God, guard my tongue from evil and my lips from speaking deceitfully.*[3] *To those who curse me, let my soul be silent; and let my soul be like dust to everyone. Open my heart to Your Torah, then my soul will pursue Your commandments. As for all those who design evil against me, speedily nullify their counsel and disrupt their design. Act for Your Name's sake; act for Your right hand's sake; act for Your sanctity's sake; act for Your Torah's sake. That Your beloved ones may be given rest; let Your right hand save, and respond to me.*[4]

Some recite verses pertaining to their names at this point. See page 1143.

May the expressions of my mouth and the thoughts of my heart find favor before You, HASHEM, *my Rock and my Redeemer.*[2] *He Who makes peace in His heights, may He make peace upon us, and upon all Israel. Now respond: Amen.*

Bow and take three steps back. Bow left and say, *'He Who makes peace . . .'*; bow right and say, *'may He make peace . . .'*; bow forward and say, *'and upon . . . Amen.'*

יְהִי רָצוֹן *May it be Your will,* HASHEM, *our God and the God of our forefathers, that the Holy Temple be rebuilt, speedily in our days. Grant us our share in Your Torah, and may we serve You there with reverence, as in days of old and in former years. Then the offering of Judah and Jerusalem will be pleasing to* HASHEM, *as in days of old and in former years.*[5]

THE INDIVIDUAL'S RECITATION OF *SHEMONEH ESREI* ENDS HERE.

FOR THOSE CONGREGATIONS THAT RECITE *PIYUTIM,* THE *CHAZZAN'S* REPETITION BEGINS:
SEVENTH DAY ON MONDAY, WEDNESDAY, OR THE SABBATH — PAGE 882
SEVENTH DAY ON FRIDAY — PAGE 910
EIGHTH DAY ON SUNDAY, TUESDAY, OR THURSDAY — PAGE 910
EIGHTH DAY ON THE SABBATH — PAGE 882
FOR THOSE CONGREGATIONS THAT DO NOT RECITE *PIYUTIM,*
THE *CHAZZAN'S* REPETITION BEGINS ON PAGE 874

(1) *Numbers* 6:24-26. (2) *Psalms* 19:15. (3) Cf. 34:14. (4) 60:7; 108:7. (5) *Malachi* 3:4.

חזרת הש״ץ לשני ימים האחרונים

FOR THE SEVENTH DAY ON MONDAY, WEDNESDAY, OR THE SABBATH AND FOR THE EIGHTH DAY ON THE SABBATH. ON OTHER DAYS TURN TO PAGE 910.

אֲדֹנָי שְׂפָתַי תִּפְתָּח, וּפִי יַגִּיד תְּהִלָּתֶךָ.[1]

אבות

The *chazzan* bends his knees at בָּרוּךְ; bows at אַתָּה; straightens up at ה׳.

בָּרוּךְ אַתָּה יהוה אֱלֹהֵינוּ וֵאלֹהֵי אֲבוֹתֵינוּ, אֱלֹהֵי אַבְרָהָם, אֱלֹהֵי יִצְחָק, וֵאלֹהֵי יַעֲקֹב, הָאֵל הַגָּדוֹל הַגִּבּוֹר וְהַנּוֹרָא, אֵל עֶלְיוֹן, גּוֹמֵל חֲסָדִים טוֹבִים וְקוֹנֵה הַכֹּל, וְזוֹכֵר חַסְדֵי אָבוֹת, וּמֵבִיא גוֹאֵל לִבְנֵי בְנֵיהֶם, לְמַעַן שְׁמוֹ בְּאַהֲבָה. מֶלֶךְ עוֹזֵר וּמוֹשִׁיעַ וּמָגֵן.

מִסּוֹד* חֲכָמִים וּנְבוֹנִים, וּמִלֶּמֶד דַּעַת מְבִינִים, אֶפְתְּחָה פִּי בְּשִׁיר וּבִרְנָנִים, לְהוֹדוֹת וּלְהַלֵּל פְּנֵי שׁוֹכֵן מְעוֹנִים.

All:

אוֹתוֹתֶיךָ* רָאִינוּ אָז בְּעַיִן, בְּעֲטוֹתְךָ כַּמְּעִיל תִּלְבֹּשֶׁת זַיִן,
גּוֹיִם נֶגְדְּךָ הָיוּ כְאַיִן, דָּחוּ וְנָפְלוּ כְּשִׁכּוֹרֵי יָיִן.
הַנָּאוָה הוֹצֵאתָ מֵאִסּוּר כֶּבֶל, וְשִׁכְמָהּ הוּסַר מֵעִנּוּי סֵבֶל,
זֵד תַּנִּין מְנָאֵץ וּמְנַבֵּל, חָפוּז אַחֲרֶיהָ לְהַשְׁחִית וּלְחַבֵּל.
טָסוּ אֲגַפָּיו כְּנֶשֶׁר לְמַהֵר, יָעֲצוּ אַבִּירָיו בְּחַיִל לְדַהֵר,
כְּסִיל בְּאִוֶּלֶת שָׁנָה לְהִתְיַהֵר, לֹא יָדַע לְהָבִין וּלְהִזָּהֵר.
מַחֲנֵהוּ קִבֵּץ וְכָל יוֹעֲצָיו, נִכְבָּדָיו שָׂרָיו וְגַם מְלִיצָיו,
סָעוּ כְאַחַת בְּהַשָּׁאַת מִפְלָצָיו,* עֲרוּכֵי מִלְחָמָה נוֹסְפוּ נִקְבָּצָיו.
פָּחֲזוּ כַּמַּיִם בְּלִי לְהוֹתִיר, צִבְאוֹת קֹדֶשׁ לִרְדּוֹף וּלְהַכְתִּיר,
קָדוֹשׁ סִבַּבְתָּם דֶּרֶךְ לְהַתְאִיר, רִחַפְתָּם בְּצִלְּךָ וּבְמָגִנְּךָ לְהַסְתִּיר.
שִׁלַּחְתָּ בְּצָרִים חֲרִי וָזַעַם, שָׁמַרְתָּ בְּאֶבְרָתְךָ יְפֵיפִי פַעַם,
❖ תֹּקֶף פְּלָאוֹת הִפְלֵאתָ בְּנֹעַם, תַּנִּין בְּעֵת שִׁלַּח אֶת הָעָם.

This *Machzor* includes those *piyutim* that are commonly recited. A few *piyutim* that are omitted by a vast majority of congregations have been included in an appendix beginning on page 1108. The text will indicate where they may be recited.

חֲזָרַת הַשַּׁ״ץ / CHAZZAN'S REPETITION

On many Festivals *piyutim* are inserted in the *chazzan's* repetition. These *piyutim* [known as *kerovos*] express the mood and theme of the day, and many of them have become highlights of the day's service. Thus, the repetition is truly a communal prayer, for it involves the entire congregation.

מסוד – *Based on the tradition.* Many prominent halachic authorities from medieval times onward have opposed the insertion of *piyutim* into the prayer order, primarily on the grounds that they are an interference with and a change in the words of the prayers as they were set forth by the Sages. Most congregations, though by no means all, follow *Rama* (*Orach Chaim* 68 and 112) who permits the recitation of *piyutim*. To justify our recitation of *piyutim* during the *chazzan's Shemoneh Esrei*, they are prefaced with the formula, מִסּוֹד חֲכָמִים וּנְבוֹנִים, *Based on the tradition of our wise and discerning teachers,* meaning that we dare to interrupt the prayer service only because these *piyutim* were transmitted to us by the wise and discerning teachers of yore, based on the 'foundation' of their great wisdom and piety.

אוֹתוֹתֶיךָ — *Your signs.* As indicated by his

CHAZZAN'S REPETITION FOR THE LAST DAYS

FOR THE SEVENTH DAY ON MONDAY, WEDNESDAY, OR THE SABBATH AND FOR THE EIGHTH DAY ON THE SABBATH. ON OTHER DAYS TURN TO PAGE 910.

My Lord, open my lips, that my mouth may declare Your praise.[1]

PATRIARCHS

The *chazzan* bends his knees at *'Blessed'*; bows at *'You'*; straightens up at *'HASHEM.'*

בָּרוּךְ *Blessed are You, HASHEM, our God and the God of our forefathers, God of Abraham, God of Isaac, and God of Jacob; the great, mighty, and awesome God, the supreme God, Who bestows beneficial kindnesses and creates everything, Who recalls the kindnesses of the Patriarchs and brings a Redeemer to their children's children, for His Name's sake, with love. O King, Helper, Savior, and Shield.*

מִסּוֹד *Based on the tradition* of our wise and discerning teachers, and the teaching derived from the knowledge of the discerning, I open my mouth in song and joyful praise, to give thanks and to offer praise before Him Who dwells in the heavens.*

All:

א *We saw your signs* with our own eyes then,*
ב *when You donned the garb of weaponry like a cloak.*
ג *Nations were like nothing before You,*
ד *they were pushed and fell like those drunk with wine.*
ה *You brought the comely nation out of its fettered imprisonment,*
ו *and removed its shoulder from the burden's pain.*
ז *[Pharaoh] the wanton, blaspheming, obscene sea-serpent,*
ח *sped after her bent on destruction and havoc.*
ט *He flapped his wings with an eagle's swiftness,*
י *for his warriors advised him to give chase with his army.*
כ *The fool in his folly once again grew arrogant,*
ל *he did not know or understand that he should have been wary.*
מ *He assembled his camp and all his advisors,*
נ *his honorable [elders], his princes, and also his spokesmen.*
ס *They traveled as one, with the urging of his idol,**
ע *and he kept adding and gathering [more soldiers] for his battle array.*
פ *Flowing rapidly like water, leaving none behind,*
צ *to pursue and encircle [Israel] the holy hosts.*
ק *But You, O Holy One, scouted a circular path for them.*
ר *Causing them to hover in Your shade, and secreting them behind Your shield.*
ש *You sent fury and wrath against the oppressors,*
ש *You guarded with Your pinion, those who travel the beautiful path.*
ת Chazzan – *With powerful wonder You pleasantly set apart [Israel],*
ת *When the sea-serpent sent forth the nation.*

(1) *Psalms* 51:17.

signature, which appears repeatedly, the *kerovos* of the seventh day were composed by *R' Shimon bar Yitzchak* (see p. 524).

בְּהַשָּׁאַת מִפְלַצְיו— *With the urging of his idol.* When Israel left Egypt, God destroyed all the idols in the land. However, He left one — *Baal Tzafon* — standing. This He did to mislead the Egyptians. Now they would think that Hashem was indeed stronger than the weaker idols, but He was no match for *Baal Tzafon*. Thus they were encouraged to pursue Israel (*Rashi* to *Exodus* 14:2 citing *Mechilta*).

All:

אָזְנַי* שָׁמְעוּ מוֹפְתֵי עִנְיָנֶיךָ, וְנֶצַח בִּרְכָתְךָ יַזְכִּירוּ צְפוּנֶיךָ,
❖ חָפַצְתָּ לִפְסֹחַ וּלְהָגֵן הֲמוֹנֶךָ, קָדוֹשׁ הֵן חֵפֶץ לְגוֹנְנִי בְּמָגִנֶּךָ.

Chazzan bends his knees at בָּרוּךְ; bows at אַתָּה; straightens up at ה'.

בָּרוּךְ אַתָּה יהוה, מָגֵן אַבְרָהָם. (Cong.– אָמֵן.)

גבורות

אַתָּה גִּבּוֹר לְעוֹלָם אֲדֹנָי, מְחַיֵּה מֵתִים אַתָּה, רַב לְהוֹשִׁיעַ. מְכַלְכֵּל חַיִּים בְּחֶסֶד, מְחַיֵּה מֵתִים בְּרַחֲמִים רַבִּים, סוֹמֵךְ נוֹפְלִים, וְרוֹפֵא חוֹלִים, וּמַתִּיר אֲסוּרִים, וּמְקַיֵּם אֱמוּנָתוֹ לִישֵׁנֵי עָפָר. מִי כָמְוֹךָ בַּעַל גְּבוּרוֹת, וּמִי דּוֹמֶה לָּךְ, מֶלֶךְ מֵמִית וּמְחַיֶּה וּמַצְמִיחַ יְשׁוּעָה. וְנֶאֱמָן אַתָּה לְהַחֲיוֹת מֵתִים.

All:

תִּרְגַּלְתָּ עֲמוּסִים מִמִּצְרַיִם בְּצֵאתָם,
שָׁרִים כַּחוֹלְלִים וּמְבָרְכִים בְּמַקְהֵלוֹתָם,
רוֹדְפֵיהֶם בִּמְצוֹלוֹת יָם הֶאֱבַדְתָּם, קְנוּיֶיךָ קַהְתָּ עַל זְרוֹעוֹתָם.
צוֹעֲנִים אֲשֶׁר נֶאֶסְפוּ לַמִּלְחָמָה, פִּגְרֵיהֶם הֲמַמְתָּ וְנִגְרְפוּ הַיָּמָּה,
עֶשֶׂר מַכּוֹת הֻכּוּ בְּמִצְרַיְמָה, סָפוּ בְּאַחַת עֶשֶׂר בְּיָד הָרָמָה.
נָבְקָה רוּחָם וְנִבְלְעָה עֲצָתָם,[1] מֶסֶךְ עִוְעִים נִמְסְכוּ לְהִתְעוֹתָם,[2]
לִבָּם נָמַס וְנָמַקּוּ גְוִיָּתָם, כָּלוּ בַּבֶּהָלוֹת הֲמוֹן שְׁאֵרִיתָם.
יָזְמוּ לִרְדּוֹף וּלְהָסִיר כֶּתֶר, טְרַח עֲבוֹדָה וְנִצּוּל חֶתֶר,
חָזְקָה לְהוֹסִיף שְׁבוּעַת בֶּתֶר, וְזָהֲבֵי תוֹרִים וּנְקֻדַּת יֶתֶר.[3]
וְטֶרֶם הַגָּעַת עִתּוֹתֵי דוֹדִים,*[4] הָפְכוּ בְּקֶרֶב אֶפְרָתִים יְדִידִים,[5]
דִּגְלָם כְּחָפַז גְּאֻלָּתָם לְהַקְדִּים, גְּדָעוּם אַנְשֵׁי גַת הַנּוֹלָדִים.[6]
בַּעֲבוּר זֹאת הֵסַבּוּ מִדֶּרֶךְ,[7] בְּמַפַּלְתָּם מַרְאוֹת לְיִרְאָם בְּמֹרֶךְ,
❖ אִמַּצְתָּ וְחִזַּקְתָּ כּוֹשְׁלֵי בֶרֶךְ, אֲשׁוּרֵינוּ כּוֹנַנְתָּ בַּהֲסִבַּת דֶּרֶךְ.

All:

אֲשׁוּרַי שָׁמַרְתָּ עֵקֶב צִדְקוֹתֶיךָ, וְנֹגַהּ כָּאוֹר פֵּאַרְתָּנוּ בְּאַהֲבָתֶךָ,
❖ בַּעֲבוּר אוֹהֲבֶיךָ שׁוֹמְרֵי בְרִיתֶךָ, תִּשְׁמְרֵנוּ וּתְחַיֵּנוּ בְּטַל תְּחִיָּתֶךָ.

Chazzan:

בָּרוּךְ אַתָּה יהוה, מְחַיֵּה הַמֵּתִים. (Cong.– אָמֵן.)

(1) Cf. *Isaiah* 19:3. (2) Cf. 19:14. (3) Cf. *Song of Songs* 1:11. (4) Cf. *Ezekiel* 16:8. (5) Cf. *Psalms* 78:9. (6) Cf. *I Chronicles* 7:21. (7) Cf. *Exodus* 13:17.

אָזְנַי — *My ears.* This final stanza contains the *paytan's* signature: שִׁמְעוֹן בַּר יִצְחָק, *Shimon son of Yitzchak.*

וְטֶרֶם הַגָּעַת עִתּוֹתֵי דוֹדִים — *And yet before the time of Divine love came [to bring redemption].* The Ephraimites premature breakout from Egypt and the disastrous consequences are discussed in the commentary to *Zavad and Sushelach* on page 911.

All:

My ears have heard about Your wonders,*
and eternally will those hidden [in Your Clouds of Glory] recall Your blessing.
Chazzan — *As You desired to pity and protect Your multitude,*
O Holy One, so may You desire to protect me with Your shield.

Chazzan bends his knees at 'Blessed'; bows at 'You'; straightens up at 'HASHEM.'

Blessed are You, HASHEM, Shield of Abraham. (Cong.—*Amen.*)

GOD'S MIGHT

אַתָּה *You are eternally mighty, my Lord, the Resuscitator of the dead are You; abundantly able to save. He sustains the living with kindness, resuscitates the dead with abundant mercy, supports the fallen, heals the sick, releases the confined, and maintains His faith to those asleep in the dust. Who is like You, O Master of mighty deeds, and who is comparable to You, O King Who causes death and restores life and makes salvation sprout! And You are faithful to resuscitate the dead.*

All:

ת *You led the borne nation from Egypt when they went forth,*
ש *singing like the flutists and blessing in their assemblages.*
ר *You destroyed their pursuers in the depths of the sea,*
ק *but Your acquired nation You took by their arms.*
צ *The Zoanite [Egyptians] who gathered for battle,*
פ *You confounded their bodies and they were shoveled into the sea.*
ע *They were smitten with ten plagues in Egypt,*
ס *their end came with the eleventh, [when they were drowned] by a great hand.*
נ *Their spirit flagged and their plans were swallowed up,*[1]
מ *He covered them with a blanket of madness, to lead them astray.*[2]
ל *Their hearts melted and their bodies disintegrated,*
כ *the remnant of their multitude was wiped out in a frenzy.*
י *They wanted to give chase and to remove the crown [of freedom from Israel],*
ט *[and place upon them] the duties of labor,*
and to retrieve [what Israel borrowed from] their hiding places.
ח *But the oath at the Covenant Between the Parts was stronger [than them] and increased [their wealth],*
ז *with bejeweled golden circlets.*[3]
ו *And yet before the time of Divine love*[4] *came [to bring redemption],**
ה *the beloved Ephraimites turned to war.*[5]
ד *When they hastened to their flag to bring their redemption prematurely,*
ג *they were cut down by the natives, the men of Gath.*[6]
ב *Because of this [when Israel left Egypt] they detoured from the [direct] road,*[7]
ב *that they not be discouraged by seeing the [Ephraimites'] downfall.*
א Chazzan — *You encouraged and strengthened those weak of knee,*
א *You prepared our footsteps by leading us on a roundabout route.*

All:

You guarded my footsteps, thanks to Your righteousness,
You glorified us with great illuminating light.
Chazzan — *For the sake of those who love You, those who observe Your covenant,*
Protect us and invigorate us with Your life-giving dew.

Chazzan:

Blessed are You, HASHEM, Who resuscitates the dead. (Cong.—*Amen.*)

All:

שִׁבְטֵי יָהּ הוֹצֵאתָ לְפִדְיוֹם, שְׁלֵמִים כַּצָּהֳרַיִם בְּעֶצֶם הַיּוֹם,
שַׁדַּי כְּמוֹ כֵן הָחִישׁ בְּצִבְיוֹן, שְׁנַת שִׁלּוּמִים לְרִיב צִיּוֹן.[1]
מִגַּרְתָּ וְנֵאַרְתָּ שֵׁבֶט הָרֶשַׁע, מַכְבִּיד אָזְנָיו וְעֵינָיו הָשַׁע,[2]
מַהֲלוּמוֹת וּכַחְתָּ לְגֵו נִפְשַׁע, מָחַצְתָּ רֹאשׁ מִבֵּית רָשָׁע.[3]
עוֹרִי עוֹרִי זְרוֹעַ יַד הַגְּדוֹלָה, עֲדִינָה[4] תִמְחַץ וְשִׁיתָהּ כָּלָה,
עֶרְיָה תֵעוֹר מֵאֱנוֹשׁ לְחַלְּלָהּ, עָרוֹת יְסוֹד עַד צַוָּאר סֶלָה.[3]
וּבְצֵאתְךָ לְיֶשַׁע בְּעֹז אָזוּר, וְצֹאן יָדְךָ בַּעֲדִי נָזוּר,
וְעוֹיְנִים נִפְרְדוּ כְּאֵפֶר פָּזוּר, וְכָשַׁל עוֹזֵר וְנָפַל עָזוּר.[5]
נָאוֹר בִּרְאוֹתְךָ בְּדָם מִתְבּוֹסֵס,[6] נָגַפְתָּ פּוֹרְכִים פְּרָיִם לְקוֹסֵס,
נֶפֶשׁ וּבָשָׂר כִּמְסוֹס נוֹסֵס,[7] נָתַתָּ לִירֵאֶיךָ נֵס לְהִתְנוֹסֵס.[8]
בְּיִטָּה וּמַהֵר שְׁנַת גְּאוּלִים, בַּגֵּד בּוֹגְדִים וְחַלֵּף אֱלִילִים,
בְּטוֹפְלֵי שֶׁקֶר הַפֵּל חֲלָלִים, בְּיוֹם הֶרֶג רַב בִּנְפוֹל מִגְדָּלִים.[9]
רַחֵם וַחֲמֹל בֵּן יַקִּיר,[10] רַוֵּה נֶפֶשׁ שׁוֹקֵקָה לְהָקִיר,
רְאֵה כִּי גָבְרָה יַד הַמַּדְקִיר, רוּחַ עָרִיצִים כְּזֶרֶם קִיר.[11]
יוֹם יוֹם נְצַפֶּה גְאֻלָּתֵנוּ, יָגַעְנוּ בְקָרְאֵנוּ נִחַר גְּרוֹנֵנוּ,[12]
יָד אָזְלָה וַתַּשׁ כֹּחֵנוּ, יהוה חָנֵּנוּ לְךָ קִוִּינוּ.[13]
צֹאנְךָ פְּקֹד וְהָשֵׁב תְּפוּצָתוֹ, צְפֵה כִּי שֻׁדְּדָה מַרְעִיתוֹ,[14]
צַמֵּת עוֹיֵן בָּתָה לַהֲשִׁיתוֹ, צִיצַת נוֹבֵל צְבִי תִפְאַרְתּוֹ.[15]
חֻפְּשׂוּ עִם מִפֶּרֶךְ בְּכֹסֶף, חֲשׁוּקֵי חֶמֶד זָהָב וָכֶסֶף,
חֵרוּת הַמְצִיא וְהַשְׁמִיעֵנוּ בְּחֹסֶף,
חִנָּם נִמְכַּרְתֶּם תִּגָּאֵלוּ וְלֹא בְכָסֶף.[16]
קְהִלּוֹת יַעֲקֹב בְּשֵׁם יִקְרָאוּךָ,
קִוִּינוּ לוֹ לָז לְלָז יַרְאוּךָ,[17]
❖ קְדֻשָּׁתְךָ יַעֲרִיצוּ וּבְרוֹן יְנַשְּׂאוּךָ,
קִרְיַת גּוֹיִם עָרִיצִים יִירָאוּךָ.[18]

Congregation aloud, then *chazzan:*

יִמְלֹךְ יהוה לְעוֹלָם, אֱלֹהַיִךְ צִיּוֹן, לְדֹר וָדֹר, הַלְלוּיָהּ.[19]
וְאַתָּה קָדוֹשׁ יוֹשֵׁב תְּהִלּוֹת יִשְׂרָאֵל,[20] אֵל נָא.

(1) *Isaiah* 34:8. (2) Cf. 6:10. (3) *Habakkuk* 3:13. (4) See *Isaiah* 47:8 with commentaries. (5) 31:3. (6) Cf. *Ezekiel* 16:6. (7) Cf. *Isaiah* 10:18. (8) *Psalms* 60:6. (9) *Isaiah* 30:25. (10) Cf. *Jeremiah* 31:19. (11) *Isaiah* 25:4. (12) Cf. *Psalms* 69:4. (13) *Isaiah* 33:2. (14) Cf. *Jeremiah* 25:36. (15) Cf. *Isaiah* 28:1. (16) Cf. 52:3. (17) See commentary, p. 811. (18) *Isaiah* 25:3. (19) *Psalms* 146:10. (20) 22:4.

All:

ש *You brought forth God's Tribes for redemption,*
ש *they were wholesome and bright like the middle of the day.*
ש *O Almighty, as then, so may You hasten Your will,*
ש *this year to recompense those who aggrieve Zion.*[1]
מ *You cast down and destroyed the scepter of the wicked,*
מ *You hardened his ear and blocked his eyes,*[2]
מ *You punished the sinner's body, smiting it with plagues.*
מ *You smashed the head of the evil house.*[3]
ע *Wake up! Wake up! O arm of the great hand.*
ע *Smash the pampered nation*[4] *and put an end to it,*
ע *for it is bare [of mitzvos]; therefore arouse [Your power] to erase their memories,*
ע *reveal [their total worthlessness] from foot to neck, Selah.*[3]
ו *When [in Egypt] You went forth to save, girded with might,*
ו *Your hand adorned Your flock with crowns.*
ו *The hated ones were separated, like scattered ashes,*
ו *the guardian angel [of Egypt] stumbled and those it guarded fell.*[5]
נ *O Illuminating One, when You saw them wallowing in blood,*[6]
נ *You plagued the taskmasters, to destroy their posterity.*
נ *While You caused their soul and flesh to disintegrate and melt,*[7]
נ *You granted miracles to elevate those who fear You.*[8]
ב *O look and hasten the year of redemptions,*
ב *destroy the rebellious and put an end to idolatry.*
ב *Make those engaged in falsehood fall as corpses,*
ב *on the day of the great slaughter when the towers fall.*[9]
ר *Pity and be compassionate with the precious son,*[10]
ר *satisfy the soul that thirsts for serenity.*
ר *See how the oppressor's hand has overwhelmed,*
ר *for the [ill] wind of the strong [causes destruction],*
like the water flowing down a wall [undermines the wall].[11]
י *Each day we hope for our Redemption*
י *We are wearied by our crying; our throats are parched.*[12]
י *Our power is gone; our strength is sapped;*
י *HASHEM, be gracious to us; to You do we hope.*[13]
צ *Recall Your flock and return its dispersion.*
צ *Observe how its pasturage [Jerusalem] has been looted.*[14]
צ *Cut down the enemy, destroy him and lay him waste.*
צ *let his desirable splendor become a wilted blossom.*[15]
ח *The people were freed from servitude with favor,*
ח *girded with desirable gold and silver.*
ח *[So] may You [now] provide [our] freedom and let us hear openly,*
ח *'You were sold for nought, you will be redeemed but not with money.'*[16]
ק *The congregations of Jacob will call You by [Your Ineffable] Name.*
ק *'We hoped for Him,' one will say to the other pointing towards You.*[17]
ק Chazzan — *They will revere Your Holiness, and exalt You with glad song;*
ק *the city of powerful nations will be in awe of You.*[18]

Congregation aloud, then *chazzan:*

HASHEM shall reign forever — your God, O Zion —
from generation to generation, Halleluyah![19]
You, O Holy One, are enthroned upon
Israel's praises[20] **— please, O God.**

Chazzan, then congregation:

כְּעַל גְּמוּלוֹת כְּעַל יְשַׁלֵּם,[1] לְחֵיק לֹא יָדְעוּ הַכֹּלֶם,[2]
לְאִיִּים גְּמוּל יְשַׁלֵּם,[1] קָדוֹשׁ.

All:

אִמְרוּ* לֵאלֹהִים אַדִּירִים, מְאֹד מַעֲשָׂיו נָאִים וַהֲדוּרִים,
בְּתִתּוֹ אוֹת וּמוֹפֵת בְּצָרִים.
נֶהֱרָגִים הוֹרְגִים אֶת הוֹרְגֵיהֶם, וְנִצְלָבִים צוֹלְבִים אֶת צוֹלְבֵיהֶם,
וְנִשְׁקָעִים שׁוֹקְעִים אֶת שׁוֹקְעֵיהֶם.
יְהִירִים אֲשֶׁר זָדוּ בְּזָדוֹן, נִמְדְּדוּ בְסַאסְּאָה כְּפָעֳלָם לָדוֹן,
וְהוּרַד גְּאוֹנָם שְׁאוֹל וַאֲבַדּוֹן.
שְׁטוּפֵי* וָעַם נִשְׁכְּחֵי רֶגֶל, הָהְפַּךְ עֲלֵיהֶם בַּלָּהוֹת לְגַלְגֵּל,
כְּהוּחַל לִקְרֹא בְּשֵׁם[3] אֱלִיל וּלְרַגֵּל.
מָרוֹם קָרָא לְמֵי הַיָּם, וַאֲרֻבּוֹת הַשָּׁמַיִם פָּתַח בַּעְיָם,
וַיִּמַּח יְקוּמָם בְּשֶׁטֶף דָּכְיָם.
עֲלֵיהֶם סִדְרֵי בְרֵאשִׁית נִשְׁתַּנּוּ, בְּשַׁחֲתָם אֶת דַּרְכָּם[4] נִתְגַּנּוּ,
בְּרוֹתְחִין קִלְקְלוּ וּבְרוֹתְחִין נִדּוֹנוּ.
וּבְנָסְעַ מִקֶּדֶם יוֹשְׁבֵי שִׁנְעָר,[5] בְּבִנְיַן הַמִּגְדָּל לִבָּם נִבְעָר,
וְיָזְמוּ לְהַגְבִּיהוּ לְאֵין מִשְׁעָר.
נוֹעֲצוּ לֵב וְנוֹסְדוּ מְזִמּוֹת, אִם נִצְטָרֵךְ לְטִפֵּי מֵימוֹת,
נַעֲלֶה לָרָקִיעַ וְנַכֶּנּוּ בְּקַרְדֻּמּוֹת.
בָּלַל לְשׁוֹנָם וְחִלְּשָׁם וְהִתִּישָׁם, וּבִנְיָנָם הִשְׁחִית עֲבוּר לְבַיְּשָׁם,
וַיָּפֶץ יהוה אֹתָם מִשָּׁם.[6]
רָעִים בְּגוּפָם וְחַטָּאִים בְּמְאֹדָם, גְּאוֹן שִׂבְעַת לֶחֶם הָיָה יְסוֹדָם,
וְעָנִי וְאֶבְיוֹן לֹא הֶחֱזִיקָה יָדָם:[7]
יָהּ בִּרְאוֹת כְּנִתְמַלֵּא סִפְקָם, פַּחִים וְרוּחַ זִלְעָפוֹת הִשִּׂיקָם,[8]
תַּחַת רְשָׁעִים סְפָקָם.[9]
צִדְקַת אֶזְרָח אָדוֹן זָכַר, וּבֶן אָחִיו נִמְלַט מִלְּהִתְמַכֵּר,
בְּשַׁחֵת אֱלֹהִים אֶת עָרֵי הַכִּכָּר.[10]
חֵרְפוּ וְגִדְּפוּ מַלְאֲכֵי תִלְגַּת,[11] בְּצִוּוּי אֲדוֹנֵיהֶם לְגַדֵּל לַעֲגַת,
וּמַלְאָךְ יָצָא וּבְעָטָם כַּגַּת.
קַנּוֹא גִּלְּחוֹ בְּתַעַר הַשְּׂכִירָה,[12] בְּעֶבְרֵי נָהָר מֶלֶךְ אַשּׁוּרָה,
וְלֹא נוֹתַר בָּם כִּי אִם עֲשָׂרָה.

אִמְרוּ ☙ — *Say.* In thirty-three triplets arranged in eleven stanzas, the *paytan* records the Scriptural accounts of blasphemy, from the generation of Enosh, grandson of Adam, until the wicked Haman. The stanzas carry the acrostic: אֲנִי שִׁמְעוֹן בַּר יִצְחָק בַּר אָבוּן חֲזַק וֶאֱמַץ בְּתוֹרָה — *I am Shimon son of Yitzchak son of Avun, may he be strong and persevere in Torah.*

שְׁטוּפֵי — *They were inundated.* The generation of Enosh was the first to practice idolatry. As a result

Chazzan, then congregation:

כְּעַל *According to their deeds, so shall they be repaid,*[1]
to the mouth of the wanton who know no shame,[2]
to the islands He shall pay recompense[1] *— He is the Holy One.*

All:

א *Say* of the powerful God, whose works are becoming and beautiful, when He places sign and wonder upon his enemy.*

נ *The slain slew their slayers, the hanged hung their hangers, the drowned drowned their drowners.*

י *The arrogant, who were purposely wanton, were measured accordingly to be judged by their deeds, and their pride was lowered to the pit, to Gehinnom.*

ש *They were inundated* by fury, forgotten by those who walk [the earth], Their life was turned, confusion rolling over them, when they profaned by calling the idols they followed by God's Name.*[3]

מ *From on high, He called to the Sea's waters, and he opened the windows of heaven with force, thus He wiped out civilization with the forceful flow of their waves.*

ע *The laws of nature were changed because of them; they were degraded for having corrupted their ways.*[4] *They sinned with heated passion and were punished with boiling water.*

ו *And when they traveled from the east to dwell in Shinar,*[5] *their hearts were foolish with the building of a tower, they wanted to raise it to an unmeasurable height.*

נ *They planned with single heart, taking perverted counsel: 'If we need the raindrops' water, let us ascend to the heaven and smite it with axes.'*

ב *He confused their language, weakening and sapping them, and He destroyed their edifice in order to shame them. Then* HASHEM *dispersed them from there.*[6]

ר *[The Sodomites were] evil with their bodies, sinful with their money, their haughtiness caused by their abundant food supply, yet they would not support the poor and needy.*[7]

י *When God saw that they were replete with sin, He battered them with coals and burning wind;*[8] *because of their wickedness He smote them.*[9]

צ *The Lord remembered Abraham's righteousness, and rescued his nephew from being given over [to the destroyers], when God destroyed the cities of the [Jordan's] plain.*[10]

ח *The emissaries of Tilgas [Sennacherib, king of Assyria] cursed and blasphemed,*[11] *when their master ordered them to heap scorn, so an angel went forth and tread on them as [on the grapes in] a winepress.*

ק *The Vengeful One 'shaved' with the huge razor,*[12] *those across the river and the king of Assyria, none of them remained save ten.*

(1) *Isaiah* 59:18. (2) Cf. *Jeremiah* 8:12. (3) Cf. *Genesis* 4:26. (4) Cf. 6:12. (5) Cf. 11:2. (6) Cf. 11:9. (7) Cf. *Ezekiel* 16:49. (8) Cf. *Psalms* 11:6. (9) *Job* 34:26. (10) *Genesis* 19:29. (11) See *II Kings*, chs. 18-19, and *Isaiah*, chs. 36-37. (12) Cf. *Isaiah* 7:20.

of their evil ways, a flood covered one-third of the earth. This stanza speaks of both that generation and the generation of Noah, since both were punished with a flood.

בְּהִשְׁתַּחֲוֹתוֹ לִנְסְרוֹךְ דַּרְכּוֹ יָרַט, וּבָנָיו הִכּוּהוּ בְּזַיִן מְמֹרָט,
וְהֵמָּה נִמְלְטוּ אֶרֶץ אֲרָרָט.[1]
רָם וְנִתְגַּדֵּל מַשּׂוֹר עַל מְנִיפוֹ,[2] וְאָמַר לַעֲלוֹת עַל מְרוֹמֵי גַּפּוֹ,[3]
כִּי פָּקַד עָלָיו חֲרוֹן אַפּוֹ.
אָדוֹן הֱסִירוֹ מִמְּלוֹךְ בִּמְלוּכָה, וּמִבְּנֵי אָדָם טְרָדוֹ לְשַׁלְּכָה,
עִם בְּהֵמוֹת שֶׁבַע* לְהַלְּכָה.
בְּבוֹא פְקוּדָּתוֹ נִסְחַב פִּגְרוֹ, וּכְנֵצֶר נִתְעָב הָשְׁלַךְ מִקִּבְרוֹ,*[4]
כְּפֶגֶר מוּבָס הָבְאַשׁ בְּשָׂרוֹ.
וּבְעַזּוּת פָּנִים הֵעִיז בֵּלְשַׁאצַּר, וְצִוָּה וְהוֹצִיא מִן הָאוֹצָר,
כֵּלִים אֲשֶׁר הֶגְלָה נְבוּכַדְנֶאצַּר.[5]
נִתְגָּאָה לִשְׁתּוֹת בָּם תִּירוֹשָׁיו, הוּא וְשָׂרָיו וַעֲבָדָיו וְנָשָׁיו וּפִלַגְשָׁיו,
וּפַסַּת יָד כָּתְבָה פֵרוּשָׁיו.
חֲמוּדוֹת[6] בֵּאֵר לוֹ הָאוֹתִיּוֹת, כִּי קָצַף עָלָיו רַב הָעֲלִילִיּוֹת,
וּבוֹ בַלַּיְלָה נֶהֱרַג בִּשְׁאִיּוֹת.
זָד אֲגָגִי לַהֲרֹג וּלְאַבֵּד, בָּנִים אֲשֶׁר בָּם אָב מִתְכַּבֵּד,
פִּתְאֹם הָיָה כִּכְלִי אוֹבֵד.
קִצֵּץ עֵץ מִשְׁנֶה לִתְלוֹת, וּלְעַצְמוֹ הֱכִינוֹ עָלָיו לְהִתָּלוֹת,
וִיהוּדִי עָשׂ מִלְחָמָה בְּתַחְבֻּלוֹת.
וּבְגוּמָּץ אֲשֶׁר חָפַר נִשְׁדַּד,[7] וּבִסְאָה אֲשֶׁר מָדַד הָמְדַּד,
וְעָנוּ עָלָיו הֵידָד הֵידָד.[8]
אָמְנָם (כָּל) אֵלּוּ הַמַּכְעִיסִים, הָיָה לָהֶם עַל לֵב לְהָשִׂים,
לְהַעֲרִים וּלְהִוָּסֵר מִמֶּלֶךְ חֲנֵסִים.
מֵאֵן לְשַׁלַּח עַם הֲמוֹנַי, וְשָׁאַג וְאָמַר מִי יהוה,
לֹא יָדַעְתִּי אֶת יהוה.[9]
צוּר נְגָפוֹ בְּעֶשֶׂר לְהַכּוֹ, וּבַעֲבוּר זֹאת הֶעֱמִידוֹ וְהֶאֱרִיכוֹ,
לְהוֹדִיעַ לַכֹּל הַגִּיעוֹ בְּכֹה.
בְּחַבּוּרוֹת וּפְצָעִים אוֹתוֹ אִלַּח, וּבִירִיַּת חִצָּיו כְּבֵדוֹ פִלַּח,[10]
וְאַחֲרֵי כֵן חָזְקָה יָדוֹ לְשַׁלַּח.
תְּחוּם מִצְרַיִם עַד לֹא הִרְחִיקוּ, הוּא וַעֲבָדָיו עֵצָה הֶעֱמִיקוּ,
לִרְדּוֹף אַחֲרֵיהֶם מָגֵן הֶחֱזִיקוּ.

שֶׁבַע — *Seven [years].* Nebuchadnezzar's seven years of madness, isolated in the forest away from humanity, is described in the Book of *Daniel* (ch. 4).

הָשְׁלַךְ מִקִּבְרוֹ — *He was cast from his grave.* When Nebuchadnezzar's madness began, the populace crowned his son Evil-merodach as king in his stead. But when Nebuchadnezzar regained his sanity and his throne, he had his son imprisoned. After Nebuchadnezzar's death, the populace released Evil-merodach from confinement and tried to crown him another time. But he refused, 'What if my father returns to power again. This time he will kill me!' The people assured him that his father had died, but this did not sway him. Finally, when they pulled Nebuchadnezzar's decaying carcass out of his grave and showed it to his son, Evil-merodach accepted the kingship. [See *Rashi* to *Isaiah* 14:19.]

ב *When he prostrated himself to Nisroch [his idol], he hastened the way*
[to his downfall], his own sons smote him with sharpened sword,
and they escaped to the land of Ararat.[1]

ד *The saw [Nebuchadnezzar] elevated and magnified itself against the One Who wielded it,*[2]
and said that he would ascend to the highest heavens,[3]
but [God] visited His fiery anger upon him.

א *The Lord removed him from reigning as king,*
driving him from humanity, flinging him far off,
to sojourn seven [years] with the animals.*

ב *When his time came, his corpse was dragged about.*
Like an uprooted plant, he was cast from his grave,[4]*
His flesh smelled like a trodden carcass.

ו *Belshazzar displayed a brazen face,*
and commanded to bring from his treasure house,
the utensils [of the Temple] that Nebuchadnezzar brought into exile.[5]

נ *With arrogance he drank his wine from them,*
he, his officers, his servants, his wives, and his concubines,
then the palm of a hand wrote his sentence.

ח *The greatly beloved [Daniel]*[6] *explained the letters to him,*
that the Master of Deeds was angered at him,
and that very night he was killed in an attack.

ז *The Agagite [Haman] sought to kill and destroy,*
the children in whom the Father takes pride,
so he suddenly became like a lost utensil.

ק *He cut a timber on which to hang the [eventual] viceroy,*
but really prepared it for himself to be hung,
and [Mordechai] the man of Judah waged war with stratagems.

ו *He was destroyed in the pit he had dug,*[7]
and against the bushel with which he measured he was measured himself,
and they cried over him, 'Hoorah! Hoorah!'[8]

א *Yet all of these who angered [God] should have taken to heart,*
to understand and learn a lesson from the Egyptian king.

מ *When he refused to send out the people of My multitude,*
and he roamed and said, 'Who is HASHEM*? I have not known* HASHEM*!'*[9]

צ *The Creator plagued him, smiting him ten times,*
and for this reason his life was extended,
that he relate to all what had happened to him.

ב *With wounds and lacerations he became depraved,*
with a shot of His arrow, his liver was pierced,[10]
then, finally, he sent [Israel] out with a strong hand.

ת *But before they were far from Egypt's border,*
he and his servants plotted a profound plan,
to pursue them strengthened with shield.

---

(1) *II Kings* 19:37; *Isaiah* 37:38. (2) Cf. 10:15. (3) Cf. 14:14. (4) Cf. 14:19.
(5) See *Daniel* 5:2. (6) See 10:11. (7) Cf. *Ecclesiastes* 10:8. (8) Cf. *Jeremiah* 51:14.
(9) *Exodus* 5:2. (10) Cf. *Proverbs* 7:23.

וְצוּר נַעֲרָץ בְּסוֹד קְדוֹשִׁים רַבָּה,[1] שָׂת אֶת הַיָּם לֶחָרָבָה,
בַּיָּם נָתַן דֶּרֶךְ וּבְמַיִם עַזִּים נְתִיבָה.[2]
רֶסֶן מַתְעֶה הִרְסִין עֲנָמִים, וְנִהֲגָם בִּכְבֵדוּת לְגַלֵּי הוֹמִים,
וְצָלְלוּ כַּעוֹפֶרֶת בְּעִמְקֵי יַמִּים.[3]
הוֹלְכֵי נְתִיבוֹת בְּמַעֲמַקֵּי מַיִם, שִׁבְּחוּ וְהוֹדוּ לָאֵל הַשָּׁמַיִם,
אֲשֶׁר נִלְחַם לָהֶם בְּמִצְרָיִם.[4]
מֵאָז וְהָלְאָה הָקְבַּע לַדּוֹרוֹת, לְסַפֵּר לָעַד כֹּחַ וּגְבוּרוֹת,
וּלְהַזְכִּיר יְצִיאַת מִצְרַיִם בְּשִׁירוֹת.

[In some congregations, the congregation pauses at the end of each of the next twenty-one paragraphs, as indicated in the text. In others, these prayers are recited straight through till page 904.]

Chazzan, then congregation:

וּבְכֵן וַיּוֹשַׁע יהוה בַּיּוֹם הַהוּא.[5]

All:

אֵילֵי הַצֶּדֶק יְדוּעִים,[6] **בָּ**נִים מְגֻדָּלִים כִּנְטִיעִים,[7]
גֶּזַע תִּפְאֶרֶת מַטָּעִים,[6] **דְּ**בוּקִים וַחֲשׁוּקִים דַּרְדַּעִים,*
הַגּוּיִם הֲגוּנִים וְנִשְׁמָעִים, **וָ**תִיקִים נִבְחָרִים מִשִּׁבְעִים,
זַרְעָם בַּגּוֹיִם נוֹדָעִים,[8] **חֲ**מוּדִים וּמַעֲשֵׂיהֶם נָעִים,
טוֹבִים בָּאֲרָצוֹת מוּדָעִים, **יוֹ**דְעִים יְדוּעִים וּמְיֻדָּעִים,
כַּחוֹתָם בִּזְרוֹעַ נִקְבָּעִים,* **לְ**מוֹדֵי נִסִּים וְנוֹשָׁעִים.
❖ נוֹשָׁעִים מִבֵּין קִצְרֵי יָד,[9] תַּתָּה לָמוֹ שֵׁם וָיָד,
All – **וַיַּרְא יִשְׂרָאֵל אֶת הַיָּד.**[10]
מְחוֹלֶלֶת תַּנִּין בִּגְעָרָה,[11] **נוֹ**תֶנֶת בַּיָּם מַעֲבָרָה,
סוֹעֶרֶת גַּלִּים בִּסְעָרָה, **עוֹ**רֶכֶת מְסִלָּה יְשָׁרָה,
פְּלָאוֹת וְנוֹרָאוֹת מַאְדִּירָה, **צוֹ**לֶלֶת קָמִים בִּגְבוּרָה,
קְנְאַת מִלְחֶמֶת מְעִירָה,[12] **רַ**הַב[11] מַחֲצֶבֶת בְּעֶבְרָה,
שׁוֹלֶפֶת חֶרֶב מִתַּעְרָהּ,[13] **תַּ**מָּתוֹ לְהוֹשִׁיעַ מִצָּרָה.
❖ מִצָּרָה נִצְּלוּ עַם אֵל, וְהִגִּידוּ צִדְקָתוֹ כְּהַרְרֵי אֵל,[14]
All – **אָז יָשִׁיר מֹשֶׁה וּבְנֵי יִשְׂרָאֵל.**[15]
שֶׁבַח וְהוֹדָאָה מְעֻלָּה, מַלְכוּת שְׂרָרָה וּמֶמְשָׁלָה,
עֹז וְתַעֲצוּמוֹת לְאַיָּלָה, וְרוֹמֵמוֹת לְמַעְלָה לְמַעְלָה,

(1) *Psalms* 89:8. (2) Cf. *Isaiah* 43:16. (3) Cf. *Exodus* 15:10. (4) 14:25. (5) 14:30. (6) Cf. *Isaiah* 61:3. (7) Cf. *Psalms* 144:12. (8) Cf. *Isaiah* 61:9. (9) Cf. *II Kings* 19:26. (10) *Exodus* 14:31. (11) Cf. *Isaiah* 51:9. (12) Cf. 42:13. (13) Cf. *Ezekiel* 21:10. (14) *Psalms* 36:7. (15) *Exodus* 15:1.

וּבְכֵן וַיּוֹשַׁע — *And so,* HASHEM *saved.* We now begin a series of twenty-one stanzas, each ten or twelve lines long. The pattern of the acrostics varies between a straight *aleph-beis* (six times), a reverse *aleph-beis* (three times) and the author's name *Shimon bar Yitzchak* (four times). The last word of each stanza is repeated as the first word of the next. The introductory line of each stanza ends with a verse from the Song of the Sea.

דַּרְדַּעִים — *The 'generation of knowledge.'* דַּרְדַּע, *Darda,* was an exceedingly wise man, as attested to in *I Kings* 5:11. The generation of the Wilderness received the Torah at Mount Sinai and therefore was called דּוֹר דֵּעָה, *the generation of knowledge.* The *paytan* plays on the terms דּוֹר דֵּעָה and דַּרְדַּע and calls the people of the Wilderness generation דַּרְדַּעִים, *Dardaites.*

בִּזְרוֹעַ נִקְבָּעִים — *Fixed on the arm [of God].* Just as Israel wears *tefillin,* so does God wear *tefillin.*

ו *The Creator Who is dreaded in the great counsel of the holy ones,*[1]
turned the sea into dry land.
He made a road through the sea, and a path through the mighty waters.[2]
ר *He harnessed the Anamite [Egyptians] with a bridle to mislead them,*
He led them heavily into the raging waves.
They sank like lead in the depths of the seas.[3]
ה *Those who traversed the paths of the watery depths,*
praised and sang to God in the heavens,
Who fought their battle against Egypt.[4]
From that time onward it was established for [all] generations,
eternally to retell the strength and mighty deeds,
and to recall the Exodus from Egypt with song.

[In some congregations, the congregation pauses at the end of each of the next twenty-one paragraphs, as indicated in the text. In others, these prayers are recited straight through till page 904.]

Chazzan, then congregation:

And so, HASHEM saved• on that day.[5]

All:

א *Renowned for oak-like righteousness,*[6]
ב *the children [of Israel] nurtured like saplings,*[7]
ג *the offshoot of [God's] glorious planting,*[6]
ד *the 'generation of knowledge,'• cleaving and bound [to God].*
ה *They ponder upon the proper and logical [words of Torah],*
ו *the scrupulous ones, chosen from the seventy [nations],*
ז *their offspring are noted among the nations,*[8]
ח *they are pleasant and their deeds are sweet.*
ט *Their beneficence is known in the lands;*
י *knowledgeable [of Torah], well-reputed [among the nations], beloved [of God].*
כ *They are fixed on the arm [of God]• as a seal;*
ל *they are well-versed in miracles and they were saved [from Egypt].*

✧ *They were saved [from Egypt] whose power is cut short,*[9]
You gave them repute and power,
All — *and Israel saw the [great] hand:*[10]

מ *Which caused [Pharaoh] the sea-serpent to tremble*[11] *with shaking.*
נ *which made a crossing in the sea,*
ס *which raged at the waves with a storm wind,*
ע *which prepared a straight road,*
פ *which is adorned with wonders and awesome deeds,*
צ *which drowned the opponents with might,*
ק *which aroused the vengeance of war,*[12]
ר *which hewed Rahab*[11] *[Egypt] with fury,*
ש *which drew a sword from its sheath,*[13]
ת *[all this] to save His wholesome nation from trouble.*

✧ *From [its] troubles God's people were rescued,*
and they retold of His righteousness that is like the mighty mountains,[14]
All — *then, when Moses and the Children of Israel chose to sing.*[15]

ש *Exalted praise and thanks,*
מ *kingship, rulership and dominion,*
ע *power and strengthening might,*
ו *and exaltation, higher and higher,*

נֶצַח גְּבוּרָה וּגְדֻלָּה, בְּרָכָה וְשִׁירָה מְהֻלָּלָה,
רִנָּה וְזִמְרָה וְצָהֳלָה, יִחוּד קְדֻשָּׁה וּתְהִלָּה,
צְפִירָה וְתִפְאֶרֶת לְסַלְסְלָה, חָסִיד לִמְאֹד נַעֲלָה,
קוֹל תּוֹדָה לְצַלְצְלָה, נֵזֶר וַעֲטָרָה לְכַלְּלָה.

❖ לְכַלְּלָה בְּרוֹן וְהוֹדָיָה, לְצוּר הָעוֹנֶה בַּמֶּרְחָב יָהּ,

All – **עָזִּי וְזִמְרָת יָהּ,**[1]

תָּמַךְ בְּמַעְגְּלוֹתָיו אֲשׁוּרַי,[2] שִׁחֵת בַּחֲמָתוֹ צוֹרְרַי,
רָאֲתָה עֵינִי בְּשׁוּרָי,[3] קָמֵי הִכְרִיעוּ וְשׁוֹרְרַי,
צוּר עוֹלָמִים בְּעוֹזְרַי, פִּתַּח מִמַּסְגֵּר אֲסִירַי,
עוֹינַי וּמַפְרִיכַי וְצוֹרְרַי, סֻגְּרוּ הֱיוֹתָם בְּעוֹכְרַי,
נֶצַח יְנַצְּחוּהוּ אַדִּירַי, מְלַמְּדַי וּמַשְׂכִּילַי וְסוֹפְרָי.

❖ וְסוֹפְרָי רוֹמְמוּ יְמִין רוֹמֵמָה,[4] כִּי לַיהוה הַמִּלְחָמָה,

All – **יהוה אִישׁ מִלְחָמָה.**[5]

לוֹבֵשׁ צְדָקָה כַּשִּׁרְיָן,[6] כֹּחַ וּגְבוּרָה מְזֻיָּן,
יוֹדֵעַ וָעֵד וְדַיָּן, טַכְסִיסֵי מַלְכוּת מְצֻיָּן,
חָצָה[7] וְדִלֵּג מִנְיָן,[8] זְמַן שִׁעְבּוּד תִּנְיָן,
וּבִרְכוּשׁ מִקְנֶה וְקִנְיָן, הוֹצִיא צְבְאוֹתָיו בְּמִנְיָן,
דֶּרֶךְ חוֹמוֹת בִּנְיָן, גְּזָרִים הִסְלִיל בְּעִנְיָן,
בְּשׁוּמוֹ מַעֲמַקֵּי יָם, אֹרַח וּמַסְלוּל מְסַיֵּם.

❖ מְסַיֵּם לְהַעֲבִיר כָּל חֵילוֹ, וַיְנַעֵר בְּאֹמֶץ גָּדְלוֹ,

All – **מַרְכְּבוֹת פַּרְעֹה וְחֵילוֹ.**[9]

אִבַּד וְשִׁבַּר וְכִלָּם, בָּאֵשׁ וּבְמַהֲמוֹרוֹת הִפִּילָם,[10]
גַּלִּים כִּסּוּ קְהָלָם, דֹּעֲכוּ כַּפִּשְׁתָּה כֻּלָּם,
הֵסִיר אוֹפַנֵּי גַלְגַּלָּם, וְנִהֲגָם בִּכְבֵדוּת[11] לְהַכְשִׁילָם,
זֹרְמוּ עָבוֹת לְמוּלָם, חֲצָצֶיךָ הָלְכוּ[12] לְשַׁכְּלָם,
טָבְעוּ בַבּוֹץ רַגְלָם,[13] יָשׁוּב בְּרֹאשָׁם עֲמָלָם,[14]
כָּרְעוּ קָרְסוּ בְּנָפְלָם,[15] לְהָסִיר מֵעֲלֵיהֶם צִלָּם.[16]

❖ צִלָּם הוּסַר וְנִזְעֲמוּ וּבוֹשׁוּ וְגַם נִכְלָמוּ,

All – **תְּהֹמֹת יְכַסְיֻמוּ.**[17]

(1) *Exodus* 15:2. (2) Cf. *Psalms* 17:5. (3) Cf. 92:12. (4) Cf. 118:16. (5) *Exodus* 15:3. (6) Cf. *Isaiah* 59:17. (7) See commentary, p. 45. (8) See commentary, p. 277. (9) *Exodus* 15:4. (10) Cf. *Psalms* 140:11. (11) Cf. *Exodus* 14:25. (12) Cf. *Psalms* 77:18. (13) Cf. *Jeremiah* 38:22. (14) Cf. *Psalms* 7:17. (15) Cf. *Isaiah* 46:2. (16) Cf. *Numbers* 14:9. (17) *Exodus* 15:5.

Just as Israel's *tefillin* declare God's Oneness, so do God's *tefillin* declare Israel's unique status (*Berachos* 6a). Thus, Israel is fixed in the *tefillin* on God's arm, so to speak.

נ *victory, strength and greatness,*
ב *blessing and praiseful song,*
ר *glad song, music and joyfulness,*
י *Oneness, holiness and praise,*
צ *crown and glory to extol,*
ח *to the exceedingly exalted Pious One,*
ק *to resound with the voice of thankfulness,*
with crown and diadem to coronate Him.

❖ *To coronate Him with joyous song and thanks,*
to the Creator Who answers with expansiveness,
All – *'God is my might and praise.'*[1]

ת *He supported my strides in His pathways,*[2]
ש *He destroyed my enemies in His anger,*
ר *my eye saw [what He did to] my vigorous foe,*[3]
ק *my opponents and watchful enemies He humbled.*
צ *The Creator of the world was my help,*
פ *He released my bound ones from confinement*
ע *[in the hands of] those who hate me, enslave me, oppress me,*
ס *You sealed [their death sentence] because they tried to destroy me,*
נ *forever shall my great ones and my strong ones praise him,*
מ *my teachers my scholars, my scribes.*

❖ *My scribes exalt His triumphant right hand,*[4] *for the battle is to* HASHEM,
All – HASHEM *is Master of war.*[5]

ל *He wears righteousness like a suit of mail,*[6]
כ *armed with strength and power,*
י *He knows, He bears a witness, He is the judge,*
ט *outstanding in the protocols of royalty.*
ח *He split the night*[7] *and hastened the count*[8]
ז *of the stipulated time of servitude,*
ו *and with a wealth of cattle and possessions,*
ה *He removed his multitudes with a census.*
ד *through [the sea which became like] the walls of a building,*
ג *He smoothed the divisions [of the sea]*
ב *when He made the depths of the sea,*
א *a road straight and paved.*

❖ *Paved that all His hosts may cross; but with his great might He emptied into it,*
All – *Pharaoh's chariots and army.*[9]

א *He destroyed, broke and eradicated them,*
ב *He cast them into fire and deep pits,*[10]
ג *waves covered their multitudes,*
ד *they were all singed like flax.*
ה *He removed the wheels of their chariots,*
ו *and led them with heaviness*[11] *to ensnare them.*
ז *The clouds streamed forth against them,*
ח *Your arrows [of lightning] went forth*[12] *to bereave them of their children.*
ט *Their feet sank in the mud,*[13]
י *their evil recoiled upon their own heads,*[14]
כ *they knelt and were bent in their fall,*[15]
ל *to remove from them their protective shade.*[16]

❖ *Their protective shade was removed and replaced with fury,*
they were embarrassed and abashed,
All – *the deep waters covered them.*[17]

מִשְּׁבָרִים נִתְחַטְּאוּ וְגַלִּים,[1] נֶגֶד שָׂרֵי אֱוִילִים,[2]
סוֹעֲרִים הוֹמִים וּמִתְנַטְּלִים, עוֹזְרֵי רַהַב מַפִּילִים,
פִּגְרֵיהֶם הֻצְּעוּ חֲלָלִים, צָלְלוּ כַּעוֹפֶרֶת[3] מִסְתּוֹלְלִים,
קְנוּיִם עָבְרוּ גְאוּלִים, רוֹמְמוֹת יְמִינְךָ מַגְדִּילִים,
שָׁרִים מְתוֹפְפִים כְּחוֹלְלִים,[4] תִּשְׁבָּחוֹת וְשִׁירִים וְהִלּוּלִים.

❖ וְהִלּוּלִים לְתוֹחַלְתִּי וְסִבְרִי, וְעַל מְשַׂנְאַי לְהַגְבִּירִי,

All – **יְמִינְךָ יהוה נֶאְדָּרִי.**[5]

שִׁתַּתָּה עוֹלָם בְּבִנְיָנֶיךָ, מָלְאָה הָאָרֶץ קִנְיָנֶיךָ,[6]
עֶלְיוֹן שַׂמְתָּ מְעוֹנֶךָ,[7] וְהוֹד וְהָדָר לְפָנֶיךָ,[8]
נְעִימוֹת נֶצַח בִּימִינֶךָ,[9] בְּצֵאתְךָ לְיֵשַׁע בָּנֶיךָ,
רָעֲשׁוּ הָרִים מִפָּנֶיךָ,[10] יָחִילוּ מַיִם מֵחֲרוֹנֶךָ,
צֶדֶק מָלְאָה יְמִינֶךָ,[11] חַיִל וָיֶשַׁע לַהֲמוֹנֶיךָ,
קַנּוֹא וְנוֹקֵם לְשׂוֹטְנֶיךָ, כִּי תָמְכָה יְמִינֶךָ.[12]

❖ יְמִינְךָ הַגְּבוּרָה שׂוֹנְאֶיךָ לַהֲרוֹס, וְאוֹתִי בֶּאֱמוּנָה לֶאֱרוֹס,[13]

All – **וּבְרֹב גְּאוֹנְךָ תַּהֲרֹס.**[14]

תַּלְמִיד לוֹמֵד וּמְלַמְּדוֹ, שׁוֹטֵר וּמוֹשֵׁל וּפְקִידוֹ,
רַכָּב סוּסוֹ וּפִרְדוֹ, קָרוֹב וְגוֹאֲלוֹ וְדוֹדוֹ,
צָעִיר וְיָשִׁישׁ וּמְכַבְּדוֹ, פּוֹעֵל וְאִכָּר וְצִמְדוֹ,
עָשִׁיר וְרֵיעוֹ וִידִידוֹ, שָׂכִיר וְשׁוֹכֵר וּמְשַׁחֲדוֹ,
נָדִיב וְנִינוֹ וְנֶכְדוֹ, מְשָׁרֵת אֲדוֹנוֹ וְעַבְדוֹ,
לַאֲבַדּוֹן הוּרַד כְּבוֹדוֹ, הָפְרַע וְכָל הַבָּא בְיָדוֹ.

❖ בְּיָדוֹ כָּל חֵיל מִצְרַיִם, בָּאוּ בָאֵשׁ וּבַמַּיִם,

All – **וּבְרוּחַ אַפֶּיךָ נֶעֶרְמוּ מַיִם.**[15]

לְכַדּוּ פְּנֵי תְהוֹמוֹת, כָּאֶבֶן נִתְחַבְּאוּ מֵימוֹת,[16]
יָשְׁרוּ מְסִלּוֹת רָמוֹת, טִירוֹת גְּבוֹהוֹת כְּחוֹמוֹת,
חָזוּם מַלְכֵי אֲדָמוֹת, זָעוּ וְנִתְפַּלְּצוּ בְּאֵימוֹת,
וְנָתְנוּ לָאֵל רוֹמְמוֹת, הַנּוֹתֵן עֹז וְתַעֲצוּמוֹת,
דִּקְדֵּק בְּצָרִים נְקָמוֹת, גָּבַר וְהִשְׁבִּית מִלְחָמוֹת,

(1) Cf. *Job* 41:17. (2) Cf. *Isaiah* 19:11. (3) *Exodus* 15:10. (4) Cf. *Psalms* 87:7.
(5) *Exodus* 15:6. (6) *Psalms* 104:24. (7) 91:9. (8) Cf. 96:6. (9) Cf. 16:11.
(10) Cf. *Nahum* 1:5. (11) *Psalms* 48:11. (12) 63:9. (13) Cf. *Hosea* 2:22.
(14) *Exodus* 15:7. (15) 15:8. (16) Cf. *Job* 38:30.

מ *Breakers and waves raced,*[1]
נ *against the prince of the foolish,*[2]
ס *storming at them, confusing them, raising them,*
ע *throwing down Egypt's guardian angels,*
פ *scattering their bodies as corpses.*
צ *The scorners sank like lead,*[3]
ק *[God's] acquired ones crossed over as redeemed ones,*
ר *they exulted in the exaltedness of Your hand,*
ש *singers, drummers, as well as flutists,*[4]
ת *praises, songs and laudings.*

❖ *And lauding to my hoped for and anticipated One,*
that I be placed above my enemies,
All – *through Your adorned right hand,* HASHEM.[5]

ש *You set the world's foundation when You built it,*
מ *the earth is full of Your possessions.*[6]
ע *You have made the highest heaven Your dwelling place,*[7]
ו *glory and majesty are before You,*[8]
נ *the delights of eternity are in Your right hand.*[9]
ב *When You went forth to save Your children,*
ר *mountains quaked before You,*[10]
י *the waters trembled at Your anger.*
צ *Righteousness fills Your right hand.*[11]
ה *It gives wealth and salvation to Your multitudes.*
ק *Jealous and avenging Your enemies.*
I have been supported by Your right hand.[12]

❖ *Your right hand overpoweringly uprooted Your enemy,*
and betrothed me with faithfulness,[13]
All – *in Your abundant grandeur You shatter [Your opponents, including]:*[14]

ת *The student who studies [idolatry] and his teacher,*
ש *officer, governor and his appointee,*
ר *charioteer, his horse and his mule,*
ק *his relative, his redeemer, his uncle,*
צ *youth, elder and those who pay him homage,*
פ *laborer, farmer and his team,*
ע *rich man, his companion and his beloved,*
ס *hiree, hirer and his foreman,*
נ *nobleman, his children and grandchildren,*
מ *servant, his master and his slave, his glory was thrown down to Gehinnom,*
Pharaoh and all who came at his hand.

❖ *At his hand the entire army of Egypt came into fire and water,*
All – *at the blast of Your anger the waters were heaped.*[15]

ל *The face of the depths solidified,*
כ *the waters were hidden like a stone,*[16]
י *straightened like a high road,*
ט *tall like parapets and walls.*
ח *When the kings of earth saw them,*
ז *they shivered and trembled with awe,*
ו *they presented God with exalting praises,*
ה *He Who grants power and potency.*
ד *He scrupulously took vengeance on the enemy,*
ג *He overpowered and destroyed with battles,*

בָּאָרֶץ שָׁם שַׁמּוֹת,[1] אִדְּרוּהוּ שִׁירוֹת נְעִימוֹת.

❖ נְעִימוֹת לְשַׁבֵּחַ וְלַעֲדֹף, בְּהַפִּילוֹ צַר לִנְדֹּף,

All – **אָמַר אוֹיֵב אֶרְדֹּף.**[2]

אוֹיְבִים נֶחְלְקוּ לְכִתּוֹת, בְּהַשָּׁאַת פֶּתֶן לְפַתּוֹת,

גִּבּוֹר הַמַּפְלִיא אוֹתוֹת, דְּרָכָם וּבְעֲטָם כַּגִּתּוֹת,

הִכָּם בְּתַחֲלוּאֵי מִיתוֹת, וְכֻלָּם בְּנֶגֶף לְכַתּוֹת,

זֵדִים עוֹרְכֵי חֲנִיתוֹת, חֲגוּרֵי חֲרָבוֹת וּקְשָׁתוֹת,

טָרְפוּ בְּמַכְמוֹרֵי רְשָׁתוֹת, יֵין הַחֵמָה לִשְׁתּוֹת,

כְּזָכְרְךָ שְׁבוּעַת בְּרִיתוֹת, לְצָרָה נִשְׂגַּבְתָּ לְעִתּוֹת.[3]

❖ לְעִתּוֹת בַּצָּרָה נִמְצֵאתָ לָמוֹ, וּבְעַזִּים הִשְׁלַכוּ צָרֵימוֹ,

All – **נָשַׁפְתָּ בְרוּחֲךָ כִּסָּמוֹ.**[4]

מֵי יַם סוּף הוּצָפוּ, נִבְכֵיהֶם לְרֹאשָׁם צָפוּ,

סִלִּיתָ צָרִים וְנִשְׁטָפוּ, עֶבְרָה וָזַעַם נֶאֱסָפוּ,

פַּחִים לְרַגְלָם הוּקָפוּ, צִירִים אֲחָזוּם וְנֶהְדָּפוּ,

קָלְעוּ נַפְשָׁם וְנִגָּפוּ, רָאוּ וּפְנֵיהֶם חָפוּ,

שֻׁבְּרוּ עַצְמוֹתָם וְשֻׁפּוּ, תְּנוּפַת שָׁוְא הוּנָפוּ.[5]

❖ הוּנְפוּ וְהוּמְכוּ חֲלָלִים, וְקוֹל הִשְׁמִיעוּ גְּאוּלִים,

All – **מִי כָמֹכָה בָּאֵלִם.**[6]

שַׁלִּיט חָסִין וְנוֹרָא, מְאֹד סְבִיבָיו נִשְׂעָרָה,[7]

עֲלִיּוֹת בַּמַּיִם קֵרָה,[8] וְשׁוֹמֵעַ וּמַאֲזִין עֲתִירָה,

נַעֲרָץ בִּקְדוֹשֵׁי טָהֳרָה,[9] בַּקֹּדֶשׁ נֶאְדָּר[6] לְפָאֲרָה,

רוֹפֵף עַמּוּדִים בְּגַעֲרָה,[10] יָרוּץ דְּבָרוֹ מְהֵרָה,[11]

צִבְאוֹתָיו אֵין לְשַׁעֲרָה,[12] חָשִׁים בְּמִשְׁלַחְתּוֹ לְמַהֲרָה,

קַנּוֹא וְנוֹקֵם בְּעֶבְרָה, וּמֵחִישׁ עֶזְרָה בַּצָּרָה.

❖ בַּצָּרָה גְּנַנְתָּם וַתְּפַלְּטֵמוֹ, וּבְפוֹרְכֵיהֶם רָאוּ עֵינֵימוֹ,

All – **נָטִיתָ יְמִינְךָ תִּבְלָעֵמוֹ.**[13]

תְּהוֹם זָרְקָן לְיַבֶּשֶׁת, שׁוּר זוּ בְּפִגְרֵי חֲשׂוּפֵי שֵׁת,[14]

רוֹעֶדֶת תֵּבֵל וּמַרְגֶּשֶׁת, קִבְרָם אֵינָהּ מְבַקֶּשֶׁת,*

צָוְחָה וּפָתְחָה בַּאֲרֶשֶׁת, פְּחֲדָה מֵהַכָּלֵם בְּבֹשֶׁת,

(1) Cf. *Psalms* 46:9. (2) *Exodus* 15:9. (3) Cf. *Psalms* 9:10. (4) *Exodus* 15:10.
(5) Cf. *Isaiah* 30:28. (6) *Exodus* 15:11. (7) Cf. *Psalms* 50:3. (8) Cf. 104:3. (9) Cf. 89:8.
(10) Cf. *Job* 26:11. (11) Cf. *Psalms* 147:15. (12) Cf. *Job* 25:3. (13) *Exodus* 15:12. (14) Cf. *Isaiah* 20:4.

קִבְרָם אֵינָהּ מְבַקֶּשֶׁת — *Not wanting to accept them for burial.* After the Egyptians had drowned, their bodies were cast out of the sea onto the shore. This served three purposes: (a) It assured the Jews that the Egyptians had not escaped from the sea to take up their pursuit once again; (b) it enabled the Jews to strip the Egyptians of their jewels and armor; and (c) it gave the

ב *He has wrought devastation in the land.*[1]
א *They praised His power with pleasant songs.*
∴ *With pleasant [songs] to praise increasingly to cast down and disperse the foe,*
All — *when the enemy declared, 'I will pursue!'*[2]
א *The enemy divided into groups,*
ב *when they were seduced by the viper's words.*
ג *The Strong One Who does wondrous deeds,*
ד *tread and trampled them like [grapes in] wine presses,*
ה *He smote them with deathly sicknesses,*
ו *He put an end to them, crumbling them with a plague,*
ז *the wanton prepared with spears,*
ח *armed with swords and bows.*
ט *He tore them in snares and nets,*
י *giving them the wine of anger to drink,*
כ *when You recalled the oaths and covenants,*
ל *You are a fortress in times of distress.*[3]
∴ *In times of distress You found them [Israel], in strong waters You cast their foe,*
All — *You blew with Your wind and covered them.*[4]
מ *The Sea of Reeds' waters inundated them,*
נ *their waves rolled over their heads,*
ס *You stepped on Your enemies and they were drowned,*
ע *anger and fury encircled them,*
פ *traps surrounded their feet,*
צ *pains grasped them and they were jostled,*
ק *their souls were cast away and they were plagued,*
ר *they saw and their faces were covered with shame,*
ש *their bones were broken and dislocated,*
ת *in vain elevation they were raised.*[5]
∴ *Raised and cast down were the corpses,*
and the redeemed ones let their voice be heard,
All — *'Who is like You among the mighty?'*[6]
ש *Mighty, awesome Ruler,*
מ *His surroundings are exceedingly turbulent,*[7]
ע *He ceiled the heavens with water,*[8]
ו *He listens and hearkens to prayer.*
נ *He is dreaded among the pure, holy ones,*[9]
ב *He is mighty in holiness*[6] *and glory,*
ר *His reproof causes pillars to tremble,*[10]
י *His commandment runs swiftly [to be fulfilled].'*[11]
צ *His armies cannot be measured,*[12]
ח *they rush to speed his errands [to completion],*
ק *He is jealous and vengeful in fury,*
and He hastens assistance in [times of] trouble.
∴ *In [times of] trouble You protected and delivered them,*
and they saw [revenge taken] against their taskmasters before their eyes,
All — *when You stretched out Your right hand, and [the earth] swallowed them.*[13]
ת *The deep waters cast them to the dry land,*
ש *that Israel may see their naked corpses,*[14]
ר *the earth trembled and shook,*
ק *not wanting to accept them for burial.**
צ *The earth began speaking its claim,*
פ *she feared she would be eternally shamed,*

עֵת לָדִין מִתְבַּקֶּשֶׁת, שִׂיחַ מָה רוֹחֶשֶׁת,
נִזְכֶּרֶת הֶבֶל וְנִרְעֶשֶׁת, מִקֶּדֶם נֶאֱרֶרֶת וְנֶחֱלֶשֶׁת,
בִּרְאוֹתָהּ יְמִינְךָ מְאַשֶּׁשֶׁת, אָז עָרְבָה לָגֶשֶׁת.
❖ לָגֶשֶׁת לִבְלוֹעַ אוּם הַלֵּזוּ, וִידִידִים עָבְרוּ וְגָזוּ,
All – **נָחִיתָ בְחַסְדְּךָ עַם זוּ.**[1]
לֹא כְמַעֲשֵׂה יְדֵיהֶם, כִּי אִם בְּחַסְדְּךָ עֲלֵיהֶם,
יָדַעְתָּ לְכָל אוֹיְבֵיהֶם, טוּבְךָ וְחַסְדְּךָ עֲלֵיהֶם,
חֹק שְׁבוּעַת אֲבוֹתֵיהֶם, זָכַרְתָּ לִפְדוֹתָם מִמְּעַנֵּיהֶם,
וּבְעַמּוּד עָנָן לִפְנֵיהֶם, הוֹלַכְתָּ וְנֵהַלְתָּ שִׁבְטֵיהֶם,
דָּתְךָ הוֹדַעְתָּ לָהֶם, גְּבוּרוֹת פָּעַלְתָּ לְמַעֲנֵיהֶם,
בַּעֲשׂוֹתְךָ נוֹרָאוֹת לְעֵינֵיהֶם, אָפְפוּ חִתַּת כָּל שׁוֹמְעֵיהֶם.
❖ שׁוֹמְעֵיהֶם מִשְׁמַנָּם יֵרָזוּן,[2] וּבְעָתָה וּפַלָּצוּת יֵאָחֵזוּן,
All – **שָׁמְעוּ עַמִּים יִרְגָּזוּן.**[3]
אוֹתוֹת וּמוֹפְתִים וְנִסִּים, בְּהוֹצִיאֲךָ מִפֶּרֶךְ אֲנוּסִים,
גָּאַלְתָּ בִּזְרוֹעַ חוֹסִים, דְּרוֹר קָרָאתָ לַעֲמוּסִים,
הוֹצֵאתָם בִּרְכוּשׁ שָׂשִׂים, וַיְנַצְּלוּ אֶת אֶרֶץ חֲנֵסִים,
זְדוֹנִים וְשָׂרֵי מִסִּים, חֵילָם בְּרַגְלָם רְמוּסִים,
טָבְעוּ וְצָלְלוּ פַּתְרוּסִים, יַמִּים עֲלֵיהֶם מְכַסִּים,
כִּקְדֹחַ אֵשׁ הֲמָסִים,[4]* לָבְשׁוּ חֲרָדוֹת מַכְעִיסִים.
❖ מַכְעִיסִים יָשְׁבוּ בָדָד לָדוּם, כִּי נִכְרְתוּ צָרִים מֵהֲדוּם,
All – **אָז נִבְהֲלוּ אַלּוּפֵי אֱדוֹם.**[5]
אַלּוּפֵי אֲדוּמִים וּמוֹאָבִים, בִּרְעָדָה וּבִדְאָגָה כּוֹאֲבִים,
גָּרֵי כְנַעַן הַיּוֹשְׁבִים, דָּמוּ בְּמַפֶּלֶת לְהָבִים,
הַגּוֹי הָעַז הַחֲשׁוּבִים, וּמַמְלְכוֹת אֶשְׁכָּרִים מְשִׁיבִים,
זְעוּכִים רְמוּסִים וְנִסְחָבִים, חֲשׁוּכִים וְכַפִּשְׁתָּה כָּבִים,
טְבוּעִים בְּגַלֵּי רְהָבִים, יִמְתְּקוּ לָמוֹ רְגָבִים,[6]
כְּמוֹ כֵן גַּם הֵם נֶחֱרָבִים, לְיוֹם תּוֹכֵחָה קְרוֹבִים.

(1) *Exodus* 15:13. (2) Cf. *Isaiah* 17:4. (3) *Exodus* 15:14.
(4) Cf. *Isaiah* 64:1. (5) *Exodus* 15:15. (6) Cf. *Job* 21:33.

Egyptians the opportunity to be buried in graves rather than at the bottom of the sea — as a reward for their statement: '*HASHEM is righteous*' (*Exodus* 9:27). Nevertheless, when God commanded the earth to open and accept their bodies for burial, the ground demurred. 'When I accepted the blood of a single victim, Abel, You cursed me and said; *You are cursed from the earth* (*Genesis* 4:11). Certainly if I accept all these corpses I will be cursed.' At this, God raised His right hand (so to speak) in an oath, and vowed that He would not curse the earth. Only then did the earth open and they were buried (*Mechilta* 15:12).

כִּקְדֹחַ אֵשׁ הֲמָסִים — *As the melting fire burns.* When the waters covered the Egyptians, they did so with a fury. It appeared as if flaming coals had been thrown into the water causing it to bubble and erupt violently (*Rashi* to *Isaiah* 64:1).

ע *when she would be hailed into court,*
ס *and her lips would dare to speak.*
נ *For she recalled how she was shaken with Abel,*
מ *in ancient time, she was cursed and weakened.*
But when she saw Your right hand raised in powerful oath,
then she obligated herself to allow them to approach [and be swallowed up].

∴ *To approach and to swallow up this [Egyptian] nation,*
while the beloved [Israel] crossed and changed [into free men],
All — *in Your kindness You guided this people.*[1]

ל *Not in merit of their deeds,*
כ *but only in Your kindness towards them.*
י *You made known to all their enemies,*
ט *Your beneficence and kindness towards them.*
ח *The decree and oath to their forefathers.*
ז *You recalled, to redeem them from their pains,*
ו *and with a pillar of cloud before them,*
ה *You led and guided their tribes.*
ד *Your Torah You made known to them,*
ג *You worked mighty acts for their sake,*
ב *when You performed awesome deeds before their eyes,*
א *trepidation encircled all those who heard of them.*

∴ *Those who heard of them, their fat turned lean,*[2]
and trembling and confusion gripped them,
All — *peoples heard and were agitated.*[3]

א *Signs, wonders and miracles,*
ב *when You removed the forced laborers from back-breaking toil.*
ג *With [outstretched] arm You redeemed those who take refuge in You,*
ד *You declared freedom for those borne by You,*
ה *You brought them forth with wealth, they rejoiced,*
ו *and they emptied the land of Chanes [Egypt],*
ז *the wanton ones and the taskmasters,*
ח *their army was trampled underfoot.*
ט *The Pasrosite [Egyptians] drowned and sank,*
י *the seas covered them over,*
כ *as the melting fire burns,*[4]*
ל *they garbed themselves with trepidation —those who anger [God].*

∴ *Those who anger [God] sat silently alone,*
for [they saw God's] enemies wiped off the [earth, His] footstool,
All — *then the chieftains of Edom was confounded.*[5]

א *The chieftains of the Edomites and the Moabites*
ב *were pained with trembling and worry,*
ג *those who sojourned in Canaan and its residents*
ד *were silenced by the downfall of the Lehavite [Egyptians].*
ה *The recognized, powerful nation,*
ו *to which the kingdoms had sent tribute,*
ז *was exiled, trampled and dragged about,*
ח *degraded and singed as flax.*
ט *The Rahabites were drowned in the waves,*
י *the clods of earth were sweetened for them*[6] *[and buried them],*
כ *similarly will they [the other oppressor nations] be destroyed,*
ל *As the day of admonition draws near.*

❖ קְרוֹבִים וּרְחוֹקִים אָחֲזוּ בְעָתָה, וְצוּר עִתְּדָם לִמְחִתָּה,

All – **תִּפֹּל עֲלֵיהֶם אֵימָתָה.**[1]

מְרוֹמְמוּתְךָ נָדְּדוּ עַמִּים, נוֹאֲלוּ שָׂרִים וַחֲכָמִים,

שָׂמוּ יָד לְפֶה וְנֶאֱלָמִים, עֲגוּמִים בְּפָנִים נִזְעָמִים,

פֶּן יִקְרָאֵם כָּעֲנָמִים, צִירִים אֲחָזוּם מִמִּתְקוֹמְמִים,

קְרוּאִים וּלְקוּחִים מֵעֲמָמִים, רָצוּ וְנִמְשְׁכוּ[2] מְשֻׁלָּמִים,

שַׁדַּי הוֹלִיכָם שְׁלֵמִים, תִּרְגְּלָם נְשָׂאָם לְבֵית עוֹלָמִים.*

❖ עוֹלָמִים הִנְחַלְתָּ לִסְגֻלָּתֶךָ, וְכַנֶּשֶׁר נְשָׂאתָם בְּאֶבְרָתֶךָ,

All – **תְּבִאֵמוֹ וְתִטָּעֵמוֹ בְּהַר נַחֲלָתְךָ.**[3]

אַרְבָּעָה נִקְרְאוּ נַחֲלָה, בְּחֵפֶץ וּבְאַהֲבָה כְּלוּלָה,

גְּבוּל אֶרֶץ הַמְּעֻלָּה,[4] דִּירַת בִּנְיַן זְבוּלָה,[5]

הַנְּתוּנָה מִימִין הַגְּדוֹלָה,[6] וּמְקַבְּלֶיהָ בְּרֶתֶת וְחִילָה,[7]

זֶה הַיּוֹם נָגִילָה,[8] חֵרוּת הַמְצִיא לִסְגֻלָּה,

טְרוּדִים עַתָּה בַּגּוֹלָה, יְזֻמְּנוּ לְיוֹם גְּאֻלָּה,

כַּאֲשֶׁר שֵׁמַע לְעֶגְלָה,[9] לְאוֹיְבָיו יַעֲשֶׂה כָלָה.

❖ כָּלָה וְנֶחֱרָצָה[10] לְהַרְעֵד, בְּיוֹם כִּי אֶקַּח מוֹעֵד,

All – **יהוה יִמְלֹךְ לְעוֹלָם וָעֶד.**[11]

מְלוּכָה וּגְבוּרָה שֶׁלּוֹ, נִשְׁתַּחֲוֶה לַהֲדֹם רַגְלוֹ,[12]

שִׂמְחַת עוֹלָם בְּהַגְדִּילוֹ, עָלַי בְּאַהַב בְּהַדְגִּילוֹ,

פַּנּוֹת אוֹיֵב וּלְהַשְׁפִּילוֹ, צֹאנוֹ לִרְעוֹת בְּצִלּוֹ,

קַרְנוֹת רְשָׁעִים בְּהַפִּילוֹ, רוֹמְמוֹתָיו לְהַגִּיד וְחֵילוֹ,

שְׁכֶם אֶחָד לַעֲבָד לוֹ, תֵּבֵל וּמְלוֹאָהּ לְהַלְּלוֹ.

❖ לְהַלְּלוֹ יְחוּדוֹ לְהַעֲרִיץ, יהוה מָלָךְ תָּגֵל הָאָרֶץ,[13]

All – **וְהָיָה יהוה לְמֶלֶךְ עַל כָּל הָאָרֶץ.**[14]

שֵׁם יִקָּרֵא כִּכְתִיבָתוֹ,* מֵחֶצְיוֹ תִּתְמַלֵּא תֵבָתוֹ,

עוֹד תִּתְנַשֵּׂא מַלְכוּתוֹ, וְכִסְאוֹ יִכּוֹן בִּמְלֵאָתוֹ,

---

בֵּית עוֹלָמִים — *The Eternal House* [or, *the House of the worlds*]. This refers to either Jerusalem in general (see *Rashi* to *Sanhedrin* 94a), or the Temple (see *Succah* 5b).

שֵׁם יִקָּרֵא כִּכְתִיבָתוֹ — *His Name will be read as it is written.* Two statements of the Sages are alluded to in this stanza, one from the Talmud, one from the Midrash.

The Talmud (*Pesachim* 50a) discusses the pronunciation of God's Name:

Moses asked God: *When I come to the Children of Israel and say to them, 'The God of your ancestors has sent me to you,' and they will respond, 'What is His Name?' What shall I tell them?*

God replied: י־ה־ו־ה, *HASHEM, God of Your ancestors,* זֶה שְּׁמִי, *this is My Name eternally,* וְזֶה זִכְרִי, *and this is My Mention in every generation* (*Exodus* 3:13,15).

The Talmud finds this last passage difficult, for although the verse records only one name — the Ineffable Four-Letter Name — it repeats the demonstrative pronoun זֶה, *this,* the repetition indicating that two Names are under discussion.

R' Avina explains the passage: God meant, 'Not as My Name is written, is it pronounced [or mentioned].' *This is My Name* alludes to the way we spell God's Name, י־ה־ו־ה; *this is My Mention* refers to our pronunciation of the Name, as if it were spelled אֲדֹנָי, *Adonai.*

[A different explanation of this question is found in *Tikkunei Zohar*. The word שְׁמִי refers to the first two letters of the Name, י and ה; while זִכְרִי refers to the last two letters, ו and ה. Furthermore, the *gematria* of שְׁמִי together with י and ה is 365, the numbers of negative commandments. And the *gematria* of זִכְרִי along with ה and ו is 248, the number of positive commandments.]

❖ *Near and far [nations] were gripped with terror,*
the Creator has prepared them for dismay,
All — *may fear befall them.*[1]

מ *From [awe of] Your exaltedness nations fled,*
נ *princes and sages became foolish,*
ס *they placed hand to mouth and remained silent,*
ע *grieving with angry faces,*
פ *lest the Anamite [Egyptian] fate befall them.*
צ *Pains gripped them because they [Israel] stood proud,*
ק *summoned and taken from among the nations,*
ר *the perfect ones ran and were drawn [after God],*[2]
ש *the Almighty led the wholesome ones,*
ת *He guided them and bore them to the Eternal House.**

❖ *The Eternal [House] You bequeathed to Your treasured [nation],*
and like an eagle You bore them on Your pinion,
All — *may You bring them and implant them on the mount of Your heritage.*[3]

א *Four [things] are called 'heritage' [in Scripture],*
ב *they are crowned with desire and love:*
ג *(a) the boundaries of the elevated land;*[4]
ד *(b) the building of the Temple in which He dwells;*[5]
ה *(c) [the Torah] which was given with the great right hand;*[6]
ו *(d) and those who accepted it with fear and trepidation.*[7]
ז *Let us rejoice on this day,*[8]
ח *when He granted freedom to His treasured nation,*
ט *they are presently exiled in the Diaspora,*
י *preparing for the day of redemption.*
כ *As the report regarding the [Egyptian] calf,*[9]
ל *so to his enemies may He bring destruction.*

❖ *Destruction and cutting down,*[10] *that they may fear Him,*
in the day I shall take as a festival,
All — *HASHEM shall reign for all eternity.*[11]

מ *Kingship and strength are His,*
נ *let us bow at His footstool,*[12]
ס *when He magnifies eternal joy,*
ע *He will raise a banner to declare His love for me,*
פ *and he will turn away and humble the enemy.*
צ *He will graze His flock in His shadow,*
ק *and will cast down the horns of the wicked.*
ר *They will retell His exaltedness and power,*
ש *to serve Him united as one,*
ת *the earth and its fill to praise Him.*

❖ *To praise Him, to extol His Oneness,*
when HASHEM shall reign, the earth shall rejoice,[13]
All — *then HASHEM will be King over all the world.*[14]

ש *His Name will be read as it is written,**
מ *from half, the Word will become complete,*
ע *His kingdom will again be exalted,*
ו *and His throne set in its fullness.*

---

(1) *Exodus* 15:16. (2) Cf. *Song of Songs* 1:4. (3) *Exodus* 15:17. (4) See *Deuteronomy* 26:1.
(5) See *Exodus* 15:17. (6) See *Deuteronomy* 33:2 and *Numbers* 21:19.
(7) See *Deuteronomy* 9:29. (8) Cf. *Psalms* 118:24. (9) Cf. *Isaiah* 23:5. (10) Cf. 10:23.
(11) *Exodus* 15:18. (12) Cf. *Psalms* 99:5. (13) *Psalms* 97:1. (14) *Zechariah* 14:9.

נֶכְדֵי שְׂעִיר בְּהַכּוֹתוֹ, בְּאוֹיְבָיו יִתֵּן נִקְמָתוֹ,
רְבוּת מוֹפְתֵי גְבוּרָתוֹ, יִתְקַע בַּשּׁוֹפָר בְּסַעֲרָתוֹ,
צִיּוֹן יְקַנֵּא בְקִנְאָתוֹ, חַיַּת קָנֶה בְּגַעֲרָתוֹ,[1]
קִרְיַת מֶלֶךְ בִּבְנוֹתוֹ, חֶבְיוֹן עֻזּוֹ וְתִפְאַרְתּוֹ,
זְרוּיִם בְּקַצְוֵי אַדְמָתוֹ, קְבוּצִים בְּבֵית תִּפְאַרְתּוֹ,
❖ וְשָׁם נְשׁוֹרֵר תְּהִלָּתוֹ, אֹמֶץ חַסְדּוֹ וְצִדְקָתוֹ,
מוֹרֶה צֶדֶק לַעֲדָתוֹ, בְּתוֹכָם יַצִּיב שְׁכִינָתוֹ.
❖ שְׁכִינָתוֹ עִמָּנוּ לְהִתְאַחֵד, וְאוֹתָנוּ יַעֲשֶׂה לְגוֹי אֶחָד,
All – **בַּיּוֹם הַהוּא יִהְיֶה יהוה אֶחָד וּשְׁמוֹ אֶחָד.**[2]

וּבְכֵן וּלְךָ תַעֲלֶה קְדֻשָּׁה כִּי אַתָּה קְדוֹשׁ יִשְׂרָאֵל וּמוֹשִׁיעַ.

Some congregations recite the prayer חַסְדֵּי ה׳ (p. 1121) before *Kedushah*.
Most congregations recite the standard *Yom Tov Kedushah* (below).
Those who recite חַסְדֵּי ה׳ omit the opening phrase in parentheses.

קדושה

When reciting *Kedushah,* one must stand with his feet together and avoid any interruptions. One should rise on his toes when saying the words קָדוֹשׁ, קָדוֹשׁ, קָדוֹשׁ; בָּרוּךְ (of בָּרוּךְ כְּבוֹד); and יִמְלֹךְ.

Cong. then *Chazzan* – (**נְקַדֵּשׁ** אֶת שִׁמְךָ בָּעוֹלָם, כְּשֵׁם שֶׁמַּקְדִּישִׁים אוֹתוֹ בִּשְׁמֵי מָרוֹם,) כַּכָּתוּב עַל יַד נְבִיאֶךָ, וְקָרָא זֶה אֶל זֶה וְאָמַר:

All – קָדוֹשׁ קָדוֹשׁ קָדוֹשׁ יהוה צְבָאוֹת, מְלֹא כָל הָאָרֶץ כְּבוֹדוֹ.[3]
❖ אָז בְּקוֹל* רַעַשׁ גָּדוֹל אַדִּיר וְחָזָק מַשְׁמִיעִים קוֹל, מִתְנַשְּׂאִים לְעֻמַּת שְׂרָפִים, לְעֻמָּתָם בָּרוּךְ יֹאמֵרוּ:

All – בָּרוּךְ כְּבוֹד יהוה, מִמְּקוֹמוֹ.[4] ❖ מִמְּקוֹמְךָ מַלְכֵּנוּ תוֹפִיעַ, וְתִמְלֹךְ עָלֵינוּ, כִּי מְחַכִּים אֲנַחְנוּ לָךְ. מָתַי תִּמְלֹךְ בְּצִיּוֹן, בְּקָרוֹב בְּיָמֵינוּ, לְעוֹלָם וָעֶד תִּשְׁכּוֹן. תִּתְגַּדַּל וְתִתְקַדַּשׁ בְּתוֹךְ יְרוּשָׁלַיִם עִירְךָ, לְדוֹר וָדוֹר וּלְנֵצַח נְצָחִים. וְעֵינֵינוּ תִרְאֶינָה מַלְכוּתֶךָ, כַּדָּבָר הָאָמוּר בְּשִׁירֵי עֻזֶּךָ, עַל יְדֵי דָוִד מְשִׁיחַ צִדְקֶךָ:

All – יִמְלֹךְ יהוה לְעוֹלָם, אֱלֹהַיִךְ צִיּוֹן לְדֹר וָדֹר, הַלְלוּיָהּ.[5]

קדושת השם

Chazzan continues:

לְדוֹר וָדוֹר נַגִּיד גָּדְלֶךָ וּלְנֵצַח נְצָחִים קְדֻשָּׁתְךָ נַקְדִּישׁ, וְשִׁבְחֲךָ אֱלֹהֵינוּ מִפִּינוּ לֹא יָמוּשׁ לְעוֹלָם וָעֶד, כִּי אֵל מֶלֶךְ גָּדוֹל וְקָדוֹשׁ אָתָּה. בָּרוּךְ אַתָּה יהוה, הָאֵל הַקָּדוֹשׁ. (Cong. – אָמֵן.)

The Midrash (*Tanchuma, Ki Seitzei,* cited in *Rashi*) expounds on the verse: *And He said, 'His hand is upon the throne* (כֵּס) *of God* (יָהּ); *HASHEM will do battle with Amalek in every generation'* (*Exodus* 17:16). In this verse the word כִּסֵּא, *seat* or *throne,* is shortened to כֵּס. Additionally, the throne is called by the abridged Name יָהּ, instead of the full Four-Letter Name. The Midrash understands *His hand is upon the throne* as an oath, much like one taking an oath on a Torah

נ *When He smites Seir's offspring,*
ב *when He places His vengeance upon His enemies,*
ר *increasing the wonders of His power,*
י *He will sound the shofar with His storm wind.*
צ *He will avenge Zion in His jealousy,*
ח *when He rebukes the beast of the reeds,*[1]
ק *when He builds the royal city,*
ח *the hidden glory of His power.*
ז *Those scattered to the ends of His earth,*
ק *gathered in the Temple of His glory,*
ו Chazzan — *there we shall sing His praises,*
א *the strength of His kindness and righteousness,*
צמ *He shall teach righteousness to His flock*
and among them station His Presence.

∴ *His Presence will unite with us,*
He will make us a united nation,
All – *on that day,* HASHEM *will be One and His Name will be One.*[2]

And so, the Kedushah prayer shall ascend to You,
for You are the Holy One of Israel, and its Savior.

Some congregations recite the prayer חַסְדֵי ה' (p. 1121) before *Kedushah.*
Most congregations recite the standard *Yom Tov Kedushah* (below).
Those who recite חַסְדֵי ה' omit the opening phrase in parentheses.

KEDUSHAH

When reciting *Kedushah*, one must stand with his feet together and avoid any interruptions. One should rise on his toes when saying the words *Holy, holy, holy; Blessed is;* and *HASHEM shall reign.*

Cong. then Chazzan – **נְקַדֵּשׁ** *(We shall sanctify Your Name in this world, just as they sanctify it in heaven above,) as it is written by Your prophet, "And one [angel] will call another and say:*

All – *'Holy, holy, holy is* HASHEM, *Master of Legions, the whole world is filled with His glory.'"*[3] ∴ *Then, with a sound* of great noise, mighty and powerful, they make heard a voice, raising themselves toward the seraphim; those facing them say 'Blessed . . .':*

All – *'Blessed is the glory of* HASHEM *from His place.'*[4] ∴ *From Your place, our King, You will appear and reign over us, for we await You. When will You reign in Zion? Soon, in our days — forever and ever — may You dwell there. May You be exalted and sanctified within Jerusalem, Your city, from generation to generation and for all eternity. May our eyes see Your kingdom, as it is expressed in the songs of Your might, written by David, Your righteous anointed:*

All – *'*HASHEM *shall reign forever — your God, O Zion — from generation to generation, Halleluyah!'*[5]

HOLINESS OF GOD'S NAME

Chazzan continues:

לְדוֹר *From generation to generation we shall relate Your greatness and for infinite eternities we shall proclaim Your holiness. Your praise, our God, shall not leave our mouth forever and ever, for You, O God, are a great and holy King. Blessed are You,* HASHEM, *the holy God.* (Cong. – *Amen.*)

(1) Cf. *Psalms* 68:31. (2) *Zechariah* 14:9. (3) *Isaiah* 6:3. (4) *Ezekiel* 3:12. (5) *Psalms* 146:10.

Scroll or while holding a pair of *tefillin.* Thus, God swore that neither His throne (כֵּס) nor His Name (יָהּ) will be complete until the seed of Amalek is eradicated from the world.

קדושת היום

אַתָּה בְחַרְתָּנוּ מִכָּל הָעַמִּים, אָהַבְתָּ אוֹתָנוּ, וְרָצִיתָ בָּנוּ, וְרוֹמַמְתָּנוּ מִכָּל הַלְּשׁוֹנוֹת, וְקִדַּשְׁתָּנוּ בְּמִצְוֹתֶיךָ, וְקֵרַבְתָּנוּ מַלְכֵּנוּ לַעֲבוֹדָתֶךָ, וְשִׁמְךָ הַגָּדוֹל וְהַקָּדוֹשׁ עָלֵינוּ קָרָאתָ.

On the Sabbath add the words in brackets. [If forgotten, see *Laws* §86-90.]

וַתִּתֶּן לָנוּ יהוה אֱלֹהֵינוּ בְּאַהֲבָה [שַׁבָּתוֹת לִמְנוּחָה וּ]מוֹעֲדִים לְשִׂמְחָה חַגִּים וּזְמַנִּים לְשָׂשׂוֹן, אֶת יוֹם [הַשַּׁבָּת הַזֶּה וְאֶת יוֹם] חַג הַמַּצּוֹת הַזֶּה, זְמַן חֵרוּתֵנוּ [בְּאַהֲבָה] מִקְרָא קֹדֶשׁ, זֵכֶר לִיצִיאַת מִצְרָיִם.

Congregation responds אָמֵן as indicated.

אֱלֹהֵינוּ וֵאלֹהֵי אֲבוֹתֵינוּ, יַעֲלֶה, וְיָבֹא, וְיַגִּיעַ, וְיֵרָאֶה, וְיֵרָצֶה, וְיִשָּׁמַע, וְיִפָּקֵד, וְיִזָּכֵר זִכְרוֹנֵנוּ וּפִקְדּוֹנֵנוּ, וְזִכְרוֹן אֲבוֹתֵינוּ, וְזִכְרוֹן מָשִׁיחַ בֶּן דָּוִד עַבְדֶּךָ, וְזִכְרוֹן יְרוּשָׁלַיִם עִיר קָדְשֶׁךָ, וְזִכְרוֹן כָּל עַמְּךָ בֵּית יִשְׂרָאֵל לְפָנֶיךָ, לִפְלֵיטָה לְטוֹבָה לְחֵן וּלְחֶסֶד וּלְרַחֲמִים, לְחַיִּים וּלְשָׁלוֹם בְּיוֹם חַג הַמַּצּוֹת הַזֶּה. זָכְרֵנוּ יהוה אֱלֹהֵינוּ בּוֹ לְטוֹבָה (.Cong – אָמֵן), וּפָקְדֵנוּ בוֹ לִבְרָכָה (.Cong – אָמֵן), וְהוֹשִׁיעֵנוּ בוֹ לְחַיִּים (.Cong – אָמֵן). וּבִדְבַר יְשׁוּעָה וְרַחֲמִים, חוּס וְחָנֵּנוּ וְרַחֵם עָלֵינוּ וְהוֹשִׁיעֵנוּ, כִּי אֵלֶיךָ עֵינֵינוּ, כִּי אֵל מֶלֶךְ חַנּוּן וְרַחוּם אָתָּה.[1]

On the Sabbath add the words in brackets. [If forgotten, see *Laws* §86-90.]

וְהַשִּׂיאֵנוּ יהוה אֱלֹהֵינוּ אֶת בִּרְכַּת מוֹעֲדֶיךָ לְחַיִּים וּלְשָׁלוֹם, לְשִׂמְחָה וּלְשָׂשׂוֹן, כַּאֲשֶׁר רָצִיתָ וְאָמַרְתָּ לְבָרְכֵנוּ. [אֱלֹהֵינוּ וֵאלֹהֵי אֲבוֹתֵינוּ רְצֵה בִמְנוּחָתֵנוּ] קַדְּשֵׁנוּ בְּמִצְוֹתֶיךָ וְתֵן חֶלְקֵנוּ בְּתוֹרָתֶךָ, שַׂבְּעֵנוּ מִטּוּבֶךָ וְשַׂמְּחֵנוּ בִּישׁוּעָתֶךָ, וְטַהֵר לִבֵּנוּ לְעָבְדְּךָ בֶּאֱמֶת, וְהַנְחִילֵנוּ יהוה אֱלֹהֵינוּ [בְּאַהֲבָה וּבְרָצוֹן] בְּשִׂמְחָה וּבְשָׂשׂוֹן [שַׁבָּת וּ]מוֹעֲדֵי קָדְשֶׁךָ, וְיִשְׂמְחוּ בְךָ יִשְׂרָאֵל מְקַדְּשֵׁי שְׁמֶךָ. בָּרוּךְ אַתָּה יהוה, מְקַדֵּשׁ [הַשַּׁבָּת וְ]יִשְׂרָאֵל וְהַזְּמַנִּים. (.Cong – אָמֵן.)

עבודה

רְצֵה יהוה אֱלֹהֵינוּ בְּעַמְּךָ יִשְׂרָאֵל וּבִתְפִלָּתָם, וְהָשֵׁב אֶת הָעֲבוֹדָה לִדְבִיר בֵּיתֶךָ. וְאִשֵּׁי יִשְׂרָאֵל וּתְפִלָּתָם בְּאַהֲבָה תְקַבֵּל בְּרָצוֹן, וּתְהִי לְרָצוֹן תָּמִיד עֲבוֹדַת יִשְׂרָאֵל עַמֶּךָ.

וְתֶחֱזֶינָה עֵינֵינוּ בְּשׁוּבְךָ לְצִיּוֹן בְּרַחֲמִים. בָּרוּךְ אַתָּה יהוה, הַמַּחֲזִיר שְׁכִינָתוֹ לְצִיּוֹן. (.Cong – אָמֵן.)

SANCTIFICATION OF THE DAY

אַתָּה *You have chosen us from all the peoples; You loved us and found favor in us; You exalted us above all the tongues and You sanctified us with Your commandments. You drew us close, our King, to Your service and proclaimed Your great and Holy Name upon us.*

On the Sabbath add the words in brackets. [If forgotten, see *Laws* §86-90.]

וַתִּתֶּן לָנוּ *And You gave us, HASHEM, our God, with love [Sabbaths for rest], appointed festivals for gladness, Festivals and times for joy, [this day of Sabbath and] this day of the Festival of Matzos, the time of our freedom [with love], a holy convocation, a memorial of the Exodus from Egypt.*

Congregation responds *Amen* as indicated.

אֱלֹהֵינוּ *Our God and God of our forefathers, may there rise, come, reach, be noted, be favored, be heard, be considered, and be remembered — the remembrance and consideration of ourselves; the remembrance of our forefathers; the remembrance of Messiah, son of David, Your servant; the remembrance of Jerusalem, the City of Your Holiness; the remembrance of Your entire people the Family of Israel — before You for deliverance, for goodness, for grace, for kindness, and for compassion, for life, and for peace on this day of the Festival of Matzos. Remember us on it, HASHEM, our God, for goodness (*Cong. – *Amen); consider us on it for blessing (*Cong. – *Amen); and help us on it for life (*Cong. – *Amen). In the matter of salvation and compassion, pity, be gracious and compassionate with us and help us, for our eyes are turned to You, because You are God, the gracious and compassionate King.*[1]

On the Sabbath add the words in brackets. [If forgotten, see *Laws* §86-90.]

וְהַשִּׂיאֵנוּ *Bestow upon us, O HASHEM, our God, the blessing of Your appointed Festivals for life and for peace, for gladness and for joy, as You desired and promised to bless us. [Our God and the God of our forefathers, may You be pleased with our rest.] Sanctify us with Your commandments and grant us our share in Your Torah; satisfy us from Your goodness and gladden us with Your salvation, and purify our heart to serve You sincerely. And grant us a heritage, O HASHEM, our God — [with love and with favor] with gladness and with joy — [the Sabbath and] the appointed festivals of Your holiness, and may Israel, the sanctifiers of Your Name, rejoice in You. Blessed are You, HASHEM, Who sanctifies [the Sabbath,] Israel and the festive seasons.* (Cong. – *Amen.)*

TEMPLE SERVICE

רְצֵה *Be favorable, HASHEM, our God, toward Your people Israel and their prayer and restore the service to the Holy of Holies of Your Temple. The fire-offerings of Israel and their prayer accept with love and favor, and may the service of Your people Israel always be favorable to You.*

וְתֶחֱזֶינָה *May our eyes behold Your return to Zion in compassion. Blessed are You, HASHEM, Who restores His Presence to Zion.*

(Cong. – *Amen.)*

---

(1) Cf. *Nehemiah* 9:31.

Chazzan bows at מוֹדִים; straightens up at 'ה. The *chazzan* recites the entire מוֹדִים aloud, while the congregation recites מוֹדִים דְּרַבָּנָן softly.

מוֹדִים אֲנַחְנוּ לָךְ, שָׁאַתָּה הוּא יהוה אֱלֹהֵינוּ וֵאלֹהֵי אֲבוֹתֵינוּ לְעוֹלָם וָעֶד. צוּר חַיֵּינוּ, מָגֵן יִשְׁעֵנוּ אַתָּה הוּא לְדוֹר וָדוֹר. נוֹדֶה לְּךָ וּנְסַפֵּר תְּהִלָּתֶךָ[1] עַל חַיֵּינוּ הַמְּסוּרִים בְּיָדֶךָ, וְעַל נִשְׁמוֹתֵינוּ הַפְּקוּדוֹת לָךְ, וְעַל נִסֶּיךָ שֶׁבְּכָל יוֹם עִמָּנוּ, וְעַל נִפְלְאוֹתֶיךָ וְטוֹבוֹתֶיךָ שֶׁבְּכָל עֵת, עֶרֶב וָבֹקֶר וְצָהֳרָיִם. הַטּוֹב כִּי לֹא כָלוּ רַחֲמֶיךָ, וְהַמְּרַחֵם כִּי לֹא תַמּוּ חֲסָדֶיךָ,[2] מֵעוֹלָם קִוִּינוּ לָךְ.

מודים דרבנן

מוֹדִים אֲנַחְנוּ לָךְ, שָׁאַתָּה הוּא יהוה אֱלֹהֵינוּ וֵאלֹהֵי אֲבוֹתֵינוּ, אֱלֹהֵי כָל בָּשָׂר, יוֹצְרֵנוּ, יוֹצֵר בְּרֵאשִׁית. בְּרָכוֹת וְהוֹדָאוֹת לְשִׁמְךָ הַגָּדוֹל וְהַקָּדוֹשׁ, עַל שֶׁהֶחֱיִיתָנוּ וְקִיַּמְתָּנוּ. כֵּן תְּחַיֵּנוּ וּתְקַיְּמֵנוּ, וְתֶאֱסוֹף גָּלֻיּוֹתֵינוּ לְחַצְרוֹת קָדְשֶׁךָ, לִשְׁמוֹר חֻקֶּיךָ וְלַעֲשׂוֹת רְצוֹנֶךָ, וּלְעָבְדְּךָ בְּלֵבָב שָׁלֵם, עַל שֶׁאֲנַחְנוּ מוֹדִים לָךְ. בָּרוּךְ אֵל הַהוֹדָאוֹת.

וְעַל כֻּלָּם יִתְבָּרַךְ וְיִתְרוֹמַם שִׁמְךָ מַלְכֵּנוּ תָּמִיד לְעוֹלָם וָעֶד.

The *chazzan* bends his knees at בָּרוּךְ; bows at אַתָּה; straightens up at 'ה.

וְכֹל הַחַיִּים יוֹדְוּךָ סֶּלָה, וִיהַלְלוּ אֶת שִׁמְךָ בֶּאֱמֶת, הָאֵל יְשׁוּעָתֵנוּ וְעֶזְרָתֵנוּ סֶלָה. בָּרוּךְ אַתָּה יהוה, הַטּוֹב שִׁמְךָ וּלְךָ נָאֶה לְהוֹדוֹת. (.Cong – אָמֵן.)

The *chazzan* recites בִּרְכַּת כֹּהֲנִים. He faces right at וְיִשְׁמְרֶךָ; faces left at אֵלֶיךָ וִיחֻנֶּךָּ; faces the Ark for the rest of the blessings.

אֱלֹהֵינוּ, וֵאלֹהֵי אֲבוֹתֵינוּ, בָּרְכֵנוּ בַבְּרָכָה הַמְּשֻׁלֶּשֶׁת בַּתּוֹרָה הַכְּתוּבָה עַל יְדֵי מֹשֶׁה עַבְדֶּךָ, הָאֲמוּרָה מִפִּי אַהֲרֹן וּבָנָיו, כֹּהֲנִים עַם קְדוֹשֶׁךָ, כָּאָמוּר: יְבָרֶכְךָ יהוה, וְיִשְׁמְרֶךָ. (.Cong – כֵּן יְהִי רָצוֹן.)

יָאֵר יהוה פָּנָיו אֵלֶיךָ וִיחֻנֶּךָּ. (.Cong – כֵּן יְהִי רָצוֹן.)

יִשָּׂא יהוה פָּנָיו אֵלֶיךָ וְיָשֵׂם לְךָ שָׁלוֹם.[3] (.Cong – כֵּן יְהִי רָצוֹן.)

שִׂים שָׁלוֹם טוֹבָה, וּבְרָכָה, חֵן, וָחֶסֶד וְרַחֲמִים עָלֵינוּ וְעַל כָּל יִשְׂרָאֵל עַמֶּךָ. בָּרְכֵנוּ אָבִינוּ, כֻּלָּנוּ כְּאֶחָד בְּאוֹר פָּנֶיךָ, כִּי בְאוֹר פָּנֶיךָ נָתַתָּ לָּנוּ, יהוה אֱלֹהֵינוּ, תּוֹרַת חַיִּים וְאַהֲבַת חֶסֶד, וּצְדָקָה, וּבְרָכָה, וְרַחֲמִים, וְחַיִּים, וְשָׁלוֹם. וְטוֹב בְּעֵינֶיךָ לְבָרֵךְ אֶת עַמְּךָ יִשְׂרָאֵל, בְּכָל עֵת וּבְכָל שָׁעָה בִּשְׁלוֹמֶךָ. בָּרוּךְ אַתָּה יהוה, הַמְּבָרֵךְ אֶת עַמּוֹ יִשְׂרָאֵל בַּשָּׁלוֹם. (.Cong – אָמֵן.)

in an undertone – יִהְיוּ לְרָצוֹן אִמְרֵי פִי וְהֶגְיוֹן לִבִּי לְפָנֶיךָ, יהוה צוּרִי וְגֹאֲלִי.[4]

THE SERVICE CONTINUES WITH הַלֵּל, PAGE 938.

Chazzan bows at *'We gratefully thank You'*; straightens up at *'HASHEM.'*
Chazzan recites the entire *Modim* aloud, while congregation recites *Modim of the Rabbis* softly.

מוֹדִים *We gratefully thank You, for it is You Who are HASHEM, our God and the God of our forefathers for all eternity; Rock of our lives, Shield of our salvation are You from generation to generation. We shall thank You and relate Your praise[1] — for our lives, which are committed to Your power and for our souls that are entrusted to You; for Your miracles that are with us every day; and for Your wonders and favors in every season — evening, morning, and afternoon. The Beneficent One, for Your compassions were never exhausted, and the Compassionate One, for Your kindnesses never ended[2] — always have we put our hope in You.*

MODIM OF THE RABBIS

מוֹדִים *We gratefully thank You, for it is You Who are HASHEM, our God and the God of our forefathers, the God of all flesh, our Molder, the Molder of the universe. Blessings and thanks are due Your great and holy Name for You have given us life and sustained us. So may You continue to give us life and sustain us and gather our exiles to the Courtyards of Your Sanctuary, to observe Your decrees, to do Your will and to serve You wholeheartedly. [We thank You] for inspiring us to thank You. Blessed is the God of thanksgivings.*

For all these, may Your Name be blessed and exalted, our King, continually forever and ever.

The *chazzan* bends his knees at *'Blessed'*; bows at *'You'*; straightens up at *'HASHEM.'*

Everything alive will gratefully acknowledge You, Selah! and praise Your Name sincerely, O God of our salvation and help, Selah! Blessed are You, HASHEM, Your Name is 'The Beneficent One' and to You it is fitting to give thanks. (Cong.— *Amen.*)

THE PRIESTLY BLESSING

The *chazzan* recites the Priestly Blessing.

אֱלֹהֵינוּ *Our God and the God of our forefathers, bless us with the three-verse blessing in the Torah that was written by the hand of Moses, Your servant, that was said by Aaron and his sons, the Kohanim, Your holy people, as it is said:*

May HASHEM bless you and safeguard you. (Cong.— *So may it be.*)

May HASHEM illuminate His countenance for you and be gracious to you. (Cong.— *So may it be.*)

May HASHEM turn His countenance to you and establish peace for you.[3] (Cong.— *So may it be.*)

שִׂים שָׁלוֹם *Establish peace, goodness, blessing, graciousness, kindness, and compassion upon us and upon all of Your people Israel. Bless us, our Father, all of us as one, with the light of Your countenance, for with the light of Your countenance You gave us, HASHEM, our God, the Torah of life and a love of kindness, righteousness, blessing, compassion, life, and peace. And may it be good in Your eyes to bless Your people Israel at every time and every hour with Your peace. Blessed are You, HASHEM, Who blesses His people Israel with peace.* (Cong.— *Amen.*)

May the expressions of my mouth and the thoughts of my heart find favor before You, HASHEM, my Rock and my Redeemer.[4]

THE SERVICE CONTINUES WITH HALLEL, PAGE 938.

(1) Cf. *Psalms* 79:13. (2) Cf. *Lamentations* 3:22. (3) *Numbers* 6:24-26. (4) *Psalms* 19:15.

חזרת הש״ץ לשני ימים האחרונים

FOR THE SEVENTH DAY ON FRIDAY, AND FOR THE EIGHTH DAY ON SUNDAY, TUESDAY, OR THURSDAY. ON OTHER DAYS TURN TO PAGE 882.

אֲדֹנָי שְׂפָתַי תִּפְתָּח, וּפִי יַגִּיד תְּהִלָּתֶךָ.[1]

אבות

The *chazzan* bends his knees at בָּרוּךְ; bows at אַתָּה; straightens up at ה׳.

בָּרוּךְ אַתָּה יהוה אֱלֹהֵינוּ וֵאלֹהֵי אֲבוֹתֵינוּ, אֱלֹהֵי אַבְרָהָם, אֱלֹהֵי יִצְחָק, וֵאלֹהֵי יַעֲקֹב, הָאֵל הַגָּדוֹל הַגִּבּוֹר וְהַנּוֹרָא, אֵל עֶלְיוֹן, גּוֹמֵל חֲסָדִים טוֹבִים וְקוֹנֵה הַכֹּל, וְזוֹכֵר חַסְדֵי אָבוֹת, וּמֵבִיא גוֹאֵל לִבְנֵי בְנֵיהֶם, לְמַעַן שְׁמוֹ בְּאַהֲבָה. מֶלֶךְ עוֹזֵר וּמוֹשִׁיעַ וּמָגֵן.

מִסּוֹד* חֲכָמִים וּנְבוֹנִים, וּמִלֶּמֶד דַּעַת מְבִינִים, אֶפְתְּחָה פִּי בְּשִׁיר וּבִרְנָנִים, לְהוֹדוֹת וּלְהַלֵּל פְּנֵי שׁוֹכֵן מְעוֹנִים.

All:

אֵימַת נוֹרְאוֹתֶיךָ* בִּשְׂדֵה צֹעַן כְּהִשְׁלַחְתָּ, בָּעַר כְּסִילָן בְּצִיר אֲשֶׁר שָׁלַחְתָּ,
גּוֹי מִקֶּרֶב גּוֹי בְּמַסּוֹת לָקַחְתָּ,[2] דְּבָרֶיךָ לְהָקִים כְּמוֹ לְאָב הִבְטַחְתָּ.
הֵעֵז יָהִיר וְנִאֵץ מוּל שְׁלוּחֶךָ, וְנָם מִי יהוה אֲשֶׁר שְׁלָחֶךָ,[3]
זָעַם וְעֶבְרָה בּוֹ בְּאַף בְּשַׁלְּחֶךָ, חָזַר בְּעַל כָּרְחוֹ עֲשׂוֹת מִשְׁלָחֶךָ.
טָפַשׁ לִבּוֹ וְנִבְעַר אַחֲרֵי זֹאת, יָעַץ רְדֹף אַחֲרֵימוֹ לָבֹז בִּזּוֹת,
כְּלֵי קְרָב נָשָׂא וַחֲרָבוֹת שְׁחוּזוֹת, לְהָשִׁיב לַעֲבְדוּת אֹם נָאוָה בַּחֲרוּזוֹת.[4]
מוֹעֵד שְׁלֹשֶׁת יָמִים חִכָּה לַחֲזוֹר, נֶהְפַּךְ לִבּוֹ בְּלֹא אָבוֹ חֲזוֹר,
סְפוּנֵי גְנָזָיו פִּנָּה לַחֲילוֹתָיו לִבְזוֹר, עֲבוּר בְּכָל לֵב אוֹתוֹ לַעֲזוֹר.
פָּרָשַׁת דְּרָכִים כְּגַע עִם מְשֻׁלָּח, צִדְּדָם מֵאֹרַח פְּלֶשֶׁת[5] טוֹב וְסַלָּח,
❖ קַלְגַּסִּים מַרְאוֹת עֲצֻמוֹת זָבַד וְשׁוּתֶלַח,*[6]
רִחֲקָם מִדֶּרֶךְ אוֹתָם צַר בְּשַׁלַּח.

This *Machzor* includes those *piyutim* that are commonly recited. A few *piyutim* that are omitted by a vast majority of congregations have been included in an appendix beginning on page 1108. The text will indicate where they may be recited.

חֲזָרַת הַשַּׁ״ץ / CHAZZAN'S REPETITION

On many Festivals *piyutim* are inserted in the *chazzan's* repetition. These *piyutim* [known as *kerovos*] express the mood and theme of the day, and many of them have become highlights of the day's service. Thus, the repetition is truly a communal prayer, for it involves the entire congregation.

מִסּוֹד — *Based on the tradition.* Many prominent halachic authorities from medieval times onward have opposed the insertion of *piyutim* into the prayer order, primarily on the grounds that they are an interference with and a change in the words of the prayers as they were set forth by the Sages. Most congregations, though by no means all, follow *Rama* (*Orach Chaim* 68 and 112) who permits the recitation of *piyutim.* To justify our recitation of *piyutim* during the *chazzan's Shemoneh Esrei,* they are prefaced with the formula, מִסּוֹד חֲכָמִים וּנְבוֹנִים, *Based on the tradition of our wise and discerning teachers,* meaning that we dare to interrupt the prayer service only because these *piyutim* were transmitted to us by the wise and discerning teachers of yore, based on the 'foundation' of their great wisdom and piety.

אֵימַת נוֹרְאוֹתֶיךָ — *Your fearsome awe.* The composer of the *kerovos* for the eighth day of Pesach was R' Moshe ben Klonimos of tenth-century Italy and Germany, a member of the well-known Klonimos family that dominated

CHAZZAN'S REPETITION FOR THE LAST DAYS

FOR THE SEVENTH DAY ON FRIDAY, AND FOR THE EIGHTH DAY ON SUNDAY, TUESDAY, OR THURSDAY. ON OTHER DAYS TURN TO PAGE 882.

My Lord, open my lips, that my mouth may declare Your praise.[1]

PATRIARCHS

The *chazzan* bends his knees at *'Blessed'*; bows at *'You'*; straightens up at *'HASHEM.'*

בָּרוּךְ *Blessed are You, HASHEM, our God and the God of our forefathers, God of Abraham, God of Isaac, and God of Jacob; the great, mighty, and awesome God, the supreme God, Who bestows beneficial kindnesses and creates everything, Who recalls the kindnesses of the Patriarchs and brings a Redeemer to their children's children, for His Name's sake, with love. O King, Helper, Savior, and Shield.*

מְסוֹד *Based on the tradition* of our wise and discerning teachers, and the teaching derived from the knowledge of the discerning, I open my mouth in song and joyful praise, to give thanks and to offer praise before Him Who dwells in the heavens.*

All:

א *When You cast Your fearsome awe* upon the fields of Zoan [Egypt],*
ב *When the boor [Pharaoh] stubbornly opposed the agent [Moses] whom You sent,*
ג *You removed one nation from among another with miracles,*[2]
ד *to fulfill Your word, as You promised the Patriarch [Abraham].*
ה *The haughty one was arrogant and blasphemed against Your emissary,*
ו *saying, 'Who is HASHEM that has sent you?'*[3]
ז *You sent wrath and fury against them in anger,*
ח *He was forced to turn about and fulfill Your message.*
ט *His heart became foolish and silly after this,*
י *he advised pursuing after them to plunder their booty.*
כ *He carried weapons of war and sharpened swords,*
ל *to return to slavery the nation wearing beautiful necklaces*[4] *[they had borrowed before leaving Egypt].*
מ *He expected them to return in three-days' time,*
נ *his heart turned [against them] when they would not return.*
ס *He emptied his treasures to distribute to his soldiers,*
ע *to persuade them to assist him wholeheartedly.*
פ *When the released nation reached the crossroads,*
צ *the Beneficent, Forgiving One turned them away from the road to Philistia.*[5]
ק Chazzan – *To prevent them from seeing the [Philistine] troops and the bones of Zavad and Shuselach,*[6]*
ר *He led them far out of their way when the enemy sent them forth.*

(1) *Psalms* 51:17. (2) Cf. *Deuteronomy* 4:34. (3) Cf. *Exodus* 5:2. (4) Cf. *Song of Songs* 1:10. (5) Cf. *Exodus* 13:17. (6) Cf. *I Chronicles* 7:21.

much of Jewish life in the tenth to thirteenth centuries. After moving to Germany, R' Moshe greatly influenced his contemporary, R' Shimon bar Yitzchak (see above).

זָבָד וְשׁוּתֶלַח — *Zavad and Shuselach.* These are two of the descendants of Ephraim, who were killed by the men of Gath (*I Chronicles* 7:21). The Midrash (*Pirkei d'Rabbi Eliezer* 48) describes the incident and the events leading up to it.

At some point during the Egyptian enslavement, Genon, an Ephraimite, claimed that he had been sent by God to take the Jews out of Egypt. His tribesmen followed him. Two hundred thousand of their number, relying on their military might (see *Psalms* 78:9), managed to escape from mighty Egypt. They thus anticipated

All:

עַבְדּוֹ שָׁלַח* לְהוֹצִיא עַמּוֹ בְּשָׂשׂוֹן,[1] שׁוֹדְדֵיהֶם שָׁת בָּם מַכּוֹת אָסוֹן,
❖ תָּמִים זָכַר מְנֻסֶּה וְנִמְצָא חָסוֹן, תּוֹלְדוֹתָיו לְהָגֵן נַחֲלַת אָב לַחֲסוֹן.

Chazzan bends his knees at בָּרוּךְ; bows at אַתָּה; straightens up at ה׳.

בָּרוּךְ אַתָּה יהוה, מָגֵן אַבְרָהָם. (Cong.– אָמֵן.)

גבורות

אַתָּה גִּבּוֹר לְעוֹלָם אֲדֹנָי, מְחַיֵּה מֵתִים אַתָּה, רַב לְהוֹשִׁיעַ. מְכַלְכֵּל חַיִּים בְּחֶסֶד, מְחַיֵּה מֵתִים בְּרַחֲמִים רַבִּים, סוֹמֵךְ נוֹפְלִים, וְרוֹפֵא חוֹלִים, וּמַתִּיר אֲסוּרִים, וּמְקַיֵּם אֱמוּנָתוֹ לִישֵׁנֵי עָפָר. מִי כָמְוֹךָ בַּעַל גְּבוּרוֹת, וּמִי דּוֹמֶה לָּךְ, מֶלֶךְ מֵמִית וּמְחַיֶּה וּמַצְמִיחַ יְשׁוּעָה. וְנֶאֱמָן אַתָּה לְהַחֲיוֹת מֵתִים.

All:

תַּחְבּוּלוֹת עָשׂ רַב עֵצָה וּגְבוּרָה, שׁוֹכְנֵי חֶלֶד לְלַמֵּד חָכְמָה מִגְּבוּרָה,[2]
רֶסֶן מַתְעֶה הִרְסִין שַׂר הַבִּירָה, קְהָלָיו לְהַקְהִיל לִרְדּוֹף יָפָה וּבָרָה.
צִלּוּל כְּחָבוּ מַשְׁלִיכֵי יְאוֹר זְכָרִים, פּוֹרֵעַ פְּלִשְׁתִּים סוֹף הֱיוֹת סְכוּרִים,
עֲצוּת מֵרָחוֹק[3] אִמֵּן לְעַם נִכְרִים, שִׂיחַ אֲשֶׁר שָׂח לְשָׁרֵשׁ בִּכּוּרִים.[4]
נוֹאֲלוּ שָׂרֵי צֹעַן עֵצָה נִבְעָרָה,[5] מִצְעֲדֵי זֹאת שֶׁגֶת לַהֲפִיצָהּ בִּסְעָרָה,
לוּלֵי אֵל שֶׁהוֹצִיא חַרְבּוֹ מִתַּעְרָהּ, כָּרְתוּ יַעְרָהּ וּבָעֲרוּ בָהּ הַבְעָרָה.
יוֹשֵׁב בַּשָּׁמַיִם שָׂחַק וְהִלְעִיג לָמוֹ,[6] טַכְסִיס גְּיָסָיו כְּגִיְּסוּ לָצֵאת עָלֵימוֹ,
חָז כִּי בָא יוֹם גְּמוּלֵימוֹ, זֹאת תַּחַת זֹאת נִקְמַת עוֹלָלֵימוֹ.
וְלַעֲשׂוֹת בָּהֶם מִשְׁפָּט הַכָּתוּב[7] בְּחִסּוּף, הָשֵׁב גְּמוּלָם כְּזָדוּ בְּעַם הַכָּסוּף,
❖ דֶּרֶךְ הֵסֵב לִגְאוּלֵי בִּזְרוֹעַ חָשׂוּף, גִּלְגְּלָם הַמִּדְבָּרָה דֶּרֶךְ יַם סוּף.[8]

All:

מַעֲלָלָיו בִּקְהַל עָם תָּמִיד אֲרַנֵּן, בַּבֹּקֶר לְהַגִּיד חַסְדּוֹ וֶאֱמוּנָתוֹ בְּהִתְלוֹנֵן,[9]
❖ אוֹרוֹת טַלְלֵי תֶחִי מֶנּוּ אֶתְחוֹנֵן, אֲטוּמִים לְהַחֲיוֹת עַם בְּצִלּוֹ מִתְלוֹנֵן.

Chazzan:

בָּרוּךְ אַתָּה יהוה, מְחַיֵּה הַמֵּתִים. (Cong.– אָמֵן.)

---

the redemption by thirty years (*Rashi*, *Sanhedrin* 92b). In doing so, they contravened the oath which Joseph's brothers had sworn to him (see *Mechilta* to *Beshalach*) that they would not attempt to leave Egypt before God would redeem them. When they did battle with the Philistines on their way to Israel they were defeated and a terrible slaughter took place.

The *paytan* adopts the Midrashic view (*Shemos Rabbah* 20:10) that it was this debacle which caused God not to take Israel up to the Promised Land by the most direct route — through Philistia (*Exodus* 13:17) — when He brought them out of Egypt. The sight of the bones of their defeated brothers would have weakened their resolve and might have caused them to want to return to Egypt.

עַבְדּוֹ שָׁלַח — *He sent [Moses] His servant.* This phrase is based on the verse שָׁלַח מֹשֶׁה עַבְדּוֹ, *He sent Moses, His servant.* It is difficult to understand why the *paytan* reversed the order of the words, especially since ש is the expected initial letter.

All:

He sent [Moses,] His servant to bring them out with joy,*[1]
and He sent terrible plagues against their despoiler,
Chazzan – *O Wholesome One, remember the tested one [Abraham] whose faith was found strong,*
protect his offspring and grant them their Patriarch's heritage.

Chazzan bends his knees at *'Blessed'*; bows at *'You'*; straightens up at *'HASHEM.'*

Blessed are You, HASHEM, Shield of Abraham. (Cong. – *Amen.*)

GOD'S MIGHT

אַתָּה *You are eternally mighty, my Lord, the Resuscitator of the dead are You; abundantly able to save. He sustains the living with kindness, resuscitates the dead with abundant mercy, supports the fallen, heals the sick, releases the confined, and maintains His faith to those asleep in the dust. Who is like You, O Master of mighty deeds, and who is comparable to You, O King Who causes death and restores life and makes salvation sprout! And You are faithful to resuscitate the dead.*

All:

ת *He Who is abundant in plan and power carried out strategies,*
ש *to teach the dwellers on earth the advantage of wisdom over strength.*[2]
ר *He harnessed [Pharaoh] the lord of the castle with a bridle and misdirected him,*
ק *that he gather his assemblages to pursue the beautiful and pure [nation of Israel].*
צ *Those who cast male infants into the Nile were judged to be drowned,*
פ *He recompensed their measure by confining them in the Sea of Reeds.*
ע *He verified the ancient plans*[3] *for the people who recognize Him,*
ס *the discussion He had spoken with [Abraham] the root of the first fruits.*[4]
נ *The princes of Tzoan [Egypt] acted foolishly with a boorish plan,*[5]
מ *to overtake these foot travelers and to scatter them as with a storm wind.*
ל *If not for God Who removed His sword from its sheath,*
כ *they would have cut down the forest and burned it in flame.*
י *He Who sits in Heaven laughed, and mocked them,*[6]
ט *when He set His [angelic] troops in battle array to go out against them,*
ח *He saw that the time had come for their recompense.*
ז *He exchanged this for that [by drowning the Egyptians] to avenge His infants [that they had drowned].*
ו *To execute upon them the clearly written judgment,*[7]
ה *He recompensed them with what they sought to do to the desirable people.*
ד Chazzan — *He led the redeemed ones on a roundabout route, with revealed might,*
ג *He turned them towards the wilderness, the way to the Sea of Reeds.*[8]

All:

In the assembly of the people I shall extol His works forever,
ב *in the morning to relate His kindness, and His faithfulness through the night.*[9]
א Chazzan – *I pray that He grant invigorating rainfall and dew, to return to the living those interred and reposing in His shade.*

Chazzan:

Blessed are You, HASHEM, Who resuscitates the dead. (Cong. – *Amen.*)

(1) Cf. *Psalms* 105:26, 43. (2) Cf. *Ecclesiastes* 9:16. (3) Cf. *Isaiah* 25:1. (4) Cf. *Hosea* 9:10. (5) Cf. *Isaiah* 19:11,13. (6) Cf. *Psalms* 2:4. (7) Cf. 149:9. (8) Cf. *Exodus* 13:18. (9) Cf. *Psalms* 92:3.

All:

אָיוֹם וְנוֹרָא* מִי לֹא יִרָאֲךָ,[1] תְּוֹעֵי לֵב לֹא הִכִּירוּ מוֹרָאֲךָ,
בַּחוּרֵי אָוֶן וּפִיבֶסֶת[2] דִּין בְּהַרְאֲךָ, שׁוֹמְעֵי שִׁמְעֲךָ רָגְזוּ וְחָלוּ מִמּוֹרָאֲךָ.[3]
גֹּדֶל נוֹרְאוֹתֶיךָ מִי יוּכַל לְסַפֵּר, רַבּוּ עַד לִמְאֹד וְעָצְמוּ מִסַּפֵּר,
דְּיוֹ הַיָּם וְכָל יְצִיר סוֹפֵר, קְצַת נוֹרְאוֹתָיו לֹא יוּכְלוּ לָחֹק בַּסֵּפֶר.
הִלּוּךְ חֲמֵשׁ מֵאוֹת קָפַצְתָּ מִמְּעוֹנֶיךָ,[4] צוֹרְרֶיךָ הִצְמַתָּ כְּהֶרְעוּ בִּטְלָאֵי עֲנֶךָ,
וּבְמַחֲמַדֵּי בִטְנָם לֹא חָסָה עֵינֶיךָ, פִּטְרֵי רֶחֶם וְרָאשֵׁי אוֹן בְּעַנֶּךָ.
זִעַכָם בְּעֶשֶׂר בְּחֹמֶשׁ יָד הַגְּדוֹלָה, עוֹלוֹת אַחַת לְחָמֵשׁ* בְּעָבוֹת גְּדֵלָה,
חָשְׂפוּ זְרוֹעַ אֲשֶׁר מְאֹד גָּדְלָה, סְעָפָם עַל אַחַת חָמֵשׁ בִּגְדוֹלָה.
טְבוּעִים בְּיָוֵן מְצוּל בְּתִלּוּל הַגְּשִׁיר, נֶגֶף אֶבֶן הָסֵר וְעָקוֹב הַיְשִׁיר,
❖ יֶשַׁע מִצִּיּוֹן שְׁלַח וְחָדָשׁ נָשִׁיר, כֶּתֶר לְךָ לִתֵּן כְּאָז יָשִׁיר.

All:

חָרְשׁוּ יוֹשְׁבֵי חֲרֹשֶׁת[5] לְאַבֵּד יָפָה וּבָרָה,
נְתוּשׁ וְאַבֵּד שֵׁם וּשְׁאָר בִּגְבוּרָה,
❖ נַחַל קִישׁוֹן גְּרָפָם[6] וּזְרוֹעָם נִשְׁבָּרָה,
אָז לָבְשָׁה רוּחַ וְשָׁרָה דְבוֹרָה.

All:

קָם עַל רַבּוֹ קָמָיו לִלְזוֹת,
לַחֲמַתְּ לוֹחֲמָיו וְהִכְנַעְתָּ אוֹתָם לְהַבְזוֹת,
❖ נֹעַם זְמִירוֹת בִּטָּה לְךָ לְהַזּוֹת,
יָחַד וְשָׁר אֶת הַשִּׁירָה הַזֹּאת.[7]

All:

מִכְלַל יְפִי עַל מִשְׁפָּטוֹ יְחֻדָּשׁ,
וְעוֹד נָוֶךָ בּוֹ כְּקֶדֶם יִתְחַדָּשׁ,
❖ שִׁיאוּ לְמַעְלָה לְמַעְלָה יָרוּם וְיִגְדָּשׁ,
סֶלָה בְּתוֹכוֹ נָשִׁיר שִׁיר חָדָשׁ.

Congregation aloud, then *chazzan:*

יִמְלֹךְ יהוה לְעוֹלָם, אֱלֹהַיִךְ צִיּוֹן, לְדֹר וָדֹר, הַלְלוּיָהּ.[8]
וְאַתָּה קָדוֹשׁ יוֹשֵׁב תְּהִלּוֹת יִשְׂרָאֵל,[9] אֵל נָא.

⊱**אָיוֹם וְנוֹרָא** — *O Revered and Awesome One.* The first five stanzas follow the א״ת ב״ש arrangement of the alphabet, pairing the first letter א with the last letter ת; the second letter ב with the second to last ש; etc. The final two stanzas bear the acrostic קְלוֹנִימוֹס, *Klonimos.*

בְּחֹמֶשׁ . . . אַחַת לְחָמֵשׁ — *By a fifth . . . fivefold.* The ten plagues that hit Egypt are called the *finger of God* (*Exodus* 8:15); their afflictions at the sea are called God's *great hand* (ibid. 14:31). A hand has five fingers; it follows that the Egyptians suffered at the sea five times what they endured in Egypt — fifty plagues.

Moreover, according to one view (see page 96), each plague consisted of five parts.

All:

א *O Revered and Awesome One,* who shall not fear You?*[1]
ת *Yet those of wandering hearts did not recognize Your fearsomeness.*
ב *When You displayed upon the youth of [the Egyptian cities] Aven and Pibeses.*[2]
ש *those who heard Your reputation were agitated and shuddered from Your fearfulness.*[3]
ג *Who can recount Your great awesome deeds?*
ר *They are extremely abundant, too numerous to relate.*
ד *Were the sea ink and every creature a scribe,*
ק *even a fraction of His awesome deed they could not inscribe in a book.*
ה *You leapt across a five-hundred-year journey You leapt from Your dwelling,*[4]
צ *to crush Your enemies as they mistreated the lambs of Your flock.*
ו *On the [Egyptians'] beloved offspring You did not look with pity,*
פ *When You punished their firstborn, their initial vigor.*
ז *You shortened their lives with ten [plagues, brought] by a fifth of the great hand;*
ע *each [plague] fivefold* like a plaited braid.*
ח *He revealed His extremely great arm [at the sea],*
ס *and struck them down with five times greater [plagues].*
ט *And now, let us who are sinking in the muddy depths ascend on a bridge,*
נ *remove the stumbling stones and smooth out the crooked road.*
ימ׳ Chazzan – *Send salvation forth from Zion, and we will sing anew,*
כל *to present You with a crown [of praise] as when they sang then [at the sea].*

All:

Those who dwell in Charoshes [Yavin and Sisera][5] *thought to destroy the beautiful and pure [nation],*
to break up and eradicate their name and remnant in a powerful way.
Chazzan – *But in the Valley of Kishon they were swept away,*[6] *with their arms broken,*
then Devorah cloaked herself with the spirit [of prophecy] and sang.

All:

ק *[David,] the one who stood exalted — his many opponents sought to besmirch.*
לו *But You battled with those who fought him, and reduced them to shame.*
נ Chazzan – *He sprinkled You with the pleasant psalms he uttered;*
י *He declared Your oneness and sang, 'This song.'*[7]

All:

מ *Renew the consummate beauty [of Zion] in its proper fashion;*
ו *and the meeting place of Your Temple renew as of old.*
Chazzan – *Raise it even higher, exalted and replete,*
ס *that eternally we may sing a new song in it.*

Congregation aloud, then *chazzan:*

HASHEM shall reign forever — your God, O Zion — from generation to generation, Halleluyah![8] You, O Holy One, are enthroned upon Israel's praises[9] — please, O God.

---

(1) Cf. *Jeremiah* 10:7. (2) Cf. *Ezekiel* 30:17. (3) Cf. *Exodus* 15:14. (4) See commentary, p. 334. (5) See commentary, p. 867. (6) *Judges* 5:21. (7) See *Psalms* 18. (8) *Psalms* 146:10. (9) 22:4.

All:

אַדְנֵי חֶלֶד עַד לֹא טְבוּעִים, וְטֶרֶם תְּלוּלֵי רוּם לְאֹהֶל קְבוּעִים,
מֵאָז הֶעֱלָה בְּמַחֲשֶׁבֶת דִּגְלֵי רְבוּעִים, הֱיוֹת לוֹ מִכָּל אֹם תְּבוּעִים.
וּבְהִמָּלֵךְ לִבְרֹאת יְצִיר רֹאשׁ טְבָעִים,
בַּעֲדָם חָלוּ מֶלֶךְ וּמְשָׁרְתָיו מַצְבִּיעִים,
וּמֵאָז בְּחֶלְקוֹ עָלוּ מֵחֲלָשִׁים שִׁבְעִים, וּסְגֻלָּם לוֹ לְחֶבֶל נַחֲלָה מְקֻבָּעִים.
וּכְחָבוּ גֵרוּת וְעִנּוּי וּקְבָעוּם קוֹבְעִים.
נִתְגַּלְגְּלוּ רַחֲמָיו לְסוֹף שְׁלֹשִׁים שָׁבוּעִים,
וַיֵּט חֶסֶד עַל בְּנֵי רְבֵעִים,[1] וְהִטָּה אֹזֶן וְסָכַת שִׂיחַ מְשַׁוְּעִים.
וַיִּקַץ כְּיָשֵׁן וַיַּךְ צָרָיו בְּגִוּוּעִים, הַכֵּה וּפָצוֹעַ בְּכָל מַכָּה וַאֲבַעְבּוּעִים,
וְאַחֲרֵי כֵן שִׁלְּחוּם בִּרְכוּשׁ גָּדוֹל[2] שְׂבֵעִים,
בְּפָז וּבְכֶסֶף וּבְזָהָב וְכָל מִינֵי צְבָעִים.
וְעוֹד מָסַךְ בְּקִרְבָּם רוּחַ עִוְעִים,[3]
וַיְסִיתֵם רְדוֹף אַחֲרֵימוֹ בְּשִׁרְיוֹנוֹת וְכוֹבָעִים,
וְאָז עָלְתָה חֲמָתוֹ וַיָּשֶׁב עֲלֵיהֶם אוֹנָם וְשִׁקְּעָם בְּטִבּוּעִים,
וְנָפְלוּ וְנִשְׁבְּרוּ כְּשֵׁבֶר נֵבֶל לְמַבּוּעִים.[4]

Chazzan, then congregation:

בִּגְזֵרַת חַי וְקַיָּם נוֹרָא וּמָרוֹם וְקָדוֹשׁ.

Chazzan, then congregation:

חֲכַם לֵבָב וְאַמִּיץ כֹּחַ,[5] מִי יוּכַל אֵלָיו לְנָכְוֹחַ,
אֲשֶׁר בְּיָדוֹ הַגְּבוּרָה וְהַכֹּחַ, קָדוֹשׁ.

All:

מַה* מּוֹעִיל רֶשַׁע בְּעָלָיו, וּמַה יָּעוֹז זֵד בְּמַעֲלָלָיו,
פְּנֵי מְשַׁלֵּם לְאִישׁ כְּמִפְעָלָיו.
מֶרֶד הֲיוּכַל עֲרוֹךְ חֹמֶר, נֹכַח יוֹצֵר כֹּל בְּאֹמֶר,
רוּחוֹ וְנִשְׁמָתוֹ בְּיָדוֹ שׁוֹמֵר.
שִׁכְנוֹ שָׁת בְּרוּם עוֹלָם, מֶמְשַׁלְתּוֹ עַל כָּל הָעוֹלָם,
מִי הִקְשָׁה אֵלָיו וַיִּשְׁלָם.
שְׁלִישִׁים פָּתְחוּ רִאשׁוֹן לְקַלְקֵל, אָצוּ סְלוּל אֹרַח לְעַקֵּל,
שָׂם אֵל בָּאֱלִיל לְהָקֵל.
הַעַל פָּרְצוּ גֶּדֶר עוֹלָם, פָּרַץ מֵי הַיָּם בִּגְבוּלָם,
וְשִׁטְּפָם וְאִבְּדָם מִן הָעוֹלָם.
הֶרְאָה בָם דִּין לְדוֹרוֹת, לְבִלְתִּי פְּלוֹחַ לְכָל יְצִירוֹת,
כִּי אִם לְקוֹרֵא הַדּוֹרוֹת.[6]

(1) Cf. *Genesis* 15:16. (2) 15:14. (3) Cf. *Isaiah* 19:14. (4) Cf. 30:14. (5) *Job* 9:4. (6) Cf. *Isaiah* 41:4.

מה ◆ — *How.* The acrostic of this *piyut* reads מֹשֶׁה בְּרַבִּי קְלוֹנִימוּס, *Moshe son of R' Klonimos,* with each letter appearing twice.

All:

Before the foundations of the earth were emplaced,
and before the heavens were set as a canopy on high,
from then He raised the thought regarding the four-bannered [Israel],
to be unto Him the most sought after of nations.
And when He took counsel to create the first creature of the mold,
the King and [seventy of] His [angelic] servants began to draw lots for them [Israel],
and thence from the lottery of seventy [Israel] arose as His portion,
He treasured them for Himself and set them as the lot of His heritage.
When they were obliged to suffer alienation and pain,
the [Egyptians] looters despoiled them,
His mercy overwhelmed after thirty septads [of years],
so He stretched kindness over the children of the fourth generation,[1]
and bent an ear to hear the words of the petitioners.
He awoke as if from sleep, and smote His foe with death plagues,
He smote and lacerated with all varieties of wounds and blisters;
after that he sent them out with great satisfying wealth,[2]
With fine gold, silver, gold and all sort of dyed garb.
Further, He covered them [the Egyptians] with a spirit of madness,[3]
and convinced them to give chase with shields and helmets,
then His anger flared and He sent their recompense,
sinking them in the drowning waters,
and they fell and broke like the sudden breaking of a vessel . . .[4]

Chazzan, then congregation:

. . . at the decree of the Living, Enduring, Awesome, Exalted and Holy One.

Chazzan, then congregation:

חָכָם *Wise of heart, mighty in strength,*[5]
who is capable of opposing Him,
in Whose hand is power and strength, *O Holy One,*

All:

מ *How* can evil help its master,*
what can the wanton one accomplish with his deeds,
before the One Who repays a man for his works?
מ *Can a corporeal being wage rebellion,*
against Him Who created everything with a word,
and in Whose hand his spirit and soul one protected?
ש *He set His Presence in the heights of the world;*
His rulership is over the entire world.
Who can be stubborn against Him and remain whole?
ש *The third generation was the first to despoil,*
they rushed to twist the road and make it crooked,
to profane, calling idols by God's name.
ה *Because they breached the world's fence,*
the sea's waters inundated their area,
drowning them and making them lost to the world.
ה *Through their punishment He showed the generation,*
not to worship any creations,
but only Him Who calls the generations.[6]

בַּעֲלֵי זְרוֹעַ הֶחֱלוּ לָרֹב, וַיֹּאמְרוּ לָאֵל סוּר מִקָּרוֹב,
כְּמַלֵּא בָתֵּיהֶם טוֹבוֹת רֹב.[1]
בָּעֲטוּ בְּאֵד עוֹלֶה מִן הָאָרֶץ,[2] וְנָאֲצוּ לְמַמְטִיר עַל הָאָרֶץ,
מַה לָּנוּ לִמְטָרוֹת עָרֶץ.
רָם מָתַח דִּין בָּהֶם, וּמְטָרוֹת עֹז שָׁפַךְ עֲלֵיהֶם,
וַיִּמַח אֶת כָּל יְקוּמֵיהֶם.[3]
רָמָה רוּחַ יוֹשְׁבֵי שִׁנְעָר, וְלַעֲלוֹת לַשַּׁחַק לִבָּם נִבְעַר,
וְהֱפִיצָם בְּרוּחַ סוֹעָה וָסָעַר.
בַּד בְּבַד פֶּרַע שְׁאוֹנָם, וְנֶפֶץ מוּל נֶפֶץ דָּנָם,[4]
וּבָטְלָה עֲצָתָם כְּפֶלֶג לְשׁוֹנָם.
בַּאֲשֶׁר[5] הֵם בְּשָׂפָה זָדוּ, וּבַאֲגֻדָּה אַחַת כֻּלָּם נוֹעָדוּ,
בָּלַל לְשׁוֹנָם וּמִשָּׁם נִפְרָדוּ.[6]
יָקְשׁוּ צָרֵי עַיִן בְּבֶצַע, וּמֵאֲנוּ פְּרוּסָה לָרָעֵב לִבְצַע,
וְהֶאֱרִיכוּ וְקִצְּרוּ* אֶת הַמַּצָּע.
יָד קָפְצוּ מֵעָנִי וָדָל, וְעוֹבֵר אֹרַח מֵעֲלֵיהֶם חָדַל,
וְכָבֵד חֵטְא וְעָוֹן גָּדַל.
קִלְקְלוּ צַעֲדֵי יֹשֶׁר לְסַלֵּף, וְאוֹצָרוֹ הַטּוֹב* עֲלֵיהֶם חִלֵּף,
וַהֲפָכָם מִשֹּׁרֶשׁ דּוֹרוֹת לְאַלֵּף.
קַחַת מוּסָר מֵאֲנוּ צוֹעֲנִים, וְלֹא לָמְדוּ דַּעַת מִקַּדְמוֹנִים,
הֵרֵעוּ מִכָּל אֲשֶׁר לְפָנִים.
לָחֲצוּ בְּמֶרֶד זֶרַע חֲסִידָיו, וְגָזְרוּ גְזֵרוֹת לִבְנֵי יְדִידָיו,
וַיַּרְא יהוה וַיְעוֹרֵר חֲסָדָיו.
לְמַלֹּאת דְּבָרוֹ וּלְהָחִישׁ עֶזְרָה, אָחוֹר הֵשִׁיב חֶשְׁבּוֹן גְּזֵרָה,
וְעַל תַּנִּין שָׁפַךְ עֶבְרָה.[7]
וְלֹא בְּכֹחַ לְפִי הַגְּדֻלָּה, הֵחֵל בְּבַעֲלֵי זְרוֹעַ תְּחִלָּה,
כִּי אִם בַּעֲנָוָה גְדוֹלָה.
וְאוֹת וּמוֹפֵת שָׁלַח לְהַרְאוֹת, וְהִקְשָׁה עֹרֶף וְהִכְבִּיד תְּלָאוֹת,
אָז הִכָּהוּ מַכּוֹת נוֹרָאוֹת.
נָאוֹר אַף לְפִי חֲמָתוֹ, לֹא עִבֵּר דִּין אֲמִתּוֹ,
כִּי אִם בְּיֹשֶׁר מִדָּתוֹ.
נֶגַע אֲשֶׁר בְּסוֹף הִבְעִיתוֹ, בּוֹ הִקְדִּים תְּחִלָּה לְהַתְרוֹתוֹ,
וּמִקֵּץ לְקֵץ הֶאֱרִיךְ עֶבְרָתוֹ.

וְהֶאֱרִיכוּ וְקִצְּרוּ — *They lengthened and shortened.* Whenever a wealthy traveler would arrive in Sodom, he would be offered a fine show of hospitality. However, he would invariably be given a bed that did not accommodate him properly. If he was tall, they would give him a very short bed and under the pretense of making him comfortable, they would nail his legs to the bed so that they would not hang over the edge. When he died of the wounds they had inflicted, they would say, 'How terrible! We tried so hard to make him comfortable, but he died. How sad!' And with mock tears they would share his belongings and depart.

Similarly, if a short visitor came, they would place him on a very long bed, and then stretch his limbs until he fit the bed properly. Thus, they would kill him with 'kindness.'

ב *Strong-armed men began to increase, and they said to God,*
'Turn away from my venue,
when He had filled their homes with abundant good.'[1]

ב *They kicked at Him Who made the cloud rise from the earth,*[2]
and blasphemed Him Who makes rain fall on the earth,
[saying,] 'We don't need the Revered One's precipitation.'

ר *The Exalted One spread punishment over them,*
and poured powerful rains upon them,
and thus destroyed everything that lived.[3]

ר *The residents of Shinar were of haughty spirit,*
their hearts burned with desire to scale the heavens,
so He scattered them with a furious storm wind.

כ *He repaid their multitudes measure for measure,*
He judged them with dispersion, because they feared dispersion,[4]
and He balked their plans when He divided their tongue.

כ *Because*[5] *they sinned with their lips,*
and they gathered together in one band,
He confused their language and from there they dispersed.[6]

י *The miserly [Sodomites] were ensnared by pelf,*
refusing to spare a crumb for the hungry;
and they lengthened and shortened the bedding.*

י *They closed their hand to the poor and needy,*
and prevented travelers from passing through,
but they were heavy with sin and great iniquity.

ק *They harmfully twisted the righteous paths,*
so He exchanged His storehouse of beneficence for them,*
and uprooted them as a lesson for generations.

ק *The Tzoanite [Egyptians] refused to take heed,*
and did not learn wisdom from the earlier ones,
they were more wicked than all who preceded them.

ל *They bitterly oppressed the offspring of His pious ones,*
and decreed harsh decrees against the children of His beloved;
HASHEM saw and aroused His kindness.

ל *To fulfill His words and to hasten assistance,*
He turned back the length of the decree,
and poured fury on [Pharaoh] the sea-serpent.[7]

ו *He did not display the greatness of His power,*
by starting immediately as the strong-armed do,
but with great humility [He gave warning first].

ו *A sign and a wonder He sent to show,*
but he [Pharaoh] stiffened his neck and made the work harder.
First then He smote him with awesome plagues.

נ *Although the Illuminating One was in anger,*
He did not overstep the truth of His judgment,
but only according to its proper measure.

נ *With the last plague that caused him to hurry,*
he first began to issue warning.
And from one end [of the year] to the other He stretched His fury.

---

(1) Cf. *Job* 22:17-18. (2) Cf. *Genesis* 2:6. (3) Cf. 7:23. (4) Cf. 11:4, 8. (5) [Some *machzorim* read כַּאֲשֶׁר, *just as*. However, that reading does not fit the acrostic.] (6) Cf. 11:9. (7) See *Ezekiel* 29:3.

אוֹצָרוֹ הַטּוֹב — *His storehouse of beneficence.* According to *Deuteronomy* (28:12), God causes rain to fall from *His storehouse of beneficence.* But Sodom forfeited this boon, and He rained

יָהּ מַכֵּה לֹא הִכָּהוּ, עַד שֶׁלֹּא קָדַם וְהִתְרָהוּ,
וְאַחֲרֵי כֵן שָׁלַח וְהִלְקָהוּ.
יֶרַח הַקָּצָב לְכָל מַכָּה, וּשְׁלֹשֶׁת חֲלָקִים הֵעִיד וְחִכָּה,
וּרְבִיעִית הַחֹדֶשׁ שִׁמְּשָׁה הַמַּכָּה.
מָחַץ בּוֹ מֶחֱצוֹת תֵּשַׁע, וְלֹא נִכְנַע וְלֹא שָׁע,
וּבָעֲשִׂירִית נִשְׁבַּר מַטֵּה הָרֶשַׁע.
מֵעֶרֶשׂ יְצוּעוֹ קָם לַיְלָה, וּבְאֶרֶץ פַּתְרוֹס צְוָחָה גְדוֹלָה,
מֵאֵין בַּיִת בְּלֹא יְלָלָה.[1]
וּפֶה שֶׁאָמַר לֹא אֲשַׁלֵּחַ,[2] הוּא הַפֶּה חִנֵּן לְשַׁלֵּחַ,
קוּמוּ צְאוּ כְּדַבֶּרְכֶם לִפְלֹחַ.[3]
וְלָמָּה זֶה לַחֲשׁוּבֵי כְאַיִן, לִקְנוֹת חָכְמָה וְלֵב אַיִן,
מַתְרִים כְּנוֹגֵעַ בְּבָבַת עַיִן.
שֵׂכֶל זֹאת לֹא יָבִינוּ, פּוֹטִים אֲשֶׁר בִּתְחִלָּה הִתְקִינוּ,*
כְּעִקְּלוּ בְּסוֹף כָּךְ נִדּוֹנוּ.
❖ שֵׂעִיר וּטְפוּלָיו אֲשֶׁר לְחָרְבָּה, נִתְכַּוְּנוּ מֵרֹאשׁ וְעַד קִצְבָּה,
מַה יַּעֲשׂוּ בְּלַהַט הַיּוֹם הַבָּא.[4]

Chazzan, then congregation:

בַּעֲטוֹתוֹ קִנְאָה בְּלָבְשׁוֹ נָקָם, לְהָרִיעַ וּלְהַצְרִיחַ מִקָּמָיו לְהִתְנַקֵּם,
שִׁבְעָתַיִם יָשִׁיב אֶל חֵיקָם,[5] קָדוֹשׁ.

[In some congregations, the congregation pauses at the end of each of the next twenty-one paragraphs, as indicated in the text. In others, these prayers are recited straight through till page 932.]

Chazzan, then congregation:

וּבְכֵן, וַיּוֹשַׁע יהוה בַּיּוֹם הַהוּא.[6]

All:

אֲצוּלִים מִפֶּרֶךְ סוֹנִים, בְּחֹזֶק יָד וְנִסְיוֹנִים,
גּוֹי שׁוֹמֵר אֱמוּנִים,[7] דֵּעָה וְחָכְמָה חֲנוּנִים,
הַהוֹגִים בִּיקָרָה מִפְּנִינִים,[8] וּמִצְוֹתֶיהָ וְהוֹרָיוֹתֶיהָ מְבִינִים,
זְמִירוֹת לָאֵל נוֹתְנִים, חֶבֶל נַחֲלָתוֹ[9] מְכֻנִּים,
טְפוּלִים בּוֹ וְעָלָיו נִשְׁעָנִים, יוֹדְעִים מַה פָּעַל[10] דַּר מְעוֹנִים,
כָּאֵזוֹר בְּמָתְנַיִם נְתוּנִים, לוֹ דְבֵקִים[11] וּבְצִלּוֹ לָנִים.
❖ לָנִים וּמִסְתּוֹפְפִים בְּצֵל אֵל,
מְשׁוּכִים אַחֲרֵי אֵל, וּבְצוּרֵיהֶם נִלְחָם הָאֵל,
All – **וַיַּרְא יִשְׂרָאֵל.[12]**

(1) Cf. *Exodus* 12:30. (2) Cf. 5:2. (3) Cf. 12:31. (4) Cf. *Malachi* 3:19. (5) *Psalms* 79:12.
(6) *Exodus* 14:30. (7) Cf. *Isaiah* 26:2. (8) Cf. *Proverbs* 3:15. (9) *Deuteronomy* 32:9.
(10) Cf. *Numbers* 23:23. (11) Cf. *Jeremiah* 13:11. (12) *Exodus* 14:31.

upon them brimstone and fire (*Genesis* 19:24).

בִּתְחִלָּה הִתְקִינוּ — *At first acted properly.* When Jacob and his sons arrived in Egypt, they were treated like royalty. Only after the last brother passed away did the enslavement and oppression begin (*Rashi* to *Exodus* 6:16).

⊷ וּבְכֵן וַיּוֹשַׁע — *And so, Hashem saved.* In a pattern similar to the seventh day's *piyutim*, the *paytan* now presents twenty stanzas that alternate between an *aleph-beis* acrostic and a reverse

י *God did not smite him with any plague,*
until he had first given him warning,
only then did He send out and smite him.

י *A month was set for each plague,*
for three quarters of it He warned and waited,
then for a quarter month the plague reigned.

מ *He hit them with nine plagues,*
they would not humble themselves, they would not listen;
with the tenth the staff of wickedness was broken.

מ *From the mattress of his bed he arose at night,*
in the land of Pasros [Egypt] there was a great screaming,
there was no home in which there was no crying.[1]

ו *And the mouth that said,*
'I shall not send out,'[2] *that is the mouth that begged to send,*
'Arise, go forth, to worship as you have said.'[3]

ו *Why should it be that worthless [nations] don't gain wisdom or take to heart?*
They have been warned [that oppressing Israel is]
like touching the pupil of the eye.

ס *This wisdom they do not understand,*
*the Putite [Egyptians] who first acted properly,**
as they later became perverse, so were they judged.

ס Chazzan – *Seir and his lackeys who intended to destroy,*
from beginning to end,
what will they do in the flame of the day that is coming?[4]

Chazzan, then congregation:

בְּעֶטוֹתוֹ *When He dons vengeance when He garbs Himself in revenge,*
to shout and to scream, to avenge His opponents,
may He recompense them sevenfold into their bosom.[5] *O Holy One!*

[In some congregations, the congregation pauses at the end of each of the next twenty-one paragraphs, as indicated in the text. In others, these prayers are recited straight through till page 932.]

Chazzan, then congregation:

And so, HASHEM saved on that day . . .[6]

All:

א *. . . those set apart from the back-breaking labor of Aswan,*
ב *with a strong hand and miracles*
ג *the nation that keeps that faith,*[7]
ד *they are graced with [Torah] knowledge and wisdom*
ה *they meditate on [the Torah,] that which is more precious than pearls*[8]
ו *they understand its mitzvos and teaching,*
ז *they give forth song to God,*
ח *they are called, 'the lot of His heritage,'*[9]
ט *they cleave to Him, and rely on Him,*
י *they know what the Dweller in Heaven has wrought,*[10]
כ *with the closeness of the girdle upon the loins,*
ל *they cleave to Him*[11] *and in His protective shades they lodge.*

❖ *They lodge and stand at the threshold in God's protective shade,*
מ *they are drawn after God, and so God battles their enemies;*
All – *and Israel saw . . .*[12]

---

aleph-beis (תשר״ק). The composer buried his name in the introductory lines to each stanza in the initial letters of either the second words or phrase, as indicated by the bold print in the text. His signature reads מֹשֶׁה בְּרַבִּי קְלוֹנִימוֹס הַקָּטָן, *Moshe son of Klonimos, the Lesser.*

מוֹתַחַת גָּבְהֵי מְרוֹמִים,[1] נוֹטַעַת אַדְנֵי הֲדוֹמִים,
סוֹעֶרֶת שְׁאוֹן יַמִּים,[2] עוֹרֶפֶת הֲמוֹן קָמִים,
פּוֹרַעַת דִּין עֲנָמִים, צוֹדָה מְחַבְּלִים כְּרָמִים,[3]
קוֹלַעַת עַד צִית רָמִים,* רוֹטֶשֶׁת עַד חוּג תְּהוֹמִים,
שׁוֹפֶטֶת דִּין יְתוֹמִים, תְּהִלָּתוֹ תָּמִיד הֱיוֹת נוֹאֲמִים.
❖ נוֹאֲמִים שְׁלוֹל חֵילָם[4] בְּלֵב מַקְשֶׁה, כְּסִכְּרוֹ בְּיַד אֲדוֹנִים קָשֶׁה,[5]

All – **אָז יָשִׁיר מֹשֶׁה.**[6]

תּוֹדָה וְקוֹל זִמְרָה,[7] שֶׁבַח וְהַלֵּל וּצְפִירָה,
רוֹן וָעוֹז וְתִפְאָרָה, קוֹל אוֹמְרִים אֲשִׁירָה,[8]
צִלְצוּל לְדָר בִּנְהוֹרָא, פּוֹדֶה וּמֵחִישׁ עֶזְרָה,
עוֹנֶה בְּעֵת צָרָה, סוֹכֵת מֵעַמּוֹ עֲתִירָה,
נוֹתֵן תְּשׁוּעָה לְעַם נִבְרָא,* מַצְלִיל קָמֵיהֶם בְּעֶבְרָה.
❖ בְּעֶבְרָה הֵשַׁח יְפֵה פִיָּה,[9] וְדָלַנִי מִשְּׁאוֹל תַּחְתִּיָּה,

All – **עָזִּי וְזִמְרָת יָהּ.**[10]

לוֹ חִכְּתָה נַפְשִׁי,[11] כְּבוֹדִי וּמֵרִים רֹאשִׁי,[12]
יוֹדֵעַ בְּצַר נַפְשִׁי, טָס עַל עָב קַל לְהַנְפִּישִׁי,[13]
חָמַל עָלַי וְשָׁע רַחֲשִׁי, זָכַר חַסְדּוֹ וֶאֱמוּנָתוֹ[14] לְהַחְפִּישִׁי,
וַיַּעֲלֵנִי מִטִּיט רִפְשִׁי, הַמּוֹצִיאִי מִמַּסְגֵּר לַחָפְשִׁי,
דֵּעֵךְ וְצִמֵּת מַבְאִישִׁי, גִּלָּה כְבוֹדוֹ עָלַי לְדָרְשִׁי,
בַּצַּר לִי קְרָאתִיו וְלֹא נְטָשִׁי, אֵילִי וְחֵילִי וְלֹא בָזָה לַחֲשִׁי.
❖ לַחֲשִׁי בָּן וַיֵּצֵא בְחֵימָה, מוּל צָר לְהִלָּחֵמָה,

All – **יהוה אִישׁ מִלְחָמָה.**[15]

אָזַר עֹז וְעָט קִנְאָה, בְּשִׁרְיוֹן וְכוֹבַע נִרְאָה,[16]
גֵּאוּת לָבֵשׁ וְנִתְגָּאָה,[17] דָּרַךְ קַשְׁתּוֹ וּבְרַק חֲנִית הֶרְאָה,
הִרְעִים רַעַשׁ וְקוֹל תְּשׁוּאָה, וַתִּתְגָּעַשׁ וַתִּרְעַשׁ אֶרֶץ וּמְלוֹאָהּ,[18]
זִלְעֵף פּוּט וְלוּד בִּמְשׁוֹאָה, חָרוֹב וְהֶחֱרִיב בְּלִי רְפוּאָה,
טָרַף זְרוֹעַ וְקָדְקֹד וּפֵאָה,[19]* יָחַד שׁוֹעַ וְקוֹעַ[20] וְשַׂר מֵאָה,

(1) Cf. *Jeremiah* 40:22. (2) Cf. *Psalms* 65:8. (3) Cf. *Song of Songs* 2:15. (4) Cf. *Exodus* 15:9. (5) Cf. *Isaiah* 19:4. (6) *Exodus* 15:1. (7) *Isaiah* 51:3. (8) *Exodus* 15:1. (9) See *Jeremiah* 46:20. (10) *Exodus* 15:2. (11) Cf. *Psalms* 33:20. (12) 3:4. (13) Cf. *Isaiah* 19:1. (14) *Psalms* 98:3. (15) *Exodus* 15:3. (16) Cf. *Isaiah* 59:17. (17) Cf. *Exodus* 15:1; *Psalms* 93:1. (18) Cf. 18:8. (19) Cf. *Deuteronomy* 33:20. (20) See *Ezekiel* 22:23 with *Radak*.

קוֹלַעַת עַד צִית רָמִים — *Who tosses [His enemies] to the heavenly heights.* Before God allows a nation or an individual to be the agent of Divine retribution for Israel's sins, He elevates that nation to an exalted position in the world. Thus none can say that He gave His children over to a lowly nation (*Chagigah* 13b).

לְעַם נִבְרָא — *To the recreated people.* Such a drastic change took hold of the nation when it went from slavery to freedom, from subjugation to redemption, that it may be considered to have been created anew.

זְרוֹעַ וְקָדְקֹד וּפֵאָה — *Arm and head and side,* i.e., the general, the king and the populace (*Targum* to *Deuteronomy* 33:20).

מ *. . . One Who spreads the highest heavens,*[1]
נ *Who implanted the foundations of the earth,*
ס *Who causes the storm winds and the roar of the seas,*[2]
ע *Who beheads the multitudes who stand against Him,*
פ *Who administers justice to the Anamite [Egyptians],*
צ *Who snares the despoilers of [Israel's] vineyards,*[3]
ק *Who tosses [enemies] to the heavenly heights,**
ר *then smashes them in the depths of the sea,*
ש *Who judges the grievance of orphans,*
ת *Who praises — eternally — they proclaim.*

❖ ש *They proclaimed that they would hard-heartedly loot [Israel's] possessions,*[4]
but they were given over to a tough master[5]
All – *then Moses chose to sing . . .*[6]

ת *. . . thanksgiving and the voice of music,*[7]
ש *lauding, praise and diadem,*
ר *glad song, might and splendor,*
ק *a voice saying, 'I shall sing . . .'*[8]
צ *resonance to Him Who dwells in light,*
פ *Who redeems to Him Who dwells in light,*
ע *Who answers in time of trouble,*
ס *Who hearkens to the prayers of His people,*
נ *Who gives salvation to the recreated people,**
מ *Who drowns their opponents in fury.*

❖ ה *In fury He humbled [Egypt,[the beautiful calf,*[9]
and He drew me from the nethermost pit,
All – *God, my might and my praise.*[10]

ל *My soul longed for Him,*[11]
כ *He is my honor and He raises my head,*[12]
י *He knows my soul's troubles,*
ט *He flies on a swift cloud to grant me rest,*[13]
ח *He pitied me and turned to my prayer,*
ז *He recalled His kindness and His faithfulness, to liberate me,*[14]
ו *He lifted me out of my mud and mire,*
ה *He brought me forth from confinement to liberty,*
ד *He extinguished and cut down those who abhor me,*
ג *He revealed His honor when He sought me [at the sea],*
ב *I called to Him in my trouble and He forsook me not,*
א *He strengthened and supplied me, and did not reject my whispered prayer.*

❖ ב *My whispered prayer He understood and went forth in anger,*
to do battle against the foe,
All – *Hashem, the Master of war.*[15]

א *He girded Himself with might, cloaked himself with vengeance,*
ב *He appeared in mail and helmet,*[16]
ג *He donned grandeur and exalted Himself,*[17]
ד *He loosed His bow and displayed His flashing spear,*
ה *He thundered with a roar, a tumultuous voice,*
ו *the earth and its fill quaked with loud noise,*[18]
ז *[The Egyptian cities] Put and Lud trembled in the stream,*
ח *He drew sword and destroyed so that there was no cure,*
ט *He tore off arm and head and side,*[19]*
י *all ranks of officers together,*[20]

כֻּלָּם נִעֵר בְּכַלָּאָה, לְבַעֲבוּר אוֹם הַנֶּהֱלָאָה.

❖ הַנֶּהֱלָאָה רִחֵף בְּצִלּוֹ, וְצָר בְּתוֹךְ יָם הִצְלִילוֹ,

All – **מַרְכְּבוֹת פַּרְעֹה וְחֵילוֹ.**[1]

מַחֲנֵה צָר וְכָל שְׁאוֹנוֹ, נְגִיד וְנוֹשֵׂא כְּלֵי זֵינוֹ,

שַׂר כָּל פֶּלֶךְ וָפֶלֶךְ וּלְגִיוֹנוֹ, עָטוּר כּוֹבַע וְלָבוּשׁ שִׁרְיוֹנוֹ,

פָּרָשׁ וְרַכָּב מְצֻמֶּדֶת עַל מָתְנוֹ, צוֹעֵד בְּרֶגֶל וְקוֹלֵעַ בְּאַבְנוֹ,

קָצִין וְנִקְלֶה וְעַבְדּוֹ וַאֲדוֹנוֹ, רוֹמֵי קֶשֶׁת וְאִטֵּר יַד יְמִינוֹ,[2]

שָׂם פַּרְעֹה וְכָל הֲמוֹנוֹ, תַּמּוּ נִכְרְתוּ וְהוּרַד שְׁאוֹל גְּאוֹנוֹ.

❖ גְּאוֹנוֹ בֻּלַּע וּשְׁאוֹנוֹ נֶחֱרָמוּ, וְיַחַד כֻּלָּם נֶהֱמָמוּ,

All – **תְּהֹמֹת יְכַסְיֻמוּ.**[3]

תְּהוֹם אֶל תְּהוֹם קָרָא,[4] שְׁאוֹן סוּף לְעֻמָּתָם נִתְגָּרָה,

רַעַם נָרַעַשׁ וְקוֹל וְעֶבְרָה, קָדִים וְסוּפָה וּסְעָרָה,[5]

צִנּוֹרוֹת מִפֹּה וּמִפֹּה מְקַלְּחִין בִּגְבוּרָה, פְּלָגִים יִבְלֵי נְהָרָה,[6]

עֶבְרָה וָזַעַם וְצָרָה,[7] סָבִיב בְּעֶתְיוּהוּ צָר עִם כָּל שְׁיָרָה,

נִשְׁקְעוּ כֻּלָּם יַחַד כַּאֲבָרָה, מִבְּלִי הוֹתִיר מוֹלִיךְ בְּשׂוֹרָה.*

❖ בְּשׂוֹרָה יָצְאָה וְחָלוּ כָּל בַּעֲלֵי מְדָנַי,

וְאִדְּרוּהוּ יַחַד צִיר וְכָל הֲמוֹנָי,

All – **יְמִינְךָ יהוה.**[8]

לְמַעַן סַפֵּר בְּכָל גֵּיא שְׁמֶךָ, כֹּחֲךָ הֶרְאֵיתָ בְּמִתְקוֹמְמֶיךָ,

יָצָאתָ לְיֵשַׁע עַמֶּךָ,[9] טִבְחָה לָשִׁית בְּקָמֶיךָ,

חָשַׂפְתָּ יְמִין תַּעֲצוּמֶיךָ, זְרוֹת כַּמּוֹץ לוֹחֲמֶיךָ,

וַתִּנְהוֹם בְּשַׁאֲגַת רְעָמֶיךָ, הֲמוֹן הוֹמִים לְעֻמֶּךָ,

דִּין גָּמוּר דַּנְתָּ כִּנְאֻמֶּךָ,[10] גּוֹי הַמַּעֲבִיר רְחוּמֶיךָ,

בְּכָל גּוֹיִם נִשְׁמַע נִקְמֶךָ, אֲשֶׁר עָשִׂיתָ לְעַמֶּךָ.

❖ לְעַמְּךָ קוֹלָם הִסְכֵּיתָ מִמְּעוֹנָךְ, וְרוֹדְפֵיהֶם הִכְנַעְתָּ בַּחֲרוֹנָךְ,

All – **וּבְרֹב גְּאוֹנְךָ.**[11]

אֶדֶר גֵּאוּת לָבַשְׁתָּ, בְּעָזְּךָ יָם כְּפוֹרַרְתָּ,

גְּאוּת עָרִיצִים הִשְׁפַּלְתָּ,[12] דַּכְאוּת דַּלִּים רוֹמַמְתָּ,

הֲלֹא מֵי יַם סוּף הוֹבַשְׁתָּ,[13] וּבְמַעֲמַקֵּי יָם דֶּרֶךְ שַׂמְתָּ,[14]

---

(1) *Exodus* 15:4. (2) Cf. *Judges* 20:16. (3) *Exodus* 15:5. (4) Cf. *Psalms* 42:8. (5) Cf. *Isaiah* 29:6. (6) Cf. *Isaiah* 30:25. (7) *Psalms* 78:49. (8) *Exodus* 15:6. (9) *Habakkuk* 3:13. (10) See *Genesis* 15:14. (11) *Exodus* 15:7. (12) Cf. *Isaiah* 13:11. (13) Cf. *Joshua* 2:10. (14) Cf. *Isaiah* 51:10.

מִבְּלִי הוֹתִיר מוֹלִיךְ בְּשׂוֹרָה — *So none remained to bring the report.* The Midrash records two views regarding Pharaoh at the sea. According to one view, he was saved in order that he might carry an eye-witness report about God's might to all the nations of the world. But the *paytan* here adopts the opposing opinion that Pharaoh also drowned in the sea, although not immediately (*Midrash Tehillim* 106: *Mechilta, Beshalach*).

כ *He tossed all of them into the prison [of the sea],*
ל *for the sake of the weary nation.*

❖ ר *The weary nation hovered in His protective shade,*
while the enemy drowned in the sea,
All — *Pharoah's chariots and army.*[1]

מ *The enemy's camp and all its multitude,*
נ *officer along with his arms bearer,*
ס *commander of each section and his legion,*
ע *crowned in helmet and clad in his main,*
פ *horseman and charioteer, [sword] sheathed on his loin,*
צ *foot soldier and artillery man*
ק *rich man and pauper, servant and master,*
ר *archers and left-handed marksmen,*[2]
ש *there Pharaoh and his entire multitude,*
ת *were wiped out, cut down; lowered into the pit was his grandeur.*

❖ ב *His grandeur was swallowed, his multitudes were destroyed*
as one they were all confounded,
All — *deep waters covered them.*[3]

ת *Watery deep called out to watery deep,*[4]
ש *the roaring Sea of Reeds was agitated against them,*
ר *thunder, earthquake and the sound of fury,*
ק *East wind, tempest and storm,*[5]
צ *heavily flowing channels from here and from there,*
פ *natural streams and canals,*[6]
ע *fury and wrath and trouble,*[7]
ס *He caused trepidation to surround the enemy and his entourage,*
נ *they all sank together like lead,*
מ *so none remained to bring the report.**

❖ י *The report went forth and all the strong armed foe trembled as one,*
the emissary [Moses] and all my multitude praised Him,
All — *'Your right hand, Hashem . . .'*[8]

ל *In order that Your Name be spoken of throughout the earth,*
כ *You displayed Your strength against those who opposed You,*
י *You went forth for the salvation of Your people,*[9]
ט *to perform the slaughter of Your adversaries,*
ח *You revealed Your mighty right hand,*
ז *to scatter like chaff those who do battle against You,*
ו *You shouted with Your thunderous roar*
ה *at the multitudes screaming defiantly at You,*
ד *You judged them with full justice, as You had said,*[10]
ג *that nation that bypassed Your attribute of kindness,*
ב *Your vengeance was heard among all the nations,*
א *that which You did for the sake of Your people.*

❖ ק *Your people's voice — You hearkened to from Your heavenly dwelling,*
and You humbled their pursuers in Your anger,
All — *in Your abundant grandeur.*[11]

א *You donned a cloak of grandeur,*
ב *when You split the sea with Your might,*
ג *You laid low the wicked ones' haughtiness,*[12]
ד *the oppressed paupers You elevated,*
ה *indeed You dried up the Sea of Reed's waters,*[13]
ו *and You placed a road in the depths of the sea,*[14]

זַכִּים בּוֹ הֶעֱבַרְתָּ, חֲנֵפִים בְּתוֹכוֹ שִׁקַּעְתָּ,
טִבְעֲךָ בָּעוֹלָם הוֹדַעְתָּ, יִרְאָתְךָ עַל פְּנֵי כָל הָעַמִּים תַּתָּה,
כַּסְלְחִים עֵת הִכְנַעְתָּ, לְבַדְּךָ עַל כָּל אֱלֹהַּ נִתְגַּדַּלְתָּ.
❖ נִתְגַּדַּלְתָּ (וְנִתְקַדַּשְׁתָּ)[1] לְשַׁבֵּר רָאשֵׁי תַנִּינִים בְּתָקְפֶּךָ,
וְהִסְעַרְתָּ לֵב יָם בְּזַעְפֶּךָ,
All – **וּבְרוּחַ אַפֶּיךָ.**[2]

מִפֹּה וּמִפֹּה עֲרֵמוֹת, נוֹזְלִים צָגוּ כַחוֹמוֹת,
סָעֲרוּ וְקָפְאוּ תְהוֹמוֹת,[2] עָמְדוּ צְרוּרִים כַּחֵמוֹת,
פָּנוּ כָּאן וְכָאן שְׁלִישׁ רוּם מֵימוֹת,* צָצוּ הַנּוֹתָרִים לְמִדְרַס פְּעָמוֹת,
קָרְעוּ אֶת שֶׁבַּנְּהָרִים וַאֲגַמּוֹת, רִבָּה בּוֹר וְשִׁיחַ וְנִקְרַת אֲדָמוֹת,
שְׁאוּבִים אַף שֶׁהָיוּ בְּכָל מְקוֹמוֹת, תִּכּוּ יַחַד בִּגְזֵרַת לוֹבֵשׁ נְקָמוֹת.
❖ נְקָמוֹת וְקִנְאָה יָעַט שׂוֹנְאָיו לַהֲדֹף, כְּמוֹ לְשֶׁעָבַר עָט לִנְדֹּף,
All – **אָמַר אוֹיֵב אֶרְדֹּף.**[3]

תַּעֲלוּלֵי צָר וְרוֹעַ מַעֲלָלֵהוּ, שֶׁקֶט וְשָׁלֵו לֹא הִנִּיחוּהוּ,
רוּחַ עָרִיצִים הִתְעָהוּ, קִיאוֹ לָשׁוּב וּלְבַלְּעֵהוּ,[4]*
צוּר עָבוּר לְגַבּוֹת שְׁטַר נְשִׁיֵּהוּ, פִּלֵּג לִבּוֹ וְהִשְׁגֵּהוּ,
עַם הַנִּתָּק מִמְּתַלְּעוֹת פִּיהוּ, שָׁח אֶרְדֹּף אַשִּׂיג וַאֲכַלֵּהוּ,[5]
נִפְרַע סְאָה בִסְאָה בְּרִשְׁעֵהוּ, מָדַד לוֹ כְּנֶגֶד מִדּוֹתֵיהוּ.
❖ מִדּוֹתֵיהוּ נִאֵץ מִי יהוה מוּל שְׁלוּחֶךָ, גְּרַרְתּוֹ בְּמֵי יָם לְהוֹדִיעוֹ כֹּחֶךָ,[6]
All – **נָשַׁפְתָּ בְרוּחֲךָ.**[7]

לְהָשִׁיב יָם לְאֵיתָנוֹ, כִּפְנוֹת בֹּקֶר לְעִנְיָנוֹ,
יָם הַגָּדוֹל פָּרַץ מֵאוֹגְנוֹ, טָרַף זֶה בְּזֶה* לְהַגְבִּיר שְׁאוֹנוֹ,
חַי כָּל אֶחָד וְאֶחָד בְּעוֹד יְשָׁנוֹ, זִלְעֵף רוּחוֹ בְּתוֹךְ נְדָנוֹ,
וַיַּעֲלֵם עַד רוּם מְעוֹנוֹ, הוֹרִידָם לְמַטָּה בְּדָכְיוֹת עֲשׁוֹנוֹ,
דִּבֵּק סוּס בְּרֶכֶב וְהִשְׁמִיט אוֹפַנּוֹ, גְּרָרָם בְּכֹבֶד בְּמֶתֶג רִסְנוֹ,[8]
בְּלֶב יָם הֱבִיאָם בְּעֶצֶם אוֹנוֹ, אֲכָלוּ כְּקַשׁ יָבֵשׁ בַּחֲרוֹנוֹ.[9]
❖ בַּחֲרוֹנוֹ יָרָה בַיָּם אֱוִילִים, וְשׁוֹרְרוּ לוֹ בְּנֵי אֵלִים,
All – **מִי כָמֹכָה בָּאֵלִים.**[10]

---

(1) Cf. *Ezekiel* 38:23. (2) *Exodus* 15:8. (3) 15:9. (4) Cf. *Proverbs* 26:11. (5) Cf. *Exodus* 15:9. (6) 5:2. (7) 15:10. (8) Cf. *Psalms* 32:9. (9) Cf. *Exodus* 15:7. (10) 15:11.

שְׁלִישׁ רוּם מֵימוֹת — *A third of the waters' height.* According to the Midrash, one-third of the Sea of Reeds' waters rose and congealed into walls. This is derived from the verse: *The deep waters congealed in the heart of the sea* (*Exodus* 15:8). Just as the heart demarcates one-third of the body (from the head down), so did one-third of the water rise (*Bamidbar Rabbah* 9:14). The *paytan* adds that the other two-thirds of the water rose into a dry, solid floor on which the Jewish nation crossed the sea.

וּלְבַלְּעֵהוּ — *And to swallow it again.* King Solomon taught, *As a dog returns to his vomit, so a fool repeats his foolishness* (*Proverbs* 26:11). The *paytan* applies this verse to Pharaoh, who after finally ridding himself of the plagues by setting the Jewish slaves free (*Exodus* 12:31), brought troubles back upon himself by saying, 'What is this we have done that we have sent Israel out from our service?' (ibid. 14:5), and giving chase to bring them back.

טָרַף זֶה בְּזֶה — *They merged with each other.* The waters of the Mediterranean Sea flooded their banks and flowed to the Sea of Reeds. There the

ז *You brought the meritorious [Israel] across on it,*
ח *while the falsifiers drowned in the sea,*
ט *You displayed Your attributes to the world*
י *You set Your awe upon the face of all peoples,*
כ *When You humbled the Kasluchite [Egyptians],*
ל *above all the mighty ones You exalted Yourself.*

❖ ל *You exalted Yourself (and sanctified Yourself)*[1]
when You broke the sea-serpents' heads with Your power,
and You made the heart of the sea rage in Your anger,
All — *and with the wind of your wrath . . .*[2]

מ *. . . [the waters] heaped up here and there,*
נ *the flowing waters stood erect like walls,*
ס *the deep waters stormed, then congealed,*[2]
ע *they stood bound as if in flasks,*
פ *a third of the waters height* turned to this side and that,*
צ *while the remainder spread out under their feet.*
ק *The waters of rivers and swamps were torn apart,*
ר *including [those] in a pit, cistern or crevice in the ground,*
ש *even the drawn waters, wherever they were [placed],*
ת *all split in their center as one, at the decree of the One Who dons vengeance.*

❖ ו *May He don vengeance and jealousy with which to overpower His enemies,*
as in the past when He donned [vengeance] to disperse [Egypt],
All — *when the enemy declared, 'I will pursue.'*[3]

ת *The oppressor's hidden actions and His openly evil works,*
ש *did not allow him to sit in quiet serenity,*
ר *ruthlessness of spirit led him astray,*
ק *to return to his vomit and to swallow it again.*[4]*
צ *The Creator, in order to collect his owing debt,*
פ *split his heart and caused him to err [and to chase]*
ע *the people that had slipped away from his fangs,*
ס *thus he said, 'I will pursue; I will overtake; I will exterminate them!'*[5]
נ *He was recompensed bushel for bushel of his wickedness,*
מ *for it was meted out to him according to his measure.*

❖ נ *His measure was to blaspheme [saying,] 'Who is* HASHEM*?'*[6] *Your emissary.*
You dragged him through the sea's water to let him know Your strength,
All — *You blew with Your wind . . .*[7]

ל *. . . to return the sea to its original power,*
כ *by dawn's arrival it should be in its usual way.*
י *Then the Mediterranean Sea flooded its banks,*
ט *they merged with each other* to increase its tumultuousness.*
ח *As long as each one of them was still alive,*
ז *He set a spirit of trepidation into his [body] cavity,*
ו *and raised them to the heights of His Heavenly dwelling,*
ה *then threw them down into the deepest depths.*
ד *He bound horse and rider together and loosed the [charioteer's] wheel,*
ג *He dragged them heavily with his muzzle and harness*[8]
ב *with His powerful might He brought them to the heart of the sea,*
א *they were consumed like straw by His burning wrath.*[9]

❖ י *His burning wrath threw the fools into the sea,*
and the sons of the Patriarchs sang to Him,
All — *'Who is like You among the powerful. . .'*[10]

אֱלֹהַּ עַל כָּל אֱלֹהִים,[1] בּוֹרֵא עֹמֶק וְרוּם גְּבֹהִים,[2]
גּוֹזֵר יָם גַּלָּיו לְבַל יְהוּ זוֹהִים, דֹּק וָחֶלֶד מֵאֵימָתוֹ נִרְהִים,
הָאוֹמֵר לַחֶרֶס וְזָהֳרָיו כֵּהִים, וְחוֹתֵם בְּעַד הַלִּים וְלֹא מַגִּיהִים,
זִקִּים וּבְרָקִים מִמֶּנּוּ נִשְׁלָחִים, חָשִׁים בִּשְׁלִיחוּתוֹ וְלֹא שׁוֹהִים,
טִכֵּס גַּלְגַּל קָבוּעַ וּמַזָּלוֹת צוֹמְחִים, יִחַד כְּסִיל וְכִימָה עִמָּם זוֹרְחִים,
כּוֹנֵן עָשׁ[3] בַּצָּפוֹן וְעַקְרָב בַּדָּרוֹם מֻנָּחִים, לְיִחוּד שְׁמוֹ כֻּלָּם מוֹכִיחִים.
❖ מוֹכִיחִים מַעֲשֶׂיךָ אַהֲבַת אֱמוּנֶיךָ, לְבַלַּע לוֹחֲצֵי הֲמוֹנֶיךָ,
All – **נָטִיתָ יְמִינְךָ.**[4]
מוּמָתִים וְלֹא מֵתִים בְּעוֹדָם, נַפְשׁוֹתָם עֲדַיִן צְרוּרוֹת בְּחֶלְדָּם,
סַעַר סוּף לְיַבֶּשֶׁת לְיַדָּם, עֵיפָתָה אַף הִיא קִלְעָתָם לְבֵית מְצוּדָם,[5]
פְּצוּעִים וְנִפְצָעִים וּמְפֻלָּח כְּבֵדָם,[6] צְנוּפִים כַּדּוּר[7] עִם מַרְכְּבוֹת כְּבוֹדָם,
קָרוּעַ וְרָקוּעַ נֶחֱרִים בַּעֲדָם, רִיב וּמַצָּה נִתְגָּרוּ עַל יָדָם,
שַׁדַּי הַמְשַׁלֵּם לְשׂוֹנְאָיו לְהַאֲבִידָם, שָׁת יְמִינוֹ לָאָרֶץ לִגְמֹל לָהֶם חַסְדָּם,
תָּפְתֶּה פָּעֲרָה פִּיהָ וּבָלְעָה הוֹדָם, תְּחַתְתּוּ יַחַד וְעִמָּם רֶכֶב וְסוּס נִרְדָּם.[8]
❖ נִרְדָּם וְאָבַד שְׁאוֹן בּוֹגְדֶיךָ. וּבְנֵי זֶרַע חֲסִידֶיךָ,
All – **נָחִיתָ בְחַסְדְּךָ.**[9]
אֹרַח עוֹלָם עֲלֵיהֶם בְּאַהַב שִׁנִּיתָ, בְּנֵי עֲבָדֶיךָ כְּדֶרֶךְ אֲדוֹנִים הִנְחֵיתָ,
גַּעְגּוּעִים כְּאָב לַבָּנִים לָמוֹ עָשִׂיתָ, דְּבַשׁ מִסֶּלַע אוֹתָם הֵינַקְתָּ,[10]*
הִרְחַקְתָּ וְהִלְבַּשְׁתָּ וְהִנְעַלְתָּ וְסַכְתָּ,[11]
וּבְסֹלֶת וּדְבַשׁ וָשֶׁמֶן אוֹתָם הִרְבֵּיתָ,[12]
זֶה בְּעַמּוּד עָנָן הִנְחֵיתָ, חֹשֶׁךְ בְּעַמּוּד אֵשׁ כְּמַנְהִיר[13] נַעֲשֵׂיתָ,
טַל מִתַּחַת וְלֶחֶם מִמַּעַל[14] לָמוֹ הֶחֱשַׁרְתָּ,
יְאוֹרִים לִצְמָאָם מִצּוּר הוֹצֵאתָ,
כְּנַסְתָּם לְהַר חֶמֶד וּמִצְוֹת וְחֻקִּים הוֹרֵיתָ,
לְמַעַנְךָ כְּגֹדֶל חַסְדְּךָ לִנְוֵה קָדְשְׁךָ נָחִיתָ.[15]
❖ נָחִיתָ סְגוּלֶיךָ יָם כְּגָזוּן, וְצוֹרְרֵיהֶם צִירִים כַּיּוֹלֵדָה אֲחָזוּן,
All – **שָׁמְעוּ עַמִּים יִרְגָּזוּן.**[16]
מִקּוֹל מַפֶּלֶת שְׁאוֹן פּוֹרְכִים, נִרְעֲשׁוּ אִיִּים וְיוֹשְׁבֵי כְרַכִּים,

(1) Cf. *Psalms* 136:2. (2) Cf. *Proverbs* 25:3. (3) Cf. *Job* 9:9. (4) *Exodus* 15:12.
(5) See commentary, p. 898. (6) Cf. *Proverbs* 7:23. (7) Cf. *Isaiah* 22:18. (8) Cf. *Psalms* 76:7.
(9) *Exodus* 15:13. (10) Cf. *Deuteronomy* 32:13. (11) Cf. *Ezekiel* 16:9-10. (12) Cf. 16:13.
(13) Cf. *Exodus* 13:21. (14) Cf. 16:13-14. (15) Cf. 15:13. (16) 15:14.

combined waters of the two seas wreaked devastation on Pharaoh and his army.

דְּבַשׁ מִסֶּלַע — *Honey from a rock.* When the time came for the Jewish women in Egypt to give birth, they would go out into the fields and have their babies there, out of sight of the Egyptian taskmasters who wished to kill every new baby. An angel would descend and perform the midwifery. Since the mother had to return to her slave labor before her absence was realized, the infants would be left in the care of the angelic midwives. Two round stones were presented to each baby: from one the baby would suck honey, and from the other would flow oil with which the baby would be anointed and cleansed — as it is written (*Deuteronomy* 32:13), *He gave him to suck honey from a rock, and oil from a flintrock* (*Sotah* 11b).

א *God over all the heavenly powers,*[1]
ב *He creates the depths [of earth] and the highest heights [of heaven],*[2]
ג *He splits the sea that its waves not become arrogant,*
ד *heaven and earth tremble from Your awesomeness,*
ה *He Who tells the sun and moon to dim their light,*
ו *and seals off the stars that they not shine,*
ז *thunder and lightning are sent forth from Him,*
ח *they hasten in their errands and tarry not.*
ט *He set the permanent sphere and revolving constellations, in order,*
י *together Orion and Pleiades shine with them,*
כ *He set Ursa*[3] *in the north and Scorpio in the south,*
ל *to the Oneness of His Name they all point.*

❖ מ *They point — Your works — to the love of Your faithful,*
to swallow up the oppressors of Your multitudes,
All – *You stretched out Your right hand.*[4]

מ *Dying, but not dead — still living,*
נ *their souls still bound to their bodies,*
ס *You caused the Sea of Reeds to storm and toss them ashore,*
ע *but the earth slung them back to their [watery] prison,*[5]
פ *wounded and lacerated, their liver pierced,*[6]
צ *tossed like a ball*[7] *with their famous chariots,*
ק *the split [sea] and the spread [earth] were angered because of them,*
ר *dispute and strife were aroused by their hand*
ש *the Omnipotent Who repays his enemies [for the little good they have done], in order to remove them forever,*
ש *placed His right hand on the earth to repay their kindness,*
ת *Gehinnom opened its mouth and swallowed their majesty,*
ת *they descended to the Pit together — and with them rider and horse — to eternal sleep.*[8]

❖ ו *Eternal sleep and extermination for the multitudes who rebel against You,*
but the children of Your pious one's offspring
All – *You guided in Your kindness.*[9]

א *You changed the ways of nature in Your love for them [Israel],*
ב *the children of Your servants You led like royalty,*
ג *You long for them like a father for his children,*
ד *You suckled them with honey from a rock,*[10]*
ה *You bathed them, dressed them, shod them and anointed them,*[11]
ו *You raised them on fine flour, honey and oil,*[12]
ז *You led this [nation] with a pillar of cloud,*
ח *You turned the darkness to light with a pillar of fire,*[13]
ט *You rained for them an underlayer of dew with manna-bread upon it,*[14]
י *You extracted streams from a rock for their thirst,*
כ *You gathered them at the desirous mount, mitzvos and decrees to teach them,*
ל *for Your sake, with Your great kindness, to Your holy abode You guided them.*[15]

❖ ס *You guided Your treasured ones as You sheared the sea,*
their oppressors were gripped with labor-like pangs,
All – *peoples heard — they were agitated.*[16]

מ *With the sound of the taskmasters' multitudes' downfall,*
נ *the residents of islands and cities were overwhelmed,*

סְלָעֲמוּ סוֹד נִמְלָכִים, עֻלְּפוּ וְנָסוֹגוּ אָחוֹר נְסִיכִים,
פַּחוֹת וּסְגָנִים נִמְרָכִים, צוֹר וְצִידוֹן וְכָל גְּלִילֵי פְּלֶשֶׁת[1] נְבֻכִים,
קָצִין וְרָשׁ וְאִישׁ תְּכָכִים,[2] רֶטֶט הֶחֱזִיקוּ[3] וְכַמַּיִם נִשְׁפָּכִים,
שָׁמְמוּ עֲלֵיהֶם הוֹלְכֵי דְרָכִים, תְּמָהוֹן קָמוּ מִכִּסְאוֹתָם מְלָכִים.
❖ מְלָכִים הוֹלָלוּ וְהָרְעָלוּ, וְשֵׂעִיר וְזִמִּי וְאַרְוָדִי חָלְחָלוּ,*
All – **אָז נִבְהֲלוּ.**[4]
תֵּימָן וְיוֹשְׁבָיו נְפוּגִים, שִׁבְרוֹן לֵב וְרִפְיוֹן יָדַיִם מַשִּׂיגִים,
רַבֵּי מוֹאָב מִתְמוֹגְגִים, קִינִים וּנְהִי בְּפִיהֶם הוֹגִים,
צְעִיר חָם וְכָל אֵלָיו זָגִים, פָּחֲדוּ וְרָעֲדוּ וְכַדּוֹנַג נְמוֹגִים,
עַרְקִי וְסִינִי כַּשִּׁכּוֹר הוֹגִים, סוֹעָה וְסַעַר בָּם מַנְהִיגִים,
נִבְעֲרוּ כֻלָּם וְנַעֲשׂוּ שׁוֹגִים, מְדַמְמִים לָאָרֶץ יָשְׁבוּ נוֹגִים.[5]
❖ נוֹגִים קְטַנִּים וּגְדוֹלִים כְּאֶחָד, וּכְאָז כֵּן עַתָּה כָּל צוֹרְרֶיךָ יַחַד,
All – **תִּפֹּל עֲלֵיהֶם אֵימָתָה וָפַחַד.**[6]
לְמַעַן לָמוּג לְבָבֵיהֶם, כּוֹס חֲמָתְךָ מְסֹךְ בֵּינֵיהֶם,
יִרְאָה וָרַעַד יָבֹא בָהֶם, טֵרוּף דַּעַת בִּלְבָבֵיהֶם,
חַלְחָלָה וּמַעַד עַל מָתְנֵיהֶם, זִיעַ וָרֶתֶת בְּכָל אֵבָרֵיהֶם,
וְכָשְׁלוּ מֵהֶם וּבָהֶם, הֹוָה עַל הֹוָה תָּבֹא עֲלֵיהֶם,[7]
דּוּמָם יֵשְׁבוּ תַחְתֵּיהֶם, גַּעַר מְלֵאִים וְאֵין מַרְפֵּא לָהֶם,
בָּנֶיךָ עַד יַעַבְרוּ לִגְבוּלֵיהֶם,[8] אֶל הָאָרֶץ אֲשֶׁר נִשְׁבַּעְתָּ לַאֲבוֹתֵיהֶם.
❖ לַאֲבוֹתֵיהֶם טוֹב פָּצְתָּ מַלֵּא לִבְנֵימוֹ, וְאֶל הַר מְרוֹם מַאֲוַיֵּמוֹ,
All – **תְּבִאֵמוֹ וְתִטָּעֵמוֹ.**[9]
אֶרֶץ מִכָּל אֲרָצוֹת עִשּׂוּר מְפֹרָשָׁה, בְּעֶשֶׂר קְדֻשּׁוֹת מְקֻדָּשָׁה,[10]
גַּם עוֹד מִמֶּנָּה מַעֲשֵׂר מִן הַמַּעֲשֵׂר מְנַת גָּבְהָהּ הַפְרָשָׁה,
דִּירַת יְבוּסִי[11] הִיא הָעִיר הַקְּדוֹשָׁה,
הֶעֱלָה מֵאָז בְּמַחֲשֶׁבֶת עַד לֹא קְרֹאת יַבָּשָׁה,[12]
וְתָמִיד עֵינֵי אֱלֹהִים בָּהּ לְדָרְשָׁה,[13]
זִמְּנָהּ לוֹ לְכֵס שֶׁבֶת וּלְיִשְׂרָאֵל יְרֻשָּׁה,
חֲנוֹת בְּתוֹכָהּ סֻכּוֹת מֵהֶם לְחִישָׁה,
טַלְלֵם בְּצֵל מֵחֹרֶב מְצוֹא נְפִישָׁה, יַחַד לְחַשְׂכָם מִזֶּרֶם וְרוּחַ קָשָׁה,[14]
כָּל נֶגַע וְכָל מַכָּה אֲנוּשָׁה,[15] לְהָסִיר מֵאֹם מְשֻׁלָּשָׁה.*

(1) Cf. *Joel* 4:4. (2) Cf. *Proverbs* 29:13. (3) Cf. *Jeremiah* 49:24. (4) *Exodus* 15:15. (5) Cf. *Lam*. 2:10. (6) *Exodus* 15:16. (7) Cf. *Ezekiel* 7:26. (8) Cf. *Jeremiah* 31:16. (9) *Exodus* 15:17. (10) Mishnah, *Keilim* 1:6. (11) See *Joshua* 18:28 and *I Chronicles* 11:4. (12) Cf. *Genesis* 1:10. (13) Cf. *Deuteronomy* 11:12. (14) Cf. *Isaiah* 25:4. (15) Cf. *Micah* 1:9; *Jeremiah* 15:18.

וְשֵׂעִיר וְזִמִּי וְאַרְוָדִי — *Seir, the Zimmites and the Arvadites.* These are three nations. Some identify them as Edom, Moab and Canaan, since those are the three listed in *Exodus* 15:15, which corresponds to this stanza of the *piyut*. Edom is often identified with Seir (e.g., *Genesis* 36:9); זִמִּי, *Zimmites*, alludes to Moab, a nation steeped in זִמָּה, *adultery;* and the Arvadites were a Canaanite tribe (ibid. 10:18). Some *machzorim* read וְאָרוּרִי, *the cursed one*, an allusion to the progenitor of Canaan who was cursed by his grandfather Noah (ibid. 9:25).

מֵאֹם מְשֻׁלָּשָׁה — *From the trebled nation.* Israel is described as a trebled nation because it comprises *Kohanim*, Levites and Israelites.

ס *they swarmed like locusts to take counsel,*
ע *but princes wearied and retreated,*
פ *sultans and viziers weakened,*
צ *Tyre, Sidon and the territories of Philistia*[1] *were confounded,*
ק *wealthy and pauper and the middle classes,*[2]
ר *trembling overcame*[3] *them, and they poured out like water,*
ש *travelers wondered about them,*
ת *and bewildered, they arose from their thrones — the kings.*

✣ ה *The kings became foolish with astonishment,*
*Seir, the Zimmites, the Arvadites, trembled,**
All – *then they were confounded.*[4]

ת *Teiman and its inhabitants became faint,*
ש *heartbreak and weakhandedness overtook them,*
ר *the chieftains of Moab melted,*
ק *their mouths uttered elegy and sobs,*
צ *Ham's youngest son (Canaan) and all his allies,*
פ *feared, trembled and melted like wax,*
ע *the Arkites and Sinites danced like drunks,*
ס *tempest and stormwind led them about,*
נ *they all became boorish and acted like fools,*
מ *silently they sat on the ground aggrieved.*[5]

✣ ק *Aggrieved, young and old alike, as then, so now, all Your enemies together,*
All – *make fear and terror befall them.*[6]

ל *in order to melt their hearts,*
כ *pour the cup of Your wrath among them,*
י *may fear and trembling come upon them,*
ט *place madness in their hearts,*
ח *shaking and weakness on their loins,*
ז *sweat and shivering in all their organs,*
ו *let each stumble over the other,*
ה *may trouble upon trouble come upon them,*[7]
ד *may they be made to sit silently in their places,*
ג *full with rebuke, with no cure for them,*
ב *until Your children return to their borders,*[8]
א *to the land You swore [to give] to their forefathers.*

✣ ט *To their forefathers You promised beneficence,*
may You fulfill it for their children,
and [take them] to the [Temple] Mount, the heights of their longing,
All – *bring them and implant them there.*[9]

א *The land set aside as a tithe from all the lands,*
ב *sanctified with ten degrees of holiness,*[10]
ג *and also from it was a tithe from the tithe set aside as the Exalted One's portion,*
ד *[Jerusalem,] the Holy City that had been the dwelling place of the Jebusite,*[11]
ה *it was in His plans even before He called the dry land ['eretz'],*[12]
ו *and God's eyes always seek it out,*[13]
ז *He prepared it as the seat of His throne and Israel's heritage,*
ח *to dwell in it, there to hearken to whispered prayer.*
ט *Protect them from the heat with shade, that they may find serenity,*
י *be a refuge to them all from the storm and harsh winds,*[14]
כ *from all plague and incurable affliction,*[15]
ל *to remove [all of these] from the trebled nation.**

❖ מְשֻׁלָּשָׁה נִבָּטָה בְּרוּחַ לְהָרֵעַד,[1] וּבִלְשׁוֹן עָתִיד פָּתְחָה וְסִיְּמָה לְהָעֵד,

All – **יהוה יִמְלֹךְ לְעוֹלָם וָעֶד.**[2]

מַלְכוּת עַד לֹא קֶדֶם קְדוּמָה, נֶצַח נְצָחִים מְקֻיָּמָה,
סוֹף וָקֶדֶם וְתָוֶךְ עֲצוּמָה, עַד עוֹלְמֵי עַד מְסֻיָּמָה,
פּוּטִים כְּכַלָּה בִּמְהוּמָה, צְנִיף מְלוּכָה הִמְלִיכְוּהוּ דִּגְלֵי אֲיֻמָּה,
קוּמוּ לָעַד דּוּמָה לְהוֹמֵמָה, רוּם וְתַחַת יַמְלִיכְוּהוּ בְּאֵימָה,
שָׁמַיִם יִפְצְחוּ רֶנֶן נְעִימָה,[3] תְּהִלָּתוֹ יִתְּנוּ כָּל מַלְכֵי אֲדָמָה.

❖ אָז יַהֲפֹךְ אֶל עַמִּים שָׂפָה בְרוּרָה יַחַד, לִקְרֹא כֻלָּם בְּשֵׁם הַמְּיֻחָד,[4]
וְיִמְאֲסוּן אִישׁ אֱלִילֵי כַסְפּוֹ וְאִישׁ אֱלִילֵי זְהָבוֹ בְּכַחַד,
וְיַטּוּ שְׁכֶם אֶחָד לְעָבְדוֹ בְּפַחַד,

❖ בְּפַחַד וּבְרַעַד יַמְלִיכְוּהוּ גּוֹי אֶחָד, וְאוֹתָנוּ יַעֲשֶׂה לְגוֹי אֶחָד,

All – **בַּיּוֹם הַהוּא יִהְיֶה יהוה אֶחָד וּשְׁמוֹ אֶחָד.**[5]

וּבְכֵן לְךָ תַעֲלֶה קְדֻשָּׁה כִּי אַתָּה קְדוֹשׁ יִשְׂרָאֵל וּמוֹשִׁיעַ.

Some congregations recite the prayer אוֹמֶץ גְּבוּרוֹתֶיךָ (p. 1123) before *Kedushah.*
Most congregations recite the standard *Yom Tov Kedushah* (below).
Those who recite אוֹמֶץ גְּבוּרוֹתֶיךָ omit the opening phrase in parentheses.

קדושה

When reciting *Kedushah,* one must stand with his feet together and avoid any interruptions. One should rise on his toes when saying the words קָדוֹשׁ, קָדוֹשׁ, קָדוֹשׁ; בָּרוּךְ (of בָּרוּךְ כְּבוֹד); and יִמְלֹךְ.

Cong. then *Chazzan* – (**נְקַדֵּשׁ** אֶת שִׁמְךָ בָּעוֹלָם, כְּשֵׁם שֶׁמַּקְדִּישִׁים אוֹתוֹ בִּשְׁמֵי מָרוֹם,) כַּכָּתוּב עַל יַד נְבִיאֶךָ, וְקָרָא זֶה אֶל זֶה וְאָמַר:

All – קָדוֹשׁ קָדוֹשׁ קָדוֹשׁ יהוה צְבָאוֹת, מְלֹא כָל הָאָרֶץ כְּבוֹדוֹ.[6]

❖ אָז בְּקוֹל* רַעַשׁ גָּדוֹל אַדִּיר וְחָזָק מַשְׁמִיעִים קוֹל, מִתְנַשְּׂאִים לְעֻמַּת שְׂרָפִים, לְעֻמָּתָם בָּרוּךְ יֹאמֵרוּ:

All – בָּרוּךְ כְּבוֹד יהוה, מִמְּקוֹמוֹ.[7] ❖ מִמְּקוֹמְךָ מַלְכֵּנוּ תוֹפִיעַ, וְתִמְלֹךְ עָלֵינוּ, כִּי מְחַכִּים אֲנַחְנוּ לָךְ. מָתַי תִּמְלֹךְ בְּצִיּוֹן, בְּקָרוֹב בְּיָמֵינוּ, לְעוֹלָם וָעֶד תִּשְׁכּוֹן. תִּתְגַּדַּל וְתִתְקַדַּשׁ בְּתוֹךְ יְרוּשָׁלַיִם עִירְךָ, לְדוֹר וָדוֹר וּלְנֵצַח נְצָחִים. וְעֵינֵינוּ תִרְאֶינָה מַלְכוּתֶךָ, כַּדָּבָר הָאָמוּר בְּשִׁירֵי עֻזֶּךָ, עַל יְדֵי דָוִד מְשִׁיחַ צִדְקֶךָ:

All – יִמְלֹךְ יהוה לְעוֹלָם, אֱלֹהַיִךְ צִיּוֹן לְדֹר וָדֹר, הַלְלוּיָהּ.[8]

קדושת השם

Chazzan continues:

לְדוֹר וָדוֹר נַגִּיד גָּדְלֶךָ וּלְנֵצַח נְצָחִים קְדֻשָּׁתְךָ נַקְדִּישׁ, וְשִׁבְחֲךָ אֱלֹהֵינוּ מִפִּינוּ לֹא יָמוּשׁ לְעוֹלָם וָעֶד, כִּי אֵל מֶלֶךְ גָּדוֹל וְקָדוֹשׁ אָתָּה. בָּרוּךְ אַתָּה יהוה, הָאֵל הַקָּדוֹשׁ. (.Cong. – אָמֵן)

---

(1) Some *machzorim* read לְהָעֵד, *to bear witness.* (2) *Exodus* 15:18. (3) Cf. *Isaiah* 44:23.
(4) Cf. *Zephaniah* 3:9. (5) *Zechariah* 14:9. (6) *Isaiah* 6:3. (7) *Ezekiel* 3:12. (8) *Psalms* 146:10.

∻ נ *The trebled [nation] peered with the [Holy] spirit to become awe-inspired,*[1]
thus they began and ended with the future tense,
All – *HASHEM shall reign for all eternity.*[2]
מ *His kingdom was before anything else began,*
נ *and it is enduring for all eternity,*
ס *it is powerful [at all times] — future, past, present,*
ע *established forever and ever.*
פ *When He wiped out the Putite [Egyptians] with destruction,*
צ *[Israel,] the nation of awesome banners crowned Him with kingship.*
ק *And when He arises to destroy Edom with finality,*
ר *[Heaven] above and [earth] below will declare Him King with awe,*
ש *the heavens will burst forth in sweet, glad song,*[3]
ת *all the kings of earth will relate His praise.*
Chazzan – *Then all the peoples will turn together to the pure language,*
that all will call in the unified Name,[4]
every man will be disgusted by his silver idol, deny his golden idol,
and will bend their shoulder as one to serve Him in awe.
∻ *In awe and trepidation they will declare Him King over them as one nation,*
and He will establish us as a unique nation,
All – *on that day HASHEM will be One and His Name will be One.*[5]

And so, the Kedushah prayer shall ascend to You,
for You are the Holy One of Israel, and its Savior.

Some congregations recite the prayer אוֹמֶץ גְּבוּרוֹתֶךָ (p. 1123) before *Kedushah*.
Most congregations recite the standard *Yom Tov Kedushah* (below).
Those who recite אוֹמֶץ גְּבוּרוֹתֶךָ omit the opening phrase in parentheses.

KEDUSHAH

When reciting *Kedushah*, one must stand with his feet together and avoid any interruptions. One should rise on his toes when saying the words *Holy, holy, holy; Blessed is;* and *HASHEM shall reign.*

Cong. then Chazzan – **נְקַדֵּשׁ** *(We shall sanctify Your Name in this world, just as they sanctify it in heaven above,) as it is written by Your prophet, "And one [angel] will call another and say:*

All – *'Holy, holy, holy is HASHEM, Master of Legions, the whole world is filled with His glory.'"*[6] ∻ *Then, with a sound* of great noise, mighty and powerful, they make heard a voice, raising themselves toward the seraphim; those facing them say 'Blessed ...':*

All – *'Blessed is the glory of HASHEM from His place.'*[7] ∻ *From Your place, our King, You will appear and reign over us, for we await You. When will You reign in Zion? Soon, in our days — forever and ever — may You dwell there. May You be exalted and sanctified within Jerusalem, Your city, from generation to generation and for all eternity. May our eyes see Your kingdom, as it is expressed in the songs of Your might, written by David, Your righteous anointed:*

All – *'HASHEM shall reign forever — your God, O Zion — from generation to generation, Halleluyah!'*[8]

HOLINESS OF GOD'S NAME

Chazzan continues:

לְדוֹר *From generation to generation we shall relate Your greatness and for infinite eternities we shall proclaim Your holiness. Your praise, our God, shall not leave our mouth forever and ever, for You, O God, are a great and holy King. Blessed are You, HASHEM, the holy God.* (Cong. – *Amen.*)

קדושת היום

אַתָּה בְחַרְתָּנוּ מִכָּל הָעַמִּים, אָהַבְתָּ אוֹתָנוּ, וְרָצִיתָ בָּנוּ, וְרוֹמַמְתָּנוּ מִכָּל הַלְּשׁוֹנוֹת, וְקִדַּשְׁתָּנוּ בְּמִצְוֹתֶיךָ, וְקֵרַבְתָּנוּ מַלְכֵּנוּ לַעֲבוֹדָתֶךָ, וְשִׁמְךָ הַגָּדוֹל וְהַקָּדוֹשׁ עָלֵינוּ קָרָאתָ.

וַתִּתֶּן לָנוּ יהוה אֱלֹהֵינוּ בְּאַהֲבָה מוֹעֲדִים לְשִׂמְחָה חַגִּים וּזְמַנִּים לְשָׂשׂוֹן, אֶת יוֹם חַג הַמַּצּוֹת הַזֶּה, זְמַן חֵרוּתֵנוּ מִקְרָא קֹדֶשׁ, זֵכֶר לִיצִיאַת מִצְרָיִם.

Congregation responds אָמֵן as indicated.

אֱלֹהֵינוּ וֵאלֹהֵי אֲבוֹתֵינוּ, יַעֲלֶה, וְיָבֹא, וְיַגִּיעַ, וְיֵרָאֶה, וְיֵרָצֶה, וְיִשָּׁמַע, וְיִפָּקֵד, וְיִזָּכֵר זִכְרוֹנֵנוּ וּפִקְדוֹנֵנוּ, וְזִכְרוֹן אֲבוֹתֵינוּ, וְזִכְרוֹן מָשִׁיחַ בֶּן דָּוִד עַבְדֶּךָ, וְזִכְרוֹן יְרוּשָׁלַיִם עִיר קָדְשֶׁךָ, וְזִכְרוֹן כָּל עַמְּךָ בֵּית יִשְׂרָאֵל לְפָנֶיךָ, לִפְלֵיטָה לְטוֹבָה לְחֵן וּלְחֶסֶד וּלְרַחֲמִים, לְחַיִּים וּלְשָׁלוֹם בְּיוֹם חַג הַמַּצּוֹת הַזֶּה. זָכְרֵנוּ יהוה אֱלֹהֵינוּ בּוֹ לְטוֹבָה (Cong. – אָמֵן), וּפָקְדֵנוּ בוֹ לִבְרָכָה (Cong. – אָמֵן), וְהוֹשִׁיעֵנוּ בוֹ לְחַיִּים (Cong. – אָמֵן). וּבִדְבַר יְשׁוּעָה וְרַחֲמִים, חוּס וְחָנֵּנוּ וְרַחֵם עָלֵינוּ וְהוֹשִׁיעֵנוּ, כִּי אֵלֶיךָ עֵינֵינוּ, כִּי אֵל מֶלֶךְ חַנּוּן וְרַחוּם אָתָּה.[1]

וְהַשִּׂיאֵנוּ יהוה אֱלֹהֵינוּ אֶת בִּרְכַּת מוֹעֲדֶיךָ לְחַיִּים וּלְשָׁלוֹם, לְשִׂמְחָה וּלְשָׂשׂוֹן, כַּאֲשֶׁר רָצִיתָ וְאָמַרְתָּ לְבָרְכֵנוּ. קַדְּשֵׁנוּ בְּמִצְוֹתֶיךָ וְתֵן חֶלְקֵנוּ בְּתוֹרָתֶךָ, שַׂבְּעֵנוּ מִטּוּבֶךָ וְשַׂמְּחֵנוּ בִּישׁוּעָתֶךָ, וְטַהֵר לִבֵּנוּ לְעָבְדְּךָ בֶּאֱמֶת, וְהַנְחִילֵנוּ יהוה אֱלֹהֵינוּ בְּשִׂמְחָה וּבְשָׂשׂוֹן מוֹעֲדֵי קָדְשֶׁךָ, וְיִשְׂמְחוּ בְךָ יִשְׂרָאֵל מְקַדְּשֵׁי שְׁמֶךָ. בָּרוּךְ אַתָּה יהוה, מְקַדֵּשׁ יִשְׂרָאֵל וְהַזְּמַנִּים. (Cong. – אָמֵן.)

עבודה

רְצֵה יהוה אֱלֹהֵינוּ בְּעַמְּךָ יִשְׂרָאֵל וּבִתְפִלָּתָם, וְהָשֵׁב אֶת הָעֲבוֹדָה לִדְבִיר בֵּיתֶךָ. וְאִשֵּׁי יִשְׂרָאֵל וּתְפִלָּתָם בְּאַהֲבָה תְקַבֵּל בְּרָצוֹן, וּתְהִי לְרָצוֹן תָּמִיד עֲבוֹדַת יִשְׂרָאֵל עַמֶּךָ.

וְתֶחֱזֶינָה עֵינֵינוּ בְּשׁוּבְךָ לְצִיּוֹן בְּרַחֲמִים. בָּרוּךְ אַתָּה יהוה, הַמַּחֲזִיר שְׁכִינָתוֹ לְצִיּוֹן. (Cong. – אָמֵן.)

SANCTIFICATION OF THE DAY

אַתָּה *You have chosen us from all the peoples; You loved us and found favor in us; You exalted us above all the tongues and You sanctified us with Your commandments. You drew us close, our King, to Your service and proclaimed Your great and Holy Name upon us.*

וַתִּתֶּן לָנוּ *And You gave us,* HASHEM, *our God, with love, appointed festivals for gladness, Festivals and times for joy, this day of the Festival of Matzos, the time of our freedom, a holy convocation, a memorial of the Exodus from Egypt.*

Congregation responds *Amen* as indicated.

אֱלֹהֵינוּ *Our God and God of our forefathers, may there rise, come, reach, be noted, be favored, be heard, be considered, and be remembered — the remembrance and consideration of ourselves; the remembrance of our forefathers; the remembrance of Messiah, son of David, Your servant; the remembrance of Jerusalem, the City of Your Holiness; the remembrance of Your entire people the Family of Israel — before You for deliverance, for goodness, for grace, for kindness, and for compassion, for life, and for peace on this day of the Festival of Matzos. Remember us on it,* HASHEM, *our God, for goodness (*Cong. – *Amen); consider us on it for blessing (*Cong. – *Amen); and help us on it for life (*Cong. – *Amen). In the matter of salvation and compassion, pity, be gracious and compassionate with us and help us, for our eyes are turned to You, because You are God, the gracious and compassionate King.*[1]

וְהַשִּׂיאֵנוּ *Bestow upon us, O* HASHEM, *our God, the blessing of Your appointed Festivals for life and for peace, for gladness and for joy, as You desired and promised to bless us. Sanctify us withYour commandments and grant us our share in Your Torah; satisfy us from Your goodness and gladden us with Your salvation, and purify our heart to serve You sincerely. And grant us a heritage, O* HASHEM, *our God — with gladness and with joy — the appointed festivals of Your holiness, and may Israel, the sanctifiers of Your Name, rejoice in You. Blessed are You,* HASHEM, *Who sanctifies Israel and the festive seasons.* (Cong. – *Amen.)*

TEMPLE SERVICE

רְצֵה *Be favorable,* HASHEM, *our God, toward Your people Israel and their prayer and restore the service to the Holy of Holies of Your Temple. The fire-offerings of Israel and their prayer accept with love and favor, and may the service of Your people Israel always be favorable to You.*

וְתֶחֱזֶינָה *May our eyes behold Your return to Zion in compassion. Blessed are You,* HASHEM, *Who restores His Presence to Zion.* (Cong. – *Amen.)*

(1) Cf. *Nehemiah* 9:31.

Chazzan bows at מוֹדִים; straightens up at ה'. The chazzan recites
the entire מוֹדִים aloud, while the congregation recites מוֹדִים דְּרַבָּנָן softly.

מוֹדִים אֲנַחְנוּ לָךְ, שָׁאַתָּה הוּא
יהוה אֱלֹהֵינוּ וֵאלֹהֵי
אֲבוֹתֵינוּ לְעוֹלָם וָעֶד. צוּר חַיֵּינוּ,
מָגֵן יִשְׁעֵנוּ אַתָּה הוּא לְדוֹר וָדוֹר.
נוֹדֶה לְּךָ וּנְסַפֵּר תְּהִלָּתֶךָ[1] עַל
חַיֵּינוּ הַמְּסוּרִים בְּיָדֶךָ, וְעַל
נִשְׁמוֹתֵינוּ הַפְּקוּדוֹת לָךְ, וְעַל נִסֶּיךָ
שֶׁבְּכָל יוֹם עִמָּנוּ, וְעַל נִפְלְאוֹתֶיךָ
וְטוֹבוֹתֶיךָ שֶׁבְּכָל עֵת, עֶרֶב וָבֹקֶר
וְצָהֳרָיִם. הַטּוֹב כִּי לֹא כָלוּ
רַחֲמֶיךָ, וְהַמְרַחֵם כִּי לֹא תַמּוּ
חֲסָדֶיךָ,[2] מֵעוֹלָם קִוִּינוּ לָךְ.

מוֹדִים דְּרַבָּנָן

מוֹדִים אֲנַחְנוּ לָךְ, שָׁאַתָּה
הוּא יהוה אֱלֹהֵינוּ
וֵאלֹהֵי אֲבוֹתֵינוּ, אֱלֹהֵי כָל
בָּשָׂר, יוֹצְרֵנוּ, יוֹצֵר בְּרֵאשִׁית.
בְּרָכוֹת וְהוֹדָאוֹת לְשִׁמְךָ הַגָּדוֹל
וְהַקָּדוֹשׁ, עַל שֶׁהֶחֱיִיתָנוּ
וְקִיַּמְתָּנוּ. כֵּן תְּחַיֵּנוּ וּתְקַיְּמֵנוּ,
וְתֶאֱסוֹף גָּלֻיּוֹתֵינוּ לְחַצְרוֹת
קָדְשֶׁךָ, לִשְׁמוֹר חֻקֶּיךָ וְלַעֲשׂוֹת
רְצוֹנֶךָ, וּלְעָבְדְּךָ בְּלֵבָב שָׁלֵם,
עַל שֶׁאֲנַחְנוּ מוֹדִים לָךְ. בָּרוּךְ
אֵל הַהוֹדָאוֹת.

וְעַל כֻּלָּם יִתְבָּרַךְ וְיִתְרוֹמַם שִׁמְךָ מַלְכֵּנוּ תָּמִיד לְעוֹלָם וָעֶד.

The chazzan bends his knees at בָּרוּךְ; bows at אַתָּה; straightens up at ה'.

וְכֹל הַחַיִּים יוֹדוּךָ סֶּלָה, וִיהַלְלוּ אֶת שִׁמְךָ בֶּאֱמֶת, הָאֵל
יְשׁוּעָתֵנוּ וְעֶזְרָתֵנוּ סֶלָה. בָּרוּךְ אַתָּה יהוה, הַטּוֹב שִׁמְךָ וּלְךָ נָאֶה
לְהוֹדוֹת. (Cong. – אָמֵן.)

The chazzan recites בִּרְכַּת כֹּהֲנִים. He faces right at וְיִשְׁמְרֶךָ;
faces left at וִיחֻנֶּךָּ; אֵלֶיךָ; faces the Ark for the rest of the blessings.

אֱלֹהֵינוּ, וֵאלֹהֵי אֲבוֹתֵינוּ, בָּרְכֵנוּ בַבְּרָכָה הַמְשֻׁלֶּשֶׁת בַּתּוֹרָה הַכְּתוּבָה
עַל יְדֵי מֹשֶׁה עַבְדֶּךָ, הָאֲמוּרָה מִפִּי אַהֲרֹן וּבָנָיו, כֹּהֲנִים עַם
קְדוֹשֶׁךָ, כָּאָמוּר: יְבָרֶכְךָ יהוה, וְיִשְׁמְרֶךָ. (Cong. – כֵּן יְהִי רָצוֹן.)
יָאֵר יהוה פָּנָיו אֵלֶיךָ וִיחֻנֶּךָּ. (Cong. – כֵּן יְהִי רָצוֹן.)
יִשָּׂא יהוה פָּנָיו אֵלֶיךָ וְיָשֵׂם לְךָ שָׁלוֹם.[3] (Cong. – כֵּן יְהִי רָצוֹן.)

שִׂים שָׁלוֹם טוֹבָה, וּבְרָכָה, חֵן, וָחֶסֶד וְרַחֲמִים עָלֵינוּ וְעַל כָּל
יִשְׂרָאֵל עַמֶּךָ. בָּרְכֵנוּ אָבִינוּ, כֻּלָּנוּ כְּאֶחָד בְּאוֹר
פָּנֶיךָ, כִּי בְאוֹר פָּנֶיךָ נָתַתָּ לָּנוּ, יהוה אֱלֹהֵינוּ, תּוֹרַת חַיִּים וְאַהֲבַת
חֶסֶד, וּצְדָקָה וּבְרָכָה, וְרַחֲמִים, וְחַיִּים, וְשָׁלוֹם. וְטוֹב בְּעֵינֶיךָ
לְבָרֵךְ אֶת עַמְּךָ יִשְׂרָאֵל, בְּכָל עֵת וּבְכָל שָׁעָה בִּשְׁלוֹמֶךָ. בָּרוּךְ
אַתָּה יהוה, הַמְבָרֵךְ אֶת עַמּוֹ יִשְׂרָאֵל בַּשָּׁלוֹם. (Cong. – אָמֵן.)
in an undertone – יִהְיוּ לְרָצוֹן אִמְרֵי פִי וְהֶגְיוֹן לִבִּי לְפָנֶיךָ, יהוה צוּרִי וְגֹאֲלִי.[4]

THE SERVICE CONTINUES WITH הַלֵּל, PAGE 938.

Chazzan bows at *'We gratefully thank You'*; straightens up at *'HASHEM.'*
Chazzan recites the entire *Modim* aloud, while congregation recites *Modim of the Rabbis* softly.

מוֹדִים *We gratefully thank You, for it is You Who are HASHEM, our God and the God of our forefathers for all eternity; Rock of our lives, Shield of our salvation are You from generation to generation. We shall thank You and relate Your praise[1] — for our lives, which are committed to Your power and for our souls that are entrusted to You; for Your miracles that are with us every day; and for Your wonders and favors in every season — evening, morning, and afternoon. The Beneficent One, for Your compassions were never exhausted, and the Compassionate One, for Your kindnesses never ended[2] — always have we put our hope in You.*

MODIM OF THE RABBIS

מוֹדִים *We gratefully thank You, for it is You Who are HASHEM, our God and the God of our forefathers, the God of all flesh, our Molder, the Molder of the universe. Blessings and thanks are due Your great and holy Name for You have given us life and sustained us. So may You continue to give us life and sustain us and gather our exiles to the Courtyards of Your Sanctuary, to observe Your decrees, to do Your will and to serve You wholeheartedly. [We thank You] for inspiring us to thank You. Blessed is the God of thanksgivings.*

For all these, may Your Name be blessed and exalted, our King, continually forever and ever.

The *chazzan* bends his knees at *'Blessed'*; bows at *'You'*; straightens up at *'HASHEM.'*

Everything alive will gratefully acknowledge You, Selah! and praise Your Name sincerely, O God of our salvation and help, Selah! Blessed are You, HASHEM, Your Name is 'The Beneficent One' and to You it is fitting to give thanks. (Cong.— *Amen.*)

THE PRIESTLY BLESSING

The *chazzan* recites the Priestly Blessing.

אֱלֹהֵינוּ *Our God and the God of our forefathers, bless us with the three-verse blessing in the Torah that was written by the hand of Moses, Your servant, that was said by Aaron and his sons, the Kohanim, Your holy people, as it is said:*

May HASHEM bless you and safeguard you. (Cong.— *So may it be.*)

May HASHEM illuminate His countenance for you and be gracious to you. (Cong.— *So may it be.*)

May HASHEM turn His countenance to you and establish peace for you.[3] (Cong.— *So may it be.*)

שִׂים שָׁלוֹם *Establish peace, goodness, blessing, graciousness, kindness, and compassion upon us and upon all of Your people Israel. Bless us, our Father, all of us as one, with the light of Your countenance, for with the light of Your countenance You gave us, HASHEM, our God, the Torah of life and a love of kindness, righteousness, blessing, compassion, life, and peace. And may it be good in Your eyes to bless Your people Israel at every time and every hour with Your peace. Blessed are You, HASHEM, Who blesses His people Israel with peace.* (Cong.— *Amen.*)

May the expressions of my mouth and the thoughts of my heart find favor before You, HASHEM, my Rock and my Redeemer.[4]

THE SERVICE CONTINUES WITH HALLEL, PAGE 938.

(1) Cf. *Psalms* 79:13. (2) Cf. *Lamentations* 3:22. (3) *Numbers* 6:24-26. (4) *Psalms* 19:15.

הלל

The *chazzan* recites the blessing. The congregation, after responding אָמֵן, repeats it, and continues with the first psalm.

בָּרוּךְ אַתָּה יהוה אֱלֹהֵינוּ מֶלֶךְ הָעוֹלָם, אֲשֶׁר קִדְּשָׁנוּ בְּמִצְוֹתָיו, וְצִוָּנוּ לִקְרוֹא אֶת הַהַלֵּל. (.Cong.– אָמֵן)

תהלים קיג

הַלְלוּיָהּ הַלְלוּ עַבְדֵי יהוה, הַלְלוּ אֶת שֵׁם יהוה. יְהִי שֵׁם יהוה מְבֹרָךְ, מֵעַתָּה וְעַד עוֹלָם. מִמִּזְרַח שֶׁמֶשׁ עַד מְבוֹאוֹ, מְהֻלָּל שֵׁם יהוה. רָם עַל כָּל גּוֹיִם יהוה, עַל הַשָּׁמַיִם כְּבוֹדוֹ. מִי כַּיהוה אֱלֹהֵינוּ, הַמַּגְבִּיהִי לָשָׁבֶת. הַמַּשְׁפִּילִי לִרְאוֹת, בַּשָּׁמַיִם וּבָאָרֶץ. ❖ מְקִימִי מֵעָפָר דָּל, מֵאַשְׁפֹּת יָרִים אֶבְיוֹן. לְהוֹשִׁיבִי עִם נְדִיבִים, עִם נְדִיבֵי עַמּוֹ. מוֹשִׁיבִי עֲקֶרֶת הַבַּיִת, אֵם הַבָּנִים שְׂמֵחָה, הַלְלוּיָהּ.

תהלים קיד

בְּצֵאת יִשְׂרָאֵל מִמִּצְרָיִם, בֵּית יַעֲקֹב מֵעַם לֹעֵז. הָיְתָה יְהוּדָה לְקָדְשׁוֹ, יִשְׂרָאֵל מַמְשְׁלוֹתָיו. הַיָּם רָאָה וַיָּנֹס, הַיַּרְדֵּן יִסֹּב לְאָחוֹר. הֶהָרִים רָקְדוּ כְאֵילִים, גְּבָעוֹת כִּבְנֵי צֹאן. ❖ מַה לְּךָ הַיָּם כִּי תָנוּס, הַיַּרְדֵּן תִּסֹּב לְאָחוֹר. הֶהָרִים תִּרְקְדוּ כְאֵילִים, גְּבָעוֹת כִּבְנֵי צֹאן. מִלִּפְנֵי אָדוֹן חוּלִי אָרֶץ, מִלִּפְנֵי אֱלוֹהַּ יַעֲקֹב. הַהֹפְכִי הַצּוּר אֲגַם מָיִם, חַלָּמִישׁ לְמַעְיְנוֹ מָיִם.

תהלים קטו:יב-יח

יהוה זְכָרָנוּ יְבָרֵךְ, יְבָרֵךְ אֶת בֵּית יִשְׂרָאֵל, יְבָרֵךְ אֶת בֵּית אַהֲרֹן. יְבָרֵךְ יִרְאֵי יהוה, הַקְּטַנִּים עִם הַגְּדֹלִים. יֹסֵף יהוה עֲלֵיכֶם, עֲלֵיכֶם וְעַל בְּנֵיכֶם. בְּרוּכִים אַתֶּם לַיהוה, עֹשֵׂה שָׁמַיִם וָאָרֶץ. ❖ הַשָּׁמַיִם שָׁמַיִם לַיהוה, וְהָאָרֶץ נָתַן לִבְנֵי אָדָם. לֹא הַמֵּתִים יְהַלְלוּ יָהּ, וְלֹא כָּל יֹרְדֵי דוּמָה. וַאֲנַחְנוּ נְבָרֵךְ יָהּ, מֵעַתָּה וְעַד עוֹלָם, הַלְלוּיָהּ.

תהלים קטז:יב-יט

מָה אָשִׁיב לַיהוה, כָּל תַּגְמוּלוֹהִי עָלָי. כּוֹס יְשׁוּעוֹת אֶשָּׂא, וּבְשֵׁם יהוה אֶקְרָא. נְדָרַי לַיהוה אֲשַׁלֵּם, נֶגְדָה נָּא לְכָל עַמּוֹ. יָקָר בְּעֵינֵי יהוה, הַמָּוְתָה לַחֲסִידָיו. אָנָּה יהוה כִּי אֲנִי עַבְדֶּךָ, אֲנִי עַבְדְּךָ, בֶּן אֲמָתֶךָ, פִּתַּחְתָּ לְמוֹסֵרָי. ❖ לְךָ אֶזְבַּח זֶבַח תּוֹדָה, וּבְשֵׁם יהוה אֶקְרָא. נְדָרַי לַיהוה אֲשַׁלֵּם, נֶגְדָה נָּא לְכָל עַמּוֹ. בְּחַצְרוֹת בֵּית יהוה, בְּתוֹכֵכִי יְרוּשָׁלָיִם הַלְלוּיָהּ.

HALLEL

The *chazzan* recites the blessing. The congregation, after responding *Amen*, repeats it, and continues with the first psalm.

בָּרוּךְ *Blessed are You,* HASHEM, *our God, King of the universe, Who has sanctified us with His commandments and has commanded us to read the Hallel.* (Cong.– *Amen.*)

Psalm 113

הַלְלוּיָהּ *Halleluyah! Give praise, you servants of* HASHEM; *praise the Name of* HASHEM! *Blessed be the Name of* HASHEM, *from this time and forever. From the rising of the sun to its setting,* HASHEM's *Name is praised. High above all nations is* HASHEM, *above the heavens is His glory. Who is like* HASHEM, *our God, Who is enthroned on high — yet deigns to look upon the heaven and the earth?* Chazzan– *He raises the needy from the dust, from the trash heaps He lifts the destitute. To seat them with nobles, with the nobles of His people. He transforms the barren wife into a glad mother of children. Halleluyah!*

Psalm 114

בְּצֵאת *When Israel went out of Egypt, Jacob's household from a people of alien tongue — Judah became His sanctuary, Israel His dominions. The sea saw and fled: the Jordan turned backward. The mountains skipped like rams, the hills like young lambs.* Chazzan– *What ails you, O sea, that you flee? O Jordan, that you turn backward? O mountains, that you skip like rams? O hills, like young lambs? Before the Lord's Presence — did I, the earth, tremble — before the presence of the God of Jacob, Who turns the rock into a pond of water, the flint into a flowing fountain.*

Psalm 115:12-18

יהוה HASHEM *Who has remembered us will bless — He will bless the House of Israel; He will bless the House of Aaron; He will bless those who fear* HASHEM, *the small as well as the great. May* HASHEM *increase upon you, upon you and upon your children! You are blessed of* HASHEM, *Maker of heaven and earth.* Chazzan– *As for the heavens — the heavens are* HASHEM's, *but the earth He has given to mankind. Neither the dead can praise God, nor any who descend into silence; but we will bless God from this time and forever. Halleluyah!*

Psalm 116:12-19

מָה אָשִׁיב *How can I repay* HASHEM *for all His kindness to me? I will raise the cup of salvations and the Name of* HASHEM *I will invoke. My vows to* HASHEM *I will pay, in the presence, now, of His entire people. Difficult in the eyes of* HASHEM *is the death of His devout ones. Please,* HASHEM *— for I am Your servant, I am Your servant, son of Your handmaid — You have released my bonds.* Chazzan– *To You I will sacrifice thanksgiving offerings, and the name of* HASHEM *I will invoke. My vows to* HASHEM *I will pay, in the presence, now, of His entire people. In the courtyards of the House of* HASHEM, *in your midst, O Jerusalem, Halleluyah!*

Congregation, then *chazzan:*

תהלים קיז

הַלְלוּ אֶת יהוה, כָּל גּוֹיִם, שַׁבְּחוּהוּ כָּל הָאֻמִּים. כִּי גָבַר עָלֵינוּ חַסְדּוֹ, וֶאֱמֶת יהוה לְעוֹלָם, הַלְלוּיָהּ.

תהלים קיח

Chazzan – **הוֹדוּ** לַיהוה כִּי טוֹב, כִּי לְעוֹלָם חַסְדּוֹ.
Cong. – הוֹדוּ לַיהוה כִּי טוֹב, כִּי לְעוֹלָם חַסְדּוֹ.
יֹאמַר נָא יִשְׂרָאֵל, כִּי לְעוֹלָם חַסְדּוֹ.
Chazzan – יֹאמַר נָא יִשְׂרָאֵל, כִּי לְעוֹלָם חַסְדּוֹ.
Cong. – הוֹדוּ לַיהוה כִּי טוֹב, כִּי לְעוֹלָם חַסְדּוֹ.
יֹאמְרוּ נָא בֵית אַהֲרֹן, כִּי לְעוֹלָם חַסְדּוֹ.
Chazzan – יֹאמְרוּ נָא בֵית אַהֲרֹן, כִּי לְעוֹלָם חַסְדּוֹ.
Cong. – הוֹדוּ לַיהוה כִּי טוֹב, כִּי לְעוֹלָם חַסְדּוֹ.
יֹאמְרוּ נָא יִרְאֵי יהוה, כִּי לְעוֹלָם חַסְדּוֹ.
Chazzan – יֹאמְרוּ נָא יִרְאֵי יהוה, כִּי לְעוֹלָם חַסְדּוֹ.
Cong. – הוֹדוּ לַיהוה כִּי טוֹב, כִּי לְעוֹלָם חַסְדּוֹ.

מִן הַמֵּצַר קָרָאתִי יָּהּ, עָנָנִי בַמֶּרְחָב יָהּ. יהוה לִי לֹא אִירָא, מַה יַּעֲשֶׂה לִי אָדָם. יהוה לִי בְּעֹזְרָי, וַאֲנִי אֶרְאֶה בְשֹׂנְאָי. טוֹב לַחֲסוֹת בַּיהוה, מִבְּטֹחַ בָּאָדָם. טוֹב לַחֲסוֹת בַּיהוה, מִבְּטֹחַ בִּנְדִיבִים. כָּל גּוֹיִם סְבָבוּנִי, בְּשֵׁם יהוה כִּי אֲמִילַם. סַבּוּנִי גַם סְבָבוּנִי, בְּשֵׁם יהוה כִּי אֲמִילַם. סַבּוּנִי כִדְבֹרִים דֹּעֲכוּ כְּאֵשׁ קוֹצִים, בְּשֵׁם יהוה כִּי אֲמִילַם. דָּחֹה דְחִיתַנִי לִנְפֹּל, וַיהוה עֲזָרָנִי. עָזִּי וְזִמְרָת יָהּ, וַיְהִי לִי לִישׁוּעָה. קוֹל רִנָּה וִישׁוּעָה, בְּאָהֳלֵי צַדִּיקִים, יְמִין יהוה עֹשָׂה חָיִל. יְמִין יהוה רוֹמֵמָה, יְמִין יהוה עֹשָׂה חָיִל. לֹא אָמוּת כִּי אֶחְיֶה, וַאֲסַפֵּר מַעֲשֵׂי יָהּ. יַסֹּר יִסְּרַנִּי יָּהּ, וְלַמָּוֶת לֹא נְתָנָנִי. ❖ פִּתְחוּ לִי שַׁעֲרֵי צֶדֶק, אָבֹא בָם אוֹדֶה יָהּ. זֶה הַשַּׁעַר לַיהוה, צַדִּיקִים יָבֹאוּ בוֹ. אוֹדְךָ כִּי עֲנִיתָנִי, וַתְּהִי לִי לִישׁוּעָה. אוֹדְךָ כִּי עֲנִיתָנִי, וַתְּהִי לִי לִישׁוּעָה. אֶבֶן מָאֲסוּ הַבּוֹנִים, הָיְתָה לְרֹאשׁ פִּנָּה. אֶבֶן מָאֲסוּ הַבּוֹנִים, הָיְתָה לְרֹאשׁ פִּנָּה. מֵאֵת יהוה הָיְתָה זֹּאת, הִיא נִפְלָאת בְּעֵינֵינוּ. מֵאֵת יהוה הָיְתָה זֹּאת, הִיא נִפְלָאת בְּעֵינֵינוּ. זֶה הַיּוֹם עָשָׂה יהוה, נָגִילָה וְנִשְׂמְחָה בוֹ. זֶה הַיּוֹם עָשָׂה יהוה, נָגִילָה וְנִשְׂמְחָה בוֹ.

Congregation, then *chazzan:*

Psalm 117

הַלְלוּ *Praise* HASHEM, *all nations; praise Him, all the states! For His kindness has overwhelmed us, and the truth of* HASHEM *is eternal, Halleluyah!*

Psalm 118

Chazzan – **הוֹדוּ** *Give thanks to* HASHEM *for He is good; His kindness endures forever!*

Cong. – *Give thanks to* HASHEM, *for He is good; His kindness endures forever!*

Let Israel say now: His kindness endures forever!

Chazzan – *Let Israel say now: His kindness endures forever!*

Cong. – *Give thanks to* HASHEM, *for He is good; His kindness endures forever!*

Let the House of Aaron say now: His kindness endures forever!

Chazzan – *Let the House of Aaron say now: His kindness endures forever!*

Cong. – *Give thanks to* HASHEM, *for He is good; His kindness endures forever!*

Let those who fear HASHEM *say now: His kindness endures forever!*

Chazzan – *Let those who fear* HASHEM *say now: His kindness endures forever!*

Cong. – *Give thanks to* HASHEM, *for He is good; His kindness endures forever!*

מִן הַמֵּצַר *From the straits did I call upon God; God answered me with expansiveness.* HASHEM *is with me, I have no fear; how can man affect me?* HASHEM *is with me through my helpers; therefore I can face my foes. It is better to take refuge in* HASHEM *than to rely on man. It is better to take refuge in* HASHEM *than to rely on nobles. All the nations surround me; in the Name of* HASHEM *I cut them down! They encircle me, they also surround me; in the Name of* HASHEM, *I cut them down! They encircle me like bees, but they are extinguished as a fire does thorns; in the Name of* HASHEM *I cut them down! You pushed me hard that I might fall, but* HASHEM *assisted me. God is my might and my praise, and He was a salvation for me. The sound of rejoicing and salvation is in the tents of the righteous: '*HASHEM*'s right hand does valiantly.* HASHEM*'s right hand is raised triumphantly;* HASHEM*'s right hand does valiantly!' I shall not die! But I shall live and relate the deeds of God. God has chastened me exceedingly, but He did not let me die.* Chazzan – *Open for me the gates of righteousness, I will enter them and thank God. This is the gate of* HASHEM; *the righteous shall enter through it. I thank You for You have answered me and become my salvation. I thank You for You have answered me and become my salvation. The stone the builders despised has become the cornerstone. The stone the builders despised has become the cornerstone. This emanated from* HASHEM; *it is wondrous in our eyes. This emanated from* HASHEM; *it is wondrous in our eyes. This is the day* HASHEM *has made; let us rejoice and be glad on it. This is the day* HASHEM *has made; let us rejoice and be glad on it.*

The next four lines are recited responsively — *chazzan,* then congregation.

אָנָּא יהוה הוֹשִׁיעָה נָּא. אָנָּא יהוה הוֹשִׁיעָה נָּא.
אָנָּא יהוה הַצְלִיחָה נָא. אָנָּא יהוה הַצְלִיחָה נָא.

בָּרוּךְ הַבָּא בְּשֵׁם יהוה, בֵּרַכְנוּכֶם מִבֵּית יהוה. בָּרוּךְ הַבָּא בְּשֵׁם יהוה, בֵּרַכְנוּכֶם מִבֵּית יהוה. אֵל יהוה וַיָּאֶר לָנוּ, אִסְרוּ חַג בַּעֲבֹתִים, עַד קַרְנוֹת הַמִּזְבֵּחַ. אֵל יהוה וַיָּאֶר לָנוּ, אִסְרוּ חַג בַּעֲבֹתִים, עַד קַרְנוֹת הַמִּזְבֵּחַ. אֵלִי אַתָּה וְאוֹדֶךָּ, אֱלֹהַי אֲרוֹמְמֶךָּ. אֵלִי אַתָּה וְאוֹדֶךָּ, אֱלֹהַי אֲרוֹמְמֶךָּ. הוֹדוּ לַיהוה כִּי טוֹב, כִּי לְעוֹלָם חַסְדּוֹ. הוֹדוּ לַיהוה כִּי טוֹב, כִּי לְעוֹלָם חַסְדּוֹ.

יְהַלְלְוּךָ יהוה אֱלֹהֵינוּ כָּל מַעֲשֶׂיךָ, וַחֲסִידֶיךָ צַדִּיקִים עוֹשֵׂי רְצוֹנֶךָ, וְכָל עַמְּךָ בֵּית יִשְׂרָאֵל בְּרִנָּה יוֹדוּ וִיבָרְכוּ וִישַׁבְּחוּ וִיפָאֲרוּ וִירוֹמְמוּ וְיַעֲרִיצוּ וְיַקְדִּישׁוּ וְיַמְלִיכוּ אֶת שִׁמְךָ מַלְכֵּנוּ. ❖ כִּי לְךָ טוֹב לְהוֹדוֹת וּלְשִׁמְךָ נָאֶה לְזַמֵּר, כִּי מֵעוֹלָם וְעַד עוֹלָם אַתָּה אֵל. בָּרוּךְ אַתָּה יהוה, מֶלֶךְ מְהֻלָּל בַּתִּשְׁבָּחוֹת.
(.Cong. – אָמֵן)

The *chazzan* recites *Kaddish:*

יִתְגַּדַּל וְיִתְקַדַּשׁ שְׁמֵהּ רַבָּא. (.Cong. – אָמֵן) בְּעָלְמָא דִּי בְרָא כִרְעוּתֵהּ. וְיַמְלִיךְ מַלְכוּתֵהּ, בְּחַיֵּיכוֹן וּבְיוֹמֵיכוֹן וּבְחַיֵּי דְכָל בֵּית יִשְׂרָאֵל, בַּעֲגָלָא וּבִזְמַן קָרִיב. וְאִמְרוּ: אָמֵן.

(.Cong. – אָמֵן. יְהֵא שְׁמֵהּ רַבָּא מְבָרַךְ לְעָלַם וּלְעָלְמֵי עָלְמַיָּא.)

יְהֵא שְׁמֵהּ רַבָּא מְבָרַךְ לְעָלַם וּלְעָלְמֵי עָלְמַיָּא.

יִתְבָּרַךְ וְיִשְׁתַּבַּח וְיִתְפָּאַר וְיִתְרוֹמַם וְיִתְנַשֵּׂא וְיִתְהַדָּר וְיִתְעַלֶּה וְיִתְהַלָּל שְׁמֵהּ דְּקֻדְשָׁא בְּרִיךְ הוּא (.Cong. – בְּרִיךְ הוּא) – לְעֵלָּא מִן כָּל בִּרְכָתָא וְשִׁירָתָא תֻּשְׁבְּחָתָא וְנֶחֱמָתָא, דַּאֲמִירָן בְּעָלְמָא. וְאִמְרוּ: אָמֵן. (.Cong. – אָמֵן.)

(.Cong. – קַבֵּל בְּרַחֲמִים וּבְרָצוֹן אֶת תְּפִלָּתֵנוּ.)

תִּתְקַבֵּל צְלוֹתְהוֹן וּבָעוּתְהוֹן דְּכָל בֵּית יִשְׂרָאֵל קֳדָם אֲבוּהוֹן דִּי בִשְׁמַיָּא. וְאִמְרוּ: אָמֵן. (.Cong. – אָמֵן.)

(.Cong. – יְהִי שֵׁם יהוה מְבֹרָךְ, מֵעַתָּה וְעַד עוֹלָם.[1])

יְהֵא שְׁלָמָא רַבָּא מִן שְׁמַיָּא, וְחַיִּים עָלֵינוּ וְעַל כָּל יִשְׂרָאֵל. וְאִמְרוּ: אָמֵן. (.Cong. – אָמֵן.)

(.Cong. – עֶזְרִי מֵעִם יהוה, עֹשֵׂה שָׁמַיִם וָאָרֶץ.[2])

Take three steps back. Bow left and say . . . עֹשֶׂה; bow right and say . . . הוּא; bow forward and say וְעַל כָּל . . . אָמֵן. Remain standing in place for a few moments, then take three steps forward.

עֹשֶׂה שָׁלוֹם בִּמְרוֹמָיו, הוּא יַעֲשֶׂה שָׁלוֹם עָלֵינוּ, וְעַל כָּל יִשְׂרָאֵל. וְאִמְרוּ: אָמֵן. (.Cong. – אָמֵן.)

ON THE SABBATH, שִׁיר הַשִּׁירִים (PAGE 566) IS RECITED AT THIS POINT.

The next four lines are recited responsively — *chazzan,* then congregation.

אָנָּא *Please, HASHEM, save now!*
Please, HASHEM, save now!
Please, HASHEM, bring success now!
Please, HASHEM, bring success now!

בָּרוּךְ *Blessed is he who comes in the Name of HASHEM; we bless you from the House of HASHEM. Blessed is he who comes in the Name of HASHEM; we bless you from the House of HASHEM. HASHEM is God, He illuminated for us; bind the festival offering with cords until the corners of the Altar. HASHEM is God, He illuminated for us; bind the festival offering with cords until the corners of the Altar. You are my God, and I will thank You; my God, I will exalt You. You are my God, and I will thank You; my God, I will exalt You. Give thanks to HASHEM, for He is good; His kindness endures forever. Give thanks to HASHEM, for He is good; His kindness endures forever.*

יְהַלְלוּךָ *All Your works shall praise You, HASHEM our God. And Your devout ones, the righteous, who do Your will, and Your entire people, the House of Israel, with glad song will thank, bless, praise, glorify, exalt, extol, sanctify, and proclaim the sovereignty of Your Name, our King.* Chazzan — *For to You it is fitting to give thanks, and unto Your Name it is proper to sing praises, for from This World to the World to Come You are God. Blessed are You, HASHEM, the King Who is lauded with praises.*

(Cong. — *Amen.*)

FULL KADDISH

The *chazzan* recites *Kaddish:*

יִתְגַּדַּל *May His great Name grow exalted and sanctified* (Cong. — *Amen.*) *in the world that He created as He willed. May He give reign to His kingship in your lifetimes and in your days, and in the lifetimes of the entire Family of Israel, swiftly and soon. Now respond: Amen.*

(Cong. — *Amen. May His great Name be blessed forever and ever.*)

May His great Name be blessed forever and ever.

Blessed, praised, glorified, exalted, extolled, mighty, upraised, and lauded be the Name of the Holy One, Blessed is He (Cong. — *Blessed is He*) — *beyond any blessing and song, praise and consolation that are uttered in the world. Now respond: Amen.* (Cong. — *Amen*).

(Cong. — *Accept our prayers with mercy and favor.*)

May the prayers and supplications of the entire Family of Israel be accepted before their Father Who is in Heaven. Now respond: Amen. (Cong. — *Amen.*)

(Cong. — *Blessed be the Name of HASHEM, from this time and forever.*[1])

May there be abundant peace from Heaven, and life, upon us and upon all Israel. Now respond: Amen. (Cong. — *Amen.*)

(Cong. — *My help is from HASHEM, Maker of heaven and earth.*[2])

Take three steps back. Bow left and say, *'He Who makes peace . . .';* bow right and say, *'may He . . .';* bow forward and say, *'and upon all Israel . . .'* Remain standing in place for a few moments, then take three steps forward.

He Who makes peace in His heights, may He make peace upon us, and upon all Israel. Now respond: Amen. (Cong. — *Amen.*)

ON THE SABBATH, SONG OF SONGS (PAGE 566) IS RECITED AT THIS POINT.

---

(1) *Psalms* 113:2. (2) 121:2.

הוצאת ספר תורה

From the moment the Ark is opened until the Torah is returned to it, one must conduct himself with the utmost respect, and avoid unnecessary conversation. It is commendable to kiss the Torah as it is carried to the *bimah* [reading table] and back to the Ark.

All rise and remain standing until the Torah is placed on the *bimah*. The congregation recites:

אֵין כָּמְוֹךָ* בָאֱלֹהִים אֲדֹנָי, וְאֵין כְּמַעֲשֶׂיךָ.*[1] מַלְכוּתְךָ מַלְכוּת כָּל עֹלָמִים, וּמֶמְשַׁלְתְּךָ בְּכָל דּוֹר וָדֹר.[2] יהוה מֶלֶךְ,[3] יהוה מָלָךְ,[4] יהוה יִמְלֹךְ לְעֹלָם וָעֶד.[5] יהוה עֹז לְעַמּוֹ יִתֵּן, יהוה יְבָרֵךְ אֶת עַמּוֹ בַשָּׁלוֹם.[6]

אַב הָרַחֲמִים, הֵיטִיבָה בִרְצוֹנְךָ אֶת צִיּוֹן,* תִּבְנֶה חוֹמוֹת יְרוּשָׁלָיִם.[7] כִּי בְךָ לְבַד בָּטָחְנוּ, מֶלֶךְ אֵל רָם וְנִשָּׂא, אֲדוֹן עוֹלָמִים.

THE ARK IS OPENED

Before the Torah is removed the congregation recites:

וַיְהִי בִּנְסֹעַ הָאָרֹן* וַיֹּאמֶר משֶׁה, קוּמָה יהוה וְיָפֻצוּ אֹיְבֶיךָ וְיָנֻסוּ מְשַׂנְאֶיךָ מִפָּנֶיךָ.[8] כִּי מִצִּיּוֹן תֵּצֵא תוֹרָה, וּדְבַר יהוה מִירוּשָׁלָיִם.[9] בָּרוּךְ שֶׁנָּתַן תּוֹרָה לְעַמּוֹ יִשְׂרָאֵל בִּקְדֻשָּׁתוֹ.

ON THE SABBATH THE FOLLOWING PRAYERS ARE OMITTED AND THE SERVICE CONTINUES WITH בְּרִיךְ שְׁמֵהּ (P. 946).

The following paragraph [the Thirteen Attributes of Mercy] is recited three times:

יהוה, יהוה, אֵל, רַחוּם, וְחַנּוּן, אֶרֶךְ אַפַּיִם, וְרַב חֶסֶד, וֶאֱמֶת, נֹצֵר חֶסֶד לָאֲלָפִים, נֹשֵׂא עָוֹן, וָפֶשַׁע, וְחַטָּאָה, וְנַקֵּה.[10]

הוֹצָאַת סֵפֶר תּוֹרָה / Removal of the Torah

אֵין כָּמְוֹךָ — *There is none like You.* On the Sabbath and Festivals, the service of removing the Torah from the Ark begins with an introductory series of verses that emphasize God's greatness and plead for the rebuilding of Zion and Jerusalem. Since we are about to read from God's word to Israel, it is fitting that we first call to mind that the One Who speaks to us is our All-powerful King.

וְאֵין כְּמַעֲשֶׂיךָ — *And there is nothing like Your works.* This refers to the work of creation. It follows, therefore, that since God is the Creator of the universe, He was and remains its King.

הֵיטִיבָה . . . אֶת צִיּוֹן — *Do good with Zion.* Only in God's chosen Sanctuary can His kingdom come to full flower among mankind. Only there can the Torah reading attain its greatest meaning.

וַיְהִי בִּנְסֹעַ הָאָרֹן — *When the Ark would travel.* When the Ark is opened we declare, as Moses did when the Ark traveled, that God's word is invincible. Having acknowledged this, we can read from the Torah with the proper awareness. We continue that it is God's will that the Torah's message go forth to the entire world, and by blessing Him for having given us the Torah, we accept our responsibility to carry out its commands and spread its message *(R' Hirsch).*

The Thirteen Attributes of Mercy

During Festivals a special prayer is inserted before בְּרִיךְ שְׁמֵהּ, *Blessed is the Name*, requesting God's help in attaining His goals for us. [Like all personal supplications, this is not recited on the Sabbath.] It is preceded by the י״ג מִדּוֹת הָרַחֲמִים, *Thirteen Attributes of Mercy*, the prayer that God Himself taught Moses after Israel worshiped the Golden Calf. Although Moses, quite understandably, thought that no prayers could help the nation that had bowed to and danced around an idol less than six weeks after hearing the Ten Commandments, God showed him that it was never too late for prayer and repentance. God made a Divine covenant with him that the prayerful, repentant recitation of the Thirteen Attributes of Mercy would never be turned back unanswered *(Rosh Hashanah* 17b).

There are various opinions among the com-

REMOVAL OF THE TORAH FROM THE ARK

From the moment the Ark is opened until the Torah is returned to it, one must conduct himself with the utmost respect, and avoid unnecessary conversation. It is commendable to kiss the Torah as it is carried to the *bimah* [reading table] and back to the Ark.

All rise and remain standing until the Torah is placed on the *bimah*. The congregation recites:

אֵין כָּמְוֹךָ *There is none like You* among the gods, my Lord, and there is nothing like Your works.*[1] Your kingdom is a kingdom spanning all eternities, and Your dominion is throughout every generation.[2] HASHEM reigns,[3] HASHEM has reigned,[4] HASHEM shall reign for all eternity.[5] HASHEM will give might to His people; HASHEM will bless His people with peace.[6]*

אַב הָרַחֲמִים *Father of compassion, do good with Zion* according to Your will; rebuild the walls of Jerusalem.[7] For we trust in You alone, O King, God, exalted and uplifted, Master of worlds.*

THE ARK IS OPENED

Before the Torah is removed the congregation recites:

וַיְהִי בִּנְסֹעַ *When the Ark would travel,* Moses would say, 'Arise, HASHEM, and let Your foes be scattered, let those who hate You flee from You.'[8] For from Zion the Torah will come forth and the word of HASHEM from Jerusalem.[9] Blessed is He Who gave the Torah to His people Israel in His holiness.*

ON THE SABBATH THE FOLLOWING PRAYERS ARE OMITTED

AND THE SERVICE CONTINUES WITH בְּרִיךְ שְׁמֵהּ, *BLESSED IS THE NAME* (P. 946).

The following paragraph [the Thirteen Attributes of Mercy] is recited three times:

יהוה HASHEM, HASHEM, God, Compassionate and Gracious, Slow to anger, and Abundant in Kindness and Truth. Preserver of kindness for thousands of generations, Forgiver of iniquity, willful sin, and error, and Who cleanses.[10]

(1) *Psalms* 86:8. (2) 145:13. (3) 10:16. (4) 93:1 et al. (5) *Exodus* 15:18.
(6) *Psalms* 29:11. (7) 51:20. (8) *Numbers* 10:35. (9) *Isaiah* 2:3. (10) *Exodus* 34:6-7.

---

mentators regarding the precise enumeration of the Thirteen Attributes. The following is the opinion of *Rabbeinu Tam* (*Rosh Hashanah* 17b). For a fuller commentary, see the ArtScroll *Tashlich* and the *Yom Kippur Machzor*.

1. ה׳ — *HASHEM*. This Name denotes mercy. God is merciful before a person sins, though He knows that future evil lies dormant in him.

2. ה׳ — *HASHEM*. God is merciful after the sinner has gone astray.

3. אֵל — *God*. This Name denotes power: the force of God's mercy sometimes surpasses even that indicated by the Name *HASHEM*.

4. רַחוּם — *Compassionate*. God eases the punishment of the guilty; and He does not put people into extreme temptation.

5. וְחַנּוּן — *and Gracious*, even to the undeserving.

6. אֶרֶךְ אַפַּיִם — *Slow to anger*, so that the sinner can reconsider long before it is too late.

7. וְרַב חֶסֶד — *and Abundant in Kindness*, toward those who lack personal merits. Also, if the scales of good and evil are evenly balanced, He tips them to the good.

8. וֶאֱמֶת — *and Truth*. God never reneges on His word.

9. נֹצֵר חֶסֶד לָאֲלָפִים — *Preserver of kindness for thousands of generations*. The deeds of the righteous benefit their offspring far into the future.

10. נֹשֵׂא עָוֹן — *Forgiver of iniquity*. God forgives the intentional sinner, if he repents.

11. וָפֶשַׁע — *[Forgiver of] willful sin*. Even those who purposely anger God are allowed to repent.

12. וְחַטָּאָה — *and [Forgiver of] error*. This is a sin committed out of carelessness or apathy.

13. וְנַקֵּה — *and Who cleanses*. God wipes away the sins of those who repent.

רִבּוֹנוֹ שֶׁל עוֹלָם מַלֵּא מִשְׁאֲלוֹת לִבִּי לְטוֹבָה,* וְהָפֵק רְצוֹנִי, וְתֵן שְׁאֵלָתִי, לִי עַבְדְּךָ (name) בֶּן/בַּת (mother's name) אֲמָתֶךָ, וְזַכֵּנִי

Insert the appropriate phrase(s) – וְאֶת אִשְׁתִּי/בַּעְלִי, וּבְנִי/וּבָנַי, וּבִתִּי/וּבְנוֹתַי

וְכָל בְּנֵי בֵיתִי לַעֲשׂוֹת רְצוֹנְךָ בְּלֵבָב שָׁלֵם. וּמַלְּטֵנוּ מִיֵּצֶר הָרָע, וְתֵן חֶלְקֵנוּ בְּתוֹרָתֶךָ. וְזַכֵּנוּ שֶׁתִּשְׁרֶה שְׁכִינָתְךָ עָלֵינוּ, וְהוֹפַע עָלֵינוּ רוּחַ חָכְמָה וּבִינָה. וְיִתְקַיֵּם בָּנוּ מִקְרָא שֶׁכָּתוּב: וְנָחָה עָלָיו רוּחַ יהוה, רוּחַ חָכְמָה וּבִינָה, רוּחַ עֵצָה וּגְבוּרָה, רוּחַ דַּעַת וְיִרְאַת יהוה.[1] וְכֵן יְהִי רָצוֹן מִלְּפָנֶיךָ, יהוה אֱלֹהֵינוּ וֵאלֹהֵי אֲבוֹתֵינוּ, שֶׁתְּזַכֵּנוּ לַעֲשׂוֹת מַעֲשִׂים טוֹבִים בְּעֵינֶיךָ, וְלָלֶכֶת בְּדַרְכֵי יְשָׁרִים לְפָנֶיךָ. וְקַדְּשֵׁנוּ בְּמִצְוֹתֶיךָ כְּדֵי שֶׁנִּזְכֶּה לְחַיִּים טוֹבִים וַאֲרוּכִים לִימוֹת הַמָּשִׁיחַ וּלְחַיֵּי הָעוֹלָם הַבָּא. וְתִשְׁמְרֵנוּ מִמַּעֲשִׂים רָעִים, וּמִשָּׁעוֹת רָעוֹת הַמִּתְרַגְּשׁוֹת לָבֹא לָעוֹלָם. וְהַבּוֹטֵחַ בַּיהוה חֶסֶד יְסוֹבְבֶנְהוּ,[2] אָמֵן. יִהְיוּ לְרָצוֹן אִמְרֵי פִי וְהֶגְיוֹן לִבִּי לְפָנֶיךָ, יהוה צוּרִי וְגֹאֲלִי.[3]

Recite the following verse three times:

וַאֲנִי תְפִלָּתִי לְךָ* יהוה עֵת רָצוֹן, אֱלֹהִים בְּרָב חַסְדֶּךָ, עֲנֵנִי בֶּאֱמֶת יִשְׁעֶךָ.[4]

ON ALL DAYS CONTINUE:

זוהר ויקהל שסט:א

בְּרִיךְ שְׁמֵהּ* דְּמָרֵא עָלְמָא, בְּרִיךְ כִּתְרָךְ וְאַתְרָךְ. יְהֵא רְעוּתָךְ עִם עַמָּךְ יִשְׂרָאֵל לְעָלַם, וּפֻרְקַן יְמִינָךְ אַחֲזֵי לְעַמָּךְ בְּבֵית מַקְדְּשָׁךְ, וּלְאַמְטוּיֵי לָנָא מִטּוּב נְהוֹרָךְ, וּלְקַבֵּל צְלוֹתָנָא בְּרַחֲמִין. יְהֵא רַעֲוָא קֳדָמָךְ, דְּתוֹרִיךְ לָן חַיִּין בְּטִיבוּתָא, וְלֶהֱוֵי אֲנָא פְקִידָא בְּגוֹ צַדִּיקַיָּא, לְמִרְחַם עָלַי וּלְמִנְטַר יָתִי וְיַת כָּל דִּי לִי, וְדִי לְעַמָּךְ יִשְׂרָאֵל. אַנְתְּ הוּא זָן לְכֹלָּא, וּמְפַרְנֵס לְכֹלָּא, אַנְתְּ הוּא שַׁלִּיט עַל כֹּלָּא. אַנְתְּ הוּא דְּשַׁלִּיט עַל מַלְכַיָּא, וּמַלְכוּתָא דִּילָךְ הִיא. אֲנָא עַבְדָּא דְקֻדְשָׁא בְּרִיךְ הוּא, דְּסָגִידְנָא קַמֵּהּ וּמִקַּמָּא דִּיקַר אוֹרַיְתֵהּ בְּכָל עִדָּן וְעִדָּן. לָא עַל אֱנָשׁ רָחִיצְנָא, וְלָא עַל בַּר אֱלָהִין סָמִיכְנָא, אֶלָּא בֶּאֱלָהָא דִשְׁמַיָּא, דְּהוּא אֱלָהָא קְשׁוֹט, וְאוֹרַיְתֵהּ קְשׁוֹט, וּנְבִיאוֹהִי קְשׁוֹט, וּמַסְגֵּא לְמֶעְבַּד טַבְוָן וּקְשׁוֹט. בֵּהּ אֲנָא

רִבּוֹנוֹ שֶׁל עוֹלָם / Master of the Universe

מַלֵּא מִשְׁאֲלוֹת לִבִּי לְטוֹבָה — *Fulfill my heartfelt requests for good.* Often man's personal goals are not to his real benefit. May my requests be filled in a way that will be truly good.

וַאֲנִי תְפִלָּתִי לְךָ — *As for me, may my prayer to You.* This verse makes three declarations: We pray to God alone; we hope that the time is proper in His eyes; and we know that only through His abundant kindness can we expect salvation.

רִבּוֹנוֹ *Master of the universe, fulfill my heartfelt requests for good,* satisfy my desire and grant my request, me—Your servant* (name) *son/daughter of* (mother's name) *Your maidservant—and privilege me*

Insert the appropriate phrase(s): *and my wife/husband, my son(s), my daughter(s)*

---

and everyone in my household to do Your will wholeheartedly. Rescue us from the Evil Inclination and grant our share in Your Torah. Privilege us that You may rest Your Presence upon us and radiate upon us a spirit of wisdom and insight. Let there be fulfilled in us the verse that is written: The spirit of HASHEM *shall rest upon him, the spirit of wisdom and insight, the spirit of counsel and strength, the spirit of knowledge and fear of* HASHEM.[1] *Similarly may it be Your will,* HASHEM, *our God and the God of our forefathers, that You privilege us to do deeds that are good in Your eyes and to walk before You in upright paths. Sanctify us with Your commandments so that we may be worthy of a good and long life, to the days of the Messiah and to the life of the World to Come. May You protect us against evil deeds and from bad times that surge upon the world. He who trusts in* HASHEM *— may kindness surround him.*[2] *Amen. May the expressions of my mouth and the thoughts of my heart find favor before You,* HASHEM, *my Rock and my Redeemer.*[3]

Recite the following verse three times:

וַאֲנִי תְפִלָּתִי *As for me, may my prayer to You,** HASHEM, *be at an opportune time; O God, in Your abundant kindness, answer me with the truth of Your salvation.*[4]

ON ALL DAYS CONTINUE:

Zohar, Vayakhel 369a

בְּרִיךְ שְׁמֵהּ *Blessed is the Name* of the Master of the universe, blessed is Your crown and Your place. May Your favor remain with Your people Israel forever; may You display the salvation of Your right hand to Your people in Your Holy Temple, to benefit us with the goodness of Your luminescence and to accept our prayers with mercy. May it be Your will that You extend our lives with goodness and that I be numbered among the righteous; that You have mercy on me and protect me, all that is mine and that is Your people Israel's. It is You Who nourishes all and sustains all; You control everything. It is You Who control kings, and kingship is Yours. I am a servant of the Holy One, Blessed is He, and I prostrate myself before Him and before the glory of His Torah at all times. Not in any man do I put trust, nor on any angel do I rely — only on the God of heaven Who is the God of truth, Whose Torah is truth and Whose prophets are true and Who acts liberally with kindness and truth. In Him do I*

(1) *Isaiah* 11:2. (2) Cf. *Psalms* 32:10. (3) 19:15. (4) 69:14.

◆§ בְּרִיךְ שְׁמֵהּ — *Blessed is the Name.* The *Zohar* declares that when the congregation prepares to read from the Torah, the heavenly gates of mercy are opened and God's love for Israel is aroused. Therefore, it is an auspicious occasion for the recital of this prayer which asks for God's compassion; pleads that He display His salvation in the finally rebuilt Holy Temple; declares our

רַחִיץ, וְלִשְׁמֵהּ קַדִּישָׁא יַקִּירָא אֲנָא אֵמַר תֻּשְׁבְּחָן. יְהֵא רַעֲוָא קֳדָמָךְ, דְּתִפְתַּח לִבָּאִי בְּאוֹרַיְתָא, וְתַשְׁלִים מִשְׁאֲלִין דְּלִבָּאִי, וְלִבָּא דְכָל עַמָּךְ יִשְׂרָאֵל, לְטַב וּלְחַיִּין וְלִשְׁלָם. (אָמֵן.)

Two Torah Scrolls are removed from the Ark; one for the main Torah reading and the second for *Maftir*. The first is presented to the *chazzan*, who accepts it in his right arm. Facing the congregation, the *chazzan* raises the Torah and, followed by congregation, recites:

שְׁמַע יִשְׂרָאֵל* יהוה אֱלֹהֵינוּ יהוה אֶחָד.[1]

Still facing the congregation, the *chazzan* raises the Torah and, followed by congregation, recites:

אֶחָד (הוּא) אֱלֹהֵינוּ גָּדוֹל אֲדוֹנֵינוּ, קָדוֹשׁ שְׁמוֹ.

The *chazzan* turns to the Ark, bows while raising the Torah, and recites:

גַּדְּלוּ* לַיהוה אִתִּי וּנְרוֹמְמָה שְׁמוֹ יַחְדָּו.[2]

The *chazzan* turns to his right and carries the Torah to the *bimah*, as the congregation responds:

לְךָ יהוה הַגְּדֻלָּה* וְהַגְּבוּרָה וְהַתִּפְאֶרֶת וְהַנֵּצַח וְהַהוֹד כִּי כֹל בַּשָּׁמַיִם וּבָאָרֶץ, לְךָ יהוה הַמַּמְלָכָה וְהַמִּתְנַשֵּׂא לְכֹל לְרֹאשׁ.[3] רוֹמְמוּ יהוה אֱלֹהֵינוּ, וְהִשְׁתַּחֲווּ לַהֲדֹם רַגְלָיו,* קָדוֹשׁ הוּא. רוֹמְמוּ יהוה אֱלֹהֵינוּ, וְהִשְׁתַּחֲווּ לְהַר קָדְשׁוֹ, כִּי קָדוֹשׁ יהוה אֱלֹהֵינוּ.[4]

As the *chazzan* carries the Torah to the *bimah*, the congregation recites:

עַל הַכֹּל,* יִתְגַּדַּל וְיִתְקַדַּשׁ וְיִשְׁתַּבַּח וְיִתְפָּאַר וְיִתְרוֹמַם וְיִתְנַשֵּׂא שְׁמוֹ שֶׁל מֶלֶךְ מַלְכֵי הַמְּלָכִים הַקָּדוֹשׁ בָּרוּךְ הוּא, בָּעוֹלָמוֹת שֶׁבָּרָא, הָעוֹלָם הַזֶּה וְהָעוֹלָם הַבָּא, כִּרְצוֹנוֹ,* וְכִרְצוֹן יְרֵאָיו, וְכִרְצוֹן כָּל בֵּית יִשְׂרָאֵל. צוּר הָעוֹלָמִים, אֲדוֹן כָּל הַבְּרִיּוֹת, אֱלוֹהַּ כָּל הַנְּפָשׁוֹת, הַיּוֹשֵׁב בְּמֶרְחֲבֵי מָרוֹם, הַשּׁוֹכֵן בִּשְׁמֵי שְׁמֵי קֶדֶם. קְדֻשָּׁתוֹ עַל הַחַיּוֹת, וּקְדֻשָּׁתוֹ עַל כִּסֵּא הַכָּבוֹד. וּבְכֵן יִתְקַדַּשׁ שִׁמְךָ בָּנוּ* יהוה אֱלֹהֵינוּ לְעֵינֵי כָּל חָי. וְנֹאמַר לְפָנָיו שִׁיר חָדָשׁ, כַּכָּתוּב: שִׁירוּ לֵאלֹהִים זַמְּרוּ שְׁמוֹ, סֹלּוּ

---

faith in Him and His Torah; and asks that He make us receptive to its wisdom.

◆§ שְׁמַע יִשְׂרָאֵל — *Hear, O Israel.* Holding the Torah Scroll, the *chazzan* leads the congregation in reciting three verses that help set the majestic tone of reading publicly from the word of God. The verses form a logical progression: God is One; He is great and holy; therefore we join in declaring His greatness.

◆§ גַּדְּלוּ — *Declare the greatness.* Our rejoicing in the Torah manifests itself in praise of its Giver. The *chazzan* calls upon the congregation to join him in praising God.

◆§ לְךָ ה' הַגְּדֻלָּה — *Yours, HASHEM, is the greatness.* This praise was first uttered by David in his ecstasy at seeing how wholeheartedly the people contributed their riches toward the eventual building of the Temple. He ascribed the greatness of that and every other achievement to God's graciousness.

לַהֲדֹם רַגְלָיו — *At His footstool*, i.e., the Temple, as if to say that God's Heavenly Presence extends earthward, like a footstool that helps support a monarch sitting on his throne. In a further sense, this represents our resolve to live in such a way that we are worthy of His Presence resting upon us *(R' Hirsch)*.

◆§ עַל הַכֹּל — *For all this.* All the praises that we

trust, and to His glorious and holy Name do I declare praises. May it be Your will that You open my heart to the Torah and that You fulfill the wishes of my heart and the heart of Your entire people Israel for good, for life, and for peace. (Amen.)

Two Torah Scrolls are removed from the Ark; one for the main Torah reading and the second for *Maftir.* The first is presented to the *chazzan,* who accepts it in his right arm. Facing the congregation, the *chazzan* raises the Torah and, followed by congregation, recites:

Hear, O Israel:* HASHEM is our God, HASHEM, the One and Only.[1]

Still facing the congregation, the *chazzan* raises the Torah and, followed by congregation, recites:

One is our God, great is our Master, Holy is His Name.

The *chazzan* turns to the Ark, bows while raising the Torah, and recites:

Declare the greatness* of HASHEM with me, and let us exalt His Name together.[2]

The *chazzan* turns to his right and carries the Torah to the *bimah,* as the congregation responds:

לְךָ *Yours, HASHEM, is the greatness,* the strength, the splendor, the triumph, and the glory; even everything in heaven and earth; Yours, HASHEM, is the kingdom, and the sovereignty over every leader.[3] Exalt HASHEM, our God, and bow at His footstool;* He is Holy! Exalt HASHEM, our God, and bow to His holy mountain; for holy is HASHEM, our God.[4]*

As the *chazzan* carries the Torah to the *bimah,* the congregation recites:

עַל הַכֹּל *For all this,* let the Name of the King of kings, the Holy One, Blessed is He, grow exalted, sanctified, praised, glorified, exalted, and extolled in the worlds that He has created — This World and the World to Come — according to His will,* the will of those who fear Him, and the will of the entire House of Israel. Rock of the eternities, Master of all creatures, God of all souls, He Who sits in the expanses on high, Who rests in the loftiest primeval heavens. His holiness is upon the Chayos; His holiness is upon the Throne of Glory. Similarly, may Your Name be sanctified within us,* HASHEM, our God, in the sight of all the living. May we chant before Him a new song as it is written: 'Sing to God, make music for His Name, extol the One Who*

(1) *Deuteronomy* 6:4. (2) *Psalms* 34:4. (3) *I Chronicles* 29:11. (4) *Psalms* 99:5,9.

---

have uttered heretofore are inadequate to describe God's greatness. May His Name continue to grow exalted (*Kol Bo*).

This paragraph is intended to express the majesty of God especially now that we are about to read from the Torah. We say that although He is sanctified in the heavens and by the spiritual beings, we long to become worthy vehicles through which His greatness can be manifested on earth, as well.

כִּרְצוֹנוֹ — *According to His will.* May He be *exalted, sanctified, praised* ... as He wishes to be. God created the universe so that His glory could be appreciated and emulated by man (see *Isaiah* 43:7). We now pray that this will indeed take place.

וּבְכֵן יִתְקַדַּשׁ שִׁמְךָ בָּנוּ — *Similarly, may Your Name be sanctified within us.* The goal of people should be to demonstrate that God's greatness should not be reserved for the 'higher, spiritual' spheres. Rather, the most noble purpose of life is for mortal man to become a bearer of Godliness.

לְרֹכֵב בָּעֲרָבוֹת בְּיָהּ שְׁמוֹ, וְעִלְזוּ לְפָנָיו.[1] וְנִרְאֵהוּ עַיִן בְּעַיִן בְּשׁוּבוֹ אֶל נָוֵהוּ, כַּכָּתוּב: כִּי עַיִן בְּעַיִן יִרְאוּ בְּשׁוּב יהוה צִיּוֹן.[2] וְנֶאֱמַר: וְנִגְלָה כְּבוֹד יהוה, וְרָאוּ כָל בָּשָׂר יַחְדָּו כִּי פִּי יהוה דִּבֵּר.[3]

אַב הָרַחֲמִים הוּא יְרַחֵם עַם עֲמוּסִים, וְיִזְכֹּר בְּרִית אֵיתָנִים, וְיַצִּיל נַפְשׁוֹתֵינוּ מִן הַשָּׁעוֹת הָרָעוֹת, וְיִגְעַר בְּיֵצֶר הָרָע מִן הַנְּשׂוּאִים, וְיָחֹן אוֹתָנוּ לִפְלֵיטַת עוֹלָמִים, וִימַלֵּא מִשְׁאֲלוֹתֵינוּ בְּמִדָּה טוֹבָה יְשׁוּעָה וְרַחֲמִים.

The Torah is placed on the *bimah* and prepared for reading.

The *gabbai* uses the following formula to call a *Kohen* to the Torah:

וְיַעֲזוֹר וְיָגֵן וְיוֹשִׁיעַ לְכֹל הַחוֹסִים בּוֹ, וְנֹאמַר, אָמֵן. הַכֹּל הָבוּ גֹדֶל לֵאלֹהֵינוּ וּתְנוּ כָבוֹד לַתּוֹרָה, כֹּהֵן° קְרָב, יַעֲמֹד (name) בֶּן (father's name) הַכֹּהֵן.

°If no *Kohen* is present, the *gabbai* says:
"אֵין כָּאן כֹּהֵן, יַעֲמֹד (insert name) יִשְׂרָאֵל (לֵוִי) בִּמְקוֹם כֹּהֵן."

בָּרוּךְ שֶׁנָּתַן תּוֹרָה לְעַמּוֹ יִשְׂרָאֵל בִּקְדֻשָּׁתוֹ. (תּוֹרַת יהוה תְּמִימָה מְשִׁיבַת נָפֶשׁ, עֵדוּת יהוה נֶאֱמָנָה מַחְכִּימַת פֶּתִי. פִּקּוּדֵי יהוה יְשָׁרִים מְשַׂמְּחֵי לֵב, מִצְוַת יהוה בָּרָה מְאִירַת עֵינָיִם.[4] יהוה עֹז לְעַמּוֹ יִתֵּן, יהוה יְבָרֵךְ אֶת עַמּוֹ בַשָּׁלוֹם.[5] הָאֵל תָּמִים דַּרְכּוֹ, אִמְרַת יהוה צְרוּפָה, מָגֵן הוּא לְכֹל הַחוֹסִים בּוֹ.[6])

Congregation, then *gabbai:*

וְאַתֶּם הַדְּבֵקִים בַּיהוה אֱלֹהֵיכֶם, חַיִּים כֻּלְּכֶם הַיּוֹם.[7]

קריאת התורה

The reader shows the *oleh* (person called to the Torah) the place in the Torah. The *oleh* touches the Torah with a corner of his *tallis,* or the belt or mantle of the Torah, and kisses it. He then begins the blessing, bowing at בָּרְכוּ, and straightening up at 'ה.

בָּרְכוּ אֶת יהוה הַמְּבֹרָךְ.

Congregation, followed by *oleh,* responds, bowing at בָּרוּךְ, and straightening up at 'ה.

בָּרוּךְ יהוה הַמְּבֹרָךְ לְעוֹלָם וָעֶד.

Oleh continues:

בָּרוּךְ אַתָּה יהוה אֱלֹהֵינוּ מֶלֶךְ הָעוֹלָם, אֲשֶׁר בָּחַר בָּנוּ מִכָּל הָעַמִּים, וְנָתַן לָנוּ אֶת תּוֹרָתוֹ. בָּרוּךְ אַתָּה יהוה, נוֹתֵן הַתּוֹרָה. (–Cong. אָמֵן.)

קְרִיאַת הַתּוֹרָה / Reading of the Torah

There is a basic difference between the reading of the Torah and the prayers. When we pray, *we* call upon *God;* that is why the *chazzan* stands in front of the congregation as its representative. But the Torah reading is reminiscent of God's revelation to Israel, when the nation gathered around Mount Sinai to hear Him communicate His word to Israel. That is why the Torah is read from a *bimah,* platform, in the center of the congregation and usually elevated, like the mountain around which Israel gathered.

The number of people called to the Torah varies in accordance with the sanctity of the day. Thus, on Monday and Thursday, fast days, Purim and Chanukah, three people are called; on Rosh Chodesh and Chol HaMoed, four; on Festivals and Rosh Hashanah, five; on Yom Kippur, six; and on the Sabbath [whether an *rides in the highest heavens with His Name YAH, and exult before Him.'[1] May we see Him with a perceptive view upon His return to His Abode, as is written: 'For they shall see with a perceptive view as HASHEM returns to Zion.'[2] And it is said: 'The glory of HASHEM shall be revealed and all flesh together shall see that the mouth of HASHEM has spoken.'[3]*

אַב הָרַחֲמִים *May the Father of compassion have mercy on the nation that is borne by Him, and may He remember the covenant of the spiritually mighty. May He rescue our souls from the bad times, and upbraid the evil inclination to leave those borne by Him, graciously make us an eternal remnant, and fulfill our requests in good measure, for salvation and mercy.*

The Torah is placed on the *bimah* and prepared for reading.

The *gabbai* uses the following formula to call a *Kohen* to the Torah:

וְיַעֲזוֹר *May He help, shield, and save all who take refuge in Him — Now let us respond: Amen. All of you ascribe greatness to our God and give honor to the Torah. Kohen,° approach. Arise* (name) *son of* (father's name) *the Kohen.*

°If no *Kohen* is present, the *gabbai* says: *'There is no Kohen present, stand* (name) *son of* (father's name) *an Israelite (Levite) in place of the Kohen.'*

Blessed is He Who gave the Torah to His people Israel in His holiness. (The Torah of HASHEM is perfect, restoring the soul; the testimony of HASHEM is trustworthy, making the simple one wise. The orders of HASHEM are upright, gladdening the heart; the command of HASHEM is clear, enlightening the eyes.[4] HASHEM will give might to His nation; HASHEM will bless His nation with peace.[5] The God Whose way is perfect, the promise of HASHEM is flawless, He is a shield for all who take refuge in Him.[6])

Congregation, then *gabbai:*

You who cling to HASHEM, your God, you are all alive today.[7]

READING OF THE TORAH

The reader shows the *oleh* (person called to the Torah) the place in the Torah. The *oleh* touches the Torah with a corner of his *tallis,* or the belt or mantle of the Torah, and kisses it. He then begins the blessing, bowing at *'Bless,'* and straightening up at 'HASHEM.'

Bless HASHEM,• the blessed One.

Congregation, followed by *oleh,* responds, bowing at 'Blessed,' and straightening up at 'HASHEM.'

Blessed is HASHEM, the blessed One, for all eternity.

Oleh continues:

בָּרוּךְ *Blessed are You, HASHEM, our God, King of the universe, Who selected us from all the peoples and gave us His Torah. Blessed are You, HASHEM, Giver of the Torah.* (Cong.— *Amen.)*

(1) *Psalms* 68:5. (2) *Isaiah* 52:8. (3) 40:5. (4) *Psalms* 19:8-9. (4) 29:11. (6) 18:31. (7) *Deuteronomy* 4:4.

---

ordinary Sabbath or a Festival that falls on the Sabbath], seven. (It should be noted that *Maftir* is not included in the above number since *Maftir* is attached to the *Haftarah* reading.) Only three are called on Sabbath afternoons since the Torah has already been read in the morning.

On most Festivals the Torah reading is a selection on either the historical narrative of the day or the commandment to observe the Festivals.

בָּרְכוּ אֶת ה׳ — *Bless HASHEM.* This call to the congregation to bless God prior to the Torah reading is based on the practice of Ezra (*Nechemiah* 8:6). Before he read from the Torah to the multitude, he blessed God and they responded in kind. Similarly, the Sages (*Berachos* 21a) derive the Scriptural requirement to recite a blessing before Torah study from the verse, *When I proclaim the Name of HASHEM, ascribe greatness to our God* (*Deuteronomy* 32:3). The implication

After his Torah portion has been read, the *oleh* recites:

בָּרוּךְ אַתָּה יהוה אֱלֹהֵינוּ מֶלֶךְ הָעוֹלָם, אֲשֶׁר נָתַן לָנוּ תּוֹרַת אֱמֶת, וְחַיֵּי עוֹלָם* נָטַע בְּתוֹכֵנוּ. בָּרוּךְ אַתָּה יהוה, נוֹתֵן הַתּוֹרָה. (Cong. – אָמֵן.)

PRAYER FOR THE OLEH / מי שברך לעולה לתורה

After each *oleh* completes his concluding blessing, the *gabbai* calls the next *oleh* to the Torah, then blesses the one who has just concluded.

מִי שֶׁבֵּרַךְ אֲבוֹתֵינוּ אַבְרָהָם יִצְחָק וְיַעֲקֹב, הוּא יְבָרֵךְ אֶת (name) בֶּן (father's name) בַּעֲבוּר שֶׁעָלָה לִכְבוֹד הַמָּקוֹם, לִכְבוֹד הַתּוֹרָה, לִכְבוֹד הַשַּׁבָּת, לִכְבוֹד הָרֶגֶל. בִּשְׂכַר זֶה, הַקָּדוֹשׁ בָּרוּךְ הוּא יִשְׁמְרֵהוּ וְיַצִּילֵהוּ מִכָּל צָרָה וְצוּקָה, וּמִכָּל נֶגַע וּמַחֲלָה, וְיִשְׁלַח בְּרָכָה וְהַצְלָחָה בְּכָל מַעֲשֵׂה יָדָיו, וְיִזְכֶּה לַעֲלוֹת לָרֶגֶל, עִם כָּל יִשְׂרָאֵל אֶחָיו. וְנֹאמַר: אָמֵן. (Cong. – אָמֵן.)

PRAYER FOR OTHERS / מי שברך לאחרים

It is customary that the following prayer be recited for the family members of the *oleh* and for anyone else that he may wish to include:

מִי שֶׁבֵּרַךְ אֲבוֹתֵינוּ אַבְרָהָם יִצְחָק וְיַעֲקֹב, הוּא יְבָרֵךְ אֶת (names of the recipients) בַּעֲבוּר שֶׁ(name of *oleh*) יִתֵּן לִצְדָקָה בַּעֲבוּרָם. בִּשְׂכַר זֶה, הַקָּדוֹשׁ בָּרוּךְ הוּא יִשְׁמְרֵם וְיַצִּילֵם מִכָּל צָרָה וְצוּקָה, וּמִכָּל נֶגַע וּמַחֲלָה, וְיִשְׁלַח בְּרָכָה וְהַצְלָחָה בְּכָל מַעֲשֵׂה יְדֵיהֶם, וְיִזְכּוּ לַעֲלוֹת לָרֶגֶל, עִם כָּל יִשְׂרָאֵל אֲחֵיהֶם. וְנֹאמַר: אָמֵן. (Cong. – אָמֵן.)

PRAYER FOR A SICK PERSON / מי שברך לחולה

מִי שֶׁבֵּרַךְ אֲבוֹתֵינוּ אַבְרָהָם יִצְחָק וְיַעֲקֹב, מֹשֶׁה אַהֲרֹן דָּוִד וּשְׁלֹמֹה,

for a man

הוּא יְבָרֵךְ וִירַפֵּא אֶת הַחוֹלֶה (patient's name) בֶּן (mother's name) בַּעֲבוּר שֶׁ(supplicant's name) יִתֵּן לִצְדָקָה בַּעֲבוּרוֹ.°° בִּשְׂכַר זֶה, הַקָּדוֹשׁ בָּרוּךְ הוּא יִמָּלֵא רַחֲמִים עָלָיו, לְהַחֲלִימוֹ וּלְרַפְּאתוֹ וּלְהַחֲזִיקוֹ וּלְהַחֲיוֹתוֹ, וְיִשְׁלַח לוֹ מְהֵרָה רְפוּאָה שְׁלֵמָה מִן הַשָּׁמַיִם, לִרְמַ״ח אֵבָרָיו, וּשְׁסָ״ה גִּידָיו, בְּתוֹךְ

for a woman

הוּא יְבָרֵךְ וִירַפֵּא אֶת הַחוֹלָה (patient's name) בַּת (mother's name) בַּעֲבוּר שֶׁ(supplicant's name) יִתֵּן לִצְדָקָה בַּעֲבוּרָהּ.°° בִּשְׂכַר זֶה, הַקָּדוֹשׁ בָּרוּךְ הוּא יִמָּלֵא רַחֲמִים עָלֶיהָ, לְהַחֲלִימָהּ וּלְרַפְּאתָהּ וּלְהַחֲזִיקָהּ וּלְהַחֲיוֹתָהּ, וְיִשְׁלַח לָהּ מְהֵרָה רְפוּאָה שְׁלֵמָה מִן הַשָּׁמַיִם, לְכָל אֵבָרֶיהָ, וּלְכָל גִּידֶיהָ, בְּתוֹךְ

שְׁאָר חוֹלֵי יִשְׂרָאֵל, רְפוּאַת הַנֶּפֶשׁ, וּרְפוּאַת הַגּוּף, [On the Sabbath – שַׁבָּת וְ] יוֹם טוֹב הוּא מִלִּזְעֹק, וּרְפוּאָה קְרוֹבָה לָבֹא, הַשְׁתָּא, בַּעֲגָלָא וּבִזְמַן קָרִיב. וְנֹאמַר: אָמֵן. (Cong. – אָמֵן.)

°°Many congregations substitute:

בַּעֲבוּר שֶׁכָּל הַקָּהָל מִתְפַּלְּלִים בַּעֲבוּרוֹ (בַּעֲבוּרָהּ)

After his Torah portion has been read, the *oleh* recites:

בָּרוּךְ *Blessed are You,* HASHEM, *our God, King of the universe, Who gave us the Torah of truth and implanted eternal life* within us. Blessed are You,* HASHEM, *Giver of the Torah.* (Cong.– *Amen.)*

PRAYER FOR THE OLEH

After each *oleh* completes his concluding blessing, the *gabbai* calls the next *oleh* to the Torah, then blesses the one who has just concluded.

מִי שֶׁבֵּרַךְ *He Who blessed our forefathers Abraham, Isaac, and Jacob — may He bless (* Hebrew name*) son of (* father's Hebrew name*) because he has come up to the Torah in honor of the Omnipresent, in honor of the Torah, in honor of the Sabbath, in honor of the pilgrimage festival. As reward for this, may the Holy One, Blessed is He, protect him and rescue him from every trouble and distress, from every plague and illness; may He send blessing and success in his every endeavor, and may he be privileged to ascend to Jerusalem for the pilgrimage, together with all Israel, his brethren. Now let us respond: Amen.* (Cong.– *Amen.)*

PRAYER FOR OTHERS

It is customary that the following prayer be recited for the family members of the *oleh* and for anyone else that he may wish to include:

מִי שֶׁבֵּרַךְ *He Who blessed our forefathers Abraham, Isaac, and Jacob — may He bless (* names of recipients*) for (* name of *oleh) will contribute to charity on their behalf. As reward for this, may the Holy One, Blessed is He, protect them and rescue them from every trouble and distress, from every plague and illness; may He send blessing and success in their every endeavor and may they be privileged to ascend to Jerusalem for the pilgrimage, together with all Israel, their brethren. Now let us respond: Amen.* (Cong.– *Amen.)*

PRAYER FOR A SICK PERSON

מִי שֶׁבֵּרַךְ *He Who blessed our forefathers Abraham, Isaac and Jacob, Moses and Aaron, David and Solomon — may He bless and heal the sick person (* patient's Hebrew name*) son/daughter of (* patient's mother's Hebrew name*) because (* name of supplicant*) will contribute to charity on his/her behalf.*°° *In reward for this, may the Holy One, Blessed is He, be filled with*

for a man	for a woman
compassion for him to restore his health, to heal him, to strengthen him, and to revivify him. And may He send him speedily a complete recovery from heaven for his two hundred forty-eight organs and three hundred sixty-five blood vessels, among the other	*compassion for her to restore her health, to heal her, to strengthen her, and to revivify her. And may He send her speedily a complete recovery from heaven for all her organs and all her blood vessels, among the other*

sick people of Israel, a recovery of the body and a recovery of the spirit though the [on the Sabbath: *Sabbath and*] *Festival prohibit*[*s*] *us from crying out, may a recovery come speedily, swiftly and soon. Now let us respond: Amen.* (Cong.– *Amen.)*

°°Many congregations substitute:
because the entire congregation prays for him (her)

---

is that public study of Torah requires a blessing.

תּוֹרַת אֱמֶת וְחַיֵּי עוֹלָם — *The Torah of truth ... eternal life. Torah of Truth* refers to the Written Torah, and *eternal life* to the Oral Law. The Oral Law is described as *implanted within us,* because Jews constantly expand their Torah knowledge through their personal study and analysis (*Tur Orach Chaim* 139).

SEVENTH DAY

קריאת התורה ליום שביעי

שמות יג:יז-טו:כו

כהן– וַיְהִ֗י בְּשַׁלַּ֣ח פַּרְעֹה֮ אֶת־הָעָם֒ וְלֹא־נָחָ֣ם אֱלֹהִ֗ים דֶּ֚רֶךְ אֶ֣רֶץ
פְּלִשְׁתִּ֔ים כִּ֥י קָר֖וֹב ה֑וּא* כִּ֣י ׀ אָמַ֣ר אֱלֹהִ֗ים פֶּֽן־יִנָּחֵ֥ם הָעָ֛ם בִּרְאֹתָ֥ם
מִלְחָמָ֖ה וְשָׁ֥בוּ מִצְרָֽיְמָה׃ וַיַּסֵּ֨ב אֱלֹהִ֧ים ׀ אֶת־הָעָ֛ם דֶּ֥רֶךְ הַמִּדְבָּ֖ר
יַם־ס֑וּף וַחֲמֻשִׁ֛ים* עָל֥וּ בְנֵֽי־יִשְׂרָאֵ֖ל מֵאֶ֥רֶץ מִצְרָֽיִם׃ וַיִּקַּ֥ח מֹשֶׁ֛ה*
אֶת־עַצְמ֥וֹת יוֹסֵ֖ף עִמּ֑וֹ כִּי֩ הַשְׁבֵּ֨עַ הִשְׁבִּ֜יעַ אֶת־בְּנֵ֤י יִשְׂרָאֵל֙* לֵאמֹ֔ר
פָּקֹ֨ד יִפְקֹ֤ד אֱלֹהִים֙ אֶתְכֶ֔ם וְהַעֲלִיתֶ֧ם אֶת־עַצְמֹתַ֛י מִזֶּ֖ה אִתְּכֶֽם׃

◆ TORAH READING FOR THE SEVENTH DAY ◆

Since the splitting of the Sea of Reeds took place on the seventh day of the Exodus, its Scriptural account forms the seventh day Torah reading.

כִּי קָרוֹב הוּא —*Because it was near.* The easiest way to go from Egypt to *Eretz Yisrael* is along the Mediterranean coast, which leads through the *land of the Philistines.* But that apparent advantage was the very reason why God chose not to lead the nation that way. Had the return journey been direct, as it would have been from Philistia, when the inevitable attacks against them took place, the people would have been tempted to return to the security and safety of Egyptian servitude. Indeed, there was once such a sentiment in the wake of an Amalekite and Canaanite attack (*Numbers* 14:4). In order to prevent that from happening, God led them on a long, difficult, and roundabout way, through the Sinai Desert.

וַחֲמֻשִׁים — *Armed.* Knowing that they would be facing battles in their future, the people took arms with them. Had they not been able to defend themselves, even the roundabout route

EIGHTH DAY

קריאת התורה ליום אחרון

דברים יד:כב-טז:יז

ON THE SABBATH THE READING BEGINS HERE;
ON WEEKDAYS THE READING BEGINS ON PAGE 964.

(בשבת כהן) – עַשֵּׂ֣ר תְּעַשֵּׂ֔ר* אֵ֖ת כָּל־תְּבוּאַ֣ת זַרְעֶ֑ךָ הַיֹּצֵ֥א הַשָּׂדֶ֖ה שָׁנָ֥ה
שָׁנָֽה׃ וְאָכַלְתָּ֞ לִפְנֵ֣י ׀ יהוה* אֱלֹהֶ֗יךָ בַּמָּק֣וֹם אֲשֶׁר־יִבְחַר֮ לְשַׁכֵּ֣ן
שְׁמ֣וֹ שָׁם֒ מַעְשַׂ֤ר דְּגָֽנְךָ֙ תִּירֹשְׁךָ֣ וְיִצְהָרֶ֔ךָ וּבְכֹרֹ֥ת בְּקָרְךָ֖ וְצֹאנֶ֑ךָ
לְמַ֣עַן תִּלְמַ֗ד לְיִרְאָ֛ה* אֶת־יהוה אֱלֹהֶ֖יךָ כָּל־הַיָּמִֽים׃ וְכִֽי־יִרְבֶּ֨ה
מִמְּךָ֜ הַדֶּ֗רֶךְ כִּ֣י לֹ֤א תוּכַל֙ שְׂאֵת֔וֹ כִּֽי־יִרְחַ֤ק מִמְּךָ֙ הַמָּק֔וֹם אֲשֶׁ֤ר
יִבְחַר֙ יהוה אֱלֹהֶ֔יךָ לָשׂ֥וּם שְׁמ֖וֹ שָׁ֑ם כִּ֥י יְבָרֶכְךָ֖* יהוה אֱלֹהֶֽיךָ׃

◆ TORAH READING FOR THE EIGHTH DAY ◆

This portion is read on the last days of Pesach and Shavuos as well on Shemini Atzeres, but there is a difference. If those days of Pesach and Shavuos fall on weekdays, the reading begins at 15:9, with כָּל הַבְּכוֹר, *Every firstborn.* Only on the Sabbath, when seven people instead of five are called to the Torah and more verses are needed, do we begin from עַשֵּׂר תְּעַשֵּׂר, *you are to take tithes.* On Shemini Atzeres, however, the reading always begins with the passage on tithes, because this is the time when people are enjoined to deliver their tithes to the needy. As the season when crops

SEVENTH DAY

TORAH READING FOR THE SEVENTH DAY

Exodus 13:17-15:26

Kohen – *It happened when Pharaoh sent out the people that God did not lead them by way of the land of the Philistines because it was near,* for God said: 'Perhaps the people will have a change of heart when they see war, and they will return to Egypt.' So God turned the people toward the way of the wilderness, to the Sea of Reeds. The Children of Israel were armed* as they went up from Egypt. Moses took* the bones of Joseph with him, for he had firmly adjured the sons of Israel* saying: 'God will surely remember you, and you shall bring up my bones from here with you.'*

through the desert would not have prevented them from retreating back to Egypt. An alternate rendering is *one-fifth*. Since only one-fifth of the people were worthy to be redeemed from Egypt, the rest died during the plague of darkness, so that the Egyptians would not see what happened to them.

וַיִּקַּח מֹשֶׁה — *Moses took*. King Solomon taught that a wise person seeks ways to perform the commandments (*Proverbs* 10:8), a teaching that the Sages apply to this act of Moses. The rest of the people were engaged in enriching themselves by borrowing vessels and garments from the Egyptians, but Moses occupied himself with the good deed of salvaging Joseph's remains.

בְּנֵי יִשְׂרָאֵל — *The sons of Israel.* Although this phrase is usually rendered *the Children of Israel*, here it is used in its literal sense, *Israel's* (i.e., *Jacob's*) *sons*. Joseph had imposed this oath upon his brothers, Israel's sons. They, in turn, passed on the oath to the later generations. Implied in the term *with you* is the additional oath that the bones of Joseph's brothers, as well, were removed from Egypt at the time of the Exodus.

EIGHTH DAY

TORAH READING FOR THE EIGHTH DAY

Deuteronomy 14:22-16:17

ON THE SABBATH THE READING BEGINS HERE;
ON WEEKDAYS THE READING BEGINS ON PAGE 964.

(On the Sabbath – Kohen) *You are to take tithes* from the entire crop of your planting; what is produced by the field year in, year out. And you are to eat it before* HASHEM,* *your God — in the place in which He will have chosen to rest His Name — the tithe of your grain, wine and oil, and the firstborn of your cattle and sheep; so that you will learn to fear** HASHEM, *your God, throughout the years. If the distance is too great for you so that you cannot carry it, because far from you is the place that* HASHEM, *your God, will have chosen to place His Name there; for* HASHEM, *your God, will have blessed you.**

are gathered in, Shemini Atzeres is the time when it is especially important for all Jews to share their prosperity with the less fortunate.

עַשֵּׂר תְּעַשֵּׂר — *You are to take tithes.* The Sages expound homiletically עַשֵּׂר בִּשְׁבִיל שֶׁתִּתְעַשֵּׁר, *give tithes in order that you should become wealthy*, i.e., God rewards charitable people with prosperity far beyond their contributions (*Shabbos* 119a).

וְאָכַלְתָּ לִפְנֵי ה׳ — *And you are to eat it before* HASHEM. This commandment applies to מַעֲשֵׂר שֵׁנִי, the *second tithe*, which is brought to Jerusalem and eaten there.

לְמַעַן תִּלְמַד לְיִרְאָה — *So that you will learn to fear.* One who comes to Jerusalem, which is saturated with holiness, learns יִרְאַת שָׁמַיִם, *fear of Heaven*.

כִּי יְבָרֶכְךָ — *For . . . will have blessed you.* God has blessed you with such abundant crops that you cannot carry all your tithes to Jerusalem, even

SEVENTH DAY

(בשבת לוי –) וַיִּסְעוּ מִסֻּכֹּת וַיַּחֲנוּ בְאֵתָם בִּקְצֵה הַמִּדְבָּר: וַיהוָה הֹלֵךְ* לִפְנֵיהֶם יוֹמָם בְּעַמּוּד עָנָן לַנְחֹתָם הַדֶּרֶךְ וְלַיְלָה בְּעַמּוּד אֵשׁ לְהָאִיר לָהֶם לָלֶכֶת יוֹמָם וָלָיְלָה: לֹא־יָמִישׁ עַמּוּד הֶעָנָן יוֹמָם וְעַמּוּד הָאֵשׁ לָיְלָה לִפְנֵי הָעָם:

לוי (בשבת שלישי) – וַיְדַבֵּר יהוָה אֶל־מֹשֶׁה לֵּאמֹר: דַּבֵּר אֶל־בְּנֵי יִשְׂרָאֵל וְיָשֻׁבוּ* וְיַחֲנוּ לִפְנֵי פִּי הַחִירֹת בֵּין מִגְדֹּל וּבֵין הַיָּם לִפְנֵי בַּעַל צְפֹן נִכְחוֹ תַחֲנוּ עַל־הַיָּם: וְאָמַר פַּרְעֹה לִבְנֵי יִשְׂרָאֵל נְבֻכִים הֵם בָּאָרֶץ סָגַר עֲלֵיהֶם הַמִּדְבָּר: וְחִזַּקְתִּי אֶת־לֵב־פַּרְעֹה וְרָדַף אַחֲרֵיהֶם וְאִכָּבְדָה* בְּפַרְעֹה וּבְכָל־חֵילוֹ וְיָדְעוּ מִצְרַיִם כִּי־אֲנִי יהוָה וַיַּעֲשׂוּ־כֵן:

וַה׳ הֹלֵךְ — *HASHEM went.* The term וה׳ always implies HASHEM and His Heavenly Court. Thus God and His Court accompanied the people, guiding them with the pillars of cloud and fire, which alternated between day and night (*Rashi* here and 12:29). According to *Ramban,* God came during the day in the pillar of cloud, and His Court came during the night in the pillar of fire.

וְיָשֻׁבוּ — *Let them turn back.* From their encampment at the border of Egypt — *at the edge of the wilderness* — God commanded them to retreat and journey back toward the interior of the

EIGHTH DAY

וְנָתַתָּה בַּכָּסֶף* וְצַרְתָּ הַכֶּסֶף בְּיָדְךָ וְהָלַכְתָּ אֶל־הַמָּקוֹם אֲשֶׁר יִבְחַר יהוָה אֱלֹהֶיךָ בּוֹ: וְנָתַתָּה הַכֶּסֶף בְּכֹל אֲשֶׁר־תְּאַוֶּה נַפְשְׁךָ בַּבָּקָר וּבַצֹּאן וּבַיַּיִן וּבַשֵּׁכָר וּבְכֹל אֲשֶׁר תִּשְׁאָלְךָ נַפְשֶׁךָ וְאָכַלְתָּ שָּׁם לִפְנֵי יהוָה אֱלֹהֶיךָ וְשָׂמַחְתָּ אַתָּה וּבֵיתֶךָ: וְהַלֵּוִי אֲשֶׁר־בִּשְׁעָרֶיךָ לֹא תַעַזְבֶנּוּ* כִּי אֵין לוֹ חֵלֶק וְנַחֲלָה עִמָּךְ: מִקְצֵה ׀ שָׁלֹשׁ שָׁנִים* תּוֹצִיא אֶת־כָּל־מַעְשַׂר תְּבוּאָתְךָ בַּשָּׁנָה הַהִוא וְהִנַּחְתָּ בִּשְׁעָרֶיךָ: וּבָא הַלֵּוִי* כִּי אֵין־לוֹ חֵלֶק וְנַחֲלָה עִמָּךְ וְהַגֵּר וְהַיָּתוֹם וְהָאַלְמָנָה אֲשֶׁר בִּשְׁעָרֶיךָ וְאָכְלוּ וְשָׂבֵעוּ לְמַעַן יְבָרֶכְךָ יהוָה אֱלֹהֶיךָ בְּכָל־מַעֲשֵׂה יָדְךָ אֲשֶׁר תַּעֲשֶׂה:

(בשבת לוי –) מִקֵּץ שֶׁבַע־שָׁנִים תַּעֲשֶׂה שְׁמִטָּה:* וְזֶה דְּבַר הַשְּׁמִטָּה שָׁמוֹט כָּל־בַּעַל מַשֵּׁה יָדוֹ אֲשֶׁר יַשֶּׁה בְּרֵעֵהוּ לֹא־יִגֹּשׂ אֶת־

though you are going there anyway.

וְנָתַתָּה בַּכָּסֶף — *Then you may exchange it for money.* When the crops of the tithe are exchanged for coins, the crops lose their sanctity and the money gets the status of the second tithe. The money is brought to Jerusalem and must be used to buy food, which must then be eaten in the city.

וְהַלֵּוִי . . . לֹא תַעַזְבֶנּוּ — *Do not forsake the Levite.* When you go to Jerusalem with your second tithe, do not forget to give your מַעֲשֵׂר רִאשׁוֹן, *first tithe,* to the Levite whom you leave behind *in your own gates,* i.e., your home town.

שָׁלֹשׁ שָׁנִים — *Three years.* Every three years is a tithe-cycle: in addition to the Levite's tithe, which

SEVENTH DAY

(On the Sabbath – Levi) *They journeyed from Succos and encamped in Etham, at the edge of the wilderness. HASHEM went* before them by day with a pillar of cloud, to cause them to be led on the way, and at night with a pillar of fire to give them light, so that they could travel day and night. He did not remove the pillar of cloud by day nor the pillar of fire by night from before the people.*

Levi (On the Sabbath – Third) *HASHEM spoke to Moses, saying: Speak to the Children of Israel and let them turn back* and encamp before Pi Hachiroth, between Migdol and the sea, before Baal Zephon; you shall encamp opposite it by the sea. Pharaoh will say of the Children of Israel: 'They are mired in the land, the wilderness has locked them in.' I shall strengthen the heart of Pharaoh and he will pursue them, and I will be glorified* through Pharaoh and his entire army, and Egypt will know that I am HASHEM; and so they did.*

country. Furthermore, they were to encamp opposite Baal Zephon, the only Egyptian idol that had not been destroyed. These moves were designed to let Pharaoh delude himself into thinking that they were lost, confused, and unable or afraid to leave the country; and to think that Baal Zephon was a god so powerful that it was responsible for Israel's inability to seize the opportunity to go free.

וְאִכָּבְדָה — *And I will be glorified*. When the wicked are punished, God's Name is glorified, because this demonstrates that He is all-powerful and no one can defy Him with impunity.

EIGHTH DAY

Then you may exchange it for money, wrap up the money and hold it in hand, and go to the place that HASHEM, your God, will have chosen. You may spend the money for anything that your soul desires — for cattle, sheep, wine, or alchoholic beverage — or for anything that your soul wishes; eat it there before HASHEM, your God, and rejoice — you and your household. And do not forsake the Levite* who is in your own gates, for he has no portion or heritage as you do.*

At the end of three years, you are to take out every tithe of your crop in that year and set it down within your gates. Then the Levite can come* — for he has no portion or heritage as you do — and the stranger, the orphan and the widow, who are in your gates, and they can eat and be satisfied; in order that HASHEM, your God, will bless you in all of your handiwork that you may undertake.*

(On the Sabbath – Levi) *At the end of seven years you are to institute a remission year.* This is the function of the remission: every creditor remits his authority over what he has lent to his neighbor; he may not press his*

must be given every year, the first tithe is taken from the crops of the first two years and in the third year, a tithe is given to the poor [מַעְשַׂר עָנִי]. When the three years are over, each householder is commanded to give to the proper parties any tithes that he may have held back up to then.

וּבָא הַלֵּוִי – *Then the Levite can come*. This verse describes all those who are entitled to receive the various tithes. The Levite gets the first tithe, the others are frequently poor and are entitled to the tithe of the poor, and all of them, including the first Levite, should be invited to share the second tithe in Jerusalem with its owner.

שְׁמִטָּה – *A remission year [Shemittah]*. The laws

SEVENTH DAY

(בשבת רביעי)– וַיֻּגַּד* לְמֶלֶךְ מִצְרַיִם כִּי בָרַח הָעָם וַיֵּהָפֵךְ לְבַב פַּרְעֹה
וַעֲבָדָיו אֶל־הָעָם וַיֹּאמְרוּ מַה־זֹּאת עָשִׂינוּ כִּי־שִׁלַּחְנוּ אֶת־
יִשְׂרָאֵל מֵעָבְדֵנוּ: וַיֶּאְסֹר* אֶת־רִכְבּוֹ וְאֶת־עַמּוֹ לָקַח עִמּוֹ: וַיִּקַּח
שֵׁשׁ־מֵאוֹת רֶכֶב בָּחוּר וְכֹל רֶכֶב מִצְרָיִם וְשָׁלִשִׁם עַל־כֻּלּוֹ: וַיְחַזֵּק
יהוה אֶת־לֵב פַּרְעֹה מֶלֶךְ מִצְרַיִם וַיִּרְדֹּף אַחֲרֵי בְּנֵי יִשְׂרָאֵל וּבְנֵי
יִשְׂרָאֵל יֹצְאִים בְּיָד רָמָה:
שלישי (בשבת חמישי)– וַיִּרְדְּפוּ מִצְרַיִם אַחֲרֵיהֶם וַיַּשִּׂיגוּ אוֹתָם חֹנִים עַל־
הַיָּם כָּל־סוּס* רֶכֶב פַּרְעֹה וּפָרָשָׁיו וְחֵילוֹ עַל־פִּי הַחִירֹת לִפְנֵי
בַּעַל צְפֹן: וּפַרְעֹה הִקְרִיב וַיִּשְׂאוּ בְנֵי־יִשְׂרָאֵל אֶת־עֵינֵיהֶם וְהִנֵּה

וַיֻּגַּד — *It was told.* The news was relayed to Pharaoh by agents whom he had sent along to spy on the Jews and report back to him. The chronology of the chapter is as follows: Day 1: Israel traveled from Rameses to Succoth. Day 2: They traveled from Succoth to Etham. Day 3: They retreated back into Egypt and camped at Pi Hachiroth. Day 4: Pharaoh's agents reported that the 'three days to serve God' had gone by and the people were not returning to their servitude. Days 5-6: Pharaoh organized his forces and pursued the Jews. Day 7: The Egyptians pursued Israel into the sea.

וַיֶּאְסֹר — *He harnessed.* Pharaoh harnessed his own chariot in order to raise the morale and

EIGHTH DAY

רֵעֵהוּ וְאֶת־אָחִיו כִּי־קָרָא שְׁמִטָּה לַיהוה: אֶת־הַנָּכְרִי תִּגֹּשׂ*
וַאֲשֶׁר יִהְיֶה לְךָ אֶת־אָחִיךָ תַּשְׁמֵט יָדֶךָ: אֶפֶס כִּי לֹא יִהְיֶה־בְּךָ
אֶבְיוֹן* כִּי־בָרֵךְ יְבָרֶכְךָ יהוה בָּאָרֶץ אֲשֶׁר יהוה אֱלֹהֶיךָ נֹתֵן־לְךָ
נַחֲלָה לְרִשְׁתָּהּ: רַק אִם־שָׁמוֹעַ תִּשְׁמַע* בְּקוֹל יהוה אֱלֹהֶיךָ
לִשְׁמֹר לַעֲשׂוֹת אֶת־כָּל־הַמִּצְוָה הַזֹּאת אֲשֶׁר אָנֹכִי מְצַוְּךָ הַיּוֹם:
כִּי־יהוה אֱלֹהֶיךָ בֵּרַכְךָ כַּאֲשֶׁר דִּבֶּר־לָךְ וְהַעֲבַטְתָּ גּוֹיִם רַבִּים
וְאַתָּה לֹא תַעֲבֹט וּמָשַׁלְתָּ בְּגוֹיִם רַבִּים וּבְךָ לֹא יִמְשֹׁלוּ: כִּי־
יִהְיֶה בְךָ אֶבְיוֹן מֵאַחַד אַחֶיךָ* בְּאַחַד שְׁעָרֶיךָ בְּאַרְצְךָ אֲשֶׁר־
יהוה אֱלֹהֶיךָ נֹתֵן לָךְ לֹא תְאַמֵּץ אֶת־לְבָבְךָ וְלֹא תִקְפֹּץ אֶת־
יָדְךָ מֵאָחִיךָ הָאֶבְיוֹן: כִּי־פָתֹחַ תִּפְתַּח אֶת־יָדְךָ לוֹ וְהַעֲבֵט
תַּעֲבִיטֶנּוּ דֵּי מַחְסֹרוֹ אֲשֶׁר יֶחְסַר לוֹ:* הִשָּׁמֶר לְךָ פֶּן־יִהְיֶה

of the Sabbatical year that relate to crops and farming are given in *Leviticus* ch. 25. This chapter deals with the law that all debts are forgiven in the seventh year.

אֶת הַנָּכְרִי תִּגֹּשׂ – *You may press the gentile.* The commandments of the seventh year do not apply to non-Jews. Just as they may work the land and collect debts from Jews, so may Jews collect their debts from gentiles.

כִּי לֹא יִהְיֶה בְּךָ אֶבְיוֹן – *There will be no destitute among you.* Even though, in observance of the *Shemittah* laws, you forgo the opportunity to collect enormous debts, God promises you that you will not suffer poverty. He will bless you with wealth and power.

רַק אִם שָׁמוֹעַ תִּשְׁמַע – *Only if you continually*

SEVENTH DAY

(On the Sabbath – Fourth) *It was told* to the king of Egypt that the people had fled; the heart of Pharaoh and his servants became transformed regarding the people, and they said: 'What is this that we have done that we have sent away Israel from serving us!'*

He harnessed his chariot and took his people with him. He took six hundred elite chariots and all the chariots of Egypt, with officers on them all. HASHEM strengthened the heart of Pharaoh the king of Egypt and he pursued the Children of Israel, and the Children of Israel went out with an upraised hand.*

Third (On the Sabbath – Fifth) *Egypt pursued them and overtook them encamped by the sea — all the horses* and chariots of Pharaoh, and his horsemen and army — by Pi Hachiroth before Baal Zephon. Pharaoh approached; the Children of Israel raised their eyes and behold! —*

inspire the enthusiasm of his warriors. And in order to *entice* them, he declared that he would lead them into battle in person, not remain behind the lines in safety, as kings usually do.

כָּל סוּס — *All the horses.* But if all the livestock of Egypt died in the fifth plague (*Exodus* 9:6), how did Pharaoh have horses for this pursuit? These were the animals of the "God-fearing" Egyptians, who took their animals indoors so that they should not be killed in the plagues (ibid. 9:20). Such were the so-called pious Egyptians — when the time came to betray God's nation, they made their animals available!

EIGHTH DAY

neighbor or brother, for the remission-time in honor of HASHEM has arrived. You may press the gentile; but you must remit the authority that you have over your kinsman. Then there will be no destitute among you;* rather HASHEM will surely bless you in the Land that HASHEM, your God, gives you as a heritage, for a possession. Only if you continually hearken* to the voice of HASHEM, your God; to observe, to perform this entire commandment that I command you today. For HASHEM, your God, will bless you as He has told you; you will lend to many nations, but you will not borrow; and you will dominate many nations, but they will not dominate you.*

If there is to be a destitute person among you, any of your brethren in any of your gates, in the Land that HASHEM, your God, gives you, do not harden your heart or close your hand against your destitute brother. Instead, you shall surely open your hand to him; you shall surely lend him his requirement, whatever he lacks.* Beware, lest there be*

hearken. Logic might dictate that you cannot be prosperous if you make loans and don't collect them or own farms and don't work them. However, the contrary is true. Only if you obey God's laws will He give you the blessings of prosperity.

מֵאַחַד אַחֶיךָ – *Any of your brethren.* From this verse, the Sages derive the priorities of charity giving: first come close relatives (*brethren*), then neighbors and townspeople (*your gates*), then countrymen (*the land . . .*).

דֵּי מַחְסֹרוֹ אֲשֶׁר יֶחְסַר לוֹ – *His requirement, whatever he lacks.* Give him what he requires, but don't make him rich. On the other hand, if someone grew up in luxury, do not begrudge him more than minimum needs — to him a degree of elegance is a necessity.

SEVENTH DAY

מִצְרַ֔יִם ׀ נֹסֵ֖עַ אַחֲרֵיהֶ֑ם וַיִּֽירְא֣וּ מְאֹ֔ד וַיִּצְעֲק֥וּ בְנֵֽי־יִשְׂרָאֵ֖ל
אֶל־יְהוָֽה: וַיֹּֽאמְרוּ֮ אֶל־מֹשֶׁה֒ הֲמִבְּלִ֤י אֵֽין־קְבָרִים֙ בְּמִצְרַ֔יִם
לְקַחְתָּ֖נוּ לָמ֣וּת בַּמִּדְבָּ֑ר מַה־זֹּאת֙ עָשִׂ֣יתָ לָּ֔נוּ לְהֽוֹצִיאָ֖נוּ מִמִּצְרָֽיִם:
הֲלֹא־זֶ֣ה הַדָּבָ֗ר אֲשֶׁר֩ דִּבַּ֨רְנוּ אֵלֶ֤יךָ בְמִצְרַ֨יִם֙ לֵאמֹ֔ר חֲדַ֥ל מִמֶּ֖נּוּ
וְנַֽעַבְדָ֣ה אֶת־מִצְרָ֑יִם כִּ֣י ט֥וֹב לָ֨נוּ֙ עֲבֹ֣ד אֶת־מִצְרַ֔יִם מִמֻּתֵ֖נוּ
בַּמִּדְבָּֽר: וַיֹּ֨אמֶר מֹשֶׁ֣ה אֶל־הָעָם֮ אַל־תִּירָאוּ֒ הִֽתְיַצְּב֗וּ וּרְאוּ֙
אֶת־יְשׁוּעַ֣ת יְהוָ֔ה אֲשֶׁר־יַֽעֲשֶׂ֥ה לָכֶ֖ם הַיּ֑וֹם כִּ֗י אֲשֶׁ֨ר רְאִיתֶ֤ם
אֶת־מִצְרַ֨יִם֙ הַיּ֔וֹם לֹ֥א תֹסִ֛פוּ לִרְאֹתָ֥ם ע֖וֹד עַד־עוֹלָֽם: יְהוָ֖ה יִלָּחֵ֣ם
לָכֶ֑ם וְאַתֶּ֖ם תַּֽחֲרִשֽׁוּן:

רביעי (בשבת ששי)– וַיֹּ֤אמֶר יְהוָה֙ אֶל־מֹשֶׁ֔ה מַה־תִּצְעַ֖ק אֵלָ֑י דַּבֵּ֥ר
אֶל־בְּנֵֽי־יִשְׂרָאֵ֖ל וְיִסָּֽעוּ:* וְאַתָּ֞ה הָרֵ֣ם אֶֽת־מַטְּךָ֗ וּנְטֵ֧ה אֶת־יָֽדְךָ֛
עַל־הַיָּ֖ם וּבְקָעֵ֑הוּ וְיָבֹ֧אוּ בְנֵֽי־יִשְׂרָאֵ֛ל בְּת֥וֹךְ הַיָּ֖ם בַּיַּבָּשָֽׁה: וַֽאֲנִ֗י
הִֽנְנִ֤י מְחַזֵּק֙ אֶת־לֵ֣ב מִצְרַ֔יִם וְיָבֹ֖אוּ אַֽחֲרֵיהֶ֑ם וְאִכָּֽבְדָ֤ה בְּפַרְעֹה֙

וַיִּסָּעוּ — *And let them journey forth.* They need not fear Egypt. The merit of their forefathers and their own faith in God, as shown by their willingness to leave Egypt for an unknown

EIGHTH DAY

דָבָ֣ר עִם־לְבָֽבְךָ֘ בְלִיַּעַל֒ לֵאמֹ֗ר קָֽרְבָ֣ה שְׁנַת־הַשֶּׁ֨בַע֙ שְׁנַ֣ת הַשְּׁמִטָּ֔ה
וְרָעָ֣ה עֵֽינְךָ֗ בְּאָחִ֨יךָ֙ הָֽאֶבְי֔וֹן וְלֹ֥א תִתֵּ֖ן ל֑וֹ וְקָרָ֤א עָלֶ֨יךָ֙* אֶל־יְהוָ֔ה
וְהָיָ֥ה בְךָ֖ חֵֽטְא: נָת֤וֹן תִּתֵּן֙ ל֔וֹ וְלֹֽא־יֵרַ֥ע לְבָֽבְךָ֖ בְּתִתְּךָ֣ ל֑וֹ כִּ֞י בִּגְלַ֣ל ׀
הַדָּבָ֣ר הַזֶּ֗ה יְבָרֶכְךָ֙ יְהוָ֣ה אֱלֹהֶ֔יךָ בְּכָֽל־מַֽעֲשֶׂ֔ךָ וּבְכֹ֖ל מִשְׁלַ֥ח יָדֶֽךָ:
כִּ֛י לֹֽא־יֶחְדַּ֥ל אֶבְי֖וֹן* מִקֶּ֣רֶב הָאָ֑רֶץ עַל־כֵּ֞ן אָֽנֹכִ֤י מְצַוְּךָ֙ לֵאמֹ֔ר
פָּתֹ֧חַ תִּפְתַּ֛ח אֶת־יָֽדְךָ֖ לְאָחִ֑יךָ לַֽעֲנִיֶּ֧ךָ וּלְאֶבְיֹֽנְךָ֛ בְּאַרְצֶֽךָ: כִּֽי־
יִמָּכֵ֨ר לְךָ֜ אָחִ֣יךָ הָֽעִבְרִ֗י א֚וֹ הָֽעִבְרִיָּ֔ה וַֽעֲבָֽדְךָ֖ שֵׁ֣שׁ שָׁנִ֑ים וּבַשָּׁנָה֙
הַשְּׁבִיעִ֔ת תְּשַׁלְּחֶ֥נּוּ חָפְשִׁ֖י מֵֽעִמָּֽךְ: וְכִֽי־תְשַׁלְּחֶ֥נּוּ חָפְשִׁ֖י מֵֽעִמָּ֑ךְ
לֹ֥א תְשַׁלְּחֶ֖נּוּ רֵיקָֽם: הַֽעֲנֵ֤יק תַּֽעֲנִיק֙ לוֹ֔* מִצֹּ֣אנְךָ֔ וּמִֽגָּרְנְךָ֖ וּמִיִּקְבֶ֑ךָ
אֲשֶׁ֧ר בֵּֽרַכְךָ֛ יְהוָ֥ה אֱלֹהֶ֖יךָ תִּתֶּן־לֽוֹ: וְזָֽכַרְתָּ֗ כִּ֣י עֶ֤בֶד הָיִ֨יתָ֙ בְּאֶ֣רֶץ
מִצְרַ֔יִם וַֽיִּפְדְּךָ֖ יְהוָ֣ה אֱלֹהֶ֑יךָ עַל־כֵּ֞ן אָֽנֹכִ֧י מְצַוְּךָ֛ אֶת־הַדָּבָ֥ר הַזֶּ֖ה

וְלֹא תִתֵּן לוֹ — *And you will refuse to give him,* i.e., you will refuse to lend him money, because you are afraid that the seventh year will render your loan worthless.

וְקָרָא עָלֶיךָ — *Then he may appeal against you.* Even if he does not appeal against you, you will

be punished for your sin, but if your victim feels aggrieved, you will be punished sooner.

כִּי לֹא יֶחְדַּל אֶבְיוֹן — *For destitute people will not cease to exist.* Let no one think he is immune from poverty or tragedy. To the extent that someone has pity on others, God will be

SEVENTH DAY

Egypt was journeying after them, and they were very frightened; the Children of Israel cried out to HASHEM.

They said to Moses: "Were there no graves in Egypt, that you took us to die in the wilderness? What have you done to us to take us out of Egypt? Is this not the statement that we made to you in Egypt, saying: 'Let us be and we will serve Egypt, for it is better for us to serve Egypt than that we should die in the wilderness!' "

Moses said to the people: 'Do not fear! Stand fast and see the salvation of HASHEM *that He will perform for you today; for you have seen Egypt only today, you will not see them ever again!* HASHEM *shall do battle for you, and you are to remain silent.'*

Fourth (On the Sabbath – Sixth) HASHEM *said to Moses: 'Why do you cry out to Me, speak to the Children of Israel and let them journey forth!* And as for you, lift up your staff and stretch out your arm over the sea and split it; then let the Children of Israel come into the midst of the sea on dry land. And as for Me, Behold I shall strengthen the heart of Egypt and they will come after them; and I will be glorified through Pharaoh*

destination, makes them worthy of a miracle.

The sea did not split until Nachshon ben Aminadav, the leader of Judah, went into the water and kept on going until it was up to his nostrils. Only after this proof of Jewish faith did the water split.

EIGHTH DAY

a lawless thought in your heart, saying, the seventh year approaches, the remission year, and you will look malevolently upon your destitute brother, and you will refuse to give him; then he may appeal against you* to* HASHEM *— and the sin will rest upon you. Give him always, and let your heart not feel bad when you give him, for in return for this,* HASHEM, *your God, will bless you in all your deeds and wherever you send your hand. For destitute people will not cease to exist* within your land, therefore I command you, 'Always open your hand to your brother, your poor, and your destitute in your land.'*

If your brother, a Hebrew man or woman, is sold to you, he is to serve you for six years; and in the seventh year you are to send him away free. But when you send him away free, do not send him empty-handed. Adorn him generously from your sheep, your threshing floor, and your wine-cellar; as* HASHEM, *your God, has blessed you, so shall you give him. You must remember that you were a slave in the land of Egypt, and* HASHEM, *your God, redeemed you; therefore, I command you today regarding this matter.*

compassionate with him when he suffers misfortune.

הַעֲנֵיק תַּעֲנִיק לוֹ – *Adorn him generously.* Do not simply set him free with gifts; present them generously and ceremoniously so that it will be clear to him and to the public that you appreciate his years of service.

SEVENTH DAY

וּבְכָל־חֵילֽוֹ בְּרִכְבּֽוֹ וּבְפָרָשָׁיו: וְיָדְעֽוּ מִצְרַֽיִם כִּי־אֲנִי יהוֹה בְּהִכָּבְדִי בְּפַרְעֹה בְּרִכְבֽוֹ וּבְפָרָשָׁיו: וַיִּסַּע מַלְאַ֤ךְ הָאֱלֹהִים* הַהֹלֵךְ֙ לִפְנֵי֙ מַחֲנֵ֣ה יִשְׂרָאֵ֔ל וַיֵּ֖לֶךְ מֵאַחֲרֵיהֶ֑ם וַיִּסַּ֞ע עַמּ֤וּד הֶֽעָנָן֙ מִפְּנֵיהֶ֔ם וַֽיַּעֲמֹ֖ד מֵאַחֲרֵיהֶֽם: וַיָּבֹ֞א בֵּ֣ין ׀ מַחֲנֵ֣ה מִצְרַ֗יִם וּבֵין֙ מַחֲנֵ֣ה יִשְׂרָאֵ֔ל וַיְהִ֤י הֶֽעָנָן֙ וְהַחֹ֔שֶׁךְ וַיָּ֖אֶר אֶת־הַלָּ֑יְלָה וְלֹא־קָרַ֥ב זֶ֛ה אֶל־זֶ֖ה כָּל־הַלָּֽיְלָה: וַיֵּ֨ט מֹשֶׁ֣ה אֶת־יָדוֹ֮ עַל־הַיָּם֒ וַיּ֣וֹלֶךְ יהוֹה ׀ אֶת־הַיָּ֡ם בְּר֣וּחַ קָדִים֩ עַזָּ֨ה כָּל־הַלַּ֜יְלָה וַיָּ֧שֶׂם אֶת־הַיָּ֛ם לֶחָרָבָ֖ה וַיִּבָּקְע֥וּ הַמָּֽיִם: וַיָּבֹ֧אוּ בְנֵֽי־יִשְׂרָאֵ֛ל בְּת֥וֹךְ הַיָּ֖ם בַּיַּבָּשָׁ֑ה* וְהַמַּ֤יִם לָהֶם֙ חֹמָ֔ה מִֽימִינָ֖ם וּמִשְּׂמֹאלָֽם: וַיִּרְדְּפ֤וּ מִצְרַ֨יִם֙ וַיָּבֹ֣אוּ אַחֲרֵיהֶ֔ם כֹּ֚ל ס֣וּס פַּרְעֹ֔ה רִכְבּ֖וֹ וּפָרָשָׁ֑יו אֶל־תּ֖וֹךְ הַיָּֽם: וַיְהִי֙ בְּאַשְׁמֹ֣רֶת הַבֹּ֔קֶר* וַיַּשְׁקֵ֤ף יהוֹה֙ אֶל־מַחֲנֵ֣ה מִצְרַ֔יִם בְּעַמּ֥וּד אֵ֖שׁ וְעָנָ֑ן* וַיָּ֕הָם אֵ֖ת מַחֲנֵ֥ה מִצְרָֽיִם: וַיָּ֗סַר אֵ֚ת אֹפַ֣ן מַרְכְּבֹתָ֔יו וַֽיְנַהֲגֵ֖הוּ בִּכְבֵדֻ֑ת וַיֹּ֣אמֶר מִצְרַ֗יִם אָנֽוּסָה֙ מִפְּנֵ֣י יִשְׂרָאֵ֔ל כִּ֣י יהוֹה נִלְחָ֥ם לָהֶ֖ם בְּמִצְרָֽיִם:

מַלְאַ֤ךְ הָאֱלֹהִים — *The angel of God.* The flow of this verse and the next is as follows: The *angel,* i.e., the pillar of cloud, moved from in front of the Jews and posted itself behind them, to prevent the Egyptians from coming close and to swallow up the arrows and stones that the Egyptians hurled at Israel. When night fell and the pillar of fire came to provide light for Israel, the cloud remained in place. — as if it once again *moved from in front of them . . .* — in order to prevent the Egyptians from benefiting from the fire's light. Thus the Egyptians suffered both from the natural *darkness* as well as the additional darkness caused by the cloud. This took place *while it* [i.e., the pillar of fire] *illuminated the night for Israel.* Thus *one* camp *did not draw near*

EIGHTH DAY

הַיּֽוֹם: וְהָיָה֙ כִּֽי־יֹאמַ֣ר אֵלֶ֔יךָ לֹ֥א אֵצֵ֖א מֵעִמָּ֑ךְ כִּ֤י אֲהֵֽבְךָ֙ וְאֶת־בֵּיתֶ֔ךָ כִּי־ט֥וֹב ל֖וֹ עִמָּֽךְ: וְלָקַחְתָּ֣ אֶת־הַמַּרְצֵ֗עַ* וְנָתַתָּ֤ה בְאָזְנוֹ֙ וּבַדֶּ֔לֶת וְהָיָ֥ה לְךָ֖ עֶ֣בֶד עוֹלָ֑ם* וְאַ֥ף לַאֲמָתְךָ֖* תַּעֲשֶׂה־ כֵּֽן: לֹא־יִקְשֶׁ֣ה בְעֵינֶ֗ךָ* בְּשַׁלֵּֽחֲךָ֙ אֹת֤וֹ חָפְשִׁי֙ מֵֽעִמָּ֔ךְ כִּ֗י מִשְׁנֶה֙ שְׂכַ֣ר שָׂכִ֔יר* עֲבָֽדְךָ֖ שֵׁ֣שׁ שָׁנִ֑ים וּבֵֽרַכְךָ֙ יהוֹה אֱלֹהֶ֔יךָ בְּכֹ֖ל אֲשֶׁ֥ר תַּעֲשֶֽׂה:

וְלָקַחְתָּ֣ אֶת־הַמַּרְצֵ֗עַ — *Then take the awl.* Every Jewish ear heard at Sinai that we are servants of God, not man. And in Egypt, it was the doorpost that we daubed with blood from the *pesach* offering, and the Jewish doorposts over which God passed when He took the lives of the Egyptian firstborn. Thus the ear and the doorpost are symbols of our freedom from every master except God. Consequently, a Jew who has tasted slavery and still consciously prefers it to freedom, is stood at the doorpost and has his ear punctured.

עֶ֣בֶד עוֹלָ֑ם — *An eternal slave,* i.e., until the next יובל, *Jubilee year,* which comes every fifty years. When that year arrives, all Jewish slaves go free, even if they prefer to remain with their masters.

SEVENTH DAY

and through his entire army, through his chariots and through his horsemen. Egypt will know that I am HASHEM, when I am glorified through Pharaoh, through his chariots, and through his horsemen.'

The angel of God who had been going in front of the Children of Israel, moved and went behind them; and the pillar of cloud moved from in front of them and went behind them. It came between the camp of Egypt and the camp of Israel and there were cloud and darkness — while it illuminated the night; and one did not draw near the other all the night. Moses stretched out his hand over the sea, and HASHEM moved back the sea with a strong east wind all the night, and He turned the sea to damp land,* and the water split. The Children of Israel came within the sea on dry land;* and the water was a wall for them, on their right and on their left. Egypt pursued and came after them — all the horses of Pharaoh, his chariots, and his horsemen — into the midst of the sea. It happened at the morning watch* that HASHEM looked down at the camp of Egypt with a pillar of fire and cloud,* and He confounded the camp of Egypt. He removed the wheels of their chariots and caused them to drive with difficulty. Egypt said: 'I shall flee before Israel, for HASHEM is waging war for them against Egypt.'*

the other one all night.

לֶחָרָבָה . . . בַּיַּבָּשָׁה — *To damp land . . . on dry land.* First the wind pushed back the water and turned the sea bed damp. Then, when the Jews marched into the sea, it turned completely dry.

בְּאַשְׁמֹרֶת הַבֹּקֶר — *At the morning watch.* The night is divided into three *watches*, during each of which a different shift of angels sings its praises to God. The watch just before morning is called the *morning watch*. Thus the Splitting of the Sea took place during the night.

אֵשׁ וְעָנָן — *Fire and cloud.* The cloud came down on the sea bed to moisten it and make it muddy. Then the fire came and boiled the mud, so that it

EIGHTH DAY

And in the event he will say to you, 'I will not leave you,' for he loves you and your household, for it goes well for him with you; then take the awl and put it through his ear and the door, and he shall be for you an eternal slave;* and do the same for your maidservant.* Do not feel distressed* when you send him away free, for he has earned you double the wages of a hired hand* in six years; and may HASHEM, your God, bless you in all that you do.*

לַאֲמָתְךָ — *For your maidservant.* This applies only to the owner's requirement to give gifts at the end of the servitude. However, a maidservant is not permitted to remain enslaved until the Jubilee year.

לֹא יִקְשֶׁה בְעֵינֶךָ — *Do not feel distressed.* Although his purchase price was for only six years of work, you may feel distressed that you are being forced to give him substantial gifts when you free him. Bear in mind, however, that he worked hard for you and that God's blessing will more than compensate you for your losses.

מִשְׁנֶה שְׂכַר שָׂכִיר — *Double the wages of a hired hand.* From this expression the Sages derive that a Jewish slave serves his master not only during the regular workday, but also at night. How so? Because his owner may require him to live with a gentile maidservant, whose children will belong to the master.

SEVENTH DAY

חמישי (שביעי בשבת) — **וַיֹּאמֶר יהוה אֶל־מֹשֶׁה נְטֵה אֶת־יָדְךָ עַל־הַיָּם**
וְיָשֻׁבוּ הַמַּיִם עַל־מִצְרַיִם עַל־רִכְבּוֹ וְעַל־פָּרָשָׁיו: וַיֵּט מֹשֶׁה
אֶת־יָדוֹ עַל־הַיָּם וַיָּשָׁב הַיָּם לִפְנוֹת בֹּקֶר לְאֵיתָנוֹ* וּמִצְרַיִם נָסִים
לִקְרָאתוֹ וַיְנַעֵר יהוה אֶת־מִצְרַיִם בְּתוֹךְ הַיָּם: וַיָּשֻׁבוּ הַמַּיִם וַיְכַסּוּ
אֶת־הָרֶכֶב וְאֶת־הַפָּרָשִׁים לְכֹל חֵיל פַּרְעֹה הַבָּאִים אַחֲרֵיהֶם בַּיָּם
לֹא־נִשְׁאַר בָּהֶם עַד־אֶחָד: וּבְנֵי יִשְׂרָאֵל הָלְכוּ בַיַּבָּשָׁה בְּתוֹךְ הַיָּם
וְהַמַּיִם לָהֶם חֹמָה מִימִינָם וּמִשְּׂמֹאלָם: וַיּוֹשַׁע יהוה* בַּיּוֹם הַהוּא
אֶת־יִשְׂרָאֵל מִיַּד מִצְרָיִם וַיַּרְא יִשְׂרָאֵל אֶת־מִצְרַיִם מֵת עַל־
שְׂפַת הַיָּם: וַיַּרְא יִשְׂרָאֵל אֶת־הַיָּד הַגְּדֹלָה אֲשֶׁר עָשָׂה יהוה
בְּמִצְרַיִם וַיִּירְאוּ הָעָם אֶת־יהוה וַיַּאֲמִינוּ* בַּיהוה וּבְמֹשֶׁה עַבְדּוֹ:

burned the hooves of the Egyptian horses. All this time, the walls of water remained firm and intact.

לְאֵיתָנוֹ —*To its power.* The water plunged down from its walls and resumed its original *power*. The Sages expound that the word contains the letters of לִתְנָאוֹ, *to its condition,* i.e., the sea returned to the original condition under which it was brought into existence. When God first created the sea, He did so on the condition that it would split when the time came for Israel to be saved.

שִׁירַת הַיָּם / The Song at the Sea

The early commentators note that the miracles of the Exodus, beginning with the Ten Plagues, illustrated that God controls every facet of nature at will. Thus, they remained the testimony to God as the all-powerful Creator: no human being saw the creation of the universe, but millions of Jews

EIGHTH DAY

ON WEEKDAYS THE READING BEGINS HERE.

כהן (בשבת שלישי) — **כָּל־הַבְּכוֹר* אֲשֶׁר יִוָּלֵד בִּבְקָרְךָ וּבְצֹאנְךָ הַזָּכָר**
תַּקְדִּישׁ לַיהוה אֱלֹהֶיךָ לֹא תַעֲבֹד בִּבְכֹר שׁוֹרֶךָ וְלֹא תָגֹז בְּכוֹר
צֹאנֶךָ: לִפְנֵי יהוה אֱלֹהֶיךָ תֹאכְלֶנּוּ* שָׁנָה בְשָׁנָה בַּמָּקוֹם
אֲשֶׁר־יִבְחַר יהוה אַתָּה וּבֵיתֶךָ: וְכִי־יִהְיֶה בוֹ מוּם פִּסֵּחַ אוֹ עִוֵּר
כֹּל מוּם רָע לֹא תִזְבָּחֶנּוּ לַיהוה אֱלֹהֶיךָ: בִּשְׁעָרֶיךָ תֹּאכְלֶנּוּ הַטָּמֵא
וְהַטָּהוֹר יַחְדָּו כַּצְּבִי וְכָאַיָּל: רַק אֶת־דָּמוֹ לֹא תֹאכֵל עַל־הָאָרֶץ
תִּשְׁפְּכֶנּוּ כַּמָּיִם:*

לוי (בשבת רביעי) — **שָׁמוֹר אֶת־חֹדֶשׁ הָאָבִיב* וְעָשִׂיתָ פֶּסַח לַיהוה**

כָּל הַבְּכוֹר — *Every firstborn male.* The previous chapter has outlined a series of commandments requiring us to be kind, from tithes to the needy to giving gifts to freed slaves. This chapter includes commandments that express our gratitude for God's kindness to us, from the consecration of our firstborn to the various festivals that symbolize gratitude for God's gifts of sustenance and prosperity *(Sforno).* The sanctification of first fruits and the gift to the *Kohen* of *terumah* before crops or dough may be eaten demonstrates our acknowledgment that the ultimate Owner and Giver is God.

תֹאכְלֶנּוּ — *Eat it.* Elsewhere (*Numbers* 18:17) the Torah tells us that the owner presents the firstborn animal to the *Kohen* of his choice. If it is unblemished, the *Kohen* brings it as an offering within the first year of its life, and he

SEVENTH DAY

Fifth (On the Sabbath – Seventh) *HASHEM said to Moses: 'Stretch out your hand over the sea, and the water will go back upon Egypt, upon its chariots and upon its horsemen.' Moses stretched out his hand over the sea, and toward morning the water went back to its power* as Egypt fled toward it; and HASHEM spilled Egypt into the midst of the sea. The water returned and covered the chariots and the horsemen, of the entire army of Pharaoh, who were coming behind them in the sea — there remained not a one of them. The Children of Israel went on dry land in the midst of the sea; the water was a wall for them, on their right and on their left.*

HASHEM saved — on that day — Israel from the hand of Egypt, and Israel saw the Egyptians dead on the seashore.* Chazzan– *Israel saw the great hand that HASHEM inflicted upon Egypt and the people feared HASHEM, and they had faith* in HASHEM and in Moses, His servant.*

witnessed the Exodus. The climax of those miraculous events was the splitting of the sea; as the Passover *Haggadah* relates, the miracles at the sea were five times as great as those that took place in Egypt itself. That event was celebrated by Moses and the entire nation in the glorious Song of the Sea, a combination of praise and faith.

וַיּוֹשַׁע ה׳ — *HASHEM saved.* The Torah sums up the miracle at the sea as a prelude to Moses' song.

וַיִּירְאוּ . . . וַיַּאֲמִינוּ — *(They) feared . . . and they had faith.* The fact that God has the power to perform miracles is unimportant; the Creator of the universe has no difficulty in stopping the flow of a sea. What *did* matter was the effect the miracle had on Israel. The people felt a new and higher degree of *fear,* in the sense of awe and reverence. And their *faith* increased immeasurably, for they had seen that, through His prophet, God promised salvation from danger and had indeed saved them.

EIGHTH DAY

ON WEEKDAYS THE READING BEGINS HERE.

Kohen (On the Sabbath–Third) *Every firstborn male* that is born in your cattle and flock you are to sanctify to HASHEM, your God; you may not work with the firstborn of your bull and you may not shear the firstborn of your sheep. Eat it* before HASHEM, your God, year in, year out, in the place that HASHEM will choose; you and your household. If it has a blemish — lameness or blindness — or any serious blemish, do not offer it to HASHEM, your God. You may eat it within your gates, clean and unclean people alike, like the gazelle and the hart. However you may not eat the blood; you are to pour it upon the ground like water.**

Levi (on the Sabbath–Fourth) *Observe the month of springtime* and perform*

may invite anyone, including non-*Kohanim,* to share its meat. If the animal is blemished and not fit for an offering, it becomes the *Kohen's* personal property; he may slaughter it wherever he wishes, sell it, or share its meat with non-*Kohanim* or even non-Jews.

תִּשְׁפְּכֶנּוּ כַּמָּיִם – *You are to pour it . . . like water.* From the comparison of blood to water, the Sages derive two laws. First, just as it is permitted to use and derive benefit from water, so one may sell or use blood as he wishes, even though it is forbidden to drink it. Second, even though the blood of fowl, harts, and gazelles must be covered after slaughter (*Leviticus* 17:13), this does not apply to cattle, sheep and goats. Their blood is likened to water, and need not be covered.

חֹדֶשׁ הָאָבִיב – *The month of springtime.* Since the Torah requires that Nissan, the month of Pesach, must fall in the springtime, the court adds a thirteenth month to the calendar at regular intervals. Since the twelve-month lunar

SEVENTH DAY

אָז יָשִׁיר־מֹשֶׁה* וּבְנֵי יִשְׂרָאֵל אֶת־הַשִּׁירָה הַזֹּאת לַיהוה וַיֹּאמְרוּ
לֵאמֹר אָשִׁירָה לַיהוה כִּי־גָאֹה גָּאָה סוּס
וְרֹכְבוֹ רָמָה בַיָּם: עָזִּי וְזִמְרָת יָהּ* וַיְהִי־לִי
לִישׁוּעָה זֶה אֵלִי וְאַנְוֵהוּ* אֱלֹהֵי
אָבִי וַאֲרֹמְמֶנְהוּ: יהוה אִישׁ מִלְחָמָה יהוה
שְׁמוֹ:* מַרְכְּבֹת פַּרְעֹה וְחֵילוֹ יָרָה בַיָּם וּמִבְחַר
שָׁלִשָׁיו טֻבְּעוּ בְיַם־סוּף: תְּהֹמֹת יְכַסְיֻמוּ יָרְדוּ בִמְצוֹלֹת כְּמוֹ־
אָבֶן: יְמִינְךָ* יהוה נֶאְדָּרִי בַּכֹּחַ יְמִינְךָ*
יהוה תִּרְעַץ אוֹיֵב: וּבְרֹב גְּאוֹנְךָ תַּהֲרֹס
קָמֶיךָ תְּשַׁלַּח חֲרֹנְךָ יֹאכְלֵמוֹ כַּקַּשׁ: וּבְרוּחַ

אָז יָשִׁיר מֹשֶׁה — *Then Moses ... chose to sing.* Rather than שָׁר, *sang,* the Torah uses the verb יָשִׁיר, literally, *will sing.* In the simple sense, the verse means that upon seeing the miracle the people decided that they *would* sing. Midrashically, the verb implies the principle that God will bring the dead back to life in Messianic times — and then they *will* sing God's praises once again *(Rashi).*

עָזִּי וְזִמְרָת יָהּ — *God is my might and my praise.* The translation follows *Targum Onkelos.* According to *Rashi* the phrase is translated: *God's might and His cutting away [of the enemy] was a salvation for me.*

זֶה אֵלִי — *This is my God.* So obvious was God's Presence, that the Jews could point to it, as it were, and say, 'This is my God.' As the Sages put it: 'A maidservant at the sea saw more than the prophet Yechezkel [saw in his heavenly prophecy]' *(Rashi).*

EIGHTH DAY

אֱלֹהֶיךָ כִּי בְּחֹדֶשׁ הָאָבִיב הוֹצִיאֲךָ יהוה אֱלֹהֶיךָ מִמִּצְרַיִם לָיְלָה:*
וְזָבַחְתָּ פֶּסַח לַיהוה אֱלֹהֶיךָ צֹאן וּבָקָר* בַּמָּקוֹם אֲשֶׁר יִבְחַר יהוה
לְשַׁכֵּן שְׁמוֹ שָׁם: לֹא־תֹאכַל עָלָיו חָמֵץ שִׁבְעַת יָמִים תֹּאכַל־עָלָיו
מַצּוֹת לֶחֶם עֹנִי* כִּי בְחִפָּזוֹן יָצָאתָ מֵאֶרֶץ מִצְרַיִם לְמַעַן תִּזְכֹּר
אֶת־יוֹם צֵאתְךָ מֵאֶרֶץ מִצְרַיִם כֹּל יְמֵי חַיֶּיךָ:
שלישי (בשבת חמישי) – וְלֹא־יֵרָאֶה לְךָ שְׂאֹר בְּכָל־גְּבֻלְךָ שִׁבְעַת יָמִים
וְלֹא־יָלִין מִן־הַבָּשָׂר אֲשֶׁר תִּזְבַּח בָּעֶרֶב בַּיּוֹם הָרִאשׁוֹן* לַבֹּקֶר:

year is about eleven days shorter than the solar year, the month of Nissan would become progressively earlier unless these months were added.

לָיְלָה — *At night.* The actual march out of Egypt took place in the morning, but Pharaoh freed the people in the middle of the night.

צֹאן וּבָקָר — *From the flock — and also offer bulls.* The *pesach* offering comes *from the flock,* i.e. lambs or kids; the קָרְבַּן חֲגִיגָה *[chagigah], festival peace-offerings,* may come from bulls as well. From the juxtaposition of *flock* and *bulls,* the Sages derive the law of an animal designated for a *pesach*-offering that had not been offered on the fourteenth of Nissan, or money designated to purchase a *pesach* offering, which was not used for that purpose. This animal or money should be used for the sort of offering that can come from both the *flock* and *bulls,* meaning peace-offerings [מוֹתַר פֶּסַח קָרֵב שְׁלָמִים].

מַצּוֹת לֶחֶם עֹנִי — *Matzos, bread of affliction.* If

SEVENTH DAY

Then Moses and the Children of Israel chose to sing this song to HASHEM, and they said the following:*

I shall sing to HASHEM for He is exalted above the arrogant, having hurled horse with its rider into the sea.

God is my might and my praise, and He was a salvation for me. This is my God,* and I will build Him a Sanctuary;* the God of my father, and I will exalt Him.*

*HASHEM is Master of war, through His Name HASHEM.**

Pharaoh's chariots and army He threw into the sea; and the pick of his officers were mired in the Sea of Reeds.

Deep waters covered them; they descended in the depths like stone.

Your right hand, HASHEM, is adorned with strength; Your right hand, HASHEM, smashes the enemy.*

In Your abundant grandeur You shatter Your opponents; You dispatch Your wrath, it consumes them like straw.

וְאַנְוֵהוּ — *And I will build Him a Sanctuary.* The root of the word is נָוֶה, *abode.* An alternative interpretation based on the same root: I will make myself into a Godly sanctuary *(Rashi)* — to remake oneself in God's image is to build the greatest of all sanctuaries.

Another translation is *I will beautify* or *glorify Him* [based on the root נאה, *fitting, beautiful*]. The Sages teach that this is done by performing the commandments in a beautiful manner, by having beautiful *tefillin*, a beautiful *succah*, a beautiful *esrog* and so on *(Shabbos* 133b).

ה׳ שְׁמוֹ — *Through His Name HASHEM.* Mortal kings require legions and armaments, but God overcomes His enemies with nothing more than His Name. Moreover, this Name of mercy applies to Him even when He is forced to vanquish the wicked *(Rashi).*

יְמִינְךָ — *Your right hand.* Of course God has no physical characteristics. All the many Scriptural references to physicality are allegorical.

EIGHTH DAY

the pesach service to HASHEM, your God, for in the month of springtime HASHEM, your God, took you out of Egypt at night. You are to slaughter the pesach offering to HASHEM, your God, from the flock — and also offer bulls* — in the place where HASHEM will choose to rest His Name. Do not eat leavened food with it, for seven days you are to eat matzos, bread of affliction,* for you departed from Egypt in haste — so that you will remember the day of your departure from Egypt all the days of your life.*

Third (on the Sabbath—Fifth) *No leaven of yours may be seen throughout your boundary for seven days; nor may any of the meat you have offered on the afternoon before the first day* remain until morning.*

you wish to eat grain products during the seven days of Pesach, they must be matzah, i.e. unleavened bread. Matzah reminds us of the *affliction* of Egyptian slavery, because it is made of unadorned, unflavored, and unleavened flour and water — the sort of food that harried, poverty-stricken slaves would prepare for themselves.

בָּעֶרֶב בַּיּוֹם הָרִאשׁוֹן — *On the afternoon before the first day.* I.e., the *pesach* offering, which comes the afternoon before the first Seder night.

Three time periods are mentioned here: (1) the *pesach* offering is offered *in the afternoon;* (2) it is eaten after *the sun sets*; and (3) if any of its meat has not been eaten by morning, i.e., *the time of your departure from Egypt*, the leftovers

SEVENTH DAY

אַפֶּיךָ נֶעֶרְמוּ מַיִם נִצְּבוּ כְמוֹ־נֵד
נֹזְלִים קָפְאוּ תְהֹמֹת בְּלֶב־יָם: אָמַר
אוֹיֵב* אֶרְדֹּף אַשִּׂיג אֲחַלֵּק שָׁלָל תִּמְלָאֵמוֹ
נַפְשִׁי אָרִיק חַרְבִּי תּוֹרִישֵׁמוֹ יָדִי: נָשַׁפְתָּ
בְרוּחֲךָ כִּסָּמוֹ יָם צָלְלוּ כַּעוֹפֶרֶת בְּמַיִם
אַדִּירִים: מִי־כָמֹכָה בָּאֵלִם יהוה מִי
כָּמֹכָה נֶאְדָּר בַּקֹּדֶשׁ נוֹרָא תְהִלֹּת עֹשֵׂה
פֶלֶא: נָטִיתָ יְמִינְךָ תִּבְלָעֵמוֹ אָרֶץ: נָחִיתָ
בְחַסְדְּךָ עַם־זוּ גָּאָלְתָּ נֵהַלְתָּ בְעָזְּךָ אֶל־נְוֵה
קָדְשֶׁךָ:* שָׁמְעוּ עַמִּים יִרְגָּזוּן חִיל
אָחַז יֹשְׁבֵי פְּלָשֶׁת: אָז נִבְהֲלוּ אַלּוּפֵי
אֱדוֹם* אֵילֵי מוֹאָב יֹאחֲזֵמוֹ רָעַד נָמֹגוּ
כֹּל יֹשְׁבֵי כְנָעַן: תִּפֹּל עֲלֵיהֶם אֵימָתָה
וָפַחַד בִּגְדֹל זְרוֹעֲךָ יִדְּמוּ כָּאָבֶן עַד־
יַעֲבֹר עַמְּךָ* יהוה עַד־יַעֲבֹר עַם־זוּ

אָמַר אוֹיֵב — *The enemy declared.* In order to coax his people to join him in pursuit of the Jews, Pharaoh *(the enemy)* spoke confidently of his ability to overtake and plunder them.

אֶל נְוֵה קָדְשֶׁךָ — *To Your holy abode,* i.e., the Holy Temple. Although the Temple would not be built for over four hundred years, prophetic song typically combines past with future, because in the Divine perception they are interrelated.

פְּלָשֶׁת . . . אֱדוֹם . . . — *Philistia . . . Edom . . .* Not all the nations were of equal status. Philistia and Canaan rightly feared conquest because their

EIGHTH DAY

לֹא תוּכַל לִזְבֹּחַ אֶת־הַפָּסַח בְּאַחַד שְׁעָרֶיךָ אֲשֶׁר־יהוה אֱלֹהֶיךָ
נֹתֵן לָךְ: כִּי אִם־אֶל־הַמָּקוֹם אֲשֶׁר־יִבְחַר יהוה אֱלֹהֶיךָ לְשַׁכֵּן
שְׁמוֹ שָׁם תִּזְבַּח אֶת־הַפֶּסַח בָּעָרֶב כְּבוֹא הַשֶּׁמֶשׁ מוֹעֵד צֵאתְךָ
מִמִּצְרָיִם: וּבִשַּׁלְתָּ וְאָכַלְתָּ בַּמָּקוֹם אֲשֶׁר יִבְחַר יהוה אֱלֹהֶיךָ בּוֹ
וּפָנִיתָ בַבֹּקֶר* וְהָלַכְתָּ לְאֹהָלֶיךָ: שֵׁשֶׁת יָמִים* תֹּאכַל מַצּוֹת וּבַיּוֹם
הַשְּׁבִיעִי עֲצֶרֶת* לַיהוה אֱלֹהֶיךָ לֹא תַעֲשֶׂה מְלָאכָה:
רביעי (בשבת ששי) – שִׁבְעָה שָׁבֻעֹת תִּסְפָּר־לָךְ מֵהָחֵל חֶרְמֵשׁ* בַּקָּמָה

must be burned.

וּפָנִיתָ בַבֹּקֶר — ***In the morning you may turn back.*** Whenever someone brings an offering, he is required to spend the following night in Jerusalem, and may not return home until morning. In the case of the *pesach* offering, since the following morning is the first festival day of Pesach when it is forbidden to travel, he may not return home until the morning of the first Intermediate Day.

שֵׁשֶׁת יָמִים — *For six days.* But earlier we were told that matzos are eaten for *seven* days?!

SEVENTH DAY

At a blast from Your nostrils the waters were heaped up; straight as a wall stood the running water, the deep waters congealed in the heart of the sea.

The enemy declared: 'I will pursue, I will overtake, I will divide plunder; I will satisfy my lust with them; I will unsheathe my sword, my hand will impoverish them.'*

You blew with Your wind — the sea enshrouded them; the mighty ones sank like lead in the waters.

Who is like You among the heavenly powers, HASHEM! Who is like You, mighty in holiness, too awesome for praise, doing wonders!

You stretched out Your right hand — the earth swallowed them.

*You guided in Your kindness this people that You redeemed; You led with Your might to Your holy abode.**

Peoples heard — they were agitated; convulsive terror gripped the dwellers of Philistia.

Then the chieftains of Edom were confounded, trembling gripped the powers of Moab, all the dwellers of Canaan dissolved.*

May fear and terror befall them, at the greatness of Your arm may they be still as stone; until Your people passes through, HASHEM, until this people You have acquired passes through.*

lands comprised *Eretz Yisrael.* Edom and Moab did not fear losing their land, but rather feared retribution because they did not and would not show compassion for Jewish suffering *(Rashi).*

עַד יַעֲבֹר עַמְּךָ — *Until Your people passes through.* This continues the previous thought; the terror of the nations would continue until Israel crossed into *Eretz Yisrael.* The term *passes through* is used twice: once in reference to the crossing of the Jordan and once in reference to the waters of the Arnon, on the border of Israel and Moab [see *Numbers* 21:13-20] *(Rashi).*

EIGHTH DAY

You may not bring the pesach offering in one of your private gates that HASHEM, your God, gives you. Only at the place that HASHEM will choose to rest His Name, there are you to slaughter the pesach offering in the afternoon, when the sun descends, the appointed time of your departure from Egypt. You are to cook and eat it in the place that HASHEM will choose; and in the morning you may turn back and go to your shelters. For six days* you are to eat matzos and the seventh day shall be an assembly* to HASHEM, your God, you may not perform labor.*

Fourth (on the Sabbath—Sixth) *You are to count for yourselves seven weeks; from when the sickle is first put* to the standing crop, you are to*

Through hermeneutical means, the Sages derive that only on the Seder night is one *required* to eat matzah. During the rest of Passover, there is no positive commandment to eat matzah; only a prohibition against eating *chometz.*

עֲצֶרֶת — *An assembly.* Since the seventh day should be dedicated to service of God, work is prohibited.

מֵהָחֵל חֶרְמֵשׁ — *From when the sickle is first put.* The first grain to be cut is the barley for the Omer offering, which is brought on the second day of Pesach. The seven-week count is begun from that day.

SEVENTH DAY

קָנִֽיתָ׃ תְּבִאֵ֗מוֹ* וְתִטָּעֵ֙מוֹ֙ בְּהַ֣ר נַחֲלָֽתְךָ֔ מָכ֛וֹן
לְשִׁבְתְּךָ֥ פָּעַ֖לְתָּ יהוָ֑ה מִקְּדָ֕שׁ אֲדֹנָ֖י כּוֹנְנ֥וּ
יָדֶֽיךָ׃ יהוָ֥ה ׀ יִמְלֹ֖ךְ לְעֹלָ֥ם וָעֶֽד׃
כִּ֣י בָא֩ ס֨וּס פַּרְעֹ֜ה בְּרִכְבּ֤וֹ וּבְפָרָשָׁיו֙ בַּיָּ֔ם וַיָּ֧שֶׁב יהוָ֛ה עֲלֵהֶ֖ם אֶת־
מֵ֣י הַיָּ֑ם וּבְנֵ֧י יִשְׂרָאֵ֛ל הָלְכ֥וּ בַיַּבָּשָׁ֖ה בְּת֥וֹךְ הַיָּֽם׃ וַתִּקַּח֩ מִרְיָ֨ם
הַנְּבִיאָ֜ה אֲח֧וֹת אַהֲרֹ֛ן אֶת־הַתֹּ֖ף בְּיָדָ֑הּ וַתֵּצֶ֤אןָ כָֽל־הַנָּשִׁים֙ אַחֲרֶ֔יהָ
בְּתֻפִּ֖ים* וּבִמְחֹלֹֽת׃ וַתַּ֥עַן לָהֶ֖ם מִרְיָ֑ם שִׁ֤ירוּ לַֽיהוָה֙ כִּֽי־גָאֹ֣ה גָּאָ֔ה
ס֥וּס וְרֹכְב֖וֹ רָמָ֥ה בַיָּֽם׃ וַיַּסַּ֨ע מֹשֶׁ֤ה אֶת־יִשְׂרָאֵל֙ מִיַּם־ס֔וּף וַיֵּצְא֖וּ
אֶל־מִדְבַּר־שׁ֑וּר וַיֵּלְכ֧וּ שְׁלֹֽשֶׁת־יָמִ֛ים בַּמִּדְבָּ֖ר וְלֹא־מָ֥צְאוּ מָֽיִם׃
וַיָּבֹ֣אוּ מָרָ֔תָה וְלֹ֣א יָֽכְל֗וּ לִשְׁתֹּ֥ת מַ֙יִם֙ מִמָּרָ֔ה כִּ֥י מָרִ֖ים הֵ֑ם עַל־כֵּ֥ן
קָרָֽא־שְׁמָ֖הּ מָרָֽה׃ וַיִּלֹּ֧נוּ* הָעָ֛ם עַל־מֹשֶׁ֥ה לֵּאמֹ֖ר מַה־נִּשְׁתֶּֽה׃

תְּבִאֵמוֹ — *You shall bring them.* Moses unconsciously prophesied that he would not enter the Land, for he said, 'You shall bring *them,*' and not 'You shall bring *us*' *(Rashi).*

בְּתֻפִּים — *With drums.* The righteous women of the generation were certain that God would perform miracles for Israel, so they took drums with them in order to celebrate.

EIGHTH DAY

תָּחֵ֣ל לִסְפֹּ֔ר שִׁבְעָ֖ה שָׁבֻעֽוֹת׃ וְעָשִׂ֜יתָ חַ֤ג שָׁבֻעוֹת֙ לַיהוָ֣ה אֱלֹהֶ֔יךָ
מִסַּ֛ת* נִדְבַ֥ת יָדְךָ֖ אֲשֶׁ֣ר תִּתֵּ֑ן כַּאֲשֶׁ֥ר יְבָרֶכְךָ֖ יהוָ֥ה אֱלֹהֶֽיךָ׃ וְשָׂמַחְתָּ֞
לִפְנֵ֣י ׀ יהוָ֣ה אֱלֹהֶ֗יךָ אַתָּ֨ה וּבִנְךָ֣* וּבִתֶּךָ֮ וְעַבְדְּךָ֣ וַאֲמָתֶךָ֒ וְהַלֵּוִי֙ אֲשֶׁ֣ר
בִּשְׁעָרֶ֔יךָ וְהַגֵּ֛ר וְהַיָּת֥וֹם וְהָאַלְמָנָ֖ה אֲשֶׁ֣ר בְּקִרְבֶּ֑ךָ בַּמָּק֗וֹם אֲשֶׁ֤ר
יִבְחַר֙ יהוָ֣ה אֱלֹהֶ֔יךָ לְשַׁכֵּ֥ן שְׁמ֖וֹ שָֽׁם׃ וְזָ֣כַרְתָּ֔ כִּי־עֶ֥בֶד הָיִ֖יתָ
בְּמִצְרָ֑יִם וְשָׁמַרְתָּ֣ וְעָשִׂ֔יתָ אֶת־הַחֻקִּ֖ים הָאֵֽלֶּה׃
חמישי (בשבת שביעי) – חַ֧ג הַסֻּכֹּ֛ת תַּעֲשֶׂ֥ה לְךָ֖ שִׁבְעַ֣ת יָמִ֑ים בְּאָ֨סְפְּךָ֔ מִגָּרְנְךָ֖
וּמִיִּקְבֶֽךָ׃ וְשָׂמַחְתָּ֖* בְּחַגֶּ֑ךָ אַתָּ֨ה וּבִנְךָ֤ וּבִתֶּ֙ךָ֙ וְעַבְדְּךָ֣ וַאֲמָתֶ֔ךָ
וְהַלֵּוִ֗י וְהַגֵּ֛ר וְהַיָּת֥וֹם וְהָאַלְמָנָ֖ה אֲשֶׁ֥ר בִּשְׁעָרֶֽיךָ׃ שִׁבְעַ֣ת יָמִ֗ים
תָּחֹג֙ לַיהוָ֣ה אֱלֹהֶ֔יךָ בַּמָּק֖וֹם אֲשֶׁר־יִבְחַ֣ר יהוָ֑ה כִּ֣י יְבָרֶכְךָ֞ יהוָ֣ה
אֱלֹהֶ֗יךָ בְּכֹ֤ל תְּבוּאָֽתְךָ֙ וּבְכֹל֙ מַעֲשֵׂ֣ה יָדֶ֔יךָ וְהָיִ֖יתָ אַ֥ךְ שָׂמֵֽחַ׃

מִסַּת — *Commensurate with.* On festivals, one is required to bring peace- and elevation-offerings. The number and value of such offerings depends on the wealth with which God has blessed him.

אַתָּה וּבִנְךָ — *You, your son.* Just as you will surely rejoice with your own family and servants, you should also see to it that the Levites, the poor and lonely are provided for. Your joy is incomplete unless you share it with others.

וְשָׂמַחְתָּ — *You are to rejoice.* Succos is the time of year when the crops are gathered in from the fields and the success of the past agricultural year is apparent. This makes it a time of great joy. In a deeper sense, Succos follows the season of

SEVENTH DAY

You shall bring them and implant them on the mount of Your heritage, the foundation of Your dwelling-place, which You, HASHEM, have made: the Sanctuary, my Lord, that Your hands established.*

HASHEM shall reign for all eternity.

When Pharaoh's cavalry came — with his chariots and horsemen — into the sea and HASHEM turned back the waters of the sea upon them, the Children of Israel walked on the dry bed amid the sea.

Miriam the prophetess, the sister of Aaron, took the drum in her hand, and all the women went forth behind her with drums and with dances. Miriam spoke up to them: 'Sing to HASHEM for He is exalted above the arrogant, having hurled horse with its rider into the sea.'*

Moses caused the Children of Israel to journey from the Sea of Reeds and they went out to the Wilderness of Shur; they went for three days in the wilderness but they did not find water. They came to Marah, but they could not drink the waters of Marah because they were bitter; therefore they named it Marah. The people complained against Moses, saying: 'What shall we drink?'*

וַיִּלֹּנוּ הָעָם — *The people complained.* The people had a right to ask for water, but the Torah reproaches them for the angry way in which they did it. After seeing so many miracles for their benefit, they should have made their request respectfully.

EIGHTH DAY

begin counting seven weeks. Then you are to observe the festival of Shavuos for HASHEM, your God; the voluntary offerings that you give should be commensurate with how much HASHEM, your God, will have blessed you. You are to rejoice before HASHEM, your God — you, your son,* your daughter, your slave, your maidservant, the Levite who is in your gates, the stranger, the orphan, and the widow who are among you — in the place where HASHEM, your God, will choose to rest His Name. And you are to remember that you were a slave in Egypt; and you are to observe and perform these decrees.*

Fifth (on the Sabbath—Seventh) *You are to observe the festival of Succos for seven days, when you gather in from your threshing floor and your wine cellar. You are to rejoice* on your festival — you, your son, your daughter, your slave, your maidservant, the Levite, the stranger, the orphan, and the widow who are in your gates. For seven days you are to celebrate to HASHEM, your God, in the place that HASHEM will choose; for HASHEM, your God, will have blessed you in all your crop and in all your handiwork, and you will be completely joyful.**

repentance and atonement, when people 'gather in' their spiritual harvest. This commandment to rejoice on Succos is expressed in the prayers, in which Succos is described as זְמַן שִׂמְחָתֵנוּ, *the time of our gladness.*

אַךְ שָׂמֵחַ — *Completely joyful.* In its simple meaning, rather than a *mitzvah*, this is a Divine promise that we will be joyful. The Sages also derive from here that Shemini Atzeres is included in the earlier commandment to rejoice on this festival.

SEVENTH DAY

וַיִּצְעַק אֶל־יהוה וַיּוֹרֵהוּ יהוה עֵץ וַיַּשְׁלֵךְ אֶל־הַמַּיִם וַיִּמְתְּקוּ הַמָּיִם שָׁם שָׂם לוֹ חֹק וּמִשְׁפָּט* וְשָׁם נִסָּהוּ:* וַיֹּאמֶר אִם־שָׁמוֹעַ תִּשְׁמַע לְקוֹל ׀ יהוה אֱלֹהֶיךָ וְהַיָּשָׁר בְּעֵינָיו תַּעֲשֶׂה וְהַאֲזַנְתָּ לְמִצְוֹתָיו וְשָׁמַרְתָּ כָּל־חֻקָּיו כָּל־הַמַּחֲלָה אֲשֶׁר־שַׂמְתִּי בְמִצְרַיִם לֹא־אָשִׂים עָלֶיךָ כִּי אֲנִי יהוה רֹפְאֶךָ:*

שָׂם לוֹ חֹק וּמִשְׁפָּט — *He established for it [the nation] a decree and an ordinance.* God gave the nation the teachings of several commandments so that they could involve themselves in Torah study. These commandments were not yet binding since they had not been formally put into effect, but the holiness of Torah study would serve as a means to elevate the people. The commandments were Sabbath, the Red Cow [פָּרָה אֲדֻמָּה], and the general laws of commerce [דִּינִים].

EIGHTH DAY

שָׁלוֹשׁ פְּעָמִים ׀ בַּשָּׁנָה יֵרָאֶה כָל־זְכוּרְךָ אֶת־פְּנֵי ׀ יהוה אֱלֹהֶיךָ בַּמָּקוֹם אֲשֶׁר יִבְחָר בְּחַג הַמַּצּוֹת וּבְחַג הַשָּׁבֻעוֹת וּבְחַג הַסֻּכּוֹת וְלֹא יֵרָאֶה אֶת־פְּנֵי יהוה רֵיקָם:* אִישׁ כְּמַתְּנַת יָדוֹ* כְּבִרְכַּת יהוה אֱלֹהֶיךָ אֲשֶׁר נָתַן־לָךְ:

חצי קדיש

After the last *oleh* has completed his closing blessing, the second Torah Scroll is placed on the *bimah* alongside the first, and the reader recites Half-*Kaddish*.

יִתְגַּדַּל וְיִתְקַדַּשׁ שְׁמֵהּ רַבָּא. (.Cong – אָמֵן.) בְּעָלְמָא דִּי בְרָא כִרְעוּתֵהּ. וְיַמְלִיךְ מַלְכוּתֵהּ, בְּחַיֵּיכוֹן וּבְיוֹמֵיכוֹן וּבְחַיֵּי דְכָל בֵּית יִשְׂרָאֵל, בַּעֲגָלָא וּבִזְמַן קָרִיב. וְאִמְרוּ: אָמֵן.

(.Cong – אָמֵן. יְהֵא שְׁמֵהּ רַבָּא מְבָרַךְ לְעָלַם וּלְעָלְמֵי עָלְמַיָּא.)

יְהֵא שְׁמֵהּ רַבָּא מְבָרַךְ לְעָלַם וּלְעָלְמֵי עָלְמַיָּא.

יִתְבָּרַךְ וְיִשְׁתַּבַּח וְיִתְפָּאַר וְיִתְרוֹמַם וְיִתְנַשֵּׂא וְיִתְהַדָּר וְיִתְעַלֶּה וְיִתְהַלָּל שְׁמֵהּ דְּקֻדְשָׁא בְּרִיךְ הוּא (.Cong – בְּרִיךְ הוּא) — לְעֵלָּא מִן כָּל בִּרְכָתָא וְשִׁירָתָא תֻּשְׁבְּחָתָא וְנֶחֱמָתָא, דַּאֲמִירָן בְּעָלְמָא. וְאִמְרוּ: אָמֵן. (.Cong – אָמֵן.)

הגבהה וגלילה

The first Torah is raised for all to see. Each person looks at the Torah and recites aloud:

וְזֹאת הַתּוֹרָה אֲשֶׁר שָׂם מֹשֶׁה לִפְנֵי בְּנֵי יִשְׂרָאֵל,[1] עַל פִּי יהוה בְּיַד מֹשֶׁה.[2]

(1) *Deuteronomy* 4:44. (2) *Numbers* 9:23.

SEVENTH DAY

He cried out to HASHEM, *and* HASHEM *showed him a stick; he threw it into the water and the water became sweet; there He established for it a decree and an ordinance,* and there He tested it.* He said: 'If you will diligently hearken to the voice of* HASHEM, *your God, do what is upright in His eyes, give ear to His commandments, and observe all His decrees, then I will not bring upon you any of the diseases that I brought upon Egypt, for I am* HASHEM, *your Healer.'**

נִסָּהוּ — *He tested it.* God tested the nation to see how it would respond to adversity, as represented by the lack of water — and it was found wanting because of the negative way in which it made its demand of Moses.

רֹפְאֶךָ — *Your Healer.* Just as God miraculously turned the water from bitter to sweet — by means of a *bitter* piece of wood — so He can be trusted to remove all illnesses from Israel, if they but heed His commandments.

EIGHTH DAY

Three times a year all your males should appear before HASHEM, *your God, in the place that He will choose: on the festival of Matzos, the festival of Shavuos, and the festival of Succos; and you are not to appear before* HASHEM *empty-handed.* Everyone according to what he can give,* according to the blessing that* HASHEM, *your God, gives you.*

רֵיקָם – *Empty-handed,* i.e., do not make your pilgrimage without bringing burnt and peace-offerings.

אִישׁ כְּמַתְּנַת יָדוֹ – *Everyone according to what he can give.* A person should give generously but not excessively, lest he become poor and require the charity of others. As the Sages say, one should not spend more than a fifth of his resources for the performance of a *mitzvah* (*Sforno*).

HALF KADDISH

After the last *oleh* has completed his closing blessing, the second Torah Scroll is placed on the *bimah* alongside the first, and the reader recites Half-*Kaddish*.

יִתְגַּדַּל *May His great Name grow exalted and sanctified* (Cong.– *Amen.*) *in the world that He created as He willed. May He give reign to His kingship in your lifetimes and in your days, and in the lifetimes of the entire Family of Israel, swiftly and soon. Now respond: Amen.*

(Cong.– *Amen. May His great Name be blessed forever and ever.*)

May His great Name be blessed forever and ever.

Blessed, praised, glorified, exalted, extolled, mighty, upraised, and lauded be the Name of the Holy One, Blessed is He (Cong.– *Blessed is He*) — *beyond any blessing and song, praise and consolation that are uttered in the world. Now respond: Amen.* (Cong.– *Amen.*)

HAGBAHAH AND GELILAH

The first Torah is raised for all to see. Each person looks at the Torah and recites aloud:

This is the Torah that Moses placed before the Children of Israel,[1] upon the command of HASHEM, through Moses' hand.[2]

Some add:

עֵץ חַיִּים הִיא לַמַּחֲזִיקִים בָּהּ, וְתֹמְכֶיהָ מְאֻשָּׁר.[1] דְּרָכֶיהָ דַרְכֵי נֹעַם, וְכָל נְתִיבוֹתֶיהָ שָׁלוֹם.[2] אֹרֶךְ יָמִים בִּימִינָהּ, בִּשְׂמֹאלָהּ עֹשֶׁר וְכָבוֹד.[3] יהוה חָפֵץ לְמַעַן צִדְקוֹ, יַגְדִּיל תּוֹרָה וְיַאְדִּיר.[4]

מפטיר

After the first Torah is wound, tied, and covered, the *oleh* for *Maftir* is called to the second Torah.

במדבר כח:יט־כה

וְהִקְרַבְתֶּם אִשֶּׁה עֹלָה לַיהוה פָּרִים בְּנֵי־בָקָר שְׁנַיִם וְאַיִל אֶחָד וְשִׁבְעָה כְבָשִׂים בְּנֵי שָׁנָה תְּמִימִם יִהְיוּ לָכֶם: וּמִנְחָתָם סֹלֶת בְּלוּלָה בַשָּׁמֶן שְׁלֹשָׁה עֶשְׂרֹנִים לַפָּר וּשְׁנֵי עֶשְׂרֹנִים לָאַיִל תַּעֲשׂוּ: עִשָּׂרוֹן עִשָּׂרוֹן תַּעֲשֶׂה לַכֶּבֶשׂ הָאֶחָד לְשִׁבְעַת הַכְּבָשִׂים: וּשְׂעִיר חַטָּאת אֶחָד לְכַפֵּר עֲלֵיכֶם: מִלְּבַד עֹלַת הַבֹּקֶר אֲשֶׁר לְעֹלַת הַתָּמִיד תַּעֲשׂוּ אֶת־אֵלֶּה: כָּאֵלֶּה תַּעֲשׂוּ לַיּוֹם שִׁבְעַת יָמִים לֶחֶם אִשֵּׁה רֵיחַ־נִיחֹחַ לַיהוה עַל־עוֹלַת הַתָּמִיד יֵעָשֶׂה וְנִסְכּוֹ: וּבַיּוֹם הַשְּׁבִיעִי מִקְרָא־קֹדֶשׁ יִהְיֶה לָכֶם כָּל־מְלֶאכֶת עֲבֹדָה לֹא תַעֲשׂוּ:

הגבהה וגלילה

The *maftir* completes his closing blessing.
Then the second Torah Scroll is raised and each person looks at the Torah and recites aloud:

וְזֹאת הַתּוֹרָה אֲשֶׁר שָׂם מֹשֶׁה לִפְנֵי בְּנֵי יִשְׂרָאֵל,[5] עַל פִּי יהוה בְּיַד מֹשֶׁה.[6]

Some add:

עֵץ חַיִּים הִיא לַמַּחֲזִיקִים בָּהּ, וְתֹמְכֶיהָ מְאֻשָּׁר.[1] דְּרָכֶיהָ דַרְכֵי נֹעַם, וְכָל נְתִיבוֹתֶיהָ שָׁלוֹם.[2] אֹרֶךְ יָמִים בִּימִינָהּ, בִּשְׂמֹאלָהּ עֹשֶׁר וְכָבוֹד.[3] יהוה חָפֵץ לְמַעַן צִדְקוֹ, יַגְדִּיל תּוֹרָה וְיַאְדִּיר.[4]

After the Torah Scroll has been wound, tied and covered,
the *maftir* recites the *Haftarah* blessings.

ברכה קודם ההפטרה

בָּרוּךְ אַתָּה יהוה אֱלֹהֵינוּ מֶלֶךְ הָעוֹלָם, אֲשֶׁר בָּחַר בִּנְבִיאִים טוֹבִים, וְרָצָה בְדִבְרֵיהֶם הַנֶּאֱמָרִים בֶּאֱמֶת, בָּרוּךְ אַתָּה יהוה, הַבּוֹחֵר בַּתּוֹרָה וּבְמֹשֶׁה עַבְדּוֹ, וּבְיִשְׂרָאֵל עַמּוֹ, וּבִנְבִיאֵי הָאֱמֶת וָצֶדֶק: (Cong.— אָמֵן.)

Some add:

עֵץ *It is a tree of life for those who grasp it, and its supporters are praiseworthy.*[1] *Its ways are ways of pleasantness and all its paths are peace.*[2] *Lengthy days are at its right; at its left are wealth and honor.*[3] *HASHEM desired, for the sake of its [Israel's] righteousness, that the Torah be made great and glorious.*[4]

MAFTIR

After the first Torah is wound, tied, and covered, the *oleh* for *Maftir* is called to the second Torah.

Numbers 28:19-25

You shall offer a fire-offering, an elevation-offering to HASHEM, two young bulls, one ram, and seven lambs within their first year, unblemished shall they be for you. And their meal-offering shall be fine flour mixed with oil; you shall make it three tenth-ephah for each bull and two tenth-ephah for each ram. One tenth-ephah shall you make for each lamb, of the seven rams. And one he-goat for a sin-offering, to provide you atonement. Aside from the elevation-offering of the morning that is for the continual elevation-offering shall you offer these. Like these shall you offer each day of the seven days, food, a fire-offering, a satisfying aroma to HASHEM; after the continual elevation-offering shall it be made, with its libation. The seventh day shall be a holy convocation for you, you shall not do any laborious work.

HAGBAHAH AND GELILAH

The *maftir* completes his closing blessing.
Then the second Torah Scroll is raised and each person looks at the Torah and recites aloud:

This is the Torah that Moses placed
before the Children of Israel,[5]
upon the command of HASHEM, through Moses' hand.[6]

Some add:

עֵץ *It is a tree of life for those who grasp it, and its supporters are praiseworthy.*[1] *Its ways are ways of pleasantness and all its paths are peace.*[2] *Lengthy days are at its right; at its left are wealth and honor.*[3] *HASHEM desired, for the sake of its [Israel's] righteousness, that the Torah be made great and glorious.*[4]

After the Torah Scroll has been wound, tied and covered,
the *maftir* recites the *Haftarah* blessings.

BLESSING BEFORE THE HAFTARAH

בָּרוּךְ *Blessed are You, HASHEM, our God, King of the universe, Who has chosen good prophets and was pleased with their words that were uttered with truth. Blessed are You, HASHEM, Who chooses the Torah; Moses, His servant; Israel, His nation; and the prophets of truth and righteousness.* (Cong.— *Amen.*)

---

(1) *Proverbs* 3:18. (2) 3:17. (3) 3:16. (4) *Isaiah* 42:21.
(5) *Deuteronomy* 4:44. (6) *Numbers* 9:23.

SEVENTH DAY

הפטרה ליום שביעי

שמואל ב כב:א-נא

וַיְדַבֵּ֥ר דָּוִד֙ לַֽיהֹוָ֔ה אֶת־דִּבְרֵ֖י הַשִּׁירָ֣ה הַזֹּ֑את בְּיוֹם֩ הִצִּ֨יל יְהֹוָ֥ה אֹת֛וֹ מִכַּ֥ף כָּל־אֹיְבָ֖יו וּמִכַּ֥ף שָׁאֽוּל: וַיֹּאמַ֑ר יְהֹוָ֥ה סַלְעִ֖י וּמְצֻדָתִ֥י וּמְפַלְטִי־לִֽי: אֱלֹהֵ֥י צוּרִ֖י אֶחֱסֶה־בּ֑וֹ מָֽגִנִּ֞י וְקֶ֣רֶן יִשְׁעִ֗י מִשְׂגַּבִּי֙ וּמְנוּסִ֔י מֹֽשִׁעִ֕י מֵֽחָמָ֖ס תֹּֽשִׁעֵֽנִי: מְהֻלָּ֖ל אֶקְרָ֣א יְהֹוָ֑ה וּמֵאֹֽיְבַ֖י אִוָּשֵֽׁעַ: כִּ֥י אֲפָפֻ֖נִי מִשְׁבְּרֵי־מָ֑וֶת נַֽחֲלֵ֥י בְלִיַּ֖עַל יְבַֽעֲתֻֽנִי: חֶבְלֵ֥י שְׁא֖וֹל סַבֻּ֑נִי קִדְּמֻ֖נִי מֹ֥קְשֵׁי־מָֽוֶת: בַּצַּר־לִ֣י אֶקְרָ֣א יְהֹוָ֗ה וְאֶל־אֱלֹהַ֖י אֶקְרָ֑א וַיִּשְׁמַ֤ע מֵהֵֽיכָלוֹ֙ קוֹלִ֔י וְשַׁוְעָתִ֖י בְּאָזְנָֽיו: וַיִּתְגָּעַ֤שׁ וַתִּרְעַשׁ֙ הָאָ֔רֶץ מֽוֹסְד֥וֹת הַשָּׁמַ֖יִם יִרְגָּ֑זוּ וַיִּֽתְגָּֽעֲשׁ֖וּ כִּֽי־חָ֥רָה לֽוֹ: עָלָ֤ה עָשָׁן֙ בְּאַפּ֔וֹ וְאֵ֥שׁ מִפִּ֖יו תֹּאכֵ֑ל גֶּֽחָלִ֖ים בָּֽעֲר֥וּ מִמֶּֽנּוּ: וַיֵּ֥ט שָׁמַ֖יִם וַיֵּרַ֑ד וַֽעֲרָפֶ֖ל תַּ֥חַת רַגְלָֽיו: וַיִּרְכַּ֥ב עַל־כְּר֖וּב וַיָּעֹ֑ף וַיֵּרָ֖א עַל־כַּנְפֵי־רֽוּחַ: וַיָּ֤שֶׁת חֹ֨שֶׁךְ֙ סְבִֽיבֹתָ֖יו סֻכּ֑וֹת חַשְׁרַת־מַ֖יִם עָבֵ֥י שְׁחָקִֽים: מִנֹּ֖גַהּ נֶגְדּ֑וֹ בָּֽעֲר֖וּ גַּֽחֲלֵי־אֵֽשׁ: יַרְעֵ֤ם מִן־שָׁמַ֨יִם֙ יְהֹוָ֔ה וְעֶלְי֖וֹן יִתֵּ֣ן קוֹל֑וֹ: וַיִּשְׁלַ֞ח

⫷ HAFTARAH FOR THE SEVENTH DAY ⫸

The *Haftarah* is David's song of gratitude to Hashem for a lifetime of kindness and salvation, during which God rescued him from a constant succession of conspiracy, danger, and attempts on his life. Thus it is a fitting complement to the song that Moses and the Children of Israel sang at the Splitting of the Sea.

EIGHTH DAY

הפטרה ליום אחרון

ישעיה י:לב-יב:ו

ע֥וֹד הַיּ֖וֹם בְּנֹ֣ב לַֽעֲמֹ֑ד יְנֹפֵ֤ף יָדוֹ֙ הַ֣ר בַּת־צִיּ֔וֹן גִּבְעַ֖ת יְרֽוּשָׁלָֽ͏ִם: הִנֵּ֤ה הָֽאָדוֹן֙ יְהֹוָ֣ה צְבָא֔וֹת מְסָעֵ֥ף פֻּארָ֖ה בְּמַֽעֲרָצָ֑ה וְרָמֵ֤י הַקּֽוֹמָה֙ גְּדֻעִ֔ים וְהַגְּבֹהִ֖ים יִשְׁפָּֽלוּ: וְנִקַּ֛ף סִֽבְכֵ֥י הַיַּ֖עַר בַּבַּרְזֶ֑ל וְהַלְּבָנ֖וֹן בְּאַדִּ֥יר יִפּֽוֹל: וְיָצָ֥א חֹ֖טֶר מִגֵּ֣זַע יִשָׁ֑י וְנֵ֖צֶר מִשָּֽׁרָשָׁ֥יו יִפְרֶֽה: וְנָחָ֥ה עָלָ֖יו ר֣וּחַ יְהֹוָ֑ה ר֧וּחַ חָכְמָ֣ה וּבִינָ֗ה ר֤וּחַ עֵצָה֙ וּגְבוּרָ֔ה ר֥וּחַ דַּ֖עַת וְיִרְאַ֥ת יְהֹוָֽה: וַהֲרִיח֖וֹ בְּיִרְאַ֣ת יְהֹוָ֑ה וְלֹֽא־לְמַרְאֵ֤ה עֵינָיו֙ יִשְׁפּ֔וֹט וְלֹֽא־לְמִשְׁמַ֥ע אָזְנָ֖יו יוֹכִֽיחַ: וְשָׁפַ֤ט בְּצֶ֨דֶק֙ דַּלִּ֔ים וְהוֹכִ֥יחַ בְּמִישׁ֖וֹר לְעַנְוֵי־אָ֑רֶץ וְהִֽכָּה־אֶ֨רֶץ֙ בְּשֵׁ֣בֶט פִּ֔יו וּבְר֥וּחַ שְׂפָתָ֖יו יָמִ֥ית רָשָֽׁע:

⫷ HAFTARAH FOR THE EIGHTH DAY ⫸

For the close of the festival that marks Israel's first redemption, a *Haftarah* was selected that gives lyrical allusions to another great salvation that took place during Pesach, and the final salvation — the coming of Messiah.

The *Haftarah* begins with the arrogant boast

SEVENTH DAY

HAFTARAH FOR THE SEVENTH DAY

II Samuel 22:1-51

David spoke to HASHEM *the words of this song on the day that* HASHEM *delivered him from the hand of all his enemies and from the hand of Saul. He said:* HASHEM *is my Rock, my Fortress, and my Rescuer. God, my Rock, I take refuge in Him; my Shield and the Horn of my Salvation, my Stronghold and my Refuge, my Savior Who saves me from violence. With praises I call unto* HASHEM, *and I am saved from my enemies. For the pains of death encircled me, and torrents of godless men would frighten me. The pains of the grave surrounded me, the snares of death confronted me. In my distress I would call upon* HASHEM, *and to my God I would call — from His abode He would hear my voice, my cry in His ears. And the earth quaked and roared, the foundations of the heaven shook; they trembled when His wrath flared. Smoke rose up in His nostrils, a devouring fire from His mouth, flaming coals burst forth from Him. He bent down the heavens and descended, with thick darkness beneath His feet. He mounted a cherub and flew, He swooped on the wings of the wind. He made darkness His shelter all around Him — the darkness of water, the clouds of heaven. From out of the brilliance that is before Him, burned fiery coals. And* HASHEM *thundered in the heavens, the Most High cried out. He sent forth*

EIGHTH DAY

HAFTARAH FOR THE EIGHTH DAY

Isaiah 10:32 -12:6

Yet today he will stand in Nob; he will wave his hand [contemptuously] toward the mountain of the daughter of Zion, the hill of Jerusalem. Behold! — the Lord, HASHEM, *Master of Legions will lop off the branches with an ax; then the lofty ones will be severed and the proud ones humbled. Forest thickets will be hewn by iron, and the Lebanon will fall through a mighty one.*

A staff will grow from the stump of Jesse, and a shoot will sprout from his roots. And a spirit of HASHEM *will rest upon him: a spirit of wisdom and understanding, a spirit of counsel and strength, a spirit of knowledge and fear of* HASHEM. *He will be censed with fear of* HASHEM; *he will not judge by what his eyes see nor will he decide by what his ears hear. He will judge the destitute with righteousness, and decide with fairness for the humble of the earth; he will strike the earth with the staff of his mouth, and with the breath of his mouth he will slay the wicked.*

of the all-victorious Sennacherib of Assyria, who was swiftly conquering *Eretz Yisrael* and was on his way to an easy conquest of Jerusalem. But instead of victory, the brazen conqueror and his entire army were cut down in a single night by the angel of God.

These two verse are followed by one of Scripture's most stirring prophecies of the End of Days. The ravages of the exile will have decimated the Davidic dynasty — but *the stump of*

SEVENTH DAY

חִצִּים וַיְפִיצֵם בָּרָק וַיָּהֹם: וַיֵּרָאוּ אֲפִקֵי יָם יִגָּלוּ מֹסְדוֹת תֵּבֵל
בְּגַעֲרַת יהוה מִנִּשְׁמַת רוּחַ אַפּוֹ: יִשְׁלַח מִמָּרוֹם יִקָּחֵנִי יַמְשֵׁנִי
מִמַּיִם רַבִּים: יַצִּילֵנִי מֵאֹיְבִי עָז מִשֹּׂנְאַי כִּי אָמְצוּ מִמֶּנִּי: יְקַדְּמֻנִי
בְּיוֹם אֵידִי וַיְהִי יהוה מִשְׁעָן לִי: וַיֹּצֵא לַמֶּרְחָב אֹתִי יְחַלְּצֵנִי
כִּי־חָפֵץ בִּי: יִגְמְלֵנִי יהוה כְּצִדְקָתִי כְּבֹר יָדַי יָשִׁיב לִי: כִּי שָׁמַרְתִּי
דַּרְכֵי יהוה וְלֹא רָשַׁעְתִּי מֵאֱלֹהָי: כִּי כָל־מִשְׁפָּטָו לְנֶגְדִּי וְחֻקֹּתָיו
לֹא־אָסוּר מִמֶּנָּה: וָאֶהְיֶה תָמִים לוֹ וָאֶשְׁתַּמְּרָה מֵעֲוֺנִי: וַיָּשֶׁב יהוה
לִי כְּצִדְקָתִי כְּבֹרִי לְנֶגֶד עֵינָיו: עִם־חָסִיד תִּתְחַסָּד עִם־גִּבּוֹר תָּמִים
תִּתַּמָּם: עִם־נָבָר תִּתָּבָר וְעִם־עִקֵּשׁ תִּתַּפָּל: וְאֶת־עַם עָנִי תּוֹשִׁיעַ
וְעֵינֶיךָ עַל־רָמִים תַּשְׁפִּיל: כִּי־אַתָּה נֵירִי יהוה וַיהוה יַגִּיהַּ חָשְׁכִּי:
כִּי בְכָה אָרוּץ גְּדוּד בֵּאלֹהַי אֲדַלֶּג־שׁוּר: הָאֵל תָּמִים דַּרְכּוֹ אִמְרַת
יהוה צְרוּפָה מָגֵן הוּא לְכֹל הַחֹסִים בּוֹ: כִּי מִי־אֵל מִבַּלְעֲדֵי יהוה
וּמִי צוּר מִבַּלְעֲדֵי אֱלֹהֵינוּ: הָאֵל מָעוּזִּי חָיִל וַיַּתֵּר תָּמִים דַּרְכִּי:
מְשַׁוֶּה רַגְלַי כָּאַיָּלוֹת וְעַל בָּמֹתַי יַעֲמִדֵנִי: מְלַמֵּד יָדַי לַמִּלְחָמָה

EIGHTH DAY

וְהָיָה צֶדֶק אֵזוֹר מָתְנָיו וְהָאֱמוּנָה אֵזוֹר חֲלָצָיו: וְגָר זְאֵב עִם־כֶּבֶשׂ
וְנָמֵר עִם־גְּדִי יִרְבָּץ וְעֵגֶל וּכְפִיר וּמְרִיא יַחְדָּו וְנַעַר קָטֹן נֹהֵג בָּם:
וּפָרָה וָדֹב תִּרְעֶינָה יַחְדָּו יִרְבְּצוּ יַלְדֵיהֶן וְאַרְיֵה כַּבָּקָר יֹאכַל־תֶּבֶן:
וְשִׁעֲשַׁע יוֹנֵק עַל־חֻר פָּתֶן וְעַל מְאוּרַת צִפְעוֹנִי גָּמוּל יָדוֹ הָדָה:
לֹא־יָרֵעוּ וְלֹא־יַשְׁחִיתוּ בְּכָל־הַר קָדְשִׁי כִּי־מָלְאָה הָאָרֶץ דֵּעָה
אֶת־יהוה כַּמַּיִם לַיָּם מְכַסִּים: וְהָיָה בַּיּוֹם הַהוּא שֹׁרֶשׁ יִשַׁי אֲשֶׁר
עֹמֵד לְנֵס עַמִּים אֵלָיו גּוֹיִם יִדְרֹשׁוּ וְהָיְתָה מְנֻחָתוֹ כָּבוֹד: וְהָיָה ׀
בַּיּוֹם הַהוּא יוֹסִיף אֲדֹנָי ׀ שֵׁנִית יָדוֹ לִקְנוֹת אֶת־שְׁאָר עַמּוֹ
אֲשֶׁר יִשָּׁאֵר מֵאַשּׁוּר וּמִמִּצְרַיִם וּמִפַּתְרוֹס וּמִכּוּשׁ וּמֵעֵילָם
וּמִשִּׁנְעָר וּמֵחֲמָת וּמֵאִיֵּי הַיָּם: וְנָשָׂא נֵס לַגּוֹיִם וְאָסַף נִדְחֵי יִשְׂרָאֵל

Jesse will remain, and from it will grow a monarch worthy of his glorious ancestors, a monarch who will once more reflect the spirit and wisdom of Jewish holiness. He will usher in the new era of history when peace will rule the world, when mortal enemies will dwell together and predators will no more molest the weak and defenseless. God will gather in His children from the ends of the earth. The once hostile factions of Judah and Ephraim will unite in brotherhood and reconquer all of *Eretz Yisrael* from the adversaries who denied them their land.

Finally, the Jews emerging from exile will recognize the underlying meaning of history. They will be grateful not only for deliverance and blessing, but even for the tribulations of exile, because they will understand that suffering was part of the series of events leading to the bliss of redemption and spiritual triumph.

SEVENTH DAY

His arrows and scattered them, lightning and He frenzied them. The channels of water became visible, the foundations of the earth were laid bare by the rebuke of HASHEM, by the breath of His nostrils. He sent from on high and took me, He drew me out of deep waters. He saved me from my mighty foe, and from my enemies for they overpowered me. They confronted me on the day of my misfortune, but HASHEM was my support. He brought me out into broad spaces, He released me for He desires me. HASHEM recompensed me according to my righteousness; He repaid me according to the cleanliness of my hands. For I have kept the ways of HASHEM, and I have not departed wickedly from my God. For all His judgments are before me, and I shall not remove myself from His statutes. I was perfectly innocent with Him, and I was vigilant against my sin. HASHEM repaid me according to my righteousness, according to my cleanliness before His eyes. With the devout You act devoutly, with the wholehearted strong you act wholeheartedly. With the pure You act purely, with the crooked You act perversely. You save the humble people, and Your eyes are upon the haughty to bring them low. For You, HASHEM, are my lamp, and HASHEM will illuminate my darkness. For with you I smash a troop, and with my God I leap a wall. The God! — His way is perfect; the promise of HASHEM is flawless, He is a shield for all who take refuge in Him. For who is God except for HASHEM, and who is a Rock except for our God. The God Who is my strong Fortress, and Who let my way be perfect. Who straightened my feet like the hind, and stood me on my heights. Who trained my hands for battle,

EIGHTH DAY

Righteousness will be the girdle round his loins, and faith will be the girdle of his waist.

A wolf will dwell with a sheep and a leopard will lie down with a kid; and a calf, a lion and a fatling together, with a young child leading them. A cow and a bear will graze, and their young will lie down together; and a lion will eat hay like a cattle. A suckling will play by the hole of a viper; and a newly weaned child will stretch his hand toward an adder's lair. They will neither injure nor destroy in all of My sacred mount; for the earth will be as filled with knowledge of HASHEM, as the water covering the sea bed. On that day the root of Jesse that remained standing will be a banner for the peoples, nations will seek him, and his resting place will be glorious.

And it will be on that day, my Lord will again show His strength to acquire the remnant of His people that will have remained, from Assyria and from Egypt and from Pathros and from Cush and from Elam and from Shinar and from Hamas and from the islands of the sea. He will raise a banner for the nations and assemble the castaways of Israel;

SEVENTH DAY

וְנִחַת קֶשֶׁת־נְחוּשָׁה זְרֹעֹתָי׃ וַתִּתֶּן־לִי מָגֵן יִשְׁעֶךָ וַעֲנֹתְךָ תַּרְבֵּנִי׃
תַּרְחִיב צַעֲדִי תַּחְתֵּנִי וְלֹא מָעֲדוּ קַרְסֻלָּי׃ אֶרְדְּפָה אֹיְבַי וָאַשְׁמִידֵם
וְלֹא אָשׁוּב עַד־כַּלּוֹתָם׃ וָאֲכַלֵּם וָאֶמְחָצֵם וְלֹא יְקוּמוּן וַיִּפְּלוּ תַּחַת
רַגְלָי׃ וַתַּזְרֵנִי חַיִל לַמִּלְחָמָה תַּכְרִיעַ קָמַי תַּחְתֵּנִי׃ וְאֹיְבַי תַּתָּה לִּי
עֹרֶף מְשַׂנְאַי וָאַצְמִיתֵם׃ יִשְׁעוּ וְאֵין מֹשִׁיעַ אֶל־יְהוָֹה וְלֹא עָנָם׃
וְאֶשְׁחָקֵם כַּעֲפַר־אָרֶץ כְּטִיט־חוּצוֹת אֲדִקֵּם אֶרְקָעֵם׃ וַתְּפַלְּטֵנִי
מֵרִיבֵי עַמִּי תִּשְׁמְרֵנִי לְרֹאשׁ גּוֹיִם עַם לֹא־יָדַעְתִּי יַעַבְדֻנִי׃ בְּנֵי
נֵכָר יִתְכַּחֲשׁוּ־לִי לִשְׁמוֹעַ אֹזֶן יִשָּׁמְעוּ לִי׃ בְּנֵי נֵכָר יִבֹּלוּ וְיַחְגְּרוּ
מִמִּסְגְּרוֹתָם׃ חַי־יְהוָֹה וּבָרוּךְ צוּרִי וְיָרֻם אֱלֹהֵי צוּר יִשְׁעִי׃ הָאֵל
הַנֹּתֵן נְקָמֹת לִי וּמוֹרִיד עַמִּים תַּחְתֵּנִי׃ וּמוֹצִיאִי מֵאֹיְבָי וּמִקָּמַי
תְּרוֹמְמֵנִי מֵאִישׁ חֲמָסִים תַּצִּילֵנִי׃ עַל־כֵּן אוֹדְךָ יְהוָֹה בַּגּוֹיִם
וּלְשִׁמְךָ אֲזַמֵּר׃ מִגְדּוֹל יְשׁוּעוֹת מַלְכּוֹ וְעֹשֶׂה־חֶסֶד לִמְשִׁיחוֹ לְדָוִד
וּלְזַרְעוֹ עַד־עוֹלָם׃

EIGHTH DAY

וּנְפֻצוֹת יְהוּדָה יְקַבֵּץ מֵאַרְבַּע כַּנְפוֹת הָאָרֶץ׃ וְסָרָה קִנְאַת אֶפְרַיִם
וְצֹרְרֵי יְהוּדָה יִכָּרֵתוּ אֶפְרַיִם לֹא־יְקַנֵּא אֶת־יְהוּדָה וִיהוּדָה
לֹא־יָצֹר אֶת־אֶפְרָיִם׃ וְעָפוּ בְכָתֵף פְּלִשְׁתִּים יָמָּה יַחְדָּו יָבֹזּוּ
אֶת־בְּנֵי־קֶדֶם אֱדוֹם וּמוֹאָב מִשְׁלוֹחַ יָדָם וּבְנֵי עַמּוֹן מִשְׁמַעְתָּם׃
וְהֶחֱרִים יְהוָֹה אֵת לְשׁוֹן יָם־מִצְרַיִם וְהֵנִיף יָדוֹ עַל־הַנָּהָר בַּעְיָם
רוּחוֹ וְהִכָּהוּ לְשִׁבְעָה נְחָלִים וְהִדְרִיךְ בַּנְּעָלִים׃ וְהָיְתָה מְסִלָּה
לִשְׁאָר עַמּוֹ אֲשֶׁר יִשָּׁאֵר מֵאַשּׁוּר כַּאֲשֶׁר הָיְתָה לְיִשְׂרָאֵל בְּיוֹם
עֲלֹתוֹ מֵאֶרֶץ מִצְרָיִם׃ וְאָמַרְתָּ בַּיּוֹם הַהוּא אוֹדְךָ יְהוָֹה כִּי אָנַפְתָּ בִּי
יָשֹׁב אַפְּךָ וּתְנַחֲמֵנִי׃ הִנֵּה אֵל יְשׁוּעָתִי אֶבְטַח וְלֹא אֶפְחָד כִּי־עָזִּי
וְזִמְרָת יָהּ יְהוָֹה וַיְהִי־לִי לִישׁוּעָה׃ וּשְׁאַבְתֶּם־מַיִם בְּשָׂשׂוֹן מִמַּעַיְנֵי
הַיְשׁוּעָה׃ וַאֲמַרְתֶּם בַּיּוֹם הַהוּא הוֹדוּ לַיהוָֹה קִרְאוּ בִשְׁמוֹ הוֹדִיעוּ
בָעַמִּים עֲלִילֹתָיו הַזְכִּירוּ כִּי נִשְׂגָּב שְׁמוֹ׃ זַמְּרוּ יְהוָֹה כִּי גֵאוּת
עָשָׂה מוּדַעַת זֹאת בְּכָל־הָאָרֶץ׃ צַהֲלִי וָרֹנִּי יוֹשֶׁבֶת צִיּוֹן כִּי־גָדוֹל
בְּקִרְבֵּךְ קְדוֹשׁ יִשְׂרָאֵל׃

SEVENTH DAY

so that an iron bow could be bent by my arms. You have given me Your shield of salvation, and Your humility made me great. You have widened my stride beneath me, and my ankles have not faltered. I pursued my foes and overtook them, and returned not until they were destroyed. I destroyed them, struck them down and they did not rise, and they fell beneath my feet. You girded me with strength for battle, You bring my adversaries to their knees beneath me. And my enemies — You gave me [their] back; my antagonists and I cut them down. They turned, but there was no savior; to HASHEM, but He answered them not. I pulverized them like dust of the earth, like the mud of the streets I thinned them and I poured them out. You rescued me from the strife of my people; You preserved me to be head of nations, a people I did not know serves me. Foreigners dissemble to me; when their ear hears of me they are obedient to me. Foreigners are withered, and they are terrified even within their strong enclosures. HASHEM lives, and blessed is my Rock; and exalted is God, Rock of my salvation. The God Who grants me vengeance, and brings peoples down beneath me. You bring me forth from my enemies, and raise me above my adversaries, from a man of violence You rescue me. Therefore, I will thank You, HASHEM, among the nations, and sing to Your Name. He is a tower of salvations to His king, and does kindness to His anointed one, to David and to his descendants forever.

EIGHTH DAY

and the dispersed ones of Judah will He gather in from the four corners of the earth.

The jealousy of Ephraim will leave and the oppressors of Judah will be cut off; Ephraim will not be jealous of Judah, and Judah will not harass Ephraim. They will fly to the Philistine boundary to the west, together they will plunder the residents of the east; their hands will be extended over Edom and Moab, and their discipline over the children of Ammon. HASHEM will dry up the tongue of the Sea of Egypt, and He will raise His hand over the River [Euphrates] with the power of His breath; He will break it into seven streams and lead them across with [dry] shoes. There will be a road for the remnant of His people that will be left from Assyria, as there was for Israel on the day it went up from the land of Egypt.

You will say on that day, 'I thank You, HASHEM, for You were angry with me, but You removed Your wrath and comforted me. Behold! — God is my salvation, I shall trust and not fear; for God is my might and my praise — HASHEM — and He was a salvation for me. You can draw water with joy from the springs of salvation." And you will say on that day, 'Give thanks to HASHEM, declare His Name, make His acts known among the peoples; remind one another, for His Name is powerful. Make music for HASHEM for He has established grandeur, make this known throughout the world.' Exult and sing for joy, O inhabitant of Zion, for the Holy One of Israel has done greatly among you.

ברכות לאחר ההפטרה

After the *Haftarah* is read, the *oleh* recites the following blessings.

בָּרוּךְ אַתָּה יהוה אֱלֹהֵינוּ מֶלֶךְ הָעוֹלָם, צוּר כָּל הָעוֹלָמִים,* צַדִּיק בְּכָל הַדּוֹרוֹת,* הָאֵל הַנֶּאֱמָן הָאוֹמֵר וְעֹשֶׂה, הַמְּדַבֵּר וּמְקַיֵּם, שֶׁכָּל דְּבָרָיו אֱמֶת וָצֶדֶק.* נֶאֱמָן אַתָּה הוּא יהוה אֱלֹהֵינוּ, וְנֶאֱמָנִים דְּבָרֶיךָ, וְדָבָר אֶחָד מִדְּבָרֶיךָ אָחוֹר לֹא יָשׁוּב רֵיקָם, כִּי אֵל מֶלֶךְ נֶאֱמָן (וְרַחֲמָן) אָתָּה. בָּרוּךְ אַתָּה יהוה, הָאֵל הַנֶּאֱמָן בְּכָל דְּבָרָיו. (–Cong. אָמֵן.)

רַחֵם עַל צִיּוֹן* כִּי הִיא בֵּית חַיֵּינוּ, וְלַעֲלוּבַת נֶפֶשׁ תּוֹשִׁיעַ בִּמְהֵרָה בְיָמֵינוּ. בָּרוּךְ אַתָּה יהוה, מְשַׂמֵּחַ צִיּוֹן בְּבָנֶיהָ. (–Cong. אָמֵן.)

שַׂמְּחֵנוּ יהוה אֱלֹהֵינוּ בְּאֵלִיָּהוּ הַנָּבִיא עַבְדֶּךָ, וּבְמַלְכוּת בֵּית דָּוִד* מְשִׁיחֶךָ, בִּמְהֵרָה יָבֹא וְיָגֵל לִבֵּנוּ, עַל כִּסְאוֹ לֹא יֵשֶׁב זָר וְלֹא יִנְחֲלוּ עוֹד אֲחֵרִים אֶת כְּבוֹדוֹ, כִּי בְשֵׁם קָדְשְׁךָ נִשְׁבַּעְתָּ לּוֹ, שֶׁלֹּא יִכְבֶּה נֵרוֹ לְעוֹלָם וָעֶד. בָּרוּךְ אַתָּה יהוה, מָגֵן דָּוִד.* (–Cong. אָמֵן.)

[On the Sabbath add the words in brackets.]

עַל הַתּוֹרָה,* וְעַל הָעֲבוֹדָה, וְעַל הַנְּבִיאִים, וְעַל יוֹם [הַשַּׁבָּת הַזֶּה, וְיוֹם] חַג הַמַּצּוֹת הַזֶּה שֶׁנָּתַתָּ לָּנוּ יהוה אֱלֹהֵינוּ, [לִקְדֻשָּׁה וְלִמְנוּחָה,] לְשָׂשׂוֹן וּלְשִׂמְחָה, לְכָבוֹד וּלְתִפְאָרֶת. עַל הַכֹּל יהוה אֱלֹהֵינוּ, אֲנַחְנוּ מוֹדִים לָךְ, וּמְבָרְכִים אוֹתָךְ, יִתְבָּרַךְ שִׁמְךָ בְּפִי כָּל חַי תָּמִיד לְעוֹלָם וָעֶד. בָּרוּךְ אַתָּה יהוה, מְקַדֵּשׁ [הַשַּׁבָּת וְ]יִשְׂרָאֵל וְהַזְּמַנִּים. (–Cong. אָמֵן.)

ON THE SABBATH THE SERVICE CONTINUES ON PAGE 984.
ON WEEKDAYS, THE SEVENTH DAY'S SERVICE CONTINUES ON PAGE 994;
AND THE EIGHTH DAY'S SERVICE CONTINUES WITH YIZKOR ON PAGE 986.

Blessings after the Haftarah

צוּר כָּל הָעוֹלָמִים — *Rock of all eternities.* In its simple meaning this term describes God as all-powerful throughout the ages; therefore, only He is worthy of our trust. Nothing diminishes His power and nothing changes His sense of justice, fairness, and mercy. The *Zohar* interprets צוּר as צַיָּר, *Molder*. Thus, the term describes God as the One Who created and fashioned all the worlds and all ages. Both interpretations are especially apt with reference to the words of the prophets which we have read in the *Haftarah*. Because God is eternal, strong, and able to mold creation to suit His goal, we should have absolute faith in the prophecies He has communicated to us. This faith in the absolute truth and constancy of God's word is the theme of the first blessing.

צַדִּיק בְּכָל הַדּוֹרוֹת — *Righteous in all generations.* Whether a generation enjoys good fortune or suffers tragic oppression, God is righteous and His judgments are justified.

אֱמֶת וָצֶדֶק — *True and righteous.* The universe was established on God's commitment to *truth* and *righteousness.* Truth is the seal of God (*Shabbos* 55a), the theme underlying His guid-

BLESSINGS AFTER THE HAFTARAH

After the *Haftarah* is read, the *oleh* recites the following blessings.

בָּרוּךְ *Blessed are You, HASHEM, King of the universe, Rock of all eternities,* Righteous in all generations,* the trustworthy God, Who says and does, Who speaks and fulfills, all of Whose words are true and righteous.* Trustworthy are You, HASHEM, our God, and trustworthy are Your words, not one of Your words is turned back to its origin unfulfilled, for You are God, trustworthy (and compassionate) King. Blessed are You, HASHEM, the God Who is trustworthy in all His words.*

(Cong.— *Amen.)*

רַחֵם *Have mercy on Zion* for it is the source of our life; to the one who is deeply humiliated bring salvation speedily, in our days. Blessed are You, HASHEM, Who gladdens Zion through her children.*

(Cong.— *Amen.)*

שַׂמְּחֵנוּ *Gladden us, HASHEM, our God, with Elijah the prophet, Your servant, and with the kingdom of the House of David,* Your anointed, may he come speedily and cause our heart to exult. On his throne let no stranger sit nor let others continue to inherit his honor, for by Your holy Name You swore to him that his heir will not be extinguished forever and ever. Blessed are You, HASHEM, Shield of David.**

(Cong.— *Amen.)*

[On the Sabbath add the words in brackets.]

עַל הַתּוֹרָה *For the Torah reading,* for the prayer service, for the reading from the Prophets [for this Sabbath day] and for this day of the Festival of Matzos that You, HASHEM, our God, have given us [for holiness and contentment,] for gladness and joy, for glory and splendor — for all this, HASHEM, our God, we gratefully thank You and bless You. May Your Name be blessed by the mouth of all the living, always, for all eternity. Blessed are You, HASHEM, Who sanctifies [the Sabbath,] Israel and the festival seasons.*

(Cong.— *Amen.)*

ON THE SABBATH THE SERVICE CONTINUES ON PAGE 984.
ON WEEKDAYS, THE SEVENTH DAY'S SERVICE CONTINUES ON PAGE 994;
AND THE EIGHTH DAY'S SERVICE CONTINUES WITH YIZKOR ON PAGE 986.

---

ance and control of the world. His truth endures because all those who violate it are brought to righteous judgment.

רַחֵם עַל צִיּוֹן – *Have mercy on Zion.* The holiness of the Temple on Mount Zion is the source of our spiritual life. Exiled and without it, we are humiliated. Without her children, Zion, too, is despondent, as it is movingly described in the beginning of *Ecclesiastes.* Without her 'children' and Temple, Zion is likened by the prophets to a widow. The Torah warns repeatedly that one dare not wrong a widow because she feels her hurt so keenly. Similarly, in this blessing we plead with God to bring salvation to Zion because she is deeply humiliated.

בְּאֵלִיָּהוּ . . . בֵּית דָּוִד – *With Elijah . . . the House of David.* The prophets teach that Elijah will appear to the Jewish people before the coming of the Messiah to announce that redemption is imminent. Since the Messiah will be descended from David and will restore the Davidic dynasty to the throne of the Jewish people — its first undisputed reign since the days of Solomon — this blessing relates Elijah with the House of David.

מָגֵן דָּוִד – *Shield of David.* In *II Samuel* (22:36) and *Psalms* (18:36), David praised God for shielding him against defeat.

עַל הַתּוֹרָה – *For the Torah [reading].* This final blessing sums up the entire service: not only the reading from the Prophets, but also the Torah reading, the prayers and the holiness of the Sabbath or Festival day.

יקום פרקן

On the Sabbath the following is recited. One praying alone omits the last two paragraphs.

יְקוּם פֻּרְקָן* מִן שְׁמַיָּא, חִנָּא וְחִסְדָּא וְרַחֲמֵי, וְחַיֵּי אֲרִיכֵי, וּמְזוֹנֵי רְוִיחֵי, וְסִיַּעְתָּא דִשְׁמַיָּא, וּבַרְיוּת גּוּפָא, וּנְהוֹרָא מַעַלְיָא, זַרְעָא חַיָּא וְקַיָּמָא, זַרְעָא דִּי לָא יִפְסוּק וְדִי לָא יִבְטוּל מִפִּתְגָּמֵי אוֹרַיְתָא. לְמָרָנָן וְרַבָּנָן חֲבוּרָתָא קַדִּישָׁתָא דִּי בְאַרְעָא דְיִשְׂרָאֵל וְדִי בְּבָבֶל,* לְרֵישֵׁי כַלֵּי,* וּלְרֵישֵׁי גַלְוָתָא,* וּלְרֵישֵׁי מְתִיבָתָא, וּלְדַיָּנֵי דִי בָבָא, לְכָל תַּלְמִידֵיהוֹן, וּלְכָל תַּלְמִידֵי תַלְמִידֵיהוֹן, וּלְכָל מָן דְּעָסְקִין בְּאוֹרַיְתָא. מַלְכָּא דְעָלְמָא יְבָרֵךְ יַתְהוֹן, יַפִּישׁ חַיֵּיהוֹן, וְיַסְגֵּא יוֹמֵיהוֹן, וְיִתֵּן אַרְכָה לִשְׁנֵיהוֹן, וְיִתְפָּרְקוּן וְיִשְׁתֵּזְבוּן מִן כָּל עָקָא וּמִן כָּל מַרְעִין בִּישִׁין. מָרָן דִּי בִשְׁמַיָּא יְהֵא בְסַעְדְּהוֹן, כָּל זְמַן וְעִדָּן. וְנֹאמַר: אָמֵן.

(.Cong. — אָמֵן)

יְקוּם פֻּרְקָן* מִן שְׁמַיָּא, חִנָּא וְחִסְדָּא וְרַחֲמֵי, וְחַיֵּי אֲרִיכֵי, וּמְזוֹנֵי רְוִיחֵי, וְסִיַּעְתָּא דִשְׁמַיָּא, וּבַרְיוּת גּוּפָא, וּנְהוֹרָא מַעַלְיָא, זַרְעָא חַיָּא וְקַיָּמָא, זַרְעָא דִּי לָא יִפְסוּק וְדִי לָא יִבְטוּל מִפִּתְגָּמֵי אוֹרַיְתָא. לְכָל קְהָלָא קַדִּישָׁא הָדֵין, רַבְרְבַיָּא עִם זְעֵרַיָּא, טַפְלָא וּנְשַׁיָּא, מַלְכָּא דְעָלְמָא יְבָרֵךְ יַתְכוֹן, יַפִּישׁ חַיֵּיכוֹן, וְיַסְגֵּא יוֹמֵיכוֹן, וְיִתֵּן אַרְכָה לִשְׁנֵיכוֹן, וְתִתְפָּרְקוּן וְתִשְׁתֵּזְבוּן מִן כָּל עָקָא וּמִן כָּל מַרְעִין בִּישִׁין, מָרָן דִּי בִשְׁמַיָּא יְהֵא בְסַעְדְּכוֹן, כָּל זְמַן וְעִדָּן. וְנֹאמַר: אָמֵן.

(.Cong. — אָמֵן)

מִי שֶׁבֵּרַךְ* אֲבוֹתֵינוּ אַבְרָהָם יִצְחָק וְיַעֲקֹב, הוּא יְבָרֵךְ אֶת כָּל הַקָּהָל הַקָּדוֹשׁ הַזֶּה, עִם כָּל קְהִלּוֹת הַקֹּדֶשׁ, הֵם, וּנְשֵׁיהֶם, וּבְנֵיהֶם, וּבְנוֹתֵיהֶם, וְכָל אֲשֶׁר לָהֶם. וּמִי שֶׁמְּיַחֲדִים בָּתֵּי כְנֵסִיּוֹת לִתְפִלָּה, וּמִי שֶׁבָּאִים בְּתוֹכָם לְהִתְפַּלֵּל, וּמִי שֶׁנּוֹתְנִים נֵר לַמָּאוֹר, וְיַיִן לְקִדּוּשׁ וּלְהַבְדָּלָה, וּפַת לָאוֹרְחִים, וּצְדָקָה לָעֲנִיִּים, וְכָל מִי שֶׁעוֹסְקִים בְּצָרְכֵי צִבּוּר בֶּאֱמוּנָה, הַקָּדוֹשׁ בָּרוּךְ הוּא יְשַׁלֵּם שְׂכָרָם, וְיָסִיר מֵהֶם כָּל מַחֲלָה, וְיִרְפָּא לְכָל גּוּפָם, וְיִסְלַח לְכָל עֲוֹנָם, וְיִשְׁלַח בְּרָכָה וְהַצְלָחָה בְּכָל מַעֲשֵׂה יְדֵיהֶם, עִם כָּל יִשְׂרָאֵל אֲחֵיהֶם. וְנֹאמַר: אָמֵן.

(.Cong. — אָמֵן)

In many congregations, a prayer for the welfare of the State is recited by the Rabbi, *chazzan,* or *gabbai* at this point.

יְקוּם פֻּרְקָן — *May salvation arise.* After reading from the Torah, a series of prayers is recited for those who teach, study, and support the Torah, and undertake the responsibilities of leadership. The first is a general prayer for all such people wherever they may be; consequently, it is recited even by people praying without a *minyan.* The second and third are prayers for the congregation with which one is praying; consequently, one praying alone omits them. The two יְקוּם פֻּרְקָן prayers were composed by the Babylonian *geonim* after the close of the Talmudic period, in Aramaic, the spoken language of that country. These prayers were instituted specifically for the Sabbath, not for Festivals, except those that fall on the Sabbath.

דִּי בְאַרְעָא דְיִשְׂרָאֵל וְדִי בְבָבֶל — *That are in Eretz Yisrael and that are in the Diaspora* [lit., *Babylonia*]. Although the Jewish community in *Eretz Yisrael* at that time was comparatively insignificant, the *geonim* gave honor and precedence to the Holy Land. Although the great

YEKUM PURKAN

On the Sabbath the following is recited. One praying alone omits the last two paragraphs.

יְקוּם פֻּרְקָן *May salvation arise* from heaven — grace, kindness, compassion, long life, abundant sustenance, heavenly assistance, physical health, lofty vision, living and surviving offspring, offspring who will neither interrupt nor cease from words of the Torah — for our masters and sages, the holy fellowships that are in Eretz Yisrael and that are in the Diaspora*: for the leaders of the Torah assemblages,* the leaders of the exile communities,* the leaders of the academies, the judges at the gateways, and all their students and to all the students of their students, and to everyone who engages in Torah study. May the King of the universe bless them, make their lives fruitful, increase their days and grant length to their years. May He save them and rescue them from every distress and from all serious ailments. May the Master in heaven come to their assistance at every season and time. Now let us respond: Amen.* (Cong.—*Amen.*)

יְקוּם פֻּרְקָן *May salvation arise* from heaven — grace, kindness, compassion, long life, abundant sustenance, heavenly assistance, physical health, lofty vision, living and surviving offspring, offspring who will neither interrupt nor cease from the words of the Torah — to this entire holy congregation, adults along with children, infants and women. May the King of the universe bless you, make your lives fruitful, increase your days, and grant length to your years. May He save you and rescue you from every distress and from all serious ailments. May the Master in heaven come to your assistance at every season and time. Now let us respond: Amen.* (Cong.—*Amen.*)

מִי שֶׁבֵּרַךְ *He Who blessed* our forefathers, Abraham, Isaac, and Jacob — may He bless this entire holy congregation along with all the holy congregations; them, their wives, sons, and daughters and all that is theirs; and those who dedicate synagogues for prayer and those who enter them to pray, and those who give lamps for illumination and wine for Kiddush and Havdalah, bread for guests and charity for the poor; and all who are involved faithfully in the needs of the community — may the Holy One, Blessed is He, pay their reward and remove from them every affliction, heal their entire body and forgive their every iniquity, and send blessing and success to all their handiwork, along with all Israel, their brethren. And let us say: Amen.* (Cong.—*Amen.*)

In many congregations, a prayer for the welfare of the State is recited by the Rabbi, *chazzan,* or *gabbai* at this point.

---

masses of Jewry no longer live in Babylonia, this timeless prayer refers to all Jewish communities; the word Babylonia is used as a general term for all Jewish communities outside of *Eretz Yisrael.*

לְרֵישֵׁי כַלֵּי — *For the leaders of the Torah assemblages.* These were the scholars who deliver Torah lectures on the Sabbath and Festivals to mass gatherings of the people.

וּלְרֵישֵׁי גַלְוָתָא — *The leaders of the exile communities.* The רֵישׁ גָּלוּתָא, *Exilarch,* was the leader of the Jewish nation, equivalent to the *Nassi* in earlier times. His headquarters was in Babylonia.

יְקוּם פֻּרְקָן ☙ — *May salvation arise.* This prayer refers to the congregation with which one is praying. Thus it omits mention of national teachers and leaders. It includes the entire congregation, young and old, men and women, because it prays for the welfare of each one.

מִי שֶׁבֵּרַךְ ☙ — *He Who blessed.* This is a prayer for this and all other congregations, and singles out the people who provide the means and services for the general good. *Bais Yosef* (284) notes that these charitable causes are stressed so that the entire community will hear of the great reward of those who study and support Torah and others will emulate their deeds.

סדר הזכרת נשמות — יזכור

Those congregants whose parents are both living do not participate in the *Yizkor* service, but leave the synagogue and return when the congregation begins אַב הָרַחֲמִים (page 992) after *Yizkor*.

Although the following verses are not part of the traditional *Yizkor* service, some congregations have adopted the custom of reciting them responsively before *Yizkor*.

יהוה, מָה אָדָם וַתֵּדָעֵהוּ, בֶּן אֱנוֹשׁ וַתְּחַשְּׁבֵהוּ.
אָדָם לַהֶבֶל דָּמָה, יָמָיו כְּצֵל עוֹבֵר.[1]
בַּבֹּקֶר יָצִיץ וְחָלָף, לָעֶרֶב יְמוֹלֵל וְיָבֵשׁ.[2]
לִמְנוֹת יָמֵינוּ כֵּן הוֹדַע, וְנָבִא לְבַב חָכְמָה.[3]
שְׁמָר תָּם וּרְאֵה יָשָׁר, כִּי אַחֲרִית לְאִישׁ שָׁלוֹם.[4]
אַךְ. אֱלֹהִים יִפְדֶּה נַפְשִׁי מִיַּד שְׁאוֹל, כִּי יִקָּחֵנִי סֶלָה.[5]
כָּלָה שְׁאֵרִי וּלְבָבִי, צוּר לְבָבִי וְחֶלְקִי אֱלֹהִים לְעוֹלָם.[6]
וְיָשֹׁב הֶעָפָר עַל הָאָרֶץ כְּשֶׁהָיָה,
וְהָרוּחַ תָּשׁוּב אֶל הָאֱלֹהִים אֲשֶׁר נְתָנָהּ.[7]

תהלים צא

יֹשֵׁב בְּסֵתֶר עֶלְיוֹן, בְּצֵל שַׁדַּי יִתְלוֹנָן. אֹמַר לַיהוה, מַחְסִי וּמְצוּדָתִי, אֱלֹהַי אֶבְטַח בּוֹ. כִּי הוּא יַצִּילְךָ מִפַּח יָקוּשׁ, מִדֶּבֶר הַוּוֹת. בְּאֶבְרָתוֹ יָסֶךְ לָךְ, וְתַחַת כְּנָפָיו תֶּחְסֶה, צִנָּה וְסֹחֵרָה אֲמִתּוֹ. לֹא תִירָא מִפַּחַד לָיְלָה, מֵחֵץ יָעוּף יוֹמָם. מִדֶּבֶר בָּאֹפֶל יַהֲלֹךְ, מִקֶּטֶב יָשׁוּד צָהֳרָיִם. יִפֹּל מִצִּדְּךָ אֶלֶף, וּרְבָבָה מִימִינֶךָ, אֵלֶיךָ לֹא יִגָּשׁ. רַק בְּעֵינֶיךָ תַבִּיט, וְשִׁלֻּמַת רְשָׁעִים תִּרְאֶה. כִּי אַתָּה יהוה מַחְסִי, עֶלְיוֹן שַׂמְתָּ מְעוֹנֶךָ. לֹא תְאֻנֶּה אֵלֶיךָ רָעָה, וְנֶגַע לֹא יִקְרַב בְּאָהֳלֶךָ. כִּי מַלְאָכָיו יְצַוֶּה לָּךְ, לִשְׁמָרְךָ בְּכָל דְּרָכֶיךָ. עַל כַּפַּיִם יִשָּׂאוּנְךָ, פֶּן תִּגֹּף בָּאֶבֶן רַגְלֶךָ. עַל שַׁחַל וָפֶתֶן תִּדְרֹךְ, תִּרְמֹס כְּפִיר וְתַנִּין. כִּי בִי חָשַׁק וַאֲפַלְּטֵהוּ, אֲשַׂגְּבֵהוּ, כִּי יָדַע שְׁמִי. יִקְרָאֵנִי וְאֶעֱנֵהוּ, עִמּוֹ אָנֹכִי בְצָרָה, אֲחַלְּצֵהוּ וַאֲכַבְּדֵהוּ. אֹרֶךְ יָמִים אַשְׂבִּיעֵהוּ, וְאַרְאֵהוּ בִּישׁוּעָתִי. אֹרֶךְ יָמִים אַשְׂבִּיעֵהוּ, וְאַרְאֵהוּ בִּישׁוּעָתִי.

YIZKOR / יִזְכֹּר

The ancient custom of recalling the souls of the departed and contributing to charity in their memory is rooted in the fundamental Jewish belief in the eternity of the soul. When physical life ends, only the body dies, but the soul ascends to the realm of the spirit where it regularly attains higher levels of purity and holiness.

When this life is over, the soul can no longer perform good deeds; that method of attaining merit is the sole province of mortal man who must struggle with the baseness and selfishness of his animal nature. But there is a way that the disembodied soul can derive new sources of merit. History is a continuum. If we, the living, give charity or do good deeds due to the lasting influence or in memory of a departed parent or other loved one, the merit is truly that of the soul in its spiritual realm. Moreover, God in His mercy credits our deeds to the departed one because he or she would have done the same were it possible. Even if the departed one was too poor to have made contributions to charity, the soul benefits nonetheless, because it may be assumed that he or she would have been charitable, had sufficient means been available. But mere intentions do not suffice; only accomplishment can achieve this purpose. The intention to give and the fulfillment of that intention are both necessary; consequently, the pledges to charity should be redeemed as soon as possible after Yom Kippur.

It should be noted that a נֶדֶר, *vow*, is a very serious matter in Jewish law, and one must be scrupulous in fulfilling his vows. In order to avoid the possibility that one may make a pledge to charity and then forget to redeem it, we follow the practice of many *machzorim* in not using the word נֶדֶר, *vow*, in the *Yizkor* text. Instead we use

YIZKOR

Those congregants whose parents are both living do not participate in the *Yizkor* service, but leave the synagogue and return when the congregation begins אַב הָרַחֲמִים (page 992) after *Yizkor*.

Although the following verses are not part of the traditional *Yizkor* service, some congregations have adopted the custom of reciting them responsively before *Yizkor*.

יהוה *HASHEM, what is man that You recognize him? The son of a frail human that You reckon with him?*
Man is like a breath, his days are like a passing shadow.[1]
In the morning it blossoms and is rejuvenated, by evening it is cut down and brittle.[2]
According to the count of our days, so may You teach us;
then we shall acquire a heart of wisdom.[3]
Safeguard the perfect and watch the upright, for the destiny of that man is peace.[4]
But God will redeem my soul from the grip of the Lower World,
for He will take me, Selah![5]
My flesh and my heart yearn — Rock of my heart, and my portion is God, forever.[6]
Thus the dust returns to the ground as it was, and the spirit returns to God who gave it.[7]

Psalm 91

יֹשֵׁב *Whoever sits in the refuge of the Most High, he shall dwell in the shadow of the Almighty. I will say of HASHEM, 'He is my refuge and my fortress, my God, I will trust in Him.' That He will deliver you from the ensnaring trap and from devastating pestilence. With His pinion He will cover you, and beneath His wings you will be protected; shield and armor is His truth. You shall not be afraid of the terror of night, nor of the arrow that flies by day; nor the pestilence that walks in gloom, nor the destroyer who lays waste at noon. Let a thousand encamp at your side and a myriad at your right hand, but to you they shall not approach. You will merely peer with your eyes and you will see the retribution of the wicked. Because [you said], 'You, HASHEM, are my refuge'; you have made the Most High your dwelling place. No evil will befall you, nor will any plague come near your tent. He will charge His angels for you, to protect you in all your ways. On their palms they will carry you, lest you strike your foot against a stone. Upon the lion and the viper you will tread; you will trample the young lion and the serpent. For he has yearned for Me and I will deliver him; I will elevate him because he knows My Name. He will call upon Me and I will answer him, I am with him in distress, I will release him and I will honor him. I will satisfy him with long life and show him My salvation. I will satisfy him with long life and show him My salvation.*

(1) *Psalms* 144:3-4. (2) 90:6. (3) 90:12. (4) 37:37. (5) 49:16. (6) 73:26. (7) *Ecclesiastes* 12:7.

---

the form שֶׁבְּלִי נֶדֶר אֶתֵּן, *without making a vow I shall give.*

It is virtually a universal custom that those whose parents are still living leave the synagogue during *Yizkor*. This is done to avoid the 'evil eye,' i.e., the resentment that might be felt by those without parents toward those whose parents are still living. *R' Elie Munk* suggests a further reason: we wish to avoid the possibility that people with living parents may mistakenly join in reciting *Yizkor*.

In most congregations children do not recite *Yizkor* in the first year after their parent's death, because they may become very emotional and disturb the prayers of others.

The earliest source of the custom to recite *Yizkor* is *Midrash Tanchuma, Haazinu,* which cites the rite of recalling the departed and pledging to contribute to charity on their behalf on Yom Kippur. In *Shulchan Aruch* (*Orach Chaim* 621:6), *Bais Yosef* records that on Yom Kippur it is customary to pledge to charity as a merit to the departed; and *Rama* adds the Ashkenazic custom of reciting *Yizkor*. However there is no mention in *Shulchan Aruch* of *Yizkor* on other days.

Ashkenazic Jewry's custom of reciting *Yizkor* on the last days of Pesach and Shavuos and on Shemini Atzeres may have begun at the time of the Crusades, when bloody massacres by the 'holy' warriors wiped out many Jewish communities, and seriously depleted many others. The general rule is that *Yizkor* is recited when the Torah portion of כָּל הַבְּכוֹר, *Every firstborn,* is read, because this portion includes the exhortation that everyone should give to charity according to the degree with which God has blessed him. Since the charity of their children and other close relatives is a source of merit for the departed, it is natural that the charity commanded by the Torah reading should be coupled with a prayer for their souls.

In addition to *Yizkor* for parents, it is also recited for other close relatives and for martyrs who have perished עַל קִדּוּשׁ הַשֵּׁם, *in sanctification of God's Name.*

Whenever the name of the deceased is mentioned in the *Yizkor* service, it is given in the following form: the Hebrew name of the deceased followed by the word בֶּן, *son of* — or, בַּת, *daughter of* — and then the deceased's father's Hebrew name.

FOR ONE'S FATHER

יִזְכֹּר אֱלֹהִים* נִשְׁמַת אָבִי מוֹרִי (name of the deceased) שֶׁהָלַךְ לְעוֹלָמוֹ, בַּעֲבוּר שֶׁבְּלִי נֶדֶר אֶתֵּן צְדָקָה בַּעֲדוֹ. בִּשְׂכַר זֶה תְּהֵא נַפְשׁוֹ צְרוּרָה בִּצְרוֹר הַחַיִּים* עִם נִשְׁמוֹת אַבְרָהָם יִצְחָק וְיַעֲקֹב, שָׂרָה רִבְקָה רָחֵל וְלֵאָה, וְעִם שְׁאָר צַדִּיקִים וְצִדְקָנִיּוֹת שֶׁבְּגַן עֵדֶן.* וְנֹאמַר: אָמֵן.

FOR ONE'S MOTHER

יִזְכֹּר אֱלֹהִים* נִשְׁמַת אִמִּי מוֹרָתִי (name of the deceased) שֶׁהָלְכָה לְעוֹלָמָהּ, בַּעֲבוּר שֶׁבְּלִי נֶדֶר אֶתֵּן צְדָקָה בַּעֲדָהּ. בִּשְׂכַר זֶה תְּהֵא נַפְשָׁהּ צְרוּרָה בִּצְרוֹר הַחַיִּים* עִם נִשְׁמוֹת אַבְרָהָם יִצְחָק וְיַעֲקֹב, שָׂרָה רִבְקָה רָחֵל וְלֵאָה, וְעִם שְׁאָר צַדִּיקִים וְצִדְקָנִיּוֹת שֶׁבְּגַן עֵדֶן.* וְנֹאמַר: אָמֵן.

FOR A RELATIVE

יִזְכֹּר אֱלֹהִים* נִשְׁמַת

wife	husband	daughter	son	sister	brother	aunt	uncle	grandmother	grandfather
אִשְׁתִּי	בַּעְלִי	בִּתִּי	בְּנִי	אֲחוֹתִי	אָחִי	דּוֹדָתִי	דּוֹדִי	זְקֶנְתִּי	זְקֵנִי

for a man

שֶׁהָלַךְ לְעוֹלָמוֹ, (name of the deceased) בַּעֲבוּר שֶׁבְּלִי נֶדֶר אֶתֵּן צְדָקָה בַּעֲדוֹ. בִּשְׂכַר זֶה תְּהֵא נַפְשׁוֹ צְרוּרָה בִּצְרוֹר הַחַיִּים* עִם נִשְׁמוֹת אַבְרָהָם יִצְחָק וְיַעֲקֹב, שָׂרָה רִבְקָה רָחֵל וְלֵאָה, וְעִם שְׁאָר צַדִּיקִים וְצִדְקָנִיּוֹת שֶׁבְּגַן עֵדֶן.* וְנֹאמַר: אָמֵן.

for a woman

שֶׁהָלְכָה (name of the deceased) לְעוֹלָמָהּ, בַּעֲבוּר שֶׁבְּלִי נֶדֶר אֶתֵּן צְדָקָה בַּעֲדָהּ. בִּשְׂכַר זֶה תְּהֵא נַפְשָׁהּ צְרוּרָה בִּצְרוֹר הַחַיִּים* עִם נִשְׁמוֹת אַבְרָהָם יִצְחָק וְיַעֲקֹב, שָׂרָה רִבְקָה רָחֵל וְלֵאָה, וְעִם שְׁאָר צַדִּיקִים וְצִדְקָנִיּוֹת שֶׁבְּגַן עֵדֶן.* וְנֹאמַר: אָמֵן.

FOR ONE'S EXTENDED FAMILY

יִזְכֹּר אֱלֹהִים* נִשְׁמוֹת זְקֵנַי וּזְקֵנוֹתַי, דּוֹדַי וְדוֹדוֹתַי, אַחַי וְאַחְיוֹתַי, הֵן מִצַּד אָבִי, הֵן מִצַּד אִמִּי, שֶׁהָלְכוּ לְעוֹלָמָם, בַּעֲבוּר שֶׁבְּלִי נֶדֶר אֶתֵּן צְדָקָה בַּעֲדָם. בִּשְׂכַר זֶה תִּהְיֶינָה נַפְשׁוֹתֵיהֶם צְרוּרוֹת בִּצְרוֹר הַחַיִּים* עִם נִשְׁמוֹת אַבְרָהָם יִצְחָק וְיַעֲקֹב, שָׂרָה רִבְקָה רָחֵל וְלֵאָה, וְעִם שְׁאָר צַדִּיקִים וְצִדְקָנִיּוֹת שֶׁבְּגַן עֵדֶן.* וְנֹאמַר: אָמֵן.

FOR MARTYRS

יִזְכֹּר אֱלֹהִים* נִשְׁמוֹת (כָּל קְרוֹבַי וּקְרוֹבוֹתַי, הֵן מִצַּד אָבִי, הֵן מִצַּד אִמִּי) הַקְּדוֹשִׁים וְהַטְּהוֹרִים שֶׁהוּמְתוּ וְשֶׁנֶּהֶרְגוּ וְשֶׁנִּשְׁחֲטוּ וְשֶׁנִּשְׂרְפוּ וְשֶׁנִּטְבְּעוּ וְשֶׁנֶּחְנְקוּ עַל קִדּוּשׁ הַשֵּׁם, בַּעֲבוּר שֶׁבְּלִי נֶדֶר אֶתֵּן צְדָקָה בְּעַד הַזְכָּרַת נִשְׁמוֹתֵיהֶם. בִּשְׂכַר זֶה תִּהְיֶינָה נַפְשׁוֹתֵיהֶם צְרוּרוֹת בִּצְרוֹר הַחַיִּים* עִם נִשְׁמוֹת אַבְרָהָם יִצְחָק וְיַעֲקֹב, שָׂרָה רִבְקָה רָחֵל וְלֵאָה, וְעִם שְׁאָר צַדִּיקִים וְצִדְקָנִיּוֹת שֶׁבְּגַן עֵדֶן.* וְנֹאמַר: אָמֵן.

Whenever the name of the deceased is mentioned in the *Yizkor* service, it is given in the following form: the Hebrew name of the deceased followed by בֶּן, *son of* — or, בַּת, *daughter of* — and then the deceased's father's Hebrew name.

FOR ONE'S FATHER

יִזְכֹּר *May God remember* the soul of my father, my teacher,* (name of the deceased) *who has gone on to his world, because, without making a vow, I shall give to charity on his behalf. As reward for this, may his soul be bound in the Bond of Life,* together with the souls of Abraham, Isaac, and Jacob; Sarah, Rebecca, Rachel, and Leah; and together with the other righteous men and women in the Garden of Eden.* Now let us respond: Amen.*

FOR ONE'S MOTHER

יִזְכֹּר *May God remember* the soul of my mother, my teacher,* (name of the deceased) *who has gone on to her world, because, without making a vow, I shall give to charity on her behalf. As reward for this, may her soul be bound in the Bond of Life,* together with the souls of Abraham, Isaac, and Jacob; Sarah, Rebecca, Rachel, and Leah; and together with the other righteous men and women in the Garden of Eden.* Now let us respond: Amen.*

FOR A RELATIVE

יִזְכֹּר *May God remember* the soul of my grandfather/grandmother/uncle/aunt/brother/sister/son/daughter/husband/wife* (name of the deceased) *who has gone on to his/her world, because, without making a vow, I shall give to charity on his/her behalf. As reward for this, may his/her soul be bound in the Bond of Life,* together with the souls of Abraham, Isaac, and Jacob; Sarah, Rebecca, Rachel, and Leah; and together with the other righteous men and women in the Garden of Eden.* Now let us respond: Amen.*

FOR ONE'S EXTENDED FAMILY

יִזְכֹּר *May God remember* the souls of my grandfathers and grandmothers, uncles and aunts, brothers and sisters both on my father's side and on my mother's side, who went on to their world, because, without making a vow, I shall give to charity on their behalf. As reward for this, may their souls be bound in the Bond of Life,* together with the souls of Abraham, Isaac, and Jacob; Sarah, Rebecca, Rachel, and Leah; and together with the other righteous men and women in the Garden of Eden.* Now let us respond: Amen.*

FOR MARTYRS

יִזְכֹּר *May God remember* the souls of (all my relatives, both on my father's side and on my mother's side), the holy and pure ones who were killed, murdered, slaughtered, burned, drowned and strangled for the sanctification of the Name, because, without making a vow, I shall give to charity on their behalf. As reward for this, may their souls be bound in the Bond of Life,* together with the souls of Abraham, Isaac, and Jacob; Sarah, Rebecca, Rachel, and Leah; and together with the other righteous men and women in the Garden of Eden.* Now let us respond: Amen.*

יִזְכֹּר אֱלֹהִים ◆§ — *May God remember.* In calling upon God to 'remember' the soul of the departed, we do not suggest that the possibility of forgetting exists before the All-Knowing One. Rather we pray that in return for our devotion and generosity, God should take cognizance of the new source of merit for the soul whose memory is now influencing our conduct.

בִּצְרוֹר הַחַיִּים — *In the Bond of Life.* The ultimate which is unlimited by the constraints of time and space and the weakness of flesh. The greater the merit achieved by a soul during its time on earth — or as a result of our good deeds in its memory — the more it is bound together with the souls of the Patriarchs and Matriarchs.

בְּגַן עֵדֶן — *In the Garden of Eden.* Although literally this is the place where Adam and Eve lived until their sin caused them to be driven out,

FOR MEMBERS OF THE ISRAEL DEFENSE FORCE

[The following text is taken from the *Minchas Yerushalayim Siddur.*]

יִזְכֹּר אֱלֹהִים אֶת נִשְׁמוֹת חַיָּלֵי צְבָא הַהֲגָנָה לְיִשְׂרָאֵל שֶׁמָּסְרוּ נַפְשָׁם עַל קְדֻשַּׁת הַשֵּׁם, הָעָם וְהָאָרֶץ, וְנָפְלוּ מוֹת גִּבּוֹרִים בְּמִלְחֶמֶת הַשִּׁחְרוּר, וּבְמַעַרְכוֹת סִינַי בְּתַפְקִידֵי הֲגָנָּה וּבִטָּחוֹן. מִנְּשָׁרִים קַלּוּ, וּמֵאֲרָיוֹת גָּבֵרוּ, בְּהֵחָלְצָם לְעֶזְרַת הָעָם, וְהִרְווּ בְּדָמָם הַטָּהוֹר אֶת רִגְבֵי אַדְמַת קָדְשֵׁנוּ וּמִדְבְּרוֹת סִינָי. זֵכֶר עֲקֵדָתָם וּמַעֲשֵׂי גְבוּרָתָם לֹא יָסוּפוּ מֵאִתָּנוּ לְעוֹלָמִים. תִּהְיֶינָה נִשְׁמוֹתֵיהֶם צְרוּרוֹת בִּצְרוֹר הַחַיִּים עִם נִשְׁמוֹת אַבְרָהָם יִצְחָק וְיַעֲקֹב, וְעִם נִשְׁמוֹת שְׁאָר גִּבּוֹרֵי יִשְׂרָאֵל וּקְדוֹשָׁיו שֶׁבְּגַן עֵדֶן. אָמֵן.

After reciting *Yizkor* it is customary to recite the following prayers. It is permitted to mention many names in this prayer, but it is preferable to recite separate prayers for men and women.

FOR AN INDIVIDUAL

אֵל מָלֵא רַחֲמִים, שׁוֹכֵן בַּמְּרוֹמִים, הַמְצֵא מְנוּחָה נְכוֹנָה* עַל כַּנְפֵי הַשְּׁכִינָה,* בְּמַעֲלוֹת קְדוֹשִׁים וּטְהוֹרִים* כְּזֹהַר הָרָקִיעַ מַזְהִירִים,

for a man

אֶת נִשְׁמַת (name of the deceased) שֶׁהָלַךְ לְעוֹלָמוֹ, בַּעֲבוּר שֶׁבְּלִי נֶדֶר אֶתֵּן צְדָקָה בְּעַד הַזְכָּרַת נִשְׁמָתוֹ, בְּגַן עֵדֶן תְּהֵא מְנוּחָתוֹ, לָכֵן בַּעַל הָרַחֲמִים יַסְתִּירֵהוּ בְּסֵתֶר כְּנָפָיו לְעוֹלָמִים, וְיִצְרוֹר בִּצְרוֹר הַחַיִּים אֶת נִשְׁמָתוֹ, יהוה הוּא נַחֲלָתוֹ, וְיָנוּחַ בְּשָׁלוֹם עַל מִשְׁכָּבוֹ. וְנֹאמַר: אָמֵן.

for a woman

אֶת נִשְׁמַת (name of the deceased) שֶׁהָלְכָה לְעוֹלָמָהּ, בַּעֲבוּר שֶׁבְּלִי נֶדֶר אֶתֵּן צְדָקָה בְּעַד הַזְכָּרַת נִשְׁמָתָהּ, בְּגַן עֵדֶן תְּהֵא מְנוּחָתָהּ, לָכֵן בַּעַל הָרַחֲמִים יַסְתִּירֶהָ בְּסֵתֶר כְּנָפָיו לְעוֹלָמִים, וְיִצְרוֹר בִּצְרוֹר הַחַיִּים אֶת נִשְׁמָתָהּ, יהוה הוּא נַחֲלָתָהּ, וְתָנוּחַ בְּשָׁלוֹם עַל מִשְׁכָּבָהּ. וְנֹאמַר: אָמֵן.

FOR A GROUP

אֵל מָלֵא רַחֲמִים, שׁוֹכֵן בַּמְּרוֹמִים, הַמְצֵא מְנוּחָה נְכוֹנָה* עַל כַּנְפֵי הַשְּׁכִינָה,* בְּמַעֲלוֹת קְדוֹשִׁים וּטְהוֹרִים* כְּזֹהַר הָרָקִיעַ מַזְהִירִים,

for men

אֶת נִשְׁמוֹת (names of the deceased) שֶׁהָלְכוּ לְעוֹלָמָם, בַּעֲבוּר שֶׁבְּלִי נֶדֶר אֶתֵּן צְדָקָה בְּעַד הַזְכָּרַת נִשְׁמוֹתֵיהֶם, בְּגַן עֵדֶן תְּהֵא מְנוּחָתָם, לָכֵן בַּעַל הָרַחֲמִים יַסְתִּירֵם בְּסֵתֶר כְּנָפָיו לְעוֹלָמִים, וְיִצְרוֹר בִּצְרוֹר הַחַיִּים אֶת נִשְׁמוֹתֵיהֶם, יהוה הוּא נַחֲלָתָם, וְיָנוּחוּ בְּשָׁלוֹם עַל מִשְׁכְּבוֹתֵיהֶם. וְנֹאמַר: אָמֵן.

for women

אֶת נִשְׁמוֹת (names of the deceased) שֶׁהָלְכוּ לְעוֹלָמָן, בַּעֲבוּר שֶׁבְּלִי נֶדֶר אֶתֵּן צְדָקָה בְּעַד הַזְכָּרַת נִשְׁמוֹתֵיהֶן, בְּגַן עֵדֶן תְּהֵא מְנוּחָתָן, לָכֵן בַּעַל הָרַחֲמִים יַסְתִּירֵן בְּסֵתֶר כְּנָפָיו לְעוֹלָמִים, וְיִצְרוֹר בִּצְרוֹר הַחַיִּים אֶת נִשְׁמוֹתֵיהֶן, יהוה הוּא נַחֲלָתָן, וְתָנוּחוּ בְּשָׁלוֹם עַל מִשְׁכְּבוֹתֵיהֶן. וְנֹאמַר: אָמֵן.

FOR MEMBERS OF THE ISRAEL DEFENSE FORCE

[The following text is translated from the *Minchas Yerushalayim Siddur.*]

יִזְכֹּר *May God remember the souls of the fighters of the Israel Defense Force who gave their lives for the sanctification of the Name, the People and the Land; who died a heroic death in the War of Independence and the battlefields of Sinai in missions of defense and safety. They were quicker than eagles and stronger than lions as they volunteered to assist the people and with their pure blood soaked the clods of our holy earth and the deserts of Sinai. The memory of their self-sacrifice and heroic deeds will never perish from us. May their souls be bound in the Bond of Life with the souls of Abraham, Isaac and Jacob, and with the souls of the other Jewish heroes and martyrs who are in the Garden of Eden. Amen.*

After reciting *Yizkor* it is customary to recite the following prayers. It is permitted to mention many names in this prayer, but it is preferable to recite separate prayers for men and women.

FOR AN INDIVIDUAL

אֵל *O God, full of mercy, Who dwells on high, grant proper rest* on the wings of the Divine Presence* — in the lofty levels of the holy and the pure ones,* who shine like the glow of the firmament — for the soul of*

for a man

(name of the deceased) *who went on to his world, because, without making a vow, I will contribute to charity in remembrance of his soul. May his resting place be in the Garden of Eden — therefore may the Master of mercy shelter him in the shelter of His wings for eternity; and may He bind his soul in the Bond of Life.* HASHEM *is his heritage, and may he repose in peace on his resting place. Now let us respond: Amen.*

for a woman

(name of the deceased) *who went on to her world, because, without making a vow, I will contribute to charity in remembrance of her soul. May her resting place be in the Garden of Eden — therefore may the Master of mercy shelter her in the shelter of His wings for eternity; and may He bind her soul in the Bond of Life.* HASHEM *is her heritage, and may she repose in peace on her resting place. Now let us respond: Amen.*

FOR A GROUP

אֵל *O God, full of mercy, Who dwells on high, grant proper rest* on the wings of the Divine Presence* — in the lofty levels of the holy and the pure ones,* who shine like the glow of the firmament — for the souls of* (names of the deceased) *who went on to their world, because, without making a vow, I will contribute to charity in remembrance of their souls. May their resting place be in the Garden of Eden — therefore may the Master of mercy shelter them in the shelter of His wings for eternity; and may He bind their souls in the Bond of Life.* HASHEM *is their heritage, and may they repose in peace on their resting places. Now let us respond: Amen.*

---

it is also used to refer to the spiritual paradise because it implies spiritual perfection and bliss.

§ אֵל ... הַמְצֵא מְנוּחָה נְכוֹנָה — *O God, ... grant proper rest.* The fact that a soul is in Paradise does not guarantee it complete contentment. Its level there depends on its prior achievements here on earth; consequently, there are as many degrees there as there are degrees of righteousness on earth. Through our prayers and deeds, we hope to earn God's compassion upon the departed soul.

עַל כַּנְפֵי הַשְּׁכִינָה — *On the wings of the Divine Presence.* When this term is used to mean Heavenly protection from danger, we say תַּחַת, *under,* the wings, using the analogy of a bird spreading its protective wings over its young. In this prayer, where we speak of spiritual elevation, we reverse the analogy, comparing God's Presence to a soaring eagle that puts its young on top of its wings and carries them aloft.

קְדוֹשִׁים וּטְהוֹרִים — *The holy and the pure ones,* a reference to the angels.

FOR MARTYRS

אֵל מָלֵא רַחֲמִים, שׁוֹכֵן בַּמְּרוֹמִים, הַמְצֵא מְנוּחָה נְכוֹנָה* עַל כַּנְפֵי הַשְּׁכִינָה,* בְּמַעֲלוֹת קְדוֹשִׁים וּטְהוֹרִים* כְּזֹהַר הָרָקִיעַ מַזְהִירִים, אֶת נִשְׁמוֹת (כָּל קְרוֹבַי וּקְרוֹבוֹתַי, הֵן מִצַּד אָבִי, הֵן מִצַּד אִמִּי) הַקְּדוֹשִׁים וְהַטְּהוֹרִים שֶׁהוּמְתוּ וְשֶׁנֶּהֶרְגוּ וְשֶׁנִּשְׁחֲטוּ וְשֶׁנִּשְׂרְפוּ וְשֶׁנִּטְבְּעוּ וְשֶׁנֶּחְנְקוּ עַל קִדּוּשׁ הַשֵּׁם, (עַל יְדֵי הַצּוֹרְרִים הַגֶּרְמָנִים, יִמַּח שְׁמָם וְזִכְרָם) בַּעֲבוּר שֶׁבְּלִי נֶדֶר אֶתֵּן צְדָקָה בְּעַד הַזְכָּרַת נִשְׁמוֹתֵיהֶם, בְּגַן עֵדֶן תְּהֵא מְנוּחָתָם, לָכֵן בַּעַל הָרַחֲמִים יַסְתִּירֵם בְּסֵתֶר כְּנָפָיו לְעוֹלָמִים, וְיִצְרוֹר בִּצְרוֹר הַחַיִּים אֶת נִשְׁמוֹתֵיהֶם, יהוה הוּא נַחֲלָתָם, וְיָנוּחוּ בְשָׁלוֹם עַל מִשְׁכְּבוֹתֵיהֶם. וְנֹאמַר: אָמֵן.

מי שברך להרב

At the conclusion of the *Yizkor* service, it is customary for the *gabbai* to recite a prayer on behalf of the rabbi of the congregation.

מִי שֶׁבֵּרַךְ אֲבוֹתֵינוּ אַבְרָהָם יִצְחָק וְיַעֲקֹב, מֹשֶׁה וְאַהֲרֹן, דָּוִד וּשְׁלֹמֹה, הוּא יְבָרֵךְ אֶת רַבִּי (name) בֶּן (father's name) שֶׁיִּתֵּן לִצְדָקָה בְּעַד הַנְּשָׁמוֹת שֶׁהִזְכִּיר הַיּוֹם, לִכְבוֹד הַמָּקוֹם, לִכְבוֹד הַתּוֹרָה, בִּשְׂכַר זֶה, הַקָּדוֹשׁ בָּרוּךְ הוּא יִשְׁמְרֵהוּ וְיַצִּילֵהוּ מִכָּל צָרָה וְצוּקָה, וּמִכָּל נֶגַע וּמַחֲלָה, וְיִשְׁלַח בְּרָכָה וְהַצְלָחָה בְּכָל מַעֲשֵׂה יָדָיו, וְיִזְכֶּה לַעֲלוֹת לְרֶגֶל, עִם כָּל יִשְׂרָאֵל אֶחָיו. וְנֹאמַר: אָמֵן. (Cong. – אָמֵן.)

Congregation and *chazzan*:

אַב הָרַחֲמִים,* שׁוֹכֵן מְרוֹמִים, בְּרַחֲמָיו הָעֲצוּמִים הוּא יִפְקוֹד בְּרַחֲמִים, הַחֲסִידִים וְהַיְשָׁרִים וְהַתְּמִימִים, קְהִלּוֹת הַקֹּדֶשׁ שֶׁמָּסְרוּ נַפְשָׁם עַל קְדֻשַּׁת הַשֵּׁם, הַנֶּאֱהָבִים וְהַנְּעִימִים בְּחַיֵּיהֶם, וּבְמוֹתָם לֹא נִפְרָדוּ. מִנְּשָׁרִים קַלּוּ, וּמֵאֲרָיוֹת גָּבֵרוּ, לַעֲשׂוֹת רְצוֹן קוֹנָם וְחֵפֶץ צוּרָם. יִזְכְּרֵם אֱלֹהֵינוּ לְטוֹבָה, עִם שְׁאָר צַדִּיקֵי עוֹלָם, וְיִנְקוֹם* לְעֵינֵינוּ נִקְמַת דַּם עֲבָדָיו הַשָּׁפוּךְ, כַּכָּתוּב בְּתוֹרַת מֹשֶׁה אִישׁ הָאֱלֹהִים: הַרְנִינוּ גוֹיִם עַמּוֹ כִּי דַם עֲבָדָיו יִקּוֹם, וְנָקָם יָשִׁיב לְצָרָיו, וְכִפֶּר אַדְמָתוֹ עַמּוֹ.[1] וְעַל יְדֵי עֲבָדֶיךָ הַנְּבִיאִים כָּתוּב לֵאמֹר: וְנִקֵּיתִי דָּמָם לֹא נִקֵּיתִי, וַיהוה שֹׁכֵן בְּצִיּוֹן.[2] וּבְכִתְבֵי הַקֹּדֶשׁ נֶאֱמַר: לָמָּה יֹאמְרוּ הַגּוֹיִם, אַיֵּה אֱלֹהֵיהֶם, יִוָּדַע בַּגּוֹיִם לְעֵינֵינוּ, נִקְמַת דַּם עֲבָדֶיךָ הַשָּׁפוּךְ.[3] וְאוֹמֵר: כִּי דֹרֵשׁ דָּמִים אוֹתָם זָכָר, לֹא שָׁכַח צַעֲקַת עֲנָוִים.[4] וְאוֹמֵר: יָדִין בַּגּוֹיִם* מָלֵא גְוִיּוֹת, מָחַץ רֹאשׁ עַל אֶרֶץ רַבָּה. מִנַּחַל בַּדֶּרֶךְ יִשְׁתֶּה, עַל כֵּן יָרִים רֹאשׁ.[5]

THE *YIZKOR* SERVICE ENDS HERE.

(1) *Deuteronomy* 32:43. (2) *Joel* 4:21. (3) *Psalms* 79:10. (4) 9:13. (5) 110:6-7.

⧼ **אַב הָרַחֲמִים** — *Father of compassion.* This is a memorial prayer, as the text makes clear, for the martyrs who died to sanctify God's Name.

וְיִנְקוֹם — *May He ... exact retribution.* We do not pray that we be strong enough to avenge our martyrs; Jews are not motivated by a lust to repay violence and murder with violence and murder. Rather we pray that God choose how and when to atone for the blood of His fallen martyrs. For the living, decency and integrity remain the primary goals of social life *(R' Hirsch).*

יָדִין בַּגּוֹיִם — *He will judge the ... nations.* God intervenes against the nations who seek to

FOR MARTYRS

אֵל *O God, full of mercy, Who dwells on high, grant proper rest* on the wings of the Divine Presence* — in the lofty levels of the holy and the pure ones,* who shine like the glow of the firmament — for the souls of (all my relatives, both on my father's side and on my mother's side,) the holy and pure ones who were killed, murdered, slaughtered, burned, drowned and strangled for the sanctification of the Name, (through the hands of the German oppressors, may their name and memory be obliterated) because, without making a vow, I will contribute to charity in remembrance of their souls. May their resting place be in the Garden of Eden — therefore may the Master of mercy shelter them in the shelter of His wings for eternity; and may He bind their souls in the Bond of Life.* HASHEM *is their heritage, and may they repose in peace on their resting places. Now let us respond: Amen.*

PRAYER FOR THE RABBI

At the conclusion of the *Yizkor* service, it is customary for the *gabbai* to recite a prayer on behalf of the rabbi of the congregation.

מִי שֶׁבֵּרַךְ *He Who blessed our forefathers Abraham, Isaac and Jacob, Moses and Aaron, David and Solomon — may He bless Rabbi (*Hebrew name*) son of (*father's Hebrew name*) because he shall contribute to charity on behalf of the souls remembered today, in honor of the Omnipresent, in honor of the Torah, in honor of the Day of Judgment. As reward for this, may the Holy One, Blessed is He, protect him and rescue him from every trouble and distress, from every plague and illness; and may He send blessing and success in his every endeavor, and may he be privileged to ascend to Jerusalem for the pilgrimage, together with all Israel, his brethren. Now let us respond: Amen.*

*(*Cong. *— Amen)*

Congregation and chazzan:

אַב הָרַחֲמִים *Father of compassion,* Who dwells on high, in His powerful compassion may He recall with compassion the devout, the upright, and the perfect ones; the holy congregations who gave their lives for the Sanctification of the Name — who were beloved and pleasant in their lifetime and in their death were not parted [from God]. They were quicker than eagles and stronger than lions to do their Creator's will and their Rock's desire. May our God remember them for good with the other righteous of the world. May He, before our eyes, exact retribution* for the spilled blood of His servants, as is written in the Torah of Moses, the man of God: O nations, sing the praise of His people for He will avenge the blood of His servants and He will bring retribution upon His foes; and He will appease His land and His people.[1] And by Your servants, the prophets, it is written saying: Though I cleanse [the enemy] — their bloodshed I will not cleanse when* HASHEM *dwells in Zion.[2] And in the Holy Writings it is said: Why should the nations say, 'Where is their God?' Let there be known among the nations, before our eyes, revenge for Your servants' spilled blood.[3] And it says: For the Avenger of blood has remembered them; He has not forgotten the cry of the humble.[4] And it says: He will judge the corpse-filled nations,* He will crush the leader of the mighty land. From a river along the way he shall drink — therefore he may proudly lift his head.[5]*

THE *YIZKOR* SERVICE ENDS HERE.

---

slaughter the Jews. He turns their army into a mass of corpses and crushes their leader. Figuratively, enemy blood flows like a river from which the rescued fugitives can 'drink.' Spared from danger and shame, Israel 'may proudly lift his head.'

יה אלי

Chazzan:

יָהּ אֵלִי* וְגוֹאֲלִי אֶתְיַצְּבָה לִקְרָאתֶךָ, הָיָה וְיִהְיֶה,* הָיָה וְהֹוֶה, כָּל גּוֹי אַדְמָתֶךָ.* וְתוֹדָה,* וְלָעוֹלָה, וְלַמִּנְחָה, וְלַחַטָּאת, וְלָאָשָׁם, וְלַשְּׁלָמִים, וְלַמִּלּוּאִים כָּל קָרְבָּנֶךָ. זְכוֹר נִלְאָה* אֲשֶׁר נָשְׂאָה וְהָשִׁיבָהּ לְאַדְמָתֶךָ. סֶלָה אֲהַלְלֶךָ,* בְּאַשְׁרֵי יוֹשְׁבֵי בֵיתֶךָ.

דַּק עַל דַּק,* עַד אֵין נִבְדַּק, וְלִתְבוּנָתוֹ אֵין חֵקֶר. הָאֵל נוֹרָא, בְּאַחַת סְקִירָה,* בֵּין טוֹב לָרַע יְבַקֵּר. וְתוֹדָה, וְלָעוֹלָה, וְלַמִּנְחָה, וְלַחַטָּאת, וְלָאָשָׁם, וְלַשְּׁלָמִים, וְלַמִּלּוּאִים כָּל קָרְבָּנֶךָ. זְכוֹר נִלְאָה אֲשֶׁר נָשְׂאָה וְהָשִׁיבָהּ לְאַדְמָתֶךָ. סֶלָה אֲהַלְלֶךָ, בְּאַשְׁרֵי יוֹשְׁבֵי בֵיתֶךָ.

אֲדוֹן צְבָאוֹת,* בְּרוֹב פְּלָאוֹת, חִבֵּר כָּל אָהֳלוֹ. בִּנְתִיבוֹת לֵב לְבַלֵּב, הַצּוּר תָּמִים פָּעֳלוֹ. וְתוֹדָה, וְלָעוֹלָה, וְלַמִּנְחָה, וְלַחַטָּאת, וְלָאָשָׁם, וְלַשְּׁלָמִים, וְלַמִּלּוּאִים כָּל קָרְבָּנֶךָ. זְכוֹר נִלְאָה אֲשֶׁר נָשְׂאָה וְהָשִׁיבָהּ לְאַדְמָתֶךָ. סֶלָה אֲהַלְלֶךָ, בְּאַשְׁרֵי יוֹשְׁבֵי בֵיתֶךָ.

יָהּ אֵלִי — *O God, my God.* Since *Ashrei* is one of the most prominent of all the psalms (see p. 8), its recitation before the Festival *Mussaf* is introduced with a joyous prayer that longs for the opportunity to sing it before God in the rebuilt Temple, along with the order of sacrificial offerings. This is in keeping with the literal meaning of אַשְׁרֵי יוֹשְׁבֵי בֵיתֶךָ, *Praiseworthy are those who dwell in Your house.* Although, in the *Siddur*, God's 'house' has the broad meaning of the synagogue or any other place where one can serve God, it also refers specifically to the Temple, where the *Kohanim* and Levites have the good fortune to serve God (*Radak* and *Ibn Ezra* to *Psalms* 84:5). The spiritual elevation of the Festival, especially before *Mussaf* when we are about to cite the unique offering of the Festival, is a logical time for this prayer that combines joy in the Temple service and longing that we will soon be able to perform it in actuality as well as in aspiration. In view of the somber nature of *Yizkor*, this *piyut* is omitted on *Yizkor* days.

הָיָה וְיִהְיֶה — *Who was and Who will be.* God's Four-letter Name contains the letters that form the words indicating past, present, and future. Thus, this Name represents Him as the One Who creates and controls history — and Who will sooner or later return our service to the Temple.

כָּל גּוֹי אַדְמָתֶךָ — *With the entire nation on Your soil.* May all Israel be united in *Eretz Yisrael*, there to praise and thank God by offering all the prescribed offerings listed below.

וְתוֹדָה — *And the thanksgiving-offering.* We ask for the privilege of being in the Temple on God's soil so that we may bring Him all the offerings mentioned in the Torah.

The order of the offerings is difficult since the thanksgiving offering has less holiness than the next four on the list. Also, the meal offering consists of flour and oil, yet it is inserted between the animal offerings. Perhaps the order can be explained this way: first comes the thanksgiving offering because the very fact that we will have

PRE-MUSSAF PIYUT

Chazzan:

יָהּ אֵלִי *O God, my God* and Redeemer, I shall stand to greet You — Who was and Who will be,* Who was and Who is — with the entire nation on Your soil;* and the thanksgiving-,* elevation-, meal-, sin-, guilt-, peace-, and inauguration-offerings — Your every offering. Remember the exhausted [nation]* that won [Your favor], and return her to Your soil. Eternally will I laud You,* saying, 'Praiseworthy are those who dwell in Your House.'*

דַּק *Painstakingly exact,* beyond calculation — to His intelligence there is no limit. The awesome God — with a single stripe,* He differentiates the good from bad. And the thanksgiving-, elevation-, meal-, sin-, guilt-, peace-, and inauguration-offerings — Your every offering. Remember the exhausted [nation] that won [Your favor], and return her to Your soil. Eternally will I laud You, saying, 'Praiseworthy are those who dwell in Your House.'*

אֲדוֹן *The Lord of Legions,* with abundant miracles He connected His entire Tabernacle; in the paths of the heart may it blossom — the Rock, His work is perfect! And the thanksgiving-, elevation-, meal-, sin-, guilt-, peace-, and inauguration-offerings — Your every offering. Remember the exhausted [nation] that won [Your favor], and return her to Your soil. Eternally will I laud You, saying, 'Praiseworthy are those who dwell in Your House.'*

---

been returned to *Eretz Yisrael* and the rebuilt Temple will be cause for an enormous sense of thanksgiving. The elevation offering, which is consumed entirely on the altar, represents Israel's longing for elevation in God's service and dedication to Him; thus it takes precedence over offerings that come to atone for sin. Of the meal offering, the Sages derive from Scripture (see *Rashi, Leviticus* 2:1) that God heaps particular praise upon a poor man who can afford no more than a bit of flour and oil, yet wishes to bring an offering to express His dedication to God. The sin and guilt offerings are of greater holiness than the peace offering. The inauguration offerings are mentioned last because they will be offered only once — when the Temple is dedicated — and then will never be needed, because the Third Temple will be eternal.

וְכוֹר נְלְאָה — *Remember the exhausted [nation].* Israel has been exhausted by long exile and much travail, but she won God's favor long ago and therefore longs for her return from exile.

סֶלָה אֲהַלְלֶךָּ — *Eternally will I laud You.* This verse is a rearrangement of the first verse of *Ashrei*. It expresses our resolve to praise God by declaring our pride at being able to serve Him.

דַּק עַל דַּק — *Painstakingly exact.* This verse and the next describe the inscrutable greatness of God's awesome judgment.

בְּאַחַת סְקִירָה — *With a single stripe.* This phrase is based on the Talmudic expression that on the Day of Judgment, 'All who walk the earth pass before Him כִּבְנֵי מָרוֹן, *like young sheep' (Rosh Hashanah* 16a, 18a). When sheep were tithed, they were released one by one through a small opening in a corral. Each tenth one was marked with a single stripe, identifying it as a tithe animal that would become an Altar offering. In the context of this prayer, it refers to God differentiating between the sinful and the righteous.

צְבָאוֹת — *Legions.* God's Legions are the entire host of the universe's components. He weaves them together to create the complex harmony of Creation. We pray that realization of His greatness will blossom in our hearts so that we will recognize His greatness and be worthy to serve Him in the rebuilt Temple.

אַשְׁרֵי יוֹשְׁבֵי בֵיתֶךָ; עוֹד יְהַלְּלוּךָ סֶּלָה.[1] אַשְׁרֵי הָעָם שֶׁכָּכָה לּוֹ, אַשְׁרֵי הָעָם שֶׁיהוה אֱלֹהָיו.[2]

תהלים קמה

תְּהִלָּה לְדָוִד,

אֲרוֹמִמְךָ אֱלוֹהַי הַמֶּלֶךְ, וַאֲבָרְכָה שִׁמְךָ לְעוֹלָם וָעֶד.
בְּכָל יוֹם אֲבָרְכֶךָּ, וַאֲהַלְלָה שִׁמְךָ לְעוֹלָם וָעֶד.
גָּדוֹל יהוה וּמְהֻלָּל מְאֹד, וְלִגְדֻלָּתוֹ אֵין חֵקֶר.
דּוֹר לְדוֹר יְשַׁבַּח מַעֲשֶׂיךָ, וּגְבוּרֹתֶיךָ יַגִּידוּ.
הֲדַר כְּבוֹד הוֹדֶךָ, וְדִבְרֵי נִפְלְאֹתֶיךָ אָשִׂיחָה.
וֶעֱזוּז נוֹרְאוֹתֶיךָ יֹאמֵרוּ, וּגְדוּלָּתְךָ אֲסַפְּרֶנָּה.
זֵכֶר רַב טוּבְךָ יַבִּיעוּ, וְצִדְקָתְךָ יְרַנֵּנוּ.
חַנּוּן וְרַחוּם יהוה, אֶרֶךְ אַפַּיִם וּגְדָל חָסֶד.
טוֹב יהוה לַכֹּל, וְרַחֲמָיו עַל כָּל מַעֲשָׂיו.
יוֹדוּךָ יהוה כָּל מַעֲשֶׂיךָ, וַחֲסִידֶיךָ יְבָרְכוּכָה.
כְּבוֹד מַלְכוּתְךָ יֹאמֵרוּ, וּגְבוּרָתְךָ יְדַבֵּרוּ.
לְהוֹדִיעַ לִבְנֵי הָאָדָם גְּבוּרֹתָיו, וּכְבוֹד הֲדַר מַלְכוּתוֹ.
מַלְכוּתְךָ מַלְכוּת כָּל עֹלָמִים, וּמֶמְשַׁלְתְּךָ בְּכָל דּוֹר וָדֹר.
סוֹמֵךְ יהוה לְכָל הַנֹּפְלִים, וְזוֹקֵף לְכָל הַכְּפוּפִים.
עֵינֵי כֹל אֵלֶיךָ יְשַׂבֵּרוּ, וְאַתָּה נוֹתֵן לָהֶם אֶת אָכְלָם בְּעִתּוֹ.
פּוֹתֵחַ אֶת יָדֶךָ,
וּמַשְׂבִּיעַ לְכָל חַי רָצוֹן.

While reciting the verse פּוֹתֵחַ, concentrate intently on its meaning.

צַדִּיק יהוה בְּכָל דְּרָכָיו, וְחָסִיד בְּכָל מַעֲשָׂיו.
קָרוֹב יהוה לְכָל קֹרְאָיו, לְכֹל אֲשֶׁר יִקְרָאֻהוּ בֶאֱמֶת.
רְצוֹן יְרֵאָיו יַעֲשֶׂה, וְאֶת שַׁוְעָתָם יִשְׁמַע וְיוֹשִׁיעֵם.
שׁוֹמֵר יהוה אֶת כָּל אֹהֲבָיו, וְאֵת כָּל הָרְשָׁעִים יַשְׁמִיד.
❖ תְּהִלַּת יהוה יְדַבֶּר פִּי,
וִיבָרֵךְ כָּל בָּשָׂר שֵׁם קָדְשׁוֹ לְעוֹלָם וָעֶד.
וַאֲנַחְנוּ נְבָרֵךְ יָהּ, מֵעַתָּה וְעַד עוֹלָם, הַלְלוּיָהּ.[3]

(1) *Psalms* 84:5. (2) 144:15. (3) 115:18.

אַשְׁרֵי *Praiseworthy are those who dwell in Your house, may they always praise You, Selah!*[1] *Praiseworthy is the people for whom this is so, praiseworthy is the people whose God is* HASHEM.[2]

Psalm 145

A psalm of praise by David:

א *I will exalt You, my God the King,*
and I will bless Your Name forever and ever.
ב *Every day I will bless You,*
and I will laud Your Name forever and ever.
ג HASHEM *is great and exceedingly lauded,*
and His greatness is beyond investigation.
ד *Each generation will praise Your deeds to the next*
and of Your mighty deeds they will tell;
ה *The splendrous glory of Your power*
and Your wondrous deeds I shall discuss.
ו *And of Your awesome power they will speak,*
and Your greatness I shall relate.
ז *A recollection of Your abundant goodness they will utter*
and of Your righteousness they will sing exultantly.
ח *Gracious and merciful is* HASHEM,
slow to anger, and great in [bestowing] kindness.
ט HASHEM *is good to all; His mercies are on all His works.*
י *All Your works shall thank You,* HASHEM,
and Your devout ones will bless You.
כ *Of the glory of Your kingdom they will speak,*
and of Your power they will tell;
ל *To inform human beings of His mighty deeds,*
and the glorious splendor of His kingdom.
מ *Your kingdom is a kingdom spanning all eternities,*
and Your dominion is throughout every generation.
ס HASHEM *supports all the fallen ones and straightens all the bent.*
ע *The eyes of all look to You with hope*
and You give them their food in its proper time;
פ *You open Your hand,* Concentrate intently while reciting the verse, *'You open. . .'*
and satisfy the desire of every living thing.
צ *Righteous is* HASHEM *in all His ways*
and magnanimous in all His deeds.
ק HASHEM *is close to all who call upon Him —*
to all who call upon Him sincerely.
ר *The will of those who fear Him He will do;*
and their cry He will hear, and save them.
ש HASHEM *protects all who love Him;*
but all the wicked He will destroy.
ת Chazzan – *May my mouth declare the praise of* HASHEM
and may all flesh bless His Holy Name forever and ever.
We will bless God from this time and forever, Halleluyah![3]

הכנסת ספר תורה

The *chazzan* takes the Torah in his right arm and recites:

יְהַלְּלוּ אֶת שֵׁם יהוה, כִּי נִשְׂגָּב שְׁמוֹ לְבַדּוֹ –

Congregation responds:

– הוֹדוֹ עַל אֶרֶץ וְשָׁמָיִם. וַיָּרֶם קֶרֶן לְעַמּוֹ, תְּהִלָּה לְכָל חֲסִידָיו, לִבְנֵי יִשְׂרָאֵל עַם קְרֹבוֹ, הַלְלוּיָהּ.[1]

As the Torah is carried to the Ark the congregation recites the appropriate psalm.

ON A WEEKDAY:

תהלים כד

לְדָוִד מִזְמוֹר, לַיהוה הָאָרֶץ וּמְלוֹאָהּ, תֵּבֵל וְיִשְׁבֵי בָהּ. כִּי הוּא עַל יַמִּים יְסָדָהּ, וְעַל נְהָרוֹת יְכוֹנְנֶהָ. מִי יַעֲלֶה בְהַר יהוה, וּמִי יָקוּם בִּמְקוֹם קָדְשׁוֹ. נְקִי כַפַּיִם וּבַר לֵבָב, אֲשֶׁר לֹא נָשָׂא לַשָּׁוְא נַפְשִׁי וְלֹא נִשְׁבַּע לְמִרְמָה. יִשָּׂא בְרָכָה מֵאֵת יהוה, וּצְדָקָה מֵאֱלֹהֵי יִשְׁעוֹ. זֶה דּוֹר דֹּרְשָׁיו, מְבַקְשֵׁי פָנֶיךָ, יַעֲקֹב, סֶלָה. שְׂאוּ שְׁעָרִים רָאשֵׁיכֶם, וְהִנָּשְׂאוּ פִּתְחֵי עוֹלָם, וְיָבוֹא מֶלֶךְ הַכָּבוֹד. מִי זֶה מֶלֶךְ הַכָּבוֹד, יהוה עִזּוּז וְגִבּוֹר, יהוה גִּבּוֹר מִלְחָמָה. שְׂאוּ שְׁעָרִים רָאשֵׁיכֶם, וּשְׂאוּ פִּתְחֵי עוֹלָם, וְיָבֹא מֶלֶךְ הַכָּבוֹד. מִי הוּא זֶה מֶלֶךְ הַכָּבוֹד, יהוה צְבָאוֹת הוּא מֶלֶךְ הַכָּבוֹד, סֶלָה.

ON THE SABBATH:

תהלים כט

מִזְמוֹר לְדָוִד, הָבוּ לַיהוה בְּנֵי אֵלִים, הָבוּ לַיהוה כָּבוֹד וָעֹז. הָבוּ לַיהוה כְּבוֹד שְׁמוֹ, הִשְׁתַּחֲווּ לַיהוה בְּהַדְרַת קֹדֶשׁ. קוֹל יהוה עַל הַמָּיִם, אֵל הַכָּבוֹד הִרְעִים, יהוה עַל מַיִם רַבִּים. קוֹל יהוה בַּכֹּחַ, קוֹל יהוה בֶּהָדָר. קוֹל יהוה שֹׁבֵר אֲרָזִים, וַיְשַׁבֵּר יהוה אֶת אַרְזֵי הַלְּבָנוֹן. וַיַּרְקִידֵם כְּמוֹ עֵגֶל, לְבָנוֹן וְשִׂרְיוֹן כְּמוֹ בֶן רְאֵמִים. קוֹל יהוה חֹצֵב לַהֲבוֹת אֵשׁ. קוֹל יהוה יָחִיל מִדְבָּר, יָחִיל יהוה מִדְבַּר קָדֵשׁ. קוֹל יהוה יְחוֹלֵל אַיָּלוֹת, וַיֶּחֱשֹׂף יְעָרוֹת, וּבְהֵיכָלוֹ, כֻּלּוֹ אֹמֵר כָּבוֹד. יהוה לַמַּבּוּל יָשָׁב, וַיֵּשֶׁב יהוה מֶלֶךְ לְעוֹלָם. יהוה עֹז לְעַמּוֹ יִתֵּן, יהוה יְבָרֵךְ אֶת עַמּוֹ בַשָּׁלוֹם.

לְדָוִד מִזְמוֹר / Psalm 24

This psalm is recited when the Torah is brought back to the Ark because its final verses: *Raise up your heads, O gates* ... were recited when King Solomon brought the Ark into the newly built Temple. Commentary to this psalm appears on pages 448-449.

מִזְמוֹר לְדָוִד / Psalm 29

Tur (284) points out that the phrase *the voice of HASHEM* appears seven times in Psalm 29. This seven-fold mention alludes to: (a) the heavenly voice heard at Mount Sinai during the Giving of the Torah; and (b) the seven blessings contained in the *[Mussaf] Shemoneh Esrei* of

RETURNING THE TORAH

The *chazzan* takes the Torah in his right arm and recites:

Let them praise the Name of HASHEM, for His Name alone will have been exalted —

Congregation responds:

— His glory is above earth and heaven. And He will have exalted the pride of His people, causing praise for all His devout ones, for the Children of Israel, His intimate people. Halleluyah![1]

As the Torah is carried to the Ark the congregation recites the appropriate psalm.

ON A WEEKDAY:

Psalm 24

לְדָוִד *Of David a psalm. HASHEM's is the earth and its fullness, the inhabited land and those who dwell in it. For He founded it upon seas, and established it upon rivers. Who may ascend the mountain of HASHEM, and who may stand in the place of His sanctity? One with clean hands and pure heart, who has not sworn in vain by My soul and has not sworn deceitfully. He will receive a blessing from HASHEM and just kindness from the God of his salvation. This is the generation of those who seek Him, those who strive for Your Presence — Jacob, Selah. Raise up your heads, O gates, and be uplifted, you everlasting entrances, so that the King of Glory may enter. Who is this King of Glory? — HASHEM, the mighty and strong, HASHEM, the strong in battle. Raise up your heads, O gates, and raise up, you everlasting entrances, so that the King of Glory may enter. Who then is the King of Glory? HASHEM, Master of Legions, He is the King of Glory. Selah!*

ON THE SABBATH:

Psalm 29

מִזְמוֹר *A psalm of David. Render unto HASHEM, you sons of the powerful; render unto HASHEM, honor and might. Render unto HASHEM the honor worthy of His Name, prostrate yourselves before HASHEM in His intensely holy place. The voice of HASHEM is upon the waters, the God of Glory thunders, HASHEM is upon vast waters. The voice of HASHEM is in power! The voice of HASHEM is in majesty! The voice of HASHEM breaks the cedars, HASHEM shatters the cedars of Lebanon! He makes them prance about like a calf; Lebanon and Siryon like young re'eimim. The voice of HASHEM carves with shafts of fire. The voice of HASHEM convulses the wilderness. HASHEM convulses the wilderness of Kadesh. The voice of HASHEM frightens the hinds, and strips the forests bare; while in His Temple all proclaim, 'Glory!' HASHEM sat enthroned at the Deluge; HASHEM sits enthroned as King forever. HASHEM will give might to His people, HASHEM will bless His people with peace.*

(1) 148:13-14.

the Sabbath. Thus, it is appriopriate to recite this psalm at the time the Torah is returned to the Ark on the Sabbath just before the recitation of *Mussaf*.

As the Torah is placed into the Ark, the congregation recites the following verses:

וּבְנֻחֹה יֹאמַר, שׁוּבָה יהוה רִבְבוֹת אַלְפֵי יִשְׂרָאֵל.[1] קוּמָה יהוה לִמְנוּחָתֶךָ, אַתָּה וַאֲרוֹן עֻזֶּךָ. כֹּהֲנֶיךָ יִלְבְּשׁוּ צֶדֶק, וַחֲסִידֶיךָ יְרַנֵּנוּ. בַּעֲבוּר דָּוִד עַבְדֶּךָ, אַל תָּשֵׁב פְּנֵי מְשִׁיחֶךָ.[2] כִּי לֶקַח טוֹב נָתַתִּי לָכֶם, תּוֹרָתִי אַל תַּעֲזֹבוּ.[3] ❖ עֵץ חַיִּים הִיא לַמַּחֲזִיקִים בָּהּ, וְתֹמְכֶיהָ מְאֻשָּׁר.[4] דְּרָכֶיהָ דַרְכֵי נֹעַם, וְכָל נְתִיבוֹתֶיהָ שָׁלוֹם.[5] הֲשִׁיבֵנוּ יהוה אֵלֶיךָ וְנָשׁוּבָה, חַדֵּשׁ יָמֵינוּ כְּקֶדֶם.[6]

The *chazzan* recites חֲצִי קַדִּישׁ.

יִתְגַּדַּל וְיִתְקַדַּשׁ שְׁמֵהּ רַבָּא. (.Cong – אָמֵן.) בְּעָלְמָא דִּי בְרָא כִרְעוּתֵהּ. וְיַמְלִיךְ מַלְכוּתֵהּ, בְּחַיֵּיכוֹן וּבְיוֹמֵיכוֹן וּבְחַיֵּי דְכָל בֵּית יִשְׂרָאֵל, בַּעֲגָלָא וּבִזְמַן קָרִיב. וְאִמְרוּ: אָמֵן.

(.Cong – אָמֵן. יְהֵא שְׁמֵהּ רַבָּא מְבָרַךְ לְעָלַם וּלְעָלְמֵי עָלְמַיָּא.)

יְהֵא שְׁמֵהּ רַבָּא מְבָרַךְ לְעָלַם וּלְעָלְמֵי עָלְמַיָּא.

יִתְבָּרַךְ וְיִשְׁתַּבַּח וְיִתְפָּאַר וְיִתְרוֹמַם וְיִתְנַשֵּׂא וְיִתְהַדָּר וְיִתְעַלֶּה וְיִתְהַלָּל שְׁמֵהּ דְּקֻדְשָׁא בְּרִיךְ הוּא (.Cong – בְּרִיךְ הוּא) – לְעֵלָּא מִן כָּל בִּרְכָתָא וְשִׁירָתָא תֻּשְׁבְּחָתָא וְנֶחֱמָתָא, דַּאֲמִירָן בְּעָלְמָא. וְאִמְרוּ: אָמֵן. (.Cong – אָמֵן.)

מוסף לשני ימים האחרונים

Take three steps backward, then three steps forward. Remain standing with the feet together while reciting *Shemoneh Esrei*. Recite it with quiet devotion and without interruption, verbal or otherwise. Although its recitation should not be audible to others, one must pray loudly enough to hear himself.

כִּי שֵׁם יהוה אֶקְרָא, הָבוּ גֹדֶל לֵאלֹהֵינוּ.[7]

אֲדֹנָי שְׂפָתַי תִּפְתָּח, וּפִי יַגִּיד תְּהִלָּתֶךָ.[8]

אבות

Bend the knees at בָּרוּךְ; bow at אַתָּה; straighten up at ה׳.

בָּרוּךְ אַתָּה יהוה אֱלֹהֵינוּ וֵאלֹהֵי אֲבוֹתֵינוּ, אֱלֹהֵי אַבְרָהָם, אֱלֹהֵי יִצְחָק, וֵאלֹהֵי יַעֲקֹב, הָאֵל הַגָּדוֹל הַגִּבּוֹר וְהַנּוֹרָא, אֵל עֶלְיוֹן, גּוֹמֵל חֲסָדִים טוֹבִים וְקוֹנֵה הַכֹּל, וְזוֹכֵר חַסְדֵי אָבוֹת, וּמֵבִיא גוֹאֵל לִבְנֵי בְנֵיהֶם, לְמַעַן שְׁמוֹ בְּאַהֲבָה. מֶלֶךְ עוֹזֵר וּמוֹשִׁיעַ וּמָגֵן.

Bend the knees at בָּרוּךְ; bow at אַתָּה; straighten up at ה׳.

בָּרוּךְ אַתָּה יהוה, מָגֵן אַבְרָהָם.

גבורות

אַתָּה גִּבּוֹר לְעוֹלָם אֲדֹנָי, מְחַיֵּה מֵתִים אַתָּה, רַב לְהוֹשִׁיעַ. מְכַלְכֵּל חַיִּים בְּחֶסֶד, מְחַיֵּה מֵתִים בְּרַחֲמִים רַבִּים, סוֹמֵךְ

As the Torah is placed into the Ark, the congregation recites the following verses:

וּבְנֻחֹה *And when it rested he would say, 'Return, HASHEM, to the myriad thousands of Israel.'*[1] *Arise, HASHEM, to Your resting place, You and the Ark of Your strength. Let Your priests be clothed in righteousness, and Your devout ones will sing joyously. For the sake of David, Your servant, turn not away the face of Your anointed.*[2] *For I have given you a good teaching, do not forsake My Torah.*[3] Chazzan– *It is a tree of life for those who grasp it, and its supporters are praiseworthy.*[4] *Its ways are ways of pleasantness and all its paths are peace.*[5] *Bring us back to You, HASHEM, and we shall return, renew our days as of old.*[6]

The *chazzan* recites Half-*Kaddish:*

יִתְגַּדַּל *May His great Name grow exalted and sanctified* (Cong.– *Amen.*) *in the world that He created as He willed. May He give reign to His kingship in your lifetimes and in your days, and in the lifetimes of the entire Family of Israel, swiftly and soon. Now respond: Amen.*

(Cong.– *Amen. May His great Name be blessed forever and ever.*)

May His great Name be blessed forever and ever.

Blessed, praised, glorified, exalted, extolled, mighty, upraised, and lauded be the Name of the Holy One, Blessed is He (Cong.– *Blessed is He*) — *beyond any blessing and song, praise and consolation that are uttered in the world. Now respond: Amen.* (Cong.– *Amen*.)

MUSSAF FOR THE LAST TWO DAYS

Take three steps backward, then three steps forward. Remain standing with the feet together while reciting *Shemoneh Esrei*. Recite it with quiet devotion and without interruption, verbal or otherwise. Although its recitation should not be audible to others, one must pray loudly enough to hear himself.

When I call out the Name of HASHEM, ascribe greatness to our God.[7]

My Lord, open my lips, that my mouth may declare Your praise.[8]

PATRIARCHS

Bend the knees at *'Blessed'*; bow at *'You'*; straighten up at *'HASHEM.'*

בָּרוּךְ *Blessed are You, HASHEM, our God and the God of our forefathers, God of Abraham, God of Isaac, and God of Jacob; the great, mighty, and awesome God, the supreme God, Who bestows beneficial kindnesses and creates everything, Who recalls the kindnesses of the Patriarchs and brings a Redeemer to their children's children, for His Name's sake, with love. O King, Helper, Savior, and Shield.*

Bend the knees at *'Blessed'*; bow at *'You'*; straighten up at *'HASHEM.'*

Blessed are You, HASHEM, Shield of Abraham.

GOD'S MIGHT

אַתָּה *You are eternally mighty, my Lord, the Resuscitator of the dead are You; abundantly able to save. He sustains the living with kindness, resuscitates the dead with abundant mercy, supports the*

(1) *Numbers* 10:36. (2) *Psalms* 132:8-10. (3) *Proverbs* 4:2. (4) 3:18.
(5) 3:17. (6) *Lamentations* 5:21. (7) *Deuteronomy* 32:3. (8) *Psalms* 51:17.

נוֹפְלִים, וְרוֹפֵא חוֹלִים, וּמַתִּיר אֲסוּרִים, וּמְקַיֵּם אֱמוּנָתוֹ לִישֵׁנֵי עָפָר. מִי כָמְוֹךָ בַּעַל גְּבוּרוֹת, וּמִי דּוֹמֶה לָּךְ, מֶלֶךְ מֵמִית וּמְחַיֶּה וּמַצְמִיחַ יְשׁוּעָה. וְנֶאֱמָן אַתָּה לְהַחֲיוֹת מֵתִים. בָּרוּךְ אַתָּה יהוה, מְחַיֵּה הַמֵּתִים.

During the *chazzan's* repetition, *Kedushah* (below) is recited at this point.

קדושת השם

INDIVIDUALS RECITE:

אַתָּה קָדוֹשׁ וְשִׁמְךָ קָדוֹשׁ, וּקְדוֹשִׁים בְּכָל יוֹם יְהַלְּלְוּךָ סֶּלָה. בָּרוּךְ אַתָּה יהוה, הָאֵל הַקָּדוֹשׁ.

CHAZZAN RECITES DURING HIS REPETITION:

לְדוֹר וָדוֹר נַגִּיד גָּדְלֶךָ וּלְנֵצַח נְצָחִים קְדֻשָּׁתְךָ נַקְדִּישׁ, וְשִׁבְחֲךָ אֱלֹהֵינוּ מִפִּינוּ לֹא יָמוּשׁ לְעוֹלָם וָעֶד, כִּי אֵל מֶלֶךְ גָּדוֹל וְקָדוֹשׁ אָתָּה. בָּרוּךְ אַתָּה יהוה, הָאֵל הַקָּדוֹשׁ.

קדושת היום

אַתָּה בְחַרְתָּנוּ מִכָּל הָעַמִּים, אָהַבְתָּ אוֹתָנוּ, וְרָצִיתָ בָּנוּ, וְרוֹמַמְתָּנוּ מִכָּל הַלְּשׁוֹנוֹת, וְקִדַּשְׁתָּנוּ בְּמִצְוֹתֶיךָ, וְקֵרַבְתָּנוּ מַלְכֵּנוּ לַעֲבוֹדָתֶךָ, וְשִׁמְךָ הַגָּדוֹל וְהַקָּדוֹשׁ עָלֵינוּ קָרָאתָ.

קדושה

When reciting *Kedushah,* one must stand with his feet together, and avoid any interruptions. One should rise on his toes when saying the words קָדוֹשׁ, קָדוֹשׁ, קָדוֹשׁ; בָּרוּךְ (of בָּרוּךְ כְּבוֹד); and יִמְלֹךְ.

Cong. then *chazzan*:

נַעֲרִיצְךָ וְנַקְדִּישְׁךָ כְּסוֹד שִׂיחַ שַׂרְפֵי קֹדֶשׁ, הַמַּקְדִּישִׁים שִׁמְךָ בַּקֹּדֶשׁ, כַּכָּתוּב עַל יַד נְבִיאֶךָ, וְקָרָא זֶה אֶל זֶה וְאָמַר:

All – קָדוֹשׁ קָדוֹשׁ קָדוֹשׁ יהוה צְבָאוֹת, מְלֹא כָל הָאָרֶץ כְּבוֹדוֹ.[1] ❖ כְּבוֹדוֹ מָלֵא עוֹלָם, מְשָׁרְתָיו שׁוֹאֲלִים זֶה לָזֶה, אַיֵּה מְקוֹם כְּבוֹדוֹ, לְעֻמָּתָם בָּרוּךְ יֹאמֵרוּ:

All – בָּרוּךְ כְּבוֹד יהוה, מִמְּקוֹמוֹ.[2] ❖ מִמְּקוֹמוֹ הוּא יִפֶן בְּרַחֲמִים, וְיָחוֹן עַם הַמְּיַחֲדִים שְׁמוֹ, עֶרֶב וָבֹקֶר בְּכָל יוֹם תָּמִיד, פַּעֲמַיִם בְּאַהֲבָה שְׁמַע אוֹמְרִים.

All – שְׁמַע יִשְׂרָאֵל, יהוה אֱלֹהֵינוּ, יהוה אֶחָד.[3] ❖ הוּא אֱלֹהֵינוּ, הוּא אָבִינוּ, הוּא מַלְכֵּנוּ, הוּא מוֹשִׁיעֵנוּ, וְהוּא יַשְׁמִיעֵנוּ בְּרַחֲמָיו שֵׁנִית, לְעֵינֵי כָּל חָי, לִהְיוֹת לָכֶם לֵאלֹהִים, אֲנִי יהוה אֱלֹהֵיכֶם.[4]

All – אַדִּיר אַדִּירֵנוּ, יהוה אֲדֹנֵינוּ, מָה אַדִּיר שִׁמְךָ בְּכָל הָאָרֶץ.[5] וְהָיָה יהוה לְמֶלֶךְ עַל כָּל הָאָרֶץ, בַּיּוֹם הַהוּא יִהְיֶה יהוה אֶחָד וּשְׁמוֹ אֶחָד.[6]

Chazzan – וּבְדִבְרֵי קָדְשְׁךָ כָּתוּב לֵאמֹר:

All – יִמְלֹךְ יהוה לְעוֹלָם, אֱלֹהַיִךְ צִיּוֹן, לְדֹר וָדֹר, הַלְּלוּיָהּ.[7]

fallen, heals the sick, releases the confined, and maintains His faith to those asleep in the dust. Who is like You, O Master of mighty deeds, and who is comparable to You, O King Who causes death and restores life and makes salvation sprout! And You are faithful to resuscitate the dead. Blessed are You, HASHEM, Who resuscitates the dead.

During the *chazzan's* repetition, *Kedushah* (below) is recited at this point.

HOLINESS OF GOD'S NAME

INDIVIDUALS RECITE:

אַתָּה *You are holy and Your Name is holy, and holy ones praise You every day, forever. Blessed are You, HASHEM, the holy God.*

CHAZZAN RECITES DURING HIS REPETITION:

לְדוֹר *From generation to generation we shall relate Your greatness and for infinite eternities we shall proclaim Your holiness. Your praise, our God, shall not leave our mouth forever and ever, for You, O God, are a great and holy King. Blessed are You, HASHEM, the holy God.*

SANCTIFICATION OF THE DAY

אַתָּה בְחַרְתָּנוּ *You have chosen us from all the peoples; You loved us and found favor in us; You exalted us above all the tongues and You sanctified us with Your commandments. You drew us close, our King, to Your service and proclaimed Your great and Holy Name upon us.*

KEDUSHAH

When reciting *Kedushah*, one must stand with his feet together and avoid any interruptions. One should rise on his toes when saying the words *'Holy, holy, holy; Blessed is; HASHEM shall reign.'*

Cong. then *chazzan:*

נַעֲרִיצְךָ *We will revere You and sanctify You according to the counsel of the holy Seraphim, who sanctify Your Name in the Sanctuary, as it is written by Your prophet: "And one [angel] will call another and say:*

All – *'Holy, holy, holy is HASHEM, Master of Legions, the whole world is filled with His glory.' "*[1] ❖*His glory fills the world. His ministering angels ask one another, 'Where is the place of His glory?' Those facing them say 'Blessed':*

All – *'Blessed is the glory of HASHEM from His place.'*[2] ❖*From His place may He turn with compassion and be gracious to the people who declare the Oneness of His Name; evening and morning, every day constantly, twice, with love, they proclaim 'Shema.'*

All – *'Hear O Israel: HASHEM is our God, HASHEM the One and Only.'*[3] ❖*He is our God; He is our Father; He is our King; He is our Savior; and He will let us hear, in His compassion, for a second time in the presence of all the living,' . . . to be a God to you, I am HASHEM, your God.'*[4]

All – *Mighty is our Mighty One, HASHEM, our Master — how mighty is Your name throughout the earth!*[5] *HASHEM will be King over all the world — on that day HASHEM will be One and His Name will be One.*[6]

Chazzan – *And in Your holy Writings the following is written:*

All – *'HASHEM shall reign forever — your God, O Zion — from generation to generation, Halleluyah!'*[7]

---

(1) *Isaiah* 6:3. (2) *Ezekiel* 3:12. (3) *Deuteronomy* 6:4.
(4) *Numbers* 15:41. (5) *Psalms* 8:2. (6) *Zechariah* 14:9. (7) *Psalms* 146:10.

On the Sabbath add the words in brackets. [If forgotten, see *Laws* §86-90.]

וַתִּתֶּן לָנוּ יהוה אֱלֹהֵינוּ בְּאַהֲבָה [שַׁבָּתוֹת לִמְנוּחָה וּ]מוֹעֲדִים לְשִׂמְחָה חַגִּים וּזְמַנִּים לְשָׂשׂוֹן, אֶת יוֹם [הַשַּׁבָּת הַזֶּה וְאֶת יוֹם] חַג הַמַּצּוֹת הַזֶּה, זְמַן חֵרוּתֵנוּ [בְּאַהֲבָה] מִקְרָא קֹדֶשׁ, זֵכֶר לִיצִיאַת מִצְרָיִם.

וּמִפְּנֵי חֲטָאֵינוּ גָּלִינוּ מֵאַרְצֵנוּ, וְנִתְרַחַקְנוּ מֵעַל אַדְמָתֵנוּ. וְאֵין אֲנַחְנוּ יְכוֹלִים לַעֲלוֹת וְלֵרָאוֹת וּלְהִשְׁתַּחֲוֹת לְפָנֶיךָ, וְלַעֲשׂוֹת חוֹבוֹתֵינוּ בְּבֵית בְּחִירָתֶךָ, בַּבַּיִת הַגָּדוֹל וְהַקָּדוֹשׁ שֶׁנִּקְרָא שִׁמְךָ עָלָיו, מִפְּנֵי הַיָּד שֶׁנִּשְׁתַּלְּחָה בְּמִקְדָּשֶׁךָ. יְהִי רָצוֹן מִלְּפָנֶיךָ יהוה אֱלֹהֵינוּ וֵאלֹהֵי אֲבוֹתֵינוּ, מֶלֶךְ רַחֲמָן, שֶׁתָּשׁוּב וּתְרַחֵם עָלֵינוּ וְעַל מִקְדָּשְׁךָ בְּרַחֲמֶיךָ הָרַבִּים, וְתִבְנֵהוּ מְהֵרָה וּתְגַדֵּל כְּבוֹדוֹ. אָבִינוּ מַלְכֵּנוּ, גַּלֵּה כְּבוֹד מַלְכוּתְךָ עָלֵינוּ מְהֵרָה, וְהוֹפַע וְהִנָּשֵׂא עָלֵינוּ לְעֵינֵי כָּל חָי. וְקָרֵב פְּזוּרֵינוּ מִבֵּין הַגּוֹיִם, וּנְפוּצוֹתֵינוּ כַּנֵּס מִיַּרְכְּתֵי אָרֶץ. וַהֲבִיאֵנוּ לְצִיּוֹן עִירְךָ בְּרִנָּה, וְלִירוּשָׁלַיִם בֵּית מִקְדָּשְׁךָ בְּשִׂמְחַת עוֹלָם. וְשָׁם נַעֲשֶׂה לְפָנֶיךָ אֶת קָרְבְּנוֹת חוֹבוֹתֵינוּ, תְּמִידִים כְּסִדְרָם, וּמוּסָפִים כְּהִלְכָתָם. וְאֶת [Weekdays– מוּסַף יוֹם] [Sabbath– מוּסְפֵי יוֹם הַשַּׁבָּת הַזֶּה וְיוֹם] חַג הַמַּצּוֹת הַזֶּה נַעֲשֶׂה וְנַקְרִיב לְפָנֶיךָ בְּאַהֲבָה כְּמִצְוַת רְצוֹנֶךָ, כְּמוֹ שֶׁכָּתַבְתָּ עָלֵינוּ בְּתוֹרָתֶךָ, עַל יְדֵי מֹשֶׁה עַבְדֶּךָ, מִפִּי כְבוֹדֶךָ כָּאָמוּר:

On the Sabbath add. [If forgotten, do not repeat *Shemoneh Esrei*. See *Laws* §86.]

וּבְיוֹם הַשַּׁבָּת שְׁנֵי כְבָשִׂים בְּנֵי שָׁנָה תְּמִימִם, וּשְׁנֵי עֶשְׂרֹנִים סֹלֶת מִנְחָה בְּלוּלָה בַשֶּׁמֶן, וְנִסְכּוֹ. עֹלַת שַׁבַּת בְּשַׁבַּתּוֹ, עַל עֹלַת הַתָּמִיד וְנִסְכָּהּ.[1] (זֶה קָרְבַּן שַׁבָּת. וְקָרְבַּן הַיּוֹם כָּאָמוּר:)

וְהִקְרַבְתֶּם אִשֶּׁה עֹלָה לַיהוה, פָּרִים בְּנֵי בָקָר שְׁנַיִם, וְאַיִל אֶחָד, וְשִׁבְעָה כְבָשִׂים בְּנֵי שָׁנָה, תְּמִימִם יִהְיוּ לָכֶם.[2] וּמִנְחָתָם וְנִסְכֵּיהֶם כִּמְדֻבָּר, שְׁלֹשָׁה עֶשְׂרֹנִים לַפָּר, וּשְׁנֵי עֶשְׂרֹנִים לָאָיִל, וְעִשָּׂרוֹן לַכֶּבֶשׂ, וְיַיִן כְּנִסְכּוֹ. וְשָׂעִיר לְכַפֵּר, וּשְׁנֵי תְמִידִים כְּהִלְכָתָם.

On the Sabbath add the words in brackets. [If forgotten, see *Laws* §86-90.]

וַתִּתֶּן לָנוּ *And You gave us, Hashem, our God, with love [Sabbaths for rest], appointed festivals for gladness, Festivals and times for joy, [this day of Sabbath and] this day of the Festival of Matzos, the time of our freedom [with love], a holy convocation, a memorial of the Exodus from Egypt.*

וּמִפְּנֵי חֲטָאֵינוּ *But because of our sins we have been exiled from our land and sent far from our soil. We cannot ascend to appear and to prostrate ourselves before You, and to perform our obligations in the House of Your choice, in the great and holy House upon which Your Name was proclaimed, because of the hand that was dispatched against Your Sanctuary. May it be Your will, Hashem, our God and the God of our forefathers, O merciful King, that You once more be compassionate upon us and upon Your Sanctuary in Your abundant mercy, and rebuild it soon and magnify its glory. Our Father, our King, reveal the glory of Your Kingship upon us, speedily; appear and be uplifted over us before the eyes of all the living. Draw our scattered ones near from among the nations, and bring in our dispersions from the ends of the earth. Bring us to Zion, Your City, in glad song, and to Jerusalem, home of Your Sanctuary, in eternal joy. There we will perform before You our obligatory offerings, the continual offerings according to their order and the additional offerings according to their law. And the additional offering[s of this day of Sabbath and] of this day of the Festival of Matzos, we will perform and bring near to You with love, according to the commandment of Your will, as You have written for us in Your Torah, through Moses, Your servant, from Your glorious expression, as it is said:*

On the Sabbath add. [If forgotten, do not repeat *Shemoneh Esrei.* See *Laws* §86.]

וּבְיוֹם הַשַּׁבָּת *On the Sabbath day: two [male] first-year lambs, unblemished; and two tenth-ephah of fine flour for a meal-offering, mixed with olive oil, and its wine-libation. The elevation-offering of the Sabbath must be on its particular Sabbath, in addition to the continual elevation-offering and its wine-libation.[1] (This is the offering of the Sabbath. And the offering of the day is as it is said:)*

וְהִקְרַבְתֶּם *You are to bring a fire-offering, an elevation-offering to Hashem, two young bulls, one ram and seven male lambs in their first year, they shall be unblemished for you.[2] And their meal-offerings and their wine-libations as mentioned: three tenth-ephah for each bull; two tenth-ephah for each ram; one tenth-ephah for each lamb; and wine for its libation. A he-goat for atonement, and two continual offerings according to their law.*

(1) *Numbers* 28:9-10. (2) 28:19.

On the Sabbath add. [If forgotten, do not repeat *Shemoneh Esrei.* See *Laws* §86.]

יִשְׂמְחוּ בְמַלְכוּתְךָ שׁוֹמְרֵי שַׁבָּת וְקוֹרְאֵי עֹנֶג, עַם מְקַדְּשֵׁי שְׁבִיעִי, כֻּלָּם יִשְׂבְּעוּ וְיִתְעַנְּגוּ מִטּוּבֶךָ, וּבַשְּׁבִיעִי רָצִיתָ בּוֹ וְקִדַּשְׁתּוֹ, חֶמְדַּת יָמִים אֹתוֹ קָרָאתָ, זֵכֶר לְמַעֲשֵׂה בְרֵאשִׁית.

On the Sabbath add the words in brackets. [If forgotten, see *Laws* §86-90.]

אֱלֹהֵינוּ וֵאלֹהֵי אֲבוֹתֵינוּ, [רְצֵה בִמְנוּחָתֵנוּ] מֶלֶךְ רַחֲמָן רַחֵם עָלֵינוּ, טוֹב וּמֵטִיב הִדָּרֶשׁ לָנוּ, שׁוּבָה אֵלֵינוּ בַּהֲמוֹן רַחֲמֶיךָ, בִּגְלַל אָבוֹת שֶׁעָשׂוּ רְצוֹנֶךָ. בְּנֵה בֵיתְךָ כְּבַתְּחִלָּה, וְכוֹנֵן מִקְדָּשְׁךָ עַל מְכוֹנוֹ, וְהַרְאֵנוּ בְּבִנְיָנוֹ, וְשַׂמְּחֵנוּ בְּתִקּוּנוֹ. וְהָשֵׁב כֹּהֲנִים לַעֲבוֹדָתָם, וּלְוִיִּם לְשִׁירָם וּלְזִמְרָם, וְהָשֵׁב יִשְׂרָאֵל לִנְוֵיהֶם. וְשָׁם נַעֲלֶה וְנֵרָאֶה וְנִשְׁתַּחֲוֶה לְפָנֶיךָ, בְּשָׁלֹשׁ פַּעֲמֵי רְגָלֵינוּ, כַּכָּתוּב בְּתוֹרָתֶךָ: שָׁלוֹשׁ פְּעָמִים בַּשָּׁנָה, יֵרָאֶה כָל זְכוּרְךָ אֶת פְּנֵי יהוה אֱלֹהֶיךָ, בַּמָּקוֹם אֲשֶׁר יִבְחָר, בְּחַג הַמַּצּוֹת, וּבְחַג הַשָּׁבֻעוֹת, וּבְחַג הַסֻּכּוֹת, וְלֹא יֵרָאֶה אֶת פְּנֵי יהוה רֵיקָם. אִישׁ כְּמַתְּנַת יָדוֹ, כְּבִרְכַּת יהוה אֱלֹהֶיךָ, אֲשֶׁר נָתַן לָךְ:[1]

On the Sabbath add the words in brackets. [If forgotten, see *Laws* §86-90.]

וְהַשִּׂיאֵנוּ יהוה אֱלֹהֵינוּ אֶת בִּרְכַּת מוֹעֲדֶיךָ לְחַיִּים וּלְשָׁלוֹם, לְשִׂמְחָה וּלְשָׂשׂוֹן, כַּאֲשֶׁר רָצִיתָ וְאָמַרְתָּ לְבָרְכֵנוּ. [אֱלֹהֵינוּ וֵאלֹהֵי אֲבוֹתֵינוּ רְצֵה בִמְנוּחָתֵנוּ] קַדְּשֵׁנוּ בְּמִצְוֹתֶיךָ וְתֵן חֶלְקֵנוּ בְּתוֹרָתֶךָ, שַׂבְּעֵנוּ מִטּוּבֶךָ וְשַׂמְּחֵנוּ בִּישׁוּעָתֶךָ, וְטַהֵר לִבֵּנוּ לְעָבְדְּךָ בֶּאֱמֶת, וְהַנְחִילֵנוּ יהוה אֱלֹהֵינוּ [בְּאַהֲבָה וּבְרָצוֹן] בְּשִׂמְחָה וּבְשָׂשׂוֹן [שַׁבָּת וּ]מוֹעֲדֵי קָדְשֶׁךָ, וְיִשְׂמְחוּ בְךָ יִשְׂרָאֵל מְקַדְּשֵׁי שְׁמֶךָ. בָּרוּךְ אַתָּה יהוה, מְקַדֵּשׁ [הַשַּׁבָּת וְ]יִשְׂרָאֵל וְהַזְּמַנִּים.

עבודה

רְצֵה יהוה אֱלֹהֵינוּ בְּעַמְּךָ יִשְׂרָאֵל וּבִתְפִלָּתָם, וְהָשֵׁב אֶת הָעֲבוֹדָה לִדְבִיר בֵּיתֶךָ. וְאִשֵּׁי יִשְׂרָאֵל וּתְפִלָּתָם בְּאַהֲבָה תְקַבֵּל בְּרָצוֹן, וּתְהִי לְרָצוֹן תָּמִיד עֲבוֹדַת יִשְׂרָאֵל עַמֶּךָ.

WHEN THE *KOHANIM* ASCEND THE *DUCHAN* TO PRONOUNCE *BIRCAS KOHANIM* [THE PRIESTLY BLESSING], THE *CHAZZAN'S* REPETITION CONTINUES ON PAGE 1012.

On the Sabbath add. [If forgotten, do not repeat *Shemoneh Esrei.* See *Laws* §86.]

יִשְׂמְחוּ *They shall rejoice in Your Kingship — those who observe the Sabbath and call it a delight. The people that sanctifies the Seventh — they will all be satisfied and delighted from Your goodness. And the Seventh — You found favor in it and sanctified it. 'Most coveted of days' You called it, a remembrance of creation.*

On the Sabbath add the words in brackets. [If forgotten, see *Laws* §86-90.]

אֱלֹהֵינוּ *Our God and the God of our forefathers, [may You be pleased with our rest] O merciful King, have mercy on us; O good and beneficent One, let Yourself be sought out by us; return to us in Your yearning mercy for the sake of the forefathers who did Your will. Rebuild Your House as it was at first, and establish Your Sanctuary on its prepared site; show us its rebuilding and gladden us in its perfection. Restore the Kohanim to their service and the Levites to their song and music; and restore Israel to their dwellings. And there we will ascend and appear and prostrate ourselves before You, during our three pilgrimage seasons, as it is written in Your Torah: Three times a year all your males are to appear before HASHEM, your God, in the place He shall choose, on the Festival of Matzos, on the Festival of Shavuos, and on the Festival of Succos, and they shall not appear before HASHEM empty-handed. Every man according to the gift of his hand, according to the blessing of HASHEM, your God, that He gave you.*[1]

On the Sabbath add the words in brackets. [If forgotten, see *Laws* §86-90.]

וְהַשִּׂיאֵנוּ *Bestow upon us, O HASHEM, our God, the blessing of Your appointed Festivals for life and for peace, for gladness and for joy, as You desired and promised to bless us. [Our God and the God of our forefathers, may You be pleased with our rest.] Sanctify us with Your commandments and grant us our share in Your Torah; satisfy us from Your goodness and gladden us with Your salvation, and purify our heart to serve You sincerely. And grant us a heritage, O HASHEM, our God — [with love and with favor] with gladness and with joy — [the Sabbath and] the appointed festivals of Your holiness, and may Israel, the sanctifiers of Your Name, rejoice in You. Blessed are You, HASHEM, Who sanctifies [the Sabbath] Israel and the festive seasons.*

TEMPLE SERVICE

רְצֵה *Be favorable, HASHEM, our God, toward Your people Israel and their prayer and restore the service to the Holy of Holies of Your Temple. The fire-offerings of Israel and their prayer accept with love and favor, and may the service of Your people Israel always be favorable to You.*

WHEN THE *KOHANIM* ASCEND THE *DUCHAN* TO PRONOUNCE *BIRCAS KOHANIM* [THE PRIESTLY BLESSING], THE *CHAZZAN'S* REPETITION CONTINUES ON PAGE 1012.

(1) *Deuteronomy* 16:16-17.

If no *Kohen* is present, the *chazzan* continues here.

וְתֶחֱזֶינָה עֵינֵינוּ בְּשׁוּבְךָ לְצִיּוֹן בְּרַחֲמִים. בָּרוּךְ אַתָּה יהוה, הַמַּחֲזִיר שְׁכִינָתוֹ לְצִיּוֹן.

הודאה

Bow at מוֹדִים; straighten up at ה׳. In his repetition the *chazzan* should recite the entire מוֹדִים aloud, while the congregation recites מוֹדִים דְּרַבָּנָן softly.

מוֹדִים אֲנַחְנוּ לָךְ, שָׁאַתָּה הוּא יהוה אֱלֹהֵינוּ וֵאלֹהֵי אֲבוֹתֵינוּ לְעוֹלָם וָעֶד. צוּר חַיֵּינוּ, מָגֵן יִשְׁעֵנוּ אַתָּה הוּא לְדוֹר וָדוֹר. נוֹדֶה לְּךָ וּנְסַפֵּר תְּהִלָּתֶךָ[1] עַל חַיֵּינוּ הַמְּסוּרִים בְּיָדֶךָ, וְעַל נִשְׁמוֹתֵינוּ הַפְּקוּדוֹת לָךְ, וְעַל נִסֶּיךָ שֶׁבְּכָל יוֹם עִמָּנוּ, וְעַל נִפְלְאוֹתֶיךָ וְטוֹבוֹתֶיךָ שֶׁבְּכָל עֵת, עֶרֶב וָבֹקֶר וְצָהֳרָיִם. הַטּוֹב כִּי לֹא כָלוּ רַחֲמֶיךָ, וְהַמְּרַחֵם כִּי לֹא תַמּוּ חֲסָדֶיךָ,[2] מֵעוֹלָם קִוִּינוּ לָךְ.

מודים דרבנן

מוֹדִים אֲנַחְנוּ לָךְ, שָׁאַתָּה הוּא יהוה אֱלֹהֵינוּ וֵאלֹהֵי אֲבוֹתֵינוּ, אֱלֹהֵי כָל בָּשָׂר, יוֹצְרֵנוּ, יוֹצֵר בְּרֵאשִׁית. בְּרָכוֹת וְהוֹדָאוֹת לְשִׁמְךָ הַגָּדוֹל וְהַקָּדוֹשׁ, עַל שֶׁהֶחֱיִיתָנוּ וְקִיַּמְתָּנוּ. כֵּן תְּחַיֵּנוּ וּתְקַיְּמֵנוּ, וְתֶאֱסוֹף גָּלֻיּוֹתֵינוּ לְחַצְרוֹת קָדְשֶׁךָ, לִשְׁמוֹר חֻקֶּיךָ וְלַעֲשׂוֹת רְצוֹנֶךָ, וּלְעָבְדְּךָ בְּלֵבָב שָׁלֵם, עַל שֶׁאֲנַחְנוּ מוֹדִים לָךְ. בָּרוּךְ אֵל הַהוֹדָאוֹת.

וְעַל כֻּלָּם יִתְבָּרַךְ וְיִתְרוֹמַם שִׁמְךָ מַלְכֵּנוּ תָּמִיד לְעוֹלָם וָעֶד.

Bend the knees at בָּרוּךְ; bow at אַתָּה; straighten up at ה׳.

וְכֹל הַחַיִּים יוֹדוּךָ סֶּלָה, וִיהַלְלוּ אֶת שִׁמְךָ בֶּאֱמֶת, הָאֵל יְשׁוּעָתֵנוּ וְעֶזְרָתֵנוּ סֶלָה. בָּרוּךְ אַתָּה יהוה, הַטּוֹב שִׁמְךָ וּלְךָ נָאֶה לְהוֹדוֹת.

ברכת כהנים

If the *Kohanim* do not ascend the *duchan*, the *chazzan* recites the following during his repetition. He faces right at וְיִשְׁמְרֶךָ; faces left at אֵלֶיךָ וִיחֻנֶּךָּ; faces the Ark for the rest of the blessings.

אֱלֹהֵינוּ, וֵאלֹהֵי אֲבוֹתֵינוּ, בָּרְכֵנוּ בַבְּּרָכָה הַמְּשֻׁלֶּשֶׁת בַּתּוֹרָה הַכְּתוּבָה עַל יְדֵי מֹשֶׁה עַבְדֶּךָ, הָאֲמוּרָה מִפִּי אַהֲרֹן וּבָנָיו, כֹּהֲנִים עַם קְדוֹשֶׁךָ, כָּאָמוּר:

יְבָרֶכְךָ יהוה, וְיִשְׁמְרֶךָ. (Cong. – כֵּן יְהִי רָצוֹן.)

יָאֵר יהוה פָּנָיו אֵלֶיךָ וִיחֻנֶּךָּ. (Cong. – כֵּן יְהִי רָצוֹן.)

יִשָּׂא יהוה פָּנָיו אֵלֶיךָ וְיָשֵׂם לְךָ שָׁלוֹם.[3] (Cong. – כֵּן יְהִי רָצוֹן.)

If no *Kohen* is present, the *chazzan* continues here.

וְתֶחֱזֶינָה *May our eyes behold Your return to Zion in compassion. Blessed are You, HASHEM, Who restores His Presence to Zion.*

THANKSGIVING [MODIM]

Bow at *'We gratefully thank You'*; straighten up at *'HASHEM.'* In his repetition the *chazzan* should recite the entire *Modim* aloud, while the congregation recites *Modim of the Rabbis* softly.

מוֹדִים *We gratefully thank You, for it is You Who are HASHEM, our God and the God of our forefathers for all eternity; Rock of our lives, Shield of our salvation are You from generation to generation. We shall thank You and relate Your praise[1] — for our lives, which are committed to Your power and for our souls that are entrusted to You; for Your miracles that are with us every day; and for Your wonders and favors in every season — evening, morning, and afternoon. The Beneficent One, for Your compassions were never exhausted, and the Compassionate One, for Your kindnesses never ended[2] — always have we put our hope in You.*

MODIM OF THE RABBIS

מוֹדִים *We gratefully thank You, for it is You Who are HASHEM, our God and the God of our forefathers, the God of all flesh, our Molder, the Molder of the universe. Blessings and thanks are due Your great and holy Name for You have given us life and sustained us. So may You continue to give us life and sustain us and gather our exiles to the Courtyards of Your Sanctuary, to observe Your decrees, to do Your will and to serve You wholeheartedly. [We thank You] for inspiring us to thank You. Blessed is the God of thanksgivings.*

For all these, may Your Name be blessed and exalted, our King, continually forever and ever.

Bend the knees at *'Blessed'*; bow at *'You'*; straighten up at *'HASHEM.'*

Everything alive will gratefully acknowledge You, Selah! and praise Your Name sincerely, O God of our salvation and help, Selah! Blessed are You, HASHEM, Your Name is 'The Beneficent One' and to You it is fitting to give thanks.

THE PRIESTLY BLESSING

If the *Kohanim* do not ascend the *duchan*, the *chazzan* recites the following during his repetition.

אֱלֹהֵינוּ *Our God and the God of our forefathers, bless us with the three-verse blessing in the Torah that was written by the hand of Moses, Your servant, that was said by Aaron and his sons, the Kohanim, Your holy people, as it is said:*

May HASHEM bless you and safeguard you. (Cong.— *So may it be.*)

May HASHEM illuminate His countenance for you and be gracious to you. (Cong.— *So may it be.*)

May HASHEM turn His countenance to you and establish peace for you.[3] (Cong.— *So may it be.*)

(1) Cf. *Psalms* 79:13. (2) Cf. *Lamentations* 3:22. (3) *Numbers* 6:24-26.

שלום

שִׂים שָׁלוֹם, טוֹבָה, וּבְרָכָה, חֵן, וָחֶסֶד וְרַחֲמִים עָלֵינוּ וְעַל כָּל יִשְׂרָאֵל עַמֶּךָ. בָּרְכֵנוּ אָבִינוּ, כֻּלָּנוּ כְּאֶחָד בְּאוֹר פָּנֶיךָ, כִּי בְאוֹר פָּנֶיךָ נָתַתָּ לָּנוּ, יהוה אֱלֹהֵינוּ, תּוֹרַת חַיִּים וְאַהֲבַת חֶסֶד, וּצְדָקָה, וּבְרָכָה, וְרַחֲמִים, וְחַיִּים, וְשָׁלוֹם. וְטוֹב בְּעֵינֶיךָ לְבָרֵךְ אֶת עַמְּךָ יִשְׂרָאֵל, בְּכָל עֵת וּבְכָל שָׁעָה בִּשְׁלוֹמֶךָ. בָּרוּךְ אַתָּה יהוה, הַמְּבָרֵךְ אֶת עַמּוֹ יִשְׂרָאֵל בַּשָּׁלוֹם.

יִהְיוּ לְרָצוֹן אִמְרֵי פִי וְהֶגְיוֹן לִבִּי לְפָנֶיךָ, יהוה צוּרִי וְגֹאֲלִי.[1]

The *chazzan's* repetition of *Shemoneh Esrei* ends here.
Individuals continue below:

אֱלֹהַי, נְצוֹר לְשׁוֹנִי מֵרָע, וּשְׂפָתַי מִדַּבֵּר מִרְמָה,[2] וְלִמְקַלְלַי נַפְשִׁי תִדּוֹם, וְנַפְשִׁי כֶּעָפָר לַכֹּל תִּהְיֶה. פְּתַח לִבִּי בְּתוֹרָתֶךָ, וּבְמִצְוֹתֶיךָ תִּרְדּוֹף נַפְשִׁי. וְכֹל הַחוֹשְׁבִים עָלַי רָעָה, מְהֵרָה הָפֵר עֲצָתָם וְקַלְקֵל מַחֲשַׁבְתָּם. עֲשֵׂה לְמַעַן שְׁמֶךָ, עֲשֵׂה לְמַעַן יְמִינֶךָ, עֲשֵׂה לְמַעַן קְדֻשָּׁתֶךָ, עֲשֵׂה לְמַעַן תּוֹרָתֶךָ. לְמַעַן יֵחָלְצוּן יְדִידֶיךָ, הוֹשִׁיעָה יְמִינְךָ וַעֲנֵנִי.[3]

Some recite verses pertaining to their names here. See page 1143.

יִהְיוּ לְרָצוֹן אִמְרֵי פִי וְהֶגְיוֹן לִבִּי לְפָנֶיךָ, יהוה צוּרִי וְגֹאֲלִי.[1]

Bow and take three steps back. Bow left and say . . . עֹשֶׂה; bow right and say . . . הוּא יַעֲשֶׂה; bow forward and say וְעַל כָּל . . . אָמֵן.

עֹשֶׂה שָׁלוֹם בִּמְרוֹמָיו, הוּא יַעֲשֶׂה שָׁלוֹם עָלֵינוּ, וְעַל כָּל יִשְׂרָאֵל. וְאִמְרוּ: אָמֵן.

יְהִי רָצוֹן מִלְּפָנֶיךָ יהוה אֱלֹהֵינוּ וֵאלֹהֵי אֲבוֹתֵינוּ, שֶׁיִּבָּנֶה בֵּית הַמִּקְדָּשׁ בִּמְהֵרָה בְיָמֵינוּ, וְתֵן חֶלְקֵנוּ בְּתוֹרָתֶךָ. וְשָׁם נַעֲבָדְךָ בְּיִרְאָה, כִּימֵי עוֹלָם וּכְשָׁנִים קַדְמוֹנִיּוֹת. וְעָרְבָה לַיהוה מִנְחַת יְהוּדָה וִירוּשָׁלָיִם, כִּימֵי עוֹלָם וּכְשָׁנִים קַדְמוֹנִיּוֹת.[4]

THE INDIVIDUAL'S RECITATION OF *SHEMONEH ESREI* ENDS HERE.

The individual remains standing in place until the *chazzan* reaches *Kedushah* — or at least until the *chazzan* begins his repetition — then he takes three steps forward. The *chazzan* himself, or one praying alone, should remain in place for at least a few moments before taking three steps forward.

PEACE

שִׂים שָׁלוֹם *Establish peace, goodness, blessing, graciousness, kindness, and compassion upon us and upon all of Your people Israel. Bless us, our Father, all of us as one, with the light of Your countenance, for with the light of Your countenance You gave us, HASHEM, our God, the Torah of life and a love of kindness, righteousness, blessing, compassion, life, and peace. And may it be good in Your eyes to bless Your people Israel at every time and every hour with Your peace. Blessed are You, HASHEM, Who blesses His people Israel with peace.*

May the expressions of my mouth and the thoughts of my heart find favor before You, HASHEM, my Rock and my Redeemer.[1]

The *chazzan's* repetition of *Shemoneh Esrei* ends here.
Individuals continue below:

אֱלֹהַי *My God, guard my tongue from evil and my lips from speaking deceitfully.*[2] *To those who curse me, let my soul be silent; and let my soul be like dust to everyone. Open my heart to Your Torah, then my soul will pursue Your commandments. As for all those who design evil against me, speedily nullify their counsel and disrupt their design. Act for Your Name's sake; act for Your right hand's sake; act for Your sanctity's sake; act for Your Torah's sake. That Your beloved ones may be given rest; let Your right hand save, and respond to me.*[3]

Some recite verses pertaining to their names at this point. See page 1143.

May the expressions of my mouth and the thoughts of my heart find favor before You, HASHEM, my Rock and my Redeemer.[1] *He Who makes peace in His heights, may He make peace upon us, and upon all Israel. Now respond: Amen.*

Bow and take three steps back. Bow left and say, *'He Who makes peace . . .'*; bow right and say, *'may He make peace . . .'*; bow forward and say, *'and upon . . . Amen.'*

יְהִי רָצוֹן *May it be Your will, HASHEM, our God and the God of our forefathers, that the Holy Temple be rebuilt, speedily in our days. Grant us our share in Your Torah, and may we serve You there with reverence, as in days of old and in former years. Then the offering of Judah and Jerusalem will be pleasing to HASHEM, as in days of old and in former years.*[4]

THE INDIVIDUAL'S RECITATION OF *SHEMONEH ESREI* ENDS HERE.

The individual remains standing in place until the *chazzan* reaches *Kedushah* — or at least until the *chazzan* begins his repetition — then he takes three steps forward. The *chazzan* himself, or one praying alone, should remain in place for at least a few moments before taking three steps forward.

(1) *Psalms* 19:15. (2) Cf. 34:14. (3) 60:7; 108:7. (4) *Malachi* 3:4.

ברכת כהנים

Congregation and *Kohanim,* then *chazzan.*

וְתֶעֱרַב לְפָנֶיךָ עֲתִירָתֵנוּ כְּעוֹלָה וּכְקָרְבָּן. אָנָּא, רַחוּם, בְּרַחֲמֶיךָ הָרַבִּים הָשֵׁב שְׁכִינָתְךָ לְצִיּוֹן עִירֶךָ, וְסֵדֶר הָעֲבוֹדָה לִירוּשָׁלָיִם. וְתֶחֱזֶינָה עֵינֵינוּ בְּשׁוּבְךָ לְצִיּוֹן בְּרַחֲמִים, וְשָׁם נַעֲבָדְךָ בְּיִרְאָה כִּימֵי עוֹלָם וּכְשָׁנִים קַדְמוֹנִיּוֹת.

Chazzan concludes:

בָּרוּךְ אַתָּה יהוה, שֶׁאוֹתְךָ לְבַדְּךָ בְּיִרְאָה נַעֲבוֹד.

(–Cong. and *Kohanim* אָמֵן.)

הודאה

The *chazzan* recites the entire מודים aloud, while the congregation recites מודים דְּרַבָּנָן softly. Bow at מודים; straighten up at 'ה.

מוֹדִים אֲנַחְנוּ לָךְ, שָׁאַתָּה הוּא יהוה אֱלֹהֵינוּ וֵאלֹהֵי אֲבוֹתֵינוּ לְעוֹלָם וָעֶד. צוּר חַיֵּינוּ, מָגֵן יִשְׁעֵנוּ אַתָּה הוּא לְדוֹר וָדוֹר. נוֹדֶה לְּךָ וּנְסַפֵּר תְּהִלָּתֶךָ[1] עַל חַיֵּינוּ הַמְּסוּרִים בְּיָדֶךָ, וְעַל נִשְׁמוֹתֵינוּ הַפְּקוּדוֹת לָךְ, וְעַל נִסֶּיךָ שֶׁבְּכָל יוֹם עִמָּנוּ, וְעַל נִפְלְאוֹתֶיךָ וְטוֹבוֹתֶיךָ שֶׁבְּכָל עֵת, עֶרֶב וָבֹקֶר וְצָהֳרָיִם. הַטּוֹב כִּי לֹא כָלוּ רַחֲמֶיךָ, וְהַמְּרַחֵם כִּי לֹא תַמּוּ חֲסָדֶיךָ,[2] מֵעוֹלָם קִוִּינוּ לָךְ.

מודים דרבנן

מוֹדִים אֲנַחְנוּ לָךְ, שָׁאַתָּה הוּא יהוה אֱלֹהֵינוּ וֵאלֹהֵי אֲבוֹתֵינוּ, אֱלֹהֵי כָל בָּשָׂר, יוֹצְרֵנוּ, יוֹצֵר בְּרֵאשִׁית. בְּרָכוֹת וְהוֹדָאוֹת לְשִׁמְךָ הַגָּדוֹל וְהַקָּדוֹשׁ, עַל שֶׁהֶחֱיִיתָנוּ וְקִיַּמְתָּנוּ. כֵּן תְּחַיֵּנוּ וּתְקַיְּמֵנוּ, וְתֶאֱסוֹף גָּלֻיּוֹתֵינוּ לְחַצְרוֹת קָדְשֶׁךָ, לִשְׁמוֹר חֻקֶּיךָ וְלַעֲשׂוֹת רְצוֹנֶךָ, וּלְעָבְדְּךָ בְּלֵבָב שָׁלֵם, עַל שֶׁאֲנַחְנוּ מוֹדִים לָךְ. בָּרוּךְ אֵל הַהוֹדָאוֹת.

וְעַל כֻּלָּם יִתְבָּרַךְ וְיִתְרוֹמַם שִׁמְךָ מַלְכֵּנוּ תָּמִיד לְעוֹלָם וָעֶד.

The *chazzan* bends his knees at בָּרוּךְ; bows at אַתָּה; and straightens up at 'ה. When the *chazzan* recites וְכֹל הַחַיִּים, the *Kohanim* recite יְהִי רָצוֹן.

וְכֹל הַחַיִּים יוֹדוּךָ סֶּלָה, וִיהַלְלוּ אֶת שִׁמְךָ בֶּאֱמֶת, הָאֵל יְשׁוּעָתֵנוּ וְעֶזְרָתֵנוּ סֶלָה. בָּרוּךְ אַתָּה יהוה, הַטּוֹב שִׁמְךָ וּלְךָ נָאֶה לְהוֹדוֹת. (–Cong. and *Kohanim* אָמֵן.)

יְהִי רָצוֹן מִלְּפָנֶיךָ, יהוה אֱלֹהֵינוּ וֵאלֹהֵי אֲבוֹתֵינוּ, שֶׁתְּהֵא הַבְּרָכָה הַזֹּאת שֶׁצִּוִּיתָנוּ לְבָרֵךְ אֶת עַמְּךָ יִשְׂרָאֵל בְּרָכָה שְׁלֵמָה, וְלֹא יִהְיֶה בָּהּ שׁוּם מִכְשׁוֹל וְעָוֹן מֵעַתָּה וְעַד עוֹלָם.

THE PRIESTLY BLESSING

Congregation and *Kohanim*, then *chazzan*.

וְתֶעָרֵב *May our entreaty be pleasing unto You as an elevation-offering and as a sacrifice. Please, O Merciful One, in Your abounding mercy return Your Shechinah to Zion, Your city, and the order of the Temple service to Jerusalem. And may our eyes behold when You return to Zion in mercy, that we may there serve You with awe as in days of old and as in earlier years.*

Chazzan concludes:

Blessed are You, HASHEM, for You alone do we serve, with awe.

(Cong. and *Kohanim*— *Amen.)*

THANKSGIVING [MODIM]

Chazzan recites the entire *Modim* aloud, while the congregation recites *Modim of the Rabbis* softly. Bow at *'We gratefully thank You'*; straighten up at *'HASHEM.'*

מוֹדִים *We gratefully thank You, for it is You Who are HASHEM, our God and the God of our forefathers for all eternity; Rock of our lives, Shield of our salvation are You from generation to generation. We shall thank You and relate Your praise[1] — for our lives, which are committed to Your power and for our souls that are entrusted to You; for Your miracles that are with us every day; and for Your wonders and favors in every season — evening, morning, and afternoon. The Beneficent One, for Your compassions were never exhausted, and the Compassionate One, for Your kindnesses never ended[2] — always have we put our hope in You.*

MODIM OF THE RABBIS

מוֹדִים *We gratefully thank You, for it is You Who are HASHEM, our God and the God of our forefathers, the God of all flesh, our Molder, the Molder of the universe. Blessings and thanks are due Your great and holy Name for You have given us life and sustained us. So may You continue to give us life and sustain us and gather our exiles to the Courtyards of Your Sanctuary, to observe Your decrees, to do Your will and to serve You wholeheartedly. [We thank You] for inspiring us to thank You. Blessed is the God of thanksgivings.*

For all these, may Your Name be blessed and exalted, our King, continually forever and ever.

When the *chazzan* recites וְכֹל הַחַיִּים, *Everything alive,* the *Kohanim* recite יְהִי רָצוֹן, *May it be Your will.*

וְכֹל *Everything alive will gratefully acknowledge You, Selah! and praise Your Name sincerely, O God of our salvation and help, Selah! Blessed are You, HASHEM, Your Name is 'The Beneficent One' and to You it is fitting to give thanks.*

(Cong. and *Kohanim*— *Amen.)*

יְהִי רָצוֹן *May it be Your will, HASHEM, our God and the God of our fathers, that this blessing which You have commanded us to bestow upon Your nation Israel be a full blessing, that there be in it neither stumbling block nor sin from now and forever.*

(1) Cf. *Psalms* 79:13. (2) Cf. *Lamentations* 3:22.

The *chazzan* recites the following in an undertone but says the word כֹּהֲנִים aloud as a formal summons to the *Kohanim** to bless the people. In some communities the congregation, but not the *Kohanim*, responds עַם קְדוֹשֶׁךָ כָּאָמוּר, aloud.

אֱלֹהֵינוּ וֵאלֹהֵי אֲבוֹתֵינוּ, בָּרְכֵנוּ בַבְּרָכָה* הַמְּשֻׁלֶּשֶׁת* בַּתּוֹרָה הַכְּתוּבָה עַל יְדֵי מֹשֶׁה עַבְדֶּךָ, הָאֲמוּרָה מִפִּי אַהֲרֹן וּבָנָיו,

כֹּהֲנִים

עַם קְדוֹשֶׁךָ* — כָּאָמוּר:

The *Kohanim* recite the following blessing aloud, in unison, and the congregation, but not the *chazzan*, responds אָמֵן.

בָּרוּךְ אַתָּה יהוה, אֱלֹהֵינוּ מֶלֶךְ הָעוֹלָם, אֲשֶׁר קִדְּשָׁנוּ בִּקְדֻשָּׁתוֹ שֶׁל אַהֲרֹן,* וְצִוָּנוּ לְבָרֵךְ אֶת עַמּוֹ יִשְׂרָאֵל בְּאַהֲבָה.*

(אָמֵן. —Cong.)

See commentary regarding the related verses* in small print that appear beside the words of the *Kohanim's* blessing.

יְבָרֶכְךָ יְבָרֶכְךָ יהוה מִצִּיּוֹן, עֹשֵׂה שָׁמַיִם וָאָרֶץ.[1]

יהוה* יהוה אֲדֹנֵינוּ, מָה אַדִּיר שִׁמְךָ בְּכָל הָאָרֶץ.[2]

וְיִשְׁמְרֶךָ.* שָׁמְרֵנִי, אֵל, כִּי חָסִיתִי בָךְ.[3]

בִּרְכַּת כֹּהֲנִים / THE PRIESTLY BLESSING

The Midrash (*Bamidbar Rabbah* 11:2) teaches that until the time of the Patriarchs, God Himself retained the power to bless people. With the advent of the Patriarchs, He gave this awesome power to them. After they died, God declared that henceforth the *Kohanim* would bless the Jewish people. Thus, the upraised hands of the *Kohanim* are the vehicle through which God's blessing flows upon His chosen people.

This section is abridged from ArtScroll's *Bircas Kohanim/The Priestly Blessings*, by Rabbi Avie Gold.

אֱלֹהֵינוּ . . . בָּרְכֵנוּ בַבְּרָכָה — *Our God . . . bless us with the ... blessing.* We ask God, not the *Kohanim*, to bless us, because, although the *Kohanim* pronounce the words, they are merely conduits through which the blessing descends from God to the nation below (*Chullin* 49a). This is made clear in the Scriptural commandment, which ends with God's pledge וַאֲנִי אֲבָרְכֵם, *and I will bless them* (*Numbers* 6:27).

הַמְּשֻׁלֶּשֶׁת — *Three-verse.* The Priestly Blessing contains three Torah verses: *Numbers* 6:24-26.

עַם קְדוֹשֶׁךָ — *Your holy people.* The *Kohanim* are so described (*I Chronicles* 23:13) because they were designated to serve God and bless Israel.

בָּרוּךְ . . . בִּקְדֻשָּׁתוֹ שֶׁל אַהֲרֹן — *Blessed . . . with the holiness of Aaron.* Just as the selection of Israel as the Holy Nation is not dependent solely upon the deeds of each individual member, but on the holiness of their forebears — indeed, it is the very sanctity of the Patriarchs which imbued their descendants with a capacity for holiness — so is the sanctity of the *Kehunah* [priesthood] unique among the descendants of Aaron.

בְּאַהֲבָה — *With love.* The *Kohanim* are to feel love for the congregation when they pronounce the blessing. The addition of this phrase is based upon *Zohar* (*Naso* 147b): 'Any *Kohen* who does not have love for the congregation or for whom the congregation has no love, may not raise his hands to bless the congregation . . .'

On his first day as *Kohen Gadol*, when he completed the service, *Aaron raised his hands toward the nation and blessed them* (*Leviticus* 9:22), but we are not told what he said (*Ramban*). This teaches that a person must rejoice in his fellow Jew's good fortune until his heart becomes filled with love, joy and blessing — a blessing so great that mere words cannot express it, so overflowing with love that the very movements of his hands express his joy and love.

Raising the hands is a symbol of a heart pouring forth blessing and joy from a treasure trove of happiness. Raising the hands is not a sterile act — it must be a wholehearted expression of the hope and blessing which are hidden in the soul. An ocean of inexpressible joy issues from a pure soul; and the purer the soul, the purer the blessing (*Ohr Chadash*).

יְבָרֶכְךָ ה׳ — *May* HASHEM *bless you,* with increasing wealth (*Rashi*) and long life (*Ibn Ezra*).

וְיִשְׁמְרֶךָ — *And safeguard you.* May the above blessings be preserved against loss or attack. Only God can guarantee that no one or nothing can

The *chazzan* recites the following in an undertone but says the word *'Kohanim'* aloud as a formal summons to the *Kohanim** to bless the people. In some communities the congregation, but not the *Kohanim*, responds, *'Your holy people — as it is said,'* aloud.

אֱלֹהֵינוּ *Our God and the God of our forefathers, bless us with the three-verse* blessing* in the Torah that was written by the hand of Moses, Your servant, that was said by Aaron and his sons, the*

Kohanim,

Your holy people — as it is said:*

The *Kohanim* recite the following blessing aloud, in unison, and the congregation, but not the *chazzan*, responds *Amen.*

בָּרוּךְ *Blessed are You,* HASHEM, *our God, King of the universe, Who has sanctified us with the holiness of Aaron,* and has commanded us to bless His people Israel with love.** (Cong.— *Amen.)*

See commentary regarding the related verses* in small print that appear beside the words of the *Kohanim's* blessing.

May [He] bless you — *May* HASHEM *bless you from Zion, Maker of heaven and earth.*[1]

— HASHEM* — — HASHEM, *our Master, how mighty is Your Name throughout the earth!*[2]

and safeguard you.* — *Safeguard me, O God, for in You have I taken refuge.*[3]

(1) *Psalms* 134:3. (2) 8:10. (3) 16:1.

tamper with the gifts He confers upon His loved ones (*Midrash Rabbah*).

Related verses appear alongside the fifteen words of *Bircas Kohanim* in most *Siddurim*. The

Laws of Bircas Kohanim

After *Kedushah*, a Levite pours water from a utensil over the *Kohen's* hands. When the *chazzan* begins רְצֵה the *Kohanim* slip off their shoes (the laces should be loosened before the hands are washed) and ascend the *duchan* [platform in front of the Ark] where they stand facing the Ark.

When the *chazzan* recites וְכֹל הַחַיִּים, the *Kohanim* quietly recite the יְהִי רָצוֹן supplication, concluding it to coincide with the ending of the *chazzan's* blessing, so that the congregational *Amen* will be in response to their prayer as well as the *chazzan's*.

In most congregations, the *chazzan* quietly recites, '. . . אֱלֹהֵינוּ וֵאלֹהֵי אֲבוֹתֵינוּ בָּרְכֵנוּ, *Our God . . . bless us . . .'* until the word כֹּהֲנִים, *Kohanim*, which he calls out in a loud voice. Then, resuming his undertone, he recites the next words, 'עַם קְדוֹשֶׁךָ כָּאָמוּר, *Your holy people, as it is said.'* Even if only one *Kohen* is present, the *chazzan* uses the word *Kohanim* in plural, since it is the established form of the prayer. In some congregations, however, the *chazzan* merely calls out *'Kohanim'* without reciting the introductory prayer. In these places the *chazzan* calls out the plural word *Kohanim* only if two or more *Kohanim* ascend the *duchan*. If only one *Kohen* is present, however, that *Kohen* does not wait for a call, but raises his hands and begins his blessing immediately.

From this point until the *chazzan* begins שִׂים שָׁלוֹם, the congregation stands, facing the *Kohanim* attentively. No one may gaze at the *Kohanim's* raised hands.

Those standing behind the *Kohanim* do not receive the benefits of the blessing. Therefore, people behind them should move up during *Bircas Kohanim*.

The *chazzan* reads each word of *Bircas Kohanim* aloud and the *Kohanim* repeat it after him. The congregation may not respond אָמֵן until the *Kohanim* have completed the initial blessing; the *chazzan* may not call out יְבָרֶכְךָ until the congregation has finished its אָמֵן; the *Kohanim* may not repeat יְבָרֶכְךָ until the *chazzan* has read the full word; etc., etc.

When the *chazzan* begins שִׂים שָׁלוֹם, the *Kohanim*, with hands still raised, turn to the Ark, then lower their hands. While the *chazzan* recites שִׂים שָׁלוֹם, the *Kohanim* recite . . . רִבּוֹנוֹ שֶׁל עוֹלָם עָשִׂינוּ and the congregation recites אַדִּיר בַּמָּרוֹם. All should conclude their respective prayers simultaneously with the *chazzan's* conclusion of שִׂים שָׁלוֹם.

It is preferable that the *Kohanim* not return to their seats until after the *chazzan* completes *Kaddish* (except on Succos when the *Hoshana* prayers are recited before *Kaddish*).

The *Kohanim* sing an extended chant before saying וְיִשְׁמְרֶךָ, and the congregation recites the following supplication in an undertone. (On the Sabbath this supplication is omitted.) When the *Kohanim* conclude וְיִשְׁמְרֶךָ, the congregation and *chazzan* respond אָמֵן.

רִבּוֹנוֹ שֶׁל עוֹלָם, אֲנִי שֶׁלָּךְ וַחֲלוֹמוֹתַי שֶׁלָּךְ. חֲלוֹם חָלַמְתִּי וְאֵינִי יוֹדֵעַ מַה הוּא. יְהִי רָצוֹן מִלְּפָנֶיךָ, יהוה אֱלֹהַי וֵאלֹהֵי אֲבוֹתַי, שֶׁיִּהְיוּ כָּל חֲלוֹמוֹתַי עָלַי וְעַל כָּל יִשְׂרָאֵל לְטוֹבָה — בֵּין שֶׁחָלַמְתִּי עַל עַצְמִי, וּבֵין שֶׁחָלַמְתִּי עַל אֲחֵרִים, וּבֵין שֶׁחָלְמוּ אֲחֵרִים עָלַי. אִם טוֹבִים הֵם, חַזְּקֵם וְאַמְּצֵם, וְיִתְקַיְּמוּ בִי וּבָהֶם כַּחֲלוֹמוֹתָיו שֶׁל יוֹסֵף הַצַּדִּיק. וְאִם צְרִיכִים רְפוּאָה, רְפָאֵם כְּחִזְקִיָּהוּ מֶלֶךְ יְהוּדָה מֵחָלְיוֹ, וּכְמִרְיָם הַנְּבִיאָה מִצָּרַעְתָּהּ, וּכְנַעֲמָן מִצָּרַעְתּוֹ, וּכְמֵי מָרָה עַל יְדֵי מֹשֶׁה רַבֵּנוּ, וּכְמֵי יְרִיחוֹ עַל יְדֵי אֱלִישָׁע. וּכְשֵׁם שֶׁהָפַכְתָּ אֶת קִלְלַת בִּלְעָם הָרָשָׁע מִקְּלָלָה לִבְרָכָה, כֵּן תַּהֲפוֹךְ כָּל חֲלוֹמוֹתַי עָלַי וְעַל כָּל יִשְׂרָאֵל לְטוֹבָה, וְתִשְׁמְרֵנִי וּתְחָנֵּנִי וְתִרְצֵנִי. אָמֵן.

יָאֵר אֱלֹהִים יְחָנֵּנוּ וִיבָרְכֵנוּ, יָאֵר פָּנָיו אִתָּנוּ, סֶלָה.[1]

יהוה יהוה יהוה, אֵל רַחוּם וְחַנּוּן, אֶרֶךְ אַפַּיִם וְרַב חֶסֶד וֶאֱמֶת.[2]

פָּנָיו פְּנֵה אֵלַי וְחָנֵּנִי, כִּי יָחִיד וְעָנִי אָנִי.[3]

אֵלֶיךָ אֵלֶיךָ יהוה נַפְשִׁי אֶשָּׂא.[4]

וִיחֻנֶּךָּ הִנֵּה כְעֵינֵי עֲבָדִים אֶל יַד אֲדוֹנֵיהֶם, כְּעֵינֵי שִׁפְחָה אֶל יַד גְּבִרְתָּהּ, כֵּן עֵינֵינוּ אֶל יהוה אֱלֹהֵינוּ עַד שֶׁיְּחָנֵּנוּ.[5]

The *Kohanim* sing an extended chant before saying וִיחֻנֶּךָּ, and the congregation recites the supplication (above) in an undertone. (On the Sabbath this supplication is omitted.) When the *Kohanim* conclude וִיחֻנֶּךָּ, the congregation and *chazzan* respond אָמֵן.

יִשָּׂא יִשָּׂא בְרָכָה מֵאֵת יהוה, וּצְדָקָה מֵאֱלֹהֵי יִשְׁעוֹ.[6] וּמְצָא חֵן וְשֵׂכֶל טוֹב בְּעֵינֵי אֱלֹהִים וְאָדָם.[7]

יהוה יהוה, חָנֵּנוּ, לְךָ קִוִּינוּ, הֱיֵה זְרֹעָם לַבְּקָרִים, אַף יְשׁוּעָתֵנוּ בְּעֵת צָרָה.[8]

פָּנָיו אַל תַּסְתֵּר פָּנֶיךָ מִמֶּנִּי בְּיוֹם צַר לִי, הַטֵּה אֵלַי אָזְנֶךָ, בְּיוֹם אֶקְרָא מַהֵר עֲנֵנִי.[9]

אֵלֶיךָ אֵלֶיךָ נָשָׂאתִי אֶת עֵינַי, הַיֹּשְׁבִי בַּשָּׁמָיִם.[10]

---

function of these verses and the propriety of reciting them presents a difficulty already dealt with in the Talmud (*Sotah* 39b,40a). Most authorities agree that no verses should be recited at all. Some permit the verses to be read in an undertone while the *chazzan* calls out the words of the blessing. In any case, the practice of the masses who read these verses aloud—and especially of those who repeat the words of *Bircas Kohanim* after the *chazzan* — is wrong and has no halachic basis (*Mishnah Berurah* 128:103).

יָאֵר ה׳ פָּנָיו אֵלֶיךָ — *May* HASHEM *illuminate His countenance for you.* This is the blessing of spiritual growth, the light of Torah, which is symbolized by God's 'countenance' (*Sifre*).

וִיחֻנֶּךָּ — *And be gracious to you.* May you find favor in God's eyes (*Ramban*); or, may you find favor in the eyes of others, for all a person's talents and qualities will avail him little if others dislike him (*Ohr HaChaim*).

יִשָּׂא ה׳ פָּנָיו אֵלֶיךָ — *May [He]* HASHEM *turn His countenance to you.* May He suppress His anger against you, even if you are sinful and deserve to be punished (*Rashi*). One's face is

The *Kohanim* sing an extended chant and the congregation recites the following supplication in an undertone. (On the Sabbath this supplication is omitted.) When the *Kohanim* conclude וְיִשְׁמְרֶךָ, *'and safeguard you,'* the congregation and *chazzan* respond *Amen*.

רִבּוֹנוֹ שֶׁל עוֹלָם *Master of the world, I am Yours and my dreams are Yours. I have dreamed a dream but I do not know what it indicates. May it be Your will, HASHEM, my God and the God of my fathers, that all my dreams regarding myself and regarding all of Israel be good ones — those I have dreamed about myself, those I have dreamed about others, and those that others dreamed about me. If they are good, strengthen them, fortify them, make them endure in me and in them like the dreams of the righteous Joseph. But if they require healing, heal them like Hezekiah, King of Judah, from his sickness; like Miriam the prophetess from her tzaraas; like Naaman from his tzaraas; like the waters of Marah through the hand of Moses our teacher; and like the waters of Jericho through the hand of Elisha. And just as You transformed the curse of the wicked Balaam from a curse to a blessing, so may You transform all of my dreams regarding myself and regarding all of Israel for goodness. May You protect me, may You be gracious to me, may You accept me. Amen.*

May [He] illuminate *May God favor us and bless us, may He illuminate His countenance with us, Selah.*[1]

HASHEM *HASHEM, HASHEM, God, Compassionate and Gracious, Slow to anger, and Abundant in Kindness and Truth.*[2]

His countenance *Turn Your face to me and be gracious to me, for alone and afflicted am I.*[3]

for you* *To You, HASHEM, I raise my soul.*[4]

and be gracious to you.* *Behold! Like the eyes of servants unto their master's hand, like the eyes of a maid unto her mistress's hand, so are our eyes unto HASHEM, our God, until He will favor us.*[5]

The *Kohanim* sing an extended chant and the congregation recites the supplication (above) in an undertone. (On the Sabbath this supplication is omitted.) When the *Kohanim* conclude וִיחֻנֶּךָּ, *'and be gracious to you,'* the congregation and *chazzan* respond *Amen*.

May [He] turn *May he receive a blessing from HASHEM, and just kindness from the God of his salvation.*[6] *And he will find favor and good understanding in the eyes of God and man.*[7]

— HASHEM — *HASHEM, find favor with us, for You have we hoped! Be their power in the mornings, and our salvation in times of distress.*[8]

His countenance *Do not hide Your countenance from me in a day that is distressing to me; lean Your ear toward me; in the day that I call, speedily answer me.*[9]

to you* *To You I raised my eyes, O You Who dwells in the Heavens.*[10]

(1) *Psalms* 67:2. (2) *Exodus* 34:6. (3) *Psalms* 25:16. (4) 25:1. (5) 123:2. (6) 24:5. (7) *Proverbs* 3:4. (8) *Isaiah* 33:2. (9) *Psalms* 102:3. (10) 123:1.

indicative of his attitude toward someone else. If he is angry, he will turn away from the one he dislikes. God 'turns His face' *toward* Israel to show that He loves them (*Maharzu*).

וְיָשֵׂם וְשָׂמוּ אֶת שְׁמִי עַל בְּנֵי יִשְׂרָאֵל, וַאֲנִי אֲבָרְכֵם.[1]

לְךָ לְךָ יהוה, הַגְּדֻלָּה וְהַגְּבוּרָה וְהַתִּפְאֶרֶת וְהַנֵּצַח וְהַהוֹד, כִּי כֹל בַּשָּׁמַיִם וּבָאָרֶץ, לְךָ יהוה, הַמַּמְלָכָה וְהַמִּתְנַשֵּׂא לְכֹל לְרֹאשׁ.[2]

שָׁלוֹם.• שָׁלוֹם שָׁלוֹם לָרָחוֹק וְלַקָּרוֹב, אָמַר יהוה, וּרְפָאתִיו.[3]

The *Kohanim* sing an extended chant before saying שָׁלוֹם, and the congregation recites the following supplication in an undertone. [The twenty-two-letter Divine Name appears here in brackets and bold type. This Name should be scanned with the eyes but not spoken.]
(On the Sabbath this supplication is omitted.)
When the *Kohanim* conclude שָׁלוֹם, congregation and *chazzan* respond אָמֵן.

יְהִי רָצוֹן מִלְּפָנֶיךָ, יהוה אֱלֹהַי וֵאלֹהֵי אֲבוֹתַי, שֶׁתַּעֲשֶׂה לְמַעַן קְדֻשַּׁת חֲסָדֶיךָ וְגֹדֶל רַחֲמֶיךָ הַפְּשׁוּטִים, וּלְמַעַן טָהֳרַת שִׁמְךָ הַגָּדוֹל הַגִּבּוֹר וְהַנּוֹרָא, בֶּן עֶשְׂרִים וּשְׁתַּיִם אוֹתִיּוֹת* הַיּוֹצְאִים מִן הַפְּסוּקִים שֶׁל בִּרְכַּת כֹּהֲנִים **[אנקת״ם פסת״ם פספסי״ם דיונסי״ם]** הָאֲמוּרָה מִפִּי אַהֲרֹן וּבָנָיו עַם קְדוֹשֶׁךָ, שֶׁתִּהְיֶה קָרוֹב לִי בְּקָרְאִי לָךְ, וְתִשְׁמַע תְּפִלָּתִי נַאֲקָתִי וְאֶנְקָתִי תָּמִיד, כְּשֵׁם שֶׁשָּׁמַעְתָּ **אֶנְקַת** יַעֲקֹב תְּמִימֶךָ הַנִּקְרָא אִישׁ **תָּם**. וְתִתֶּן לִי וּלְכָל נַפְשׁוֹת בֵּיתִי מְזוֹנוֹתֵינוּ וּפַרְנָסָתֵנוּ – בְּרֶוַח וְלֹא בְצִמְצוּם, בְּהֶתֵּר וְלֹא בְאִסּוּר, בְּנַחַת וְלֹא בְצַעַר – מִתַּחַת יָדְךָ הָרְחָבָה, כְּשֵׁם שֶׁנָּתַתָּ **פִּסַּת** לֶחֶם לֶאֱכוֹל וּבֶגֶד לִלְבּוֹשׁ לְיַעֲקֹב אָבִינוּ הַנִּקְרָא אִישׁ **תָּם**. וְתִתְּנֵנוּ לְאַהֲבָה, לְחֵן וּלְחֶסֶד וּלְרַחֲמִים בְּעֵינֶיךָ וּבְעֵינֵי כָל רוֹאֵינוּ, וְיִהְיוּ דְבָרַי נִשְׁמָעִים לַעֲבוֹדָתֶךָ, כְּשֵׁם שֶׁנָּתַתָּ אֶת יוֹסֵף צַדִּיקֶךָ – בְּשָׁעָה שֶׁהִלְבִּישׁוֹ אָבִיו כְּתֹנֶת **פַּסִּים** – לְחֵן וּלְחֶסֶד וּלְרַחֲמִים בְּעֵינֶיךָ וּבְעֵינֵי כָל רוֹאָיו. וְתַעֲשֶׂה עִמִּי נִפְלָאוֹת **וְנִסִּים**, וּלְטוֹבָה אוֹת, וְתַצְלִיחֵנִי בִּדְרָכַי, וְתֵן בְּלִבִּי בִּינָה לְהָבִין וּלְהַשְׂכִּיל וּלְקַיֵּם אֶת כָּל דִּבְרֵי תַלְמוּד תּוֹרָתֶךָ וְסוֹדוֹתֶיהָ, וְתַצִּילֵנִי מִשְּׁגִיאוֹת, וּתְטַהֵר רַעְיוֹנַי וְלִבִּי לַעֲבוֹדָתֶךָ וּלְיִרְאָתֶךָ. וְתַאֲרִיךְ יָמַי (insert the appropriate words – וִימֵי אָבִי וְאִמִּי וְאִשְׁתִּי וּבָנַי וּבְנוֹתַי) בְּטוֹב וּבִנְעִימוֹת, בְּרֹב עֹז וְשָׁלוֹם, אָמֵן סֶלָה.

The *chazzan* immediately begins שִׂים שָׁלוֹם; the *Kohanim* turn back to the Ark, lower their hands and recite their concluding prayer רִבּוֹנוֹ שֶׁל עוֹלָם; and the congregation recites אַדִּיר בַּמָּרוֹם. All should conclude their respective prayers simultaneously with the *chazzan's* conclusion of שִׂים שָׁלוֹם.

Kohanim:

רִבּוֹנוֹ שֶׁל עוֹלָם, עָשִׂינוּ מַה שֶּׁגָּזַרְתָּ עָלֵינוּ, אַף אַתָּה עֲשֵׂה עִמָּנוּ כְּמָה שֶׁהִבְטַחְתָּנוּ: הַשְׁקִיפָה מִמְּעוֹן קָדְשְׁךָ, מִן הַשָּׁמַיִם, וּבָרֵךְ אֶת עַמְּךָ אֶת יִשְׂרָאֵל, וְאֵת הָאֲדָמָה אֲשֶׁר נָתַתָּה לָנוּ – כַּאֲשֶׁר נִשְׁבַּעְתָּ לַאֲבוֹתֵינוּ – אֶרֶץ זָבַת חָלָב וּדְבָשׁ.[4]

Congregation:

אַדִּיר בַּמָּרוֹם, שׁוֹכֵן בִּגְבוּרָה, אַתָּה שָׁלוֹם וְשִׁמְךָ שָׁלוֹם. יְהִי רָצוֹן שֶׁתָּשִׂים עָלֵינוּ וְעַל כָּל עַמְּךָ בֵּית יִשְׂרָאֵל חַיִּים וּבְרָכָה לְמִשְׁמֶרֶת שָׁלוֹם.

וְיָשֵׂם לְךָ שָׁלוֹם — *And establish for you peace.* Peace is the seal of all blessings, because without peace — prosperity, health, food, and drink are worthless *(Sifre).*

שִׁמְךָ ... בֶּן עֶשְׂרִים וּשְׁתַּיִם אוֹתִיּוֹת — *Your Name ... composed of twenty-two letters.* Scripture uses many appellations for God. Each of these Divine Names represents an attribute by which God allows man to perceive Him. י־ה־ו־ה represents the attribute of Divine Kindness. Since this Name is composed of the letters of הָיָה הֹוֶה יִהְיֶה, *He was, He is, He will be,* it is also an

and establish *And they shall place My Name upon the Children of Israel, and I shall bless them.*[1]

for you *Yours, HASHEM, is the greatness, the strength, the splendor, the triumph, and the glory, even all that is in heaven and earth; Yours, HASHEM, is the kingdom and the sovereignty over every leader.*[2]

peace.* *'Peace, peace, for far and near,' says HASHEM, 'and I shall heal him.'*[3]

The *Kohanim* sing an extended chant and the congregation recites the following supplication in an undertone. [The twenty-two-letter Divine Name appears here in brackets and bold type. This Name should be scanned with the eyes but not spoken.] (On the Sabbath this supplication is omitted.) When the *Kohanim* conclude שָׁלוֹם, *'peace,'* congregation and *chazzan* respond *Amen.*

יְהִי רָצוֹן *May it be Your will, HASHEM, my God and the God of my forefathers, that You act for the sake of the holiness of Your kindness and the greatness of Your mercies which reach out, and for the sake of the sanctity of Your Name — the great, the mighty and the awesome; composed of twenty-two letters* which derive from the verses of Bircas Kohanim* [**אנקת״ם פסת״ם פספסי״ם דיונסי״ם**]*; spoken by Aaron and his sons, Your holy people — that You be near to me when I call to You; that You listen to my prayer, my plea and my cry at all times, just as You listened to the cry* [**אֶנְקַת**] *of Jacob, Your perfect one, who is called 'a wholesome man'* [**תָּם**]*. And may You bestow upon me and upon all the souls of my household, our food and our sustenance — generously and not sparsely, honestly and not in forbidden fashion, pleasurably and not in pain — from beneath Your generous hand, just as You gave a portion* [**פַּסַּת**] *of bread to eat and clothing to wear to our father Jacob who is called 'a wholesome man'* [**תָּם**]*. And may You grant that we find love, favor, kindness and mercy in Your eyes and in the eyes of all who behold us; and that my words in Your service be heard; just as You granted Joseph, Your righteous one — at the time that his father garbed him in a fine woolen tunic* [**פַּסִּים**] *— that he find favor, kindness and mercy in Your eyes and in the eyes of all who beheld him. May You perform wonders and miracles* [**וְנִסִּים**] *with me, and a goodly sign; grant me success in my ways; place in my heart the power of understanding, to understand, to be wise, to fulfill all the words of Your Torah's teaching and its mysteries; save me from errors; and purify my thinking and my heart for Your service and Your awe. May You prolong my days [*insert the appropriate words*— and the days of my father, my mother, my wife, my son(s), my daughter(s)] with goodness, with sweetness, with an abundance of strength and peace. Amen: Selah.*

The *chazzan* immediately begins שִׂים שָׁלוֹם, *Establish* peace; the *Kohanim* turn back to the Ark, lower their hands and recite their concluding prayer רִבּוֹנוֹ שֶׁל עוֹלָם, *Master of the World;* and the congregation recites אַדִּיר, *Mighty One*. All should conclude their respective prayers simultaneously with the *chazzan's* conclusion of שִׂים שָׁלוֹם.

Kohanim:

רִבּוֹנוֹ שֶׁל עוֹלָם *Master of the world, we have done what You have decreed upon us, now may You also do as You have promised us: Look down from Your sacred dwelling, from the heavens, and bless Your people, Israel, and the earth which You have given us — just as You have sworn to our fathers — a land that flows with milk and honey.*[4]

Congregation:

אַדִּיר *Mighty One on high, He Who dwells in power! You are Peace and Your Name is Peace! May it be acceptable that You grant us and all of Your people, the house of Israel, life and blessing for a safeguard of peace.*

(1) *Numbers* 6:27. (2) *II Chronicles* 29:11. (3) *Isaiah* 57:19. (4) *Deuteronomy* 26:15.

indication of God's Eternality. אֱלֹהִים, *ELOHIM,* represents Divine Justice. This word can also mean *judge* and *power*. Similarly, each Name found in Scripture is but an allusion to a

Chazzan:

שִׂים שָׁלוֹם, טוֹבָה וּבְרָכָה, חֵן, וָחֶסֶד וְרַחֲמִים עָלֵינוּ וְעַל כָּל יִשְׂרָאֵל עַמֶּךָ. בָּרְכֵנוּ אָבִינוּ, כֻּלָּנוּ כְּאֶחָד בְּאוֹר פָּנֶיךָ, כִּי בְאוֹר פָּנֶיךָ נָתַתָּ לָּנוּ, יהוה אֱלֹהֵינוּ, תּוֹרַת חַיִּים וְאַהֲבַת חֶסֶד, וּצְדָקָה, וּבְרָכָה, וְרַחֲמִים, וְחַיִּים, וְשָׁלוֹם. וְטוֹב בְּעֵינֶיךָ לְבָרֵךְ אֶת עַמְּךָ יִשְׂרָאֵל, בְּכָל עֵת וּבְכָל שָׁעָה בִּשְׁלוֹמֶךָ. בָּרוּךְ אַתָּה יהוה, הַמְּבָרֵךְ אֶת עַמּוֹ יִשְׂרָאֵל בַּשָּׁלוֹם.

(.אָמֵן – Cong. and *Kohanim*)

Chazzan, in an undertone:

יִהְיוּ לְרָצוֹן אִמְרֵי פִי וְהֶגְיוֹן לִבִּי לְפָנֶיךָ, יהוה צוּרִי וְגֹאֲלִי.[1]

קדיש שלם

The *chazzan* recites קַדִּישׁ שָׁלֵם.

יִתְגַּדַּל וְיִתְקַדַּשׁ שְׁמֵהּ רַבָּא. (.Cong – אָמֵן.) בְּעָלְמָא דִּי בְרָא כִרְעוּתֵהּ. וְיַמְלִיךְ מַלְכוּתֵהּ, בְּחַיֵּיכוֹן וּבְיוֹמֵיכוֹן וּבְחַיֵּי דְכָל בֵּית יִשְׂרָאֵל, בַּעֲגָלָא וּבִזְמַן קָרִיב. וְאִמְרוּ: אָמֵן.

(.Cong – אָמֵן. יְהֵא שְׁמֵהּ רַבָּא מְבָרַךְ לְעָלַם וּלְעָלְמֵי עָלְמַיָּא.)

יְהֵא שְׁמֵהּ רַבָּא מְבָרַךְ לְעָלַם וּלְעָלְמֵי עָלְמַיָּא.

יִתְבָּרַךְ וְיִשְׁתַּבַּח וְיִתְפָּאַר וְיִתְרוֹמַם וְיִתְנַשֵּׂא וְיִתְהַדָּר וְיִתְעַלֶּה וְיִתְהַלָּל שְׁמֵהּ דְּקֻדְשָׁא בְּרִיךְ הוּא (.Cong – בְּרִיךְ הוּא) – לְעֵלָּא מִן כָּל בִּרְכָתָא וְשִׁירָתָא תֻּשְׁבְּחָתָא וְנֶחֱמָתָא, דַּאֲמִירָן בְּעָלְמָא. וְאִמְרוּ: אָמֵן. (.Cong – אָמֵן.)

(.Cong – קַבֵּל בְּרַחֲמִים וּבְרָצוֹן אֶת תְּפִלָּתֵנוּ.)

תִּתְקַבֵּל צְלוֹתְהוֹן וּבָעוּתְהוֹן דְּכָל בֵּית יִשְׂרָאֵל קֳדָם אֲבוּהוֹן דִּי בִשְׁמַיָּא. וְאִמְרוּ: אָמֵן. (.Cong – אָמֵן.)

(.Cong – יְהִי שֵׁם יהוה מְבֹרָךְ, מֵעַתָּה וְעַד עוֹלָם.[2])

יְהֵא שְׁלָמָא רַבָּא מִן שְׁמַיָּא, וְחַיִּים עָלֵינוּ וְעַל כָּל יִשְׂרָאֵל. וְאִמְרוּ: אָמֵן. (.Cong – אָמֵן.)

(.Cong – עֶזְרִי מֵעִם יהוה, עֹשֵׂה שָׁמַיִם וָאָרֶץ.[3])

Take three steps back. Bow left and say . . . עֹשֶׂה; bow right and say . . . הוּא; bow forward and say וְעַל כָּל . . . אָמֵן. Remain standing in place for a few moments, then take three steps forward.

עֹשֶׂה שָׁלוֹם בִּמְרוֹמָיו, הוּא יַעֲשֶׂה שָׁלוֹם עָלֵינוּ, וְעַל כָּל יִשְׂרָאֵל. וְאִמְרוּ: אָמֵן. (.Cong – אָמֵן.)

---

different Divine attribute. Kaballah records many Divine Names which are not found explicitly in Scripture but may be derived through various Kaballistic principles. One of the Names is described in Kabballistic literature as the Twenty-two-letter Name, and the letters of *Bircas Kohanim* are said to allude to it.

The well-known Kabbalist Rabbi Moshe Cor-

Chazzan:

שִׂים שָׁלוֹם *Establish peace, goodness, blessing, graciousness, kindness, and compassion upon us and upon all of Your people Israel. Bless us, our Father, all of us as one, with the light of Your countenance, for with the light of Your countenance You gave us, HASHEM, our God, the Torah of life and a love of kindness, righteousness, blessing, compassion, life, and peace. And may it be good in Your eyes to bless Your people Israel, in every season and in every hour with Your Peace. Blessed are You, HASHEM, Who blesses His people Israel with peace.*

(Cong. and *Kohanim*— *Amen.*)

Chazzan, in an undertone:

May the expressions of my mouth and the thoughts of my heart find favor before You, HASHEM, my Rock and my Redeemer.[1]

FULL KADDISH

The *chazzan* recites the Full *Kaddish*.

יִתְגַּדַּל *May His great Name grow exalted and sanctified* (Cong.— *Amen.*) *in the world that He created as He willed. May He give reign to His kingship in your lifetimes and in your days, and in the lifetimes of the entire Family of Israel, swiftly and soon. Now respond: Amen.*

(Cong.— *Amen. May His great Name be blessed forever and ever.*)

May His great Name be blessed forever and ever.

Blessed, praised, glorified, exalted, extolled, mighty, upraised, and lauded be the Name of the Holy One, Blessed is He (Cong.— *Blessed is He*) — *beyond any blessing and song, praise and consolation that are uttered in the world. Now respond: Amen.* (Cong.— *Amen.*)

(Cong.— *Accept our prayers with mercy and favor.*)

May the prayers and supplications of the entire Family of Israel be accepted before their Father Who is in Heaven. Now respond: Amen. (Cong.— *Amen.*)

(Cong.— *Blessed be the Name of HASHEM, from this time and forever.*[2])

May there be abundant peace from Heaven, and life, upon us and upon all Israel. Now respond: Amen. (Cong.— *Amen.*)

(Cong.— *My help is from HASHEM, Maker of heaven and earth.*[3])

Take three steps back. Bow left and say, *'He Who makes peace . . .'*; bow right and say, *'may He . . .'*; bow forward and say, *'and upon all Israel . . .'* Remain standing in place for a few moments, then take three steps forward.

He Who makes peace in His heights, may He make peace upon us, and upon all Israel. Now respond: Amen. (Cong.— *Amen.*)

(1) *Psalms* 19:15. (2) 113:2. (3) 121:2.

dovero *[Ramak]* explains that this Twenty-two-letter Name comprises four individual Names [אנקת״ם פסת״ם פספסי״ם דיונסי״ם], each capable of effecting the fulfillment of a particular human need. The first Name, אנקת״ם, — a contraction of אֶנְקַת תָּמִים, literally *the cry of the perfect ones* — is efficacious in making one's prayer accepted in Heaven; the second, פסת״ם, is the Name through which God distributes פַּת בַּר, *portions of bread,* to the hungry; through the Name פספסי״ם — related to כְּתֹנֶת פַּסִּים, *woolen tunic,* that Jacob made for Joseph (*Genesis* 37:3) — He clothes the naked; and דיונסי״ם indicates that He performs נִסִּים, *miracles,* and wonders. These four Names were invoked by Jacob when he prayed (*Genesis* 28:21) that *God be with me and guard me on this way which I am going; and give me bread to eat and clothes to wear; and that I return in peace* ... (*Pardes,* cited in *Siddur Amudei Shamayim*).

קַוֵּה אֶל יהוה, חֲזַק וְיַאֲמֵץ לִבֶּךָ, וְקַוֵּה אֶל יהוה.[1] אֵין קָדוֹשׁ כַּיהוה, כִּי אֵין בִּלְתֶּךָ, וְאֵין צוּר כֵּאלֹהֵינוּ.[2] כִּי מִי אֱלוֹהַּ מִבַּלְעֲדֵי יהוה, וּמִי צוּר זוּלָתִי אֱלֹהֵינוּ.[3]

אֵין כֵּאלֹהֵינוּ, אֵין כַּאדוֹנֵינוּ, אֵין כְּמַלְכֵּנוּ, אֵין כְּמוֹשִׁיעֵנוּ. מִי כֵאלֹהֵינוּ, מִי כַאדוֹנֵינוּ, מִי כְמַלְכֵּנוּ, מִי כְמוֹשִׁיעֵנוּ. נוֹדֶה לֵאלֹהֵינוּ, נוֹדֶה לַאדוֹנֵינוּ, נוֹדֶה לְמַלְכֵּנוּ, נוֹדֶה לְמוֹשִׁיעֵנוּ. בָּרוּךְ אֱלֹהֵינוּ, בָּרוּךְ אֲדוֹנֵינוּ, בָּרוּךְ מַלְכֵּנוּ, בָּרוּךְ מוֹשִׁיעֵנוּ. אַתָּה הוּא אֱלֹהֵינוּ, אַתָּה הוּא אֲדוֹנֵינוּ, אַתָּה הוּא מַלְכֵּנוּ, אַתָּה הוּא מוֹשִׁיעֵנוּ. אַתָּה הוּא שֶׁהִקְטִירוּ אֲבוֹתֵינוּ לְפָנֶיךָ אֶת קְטֹרֶת הַסַּמִּים.

כריתות ו.

פִּטּוּם הַקְּטֹרֶת: (א) הַצֳּרִי, (ב) וְהַצִּפֹּרֶן, (ג) הַחֶלְבְּנָה, (ד) וְהַלְּבוֹנָה, מִשְׁקַל שִׁבְעִים שִׁבְעִים מָנֶה; (ה) מוֹר, (ו) וּקְצִיעָה, (ז) שִׁבֹּלֶת נֵרְדְּ, (ח) וְכַרְכֹּם, מִשְׁקַל שִׁשָּׁה עָשָׂר שִׁשָּׁה עָשָׂר מָנֶה; (ט) הַקֹּשְׁטְ שְׁנֵים עָשָׂר, (י) וְקִלּוּפָה שְׁלֹשָׁה, (יא) וְקִנָּמוֹן תִּשְׁעָה. בֹּרִית כַּרְשִׁינָה תִּשְׁעָה קַבִּין, יֵין קַפְרִיסִין סְאִין תְּלָתָא וְקַבִּין תְּלָתָא; וְאִם אֵין לוֹ יֵין קַפְרִיסִין, מֵבִיא חֲמַר חִוַּרְיָן עַתִּיק; מֶלַח סְדוֹמִית רֹבַע הַקָּב; מַעֲלֶה עָשָׁן כָּל שֶׁהוּא. רַבִּי נָתָן הַבַּבְלִי אוֹמֵר: אַף כִּפַּת הַיַּרְדֵּן כָּל שֶׁהוּא. וְאִם נָתַן בָּהּ דְּבַשׁ פְּסָלָהּ. וְאִם חִסַּר אַחַת מִכָּל סַמָּנֶיהָ, חַיָּב מִיתָה.

רַבָּן שִׁמְעוֹן בֶּן גַּמְלִיאֵל אוֹמֵר: הַצֳּרִי אֵינוֹ אֶלָּא שְׂרָף הַנּוֹטֵף מֵעֲצֵי הַקְּטָף. בֹּרִית כַּרְשִׁינָה שֶׁשָּׁפִין בָּהּ אֶת הַצִּפֹּרֶן כְּדֵי שֶׁתְּהֵא נָאָה; יֵין קַפְרִיסִין שֶׁשּׁוֹרִין בּוֹ אֶת הַצִּפֹּרֶן כְּדֵי שֶׁתְּהֵא עַזָּה; וַהֲלֹא מֵי רַגְלַיִם יָפִין לָהּ, אֶלָּא שֶׁאֵין מַכְנִיסִין מֵי רַגְלַיִם בָּעֲזָרָה מִפְּנֵי הַכָּבוֹד.

משנה, תמיד ז:ד

הַשִּׁיר שֶׁהַלְוִיִּם הָיוּ אוֹמְרִים בְּבֵית הַמִּקְדָּשׁ. בַּיּוֹם הָרִאשׁוֹן הָיוּ אוֹמְרִים: לַיהוה הָאָרֶץ וּמְלוֹאָהּ, תֵּבֵל וְיֹשְׁבֵי בָהּ.[4] בַּשֵּׁנִי הָיוּ אוֹמְרִים: גָּדוֹל יהוה וּמְהֻלָּל מְאֹד, בְּעִיר אֱלֹהֵינוּ הַר קָדְשׁוֹ.[5] בַּשְּׁלִישִׁי הָיוּ אוֹמְרִים: אֱלֹהִים נִצָּב בַּעֲדַת אֵל, בְּקֶרֶב אֱלֹהִים יִשְׁפֹּט.[6] בָּרְבִיעִי הָיוּ אוֹמְרִים: אֵל נְקָמוֹת יהוה, אֵל נְקָמוֹת הוֹפִיעַ.[7] בַּחֲמִישִׁי הָיוּ אוֹמְרִים: הַרְנִינוּ לֵאלֹהִים עוּזֵּנוּ, הָרִיעוּ לֵאלֹהֵי יַעֲקֹב.[8] בַּשִּׁשִּׁי הָיוּ אוֹמְרִים: יהוה מָלָךְ גֵּאוּת לָבֵשׁ, לָבֵשׁ יהוה עֹז

קַוֵּה *Hope to HASHEM, strengthen yourself and He will give you courage; and hope to HASHEM.[1] There is none holy as HASHEM, for there is none beside You, and there is no Rock like our God.[2] For who is a god beside HASHEM, and who is a Rock except for our God.[3]*

אֵין *There is none like our God; there is none like our Master;*
there is none like our King; there is none like our Savior.
Who is like our God? Who is like our Master?
Who is like our King? Who is like our Savior?
Let us thank our God; let us thank our Master;
let us thank our King; let us thank our Savior.
Blessed is our God; blessed is our Master;
blessed is our King; blessed is our Savior.
It is You Who is our God; it is You Who is our Master;
it is You Who is our King; it is You Who is our Savior.
It is You before Whom our forefathers burned the spice-incense.

Talmud, *Kereisos* 6a

פִּטּוּם הַקְּטֹרֶת *The incense mixture was formulated of [eleven spices]: (1) stacte, (2) onycha, (3) galbanum, (4) frankincense — each weighing seventy maneh; (5) myrrh, (6) cassia, (7) spikenard, (8) saffron — each weighing sixteen maneh; (9) costus — twelve [maneh]; (10) aromatic bark — three; and (11) cinnamon — nine. [Additionally] Carshina lye — nine kab; Cyprus wine, three se'ah and three kab — if he has no Cyprus wine, he brings old white wine; Sodom salt, a quarter kab; and a minute amount of smoke-raising herb. Rabbi Nassan the Babylonian says: Also a minute amount of Jordan amber. If he placed fruit-honey into it, he invalidated it. And if he left out any of its spices, he is liable to the death penalty.*

רַבָּן שִׁמְעוֹן *Rabban Shimon ben Gamliel says: The stacte is simply the sap that drips from balsam trees. Carshina lye is used to bleach the onycha to make it pleasing. Cyprus wine is used to soak the onycha to make it pungent. Even though urine is suitable for that, nevertheless they do not bring urine into the Temple out of respect.*

Mishnah, *Tamid* 7:4

הַשִּׁיר *The daily song that the Levites would recite in the Temple was as follows: On the first day [of the week] they would say: 'HASHEM's is the earth and its fullness, the inhabited land and those who dwell in it.'[4] On the second day they would say: 'Great is HASHEM and much praised, in the city of our God, Mount of His Holiness.'[5] On the third day they would say: 'God stands in the Divine assembly, in the midst of judges shall He judge.'[6] On the fourth day they would say: 'O God of vengeance, HASHEM, O God of vengeance, appear.'[7] On the fifth day they would say: 'Sing joyously to the God of our might, call out to the God of Jacob.'[8] On the sixth day they would say: 'HASHEM will have reigned, He will have donned grandeur; He will have donned might*

---

(1) *Psalms* 27:14. (2) *I Samuel* 2:2. (3) *Psalms* 18:32. (4) 24:1. (5) 48:2. (6) 82:1. (7) 94:1. (8) 81:2.

הִתְאַזָּר, אַף תִּכּוֹן תֵּבֵל בַּל תִּמּוֹט.[1] בַּשַּׁבָּת הָיוּ אוֹמְרִים: מִזְמוֹר שִׁיר לְיוֹם הַשַּׁבָּת.[2] מִזְמוֹר שִׁיר לֶעָתִיד לָבֹא, לְיוֹם שֶׁכֻּלּוֹ שַׁבָּת וּמְנוּחָה לְחַיֵּי הָעוֹלָמִים.

מגילה כח:

תָּנָא דְבֵי אֵלִיָּהוּ: כָּל הַשּׁוֹנֶה הֲלָכוֹת בְּכָל יוֹם, מֻבְטָח לוֹ שֶׁהוּא בֶּן עוֹלָם הַבָּא, שֶׁנֶּאֱמַר: הֲלִיכוֹת עוֹלָם לוֹ,[3] אַל תִּקְרֵי הֲלִיכוֹת, אֶלָּא הֲלָכוֹת.

ברכות סד.

אָמַר רַבִּי אֶלְעָזָר אָמַר רַבִּי חֲנִינָא: תַּלְמִידֵי חֲכָמִים מַרְבִּים שָׁלוֹם בָּעוֹלָם, שֶׁנֶּאֱמַר: וְכָל בָּנַיִךְ לִמּוּדֵי יהוה, וְרַב שְׁלוֹם בָּנָיִךְ,[4] אַל תִּקְרֵי בָּנָיִךְ אֶלָּא בּוֹנָיִךְ. ❖ שָׁלוֹם רָב לְאֹהֲבֵי תוֹרָתֶךָ, וְאֵין לָמוֹ מִכְשׁוֹל.[5] יְהִי שָׁלוֹם בְּחֵילֵךְ, שַׁלְוָה בְּאַרְמְנוֹתָיִךְ. לְמַעַן אַחַי וְרֵעָי, אֲדַבְּרָה נָּא שָׁלוֹם בָּךְ. לְמַעַן בֵּית יהוה אֱלֹהֵינוּ, אֲבַקְשָׁה טוֹב לָךְ.[6] יהוה עֹז לְעַמּוֹ יִתֵּן, יהוה יְבָרֵךְ אֶת עַמּוֹ בַשָּׁלוֹם.[7]

קדיש דרבנן

In the presence of a *minyan,* mourners recite קַדִּישׁ דְּרַבָּנָן (see *Laws* §84-85).

יִתְגַּדַּל וְיִתְקַדַּשׁ שְׁמֵהּ רַבָּא. (.Cong – אָמֵן.) בְּעָלְמָא דִּי בְרָא כִרְעוּתֵהּ. וְיַמְלִיךְ מַלְכוּתֵהּ, בְּחַיֵּיכוֹן וּבְיוֹמֵיכוֹן וּבְחַיֵּי דְכָל בֵּית יִשְׂרָאֵל, בַּעֲגָלָא וּבִזְמַן קָרִיב. וְאִמְרוּ: אָמֵן.

(.Cong – אָמֵן. יְהֵא שְׁמֵהּ רַבָּא מְבָרַךְ לְעָלַם וּלְעָלְמֵי עָלְמַיָּא.)

יְהֵא שְׁמֵהּ רַבָּא מְבָרַךְ לְעָלַם וּלְעָלְמֵי עָלְמַיָּא.

יִתְבָּרַךְ וְיִשְׁתַּבַּח וְיִתְפָּאַר וְיִתְרוֹמַם וְיִתְנַשֵּׂא וְיִתְהַדָּר וְיִתְעַלֶּה וְיִתְהַלָּל שְׁמֵהּ דְּקֻדְשָׁא בְּרִיךְ הוּא (.Cong – בְּרִיךְ הוּא) — לְעֵלָּא מִן כָּל בִּרְכָתָא וְשִׁירָתָא תֻּשְׁבְּחָתָא וְנֶחֱמָתָא, דַּאֲמִירָן בְּעָלְמָא. וְאִמְרוּ: אָמֵן. (.Cong – אָמֵן.)

עַל יִשְׂרָאֵל וְעַל רַבָּנָן, וְעַל תַּלְמִידֵיהוֹן וְעַל כָּל תַּלְמִידֵי תַלְמִידֵיהוֹן, וְעַל כָּל מָאן דְּעָסְקִין בְּאוֹרַיְתָא, דִּי בְאַתְרָא הָדֵין וְדִי בְכָל אֲתַר וַאֲתַר. יְהֵא לְהוֹן וּלְכוֹן שְׁלָמָא רַבָּא, חִנָּא וְחִסְדָּא וְרַחֲמִין, וְחַיִּין אֲרִיכִין, וּמְזוֹנֵי רְוִיחֵי, וּפֻרְקָנָא, מִן קֳדָם אֲבוּהוֹן דִּי בִשְׁמַיָּא (וְאַרְעָא). וְאִמְרוּ: אָמֵן.

(.Cong – אָמֵן.)

יְהֵא שְׁלָמָא רַבָּא מִן שְׁמַיָּא, וְחַיִּים (טוֹבִים) עָלֵינוּ וְעַל כָּל יִשְׂרָאֵל. וְאִמְרוּ: אָמֵן. (.Cong – אָמֵן.)

Take three steps back. Bow left and say . . . עֹשֶׂה; bow right and say . . . הוּא; bow forward and say וְעַל כָּל . . . אָמֵן. Remain standing in place for a few moments, then take three steps forward.

עֹשֶׂה שָׁלוֹם בִּמְרוֹמָיו, הוּא בְּרַחֲמָיו יַעֲשֶׂה שָׁלוֹם עָלֵינוּ, וְעַל כָּל יִשְׂרָאֵל. וְאִמְרוּ: אָמֵן. (.Cong – אָמֵן.)

and girded Himself; He even made the world firm so that it should not falter.'[1] *On the Sabbath they would say: 'A psalm, a song for the Sabbath day.'*[2] *A psalm, a song for the time to come, to the day that will be entirely Sabbath and contentment for the eternal life.*

Talmud, *Megillah* 28b

תָּנָא *The Academy of Elijah taught: He who studies Torah laws every day, has the assurance that he will be in the World to Come, as it is said, 'The ways of the world are His'*[3] *— do not read* [הֲלִיכוֹת] *'ways,' but* [הֲלָכוֹת] *'laws.'*

Talmud, *Berachos* 64a

אָמַר *Rabbi Elazar said on behalf of Rabbi Chanina: Torah scholars increase peace in the world, as it is said: 'And all your children will be students of* H*ASHEM, and your children will have peace'*[4] *— do not read* [בָּנָיִךְ] *'your children,' but* [בּוֹנָיִךְ] *'your builders.'* Chazzan— *There is abundant peace for the lovers of Your Torah, and there is no stumbling block for them.*[5] *May there be peace within your wall, serenity within your palaces. For the sake of my brethren and comrades I shall speak of peace in your midst. For the sake of the House of* H*ASHEM, our God, I will request your good.*[6] H*ASHEM will give might to His people,* H*ASHEM will bless His people with peace.*[7]

RABBIS' KADDISH

In the presence of a *minyan,* mourners recite the Rabbis' *Kaddish* (see *Laws* §84-85).
[A transliteration of this *Kaddish* appears on p. 1146.]

יִתְגַּדַּל *May His great Name grow exalted and sanctified* (Cong.— *Amen.*) *in the world that He created as He willed. May He give reign to His kingship in your lifetimes and in your days, and in the lifetimes of the entire Family of Israel, swiftly and soon. Now respond: Amen.*

(Cong.— *Amen. May His great Name be blessed forever and ever.*)
May His great Name be blessed forever and ever.

Blessed, praised, glorified, exalted, extolled, mighty, upraised, and lauded be the Name of the Holy One, Blessed is He (Cong.— *Blessed is He*) *— beyond any blessing and song, praise and consolation that are uttered in the world. Now respond: Amen.* (Cong.— *Amen.*)

Upon Israel, upon the teachers, their disciples and all of their disciples and upon all those who engage in the study of Torah, who are here or anywhere else; may they and you have abundant peace, grace, kindness, and mercy, long life, ample nourishment, and salvation, from before their Father Who is in Heaven (and on earth). Now respond: Amen. (Cong. — *Amen.*)

May there be abundant peace from Heaven, and (good) life, upon us and upon all Israel. Now respond: Amen. (Cong.— *Amen.*)

Take three steps back. Bow left and say, *'He Who makes peace . . .';* bow right and say, *'may He . . .';* bow forward and say, *'and upon all Israel . . .'* Remain standing in place for a few moments, then take three steps forward.

He Who makes peace in His heights, may He, in His compassion, make peace upon us, and upon all Israel. Now respond: Amen. (Cong.— *Amen.*)

(1) *Psalms* 93:1. (2) 92:1. (3) *Habakkuk* 3:6. (4) *Isaiah* 54:13. (5) *Psalms* 119:165. (6) 122:7-9. (7) 29:11.

Stand while reciting עָלֵינוּ.

עָלֵינוּ לְשַׁבֵּחַ לַאֲדוֹן הַכֹּל, לָתֵת גְּדֻלָּה לְיוֹצֵר בְּרֵאשִׁית, שֶׁלֹּא עָשָׂנוּ כְּגוֹיֵי הָאֲרָצוֹת, וְלֹא שָׂמָנוּ כְּמִשְׁפְּחוֹת הָאֲדָמָה. שֶׁלֹּא שָׂם חֶלְקֵנוּ כָּהֶם, וְגוֹרָלֵנוּ כְּכָל הֲמוֹנָם. (שֶׁהֵם מִשְׁתַּחֲוִים לְהֶבֶל וָרִיק, וּמִתְפַּלְּלִים אֶל אֵל לֹא יוֹשִׁיעַ.[1]) וַאֲנַחְנוּ כּוֹרְעִים וּמִשְׁתַּחֲוִים וּמוֹדִים, לִפְנֵי מֶלֶךְ מַלְכֵי הַמְּלָכִים הַקָּדוֹשׁ בָּרוּךְ הוּא. שֶׁהוּא נוֹטֶה שָׁמַיִם וְיֹסֵד אָרֶץ,[2] וּמוֹשַׁב יְקָרוֹ בַּשָּׁמַיִם מִמַּעַל, וּשְׁכִינַת עֻזּוֹ בְּגָבְהֵי מְרוֹמִים. הוּא אֱלֹהֵינוּ, אֵין עוֹד. אֱמֶת מַלְכֵּנוּ, אֶפֶס זוּלָתוֹ, כַּכָּתוּב בְּתוֹרָתוֹ: וְיָדַעְתָּ הַיּוֹם וַהֲשֵׁבֹתָ אֶל לְבָבֶךָ, כִּי יהוה הוּא הָאֱלֹהִים בַּשָּׁמַיִם מִמַּעַל וְעַל הָאָרֶץ מִתָּחַת, אֵין עוֹד.[3]

Bow while reciting וַאֲנַחְנוּ כּוֹרְעִים וּמִשְׁתַּחֲוִים.

עַל כֵּן נְקַוֶּה לְּךָ יהוה אֱלֹהֵינוּ לִרְאוֹת מְהֵרָה בְּתִפְאֶרֶת עֻזֶּךָ, לְהַעֲבִיר גִּלּוּלִים מִן הָאָרֶץ, וְהָאֱלִילִים כָּרוֹת יִכָּרֵתוּן, לְתַקֵּן עוֹלָם בְּמַלְכוּת שַׁדַּי. וְכָל בְּנֵי בָשָׂר יִקְרְאוּ בִשְׁמֶךָ, לְהַפְנוֹת אֵלֶיךָ כָּל רִשְׁעֵי אָרֶץ. יַכִּירוּ וְיֵדְעוּ כָּל יוֹשְׁבֵי תֵבֵל, כִּי לְךָ תִּכְרַע כָּל בֶּרֶךְ, תִּשָּׁבַע כָּל לָשׁוֹן.[4] לְפָנֶיךָ יהוה אֱלֹהֵינוּ יִכְרְעוּ וְיִפֹּלוּ, וְלִכְבוֹד שִׁמְךָ יְקָר יִתֵּנוּ. וִיקַבְּלוּ כֻלָּם אֶת עוֹל מַלְכוּתֶךָ, וְתִמְלֹךְ עֲלֵיהֶם מְהֵרָה לְעוֹלָם וָעֶד. כִּי הַמַּלְכוּת שֶׁלְּךָ הִיא וּלְעוֹלְמֵי עַד תִּמְלוֹךְ בְּכָבוֹד, כַּכָּתוּב בְּתוֹרָתֶךָ: יהוה יִמְלֹךְ לְעֹלָם וָעֶד.[5] ❖ וְנֶאֱמַר: וְהָיָה יהוה לְמֶלֶךְ עַל כָּל הָאָרֶץ, בַּיּוֹם הַהוּא יִהְיֶה יהוה אֶחָד וּשְׁמוֹ אֶחָד.[6]

Some congregations recite the following after עָלֵינוּ:

אַל תִּירָא מִפַּחַד פִּתְאֹם, וּמִשֹּׁאַת רְשָׁעִים כִּי תָבֹא.[7] עֻצוּ עֵצָה וְתֻפָר, דַּבְּרוּ דָבָר וְלֹא יָקוּם, כִּי עִמָּנוּ אֵל.[8] וְעַד זִקְנָה אֲנִי הוּא, וְעַד שֵׂיבָה אֲנִי אֶסְבֹּל, אֲנִי עָשִׂיתִי וַאֲנִי אֶשָּׂא, וַאֲנִי אֶסְבֹּל וַאֲמַלֵּט.[9]

קדיש יתום

In the presence of a *minyan*, mourners recite קַדִּישׁ יָתוֹם, the Mourner's *Kaddish* (see *Laws* §81-83).

יִתְגַּדַּל וְיִתְקַדַּשׁ שְׁמֵהּ רַבָּא. (Cong. – אָמֵן.) בְּעָלְמָא דִּי בְרָא כִרְעוּתֵהּ. וְיַמְלִיךְ מַלְכוּתֵהּ, בְּחַיֵּיכוֹן וּבְיוֹמֵיכוֹן וּבְחַיֵּי דְכָל בֵּית יִשְׂרָאֵל, בַּעֲגָלָא וּבִזְמַן קָרִיב. וְאִמְרוּ: אָמֵן.

(Cong. – אָמֵן. יְהֵא שְׁמֵהּ רַבָּא מְבָרַךְ לְעָלַם וּלְעָלְמֵי עָלְמַיָּא.)

Stand while reciting עָלֵינוּ, *'It is our duty . . .'*

עָלֵינוּ *It is our duty to praise the Master of all, to ascribe greatness to the Molder of primeval creation, for He has not made us like the nations of the lands, and has not emplaced us like the families of the earth; for He has not assigned our portion like theirs nor our lot like all their multitudes. (For they bow to vanity and emptiness and pray to a god which helps not.[1]) But we bend our knees, bow, and acknowledge our thanks before the King Who reigns over kings, the Holy One, Blessed is He. He stretches out heaven and establishes earth's foundation,[2] the seat of His homage is in the heavens above and His powerful Presence is in the loftiest heights. He is our God and there is none other. True is our King, there is nothing beside Him, as it is written in His Torah: 'You are to know this day and take to your heart that* HASHEM *is the only God — in heaven above and on the earth below — there is none other.'[3]*

Bow while reciting 'But we bend our knees.'

עַל כֵּן *Therefore we put our hope in You,* HASHEM, *our God, that we may soon see Your mighty splendor, to remove detestable idolatry from the earth, and false gods will be utterly cut off, to perfect the universe through the Almighty's sovereignty. Then all humanity will call upon Your Name, to turn all the earth's wicked toward You. All the world's inhabitants will recognize and know that to You every knee should bend, every tongue should swear.[4] Before You,* HASHEM, *our God, they will bend every knee and cast themselves down and to the glory of Your Name they will render homage, and they will all accept upon themselves the yoke of Your kingship that You may reign over them soon and eternally. For the kingdom is Yours and You will reign for all eternity in glory as it is written in Your Torah:* HASHEM *shall reign for all eternity.[5]*
Chazzan– *And it is said:* HASHEM *will be King over all the world — on that day* HASHEM *will be One and His Name will be One.[6]*

Some congregations recite the following after *Aleinu.*

אַל תִּירָא *Do not fear sudden terror, or the holocaust of the wicked when it comes.[7] Plan a conspiracy and it will be annulled; speak your piece and it shall not stand, for God is with us.[8] Even till your seniority, I remain unchanged; and even till your ripe old age, I shall endure. I created you and I shall bear you; I shall endure and rescue.[9]*

MOURNER'S KADDISH

In the presence of a *minyan,* mourners recite קַדִּישׁ יָתוֹם, the Mourner's *Kaddish* (see *Laws* 81-83).
[A transliteration of this *Kaddish* appears on page 1147.]

יִתְגַּדַּל *May His great Name grow exalted and sanctified* (Cong.– *Amen.*) *in the world that He created as He willed. May He give reign to His kingship in your lifetimes and in your days, and in the lifetimes of the entire Family of Israel, swiftly and soon. Now respond: Amen.*

(Cong.– *Amen. May His great Name be blessed forever and ever.*)

---

(1) *Isaiah* 45:20. (2) 51:13. (3) *Deuteronomy* 4:39. (4) Cf. *Isaiah* 45:23.
(5) *Exodus* 15:18. (6) *Zechariah* 14:9. (7) *Proverbs* 3:25. (8) *Isaiah* 8:10. (9) 46:4.

יְהֵא שְׁמֵהּ רַבָּא מְבָרַךְ לְעָלַם וּלְעָלְמֵי עָלְמַיָּא.

יִתְבָּרַךְ וְיִשְׁתַּבַּח וְיִתְפָּאַר וְיִתְרוֹמַם וְיִתְנַשֵּׂא וְיִתְהַדָּר וְיִתְעַלֶּה וְיִתְהַלָּל שְׁמֵהּ דְּקֻדְשָׁא בְּרִיךְ הוּא (.Cong – בְּרִיךְ הוּא) – לְעֵֽלָּא מִן כָּל בִּרְכָתָא וְשִׁירָתָא תֻּשְׁבְּחָתָא וְנֶחֱמָתָא, דַּאֲמִירָן בְּעָלְמָא. וְאִמְרוּ: אָמֵן. (.Cong – אָמֵן.)

יְהֵא שְׁלָמָא רַבָּא מִן שְׁמַיָּא, וְחַיִּים עָלֵינוּ וְעַל כָּל יִשְׂרָאֵל. וְאִמְרוּ: אָמֵן. (.Cong – אָמֵן.)

Take three steps back. Bow left and say . . . עֹשֶׂה; bow right and say . . . הוּא; bow forward and say וְעַל כָּל . . . אָמֵן. Remain standing in place for a few moments, then take three steps forward.

עֹשֶׂה שָׁלוֹם בִּמְרוֹמָיו, הוּא יַעֲשֶׂה שָׁלוֹם עָלֵינוּ, וְעַל כָּל יִשְׂרָאֵל. וְאִמְרוּ: אָמֵן. (.Cong – אָמֵן.)

שיר הכבוד

The Ark is opened and שִׁיר הַכָּבוֹד, *The Song of Glory,* is recited responsively – the *chazzan* reciting the first verse, the congregation reciting the second and so on.

אַנְעִים זְמִירוֹת וְשִׁירִים אֶאֱרוֹג, כִּי אֵלֶיךָ נַפְשִׁי תַעֲרוֹג.

נַפְשִׁי חָמְדָה בְּצֵל יָדֶךָ, לָדַעַת כָּל רָז סוֹדֶךָ.

❖ מִדֵּי דַבְּרִי בִּכְבוֹדֶךָ, הוֹמֶה לִבִּי אֶל דּוֹדֶיךָ.

עַל כֵּן אֲדַבֵּר בְּךָ נִכְבָּדוֹת, וְשִׁמְךָ אֲכַבֵּד בְּשִׁירֵי יְדִידוֹת.

❖ אֲסַפְּרָה כְבוֹדְךָ וְלֹא רְאִיתִיךָ, אֲדַמְּךָ אֲכַנְּךָ וְלֹא יְדַעְתִּיךָ.

בְּיַד נְבִיאֶיךָ בְּסוֹד עֲבָדֶיךָ, דִּמִּיתָ הֲדַר כְּבוֹד הוֹדֶךָ.

❖ גְּדֻלָּתְךָ וּגְבוּרָתֶךָ, כִּנּוּ לְתֹקֶף פְּעֻלָּתֶךָ.

דִּמּוּ אוֹתְךָ וְלֹא כְּפִי יֶשְׁךָ, וַיְשַׁוּוּךָ לְפִי מַעֲשֶׂיךָ.

❖ הִמְשִׁילוּךָ בְּרֹב חֶזְיוֹנוֹת, הִנְּךָ אֶחָד בְּכָל דִּמְיוֹנוֹת.

וַיֶּחֱזוּ בְךָ זִקְנָה וּבַחֲרוּת, וּשְׂעַר רֹאשְׁךָ בְּשֵׂיבָה וְשַׁחֲרוּת.

❖ זִקְנָה בְּיוֹם דִּין וּבַחֲרוּת בְּיוֹם קְרָב, כְּאִישׁ מִלְחָמוֹת יָדָיו לוֹ רָב.

חָבַשׁ כּֽוֹבַע יְשׁוּעָה בְּרֹאשׁוֹ, הוֹשִׁיעָה לּוֹ יְמִינוֹ וּזְרוֹעַ קָדְשׁוֹ.

❖ טַלְלֵי אוֹרוֹת רֹאשׁוֹ נִמְלָא, קְוֻצּוֹתָיו רְסִיסֵי לָיְלָה.

יִתְפָּאֵר בִּי כִּי חָפֵץ בִּי. וְהוּא יִהְיֶה לִּי לַעֲטֶרֶת צְבִי.

❖ כֶּתֶם טָהוֹר פָּז דְּמוּת רֹאשׁוֹ, וְחַק עַל מֵצַח כְּבוֹד שֵׁם קָדְשׁוֹ.

לְחֵן וּלְכָבוֹד צְבִי תִפְאָרָה, אֻמָּתוֹ לוֹ עִטְּרָה עֲטָרָה.

❖ מַחְלְפוֹת רֹאשׁוֹ כְּבִימֵי בְחֻרוֹת, קְוֻצּוֹתָיו תַּלְתַּלִּים שְׁחוֹרוֹת.

נְוֵה הַצֶּדֶק צְבִי תִפְאַרְתּוֹ, יַעֲלֶה נָּא עַל רֹאשׁ שִׂמְחָתוֹ.

May His great Name be blessed forever and ever.

Blessed, praised, glorified, exalted, extolled, mighty, upraised, and lauded be the Name of the Holy One, Blessed is He (Cong.— *Blessed is He*) — *beyond any blessing and song, praise and consolation that are uttered in the world. Now respond: Amen.* (Cong.— *Amen*).

May there be abundant peace from Heaven, and life, upon us and upon all Israel. Now respond: Amen. (Cong.— *Amen.*)

Take three steps back. Bow left and say, *'He Who makes peace . . .'*; bow right and say, *'may He . . .'*; bow forward and say, *'and upon all Israel . . .'* Remain standing in place for a few moments, then take three steps forward.

He Who makes peace in His heights, may He make peace upon us, and upon all Israel. Now respond: Amen. (Cong.— *Amen.*)

SONG OF GLORY

The Ark is opened and the *Song of Glory* is recited responsively — the *chazzan* reciting the first verse, the congregation reciting the second and so on.

אַנְעִים זְמִירוֹת *I shall compose pleasant psalms and weave hymns,*
because for You shall my soul pine.

My soul desired the shelter of Your hand,
to know every mystery of Your secret.
∴ *As I speak of Your glory, my heart yearns for Your love.*
Therefore I shall speak of Your glories,
and Your Name I shall honor with loving songs.
∴ *I shall relate Your glory, though I see You not;*
I shall allegorize You, I shall describe You, though I know You not.
Through the hand of Your prophets, through the counsel of Your servants;
You allegorized the splendrous glory of Your power.
∴ *Your greatness and Your strength,*
they described the might of Your works.
They allegorized You, but not according to Your reality,
and they portrayed You according to Your deeds.
∴ *They symbolized You in many varied visions;*
yet You are a Unity containing all the allegories.
They envisioned in You agedness and virility,
and the hair of Your head as hoary and jet black.
∴ *Aged on judgment day and virile on the day of battle,*
like a man of war whose powers are many.
The hat of salvation He put on His head;
salvation for Him, His right hand and His sacred arm.
∴ *With illuminating dew drops His head is filled,*
His locks are the rains of the night.
He shall glory in me for He desires me,
and He shall be for me a crown of pride.
∴ *A form of the very finest gold upon his head,*
and carved on his forehead is His glorious, sacred Name.
For grace and for glory the pride of His splendor;
His nation crowns Him with its prayers.
∴ *The tresses of His head are like His youthful days;*
His locks are jet-black ringlets.
The Abode of righteousness is the pride of His splendor;
may He elevate it to His foremost joy.

❖ סְגֻלָּתוֹ תְּהִי בְיָדוֹ עֲטֶרֶת, וּצְנִיף מְלוּכָה צְבִי תִפְאָרֶת.
עֲמוּסִים נְשָׂאָם עֲטֶרֶת עִנְּדָם, מֵאֲשֶׁר יָקְרוּ בְעֵינָיו כִּבְּדָם.
❖ פְּאֵרוֹ עָלַי וּפְאֵרִי עָלָיו, וְקָרוֹב אֵלַי בְּקָרְאִי אֵלָיו.
צַח וְאָדוֹם לִלְבוּשׁוֹ אָדוֹם, פּוּרָה בְדָרְכוֹ בְּבוֹאוֹ מֵאֱדוֹם.
❖ קֶשֶׁר תְּפִלִּין הֶרְאָה לֶעָנָו, תְּמוּנַת יהוה לְנֶגֶד עֵינָיו.
רוֹצֶה בְעַמּוֹ עֲנָוִים יְפָאֵר, יוֹשֵׁב תְּהִלּוֹת בָּם לְהִתְפָּאֵר.
❖ רֹאשׁ דְּבָרְךָ אֱמֶת קוֹרֵא מֵרֹאשׁ, דּוֹר וָדוֹר עַם דּוֹרֶשְׁךָ דְּרוֹשׁ.
שִׁית הֲמוֹן שִׁירַי נָא עָלֶיךָ, וְרִנָּתִי תִּקְרַב אֵלֶיךָ.
❖ תְּהִלָּתִי תְּהִי לְרֹאשְׁךָ עֲטֶרֶת, וּתְפִלָּתִי תִּכּוֹן קְטֹרֶת.
תִּיקַר שִׁירַת רָשׁ בְּעֵינֶיךָ, כַּשִּׁיר יוּשַׁר עַל קָרְבָּנֶיךָ.
❖ בִּרְכָתִי תַעֲלֶה לְרֹאשׁ מַשְׁבִּיר, מְחוֹלֵל וּמוֹלִיד צַדִּיק כַּבִּיר.
וּבְבִרְכָתִי תְנַעֲנַע לִי רֹאשׁ, וְאוֹתָהּ קַח לְךָ כִּבְשָׂמִים רֹאשׁ.
❖ יֶעֱרַב נָא שִׂיחִי עָלֶיךָ, כִּי נַפְשִׁי תַעֲרוֹג אֵלֶיךָ.

לְךָ יהוה הַגְּדֻלָּה וְהַגְּבוּרָה וְהַתִּפְאֶרֶת וְהַנֵּצַח וְהַהוֹד, כִּי כֹל בַּשָּׁמַיִם וּבָאָרֶץ; לְךָ יהוה הַמַּמְלָכָה וְהַמִּתְנַשֵּׂא לְכֹל לְרֹאשׁ.[1] מִי יְמַלֵּל גְּבוּרוֹת יהוה, יַשְׁמִיעַ כָּל תְּהִלָּתוֹ.[2]

קדיש יתום

In the presence of a *minyan,* mourners recite קַדִּישׁ יָתוֹם, the Mourner's *Kaddish* (see *Laws* §81-83):

יִתְגַּדַּל וְיִתְקַדַּשׁ שְׁמֵהּ רַבָּא. (.Cong – אָמֵן) בְּעָלְמָא דִּי בְרָא כִרְעוּתֵהּ. וְיַמְלִיךְ מַלְכוּתֵהּ, בְּחַיֵּיכוֹן וּבְיוֹמֵיכוֹן וּבְחַיֵּי דְכָל בֵּית יִשְׂרָאֵל, בַּעֲגָלָא וּבִזְמַן קָרִיב. וְאִמְרוּ: אָמֵן.

(.Cong – אָמֵן. יְהֵא שְׁמֵהּ רַבָּא מְבָרַךְ לְעָלַם וּלְעָלְמֵי עָלְמַיָּא.)

יְהֵא שְׁמֵהּ רַבָּא מְבָרַךְ לְעָלַם וּלְעָלְמֵי עָלְמַיָּא.

יִתְבָּרַךְ וְיִשְׁתַּבַּח וְיִתְפָּאַר וְיִתְרוֹמַם וְיִתְנַשֵּׂא וְיִתְהַדָּר וְיִתְעַלֶּה וְיִתְהַלָּל שְׁמֵהּ דְּקֻדְשָׁא בְּרִיךְ הוּא (.Cong – בְּרִיךְ הוּא) — לְעֵלָּא מִן כָּל בִּרְכָתָא וְשִׁירָתָא תֻּשְׁבְּחָתָא וְנֶחֱמָתָא, דַּאֲמִירָן בְּעָלְמָא. וְאִמְרוּ: אָמֵן. (.Cong – אָמֵן.)

יְהֵא שְׁלָמָא רַבָּא מִן שְׁמַיָּא, וְחַיִּים עָלֵינוּ וְעַל כָּל יִשְׂרָאֵל. וְאִמְרוּ: אָמֵן. (.Cong – אָמֵן.)

Take three steps back. Bow left and say . . . עֹשֶׂה; bow right and say . . . הוּא; bow forward and say וְעַל כָּל . . . אָמֵן. Remain standing in place for a few moments, then take three steps forward.

עֹשֶׂה שָׁלוֹם בִּמְרוֹמָיו, הוּא יַעֲשֶׂה שָׁלוֹם עָלֵינוּ, וְעַל כָּל יִשְׂרָאֵל. וְאִמְרוּ: אָמֵן. (.Cong – אָמֵן.)

∴ *May His treasured nation be in His hand like a crown,*
and like a royal tiara the pride of His splendor.
From infancy He bore them and affixed them as a crown,
because they are precious in His eyes He honored them.
∴ *His tefillin-splendor is upon me and my tefillin-splendor is upon Him,*
and He is near to me when I call to Him.
He is white and crimson; His garment will be bloody red,
when He tramples as in a press on His coming from Edom.
∴ *He showed the tefillin-knot to the humble [Moses],*
the likeness of HASHEM *before his eyes.*
He desires His people, He will glorify the humble;
enthroned upon praises, He glories with them.
∴ *The very beginning of Your word is truth — one reads it from the Torah's start; the people that seeks You expounds each generation's fate.*
Place the multitude of my songs before You, please;
and my glad song bring near to You.
∴ *May my praise be a crown for Your head,*
and may my prayer be accepted like incense.
May the poor man's song be dear in Your eyes,
like the song that is sung over Your offerings.
∴ *May my blessing rise up upon the head of the Sustainer —*
Creator, Giver of life, mighty Righteous One.
And to my blessing, nod Your head to me,
and take it to Yourself like the finest incense.
∴ *May my prayer be sweet to You, for my soul shall pine for You.*

לְךָ *Yours,* HASHEM, *is the greatness, the strength, the splendor, the triumph, and the glory; even everything in heaven and earth; Yours,* HASHEM, *is the kingdom, and the sovereignty over every leader.*[1] *Who can express the mighty acts of* HASHEM*? Who can declare all His praise?*[2]

MOURNER'S KADDISH

In the presence of a *minyan,* mourners recite the Mourner's *Kaddish* (see *Laws* §81-83).

יִתְגַּדַּל *May His great Name grow exalted and sanctified* (Cong.– *Amen.*) *in the world that He created as He willed. May He give reign to His kingship in your lifetimes and in your days, and in the lifetimes of the entire Family of Israel, swiftly and soon. Now respond: Amen.*

(Cong.– *Amen. May His great Name be blessed forever and ever.*)

May His great Name be blessed forever and ever.

Blessed, praised, glorified, exalted, extolled, mighty, upraised, and lauded be the Name of the Holy One, Blessed is He (Cong.– *Blessed is He*) *— beyond any blessing and song, praise and consolation that are uttered in the world. Now respond: Amen.* (Cong.– *Amen.*)

May there be abundant peace from Heaven, and life, upon us and upon all Israel. Now respond: Amen. (Cong.– *Amen.*)

Take three steps back. Bow left and say, *'He Who makes peace . . .';* bow right and say, *'may He . . .';* bow forward and say, *'and upon all Israel . . .'* Remain standing in place for a few moments, then take three steps forward.

He Who makes peace in His heights, may He make peace upon us, and upon all Israel. Now respond: Amen. (Cong.– *Amen.*)

(1) *I Chronicles* 29:11. (2) *Psalms* 106:2.

שיר של יום

A different psalm is assigned as the שִׁיר שֶׁל יוֹם, *Song of the Day,* for each day of the week.

SUNDAY

הַיּוֹם יוֹם רִאשׁוֹן בְּשַׁבָּת, שֶׁבּוֹ הָיוּ הַלְוִיִּם אוֹמְרִים בְּבֵית הַמִּקְדָּשׁ:

תהלים כד

לְדָוִד מִזְמוֹר, לַיהוה הָאָרֶץ* וּמְלוֹאָהּ, תֵּבֵל וְיִשְׁבֵי בָהּ. כִּי הוּא עַל יַמִּים יְסָדָהּ,* וְעַל נְהָרוֹת יְכוֹנְנֶהָ. מִי יַעֲלֶה* בְהַר יהוה, וּמִי יָקוּם בִּמְקוֹם קָדְשׁוֹ. נְקִי כַפַּיִם* וּבַר לֵבָב, אֲשֶׁר לֹא נָשָׂא לַשָּׁוְא נַפְשִׁי,* וְלֹא נִשְׁבַּע לְמִרְמָה. יִשָּׂא בְרָכָה* מֵאֵת יהוה, וּצְדָקָה מֵאֱלֹהֵי יִשְׁעוֹ. זֶה דּוֹר דֹּרְשָׁיו, מְבַקְשֵׁי פָנֶיךָ יַעֲקֹב סֶלָה. שְׂאוּ שְׁעָרִים* רָאשֵׁיכֶם, וְהִנָּשְׂאוּ פִּתְחֵי עוֹלָם,* וְיָבוֹא מֶלֶךְ הַכָּבוֹד.* מִי זֶה מֶלֶךְ הַכָּבוֹד, יהוה עִזּוּז וְגִבּוֹר, יהוה גִּבּוֹר מִלְחָמָה. ❖ שְׂאוּ שְׁעָרִים רָאשֵׁיכֶם, וּשְׂאוּ פִּתְחֵי עוֹלָם, וְיָבֹא מֶלֶךְ הַכָּבוֹד. מִי הוּא זֶה מֶלֶךְ הַכָּבוֹד, יהוה צְבָאוֹת, הוּא מֶלֶךְ הַכָּבוֹד סֶלָה.

The service continues with קַדִּישׁ יָתוֹם, *the Mourner's Kaddish* (page 1030).

MONDAY

הַיּוֹם יוֹם שֵׁנִי בְּשַׁבָּת, שֶׁבּוֹ הָיוּ הַלְוִיִּם אוֹמְרִים בְּבֵית הַמִּקְדָּשׁ:

תהלים מח

שִׁיר מִזְמוֹר לִבְנֵי קֹרַח. גָּדוֹל יהוה וּמְהֻלָּל מְאֹד, בְּעִיר אֱלֹהֵינוּ, הַר קָדְשׁוֹ. יְפֵה נוֹף, מְשׂוֹשׂ כָּל הָאָרֶץ,* הַר צִיּוֹן* יַרְכְּתֵי צָפוֹן,* קִרְיַת מֶלֶךְ רָב. אֱלֹהִים בְּאַרְמְנוֹתֶיהָ נוֹדַע לְמִשְׂגָּב. כִּי הִנֵּה הַמְּלָכִים נוֹעֲדוּ,* עָבְרוּ יַחְדָּו. הֵמָּה רָאוּ כֵּן תָּמָהוּ, נִבְהֲלוּ נֶחְפָּזוּ. רְעָדָה אֲחָזָתַם שָׁם, חִיל כַּיּוֹלֵדָה. בְּרוּחַ קָדִים תְּשַׁבֵּר אֳנִיּוֹת

שִׁיר שֶׁל יוֹם / SONG OF THE DAY

As part of the morning Temple service, the Levites chanted a psalm that was suited to the significance of that particular day of the week (*Tamid* 7:4). As a memorial to the Temple, these psalms have been incorporated into daily *Shacharis*. The Talmud (*Rosh Hashanah* 31a) explains how each psalm was appropriate to its respective day; we will note the reasons in the commentary. The introductory sentence, *'Today is the first day of the Sabbath . . .,'* helps fulfill the Torah's command to remember the Sabbath always. By counting the days of the week with reference to the forthcoming Sabbath we tie our existence to the Sabbath. This is in sharp contrast to the non-Jewish custom of assigning names to the days in commemoration of events or gods, such as Sunday for the sun, Monday for the moon and so on (*Ramban, Exodus* 20:8).

יוֹם רִאשׁוֹן / The First Day

The first day's psalm teaches that everything belongs to God, because on the first day of creation, God was the sole Power — even the angels had not yet been created. He took possession of His newly created world with the intention of ceding it to man (*Rosh Hashanah* 31a).

לַה׳ הָאָרֶץ — *HASHEM's is the earth.* Since the world belongs to God, anyone who derives pleasure from His world without reciting the proper blessing expressing thanks to the Owner is regarded as a thief (*Berachos* 35a).

כִּי הוּא עַל יַמִּים יְסָדָהּ — *For He founded it upon seas.* The entire planet was covered with water until God commanded it to gather in seas and rivers and to expose the dry land (*Ibn Ezra*).

מִי יַעֲלֶה . . . — *Who may ascend . . .* God's most intense Presence is in the Temple, so those who wish to draw near and to perceive His splendor must be especially worthy (*Rashi*). By extension, one who wishes to enjoy spiritual elevation must refine his behavior.

נְקִי כַפַּיִם — *One with clean hands.* This verse answers the previous questions. To 'ascend,' one's hands may not be soiled by dishonest gain. He must be honest in his dealings with man, and reverent in his attitude toward God.

נַפְשִׁי — *My soul.* God is the 'speaker.' He refers to

SONG OF THE DAY

A different psalm is assigned as the Song of the Day for each day of the week.

SUNDAY

*Today is the first day of the Sabbath,
on which the Levites would recite in the Holy Temple:*

Psalm 24

לְדָוִד *Of David a psalm. HASHEM's is the earth* and its fullness, the inhabited land and those who dwell in it. For He founded it upon seas,* and established it upon rivers. Who may ascend* the mountain of HASHEM, and who may stand in the place of His sanctity? One with clean hands* and pure heart, who has not sworn in vain by My soul* and has not sworn deceitfully. He will receive a blessing* from HASHEM and just kindness from the God of his salvation. This is the generation of those who seek Him, those who strive for Your Presence — Jacob, Selah. Raise up your heads, O gates,* and be uplifted, you everlasting entrances,* so that the King of Glory* may enter. Who is this King of Glory? — HASHEM, the mighty and strong, HASHEM, the strong in battle.* Chazzan— *Raise up your heads, O gates, and raise up, you everlasting entrances, so that the King of Glory may enter. Who then is the King of Glory? HASHEM, Master of Legions, He is the King of Glory. Selah!*

The service continues with קַדִּישׁ יָתוֹם, *the Mourner's Kaddish* (p. 1030).

MONDAY

*Today is the second day of the Sabbath,
on which the Levites would recite in the Holy Temple:*

Psalm 48

שִׁיר מִזְמוֹר *A song, a psalm, by the sons of Korach. Great is HASHEM and much praised, in the city of our God, Mount of His Holiness. Fairest of sites, joy of all the earth* is Mount Zion,* by the northern sides* of the great king's city. In her palaces God is known as the Stronghold. For behold — the kings assembled,* they came together. They saw and they were astounded, they were confounded and hastily fled. Trembling gripped them there, convulsions like a woman in birth travail. With an east wind You smashed the ships*

---

one who swears falsely as having treated God's 'soul,' as it were, with disrespect.

יִשָּׂא בְרָכָה ... — *He will receive a blessing.* Because he honors God's Name in heart and behavior, such a person earns God's *blessing, kindness,* and *salvation* (*R' Hirsch*).

שְׂאוּ שְׁעָרִים — *Raise up ... O gates.* When Solomon sought to bring the Ark into the Temple, the gates remained shut despite all his pleas, until he prayed that God open the gates in the merit of David, who made all the preparations to build the Temple. Thus, this verse alludes to Solomon's future prayer (*Shabbos* 30a). The plea to the gates is repeated later to allude to the Ark's re-entry when the Third Temple will be built (*Ibn Ezra*).

פִּתְחֵי עוֹלָם — *Everlasting entrances,* i.e. the holiness of the Temple gates is eternal.

מֶלֶךְ הַכָּבוֹד — *The King of Glory.* God is given this title because He gives glory to those who revere Him (*Midrash*).

יוֹם שֵׁנִי / The Second Day

On this day, God separated between the heavenly and earthly components of the universe and ruled over both. Nevertheless, the psalm specifies Jerusalem because the seat of His holiness is Jerusalem (*Rosh Hashanah* 31a). *Resisei Laylah* comments that this day's separation between heaven and earth initiated the eternal strife between the spiritual and the physical. This is why the Levites recited a psalm composed by the sons of Korach, the man who instigated a quarrel against Moses.

מְשׂוֹשׂ כָּל הָאָרֶץ — *Joy of all the earth.* Jerusalem was given this title because the Holy City gave joy to the troubled who were atoned through the Temple service, and because the spiritual uplift of its holiness eased troubles (*Rashi*).

הַר צִיּוֹן — *Mount Zion.* The word Zion comes from צִיּוּן, a *monument.* The site of God's Sanctuary remains an eternal memorial to truth and sanctity (*R' Hirsch*).

יַרְכְּתֵי צָפוֹן — *The northern sides.* Mount Zion was north of the City of David, the *great king* (*Radak*).

הַמְּלָכִים נוֹעֲדוּ — *The kings assembled.* When

תַּרְשִׁישׁ.* כַּאֲשֶׁר שָׁמַעְנוּ* כֵּן רָאִינוּ בְּעִיר יהוה צְבָאוֹת, בְּעִיר אֱלֹהֵינוּ, אֱלֹהִים יְכוֹנְנֶהָ עַד עוֹלָם סֶלָה. דִּמִּינוּ אֱלֹהִים חַסְדֶּךָ, בְּקֶרֶב הֵיכָלֶךָ. כְּשִׁמְךָ אֱלֹהִים* כֵּן תְּהִלָּתְךָ, עַל קַצְוֵי אֶרֶץ, צֶדֶק מָלְאָה יְמִינֶךָ. יִשְׂמַח הַר צִיּוֹן, תָּגֵלְנָה בְּנוֹת יְהוּדָה, לְמַעַן מִשְׁפָּטֶיךָ. סֹבּוּ צִיּוֹן וְהַקִּיפוּהָ, סִפְרוּ מִגְדָּלֶיהָ. ❖ שִׁיתוּ לִבְּכֶם לְחֵילָה, פַּסְּגוּ אַרְמְנוֹתֶיהָ, לְמַעַן תְּסַפְּרוּ לְדוֹר אַחֲרוֹן. כִּי זֶה אֱלֹהִים אֱלֹהֵינוּ עוֹלָם וָעֶד, הוּא יְנַהֲגֵנוּ עַל־מוּת.*

The service continues with קַדִּישׁ יָתוֹם, *the Mourner's Kaddish* (page 1030).

TUESDAY

הַיּוֹם יוֹם שְׁלִישִׁי בְּשַׁבָּת, שֶׁבּוֹ הָיוּ הַלְוִיִּם אוֹמְרִים בְּבֵית הַמִּקְדָּשׁ:

תהלים פב

מִזְמוֹר לְאָסָף,* אֱלֹהִים נִצָּב בַּעֲדַת אֵל,* בְּקֶרֶב אֱלֹהִים יִשְׁפֹּט. עַד מָתַי* תִּשְׁפְּטוּ עָוֶל, וּפְנֵי רְשָׁעִים תִּשְׂאוּ סֶלָה. שִׁפְטוּ דַל וְיָתוֹם, עָנִי וָרָשׁ הַצְדִּיקוּ. פַּלְּטוּ דַל וְאֶבְיוֹן, מִיַּד רְשָׁעִים הַצִּילוּ. לֹא יָדְעוּ וְלֹא יָבִינוּ, בַּחֲשֵׁכָה יִתְהַלָּכוּ, יִמּוֹטוּ כָּל מוֹסְדֵי אָרֶץ. אֲנִי אָמַרְתִּי אֱלֹהִים אַתֶּם, וּבְנֵי עֶלְיוֹן כֻּלְּכֶם. אָכֵן כְּאָדָם תְּמוּתוּן, וּכְאַחַד הַשָּׂרִים תִּפֹּלוּ. ❖ קוּמָה אֱלֹהִים שָׁפְטָה הָאָרֶץ, כִּי אַתָּה תִנְחַל בְּכָל הַגּוֹיִם.

The service continues with קַדִּישׁ יָתוֹם, *the Mourner's Kaddish* (page 1030).

WEDNESDAY

הַיּוֹם יוֹם רְבִיעִי בְּשַׁבָּת, שֶׁבּוֹ הָיוּ הַלְוִיִּם אוֹמְרִים בְּבֵית הַמִּקְדָּשׁ:

תהלים צד:א-צה:ג

אֵל נְקָמוֹת יהוה, אֵל נְקָמוֹת הוֹפִיעַ. הִנָּשֵׂא שֹׁפֵט הָאָרֶץ, הָשֵׁב גְּמוּל עַל גֵּאִים. עַד מָתַי רְשָׁעִים, יהוה, עַד מָתַי רְשָׁעִים יַעֲלֹזוּ. יַבִּיעוּ יְדַבְּרוּ עָתָק, יִתְאַמְּרוּ כָּל פֹּעֲלֵי אָוֶן. עַמְּךָ יהוה יְדַכְּאוּ, וְנַחֲלָתְךָ יְעַנּוּ. אַלְמָנָה וְגֵר יַהֲרֹגוּ, וִיתוֹמִים יְרַצֵּחוּ. וַיֹּאמְרוּ לֹא יִרְאֶה יָּהּ,* וְלֹא יָבִין אֱלֹהֵי יַעֲקֹב. בִּינוּ* בֹּעֲרִים בָּעָם, וּכְסִילִים מָתַי תַּשְׂכִּילוּ. הֲנֹטַע

---

kings assembled at various times to attack Jerusalem, they saw that God was its *stronghold*. Seeing His miracles (next verse), they were astounded and fled *(Radak)*.

אֳנִיּוֹת תַּרְשִׁישׁ — *The ships of Tarshish.* A sea near Africa, Tarshish represents invading fleets that were dispatched against *Eretz Yisrael*.

כַּאֲשֶׁר שָׁמַעְנוּ — *As we heard.* From our ancestors we heard of God's miraculous salvations — but we will see similar wonders as well *(Rashi)*.

כְּשִׁמְךָ אֱלֹהִים — *Like Your Name, O God.* The prophets gave You exalted Names, but we can testify that *Your praise*, given You for actual deeds, justifies those glorious titles *(Radak)*.

עַל־מוּת — *Like children.* The two words are rendered as one: עַלְמוּת, *youth.* God will guide us like a father caring for his young *(Targum; Rashi)*; or He will preserve the enthusiasm and vigor of our youth *(Meiri)*. According to the Masoretic tradition that these are two words, they mean that God will continue to guide us *beyond death*, i.e., in the World to Come.

יוֹם שְׁלִישִׁי / The Third Day

On the third day, God caused the dry land to become visible and fit for habitation. He did so in order that man follow the Torah's laws and deal justly with other people. Therefore the psalm speaks of justice *(Rosh Hashanah* 31a). *Maharsha* explains that the theme of this psalm — the maintenance of equity and justice — is a prerequisite for the continued existence of the world that was revealed on the third day. But this message is not limited only to courts. In his own personal life, every Jew is a judge, for his opinions and decisions about people can affect their lives in a thousand different ways.

לְאָסָף — *Of Assaf.* A descendant of Korach, Assaf was one of the psalmists whose composi-

of Tarshish. As we heard,* so we saw in the city of* HASHEM, *Master of Legions, in the city of our God — may God establish it to eternity, Selah! We hoped, O God, for Your kindness, in the midst of Your Sanctuary. Like Your Name, O God,* so is Your praise — to the ends of the earth; righteousness fills Your right hand. May Mount Zion be glad, may the daughters of Judah rejoice, because of Your judgments. Walk about Zion and encircle her, count her towers.* Chazzan– *Mark well in your hearts her ramparts, raise up her palaces, that you may recount it to the succeeding generation: that this is God, our God, forever and ever, He will guide us like children.**

The service continues with קַדִּישׁ יָתוֹם, *the Mourner's Kaddish* (p. 1030).

TUESDAY

Today is the third day of the Sabbath,
on which the Levites would recite in the Holy Temple:

Psalm 82

מִזְמוֹר *A psalm of Assaf:* God stands in the Divine assembly,* in the midst of judges shall He judge. Until when* will you judge lawlessly and favor the presence of the wicked, Selah? Judge the needy and the orphan, vindicate the poor and impoverished. Rescue the needy and destitute, from the hand of the wicked deliver them. They do not know nor do they understand, in darkness they walk; all foundations of the earth collapse. I said, 'You are angelic, sons of the Most High are you all.' But like men you shall die, and like one of the princes you shall fall.* Chazzan– *Arise, O God, judge the earth, for You allot the heritage among all the nations.*

The service continues with קַדִּישׁ יָתוֹם, *the Mourner's Kaddish* (p. 1030).

WEDNESDAY

Today is the fourth day of the Sabbath,
on which the Levites would recite in the Holy Temple:

Psalm 94:1-95:3

אֵל נְקָמוֹת *O God of vengeance,* HASHEM; *O God of vengeance, appear! Arise, O Judge of the earth, render recompense to the haughty. How long shall the wicked —* O HASHEM *— how long shall the wicked exult? They speak freely, they utter malicious falsehood, they glorify themselves, all workers of iniquity. Your nation,* HASHEM, *they crush, and they afflict Your heritage. The widow and the stranger they slay, and the orphans they murder. And they say, 'God will not see,* nor will the God of Jacob understand.' Understand,* you boors among the people; and you fools, when will you gain wisdom? He Who implants*

---

tions David incorporated into the Book of Psalms.

בַּעֲדַת אֵל — *In the Divine assembly.* Judges who seek truth and justice are the *Divine assembly,* because they represent God's justice on earth. As a result of their sincerity, God Himself penetrates into their hearts — בְּקֶרֶב אֱלֹהִים, *in the midst of judges* — to assure them of reaching a just verdict *(Alshich).*

עַד מָתַי — *Until when . . .?* The next three verses address directly the judges who do not carry out their responsibilities. Included in this exhortation is the clear message for the judges to take the initiative in seeking out and correcting injustice.

יוֹם רְבִיעִי / The Fourth Day

On the fourth day, God created the sun, moon, and stars, but instead of recognizing them as God's servants, man eventually came to regard the luminaries as independent gods that should be worshiped. Because of this idolatry, God showed Himself to be, as this psalm describes Him, the *God of vengeance,* for despite His almost endless patience and mercy, He does not tolerate evil forever.

וַיֹּאמְרוּ לֹא יִרְאֶה יָּהּ — *And they say, 'God will not see . . .'* When the Temple was destroyed, it was as if God's power had been diminished and His Four-letter Name abbreviated to the two letters of יָהּ *(Eruvin* 18b). This gives evildoers the pretext to claim that God was detached from the world and unable to see the wickedness being done on earth *(Zera Yaakov).*

בִּינוּ — *Understand.* If only the boors would

אֹזֶן הֲלֹא יִשְׁמָע, אִם יֹצֵר עַיִן הֲלֹא יַבִּיט. הֲיֹסֵר גּוֹיִם הֲלֹא יוֹכִיחַ, הַמְלַמֵּד אָדָם דָּעַת. יהוה יֹדֵעַ מַחְשְׁבוֹת אָדָם, כִּי הֵמָּה הָבֶל. אַשְׁרֵי הַגֶּבֶר* אֲשֶׁר תְּיַסְּרֶנּוּ יָּהּ, וּמִתּוֹרָתְךָ תְלַמְּדֶנּוּ. לְהַשְׁקִיט לוֹ* מִימֵי רָע, עַד יִכָּרֶה לָרָשָׁע שָׁחַת. כִּי לֹא יִטֹּשׁ יהוה עַמּוֹ, וְנַחֲלָתוֹ* לֹא יַעֲזֹב. כִּי עַד צֶדֶק יָשׁוּב מִשְׁפָּט,* וְאַחֲרָיו כָּל יִשְׁרֵי לֵב. מִי יָקוּם לִי עִם מְרֵעִים, מִי יִתְיַצֵּב לִי עִם פֹּעֲלֵי אָוֶן. לוּלֵי יהוה עֶזְרָתָה לִּי, כִּמְעַט שָׁכְנָה דוּמָה נַפְשִׁי. אִם אָמַרְתִּי מָטָה רַגְלִי,* חַסְדְּךָ יהוה יִסְעָדֵנִי. בְּרֹב שַׂרְעַפַּי בְּקִרְבִּי, תַּנְחוּמֶיךָ יְשַׁעַשְׁעוּ נַפְשִׁי. הַיְחָבְרְךָ כִּסֵּא הַוּוֹת, יֹצֵר עָמָל* עֲלֵי חֹק. יָגוֹדּוּ עַל נֶפֶשׁ צַדִּיק, וְדָם נָקִי יַרְשִׁיעוּ. וַיְהִי יהוה לִי לְמִשְׂגָּב, וֵאלֹהַי לְצוּר מַחְסִי. וַיָּשֶׁב עֲלֵיהֶם אֶת אוֹנָם, וּבְרָעָתָם יַצְמִיתֵם, יַצְמִיתֵם יהוה אֱלֹהֵינוּ.

❖ לְכוּ נְרַנְּנָה* לַיהוה, נָרִיעָה לְצוּר יִשְׁעֵנוּ. נְקַדְּמָה פָנָיו בְּתוֹדָה, בִּזְמִרוֹת נָרִיעַ לוֹ. כִּי אֵל גָּדוֹל יהוה, וּמֶלֶךְ גָּדוֹל עַל כָּל אֱלֹהִים.

The service continues with קַדִּישׁ יָתוֹם, *the Mourner's Kaddish* (page 1030).

THURSDAY

הַיּוֹם יוֹם חֲמִישִׁי בַּשַּׁבָּת, שֶׁבּוֹ הָיוּ הַלְוִיִּם אוֹמְרִים בְּבֵית הַמִּקְדָּשׁ:

תהלים פא

לַמְנַצֵּחַ עַל הַגִּתִּית* לְאָסָף. הַרְנִינוּ לֵאלֹהִים עוּזֵּנוּ, הָרִיעוּ לֵאלֹהֵי יַעֲקֹב.* שְׂאוּ זִמְרָה וּתְנוּ תֹף, כִּנּוֹר נָעִים עִם נָבֶל. תִּקְעוּ בַחֹדֶשׁ שׁוֹפָר,* בַּכֵּסֶה לְיוֹם חַגֵּנוּ. כִּי חֹק לְיִשְׂרָאֵל הוּא, מִשְׁפָּט* לֵאלֹהֵי יַעֲקֹב. עֵדוּת בִּיהוֹסֵף שָׂמוֹ,* בְּצֵאתוֹ עַל אֶרֶץ מִצְרָיִם, שְׂפַת לֹא יָדַעְתִּי אֶשְׁמָע. הֲסִירוֹתִי מִסֵּבֶל שִׁכְמוֹ, כַּפָּיו מִדּוּד תַּעֲבֹרְנָה. בַּצָּרָה קָרָאתָ, וָאֲחַלְּצֶךָּ, אֶעֶנְךָ בְּסֵתֶר רַעַם, אֶבְחָנְךָ עַל מֵי מְרִיבָה, סֶלָה. שְׁמַע עַמִּי וְאָעִידָה בָּךְ, יִשְׂרָאֵל אִם תִּשְׁמַע לִי. לֹא יִהְיֶה בְךָ אֵל זָר, וְלֹא תִשְׁתַּחֲוֶה לְאֵל נֵכָר.

---

realize that God cannot be fooled or ignored! *(Radak)*.

אַשְׁרֵי הַגֶּבֶר — *Praiseworthy is the man.* The wicked ask why the righteous suffer, if God truly controls everything. The Psalmist answers that God afflicts the righteous only when it is to their benefit, to correct them, to make them realize the futility of physical pleasures, or to atone for their sins *(Radak; Meiri)*.

לְהַשְׁקִיט לוֹ — *To give him rest.* The suffering of good people on earth spares them from the far worse *days of evil* in *Gehinnom,* but they will not suffer forever — only until evil is purged from the world and *a pit is dug for the wicked (Rashi)*.

וְנַחֲלָתוֹ — *His heritage.* Even in exile, Israel knows it will survive, because it is God's *heritage (Radak)*.

יָשׁוּב מִשְׁפָּט — *Shall revert to righteousness.* For the good person who has sinned, God's punishment will cause him to repent *(Rashi)*.

מָטָה רַגְלִי — *'My foot falters.'* When Israel fears it will falter, God's goodness supports it *(Radak)*.

יֹצֵר עָמָל . . . — *Those who fashion evil* . . . Would God associate with those who legitimize their evil by turning it into a code of law? *(Radak)*.

לְכוּ נְרַנְּנָה — *Come — let us sing.* The next three verses are not part of the psalm of the day, and are not recited in all congregations. They are the beginning of the next psalm and are recited because of their inspiring message that is an apt climax to the song of the day.

⊰ יוֹם חֲמִישִׁי / The Fifth Day

On the fifth day of creation, God made the birds and the fish, which bring joy to the world. When people observe the vast variety of colorful birds and fish, they are awed by the tremendous scope of God's creative ability, and they are stirred to praise Him with song *(Rosh Hashanah* 31a).

הַגִּתִּית — *The gittis.* A musical instrument named after the town of Gath, where it was made *(Rashi)*.

הָרִיעוּ לֵאלֹהֵי יַעֲקֹב — *Call out to the God of Jacob.*

the ear, shall He not hear? He Who fashions the eye, shall He not see? He Who chastises nations, shall He not rebuke? — He Who teaches man knowledge. HASHEM knows the thoughts of man, that they are futile. Praiseworthy is the man whom God disciplines, and whom You teach from Your Torah. To give him rest* from the days of evil, until a pit is dug for the wicked. For HASHEM will not cast off His people, nor will He forsake His heritage.* For justice shall revert to righteousness,* and following it will be all of upright heart. Who will rise up for me against evildoers? Who will stand up for me against the workers of iniquity? Had HASHEM not been a help to me, my soul would soon have dwelt in silence. If I said, 'My foot falters,'* Your kindness, HASHEM, supported me. When my forebodings were abundant within me, Your comforts cheered my soul. Can the throne of destruction be associated with You? — those who fashion evil* into a way of life. They join together against the soul of the righteous, and the blood of the innocent they condemn. Then HASHEM became a stronghold for me, and my God, the Rock of my refuge. He turned upon them their own violence, and with their own evil He will cut them off, HASHEM, our God, will cut them off.*

Chazzan— *Come — let us sing* to HASHEM, let us call out to the Rock of our salvation. Let us greet Him with thanksgiving, with praiseful songs let us call out to Him. For a great God is HASHEM, and a great King above all heavenly powers.*

The service continues with קַדִּישׁ יָתוֹם, *the Mourner's Kaddish* (p. 1030).

THURSDAY

Today is the fifth day of the Sabbath,
on which the Levites would recite in the Holy Temple:

Psalm 81

לַמְנַצֵּחַ *For the Conductor, upon the gittis,* by Assaf. Sing joyously to the God of our might, call out to the God of Jacob.* Raise a song and sound the drum, the sweet harp with the lyre. Blow the shofar at the moon's renewal,* at the time appointed for our festive day. Because it is a decree for Israel, a judgment day* for the God of Jacob. He imposed it as a testimony for Joseph* when he went forth over the land of Egypt — 'I understood a language I never knew!' I removed his shoulder from the burden, his hands let go of the kettle. In distress you called out, and I released you, I answered you with thunder when you hid, I tested you at the Waters of Strife, Selah. Listen, My nation, and I will attest to you; O Israel, if you would but listen to Me. There shall be no strange god within you, nor shall you bow before an alien god.*

The Patriarch Jacob is singled out because he went down to Egypt with his sons and their families. The two hundred and ten years of bondage are counted from the moment Jacob arrived in Egypt. During this period the children of Jacob called out to God in their distress (*Radak*).

תִּקְעוּ בַחֹדֶשׁ שׁוֹפָר — *Blow the shofar at the moon's renewal.* The *moon's renewal* is a poetic term for the first day of the lunar month, when the moon becomes visible again. This refers to Rosh Hashanah, the only Festival that occurs on the first day of the month and when the *shofar* is blown.

Homiletically Rosh Hashanah is the time for חֹדֶשׁ, *renewal,* of one's dedication and שׁוֹפָר [cognate with שִׁיפּוּר, *beautification*] *improvement,* of one's deeds (*Midrash Shocher Tov*).

חֹק ... מִשְׁפָּט — *Decree ... judgment [day].* It is a Divine decree that Israel blow the *shofar* on Rosh Hashanah, the day when God sits in judgment (*Rashi*).

The Talmud (*Beitzah* 16a) translates חֹק as a *fixed ration.* On Rosh Hashanah the heavenly tribunal fixes each person's sustenance for the coming year.

עֵדוּת בִּיהוֹסֵף שָׂמוֹ — *He imposed it as a testimony for Joseph.* This entire verse is based on the life of Joseph. The Talmud (*Rosh Hashanah* 10b) teaches that Joseph was released from prison and appointed viceroy of Egypt on Rosh Hashanah. In honor of that event, God ordained the *mitzvah* of shofar on Rosh Hashanah as a *testimony,* i.e.,

אָנֹכִי יהוה אֱלֹהֶיךָ, הַמַּעַלְךָ מֵאֶרֶץ מִצְרָיִם, הַרְחֶב פִּיךָ* וַאֲמַלְאֵהוּ. וְלֹא שָׁמַע עַמִּי לְקוֹלִי, וְיִשְׂרָאֵל לֹא אָבָה לִי. וָאֲשַׁלְּחֵהוּ בִּשְׁרִירוּת לִבָּם, יֵלְכוּ בְּמוֹעֲצוֹתֵיהֶם. לוּ עַמִּי שֹׁמֵעַ לִי, יִשְׂרָאֵל בִּדְרָכַי יְהַלֵּכוּ. כִּמְעַט אוֹיְבֵיהֶם אַכְנִיעַ, וְעַל צָרֵיהֶם אָשִׁיב יָדִי. מְשַׂנְאֵי יהוה יְכַחֲשׁוּ לוֹ,* וִיהִי עִתָּם לְעוֹלָם.* ❖ וַיַּאֲכִילֵהוּ* מֵחֵלֶב חִטָּה, וּמִצּוּר דְּבַשׁ אַשְׂבִּיעֶךָ.

The service continues with קַדִּישׁ יָתוֹם, *the Mourner's Kaddish* (page 1030).

FRIDAY

הַיּוֹם יוֹם שִׁשִּׁי בְּשַׁבָּת, שֶׁבּוֹ הָיוּ הַלְוִיִּם אוֹמְרִים בְּבֵית הַמִּקְדָּשׁ:

תהלים צג

יהוה מָלָךְ, גֵּאוּת לָבֵשׁ, לָבֵשׁ יהוה עֹז הִתְאַזָּר, אַף תִּכּוֹן תֵּבֵל בַּל תִּמּוֹט. נָכוֹן כִּסְאֲךָ מֵאָז, מֵעוֹלָם אָתָּה. נָשְׂאוּ נְהָרוֹת יהוה, נָשְׂאוּ נְהָרוֹת קוֹלָם, יִשְׂאוּ נְהָרוֹת דָּכְיָם. מִקֹּלוֹת מַיִם רַבִּים, אַדִּירִים מִשְׁבְּרֵי יָם, אַדִּיר בַּמָּרוֹם יהוה. ❖ עֵדֹתֶיךָ נֶאֶמְנוּ מְאֹד לְבֵיתְךָ נַאֲוָה קֹדֶשׁ, יהוה לְאֹרֶךְ יָמִים.

The service continues with קַדִּישׁ יָתוֹם, *the Mourner's Kaddish* (page 1030).

THE SABBATH

הַיּוֹם יוֹם שַׁבַּת קֹדֶשׁ שֶׁבּוֹ הָיוּ הַלְוִיִּם אוֹמְרִים בְּבֵית הַמִּקְדָּשׁ:

תהלים צב

מִזְמוֹר שִׁיר לְיוֹם הַשַּׁבָּת. טוֹב לְהֹדוֹת לַיהוה, וּלְזַמֵּר לְשִׁמְךָ עֶלְיוֹן. לְהַגִּיד בַּבֹּקֶר חַסְדֶּךָ, וֶאֱמוּנָתְךָ בַּלֵּילוֹת. עֲלֵי עָשׂוֹר וַעֲלֵי נָבֶל, עֲלֵי הִגָּיוֹן בְּכִנּוֹר. כִּי שִׂמַּחְתַּנִי יהוה בְּפָעֳלֶךָ, בְּמַעֲשֵׂי יָדֶיךָ אֲרַנֵּן. מַה גָּדְלוּ מַעֲשֶׂיךָ יהוה, מְאֹד עָמְקוּ מַחְשְׁבֹתֶיךָ. אִישׁ בַּעַר לֹא יֵדָע, וּכְסִיל לֹא יָבִין אֶת זֹאת. בִּפְרֹחַ רְשָׁעִים כְּמוֹ עֵשֶׂב, וַיָּצִיצוּ כָּל פֹּעֲלֵי אָוֶן, לְהִשָּׁמְדָם עֲדֵי עַד. וְאַתָּה מָרוֹם לְעֹלָם יהוה. כִּי הִנֵּה אֹיְבֶיךָ יהוה, כִּי הִנֵּה אֹיְבֶיךָ יֹאבֵדוּ, יִתְפָּרְדוּ כָּל פֹּעֲלֵי אָוֶן. וַתָּרֶם כִּרְאֵים קַרְנִי, בַּלֹּתִי בְּשֶׁמֶן רַעֲנָן. וַתַּבֵּט עֵינִי בְּשׁוּרָי, בַּקָּמִים עָלַי מְרֵעִים, תִּשְׁמַעְנָה אָזְנָי. ❖ צַדִּיק כַּתָּמָר יִפְרָח, כְּאֶרֶז בַּלְּבָנוֹן יִשְׂגֶּה. שְׁתוּלִים בְּבֵית יהוה, בְּחַצְרוֹת אֱלֹהֵינוּ יַפְרִיחוּ. עוֹד יְנוּבוּן בְּשֵׂיבָה, דְּשֵׁנִים וְרַעֲנַנִּים יִהְיוּ. לְהַגִּיד כִּי יָשָׁר יהוה, צוּרִי וְלֹא עַוְלָתָה בּוֹ.

The service continues with קַדִּישׁ יָתוֹם, *the Mourner's Kaddish* (p. 1030).

---

a reminder of Joseph's freedom. In order to qualify as a ruler under Egyptian law, Joseph had to know all the languages — a requirement that was fulfilled when the angel Gabriel taught them to him. Thus Joseph exclaimed, *'I understood a language I never knew' (Rashi).*

הַרְחֶב פִּיךָ — *Open wide your mouth,* with requests, and I will fulfill them. God urges Israel to ask all that its heart desires *(Ibn Ezra).* By asking God for *everything* that he needs, a person demonstrates his faith that God's power and generosity know no bounds *(Taanis 3:6).*

מְשַׂנְאֵי ה׳ יְכַחֲשׁוּ לוֹ — *Those who hate* HASHEM [i.e., because Israel's enemies are God's as well] *lie to Him.* They deny that they ever harmed Israel *(Rashi).*

וִיהִי עִתָּם לְעוֹלָם — *So their destiny is eternal.* Israel's tormentors will be condemned to eternal suffering. In contrast, concerning Israel, God promises that:

וַיַּאֲכִילֵהוּ — *But He would feed him.* In the Wilderness, God provided Israel with manna that

I am HASHEM, *your God, Who elevated you from the land of Egypt, open wide your mouth* and I will fill it. But My people did not heed My voice and Israel did not desire Me. So I let them follow their heart's fantasies, they follow their own counsels. If only My people would heed Me, if Israel would walk in My ways. In an instant I would subdue their foes, and against their tormentors turn My hand. Those who hate* HASHEM *lie to Him* — so their destiny is eternal.** Chazzan— *But He would feed him* with the cream of the wheat, and with honey from a rock sate you.*

The service continues with קַדִּישׁ יָתוֹם, *the Mourner's Kaddish* (p. 1030).

FRIDAY

Today is the sixth day of the Sabbath,
on which the Levites would recite in the Holy Temple:

Psalm 93

יהוה מָלָךְ HASHEM *will have reigned, He will have donned grandeur; He will have donned might and girded Himself; He even made the world firm so that it should not falter. Your throne was established from of old, eternal are You. Like rivers they raised, O* HASHEM, *like rivers they raised their voice; like rivers they shall raise their destructiveness. More than the roars of many waters, mightier than the waves of the sea — You are mighty on high,* HASHEM. Chazzan— *Your testimonies are exceedingly trustworthy about Your House, the Sacred Dwelling — O* HASHEM, *may it be for long days.*

The service continues with קַדִּישׁ יָתוֹם, *the Mourner's Kaddish* (p. 1030).

THE SABBATH

Today is the Holy Sabbath day,
on which the Levites would sing in the Holy Temple:

Psalm 92

מִזְמוֹר שִׁיר *A psalm, a song for the Sabbath day. It is good to thank* HASHEM *and to sing praise to Your Name, O Exalted One; to relate Your kindness in the dawn and Your faith in the nights. Upon ten-stringed instrument and lyre, with singing accompanied by a harp. For You have gladdened me,* HASHEM, *with Your deeds; at the works of Your Hands I sing glad song. How great are Your deeds,* HASHEM; *exceedingly profound are Your thoughts. A boor cannot know, nor can a fool understand this: when the wicked bloom like grass and all the doers of iniquity blossom — it is to destroy them till eternity. But You remain exalted forever,* HASHEM. *For behold! — Your enemies,* HASHEM, *for behold! — Your enemies shall perish, dispersed shall be all doers of iniquity. As exalted as a re'eim's shall be my pride, I will be saturated with ever-fresh oil. My eyes have seen my vigilant foes; when those who would harm me rise up against me, my ears have heard their doom.* Chazzan— *A righteous man will flourish like a date palm, like a cedar in the Lebanon he will grow tall. Planted in the house of* HASHEM, *in the courtyards of our God they will flourish. They will still be fruitful in old age, vigorous and fresh they will be — to declare that* HASHEM *is just, my Rock in Whom there is no wrong.*

The service continues with קַדִּישׁ יָתוֹם, *the Mourner's Kaddish* (p. 1030).

---

was finer than *the cream of the wheat* and with honey-sweet water from a rock *(Ibn Ezra).*

יום ששי / The Sixth Day

Because it describes God in His full grandeur and power as He was when He completed the six days of Creation, and because it describes Him as 'donning' grandeur and 'girding' Himself like one dressing in his Sabbath finery, this psalm was designated as the song of Friday, when the footsteps of the Sabbath begin to be heard. [Commentary appears on page 40.]

שַׁבָּת / The Sabbath

Although this psalm is identified as belonging to the theme of the Sabbath and was the Levites'

קידושא רבא

ON THE SABBATH BEGIN HERE.

Many omit some or all of these verses and begin with עַל כֵּן.

אִם תָּשִׁיב* מִשַּׁבָּת רַגְלֶךָ, עֲשׂוֹת חֲפָצֶךָ בְּיוֹם קָדְשִׁי, וְקָרָאתָ לַשַּׁבָּת עֹנֶג, לִקְדוֹשׁ יהוה מְכֻבָּד, וְכִבַּדְתּוֹ מֵעֲשׂוֹת דְּרָכֶיךָ, מִמְּצוֹא חֶפְצְךָ וְדַבֵּר דָּבָר. אָז תִּתְעַנַּג עַל יהוה, וְהִרְכַּבְתִּיךָ עַל בָּמֳתֵי אָרֶץ, וְהַאֲכַלְתִּיךָ נַחֲלַת יַעֲקֹב אָבִיךָ,* כִּי פִּי יהוה דִּבֵּר.[1]

וְשָׁמְרוּ בְנֵי יִשְׂרָאֵל אֶת הַשַּׁבָּת, לַעֲשׂוֹת אֶת הַשַּׁבָּת לְדֹרֹתָם בְּרִית עוֹלָם. בֵּינִי וּבֵין בְּנֵי יִשְׂרָאֵל אוֹת הִיא לְעֹלָם, כִּי שֵׁשֶׁת יָמִים עָשָׂה יהוה אֶת הַשָּׁמַיִם וְאֶת הָאָרֶץ, וּבַיּוֹם הַשְּׁבִיעִי שָׁבַת וַיִּנָּפַשׁ.[2]

זָכוֹר* אֶת יוֹם הַשַּׁבָּת לְקַדְּשׁוֹ. שֵׁשֶׁת יָמִים תַּעֲבֹד וְעָשִׂיתָ כָּל מְלַאכְתֶּךָ. וְיוֹם הַשְּׁבִיעִי שַׁבָּת לַיהוה אֱלֹהֶיךָ, לֹא תַעֲשֶׂה כָל מְלָאכָה, אַתָּה וּבִנְךָ וּבִתֶּךָ עַבְדְּךָ וַאֲמָתְךָ וּבְהֶמְתֶּךָ, וְגֵרְךָ אֲשֶׁר בִּשְׁעָרֶיךָ. כִּי שֵׁשֶׁת יָמִים עָשָׂה יהוה אֶת הַשָּׁמַיִם וְאֶת הָאָרֶץ אֶת הַיָּם וְאֶת כָּל אֲשֶׁר בָּם, וַיָּנַח בַּיּוֹם הַשְּׁבִיעִי —

עַל כֵּן בֵּרַךְ יהוה אֶת יוֹם הַשַּׁבָּת וַיְקַדְּשֵׁהוּ.[3]

(אֵלֶּה מוֹעֲדֵי יהוה מִקְרָאֵי קֹדֶשׁ אֲשֶׁר תִּקְרְאוּ אֹתָם בְּמוֹעֲדָם.[4])

וַיְדַבֵּר מֹשֶׁה* אֶת מֹעֲדֵי יהוה, אֶל בְּנֵי יִשְׂרָאֵל.[5]

סַבְרִי מָרָנָן וְרַבָּנָן וְרַבּוֹתַי:

בָּרוּךְ אַתָּה יהוה אֱלֹהֵינוּ מֶלֶךְ הָעוֹלָם, בּוֹרֵא פְּרִי הַגָּפֶן.

(All present – אָמֵן.)

---

song for the Sabbath Temple service, the text contains not a single direct reference to the Sabbath. Among the explanations given are:

— The psalm refers not to the weekly Sabbath, but to the World to Come, when man will achieve the spiritual perfection we only glimpse during the Sabbath. The psalm is thus well suited to the Sabbath which is a semblance of that future spiritual perfection *(Rashi)*.

— Praise of God is necessary, but difficult on weekdays when people must struggle for a livelihood. On the Sabbath, free from the strictures of the week, Jews can turn their minds to the perception of God's ways and His praise — which are the topics of this psalm *(Radak)*.

Additional commentary to this psalm appears on page 38.

קִדּוּשָׁא רַבָּא / The Morning Kiddush

The morning *Kiddush* was introduced by the Sages, and its status is thus inferior to the evening *Kiddush* which is Scriptural in origin *(Pesachim* 106b). Therefore, it is euphemistically called קִידּוּשָׁא רַבָּא, the *Great Kiddush*. Originally, the *Kiddush* consisted only of the blessing over wine *(Pesachim* 106b), the Scriptural verses

KIDDUSHA RABBA

ON THE SABBATH BEGIN HERE.

Many omit some or all of these verses and begin with *'therefore HASHEM blessed.'*

אִם תָּשִׁיב *If you restrain,* because of the Sabbath, your feet, refrain from accomplishing your own needs on My holy day; if you proclaim the Sabbath 'a delight,' the holy one of HASHEM, 'honored one,' and you honor it by not doing your own ways, from seeking your needs or discussing the forbidden. Then you shall be granted pleasure with HASHEM and I shall mount you astride the heights of the world, and provide you the heritage of your forefather Jacob* — for the mouth of HASHEM has spoken.*[1]

וְשָׁמְרוּ *And the Children of Israel observed the Sabbath, to make the Sabbath for their generations an eternal covenant. Between Me and the Children of Israel it is a sign forever, that in six days did HASHEM make the heaven and the earth, and on the seventh day He rested and was refreshed.*[2]

זָכוֹר *Always remember* the Sabbath day to hallow it. For six days you may labor and do all your work. But the seventh day is the Sabbath for HASHEM, Your God; you may do no work — you, your son and your daughter, your slave and your maidservant, your animal, and the stranger who is in your gates. For in six days did HASHEM make the heaven and the earth, the sea and all that is in them and He rested on the seventh day;*

therefore HASHEM blessed the Sabbath day and sanctified it.[3]

(These are the appointed festivals of HASHEM, holy convocations, which you are to proclaim in their appointed times.[4]*)*

And Moses declared HASHEM's appointed festivals to the Children of Israel.*[5]

By your leave, my masters and teachers:

בָּרוּךְ *Blessed are You, HASHEM, our God, King of the universe, Who creates the fruit of the vine.* (All present — *Amen.)*

(1) *Isaiah* 58:13-14. (2) *Exodus* 31:16-17. (3) 20:8-11. (4) *Leviticus* 23:4. (5) 23:44.

having been added over the centuries. However, not everyone says all the verses.

אִם תָּשִׁיב — *If you restrain.* These verses from *Isaiah* conclude a chapter that urges a variety of good practices upon people and assures them of God's blessings in return for compliance.

נַחֲלַת יַעֲקֹב אָבִיךָ — *The heritage of your forefather Jacob.* The land promised Abraham and Isaac was delineated by borders, but Jacob's blessing had no limitation.

זָכוֹר — *Always remember.* The fourth of the Ten Commandments, this passage implies the positive commandments of the day.

אֵלֶּה מוֹעֲדֵי ... וַיְדַבֵּר מֹשֶׁה — *These are the appointed festivals ... And Moses declared.* These two verses bracket the Scriptural passage that delineates the laws pertaining to each Festival. Thus, they are an appropriate selection for the Festival *Kiddush.*

Laws of Kiddush

The laws for *Kiddush* on *Yom Tov* are the same as on Shabbos. It is essential that *Kiddush*

מעין שלש

The following blessing is recited after partaking of (a) grain products such as foods made with matzah meal (but not matzah itself which requires the full *Bircas HaMazon*); (b) grape wine or grape juice; (c) grapes, figs, pomegranates, olives, or dates. (If foods from two or three of these groups were consumed, then the insertions for each group are connected with the conjunctive ו, thus וְעַל.) The order of insertion in such a case is grain, wine, fruit.)

בָּרוּךְ אַתָּה יהוה אֱלֹהֵינוּ מֶלֶךְ הָעוֹלָם,

After grain products:	After wine:	After fruits:
עַל הַמִּחְיָה	עַל הַגֶּפֶן	עַל הָעֵץ
וְעַל הַכַּלְכָּלָה,	וְעַל פְּרִי הַגֶּפֶן,	וְעַל פְּרִי הָעֵץ,

וְעַל תְּנוּבַת הַשָּׂדֶה, וְעַל אֶרֶץ חֶמְדָּה טוֹבָה וּרְחָבָה, שֶׁרָצִיתָ וְהִנְחַלְתָּ לַאֲבוֹתֵינוּ, לֶאֱכוֹל מִפִּרְיָהּ וְלִשְׂבּוֹעַ מִטּוּבָהּ. רַחֵם יהוה אֱלֹהֵינוּ עַל יִשְׂרָאֵל עַמֶּךָ, וְעַל יְרוּשָׁלַיִם עִירֶךָ, וְעַל צִיּוֹן מִשְׁכַּן כְּבוֹדֶךָ, וְעַל מִזְבְּחֶךָ וְעַל הֵיכָלֶךָ. וּבְנֵה יְרוּשָׁלַיִם עִיר הַקֹּדֶשׁ בִּמְהֵרָה בְיָמֵינוּ, וְהַעֲלֵנוּ לְתוֹכָהּ, וְשַׂמְּחֵנוּ בְּבִנְיָנָהּ, וְנֹאכַל מִפִּרְיָהּ, וְנִשְׂבַּע מִטּוּבָהּ, וּנְבָרֶכְךָ עָלֶיהָ בִּקְדֻשָּׁה וּבְטָהֳרָה. [On the Sabbath– וּרְצֵה וְהַחֲלִיצֵנוּ בְּיוֹם הַשַּׁבָּת הַזֶּה.] וְשַׂמְּחֵנוּ בְּיוֹם חַג הַמַּצּוֹת הַזֶּה. כִּי אַתָּה יהוה טוֹב וּמֵטִיב לַכֹּל, וְנוֹדֶה לְּךָ עַל הָאָרֶץ

After grain products	After wine:	After fruit:
וְעַל הַמִּחְיָה.	וְעַל פְּרִי הַגֶּפֶן.	וְעַל הַפֵּרוֹת.°

בָּרוּךְ אַתָּה יהוה, עַל הָאָרֶץ

וְעַל הַמִּחְיָה.	וְעַל פְּרִי הַגֶּפֶן.	וְעַל הַפֵּרוֹת.°

°If the fruit grew in *Eretz Yisrael*, substitute פֵּירוֹתֶיהָ for הַפֵּרוֹת.

בורא נפשות

After eating or drinking any food for which neither *Bircas HaMazon* nor the Three-Faceted Blessing applies, such as fruits other than the above, vegetables or beverages other than wine, recite:

בָּרוּךְ אַתָּה יהוה אֱלֹהֵינוּ מֶלֶךְ הָעוֹלָם, בּוֹרֵא נְפָשׁוֹת רַבּוֹת וְחֶסְרוֹנָן, עַל כָּל מַה שֶּׁבָּרָא(תָ) לְהַחֲיוֹת בָּהֶם נֶפֶשׁ כָּל חָי. בָּרוּךְ חֵי הָעוֹלָמִים.

---

be followed by a meal at the site of the *Kiddush* (*Shulchan Aruch, Orach Chaim* 273:1). The Talmud (*Pesachim* 101a) states: אֵין קִידּוּשׁ אֶלָּא בְּמְקוֹם סְעוּדָה, *Kiddush is valid only at a meal.* It is also forbidden to eat or drink (even water) before one has recited *Kiddush* (O.C. 271:4). It follows from this that if one did say the *Kiddush*, but did not follow it with a meal, his *Kiddush* is not valid, and he may not eat or drink (see O.C. 269:1). These rules apply to the *Kiddush* recited at night and the one said in the morning as well (see O.C. 289:1).

Many *poskim* assert that a meal in this

THE THREE-FACETED BLESSING

The following blessing is recited after partaking of (a) grain products such as foods made with matzah meal (but not matzah itself which requires the full *Bircas HaMazon*); (b) grape wine or grape juice; (c) grapes, figs, pomegranates, olives, or dates. (If foods from two or three of these groups were consumed, then the insertions for each group are connected with the conjunctive ו, thus וְעַל.) The order of insertion in such a case is grain, wine, fruit.)

בָּרוּךְ *Blessed are You, HASHEM, our God, King of the universe, for the*

After grain products:	After wine:	After fruits:
nourishment and the sustenance,	*vine and the fruit of the vine,*	*tree and the fruit of the tree,*

and for the produce of the field; for the desirable, good and spacious Land that You were pleased to give our forefathers as a heritage, to eat of its fruit and to be satisfied with its goodness. Have mercy, HASHEM, our God, on Israel, Your people; on Jerusalem, Your city; and on Zion, the resting place of Your glory; upon Your altar, and upon Your Temple. Rebuild Jerusalem, the city of holiness, speedily in our days. Bring us up into it and gladden us in its rebuilding and let us eat from its fruit and be satisfied with its goodness and bless You upon it in holiness and purity. [On the Sabbath— *And be pleased to let us rest on this Sabbath day.]* *And gladden us on this day of the Festival of Matzos. For You, HASHEM, are good and do good to all and we thank You for the land and for the*

After grain products:	After wine:	After fruit:
nourishment.	*fruit of the vine.*	*fruit.*°

Blessed are You, HASHEM, for the land and for the

nourishment.	*fruit of the vine.*	*fruit.*°

°If the fruit grew in *Eretz Yisrael,* substitute *'its fruit.'*

BOREI NEFASHOS

After eating or drinking any food for which neither *Bircas HaMazon* nor the Three-Faceted Blessing applies, such as fruits other than the above, vegetables or beverages other than wine, recite:

בָּרוּךְ *Blessed are You, HASHEM, our God, King of the universe, Who creates numerous living things with their deficiencies; for all that You have created with which to maintain the life of every being. Blessed is He, the life of the worlds.*

---

context need not consist of bread (i.e., matzah), but that it is sufficient to eat an olive's volume of cake made of one of the five grains (wheat, barley, oats, rye, and spelt), or to drink — besides the wine which is drunk for *Kiddush* — a *revi'is* of wine or grape juice. Other foods or drinks do not qualify as a meal in this regard (see O.C. 273:5 with *Mishnah Berurah*). Some *poskim* rule that one can be lenient in cases of emergency — e.g., a person feels faint but has no cake or extra wine/grape juice — and rely on the view of the *Shiltei HaGibborim* that fruit is also considered a meal concerning the morning *Kiddush.* Hence, if one goes to a *bris* or social function where *Kiddush* is made but no cake is served, he should drink an extra *revi'is* of wine or grape juice, otherwise he should not partake of any food, since he will, in essence, be eating before *Kiddush* (M.B. #26).

This law has special relevancy on Pesach, when the cake that is served at a *Kiddush* often will be made of potato flour. In case of emergency, however, one can follow the *Kiddush* with other foods, as stated above.

❧ מנחה לשני ימים האחרונים ☙

אַשְׁרֵי יוֹשְׁבֵי בֵיתֶךָ, עוֹד יְהַלְלוּךָ סֶּלָה.[1] אַשְׁרֵי הָעָם שֶׁכָּכָה לּוֹ, אַשְׁרֵי הָעָם שֶׁיהוה אֱלֹהָיו.[2]

תהלים קמה

תְּהִלָּה לְדָוִד,

אֲרוֹמִמְךָ אֱלוֹהַי הַמֶּלֶךְ, וַאֲבָרְכָה שִׁמְךָ לְעוֹלָם וָעֶד.
בְּכָל יוֹם אֲבָרְכֶךָּ, וַאֲהַלְלָה שִׁמְךָ לְעוֹלָם וָעֶד.
גָּדוֹל יהוה וּמְהֻלָּל מְאֹד, וְלִגְדֻלָּתוֹ אֵין חֵקֶר.
דּוֹר לְדוֹר יְשַׁבַּח מַעֲשֶׂיךָ, וּגְבוּרֹתֶיךָ יַגִּידוּ.
הֲדַר כְּבוֹד הוֹדֶךָ, וְדִבְרֵי נִפְלְאֹתֶיךָ אָשִׂיחָה.
וֶעֱזוּז נוֹרְאוֹתֶיךָ יֹאמֵרוּ, וּגְדוּלָּתְךָ אֲסַפְּרֶנָּה.
זֵכֶר רַב טוּבְךָ יַבִּיעוּ, וְצִדְקָתְךָ יְרַנֵּנוּ.
חַנּוּן וְרַחוּם יהוה, אֶרֶךְ אַפַּיִם וּגְדָל חָסֶד.
טוֹב יהוה לַכֹּל, וְרַחֲמָיו עַל כָּל מַעֲשָׂיו.
יוֹדוּךָ יהוה כָּל מַעֲשֶׂיךָ, וַחֲסִידֶיךָ יְבָרְכוּכָה.
כְּבוֹד מַלְכוּתְךָ יֹאמֵרוּ, וּגְבוּרָתְךָ יְדַבֵּרוּ.
לְהוֹדִיעַ לִבְנֵי הָאָדָם גְּבוּרֹתָיו, וּכְבוֹד הֲדַר מַלְכוּתוֹ.
מַלְכוּתְךָ מַלְכוּת כָּל עֹלָמִים, וּמֶמְשַׁלְתְּךָ בְּכָל דּוֹר וָדֹר.
סוֹמֵךְ יהוה לְכָל הַנֹּפְלִים, וְזוֹקֵף לְכָל הַכְּפוּפִים.
עֵינֵי כֹל אֵלֶיךָ יְשַׂבֵּרוּ, וְאַתָּה נוֹתֵן לָהֶם אֶת אָכְלָם בְּעִתּוֹ.

While reciting the verse פּוֹתֵחַ, concentrate intently on its meaning.

פּוֹתֵחַ אֶת יָדֶךָ,
וּמַשְׂבִּיעַ לְכָל חַי רָצוֹן.

צַדִּיק יהוה בְּכָל דְּרָכָיו, וְחָסִיד בְּכָל מַעֲשָׂיו.
קָרוֹב יהוה לְכָל קֹרְאָיו, לְכֹל אֲשֶׁר יִקְרָאֻהוּ בֶאֱמֶת.
רְצוֹן יְרֵאָיו יַעֲשֶׂה, וְאֶת שַׁוְעָתָם יִשְׁמַע וְיוֹשִׁיעֵם.
שׁוֹמֵר יהוה אֶת כָּל אֹהֲבָיו, וְאֵת כָּל הָרְשָׁעִים יַשְׁמִיד.
❖ תְּהִלַּת יהוה יְדַבֶּר פִּי, וִיבָרֵךְ כָּל בָּשָׂר שֵׁם קָדְשׁוֹ לְעוֹלָם וָעֶד.
וַאֲנַחְנוּ נְבָרֵךְ יָהּ, מֵעַתָּה וְעַד עוֹלָם, הַלְלוּיָהּ.[3]

(1) *Psalms* 84:5. (2) 144:15. (3) 115:18.

❧ MINCHAH / מִנְחָה ☙

Minchah is usually recited in the late afternoon, a particularly apt time for prayer, for it is a time of Divine mercy. Thus, both Isaac (*Genesis* 24:63) and Elijah (*I Kings* 18:36) prayed in the afternoon. Prefatory remarks to *Minchah* and commentary to אַשְׁרֵי appear on page 8.

MINCHAH FOR THE LAST TWO DAYS

אַשְׁרֵי *Praiseworthy are those who dwell in Your house; may they always praise You, Selah![1] Praiseworthy is the people for whom this is so, praiseworthy is the people whose God is HASHEM.[2]*

Psalm 145 *A psalm of praise by David:*

א *I will exalt You, my God the King,*
and I will bless Your Name forever and ever.
ב *Every day I will bless You,*
and I will laud Your Name forever and ever.
ג *HASHEM is great and exceedingly lauded,*
and His greatness is beyond investigation.
ד *Each generation will praise Your deeds to the next*
and of Your mighty deeds they will tell.
ה *The splendrous glory of Your power*
and Your wondrous deeds I shall discuss.
ו *And of Your awesome power they will speak,*
and Your greatness I shall relate.
ז *A recollection of Your abundant goodness they will utter*
and of Your righteousness they will sing exultantly.
ח *Gracious and merciful is HASHEM,*
slow to anger, and great in [bestowing] kindness.
ט *HASHEM is good to all; His mercies are on all His works.*
י *All Your works shall thank You, HASHEM,*
and Your devout ones will bless You.
כ *Of the glory of Your kingdom they will speak,*
and of Your power they will tell;
ל *To inform human beings of His mighty deeds,*
and the glorious splendor of His kingdom.
מ *Your kingdom is a kingdom spanning all eternities,*
and Your dominion is throughout every generation.
ס *HASHEM supports all the fallen ones and straightens all the bent.*
ע *The eyes of all look to You with hope*
and You give them their food in its proper time;
פ *You open Your hand,*
and satisfy the desire of every living thing.

While reciting the verse, *'You open . . .'* concentrate intently on its meaning.

צ *Righteous is HASHEM in all His ways*
and magnanimous in all His deeds.
ק *HASHEM is close to all who call upon Him —*
to all who call upon Him sincerely.
ר *The will of those who fear Him He will do;*
and their cry He will hear, and save them.
ש *HASHEM protects all who love Him;*
but all the wicked He will destroy.
ת Chazzan– *May my mouth declare the praise of HASHEM*
and may all flesh bless His Holy Name forever and ever.

We will bless God from this time and forever, Halleluyah![3]

The primary part of וּבָא לְצִיּוֹן is the *Kedushah* recited by the angels. These verses are presented in bold type and it is preferable that the congregation recite them aloud and in unison. However, the interpretive translation in Aramaic (which follows the verses in bold type) should be recited softly.

וּבָא לְצִיּוֹן גּוֹאֵל,* וּלְשָׁבֵי פֶשַׁע בְּיַעֲקֹב, נְאֻם יהוה. וַאֲנִי, זֹאת בְּרִיתִי* אוֹתָם, אָמַר יהוה, רוּחִי אֲשֶׁר עָלֶיךָ, וּדְבָרַי אֲשֶׁר שַׂמְתִּי בְּפִיךָ, לֹא יָמוּשׁוּ מִפִּיךָ וּמִפִּי זַרְעֲךָ* וּמִפִּי זֶרַע זַרְעֲךָ, אָמַר יהוה, מֵעַתָּה וְעַד עוֹלָם:[1] ❖ וְאַתָּה קָדוֹשׁ יוֹשֵׁב תְּהִלּוֹת יִשְׂרָאֵל.*[2] וְקָרָא זֶה אֶל זֶה וְאָמַר:

קָדוֹשׁ, קָדוֹשׁ, קָדוֹשׁ יהוה צְבָאוֹת, מְלֹא כָל הָאָרֶץ כְּבוֹדוֹ.[3]

וּמְקַבְּלִין דֵּין מִן דֵּין וְאָמְרִין:
קַדִּישׁ בִּשְׁמֵי מְרוֹמָא עִלָּאָה בֵּית שְׁכִינְתֵּהּ,
קַדִּישׁ עַל אַרְעָא עוֹבַד גְּבוּרְתֵּהּ,
קַדִּישׁ לְעָלַם וּלְעָלְמֵי עָלְמַיָּא, יהוה צְבָאוֹת,
מַלְיָא כָל אַרְעָא זִיו יְקָרֵהּ.[4]

❖ וַתִּשָּׂאֵנִי רוּחַ,* וָאֶשְׁמַע אַחֲרַי קוֹל רַעַשׁ גָּדוֹל:

בָּרוּךְ כְּבוֹד יהוה מִמְּקוֹמוֹ.[5]

וּנְטָלַתְנִי רוּחָא, וּשְׁמָעִית בַּתְרַי קָל זִיעַ סַגִּיא דִּמְשַׁבְּחִין וְאָמְרִין:
בְּרִיךְ יְקָרָא דַיהוה מֵאֲתַר בֵּית שְׁכִינְתֵּהּ.[6]

יהוה יִמְלֹךְ לְעֹלָם וָעֶד.[7]

יהוה מַלְכוּתֵהּ קָאֵם לְעָלַם וּלְעָלְמֵי עָלְמַיָּא.[8]

יהוה אֱלֹהֵי אַבְרָהָם יִצְחָק וְיִשְׂרָאֵל אֲבֹתֵינוּ, שָׁמְרָה זֹּאת* לְעוֹלָם, לְיֵצֶר מַחְשְׁבוֹת לְבַב עַמֶּךָ, וְהָכֵן לְבָבָם אֵלֶיךָ.[9] וְהוּא רַחוּם,

---

⊰ וּבָא לְצִיּוֹן / Uva Letzion

The most important part of the וּבָא לְצִיּוֹן prayer is the recitation of the angel's praises of God.

The Talmud (*Sotah* 49a) declares that since the destruction of the Temple, even the physical beauty and pleasures of the world began deteriorating. If so, by what merit does the world endure? Rava teaches: the *Kedushah* in the prayer *Uva Letzion*, and the recitation of *Kaddish* following the public study of Torah. *Rashi* explains that after the Destruction, the primary focus of holiness in the universe is Torah study. In *Uva Letzion*, the Sages combined the Scriptural verses containing the angel's praise of God with the interpretive translation of *Yonasan ben Uziel*. Thus, this prayer itself constitutes Torah study and its recitation involves the entire congregation in Torah study. This emphasis on Torah study is further stressed by the latter part of *Uva Letzion* which lauds the study and observance of the Torah. The *Kaddish* recited after public Torah study is a further affirmation of the Torah's central role in Jewish existence.

וּבָא לְצִיּוֹן גּוֹאֵל — *A redeemer shall come to Zion.* God pledges that the Messiah will come to redeem the city Zion and the people of Israel. Not only those who remained righteous throughout the ordeal of exile will be saved, but even those who had sinned will join in the glorious future, if they return to the ways of God (*Etz Yosef*).

בְּרִיתִי — *My covenant.* God affirms that His covenant, i.e., His *spirit* of prophecy and *words* of Torah, will remain with Israel forever (*Metzudos*).

מִפִּיךָ וּמִפִּי זַרְעֲךָ . . . — *From your mouth, nor from*

The primary part of וּבָא לְצִיּוֹן, *'A redeemer shall come . . .'*, is the *Kedushah* recited by the angels. These verses are presented in bold type and it is preferable that the congregation recite them aloud and in unison. However, the interpretive translation in Aramaic (which follows the verses in bold type) should be recited softly.

וּבָא לְצִיּוֹן *'A redeemer shall come to Zion* and to those of Jacob who repent from willful sin,' the words of* HASHEM. *'And as for Me, this is My covenant* with them,' said* HASHEM, *'My spirit that is upon you and My words that I have placed in your mouth shall not be withdrawn from your mouth, nor from the mouth of your offspring,* nor from the mouth of your offspring's offspring,' said* HASHEM, *'from this moment and forever.'*[1] Chazzan– *You are the Holy One, enthroned upon the praises of Israel.**[2] *And one [angel] will call another and say:*

'Holy, holy, holy is HASHEM, Master of Legions,
the whole world is filled with His glory.'[3]

And they receive permission from one another and say:
'Holy in the most exalted heaven, the abode of His Presence;
holy on earth, product of His strength;
holy forever and ever is HASHEM, *Master of Legions —*
the entire world is filled with the radiance of His glory.'[4]
Chazzan– *And a wind lifted me;* and I heard behind me*
the sound of a great noise:

'Blessed is the glory of HASHEM from His place.'[5]

And a wind lifted me and I heard behind me the sound
of the powerful movement of those who praised saying:
'Blessed is the honor of HASHEM
from the place of the abode of His Presence.'[6]

HASHEM shall reign for all eternity.[7]

HASHEM *— His kingdom is established forever and ever.*[8]

HASHEM, *God of Abraham, Isaac, and Israel, our forefathers, may You preserve this* forever as the realization of the thoughts in Your people's heart, and may You direct their heart to You.*[9] *He, the Merciful One,*

(1) *Isaiah* 59:20-21. (2) *Psalms* 22:4. (3) *Isaiah* 6:3. (4) *Targum Yonasan.* (5) *Ezekiel* 3:12. (6) *Targum Yonasan.* (7) *Exodus* 15:18. (8) *Targum Onkelos.* (9) *I Chronicles* 29:18.

the mouth of your offspring . . . This is a Divine assurance that if a family produces three consecutive generations of profound Torah scholars, the blessing of Torah knowledge will not be withdrawn from its posterity (*Bava Metzia* 85a). In a broader sense, we see the fulfillment of this blessing in the miracle that Torah greatness has remained with Israel throughout centuries of exile and flight from country to country and from continent to continent (*Siach Yitzchak*).

יוֹשֵׁב תְּהִלּוֹת יִשְׂרָאֵל — *Enthroned upon the praises of Israel.* Although God is praised by myriad angels, He values the praises of Israel above all; as the Sages teach (*Chullin* 90b), the angels are not permitted to sing their praises above until the Jews sing theirs below (*Abudraham*).

וַתִּשָּׂאֵנִי רוּחַ — *And a wind lifted me.* This was uttered by the prophet Ezekiel, who had just been commanded to undertake a difficult mission on behalf of the exiled Jews. God sent a wind to transport him to Babylon, and as he was lifted, he heard the song of the angels. This suggests that the person who ignores his own convenience in order to serve God can expect to climb spiritual heights beyond his normal capacity.

שָׁמְרָה זֹּאת — *May You preserve this.* May God help us remain permanently with the above fervent declaration of His holiness and kingship (*Abudraham*).

יְכַפֵּר עָוֹן וְלֹא יַשְׁחִית, וְהִרְבָּה לְהָשִׁיב אַפּוֹ, וְלֹא יָעִיר כָּל חֲמָתוֹ.[1] כִּי אַתָּה אֲדֹנָי טוֹב וְסַלָּח, וְרַב חֶסֶד לְכָל קֹרְאֶיךָ.[2] צִדְקָתְךָ צֶדֶק לְעוֹלָם, וְתוֹרָתְךָ אֱמֶת.[3] תִּתֵּן אֱמֶת לְיַעֲקֹב, חֶסֶד לְאַבְרָהָם, אֲשֶׁר נִשְׁבַּעְתָּ לַאֲבֹתֵינוּ מִימֵי קֶדֶם.[4] בָּרוּךְ אֲדֹנָי יוֹם יוֹם יַעֲמָס לָנוּ, הָאֵל יְשׁוּעָתֵנוּ סֶלָה.[5] יהוה צְבָאוֹת עִמָּנוּ, מִשְׂגָּב לָנוּ אֱלֹהֵי יַעֲקֹב סֶלָה.[6] יהוה צְבָאוֹת, אַשְׁרֵי אָדָם בֹּטֵחַ בָּךְ.[7] יהוה הוֹשִׁיעָה, הַמֶּלֶךְ יַעֲנֵנוּ בְיוֹם קָרְאֵנוּ.[8]

בָּרוּךְ הוּא אֱלֹהֵינוּ שֶׁבְּרָאָנוּ לִכְבוֹדוֹ, וְהִבְדִּילָנוּ מִן הַתּוֹעִים, וְנָתַן לָנוּ תּוֹרַת אֱמֶת, וְחַיֵּי עוֹלָם נָטַע בְּתוֹכֵנוּ. הוּא יִפְתַּח לִבֵּנוּ בְּתוֹרָתוֹ, וְיָשֵׂם בְּלִבֵּנוּ אַהֲבָתוֹ וְיִרְאָתוֹ וְלַעֲשׂוֹת רְצוֹנוֹ וּלְעָבְדוֹ בְּלֵבָב שָׁלֵם, לְמַעַן לֹא נִיגַע לָרִיק, וְלֹא נֵלֵד לַבֶּהָלָה.[9]

יְהִי רָצוֹן מִלְּפָנֶיךָ יהוה אֱלֹהֵינוּ וֵאלֹהֵי אֲבוֹתֵינוּ, שֶׁנִּשְׁמֹר חֻקֶּיךָ בָּעוֹלָם הַזֶּה, וְנִזְכֶּה וְנִחְיֶה וְנִרְאֶה וְנִירַשׁ טוֹבָה וּבְרָכָה לִשְׁנֵי יְמוֹת הַמָּשִׁיחַ וּלְחַיֵּי הָעוֹלָם הַבָּא. לְמַעַן יְזַמֶּרְךָ כָבוֹד וְלֹא יִדֹּם, יהוה אֱלֹהַי לְעוֹלָם אוֹדֶךָּ.[10] בָּרוּךְ הַגֶּבֶר אֲשֶׁר יִבְטַח בַּיהוה, וְהָיָה יהוה מִבְטַחוֹ.[11] בִּטְחוּ בַיהוה עֲדֵי עַד, כִּי בְּיָהּ יהוה צוּר עוֹלָמִים.[12] ❖ וְיִבְטְחוּ בְךָ יוֹדְעֵי שְׁמֶךָ, כִּי לֹא עָזַבְתָּ דֹּרְשֶׁיךָ, יהוה.[13] יהוה חָפֵץ לְמַעַן צִדְקוֹ, יַגְדִּיל תּוֹרָה וְיַאְדִּיר.[14]

חצי קדיש

Chazzan recites חֲצִי קַדִּישׁ.

יִתְגַּדַּל וְיִתְקַדַּשׁ שְׁמֵהּ רַבָּא. (.Cong – אָמֵן.) בְּעָלְמָא דִּי בְרָא כִרְעוּתֵהּ. וְיַמְלִיךְ מַלְכוּתֵהּ, בְּחַיֵּיכוֹן וּבְיוֹמֵיכוֹן וּבְחַיֵּי דְכָל בֵּית יִשְׂרָאֵל, בַּעֲגָלָא וּבִזְמַן קָרִיב. וְאִמְרוּ: אָמֵן.

(.Cong – אָמֵן. יְהֵא שְׁמֵהּ רַבָּא מְבָרַךְ לְעָלַם וּלְעָלְמֵי עָלְמַיָּא.)

יְהֵא שְׁמֵהּ רַבָּא מְבָרַךְ לְעָלַם וּלְעָלְמֵי עָלְמַיָּא.

יִתְבָּרַךְ וְיִשְׁתַּבַּח וְיִתְפָּאַר וְיִתְרוֹמַם וְיִתְנַשֵּׂא וְיִתְהַדָּר וְיִתְעַלֶּה וְיִתְהַלָּל שְׁמֵהּ דְּקֻדְשָׁא בְּרִיךְ הוּא (.Cong – בְּרִיךְ הוּא) — לְעֵלָּא מִן כָּל בִּרְכָתָא וְשִׁירָתָא תֻּשְׁבְּחָתָא וְנֶחֱמָתָא, דַּאֲמִירָן בְּעָלְמָא. וְאִמְרוּ: אָמֵן. (.Cong – אָמֵן.)

ON WEEKDAYS CONTINUE WITH *SHEMONEH ESREI*, PAGE 1062.
ON THE SABBATH THE TORAH IS READ, PAGE 1050.

is forgiving of iniquity and does not destroy; frequently He withdraws His anger, not arousing His entire rage.[1] *For You, my Lord, are good and forgiving, and abundantly kind to all who call upon You.*[2] *Your righteousness remains righteous forever, and Your Torah is truth.*[3] *Grant truth to Jacob, kindness to Abraham, as You swore to our forefathers from ancient times.*[4] *Blessed is my Lord for every single day, He burdens us with blessings, the God of our salvation, Selah.*[5] *HASHEM, Master of Legions, is with us, a stronghold for us is the God of Jacob, Selah.*[6] *HASHEM, Master of Legions, praiseworthy is the man who trusts in You.*[7] *HASHEM, save! May the King answer us on the day we call.*[8]

Blessed is He, our God, Who created us for His glory, separated us from those who stray, gave us the Torah of truth and implanted eternal life within us. May He open our heart through His Torah and imbue our heart with love and awe of Him and that we may do His will and serve Him wholeheartedly, so that we do not struggle in vain nor produce for futility.[9]

May it be Your will, HASHEM, our God and the God of our forefathers, that we observe Your decrees in This World, and merit that we live and see and inherit goodness and blessing in the years of Messianic times and for the life of the World to Come. So that my soul might sing to You and not be stilled, HASHEM, my God, forever will I thank You.[10] *Blessed is the man who trusts in HASHEM, then HASHEM will be his security.*[11] *Trust in HASHEM forever, for in God, HASHEM, is the strength of the worlds.*[12] Chazzan– *Those knowing Your Name will trust in You, and You forsake not those Who seek You, HASHEM.*[13] *HASHEM desired, for the sake of its [Israel's] righteousness, that the Torah be made great and glorious.*[14]

HALF-KADDISH

Chazzan recites Half-*Kaddish*.

יִתְגַּדַּל *May His great Name grow exalted and sanctified* (Cong.– *Amen.*) *in the world that He created as He willed. May He give reign to His kingship in your lifetimes and in your days, and in the lifetimes of the entire Family of Israel, swiftly and soon. Now respond: Amen.*

(Cong.– *Amen. May His great Name be blessed forever and ever.*)

May His great Name be blessed forever and ever.

Blessed, praised, glorified, exalted, extolled, mighty, upraised, and lauded be the Name of the Holy One, Blessed is He (Cong.– *Blessed is He*) — *beyond any blessing and song, praise and consolation that are uttered in the world. Now respond: Amen.* (Cong.– *Amen.*)

ON WEEKDAYS CONTINUE WITH *SHEMONEH ESREI*, PAGE 1062.

ON THE SABBATH THE TORAH IS READ, PAGE 1050.

(1) *Psalms* 78:38. (2) 86:5. (3) 119:142. (4) *Micah* 7:20. (5) *Psalms* 68:20. (6) 46:8. (7) 84:13. (8) 20:10. (9) Cf. *Isaiah* 65:23. (10) *Psalms* 30:13. (11) *Jeremiah* 17:7. (12) *Isaiah* 26:4. (13) *Psalms* 9:11. (14) *Isaiah* 42:21.

Congregation, then *chazzan:*

וַאֲנִי תְפִלָּתִי לְךָ יהוה עֵת רָצוֹן, אֱלֹהִים בְּרָב חַסְדֶּךָ, עֲנֵנִי בֶּאֱמֶת יִשְׁעֶךָ.[1]

הוצאת ספר תורה

From the moment the Ark is opened until the Torah is returned to it, one must conduct himself with the utmost respect, and avoid unnecessary conversation. It is commendable to kiss the Torah as it is carried to the *bimah* [reading table] and back to the Ark.

All rise and remain standing until the Torah is placed on the *bimah*.
The Ark is opened; before the Torah is removed the congregation recites:

וַיְהִי בִּנְסֹעַ הָאָרֹן, וַיֹּאמֶר מֹשֶׁה, קוּמָה יהוה וְיָפֻצוּ אֹיְבֶיךָ, וְיָנֻסוּ מְשַׂנְאֶיךָ מִפָּנֶיךָ.[2] כִּי מִצִּיּוֹן תֵּצֵא תוֹרָה, וּדְבַר יהוה מִירוּשָׁלָיִם.[3] בָּרוּךְ שֶׁנָּתַן תּוֹרָה לְעַמּוֹ יִשְׂרָאֵל בִּקְדֻשָּׁתוֹ.

זוהר ויקהל שסט:א

בְּרִיךְ שְׁמֵהּ דְּמָרֵא עָלְמָא, בְּרִיךְ כִּתְרָךְ וְאַתְרָךְ. יְהֵא רְעוּתָךְ עִם עַמָּךְ יִשְׂרָאֵל לְעָלַם, וּפֻרְקַן יְמִינָךְ אַחֲזֵי לְעַמָּךְ בְּבֵית מַקְדְּשָׁךְ, וּלְאַמְטוּיֵי לָנָא מִטּוּב נְהוֹרָךְ, וּלְקַבֵּל צְלוֹתָנָא בְּרַחֲמִין. יְהֵא רַעֲוָא קֳדָמָךְ, דְּתוֹרִיךְ לָן חַיִּין בְּטִיבוּתָא, וְלֶהֱוֵי אֲנָא פְקִידָא בְּגוֹ צַדִּיקַיָּא, לְמִרְחַם עָלַי וּלְמִנְטַר יָתִי וְיַת כָּל דִּי לִי וְדִי לְעַמָּךְ יִשְׂרָאֵל. אַנְתְּ הוּא זָן לְכֹלָּא, וּמְפַרְנֵס לְכֹלָּא, אַנְתְּ הוּא שַׁלִּיט עַל כֹּלָּא. אַנְתְּ הוּא דְּשַׁלִּיט עַל מַלְכַיָּא, וּמַלְכוּתָא דִּילָךְ הִיא. אֲנָא עַבְדָּא דְקֻדְשָׁא בְּרִיךְ הוּא, דְּסָגִידְנָא קַמֵּהּ וּמִקַּמָּא דִּיקַר אוֹרַיְתֵהּ בְּכָל עִדָּן וְעִדָּן. לָא עַל אֱנָשׁ רָחִיצְנָא, וְלָא עַל בַּר אֱלָהִין סָמִיכְנָא, אֶלָּא בֶּאֱלָהָא דִשְׁמַיָּא, דְּהוּא אֱלָהָא קְשׁוֹט, וְאוֹרַיְתֵהּ קְשׁוֹט, וּנְבִיאוֹהִי קְשׁוֹט, וּמַסְגֵּא לְמֶעְבַּד טַבְוָן וּקְשׁוֹט. בֵּהּ אֲנָא רָחִיץ, וְלִשְׁמֵהּ קַדִּישָׁא יַקִּירָא אֲנָא אֵמַר תֻּשְׁבְּחָן. יְהֵא רַעֲוָא קֳדָמָךְ, דְּתִפְתַּח לִבָּאִי בְּאוֹרַיְתָא, וְתַשְׁלִים מִשְׁאֲלִין דְּלִבָּאִי, וְלִבָּא דְכָל עַמָּךְ יִשְׂרָאֵל, לְטַב וּלְחַיִּין וְלִשְׁלָם. (אָמֵן.)

The Torah is removed from the Ark and presented to the *chazzan*, who accepts it in his right arm. He then turns to the Ark and raises the Torah slightly as he bows and recites:

גַּדְּלוּ לַיהוה אִתִּי, וּנְרוֹמְמָה שְׁמוֹ יַחְדָּו.[4]

The *chazzan* turns to his right and carries the Torah to the *bimah*, as the congregation responds:

לְךָ יהוה הַגְּדֻלָּה וְהַגְּבוּרָה וְהַתִּפְאֶרֶת וְהַנֵּצַח וְהַהוֹד, כִּי כֹל בַּשָּׁמַיִם וּבָאָרֶץ, לְךָ יהוה הַמַּמְלָכָה וְהַמִּתְנַשֵּׂא לְכֹל לְרֹאשׁ.[5] רוֹמְמוּ יהוה אֱלֹהֵינוּ וְהִשְׁתַּחֲווּ לַהֲדֹם רַגְלָיו, קָדוֹשׁ הוּא. רוֹמְמוּ יהוה אֱלֹהֵינוּ וְהִשְׁתַּחֲווּ לְהַר קָדְשׁוֹ, כִּי קָדוֹשׁ יהוה אֱלֹהֵינוּ.[6]

Congregation, then *chazzan:*

וַאֲנִי תְפִלָּתִי *As for me, may my prayer to You, HASHEM, be at an opportune time; O God, in Your abundant kindness, answer me with the truth of Your salvation.*[1]

REMOVAL OF THE TORAH FROM THE ARK

From the moment the Ark is opened until the Torah is returned to it, one must conduct himself with the utmost respect, and avoid unnecessary conversation. It is commendable to kiss the Torah as it is carried to the *bimah* [reading table] and back to the Ark.

All rise and remain standing until the Torah is placed on the *bimah.* The Ark is opened; before the Torah is removed the congregation recites:

וַיְהִי בִּנְסֹעַ *When the Ark would travel, Moses would say, 'Arise, HASHEM, and let Your foes be scattered, let those who hate You flee from You.'*[2] *For from Zion will the Torah come forth and the word of HASHEM from Jerusalem.*[3] *Blessed is He Who gave the Torah to His people Israel in His holiness.*

Zohar, Vayakhel 369a

בְּרִיךְ שְׁמֵהּ *Blessed is the Name of the Master of the universe, blessed is Your crown and Your place. May Your favor remain with Your people Israel forever; may You display the salvation of Your right hand to Your people in Your Holy Temple, to benefit us with the goodness of Your luminescence and to accept our prayers with mercy. May it be Your will that You extend our lives with goodness and that I be numbered among the righteous; that You have mercy on me and protect me, all that is mine and that is Your people Israel's. It is You Who nourishes all and sustains all, You control everything. It is You Who control kings, and Kingship is Yours. I am a servant of the Holy One, Blessed is He, and I prostrate myself before Him and before the glory of His Torah at all times. Not in any man do I put trust, nor on any angel do I rely — only on the God of heaven Who is the God of truth, Whose Torah is truth and Whose prophets are true and Who acts liberally with kindness and truth. In Him do I trust, and to His glorious and Holy Name do I declare praises. May it be Your will that You open my heart to the Torah and that You fulfill the wishes of my heart and the heart of Your entire people Israel for good, for life, and for peace. (Amen.)*

The Torah is removed from the Ark and presented to the *chazzan,* who accepts it in his right arm He then turns to the Ark and raises the Torah slightly as he bows and recites:

Declare the greatness of HASHEM with me, and let us exalt His Name together.[4]

The *chazzan* turns to his right and carries the Torah to the *bimah,* as the congregation responds:

לְךָ *Yours, HASHEM, is the greatness, the strength, the splendor, the triumph, and the glory; even everything in heaven and earth; Yours, HASHEM, is the kingdom, and the sovereignty over every leader.*[5] *Exalt HASHEM, our God, and bow at His footstool; He is Holy! Exalt HASHEM, our God, and bow at His holy mountain; for holy is HASHEM, our God.*[6]

(1) *Psalms* 69:14. (2) *Numbers* 10:35. (3) *Isaiah* 2:3.
(4) *Psalms* 34:4. (5) *I Chronicles* 29:11. (6) *Psalms* 99:5,9.

אַב הָרַחֲמִים הוּא יְרַחֵם עַם עֲמוּסִים, וְיִזְכֹּר בְּרִית אֵיתָנִים, וְיַצִּיל נַפְשׁוֹתֵינוּ מִן הַשָּׁעוֹת הָרָעוֹת, וְיִגְעַר בְּיֵצֶר הָרַע מִן הַנְּשׂוּאִים, וְיָחֹן אוֹתָנוּ לִפְלֵיטַת עוֹלָמִים, וִימַלֵּא מִשְׁאֲלוֹתֵינוּ בְּמִדָּה טוֹבָה יְשׁוּעָה וְרַחֲמִים.

The Torah is placed on the *bimah* and prepared for reading.
The *gabbai* uses the following formula to call a *Kohen* to the Torah:

וְתִגָּלֶה וְתֵרָאֶה מַלְכוּתוֹ עָלֵינוּ בִּזְמַן קָרוֹב, וְיָחֹן פְּלֵיטָתֵנוּ וּפְלֵיטַת עַמּוֹ בֵּית יִשְׂרָאֵל לְחֵן וּלְחֶסֶד וּלְרַחֲמִים וּלְרָצוֹן. וְנֹאמַר אָמֵן. הַכֹּל הָבוּ גֹדֶל לֵאלֹהֵינוּ וּתְנוּ כָבוֹד לַתּוֹרָה. כֹּהֵן° קְרָב, יַעֲמֹד (insert name) הַכֹּהֵן.

°If no *Kohen* is present, the *gabbai* says: "אֵין כַּאן כֹּהֵן, יַעֲמֹד (name) יִשְׂרָאֵל (לֵוִי) בִּמְקוֹם כֹּהֵן."

בָּרוּךְ שֶׁנָּתַן תּוֹרָה לְעַמּוֹ יִשְׂרָאֵל בִּקְדֻשָּׁתוֹ. (תּוֹרַת יהוה תְּמִימָה מְשִׁיבַת נָפֶשׁ, עֵדוּת יהוה נֶאֱמָנָה מַחְכִּימַת פֶּתִי. פִּקּוּדֵי יהוה יְשָׁרִים מְשַׂמְּחֵי לֵב, מִצְוַת יהוה בָּרָה מְאִירַת עֵינָיִם.[1] יהוה עֹז לְעַמּוֹ יִתֵּן, יהוה יְבָרֵךְ אֶת עַמּוֹ בַשָּׁלוֹם.[2] הָאֵל תָּמִים דַּרְכּוֹ, אִמְרַת יהוה צְרוּפָה, מָגֵן הוּא לְכֹל הַחֹסִים בּוֹ.[3])

Congregation, then *gabbai:*

וְאַתֶּם הַדְּבֵקִים בַּיהוה אֱלֹהֵיכֶם, חַיִּים כֻּלְּכֶם הַיּוֹם:[4]

קריאת התורה

The reader shows the *oleh* (person called to the Torah) the place in the Torah. The *oleh* touches the Torah with a corner of his *tallis,* or the belt or mantle of the Torah, and kisses it. He then begins the blessing, bowing at בָּרְכוּ, and straightening up at ה׳.

בָּרְכוּ אֶת יהוה הַמְּבֹרָךְ.

Congregation, followed by *oleh,* responds, bowing at בָּרוּךְ, and straightening up at ה׳:

בָּרוּךְ יהוה הַמְּבֹרָךְ לְעוֹלָם וָעֶד.

Oleh continues:

בָּרוּךְ אַתָּה יהוה אֱלֹהֵינוּ מֶלֶךְ הָעוֹלָם, אֲשֶׁר בָּחַר בָּנוּ מִכָּל הָעַמִּים, וְנָתַן לָנוּ אֶת תּוֹרָתוֹ. בָּרוּךְ אַתָּה יהוה, נוֹתֵן הַתּוֹרָה.

(—Cong. אָמֵן.)

After his Torah portion has been read, the *oleh* recites:

בָּרוּךְ אַתָּה יהוה אֱלֹהֵינוּ מֶלֶךְ הָעוֹלָם, אֲשֶׁר נָתַן לָנוּ תּוֹרַת אֱמֶת, וְחַיֵּי עוֹלָם נָטַע בְּתוֹכֵנוּ. בָּרוּךְ אַתָּה יהוה, נוֹתֵן הַתּוֹרָה.

(—Cong. אָמֵן.)

THE VARIOUS מִי שֶׁבֵּרַךְ PRAYERS APPEAR ON PAGE 368.

THE TORAH READING ON THE SABBATH

The Torah reading during the Sabbath *Minchah* includes the calling to the Torah of *Kohen,* Levite, and Israelite. The reading is the first section of the next *sidrah* in the regular order of weekly Torah reading. Since the Sabbath following Pesach can be either *Shemini, Acharei,* or *Kedoshim,* the first section from one of these *sidrahs* is read.

אַב הָרַחֲמִים *May the Father of mercy have mercy on the nation that is borne by Him, and may He remember the covenant of the spiritually mighty. May He rescue our souls from the bad times, and upbraid the evil inclination to leave those borne by Him, graciously make us an eternal remnant, and fulfill our requests in good measure, for salvation and mercy.*

The Torah is placed on the *bimah* and prepared for reading.
The *gabbai* uses the following formula to call a *Kohen* to the Torah:

וְתִגָּלֶה *And may His kingship over us be revealed and become visible soon, and may He be gracious to our remnant and the remnant of His people the Family of Israel, for graciousness, kindness, mercy, and favor. And let us respond, Amen. All of you ascribe greatness to our God and give honor to the Torah. Kohen,° approach. Stand* (name) *son of* (father's name) *the Kohen.*

°If no *Kohen* is present, the *gabbai* says: *'There is no Kohen present, stand* (name) *son of* (father's name) *an Israelite (Levite) in place of the Kohen.'*

Blessed is He Who gave the Torah to His people Israel in His holiness (The Torah of HASHEM is perfect, restoring the soul; the testimony of HASHEM is trustworthy, making the simple one wise. The orders of HASHEM are upright, gladdening the heart; the command of HASHEM is clear, enlightening the eyes.[1] *HASHEM will give might to His people; HASHEM will bless His people with peace.*[2] *The God Whose way is perfect, the promise of HASHEM is flawless, He is a shield for all who take refuge in Him.*[3]*)*

Congregation, then *gabbai:*

You who cling to HASHEM your God—you are all alive today.[4]

READING OF THE TORAH

The reader shows the *oleh* (person called to the Torah) the place in the Torah. The *oleh* touches the Torah with a corner of his *tallis,* or the belt or mantle of the Torah, and kisses it. He then begins the blessing, bowing at *'Bless,'* and straightening up at 'HASHEM':

Bless HASHEM, the blessed One.

Congregation, followed by *oleh,* responds, bowing at 'Blessed,' and straightening up at 'HASHEM.'

Blessed is HASHEM, the blessed One, for all eternity.

Oleh continues:

בָּרוּךְ *Blessed are You, HASHEM, our God, King of the universe, Who selected us from all the peoples and gave us His Torah. Blessed are You, HASHEM, Giver of the Torah.* (Cong.– *Amen.)*

After his Torah portion has been read, the *oleh* recites:

בָּרוּךְ *Blessed are You, HASHEM, our God, King of the universe, Who gave us the Torah of truth and implanted eternal life within us. Blessed are You, HASHEM, Giver of the Torah.* (Cong.– *Amen.)*

THE VARIOUS *MI SHEBEIRACH* PRAYERS APPEAR ON PAGE 368.

(1) *Psalms* 19:8-9. (2) 29:11. (3) 18:31. (4) *Deuteronomy* 4:4.

The Torah reading just before the end of the Sabbath symbolizes that we will take the Torah-imbued spirit of the Sabbath with us into the next week.

The Torah reading at *Minchah* on *Shabbos* corresponds to the *sidrah* read on the *Shabbos* following Pesach. This reading is from *Shemini, Acharei Mos,* or *Kedoshim.*

פרשת שמיני

ויקרא ט:א-טז

כהן – וַיְהִי֙ בַּיּ֣וֹם הַשְּׁמִינִ֔י קָרָ֣א מֹשֶׁ֔ה לְאַהֲרֹ֖ן וּלְבָנָ֑יו וּלְזִקְנֵ֖י יִשְׂרָאֵֽל: וַיֹּ֣אמֶר אֶֽל־אַהֲרֹ֗ן קַח־לְ֠ךָ עֵ֣גֶל בֶּן־בָּקָ֧ר לְחַטָּ֛את וְאַ֥יִל לְעֹלָ֖ה תְּמִימִ֑ם וְהַקְרֵ֖ב לִפְנֵ֥י יְהֹוָֽה: וְאֶל־בְּנֵ֥י יִשְׂרָאֵ֖ל תְּדַבֵּ֣ר לֵאמֹ֑ר קְח֤וּ שְׂעִיר־עִזִּים֙ לְחַטָּ֔את וְעֵ֨גֶל וָכֶ֧בֶשׂ בְּנֵֽי־שָׁנָ֛ה תְּמִימִ֖ם לְעֹלָֽה: וְשׁ֨וֹר וָאַ֜יִל לִשְׁלָמִ֗ים לִזְבֹּ֨חַ֙ לִפְנֵ֣י יְהֹוָ֔ה וּמִנְחָ֖ה בְּלוּלָ֣ה בַשָּׁ֑מֶן כִּ֣י הַיּ֔וֹם יְהֹוָ֖ה נִרְאָ֥ה אֲלֵיכֶֽם: וַיִּקְח֗וּ אֵ֚ת אֲשֶׁ֣ר צִוָּ֣ה מֹשֶׁ֔ה אֶל־פְּנֵ֖י אֹ֣הֶל מוֹעֵ֑ד וַיִּקְרְבוּ֙ כָּל־הָ֣עֵדָ֔ה וַיַּֽעַמְד֖וּ לִפְנֵ֥י יְהֹוָֽה: וַיֹּ֣אמֶר מֹשֶׁ֔ה זֶ֧ה הַדָּבָ֛ר אֲשֶׁר־צִוָּ֥ה יְהֹוָ֖ה תַּעֲשׂ֑וּ וְיֵרָ֥א אֲלֵיכֶ֖ם כְּב֥וֹד יְהֹוָֽה:

לוי – וַיֹּ֨אמֶר מֹשֶׁ֜ה אֶֽל־אַהֲרֹ֗ן קְרַ֤ב אֶל־הַמִּזְבֵּ֨חַ֙ וַעֲשֵׂ֞ה אֶת־חַטָּֽאתְךָ֙ וְאֶת־עֹ֣לָתֶ֔ךָ וְכַפֵּ֥ר בַּֽעַדְךָ֖ וּבְעַ֣ד הָעָ֑ם וַעֲשֵׂ֞ה אֶת־קָרְבַּ֤ן הָעָם֙ וְכַפֵּ֣ר בַּֽעֲדָ֔ם כַּאֲשֶׁ֖ר צִוָּ֥ה יְהֹוָֽה: וַיִּקְרַ֣ב אַהֲרֹן֮ אֶל־הַמִּזְבֵּ֒חַ֒ וַיִּשְׁחַ֛ט אֶת־עֵ֥גֶל הַֽחַטָּ֖את אֲשֶׁר־לֽוֹ: וַ֠יַּקְרִ֠בוּ בְּנֵ֨י אַהֲרֹ֣ן אֶת־הַדָּם֮ אֵלָיו֒ וַיִּטְבֹּ֤ל אֶצְבָּעוֹ֙ בַּדָּ֔ם וַיִּתֵּ֖ן עַל־קַרְנ֣וֹת הַמִּזְבֵּ֑חַ וְאֶת־הַדָּ֣ם יָצַ֔ק אֶל־יְס֖וֹד הַמִּזְבֵּֽחַ: וְאֶת־הַחֵ֨לֶב וְאֶת־הַכְּלָיֹ֜ת וְאֶת־הַיֹּתֶ֤רֶת מִן־הַכָּבֵד֙ מִן־הַ֣חַטָּ֔את הִקְטִ֖יר הַמִּזְבֵּ֑חָה כַּאֲשֶׁ֛ר צִוָּ֥ה יְהֹוָ֖ה אֶת־מֹשֶֽׁה:

ישראל – וְאֶת־הַבָּשָׂ֖ר וְאֶת־הָע֑וֹר שָׂרַ֣ף בָּאֵ֔שׁ מִח֖וּץ לַֽמַּחֲנֶֽה: וַיִּשְׁחַ֖ט אֶת־הָעֹלָ֑ה וַ֠יַּמְצִ֠אוּ בְּנֵ֨י אַהֲרֹ֤ן אֵלָיו֙ אֶת־הַדָּ֔ם וַיִּזְרְקֵ֥הוּ עַל־הַמִּזְבֵּ֖חַ סָבִֽיב: וְאֶת־הָ֣עֹלָ֔ה הִמְצִ֥יאוּ אֵלָ֖יו לִנְתָחֶ֑יהָ וְאֶת־הָרֹ֑אשׁ וַיַּקְטֵ֖ר עַל־הַמִּזְבֵּֽחַ: וַיִּרְחַ֥ץ אֶת־הַקֶּ֖רֶב וְאֶת־הַכְּרָעָ֑יִם וַיַּקְטֵ֥ר עַל־הָעֹלָ֖ה הַמִּזְבֵּֽחָה: וַיַּקְרֵ֕ב אֵ֖ת קָרְבַּ֣ן הָעָ֑ם וַיִּקַּ֞ח אֶת־שְׂעִ֤יר הַֽחַטָּאת֙ אֲשֶׁ֣ר לָעָ֔ם וַיִּשְׁחָטֵ֥הוּ וַֽיְחַטְּאֵ֖הוּ כָּרִאשֽׁוֹן: וַיַּקְרֵ֖ב אֶת־הָֽעֹלָ֑ה וַיַּֽעֲשֶׂ֖הָ כַּמִּשְׁפָּֽט:

The Torah reading at *Minchah* on *Shabbos* corresponds to the *sidrah* read on the *Shabbos* following Pesach. This reading is from *Shemini, Acharei Mos,* or *Kedoshim.*

PARASHAS SHEMINI

Leviticus 9:1-16

Kohen – *It was on the eighth day, Moses summoned Aaron and his sons, and the elders of Israel. He said to Aaron: Take yourself a young bull for a sin-offering and a ram for an elevation-offering — unblemished; and offer them before* HASHEM. *And to the Children of Israel speak as follows: Take a he-goat for a sin-offering, and a calf and a sheep in their first year — unblemished — for an elevation-offering. And a bull and a ram for a peace-offering to slaughter before* HASHEM, *and a meal-offering mixed with oil; for today* HASHEM *appears to you.*

They took what Moses had commanded to the front of the Tent of Meeting; the entire assembly approached and stood before HASHEM. *Moses said: This is the thing that* HASHEM *has commanded you to do; then the glory of* HASHEM *will appear to you.*

Levi – *Moses said to Aaron: Come near to the Altar and perform the service of your sin-offering and your elevation-offering and effect atonement for yourself and for the people; then perform the service of the people's offering and effect atonement for them, as* HASHEM *has commanded.*

Aaron came near to the Altar, and slaughtered the sin-offering calf that was his own. The sons of Aaron brought the blood to him. He dipped his finger into the blood and placed it upon the corners of the Altar, and he poured the blood upon the foundation of the Altar. The fats, the kidneys, and the diaphragm with the liver of the sin-offering, he caused to go up in smoke on the Altar, as HASHEM *had commanded Moses.*

Third – *The flesh and the hide he burned in fire outside the camp. He slaughtered the elevation- offering; the sons of Aaron presented the blood to him and he threw it upon the Altar, all around. They presented the elevation-offering to him in its pieces with the head; and he caused it to go up in smoke on the Altar. He washed the innards and the feet, and caused them to go up in smoke on the elevation-offering on the Altar.*

He brought near the offering of the people. He took the sin-offering goat that was for the people, and slaughtered it and performed the sin-offering service, as for the first one. He brought near the elevation-offering and performed its service as prescribed.

פרשת אחרי מות

ויקרא טז:א-יז

כהן – וַיְדַבֵּ֣ר יְהוָה֮ אֶל־מֹשֶׁה֒ אַחֲרֵ֣י מ֔וֹת שְׁנֵ֖י בְּנֵ֣י אַהֲרֹ֑ן בְּקָרְבָתָ֥ם לִפְנֵֽי־יְהוָ֖ה וַיָּמֻֽתוּ: וַיֹּ֨אמֶר יְהוָ֜ה אֶל־מֹשֶׁ֗ה דַּבֵּר֙ אֶל־אַהֲרֹ֣ן אָחִ֔יךָ וְאַל־יָבֹ֤א בְכָל־עֵת֙ אֶל־הַקֹּ֔דֶשׁ מִבֵּ֖ית לַפָּרֹ֑כֶת אֶל־פְּנֵ֨י הַכַּפֹּ֜רֶת אֲשֶׁ֤ר עַל־הָֽאָרֹן֙ וְלֹ֣א יָמ֔וּת כִּ֚י בֶּֽעָנָ֔ן אֵרָאֶ֖ה עַל־הַכַּפֹּֽרֶת: בְּזֹ֛את יָבֹ֥א אַהֲרֹ֖ן אֶל־הַקֹּ֑דֶשׁ בְּפַ֧ר בֶּן־בָּקָ֛ר לְחַטָּ֖את וְאַ֥יִל לְעֹלָֽה: כְּתֹֽנֶת־בַּ֨ד קֹ֜דֶשׁ יִלְבָּ֗שׁ וּמִֽכְנְסֵי־בַד֮ יִהְי֣וּ עַל־בְּשָׂרוֹ֒ וּבְאַבְנֵ֥ט בַּד֙ יַחְגֹּ֔ר וּבְמִצְנֶ֥פֶת בַּ֖ד יִצְנֹ֑ף בִּגְדֵי־קֹ֣דֶשׁ הֵ֔ם וְרָחַ֥ץ בַּמַּ֛יִם אֶת־בְּשָׂר֖וֹ וּלְבֵשָֽׁם: וּמֵאֵ֗ת עֲדַת֙ בְּנֵ֣י יִשְׂרָאֵ֔ל יִקַּ֛ח שְׁנֵֽי־שְׂעִירֵ֥י עִזִּ֖ים לְחַטָּ֑את וְאַ֥יִל אֶחָ֖ד לְעֹלָֽה: וְהִקְרִ֧יב אַהֲרֹ֛ן אֶת־פַּ֥ר הַֽחַטָּ֖את אֲשֶׁר־ל֑וֹ וְכִפֶּ֥ר בַּעֲד֖וֹ וּבְעַ֥ד בֵּיתֽוֹ:

לוי – וְלָקַ֖ח אֶת־שְׁנֵ֣י הַשְּׂעִירִ֑ם וְהֶעֱמִ֤יד אֹתָם֙ לִפְנֵ֣י יְהוָ֔ה פֶּ֖תַח אֹ֥הֶל מוֹעֵֽד: וְנָתַ֧ן אַהֲרֹ֛ן עַל־שְׁנֵ֥י הַשְּׂעִירִ֖ם גֹּֽרָל֑וֹת גּוֹרָ֤ל אֶחָד֙ לַֽיהוָ֔ה וְגוֹרָ֥ל אֶחָ֖ד לַעֲזָאזֵֽל: וְהִקְרִ֤יב אַהֲרֹן֙ אֶת־הַשָּׂעִ֔יר אֲשֶׁ֨ר עָלָ֥ה עָלָ֛יו הַגּוֹרָ֖ל לַיהוָ֑ה וְעָשָׂ֖הוּ חַטָּֽאת: וְהַשָּׂעִ֗יר אֲשֶׁר֩ עָלָ֨ה עָלָ֤יו הַגּוֹרָל֙ לַעֲזָאזֵ֔ל יָֽעֳמַד־חַ֛י לִפְנֵ֥י יְהוָ֖ה לְכַפֵּ֣ר עָלָ֑יו לְשַׁלַּ֥ח אֹת֛וֹ לַעֲזָאזֵ֖ל הַמִּדְבָּֽרָה: וְהִקְרִ֨יב אַהֲרֹ֜ן אֶת־פַּ֤ר הַֽחַטָּאת֙ אֲשֶׁר־ל֔וֹ וְכִפֶּ֥ר בַּֽעֲד֖וֹ וּבְעַ֣ד בֵּית֑וֹ וְשָׁחַ֛ט אֶת־פַּ֥ר הַֽחַטָּ֖את אֲשֶׁר־לֽוֹ:

ישראל – וְלָקַ֣ח מְלֹֽא־הַ֠מַּחְתָּה גַּֽחֲלֵי־אֵ֞שׁ מֵעַ֤ל הַמִּזְבֵּ֙חַ֙ מִלִּפְנֵ֣י יְהוָ֔ה וּמְלֹ֣א חָפְנָ֔יו קְטֹ֥רֶת סַמִּ֖ים דַּקָּ֑ה וְהֵבִ֖יא מִבֵּ֥ית לַפָּרֹֽכֶת: וְנָתַ֧ן אֶת־הַקְּטֹ֛רֶת עַל־הָאֵ֖שׁ לִפְנֵ֣י יְהוָ֑ה וְכִסָּ֣ה ׀ עֲנַ֣ן הַקְּטֹ֗רֶת אֶת־הַכַּפֹּ֛רֶת אֲשֶׁ֥ר עַל־הָעֵד֖וּת וְלֹ֥א יָמֽוּת: וְלָקַח֙ מִדַּ֣ם הַפָּ֔ר וְהִזָּ֧ה בְאֶצְבָּע֛וֹ עַל־פְּנֵ֥י הַכַּפֹּ֖רֶת קֵ֑דְמָה וְלִפְנֵ֣י הַכַּפֹּ֗רֶת יַזֶּ֧ה שֶֽׁבַע־פְּעָמִ֛ים מִן־הַדָּ֖ם בְּאֶצְבָּעֽוֹ: וְשָׁחַ֞ט אֶת־שְׂעִ֤יר הַֽחַטָּאת֙ אֲשֶׁ֣ר לָעָ֔ם וְהֵבִיא֙ אֶת־דָּמ֔וֹ אֶל־מִבֵּ֖ית לַפָּרֹ֑כֶת וְעָשָׂ֣ה אֶת־דָּמ֗וֹ כַּֽאֲשֶׁ֤ר עָשָׂה֙ לְדַ֣ם הַפָּ֔ר וְהִזָּ֤ה אֹתוֹ֙ עַל־הַכַּפֹּ֖רֶת וְלִפְנֵ֥י הַכַּפֹּֽרֶת: וְכִפֶּ֣ר עַל־הַקֹּ֗דֶשׁ מִטֻּמְאֹת֙ בְּנֵ֣י יִשְׂרָאֵ֔ל וּמִפִּשְׁעֵיהֶ֖ם לְכָל־חַטֹּאתָ֑ם וְכֵ֤ן יַֽעֲשֶׂה֙ לְאֹ֣הֶל מוֹעֵ֔ד הַשֹּׁכֵ֣ן אִתָּ֔ם בְּת֖וֹךְ טֻמְאֹתָֽם: וְכָל־אָדָ֞ם לֹא־יִהְיֶ֣ה ׀ בְּאֹ֣הֶל מוֹעֵ֗ד בְּבֹא֛וֹ

PARASHAS ACHAREI MOS

Leviticus 16:1-17

Kohen – *HASHEM spoke to Moses after the death of Aaron's two sons, when they approached before HASHEM, and they died. And HASHEM said to Moses : Speak to Aaron, your brother — he may not come at any time into the Sanctuary, within the Curtain, in front of the cover that is upon the Ark, so that he should not die; for in a cloud will I appear upon the Ark-cover. With this shall Aaron come into the Sanctuary: with a young bull for a sin-offering and a ram for an elevation-offering. He shall don a sacred linen tunic; linen breeches shall be upon his flesh, he shall gird himself with a linen sash, and cover his head with a linen turban; they are sacred vestments — he shall immerse himself in water and then don them. From the assembly of the Children of Israel he shall take two he-goats for a sin-offering and one ram for an elevation-offering. Aaron shall bring near his own sin-offering bull, and atone for himself and for his household.*

Levi – *He shall take the two he-goats and stand them before HASHEM at the entrance of the Tent of Meeting. Aaron shall place lots upon the two he-goats: one lot "for HASHEM" and one lot "for Azazel". Aaron shall bring near the he-goat designated by lot for HASHEM, and which he was to declare as a sin-offering. And the he-goat designated by lot for Azazel shall be stood alive before HASHEM, to make atonement through it, to send it to Azazel to the Wilderness. Aaron shall have brought near his own sin-offering bull and he shall atone for himself and for his household; then he shall slaughter his own sin-offering bull.*

Third – *He shall take a shovelful of fiery coals from atop the Altar that is before HASHEM, and his cupped handsful of finely ground incense-spices, and bring it within the Curtain. He shall place the incense upon the fire before HASHEM; so that the cloud of the incense shall blanket the Ark-cover that is atop the [Tablets of the] Testimony — so that he shall not die.*

He shall take of the blood of the bull and sprinkle with his finger upon the eastern front of the Ark-cover; and in front of the Ark-cover he shall sprinkle seven times from the blood with his finger. He shall slaughter the sin-offering he-goat of the people, and bring its blood within the Curtain; he shall do with its blood as he had done with the blood of the bull, and sprinkle it upon the Ark-cover and in front of the Ark-cover. Thus shall he bring atonement upon the Sanctuary for the contaminations of the Children of Israel, even for their willful sins among all their sins; and so shall he do for the Tent of Meeting that dwells with them amid their contamination. Every person is forbidden to be in the Tent of Meeting when he comes

לְכַפֵּר בַּקֹּדֶשׁ עַד־צֵאתוֹ וְכִפֶּר בַּעֲדוֹ וּבְעַד בֵּיתוֹ וּבְעַד
כָּל־קְהַל יִשְׂרָאֵל׃

פרשת קדושים

ויקרא יט:א־יד

כהן – וַיְדַבֵּר יהוה אֶל־מֹשֶׁה לֵּאמֹר׃ דַּבֵּר אֶל־כָּל־עֲדַת בְּנֵי־
יִשְׂרָאֵל וְאָמַרְתָּ אֲלֵהֶם קְדֹשִׁים תִּהְיוּ כִּי קָדוֹשׁ אֲנִי יהוה
אֱלֹהֵיכֶם׃ אִישׁ אִמּוֹ וְאָבִיו תִּירָאוּ וְאֶת־שַׁבְּתֹתַי תִּשְׁמֹרוּ אֲנִי
יהוה אֱלֹהֵיכֶם׃ אַל־תִּפְנוּ אֶל־הָאֱלִילִם וֵאלֹהֵי מַסֵּכָה לֹא
תַעֲשׂוּ לָכֶם אֲנִי יהוה אֱלֹהֵיכֶם׃

לוי – וְכִי תִזְבְּחוּ זֶבַח שְׁלָמִים לַיהוה לִרְצֹנְכֶם תִּזְבָּחֻהוּ׃ בְּיוֹם
זִבְחֲכֶם יֵאָכֵל וּמִמָּחֳרָת וְהַנּוֹתָר עַד־יוֹם הַשְּׁלִישִׁי בָּאֵשׁ יִשָּׂרֵף׃
וְאִם הֵאָכֹל יֵאָכֵל בַּיּוֹם הַשְּׁלִישִׁי פִּגּוּל הוּא לֹא יֵרָצֶה׃ וְאֹכְלָיו
עֲוֹנוֹ יִשָּׂא כִּי־אֶת־קֹדֶשׁ יהוה חִלֵּל וְנִכְרְתָה הַנֶּפֶשׁ הַהִוא
מֵעַמֶּיהָ׃ וּבְקֻצְרְכֶם אֶת־קְצִיר אַרְצְכֶם לֹא תְכַלֶּה פְּאַת שָׂדְךָ
לִקְצֹר וְלֶקֶט קְצִירְךָ לֹא תְלַקֵּט׃ וְכַרְמְךָ לֹא תְעוֹלֵל וּפֶרֶט
כַּרְמְךָ לֹא תְלַקֵּט לֶעָנִי וְלַגֵּר תַּעֲזֹב אֹתָם אֲנִי יהוה אֱלֹהֵיכֶם׃

ישראל – לֹא תִּגְנֹבוּ וְלֹא־תְכַחֲשׁוּ וְלֹא־תְשַׁקְּרוּ אִישׁ בַּעֲמִיתוֹ׃
וְלֹא־תִשָּׁבְעוּ בִשְׁמִי לַשָּׁקֶר וְחִלַּלְתָּ אֶת־שֵׁם אֱלֹהֶיךָ אֲנִי יהוה׃
לֹא־תַעֲשֹׁק אֶת־רֵעֲךָ וְלֹא תִגְזֹל לֹא־תָלִין פְּעֻלַּת שָׂכִיר אִתְּךָ
עַד־בֹּקֶר׃ לֹא־תְקַלֵּל חֵרֵשׁ וְלִפְנֵי עִוֵּר לֹא תִתֵּן מִכְשֹׁל וְיָרֵאתָ
מֵּאֱלֹהֶיךָ אֲנִי יהוה׃

When the Torah reading has been completed, the Torah is raised for all to see.
Each person looks at the Torah and recites aloud:

וְזֹאת הַתּוֹרָה אֲשֶׁר שָׂם מֹשֶׁה לִפְנֵי בְּנֵי יִשְׂרָאֵל,[1]
עַל פִּי יהוה בְּיַד מֹשֶׁה.[2]

Some add the following verses:

עֵץ חַיִּים הִיא לַמַּחֲזִיקִים בָּהּ, וְתֹמְכֶיהָ מְאֻשָּׁר.[3] דְּרָכֶיהָ דַרְכֵי נֹעַם,
וְכָל נְתִיבוֹתֶיהָ שָׁלוֹם.[4] אֹרֶךְ יָמִים בִּימִינָהּ, בִּשְׂמֹאלָהּ עֹשֶׁר
וְכָבוֹד.[5] יהוה חָפֵץ לְמַעַן צִדְקוֹ, יַגְדִּיל תּוֹרָה וְיַאְדִּיר.[6]

to bring atonement in the Sanctuary until his departure; he shall atone for himself, for his household, and for the entire congregation of Israel.

PARASHAS KEDOSHIM

Leviticus 19:1-14

Kohen – *HASHEM spoke to Moses, saying: Speak to the entire assembly of the Children of Israel and say to them: Be holy, for I, HASHEM, your God, am holy.*

Every man: You shall revere your father and mother, and you shall observe My Sabbaths — I am HASHEM, your God. Do not turn to the idols and do not make molten gods for yourselves — I am HASHEM, your God.

Levi – *When you slaughter a feast peace-offering to HASHEM, you shall slaughter it to find favor for yourselves. It shall be eaten on the day you slaughter it and on the next day, and whatever remains until the third day shall be burned in fire. But if it was eaten on the third day, it is rejected — it does not find favor. Each of those who eat it will bear his iniquity, for he has desecrated what is sacred to HASHEM; and that soul will be cut off from its people.*

When you reap the harvest of your land, do not complete the reaping to the corner of your field, and do not take the gleanings of your harvest. Do not pick from the undeveloped twigs of your vineyard and do not gather the fallen fruit of your vineyard; for the poor and the proselyte shall you leave them — I am HASHEM, your God.

Third – *Do not steal, do not deny falsely, and do not lie to one another. Do not swear falsely by My Name, thereby desecrating the Name of your God — I am HASHEM. Do not cheat your fellow and do not rob; and do not withhold a worker's wage with you until morning. Do not curse a deaf person, do not place a stumbling-block before a blind person; you shall fear your God — I am HASHEM.*

When the Torah reading has been completed, the Torah is raised for all to see. Each person looks at the Torah and recites aloud:

This is the Torah that Moses placed before the Children of Israel,[1] upon the command of HASHEM, through Moses' hand.[2]

Some add the following verses:

עֵץ *It is a tree of life for those who grasp it, and its supporters are praiseworthy.[3] Its ways are ways of pleasantness and all its paths are peace.[4] Lengthy days are at its right; at its left are wealth and honor.[5] HASHEM desired, for the sake of its [Israel's] righteousness, that the Torah be made great and glorious.[6]*

(1) *Deuteronomy* 4:44. (2) *Numbers* 9:23. (3) *Proverbs* 3:18. (4) 3:17. (5) 3:16. (6) *Isaiah* 42:21.

Chazzan takes the Torah in his right arm and recites:

יְהַלְּלוּ אֶת שֵׁם יהוה, כִּי נִשְׂגָּב שְׁמוֹ לְבַדּוֹ –

Congregation responds:

– הוֹדוֹ עַל אֶרֶץ וְשָׁמָיִם. וַיָּרֶם קֶרֶן לְעַמּוֹ, תְּהִלָּה לְכָל חֲסִידָיו, לִבְנֵי יִשְׂרָאֵל עַם קְרֹבוֹ, הַלְלוּיָהּ.[1]

As the Torah is carried to the Ark, congregation recites Psalm 24, לְדָוִד מִזְמוֹר.

לְדָוִד מִזְמוֹר, לַיהוה הָאָרֶץ וּמְלוֹאָהּ, תֵּבֵל וְיִשְׁבֵי בָהּ. כִּי הוּא עַל יַמִּים יְסָדָהּ, וְעַל נְהָרוֹת יְכוֹנְנֶהָ. מִי יַעֲלֶה בְהַר יהוה, וּמִי יָקוּם בִּמְקוֹם קָדְשׁוֹ. נְקִי כַפַּיִם וּבַר לֵבָב, אֲשֶׁר לֹא נָשָׂא לַשָּׁוְא נַפְשִׁי וְלֹא נִשְׁבַּע לְמִרְמָה. יִשָּׂא בְרָכָה מֵאֵת יהוה, וּצְדָקָה מֵאֱלֹהֵי יִשְׁעוֹ. זֶה דּוֹר דֹּרְשָׁיו, מְבַקְשֵׁי פָנֶיךָ, יַעֲקֹב, סֶלָה. שְׂאוּ שְׁעָרִים רָאשֵׁיכֶם, וְהִנָּשְׂאוּ פִּתְחֵי עוֹלָם, וְיָבוֹא מֶלֶךְ הַכָּבוֹד. מִי זֶה מֶלֶךְ הַכָּבוֹד, יהוה עִזּוּז וְגִבּוֹר, יהוה גִּבּוֹר מִלְחָמָה. שְׂאוּ שְׁעָרִים רָאשֵׁיכֶם, וּשְׂאוּ פִּתְחֵי עוֹלָם, וְיָבֹא מֶלֶךְ הַכָּבוֹד. מִי הוּא זֶה מֶלֶךְ הַכָּבוֹד, יהוה צְבָאוֹת הוּא מֶלֶךְ הַכָּבוֹד, סֶלָה.

As the Torah is placed into the Ark, congregation recites the following verses:

וּבְנֻחֹה יֹאמַר, שׁוּבָה יהוה רִבְבוֹת אַלְפֵי יִשְׂרָאֵל.[2] קוּמָה יהוה לִמְנוּחָתֶךָ, אַתָּה וַאֲרוֹן עֻזֶּךָ. כֹּהֲנֶיךָ יִלְבְּשׁוּ צֶדֶק, וַחֲסִידֶיךָ יְרַנֵּנוּ. בַּעֲבוּר דָּוִד עַבְדֶּךָ אַל תָּשֵׁב פְּנֵי מְשִׁיחֶךָ.[3] כִּי לֶקַח טוֹב נָתַתִּי לָכֶם, תּוֹרָתִי אַל תַּעֲזֹבוּ.[4] ❖ עֵץ חַיִּים הִיא לַמַּחֲזִיקִים בָּהּ, וְתֹמְכֶיהָ מְאֻשָּׁר.[5] דְּרָכֶיהָ דַרְכֵי נֹעַם, וְכָל נְתִיבֹתֶיהָ שָׁלוֹם.[6] הֲשִׁיבֵנוּ יהוה אֵלֶיךָ וְנָשׁוּבָה, חַדֵּשׁ יָמֵינוּ כְּקֶדֶם.[7]

חצי קדיש

The Ark is closed and the *chazzan* recites חֲצִי קַדִּישׁ.

יִתְגַּדַּל וְיִתְקַדַּשׁ שְׁמֵהּ רַבָּא. (.Cong – אָמֵן.) בְּעָלְמָא דִּי בְרָא כִרְעוּתֵהּ. וְיַמְלִיךְ מַלְכוּתֵהּ, בְּחַיֵּיכוֹן וּבְיוֹמֵיכוֹן וּבְחַיֵּי דְכָל בֵּית יִשְׂרָאֵל, בַּעֲגָלָא וּבִזְמַן קָרִיב. וְאִמְרוּ: אָמֵן.

(.Cong – אָמֵן. יְהֵא שְׁמֵהּ רַבָּא מְבָרַךְ לְעָלַם וּלְעָלְמֵי עָלְמַיָּא.)

יְהֵא שְׁמֵהּ רַבָּא מְבָרַךְ לְעָלַם וּלְעָלְמֵי עָלְמַיָּא.

יִתְבָּרַךְ וְיִשְׁתַּבַּח וְיִתְפָּאַר וְיִתְרוֹמַם וְיִתְנַשֵּׂא וְיִתְהַדָּר וְיִתְעַלֶּה וְיִתְהַלָּל שְׁמֵהּ דְּקֻדְשָׁא בְּרִיךְ הוּא (.Cong – בְּרִיךְ הוּא) – לְעֵלָּא מִן כָּל בִּרְכָתָא וְשִׁירָתָא תֻּשְׁבְּחָתָא וְנֶחֱמָתָא, דַּאֲמִירָן בְּעָלְמָא. וְאִמְרוּ: אָמֵן. (.Cong – אָמֵן.)

(1) *Psalms* 148:13-14. (2) *Numbers* 10:36. (3) *Psalms* 132:8-10.
(4) *Proverbs* 4:2. (5) 3:18. (6) 3:17. (7) *Lamentations* 5:21.

Chazzan takes the Torah in his right arm and recites:

Let them praise the Name of HASHEM, for His Name alone will have been exalted —

Congregation responds:

— His glory is above earth and heaven. And He will have exalted the pride of His people, causing praise for all His devout ones, for the Children of Israel, His intimate nation. Halleluyah![1]

As the Torah is carried to the Ark, congregation recites Psalm 24, *'Of David a psalm.'*

לְדָוִד *Of David a psalm.* HASHEM*'s is the earth and its fullness, the inhabited land and those who dwell in it. For He founded it upon seas, and established it upon rivers. Who may ascend the mountain of* HASHEM*, and who may stand in the place of His sanctity? One with clean hands and pure heart, who has not sworn in vain by My soul and has not sworn deceitfully. He will receive a blessing from* HASHEM *and just kindness from the God of his salvation. This is the generation of those who seek Him, those who strive for Your Presence — Jacob, Selah. Raise up your heads, O gates, and be uplifted, you everlasting entrances, so that the King of Glory may enter. Who is this King of Glory? —* HASHEM*, the mighty and strong,* HASHEM*, the strong in battle. Raise up your heads, O gates, and raise up, you everlasting entrances, so that the King of Glory may enter. Who then is the King of Glory?* HASHEM*, Master of Legions, He is the King of Glory. Selah!*

As the Torah is placed into the Ark, congregation recites the following verses:

וּבְנֻחֹה *And when it rested he would say, 'Return,* HASHEM*, to the myriad thousands of Israel.'*[2] *Arise,* HASHEM*, to Your resting place, You and the Ark of Your strength. Let Your priests be clothed in righteousness, and Your devout ones will sing joyously. For the sake of David, Your servant, turn not away the face of Your anointed.*[3] *For I have given you a good teaching, do not forsake My Torah.*[4] Chazzan— *It is a tree of life for those who grasp it, and its supporters are praiseworthy.*[5] *Its ways are ways of pleasantness and all its paths are peace.*[6] *Bring us back to You,* HASHEM*, and we shall return, renew our days as of old.*[7]

HALF KADDISH

The Ark is closed and the *chazzan* recites Half-*Kaddish*.

יִתְגַּדַּל *May His great Name grow exalted and sanctified* (Cong.— *Amen.*) *in the world that He created as He willed. May He give reign to His kingship in your lifetimes and in your days, and in the lifetimes of the entire Family of Israel, swiftly and soon. Now respond: Amen.*

(Cong.— *Amen. May His great Name be blessed forever and ever.*)

May His great Name be blessed forever and ever.

Blessed, praised, glorified, exalted, extolled, mighty, upraised, and lauded be the Name of the Holy One, Blessed is He (Cong.— *Blessed is He*) *— beyond any blessing and song, praise and consolation that are uttered in the world. Now respond: Amen.* (Cong.— *Amen.*)

שמונה עשרה – עמידה

Take three steps backward, then three steps forward. Remain standing with feet together while reciting *Shemoneh Esrei.* Recite it with quiet devotion and without interruption, verbal or otherwise. Although it should not be audible to others, one must pray loudly enough to hear himself.

כִּי שֵׁם יהוה אֶקְרָא, הָבוּ גֹדֶל לֵאלֹהֵינוּ.[1]
אֲדֹנָי שְׂפָתַי תִּפְתָּח, וּפִי יַגִּיד תְּהִלָּתֶךָ.[2]

אבות

Bend the knees at בָּרוּךְ; bow at אַתָּה; straighten up at 'ה.

בָּרוּךְ אַתָּה יהוה אֱלֹהֵינוּ וֵאלֹהֵי אֲבוֹתֵינוּ, אֱלֹהֵי אַבְרָהָם, אֱלֹהֵי יִצְחָק, וֵאלֹהֵי יַעֲקֹב, הָאֵל הַגָּדוֹל הַגִּבּוֹר וְהַנּוֹרָא, אֵל עֶלְיוֹן, גּוֹמֵל חֲסָדִים טוֹבִים וְקוֹנֵה הַכֹּל, וְזוֹכֵר חַסְדֵי אָבוֹת, וּמֵבִיא גוֹאֵל לִבְנֵי בְנֵיהֶם, לְמַעַן שְׁמוֹ בְּאַהֲבָה. מֶלֶךְ עוֹזֵר וּמוֹשִׁיעַ וּמָגֵן.

Bend the knees at בָּרוּךְ; bow at אַתָּה; straighten up at 'ה.

בָּרוּךְ אַתָּה יהוה, מָגֵן אַבְרָהָם.

גבורות

אַתָּה גִּבּוֹר לְעוֹלָם אֲדֹנָי, מְחַיֵּה מֵתִים אַתָּה, רַב לְהוֹשִׁיעַ. מְכַלְכֵּל חַיִּים בְּחֶסֶד, מְחַיֵּה מֵתִים בְּרַחֲמִים רַבִּים, סוֹמֵךְ נוֹפְלִים, וְרוֹפֵא חוֹלִים, וּמַתִּיר אֲסוּרִים, וּמְקַיֵּם אֱמוּנָתוֹ לִישֵׁנֵי עָפָר. מִי כָמוֹךָ בַּעַל גְּבוּרוֹת, וּמִי דּוֹמֶה לָּךְ, מֶלֶךְ מֵמִית וּמְחַיֶּה וּמַצְמִיחַ יְשׁוּעָה. וְנֶאֱמָן אַתָּה לְהַחֲיוֹת מֵתִים. בָּרוּךְ אַתָּה יהוה, מְחַיֵּה הַמֵּתִים.

During the *chazzan's* repetition, *Kedushah* (below) is recited at this point.

קְדֻשָּׁה

When reciting *Kedushah,* one must stand with his feet together and avoid any interruptions. One should rise on his toes when saying the words קָדוֹשׁ, קָדוֹשׁ, קָדוֹשׁ; בָּרוּךְ (of בָּרוּךְ כְּבוֹד); and יִמְלֹךְ.

Cong. then *Chazzan* – **נְקַדֵּשׁ** אֶת שִׁמְךָ בָּעוֹלָם, כְּשֵׁם שֶׁמַּקְדִּישִׁים אוֹתוֹ בִּשְׁמֵי מָרוֹם, כַּכָּתוּב עַל יַד נְבִיאֶךָ, וְקָרָא זֶה אֶל זֶה וְאָמַר:

All – קָדוֹשׁ קָדוֹשׁ קָדוֹשׁ יהוה צְבָאוֹת, מְלֹא כָל הָאָרֶץ כְּבוֹדוֹ.[3]

Chazzan – לְעֻמָּתָם בָּרוּךְ יֹאמֵרוּ:

All – בָּרוּךְ כְּבוֹד יהוה, מִמְּקוֹמוֹ.[4]

Chazzan – וּבְדִבְרֵי קָדְשְׁךָ כָּתוּב לֵאמֹר:

All – יִמְלֹךְ יהוה לְעוֹלָם, אֱלֹהַיִךְ צִיּוֹן לְדֹר וָדֹר, הַלְלוּיָהּ.[5]

Chazzan only concludes – לְדוֹר וָדוֹר נַגִּיד גָּדְלֶךָ וּלְנֵצַח נְצָחִים קְדֻשָּׁתְךָ נַקְדִּישׁ, וְשִׁבְחֲךָ אֱלֹהֵינוּ מִפִּינוּ לֹא יָמוּשׁ לְעוֹלָם וָעֶד, כִּי אֵל מֶלֶךְ גָּדוֹל וְקָדוֹשׁ אָתָּה. בָּרוּךְ אַתָּה יהוה, הָאֵל הַקָּדוֹשׁ.

Chazzan continues . . . אַתָּה בְחַרְתָּנוּ (page 1064).

SHEMONEH ESREI — AMIDAH

Take three steps backward, then three steps forward. Remain standing with feet together while reciting *Shemoneh Esrei*. Recite it with quiet devotion and without interruption, verbal or otherwise. Although it should not be audible to others, one must pray loudly enough to hear himself.

When I call out the Name of HASHEM, ascribe greatness to our God.[1]
My Lord, open my lips, that my mouth may declare Your praise.[2]

PATRIARCHS

Bend the knees at *'Blessed'*; bow at *'You'*; straighten up at *'HASHEM.'*

בָּרוּךְ *Blessed are You, HASHEM, our God and the God of our forefathers, God of Abraham, God of Isaac, and God of Jacob; the great, mighty, and awesome God, the supreme God, Who bestows beneficial kindnesses and creates everything, Who recalls the kindnesses of the Patriarchs and brings a Redeemer to their children's children, for His Name's sake, with love. O King, Helper, Savior, and Shield.*

Bend the knees at *'Blessed'*; bow at *'You'*; straighten up at *'HASHEM.'*

Blessed are You, HASHEM, Shield of Abraham.

GOD'S MIGHT

אַתָּה *You are eternally mighty, my Lord, the Resuscitator of the dead are You; abundantly able to save. He sustains the living with kindness, resuscitates the dead with abundant mercy, supports the fallen, heals the sick, releases the confined, and maintains His faith to those asleep in the dust. Who is like You, O Master of mighty deeds, and who is comparable to You, O King Who causes death and restores life and makes salvation sprout! And You are faithful to resuscitate the dead. Blessed are You, HASHEM, Who resuscitates the dead.*

During the *chazzan's* repetition, *Kedushah* (below) is recited at this point.

KEDUSHAH

When reciting *Kedushah*, one must stand with his feet together and avoid any interruptions. One should rise on his toes when saying *Holy, holy, holy; Blessed is;* and *HASHEM shall reign.*

Cong. then Chazzan — **נְקַדֵּשׁ** *We shall sanctify Your Name in this world, just as they sanctify it in heaven above, as it is written by Your prophet, "And one [angel] will call another and say:*

All — *'Holy, holy, holy is HASHEM, Master of Legions, the whole world is filled with His glory.' "*[3]

Chazzan — *Those facing them say 'Blessed':*

All — *'Blessed is the glory of HASHEM from His place.'*[4]

Chazzan — *And in Your holy Writings the following is written:*

All — *'HASHEM shall reign forever — your God, O Zion — from generation to generation, Halleluyah!'*[5]

Chazzan only concludes — *From generation to generation we shall relate Your greatness and for infinite eternities we shall proclaim Your holiness. Your praise, our God, shall not leave our mouth forever and ever, for You, O God, are a great and holy King. Blessed are You, HASHEM, the holy God.*

Chazzan continues אַתָּה בְחַרְתָּנוּ, *You have chosen us . . .* (page 1064).

---

(1) *Deuteronomy* 32:3. (2) *Psalms* 51:17. (3) *Isaiah* 6:3. (4) *Ezekiel* 3:12. (5) *Psalms* 146:10.

קדושת השם

אַתָּה קָדוֹשׁ וְשִׁמְךָ קָדוֹשׁ, וּקְדוֹשִׁים בְּכָל יוֹם יְהַלְלוּךָ סֶּלָה. בָּרוּךְ אַתָּה יהוה, הָאֵל הַקָּדוֹשׁ.

קדושת היום

אַתָּה בְחַרְתָּנוּ מִכָּל הָעַמִּים, אָהַבְתָּ אוֹתָנוּ, וְרָצִיתָ בָּנוּ, וְרוֹמַמְתָּנוּ מִכָּל הַלְּשׁוֹנוֹת, וְקִדַּשְׁתָּנוּ בְּמִצְוֹתֶיךָ, וְקֵרַבְתָּנוּ מַלְכֵּנוּ לַעֲבוֹדָתֶךָ, וְשִׁמְךָ הַגָּדוֹל וְהַקָּדוֹשׁ עָלֵינוּ קָרָאתָ.

On the Sabbath add the words in brackets. [If forgotten, see *Laws* §86-90.]

וַתִּתֶּן לָנוּ יהוה אֱלֹהֵינוּ בְּאַהֲבָה [שַׁבָּתוֹת לִמְנוּחָה וּ]מוֹעֲדִים לְשִׂמְחָה חַגִּים וּזְמַנִּים לְשָׂשׂוֹן, אֶת יוֹם [הַשַּׁבָּת הַזֶּה וְאֶת יוֹם] חַג הַמַּצּוֹת הַזֶּה, זְמַן חֵרוּתֵנוּ [בְּאַהֲבָה] מִקְרָא קֹדֶשׁ, זֵכֶר לִיצִיאַת מִצְרָיִם.

During the *chazzan's* repetition, congregation responds אָמֵן as indicated.

אֱלֹהֵינוּ וֵאלֹהֵי אֲבוֹתֵינוּ, יַעֲלֶה, וְיָבֹא, וְיַגִּיעַ, וְיֵרָאֶה, וְיֵרָצֶה, וְיִשָּׁמַע, וְיִפָּקֵד, וְיִזָּכֵר זִכְרוֹנֵנוּ וּפִקְדוֹנֵנוּ, וְזִכְרוֹן אֲבוֹתֵינוּ, וְזִכְרוֹן מָשִׁיחַ בֶּן דָּוִד עַבְדֶּךָ, וְזִכְרוֹן יְרוּשָׁלַיִם עִיר קָדְשֶׁךָ, וְזִכְרוֹן כָּל עַמְּךָ בֵּית יִשְׂרָאֵל לְפָנֶיךָ, לִפְלֵיטָה לְטוֹבָה לְחֵן וּלְחֶסֶד וּלְרַחֲמִים, לְחַיִּים וּלְשָׁלוֹם בְּיוֹם חַג הַמַּצּוֹת הַזֶּה. זָכְרֵנוּ יהוה אֱלֹהֵינוּ בּוֹ לְטוֹבָה (.Cong – אָמֵן), וּפָקְדֵנוּ בוֹ לִבְרָכָה (.Cong – אָמֵן), וְהוֹשִׁיעֵנוּ בוֹ לְחַיִּים (.Cong – אָמֵן). וּבִדְבַר יְשׁוּעָה וְרַחֲמִים, חוּס וְחָנֵּנוּ וְרַחֵם עָלֵינוּ וְהוֹשִׁיעֵנוּ, כִּי אֵלֶיךָ עֵינֵינוּ, כִּי אֵל מֶלֶךְ חַנּוּן וְרַחוּם אָתָּה.[1]

On the Sabbath add the words in brackets. [If forgotten, see *Laws* §86-90.]

וְהַשִּׂיאֵנוּ יהוה אֱלֹהֵינוּ אֶת בִּרְכַּת מוֹעֲדֶיךָ לְחַיִּים וּלְשָׁלוֹם, לְשִׂמְחָה וּלְשָׂשׂוֹן, כַּאֲשֶׁר רָצִיתָ וְאָמַרְתָּ לְבָרְכֵנוּ. [אֱלֹהֵינוּ וֵאלֹהֵי אֲבוֹתֵינוּ רְצֵה בִמְנוּחָתֵנוּ] קַדְּשֵׁנוּ בְּמִצְוֹתֶיךָ וְתֵן חֶלְקֵנוּ בְּתוֹרָתֶךָ, שַׂבְּעֵנוּ מִטּוּבֶךָ וְשַׂמְּחֵנוּ בִּישׁוּעָתֶךָ, וְטַהֵר לִבֵּנוּ לְעָבְדְּךָ בֶּאֱמֶת, וְהַנְחִילֵנוּ יהוה אֱלֹהֵינוּ [בְּאַהֲבָה וּבְרָצוֹן] בְּשִׂמְחָה וּבְשָׂשׂוֹן [שַׁבָּת וּ]מוֹעֲדֵי קָדְשֶׁךָ, וְיִשְׂמְחוּ בְךָ יִשְׂרָאֵל מְקַדְּשֵׁי שְׁמֶךָ. בָּרוּךְ אַתָּה יהוה, מְקַדֵּשׁ [הַשַּׁבָּת וְ]יִשְׂרָאֵל וְהַזְּמַנִּים.

HOLINESS OF GOD'S NAME

אַתָּה *You are holy and Your Name is holy, and holy ones praise You every day, forever. Blessed are You,* H*ASHEM, the holy God.*

SANCTIFICATION OF THE DAY

אַתָּה בְחַרְתָּנוּ *You have chosen us from all the peoples; You loved us and found favor in us; You exalted us above all the tongues and You sanctified us with Your commandments. You drew us close, our King, to Your service and proclaimed Your great and Holy Name upon us.*

On the Sabbath add the words in brackets. [If forgotten, see *Laws* §86-90.]

וַתִּתֶּן לָנוּ *And You gave us,* H*ASHEM, our God, with love [Sabbaths for rest], appointed festivals for gladness, Festivals and times for joy, [this day of Sabbath and] this day of the Festival of Matzos, the time of our freedom [with love], a holy convocation, a memorial of the Exodus from Egypt.*

During the *chazzan's* repetition, congregation responds *Amen* as indicated.

אֱלֹהֵינוּ *Our God and God of our forefathers, may there rise, come, reach, be noted, be favored, be heard, be considered, and be remembered — the remembrance and consideration of ourselves; the remembrance of our forefathers; the remembrance of Messiah, son of David, Your servant; the remembrance of Jerusalem, the City of Your Holiness; the remembrance of Your entire people the Family of Israel — before You for deliverance, for goodness, for grace, for kindness, and for compassion, for life, and for peace on this day of the Festival of Matzos. Remember us on it,* H*ASHEM, our God, for goodness (*Cong. – *Amen); consider us on it for blessing (*Cong. – *Amen); and help us on it for life (*Cong. – *Amen). In the matter of salvation and compassion, pity, be gracious and compassionate with us and help us, for our eyes are turned to You, because You are God, the gracious and compassionate King.*[1]

On the Sabbath add the words in brackets. [If forgotten, see *Laws* §86-90.]

וְהַשִּׂיאֵנוּ *Bestow upon us, O* H*ASHEM, our God, the blessing of Your appointed Festivals for life and for peace, for gladness and for joy, as You desired and promised to bless us. [Our God and the God of our forefathers, may You be pleased with our rest.] Sanctify us with Your commandments and grant us our share in Your Torah; satisfy us from Your goodness and gladden us with Your salvation, and purify our heart to serve You sincerely. And grant us a heritage, O* H*ASHEM, our God — [with love and with favor] with gladness and with joy — [the Sabbath and] the appointed festivals of Your holiness, and may Israel, the sanctifiers of Your Name, rejoice in You. Blessed are You,* H*ASHEM, Who sanctifies [the Sabbath,] Israel and the festive seasons.*

---

(1) Cf. *Nehemiah* 9:31.

עבודה

רְצֵה יהוה אֱלֹהֵינוּ בְּעַמְּךָ יִשְׂרָאֵל וּבִתְפִלָּתָם, וְהָשֵׁב אֶת הָעֲבוֹדָה לִדְבִיר בֵּיתֶךָ. וְאִשֵּׁי יִשְׂרָאֵל וּתְפִלָּתָם בְּאַהֲבָה תְקַבֵּל בְּרָצוֹן, וּתְהִי לְרָצוֹן תָּמִיד עֲבוֹדַת יִשְׂרָאֵל עַמֶּךָ.

וְתֶחֱזֶינָה עֵינֵינוּ בְּשׁוּבְךָ לְצִיּוֹן בְּרַחֲמִים. בָּרוּךְ אַתָּה יהוה, הַמַּחֲזִיר שְׁכִינָתוֹ לְצִיּוֹן.

הודאה

Bow at מוֹדִים; straighten up at 'ה. In his repetition the *chazzan* should recite the entire מוֹדִים aloud, while the congregation recites מוֹדִים דְּרַבָּנָן softly.

מוֹדִים אֲנַחְנוּ לָךְ, שָׁאַתָּה הוּא יהוה אֱלֹהֵינוּ וֵאלֹהֵי אֲבוֹתֵינוּ לְעוֹלָם וָעֶד. צוּר חַיֵּינוּ, מָגֵן יִשְׁעֵנוּ אַתָּה הוּא לְדוֹר וָדוֹר. נוֹדֶה לְּךָ וּנְסַפֵּר תְּהִלָּתֶךָ[1] עַל חַיֵּינוּ הַמְּסוּרִים בְּיָדֶךָ, וְעַל נִשְׁמוֹתֵינוּ הַפְּקוּדוֹת לָךְ, וְעַל נִסֶּיךָ שֶׁבְּכָל יוֹם עִמָּנוּ, וְעַל נִפְלְאוֹתֶיךָ וְטוֹבוֹתֶיךָ שֶׁבְּכָל עֵת, עֶרֶב וָבֹקֶר וְצָהֳרָיִם. הַטּוֹב כִּי לֹא כָלוּ רַחֲמֶיךָ, וְהַמְרַחֵם כִּי לֹא תַמּוּ חֲסָדֶיךָ,[2] מֵעוֹלָם קִוִּינוּ לָךְ.

מודים דרבנן

מוֹדִים אֲנַחְנוּ לָךְ, שָׁאַתָּה הוּא יהוה אֱלֹהֵינוּ וֵאלֹהֵי אֲבוֹתֵינוּ, אֱלֹהֵי כָל בָּשָׂר, יוֹצְרֵנוּ, יוֹצֵר בְּרֵאשִׁית. בְּרָכוֹת וְהוֹדָאוֹת לְשִׁמְךָ הַגָּדוֹל וְהַקָּדוֹשׁ, עַל שֶׁהֶחֱיִיתָנוּ וְקִיַּמְתָּנוּ. כֵּן תְּחַיֵּנוּ וּתְקַיְּמֵנוּ, וְתֶאֱסוֹף גָּלֻיּוֹתֵינוּ לְחַצְרוֹת קָדְשֶׁךָ, לִשְׁמוֹר חֻקֶּיךָ וְלַעֲשׂוֹת רְצוֹנֶךָ, וּלְעָבְדְּךָ בְּלֵבָב שָׁלֵם, עַל שֶׁאֲנַחְנוּ מוֹדִים לָךְ. בָּרוּךְ אֵל הַהוֹדָאוֹת.

וְעַל כֻּלָּם יִתְבָּרַךְ וְיִתְרוֹמַם שִׁמְךָ מַלְכֵּנוּ תָּמִיד לְעוֹלָם וָעֶד.

Bend the knees at בָּרוּךְ; bow at אַתָּה; straighten up at 'ה.

וְכֹל הַחַיִּים יוֹדוּךָ סֶּלָה, וִיהַלְלוּ אֶת שִׁמְךָ בֶּאֱמֶת, הָאֵל יְשׁוּעָתֵנוּ וְעֶזְרָתֵנוּ סֶלָה. בָּרוּךְ אַתָּה יהוה, הַטּוֹב שִׁמְךָ וּלְךָ נָאֶה לְהוֹדוֹת.

שלום

שָׁלוֹם רָב עַל יִשְׂרָאֵל עַמְּךָ תָּשִׂים לְעוֹלָם, כִּי אַתָּה הוּא מֶלֶךְ אָדוֹן לְכָל הַשָּׁלוֹם. וְטוֹב בְּעֵינֶיךָ לְבָרֵךְ אֶת עַמְּךָ יִשְׂרָאֵל בְּכָל עֵת וּבְכָל שָׁעָה בִּשְׁלוֹמֶךָ. בָּרוּךְ אַתָּה יהוה, הַמְּבָרֵךְ אֶת עַמּוֹ יִשְׂרָאֵל בַּשָּׁלוֹם.

יִהְיוּ לְרָצוֹן אִמְרֵי פִי וְהֶגְיוֹן לִבִּי לְפָנֶיךָ, יהוה צוּרִי וְגֹאֲלִי.[3]

The *chazzan's* repetition of *Shemoneh Esrei* ends here. Individuals continue on page 1068.

TEMPLE SERVICE

רְצֵה *Be favorable, HASHEM, our God, toward Your people Israel and their prayer and restore the service to the Holy of Holies of Your Temple. The fire-offerings of Israel and their prayer accept with love and favor, and may the service of Your people Israel always be favorable to You.*

וְתֶחֱזֶינָה *May our eyes behold Your return to Zion in compassion. Blessed are You, HASHEM, Who restores His Presence to Zion.*

THANKSGIVING [MODIM]

Bow at *'We gratefully thank You'*; straighten up at *'HASHEM.'* In his repetition the *chazzan* should recite the entire *Modim* aloud, while the congregation recites *Modim of the Rabbis* softly.

מוֹדִים *We gratefully thank You, for it is You Who are HASHEM, our God and the God of our forefathers for all eternity; Rock of our lives, Shield of our salvation are You from generation to generation. We shall thank You and relate Your praise[1] — for our lives, which are committed to Your power and for our souls that are entrusted to You; for Your miracles that are with us every day; and for Your wonders and favors in every season — evening, morning, and afternoon. The Beneficent One, for Your compassions were never exhausted, and the Compassionate One, for Your kindnesses never ended[2] — always have we put our hope in You.*

MODIM OF THE RABBIS

מוֹדִים *We gratefully thank You, for it is You Who are HASHEM, our God and the God of our forefathers, the God of all flesh, our Molder, the Molder of the universe. Blessings and thanks are due Your great and holy Name for You have given us life and sustained us. So may You continue to give us life and sustain us and gather our exiles to the Courtyards of Your Sanctuary, to observe Your decrees, to do Your will and to serve You wholeheartedly. [We thank You] for inspiring us to thank You. Blessed is the God of thanksgivings.*

For all these, may Your Name be blessed and exalted, our King, continually forever and ever.

Bend the knees at *'Blessed'*; bow at *'You'*; straighten up at *'HASHEM.'*

Everything alive will gratefully acknowledge You, Selah! and praise Your Name sincerely, O God of our salvation and help, Selah! Blessed are You, HASHEM, Your Name is 'The Beneficent One' and to You it is fitting to give thanks.

PEACE

שָׁלוֹם רָב *Establish abundant peace upon Your people Israel forever, for You are King, Master of all peace. May it be good in Your eyes to bless Your people Israel at every time and every hour with Your peace. Blessed are You, HASHEM, Who blesses His people Israel with peace.*

May the expressions of my mouth and the thoughts of my heart find favor before You, HASHEM, my Rock and my Redeemer.[3]

The *chazzan's* repetition of *Shemoneh Esrei* ends here. Individuals continue on page 1068.

---

(1) Cf. *Psalms* 79:13. (2) Cf. *Lamentations* 3:22. (3) *Psalms* 19:15.

אֱלֹהַי, נְצוֹר לְשׁוֹנִי מֵרָע, וּשְׂפָתַי מִדַּבֵּר מִרְמָה,[1] וְלִמְקַלְלַי נַפְשִׁי תִדּוֹם, וְנַפְשִׁי כֶּעָפָר לַכֹּל תִּהְיֶה. פְּתַח לִבִּי בְּתוֹרָתֶךָ, וּבְמִצְוֹתֶיךָ תִּרְדּוֹף נַפְשִׁי. וְכֹל הַחוֹשְׁבִים עָלַי רָעָה, מְהֵרָה הָפֵר עֲצָתָם וְקַלְקֵל מַחֲשַׁבְתָּם. עֲשֵׂה לְמַעַן שְׁמֶךָ, עֲשֵׂה לְמַעַן יְמִינֶךָ, עֲשֵׂה לְמַעַן קְדֻשָּׁתֶךָ, עֲשֵׂה לְמַעַן תּוֹרָתֶךָ. לְמַעַן יֵחָלְצוּן יְדִידֶיךָ, הוֹשִׁיעָה יְמִינְךָ וַעֲנֵנִי.[2] Some recite verses pertaining to their names at this point. See p. 1143. יִהְיוּ לְרָצוֹן אִמְרֵי פִי וְהֶגְיוֹן לִבִּי לְפָנֶיךָ, יהוה צוּרִי וְגֹאֲלִי.[3] עֹשֶׂה שָׁלוֹם בִּמְרוֹמָיו, הוּא יַעֲשֶׂה שָׁלוֹם עָלֵינוּ, וְעַל כָּל יִשְׂרָאֵל. וְאִמְרוּ: אָמֵן.

יְהִי רָצוֹן מִלְּפָנֶיךָ יהוה אֱלֹהֵינוּ וֵאלֹהֵי אֲבוֹתֵינוּ, שֶׁיִּבָּנֶה בֵּית הַמִּקְדָּשׁ בִּמְהֵרָה בְיָמֵינוּ, וְתֵן חֶלְקֵנוּ בְּתוֹרָתֶךָ. וְשָׁם נַעֲבָדְךָ בְּיִרְאָה, כִּימֵי עוֹלָם וּכְשָׁנִים קַדְמוֹנִיּוֹת. וְעָרְבָה לַיהוה מִנְחַת יְהוּדָה וִירוּשָׁלָיִם, כִּימֵי עוֹלָם וּכְשָׁנִים קַדְמוֹנִיּוֹת.[4]

THE INDIVIDUAL'S RECITATION OF שְׁמוֹנֶה עֶשְׂרֵה ENDS HERE.

The individual remains standing in place until the *chazzan* reaches *Kedushah* – or at least until the *chazzan* begins his repetition – then he takes three steps forward. The *chazzan* himself, or one praying alone, should remain in place for a few moments before taking three steps forward.

The *chazzan* recites קַדִּישׁ שָׁלֵם.

יִתְגַּדַּל וְיִתְקַדַּשׁ שְׁמֵהּ רַבָּא. (.Cong – אָמֵן.) בְּעָלְמָא דִּי בְרָא כִרְעוּתֵהּ. וְיַמְלִיךְ מַלְכוּתֵהּ, בְּחַיֵּיכוֹן וּבְיוֹמֵיכוֹן וּבְחַיֵּי דְכָל בֵּית יִשְׂרָאֵל, בַּעֲגָלָא וּבִזְמַן קָרִיב. וְאִמְרוּ: אָמֵן.

(.Cong – אָמֵן. יְהֵא שְׁמֵהּ רַבָּא מְבָרַךְ לְעָלַם וּלְעָלְמֵי עָלְמַיָּא.)

יְהֵא שְׁמֵהּ רַבָּא מְבָרַךְ לְעָלַם וּלְעָלְמֵי עָלְמַיָּא.

יִתְבָּרַךְ וְיִשְׁתַּבַּח וְיִתְפָּאַר וְיִתְרוֹמַם וְיִתְנַשֵּׂא וְיִתְהַדָּר וְיִתְעַלֶּה וְיִתְהַלָּל שְׁמֵהּ דְּקֻדְשָׁא בְּרִיךְ הוּא (.Cong – בְּרִיךְ הוּא) – לְעֵלָּא מִן כָּל בִּרְכָתָא וְשִׁירָתָא תֻּשְׁבְּחָתָא וְנֶחֱמָתָא, דַּאֲמִירָן בְּעָלְמָא. וְאִמְרוּ: אָמֵן. (.Cong – אָמֵן.)

(.Cong – קַבֵּל בְּרַחֲמִים וּבְרָצוֹן אֶת תְּפִלָּתֵנוּ.)

תִּתְקַבֵּל צְלוֹתְהוֹן וּבָעוּתְהוֹן דְּכָל בֵּית יִשְׂרָאֵל קֳדָם אֲבוּהוֹן דִּי בִשְׁמַיָּא. וְאִמְרוּ: אָמֵן. (.Cong – אָמֵן.)

(.Cong – יְהִי שֵׁם יהוה מְבֹרָךְ, מֵעַתָּה וְעַד עוֹלָם.[5])

יְהֵא שְׁלָמָא רַבָּא מִן שְׁמַיָּא, וְחַיִּים עָלֵינוּ וְעַל כָּל יִשְׂרָאֵל. וְאִמְרוּ: אָמֵן. (.Cong – אָמֵן.)

(.Cong – עֶזְרִי מֵעִם יהוה, עֹשֵׂה שָׁמַיִם וָאָרֶץ.[6])

Take three steps back. Bow left and say . . . עֹשֶׂה; bow right and say . . . הוּא; bow forward and say וְעַל כָּל . . . אָמֵן. Remain standing in place for a few moments, then take three steps forward.

עֹשֶׂה שָׁלוֹם בִּמְרוֹמָיו, הוּא יַעֲשֶׂה שָׁלוֹם עָלֵינוּ, וְעַל כָּל יִשְׂרָאֵל. וְאִמְרוּ: אָמֵן. (.Cong – אָמֵן.)

אֱלֹהַי *My God, guard my tongue from evil and my lips from speaking deceitfully.*[1] *To those who curse me, let my soul be silent; and let my soul be like dust to everyone. Open my heart to Your Torah, then my soul will pursue Your commandments. As for all those who design evil against me, speedily nullify their counsel and disrupt their design. Act for Your Name's sake; act for Your right hand's sake; act for Your sanctity's sake; act for Your Torah's sake. That Your beloved ones may be given rest; let Your right hand save, and respond to me.*[2] Some recite verses pertaining to their names at this point. See page 1143. *May the expressions of my mouth and the thoughts of my heart find favor before You, HASHEM, my Rock and my Redeemer.*[3] *He Who makes peace in His heights, may He make peace upon us, and upon all Israel. Now respond: Amen.*

יְהִי רָצוֹן *May it be Your will, HASHEM, our God and the God of our forefathers, that the Holy Temple be rebuilt, speedily in our days. Grant us our share in Your Torah, and may we serve You there with reverence, as in days of old and in former years. Then the offering of Judah and Jerusalem will be pleasing to HASHEM, as in days of old and in former years.*[4]

THE INDIVIDUAL'S RECITATION OF *SHEMONEH ESREI* ENDS HERE.

The individual remains standing in place until the *chazzan* reaches *Kedushah* — or at least until the *chazzan* begins his repetition — then he takes three steps forward. The *chazzan* himself, or one praying alone, should remain in place for a few moments before taking three steps forward.

FULL KADDISH

The *chazzan* recites the Full *Kaddish*.

יִתְגַּדַּל *May His great Name grow exalted and sanctified* (Cong.— *Amen.*) *in the world that He created as He willed. May He give reign to His kingship in your lifetimes and in your days, and in the lifetimes of the entire Family of Israel, swiftly and soon. Now respond: Amen.*

(Cong.— *Amen. May His great Name be blessed forever and ever.*)

May His great Name be blessed forever and ever.

Blessed, praised, glorified, exalted, extolled, mighty, upraised, and lauded be the Name of the Holy One, Blessed is He (Cong.— *Blessed is He*) — *beyond any blessing and song, praise and consolation that are uttered in the world. Now respond: Amen.* (Cong.— *Amen.*)

(Cong.— *Accept our prayers with mercy and favor.*)

May the prayers and supplications of the entire Family of Israel be accepted before their Father Who is in Heaven. Now respond: Amen. (Cong.— *Amen.*)

(Cong.— *Blessed be the Name of HASHEM, from this time and forever.*[5])

May there be abundant peace from Heaven, and life, upon us and upon all Israel. Now respond: Amen. (Cong.— *Amen.*)

(Cong.— *My help is from HASHEM, Maker of heaven and earth.*[6])

Take three steps back. Bow left and say, *'He Who makes peace . . .'*; bow right and say, *'may He . . .'*; bow forward and say, *'and upon all Israel . . .'* Remain standing in place for a few moments, then take three steps forward.

He Who makes peace in His heights, may He make peace upon us, and upon all Israel. Now respond: Amen. (Cong.— *Amen.*)

---

(1) *Psalms* 60:7; 108:7. (2) Cf. 34:14. (3) 19:15. (4) *Malachi* 3:4. (5) *Psalms* 113:2. (6) 121:2.

Stand while reciting עָלֵינוּ.

עָלֵינוּ לְשַׁבֵּחַ לַאֲדוֹן הַכֹּל, לָתֵת גְּדֻלָּה לְיוֹצֵר בְּרֵאשִׁית, שֶׁלֹּא עָשָׂנוּ כְּגוֹיֵי הָאֲרָצוֹת, וְלֹא שָׂמָנוּ כְּמִשְׁפְּחוֹת הָאֲדָמָה. שֶׁלֹּא שָׂם חֶלְקֵנוּ כָּהֶם, וְגוֹרָלֵנוּ כְּכָל הֲמוֹנָם. (שֶׁהֵם מִשְׁתַּחֲוִים לְהֶבֶל וָרִיק, וּמִתְפַּלְּלִים אֶל אֵל לֹא יוֹשִׁיעַ.[1]) וַאֲנַחְנוּ כּוֹרְעִים וּמִשְׁתַּחֲוִים וּמוֹדִים, לִפְנֵי מֶלֶךְ מַלְכֵי הַמְּלָכִים הַקָּדוֹשׁ בָּרוּךְ הוּא. שֶׁהוּא נוֹטֶה שָׁמַיִם וְיֹסֵד אָרֶץ,[2] וּמוֹשַׁב יְקָרוֹ בַּשָּׁמַיִם מִמַּעַל, וּשְׁכִינַת עֻזּוֹ בְּגָבְהֵי מְרוֹמִים. הוּא אֱלֹהֵינוּ, אֵין עוֹד. אֱמֶת מַלְכֵּנוּ, אֶפֶס זוּלָתוֹ, כַּכָּתוּב בְּתוֹרָתוֹ: וְיָדַעְתָּ הַיּוֹם וַהֲשֵׁבֹתָ אֶל לְבָבֶךָ, כִּי יהוה הוּא הָאֱלֹהִים בַּשָּׁמַיִם מִמַּעַל וְעַל הָאָרֶץ מִתָּחַת, אֵין עוֹד.[3]

Bow while reciting וַאֲנַחְנוּ כּוֹרְעִים וּמִשְׁתַּחֲוִים.

עַל כֵּן נְקַוֶּה לְּךָ יהוה אֱלֹהֵינוּ לִרְאוֹת מְהֵרָה בְּתִפְאֶרֶת עֻזֶּךָ, לְהַעֲבִיר גִּלּוּלִים מִן הָאָרֶץ, וְהָאֱלִילִים כָּרוֹת יִכָּרֵתוּן, לְתַקֵּן עוֹלָם בְּמַלְכוּת שַׁדַּי. וְכָל בְּנֵי בָשָׂר יִקְרְאוּ בִשְׁמֶךָ, לְהַפְנוֹת אֵלֶיךָ כָּל רִשְׁעֵי אָרֶץ. יַכִּירוּ וְיֵדְעוּ כָּל יוֹשְׁבֵי תֵבֵל, כִּי לְךָ תִּכְרַע כָּל בֶּרֶךְ, תִּשָּׁבַע כָּל לָשׁוֹן.[4] לְפָנֶיךָ יהוה אֱלֹהֵינוּ יִכְרְעוּ וְיִפֹּלוּ, וְלִכְבוֹד שִׁמְךָ יְקָר יִתֵּנוּ. וִיקַבְּלוּ כֻלָּם אֶת עוֹל מַלְכוּתֶךָ, וְתִמְלֹךְ עֲלֵיהֶם מְהֵרָה לְעוֹלָם וָעֶד. כִּי הַמַּלְכוּת שֶׁלְּךָ הִיא וּלְעוֹלְמֵי עַד תִּמְלוֹךְ בְּכָבוֹד, כַּכָּתוּב בְּתוֹרָתֶךָ: יהוה יִמְלֹךְ לְעֹלָם וָעֶד.[5] ❖ וְנֶאֱמַר: וְהָיָה יהוה לְמֶלֶךְ עַל כָּל הָאָרֶץ, בַּיּוֹם הַהוּא יִהְיֶה יהוה אֶחָד וּשְׁמוֹ אֶחָד.[6]

Some congregations recite the following after עָלֵינוּ:

אַל תִּירָא מִפַּחַד פִּתְאֹם, וּמִשֹּׁאַת רְשָׁעִים כִּי תָבֹא.[7] עֻצוּ עֵצָה וְתֻפָר, דַּבְּרוּ דָבָר וְלֹא יָקוּם, כִּי עִמָּנוּ אֵל.[8] וְעַד זִקְנָה אֲנִי הוּא, וְעַד שֵׂיבָה אֲנִי אֶסְבֹּל, אֲנִי עָשִׂיתִי וַאֲנִי אֶשָּׂא, וַאֲנִי אֶסְבֹּל וַאֲמַלֵּט.[9]

קדיש יתום

In the presence of a *minyan,* mourners recite קַדִּישׁ יָתוֹם, the Mourner's *Kaddish* (see *Laws* §81-83).

יִתְגַּדַּל וְיִתְקַדַּשׁ שְׁמֵהּ רַבָּא. (.Cong – אָמֵן.) בְּעָלְמָא דִּי בְרָא כִרְעוּתֵהּ. וְיַמְלִיךְ מַלְכוּתֵהּ, בְּחַיֵּיכוֹן וּבְיוֹמֵיכוֹן וּבְחַיֵּי דְכָל בֵּית יִשְׂרָאֵל, בַּעֲגָלָא וּבִזְמַן קָרִיב. וְאִמְרוּ: אָמֵן.

(.Cong – אָמֵן. יְהֵא שְׁמֵהּ רַבָּא מְבָרַךְ לְעָלַם וּלְעָלְמֵי עָלְמַיָּא.)

יְהֵא שְׁמֵהּ רַבָּא מְבָרַךְ לְעָלַם וּלְעָלְמֵי עָלְמַיָּא.

יִתְבָּרַךְ וְיִשְׁתַּבַּח וְיִתְפָּאַר וְיִתְרוֹמַם וְיִתְנַשֵּׂא וְיִתְהַדָּר וְיִתְעַלֶּה וְיִתְהַלָּל

Stand while reciting עָלֵינוּ, *'It is our duty . . .'*

עָלֵינוּ *It is our duty to praise the Master of all, to ascribe greatness to the Molder of primeval creation, for He has not made us like the nations of the lands, and has not emplaced us like the families of the earth; for He has not assigned our portion like theirs nor our lot like all their multitudes. (For they bow to vanity and emptiness and pray to a god which helps not.*[1]*) But we bend our knees, bow, and acknowledge our thanks before the King Who reigns over kings, the Holy One, Blessed is He. He stretches out heaven and establishes earth's foundation,*[2] *the seat of His homage is in the heavens above and His powerful Presence is in the loftiest heights. He is our God and there is none other. True is our King, there is nothing beside Him, as it is written in His Torah: 'You are to know this day and take to your heart that* HASHEM *is the only God — in heaven above and on the earth below — there is none other.'*[3]

Bow while reciting 'But we bend our knees.'

עַל כֵּן *Therefore we put our hope in You,* HASHEM, *our God, that we may soon see Your mighty splendor, to remove detestable idolatry from the earth, and false gods will be utterly cut off, to perfect the universe through the Almighty's sovereignty. Then all humanity will call upon Your Name, to turn all the earth's wicked toward You. All the world's inhabitants will recognize and know that to You every knee should bend, every tongue should swear.*[4] *Before You,* HASHEM, *our God, they will bend every knee and cast themselves down and to the glory of Your Name they will render homage, and they will all accept upon themselves the yoke of Your kingship that You may reign over them soon and eternally. For the kingdom is Yours and You will reign for all eternity in glory as it is written in Your Torah:* HASHEM *shall reign for all eternity.*[5] Chazzan— *And it is said:* HASHEM *will be King over all the world — on that day* HASHEM *will be One and His Name will be One.*[6]

Some congregations recite the following after *Aleinu.*

אַל תִּירָא *Do not fear sudden terror, or the holocaust of the wicked when it comes.*[7] *Plan a conspiracy and it will be annulled; speak your piece and it shall not stand, for God is with us.*[8] *Even till your seniority, I remain unchanged; and even till your ripe old age, I shall endure. I created you and I shall bear you; I shall endure and rescue.*[9]

MOURNER'S KADDISH

In the presence of a *minyan,* mourners recite קַדִּישׁ יָתוֹם, the Mourner's *Kaddish* (see *Laws* 81-83).

[A transliteration of this *Kaddish* appears on page 1147.]

יִתְגַּדַּל *May His great Name grow exalted and sanctified* (Cong.— *Amen.*) *in the world that He created as He willed. May He give reign to His kingship in your lifetimes and in your days, and in the lifetimes of the entire Family of Israel, swiftly and soon. Now respond: Amen.*

(Cong.— *Amen. May His great Name be blessed forever and ever.*)

May His great Name be blessed forever and ever.

Blessed, praised, glorified, exalted, extolled, mighty, upraised, and lauded be

(1) *Isaiah* 45:20. (2) 51:13. (3) *Deuteronomy* 4:39. (4) Cf. *Isaiah* 45:23. (5) *Exodus* 15:18. (6) *Zechariah* 14:9. (7) *Proverbs* 3:25. (8) *Isaiah* 8:10. (9) 46:4.

שְׁמֵהּ דְּקֻדְשָׁא בְּרִיךְ הוּא (.Cong – בְּרִיךְ הוּא) – לְעֵלָּא מִן כָּל בִּרְכָתָא וְשִׁירָתָא תֻּשְׁבְּחָתָא וְנֶחֱמָתָא, דַּאֲמִירָן בְּעָלְמָא. וְאִמְרוּ: אָמֵן. (.Cong – אָמֵן.)

יְהֵא שְׁלָמָא רַבָּא מִן שְׁמַיָּא, וְחַיִּים עָלֵינוּ וְעַל כָּל יִשְׂרָאֵל. וְאִמְרוּ: אָמֵן. (.Cong – אָמֵן.)

Take three steps back. Bow left and say . . . עֹשֶׂה; bow right and say . . . הוּא; bow forward and say וְעַל כָּל . . . אָמֵן. Remain standing in place for a few moments, then take three steps forward.

עֹשֶׂה שָׁלוֹם בִּמְרוֹמָיו, הוּא יַעֲשֶׂה שָׁלוֹם עָלֵינוּ, וְעַל כָּל יִשְׂרָאֵל. וְאִמְרוּ: אָמֵן. (.Cong – אָמֵן.)

מעריב למוצאי יום טוב

Congregation, then *chazzan:*

וְהוּא רַחוּם יְכַפֵּר עָוֹן וְלֹא יַשְׁחִית, וְהִרְבָּה לְהָשִׁיב אַפּוֹ, וְלֹא יָעִיר כָּל חֲמָתוֹ.[1] יהוה הוֹשִׁיעָה, הַמֶּלֶךְ יַעֲנֵנוּ בְיוֹם קָרְאֵנוּ.[2]

In some congregations the *chazzan* chants a melody during his recitation of בָּרְכוּ, so that the congregation can then recite יִתְבָּרַךְ.

Chazzan bows at בָּרְכוּ and straightens up at 'ה.

בָּרְכוּ אֶת יהוה הַמְּבֹרָךְ.

Congregation, followed by *chazzan*, responds, bowing at בָּרוּךְ and straightening up at 'ה.

בָּרוּךְ יהוה הַמְּבֹרָךְ לְעוֹלָם וָעֶד.

יִתְבָּרַךְ וְיִשְׁתַּבַּח וְיִתְפָּאַר וְיִתְרוֹמַם וְיִתְנַשֵּׂא שְׁמוֹ שֶׁל מֶלֶךְ מַלְכֵי הַמְּלָכִים, הַקָּדוֹשׁ בָּרוּךְ הוּא. שֶׁהוּא רִאשׁוֹן וְהוּא אַחֲרוֹן, וּמִבַּלְעָדָיו אֵין אֱלֹהִים.[3] סֹלּוּ, לָרֹכֵב בָּעֲרָבוֹת, בְּיָהּ שְׁמוֹ, וְעִלְזוּ לְפָנָיו.[4] וּשְׁמוֹ מְרוֹמָם עַל כָּל בְּרָכָה וּתְהִלָּה.[5] בָּרוּךְ שֵׁם כְּבוֹד מַלְכוּתוֹ לְעוֹלָם וָעֶד. יְהִי שֵׁם יהוה מְבֹרָךְ, מֵעַתָּה וְעַד עוֹלָם.[6]

ברכות קריאת שמע

בָּרוּךְ אַתָּה יהוה אֱלֹהֵינוּ מֶלֶךְ הָעוֹלָם, אֲשֶׁר בִּדְבָרוֹ מַעֲרִיב עֲרָבִים, בְּחָכְמָה פּוֹתֵחַ שְׁעָרִים, וּבִתְבוּנָה מְשַׁנֶּה עִתִּים, וּמַחֲלִיף אֶת הַזְּמַנִּים, וּמְסַדֵּר אֶת הַכּוֹכָבִים בְּמִשְׁמְרוֹתֵיהֶם בָּרָקִיעַ כִּרְצוֹנוֹ. בּוֹרֵא יוֹם וָלָיְלָה, גּוֹלֵל אוֹר מִפְּנֵי חֹשֶׁךְ וְחֹשֶׁךְ מִפְּנֵי אוֹר. וּמַעֲבִיר יוֹם וּמֵבִיא לָיְלָה, וּמַבְדִּיל בֵּין יוֹם וּבֵין לָיְלָה, יהוה צְבָאוֹת שְׁמוֹ. ❖ אֵל חַי וְקַיָּם, תָּמִיד יִמְלוֹךְ עָלֵינוּ, לְעוֹלָם וָעֶד. בָּרוּךְ אַתָּה יהוה, הַמַּעֲרִיב עֲרָבִים. (.Cong – אָמֵן.)

אַהֲבַת עוֹלָם בֵּית יִשְׂרָאֵל עַמְּךָ אָהָבְתָּ. תּוֹרָה וּמִצְוֹת, חֻקִּים וּמִשְׁפָּטִים, אוֹתָנוּ לִמַּדְתָּ. עַל כֵּן יהוה אֱלֹהֵינוּ, בְּשָׁכְבֵנוּ וּבְקוּמֵנוּ נָשִׂיחַ בְּחֻקֶּיךָ, וְנִשְׂמַח בְּדִבְרֵי

the Name of the Holy One, Blessed is He (Cong.– *Blessed is He*) — *beyond any blessing and song, praise and consolation that are uttered in the world. Now respond: Amen.* (Cong.– *Amen*).

May there be abundant peace from Heaven, and life, upon us and upon all Israel. Now respond: Amen. (Cong.– *Amen.*)

Take three steps back. Bow left and say, *'He Who makes peace . . .';* bow right and say, *'may He . . .';* bow forward and say, *'and upon all Israel . . .'* Remain standing in place for a few moments, then take three steps forward.

He Who makes peace in His heights, may He make peace upon us, and upon all Israel. Now respond: Amen. (Cong.– *Amen.*)

MAARIV FOR THE CONCLUSION OF YOM TOV

Congregation, then *chazzan:*

וְהוּא רַחוּם *He, the Merciful One, is forgiving of iniquity and does not destroy. Frequently He withdraws His anger, not arousing His entire rage.*[1] *HASHEM, save! May the King answer us on the day we call.*[2]

In some congregations the *chazzan* chants a melody during his recitation of *Borchu,* so that the congregation can then recite *'Blessed, praised . . .'*

Chazzan bows at *'Bless,'* and straightens up at *'HASHEM.'*

Bless HASHEM, the blessed One.

Congregation, followed by *chazzan,* responds, bowing at *'Blessed'* and straightening up at *'HASHEM.'*

Blessed is HASHEM, the blessed One, for all eternity.

Blessed, praised, glorified, exalted and upraised is the Name of the King Who rules over kings — the Holy One, Blessed is He. For He is the First and He is the Last and aside from Him there is no god.[3] *Extol Him — Who rides the highest heavens — with His Name, YAH, and exult before Him.*[4] *His Name is exalted beyond every blessing and praise.*[5] *Blessed is the Name of His glorious kingdom for all eternity. Blessed be the Name of HASHEM from this time and forever.*[6]

BLESSINGS OF THE SHEMA

בָּרוּךְ *Blessed are You, HASHEM, our God, King of the universe, Who by His word brings on evenings, with wisdom opens gates, with understanding alters periods, changes the seasons, and orders the stars in their heavenly constellations as He wills. He creates day and night, removing light before darkness and darkness before light. He causes day to pass and brings night, and separates between day and night — HASHEM, Master of Legions, is His Name.* Chazzan– *May the living and enduring God continuously reign over us, for all eternity. Blessed are You, HASHEM, Who brings on evenings.* (Cong.– *Amen.*)

אַהֲבַת *With an eternal love have You loved the House of Israel, Your nation. Torah and commandments, decrees and ordinances have You taught us. Therefore HASHEM, our God, upon our retiring and arising, we will discuss Your decrees and we will rejoice with the words*

(1) *Psalms* 78:38. (2) 20:10. (3) Cf. *Isaiah* 44:6. (4) *Psalms* 68:5. (5) Cf. *Nehemiah* 9:5. (6) *Psalms* 113.2.

תּוֹרָתֶךָ, וּבְמִצְוֹתֶיךָ לְעוֹלָם וָעֶד. ❖ כִּי הֵם חַיֵּינוּ, וְאֹרֶךְ יָמֵינוּ, וּבָהֶם נֶהְגֶּה יוֹמָם וָלָיְלָה. וְאַהֲבָתְךָ, אַל תָּסִיר מִמֶּנּוּ לְעוֹלָמִים. בָּרוּךְ אַתָּה יהוה, אוֹהֵב עַמּוֹ יִשְׂרָאֵל. (Cong. – אָמֵן.)

שמע

Immediately before its recitation, concentrate on fulfilling the positive commandment of reciting the *Shema* twice daily. It is important to enunciate each word clearly and not to run words together. For this reason, vertical lines have been placed between two words that are prone to be slurred into one and are not separated by a comma or a hyphen. See *Laws* §40-52.

When praying without a *minyan*, begin with the following three-word formula:

אֵל מֶלֶךְ נֶאֱמָן.

Recite the first verse aloud, with the right hand covering the eyes, and concentrate intently upon accepting God's absolute sovereignty.

שְׁמַע | יִשְׂרָאֵל, יהוה | אֱלֹהֵינוּ, יהוה | אֶחָד:[1]

In an undertone – בָּרוּךְ שֵׁם כְּבוֹד מַלְכוּתוֹ לְעוֹלָם וָעֶד.

While reciting the first paragraph (דברים ו:ה-ט), concentrate on accepting the commandment to love God.

וְאָהַבְתָּ אֵת | יהוה | אֱלֹהֶיךָ, בְּכָל־לְבָבְךָ, וּבְכָל־נַפְשְׁךָ, וּבְכָל־מְאֹדֶךָ: וְהָיוּ הַדְּבָרִים הָאֵלֶּה, אֲשֶׁר | אָנֹכִי מְצַוְּךָ הַיּוֹם, עַל־לְבָבֶךָ: וְשִׁנַּנְתָּם לְבָנֶיךָ, וְדִבַּרְתָּ בָּם, בְּשִׁבְתְּךָ בְּבֵיתֶךָ, וּבְלֶכְתְּךָ בַדֶּרֶךְ, וּבְשָׁכְבְּךָ וּבְקוּמֶךָ: וּקְשַׁרְתָּם לְאוֹת | עַל־יָדֶךָ, וְהָיוּ לְטֹטָפֹת בֵּין | עֵינֶיךָ: וּכְתַבְתָּם | עַל־מְזֻזוֹת בֵּיתֶךָ, וּבִשְׁעָרֶיךָ:

While reciting the second paragraph (דברים יא:יג-כא), concentrate on accepting all the commandments and the concept of reward and punishment.

וְהָיָה, אִם־שָׁמֹעַ תִּשְׁמְעוּ אֶל־מִצְוֹתַי, אֲשֶׁר | אָנֹכִי מְצַוֶּה | אֶתְכֶם הַיּוֹם, לְאַהֲבָה אֶת־יהוה | אֱלֹהֵיכֶם וּלְעָבְדוֹ, בְּכָל־לְבַבְכֶם, וּבְכָל־נַפְשְׁכֶם: וְנָתַתִּי מְטַר־אַרְצְכֶם בְּעִתּוֹ, יוֹרֶה וּמַלְקוֹשׁ, וְאָסַפְתָּ דְגָנֶךָ וְתִירֹשְׁךָ וְיִצְהָרֶךָ: וְנָתַתִּי | עֵשֶׂב | בְּשָׂדְךָ לִבְהֶמְתֶּךָ, וְאָכַלְתָּ וְשָׂבָעְתָּ: הִשָּׁמְרוּ לָכֶם, פֶּן־יִפְתֶּה לְבַבְכֶם, וְסַרְתֶּם וַעֲבַדְתֶּם | אֱלֹהִים | אֲחֵרִים, וְהִשְׁתַּחֲוִיתֶם לָהֶם: וְחָרָה | אַף־יהוה בָּכֶם, וְעָצַר | אֶת־הַשָּׁמַיִם, וְלֹא־יִהְיֶה מָטָר, וְהָאֲדָמָה לֹא תִתֵּן אֶת־יְבוּלָהּ, וַאֲבַדְתֶּם | מְהֵרָה מֵעַל הָאָרֶץ הַטֹּבָה | אֲשֶׁר | יהוה נֹתֵן לָכֶם: וְשַׂמְתֶּם | אֶת־דְּבָרַי | אֵלֶּה, עַל־לְבַבְכֶם וְעַל־נַפְשְׁכֶם, וּקְשַׁרְתֶּם | אֹתָם לְאוֹת | עַל־יֶדְכֶם, וְהָיוּ לְטוֹטָפֹת בֵּין | עֵינֵיכֶם: וְלִמַּדְתֶּם | אֹתָם | אֶת־בְּנֵיכֶם, לְדַבֵּר בָּם, בְּשִׁבְתְּךָ בְּבֵיתֶךָ, וּבְלֶכְתְּךָ בַדֶּרֶךְ, וּבְשָׁכְבְּךָ וּבְקוּמֶךָ: וּכְתַבְתָּם | עַל־מְזוּזוֹת בֵּיתֶךָ, וּבִשְׁעָרֶיךָ: לְמַעַן | יִרְבּוּ | יְמֵיכֶם וִימֵי בְנֵיכֶם, עַל הָאֲדָמָה | אֲשֶׁר נִשְׁבַּע | יהוה לַאֲבֹתֵיכֶם לָתֵת לָהֶם, כִּימֵי הַשָּׁמַיִם | עַל־הָאָרֶץ:

of Your Torah and with Your commandments for all eternity. Chazzan– *For they are our life and the length of our days and about them we will meditate day and night. May You not remove Your love from us forever. Blessed are You, HASHEM, Who loves His nation Israel.* (Cong.– *Amen.)*

THE SHEMA

Immediately before its recitation, concentrate on fulfilling the positive commandment of reciting the *Shema* twice daily. It is important to enunciate each word clearly and not to run words together. See *Laws* §40-52.

When praying without a *minyan*, begin with the following three-word formula:

God, trustworthy King.

Recite the first verse aloud, with the right hand covering the eyes, and concentrate intently upon accepting God's absolute sovereignty.

Hear, O Israel: HASHEM is our God, HASHEM, the One and Only.[1]

In an undertone– *Blessed is the Name of His glorious kingdom for all eternity.*

While reciting the first paragraph (*Deuteronomy* 6:5-9), concentrate on accepting the commandment to love God.

וְאָהַבְתָּ *You shall love HASHEM, your God, with all your heart, with all your soul and with all your resources. Let these matters that I command you today be upon your heart. Teach them thoroughly to your children and speak of them while you sit in your home, while you walk on the way, when you retire and when you arise. Bind them as a sign upon your arm and let them be tefillin between your eyes. And write them on the doorposts of your house and upon your gates.*

While reciting the second paragraph (*Deuteronomy* 11:13-21), concentrate on accepting all the commandments and the concept of reward and punishment.

וְהָיָה *And it will come to pass that if you continually hearken to My commandments that I command you today, to love HASHEM, your God, and to serve Him, with all your heart and with all your soul — then I will provide rain for your land in its proper time, the early and late rains, that you may gather in your grain, your wine, and your oil. I will provide grass in your field for your cattle and you will eat and be satisfied. Beware lest your heart be seduced and you turn astray and serve gods of others and bow to them. Then the wrath of HASHEM will blaze against you. He will restrain the heaven so there will be no rain and the ground will not yield its produce. And you will swiftly be banished from the goodly land which HASHEM gives you. Place these words of Mine upon your heart and upon your soul; bind them for a sign upon your arm and let them be tefillin between your eyes. Teach them to your children, to discuss them, while you sit in your home, while you walk on the way, when you retire and when you arise. And write them on the doorposts of your house and upon your gates. In order to prolong your days and the days of your children upon the ground that HASHEM has sworn to your ancestors to give them, like the days of the heaven on the earth.*

---

(1) *Deuteronomy* 6:4.

במדבר טו:לז-מא

וַיֹּאמֶר | יְהוָה | אֶל־מֹשֶׁה לֵּאמֹר: דַּבֵּר | אֶל־בְּנֵי | יִשְׂרָאֵל, וְאָמַרְתָּ אֲלֵהֶם, וְעָשׂוּ לָהֶם צִיצִת, עַל־כַּנְפֵי בִגְדֵיהֶם לְדֹרֹתָם, וְנָתְנוּ | עַל־צִיצִת הַכָּנָף, פְּתִיל תְּכֵלֶת: וְהָיָה לָכֶם לְצִיצִת, וּרְאִיתֶם | אֹתוֹ, וּזְכַרְתֶּם | אֶת־כָּל־מִצְוֹת | יְהוָה, וַעֲשִׂיתֶם | אֹתָם, וְלֹא תָתֻרוּ | אַחֲרֵי לְבַבְכֶם וְאַחֲרֵי | עֵינֵיכֶם, אֲשֶׁר־אַתֶּם זֹנִים | אַחֲרֵיהֶם: לְמַעַן תִּזְכְּרוּ, וַעֲשִׂיתֶם | אֶת־כָּל־מִצְוֹתָי, וִהְיִיתֶם קְדֹשִׁים לֵאלֹהֵיכֶם: אֲנִי יְהוָה | אֱלֹהֵיכֶם, אֲשֶׁר הוֹצֵאתִי | אֶתְכֶם | מֵאֶרֶץ מִצְרַיִם, לִהְיוֹת לָכֶם לֵאלֹהִים, אֲנִי | יְהוָה | אֱלֹהֵיכֶם: אֱמֶת —

Concentrate on fulfilling the commandment of remembering the Exodus from Egypt.

Although the word אֱמֶת belongs to the next paragraph, it is appended to the conclusion of the previous one, as explained in the commentary on page 50.

Chazzan repeats — **יְהוָה אֱלֹהֵיכֶם אֱמֶת.**

וֶאֱמוּנָה כָּל זֹאת, וְקַיָּם עָלֵינוּ, כִּי הוּא יְהוָה אֱלֹהֵינוּ וְאֵין זוּלָתוֹ, וַאֲנַחְנוּ יִשְׂרָאֵל עַמּוֹ. הַפּוֹדֵנוּ מִיַּד מְלָכִים, מַלְכֵּנוּ הַגּוֹאֲלֵנוּ מִכַּף כָּל הֶעָרִיצִים. הָאֵל הַנִּפְרָע לָנוּ מִצָּרֵינוּ, וְהַמְשַׁלֵּם גְּמוּל לְכָל אֹיְבֵי נַפְשֵׁנוּ. הָעֹשֶׂה גְדֹלוֹת עַד אֵין חֵקֶר, וְנִפְלָאוֹת עַד אֵין מִסְפָּר.[1] הַשָּׂם נַפְשֵׁנוּ בַּחַיִּים, וְלֹא נָתַן לַמּוֹט רַגְלֵנוּ.[2] הַמַּדְרִיכֵנוּ עַל בָּמוֹת אוֹיְבֵינוּ, וַיָּרֶם קַרְנֵנוּ עַל כָּל שׂנְאֵינוּ. הָעֹשֶׂה לָּנוּ נִסִּים וּנְקָמָה בְּפַרְעֹה, אוֹתוֹת וּמוֹפְתִים בְּאַדְמַת בְּנֵי חָם. הַמַּכֶּה בְעֶבְרָתוֹ כָּל בְּכוֹרֵי מִצְרָיִם, וַיּוֹצֵא אֶת עַמּוֹ יִשְׂרָאֵל מִתּוֹכָם לְחֵרוּת עוֹלָם. הַמַּעֲבִיר בָּנָיו בֵּין גִּזְרֵי יַם סוּף, אֶת רוֹדְפֵיהֶם וְאֶת שׂוֹנְאֵיהֶם בִּתְהוֹמוֹת טִבַּע. וְרָאוּ בָנָיו גְּבוּרָתוֹ, שִׁבְּחוּ וְהוֹדוּ לִשְׁמוֹ. ❖ וּמַלְכוּתוֹ בְּרָצוֹן קִבְּלוּ עֲלֵיהֶם. מֹשֶׁה וּבְנֵי יִשְׂרָאֵל לְךָ עָנוּ שִׁירָה, בְּשִׂמְחָה רַבָּה, וְאָמְרוּ כֻלָּם:

מִי כָמֹכָה בָּאֵלִם יְהוָה, מִי כָּמֹכָה נֶאְדָּר בַּקֹּדֶשׁ, נוֹרָא תְהִלֹּת, עֹשֵׂה פֶלֶא.[3] ❖ מַלְכוּתְךָ רָאוּ בָנֶיךָ בּוֹקֵעַ יָם לִפְנֵי מֹשֶׁה, זֶה אֵלִי[4] עָנוּ וְאָמְרוּ:

יְהוָה יִמְלֹךְ לְעֹלָם וָעֶד.[5] ❖ וְנֶאֱמַר: כִּי פָדָה יְהוָה אֶת יַעֲקֹב, וּגְאָלוֹ מִיַּד חָזָק מִמֶּנּוּ.[6] בָּרוּךְ אַתָּה יְהוָה, גָּאַל יִשְׂרָאֵל.

(Cong. — אָמֵן.)

---

(1) *Job* 9:10. (2) *Psalms* 66:9. (3) *Exodus* 15:11. (4) 15:2. (5) 15:18. (6) *Jeremiah* 31:10.

Numbers 15:37-41

וַיֹּאמֶר *And HASHEM said to Moses saying: Speak to the Children of Israel and say to them that they are to make themselves tzitzis on the corners of their garments, throughout their generations. And they are to place upon the tzitzis of each corner a thread of techeiles. And it shall constitute tzitzis for you, that you may see it and remember all the commandments of HASHEM and perform them; and not explore after your heart and after your eyes after which you stray. So that you may remember and perform all My commandments; and be holy to your God. I am HASHEM, your God, Who has removed you from the land of Egypt to be a God to you; I am HASHEM your God — it is true —*

Concentrate on fulfilling the commandment of remembering the Exodus from Egypt.

Although the word אֱמֶת, *'it is true,'* belongs to the next paragraph, it is appended to the conclusion of the previous one, as explained in the commentary on page 50.

Chazzan repeats: **HASHEM, your God, is true.**

וֶאֱמוּנָה *And faithful is all this, and it is firmly established for us that He is HASHEM our God, and there is none but Him, and we are Israel, His nation. He redeems us from the power of kings, our King Who delivers us from the hand of all the cruel tyrants. He is the God Who exacts vengeance for us from our foes and Who brings just retribution upon all enemies of our soul; Who performs great deeds that are beyond comprehension, and wonders beyond number.*[1] *Who set our soul in life and did not allow our foot to falter.*[2] *Who led us upon the heights of our enemies and raised our pride above all who hate us; Who wrought for us miracles and vengeance upon Pharaoh; signs and wonders on the land of the offspring of Ham; Who struck with His anger all the firstborn of Egypt and removed His nation Israel from their midst to eternal freedom; Who brought His children through the split parts of the Sea of Reeds while those who pursued them and hated them He caused to sink into the depths. When His children perceived His power, they lauded and gave grateful praise to His Name.* Chazzan– *And His Kingship they accepted upon themselves willingly. Moses and the Children of Israel raised their voices to You in song with abundant gladness — and said unanimously:*

מִי כָמֹכָה *Who is like You among the heavenly powers, HASHEM! Who is like You, mighty in holiness, too awesome for praise, doing wonders!*[3] Chazzan– *Your children beheld Your majesty, as You split the sea before Moses: 'This is my God!'*[4] *they exclaimed, then they said:*

יהוה *'HASHEM shall reign for all eternity!'*[5] Chazzan– *And it is further said: 'For HASHEM has redeemed Jacob and delivered him from a power mightier than he.'*[6] *Blessed are You, HASHEM, Who redeemed Israel.*

(Cong.– *Amen.)*

הַשְׁכִּיבֵנוּ יהוה אֱלֹהֵינוּ לְשָׁלוֹם, וְהַעֲמִידֵנוּ מַלְכֵּנוּ לְחַיִּים, וּפְרוֹשׂ עָלֵינוּ סֻכַּת שְׁלוֹמֶךָ, וְתַקְּנֵנוּ בְּעֵצָה טוֹבָה מִלְּפָנֶיךָ, וְהוֹשִׁיעֵנוּ לְמַעַן שְׁמֶךָ. וְהָגֵן בַּעֲדֵנוּ, וְהָסֵר מֵעָלֵינוּ אוֹיֵב, דֶּבֶר, וְחֶרֶב, וְרָעָב, וְיָגוֹן, וְהָסֵר שָׂטָן מִלְּפָנֵינוּ וּמֵאַחֲרֵינוּ, וּבְצֵל כְּנָפֶיךָ תַּסְתִּירֵנוּ,[1] כִּי אֵל שׁוֹמְרֵנוּ וּמַצִּילֵנוּ אָתָּה, כִּי אֵל מֶלֶךְ חַנּוּן וְרַחוּם אָתָּה.[2] ❖ וּשְׁמוֹר צֵאתֵנוּ וּבוֹאֵנוּ, לְחַיִּים וּלְשָׁלוֹם מֵעַתָּה וְעַד עוֹלָם.[3] בָּרוּךְ אַתָּה יהוה, שׁוֹמֵר עַמּוֹ יִשְׂרָאֵל לָעַד.

(.Cong. – אָמֵן)

Some congregations omit the following prayers and continue with Half-*Kaddish* (p. 1080).

בָּרוּךְ יהוה לְעוֹלָם, אָמֵן וְאָמֵן.[4] בָּרוּךְ יהוה מִצִּיּוֹן, שֹׁכֵן יְרוּשָׁלָיִם, הַלְלוּיָהּ.[5] בָּרוּךְ יהוה אֱלֹהִים אֱלֹהֵי יִשְׂרָאֵל, עֹשֵׂה נִפְלָאוֹת לְבַדּוֹ. וּבָרוּךְ שֵׁם כְּבוֹדוֹ לְעוֹלָם, וְיִמָּלֵא כְבוֹדוֹ אֶת כָּל הָאָרֶץ, אָמֵן וְאָמֵן.[6] יְהִי כְבוֹד יהוה לְעוֹלָם, יִשְׂמַח יהוה בְּמַעֲשָׂיו.[7] יְהִי שֵׁם יהוה מְבֹרָךְ, מֵעַתָּה וְעַד עוֹלָם.[8] כִּי לֹא יִטֹּשׁ יהוה אֶת עַמּוֹ בַּעֲבוּר שְׁמוֹ הַגָּדוֹל, כִּי הוֹאִיל יהוה לַעֲשׂוֹת אֶתְכֶם לוֹ לְעָם.[9] וַיַּרְא כָּל הָעָם וַיִּפְּלוּ עַל פְּנֵיהֶם, וַיֹּאמְרוּ, יהוה הוּא הָאֱלֹהִים, יהוה הוּא הָאֱלֹהִים.[10] וְהָיָה יהוה לְמֶלֶךְ עַל כָּל הָאָרֶץ, בַּיּוֹם הַהוּא יִהְיֶה יהוה אֶחָד וּשְׁמוֹ אֶחָד.[11] יְהִי חַסְדְּךָ יהוה עָלֵינוּ, כַּאֲשֶׁר יִחַלְנוּ לָךְ.[12] הוֹשִׁיעֵנוּ יהוה אֱלֹהֵינוּ, וְקַבְּצֵנוּ מִן הַגּוֹיִם, לְהוֹדוֹת לְשֵׁם קָדְשֶׁךָ, לְהִשְׁתַּבֵּחַ בִּתְהִלָּתֶךָ.[13] כָּל גּוֹיִם אֲשֶׁר עָשִׂיתָ יָבוֹאוּ וְיִשְׁתַּחֲווּ לְפָנֶיךָ אֲדֹנָי, וִיכַבְּדוּ לִשְׁמֶךָ. כִּי גָדוֹל אַתָּה וְעֹשֵׂה נִפְלָאוֹת, אַתָּה אֱלֹהִים לְבַדֶּךָ.[14] וַאֲנַחְנוּ עַמְּךָ וְצֹאן מַרְעִיתֶךָ, נוֹדֶה לְּךָ לְעוֹלָם, לְדוֹר וָדֹר נְסַפֵּר תְּהִלָּתֶךָ.[15] בָּרוּךְ יהוה בַּיּוֹם. בָּרוּךְ יהוה בַּלָּיְלָה. בָּרוּךְ יהוה בְּשָׁכְבֵנוּ. בָּרוּךְ יהוה בְּקוּמֵנוּ. כִּי בְיָדְךָ נַפְשׁוֹת הַחַיִּים וְהַמֵּתִים. אֲשֶׁר בְּיָדוֹ נֶפֶשׁ כָּל חָי, וְרוּחַ כָּל בְּשַׂר אִישׁ.[16] בְּיָדְךָ אַפְקִיד רוּחִי, פָּדִיתָה אוֹתִי, יהוה אֵל אֱמֶת.[17] אֱלֹהֵינוּ שֶׁבַּשָּׁמַיִם יַחֵד שִׁמְךָ, וְקַיֵּם מַלְכוּתְךָ תָּמִיד, וּמְלוֹךְ עָלֵינוּ לְעוֹלָם וָעֶד.

יִרְאוּ עֵינֵינוּ וְיִשְׂמַח לִבֵּנוּ וְתָגֵל נַפְשֵׁנוּ בִּישׁוּעָתְךָ בֶּאֱמֶת, בֶּאֱמֹר לְצִיּוֹן מָלַךְ אֱלֹהָיִךְ.[18] יהוה מֶלֶךְ,[19] יהוה מָלָךְ,[20] יהוה יִמְלֹךְ לְעֹלָם וָעֶד.[21] כִּי הַמַּלְכוּת שֶׁלְּךָ הִיא, וּלְעוֹלְמֵי עַד

הַשְׁכִּיבֵנוּ *Lay us down to sleep,* HASHEM *our God, in peace, raise us erect, our King, to life; and spread over us the shelter of Your peace. Set us aright with good counsel from before Your Presence, and save us for Your Name's sake. Shield us, remove from us foe, plague, sword, famine, and woe; and remove spiritual impediment from before us and behind us, and in the shadow of Your wings shelter us*[1] *— for God Who protects and rescues us are You; for God, the Gracious and Compassionate King, are You.*[2] Chazzan– *Safeguard our going and coming, for life and for peace from now to eternity.*[3] *Blessed are You,* HASHEM, *Who protects His people Israel forever.* (Cong.– *Amen.)*

Some congregations omit the following prayers and continue with Half-*Kaddish* (p. 1080).

בָּרוּךְ *Blessed is* HASHEM *forever, Amen and Amen.*[4] *Blessed is* HASHEM *from Zion, Who dwells in Jerusalem, Halleluyah!*[5] *Blessed is* HASHEM, *God, the God of Israel, Who alone does wondrous things. Blessed is His glorious Name forever, and may all the earth be filled with His glory, Amen and Amen.*[6] *May the glory of* HASHEM *endure forever, let* HASHEM *rejoice in His works.*[7] *Blessed be the Name of* HASHEM *from this time and forever.*[8] *For* HASHEM *will not cast off His nation for the sake of His Great Name, for* HASHEM *has vowed to make you His own people.*[9] *Then the entire nation saw and fell on their faces and said, '*HASHEM *— only He is God!* HASHEM *— only He is God!'*[10] *Then* HASHEM *will be King over all the world, on that day* HASHEM *will be One and His Name will be One.*[11] *May Your kindness,* HASHEM, *be upon us, just as we awaited You.*[12] *Save us,* HASHEM, *our God, gather us from the nations, to thank Your Holy Name and to glory in Your praise!*[13] *All the nations that You made will come and bow before You, My Lord, and shall glorify Your Name. For You are great and work wonders; You alone, O God.*[14] *Then we, Your nation and the sheep of Your pasture, shall thank You forever; for generation after generation we will relate Your praise.*[15] *Blessed is* HASHEM *by day; Blessed is* HASHEM *by night; Blessed is* HASHEM *when we retire; Blessed is* HASHEM *when we arise. For in Your hand are the souls of the living and the dead. He in Whose hand is the soul of all the living and the spirit of every human being.*[16] *In Your hand I shall entrust my spirit, You redeemed me,* HASHEM, *God of truth.*[17] *Our God, Who is in heaven, bring unity to Your Name; establish Your kingdom forever and reign over us for all eternity.*

יִרְאוּ *May our eyes see, our heart rejoice and our soul exult in Your salvation in truth, when Zion is told, 'Your God has reigned!'*[18] HASHEM *reigns,*[19] HASHEM *has reigned,*[20] HASHEM *will reign for all eternity.*[21] Chazzan– *For the kingdom is Yours and for all eternity*

(1) Cf. *Psalms* 17:8. (2) Cf. *Nehemiah* 9:31. (3) Cf. *Psalms* 121:8. (4) *Psalms* 89:53. (5) 135:21. (6) 72:18-19. (7) 104:31. (8) 113:2. (9) *I Samuel* 12:22. (10) *I Kings* 18:39. (11) *Zechariah* 14:9. (12) *Psalms* 33:22. (13) 106:47. (14) 86:9-10. (15) 79:13. (16) *Job* 12:10. (17) *Psalms* 31:6. (18) Cf. *Isaiah* 52:7. (19) *Psalms* 10:16. (20) 93:1 et al. (21) *Exodus* 15:18.

תִּמְלוֹךְ בְּכָבוֹד, כִּי אֵין לָנוּ מֶלֶךְ אֶלָּא אָתָּה. בָּרוּךְ אַתָּה יהוה, הַמֶּלֶךְ בִּכְבוֹדוֹ תָּמִיד יִמְלוֹךְ עָלֵינוּ לְעוֹלָם וָעֶד, וְעַל כָּל מַעֲשָׂיו. (–Cong. אָמֵן.)

The *chazzan* recites חֲצִי קַדִּישׁ.

יִתְגַּדַּל וְיִתְקַדַּשׁ שְׁמֵהּ רַבָּא. (–Cong. אָמֵן.) בְּעָלְמָא דִּי בְרָא כִרְעוּתֵהּ, וְיַמְלִיךְ מַלְכוּתֵהּ, בְּחַיֵּיכוֹן וּבְיוֹמֵיכוֹן וּבְחַיֵּי דְכָל בֵּית יִשְׂרָאֵל, בַּעֲגָלָא וּבִזְמַן קָרִיב. וְאִמְרוּ: אָמֵן.

(–Cong. אָמֵן. יְהֵא שְׁמֵהּ רַבָּא מְבָרַךְ לְעָלַם וּלְעָלְמֵי עָלְמַיָּא.)

יְהֵא שְׁמֵהּ רַבָּא מְבָרַךְ לְעָלַם וּלְעָלְמֵי עָלְמַיָּא.

יִתְבָּרַךְ וְיִשְׁתַּבַּח וְיִתְפָּאַר וְיִתְרוֹמַם וְיִתְנַשֵּׂא וְיִתְהַדָּר וְיִתְעַלֶּה וְיִתְהַלָּל שְׁמֵהּ דְּקֻדְשָׁא בְּרִיךְ הוּא (–Cong. בְּרִיךְ הוּא) — לְעֵלָּא מִן כָּל בִּרְכָתָא וְשִׁירָתָא תֻּשְׁבְּחָתָא וְנֶחֱמָתָא, דַּאֲמִירָן בְּעָלְמָא. וְאִמְרוּ: אָמֵן. (–Cong. אָמֵן.)

שמונה עשרה – עמידה

Take three steps backward, then three steps forward. Remain standing with the feet together while reciting *Shemoneh Esrei*. Recite it with quiet devotion and without interruption, verbal or otherwise. Although its recitation should not be audible to others, one must pray loudly enough to hear himself.

אֲדֹנָי שְׂפָתַי תִּפְתָּח, וּפִי יַגִּיד תְּהִלָּתֶךָ.¹

אבות

Bend the knees at בָּרוּךְ; bow at אַתָּה; straighten up at ה׳.

בָּרוּךְ אַתָּה יהוה אֱלֹהֵינוּ וֵאלֹהֵי אֲבוֹתֵינוּ, אֱלֹהֵי אַבְרָהָם, אֱלֹהֵי יִצְחָק, וֵאלֹהֵי יַעֲקֹב, הָאֵל הַגָּדוֹל הַגִּבּוֹר וְהַנּוֹרָא, אֵל עֶלְיוֹן, גּוֹמֵל חֲסָדִים טוֹבִים וְקוֹנֵה הַכֹּל, וְזוֹכֵר חַסְדֵי אָבוֹת, וּמֵבִיא גוֹאֵל לִבְנֵי בְנֵיהֶם, לְמַעַן שְׁמוֹ בְּאַהֲבָה. מֶלֶךְ עוֹזֵר וּמוֹשִׁיעַ וּמָגֵן.

Bend the knees at בָּרוּךְ; bow at אַתָּה; straighten up at ה׳.

בָּרוּךְ אַתָּה יהוה, מָגֵן אַבְרָהָם.

גבורות

אַתָּה גִּבּוֹר לְעוֹלָם אֲדֹנָי, מְחַיֵּה מֵתִים אַתָּה, רַב לְהוֹשִׁיעַ. מְכַלְכֵּל חַיִּים בְּחֶסֶד, מְחַיֵּה מֵתִים בְּרַחֲמִים רַבִּים, סוֹמֵךְ נוֹפְלִים, וְרוֹפֵא חוֹלִים, וּמַתִּיר אֲסוּרִים, וּמְקַיֵּם אֱמוּנָתוֹ לִישֵׁנֵי עָפָר. מִי כָמוֹךָ בַּעַל גְּבוּרוֹת, וּמִי דּוֹמֶה לָּךְ, מֶלֶךְ מֵמִית וּמְחַיֶּה וּמַצְמִיחַ יְשׁוּעָה. וְנֶאֱמָן אַתָּה לְהַחֲיוֹת מֵתִים. בָּרוּךְ אַתָּה יהוה, מְחַיֵּה הַמֵּתִים.

קדושת השם

אַתָּה קָדוֹשׁ וְשִׁמְךָ קָדוֹשׁ, וּקְדוֹשִׁים בְּכָל יוֹם יְהַלְלוּךָ סֶּלָה. בָּרוּךְ אַתָּה יהוה, הָאֵל הַקָּדוֹשׁ.

You will reign in glory, for we have no King but You. Blessed are You, HASHEM, the King in His glory — He shall constantly reign over us forever and ever, and over all His creatures. (Cong.– *Amen.*)

The chazzan recites Half-*Kaddish*.

יִתְגַּדַּל *May His great Name grow exalted and sanctified* (Cong.– *Amen.*) *in the world that He created as He willed. May He give reign to His kingship in your lifetimes and in your days, and in the lifetimes of the entire Family of Israel, swiftly and soon. Now respond: Amen.*

(Cong.– *Amen. May His great Name be blessed forever and ever.*)

May His great Name be blessed forever and ever.

Blessed, praised, glorified, exalted, extolled, mighty, upraised, and lauded be the Name of the Holy One, Blessed is He (Cong.– *Blessed is He*) — *beyond any blessing and song, praise and consolation that are uttered in the world. Now respond: Amen.* (Cong.– *Amen.*)

SHEMONEH ESREI – AMIDAH

Take three steps backward, then three steps forward. Remain standing with the feet together while reciting *Shemoneh Esrei*. Recite it with quiet devotion and without interruption, verbal or otherwise. Although its recitation should not be audible to others, one must pray loudly enough to hear himself.

My Lord, open my lips, that my mouth may declare Your praise.[1]

PATRIARCHS

Bend the knees at *'Blessed'*; bow at *'You'*; straighten up at *'HASHEM.'*

בָּרוּךְ *Blessed are You, HASHEM, our God and the God of our forefathers, God of Abraham, God of Isaac, and God of Jacob; the great, mighty, and awesome God, the supreme God, Who bestows beneficial kindnesses and creates everything, Who recalls the kindnesses of the Patriarchs and brings a Redeemer to their children's children, for His Name's sake, with love.*

Bend the knees at *'Blessed'*; bow at *'You'*; straighten up at 'HASHEM.'

O King, Helper, Savior, and Shield. Blessed are You, HASHEM, Shield of Abraham.

GOD'S MIGHT

אַתָּה *You are eternally mighty, my Lord, the Resuscitator of the dead are You; abundantly able to save. He sustains the living with kindness, resuscitates the dead with abundant mercy, supports the fallen, heals the sick, releases the confined, and maintains His faith to those asleep in the dust. Who is like You, O Master of mighty deeds, and who is comparable to You, O King Who causes death and restores life and makes salvation sprout! And You are faithful to resuscitate the dead. Blessed are You, HASHEM, Who resuscitates the dead.*

HOLINESS OF GOD'S NAME

אַתָּה *You are holy and Your Name is holy, and holy ones praise You every day, forever. Blessed are You, HASHEM, the holy God.*

(1) *Psalms* 51:17.

בינה

אַתָּה חוֹנֵן לְאָדָם דַּעַת, וּמְלַמֵּד לֶאֱנוֹשׁ בִּינָה. אַתָּה חוֹנַנְתָּנוּ לְמַדַּע תּוֹרָתֶךָ, וַתְּלַמְּדֵנוּ לַעֲשׂוֹת חֻקֵּי רְצוֹנֶךָ וַתַּבְדֵּל יהוה אֱלֹהֵינוּ בֵּין קֹדֶשׁ לְחוֹל בֵּין אוֹר לְחֹשֶׁךְ, בֵּין יִשְׂרָאֵל לָעַמִּים בֵּין יוֹם הַשְּׁבִיעִי לְשֵׁשֶׁת יְמֵי הַמַּעֲשֶׂה. אָבִינוּ מַלְכֵּנוּ הָחֵל עָלֵינוּ הַיָּמִים הַבָּאִים לִקְרָאתֵנוּ לְשָׁלוֹם חֲשׂוּכִים מִכָּל חֵטְא וּמְנֻקִּים מִכָּל עָוֹן וּמְדֻבָּקִים בְּיִרְאָתֶךָ. וְחָנֵּנוּ מֵאִתְּךָ דֵּעָה בִּינָה וְהַשְׂכֵּל. בָּרוּךְ אַתָּה יהוה, חוֹנֵן הַדָּעַת.

תשובה

הֲשִׁיבֵנוּ אָבִינוּ לְתוֹרָתֶךָ, וְקָרְבֵנוּ מַלְכֵּנוּ לַעֲבוֹדָתֶךָ, וְהַחֲזִירֵנוּ בִּתְשׁוּבָה שְׁלֵמָה לְפָנֶיךָ. בָּרוּךְ אַתָּה יהוה, הָרוֹצֶה בִּתְשׁוּבָה.

סליחה

Strike the left side of the chest with the right fist while reciting the words חָטָאנוּ and פָּשָׁעְנוּ.

סְלַח לָנוּ אָבִינוּ כִּי חָטָאנוּ, מְחַל לָנוּ מַלְכֵּנוּ כִּי פָשָׁעְנוּ, כִּי מוֹחֵל וְסוֹלֵחַ אָתָּה. בָּרוּךְ אַתָּה יהוה, חַנּוּן הַמַּרְבֶּה לִסְלֹחַ.

גאולה

רְאֵה בְעָנְיֵנוּ, וְרִיבָה רִיבֵנוּ, וּגְאָלֵנוּ[1] מְהֵרָה לְמַעַן שְׁמֶךָ, כִּי גוֹאֵל חָזָק אָתָּה. בָּרוּךְ אַתָּה יהוה, גּוֹאֵל יִשְׂרָאֵל.

רפואה

רְפָאֵנוּ יהוה וְנֵרָפֵא, הוֹשִׁיעֵנוּ וְנִוָּשֵׁעָה, כִּי תְהִלָּתֵנוּ אָתָּה,[2] וְהַעֲלֵה רְפוּאָה שְׁלֵמָה לְכָל מַכּוֹתֵינוּ, °°כִּי אֵל מֶלֶךְ רוֹפֵא נֶאֱמָן וְרַחֲמָן אָתָּה. בָּרוּךְ אַתָּה יהוה, רוֹפֵא חוֹלֵי עַמּוֹ יִשְׂרָאֵל.

ברכת השנים

בָּרֵךְ עָלֵינוּ יהוה אֱלֹהֵינוּ אֶת הַשָּׁנָה הַזֹּאת וְאֶת כָּל מִינֵי תְבוּאָתָהּ לְטוֹבָה, וְתֵן בְּרָכָה עַל פְּנֵי הָאֲדָמָה, וְשַׂבְּעֵנוּ מִטּוּבֶךָ, וּבָרֵךְ שְׁנָתֵנוּ כַּשָּׁנִים הַטּוֹבוֹת. בָּרוּךְ אַתָּה יהוה, מְבָרֵךְ הַשָּׁנִים.

°°At this point one may interject a prayer for one who is ill:

יְהִי רָצוֹן מִלְּפָנֶיךָ יהוה אֱלֹהַי וֵאלֹהֵי אֲבוֹתַי, שֶׁתִּשְׁלַח מְהֵרָה רְפוּאָה שְׁלֵמָה מִן הַשָּׁמַיִם, רְפוּאַת הַנֶּפֶשׁ וּרְפוּאַת הַגּוּף

לַחוֹלֶה (patient's name) בֶּן (mother's name) בְּתוֹךְ שְׁאָר חוֹלֵי יִשְׂרָאֵל.—for a male

לַחוֹלָה (patient's name) בַּת (mother's name) בְּתוֹךְ שְׁאָר חוֹלֵי יִשְׂרָאֵל.—for a female

continue—כִּי אֵל . . .

INSIGHT

אַתָּה *You graciously endow man with wisdom and teach insight to a frail mortal. You have graced us with intelligence to study Your Torah and You have taught us to perform the decrees You have willed.* HASHEM, *our God, You have distinguished between the sacred and the secular, between light and darkness, between Israel and the peoples, between the seventh day and the six days of labor. Our Father, our King, begin for us the days approaching us for peace, free from all sin, cleansed from all iniquity and attached to fear of You. And endow us graciously from Yourself with wisdom, insight, and discernment. Blessed are You,* HASHEM, *gracious Giver of wisdom.*

REPENTANCE

הֲשִׁיבֵנוּ *Bring us back, our Father, to Your Torah, and bring us near, our King, to Your service, and influence us to return in perfect repentance before You. Blessed are You,* HASHEM, *Who desires repentance.*

FORGIVENESS

Strike the left side of the chest with the right fist while reciting the words *'erred'* and *'sinned.'*

סְלַח *Forgive us, our Father, for we have erred; pardon us, our King, for we have willfully sinned; for You pardon and forgive. Blessed are You,* HASHEM, *the gracious One Who pardons abundantly.*

REDEMPTION

רְאֵה *Behold our affliction, take up our grievance, and redeem us*[1] *speedily for Your Name's sake, for You are a powerful Redeemer. Blessed are You,* HASHEM, *Redeemer of Israel.*

HEALTH AND HEALING

רְפָאֵנוּ *Heal us,* HASHEM *— then we will be healed; save us — then we will be saved, for You are our praise.*[2] *Bring complete recovery for all our ailments,* °°*for You are God, King, the faithful and compassionate Healer. Blessed are You,* HASHEM, *Who heals the sick of His people Israel.*

YEAR OF PROSPERITY

בָּרֵךְ *Bless on our behalf — O* HASHEM, *our God — this year and all its kinds of crops for the best, and give a blessing on the face of the earth, and satisfy us from Your bounty, and bless our year like the best years. Blessed are You,* HASHEM, *Who blesses the years.*

°°At this point one may interject a prayer for one who is ill:

May it be Your will, HASHEM, *my God, and the God of my forefathers, that You quickly send a complete recovery from heaven, spiritual healing and physical healing to the patient* (name) *son/daughter of* (mother's name) *among the other patients of Israel.* Continue: *For You are God . . .*

(1) Cf. *Psalms* 119:153-154. (2) Cf. *Jeremiah* 17:14.

קיבוץ גליות

תְּקַע בְּשׁוֹפָר גָּדוֹל לְחֵרוּתֵנוּ, וְשָׂא נֵס לְקַבֵּץ גָּלֻיּוֹתֵינוּ, וְקַבְּצֵנוּ יַחַד מֵאַרְבַּע כַּנְפוֹת הָאָרֶץ.[1] בָּרוּךְ אַתָּה יהוה, מְקַבֵּץ נִדְחֵי עַמּוֹ יִשְׂרָאֵל.

דין

הָשִׁיבָה שׁוֹפְטֵינוּ כְּבָרִאשׁוֹנָה, וְיוֹעֲצֵינוּ כְּבַתְּחִלָּה,[2] וְהָסֵר מִמֶּנּוּ יָגוֹן וַאֲנָחָה, וּמְלוֹךְ עָלֵינוּ אַתָּה יהוה לְבַדְּךָ בְּחֶסֶד וּבְרַחֲמִים, וְצַדְּקֵנוּ בַּמִּשְׁפָּט. בָּרוּךְ אַתָּה יהוה, מֶלֶךְ אוֹהֵב צְדָקָה וּמִשְׁפָּט.

ברכת המינים

וְלַמַּלְשִׁינִים אַל תְּהִי תִקְוָה, וְכָל הָרִשְׁעָה כְּרֶגַע תֹּאבֵד, וְכָל אֹיְבֶיךָ מְהֵרָה יִכָּרֵתוּ, וְהַזֵּדִים מְהֵרָה תְעַקֵּר וּתְשַׁבֵּר וּתְמַגֵּר וְתַכְנִיעַ בִּמְהֵרָה בְיָמֵינוּ. בָּרוּךְ אַתָּה יהוה, שׁוֹבֵר אֹיְבִים וּמַכְנִיעַ זֵדִים.

צדיקים

עַל הַצַּדִּיקִים וְעַל הַחֲסִידִים, וְעַל זִקְנֵי עַמְּךָ בֵּית יִשְׂרָאֵל, וְעַל פְּלֵיטַת סוֹפְרֵיהֶם, וְעַל גֵּרֵי הַצֶּדֶק וְעָלֵינוּ, יֶהֱמוּ רַחֲמֶיךָ יהוה אֱלֹהֵינוּ, וְתֵן שָׂכָר טוֹב לְכָל הַבּוֹטְחִים בְּשִׁמְךָ בֶּאֱמֶת, וְשִׂים חֶלְקֵנוּ עִמָּהֶם לְעוֹלָם, וְלֹא נֵבוֹשׁ כִּי בְךָ בָּטָחְנוּ. בָּרוּךְ אַתָּה יהוה, מִשְׁעָן וּמִבְטָח לַצַּדִּיקִים.

בנין ירושלים

וְלִירוּשָׁלַיִם עִירְךָ בְּרַחֲמִים תָּשׁוּב, וְתִשְׁכּוֹן בְּתוֹכָהּ כַּאֲשֶׁר דִּבַּרְתָּ, וּבְנֵה אוֹתָהּ בְּקָרוֹב בְּיָמֵינוּ בִּנְיַן עוֹלָם, וְכִסֵּא דָוִד מְהֵרָה לְתוֹכָהּ תָּכִין. בָּרוּךְ אַתָּה יהוה, בּוֹנֵה יְרוּשָׁלָיִם.

מלכות בית דוד

אֶת צֶמַח דָּוִד עַבְדְּךָ מְהֵרָה תַצְמִיחַ, וְקַרְנוֹ תָּרוּם בִּישׁוּעָתֶךָ, כִּי לִישׁוּעָתְךָ קִוִּינוּ כָּל הַיּוֹם. בָּרוּךְ אַתָּה יהוה, מַצְמִיחַ קֶרֶן יְשׁוּעָה.

קבלת תפלה

שְׁמַע קוֹלֵנוּ יהוה אֱלֹהֵינוּ, חוּס וְרַחֵם עָלֵינוּ, וְקַבֵּל בְּרַחֲמִים וּבְרָצוֹן אֶת תְּפִלָּתֵנוּ, כִּי אֵל שׁוֹמֵעַ תְּפִלּוֹת וְתַחֲנוּנִים אָתָּה. וּמִלְּפָנֶיךָ מַלְכֵּנוּ רֵיקָם אַל תְּשִׁיבֵנוּ,

INGATHERING OF EXILES

תְּקַע *Sound the great shofar for our freedom, raise the banner to gather our exiles and gather us together from the four corners of the earth.*[1] *Blessed are You,* HASHEM, *Who gathers in the dispersed of His people Israel.*

RESTORATION OF JUSTICE

הָשִׁיבָה *Restore our judges as in earliest times and our counselors as at first;*[2] *remove from us sorrow and groan; and reign over us — You,* HASHEM, *alone — with kindness and compassion, and justify us through judgment. Blessed are You,* HASHEM, *the King Who loves righteousness and judgment.*

AGAINST HERETICS

וְלַמַּלְשִׁינִים *And for slanderers let there be no hope; and may all wickedness perish in an instant; and may all Your enemies be cut down speedily. May You speedily uproot, smash, cast down, and humble the wanton sinners — speedily in our days. Blessed are You,* HASHEM, *Who breaks enemies and humbles wanton sinners.*

THE RIGHTEOUS

עַל הַצַּדִּיקִים *On the righteous, on the devout, on the elders of Your people the Family of Israel, on the remnant of their scholars, on the righteous converts and on ourselves — may Your compassion be aroused,* HASHEM, *our God, and give goodly reward to all who sincerely believe in Your Name. Put our lot with them forever, and we will not feel ashamed, for we trust in You. Blessed are You,* HASHEM, *Mainstay and Assurance of the righteous.*

REBUILDING JERUSALEM

וְלִירוּשָׁלַיִם *And to Jerusalem, Your city, may You return in compassion, and may You rest within it, as You have spoken. May You rebuild it soon in our days as an eternal structure, and may You speedily establish the throne of David within it. Blessed are You,* HASHEM, *the Builder of Jerusalem.*

DAVIDIC REIGN

אֶת צֶמַח *The offspring of Your servant David may You speedily cause to flourish, and enhance his pride through Your salvation, for we hope for Your salvation all day long. Blessed are You,* HASHEM, *Who causes the pride of salvation to flourish.*

ACCEPTANCE OF PRAYER

שְׁמַע *Hear our voice,* HASHEM *our God, pity and be compassionate to us, and accept — with compassion and favor — our prayer, for God Who hears prayers and supplications are You. From before Yourself, our King, turn us not away empty-handed,*

---

(1) Cf. *Isaiah* 11:12. (2) Cf. 1:26.

°°כִּי אַתָּה שׁוֹמֵעַ תְּפִלַּת עַמְּךָ יִשְׂרָאֵל בְּרַחֲמִים. בָּרוּךְ אַתָּה יהוה, שׁוֹמֵעַ תְּפִלָּה.

עבודה

רְצֵה יהוה אֱלֹהֵינוּ בְּעַמְּךָ יִשְׂרָאֵל וּבִתְפִלָּתָם, וְהָשֵׁב אֶת הָעֲבוֹדָה לִדְבִיר בֵּיתֶךָ. וְאִשֵּׁי יִשְׂרָאֵל וּתְפִלָּתָם בְּאַהֲבָה תְקַבֵּל בְּרָצוֹן, וּתְהִי לְרָצוֹן תָּמִיד עֲבוֹדַת יִשְׂרָאֵל עַמֶּךָ.

וְתֶחֱזֶינָה עֵינֵינוּ בְּשׁוּבְךָ לְצִיּוֹן בְּרַחֲמִים. בָּרוּךְ אַתָּה יהוה, הַמַּחֲזִיר שְׁכִינָתוֹ לְצִיּוֹן.

הודאה

Bow at מוֹדִים; straighten up at ה׳.

מוֹדִים אֲנַחְנוּ לָךְ שָׁאַתָּה הוּא יהוה אֱלֹהֵינוּ וֵאלֹהֵי אֲבוֹתֵינוּ לְעוֹלָם וָעֶד. צוּר חַיֵּינוּ, מָגֵן יִשְׁעֵנוּ אַתָּה הוּא לְדוֹר וָדוֹר. נוֹדֶה לְּךָ וּנְסַפֵּר תְּהִלָּתֶךָ[1] עַל חַיֵּינוּ הַמְּסוּרִים בְּיָדֶךָ, וְעַל נִשְׁמוֹתֵינוּ הַפְּקוּדוֹת לָךְ, וְעַל נִסֶּיךָ שֶׁבְּכָל יוֹם עִמָּנוּ, וְעַל נִפְלְאוֹתֶיךָ וְטוֹבוֹתֶיךָ שֶׁבְּכָל עֵת, עֶרֶב וָבֹקֶר וְצָהֳרָיִם. הַטּוֹב כִּי לֹא כָלוּ רַחֲמֶיךָ, וְהַמְּרַחֵם כִּי לֹא תַמּוּ חֲסָדֶיךָ,[2] מֵעוֹלָם קִוִּינוּ לָךְ.

וְעַל כֻּלָּם יִתְבָּרַךְ וְיִתְרוֹמַם שִׁמְךָ מַלְכֵּנוּ תָּמִיד לְעוֹלָם וָעֶד.

Bend the knees at בָּרוּךְ; bow at אַתָּה; straighten up at ה׳.

וְכֹל הַחַיִּים יוֹדוּךָ סֶּלָה, וִיהַלְלוּ אֶת שִׁמְךָ בֶּאֱמֶת, הָאֵל יְשׁוּעָתֵנוּ וְעֶזְרָתֵנוּ סֶלָה. בָּרוּךְ אַתָּה יהוה, הַטּוֹב שִׁמְךָ וּלְךָ נָאֶה לְהוֹדוֹת.

°°During the silent *Shemoneh Esrei* one may insert either or both of these personal prayers.

For forgiveness:

אָנָּא יהוה, חָטָאתִי עָוִיתִי וּפָשַׁעְתִּי לְפָנֶיךָ, מִיּוֹם הֱיוֹתִי עַל הָאֲדָמָה עַד הַיּוֹם הַזֶּה (וּבִפְרַט בַּחֵטְא ....). אָנָּא יהוה, עֲשֵׂה לְמַעַן שִׁמְךָ הַגָּדוֹל, וּתְכַפֶּר לִי עַל עֲוֹנַי וַחֲטָאַי וּפְשָׁעַי שֶׁחָטָאתִי וְשֶׁעָוִיתִי וְשֶׁפָּשַׁעְתִּי לְפָנֶיךָ, מִנְּעוּרַי עַד הַיּוֹם הַזֶּה. וּתְמַלֵּא כָּל הַשֵּׁמוֹת שֶׁפָּגַמְתִּי בְּשִׁמְךָ הַגָּדוֹל.

For livelihood:

אַתָּה הוּא יהוה הָאֱלֹהִים, הַזָּן וּמְפַרְנֵס וּמְכַלְכֵּל מִקַּרְנֵי רְאֵמִים עַד בֵּיצֵי כִנִּים. הַטְרִיפֵנִי לֶחֶם חֻקִּי, וְהַמְצֵא לִי וּלְכָל בְּנֵי בֵיתִי מְזוֹנוֹתַי קוֹדֶם שֶׁאֶצְטָרֵךְ לָהֶם, בְּנַחַת וְלֹא בְצַעַר, בְּהֶתֵּר וְלֹא בְאִסּוּר, בְּכָבוֹד וְלֹא בְבִזָּיוֹן, לְחַיִּים וּלְשָׁלוֹם, מִשֶּׁפַע בְּרָכָה וְהַצְלָחָה, וּמִשֶּׁפַע בְּרֵכָה עֶלְיוֹנָה, כְּדֵי שֶׁאוּכַל לַעֲשׂוֹת רְצוֹנֶךָ וְלַעֲסוֹק בְּתוֹרָתֶךָ וּלְקַיֵּם מִצְוֹתֶיךָ. וְאַל תַּצְרִיכֵנִי לִידֵי מַתְּנַת בָּשָׂר וָדָם. וִיקֻיַּם בִּי מִקְרָא שֶׁכָּתוּב: פּוֹתֵחַ אֶת יָדֶךָ, וּמַשְׂבִּיעַ לְכָל חַי רָצוֹן.[3] וְכָתוּב: הַשְׁלֵךְ עַל יהוה יְהָבְךָ וְהוּא יְכַלְכְּלֶךָ.[4]

Continue— כִּי אַתָּה . . .

(1) Cf. *Psalms* 79:13. (2) Cf. *Lamentations* 3:22. (3) *Psalms* 145:16. (4) 55:23.

°° *for You hear the prayer of Your people Israel with compassion. Blessed are You, Hashem, Who hears prayer.*

TEMPLE SERVICE

רְצֵה *Be favorable, Hashem, our God, toward Your people Israel and their prayer and restore the service to the Holy of Holies of Your Temple. The fire-offerings of Israel and their prayer accept with love and favor, and may the service of Your people Israel always be favorable to You.*

וְתֶחֱזֶינָה *May our eyes behold Your return to Zion in compassion. Blessed are You, Hashem, Who restores His Presence to Zion.*

THANKSGIVING [MODIM]

Bow at *'We gratefully thank You'*; straighten up at *'Hashem.'*

מוֹדִים *We gratefully thank You, for it is You Who are Hashem, our God and the God of our forefathers for all eternity; Rock of our lives, Shield of our salvation are You from generation to generation. We shall thank You and relate Your praise[1] — for our lives, which are committed to Your power and for our souls that are entrusted to You; for Your miracles that are with us every day; and for Your wonders and favors in every season — evening, morning, and afternoon. The Beneficent One, for Your compassions were never exhausted, and the Compassionate One, for Your kindnesses never ended[2] — always have we put our hope in You.*

For all these, may Your Name be blessed and exalted, our King, continually forever and ever.

Bend the knees at *'Blessed'*; bow at *'You'*; straighten up at *'Hashem.'*

Everything alive will gratefully acknowledge You, Selah! and praise Your Name sincerely, O God of our salvation and help, Selah! Blessed are You, Hashem, Your Name is 'The Beneficent One' and to You it is fitting to give thanks.

°°During the silent *Shemoneh Esrei* one may insert either or both of these personal prayers.

For forgiveness:

אָנָּא *Please, O Hashem, I have erred, been iniquitous, and willfully sinned before You, from the day I have existed on earth until this very day (and especially with the sin of . . .). Please, Hashem, act for the sake of Your Great Name and grant me atonement for my iniquities, my errors, and my willful sins through which I have erred, been iniquitous, and willfully sinned before You, from my youth until this day. And make whole all the Names that I have blemished in Your Great Name.*

For livelihood:

אַתָּה *It is You, Hashem the God, Who nourishes, sustains, and supports, from the horns of re'eimim to the eggs of lice. Provide me with my allotment of bread; and bring forth for me and all members of my household, my food, before I have need for it; in contentment but not in pain, in a permissible but not a forbidden manner, in honor but not in disgrace, for life and for peace; from the flow of blessing and success and from the flow of the Heavenly spring, so that I be enabled to do Your will and engage in Your Torah and fulfill Your commandments. Make me not needful of people's largesse; and may there be fulfilled in me the verse that states, 'You open Your hand and satisfy the desire of every living thing'[3] and that states, 'Cast Your burden upon Hashem and He will support you.'[4]*

Continue: *For You hear the prayer . . .*

שלום

שָׁלוֹם רָב עַל יִשְׂרָאֵל עַמְּךָ תָּשִׂים לְעוֹלָם, כִּי אַתָּה הוּא מֶלֶךְ אָדוֹן לְכָל הַשָּׁלוֹם. וְטוֹב בְּעֵינֶיךָ לְבָרֵךְ אֶת עַמְּךָ יִשְׂרָאֵל, בְּכָל עֵת וּבְכָל שָׁעָה בִּשְׁלוֹמֶךָ. בָּרוּךְ אַתָּה יהוה, הַמְּבָרֵךְ אֶת עַמּוֹ יִשְׂרָאֵל בַּשָּׁלוֹם.

יִהְיוּ לְרָצוֹן אִמְרֵי פִי וְהֶגְיוֹן לִבִּי לְפָנֶיךָ, יהוה צוּרִי וְגֹאֲלִי.[1]

אֱלֹהַי, נְצוֹר לְשׁוֹנִי מֵרָע, וּשְׂפָתַי מִדַּבֵּר מִרְמָה,[2] וְלִמְקַלְלַי נַפְשִׁי תִדּוֹם, וְנַפְשִׁי כֶּעָפָר לַכֹּל תִּהְיֶה. פְּתַח לִבִּי בְּתוֹרָתֶךָ, וּבְמִצְוֹתֶיךָ תִּרְדּוֹף נַפְשִׁי. וְכֹל הַחוֹשְׁבִים עָלַי רָעָה, מְהֵרָה הָפֵר עֲצָתָם וְקַלְקֵל מַחֲשַׁבְתָּם. עֲשֵׂה לְמַעַן שְׁמֶךָ, עֲשֵׂה לְמַעַן יְמִינֶךָ, עֲשֵׂה לְמַעַן קְדֻשָּׁתֶךָ, עֲשֵׂה לְמַעַן תּוֹרָתֶךָ. לְמַעַן יֵחָלְצוּן יְדִידֶיךָ, הוֹשִׁיעָה יְמִינְךָ וַעֲנֵנִי.[3]

Some recite verses pertaining to their names here. See page 1143.

יִהְיוּ לְרָצוֹן אִמְרֵי פִי וְהֶגְיוֹן לִבִּי לְפָנֶיךָ, יהוה צוּרִי וְגֹאֲלִי.[1]

Bow and take three steps back. Bow left and say . . . עֹשֶׂה; bow right and say . . . הוּא יַעֲשֶׂה; bow forward and say וְעַל כָּל . . . אָמֵן.

עֹשֶׂה שָׁלוֹם בִּמְרוֹמָיו, הוּא יַעֲשֶׂה שָׁלוֹם עָלֵינוּ, וְעַל כָּל יִשְׂרָאֵל. וְאִמְרוּ: אָמֵן.

יְהִי רָצוֹן מִלְּפָנֶיךָ יהוה אֱלֹהֵינוּ וֵאלֹהֵי אֲבוֹתֵינוּ, שֶׁיִּבָּנֶה בֵּית הַמִּקְדָּשׁ בִּמְהֵרָה בְיָמֵינוּ, וְתֵן חֶלְקֵנוּ בְּתוֹרָתֶךָ. וְשָׁם נַעֲבָדְךָ בְּיִרְאָה, כִּימֵי עוֹלָם וּכְשָׁנִים קַדְמוֹנִיּוֹת. וְעָרְבָה לַיהוה מִנְחַת יְהוּדָה וִירוּשָׁלָיִם, כִּימֵי עוֹלָם וּכְשָׁנִים קַדְמוֹנִיּוֹת.[4]

SHEMONEH ESREI ENDS HERE.

Remain standing in place for at least a few moments before taking three steps forward.

ON SATURDAY NIGHT THE SERVICE CONTINUES HERE.
ON OTHER NIGHTS TURN TO PAGE 1092.

The *chazzan* recites חֲצִי קַדִּישׁ.

יִתְגַּדַּל וְיִתְקַדַּשׁ שְׁמֵהּ רַבָּא. (.Cong.– אָמֵן) בְּעָלְמָא דִּי בְרָא כִרְעוּתֵהּ. וְיַמְלִיךְ מַלְכוּתֵהּ, בְּחַיֵּיכוֹן וּבְיוֹמֵיכוֹן וּבְחַיֵּי דְכָל בֵּית יִשְׂרָאֵל, בַּעֲגָלָא וּבִזְמַן קָרִיב. וְאִמְרוּ: אָמֵן.

(.Cong.– אָמֵן. יְהֵא שְׁמֵהּ רַבָּא מְבָרַךְ לְעָלַם וּלְעָלְמֵי עָלְמַיָּא.)

יְהֵא שְׁמֵהּ רַבָּא מְבָרַךְ לְעָלַם וּלְעָלְמֵי עָלְמַיָּא.

יִתְבָּרַךְ וְיִשְׁתַּבַּח וְיִתְפָּאַר וְיִתְרוֹמַם וְיִתְנַשֵּׂא וְיִתְהַדָּר וְיִתְעַלֶּה וְיִתְהַלָּל שְׁמֵהּ דְּקֻדְשָׁא בְּרִיךְ הוּא (.Cong.– בְּרִיךְ הוּא) — לְעֵלָּא מִן כָּל בִּרְכָתָא וְשִׁירָתָא תֻּשְׁבְּחָתָא וְנֶחֱמָתָא, דַּאֲמִירָן בְּעָלְמָא. וְאִמְרוּ: אָמֵן. (.Cong.– אָמֵן)

PEACE

שָׁלוֹם *Establish abundant peace upon Your people Israel forever, for You are King, Master of all peace. May it be good in Your eyes to bless Your people Israel at every time and every hour with Your peace. Blessed are You, HASHEM, Who blesses His people Israel with peace.*

May the expressions of my mouth and the thoughts of my heart find favor before You, HASHEM, my Rock and my Redeemer.[1]

אֱלֹהַי *My God, guard my tongue from evil and my lips from speaking deceitfully.*[2] *To those who curse me, let my soul be silent; and let my soul be like dust to everyone. Open my heart to Your Torah, then my soul will pursue Your commandments. As for all those who design evil against me, speedily nullify their counsel and disrupt their design. Act for Your Name's sake; act for Your right hand's sake; act for Your sanctity's sake; act for Your Torah's sake. That Your beloved ones may be given rest; let Your right hand save, and respond to me.*[3]

Some recite verses pertaining to their names at this point. See page 1143.

May the expressions of my mouth and the thoughts of my heart find favor before You, HASHEM, my Rock and my Redeemer.[1] *He Who makes peace in His heights, may He make peace upon us, and upon all Israel. Now respond: Amen.*

Bow and take three steps back. Bow left and say, *'He Who makes peace . . .'*; bow right and say, *'may He make peace . . .'*; bow forward and say, *'and upon . . . Amen.'*

יְהִי רָצוֹן *May it be Your will, HASHEM, our God and the God of our forefathers, that the Holy Temple be rebuilt, speedily in our days. Grant us our share in Your Torah, and may we serve You there with reverence, as in days of old and in former years. Then the offering of Judah and Jerusalem will be pleasing to HASHEM, as in days of old and in former years.*[4]

SHEMONEH ESREI ENDS HERE.

Remain standing in place for at least a few moments before taking three steps forward.

ON SATURDAY NIGHT THE SERVICE CONTINUES HERE.
ON OTHER NIGHTS TURN TO PAGE 1092.

The *chazzan* recites Half *Kaddish*.

יִתְגַּדַּל *May His great Name grow exalted and sanctified* (Cong.– *Amen.*) *in the world that He created as He willed. May He give reign to His kingship in your lifetimes and in your days, and in the lifetimes of the entire Family of Israel, swiftly and soon. Now respond: Amen.*

(Cong.– *Amen. May His great Name be blessed forever and ever.*)

May His great Name be blessed forever and ever.

Blessed, praised, glorified, exalted, extolled, mighty, upraised, and lauded be the Name of the Holy One, Blessed is He (Cong.– *Blessed is He*) *— beyond any blessing and song, praise and consolation that are uttered in the world. Now respond: Amen.* (Cong.– *Amen.*)

(1) *Psalms* 19:15. (2) Cf. 34:14. (3) 60:7; 108:7. (4) *Malachi* 3:4.

וִיהִי נֹעַם אֲדֹנָי אֱלֹהֵינוּ עָלֵינוּ, וּמַעֲשֵׂה יָדֵינוּ כּוֹנְנָה עָלֵינוּ, וּמַעֲשֵׂה יָדֵינוּ כּוֹנְנֵהוּ.[1]

תהלים צא

יֹשֵׁב בְּסֵתֶר עֶלְיוֹן, בְּצֵל שַׁדַּי יִתְלוֹנָן. אֹמַר לַיהוה מַחְסִי וּמְצוּדָתִי, אֱלֹהַי אֶבְטַח בּוֹ. כִּי הוּא יַצִּילְךָ מִפַּח יָקוּשׁ, מִדֶּבֶר הַוּוֹת. בְּאֶבְרָתוֹ יָסֶךְ לָךְ, וְתַחַת כְּנָפָיו תֶּחְסֶה, צִנָּה וְסֹחֵרָה אֲמִתּוֹ. לֹא תִירָא מִפַּחַד לָיְלָה, מֵחֵץ יָעוּף יוֹמָם. מִדֶּבֶר בָּאֹפֶל יַהֲלֹךְ, מִקֶּטֶב יָשׁוּד צָהֳרָיִם. יִפֹּל מִצִּדְּךָ אֶלֶף, וּרְבָבָה מִימִינֶךָ, אֵלֶיךָ לֹא יִגָּשׁ. רַק בְּעֵינֶיךָ תַבִּיט, וְשִׁלֻּמַת רְשָׁעִים תִּרְאֶה. כִּי אַתָּה יהוה מַחְסִי, עֶלְיוֹן שַׂמְתָּ מְעוֹנֶךָ. לֹא תְאֻנֶּה אֵלֶיךָ רָעָה, וְנֶגַע לֹא יִקְרַב בְּאָהֳלֶךָ. כִּי מַלְאָכָיו יְצַוֶּה לָּךְ, לִשְׁמָרְךָ בְּכָל דְּרָכֶיךָ. עַל כַּפַּיִם יִשָּׂאוּנְךָ, פֶּן תִּגֹּף בָּאֶבֶן רַגְלֶךָ. עַל שַׁחַל וָפֶתֶן תִּדְרֹךְ, תִּרְמֹס כְּפִיר וְתַנִּין. כִּי בִי חָשַׁק וַאֲפַלְּטֵהוּ, אֲשַׂגְּבֵהוּ כִּי יָדַע שְׁמִי. יִקְרָאֵנִי וְאֶעֱנֵהוּ, עִמּוֹ אָנֹכִי בְצָרָה, אֲחַלְּצֵהוּ וַאֲכַבְּדֵהוּ. ❖ אֹרֶךְ יָמִים אַשְׂבִּיעֵהוּ, וְאַרְאֵהוּ בִּישׁוּעָתִי. אֹרֶךְ יָמִים אַשְׂבִּיעֵהוּ, וְאַרְאֵהוּ בִּישׁוּעָתִי.

וְאַתָּה קָדוֹשׁ יוֹשֵׁב תְּהִלּוֹת יִשְׂרָאֵל.[2] וְקָרָא זֶה אֶל זֶה וְאָמַר:

קָדוֹשׁ, קָדוֹשׁ, קָדוֹשׁ יהוה צְבָאוֹת, מְלֹא כָל הָאָרֶץ כְּבוֹדוֹ.[3]

וּמְקַבְּלִין דֵּין מִן דֵּין וְאָמְרִין:

קַדִּישׁ בִּשְׁמֵי מְרוֹמָא עִלָּאָה בֵּית שְׁכִינְתֵּהּ,
קַדִּישׁ עַל אַרְעָא עוֹבַד גְּבוּרְתֵּהּ,
קַדִּישׁ לְעָלַם וּלְעָלְמֵי עָלְמַיָּא, יהוה צְבָאוֹת,
מַלְיָא כָל אַרְעָא זִיו יְקָרֵהּ.[4]

❖ וַתִּשָּׂאֵנִי רוּחַ, וָאֶשְׁמַע אַחֲרַי קוֹל רַעַשׁ גָּדוֹל:

בָּרוּךְ כְּבוֹד יהוה מִמְּקוֹמוֹ.[5]

וּנְטָלַתְנִי רוּחָא, וּשְׁמָעִית בַּתְרַי קָל זִיעַ סַגִּיא דִּמְשַׁבְּחִין וְאָמְרִין:

בְּרִיךְ יְקָרָא דַיהוה מֵאֲתַר בֵּית שְׁכִינְתֵּהּ.[6]

יהוה יִמְלֹךְ לְעֹלָם וָעֶד.[7]

יהוה מַלְכוּתֵהּ קָאֵם לְעָלַם וּלְעָלְמֵי עָלְמַיָּא.[8]

---

(1) *Psalms* 90:17. (2) 22:4. (3) *Isaiah* 6:3. (4) *Targum Yonasan.* (5) *Ezekiel* 3:12. (6) *Targum Yonasan.* (7) *Exodus* 15:18. (8) *Targum Onkelos.*

וִיהִי נֹעַם *May the pleasantness of my Lord, our God, be upon us — our handiwork, may He establish for us; our handiwork, may He establish.*[1]

Psalm 91

יֹשֵׁב *Whoever sits in the refuge of the Most High, he shall dwell in the shadow of the Almighty. I will say of* HASHEM, *'He is my refuge and my fortress, my God, I will trust in Him.' For He will deliver you from the ensnaring trap, from devastating pestilence. With His pinion He will cover you, and beneath His wings you will be protected; shield and armor is His truth. You shall not fear the terror of night; nor of the arrow that flies by day; nor the pestilence that walks in gloom; nor the destroyer who lays waste at noon. Let a thousand encamp at your side and a myriad at your right hand, but to you they shall not approach. You will merely peer with your eyes and you will see the retribution of the wicked. Because [you said], 'You,* HASHEM, *are my refuge,' you have made the Most High your dwelling place. No evil will befall you, nor will any plague come near your tent. He will charge His angels for you, to protect you in all your ways. On your palms they will carry you, lest you strike your foot against a stone. Upon the lion and the viper you will tread; you will trample the young lion and the serpent. For he has yearned for Me and I will deliver him; I will elevate him because he knows My Name. He will call upon Me and I will answer him, I am with him in distress, I will release him and I will honor him.* Chazzan– *With long life will I satisfy him, and I will show him My salvation. With long life will I satisfy him, and I will show him My salvation.*

וְאַתָּה קָדוֹשׁ *You are the Holy One, enthroned upon the praises of Israel.*[2] *And one [angel] will call another and say:*

'Holy, holy, holy is HASHEM, Master of Legions,
the whole world is filled with His glory.'[3]

And they receive permission from one another and say:
'Holy in the most exalted heaven, the abode of His Presence;
holy on earth, product of His strength;
holy forever and ever is HASHEM, *Master of Legions —*
the entire world is filled with the radiance of His glory.'[4]
Chazzan– *And a wind lifted me; and I heard behind me*
the sound of a great noise:

'Blessed is the glory of HASHEM from His place.'[5]

And a wind lifted me and I heard behind me the sound
of the powerful movement of those who praised saying:
'Blessed is the honor of HASHEM
from the place of the abode of His Presence.'[6]

HASHEM shall reign for all eternity.[7]

HASHEM — *His kingdom is established forever and ever.*[8]

יהוה אֱלֹהֵי אַבְרָהָם יִצְחָק וְיִשְׂרָאֵל אֲבֹתֵינוּ, שָׁמְרָה זֹּאת לְעוֹלָם, לְיֵצֶר מַחְשְׁבוֹת לְבַב עַמֶּךָ, וְהָכֵן לְבָבָם אֵלֶיךָ.[1] וְהוּא רַחוּם, יְכַפֵּר עָוֹן וְלֹא יַשְׁחִית, וְהִרְבָּה לְהָשִׁיב אַפּוֹ, וְלֹא יָעִיר כָּל חֲמָתוֹ.[2] כִּי אַתָּה אֲדֹנָי טוֹב וְסַלָּח, וְרַב חֶסֶד לְכָל קֹרְאֶיךָ.[3] צִדְקָתְךָ צֶדֶק לְעוֹלָם, וְתוֹרָתְךָ אֱמֶת.[4] תִּתֵּן אֱמֶת לְיַעֲקֹב, חֶסֶד לְאַבְרָהָם, אֲשֶׁר נִשְׁבַּעְתָּ לַאֲבֹתֵינוּ מִימֵי קֶדֶם.[5] בָּרוּךְ אֲדֹנָי יוֹם יוֹם יַעֲמָס לָנוּ, הָאֵל יְשׁוּעָתֵנוּ סֶלָה.[6] יהוה צְבָאוֹת עִמָּנוּ, מִשְׂגָּב לָנוּ אֱלֹהֵי יַעֲקֹב סֶלָה.[7] יהוה צְבָאוֹת, אַשְׁרֵי אָדָם בֹּטֵחַ בָּךְ.[8] יהוה הוֹשִׁיעָה, הַמֶּלֶךְ יַעֲנֵנוּ בְיוֹם קָרְאֵנוּ.[9]

בָּרוּךְ הוּא אֱלֹהֵינוּ שֶׁבְּרָאָנוּ לִכְבוֹדוֹ, וְהִבְדִּילָנוּ מִן הַתּוֹעִים, וְנָתַן לָנוּ תּוֹרַת אֱמֶת, וְחַיֵּי עוֹלָם נָטַע בְּתוֹכֵנוּ. הוּא יִפְתַּח לִבֵּנוּ בְּתוֹרָתוֹ, וְיָשֵׂם בְּלִבֵּנוּ אַהֲבָתוֹ וְיִרְאָתוֹ וְלַעֲשׂוֹת רְצוֹנוֹ וּלְעָבְדוֹ בְּלֵבָב שָׁלֵם, לְמַעַן לֹא נִיגַע לָרִיק, וְלֹא נֵלֵד לַבֶּהָלָה.[10]

יְהִי רָצוֹן מִלְּפָנֶיךָ יהוה אֱלֹהֵינוּ וֵאלֹהֵי אֲבוֹתֵינוּ, שֶׁנִּשְׁמֹר חֻקֶּיךָ בָּעוֹלָם הַזֶּה, וְנִזְכֶּה וְנִחְיֶה וְנִרְאֶה וְנִירַשׁ טוֹבָה וּבְרָכָה לִשְׁנֵי יְמוֹת הַמָּשִׁיחַ וּלְחַיֵּי הָעוֹלָם הַבָּא. לְמַעַן יְזַמֶּרְךָ כָבוֹד וְלֹא יִדֹּם, יהוה אֱלֹהַי לְעוֹלָם אוֹדֶךָּ.[11] בָּרוּךְ הַגֶּבֶר אֲשֶׁר יִבְטַח בַּיהוה, וְהָיָה יהוה מִבְטַחוֹ.[12] בִּטְחוּ בַיהוה עֲדֵי עַד, כִּי בְּיָהּ יהוה צוּר עוֹלָמִים.[13] ❖ וְיִבְטְחוּ בְךָ יוֹדְעֵי שְׁמֶךָ, כִּי לֹא עָזַבְתָּ דֹּרְשֶׁיךָ, יהוה.[14] יהוה חָפֵץ לְמַעַן צִדְקוֹ, יַגְדִּיל תּוֹרָה וְיַאְדִּיר.[15]

ON ALL NIGHTS CONTINUE HERE.

קדיש שלם

Chazzan recites קַדִּישׁ שָׁלֵם.

יִתְגַּדַּל וְיִתְקַדַּשׁ שְׁמֵהּ רַבָּא. (.Cong – אָמֵן.) בְּעָלְמָא דִּי בְרָא כִרְעוּתֵהּ. וְיַמְלִיךְ מַלְכוּתֵהּ, בְּחַיֵּיכוֹן וּבְיוֹמֵיכוֹן וּבְחַיֵּי דְכָל בֵּית יִשְׂרָאֵל, בַּעֲגָלָא וּבִזְמַן קָרִיב. וְאִמְרוּ: אָמֵן.

(.Cong – אָמֵן. יְהֵא שְׁמֵהּ רַבָּא מְבָרַךְ לְעָלַם וּלְעָלְמֵי עָלְמַיָּא.)

יְהֵא שְׁמֵהּ רַבָּא מְבָרַךְ לְעָלַם וּלְעָלְמֵי עָלְמַיָּא.

Hashem, God of Abraham, Isaac, and Israel, our forefathers, may You preserve this forever as the realization of the thoughts in Your people's heart, and may You direct their heart to You.[1] *He, the Merciful One, is forgiving of iniquity and does not destroy; frequently He withdraws His anger, not arousing His entire rage.*[2] *For You, my Lord, are good and forgiving, and abundantly kind to all who call upon You.*[3] *Your righteousness remains righteous forever, and Your Torah is truth.*[4] *Grant truth to Jacob, kindness to Abraham, as You swore to our forefathers from ancient times.*[5] *Blessed is my Lord for every single day, He burdens us with blessings, the God of our salvation, Selah.*[6] *Hashem, Master of Legions, is with us, a stronghold for us is the God of Jacob, Selah.*[7] *Hashem, Master of Legions, praiseworthy is the man who trusts in You.*[8] *Hashem, save! May the King answer us on the day we call.*[9]

Blessed is He, our God, Who created us for His glory, separated us from those who stray, gave us the Torah of truth and implanted eternal life within us. May He open our heart through His Torah and imbue our heart with love and awe of Him and that we may do His will and serve Him wholeheartedly, so that we do not struggle in vain nor produce for futility.[10]

May it be Your will, Hashem, our God and the God of our forefathers, that we observe Your decrees in This World, and merit that we live and see and inherit goodness and blessing in the years of Messianic times and for the life of the World to Come. So that my soul might sing to You and not be stilled, Hashem, my God, forever will I thank You.[11] *Blessed is the man who trusts in Hashem, then Hashem will be his security.*[12] *Trust in Hashem forever, for in God, Hashem, is the strength of the worlds.*[13] Chazzan– *Those knowing Your Name will trust in You, and You forsake not those Who seek You, Hashem.*[14] *Hashem desired, for the sake of its [Israel's] righteousness, that the Torah be made great and glorious.*[15]

ON ALL NIGHTS CONTINUE HERE.

FULL KADDISH

Chazzan recites the Full *Kaddish*.

יִתְגַּדַּל *May His great Name grow exalted and sanctified* (Cong.– *Amen.*) *in the world that He created as He willed. May He give reign to His kingship in your lifetimes and in your days, and in the lifetimes of the entire Family of Israel, swiftly and soon. Now respond: Amen.*

(Cong.– *Amen. May His great Name be blessed forever and ever.*)
May His great Name be blessed forever and ever.

(1) *I Chronicles* 29:18. (2) *Psalms* 78:38. (3) 86:5. (4) 119:142. (5) *Micah* 7:20.
(6) *Psalms* 68:20. (7) 46:8. (8) 84:13. (9) 20:10. (10) Cf. *Isaiah* 65:23. (11) *Psalms* 30:13.
(12) *Jeremiah* 17:7. (13) *Isaiah* 26:4. (14) *Psalms* 9:11. (15) *Isaiah* 42:21.

יִתְבָּרַךְ וְיִשְׁתַּבַּח וְיִתְפָּאַר וְיִתְרוֹמַם וְיִתְנַשֵּׂא וְיִתְהַדָּר וְיִתְעַלֶּה וְיִתְהַלָּל שְׁמֵהּ דְּקֻדְשָׁא בְּרִיךְ הוּא (.Cong – בְּרִיךְ הוּא) – לְעֵלָּא מִן כָּל בִּרְכָתָא וְשִׁירָתָא תֻּשְׁבְּחָתָא וְנֶחֱמָתָא, דַּאֲמִירָן בְּעָלְמָא. וְאִמְרוּ: אָמֵן. (.Cong – אָמֵן.)

(.Cong – קַבֵּל בְּרַחֲמִים וּבְרָצוֹן אֶת תְּפִלָּתֵנוּ.)

תִּתְקַבֵּל צְלוֹתְהוֹן וּבָעוּתְהוֹן דְּכָל בֵּית יִשְׂרָאֵל קֳדָם אֲבוּהוֹן דִּי בִשְׁמַיָּא. וְאִמְרוּ: אָמֵן. (.Cong – אָמֵן.)

(.Cong – יְהִי שֵׁם יהוה מְבֹרָךְ, מֵעַתָּה וְעַד עוֹלָם.[1])

יְהֵא שְׁלָמָא רַבָּא מִן שְׁמַיָּא, וְחַיִּים עָלֵינוּ וְעַל כָּל יִשְׂרָאֵל. וְאִמְרוּ: אָמֵן. (.Cong – אָמֵן.)

(.Cong – עֶזְרִי מֵעִם יהוה, עֹשֵׂה שָׁמַיִם וָאָרֶץ.[2])

Take three steps back. Bow left and say . . . עֹשֶׂה; bow right and say . . . הוּא; bow forward and say וְעַל כָּל . . . אָמֵן. Remain standing in place for a few moments, then take three steps forward.

עֹשֶׂה שָׁלוֹם בִּמְרוֹמָיו, הוּא יַעֲשֶׂה שָׁלוֹם עָלֵינוּ, וְעַל כָּל יִשְׂרָאֵל. וְאִמְרוּ: אָמֵן. (.Cong – אָמֵן.)

ספירת העומר

Most congregations count the *Omer* at this point; some count after *Aleinu* (p. 1106). See page 79 and *Laws* §109-134 for pertinent laws.

In some congregations the following Kabbalistic prayer precedes the counting of the *Omer*.

לְשֵׁם יִחוּד קוּדְשָׁא בְּרִיךְ הוּא וּשְׁכִינְתֵּיהּ, בִּדְחִילוּ וּרְחִימוּ לְיַחֵד שֵׁם יוּ״ד הֵ״א בְּוָא״ו הֵ״א בְּיִחוּדָא שְׁלִים, בְּשֵׁם כָּל יִשְׂרָאֵל. הִנְנִי מוּכָן וּמְזוּמָן לְקַיֵּם מִצְוַת עֲשֵׂה שֶׁל סְפִירַת הָעוֹמֶר, כְּמוֹ שֶׁכָּתוּב בַּתּוֹרָה: וּסְפַרְתֶּם לָכֶם מִמָּחֳרַת הַשַּׁבָּת, מִיּוֹם הֲבִיאֲכֶם אֶת עֹמֶר הַתְּנוּפָה, שֶׁבַע שַׁבָּתוֹת תְּמִימֹת תִּהְיֶינָה. עַד מִמָּחֳרַת הַשַּׁבָּת הַשְּׁבִיעִת תִּסְפְּרוּ חֲמִשִּׁים יוֹם, וְהִקְרַבְתֶּם מִנְחָה חֲדָשָׁה לַיהוה.[3] וִיהִי נֹעַם אֲדֹנָי אֱלֹהֵינוּ עָלֵינוּ, וּמַעֲשֵׂה יָדֵינוּ כּוֹנְנָה עָלֵינוּ, וּמַעֲשֵׂה יָדֵינוּ כּוֹנְנֵהוּ.[4]

Chazzan, followed by congregation, recites the blessing and counts. One praying without a *minyan* should, nevertheless, recite the entire *Omer* service.

בָּרוּךְ אַתָּה יהוה אֱלֹהֵינוּ מֶלֶךְ הָעוֹלָם, אֲשֶׁר קִדְּשָׁנוּ בְּמִצְוֹתָיו וְצִוָּנוּ עַל סְפִירַת הָעוֹמֶר.

הַיּוֹם שְׁמוֹנָה יָמִים,

שֶׁהֵם שָׁבוּעַ אֶחָד וְיוֹם אֶחָד, לָעוֹמֶר.

הָרַחֲמָן הוּא יַחֲזִיר לָנוּ עֲבוֹדַת בֵּית הַמִּקְדָּשׁ לִמְקוֹמָהּ, בִּמְהֵרָה בְיָמֵינוּ. אָמֵן סֶלָה.

Blessed, praised, glorified, exalted, extolled, mighty, upraised, and lauded be the Name of the Holy One, Blessed is He (Cong.– *Blessed is He*) — *beyond any blessing and song, praise and consolation that are uttered in the world. Now respond: Amen.* (Cong.– *Amen.*)

(Cong.– *Accept our prayers with mercy and favor.*)

May the prayers and supplications of the entire Family of Israel be accepted before their Father Who is in Heaven. Now respond: Amen. (Cong.– *Amen.*)

(Cong.– *Blessed be the Name of* HASHEM, *from this time and forever.*[1])

May there be abundant peace from Heaven, and life, upon us and upon all Israel. Now respond: Amen. (Cong.– *Amen.*)

(Cong.– *My help is from* HASHEM, *Maker of heaven and earth.*[2])

Take three steps back. Bow left and say, *'He Who makes peace . . .'*; bow right and say, *'may He . . .'*; bow forward and say, *'and upon all Israel . . .'* Remain standing in place for a few moments, then take three steps forward.

He Who makes peace in His heights, may He make peace upon us, and upon all Israel. Now respond: Amen. (Cong.– *Amen.*)

COUNTING THE OMER

Most congregations count the *Omer* at this point; some count after *Aleinu* (p. 1106). See page 79 and *Laws* §109-134 for pertinent laws.

In some congregations the following Kabbalistic prayer precedes the counting of the *Omer*.

לְשֵׁם *For the sake of the unification of the Holy One, Blessed is He, and His Presence, in fear and love to unify the Name Yud-Kei with Vav-Kei in perfect unity, in the name of all Israel. Behold I am prepared and ready to perform the commandment of counting the Omer, as it is written in the Torah: 'You are to count from the morrow of the rest day, from the day you brought the Omer-offering that is waved — they are to be seven complete weeks — until the morrow of the seventh week you are to count fifty days, and then offer a new meal-offering to* HASHEM.'[3] *May the pleasantness of my Lord, our God, be upon us — may He establish our handiwork for us; our handiwork, may He establish.*[4]

Chazzan, followed by congregation, recites the blessing and counts. One praying without a *minyan* should, nevertheless, recite the entire *Omer* service.

בָּרוּךְ *Blessed are You,* HASHEM, *our God, King of the universe, Who has sanctified us with His commandments and has commanded us regarding the counting of the Omer.*

Today is eight days, which are one week and one day, of the Omer.

הָרַחֲמָן *The Compassionate One! May He return for us the service of the Temple to its place, speedily in our days. Amen, selah!*

(1) *Psalms* 113:2. (2) 121:2. (3) *Leviticus* 23:15-16. (4) *Psalms* 90:17.

תהלים סז

לַמְנַצֵּחַ בִּנְגִינֹת מִזְמוֹר שִׁיר. אֱלֹהִים יְחָנֵּנוּ וִיבָרְכֵנוּ, יָאֵר פָּנָיו אִתָּנוּ סֶלָה. לָדַעַת בָּאָרֶץ דַּרְכֶּךָ, בְּכָל גּוֹיִם יְשׁוּעָתֶךָ. יוֹדוּךָ עַמִּים אֱלֹהִים, יוֹדוּךָ עַמִּים כֻּלָּם. יִשְׂמְחוּ וִירַנְּנוּ לְאֻמִּים, כִּי תִשְׁפֹּט עַמִּים מִישֹׁר, וּלְאֻמִּים בָּאָרֶץ תַּנְחֵם סֶלָה. יוֹדוּךָ עַמִּים, אֱלֹהִים, יוֹדוּךָ עַמִּים כֻּלָּם. אֶרֶץ נָתְנָה יְבוּלָהּ, יְבָרְכֵנוּ אֱלֹהִים אֱלֹהֵינוּ. יְבָרְכֵנוּ אֱלֹהִים, וְיִירְאוּ אוֹתוֹ כָּל אַפְסֵי אָרֶץ.

אָנָּא בְּכֹחַ גְּדֻלַּת יְמִינְךָ תַּתִּיר צְרוּרָה. אב״ג ית״ץ
קַבֵּל רִנַּת עַמְּךָ שַׂגְּבֵנוּ טַהֲרֵנוּ נוֹרָא. קר״ע שט״ן
נָא גִבּוֹר דּוֹרְשֵׁי יִחוּדְךָ כְּבָבַת שָׁמְרֵם. נג״ד יכ״ש
בָּרְכֵם טַהֲרֵם רַחֲמֵם צִדְקָתְךָ תָּמִיד גָּמְלֵם. בט״ר צת״ג
חֲסִין קָדוֹשׁ בְּרוֹב טוּבְךָ נַהֵל עֲדָתֶךָ. חק״ב טנ״ע
יָחִיד גֵּאֶה לְעַמְּךָ פְּנֵה זוֹכְרֵי קְדֻשָּׁתֶךָ. יג״ל פז״ק
שַׁוְעָתֵנוּ קַבֵּל וּשְׁמַע צַעֲקָתֵנוּ יוֹדֵעַ תַּעֲלֻמוֹת. שק״ו צי״ת
בָּרוּךְ שֵׁם כְּבוֹד מַלְכוּתוֹ לְעוֹלָם וָעֶד.

רִבּוֹנוֹ שֶׁל עוֹלָם, אַתָּה צִוִּיתָנוּ עַל יְדֵי מֹשֶׁה עַבְדֶּךָ לִסְפּוֹר סְפִירַת הָעֹמֶר, כְּדֵי לְטַהֲרֵנוּ מִקְּלִפּוֹתֵינוּ וּמִטֻּמְאוֹתֵינוּ, כְּמוֹ שֶׁכָּתַבְתָּ בְּתוֹרָתֶךָ: וּסְפַרְתֶּם לָכֶם מִמָּחֳרַת הַשַּׁבָּת מִיּוֹם הֲבִיאֲכֶם אֶת עֹמֶר הַתְּנוּפָה, שֶׁבַע שַׁבָּתוֹת תְּמִימֹת תִּהְיֶינָה. עַד מִמָּחֳרַת הַשַּׁבָּת הַשְּׁבִיעִת תִּסְפְּרוּ חֲמִשִּׁים יוֹם.[1] כְּדֵי שֶׁיִּטָּהֲרוּ נַפְשׁוֹת עַמְּךָ יִשְׂרָאֵל מִזֻּהֲמָתָם. וּבְכֵן יְהִי רָצוֹן מִלְּפָנֶיךָ יהוה אֱלֹהֵינוּ וֵאלֹהֵי אֲבוֹתֵינוּ, שֶׁבִּזְכוּת סְפִירַת הָעֹמֶר שֶׁסָּפַרְתִּי הַיּוֹם, יְתֻקַּן מַה שֶּׁפָּגַמְתִּי בִּסְפִירָה חֶסֶד שֶׁבִּגְבוּרָה. וְאֶטָּהֵר וְאֶתְקַדֵּשׁ בִּקְדֻשָּׁה שֶׁל מַעְלָה, וְעַל יְדֵי זֶה יֻשְׁפַּע שֶׁפַע רַב בְּכָל הָעוֹלָמוֹת. וּלְתַקֵּן אֶת נַפְשׁוֹתֵינוּ, וְרוּחוֹתֵינוּ, וְנִשְׁמוֹתֵינוּ, מִכָּל סִיג וּפְגַם, וּלְטַהֲרֵינוּ וּלְקַדְּשֵׁנוּ בִּקְדֻשָּׁתְךָ הָעֶלְיוֹנָה. אָמֵן סֶלָה.

In some congregations, if a mourner is present, the Mourner's *Kaddish* (p. 1104) is recited, followed by *Aleinu*. In others, *Aleinu* is recited immediately.

AT THE CONCLUSION OF THE SABBATH THE SERVICE CONTINUES BELOW.

פסוקי ברכה

וְיִתֶּן לְךָ הָאֱלֹהִים מִטַּל הַשָּׁמַיִם וּמִשְׁמַנֵּי הָאָרֶץ, וְרֹב דָּגָן וְתִירֹשׁ. יַעַבְדוּךָ עַמִּים, וְיִשְׁתַּחֲווּ לְךָ לְאֻמִּים, הֱוֵה גְבִיר לְאַחֶיךָ, וְיִשְׁתַּחֲווּ לְךָ בְּנֵי אִמֶּךָ, אֹרְרֶיךָ אָרוּר, וּמְבָרְכֶיךָ בָּרוּךְ.[2] וְאֵל שַׁדַּי

Psalm 67

לַמְנַצֵּחַ *For the Conductor, upon Neginos, a psalm, a song. May God favor us and bless us, may He illuminate His countenance with us, Selah. To make known Your way on earth, among all the nations Your salvation. The peoples will acknowledge You, O God, the peoples will acknowledge You, all of them. Nations will be glad and sing for joy, because You will judge the peoples fairly and guide the nations on earth, Selah. The peoples will acknowledge You, O God, the peoples will acknowledge You, all of them. The earth has yielded its produce, may God, our own God, bless us. May God bless us and may all the ends of the earth fear him.*

אָנָּא *We beg You! With the strength of Your right hand's greatness, untie the bundled sins. Accept the prayer of Your nation; strengthen us, purify us, O Awesome One. Please, O Strong One — those who foster Your Oneness, guard them like the apple of an eye. Bless them, purify them, show them pity, may Your righteousness always recompense them. Powerful Holy One, with Your abundant goodness guide Your congregation. One and only Exalted One, turn to Your nation, which proclaims Your holiness. Accept our entreaty and hear our cry, O Knower of mysteries. Blessed is the Name of His glorious Kingdom for all eternity.*

רִבּוֹנוֹ שֶׁל עוֹלָם *Master of the universe, You commanded us through Moses, Your servant, to count the Omer Count in order to cleanse us from our encrustations of evil and from our contaminations, as You have written in Your Torah: You are to count from the morrow of the rest day, from the day you brought the Omer-offering that is waved — they are to be seven complete weeks. Until the morrow of the seventh week you are to count fifty days,[1] so that the souls of Your people Israel be cleansed from their contamination. Therefore, may it be You will, HASHEM, our God and the God of our forefathers, that in the merit of the Omer Count that I have counted today, may there be corrected whatever blemish I have caused in the sefirah chesed shebigvurah. May I be cleansed and sanctified with the holiness of Above, and through this may abundant bounty flow in all the worlds. And may it correct our lives, spirits, and souls from all sediment and blemish; may it cleanse us and sanctify us with Your exalted holiness. Amen, Selah!*

In some congregations, if a mourner is present, the Mourner's *Kaddish* (p. 1104) is recited, followed by *Aleinu*. In others, *Aleinu* is recited immediately.

AT THE CONCLUSION OF THE SABBATH THE SERVICE CONTINUES BELOW.

VERSES OF BLESSING

וְיִתֶּן *And may God give you of the dew of the heavens and of the fatness of the earth, and abundant grain and wine. Peoples will serve you, and regimes will prostrate themselves to you; be a lord to your kinsmen, and your mother's sons will prostrate themselves to you; they who curse you are cursed, and they who bless you are blessed.[2] And may El Shaddai*

(1) *Leviticus* 23:15-16. (2) *Genesis* 27:28-29.

יְבָרֵךְ אֹתְךָ וְיַפְרְךָ וְיַרְבֶּךָ, וְהָיִיתָ לִקְהַל עַמִּים. וְיִתֶּן לְךָ אֶת בִּרְכַּת אַבְרָהָם, לְךָ וּלְזַרְעֲךָ אִתָּךְ, לְרִשְׁתְּךָ אֶת אֶרֶץ מְגֻרֶיךָ, אֲשֶׁר נָתַן אֱלֹהִים לְאַבְרָהָם.[1] מֵאֵל אָבִיךָ וְיַעְזְרֶךָּ, וְאֵת שַׁדַּי וִיבָרְכֶךָּ, בִּרְכֹת שָׁמַיִם מֵעָל, בִּרְכֹת תְּהוֹם רֹבֶצֶת תָּחַת, בִּרְכֹת שָׁדַיִם וָרָחַם. בִּרְכֹת אָבִיךָ גָּבְרוּ עַל בִּרְכֹת הוֹרַי, עַד תַּאֲוַת גִּבְעֹת עוֹלָם, תִּהְיֶיןָ לְרֹאשׁ יוֹסֵף, וּלְקָדְקֹד נְזִיר אֶחָיו.[2] וַאֲהֵבְךָ וּבֵרַכְךָ וְהִרְבֶּךָ, וּבֵרַךְ פְּרִי בִטְנְךָ וּפְרִי אַדְמָתֶךָ, דְּגָנְךָ וְתִירֹשְׁךָ וְיִצְהָרֶךָ, שְׁגַר אֲלָפֶיךָ וְעַשְׁתְּרֹת צֹאנֶךָ, עַל הָאֲדָמָה אֲשֶׁר נִשְׁבַּע לַאֲבֹתֶיךָ לָתֶת לָךְ. בָּרוּךְ תִּהְיֶה מִכָּל הָעַמִּים, לֹא יִהְיֶה בְךָ עָקָר וַעֲקָרָה, וּבִבְהֶמְתֶּךָ. וְהֵסִיר יהוה מִמְּךָ כָּל חֹלִי, וְכָל מַדְוֵי מִצְרַיִם הָרָעִים אֲשֶׁר יָדַעְתָּ, לֹא יְשִׂימָם בָּךְ, וּנְתָנָם בְּכָל שֹׂנְאֶיךָ.[3]

הַמַּלְאָךְ הַגֹּאֵל אֹתִי מִכָּל רָע יְבָרֵךְ אֶת הַנְּעָרִים וְיִקָּרֵא בָהֶם שְׁמִי, וְשֵׁם אֲבֹתַי אַבְרָהָם וְיִצְחָק, וְיִדְגּוּ לָרֹב בְּקֶרֶב הָאָרֶץ.[4] יהוה אֱלֹהֵיכֶם הִרְבָּה אֶתְכֶם, וְהִנְּכֶם הַיּוֹם כְּכוֹכְבֵי הַשָּׁמַיִם לָרֹב. יהוה אֱלֹהֵי אֲבוֹתֵכֶם יֹסֵף עֲלֵיכֶם כָּכֶם אֶלֶף פְּעָמִים, וִיבָרֵךְ אֶתְכֶם כַּאֲשֶׁר דִּבֶּר לָכֶם.[5]

בָּרוּךְ אַתָּה בָּעִיר, וּבָרוּךְ אַתָּה בַּשָּׂדֶה. בָּרוּךְ אַתָּה בְּבֹאֶךָ, וּבָרוּךְ אַתָּה בְּצֵאתֶךָ. בָּרוּךְ טַנְאֲךָ וּמִשְׁאַרְתֶּךָ. בָּרוּךְ פְּרִי בִטְנְךָ וּפְרִי אַדְמָתְךָ וּפְרִי בְהֶמְתֶּךָ, שְׁגַר אֲלָפֶיךָ וְעַשְׁתְּרוֹת צֹאנֶךָ.[6] יְצַו יהוה אִתְּךָ אֶת הַבְּרָכָה בַּאֲסָמֶיךָ וּבְכֹל מִשְׁלַח יָדֶךָ, וּבֵרַכְךָ בָּאָרֶץ אֲשֶׁר יהוה אֱלֹהֶיךָ נֹתֵן לָךְ. יִפְתַּח יהוה לְךָ אֶת אוֹצָרוֹ הַטּוֹב, אֶת הַשָּׁמַיִם, לָתֵת מְטַר אַרְצְךָ בְּעִתּוֹ, וּלְבָרֵךְ אֵת כָּל מַעֲשֵׂה יָדֶךָ, וְהִלְוִיתָ גּוֹיִם רַבִּים, וְאַתָּה לֹא תִלְוֶה.[7] כִּי יהוה אֱלֹהֶיךָ בֵּרַכְךָ כַּאֲשֶׁר דִּבֶּר לָךְ, וְהַעֲבַטְתָּ גּוֹיִם רַבִּים, וְאַתָּה לֹא תַעֲבֹט, וּמָשַׁלְתָּ בְּגוֹיִם רַבִּים, וּבְךָ לֹא יִמְשֹׁלוּ.[8] אַשְׁרֶיךָ יִשְׂרָאֵל, מִי כָמוֹךָ, עַם נוֹשַׁע בַּיהוה, מָגֵן עֶזְרֶךָ, וַאֲשֶׁר חֶרֶב גַּאֲוָתֶךָ, וְיִכָּחֲשׁוּ אֹיְבֶיךָ לָךְ, וְאַתָּה עַל בָּמוֹתֵימוֹ תִדְרֹךְ.[9]

גאולה

מָחִיתִי כָעָב פְּשָׁעֶיךָ וְכֶעָנָן חַטֹּאתֶיךָ, שׁוּבָה אֵלַי כִּי גְאַלְתִּיךָ. רָנּוּ שָׁמַיִם, כִּי עָשָׂה יהוה, הָרִיעוּ תַּחְתִּיּוֹת אָרֶץ, פִּצְחוּ הָרִים רִנָּה, יַעַר וְכָל עֵץ בּוֹ, כִּי גָאַל יהוה יַעֲקֹב וּבְיִשְׂרָאֵל יִתְפָּאָר.[10] גֹּאֲלֵנוּ יהוה צְבָאוֹת שְׁמוֹ, קְדוֹשׁ יִשְׂרָאֵל.[11]

ישועה

יִשְׂרָאֵל נוֹשַׁע בַּיהוה תְּשׁוּעַת עוֹלָמִים, לֹא תֵבֹשׁוּ וְלֹא תִכָּלְמוּ עַד עוֹלְמֵי עַד.[12] וַאֲכַלְתֶּם אָכוֹל וְשָׂבוֹעַ, וְהִלַּלְתֶּם אֶת שֵׁם יהוה אֱלֹהֵיכֶם אֲשֶׁר עָשָׂה עִמָּכֶם לְהַפְלִיא, וְלֹא יֵבֹשׁוּ עַמִּי לְעוֹלָם.

(1) *Genesis* 28:3-4. (2) 49:25-26. (3) *Deuteronomy* 7:13-15. (4) *Genesis* 48:16. (5) *Deuteronomy* 1:10-11. (6) 28:3,6,5,4. (7) 28:8,12. (8) 15:6. (9) 33:29. (10) *Isaiah* 44:22-23. (11) 47:4. (12) 45:17.

bless you, make you fruitful and make you numerous, and may you be a congregation of peoples. May He grant you the blessing of Abraham, to you and to your offspring with you, that you may possess the land of your sojourns which God gave to Abraham.[1] *It is from the God of your father and He will help you, and with Shaddai and He will bless you — blessings of heaven from above, blessings of the deep crouching below, blessings of the bosom and womb. The blessings of your father surpassed the blessings of my fathers, to the endless bounds of the world's hills; let them be upon Joseph's head and upon the head of the one separated from his brothers.*[2] *And He shall love you, and He shall bless you, and He shall make you numerous; may He bless the fruit of your womb and the fruit of your land, your grain, your wine and your oil, the offspring of your cattle and the flocks of your sheep, on the land that He swore to your forefathers to give to you. Blessed shall you be above all peoples; there shall not be among you a barren man or woman, nor among your cattle. HASHEM shall remove from you all illness; and all the evil sufferings of Egypt that you knew, He will not place upon you, but He will set them upon all your enemies.*[3]

הַמַּלְאָךְ *May the angel who redeems me from all evil bless the lads, and may my name be declared upon them — and the names of my forefathers Abraham and Isaac — and may they proliferate abundantly like fish within the land.*[4] *HASHEM, your God, has made you numerous, and behold! you are today like the stars of heaven in abundance. May HASHEM, the God of your forefathers, increase you a thousandfold and bless you as He spoke to you.*[5]

בָּרוּךְ *Blessed are you in the city; blessed are you in the field. Blessed are you upon your arrival; blessed are you upon your departure. Blessed is your fruit basket and your kneading trough. Blessed is the fruit of your womb, the fruit of your land and the fruit of your animal, the offspring of your cattle and the flocks of your sheep.*[6] *May HASHEM command that the blessing accompany you in your storehouse and wherever you set your hand, and may He bless you in the land that HASHEM, your God, gives you. May HASHEM open for you His good treasury, the heaven, to give you rain for your land in its time and to bless your every handiwork; and may you lend many nations, but may you not borrow.*[7] *For HASHEM, your God, will have blessed you as He spoke to you; and may you make many nations indebted to you, but may you not become indebted; and you will dominate many nations, but they will not dominate you.*[8] *Praiseworthy are you, O Israel, who is like you! — a people saved by God, Who is the Shield of your help, and Who is the Sword of your majesty. Your enemies will be false with you, but you will tread upon their heights.*[9]

REDEMPTION

מָחִיתִי *I have blotted out your willful sins like a thick mist and your errors like a cloud — return to Me for I have redeemed you. Sing gladly, O heaven, for HASHEM has done so; exult O depths of the earth; break out, O mountains, in glad song, forest and every tree within it, for HASHEM has redeemed Jacob and will take pride in Israel.*[10] *Our Redeemer — HASHEM, Master of Legions, is His Name — is the Holy One of Israel.*[11]

SALVATION

יִשְׂרָאֵל *Israel is saved by God in an everlasting salvation; they will not be shamed nor humiliated forever and ever.*[12] *You shall eat food and be satisfied, and you shall praise the Name of HASHEM, your God, Who has done wondrously with you, and My people shall not be shamed forever.*

וִידַעְתֶּם כִּי בְקֶרֶב יִשְׂרָאֵל אָנִי, וַאֲנִי יהוה אֱלֹהֵיכֶם, וְאֵין עוֹד, וְלֹא יֵבֹשׁוּ עַמִּי לְעוֹלָם.[1] כִּי בְשִׂמְחָה תֵצֵאוּ וּבְשָׁלוֹם תּוּבָלוּן, הֶהָרִים וְהַגְּבָעוֹת יִפְצְחוּ לִפְנֵיכֶם רִנָּה, וְכָל עֲצֵי הַשָּׂדֶה יִמְחֲאוּ כָף.[2] הִנֵּה אֵל יְשׁוּעָתִי, אֶבְטַח וְלֹא אֶפְחָד, כִּי עָזִּי וְזִמְרָת יָהּ יהוה וַיְהִי לִי לִישׁוּעָה. וּשְׁאַבְתֶּם מַיִם בְּשָׂשׂוֹן, מִמַּעַיְנֵי הַיְשׁוּעָה. וַאֲמַרְתֶּם בַּיּוֹם הַהוּא, הוֹדוּ לַיהוה קִרְאוּ בִשְׁמוֹ, הוֹדִיעוּ בָעַמִּים עֲלִילֹתָיו, הַזְכִּירוּ כִּי נִשְׂגָּב שְׁמוֹ. זַמְּרוּ יהוה כִּי גֵאוּת עָשָׂה, מוּדַעַת זֹאת בְּכָל הָאָרֶץ. צַהֲלִי וָרֹנִּי יוֹשֶׁבֶת צִיּוֹן, כִּי גָדוֹל בְּקִרְבֵּךְ קְדוֹשׁ יִשְׂרָאֵל.[3] וְאָמַר בַּיּוֹם הַהוּא, הִנֵּה אֱלֹהֵינוּ זֶה, קִוִּינוּ לוֹ וְיוֹשִׁיעֵנוּ, זֶה יהוה קִוִּינוּ לוֹ, נָגִילָה וְנִשְׂמְחָה בִּישׁוּעָתוֹ.[4]

דעת ה'

בֵּית יַעֲקֹב, לְכוּ וְנֵלְכָה בְּאוֹר יהוה.[5] וְהָיָה אֱמוּנַת עִתֶּיךָ חֹסֶן יְשׁוּעֹת חָכְמַת וָדָעַת, יִרְאַת יהוה הִיא אוֹצָרוֹ.[6] וַיְהִי דָוִד לְכָל דְּרָכָיו מַשְׂכִּיל, וַיהוה עִמּוֹ.[7]

פדיום

פָּדָה בְשָׁלוֹם נַפְשִׁי מִקְּרָב לִי, כִּי בְרַבִּים הָיוּ עִמָּדִי.[8] וַיֹּאמֶר הָעָם אֶל שָׁאוּל, הֲיוֹנָתָן יָמוּת אֲשֶׁר עָשָׂה הַיְשׁוּעָה הַגְּדוֹלָה הַזֹּאת בְּיִשְׂרָאֵל, חָלִילָה, חַי יהוה, אִם יִפֹּל מִשַּׂעֲרַת רֹאשׁוֹ אַרְצָה, כִּי עִם אֱלֹהִים עָשָׂה הַיּוֹם הַזֶּה, וַיִּפְדּוּ הָעָם אֶת יוֹנָתָן וְלֹא מֵת.[9] וּפְדוּיֵי יהוה יְשֻׁבוּן, וּבָאוּ צִיּוֹן בְּרִנָּה, וְשִׂמְחַת עוֹלָם עַל רֹאשָׁם, שָׂשׂוֹן וְשִׂמְחָה יַשִּׂיגוּ וְנָסוּ יָגוֹן וַאֲנָחָה.[10]

הפוך צרה

הָפַכְתָּ מִסְפְּדִי לְמָחוֹל לִי, פִּתַּחְתָּ שַׂקִּי, וַתְּאַזְּרֵנִי שִׂמְחָה.[11] וְלֹא אָבָה יהוה אֱלֹהֶיךָ לִשְׁמֹעַ אֶל בִּלְעָם, וַיַּהֲפֹךְ יהוה אֱלֹהֶיךָ לְּךָ אֶת הַקְּלָלָה לִבְרָכָה, כִּי אֲהֵבְךָ יהוה אֱלֹהֶיךָ.[12] אָז תִּשְׂמַח בְּתוּלָה בְּמָחוֹל, וּבַחֻרִים וּזְקֵנִים יַחְדָּו, וְהָפַכְתִּי אֶבְלָם לְשָׂשׂוֹן, וְנִחַמְתִּים וְשִׂמַּחְתִּים מִיגוֹנָם.[13]

שלום

בּוֹרֵא נִיב שְׂפָתָיִם, שָׁלוֹם שָׁלוֹם לָרָחוֹק וְלַקָּרוֹב, אָמַר יהוה וּרְפָאתִיו.[14] וְרוּחַ לָבְשָׁה אֶת עֲמָשַׂי, רֹאשׁ הַשָּׁלִישִׁים, לְךָ דָוִיד וְעִמְּךָ בֶן יִשַׁי שָׁלוֹם, שָׁלוֹם לְךָ, וְשָׁלוֹם לְעֹזְרֶךָ כִּי עֲזָרְךָ אֱלֹהֶיךָ וַיְקַבְּלֵם דָּוִיד וַיִּתְּנֵם בְּרָאשֵׁי הַגְּדוּד.[15] וַאֲמַרְתֶּם, כֹּה לֶחָי, וְאַתָּה שָׁלוֹם וּבֵיתְךָ שָׁלוֹם וְכֹל אֲשֶׁר לְךָ שָׁלוֹם.[16] יהוה עֹז לְעַמּוֹ יִתֵּן יהוה יְבָרֵךְ אֶת עַמּוֹ בַשָּׁלוֹם.[17]

מסכת מגילה לא.

אָמַר רַבִּי יוֹחָנָן: בְּכָל מָקוֹם שֶׁאַתָּה מוֹצֵא גְּדֻלָּתוֹ שֶׁל הַקָּדוֹשׁ בָּרוּךְ הוּא, שָׁם אַתָּה מוֹצֵא עַנְוְתָנוּתוֹ. דָּבָר זֶה כָּתוּב בַּתּוֹרָה, וְשָׁנוּי

(1) *Joel* 2:26-27. (2) *Isaiah* 55:12. (3) 12:2-6. (4) 25:9. (5) 2:5. (6) 33:6. (7) *I Samuel* 18:14. (8) *Psalms* 55:19. (9) *I Samuel* 14:45. (10) *Isaiah* 35:10. (11) *Psalms* 30:12. (12) *Deuteronomy* 23:6. (13) *Jeremiah* 31:12. (14) *Isaiah* 57:19. (15) *I Chronicles* 12:19. (16) *I Samuel* 25:6. (17) *Psalms* 29:11.

And you shall know that in the midst of Israel am I, and I am HASHEM, *your God — there is none other; and My people shall not be shamed forever.*[1] *For in gladness shall you go out and in peace shall you arrive; the mountains and the hills will break out before you in glad song and all the trees of the field will clap hands.*[2] *Behold! God is my help, I shall trust and not fear — for God is my might and my praise —* HASHEM *— and He was a salvation to me. You can draw water in joy, from the springs of salvation. And you shall say on that day, 'Give thanks to* HASHEM, *declare His name, make His acts known among the peoples;' remind one another, for His Name is powerful. Make music to* HASHEM *for He has established grandeur — this is known throughout the earth. Exult and sing for joy, O inhabitant of Zion, for the Holy One of Israel has done greatly among you.*[3] *And he shall say on that day, 'Behold! this is our God, we have hoped for Him, that He would save us — this is* HASHEM, *we have hoped for Him, we shall rejoice and be glad at His salvation.'*[4]

KNOWLEDGE OF GOD

בֵּית *O House of Jacob — come let us go by the light of* HASHEM.[5] *The stability of your times, the strength of your salvations shall be through knowledge and wisdom, fear of God — that is one's treasure.*[6] *And David was successful in all his ways, and* HASHEM *was with him.*[7]

RESCUE

פָּדָה *He redeemed my soul in peace from the battles that were upon me, for the sake of the multitudes who were with me.*[8] *And the people said to Saul, 'Shall Jonathan die, who performed this great salvation for Israel? A sacrilege! — as* HASHEM *lives, if a hair of his head falls to the ground, for with* HASHEM *has he acted this day!' And the people redeemed Jonathan and he did not die.*[9] *Those redeemed by God will return and arrive at Zion with glad song and eternal gladness on their heads; joy and gladness shall they attain, and sorrow and groan shall flee.*[10]

TRANSFORMATION OF DISTRESS TO RELIEF

הָפַכְתָּ *You have changed for me my lament into dancing; You undid my sackcloth and girded me with gladness.*[11] HASHEM, *your God, did not wish to pay heed to Balaam, and* HASHEM, *your God, transformed for you the curse to blessing, for* HASHEM, *your God, loves you.*[12] *Then the maiden shall rejoice in a dance, and lads and elders together; and I shall change their mourning to joy, and I shall console them and gladden them from their sorrow.*[13]

PEACE

בּוֹרֵא *I create fruit of the lips: 'Peace, peace, for far and near,' says* HASHEM, *'and I shall heal him.'*[14] *A spirit clothed Amasai, head of the officers, 'For your sake, David, and to be with you, son of Jesse; peace, peace to you, and peace to him who helps you, for your God has helped you.' David accepted them and appointed them heads of the band.*[15] *And you shall say: 'So may it be as long as you live; peace for you, peace for your household and peace for all that is with you.'*[16] HASHEM *will give might to His people,* HASHEM *will bless His people with peace.*[17]

Talmud, Tractate *Megillah* 31a

אָמַר *Rabbi Yochanan said: Wherever you find the greatness of the Holy One, Blessed is He, there you find His humility. This phenomenon is written in the Torah, repeated in the Prophets and stated a third time in the*

בַּנְּבִיאִים, וּמְשֻׁלָּשׁ בַּכְּתוּבִים. כָּתוּב בַּתּוֹרָה: כִּי יהוה אֱלֹהֵיכֶם הוּא אֱלֹהֵי הָאֱלֹהִים וַאֲדֹנֵי הָאֲדֹנִים, הָאֵל הַגָּדֹל הַגִּבֹּר וְהַנּוֹרָא אֲשֶׁר לֹא יִשָּׂא פָנִים וְלֹא יִקַּח שֹׁחַד.[1] וּכְתִיב בַּתְרֵהּ: עֹשֶׂה מִשְׁפַּט יָתוֹם וְאַלְמָנָה, וְאֹהֵב גֵּר לָתֶת לוֹ לֶחֶם וְשִׂמְלָה.[2] שָׁנוּי בַּנְּבִיאִים, דִּכְתִיב: כִּי כֹה אָמַר רָם וְנִשָּׂא שֹׁכֵן עַד וְקָדוֹשׁ שְׁמוֹ, מָרוֹם וְקָדוֹשׁ אֶשְׁכּוֹן, וְאֶת דַּכָּא וּשְׁפַל רוּחַ, לְהַחֲיוֹת רוּחַ שְׁפָלִים וּלְהַחֲיוֹת לֵב נִדְכָּאִים.[3] מְשֻׁלָּשׁ בַּכְּתוּבִים, דִּכְתִיב: שִׁירוּ לֵאלֹהִים, זַמְּרוּ שְׁמוֹ, סֹלּוּ לָרֹכֵב בָּעֲרָבוֹת, בְּיָהּ שְׁמוֹ, וְעִלְזוּ לְפָנָיו.[4] וּכְתִיב בַּתְרֵהּ: אֲבִי יְתוֹמִים וְדַיַּן אַלְמָנוֹת, אֱלֹהִים בִּמְעוֹן קָדְשׁוֹ.[5]

יְהִי יהוה אֱלֹהֵינוּ עִמָּנוּ כַּאֲשֶׁר הָיָה עִם אֲבֹתֵינוּ, אַל יַעַזְבֵנוּ וְאַל יִטְּשֵׁנוּ.[6] וְאַתֶּם הַדְּבֵקִים בַּיהוה אֱלֹהֵיכֶם חַיִּים כֻּלְּכֶם הַיּוֹם.[7] כִּי נִחַם יהוה צִיּוֹן, נִחַם כָּל חָרְבֹתֶיהָ, וַיָּשֶׂם מִדְבָּרָהּ כְּעֵדֶן וְעַרְבָתָהּ כְּגַן יהוה, שָׂשׂוֹן וְשִׂמְחָה יִמָּצֵא בָהּ, תּוֹדָה וְקוֹל זִמְרָה.[8] יהוה חָפֵץ לְמַעַן צִדְקוֹ, יַגְדִּיל תּוֹרָה וְיַאְדִּיר.[9]

תהלים קכח

שִׁיר הַמַּעֲלוֹת אַשְׁרֵי כָּל יְרֵא יהוה, הַהֹלֵךְ בִּדְרָכָיו. יְגִיעַ כַּפֶּיךָ כִּי תֹאכֵל, אַשְׁרֶיךָ וְטוֹב לָךְ. אֶשְׁתְּךָ כְּגֶפֶן פֹּרִיָּה בְּיַרְכְּתֵי בֵיתֶךָ, בָּנֶיךָ כִּשְׁתִלֵי זֵיתִים, סָבִיב לְשֻׁלְחָנֶךָ. הִנֵּה כִי כֵן יְבֹרַךְ גָּבֶר יְרֵא יהוה. יְבָרֶכְךָ יהוה מִצִּיּוֹן וּרְאֵה בְּטוּב יְרוּשָׁלָיִם, כֹּל יְמֵי חַיֶּיךָ. וּרְאֵה בָנִים לְבָנֶיךָ, שָׁלוֹם עַל יִשְׂרָאֵל.

In some congregations mourners recite קַדִּישׁ יָתוֹם (p. 1104) at this point.

הבדלה בבית הכנסת

סַבְרִי מָרָנָן וְרַבָּנָן וְרַבּוֹתַי:

בָּרוּךְ אַתָּה יהוה אֱלֹהֵינוּ מֶלֶךְ הָעוֹלָם, בּוֹרֵא פְּרִי הַגָּפֶן.

(.Cong. – אָמֵן)

At the departure of the Sabbath the following two blessings are recited.

After the following blessing smell the spices.

בָּרוּךְ אַתָּה יהוה אֱלֹהֵינוּ מֶלֶךְ הָעוֹלָם, בּוֹרֵא מִינֵי בְשָׂמִים.

(.Cong. – אָמֵן)

After the following blessing hold fingers up to the flame to see the reflected light:

בָּרוּךְ אַתָּה יהוה אֱלֹהֵינוּ מֶלֶךְ הָעוֹלָם, בּוֹרֵא מְאוֹרֵי הָאֵשׁ.

(.Cong. – אָמֵן)

בָּרוּךְ אַתָּה יהוה אֱלֹהֵינוּ מֶלֶךְ הָעוֹלָם, הַמַּבְדִּיל בֵּין קֹדֶשׁ לְחוֹל, בֵּין אוֹר לְחֹשֶׁךְ, בֵּין יִשְׂרָאֵל לָעַמִּים, בֵּין יוֹם הַשְּׁבִיעִי לְשֵׁשֶׁת יְמֵי הַמַּעֲשֶׂה. בָּרוּךְ אַתָּה יהוה, הַמַּבְדִּיל בֵּין קֹדֶשׁ לְחוֹל.

(.Cong. – אָמֵן)

The *chazzan,* or someone else present for *Havdalah,* should drink most of the cup.

Writings. It is written in the Torah: 'For HASHEM, your God, He is the God of heavenly forces and the Master of masters, the great, mighty and awesome God, Who shows no favoritism and accepts no bribe.'[1] Afterwards it is written: 'He performs justice for orphan and widow, and loves the stranger, to give him food and clothing.'[2] It is repeated in the Prophets, as it is written: "For so says the exalted and uplifted One, Who abides forever, and Whose Name is holy, 'I abide in exaltedness and holiness — but am with the contrite and lowly of spirit, to revive the spirit of the lowly and to revive the heart of the contrite.' "[3] And it is stated a third time in the Writings, as it is written: 'Sing to God, make music for His Name, extol Him Who rides in the highest heaven, with His Name — God — and exult before Him.'[4] Afterwards it is written: 'Father of orphans and Judge of widows, God in the habitation of His holiness.'[5]

May HASHEM, our God, be with us as He was with our forefathers, may He not forsake us nor cast us off.[6] You who cling to HASHEM, our God, are all alive today.[7] For HASHEM comforts Zion, He comforts all her ruins, He will make her wilderness like Eden and her wastes like a garden of HASHEM — joy and gladness will be found there, thanksgiving and the sound of music.[8] HASHEM desired, for the sake of its [Israel's] righteousness, that the Torah be made great and glorious.[9]

Psalm 128

שִׁיר הַמַּעֲלוֹת *A song of ascents. Praiseworthy is each person who fears HASHEM, who walks in His paths. When you eat the labor of your hands, you are praiseworthy, and it is well with you. Your wife shall be like a fruitful vine in the inner chambers of your home; your children shall be like olive shoots surrounding your table. Behold! For so is blessed the man who fears HASHEM. May HASHEM bless you from Zion, and may you gaze upon the goodness of Jerusalem, all the days of your life. And may you see children born to children, peace upon Israel.*

In some congregations mourners recite the Mourner's *Kaddish* (page 1104) at this point.

HAVDALAH IN THE SYNAGOGUE

By your leave, my masters and teachers:

בָּרוּךְ *Blessed are You, HASHEM, our God, King of the universe, Who creates the fruit of the vine.* (Cong. – *Amen.)*

At the departure of the Sabbath the following two blessings are recited.

After the following blessing smell the spices.

בָּרוּךְ *Blessed are You, HASHEM, our God, King of the universe, Who creates species of fragrance.* (Cong. – *Amen.)*

After the following blessing hold fingers up to the flame to see the reflected light:.

בָּרוּךְ *Blessed are You, HASHEM, our God, King of the universe, Who creates the illuminations of the fire.* (Cong.– *Amen.)*

בָּרוּךְ *Blessed are You, HASHEM our God, King of the universe, Who separates between holy and secular, between light and darkness, between Israel and the nations, between the seventh day and the six days of labor. Blessed are You, HASHEM, Who separates between holy and secular.* (Cong. – *Amen.)*

The *chazzan* or someone else present for *Havdalah,* should drink most of the cup.

---

(1) *Deuteronomy* 10:17. (2) 10:18. (3) *Isaiah* 57:15. (4) *Psalms* 68:5. (5) 68:6.
(6) *I Kings* 8:57. (7) *Deuteronomy* 4:4. (8) *Isaiah* 51:3. (9) 42:21.

The congregation stands while reciting עָלֵינוּ.

עָלֵינוּ לְשַׁבֵּחַ לַאֲדוֹן הַכֹּל, לָתֵת גְּדֻלָּה לְיוֹצֵר בְּרֵאשִׁית, שֶׁלֹּא עָשָׂנוּ כְּגוֹיֵי הָאֲרָצוֹת, וְלֹא שָׂמָנוּ כְּמִשְׁפְּחוֹת הָאֲדָמָה. שֶׁלֹּא שָׂם חֶלְקֵנוּ כָּהֶם, וְגוֹרָלֵנוּ כְּכָל הֲמוֹנָם. (שֶׁהֵם מִשְׁתַּחֲוִים לְהֶבֶל וָרִיק, וּמִתְפַּלְלִים אֶל אֵל לֹא יוֹשִׁיעַ.[1]) וַאֲנַחְנוּ כּוֹרְעִים וּמִשְׁתַּחֲוִים וּמוֹדִים, לִפְנֵי מֶלֶךְ מַלְכֵי הַמְּלָכִים הַקָּדוֹשׁ בָּרוּךְ הוּא. שֶׁהוּא נוֹטֶה שָׁמַיִם וְיֹסֵד אָרֶץ,[2] וּמוֹשַׁב יְקָרוֹ בַּשָּׁמַיִם מִמַּעַל, וּשְׁכִינַת עֻזּוֹ בְּגָבְהֵי מְרוֹמִים. הוּא אֱלֹהֵינוּ, אֵין עוֹד. אֱמֶת מַלְכֵּנוּ, אֶפֶס זוּלָתוֹ, כַּכָּתוּב בְּתוֹרָתוֹ: וְיָדַעְתָּ הַיּוֹם וַהֲשֵׁבֹתָ אֶל לְבָבֶךָ, כִּי יהוה הוּא הָאֱלֹהִים בַּשָּׁמַיִם מִמַּעַל וְעַל הָאָרֶץ מִתָּחַת, אֵין עוֹד.[3]

Bow while reciting וַאֲנַחְנוּ כּוֹרְעִים וּמִשְׁתַּחֲוִים.

עַל כֵּן נְקַוֶּה לְּךָ יהוה אֱלֹהֵינוּ לִרְאוֹת מְהֵרָה בְּתִפְאֶרֶת עֻזֶּךָ, לְהַעֲבִיר גִּלּוּלִים מִן הָאָרֶץ, וְהָאֱלִילִים כָּרוֹת יִכָּרֵתוּן, לְתַקֵּן עוֹלָם בְּמַלְכוּת שַׁדַּי. וְכָל בְּנֵי בָשָׂר יִקְרְאוּ בִשְׁמֶךָ, לְהַפְנוֹת אֵלֶיךָ כָּל רִשְׁעֵי אָרֶץ. יַכִּירוּ וְיֵדְעוּ כָּל יוֹשְׁבֵי תֵבֵל, כִּי לְךָ תִּכְרַע כָּל בֶּרֶךְ, תִּשָּׁבַע כָּל לָשׁוֹן.[4] לְפָנֶיךָ יהוה אֱלֹהֵינוּ יִכְרְעוּ וְיִפֹּלוּ, וְלִכְבוֹד שִׁמְךָ יְקָר יִתֵּנוּ. וִיקַבְּלוּ כֻלָּם אֶת עוֹל מַלְכוּתֶךָ, וְתִמְלֹךְ עֲלֵיהֶם מְהֵרָה לְעוֹלָם וָעֶד. כִּי הַמַּלְכוּת שֶׁלְּךָ הִיא וּלְעוֹלְמֵי עַד תִּמְלוֹךְ בְּכָבוֹד, כַּכָּתוּב בְּתוֹרָתֶךָ: יהוה יִמְלֹךְ לְעֹלָם וָעֶד.[5] ❖ וְנֶאֱמַר: וְהָיָה יהוה לְמֶלֶךְ עַל כָּל הָאָרֶץ, בַּיּוֹם הַהוּא יִהְיֶה יהוה אֶחָד וּשְׁמוֹ אֶחָד.[6]

אַל תִּירָא מִפַּחַד פִּתְאֹם, וּמִשֹּׁאַת רְשָׁעִים כִּי תָבֹא.[7] עֻצוּ עֵצָה וְתֻפָר, דַּבְּרוּ דָבָר וְלֹא יָקוּם, כִּי עִמָּנוּ אֵל.[8] וְעַד זִקְנָה אֲנִי הוּא, וְעַד שֵׂיבָה אֲנִי אֶסְבֹּל, אֲנִי עָשִׂיתִי וַאֲנִי אֶשָּׂא, וַאֲנִי אֶסְבֹּל וַאֲמַלֵּט.[9]

קדיש יתום

Mourners recite קַדִּישׁ יָתוֹם.

יִתְגַּדַּל וְיִתְקַדַּשׁ שְׁמֵהּ רַבָּא. (.Cong – אָמֵן.) בְּעָלְמָא דִּי בְרָא כִרְעוּתֵהּ. וְיַמְלִיךְ מַלְכוּתֵהּ, בְּחַיֵּיכוֹן וּבְיוֹמֵיכוֹן וּבְחַיֵּי דְכָל בֵּית יִשְׂרָאֵל, בַּעֲגָלָא וּבִזְמַן קָרִיב. וְאִמְרוּ: אָמֵן.

(.Cong – אָמֵן. יְהֵא שְׁמֵהּ רַבָּא מְבָרַךְ לְעָלַם וּלְעָלְמֵי עָלְמַיָּא.)

יְהֵא שְׁמֵהּ רַבָּא מְבָרַךְ לְעָלַם וּלְעָלְמֵי עָלְמַיָּא.

---

(1) *Isaiah* 45:20. (2) 51:13. (3) *Deuteronomy* 4:39. (4) Cf. *Isaiah* 45:23. (5) *Exodus* 15:18. (6) *Zechariah* 14:9. (7) *Proverbs* 3:25. (8) *Isaiah* 8:10. (9) 46:4.

The congregation stands while reciting עָלֵינוּ, *'It is our duty . . .'*

עָלֵינוּ *It is our duty to praise the Master of all, to ascribe greatness to the Molder of primeval creation, for He has not made us like the nations of the lands, and has not emplaced us like the families of the earth; for He has not assigned our portion like theirs nor our lot like all their multitudes. (For they bow to vanity and emptiness and pray to a god which helps not.*[1]*) But we bend our knees, bow, and acknowledge our thanks before the King Who reigns over kings, the Holy One, Blessed is He. He stretches out heaven and establishes earth's foundation,*[2] *the seat of His homage is in the heavens above and His powerful Presence is in the loftiest heights. He is our God and there is none other. True is our King, there is nothing beside Him, as it is written in His Torah: 'You are to know this day and take to your heart that* HASHEM *is the only God — in heaven above and on the earth below — there is none other.'*[3]

Bow while reciting *'But we bend our knees.'*

עַל כֵּן *Therefore we put our hope in You,* HASHEM, *our God, that we may soon see Your mighty splendor, to remove detestable idolatry from the earth, and false gods will be utterly cut off, to perfect the universe through the Almighty's sovereignty. Then all humanity will call upon Your Name, to turn all the earth's wicked toward You. All the world's inhabitants will recognize and know that to You every knee should bend, every tongue should swear.*[4] *Before You,* HASHEM, *our God, they will bend every knee and cast themselves down and to the glory of Your Name they will render homage, and they will all accept upon themselves the yoke of Your kingship that You may reign over them soon and eternally. For the kingdom is Yours and You will reign for all eternity in glory as it is written in Your Torah:* HASHEM *shall reign for all eternity.*[5] Chazzan– *And it is said:* HASHEM *will be King over all the world — on that day* HASHEM *will be One and His Name will be One.*[6]

אַל תִּירָא *Do not fear sudden terror, or the holocaust of the wicked when it comes.*[7] *Plan a conspiracy and it will be annulled; speak your piece and it shall not stand, for God is with us.*[8] *Even till your seniority, I remain unchanged; and even till your ripe old age, I shall endure. I created you and I shall bear you; I shall endure and rescue.*[9]

MOURNER'S KADDISH

Mourners recite the Mourners' *Kaddish*. See *Laws* §81-83.

[A transliteration of this *Kaddish* appears on page 1147.]

יִתְגַּדַּל *May His great Name grow exalted and sanctified* (Cong.– *Amen.*) *in the world that He created as He willed. May He give reign to His kingship in your lifetimes and in your days, and in the lifetimes of the entire Family of Israel, swiftly and soon. Now respond: Amen.*

(Cong.– *Amen. May His great Name be blessed forever and ever.*)

May His great Name be blessed forever and ever.

יִתְבָּרַךְ וְיִשְׁתַּבַּח וְיִתְפָּאַר וְיִתְרוֹמַם וְיִתְנַשֵּׂא וְיִתְהַדָּר וְיִתְעַלֶּה וְיִתְהַלָּל שְׁמֵהּ דְּקֻדְשָׁא בְּרִיךְ הוּא (Cong. – בְּרִיךְ הוּא) – לְעֵלָּא מִן כָּל בִּרְכָתָא וְשִׁירָתָא תֻּשְׁבְּחָתָא וְנֶחֱמָתָא, דַּאֲמִירָן בְּעָלְמָא. וְאִמְרוּ: אָמֵן. (Cong. – אָמֵן.)

יְהֵא שְׁלָמָא רַבָּא מִן שְׁמַיָּא, וְחַיִּים עָלֵינוּ וְעַל כָּל יִשְׂרָאֵל. וְאִמְרוּ: אָמֵן. (Cong. – אָמֵן.)

Take three steps back. Bow left and say . . . עֹשֶׂה; bow right and say . . . הוּא; bow forward and say וְעַל כָּל . . . אָמֵן. Remain standing in place for a few moments, then take three steps forward.

עֹשֶׂה שָׁלוֹם בִּמְרוֹמָיו, הוּא יַעֲשֶׂה שָׁלוֹם עָלֵינוּ, וְעַל כָּל יִשְׂרָאֵל. וְאִמְרוּ: אָמֵן. (Cong. – אָמֵן.)

Some congregations count the *Omer* (page 1094) at this point.

הבדלה

At the departure of the Sabbath begin here.

הִנֵּה אֵל יְשׁוּעָתִי אֶבְטַח וְלֹא אֶפְחָד, כִּי עָזִּי וְזִמְרָת יָהּ יהוה, וַיְהִי לִי לִישׁוּעָה. וּשְׁאַבְתֶּם מַיִם בְּשָׂשׂוֹן, מִמַּעַיְנֵי הַיְשׁוּעָה.[1] לַיהוה הַיְשׁוּעָה, עַל עַמְּךָ בִרְכָתֶךָ סֶּלָה.[2] יהוה צְבָאוֹת עִמָּנוּ, מִשְׂגָּב לָנוּ אֱלֹהֵי יַעֲקֹב סֶלָה.[3] יהוה צְבָאוֹת, אַשְׁרֵי אָדָם בֹּטֵחַ בָּךְ.[4] יהוה הוֹשִׁיעָה, הַמֶּלֶךְ יַעֲנֵנוּ בְיוֹם קָרְאֵנוּ.[5] לַיְּהוּדִים הָיְתָה אוֹרָה וְשִׂמְחָה, וְשָׂשֹׂן וִיקָר,[6] כֵּן תִּהְיֶה לָּנוּ. כּוֹס יְשׁוּעוֹת אֶשָּׂא, וּבְשֵׁם יהוה אֶקְרָא.[7]

סַבְרִי מָרָנָן וְרַבָּנָן וְרַבּוֹתַי:

בָּרוּךְ אַתָּה יהוה אֱלֹהֵינוּ מֶלֶךְ הָעוֹלָם, בּוֹרֵא פְּרִי הַגָּפֶן. (all present respond– אָמֵן.)

At the departure of the Sabbath the following two blessings are recited.

After the following blessing smell the spices.

בָּרוּךְ אַתָּה יהוה אֱלֹהֵינוּ מֶלֶךְ הָעוֹלָם, בּוֹרֵא מִינֵי בְשָׂמִים. (all present respond– אָמֵן.)

After the following blessing hold fingers up to the flame to see the reflected light.

בָּרוּךְ אַתָּה יהוה אֱלֹהֵינוּ מֶלֶךְ הָעוֹלָם, בּוֹרֵא מְאוֹרֵי הָאֵשׁ. (all present respond– אָמֵן.)

בָּרוּךְ אַתָּה יהוה אֱלֹהֵינוּ מֶלֶךְ הָעוֹלָם, הַמַּבְדִּיל בֵּין קֹדֶשׁ לְחוֹל, בֵּין אוֹר לְחֹשֶׁךְ, בֵּין יִשְׂרָאֵל לָעַמִּים, בֵּין יוֹם הַשְּׁבִיעִי לְשֵׁשֶׁת יְמֵי הַמַּעֲשֶׂה. בָּרוּךְ אַתָּה יהוה, הַמַּבְדִּיל בֵּין קֹדֶשׁ לְחוֹל. (all present respond– אָמֵן.)

The one who recited *Havdalah,* or someone else present for *Havdalah,* should drink most of the wine from the cup.

At the departure of the Sabbath extinguish the flame by pouring leftover wine over it into a dish. It is customary to dip the fingers into the wine-dish and touch the eyelids and inner pockets with them. This symbolizes that the 'light of the *mitzvah*' will guide us and it invokes blessing for the week.

Blessed, praised, glorified, exalted, extolled, mighty, upraised, and lauded be the Name of the Holy One, Blessed is He (Cong.– *Blessed is He*) *— beyond any blessing and song, praise and consolation that are uttered in the world. Now respond: Amen.* (Cong.– *Amen.*)

May there be abundant peace from Heaven, and life, upon us and upon all Israel. Now respond: Amen. (Cong.– *Amen.*)

Take three steps back. Bow left and say, *'He Who makes peace . . .'*; bow right and say, *'may He . . .'*; bow forward and say, *'and upon all Israel . . .'* Remain standing in place for a few moments, then take three steps forward.

He Who makes peace in His heights, may He make peace upon us, and upon all Israel. Now respond: Amen. (Cong.– *Amen.*)

Some congregations count the *Omer* (page 1094) at this point.

HAVDALAH

At the departure of the Sabbath begin here.

הִנֵּה *Behold! God is my salvation, I shall trust and not fear — for God is my might and my praise — HASHEM — and He was a salvation for me. You can draw water with joy, from the springs of salvation.*[1] *Salvation is HASHEM's, upon Your people is Your blessing, Selah.*[2] *HASHEM, Master of legions, is with us, a stronghold for us is the God of Jacob, Selah.*[3] *HASHEM, Master of legions, praised is the man who trusts in You.*[4] *HASHEM save! May the King answer us on the day we call.*[5] *For the Jews there was light, gladness, joy, and honor*[6] *— so may it be for us. I will raise the cup of salvations, and I shall invoke the Name of HASHEM.*[7]

By your leave, my masters and teachers:

בָּרוּךְ *Blessed are You, HASHEM, our God, King of the universe, Who creates the fruit of the vine.* (All present respond– *Amen.*)

At the departure of the Sabbath the following two blessings are recited. After the following blessing smell the spices.

בָּרוּךְ *Blessed are You, HASHEM, our God, King of the universe, Who creates species of fragrance.* (All present respond– *Amen.*)

After the following blessing hold fingers up to the flame to see the reflected light.

בָּרוּךְ *Blessed are You, HASHEM, our God, King of the universe, Who creates the illuminations of the fire.* (All present respond– *Amen.*)

בָּרוּךְ *Blessed are You, HASHEM our God, King of the universe, Who separates between holy and secular, between light and darkness, between Israel and the nations, between the seventh day and the six days of labor. Blessed are You, HASHEM, Who separates between holy and secular.* (All present respond– *Amen.*)

The one who recited *Havdalah,* or someone else present for *Havdalah,* should drink most of the wine from the cup.

At the departure of the Sabbath extinguish the flame by pouring leftover wine over it into a dish. It is customary to dip the fingers into the wine-dish and touch the eyelids and inner pockets with them. This symbolizes that the 'light of the *mitzvah*' will guide us and it invokes blessing for the week.

---

(1) *Isaiah* 12:2-3. (2) *Psalms* 3:9. (3) 46:12. (4) 84:13. (5) 20:10. (6) *Esther* 8:16. (7) *Psalms* 116:13.

Appendices

- פיוטים נוספים

  Additional Piyutim

- הלכות

  Selected Laws

- פסוקים לשמות אנשים

  Verses for People's Names

- קדיש באותיות אנגלית

  Kaddish Transliterated

Some recite the following ten Scriptural passages as part of the recital of the *pesach* offering (page 32).

שמות יב:כא-כח / *Exodus* 12:21-28

וַיִּקְרָא מֹשֶׁה לְכָל זִקְנֵי יִשְׂרָאֵל וַיֹּאמֶר אֲלֵיהֶם מִשְׁכוּ וּקְחוּ לָכֶם צֹאן לְמִשְׁפְּחֹתֵיכֶם וְשַׁחֲטוּ הַפָּסַח. וּלְקַחְתֶּם אֲגֻדַּת אֵזוֹב וּטְבַלְתֶּם בַּדָּם אֲשֶׁר בַּסַּף וְהִגַּעְתֶּם אֶל הַמַּשְׁקוֹף וְאֶל שְׁתֵּי הַמְּזוּזֹת מִן הַדָּם אֲשֶׁר בַּסָּף וְאַתֶּם לֹא תֵצְאוּ אִישׁ מִפֶּתַח בֵּיתוֹ עַד בֹּקֶר. וְעָבַר יהוה לִנְגֹּף אֶת מִצְרַיִם וְרָאָה אֶת הַדָּם עַל הַמַּשְׁקוֹף וְעַל שְׁתֵּי הַמְּזוּזֹת וּפָסַח יהוה עַל הַפֶּתַח וְלֹא יִתֵּן הַמַּשְׁחִית לָבֹא אֶל בָּתֵּיכֶם לִנְגֹּף. וּשְׁמַרְתֶּם אֶת הַדָּבָר הַזֶּה לְחָק לְךָ וּלְבָנֶיךָ עַד עוֹלָם. וְהָיָה כִּי תָבֹאוּ אֶל הָאָרֶץ אֲשֶׁר יִתֵּן יהוה לָכֶם כַּאֲשֶׁר דִּבֵּר וּשְׁמַרְתֶּם אֶת הָעֲבֹדָה הַזֹּאת. וְהָיָה כִּי יֹאמְרוּ אֲלֵיכֶם בְּנֵיכֶם מָה הָעֲבֹדָה הַזֹּאת לָכֶם. וַאֲמַרְתֶּם זֶבַח פֶּסַח הוּא לַיהוה אֲשֶׁר פָּסַח עַל בָּתֵּי בְנֵי יִשְׂרָאֵל בְּמִצְרַיִם בְּנָגְפּוֹ אֶת מִצְרַיִם וְאֶת בָּתֵּינוּ הִצִּיל וַיִּקֹּד הָעָם וַיִּשְׁתַּחֲווּ. וַיֵּלְכוּ וַיַּעֲשׂוּ בְּנֵי יִשְׂרָאֵל כַּאֲשֶׁר צִוָּה יהוה אֶת מֹשֶׁה וְאַהֲרֹן כֵּן עָשׂוּ.

שמות יב:מג-נ / *Exodus* 12:43-50

וַיֹּאמֶר יהוה אֶל מֹשֶׁה וְאַהֲרֹן זֹאת חֻקַּת הַפָּסַח כָּל בֶּן נֵכָר לֹא יֹאכַל בּוֹ. וְכָל עֶבֶד אִישׁ מִקְנַת כָּסֶף וּמַלְתָּה אֹתוֹ אָז יֹאכַל בּוֹ. תּוֹשָׁב וְשָׂכִיר לֹא יֹאכַל בּוֹ. בְּבַיִת אֶחָד יֵאָכֵל לֹא תוֹצִיא מִן הַבַּיִת מִן הַבָּשָׂר חוּצָה וְעֶצֶם לֹא תִשְׁבְּרוּ בוֹ. כָּל עֲדַת יִשְׂרָאֵל יַעֲשׂוּ אֹתוֹ. וְכִי יָגוּר אִתְּךָ גֵּר וְעָשָׂה פֶסַח לַיהוה הִמּוֹל לוֹ כָל זָכָר וְאָז יִקְרַב לַעֲשֹׂתוֹ וְהָיָה כְּאֶזְרַח הָאָרֶץ וְכָל עָרֵל לֹא יֹאכַל בּוֹ. תּוֹרָה אַחַת יִהְיֶה לָאֶזְרָח וְלַגֵּר הַגָּר בְּתוֹכְכֶם. וַיַּעֲשׂוּ כָּל בְּנֵי יִשְׂרָאֵל כַּאֲשֶׁר צִוָּה יהוה אֶת מֹשֶׁה וְאֶת אַהֲרֹן כֵּן עָשׂוּ.

ויקרא כג:ד-ה / *Leviticus* 23:4-5

אֵלֶּה מוֹעֲדֵי יהוה מִקְרָאֵי קֹדֶשׁ אֲשֶׁר תִּקְרְאוּ אֹתָם בְּמוֹעֲדָם. בַּחֹדֶשׁ הָרִאשׁוֹן בְּאַרְבָּעָה עָשָׂר לַחֹדֶשׁ בֵּין הָעַרְבָּיִם פֶּסַח לַיהוה.

במדבר ט:א-יד / *Numbers* 9:1-14

וַיְדַבֵּר יהוה אֶל מֹשֶׁה בְמִדְבַּר סִינַי בַּשָּׁנָה הַשֵּׁנִית לְצֵאתָם מֵאֶרֶץ מִצְרַיִם בַּחֹדֶשׁ הָרִאשׁוֹן לֵאמֹר. וְיַעֲשׂוּ בְנֵי יִשְׂרָאֵל אֶת הַפָּסַח בְּמוֹעֲדוֹ. בְּאַרְבָּעָה עָשָׂר יוֹם בַּחֹדֶשׁ הַזֶּה בֵּין הָעַרְבַּיִם תַּעֲשׂוּ אֹתוֹ בְּמֹעֲדוֹ כְּכָל חֻקֹּתָיו וּכְכָל מִשְׁפָּטָיו תַּעֲשׂוּ אֹתוֹ. וַיְדַבֵּר מֹשֶׁה אֶל בְּנֵי יִשְׂרָאֵל לַעֲשֹׂת הַפָּסַח. וַיַּעֲשׂוּ אֶת הַפֶּסַח בָּרִאשׁוֹן בְּאַרְבָּעָה עָשָׂר יוֹם לַחֹדֶשׁ בֵּין הָעַרְבַּיִם בְּמִדְבַּר סִינָי כְּכֹל אֲשֶׁר צִוָּה יהוה אֶת מֹשֶׁה כֵּן עָשׂוּ בְּנֵי יִשְׂרָאֵל. וַיְהִי אֲנָשִׁים אֲשֶׁר הָיוּ טְמֵאִים לְנֶפֶשׁ אָדָם וְלֹא יָכְלוּ לַעֲשֹׂת הַפֶּסַח בַּיּוֹם הַהוּא וַיִּקְרְבוּ לִפְנֵי מֹשֶׁה וְלִפְנֵי אַהֲרֹן בַּיּוֹם הַהוּא. וַיֹּאמְרוּ הָאֲנָשִׁים הָהֵמָּה אֵלָיו אֲנַחְנוּ טְמֵאִים לְנֶפֶשׁ אָדָם לָמָּה נִגָּרַע לְבִלְתִּי הַקְרִיב אֶת קָרְבַּן יהוה בְּמֹעֲדוֹ בְּתוֹךְ בְּנֵי יִשְׂרָאֵל. וַיֹּאמֶר אֲלֵהֶם מֹשֶׁה

עִמְדוּ וְאֶשְׁמְעָה מַה יְצַוֶּה יהוה לָכֶם. וַיְדַבֵּר יהוה אֶל מֹשֶׁה לֵּאמֹר. דַּבֵּר אֶל בְּנֵי יִשְׂרָאֵל לֵאמֹר אִישׁ אִישׁ כִּי יִהְיֶה טָמֵא לָנֶפֶשׁ אוֹ בְדֶרֶךְ רְחֹקָה לָכֶם אוֹ לְדֹרֹתֵיכֶם וְעָשָׂה פֶסַח לַיהוה. בַּחֹדֶשׁ הַשֵּׁנִי בְּאַרְבָּעָה עָשָׂר יוֹם בֵּין הָעַרְבַּיִם יַעֲשׂוּ אֹתוֹ עַל מַצּוֹת וּמְרֹרִים יֹאכְלֻהוּ. לֹא יַשְׁאִירוּ מִמֶּנּוּ עַד בֹּקֶר וְעֶצֶם לֹא יִשְׁבְּרוּ בוֹ כְּכָל חֻקַּת הַפֶּסַח יַעֲשׂוּ אֹתוֹ: וְהָאִישׁ אֲשֶׁר הוּא טָהוֹר וּבְדֶרֶךְ לֹא הָיָה וְחָדַל לַעֲשׂוֹת הַפֶּסַח וְנִכְרְתָה הַנֶּפֶשׁ הַהִוא מֵעַמֶּיהָ כִּי קָרְבַּן יהוה לֹא הִקְרִיב בְּמֹעֲדוֹ חֶטְאוֹ יִשָּׂא הָאִישׁ הַהוּא. וְכִי יָגוּר אִתְּכֶם גֵּר וְעָשָׂה פֶסַח לַיהוה כְּחֻקַּת הַפֶּסַח וּכְמִשְׁפָּטוֹ כֵּן יַעֲשֶׂה חֻקָּה אַחַת יִהְיֶה לָכֶם וְלַגֵּר וּלְאֶזְרַח הָאָרֶץ.

Numbers 28:16 / במדבר כח:טז

וּבַחֹדֶשׁ הָרִאשׁוֹן בְּאַרְבָּעָה עָשָׂר יוֹם לַחֹדֶשׁ פֶּסַח לַיהוה.

Deuteronomy 16:1-8 / דברים טז:א-ח

שָׁמוֹר אֶת חֹדֶשׁ הָאָבִיב וְעָשִׂיתָ פֶּסַח לַיהוה אֱלֹהֶיךָ כִּי בְּחֹדֶשׁ הָאָבִיב הוֹצִיאֲךָ יהוה אֱלֹהֶיךָ מִמִּצְרַיִם לָיְלָה. וְזָבַחְתָּ פֶּסַח לַיהוה אֱלֹהֶיךָ צֹאן וּבָקָר בַּמָּקוֹם אֲשֶׁר יִבְחַר יהוה לְשַׁכֵּן שְׁמוֹ שָׁם. לֹא תֹאכַל עָלָיו חָמֵץ שִׁבְעַת יָמִים תֹּאכַל עָלָיו מַצּוֹת לֶחֶם עֹנִי כִּי בְחִפָּזוֹן יָצָאתָ מֵאֶרֶץ מִצְרַיִם לְמַעַן תִּזְכֹּר אֶת יוֹם צֵאתְךָ מֵאֶרֶץ מִצְרַיִם כֹּל יְמֵי חַיֶּיךָ. וְלֹא יֵרָאֶה לְךָ שְׂאֹר בְּכָל גְּבֻלְךָ שִׁבְעַת יָמִים וְלֹא יָלִין מִן הַבָּשָׂר אֲשֶׁר תִּזְבַּח בָּעֶרֶב בַּיּוֹם הָרִאשׁוֹן לַבֹּקֶר. לֹא תוּכַל לִזְבֹּחַ אֶת הַפָּסַח בְּאַחַד שְׁעָרֶיךָ אֲשֶׁר יהוה אֱלֹהֶיךָ נֹתֵן לָךְ. כִּי אִם אֶל הַמָּקוֹם אֲשֶׁר יִבְחַר יהוה אֱלֹהֶיךָ לְשַׁכֵּן שְׁמוֹ שָׁם תִּזְבַּח אֶת הַפֶּסַח בָּעָרֶב כְּבוֹא הַשֶּׁמֶשׁ מוֹעֵד צֵאתְךָ מִמִּצְרָיִם. וּבִשַּׁלְתָּ וְאָכַלְתָּ בַּמָּקוֹם אֲשֶׁר יִבְחַר יהוה אֱלֹהֶיךָ בּוֹ וּפָנִיתָ בַבֹּקֶר וְהָלַכְתָּ לְאֹהָלֶיךָ. שֵׁשֶׁת יָמִים תֹּאכַל מַצּוֹת וּבַיּוֹם הַשְּׁבִיעִי עֲצֶרֶת לַיהוה אֱלֹהֶיךָ לֹא תַעֲשֶׂה מְלָאכָה.

Joshua 5:10-11 / יהושע ה:י-יא

וַיַּחֲנוּ בְנֵי יִשְׂרָאֵל בַּגִּלְגָּל וַיַּעֲשׂוּ אֶת הַפֶּסַח בְּאַרְבָּעָה עָשָׂר יוֹם לַחֹדֶשׁ בָּעֶרֶב בְּעַרְבוֹת יְרִיחוֹ. וַיֹּאכְלוּ מֵעֲבוּר הָאָרֶץ מִמָּחֳרַת הַפֶּסַח מַצּוֹת וְקָלוּי בְּעֶצֶם הַיּוֹם הַזֶּה.

II Kings 23:21, 22 / מלכים ב כג:כא-כב

וַיְצַו הַמֶּלֶךְ אֶת כָּל הָעָם לֵאמֹר עֲשׂוּ פֶסַח לַיהוה אֱלֹהֵיכֶם כַּכָּתוּב עַל סֵפֶר הַבְּרִית הַזֶּה. כִּי לֹא נַעֲשָׂה כַּפֶּסַח הַזֶּה מִימֵי הַשֹּׁפְטִים אֲשֶׁר שָׁפְטוּ אֶת יִשְׂרָאֵל וְכֹל יְמֵי מַלְכֵי יִשְׂרָאֵל וּמַלְכֵי יְהוּדָה: כִּי אִם בִּשְׁמֹנֶה עֶשְׂרֵה שָׁנָה לַמֶּלֶךְ יֹאשִׁיָּהוּ נַעֲשָׂה הַפֶּסַח הַזֶּה לַיהוה בִּירוּשָׁלָם:

II Chronicles 30:1-20 / דברי הימים ב ל:א-כ

וַיִּשְׁלַח יְחִזְקִיָּהוּ עַל כָּל יִשְׂרָאֵל וִיהוּדָה וְגַם אִגְּרוֹת כָּתַב עַל אֶפְרַיִם וּמְנַשֶּׁה לָבוֹא לְבֵית יהוה בִּירוּשָׁלָם לַעֲשׂוֹת פֶּסַח לַיהוה אֱלֹהֵי יִשְׂרָאֵל. וַיִּוָּעַץ הַמֶּלֶךְ וְשָׂרָיו וְכָל הַקָּהָל בִּירוּשָׁלָם לַעֲשׂוֹת הַפֶּסַח

בַּחֹדֶשׁ הַשֵּׁנִי. כִּי לֹא יָכְלוּ לַעֲשֹׂתוֹ בָּעֵת הַהִיא כִּי הַכֹּהֲנִים לֹא הִתְקַדְּשׁוּ לְמַדַּי וְהָעָם לֹא נֶאֶסְפוּ לִירוּשָׁלִָם. וַיִּישַׁר הַדָּבָר בְּעֵינֵי הַמֶּלֶךְ וּבְעֵינֵי כָּל הַקָּהָל: וַיַּעֲמִידוּ דָבָר לְהַעֲבִיר קוֹל בְּכָל יִשְׂרָאֵל מִבְּאֵר שֶׁבַע וְעַד דָּן לָבוֹא לַעֲשׂוֹת פֶּסַח לַיהוה אֱלֹהֵי יִשְׂרָאֵל בִּירוּשָׁלִָם כִּי לֹא לָרֹב עָשׂוּ כַּכָּתוּב: וַיֵּלְכוּ הָרָצִים בָּאִגְּרוֹת מִיַּד הַמֶּלֶךְ וְשָׂרָיו בְּכָל יִשְׂרָאֵל וִיהוּדָה וּכְמִצְוַת הַמֶּלֶךְ לֵאמֹר בְּנֵי יִשְׂרָאֵל שׁוּבוּ אֶל יהוה אֱלֹהֵי אַבְרָהָם יִצְחָק וְיִשְׂרָאֵל וְיָשֹׁב אֶל הַפְּלֵיטָה הַנִּשְׁאֶרֶת לָכֶם מִכַּף מַלְכֵי אַשּׁוּר. וְאַל תִּהְיוּ כַּאֲבוֹתֵיכֶם וְכַאֲחֵיכֶם אֲשֶׁר מָעֲלוּ בַּיהוה אֱלֹהֵי אֲבוֹתֵיהֶם וַיִּתְּנֵם לְשַׁמָּה כַּאֲשֶׁר אַתֶּם רֹאִים: עַתָּה אַל תַּקְשׁוּ עָרְפְּכֶם כַּאֲבוֹתֵיכֶם תְּנוּ יָד לַיהוה וּבֹאוּ לְמִקְדָּשׁוֹ אֲשֶׁר הִקְדִּישׁ לְעוֹלָם וְעִבְדוּ אֶת יהוה אֱלֹהֵיכֶם וְיָשֹׁב מִכֶּם חֲרוֹן אַפּוֹ: כִּי בְשׁוּבְכֶם עַל יהוה אֲחֵיכֶם וּבְנֵיכֶם לְרַחֲמִים לִפְנֵי שׁוֹבֵיהֶם וְלָשׁוּב לָאָרֶץ הַזֹּאת כִּי חַנּוּן וְרַחוּם יהוה אֱלֹהֵיכֶם וְלֹא יָסִיר פָּנִים מִכֶּם אִם תָּשׁוּבוּ אֵלָיו: וַיִּהְיוּ הָרָצִים עֹבְרִים מֵעִיר לָעִיר בְּאֶרֶץ אֶפְרַיִם וּמְנַשֶּׁה וְעַד זְבֻלוּן וַיִּהְיוּ מַשְׂחִיקִים עֲלֵיהֶם וּמַלְעִגִים בָּם. אַךְ אֲנָשִׁים מֵאָשֵׁר וּמְנַשֶּׁה וּמִזְּבֻלוּן נִכְנְעוּ וַיָּבֹאוּ לִירוּשָׁלִָם. גַּם בִּיהוּדָה הָיְתָה יַד הָאֱלֹהִים לָתֵת לָהֶם לֵב אֶחָד לַעֲשׂוֹת מִצְוַת הַמֶּלֶךְ וְהַשָּׂרִים בִּדְבַר יהוה. וַיֵּאָסְפוּ יְרוּשָׁלִַם עַם רָב לַעֲשׂוֹת אֶת חַג הַמַּצּוֹת בַּחֹדֶשׁ הַשֵּׁנִי קָהָל לָרֹב מְאֹד. וַיָּקֻמוּ וַיָּסִירוּ אֶת הַמִּזְבְּחוֹת אֲשֶׁר בִּירוּשָׁלִָם וְאֵת כָּל הַמְקַטְּרוֹת הֵסִירוּ וַיַּשְׁלִיכוּ לְנַחַל קִדְרוֹן. וַיִּשְׁחֲטוּ הַפֶּסַח בְּאַרְבָּעָה עָשָׂר לַחֹדֶשׁ הַשֵּׁנִי וְהַכֹּהֲנִים וְהַלְוִיִּם נִכְלְמוּ וַיִּתְקַדְּשׁוּ וַיָּבִיאוּ עֹלוֹת בֵּית יהוה: וַיַּעַמְדוּ עַל עָמְדָם כְּמִשְׁפָּטָם כְּתוֹרַת מֹשֶׁה אִישׁ הָאֱלֹהִים הַכֹּהֲנִים זֹרְקִים אֶת הַדָּם מִיַּד הַלְוִיִּם. כִּי רַבַּת בַּקָּהָל אֲשֶׁר לֹא הִתְקַדָּשׁוּ וְהַלְוִיִּם עַל שְׁחִיטַת הַפְּסָחִים לְכֹל לֹא טָהוֹר לְהַקְדִּישׁ לַיהוה. כִּי מַרְבִּית הָעָם רַבַּת מֵאֶפְרַיִם וּמְנַשֶּׁה יִשָּׂשכָר וּזְבֻלוּן לֹא הִטֶּהָרוּ כִּי אָכְלוּ אֶת הַפֶּסַח בְּלֹא כַכָּתוּב כִּי הִתְפַּלֵּל יְחִזְקִיָּהוּ עֲלֵיהֶם לֵאמֹר יהוה הַטּוֹב יְכַפֵּר בְּעַד. כָּל לְבָבוֹ הֵכִין לִדְרוֹשׁ הָאֱלֹהִים יהוה אֱלֹהֵי אֲבוֹתָיו וְלֹא כְּטָהֳרַת הַקֹּדֶשׁ. וַיִּשְׁמַע יהוה אֶל יְחִזְקִיָּהוּ וַיִּרְפָּא אֶת הָעָם.

II Chronicles 35:1-19 / דברי הימים ב לה:א-יט

וַיַּעַשׂ יֹאשִׁיָּהוּ בִירוּשָׁלִַם פֶּסַח לַיהוה וַיִּשְׁחֲטוּ הַפֶּסַח בְּאַרְבָּעָה עָשָׂר לַחֹדֶשׁ הָרִאשׁוֹן: וַיַּעֲמֵד הַכֹּהֲנִים עַל מִשְׁמְרוֹתָם וַיְחַזְּקֵם לַעֲבוֹדַת בֵּית יהוה: וַיֹּאמֶר לַלְוִיִּם הַמְּבִינִים לְכָל יִשְׂרָאֵל הַקְּדוֹשִׁים לַיהוה תְּנוּ אֶת אֲרוֹן הַקֹּדֶשׁ בַּבַּיִת אֲשֶׁר בָּנָה שְׁלֹמֹה בֶן דָּוִיד מֶלֶךְ יִשְׂרָאֵל אֵין לָכֶם מַשָּׂא בַּכָּתֵף עַתָּה עִבְדוּ אֶת יהוה אֱלֹהֵיכֶם וְאֵת עַמּוֹ יִשְׂרָאֵל. וְהָכִינוּ לְבֵית אֲבוֹתֵיכֶם כְּמַחְלְקוֹתֵיכֶם בִּכְתָב דָּוִיד מֶלֶךְ יִשְׂרָאֵל וּבְמִכְתַּב שְׁלֹמֹה בְנוֹ. וְעִמְדוּ בַקֹּדֶשׁ לִפְלֻגּוֹת בֵּית הָאָבוֹת לַאֲחֵיכֶם בְּנֵי הָעָם וַחֲלֻקַּת בֵּית אָב לַלְוִיִּם. וְשַׁחֲטוּ הַפָּסַח וְהִתְקַדְּשׁוּ וְהָכִינוּ לַאֲחֵיכֶם לַעֲשׂוֹת כִּדְבַר יהוה בְּיַד מֹשֶׁה. וַיָּרֶם יֹאשִׁיָּהוּ לִבְנֵי הָעָם צֹאן כְּבָשִׂים

וּבְנֵי עִזִּים הַכֹּל לַפְּסָחִים לְכָל הַנִּמְצָא לְמִסְפַּר שְׁלֹשִׁים אֶלֶף וּבָקָר שְׁלֹשֶׁת אֲלָפִים אֵלֶּה מֵרְכוּשׁ הַמֶּלֶךְ. וְשָׂרָיו לִנְדָבָה לָעָם לַכֹּהֲנִים וְלַלְוִיִּם הֵרִימוּ חִלְקִיָּה וּזְכַרְיָהוּ וִיחִיאֵל נְגִידֵי בֵּית הָאֱלֹהִים לַכֹּהֲנִים נָתְנוּ לַפְּסָחִים אַלְפַּיִם וְשֵׁשׁ מֵאוֹת וּבָקָר שְׁלֹשׁ מֵאוֹת. וְכָנַנְיָהוּ וּשְׁמַעְיָהוּ וּנְתַנְאֵל אֶחָיו וַחֲשַׁבְיָהוּ וִיעִיאֵל וְיוֹזָבָד שָׂרֵי הַלְוִיִּם הֵרִימוּ לַלְוִיִּם לַפְּסָחִים חֲמֵשֶׁת אֲלָפִים וּבָקָר חֲמֵשׁ מֵאוֹת. וַתִּכּוֹן הָעֲבוֹדָה וַיַּעַמְדוּ הַכֹּהֲנִים עַל עָמְדָם וְהַלְוִיִּם עַל מַחְלְקוֹתָם כְּמִצְוַת הַמֶּלֶךְ. וַיִּשְׁחֲטוּ הַפָּסַח וַיִּזְרְקוּ הַכֹּהֲנִים מִיָּדָם וְהַלְוִיִּם מַפְשִׁיטִים. וַיָּסִירוּ הָעֹלָה לְתִתָּם לְמִפְלַגּוֹת לְבֵית אָבוֹת לִבְנֵי הָעָם לְהַקְרִיב לַיהוה כַּכָּתוּב בְּסֵפֶר מֹשֶׁה וְכֵן לַבָּקָר. וַיְבַשְּׁלוּ הַפֶּסַח בָּאֵשׁ כַּמִּשְׁפָּט וְהַקֳּדָשִׁים בִּשְּׁלוּ בַּסִּירוֹת וּבַדְּוָדִים וּבַצֵּלָחוֹת וַיָּרִיצוּ לְכָל בְּנֵי הָעָם. וְאַחַר הֵכִינוּ לָהֶם וְלַכֹּהֲנִים כִּי הַכֹּהֲנִים בְּנֵי אַהֲרֹן בְּהַעֲלוֹת הָעוֹלָה וְהַחֲלָבִים עַד לָיְלָה וְהַלְוִיִּם הֵכִינוּ לָהֶם וְלַכֹּהֲנִים בְּנֵי אַהֲרֹן. וְהַמְשֹׁרְרִים בְּנֵי אָסָף עַל מַעֲמָדָם כְּמִצְוַת דָּוִיד וְאָסָף וְהֵימָן וִידֻתוּן חוֹזֵה הַמֶּלֶךְ וְהַשֹּׁעֲרִים לְשַׁעַר וָשָׁעַר אֵין לָהֶם לָסוּר מֵעַל עֲבֹדָתָם כִּי אֲחֵיהֶם הַלְוִיִּם הֵכִינוּ לָהֶם. וַתִּכּוֹן כָּל עֲבוֹדַת יהוה בַּיּוֹם הַהוּא לַעֲשׂוֹת הַפֶּסַח וְהַעֲלוֹת עֹלוֹת עַל מִזְבַּח יהוה כְּמִצְוַת הַמֶּלֶךְ יֹאשִׁיָּהוּ. וַיַּעֲשׂוּ בְנֵי יִשְׂרָאֵל הַנִּמְצְאִים אֶת הַפֶּסַח בָּעֵת הַהִיא וְאֶת חַג הַמַּצּוֹת שִׁבְעַת יָמִים. וְלֹא נַעֲשָׂה פֶסַח כָּמֹהוּ בְּיִשְׂרָאֵל מִימֵי שְׁמוּאֵל הַנָּבִיא וְכָל מַלְכֵי יִשְׂרָאֵל לֹא עָשׂוּ כַּפֶּסַח אֲשֶׁר עָשָׂה יֹאשִׁיָּהוּ וְהַכֹּהֲנִים וְהַלְוִיִּם וְכָל יְהוּדָה וְיִשְׂרָאֵל הַנִּמְצָא וְיוֹשְׁבֵי יְרוּשָׁלָיִם. בִּשְׁמוֹנֶה עֶשְׂרֵה שָׁנָה לְמַלְכוּת יֹאשִׁיָּהוּ נַעֲשָׂה הַפֶּסַח הַזֶּה.

The recital of the *pesach* offering continues כָּךְ הָיְתָה, page 34.

ליל ראשון

Some congregations recite this alphabetically arranged *piyut* during *Maariv* of the first night (page 62). The last stanza indicates that it was composed by מֵאִיר בַּר יִצְחָק, *Meir bar Yitzchak.*

אֶזְכְּרָה שְׁנוֹת עוֹלָמִים יָמִים מִקֶּדֶם, בַּנְּעָלִים יָפְיָפִית בַּת נָדִיב הַקֹּדֶם,
גְּבוּל גָּבְהָהּ תְּחוּם צָעִיר רֹדֵם, דְּגְמַת מְלָכִים בֵּית אֱלֹהִים אֲדַדֵּם,
הֵרָאוֹת בָּעֲזָרָה בְּקָרְבָּן פָּנִים לְקַדֵּם, וּבִדְמֵי פִסְחֵי מִזְבֵּחַ הַקֹּדֶשׁ לְאַדֵּם.
זֶבַח הַמְיֻחָד לַשֵּׁם בֹּקֶר וָעֶרֶב, חֹק הֲלִיכָתוֹ כָּל הַשָּׁנָה קָרֵב,
טָעוּן הַקְדָּמָה עֶרֶב פְּסָחִים לְהִתְקָרֵב,
 יְרוּשָׁלַיִם הַבְּנוּיָה צֶדֶק יָלִין בָּהּ בְּקֶרֶב,
כְּאֵין אַחֲרֶיהָ הַתֵּר וְהַמִּקְדָּשׁ חָרֵב, לַעֲבוֹד בַּפֶּה נִכְסַפְתִּי לְרֵיחַ עָרֵב.
מִדְבָּר נָוֶה מְשׂוֹשׂ כָּל הָאָרֶץ וְעַלּוּסֶיהָ,
 נִשְׁחַט בָּהּ הַפֶּסַח בִּשְׁלוֹשׁ אוֹכְלוּסֶיהָ,
סוֹדֶרֶת עֲנִיַּת הַלֵּל לְוִיָּה בְּקִלּוּסֶיהָ, פִּרְחֵי אַהֲרֹן עוֹמְדִים בְּשׁוּרוֹת פְּלוּסֶיהָ,
צִדֵּי הַיְסוֹד זְרוֹק דְּמֵי מְקוּלָסֶיהָ, קַטֵּר אֵמוּרִין עַל מִזְבַּח מְלוּסֶיהָ.
רֵעִים לִמְנוּיָו בַּלַּיְלָה נֶאֱכָל צָלִיל, שִׁשִּׁים מִצְוֹת טָעוּן וְרִבּוּעַ הַכְלִיל,
תּוֹף וְחָלִיל יִשְׂאוּ יְהוּדָה וְגָלִיל, מֵקִים דְּבַר עַבְדּוֹ וַעֲצָתוֹ בַּעֲלִיל,

אוֹמֵר לִירוּשָׁלַיִם תּוּשַׁב וְחָרְבוֹתֶיהָ אַתְלִיל,
בְּרִבְיוֹן יְוֹפִי צִיּוֹן חֵיק תַּכְלִיל,
חֵלָה וְאַרְמְנוֹתֶיהָ בְּסֻכַּת שָׁלֵם תַּטְלִיל,
אָז תַּחְפֹּץ זִבְחֵי צֶדֶק עוֹלָה וְכָלִיל.

The service continues בָּרוּךְ אַתָּה, page 66.

תפלת טל

Some congregations recite the following *piyutim* during the prayer for dew (p. 416) on the first day.

אֶרֶשֶׁה אֱרוֹשׁ רַחֲשׁוֹן, בְּאֶרֶשׁ נִיב וְלָשׁוֹן,
אַתְחִין בְּחִין לַחֲשׁוֹן, דִּבְּבֵי מִלַּעֲשׁוֹן.
בְּעַד נְצוּרֵי כְּאִישׁוֹן, אֶפְגְּעָה בְּלִי לִישׁוֹן,
בַּקָּשָׁה כְּשַׁי נַחְשׁוֹן, אֵרָצֶה בָּרִאשׁוֹן.
גְּרֹנִי בַּל יְנֻטַּל, מִקְּרוֹא לְרָם וְנִטָּל, גֵּוִי בַּל יְבֻטַּל, מֵהַזְכִּיר גְּבוּרוֹת טָל.
דֵּעִי בַּל יוּטַל, רְשׁוּת מִלְטַל, דּוֹדִי יִתְנַטַּל, בְּשִׂיחַ, תְּפִלַּת טָל.
הֲמוֹן לוֹ נִכְסָף, לַעֲדַת אֵל אֶאֱסַף, הוּא אִתָּם יִתְאַסַּף, וּלְמַעֲשָׂיו יִכְסֹף.
וְאֶתְיַצְּבָה בַּסַּף, לְחַלּוֹת פְּנֵי יָסַף, וְאִמְרַת טַל אֶחֱסַף, לְחַבְּרֶנָּה בְּמוּסָף.
זֶבֶד מַשְׂאַת בָּר, וְאָבִיב נְשִׁיקוֹת בָּר, זַעַק פִּי יֻגְבַּר, וְשִׂיחַ לְשׁוֹנִי יְכֻבַּר.
חֵן וָחֶסֶד יְחֻבַּר, לְחַנְּנִי עַל דָּבָר, חַשְׁרַת מַיִם יַעֲבָר, כִּי הִנֵּה הַסְּתָו עָבָר.
טַעַם רִנּוּן, וְשַׁאַג שִׁנּוּן, טַלְתִּי בְּתַחֲנוּן, אֶת פְּנֵי חַנּוּן.
יְשִׁישַׁי לַחֲנוּן, בְּזֵכֶר יֵין לְבָנוֹן, יְדוּעַי לִגְנוֹן, בְּפָסוֹחַ וְגָנוֹן.
כִּשָׁרִים וְכַחוֹלְלִים אֲהַלֵּל כְּבַחֲלִילִים, כְּמִפִּי עוֹלְלִים, אֲשׁוֹרֵר הִלּוּלִים.
לְשָׂא דֵּעַ פְּלִילִים, צַגְתִּי בְּמַסְלוּלִים,
לְהִזָּכֵר בִּפְלוּלִים, שֶׁוַע גְּבוּרוֹת טְלָלִים.
מִטַּעַם זְקֵנִים, אֶתְבּוֹנֵן עַד זְקֵנִים, מוֹרִים תִּקּוּנִים, כַּדָּת מְתֻקָּנִים.
נֹפֶת נְבוֹנִים, בִּינַת עַם מְבִינִים,
נְטִיעַת דַּרְבָנִים, תְּוֹכְוֹנִי בֵּין שְׁנֵי לֻחוֹת אֲבָנִים.
שְׂפָתַי בְּשֶׁוַע אֶפְתַּח, כְּאוּלָם הַמְּפֻתָּח,
שִׂיחוֹת פִּי אֶפְתַּח, כְּאִיתוֹן אֲשֶׁר נִפְתָּח.
עֹז וְכֹחַ לִי יִמְתַּח, כַּדֹּק אֲשֶׁר מָתַח, עַב טַל יְפַתַּח, וְחֹרֶב בַּל יֻרְתָּח.
פְּנֵי רָם וְנִשָּׂא, עַיִן בְּחִין אֶשָּׂא, פְּאֵרוֹ לְנוֹסְסָה, כְּמוֹ בְּטַל נֻסָּה.
צְבָאָיו לוֹ אֲגַיְּסָה, וְאִתָּם אֶתְגַּיְּסָה,
צְעוֹק בַּעֲדָם אֶתְנַגְּשָׁה, וְלֹא בְרוּחַ גַּסָּה.
קַמְתִּי מִמִּשְׁפְּתַיִם, לְהַפְגִּיעַ בְּעַד לָנֵי שְׁפַתַּיִם,
קוֹל מָה אֶתֵּן בְּשִׁפְתּוֹתַיִם, הֵן אֲנִי עֲרַל שְׂפָתָיִם.
רוֹן בְּלִי עֲצַלְתַּיִם, עָרַכְתִּי בְּמַחֲנוֹתַיִם,
רָחַשְׁתִּי גִּישׁוֹת שְׁתַּיִם, בְּעַד שְׁאֵלוֹת שְׁתָּיִם.
שַׁחֲרִית חִנּוֹתִי לַמָּטָר, בְּלָקְשׁוֹ גֵּיא לַעֲטַר,
שַׁבְתִּי לְקָחִי עוֹד לִנְטַר, מִתְּבוֹעַ עֶרֶף מָטָר.

תְּפִלַּת גְּבוּרוֹת טַל, חִלּוֹתִי בְּצֹהַר לִנְטַל,
תִּזַּל אִמְרָתִי כַּטַּל, לְקוֹי רְסִיסֵי טָל.
אֶאֱגְרָה בְּנֵי אִישׁ הַמְשֻׁרָר בְּטַל, אִוָּעֵד אִתָּם לְחַנֵּן בְּעַד טַל,
אֲבַשֵּׂר בִּקְהָל רָב זֵכֶר גְּבוּרוֹת טַל, אֲחַלֶּה פְּנֵי צוּרִי בְּזִיל אִמְרַת טָל.
בְּפִתְחוֹן פִּי אֲחַלֶּנּוּ עֲלֵי טַל, בְּמַעֲנֵה לְשׁוֹנִי אֲפַתֶּנּוּ עֲדֵי טַל,
בַּהֲפִיקִי מַעַן אַרְצָה כִּרְסִיס טַל, בְּגִשְׁתִּי צְקוּנִי יַעַל כְּשִׁכְבַת טָל.
גַּל בֵּינוּ לְבֵינִי סִיּוּם אוֹת טַל, גָּלוּי לַכֹּל כְּאֵשׁ אוֹכְלָה וְלִי כִּפְרִיחַת טַל,
גָּמַר מֵאָז אֹמֶר הֱיוֹת לִי כַּטַּל, גַּם בְּהוֹפִיעוֹ בִּי דָּפַק בְּרֹאשׁ נִמְלָא טָל.
דָּרַשׁ וְחָקַר מֵאָז וְחֶלֶשׁ הֵטַל, דַּק וָחֶלֶד לְכוֹנֵן בְּקֵץ עִתּוֹתֵי טַל,
דָּת קְנוּיַת קֶדֶם רְשׁוּת מֶנָּה נָטַל, דֵּעַ בָּהּ נוֹעַץ וּמְאוּם לֹא בְטַל.
הִטְבִּיעַ אַדְנֵי נְשִׁי הֲדוֹם וְכֵס הַמְנֻטָּל,
הוֹלִיד בְּתוֹלְדוֹתָם תּוֹלְדוֹת אֶגְלֵי טַל,
הִשְׁתִּיל שְׁתִילֵי עֵדֶן בִּרְווּי עֲנִינַת טַל, הֵכִין וְתִקֵּן בַּשַּׁחַק אֹסֶם אֹצְרוֹת טָל.
וּמִשְׁתִּיַּת אֶבֶן מְקוֹם חֶרְמוֹן טַל, וּתֵּק לְהַשְׁתּוֹת שְׁתִוֹתֵי טַל,
וּמִשָּׁם צָר חֹמֶר גֹּלֶם מְטַּל, וְנָפַח בּוֹ נֶשֶׁם חִיּוּת בְּחַיֵּי טָל.
זָבַת מִקֶּדֶם אִשֵּׁשׁ בְּאֵד טַל, זֶרַע וָדֶשֶׁא וָפֶרַח לְפַרְנֵס בְּמַתַּן טַל,
זֶרֶם עַד לֹא הִמְטִיר וְגֶשֶׁם הֵטַל, זְבָדָהּ וְעִדְּנָהּ חֲיוּת בְּטִפֵּי טָל.
חֲבָלִים נָפְלוּ לָהּ אֲסָמֵי אוֹרוֹת טַל, חַיַּת יְשֵׁנֶיהָ לְהַחֲיוֹת בְּאֵד טַל,
חַשְׁרַת מֵי גֶשֶׁם עָלֶיהָ לְהֵטַל, חָזוּז לְאַרְבָּעִים שָׁנָה לְפָקְדָהּ יֻטָּל.
טֹרַח מִטְרוֹת עֹז עַד עַתָּה לֹא הֻטַּל, טְלָלָהּ עַד דּוֹר עֲשִׂירִי מִתְנוֹבֶבֶת בְּטַל,
טָפְשׁוּ דָרֶיהָ וְגָאוּ בְּאֵד טַל, טִרְחוֹת גְּשָׁמִים מַה צֹּרֶךְ דַּיֵּנוּ בְטָל.
יַעַן כַּאֲשֶׁר מַדּוּ מָדַד וְהֵטַל, יְקוּמָם מָחָה וְזִכְרָם בִּטַּל,
יָקָר כַּעֲסָם כַּחוֹל וְכָאֶבֶן נֵטֶל, יְזֹרְבוּ נִצְמָתוּ בְּחֹרֶב וְחֹם טָל.
כָּמוֹס גֹּפֶר וְלִוּוּיָו מִכֹּל נֻטַּל, כִּי מֵי נֹחַ זֹאת לִי לְעוֹלָם בְּלִי לְבַטַּל,
כָּרַת לוֹ וּלְנֶשִׁי עוֹד בַּל יְבֻטַּל, כָּל יְמֵי הָאָרֶץ לְהַקְווֹת בְּקִוּוּי מָטָר וָטָל.
לֹא בָנוּ נוֹסְעֵי קֶדֶם מִשְׁאוֹן הַמְּקֻטָּל, לְהָקוּ וְיָזְמוּ עֲלוֹת לְדַק הַמְּנֻטַּל,
לִבָּם חָלַק וַעֲצָתָם בִּטַּל, לְנֶפֶץ וּלְזֶרֶם לְצוּל לְהֵטַל.
מוֹט הִתְמוֹטְטָה גֵּיא בְּחֹרֶב בְּלִי טַל, מֵאֲסָה עַד צָץ אָב וְהִפְרִיחָהּ כְּטַל,
מָטֵי הֶרֶג הִסְלִיל וְהִטְלִילָם בְּטַל, מִשָּׁם צָדַק נְחוֹל לְיַלְדוֹתָיו טָל.
נֶחְצַב כְּצוּר אִטֵּם זֶרֶם מִלְּהֵטַל, נֶחְשַׁב אֵת עֶדְנוֹ לְהִפָּקֵד בְּעֵת טַל,
נִפְקְדוּ בְּמוֹעֵד זֶה בְּקֵץ זְכִירַת טַל, נֶעֱקַד לְהַפְרִיחַ כְּשׁוֹשַׁנָּה בְּטָל.
שֵׁדֵד תֶּלֶם לְזֶרַע וּבִקְצִירוֹ לָן טַל, שָׂדֶה מְבֹרָךְ כְּהֵרִיחַ בֵּרְכוֹ בְּמַתַּן טַל,
סָכַם אִתּוֹ צִיר חָתוּם בְּבִרְכַּת טַל, שְׂרִידָיו לְהִתְבּוֹדֵד בְּבֶטַח עֶרֶךְ שְׁמֵי טָל.
עֲנָפָיו שָׂרְדוּ הֱיוֹת בַּגּוֹיִם כְּטַל, עֲלֵי עַיִן לְבָרֵךְ מִמֶּגֶד וּמִטַּל,
עָדָיו נָעוּ לְוּדָה וְנָם טִלְטַל, עַל בַּרְזֶל שָׁם עָלֵימוֹ לְהֵטַל.
פָּסַע וְדִלֵּג קֵץ כְּזֵכֶר בְּרִית טַל, פִּתְחֵי דֶּפֶק בְּרֹאשׁ נִמְלָא טַל,
פְּדוּת שָׁלַח לְיֵשַׁע בָּרִאשׁוֹן לְהַרְסִיס טַל,
פֶּגַע בְּכֵן חִקּוּתִי בָּרִאשׁוֹן לְהַזְכִּיר גְּבוּרוֹת טָל.

צֵאתִי לֶאֱלוֹשׁ עֻדַּנְתִּי בְּרֶדֶת טַל. צָעַקְתִּי וְהָזְכַּר לִי בְּרִית יַלְדוּת טַל,
צְבָאַי כִּלְכְּלוּ בְּמַן אֵבוּר טַל, צֵדָה שָׁלַח לָהֶם לָשֹׂבַע כַּעֲלוֹת שִׁכְבַת טָל.
קִבַּצְתִּי לְהַר חֶמֶד נְחוֹל אִמְרֵי טַל, קְהָלִי עַל אֶבְרַת נְשָׁרִים נְטַל,
קוֹל וּבָרָק וָנֶטֶף וְזֵילַת טַל, קוֹנִי עָלַי הִזִּיל עֲיֵפוֹת לְהָקֵר בְּטָל.
רִשְׁפֵּי לַהַב וְקוֹל כֹּחַ הֵירַד לִי בְּטַל, רַעַשׁ בְּשׁוּרִי חַלְתִּי וַיְעוֹרְרֵנִי בְּטַל,
רֶגֶשׁ שִׁבְעַת עֲנָנֵי הוֹד מָסַךְ וְהֵטַל,
רָצִים לְפָנַי תּוּר אֶרֶץ שִׁבְעַת מִשְׁמַנֵּי טָל.
שְׁכִינָה אִהֵל צִיר בֵּין שָׁדַי בְּלִין טַל, שֶׁמֶן מָשַׁח אָח שֶׁיּוֹרֵד כְּטַל,
שְׁבָטַי בֵּרַךְ בְּעֵקֶב כְּעֵין נִתְבָּרַךְ בְּטַל, שִׁירָה שָׁר לָמוֹ בְּאֹמֶר זִיל טָל.
תַּחְתָּיו צָג נֶצֶר מִגֶּזַע מְבֹרָךְ בְּטַל, תֵּבֵל עָם לְהַנְחִיל בְּתוֹךְ עֵינוֹת טַל.
תִּרְגַּלְתָּם נְשָׂאָם בְּשֶׁכֶם כְּאוֹמֵן בֵּן נָטַל, תְּקוּפַת צַר וְאוֹר בְּשֶׁלָם בְּטַל.

תַּחַת אֵילַת עֹפֶר בֹּרַךְ מוֹשִׁיעַ בְּטַל,
אֻמַּץ וְנֻסַּס כְּאֵיתָן בְּחֹרֶב וְגִזַּת טַל,
שֻׁעֲנְתִּי מֵאָז וְעַד עַתָּה בְּהַבְטָחַת טַל,
לָעַד בְּלִי לְהִמָּנַע מֵאִתִּי טָל.
רָגַז תִּשְׁבִּי כְּחָר וְעָצַר טַל,
עַל פַּת לֶחֶם וָטֶרֶף טֹרַד וְטֻלְטַל,
קָדוֹשׁ כְּהִבִּיט לְבַל תּוּפַר בְּרִית טַל,
זִלְעַף רוּחַ לַיֶּלֶד וְנַפְשׁוֹ נָטָל.
צָרְפִית בְּצִיר רָגְנָה תְּנוּאוֹת לְהֵטַל,
רְאוֹתוֹ כִּי פָּס בֵּן הִתִּיר נֶדֶר טַל,
פֶּשַׁע אִם הֶעֱוָה עֲדֵי עֲצִירַת טַל,
בְּכֵן עָרַךְ תַּחַן לְמוֹלִיד אֶגְלֵי טָל.
עָתַר לִפְנֵי חַי מְחַיֶּה כֹּל בְּטַל,
יְחִידַת יֶלֶד הֵשִׁיב בְּהַתָּרַת טַל,
סָדַר וְחָשַׂף לַכֹּל כֹּחַ גְּבוּרוֹת טַל,
רָמַז כִּי שְׁכוּנִים יָקִיצוּ בְטָל.
נִכְרַתָה זֹאת לְהַרְרֵי קֶדֶם בְּמַתְּנַת טַל,
בְּלֹא יְקַוֶּה לְאִישׁ לְיַחֵל עֲלֵי טַל,
מִמָּחֳרַת הַפֶּסַח יְחַנְּנוּ בְּעַד טַל,
יָנִיפוּ בְּמַעֲלֶה וּמוֹרִיד לְהָנִיף רוֹעַ טָל.
לָכֵן מִלִּפְנֵי עֹמֶר אַזְכִּיר בְּתַחַן טַל,
קָדוּם לַיְלָה אֶחָד לְהָלִין בּוֹ טַל,
כּוֹרְתָה לְחַיִּים מְחִיַּת יְרִידַת טַל,
לַמֵּתִים חָפְשִׁי הוּכָנָה תְּחִיַּת טָל.
יְעוֹרְרוּ יְזוֹרְרוּ יִחְיוּ בְּרֶדֶת טַל,
יַעַמְדוּ יָקוּמוּ יַעֲלוּ בְשִׁכְבַת טַל,

טַעַם זְמִרוֹת יַשְׁמִיעוּ בְּטַל אוֹרוֹת טַל,
רוֹן יוֹשְׁבֵי סֶלַע אֲשֶׁר יִחְיוּ בְּטָל.
חֲבַצֶּלֶת וַעֲרָבָה תָּגֵלְנָה בִּפְרִיחַת טַל,
מִדְבָּר וְצִיָּה יְשֻׂשׂוּם בְּטִלּוּל טַל,
זָרֶב וְשָׁרָב וְשֶׁמֶשׁ וָחֹרֶב וְחֵמַת טַל,
קָמוֹת לֹא יַקְדִּירוּ בְּגֵיא טְלוּלַת טָל.
וְסֻכָּה תִּהְיֶה לְצֵל קָרִיב מִלְּהֵטַל,
רְבוּצִים עַל כָּבוֹד חֻפַּת עָב טַל,
הוֹגֵי הֲמֻלָּה יָנִיפוּ רְסִיסֵי טַל,
יִפָּתְדוּ אֲסָמִים לְהַטִּיף נִזְלֵי טָל.
דּוֹדֵי הָמוֹן חוֹגֵג שְׁאֵרִיתָם כְּטַל,
תַּרְשִׁישִׁים יְנַהֲלוּם בְּמַרְפֵּא כְּנַף טַל,
גִּיל קוֹל רִנָּה לַעֲבוֹר בַּסָּךְ וְטַל,
סְלוּלִים עֲלוֹת אֶל נָכוֹן וְנִשָּׂא וְנִטָּל.
בְּשׁוּרָם מֵאֲמָנָה עַל חֶרְמוֹן טַל,
פָּרוֹחַ יִפְרְחוּ כְּשׁוֹשַׁנָּה בְּטָל.
אֶל אֶרֶץ דָּגָן וְתִירוֹשׁ אַף שָׁמָיו יַעַרְפוּ טָל,
רְאוּתָם אֵשׁ אוֹכֶלֶת כִּי נִהְיֶה כְּטָל.

אֵלִים בְּיוֹם מְחֻסָּן, חִלּוּ פְּנֵי מְנוּסָן, טַל אוֹרוֹת לְנוֹסְסָן, לְהַזִּילָם בְּעֶצֶם נִיסָן. אֲשְׁאֲלָה בְּעָדָם מָעַן, גְּבוּרוֹת טַל לְהַעַן. טַל זָב הֶבְטַח לִשְׁעַן, יִתֵּן לְהַמְתִּיק לַעַן.

מזל ניסן

טלה

בְּשִׁמְךָ טַל אֲטַלֶּה, בְּיַלְדוּת טַל לְהִטָּלֶה. טַל בּוֹ אֵיתָן מְטֻלֶּה, בַּדָּיו יִרְעוּ כְּמוֹ טָלֶה. בְּרִית כְּרוּתָה לְרֹאשׁ אָבוֹת, חֲיָלָיו בְּטַל לְהַרְבּוֹת, טַל בַּל יָזִיז מִבְּנֵי אָבוֹת, לְהַרְסִיס עִם נְדָבוֹת.

גֶּזַע כִּרְבִיב טַל מְשִׁיר, שִׁשִּׁים וְאַחַת אָרְחוּ בִּמְשִׁיר, טַל גַּד לְצֵדָם תְּיַר, מֵחֲמִשָּׁה עָשָׂר בְּאִיָּר. גִּיל טַל לְכָל יְגֵעִים, וְדוּדָאֵי בְכוֹר בּוֹ רוֹגְעִים. טַל גְּאוּלִים בּוֹ גֵאִים, עִם כְּטַל נִשְׁאֲרוּ בַגּוֹיִם.

מזל אייר

שור

דוֹפְקֵי דְּלָתֶיךָ לָשׁוּר, הַטְלִילֵם בְּמַעְגַּל מִישׁוֹר, טַל דוֹק לָמוֹ חָשׁוּר, עַד קֵץ לְחִיכַּת שׁוֹר. דִּגְלֵי אֲסוּר מוּף עֲנֵה, גֵּיא וּדְשָׁאֶיהָ תְּעַנֶּה. טַל דְּשָׁאֵימוֹ יַחֲנֶה, כְּטַל סְבִיבוֹת הַמַּחֲנֶה.

הַפְגָּעַת טַל תְּכֻנָּן, מוּל מְכוֹן שֶׁבֶת כֻּנָּן, טַל הֲנָפַת עָב תִּתְכּוֹנָן, בְּמַתְּנַת טַל סִיוָן. הִלּוּל קֹדֶשׁ תִּירוֹשִׁי, יַמְגִּיד בְּטַל קְדוֹשִׁי. טַל הֲלָנַת קְצִיר שָׁרְשִׁי, יָלִין בְּטַל לְהַשְׁרִישִׁי.

מזל סיון

תאומים

וְאוֹת לַחֲשׂוֹף חֲתוּמִים, וְרֶמֶז לְצַחְצֵחַ כְּתָמִים, טַל וַתֵּר לִתְמִימִים, לְהֵאָחוֹת בּוֹ כִּ**תְאוֹמִים**. וְרַד עִם אֵל לְהָכֵן, וְנֵס מְנַשִּׁי לְתַכֵּן. טַל וָעַד צוּר לְשַׁכֵּן, אִתּוֹ כְּנָם לַעֲשׂוֹת כֵּן.

זַעֲקִי בַּל תָּבוֹז, לְהַטְלִילֵי מֵעוֹז וּמִבּוֹז, טַל זְמַנְתִּי לְרָמוֹז, לְהַחֵל כְּאֵב **תַּמּוּז**. זֶרַע בֶּן עֶתִין חִפֵּשׂ. לָעַד בְּלִי יֶאְפַּס. טַל זוֹרֵר עַל פַּס, כְּבַמִּדְבָּר דַּק מְחֻסְפָּס.

מזל תמוז

סרטן

חַבֵּא מִשַּׂד שָׂטָן, פְּסוּחֶיךָ בְּלִי לְסָטָן, טַל חַיֵּיב יַרְטָן, לְהִפָּסֵחַ כְּגוֹן **סַרְטָן**. חוֹף יַמִּים בְּצִיָּנוֹ, מַרְאִית טְלָלֵי נִצָּנוֹ. טַל חֲשׁוֹר לְרֶבֶץ צֹאנוֹ, וּכְטַל עַל עֵשֶׂב רְצוֹנוֹ.

טַלְלֵי יֶשַׁע אֶשְׁאָב, בְּמָשׁוֹשׂ מִמַּשְׁאָב, טַל טַעַם אָב יַטְעִימֵנוּ אֵל וָ**אָב**. טִלּוּל יְדִידוּת שִׁכְנִי, יִשְׁכֹּן לָבֶטַח לְשָׁכְנִי, טַל טֹהַר מִשְׁכָּנִי, יִשְׁקֹט כְּעָב טַל עַל מְכוֹנִי.

מזל אב

אריה

יַלְדוּת טַל תְּאֳרִי, כְּמֵאָז בּוֹ לְפָאֲרִי, טַל יָפִיק לְבֵית יַעֲרִי, לִשְׁאָג בּוֹ כָּ**אֲרִי**. יוֹם טוֹבָה בְּטוֹב אַבְלִילָה, בְּזִנּוּק בָּשָׁן לְהִתְהַלְּלָה, טַל יְבוּלֵי אֵל הַטְלִילָה, כְּעַל הַמַּחֲנֶה לָיְלָה.

כְּרְיֵס רַד בְּרֹאשׁ תָּלוּל, בְּקֵץ רִאשׁוֹן לְטִלּוּל, טַל כֵּן יְהֵא כָלוּל, לְהַדְשִׁיא פִּרְחֵי **אֱלוּל**. כְּמֵהִים שְׂבַע רָצוֹן לְהַסְפֵּק, בְּלַחֲלוּחַ נֶגֶב לְהֵאָפֵק. טַל כְּנֶסֶת עַל דּוֹדָהּ תְּרַפֵּק, לְעוֹרְרָהּ בְּקוֹל דּוֹפֵק.

מזל אלול

בתולה

לְאוֹת טוֹב טַל נִתְלָה, תֵּת לְעוֹלָם חַתְלָה, טַל לְנוֹבֵב תְּנוּב שְׁתוּלָה, לְהָגִיל בְּמָשׂוֹשׂ **בְּתוּלָה**. לֶאֱגֹד גְּדוּד יְשַׁפֵּר, לְהַעֲצִים גְּדוּדָיו בְּלִי מִסְפָּר, טַל לְהָקִיץ בְּקוֹל שׁוֹפָר, אֲטוּמִים שׁוֹכְנֵי עָפָר.

מִכָּל אוֹם יְאַשְּׁרִי, וַאֲהוֹדֶנּוּ מְשִׁירִי, טַל מֵאֶגְלוֹ יְעַשְּׁרִי, לְהַסְפִּיק עַד קֵץ **תִּשְׁרִי**. מִשְׁמַן לֶחֶם מַקָּחִי, מֵעֲסִיס יֵין רִקּוּחִי. טַל מַלֵּא מִשְׁאֲלוֹת מַלְקוּחִי, יַעֲרֹף כַּמָּטָר לִקְחִי.

מזל תשרי

מאזנים

נָאַק נוֹשְׂאֵי לְךָ עֵינַיִם, לַעֲנוּתָם הַט אָזְנַיִם, טַל נוֹפֵף לִמְחוֹלַת מַחֲנַיִם, לְהַכְרִיעַ צִדְקָם בְּ**מֹאזְנַיִם**. נִתְבָּרֵךְ מִמֶּגֶד וּמִטַּל כְּבְאַחִים מְנֻשָּׂא וּמְנֻטָּל. טַל נֶשֶׁב אֶגְלִים תִּטַּל, מוֹלִיד אֶגְלֵי טָל.

שִׂיחַ זוּ אֱזֹן לַיִּשְׁבָן, בֶּטַח לְהוֹשִׁיבָן, טַל שְׂעִירִים לְחַשְּׁבָן, מֵעֵת **מַרְחֶשְׁוָן**. סִדּוּר עָבִים לְהַטְלִילָם, כְּיֶלֶד שַׁעֲשׁוּעִים לְנַטְּלָם. טַל שְׂבַע לְטַלְּלָם, צַו לַשָּׁמַיִם תֵּת טַלָּם.

מזל חשון

עקרב

עֲתִירַת טַל תֶּעֱרַב, וּלְפָנֶיךָ תִּקְרַב, טַל עֲלֵי שָׁרָב, יִפְרַח כְּבִמְקוֹם **עַקְרָב**. עֲלוֹת שִׁכְבַת מַפְרַחַת, בְּאִבֵּי נַחַל מַאֲרַחַת, טַל עֲלֵי עַיִן לְבָרֵךְ מֵרוּם וּמִתַּחַת, וּמִתְּהוֹם רוֹבֶצֶת תָּחַת.

פִּרְחֵי חֶלֶד תַּשְׁלֵו, בְּטַל שַׁלְאֲנָן וְשָׁלֵו, טַל פֶּרַח לְהַדְגֹּא וּלְהַשְׁלֵו, צִמְחֵי תְנוּב **כִּסְלֵו**. פְּקֹד חֹרֶב בְּצָיוֹן, לְמִלְּטָם מֵחֹרֶב צִחָיוֹן. טַל פֵּרוֹת לְבָרֵךְ בְּצִבְיוֹן, כְּטַל חֶרְמוֹן שֶׁיּוֹרֵד עַל הַרְרֵי צִיּוֹן.

מזל כסלו

קשת

צִיָּה אִם מְלֻקֶּשֶׁת, וּמַלְקוֹשׁ אִם מְבֻקֶּשֶׁת, טַל צוּק עָבִים תְּהֵא מְאַשֶּׁשֶׁת, כְּבַעֲנִינַת **קֶשֶׁת**. צִמְאוֹן צָהֳרַיִם, בַּל יַשְׁזִיף עֲדָנִים אֲחוֹרַיִם. טַל צְלִיחַת אֱתוּי נַהֲרַיִם תַּצְלִיחַ בּוֹ יְהוּדָה וְאֶפְרָיִם.

מזל טבת

גדי

קָלֵי בַּל יִצְבַּט, בְּלִי בְּחֹרֶב יֻלְבַּט, טַל קֶרַח בַּל יֻחְבַּט, לְזֵרְעוֹנֵי **טֵבֵת וּשְׁבָט**. קוֹרְאֶיךָ לְטוּב תִּקּוֹב, לְהָסִיר מֵהֶם לֵב הֶעָקוֹב. טַל קָמוֹת בְּלִי לִרְקוֹב, לִשְׁכֹּן בֶּטַח בָּדָד עֵין יַעֲקֹב.

מזל שבט

דלי

רֶשַׁע מַר מִדְּלִי, מִצִּלָּם הַחֲדִילִי, טַל רְסִיסִים תִּדְלִי, לְהַזִּיל לִגְדָאֵי כְּמִ**דְּלִי**. רֶשֶׁף נְצוּצִים בְּאוּר חֵדֶק, בְּצֵל צַלְמוֹן צוּרָם לְהַדֵּק. טַל רַחֵף עֲלֵי זוּ בְּצֶדֶק, וּשְׁחָקִים יִרְעֲפוּ טַל וְיִזְּלוּ צֶדֶק.

מזל אדר

דגים

שַׁפֵּר אֲסָמֵי טַל דָּר, בַּקֹּדֶשׁ נֶאְדָּר, טַל שְׁתִילִים יְהֻדָּר, הַחֲנוּטִים מֵ**אֲדָר**. תַּדְגִּיא תְּנוּב שָׁנָה, בְּשַׁעַר **דָּגִים** מְדֻשָּׁנָה. טַל תַּשְׁרִישׁ אִבֵּי יְשֵׁנָה, לְהַפְרִיחַ כְּטַל שׁוֹשַׁנָּה.

The Ark is opened and the service continues on p. 418.

יום שני – שחרית

Some congregations recite this alphabetically arranged *piyut* during the *chazzan's* repetition of the *Amidah* of *Shacharis* on the second day (page 340).

וּבְכֵן שׁוֹר אוֹ כֶשֶׂב אוֹ עֵז כִּי יִוָּלֵד.

שׁוֹר אֲשֶׁר מֵאָז עֲלֵי עֹפֶר פָּסַח,
בְּמַקְרִין וּמַפְרִיס תֵּת כָּפְרוֹ שָׂח,
גְּמוּלָיו צוּר צָו עֲלֵימוֹ לִפְסָח,
בְּאֹמֶר וַאֲמַרְתֶּם זֶבַח פֶּסַח הוּא לַיהוה אֲשֶׁר פָּסַח. (שׁוֹר)

שׁוֹר דָּרַשׁ אָב לְהַאֲרִיחַ קְרוּאֵי אֵל,
הֵכִין עֻגּוֹת מֵאָז לְהַמְשְׁכוֹ אַחֲרֵי אֵל,
וּבְצִדְקוֹ חֻפְּשׂוּ יִשְׁרֵי אֵל,
אֲשֶׁר פָּסַח עַל בָּתֵּי בְנֵי יִשְׂרָאֵל. (שׁוֹר)

שׁוֹר זְעֵם יְחוּמֵי אֲרַם נַהֲרַיִם,
חִיְּבוּ בְּתַבְנִיתוֹ לָשׁוּב אֲחוֹרַיִם,
טוֹב זָכַר לָמוֹ יוֹשֵׁב כְּחֹם צָהֳרַיִם,
בְּמִצְרַיִם בְּנָגְפוֹ אֶת מִצְרָיִם. (שור)
שׁוֹר יִמַּן מַעֲשֵׂה שׁוֹר בּוֹ לְהַצִּיל,
כּוֹנְנוּ בְּמִלּוּאִים פְּסוּחִים בּוֹ לְהַצִּיל,
לְהָגֵן לְמַלֵּט לִפְסֹחַ וּלְהַצִּיל,
כְּמוֹ בְחָם וְאֶת בָּתֵּינוּ הִצִּיל. (שור)
שׁוֹר מְכַפֵּר בֶּעָשׂוֹר מְשׁוּחִים בּוֹ כְּחִיְּבוֹ,
נֶעְלַם דָּבָר בָּעֵדָה בּוֹ יֶאֱהָבוּ,
סְלִיחָה מָצְאוּ בוֹ שׁוֹבְבִים כְּהֶעֱווּ,
וַיִּקּוֹד הָעָם וַיִּשְׁתַּחֲווּ. (שור)
שׁוֹר עֲלֵי מְשׁוֹרְרִים בְּהַדְרַת קֹדֶשׁ,
פִּשְׁעָם לִמְחֹל לְשָׁרֵת בַּקֹּדֶשׁ,
צָדַק הֱיוֹת רֹאשׁ לְנִיחֹחֵי קֹדֶשׁ,
בְּאֵלֶּה מוֹעֲדֵי יהוה מִקְרָאֵי קֹדֶשׁ. (שור)
שׁוֹר קָצַב לְחֶגֶג וְכֶשֶׂב וָעֵז בְּמֶלֶל,
רֶנֶן עָלֵימוֹ קְרִיאַת הַלֵּל,
שָׁלֹשׁ כִּתּוֹת גְּבוּרוֹת בָּם לְמַלֵּל,
❖ תּוֹדָה וְקוֹל זִמְרָה לְהוֹדוֹת וּלְהַלֵּל. (שור)
יוֹצְאֵי חִפָּזוֹן, סִפְּקָם מָזוֹן, לִשְׂבֹּעַ וְלֹא לְרָזוֹן. קָדוֹשׁ.

The service continues וּבְכֵן, page 340.

Some congregations recite this *piyut* before the *Kedushah* of *Shacharis* (page 342) of the second day.

בְּעֶשֶׂר מַכּוֹת פַּתְרוּסִים הִפְרַכְתָּ, וְאַרְכָּא לָמוֹ הֶאֱרַכְתָּ. לְשַׁלַּח בְּלִי עִכּוּב עִם אֲשֶׁר בֵּרַרְתָּ, וְכַמָּה פְעָמִים בָּמוֹ הֵעַרְתָּ, וְכָאֵלֶּה כַּמֶּה בָּם הִתְרֵיתָ, וְכִלָּיוֹן עֲלֵיהֶם לֹא גָמַרְתָּ, עַד כִּי גָמְרוּ רִשְׁעָם כַּאֲשֶׁר גָּזַרְתָּ, וְנִאֲצוּ לְמוּל צִיר אֲשֶׁר בָּחַרְתָּ, וְנָם מִי יהוה אֲשֶׁר אָמַרְתָּ, לְשַׁלַּח אֶת הָעָם אֲשֶׁר דִּבַּרְתָּ, וְאַתָּה לְעֻמָּם קִנְאָה אָזַרְתָּ, וּכְגִבּוֹר מִתְרוֹנֵן מִשֵּׁנָה הֵעַרְתָּ, כְּלֵי קְרָב חָגַרְתָּ, בְּאַרְצָם עָבַרְתָּ, בְּכוֹרֵיהֶם פִּגַּרְתָּ, רָהֲבֵיהֶם שִׁבַּרְתָּ, רֵאשִׁית אוֹנָם הִדְבַּרְתָּ.

בְּשׁוֹפְטֵיהֶם שְׁפָטִים עָשִׂיתָ, לַיְלָה חַצְתָּ, רֹאשׁ מָחַצְתָּ, תַּנִּין רִעַצְתָּ, רֹאשׁ לִוְיָתָן רִצַּצְתָּ, בְּכָל גַּיְא אוֹתוֹ הֵפַצְתָּ, לְמַעַן סַפֵּר שִׁמְךָ עַצְתָּ, חָמֵשׁ מֵאוֹת מַהֲלָךְ רַצְתָּ, וּלְסוּף בַּסּוּף לְחָמוֹ נִפַּצְתָּ, וְכָל שְׁאוֹנוֹ בְּסַאסְּאָה לָחַצְתָּ, וְעַל הֶהָרִים קִפַּצְתָּ, וּלְיֵשַׁע עַמְּךָ יָצָאתָ, וְאוֹתָם בִּזְרוֹעַ הוֹצֵאתָ, וְכָל הֲמוֹנֵי חָם כְּחוֹחִים הִצַּתָּ, כִּי כְּמִדָּתָם לָמוֹ מָדַדְתָּ, וְכָל הַיְקוּם בָּם לִמַּדְתָּ, וּכְמוֹ עִנּוּ עִם אֲשֶׁר חָמַדְתָּ, בָּהּ בְּמִדָּה אוֹתָם הִשְׁמַדְתָּ.

הֵם שָׁפְכוּ כַּמַּיִם דַּם עוֹלְלֵיהֶם, לָכֵן לְדָם נֶהֶפְכוּ נוֹזְלֵיהֶם.
הֵם מֵעֲכוּם לְמַעַן הַשְׁחִיתָם, לָכֵן עָלְתָה צְפַרְדֵּעַ וַתַּשְׁחִיתֵם.

הֵם לְחָצוּם בְּעָפָר וָחֹמֶר לִלְבּוֹן לְבֵנִים, לָכֵן הוּמַר עֲפָרָם לְכִנִּים.
הֵם הֶגְלוּם לְהָבִיא חַיּוֹת לְהַצְדָּאוֹת, לָכֵן עָרוֹב בָּא בִגְבוּלָם לְהַצְדּוֹת.
הֵם הֶשִׁיתוּם כְּמוֹ חַלְלֵי קֶבֶר, לָכֵן חַיָּתָם סֻגְּרָה לַדֶּבֶר.
הֵם אֲסָרוּם לְהָבִיא רִבּוּעוֹת, לָכֵן מַס חֲמוּדָם בַּאֲבַעְבֻּעוֹת.
הֵם הֶעֱבִידוּם בְּחֹם וָנֶשֶׁף, לָכֵן סֻגַּר מִקְנֵיהֶם לַבָּרָד וְגַם רֶשֶׁף.
הֵם גָּאוּ בְּמֶלֶךְ אֵין לָאַרְבֶּה, לָכֵן לֹא הָיָה כֵן אַרְבֶּה.
הֵם הֶאֱפִילוּ בָּרָה כַּשֶּׁמֶשׁ, לָכֵן חָשַׁךְ אוֹרָם לָאֶמֶשׁ.
הֵם יָעֲצוּ לְאַבֵּד בֵּן בְּכוֹר לָכֵן חֲצוֹת לַיְלָה נֻגַּף בָּם כָּל בְּכוֹר.
הֵם זָמְמוּ לְאַבְּדָם בַּמַּיִם, לָכֵן בָּאוּ בָּאֵשׁ וּבַמָּיִם.

וְאַתָּה פָּסַחְתָּ בַּחֲצִי לֵיל עַל פְּתָחִים, בְּאָכְלָם זִבְחֵי פְסָחִים, וּבְעֶצֶם הַיּוֹם הוֹצֵאתָם שְׂמֵחִים, לְעֵין פַּתְרוּסִים וְכַסְלוּחִים, וְהֶצָּתוּ כְּקוֹצִים כְּסוּחִים, וְשׁוֹשַׁנִּים כִּלְקָטוּ מִבֵּין הַחוֹחִים, רֶנֶן וְהַלֵּל וְשִׁיר מְשׂוֹחֲחִים, רְנָנוֹת לְךָ מְשִׂיחִים, תּוֹדָה וְקוֹל זִמְרָה פּוֹצְחִים.

וְאַתָּה בְּשִׂמְחָתָם שָׂמַחְתָּ, וּבִישׁוּעָתָם נוֹשַׁעְתָּ, וּבְכָל צָרָתָם צַרְתָּ, בְּכֵן קִצָּם קָצַרְתָּ.
וּכְמוֹ הָיוּ בֵּין הַחוֹחִים, לְנֶאֱמַן בַּיִת נִגְלֵיתָ בַּסְּנֶה בְחוֹחִים.
וּכְמוֹ לְחָצוּ בִלְבֵנִים וָחֹמֶר, כֵּן נִגְלֵיתָ בִּלְבְנַת סַפִּיר בָּאֹמֶר.
וּכְהוֹצֵאתָם מִתַּחַת סִבְלוֹת, אִתָּם הוֹצֵאתָ מִסִּבְלוֹת.
וּכְהוּבָאוּ בָּבֶלָה, לְמַעֲנָם שִׁלַּחְתָּ בָּבֶלָה.
וּכְנָדוּ לְעֵילָם, כִּסְאֲךָ הוּשַׂם בְּעֵילָם.
וּכְנָעוּ לְיָוָן, עוֹרַרְתָּ בּוֹא לְיָוָן.
וְכִגְלוּתָם לְשֵׂעִיר, אֵלַי קוֹרֵא מִשֵּׂעִיר.
וּבְשׁוּבָם מֵאֱדוֹם, אִתָּם תָּבֹא אָדוֹם, כָּאָמוּר מִי זֶה בָּא מֵאֱדוֹם.
וּבְבוֹאֲךָ לְדַלְתֵי לְבָנוֹן, אִתְּךָ יָבֹאוּ לַלְּבָנוֹן.

כִּי מֵרֶחֶם אוֹתָם נָשָׂאתָ, וּמִבֶּטֶן אוֹתָם הֶעֱמַסְתָּ, כְּרֵעִים וְאַחִים הֵם לְךָ הִתְאַמְתָּ, בְּרִדְתָּם לְחָם עִמָּם יָרַדְתָּ, וְכָל מַחֲנֶיךָ הוֹרַדְתָּ, וּבַעֲלוֹתָם אִתָּם עָלִיתָ, וְכָל מְשָׁרְתֶיךָ הֶעֱלִיתָ, וּבְצֵאתָם יָצָאתָ, וּבְעִנּוּיָם נִמְצֵאתָ, וּבְנוּחָם מְנוּחָה מָצָאתָ, וְצִבְאוֹתֶיךָ אֲשֶׁר בְּמַעְלָה הוֹצֵאתָ, לְהוֹדִיעָם כִּי בָמוֹ נִרְצֵיתָ וּבִשְׁבִילָם גֵּיא וָדוֹק יָצַרְתָּ, וּבְקִרְבָּם נִתְקַדַּשְׁתָּ וְנִשְׂגַּבְתָּ וְנֶעֱרַצְתָּ, וְנִתְהַדַּרְתָּ וְנִתְאַדַּרְתָּ, וְכִפְאֵר מַעְלָה פְּאֵרָם אִמַּצְתָּ, וּכְשִׁירוֹת רוּם שִׁירָתָם חָפַצְתָּ, וְכִקְדֻשַּׁת מָרוֹם קְדֻשָּׁתָם הֱיוֹת פָּצְתָּ, וּבְכִנּוּי שֵׁם גָּבְהֲךָ שְׁמוֹתָם חָצַצְתָּ.

אֵלִים בְּשֵׁם אֵלִים,	אֱלֹהִים בְּשֵׁם אֱלֹהִים,	בָּנִים בְּשֵׁם בָּנִים,
מַחֲנוֹת בְּשֵׁם מַחֲנוֹת,	מְחִיצוֹת בְּשֵׁם מְחִיצוֹת,	שֵׁמוֹת בְּשֵׁם שֵׁמוֹת.
אֵין כָּאֵל בְּשֵׁם מִיכָאֵל,		גִּבּוֹרֵי אֵל בְּשֵׁם גַּבְרִיאֵל,
בְּנֵי יַעֲקֹב בְּשֵׁם אֱלֹהֵי יַעֲקֹב,		קְדוֹשׁ יַעֲקֹב בְּשֵׁם קְדוֹשׁ יַעֲקֹב,

מְשַׁלְּשֵׁי קָדוֹשׁ בְּשֵׁם מְשַׁלְּשֵׁי קָדוֹשׁ.

The service continues with *Kedushah*, page 342.

שני ימים האחרונים

Some congregations recite this *piyut* instead of [or in addition to] וַיּוֹשַׁע (p. 858) on the seventh day. The author's name — יַעֲקֹב, *Yaakov* — appears as the initial letters of the verses in the first stanza. It also forms the acrostic of the five stanzas, but this time it is spelled יַעֲקוּב.

יְדוּעֵי שֵׁם בְּכוֹר נֶשֶׁם, וּבְנִקְיוֹן רַעְיוֹנִים,
עֵת פֻּלְּטוּ וְנִתְמַלָּטוּ, מִכּוּר בַּרְזֶל סוֹנְנִים,
קוֹל נוֹפְפוּ וְלֹא רוֹפְפוּ, כְּמוֹ אָבוֹת כֵּן בָּנִים,
בְּכֵן יַחַד קוֹל אֶחָד, כִּי צוּר שׁוֹכֵן מְעוֹנִים.
הוּא אֱלֹהֵי הָאֱלֹהִים, וַאֲדוֹנֵי הָאֲדוֹנִים.

עֲדַת עֲנָמִים עֲבוּר עֲגוּמִים, עֲלֵיהֶם מָרוֹם הִרְעִים,
וּשְׁפָטָם וַחֲבָטָם, בַּעֲשָׂרָה נְגָעִים,
וַיְשַׁמֵּם וַיְשִׁימֵם, בְּלֵב יַמִּים נִטְבָּעִים,
וְנִצְּלוּ וְנִגְאֲלוּ, פְּלֵיטֵי הֲמוֹן נוֹשָׁעִים.
אָז שׁוֹרְרוּ וְאָז פֵּאֲרוּ, בִּזְמָרִים וּבִרְנָנִים,
הוּא אֱלֹהֵי הָאֱלֹהִים, וַאֲדוֹנֵי הָאֲדוֹנִים.

קָבֵל מְרוֹמוֹ יוֹם בְּיוֹמוֹ, כֵּן יְבָרְכוּ שֵׁם כְּבוֹדוֹ,
וּכְשָׁמְעָם כֵּן בְּרַעַם, מֵאֲחוֹרֵי פַּרְגּוֹדוֹ,
יִסְגּוֹדוּן וְיִקּוֹדוּן מֵחֲזוֹת שְׁכִינַת הוֹדוֹ.
וּמִי יֶחֱזֶה זֶה אוֹ זֶה, נִסְתָּר בְּעָבֵי עֲנָנִים,
הוּא אֱלֹהֵי הָאֱלֹהִים וַאֲדוֹנֵי הָאֲדוֹנִים.

וְהַחַיּוֹת בְּרוּם עֶלְיוֹת, כֵּס יְקָרוֹ תְּשָׁאֶנָּה,
בְּכַנְפֵיהֶן גַּבֵּיהֶן וּגְוִיּוֹתֵיהֶן תְּכַסֶּינָה,
בְּקוֹל נוֹשְׁקָן בְּהַחֲזִיקָן בְּכַנְפֵיהֶם תְּרִימֶנָּה,
בְּעֵת עָמְדָם בְּמַעֲמָדָם כַּנְפֵיהֶם תְּרַפֶּינָה.
גַּם בְּלֶכְתָּם לְעֻמָּתָם יֵלְכוּ הָאוֹפַנִּים.
הוּא אֱלֹהֵי הָאֱלֹהִים וַאֲדוֹנֵי הָאֲדוֹנִים.

בְּנֵי סְגֻלָּה מִתְּחִלָּה הֵמָּה יְשַׂגְּבוּ בְּמַטָּה,
בְּרוּם קוֹלָם אֲדוֹן עוֹלָם אֲשֶׁר אוֹר לָבַשׁ וְעָטָה,
וְאָז הֲמֻלָּה מִלְּמַעְלָה יַעֲרִיצוּהוּ בְּמִבְטָא,
חֲבוּרַת אֵל כְּנֶגֶד אֵל, מְסַדְּרִים כְּמוֹ שִׁיטָה.
אֵל מְפָאֲרִים וּמְהַדְּרִים, וְהֵם אוֹמְרִים וְגַם עוֹנִים,
הוּא אֱלֹהֵי הָאֱלֹהִים וַאֲדוֹנֵי הָאֲדוֹנִים.

The service continues on page 860.

Some congregations recite this *piyut* instead of [or in addition to] מְחוֹלֶלֶת (p. 858) on the eighth day. The author's name בִּנְיָמִן, *Binyamin,* appears as the second letter of each stanza.

לְבַעַל הַתִּפְאֶרֶת, מְתַקֵּן רוּם בְּזֶרֶת, מֵעֲצִימִים אַדֶּרֶת,
מַלְאֲכֵי הַשָּׁרֵת נוֹחִים לוֹ לְתִשְׁחֹרֶת, כַּהֲלָכָה וּמַסֹּרֶת,
וַאֲנִי שְׁחַרְחֹרֶת, תְּהִלָּה בְּפִי סוֹדֶרֶת.

לְנִקְרָא רִאשׁוֹן וְאַחֲרוֹן, מֶלֶךְ אַדִּירִירוֹן, מַבִּיעִים סֶלֶד וָרוֹן,
בְּיֹשֶׁר וְכִשְׁרוֹן וְאִתָּם מְטַטְרוֹן, פִּסְקוֹן אִטְמוֹן וְסִגְרוֹן,
וַאֲנִי חֲבַצֶּלֶת הַשָּׁרוֹן, מִשְׁתַּחֲוָה פְּנֵי הָאָרוֹן.
לְיָהּ חוֹצֵב לֶהָבָה, נַעֲרָץ בְּסוֹד קְדוֹשִׁים רַבָּה,
וְעִירֵי מֶרְכָּבָה וְקַדִּישֵׁי שַׁלְהֶבָה, מִתְגַּבְּרִים לְהַקְשִׁיבָה,
קְדֻשָּׁה כְּאַחַת חֲטִיבָה, וַאֲנִי חוֹלַת אַהֲבָה, בְּבַקָּשָׁה עֲרֵבָה.
לְמַפְלִיא פְּלָאוֹת, אֲדוֹן כָּל הַנִּפְלָאוֹת, כִּתִּים וַחֲיָלוֹת,
בְּחַדְרֵי הֵיכָלוֹת, רוֹעֲשִׁים בְּקוֹלוֹת, נוֹעָדִים בְּמַקְהֵלוֹת,
וַאֲנִי חוֹמָה וְשָׁדַי כַּמִּגְדָּלוֹת, תִּשְׁבָּחוֹת וּתְהִלּוֹת.
לְנֶאֱמָן בִּבְרִיתוֹ וְקַיָּם בִּשְׁבוּעָתוֹ, חַשְׁמַלֵּי שֵׁרוּתוֹ,
מִתְבַּהֲלִים מִשְּׂאֵתוֹ, מִתְנַטְּלִים מֵאֵימָתוֹ, וּמַגִּידִים אֱיָלוּתוֹ,
וַאֲנִי לְדוֹדִי, וְעָלַי תְּשׁוּקָתוֹ, בָּרוּךְ שֵׁם כְּבוֹד מַלְכוּתוֹ.

The service continues on page 860.

Some congregations recite the following *piyut* before *Kedushah* of *Shacharis* (p. 904) on the seventh day that falls on Monday, Wednesday or the Sabbath; and on the eighth day that falls on the Sabbath.

חַסְדֵי יהוה אַזְכִּיר תְּהִלּוֹת יהוה, כְּעַל כֹּל אֲשֶׁר גְּמָלָנוּ יהוה, וְרַב טוּב לְבֵית אֵיתָנַי, אֲשֶׁר גְּמָלָנוּ כְּרַחֲמָיו וּכְרֹב חֲסָדָיו לְעֵינַי, וַיֹּאמֶר אַךְ עַמִּי הֵמָּה וּבָנַי, בָּנִים לֹא יְשַׁקֵּרוּ נֶאֱמָנַי, בְּנֵי אֱמוּנַי בְּנֵי בְחוּנַי, וַיְהִי לָהֶם לְמוֹשִׁיעַ מִיגוֹנַי, בְּכָל צָרָתָם לוֹ צָר בְּעִנְיָנַי, וּמַלְאַךְ פָּנָיו הוֹשִׁיעַ הֲמוֹנַי, בְּאַהֲבָתוֹ וּבְחֶמְלָתוֹ גְּאָלָם מִמְּעַנַּי, וַיְנַטְּלֵם וַיְנַשְּׂאֵם עַד הֵנָּה עֲזָרָנוּ יהוה.

וְלֹא הֵסִיר חַסְדּוֹ מֵהֶם בְּכָל מְקוֹם גָּלוּתָם, וְלֹא מְאָסָם וְלֹא גְעָלָם לְכַלּוֹתָם, גָּלוּ תְחִלָּה לְמִצְרַיִם בְּשִׁבְעִים נַפְשׁוֹתָם, וַיִּפְרוּ וַיִּרְבּוּ בִּמְאֹד מְאֹד לְהַרְבּוֹתָם, וַיִּתְחַכְּמוּ עֲלֵיהֶם פּוֹטִים לְהַשְׁחִיתָם, הָפַךְ לִבָּם לִשְׂנֹאתָם, וּלְהִתְנַכֵּל בְּסִבְלוֹתָם, וַיַּעֲבִידוּם בְּפֶרֶךְ בְּכָל עֲבוֹדָתָם, וַיָּשִׂימוּ עֲלֵיהֶם שָׂרֵי מִסִּים לְעַנּוֹתָם, וַיִּצְעֲקוּ אֶל יהוה בַּצַּר לָהֶם מִמְּצוּקוֹתָם, וְלִמְעוֹן קָדְשׁוֹ הַשָּׁמַיְמָה עָלְתָה שַׁוְעָתָם, וַיָּקֶם לָהֶם מוֹשִׁיעִים לְהוֹשִׁיעָם מִצָּרָתָם, שָׁלַח מֹשֶׁה וְאַהֲרֹן אֲשֶׁר בָּחַר בָּהֶם וּבִשְׁלִיחוּתָם, וְשָׂם בְּמִצְרַיִם אוֹתוֹתָיו וּמוֹפְתָיו לְהַרְאוֹתָם, וַיַּהֲפוֹךְ לְדָם יְאֹרֵיהֶם וְכָל נַהֲרוֹתָם, הָפַךְ אֶת מֵימֵיהֶם לְדָם וַיָּמֶת אֶת דְּגָתָם, אָמַר וַיָּבֹא עָרוֹב וְכִנִּים בְּכָל עַפְרוֹתָם, וְשִׁלַּח בָּם עָרוֹב וַיֹּאכְלֵם וּצְפַרְדֵּעַ וְהִשְׁחִיתָם, וַיִּתֵּן לֶחָסִיל יְבוּלָם וּלְאַרְבֶּה תְּבוּאָתָם, וַיֹּאכַל כָּל עֵשֶׂב בְּאַרְצָם וְכָל פְּרִי אַדְמָתָם, וַיַּהֲרֹג בַּבָּרָד גַּפְנָם וּבַחֲנָמַל שִׁקְמָתָם, וַיַּסְגֵּר לַבָּרָד בְּעִירָם וְלָרְשָׁפִים בְּהֶמְתָּם, וְשִׁלַּח בָּם חֲרוֹן אַפּוֹ עֶבְרָה וָזַעַם וְצָרָה לְהַבְעִיתָם, וּמַלְאֲכֵי רָעִים הָיוּ בְּמִשְׁלַחְתָּם, וְלֹא חָשַׂךְ מִמָּוֶת נַפְשָׁם וְחַיָּתָם, וַיַּךְ כָּל בְּכוֹר בְּמִצְרַיִם וְאוֹנֵי רֵאשִׁיתָם, וַיּוֹצִיאֵם בְּכֶסֶף וְזָהָב וְאֵין כּוֹשֵׁל בְּמַחֲנוֹתָם, נָפַל פַּחְדָּם עַל מִצְרַיִם וְשָׂמְחוּ בְּצֵאתָם, פָּרַשׂ עָנָן לְמָסָךְ וְאֵשׁ לְהָאִיר אֲפֵלָתָם, וַיּוֹצֵא עַמּוֹ בְּשָׂשׂוֹן בְּחִירָיו בְּרִנָּתָם, וַיִּסְעוּ מֵרַעְמְסֵס לְסֻכּוֹת וּמִסֻּכּוֹת לְאֵתָם, וּמֵאֵתָם לִפְנֵי פִּי הַחִירוֹת הָיְתָה חֲנָיָתָם, בֵּין מִגְדֹּל וּבֵין הַיָּם בְּאֶמְצָעִיתָם, לִפְנֵי בַּעַל צְפוֹן הַנִּשְׁאָר מִכָּל

אֱלִילֵי פַּחֲזוּתָם, וְלָמָּה נִשְׁאַר הוּא כְּדֵי לְהַשִּׁיאָם וּלְהַטְעוֹתָם, שֶׁיֹּאמְרוּ קָשָׁה יִרְאָתָם, שֶׁלֹּא לָקְתָה כְּמוֹתָם, שָׁם חָנוּ בַּיּוֹם הַשְּׁלִישִׁי לִנְסִיעָתָם, וּבָרְבִיעִי מְתַקְּנִים כְּלֵיהֶם וּמַצִּיעִין בְּהֶמְתָּם, וְאָמְרוּ לָהֶם הָאוֹקְטוֹרִין בְּמִלָּתָם, הִגַּעְתֶּם תְּחוּם אֲשֶׁר קָבְעוּ לָכֶם צְעָנִים בְּטוֹבָתָם, אֲשֶׁר אֲמַרְתֶּם דֶּרֶךְ שְׁלֹשֶׁת יָמִים נֵלֵךְ וְנָשׁוּב לְעַבְדוּתָם, וּגְאוּלִים הֵשִׁיבוּ לֹא יָצָאנוּ בִּרְשׁוּתָם, כִּי אִם בְּיָד רָמָה בְּעַל כָּרְחָם שֶׁלֹּא בְטוֹבָתָם, וְהֵם עָנוּ רוֹצִים וְלֹא רוֹצִים אִישׁ כְּפִי שִׂיחָתָם, סוֹפְּכֶם לְקַיֵּם דְּבַר מַלְכוּת וְלֹא לַעֲבֹר עַל דַּעְתָּם, וְעָמְדוּ עֲלֵיהֶם וְהִכּוּם וּפְצָעוּם וְהָרְגוּ מִקְצָתָם, וְהֵם הָלְכוּ וְהִגִּידוּ לְפַרְעֹה כָּל קוֹרוֹתָם, וַיֵּהָפֵךְ לִבּוֹ וּלְבַב עַמּוֹ לִרְדּוֹף אוֹתָם, וַיֹּאמְרוּ מַה זֹּאת עָשִׂינוּ וַיָּשִׂמוּ עַל עֵקֶב בָּשְׁתָּם, וְאָמְרוּ נְבֻכִים הֵם וְעָבְטוּ אָרְחוֹתָם, נִרְדְּפָה אַחֲרֵיהֶם וְנִרְאֶה בְּרָעָתָם, וַיֶּאְסֹר אֶת רִכְבּוֹ בְּעַצְמוֹ כְּדֵי לְזָרְזָם וּלְפַתּוֹתָם, וְאֶת עַמּוֹ לָקַח עִמּוֹ בִּדְבָרִים לְרַמּוֹתָם, דֶּרֶךְ מְלָכִים לְהִתְנַהֵג אַחֲרֵי חֲיָלוֹתָם, וַאֲנִי אַקְדִּים רִאשׁוֹן לְהִלָּחֵם בְּמִלְחַמְתָּם, דֶּרֶךְ מְלָכִים לִטֹּל חֵלֶק רֵאשִׁית בִּזָּתָם, וַאֲנִי אַשְׁוֶה עִמָּכֶם בִּשְׁלַל צִבְעֵי רִקְמָתָם, וְעוֹד אֶפְתַּח אוֹצְרוֹתַי וּקְחוּ כָּל שְׂכִיּוֹת חֶמְדָּתָם, מִיַּד יָצְאוּ כֻלָּם בְּלֵב שָׁלֵם וְעָרְכוּ מַעַרְכוֹתָם, וַיִּקַּח שֵׁשׁ מֵאוֹת רֶכֶב בָּחוּר עִם כָּל כְּלֵי מַשְׁחִיתָם, וְכָל רֶכֶב מִצְרַיִם עִמָּהֶם בְּעֶזְרָתָם, וַיַּשִּׂיגוּ אוֹתָם חוֹנִים עַל הַיָּם בְּמַקְהֲלוֹתָם, וְנָשְׂאוּ עֵינֵיהֶם וְרָאוּ צָרֵיהֶם בְּקִרְבָּתָם, חִיל וּרְעֶדֶת שָׁם אֲחָזָתָם, וְזָעֲקוּ בִּתְפִלָּה וְתָפְשׂוּ אֻמָּנוּת אֲבוֹתָם, וּגְאָלָם חָזָק וְנוֹקֵם נִקְמָתָם, וַיַּרְא בַּצַּר לָהֶם בְּשָׁמְעוֹ אֶת רִנָּתָם, וַיּוֹשִׁיעֵם לְמַעַן שְׁמוֹ וַיִּגְאָלֵם מִצָּרָתָם, מִנֹּגַהּ נֶגְדּוֹ עָבָיו עָבְרוּ בָּרָד וְאֵשׁ גַּחֲלָתָם, וַיִּשְׁלַח חִצָּיו וַיְפִיצֵם וּבְרָקִים רָב לְהָמוֹתָם, וַיִּגְעַר בְּיַם סוּף וַיֶּחֱרַב וַיּוֹלִיכֵם בִּתְהוֹמוֹת בִּמְסִלָּתָם, וְשִׁבְטֵי יָהּ עָמְדוּ עַל הַיָּם לֵירֵד בִּירִידָתָם, וְשָׁם בִּנְיָמִין צָעִיר רֹדֵם וְשָׂרֵי יְהוּדָה רִגְמָתָם, וְכֻלָּם עָבְרוּ בַּיַּבָּשָׁה בְּמַיִם עַזִּים נְתִיבָתָם, וְהַמַּיִם לָהֶם חוֹמָה מִימִינָם וּמִשְּׂמֹאלָם בַּהֲלִיכָתָם, וְרֶסֶן מַתְעֶה עַל לְחָיֵי עֲנָמִים לַהֲבִיאָם בַּמַּיִם לְכַלּוֹתָם, וְנִהֲגָם בִּכְבֵדוּת וַיָּסַר אֵת אוֹפַנֵּי מַרְכְּבוֹתָם, וַיָּשׁוּבוּ הַמַּיִם וַיְכַסּוּ אֶת הָרֶכֶב וְאֶת הַפָּרָשִׁים בִּשְׁטִיפָתָם, וְנִעֵר פַּרְעֹה וְחֵילוֹ בְּיַם סוּף וְכָל צִבְאוֹתָם, וַיְכַסּוּ מַיִם צָרֵיהֶם אֶחָד מֵהֶם לֹא נוֹתַר בִּשְׁאֵרִיתָם, וִידִידִים עָבְרוּ וְגָזוּ וְרָאוּ פִּגְרֵי שׂוֹנְאֵיהֶם בְּמַפַּלְתָּם, וַיַּאֲמִינוּ בִדְבָרָיו וַיָּשִׁירוּ תְּהִלָּתוֹ בִּישׁוּעָתָם.

וְאִלּוּ כָּל הַיַּמִּים דְּיוֹ וַאֲגַמִּים קוּלְמוּסִים, וּבְנֵי אָדָם לַבְלָרִים וִירִיעוֹת אֲרָצוֹת פְּרוּסִים, וְכָל שַׂעֲרוֹת אָדָם פִּיּוֹת וּלְשׁוֹנוֹת מְקַלְּסִים, אֵינָן מַסְפִּיקִין לַחְקֹר פְּלָאוֹת וְנִסִּים, אַחַת מֵאֶלֶף אַלְפֵי אֲלָפִים וְרִבֵּי רְבָבוֹת הַנַּעֲשִׂים, אֲשֶׁר פָּעַל אָדוֹן לְעַם מִבֶּטֶן עֲמוּסִים, כִּי מִי גוֹי גָּדוֹל אֲשֶׁר בְּנִסִּים מִתְנוֹסְסִים, אוֹ הֲנִסָּה אֱלֹהִים לָבֹא לָקַחַת לוֹ גוֹי מִקֶּרֶב שׂוֹסִים, בְּמַסּוֹת בְּאוֹתוֹת וּבְמוֹפְתִים וּבְמִלְחָמָה נֶהֱרָסִים, כְּכֹל אֲשֶׁר עָשָׂה לָנוּ אֲדוֹן כָּל הַמַּעֲשִׂים.

חַסְדֵי יהוה כִּי לֹא תָמְנוּ, וְלֹא כָלוּ רַחֲמָיו מִמֶּנּוּ, יוֹם יוֹם יַעֲמָס לָנוּ, הָאֵל יְשׁוּעָתֵנוּ, בְּמִצְרַיִם נִגְלָה עֲבוּר לְגָאֳלֵנוּ, וּבְכָל צָרָה עִמָּנוּ לְהוֹשִׁיעֵנוּ, לֹא

מְאָסָנוּ וְלֹא גְעָלָנוּ לְכַלּוֹתֵנוּ, וְלֹא עָשָׂה עִמָּנוּ כָלָה כְּחַטֹּאתֵינוּ, וּבְכָל עֵת יָדוֹ נְטוּיָה עָלֵינוּ, בְּגָלוּת שִׁנְעָר שִׁלַּח לְמַעֲנֵנוּ, וּבְעֵילָם שָׂם כִּסְאוֹ לְרַחֲמֵנוּ, וּבְעַבְדוּתֵנוּ לֹא עֲזָבָנוּ אֱלֹהֵינוּ, וַיֵּט עָלֵינוּ חֶסֶד לִפְנֵי שׁוֹבֵינוּ, לָתֶת לָנוּ מִחְיָה וּלְרוֹמֵם בֵּית מַאֲוַיֵּנוּ, גַּרְנוּ מֶשֶׁךְ עִם קֵדָר לִשְׁכֵנֵינוּ, וְלֹא עָשָׂה כָלָה עִם שְׁאֵרִיתֵנוּ, וּבְאֶרֶץ נָכְרִיָּה כִּמְעַט שָׁכְנָה דוּמָה נַפְשֵׁנוּ, לוּלֵי יהוה שֶׁהָיָה בְּעֶזְרָתֵנוּ, כִּי בְּכָל פֶּה אֲכָלוּנוּ לְהַדִּיקֵנוּ, וְעֻלָּם הַכָּבֵד הִכְבִּידוּ עָלֵינוּ, עַד יֵעָרֶה מִמָּרוֹם רוּחַ לְנַחֲמֵנוּ, כִּי יהוה שׁוֹפְטֵנוּ יהוה מְחוֹקְקֵנוּ, יהוה מַלְכֵּנוּ הוּא יוֹשִׁיעֵנוּ, קוֹל גְּאֻלָּה יִשָּׁמַע בְּאַרְצֵנוּ, יהוה חָנֵּנוּ לְךָ קִוִּינוּ, הֱיֵה זְרוֹעָם לַבְּקָרִים אַף יְשׁוּעָתֵנוּ, וְלֹא נָסוֹג אָחוֹר מִמֶּךָּ וּתְחַיֵּנוּ, תְּמַהֵר לִשְׁכֹּן כָּבוֹד בְּאַרְצֵנוּ, וְיָבֹא מְבַשֵּׂר שָׁלוֹם לְבַשְּׂרֵנוּ, וְיִשְׂאוּ קוֹל לְרַנֵּן כָּל צוֹפֵינוּ, בַּבֹּקֶר חַסְדְּךָ שַׂבְּעֵנוּ, וּנְרַנְּנָה וְנִשְׂמְחָה בְּכָל יָמֵינוּ, וְכִימוֹת עִנִּיתָנוּ שַׂמְּחֵנוּ, וּמַעֲשֵׂה יָדֵינוּ כּוֹנְנָה עָלֵינוּ, הוֹשִׁיעָה יְמִינְךָ וַעֲנֵנוּ, וּמִתְּהוֹמוֹת הָאָרֶץ תָּשׁוּב תַּעֲלֵנוּ, יְשׁוּעָתְךָ אֱלֹהִים תְּשַׂגְּבֵנוּ, וּנְהַלְלָה שִׁמְךָ בְּשִׁיר וּנְגַדְּלֶנּוּ, כִּי אֱלֹהִים יוֹשִׁיעַ צִיּוֹן בְּיָמֵינוּ, וְיִבְנֶה עָרֵי יְהוּדָה וָהֶם יוֹשִׁיבֵנוּ, וְזֶרַע עֲבָדָיו וְאוֹהֲבֵי שְׁמוֹ בָהֶם יִשְׁכְּנוּ, וּמִבָּשָׁן וּמִמְּצֻלוֹת יָם עֵת תַּעֲלֵנוּ, עֻזָּה אֱלֹהִים זוּ פָּעַלְתָּ לָּנוּ, הַשָּׂם בַּחַיִּים נַפְשֵׁנוּ, וְלֹא נָתַן לַמּוֹט רַגְלֵנוּ, כִּי בְחַנְתָּנוּ כַּכֶּסֶף לְצָרְפֵנוּ, הֲבֵאתָנוּ בַמְּצוּדָה שַׂמְתָּ מוּעָקָה בְמָתְנֵינוּ, הִרְכַּבְתָּ אֱנוֹשׁ לְרֹאשֵׁנוּ, בָּאנוּ בָאֵשׁ וּבַמַּיִם לָרְוָיָה תּוֹצִיאֵנוּ, תְּחָנֵּנוּ וּתְבָרְכֵנוּ וְתָאִיר פָּנֶיךָ אֵלֵינוּ, תָּאִיר נֵרֵנוּ וְתַגִּיהַּ חָשְׁכֵּנוּ, חֲזֵה צִיּוֹן קִרְיַת מוֹעֲדֵינוּ, כִּי אִם שָׁם אַדִּיר יהוה אֲדוֹנֵנוּ, חָרְבוֹת יְרוּשָׁלַיִם יִפְצְחוּ רִנּוּנֵינוּ, כִּי נִחַם יהוה צִיּוֹן בֵּית מִקְדָּשֵׁנוּ, חָשַׂף זְרוֹעַ קָדְשׁוֹ לִנְקֹם נִקְמָתֵנוּ, וְרָאוּ כָל אַפְסֵי אָרֶץ אֵת יְשׁוּעַת אֱלֹהֵינוּ, בְּשׁוּבוֹ עִמָּנוּ מִגָּלוּתֵנוּ, וְיִצְמַח צֶמַח צַדִּיק לַעֲדָתֵנוּ, וְזֶה שְׁמוֹ אֲשֶׁר יִקְרְאוּ יהוה צִדְקֵנוּ.

וְאָז תִּתְגַּדַּל וְתִתְקַדַּשׁ, אֵלִי מַלְכִּי בַּקֹּדֶשׁ, נוֹרָא אֱלֹהִים מִמִּקְדָּשׁ קֹדֶשׁ, אֱלֹהִים דַּרְכְּךָ בַּקֹּדֶשׁ, מִי כָּמֹכָה נֶאְדָּר בַּקֹּדֶשׁ, הַנַּעֲרָץ בְּאֶרְאֶלֵּי קֹדֶשׁ, וִיהֻלְּלוּךָ בְּהַדְרַת קֹדֶשׁ, וְיִשְׁתַּחֲווּ בְּהַר הַקֹּדֶשׁ, אֶרְאֶלֵּי וְחַשְׁמַלֵּי קֹדֶשׁ, יַקְדִּישׁוּ וְיַעֲרִיצוּ בַּקֹּדֶשׁ, וְקוֹל כַּנְפֵי חַיּוֹת הַקֹּדֶשׁ, כְּקוֹל מַיִם רַבִּים בַּקֹּדֶשׁ, וְקוֹל אוֹפַנֵּי הַקֹּדֶשׁ, לְעֻמָּתָם מִנַּשְּׂאִים בַּקֹּדֶשׁ, קוֹל רַעַשׁ גָּדוֹל בַּקֹּדֶשׁ, וְקוֹל דְּמָמָה דַקָּה בַּקֹּדֶשׁ.

קוֹרְאִים זֶה לָזֶה, וְשׁוֹאֲלִים זֶה לָזֶה, וְנִרְשִׁים זֶה מִזֶּה, וְזֶה לְעֻמַּת זֶה, וְזֶה כְּנֶגֶד זֶה, וְזֶה מוּל זֶה, מִזֶּה וּמִזֶּה, מְשַׁלְּשִׁים בְּשִׁלּוּשׁ קָדוֹשׁ.

The service continues with *Kedushah,* p. 904.

Some congregations recite the following *piyut* before *Kedushah* of *Shacharis* (page 932) on the seventh day that falls on Friday; and the eighth day that falls on Sunday, Tuesday or Thursday.

אָמֵץ גְּבוּרוֹתֶיךָ מִי יְמַלֵּל, וּמִי יַעֲצָר כֹּחַ שִׁבְחֲךָ לְמַלֵּל, אִלּוּ פִינוּ מָלֵא כַיָּם שִׁירָה וְהַלֵּל, וְכָל שַׂעֲרוֹת רֹאשֵׁנוּ לְשׁוֹנוֹת לְהִתְפַּלֵּל, וּבָם אָנוּ עֲסוּקִים יוֹמָם וָלֵיל, לֹא נוּכַל לְהַסְפִּיק מֶלֶל, עַל אַחַת מֵרִבֵּי רְבָבוֹת שִׁמְךָ לְהַלֵּל, אֲשֶׁר הִפְלֵאתָ וְחִשַּׁבְתָּ לְהִתְעוֹלֵל, עַל עַם אֲשֶׁר לְךָ מִתְחוֹלֵל,

בְּטֶרֶם הָרִים יֻלָּדוּ וְאֶרֶץ תְּחוֹלֵל, חֲשַׁקְתָּם לְשִׁמְךָ בְּאַהַב לְכַלֵּל, הֱיוֹת לְךָ לְבָנִים וְאַתָּה לָמוֹ מְחוֹלֵל, בְּצֵל יָדְךָ אוֹתָם לְטַלֵּל, עַל כָּל עַם וְלָשׁוֹן רֹאשָׁם לְהַתְלֵל, בְּאֹרַח חַיִּים אוֹתָם לְהַסְלֵל, בְּלִי לְהַחֲלִיפָם בְּאֻמָּה אַחֶרֶת אוֹתָם לְחַלֵּל, לְהִתְפָּאֵר בָּם וְהֵם בְּךָ לְהִתְהַלֵּל.

כִּי מִי אֱלֹהַּ זוּלָתְךָ בָּעֶלְיוֹנִים, וּמִי כְעַמְּךָ יִשְׂרָאֵל גּוֹי אֶחָד בַּתַּחְתּוֹנִים, אֲשֶׁר הָלְכוּ אֱלֹהִים לִפְדוֹתָם מִמְּעַנִּים, בְּמַסּוֹת בְּאוֹתוֹת וּבְמוֹפְתִים מְשֻׁנִּים, כַּאֲשֶׁר עָשִׂיתָ אֲדוֹנֵי הָאֲדוֹנִים, לִבְנֵי שְׁלֹשֶׁת אֵיתָנִים, אֲשֶׁר בִּשְׁבִילָם טַסְתָּ מִמְּעוֹנִים, בִּרְכוּב כְּרוּב וְרוּחַ וַעֲנָנִים, וְנִגְלֵיתָ בִּכְבוֹדְךָ בְּאַדְמַת צֹעֲנִים, וְנָעוּ מִלְּפָנֶיךָ אֲשֵׁרִים וְחַמָּנִים, וְלֵב מִצְרַיִם הִמְסֵיתָ בְּדִבְיוֹנִים, בְּמַכּוֹת גְּדוֹלוֹת וָחֳלָיִם רָעִים וְנֶאֱמָנִים, וַתּוֹצִיא אֶת עַמְּךָ יִשְׂרָאֵל מִקֶּרֶב מוֹנִים, כְּעֶבֶר הַנִּשְׁמָט מֵרֶחֶם בְּתוֹךְ זְמַנִּים, בְּלֹא פְגַם וָנֶזֶק וְצַעַר בָּנִים, וְשֶׁלֹּא לִתֵּן פִּתְחוֹן פֶּה לַמִּינִים, לוֹמַר כְּעֶבֶד שֶׁבָּרַח מֵאֲדוֹנָיו כֵּן בָּרְחוּ אֱמוּנִים, וְלֹא הוֹצֵאתָם בְּשָׁעָה שֶׁבְּנֵי אָדָם יְשֵׁנִים, כִּי אִם לְאוֹר הַבֹּקֶר לְעֵין כָּל הֲמוֹנִים, כְּתוֹעֲפוֹת רְאֵם רָמִים וְעֶלְיוֹנִים, וְעַל כַּנְפֵי נֶשֶׁר נִטְעָנִים, שִׁיר וָשֶׁבַח וְהַלֵּל רוֹנְנִים, בְּתֹף וְכִנּוֹר וְעֻגָב וּמִנִּים, וּלְקַיֵּם דְּבָרְךָ אֲשֶׁר עֲצַתָּ לְרֹאשׁ מַאֲמִינִים, לֹא הוֹצֵאתָם בְּפַחֵי נֶפֶשׁ רֵיקָנִים, כִּי אִם מְלֵאִים כָּל טוּב כָּרִמּוֹנִים, כְּלֵי כֶסֶף וּכְלֵי זָהָב וְטוֹבוֹת אֲבָנִים, וּבִגְדֵי חֹפֶשׁ וְרִקְמַת צִבְעוֹנִים, כְּדֵי לְשַׁלֵּם שְׂכַר שִׁעְבּוּד חֹמֶר וּלְבֵנִים, חוֹפַפְתָּם בְּטִלּוּל שִׁבְעַת עֲנָנִים, מַעְלָה וּמַטָּה וּמֵאַרְבַּע רוּחוֹת גְּנוּנִים, לְחָשְׂכָם מִזֶּרֶם וְחֹרֶב וְצִנִּים, וּמִפְּנֵי חַיּוֹת וּנְשִׁיכַת צִפְעוֹנִים, וְעַיִן בְּעַיִן כְּבוֹדְךָ מְהַלֵּךְ לְפָנִים, בֶּעָנָן יוֹמָם לַנְחוֹתָם נְתִיבוֹת מְתֻקָּנִים, וּבָאֵשׁ לַיְלָה בְּלִי לְהִכָּשֵׁל בְּאִישׁוֹנִים, מִנָּוֶה טוֹב לְנָוֶה טוֹב נוֹסְעִים וְחוֹנִים, לֹא צְמֵאִים וְלֹא מְכֻפָּנִים, כִּי מְרַחֲמָם יְנַהֲגֵם עַל מַבּוּעֵי שְׁמָנִים, וְהוּא יְנַהֲלֵם עַל מַבּוּעֵי עֲיָנִים, וְשַׂר נוֹא יוֹשֵׁב עַל מִפְתַּן אַרְמוֹנִים, מְצַפֶּה יַד דֶּרֶךְ לְיָמִים הַנִּתָּנִים, וְהִנֵּה כְּתָב אֵלָיו מֵאֶרֶץ תֵּימָנִים, וְשׁוֹמְרִים שֶׁהִפְקִיד עֲלֵיהֶם מְמֻנִּים, הִתְחִילוּ כָּזֹאת אֵלָיו מְתַנִּים, וְהֶרְאוּהוּ פְצָעִים שֶׁפְּצָעוּם פִּרְחֵי נֶאֱמָנִים, וְצָוַח וַי וַי וְכָל עֲבָדָיו אַחֲרָיו עוֹנִים, וְנָמוּ מַה זֹּאת עָשִׂינוּ כְּסִכְלוֹנִים, כִּי שִׁלַּחְנוּ עֲבָדִים שֶׁתַּחַת יָדֵינוּ מְכֻדָּנִים, מִי יִרְמָס לָנוּ חֹמֶר וּמִי יַחֲזִיק לָנוּ מַלְבֵּנִים, מִי יִבְנֶה לָנוּ חוֹמוֹת וּבִנְיָנִים, הָעֵת יַגְדִּילוּ עָלֵינוּ שְׁכֵנִים, וְגַם הַמְּלָכִים שֶׁמַּס לָנוּ נוֹתְנִים, שׁוּב לֹא יִהְוּ אֵלֵינוּ פוֹנִים, כִּי יֹאמְרוּ הִנֵּה עֲבָדִים שֶׁתַּחַת יְדֵיהֶם נְתוּנִים, הֵם פָּשְׁעוּ בָם וּבָהֶם לֹא סוֹפְנִים, אַף כִּי אֲנַחְנוּ חוֹרֵי הָאָרֶץ וּקְצִינִים, וּבְכֵן שָׁלַח וְקִבֵּץ אֶת כָּל חַרְטֻמֵּי מִצְרַיִם וְאִצְטַגְנִינִים, וְגַם אֶת הָאוֹבוֹת וְאֶת הַיִּדְּעוֹנִים, וַיִּוָּעֵץ בָּם וּבִזְקֵנִים, וַיֵּצְאוּ כֻלָּם בְּעֵצָה אַחַת מְכֻוָּנִים, לִרְדֹּף אַחֲרֵיהֶם וּלְבַלְּעָם כְּתַנִּינִים, וַיְצַו וַיַּעֲבִירוּ קוֹל בְּאֶרֶץ סְוֵנִים, כָּל שׁוֹלֵף חֶרֶב הֱיוֹת מוּכָנִים, וַיֵּאָסְפוּ כֻלָּם כְּאִישׁ אֶחָד מְזֻמָּנִים וְהָאֲחַשְׁדַּרְפְּנִים וְהַפַּחוֹת וְהַסְּגָנִים, וְאַנְשֵׁי הַצָּבָא אִישׁ וְאִישׁ בִּכְלֵי זְיָנִים, אָז פָּתַח אוֹצְרוֹת גִּנְזֵי מַטְמוֹנִים, אֲשֶׁר גָּנַז הוּא וּמְלָכִים קַדְמוֹנִים, וְהוֹצִיא כְּלֵי יְקָר וְדַרְכְּמוֹנִים, וְחָלַק לְכָל אֶחָד וְאֶחָד כְּפִי הֲגוּנִים, וְשִׁדְּלָם בִּדְבָרִים

וְהִסְבִּיר לָמוֹ פָּנִים, וְכֹה אָמַר לָהֶם בְּשִׂיחַ מַעֲנִים, מִשְׁפַּט הַמֶּלֶךְ כָּל הָעָם בּוֹזְזִים וּלְפָנָיו נוֹתְנִים, וַאֲנִי כְּאֶחָד מִכֶּם אֶטֹּל מָנִים, מִשְׁפַּט הַמֶּלֶךְ עֲבָדָיו יוֹצְאִים רִאשׁוֹנִים, וַאֲנִי אֵצֵא רִאשׁוֹן וְאַתֶּם צְאוּ אַחֲרוֹנִים, מִשְׁפַּט הַמֶּלֶךְ עֲבָדָיו אוֹסְרִים מֶרְכַּבְתּוֹ וּמְתַקְּנִים, וַאֲנִי בְּעַצְמִי אֶאֱסֹר רִכְבִּי וְאָשִׁים רְסָנִים, וְנִתְרַצּוּ יַחַד גְּדוֹלִים וּקְטַנִּים, וַיָּשִׂימוּ כּוֹבַע עַל רָאשֵׁיהֶם וְלָבְשׁוּ שִׁרְיוֹנִים, וַיַּחְגְּרוּ אִישׁ חַרְבּוֹ וְנָטְלוּ כִידוֹנִים, וַיִּקְחוּ אִישׁ רֹמַח בְּיָדוֹ וַיַּחֲזִיקוּ מָגִנִּים, וְנָשְׂאוּ קֶשֶׁת וּמָלְאוּ שִׁלְטֵיהֶם חִצִּים שְׁנוּנִים, וְהַקַּלָּעִים אִישׁ קַלְעוֹ בְּיָדוֹ לְקַלַּע בָּאֲבָנִים, וַיֵּצְאוּ יַחַד בְּלֵב שָׁלֵם וּבִצְבִיוֹנִים, וְלֹא נִכְשַׁל אֶחָד מֵהֶם וְלֹא אֵרְעוּהוּ סִמָּנִים, לְבִלְתִּי לְנַחֵשׁ לָשׁוּב לְמְלוֹנִים, כִּי חֻקּוֹת הָעַמִּים מְנַחֲשִׁים וּמְעוֹנְנִים, וְאִישׁ יִשְׂרָאֵל עַל שְׂפַת יָם חוֹנִים, וַיִּשְׂאוּ עֵינֵיהֶם וְהִנֵּה מִצְרַיִם נוֹסְעִים כַּעֲנָנִים, וְאֵין מָקוֹם לָנוּס לֹא לְאָחוֹר וְלֹא לְפָנִים, וְאַף לֹא מִדַּפְּנוֹת מִפְּנֵי חַיּוֹת וּפְתָנִים, וַיִּצְעֲקוּ אֶל יהוה וְהִפִּילוּ לְפָנָיו תַּחֲנוּנִים, וַיִּמָּצֵא לָהֶם הַמָּצוּי בְּכָל עִדָּנִים, וַיִּגְעַר בְּיַם סוּף וְחָרְבוּ זֵידוֹנִים, וַיֵּלְכוּ בִתְהוֹמוֹת כְּעַל דְּרָכִים מְפֻנִּים, מִזֶּה וּמִזֶּה הֶעֱלָה אִילָנוֹת טְעוּנִים, וּבְתוֹךְ תְּהוֹמוֹת הִמְתִּיק לָמוֹ מַעְיָנִים, וְעִשֵּׁן לִפְנֵיהֶם קְטֹרֶת סַמָּמָנִים, וַיַּנְחֵם אֶל מְחוֹז חֶפְצָם שַׁאֲנַנִּים, וְכַעֲלוֹת לְצַד זֶה עַל שְׂפַת יָם כֵּנִים, בָּאוּ מִצַּד זֶה בְּתוֹךְ יָם סְוֵנִים, תְּחִלָּה בְּרָצוֹן וְסוֹף בְּרֶסֶן מְרֻסָּנִים, כִּי סִדְרֵי בְרֵאשִׁית עֲלֵיהֶם מִשְׁתַּנִּים, דֶּרֶךְ אֶרֶץ סוּסִים מוֹשְׁכִים אוֹפַנִּים, וְנֶהְפַּךְ בָּם וְנִמְשְׁכוּ סוּסִים אַחַר הַסַּדָּנִים, דֶּרֶךְ אֶרֶץ מָקוֹם שֶׁרַכָּב מַנְהִיג שָׁם מוֹשְׁכִים וּפוֹנִים, וְכַאן מַנְהִיג וּמוֹשֵׁךְ בְּעַל כָּרְחָם נִפְנִים, וּבָאוּ לְתוֹךְ יָם בְּאֶמְצַע שְׁאוֹנִים, וְהִנֵּה כְּבוֹד יהוה אֱלֹהֵי יִשְׂרָאֵל בָּא בְּרֹב לִגְיוֹנִים, נִיִּרְכַּב עַל כְּרוּב וַיֵּדֶא מוּל בַּעֲלֵי מְדָנִים, וְעִמּוֹ שַׂרְפֵי הַקֹּדֶשׁ וְחַיּוֹת וְאוֹפַנִּים, וְאֶלֶף אַלְפִין וְרִבּוֹ רִבְבָן גְּדוּדֵי שִׁנְאַנִּים, וְרֶכֶב אֵשׁ וְסוּסֵי אֵשׁ וְכָל דִּמְיוֹנִים, כַּמַּרְאֶה אֲשֶׁר רָאָה צִיר בְּחֶזְיוֹנִים, סוּסִים אֲדֻמִּים וְסוּסִים שְׁחוֹרִים שְׂרֻקִּים וּלְבָנִים, וַיַּחֲנוּ אֵלֶּה נֹכַח אֵלֶּה אֲפוּנִים, מַחֲנֶה אֵשׁ מוּל מַחֲנֶה קַשׁ פָּנִים בְּפָנִים, וּלְפִי שָׁעָה הִרְגִּישׁוּ כָּל צְבָא מְעוֹנִים, בִּזְרוֹעַ עֻזּוֹ נִלְחָם רַב אוֹנִים, לֹא בְּעֹצֶם יַד חֵיל שׁוֹטְנִים, הֲלֹא הַנְּפִילִים וְאַנְשֵׁי הַשֵּׁם מְכֻנִּים, מֵרוּחַ אַפּוֹ כָּלוּ וְהִנָּם טְמוּנִים, וְאַף כִּי מְשׁוּלִים לְמִשְׁעֶנֶת קָנִים, אֲשֶׁר הֶבֶל וָרִיק לְעֶזְרָה מְתֻקָּנִים, כִּי אִם לְהוֹדִיעַ חִבַּת אָב לְבָנִים, וַיַּרְעֵם בְּקוֹל גְּאוֹנוֹ עַל גְּאוֹנִים, וַיָּרָץ לִקְרָאתָם בְּמָגֵן וְצִנִּים, וַיַּדְרִיכֵם בְּאַפּוֹ וַיִּרְמְסֵם בַּחֲמָתוֹ כְּחֹמֶר טִינִים, וְהִדִּישָׁם כְּהִדּוּשׁ מַתְבֵּן בְּמוֹ מַדְמֵנִים, וְאָז שַׂר יָם עִם שַׂר חָם יַחַד נִדּוֹנִים, זֶה לְעֻמַּת זֶה נֶאֱבָקוּ בִּמְעוֹנִים, וַיֶּחֱזַק רַהַב עַל שַׂר אֲוֵנִים, וַיַּשְׁלִיכֵהוּ אַרְצָה וַיִּרְמְסֵהוּ בְּעֶזְרַת דַּר אוֹפַנִּים, וְעַם זוּ בְּשׁוּרָם בְּאֵלֶּה דִינִים, עוֹזֵר וְעָזוּר בְּקַו נִדּוֹנִים, פָּתְחוּ פִיהֶם בְּשִׁיר וּבִרְנָנִים, עָזִּי וְזִמְרָת יָהּ פָּצְחוּ בִּרְנוּנִים, לְרָם עַל רָמִים וּמִתְגָּאֶה עַל גֵּוְתָנִים, לְשׁוֹמֵעַ אֶנְקַת אֶבְיוֹנִים, לְמַשְׁפִּיל רָמִים וּמֵרִים מִסְכֵּנִים, וְקִדְּמוּ שָׂרִים אַחַר נוֹגְנִים, וּבְתוֹךְ עֲלָמוֹת תּוֹפְפוּ נִגּוּנִים, וְאַחַר כָּךְ הִרְשׁוּ שִׁנְאַנִּים.

The service continues with *Kedushah,* page 932.

☙ Selected Laws and Customs

compiled by Rabbi Hersh Goldwurm

Although most of the applicable laws are cited in the main text of the *Machzor,* in some cases they are too involved or lengthy to be given fully where they apply. A selection of such laws is compiled here. This digest cannot cover all eventualities and should be regarded merely as a guide; in case of doubt, one should consult a competent halachic authority. When a particular *halachah* is in dispute, we generally follow the ruling of *Mishnah Berurah.* On occasion, however (usually when *Mishnah Berurah* does not give a definitive ruling or when a significant number of congregations do not follow *Mishnah Berurah's* ruling), we cite more than one opinion. As a general rule, each congregation is bound by its tradition and the ruling of its authorities.

These laws and customs have been culled, in the main, from the most widely accepted authorities: the *Shulchan Aruch Orach Chaim* [here abbreviated *O.C.*] and *Mishnah Berurah* [*M.B.*]. We have also included many of the general laws of prayer that apply to the *Yom Tov.*

Special sections have been added on: the laws pertaining to Erev Pesach (§1-12); the Blessing for Dew (טַל) and the deletion of the passage מַשִּׁיב הָרוּחַ וּמוֹרִיד הַגֶּשֶׁם (§98-108); *Sefiras HaOmer* (§109-134); the recitation of וְתֵן בְּרָכָה during *Chol HaMoed* and after Pesach (§135-139); and Erev Pesach that falls on the Sabbath (§140-149).

These digests, too, are not a substitute for the source texts. They are meant only as a learning and familiarizing tool. For halachic questions, one should consult the *Shulchan Aruch* and its commentaries and/or a halachic authority.

EREV PESACH

1. The search for *chametz* should start immediately at the beginning of the night of 14 Nissan (*O.C.* 431:1, *M.B.* §1). [Beginning of the night — halachically synonymous with צֵאת הַכּוֹכָבִים, *emergence of the stars* — is interpreted variously by different *poskim*; each person should follow the tradition of his community.] No other activity — not even learning Torah — should be started from half an hour before the beginning of the night until the search is done (*O.C.* 431:2). One may however recite the *Maariv* prayer with a *minyan* prior to the search. If one will pray without a *minyan* there is question as to what he should do first — the search or the prayer; there is not a conclusive ruling on this question and one may follow either sequence (*M.B.* 431:4).

2. One must search all the places into which *chametz* may conceivably have been brought (*O.C.* 433:3). If one owns a business he must conduct a search at his place of business as well; he should consult a halachic authority as to when and how he should conduct the search. Before starting the search one recites the *berachah*, ... בָּרוּךְ אַתָּה ... מֶלֶךְ הָעוֹלָם אֲשֶׁר קִדְּשָׁנוּ ... עַל בִּעוּר חָמֵץ, *Blessed are You ... Who has sanctified us ... concerning the removal of chametz* (*O.C.* 432:1). Although the removal of *chametz* — its destruction — only takes place on the morrow, the *berachah* for it is recited now, because the purpose of the search is the ultimate removal of *chametz* (*M.B.* §2). Just as with other *mitzvos*, one may not interpose between the *berachah* and the beginning of the search with extraneous talk; if one did talk he must recite the *berachah* again. Moreover, one should refrain from extraneous talk during the entire search in order to concentrate totally on the search (*O.C.* 432:1 with *M.B.*). It is customary to put out [ten] pieces of *chametz* where they will be found during the search so that the *berachah* should not have been recited in vain in case no *chametz* is found (*O.C.* 432:2). The search must be done with a candle (*O.C.* 433:2).

3. After the search is completed one must formally nullify any *chametz* he has not found and may still have. [The formula appears on page 2.] If one does not understand the language of the formula he must recite it in a language he understands. Since the Hebrew term חָמֵץ, *chametz*, includes both leavened doughs and leavening agents — שְׂאוֹר — made from grain, when the formula is said in other languages both of these types of *chametz* must be specified (*O.C.* 434:2).

☙ Shacharis on Erev Pesach

4. In *Shacharis*, psalm 100, מִזְמוֹר לְתוֹדָה, *A psalm of thanksgiving*, is omitted. *Tachanun* is not said, just as it is not said for the entire month of Nissan. The short prayer קֵל אֶרֶךְ אַפַּיִם, usually said on Monday and Thursday before the Torah reading, and the יְהִי רָצוֹן prayers, said after the Torah reading, are omitted. Psalm 20 which is usually said before וּבָא לְצִיּוֹן is also omitted (*O.C.* 429:2).

☙ The Fast of the Firstborn and the Siyum

5. It is a time honored tradition for all firstborn males to fast on the eve of Pesach in commemoration of the miracle which was experienced by the firstborn on the night of Pesach in Egypt. [As the Torah relates (*Ex.* 11:4-7, 12:29-30), all the firstborn in Egypt died at midnight of 15 Nissan while all the Israelite firstborn were spared.] The fast is mentioned in *Yerushalmi* (*Pesachim* 10:1) and *Maseches Soferim* (21:3; see *Tur and Bais Yosef* O.C. 470). One fasts whether he is his mother's firstborn or his father's. A father fasts for his minor male firstborn. When the Pesach eve falls on the Sabbath, the fast is observed on the preceding Thursday (*O.C.* 470:1-2). Someone who has difficulty fasting, e.g., he suffers from headaches, or it is difficult for him to eat after a fast so that he might find it hard to eat *matzah* and *maror* at the *Seder*, need not fast (*M.B.* §2). Some *poskim* assert that a firstborn may participate in a סְעוּדַת מִצְוָה, *feast celebrating the performance of a mitzvah,* e.g., a *bris* or a *pidyon haben.* Some extend this dispensation even to celebration of a *siyum* — the completion of the study of a tractate of *Gemara.* Custom accepts the more lenient opinion. Moreover, even if the firstborn has not participated in the learning, he may participate in the meal. In such a case it is customary for those who have not participated in the learning to be present at least when the last passage of the tractate is studied (*M.B.* §10).

◄§ Chametz on the Eve of Pesach

6. It is forbidden to eat *chametz* later than two hours before noon on the eve of Pesach. It is also forbidden to derive benefit from *chametz* in the hour before noon. Hence one must be sure to sell or give his *chametz* to a gentile, or to destroy it, earlier than one hour before noon. [According to most *poskim,* an hour in this regard is not an hour on the clock but a twelfth of the day — a halachic hour (see below), which is often somewhat longer than a clock hour.] One who neglected to sell his *chametz* on time should ask a competent halachic authority, since the laws governing such cases are very complex. [Moreover, the sale of *chametz* to a gentile should never be attempted by a layman.] There is disagreement among the *poskim* regarding how the day is reckoned with regard to these laws. Either the day begins with dawn and ends with the emergence of the stars, or it begins at sunup and ends with sundown. Ideally one should comply with the first, more stringent, view (*O.C.* 443:1 with *M.B.*).

◄§ Matzah on the Eve of Pesach

7. *Matzah* may not be eaten from dawn on the fourteenth of Nissan, to highlight the *mitzvah* aspect of the *matzah* eaten at the *Seder*. This applies only to *matzah* which is fit to be used for the fulfillment of the *mitzvah* of eating *matzah* at the *Seder*. *Matzah* which was prepared with fruit-juice or eggs may be eaten (*O.C.* 471:2). However, it is customary among Ashkenazim to refrain from eating such *matzos* throughout Pesach because of their greater susceptibility to becoming *chametz*, [so that such *matzos* are not eaten whenever *chametz* is prohibited] (*M.B.* §11; see *O.C.* 462:4, 444:1, *Shaarei Teshuvah* there).

◄§ Burning the Chametz

8. The *chametz* which has been found during the search and any other *chametz* which has not been sold may be destroyed either through burning (the preferred way, see below), reducing it to crumbs and strewing the crumbs to the wind, or in the case of *chametz* grain, cutting or grinding it up and then strewing it to the wind (*O.C.* 445:1). One may also cast the *chametz* into a river or sea, but should first reduce it to crumbs or small pieces (*O.C.* 445:1 with *M.B.* §5). However, in deference to the opinion of R' Yehudah (*Pesachim* 21a), it is customary to destroy the *chametz* only through burning. Although technically the *chametz* may be destroyed anytime before noon of 14 Nissan (see *M.B.* 443:1 with *Shaar Hatziyun*), nevertheless custom has adopted two strictures in this regard: (a) the *chametz* should not be burned before sunup of the fourteenth of Nissan (*O.C.* 445:1); (b) since it is customary to again nullify the *chametz* after one has destroyed it, and this second nullification is valid only until one halachic hour before noon (*Gemara Pesachim* 7a; for a definition of the term *halachic hour*, see §6), one must allow enough time when burning the *chametz* to enable him to nullify it within the appropriate time after it has been consumed by the fire (*M.B.* 434:12).

◄§ The Second Nullification of Chametz

9. It is customary to again nullify the *chametz* after one has destroyed it, and to include in this nullification even the *chametz* one has found during the search and has set aside to be burned (*O.C.* 434:2). The reason for this is because one may have acquired *chametz* between the first nullification and the destruction and neglect to burn some of it. Also, he may neglect to burn some of the *chametz* he put aside for use last night or this morning. The formula for this nullification is modified to include the *chametz* one has found and will burn. It appears on page 2.

◄§ Work on the Eve of Pesach

10. The day before the Pesach festival, more so than the eve of any other festival, has a quasi-festive aspect. In the Temple era, since every Jew was obligated to participate in a *pesach* offering, the period from noon till night — the time in which the *pesach* offering may be brought — was a festival in regard to doing work (*Yerushalmi Pesachim 4:1*). Even in the post-Temple era this prohibition was continued (*Tosafos Pesachim 50a; O.C.* 468:1). Furthermore, as reported by the Mishnah, some localities extended the prohibition to the morning of the fourteenth of Nissan. Everyone must conform to the custom followed in the locality he happens to be in (*Pesachim* 50a; *O.C.* 468:4). *Rama* (*O.C.* 468:3) reports that the custom is to refrain from work in the morning, but later *poskim* assert that this custom is not universal (*M.B.* §12). [Nowadays the custom has been virtually forgotten.]

11. The prohibition against work in the afternoon is similar to the law regarding work on *Chol HaMoed*. All of the leniencies — e.g., work done to avert monetary loss — which apply to *Chol HaMoed*, apply also to the Pesach eve (*M.B.* 468:7). [It is impossible to summarize these laws in detail here.] Any work done for gain [which is prohibited on *Chol HaMoed*] is prohibited even if it is needed for the festival. Also any מְלָאכָה גְמוּרָה may not be done even if it is needed for the festival. Hence, it is prohibited to sew new clothes, even for the festival. One may not wash clothing for the festival. However one may mend clothing needed for the festival, but may not do so for money (*O.C.* 468:2 with *M.B.* §6-8). One may not cut his hair or have it cut (by a fellow Jew) even though this is done for the festival, but may cut his fingernails if he has forgotten to do so in the morning (*M.B.* §5). [Ideally though, the fingernails should be cut in the morning.] *Rama* states that it is permissible to ask a gentile to do work for him (*O.C.* 468:1). Hence one may have his hair cut by a gentile even though it is impossible to avoid a minimal amount of assistance, such as bending the head to facilitate the work (*M.B.* §5). One may bring materials to an artisan to be fixed and may pick them up from him in the afternoon, even if these materials are not needed for the festival (*O.C.* 468:10).

☙§ Meals during the Afternoon of the Eve of Pesach

12. Ideally, the *matzah* and *maror* should be eaten at the *Seder* with appetite. To ensure compliance with this, the Sages instituted a safeguard and restricted food intake during the three halachic hours before sundown (for a definition of *halachic hours* see §6) — i.e., halfway between the true noon and sundown. During this time one may not eat anything made of grain (*O.C.* 471:1). This includes ordinary *matzah* [which may not be eaten the entire day] *matzah* kneaded with fruit-juice or egg [which Ashkenazic custom forbids whenever *chametz* may not be eaten], or foods prepared with matzah meal. One may eat a small amount of fruit, vegetable, meat, fish, egg, etc., but should be careful not fill himself with these foods. A person whose appetite is dulled by eating even a small amount of food should refrain from eating at all (*O.C.* 471:1 with *M.B.*§3).

GENERAL LAWS OF PRAYER

☙§ The Obligation

13. Prayer is a major ingredient of every Jew's daily religious life. The Sages teach us that in the post-Temple era, prayer was substituted for the Temple service, and according to some authorities it is a Scriptural obligation to pray every single day (see *Rambam, Hil. Tefillah*).

14. Before praying, one should set aside a few minutes to collect his thoughts and to prepare himself mentally to stand before his Maker. Also, one should not rush away immediately after ending his prayer so as not to give the impression that he regards prayer as a burdensome task (*O.C.* 93:1).

15. Before beginning to pray, one should meditate upon God's infinite greatness and man's insignificance, and thereby remove from his heart any thoughts of physical pleasure (*O.C.* 98:1). By pondering God's works, man recognizes His infinite wisdom and comes to love and laud Him. This makes man cognizant of his own puny intelligence and flawed nature and puts him in a proper frame of mind to plead for God's mercy (*Rambam, Yesodei HaTorah* 2:2).

16. The prayers should be said with a feeling of awe and humility, and surely not in an atmosphere of levity, frivolity, or mundane concerns, nor should one pray while angry. Rather one should pray with the feeling of happiness brought on by the knowledge of God's historic kindness to Israel and His mercy to all creatures (*O.C.* 93:2).

☙§ Concentration on the Prayers

17. During *Shemoneh Esrei* one should imagine that he is in the Holy Temple and concentrate his feelings and thoughts toward Heaven, clearing his mind of all extraneous matters (*O.C.* 95:2). His eyes should be directed downward, either closed or reading from the *machzor* (*O.C.* 95:2, *M.B.* 5). One should not look up during *Shemoneh Esrei*, but when he feels his concentration failing he should raise his eyes heavenward to renew his inspiration (*M.B.* 90:8).

18. One should know the meaning of his prayers. If one had an audience with a human ruler he would take the utmost care in his choice of words and be aware of their meaning. Surely, therefore, when one stands before the King of Kings Who knows his innermost thoughts, he must be careful how he speaks (*O.C.* 98:1). Especially in regard to the benedictions of *Shemoneh Esrei*, one should at least meditate on the meaning of the concluding sentence of each benediction, which summarizes its theme (e.g., בָּרוּךְ ... הָאֵל הַקָּדוֹשׁ, *Blessed ... the holy God; M.B.* 101 §1). The first benediction of the *Shemoneh Esrei* is treated with special stringency in this regard. According to the *halachah* as stated in the Talmud, this benediction must be repeated if it was said without concentration on its meaning (*O.C.* 101:1). However, *Rama (loc. cit.)* rules that it is best *not* to repeat the benediction because it is likely that one will not concentrate properly even during the repetition. *Chayei Adam* (cited in *M.B.* 101:4) advises that if one realized his inattentiveness before saying the word HASHEM in the concluding formula of the first blessing (בָּרוּךְ ... מָגֵן אַבְרָהָם), he should start over from אֱלֹהֵי אַבְרָהָם. Thus it is of utmost importance that one learn the meaning of the prayers in order to develop his power of concentration (*M.B.* 101:2).

19. The prayers of *Yom Tov* differ from the regular weekday prayers. This is especially true in communities where *piyutim* are said. Thus it is desirable that one learn the meaning of the prayers before *Yom Tov* so that he will understand what he is reciting. One should also leaf through the *machzor* to familiarize himself with the relatively unfamiliar sequence of the prayers, so that he not have to interrupt the flow of the prayer to find the place. This is especially important in congregations that skip some of the *piyutim.* Likewise one should teach his children where to find the prayers so that they will not distract him during the services (*Matteh Ephraim* 625:26).

☙ Women's Obligation to Pray

20. Women are obligated to pray, and according to *Rambam* and *Shulchan Aruch* (*O.C.* 106:1) this obligation has Scriptural status. However, there are various opinions regarding the extent of their obligation.

According to the views preferred by *M.B.* (106:4), women are required to recite the *Shemoneh Esrei* of *Shacharis* and *Minchah;* they must recall the Exodus by reciting אֱמֶת וְיַצִּיב, *true and certain* (the prayer after the *Shacharis* recitation of *Shema)*, and אֱמֶת וֶאֱמוּנָה, *true and faithful* (the parallel prayer after the *Maariv* recitation of *Shema)*, because it recalls the Exodus (*M.B.* 70:2); and it is urged that they recite at least the first verse of *Shema* because it constitutes קַבָּלַת עוֹל מַלְכוּת שָׁמַיִם, *acceptance of God's sovereignty* (*O.C.* 70:1).

Some authorities rule that women should also recite all the morning benedictions. According to one view, *Pesukei D'zimrah* is introductory to *Shemoneh Esrei* and, consequently, is obligatory upon women too (*M.B.* 70:2).

Women should recite בִּרְכַּת הַתּוֹרָה, *blessings of the Torah* (O.C. 47:14, see *Be'ur Halachah)*.

According to *Magen Avraham* (*O.C.* 106:2), women are required by the Torah to pray once a day and they may formulate the prayer as they wish. In many countries, this ruling became the basis for the custom that women recite a brief prayer early in the morning and do not recite any of the formal prayers from the *Siddur*.

☙ Miscellaneous Laws

21. One should not eat nor drink in the morning before praying (*O.C.* 89:3). However, it is permitted to drink water, tea, or coffee (*M.B.* 89:22) with milk (*Daas Torah* 89:5).

22. One may not pray in the presence of immodestly clad women, or facing a window through which they can be observed (see *O.C.* 75 for details).

23. It is forbidden to pray while one feels the need to discharge his bodily functions (*O.C.* 92:1-3).

24. One must wash his hands before praying, but no benediction is required (*O.C.* 92:4).

PRAYER WITH THE CONGREGATION

☙ Prayer with a Minyan of Ten

25. One should do his utmost to pray in the synagogue together with the congregation (*O.C.* 90:9), for the Almighty does not reject the prayer of the many. Contrary to the popular misconception that it is sufficient to respond to בָּרְכוּ and קְדוּשָׁה, the main objective of prayer with a *minyan* is to recite *Shemoneh Esrei* with the *minyan*. Therefore one must arrive at the synagogue early enough to keep up with the congregation (*M.B.* §28).

☙ Instructions for Latecomers

26. If one arrived at the synagogue too late to recite the entire order of the prayer and still recite the *Shemoneh Esrei* together with the congregation, he may omit certain parts of the service and recite them after the end of *Shacharis.* If time is extremely short, it suffices to recite the benedictions עַל נְטִילַת יָדַיִם; אֲשֶׁר יָצַר; אֱלֹהַי נְשָׁמָה; the benedictions over the Torah; בָּרוּךְ שֶׁאָמַר; אַשְׁרֵי; נִשְׁמַת; and from יִשְׁתַּבַּח through *Shemoneh Esrei.* If time permits, the following sections (listed in descending order of importance) should be recited:

(1) הַלְלוּיָהּ הַלְלוּ אֵל בְּקָדְשׁוֹ;

(2) הַלְלוּיָהּ הַלְלוּ אֶת ה׳ מִן הַשָּׁמַיִם;

(3) the other three הַלְלוּיָהּ psalms;

(4) from וַיְבָרֶךְ דָּוִיד until לְשֵׁם תִּפְאַרְתֶּךָ;

(5) הודו until וְהוּא רַחוּם;

(6) the rest of *Pesukei D'zimrah* (*O.C.* 52:1, *M.B.* 4, *Ba'er Heitev* §3).

27. All of the psalms that are recited daily take precedence over those that are added on the Sabbath and Festival (with the exception of נִשְׁמַת, as noted above). Among the Sabbath additions themselves, some selections have priority over the others. They are: לְדָוִד בְּשַׁנּוֹתוֹ, לַמְנַצֵּחַ, and תְּפִלָּה לְמֹשֶׁה (*M.B.* 52:5).

28. The above is only an emergency solution. One should not rely on this to arrive late for the *Pesukei D'zimrah,* because the proper order of the prayers is of utmost importance. Indeed, some authorities contend that recitation of the prayers in their proper order takes priority over the obligation to recite *Shemoneh Esrei* together with the congregation (*M.B.* 52:1).

RESPONSES DURING THE PRAYER

◆§ During Pesukei D'zimrah

29. Other than the exceptions noted below, it is prohibited to interrupt from the beginning of בָּרוּךְ שֶׁאָמַר until the conclusion of the *Shemoneh Esrei* (O.C. 51:4). Wherever one may not talk, it is forbidden to do so even in Hebrew (*M.B.* 51:7).

30. With the exception of *Shemoneh Esrei*, parts of *Shacharis* may be interrupted for certain responses to the *chazzan* or for certain blessings, but the rules vary widely, depending on the section of *Shacharis* and the response. In this regard, the most lenient part of *Shacharis* is *Pesukei D'zimrah*, i.e., the unit that includes the verses between בָּרוּךְ שֶׁאָמַר and יִשְׁתַּבַּח. There, one may respond with *Amen* to any benediction, but may not say בָּרוּךְ הוּא וּבָרוּךְ שְׁמוֹ. It is permitted to respond to *Kedushah* and מוֹדִים (in the repetiton of *Shemoneh Esrei*), בָּרְכוּ, and *Kaddish*. If the congregation is reciting the *Shema*, one should recite the first verse (*Shema Yisrael* ...) together with them. If one discharged his bodily functions, he may recite the benediction אֲשֶׁר יָצַר (*M.B.* 51:8).

31. If one did not yet recite the *Shema* and calculates that the congregation will reach it after the deadline (see §55 below) or if he had forgotten to say the daily *berachos* on the Torah, he should say them in the *Pesukei D'zimrah* (*M.B.* 51:10).

◆§ During the Pesukei D'zimrah Blessings

32. The second level of stringency regarding interruptions includes the two benedictions of *Pesukei D'zimrah* — בָּרוּךְ שֶׁאָמַר and יִשְׁתַּבַּח.

בָּרוּךְ שֶׁאָמַר is composed of three parts:

(a) From בָּרוּךְ שֶׁאָמַר until the first בָּרוּךְ אַתָּה ה׳ is but a preamble; all responses are permitted.

(b) From the first בָּרוּךְ אַתָּה ה׳ until the final one, all the interruptions permitted in §30 for the rest of *Pesukei D'zimrah* are also permitted here. However, the following interruptions are *not* permitted at this point: אֲשֶׁר יָצַר and the *Amen* after the benedictions בָּרוּךְ שֶׁאָמַר and יִשְׁתַּבַּח.

(c) The last, brief blessing, בָּרוּךְ ... בַּתִּשְׁבָּחוֹת, during which no interruption at all is permitted (*M.B.* 51:2).

יִשְׁתַּבַּח is composed of two parts:

(a) From the beginning of יִשְׁתַּבַּח to בָּרוּךְ אַתָּה ה׳, which has the same rules as (b) above.

(b) From בָּרוּךְ אַתָּה ה׳ to the end, which has the same rules as (c) above (*M.B.* 51:2, 65:11, 54:11).

◆§ Between the Shema Blessings of Shacharis and Maariv

33. The third level of stringency concerns the 'intervals' between the various sections of the *Shema* and the benedictions bracketing it. The intervals are as follows: After בָּרוּךְ ... יוֹצֵר הַמְּאוֹרוֹת; after בָּרוּךְ ... בְּאַהֲבָה; and after the first and second sections of the *Shema*. [The end of the *Shema* is immediately followed by the first word of the following paragraph (אֱמֶת) so that there is no 'interval' there. Similarly, it is forbidden to interrupt between the benediction גָּאַל יִשְׂרָאֵל and *Shemoneh Esrei* (O.C. 66:5,9).]

Corresponding 'intervals' exist in *Maariv* following each blessing and after the first and second sections of the *Shema* (*M.B.* 66:27; *Be'ur Halachah* there).

34. During the 'intervals' one may respond with *Amen* to all benedictions (*M.B.* 66:23). Regarding קַדִּישׁ, קְדוּשָׁה, בָּרְכוּ, and other interruptions, the 'intervals' are treated in the same way as are interruptions in the fourth level (see below §35). During the interval between בְּאַהֲבָה and שְׁמַע, however, only the *Amen* after בְּאַהֲבָה is permitted (*Derech HaChaim*; see *M.B.* 59:25).

◆§ During the Shema and Its Blessings in Shacharis and Maariv

35. The fourth level concerns the *Shema* itself and the benedictions bracketing it. The benedictions may be separated into two parts for this purpose: (1) During the concluding, brief blessing, and during the verses of שְׁמַע ... אֶחָד and בָּרוּךְ שֵׁם, no interruption whatever is permitted (O.C. 66:1; *M.B.* §11, 12). (2) During the rest of the fourth level, one may respond with *Amen* only to the two blessings הָאֵל הַקָּדוֹשׁ and שׁוֹמֵעַ תְּפִלָּה in *Shemoneh Esrei*. It is permitted to respond to בָּרְכוּ of both the *chazzan* and one who is called up to the Torah. In *Kaddish* one may respond with ... אָמֵן יְהֵא שְׁמֵהּ רַבָּא and with the *Amen* to דַּאֲמִירָן בְּעָלְמָא. In *Kedushah* one may say only the verses beginning קָדוֹשׁ and בָּרוּךְ. To *Modim*, one may respond only with the three words מוֹדִים אֲנַחְנוּ לָךְ (O.C 66:3; *M.B.* §17,18).

A person who is reciting the *Shema* or its benedictions should not be called up to the Torah, even if he is the only *Kohen* or Levite present; in such a case it is preferable that he leave the room. However, if he *was* called up to the Torah, he may recite the benedictions, but should not read along with the reader. If possible he should attempt to get to an 'interval' in his prayers before doing so (*M.B.* 66:26).

If one had to discharge his bodily functions he should merely wash his hands and defer the recitation of אֲשֶׁר יָצַר until after *Shemoneh Esrei* (*M.B.* 66:23).

36. If one has not yet responded to בָּרְכוּ, קְדוּשָׁה or מוֹדִים and is nearly up to *Shemoneh Esrei*, he should stop before שִׁירָה חֲדָשָׁה in order to make the responses. If he has already said שִׁירָה חֲדָשָׁה, but has not yet concluded the benediction, he may respond, but after the response he should start again from

שִׁירָה חֲדָשָׁה (*M.B.* 66:52).

37. Regarding גָּאַל יִשְׂרָאֵל of *Shacharis, Rama,* followed by most Ashkenazi congregations, rules that it is permitted to answer *Amen,* while others, particularly Chassidic congregations, follow R' Yosef Caro's ruling against *Amen* at this point. To avoid the controversy, many individuals recite the blessing in unison with the *chazzan* (*O.C.* 66:7, *M.B.* §35).

38. The fifth level concerns the *Shemoneh Esrei* prayer. Here any interruption is forbidden. Even motioning to someone is prohibited (*O.C.* 104:1; *M.B.* §1). If the *chazzan* is up to קַדִּישׁ, קְדוּשָּׁה, or בָּרְכוּ, one should stop and listen silently to the *chazzan's* recitation; his own silent concentration is considered as if he had responded (*O.C.* 104:7; *M.B.* §26-28).

39. From the time one has concluded the last benediction of *Shemoneh Esrei* with בַּשָּׁלוֹם until the end of the standard prayers (i.e., יִהְיוּ לְרָצוֹן at the end of אֱלֹהַי נְצוֹר), one is restricted to the responses listed in level four. However, whenever possible, one should hurry to say the verse יִהְיוּ לְרָצוֹן ... וְגוֹאֲלִי before making any kind of response. It is preferable to take the usual three steps backward before making the responses (*O.C.* 122:1; *M.B.* §2-4).

LAWS OF RECITING THE SHEMA

40. It is a Scriptural precept to recite the *Shema* twice daily, once in the morning and again in the evening. When one recites the *Shema* he must have in mind that he is fulfilling a Scriptural precept; otherwise it must be repeated (*O.C.* 60:4). However, if the circumstances make it obvious that the intention was present — e.g., he recited it during the prayer with the benedictions preceding and following it — he need not repeat the *Shema* even if he did not make a mental declaration of purpose (*M.B.* 60:10).

41. The third section of *Shema,* whose recitation is Rabbinical in origin according to almost all authorities, contains a verse whose recitation fulfills the Scriptural obligation to commemorate the Exodus from Egypt twice daily (see *Berachos* 12b; *Rambam, Hil. Kerias Shema* 1:3). The above rule concerning a mental declaration of intent applies here, too.

42. One should concentrate on the meaning of all the words, and read them with awe and trepidation (*O.C.* 61:1). He should read the *Shema* as if it were a new proclamation containing teachings never yet revealed (*O.C.* 61:2). The first verse of *Shema* is the essential profession of our faith. Therefore the utmost concentration on its meaning is necessary. If one said it without such concentration, he has not fulfilled his obligation and must repeat it (*O.C.* 60:5, 63:4), but he should repeat the verse quietly, for one may not (publicly) say the first verse of *Shema* repeatedly (ibid.).

43. While reciting the first verse, it is customary to cover the eyes with the right hand to avoid distraction and to enhance concentration (*O.C.* 61:5).

44. Although *Shema* may be recited quietly, one should recite it loudly enough to hear himself. However, one has discharged his obligation even if he does not hear himself, as long as he has enunciated the words (*O.C.* 62:3).

45. The last word of the first verse, אֶחָד, must be pronounced with special emphasis, while one meditates on God's exclusive sovereignty over the seven heavens and earth, and the four directions — east, south, west, and north (*O.C.* 61:6).

46. Some consider it preferable to recite the entire *Shema* aloud (except for the passage בָּרוּךְ שֵׁם) while others say it quietly; our custom follows the latter usage. However, the first verse should be said aloud in order to arouse one's full concentration (*O.C.* 61:4,26). It is customary for the *chazzan* to lead the congregation in the recitation of the first verse so that they all proclaim the Kingdom of Heaven together (*Kol Bo* cited in *Darkei Moshe* to *O.C.* 61; *Levush*).

47. Every word must be enunciated clearly and uttered with the correct grammatical pronunciation (*O.C.* 62:1, 61:23, 16-19). It is especially important to enunciate each word clearly and to avoid run-on words by pausing briefly between words ending and beginning with the same consonant, such as וַאֲבַדְתֶּם מְהֵרָה, בְּכָל לְבַבְכֶם, and to pause between a word that ends with a consonant and the next one that begins with a silent letter [i.e., א or ע], such as אֲשֶׁר אָנֹכִי, הַיּוֹם עַל, וּרְאִיתֶם אֹתוֹ (*O.C.* 61:20, 21).

48. Although it is not the universal custom to chant the *Shema* with the cantillation melody used during the synagogue Torah reading, it is laudable to do so, unless one finds that such chanting interferes with his concentration. In any event, the proper punctuation must be followed so that words are grouped into the proper phrases in accordance with the syntax of each word-group and verse (*O.C.* 61:24, *M.B.* §37,38).

49. While reciting the first two portions of the *Shema,* one may not communicate with someone else by winking or motioning with his lips or fingers (*O.C.* 63:6, *M.B.* §18).

50. It is incumbent that each paragraph of the *Shema* be read word for word as it appears in the Torah. If one erred and skipped a word, he must return to the place of his error and continue the section from there (*O.C.* 64:1-2).

51. The *Shema* should be said in one uninterrupted recitation, but, if one interrupted, whether by talking or waiting silently, he does not have to repeat the *Shema*. However, if the interruption was involuntary in nature [e.g., one had to relieve himself], and the interruption was long enough for him to have recited all three paragraphs of the *Shema* at his own normal speed, he must repeat the entire *Shema* (*Rama* O.C. 65:1). Multiple interruptions interspersed in the recitation of *Shema* are not added together to constitute one long, invalidating interruption (*M.B.* 65:4).

52. If one is present in the synagogue when the congregation recites the *Shema*, he must recite at least the first verse and the verse בָּרוּךְ שֵׁם together with them. If he is in the midst of a prayer that he may not interrupt (see above §29-39), he should at least give the appearance of saying *Shema* by praying loudly in the tune the congregation uses for the *Shema* (O.C. 65:2,3; *M.B.* §10).

53. During morning services, one should gather together the four *tzitzis* when he says the words וַהֲבִיאֵנוּ לְשָׁלוֹם מֵאַרְבַּע כַּנְפוֹת הָאָרֶץ, *Bring us in peacefulness from the four corners of the earth*, in the paragraph preceding the *Shema*. From then on and throughout the *Shema*, he should hold the *tzitzis* — according to some customs, between the fourth and little fingers of the left hand — against the heart (*Ba'er Heitev*, O.C. 59:3; *Derech HaChaim*).

54. When reciting the third portion of the *Shema*, וַיֹּאמֶר ה׳, during the morning services, one should grasp the *tzitzis* with the right hand also, and look at them, until after he has said the words נֶאֱמָנִים וְנֶחֱמָדִים לָעַד in the אֱמֶת וְיַצִּיב prayer following *Shema*. At that point one should kiss the *tzitzis* and release them from his hand (ibid.). [According to the prevalent custom, one also kisses the *tzitzis* every time he says the word צִיצִת, at the end of *Shema*, and at לָעַד קַיֶּמֶת.]

☙ K'rias Shema on Yom Tov

55. It is absolutely required that the *Shema* be recited within the requisite time — the first quarter of the day. There are various opinions among the *poskim* as to how to calculate the first quarter of a day, and these are noted in many Jewish calendars. Since many congregations begin *Shacharis* late on *Yom Tov*, one should be careful to check the deadline for *K'rias Shema* and, if necessary, recite all three passages of the *Shema* before the communal prayers.

☙ Shemoneh Esrei

56. On Chol HaMoed the prayer יַעֲלֶה וְיָבֹא is inserted in the benediction רְצֵה, *Be favorable*, of *Shemoneh Esrei*. If it is forgotten, the *Shemoneh Esrei* must be repeated. [The omission of יַעֲלֶה וְיָבֹא on *Yom Tov* is a rare occurrence, since it is an integral part of the *Yom Tov* *Shemoneh Esrei*. On Chol HaMoed, however, it is merely an insertion in the standard weekday prayer.]

Thus, if one realized his error before uttering the word HASHEM in the formula concluding the benediction, he returns to יַעֲלֶה וְיָבֹא. If he has already concluded with הַמַּחֲזִיר שְׁכִינָתוֹ לְצִיּוֹן but not yet begun the benediction מוֹדִים, he should recite יַעֲלֶה וְיָבֹא there (till מֶלֶךְ חַנּוּן וְרַחוּם אָתָּה) and continue with מוֹדִים. If he had already begun to say מוֹדִים, he must return to the beginning of the benediction רְצֵה. If he had concluded *Shemoneh Esrei*, he must repeat it in its entirety (O.C. 422:1; 490:2).

One is considered to have 'concluded' in this context when one has recited the verse יִהְיוּ לְרָצוֹן at the conclusion of the prayer אֱלֹהַי (before עֹשֶׂה שָׁלוֹם; see *M.B.* 422:9).

If one is in doubt whether he has said יַעֲלֶה וְיָבֹא, he must assume he has not said it. However, if he knows that while praying he was aware that he had to recite יַעֲלֶה וְיָבֹא, but is in doubt some time after concluding the prayer, he may assume that he fulfilled his intention and recited יַעֲלֶה וְיָבֹא (*M.B.* 422:10).

☙ The Chazzan's Repetition of the Shemoneh Esrei

57. The *chazzan*'s repetition of *Shemoneh Esrei* is a congregational, rather than an individual, worship. By definition a 'congregation' consists of a *minyan* (quorum of at least ten males over *bar mitzvah*, including the *chazzan*), present and listening to the recitation. If the congregants do not pay attention, it is almost as if the *chazzan* were taking God's Name in vain. Every person should imagine that there are only ten congregants present and that he is one of the nine whose attentive listening is vital to the recitation (O.C. 124:4).

If one of the ten is in the middle of the silent *Amidah*, he may still be counted as part of the *minyan*. However, it is preferable that not more than one such person be included (*M.B.* 55:32-34).

58. One should respond with *Amen* to every benediction he hears, and should teach his young children to do so (O.C. 124:6,7).

59. When one says *Amen*, it is important to enunciate all of the vowels and consonants distinctly. One should not respond until the *chazzan* has concluded the benediction, and then the response should be immediate (O.C. 124:8). *Mishnah Berurah* (§17) cautions even against Torah study or recitation of psalms and other prayers during the *chazzan*'s recitation of the *Shemoneh Esrei*.

60. It is absolutely forbidden to talk during the repetition of *Shemoneh Esrei* even if one makes sure to respond with *Amen* at the conclusion of each benediction (O.C. 124:7).

THE READING OF THE TORAH

61. On Pesach, as on every Festival, five people are called to the Torah. If the first day of Pesach falls on the Sabbath, the same Torah portion is divided into seven *aliyos* to allow for the mandatory number of seven people who must be called to the Torah on the Sabbath. It is customary not to add to the prescribed amount of *aliyos* on Festivals. However, when it falls on the Sabbath it is permitted to add *aliyos* although it is rarely done (O.C. 282:1, M.B. §6).

62. The first *aliyah* belongs to a *Kohen* and the second to a *Levi* (if any are present). If no *Kohen* is present, there is no obligation to call a *Levi* in his place, but if no *Levi* is present the same *Kohen* who has been called for his own *aliyah* is called again to replace the *Levi*. He recites both blessings again. According to the prevalent custom, a *Kohen* or *Levi* may not be called up for any other regular *aliyah* except *Maftir*. They may also be called for *Acharon*, the last *aliyah* of the weekly Sabbath portion *(sidra)*, after the prescribed number of seven *aliyos* has been completed (O.C. 135:10, M.B. §35).

63. Time-honored custom has established that certain occasions entitle one to an *aliyah*. These are listed in *Levush* and *Magen Avraham* to *Orach Chaim* 282, and in *Be'ur Halachah* to O.C. 136. [They are summarized in the *Laws* section of the ArtScroll *Siddur* §99-101.]

◆§ Close Relatives in Successive Aliyos

64. Two brothers, or a father and a son, should not be called up to the Torah in succession. Some authorities feel that this stringency should be followed even in regard to a grandfather and his grandson (O.C. 141:6; M.B. there). However, when *Maftir* is read from a second Torah scroll, as on Festivals, even a father and son may be called up in succession *(Ba'er Heitev* 141:6).

◆§ Procedure of the Aliyah

65. Before the person called to the Torah for an *aliyah* recites the benediction, he must open the Torah and find the passage that will be read for him (O.C. 139:4). In order to dispel any notion that he is reading the benedictions from the Torah, one should avert his face while reciting them; it is preferable to turn to the left side *(Rama* there). Some authorities maintain that it is better to face the Torah while saying the benedictions but to close his eyes *(M.B.* §19). Others say that it is better to close the Torah during the recitation of the benedictions *(Be'ur Halachah* there). All three modes are practiced today in various congregations.

66. In many congregations it is customary to touch the Torah with the *tallis* (or the Torah's mantle or girdle) at the beginning of the passage to be read, and to kiss the edge which touched the Torah (*Sha'arei Ephraim* 4:3). One should be careful not to rub on the Torah script forcefully for this can cause words to become erased and thus invalidate the Torah scroll.

67. It is extremely important that the benedictions be said loud enough for the congregation to hear (O.C. 139:6). If the congregation did not hear the recitation of בָּרְכוּ, they may not respond with בָּרוּךְ . . . וָעֶד *(Be'ur Halachah* to O.C. 57:1). However, if the congregation (or at least a *minyan)* heard בָּרְכוּ, then even someone who has not heard בָּרְכוּ may respond along with the congregation *(M.B.* 57:2).

68. While reciting the benedictions, one should hold the poles *(atzei chaim)* upon which the Torah is rolled. During the reading the reader holds one pole and the person called to the Torah holds the other one (O.C. 139:11; M.B. §35). *Arizal* says one should hold the *atzei chaim* with both hands during the benedictions and with the right hand only during the reading (cited in *Magen Avraham* 139:13).

69. Upon completion of the reading it is customary for the person who has been called up to touch the Torah with his *tallis* (or the Torah's mantle or girdle) and to kiss the edge that has touched the Torah (see M.B. 139:35).

70. After the Torah passage has been read, he closes the Torah scroll and then recites the benediction *(Rama* O.C. 139:5). If the Torah reading will not be resumed immediately (e.g., a מִי שֶׁבֵּרַךְ is said), then a covering should be spread out over the Torah *(M.B.* 139:21).

71. In Talmudic times the person called for an *aliyah* would also read aloud from the Torah. This practice was still followed in Greek and Turkish communities up to the sixteenth century (see *Beis Yosef* to *Tur* O.C. 141), and the tradition persists to this day in Yemenite communities. However, since ancient times the Ashkenazic custom has been for a designated reader *(baal korei)* to read the Torah aloud to the congregation (see *Rosh* cited in *Tur* loc. cit). Nevertheless, the person who recites the benedictions should read quietly along with the reader (O.C. 141:2).

72. The reader and the one called up to the Torah must stand while reading the Torah in public. It is forbidden even to lean upon something (O.C. 141:1).

73. When going up to the *bimah* to recite the benedictions one should pick the shortest route possible, and when returning to his seat, he should take a longer route. If two routes are equidistant, one should go to the *bimah* via the route which is to his right and descend via the opposite route (O.C. 141:7).

74. After one has finished reciting the concluding benediction he should not return to his place at least until the next person called up to the Torah has come to the *bimah* (O.C. 141:7). However, it is customary to wait until the next person has finished his passage of the Torah (*M.B.* §26).

75. It is forbidden to talk or even to discuss Torah topics while the Torah is being read (O.C. 146:2).

76. It is forbidden to leave the synagogue while the Torah is being read (O.C. 146:1), even if one has already heard the reading of the passage elsewhere (*M.B.* §1). However, if necessary, one may leave during the pause between one portion and the next (O.C. 146:1), provided that a *minyan* remains in the synagogue (*M.B.* §2).

KADDISH

77. The conclusion of a section of prayer is usually signified by the recitation of the *Kaddish*. Many of these *Kaddish* recitations are the privilege of mourners (within the eleven months following the death or burial of a parent, or in some instances, of other close relatives), or of those observing *yahrzeit*, i.e., the anniversary of the death of a parent (and in some congregations, of a grandparent who has no living sons; see *Matteh Ephraim, Dinei Kaddish* 3:14). However, many recitations of *Kaddish* are exclusively the prerogative of the *chazzan*.

78. Basically there are four types of *Kaddish:*

(a) חֲצִי קַדִּישׁ, Half-*Kaddish*, which ends with דַּאֲמִירָן בְּעָלְמָא וְאִמְרוּ אָמֵן;

(b) קַדִּישׁ יָתוֹם, the Mourner's *Kaddish*, which consists of Half *Kaddish*, with the addition of יְהֵא שְׁלָמָא and עוֹשֶׂה שָׁלוֹם;

(c) קַדִּישׁ שָׁלֵם, the Full *Kaddish*, the same as the Mourner's *Kaddish* with the addition of תִּתְקַבַּל before יְהֵא שְׁלָמָא; and

(d) קַדִּישׁ דְּרַבָּנָן, the Rabbis' *Kaddish*, the same as the Mourner's *Kaddish* with the addition of עַל יִשְׂרָאֵל.

79. The function of the Half-*Kaddish* is to link different segments of the prayer, e.g., it is recited between *Pesukei D'zimrah* and the *Shema* benedictions, between *Shemoneh Esrei* (or *Tachanun*) and the prayers that conclude the service (*Pri Megadim* in *Mishbetzos Zahav, Orach Chaim* 55:1). Thus it is recited by the *chazzan*.

Nevertheless, in some congregations it is customary for a mourner to recite the *Kaddish* following the reading of the Torah if he has been called to the Torah for the concluding segment (*Sha'arei Ephraim* 10:9). The rationale for this custom is that the person called to the Torah is also a *chazzan* of sorts, since he too must read from the Torah, albeit quietly. In some congregations, a mourner recites this *Kaddish* even if he was not called to the Torah.

80. The Full *Kaddish* is recited only after the communal recitation of *Shemoneh Esrei* (or *Selichos*). It includes the *chazzan's* prayer that the just-concluded service be accepted by God. Consequently it must be recited by the *chazzan*.

81. The Mourner's *Kaddish* is recited after the recital of Scriptural verses that supplement the main body of prayer. The recital of *Kaddish* after this portion of the service is not obligatory, and is not recited if no mourners are present. Since *Kaddish* in these parts of the service is recited exclusively by mourners, it has become customary that one whose parents are living should not recite it, since this would be a mark of disrespect to his parents (see *Rama* O.C. 132:2; *Pis'chei Teshuvah, Yoreh Deah* 376:4).

If no mourners are present, the Mourner's *Kaddish* is not recited, with one exception. After *Aleinu*, which also contains Scriptural verses, *Kaddish* should be recited even if no mourner is present. In such a case, it should be recited by the *chazzan* or one of the congregants, preferably one whose parents are no longer alive, or one whose parents have not explicitly expressed their opposition to his recitation of *Kaddish* (O.C. 132:2 with *M.B.* §11).

82. Ideally, each Mourner's *Kaddish* should be recited by only one person. Where more than one mourner is present, the *poskim* developed a system of rules establishing an order of priorities for those who must recite *Kaddish* (see *M.B.* in *Be'ur Halachah* to O.C. 132, et al.). However, since adherence to these rules can often cause discord in the congregation, it has become widely accepted for all the mourners to recite the *Kaddish* simultaneously (see *Aruch HaShulchan* O.C. 132:8; *Siddur R' Yaakov Emden*; *Teshuvos Chasam Sofer*, O. C. 159).

83. In many congregations it is customary that someone observing a *yahrzeit* is given the exclusive privilege of reciting a *Kaddish*, usually the one after *Aleinu*. In that case, an additional psalm (usually *Psalm* 24) is recited at the conclusion of the services so that all the mourners can recite *Kaddish* after it.

84. The Rabbis' *Kaddish* (*Kaddish D'Rabbanan*) is recited after segments of the Oral Torah (e.g., Talmud) have been studied or recited by a quorum of ten adult males (*Rambam, Seder Tefilos Kol HaShanah*). The Talmud (*Sotah* 49a) refers to the great significance of יְהֵא שְׁמֵיהּ רַבָּא (a reference to *Kaddish*) that is said after *Aggadah*, indicating that this *Kaddish* has a special relevance to the Midrashic portion of the Torah. Therefore, it is customary to append a brief *Aggadic* selection to Torah study and then to recite the Rabbis' *Kaddish* (*M.B.* 54:9).

85. Although *Kaddish D'Rabbanan* is not reserved for mourners and may be recited even by one whose parents are alive (*Pis'chei Teshuvah, Yoreh Deah* 376:4), it is generally recited by mourners. However, when one celebrates the completion of a tractate of the Talmud, or when the rabbi delivers a *derashah* (homiletical discourse), it is customary for the celebrant or the rabbi to recite the *Kaddish* himself.

THE SABBATH

86. If *Yom Tov* falls on the Sabbath, several additions are made to the liturgy of the *Shemoneh Esrei* and *Kiddush*. Some of them are essential and, if omitted, the *Amidah* must be repeated, while others are not. In the passage beginning וַתִּתֶּן לָנוּ, *and You gave us*, the word בְּאַהֲבָה, *with love*, is added after the mention of the Sabbath and *Yom Tov*. This addition is not essential, and the prayer need not be repeated if it has been omitted (see *O.C.* 587:3). Also, if one erred and added בְּאַהֲבָה on a weekday, he need not repeat the phrase. The same applies if יִשְׂמְחוּ is omitted from *Mussaf* or וַיְכֻלּוּ from *Kiddush*.

87. A different group of additions, essential in nature, consists of the inclusion of the Sabbath wherever the *Yom Tov* is mentioned (except in יַעֲלֶה וְיָבֹא where our custom omits the mention of the Sabbath). Thus we say וַתִּתֶּן לָנוּ **אֶת יוֹם הַשַּׁבָּת הַזֶּה** וְאֶת יוֹם חַג הַמַּצּוֹת הַזֶּה זְמַן חֵרוּתֵנוּ ... and בָּרוּךְ אַתָּה ה' ... מְקַדֵּשׁ **הַשַּׁבָּת** וְיִשְׂרָאֵל וְהַזְּמַנִּים. If *both* of these additions were omitted — so that the Sabbath was not mentioned at all — then that blessing (beginning with אַתָּה בְחַרְתָּנוּ) must be repeated. Thus if one has not yet finished the *Shemoneh Esrei* [or *Kiddush*], he returns to the beginning of that blessing, and continues from there. If he has already concluded it he must start again from the beginning of *Shemoneh Esrei* [or *Kiddush*]. The 'conclusion of *Shemoneh Esrei*' in this regard is defined as the recitation of the verse יִהְיוּ לְרָצוֹן ... וְגֹאֲלִי just before ... עֹשֶׂה שָׁלוֹם.

88. There are cases, however, regarding both *Shemoneh Esrei* and *Kiddush*, where it is not clear whether or not the blessing must be repeated. If one mentioned the Sabbath at the beginning of the blessing [i.e., in וַתִּתֶּן לָנוּ], but failed to do so in the concluding formula [i.e., ... בָּרוּךְ אַתָּה ה'], it is questionable whether the blessing has to be repeated (see *M.B.* 487:7, *Be'ur Halachah* there). *Mishnah Berurah* does not give a clear ruling on these questions (although he implies his preference for some of the views). In the absence of a ruling from a competent halachic authority, one should not repeat *Shemoneh Esrei* in this case, since the general rule is that סָפֵק בְּרָכוֹת לְהָקֵל, *when there is doubt whether a blessing should be repeated, we rule leniently*, in order to avoid the possibility of reciting a blessing that is not required.

89. Conversely, if one mentioned the *Yom Tov* in וַתִּתֶּן לָנוּ but concluded the blessing with a mention only of the Sabbath, there is controversy over whether the blessing must be repeated. According to *Magen Avraham* (*O.C.* 487:2), in this case one should not repeat the blessing. However, many authorities differ (*Pri Chadash, Be'ur Halachah*, et al.; see *Hagahos R' Akiva Eiger*).

If the omission occurred in the concluding formula, one can correct it by immediately saying only the words הַשַּׁבָּת וְיִשְׂרָאֵל וְהַזְּמַנִּים. This correction is valid only if it was begun before enough time to say the words שָׁלוֹם עָלֶיךָ רַבִּי has elapsed from when the erroneously phrased formula was concluded.

90. If, however, the blessing has not yet been completed, there are cases where the error can be corrected and the above halachic problem avoided. If one omitted the Sabbath in וַתִּתֶּן לָנוּ, he simply goes back to וַתִּתֶּן לָנוּ and continues from there. If he has said the three words בָּרוּךְ אַתָּה ה' of the concluding formula, he should add the words לַמְּדֵנִי חֻקֶּיךָ. [By doing so he has recited the verse בָּרוּךְ אַתָּה ה' לַמְּדֵנִי חֻקֶּיךָ, *Blessed are you* HASHEM, *teach me Your statutes* (*Psalms* 119:12); thus no wrong or needless blessing has been recited.] Then he can go back to וַתִּתֶּן לָנוּ and correct his omission. However, if he has recited more than three words of the blessing [i.e., ... בָּרוּךְ אַתָּה ה' מְקַדֵּשׁ], he must finish the blessing.

The End of Sabbath

91. When the first or second day of *Yom Tov* follows the Sabbath, it is necessary to recite a prayer differentiating between the greater sanctity of the Sabbath and the lesser sanctity of the Festival. In the *Amidah*, this prayer — וַתּוֹדִיעֵנוּ — is recited in the fourth benediction. The rules outlined for אַתָּה חוֹנַנְתָּנוּ (see below §93) apply here as well (*Be'ur Halachah* to *O.C.* 294:1). If the Sabbath has already ended and one wishes to do work permitted on the Festival, but he has not said וַתּוֹדִיעֵנוּ, he must say the following formula: בָּרוּךְ הַמַּבְדִּיל בֵּין קֹדֶשׁ לְקֹדֶשׁ, *Blessed is He Who separates between holy and holy* (*M.B.* 299:36).

92. One should not begin to eat a meal in the three-hour period preceding the Sabbath or *Yom Tov* (*O.C.* 249:2, 429:1). If the second day of Pesach follows immediately after the Sabbath it is preferable to eat the *seudah shlishis* prior to the three-hour period (*Sha'ar HaTziyun* 529:9, see *M.B.* §9). However, if this period has already passed, one should still eat the meal. In this case he should eat only a minimal meal — slightly more than an egg's volume of *matzah* (regarding foods other than *matzah* see above §12) — at this time (*M.B.* 429:8). The same stricture applies if the Sabbath falls on the seventh day of *Yom Tov* and is thus followed by another day of *Yom Tov* (*M.B.* 429:8). If the first day of *Yom Tov* is on Sunday, see §149 regarding how to fulfill the *mitzvah* of *seudah shlishis*.

SABBATH, HAVDALAH, THE SECOND NIGHT

◆§ The End of Yom Tov

93. In the first weekday *Maariv* prayer following the first two-day Festival, a special prayer אַתָּה חוֹנַנְתָּנוּ, *You have favored us,* is inserted in the fourth benediction of *Shemoneh Esrei.* The function of this prayer is to declare the distinction between the higher holiness of the Festivals and the more mundane nature of Chol HaMoed [Intermediate Days]. If one forgets to insert this prayer he may not repeat the benediction, nor should he insert this prayer in the benediction שְׁמַע קוֹלֵנוּ. Rather, he should rely on the *Havdalah* which will be recited over wine after *Maariv* (*O.C.* 294:1; *M.B.* §6).

Even after the *Yom Tov* has ended, it is prohibited to do any forbidden work before reciting אַתָּה חוֹנַנְתָּנוּ or *Havdalah.* Therefore, if one has not yet recited either, one should be very careful not to do any work even after dark. Since women generally do not recite *Maariv,* they should be careful not do any work before hearing *Havdalah.* However, by saying the words: בָּרוּךְ הַמַּבְדִּיל בֵּין קֹדֶשׁ לְחוֹל, *Blessed is He Who separates between holy and secular,* one becomes permitted to do work (*O.C.* 299:10; see *Sha'ar HaTziyun* §51).

◆§ Preparing for the Second Day

94. It is forbidden to cook on the first day of *Yom Tov* for the second day, or to make any kind of preparations on one day for the other *(O.C.* 503:1 with *M.B.).* Even in the twilight period between the two days [בֵּין הַשְּׁמָשׁוֹת] it is forbidden to make any preparations for the night; one must wait until it is definitely night *(Pri Megadim* cited in *Be'ur Halachah* to 503:1).

[See page 2 for laws regarding preparations for the Sabbath when *Yom Tov* falls on Friday.]

95. It is customary not to begin *Maariv* until it is definitely night because most families assume that they are permitted to prepare for the Seder upon commencement of the service *(Matteh Ephraim* 599:2).

96. One may light candles at the end of the afternoon of the first day (except on the Sabbath) if their light is needed at the time they are lit, even though their main use will be at night *(Matteh Ephraim* 598:8). However, the Festival candles, which are lit with the recitation of a blessing, should be lit only after it is definitely night (preface of *Prishah* to *Yoreh Deah;* see *Eleph LaMatteh* 625:51 and *K'tzei HaMatteh* there). [The candles may only be lit from an existing fire, such as a gas pilot light; in no case may a match or cigarette lighter be struck on the Festival.]

97. Likewise it should be noted that Chol HaMoed, too, has restrictions on the types of labor which may be performed. However, as already noted, these laws are not within the purview of this digest.

MUSSAF ON THE FIRST DAY OF PESACH

98. Beginning with the recitation of *Mussaf* on the first day of Pesach, and continuing until the *Mussaf* prayer of *Shemini Atzeres,* the passage מַשִּׁיב הָרוּחַ וּמוֹרִיד הַגָּשֶׁם, *He makes the wind blow and He makes the rain descend,* is omitted from the second benediction of *Shemoneh Esrei* (*O.C.* 114:1). Although rain is necessary in some latitudes during the spring and summer, the mention of rain is omitted because of the regions near the equator where rain in the summer is harmful to the crop which is reaped and left to dry in the fields (*O.C.* 114:4; see *Taanis* 3a with *Rashi).* The mention of rain in the second benediction (in contrast with the *prayer* for rain in the ninth benediction of the weekday *Shemoneh Esrei*) is not based on the need for rain in a particular region, but rather on a general, broad-based need which prevails in the entire hemisphere (*Pri Megadim* in *Eishel Avraham* 114:6; see the responsum of *Rosh* cited by *Tur O.C.* 117; *Be'ur Halachah* to 114:4).

99. [Upon ceasing the recital of מַשִּׁיב הָרוּחַ וּמוֹרִיד הַגָּשֶׁם, most Ashkenazic congregations do not recite anything else in its place. However, some, especially in *Eretz Yisrael,* practice the Sephardic custom and recite מוֹרִיד הַטָּל in place of מַשִּׁיב הָרוּחַ וּמוֹרִיד הַגָּשֶׁם.] All agree, however, that the recitation of מוֹרִיד הַטָּל is not essential, and the prayer need not be repeated if it was omitted (*O.C.* 114:3).

100. In contrast to *Shemini Atzeres* when an announcement to begin saying מַשִּׁיב הָרוּחַ וּמוֹרִיד הַגָּשֶׁם is made prior to the silent *Mussaf Shemoneh Esrei,* no such announcement is made on the first day of Pesach for מוֹרִיד הַטָּל *(Rama O.C.* 114:3). This is because the only announcement that it is possible to proclaim is, 'מַשִּׁיב הָרוּחַ וּמוֹרִיד הַגָּשֶׁם is no longer said.' This would seem ungrateful and would appear to be a rejection of God's bounty of rain (*Magen Avraham* 114:5 citing *Levush*). [This does not apply to the Sephardic custom in which an announcement can be made to begin to say מוֹרִיד הַטָּל. Hence the Sephardic custom is to announce the recitation of מוֹרִיד הַטָּל within the framework of *piyutim* which are said before the silent *Shemoneh Esrei.*] The purpose of this announcement is to ensure that everyone will recite or omit מַשִּׁיב הָרוּחַ וּמוֹרִיד הַגָּשֶׁם, consistently with the congregation. Since many people [e.g., women and children and those who live in unsafe areas] are not present at *Maariv,* they may not remember to omit the passage. Since the greatest number of people are present at *Mussaf,* that service was chosen for the announcement (*M.B.* 114:3).

101. The passage מַשִּׁיב הָרוּחַ וּמוֹרִיד הַגָּשֶׁם is said in the silent *Mussaf Shemoneh Esrei,* since no formal public announcement has been made to omit it. The *chazzan's* omission of the passage during his repetition serves as an announcement, and the congregation omits the passage during *Minchah* and thereafter (*Rama O.C.* 114:3).

102. If one omitted מַשִּׁיב הָרוּחַ וּמוֹרִיד הַגֶּשֶׁם on the first day of Pesach (or substituted מוֹרִיד הַטָּל for it), even in the first *Maariv* of the festival, he does not have to repeat the *Shemoneh Esrei* (*M.B.* 114:3). [But if he has not yet said וְנֶאֱמָן אַתָּה, he should insert the formula at whichever point he remembers; if he has said וְנֶאֱמָן, but has not yet said the word HASHEM in the concluding formula of the benediction — בָּרוּךְ . . . מְחַיֵּה הַמֵּתִים, he should insert the omitted formula, return to וְנֶאֱמָן, and conclude the benediction.]

103. Conversely, if one said מַשִּׁיב הָרוּחַ וּמוֹרִיד הַגֶּשֶׁם after the announcement was made, or if the *chazzan* forgot to omit it in his repetition of the prayer, the *Shemoneh Esrei* must be repeated (*M.B.* 114:17). [Rain in the summer is considered harmful (see §98 above) and its mention in the prayer invalidates the *Shemoneh Esrei* (*M.B.* 114:18). The first day of Pesach is considered the beginning of summer in this regard, so that the mention of rain in the prayer, after the announcement has been made, invalidates the prayer. Conversely, even the part of the first day which elapses before the announcement is made is technically summer in this regard. The reason for waiting until *Mussaf* for the announcement is conventional as explained in §100 above (see *M.B.* 114:3), so that recitation of this passage during this period is not essential.]

104. An individual who delayed his silent *Mussaf* prayer until after the *chazzan* had already recited the second benediction omitting מַשִּׁיב הָרוּחַ וּמוֹרִיד הַגֶּשֶׁם should himself omit the passage (*M.B.* 114:16). *Daas Torah* (*O.C.* 488:3) asserts that the same is true if one had not yet recited his *Shacharis* prayer until after the *chazzan* has recited the second benediction of *Mussaf*.

105. An individual who prays at home should time his *Mussaf* prayer so that he recites it before the *chazzan* in the synagogue repeats the prayer. [However, someone whose custom it is to say מוֹרִיד הַטָּל in the silent *Mussaf* prayer should time his prayer so that he says it after the announcement is made in the synagogue.] If he is in doubt whether the *chazzan* has already repeated the prayer he should omit the passage, since its recitation is not essential now (*M.B.* 114:16).

106. As already mentioned, the recitation of מַשִּׁיב הָרוּחַ וּמוֹרִיד הַגֶּשֶׁם after the announcement was made necessitates that the prayer be repeated. If he had not yet said the word HASHEM in the concluding formula of the benediction — בָּרוּךְ . . . מְחַיֵּה הַמֵּתִים — when he realized his error, he should return to the beginning of the benediction (אַתָּה גִבּוֹר) and repeat the passage with the omission of מַשִּׁיב הָרוּחַ וּמוֹרִיד הַגֶּשֶׁם. If he had already said the word HASHEM (but nothing further) in the concluding formula of the benediction, he may conclude with לַמְּדֵנִי חֻקֶּיךָ, thereby converting the benediction into a verse of *Psalms* (119:12). He should then return to the beginning of the benediction. If he had already said even one word after the word HASHEM, he must return to the beginning of the *Shemoneh Esrei*. He need not however, repeat the prefatory passage . . . ד׳ שְׂפָתַי (*M.B.* 114:19-20). The above is true even if he said both מוֹרִיד הַגֶּשֶׁם and מוֹרִיד הַטָּל (*O.C.* 114:4).

107. If one is not sure that he has omitted מוֹרִיד הַגֶּשֶׁם, the rule is as follows: It is assumed that someone has recited whatever he has been accustomed to, until a different recitation becomes habitual. The Sages set down the presumption that until someone has recited a new addition for thirty days, it has not yet become habitual with him. Consequently, until thirty days after Pesach began, if one is uncertain whether he recited or omitted the passage, he must assume that he recited it, and must conduct himself as outlined in §103 above (*O.C.* 114:8).

108. For those who say מוֹרִיד הַטָּל, *He makes the dew descend*, in place of מַשִּׁיב הָרוּחַ וּמוֹרִיד הַגֶּשֶׁם during the summer months, there is a way to spare oneself the necessity to repeat the *Shemoneh Esrei* in cases of doubtful recitation of מוֹרִיד הַגֶּשֶׁם. He may repeat the passage מְחַיֵּה מֵתִים אַתָּה רַב לְהוֹשִׁיעַ מוֹרִיד הַטָּל . . . one hundred and one times [if he said this only ninety times it is sufficient *post facto*], thereby assuring himself that he will henceforth insert מוֹרִיד הַטָּל and omit מוֹרִיד הַגֶּשֶׁם. Some authorities rule that the same is true for those who do not say מוֹרִיד הַטָּל in the summer. They too may repeat מְחַיֵּה מֵתִים אַתָּה רַב לְהוֹשִׁיעַ מְכַלְכֵּל חַיִּים, omitting מַשִּׁיב . . . הַגֶּשֶׁם, for the required number of times and be assured of saying the correct formula henceforth. However, *Derech Chaim* disputes this analogy and cautions that it not be relied upon (*O.C.* 114:9, *M.B.* there).

THE COUNTING OF THE OMER

109. When the Temple stood, there was a *mitzvah* to offer up an *omer* — the volume of 43.2 eggs — of coarsely ground barley flour as a meal offering on the second day of Pesach, together with a group of animal offerings. The bringing of the offering rendered the new crop of grain permissible for consumption (see *Leviticus* 23:9-14). On the day the offering was brought a count of days was begun, culminating on the forty-ninth day. The following day — the fiftieth day — is the Shavuos festival (ibid. vs. 15-16). The Torah repeats the *mitzvah* to *count from the Omer*, expressing the commandment in a different way each time. In verse 15 we are told to count seven weeks, while in the next verse the *mitzvah* is expressed in terms of days. Because of this the *Gemara* (*Menachos* 66a) concludes that one must count both forty-nine days and seven weeks (as explained below).

◆§ The Obligation

110. There is disagreement whether the Scriptural *mitzvah* applies in post-Temple days, or whether it is only a rabbinic obligation in our days, enacted in commemoration of the Temple (see a summary of the views in *Be'ur Halachah* to O.C. 489:1). This disagreement has halachic ramifications, as in the case where one counted the *Omer* in the twilight period, when there is question whether or not it is already night (see below §126).

111. Only men are obligated to perform this *mitzvah*. Women are exempt since this is a מִצְוַת עֲשֵׂה שֶׁהַזְּמַן גְּרָמָא, *a positive commandment caused by time* — i.e., a *mitzvah* which one is obligated to perform in a specific time — from which women are exempt. However, *Magen Avraham* (O.C. 489:1) testifies that women have accepted this *mitzvah* as an obligation. *Mishnah Berurah* (§3) avers that it is generally not customary for women to perform this *mitzvah*. No doubt the custom regarding this varied from place to place. *Mishnah Berurah* (ibid.) adds that when women do fulfill this *mitzvah* they should not recite the *berachah* before it (the *berachah* is not essential to the fulfillment of the *mitzvah*) because of the apprehension that they (because they are not obligated to do this *mitzvah*) may forget to count on one of the days, thereby invalidating the previous count (see §123, 129) and causing the *berachos* previously recited to have been in vain.

112. The *mitzvah* to count the *Omer* obligates every individual male to count (O.C. 489:1). The *poskim* differ on the question whether the principle of שׁוֹמֵעַ כְּעוֹנֶה, *one who hears is considered as if he has voiced* — i.e., it is possible to discharge one's obligation to say something, e.g., *Kiddush* or the recitation of *berachos*, by listening to another's recitation. Some hold that the counting of the *Omer* is no exception to this rule, while others assert that the obligation for every individual to count negates the application of this principle. All agree however, that this principle can be applied to the benediction. The custom is for everyone to recite his own benediction, but where one cannot do so — e.g., he has forgotten to count one day (see below §129,130) — he may rely upon hearing the benediction from someone else and then perform the count himself (*M.B.* §5).

◆§ The Performance of the Mitzvah

113. As before most *mitzvos*, the counting of the *Omer* is preceded by a *berachah* (O.C. 489:1). The recitation of the *berachah* is not essential to the fulfillment of the *mitzvah;* if one did not preface the count with a *berachah*, he has fulfilled his obligation regarding the *mitzvah* and may not repeat the count with a *berachah* (see O.C. 489:4).

114. Every count is bracketed by the words הַיּוֹם ... לָעוֹמֶר, *Today is ... of the Omer* (O.C. 489:1). The word *today* is essential to the performance of the *mitzvah*; if omitted, the count must be repeated and another *berachah* recited (see *M.B.* 489:20). The word לָעוֹמֶר, however, is not essential (*M.B.* 489:8).

115. The *Shulchan Aruch's* (O.C. 489:1) version of the last word of the formula is not לָעוֹמֶר, but בָּעוֹמֶר, lit., *in the Omer*, i.e., in the days of the *Omer* count. *Turei Zahav* (489:3) argues that the version לָעוֹמֶר, lit., *from the Omer*, implies that the count begins after the offering of the *Omer* offering, i.e., on the seventeenth of Nissan instead of the sixteenth. However, many *poskim* accept the version לָעוֹמֶר (489:8, *M.B.* §8), and argue that this form, too, refers to the *Omer* count and not to the *Omer* offering (*Chok Yaakov* 489:3).

116. The count is valid in any language [but of course Hebrew is preferable], provided one understands what he is saying. Even when said in Hebrew the count is valid only when one understands the words (*M.B.* 489:5).

117. One must stand while reciting the *berachah* and the count, but this is not essential; if one performed the rite while sitting he need not repeat it (O.C. 489:1, *M.B.* §6).

118. Because of the connection of this *mitzvah* with the *Omer* meal offering, it is customary to conclude with a short prayer for the rebuilding of the Holy Temple, conveying our wish to perform the *mitzvah* of offering the flour offering as well. Because of the kabbalistic nuances inherent in the sevenfold nature of the count, many recite psalm 67 and other prayers which re-enforce this aspect of the *mitzvah* (*M.B.* 489:10).

◆§ Days and Weeks

119. As already mentioned earlier, both the days and the weeks must be counted. If one counted only the days and omitted the count of the weeks (at the end of a week; see further §120-121), there is question whether one must repeat the count — i.e., to repeat the count of the days together with that of the weeks. Some rely on a statement of the *amora* Ameimar (*Menachos* 66a) that in the post-Temple era the count is merely a rabbinic obligation enacted as a commemoration of the Temple, and that the count of the days alone suffices to effect a commemoration. Others argue that other *amoraim* disagree with Ameimar and hold that the count of both the days and the weeks is necessary, and their view should be accepted. This divergent *amoraic* view holds either that the counting of the *Omer* is a Scriptural obligation, or both counts are essential even if the entire obligation is rabbinic. Hence if one did count only the days, he should repeat the count of the days together with that of the weeks but should not repeat the *berachah* since the recitation of a *berachah* is never essential to the fulfillment of a *mitzvah* (*M.B.* 489:7 with *Shaar Hatziyun*).

120. The count of the days and that of the weeks differ in that every day is counted as it begins, whereas the week is counted only on the day it ends. Thus on the first six days of the count no mention of the week is made. Only on the seventh and final day of the week the formula for counting is: הַיּוֹם שִׁבְעָה יָמִים שֶׁהֵם שָׁבוּעַ אֶחָד לָעוֹמֶר, *Today is seven days, which are one week, of the Omer.* The same procedure is repeated in the second week; only on the fourteenth day do we count the second week (*O.C.* 489:1).

121. From the seventh day and further, the number of the week is included in every counting. Thus we say, *Today is eight days, which are one week and one day . . .* and so on (*O.C.* 489:1). However, this is not essential, and if omitted, the count need not be repeated. Only at the conclusion of every week is the count of weeks possibly essential (*M.B.* §9).

☙ The Time

122. The ideal time for the count is at the beginning of the night, immediately after *Maariv* (*O.C.* 489:1). [The count is inserted after the full *Kaddish*, before *Aleinu* (*M.B.* §2). On the Sabbath or *Yom Tov* (as on the latter days of Pesach), the count is deferred to after *Kiddush* in the synagogue. When *Havdalah* is said, the count precedes it, immediately after the full *Kaddish;* on Sabbath night, it is followed by וְיִתֶּן לְךָ, after which *Havdalah* is said. When the Sabbath is followed by *Yom Tov* (as when the eighth, final day of Pesach is on Sunday), *Kiddush* and *Havdalah* are said together in the synagogue; the count is made afterward (*O.C.* 489:9, *M.B.* §41-43). However when one makes the count in his own house, it should precede *Kiddush* since one may not begin a meal before performing this *mitzvah* (*M.B.* §39).

123. The Torah insists in regard to the seven counted weeks that *they shall be complete* (*Leviticus* 23:15). Therefore it is essential that the count be done during the night; were the count conducted during the day [i.e., the next morning or afternoon], it could be said that only the day and not the preceding night had been included in the count, and the seven weeks are not *complete* (see *Tosafos Megillah* 20b; *M.B.* §4).

If one forgot to count during the night, there is question among the *poskim* if he can still perform the *mitzvah* during the following day (and still have it considered that he had counted *complete* weeks). Because of this doubt, he should count during the day but without reciting a *berachah* (*O.C.* 489:7). On the following days he may again recite a *berachah* when he counts. Although no *berachah* is recited when a count is not *complete* (see below §129), it is recited when there is only a question whether the count is complete (*M.B.* §34 with *Shaar Hatziyun*).

124. The count cannot be done prior to the beginning of the day being counted, i.e., it cannot be done before nightfall. If a congregation erred on a cloudy day and said the *Maariv* prayer and made the count while it was yet surely day, they must again recite the *berachah* and repeat the count (*O.C.* 489:2, *M.B.* §13).

125. It is permissible to recite the *Maariv* prayer before night if it is after the *plag haminchah* — a halachic hour and a quarter before night (*O.C.* 232; see above §6 for a definition of *halachic hours* and how they are calculated). Although the time after the *plag haminchah* is considered night concerning the *Maariv* prayer, one should not recite the *berachah* and the count then. This is so even on the Sabbath eve when one has already accepted the Sabbath upon oneself (see *Magen Avraham* 489:8, *Chok Yaakov* §12, 14). However, many congregations follow a time honored custom and do make the count immediately after the *Maariv* prayer, even if it is still day, as long as it is after the *plag haminchah*. Some of the greatest *Acharonim* defend the custom, arguing that the dispensation afforded for the *Maariv* prayer after the *plag haminchah* can be extended to the *Omer* count as well (*Be'ur Halachah* to 489:3). Consequently, if one did make the count before night but after *plag haminchah*, he should repeat the count at night but should not again recite the *berachah* (*Eliyah Rabbah*, cited in *Shaar Hatziyun* 489:17).

126. One should wait with the count until it is definitely night — until after *the emergence of the stars* (*O.C.* 489:2; various halachic interpretations are given for the term *emergence of the stars* and congregations vary in the practices affected by this). However, many *poskim* rule that if one counted during the twilight period between sundown and the *emergence of the stars*, he need not repeat the count, in keeping with the principle that סְפֵיקָא דְרַבָּנָן לְקוּלָא, *in cases of doubt affecting rabbinic enactments one can opt for leniency;* this ruling accepts the premise that the obligation to count the *Omer* in the post-Temple era is rabbinic (see above §110). Others argue that the view which ascribes Scriptural status to the count even in the post-Temple era should be deferred to, and that the count be repeated after the *emergence of the stars* but without a *berachah* (*M.B.* §14-15).

127. If the congregation makes the count during the twilight period, even an individual who wishes to perform the *mitzvah* in an ideal fashion — after *the emergence of the stars* — should count with the congregation because of the apprehension that he may forget to count later. He should not recite the *berachah* now, and mentally declare the following condition regarding the count: 'If I will remember to make the count later — after *the emergence of the stars* — I intend not to fulfill the *mitzvah* with the count I am about to make now.' Thus if he does remember to repeat the count later, the first count is invalid, and he can recite the *berachah* over the second counting, and perform the *mitzvah* in the ideal manner. If this condition is not declared, the count performed during the twilight is valid, and although one can repeat the count later, he cannot recite the *berachah* again because of the probability that he has already discharged his obligation with the first counting (O.C. 489:3 with M.B.). Some *poskim* assert that the same procedure be followed if the congregation makes the count before twilight but after the *plag haminchah* (*Be'ur Halachah to* 489:3).

◆§ Eating and Work before the Omer Count

128. It is forbidden to eat a meal or do work from half an hour before the beginning of the (ideal) time designated for the counting — from half an hour before *the emergence of the stars* — until one has made the count. This is so even if one has already recited the *Maariv* prayer. This prohibition parallels the prohibition to eat before the *Maariv* prayer [and all the leniencies accepted for it apply also to the *Omer* count] (O.C. 489:4, M.B.23-27).

◆§ Forgetting to Count

129. As already mentioned (§123), the Torah insists in regard to the seven counted weeks that *they shall be complete (Leviticus* 23:15). Some *poskim* derive from this that if one has missed a day in the count, he can no longer fulfill the *mitzvah* since the days he will now count will not be part of a complement of seven *complete* weeks. The *Shulchan Aruch (O.C.* 489:8) rules that in case of a forgotten count, one should count the following days, but, in deference to the view which insists on *complete* weeks, should not recite a *berachah*. He should try to hear the *berachah* from the *chazzan* or another person and intend to fulfill the obligation to recite a *berachah* through hearing. [He should also apprise the other person of his intention and instruct him to have in mind that his recitation fulfill the hearer's obligation.] If, however, one is not sure he has skipped a day, he may count further with a *berachah* (O.C. 489:8). [Forgetting a count as stated in the above ruling refers to forgetting for an entire day. If one merely forgot during the night but was reminded during the day, see §123.]

130. Consequently, if an individual who has forgotten to count for one day serves as a *chazzan* for the *Maariv* prayers during the *Omer* period, he may not recite the *berachah* before the count. He should appoint another to recite the *berachah* and the count. There are conflicting views among the *poskim* if such an individual can recite the *berachah* for another who has not forgotten. They dispute whether such an individual is considered as one who is not obligated in the *mitzvah* (such as a woman or a minor whose recitation cannot be utilized by an obligated hearer to fulfill his obligation; see O.C. 186:6), or if he can still be considered as one who is obligated in the *mitzvah* (see *Mikra'ei Kodesh, Pesach* v.2, p.222; *Pri Chadash* to O.C. 489).

◆§ Mistakes in Counting

131. One should know which day of the count it is when he recites the *berachah* so that he should not have to wait between the *berachah* and the count. One should not interpose, between the *berachah* and the count, a waiting period longer than a כְּדֵי דִיבּוּר, *a minimal phrase*, i.e., the time it takes to say the phrase שָׁלוֹם עָלֶיךָ רַבִּי, or at the most the phrase שָׁלוֹם עָלֶיךָ רַבִּי וּמוֹרִי. However if one did wait longer than this between the *berachah* and the count he has, *post facto*, fulfilled his obligation (O.C. 489:5, M.B. §29).

132. Even if one was mistaken about the correct number of the day during his recitation of the *berachah* and intended to make an erroneous count, he nevertheless fulfills his obligation if he realizes his error while making the count and counts correctly [he need not repeat the *berachah*] (O.C. 489:6). Moreover, even if he actually counted wrongly, he can rectify his error by correcting himself within the time necessary to say *a minimal phrase* (see above §131). He need not repeat the word הַיּוֹם, *today is*, since it is yet within the time span of *a minimal phrase* (M.B. §32). [If, however, a time span greater than *a minimal phrase* has elapsed after the end of the erroneous count, the *berachah* must be repeated before one commences to count correctly. This is so even if the correct count was known during the recitation of the initial *berachah* and the error occurred only during the count.]

◆§ Inadvertent Count

133. If one inadvertently made the count at a time when one can perform the *mitzvah* — any time after the beginning of twilight — he may have thereby fulfilled his obligation. There is a disagreement in the *Gemara (Rosh Hashanah 28a-b)* whether intent to perform a *mitzvah* is essential to the fulfillment of one's obligation; the halachic outcome of this question is in doubt. Therefore, if one did not have in mind to fulfill the *mitzvah* when he made the count, one should repeat the count but not the *berachah* (see O.C. 489:4).

134. Because of the view that one may fulfill his obligation even without intending to do so, if one who had not yet counted was asked — after the beginning of twilight — which day of the *Omer* it is, he should not answer, *'Today is such and such a day,'* for he would thereby forfeit his chance to recite the *berachah*. Rather he should say, *'Yesterday was such and such a day'* (O.C. 489:4). However, if he responded by merely giving the number of days, without saying, *'Today is ...,'* he may still recite the *berachah*, since the phrase *'Today is'* is essential to the fulfillment of the *mitzvah* (see above §114). Also, if he made an explicit (mental) declaration that he does not want to fulfill his obligation with his response, he does not forfeit the *berachah*. There is yet a third exception to the above ruling. If this occurred at the end of a week when the count of the week is essential (see above §119), the *berachah* is also not forfeited (*M.B.* §22).

SHEMONEH ESREI DURING CHOL HAMOED

135. From after the last *Minchah* prayer said before Pesach and further, the passage וְתֵן טַל וּמָטָר לִבְרָכָה, *and give rain and dew for a blessing*, in the *berachah* בָּרֵךְ עָלֵינוּ, *bless on our behalf*, is changed to וְתֵן בְּרָכָה, *and give a blessing* (*O.C.* 117:1). In general this change is theoretical until *Chol HaMoed* (see *Be'ur Halachah* to 117:1 for a practical, though unusual, application).

136. If טַל וּמָטָר was said in the wrong season of the year, one must go back to the beginning of בָּרֵךְ עָלֵינוּ and continue from there. If he has concluded the *Shemoneh Esrei*, he must repeat it from the beginning. Conclusion of *Shemoneh Esrei* is defined here as in §87 above (*O.C.* 114:8).

137. When one is not sure what he said, he must assume that he had recited whatever he had become accustomed to. A new "habit" is not established firmly until the recitation has been in effect for a thirty-day period of recitation (*O.C.* 114:8); see §108.

138. According to some *poskim*, a ninety-fold repetition of וְאֶת כָּל מִינֵי תְבוּאָתָהּ לְטוֹבָה וְתֵן בְּרָכָה, omitting טַל וּמָטָר, is efficacious to remove doubts of incorrect recitation (*O.C.* 114:9 *M.B.* there; see above §108).

139. If an entire country experienced a drought and was in special need of rain during a period when טַל וּמָטָר is not recited, but someone erred and *did* recite טַל וּמָטָר, he need not repeat the *Shemoneh Esrei* (*O.C.* 117:2; see *Be'ur Halachah*, s.v. ושאל, and *Shoneh Halachos*). [For some of the refinements of this rule in regard to a country not in a state of drought but in which rain is not unwelcome during this period, see *Be'ur Halachah* to *O.C.* 117:2, s.v. הצריכין, *M.B.* §10.]

EREV PESACH ON THE SABBATH

140. It is not often that *Erev Pesach* falls on the Sabbath, but when it does, it creates a number of unique halachic problems and deviations from the norm. Quite a number of monographs have been written on this topic, and it is usually treated in detail by *rabbanim* in their *Shabbas Hagadol* sermons, and in instructional pamphlets which are circulated upon such an occurrence. Nevertheless, we will attempt to summarize briefly the rules set down by the *Shulchan Aruch* and its commentators, to familiarize the reader with the problems, and some of the accepted solutions.

141. The search for *chametz* is conducted, in the usual manner, on the night preceding the thirteenth of Nissan. It is preceded, as usual, by the *berachah*, and is followed by the nullification (*O.C.* 444:1, *M.B.* §1; see above §2).

142. [The *Shacharis* prayer on Friday is said in the usual manner. Psalms 100, 20, are not omitted (see above §4).] The fast of the firstborn (or the *siyum* customary in our days) is conducted on Thursday (*O.C.* 472:2).

143. Although none of the prohibitions against having or eating *chametz* apply on this day, the *chametz* should be burnt before noon, as usual, so that people not err in other years when the burning is done on the fourteenth of Nissan. However, the second nullification should not be done immediately after the burning, but rather on the Sabbath (*O.C.* 444:2; see further §148).

144. [Regarding work, eating *matzah*, or *chametz*, this Friday is not different from an ordinary Friday.]

145. One should leave over for the Sabbath only as much *chametz* as he needs for the two Sabbath meals [Friday night and Saturday morning] (*O.C.* 444:1). The food one cooks for the meals should not contain any *chametz* which will adhere to the pots, thereby creating a problem concerning their cleaning after the meal (*O.C.* 444:2). Moreover, the *poskim* advise that the food be cooked in the Pesach pots, [free of any *chametz*]. If one follows this stricture, he should be careful not to spill any hot liquid from a Pesach pot onto a *chametz* plate (*M.B.* §14 with *Shaar Hatziyun*).

146. On the Sabbath morning one may not eat *matzah*, just as on any *Erev Pesach*. The prohibitions against eating and deriving benefit from *chametz* take effect at the same time as they would on a weekday (see above §6). Therefore, it is customary to conduct the *Shacharis* and *Mussaf* prayers very early and with dispatch, to enable the people to finish the morning Sabbath meal within the time allowed for consumption of *chametz* (*M.B.* 444:4).

147. After the meal the bread crumbs should be shaken out of the tablecloth [in such a manner as not to let the crumbs fall about the house], the plates wiped clean of any food residue, and then they should be put away with the *chametz* utensils (*O.C.* 444:4). Any leftover *chametz* should be disposed of; the most convenient way is to flush it down the drain (*O.C.* 444:5 with *M.B.*). If one has a large amount of *chametz* which he has forgotten to sell to a gentile he should consult a competent halachic authority as soon as possible early in the morning (see *M.B.* §20).

148. Even if one thinks he has disposed of all his *chametz*, he must nevertheless repeat the nullification of the *chametz* after the meal, just as this is done in a regular year after the burning of the *chametz* (*O.C.* 444:6; see above §9). [One must be careful to do this before the prohibition against deriving benefit from *chametz* takes effect (see above §8).]

149. As already mentioned, one may not eat *matzah* on this Sabbath just as on any Pesach eve. This creates a problem in regard to the *seudah shlishis*, the third meal which should be eaten on the Sabbath afternoon. Some advise that *matzah* kneaded with fruit juice or eggs be used; this type of *matzah* cannot be used for the *mitzvah* of *matzah* at the *Seder*, and may consequently be eaten on *Erev Pesach*. However, *Rama* objects to this on the grounds that the Ashkenazim have accepted a stricture to view such *matzos* as סָפֵק חָמֵץ, *possibly chametz*, and consequently forbids them to be eaten on the afternoon of *Erev Pesach*, when *chametz* may not be eaten. *Rama* concludes that one should in this instance rely on the lenient opinions which allow one to fulfill the *mitzvah* of *seudah shlishis* with fruit, meat or eggs (O.C. 444:1). One may also eat cooked foods made from matzah meal — e.g., matzah balls — but these may not be eaten during the last three halachic hours of the afternoon (*M.B.*§8). Many later *poskim* caution that it is better to split the morning meal into two meals — provided there is time to wait a while between the two meals — and thereby fulfill the *mitzvah* of *seudah shlishis* with bread, since there are authorities who hold that the time of the meal is not essential (ibid.).

VERSES FOR PEOPLE'S NAMES / פסוקים לשמות אנשים

Kitzur Sh'lah teaches that it is a source of merit to recite a Scriptural verse symbolizing one's name before יִהְיוּ לְרָצוֹן at the end of *Shemoneh Esrei.* The verse should either contain the person's name, or else begin and end with the first and last letters of the name.

Following is a selection of first and last letters of names, with appropriate verses:

א...א אָנָּא יהוה הוֹשִׁיעָה נָּא, אָנָּא יהוה הַצְלִיחָה נָּא.[1]

א...ה אַשְׁרֵי מַשְׂכִּיל אֶל דָּל, בְּיוֹם רָעָה יְמַלְּטֵהוּ יהוה.[2]

א...ו אַשְׁרֵי שֶׁאֵל יַעֲקֹב בְּעֶזְרוֹ, שִׂבְרוֹ עַל יהוה אֱלֹהָיו.[3]

א...י אֲמָרַי הַאֲזִינָה יהוה בִּינָה הֲגִיגִי.[4]

א...ך אָמַרְתְּ לַיהוה אֲדֹנָי אָתָּה, טוֹבָתִי בַּל עָלֶיךָ.[5]

א...ל אֶרֶץ רָעָשָׁה אַף שָׁמַיִם נָטְפוּ מִפְּנֵי אֱלֹהִים זֶה סִינַי, מִפְּנֵי אֱלֹהִים אֱלֹהֵי יִשְׂרָאֵל.[6]

א...ם אַתָּה הוּא יהוה הָאֱלֹהִים, אֲשֶׁר בָּחַרְתָּ בְּאַבְרָם, וְהוֹצֵאתוֹ מֵאוּר כַּשְׂדִּים, וְשַׂמְתָּ שְׁמוֹ אַבְרָהָם.[7]

א...ן אֵלֶיךָ יהוה אֶקְרָא, וְאֶל אֲדֹנָי אֶתְחַנָּן.[8]

א...ע אָמַר בְּלִבּוֹ בַּל אֶמּוֹט, לְדֹר וָדֹר אֲשֶׁר לֹא בְרָע.[9]

א...ר אֵלֶּה בָרֶכֶב וְאֵלֶּה בַסּוּסִים, וַאֲנַחְנוּ בְּשֵׁם יהוה אֱלֹהֵינוּ נַזְכִּיר.[10]

ב...א בְּרִיתִי הָיְתָה אִתּוֹ הַחַיִּים וְהַשָּׁלוֹם, וָאֶתְּנֵם לוֹ מוֹרָא וַיִּירָאֵנִי, וּמִפְּנֵי שְׁמִי נִחַת הוּא.[11]

ב...ה בַּעֲבוּר יִשְׁמְרוּ חֻקָּיו, וְתוֹרֹתָיו יִנְצֹרוּ, הַלְלוּיָהּ.[12]

ב...ז בְּיוֹם קָרָאתִי וַתַּעֲנֵנִי, תַּרְהִבֵנִי בְנַפְשִׁי עֹז.[13]

ב...ך בָּרוּךְ אַתָּה יהוה, לַמְּדֵנִי חֻקֶּיךָ.[14]

ב...ל בְּמַקְהֵלוֹת בָּרְכוּ אֱלֹהִים, אֲדֹנָי מִמְּקוֹר יִשְׂרָאֵל.[15]

ב...ן בָּרוּךְ יהוה אֱלֹהֵי יִשְׂרָאֵל מֵהָעוֹלָם וְעַד הָעוֹלָם, אָמֵן וְאָמֵן.[16]

ב...ע בְּחֶסֶד וֶאֱמֶת יְכֻפַּר עָוֹן, וּבְיִרְאַת יהוה סוּר מֵרָע.[17]

ג...ה גּוֹל עַל יהוה דַּרְכֶּךָ, וּבְטַח עָלָיו וְהוּא יַעֲשֶׂה.[18]

ג...ל גַּם אֲנִי אוֹדְךָ בִכְלִי נֶבֶל, אֲמִתְּךָ אֱלֹהָי אֲזַמְּרָה לְךָ בְכִנּוֹר, קְדוֹשׁ יִשְׂרָאֵל.[19]

ג...ן גַּם בְּנֵי אָדָם גַּם בְּנֵי אִישׁ, יַחַד עָשִׁיר וְאֶבְיוֹן.[20]

ד...ב דִּרְשׁוּ יהוה בְּהִמָּצְאוֹ, קְרָאֻהוּ בִּהְיוֹתוֹ קָרוֹב.[21]

ד...ד דִּרְשׁוּ יהוה וְעֻזּוֹ, בַּקְּשׁוּ פָנָיו תָּמִיד.[22]

ד...ה דְּאָגָה בְלֶב אִישׁ יַשְׁחֶנָּה, וְדָבָר טוֹב יְשַׂמְּחֶנָּה.[23]

ד...ל דָּן יָדִין עַמּוֹ, כְּאַחַד שִׁבְטֵי יִשְׂרָאֵל.[24]

ה...א הַצּוּר תָּמִים פָּעֳלוֹ, כִּי כָל דְּרָכָיו מִשְׁפָּט, אֵל אֱמוּנָה וְאֵין עָוֶל, צַדִּיק וְיָשָׁר הוּא.[25]

ה...ה הַסְתֵּר פָּנֶיךָ מֵחֲטָאָי, וְכָל עֲוֹנֹתַי מְחֵה.[26]

ה...ל הַקְשִׁיבָה לְקוֹל שַׁוְעִי מַלְכִּי וֵאלֹהָי, כִּי אֵלֶיךָ אֶתְפַּלָּל.[27]

ז...ב זֵכֶר צַדִּיק לִבְרָכָה, וְשֵׁם רְשָׁעִים יִרְקָב.[28]

ז...ה זֹאת מְנוּחָתִי עֲדֵי עַד, פֹּה אֵשֵׁב כִּי אִוִּתִיהָ.[29]

ז...ח זָכַרְתִּי יָמִים מִקֶּדֶם, הָגִיתִי בְכָל פָּעֳלֶךָ, בְּמַעֲשֵׂה יָדֶיךָ אֲשׂוֹחֵחַ.[30]

ז...ן זְבוּלֻן לְחוֹף יַמִּים יִשְׁכֹּן, וְהוּא לְחוֹף אֳנִיֹּת, וְיַרְכָתוֹ עַל צִידֹן.[31]

---

(1) *Psalms* 118:25. (2) 41:2. (3) 146:5. (4) 5:2. (5) 16:2. (6) 68:9. (7) *Nehemiah* 9:7. (8) *Psalms* 30:9. (9) 10:6. (10) 20:8. (11) *Malachi* 2:5. (12) *Psalms* 105:45. (13) 138:3. (14) 119:12. (15) 68:27. (16) 41:14. (17) *Proverbs* 16:6. (18) *Psalms* 37:5. (19) 71:22. (20) 49:3. (21) *Isaiah* 55:6. (22) *Psalms* 105:4. (23) *Proverbs* 12:25. (24) *Genesis* 49:16. (25) *Deuteronomy* 32:4. (26) *Psalms* 51:11. (27) 5:3. (28) *Proverbs* 10:7. (29) *Psalms* 132:14. (30) 143:5. (31) *Genesis* 49:13.

ח...ה חָגְרָה בְעוֹז מָתְנֶיהָ, וַתְּאַמֵּץ זְרוֹעֹתֶיהָ.[1]
ח...ך חֲצוֹת לַיְלָה אָקוּם לְהוֹדוֹת לָךְ, עַל מִשְׁפְּטֵי צִדְקֶךָ.[2]
ח...ם חֹנֶה מַלְאַךְ יהוה סָבִיב לִירֵאָיו, וַיְחַלְּצֵם.[3]
ט...א טוֹב יַנְחִיל בְּנֵי בָנִים, וְצָפוּן לַצַּדִּיק חֵיל חוֹטֶא.[4]
ט...ה טָמְנוּ גֵאִים פַּח לִי, וַחֲבָלִים פָּרְשׂוּ רֶשֶׁת לְיַד מַעְגָּל, מֹקְשִׁים שָׁתוּ לִי סֶלָה.[5]
י...א יִשְׂרָאֵל בְּטַח בַּיהוה, עֶזְרָם וּמָגִנָּם הוּא.[6]
י...ב יַעַנְךָ יהוה בְּיוֹם צָרָה, יְשַׂגֶּבְךָ שֵׁם אֱלֹהֵי יַעֲקֹב.[7]
י...ד יָסַד אֶרֶץ עַל מְכוֹנֶיהָ, בַּל תִּמּוֹט עוֹלָם וָעֶד.[8]
י...ה יהוה הַצִּילָה נַפְשִׁי מִשְּׂפַת שֶׁקֶר, מִלָּשׁוֹן רְמִיָּה.[9]
י...י יהוה לִי בְּעֹזְרָי, וַאֲנִי אֶרְאֶה בְשֹׂנְאָי.[10]
י...ל יְמִין יהוה רוֹמֵמָה, יְמִין יהוה עֹשָׂה חָיִל.[11]
י...ם יַעְלְזוּ חֲסִידִים בְּכָבוֹד, יְרַנְּנוּ עַל מִשְׁכְּבוֹתָם.[12]
י...ן יָשֵׂם נְהָרוֹת לְמִדְבָּר, וּמֹצָאֵי מַיִם לְצִמָּאוֹן.[13]
י...ע יָחֹס עַל דַּל וְאֶבְיוֹן, וְנַפְשׁוֹת אֶבְיוֹנִים יוֹשִׁיעַ.[14]
י...ף יהוה יִגְמֹר בַּעֲדִי, יהוה חַסְדְּךָ לְעוֹלָם, מַעֲשֵׂי יָדֶיךָ אַל תֶּרֶף.[15]
י...ץ יְבָרְכֵנוּ אֱלֹהִים וְיִירְאוּ אוֹתוֹ כָּל אַפְסֵי אָרֶץ.[16]
י...ק יוֹצִיאֵם מֵחֹשֶׁךְ וְצַלְמָוֶת, וּמוֹסְרוֹתֵיהֶם יְנַתֵּק.[17]
י...ר יהוה שִׁמְךָ לְעוֹלָם, יהוה זִכְרְךָ לְדֹר וָדֹר.[18]
י...ת יהוה שֹׁמֵר אֶת גֵּרִים, יָתוֹם וְאַלְמָנָה יְעוֹדֵד, וְדֶרֶךְ רְשָׁעִים יְעַוֵּת.[19]
כ...ב כִּי לֹא יִטֹּשׁ יהוה עַמּוֹ, וְנַחֲלָתוֹ לֹא יַעֲזֹב.[20]
כ...ל כִּי מֶלֶךְ כָּל הָאָרֶץ אֱלֹהִים, זַמְּרוּ מַשְׂכִּיל.[21]
ל...א לֹא תִהְיֶה מְשַׁכֵּלָה וַעֲקָרָה בְּאַרְצֶךָ, אֶת מִסְפַּר יָמֶיךָ אֲמַלֵּא.[22]
ל...ה לְדָוִד בָּרוּךְ יהוה צוּרִי הַמְלַמֵּד יָדַי לַקְרָב, אֶצְבְּעוֹתַי לַמִּלְחָמָה.[23]
ל...י לוּלֵי תוֹרָתְךָ שַׁעֲשֻׁעָי, אָז אָבַדְתִּי בְעָנְיִי.[24]
ל...ת לַמְנַצֵּחַ עַל שֹׁשַׁנִּים לִבְנֵי קֹרַח, מַשְׂכִּיל שִׁיר יְדִידֹת.[25]
מ...א מִי כָמֹכָה בָּאֵלִם יהוה מִי כָּמֹכָה נֶאְדָּר בַּקֹּדֶשׁ, נוֹרָא תְהִלֹּת עֹשֵׂה פֶלֶא.[26]
מ...ה מַחֲשָׁבוֹת בְּעֵצָה תִכּוֹן, וּבְתַחְבֻּלוֹת עֲשֵׂה מִלְחָמָה.[27]
מ...ו מַה דּוֹדֵךְ מִדּוֹד הַיָּפָה בַּנָּשִׁים, מַה דּוֹדֵךְ מִדּוֹד שֶׁכָּכָה הִשְׁבַּעְתָּנוּ.[28]
מ...י מָה אָהַבְתִּי תוֹרָתֶךָ, כָּל הַיּוֹם הִיא שִׂיחָתִי.[29]
מ...ל מַה טֹּבוּ אֹהָלֶיךָ יַעֲקֹב, מִשְׁכְּנֹתֶיךָ יִשְׂרָאֵל.[30]
מ...ם מְאוֹר עֵינַיִם יְשַׂמַּח לֵב, שְׁמוּעָה טוֹבָה תְּדַשֶּׁן עָצֶם.[31]
מ...ר מִי זֶה הָאִישׁ יְרֵא יהוה, יוֹרֶנּוּ בְּדֶרֶךְ יִבְחָר.[32]
נ...א נַפְשֵׁנוּ חִכְּתָה לַיהוה עֶזְרֵנוּ וּמָגִנֵּנוּ הוּא.[33]
נ...ה נָחַלְתִּי עֵדְוֹתֶיךָ לְעוֹלָם, כִּי שְׂשׂוֹן לִבִּי הֵמָּה.[34]
נ...י נִדְבוֹת פִּי רְצֵה נָא יהוה, וּמִשְׁפָּטֶיךָ לַמְּדֵנִי.[35]
נ...ל נֶחְשַׁבְתִּי עִם יוֹרְדֵי בוֹר, הָיִיתִי כְּגֶבֶר אֵין אֱיָל.[36]
נ...ם נַחֲמוּ נַחֲמוּ עַמִּי, יֹאמַר אֱלֹהֵיכֶם.[37]

---

(1) *Proverbs* 31:17. (2) *Psalms* 119:62. (3) 34:8. (4) *Proverbs* 13:22. (5) *Psalms* 140:6. (6) 115:9. (7) 20:2. (8) 104:5. (9) 120:2. (10) 118:7. (11) 118:16. (12) 149:5. (13) 107:33. (14) 72:13. (15) 138:8. (16) 67:8. (17) 107:14. (18) 135:13. (19) 146:9. (20) 94:14. (21) 47:8. (22) *Exodus* 23:26. (23) *Psalms* 144:1. (24) 119:92. (25) 45:1. (26) *Exodus* 15:11. (27) *Proverbs* 20:18. (28) *Song of Songs* 5:9. (29) *Psalms* 119:97. (30) *Numbers* 24:5. (31) *Proverbs* 15:30. (32) *Psalms* 25:12. (33) 33:20. (34) 119:111. (35) 119:108. (36) 88:5. (37) *Isaiah* 40:1.

נ...ן נֵר יהוה נִשְׁמַת אָדָם, חֹפֵשׂ כָּל חַדְרֵי בָטֶן.[1]
ס...ה סֹבּוּ צִיּוֹן וְהַקִּיפוּהָ סִפְרוּ מִגְדָּלֶיהָ.[2]
ס...י סֵעֲפִים שָׂנֵאתִי, וְתוֹרָתְךָ אָהָבְתִּי.[3]
ע...א עַתָּה אָקוּם, יֹאמַר יהוה, עַתָּה אֵרוֹמָם, עַתָּה אֶנָּשֵׂא.[4]
ע...ב עַד אֶמְצָא מָקוֹם לַיהוה, מִשְׁכָּנוֹת לַאֲבִיר יַעֲקֹב.[5]
ע...ה עָזִּי וְזִמְרָת יָהּ, וַיְהִי לִי לִישׁוּעָה.[6]
ע...ל עַל דַּעְתְּךָ כִּי לֹא אֶרְשָׁע, וְאֵין מִיָּדְךָ מַצִּיל.[7]
ע...ם עֲרֹב עַבְדְּךָ לְטוֹב, אַל יַעַשְׁקֻנִי זֵדִים.[8]
ע...ר עֹשֶׂה גְדֹלוֹת וְאֵין חֵקֶר, נִפְלָאוֹת עַד אֵין מִסְפָּר.[9]
פ...ה פִּתְחוּ לִי שַׁעֲרֵי צֶדֶק, אָבֹא בָם אוֹדֶה יָהּ.[10]
פ...ל פֶּן יִטְרֹף כְּאַרְיֵה נַפְשִׁי, פֹּרֵק וְאֵין מַצִּיל.[11]
פ...ס פֶּלֶס וּמֹאזְנֵי מִשְׁפָּט לַיהוה, מַעֲשֵׂהוּ כָּל אַבְנֵי כִיס.[12]
פ...ץ פִּנִּיתָ לְפָנֶיהָ וַתַּשְׁרֵשׁ שָׁרָשֶׁיהָ וַתְּמַלֵּא אָרֶץ.[13]
צ...ה צִיּוֹן בְּמִשְׁפָּט תִּפָּדֶה, וְשָׁבֶיהָ בִּצְדָקָה.[14]
צ...ח צִיּוֹן יִשְׁאָלוּ דֶּרֶךְ הֵנָּה פְנֵיהֶם, בֹּאוּ וְנִלְווּ אֶל יהוה, בְּרִית עוֹלָם לֹא תִשָּׁכֵחַ.[15]
צ...י צַר וּמָצוֹק מְצָאוּנִי, מִצְוֹתֶיךָ שַׁעֲשֻׁעָי.[16]
ק...ל קַמְתִּי אֲנִי לִפְתֹּחַ לְדוֹדִי, וְיָדַי נָטְפוּ מוֹר וְאֶצְבְּעֹתַי מוֹר עֹבֵר עַל כַּפּוֹת הַמַּנְעוּל.[17]
ק...ן קוֹלִי אֶל יהוה אֶזְעָק, קוֹלִי אֶל יהוה אֶתְחַנָּן.[18]
ק...ת קָרוֹב אַתָּה יהוה, וְכָל מִצְוֹתֶיךָ אֱמֶת.[19]
ר...ה רִגְזוּ וְאַל תֶּחֱטָאוּ, אִמְרוּ בִלְבַבְכֶם עַל מִשְׁכַּבְכֶם, וְדֹמּוּ סֶלָה.[20]
ר...ל רְאוּ עַתָּה כִּי אֲנִי אֲנִי הוּא, וְאֵין אֱלֹהִים עִמָּדִי, אֲנִי אָמִית וַאֲחַיֶּה, מָחַצְתִּי וַאֲנִי אֶרְפָּא, וְאֵין מִיָּדִי מַצִּיל.[21]
ר...ן רְאֵה זֶה מָצָאתִי, אָמְרָה קֹהֶלֶת, אַחַת לְאַחַת לִמְצֹא חֶשְׁבּוֹן.[22]
ש...א שַׂמֵּחַ נֶפֶשׁ עַבְדֶּךָ, כִּי אֵלֶיךָ אֲדֹנָי נַפְשִׁי אֶשָּׂא.[23]
ש...ה שְׂאוּ יְדֵכֶם קֹדֶשׁ, וּבָרְכוּ אֶת יהוה.[24]
ש...ח שָׁמַע יהוה תְּחִנָּתִי, יהוה תְּפִלָּתִי יִקָּח.[25]
ש...י שָׂנֵאתִי הַשֹּׁמְרִים הַבְלֵי שָׁוְא, וַאֲנִי אֶל יהוה בָּטָחְתִּי.[26]
ש...ל שָׁלוֹם רָב לְאֹהֲבֵי תוֹרָתֶךָ וְאֵין לָמוֹ מִכְשׁוֹל.[27]
ש...ם שְׁמָר תָּם וּרְאֵה יָשָׁר, כִּי אַחֲרִית לְאִישׁ שָׁלוֹם.[28]
ש...ן שִׁיתוּ לִבְּכֶם לְחֵילָה פַּסְּגוּ אַרְמְנוֹתֶיהָ, לְמַעַן תְּסַפְּרוּ לְדוֹר אַחֲרוֹן.[29]
ש...ר שְׂפַת אֱמֶת תִּכּוֹן לָעַד, וְעַד אַרְגִּיעָה לְשׁוֹן שָׁקֶר.[30]
ש...ת שִׁיר הַמַּעֲלוֹת, הִנֵּה בָּרְכוּ אֶת יהוה כָּל עַבְדֵי יהוה, הָעֹמְדִים בְּבֵית יהוה בַּלֵּילוֹת.[31]
ת...ה תַּעֲרֹךְ לְפָנַי שֻׁלְחָן נֶגֶד צֹרְרָי, דִּשַּׁנְתָּ בַשֶּׁמֶן רֹאשִׁי, כּוֹסִי רְוָיָה.[32]
ת...י תּוֹצִיאֵנִי מֵרֶשֶׁת זוּ, טָמְנוּ לִי, כִּי אַתָּה מָעוּזִּי.[33]
ת...ם תְּנוּ עֹז לֵאלֹהִים עַל יִשְׂרָאֵל גַּאֲוָתוֹ, וְעֻזּוֹ בַּשְּׁחָקִים.[34]

(1) *Proverbs* 20:27. (2) *Psalms* 48:13. (3) 119:113. (4) *Isaiah* 33:10. (5) *Psalms* 132:5. (6) 118:14. (7) *Job* 10:7. (8) *Psalms* 119:122. (9) *Job* 5:9. (10) *Psalms* 118:19. (11) 7:3. (12) *Proverbs* 16:11. (13) *Psalms* 80:10. (14) *Isaiah* 1:27. (15) *Jeremiah* 50:5. (16) *Psalms* 119:143. (17) *Song of Songs* 5:5. (18) *Psalms* 142:2. (19) 119:151. (20) 5:4. (21) *Deuteronomy* 32:39. (22) *Ecclesiastes* 7:27. (23) *Psalms* 86:4. (24) 134:2. (25) 6:10. (26) 31:7. (27) 119:165. (28) 37:37. (29) 48:14. (30) *Proverbs* 12:19. (31) *Psalms* 134:1. (32) 23:5. (33) 31:5. (34) 68:35.

THE RABBIS' KADDISH / KADDISH D'RABBANAN

TRANSLITERATED WITH ASHKENAZIC PRONUNCIATION

Yisgadal v'yiskadash sh'mei rabbaw (Cong. — *Amein*).
B'allmaw dee v'raw chir'usei v'yamlich malchusei,
b'chayeichon, uv'yomeichon, uv'chayei d'chol beis yisroel,
ba'agawlaw u'vizman kawriv, v'imru: Amein.
(Cong. – *Amein. Y'hei sh'mei rabbaw m'vawrach l'allam u'l'allmei allmayaw.*)
Y'hei sh'mei rabbaw m'vawrach, l'allam u'l'allmei allmayaw.

Yis'bawrach, v'yishtabach, v'yispaw'ar, v'yisromam, v'yis'nasei,
v'yis'hadar, v'yis'aleh, v'yis'halawl
sh'mei d'kudshaw b'rich hu (Cong. – *b'rich hu*).
L'aylaw min kol
bir'chawsaw v'shirawsaw,
tush'b'chawsaw v'nechemawsaw,
da'ami'rawn b'allmaw, v'imru: Amein (Cong. – *Amein*).

Al yisroel v'al rabaw'nawn v'al talmidei'hon,
v'al kol talmidei salmidei'hon,
v'al kol mawn d'awskin b'oray'saw,
dee v'as'raw haw'dain, v'dee b'chol asar va'asar.
Y'hei l'hon u'l'chon shlaw'maw rabbaw,
chee'naw v'chisdaw v'rachamin,
v'chayin arichin, u'm'zonei r'vichei,
u'furkawnaw min kaw'dawm a'vu'hone dee vi'sh'ma'yaw
v'imru: Amein (Cong. – *Amein*).
Y'hei shlawmaw rabbaw min sh'mayaw,
v'chayim awleinu v'al kol yisroel, v'imru: Amein (Cong. – *Amein*).

Take three steps back, bow left and say, *'Oseh . . .'*; bow right and say, *'hu b'rachamawv ya'aseh . . .'*; bow forward and say, *'v'al kol yisroel v'imru: Amein.'*

Oseh shawlom bim'ro'mawv,
hu b'rachamawv ya'aseh shawlom awleinu,
v'al kol yisroel v'imru: Amein (Cong. – *Amein*).

Remain standing in place for a few moments, then take three steps forward.

THE MOURNER'S KADDISH

TRANSLITERATED WITH ASHKENAZIC PRONUNCIATION

Yisgadal v'yiskadash sh'mei rabbaw (Cong. — *Amein*).
B'allmaw dee v'raw chir'usei v'yamlich malchusei,
b'chayeichon, uv'yomeichon, uv'chayei d'chol beis yisroel,
ba'agawlaw u'vizman kawriv, v'imru: Amein.
(Cong. — *Amein. Y'hei sh'mei rabbaw m'vawrach l'allam u'l'allmei allmayaw.*)
Y'hei sh'mei rabbaw m'vawrach, l'allam u'l'allmei allmayaw.

Yis'bawrach, v'yishtabach, v'yispaw'ar,
v'yisromam, v'yis'nasei,
v'yis'hadar, v'yis'aleh, v'yis'halawl
sh'mei d'kudshaw b'rich hu (Cong. – *b'rich hu*).
L'aylaw min kol
bir'chawsaw v'shirawsaw,
tush'b'chawsaw v'nechemawsaw,
da'ami'rawn b'allmaw, v'imru: Amein (Cong. – *Amein*).
Y'hei shlawmaw rabbaw min sh'mayaw,
v'chayim awleinu v'al kol yisroel, v'imru: Amein (Cong. – *Amein*).

Take three steps back, bow left and say, '*Oseh . . .*'; bow right and say, '*hu ya'aseh . . .*'; bow forward and say, '*v'al kol yisroel v'imru: Amein.*'

Oseh shawlom bim'ro'mawv,
hu ya'aseh shawlom awleinu,
v'al kol yisroel v'imru: Amein (Cong. – *Amein*).

Remain standing in place for a few moments, then take three steps forward.